Contents

Published by Collins
An imprint of HarperCollins Publishers
77-85 Fulham Palace Road, Hammersmith, London W6 8JB

www.collins.co.uk

Copyright © HarperCollins Publishers Ltd 2005

Collins® is a registered trademark of HarperCollins Publishers Limited

Mapping generated from Collins Bartholomew digital databases

London Underground Map by permission of Transport Trading Limited
Registered User No. 06/4302

Spiral: ISBN-13 978 0 00 719202 1
ISBN-10 0 00 719202 9 Imp 002
SM11945 / BDB

Hardback: ISBN-13 978 0 00 719201 4
ISBN-10 0 00 719201 0 Imp 002
SM11953 / BDB

Printed in China by South China Printing Co. Ltd.

e-mail: roadcheck@harpercollins.co.uk

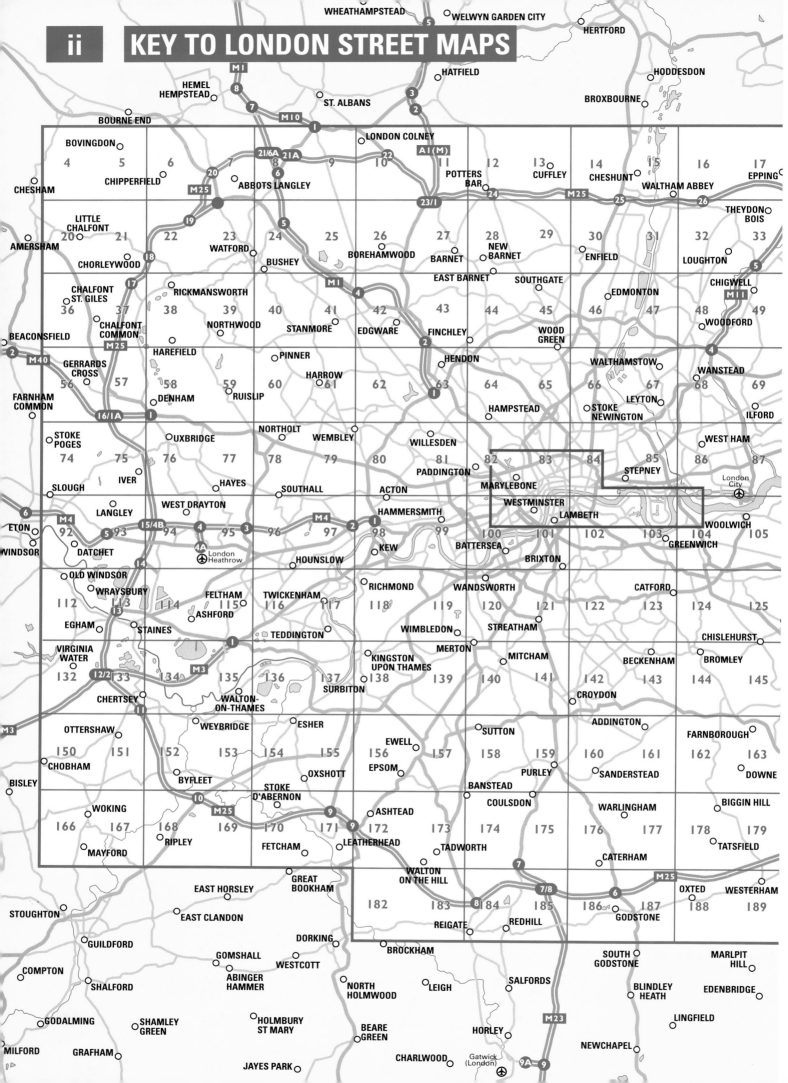

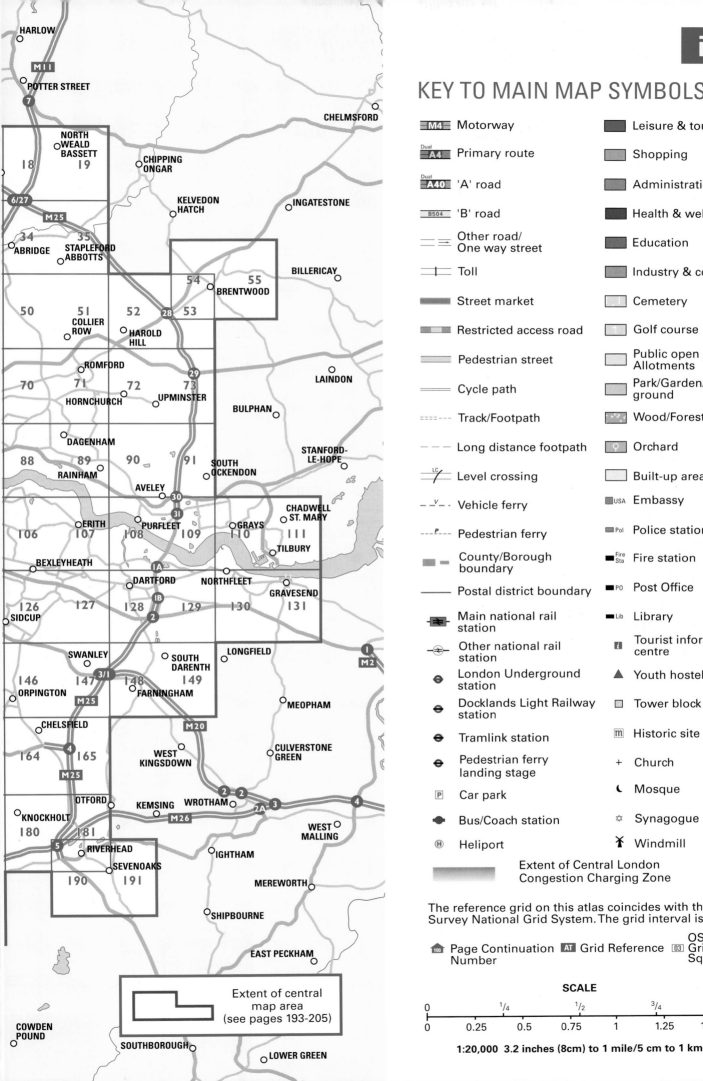

KEY TO MAIN MAP SYMBOLS

Symbol	Description	Symbol	Description
M4	Motorway		Leisure & tourism
Dual **A4**	Primary route		Shopping
Dual **A40**	'A' road		Administration & law
B504	'B' road		Health & welfare
	Other road/ One way street		Education
	Toll		Industry & commerce
	Street market		Cemetery
	Restricted access road		Golf course
	Pedestrian street		Public open space/ Allotments
	Cycle path		Park/Garden/Sports ground
	Track/Footpath		Wood/Forest
	Long distance footpath		Orchard
LC	Level crossing		Built-up area
V	Vehicle ferry	USA	Embassy
P	Pedestrian ferry	Pol	Police station
	County/Borough boundary	Fire Sta	Fire station
	Postal district boundary	PO	Post Office
	Main national rail station	Lib	Library
	Other national rail station	i	Tourist information centre
	London Underground station	▲	Youth hostel
	Docklands Light Railway station	□	Tower block
	Tramlink station	m	Historic site
	Pedestrian ferry landing stage	+	Church
P	Car park	C	Mosque
	Bus/Coach station	✡	Synagogue
H	Heliport	✗	Windmill

Extent of Central London Congestion Charging Zone

The reference grid on this atlas coincides with the Ordnance Survey National Grid System. The grid interval is 500 metres.

100 Page Continuation Number	AT Grid Reference	03 OS National Grid Kilometre Square

SCALE

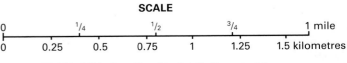

0	¼	½	¾	1 mile
0	0.25	0.5	0.75	1	1.25	1.5 kilometres

1:20,000   3.2 inches (8cm) to 1 mile/5 cm to 1 km

Extent of central map area (see pages 193-205)

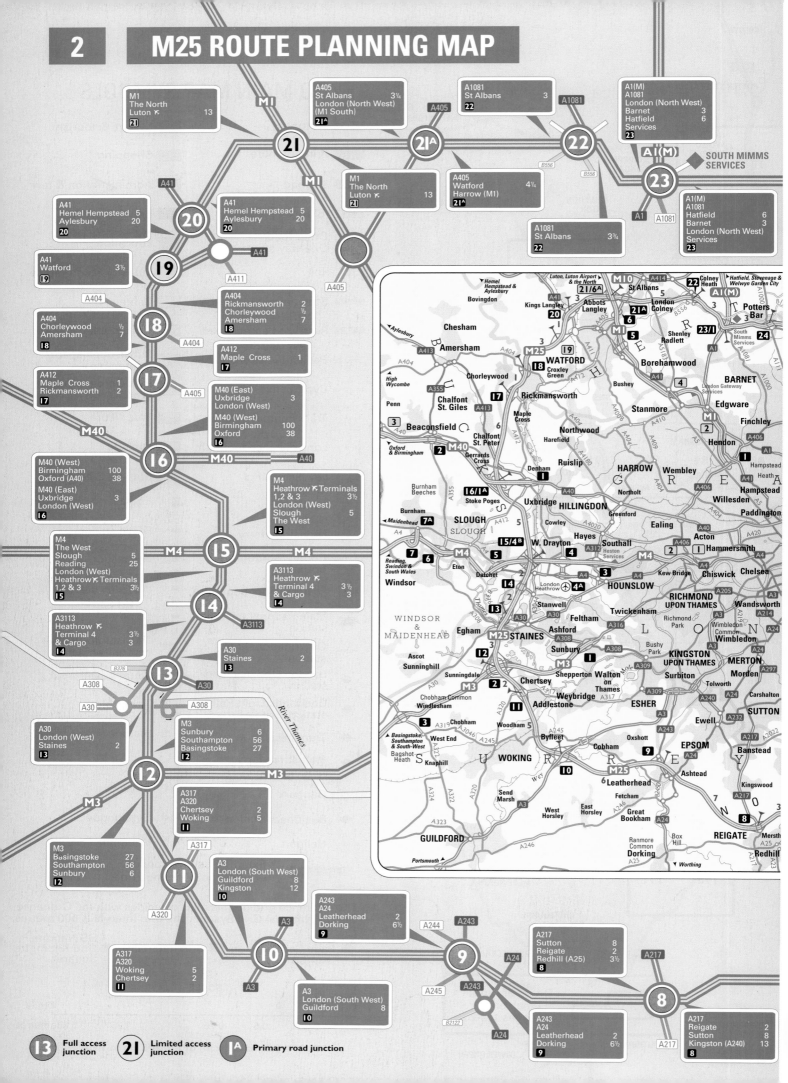

M1
The North
Luton ✈   13
21

A405
St Albans   3¼
London (North West)
(M1 South)
21ᴬ

A1081
St Albans   3
22

A1(M)
A1081
London (North West)
Barnet   3
Hatfield   6
Services
23

21

21ᴬ

22

A1(M)

SOUTH MIMMS SERVICES

M1
The North
Luton ✈   13
21

A405
Watford   4¼
Harrow (M1)
21ᴬ

23

A41
Hemel Hempstead 5
Aylesbury   20
20

A41
Hemel Hempstead 5
Aylesbury   20
20

A1081
St Albans   3¾
22

A1(M)
A1081
Hatfield   6
Barnet   3
London (North West)
Services
23

20

19

A41

A41
Watford   3½
19

A411

A405

A404

A404
Chorleywood   ½
Amersham   7
18

A404
Rickmansworth   2
Chorleywood   ½
Amersham   7
18

18

A404

A412
Maple Cross   1
17

A412
Maple Cross   1
Rickmansworth   2
17

17

A405

M40 (East)
Uxbridge   3
London (West)
M40 (West)
Birmingham   100
Oxford   38
16

M40

M40

M40   **A40**

M40 (West)
Birmingham   100
Oxford (A40)   38
M40 (East)
Uxbridge   3
London (West)
16

16

M4
Heathrow ✈ Terminals
1,2 & 3   3½
London (West)
Slough   5
The West
15

M4

15

M4

M4
The West
Slough   5
Reading   25
London (West)
Heathrow ✈ Terminals
1,2 & 3   3½
15

A3113
Heathrow ✈
Terminal 4   3½
& Cargo   3
14

14

A3113

A3113
Heathrow ✈
Terminal 4   3½
& Cargo   3
14

A30
Staines   2
13

B376

13

A30

A308

A30

A308

River Thames

A308
London (West)
Staines   2
13

M3
Sunbury   6
Southampton   56
Basingstoke   27
12

12

M3

A317
A320
Chertsey   2
Woking   5
11

M3
Basingstoke   27
Southampton   56
Sunbury   6
12

A317

11

A3
London (South West)
Guildford   8
Kingston   12
10

A320

A317
A320
Woking   5
Chertsey   2
11

A3

A243
A24
Leatherhead   2
Dorking   6½
9

A244 **A243**

A217
Sutton   8
Reigate   2
Redhill (A25)   3½
8

A217

10

A3

A3
London (South West)
Guildford   8
10

A245 **A243**

9

A24

B2122

A243
A24
Leatherhead   2
Dorking   6½
9

A24

A217

8

A217
Reigate   2
Sutton   8
Kingston (A240) 13
8

13 Full access junction   **21** Limited access junction   **1ᴬ** Primary road junction

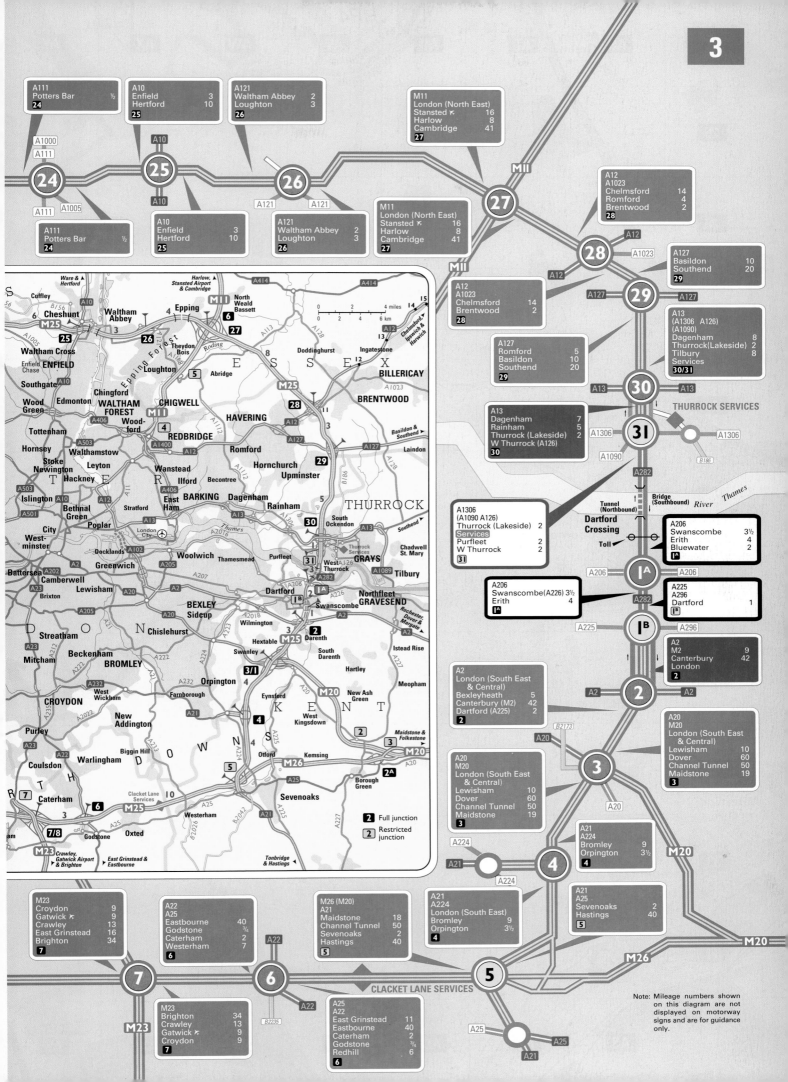
A111
Potters Bar ½
24
A10
Enfield 3
Hertford 10
25
A121
Waltham Abbey 2
Loughton 3
26
M11
London (North East)
Stansted 16
Harlow 8
Cambridge 41
27
A111
Potters Bar ½
24
A10
Enfield 3
Hertford 10
25
A121
Waltham Abbey 2
Loughton 3
26
M11
London (North East)
Stansted 16
Harlow 8
Cambridge 41
27
A12
A1023
Chelmsford 14
Romford 4
Brentwood 2
28
A127
Basildon 10
Southend 20
29
A12
A1023
Chelmsford 14
Brentwood 2
28
A13
(A1306 A126)
(A1090)
Dagenham 8
Thurrock(Lakeside) 2
Tilbury 8
Services
30/31
A127
Romford 5
Basildon 10
Southend 20
29
THURROCK SERVICES
A13
Dagenham 7
Rainham 5
Thurrock (Lakeside) 2
W Thurrock (A126)
30
A1306
(A1090 A126)
Thurrock (Lakeside) 2
Services
Purfleet 2
W Thurrock 2
31
Dartford Crossing
Tunnel (Northbound)
Bridge (Southbound)
River Thames
Toll
A206
Swanscombe 3½
Erith 4
Bluewater 2
1A
A206
Swanscombe(A226) 3½
Erith 4
1A
A225
A296
Dartford 1
1B
A2
M2
Canterbury 9
London 42
2
A2
London (South East & Central)
Bexleyheath 5
Canterbury (M2) 42
Dartford (A225) 2
2
A20
M20
London (South East & Central)
Lewisham 10
Dover 60
Channel Tunnel 50
Maidstone 19
3
A20
M20
London (South East & Central)
Lewisham 10
Dover 60
Channel Tunnel 50
Maidstone 19
3
A21
A224
Bromley 9
Orpington 3½
4
M23
Croydon 9
Gatwick 9
Crawley 13
East Grinstead 16
Brighton 34
7
A22
A25
Eastbourne 40
Godstone ¾
Caterham 2
Westerham 7
6
M26 (M20)
A21
Maidstone 18
Channel Tunnel 50
Sevenoaks 2
Hastings 40
5
A21
A224
London (South East)
Bromley 9
Orpington 3½
4
A21
A25
Sevenoaks 2
Hastings 40
5
CLACKET LANE SERVICES
M23
Brighton 34
Crawley 13
Gatwick 9
Croydon 9
7
A25
A22
East Grinstead 11
Eastbourne 40
Caterham 2
Godstone ¾
Redhill 6
6
2 Full junction
2 Restricted junction
Note: Mileage numbers shown on this diagram are not displayed on motorway signs and are for guidance only.

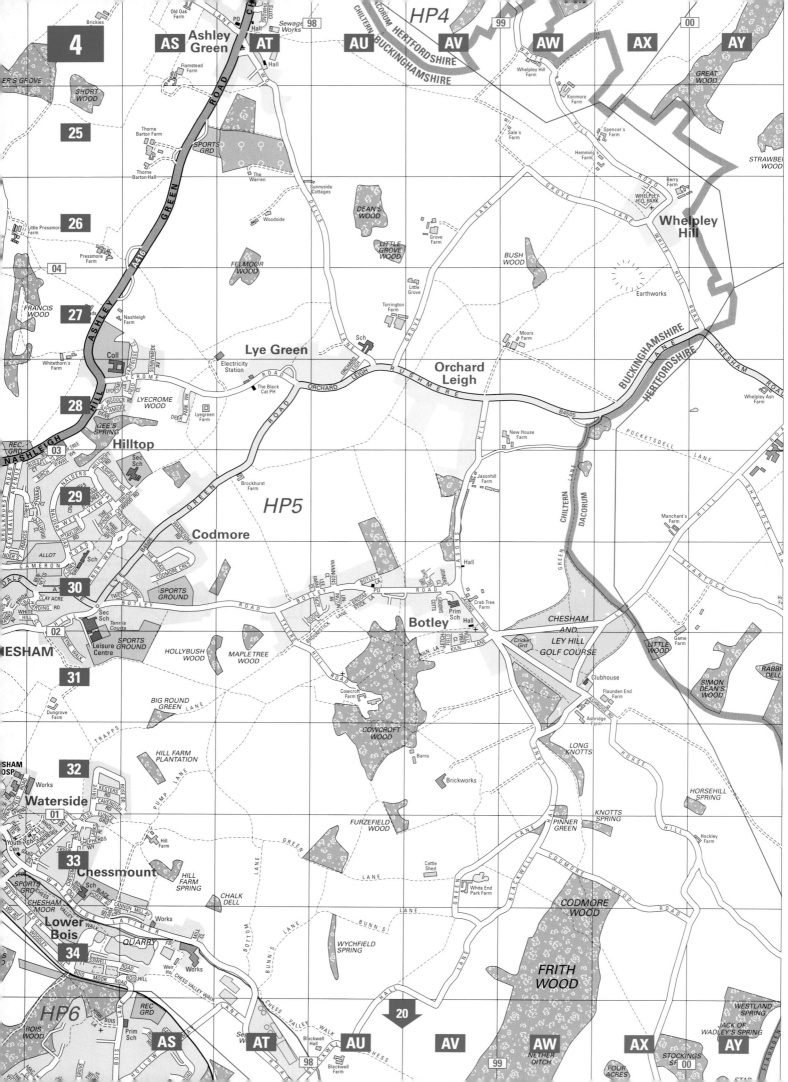

4
AS
AT
AU
AV
AW
AX
AY
HP4
HP5
HP6
98
99
00
04
03
02
01
25
26
27
28
29
30
31
32
33
34
20
Ashley Green
Old Oak Farm
Brickies
Sewage Works
Hall
PO
Flamstead Farm
SHORT WOOD
Thorne Barton Farm
Thorne Barton Hall
SPORTS GRD
The Warren
Sunnyside Cottages
Woodside
DELLS
DEAN'S WOOD
LITTLE GROVE WOOD
FELMOOR WOOD
Little Pressmore Farm
Pressmore Farm
FRANCIS WOOD
Nashleigh Farm
ASHLEY GREEN ROAD
A416
DACORUM HERTFORDSHIRE
CHILTERN BUCKINGHAMSHIRE
Whelpley Hill Farm
Kenmore Farm
Sale's Farm
Spencer's Farm
Hemming's Farm
Berry Farm
WHELPLEY HILL PARK
GREAT WOOD
STRAWBERRY WOOD
Whelpley Hill
GROVE LANE
WHITE HILL ROAD
Grove Farm
BUSH WOOD
Earthworks
Little Grove
Torrington Farm
Moors Farm
Lye Green
Sch
Orchard Leigh
Electricity Station
The Black Cat PH
ORCHARD LEIGH
RUSHMERE
B4505
BUCKINGHAMSHIRE LANE
HERTFORDSHIRE
CHESHAM ROAD
Whelpley Ash Farm
POCKETSDELL LANE
Coll
Whitethorn's Farm
LYECROME WOOD
Lyegreen Farm
GEE'S SPRING
Hilltop
NASHLEIGH HILL
REC GRD
Sec Sch
New House Farm
Jasonhill Farm
Brockhurst Farm
Codmore
CHILTERN LANE
DACORUM
Manchant's Farm
SHANTOCK
ALLOT
CAMERON
CODMORE CRES
SPORTS GROUND
Hall
Crab Tree Farm
Prim Sch
Botley
BOTLEY ROAD
CHESHAM AND LEY HILL GOLF COURSE
Cricket Grd
Clubhouse
LITTLE WOOD
Game Farm
SIMON DEAN'S WOOD
ESHAM
Leisure Centre
Tennis Courts
SPORTS GROUND
HOLLYBUSH WOOD
MAPLE TREE WOOD
Cowcroft Farm
BIG ROUND GREEN
Dungrove Farm
COWCROFT WOOD
Flaunden End Farm
Ashridge Farm
ASHRIDGE RD
LONG KNOTTS
HORSE HILL
HORSEHILL SPRING
TRAPPS
HILL FARM PLANTATION
Barns
Brickworks
Works
Waterside
PUMP LANE
Hill Farm
FURZEFIELD WOOD
PINNER GREEN
KNOTTS SPRING
Hockley Farm
Chessmount
HILL FARM SPRING
CHALK DELL
Cattle Shed
White End Park Farm
CODMORE WOOD ROAD
CODMORE WOOD
Lower Bois
QUARRY
Works
WYCHFIELD SPRING
BUNN'S LANE
BOTTOM
FRITH WOOD
REC GRD
BOIS WOOD
Prim Sch
CHESS VALLEY WALK
Blackwell Hall
Blackwell Farm
NETHER DITCH
FOUR ACRES
STOCKINGS SF
WESTLAND SPRING
JACK OF WADLEY'S SPRING

5
6
21
25
26
27
28
29
30
31
32
33
34
AZ
BA
BB
BC
BD
BE
BF
HP1
HP3
WD3
WD4
Bovingdon
Hogpits Bottom
Flaunden
Belsize
H.M. THE MOUNT PRISON
Disused Airfield
COLESHILL WOOD
HANGING WOOD
LITTLE HAY GOLF COMPLEX
BOXMOOR GOLF CLUB
SHEETHANGER COMMON
RAMACRE WOOD
GORSEFIELD WOOD
BURY WOOD
HAY WOOD
RAINHILL SPRING
RAINHILL DELL
KINGSHILL DELL
SHORTRIDGE WOOD
OLD DEAN
HOMEFIELD SPRING
BAKER'S WOOD
BOVINGDON GREEN
Bryants Nurseries
WOODMAN'S WOOD
LOWER PLANTATION
FLAUNDEN SPRING
LIMEDELL SPRING
HANGING CROFT
TOP SPRING
OLDCROFT WOOD
HANGINGLANE WOOD
BRAMBLE CROFT
DAFFODIL SPRING
ROSEHALL WOOD
DEBARDINE WOOD
PLOUGH WOOD
HILLMEADS SPRING
PENMAN'S GREEN
FIR WOOD
Felden
Chipperfield
Sarratt
DACORUM
THREE RIVERS
B4505
CHESHAM ROAD
HEMPSTEAD ROAD
BOX LANE
SHOTHANGER WAY
LONGCROFT LANE
FLAUNDEN LANE
BULSTRODE LANE
RUCKLERS LANE
CHIPPERFIELD ROAD
TOWER HILL
HOLLY HEDGES LANE
HOGPITS BOTTOM
BRAGMANS LANE
PLOUGH LANE
RED LION LANE
FLAUNDEN HILL
VENUS HILL
LONG LANE
BIRCH LANE
CHENIES HILL
OLLEBERRIE LANE
WINDMILL HILL
LITTLE WINDMILL HILL
Bricklayer's Arms PH
Bobsleigh Inn PH
The Boot PH
The Plough PH
Two Brewers PH
Cricket Ground
R.A.F. Chenies
Wyevale Garden Centre
Stoney Lane Nursery

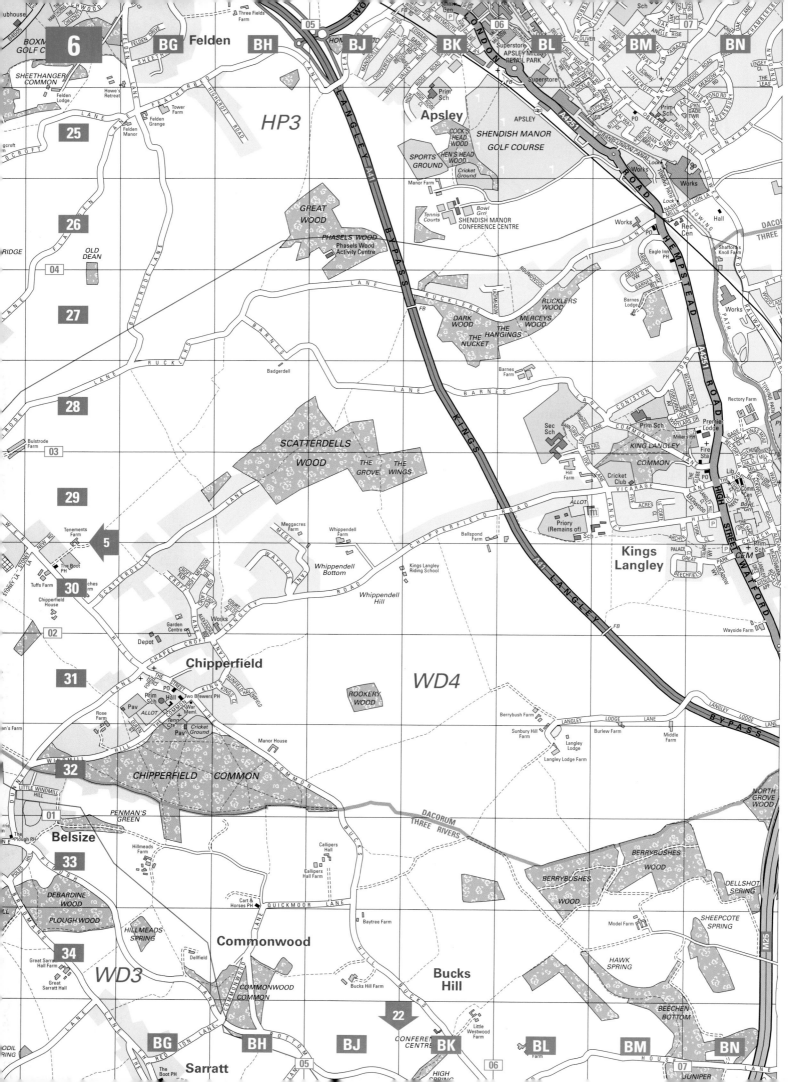
Felden
Apsley
HP3
SHENDISH MANOR GOLF COURSE
GREAT WOOD
PHASELS WOOD
SCATTERDELLS WOOD
Kings Langley
Chipperfield
WD4
CHIPPERFIELD COMMON
Belsize
Commonwood
Bucks Hill
WD3
Sarratt
BERRYBUSHES WOOD
DACORUM
THREE RIVERS
LANGLEY BYPASS A41
KINGS LANGLEY BYPASS
LONDON ROAD
HEMPSTEAD ROAD
A4251
M25
BG BH BJ BK BL BM BN
25 26 27 28 29 30 31 32 33 34
05 06 07
04 03 02 01
5
22

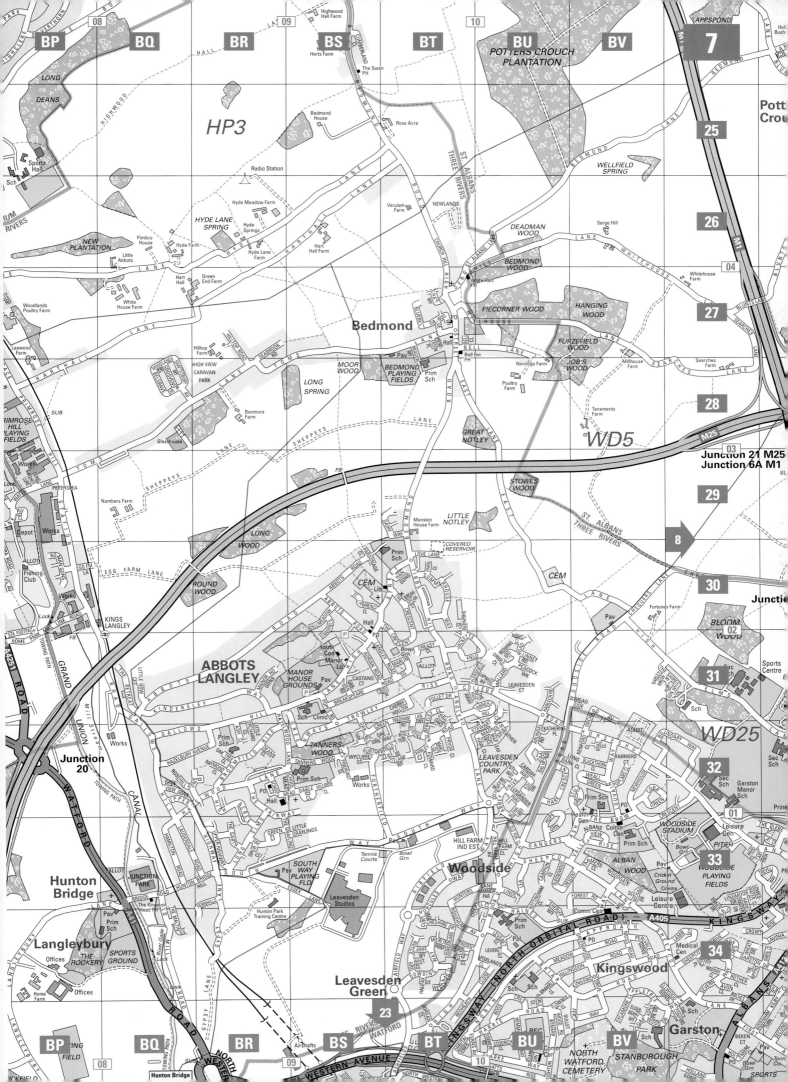

7
BP
BQ
BR
BS
BT
BU
BV
08
09
10
HP3
WD5
WD25
POTTERS CROUCH PLANTATION
LONG DEANS
NEW PLANTATION
HYDE LANE SPRING
Radio Station
Bedmond
BEDMOND WOOD
PIECORNER WOOD
HANGING WOOD
FURZEFIELD WOOD
JOB'S WOOD
DEADMAN WOOD
WELLFIELD SPRING
MOOR WOOD
LONG SPRING
BEDMOND PLAYING FIELDS
GREAT NOTLEY
LITTLE NOTLEY
STOWES WOOD
LONG WOOD
ROUND WOOD
BLOOM WOOD
Junction 21 M25
Junction 6A M1
M25
M1
ABBOTS LANGLEY
MANOR HOUSE GROUNDS
TANNERS WOOD
LEAVESDEN COUNTRY PARK
KINGS LANGLEY
Junction 20
Hunton Bridge
JUNCTION PARK
Langleybury
THE ROOKERY
SPORTS GROUND
SOUTH WAY PLAYING FLD
Leavesden Studios
Woodside
WOODSIDE STADIUM
WOODSIDE PLAYING FIELDS
ALBAN WOOD
Leavesden Green
Kingswood
Garston
NORTH WATFORD CEMETERY
STANBOROUGH PARK
GRAND UNION CANAL
WATFORD ROAD
NORTH ORBITAL ROAD
A405
KINGSWAY
NORTH WESTERN AVENUE
25
26
27
28
29
30
31
32
33
34
23
8

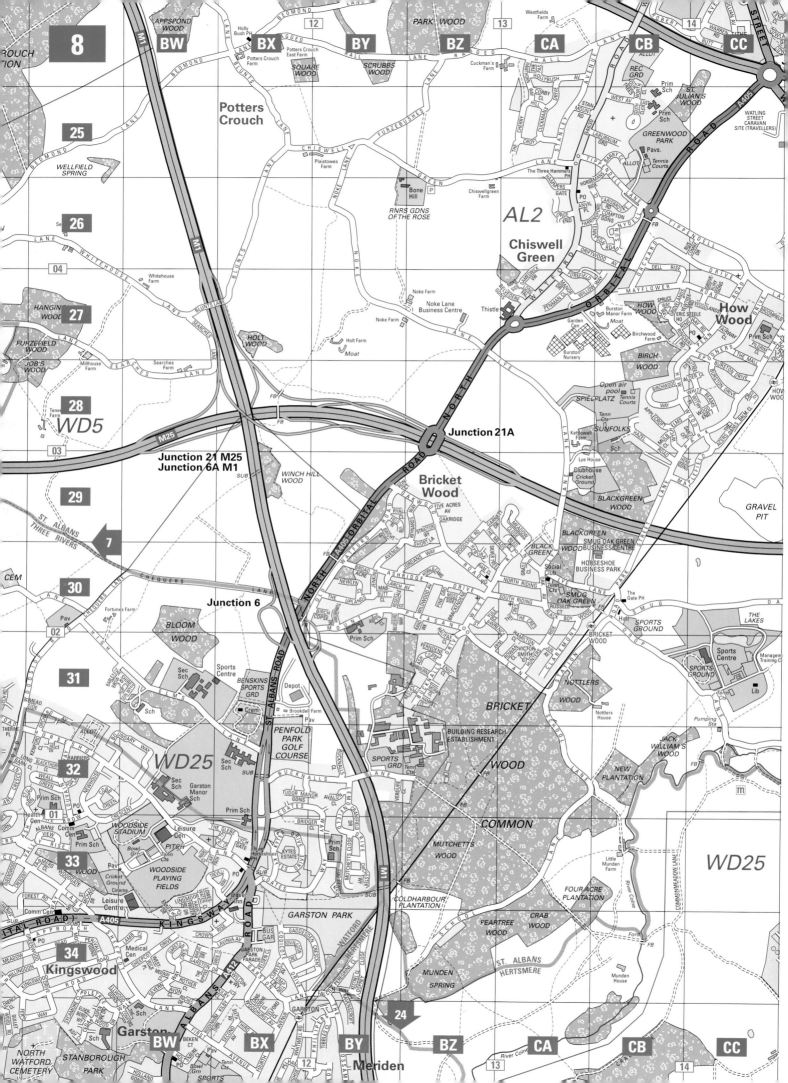

8
BW
BX
BY
BZ
CA
CB
CC
12
13
14
25
26
27
28
29
30
31
32
33
34
04
03
02
01
7
24
M1
M25
A405
A412
B4630
APPSPOND WOOD
PARK WOOD
Westfields Farm
Holly Bush PH
Potters Crouch East Farm
Potters Crouch Farm
SQUARE WOOD
SCRUBBS WOOD
Cuckman's Farm
REC GRD
Prim Sch
ST. JULIAN'S WOOD
WATLING STREET CARAVAN SITE (TRAVELLERS)
Potters Crouch
BEDMOND LANE
RAGGED HALL LANE
BLUNTS LANE
CHISWELL GREEN
FURZEBUSHES
GREENWOOD PARK
Pavs.
Tennis Courts
ALLOT
WELLFIELD SPRING
Plaistowes Farm
Bone Hill
RNRS GDNS OF THE ROSE
Chiswellgreen Farm
The Three Hammers PH
AL2
Chiswell Green
WHITEHOUSE LANE
Whitehouse Farm
Noke Farm
Noke Lane Business Centre
Thistle
HANGING WOOD
FURZEFIELD WOOD
JOB'S WOOD
Millhouse Farm
SEARCHES LANE
Searches Farm
HOLT WOOD
Holt Farm
Moat
Garden Cen
Burston Manor Farm
Burston Nursery
Birchwood Farm
How Wood
Prim Sch
BIRCH WOOD
Open air pool
SPIELPLATZ
Tennis Courts
SUNFOLKS
Tenner Farm
WD5
Junction 21A
Junction 21 M25
Junction 6A M1
WINCH HILL WOOD
Bricket Wood
Kettlewell Farm
Lye House
Clubhouse
Cricket Ground
BLACKGREEN WOOD
GRAVEL PIT
ST. ALBANS
THREE RIVERS
NORTH ORBITAL ROAD
SMUG OAK GREEN BUSINESS CENTRE
HORSESHOE BUSINESS PARK
Social Club
SMUG OAK GREEN
The Gate PH
THE LAKES
SPORTS GROUND
CEM
CHEQUERS LANE
Junction 6
Fortunes Farm
Pav
BLOOM WOOD
Prim Sch
BRICKET WOOD
Hall
Sports Centre
Management Training Centre
Lib
Sec Sch
Sports Centre
BENSKINS SPORTS GRD
Depot
Crem
Brookdell Farm
Pav
NOTTLERS WOOD
Nottlers House
BRICKET WOOD COMMON
Pumping Sta
JACK WILLIAM'S WOOD
ALLOT.
PENFOLD PARK GOLF COURSE
BUILDING RESEARCH ESTABLISHMENT
SPORTS GRD
WD25
Sec Sch
Garston Manor Sch
NEW PLANTATION
BUCKNALLS LANE
Prim Sch
Health Cen
Comm Cen
WOODSIDE STADIUM
Leisure Cen
PITCH
Three Horseshoes PH
KYTES ESTATE
Prim Sch
MUTCHETTS WOOD
Little Munden Farm
River Colne
COMMONMEADOW LANE
WD25
WOODSIDE PLAYING FIELDS
Cricket Ground
Cinema
Leisure Centre
Travel Inn
GARSTON PARK
COLDHARBOUR PLANTATION
FOUR ACRE PLANTATION
Comm Cen
KINGSWAY
BUS GAR
GARSTON PARK PARADE
PEARTREE WOOD
CRAB WOOD
Ford
FB
Medical Cen
WATFORD
HERTSMERE
ST. ALBANS
HERTSMERE
MUNDEN SPRING
Munden House
Kingswood
Sch
Garston
Sch
GARSTON
Meriden
BEKEN CT
NORTH WATFORD CEMETERY
STANBOROUGH PARK
Bowl Grn
Tenn Cts
SPORTS
River Colne

AL1
AL2
AL4
WD7
Park Street
Frogmore
Colney Street
LONDON COLNEY
RADLETT
HARPERBURY HOSPITAL
ALL SAINTS PASTORAL CENTRE
PORTERS PARK GOLF COURSE
SHENLEY PARK
Radlett Aerodrome (Disused)
GRAVEL PIT
QUARRY
COLNEY PARK
BROAD COLNEY LAKES NATURE RESERVE
NINE ACRES
HOUND'S WOOD
COW BANKS
Oakridge Lane Sewage Treatment Works
VERULAM GOLF COURSE
PARK INDUSTRIAL ESTATE
VENTURA PARK
Harper Lane Rail Depot
RADLETT GOLF CENTRE
Arsenal F.C. Training Grounds
NORTH ORBITAL ROAD
M25
A5183
A414
A1081
B556
B5378
WATLING STREET
RADLETT ROAD
HARPER LANE
SHENLEY LANE
SHENLEYBURY
BLACK LION
CD
CE
CF
CG
CH
CJ
CK
10
25
26
27
28
29
30
31
32
33
34

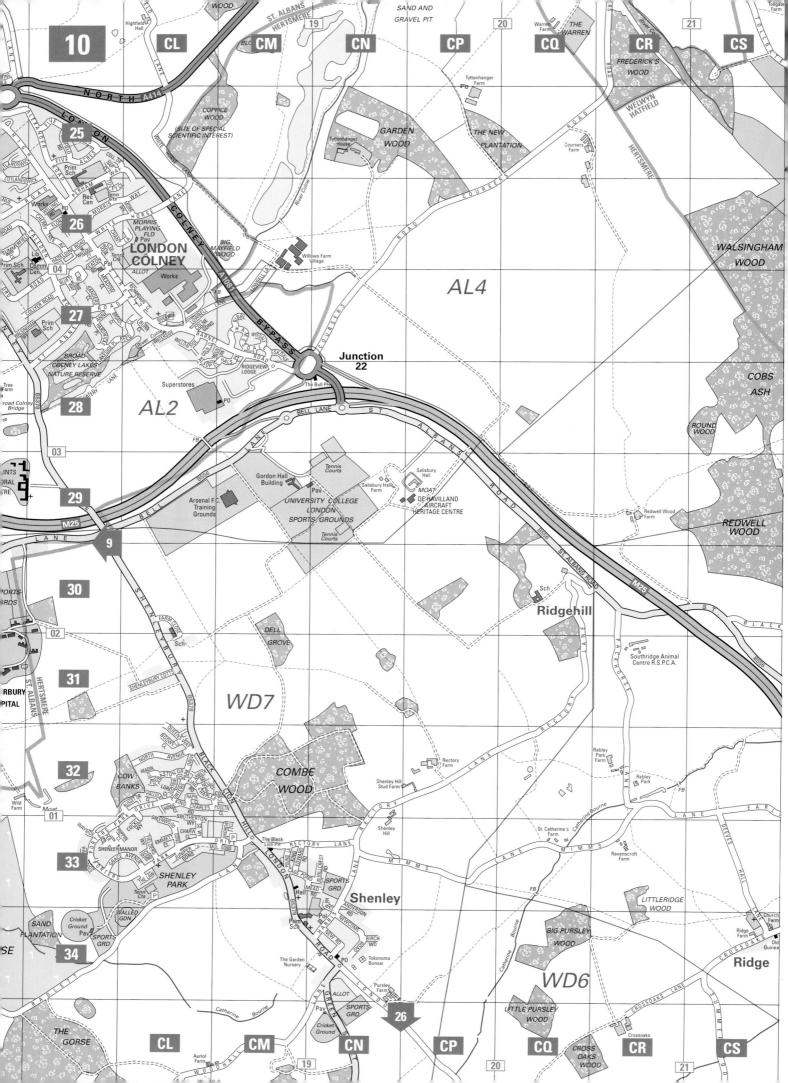

LONDON COLNEY
Shenley
Ridgehill
Ridge
AL4
AL2
WD7
WD6
Junction 22
NORTH ORBITAL A414
LONDON COLNEY BYPASS A1081
M25
COPPICE WOOD (SITE OF SPECIAL SCIENTIFIC INTEREST)
GARDEN WOOD
THE NEW PLANTATION
THE WARREN
FREDERICK'S WOOD
WELWYN HATFIELD
HERTSMERE
ST. ALBANS
WALSINGHAM WOOD
COBS ASH
ROUND WOOD
REDWELL WOOD
BROAD COLNEY LAKES NATURE RESERVE
BIG MAYFIELD WOOD
Willows Farm Village
Tyttenhanger Farm
Tyttenhanger House
Coursers Farm
COURSERS ROAD
SAND AND GRAVEL PIT
Superstores
The Bull PH
BELL LANE
Gordon Hall Building
UNIVERSITY COLLEGE LONDON SPORTS GROUNDS
Arsenal F.C. Training Grounds
Salisbury Hall
Salisbury Hall Farm
MOAT
DE HAVILLAND AIRCRAFT HERITAGE CENTRE
ST ALBANS ROAD
Redwell Wood Farm
Southridge Animal Centre R.S.P.C.A.
DELL GROVE
SHENLEYBURY
COMBE WOOD
COW BANKS
SHENLEY PARK
SHENLEY MANOR
SAND PLANTATION
THE GORSE
RECTORY LANE
Rectory Farm
Shenley Hill Stud Farm
Shenley Hill
St. Catherine's Farm
Ravenscroft Farm
Rabley Park Farm
Rabley Park
PACKHORSE LANE
MIMMS LANE
EARLS LANE
LITTLERIDGE WOOD
BIG PURSLEY WOOD
LITTLE PURSLEY WOOD
CROSS OAKS WOOD
CROSSOAKS LANE
Crossoaks
Church Farm
Ridge Farm
Old Guinea
The Black Lion PH
LONDON ROAD
The Garden Nursery
Tokonoma Bonsai
Pursley Farm
Auriol Farm
WOODHALL LANE
RADLETT LANE
Catherine Bourne
CL CM CN CP CQ CR CS
19 20 21
25 26 27 28 29 30 31 32 33 34
04 03 02 01
9
26

11
CT
CU
CV
CW
CX
CY
CZ
NORTH MYMMS PARK
Water End
BROOKMANS PARK
BROOKMANS PARK GOLF COURSE
PELPIN'S WOOD
ROUND WOOD
THE LEGG
BRICK KILN WOOD
CANGSLEY WOOD
HAWKSHEAD WOOD
MYMMSHALL WOOD
PILVAGE WOOD
FURZEFIELD WOOD
Royal Veterinary College (Hawkshead)
Royal Veterinary College (Boltons Park Farm)
GOBIONS OPEN SPACE
GOBIONS GARDEN
GOBIONS POND
SWALLOW HOLES
AL9
EN6
POTTERS BAR GOLF COURSE
KING GEORGE V PLAYING FLDS
CRANBORNE INDUSTRIAL ESTATE
SPORTS GROUND
South Mimms
South Mimms Services
Holiday Inn South Mimms
Days Inn
Cancer Research UK
Nat Inst for Biological Standards & Control
North Mymms Park Training Centre
Site of Motte & Baileys
Junction 23 (M25) Junction 1 A1(M)
Bentley Heath
POTTERS BAR
WELWYN HATFIELD
HERTSMERE
A1(M)
M25
B556
12
25
26
27
28
29
30
31
32
33
34
27

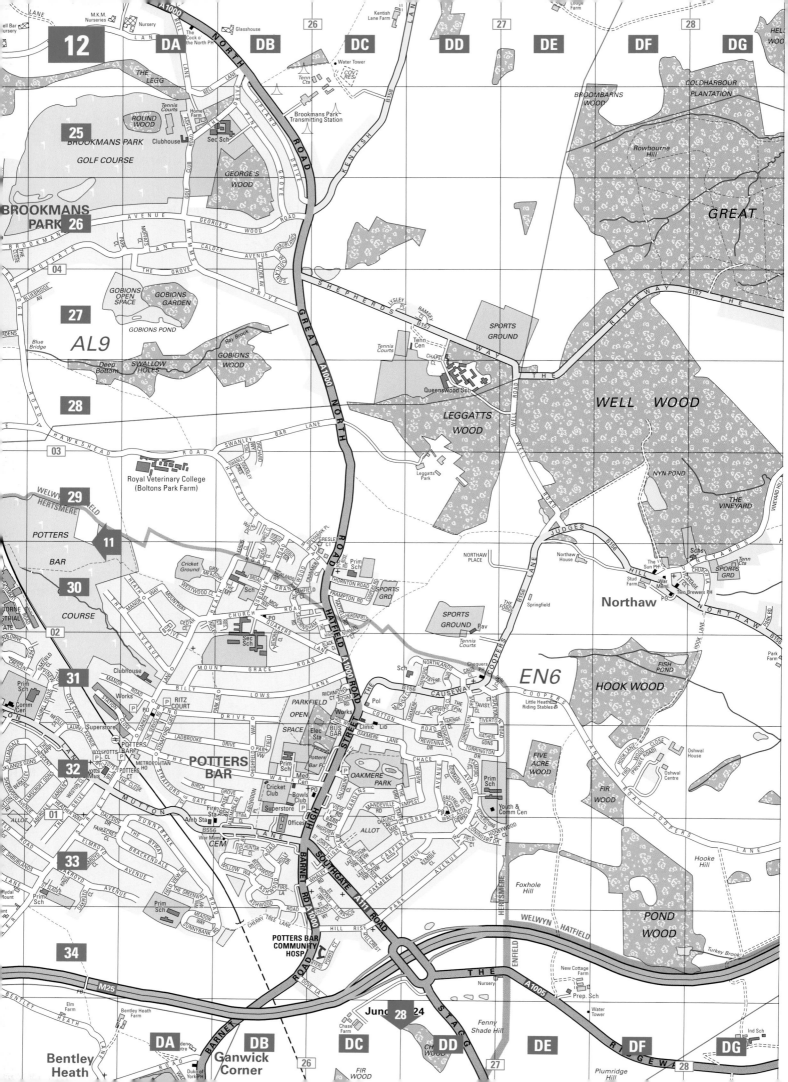

DA
DB
DC
DD
DE
DF
DG
26
27
28
A1000
NORTH
M.K.M. Nurseries
Nursery
Glasshouse
The Cock o' the North PH
Kentish Lane Farm
Water Tower
COV. RES.
Tenn Cts
THE LEGG
BELL LANE
Tennis Courts
Home Farm
ROUND WOOD
Clubhouse
Sec Sch
Brookmans Park Transmitting Station
BROOMBARNS WOOD
COLDHARBOUR PLANTATION
Rowbourne Hill
25
BROOKMANS PARK
GOLF COURSE
GEORGE'S WOOD
KENTISH
B158
GREAT
BROOKMANS PARK
26
AVENUE
GEORGE'S WOOD ROAD
CALDER AVENUE
MOFFATS LANE
THE GROVE
04
SHEPHERDS WAY
B157
RIDGEWAY
GOBIONS OPEN SPACE
GOBIONS GARDEN
27
GOBIONS POND
SPORTS GROUND
AL9
Blue Bridge
Ray Brook
GOBIONS WOOD
Deep Bottom
SWALLOW HOLES
Tennis Courts
Tenn Cen
Queenswood Sch
WELL WOOD
LEGGATTS WOOD
28
HAWKSHEAD ROAD
SWANLEY BAR LANE
03
Royal Veterinary College (Boltons Park Farm)
Leggatts Park
NYN POND
THE VINEYARD
29
WELWYN HATFIELD
HERTSMERE
POTTERS BAR
11
JUDGES HILL
B156
NORTHAW PLACE
Northaw House
The Sun PH
Schs
Stud Farm
War Meml
Two Brewers PH
SPORTS GRD
Tenn Cts
Northaw
Cricket Ground
30
COURSE
Prim Sch
Sch
THORNTON ROAD
FRAMPTON RD
SPORTS GRD
Springfield
THE FORGE
SPORTS GROUND
Pav
Tennis Courts
02
CHURCH ROAD
Sec Sch
MOUNT GRACE ROAD
Clubhouse
31
Prim Sch
Comm Cen
Works
RITZ COURT
BILLY LOWS LANE
PARKFIELD OPEN SPACE
Pol
Sch
CAUSEWAY
Chequers PH
EN6
HOOK WOOD
FISH POND
COOPERS LANE
Little Heath Riding Stables
Superstore
POTTERS BAR
Elec Sta
BUS GAR
Clinic
Lib
FIVE ACRE WOOD
Oshwal House
Oshwal Centre
32
Prim Sch
Potters Bar FC
OAKMERE PARK
Prim Sch
FIR WOOD
Cricket Club
Bowls Club
Superstore
Offices
Youth & Comm Cen
01
Fire Sta
Amb Sta
MUTTON LANE
B556
War Meml
CEM
ALLOT
33
Hooke Hill
Foxhole Hill
Prim Sch
Prim Sch
SOUTHGATE A111 ROAD
HIGH STREET
BARNET RD A1000
POND WOOD
34
POTTERS BAR COMMUNITY HOSP
HERTSMERE
ENFIELD
WELWYN HATFIELD
Turkey Brook
M25
New Cottage Farm
Nursery
Prep. Sch
Elm Farm
Bentley Heath Farm
Junc 28 24
Chase Farm
Fenny Shade Hill
Water Tower
THE RIDGEWAY
A1005
STAGG
Bentley Heath
Ganwick Corner
BARNET
FIR WOOD
Duke of York PH
Plumridge Hill
Ind Sch
27
28

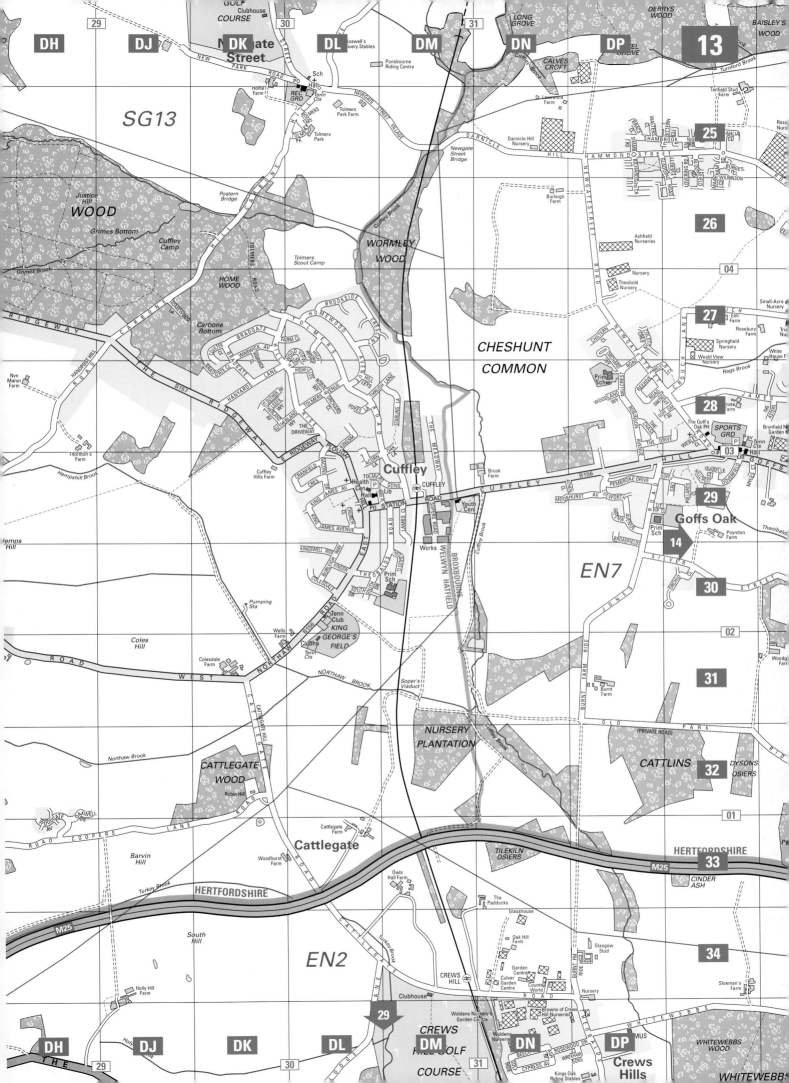
DH
DJ
DK
DL
DM
DN
DP
29
30
31
Newgate Street
GOLF COURSE
Clubhouse
Goswell's Livery Stables
Ponsbourne Riding Centre
LONG GROVE
DERRYS WOOD
BAISLEY'S WOOD
CALVES CROFT
Turnford Brook
Tanfield Stud Farm
NEW PARK ROAD
Home Farm
Sch
Hall
PO
REC GRD
Tenn Cts
Tolmers Park Farm
NEWGATE STREET VILLAGE
TOLMERS MS
TOLMERS PK
Tolmers Park
St. Lawrence Farm
Darnicle Hill Nursery
DARNICLE HILL
Newgate Street Bridge
HAMMOND STREET
SHAMBROOK
WALTERS CL
BUTTERN CL
BRACE CL
RICHARDSON CR
GLADDING RD
EVERETT CL
LOVERING RD
BLOOMFIELD RD
MARKHAM RD
BURGES CL
WILKINSON CL
DAHLIA CL
25
SG13
Justice Hill
WOOD
Grimes Bottom
Cuffley Camp
Grimes Brook
Postern Bridge
CARBONE HILL
TOLMERS ROAD
HOME WOOD
Tolmers Scout Camp
Cuffley Brook
WORMLEY WOOD
Burleigh Farm
NEWGATE STREET ROAD
Ashfield Nurseries
26
04
Nursery
Theobold Nursery
27
Small-Acre Nursery
Elm Farm
Rosebury Farm
Springfield Nursery
Weald View Nursery
Rags Brook
RIDGEWAY
HOMEWOOD LA
Carbone Bottom
HANDPOST HILL ROAD
Nyn Manor Farm
BROOKSIDE
HOMEWOOD
TOLMERS
CRESCENT
BRADGATE
FARM CL
COULTER
WARWICK AV
WOOD VIEW
RIDGE
HIGHFIELDS
ROBIN WY
TOLMERS AVENUE
ORCHARD CL
HANYARDS LANE
SUTHERLAND WY
THE DRIVEWAY
KINGSMEAD
FOXES LA
STARLING LA
THRUSH LANE
CHESHUNT COMMON
CHILTERN CL
NEWGATE STREET
COLSTON CRES
ORCHARD RD
MILLCREST
BEEHIVE LA
WOODLAND WY
ROBINSON AVENUE
THE CHASE
THE DRIVE
CROUCH LANE
Prim Sch
28
JAMES
Brynfield Nursery Garden
The Goff's Oak PH
SPORTS GRD
Pav
Tenn Cts
Hall
Lib
03
WESLEY CL
GOFFS
B157
THE RIDGEWAY
Thornton's Farm
Hempshill Brook
Cuffley Hills Farm
PLOUGH HILL
CRANFIELD CRES
BACONS DR
ACORN LA
OAK LA
Cuffley
CUFFLEY
Health Cen
P
Hall
Lib
TOLMERS GDNS
KING JAMES AV
CHURCH CL
STATION ROAD
PO
THE MEADWAY
SOPERS ROAD
Brook Farm
Youth Cen
CUFFLEY ROAD
B156
ATHEN CL
MOORHURST AV
PEMBROKE DRIVE
ISABELLE CL
HILLCREST
DOVERFIELD
POLLARDS
29
Goffs Oak
Prim Sch
14
Poynden Farm
Theobalds
BROADFIELDS
SILVER ST
Hemps Hill
JAMES AVENUE
KINGSWELL RIDE
BURLEIGH WAY
KINGSW
COLESDALE
EAST RIDGEWAY
THEOBALDS
SOUTH DR
Prim Sch
Works
Cuffley Brook
WELWYN HATFIELD
BROXBOURNE
EN7
JONES
ORCHARD CL
30
STREET
Pumping Sta
Coles Hill
Wells Farm
Tenn Club
KING GEORGE'S FIELD
Clubho
Tenn Cts
NORTHAW ROAD
02
Colesdale Farm
ROAD WEST
BURNT FARM RIDE
Burnt Farm
31
NORTHAW BROOK
Soper's Viaduct
CATTLEGATE HILL
OLD PARK RIDE
(PRIVATE ROAD)
NURSERY PLANTATION
Northaw Brook
CATTLEGATE WOOD
Robin Hill
CATTLINS
32
DYSONS OSIERS
01
WOODGATE AV
OAKWELL DR
COOPERS LANE ROAD
Cattlegate Farm
Cattlegate
TILEKILN OSIERS
HERTFORDSHIRE
M25
33
CINDER ASH
Barvin Hill
Woodhurst Farm
Owls Hall Farm
Turkey Brook
HERTFORDSHIRE
M25
The Paddocks
Glasshouse
Oak Hill Farm
Glasgow Stud
34
South Hill
EN2
CATTLEGATE ROAD
Turkey Brook
CREWS HILL
Garden Centre
Culver Garden Centre
Country World
BURNT FM RIDE
Nursery
Sloeman's Farm
Holly Hill Farm
Clubhouse
ROAD
29
Woldens Nursery & Garden Centre
Browns of Crews Hill Nurseries
WHITEWEBBS
CREWS HILL GOLF COURSE
Woldens Nurseries
ROSEWOOD DR
WROXHAM GDNS
MUS
WHITEWEBBS WOOD
DH
DJ
DK
DL
DM
DN
DP
THE
29
30
31
BEECH
CYPRESS AV
Kings Oak Riding Stables
Crews Hills
WHITEWEBBS

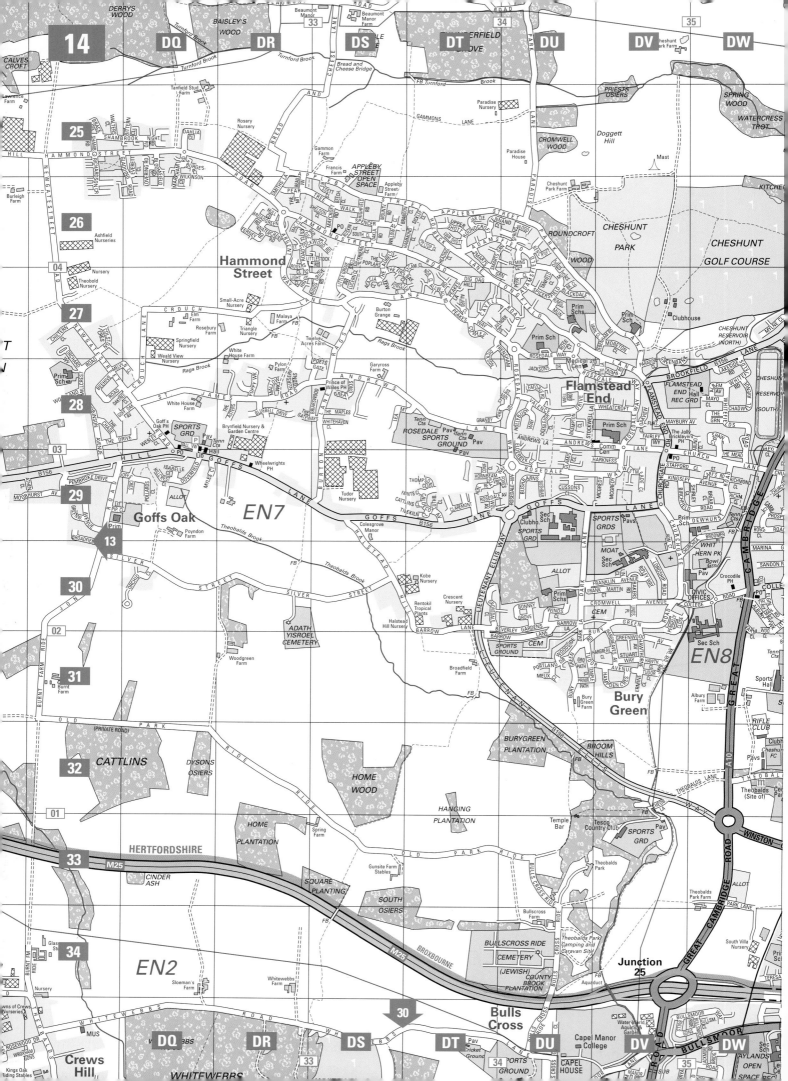
DQ
DR
DS
DT
DU
DV
DW
33
34
35
DERRYS WOOD
BAISLEY'S WOOD
CALVES CROFT
Turnford Brook
Beaumont Manor
Beaumont Manor Farm
Bread and Cheese Bridge
FB Turnford
Brook
Tanfield Stud Farm
Lawrence Farm
PRIESTS OSIERS
SPRING WOOD
WATERCRESS TROT
Paradise Nursery
GAMMONS
LANE
Rosary Nursery
25
SHAMBROOK
HAMMOND STREET
HILL
NEWGATESTREET
DAHLIA CL
Gammon Farm
Francis Farm
APPLEBY STREET OPEN SPACE
Appleby Street Farm
CROMWELL WOOD
Doggett Hill
Paradise House
Mast
Cheshunt Park Farm
Burleigh Farm
KITCHEN
26
Ashfield Nurseries
APPLEBY STREET
ROUNDCROFT
CHESHUNT PARK
CHESHUNT GOLF COURSE
WOOD
Hammond Street
04
Nursery
Theobold Nursery
Small-Acre Nursery
DIG DAG HILL
Prim Schs
Prim Sch
Clubhouse
27
CROUCH
Elm Farm
Rosebury Farm
Malaya Farm
Burton Grange
Triangle Nursery
Springfield Nursery
Weald View Nursery
Twelve Acres Farm
Rags Brook
White House Farm
CHESHUNT RESERVOIR (NORTH)
Prim Sch
Pylon Farm
POETS GATE
Garyross Farm
ROSEDALE WAY
Medical Cen
BROOKFIELD
B156
Prince of Wales PH
ANDREWS
Flamstead End
FLAMSTEAD END REC GRD
CHESHUNT RESERVOIR (SOUTH)
28
ST JAMES
White House Farm
Goff's Oak PH
SPORTS GRD
Pav
Tenn Cts
Hall
Lib
PO
Brynfield Nursery & Garden Centre
Tenn Cts
ROSEDALE SPORTS GROUND
Pav
Prim Sch
MAYBURY AV
The Jolly Bricklayers PH
03
B156
PEMBROKE DRIVE
HILL
GOFFS
Wheelwrights PH
LANE
Tudor Nursery
ROSEDALE
CHURCH
29
ALLOT
EN7
GOFFS
B156
Goffs Oak
Poyndon Farm
Colesgrove Manor
Theobalds Brook
13
Sec Sch
Clubho
SPORTS GRD
SPORTS GRDS
Pavs
MOAT
Sec Sch
Prim Sch
30
SILVER STREET
FB
Theobalds Brook
Kobe Nursery
Crescent Nursery
Rentokil Tropical Plants
Halstead Hill Nursery
ADATH YISROEL CEMETERY
ALLOT
Prim Schs
CEM
CIVIC OFFICES
Crocodile PH
02
BARROW LANE
BEVERLEY GARDENS
SPORTS GROUND
CEM
Sec Sch
EN8
Woodgreen Farm
Broadfield Farm
31
Burnt Farm
Bury Green Farm
Bury Green
Albury Farm
Sports Hall
LIEUTENANT ELLIS WAY
OLD PARK
(PRIVATE ROAD)
BURYGREEN PLANTATION
BROOM HILLS
RIFLE CLUB
Cheshunt FC
Pavs
32
CATTLINS
DYSONS OSIERS
HOME WOOD
THEOBALDS LANE
Theobalds (Site of)
A10
01
HANGING PLANTATION
Temple Bar
Tesco Country Club
SPORTS GRD
Pav
WINSTON
HOME PLANTATION
Spring Farm
HERTFORDSHIRE
33
M25
OLD PARK RIDE
CINDER ASH
Gunsite Farm Stables
Theobalds Park
SQUARE PLANTING
SOUTH OSIERS
Theobalds Park Farm
PARK LANE
ALLOT
GREAT CAMBRIDGE ROAD
Bullscross Farm
BULLSCROSS RIDE CEMETERY (JEWISH)
Theobalds Park Camping and Caravan Site
34
EN2
BROXBOURNE
M25
COUNTY BROOK PLANTATION
Junction 25
South Villa Nursery
Nursery
Sloeman's Farm
Whitewebbs Farm
Aquaduct
30
WHITEWEBBS ROAD
Bulls Cross
Water World, Aquatics & Garden
BULLSMOOR
MUS
DQ
DR
DS
DT
DU
DV
DW
Pav
Cricket Ground
Capel Manor College
Crews Hill
33
34
SPORTS GROUND
CAPEL HOUSE
35
WHITEWEBBS

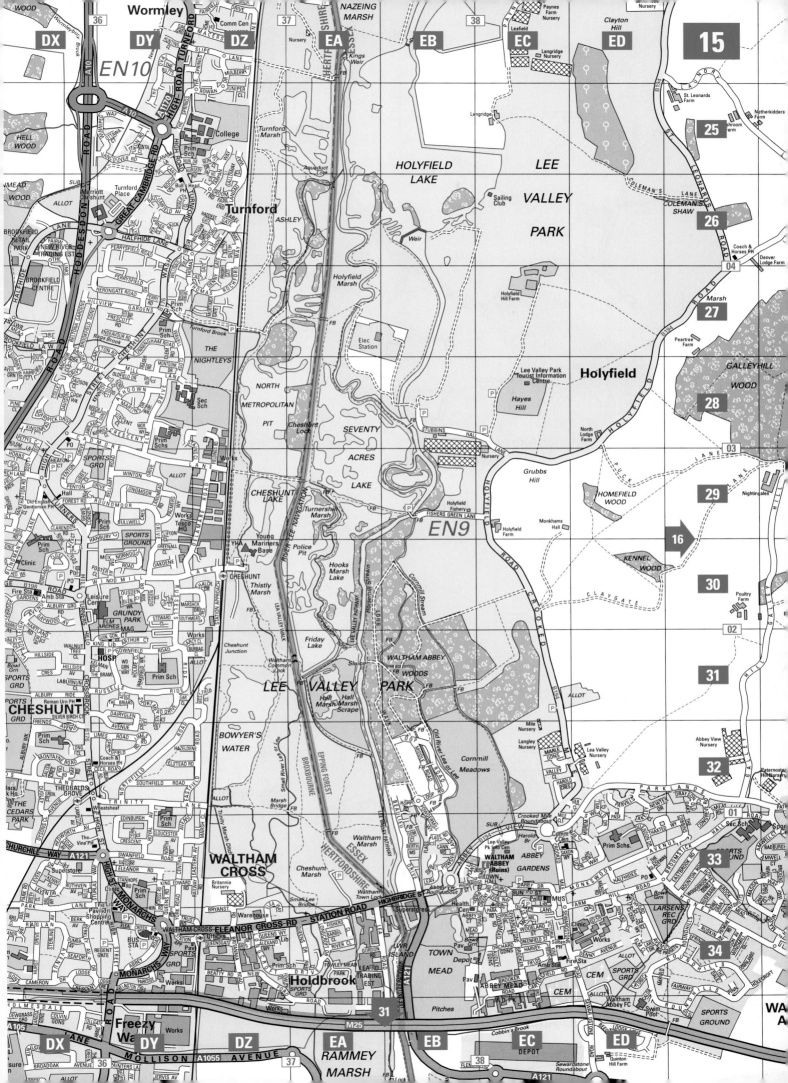
15
DX
DY
DZ
EA
EB
EC
ED
36
37
38
Wormley
NAZEING MARSH
Paynes Farm Nursery
Leafield
Clayton Hill
Langridge Nursery
Kings Weir
EN10
HELL WOOD
College
Turnford Marsh
St. Leonards Farm
Netherkidders Farm
25
HOLYFIELD LAKE
LEE VALLEY PARK
Sailing Club
Turnford
ASHLEY
Weir
COLEMAN'S SHAW
26
Coach & Horses PH
Denver Lodge Farm
04
BROOKFIELD RETAIL PARK
NEW RIVER TRADING EST
BROOKFIELD CENTRE
Holyfield Marsh
Holyfield Hill Farm
Marsh
27
Peartree Farm
THE NIGHTLEYS
Elec Station
Lee Valley Park Tourist Information Centre
Holyfield
GALLEYHILL WOOD
NORTH METROPOLITAN PIT
Cheshunt Lock
Hayes Hill
28
SEVENTY ACRES LAKE
North Lodge Farm
03
CHESHUNT LAKE
Turnershill Marsh
Grubbs Hill
HOMEFIELD WOOD
29
Nightingales
EN9
Holyfield Fishery
Holyfield Farm
Monkhams Hall
16
Young Mariners Base
Police Pit
Hooks Marsh Lake
KENNEL WOOD
Thistly Marsh
CHESHUNT
30
Poultry Farm
GRUNDY PARK
Friday Lake
Cheshunt Junction
02
WALTHAM ABBEY WOODS
31
CHESHUNT
LEE VALLEY PARK
Hall Marsh
Hall Marsh Scrape
BOWYER'S WATER
Mile Nursery
Langley Nursery
Abbey View Nursery
Cornmill Meadows
Lea Valley Nursery
32
Paternoster Hill Nursery
THE CEDARS PARK
Marsh Bridge
01
Crooked Mile Roundabout
Waltham Marsh
WALTHAM CROSS
Cheshunt Marsh
Lee Valley Pk Info Cen
WALTHAM ABBEY (Ruins)
ABBEY GARDENS
Prim Schs.
33
Britannia Nursery
Waltham Town Lock
LARSENS REC GRD
TOWN MEAD
34
Holdbrook
LEA ROAD TRADING EST
CEM
Pitches
Waltham Abbey FC
SPORTS GROUND
31
M25
Freezy Water
Works
DX
DY
DZ
EA
EB
EC
ED
RAMMEY MARSH
DEPOT
Sewardstone Roundabout
Quinton Hill Farm
MOLLISON AVENUE
A1055
A121
A10
A105
B194
B198
B176
36
37
38

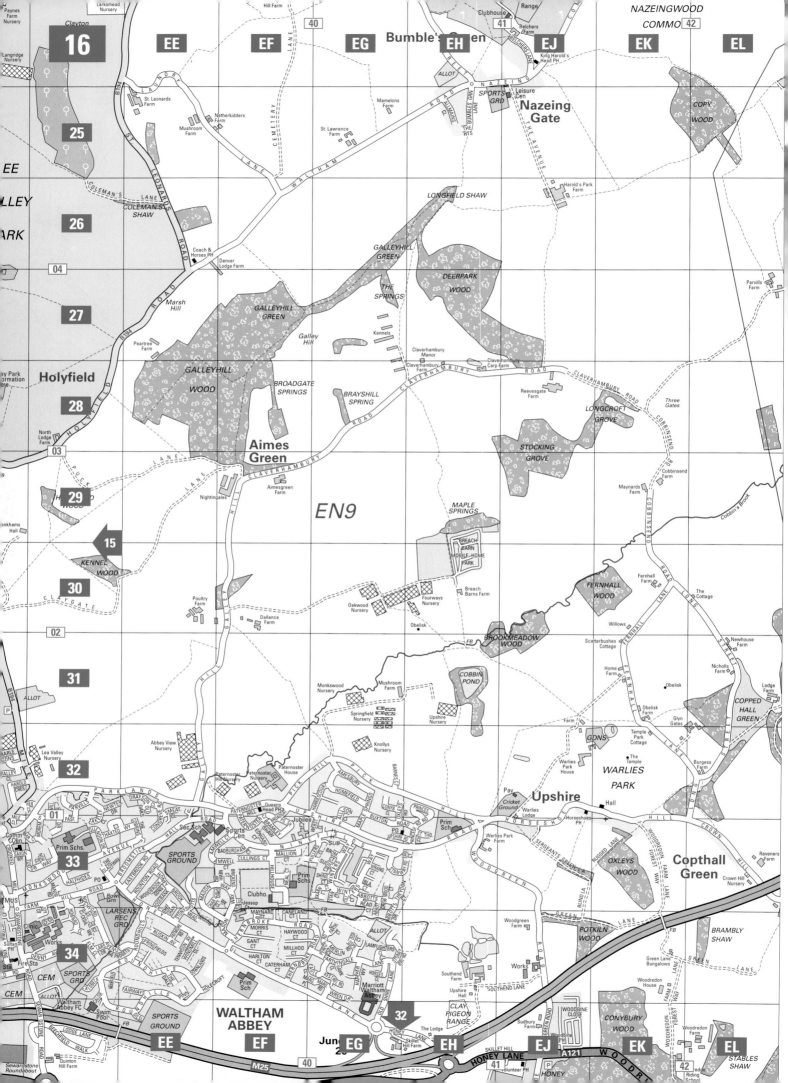
16
EE
EF
EG
EH
EJ
EK
EL
40
41
42
Bumble's Green
Nazeing Gate
NAZEINGWOOD COMMO
Clayton
Holyfield
Aimes Green
EN9
Upshire
WARLIES PARK
Copthall Green
WALTHAM ABBEY
Marsh Hill
Galley Hill
GALLEYHILL WOOD
GALLEYHILL GREEN
BROADGATE SPRINGS
BRAYSHILL SPRING
DEERPARK WOOD
THE SPRINGS
LONGFIELD SHAW
COLEMAN'S SHAW
LONGCROFT GROVE
STOCKING GROVE
MAPLE SPRINGS
FERNHALL WOOD
BROOKMEADOW WOOD
COBBIN POND
COPPED HALL GREEN
OXLEYS WOOD
POTKILN WOOD
BRAMBLY SHAW
CONYBURY WOOD
STABLES SHAW
COPY WOOD
KENNEL WOOD
25
26
27
28
29
30
31
32
33
34
15
04
03
02
01
Honey Lane
M25
A121
B194
Cobbin's Brook

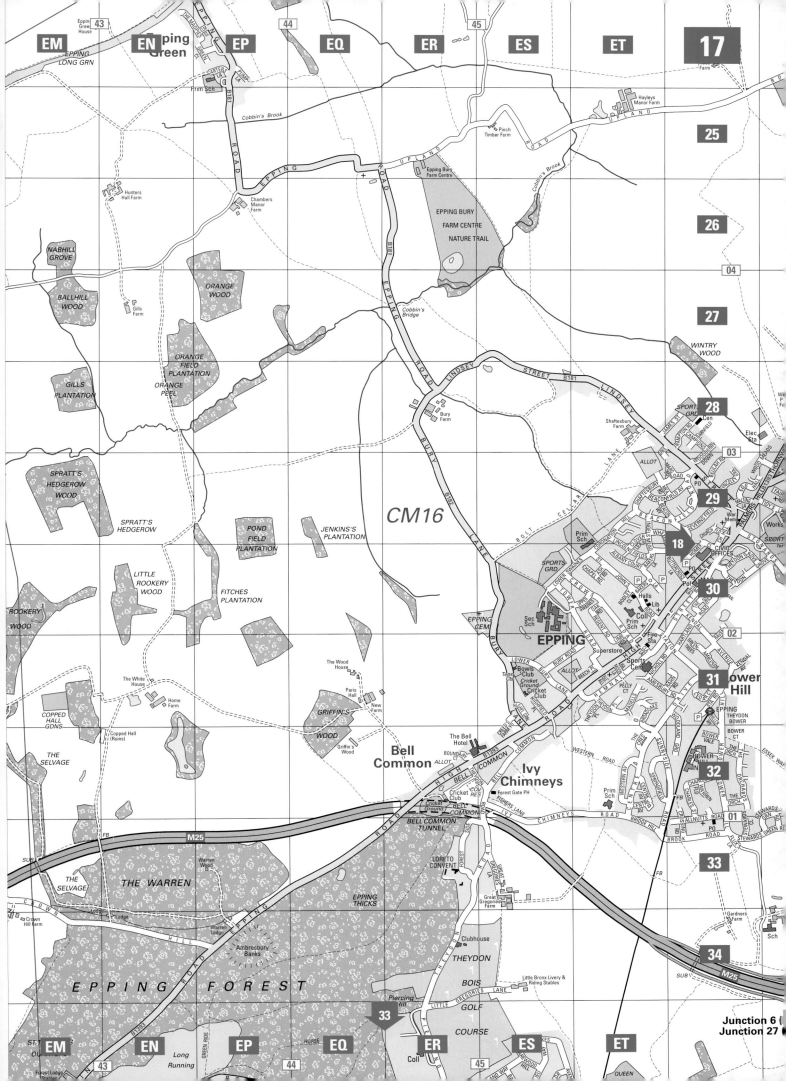

17
EM
EN
EP
EQ
ER
ES
ET
Epping Green
EPPING LONG GRN
Prim Sch
Cobbin's Brook
EPPING ROAD
EPPING UPLAND
UPLAND ROAD
Hayleys Manor Farm
Pinch Timber Farm
Epping Bury Farm Centre
EPPING BURY FARM CENTRE NATURE TRAIL
Hunters Hall Farm
Chambers Manor Farm
NABHILL GROVE
BALLHILL WOOD
ORANGE WOOD
Gills Farm
Cobbin's Bridge
ORANGE FIELD PLANTATION
ORANGE PEEL
GILLS PLANTATION
WINTRY WOOD
LINDSEY STREET
Bury Farm
Shaftesbury Farm
SPRATT'S HEDGEROW WOOD
SPRATT'S HEDGEROW
POND FIELD PLANTATION
JENKINS'S PLANTATION
CM16
BURY LANE
BOLT CELLAR LANE
LITTLE ROOKERY WOOD
FITCHES PLANTATION
ROOKERY WOOD
EPPING CEM
Sec Sch
EPPING
Superstore
Sports Cen
CIVIC OFFICES
The Wood House
Paris Hall
New Farm
The White House
Home Farm
GRIFFIN'S WOOD
Griffin's Wood
COPPED HALL GDNS
Copped Hall (Ruins)
THE SELVAGE
The Bell Hotel
Bell Common
Ivy Chimneys
Forest Gate PH
IVY CHIMNEYS ROAD
BELL COMMON TUNNEL
M25
THE WARREN
THE SELVAGE
LORETO CONVENT
Great Gregories Farm
EPPING THICKS
Crown Hill Farm
Ambresbury Banks
Clubhouse
THEYDON BOIS GOLF COURSE
Little Bronx Livery & Riding Stables
EPPING FOREST
Piercing Hill
Gardners Farm
Junction 6
Junction 27
Long Running
Coll
18
25
26
27
28
29
30
31
32
33
34
43
44
45
04
03
02
01

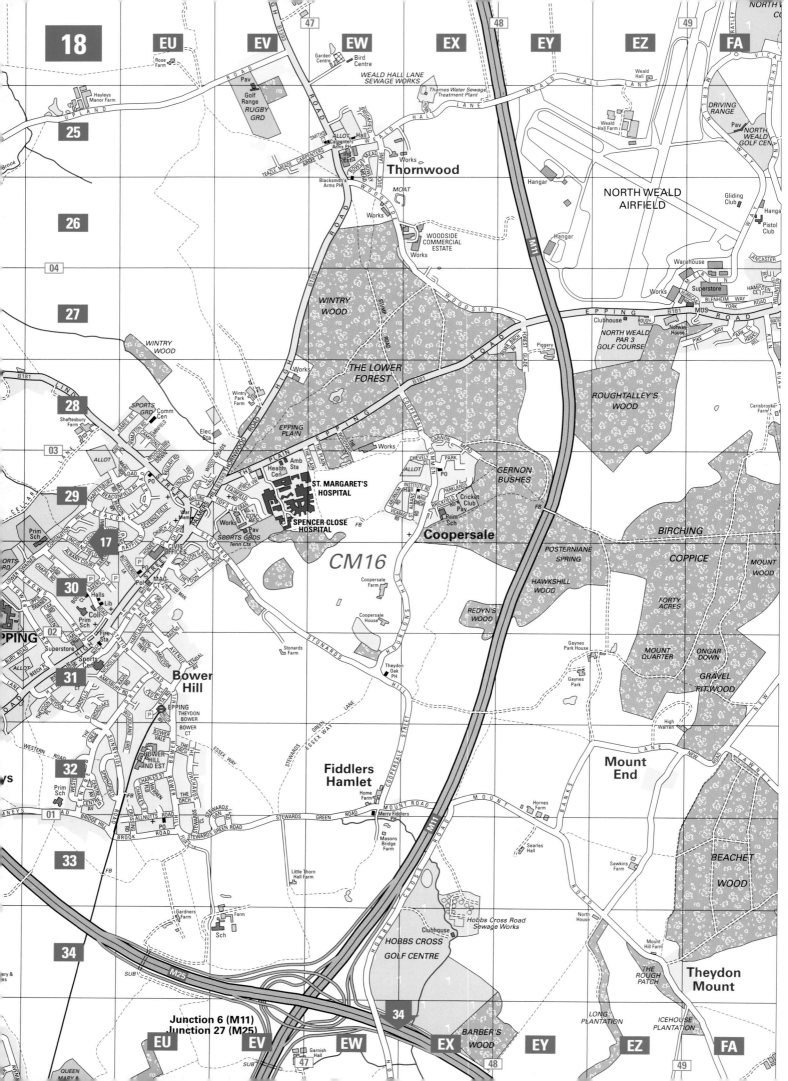
EU
EV
EW
EX
EY
EZ
FA
47
48
49
Rose Farm
Hayleys Manor Farm
UPLAND ROAD
Pav
Golf Range
RUGBY GRD
Garden Centre
Bird Centre
WEALD HALL LANE SEWAGE WORKS
Thames Water Sewage Treatment Plant
WEALD HALL LANE
Weald Hall
Weald Hall Farm
DRIVING RANGE
NORTH WEALD GOLF CEN
Thornwood
Works
MOAT
Blacksmith's Arms PH
Carpenters Arms PH
ALLOT
Hall
Ind Est
TEAZLE MEADE
CARPENTERS ARMS LA
BROOKFIELD
ROWLEY MEAD
DUCK LANE
Hangar
NORTH WEALD AIRFIELD
Gliding Club
Pistol Club
WOODSIDE COMMERCIAL ESTATE
Works
M11
Warehouse
Superstore
BLENHEIM WAY
YORK ROAD
EPPING ROAD
B181
MUS
Clubhouse
NORTH WEALD PAR 3 GOLF COURSE
Norway House
PIKE WAY
WINTRY WOOD
STUMP ROAD
WOODSIDE
B1393
HIGH ROAD
THE LOWER FOREST
SILVER BIRCH AV
FOREST GLADE
Piggery
ROUGHTALLEY'S WOOD
Carisbrooke Farm
Wintry Park Farm
Works
SPORTS GRD
Comm Cen
Shaftesbury Farm
Elec Sta
EPPING PLAIN
THORNWOOD ROAD
COOPERSALE COMMON
GARNON MEAD
CHEVELY CL
ALLOT
PARK
PO
GERNON BUSHES
Amb Sta
Health Cen
ST. MARGARET'S HOSPITAL
SPENCER CLOSE HOSPITAL
INSTITUTE RD
Hall
Cricket Club
Pav
Prim Sch
FB
Coopersale
SPORTS GRDS
Tenn Cts
CM16
BIRCHING COPPICE
POSTERNIANE SPRING
HAWKSHILL WOOD
MOUNT WOOD
FORTY ACRES
REDYN'S WOOD
Coopersale Farm
Coopersale House
Gaynes Park House
Gaynes Park
MOUNT QUARTER
ONGAR DOWN
GRAVEL PITWOOD
Stonards Farm
STONARDS HILL
HOUBLONS HILL
Theydon Oak PH
High Warren
EPPING
Superstore
Sports Cen
Prim Sch
Coll
Lib
Halls
Fire Sta
CIVIC OFFICES
MAG CT
Pol
PO
War Mem
Bower Hill
EPPING
THEYDON BOWER
BOWER CT
BOWER VALE
BOWER HILL IND EST
ESSEX WAY
STEWARDS GREEN
LANE
WESTERN ROAD
Fiddlers Hamlet
COOPERSALE STREET
Home Farm
Mount End
LANE
NEW ROAD
TAWNEY
MOUNT ROAD
Merry Fiddlers
STEWARDS GREEN ROAD
Hornes Farm
BANKS
Searles Hall
Masons Bridge Farm
Prim Sch
BRIDGE HILL
BROOK ROAD
PO
Sawkins Farm
BEACHET WOOD
Little Thorn Hall Farm
FB
HOBBS CROSS ROAD
Hobbs Cross Road Sewage Works
North House
Gardners Farm
Farm
Sch
Clubhouse
HOBBS CROSS GOLF CENTRE
Mount Hill Farm
THE ROUGH PATCH
Theydon Mount
M25
SUB
Junction 6 (M11)
Junction 27 (M25)
34
LONG PLANTATION
ICEHOUSE PLANTATION
BARBER'S WOOD
Garnish Hall
25
26
27
28
29
30
31
32
33
34
04
03
02
01
17

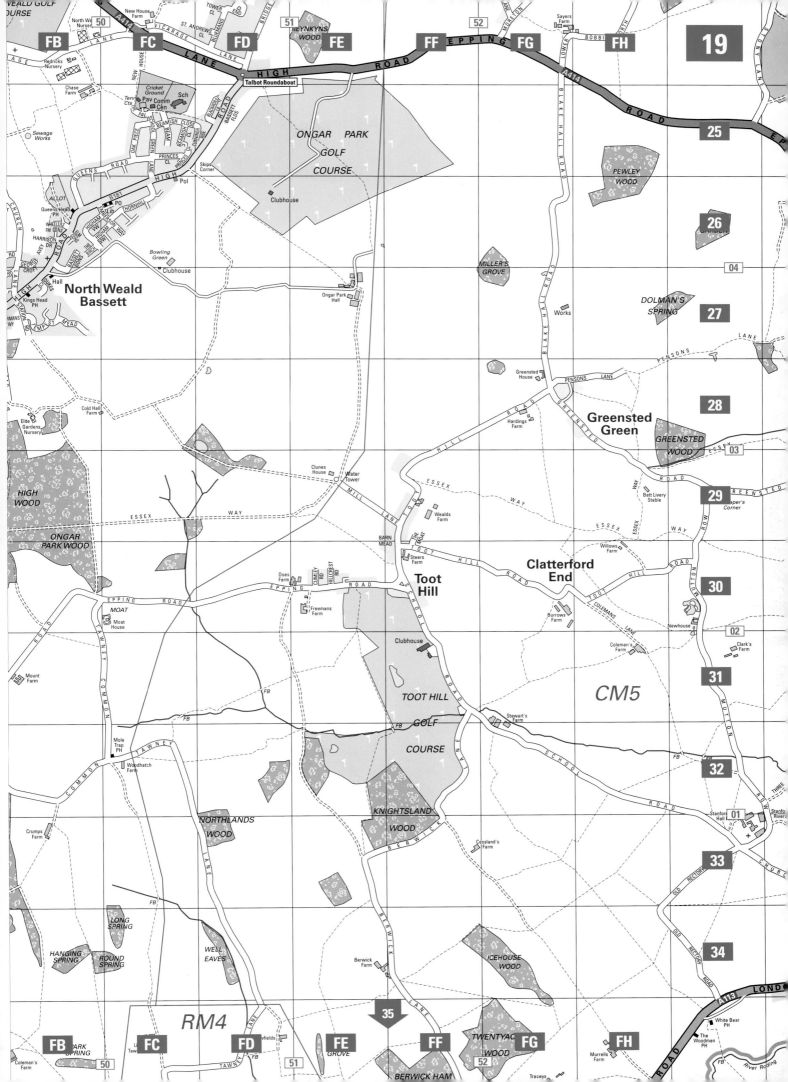
19
FB
FC
FD
FE
FF
FG
FH
50
51
52
North Weald Bassett
Talbot Roundabout
ONGAR PARK GOLF COURSE
Clubhouse
HIGH ROAD
EPPING ROAD
A414
LANE
VICARAGE LANE
New House Farm
Chase Farm
Sewage Works
Cricket Ground
Pav
Comm Cen
Sch
ALLOT
Queens Head PH
PO
Lib
Pol
Bowling Green
Clubhouse
Hall
Kings Head PH
Ongar Park Hall
Skips Corner
PEWLEY WOOD
MILLER'S GROVE
DOLMAN'S SPRING
Works
Sayers Farm
BLAKE HALL ROAD
Greensted House
PENSONS LANE
Hardings Farm
Greensted Green
GREENSTED WOOD
Cold Hall Farm
Elite Gardens Nursery
HIGH WOOD
ONGAR PARK WOOD
ESSEX WAY
Clunes House
Water Tower
MILL LANE
TOOT HILL ROAD
Wealds Farm
Batt Livery Stable
Willows Farm
Clatterford End
Toot Hill
BARN MEAD
THE MOAT
Steers Farm
Does Farm
CUMLEY RD
HILLCREST RD
Freemans Farm
MOAT
Moat House
Mount Farm
TAWNEY COMMON
Burrows Farm
Coleman's Farm
Newhouse
Clark's Farm
CM5
TOOT HILL GOLF COURSE
Stewart's Farm
SCHOOL ROAD
Mole Trap PH
Woodhatch Farm
KNIGHTSLAND WOOD
NORTHLANDS WOOD
Crumps Farm
Cessland's Farm
BERWICK LANE
MUTTON ROW
OLD RECTORY ROAD
LONG SPRING
HANGING SPRING
ROUND SPRING
WELL EAVES
ICEHOUSE WOOD
Berwick Farm
RM4
35
A113
White Bear PH
The Woodman PH
Murrells Farm
River Roding
TWENTYAC WOOD
BERWICK HAM
25
26
27
28
29
30
31
32
33
34
04
03
02
01
FB

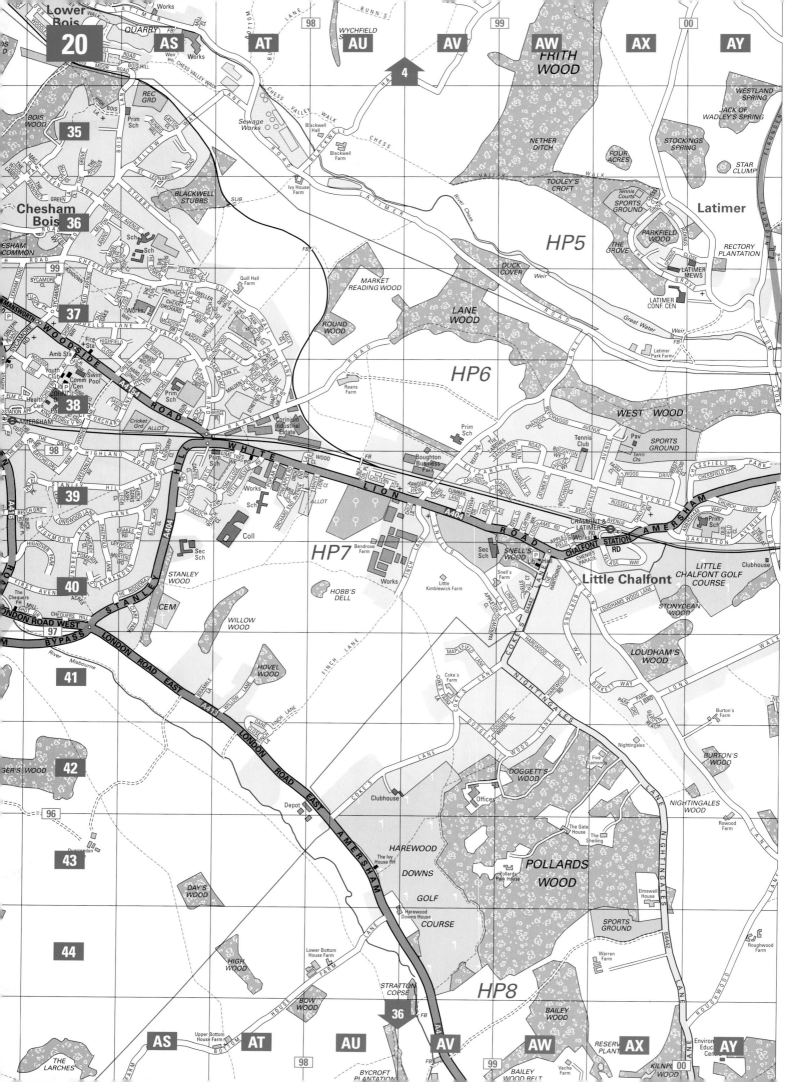
20
Lower Bois
AS
AT
AU
AV
AW
AX
AY
98
99
00
4
FRITH WOOD
WYCHFIELD
QUARRY
Works
Weir Ho
CHESS VALLEY WALK
REC GRD
Prim Sch
BOIS WOOD
35
Sewage Works
Blackwell Hall
Blackwell Farm
CHESS VALLEY WALK
WESTLAND SPRING
JACK OF WADLEY'S SPRING
NETHER DITCH
FOUR ACRES
STOCKINGS SPRING
STAR CLUMP
BLACKWELL STUBBS
Ivy House Farm
TOOLEY'S CROFT
Tennis Courts
SPORTS GROUND
Latimer
Chesham Bois
36
ESHAM COMMON
HP5
PARKFIELD WOOD
RECTORY PLANTATION
THE GROVE
LATIMER MEWS
LATIMER CONF. CEN
DUCK COVER
Weir
Quill Hall Farm
MARKET READING WOOD
99
37
LANE WOOD
Great Water
Weir
ROUND WOOD
Latimer Park Farm
WOODSIDE ROAD
A4154
Fire Sta
Amb Sta
Youth Club
Swim Pool
Comm Cen
Lib
Health Cen
38
AMERSHAM
HP6
Raans Farm
Prim Sch
Cricket Grd
ALLOT
Corinium Industrial Estate
WEST WOOD
Prim Sch
Tennis Club
Pav
SPORTS GROUND
Tenn Cts
98
Prim Sch
WHITE LION ROAD
A404
Boughton Business Park
CHESSFIELD PARK
39
Works
Sch
ALLOT
CHALFONT & LATIMER
CHALFONT STATION RD
AMERSHAM ROAD
Prim Sch
Coll
A404
HP7
Bendrose Farm
Sec Sch
SNELL'S WOOD
Lib
Hall
Clubhouse
Sec Sch
STANLEY WOOD
Works
Snell's Farm
Little Chalfont
LITTLE CHALFONT GOLF COURSE
HOBB'S DELL
Little Kimblewick Farm
40
The Chequers PH
CEM
STONYDEAN WOOD
LONDON ROAD WEST
97
BYPASS
STANLEY HILL
A416
WILLOW WOOD
LOUDHAM'S WOOD
River Misbourne
41
HOVEL WOOD
LONDON ROAD EAST
NIGHTINGALES LANE
Coke's Farm
A413
Burton's Farm
Nightingales
BURTON'S WOOD
42
DOGGETT'S WOOD
Five Diamonds
Clubhouse
Offices
NIGHTINGALES WOOD
Depot
Rowood Farm
96
The Gate House
The Sheiling
Quarrendon
43
HAREWOOD DOWNS GOLF COURSE
The Ivy House PH
POLLARDS WOOD
Pollards Park House
DAY'S WOOD
Elmswell House
Harewood Downs House
SPORTS GROUND
B4442
44
Lower Bottom House Farm
HIGH WOOD
Warren Farm
Roughwood Farm
STRATTON COPSE
HP8
BOW WOOD
36
FB
BAILEY WOOD
Upper Bottom House Farm
AS
AT
AU
AV
AW
AX
AY
THE LARCHES
98
99
00
BYCROFT PLANTATION
BAILEY WOOD BELT
Vache Farm
KILNPO WOOD
Environ Educ Cen

21
5
22
37
AZ
BA
BB
BC
BD
BE
BF
01
02
03
35
36
37
38
39
40
41
42
43
44
96
97
98
99
HP3
WD3
Chenies
Sarratt
Chorleywood
Chorleywood Bottom
The Swillet
Heronsgate
FLAUNDEN GROVE
BALDWIN'S WOOD
LONG WOOD
HANGING CROFT
MOUNT WOOD
HANGINGLANE WOOD
BRAMBLE CROFT
LIMESHILL WOOD
OLDFIELD SPRING
WALLACE'S WOOD
TOP SPRING
OLDCROFT WOOD
DAFFODIL SPRING
PLOUGH WOOD
HILLMEADS SPRING
DAWES COMMON
SANDFIELD WOOD
NICHOLAS SPRING
TURVEYLANE WOOD
WYBURN WOOD
CHILTON'S WOOD
PLACEHOUSE COPSE
CONEY WOOD
WALK WOOD
OLD HANGING WOOD
NEW HANGING WOOD
LODGE COPSE
HALSEY'S WOOD
WHITELANDS WOOD
HILLAS WOOD
CARPENTER'S WOOD
CROSSLANE WOOD
DELL WOOD
SCRUBBS WOOD
BLUNTS WOOD
MEAD SPRING
MILLFIELD PLANTATIO
LITTLE LADY'S WOOD
CHORLEYWOOD COMMON
CHORLEYWOOD GOLF COURSE
HOME WOOD
THE SCREEN
SOLOMON'S WOOD
PHEASANTS WOOD
Junction 18
AMERSHAM ROAD
A404
CHENIES ROAD
RICKMANSWORTH ROAD
LATIMER ROAD
CHESS VALLEY WALK
River Chess
BUCKINGHAMSHIRE
HERTFORDSHIRE
DACORUM
THREE RIVERS
CHILTERN
M25
Manor House
Bedford Arms PH
Cricket Ground
Football Ground
Chenies Garden Centre
Sec Sch
Field Study Centre
Tennis Club
Prim Sch
Arts Centre
Clubhouse
CHORLEYWOOD
White Horse PH
Black Horse PH
Berry Farm
The Hall Farm
West Herts Riding School
Penn Farm
Hill Farm
Bullsland Farm
Newhouse Farm
Fairfield Farm & Livery Stables
Roughwood Park
Lodge Farm
Great Greenstreet Farm
Little Greenstreet Farm
Stubbs Farm
Mountwood Farm
Valley Farm
Watercress Beds
Moor Cottage
Sarratt Bottom Cottages
Goldingtons
Sarrattmill Bridge
Water Works
Weirs
Model Farm
End Farm
Adams Nurseries
Ward's Nurseries
The Boot PH
Cricketers Inn PH
Great Sarratt Hall Farm
Great Sarratt Hall
Moonshine Farm
R.A.F. Chenies
Martin Top Farm
Mill Farm
Chenies Place
Greathouse Farm
Highlands Water Gardens
Solesbridge Mill Water Gardens

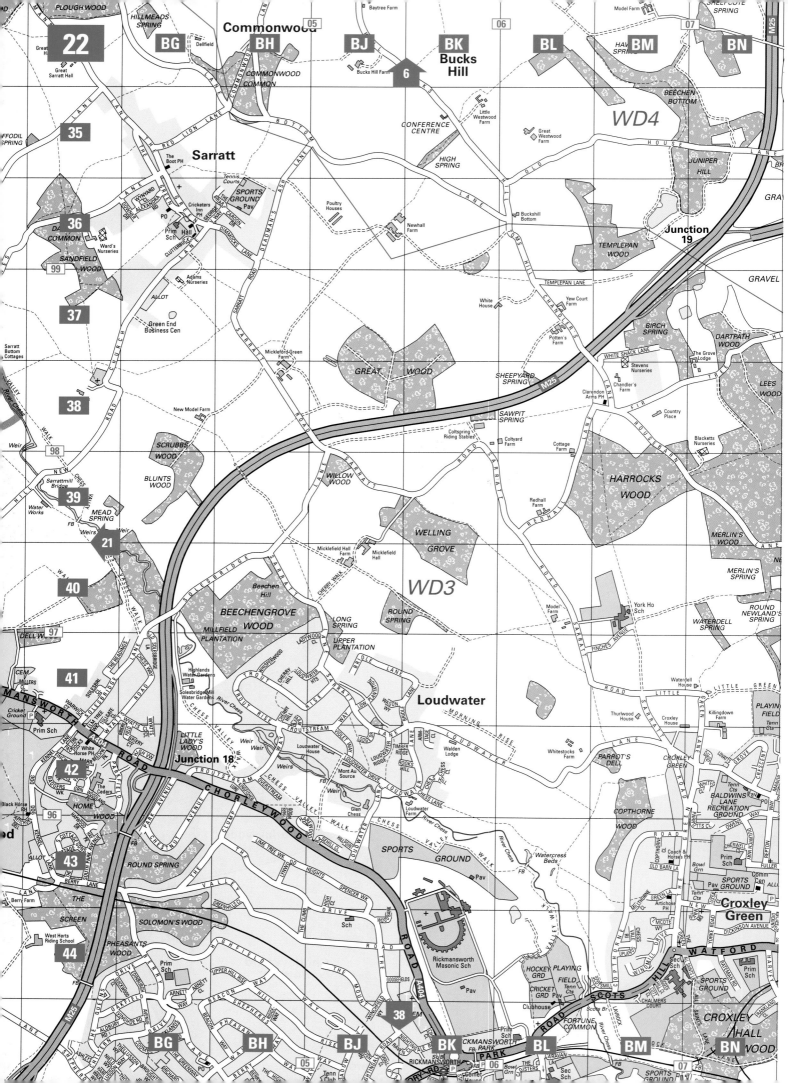
22
Commonwood
Bucks Hill
Sarratt
WD4
Junction 19
WD3
Loudwater
Junction 18
Croxley Green
Rickmansworth Masonic Sch
BG
BH
BJ
BK
BL
BM
BN
05
06
07
6
21
38
35
36
37
38
39
40
41
42
43
44
99
98
97
96
PLOUGH WOOD
HILLMEADS SPRING
COMMONWOOD COMMON
GREAT WOOD
HARROCKS WOOD
WELLING GROVE
BEECHENGROVE WOOD
TEMPLEPAN WOOD
JUNIPER HILL
BEECHEN BOTTOM
SCRUBBS WOOD
BLUNTS WOOD
WILLOW WOOD
ROUND SPRING
LONG SPRING
UPPER PLANTATION
MILLFIELD PLANTATION
COPTHORNE WOOD
SOLOMON'S WOOD
PHEASANTS WOOD
SPORTS GROUND
CHORLEYWOOD ROAD
M25
A404

23
Langleybury
Kingswood
Garston
Leavesden Green
NORTH WATFORD
WATFORD
WEST WATFORD
Holywell
WD24
WD17
WD18
NORTH WESTERN AVENUE
HEMPSTEAD ROAD
ST. ALBANS ROAD
RICKMANSWORTH ROAD
KINGSWAY
NORTH ORBITAL ROAD
WHIPPENDELL WOOD
WEST HERTS GOLF COURSE
GROVE PARK
CASSIOBURY PARK
HEATH WOOD
ROUGH WOOD
CHARLOTTE'S VALE
GRAND UNION CANAL
NORTH WATFORD CEMETERY
STANBOROUGH PARK
VICARAGE RD CEMETERY
WATFORD GENERAL HOSP
WATFORD JUNCTION
WATFORD HIGH STREET
Harlequin Centre
TRIDENT CENTRE
MOWAT INDUSTRIAL EST
COMMON MOOR
LONG VALLEY WOOD
KING GEORGE V PLAYING FIELDS
RIVERSIDE PARK
OXHEY PARK
Hunton Bridge Interchange
BP
BQ
BR
BS
BT
BU
BV
08
09
10

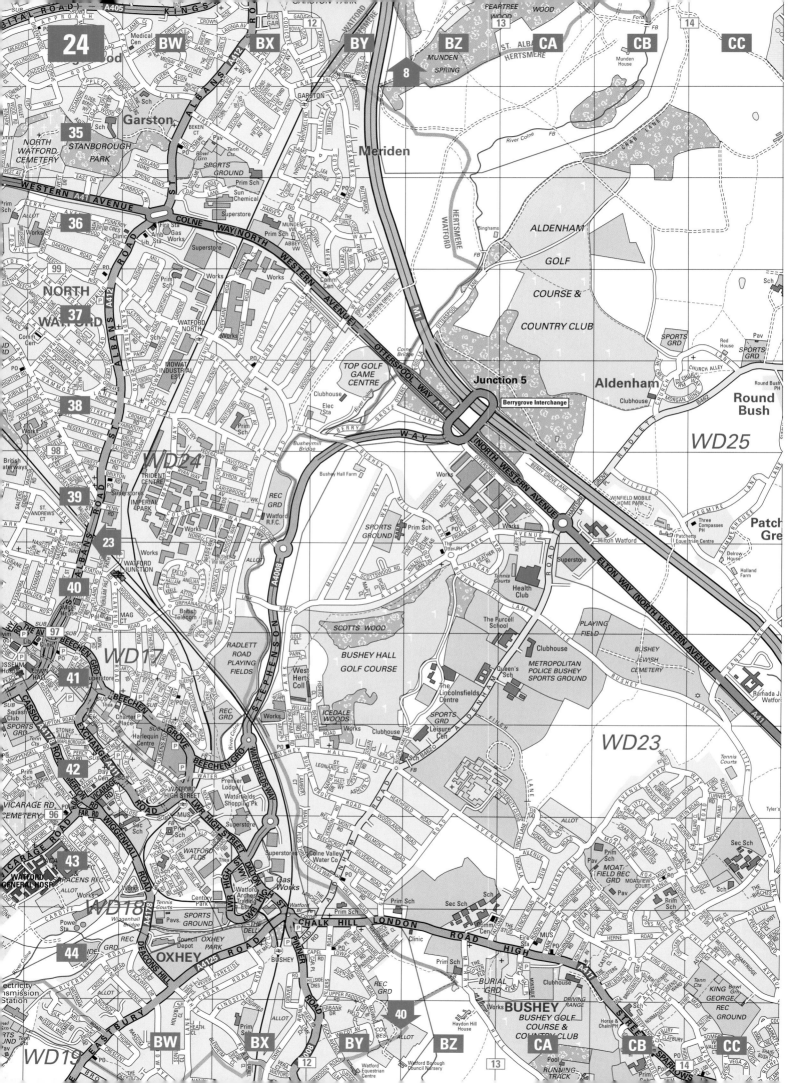

24
BW
BX
BY
BZ
CA
CB
CC
8
12
13
14
Garston
NORTH WATFORD CEMETERY
STANBOROUGH PARK
Meriden
WESTERN A41 AVENUE
COLNE WAY (NORTH WESTERN AVENUE)
NORTH WATFORD
WATFORD NORTH
MOWAT INDUSTRIAL EST
ALDENHAM GOLF COURSE & COUNTRY CLUB
TOP GOLF GAME CENTRE
Junction 5
Berrygrove Interchange
Aldenham
Round Bush
WD25
WD24
TRIDENT CENTRE
IMPERIAL PARK
WATFORD JUNCTION
Watford R.F.C.
REC GRD
SPORTS GROUND
Hilton Watford
ELTON WAY (NORTH WESTERN AVENUE)
Superstore
Health Club
The Purcell School
PLAYING FIELD
BUSHEY JEWISH CEMETERY
METROPOLITAN POLICE BUSHEY SPORTS GROUND
Ramada Jarvis Watford
SCOTTS WOOD
BUSHEY HALL GOLF COURSE
RADLETT ROAD PLAYING FIELDS
WD17
West Herts Coll
ICEDALE WOODS
The Lincolnsfields Centre
Leisure Cen
WD23
Harlequin Centre
WATFORD HIGH STREET
Waterfields Shopping Pk
VICARAGE RD. CEMETERY
WATFORD GENERAL HOSP
SARACENS RFC
WATFORD FLDS
Colne Valley Water Co
MOAT FIELD REC GRD
WD18
SPORTS GROUND
OXHEY PARK
OXHEY
CHALK HILL
LONDON ROAD
HIGH STREET
BUSHEY
BUSHEY GOLF COURSE & COUNTRY CLUB
KING GEORGE REC GROUND
RUNNING TRACK
WD19
40
Haydon Hill House
Watford Equestrian Centre
Watford Borough Council Nursery

RADLETT
Letchmore Heath
WD7
WD6
ELSTREE
ELSTREE AERODROME
HILFIELD PARK RESERVOIR
ALDENHAM COUNTRY PARK
ALDENHAM RESERVOIR
ALDENHAM PARK
ALDENHAM PARK WOODLAND
ELSTREE GOLF COURSE
THE GORSE
WATLING STREET
COBDEN HILL
THEOBALD STREET
WATFORD ROAD
ELSTREE ROAD
BARNET LANE
ELSTREE HILL NORTH
ELSTREE HILL SOUTH
TYLERS WAY (NORTH WESTERN AV)
M1
A411
A5183
KENDAL WOOD
LITTLE KENDALS WOOD
MOSES DELL
COBDENHILL DELL
WELLHOUSE DELL
SCRUBBITTS WOOD
Electricity Transfer Station
The Haberdasher's Aske's Sch for Boys
The Haberdasher's Aske's Sch for Girls
Lister Institute
ELSTREE HILL OPEN SPACE
ELSTREE OPEN SPACE
CENTENNIAL PARK
Bhaktivedanta Manor Hare Krishna Temple
Oakridge Lane Sewage Treatment Works
CD
CE
CF
CG
CH
CJ
CK
35
36
37
38
39
40
41
42
43
44
99
98
97
96
15
16
17
9
26
41

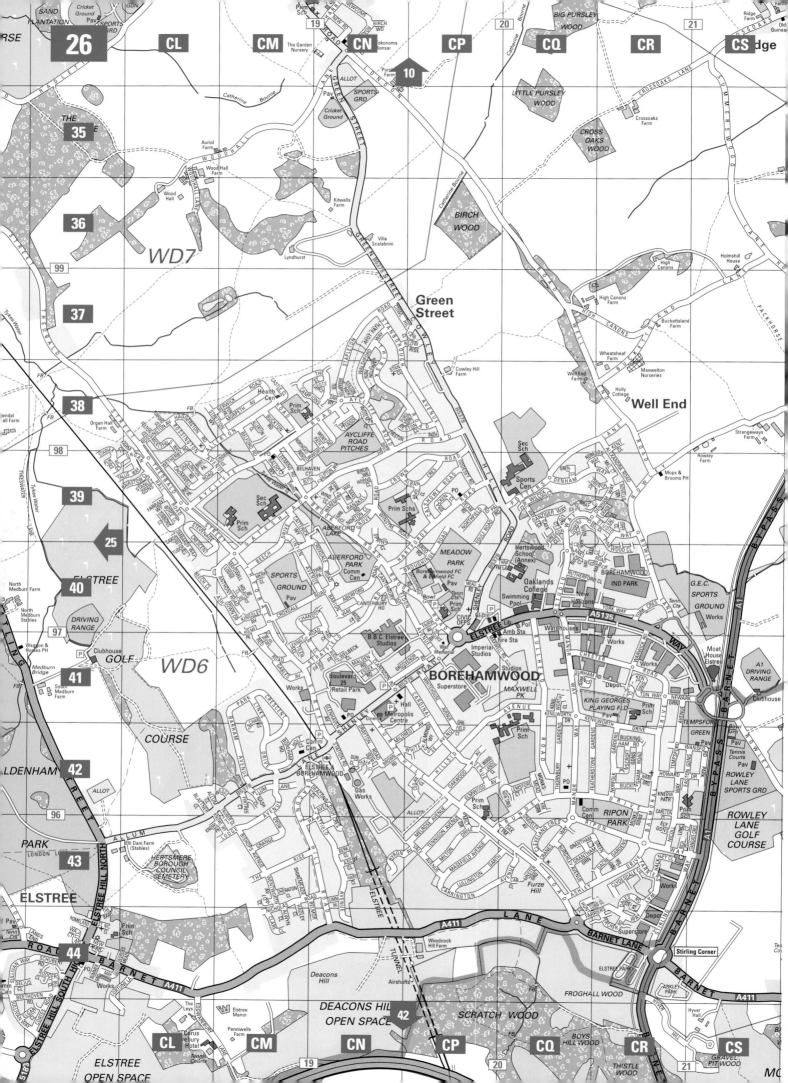

26
CL
CM
CN
CP
CQ
CR
CS
19
20
21
10
35
36
37
38
39
40
41
42
43
44
99
98
97
96
25
WD7
WD6
SAND PLANTATION
Cricket Ground
Pav
SPORTS GRD
The Garden Nursery
Tokonoma Bonsai
BIG PURSLEY WOOD
LITTLE PURSLEY WOOD
CROSS OAKS WOOD
Crossoaks Farm
CROSSOAKS LANE
Ridge Farm
Catherine Bourne
Pursley Farm
ALLOT
Auriol Farm
Wood Hall Farm
Wood Hall
WOODHALL LANE
Kitwells Farm
BIRCH WOOD
Villa Scalabrini
Lyndhurst
Holmshill House
High Canons
High Canons Farm
Bucketsland Farm
Wheatsheaf Farm
Maxwelton Nurseries
Well End Farm
Holly Cottage
Green Street
Well End
Cowley Hill Farm
Organ Hall Farm
Strangeways Farm
Rowley Farm
Mops & Brooms PH
Sec Sch
Sports Cen
AYCLIFFE ROAD PITCHES
ABERFORD LAKE
ABERFORD PARK Comm Cen
SPORTS GROUND
MEADOW PARK
Borehamwood FC & Enfield FC
Hertswood School (Annex)
Oaklands College
Swimming Pool
New Horizons
BOREHAMWOOD IND PARK
G.E.C. SPORTS GROUND
Works
Moat House Elstree
A1 DRIVING RANGE
Clubhouse
North Medburn Farm
North Medburn Stables
DRIVING RANGE
Waggon & Horses PH
Clubhouse
GOLF
COURSE
Medburn Bridge
South Medburn Farm
ELSTREE
B.B.C. Elstree Studios
Imperial Studios
Studios
War Memorial
CIVIC OFFS
Lib
Pol
Amb Sta
Fire Sta
Warehouses
Boulevard 25 Retail Park
BOREHAMWOOD
Superstore
MAXWELL PK
KING GEORGES PLAYING FLD
Metropolis Centre
Cinema
Hall
ELSTREE & BOREHAMWOOD
Comm Cen
Gas Works
RIPON PARK
TEMPSFORD GREEN
Tennis Courts
ROWLEY LANE SPORTS GRD
ROWLEY LANE GOLF COURSE
Furze Hill
ALDENHAM
PARK
Elli Dani Farm (Stables)
HERTSMERE BOROUGH COUNCIL CEMETERY
ELSTREE
Prim Sch
Woodcock Hill Farm
Deacons Hill
Airshafts
TUNNEL
DEACONS HILL OPEN SPACE
SCRATCH WOOD
FROGHALL WOOD
BOYS HILL WOOD
THISTLE WOOD
GRAVEL PIT WOOD
Stirling Corner
ELSTREE PARK
ARKLEY PARK
Hyver Hall
Elstree Manor
Penniwells Farm
Corus Edgwarebury Hotel
Tennis Courts
ELSTREE OPEN SPACE
A411
A5135
A1
B5378
BARNET BYPASS
BARNET LANE
ELSTREE HILL NORTH
ELSTREE HILL SOUTH
WATLING STREET
THEOBALD STREET
SHENLEY ROAD
ALLUM LANE
LONDON ROAD
BARNET ROAD
ROWLEY LANE
BUCKETTS LAND
HIGH CANONS
WELL END ROAD
COWLEY HILL
AYCLIFFE ROAD
GATESHEAD ROAD
MANOR WAY
BALMORAL DRIVE
STIRLING WAY
5183

27
CT
CU
CV
CW
CX
CY
CZ
11
43
28
35
36
37
38
39
40
41
42
43
44
22
23
24
99
98
97
96
M25
A1(M)
A1
A411
A1000
A1081
EN6
EN5
N20
Junction 23
(M25)
Junction 1
A1(M)
South Mimms
Depot
Works
Nat Inst for Biological Standards & Control
Blanche Farm
Summerswood Farm
Dancers Hill
Laurel Lodge
Laurel House
Dancershill House
Dyrham Park Farm
BARNET BY-PASS
ST. ALBANS ROAD
DANCERS HILL ROAD
DYRHAM LANE
BENTLEY HEATH LANE
Elm Farm
Bentley Heath Farm
Bentley Heath
Norfolk Lodge
Mausoleum
Wrotham Park
Tennis Courts
Pool
WROTHAM PARK
Duke of York PH
Cricket Ground
Pav
Deadman's Bottom
DYRHAM PARK GOLF COURSE
Country Club
DYRHAM PARK
Green Dragon Inn PH
Knightsland Farm
Valentine's Farm
Lower Kitt's End Farm
Home Farm
Kitt's End
Kitt's End Farm
GREAT NORTH ROAD
BRIDGEDOWN GOLF COURSE
ALLOTMENTS
OLD FOLD MANOR GOLF COURSE
MOAT
Clubhouse
Old Fold Manor
Monken Hadley
Battle of Barnet 1471
Hadley High Stone
HADLEY HIGHSTONE
HADLEY GREEN
ST. MARTHA'S CONVENT
Fold Farm
WROTHAM PARK OPEN SPACE
Electricity Sta
Homestead Farm
POOR CLARE MONASTERY
HERTFORDSHIRE
HERTSMERE
BARNET
BYNG ROAD PLAYING FIELDS
ALLOT
Barnet R.F.C.
Prim Sch
High Barnet
Hadley
Curriculum Centre
SPORTS GROUND
ARKLEY LANE OPEN SPACE
Woodlands Farm
KING GEORGE'S FIELD
BARNET
Sec Sch
Swim Pool
Works
TA Cen
Mkt
Lib
The Spires Shop Cen
Tenn Cts
BARNET TRADING EST
Sports Cen
Rowley Green Farm
ARKLEY OPEN SPACE
Nursery
Three Elms Farm
WOOD STREET
HIGH STREET
THE BULL THEATRE
MUS
Barnet Coll
Pol
WHALEBONE PARK
BARNET GENERAL HOSP
REC GRD
Bowl Grn
CHIPPING BARNET
HIGH BARNET
Rowley Green
ARKLEY GOLF COURSE
ARKLEY RISE ESTATE OPEN SPACE
CEMETERY
Arkley Manor Farm
Rowley Bank Nurseries
Clubhouse
War Memorial
Water Tower
PO
Arkley
BARNET ROAD
Prim Schs
Comm Cen
Valley Cen
Underhill
SPORTS GROUND
Cinema
BARNET HILL
WHITINGS HILL OPEN SPACE
BARNET GATE SPORTS GRD
The Gate PH
Barnet Gate
Whitings Hill Farm
Cottage Farm
Ducks Island
GRANGE PLAYING FIELDS
PLAYING FIELD
Dollis Brook
OLD ELIZABETHANS (BARNET) MEMORIAL PLAYING FIELDS
Brent Lodge Farm
MAYS LANE
BARNET PLAYING FIELDS
KING GEORGE V PLAYING FIELDS
Sec Sch
SOUTH HERTS GOLF

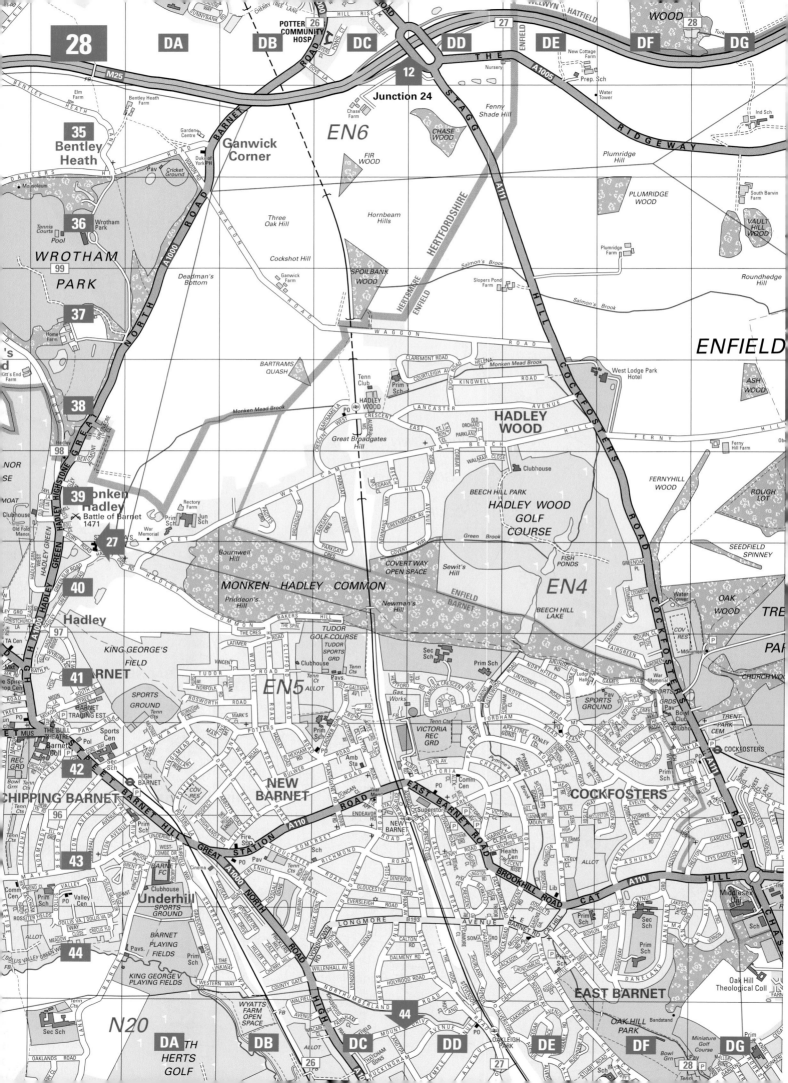
28
DA
DB
DC
DD
DE
DF
DG
Junction 24
EN6
Ganwick Corner
Bentley Heath
WROTHAM PARK
HADLEY WOOD
HADLEY WOOD GOLF COURSE
MONKEN HADLEY COMMON
EN4
EN5
ENFIELD
NEW BARNET
COCKFOSTERS
CHIPPING BARNET
EAST BARNET
Underhill
Hadley
N20
Battle of Barnet 1471
West Lodge Park Hotel
OAK HILL PARK
Oak Hill Theological Coll
BARNET PLAYING FIELDS
KING GEORGE V PLAYING FIELDS
WYATTS FARM OPEN SPACE
VICTORIA REC GRD
COVERT WAY OPEN SPACE
TUDOR GOLF COURSE
KING GEORGE'S FIELD
27
44

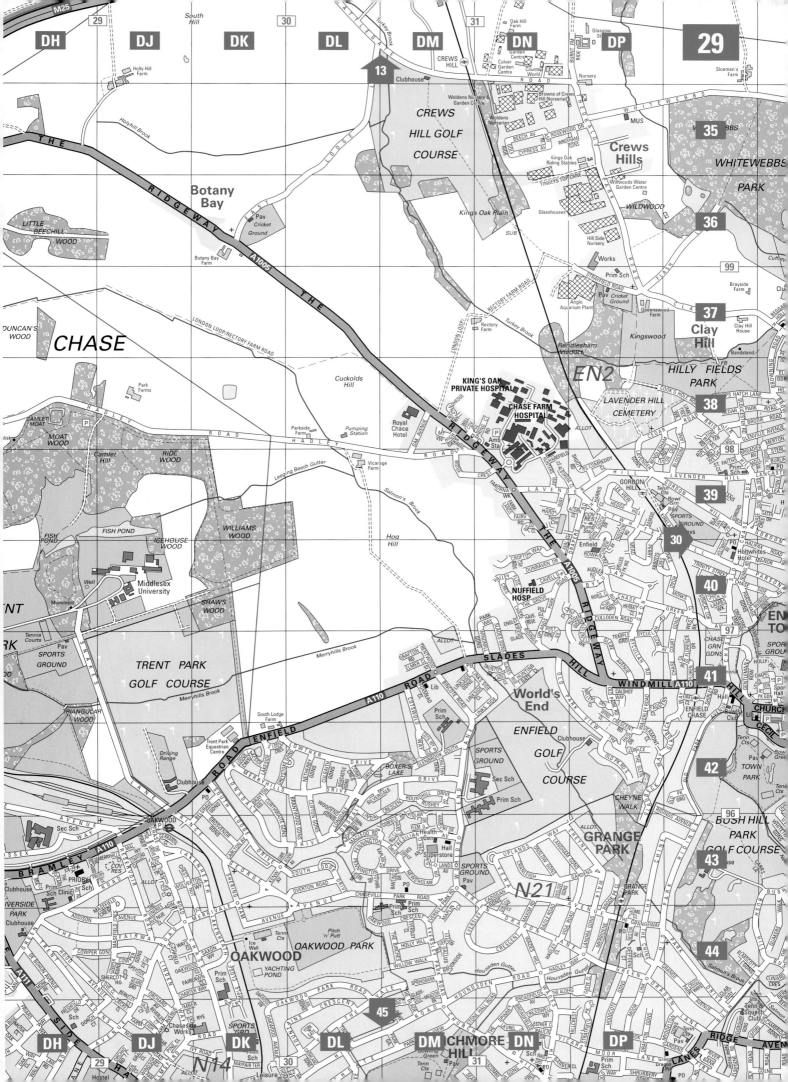

29
CREWS HILL GOLF COURSE
Crews Hills
WHITEWEBBS PARK
Botany Bay
LITTLE BEECHILL WOOD
CHASE
THE RIDGEWAY
A1005
Clay Hill
HILLY FIELDS PARK
EN2
KING'S OAK PRIVATE HOSPITAL
CHASE FARM HOSPITAL
LAVENDER HILL CEMETERY
MOAT WOOD
RIDE WOOD
WILLIAMS WOOD
FISH POND
Middlesex University
TRENT PARK GOLF COURSE
World's End
ENFIELD GOLF COURSE
GRANGE PARK
N21
OAKWOOD
OAKWOOD PARK
BUSH HILL PARK GOLF COURSE
TOWN PARK
N14

30
DQ
DR
DS
DT
DU
DV
DW
14
M25
Junction 25
Bulls Cross
Crews Hill
WHITEWEBBS WOOD
WHITEWEBBS PARK
WHITEWEBBS GOLF COURSE
White Webbs House
Capel Manor College
CAPEL HOUSE
BULLS CROSS FIELD
SPORTS GROUND
BULLSMOOR LANE
FORTY HALL COUNTRY PARK
FORTY HALL & MUSEUM
Forty Hill
Clay Hill
HILLY FIELDS PARK
Bullsmoor
CEMETERY
Crematorium
EN2
EN1
N9
N21
ENFIELD TOWN
ENFIELD
QUEEN ELIZABETH STADIUM
ENFIELD PLAYING FIELDS
BASEBALL GROUND
ENFIELD CEMETERY (JEWISH)
ST. GEORGE'S FIELD
TOWN PARK
BUSH HILL PARK
BUSH HILL PARK GOLF COURSE
GRANGE PARK
ENFIELD RETAIL PK
MARTINBRIDGE TRADING ESTATE
SOUTHBURY ROAD
GREAT CAMBRIDGE ROAD
HERTFORD ROAD
WINDMILL HILL
LONDON ROAD
Middlesex University
JUBILEE PARK
ALLOTMENTS
29
46
33
34
35
35
36
37
38
39
40
41
42
43
44
96
97
98
99

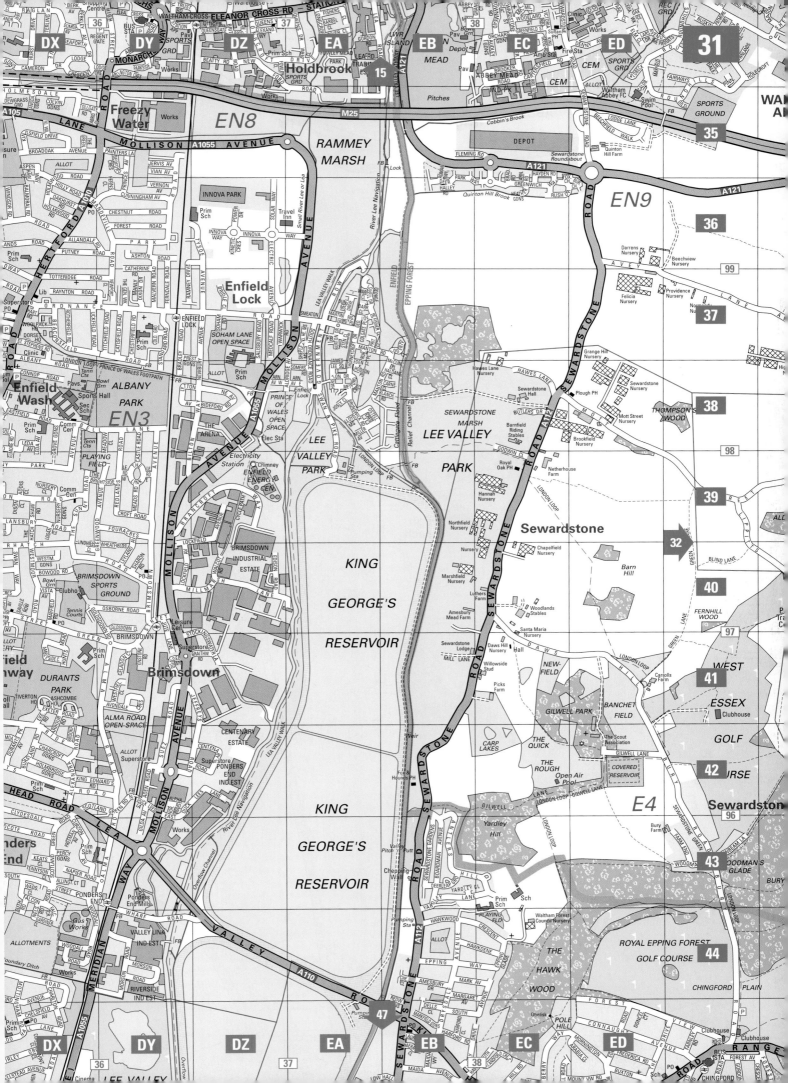

DX
DY
DZ
EA
EB
EC
ED
31
15
35
36
37
38
39
40
41
42
43
44
32
47
Holdbrook
Freezy Water
EN8
EN9
EN3
E4
M25
A121
A1055
A1010
A105
A110
A112
RAMMEY MARSH
INNOVA PARK
Enfield Lock
MOLLISON AVENUE
ALBANY PARK
Enfield Wash
SOHAM LANE OPEN SPACE
PRINCE OF WALES OPEN SPACE
LEE VALLEY PARK
ENFIELD ENERGY CEN
BRIMSDOWN INDUSTRIAL ESTATE
BRIMSDOWN SPORTS GROUND
Brimsdown
DURANTS PARK
ALMA ROAD OPEN-SPACE
CENTENARY ESTATE
PONDERS END IND EST
VALLEY LINK IND EST
RIVERSIDE IND EST
KING GEORGE'S RESERVOIR
River Lee Navigation
Relief Channel
Cattlegate Flood
EPPING FOREST
SEWARDSTONE MARSH
SEWARDSTONE ROAD
Sewardstone
Sewardstone Roundabout
DEPOT
Cobbin's Brook
Quinton Hill Brook
THOMPSON'S WOOD
Barn Hill
FERNHILL WOOD
NEW-FIELD
GILWELL PARK
BANCHET FIELD
CARP LAKES
THE QUICK
THE ROUGH
Open Air Pool
COVERED RESERVOIR
Yardley Hill
THE HAWK WOOD
WEST ESSEX GOLF COURSE
ROYAL EPPING FOREST GOLF COURSE
CHINGFORD PLAIN
POLE HILL
WOODMAN'S GLADE
LOWER ISLAND
MEAD
SPORTS GROUND
Waltham Abbey FC
MERIDIAN WAY
HERTFORD ROAD
LEA VALLEY ROAD
CHINGFORD

32
EE
EF
EG
EH
EJ
EK
EL
16
WALTHAM ABBEY
Junction 26
M25
A121
HONEY LANE
WOODRIDDEN HILL
SPORTS GROUND
CLAY PIGEON RANGE
CONYBURY WOOD
STABLES SHAW
BRAMBLY SHAW
POTKILN WOOD
Sewardstone Roundabout
35
36
37
38
39
40
41
42
43
44
EN9
99
98
97
96
40
41
42
LORD PADGETS WOOD
POPLARS SHAW
WALTHAM ABBEY CEMETERY (JEWISH)
HONEY LANE PLAIN
HONEY LANE QUARTERS
SUNSHINE PLAIN
Round Hills
BEECH HILL PARK
HIGH BEECH GOLF COURSE
PYNEST GRN
AVEY LANE
SEWARDSTONE ROAD
MOTT STREET
THOMPSON'S WOOD
Wake Valley
LITTLE MONK WOOD
Court Hill
Bellringers
Mount Pleasant
EPPING FOREST
IG10
Blackweir Hill
BLACKWEIR POND
Loughton Camp
BALDWINS POND
Broom Hill
Kate's Cellar
Shelley's Hill
Staples Hill
Strawberry Hill
STRAWBERRY HILL PONDS
ALDERGROVE WOOD
High Beach
HILL WOOD
vardstone
31
Barn Hill
FERNHILL WOOD
Police Training Centre
WHITEHOUSE PLAIN
ROUND THICKET
FAIRMEAD POND
Fairmead Bottom
North Long Hills
WEST ESSEX GOLF COURSE
ALMHOUSE PLAIN
Long Hills
BANCHET FIELD
GILWELL PARK
E4
Sewardstonebury
WOODMAN'S GLADE
BURY WOOD
Cuckoo Pits
Grimston's Oak
Magpie Hill
CONNAUGHT WATER
Warren Hill
ROYAL EPPING FOREST GOLF COURSE
CHINGFORD PLAIN
EPPING NEW ROAD A104
A1069
RANGERS ROAD
48
QUEEN ELIZABETH'S HUNTING LODGE
THE WARREN
Buckhurst Hill
HIGH ROAD
LOUGHTON
Oaklands Sch
CHINGFORD

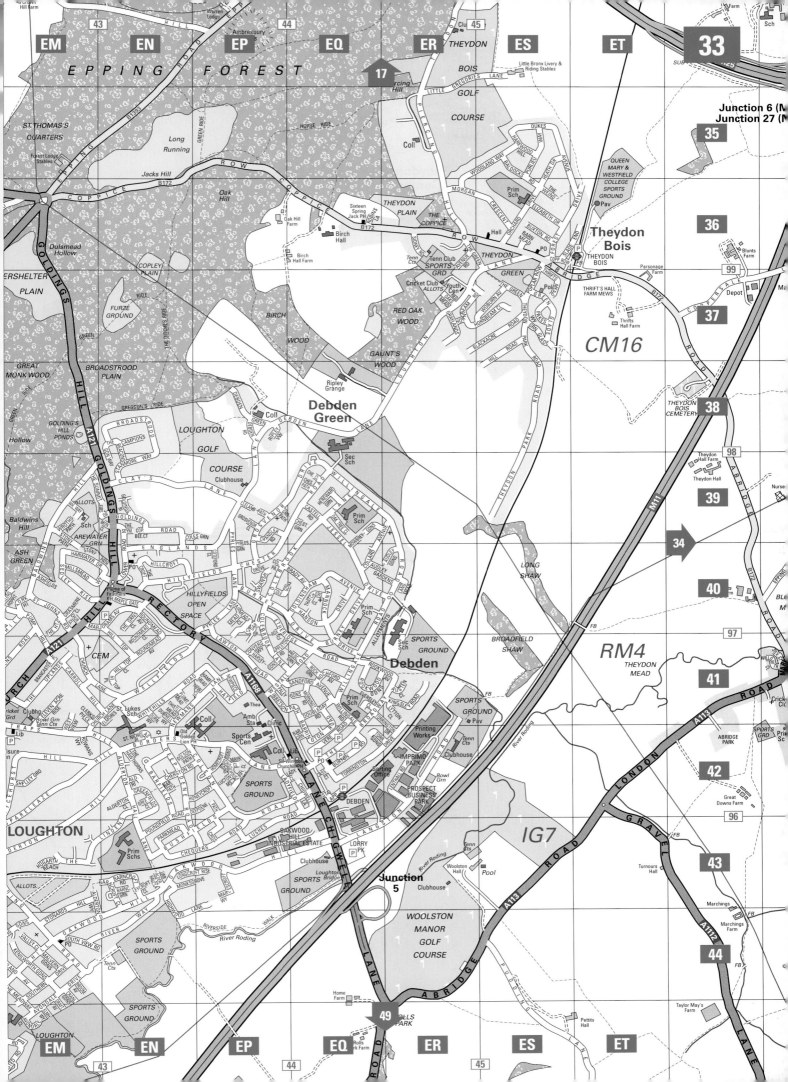

33
EM
EN
EP
EQ
ER
ES
ET
EPPING FOREST
17
THEYDON BOIS GOLF COURSE
Little Bronx Livery & Riding Stables
Junction 6 (M
Junction 27 (M
35
36
37
38
39
34
40
41
42
43
44
49
43
44
45
99
98
97
96
ST. THOMAS'S QUARTERS
Forest Lodge Stables
Long Running
Jacks Hill
Oak Hill
COPPICE ROW
B172
B1393
HORSE RIDE
Dulsmead Hollow
COPLEY PLAIN
FURZE GROUND
BIRCH WOOD
Birch Hall
Oak Hill Farm
Birch Hall Farm
Sixteen Spring Jack PH
THEYDON PLAIN
THE COPPICE
QUEEN MARY & WESTFIELD COLLEGE SPORTS GROUND
Pav
Theydon Bois
THEYDON BOIS
Parsonage Farm
Blunts Farm
THRIFT'S HALL FARM MEWS
Thrifts Hall Farm
Depot
COPPERSALE
ABRIDGE ROAD
CM16
RED OAK WOOD
GAUNT'S WOOD
Ripley Grange
Debden Green
Sec Sch
THEYDON BOIS CEMETERY
Theydon Hall Farm
Theydon Hall
Nursery
GREAT MONK WOOD
BROADSTROOD PLAIN
GOLDING'S HILL PONDS
GOLDINGS HILL
A121
LOUGHTON GOLF COURSE
Clubhouse
Baldwins Hill
ASH GREEN
LONG SHAW
M11
FB
BROADFIELD SHAW
RM4
THEYDON MEAD
HILLYFIELDS OPEN SPACE
CEM
RECTORY LANE
A1168
Debden
SPORTS GROUND
Printing Works
IMPRIMO PARK
PROSPECT BUSINESS PARK
Sorting Office
DEBDEN
A113
LONDON ROAD
ABRIDGE PARK
Great Downs Farm
GRAVEL LANE
Turnours Hall
Marchings
Marchings Farm
A1112
Taylor May's Farm
LOUGHTON
IG7
OAKWOOD HILL INDUSTRIAL ESTATE
LORRY PK
Loughton Bridge
Junction 5
Woolston Hall
Pool
WOOLSTON MANOR GOLF COURSE
River Roding
RIVERSIDE WALK
Home Farm
Pettits Hall
PUDDING LANE
ABRIDGE ROAD
CHIGWELL LANE
LOUGHTON

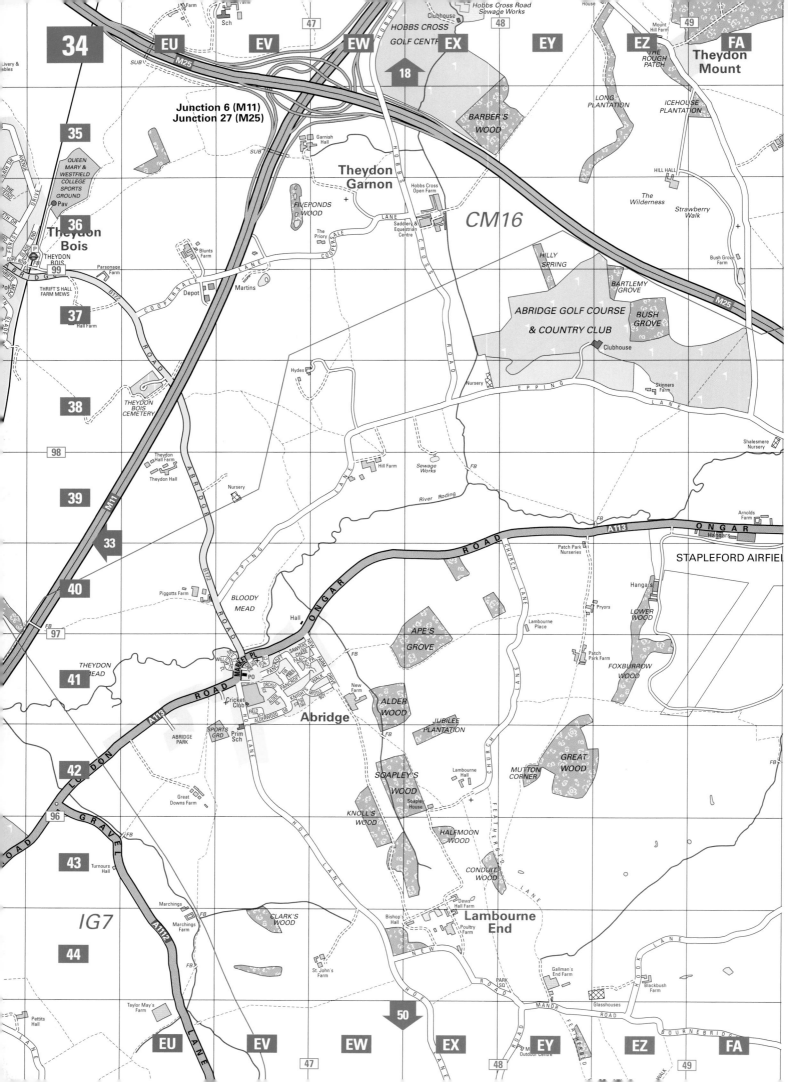
34
EU
EV
EW
EX
EY
EZ
FA
47
48
49
18
50
33
35
36
37
38
39
40
41
42
43
44
98
99
97
96
M25
M11
Junction 6 (M11)
Junction 27 (M25)
HOBBS CROSS GOLF CENTRE
Hobbs Cross Road Sewage Works
Clubhouse
BARBER'S WOOD
Theydon Mount
THE ROUGH PATCH
Mount Hill Farm
LONG PLANTATION
ICEHOUSE PLANTATION
HILL HALL
The Wilderness
Strawberry Walk
Bush Grove Farm
Theydon Garnon
Garnish Hall
FIVEPONDS WOOD
The Priory
Hobbs Cross Open Farm
Saddlery & Equestrian Centre
CM16
QUEEN MARY & WESTFIELD COLLEGE SPORTS GROUND
Pav
Theydon Bois
THEYDON BOIS
Blunts Farm
Parsonage Farm
THRIFT'S HALL FARM MEWS
Hall Farm
Depot
Martins
COOPERSALE LANE
HOBBS CROSS ROAD
HILLY SPRING
BARTLEMY GROVE
ABRIDGE GOLF COURSE & COUNTRY CLUB
BUSH GROVE
Clubhouse
Hydes
Nursery
EPPING LANE
Skinners Farm
Shalesmere Nursery
THEYDON BOIS CEMETERY
Theydon Hall Farm
Theydon Hall
Hill Farm
Sewage Works
River Roding
ABRIDGE ROAD
Arnolds Farm
ONGAR ROAD
A113
Hangars
STAPLEFORD AIRFIEL
Patch Park Nurseries
CHURCH LANE
Piggotts Farm
BLOODY MEAD
Hall
Pryors
LOWER WOOD
Lambourne Place
APE'S GROVE
THEYDON MEAD
Patch Park Farm
FOXBURROW WOOD
MARKET PL
PO
New Farm
ALDER WOOD
Cricket Club
Abridge
JUBILEE PLANTATION
ABRIDGE PARK
SPORTS GRD
Prim Sch
HOE LANE
LONDON ROAD
GREAT WOOD
MUTTON CORNER
SOAPLEY'S WOOD
Lambourne Hall
Great Downs Farm
Soapley House
KNOLL'S WOOD
HALFMOON WOOD
GRAVEL LANE
Turnours Hall
CONDUIT WOOD
FEATHERBED LANE
Marchings
Marchings Farm
CLARK'S WOOD
Dews Hall Farm
IG7
Bishop's Hall
Lambourne End
Poultry Farm
A1112
NEW ROAD
St. John's Farm
HOOK LANE
PARK SQ
Gallman's End Farm
Blackbush Farm
MANOR ROAD
Glasshouses
BOURNEBRIDGE
Taylor May's Farm
Pettits Hall
Outdoor Centre
FB
SUB

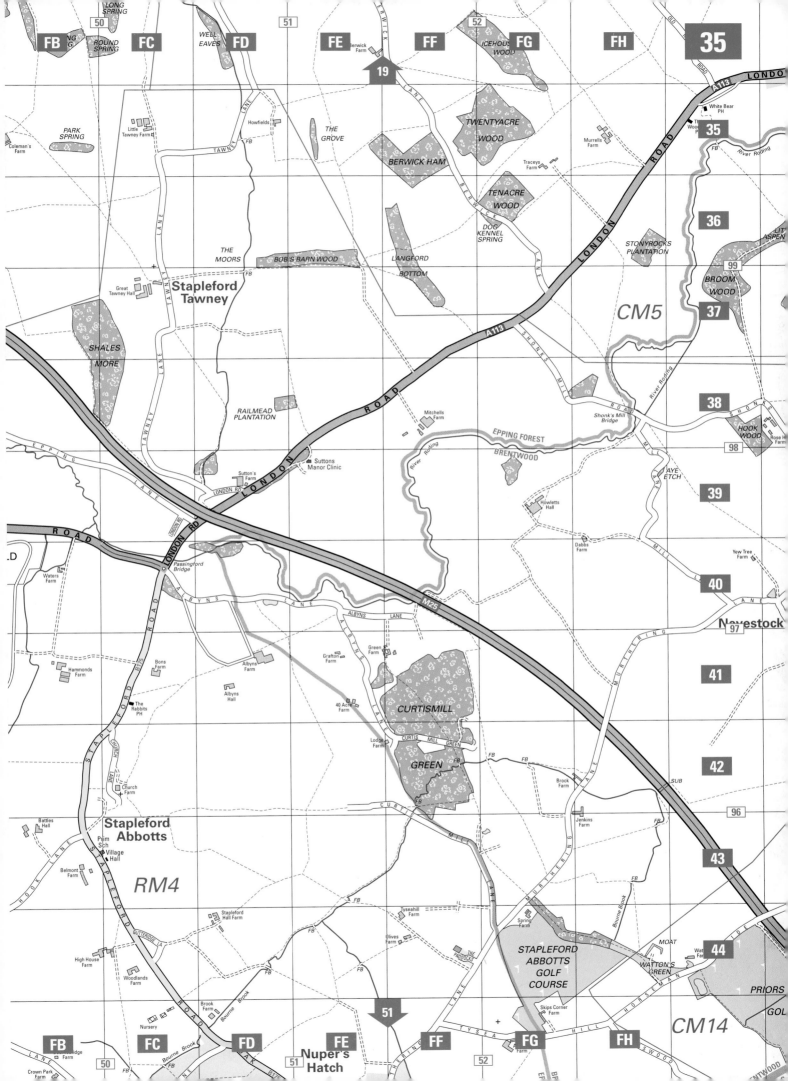

35
LONG SPRING
ROUND SPRING
WELL EAVES
Berwick Farm
19
ICEHOUSE WOOD
LONDON ROAD
A113
White Bear PH
Little Tawney Farm
TAWNEY LANE
Howfields
THE GROVE
PARK SPRING
Coleman's Farm
TWENTYACRE WOOD
Murrells Farm
River Roding
BERWICK HAM
Traceys Farm
BERWICK LANE
TENACRE WOOD
DOG KENNEL SPRING
STONYROCKS PLANTATION
THE MOORS
BOB'S BARN WOOD
LANGFORD BOTTOM
BROOM WOOD
Great Tawney Hall
Stapleford Tawney
CM5
SHALES MORE
SHONKS MILL ROAD
RAILMEAD PLANTATION
Mitchells Farm
Shonk's Mill Bridge
HOOK WOOD
Rose Hill Farm
EPPING FOREST
BRENTWOOD
EPPING LANE
Suttons Manor Clinic
Sutton's Farm
LONDON RD
Howletts Hall
MILL LANE
Dabbs Farm
Yew Tree Farm
Waters Farm
Passingford Bridge
ALBYNS LANE
M25
Navestock
MURTHERING LANE
Hammonds Farm
Bons Farm
Albyns Farm
Grafton Farm
Green Farm
Albyns Hall
The Rabbits PH
40 Acre Farm
CURTISMILL GREEN
Lodge Farm
CHURCH LANE
STAPLEFORD ROAD
B175
Church Farm
Brook Farm
SUB
Battles Hall
Stapleford Abbotts
Prim Sch
Village Hall
Jenkins Farm
CURTIS MILL LANE
Belmont Farm
RM4
HOOK LANE
Bourne Brook
Stapleford Hall Farm
Tyseahill Farm
Spring Farm
GUTTERIDGE LA
Olives Farm
THE PADDOCKS
MOAT
STAPLEFORD ABBOTTS GOLF COURSE
WATTON'S GREEN
High House Farm
Woodlands Farm
PRIORS
Brook Farm
Skips Corner Farm
HORSEMAN SIDE
Nursery
51
TYSEA HILL
CM14
Crown Park Farm
Nuper's Hatch
FB FC FD FE FF FG FH
36 37 38 39 40 41 42 43 44
50 51 52 96 97 98 99

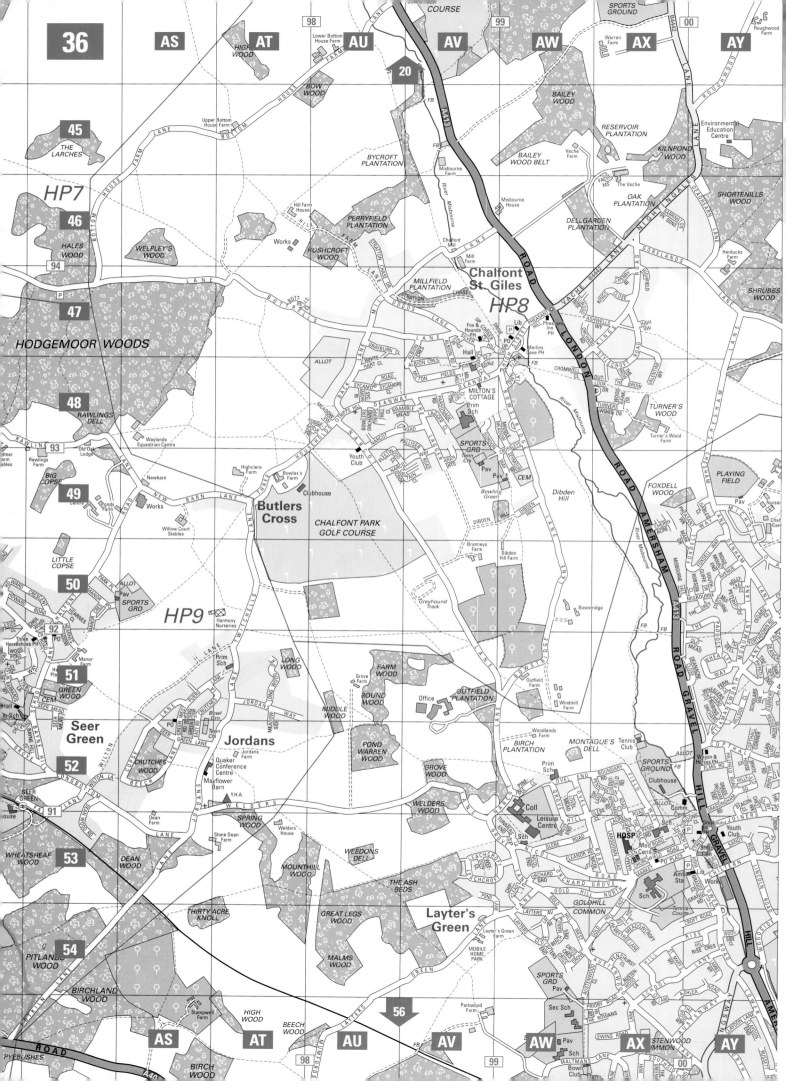
AS
AT
AU
AV
AW
AX
AY
98
99
00
20
45
46
47
48
49
50
51
52
53
54
56
94
93
92
91
HP7
HP8
HP9
HIGH WOOD
Lower Bottom House Farm
BOW WOOD
COURSE
SPORTS GROUND
Warren Farm
Roughwood Farm
BAILEY WOOD
RESERVOIR PLANTATION
Environmental Education Centre
KILNPOND WOOD
BAILEY WOOD BELT
Vache Farm
The Vache
SHORTENILLS WOOD
OAK PLANTATION
DELLGARDEN PLANTATION
Hentucks Farm
SHRUBBS WOOD
THE LARCHES
Upper Bottom House Farm
BYCROFT PLANTATION
Misbourne Farm
Misbourne House
River Misbourne
Hill Farm House
PERRYFIELD PLANTATION
HALES WOOD
WELPLEY'S WOOD
Works
RUSHCROFT WOOD
Chalfont Mill
Mill Farm
MILLFIELD PLANTATION
Chalfont St. Giles
HODGEMOOR WOODS
ALLOT
MILTON'S COTTAGE
Prim Sch
RAWLINGS DELL
Waylands Equestrian Centre
Old Oak Lodge
Rawlings Farm
Youth Club
SPORTS GRD
Pav
CEM
Bowling Green
TURNER'S WOOD
Turner's Wood Farm
PLAYING FIELD
FOXDELL WOOD
BIG COPSE
Newbarn
Highclere Farm
Bowles's Farm
Clubhouse
Butlers Cross
CHALFONT PARK GOLF COURSE
Dibden Hill
Works
Ponds Farm
Willow Court Stables
Bramleys Farm
Dibden Hill Farm
LITTLE COPSE
Greyhound Track
Bowstridge
Harmony Nurseries
LONG WOOD
FARM WOOD
Grove Farm
ROUND WOOD
Office
OUTFIELD PLANTATION
Outfield Farm
Windmill Farm
GREEN WOOD
MIDDLE WOOD
Seer Green
Jordans
POND WARREN WOOD
Woodlands Farm
BIRCH PLANTATION
MONTAGUE'S DELL
Tennis Club
SPORTS GROUND
CRUTCHES WOOD
Jordans Farm
Quaker Conference Centre
Mayflower Barn
Y.H.A.
GROVE WOOD
WELDERS WOOD
Coll
Leisure Centre
HOSP
Youth Club
SEER GREEN
Dean Farm
SPRING WOOD
Welders House
Stone Dean Farm
WHEATSHEAF WOOD
DEAN WOOD
WEEDONS DELL
MOUNTHILL WOOD
THE ASH BEDS
GOLDHILL COMMON
THIRTY ACRE KNOLL
GREAT LEGS WOOD
Layter's Green
Layter's Green Farm
MOBILE HOME PARK
PITLANDS WOOD
MALMS WOOD
SPORTS GRD
BIRCHLAND WOOD
Stampwell Farm
HIGH WOOD
BEECH WOOD
Parkwood Farm
Sec Sch
STENWOOD COMMON
PYEBUSHES
BIRCH WOOD
LONDON ROAD
AMERSHAM ROAD
GRAVEL HILL
A413
A40

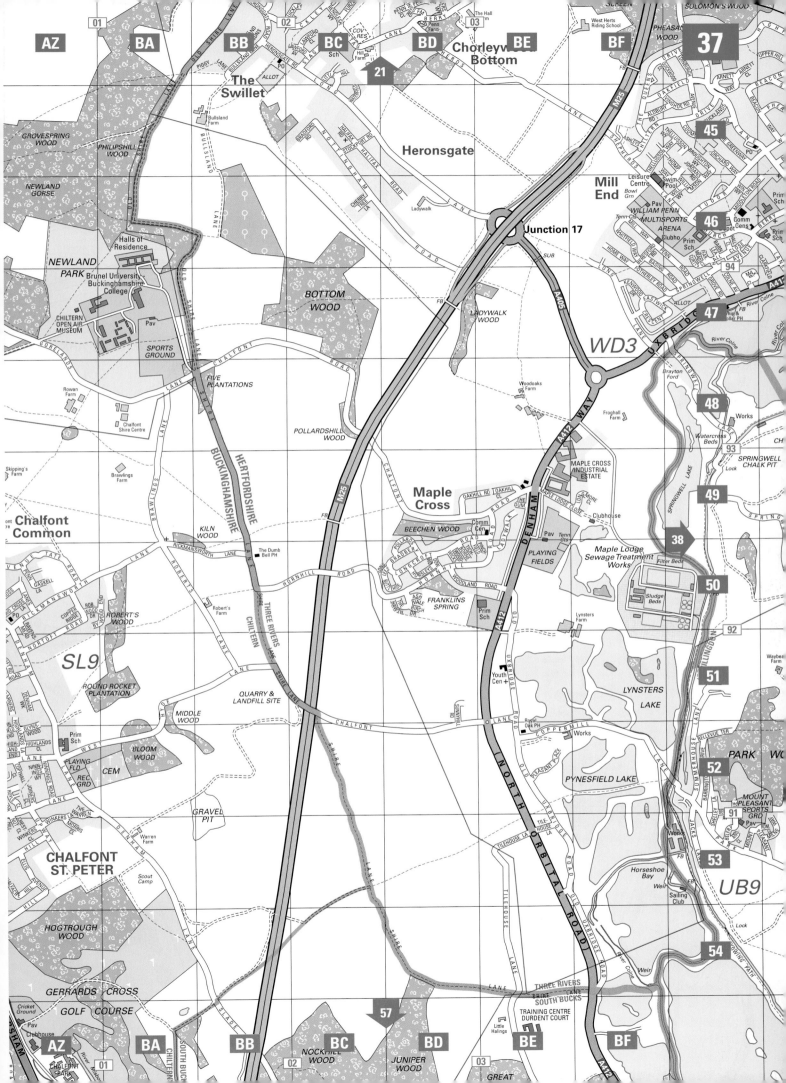
37
21
57
38
Chorleywood Bottom
The Swillet
Heronsgate
Mill End
Junction 17
WD3
Maple Cross
Chalfont Common
SL9
CHALFONT ST. PETER
UB9
NEWLAND PARK
Brunel University-Buckinghamshire College
CHILTERN OPEN AIR MUSEUM
BOTTOM WOOD
LADYWALK WOOD
POLLARDSHILL WOOD
FIVE PLANTATIONS
SPORTS GROUND
GROVESPRING WOOD
PHILIPSHILL WOOD
NEWLAND GORSE
KILN WOOD
BEECHEN WOOD
FRANKLINS SPRING
ROBERT'S WOOD
ROUND ROCKET PLANTATION
QUARRY & LANDFILL SITE
MIDDLE WOOD
BLOOM WOOD
GRAVEL PIT
HOGTROUGH WOOD
GERRARDS CROSS GOLF COURSE
NOCKHILL WOOD
JUNIPER WOOD
MAPLE CROSS INDUSTRIAL ESTATE
Maple Lodge Sewage Treatment Works
PLAYING FIELDS
LYNSTERS LAKE
PYNESFIELD LAKE
SPRINGWELL LAKE
SPRINGWELL CHALK PIT
MOUNT PLEASANT SPORTS GRD
TRAINING CENTRE DURDENT COURT
THREE RIVERS
SOUTH BUCKS
HERTFORDSHIRE
BUCKINGHAMSHIRE
NORTH ORBITAL ROAD
DENHAM WAY
M25
A412
A405

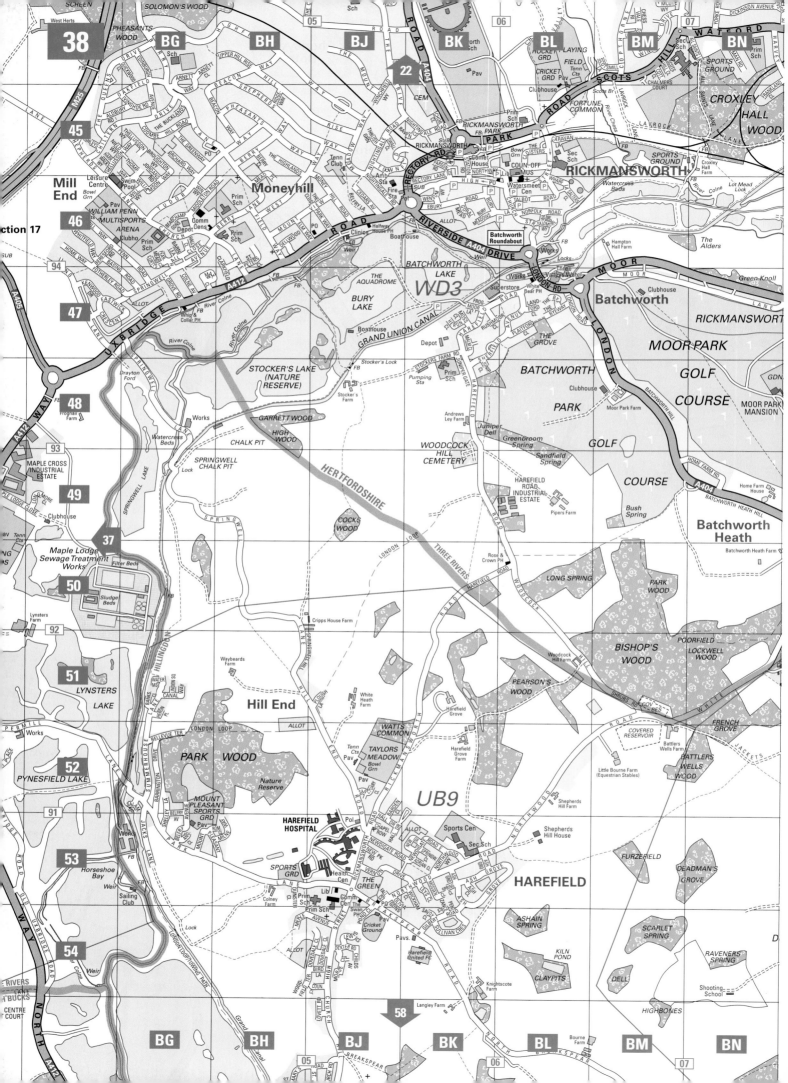

38
BG
BH
BJ
BK
BL
BM
BN
22
45
46
47
48
49
50
51
52
53
54
37
58
Section 17
Mill End
Moneyhill
RICKMANSWORTH
Batchworth
WD3
Batchworth Roundabout
BATCHWORTH LAKE
THE AQUADROME
BURY LAKE
GRAND UNION CANAL
STOCKER'S LAKE (NATURE RESERVE)
RICKMANSWORTH
MOOR PARK
GOLF
COURSE
BATCHWORTH
PARK
MOOR PARK MANSION
WOODCOCK HILL CEMETERY
HERTFORDSHIRE
THREE RIVERS
HILLINGDON
Batchworth Heath
BISHOP'S WOOD
PEARSON'S WOOD
Hill End
PARK WOOD
UB9
HAREFIELD
HAREFIELD HOSPITAL
LYNSTERS LAKE
PYNESFIELD LAKE
Maple Lodge Sewage Treatment Works
MAPLE CROSS INDUSTRIAL ESTATE
CROXLEY HALL WOOD
SPRINGWELL LAKE
LONG SPRING
PARK WOOD
DEADMAN'S GROVE
SCARLET SPRING
RAVENERS SPRING
HIGHBONES
ASHAIN SPRING
KILN POND
CLAYPITS
FURZEFIELD
FRENCH GROVE
BATTLERS WELLS WOOD
COCKS WOOD
GARRETT WOOD
HIGH WOOD
CHALK PIT
SPRINGWELL CHALK PIT
A404
A412
A405
M25

39
BP
BQ
BR
BS
BT
BU
BV
08
09
10
23
45
46
47
48
49
40
50
51
52
53
54
59
91
92
93
94
Holywell
HOLYWELL IND EST
WATFORD BUSINESS PARK
LONG VALLEY WOOD
COMMON MOOR
Moor Park Crossing
River Gade
THE EBURY WAY CYCLE PATH
WOLSEY BUSINESS PARK
MOOR PARK INDUSTRIAL ESTATE
VALE INDUSTRIAL ESTATE
TOLPITS LANE
Tolpits House
Tolpits Plantation
The Withey Bed Wood
KING GEORGE V PLAYING FIELDS
WD18
Brightwells Farm Cottage
Brightwells Farm
Brightwells Spring
HAMPERMILL LAKE
River Colne
RUNNING TRACK
Merchant Taylor's Sch
Prep. Sch
Electricity Transmission Station
SPORTS GROUND
Oxhey Hall
MOAT
Power Sta
Wiggenhall Bridge
OXHEY PARK
EASTBURY LANE
BROOKDENE AVENUE
NANCY DOWNS
HAMPERMILL LANE
WD19
HAMPERMILL WOOD
BIG WOOD
Ox Pasture Spring
SOUTH OXHEY PLAYING FIELDS
OXHEY PARK GOLF COURSE
Warren Dell
Brookdene Arms PH
Hampermill Spring
Round Spring
SANDY LODGE ROAD
GOLF COURSE
SANDY LODGE GOLF COURSE
MOOR PARK
Clubhouse
Elec Sta
OLD FURZE FIELD
YOUNG HANGINGS
OLD HANGINGS
SOUTH OXHEY
The Roughs
LONDON LOOP
Moor Park
MOOR PARK ESTATE
BATHEND CLUMP
Eastbury
OXHEY
THE PLANTATION
BECK MASON'S WOOD
WOOD
H.M.S. Warrior
Olde Green Manne PH
Prince of Wales PH
BATCHWORTH LANE
PRESTWICK ROAD
THREE RIVERS
WILD WOODS
NANSON WOOD
Pocklington House (Blind Home)
BISHOPSWOOD PRIVATE HOSP
MOUNT VERNON HOSPITAL
NORTHWOOD
FRITHWOOD PARK
Tennis Club
St. Helen's Sch
St. John's C of E Boys Sch
Cricket Ground
Sports Cen
THE GRAVEL PITS
The Grange
Northwood Coll
NORTHWOOD
Superstore
War Memorial
GREEN LANE
HA6
HILLINGDON
HARROW
PINNER WOOD
PINNER WOOD GOLF COURSE
PINNERWOOD PARK
RICKMANSWORTH ROAD
HIGH STREET
HOGS BACK OPEN SPACE
NORTHWOOD GOLF COURSE
Ducks Hill Farm
Ducks Hill Grange
DUCKS HILL
NORTHWOOD & PINNER COMMUNITY HOSP
Sports Centre
HA5
MONTESOLE PLAYING FIELDS
Northwood Hills
NORTHWOOD HILLS
NORTHWOOD CEMETERY
HASTE HILL GOLF COURSE
RUISLIP NATURE RESERVE
COPSE WOOD
Ashby Farm
YOUNG WOOD
POOR'S FIELD
HOSPITAL (closed)
The Starling PH
Superstore
PINNER GREEN
UXBRIDGE

40
BW
BX
BY
BZ
CA
CB
CC
12
13
14
45
46
47
48
49
50
51
52
53
54
91
92
93
94
24
39
60
CHALK HILL
LONDON ROAD
HIGH STREET
SPARROWS HERNE
A411
A4125
A4008
A404
A410
B4542
DEACONS HILL
EASTBURY LANE
BROOKDENE AVENUE
PINNER ROAD
OXHEY LANE
BUSHEY
BUSHEY GOLF COURSE & COUNTRY CLUB
KING GEORGE REC GROUND
RUNNING TRACK
MERRY HILL
WD23
WD19
WATFORD HEATH
SHERWOODS WOOD
MARGEHOLES WOOD
GOLF DRIVING RANGE
OXHEY PARK GOLF COURSE
Warren Dell
Ox Pasture Spring
SOUTH OXHEY PLAYING FIELDS
BIG WOOD
CARPENDERS PARK
CARPENDERS PARK CEMETERY
WOODWALKS
HARTSBOURNE GOLF COURSE & COUNTRY CLUB
HERTSMERE
MUTTON WOOD
LEVELS WOOD
Grim's Dyke Hotel
GRIMSTONE LAKE
THE CITY OPEN SPACE
WEALD WOOD
GRIM'S DYKE GOLF COURSE
STONY WOOD
SOUTH OXHEY
OXHEY
POND WOOD
SANDPIT WOOD
OXHEY WOOD
HERTFORDSHIRE
HARROW
THREE RIVERS
NANSCOT WOOD
SPORTS GROUND
SADDLERS MEAD REC GROUND
HATCH END
SHAFTESBURY PLAYING FIELDS
PINNER WOOD
PINNER HILL GOLF COURSE
HA5
PINNERWOOD PARK
UXBRIDGE ROAD
HARROW ARTS CENTRE
HATCH END PLAYING FIELD
RAGHUVANSHI CHARITABLE TRUST SPORTS GROUND
PINNER PARK
HEADSTONE LANE
BANNISTER STADIUM
THE CEDARS
MONTESOLE PLAYING FIELDS
PINNER GREEN
LITTLE COMMON
ST. THOMAS' DRIVE
RICKMANSWORTH RD
HA2
SPORTS GROUND
RECREATION

41
CD
CE
CF
CG
CH
CJ
CK
15
16
17
25
42
45
46
47
48
49
50
51
52
53
54
61
94
93
92
91
ALDENHAM RESERVOIR
SPORTS GROUND
ELSTREE HILL OPEN SPACE
BARNET
A411
ELSTREE ROAD
WATFORD BYPASS
A41
M1
CENTENNIAL PARK
ELSTREE OPEN SPACE
WD6
HERTSMERE
HARROW
Junction 4
Brockley Grange
Site of Sulloniace Roman Settlement
ROYAL NATIONAL ORTHOPAEDIC HOSP
Mike Heaffey Sports & Rehabilitation Centre
Aspire Centre
HELIPAD
LONDON LOOP
B.U.P.A. HOSPITAL
CONVENT Coll
Caldecote Farm
Berkeley Cottage
Gas Pumping Sta
BUSHEY HEATH
HEATHBOURNE ROAD
A409
A4140
MAGPIE HALL RD
THE COMMON
STANMORE COMMON
PEAR WOOD
BROCKLEY HILL
DRIVING RANGE
GOLF PARK
WATLING STREET (ROMAN ROAD)
EDGWARE WAY
BROCKLEY HILL
A5
GOVT OFFICES
Canons Corner
SPUR ROAD
STONEGROVE
High Sch for Girls
BENTLEY PRIORY
The Cedars
HARROW WEALD COMMON
Retirement Home
The Old Barn
The Kiln Nurseries
Priory House
BENTLEY PRIORY OPEN SPACE
BENTLEY PRIORY NATURE RESERVE
HERIOTS WOOD
DEER PARK
HA7
GROVE FIELDS
LITTLE COMMON
Harrow R.F.C.
CLOISTERS WOOD
STANMORE HALL
Abercorn Arms PH
STANMORE HILL
A410
LONDON ROAD
THE BDY
CHURCH RD
STANMORE
Lower Priory Farm
Suzanne's Riding School
HA3
BROOKSHILL
HARROW WEALD CEMETERY
HARROW WEALD LAKE
Harrow College
UXBRIDGE ROAD
N London Collegiate Sch
HA8
KING GEORGE V MEML GDNS
CANONS PARK
THE LAKE
Stanmore College
TEMPLE POND
MARSH LANE
A4140
HONEYPOT LANE
STANMORE GOLF COURSE
Clubhouse
PLAYING FIELD
CANONS PARK SPORTS GROUND
GOVT BUILDINGS
PRINCE EDWARD PLAYING FIELD
SPORTS GROUND
HARROW WEALD
RECREATION GROUND
HIGH ROAD
HIGH STREET
BELMONT
BELMONT CIRCLE
Kenton Lane Farm
CENTENARY PARK
SPORTS GRD
Pitch 'n' Putt
QUEENSBURY
WEALDSTONE
GEORGE STREET
BYRON REC GRD

42
CL
CM
CN
CP
CQ
CR
CS
19
20
21
Stirling Corner
A411
BARNET LANE
26
DEACONS HILL OPEN SPACE
Deacons Hill
SCRATCH WOOD
FROGHALL WOOD
BOYS HILL WOOD
THISTLE WOOD
GRAVEL PIT WOOD
ELSTREE OPEN SPACE
ELSTREE HILL SOUTH
45
WD6
HERTSMERE
BARNET
M1
46
Junction 4
Brockley Grange
Site of Sulloniacae Roman Settlement
94
47
CLUMP OF TREES WOOD
TARGET WOOD
LEG OF MUTTON POND
MILL HILL GOLF COURSE
NUT WOOD
London Gateway Services
HEMMINGS WOOD
STONEY WOOD LAKE
STONEY WOOD
EDGWAREBURY CEMETERY
REC GRD
SPORTS GRD
Bury Farm
EDGWAREBURY PARK
BROCKLEY HILL
DRIVING RANGE
48
EDGWAREBURY GOLF COURSE
A41 (WATFORD BYPASS)
EDGWARE WAY
A5 HILL
SPORTS GROUND Canons Corner
SPUR ROAD
93
GOVT OFFICES
49
A410 ROAD
STANMORE
41
STONEGROVE
Apex Corner
A5109
A5100
WATFORD WAY
A1
EDGWARE
HA8
CONVENT
50
HALE LANE
SELVAGE LANE
STONEGROVE PARK
N London Collegiate Sch
THE LAKE
92
KING GEORGE V MEML GDNS
CANONS PARK
THE SPINNEY
51
EDGWARE
BUS STA
Broadwalk Shopping Centre
BUS DEPOT
ALLOTMENTS
LYNDHURST PARK
HIGH STREET
STATION ROAD
DEANS LANE
MILL HILL BROADWAY
CANONS PARK
SPORTS GROUND
PLAYING FIELD
52
STANMORE MARSH
DEANSBROOK ROAD
EDGWARE COMMUNITY HOSPITAL
Hendon Coll
SPORTS GROUND
WATLING PARK
WOODCROFT PARK
CHANDOS RECREATION GROUND
GOVT BUILDINGS
91
HA7
53
PRINCE EDWARD PLAYING FIELD
SPORTS GROUND
BURNT OAK
BURNT OAK
A4140
HONEYPOT LANE
SILKSTREAM PARK
ADASTRAL ESTATE
GRAHAME PARK
54
CENTENARY PARK
Pitch 'n' Putt
BRIXTON EST
MONTROSE PLAYING FIELDS
COLINDALE HOSP
BLOOD TRANSFUSION CENTRE
PUBLIC HEALTH LAB
COLINDALE
COLINDALE BUSINESS PK
BURNT OAK BROADWAY
EDGWARE ROAD
62
QUEENSBURY
CAPITOL IND PK
Yaohan Plaza
BRIT. LIB NEWSPAPER COLLECTION

43
CT
CU
CV
CW
CX
CY
CZ
Barnet Gate
EN5
Ducks Island
27
GRANGE PLAYING FIELDS
OLD ELIZABETHANS (BARNET) MEMORIAL PLAYING FIELDS
KING GEORGE V PLAYING FIELDS
N20
45
SOUTH HERTS GOLF COURSE
OLD CHOLMELEIAN SPORTS GROUND
TOTTERIDGE FIELDS NATURE RESERVE
TOTTERIDGE COMMON
TOTTERIDGE
46
St. Edward's College
TOTTERIDGE VILLAGE
A5109
47
TOTTERIDGE GREEN
Highwood Hill
HIGHWOOD HILL
Holcombe Dales
Consolata Missionary Coll
48
DARLANDS LAKE NATURE RESERVE
Folly Brook
Dollis Brook
THE RIDGEWAY
NW7
St. Joseph's RC College
SPORTS GROUND
N12
49
44
Nat Inst for Medical Research
50
MILL HILL
ARRANDENE OPEN SPACE
INGLIS BARRACKS
FINCHLEY GOLF COURSE
92
51
MILL HILL PARK
MILL HILL CEM
BITTACY HILL PARK
Council Depot
MILL HILL EAST
52
CHASE LODGE PLAYING FIELD
METRO GOLF RANGE
HENDON GOLF COURSE
HENDON CEMETERY
91
N3
53
Junction 2
Five Ways Corner
BARNET COPTHALL STADIUM
COPTHALL PLAYING FIELDS
CHURCH END
FINCHLEY CENTRAL
HOLDERS HILL
NW4
SUNNY HILL PARK
54
RAF MUSEUMS
WINDSOR OPEN SPACE
EAST END ROAD
NW9
63
GREAT NORTH WAY
WATFORD WAY
M1
A1
A41
A504
REGENTS PARK
22
23
24

44
DA
DB
DC
DD
DE
DF
DG
28
26
27
45
46
47
48
49
50
51
52
53
54
43
64
94
93
92
91
EAST BARNET
Oak Hill Theological Coll
OAK HILL PARK
EN4
SOUTH HERTS GOLF COURSE
BROOK FARM OPEN SPACE
N20
KING GEORGE V PLAYING FIELDS
BARNET PLAYING FIELDS
WYATTS FARM OPEN SPACE
DAME ALICE OWEN'S GRD
OAKLEIGH PARK
TOTTERIDGE & WHETSTONE
TOTTERIDGE GREEN
WHETSTONE
SWAN LANE OPEN SPACE
NORTH MIDDLESEX GOLF COURSE
BRUNSWICK PARK
BETHUNE PARK GOLF COURSE
NEW SOUTHGATE REC GRD
FRIARY PARK
FRIERN BARNET
Consolata Missionary Coll
WOODSIDE PARK
N12
NORTH FINCHLEY
FINCHLEY
COPPETTS WOOD
WEST FINCHLEY
FINCHLEY MEMORIAL HOSP
GLEBELANDS OPEN SPACE
Great North Leisure Park
MUSWELL HILL SPORTS GROUND
COPPETTS WOOD HOSP
ST PANCRAS & ISLINGTON CEMETERY
N2
N3
FINCHLEY CENTRAL
CHURCH END
AVENUE HOUSE GRDS
COLDFALL WOOD
N10
A1000
A5109
A109
A1003
A406
A598
A504
B550
TOTTERIDGE LANE
OAKLEIGH ROAD
HIGH ROAD
BALLARDS LANE
WOODHOUSE ROAD
FRIERN BARNET ROAD
NORTH CIRCULAR ROAD
EAST END ROAD
REGENTS PARK ROAD
OAKLEIGH ROAD NORTH

45
DH
DJ
DK
DL
DM
DN
DP
29
30
31
OAKWOOD PARK
OAKWOOD
WINCHMORE HILL
GROVELANDS PARK
BOATING LAKE
PRIORY HOSPITAL
N14
N21
N13
N11
N22
OSIDGE
SOUTHGATE
Southgate Technical Coll
SOUTHGATE CEMETERY
CREMATORIUM
THE PAULIN GROUND
CLOWES SPORTS GROUND
FIRS FARM PLAYING FIELD
PALMERS GREEN
ARNOS PARK
NEW SOUTHGATE
BROOMFIELD PARK
TATEM PARK REC GRD
HAZELWOOD SPORTS GRD
HOLLYWOOD GDNS
BOWES PARK
FRIERN BRIDGE RETAIL PARK
Middlesex Uni
TOTTENHALL SPORTS GROUND
BOUNDARY PLAYING FIELDS
NEW RIVER SPORTS CENTRE
MUSWELL HILL GOLF COURSE
SCOUT PARK
TRAIN DEPOT
WOOD GREEN
NOEL PARK
LORDSHIP RECREATION GROUND
ALEXANDRA PALACE
ALEXANDRA PARK
HORNSEY WATER TREATMENT WORKS
BELMONT REC GRD
DOWNHILLS PARK
MUSWELL HILL
HORNSEY
TURNPIKE LANE
46
47
48
49
50
51
52
53
54
65
91
92
93
94
A111
A1004
A1003
A105
A406
A109
A1110
A10
A1080
CHASE SIDE
HIGH STREET
THE BOURNE
BOURNE HILL
WATERFALL ROAD
CANNON HILL
ALDERMANS HILL
GREEN LANES
HEDGE LANE
NORTH CIRCULAR ROAD
BOWES ROAD
TELFORD ROAD
BOUNDS GREEN ROAD
HIGH ROAD
LORDSHIP LANE
WESTBURY AVENUE
THE BROADWAY
GREAT CAMBRIDGE ROAD
BOREHAM AVENUE

46
DQ
DR
DS
DT
DU
DV
DW
33
34
35
30
45
46
47
48
49
50
51
52
53
54
94
93
92
91
66
N21
N13
N9
N18
N17
N22
LOWER EDMONTON
EDMONTON
UPPER EDMONTON
TOTTENHAM
TOTTENHAM HALE
TOTTENHAM MARSHES
NOEL PARK
WINCHMORE HILL
RIDGE AVENUE
GREEN LANES
GREAT CAMBRIDGE ROAD
NORTH CIRCULAR ROAD
STERLING WAY
ANGEL ROAD
HERTFORD ROAD
FORE STREET
HIGH ROAD
MERIDIAN WAY
WATERMEAD WAY
LORDSHIP LANE
BRUCE GROVE
THE ROUNDWAY
WESTBURY AVENUE
HEDGE LANE
VILLAGE ROAD
CHURCH STREET
SILVER STREET
CONDUIT LANE
KING GEORGE'S FLD
JUBILEE PARK
THE PAULIN GROUND
EDMONTON CEMETERY
FIRS FARM PLAYING FIELDS
CLOWES SPORTS GROUND
CHURCH STREET REC GRD
CHURCHFIELD REC GRD
PYMMES PARK
TATEM PARK REC GRD
HOLLYWOOD GDNS
NORTH MIDDLESEX HOSPITAL
EDMONTON FEDERATION CEMETERY (JEWISH)
WESTERN SYNAGOGUE CEMETERY
TOTTENHAM PARK CEMETERY
MONTAGU RECREATION GROUND
CRAIG PARK
TOTTENHALL SPORTS GROUND
BOUNDARY PLAYING FIELDS
NEW RIVER SPORTS CENTRE
TOTTENHAM CEMETERY
BRUCE CASTLE PARK
BRUCE CASTLE MUS
LORDSHIP RECREATION GROUND
BROADWATER FARM EST
TOWER GDNS
BELMONT REC GRD
DOWNHILLS PARK
WHITE HART LANE TOTTENHAM HOTSPUR FC
THE ROYAL LONDON ESTATE
MOWLEM TRADING ESTATE
WINGATE TRADING EST
NORTHUMBERLAND PARK
LEE VALLEY PARK
LOCKWOOD RESERVOIR
DOWN LANE REC GRD
LEE VALLEY TECHNOPARK
MILLMEAD INDUSTRIAL CENTRE
EDMONTON GREEN
Edmonton Green Shopping Cen
SALISBURY HO ARTS CEN
Salmon's Brook
Pymme's Brook
The Moselle
Kenninghall
Angel Rd Works
Electricity Station
LRT DEPOT
Superstore

DX
DY
DZ
EA
EB
EC
ED
36
37
38
31
45
46
47
48
49
50
51
52
53
54
67
91
92
93
94
ROYAL EPPING FOREST GOLF COURSE
THE HAWK WOOD
POLE HILL
CHINGFORD PLAIN
CHINGFORD
LEE VALLEY
WILLIAM GIRLING RESERVOIR
GOLF COURSE
DEEPHAMS SEWAGE TREATMENT WORKS
LEE VALLEY PARK
MANSFIELD PARK
RIDGEWAY PARK
FRIDAY HILL
PIMP HALL PARK
E4
CHINGFORD MOUNT CEMETERY
CHINGFORD HATCH
LARKSWOOD PLAYING FIELDS
LARKS WOOD
CHINGFORD HALL PARK
SOUTH CHINGFORD
HIGHAMS PARK
HALE END
JUBILEE SPORTS GRD
THE HIGHAMS PARK
BOATING LAKE
WOODFORD GOLF COURSE
WOODFORD R.F.C.
EPPING FOREST
IG8
Cooks Wharf Roundabout
Hall La
LEA VALLEY VIADUCT
BANBURY RESERVOIR
NORTH CIRCULAR RD
WALTHAMSTOW STADIUM
Crooked Billet Roundabout
SOUTHEND RD
WALTHAMSTOW FOREST
Waterworks Cor
HIGHAM HILL
E17
LLOYD PARK
Sir George Monoux Coll
WALTHAMSTOW
WALTHAM FOREST TRACK
CHESTNUTS SHOWGROUND
Waltham Forest Coll
THORPE COOMBE HOSP
UPLANDS BUSINESS PARK
HIGHAMS LODGE BUSINESS CEN
KINGS HEAD HILL
NEW ROAD
HATCH LA
OLD CHURCH ROAD
CHINGFORD MOUNT ROAD
WALTHAM WAY
LARKSHALL ROAD
FOREST ROAD
WOODFORD NEW ROAD
MERIDIAN WAY
SOUTH ROUTE

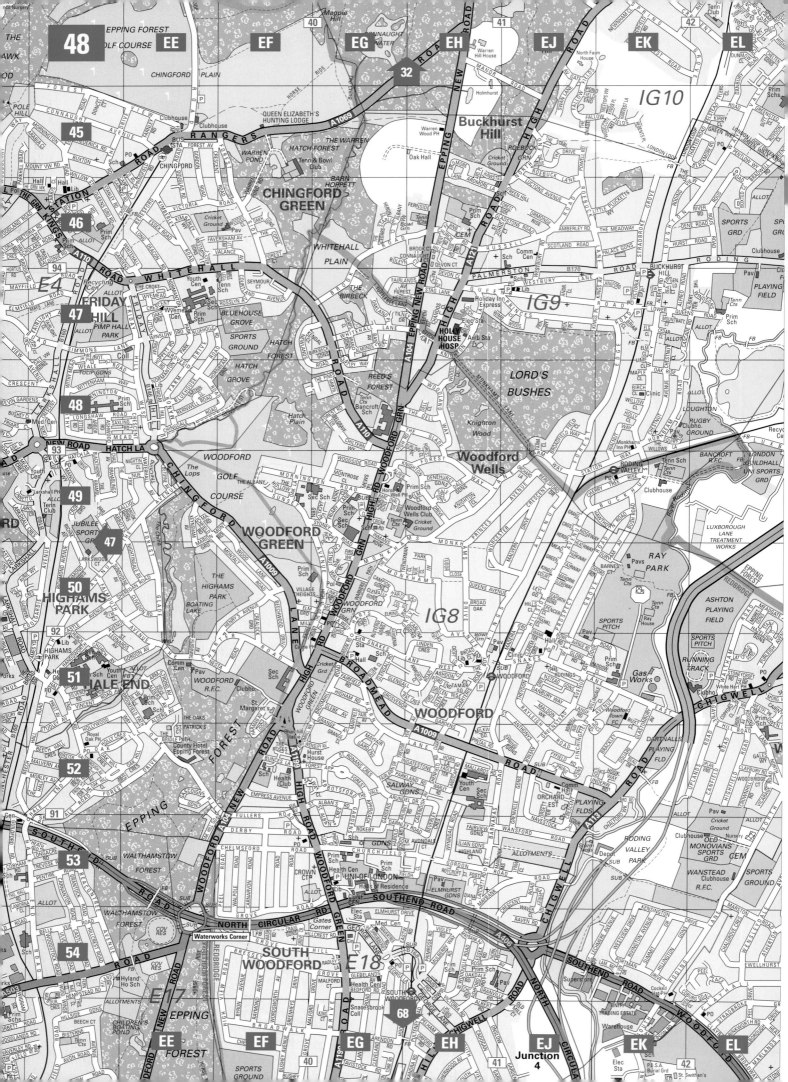

48
EE
EF
EG
EH
EJ
EK
EL
32
40
41
42
EPPING FOREST GOLF COURSE
CHINGFORD PLAIN
CONNAUGHT WATER
Magpie Hill
Warren Hill House
North Farm House
IG10
Holmhurst
Buckhurst Hill
QUEEN ELIZABETH'S HUNTING LODGE
A1069
RANGERS ROAD
CHINGFORD
HATCH FOREST
THE WARREN
WARREN POND
Tenn & Bowl Club
BARN HOPPETT
CHINGFORD GREEN
Oak Hall
Warren Wood PH
EPPING NEW ROAD
HIGH ROAD
STATION ROAD
KINGS ROAD
45
46
47
48
49
50
51
52
53
54
94
93
92
91
E4
FRIDAY HILL
PIMP HALL PARK
WHITEHALL ROAD
WHITEHALL PLAIN
BLUEHOUSE GROVE
SPORTS GROUND
HATCH FOREST
HATCH GROVE
THE BIRBECK
REED'S FOREST
Bancroft Sch
Hatch Plain
A110
A104
A121
IG9
Holiday Inn Express
HOLLY HOUSE HOSP
LORD'S BUSHES
Knighton Wood
Woodford Wells
PALMERSTON ROAD
QUEENS ROAD
BUCKHURST HILL
PLAYING FIELD
SPORTS GRD
LOUGHTON
RUGBY GROUND
BANCROFT R.F.C.
LONDON GUILDHALL UNI SPORTS GRD
RODING VALLEY
River Roding
LUXBOROUGH LANE TREATMENT WORKS
RAY PARK
EPPING FOREST
REDBRIDGE
ASHTON PLAYING FIELD
RUNNING TRACK
NEW ROAD
HATCH LA
CHINGFORD LANE
WOODFORD GOLF COURSE
The Lops
WOODFORD GREEN
Woodford Wells Club
Cricket Ground
A1009
THE HIGHAMS PARK
BOATING LAKE
HIGHAMS PARK
JUBILEE SPORTS GRD
IG8
HALE END
WOODFORD R.F.C.
BROADMEAD ROAD
WOODFORD
Gas Works
Woodford Town FC
DARTNALLS PLAYING FLD
CHIGWELL ROAD
A113
ORCHARD EST
PLAYING FLDS
RODING VALLEY PARK
OLD MONOVIANS SPORTS GRD
CEM
WANSTEAD Clubhouse R.F.C.
SPORTS GROUND
County Hotel Epping Forest
EPPING FOREST
WALTHAMSTOW FOREST
SOUTHEND ROAD
NORTH CIRCULAR RD
Waterworks Corner
Gates Corner
UNI OF LONDON
Halls of Residence
A406
SOUTH WOODFORD
E18
E17
68
Snaresbrook Coll
CHILDREN'S BOATING POND
Superstore
TRADING ESTATE
Warehouse
Junction 4
SPORTS GROUND

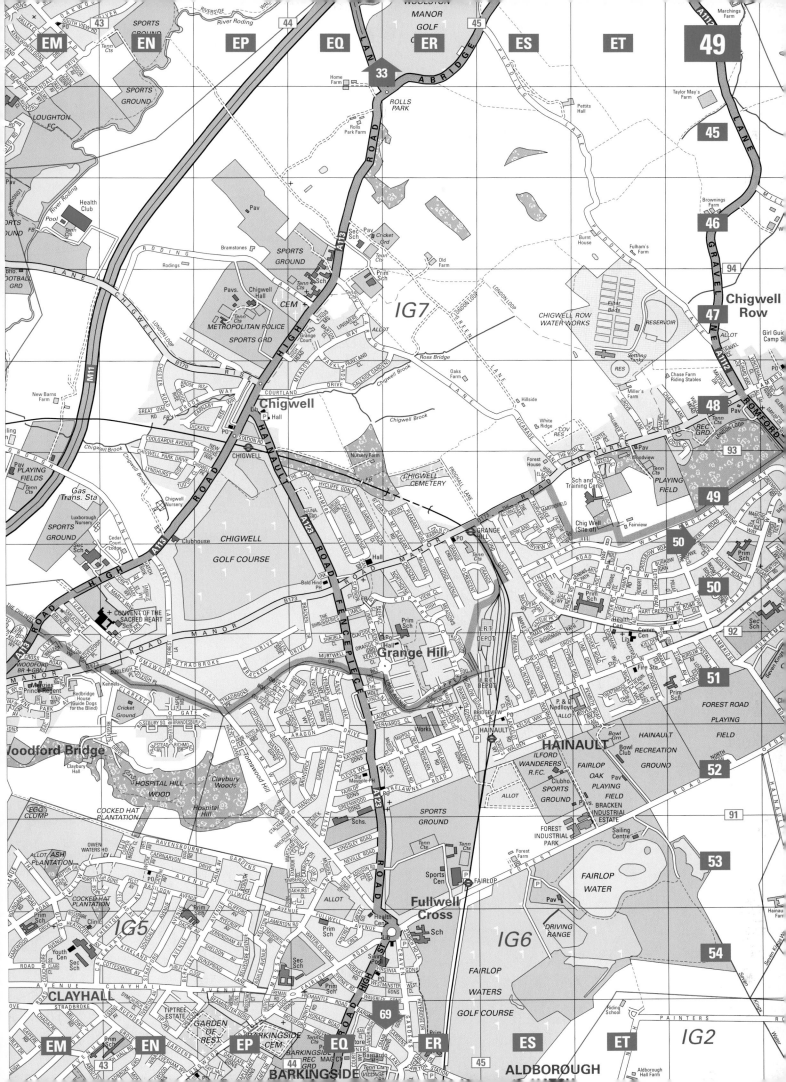49
EM
EN
EP
EQ
ER
ES
ET
43
44
45
33
WOOLSTON MANOR GOLF COURSE
River Roding
SPORTS GROUND
LOUGHTON FC
ROLLS PARK
Rolls Park Farm
Home Farm
Pettits Hall
Taylor May's Farm
Marchings Farm
Health Club
Pool
Bramstones
Rodings
SPORTS GROUND
METROPOLITAN POLICE SPORTS GRD
Chigwell Hall
CEM
IG7
Old Farm
Burnt House
Fulham's Farm
Brownings Farm
CHIGWELL ROW WATER WORKS
Filter Beds
RESERVOIR
Settling Tanks
RES
Chigwell Row
Girl Guide Camp Site
Chase Farm Riding Stables
Miller's Farm
Oaks Farm
Hillside
White Ridge
Ross Bridge
Chigwell Brook
Chigwell
CHIGWELL
New Barns Farm
Gas Trans. Sta
PLAYING FIELDS
SPORTS GROUND
Luxborough Nursery
Chigwell Nursery
Nursery Farm
CHIGWELL CEMETERY
CHIGWELL GOLF COURSE
Clubhouse
Cedar Court Lodge
CONVENT OF THE SACRED HEART
Forest House
Sch and Training Cen
PLAYING FIELD
Chig Well (Site of)
Fairview
GRANGE HILL
Grange Hill
Bald Hind PH
L.R.T. DEPOT
Woodford Bridge
Menzies Prince Regent
Redbridge House (Guide Dogs for the Blind)
Cricket Ground
Claybury Hall
HOSPITAL HILL WOOD
Claybury Woods
Hospital Hill
Tomswood Hill
EGG CLUMP
COCKED HAT PLANTATION
ASH PLANTATION
HAINAULT
ILFORD WANDERERS R.F.C.
FAIRLOP OAK PLAYING FIELD
HAINAULT RECREATION GROUND
FOREST ROAD PLAYING FIELD
BRACKEN INDUSTRIAL ESTATE
FOREST INDUSTRIAL PARK
Sailing Centre
FAIRLOP WATER
DRIVING RANGE
SPORTS GROUND
Sports Cen
FAIRLOP
Fullwell Cross
IG5
IG6
FAIRLOP WATERS GOLF COURSE
CLAYHALL
TIPTREE ESTATE
GARDEN OF REST
BARKINGSIDE CEM
BARKINGSIDE REC GRD
BARKINGSIDE
ALDBOROUGH
Aldborough Hall Farm
Riding School
IG2
A113
A123
A1112
B173
B170
M11
HIGH ROAD
HAINAULT ROAD
FENCEPIECE ROAD
MANOR ROAD
ABRIDGE ROAD
LAMBOURNE ROAD
ROMFORD ROAD
GRAVEL LANE
PUDDING LANE
VICARAGE LANE
GREEN LANE
FOREST ROAD
CHIGWELL LANE
CHIGWELL RISE
BROCKET WAY
LONDON LOOP
45
46
47
48
49
50
51
52
53
54
69
91
92
93
94

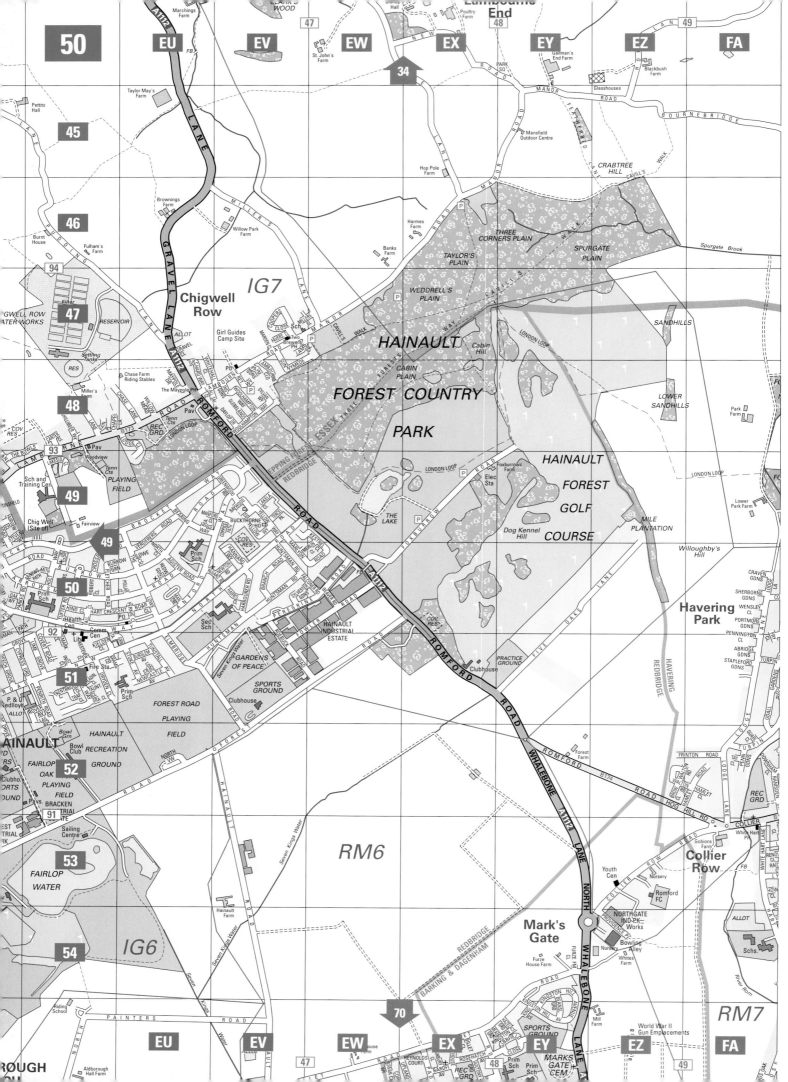
Chigwell Row
IG7
HAINAULT
FOREST COUNTRY
PARK
HAINAULT
FOREST
GOLF
COURSE
Havering Park
Collier Row
Mark's Gate
RM6
IG6
RM7
FAIRLOP WATER
FOREST ROAD PLAYING FIELD
HAINAULT RECREATION GROUND
FAIRLOP OAK PLAYING FIELD
HAINAULT INDUSTRIAL ESTATE
GARDENS OF PEACE
SPORTS GROUND
THREE CORNERS PLAIN
SPURGATE PLAIN
TAYLOR'S PLAIN
WEDDRELL'S PLAIN
CABIN PLAIN
Cabin Hill
THE LAKE
Dog Kennel Hill
SANDHILLS
LOWER SANDHILLS
MILE PLANTATION
Willoughby's Hill
CRABTREE HILL
ROMFORD ROAD
GRAVEL LANE
WHALEBONE LANE NORTH
MANOR ROAD
PAINTERS ROAD
HAINAULT ROAD
FOXBURROW ROAD
FIVE OAKS LANE
LONDON LOOP
Spurgate Brook
Seven Kings Water
EU
EV
EW
EX
EY
EZ
FA
34
70
49

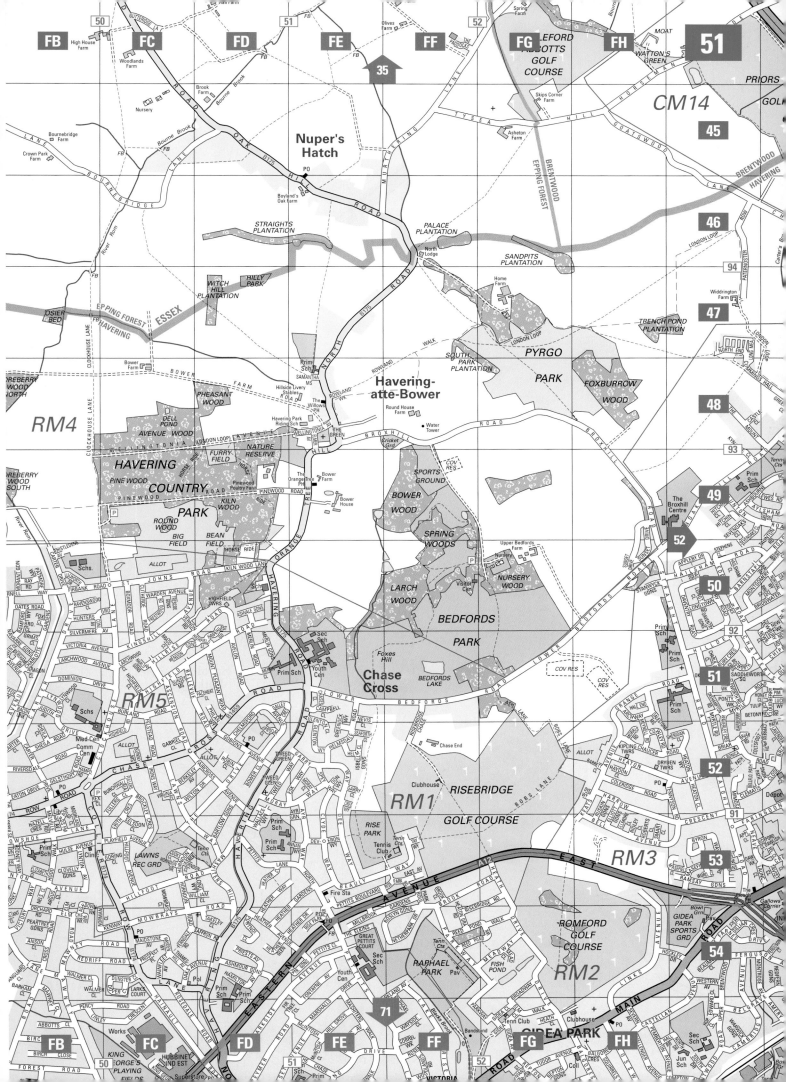

51
FB
FC
FD
FE
FF
FG
FH
50
51
52
35
71
45
46
47
48
49
50
51
52
53
54
91
92
93
94
CM14
RM1
RM2
RM3
RM4
RM5
Nuper's Hatch
Havering-atte-Bower
Chase Cross
GIDEA PARK
PRIORS
NOAK HILL ROAD
NORTH ROAD
B175
HAVERING ROAD
ORANGE TREE HILL
LOWER BEDFORDS ROAD
BROXHILL ROAD
BOURNEBRIDGE LANE
TYSEA HILL
GOATSWOOD LANE
HORSEMAN
MURTHERING LANE
EASTERN AVENUE
EAST AVENUE
A12
MAIN ROAD
CHASE CROSS ROAD
COLLIER ROW LANE
CLOCKHOUSE LANE
BOWER FARM ROAD
PINEWOOD ROAD
WELLINGTONIA AVENUE
ST JOHNS ROAD
KILN WOOD LANE
BOBS LANE
ASH LANE
STRAIGHT ROAD
HAVERING COUNTRY PARK
BEDFORDS PARK
PYRGO PARK
FOXBURROW WOOD
BOWER WOOD
SPRING WOODS
LARCH WOOD
NURSERY WOOD
ROUND WOOD
KILN WOOD
PINE WOOD
PHEASANT WOOD
DELL POND
AVENUE WOOD
FURRY FIELD
NATURE RESERVE
BIG FIELD
BEAN FIELD
WITCH HILL PLANTATION
HILLY PARK
STRAIGHTS PLANTATION
PALACE PLANTATION
SANDPITS PLANTATION
SOUTH PARK PLANTATION
TRENCH POND PLANTATION
OREBERRY WOOD NORTH
OREBERRY WOOD SOUTH
OSIER BED
EPPING FOREST
ESSEX
HAVERING
BRENTWOOD
LONDON LOOP
STAPLEFORD ABBOTTS GOLF COURSE
RISEBRIDGE GOLF COURSE
ROMFORD GOLF COURSE
RAPHAEL PARK
RISE PARK
LAWNS REC GRD
GIDEA PARK SPORTS GRD
BEDFORDS LAKE
FISH POND
SPORTS GROUND
High House Farm
Woodlands Farm
Brook Farm
Nursery
Bournebridge Farm
Crown Park Farm
Boyland's Oak Farm
Olives Farm
Spring Farm
Skips Corner Farm
Asheton Farm
Home Farm
Widdrington Farm
North Lodge
Bower Farm
Round House Farm
Water Tower
Bower House
Pinewood Poultry Farm
Upper Bedfords Farm
The Broxhill Centre
Chase End
Clubhouse
Tennis Club
Fire Sta
Youth Cen
Sec Sch
Prim Sch
Schs
Med Cen
Works
HUBBINET IND EST
Superstore
Bandstand
Tenn Club
WATTON'S GREEN
MOAT
Foxes Hill
Gallows Corner

52
FJ
FK
FL
FM
FN
FP
FQ
54
55
56
45
46
47
48
49
50
51
52
53
54
94
93
92
91
PRIORS
GOLF
COURSE
ESSEX
BRENTWOOD
HAVERING
RM4
CURTIS PLANTATION
WABBING'S PLANTATION
SEVENACRE PLANTATION
CM14
LOCKSMITH WOOD
GOLDSMITH WOOD
Frieze Hall
The Chequers PH
Weald Bridge
Weald Brook
Wright's Bridge
Old Macdonalds Farm
Wrightsbridge Farm
Wealdside
Rochetts Farm
St. Vincent's Hamlet
M25
Pentowan Farm
SPICE PITS WOOD
Spice Pits Farm
Hill Farm
NOAK HILL SPORTS GRD
Hall
Noak Hill
Widdrington Farm
TRENCH POND PLANTATION
FOXBURROW
Carter's Brook
Manor Farm
The Bear PH
THE OSIERS
BURNTWOOD
FIR WOOD
COCK WOOD
ALDER WOOD
DAGNAM PARK
MAYLANDS
GOLF
COURSE
HATTER'S
WOOD
Coll
Dycorts Sch
Sec Sch
Prim Sch
DUCK WOOD NATURE RESERVE
The Broxhill Centre
CENTRAL PARK
Harold Hill
LONG WOOD
SALE WOOD
Swim Pool
Health Cen
Youth Club
Comm Cen
Pol
Youth Centre
Cricket Ground
SHOULDER OF MUTTON WOOD
Clubhouse
Maylands
Putwell Bridge
SPORTS GRD
RM3
Harold Park
The Saxon King PH
PLAYING FIELD
COLCHESTER ROAD
A12
NAGS HEAD SEWAGE
Sludge Beds
BATES INDUSTRIAL EST
Harold Court
HAROLD HILL INDUSTRIAL ESTATE
Depot
Superstore
Works
Roots & Shoots Nursery
HAROLD WOOD HOSPITAL
King Harold PH
HAROLD WOOD
Ivy Lodge Farm
The Shepherd & Dog PH
Cockabourne Bridge
Pages Farm
Riding Stables
RM14
RM2
ROMFORD GOLF COURSE
GIDEA PARK SPORTS GRD
Gallows Corner
AVENUE INDUSTRIAL ESTATE
The Plough
Clinic
Comm Cen
Cricket Ground
HAROLD WOOD PARK
Sec Sch
Prim Sch
72
Prospect Farm
Tyes Farm
Abattoir
Ingrebourne
Ingrebourne River
SOUTHEND ARTERIAL ROAD
A127
MAIN ROAD
Clubhouse
PO
Coll
Jun Sch

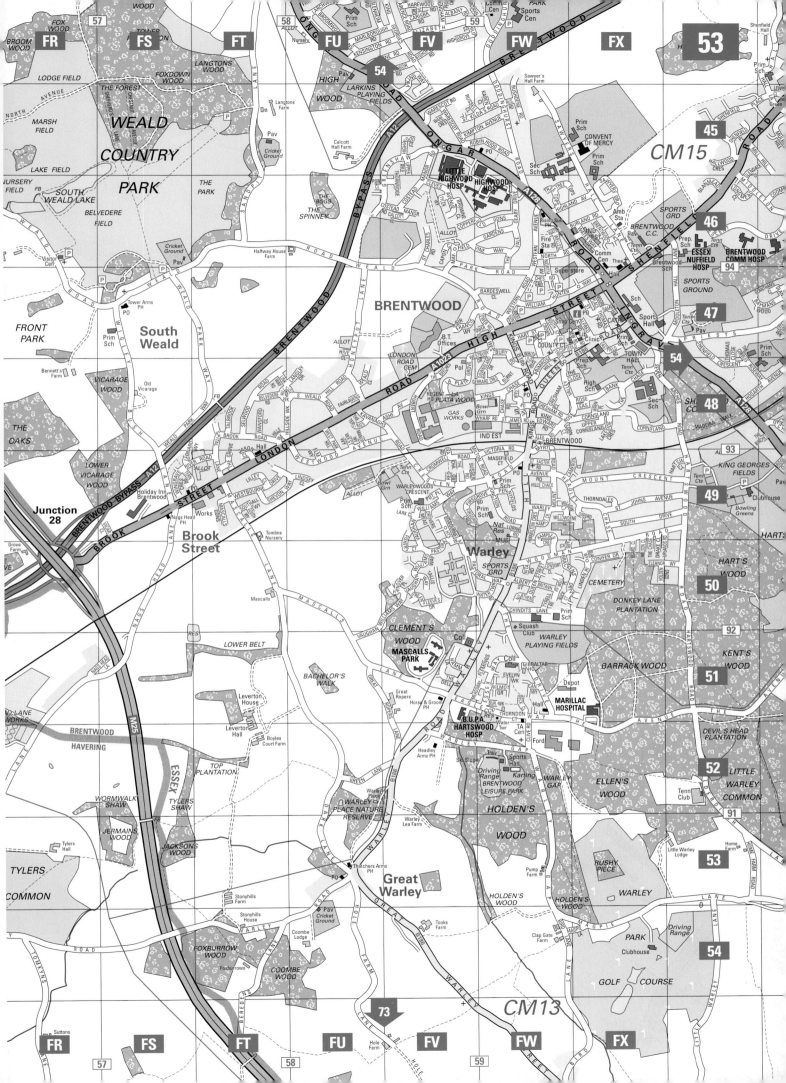

53
FR
FS
FT
FU
FV
FW
FX
57
58
59
WEALD COUNTRY PARK
BRENTWOOD
South Weald
Brook Street
Warley
Great Warley
Junction 28
CM15
CM13
LITTLE HIGHWOOD HOSP
HIGHWOOD HOSP
CONVENT OF MERCY
ESSEX NUFFIELD HOSP
BRENTWOOD COMM HOSP
MARILLAC HOSPITAL
B.U.P.A. HARTSWOOD HOSP
MASCALLS PARK
CLEMENT'S WOOD
WARLEY PLAYING FIELDS
BARRACK WOOD
HART'S WOOD
KENT'S WOOD
DONKEY LANE PLANTATION
DEVIL'S HEAD PLANTATION
LITTLE WARLEY COMMON
ELLEN'S WOOD
HOLDEN'S WOOD
WARLEY PLACE NATURE RESERVE
BRENTWOOD LEISURE PARK
TYLERS COMMON
FOXBURROW WOOD
COOMBE WOOD
JACKSONS WOOD
JERMAINS WOOD
WORMWALK SHAW
TYLERS SHAW
TOP PLANTATION
BACHELOR'S WALK
LOWER BELT
VICARAGE WOOD
LOWER VICARAGE WOOD
THE OAKS
FRONT PARK
KING GEORGES FIELDS
WARLEY PARK GOLF COURSE
HIGH WOOD
LARKINS PLAYING FIELDS
LANGTONS WOOD
FOXDOWN WOOD
MARSH FIELD
LAKE FIELD
SOUTH WEALD LAKE
BELVEDERE FIELD
THE PARK
THE SPINNEY
BRENTWOOD BYPASS A12
M25
A128
A1023
B186
BRENTWOOD
HAVERING
ESSEX
45
46
47
48
49
50
51
52
53
54
54
73
91
92
93
94

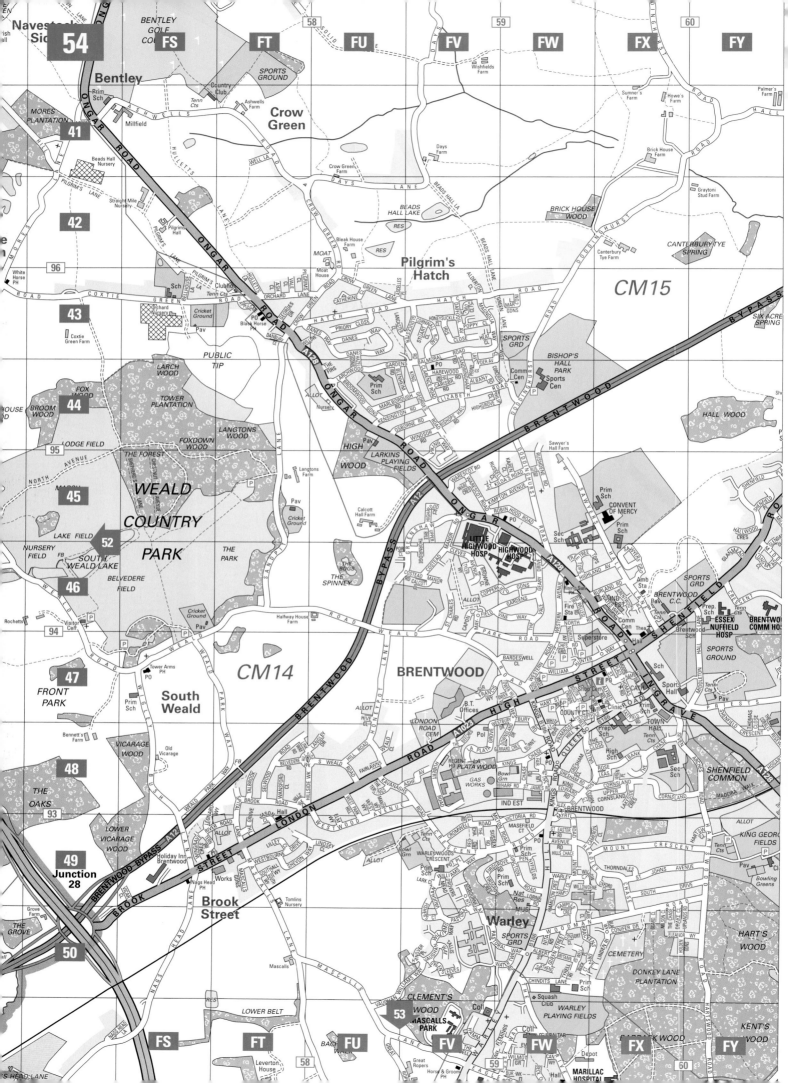
Bentley
Crow Green
Pilgrim's Hatch
CM15
WEALD COUNTRY PARK
CM14
BRENTWOOD
South Weald
Brook Street
Warley
ONGAR ROAD
BRENTWOOD BYPASS
LONDON ROAD
HIGH STREET
SHENFIELD ROAD
INGRAVE ROAD
DODDINGHURST ROAD
WEALD ROAD
Junction 28
LITTLE HIGHWOOD HOSP
HIGHWOOD HOSP
CONVENT OF MERCY
ESSEX NUFFIELD HOSP
MARILLAC HOSPITAL
SHENFIELD COMMON
HART'S WOOD
DONKEY LANE PLANTATION
CEMETERY
BISHOP'S HALL PARK
HALL WOOD
CANTERBURY TYE SPRING
BRICK HOUSE WOOD
BEADS HALL LAKE
SOUTH WEALD LAKE
FRONT PARK
THE OAKS
LOWER VICARAGE WOOD
VICARAGE WOOD
CLEMENT'S WOOD
MASCALLS PARK
WARLEY PLAYING FIELDS
FS
FT
FU
FV
FW
FX
FY
58
59
60
96
95
94
93
41
42
43
44
45
46
47
48
49
50
52
53

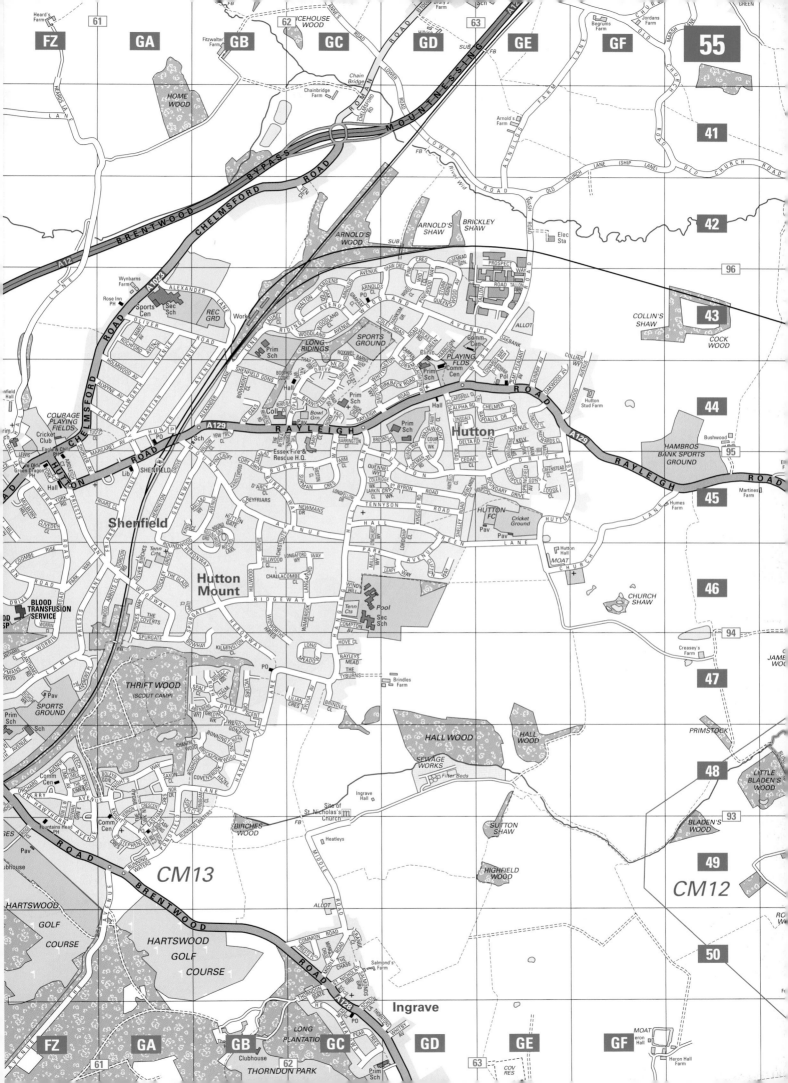
FZ
GA
GB
GC
GD
GE
GF
61
62
63
41
42
43
44
45
46
47
48
49
50
96
95
94
93
Shenfield
Hutton
Hutton Mount
Ingrave
CM13
CM12
HOME WOOD
ICEHOUSE WOOD
ARNOLD'S WOOD
ARNOLD'S SHAW
BRICKLEY SHAW
COLLIN'S SHAW
COCK WOOD
HAMBROS BANK SPORTS GROUND
CHURCH SHAW
THRIFT WOOD
(SCOUT CAMP)
HALL WOOD
SEWAGE WORKS
Filter Beds
SUTTON SHAW
HIGHFIELD WOOD
BIRCHES WOOD
LITTLE BLADEN'S WOOD
BLADEN'S WOOD
PRIMSTOCK
HARTSWOOD GOLF COURSE
LONG PLANTATIO
THORNDON PARK
BLOOD TRANSFUSION SERVICE
COURAGE PLAYING FIELDS
SPORTS GROUND
LONG RIDINGS
PLAYING FLDS
HUTTON FC
Cricket Ground
Essex Fire & Rescue H.Q.
BRENTWOOD BYPASS
MOUNTNESSING
CHELMSFORD ROAD
RAYLEIGH ROAD
BRENTWOOD ROAD
A12
A1023
A129
A128
Heard's Farm
Fitzwalter's Farm
Chainbridge Farm
Chain Bridge
Begrums Farm
Jordans Farm
Arnold's Farm
Wynbarns Farm
Rose Inn PH
Hutton Stud Farm
Bushwood
Martines Farm
Humes Farm
Hutton Hall
MOAT
Creasey's Farm
Brindles Farm
Ingrave Hall
Site of St Nicholas's Church
Heatleys
Salmond's Farm
Heron Hall
Heron Hall Farm
Fountains Head PH
Ye Olde Green Dragon PH
Eagle & Child PH
Elec Sta
River Wid
ALLOT
Clubhouse
COV RES

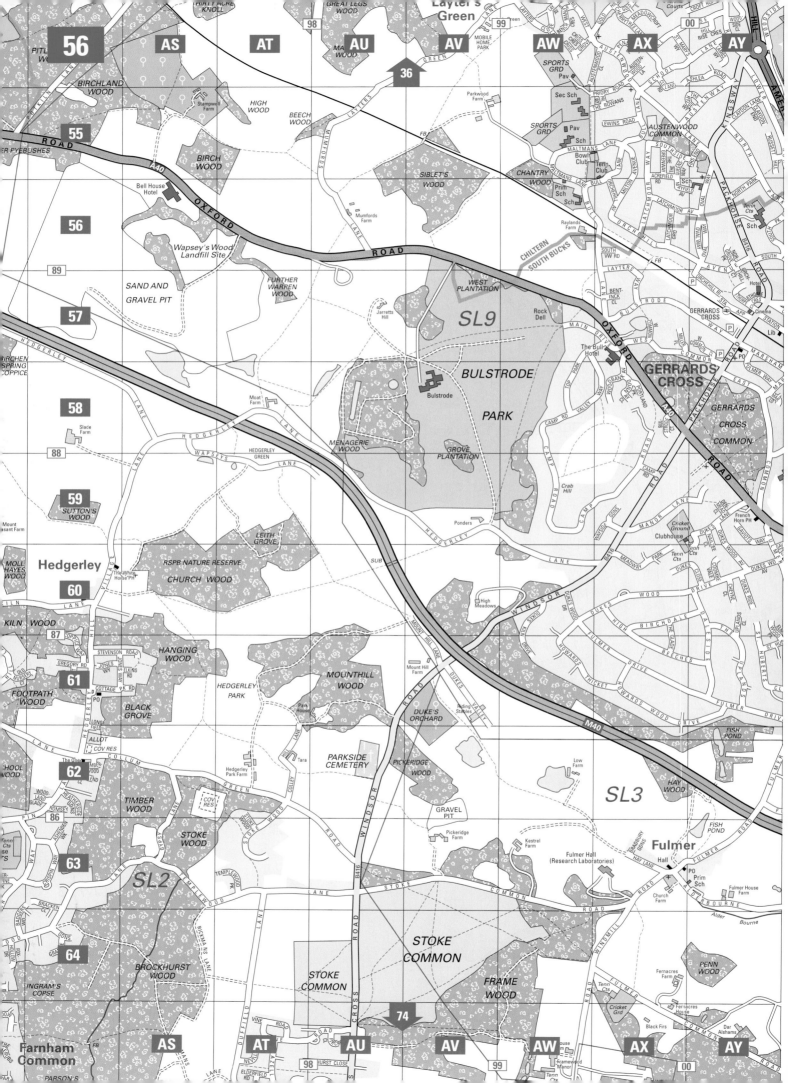
AS
AT
AU
AV
AW
AX
AY
36
74
55
56
57
58
59
60
61
62
63
64
89
88
87
86
98
99
00
Layter's Green
BIRCHLAND WOOD
HIGH WOOD
BEECH WOOD
BIRCH WOOD
SIBLET'S WOOD
CHANTRY WOOD
AUSTENWOOD COMMON
OXFORD ROAD
A40
Bell House Hotel
Wapsey's Wood Landfill Site
SAND AND GRAVEL PIT
FURTHER WARREN WOOD
WEST PLANTATION
SL9
CHILTERN
SOUTH BUCKS
Rock Dell
BULSTRODE
Bulstrode
PARK
The Bull Hotel
GERRARDS CROSS
GERRARDS CROSS COMMON
MENAGERIE WOOD
GROVE PLANTATION
HEDGERLEY LANE
HEDGERLEY GREEN
SUTTON'S WOOD
LEITH GROVE
Hedgerley
RSPB NATURE RESERVE
CHURCH WOOD
MOLL HAYES WOOD
KILN WOOD
HANGING WOOD
MOUNTHILL WOOD
HEDGERLEY PARK
FOOTPATH WOOD
BLACK GROVE
DUKE'S ORCHARD
PARKSIDE CEMETERY
PICKERIDGE WOOD
TIMBER WOOD
STOKE WOOD
GRAVEL PIT
M40
SL3
HAY WOOD
FISH POND
Fulmer
Fulmer Hall (Research Laboratories)
SL2
STOKE COMMON
BROCKHURST WOOD
INGRAM'S COPSE
FRAME WOOD
PENN WOOD
Farnham Common
WINDSOR ROAD
B416
STOKE COMMON ROAD
FULMER COMMON ROAD
Alder Bourne
Crab Hill
Cricket Ground
Clubhouse

57
AZ
BA
BB
BC
BD
BE
BF
01
02
03
37
75
HOGTROUGH WOOD
GERRARDS CROSS GOLF COURSE
Cricket Ground
Pav
Clubhouse
Tenn Cts
CHALFONT PARK
River Misbourne
CHILTERNS
SOUTH BUCKS
SQUARE COPSE
Coldharbour Farm
ROUND COPSE
Cricket Ground
NOCKHILL WOOD
JUNIPER WOOD
QUARTERS WOOD
OAKEND WOOD
Meadow Grange
Castleman's Farm
Stables
OAKEND WOOD
DENHAM MARSH WOOD
Owls Oak
MARISH LANE
MIRRIE LANE
Isle of Wight Farm
OVER THE MISBOURNE
SLADE OAK LANE
THREE RIVERS
SOUTH BUCKS
TRAINING CENTRE DURDENT COURT
Little Halings
TILEHOUSE LANE
GREAT HALINGS WOOD
HALINGS LANE
Wyatts Covert Caravan Park
NORTHMOOR HILL (NATURE RESERVE)
Denham Park Farm
Pilot Centre
Hangars
DENHAM AERODROME
Flying Schools
UXBRIDGE ROAD
Colne
Weir
Lock
55
56
BATTLESFORD WOOD
89
RANSTON COVERT
57
Rank Film Laboratories
WADLEY COVERT
NIGHTINGALE WOOD
HOLLY HILL WOOD
NORTH ORBITAL ROAD
A412
Sherwood House
Denham Green
NEWSTEAD WOOD
Prim Sch
DENHAM GOLF COURSE
COLLSELS WOOD
Clubhouse
DENHAM GOLF CLUB
58
Green Bridge
Savay Farm
88
Medical Cen
PO
59
UB9
MARTINSFIELD SPORTS GRD
Clubhouse
58
BUCKINGHAMS
60
THE PYGHTLE
Denham Place
87
Hall
VILLAGE
61
Wellers Mead
Prim Sch
Bowl Club
REC GRD
Tenn Cts
Denham
62
SPORTS GROUND
PRIORY CLOSE
86
Junc
63
64
Ivy House Farm
Oxford Rd Nursery
PLAYING FIELD
Brickfield Farm
A412 ROAD
Higher Denham
DOGGETTS FARM RD
UPPER ROAD
MIDDLE ROAD
LOWER ROAD
River Misbourne
Elec Sta
Sewage Works
Gas Works
Works
TOM WILLIAM'S WOOD
Moor House Farm
Comm Cen
BRADBURY'S ISLAND
OLD RECTORY LANE
The Prescotts
Mushroom Farm
CAPS WOOD
MISBOURNE MEADOWS
BAKER'S WOOD
RED HILL
AMERSHAM ROAD
A413
M25
OXFORD ROAD
A40
Fire Sta
Pol
Gas Pipeline Sta
Tatling End
SKYLARK RD
PINSTONE WAY
HOLLYBUSH LANE
Hollybush Farm
BLACKSMITHS LANE
MOUNT LANE
Glasshouse
Denham Mount
FROGGY LANE
Holly Bush
FIELD ROAD
DENHAM AVENUE
BRONSDON WAY
Little Acres Farm
Farm
Glasshouses
SOUTHLANDS ROAD
MILL WOOD
GALLOWS WOOD
LITTLE GALLOWS WOOD
THE RANCHO
HEUSDEN WAY
St. Hubert's
St. Hubert's Home Farm
Little Prestwick
Old Prestwick
Prestwick Cottage
NABOTH
Grayleigh
Alderbourne Manor
FULMER LANE
GALDWINS WOOD
BROADSPRING WOOD
Oldhouse Farm
HAWKS WOOD
Hawkswood
Furzeney
FURZENEY WOOD
Junction 16 (M25)
M40
FURZENEY WOOD
HAWKS WOOD
Alderbourne Arches
Junction 1a (M40)
BROADSPRING WOOD
Rush Green Farm
GOSSAMS WOOD
New House Farm
WILLETTS LANE
Durham House
Cornerfields
Watersplash Farm
Fulmer Rise Manor
HOME WOOD
PARKSPRING WOOD
MOUNT FIDGET WOOD
FULMER RISE ESTATE
BRIDGETTINE CONVENT
LANGLEY COMMON
Langley Corner
BROWN'S WOOD
Field End Farm
Ways Farm
Alderbourne Farm
Saul's Farm
SEVEN HILLS
SL0
Cherry Orchard Farm
Blanchard's Farm
Alder Bourne
OLDHOUSE WOOD
Kingcup Farm
LONG COPPICE
Copse Hill Farm
Southlands Manor
PINEWOOD
OXFORD ROAD

58
38
76
BG
BH
BJ
BK
BL
BM
BN
05
06
07
89
88
87
86
55
56
57
58
59
57
60
61
62
63
64
SOUTH HAREFIELD
UB9
UB8
UB10
Denham Green
Denham
Newyears Green
Junction 1
BUCKINGHAMSHIRE GOLF COURSE
DENHAM COUNTRY PARK
UXBRIDGE GOLF COURSE
BAYHURST WOOD COUNTRY PARK
NORTH ORBITAL ROAD
WESTERN AVENUE
OXFORD ROAD
DENHAM ROAD
Grand Union Canal
HARVIL ROAD
SWAKELEYS ROAD
NORTH BREAKSPEAR ROAD
NEW YEARS GREEN LANE
CIVIC AMENITY SITE
HAREFIELD MOOR
Rank Film Laboratories
BROADWATER PARK
RIVERSIDE WALK
HILLINGDON HOUSE FARM
Hillingdon Ski Centre
UXBRIDGE ATHLETICS TRACK
UXBRIDGE COMMON
Glaxo Research Farm
COPTHALL COVERT
NEWYEARS GREEN COVERT

59
BP
BQ
BR
BS
BT
BU
BV
08
09
10
39
Northwood Hills
NORTH CEMETERY
HILL GOLF COURSE
RUISLIP NATURE RESERVE
COPSE WOOD
HA6
YOUNG WOOD
MAD BESS WOOD
POOR'S FIELD
HOSPITAL (closed)
RUISLIP LIDO
PARK WOOD
RUISLIP COMMON
Breakspear Crematorium
Hillingdon Borough FC
DUCKS HILL
BURY ROAD
RICKMANSWORTH RD
A404
HA5
55
56
57
58
59
60
61
62
63
64
89
88
87
86
EASTCOTE VILLAGE
EASTCOTE HO GRD
EASTCOTE
CUCKOO HILL
Haydon Hall
Grangewood Sch
Eastcote Hockey & Badminton Club
KINGS COLLEGE PLAYING FIELDS
HA4
GOVERNMENT OFFICES
Swim Pool & Fitness Cen
WARRENDER PARK
RUISLIP
RUISLIP MANOR
CAVENDISH REC GRD
PINE GDNS
BESSINGBY FIELD
HIGH STREET
A4180
WEST END ROAD
RUISLIP GOLF COURSE
DRIVING RANGE
KING GEORGE V PLAYING FIELD
MAD FIELD COVERT
WEST RUISLIP
ICKENHAM
Compass Theatre
SPORTS GROUND
DEPOT
NEW POND FARM FIELDS
RUISLIP GARDENS
PLAYING FIELD
BRAINTREE INDUSTRIAL ESTATE
SOUTH RUISLIP
ODYSSEY BUSINESS PARK
Ickenham Marsh
Warehouse Hangar
Hangars
RAF NORTHOLT AERODROME
77
FREEZELAND COVERT
Master Brewer Hotel
WESTERN AVENUE
Long Lane Farm
Yeading Brook
Canal Feeder
Old Clack Farm
Crows Nest Farm
Kennels
Ashby Farm
Youngwood Farm
Ducks Hill Grange

60
BW
BX
BY
BZ
CA
CB
CC
12
13
14
40
55
56
57
58
59
60
61
62
63
64
78
86
87
88
89
PINNER
PINNER GREEN
HA5
HA2
HA4
UB5
EASTCOTE VILLAGE
EASTCOTE
HEADSTONE
NORTH HARROW
WEST HARROW
RAYNERS LANE
SOUTH HARROW
SOUTH RUISLIP
PINNER NEW CEMETERY
PINNER MEMORIAL PARK
PINNER VILLAGE GARDENS
RECREATION GROUND
LITTLE COMMON
CUCKOO HILL
THE CROFT PLAYING FIELD
ROXBOURNE PARK
CAVENDISH REC GRD
WARRENDER PARK
BESSINGBY FIELD
PINE GDNS
NEWTON PARK WEST
NEWTON FM ECOLOGY PK
ALEXANDRA PARK
ROXETH REC GRD
NORTHOLT RECREATION GRD
DEANE PARK
LORD HALSBURY MEMORIAL GRD
BRAINTREE INDUSTRIAL ESTATE
ODYSSEY BUSINESS PARK
VICTORIA RETAIL PARK
FROGMORE ESTATE
Civic Amenity Site
Streamside Reservation
WEST HARROW REC GRD
Old Lyonian Sports Club
Harrow Mus & Heritage Cen
Harrow Borough FC
EARLSMEAD STADIUM
Air Traffic Radio Sta
GEORGE V AVENUE
PINNER ROAD
ALEXANDRA AVENUE
IMPERIAL DRIVE
STATION RD
WEST END ROAD
NORTHOLT ROAD
WHITTON AV W
A404
A4090
A4180
A312
UXBRIDGE ROAD
RAYNERS LANE
EASTCOTE
NORTH HARROW
WEST HARROW
SOUTH HARROW
SOUTH RUISLIP
NORTHOLT PARK
HILLINGDON
EALING

61
CD
CE
CF
CG
CH
CJ
CK
WEALDSTONE
QUEENSBURY
KENTON
HARROW
ROXETH
HARROW ON THE HILL
NORTH WEMBLEY
SUDBURY
PRESTON
HA7
HA3
HA1
HA9
HA0
UB6
NORTHWICK PARK
HARROW SCHOOL PLAYING FIELDS
NORTHWICK PARK & ST. MARK'S HOSPITALS
University of Westminster
CLEMENTINE CHURCHILL HOSPITAL
ST. ANDREW'S AT HARROW HOSP
KENTON RECREATION GROUND
WOODCOCK PARK
PRESTON PARK
VALE FARM SPORTS GROUND
BARHAM PARK
KING EDWARD VII PARK
FORTY FARM SPORTS GROUND
JOHN BILLAM SPORTS GRD
WAVERLEY INDUSTRIAL ESTATE
WEMBLEY COMMERCIAL CENTRE
G.E.C. ESTATE
WEMBLEY FC

62
CL
CM
CN
CP
CQ
CR
CS
19
20
21
HA7
HA8
HA3
HA9
NW9
NW10
42
61
80
QUEENSBURY
KINGSBURY
PRESTON
WEMBLEY PARK
WEMBLEY
WEST HENDON
KYNGTON
CHURCH END
KINGSBURY FRYENT COUNTRY PARK
FRYENT COUNTRY PARK
BARN HILL OPEN SPACE
ROE GREEN PARK
ETON GROVE OPEN SPACE
QUEENSBURY PARK
WOODCOCK PARK
SILVER JUBILEE PARK
WEST HENDON PLAYING FIELDS
WOODFIELD PARK
WELSH HARP OPEN SPACE
NEASDEN RECREATION GRD
KING EDWARD VII PARK
SHERRINS FARM OPEN SPACE
FORTY FARM SPORTS GROUND
PRESTON PARK
JOHN BILLAM SPORTS GRD
CHURCH LANE REC GRD
TOKYNGTON REC GRD
GIBBONS REC GRD
KINGSBURY COMMUNITY HOSPITAL
COLINDALE HOSP
BLOOD TRANSFUSION CENTRE
PUBLIC HEALTH LAB.
BRIT. LIB NEWSPAPER COLLECTION
COLINDALE BUSINESS PK
CAPITOL IND PK
KINGSBURY TRADING EST
BRENT TOWN HALL
WEMBLEY ARENA
Palace of Industry
CONFERENCE CEN
EXHIB CEN
WEMBLEY STADIUM REDEVELOPMENT open 2006
WEMBLEY STADIUM
Sunday Market
CANNON TRADING EST
DRURY WAY IND EST
BRENT PARK
NEASDEN RAIL DEPOT
WEMBLEY COMMERCIAL CENTRE
G.E.C. ESTATE
WEMBLEY CENTRAL
PRESTON ROAD
Stanmore Junction
Welsh Harp Environmental Education Centre
Wembley Sailing Club
KENTON ROAD
KINGSBURY ROAD
HONEYPOT LANE
FRYENT WAY
SALMON STREET
FORTY AVENUE
FORTY LANE
BLACKBIRD HILL
NEASDEN LANE
EDGWARE ROAD
COLINDEEP LANE
BARNET ROAD
NORTH CIRCULAR ROAD
GREAT CENTRAL WAY
HARROW ROAD
HIGH ROAD
EALING ROAD
WEMBLEY PARK DRIVE
A4140
A4006
A4088
A4089
A404
B4557
B454

CT
CU
CV
CW
CX
CY
CZ
22
23
24
43
HOLDERS HILL
SUNNY HILL PARK
RAF MUSEUM
Peel Cen (Metropolitan Pol Training & Driving School)
SPORTS GRD
GARDEN HOSP
CHURCH FARM HOUSE MUS
Middlesex Uni
TOWN HALL
THE HYDE
HENDON
N3
NW4
NW11
NW2
HENDON PARK
HENDON CENTRAL
MALCOLM PARK
Uni of London
CARMELITE MONASTERY
PRINCES PARK
HOOP LANE CEMETERY (JEWISH)
GARDEN OF REMEMBRANCE
GOLDERS GREEN
GOLDERS GREEN DEPOT
Golders Green Hippodrome
GREEK CATH
BRENT CROSS
Brent Cross Shopping Centre
Junction 1
Welsh Harp
BRENT RESERVOIR
YORK PARK
AQUARIUS BUSINESS PARK
STAPLES CORNER BUSINESS PK
WELLINGTON PARK EST
Holiday Inn
Refuse Disposal Works
TRAIN DEPOT
CLITTERHOUSE PLAYING FIELDS
BASING HILL PK
CHILDS HILL PK
CHILDS HILL
SWAN POND
EVANS BUSINESS CEN
DOLLIS HILL
GLADSTONE PARK
CRICKLEWOOD
UNIVERSITY COLLEGE SCHOOL SPORTS GRD
HAMPSTEAD CEMETERY
BARNET
CAMDEN
WILLESDEN
KILBURN
WEST HAMPSTEAD
NORTH CIRCULAR ROAD
WATFORD WAY
HENDON WAY
EDGWARE ROAD
FINCHLEY ROAD
GOLDERS GREEN ROAD
CRICKLEWOOD BROADWAY
SHOOT UP HILL
55
56
57
58
59
60
61
62
63
64
81
86
87
88
89

64
DA
DB
DC
DD
DE
DF
DG
26
27
28
44
N3
N2
N6
N10
NW11
NW3
55
56
57
58
59
60
61
62
63
64
86
87
88
89
82
EAST FINCHLEY
FORTIS GREEN
HAMPSTEAD GARDEN SUBURB
GOLDERS GREEN
CHILDS HILL
HAMPSTEAD HEATH
HAMPSTEAD
WEST HAMPSTEAD
PARLIAMENT HILL
HAMPSTEAD HEATH EXTENSION
HAMPSTEAD GOLF COURSE
HIGHGATE GOLF COURSE
HIGHGATE WOOD
COLDFALL WOOD
BIG WOOD
EAST FINCHLEY CEMETERY
HOOP LANE CEMETERY (JEWISH)
GOLDERS HILL PARK
SANDY HEATH
WEST HEATH
KENWOOD
VALE OF HEALTH
HIGHGATE PONDS
ATHLONE HOUSE
ROYAL FREE HOSP
QUEEN MARY'S HOSP
ST.LUKE'S WOODSIDE HOSPITAL
NORTH CIRCULAR ROAD
FINCHLEY ROAD
NORTH END ROAD
LYTTELTON ROAD
AYLMER ROAD
FALLODEN WAY
EAST END ROAD
GREAT NORTH ROAD
HAMPSTEAD LANE
SPANIARDS ROAD
HAVERSTOCK HILL
ROSSLYN HILL
HAMPSTEAD HIGH ST
HEATH STREET
ARCHWAY
FORTIS GREEN

65
DH
DJ
DK
DL
DM
DN
DP
29
30
31
45
NOEL PARK
LORDSHIP RECREATION GROUND
ALEXANDRA PALACE
ALEXANDRA PARK
N22
MUSWELL HILL
HORNSEY
WEST GREEN
55
56
57
58
59
60
61
62
63
64
66
83
CROUCH END
N8
HARRINGAY
QUEEN'S WOOD
STROUD GREEN
FINSBURY PARK
N4
N19
WHITTINGTON HOSPITAL
HIGHGATE CEMETERY
WATERLOW PARK
UPPER HOLLOWAY
DARTMOUTH PARK
TUFNELL PARK
HOLLOWAY
LOWER HOLLOWAY
N7
KENTISH TOWN
NW5
HIGHBURY
N5
CANONBURY
ARSENAL STADIUM
PENTONVILLE PRISON
H.M. PRISON HOLLOWAY
ST. ANN'S HOSPITAL
CHESTNUTS PARK
SPORTS GROUND
ALEXANDRA PARK

66
DQ
DR
DS
DT
DU
DV
DW
33
34
35
46
55
56
57
58
59
60
61
62
63
64
65
84
86
87
88
89
NOEL PARK
N22
N17
N15
N16
N4
N5
E5
E8
LORDSHIP RECREATION GROUND
BELMONT REC GRD
WEST GREEN
DOWNHILLS PARK
TURNPIKE LANE
CHESTNUTS PARK
ST ANN'S HOSPITAL
SEVEN SISTERS
SOUTH TOTTENHAM
TOTTENHAM HALE
TOTTENHAM MARSHES
LEE VALLEY TECHNOPARK
DOWN LANE REC GRD
MARKFIELD REC GRD
MONUMENT WAY
FERRY LANE
RESERVOIR NUMBER FOUR
RESERVOIR NUMBER TWO
RESERVOIR NUMBER ONE
RESERVOIR NUMBER THREE
RESERVOIR NUMBER FIVE
WARWICK RESERVOIR EAST
WARWICK RESERVOIR WEST
LOW MAYNARD RESERVOIR
COPPERMILL PLAYING FIELD
HARRINGAY GREEN LANES
RAILWAY FLDS
FINSBURY PARK
AMERICAN GDNS
WOODBERRY DOWN ESTATE
EAST RESERVOIR
WEST RESERVOIR
STAMFORD HILL
SPRINGHILL SPORTS GRD
SPRINGFIELD PARK
Walthamstow Marsh Nature Reserve
UPPER CLAPTON
ABNEY PARK CEMETERY
STOKE NEWINGTON
CLISSOLD PARK
SPORTS GROUND
NORTH MILLFIELDS RECREATION GROUND
SHACKLEWELL
HACKNEY DOWNS
BUTTERFIELD GREEN
ARSENAL STADIUM
HIGHBURY
CANONBURY
KINGSLAND
SEVEN SISTERS ROAD
GREEN LANES
STAMFORD HILL
HIGH ROAD
AMHURST PARK
CLAPTON COMMON
UPPER CLAPTON ROAD
LOWER CLAPTON ROAD
STOKE NEWINGTON HIGH ST
STOKE NEWINGTON CH ST
RECTORY ROAD
NORTHWOLD ROAD
BROAD LANE
WEST GREEN ROAD
PAUL'S ROAD
BALLS POND ROAD
DALSTON LANE
GRAHAM ROAD

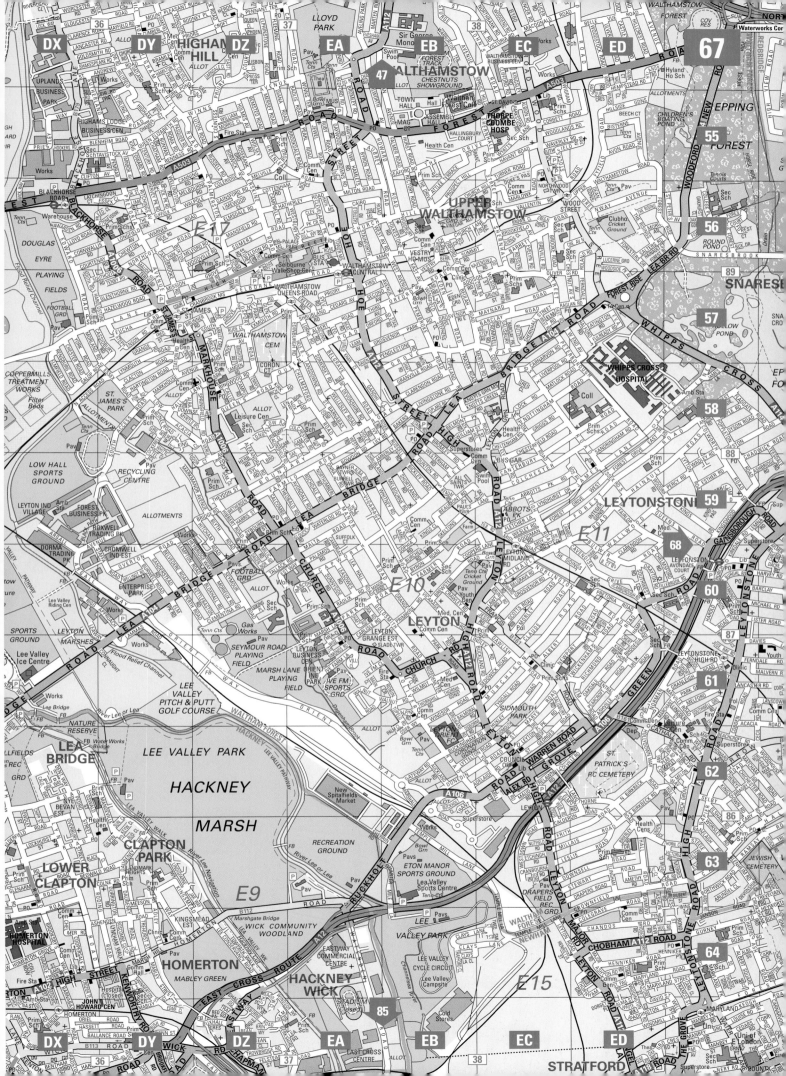

DX
DY
DZ
EA
EB
EC
ED
36
37
38
67
47
55
56
57
58
59
60
61
62
63
64
68
85
86
87
88
89
HIGHAM HILL
LLOYD PARK
WALTHAMSTOW
CHESTNUTS SHOWGROUND
UPLANDS BUSINESS PARK
HIGHAMS LODGE BUSINESS CEN
EPPING FOREST
E17
UPPER WALTHAMSTOW
THORPE COOMBE HOSP
WOOD STREET
WALTHAMSTOW CENTRAL
WALTHAMSTOW QUEENS ROAD
Selbourne Walk Shop Cen
ST. JAMES ST
WALTHAMSTOW CEM
DOUGLAS EYRE PLAYING FIELDS
SNARESBROOK
WHIPPS CROSS HOSPITAL
COPPERMILLS TREATMENT WORKS
ST. JAMES'S PARK
LOW HALL SPORTS GROUND
RECYCLING CENTRE
ALLOTMENTS
LEYTON IND VILLAGE
FOREST BUSINESS PK
ROXWELL TRADING PK
DORMA TRADING PK
CROMWELL IND EST
ENTERPRISE PARK
LEYTONSTONE
E11
E10
LEYTON
LEYTON MIDLAND RD
SEYMOUR ROAD PLAYING FIELD
MARSH LANE PLAYING FIELD
LEYTON BUSINESS CEN
LEYTON GRANGE EST
IVE FM SPORTS GRD
LEYTON ORIENT FC
SIDMOUTH PARK
ST. PATRICK'S RC CEMETERY
LEYTON MARSHES
SPORTS GROUND
Lee Valley Ice Centre
Lee Valley Riding Cen
LEE VALLEY PITCH & PUTT GOLF COURSE
NATURE RESERVE
LEA BRIDGE
LEE VALLEY PARK
HACKNEY MARSH
New Spitalfields Market
RECREATION GROUND
ETON MANOR SPORTS GROUND
Lea Valley Sports Centre
LEE VALLEY PARK
LEE VALLEY CYCLE CIRCUIT
Lee Valley Campsite
CLAPTON PARK
LOWER CLAPTON
E9
WICK COMMUNITY WOODLAND
EASTWAY COMMERCIAL CENTRE
HACKNEY WICK
STADIUM (Closed)
HOMERTON
MABLEY GREEN
HOMERTON HOSPITAL
JOHN HOWARD CEN
EAST CROSS CENTRE
E15
DRAPERS FIELD REC. GRD
JEWISH CEMETERY
Uni of E London
STRATFORD
WALTHAM FOREST
NEWHAM
HACKNEY
Waterworks Cor
EAST CROSS ROUTE
LEA BRIDGE ROAD
HOE STREET
FOREST ROAD
WHIPPS CROSS ROAD
HIGH ROAD LEYTON
LEYTONSTONE HIGH ROAD
CHURCH ROAD
MARKHOUSE ROAD
BLACKHORSE ROAD
RUCKHOLT ROAD
CHOBHAM ROAD
WOODFORD NEW ROAD
A503
A112
A104
A106
A12
A102

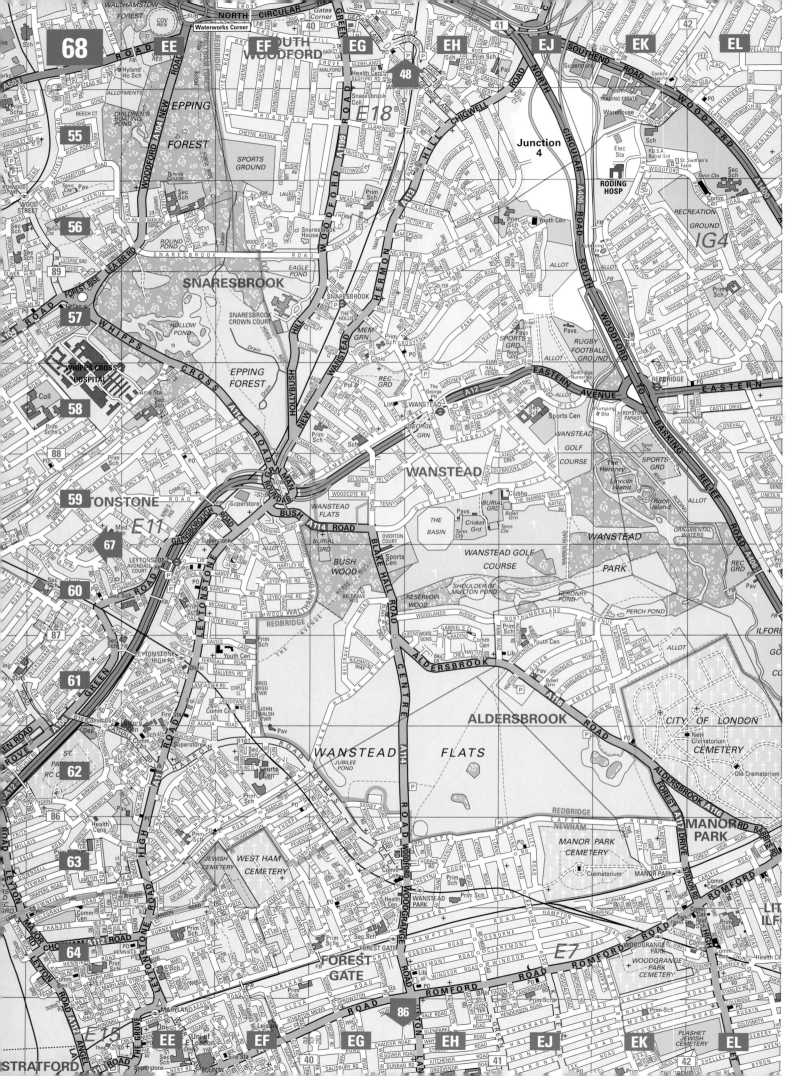
68
EE
EF
EG
EH
EJ
EK
EL
40
41
42
48
SOUTH WOODFORD
E18
EPPING FOREST
Junction 4
RODING HOSP
IG4
SNARESBROOK
SNARESBROOK CROWN COURT
WHIPPS CROSS HOSPITAL
EPPING FOREST
WANSTEAD
LEYTONSTONE
E11
67
WANSTEAD FLATS
BUSH WOOD
WANSTEAD GOLF COURSE
WANSTEAD PARK
ALDERSBROOK
CITY OF LONDON CEMETERY
WANSTEAD FLATS
MANOR PARK
MANOR PARK CEMETERY
WEST HAM CEMETERY
JEWISH CEMETERY
FOREST GATE
E7
WOODGRANGE PARK CEMETERY
PLASHET JEWISH CEMETERY
E15
STRATFORD
86
55
56
57
58
59
60
61
62
63
64
88
89
87
86
Waterworks Corner
NORTH CIRCULAR ROAD
SOUTHEND ROAD
EASTERN AVENUE
ROMFORD ROAD
ALDERSBROOK ROAD
WHIPPS CROSS ROAD
BLAKE HALL ROAD
CENTRE ROAD
WOODFORD NEW ROAD
REDBRIDGE
NEWHAM

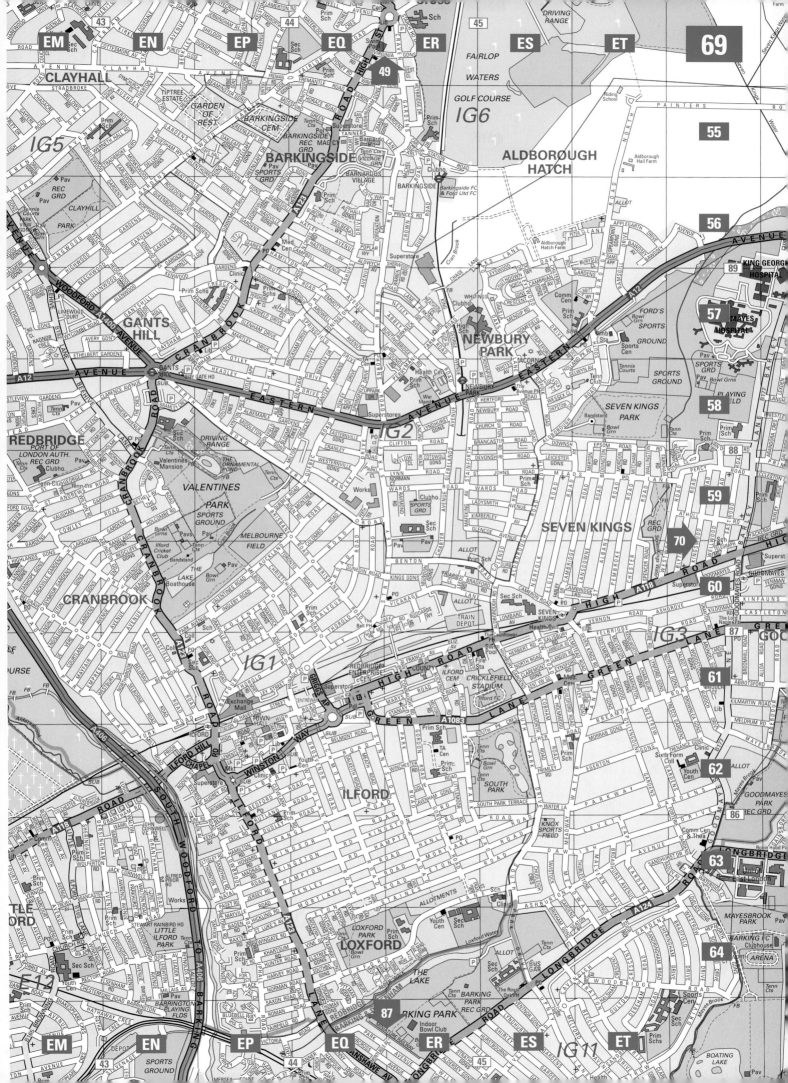
EM
EN
EP
EQ
ER
ES
ET
CLAYHALL
FAIRLOP WATERS GOLF COURSE
IG6
IG5
GARDEN OF REST
BARKINGSIDE CEM
BARKINGSIDE
BARKINGSIDE REC GRD
ALDBOROUGH HATCH
CLAYHILL PARK
BARNARDOS VILLAGE
GANTS HILL
NEWBURY PARK
FORD'S SPORTS GROUND
KING GEORGE HOSPITAL
MAYES HOSPITAL
SEVEN KINGS PARK
SPORTS GROUND
IG2
REDBRIDGE
VALENTINES PARK
MELBOURNE FIELD
SEVEN KINGS
CRANBROOK
IG1
IG3
ILFORD
SOUTH PARK
LOXFORD
KNOX SPORTS FIELD
MAYESBROOK PARK
LITTLE ILFORD PARK
E12
IG11
BARKING PARK
GOODMAYES PARK
EASTERN AVENUE
CRANBROOK ROAD
HIGH ROAD
GREEN LANE
WOODFORD AVENUE
ILFORD LANE
LONGBRIDGE ROAD
A12
A123
A118
A1083
A124
A406
A1400
49
70
87
55
56
57
58
59
60
61
62
63
64
43
44
45
86
88
89

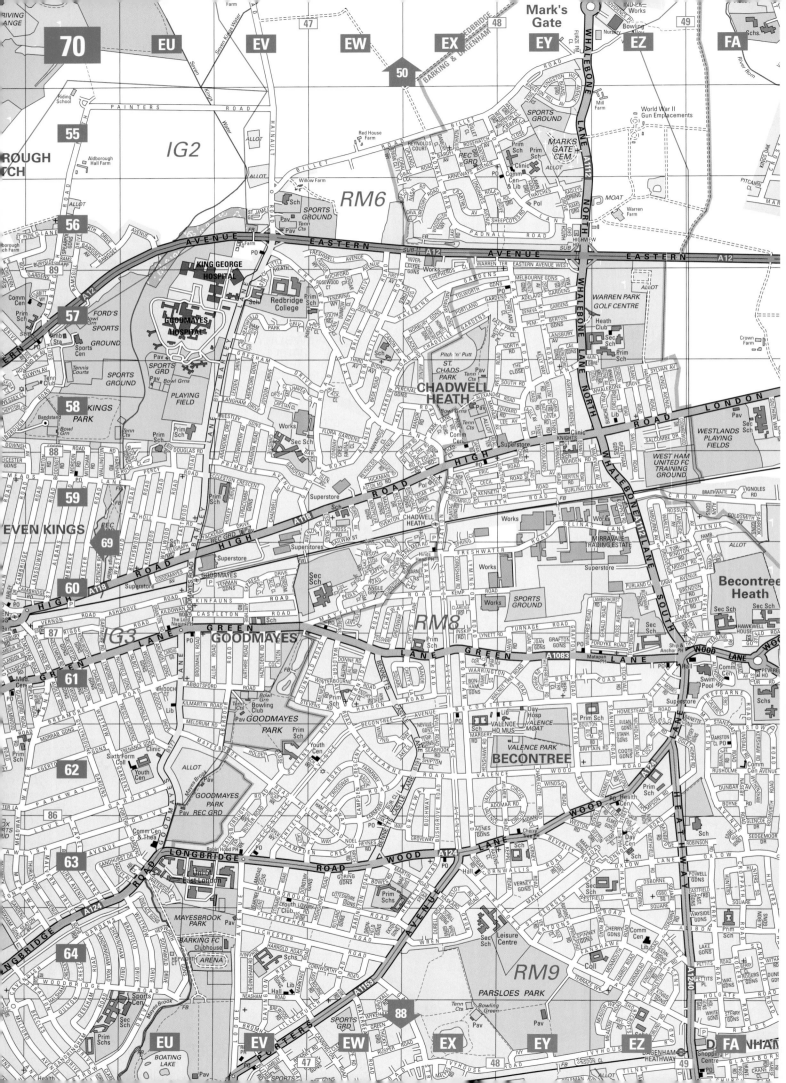
70
EU
EV
EW
EX
EY
EZ
FA
47
48
49
50
Mark's Gate
IG2
RM6
RM8
RM9
IG3
55
56
57
58
59
60
61
62
63
64
69
88
89
87
86
EASTERN AVENUE
A12
KING GEORGE HOSPITAL
GOODMAYES HOSPITAL
Redbridge College
CHADWELL HEATH
HIGH ROAD
A118
GOODMAYES
GREEN LANE
A1083
WHALEBONE LANE NORTH
WHALEBONE LANE SOUTH
A1112
BARKING & DAGENHAM
REDBRIDGE
KINGS PARK
FORD'S SPORTS GROUND
SPORTS GROUND
PLAYING FIELD
WARREN PARK GOLF CENTRE
WESTLANDS PLAYING FIELDS
WEST HAM UNITED FC TRAINING GROUND
MIRRAVALE TRADING ESTATE
Becontree Heath
BECONTREE
VALENCE PARK
VALENCE HO MUS
GOODMAYES PARK
GOODMAYES PARK REC GRD
MAYESBROOK PARK
BARKING FC Clubhouse
ARENA
BOATING LAKE
PARSLOES PARK
Leisure Centre
Uni of East London
LONGBRIDGE ROAD
WOOD LANE
A124
HEATHWAY
A1240
A1153
PORTERS AVENUE
MARKS GATE CEM
World War II Gun Emplacements
Red House Farm
Willow Farm
Warren Farm
MOAT
ST. CHADS PARK
Pitch 'n' Putt
SEVEN KINGS
Dagenham Heathway
DAGENHAM

72
ROMFORD GOLF COURSE
GIDEA PARK SPORTS GRD
AVENUE INDUSTRIAL ESTATE
HAROLD WOOD
54
55
56
FJ
FK
FL
FM
FN
FP
FQ
52
RM2
RM3
HAROLD WOOD PARK
SOUTHEND ARTERIAL ROAD
A127
MAIN ROAD
Gidea Park
55
56
57
58
59
60
61
62
63
64
89
88
87
86
GIDEA PARK
STATION
Ardleigh Green
SPORTS GRD
HAYNES PARK
Havering College of Further Educ
ST. MARY'S CONVENT
ELLIOT PLAYING FIELDS
Emerson Park
EMERSON PARK
RM11
HYLANDS PARK
Havering College
71
FIELDERS SPORTS GRD
LANGTON GDNS
ST. ANDREW'S PARK
UPMINSTER GOLF COURSE
HIGH STREET
A124
HORNCHURCH
UPMINSTER ROAD
UPMINSTER BRIDGE
HORNCHURCH CEM
HORN CHURCH STADIUM
UPMINSTER PARK
ST MARY'S LANE
UPMINSTER
UPMINSTER STATION
HORNCHURCH
RM12
ELM PARK
ST. GEORGES HOSPITAL
GAYNES PARKWAY
Hacton
PARKLANDS OPEN SPACE
Corbets Tey
90
LONDON LOOP / INGREBOURNE VALLEY GREEN WAY

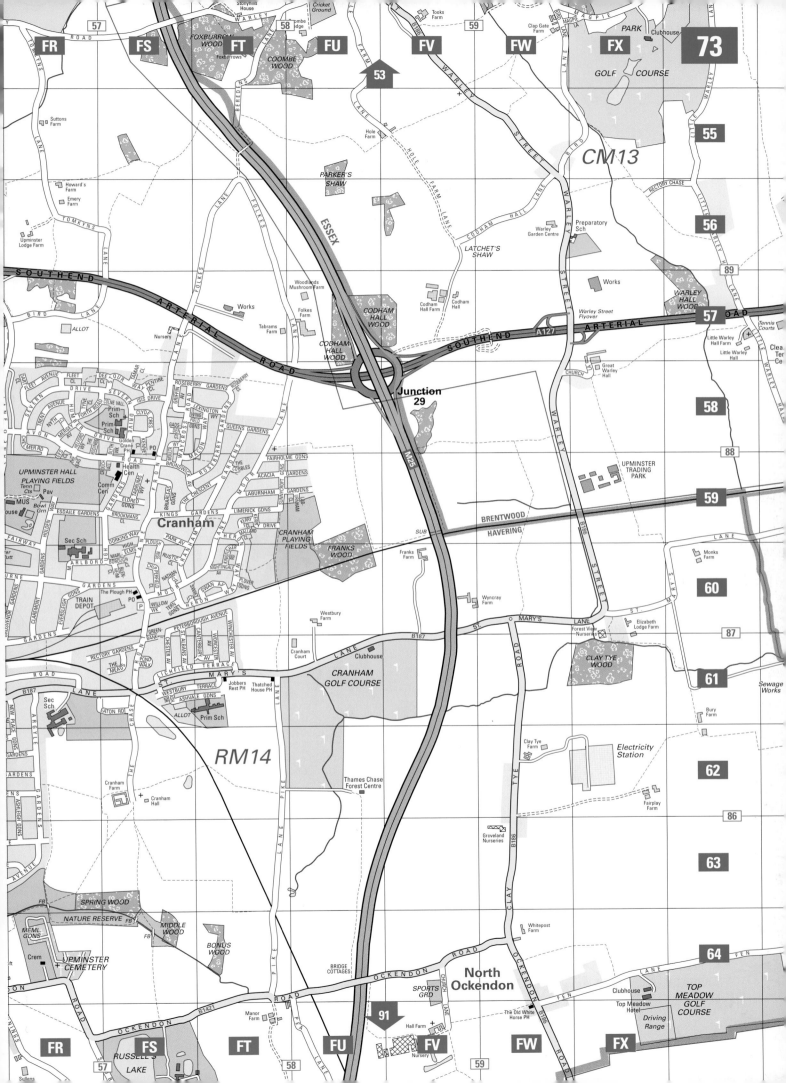

73
Cranham
North Ockendon
CM13
RM14
Junction 29
ESSEX
BRENTWOOD
HAVERING
UPMINSTER HALL PLAYING FIELDS
CRANHAM PLAYING FIELDS
CRANHAM GOLF COURSE
GOLF COURSE
TOP MEADOW GOLF COURSE
UPMINSTER TRADING PARK
UPMINSTER CEMETERY
NATURE RESERVE
FOXBURROW WOOD
COOMBE WOOD
CODHAM HALL WOOD
FRANKS WOOD
CLAY TYE WOOD
WARLEY HALL WOOD
SPRING WOOD
MIDDLE WOOD
BONUS WOOD
PARKER'S SHAW
LATCHET'S SHAW
Electricity Station
Thames Chase Forest Centre
SOUTHEND ARTERIAL ROAD
WARLEY STREET
CLAY TYE ROAD
OCKENDON ROAD
ST. MARY'S LANE
FRONT LANE
PIKE LANE
M25
A127
B186
B187
B1421
53
91
FR
FS
FT
FU
FV
FW
FX
55
56
57
58
59
60
61
62
63
64
86
87
88
89

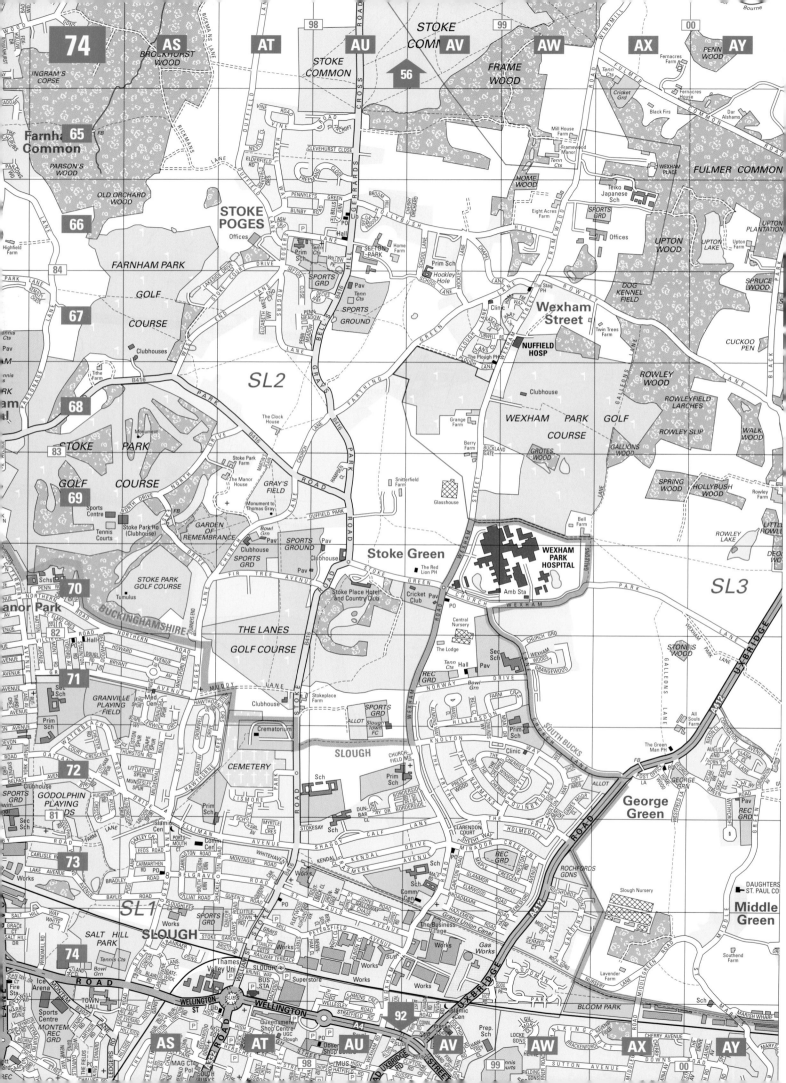

74
AS
AT
AU
AV
AW
AX
AY
56
STOKE COMMON
FRAME WOOD
PENN WOOD
BROCKHURST WOOD
INGRAM'S COPSE
Farnham Common
PARSON'S WOOD
OLD ORCHARD WOOD
STOKE POGES
FULMER COMMON
UPTON WOOD
UPTON PLANTATION
DOG KENNEL FIELD
SPRUCE WOOD
Wexham Street
NUFFIELD HOSP
CUCKOO PEN
ROWLEY WOOD
ROWLEYFIELD LARCHES
ROWLEY SLIP
WALK WOOD
WEXHAM PARK GOLF COURSE
GROTES WOOD
SPRING WOOD
HOLLYBUSH WOOD
ROWLEY LAKE
FARNHAM PARK GOLF COURSE
SL2
STOKE PARK GOLF COURSE
GRAY'S FIELD
GARDEN OF REMEMBRANCE
Stoke Green
WEXHAM PARK HOSPITAL
SL3
THE LANES GOLF COURSE
BUCKINGHAMSHIRE
SLOUGH
SOUTH BUCKS
CEMETERY
GRANVILLE PLAYING FIELD
GODOLPHIN PLAYING FIELDS
George Green
STONES WOOD
SL1
SLOUGH
SALT HILL PARK
Middle Green
Grand Union Canal
BLOOM PARK
92
98
99
00
65
66
67
68
69
70
71
72
73
74
81
82
83
84

75
57
76
93
AZ
BA
BB
BC
BD
BE
BF
01
02
03
84
83
82
81
65
66
67
68
69
70
71
72
73
74
UB9
SL0
Watersplash Farm
Fulmer Rise Manor
HOME WOOD
MOUNT FIDGET WOOD
PARKSPRING WOOD
FULMER RISE ESTATE
Fulmer Plant Park
BRIDGETTINE CONVENT
Downings
Langley Corner
LANGLEY COMMON
STRAWBERRY WOOD
HEATHFIELD PLANTATION
NATURE RESERVE
BOWLERS PLANTATION
BROWN'S WOOD
Ways Farm
Alderbourne Farm
Saul's Farm
SEVEN HILLS ROAD
PINEWOOD ROAD
Pinewood Film Studios
Heatherden Hall
Park Lodge Farm
Brackenwood
BLACK PARK COUNTRY PARK
DIAMOND WOOD
BLACKPARK LAKE
Centenary Lodge Visitors Centre
RHODODENDRON RIDE
CHESTNUT WOOD
FOXES GUTTER
COLUMN LARCHES
LANGLEY PARK WOOD
RHODODENDRON GARDENS
LANGLEY PARK COUNTRY PARK
ROUGHGROUND WOOD
ARBORETUM
Environmental Studies Centre
Langley Park House
Treal Farm
Ashen Cross
BELLSWOOD LANE
Shreding Green
Red Lion PH
HOLLYBUSH LANE
LANGLEY PARK ROAD
Love Hill House Farm
Shredding Green Farm
Moat House
Clubhouse
Glasshouse
IVER GOLF COURSE
Trenches Farm
THE ORCHARDS RESIDENTIAL PARK
Grand Union Canal (Slough Arm)
TOWING PATH
BUCKINGHAMSHIRE
SLOUGH
SOUTH BUCKS
CARAVAN SITE
Chequer Bridge
Depot
LANGLEY BUSINESS CENTRE
Works
OLDHOUSE WOOD
Cherry Orchard Farm
Belle Farm
LONG COPPICE
Sevenhills Farm
Taidswood
Copse Hill Farm
PLAYING FIELD
Dromenagh Farm
THE CLUMP
DENHAM ROAD
M25
Round Coppice Farm
Southlands Manor
Kingcup Farm
Durham House
Cornerfields
Ivy House Farm
Oxford Road Nursery
Brickfield Farm
BROOM WARREN
Stag & Hounds PH
Medical Cen
SPORTS GRD
Tenn Cts
Bowl Grn
Health Cen
Hall
Lib
Prim Sch
Warren Lodge
Warren House
Warren House Farm
Park Lodge
Five Points
Crooked Billet PH
Fernleigh
Tennis Cts
Pav
SPORTS GROUND
IVER HEATH
Home Cottage Farm
Norwood Grange
NORWOOD LANE
Nursery
Eureham Centre
Sports Centre
Whip & Collar PH
SLOUGH ROAD
A4007
A412
CHURCH ROAD
BANGORS ROAD NORTH
BANGORS ROAD SOUTH
CHANDLERS HILL
Perivale Livery Stables
Moorwards
Bangors Park Farm
Woodlands Park
Mansfield Farm
Watergate Farm
UXBRIDGE ROAD
Alder Bourne
Colne Brook
Delaford Manor
Coppins Farm
Coppins Cottages
Lower Delaford
Iver Lodge
Delaford Park
IVER
HIGH STREET
IVER LANE
SPORTS GROUND
ALLOT
MARINA WY
ORCHARD
Huntsmoor Park Farm
Filter Beds
FARLOWS LAKE
Sewage Works
THE RIDGEWAY ESTATE
THORNEY LANE
THORNEY PARK GOLF COURSE
IVER WALK
Water Treatment Works

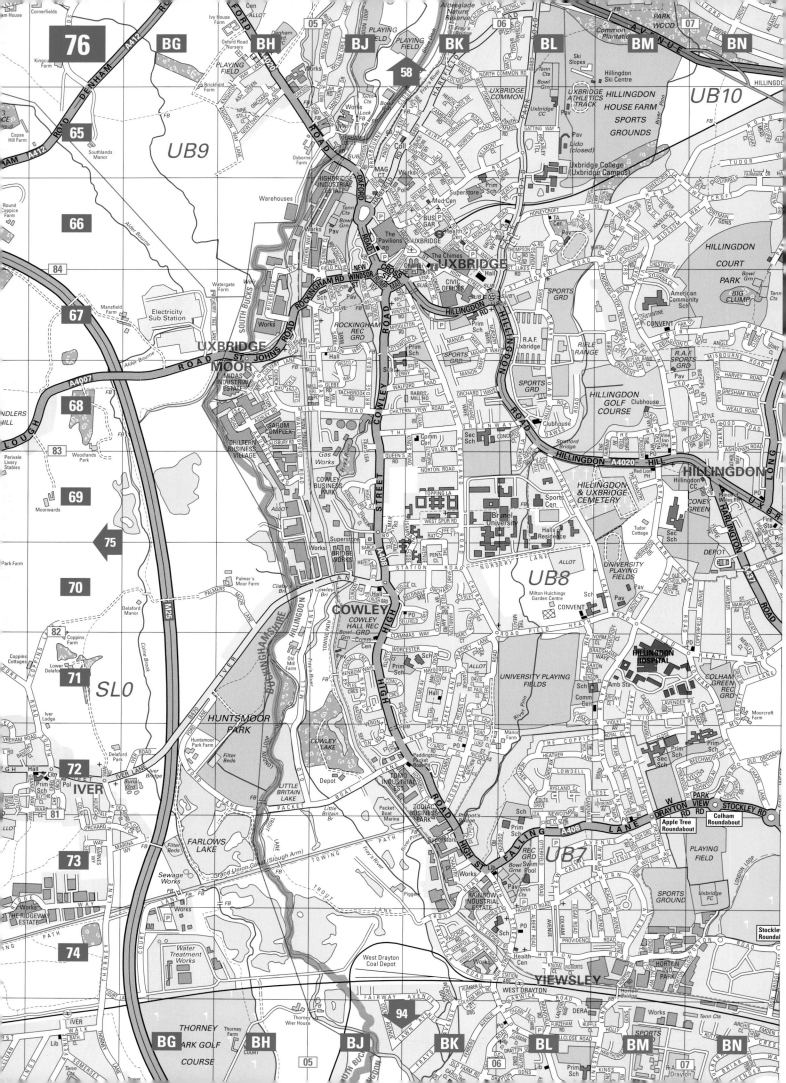

76
BG
BH
BJ
BK
BL
BM
BN
58
65
66
67
68
69
70
71
72
73
74
75
94
05
06
07
84
83
82
81
UB9
UB10
UB8
UB7
SL0
UXBRIDGE
UXBRIDGE MOOR
COWLEY
HILLINGDON
YIEWSLEY
IVER
WEST DRAYTON
DENHAM ROAD
OXFORD ROAD
ROCKINGHAM RD
ST. JOHNS ROAD
COWLEY ROAD
COWLEY HIGH ROAD
HIGH ST
HILLINGDON RD
HILLINGDON HILL
FALLING LANE
DRAYTON LANE
STOCKLEY RD
IVER LANE
HORTON ROAD
UXBRIDGE COMMON
HILLINGDON HOUSE FARM SPORTS GROUNDS
HILLINGDON GOLF COURSE
HILLINGDON COURT PARK
HILLINGDON & UXBRIDGE CEMETERY
Brunel University
UNIVERSITY PLAYING FIELDS
HILLINGDON HOSPITAL
HUNTSMOOR PARK
FARLOWS LAKE
LITTLE BRITAIN LAKE
COWLEY LAKE
THORNEY PARK GOLF COURSE
Electricity Sub Station
Water Treatment Works
West Drayton Coal Depot
Grand Union Canal (Slough Arm)
Apple Tree Roundabout
Colham Roundabout
Uxbridge College (Uxbridge Campus)
Hillingdon Ski Centre
UXBRIDGE ATHLETICS TRACK
The Pavilions
The Chimes
CIVIC OFFICES
R.A.F. Uxbridge
HIGHBRIDGE INDUSTRIAL ESTATE
MIDAS INDUSTRIAL ESTATE
CHILTERN BUSINESS VILLAGE
COWLEY BUSINESS PARK
ZODIAC BUSINESS PARK
TOMO INDUSTRIAL EST
RAINBOW INDUSTRIAL ESTATE
THE RIDGEWAY ESTATE
M25
A4020
A4007
A412
A408
A437
B470
B483

77
59
RAF NORTHOLT AERODROME
HA4
NORTH HILLINGDON
UB5
UB4
UB3
UB11
YEADING
HAYES
HAYES END
HAYES TOWN
STOCKLEY PARK GOLF COURSE
MINET COUNTRY PARK
WEST LONDON SHOOTING GROUNDS
YEADING BROOK MEADOWS NATURE RESERVE
LONDON GOLF CENTRE
BELMORE PLAYING FIELDS
HAYES PARK
WESTERN AVENUE
UXBRIDGE ROAD
A4020
A40
A437
A312
A4180
78
95
BP
BQ
BR
BS
BT
BU
BV
08
09
10
65
66
67
68
69
70
71
72
73
74
81
82
83
84

BW
BX
BY
BZ
CA
CB
CC
HA4
UB5
UB4
UB1
60
77
96
12
13
14
65
66
67
68
69
70
71
72
73
74
81
82
83
84
ODYSSEY BUSINESS PARK
FROGMORE ESTATE
Civic Amenity Site
NORTHOLT RECREATION GRD
PLAYING FIELD
LORD HALSBURY MEMORIAL REC GRD
HILLINGDON
EALING
NORTHOLT
ISLIP MANOR PARK
WESTERN AVENUE
WEST END ROAD
RUISLIP ROAD
CHURCH ROAD
MANDEVILLE ROAD
LONDON GOLF CENTRE
SPORTS GROUND
LIME TREE PARK GOLF COURSE
LIME TREE PARK
Polish War Memorial
Yeading Brook
Down Barns Moated Site
WEST LONDON SHOOTING GROUNDS
BELVUE PARK
EALING GOLF RANGE
KELVIN INDUSTRIAL ESTATE
THE METROPOLITAN CENTRE
BIRKBECK COLLEGE SPORTS GROUND
KENSINGTON & CHELSEA PLAYING FIELDS
MARNHAM FIELDS
NORTHOLT GOLF COURSE
SMITHS FARM EST
RECTORY PARK
GREENFORD
RAVENOR PARK
YEADING
BELMORE PLAYING FIELDS
THE PARKWAY (HAYES BYPASS)
Taylor Woodrow
Cricket Club
KING GEORGE'S FIELD
SPORTS GROUND
GREENFORD PARK REC GRD
GREENFORD PARK CEMETERY
JUBILEE PARK
WARREN PARK
BROOKSIDE
HGV Test Sta
WILLOWTREE MARINA
DORMER'S WELLS
WEST MIDDLESEX GOLF COURSE
GREENFORD ROAD
UXBRIDGE ROAD
THE BROADWAY
HIGH STREET
SOUTHALL
SOUTHALL PARK
Lombardy Retail Park
Uxbridge College Hayes Community Campus
ELYSTAN BUSINESS CENTRE
HAYES METRO CENTRE
HEATHROW INTERCHANGE
BROOK INDUSTRIAL ESTATE
MINET COUNTRY PARK
HEATHROW PURPLE PARKING
BARRATT INDUSTRIAL PARK
SOUTHALL RAILWAY CENTRE
GRAND UNION CANAL (PADDINGTON BRANCH)
Sunrise Radio
WHITTON AVENUE
A312
A40
A4020
A4180
A3005
B455

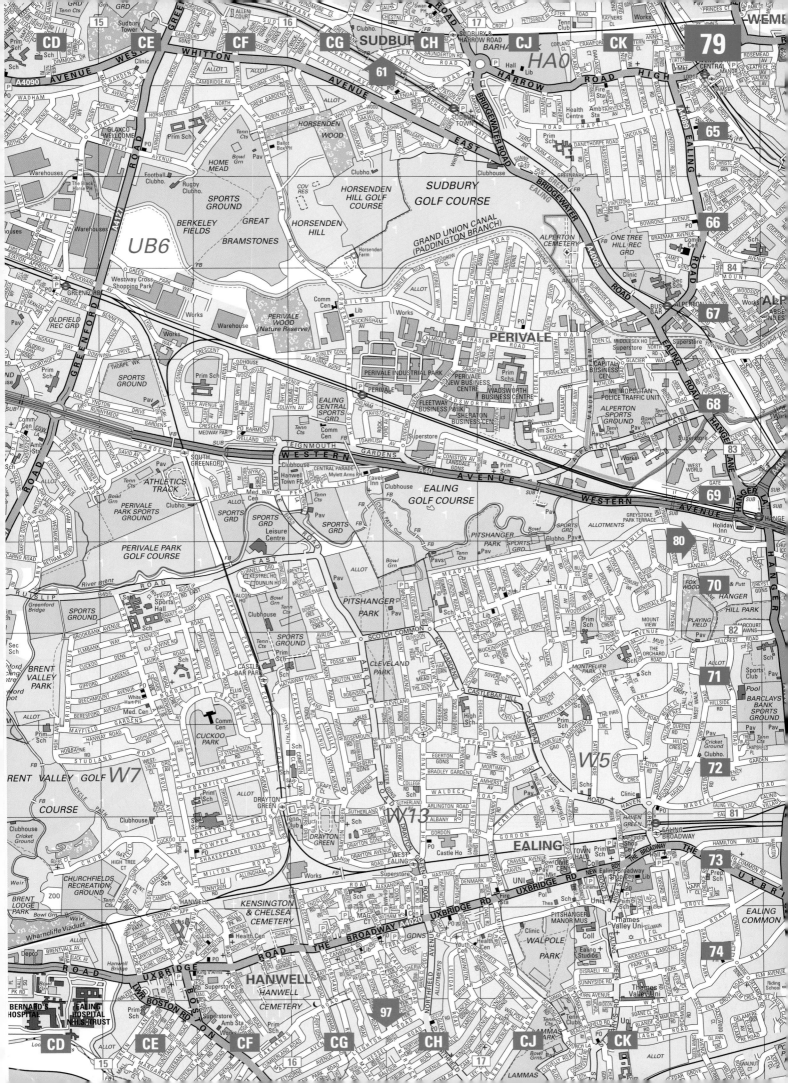

79
CD
CE
CF
CG
CH
CJ
CK
15
16
17
61
97
80
65
66
67
68
69
70
71
72
73
74
81
82
83
84
SUDBURY
HA0
UB6
W7
W13
W5
PERIVALE
EALING
HANWELL
WHITTON AVENUE WEST
A4090
A4127
GREENFORD ROAD
EASTCOTE AVENUE
HARROW ROAD
BRIDGEWATER ROAD
A4005
EALING ROAD
A4089
WESTERN AVENUE
A40
UXBRIDGE RD
A4020
THE BROADWAY
HANGER LANE
SPORTS GROUND
BERKELEY FIELDS
GREAT BRAMSTONES
HOME MEAD
HORSENDEN HILL GOLF COURSE
HORSENDEN HILL
HORSENDEN WOOD
SUDBURY GOLF COURSE
GRAND UNION CANAL (PADDINGTON BRANCH)
ALPERTON CEMETERY
ONE TREE HILL REC GRD
PERIVALE WOOD (Nature Reserve)
Westway Cross Shopping Park
OLDFIELD REC GRD
PERIVALE INDUSTRIAL PARK
PERIVALE NEW BUSINESS CENTRE
WADSWORTH BUSINESS CENTRE
FLEETWAY BUSINESS PARK
SHERATON BUSINESS CEN
CAPITAL BUSINESS CEN
METROPOLITAN POLICE TRAFFIC UNIT
ALPERTON SPORTS GROUND
EALING CENTRAL SPORTS GRD
ATHLETICS TRACK
PERIVALE PARK SPORTS GROUND
PERIVALE PARK GOLF COURSE
EALING GOLF COURSE
PITSHANGER PARK
HANGER HILL PARK
BRENT VALLEY PARK
BRENT VALLEY GOLF COURSE
CUCKOO PARK
CLEVELAND PARK
DRAYTON GREEN
CHURCHFIELDS RECREATION GROUND
BRENT LODGE PARK
KENSINGTON & CHELSEA CEMETERY
HANWELL CEMETERY
WALPOLE PARK
EALING COMMON
BARCLAYS BANK SPORTS GROUND
Wharncliffe Viaduct
EALING HOSPITAL NHS TRUST
ST BERNARD'S HOSPITAL
PITSHANGER MANOR MUS
Thames Valley Uni
EALING BROADWAY
WEST EALING
CASTLE BAR PARK
SOUTH GREENFORD
GREENFORD
SUDBURY TOWN
SUDBURY & HARROW ROAD
ALPERTON

80
CL
CM
CN
CP
CQ
CR
CS
WEMBLEY
TOKYNGTON
CHURCH END
HA0
HA9
ALPERTON
STONEBRIDGE
HARLESDEN
PARK ROYAL
NORTH ACTON
WEST ACTON
ACTON
EAST ACTON
EALING
W3
W5
EALING COMMON
HANGER HILL PARK
ACTON PARK
WEMBLEY CENTRAL
STONEBRIDGE PARK
HANGER LANE
PARK ROYAL
NORTH EALING
EALING BROADWAY
ACTON MAIN LINE
ACTON CENTRAL
ACTON TOWN
ONE TREE HILL REC GRD
TOKYNGTON RECREATION GROUND
GIBBONS REC GRD
CENTRAL MIDDLESEX HOSPITAL
NORTH ACTON PLAYING FIELDS
NORTH THAMES GAS BOARD SPORTS GRD
BARCLAYS BANK SPORTS GROUND
ACTON CEMETERY
Gypsy Corner
NORTH CIRCULAR ROAD
WESTERN AVENUE
HANGER LANE
GUNNERSBURY AVENUE
UXBRIDGE ROAD
HIGH STREET
A406
A40
A4020
A404
A4000
A4089
62
79
98
19
20
21
65
66
67
68
69
70
71
72
73
74
81
82
83
84

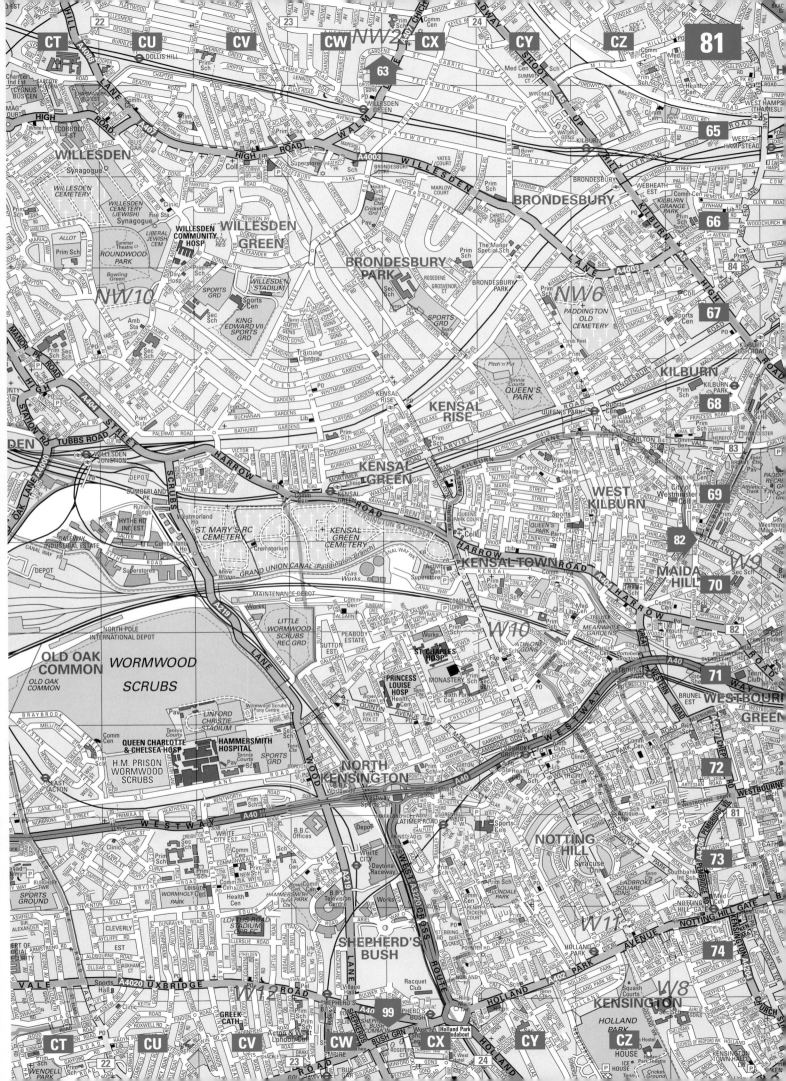
CT
CU
CV
CW
CX
CY
CZ
NW2
63
22
23
24
DOLLIS HILL
WILLESDEN
WILLESDEN CEMETERY
WILLESDEN GREEN
WILLESDEN COMMUNITY HOSP
ROUNDWOOD PARK
KING EDWARD VII SPORTS GRD
BRONDESBURY
BRONDESBURY PARK
NW10
NW6
PADDINGTON OLD CEMETERY
QUEEN'S PARK
KENSAL RISE
KILBURN
KENSAL GREEN
WEST KILBURN
WILLESDEN JUNCTION
ST. MARY'S RC CEMETERY
KENSAL GREEN CEMETERY
GRAND UNION CANAL (Paddington Branch)
KENSAL TOWN
MAIDA HILL
W9
W10
OLD OAK COMMON
WORMWOOD SCRUBS
LITTLE WORMWOOD SCRUBS REC GRD
ST CHARLES HOSP
PRINCESS LOUISE HOSP
LINFORD CHRISTIE STADIUM
QUEEN CHARLOTTE & CHELSEA HOSP
HAMMERSMITH HOSPITAL
H.M. PRISON WORMWOOD SCRUBS
NORTH KENSINGTON
WESTWAY
WESTBOURNE GREEN
NOTTING HILL
W11
LOFTUS ROAD STADIUM QPR FC
SHEPHERD'S BUSH
W12
HOLLAND PARK
W8
KENSINGTON
Holland Park Roundabout
65
66
67
68
69
70
71
72
73
74
81
82
83
84
99

82
DA
DB
DC
DD
DE
DF
DG
64
65
66
67
68
69
70
71
72
73
74
81
100
26
27
28
WEST HAMPSTEAD
SOUTH HAMPSTEAD
BELSIZE PARK
PRIMROSE HILL
NW3
NW6
NW8
NW1
W9
W2
W8
W11
KILBURN
MAIDA HILL
MAIDA VALE
ST. JOHN'S WOOD
LISSON GROVE
REGENT'S PARK
LONDON ZOO
QUEEN MARY'S GARDENS
BOATING LAKE
LORD'S CRICKET GROUND
WESTBOURNE GREEN
PADDINGTON
MARYLEBONE
BAYSWATER
KENSINGTON GARDENS
HYDE PARK
THE SERPENTINE
ROUND POND
KENSINGTON PALACE
KENSINGTON
HOLLAND PARK
TAVISTOCK CEN
SWISS COTTAGE
HOSPITAL OF ST. JOHN & ST. ELIZ
WELLINGTON HOSP
ST. MARY'S HOSP
ROYAL FREE HOSP
KILBURN HIGH ROAD
MAIDA VALE
EDGWARE ROAD
FINCHLEY ROAD
WELLINGTON RD
ST. JOHN'S WOOD ROAD
PRINCE ALBERT ROAD
WESTWAY
HARROW ROAD
BAYSWATER ROAD
NOTTING HILL GATE
KENSINGTON ROAD
KENSINGTON GORE
KNIGHTSBRIDGE
PARK LANE
OXFORD STREET
MARYLEBONE ROAD
BAKER ST
GLOUCESTER PL
HAVERSTOCK HILL
CHALK FARM
BELSIZE
ADELAIDE ROAD
OXFORD STREET where marked is closed to through traffic (except buses & taxis) from 7a.m.-7p.m. Monday - Saturday

83
NW5
N7
N1
WC1
EC1
W1
WC2
SE1
SW1
DH
DJ
DK
DL
DM
DN
DP
29
30
31
65
66
67
68
69
70
71
72
73
74
84
101
KENTISH TOWN
CAMDEN TOWN
KING'S CROSS
BARNSBURY
ISLINGTON
CANONBURY
SOMERS TOWN
ST. PANCRAS
PENTONVILLE
FINSBURY
CLERKENWELL
ST. LUKE'S
BARBICAN
REGENT'S PARK
BLOOMSBURY
HOLBORN
SOHO
STRAND
MAYFAIR
ST. JAMES'S
SOUTHWARK
THE BOROUGH
GREEN PARK
ST. JAMES'S PARK
RIVER
CALEDONIAN PARK
PENTONVILLE PRISON
KING'S CROSS ST. PANCRAS
EUSTON
WATERLOO
CHARING CROSS
BRITISH MUSEUM
LINCOLN'S INN FIELDS
RUSSELL SQUARE GDNS
CORAM'S FIELDS
GRAY'S INN GDNS
TATE MODERN
SHAKESPEARE GLOBE THEATRE
ST. PAUL'S CATH
ST. BART'S HOSP
BUCKINGHAM PALACE GDNS
VICTORIA EMBANKMENT
PICCADILLY CIRCUS
OXFORD CIRCUS
COVENT GARDEN
ALDWYCH
ROYAL COURTS OF JUSTICE
ST. GEORGE'S CATHEDRAL
MIDDLESEX HOSP
EASTMAN DENTAL HOSP
ROYAL FESTIVAL HALL
QUEEN ELIZABETH HALL
BLACKFRIARS MILLENNIUM PIER
WESTMINSTER MILLENNIUM PIER

84
DQ
DR
DS
DT
DU
DV
DW
33
34
35
66
65
67
68
69
70
71
72
73
74
83
82
81
84
102
HIGHBURY
CANONBURY
KINGSLAND
DALSTON
HACKNEY
SOUTH HACKNEY
DE BEAUVOIR TOWN
HOXTON
HAGGERSTON
BETHNAL GREEN
SHOREDITCH
ST. LUKE'S
CLERKENWELL
BARBICAN
BROADGATE
WHITECHAPEL
STEPNEY
SHADWELL
WAPPING
SOUTHWARK
THE BOROUGH
N1
E8
E2
E1
EC1
EC2
EC3
EC4
SE1
RIVER THAMES
LONDON FIELDS
REGENT'S CANAL
TOWER OF LONDON
ST. PAUL'S CATH
GUY'S HOSPITAL
LONDON BRIDGE HOSP
MOORFIELDS EYE HOSP
ROYAL LONDON HOSP
BUNHILL FIELDS
HOXTON SHOREDITCH PARK
HAGGERSTON PARK
WEAVERS FLDS
ST. KATHARINE'S DOCK
TATE MODERN
SHAKESPEARE GLOBE THEATRE
CITY HALL
POTTERS FIELDS PARK
THE POOL

DX
DY
DZ
EA
EB
EC
ED
36
37
38
67
65
66
84
68
83
69
86
70
82
71
72
81
73
74
103
HOMERTON
HOMERTON HOSPITAL
MABLEY GREEN
E9
HACKNEY WICK
EAST CROSS ROUTE
EASTWAY
WICK COMMUNITY WOODLAND
VALLEY PARK
CYCLE CIRCUIT
Lee Valley Campsite
Cold Stores
E15
STRATFORD
WELL STREET COMMON
VICTORIA PARK
OLD FORD
HERTFORD UNION CANAL
BOW INDUSTRIAL PARK
CARPENTERS ROAD
WHITE POST LA
PUDDING MILL LANE
GROVE HALL PARK
MILE END
MILE END PARK
BOW
BOW CHURCH
ROYAL LONDON HOSP (MILE END)
Queen Mary University of London
ROYAL LON. HOSP (ST. CLEMENTS)
TOWER HAMLETS CEMETERY PARK
E3
BROMLEY
ST. ANDREW'S HOSP
THREE MILLS GREEN
LEE VALLEY PARK
Three Mills Studios
MEMORIAL GDNS
WEST HAM
MEMORIAL RECREATION GROUND
E16
NEWHAM
TOWER HAMLETS
Mail Centre
MILE END STADIUM
STEPNEY GREEN
LIMEHOUSE
LANGDON PARK
BARTLETT PARK
LANSBURY EST
E14
EAST INDIA DOCK RD
CANNING TOWN
LIMMO PENINSULA ECOLOGICAL PARK
EAST INDIA DOCK BASIN
POPLAR
Billingsgate Fish Mkt
CANARY WHARF
HERON QUAYS
ISLE
WEST INDIA DOCKS
SOUTH QUAY
RIVER THAMES
SOUTHWARK
SURREY WATER
SE16
RUSSIA DOCK WOODLAND
BLACKWALL
Blackwall Reach
BLACKWALL TUNNEL
MERIDIAN GARDENS
THE DOME
SE10
NORTH GREENWICH

86
EE
EF
EG
EH
EJ
EK
EL
FOREST GATE
E7
68
ROMFORD ROAD
GRANGE PARK CEMETERY
PLASHET JEWISH CEMETERY
E15
STRATFORD
65
66
67
68
69
70
71
72
73
74
WEST HAM PARK
UPTON
WEST HAM
UPTON LANE
STOPFORD ROAD
CHILDRENS ZOO
PLASHET PARK
EAST HAM MEM HOSP
HIGH STREET NORTH
UPTON PARK
BOLEYN GRD WEST HAM UTD F.C.
BARKING ROAD
PLAISTOW
PLAISTOW HOSP
EAST LONDON CEMETERY
MEMORIAL RECREATION GROUND
SPORTS GROUND
HERMIT RD REC GRD
E13
NEWHAM GENERAL HOSPITAL
E6
EAST HAM JEWISH CEMETERY
BRAMPTON PARK
85
TERENCE McMILLAN STADIUM
PLAYING FIELDS
NEWHAM WAY
BECKTON DISTRICT PARK NORTH
MANOR ROAD
PRINCE REGENT LANE
CANNING TOWN REC GRD
CANNING TOWN
KING GEORGE V PARK
CUSTOM HOUSE
BECKTON DISTRICT PARK SOUTH
LIMMO PENINSULA ECOLOGICAL PARK
EAST INDIA DOCK BASIN NATURE RESERVE
LOWER LEA CROSSING
VICTORIA DOCK RD
ROYAL VICTORIA
ExCeL
ROYAL VICTORIA DOCK
PRINCE REGENT
CONNAUGHT BRIDGE
ROYAL ALBERT
London Regatta Centre
E16
HART RD
LONDON
Millennium Mills
Pontoon Dock
SILVERTOWN WAY
NORTH WOOLWICH ROAD
DLR under construction (opens 2005)
SILVERTOWN & LONDON CITY AIRPORT
THAMES BARRIER PARK
SILVERTOWN
THAMESIDE INDUSTRIAL EST
BLACKWALL TUNNEL
MERIDIAN GARDENS
THE DOME
SE10
NORTH GREENWICH
104
RIVER
WOOLWICH REACH
THAMES FLOOD
40
41
42

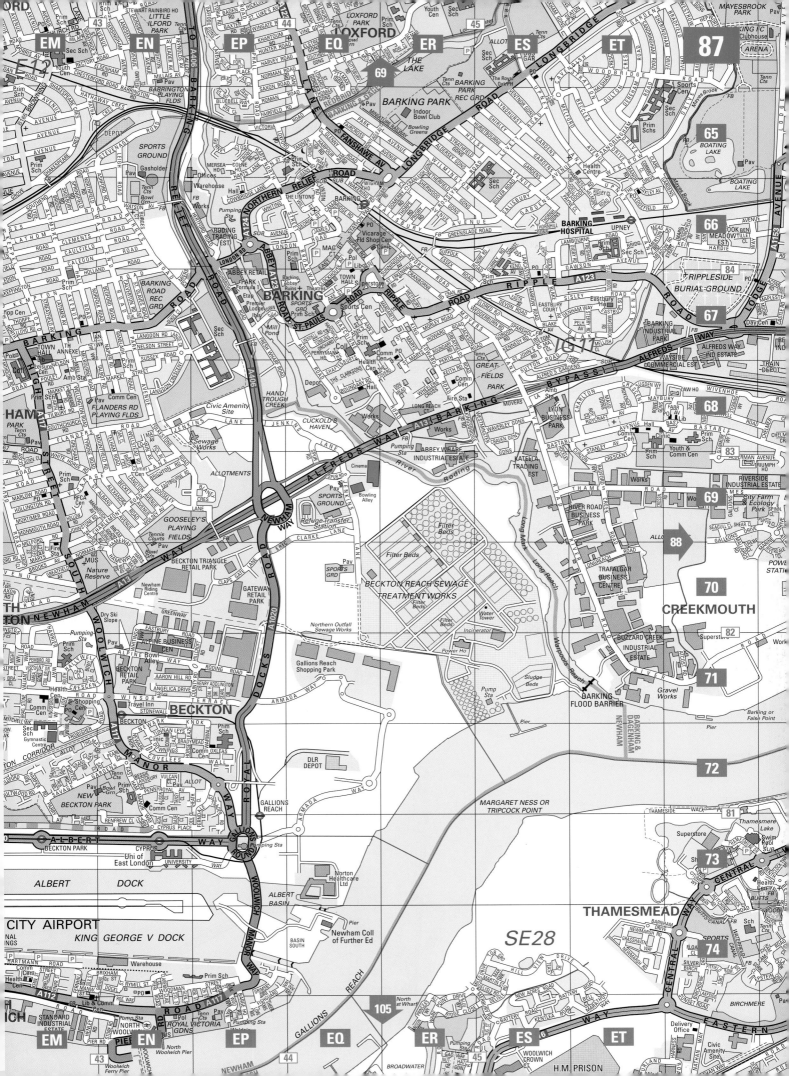
87
EM
EN
EP
EQ
ER
ES
ET
43
44
45
69
88
105
65
66
67
68
69
70
71
72
73
74
81
82
83
84
LITTLE ILFORD PARK
LOXFORD PARK
LOXFORD
THE LAKE
MAYESBROOK PARK
BARKING PARK
BARKING PARK REC GRD
BARRINGTON PLAYING FLDS
SPORTS GROUND
BOATING LAKE
BARKING HOSPITAL
UPNEY
RODING TRADING EST
ABBEY RETAIL PARK
BARKING
TOWN HALL
BARKING ROAD REC GRD
RIPPLESIDE BURIAL GROUND
BARKING INDUSTRIAL PARK
IG11
ALFREDS WAY IND ESTATE
WAYSIDE COMMERCIAL EST
GREAT FIELDS PARK
LYON BUSINESS PARK
E12
HAM PARK
FLANDERS RD PLAYING FLDS
Civic Amenity Site
HAND TROUGH CREEK
CUCKOLD'S HAVEN
ABBEY WHARF INDUSTRIAL ESTATE
KATELLA TRADING EST
RIVERSIDE INDUSTRIAL ESTATE
City Farm & Ecology Park
RIVER ROAD BUSINESS PARK
TRAFALGAR BUSINESS CENTRE
CREEKMOUTH
BUZZARD CREEK INDUSTRIAL ESTATE
BARKING FLOOD BARRIER
Barking or False Point
GOOSELEY'S PLAYING FIELDS
Nature Reserve
BECKTON TRIANGLE RETAIL PARK
GATEWAY RETAIL PARK
ALLOTMENTS
SPORTS GROUND
Refuge Transfer Station
Filter Beds
BECKTON REACH SEWAGE TREATMENT WORKS
Northern Outfall Sewage Works
Long Reach
Warpools Reach
NEWHAM
BARKING & DAGENHAM
ALPINE BUSINESS CEN
BECKTON RETAIL PARK
Gallions Reach Shopping Park
BECKTON
DLR DEPOT
NEW BECKTON PARK
GALLIONS REACH
MARGARET NESS OR TRIPCOCK POINT
BECKTON PARK
Uni of East London
ALBERT DOCK
ALBERT BASIN
Norton Healthcare Ltd
CITY AIRPORT
KING GEORGE V DOCK
BASIN SOUTH
Newham Coll of Further Ed
SE28
THAMESMEAD
Thamesmere Lake
BIRCHMERE
STANDARD INDUSTRIAL ESTATE
ROYAL VICTORIA GDNS
North Woolwich Pier
Woolwich Ferry Pier
WOOLWICH CROWN CT
H.M. PRISON
BROADWATER
A406
A124
A123
A13
A117
A1020
A112
A1153
ALFREDS WAY
NEWHAM WAY
ROYAL DOCKS ROAD
WOOLWICH MANOR WAY
ALBERT WAY
EASTERN WAY
CENTRAL WAY
LONGBRIDGE ROAD
RIPPLE ROAD
RIVER ROAD
BARKING ROAD
HIGH STREET SOUTH
NORTHERN RELIEF ROAD
FANSHAWE AV

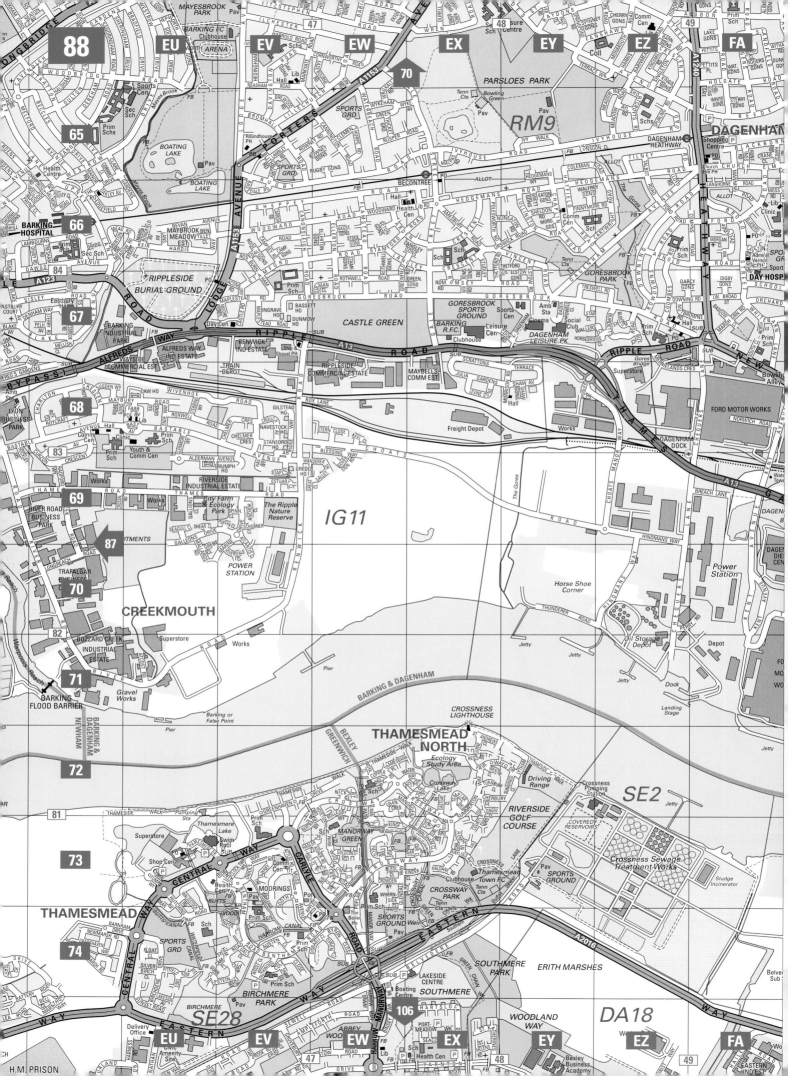
EU
EV
EW
EX
EY
EZ
FA
47
48
49
70
65
66
67
68
69
70
71
72
73
74
84
83
82
81
87
106
MAYESBROOK PARK
BARKING FC
Clubhouse
ARENA
PARSLOES PARK
RM9
DAGENHAM
DAGENHAM HEATHWAY
BOATING LAKE
BARKING HOSPITAL
BECONTREE
MAYBROOK MEADOW EST
RIPPLESIDE BURIAL GROUND
GORESBROOK PARK
CASTLE GREEN
GORESBROOK SPORTS GROUND
BARKING R.F.C.
DAGENHAM LEISURE PK
BARKING INDUSTRIAL PARK
ALFREDS WAY IND ESTATE
WAYSIDE COMMERCIAL EST
RENWICK IND ESTATE
RIPPLESIDE COMMERCIAL ESTATE
MAYBELLS COMM EST
TRAIN DEPOT
Freight Depot
FORD MOTOR WORKS
DAGENHAM DOCK
LYON BUSINESS PARK
RIVERSIDE INDUSTRIAL ESTATE
City Farm & Ecology Park
The Ripple Nature Reserve
IG11
RIVER ROAD BUSINESS PARK
POWER STATION
Horse Shoe Corner
Power Station
Oil Storage Depot
TRAFALGAR BUSINESS
CREEKMOUTH
BUZZARD CREEK INDUSTRIAL ESTATE
Superstore
BARKING FLOOD BARRIER
Gravel Works
BARKING & DAGENHAM
CROSSNESS LIGHTHOUSE
THAMESMEAD NORTH
Ecology Study Area
Crossway Lake
Driving Range
RIVERSIDE GOLF COURSE
Crossness Pumping Station
SE2
COVERED RESERVOIRS
Crossness Sewage Treatment Works
Sludge Incinerator
Thamesmere Lake
MANORWAY GREEN
MOORINGS
THAMESMEAD
CROSSWAY PARK
Thamesmead Town FC
SPORTS GROUND
SOUTHMERE PARK
ERITH MARSHES
LAKESIDE CENTRE
SOUTHMERE
BIRCHMERE PARK
SE28
WOODLAND WAY
DA18
Bexley Business Academy
H.M. PRISON
EASTERN WAY
A13
A2016
A1153
A123
A1240

FB
FC
FD
FE
FF
FG
FH
50
51
52
71
South Hornchurch
RAINHAM
RM10
RM12
RM13
DA17
HORNCHURCH
COUNTRY
PARK
SPORTS GROUND
BRITTONS PLAYING FIELD
OLD DAGENHAM PARK
HORNCHURCH MARSHES
RAINHAM MARSHES
Silt Lagoons
Riverside Sewage Works
FAIRVIEW INDUSTRIAL PARK
ALBRIGHT INDUSTRIAL ESTATE
DENVER INDUSTRIAL ESTATE
BELVEDERE INDUSTRIAL ESTATE
JENNINGTREE POINT LIGHTHOUSE
Newtons Corner
Dovers Corner
RAINHAM ROAD SOUTH
DAGENHAM ROAD
RAINHAM ROAD
NEW ROAD
A1306
A125
A13
THAMES
WESTERN AVENUE
Rainham Sunday Market
Centre for Engineering & Manufacturing Excellence
Old Man's Head
Hornchurch Shoot
WENNINGTON MARSHES
65
66
67
68
69
70
71
72
73
74
81
82
83
84
90
107

90
FJ
FK
FL
FM
FN
FP
FQ
Hacton
72
Corbets Tey
Corbets Tey Sch
PARKLANDS OPEN SPACE
Park Corner Farm
White Hart PH
Lodge Farm
Rainham Lodge Farm
Gardners Cor Hall
Central Farm
Harwood Hall
Poultry Farm
Huntsman & Hounds PH
Stables
SAND & GRAVEL PIT
Civic Amenity Site
Gerpins Farm
RM12
HORNCHURCH
COUNTRY
PARK
AIRFIELD WOOD
FLIGHTWAY WOOD
PINEWOOD
FARMFIELD WOOD
LOWFIELD WOOD
ABBEY WOOD
BERWICK POND
Berwick Ponds Farm
SAND AND GRAVEL PIT
Berwick Manor
Berwick Manor Farm
White Post Corner
SAND AND GRAVEL PIT
WARWICK WOOD
WHITE POST WOOD
Hunts Hill Farm
AINHAM
RAINHAM CEMETERY (JEWISH)
SPRING FARM PARK
IMPERIAL TRADING EST
Tennis Cts
Pav
Saxon Horn PH
Prim Sch
CEM
Health Cen
ALLOT
REC GRD
Sec Sch
Swim Pool
Prim Sch
RM13
South Hall Farm
Southall Bridge
NEW COTTAGES
East Hall Farm
MOAT
Bretts Farm
MOAT
Sir Henry Gurnett PH
Moor Hall
The Marisco PH
Prim Sch
Travel Inn
Willow Farm
Wennington Hall
Hall
Fire Sta
Wennington
New Farm
Sandy Lane Farm
SANDY LANE B1335
RAINHAM MARSHES
Silt Lagoons
Common Watercourse
Works
108
PURFLEET
Nursery
Clubhouse
SPORTS GROUND
WENNINGTON MARSHES
A13
A1306
NEW ROAD
GATEWAY
LONDON ROAD
89
65
66
67
68
69
70
71
72
73
74
54
55
56
84
83
82
81

91
FR
FS
FT
FU
FV
FW
FX
57
58
59
73
North Ockendon
UPMINSTER CEMETERY
MIDDLE WOOD
BONUS WOOD
OCKENDON ROAD
Whitepost Farm
SPORTS GRD
Manor Farm
Hall Farm
Nursery
The Old White Horse PH
Clubhouse
Top Meadow Hotel
TOP MEADOW GOLF COURSE
Driving Range
65
RUSSELL'S LAKE
Adventure Centre
COYS LAKE
Sullens Farm
RM14
HAVERING
THURROCK
M25
66
Groves Barns
THE WILDERNESS
84
67
SAND AND GRAVEL PIT
FREEMAN'S SHAW
Kemp's Farm
CLAY PIT
Tumulus
South Ockendon Hall
MOAT
68
South Ockendon Hall Farm
83
Prim Sch
Royal Oak PH
ALLOT
WEST ROAD
OCKENDON
Works
Comm Cen
Pav
SOUTH OCKENDON REC GRD
69
WHITEHALL WOOD
BELHUS COUNTRY PARK
Visitor Centre
LITTLE BRICKKILN WOOD
BRICKKILN WOOD
Running Water Brook
FORD AVELEY PLANT
70
Bensons Farm
Little Mollands Farm
SOUTH OCKENDON
82
BELHUS PARK
RM15
LONG POND
OAK WOOD
The Ockendon Complex
Sec Sch
BONNYGATE WOOD
South Ockendon Garden Centre
71
ASH PLANTATION
ROOKERY
BUCKLES LANE
LITTLE PALMER'S SHAW
GREAT PALMER'S SHAW
72
SPORTS GROUND
THE SHRUBBERY
BELHUS PARK GOLF COURSE
Driving Range
Swimming Pool
Clubhouse
DILKES PARK
Culver Centre
Health Cen
Knight of Aveley PH
The Archer PH
81
SPORTS GROUND
Tennis Cts
Sec Sch
The Troubadour PH
Clubhouse
MARDYKE VALLEY GOLF COURSE
Hill Farm
73
North Stifford
Aveley
B1335
BYPASS
STIFFORD ROAD
Works
HANGMAN'S WOOD
MILLARD'S GARDEN
BRANNETT'S WOOD
Stifford Bridge
Depot
LOW WELL WOOD
Mar Dyke
The Dog & Partridge PH
74
Stifford Interchange
Hall
SPORTS GROUND
Prince Albert PH
Prim Sch
Junction 30
LOW WELL WOOD
BRICKBARN WOOD
COMBE WOOD
109
A13
THURROCK ARTERIAL ROAD NORTH
Clinic
ARENA ESSEX RACEWAY
KARTING CEN
SPORTS GRD
LAKESIDE COACH PARK
PILGRIMS CARAVAN PARK
PILGRIMS LANE
Thurrock

92
SLOUGH
SALT HILL PARK
AS
AT
AU
AV
AW
AX
AY
98
99
00
74
Thames Valley Uni
Superstore
Works
The Business Village
Grand Union Canal
Gas Works
WELLINGTON ST
WELLINGTON
MONTEM ROAD
TOWN HALL
Sports Centre
MONTEM REC GRD
Ice Arena
Queensmere Shop Centre
Observatory Shop Centre
Royal Mail
HIGH STREET
UXBRIDGE ROAD
Islamic Cen
Prep. Sch
Tennis Courts
BLOOM PARK
Lavender Farm
NURSERY LANE
MIDDLEGREEN ROAD
SUTTON AVENUE
DOWNS ROAD
LANGLEY ROAD
SPORTS GROUND
Prim Sch
Sports Centre
Sec Sch
TRELAWNEY AVENUE
KEDERMISTER PARK
75
76
alvey
UPTON HOSP
SOUTH BUCKS COUNCIL
ALBERT ST A412
MERE RD
YEW TREE ROAD
Upton Park
HERSCHEL PARK
Upton
LASCELLES PLAYING FIELD
SUSSEX PLACE
LONDON ROAD
LONDON
79
SL1
77
A332
AGARS PLOUGH PLAYING FIELDS
Agars Plough
UPTON COURT PARK
MOTOCROSS TRACK
SLOUGH
WINDSOR & MAIDENHEAD
B.M.X. TRACK
Pumping Station
Clubhouse
Cricket Ground
SLOUGH R.F.C.
DITTON PARK
PLAYING FIELD
ETON GOLF COURSE
Open Air Pool
Fifteen Arch Bri
78
PLAYING FIELDS
POCOCKS LANE
ATHLETICS CENTRE
Eton Coll
Eton College
COV RES
Riding Court Farm
KINGS OAK
Computer Associates
DITTON PARK
FISH POND
M4
79
THE HOME PARK RECREATION GROUND
DATCHET GOLF COURSE
Victoria Bri
KING EDWARD VII AVENUE
WINDSOR ROAD
Romney Lock
CUTLERS AIT
ETON
80
WINDSOR & ETON RIVERSIDE
Eton Coll Boathouse
WATER FIREWORK AIT
SUMPTERMEAD AIT
Clubhouse
Sec Sch
Cricket Grd
MAJORS ROAD
B470
HORTON ROAD
DATCHET CEMETERY
77
WINDSOR & ETON CENTRAL
ROYAL STATION
WINDSOR CASTLE
EAST TER LAWN
EAST LAWN
Royal Mews Riding Sch
South Slopes
LIME AVENUE
QUEEN VICTORIA'S CORONATION WALK
RIVER THAMES
DATCHET
Med Cen
Lib
Tenn Cts
DATCHET SPORTS GROUND
The Rising Sun PH
81
GOLF COURSE
Tenn Cts Cambridge Gate
Adelaide Lodge
WINDSOR
Victoria Barracks
Cricket Ground
Bowl Grn
QUEEN ELIZABETH WALK
MILL PLACE CARAVAN PARK
82
Pavs.
Long Walk Gate
THE HOME PARK
SL4
FROGMORE GARDENS
Frogmore House
Royal Mausoleum
Mausoleum
Southlea
Southlea Farm
Pumping Station
76
PRINCESS MARGARET HOSP
Prince Consort's Home Farm
83
Albert Bridge
Windsor Hall
Glasshouses
ROYAL GARDENS
EVERGREEN OAK AV
NICKCROFT AIT
Sludge Lagoon
Sludge Lagoons
Filter Beds
HAM ISLAND
SUNNYMEADS
84
GARRISON SPORTS GROUND
Shaw Farm
ALBERT ROAD
A308
The Lord Nelson PH
Weir
NEW CUT
Sludge Beds
Pumping Sta
Sunnymeads
Sailing Club
Manor Farm
Ham Bridge
HAM LANE
Clayhall Farm
Queen's Cottages
Battle Bourne
112
St. George's Farm
Old Windsor Lock
The Manor
REMENHAM PARK
TW19
GREAT PARK
Hall
Lib

AZ
BA
BB
BC
BD
BE
BF
01
02
03
IVER GOLF COURSE
BUCKINGHAMSHIRE
SOUTH BUCKS
SLOUGH
75
Grand Union Canal (Slough Arm)
TOWING PATH
Trenches Farm
THE ORCHARDS RESIDENTIAL PARK
Glasshouse
Clubhouse
Moat House
THE RIDGEWAY ESTATE
Works
Depot
Chequer Bridge
Withy Bridge
LANGLEY
LANGLEY BUSINESS CENTRE
College
SPORTS GRD
Pav
Hall
Market
PO
LANGLEY MEMORIAL GROUND
Prim Sch
Tennis Courts
Comm Cen
IVER
THORNEY PARK GOLF COURSE
Thorney Farm
Richings Park
Glasshouses
SPORTS GRD
Clubhouse
Bowl Grn
Tower Arms PH
SL0
RICHINGS PARK GOLF COURSE
HOME WOOD
Old Slade Farm
Junction 15 (M25)
Junction 4B (M4)
76
77
78
79
80
81
82
83
84
HARVEY PARK
AXIS PARK
Swimming Pool
Sutton Court Farm
Warehouses
Garden Centre
OAK PLANTATION
M4
SLOUGH OLD WOOD
Sewage Works
Filter Beds
Marriott Hotel
Prim Sch
Health Centre
ALLOT
Grammar Sch
LONDON ROAD
Junction 5
Brands Hill
Quality Hotel Heathrow
COLNBROOK BYPASS
A4
94
Depot
Greyhound PH
Sailing Club
REC GRD
Brook Farm
Colnbrook
Comm Cen
Tanhouse Farm
Prim Sch
Colnbrook Bridge
GRAVEL PIT
SPORTS GRD
Warehouses
GOLF DRIVING RANGE
Longford Roundabout
Mad Bridge
Moor Bridge
HILLINGDON
M25
STANWELL
THE QUEEN MOTHER RESERVOIR
SL3
Poyle
Poyle Lodge
Poyle Channel
BRITANNIA INDUSTRIAL EST
Manor Farm
POYLE TECH CEN
MCKAY TRADING ESTATE
Poyle Farm
TRIDENT INDUSTRIAL ESTATE
Golden Cross PH
POYLE PARK
BEDFONT COURT ESTATE
Colne Brook
Wraysbury River
River Colne
Ashgood Farm
Berkyn Manor Farm
Works
Crown PH
Five Bells PH
Horton
Sailing Club
Arthur Jacob Nature Reserve
Weir
STANWELL ROAD
Lintells Bridge
Junction 14
HILLINGDON
AIRPORT WAY
A3113
TW19
SPORTS GROUND
STANWELL MOOR
Hall
PO
WINDSOR & MAIDENHEAD
SURREY
COPPERMILL ROAD
Inlet Pier
113
WRAYSBURY

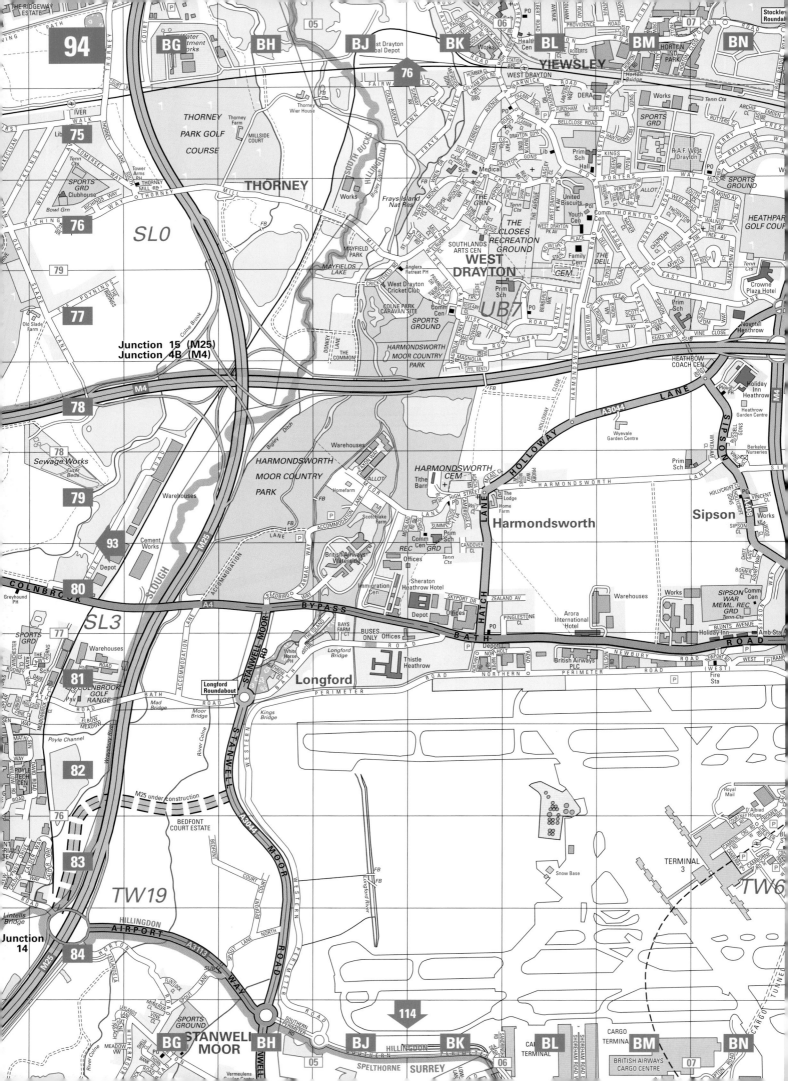
THORNEY PARK GOLF COURSE
THORNEY
SL0
SL3
TW19
UB7
TW6
WEST DRAYTON
YIEWSLEY
Harmondsworth
Sipson
Longford
HARMONDSWORTH MOOR COUNTRY PARK
Junction 15 (M25)
Junction 4B (M4)
Junction 14
M25 under construction
Longford Roundabout
STANWELL MOOR
BEDFONT COURT ESTATE
TERMINAL 3
Sewage Works
HILLINGDON AIRPORT WAY
SPELTHORNE SURREY
BRITISH AIRWAYS CARGO CENTRE

76
93
114

95
BP
BQ
BR
BS
BT
BU
BV
UB11
UB3
TW4
TW5
TW14
HAYES TOWN
MINET COUNTRY PARK
STOCKLEY PARK
Grand Union Canal
ADLER IND EST
WARNFORD IND EST
ABERGLEN INDUSTRIAL ESTATE
E.M.I. SPORTS GROUND
PROVIDENT INDUSTRIAL ESTATE
PETER JAMES BUSINESS CENTRE
HAYES & HARLINGTON
Speedmarque Centre
THE SQUIRRELS TRADING ESTATE
INTERNATIONAL TRADING EST
BULLS BRIDGE IND EST
Western International Market
HARLEQUIN CENTRE
GOVERNMENT BUILDINGS
BOURNE FARM FIELD
ALLOTMENTS
PINKWELL PARK
CHERRY LANE CEMETERY
Cherry Lane Roundabout
SAM PHILIP REC GRD
NORTH HYDE ROAD
HIGH STREET
THE PARKWAY
M4
Junction 4
Junction 3
Junction 4A
IMPERIAL COLLEGE SPORTS GROUND
LITTLE HARLINGTON FIELD
SIPSON MEADOW
SPORTS GROUND
HARLINGTON
CRANE MEADOW
CRANFORD PARK
AVENUE PARK
CRANFORD
TRAVELLERS SITE
BRITISH AIRWAYS SPORTS GROUND
PARKWAY TRADING ESTATE
REDWOOD ESTATE
AIR LINKS INDUSTRIAL ESTATE
SPITFIRE ESTATE
Radisson Edwardian Hotel
Marriott Hotel
Sheraton Skyline
Holiday Inn Ariel
Ibis
Bowling Alley
Renaissance Hotel
Heathrow Airport Visitor Cen
Cardinal Pt
BATH ROAD
A4
HEATHROW AIRPORT (LONDON)
TERMINAL 1
TERMINAL 2
Queen's Building
Maintenance Area
Hangar
Perishable Handling Facility
Parking Express
HATTON
HATTON CROSS
RADIUS PARK
GREAT SOUTH WEST ROAD
A30
BALANCING RESERVOIR
HASLEMERE HEATHROW ESTATE
British Airways PLC
HEATHROW INT TRADING ESTATE
RIFLE RANGE
GREEN LANE OPEN SPACE
MERCURY CENTRE
HOUNSLOW HEATH GOLF COURSE
DONKEY WOOD
Hounslow Urban Farm
THE CAUSEWAY
RIVER CRANE
115
77
96
75
76
78
79
80
81
82
83
84
08
09
10
BP
BQ
BR
BS
BT
BU
BV

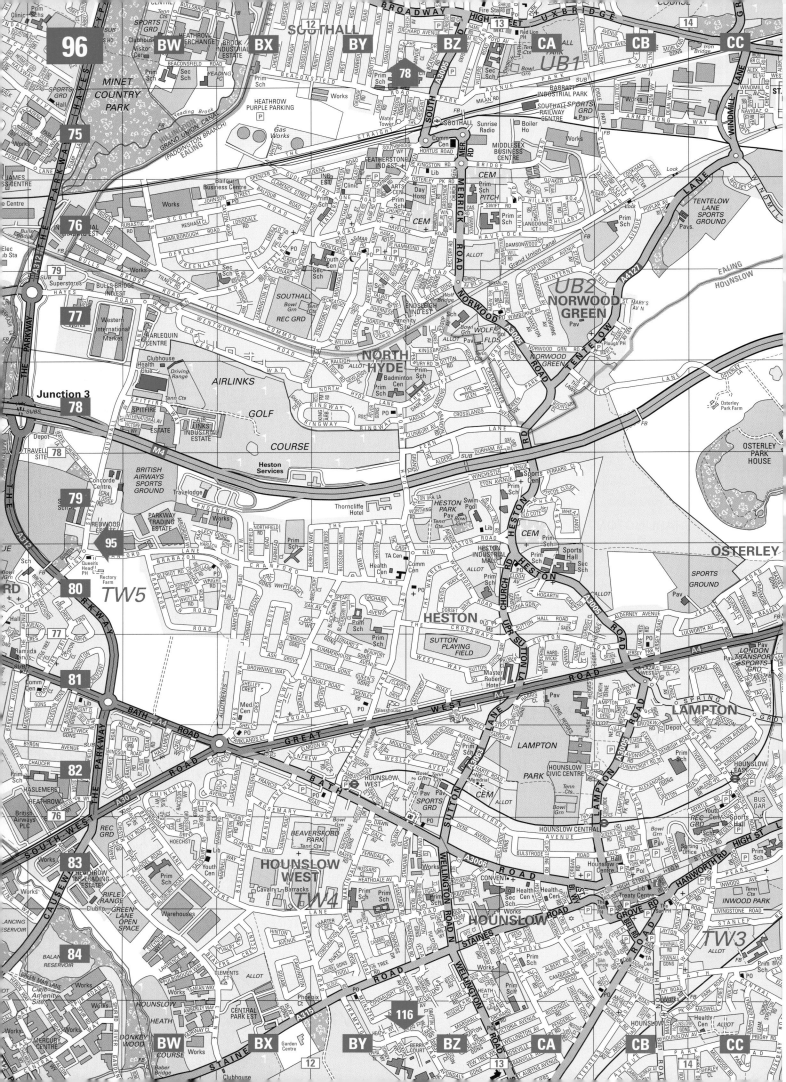

96
BW
BX
BY
BZ
CA
CB
CC
SOUTHALL
UB1
78
MINET COUNTRY PARK
HEATHROW PURPLE PARKING
GRAND UNION CANAL (PADDINGTON BRANCH)
HILLINGDON
EALING
BROADWAY
HIGH STREET
UXBRIDGE
THE STRAIGHT
THE PARKWAY
75
76
77
78
79
80
81
82
83
84
Junction 3
M4
A312
A4
A30
A3005
A4127
A3006
A3063
A315
SOUTHALL RAILWAY CENTRE
BARRATT INDUSTRIAL PARK
MIDDLESEX BUSINESS CENTRE
FEATHERSTONE IND EST
SOUTHALL REC GRD
NORWOOD GREEN
UB2
TENTELOW LANE SPORTS GROUND
EALING
HOUNSLOW
WESTERN INTERNATIONAL MARKET
HARLEQUIN CENTRE
NORTH HYDE
AIRLINKS GOLF COURSE
Heston Services
SPITFIRE ESTATE
AIR LINKS INDUSTRIAL ESTATE
BRITISH AIRWAYS SPORTS GROUND
PARKWAY TRADING ESTATE
Thorncliffe Hotel
OSTERLEY PARK HOUSE
Osterley Park Farm
OSTERLEY
95
TW5
HESTON
HESTON PARK
HESTON INDUSTRIAL MALL
SUTTON PLAYING FIELD
LAMPTON
LAMPTON PARK
HOUNSLOW CIVIC CENTRE
HOUNSLOW WEST
BEAVERSFORD PARK
HOUNSLOW WEST
TW4
Cavalry Barracks
RIFLE RANGE
GREEN LANE OPEN SPACE
HEATHROW INT TRADING ESTATE
BALANCING RESERVOIR
HOUNSLOW HEATH
DONKEY WOOD
MERCURY CENTRE
CENTRAL PARK EST
HOUNSLOW
HOUNSLOW CENTRAL
HOUNSLOW EAST
INWOOD PARK
TW3
Treaty Centre
BATH ROAD
GREAT WEST ROAD
STAINES ROAD
WELLINGTON ROAD N
116
12
13
14

CD
CE
CF
CG
CH
CJ
CK
97
79
75
76
77
78
79
80
81
82
83
84
98
117
15
16
17
HANWELL
HANWELL CEMETERY
W7
W13
W5
TW7
TW8
TW9
TW1
ELTHORNE PARK
BRENT RIVER PARK
ELTHORNE PARK EXTENSION
LAMMAS PARK
WALPOLE PARK
SOUTH EALING CEMETERY
LITTLE EALING
SOUTH EALING
NORTHFIELDS
BOSTON MANOR
LONDON PLAYING FIELDS
BOSTON MANOR HOUSE
BOSTON MANOR PARK
WYKE GREEN GOLF COURSE
OSTERLEY PARK NT
SPORTS GROUND
LONG WOOD (Nature Reserve)
M4
Junction 2
Grand Union Canal
BRENTFORD
BRENTFORD FC
SYON PARK
SYON HOUSE
Battles of Brentford 1016 & 1642
ROYAL BOTANIC GARDENS
KEW
KEW PALACE
QUEEN'S COTTAGE GARDENS
RIVER THAMES
ROYAL MID-SURREY GOLF COURSE
OLD DEER PARK RECREATION GROUND
OBSERVATORY GARDENS
RICHMOND ATHLETIC GROUND
RICHMOND GREEN
SPRING GROVE
ISLEWORTH
WOODLANDS
MOGDEN WATER TREATMENT WORKS
WEST MIDDLESEX UNIVERSITY HOSP
Brunel University (Osterley Campus)
ST. MARGARETS
GREAT WEST ROAD
LONDON ROAD
TWICKENHAM ROAD
BOSTON MANOR ROAD
UXBRIDGE ROAD
THE BROADWAY
A4020
A3002
A4
A315
A310
A316
A3004
A305
B454
B455
B363
B4491

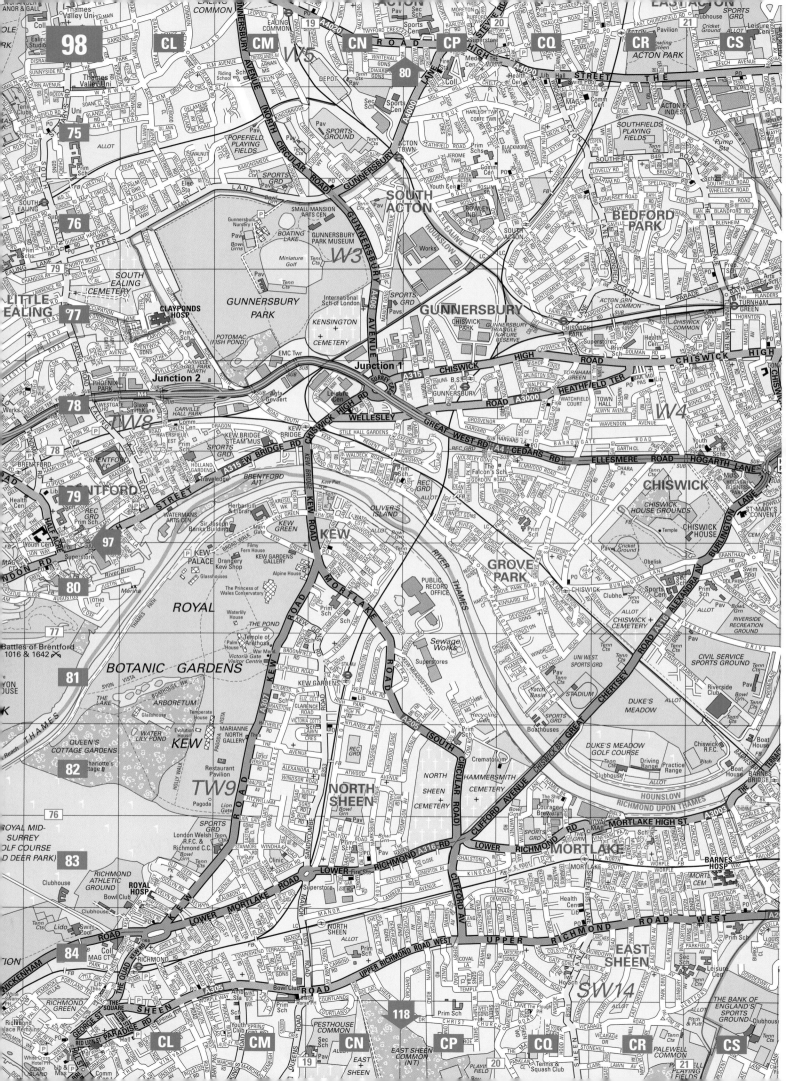
98
CL
CM
CN
CP
CQ
CR
CS
80
W5
W3
W4
TW8
TW9
SW14
ACTON PARK
SOUTH ACTON
BEDFORD PARK
GUNNERSBURY
GUNNERSBURY PARK
KENSINGTON CEMETERY
LITTLE EALING
SOUTH EALING CEMETERY
CLAYPONDS HOSP
Junction 1
Junction 2
BRENTFORD
BRENTFORD AIT
KEW BRIDGE STEAM MUS
KEW
KEW GREEN
KEW PALACE
ROYAL BOTANIC GARDENS
OLIVER'S ISLAND
RIVER THAMES
PUBLIC RECORD OFFICE
GROVE PARK
CHISWICK
CHISWICK HOUSE GROUNDS
CHISWICK HOUSE
DUKE'S MEADOW
DUKE'S MEADOW GOLF COURSE
CHISWICK CEMETERY
RIVERSIDE RECREATION GROUND
CIVIL SERVICE SPORTS GROUND
BARNES BRIDGE
HOUNSLOW
RICHMOND UPON THAMES
NORTH SHEEN
NORTH SHEEN CEMETERY
HAMMERSMITH CEMETERY
MORTLAKE
EAST SHEEN
RICHMOND
RICHMOND GREEN
ROYAL MID-SURREY GOLF COURSE
RICHMOND ATHLETIC GROUND
PESTHOUSE COMMON
EAST SHEEN COMMON (NT)
THE BANK OF ENGLAND'S SPORTS GROUND
Battles of Brentford 1016 & 1642
QUEEN'S COTTAGE GARDENS
ARBORETUM
WATER LILY POND
THE POND
THE LAKE
75
76
77
78
79
80
81
82
83
84
97
118
19
20
21

99
CT
CU
CV
CW
CX
CY
CZ
22
23
24
81
75
76
77
78
79
80
81
82
83
84
100
119
SHEPHERD'S BUSH
W12
W11
W8
KENSINGTON
HOLLAND PARK
W6
W14
OLYMPIA
HAMMERSMITH
SW5
EARLS COURT
SW6
SW13
THE WETLANDS CENTRE
SW15
SW18
CASTELNAU
BARNES
FULHAM
PARSONS GREEN
PUTNEY
WANDSWORTH
ROEHAMPTON
UXBRIDGE ROAD
GOLDHAWK ROAD
KING STREET
GREAT WEST ROAD
TALGARTH ROAD
HAMMERSMITH FLYOVER
FULHAM PALACE ROAD
LILLIE ROAD
DAWES ROAD
HOLLAND PARK AVENUE
KENSINGTON HIGH ST
UPPER RICHMOND ROAD
SOUTH CIRCULAR ROAD
PUTNEY BRIDGE
WANDSWORTH BRIDGE
RIVER THAMES
HAMMERSMITH & FULHAM
RICHMOND UPON THAMES
BARN ELMS PLAYING FIELDS
BARNES COMMON
PUTNEY COMMON
FULHAM PALACE GARDENS
BISHOP'S PARK
HURLINGHAM PARK
SOUTH PARK
WANDSWORTH PARK
EEL BROOK COMMON
CHARING CROSS HOSP
QUEENS CLUB
EARLS COURT EXHIBITION CENTRE
ROEHAMPTON PRIORY HOSPITAL
Hogarth Roundabout
Holland Park Roundabout

100
W11
W8
KENSINGTON
HOLLAND PARK
KENSINGTON GARDENS
ROUND POND
KENSINGTON PALACE
HYDE PARK
THE SERPENTINE
The Lido
SERPENTINE GALLERY
ROTTEN ROW
KENSINGTON ROAD
KENSINGTON GORE
KNIGHTSBRIDGE
SW7
SOUTH KENSINGTON
NATURAL HISTORY MUSEUM
SCIENCE MUSEUM
VICTORIA & ALBERT MUSEUM
CROMWELL ROAD
HARRODS
BELGRAVIA
BROMPTON
SW5
EARLS COURT
EARLS COURT EXHIBITION CENTRE
SW10
SW3
ROYAL MARSDEN HOSP
ROYAL BROMPTON HOSP
ROYAL HOSPITAL CHELSEA
WEST BROMPTON
BROMPTON CEMETERY
CHELSEA
CHELSEA & WEST HOSP
STAMFORD BRIDGE CHELSEA FC
KING'S ROAD
CHEYNE WALK
CHELSEA EMBANKMENT
BATTERSEA PARK
CHILDREN'S ZOO
BOATING LAKE
FULHAM BROADWAY
WALHAM GREEN
PARSONS GREEN
EEL BROOK COMMON
SANDS END
Gas Works
Chelsea Harbour
Chelsea Coll of Art & Design
LONDON BATTERSEA HELIPORT
SW6
HURLINGHAM PARK
HURLINGHAM CLUB
SW11
SW15
SW18
WANDSWORTH
WANDSWORTH BRIDGE
CLAPHAM JUNCTION
LAVENDER HILL
CLAPHAM COMMON
BATTERSEA RISE
BOLINGBROKE HOSP
HAMMERSMITH & FULHAM
DA
DB
DC
DD
DE
DF
DG
26
27
28
75
76
77
78
79
80
81
82
83
84
82
99
120

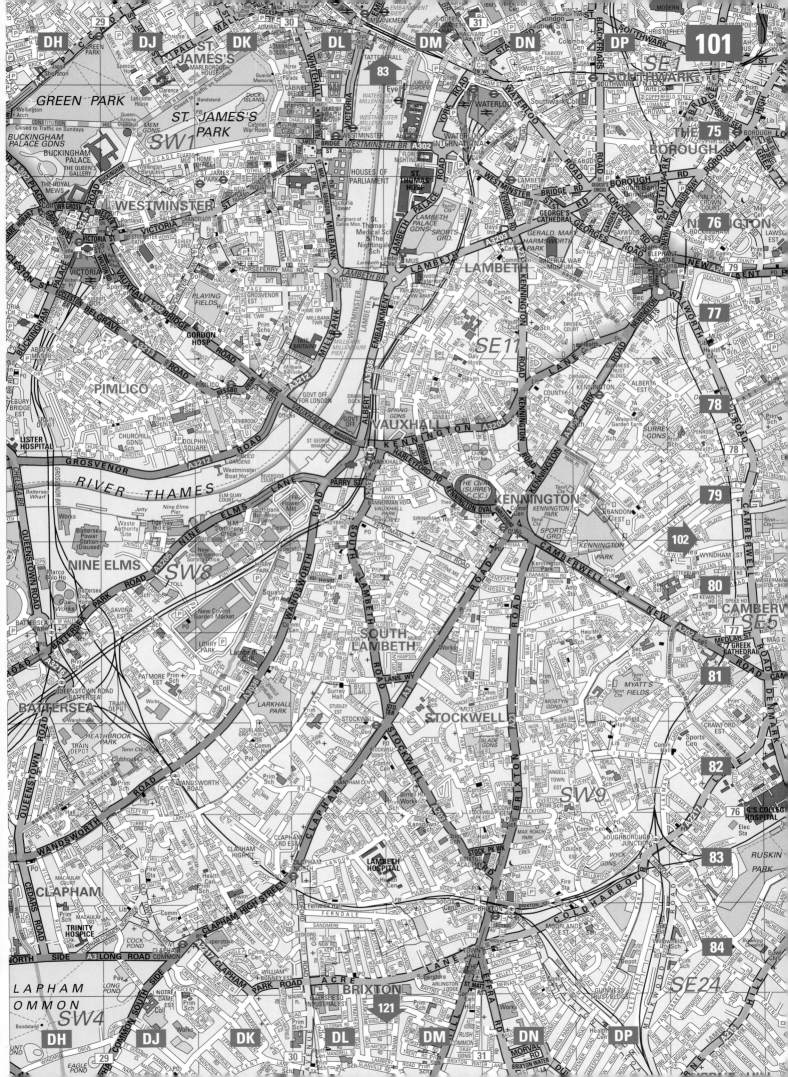

101
DH
DJ
DK
DL
DM
DN
DP
29
30
31
83
102
121
75
76
77
78
79
80
81
82
83
84
GREEN PARK
ST. JAMES'S PARK
ST. JAMES'S
SW1
BUCKINGHAM PALACE GDNS
BUCKINGHAM PALACE
THE QUEEN'S GALLERY
THE ROYAL MEWS
WESTMINSTER
VICTORIA
PIMLICO
LISTER HOSPITAL
CHURCHILL GDNS
DOLPHIN SQUARE
GROSVENOR ROAD
RIVER THAMES
HOUSES OF PARLIAMENT
ST. THOMAS' HOSP
LAMBETH PALACE
WATERLOO
WATERLOO INTERNATIONAL
SE1
SOUTHWARK
THE BOROUGH
NEWINGTON
ELEPHANT & CASTLE
IMPERIAL WAR MUSEUM
LAMBETH
SE11
KENNINGTON
KENNINGTON PARK
THE OVAL (SURREY C.C.C.)
VAUXHALL
VAUXHALL BR
LAMBETH BR
WESTMINSTER BR
TATE BRITAIN
GORDON HOSP
NINE ELMS
NINE ELMS LANE
Battersea Power Station (Disused)
New Covent Garden Market
SW8
BATTERSEA
BATTERSEA PARK
QUEENSTOWN ROAD
SOUTH LAMBETH
STOCKWELL
SW9
BRIXTON
BRIXTON ROAD
CLAPHAM
CLAPHAM HIGH STREET
CLAPHAM COMMON
SW4
LAMBETH HOSPITAL
WANDSWORTH ROAD
CAMBERWELL
CAMBERWELL NEW ROAD
SE5
MYATT'S FIELDS
RUSKIN PARK
SE24
COLDHARBOUR LANE
LOUGHBOROUGH JUNCTION
K.G'S COLLEGE HOSPITAL
GREEK CATHEDRAL
TRINITY HOSPICE
ACRE LANE
LARKHALL PARK
BURGESS PARK

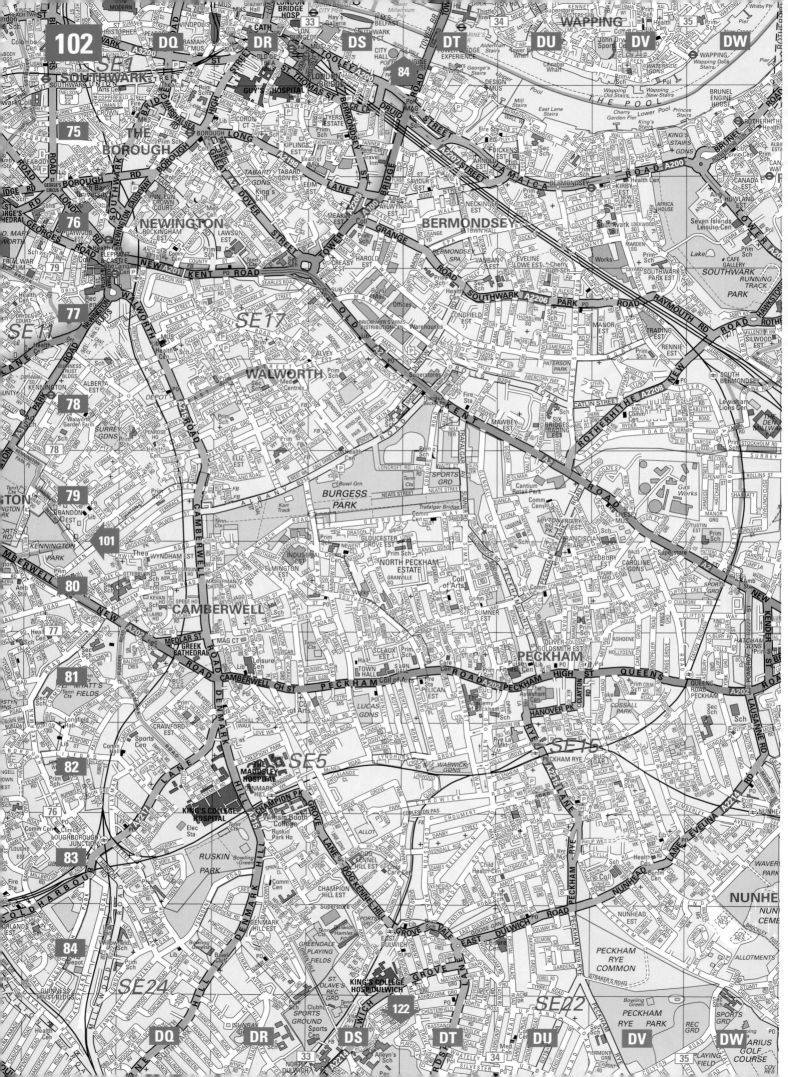

102
DQ
DR
DS
DT
DU
DV
DW
33
34
35
84
75
76
77
78
79
80
81
82
83
84
101
122
SE1
SE11
SE17
SE5
SE15
SE22
SE24
SOUTHWARK
THE BOROUGH
NEWINGTON
ELEPHANT & CASTLE
WALWORTH
CAMBERWELL
BERMONDSEY
WAPPING
PECKHAM
NUNHEAD
EAST DULWICH
BURGESS PARK
RUSKIN PARK
PECKHAM RYE COMMON
PECKHAM RYE PARK
SOUTHWARK PARK
KENNINGTON PARK
LUCAS GDNS
COSSALL PARK
GREENDALE PLAYING FIELDS
GUY'S HOSPITAL
KING'S COLLEGE HOSPITAL
KING'S COLLEGE HOSP DULWICH
THE MAUDSLEY HOSPITAL
LONDON BRIDGE HOSP
TOWER BRIDGE EXPERIENCE
CITY HALL
GREEK CATHEDRAL
THE POOL
NEW KENT ROAD
OLD KENT ROAD
JAMAICA ROAD
SOUTHWARK PARK ROAD
CAMBERWELL NEW ROAD
CAMBERWELL ROAD
DENMARK HILL
PECKHAM ROAD
PECKHAM HIGH ST
QUEENS ROAD
EAST DULWICH ROAD
COLDHARBOUR LANE
ROTHERHITHE NEW ROAD
TOWER BRIDGE ROAD
WALWORTH ROAD
BOROUGH HIGH STREET
LONG LANE
GREAT DOVER STREET
TOOLEY STREET
EVELINA ROAD
NUNHEAD LANE
RYE LANE
LORDSHIP LANE
GROVE VALE
DOG KENNEL HILL
CHAMPION PK

103
DX
DY
DZ
EA
EB
EC
ED
85
ISLE
OF
DOGS
WEST INDIA DOCKS
MILLWALL
MILLWALL OUTER DOCK
MUDCHUTE PARK
E14
CUBITT TOWN
SE16
ROTHERHITHE
SURREY QUAYS
GREENLAND DOCK
SOUTH DOCK
DEPTFORD
SE8
DEPTFORD PARK
PEPYS PARK
SE14
NEW CROSS GATE
NEW CROSS
ST JOHN'S
SE4
HILLY FIELDS
LEWISHAM
SE13
GREENWICH
GREENWICH PARK
SE10
BLACKHEATH
NORTH GREENWICH
THE DOME
MERIDIAN GARDENS
NATIONAL MARITIME MUSEUM
QUEEN'S HOUSE
CUTTY SARK
FLAMSTEED HOUSE (Old Royal Observatory)
THE WILDERNESS (DEER PARK)
BROCKLEY CEMETERY
LADYWELL CEMETERY
LADYWELL
BROCKLEY
TELEGRAPH HILL PARK
MANOR HOUSE GARDENS
MANOR PARK
THAMES
GREENWICH REACH
EVELYN STREET
CREEK ROAD
ROMNEY RD
TRAFALGAR RD
SHOOTER'S HILL
BLACKHEATH ROAD
BLACKHEATH HILL
LEWISHAM WAY
LOAMPIT HILL
LOAMPIT VALE
MANCHESTER ROAD
WESTFERRY ROAD
BLACKWALL TUNNEL APPROACH
75
76
77
78
79
80
81
82
83
84
104
123
36
37
38

104
LONDON
EE
EF
EG
EH
EJ
EK
EL
E16
THE DOME
NORTH GREENWICH
BUS STA
Millennium Pier
Blackwall Beach
Phoenix Wharf
Manhattan Wharf
RIVER
NEWHAM
GREENWICH
THAMES
WOOLWICH REACH
THAMES FLOOD BARRIER
Barrier Control Building
Barrier Gardens Pier
Tate & Lyle Jetty
SILVERTOWN
THAMES BARRIER PARK
LYLE PARK
THAMESIDE INDUSTRIAL EST
SILVERTOWN & LONDON CITY AIRPORT
DLR under construction (opens 2005)
NORTH WOOLWICH ROAD
A1020
CONNAUGHT RD
ALBERT
HART RD
Grain Mills
Pontoon Dock
Fire Sta
86
40
41
42
SE10
Gas Works
Mudlark Pier
Greenwich Yacht Club
GREENWICH PENINSULA ECOLOGY PARK
BLACKWALL TUNNEL APPROACH
A102
A2203
Holiday Inn Express
COUNCIL DEPOT
Cinema
Superstores
THAMES ANCHORAGE POINT IND EST
MERIDIAN TRADING ESTATE
NEW CHARLTON
CABLE TRADE PARK
GREENWICH INDUSTRIAL ESTATE
Stone Lake Retail Pk
VISITORS CEN
MELLISH IND EST
WOOLWICH ROAD
A206
MARYON PARK
MARYON WILSON PARK
CHILDRENS ZOO
THE VALLEY CHARLTON ATHLETIC FC
CHARLTON
SE7
Charlton House
CHARLTON PARK
QUEEN ELIZABETH HOSPITAL
75
76
77
78
79
80
81
82
83
84
103
Trafalgar Rowing Cen
Power Sta
EAST GREENWICH PLEASAUNCE
WESTCOMBE PARK
TRAFALGAR
ROMNEY RD
NATIONAL MARITIME MUSEUM
GREENWICH PARK
One Tree Hill
FLAMSTEED HOUSE
FAN MUS
The Gardens
THE WILDERNESS (DEER PARK)
RANGER'S HOUSE
Blackheath Gate
MAZE HILL
RECTORY FIELD
Blackheath R.F.C.
HORNFAIR PARK
SHOOTER'S HILL ROAD
A2
A207
BLACKHEATH
SE3
Christ's Coll for Boys
Morden College
Clarendon Hotel
ROCHESTER WAY RELIEF RD
A2213
SPORTS GROUND
GREENWICH CEMETERY
KIDBROOKE
BLACKHEATH HOSP
BLACKHEATH PARK
SPORTS GROUNDS
FOOTBALL PITCHES
SE12
SE13
LEE
LEE HIGH ROAD
A20
Lee Green
MANOR HOUSE GARDENS
MANOR PARK
SUTCLIFFE PARK
Athletics Track
KIDBROOKE GREEN (NAT RES)
UNI OF GREENWICH ATHLETIC GRD
WELL HALL PLEASAUNCE
124
ELTHAM ROAD
A210

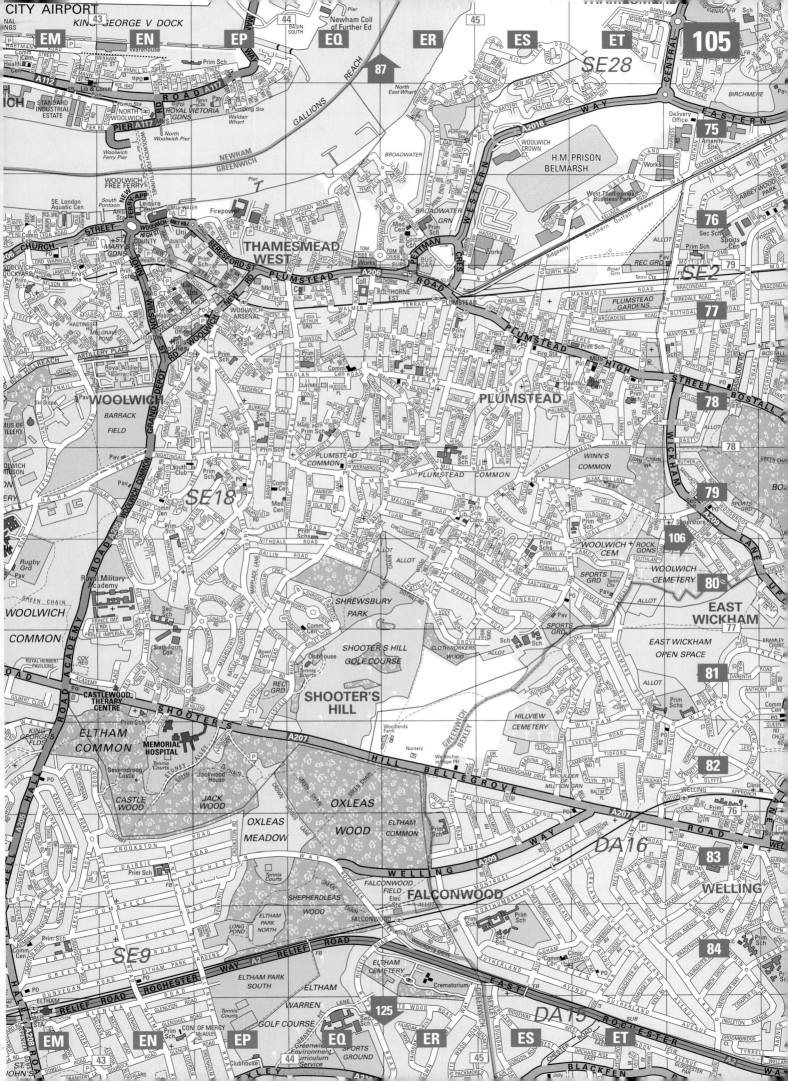

CITY AIRPORT
KING GEORGE V DOCK
Newham Coll of Further Ed
105
SE28
87
GALLIONS REACH
NEWHAM
GREENWICH
North Woolwich Pier
Woolwich Ferry Pier
WOOLWICH FREE FERRY
WOOLWICH FOOT TUNNEL
H.M. PRISON BELMARSH
West Thamesmead Business Park
BROADWATER
THAMESMEAD WEST
WOOLWICH
BARRACK FIELD
PLUMSTEAD
SE2
SE18
PLUMSTEAD COMMON
WINN'S COMMON
WOOLWICH CEM
WOOLWICH CEMETERY
EAST WICKHAM
EAST WICKHAM OPEN SPACE
WOOLWICH COMMON
Royal Military Academy
SHREWSBURY PARK
SHOOTER'S HILL GOLF COURSE
SHOOTER'S HILL
HILLVIEW CEMETERY
ELTHAM COMMON
MEMORIAL HOSPITAL
CASTLE WOOD
JACK WOOD
OXLEAS WOOD
OXLEAS MEADOW
ELTHAM COMMON
SHEPHERDLEAS WOOD
FALCONWOOD FIELD
FALCONWOOD
DA16
WELLING
SE9
ELTHAM PARK SOUTH
ELTHAM WARREN GOLF COURSE
ELTHAM CEMETERY
Crematorium
DA15
125
106
EM
EN
EP
EQ
ER
ES
ET

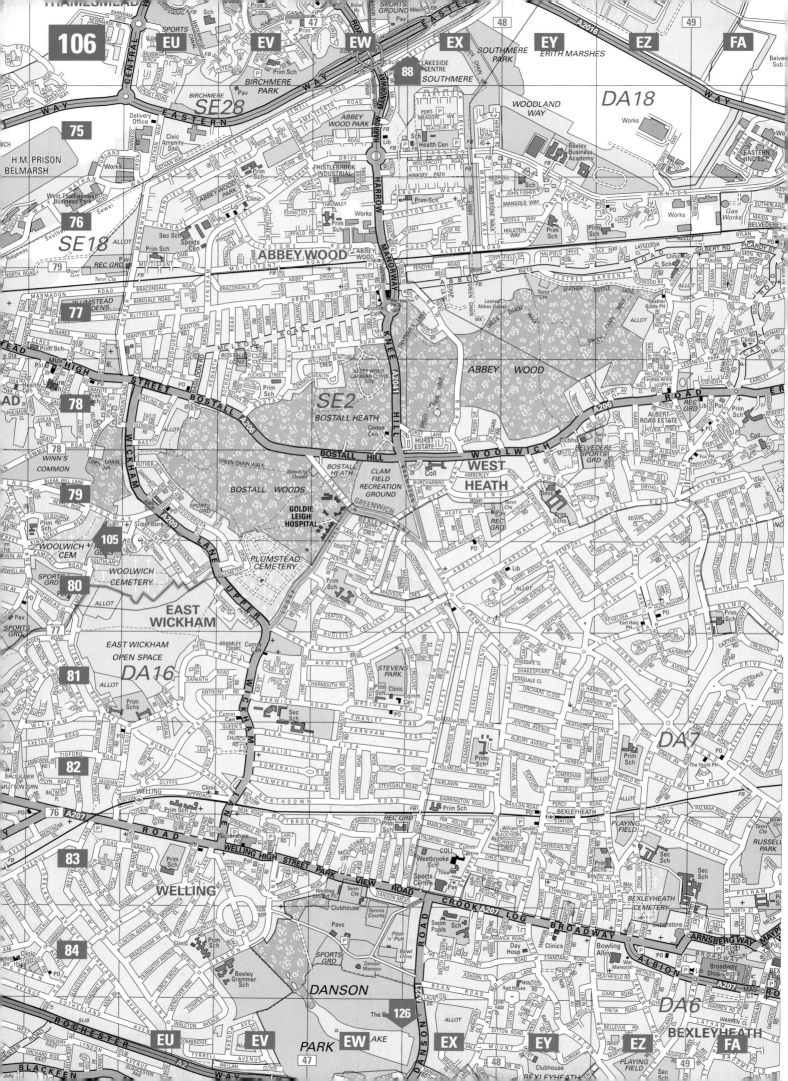

EU
EV
EW
EX
EY
EZ
FA
47
48
49
SE28
DA18
SE18
SE2
DA16
DA7
DA6
75
76
77
78
79
80
81
82
83
84
88
105
126
ABBEY WOOD
WEST HEATH
EAST WICKHAM
WELLING
DANSON
PARK
BEXLEYHEATH
H.M. PRISON BELMARSH
BIRCHMERE PARK
ABBEY WOOD PARK
THISTLEBROOK INDUSTRIAL EST
SOUTHMERE PARK
ERITH MARSHES
WOODLAND WAY
LAKESIDE CENTRE
SOUTHMERE
Bexley Business Academy
EASTERN IND EST
BOSTALL HEATH
BOSTALL WOODS
GOLDIE LEIGH HOSPITAL
CLAM FIELD RECREATION GROUND
WINN'S COMMON
WOOLWICH CEMETERY
PLUMSTEAD CEMETERY
EAST WICKHAM OPEN SPACE
STEVENS PARK
BEXLEYHEATH CEMETERY
RUSSELL PARK
Bexley Grammer Sch
Danson Mansion
ALBERT ROAD ESTATE
HURST ESTATE
BELVEDERE SPORTS GRD
EASTERN WAY
HARROW MANORWAY
KNEE HILL
BOSTALL HILL
WOOLWICH ROAD
WICKHAM LANE
UPPER WICKHAM LANE
WELLING HIGH STREET
BELLEGROVE ROAD
PARK VIEW ROAD
CROOK LOG
BROADWAY
ARNSBERG WAY
ALBION ROAD
DANSON ROAD
ROCHESTER WAY
BLACKFEN
A2016
A206
A2041
A207
A209
A221
A2

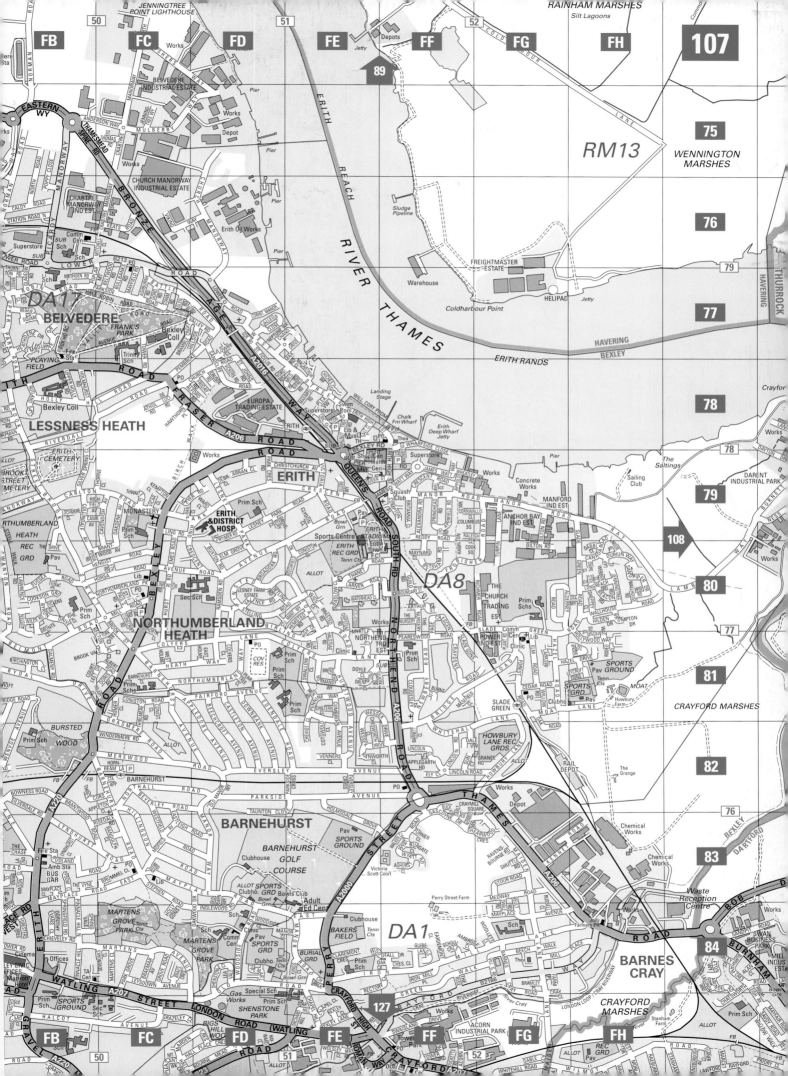
FB
FC
FD
FE
FF
FG
FH
50
51
52
89
108
127
75
76
77
78
79
80
81
82
83
84
JENNINGTREE POINT LIGHTHOUSE
RAINHAM MARSHES
Silt Lagoons
RM13
WENNINGTON MARSHES
BELVEDERE INDUSTRIAL ESTATE
CHURCH MANORWAY INDUSTRIAL ESTATE
CRABTREE MANORWAY IND EST
Erith Oil Works
ERITH REACH
RIVER THAMES
Sludge Pipeline
FREIGHTMASTER ESTATE
Coldharbour Point
HELIPAD
Warehouse
HAVERING
BEXLEY
THURROCK
ERITH RANDS
DA17
BELVEDERE
FRANK'S PARK
Bexley Coll
LESSNESS HEATH
EUROPA TRADING ESTATE
ERITH
ERITH CEMETERY
BROOK STREET CEMETERY
ERITH & DISTRICT HOSP
ERITH STADIUM
ERITH REC GRD
Erith Deep Wharf Jetty
Concrete Works
MANFORD IND EST
ANCHOR BAY IND EST
The Saltings
Sailing Club
DARENT INDUSTRIAL PARK
DA8
THE CHURCH TRADING EST
SLADE GREEN
NORTHUMBERLAND HEATH
BURSTED WOOD
HOWBURY LANE REC GRDS
CRAYFORD MARSHES
RAIL DEPOT
The Grange
BARNEHURST
BARNEHURST GOLF COURSE
SPORTS GROUND
Chemical Works
Waste Reception Centre
Perry Street Farm
MARTENS GROVE PARK
BAKERS FIELD
DA1
BARNES CRAY
SWAN BUSINESS PARK
SHENSTONE PARK
ACORN INDUSTRIAL PARK
CRAYFORD MARSHES
BIGS HILL WOOD
A206
A2016
A220
A207
A2000
B2186
B213
THAMES ROAD
BRONZE AGE WAY
FRASER ROAD
BEXLEY ROAD
NORTHEND ROAD
QUEEN'S ROAD
WATLING STREET
LONDON ROAD
CRAYFORD WAY
PERRY STREET
BOURNE ROAD
EASTERN WAY
THAMESMEAD SPINE RD

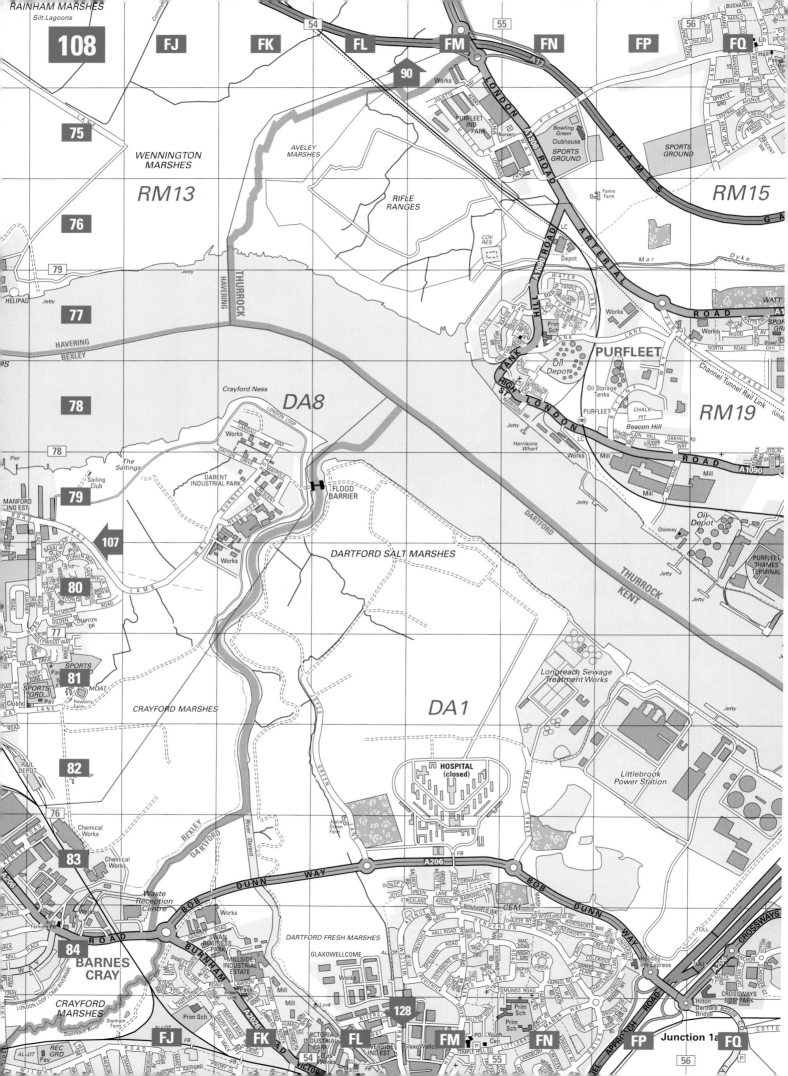

RAINHAM MARSHES
Silt Lagoons
108
FJ
FK
FL
FM
FN
FP
FQ
54
55
56
90
75
76
77
78
79
80
81
82
83
84
WENNINGTON MARSHES
RM13
AVELEY MARSHES
RIFLE RANGES
PURFLEET IND PARK
Works
Nursery
LONDON ROAD
A1306
A13
THAMES
ARTERIAL
Bowling Green
Clubhouse
SPORTS GROUND
Fanns Farm
RM15
COV RES
Depot
Mar Dyke
HELIPAD
Jetty
HAVERING
THURROCK
BEXLEY
A1090
TANK HILL ROAD
WATER LANE
Prim Sch
PO
Oil Depot
PURFLEET
Oil Storage Tanks
Channel Tunnel Rail Link
PURFLEET BYPASS
CHALK PIT
Beacon Hill
RM19
HIGH ST
HARRISONS WF
Harrisons Wharf
LC
Mill
Crayford Ness
DA8
LONDON LOOP
Works
DARENT INDUSTRIAL PARK
The Saltings
Sailing Club
Pier
MANFORD IND EST
FLOOD BARRIER
NESS ROAD
LAMB WAY
107
DARTFORD
KENT
DARTFORD SALT MARSHES
Chimney
PURFLEET THAMES TERMINAL
SPORTS GRD
Clubho
Pav
MOAT
Howbury Farm
CRAYFORD MARSHES
Longreach Sewage Treatment Works
DA1
JOYCE GREEN LANE
HOSPITAL (closed)
MARSH STREET
Littlebrook Power Station
RAIL DEPOT
Chemical Works
Joyce Green Farm
River Darent
A206
BOB DUNN WAY
FB
Waste Reception Centre
CEM
DARTFORD FRESH MARSHES
GLAXOWELLCOME
SWAN BUSINESS PARK
MILLSIDE INDUSTRIAL ESTATE
BURNHAM ROAD
A2026
BARNES CRAY
CRAYFORD MARSHES
Stanham River
Stanham Farm
Prim Sch
Lock
128
VICTORIA INDUSTRIAL PARK
RIVERSIDE IND EST
Gas Works
TEMPLE HILL SQ
Youth Cen
Holiday Inn Express
TOLL
CROSSWAYS BUS PARK
Hilton Dartford Bridge
Junction 1a
APPROACH ROAD
REC GRD
ALLOT

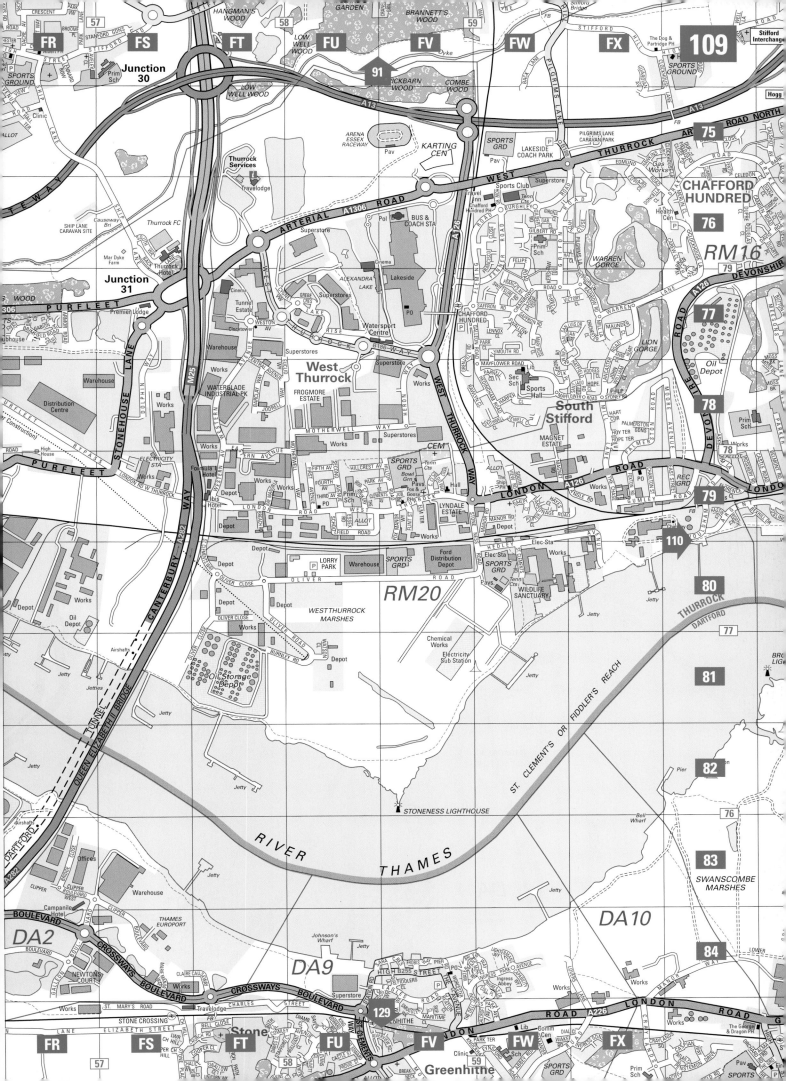

109
FR
FS
FT
FU
FV
FW
FX
57
58
59
91
Junction 30
Junction 31
HANGMAN'S WOOD
BRANNETT'S WOOD
LOW WELL WOOD
RICKBARN WOOD
COMBE WOOD
STIFFORD HILL
Stifford Interchange
The Dog & Partridge PH
SPORTS GROUND
A13
ARENA ESSEX RACEWAY
KARTING CEN
SPORTS GRD
LAKESIDE COACH PARK
PILGRIMS LANE CARAVAN PARK
PILGRIMS LANE
ARTERIAL ROAD NORTH
WEST THURROCK
ARTERIAL A1306 ROAD
Thurrock Services
Travelodge
SHIP LANE CARAVAN SITE
Thurrock FC
Mar Dyke Farm
Thurrock Hotel
BUS & COACH STA
Lakeside
ALEXANDRA LAKE
Superstore
Superstores
Tunnel Estate
Clocktower
Watersport Centre
CHAFFORD HUNDRED
RM16
WARREN GORGE
LION GORGE
Oil Depot
Premier Lodge
PURFLEET
HURROCK B186 WAY
West Thurrock
FROGMORE ESTATE
WATERGLADE INDUSTRIAL PK
Warehouse
Distribution Centre
STONEHOUSE LANE
M25
MOTHERWELL WAY
South Stifford
MAGNET ESTATE
Formula 1 Hotel
Ibis Hotel
LONDON ROAD
LYNDALE ESTATE
A126
A282
CANTERBURY WAY
ELECTRICITY STA
DEVONSHIRE ROAD
75
76
77
78
79
80
81
82
83
84
110
LORRY PARK
Ford Distribution Depot
OLIVER ROAD
RM20
WILDLIFE SANCTUARY
WEST THURROCK MARSHES
Chemical Works
Electricity Sub Station
Oil Storage Depot
QUEEN ELIZABETH II BRIDGE
TUNNEL
DARTFORD
THURROCK
ST. CLEMENT'S OR FIDDLER'S REACH
STONENESS LIGHTHOUSE
RIVER THAMES
SWANSCOMBE MARSHES
DA10
DA2
DA9
THAMES EUROPORT
Johnson's Wharf
Bell Wharf
Campanile Hotel
CROSSWAYS BOULEVARD
NEWTONS COURT
HIGH B255 STREET
Superstore
Travelodge
ST. MARY'S ROAD
STONE CROSSING
129
Stone
Greenhithe
LONDON ROAD A226
The George & Dragon PH
Jetty
Works
Depot

110
FY
FZ
GA
GB
GC
GD
GE
61
62
63
Stifford Interchange
Hogg Lane Roundabout
A13
THURROCK ARTERIAL ROAD NORTH STIFFORD
A1012
RM16
THURROCK COMMUNITY HOSPITAL
Thurrock R.F.C.
SPORTS GROUND
THURROCK ATHLETICS STADIUM
KING GEORGE'S FIELD
Blackshots Leisure Centre
Sockett's Heath
HANGMAN'S WOOD
Little Thurrock
A1013
STANFORD
LODGE LANE
CHAFFORD HUNDRED
ELIZABETH ROAD
HOGG LANE
DEVONSHIRE ROAD
A126
Badgers Mere
WARREN GORGE
LION GORGE
Oil Depot
GRAYS
RM17
South Stifford
MAGNET ESTATE
75
76
77
78
79
80
81
82
83
84
LONDON ROAD
ORSETT ROAD
PALMERS AV
SOUTHEND ROAD
EAST THURROCK RD
BROADWAY
DOCK ROAD
CIVIC OFFICES
GRAYS PARK
GLOBE IND ESTATES
GRAYS NEW CEMETERY
Rookery Hill
Marshfoot Interchange
A1089
109
Thurrock Yacht Club
Grays Beach Riverside Park
MANOR WAY IND EST
LITTLE THURROCK MARSHES
Capstan Centre
Finnish Terminal
Grain Terminal
Warehouses
RIVER THAMES
THURROCK
DARTFORD
NORTHFLEET HOPE
BROADNESS LIGHTHOUSE
Radar Mast
BROADNESS SALT MARSHES
SWANSCOMBE MARSHES
BOTANY MARSHES
DA10
DA11
KENT
GRAVESHAM
TILBURY DOCKS
A226
LONDON ROAD
GALLEY HILL ROAD
SWANSCOMBE
EBBSFLEET INDUSTRIAL ESTATE
ROBINS CREEK
Northfleet Hope
130

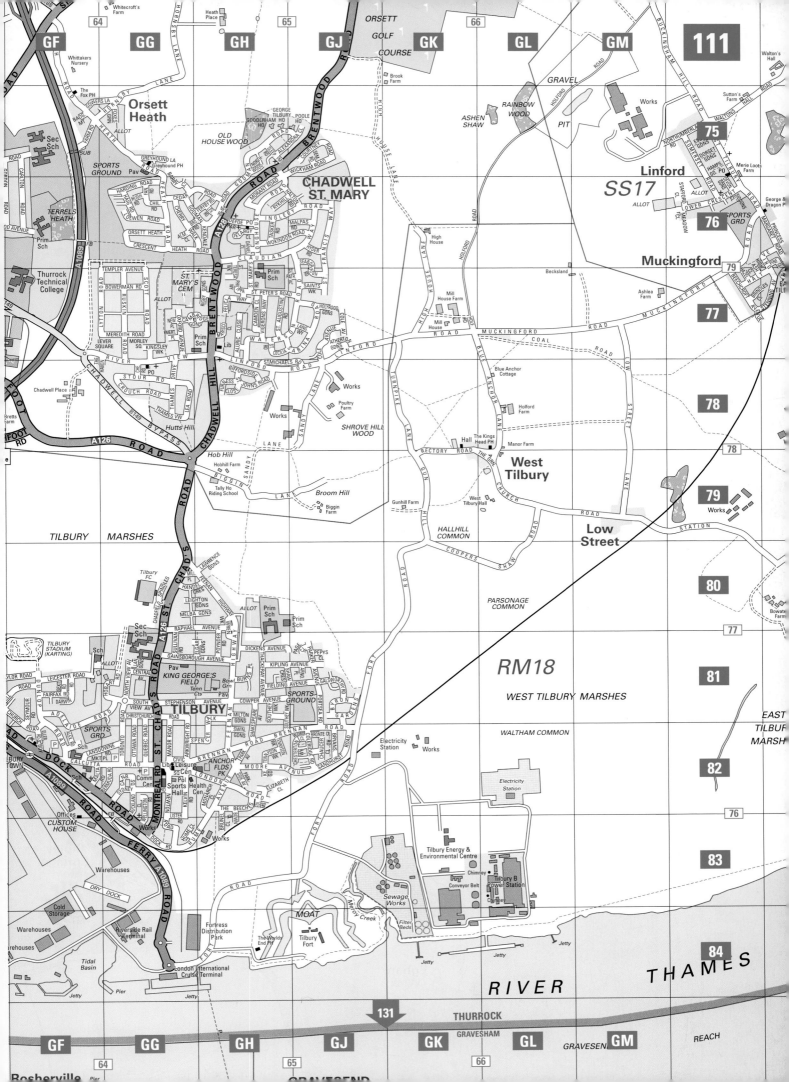

Orsett Heath
CHADWELL ST. MARY
Linford
SS17
Muckingford
West Tilbury
Low Street
TILBURY
RM18
TILBURY MARSHES
WEST TILBURY MARSHES
WALTHAM COMMON
PARSONAGE COMMON
HALLHILL COMMON
SHROVE HILL WOOD
OLD HOUSE WOOD
RAINBOW WOOD
ASHEN SHAW
GRAVEL PIT
ORSETT GOLF COURSE
SPORTS GROUND
KING GEORGE'S FIELD
Thurrock Technical College
Tilbury Energy & Environmental Centre
Tilbury B Power Station
Electricity Station
Sewage Works
Tilbury Fort
MOAT
Fortress Distribution Park
London International Cruise Terminal
Riverside Rail Terminal
Tidal Basin
CUSTOM HOUSE
DRY DOCK
Cold Storage
Warehouses
RIVER THAMES
THURROCK
GRAVESHAM
REACH
Hob Hill
Broom Hill
Hutts Hill
BRENTWOOD ROAD
CHADWELL HILL
ST. CHAD'S ROAD
MUCKINGFORD ROAD
LINFORD ROAD
FORT ROAD
DOCK ROAD
FERRY ROAD
A126
A128
A1089
B149
GF
GG
GH
GJ
GK
GL
GM
64
65
66
75
76
77
78
79
80
81
82
83
84
131

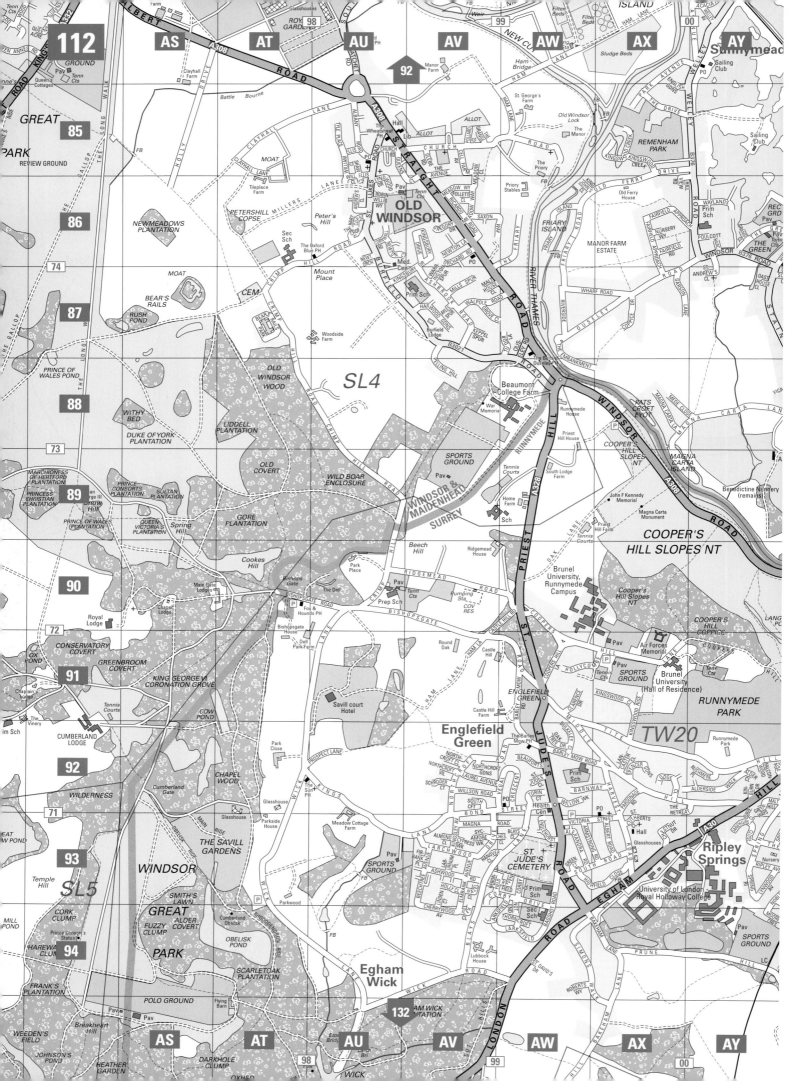

112
AS
AT
AU
AV
AW
AX
AY
92
132
98
99
00
85
86
87
88
89
90
91
92
93
94
74
73
72
71
GREAT
PARK
REVIEW GROUND
GROUND
ALBERT
A308
ROAD
Battle Bourne
Clayhall Farm
HOLLY DRIVE
THE LONG WALK
THE GALLOP
NEWMEADOWS PLANTATION
MOAT
BEAR'S RAILS
RUSH POND
CEM
PETERSHILL COPSE
MILLERS LANE
Peter's Hill
Tileplace Farm
CLAYHALL LANE
Sec Sch
The Oxford Blue PH
CRIMP HILL ROAD
Mount Place
Woodside Farm
OLD WINDSOR
STRAIGHT ROAD
Manor Farm
ALLOT
CHURCH ROAD
Hall
Lib
PO
Pav
Tenn Cts
Med. Cen
Prim Sch
Burfield Lodge
B3021
BURFIELD ROAD
KINGSBURY DRIVE
OUSELEY RD
The Bells of Ouseley PH
HAM LANE
NEW CUT
Ham Bridge
St. George's Farm
Old Windsor Lock
The Manor
The Priory
Priory Stables
FRIARY ISLAND
RIVER THAMES
MANOR FARM ESTATE
WHARF ROAD
OUSELEY ROAD
THE EMBANKMENT
Filter Beds
Sludge Beds
Weir
Sunnymead
Sailing Club
REMENHAM PARK
WELLEY ROAD
B376
KINGSWOOD CREEK
OLD FERRY DRIVE
Old Ferry House
WAYLANDS
Prim Sch
FAIRFIELD APPROACH
WINDSOR ROAD
THE GREEN
REC GRD
SL4
OLD WINDSOR WOOD
WITHY BED
DUKE OF YORK PLANTATION
LIDDELL PLANTATION
OLD COVERT
WILD BOAR ENCLOSURE
PRINCE OF WALES POND
MARCHIONESS OF HERTFORD PLANTATION
PRINCESS CHRISTIAN PLANTATION
PRINCE CONSORTS PLANTATION
SULTAN PLANTATION
QUEEN VICTORIA'S PLANTATION
Spring Hill
Snow Hill
GORE PLANTATION
Cookes Hill
WINDSOR & MAIDENHEAD
SURREY
RUNNYMEDE
Beaumont College Farm
War Memorial
Runnymede House
Priest Hill House
SPORTS GROUND
Tennis Courts
South Lodge Farm
Home Farm
Sch
A328
PRIEST HILL
WINDSOR ROAD
PATS CROFT EYOT
MAGNA CARTA ISLAND
MAGNA CARTA LANE
COOPER'S HILL SLOPES NT
John F Kennedy Memorial
Magna Carta Monument
Benedictine Nunnery (remains)
Priest Hill Farm
OAK LANE
Beech Hill
Ridgemead House
RIDGEMEAD ROAD
Park Place
Bishops Gate
The Dell
BISHOPSGATE ROAD
Fox & Hounds PH
Bishopsgate House
Dell Park Farm
Prep Sch
Pumping Sta
COV RES
Brunel University, Runnymede Campus
Cooper's Hill Slopes NT
COOPER'S HILL COPPICE
COOPERS HILL LANE
Air Forces Memorial
Brunel University (Hall of Residence)
SPORTS GROUND
HOLLYCOMBE
RUNNYMEDE PARK
TW20
Main Gate Lodges
Chapel Lodge
Royal Lodge
CONSERVATORY COVERT
GREENBROOM COVERT
OX POND
KING GEORGE VI CORONATION GROVE
Chaplain's Lodge
The Vinery
CUMBERLAND LODGE
Tennis Courts
COW POND
Round Oak
Castle Hill
HAM LANE
Savill court Hotel
ENGLEFIELD GREEN
Castle Hill Farm
Englefield Green
The Barley Mow PH
BARLEY MOW ROAD
MIDDLE HILL
ST. JUDE'S ROAD
Prim Sch
Health Cen
VICTORIA STREET
Hall
Glasshouses
Park Close
PROSPECT LANE
The Sun PH
WICK LANE
KINGS LANE
Glasshouse
Parkside House
Meadow Cottage Farm
MAGNA ROAD
LARCHWOOD
ST. JUDE'S CEMETERY
Sec Sch
BAGSHOT ROAD
EGHAM ROAD
Ripley Springs
University of London - Royal Holloway College
A30
Pav
SPORTS GROUND
PRUNE HILL
BAKEHAM LANE
Lubbock House
Egham Wick
WICK ROAD
LONDON ROAD
WILDERNESS
Cumberland Gate
CHAPEL WOOD
Glasshouse
OBELISK RIDE
THE SAVILL GARDENS
WINDSOR GREAT PARK
SL5
Temple Hill
SMITH'S LAWN
ALDER COVERT
FUZZY CLUMP
CORK CLUMP
Prince Consort's Statue
Cumberland Obelisk
OBELISK POND
SCARLETOAK PLANTATION
FRANK'S PLANTATION
POLO GROUND
Flying Barn
Breakheart Hill
WEEDEN'S FIELD
JOHNSON'S POND
HEATHER GARDEN
DARKHOLE CLUMP
Parkwood
FB
P

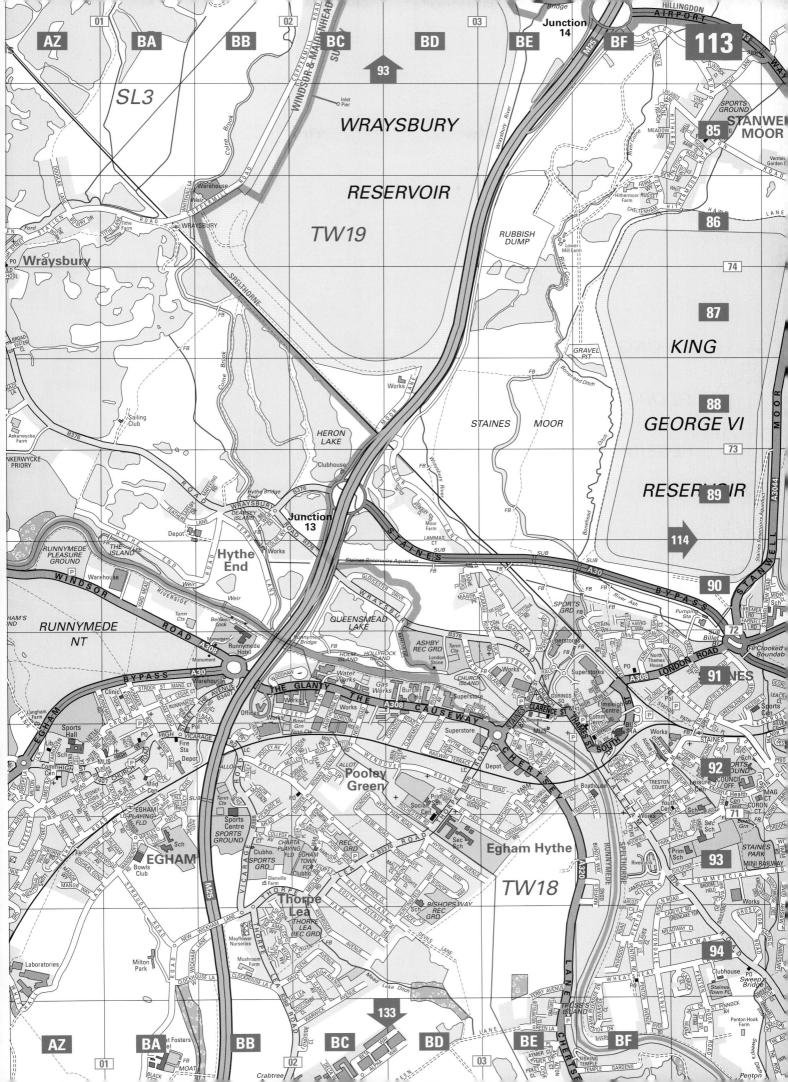

113
AZ
BA
BB
BC
BD
BE
BF
01
02
03
93
133
114
SL3
WRAYSBURY
RESERVOIR
TW19
TW18
Wraysbury
WRAYSBURY
KING
GEORGE VI
RESERVOIR
STAINES
MOOR
Junction 14
Junction 13
Hythe End
RUNNYMEDE NT
RUNNYMEDE PLEASURE GROUND
HERON LAKE
QUEENSMEAD LAKE
RUBBISH DUMP
GRAVEL PIT
Pooley Green
Egham Hythe
EGHAM
Thorpe Lea
STANWELL MOOR
HILLINGDON AIRPORT
M25
A30
A308
A320
B376
B3376
B388
A3044
WINDSOR ROAD
EGHAM BYPASS
THE CAUSEWAY
THE GLANTY
CHERTSEY LANE
STAINES BYPASS
LONDON ROAD
STANWELL MOOR ROAD
WRAYSBURY ROAD
SPELTHORNE
RUNNYMEDE
Runnymede Hotel
Bellweir Lock
Staines Reservoirs Aquaduct
85
86
87
88
89
90
91
92
93
94
74
73
72
71

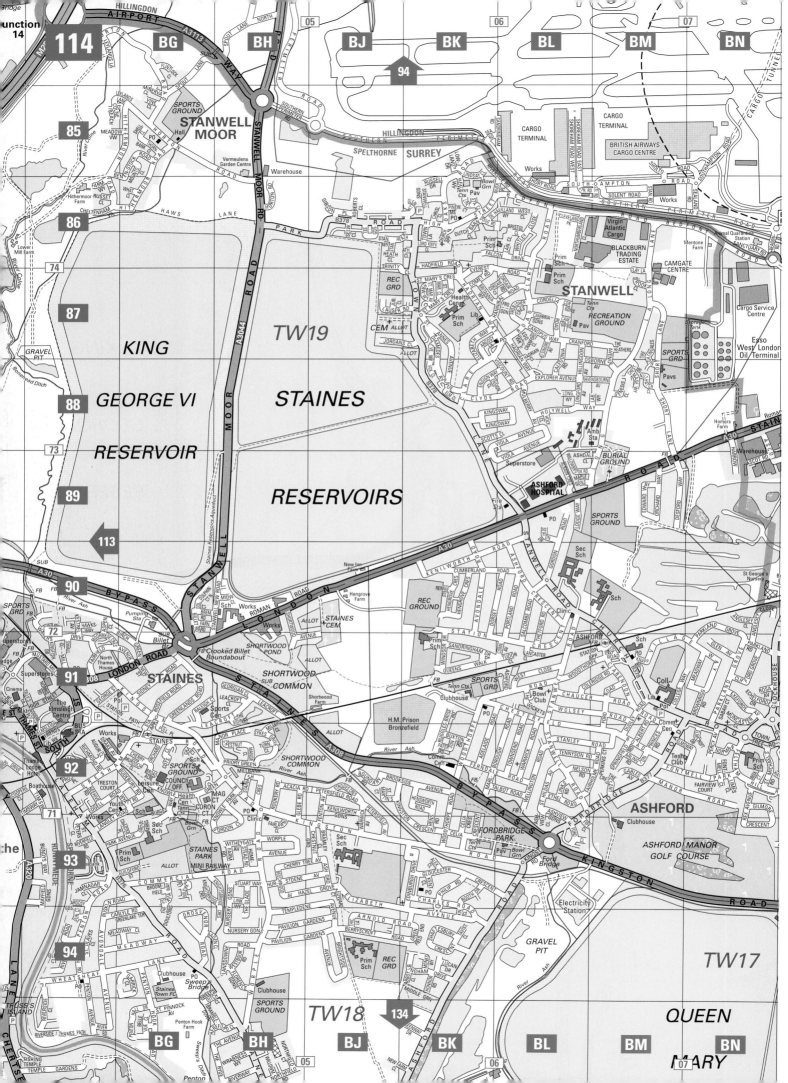
114
Junction 14
HILLINGDON
AIRPORT WAY
BG
BH
BJ
BK
BL
BM
BN
05
06
07
94
STANWELL MOOR
SPORTS GROUND
CARGO TERMINAL
BRITISH AIRWAYS CARGO CENTRE
SPELTHORNE
SURREY
SOUTHERN PERIMETER ROAD
HILLINGDON
Vermeulens Garden Centre
Warehouse
Hithermoor Farm
HAWS LANE
PARK ROAD
B378
STANWELL MOOR ROAD
A3044
Virgin Atlantic Cargo
BLACKBURN TRADING ESTATE
CAMGATE CENTRE
STANWELL
RECREATION GROUND
Cargo Service Centre
Esso West London Oil Terminal
85
86
87
88
89
90
91
92
93
94
74
73
72
71
KING GEORGE VI RESERVOIR
TW19
STAINES RESERVOIRS
GRAVEL PIT
113
ASHFORD HOSPITAL
BURIAL GROUND
SPORTS GROUND
A30
LONDON ROAD
STAINES BYPASS
Crooked Billet Roundabout
STAINES
SHORTWOOD COMMON
STAINES CEM
H.M. Prison Bronzefield
A308
STAINES BYPASS
REC GROUND
ASHFORD
ASHFORD MANOR GOLF COURSE
FORDBRIDGE PARK
KINGSTON ROAD
Electricity Station
GRAVEL PIT
TW17
QUEEN MARY
TW18
134
STAINES PARK MINI RAILWAY
SPORTS GROUND
Staines Town FC
Penton Hook Farm
TRUSS'S ISLAND
A320
CHERTSEY LANE

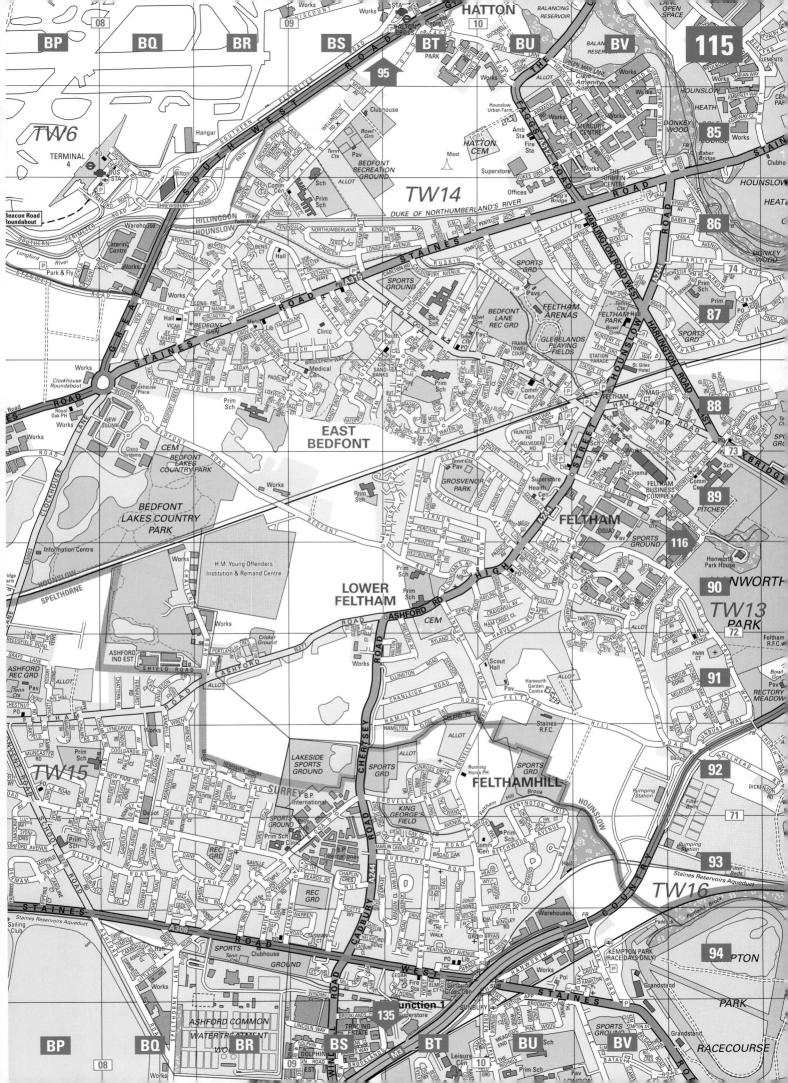
115
HATTON
BP
BQ
BR
BS
BT
BU
BV
08
09
10
95
TW6
TERMINAL 4
TW14
HATTON CEM
BEDFONT RECREATION GROUND
DUKE OF NORTHUMBERLAND'S RIVER
HILLINGDON
HOUNSLOW
STAINES ROAD
SOUTHERN PERIMETER ROAD
GREAT SOUTH WEST ROAD
Beacon Road Roundabout
Clockhouse Roundabout
HOUNSLOW HEATH
DONKEY WOOD
MERCURY CENTRE
THE GRIFFIN CENTRE
85
86
87
88
89
90
91
92
93
94
116
135
FELTHAM ARENAS
BEDFONT LANE REC GRD
GLEBELANDS PLAYING FIELDS
HARLINGTON ROAD WEST
HARLINGTON ROAD EAST
HOUNSLOW ROAD
EAST BEDFONT
BEDFONT LAKES COUNTRY PARK
H.M. Young Offenders Institution & Remand Centre
GROSVENOR PARK
FELTHAM
FELTHAM BUSINESS COMPLEX
HANWORTH
Hanworth Park House
TW13
LOWER FELTHAM
HIGH STREET
ASHFORD RD
CEM
ASHFORD IND EST
ASHFORD REC GRD
TW15
LAKESIDE SPORTS GROUND
SURREY
FELTHAMHILL
KING GEORGE'S FIELD
CHERTSEY ROAD
TW16
Staines Reservoirs Aqueduct
STAINES ROAD WEST
KEMPTON PARK (RACE DAYS ONLY)
KEMPTON PARK RACECOURSE
SUNBURY
Junction 1
ASHFORD COMMON WATER TREATMENT WORKS
M3

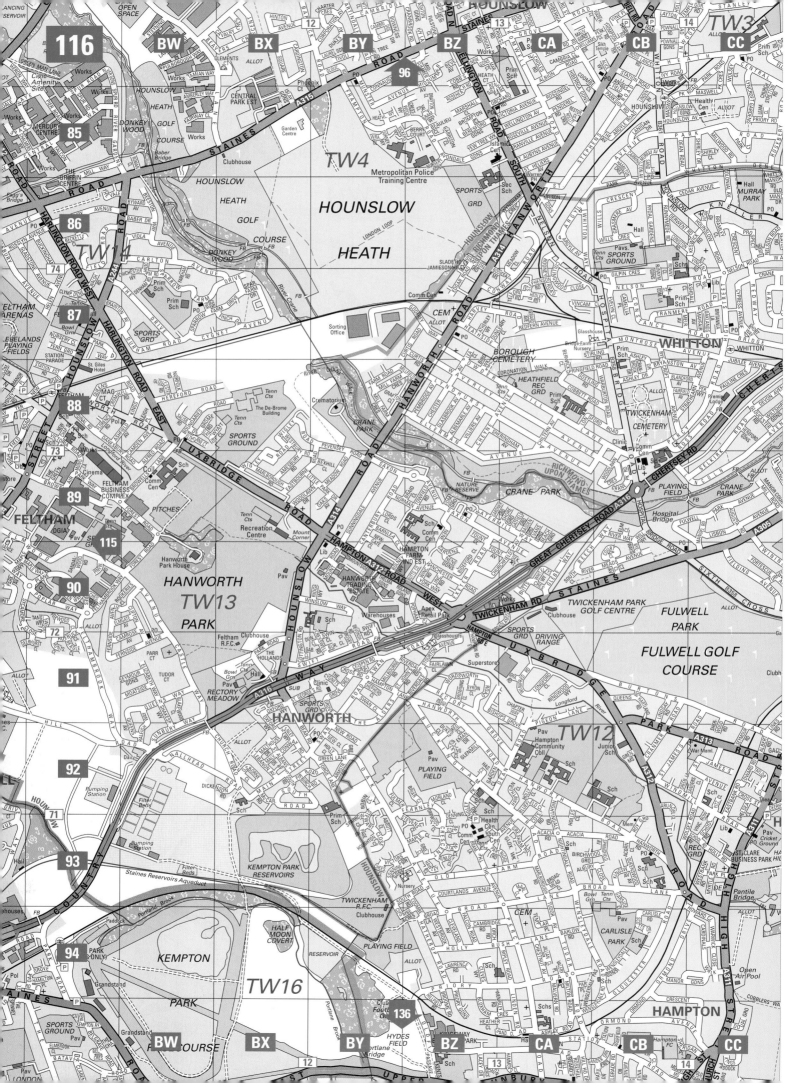
116
BW
BX
BY
BZ
CA
CB
CC
96
85
86
87
88
89
90
91
92
93
94
115
136
TW3
TW4
TW12
TW13
TW14
TW16
HOUNSLOW HEATH
HOUNSLOW HEATH GOLF COURSE
Metropolitan Police Training Centre
DONKEY WOOD
WHITTON
BOROUGH CEMETERY
HEATHFIELD REC GRD
TWICKENHAM CEMETERY
CRANE PARK
FELTHAM
HANWORTH PARK
Hanworth Park House
HANWORTH
FULWELL PARK
FULWELL GOLF COURSE
TWICKENHAM PARK GOLF CENTRE
KEMPTON PARK RESERVOIRS
KEMPTON PARK
HALF MOON COVERT
CARLISLE PARK
HAMPTON
HYDES FIELD
RECTORY MEADOW
Staines Reservoirs Aqueduct
STAINES ROAD
UXBRIDGE ROAD
HANWORTH ROAD
HAMPTON ROAD WEST
GREAT CHERTSEY ROAD
TWICKENHAM RD
HARLINGTON ROAD WEST
HARLINGTON ROAD EAST
A315
A314
A312
A316
A244
A313
A311
A305
B358
12
13
14
71
72
73
74

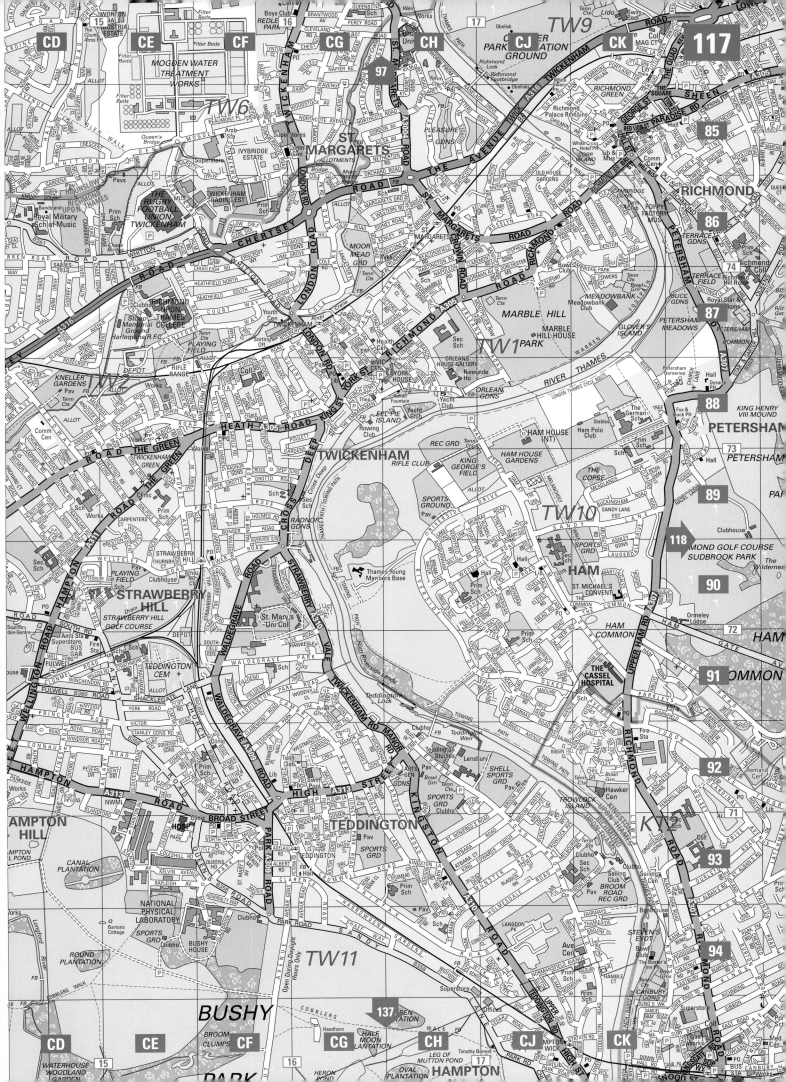
117
CD
CE
CF
CG
CH
CJ
CK
15
16
17
97
TW9
TW6
TW1
TW2
TW10
TW11
KT2
MOGDEN WATER TREATMENT WORKS
OLD DEER PARK RECREATION GROUND
ST. MARGARETS
RICHMOND
RICHMOND GREEN
TWICKENHAM
STRAWBERRY HILL
TEDDINGTON
HAM
PETERSHAM
HAM COMMON
BUSHY PARK
HAMPTON
HAMPTON HILL
THE RUGBY FOOTBALL UNION TWICKENHAM
RICHMOND UPON THAMES COLLEGE
MARBLE HILL PARK
MARBLE HILL HOUSE
HAM HOUSE (NT)
HAM HOUSE GARDENS
KING GEORGE'S FIELD
EEL PIE ISLAND
RIVER THAMES
PETERSHAM MEADOWS
GLOVER'S ISLAND
KING HENRY VIII MOUND
RICHMOND GOLF COURSE SUDBROOK PARK
THE CASSEL HOSPITAL
NATIONAL PHYSICAL LABORATORY
BUSHY HOUSE
TROWLOCK ISLAND
STEVEN'S EYOT
Teddington Lock
Teddington Weir
Thames Young Mariners Base
St. Mary's Uni Coll
ST. MICHAEL'S CONVENT
CANAL PLANTATION
ROUND PLANTATION
WATERHOUSE WOODLAND GARDEN
HALF MOON PLANTATION
LEG OF MUTTON POND
OVAL PLANTATION
HERON POND
BROOM CLUMPS
Open During Daylight Hours Only
85
86
87
88
89
90
91
92
93
94
118
137
72
73
74
71

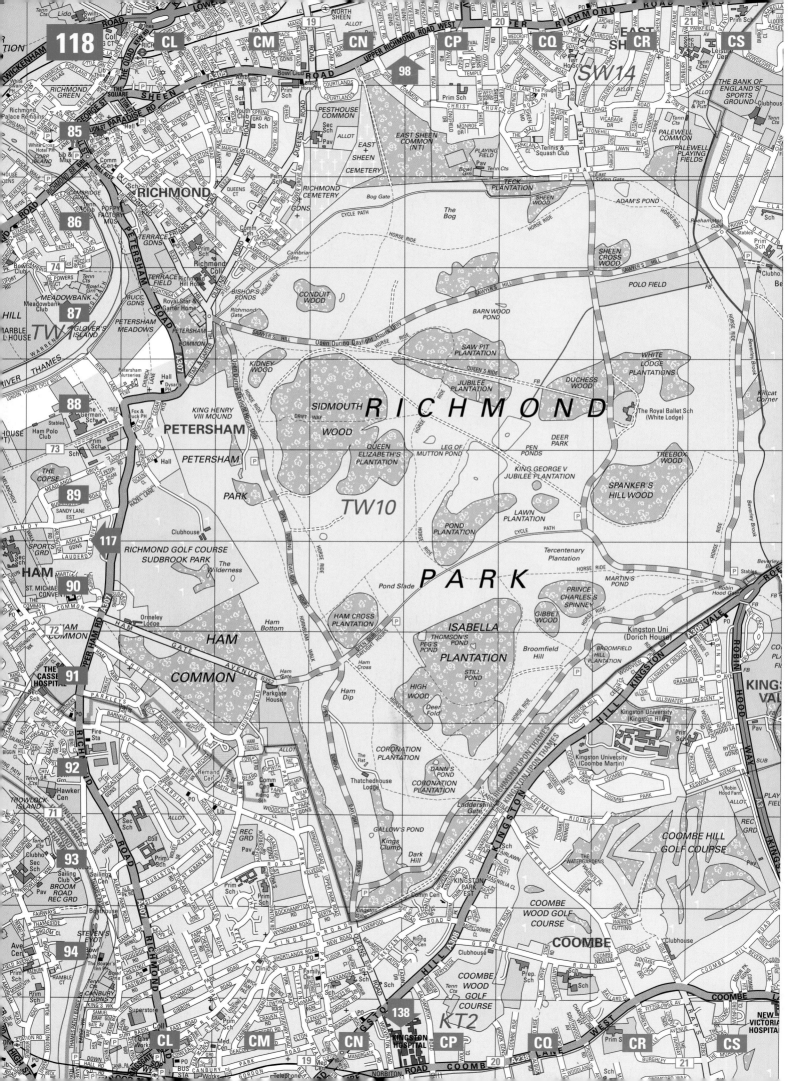
CL
CM
CN
CP
CQ
CR
CS
98
RICHMOND
RICHMOND GREEN
THE SQUARE
SHEEN ROAD
UPPER RICHMOND ROAD WEST
EAST SHEEN
SW14
PESTHOUSE COMMON
EAST SHEEN CEMETERY
EAST SHEEN COMMON (NT)
RICHMOND CEMETERY
PALEWELL COMMON
PALEWELL PLAYING FIELDS
THE BANK OF ENGLAND'S SPORTS GROUND
TECK PLANTATION
SHEEN WOOD
ADAM'S POND
The Bog
Bog Gate
East Sheen Gate
Roehampton Gate
SHEEN CROSS WOOD
SAWYER'S HILL
POLO FIELD
CONDUIT WOOD
BISHOP'S PONDS
Cambrian Gate
Richmond Gate
TERRACE GDNS
TERRACE FIELD
Richmond Hill Hotel
Royal Star & Garter Home
PETERSHAM MEADOWS
PETERSHAM COMMON
GLOVER'S ISLAND
MEADOWBANK
RIVER THAMES
TW1
85
86
87
88
89
90
91
92
93
94
BARN WOOD POND
SAW PIT PLANTATION
KIDNEY WOOD
QUEEN'S RIDE
JUBILEE PLANTATION
WHITE LODGE PLANTATIONS
DUCHESS WOOD
Killcat Corner
RICHMOND
SIDMOUTH WOOD
The Royal Ballet Sch (White Lodge)
KING HENRY VIII MOUND
PETERSHAM
DEER PARK
PEN PONDS
LEG OF MUTTON POND
QUEEN ELIZABETH'S PLANTATION
KING GEORGE V JUBILEE PLANTATION
TREEBOX WOOD
SPANKER'S HILL WOOD
PETERSHAM PARK
TW10
LAWN PLANTATION
POND PLANTATION
117
RICHMOND GOLF COURSE SUDBROOK PARK
The Wilderness
Tercentenary Plantation
PARK
Pond Slade
MARTIN'S POND
Robin Hood Gate
HAM
PRINCE CHARLES'S SPINNEY
GIBBET WOOD
HAM CROSS PLANTATION
Ham Bottom
ISABELLA PLANTATION
THOMSON'S POND
PEG'S POND
Broomfield Hill
Kingston Uni (Dorich House)
HAM COMMON
Ormeley Lodge
Ham Gate
Ham Cross
STILL POND
BROOMFIELD HILL PLANTATION
Ham Dip
HIGH WOOD
Deer Fold
Parkgate House
KINGSTON VALE
Kingston University (Kingston Hill)
CORONATION PLANTATION
The Flat
DANN'S POND
Thatchedhouse Lodge
Kingston University (Coombe Martin)
Remand Cen
Ladderstile Gate
TROWLOCK ISLAND
GALLOW'S POND
Kings Clump
Dark Hill
COOMBE HILL GOLF COURSE
THE WATERGARDENS
BROOM ROAD REC GRD
KINGSTON PARK EST
Kingston Gate
COOMBE WOOD GOLF COURSE
STEVEN'S EYOT
COOMBE
COOMBE WOOD GOLF COURSE
138
KT2
KINGSTON HOSPITAL
NEW VICTORIA HOSPITAL
NORBITON
COOMBE LANE WEST
19
20
21

119
CT
CU
CV
CW
CX
CY
CZ
22
23
24
99
120
139
85
86
87
88
89
90
91
92
93
94
71
72
73
74
WANDSWORTH
PUTNEY
ROEHAMPTON
ROEHAMPTON PRIORY HOSPITAL
Southlands College
ROEHAMPTON GOLF COURSE
Digby Stuart College
University of Surrey
Froebel College
QUEEN MARY'S UNI HOSP
ROEHAMPTON PLAYING FIELDS
South Thames Coll
Wandsworth Adult Ed Coll
MARYFIELD CONVENT
ST. MARY'S CONVENT
Whitelands College
Kingsfarm Plantation
RICHMOND PARK GOLF COURSE
Silver Hill
Chohole Gate
Crematorium
PUTNEY VALE CEMETERY
Superstore
Roehampton Vale Campus
PLAYING FIELDS
War Memorial GDNS
PUTNEY VALE
SW15
SW18
SW19
SW20
PUTNEY HEATH
Tibbet's Corner
Cricket Ground
SCIO POND
KING'S MERE
Jerry's Hill
WINDMILL MUSEUM
QUEEN'S MERE
Clubhouse
PARKSIDE CLINIC
LONDON SCOTTISH GOLF COURSE
Silent Pools
Stag Bog
WIMBLEDON
BLUEGATE GRAVEL PIT (DISUSED)
HOOKHAMSLADE POND
Queen's Butt (Site off)
Gravelly Hill
COMMON
White Cottage
Thatched Cottage
Springwell Cottage
Farm Bog
Farm Ravine
Caesar's Camp
Warren Farm
Fishponds Wood Nature Reserve
Mill Corner
ROYAL WIMBLEDON GOLF COURSE
Shadwell Wood
CANNIZARO PARK
Thistle Cannizaro House
RUSHMERE POND
LADY JANE'S WOOD
ROYAL HOSPITAL
Univ of Surrey-Whitelands Coll
WANDSWORTH
EAST PUTNEY
SOUTHFIELDS
WIMBLEDON PARK EST
WIMBLEDON PARK Stadium
WIMBLEDON PARK GOLF COURSE
WIMBLEDON PARK
ALL ENGLAND LAWN TENNIS & CROQUET CLUB
SOUTHFIELDS
Metropolitan Club
KING GEORGE'S PARK
WIMBLEDON
MUS OF LOCAL HISTORY
King's Coll Sch
WOLFSON MED. REHAB CENTRE
COPSE HILL
OBERON PLAYING FIELD
SPORTS GROUND
COTTENHAM PARK
DUNDONALD REC GRD
DUNDONALD ROAD
MERTON PARK
MERTON
TRAIN DEPOT
KINGSTON ROAD
UPPER RICHMOND ROAD
WEST HILL
KINGSTON VALE
ROEHAMPTON LANE
PUTNEY HILL
WIMBLEDON PARK SIDE
PARKSIDE
HIGH ST WIMBLEDON
WIMBLEDON HILL RD
THE BROADWAY
DURNSFORD ROAD
BUCKHOLD ROAD
A3
A205
A219
A218
A238
A3209

120
DA
DB
DC
DD
DE
DF
DG
100
85
86
87
88
89
90
91
92
93
94
119
140
WANDSWORTH
SW18
SW11
SW12
SW17
SW19
SOUTHFIELDS
EARLSFIELD
BALHAM
SUMMERSTOWN
WIMBLEDON PARK
UPPER TOOTING
TOOTING GRAVENEY
COLLIER'S WOOD
SOUTH WIMBLEDON
MERTON
FURZEDOWN
WANDSWORTH COMMON
BOLINGBROKE HOSP
H.M. PRISON WANDSWORTH
WANDSWORTH CEMETERY
SPRINGFIELD HOSPITAL
CENTRAL LONDON GOLF CENTRE
STREATHAM CEMETERY
WIMBLEDON STADIUM
WIMBLEDON CEMETERY
LAMBETH CEMETERY
ST. GEORGE'S HOSPITAL
LONDON ROAD CEMETERY
SPENCER PARK
KING GEORGE'S PARK
GARRATT PARK
GARRATT GREEN
WANDLE PARK
FIGGE'S MARSH
CLAPHAM JUNCTION
DURNSFORD ROAD
MERTON ROAD
GARRATT LANE
TRINITY ROAD
HAYDONS ROAD
MERTON HIGH STREET
TOOTING HIGH STREET
UPPER TOOTING ROAD
MITCHAM ROAD
BALHAM HIGH ROAD
WEST HILL
WANDSWORTH HIGH ST
BATTERSEA RISE
CLAPHAM COMMON W SIDE
BURNTWOOD LANE
THE BROADWAY
MERANTUN WAY
KINGSTON ROAD
A3
A24
A205
A214
A217
A218
A219
A238
B229
B235
26
27
28
71
72
73
74

DH
DJ
DK
DL
DM
DN
DP
101
CLAPHAM COMMON
SW4
CLAPHAM PARK
BRIXTON
SW2
SE24
BROCKWELL PARK
HERNE HILL
85
86
87
88
89
90
91
92
93
94
122
141
STREATHAM HILL
SE21
TULSE HILL
TOOTING BEC COMMON
STREATHAM PARK
STREATHAM
SE27
WEST NORWOOD
WEST NORWOOD CEMETERY
STREATHAM COMMON
SW16
NORWOOD GROVE RECREATION GROUND
STREATHAM VALE
SE19
NORBURY PARK
NORBURY
BIGGIN WOOD
TOOTING GRAVENEY COMMON
TOOTING BEC ATHLETICS TRACK
HAYES COURT
OAKLANDS ESTATE
WEIR ESTATE
SACKVILLE ESTATE
NATIONAL WESTMINSTER BANK SPORTS GROUND
29
30
31
71
72
73
74

122
DQ
DR
DS
DT
DU
DV
DW
SE24
HERNE HILL
BROCKWELL PARK
TULSE HILL
SE27
WEST NORWOOD
WEST NORWOOD CEMETERY
NORWOOD NEW TOWN
NORWOOD
UPPER NORWOOD
SE19
WEST DULWICH
DULWICH
SE21
DULWICH PARK
DULWICH & SYDENHAM HILL GOLF COURSE
SYDENHAM HILL WOOD (NATURE RESERVE)
DULWICH WOOD
EAST DULWICH
SE22
PECKHAM RYE COMMON
PECKHAM RYE PARK
CAMBERWELL OLD CEMETERY
HORNIMAN GDNS
UPPER SYDENHAM
SYDENHAM WELLS PARK
SE26
SYDENHAM
CRYSTAL PALACE PARK
CRYSTAL PALACE NATIONAL SPORTS CENTRE
PENGE
SE20
ANERLEY
BEAULIEU HEIGHTS
HERNE HILL STADIUM
SOUTH BANK UNIVERSITY SPORTS GROUND
NORWOOD PARK
WESTOW PARK
KING'S COLL HOSP
AQUARIUS GOLF COURSE
102
142
121
33
34
35
74
73
72
71
85
86
87
88
89
90
91
92
93
94

123
DX
DY
DZ
EA
EB
EC
ED
103
85
86
87
88
89
124
90
91
92
93
94
143
36
37
38
74
73
72
71
BROCKLEY
HONOR OAK PARK
FOREST HILL
LADYWELL
CATFORD
BELL GREEN
BELLINGHAM
SOUTHEND
LOWER SYDENHAM
NEW BECKENHAM
BECKENHAM
BROMLEY PARK
HITHER GREEN
SE4
SE13
SE23
SE6
BR1
BR2
BR3
LEWISHAM
HILLY FIELDS
LADYWELL CEMETERY
BROCKLEY CEMETERY
CAMBERWELL NEW CEMETERY
UNIVERSITY HOSPITAL LEWISHAM
LEWISHAM PARK
MOUNTFIELD PARK PLAYING FIELDS
CATFORD GREYHOUND STADIUM
LADYWELL FIELDS
BLYTHE HILL FIELDS
BROCKLEY HILL PARK
GARTHORNE ROAD NATURE RESERVE
PRIVATE BANKS SPORTS GRD
FORSTER MEMORIAL PARK
MANOR PARK
MANOR HOUSE GARDENS
MAYOW PARK
HOME PARK
BELLINGHAM PARK
SOUTHEND PARK
BECKENHAM PLACE PARK
GOLF COURSE
SUMMERHOUSE HILL WOOD
ASH PLANTATION
Stumpshill Wood
LEWISHAM BOROUGH SPORTS GROUND
MIDLAND BANK SPORTS GROUND
WARREN AVE PLAYING FIELDS
SHORTLANDS GOLF COURSE
NAT WEST BANK SPORTS GRD
KENT C.C.C.
C.G.U. CUACO SPORTS GRD
H.S.B.C. GROUP SPORTS GRD
CATOR PARK
ALEXANDRA REC GRD
BECKENHAM BUSINESS CEN
LOWER SYDENHAM IND EST
BECKENHAM JUNCTION
BECKENHAM HILL
NEW BECKENHAM
KENT HOUSE
RAVENSBOURNE
THE SLOANE HOSPITAL
DOWNHAM
STANSTEAD ROAD
SOUTH CIRCULAR ROAD
BROWNHILL ROAD
CATFORD ROAD
CATFORD HILL
PERRY HILL
RUSHEY GRN
LEWISHAM HIGH STREET
BROMLEY ROAD
SOUTHEND LANE
BECKENHAM HILL ROAD
SOUTHEND ROAD
BROMLEY HILL
A205
A212
A21
A2218
A2015
A20
A234
B218
B227
B236
B238

EE
EF
EG
EH
EJ
EK
EL
40
41
42
104
Lee Green
SE13
HITHER GREEN
SE12
SE6
LEE
MANOR HOUSE GARDENS
MANOR PARK
SPORTS GROUNDS
FOOTBALL PITCHES
SUTCLIFFE PARK
OLD COLFEIANS SPORTS GROUND
MIDDLE PARK FIELD
QUEENSCROFT REC GRD
ELTHAM
ELTHAM PALACE
UNI OF GREENWICH ATHLETIC GRD
CIVIL SERVICE SPORTS GROUNDS
KING JOHN PLAYING FIELDS
CHILTONIAN INDIESTATE
ELTHAM ROAD
A20
A210
SIDCUP ROAD
WESTHORNE AVENUE
A205
S CIRCULAR ROAD
ST. MILDREDS ROAD
BURNT ASH HILL
BARING ROAD
A2212
NORTHBROOK PARK
GROVE PARK
HITHER GREEN CEMETERY
Crematorium
MOTTINGHAM
UNI OF WESTMINSTER SPORTS GROUND
MOTTINGHAM SPORTS GROUND
CHINBROOK ESTATE
CHINBROOK MEADOWS
LOWER MARVELS WOOD
MARVELS WOOD
GROVE PARK CEMETERY
ELMSTEAD WOOD
ELMSTEAD
DOWNHAM
DOWNHAM FIELDS
DOWNHAM PLAYING FIELDS
SHAFTESBURY PARK REC GRD
PLAISTOW
KING'S MEADOW PLAYING FIELDS
BR1
SUNDRIDGE PARK GOLF COURSE
SUNDRIDGE
Sundridge Park
ELMSTEAD WOODS
ROCKPIT WOOD
LOGSHILL WOOD
LEWISHAM BOROUGH SPORTS GROUND
MIDLAND BANK SPORTS GROUND
WARREN AVE PLAYING FIELDS
BR2
SHORTLANDS GOLF CO
BROMLEY HILL
LONDON ROAD
A21
COLLEGE RD
SUNDRIDGE PARK
PLAISTOW
Bus Sta
THE SLOANE HOSPITAL
BROMLEY PARK
Widmore
85
86
87
88
89
90
91
92
93
94
123
144
71
72
73
74

125
DA16
DA15
DA14
SE9
BR7
ELTHAM PARK SOUTH
ELTHAM WARREN GOLF COURSE
ELTHAM CEMETERY
Crematorium
ROCHESTER WAY RELIEF ROAD
BEXLEY ROAD
BLACKFEN ROAD
AVERY HILL
AVERY HILL PARK
University of Greenwich Avery Hill Campus
CAMBRIDGE MISSION SPORTS GROUND
CHARLTON ATHLETIC FC TRAINING GRD
FOOTSCRAY PLAYING FIELDS
MILLWALL FC TRAINING GRD
ROYAL BLACKHEATH GOLF COURSE
TARN BIRD SANCTUARY
FAIRY HILL REC GRD
NEW ELTHAM
BLACKFEN
HOLLY OAK WOOD PK
LAMORBEY
OLD FARM PARK
KING GEORGE'S REC GRD
SIDCUP
LONGLANDS
JACK NICKLAUS GOLF CENTRE
FLAMINGO PK SPORTS GRD
LONGLANDS REC GRD
BELMONT LANE OPEN SPACE
DOG RACING TRACK
CHISLEHURST CEMETERY
OLD ELTHAMIANS SPORTS GRD
UNIVERSITY COLLEGE LONDON SPORTS GRD
SIDCUP PLACE
QUEEN MARY'S HOSP
SCADBURY PARK NATURE RESERVE
PARK WOOD
CHISLEHURST WEST
WHYTES WOODLAND
CHISLEHURST
CAMDEN PARK
CHISLEHURST GOLF COURSE
CHISLEHURST COMMON
SIDCUP BYPASS
SIDCUP ROAD
MAIN ROAD
FOOTSCRAY ROAD
WHITEHORSE HILL
PERRY STREET
BROMLEY LANE
EM EN EP EQ ER ES ET
43 44 45
105 126 145
85 86 87 88 89 90 91 92 93 94

126
EU
EV
EW
EX
EY
EZ
FA
106
DANSON
PARK
THE LAKE
The Boathouse
DA16
DA6
BEXLEYHEATH
BEXLEYHEATH GOLF COURSE
BROADWAY
ROCHESTER WAY
BLACKFEN ROAD
A2
A210
A221
A222
A223
A224
A20
A211
B2214
B2210
BEXLEY
BLACKFEN
HOLLY OAK WOOD PK
PENHILL PARK
RIVERSIDE WALK
BEXLEY PARK WOOD
SIDCUP GOLF COURSE
DA15
Rose Bruford College
LAMORBEY PARK
HURST ROAD
DA5
KING GEORGE'S REC GRD
125
SIDCUP
WARING PARK
Sidcup Arts Cen
GOLDSMITH COLLEGE SPORTS GRD
NORTH CRAY
THE ALDERS
STABLE MEADOW
NORTH CRAY WOOD
DA14
FOOTS CRAY MEADOWS
Foots Cray Place
GATTONS WOOD
GATTONS PLANTATION
SIDCUP PLACE
QUEEN MARY'S HOSP
GARDEN SHAW
FOOTS CRAY
SCADBURY PARK
NATURE RESERVE
LITTLE WOOD
RUXLEY WOOD
Ruxley Corner
Crittall's Corner
BR5
SIDCUP BYPASS
146
RUXLEY PARK
85
86
87
88
89
90
91
92
93
94
47
48
49
71
72
73
74

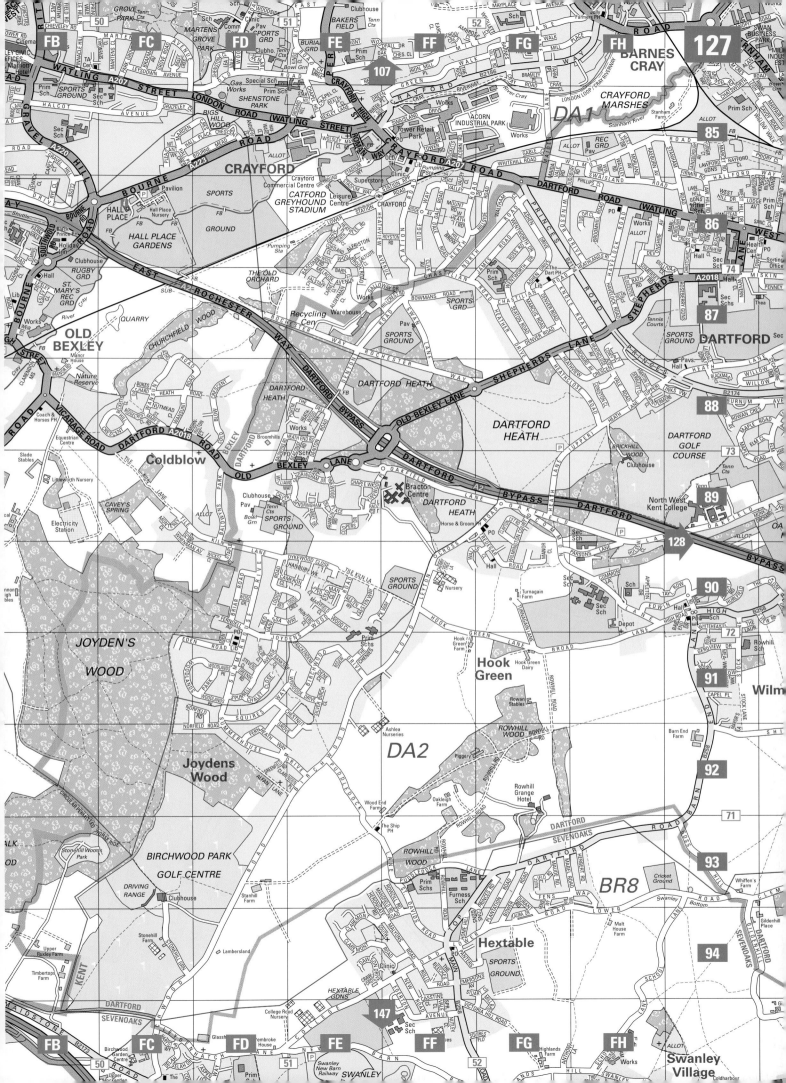
127
FB
FC
FD
FE
FF
FG
FH
50
51
52
107
147
128
85
86
87
88
89
90
91
92
93
94
74
73
72
71
BARNES CRAY
CRAYFORD MARSHES
DA1
DA2
BR8
CRAYFORD
OLD BEXLEY
DARTFORD
Coldblow
JOYDEN'S WOOD
Joydens Wood
Hook Green
Hextable
Swanley Village
SWANLEY
DARTFORD HEATH
HALL PLACE GARDENS
HALL PLACE
SPORTS GROUND
SHENSTONE PARK
BAKERS FIELD
MARTENS GROVE PARK
GROVE PARK
ACORN INDUSTRIAL PARK
Tower Retail Park
CATFORD GREYHOUND STADIUM
Crayford Commercial Centre
Leisure Centre
RUGBY GRD
ST. MARY'S REC GRD
THE OLD ORCHARD
QUARRY
CHURCHFIELD WOOD
Recycling Cen
Bracton Centre
DARTFORD GOLF COURSE
BRICKHILL WOOD
North West Kent College
Turnagain Farm
Hook Green Farm
Hook Green Dairy
Rowan Stables
ROWHILL WOOD
Rowhill Grange Hotel
Oakleigh Farm
Wood End Farm
The Ship PH
Ashlea Nurseries
BIRCHWOOD PARK GOLF CENTRE
DRIVING RANGE
Stonehill Woods Park
Stonehill Farm
Upper Ruxley Farm
Timbertops Farm
Lambersland
Stanhill Farm
HEXTABLE GDNS
College Road Nursery
Pembroke House
Swanley New Barn Railway
Birchwood Garden Centre
Highlands Farm
Malt House Farm
Barn End Farm
Whiffen's Farm
Gildenhill Place
Cricket Ground
Furness Sch
ROWHILL WOOD
Littleworth Nursery
Electricity Station
CAVEY'S SPRING
Slade Stables
Equestrian Centre
Coach & Horses PH
Nature Reserve
Manor House
Horse & Groom PH
Stanham Farm
Jolly Farmers PH
SWAN BUSINESS PARK
WATLING STREET
A207
A220
A223
A2
A2018
B2186
B2174
B258
B2173
ROCHESTER WAY
DARTFORD BYPASS
OLD BEXLEY LANE
SHEPHERDS LANE
DARTFORD ROAD
CRAYFORD ROAD
LONDON ROAD
BOURNE ROAD
GRAVEL HILL
PRINCES ROAD
HEATH LANE
HOOK GREEN LANE
PUDDLEDOCK LANE
SWANLEY LANE
SCHOOL LANE
KENT
DARTFORD
SEVENOAKS

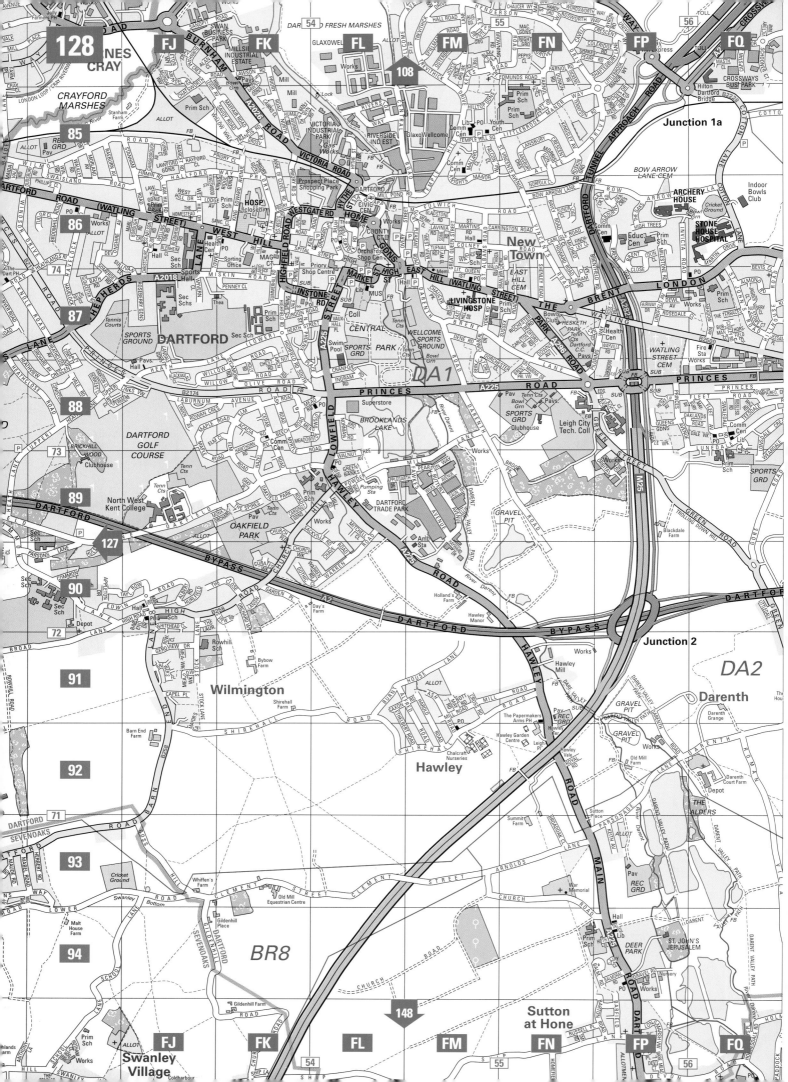

128
FJ
FK
FL
FM
FN
FP
FQ
54
55
56
108
CRAYFORD MARSHES
DARTFORD FRESH MARSHES
SWAN BUSINESS PARK
MILLSIDE INDUSTRIAL ESTATE
GLAXOWELLCOME
VICTORIA INDUSTRIAL PARK
RIVERSIDE IND EST
GlaxoWellcome
BURNHAM ROAD
VICTORIA ROAD
HENDERSON DRIVE
WORDSWORTH WAY
TEMPLE HILL
LITTLEBROOK MANOR WAY
EDMUNDS ROAD
BOW ARROW LANE
BOW ARROW LANE CEM
Junction 1a
CROSSWAYS BUS. PARK
Hilton Dartford Bridge
ARCHERY HOUSE
STONE HOUSE HOSPITAL
Indoor Bowls Club
Cricket Ground
85
86
87
88
89
90
91
92
93
94
74
73
72
71
Prospect Place Shopping Park
DARTFORD
CIVIC CEN
COUNTY CT
Orchards Shop Cen
Priory Shop Centre
WEST HILL
WATLING STREET
EAST HILL
HIGH ST
HYTHE ST
HOME GDNS
WESTGATE RD
HIGHFIELD ROAD
SPITAL STREET
MARKET ST
INSTONE RD
HOSP (closed)
New Town
EAST HILL CEM
LIVINGSTONE HOSP
LONDON ROAD
THE BRENT
SHEPHERDS LANE
MISKIN ROAD
DARTFORD
SPORTS GROUND
CENTRAL PARK
WELLCOME SPORTS GROUND
DA1
PRINCES ROAD
A225
A2018
B2174
A226
A296
A282
M25
A2
WATLING STREET CEM
PRINCES
BROOKLANDS LAKE
Superstore
LOWFIELD STREET
HAWLEY ROAD
DARTFORD GOLF COURSE
North West Kent College
OAKFIELD PARK
DARTFORD TRADE PARK
Leigh City Tech. Coll
SPORTS GRD
GRAVEL PIT
GREEN STREET GREEN ROAD
TROLLING DOWN HILL
Blackdale Farm
127
DARTFORD BYPASS
Junction 2
DA2
Holland's Farm
Hawley Manor
Day's Farm
Wilmington
Bybow Farm
Shirehall Farm
SHIREHALL ROAD
Barn End Farm
BARN END LANE
Hawley
Hawley Mill
The Papermakers Arms PH
Hawley Garden Centre
Chalcraft Nurseries
Darenth
Darenth Grange
DARENTH ROAD
Old Mill Farm
Darenth Court Farm
THE ALDERS
DARENT VALLEY PATH
Sutton Place
Summit Farm
PARSONAGE LANE
CLEMENT STREET
ARNOLDS LANE
CHURCH ROAD
MAIN ROAD
War Memorial
Whiffen's Farm
Old Mill Equestrian Centre
Gildenhill Place
Gildenhill Farm
BR8
DEER PARK
ST. JOHN'S JERUSALEM
Sutton at Hone
DARTFORD ROAD
148
Malt House Farm
Swanley Village
Cricket Ground
DARTFORD
SEVENOAKS

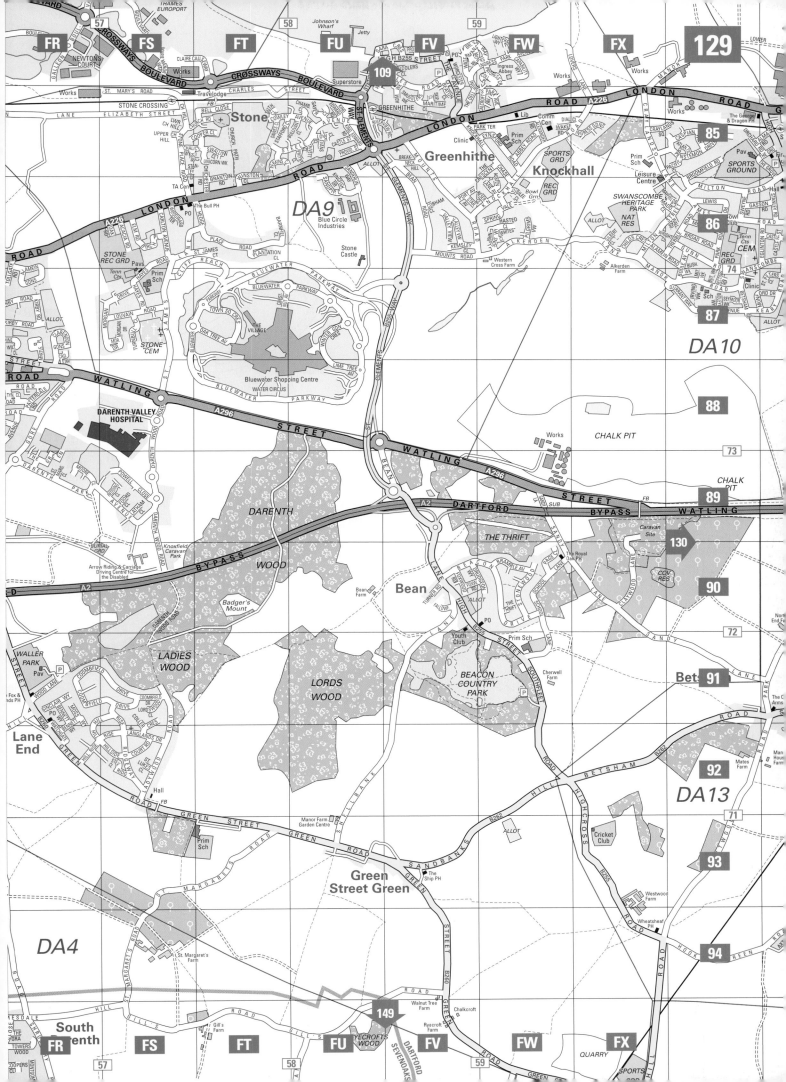
FR
FS
FT
FU
FV
FW
FX
57
58
59
Thames Europort
Johnson's Wharf
Jetty
Newtons Court
Works
Superstore
109
Travelodge
Crossways Boulevard
Stone Crossing
Stone
Greenhithe
Knockhall
London Road
A226
St. Clements Way
Lib
Comm Cen
Clinic
Prim Sch
Sports Grd
Rec Grd
Bowl Grn
TA Cen
PO
The Bull PH
DA9
Blue Circle Industries
Stone Castle
Stone Rec Grd
Pavs.
Tenn Cts
Allot
Western Cross Farm
Alkerden Farm
Swanscombe Heritage Park
Nat Res
Leisure Centre
Sports Ground
Pav
The George & Dragon PH
Tenn Cts
Cem
Rec Grd
Clinic
Sch
85
86
87
88
89
90
91
92
93
94
74
73
72
71
DA10
Bluewater Parkway
The Village
Bluewater Shopping Centre
Water Circus
Stone Cem
Watling Street
A296
Darenth Valley Hospital
St. Clements Way
B255
Chalk Pit
Works
A2
Dartford Bypass
Darenth Wood
The Thrift
Caravan Site
130
The Royal Oak PH
Cov Res
Knoxfield Caravan Park
Burial Grd
Arrow Riding & Carriage Driving Centre for the Disabled
Bean Farm
Bean
Badger's Mount
Ladies Wood
Lords Wood
Youth Club
Beacon Country Park
Cherwell Farm
Waller Park
Pav
Lane End
B260
Hall
FB
Prim Sch
Manor Farm Garden Centre
Betsham Road
B262
DA13
Allot
Cricket Club
Green Street Green
The Ship PH
Sandbanks
Westwood Farm
Wheatsheaf PH
Highcross Road
Hook Green Road
DA4
St. Margaret's Farm
St. Margaret's Road
Walnut Tree Farm
Chalkcroft
Ryecroft Farm
Gill's Farm
Gill's Road
149
Ryecrofts Wood
Dartford
Sevenoaks
South Darenth
Quarry

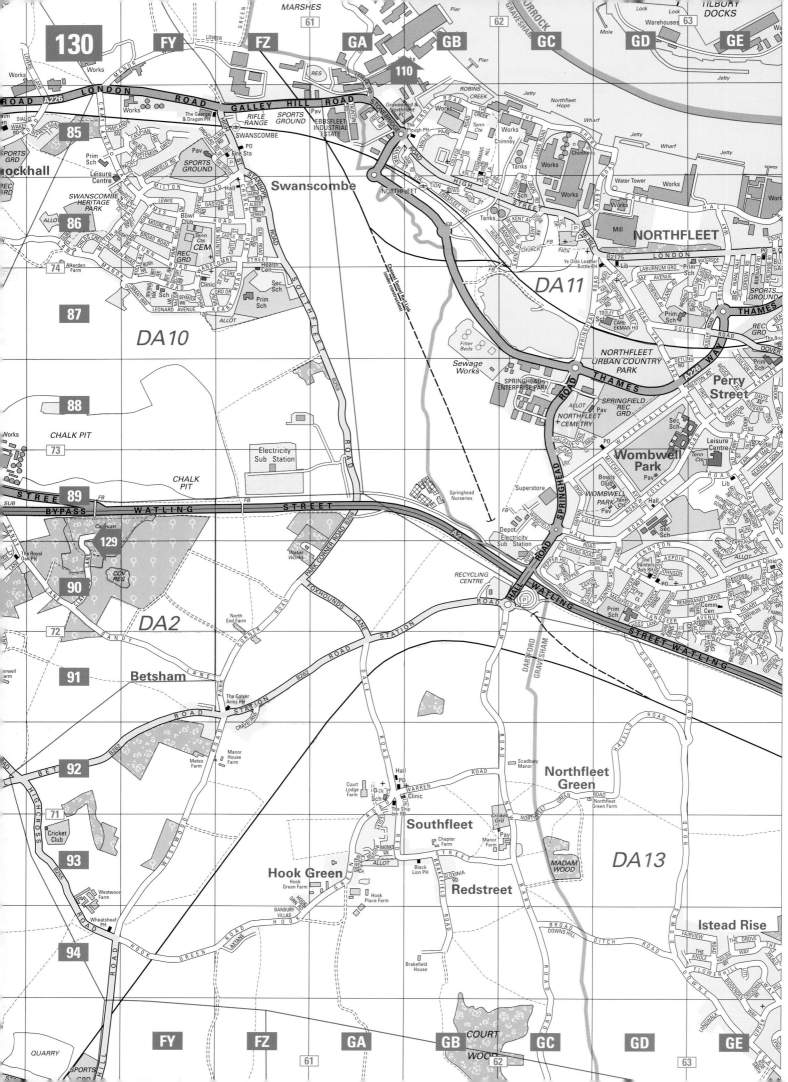
FY
FZ
GA
GB
GC
GD
GE
61
62
63
110
MARSHES
TILBURY DOCKS
Warehouses
Lock
Mole
Pier
Jetty
Wharf
LONDON ROAD
A226
GALLEY HILL ROAD
RIFLE RANGE
SPORTS GROUND
EBBSFLEET INDUSTRIAL ESTATE
SWANSCOMBE
Swanscombe
ROBINS CREEK
Northfleet Hope
Gravesend & Northfleet FC
The Plough PH
The George & Dragon PH
Works
STONEBRIDGE
HIGH STREET
Water Tower
Mill
NORTHFLEET
Chimney
Chimneys
Tanks
85
86
87
88
89
90
91
92
93
94
74
73
72
71
SWANSCOMBE HERITAGE PARK
Leisure Centre
Prim Sch
Pav
Fire Sta
PO
Hall
CEM
REC GRD
Bowl Club
Tenn Cts
Health Cen
Sec Sch
Clinic
ALLOT
Alkerden Farm
STANHOPE ROAD
SOUTHFLEET ROAD
B259
DA10
DA11
DA2
DA13
B2175
Ye Olde Leather Bottle PH
Lib
NORTHFLEET URBAN COUNTRY PARK
SPRINGHEAD ROAD
THAMES WAY
Filter Beds
Sewage Works
SPRINGHEAD ENTERPRISE PARK
NORTHFLEET CEMETRY
SPRINGFIELD REC GRD
Perry Street
Wombwell Park
Leisure Centre
Superstore
Springhead Nurseries
Depot
Electricity Sub Station
RECYCLING CENTRE
Channel Tunnel Rail Link (under construction)
Electricity Sub Station
CHALK PIT
WATLING STREET
BYPASS
A2
STATION ROAD
PARK CORNER ROAD
FOXHOUNDS LANE
SANDY LANE
North End Farm
Water Works
129
COV RES
The Royal Oak PH
Caravan
Betsham
The Colyer Arms PH
B262
Mates Farm
Manor House Farm
HIGHCROSS
B255
Cricket Club
Westwood Farm
Wheatsheaf PH
WESTWOOD
HOOK GREEN ROAD
Hook Green
Hook Green Farm
Hook Place Farm
BANBURY VILLAS
Southfleet
The Ship Inn PH
Court Lodge Farm
Chapter Farm
Manor Farm
Black Lion PH
Redstreet
Brakefield House
NEW BARN ROAD
Scadbury Manor
Northfleet Green
Northfleet Green Farm
DARTFORD
GRAVESHAM
MADAM WOOD
COURT WOOD
Istead Rise
BROAD DITCH ROAD
DOWNS ROAD
QUARRY
SPORTS GRD

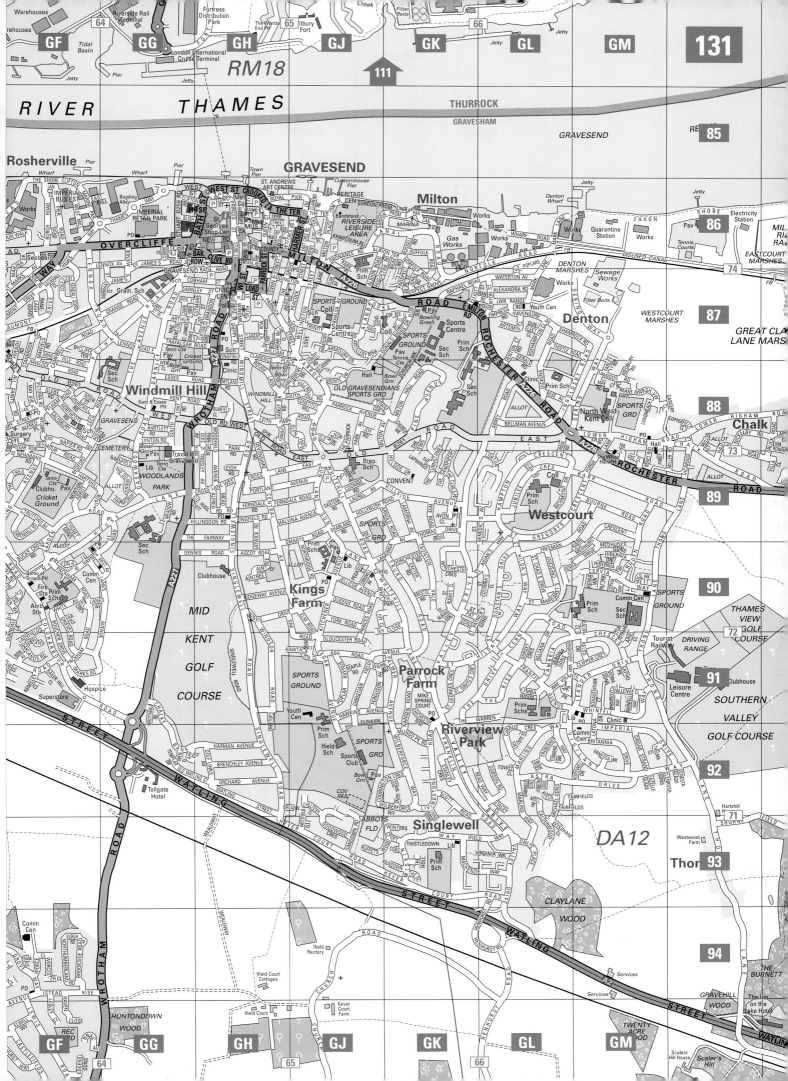

131
GF
GG
GH
GJ
GK
GL
GM
64
65
66
111
RM18
RIVER THAMES
THURROCK
GRAVESHAM
GRAVESEND
85
86
87
88
89
90
91
92
93
94
74
73
72
71
Warehouses
Riverside Rail Terminal
Fortress Distribution Park
Tidal Basin
London International Cruise Terminal
The Worlds End PH
Tilbury Fort
Filter Beds
Jetty
Pier
Rosherville
Wharf
Town Pier
IMPERIAL BUS EST
IMPERIAL RETAIL PARK
Bowling Alley
Works
St. Georges Shop Cen
HOSP
ST. ANDREWS ART CENTRE
Customhouse Pier
HERITAGE CEN
RIVERSIDE LEISURE AREA
Milton
Gas Works
Denton Wharf
Quarantine Station
Electricity Station
Tennis Courts
EASTCOURT MARSHES
DENTON MARSHES
Sewage Works
Filter Beds
Youth Cen
Denton
WESTCOURT MARSHES
GREAT CLA LANE MARS
OVERCLIFFE
MILTON ROAD
A226
ROCHESTER ROAD
CIVIC CEN
Gram. Sch
SPORTS GROUND
Coll
Sports Centre
Bowling Green
Sec Sch
Prim Sch
Windmill Hill
OLD GRAVESENDIANS SPORTS GRD
Clinic
North West Kent Coll
SPORTS GRD
Chalk
HIGHAM ROAD
ALLOT
Kent & Essex PH
GRAVESEND CEMETERY
Travel Inn Gravesend
WOODLANDS PARK
Cricket Ground
Clubho.
Prep. Sch
CONVENT
Westcourt
Prim Sch
SPORTS GRD
Kings Farm
Clubhouse
MID KENT GOLF COURSE
A227
WROTHAM ROAD
Prim Schs
Lib
Comm Cen
SPORTS GROUND
THAMES VIEW GOLF COURSE
Tourist Railway
DRIVING RANGE
Leisure Centre
Clubhouse
SOUTHERN VALLEY GOLF COURSE
Parrock Farm
MIKE SPRING COURT
Riverview Park
Youth Cen
Ifield Sch
Sports Club
Hospice
Superstore
Battle of Britain PH
Fire Sta
Amb Sta
Tollgate Hotel
WATLING STREET
ABBOTS FLD
Singlewell
DA12
Hartshill
Westwood Farm
Thor
CLAYLANE WOOD
Ifield Rectory
Ifield Court Cottages
Ifield Court
Kever Court Farm
Services
A2
GRAVEHILL WOOD
THE BURNETT
The Inn on the Lake Hotel
TWENTY ACRE WOOD
HUNTONDOWN WOOD
Comm Cen
Scalers Hill House
Scaler's Hill
WEALDWAY
HENHURST RD
CHURCH ROAD

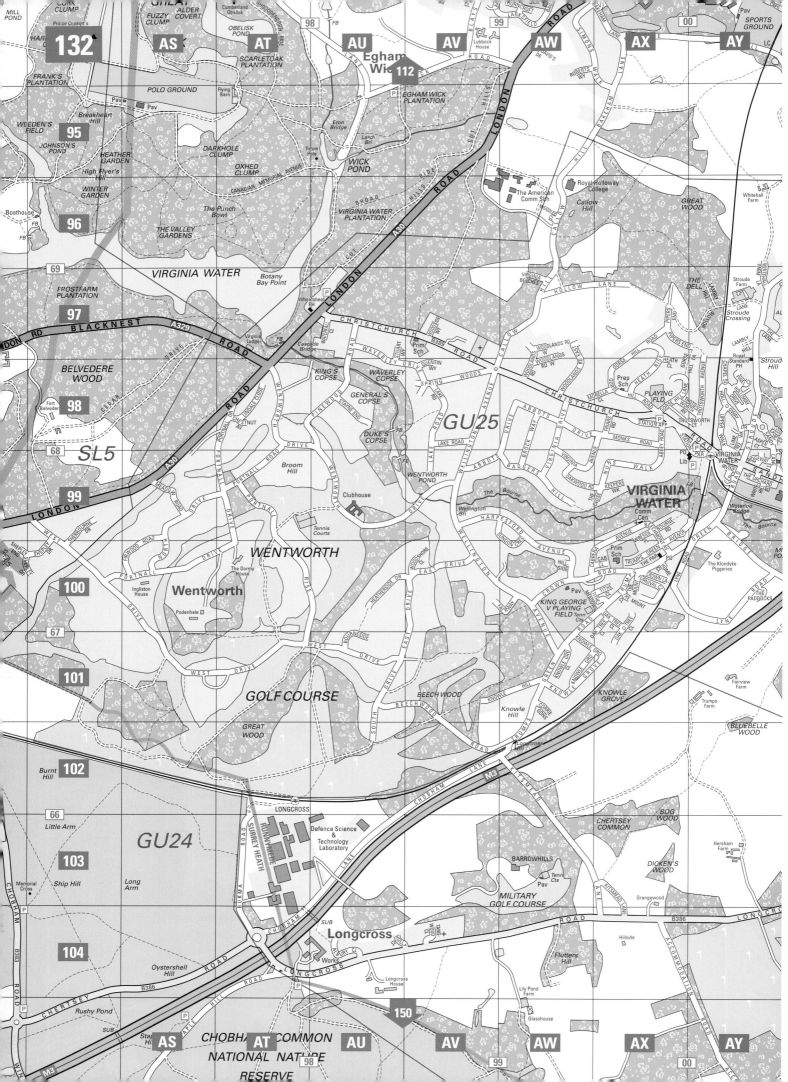
AS
AT
AU
AV
AW
AX
AY
112
95
96
97
98
99
100
101
102
103
104
150
VIRGINIA WATER
WENTWORTH
Wentworth
GOLF COURSE
GU25
GU24
SL5
VIRGINIA WATER
Longcross
LONGCROSS
Egham Wick
CHOBHAM COMMON NATIONAL NATURE RESERVE
Defence Science & Technology Laboratory
MILITARY GOLF COURSE
CHERTSEY COMMON
Royal Holloway College
The American Comm Sch
BELVEDERE WOOD
POLO GROUND
THE VALLEY GARDENS
VIRGINIA WATER PLANTATION
EGHAM WICK PLANTATION
SCARLETOAK PLANTATION
FRANK'S PLANTATION
FROSTFARM PLANTATION
GREAT WOOD
KNOWLE GROVE
BLUEBELLE WOOD
BOG WOOD
DICKEN'S WOOD
BARROWHILLS
KING GEORGE V PLAYING FIELD
BLACKNEST ROAD
LONDON ROAD
CHRISTCHURCH ROAD
WELLINGTON AVENUE
CHOBHAM LANE
CHERTSEY ROAD
ACCOMMODATION ROAD
M3
A30
A329
B389
B386
B383

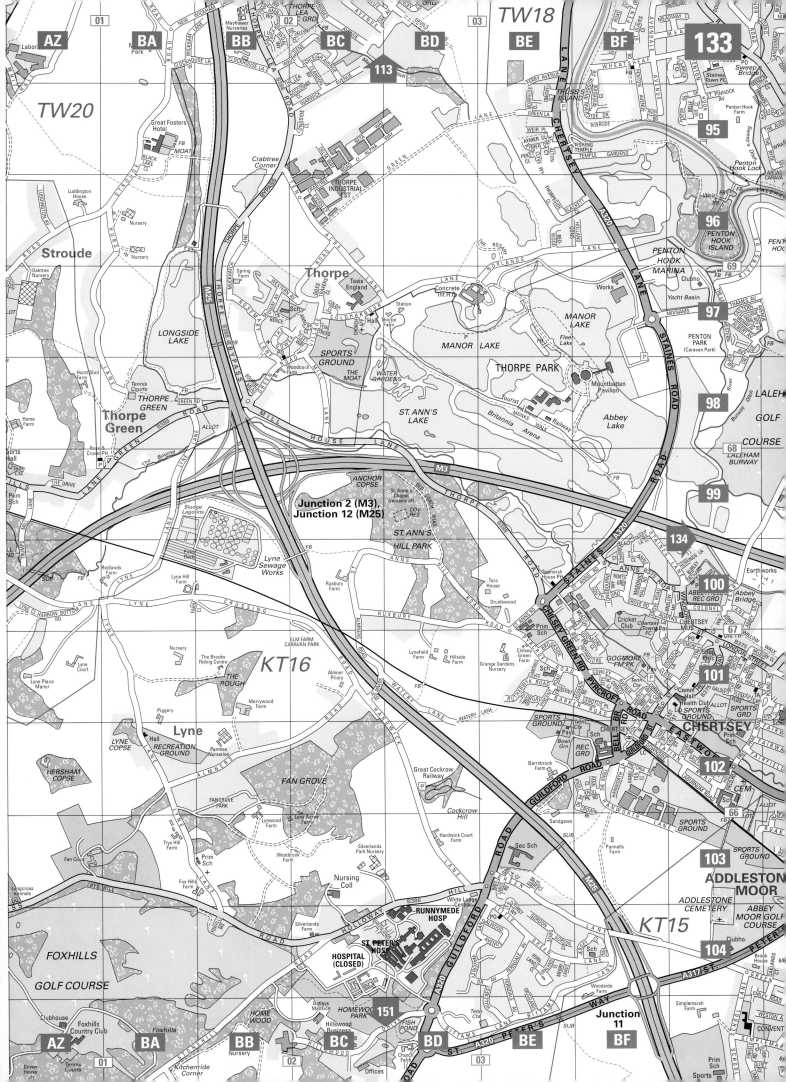

133
113
134
151
AZ
BA
BB
BC
BD
BE
BF
01
02
03
TW20
TW18
KT16
KT15
Stroude
Thorpe
Thorpe Green
Lyne
CHERTSEY
ADDLESTONE MOOR
Great Fosters Hotel
MOAT
LONGSIDE LAKE
THORPE GREEN
Luddington House
Nursery
Oaktree Nursery
Hurst Stud Farm
Tennis Courts
Home Farm
Rose & Crown PH
Crabtree Corner
THORPE INDUSTRIAL EST
THORPE BYPASS
M25
M3
A320
B388
B389
B386
B375
Spring Farm
Tasis England
Sch
Hall
Thorpe Farm
Station
SPORTS GROUND
THE MOAT
WATER GARDENS
Woodcock Farm
Concrete Int H.Q.
MANOR LAKE
Fleet Lake
THORPE PARK
Mountbatten Pavilion
Tourist
Railway
Britannia Arena
ST. ANN'S LAKE
Abbey Lake
Works
PENTON HOOK MARINA
Yacht Basin
PENTON HOOK ISLAND
Penton Hook Lock
Penton Hook Farm
Staines Town FC
Sweep's Bridge
TRUSS'S ISLAND
FISHING TEMPLE
PENTON PARK (Caravan Park)
LALEHAM GOLF COURSE
LALEHAM BURWAY
Burway Ditch
ANCHOR COPSE
Junction 2 (M3), Junction 12 (M25)
St. Anne's Chapel (remains of)
COV RES
ST. ANN'S HILL PARK
Sludge Lagoons
Filter Beds
Lyne Sewage Works
Redlands Farm
Lyne Hill Farm
Ruxbury Farm
Tara House
Druidswood
Twynersh House PH
Prim Sch
Cricket Club
Chertsey Town FC
CHERTSEY MUS
Abbey Bridge
Earthworks
ABBEYFIELDS REC GRD
GOGMORE FM PK
Chilsey Green Farm
Lynefield Farm
Hillside Farm
Grange Gardens Nursery
ELM FARM CARAVAN PARK
Nursery
The Brooks Riding Centre
Lyne Court
Lyne Place Manor
THE ROUGH
Almner Priory
Merrywood Farm
Piggery
Pantiles Nurseries
RECREATION GROUND
LYNE COPSE
HERSHAM COPSE
FAN GROVE
FANGROVE PARK
Lynwood Farm
Lyne Acres Farm
Great Cockrow Railway
Cockcrow Hill
Hardwick Court Farm
Trys Hill Farm
Fan Court
Westbrook Farm
Silverlands Park Nursery
Nursing Coll
Fox Hills Farm
Longcross Kennels
RUNNYMEDE HOSP
White Lodge Centre
ST. PETER'S HOSP
HOSPITAL (CLOSED)
Silverlands Farm
FOXHILLS GOLF COURSE
Clubhouse
Foxhills Country Club
Foxhills
Tennis Courts
Dower House
HOME WOOD
Botleys Mansion
HOMEWOOD PARK
Hillswood Business
FISH POND
Church Farm
Offices
Kitchenride Corner
Nursery
Sec Sch
Sandgates
Pannells Farm
Barrsbrook Farm
SPORTS GROUND
REC GRD
Bowl Grn
Health Club
Comm Hall
Lib
SPORTS GRD
CEM
ADDLESTONE CEMETERY
ABBEY MOOR GOLF COURSE
Woodside Farm
Simplemarsh Farm
Junction 11
Brook House
CONVENT
Sports
ST. PETER'S WAY
A317
GUILDFORD ROAD
CHERTSEY LANE
STAINES ROAD
THORPE ROAD
MILL HOUSE LANE
HOLLOWAY HILL
STONEHILL ROAD
LYNE LANE
LYNE CROSSING
RUXBURY ROAD
ALMNERS ROAD
HARDWICK LANE
WATERY LANE
GREEN ROAD
COLDHARBOUR LANE
NORLANDS LANE
MIXNAMS LANE
LONDON STREET
EASTWORTH ROAD
PYRCROFT ROAD
CHILSEY GREEN RD
BITTAMS LANE
68
69
67
66
95
96
97
98
99
100
101
102
103
104

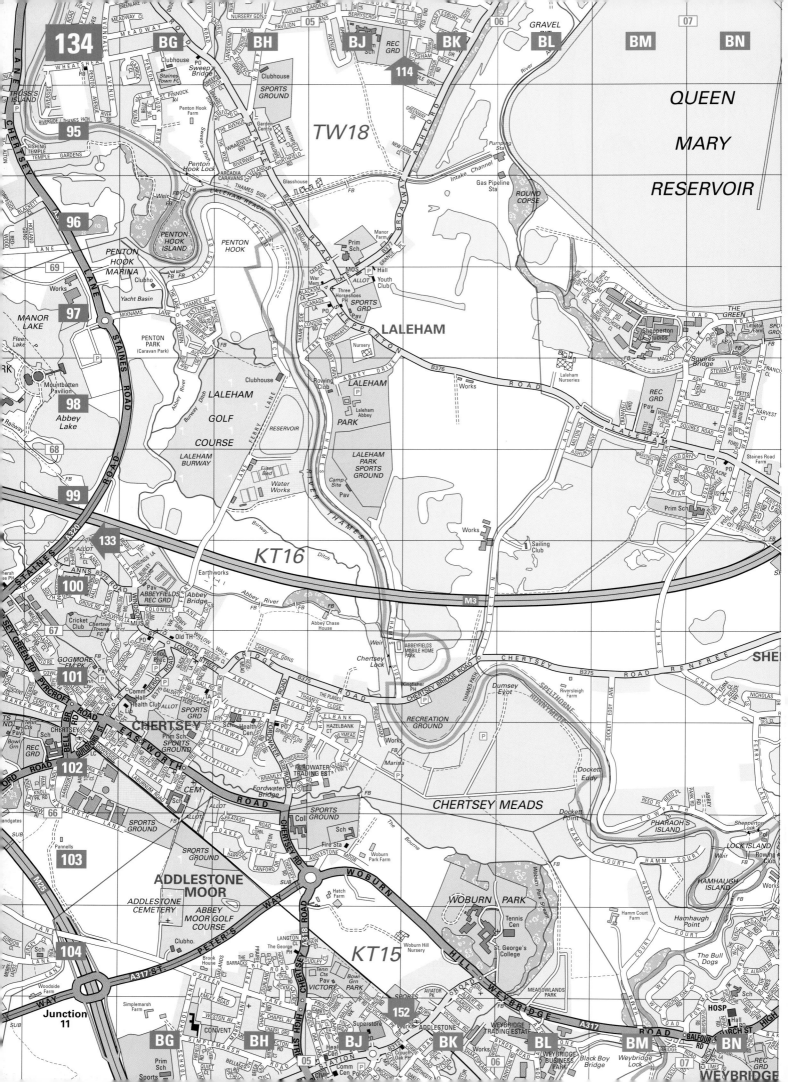

134
BG
BH
BJ
BK
BL
BM
BN
05
06
07
114
QUEEN MARY RESERVOIR
TW18
KT16
KT15
LALEHAM
LALEHAM PARK
LALEHAM GOLF COURSE
LALEHAM BURWAY
LALEHAM PARK SPORTS GROUND
PENTON HOOK
PENTON HOOK ISLAND
PENTON HOOK MARINA
Penton Hook Lock
PENTON PARK (Caravan Park)
Manor Lake
Abbey Lake
Mountbatten Pavilion
Shepperton Studios
Squires Bridge
Staines Town FC
Sweep's Bridge
Round Copse
Gas Pipeline Sta
Intake Channel
Laleham Nurseries
Water Works
Reservoir
Sailing Club
Abbey River
River Thames
Thames Side
Burway Ditch
Earthworks
M3
133
CHERTSEY
Chertsey Lock
Chertsey Bridge Road
Abbeyfields Mobile Home Park
Abbey Chase House
Dumsey Eyot
Recreation Ground
CHERTSEY MEADS
Dockett Eddy
Dockett Point
Spelthorne
Runnymede
Pharaoh's Island
Lock Island
Hamhaugh Island
Hamhaugh Point
Shepperton Lock
The Bourne
Woburn Park Farm
WOBURN PARK
St. George's College
Woburn Hill Nursery
Fordwater Trading Est
Fordwater Bridge
ADDLESTONE MOOR
ADDLESTONE CEMETERY
ABBEY MOOR GOLF COURSE
Addlestone
Weybridge Trading Estate
Weybridge Business Park
Black Boy Bridge
Weybridge Lock
WEYBRIDGE
Junction 11
M25
152
Chertsey Lane
Staines Road
Laleham Road
Shepperton Road
Chertsey Road
Woburn Hill
Weybridge Road
St. Peter's Way
Eastworth Road
London Street
Guildford Street
Pyrcroft Road
66
67
68
69
95
96
97
98
99
100
101
102
103
104

 135
BP
BQ
BR
BS
BT
BU
BV
115
153
136
Junction 1
ASHFORD COMMON
WATER TREATMENT
WORKS
TRADING
ESTATE
DOLPHIN
EST
Superstore
Sunbury
Cross Cen
SUNBURY
PARK
Grandstand
SPORTS
GROUND
Sec Sch
Leisure
Cen
Prim Sch
LONDON
IRISH
RUGBY
GROUND
GAFLAC
SPORTS
GROUND
CEDARS
REC
GRD
TW16
SUNBURY
SUNBURY PARK
RIVERSIDE
ARTS
CENTRE
Sunbury
Locks
WATER
TREATMENT
WORKS
LITTLETON
The Hidden Garden
(Garden Centre)
Civil
Amenity
Site
Caravan
Site
The
Bugle PH
UPPER
HALLIFORD
HAZELWOOD
GOLF COURSE
DRIVING
RANGE
SUNBURY
CEM
Police
Coll
SUNBURY LOCK
AIT
Gas
Works
SUNBURY
GOLF
COURSE
TW17
Grange
Farm
Vicarage
Farm
The Weir
PH
GRAVEL
PIT
SPORTS
GRD
Squires
Garden
Centre
Longmere
Farm
WHEATLEY'S
AIT
Gaston
Bridge
SHEPPERTON
BUSINESS PARK
LONGWOOD
BUSINESS PARK
Leisure Cen
KT12
Riverncok
Farm
Bramble
Hill Farm
APPLE
COURT
GREEN
Oil
Terminal
Watersplash
Farm
Glasshouses
Riding
School
Thamesfield
Farm
ALLOT
SHEPPERTON
Shepperton
Moat House
Sailing
Club
Shepperton
Marina
REC
GRD
PPERTON
BISHOP
DUPPA'S
REC GRD
RIVER ASH
EST
The
Anglers
PH
SPORTS
GRD
The Hut
LAS
PALMAS
ESTATE
Gibbs
Marina
SPORTS
GROUND
Clubhouse
Bridge
Marina
CEM
THAMES
MEADOW
COWAY
SALE
DESBOROUGH
ISLAND
Water
Works
Pumping
Sta
Superstores
MAG
CT
Coll
ELM
GROVE
REC
GRD
Swim
Pool
GEORGE
FROUDE PK
D'OYLY
CARTE ISLAND
THAMES PATH
ASHLEY
PARK
SPORTS
GRD
Cricket
Club
Health Cen
HOSP
KT13
WALTON-ON
THAMES
WALTON &
HERSHAM FC
RYDENS
Broadwater
Farm
Greenlands
Farm
BROAD WATER
ST.
MAUR'S
CONV
PLAYING
FIELDS
Oatlands
Park Hotel
ASHLEY
PARK
Offices
Amb
Sta
Fire
Sta
Sec
Sch
Prim Sch
WALTON-ON-
THAMES
OATLANDS
PARK
QUEENS
A308
A3050
A244
A317
B376
B375
B365
M3
08
09
10

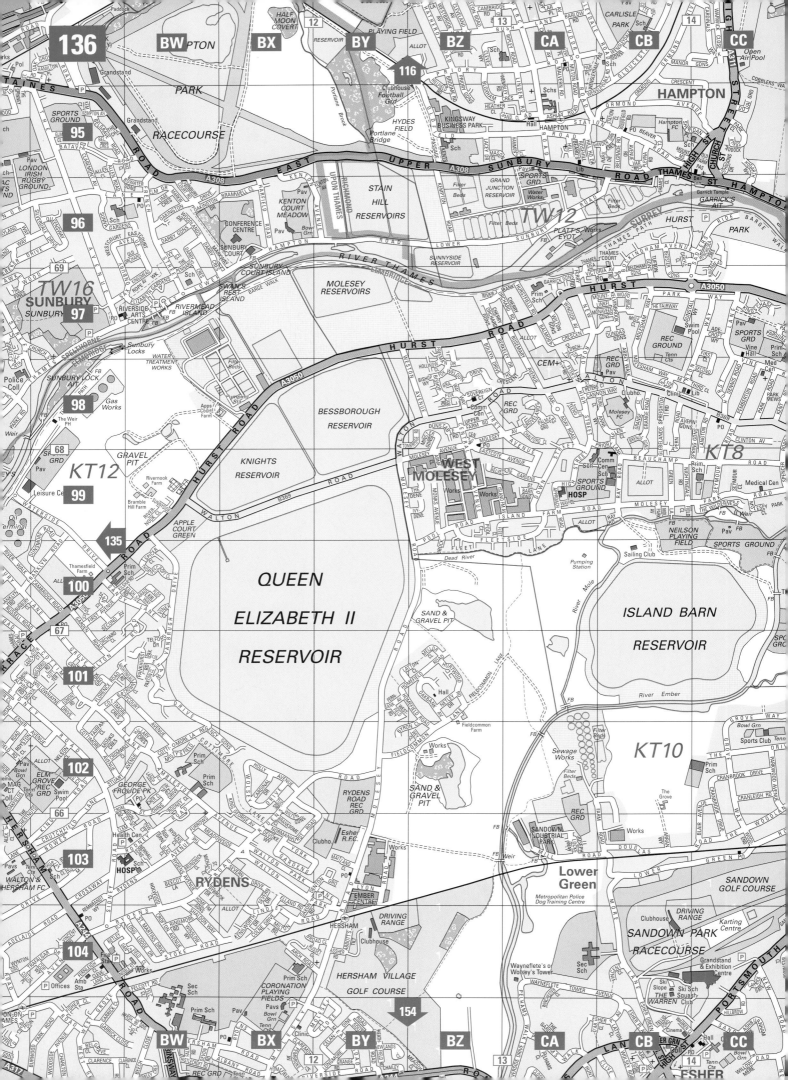
BW
BX
BY
BZ
CA
CB
CC
116
HAMPTON
KEMPTON PARK
RACECOURSE
HALF MOON COVERT
PLAYING FIELD
HYDES FIELD
Portlane Bridge
KINGSWAY BUSINESS PARK
UPPER SUNBURY ROAD
GRAND JUNCTION RESERVOIR
STAIN HILL RESERVOIRS
KENTON COURT MEADOW
CONFERENCE CENTRE
SUNBURY COURT
TW12
PLATT'S EYOT
GARRICK'S AIT
HURST PARK
RIVER THAMES
SUNNYSIDE RESERVOIR
MOLESEY RESERVOIRS
SUNBURY COURT ISLAND
SWAN'S REST ISLAND
RIVERMEAD ISLAND
TW16
SUNBURY
RIVERSIDE ARTS CENTRE
LONDON IRISH RUGBY GROUND
Sunbury Locks
SUNBURY LOCK AIT
WATER TREATMENT WORKS
Gas Works
HURST ROAD
A3050
BESSBOROUGH RESERVOIR
KNIGHTS RESERVOIR
WALTON ROAD
GRAVEL PIT
KT12
APPLE COURT GREEN
WEST MOLESEY
SPORTS GROUND
HOSP
KT8
REC GROUND
Molesey FC
NEILSON PLAYING FIELD
SPORTS GROUND
Sailing Club
Dead River
QUEEN ELIZABETH II RESERVOIR
SAND & GRAVEL PIT
ISLAND BARN RESERVOIR
River Mole
River Ember
Fieldcommon Farm
Sewage Works
KT10
SAND & GRAVEL PIT
RYDENS ROAD REC GRD
Esher R.F.C.
SANDOWN INDUSTRIAL PARK
Lower Green
Metropolitan Police Dog Training Centre
SANDOWN GOLF COURSE
DRIVING RANGE
SANDOWN PARK RACECOURSE
Karting Centre
Grandstand & Exhibition Centre
RYDENS
GEORGE FROUDE PK
ELM GROVE REC GRD
WALTON & HERSHAM FC
HERSHAM
EMBER CENTRE
DRIVING RANGE
HERSHAM VILLAGE GOLF COURSE
CORONATION PLAYING FIELDS
Wayneflete's or Wolsey's Tower
THE WARREN
ESHER
154
HERSHAM ROAD
PORTSMOUTH ROAD
95
96
97
98
99
100
101
102
103
104
69
68
67
66
135
12
13
14

137
CD
CE
CF
CG
CH
CJ
CK
117
155
138
95
96
97
98
99
100
101
102
103
104
TW11
BUSHY
PARK
BROOM CLUMPS
WATERHOUSE WOODLAND GARDEN
WATERHOUSE POND
FISHER'S POND
Red Brick Bridge
HERON POND
Boating Pool
Diana Fountain
WARREN PLANTATION
HALF MOON PLANTATION
LEG OF MUTTON POND
OVAL PLANTATION
Hawthorn Lodge
Timothy Bennet Memorial
HAMPTON WICK
Cricket Club
THE KINGSFIELD
Superstore
Offices
COBBLERS WALK
CHESTNUT AVENUE
Open During Daylight Hours Only
SANDY LANE
PARK ROAD
UPPER TEDDINGTON RD
HIGH ST
KINGSTON BR
HORSE FAIR
WOOD ST
CROMWELL RD
KINGSTON UPON THAMES
KT1
Bentalls Cen
Eden Walk Shop Cen
Market Ho
Coronation Stone
GUILDHALL
KINGS HALL RD
Kingston Coll
Kingston Uni
SURREY COUNTY HALL
PENRHYN ROAD
SURBITON RD
Kingston University
THE ROYAL PADDOCKS
HAMPTON WICK POND
The Old Ice House
Hampton Court House
Hampton Court Gate
Lion Gate Hotel
HAMPTON COURT ROAD
A308
TAGG'S ISLAND
ASH ISLAND
Cricket Ground
Royal Mews
Molesey Lock
Mitre Hotel
Hampton Court Bri
HAMPTON COURT PALACE
MAZE
HAMPTON COURT GDNS
NORTH CANAL
SOUTH CANAL
THE BROAD WK
PRIVY GDN
Glasshouse
Stud House
The Long Water
HAMPTON COURT PARK
(HOME PARK)
HAMPTON COURT PALACE GOLF COURSE
THE RICK POND
Clubhouse
RAVENS AIT
Watersports Cen
Yacht Club
Sailing Club
Water Works
Filter Beds
The Wilderness
Parkfield
River Thames
THAMES PATH / LONDON LOOP
BARGE WALK
PORTSMOUTH ROAD
A307
EAST MOLESEY
HAMPTON COURT CIGARETTE ISLAND PARK
River Mole
River Ember
DITTON FIELD
SPORTS GRD
SPORTS GROUND
HAMPTON COURT WAY
A309
THAMES DITTON ISLAND
THAMES DITTON
BOYLE FM ISLAND
Thames Marina
RICHMOND UPON THAMES
City Wharf House
THAMES DITTON
KT7
WESTON GREEN
EMBER COURT TRADING ESTATE
Met. Police Training Coll
Met. Police Sports Club
THAMES DITTON & ESHER GOLF COURSE
DITTON COMMON
ESHER
Marquis of Granby PH
Scilly Isles
LITTLEWORTH COMMON
KINGSTON BYPASS
A309
HINCHLEY WOOD
Telegraph Hill
The Waffrons
Surbiton
D.S.S. OFFICES
LONG DITTON REC GRD
VICTORIA REC GRD
KT6
LONG DITTON
Cockcrow Hill
Management Training Cen
Woodstock Garden Centre
Hill Park Nursery
Ditton Nurseries
Manor House
CEM
SURREY
KT9
KING EDWARD REC GRD
HOOK
SURBITON
SURBITON GENERAL HOSP
BRIGHTON ROAD
A243
EWELL ROAD
UPPER BRIGHTON RD
HOOK ROAD
RUGBY GRD

138
CL
CM
CN
CP
CQ
CR
CS
19
20
21
118
COOMBE
COOMBE WOOD GOLF COURSE
KT2
KINGSTON HOSPITAL
NEW VICTORIA HOSPITAL
COOMBE LANE WEST
A238
NORBITON
KINGSTON UPON THAMES
KINGSTON CEMETERY
KT1
NEW MALDEN
KT8
95
96
97
98
99
100
101
102
103
104
68
69
67
66
CROMWELL RD
LONDON ROAD
CAMBRIDGE ROAD
KINGSTON ROAD
A2043
A308
A307
A240
A243
A3
SURBITON CEMETERY
Sewage Works
GREEN LANE REC GRD
BERRYLANDS
KT3
137
HOGSMILL PUBLIC OPEN SPACE
KT5
SURBITON GENERAL HOSP
SURBITON
KT6
ALEXANDRA REC GRD
HOGSMILL OPEN SPACE
OLD MALDEN
MALDEN MANOR
MALDEN WAY
KINGSTON BYPASS
TOLWORTH HOSPITAL
TOLWORTH
MAORI SPORTS GROUND
KINGSTON UNIVERSITY SPORTS GRD
RIVERHILL SPORTS GRD
WANDGAS ATHLETIC GROUND
KING GEORGES FIELD
KING GEORGE'S FIELD AURIOL PARK
KING GEORGE'S TRADING EST
HOOK RISE SOUTH IND PK
KING EDWARD REC GRD
156
KT9
HOOK
SURREY
NG DITTON
Cockcrow Hill
HAMPTON WICK POND
River Thames
PORTSMOUTH ROAD
EWELL ROAD
HOOK ROAD
UPPER BRIGHTON ROAD
RICHMOND ROAD
KINGSTON HILL

139
CT
CU
CV
CW
CX
CY
CZ
22
23
24
WOLFSON MED. REHAB CENTRE
COPSE HILL
SW20
OBERON PLAYING FIELD
COTTENHAM PARK
COTTENHAM PK REC GRD
PLAYING FIELDS
SPORTS GROUND
GOLF COURSE
COOMBE LANE
KINGSTON BY-PASS
A238
A298
A3
A24
A217
A2043
B282
B279
B285
B286
WEST BARNES LA
RAYNES PARK
RAYNES PARK SPORTS GRD
KINGSTON ROAD
WORPLE RD
PEPYS RD
WIMBLEDON CHASE
NELSON HOSP
JOHN INNES REC GRD
DUNDONALD REC GRD
MERTON
MERTON PARK
SW19
95
96
97
98
99
100
101
102
103
104
119
140
157
66
67
68
69
PRINCE GEORGE'S PLAYING FIELD
MESSINES PLAYING FLD
JOSEPH HOOD RECREATION GROUND
BUSHEY MEAD
CANNON HILL COMMON
SOUTH MERTON
MORDEN
MOSTYN GARDENS
BEVERLEY PARK
KINGSTON UPON THAMES
BURLINGTON ROAD
WEST BARNES
MOTSPUR PARK
RAYNES PARK PLAYING FIELDS
OLD BLUES R.F.C.
UNIVERSITY OF LONDON ATHLETIC GROUND
THE SIR JOSEPH HOOD MEMORIAL PLAYING FIELDS
B.B.C. SPORTS GRD
Crematorium
MORDEN CEMETERY
SPORTS GROUND
MERTON & SUTTON JOINT CEMETERY
MANOR PARK REC GRD
MORDEN PARK
MORDEN SPORTS GROUND
SM4
Merton Coll
KING GEORGE'S FIELD
Beverley Brook
MALDEN ROAD
MALDEN WAY
CENTRAL ROAD
EPSOM ROAD
STONECOT HILL
SUTTON COMMON ROAD
GARTH ROAD IND CEN
ST. ANTHONY'S HOSP
St. Raphael's Hospice
SM3
SUTTON CEMETERY
KIMPTON TRADE BUSINESS CENTRE
REIGATE AVENUE REC GRD
Oldfields Trading Est
WORCESTER PARK
CHEAM COMMON ROAD
LONDON ROAD
KT4
CUDDINGTON
REC GRD
NORTH CHEAM
ST. DUNSTAN'S HILL
OLDFIELDS ROAD
SM1
COLLINGWOOD PARK
Sutton Utd. FC
ST. HELIER
MORDEN SOUTH
EPSOM & EWELL
SUTTON

140
DA
DB
DC
DD
DE
DF
DG
26
27
28
SOUTH WIMBLEDON
COLLIER'S WOOD
120
MERTON
MERTON PARK
SW19
MERTON HIGH STREET
MERANTUN WAY
NELSON HOSP
ABBEY REC GRD
MERTON INDUSTRIAL PARK
LOMBARD BUSINESS PARK
LONDON ROAD CEMETERY
FIGGE'S MARSH
GREENLEA PARK
WESTERN ROAD
STREATHAM ROAD
MORDEN ROAD
MORDEN
MORDEN HALL PARK
Snuff Mill Enviromental Cen
PHIPPS BRIDGE
MITCHAM
CR4
MORDEN HALL ROAD
MOSTYN GARDENS
SOUTH MERTON
SM4
MORDEN PARK
MORDEN SOUTH
LONDON ROAD
RAVENSBURY PARK
WATERMEADS NT.
MITCHAM GOLF COURSE
MITCHAM JUNCTION
POULTER PARK
EAGLE TRADING EST
GRACE BUSINESS CENTRE
SPORTS GROUND
MILL GREEN
CENTRAL ROAD
MORDEN REC GRD
ST. HELIER AVENUE
MORETON GREEN
BISHOPSFORD ROAD
ST. HELIER
THOMAS WALL PARK
CARSHALTON SPORTS ARENA
ST HELIER OPEN SPACE
SM5
REIGATE AVENUE
ROSEHILL
ROSEHILL PARK EAST
GREENSHAW WOOD
ST. HELIER HOSP
QUEEN MARY'S HOSP FOR CHILDREN
ROSEHILL RECREATION GROUND
SUTTON CEMETERY
SM3
BENHILTON
THE WRYTHE
ROYSTON PARK
LIMES GRN
DALE PARK
FELNEX TRADING ESTATE
WILDERNESS ISLAND
WRYTHE REC GRD
SUTTON COMMON
SM1
COLLINGWOOD PARK
CARSHALTON
158
139
95
96
97
98
99
100
101
102
103
104
66
67
68
69

DH
DJ
DK
DL
DM
DN
DP
STREATHAM VALE
NORBURY
NORBURY PARK
SE19
SW16
STREATHAM PARK CEMETERY
MITCHAM
COMMON
CROYDON CEMETERY
THORNTON HEATH
CR7
BROAD GREEN
MAYDAY HOSPITAL
QUEEN'S ROAD CEMETERY
CR0
WADDON
HACKBRIDGE
BEDDINGTON
SM6
BEDDINGTON PARK
POLLARDS HILL
NATIONAL WESTMINSTER BANK SPORTS GROUND
GREEN LANE SPORTS GROUND
LONDON ROAD
MITCHAM ROAD
PURLEY WAY
CROYDON ROAD
A23
A236
A232
121
142
159
95
96
97
98
99
100
101
102
103
104
29
30
31
66
67
68
69

DQ
DR
DS
DT
DU
DV
DW
33
34
35
122
UPPER NORWOOD
PENGE
SE19
SE20
ANERLEY
BETTS PARK
THE LAWNS
BEAULIEU HEIGHTS
SYLVAN ESTATE
SOUTH NORWOOD GROUNDS
SPORTS GROUND
SOUTH NORWOOD LAKE
ORCHARD SCHOOL SPORTS CENTRE
WESTOW PARK
GRANGEWOOD PARK
SOUTH NORWOOD
BECKENHAM CEMETERY
Crematorium
BIRKBECK
HARRINGTON ROAD
SOUTH NORWOOD COUNTRY PARK
SE25
SELHURST PARK CRYSTAL PALACE FC
CR7
THORNTON HEATH
NORWOOD JUNCTION
SOUTH NORWOOD REC GRD
CROYDON AND RYLANDS FIELDS
CROYDON SPORTS ARENA
Croydon FC
CROYDON DRIVING RANGE
WOODSIDE
SELHURST
HEAVERS MEADOW
RAIL DEPOT
QUEEN'S ROAD CEMETERY
MAYDAY HOSPITAL
BROAD GREEN
ASHBURTON PARK
SHIRLEY OAKS HOSPITAL
Davidson Centre
ROMAN IND EST
CR0
ADDISCOMBE
CROYDON
EAST CROYDON
WEST CROYDON
Whitgift Centre
FAIRFIELD HALLS
WANDLE PARK
WHITGIFT PLAYING FIELDS
SHIRLEY PARK
GOLF COURSE
HOCKEY PITCH
LLOYD PARK
SPORTS GROUND
PARK HILL
DUPPAS HILL
Croydon Flyover
COOMBE FARM
160
141
95
96
97
98
99
100
101
102
103
104
A212
A213
A214
A215
A222
A232
A235
A2039
B266
B273
CROYDON ROAD
PORTLAND ROAD
LOWER ADDISCOMBE ROAD
ADDISCOMBE ROAD
WHITEHORSE ROAD
WINDMILL ROAD
NORTHCOTE RD
SELHURST ROAD
SOUTH NORWOOD HILL
HIGH STREET
SPRING LANE
LONG LANE
SHIRLEY ROAD
WICKHAM ROAD
PARK LANE
COOMBE ROAD
DUPPAS HILL RD
ROMAN WAY
BEULAH HILL
CHURCH ROAD
ELMERS END ROAD
SUMNER ROAD
ST. JAMES'S ROAD
WELLESLEY ROAD

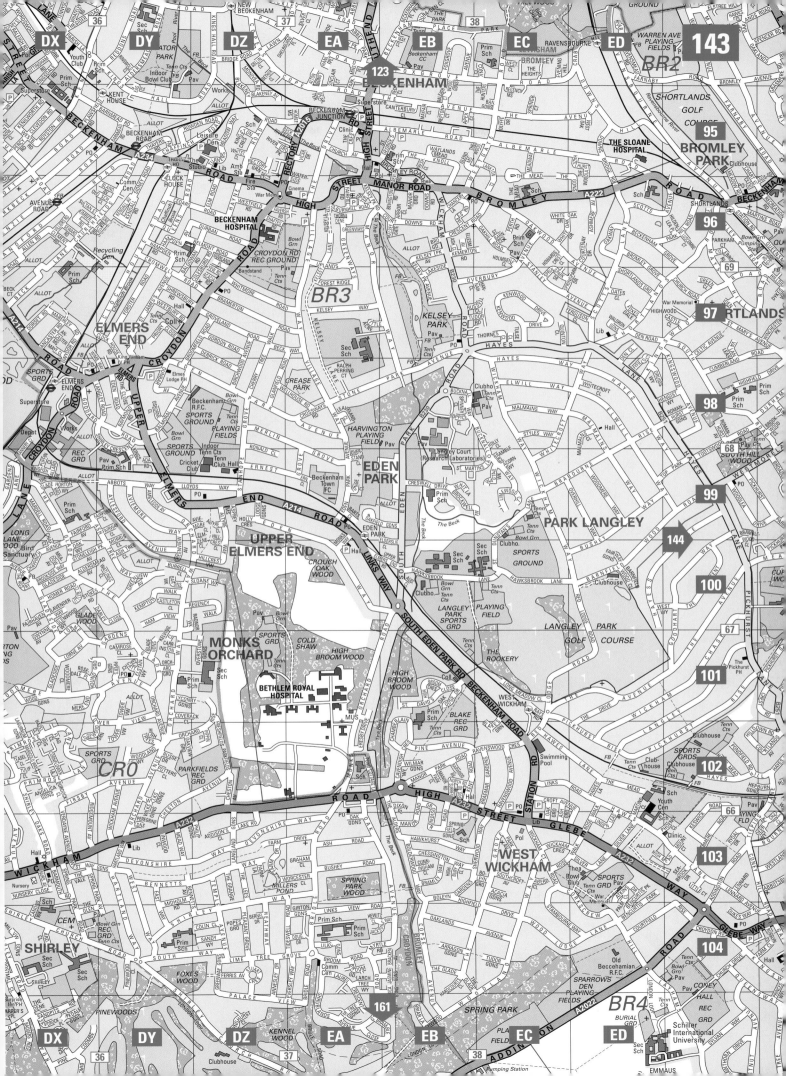

143
DX
DY
DZ
EA
EB
EC
ED
36
37
38
123
BECKENHAM
BR2
BR3
BR4
CR0
SHORTLANDS GOLF COURSE
THE SLOANE HOSPITAL
BROMLEY PARK
95
96
97
98
99
100
101
102
103
104
144
161
BECKENHAM HOSPITAL
ELMERS END
KELSEY PARK
EDEN PARK
PARK LANGLEY
UPPER ELMERS END
MONKS ORCHARD
BETHLEM ROYAL HOSPITAL
LANGLEY PARK GOLF COURSE
WEST WICKHAM
SHIRLEY
SPRING PARK
Schiller International University
EMMAUS

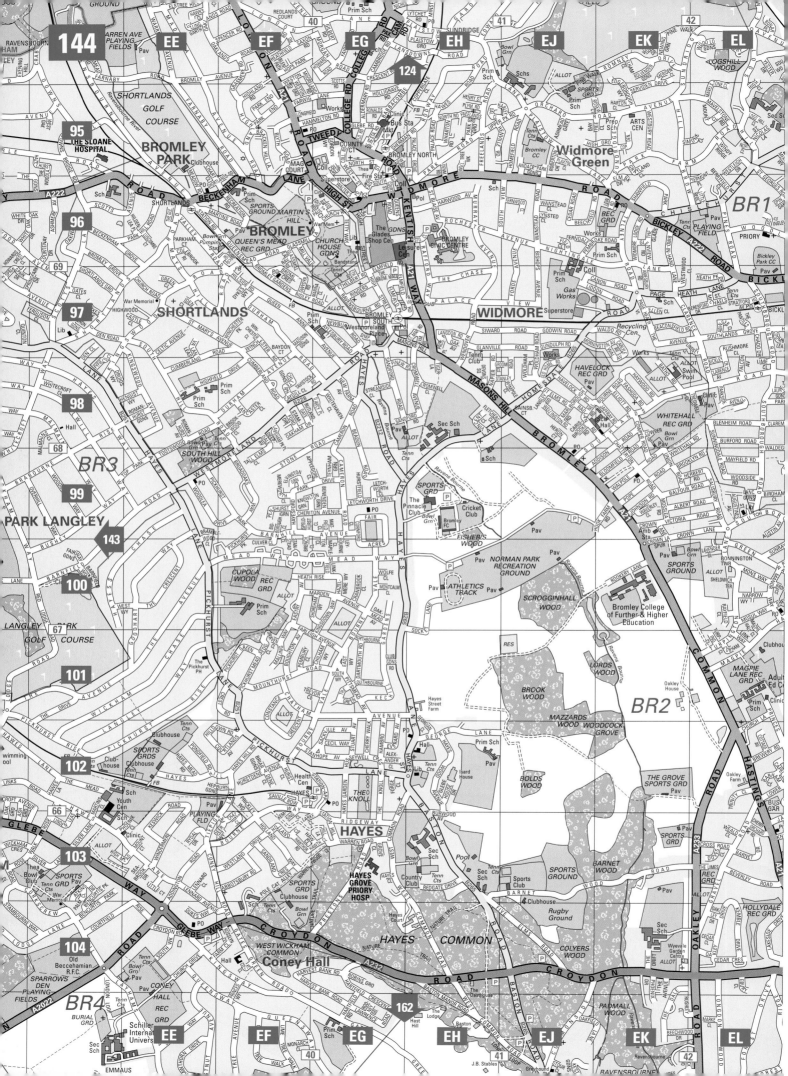
144
EE
EF
EG
EH
EJ
EK
EL
40
41
42
124
143
162
95
96
97
98
99
100
101
102
103
104
69
68
67
66
BR1
BR2
BR3
BR4
BROMLEY
BROMLEY PARK
SHORTLANDS
WIDMORE
Widmore Green
PARK LANGLEY
HAYES
Coney Hall
HAYES COMMON
SHORTLANDS GOLF COURSE
LANGLEY PARK GOLF COURSE
THE SLOANE HOSPITAL
BROMLEY CIVIC CENTRE
The Glades Shop Cen
QUEEN'S MEAD REC GRD
CHURCH HOUSE GDNS
MARTIN'S HILL
SOUTH HILL WOOD
HAVELOCK REC GRD
WHITEHALL REC GRD
NORMAN PARK RECREATION GROUND
ATHLETICS TRACK
FISHER'S WOOD
SCROGGINHALL WOOD
Bromley College of Further & Higher Education
LORDS WOOD
BROOK WOOD
MAZZARDS WOOD
WOODCOCK GROVE
BOLDS WOOD
THE GROVE SPORTS GRD
BARNET WOOD
COLYERS WOOD
PADMALL WOOD
CUPOLA WOOD
THE KNOLL
HAYES GROVE PRIORY HOSP
WEST WICKHAM COMMON
CONEY HALL REC GRD
MAGPIE LANE REC GRD
HOLLYDALE REC GRD
LOGSHILL WOOD
Bickley Park CC
Bromley CC
The Pinnacle Club
Bromley FC
Cricket Club
SPARROWS DEN PLAYING FIELDS
Old Beccehamian R.F.C.
Schiller Internat Univers
EMMAUS
Hast Hill
The Lodge
J.B. Stables
Ravensbourne
A21
A222
A232
A233
A2022
B228
B251
B265
B2212
CROYDON ROAD
HASTINGS ROAD
COMMON ROAD
OAKLEY ROAD
MASONS HILL
BROMLEY COMMON
KENTISH WAY
WIDMORE ROAD
BECKENHAM LANE
WESTMORELAND ROAD
HAYES LANE
PICKHURST LANE
BASTON ROAD
GLEBE WAY
BICKLEY ROAD
CHISLEHURST ROAD
HIGH ST
TWEEDY ROAD
LONDON ROAD
COLLEGE ROAD
MEAD WAY
WICKHAM WAY
CHASE
THE AVENUE
Ravensbourne River

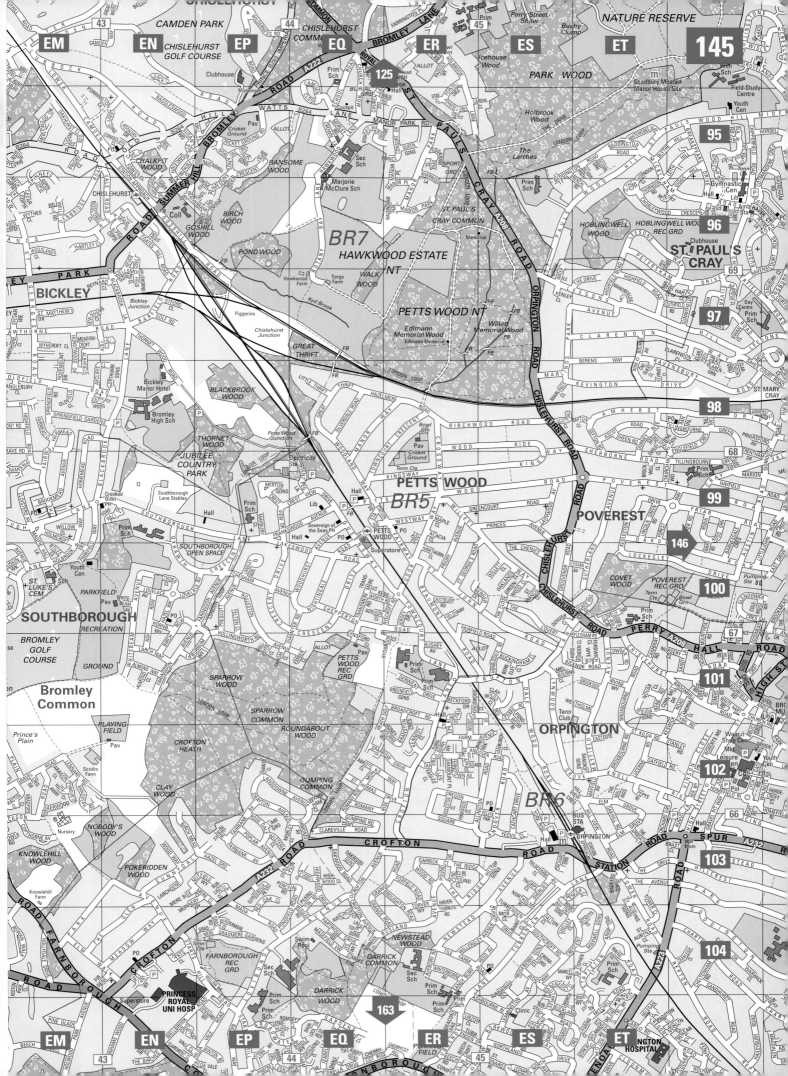
EM
EN
EP
EQ
ER
ES
ET
43
44
45
125
163
146
95
96
97
98
99
100
101
102
103
104
69
68
67
66
CAMDEN PARK
CHISLEHURST GOLF COURSE
CHISLEHURST COMMON
NATURE RESERVE
Perry Street Shaw
Bushy Clump
Icehouse Wood
PARK WOOD
Scadbury Moated Manor House Site
Field Study Centre
Youth Cen
Holbrook Wood
The Larches
Clubhouse
Monument
Cricket Ground
Pav
CHALKPIT WOOD
BANSOME WOOD
Sec Sch
Marjorie McClure Sch
CHISLEHURST
Coll
BIRCH WOOD
GOSHILL WOOD
ST. PAUL'S CRAY COMMON
HOBLINGWELL WOOD
HOBLINGWELL WOOD REC GRD
ST. PAUL'S CRAY
Gymnastic Cen
BR7
HAWKWOOD ESTATE NT
POND WOOD
Hawkwood Farm
Tongs Farm
WALK WOOD
PETTS WOOD NT
Edlmann Memorial Wood
Willett Memorial Wood
Kyd Brook
Piggeries
Chislehurst Junction
Bickley Junction
BICKLEY
GREAT THRIFT
LONDON LOOP
BLACKBROOK WOOD
Bickley Manor Hotel
Bromley High Sch
Petts Wood Junction
THORNET WOOD
JUBILEE COUNTRY PARK
Electricity Sta
Southborough Lane Stables
Crooked Billet PH
PETTS WOOD
BR5
Sovereign of the Seas PH
Superstore
SOUTHBOROUGH OPEN SPACE
POVEREST
COVET WOOD
POVEREST REC GRD
ST. LUKE'S CEM
PARKFIELD
SOUTHBOROUGH RECREATION GROUND
BROMLEY GOLF COURSE
Bromley Common
Prince's Plain
PLAYING FIELD
SPARROW WOOD
SPARROW COMMON
ROUNDABOUT WOOD
CROFTON HEATH
PETTS WOOD REC GRD
ORPINGTON
Tenn Club
BR6
CLAY WOOD
GUMPING COMMON
Scrubs Farm
Nursery
NOBODY'S WOOD
KNOWLEHILL WOOD
Knowlehill Farm
POKERIDDEN WOOD
BUS STA
ORPINGTON
Walnut Shop Cen
Mkt
Leisure Cen
NEWSTEAD WOOD
FARNBOROUGH REC GRD
DARRICK COMMON
DARRICK WOOD
PRINCESS ROYAL UNI HOSP
Superstore
Clinic
Pumping Sta
ORPINGTON HOSPITAL
BROMLEY LANE
PRINCE IMPERIAL ROAD
A222
B264
WATTS LANE
MANOR PARK RD
ST. PAULS CRAY ROAD
A208
ORPINGTON ROAD
CHISLEHURST ROAD
SUMMER HILL
BICKLEY PARK ROAD
SOUTHBOROUGH LANE
PERRY HALL ROAD
CROFTON ROAD
A232
SPUR ROAD
STATION ROAD
FARNBOROUGH ROAD
A223
BIRCHWOOD ROAD
WOOD RIDE
KINGS WAY
POVEREST ROAD
WILLETT WAY
CROFTON LANE
TUBBENDEN LANE
HIGH STREET

146
NATURE RESERVE
EU
EV
EW
EX
EY
EZ
FA
126
DA14
SIDCUP
A20
BYPASS
MAIDSTONE ROAD
EDGINGTON
Crittall's Corner
RUXLEY
BROMLEY
Ruxley Manor Nursery
Scadbury Moated Manor House Site
Field-Study Centre
95
96
97
98
99
100
101
102
103
104
145
164
ST. PAUL'S CRAY
HOBLINGWELL WOOD REC GRD
BR7
BR5
BR6
RUXLEY PARK GOLF COURSE
CRAY VALLEY GOLF COURSE
Barnfield Bank
Pilgrim Hill
CHAPMANS LANE
Simon's Field Shaw
PAULS CRAY HILL PARK
HIGHLANDS WOOD
HOCKENDEN WOOD
Hockenden Farm
Hogspring Cottages
Milewood
Wycoombe
SPRINGVALE RETAIL PARK
MURRAY BUSINESS CEN
CRAYFIELD IND PARK
ST. MARY CRAY
STAR LANE
POVEREST
THE WARREN
CHILD'S WOOD
Ringland Farm
Sheepcote Farm
Blueberry Farm
Kevington Farm
CROCKENHILL ROAD
Shawcroft Sch
ST. MARY CRAY REC GRD
RIVERSIDE GDNS
Derry Downs
GRIGG'S CROSS
KYNASTON WOOD
Waldens Farm
Crouch Farm
Walden Manor
Heather's Holdings
Depot
Bleak House Farm
POVEREST REC GRD
PERRY HALL ROAD
A208
PRIORY GARDENS
BROMLEY MUS
GRASSMEADE RECREATION GROUND
ORPINGTON
RAMSDEN
Eastwood Farm
GRIFF'S WOOD
HOLLINGBOURNE TWR
BEKESBOURNE TWR
Piggery
Byways Nurseries
SAGE WENTS
Crownwood Farm
Cookham Hill Farm
Cookham Farm
SPUR ROAD
A232
COURT ROAD (ORPINGTON BYPASS)
A224
A223
ORPINGTON HOSPITAL
Goddington
Goddington House
GODDINGTON PARK
ROUNDS SMALLAMS
LILLY'S WOOD
BLACK BUSH WOOD
SKEET HILL LANE
SKIBBS LANE
CHELSFIELD LANE
NUT TREE CLOSE
47
48
49
66
67
68
69

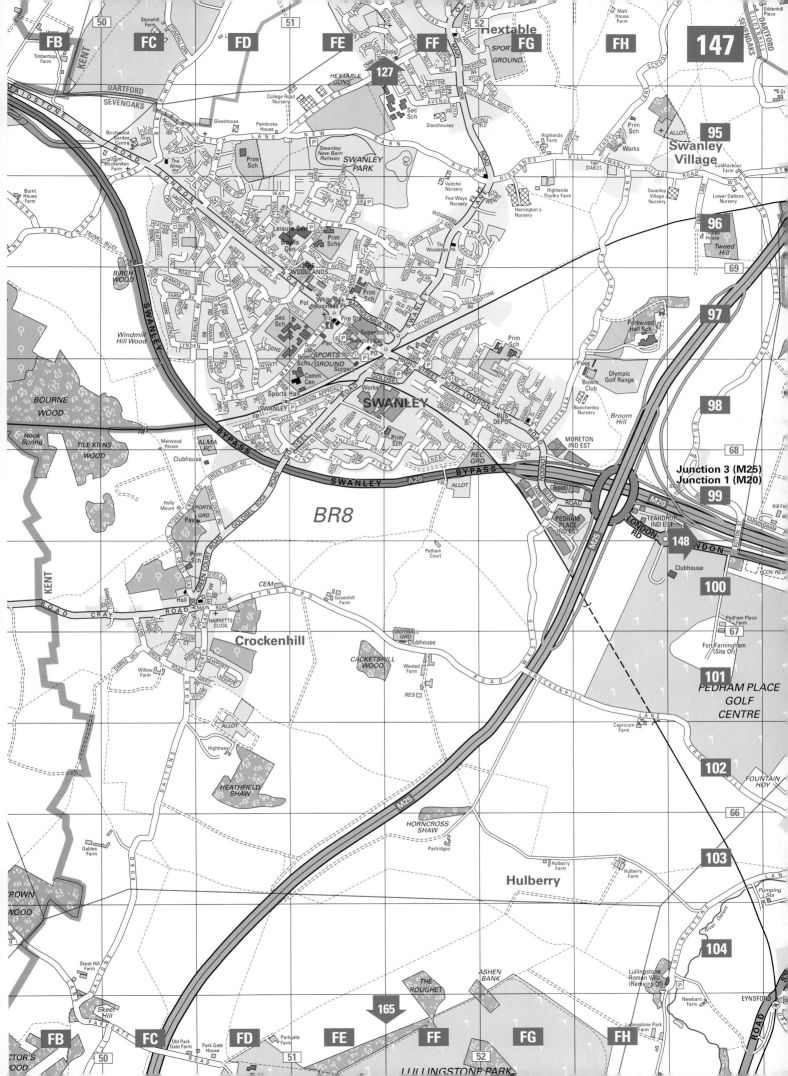
FB
FC
FD
FE
FF
FG
FH
50
51
52
127
Hextable
SPORT GROUND
KENT
DARTFORD
SEVENOAKS
MAIDSTONE ROAD
Stonehill Farm
Timbertops Farm
HEXTABLE GDNS
College Road Nursery
Glasshouse
Pembroke House
Birchwood Garden Centre
Upper Hockenden Farm
The Alma PH
Prim Sch
Swanley New Barn Railway
SWANLEY PARK
Glasshouses
Sec Sch
Clinic
Highlands Farm
Highlands Poultry Farm
Veitchii Nursery
Five Ways Nursery
Harrington's Nursery
Hall
Works
Swanley Village
Coldharbour Farm
Swanley Village Nursery
Lower Daltons Nursery
95
96
Tweed House
Tweed Hill
69
Burnt House Farm
HOCKENDEN LANE
TRUNKS ALLEY
BIRCH WOOD
Windmill Hill Wood
Leisure Cen
Bowls Cen
Prim Schs
THE WOODLANDS
The Woodman PH
White Oak Business Pk
Pol
Lib
Fire Sta
Superstore
Swanley Cen
Sec Sch
Sports Hall
Prim Schs
Comm Cen
Surgery
SPORTS GROUND
Pav
SWANLEY
Works
BUS DEPOT
Prim Sch
Parkwood Hall Sch
Olympic Golf Range
Pavs
Bowls Club
Beechenley Nursery
Broom Hill
MORETON IND EST
97
98
68
BOURNE WOOD
Hook Spring
TILE KILNS WOOD
Marwood House
ALMA FC
Clubhouse
REC GRD
ALLOT
SWANLEY BYPASS
A20
Junction 3 (M25)
Junction 1 (M20)
99
M20
M25
Depot
PEDHAM PLACE IND EST
TEARDROP IND EST
148
LONDON RD
Clubhouse
BR8
Holly Mount
SPORTS GRD
Pavs
Prim Sch
Petham Court
100
CEM
Gosenhill Farm
Hall
PO
HARNETTS CLOSE
CRAY ROAD
EYNSFORD ROAD
Crockenhill
FOOTBALL GRD
Clubhouse
CACKETSHILL WOOD
Wested Farm
RES
Willow Farm
Pedham Place Farm
67
Fort Farningham (Site Of)
101
PEDHAM PLACE GOLF CENTRE
CROCKENHILL LANE
Capricorn Farm
ALLOT
Hightrees
HEATHFIELD SHAW
102
FOUNTAIN HOY
66
HORNCROSS SHAW
Partridges
Gables Farm
Hulberry Farm
Hulberry Farm
Hulberry
103
CROWN WOOD
Pumping Sta
River Darent
104
Skeet Hill Farm
DALTONS ROAD
ASHEN BANK
THE ROUGHET
165
Lullingstone Roman Villa (Remains Of)
Newbarn Farm
EYNSFORD
Skeet Hill
PARKGATE ROAD
Old Park Gate Farm
Park Gate House
Parkgate Farm
Lullingstone Park Farm
LULLINGSTONE PARK

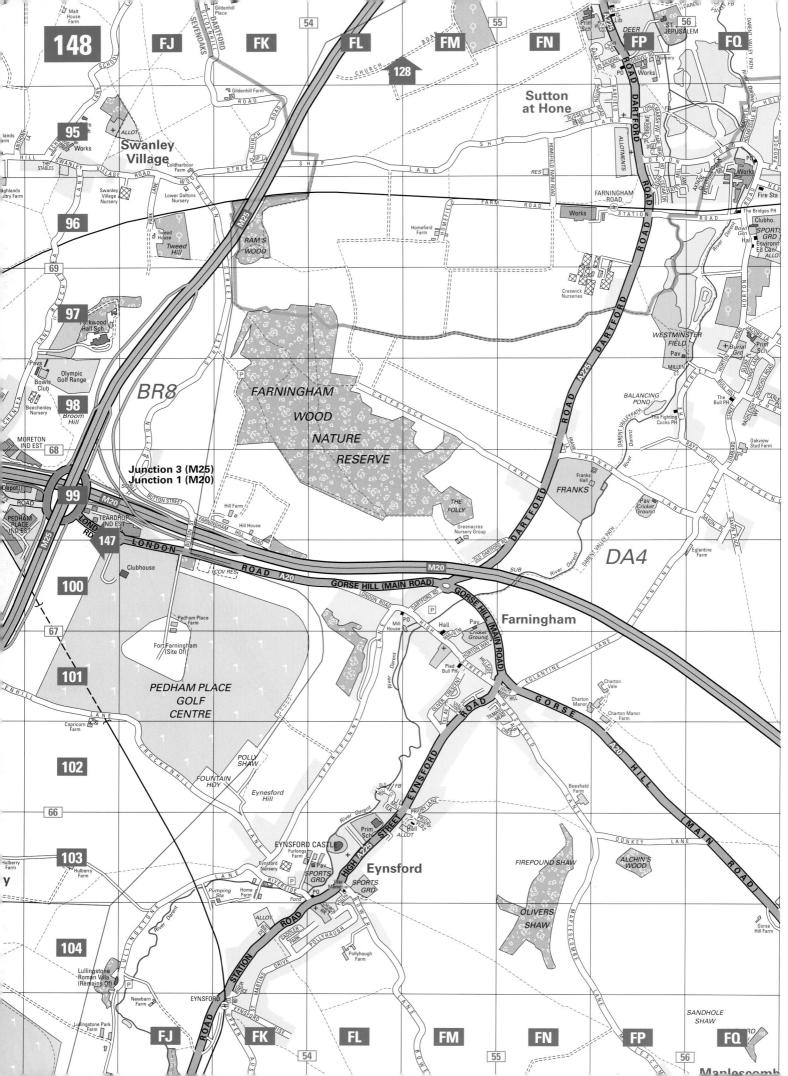
FJ
FK
FL
FM
FN
FP
FQ
128
Sutton at Hone
Swanley Village
BR8
FARNINGHAM WOOD NATURE RESERVE
Junction 3 (M25)
Junction 1 (M20)
147
DA4
Farningham
PEDHAM PLACE GOLF CENTRE
Eynsford
EYNSFORD CASTLE
FIREPOUND SHAW
OLIVERS SHAW
ALCHIN'S WOOD
SANDHOLE SHAW
FRANKS
WESTMINSTER FIELD
RAM'S WOOD
Tweed Hill
Broom Hill
Eynesford Hill
POLLY SHAW
FOUNTAIN HOY
THE FOLLY
BALANCING POND
DARTFORD ROAD
GORSE HILL (MAIN ROAD)
LONDON ROAD
EYNSFORD ROAD
HIGH STREET
STATION ROAD
CALFSTOCK LANE
SHIP LANE
FARM ROAD
STATION ROAD
CROCKENHILL LANE
SPAREPENNY LANE
DONKEY LANE
EGLANTINE LANE
Olympic Golf Range
Parkwood Hall Sch
Pedham Place Farm
Fort Farningham (Site Of)
Lullingstone Roman Villa (Remains Of)
Creswick Nurseries
Greenacres Nursery Group
Charton Manor Farm
Beesfield Farm
Pollyhaugh Farm
Eglantine Farm
Oakview Stud Farm
The Fighting Cocks PH
The Bull PH
The Bridges PH
Pied Bull PH
95
96
97
98
99
100
101
102
103
104
54
55
56
66
67
68
69

FR
FS
FT
FU
FV
FW
FX
57
58
59
129
95
96
97
98
99
100
101
102
103
104
69
68
67
66
DA2
DA3
TN15
South Darenth
Horton Kirby
Dean Bottom
Pinden
Mile End Green
Longfield
Hartley Green
New Ash Green
Fawkham Green
St. Margaret's Farm
Gill's Farm
Walnut Tree Farm
Chalkcroft
Ryecroft Farm
Orchard View
RYECROFTS WOOD
DARTFORD
SEVENOAKS
QUARRY
SPORTS GRD
Works
Pinden End Farm
Rabbits Farm
Tuppence Farm
SOUTHDOWNS
Wheatsheaf PH
Dean Bottom Farm
LONGFIELD
Sec Sch
CHURCHDOWN WOOD
Churchdown Farm
Northdown Country Riding Club
Beeches Farm
Canada Farm
Hill Barn Farm
FAWKHAM VALLEY GOLF COURSE
Country Club
Bowl Grn
Sports Ground
Sports Cen
Clubho
SPORTS GRD
Gay Dawn Farm
Pennis Farm
Prim Sch
Lone Oak Farm
Kentdown Mushroom Farm
Nursery
Elec Sta
PENNIS WOOD
YEWFIELD SHAW
GROVE WOOD
Grove Farm
HORTON WOOD
Hall
Prim Sch
REDLIBBETS GOLF COURSE
Clubhouse
FAWKHAM MANOR HOSPITAL
Fawkham Manor Farm
HOPKINS SPRING WOOD
HATCHFIELD WOOD
Radio Mast
The Rookery Pig Farm
White House Farm
Speedgate Farm
GABRIEL SPRING WOOD
CHOAKS WOOD
The Rising Sun PH
War Memorial
PO
Greyhound Schooling Establishment
Westyoke Farm
Eaglesfield Equestrian Centre
Beechcroft Farm Industries
The Black Lion PH
The Royal Oak PH
Woodhall Farm
Works
BRANDS HATCH KARTING
Leisure Cen
Brands Hatch Place Hotel
SAXTEN'S WOOD
Landway Farm
Stewart Cen
SHETLEY SHAWS
Thistle Brands Hatch
BRANDS HATCH MOTOR RACING
ASHEN GROVE
Ash Place Farm
Bovis Offices
SPORTS GROUND
M20
GORSE HILL (MAIN ROAD)
STACK ROAD
RABBITS ROAD
CANADA FARM ROAD
GREEN STREET GREEN ROAD
SCUDDERS HILL
VALLEY ROAD
MANOR LANE
SCHOOL LANE
MUSSENDEN LANE
THREE GATES ROAD
SPEEDGATE HILL
GABRIEL SPRING ROAD (EAST)
SCRATCHERS LANE
SUN HILL
FAWKHAM ROAD
HATCH ROAD
WEST YOKE
CHAPEL WOOD ROAD
CASTLE HILL
ASH ROAD
WHITEHILL ROAD
MAIN ROAD

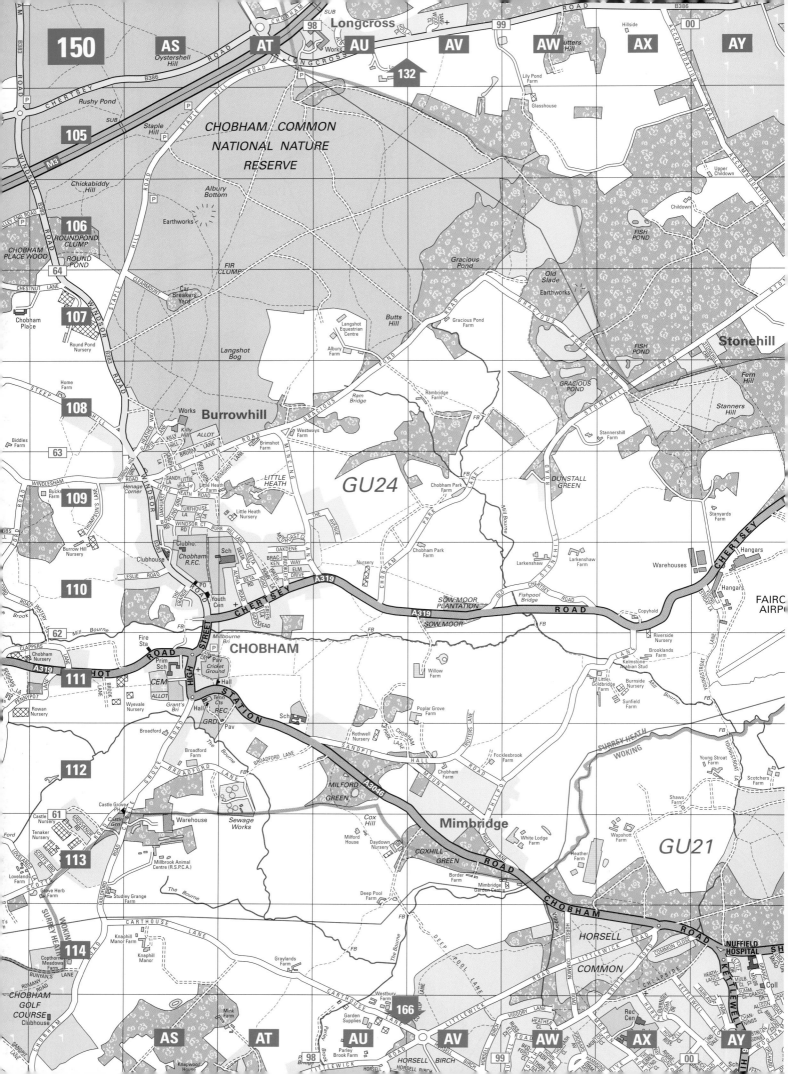
150
132
166
AS
AT
AU
AV
AW
AX
AY
105
106
107
108
109
110
111
112
113
114
Longcross
CHOBHAM COMMON
NATIONAL NATURE
RESERVE
Burrowhill
CHOBHAM
Mimbridge
Stonehill
HORSELL
COMMON
GU24
GU21
Chickabiddy
Hill
Albury
Bottom
Earthworks
Fir
Clump
Langshot
Bog
Butts
Hill
Gracious
Pond
Old
Slade
Earthworks
Fish
Pond
Gracious
Pond
Stanners
Hill
Fern
Hill
Dunstall
Green
Little
Heath
Sow Moor
Plantation
Sow Moor
Milford
Green
Coxhill
Green
Cox
Hill
Oystershell
Hill
Rushy Pond
Staple
Hill
Roundpond
Clump
Chobham
Place Wood
Round
Pond
Chobham
Golf
Course
Clubhouse
Surrey Heath
Woking
Nuffield
Hospital
Chertsey Road
Windsor Road
Staple Hill
Gracious Pond Road
Stonehill Road
Station Road
Chobham Road
Carthouse Lane
Littlewick Road
Deep Pool Lane
High Street
Accommodation Road
M3
A319
A3046
B383
B386

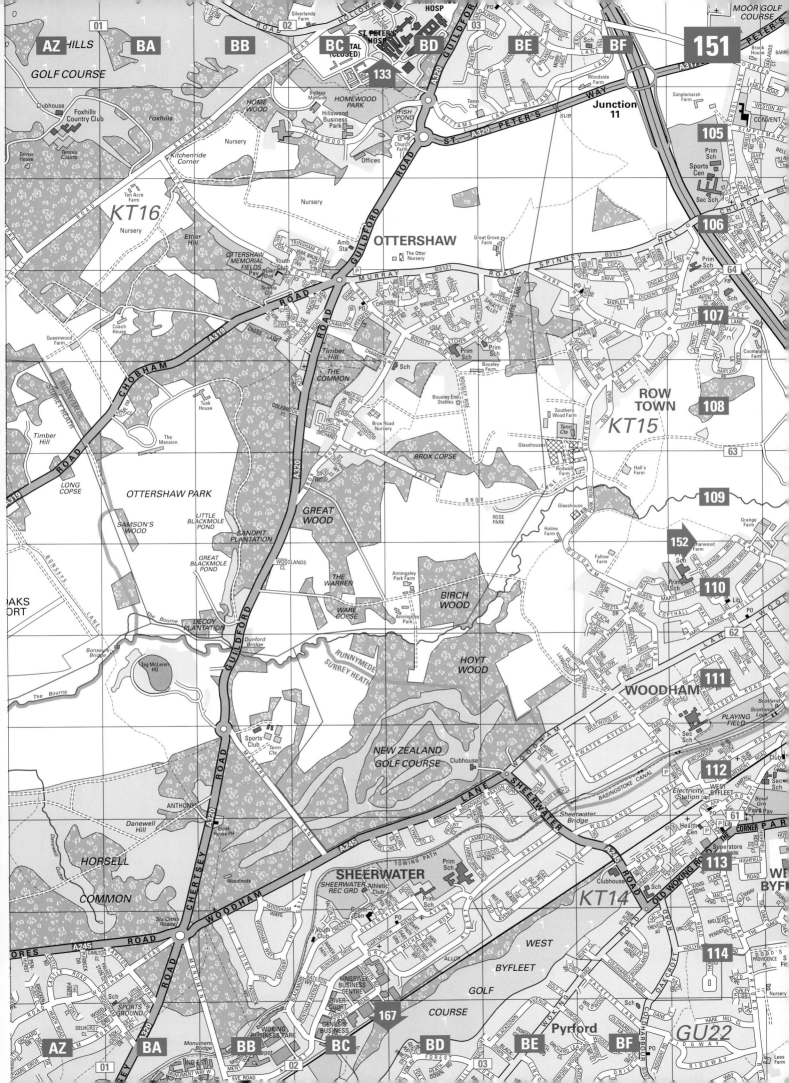
151
133
167
152
AZ
BA
BB
BC
BD
BE
BF
01
02
03
105
106
107
108
109
110
111
112
113
114
64
63
62
61
FOXHILLS
GOLF COURSE
Clubhouse
Foxhills Country Club
Foxhills
Tennis Courts
Dower House
Kitchenride Corner
Ten Acre Farm
KT16
Nursery
Ether Hill
ST PETER'S HOSP
HOSP
Silverlands Farm
Botleys Mansion
HOMEWOOD PARK
HOME WOOD
Hillswood Business Park
FISH POND
Church Farm
Offices
Woodside Farm
Junction 11
ST. PETER'S WAY
A320
A319
A317
B3121
MOOR GOLF COURSE
Brook House
Simplemarsh Farm
CONVENT
Prim Sch
Sports Cen
Sec Sch
OTTERSHAW
The Otter Nursery
Amb Sta
Great Grove Farm
OTTERSHAW MEMORIAL FIELDS
Youth Club
Bowl Grn
Tennis Cts
MURRAY ROAD
SPINNEY HILL
GUILDFORD ROAD
CHOBHAM ROAD
Coach House
Queenwood Farm
Timber Hill
THE COMMON
Sch
Prim Sch
Bousley Farm
Bousley End Stables
Brox Road Nursery
BROX COPSE
BROX LANE
Southern Wood Farm
Tenn Cts
Glasshouses
Rodwell Farm
Hall's Farm
ROW TOWN
KT15
Coomelands Farm
Tusk House
The Mansion
Timber Hill
LONG COPSE
OTTERSHAW PARK
SAMSON'S WOOD
LITTLE BLACKMOLE POND
GREAT BLACKMOLE POND
SANDPIT PLANTATION
GREAT WOOD
THE WARREN
Anningsley Park Farm
WARE COPSE
Anningsley Park
BIRCH WOOD
ROSE PARK
Glasshouse
Holme Farm
Fallow Farm
Grange Farm
Sharwood Farm
WOODHAM PARK ROAD
DECOY PLANTATION
The Bourne
Dunford Bridge
Bonsey's Bridge
Tag McLaren HQ
RUNNYMEDE
SURREY HEATH
HOYT WOOD
WOODHAM
PLAYING FIELD
Scotland Bridge
Scotland Lock
Sports Club
Tenn Cts
NEW ZEALAND GOLF COURSE
Clubhouse
SHEERWATER ROAD
BASINGSTOKE CANAL
Sheerwater Bridge
WEST BYFLEET
Electricity Station
Health Cen
Lib
Superstore
ANTHONYS
Bleak House PH
Danewell Hill
HORSELL COMMON
Danewell Gutter
Woodlands
Six Cross Roads
CHERTSEY ROAD
WOODHAM LANE
A245
SHEERWATER
SHEERWATER REC GRD
Athletic Club
Comm Cen
Youth Club
TOWING PATH
KINGSWEY BUSINESS CENTRE
RIVER-COURT
GENESIS BUSINESS
WOKING BUSINESS PARK
Depot
IND EST
Monument Bridge
MONUMENT WAY W
WEST BYFLEET GOLF COURSE
KT14
Clubhouse
OLD WOKING ROAD
Pyrford
GU22
SPORTS GROUND
Sch
Nursery
Lees Farm

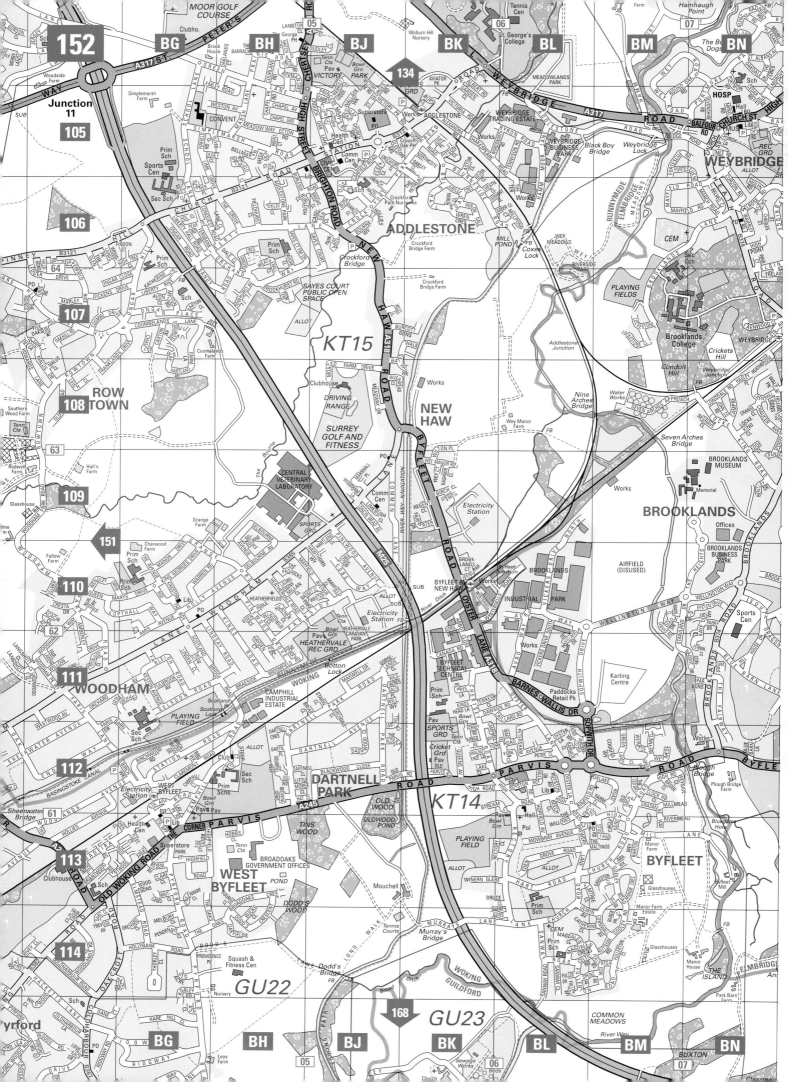

152
BG
BH
BJ
BK
BL
BM
BN
05
06
07
134
105
106
107
108
109
110
111
112
113
114
151
168
64
63
62
61
Junction 11
MOOR GOLF COURSE
St. George's College
Hamhaugh Point
Woburn Hill Nursery
ADDLESTONE
WEYBRIDGE
WEYBRIDGE TRADING ESTATE
WEYBRIDGE BUSINESS PARK
Black Boy Bridge
Weybridge Lock
KT15
ROW TOWN
NEW HAW
SURREY GOLF AND FITNESS
CENTRAL VETERINARY LABORATORY
SAYES COURT PUBLIC OPEN SPACE
Crockford Bridge
Coxes Lock
Brooklands College
Crickets Hill
Nine Arches Bridge
Seven Arches Bridge
BROOKLANDS MUSEUM
BROOKLANDS
BROOKLANDS BUSINESS PARK
AIRFIELD (DISUSED)
BROOKLANDS INDUSTRIAL PARK
Electricity Station
Byfleet & New Haw
WOODHAM
HEATHERVALE REC GRD
CAMPHILL INDUSTRIAL ESTATE
BYFLEET TECHNICAL CENTRE
Paddocks Retail Pk
Karting Centre
DARTNELL PARK
KT14
WEST BYFLEET
BROADOAKS GOVERNMENT OFFICES
BYFLEET
Plough Bridge
Sheerwater Bridge
BASINGSTOKE CANAL
Dodd's Bridge
GU22
GU23
Murray's Bridge
COMMON MEADOWS
Pyrford
BUXTON
A317
A318
A245
B3121
M25
ST. PETER'S WAY
WEYBRIDGE ROAD
HIGH STREET
CHERTSEY ROAD
BRIGHTON ROAD
NEW HAW ROAD
BYFLEET ROAD
OYSTER LANE
BARNES WALLIS DR
SOPWITH DR
PARVIS ROAD
OLD WOKING ROAD
WOODHAM LANE
RIVER WEY NAVIGATION

153
ASHLEY PARK
OATLANDS PARK
BURWOOD PARK
KT12
KT13
WALTON COMMON
BURHILL GOLF COURSE
BURHILL GOLF COURSE (NEW COURSE)
ST. GEORGE'S HILL
WHITELEY VILLAGE
ST. GEORGE'S HILL GOLF COURSE
WALTON COMMON
SILVERMERE GOLF COURSE
KT11
PAINSHILL PARK
COBHAM
BP
BQ
BR
BS
BT
BU
BV
135
154
169
105
106
107
108
109
110
111
112
113
114

LITTLEWORTH COMMON
HINCHLEY WOOD
KINGSTON BYPASS
A309
CD
CE
CF
CG
CH
CJ
CK
15
16
17
137
D.S.S. OFFICES
HINCHLEY
Telegraph Hill
Semaphore House
Clubhouse RUGBY GRD
SPORTS GRD
WOOD
ALLOT
The Waffrons
Clubhouse
SURBITON GOLF COURSE
MEML. GRD
Pav
SPORTS GROUND
KING EDWARD REC GRD
HOOK
105
106
107
108
109
110
111
112
113
114
156
171
LOVELACE PLAYING FIELD
Youth Cen
Prim Sch
Cricket Club
Cricket Ground
Garden Centre
Wingham
Wingham Lodge
Slough Farm
Manor Farm
Elm Farm
LOWER WOOD
Telephone Exchange
Loseberry
CLAYGATE
Sec Sch
Loseberry Farm
SPORTS GRD
KT10
Surgery
Comm Cen
Hare & Hounds PH
Foley Arms PH
Hall
Prim Sch
SPORTS GROUND
CLAYGATE
Sch
Sch
THE MAPLES
CLAYGATE COMMON
Oak Cottages
ALLOT
Vale Farm
Horringdon Farm
THE GRAPSOME
ESHER
ELMBRIDGE
A3
Barwell Court
Winey Hill
KT9
BARWELL LAKE
SURREY
KINGSTON UPON THAMES
CHESSINGTON NORTH
CHESSINGTON
CHURCH FIELDS
Bowl Club
CHESSINGTON SOUTH
Comm Coll
REC GRD
Cricket Club
SPORTS GROUND
CHESSINGTON GOLF CENTRE
Driving Range
Clubhouse
BARWELL BUSINESS PARK
SPORTS GROUND
64
63
62
61
Bonesgate Stream
BYPASS
Mini Railway
CHESSINGTON WORLD OF ADVENTURE
Travel Inn
LEATHERHEAD ROAD
A243
CHALKY LANE
Park Farm
POND WOOD
HOLROYDS PLANTATION
SIXTY ACRE WOOD
BIRCH WOOD
MILBOURNEHOLD PLANTATION
GREAT OAK
KT22
LIMEKILN WOOD
JUBILEE WOOD
Electricity Station
Garden Centre
CHESSINGTON WOOD
JUBILEE WOOD
OLD CARPENTERS PLANTATION
FAIROAK LANE
B280
Malden Rushett
RUSHETT LANE
BRICKYARD PLANTATION
MILBOURNEHOLD WOOD
SPORTS GROUND
Bowling Green
Glanmire Farm
NEW WOOD
Jessop's Well
THE AVENUE
Byhurst Farm
STEW POND
Woodcock Corner
Bunkers Hill
Rushett Farm
STOKE WOOD
PRINCE'S COVERTS
OXSHOTT
Telegraph Hill
COV RES
KT21
THE FOREST
NEWTON WOOD
Sch
The Star PH
Horns Hill
Willoughby's Nurseries
LEATHERHEAD GOLF COURSE
MOLE VALLEY
EPSOM
ASHTEAD COMMON

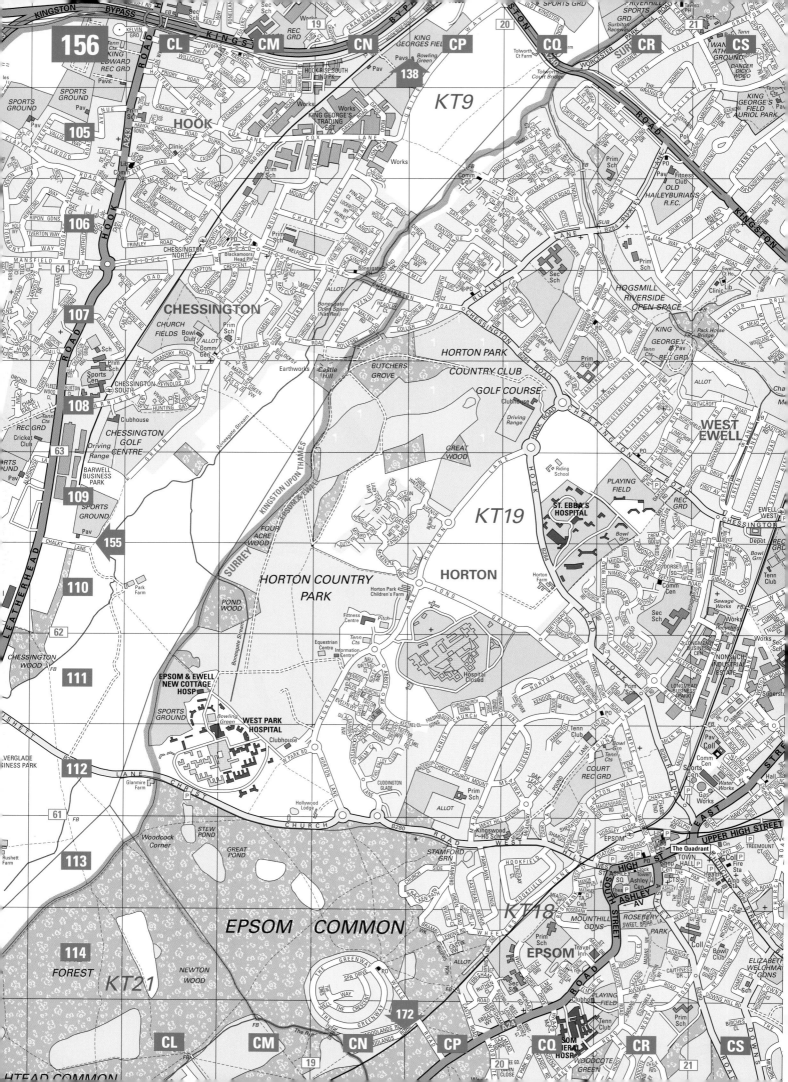

KINGSTON BYPASS
CL
CM
CN
CP
CQ
CR
CS
19
20
21
KING GEORGES FIELD
138
KT9
KING EDWARD REC GRD
SPORTS GROUND
HOOK
105
106
107
108
109
110
111
112
113
114
155
172
64
63
62
61
A243
HOOK ROAD
KING GEORGE'S TRADING EST
HOOK RISE SOUTH IND PK
Works
Prim Sch
CHESSINGTON NORTH
CHESSINGTON
CHURCH FIELDS
CHESSINGTON SOUTH
CHESSINGTON GOLF CENTRE
BARWELL BUSINESS PARK
SPORTS GROUND
CHALKY LANE
Park Farm
CHESSINGTON WOOD
LEATHERHEAD ROAD
Bonesgate Open Space (Nat Res)
Castle Hill
Earthworks
BUTCHERS GROVE
HORTON PARK COUNTRY CLUB GOLF COURSE
Clubhouse
Driving Range
GREAT WOOD
KINGSTON UPON THAMES
EPSOM & EWELL
SURREY
FOUR ACRE WOOD
HORTON COUNTRY PARK
POND WOOD
Bonesgate Stream
KT19
ST. EBBA'S HOSPITAL
PLAYING FIELD
Riding School
HORTON
Horton Farm
Horton Park Children's Farm
Fitness Centre
Equestrian Centre
Information Centre
Hospital Closed
EPSOM & EWELL NEW COTTAGE HOSP
SPORTS GROUND
WEST PARK HOSPITAL
Clubhouse
Glanmire Farm
Hollywood Lodge
CUDDINGTON GLADE
CHRIST CHURCH ROAD
B280
Woodcock Corner
STEW POND
GREAT POND
Rushett Farm
EPSOM COMMON
FOREST
KT21
NEWTON WOOD
THE GREENWAY
SPA DRIVE
The Rye
HOGSMILL RIVERSIDE OPEN SPACE
KING GEORGE V REC GRD
Pack Horse Bridge
Hogsmill River
OLD HAILEYBURIANS R.F.C.
KING GEORGE'S FIELD AURIOL PARK
DANCER DICK WOOD
WEST EWELL
REC GRD
NONSUCH INDUSTRIAL ESTATE
LONGMEAD BUSINESS CENTRE
LONGMEAD BUSINESS PARK
Sewage Works
COURT REC GRD
Gas Works
Water Works
KT18
EPSOM
The Quadrant
TOWN HALL
UPPER HIGH STREET
HIGH ST
SOUTH STREET
ASHLEY AV
ROSEBERY PARK
MOUNTHILL GDNS
Travel Inn
PLAYING FIELD
EPSOM GENERAL HOSP
WOODCOTE GREEN
ELIZABETH WELCHMAN GDNS
Kingswood Ho Sch
STAMFORD GRN
KINGSTON ROAD

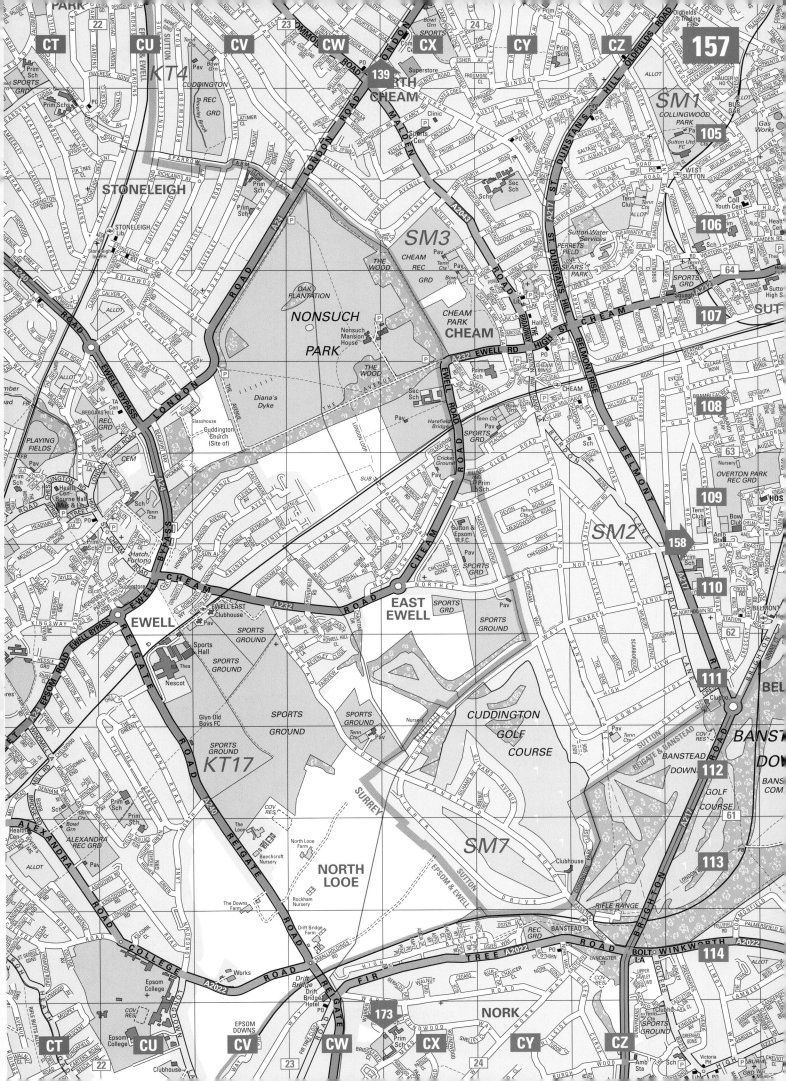
157
CT
CU
CV
CW
CX
CY
CZ
22
23
24
139
KT4
CUDDINGTON
REC GRD
STONELEIGH
NORTH CHEAM
SM1
COLLINGWOOD PARK
WEST SUTTON
105
106
107
108
109
110
111
112
113
114
SM3
CHEAM REC GRD
NONSUCH PARK
Nonsuch Mansion House
OAK PLANTATION
THE WOOD
Diana's Dyke
CHEAM PARK
CHEAM
SEARS PARK
PERRETS FIELD
Sutton Water Services
SM2
158
OVERTON PARK REC GRD
PLAYING FIELDS
EWELL BYPASS
LONDON ROAD
EWELL ROAD
CHEAM ROAD
BELMONT RISE
ST. DUNSTAN'S HILL
BELMONT LANE
HIGH ST
A24
A232
A217
A2043
A240
A2022
EAST EWELL
EWELL
Hatch Furlong
Cuddington Church (Site of)
Glasshouse
SPORTS GROUND
Nescot
Glyn Old Boys FC
KT17
REIGATE ROAD
SURREY
CUDDINGTON GOLF COURSE
SM7
EPSOM & EWELL
SUTTON
REIGATE & BANSTEAD
BANSTEAD DOWNS
GOLF COURSE
RIFLE RANGE
NORTH LOOE
North Looe Farm
Beechcroft Nursery
Rockham Nursery
The Downs Farm
Drift Bridge Farm
Drift Bridge Hotel
ALEXANDRA REC GRD
ALEXANDRA ROAD
COLLEGE ROAD
Epsom College
EPSOM DOWNS
NORK
FIR TREE ROAD
WINKWORTH ROAD
BRIGHTON ROAD
BOLTERS LA
BELMONT
173
61
62
63
64

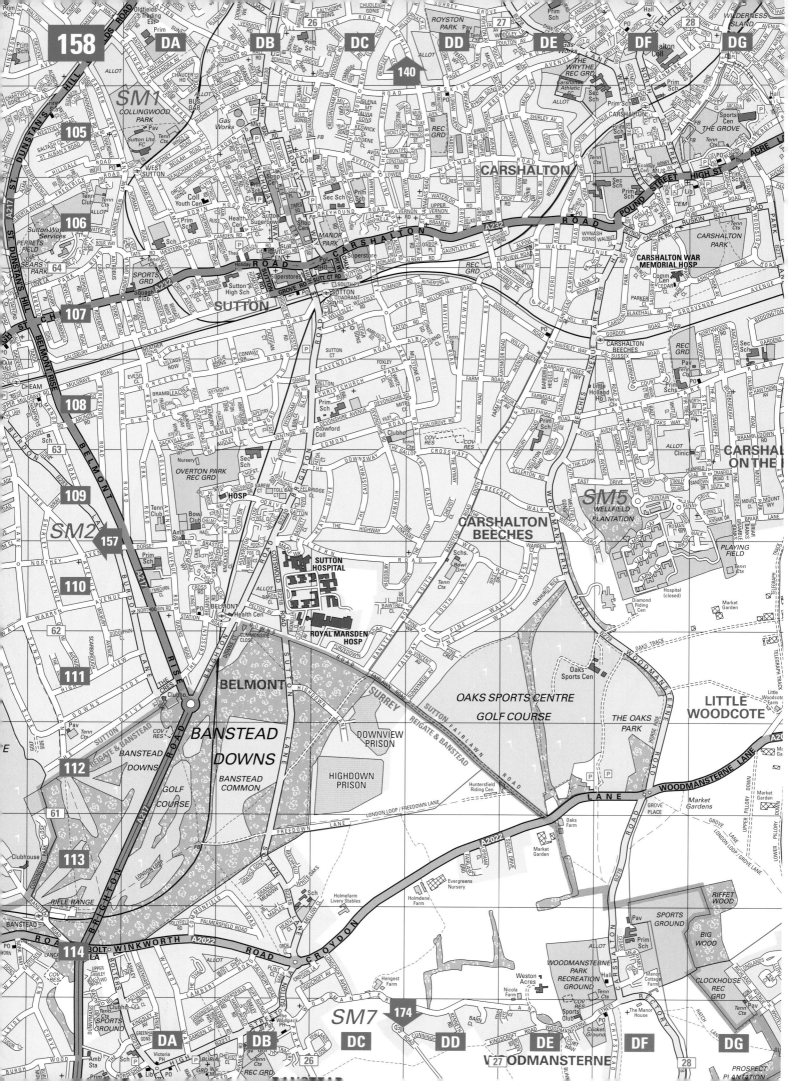

158
DA
DB
DC
DD
DE
DF
DG
140
157
174
SM1
SM2
SM5
SM7
COLLINGWOOD PARK
ROYSTON PARK
THE WRYTHE REC GRD
CARSHALTON
THE GROVE
CARSHALTON PARK
CARSHALTON WAR MEMORIAL HOSP
SUTTON
WEST SUTTON
CHEAM
SUTTON HOSPITAL
ROYAL MARSDEN HOSP
OVERTON PARK REC GRD
CARSHALTON BEECHES
CARSHALTON ON THE HILL
WELLFIELD PLANTATION
BELMONT
BANSTEAD DOWNS
BANSTEAD COMMON
GOLF COURSE
DOWNVIEW PRISON
HIGHDOWN PRISON
OAKS SPORTS CENTRE GOLF COURSE
THE OAKS PARK
LITTLE WOODCOTE
WOODMANSTERNE PARK RECREATION GROUND
SPORTS GROUND
BIG WOOD
RIFFET WOOD
CLOCKHOUSE REC GRD
WOODMANSTERNE
PROSPECT PLANTATION
BANSTEAD
ST. DUNSTAN'S HILL
BELMONT RISE
BRIGHTON ROAD
CARSHALTON ROAD
POUND STREET
HIGH ST
WOODMANSTERNE LANE
WINKWORTH ROAD
CROYDON LANE

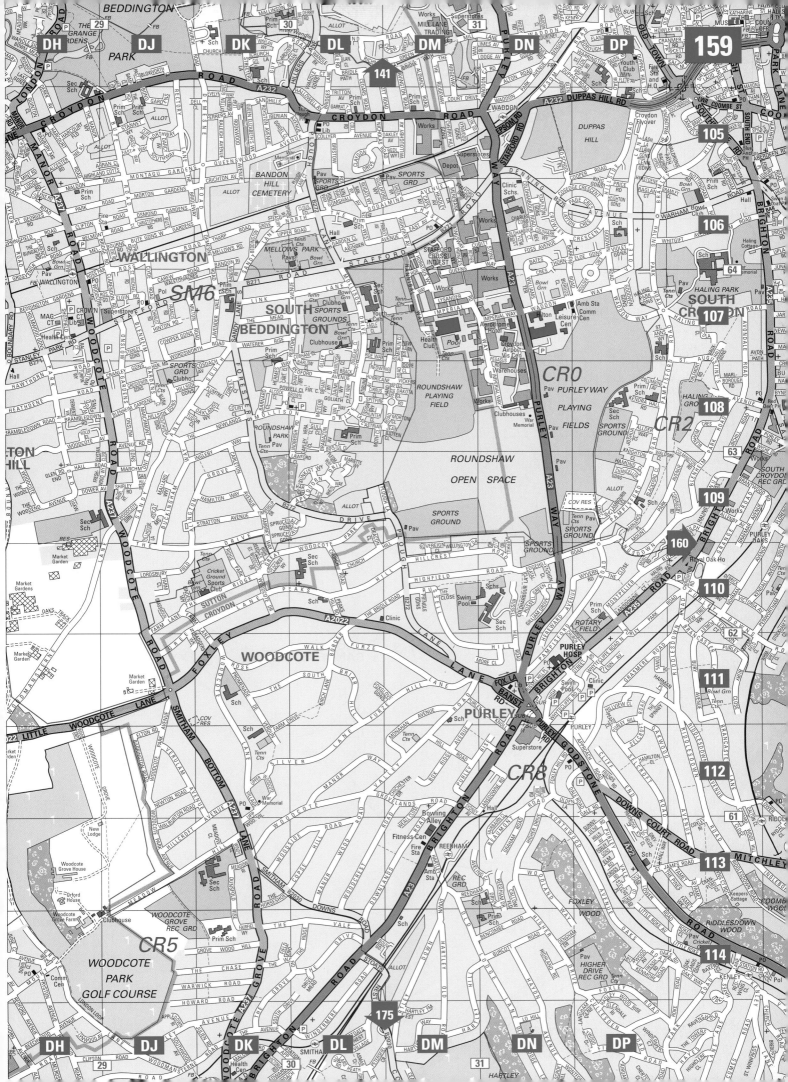
159
DH
DJ
DK
DL
DM
DN
DP
29
30
31
141
175
160
105
106
107
108
109
110
111
112
113
114
61
62
63
64
BEDDINGTON
BEDDINGTON PARK
THE GRANGE GARDENS
WALLINGTON
SM6
SOUTH BEDDINGTON
BANDON HILL CEMETERY
MELLOWS PARK
SOUTH BEDDINGTON SPORTS GROUNDS
DUPPAS HILL
STAFFORD CROSS IND EST
CR0
PURLEY WAY PLAYING FIELDS
ROUNDSHAW PLAYING FIELD
ROUNDSHAW PARK
ROUNDSHAW OPEN SPACE
SOUTH CROYDON
HALING PARK
CR2
SOUTH CROYDON REC GRD
PURLEY OAKS
WOODCOTE
PURLEY
PURLEY HOSP
CR8
REEDHAM
FOXLEY WOOD
RIDDLESDOWN WOOD
HIGHER DRIVE REC GRD
WOODCOTE GROVE REC GRD
CR5
WOODCOTE PARK GOLF COURSE
SMITHAM
KENLEY
HARTLEY
CROYDON ROAD
A232
DUPPAS HILL RD
PURLEY WAY
A23
STAFFORD ROAD
B271
WOODCOTE ROAD
A237
MANOR ROAD
LONDON ROAD
FOXLEY LANE
A2022
BRIGHTON ROAD
A235
GODSTONE ROAD
A22
DOWNS COURT ROAD
SMITHAM BOTTOM LANE
GROVE ROAD
LITTLE WOODCOTE LANE
PLOUGH LANE
B272
MOLLISON DRIVE
SANDY LANE SOUTH
FORESTERS DRIVE
CROYDON LANE
SUTTON

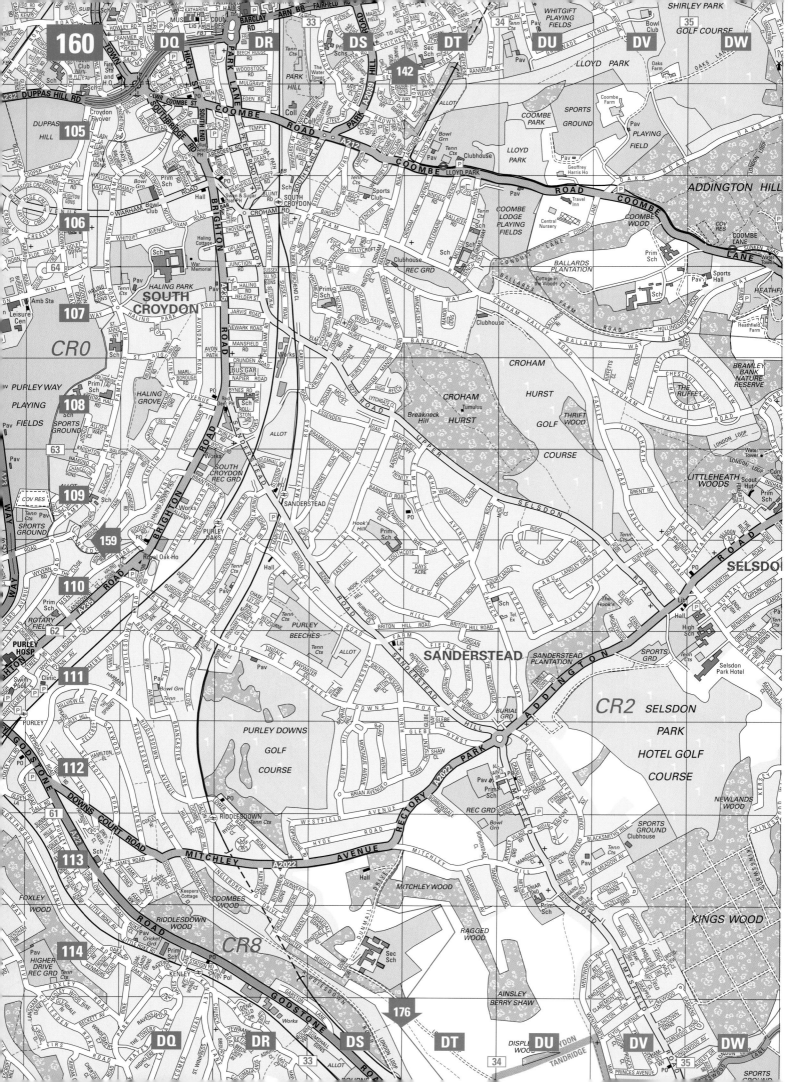

160
DQ
DR
DS
DT
DU
DV
DW
33
34
35
142
WHITGIFT PLAYING FIELDS
SHIRLEY PARK GOLF COURSE
LLOYD PARK
DUPPAS HILL RD
DUPPAS HILL
105
106
107
108
109
110
111
112
113
114
64
63
62
61
HIGH ST
PARK LANE
BARCLAY RD
COOMBE ROAD
A212
A2039
PARK HILL
Croydon Flyover
SOUTHBRIDGE RD
SOUTH END
BRIGHTON ROAD
A235
COOMBE PARK
SPORTS GROUND
PLAYING FIELD
ADDINGTON HILLS
COOMBE WOOD
COOMBE LANE
Travel Inn
Central Nursery
Geoffrey Harris Ho
LLOYD PARK
COOMBE LODGE PLAYING FIELDS
BALLARDS PLANTATION
Cottage in the Woods
BALLARDS WAY
CROHAM VALLEY ROAD
HEATHFIELD
Heathfield Farm
SOUTH CROYDON
HALING PARK
HALING GROVE
CR0
PURLEY WAY PLAYING FIELDS
SPORTS GROUND
COV RES
CROHAM HURST
CROHAM HURST GOLF COURSE
THRIFT WOOD
Breakneck Hill
Tumulus
BRAMLEY BANK NATURE RESERVE
THE RUFFETT
LITTLEHEATH WOODS
SOUTH CROYDON REC GRD
SANDERSTEAD
159
PURLEY OAKS
Royal Oak Ho
SELSDON ROAD
SELSDON
PURLEY BEECHES
SANDERSTEAD
SANDERSTEAD PLANTATION
ADDINGTON ROAD
Selsdon Park Hotel
CR2
SELSDON PARK HOTEL GOLF COURSE
PURLEY HOSP
PURLEY
PURLEY DOWNS GOLF COURSE
RECTORY PARK
A2022
MITCHLEY AVENUE
DOWNS COURT ROAD
GODSTONE ROAD
A22
RIDDLESDOWN
MITCHLEY WOOD
COOMBES WOOD
RIDDLESDOWN WOOD
CR8
FOXLEY WOOD
HIGHER DRIVE REC GRD
KENLEY
RAGGED WOOD
AINSLEY BERRY SHAW
NEWLANDS WOOD
KINGS WOOD
SPORTS GROUND
176
TANDRIDGE
LONDON LOOP

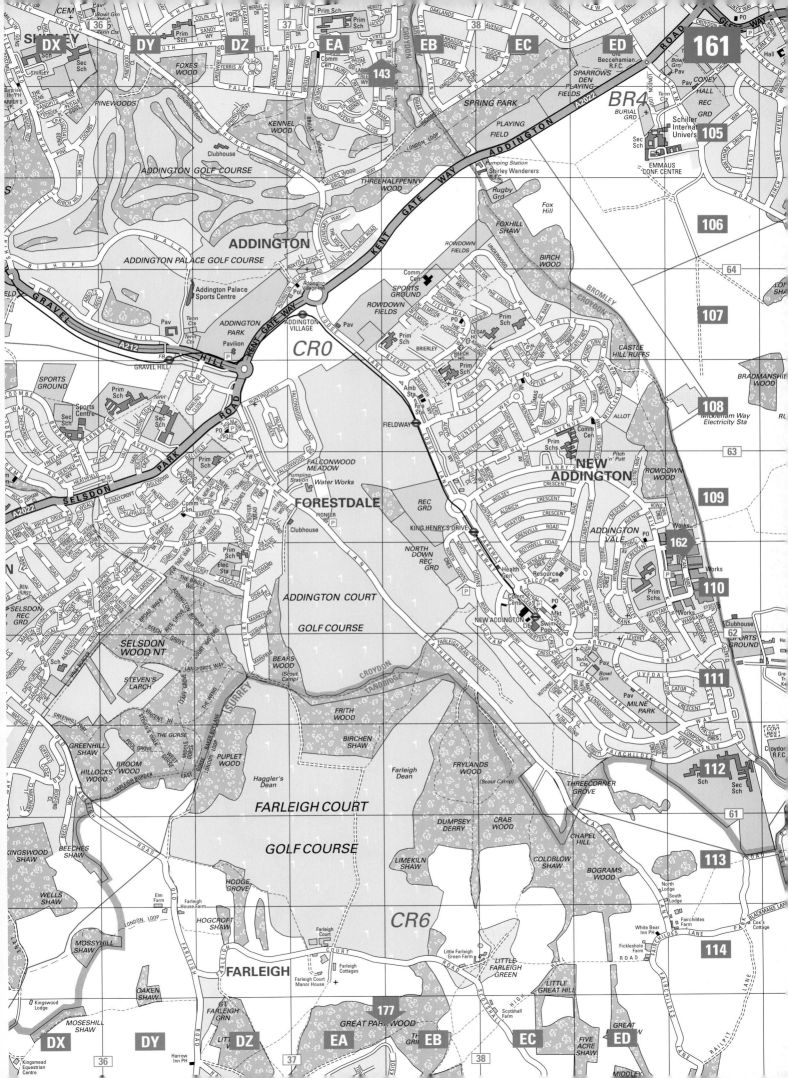
161
DX
DY
DZ
EA
EB
EC
ED
36
37
38
143
SHIRLEY
FOXES WOOD
PINEWOODS
KENNEL WOOD
Clubhouse
ADDINGTON GOLF COURSE
THREEHALFPENNY WOOD
SPRING PARK
PLAYING FIELD
SPARROWS DEN PLAYING FIELDS
Old Beccehamian R.F.C.
BR4
BURIAL GRD
Schiller Internat Univers
EMMAUS CONF. CENTRE
CONEY HALL REC GRD
105
106
107
108
109
110
111
112
113
114
64
63
62
61
A2022
ADDINGTON ROAD
KENT GATE WAY
Pumping Station
Shirley Wanderers R.F.C.
Rugby Grd
Fox Hill
FOXHILL SHAW
BIRCH WOOD
ROWDOWN FIELDS
ADDINGTON
ADDINGTON PALACE GOLF COURSE
BISHOPS WALK
GRAVEL HILL
A212
Addington Palace Sports Centre
Addington Village Inn
ADDINGTON VILLAGE
ADDINGTON PARK
Pavilion
CR0
GRAVEL HILL
SPORTS GROUND
Sports Centre
SELSDON PARK ROAD
SPORTS GROUND
Comm Cen
BROMLEY
CROYDON
CASTLE HILL RUFFS
BRADMANSHILL WOOD
Micklenam Way Electricity Sta
FIELDWAY
NEW ADDINGTON
ROWDOWN WOOD
Pitch 'n' Putt
FALCONWOOD MEADOW
Pumping Station
Water Works
FORESTDALE
REC GRD
KING HENRY'S DRIVE
NORTH DOWN REC GRD
ADDINGTON VALE
162
Clubhouse
Works
Health Cen
Resource Cen
NEW ADDINGTON
Mkt
Swim Pool
ADDINGTON COURT GOLF COURSE
SELSDON REC GRD
SELSDON WOOD NT
STEVEN'S LARCH
BEARS WOOD
(Scout Camp)
CROYDON
TANDRIDGE
SURREY
FRITH WOOD
BIRCHEN SHAW
MILNE PARK
Croydon R.F.C.
GREENHILL SHAW
BROOM WOOD
HILLOCKS WOOD
PUPLET WOOD
Haggler's Dean
Farleigh Dean
FRYLANDS WOOD
(Scout Camp)
THREECORNER GROVE
FARLEIGH COURT GOLF COURSE
DUMPSEY DERRY
CRAB WOOD
CHAPEL HILL
KINGSWOOD SHAW
BEECHES SHAW
LIMEKILN SHAW
COLDBLOW SHAW
BOGRAMS WOOD
WELLS SHAW
HODGE GROVE
Elm Farm
Farleigh House Farm
HOGCROFT SHAW
CR6
North Lodge
South Lodge
Fairchildes Farm
White Bear Inn PH
Fickleshole Farm
Cox's Cottage
MOSSYHILL SHAW
Farleigh Court
FARLEIGH
Farleigh Court Manor House
Farleigh Cottages
Little Farleigh Green Farm
LITTLE FARLEIGH GREEN
LITTLE GREAT HILL
OAKEN SHAW
Kingswood Lodge
MOSESHILL SHAW
GT FARLEIGH GRN
177
GREAT PARK WOOD
Scotshall Farm
FIVE ACRE SHAW
Harrow Inn PH
Kingsmead Equestrian Centre
MIDDLEY

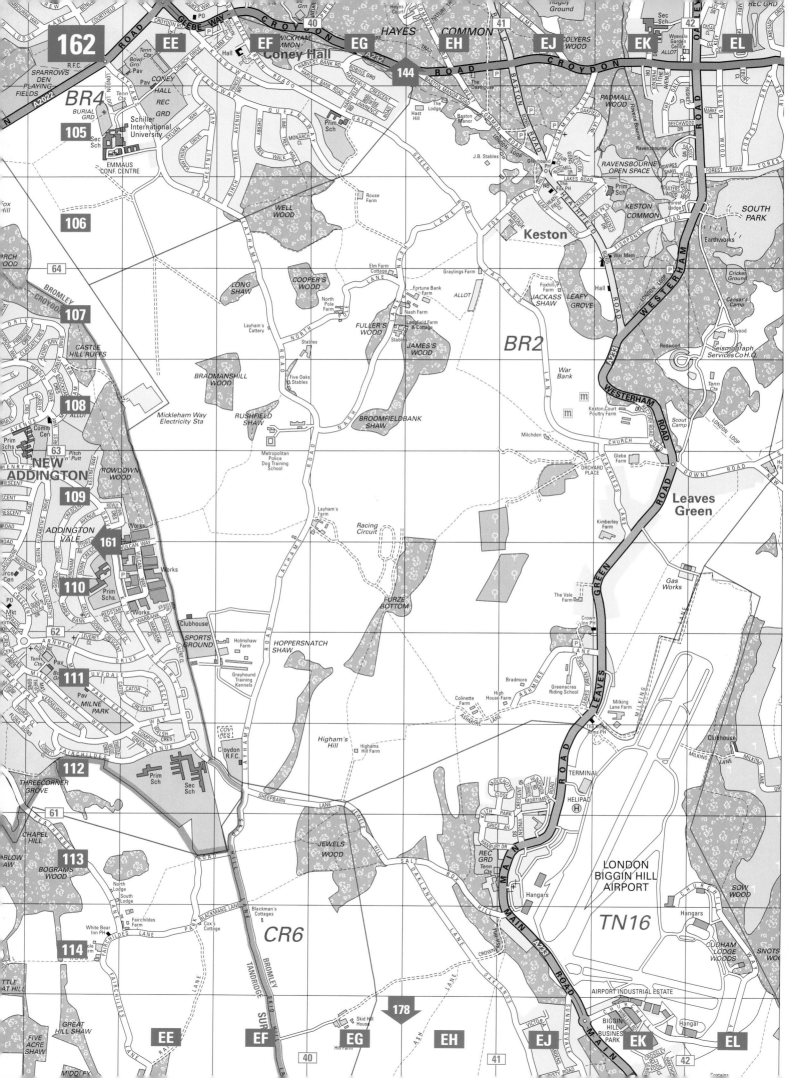
162
EE
EF
EG
EH
EJ
EK
EL
144
HAYES
COMMON
Coney Hall
WICKHAM COMMON
COLYERS WOOD
BR4
Schiller International University
EMMAUS CONF. CENTRE
SPARROWS DEN PLAYING FIELDS
CONEY HALL REC GRD
105
106
107
108
109
110
111
112
113
114
161
178
64
63
62
61
40
41
42
PADMALL WOOD
RAVENSBOURNE OPEN SPACE
KESTON COMMON
SOUTH PARK
Keston
WELL WOOD
COOPER'S WOOD
LONG SHAW
FULLER'S WOOD
JAMES'S WOOD
JACKASS SHAW
LEAFY GROVE
BR2
CASTLE HILL RUFFS
BRADMANSHILL WOOD
RUSHFIELD SHAW
BROOMFIELDBANK SHAW
Mickleham Way Electricity Sta
NEW ADDINGTON
ROWDOWN WOOD
ADDINGTON VALE
Leaves Green
Racing Circuit
FURZE BOTTOM
Gas Works
SPORTS GROUND
HOPPERSNATCH SHAW
MILNE PARK
Higham's Hill
Croydon R.F.C.
THREECORNER GROVE
CHAPEL HILL
BOGRAMS WOOD
JEWELS WOOD
LONDON BIGGIN HILL AIRPORT
TERMINAL
HELIPAD
SOW WOOD
TN16
CUDHAM LODGE WOODS
CR6
AIRPORT INDUSTRIAL ESTATE
BIGGIN HILL BUSINESS PARK
GREAT HILL SHAW
FIVE ACRE SHAW
CROYDON ROAD
WESTERHAM ROAD
LAYHAMS ROAD
NASH LANE
JACKASS LANE
LEAVES GREEN ROAD
MAIN ROAD
A233
A232
A2022
SHEEPBARN LANE
SALT BOX HILL
SKID HILL LANE
FAIRCHILDES LANE
TANDRIDGE
BROMLEY
SURREY

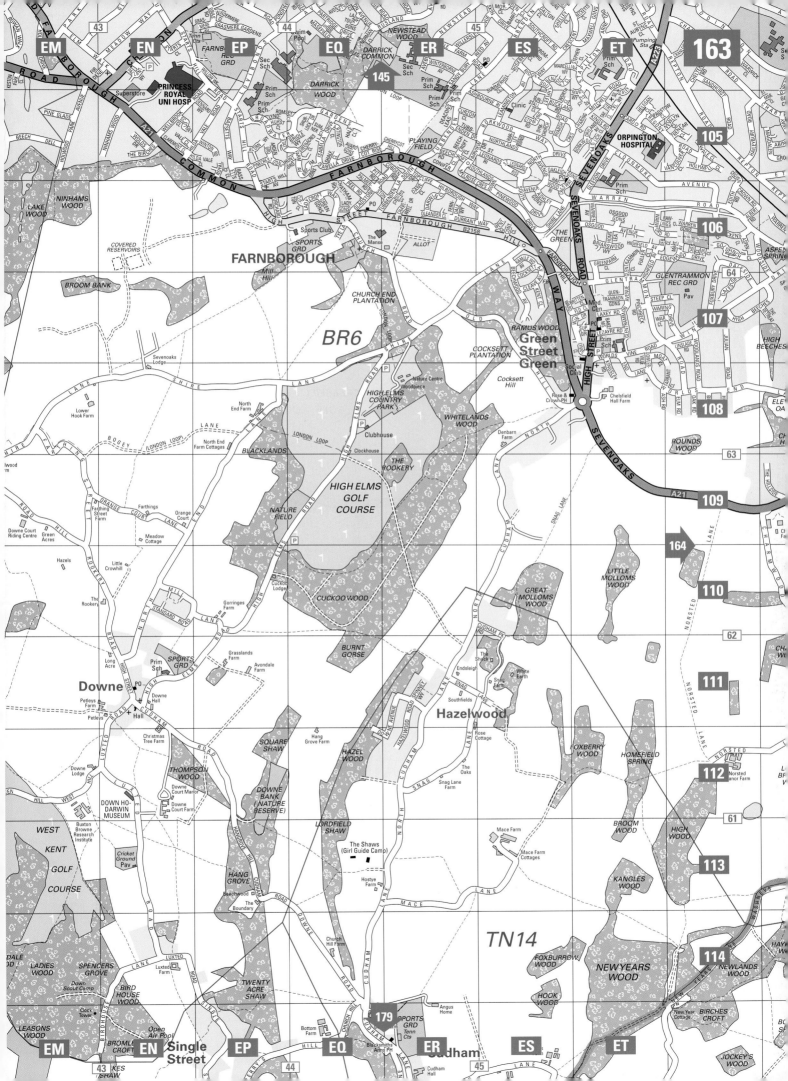

163
FARNBOROUGH
BR6
Green Street Green
Downe
Hazelwood
TN14
Cudham
Single Street
HIGH ELMS GOLF COURSE
HIGH ELMS COUNTRY PARK
PRINCESS ROYAL UNI HOSP
ORPINGTON HOSPITAL
DOWN HO DARWIN MUSEUM
WEST KENT GOLF COURSE
NEW YEARS WOOD
CUCKOO WOOD
145
164
179

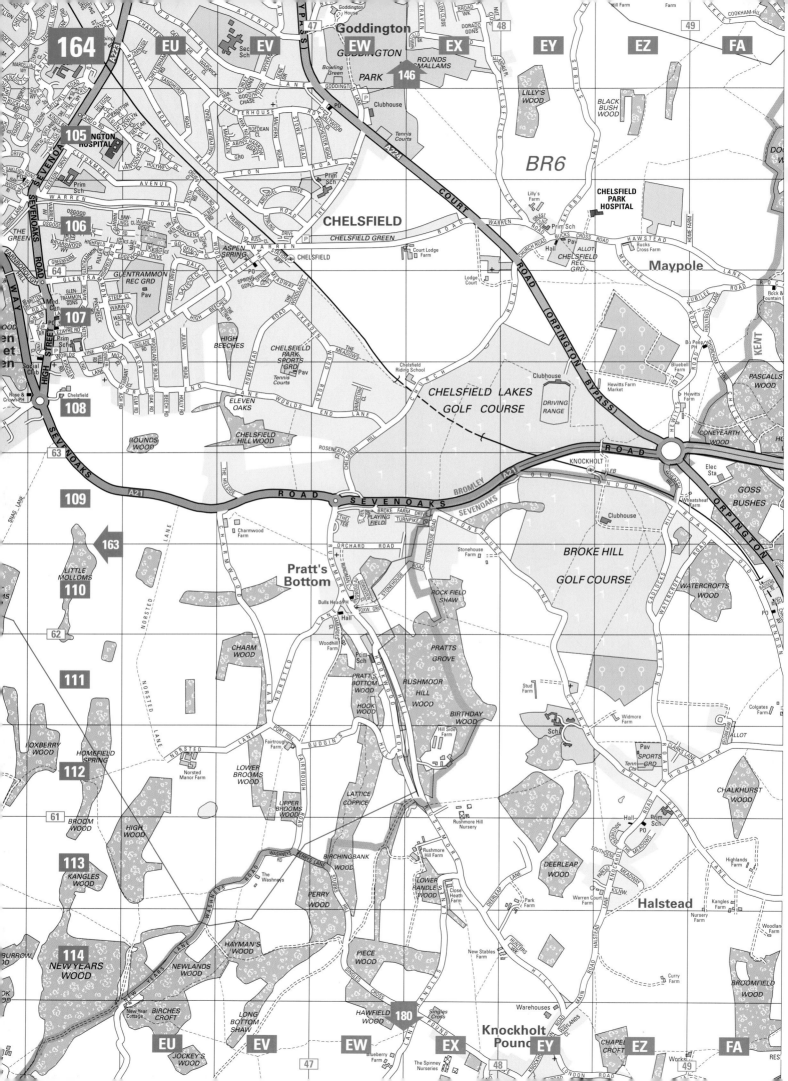
Goddington
GODDINGTON PARK
ROUNDS SMALLAMS
146
CHELSFIELD
CHELSFIELD GREEN
BR6
CHELSFIELD PARK HOSPITAL
Maypole
CHELSFIELD LAKES GOLF COURSE
DRIVING RANGE
HIGH BEECHES
CHELSFIELD PARK SPORTS GRD
ELEVEN OAKS
CHELSFIELD HILL WOOD
ROUNDS WOOD
GLENTRAMMON REC GRD
ASPEN SPRING
LILLY'S WOOD
BLACK BUSH WOOD
PASCALLS WOOD
CONEYEARTH WOOD
GOSS BUSHES
KNOCKHOLT
SEVENOAKS ROAD
A21
A224
COURT ROAD (ORPINGTON BYPASS)
BROKE HILL GOLF COURSE
WATERCROFTS WOOD
Pratt's Bottom
163
LITTLE MOLLOMS
ROCK FIELD SHAW
CHARM WOOD
PRATTS GROVE
RUSHMOOR HILL WOOD
BIRTHDAY WOOD
PRATT'S BOTTOM WOOD
HOOK WOOD
FOXBERRY WOOD
HOMEFIELD SPRING
LOWER BROOMS WOOD
UPPER BROOMS WOOD
LATTICE COPPICE
BROOM WOOD
HIGH WOOD
CHALKHURST WOOD
BIRCHINGBANK WOOD
KANGLES WOOD
PERRY WOOD
LOWER RANDLE'S WOOD
DEERLEAP WOOD
Halstead
HAYMAN'S WOOD
NEWLANDS WOOD
NEW YEARS WOOD
PIECE WOOD
BROOMFIELD WOOD
BIRCHES CROFT
LONG BOTTOM SHAW
HAWFIELD WOOD
180
Knockholt Pound
CHAPEL CROFT
JOCKEY'S WOOD
EU
EV
EW
EX
EY
EZ
FA
47
48
49
63
62
61
64
105
106
107
108
109
110
111
112
113
114

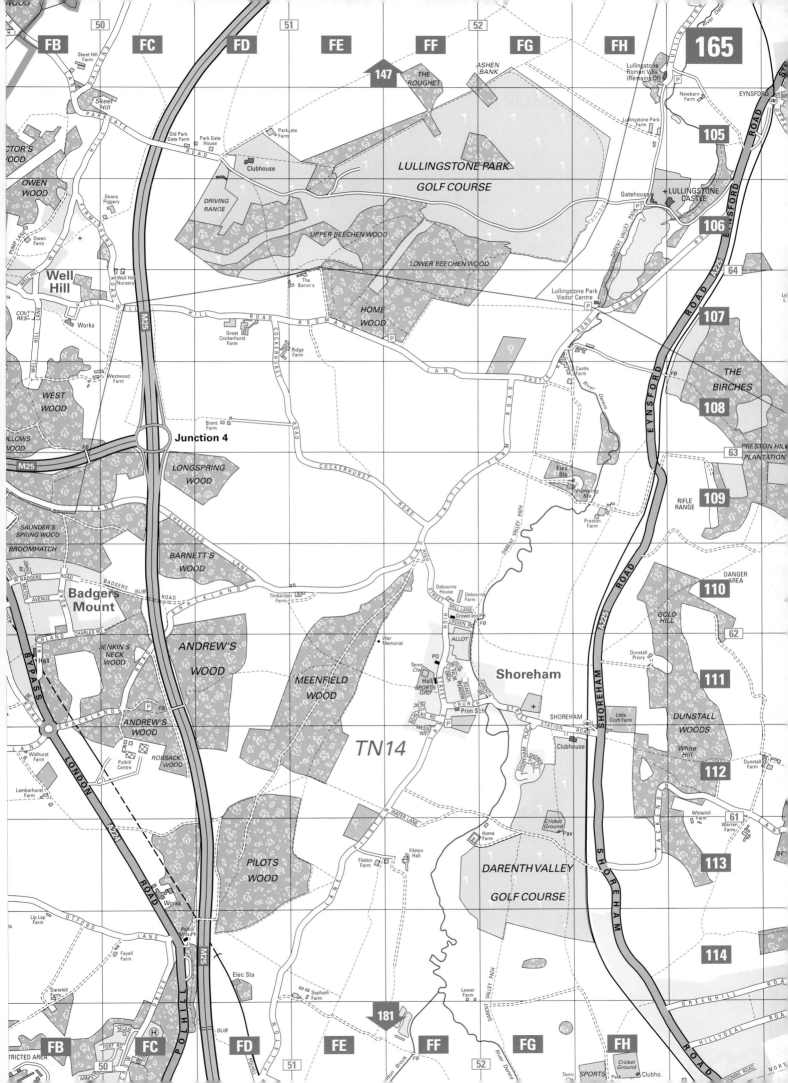
165
FB
FC
FD
FE
FF
FG
FH
50
51
52
147
181
THE ROUGHET
ASHEN BANK
Lullingstone Roman Villa (Remains Of)
Newbarn Farm
EYNSFORD
Lullingstone Park Farm
LULLINGSTONE PARK GOLF COURSE
Clubhouse
DRIVING RANGE
UPPER BEECHEN WOOD
LOWER BEECHEN WOOD
Gatehouse
LULLINGSTONE CASTLE
DARENT VALLEY PATH
Lullingstone Park Visitor Centre
Skeet Hill Farm
Skeet Hill
PARKGATE ROAD
Old Park Gate Farm
Park Gate House
Parkgate Farm
OWEN WOOD
Deans Piggery
Owen Farm
PUMP LANE
Well Hill
Well Hill Nursery
WELL HILL
Works
HOME WOOD
The Baron's
REDMANS LANE
Great Cockerhurst Farm
Ridge Farm
COCKERHURST ROAD
Westwood Farm
WEST WOOD
Castle Farm
River Darent
CASTLE ROAD
THE BIRCHES
Brent Farm
Junction 4
M25
LONGSPRING WOOD
Elec Sta
Pumping Sta
PRESTON HILL PLANTATION
RIFLE RANGE
Preston Farm
SAUNDER'S SPRING WOOD
BROOMHATCH
CHELSFIELD LANE
BARNETT'S WOOD
BADGERS ROAD
BADGERS SUB ROAD
Badgers Mount
SHACKLANDS ROAD
Timberden Farm
Oxbourne House
Oxbourne Farm
MILL LANE
Crown Inn PH
CROWN RD
ALLOT
DANGER AREA
GOLD HILL
HIGH STREET
HIGHLAND
CHARLES RD
JENKIN'S NECK WOOD
ANDREW'S WOOD
MEENFIELD WOOD
War Memorial
PO
Hall
SPORTS GRD
Shoreham
Dunstall Priory
CHURCH STREET
Prim Sch
SHOREHAM
STATION ROAD
Little Croft Farm
DUNSTALL WOODS
White Hill
BYPASS
LONDON ROAD
A224
Widhurst Farm
Polhill Centre
ROBSACK WOOD
TN14
Clubhouse
SHOREHAM PLACE
Dunstall Farm
Lamberhurst Farm
WATER LANE
FILSTON LANE
Cricket Ground
Pav
Home Farm
Whitehill Farm
Warren Farm
FACKENDEN LANE
PILOTS WOOD
Filston Farm
Filston Hall
DARENTH VALLEY GOLF COURSE
Works
Lip Lap Farm
OTFORD LANE
Polhill Arms PH
Fayell Farm
Elec Sta
Danehill Farm
Sepham Farm
Lower Farm
GREENHILL ROAD
HILLYDEAL ROAD
POLHILL
SHOREHAM ROAD
EYNSFORD ROAD
A225
64
63
62
61
105
106
107
108
109
110
111
112
113
114
FB

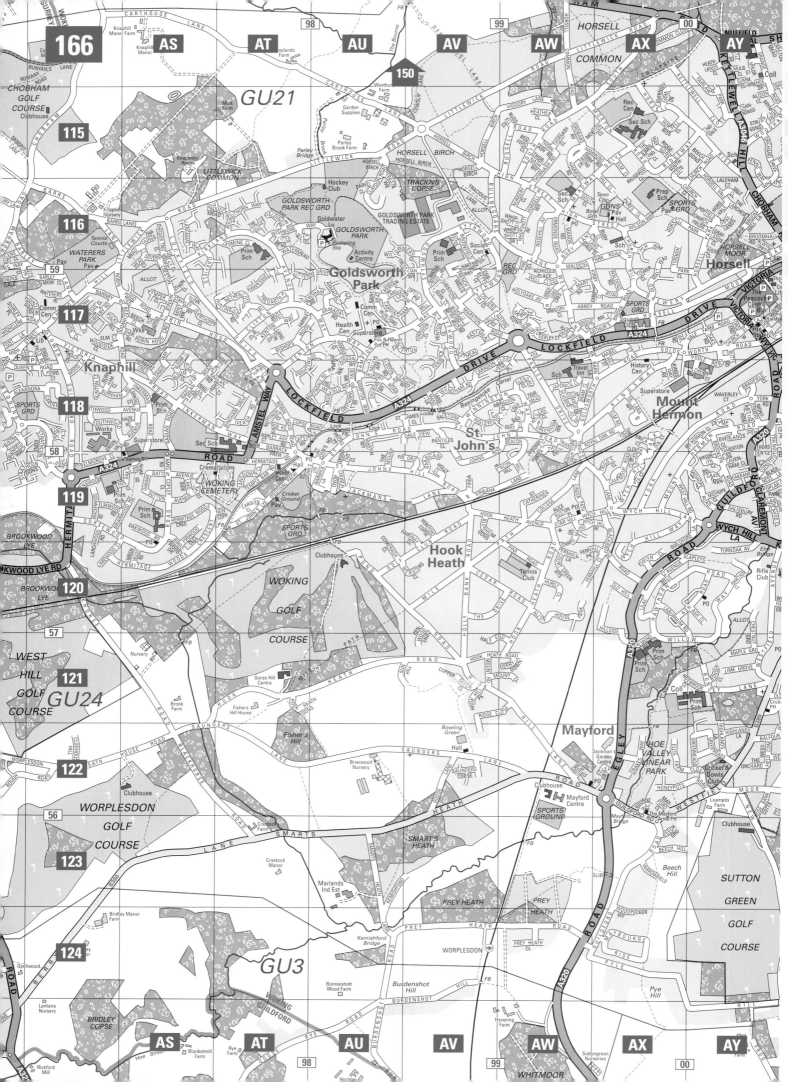

AS
AT
AU
AV
AW
AX
AY
98
99
00
150
GU21
GU24
GU3
115
116
117
118
119
120
121
122
123
124
59
58
57
56
CHOBHAM GOLF COURSE
Clubhouse
HORSELL COMMON
LITTLEWICK COMMON
Knaphill Manor Farm
Knaphill Manor
Haylands Farm
Westbury Farm
Garden Supplies
Mink Farm
Parley Brook Farm
Parley Bridge
Knapwood House
Knaphill Nursery
Tennis Courts
WATERERS PARK
Horsell
HORSELL BIRCH
HORSELL MOOR
TRACIOVS COPSE
GOLDSWORTH PARK REC GRD
GOLDSWORTH PARK TRADING ESTATE
Hockey Club
Goldwater Lo
GOLDSWORTH PARK
Pumping Sta
Activity Centre
Goldsworth Park
Health Cen
Superstore
Fox & Flower Pot PH
Knaphill
Mount Hermon
St. John's
Hook Heath
Mayford
Travel Inn
History Cen
The Peacocks Centre
LOCKFIELD DRIVE
A324
A320
A3046
Basingstoke Canal
WOKING CEMETERY
Crematorium
The Surrey BH
Cricket Ground
SPORTS GRD
BROOKWOOD LYE
WOKING GOLF COURSE
Clubhouse
Gorse Hill Centre
WEST HILL GOLF COURSE
Brook Farm
Fishers Hill House
Fisher's Hill
Bowling Green
Hall
Tennis Club
Briarwood Nursery
SAUNDERS COPSE
Jackman's Garden Centre
Mayford Centre
SPORTS GROUND
HOE VALLEY LINEAR PARK
Cricket & Bowls Club
Loampits Farm
The Mayford Arms PH
Mayford Bridge
WORPLESDON GOLF COURSE
Crastock Farm
Crastock Manor
SMART'S HEATH
Marlands Ind Est
PREY HEATH
Beech Hill
SUTTON GREEN GOLF COURSE
Bridley Manor Farm
Kemishford Bridge
WORPLESDON
Bonnieshott Wood Farm
Burdenshot Hill
Pye Hill
Havering Farm
Openwood
Lantana Nursery
BRIDLEY COPSE
Blanketmill Farm
Rye Farm
Rickford Mill
Hoe Stream
WOKING GUILDFORD
Suttongreen Nurseries
WHITMOOR
Rifle Club
Elm Bridge

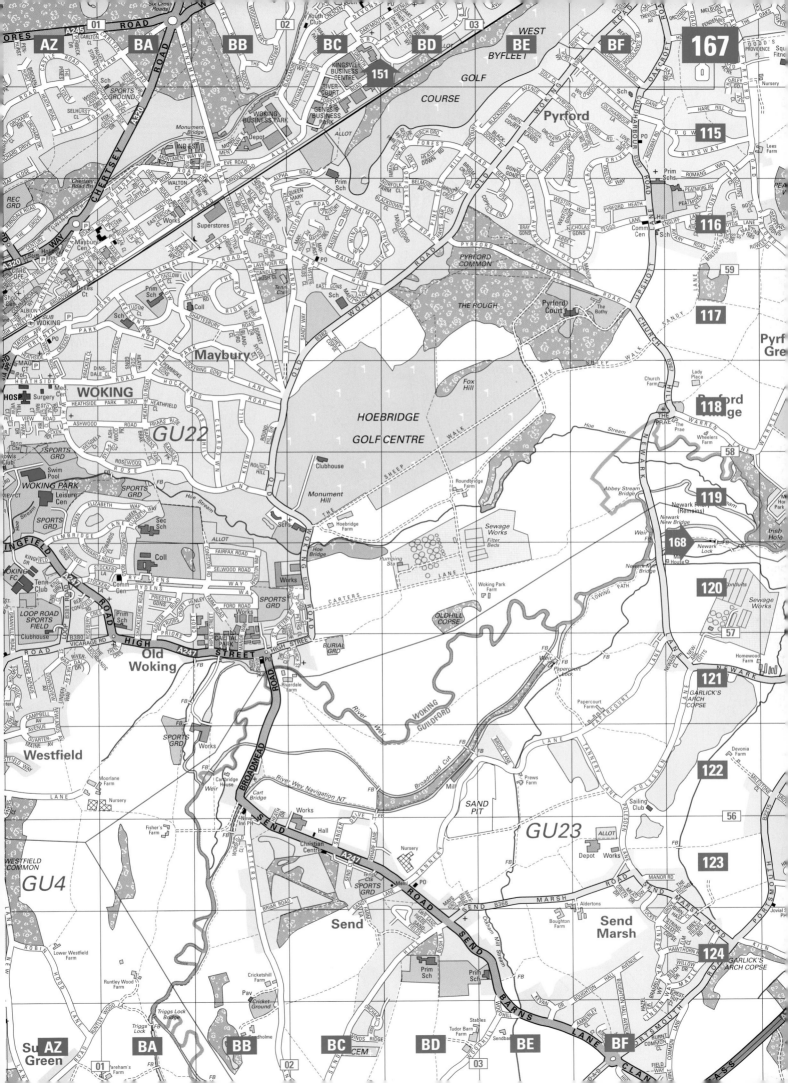

167
151
168
AZ
BA
BB
BC
BD
BE
BF
01
02
03
WEST BYFLEET
GOLF COURSE
Pyrford
WOKING
Maybury
GU22
HOEBRIDGE GOLF CENTRE
PYRFORD COMMON
THE ROUGH
Pyrford Court
WOKING PARK
Old Woking
Westfield
WESTFIELD COMMON
GU4
GU23
Send
Send Marsh
Sewage Works
Newark Priory (Remains)
River Wey
Broadmead Cut
River Wey Navigation NT
OLDHILL COPSE
SAND PIT
GARLICK'S ARCH COPSE
115
116
117
118
119
120
121
122
123
124
59
58
57
56

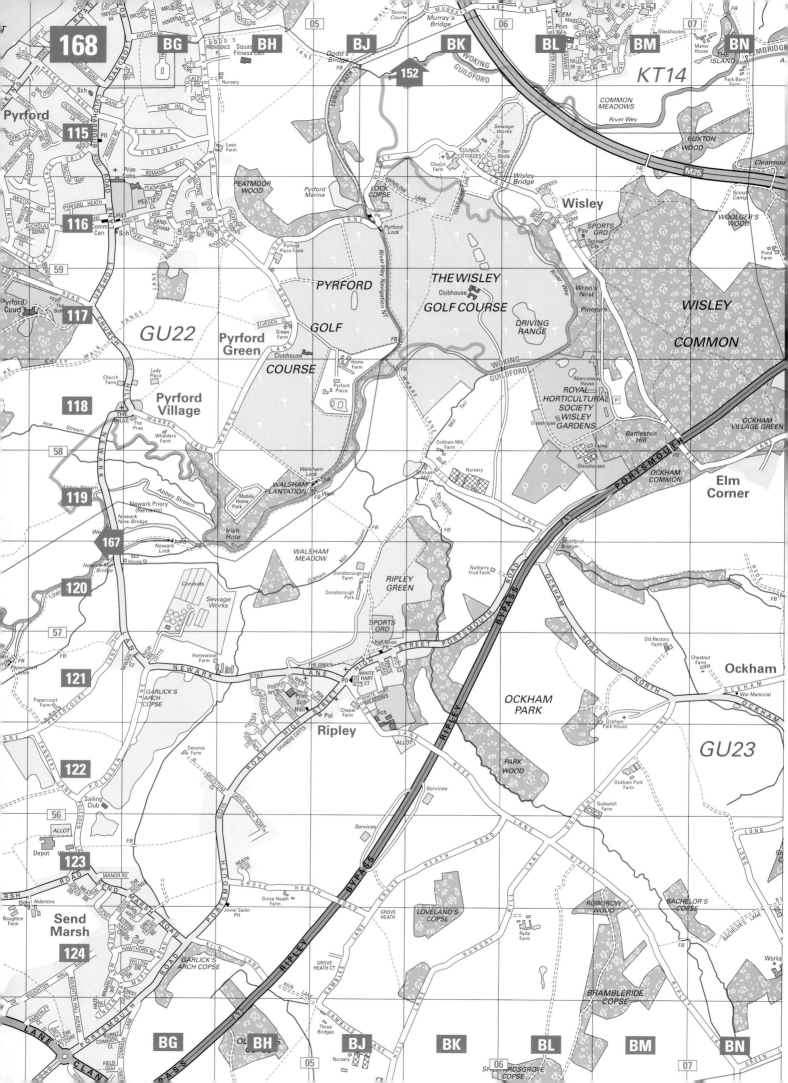
BG
BH
BJ
BK
BL
BM
BN
05
06
07
152
167
59
58
57
56
115
116
117
118
119
120
121
122
123
124
KT14
GU22
GU23
Pyrford
Pyrford Green
Pyrford Village
Pyrford Court
Wisley
Elm Corner
Ockham
Ripley
Send Marsh
Dodd's Bridge
Murray's Bridge
Wisley Bridge
Newark New Bridge
Newark Mill Bridge
Stratford Bridge
Three Bridges
Squash Fitness Cen
Nursery
Lees Farm
Prim Schs
Hall
Comm Cen
Sch
PO
Pyrford Marina
Pyrford Lock
The Anchor PH
LOCK COPSE
PEATMOOR WOOD
Pyrford Place Farm
PYRFORD GOLF COURSE
Green Farm
Clubhouse
Home Farm
Pyrford Place
THE WISLEY GOLF COURSE
DRIVING RANGE
Church Farm
Lady Place
The Prae
Wheelers Farm
Hoe Stream
Abbey Stream
Newark Priory (Remains)
Newark Lock
Mill House
Walsham Lock
WALSHAM PLANTATION
Weir
Mobile Home Park
Irish Hole
WALSHAM MEADOW
Ockham Mill Stream
Dunsborough Farm
Dunsborough Park
RIPLEY GREEN
SPORTS GRD
Half Moon PH
Conduits
Sewage Works
Homewood Farm
GARLICK'S ARCH COPSE
Papercourt Farm
Papercourt Lock
Devonia Farm
Sailing Club
ALLOT
Depot
Aldertons
Boughton Farm
Grove Heath Farm
Jovial Sailor PH
GROVE HEATH
GROVE HEATH CT
LOVELAND'S COPSE
Services
Ryde Farm
ROBOROW WOOD
BRAMBLERIDE COPSE
BACHELOR'S COPSE
SHEPHERDSGROVE COPSE
OCKHAM PARK
Ockham Park House
Ockham Park Farm
PARK WOOD
Guileshill Farm
Old Rectory Farm
Chestnut Farm
War Memorial
Nutberry Fruit Farm
Ockham Mill Farm
Ockham Mill
ROYAL HORTICULTURAL SOCIETY WISLEY GARDENS
Aberconway House
Glasshouses
Battleston Hill
OCKHAM COMMON
OCKHAM VILLAGE GREEN
WISLEY COMMON
Wren's Nest
Pinetum
SPORTS GRD
Pav
Tennis Cts
WOOLGER'S WOOD
Scout Camp
Pond Farm
BUXTON WOOD
COMMON MEADOWS
River Wey
River Wey Navigation NT
Sewage Works
Filter Beds
COUNCIL COTTAGES
Church Farm
Manor House
THE ISLAND
Park Barn Farm
Tennis Courts
WOKING
GUILDFORD
M25
A3
PORTSMOUTH ROAD
RIPLEY BYPASS
B367
B2215
B2039
NEWARK LANE
HIGH STREET
ROSE LANE
OCKHAM ROAD NORTH
OCKHAM LANE
GUILESHILL LANE
RIPLEY LANE
HUNGRY HILL LANE
GROVE HEATH ROAD
GROVE HEATH NORTH
KILN LANE
GAMBLES LANE
POLESDEN LANE
PAPERCOURT LANE
TANNERY LANE
SEND MARSH ROAD
BOUGHTON HALL AVENUE
CHURCH HILL
UPSHOTT LANE
COLDHARBOUR ROAD
PYRFORD ROAD
WARREN LANE
SANDY LANE
SHEEP WALK
WISLEY LANE
TOWNSLOW LANE
WHARF LANE
MILL LANE
HOLLYBUSH LANE
LONG LANE
ELM LANE
HYDE LANE
BACHELOR'S LANE
CLANDON

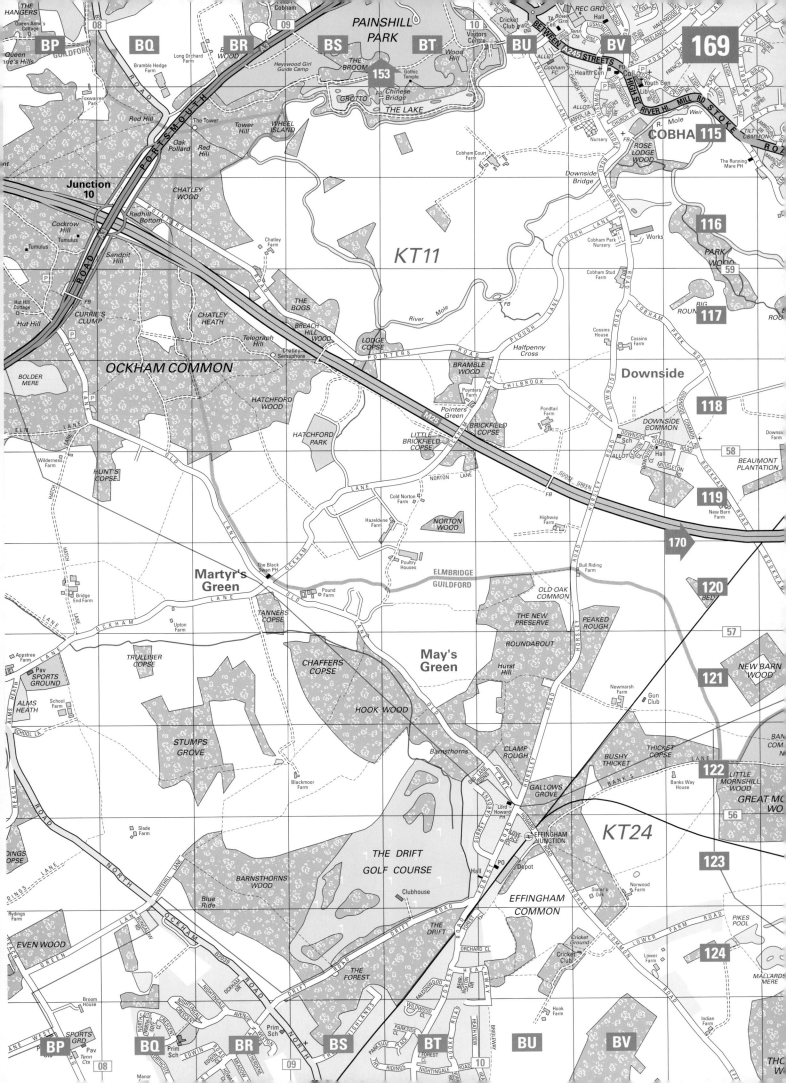
169
BP
BQ
BR
BS
BT
BU
BV
08
09
10
PAINSHILL PARK
153
Junction 10
PORTSMOUTH ROAD
CHATLEY WOOD
CHATLEY HEATH
OCKHAM COMMON
BOLDER MERE
HATCHFORD WOOD
HATCHFORD PARK
KT11
River Mole
LODGE COPSE
POINTERS ROAD
BRAMBLE WOOD
Downside
DOWNSIDE COMMON
COBHAM
115
116
117
118
119
120
121
122
123
124
170
59
58
57
56
M25
NORTON WOOD
Martyr's Green
ELMBRIDGE
GUILDFORD
OLD OAK COMMON
THE NEW PRESERVE
May's Green
CHAFFERS COPSE
HOOK WOOD
STUMPS GROVE
TRULLIBER COPSE
ALMS HEATH
THE DRIFT GOLF COURSE
BARNSTHORNS WOOD
EFFINGHAM JUNCTION
EFFINGHAM COMMON
KT24
EVEN WOOD
THE FOREST
NEW BARN WOOD
BEAUMONT PLANTATION
ROUNDABOUT
PEAKED ROUGH
CLAMP ROUGH
GALLOWS GROVE
BUSHY THICKET
THICKET COPSE
LITTLE MORNSHILL WOOD
PIKES POOL
MALLARDS MERE

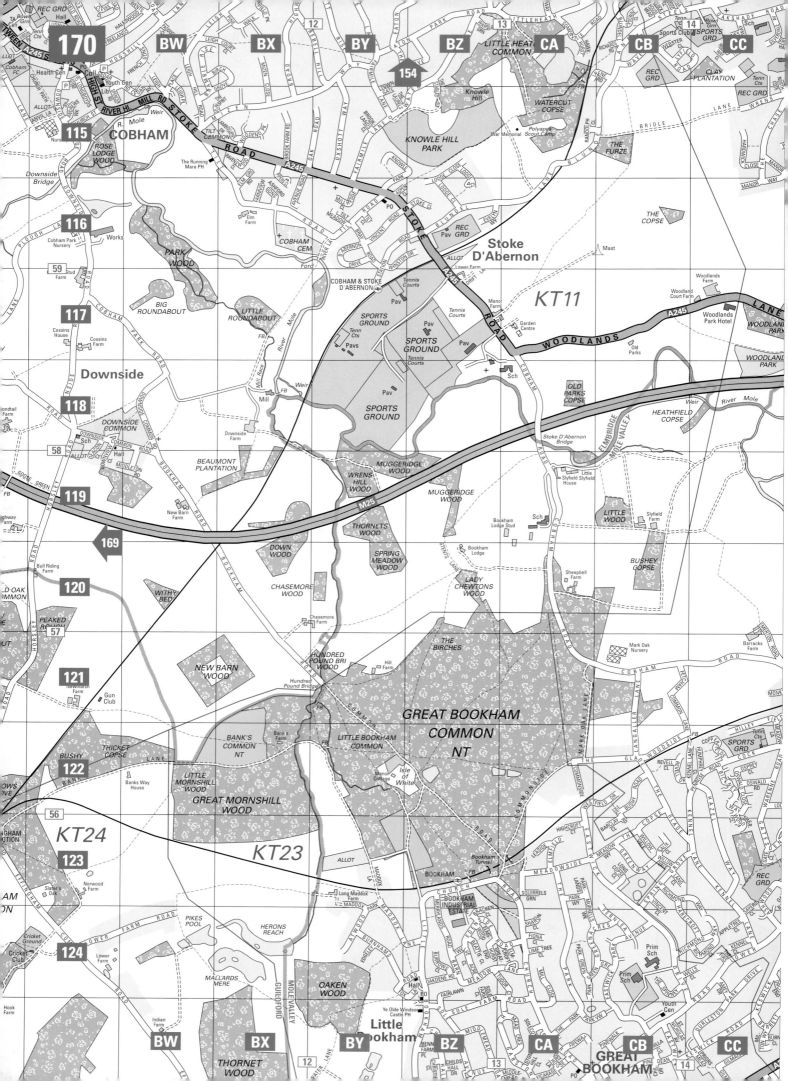

170
BW
BX
BY
BZ
CA
CB
CC
154
169
COBHAM
Stoke D'Abernon
Downside
Little Bookham
GREAT BOOKHAM
KT11
KT23
KT24
KNOWLE HILL PARK
LITTLE HEATH COMMON
WATERCUT COPSE
THE FURZE
THE COPSE
ROSE LODGE WOOD
PARK WOOD
BIG ROUNDABOUT
LITTLE ROUNDABOUT
COBHAM CEM
SPORTS GROUND
DOWNSIDE COMMON
BEAUMONT PLANTATION
MUGGERIDGE WOOD
WRENS HILL WOOD
THORNETS WOOD
SPRING MEADOW WOOD
DOWN WOOD
CHASEMORE WOOD
LADY CHEWTONS WOOD
OLD PARKS COPSE
HEATHFIELD COPSE
LITTLE WOOD
BUSHEY COPSE
WOODLANDS PARK
Woodlands Park Hotel
WITHY BED
PEAKED ROUGH
NEW BARN WOOD
HUNDRED POUND BRI WOOD
THE BIRCHES
GREAT BOOKHAM COMMON NT
LITTLE BOOKHAM COMMON
BANK'S COMMON NT
THICKET COPSE
BUSHY
LITTLE MORNSHILL WOOD
GREAT MORNSHILL WOOD
Isle of White
BOOKHAM INDUSTRIAL ESTATE
HERONS REACH
PIKES POOL
MALLARDS MERE
OAKEN WOOD
THORNET WOOD
River Mole
M25
A245
STOKE ROAD
WOODLANDS LANE
COBHAM ROAD
BOOKHAM ROAD
CHURCH ROAD
Cobham & Stoke D'Abernon
Bookham
The Running Mare PH
Ye Olde Windsor Castle PH
Mark Oak Nursery
Bookham Tunnel

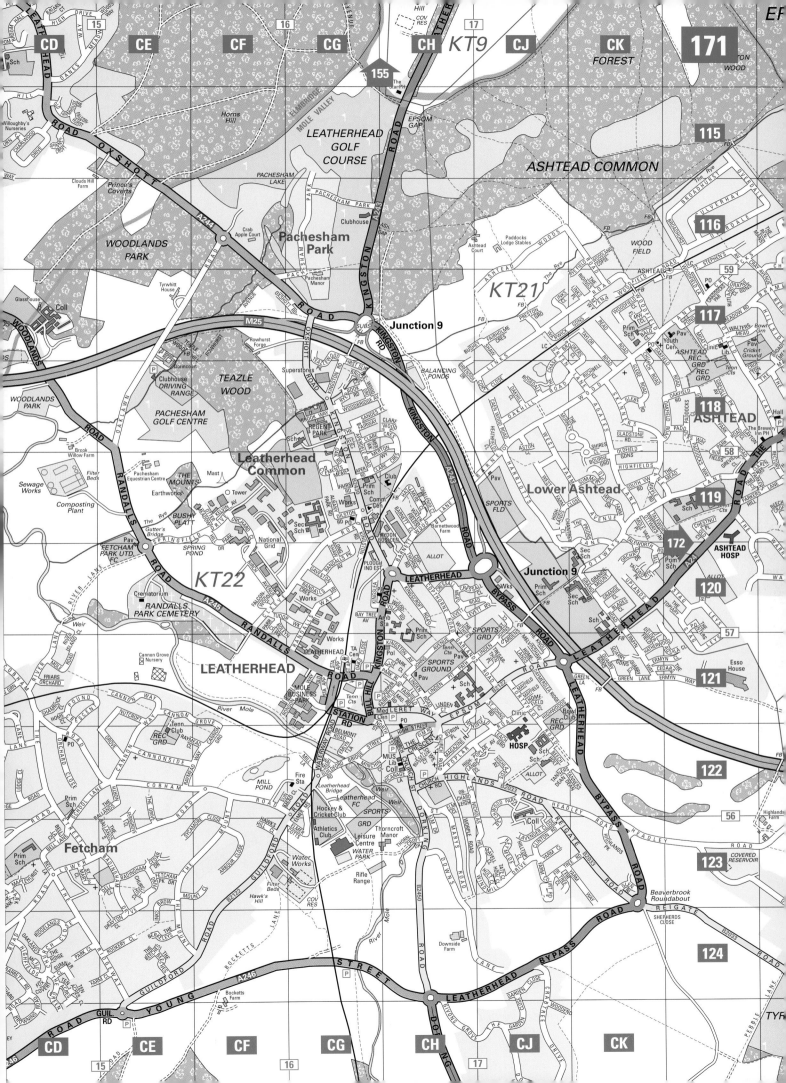
171
155
172
LEATHERHEAD GOLF COURSE
ASHTEAD COMMON
Pachesham Park
WOODLANDS PARK
TEAZLE WOOD
PACHESHAM GOLF CENTRE
Leatherhead Common
Lower Ashtead
ASHTEAD
LEATHERHEAD
Fetcham
KT9
KT21
KT22
Junction 9
RANDALLS PARK CEMETERY
ASHTEAD HOSP
Beaverbrook Roundabout
LEATHERHEAD BYPASS ROAD
OXSHOTT ROAD
KINGSTON ROAD
RANDALLS ROAD
YOUNG STREET
REIGATE ROAD
EPSOM ROAD
HEADLEY ROAD
GUILDFORD ROAD
COBHAM ROAD
M25
A24
A243
A244
A245
A246
B2033
B2122
B2430
B2450

172
EPSOM COMMON
CL
CM
CN
CP
CQ
CR
CS
156
NEWTON WOOD
EPSOM
EPSOM GENERAL HOSP
ASHTEAD COMMON
115
116
117
118
119
120
121
122
123
124
WOOD FIELD
ASHTEAD
Ashtead Park
ASHTEAD PARK
ASHTEAD HOSP
City of London Freemen's School
Woodcote
WOODCOTE GREEN
WOODCOTE PARK GOLF COURSE
Woodcote Park Country Club
HALFMOON CLUMP
WORLDS END
THE GROVE
KT21
KT18
KT22
Langley Vale
THE WARREN
LANGLEY BOTTOM WOOD
EPSOM & EWELL
MOLE VALLEY
ADDLESTEAD WOOD
LITTLE HURST WOOD
HEADLEY COURT
HAMBLETON WOOD
Tyrrell's Wood
TYRRELL'S WOOD
HOOK WOOD
GREAT HURST WOOD
PIGNUT WOOD
OYSTER HILL NT
NOWER WOOD
182
TYRRELL'S WOOD GOLF COURSE
COSTAL WOOD
Headley
Beaverbrook Roundabout
LEATHERHEAD BYPASS ROAD
M25
DORKING ROAD
A24
171
Esso House
Chase Farm Stud
Highlands Farm
COVERED RESERVOIR
Clubhouse
19
20
21
56
57
58
59

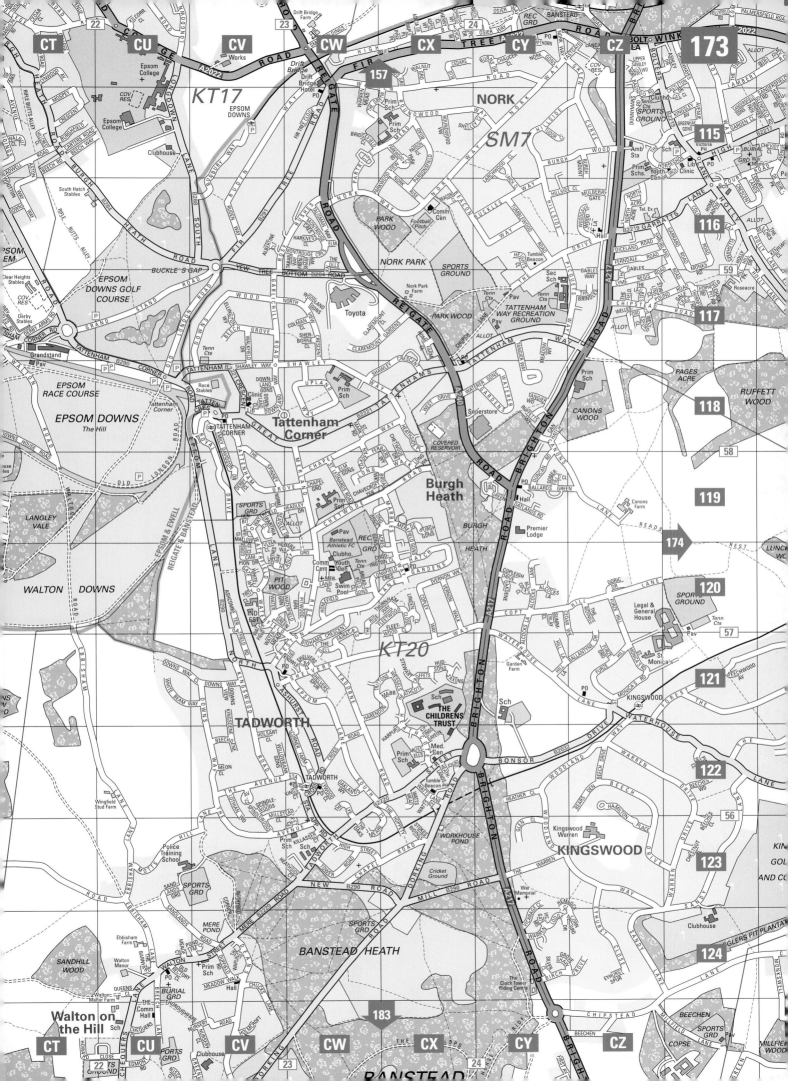

173
CT
CU
CV
CW
CX
CY
CZ
157
174
183
115
116
117
118
119
120
121
122
123
124
22
23
24
56
57
58
59
KT17
SM7
KT20
NORK
Tattenham Corner
Burgh Heath
TADWORTH
KINGSWOOD
Walton on the Hill
EPSOM DOWNS
The Hill
EPSOM RACE COURSE
EPSOM DOWNS GOLF COURSE
WALTON DOWNS
LANGLEY VALE
NORK PARK
PARK WOOD
PARK WOOD
SPORTS GROUND
TATTENHAM WAY RECREATION GROUND
CANONS WOOD
PAGES ACRE
RUFFETT WOOD
BURGH HEATH
BANSTEAD HEATH
SANDHILL WOOD
MERE POND
WORKHOUSE POND
PIT WOOD
THE CHILDRENS TRUST
Epsom College
Epsom College
EPSOM DOWNS
Drift Bridge Hotel
Drift Bridge Farm
Toyota
Grandstand
Race Stables
Tattenham Corner
COVERED RESERVOIR
Superstore
Premier Lodge
Canons Farm
Legal & General House
Kingswood Warren
Police Training School
Ebbisham Farm
Walton Manor
Wingfield Stud Farm
Banstead Athletic FC
Clear Heights Stables
Derby Stables
South Hatch Stables
Buckle's Gap
Clubhouse
REIGATE ROAD
BRIGHTON ROAD
EPSOM LANE
TATTENHAM WAY
CHIPSTEAD
BANSTEAD

174
DA
DB
DC
DD
DE
DF
DG
158
26
27
28
BANSTEAD
SM7
WOODMANSTERNE
CROYDON
A2022
WINKWORTH
A217
B2217
B2219
B2032
B278
115
116
117
118
119
120
121
122
123
124
173
184
59
58
57
56
BANSTEAD WOOD
PARK DOWNS
GREAT SOLOM'S WOOD
SCRATCH WOOD
THE SHRUBBERY
RUFFETT WOOD
PAGES ACRE
CANONS WOOD
LUNCH WOOD
FAMES ROUGH
CHIPSTEAD BOTTOM
CHIPHOUSE WOOD
WELL COPSE
NATURE RESERVE
DEPOT
Banstead Place
Courtlands Farm
Tall Trees
New Place
Little Haugh
Mint Farm
The Mint PH
Perrotts Farm
Canons Farm
KT20
KINGSWOOD
Kingswood Warren
Legal & General House
SPORTS GROUND
St. Monica's
OUTWOOD
OUTWOOD SHAW
KINGSWOOD GOLF COURSE AND COUNTRY CLUB
SMUGGLERS PIT PLANTATION
Clubhouse
Eyhurst Farm
Eyhurst Park
Pigeonhouse Farm
Well House PH
WELLFIELD SHAW
HOMEFIELD SHAWS
TOP SHAW
ROUND WOOD
THE LONG PLANTATION
POORFIELD WOOD
Chipstead Bottom
Chipstead
CHIPSTEAD GOLF COURSE
How Hills
COVERED RESERVOIR
West Ridge
CHALK WORKS
Water Works
Midday Sun PH
Tennis Club
CHIPSTEAD MEADS REC GRD
Chipstead R.F.C.
Bowl Club
EMBERS SHAW
STARROCK SHAW
Longshaw
Elmore
Chipstead FC
Cricket Ground
Shabden Park
THE BELT
THE GROVE
Hooley
FOURTEEN ACRE SHAW
Noke Farm Barns
THE RUFFETT
RUFFETTS WOOD
ROUND WOOD
COALROAST SHAW
HEDGELAND SHAW
Manor Park
South Lodge
Reeves Rest
Court Lodge
War Memorial
BIG WOOD
CLOCKHOUSE REC GRD
PROSPECT PLANTATION
WOODMANSTERNE PARK RECREATION GROUND
Weston Acres
Nicola Farm
The Manor House
Manor Cottage Farm
Victoria PH
The Woolpack PH
REC GRD
Cricket Club
BEECHEN
COPSE
MILLFIELD WOOD
Mugswell
Park Farm
HARPS OAK SHAW
BOARS GREEN

175
WOODCOTE PARK GOLF COURSE
COULSDON
Old Coulsdon
KENLEY
CR8
CR5
CR3
RH1
Chaldon
SMITHAM
COULSDON SOUTH
COULSDON COURT PUBLIC GOLF COURSE
COULSDON MANOR GOLF COURSE
HARTLEY BUSHES
FARTHING OR FAIRDEAN DOWNS
HAPPY VALLEY PARK
HAPPY VALLEY GOLF COURSE
THE GULLET
DEVILS DEN WOOD
SPARKLIE WOOD
BOXERS WOOD
FIGGS WOOD
BROAD WOOD
PILES WOOD
FRYERN BROOM WOOD
WILLEY BROOM WOOD
FURZEFIELD WOOD
ALDERSTEAD HEATH
LORD'S WOOD
GRASSCUTS SHAW
NETHERNE WOOD
PETERSHOLE SHAW
THREE CORNERED SHAW
STAR SHAW
DITCHES SHAW
STONYFIELD SHAW
TWINERS WOOD
POSTERN WOOD
DUNSTAN'S WOOD
MARLFIELD SHAW
SPARTICLES WOOD
RICKMAN HILL REC GRD
GRANGE PARK
COULSDON COMMON
ULLSWATER BUSINESS PARK
HOSPITAL (closed)
BRIGHTON ROAD
A23
A237
B2030
B2031
B2032
B276
SURREY
CROYDON
TANDRIDGE
REIGATE & BANSTEAD
CHURCH GREEN
ROOK LANE
DEAN LANE
159
176
185
115
116
117
118
119
120
121
122
123
124
DH
DJ
DK
DL
DM
DN
DP
29
30
31
56
57
58
59

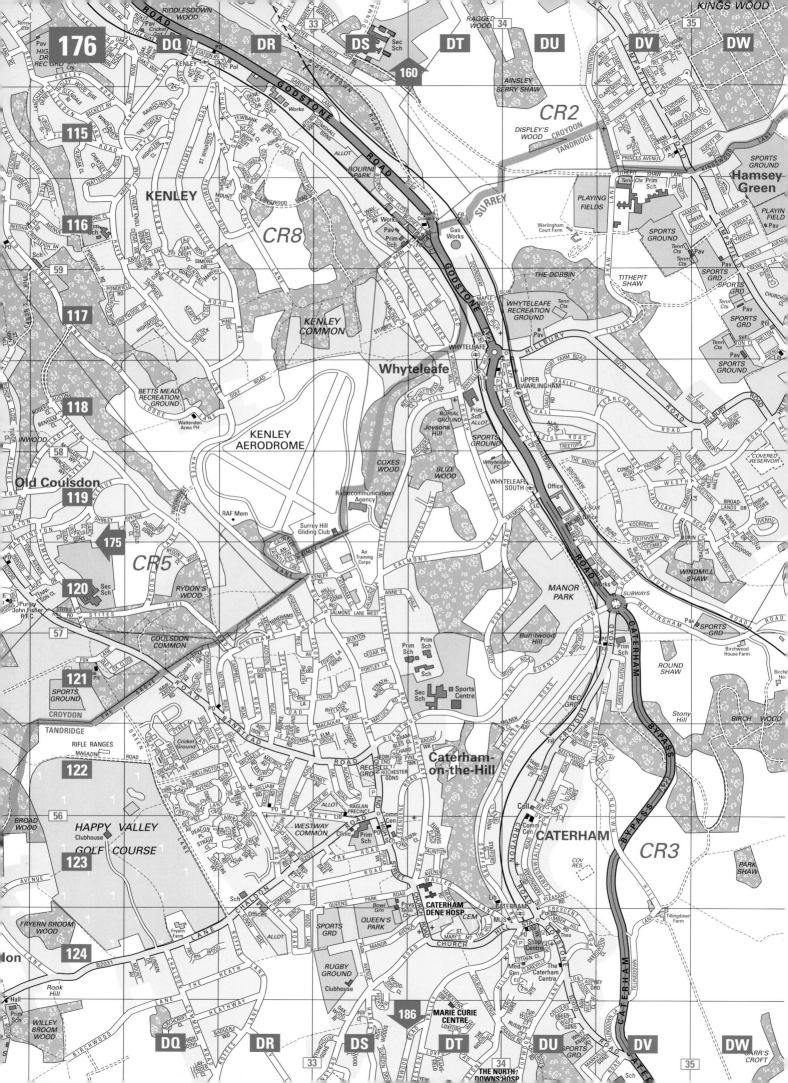

176
DQ
DR
DS
DT
DU
DV
DW
160
KINGS WOOD
RIDDLESDOWN WOOD
RAGGED WOOD
AINSLEY BERRY SHAW
CR2
DISPLEY'S WOOD
CROYDON
TANDRIDGE
SURREY
KENLEY
CR8
GODSTONE ROAD
BOURNE PARK
Hamsey Green
SPORTS GROUND
PLAYING FIELDS
Warlingham Court Farm
Gas Works
THE DOBBIN
TITHEPIT SHAW
WHYTELEAFE RECREATION GROUND
KENLEY COMMON
Whyteleafe
UPPER WARLINGHAM
BETTS MEAD RECREATION GROUND
Wattenden Arms PH
KENLEY AERODROME
COXES WOOD
BLIZE WOOD
Joysons Hill
BURIAL GROUND
WHYTELEAFE SOUTH
Radiocommunications Agency
RAF Mem
Surrey Hill Gliding Club
Air Training Corps
Old Coulsdon
175
CR5
RYDON'S WOOD
Purley John Fisher R.F.C.
MANOR PARK
WINDMILL SHAW
COVERED RESERVOIR
Burntwood Hill
ROUND SHAW
Birchwood House Farm
COULSDON COMMON
SPORTS GROUND
CROYDON
TANDRIDGE
RIFLE RANGES
MAGAZINE
Caterham-on-the-Hill
Sports Centre
Stony Hill
BIRCH WOOD
CATERHAM BYPASS
HAPPY VALLEY
Clubhouse
GOLF COURSE
BROAD WOOD
WESTWAY COMMON
CATERHAM
CR3
PARK SHAW
FRYERN BROOM WOOD
Fryern Farm
CATERHAM DENE HOSP
QUEEN'S PARK
SPORTS GRD
RUGBY GROUND
Clubhouse
The Caterham Centre
Tillingdown Farm
Rook Hill
WILLEY BROOM WOOD
186
MARIE CURIE CENTRE
THE NORTH DOWNS HOSP
CARR'S CROFT
33
34
35

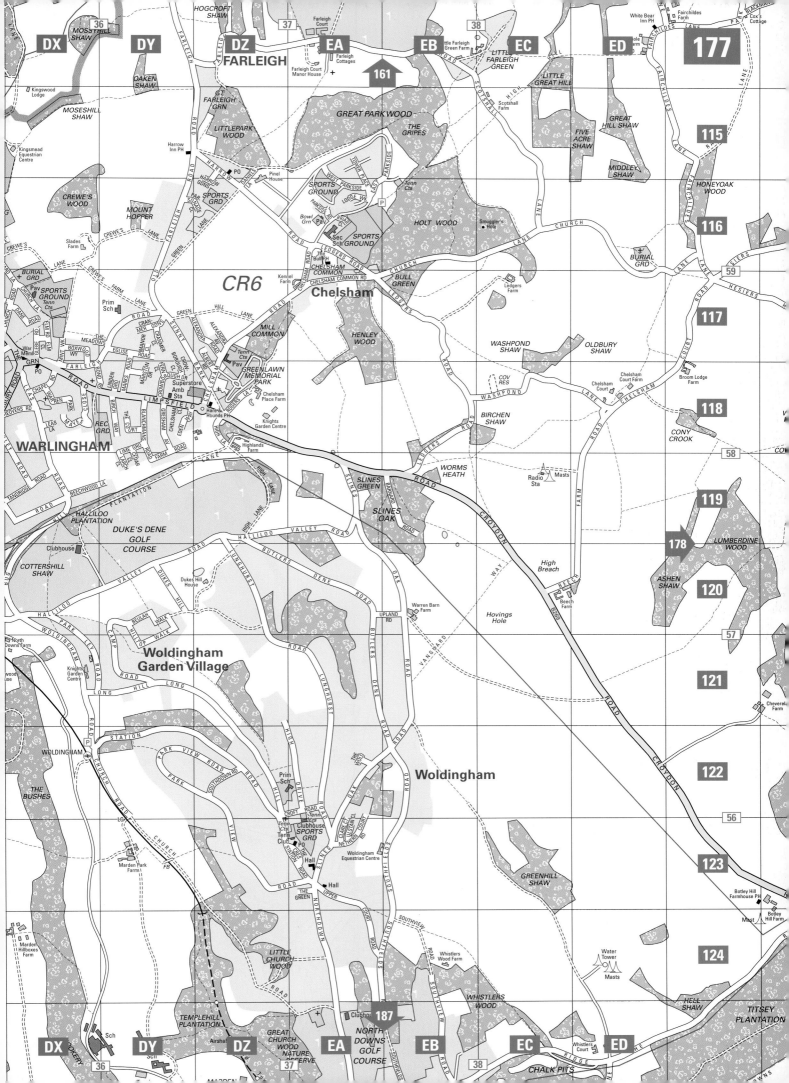
177
DX
DY
DZ
EA
EB
EC
ED
36
37
38
161
FARLEIGH
Farleigh Court
Farleigh Cottages
Farleigh Court Manor House
HOGCROFT SHAW
MOSSYHILL SHAW
OAKEN SHAW
Kingswood Lodge
MOSESHILL SHAW
Little Farleigh Green Farm
LITTLE FARLEIGH GREEN
LITTLE GREAT HILL
White Bear Inn PH
Fairchildes Farm
Cox's Cottage
GT FARLEIGH GRN
LITTLEPARK WOOD
GREAT PARK WOOD
THE GRIPES
Scotshall Farm
FIVE ACRE SHAW
GREAT HILL SHAW
MIDDLEY SHAW
115
HONEYOAK WOOD
Kingsmead Equestrian Centre
Harrow Inn PH
Pinel House
SPORTS GROUND
SPORTS GRD
CREWE'S WOOD
MOUNT HOPPER
Bowl Grn
Pav
Sec Sch
SPORTS GROUND
HOLT WOOD
Smuggler's Hole
116
BURIAL GRD
Slades Farm
BURIAL GRD
SPORTS GROUND
Tenn Cts
Kennel Farm
The Bull PH
CHELSHAM COMMON
CR6
Chelsham
BULL GREEN
Ledgers Farm
59
117
Prim Sch
MILL COMMON
HENLEY WOOD
WASHPOND SHAW
OLDBURY SHAW
GREENLAWN MEMORIAL PARK
Superstore
Amb Sta
Chelsham Place Farm
COV RES
Chelsham Court Farm
Broom Lodge Farm
Chelsham Court
118
War Memorial
Hare & Hounds PH
Knights Garden Centre
BIRCHEN SHAW
CONY CROOK
REC GRD
WARLINGHAM
Highlands Farm
WORMS HEATH
Radio Sta
Masts
58
SLINES GREEN
SLINES OAK
119
HALLILOO PLANTATION
DUKE'S DENE GOLF COURSE
Clubhouse
178
LUMBERDINE WOOD
COTTERSHILL SHAW
High Breach
ASHEN SHAW
120
Dukes Hill House
Beech Farm
Warren Barn Farm
Hovings Hole
57
North Downs Farm
Woldingham Garden Village
Knights Garden Centre
121
Cheverells Farm
WOLDINGHAM
THE BUSHES
Prim Sch
Woldingham
122
56
Clubhouse
SPORTS GRD
Tenn Club
Woldingham Equestrian Centre
Hall
123
Marden Park Farm
GREENHILL SHAW
Botley Hill Farmhouse PH
Botley Hill Farm
Mast
Marden Hillboxes Farm
LITTLE CHURCH WOOD
Whistlers Wood Farm
Water Tower
Masts
124
WHISTLERS WOOD
HELL SHAW
TITSEY PLANTATION
TEMPLEHILL PLANTATION
187
GREAT CHURCH WOOD NATURE RESERVE
NORTH DOWNS GOLF COURSE
Sch
Whistlers Court
CHALK PITS
CROYDON ROAD
LIMPSFIELD ROAD
HALLILOO VALLEY ROAD
CHELSHAM ROAD
LEDGERS ROAD
CHURCH LANE
FARLEIGH ROAD
BUTLERS DENE ROAD
LUNGHURST ROAD
STATION ROAD
CHURCH ROAD
LONG HILL
PARK VIEW ROAD
UPLAND RD
SOUTHFIELDS
SOUTHVIEW ROAD
NORTHDOWN
WASHPOND LANE
FARM ROAD
BEECH
B269

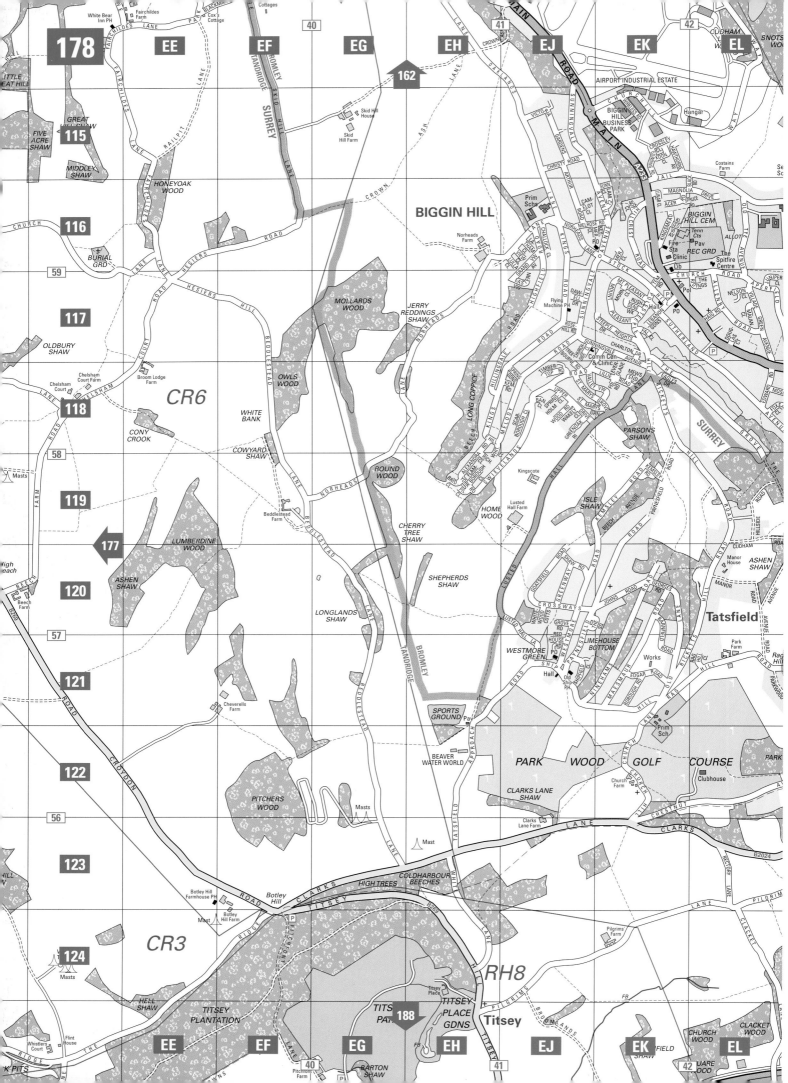
178
EE
EF
EG
EH
EJ
EK
EL
40
41
42
162
115
116
117
118
119
120
121
122
123
124
177
188
59
58
57
56
White Bear Inn PH
Fairchildes Farm
Cox's Cottage
Cottages
FAIRCHILDES LANE
BLACKMAN
PARK
CROWN ASH
OAKLANDS
MAIN ROAD
CUDHAM LANE
SNOTS WOOD
LITTLE HEAT HILL
FIVE ACRE SHAW
GREAT HILL SHAW
MIDDLEY SHAW
HONEYOAK WOOD
RAILPIT LANE
FAIRCHILDES
BROMLEY
TANDRIDGE
SURREY
SKID HILL LANE
Skid Hill House
Skid Hill Farm
AIRPORT INDUSTRIAL ESTATE
BIGGIN HILL BUSINESS PARK
CHURCHILL WAY
Hangar
Costains Farm
VICTORIA
SUNNINGVALE
GARDENS
CHRISTY ROAD
CROSSLEY CL
KOON CL
HAWTHORNE AV
A233
JAIL LANE
MAGNOLIA DRIVE
SPRUCE RD
ACER RD
BIGGIN HILL
Prim Schs
BIGGIN HILL CEM
Tenn Cts
Pav
REC GRD
ALLOTS
The Spitfire Centre
Fire Sta
Clinic
Lib
PO
Pol
CHURCH ROAD
CROWN ROAD
CHURCH
BURIAL GRD
LANE
HESIERS ROAD
HESIERS HILL
Norheads Farm
NORHEADS LANE
STOCK HILL
KINGS ROAD
HIGHFIELD ROAD
GRAND VW AV
MELROSE RD
NORHEADS LANE
MOLLARDS WOOD
JERRY REDDINGS SHAW
Flying Machine PH
SUNNINGVALE
MT PLEASANT
PLEASANT
SUTHERLAND
HAIG RD
NELSON CL
MALAN CL
DOUGLAS CT
STEEPLE HEIGHTS DR
CHARLTON DR
SUNNINGVALE AVENUE
Comm Cen & Clinic
OLDBURY SHAW
Chelsham Court Farm
Broom Lodge Farm
Chelsham Court
CHELSHAM COURT ROAD
CR6
BEDDLESTEAD LANE
OWLS WOOD
HILLINGDALE
LONG COPPICE
TIMBER TOP RD
EAGLES DR
THE GROVE
RICKETTS HILL
SURREY
WHITE BANK
CONY CROOK
COWYARD SHAW
ROUND WOOD
PARSONS SHAW
KINGS
MELODY
SCARBOROUGH CL
SWIEVELANDS
Kingscote
LUSTED HALL LANE
ISLE SHAW
KEMSLEY
PAINESFIELD ROAD
Masts
FARM ROAD
Beddlestead Farm
HOME WOOD
Lusted Hall Farm
CHERRY TREE SHAW
LUMBERDINE WOOD
ASHEN SHAW
High Beach
BEECH
Beech Farm
B269
SHEPHERDS SHAW
CUDHAM
Manor House
ASHEN SHAW
MANOR ROAD
LONGLANDS SHAW
CROSSWAYS
JOHNS ROAD
GEORGES RD
Tatsfield
WESTMORE GREEN
LIMEHOUSE BOTTOM
Works
Park Farm
RAG HILL ROAD
Hall
Old Ship PH
NINEHAMS
MAESMAUR
EDGAR ROAD
BOROUGH HILL
PARKWOOD
Cheverells Farm
BEDDLESTEAD LANE
TANDRIDGE
BROMLEY
SPORTS GROUND
Pav
APPROACH ROAD
Prim Sch
BEAVER WATER WORLD
PARK WOOD GOLF COURSE
Clubhouse
CROYDON ROAD
PITCHERS WOOD
CLARKS LANE SHAW
Church Farm
CHURCH HILL
Masts
Clarks Lane Farm
CHESTNUT
CLARKS LANE
Mast
TATSFIELD
B2024
RECTORY LANE
Botley Hill Farmhouse PH
Botley Hill
CLARKS
HIGH TREES
COLDHARBOUR BEECHES
WHITE LANE
TITSEY
Botley Hill Farm
Mast
PITCHFONT LANE
RIDGE
Pilgrims Farm
PILGRIMS LANE
CLACKET LANE
CR3
RH8
Masts
HILL SHAW
TITSEY PLANTATION
TITSEY PARK
Titsey Place
TITSEY PLACE GDNS
Titsey
BROOMLANDS
FB
PILGRIMS
CHURCH WOOD
CLACKET WOOD
Whistlers Court
Flint House
THE RIDGE
Pitchfont Farm
BARTON SHAW
TITSEY HILL

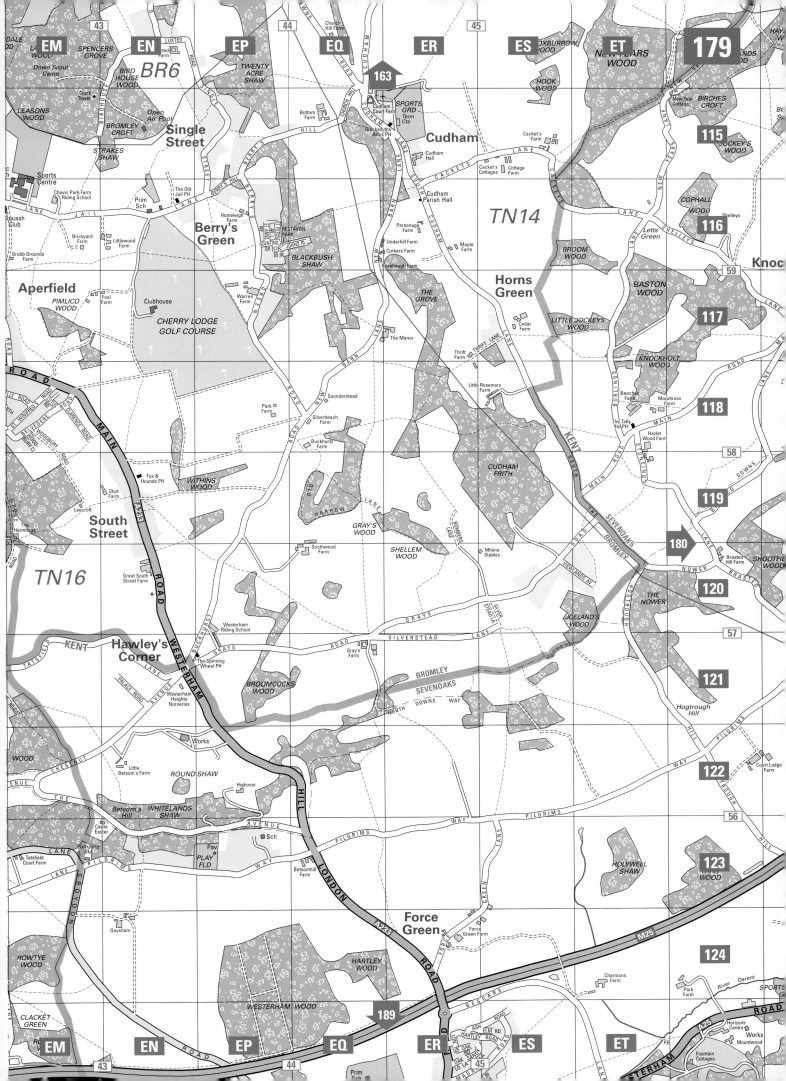
179
Cudham
Single Street
Berry's Green
Aperfield
Horns Green
South Street
Hawley's Corner
Force Green
TN14
TN16
BR6
CHERRY LODGE GOLF COURSE
CUDHAM FRITH
WESTERHAM WOOD
HARTLEY WOOD
HOLYWELL SHAW
BROOMCOCKS WOOD
WHITELANDS SHAW
ROUND SHAW
THE NOWER
KNOCKHOLT WOOD
BASTON WOOD
Hogtrough Hill
WESTERHAM ROAD
MAIN ROAD
LONDON ROAD
PILGRIMS WAY
NORTH DOWNS WAY
M25
A233

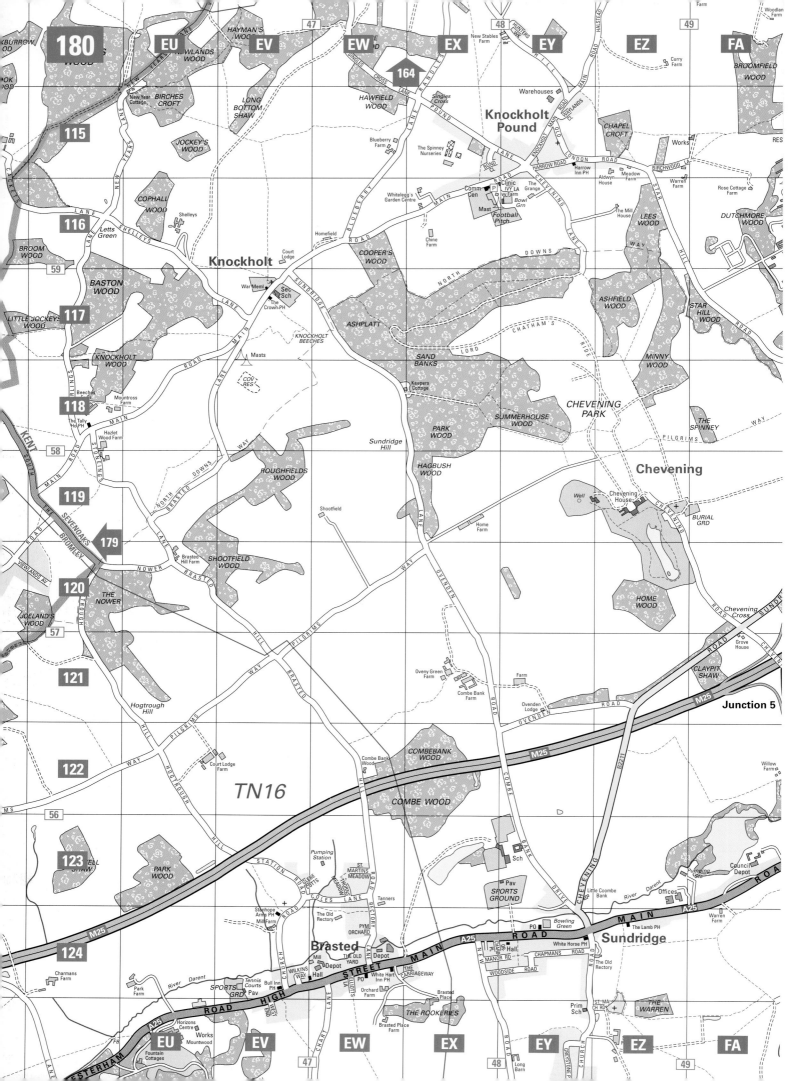
180
EU
EV
EW
EX
EY
EZ
FA
164
179
Knockholt Pound
Knockholt
Chevening
Brasted
Sundridge
Letts Green
CHEVENING PARK
TN16
Junction 5
KENT
115
116
117
118
119
120
121
122
123
124
47
48
49
56
57
58
59
NEWLANDS WOOD
HAYMAN'S WOOD
BIRCHES CROFT
LONG BOTTOM SHAW
HAWFIELD WOOD
JOCKEY'S WOOD
COPHALL WOOD
BROOM WOOD
BASTON WOOD
LITTLE JOCKEYS WOOD
KNOCKHOLT WOOD
KNOCKHOLT BEECHES
COOPER'S WOOD
ASHPLATT
SAND BANKS
PARK WOOD
SUMMERHOUSE WOOD
HAGBUSH WOOD
ROUGHFIELDS WOOD
SHOOTFIELD WOOD
THE NOWER
JOELAND'S WOOD
CHAPEL CROFT
BROOMFIELD WOOD
DUTCHMORE WOOD
LEES WOOD
ASHFIELD WOOD
STAR HILL WOOD
MINNY WOOD
THE SPINNEY
HOME WOOD
CLAYPIT SHAW
COMBEBANK WOOD
COMBE WOOD
PARK WOOD
THE ROOKERIES
THE WARREN
SPORTS GROUND
Sundridge Hill
Hogtrough Hill
Singles Cross
Chevening Cross
New Stables Farm
Curry Farm
Warehouses
Works
Blueberry Farm
The Spinney Nurseries
Harrow Inn PH
Aldwyn House
Meadow Farm
Warren Farm
Rose Cottage Farm
Whitelegg's Garden Centre
Comm Cen
Clinic
Ivy Farm
The Grange
Mast
Football Pitch
Bowl Grn
The Mill House
Chine Farm
Homefield
Court Lodge
War Meml
Sec Sch
The Crown PH
Masts
COV RES
Keepers Cottage
Shelleys
New Year Cottage
Beeches
Mountross Farm
The Tally Ho PH
Hazlet Wood Farm
Brasted Hill Farm
Shootfield
Home Farm
Well
Chevening House
BURIAL GRD
Grove House
Oveny Green Farm
Combe Bank Farm
Farm
Ovenden Lodge
Combe Bank Wood
Court Lodge Farm
Willow Farm
Pumping Station
Sch
Pav
Little Coombe Bank
Offices
Council Depot
Warren Farm
The Lamb PH
White Horse PH
Bowling Green
The Old Rectory
Prim Sch
Stanhope Arms PH
Mill Farm
The Old Rectory
Tanners
PYM ORCHARD
THE OLD YARD
Depot
Mill
Hall
Bull Inn PH
Tennis Courts
White Hart Inn PH
Orchard Farm
Brasted Place
Brasted Place Farm
Charmans Farm
Park Farm
Horizons Centre
Works
Mountwood
Fountain Cottages
Long Barn
River Darent
M25
A25
B2211
NEW YEARS LANE
CACKETS LANE
SHELLEYS LANE
SINGLES CROSS LANE
RANDLES LANE
POUND LANE
BLUEBERRY LANE
MAIN ROAD
HUNTERS WK
HALSTEAD ROAD
MAIN ROAD
WAYLANDS CL
OLD LONDON ROAD
HARROW ROAD
BOND CL
IVY LA
CHEVENING LANE
BIRCHWOOD LA
STAR HILL ROAD
NORTH DOWNS WAY
LORD CHATHAM'S RIDE
SUNDRIDGE LANE
PILGRIMS WAY
RRINGS
STONINGS
NORTH DOWNS
BRASTED LANE
NOWER
BRASTED HILL
OVENDEN ROAD
CHEVENING ROAD
SUNDRIDGE ROAD
HOGTROUGH HILL
STATION ROAD
GLEBE COTTS
ST. MARTINS MEADOW
THORNS MEADOW
COLES LANE
RECTORY LANE
COMBE BANK DRIVE
MAIN ROAD
HIGH STREET
ROAD
WEST END
WILKINS WAY
ELLIOTTS LA
THE CARRIAGEWAY
NEW ROAD
MANOR RD
CHAPMANS ROAD
WOODSIDE ROAD
CHURCH ROAD
GREYSTONE PK
ST. MARTIN'S CH RD
CHART LANE
SOUTH
THE SEVENOAKS BROMLEY
VIEWLANDS AV

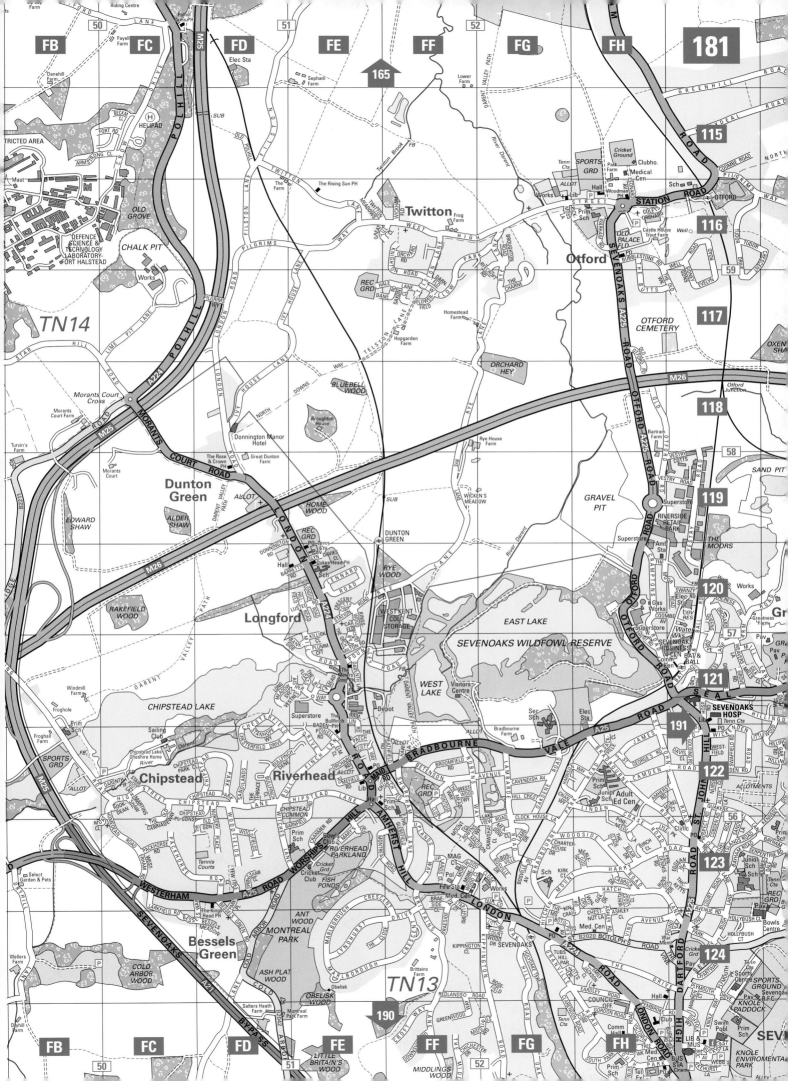
FB
FC
FD
FE
FF
FG
FH
165
115
116
117
118
119
120
121
122
123
124
191
190
50
51
52
56
57
58
59
TN14
TN13
Twitton
Otford
Dunton Green
Longford
Chipstead
Riverhead
Bessels Green
SEVENOAKS WILDFOWL RESERVE
EAST LAKE
WEST LAKE
CHIPSTEAD LAKE
GRAVEL PIT
OTFORD CEMETERY
ORCHARD HEY
BLUEBELL WOOD
HOME WOOD
RYE WOOD
ALDER SHAW
EDWARD SHAW
RAKEFIELD WOOD
OLD GROVE
CHALK PIT
DEFENCE SCIENCE & TECHNOLOGY LABORATORY FORT HALSTEAD
HELIPAD
MONTREAL PARK
ANT WOOD
ASH PLAT WOOD
OBELISK WOOD
COLD ARBOR WOOD
LITTLE BRITAIN'S WOOD
MIDDLINGS WOOD
RIVERHEAD PARKLAND
FISH PONDS
THE MOORS
SEVENOAKS HOSP
KNOLE PADDOCK
KNOLE ENVIROMENTAL PARK
SPORTS GROUND
Donnington Manor Hotel
WEST KENT COLD STORAGE
Sevenoaks Business Cen
Riverside Retail Park
M25
M26
A224
A225
A25
A21
SEVENOAKS BY-PASS
POLHILL
MORANTS COURT ROAD
LONDON ROAD
BRADBOURNE VALE ROAD
WESTERHAM ROAD
OTFORD ROAD
STATION ROAD
HIGH STREET
DARTFORD ROAD
ST. JOHN'S HILL
AMHERST HILL
PILGRIMS WAY
TWITTON LANE
SEAL ROAD
Morants Court Cross
Otford Junction
DUNTON GREEN
SEVENOAKS

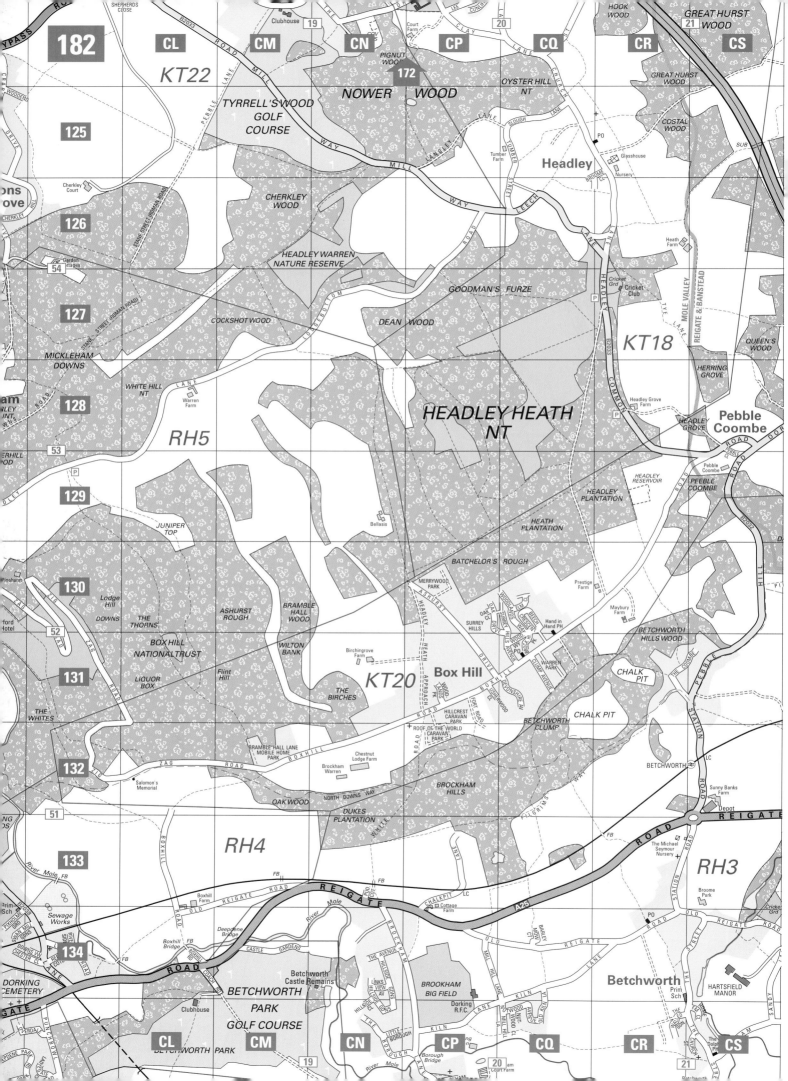

KT22
TYRRELL'S WOOD GOLF COURSE
NOWER WOOD
172
OYSTER HILL NT
Headley
CHERKLEY WOOD
HEADLEY WARREN NATURE RESERVE
GOODMAN'S FURZE
COCKSHOT WOOD
DEAN WOOD
MICKLEHAM DOWNS
WHITE HILL NT
KT18
HEADLEY HEATH NT
Pebble Coombe
RH5
HEADLEY PLANTATION
HEATH PLANTATION
JUNIPER TOP
BATCHELOR'S ROUGH
ASHURST ROUGH
BRAMBLE HALL WOOD
BOX HILL NATIONAL TRUST
WILTON BANK
KT20
Box Hill
THE BIRCHES
CHALK PIT
BETCHWORTH CLUMP
BETCHWORTH HILLS WOOD
BROCKHAM HILLS
OAK WOOD
DUKES PLANTATION
RH4
RH3
BETCHWORTH PARK GOLF COURSE
BROOKHAM BIG FIELD
Betchworth
HARTSFIELD MANOR
REIGATE ROAD
A25
GREAT HURST WOOD
COSTAL WOOD
QUEEN'S WOOD
HERRING GROVE
MOLE VALLEY
REIGATE & BANSTEAD

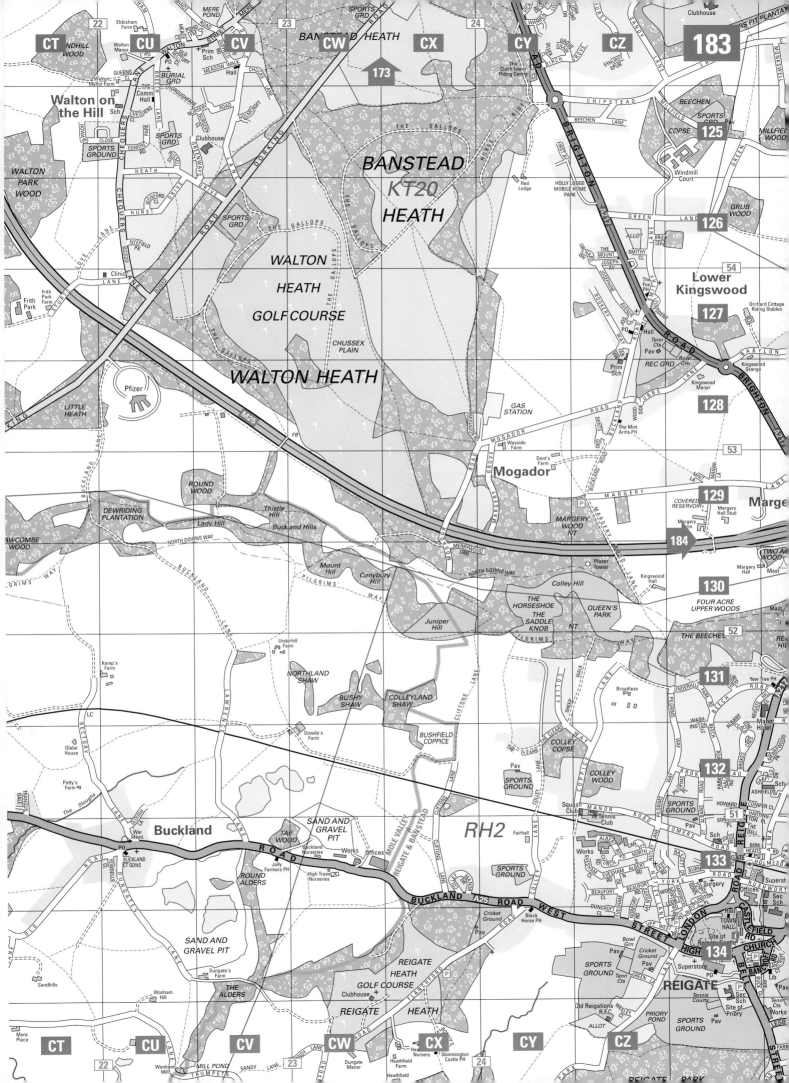
CT
CU
CV
CW
CX
CY
CZ
173
125
126
127
128
129
130
131
132
133
134
184
Walton on the Hill
WALTON PARK WOOD
BANSTEAD HEATH
KT20
WALTON HEATH GOLF COURSE
CHUSSEX PLAIN
WALTON HEATH
Pfizer
LITTLE HEATH
M25
Lower Kingswood
GAS STATION
Mogador
ROUND WOOD
DEWRIDING PLANTATION
Lady Hill
Thistle Hill
Buckland Hills
NORTH DOWNS WAY
Mount Hill
Conybury Hill
Juniper Hill
Colley Hill
THE HORSESHOE
THE SADDLE KNOB
QUEEN'S PARK
MARGERY WOOD NT
Water Tower
FOUR ACRE UPPER WOODS
THE BEECHES
NORTHLAND SHAW
BUSHY SHAW
COLLEYLAND SHAW
BUSHFIELD COPPICE
COLLEY COPSE
COLLEY WOOD
RH2
Buckland
TAP WOOD
SAND AND GRAVEL PIT
ROUND ALDERS
BUCKLAND ROAD A25
ROAD WEST STREET
REIGATE HEATH GOLF COURSE
REIGATE HEATH
THE ALDERS
REIGATE
PRIORY POND
SPORTS GROUND
MILL POND
22
23
24
51
52
53
54

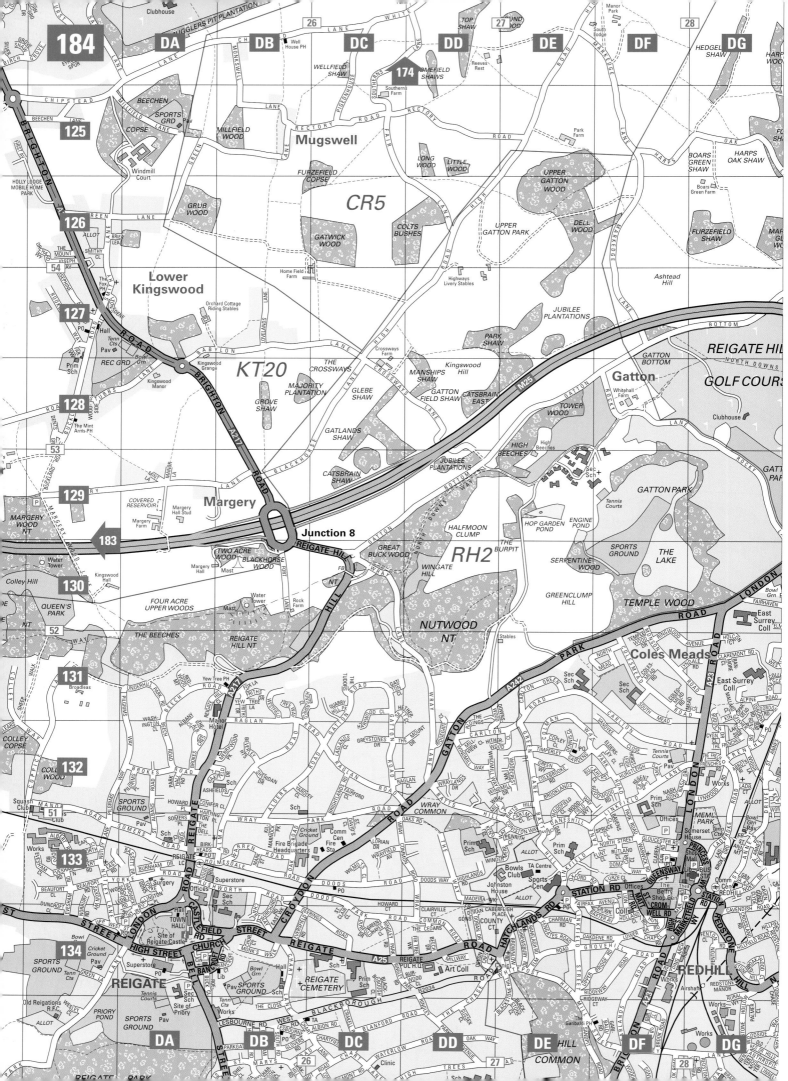
184
DA
DB
DC
DD
DE
DF
DG
174
183
Mugswell
CR5
Lower Kingswood
KT20
Margery
Junction 8
RH2
Gatton
REIGATE HILL
GOLF COURSE
Coles Meads
REIGATE
REDHILL
NUTWOOD NT
GATTON PARK
THE LAKE
TEMPLE WOOD
UPPER GATTON WOOD
UPPER GATTON PARK
REIGATE CEMETERY
M25
A217
A242
A23
A25

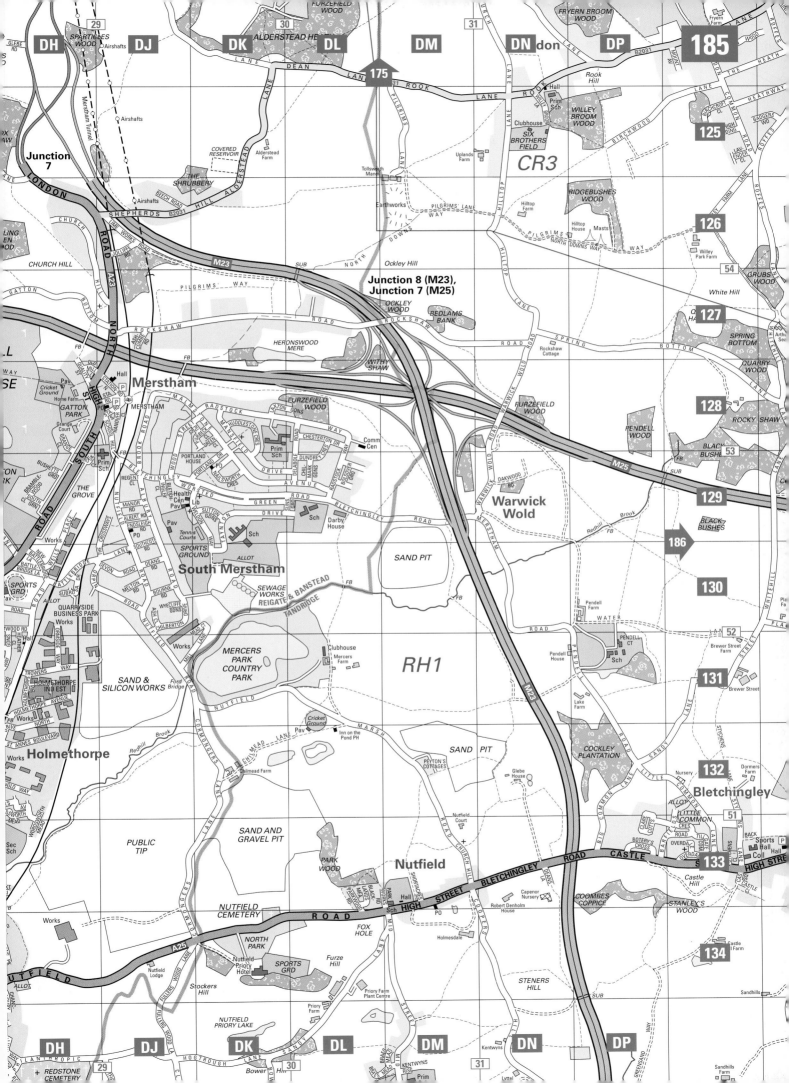
185
175
186
DH
DJ
DK
DL
DM
DN
DP
Merstham
South Merstham
Holmethorpe
Nutfield
Bletchingley
Warwick Wold
CR3
RH1
Junction 7
Junction 8 (M23), Junction 7 (M25)
M23
M25
A23
A25
B2031
ALDERSTEAD HEATH
FURZEFIELD WOOD
SPARTICLES WOOD
FRYERN BROOM WOOD
WILLEY BROOM WOOD
SIX BROTHERS FIELD
RIDGEBUSHES WOOD
THE SHRUBBERY
COVERED RESERVOIR
Alderstead Farm
Uplands Farm
Tollsworth Manor
Earthworks
Hilltop Farm
Hilltop House
Masts
Willey Park Farm
GRUBS WOOD
White Hill
CHURCH HILL
Ockley Hill
OCKLEY WOOD
BEDLAMS BANK
HERONSWOOD MERE
WITHY SHAW
SPRING BOTTOM
QUARRY WOOD
Rockshaw Cottage
ROCKY SHAW
PENDELL WOOD
BLACK BUSHES
Merstham Tunnel
Airshafts
GATTON PARK
Cricket Ground
Home Farm
Grange Court
THE GROVE
SPORTS GROUND
SAND PIT
SEWAGE WORKS
REIGATE & BANSTEAD
TANDRIDGE
MERCERS PARK COUNTRY PARK
Clubhouse
Mercers Farm
SAND & SILICON WORKS
Ford Bridge
QUARRYSIDE BUSINESS PARK
HOLMETHORPE IND EST
Pendell Farm
Pendell House
PENDELL CT
Lake Farm
COCKLEY PLANTATION
Brewer Street Farm
Brewer Street
Nursery
Dormers Farm
LITTLE COMMON
Castle Hill
COOMBES COPPICE
STANLEY'S WOOD
Castle Hill Farm
Sandhills
Sandhills Farm
Chilmead Farm
Inn on the Pond PH
Cricket Ground
PEYTON'S COTTAGES
Glebe House
Nutfield Court
SAND AND GRAVEL PIT
PUBLIC TIP
PARK WOOD
Capenor Nursery
Robert Denholm House
Holmesdale
NUTFIELD CEMETERY
FOX HOLE
NORTH PARK
Nutfield Priory Hotel
SPORTS GRD
Furze Hill
Priory Farm Plant Centre
Priory Farm
Nutfield Lodge
Stockers Hill
NUTFIELD PRIORY LAKE
STENERS HILL
Kentwyns
REDSTONE CEMETERY
Bower Hill
PILGRIMS' WAY
NORTH DOWNS WAY
ROCKSHAW ROAD
SPRING BOTTOM
NUTFIELD ROAD
BLETCHINGLEY ROAD
HIGH STREET
CASTLE STREET
MERSTHAM ROAD
PENDELL ROAD
WATER LANE
BIG COMMON LANE
HOGTROUGH LANE
FULLERS WOOD LANE
CORMONGERS LANE
CHILMEAD LANE
MARSH LANE
SANDY LANE
MID STREET
COOPERS HILL ROAD
CHURCH HILL ROAD
HILLTOP LANE
ROOK LANE
DEAN LANE
ALDERSTEAD HILL
SHEPHERDS HILL
NORTH ROAD
HIGH ST
SOUTH ROAD
GATTON BOTTOM
WHITEHILL LANE
ROFFES LANE
HEATHWAY
BIRCHWOOD LANE
GREEN ROAD
WORSTED GREEN
DRIVE
AVENUE
25
26
27
28
29
30
31
51
52
53
54
125
126
127
128
129
130
131
132
133
134

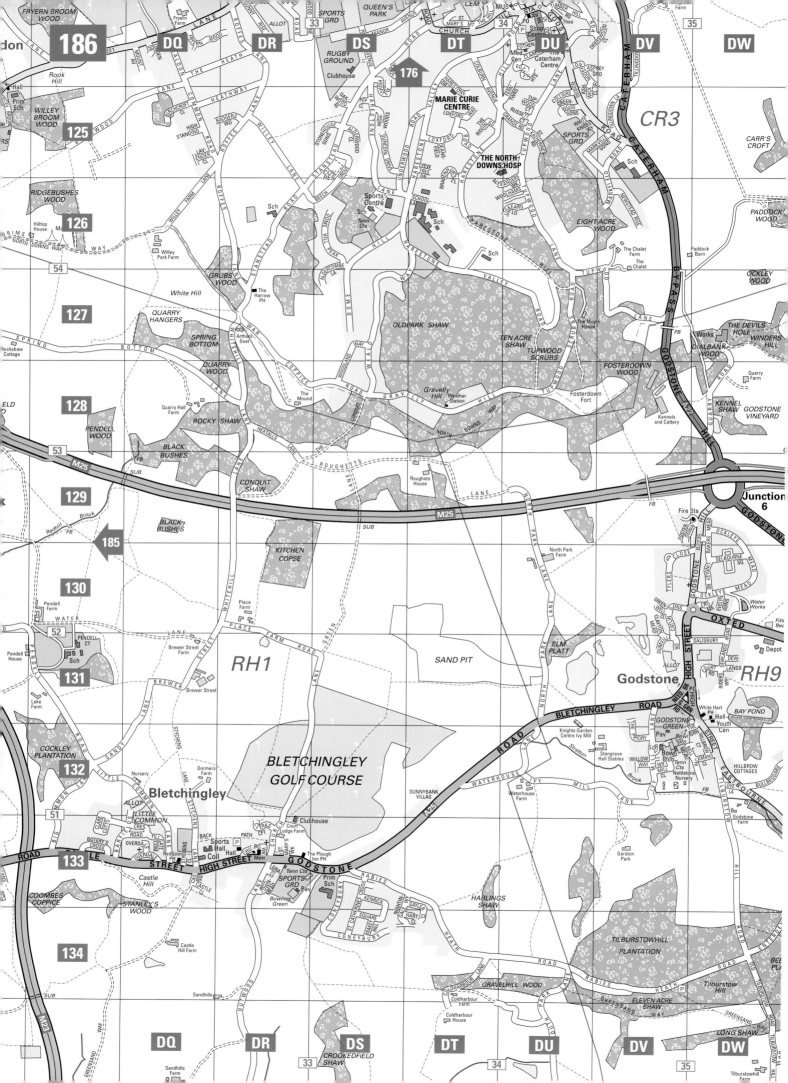
186
FRYERN BROOM WOOD
Fryern Farm
DQ
DR
DS
DT
DU
DV
DW
SPORTS GRD
QUEEN'S PARK
RUGBY GROUND
Clubhouse
176
MARIE CURIE CENTRE
THE NORTH DOWNS HOSP
Caterham Centre
CATERHAM
CR3
SPORTS GRD
CARR'S CROFT
Rook Hill
Hall
Prim Sch
WILLEY BROOM WOOD
125
RIDGEBUSHES WOOD
126
Hilltop House
NORTH DOWNS WAY
Willey Park Farm
54
White Hill
GRUBS WOOD
The Harrow PH
Sports Centre
Sch
Tenn Cts
EIGHT ACRE WOOD
The Chalet Farm
The Chalet
Paddock Barn
PADDOCK WOOD
OCKLEY WOOD
127
QUARRY HANGERS
SPRING BOTTOM
Arthurs Seat
OLDPARK SHAW
TEN ACRE SHAW
TUPWOOD SCRUBS
The Moyle House
THE DEVILS HOLE
WINDERS HILL
DIALBANK WOOD
Works
Rockshaw Cottage
QUARRY WOOD
FOSTERDOWN WOOD
Quarry Farm
Gravelly Hill
Weather Station
Fosterdown Fort
The Mound
128
Quarry Hall Farm
ROCKY SHAW
PENDELL WOOD
KENNEL SHAW
GODSTONE VINEYARD
Kennels and Cattery
53
M25
BLACK BUSHES
CONDUIT SHAW
Roughets House
Junction 6
129
BLACK BUSHES
185
KITCHEN COPSE
North Park Farm
Fire Sta
130
Pendell Farm
Place Farm
SAND PIT
Water Works
52
PENDELL CT
Pendell House
Sch
Brewer Street Farm
RH1
ELM PLATT
131
Brewer Street
Godstone
RH9
Depot
Lake Farm
BLETCHINGLEY ROAD
White Hart PH
Hall
Youth Cen
BAY POND
GODSTONE GREEN
Knights Garden Centre Ivy Mill
Stangrave Hall Stables
COCKLEY PLANTATION
132
BLETCHINGLEY GOLF COURSE
Dormers Farm
Nursery
Bletchingley
SUNNYBANK VILLAS
Waterhouse Farm
Nettletons Nursery
HILLBROW COTTAGES
51
LITTLE COMMON
Clubhouse
Court Lodge Farm
Godstone Farm
A25
Sports Hall
Coll
Red Lion PH
The Plough Inn PH
Garston Park
133
HIGH STREET
GODSTONE ROAD
Castle Hill
SPORTS GRD
Bowling Green
Prim Sch
COOMBES COPPICE
STANLEY'S WOOD
HARLINGS SHAW
TILBURSTOWHILL PLANTATION
134
Castle Hill Farm
GRAVELHILL WOOD
Coldharbour Farm
Tilburstow Hill
Sandhills
ELEVEN ACRE SHAW
Coldharbour House
M23
LONG SHAW
33
34
35
CROOKEDFIELD SHAW
Sandhills Farm
Tilburstowhill Farm

DX
DY
DZ
EA
EB
EC
ED
177
Marden Hillboxes Farm
LITTLE CHURCH WOOD
Whistlers Wood Farm
Masts
Mast
Hill Farm
HELL SHAW
TITSEY PLANTATION
125
TEMPLEHILL PLANTATION
GREAT CHURCH WOOD NATURE RESERVE
NORTH DOWNS GOLF COURSE
Clubhouse
WHISTLERS WOOD
Whistlers Court
Flint House
ROOKERY
Sch
Airshaft
Oxted Tunnel
Tennis Courts
MARDEN PARK
CHALK PITS
OXTED QUARRY
CHALK PIT
Works
BEECH PLANTATION NT
OXTED DOWNS NT
NORTH DOWNS
Paddock Barn
STUBBS COPSE
126
SPORTS GROUND
THE RUMPS
SOUTH HAWKE
NT
54
CHALKPIT WOOD
WHITFIELD PLANTATION
HAZEL SHAW
HORSE SHAW
Chaldens Farm
RYE SHAW
LODGE WOOD
ARMITAGE WOOD
HAMFIELD SHAW
FIVE ACRE SHAW
127
HOSP (closed)
BARNETT'S SHAW
Prim Schs
HANGING WOOD
RYE WOOD
HOGTROUGH LANE
NORTH DOWNS WAY
GANGERS HILL
Flint Hall Farm
Tandridge Hill Farm
ROBINS GROVE WOOD
Barrow Green Court
Coach Depot
128
Tennis Courts
Sch
Thea
Sec Schs
GENERALS GROVE
M25
BURIAL GRD
Blunt House
BLUEHOUSE
53
THE ABBEYS
Barrow Green Farm
RH8
THE MOUNT
THE BOGS
MASTER PARK
OXTED
Tenn Cts
PO
Cine
Swim Pool
Gas Holder
Superstore
Pol
Clubhouse
129
MAG CT
PALMERS WOOD OILFIELD
FLOWER WOOD
188
EAST
WEST ROAD
130
Tandridge Priory
Riding Centre
Works
Flower Farm
SAND PIT
SPORTS GROUND
A22
A25
BYPASS
ROAD
OXTED
GODSTONE ROAD
52
BUSHEY CROFT REC GRD
Clubhouse
Mill Barn
Round Lodge
Knights Garden Centre
Church Town
MOORE'S SHAW
TANDRIDGE GOLF COURSE
131
Stonehall Farm
Stonehamme
River Eden
GLEBE WATER
THE BIRCHES
Beechwood Hill
NEW BUSTONS WOOD
Little Court Farm
BUSTONS WOOD
Tandridge Court
BROADHAM GREEN
Haycutter PH
Health Centre
132
The Glebe House
LEIGH PLACE LANE
Oxted Place
Leigh Place
51
Tandridge Court Farm
ROUND WOOD
STONEPIT SHAW
OLDPARK WOOD
Leigh Mill House
CASTLEHILL WOOD
THE ENTERDENT
B2236
Southlands
Perrysfield Farm
Perrysfield
133
MAIZENHALL SHAW
REDDINGS WOOD
Tandridge
Barley Mow PH
Hall
Prim Sch
DEAN SHAW
TILBURSTOWHILL COMMON
Tandridge Hall
SOUTHLANDS SHAWS
Stockett's Manor
HOPGARDEN WOOD
Sewage Works
Filter Beds
Gibbs Brook
Southlands Lodge
134
BEECHWOOD PLANTATION
SOUTHLANDS WOOD
Rose Farm
BRACKEY HILL
STOW COPPICE
FB
EASTBOURNE ROAD
Orme House
36
37
38
Newhouse Farm
Hollybush

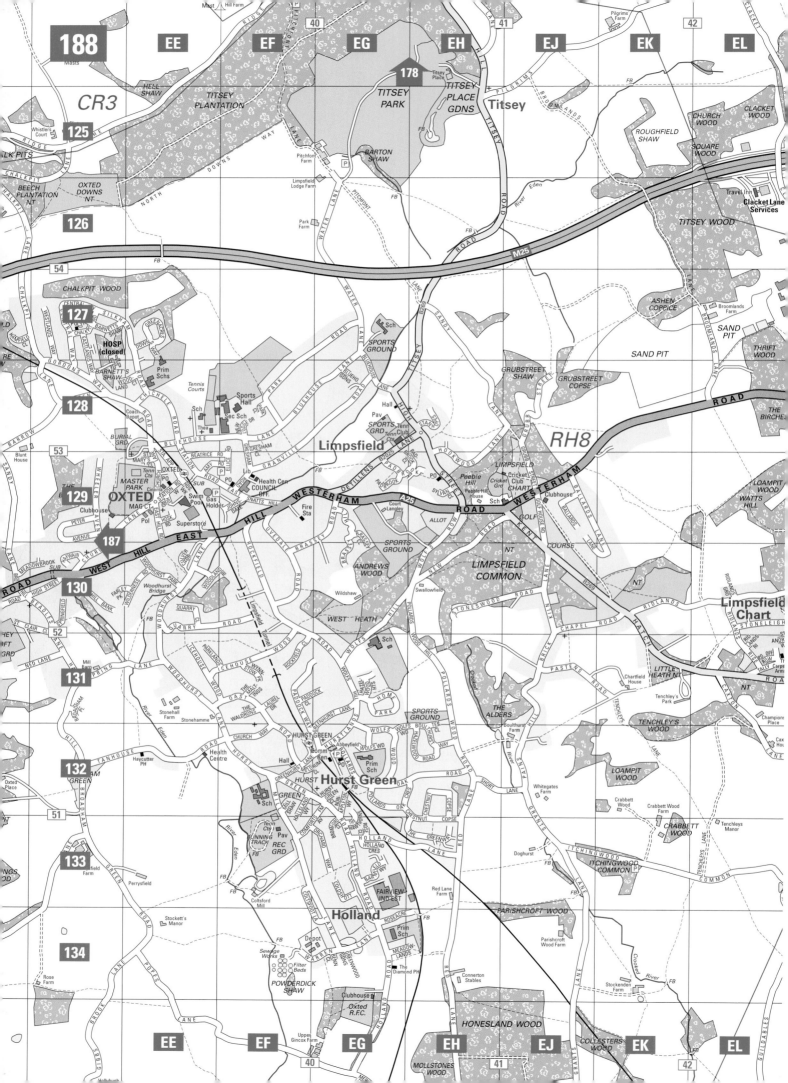
EE
EF
EG
EH
EJ
EK
EL
40
41
42
178
CR3
RH8
HELL SHAW
TITSEY PLANTATION
TITSEY PARK
TITSEY PLACE GDNS
Titsey
Titsey Place
PILGRIMS
BROOMLANDS
CHURCH WOOD
CLACKET WOOD
ROUGHFIELD SHAW
SQUARE WOOD
Travel Inn
Clacket Lane Services
TITSEY WOOD
Pilgrims Farm
Whistlers Court
125
126
127
128
129
130
131
132
133
134
187
54
53
52
51
LK PITS
CHALKPIT
BEECH PLANTATION NT
OXTED DOWNS NT
NORTH DOWNS WAY
BARTON SHAW
Pitchfont Farm
Limpsfield Lodge Farm
Park Farm
PITCHFONT
WATER LANE
TITSEY ROAD
River Eden
M25
FB
CHALKPIT WOOD
ASHEN COPPICE
Broomlands Farm
SAND PIT
THRIFT WOOD
GRUBSTREET SHAW
GRUBSTREET COPSE
THE BIRCHES
HOSP (closed)
BARNETT'S SHAW
Prim Schs
Tennis Courts
Sports Hall
Sec Sch
SPORTS GROUND
Sch
Hall
Pav
SPORTS GRD
Tenn Club
Limpsfield
BURIAL GRD
Blunt House
OXTED
MASTER PARK
Cinema
Swim Pool
Gas Holder
Superstore
Lib
Health Cen
COUNCIL OFF.
Fire Sta
Court Langley
ALLOT
WESTERHAM ROAD
A25
B269
B2025
LIMPSFIELD CHART
Cricket Grd
Cricket Club
Peeble Hill
Clubhouse
GOLF COURSE
LOAMPIT WOOD
WATTS HILL
EAST HILL
WEST HILL ROAD
SPORTS GROUND
ANDREWS WOOD
LIMPSFIELD COMMON
NT
Swallowfield
Limpsfield Chart
Woodhurst Bridge
Wildshaw
WEST HEATH
Limpsfield Tunnel
CHAPEL ROAD
STONESWOOD ROAD
Mill Barn
Stonehall Farm
Stonehamme
THE ALDERS
Chartfield House
LITTLE HEATH NT
Tenchley's Park
TENCHLEY'S WOOD
Champions Place
SPORTS GROUND
HURST GREEN
Hurst Green
Abbeyfield
Comm Cen
Prim Sch
Haycutter PH
Health Centre
Boulthurst Farm
LOAMPIT WOOD
Whitegates Farm
Crabbett Wood
Crabbett Wood Farm
CRABBETT WOOD
Tenchleys Manor
Oxted Place
Tenn Cts
RUNNING TRACK
REC GRD
Doghurst
ITCHINGWOOD COMMON
Red Lane Farm
FAIRVIEW IND EST
Perrysfield
Coltsford Mill
Holland
PARISHCROFT WOOD
Parishcroft Wood Farm
Stockett's Manor
Depot
Sewage Works
Filter Beds
The Diamond PH
Connerton Stables
Stockenden Farm
Crooked River
POWDERDICK SHAW
Rose Farm
Clubhouse
Oxted R.F.C.
HONESLAND WOOD
COLLESTERS WOOD
Upper Gincox Farm
MOLLSTONES WOOD

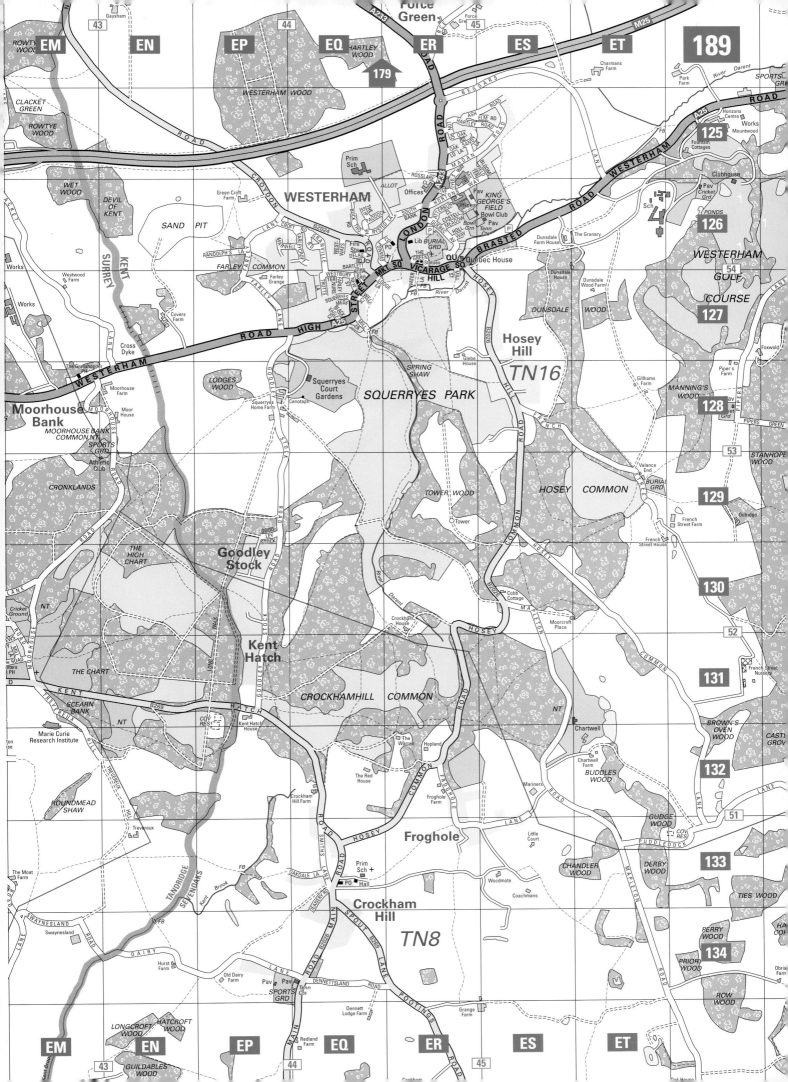
Force Green
Gaysham
43
44
45
EM
EN
EP
EQ
ER
ES
ET
ROWTYE WOOD
HARTLEY WOOD
179
M25
A233
LONDON ROAD
Charmans Farm
Park Farm
River Darent
SPORTS GRD
CLACKET GREEN
WESTERHAM WOOD
BEGGARS LANE
ASH ELM RD
HARTLEY ROAD
OAK RD
SAND LA
LO LA
MADAN
A25
WESTERHAM ROAD
Horizons Centre
Works
Mountwood
125
Fountain Cottages
Clubhouse
Pav
Cricket Grd
PONDS
126
WET WOOD
DEVIL OF KENT
CROYDON ROAD
Prim Sch
ALLOT
Green Croft Farm
WESTERHAM
Offices
ROSSLARE CL
HORTONS WAY
KING GEORGE'S FIELD
Bowl Club
Pav Tenn Cts
Bowl Grn
SAND PIT
B2024
Fire Sta
PO
Lib
BURIAL GRD
THE GREEN
Statues
BRASTED
Quebec House
Dunsdale Farm House
The Granary
Sch
WESTERHAM GOLF COURSE
54
RANDOLPH'S LA
FARLEY COMMON
Farley Grange
MKT. SQ
VICARAGE HILL
HOSEY HILL
Works
Westwood Farm
SURREY
KENT
Dunsdale House
Dunsdale Wood Farm
DUNSDALE WOOD
127
Works
Covers Farm
HIGH STREET
FB
B2026
Hosey Hill
Cross Dyke
Glebe House
TN16
Foxwold
The Grasshopper PH
WESTERHAM ROAD
SPRING SHAW
Piper's Farm
LODGES WOOD
Squerryes Court Gardens
Gillhams Farm
MANNING'S WOOD
Moorhouse Farm
SQUERRYES PARK
Cenotaph
Squerryes Home Farm
128
Moorhouse Bank
Moor House
MOORHOUSE BANK COMMON NT
FRENCH STREET
PIPERS GREEN
SPORTS GRD
53
STANHOPE WOOD
Athletic Club
CRONKLANDS
Valence End
BURIAL GRD
TOWER WOOD
HOSEY COMMON
129
Outridge
Tower
French Street Farm
French Street House
THE HIGH CHART
GOODLEY STOCK ROAD
Goodley Stock
130
Cobb Cottage
HOSEY COMMON ROAD
Cricket Ground
NT
Crockham House
Moorcroft Place
MAPLETON
52
Kent Hatch
French Street Nursery
131
THE CHART
MOORHOUSE ROAD
CROCKHAMHILL COMMON
KENT HATCH ROAD
B269
SCEARN BANK
NT
Kent Hatch House
NT
Chartwell
BROWN'S OVEN WOOD
Marie Curie Research Institute
TREVEREUX HILL
The Warren
Hopland
Chartwell Farm
BUDDLES WOOD
132
The Red House
Mariners
ROUNDMEAD SHAW
Crockham Hill Farm
Froghole Farm
FROGHOLE LANE
LANE
51
GUDGE WOOD
Trevereux
Froghole
Little Court
PUDDLEDOCK
HOSEY ROAD
SMITHS LANE
133
The Moat Farm
FB
Prim Sch
OAKDALE LA
CHANDLER WOOD
DERBY WOOD
PO
Hall
Woodmote
Coachmans
Kent Brook
TANDRIDGE
SEVENOAKS
Crockham Hill
TIES WOOD
SWAYNESLAND
Swaynesland
DEANERY RD
MAIN ROAD
SPOUT LANE
TN8
PERRY WOOD
134
DAIRY LANE
Hurst Farm
Old Dairy Farm
Pav
Tenn Cts
SPORTS GRD
DENNETTSLAND ROAD
PRIORY WOOD
ROW WOOD
Dennett Lodge Farm
Grange Farm
POOTINGS ROAD
LONGCROFT WOOD
HATCROFT WOOD
Redland Farm
GUILDABLES WOOD
Oak House

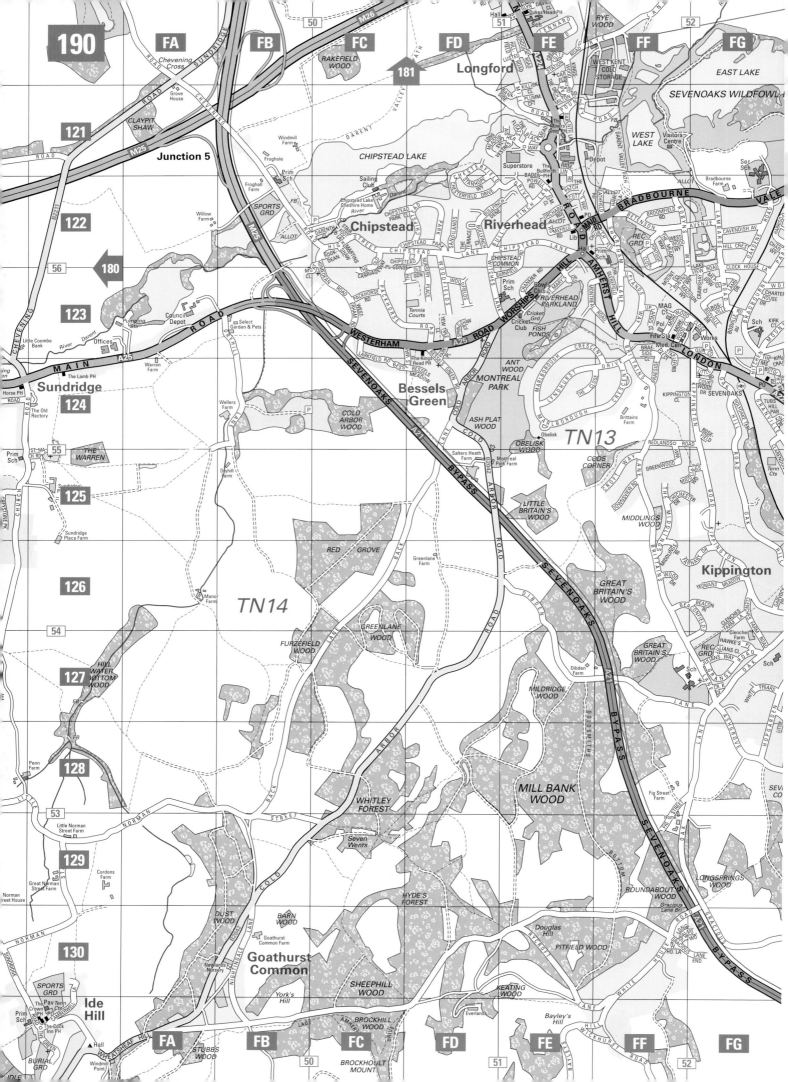

FA
FB
FC
FD
FE
FF
FG
181
180
121
122
123
124
125
126
127
128
129
130
50
51
52
53
54
55
56
Chevening Cross
Longford
Junction 5
CHIPSTEAD LAKE
Chipstead
Riverhead
Sundridge
Bessels Green
MONTREAL PARK
TN13
TN14
Kippington
SEVENOAKS WILDFOWL
EAST LAKE
WEST LAKE
RIVERHEAD PARKLAND
WESTERHAM ROAD
MAIN ROAD
SEVENOAKS BYPASS
RED GROVE
GREAT BRITAIN'S WOOD
MILL BANK WOOD
WHITLEY FOREST
HYDE'S FOREST
Goathurst Common
Ide Hill
SHEEPHILL WOOD
PITFIELD WOOD
DUST WOOD
BARN WOOD
STUBBS WOOD
BROCKHOULT MOUNT
KEATING WOOD
Everlands
Bayley's Hill
LONGSPRINGS WOOD
ROUNDABOUT WOOD
MILDRIDGE WOOD
GREENLANE WOOD
FURZEFIELD WOOD
HILL WATER BOTTOM WOOD
COLD ARBOR WOOD
ASH PLAT WOOD
ANT WOOD
OBELISK WOOD
LITTLE BRITAIN'S WOOD
CODS CORNER
MIDDLINGS WOOD
THE WARREN
CLAYPIT SHAW
RAKEFIELD WOOD
RYE WOOD
Seven Wents
Douglas Hill
York's Hill

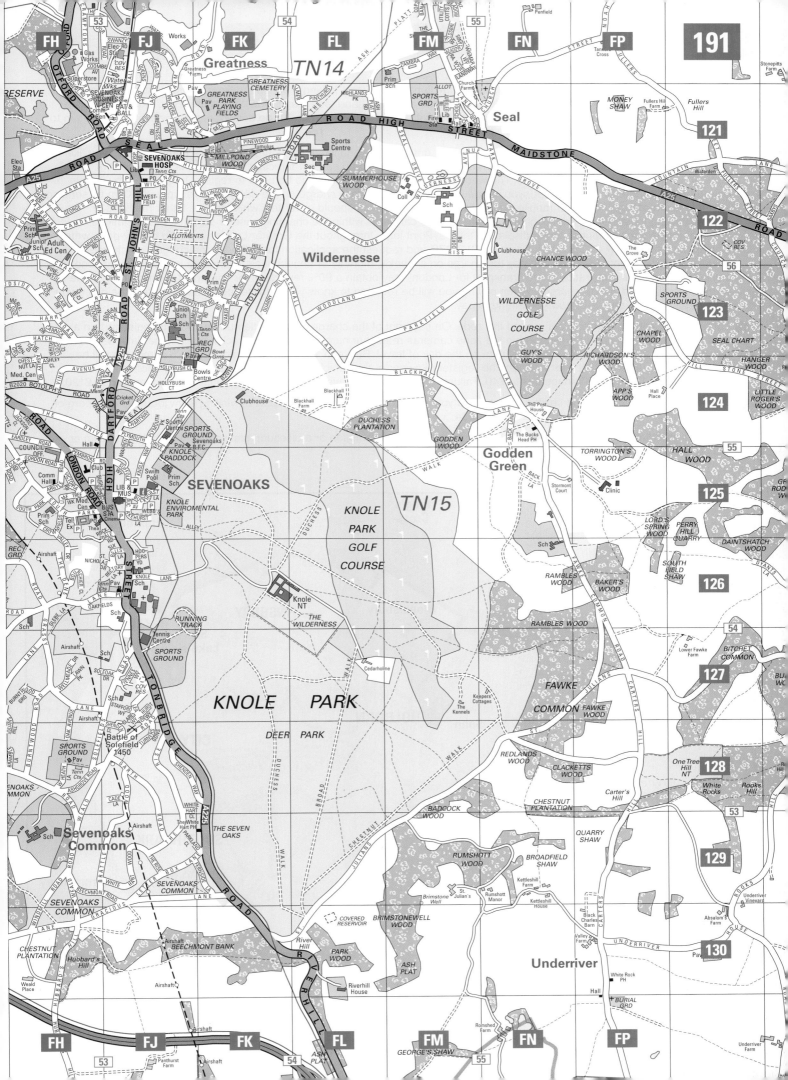

191
FH
FJ
FK
FL
FM
FN
FP
TN14
TN15
Greatness
Seal
Wildernesse
SEVENOAKS
Godden Green
KNOLE PARK
DEER PARK
KNOLE PARK GOLF COURSE
WILDERNESSE GOLF COURSE
FAWKE COMMON
Sevenoaks Common
SEVENOAKS COMMON
Underriver
SEAL ROAD
HIGH STREET
MAIDSTONE ROAD
TONBRIDGE ROAD
LONDON ROAD
DARTFORD ROAD
ST. JOHN'S HILL
RIVER HILL
A25
A225
121
122
123
124
125
126
127
128
129
130
53
54
55
56

- London's congestion charging zone operates inside the 'Inner Ring Road' linking Marylebone Road, Euston Road, Pentonville Road, Tower Bridge, Elephant and Castle, Vauxhall Bridge and Park Lane (see map below). The 'Inner Ring Road' provides a route around the charging zone and charges do not apply to vehicles travelling on it. The daily operating time is from 7.00 am to 6.30 pm, Monday to Friday, excluding public holidays.

- Payment of a £5 congestion charge allows you to enter, drive around and leave the charging zone as many times as you like that day. Payments can be made online at www.cclondon.com where you can get a receipt if required, or by phone on 0845 900 1234 charged at the local rate. The web site or phone number may also be used to register for payment by mobile phone text message. Once registered, you will be able to pay the £5 daily charge on the day you travel up until 10pm by sending a simple text message from your mobile phone. Please remember you should never text while driving. Other methods of payment are at most self service machines in major public car parks within the charging zone or selected petrol stations, newsagents and convenience stores, displaying the PayPoint logo, throughout the Greater London area. To pay by post, write to: Congestion charging, P O Box 2982, Coventry CV7 8ZR and request the application form 'Paying the congestion charge'. Regular drivers in central London can pay the charge on a weekly, monthly or annual basis. Residents in the charging zone, by paying a £10 annual registration fee to Transport for London, may obtain a 90% reduction, for one private vehicle only, in the weekly, monthly and annual charges. When paying you will be required to know your vehicle registration number, the dates you want to pay for and details of how you intend to pay.

- There are no tollbooths or barriers around the zone. On payment of the charge your vehicle number plate is registered on a database and on entering or driving within the zone cameras read your number plate and check it against the database. You can pay the charge, without penalty, until 10.00 pm on the day of travel. Between 10.00 pm and midnight a £5 surcharge will be made, making a total of £10; after midnight the registered owner of the vehicle will be sent a penalty charge notice for £80, payment within 14 days will reduce this to £40. Failure to pay within 28 days will result in the penalty being increased to £120.

- To avoid paying the congestion charge you can find your easiest route by public transport by visiting www.journeyplanner.org or calling London Travel Information on 020 7222 1234.

  For any further information, including a list of vehicles eligible for exemption or a discount, please visit www.cclondon.com or call 0845 900 1234.

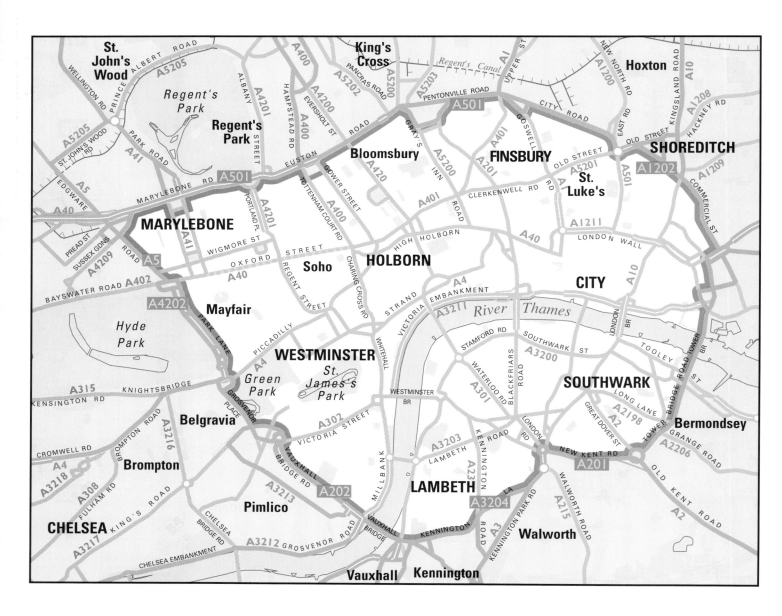

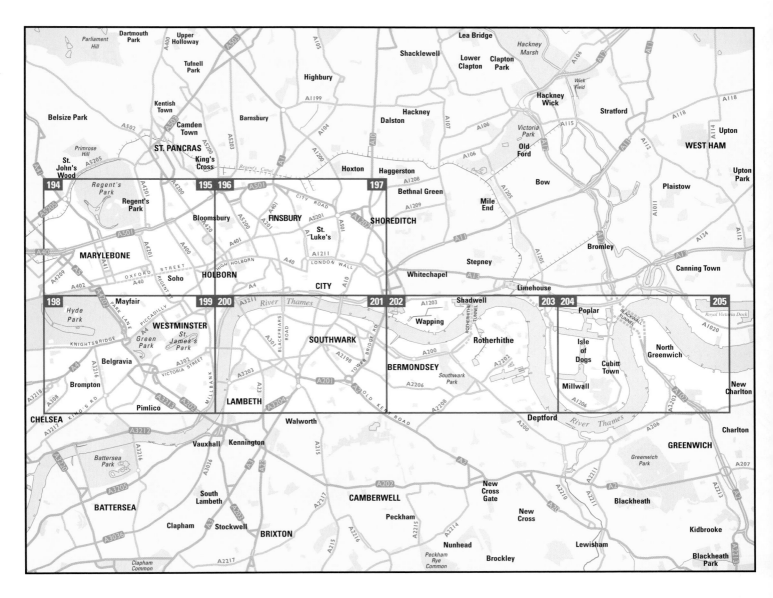

KEY TO MAP SYMBOLS

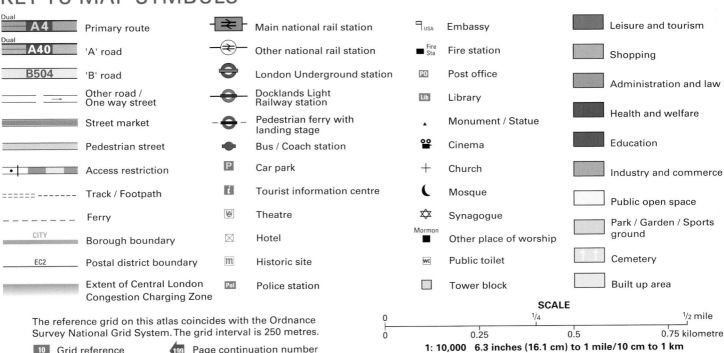

	Primary route
A4 Dual	
A40 Dual	'A' road
B504	'B' road
	Other road / One way street
	Street market
	Pedestrian street
	Access restriction
	Track / Footpath
	Ferry
CITY	Borough boundary
EC2	Postal district boundary
	Extent of Central London Congestion Charging Zone

Main national rail station

Other national rail station

London Underground station

Docklands Light Railway station

Pedestrian ferry with landing stage

Bus / Coach station

Car park

Tourist information centre

Theatre

Hotel

Historic site

Police station

Embassy

Fire station

Post office

Library

Monument / Statue

Cinema

Church

Mosque

Synagogue

Other place of worship

Public toilet

Tower block

Leisure and tourism

Shopping

Administration and law

Health and welfare

Education

Industry and commerce

Public open space

Park / Garden / Sports ground

Cemetery

Built up area

SCALE

The reference grid on this atlas coincides with the Ordnance Survey National Grid System. The grid interval is 250 metres.

10 Grid reference

199 Page continuation number

0   1/4   1/2 mile

0   0.25   0.5   0.75 kilometre

1: 10,000   6.3 inches (16.1 cm) to 1 mile/10 cm to 1 km

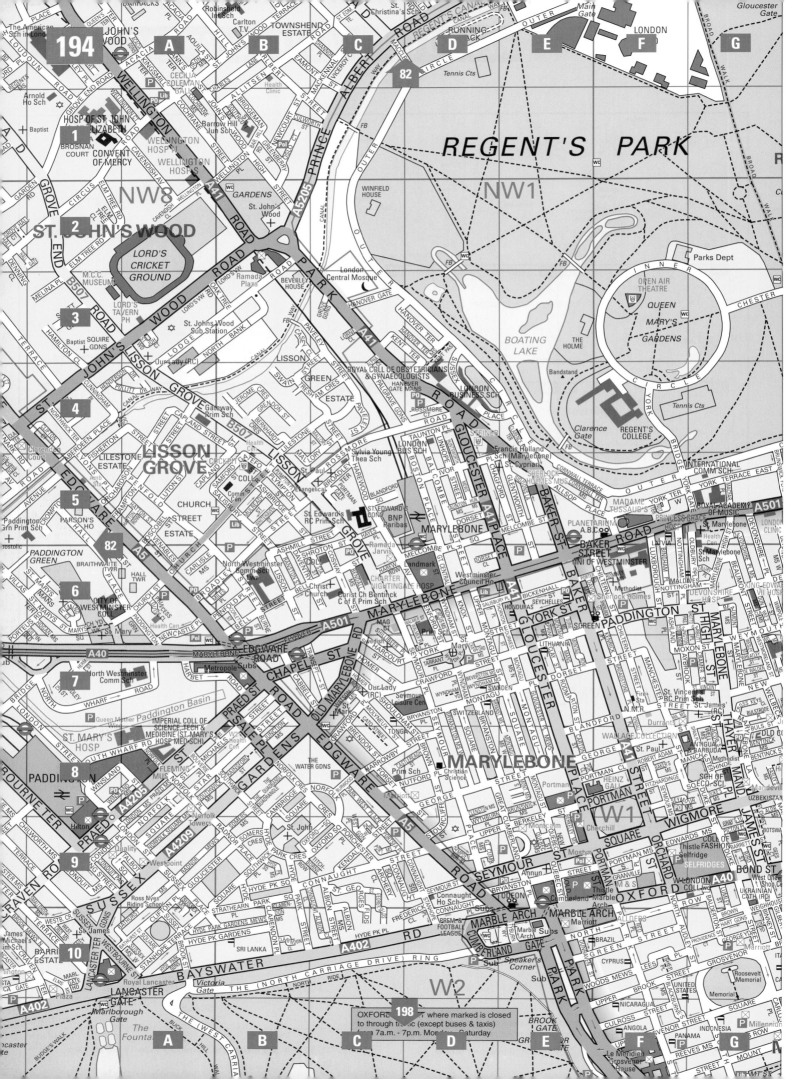
194
82
198
A
B
C
D
E
F
G
1
2
3
4
5
6
7
8
9
10
REGENT'S PARK
NW1
NW8
W1
W2
ST. JOHN'S WOOD
LORD'S CRICKET GROUND
M.C.C. MUSEUM
LORD'S TAVERN PH
LISSON GROVE
MARYLEBONE
PADDINGTON
PADDINGTON GREEN
LONDON ZOO
Gloucester Gate
Main Gate
REGENT'S CANAL
RUNNING TRACK
Tennis Cts
WINFIELD HOUSE
London Central Mosque
HANOVER GATE
BOATING LAKE
OPEN AIR THEATRE
QUEEN MARY'S GARDENS
THE HOLME
Bandstand
Parks Dept
Clarence Gate
REGENT'S COLLEGE
LONDON BUSINESS SCH
ROYAL COLL OF OBSTETRICIANS & GYNAECOLOGISTS
INTERNATIONAL COMM SCH
SHERLOCK HOLMES MUS
MADAME TUSSAUD'S
PLANETARIUM
ROYAL ACADEMY OF MUSIC
PRINCESS GRACE HOSP
BAKER STREET
UNI OF WESTMINSTER
HOSP OF ST. JOHN & ELIZABETH
CONVENT OF MERCY
WELLINGTON HOSP
CHARTER NIGHTINGALE HOSP
ST. MARY'S HOSP
IMPERIAL COLL OF SCIENCE, TECH & MEDICINE (ST MARY'S HOSP MED SCH)
Paddington Basin
CITY OF WESTMINSTER COLL
North Westminster Comm Sch
Landmark
Westminster Council Ho
WALLACE COLLECTION
SELFRIDGES
MARBLE ARCH
Speaker's Corner
Cumberland Gate
Victoria Gate
Lancaster Gate
Marlborough Gate
The Fountains
Royal Lancaster
Hilton
PRINCE ALBERT ROAD
PARK ROAD
WELLINGTON ROAD
ST. JOHN'S WOOD ROAD
LISSON GROVE
EDGWARE ROAD
MARYLEBONE ROAD
BAKER ST
GLOUCESTER PLACE
OXFORD STREET
BAYSWATER ROAD
SUSSEX GARDENS
PRAED ST
SEYMOUR PLACE
PORTMAN SQUARE
WIGMORE ST
GEORGE ST
PARK LANE
NORTH CARRIAGE DRIVE
OUTER CIRCLE
INNER CIRCLE
A41
A5
A40
A501
A402
A4205
A4209
A5205
B507
OXFORD ST where marked is closed to through traffic (except buses & taxis) from 7a.m. - 7p.m. Monday - Saturday

195
H
J
K
L
M
N
P
83
196
199
1
2
3
4
5
6
7
8
9
10
REGENT'S PARK
MORNINGTON CRESCENT
SOMERS TOWN
BRITISH LIBRARY
ST. PANCRAS
KING'S CROSS
KING'S CROSS & ST. PANCRAS
KING'S CROSS THAMESLINK
EUSTON
EUSTON SQUARE
WARREN ST
GT. PORTLAND ST
REGENT'S PARK
ST. PANCRAS
BLOOMSBURY
THE BRITISH MUSEUM
RUSSELL SQUARE GARDENS
UNIVERSITY OF LONDON
WC1
WC2
GOODGE ST
TOTTENHAM COURT RD
OXFORD CIRCUS
SOHO
COVENT GARDEN
LEICESTER SQ.
STRAND
HOLBORN
MAYFAIR
PICCADILLY CIRCUS
HAMPSTEAD ROAD
EUSTON ROAD
OXFORD ST
REGENT ST
TOTTENHAM CT RD
GOWER ST
CHARING CROSS RD
SHAFTESBURY AV
NEW OXFORD ST
ALBANY STREET
PORTLAND PLACE
WOBURN PL
SOUTHAMPTON ROW
A400
A4200
A501
A40
A4201
A5204
A5202
A401
B506
B504
B502
B406

196
A
B
C
D
E
F
G
1
2
3
4
5
6
7
8
9
10
83
195
200
KING'S CROSS
ST. PANCRAS
PENTONVILLE
PENTONVILLE ROAD
A501
CITY ROAD
FINSBURY
EC1
CLERKENWELL
CLERKENWELL RD
A5201
ST. PANCRAS
WC1
CORAM'S FIELDS
RUSSELL SQUARE GARDENS
BLOOMSBURY
THE BRITISH MUSEUM
HOLBORN
LINCOLN'S INN FIELDS
CAMDEN
GRAY'S INN GARDENS
FARRINGDON
FARRINGDON ROAD
MOUNT PLEASANT MAIL CENTRE
ISLINGTON
WC2
COVENT GARDEN
STRAND
EC4
BLACKFRIARS
VICTORIA EMBANKMENT
ROYAL COURTS OF JUSTICE
FLEET STREET
SOMERSET HOUSE
ST. BARTHOLOMEW'S HOSPITAL
CHANCERY LANE
GRAY'S INN ROAD
KINGSWAY
ALDWYCH
EUSTON RD
GUILFORD ST
B502
SOUTHAMPTON ROW
THEOBALD'S RD
A401
A5200
A201
B500
CHARTERHOUSE
ANGEL
THAMESLINK
BLACKFRIARS MILLENNIUM PIER
H.M.S. PRESIDENT
KING'S REACH

197
H
J
K
L
M
N
P
1
2
3
4
5
6
7
8
9
10
84
201
HOXTON
SHOREDITCH
ST. LUKE'S
BROADGATE
BARBICAN
CITY
N1
E2
E1
EC2
EC3
HAGGERSTON
CITY ROAD
OLD STREET
GREAT EASTERN STREET
COMMERCIAL STREET
BISHOPSGATE
KINGSLAND ROAD
HACKNEY ROAD
COLUMBIA RD
BETHNAL GREEN ROAD
NEW NORTH RD
EAST ROAD
CITY ROAD BASIN
WENLOCK BASIN
REGENT'S CANAL
BUNHILL FIELDS
FINSBURY SQ
LIVERPOOL STREET
MOORGATE
LONDON WALL
HOUNDSDITCH
ALDGATE
MINORIES
FENCHURCH
TOWER HILL
MONUMENT
BANK
MANSION HOUSE
ST. PAUL'S CATHEDRAL
CHEAPSIDE
CANNON STREET
LEADENHALL
GRACECHURCH ST
TOWER OF LONDON
OLD SPITALFIELDS MARKET
HACKNEY COMMUNITY COLL
MOORFIELDS EYE HOSP
TOWER 42
Bank of England
Royal Ex
Swiss Re
Lloyds of London

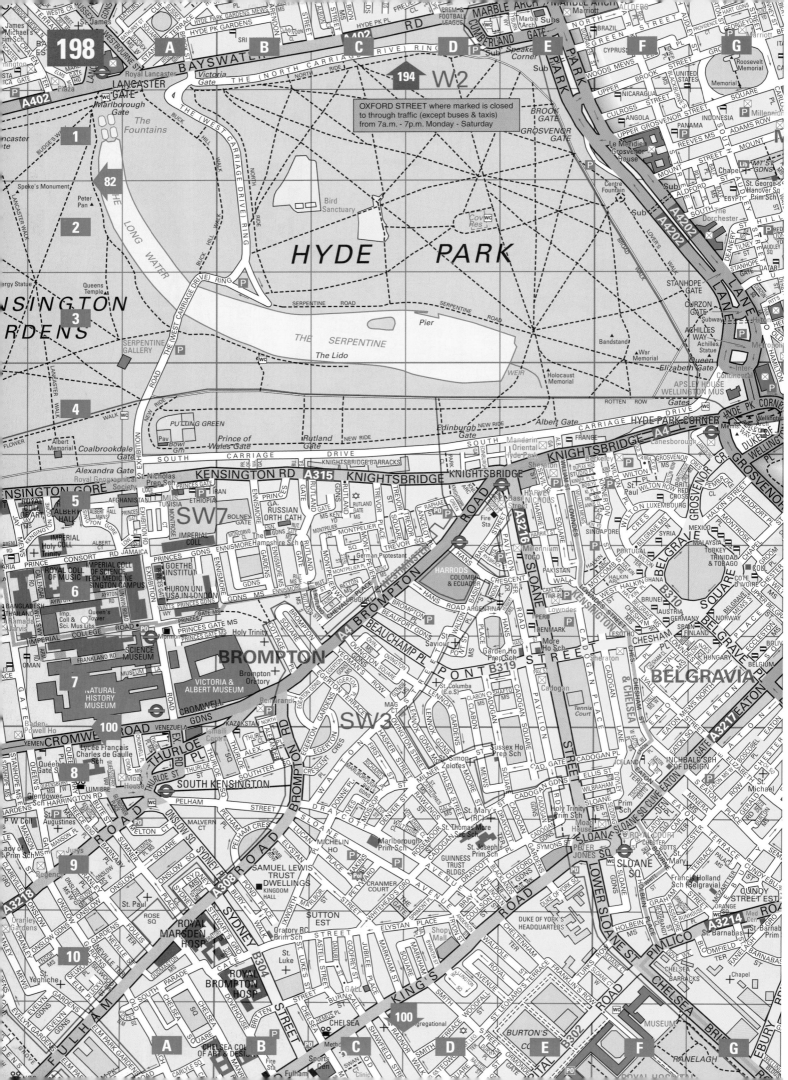

198
194
82
100
W2
SW7
SW3
A
B
C
D
E
F
G
1
2
3
4
5
6
7
8
9
10
OXFORD STREET where marked is closed to through traffic (except buses & taxis) from 7a.m. - 7p.m. Monday - Saturday
HYDE PARK
KENSINGTON GARDENS
THE SERPENTINE
The Lido
THE LONG WATER
The Fountains
Speke's Monument
Peter Pan
Queens Temple
SERPENTINE GALLERY
Albert Memorial
Bird Sanctuary
Pier
Bandstand
War Memorial
Holocaust Memorial
Achilles Statue
Centre Fountain
APSLEY HOUSE WELLINGTON MUS
MARBLE ARCH
Speakers Corner
Victoria Gate
LANCASTER GATE
Marlborough Gate
BROOK GATE
GROSVENOR GATE
STANHOPE GATE
CURZON GATE
Queen Elizabeth Gate
Albert Gate
Edinburgh Gate
Rutland Gate
Prince of Wales Gate
Alexandra Gate
Coalbrookdale Gate
PUTTING GREEN
BAYSWATER RD
NORTH CARRIAGE DRIVE
SOUTH CARRIAGE DRIVE
SERPENTINE ROAD
ROTTEN ROW
PARK LANE
A4202
A402
HYDE PARK CORNER
KENSINGTON RD
A315
KNIGHTSBRIDGE
KENSINGTON GORE
ROYAL ALBERT HALL
IMPERIAL COLL
ROYAL COLL OF MUSIC
SCIENCE MUSEUM
NATURAL HISTORY MUSEUM
VICTORIA & ALBERT MUSEUM
BROMPTON
Brompton Oratory
Holy Trinity
HARRODS
BROMPTON ROAD
A4
CROMWELL ROAD
SOUTH KENSINGTON
THURLOE PL
PELHAM STREET
ONSLOW SQ
SLOANE STREET
A3216
PONT STREET
B319
BELGRAVIA
BELGRAVE SQUARE
B310
EATON SQUARE
EATON PL
A3217
CHESHAM ST
SLOANE SQ
LOWER SLOANE ST
DUKE OF YORK'S HEADQUARTERS
KING'S ROAD
FULHAM ROAD
A308
SYDNEY ST
B304
ROYAL MARSDEN HOSP
ROYAL BROMPTON HOSP
CHELSEA COLL OF ART & DESIGN
SAMUEL LEWIS TRUST DWELLINGS
SUTTON EST
GUINNESS TRUST BLDGS
CADOGAN SQUARE
CADOGAN PL
CHELSEA BARRACKS
PIMLICO RD
A3214
A3218
B302
BURTON'S COURT
MUSEUM
Royal Lancaster
Le Meridien Grosvenor House
The Dorchester
Roosevelt Memorial
Mandarin Oriental Hyde Park
Lanesborough
Sheraton
Lycee Francais Charles de Gaulle Sch
Peter Jones
Sloane Sq

199
H
J
K
L
M
N
P
SOHO
195
STRAND
MAYFAIR
W1
PICCADILLY
PICCADILLY CIRCUS
ROYAL ACAD. OF ARTS
NATIONAL GALLERY
TRAFALGAR
CHARING CROSS
EMBANKMENT
GREEN PARK
ST. JAMES'S
ST. JAMES'S PARK
PALL MALL
THE MALL
HAYMARKET
REGENT ST
WHITEHALL
MINISTRY OF DEFENCE
HORSE GUARDS
DOWNING ST
FOREIGN & COMMONWEALTH OFFICE
H.M. TREASURY
WESTMINSTER
WESTMINSTER MILLENNIUM PIER
CONSTITUTION HILL
Closed to Traffic on Sundays
BUCKINGHAM PALACE GARDENS
BUCKINGHAM PALACE
THE QUEEN'S GALLERY
THE ROYAL MEWS
SW1
BIRDCAGE WALK
WELLINGTON BARRACKS
GUARDS MUS
HOME OFFICE
WESTMINSTER ABBEY
200
HOUSES OF PARLIAMENT
VICTORIA TOWER GARDENS
ST. THOMAS' HOSP
VICTORIA
BUS STA
VICTORIA STREET
WESTMINSTER CATH (RC)
NEW SCOTLAND YARD
HORSEFERRY RD
LAMBETH BRI
MILLBANK
THAMES HOUSE
TATE BRITAIN
MILLBANK TOWER
MILLBANK MILLENNIUM PIER
PLAYING FIELDS
GORDON HOSP
VAUXHALL BRIDGE ROAD
BELGRAVE ROAD
PIMLICO
COACH STA
ECCLESTON ST
BUCKINGHAM PALACE RD
LILLINGTON GARDENS EST
RIVERSIDE GARDENS
ALBERT EMBANKMENT
VAUXHALL BRIDGE
101
CHURCHILL GARDENS
DOLPHIN
1
2
3
4
5
6
7
8
9
10

A
B
C
D
E
F
G
1
2
3
4
5
6
7
8
9
10
196
199
101
STRAND
WC2
EC4
SW1
SE11
RIVER THAMES
KING'S REACH
VICTORIA EMBANKMENT
WATERLOO BRI
BLACKFRIARS BRI
BLACKFRIARS
BLACKFRIARS MILLENNIUM PIER
H.M.S. PRESIDENT
H.Q.S. WELLINGTON MASTER MARINERS'
SOMERSET HOUSE
KING'S COLL (STRAND CAMPUS)
TEMPLE
Inner Temple
Middle Temple
CHARING CROSS
EMBANKMENT
EMBANKMENT PIER
Charing Cross Pier
Cleopatra's Needle
SAVOY PIER
T.S. QUEEN MARY
NATIONAL GALLERY
TRAFALGAR
WHITEHALL
MINISTRY OF DEFENCE
HORSE GUARDS AV
Royal Horseguards Thistle
PS TATTERSHALL CASTLE
HISPANIOLA
HUNGERFORD BRI
Golden Jubilee Bri
Festival Pier
ROYAL FESTIVAL HALL
QUEEN ELIZABETH HALL & PURCELL ROOM
HAYWARD GALLERY
NAT FILM THEA
ROYAL NATIONAL
IBM
The London Television Centre
GABRIEL'S WHARF
OXO TWR WHARF
H.M. CUSTOMS AND EXCISE
STAMFORD STREET
A3200
IMAX
Shell Centre
JUBILEE GDNS
LONDON EYE
County Hall
London Aquarium
SAATCHI GALL
WATERLOO MILLENNIUM PIER
WATERLOO
WATERLOO INTERNATIONAL
WATERLOO EAST
THE CUT
THE YOUNG VIC
THE OLD VIC
SOUTHWARK
UNION
BLACKFRIARS ROAD
A201
DOWNING ST
RICHMOND TER
FOREIGN & COMMONWEALTH OFFICE
H.M. TREASURY
KING CHARLES ST
WESTMINSTER
WESTMINSTER MILLENNIUM PIER
PARLIAMENT SQUARE
BRIDGE ST
WESTMINSTER BRI
A302
St. Stephen's Tower (Big Ben)
HOUSES OF PARLIAMENT
WESTMINSTER ABBEY
Victoria Tower
VICTORIA TOWER GARDENS
FLORENCE NIGHTINGALE MUS
ST. THOMAS' HOSP
LAMBETH
LAMBETH PALACE GDNS
ARCHBISHOP'S PARK
Lambeth Palace
LAMBETH BRI
Lambeth Pier
MUS OF GARDEN HISTORY
LAMBETH NORTH
WESTMINSTER BRIDGE ROAD
ST. GEORGE'S CATH (RC)
ST. GEORGE'S CIRCUS
ST. GEORGE'S ROAD
BOROUGH
SOUTH BANK UNI
LONDON ROAD
GERALDINE MARY HARMSWORTH PARK
IMPERIAL WAR MUS
KENNINGTON ROAD
A23
LAMBETH ROAD
A3203
MILLBANK
A3212
THAMES HOUSE
MILLBANK TOWER
MILLBANK MILLENNIUM PIER
TATE BRITAIN
RIVERSIDE GARDENS
VAUXHALL BRI
A202
VAUXHALL
A3036
ALBERT EMBANKMENT
KENNINGTON LANE
A3204
KENNINGTON PARK ROAD
A3
KENNINGTON
NEWINGTON BUTTS
ELEPHANT & CASTLE
LONDON COLL OF PRINTING
SOUTHWARK PARK
Lilian Baylis Sch
SE11
Michael Tippett Sch
ALBERTA EST
Kennington
CITY & GUILDS OF LONDON ART SCH
SURREY GDNS

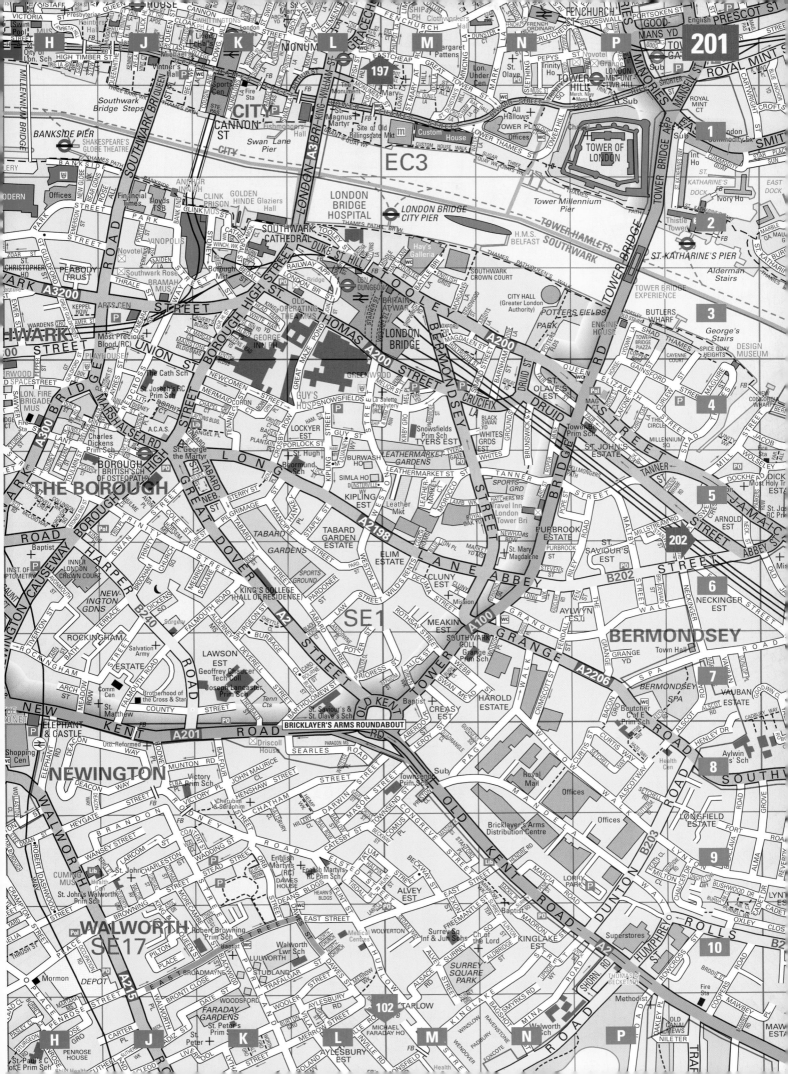

201
197
202
102
H
J
K
L
M
N
P
1
2
3
4
5
6
7
8
9
10
FENCHURCH ST
MONUMENT
CITY
CANNON ST
EASTCHEAP
GREAT TOWER ST
TOWER HILL
MINORIES
ROYAL MINT ST
ROYAL MINT CT
TOWER OF LONDON
Custom House
Site of Old Billingsgate Mkt
St. Magnus Martyr
Fishmongers Hall
Swan Lane Pier
LOWER THAMES ST
Offices
All Hallows
Tower Millennium Pier
EC3
LONDON BRIDGE CITY PIER
LONDON BRIDGE HOSPITAL
H.M.S. BELFAST
TOWER HAMLETS
SOUTHWARK
ST. KATHARINE'S PIER
Alderman Stairs
TOWER BRIDGE
TOWER BRIDGE APP
TOWER BRIDGE EXPERIENCE
BUTLERS WHARF
George's Stairs
DESIGN MUSEUM
SOUTHWARK CROWN COURT
CITY HALL (Greater London Authority)
POTTERS FIELDS PARK
Hay's Galleria
SOUTHWARK CATHEDRAL
Southwark Bridge Steps
MILLENNIUM BRIDGE
BANKSIDE PIER
SHAKESPEARE'S GLOBE THEATRE
SOUTHWARK BRIDGE
SOUTHWARK BR RD
LONDON BR
CLINK PRISON
GOLDEN HINDE
VINOPOLIS
Borough Mkt
TOOLEY ST
ST THOMAS ST
GUY'S HOSP
LONDON BRIDGE
BRITAIN AT WAR
LDN DUNGEON
BOROUGH HIGH ST
MARSHALSEA RD
THE BOROUGH
SOUTHWARK ST
UNION ST
LONG LANE
BERMONDSEY ST
DRUID ST
QUEEN ELIZABETH ST
JAMAICA RD
ABBEY ST
TANNER ST
LEATHERMARKET GARDENS
KIPLING EST
TABARD GARDEN ESTATE
TABARD GARDENS
GREAT DOVER ST
A2198
A200
A100
A2206
A2
A201
A215
A3200
A300
B202
B203
B240
SE1
SE17
BERMONDSEY
Town Hall
GRANGE RD
NECKINGER EST
BERMONDSEY SPA
VAUBAN ESTATE
SOUTHWARK PARK RD
LONGFIELD ESTATE
HAROLD ESTATE
Royal Mail
Bricklayer's Arms Distribution Centre
BRICKLAYER'S ARMS ROUNDABOUT
OLD KENT ROAD
NEW KENT ROAD
ELEPHANT & CASTLE
NEWINGTON
WALWORTH
WALWORTH RD
EAST STREET
ALVEY EST
KINGLAKE EST
SURREY SQUARE PARK
LAWSON EST
ROCKINGHAM ESTATE
NEWINGTON GDNS
INNER LONDON CROWN COURT
HARPER RD
NEWINGTON CAUSEWAY
BOROUGH RD
FALMOUTH ROAD
King's College (Hall of Residence)
Geoffrey Chaucer Tech Coll
DUNTON RD
ROLLS RD
HUMPHREY ST
FARADAY GARDENS
AYLESBURY EST
DEPOT
Superstores
Methodist

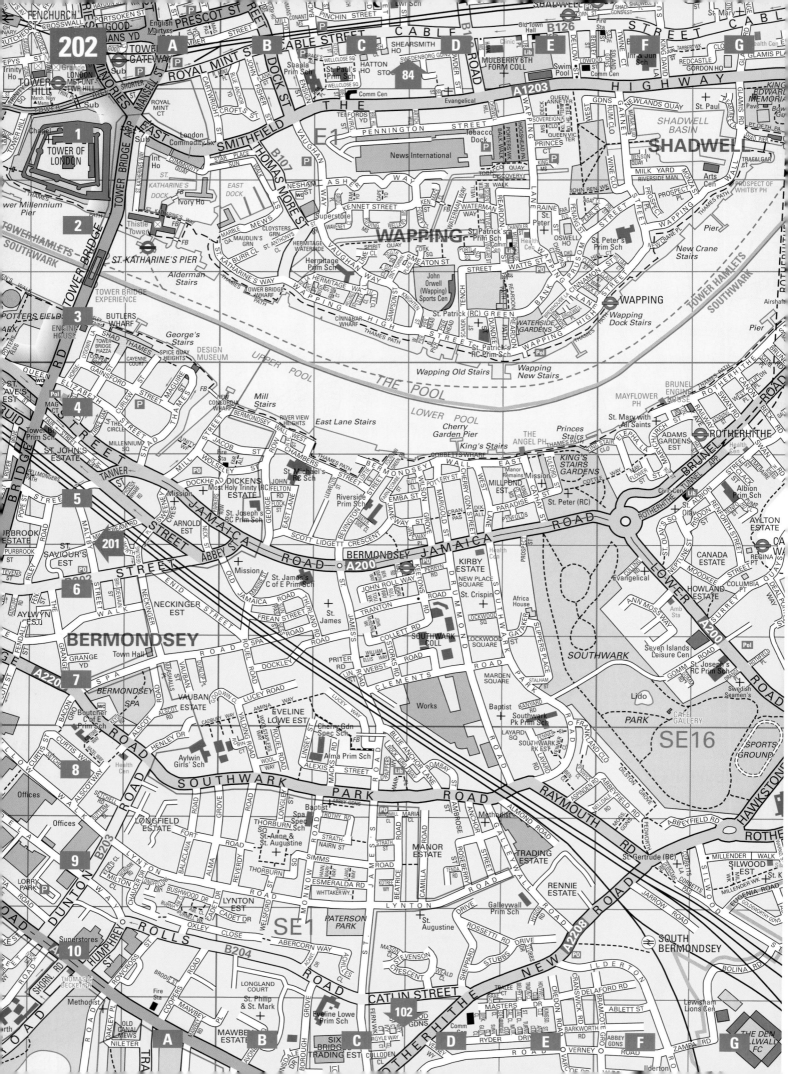

203
LIMEHOUSE
H
J
K
L
M
N
P
85
204
103
RIVER THAMES
LIMEHOUSE REACH
ROTHERHITHE
DEPTFORD
E14
SE8
SOUTHWARK
TOWER HAMLETS
LEWISHAM
WESTFERRY
CANARY WHARF
HERON QUAYS
WEST INDIA
MILLWALL
SIR JOHN MCDOUGALL GDNS
GREENLAND DOCK
SOUTH DOCK
NORWAY DOCK
SURREY WATER
CANADA WATER
RUSSIA DOCK WOODLAND
ECOLOGICAL PARK
Stave Hill
MELLISH SPORTS GROUND
DEPTFORD PARK
PEPYS PARK
SURREY QUAYS
Surrey Quays Retail Centre
MULBERRY BUSINESS CENTRE
CANNON WHARF BUSINESS CENTRE
MUSEUM IN DOCKLANDS
Telegraph & Express Print Works
Royal Naval Yd
SALTER ROAD
LOWER ROAD
EVELYN STREET
GROVE STREET
PLOUGH WAY
ROTHERHITHE STREET
REDRIFF ROAD
NARROW STREET
WESTFERRY ROAD
MARSH WALL
A13
A1203
A1206
A2202
A200
B205
B206
B207
1
2
3
4
5
6
7
8
9
10

204
A
B
C
D
E
F
G
1
2
3
4
5
6
7
8
9
10
85
203
103
EAST INDIA DOCK ROAD
A13
FOUNDATION
ROSEFIELD GDNS
PENNYFIELDS
Holy Family RC Prim Sch
MING ST
WESTFERRY
Comm Cen
Tenn Cts
REC GRD
St. Matthias
Bowl Grn
WOODSTOCK TERRACE
HALE STREET
ALL SAINTS
COTTON ST
Woolmore Prim Sch
COUNCIL OFFICES
SAFFRON
EAST INDIA
ROBIN HOOD GDNS
NAVAL ROW
B123
POPLAR HIGH STREET
DINGLE GDNS
Sports Cen
TOWER HAMLETS COLL (POPLAR CEN)
CASTOR LANE
TRAIN DEPOT
HARROW LA
POPLAR BUSINESS PARK
BLACKWALL
A1206
A1261
ASPEN WAY
NEWPORT AVENUE
JAMESTOWN WAY
PAUL JULIUS CL
Reuters
Jetty
LINK
GARFORD ST
HERTSMERE ROAD
CANNON DRIVE
UGC
POPLAR
MUSEUM IN DOCKLANDS
WEST INDIA QUAY
POPLAR
Billingsgate Fish Mkt
E14
TRAFALGAR WAY
BROADWALK PLACE
POPLAR DOCK
Ibis
BLACKWALL WAY
A102
BLACKWALL TUNNEL
ONTARIO WAY
WEST INDIA AVE
Fisherman's Offices
WESTFERRY CIRCUS
CABOT SQ
Cabot Place
NORTH COLONNADE
CANARY WHARF
HSBC
Barclays
SOUTH COLONNADE
Offices
MACKENZIE WK
No1 CANADA SQ
Canada Square
Citygroup
Superstore
CHURCHILL PL
CARTIER CIRCLE
BLACKWALL BASIN
CIVIC AMENITY SITE
LANDONS CL
PRESTONS ROAD
BLACKWALL REACH
Airy's Point
MERIDIAN GARDENS
ABERDEEN SQ
PARK PL
HERON QUAY
JUBILEE PK
UPR BANK ST
MONTGOMERY ST
HERON QUAYS
BANK STREET
Works
COLD HARBOUR
Pier
WEST INDIA DOCKS
MARSH WALL
The International Hotel
South Quay Plaza
THE GUN PH
DRAWDOCK RD
CHANDLERS MS
ANCHORAGE POINT
CUBA ST
MANILLA ST
ADMIRALS WAY
SOUTH QUAY
Thames Quay (L.D.D.C.)
Lock
MILLENNIUM HARBOUR
BYNG STREET
MERIDIAN PL
MERIDIAN GATE
LAWN HO CL
THAMES PATH
Jetty
STRAFFORD STREET
TOPMAST POINT
St. Luke
ISLE
MASTMAKER RD
SKYLINES VILLAGE
HARBOUR EX SQUARE
LIMEHARBOUR
STEWART ST
Pumping Sta
Delta Wharf
QUARTERDECK
MIDSHIP POINT
ALPHA GROVE
LIGHTERMANS RD
INDESCON COURT
MILLWALL
MILLHARBOUR
CHIPKA ST
ROFFEY ST
ASTE ST
MANCHESTER ROAD
FOLLY WALL
OCEAN WHARF
Seven Mills Prim Sch
LANTERNS COURT
Great Eastern Enterprise Cen
RIVER BARGE CL
Comm Cen
CASTALIA SQ
Clinic
KNIGHTHEAD POINT
INNER
LONDON ARENA (closed)
PLEVNA STREET
CUBITT TOWN
SIR JOHN MCDOUGALL GDNS
MELLISH STREET
OF
DOCK
EAST FERRY ROAD
Tenn Cts
KELSON HO
NEW UNION CL
TILLER ROAD
Swim Pool
PEPPER ST
CROSSHARBOUR & LONDON ARENA
Lib
GLENGALL GROVE
GLENGALL CAUSEWAY
CLAIRE PL
STARBOARD WAY
MILLWALL DOCK RD
TURNBERRY QUAY
MARSHFIELD ST
AMSTERDAM RD
ARNHEM PL
Telegraph & Express Print Works
SELSDON WAY
Cubitt Town Jun & Inf Sch
New Atlas Wharf
Arnhem Wf Prim Sch
GREENWICH VIEW PL
Superstore
FRIARS MEAD
JUBILEE CRES
SCHOONER CL
Pier
TOWER HAMLETS
GREENWICH
Docklands Sailing & Watersport Cen
DOGS
MILLWALL OUTER DOCK
MILLENNIUM DRIVE
ARDEN CRES
MILLWALL
SEVERNAKE CL
WHEAT SHEAF CL
TAEPING STREET
TELEGRAPH PL
BARNSDALE AVE
WHITEADDER WAY
FALCON WAY
UNDINE ROAD
Mudchute Farm
PIER STREET
ALLOT
MUDCHUTE PARK
SEXTANT AVE
CREWS ST
WINDMILL HO
HOMER DR
St. Edmund (RC)
SPINDRIFT AVENUE
MUDCHUTE
SEYSSEL ST
KINGFIELD ST
BILLSON ST
PLYMOUTH WF
STORERS QUAY
St. Edmund's RC Prim Sch
Works
Medical Cen
GLOBE ROPE WALK
St. Luke's Prim Sch
LEWISHAM
FERGUSON CLOSE
MASTHOUSE TER
BARNFIELD PL
HARBINGER RD
HESPERUS CRESCENT
THERMOPYLAE GATE
MACQUARIE WAY
MILLWALL PARK
PARSONAGE ST
Pol
CALEDONIAN WHARF
WESTFERRY ROAD
Harbinger Prim Sch
Works
HOUSE ST
Comm Cen
Bowling Green
SPORTS GROUND
GLENGARNOCK AVE
Christ & St. John
EMPIRE WF RD
GROSVENOR WF RD
CAHIR STREET
NAPIER AVE
CHAPEL HOUSE
ISLAND GARDENS
STEBONDALE ST
Leisure Cen
Newcastle Draw Dock
Granite Wharf
MARITIME QUAY
LOCKESFIELD PL
Fire Sta
MANCHESTER GRO
George Green's Sec Sch
SAUNDERS NESS RD
CUMBERLAND MILLS SQ
MASTHOUSE TERRACE
BLASKER WALK
RAINBOW AVE
WYNAN RD
MANCHESTER ROAD
HORSESHOE CL
ISLAND GARDENS
Lovell's Wharf
BALLAST QUAY
Palmer's Wharf
THAMES PATH
ST. DAVIDS SQUARE
FERRY HOUSE PH
FERRY STREET
Comm Cen
Rowing Club
LASSELL ST
HOSKINS ST
Royal Naval Yd
Payne's Wharf
TOWER HAMLETS
GREENWICH
GREENWICH
GREENWICH FOOT TUNNEL
High Bridge Wharf
Trafalgar Rowing Cen
Landing Stage

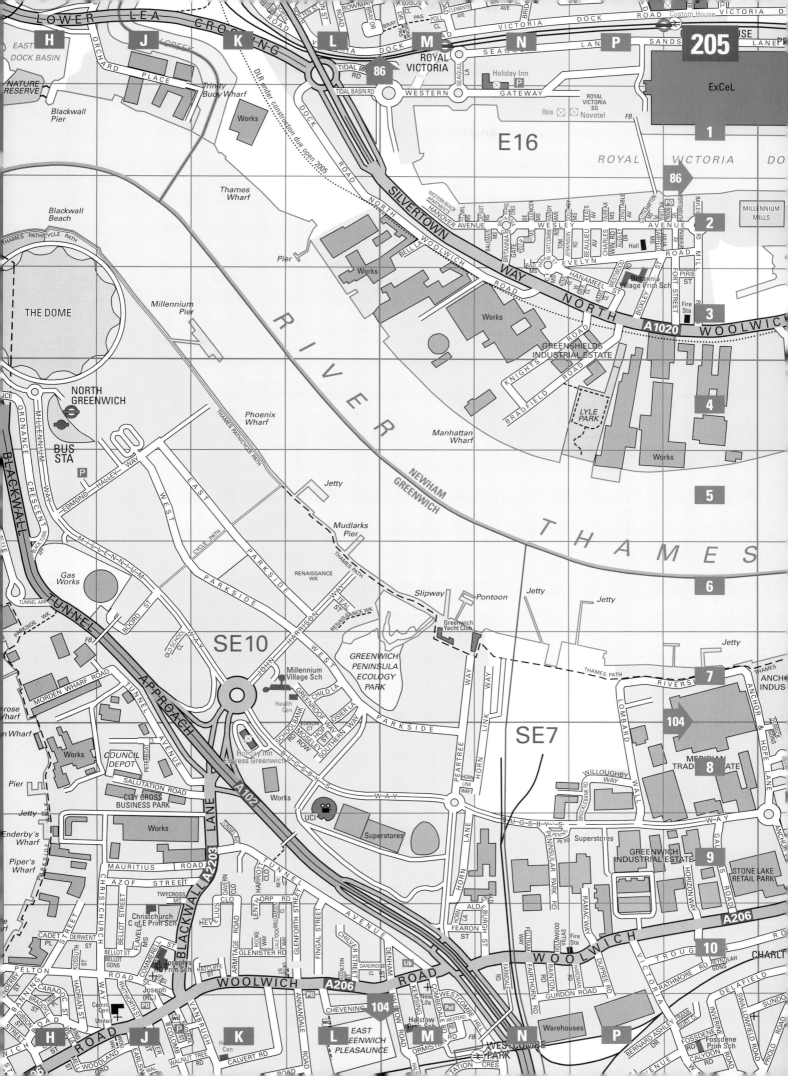
205
H
J
K
L
M
N
P
86
104
1
2
3
4
5
6
7
8
9
10
ExCeL
E16
SE10
SE7
ROYAL VICTORIA DOCK
RIVER THAMES
NEWHAM
GREENWICH
THE DOME
NORTH GREENWICH
BUS STA
LOWER LEA CROSSING
SILVERTOWN WAY
NORTH WOOLWICH ROAD
A1020
BLACKWALL TUNNEL APPROACH
A102
A2203
A206
WOOLWICH ROAD
ROYAL VICTORIA
Holiday Inn
Ibis
Novotel
Trinity Buoy Wharf
Blackwall Pier
Blackwall Beach
Thames Wharf
Millennium Pier
Phoenix Wharf
Manhattan Wharf
Mudlarks Pier
GREENSHIELDS INDUSTRIAL ESTATE
LYLE PARK
MILLENNIUM MILLS
Britannia Village Prim Sch
Gas Works
Greenwich Yacht Club
GREENWICH PENINSULA ECOLOGY PARK
Millennium Village Sch
Holiday Inn Express Greenwich
COUNCIL DEPOT
CITY CROSS BUSINESS PARK
GREENWICH INDUSTRIAL ESTATE
STONE LAKE RETAIL PARK
MERIDIAN TRADE ESTATE
Christchurch C of E Prim Sch
St. Josephs RC Prim Sch
EAST GREENWICH PLEASAUNCE
Fossdene Prim Sch
WESTCOMBE PARK
DLR under construction due open 2005

Notes on how to use the index

The index starting on page 282 combines entries for street names, place names, places of interest, stations and hospitals.

Place names are shown in capital letters,
        e.g. **ACTON**, W3 . . . .**80**CN74
These include towns, villages and other localities within the area covered by this atlas.

Places of interest are shown with a star symbol,
        e.g. ★ **British Mus**, WC1 . . . .**195**   P7
These include parks, museums, galleries, other important buildings and tourist attractions.

Hospitals, schools and types of station are shown by symbols as listed :-
    H   Hospital
    ⇄   Railway station
    ⊖   London Underground station
    DLR   Docklands Light Railway station
    Tra   Tramlink station
    Riv   Pedestrian ferry landing stage

All other entries are for street names. When there is more than one street with exactly the same name then that name is shown only once in the index. It is then followed by a list of entries for each postal district that contains a street with that same name. For example, there are three streets called **Ardley Close** in this atlas and the index entry shows that one of these is in London postal district NW10, one is in London postal district SE6 and one is in Ruislip HA4.
        e.g. **Ardley Cl**, NW10 . . . .**62**   CS62
                SE6 . . . .**123**   DY90
                Ruislip HA4 . . . .**59**   BQ59
All entries are followed by the page number and grid reference on which the name will be found. So, in the example above, **Ardley Close**, NW10 will be found on page **62** in square CS62.
All entries are indexed to the largest scale map on which they are shown.

The index also contains some streets which are not actually named on the maps because there is not enough space. In these cases the adjoining or nearest named thoroughfare to such a street is shown in *italic*. The reference indicates where the unnamed street is located *off* the named thoroughfare.
        e.g. **Bacton St**, E2 *off Roman Rd* **84**   DW69
This means that **Bacton Street** is not named on the map, but it is located *off Roman Road* on page **84** in square DW69.

A strict letter-by-letter alphabetical order is followed in this index. All non-alphabetic characters such as spaces, hyphens or apostrophes have not been included in the index order. For example **Belle Vue Road** and **Bellevue Road** will be found listed together.

Standard terms such as **Avenue, Close, Rise** and **Road** are abbreviated in the index but are ordered alphabetically as if given in full. So, for example, **Abbots Ri** comes before **Abbots Rd**.

Names beginning with a definite article (i.e. **The**) are indexed from their second word onwards with the definite article being placed at the end of the name.
        e.g. **Avenue, The**, E4 . . . .**47**   ED51

The alphabetical order extends to include postal information so that where two or more streets have exactly the same name, London postal district references are given first in alpha-numeric order and are followed by non-London post town references in alphabetical order, e.g. **Ardley Close**, NW10 is followed by **Ardley Close**, SE6 and then **Ardley Close**, Ruislip HA4.

In cases where there are two or more streets of the same name in the same postal area, extra information is given in brackets to aid location. For example, **High St**, Orpington BR6 (Farnborough), and **High St**, Orpington BR6 (Green St Grn), distinguishes between two streets called **High Street** which are both in the post town of Orpington and within the same postal district of BR6.

Extra locational information is also given for some localities within large post towns. This is also to aid location.
        e.g. **Acer Rd**, West. (Bigg.H.) TN16 . . .**178**   EK116
This street is within the locality of Biggin Hill which is part of the post town of Westerham, and it is within postal district TN16.

A full list of locality and post town abbreviations used in this atlas is given on the following page.

General abbreviations

Acad	Academy	Coron	Coroners	Grd	Ground	Mus	Museum	Shop	Shopping
All	Alley	Cors	Corners	Grds	Grounds	N	North	Spec	Special
Allot	Allotments	Cotts	Cottages	Grn	Green	NHS	National Health	Sq	Square
Amb	Ambulance	Cov	Covered	Grns	Greens		Service	St	Street
App	Approach	Crem	Crematorium	Gro	Grove	NT	National Trust	St.	Saint
Arc	Arcade	Cres	Crescent	Gros	Groves	Nat	National	Sta	Station
Av	Avenue	Ct	Court	Gt	Great	Nurs	Nursery	Sts	Streets
BUPA	British United	Cts	Courts	HQ	Headquarters	PH	Public House	Sub	Subway
	Provident Association	Ctyd	Courtyard	Ho	House	PO	Post Office	Swim	Swimming
Bdy	Broadway	Dep	Depot	Hos	Houses	PRU	Pupil Referral Unit	TA	Territorial Army
Bk	Bank	Dept	Department	Hosp	Hospital	Par	Parade	TH	Town Hall
Bldg	Building	Dev	Development	Hts	Heights	Pas	Passage	Tech	Technical, Technology
Bldgs	Buildings	Dr	Drive	Ind	Industrial	Pav	Pavilion	Tenn	Tennis
Boul	Boulevard	Dws	Dwellings	Indep	Independent	Pk	Park	Ter	Terrace
Bowl	Bowling	E	East	Inf	Infant(s)	Pl	Place	Thea	Theatre
Br	Bridge	Ed	Education, Educational	Int	International	Pol	Police	Trd	Trading
C of E	Church of England	Elec	Electricity	JM	Junior Mixed	Poly	Polytechnic	Twr	Tower
Cath	Cathedral	Embk	Embankment	JMI	Junior Mixed	Prec	Precinct	Twrs	Towers
Cem	Cemetery	Est	Estate		& Infant(s)	Prep	Preparatory	Uni	University
Cen	Central, Centre	Ex	Exchange	Jun	Junior	Prim	Primary	Upr	Upper
Cft	Croft	Exhib	Exhibition	Junct	Junction	Prom	Promenade	VA	Voluntary Aided
Cfts	Crofts	FB	Footbridge	La	Lane	Pt	Point	VC	Voluntary Controlled
Ch	Church	FC	Football Club	Las	Lanes	Quad	Quadrant	Vil	Villas
Chyd	Churchyard	Fld	Field	Lib	Library	RC	Roman Catholic	Vil	Villa
Cin	Cinema	Flds	Fields	Ln	Loan	Rd	Road	Vw	View
Circ	Circus	Fm	Farm	Lo	Lodge	Rds	Roads	W	West
Cl	Close	GM	Grant Maintained	Lwr	Lower	Rec	Recreation	Wd	Wood
Co	County	Gall	Gallery	Mag	Magistrates	Rehab	Rehabilitation	Wds	Woods
Coll	College	Gar	Garage	Mans	Mansions	Res	Reservoir, Residence	Wf	Wharf
Comb	Combined	Gdn	Garden	Med	Medical, Medicine	Ri	Rise	Wk	Walk
Comm	Community	Gdns	Gardens	Mem	Memorial	S	South	Wks	Works
Comp	Comprehensive	Gen	General	Mid	Middle	SM	Secondary Mixed	Yd	Yard
Conf	Conference	Govt	Government	Mkt	Market	Sch	School		
Cont	Continuing	Gra	Grange	Mkts	Markets	Schs	Schools		
Conv	Convent	Grad	Graduate	Ms	Mews	Sec	Secondary		
Cor	Corner	Gram	Grammar	Mt	Mount	Sen	Senior		

Locality & post town abbreviations

Note: Post towns are shown below in bold type.

Abbreviation	Locality / Post town
Abb.L.	**Abbots Langley**
Add.	**Addlestone**
Ald.	Aldenham
Amer.	**Amersham**
Ashf.	**Ashford**
Ashtd.	**Ashtead**
Bad.Dene	Badgers Dene
Bad.Mt	Badgers Mount
Bans.	**Banstead**
Bark.	**Barking**
Barn.	**Barnet**
Barne.	Barnehurst
Beac.	**Beaconsfield**
Beck.	**Beckenham**
Bedd.	Beddington
Bedd.Cor.	Beddington Corner
Belv.	**Belvedere**
Berry's Grn	Berry's Green
Bet.	**Betchworth**
Bex.	**Bexley**
Bexh.	**Bexleyheath**
Bigg.H.	**Biggin Hill**
Bkhm	Bookham
Bletch.	Bletchingley
Borwd.	**Borehamwood**
Bov.	Bovingdon
Box H.	Box Hill
Brent.	**Brentford**
Brick.Wd	Bricket Wood
Brock.	Brockham
Brom.	**Bromley**
Brook.Pk	Brookmans Park
Brox.	**Broxbourne**
Brwd.	**Brentwood**
Buck.H.	**Buckhurst Hill**
Burgh Hth	Burgh Heath
Bushey Hth	Bushey Heath
Carp.Pk	Carpenders Park
Cars.	**Carshalton**
Cat.	**Caterham**
Ch.End	Church End
Ch.St.G.	**Chalfont St. Giles**
Chad.Hth	Chadwell Heath
Chad.St.M.	Chadwell St. Mary
Chaff.Hun.	Chafford Hundred
Chal.St.P.	Chalfont St. Peter
Chel.	Chelsham
Chels.	Chelsfield
Cher.	**Chertsey**
Chesh.	**Chesham**
Chess.	**Chessington**
Chev.	Chevening
Chig.	**Chigwell**
Chipper.	Chipperfield
Chis.	**Chislehurst**
Chob.Com.	Chobham Common
Chorl.	Chorleywood
Chsht	Cheshunt
Clay.	Claygate
Cob.	**Cobham**
Cockfos.	Cockfosters
Coll.Row	Collier Row
Coln.Hth	Colney Heath
Coln.St	Colney Street
Colnbr.	Colnbrook
Cooper.	Coopersale
Couls.	**Coulsdon**
Cran.	Cranford
Cray.	Crayford
Crock.	Crockenhill
Crock.H.	Crockham Hill
Crox.Grn	Croxley Green
Croy.	**Croydon**
Dag.	**Dagenham**
Dance.H.	Dancers Hill
Dart.	**Dartford**
Denh.	Denham
Dor.	**Dorking**
Down.	Downside
Dunt.Grn	Dunton Green
E.Bed.	East Bedfont
E.Croy.	East Croydon
E.Ewell	East Ewell
E.Hors.	East Horsley
E.Mol.	**East Molesey**
E.Til.	East Tilbury
Ealing Com.	Ealing Common
Eastcote Vill.	Eastcote Village

Abbreviation	Locality / Post town
Eden.	**Edenbridge**
Edg.	**Edgware**
Eff.	Effingham
Eff.Junct.	Effingham Junction
Egh.	**Egham**
Egh.H.	Egham Hythe
Elm Pk	Elm Park
Elm.Wds	Elmstead Woods
Enf.	**Enfield**
Eng.Grn	Englefield Green
Epp.	**Epping**
Epp.Grn	Epping Green
Epsom Com.	Epsom Common
Ewell E.	Ewell East
Ewell W.	Ewell West
Eyns.	Eynsford
Farnboro.	Farnborough
Fawk.	Fawkham
Fawk.Grn	Fawkham Green
Felt.	**Feltham**
Fetch.	Fetcham
Flam.	Flamstead
Flaun.	Flaunden
Fnghm	Farningham
Frog.	Frogmore
Gdse.	**Godstone**
Geo.Grn	George Green
Ger.Cr.	**Gerrards Cross**
Gidea Pk	Gidea Park
Godden Grn	Godden Green
Grav.	**Gravesend**
Green.	**Greenhithe**
Grn St Grn	Green Street Green
Grnf.	**Greenford**
Gt Warley	Great Warley
Guil.	**Guildford**
Hackbr.	Hackbridge
Had.Wd	Hadley Wood
Halst.	Halstead
Han.	Hanworth
Har.	**Harrow**
Har.Hill	Harrow on the Hill
Har.Wld	Harrow Weald
Hare.	Harefield
Harm.	Harmondsworth
Harold Wd	Harold Wood
Hat.	**Hatfield**
Hatt.Cr.	Hatton Cross
Hav.at.Bow.	Havering-atte-Bower
Headley Ct	Headley Court
Hedg.	Hedgerley
Hem.H.	**Hemel Hempstead**
Herons.	Heronsgate
Hert.	**Hertford**
Hext.	Hextable
High Barn.	High Barnet
Highams Pk	Highams Park
Hinch.Wd	Hinchley Wood
Hlgdn	Hillingdon
Hmptn.	Hampton
Hmptn H.	Hampton Hill
Hmptn W.	Hampton Wick
Hook Grn	Hook Green
Horn.	**Hornchurch**
Hort.Kir.	Horton Kirby
Houns.	**Hounslow**
Houns.W.	Hounslow West
Hthrw Air.	**Heathrow Airport**
Hthrw Air.N.	Heathrow Airport North
Hutt.	Hutton
Ickhm	Ickenham
Ilf.	**Ilford**
Islw.	**Isleworth**
Junct	Junction
Ken.	**Kenley**
Kes.	**Keston**
Kgfld	Kingfield
Kgswd	Kingswood
Kings L.	**Kings Langley**
Kings.T.	**Kingston upon Thames**
Knap.	Knaphill
Knock.	Knockholt
Knock.P.	Knockholt Pound
Lamb.End	Lambourne End
Let.Hth	Letchmore Heath
Lmpfld	Limpsfield

Abbreviation	Locality / Post town
Lmpfld Cht.	Limpsfield Chart
Lon.Col.	London Colney
Long Dit.	Long Ditton
Long.	**Longfield**
Longcr.	Longcross
Loud.	Loudwater
Loug.	**Loughton**
Lt.Chal.	Little Chalfont
Lt.Hth	Little Heath
Lt.Warley	Little Warley
Lthd.	**Leatherhead**
Lwr Kgswd	Lower Kingswood
Lwr Sydenham	Lower Sydenham
Map.Cr.	Maple Cross
Mdgrn	Middlegreen
Merst.	Merstham
Mick.	Mickleham
Mimbr.	Mimbridge
Mitch.	**Mitcham**
Mitch.Com.	Mitcham Common
Mord.	**Morden**
Mots.Pk	Motspur Park
Mtnsg	Mountnessing
N.Finchley	North Finchley
N.Har.	North Harrow
N.Mal.	**New Malden**
N.Mymms	North Mymms
N.Ock.	North Ockendon
N.Stfd	North Stifford
N.Wld Bas.	North Weald Bassett
Nave.	Navestock
Nave.S.	Navestock Side
New Adgtn	New Addington
New Barn.	New Barnet
Newgate St	Newgate Street
Northumb.Hth	Northumberland Heath
Norwood Junct.	Norwood Junction
Nthflt	Northfleet
Nthlt.	**Northolt**
Nthwd.	**Northwood**
Nutfld	Nutfield
Old Wind.	Old Windsor
Old Wok.	Old Woking
Ong.	**Ongar**
Orch.L.	Orchard Leigh
Orp.	**Orpington**
Ott.	Ottershaw
Oxt.	**Oxted**
Park St	Park Street
Perry St	Perry Street
Petts Wd	Petts Wood
Pilg.Hat.	Pilgrim's Hatch
Pnr.	**Pinner**
Pot.B.	**Potters Bar**
Pr.Bot.	Pratt's Bottom
Pur.	**Purley**
Purf.	**Purfleet**
Rad.	**Radlett**
Rain.	**Rainham**
Red.	**Redhill**
Reig.	**Reigate**
Rich.	**Richmond**
Rick.	**Rickmansworth**
Rod.Val.	Roding Valley
Rom.	**Romford**
Rosh.	Rosherville
Ruis.	**Ruislip**
Runny.	Runnymede
Rush Grn	Rush Green
Russ.Hill	Russell Hill
Rvrhd	Riverhead
S.Croy.	**South Croydon**
S.Darenth	South Darenth
S.Har.	South Harrow
S.Merst.	South Merstham
S.Mimms	South Mimms
S.Norwood	South Norwood
S.Nutfld	South Nutfield
S.Ock.	**South Ockendon**
S.Oxhey	South Oxhey
S.Ruis.	South Ruislip
S.Stfd	South Stifford
S.Wld	South Weald
S.le H.	**Stanford-le-Hope**
Scad.Pk	Scadbury Park
Send M.	Send Marsh
Sev.	**Sevenoaks**

Abbreviation	Locality / Post town
Sheer.	Sheerwater
Shenf.	Shenfield
Shep.	**Shepperton**
Shore.	Shoreham
Short.	Shortlands
Sid.	**Sidcup**
Slade Grn	Slade Green
Slou.	**Slough**
St.Alb.	**St. Albans**
St.Clements	St. Clements
St.Geo.H	St. George's Hill
St.John's	St. John's
St.M.Cray	St. Mary Cray
St.P.Cray	St. Paul's Cray
Stai.	**Staines**
Stan.	**Stanmore**
Stanw.	**Stanwell**
Stap.Abb.	Stapleford Abbotts
Stap.Taw.	Stapleford Tawney
Sthflt	Southfleet
Sthl Grn	Southall Green
Sthl.	**Southall**
Stoke D'Ab.	Stoke D'Abernon
Stoke P.	Stoke Poges
Sun.	**Sunbury-on-Thames**
Sund.	Sundridge
Surb.	**Surbiton**
Sutt.	**Sutton**
Sutt.Grn	Sutton Green
Sutt.H.	Sutton at Hone
Swan.	**Swanley**
Swans.	**Swanscombe**
T.Ditt.	**Thames Ditton**
Tad.	**Tadworth**
Tand.	Tandridge
Tats.	Tatsfield
Tedd.	**Teddington**
Th.Hth.	**Thornton Heath**
They.B.	Theydon Bois
They.Gar.	Theydon Garnon
They.Mt	Theydon Mount
Thnwd	Thornwood
Til.	**Tilbury**
Tkgtn	Tokyngton
Turnf.	Turnford
Twick.	**Twickenham**
Tyr.Wd	Tyrrell's Wood
Undrvr	Underriver
Upmin.	**Upminster**
Uxb.	**Uxbridge**
Vir.W.	**Virginia Water**
W.Byf.	**West Byfleet**
W.Croy.	West Croydon
W.Ealing	West Ealing
W.Ewell	West Ewell
W.Hors.	West Horsley
W.Mol.	**West Molesey**
W.Thur.	West Thurrock
W.Til.	West Tilbury
W.Wick.	**West Wickham**
Wal.Abb.	**Waltham Abbey**
Wal.Cr.	**Waltham Cross**
Wall.	**Wallington**
Walt.	**Walton-on-Thames**
Warl.	**Warlingham**
Wat.	**Watford**
Wdf.Grn.	**Woodford Green**
Wdhm	Woodham
Well.	**Welling**
Wem.	**Wembley**
Wenn.	Wennington
West Dr.	**West Drayton**
West.	**Westerham**
Wey.	**Weybridge**
Whel.Hill	Whelpley Hill
Whiteley Vill.	Whiteley Village
Whyt.	**Whyteleafe**
Wilm.	Wilmington
Wind.	**Windsor**
Wldste	Wealdstone
Wok.	**Woking**
Wold.	Woldingham
Woodside Pk	Woodside Park
Wor.Pk.	**Worcester Park**
Wrays.	Wraysbury
Yiew.	Yiewsley

1 Canada Sq, E14 85 EB74
30 St. Mary Axe, EC3
off St. Mary Axe 84 DS72
99 Bishopsgate, EC2
off Bishopsgate 84 DS72

A

Aaron Hill Rd, E6 87 EN71
Abberley Ms, SW4
off Cedars Rd 101 DH83
Abberton Wk, Rain. RM13
off Ongar Way 89 FE66
Abbess Cl, E6
off Oliver Gdns 86 EL71
SW2 121 DP88
Abbeville Ms, SW4
off Clapham Pk Rd 101 DK84
Abbeville Rd, N8
off Barrington Rd 65 DK56
SW4 121 DJ86
Abbey Av, Wem. HA0 80 CL68
Abbey Business Cen, SW8
off Ingate Pl 101 DH81
Abbey Cl, E5 66 DU63
SW8 101 DK81
Hayes UB3 77 BV74
Northolt UB5
off Invicta Gro 78 BZ69
Pinner HA5 59 BV55
Romford RM1 71 FG58
Woking GU22 167 BE116
Abbey Ct, Wal.Abb. EN9 15 EB34
Abbey Cres, Belv. DA17 106 FA77
Abbeydale Rd, Wem. HA0 80 CN67
Abbey Dr, SW17
off Church La 120 DG92
Abbots Langley WD5 7 BU32
Dartford DA2
off Old Bexley La 127 FE89
Staines TW18 134 BJ98
Abbeyfield Rd, SE16 202 F8
Abbeyfields Cl, NW10 80 CN68
Abbeyfields Mobile Home Pk,
Cher. KT16 134 BK101
Abbey Gdns, NW8 82 DC68
SE16 202 C8
W6 99 CY79
Chertsey KT16 134 BG100
Chislehurst BR7 145 EN95
Waltham Abbey EN9 15 EC33
Abbey Grn, Cher. KT16 134 BG100
Abbey Gro, SE2 106 EV77
Abbeyhill Rd, Sid. DA15 126 EW89
Abbey Ind Est, Mitch. CR4 140 DF99
Wembley HA0 80 CM67
Abbey La, E15 85 EC68
Beckenham BR3 123 EA94
Abbey Mead Ind Pk,
Wal.Abb. EN9 15 EC34
Abbey Ms, E17
off Leamington Av 67 EA57
Abbey Orchard St, SW1 199 N6
Abbey Par, SW19
off Merton High St 120 DC94
W5 off Hanger La 80 CM69
Abbey Pk, Beck. BR3 123 EA94
Abbey Pl, Dart. DA1
off Priory Rd N 128 FK85
Abbey Retail Pk, Bark. IG11 87 EP67
Abbey Rd, E15 86 EE68
NW6 82 DB66
NW8 82 DC68
NW10 80 CP68
SE2 106 EX77
SW19 120 DC94
Barking IG11 87 EP66
Belvedere DA17 106 EX77
Bexleyheath DA7 106 EY84
Chertsey KT16 134 BH101
Croydon CR0 141 DP104
Enfield EN1 30 DS43
Gravesend DA12 131 GL88
Greenhithe DA9 129 FW85
Ilford IG2 69 ER57
Shepperton TW17 134 BN102
South Croydon CR2 161 DX110
Virginia Water GU25 132 AX99
Waltham Cross EN8 15 DY34
Woking GU21 166 AW117
Abbey Rd Est, NW8 82 DB67
Abbey St, E13 86 EG70
SE1 201 N6
Abbey Ter, SE2 106 EW77
Abbey Vw, NW7 43 CT48
Radlett WD7 25 CF35
Waltham Abbey EN9 15 EB33
Watford WD25 24 BX36
Abbey Vw Roundabout,
Wal.Abb. EN9 15 EB33
Abbey Wk, W.Mol. KT8 136 CB97
Abbey Way, SE2 106 EX76
Abbey Wf Ind Est, Bark. IG11 87 ER68
ABBEY WOOD, SE2 106 EV76
⇌ Abbey Wood 106 EW76
Abbey Wd Caravan Club Site,
SE2 off Federation Rd 106 EW78
Abbey Wd La, Rain. RM13 90 FK68
Abbey Wd Rd, SE2 106 EV77
Abbot Cl, Stai. TW18 114 BK94
West Byfleet (Byfleet)
KT14 152 BK110
Abbots Av, Epsom KT19 156 CN111
Abbotsbury Cl, E15 85 EC68
W14 off Abbotsbury Rd 99 CZ75
Abbotsbury Gdns, Pnr. HA5 60 BW58
Abbotsbury Ms, SE15 102 DW83
Abbotsbury Rd, W14 99 CY75
Bromley BR2 144 EF103
Morden SM4 140 DB99
Abbots Cl, N1 off Alwyne Rd 84 DQ65
Brentwood (Shenf.) CM15 55 GA46
Abbots Cl, Orpington BR5 145 EQ102
Rainham RM13 90 FJ68
Ruislip HA4 60 BX62
Abbots Dr, Har. HA2 60 CA61
Virginia Water GU25 132 AW98
Abbots Fld, Grav. DA12
off Ruffets Wd 131 GJ93
Abbotsford Av, N15 66 DQ56
Abbotsford Cl, Wok. GU22
off Onslow Cres 167 BA117
Abbotsford Gdns, Wdf.Grn.
IG8 48 EG52
Abbotsford Lo, Nthwd. HA6 39 BS50
Abbotsford Rd, Ilf. IG3 70 EU61
Abbots Gdns, N2 64 DD56
W8 off St. Mary's Pl 100 DB76
Abbots Grn, Croy. CR0 161 DX107
Abbotshade Rd, SE16 203 J2
Abbotshall Av, N14 45 DJ48
Abbotshall Rd, SE6 123 ED88
Abbots La, SE1 201 N3
Kenley CR8 176 DQ116
ABBOTS LANGLEY 7 BR31
Abbotsleigh Cl, Sutt. SM2 158 DB108
Abbotsleigh Rd, SW16 121 DJ91
Abbots Manor Est, SW1 199 H9
Abbotsmede Cl, Twick. TW1 117 CF89
Abbots Pk, SW2 121 DN88
Abbot's Pl, NW6 82 DB67
Abbots Ri, Kings L. WD4 6 BM26
Redhill RH1 184 DG132
Abbot's Rd, E6 86 EK67
Abbots Rd, Abb.L. WD5 7 BS30
Edgware HA8 42 CQ52
Abbots Ter, N8 65 DL58
Abbotstone Rd, SW15 99 CW83
Abbot St, E8 84 DT65
Abbots Vw, Kings L. WD4 6 BM27
Abbots Wk, W8
off St. Mary's Pl 100 DB76
Caterham CR3
off Tillingdown Hill 176 DU122
Abbots Way, Beck. BR3 143 DY99
Chertsey KT16 133 BF101
Abbotswell Rd, SE4 123 DZ85
Abbotswood Cl, Belv. DA17
off Coptefield Dr 106 EY76
Abbotswood Dr, Wey. KT13 153 BR110
Abbotswood Gdns, Ilf. IG5 69 EM55
Abbotswood Rd, SE22 102 DS84
SW16 121 DK90
Abbotswood Way, Hayes UB3 77 BV74
Abbott Av, SW20 139 CX96
Abbott Cl, Hmptn. TW12 116 BY93
Northolt UB5 78 BZ65
Abbott Rd, E14 85 EC71
Abbotts Cl, SE28 88 EW73
Romford RM7 71 FB55
Swanley BR8 147 FG98
Uxbridge UB8 76 BK71
Abbotts Cres, E4 47 ED49
Enfield EN2 29 DP40
Abbotts Dr, Wal.Abb. EN9 16 EG34
Wembley HA0 61 CH61
Abbotts Pk Rd, E10 67 EC59
Abbotts Rd, Barn. EN5 28 DB42
Mitcham CR4 141 DJ98
Southall UB1 78 BY74
Sutton SM3 139 CZ104
Abbott's Tilt, Walt. KT12 136 BY104
Abbotts Wk, Bexh. DA7 106 EX80
Abbs Cross Gdns, Horn. RM12 72 FJ60
Abbs Cross La, Horn. RM12 72 FJ63
Abchurch La, EC4 197 L10
Abchurch Yd, EC4 197 K10
Abdale Rd, W12 81 CV74
Abenberg Way, Brwd.
(Hutt.) CM13 55 GB47
Aberavon Rd, E3 85 DY69
Abercairn Rd, SW16 121 DJ94
Aberconway Rd, Mord. SM4 140 DB97
Abercorn Cl, NW7 43 CY52
NW8 82 DC69
South Croydon CR2 161 DX112
Abercorn Cres, Har. HA2 60 CB60
Abercorn Gdns, Har. HA3 61 CK59
Romford RM6 70 EV58
Abercorn Gro, Ruis. HA4 59 BR56
Abercorn Pl, NW8 82 DC69
Abercorn Rd, NW7 43 CY52
Stanmore HA7 41 CJ52
Abercorn Way, SE1 202 B10
Woking GU21 166 AU118
Abercrombie Dr, Enf. EN1
off Linwood Cres 30 DU39
Abercrombie St, SW11 100 DE82
Aberdale Ct, SE16
off Poolmans St 103 DX75
Aberdale Gdns, Pot.B. EN6 11 CZ33
Aberdare Cl, W.Wick. BR4 143 EC103
Aberdare Gdns, NW6 82 DB66
NW7 43 CX52
Aberdare Rd, Enf. EN3 30 DW42
Aberdeen La, N5 65 DP64
Aberdeen Par, N18
off Angel Rd 46 DV50
Aberdeen Pk, N5 65 DP64
Aberdeen Pk Ms, N5 66 DQ63
Aberdeen Pl, NW8 82 DD70
Aberdeen Rd, N5 66 DQ63
N18 46 DV50
NW10 63 CT64
Croydon CR0 160 DQ105
Harrow HA3 41 CF54
Aberdeen Sq, E14 203 P2
Aberdeen Ter, SE3 103 ED82
Aberdour Rd, Ilf. IG3 70 EV62
Aberdour St, SE1 201 M8
Aberfeldy St, E14 85 EC72
Aberford Gdns, SE18 104 EL81
Aberford Rd, Borwd. WD6 26 CN40
Aberfoyle Rd, SW16 121 DK93
Abergeldie Rd, SE12 124 EH86
Aberglen Ind Est,
Hayes UB3 95 BR75
Abernethy Rd, SE13 104 EE84
Abersham Rd, E8 66 DT64
Abery St, SE18 105 ES77
Abigail Ms, Rom. RM3
off King Alfred Rd 52 FM54
Abingdon Cl, NW1
off Camden Sq 83 DK65
SE1 202 A10
SW19 120 DC93
Uxbridge UB10 76 BM67
Woking GU21 166 AV118
Abingdon Pl, Pot.B. EN6 12 DB32
Abingdon Rd, N3 44 DC54
SW16 141 DL96
W8 100 DA76
Abingdon St, SW1 199 P6
Abingdon Vil, W8 100 DA76
Abingdon Way, Orp. BR6 164 EV105
Abinger Av, Sutt. SM2 157 CW109
Abinger Cl, Bark. IG11 70 EU63
Bromley BR1 144 EL97
Croydon CR0 161 EC107
Wallington SM6 159 DL106
Abinger Gdns, Islw. TW7 97 CE83
Abinger Gro, SE8 103 DZ79
Abinger Ms, W9
off Warlock Rd 82 DA70
Abinger Rd, W4 98 CS76
Ablett St, SE16 102 DW78
Abney Gdns, N16
off Stoke Newington
High St 66 DT61
Aboyne Dr, SW20 139 CU96
Aboyne Est, SW17 120 DD90
Aboyne Rd, NW10 62 CS62
SW17 120 DD90
Abraham Cl, Wat. WD19 39 BV49
ABRIDGE, Rom. RM4 34 EV41
Abridge Cl, Wal.Cr. EN8 31 DX35
Abridge Gdns, Rom. RM5 50 FA51
Abridge Pk, Rom. (Abridge)
RM4 34 EU42
Abridge Rd, Chig. IG7 33 ER44
Epping (They.B.) CM16 33 ES36
Romford (Abridge) RM4 34 EU39
Abridge Way, Bark. IG11 88 EV68
Abyssinia Cl, SW11
off Cairns Rd 100 DE84
Abyssinia Rd, SW11
off Auckland Rd 100 DE84
Acacia Av, N17 46 DR52
Brentford TW8 97 CH80
Hayes UB3 77 BT72
Hornchurch RM12 71 FF61
Mitcham CR4 off Acacia Rd 141 DH96
Ruislip HA4 59 BU60
Shepperton TW17 134 BN99
Staines (Wrays.) TW19 92 AY84
Wembley HA9 62 CL64
West Drayton UB7 76 BM73
Woking GU22 166 AX120
Acacia Cl, SE8 203 K9
SE20 off Selby Rd 142 DU96
Addlestone (Wdhm) KT15 151 BF110
Orpington BR5 145 ER99
Stanmore HA7 41 CE51
Waltham Cross EN7 14 DS27
Acacia Ct, Wal.Abb. EN9
off Farthingale La 16 EG34
Acacia Dr, Add. (Wdhm) KT15 151 BF110
Banstead SM7 157 CX114
Sutton SM3 139 CZ102
Upminster RM14 72 FN63
Acacia Gdns, NW8
off Acacia Rd 82 DD68
Upminster RM14 73 FT59
West Wickham BR4 143 EC103
Acacia Gro, SE21 122 DR89
New Malden KT3 138 CR97
Acacia Ms, West Dr. UB7 94 BK79
Acacia Pl, NW8 82 DD68
Acacia Rd, E11 68 EE61
E17 67 DY58
N22 45 DN53
NW8 82 DD68
SW16 141 DL95
W3 80 CQ73
Beckenham BR3 143 DZ97
Dartford DA1 128 FK88
Enfield EN2 30 DR39
Greenhithe DA9 129 FS86
Hampton TW12 116 CA93
Mitcham CR4 141 DH96
Staines TW18 114 BH92
Acacia Wk, Swan. BR8 147 FD96
Acacia Way, Sid. DA15 125 ET88
Academy Gdns, Croy. CR0 142 DT102
Northolt UB5 78 BX68
Academy Pl, SE18 105 EM81
Academy Rd, SE18 105 EM81
Acanthus Dr, SE1 202 B10
Acanthus Rd, SW11 100 DG83
Accommodation La,
West Dr. UB7 94 BJ79
Accommodation Rd, NW11 63 CZ59
Chertsey (Longcr.) KT16 132 AX104
A.C. Ct, T.Ditt. KT7
off Harvest La 137 CG100
Acer Av, Hayes UB4 78 BY71
Rainham RM13 90 FK69
Acer Rd, West. (Bigg.H.) TN16 178 EK116
Acers, St.Alb. (Park St) AL2 8 CC28
Acfold Rd, SW6 100 DB81
Achilles Cl, SE1 202 C10
Achilles Pl, Wok. GU21 166 AW117
Achilles Rd, NW6 64 DA64
Achilles St, SE14 103 DY80
Achilles Way, W1 198 G3
Acklam Rd, W10 81 CZ71
Acklington Dr, NW9 42 CS53
Ackmar Rd, SW6 100 DA81
Ackroyd Dr, E3 85 DZ71
Ackroyd Rd, SE23 123 DX87
Acland Cl, SE18
off Clothworkers Rd 105 ER80
Acland Cres, SE5 102 DR84
Acland Rd, NW2 81 CV65
Acle Cl, Ilf. IG6 49 EP52
Acme Rd, Wat. WD24 23 BU38
Acock Gro, Nthlt. UB5 60 CB63
Acol Cres, Ruis. HA4 59 BV64
Acol Rd, NW6 82 DA66
Aconbury Rd, Dag. RM9 88 EV67
Acorn Cl, E4 47 EA50
Chislehurst BR7 125 EQ92
Acorn Cl, Enfield EN2 29 DP39
Hampton TW12 116 CB93
Slough SL3 off Tamar Way 93 BB78
Stanmore HA7 41 CH52
Acorn Ct, Ilf. IG2 69 ES58
Acorn Gdns, SE19 142 DT95
W3 80 CR71
Acorn Gro, Hayes UB3 95 BT80
Ruislip HA4 59 BT63
Tadworth KT20 173 CY124
Woking GU22
off Old Sch Pl 166 AY121
Acorn Ind Pk, Dart. DA1 127 FG85
Acorn La, Pot.B. (Cuffley) EN6 13 DL29
Acorn Par, SE15
off Carlton Gro 102 DV80
Acorn Pl, Wat. WD24 23 BU37
Acorn Rd, Dart. DA1 127 FF85
Acorns, The, Chig. IG7 49 ES49
Acorns Way, Esher KT10 154 CC106
Acorn Wk, SE16 203 L2
Acorn Way, SE23 123 DX90
Beckenham BR3 143 EC99
Orpington BR6 163 EP105
Acre Dr, SE22 102 DU84
Acrefield Rd,
Ger.Cr. (Chal.St.P.) SL9 56 AX55
Acre La, SW2 101 DL84
Carshalton SM5 158 DG105
Wallington SM6 158 DG105
Acre Path, Nthlt. UB5
off Arnold Rd 78 BY65
Acre Rd, SW19 120 DD93
Dagenham RM10 89 FB66
Kingston upon Thames
KT2 138 CL95
Acres End, Amer. HP7 20 AS39
Acres Gdns, Tad. KT20 173 CX119
Acre Vw, Horn. RM11 72 FL56
Acre Way, Nthwd. HA6 39 BT53
Acris St, SW18 120 DC85
ACTON, W3 80 CN74
⇌ Acton Central 80 CR74
Acton Cl, N9 46 DU47
Waltham Cross (Chsht) EN8 15 DY31
Acton Hill Ms, W3
off Uxbridge Rd 80 CP74
Acton La, NW10 80 CS68
W3 98 CQ75
W4 98 CR76
⇌ Acton Main Line 80 CQ72
Acton Ms, E8 84 DT67
Acton Pk Ind Est, W3 98 CR75
Acton St, WC1 196 B3
⊖ Acton Town 98 CN75
Acuba Rd, SW18 120 DB89
Acworth Cl, N9 off Turin Rd 46 DW45
Ada Gdns, E14 85 ED72
E15 86 EF67
Adair Cl, SE25 142 DV97
Adair Rd, W10 81 CY70
Adair Twr, W10
off Appleford Rd 81 CY70
Adam & Eve Ct, W1 195 L8
Adam & Eve Ms, W8 100 DA76
Adam Cl, SE6 123 DZ91
Adam Ct, SW7
off Gloucester Rd 100 DC77
Adam Pl, N16
off Stoke Newington
High St 66 DT61
Adam Rd, E4 47 DZ51
Adams Cl, N3 off Falkland Av 44 DA52
NW9 62 CP61
Surbiton KT5 138 CM100
Adams Ct, EC2 197 L8
Adamsfield, Wal.Cr. EN7 14 DU27
Adams Gdns Est, SE16 202 F4
Adams Ms, N22 45 DL52
SW17 120 DF89
Adamson Rd, E16 86 EG72
NW3 82 DD66
Adamson Way, Beck. BR3
off Creswell Dr 143 EB99
Adams Pl, N7 off George's Rd 65 DM64
Adamsrill Cl, Enf. EN1 30 DR44
Adamsrill Rd, SE26 123 DY91
Adams Rd, N17 46 DR54
Beckenham BR3 143 DY99
Adams Row, W1 198 G1
Adams Sq, Bexh. DA6
off Regency Way 106 EY83
Adam St, WC2 200 A1
Adams Wk, Kings.T. KT1 138 CL96
Adams Way, Croy. CR0 142 DT100
Adam Wk, SW6 99 CW80
Ada Pl, E2 84 DU67
Adare Wk, SW16 121 DM90
Ada Rd, SE5 102 DS80
Wembley HA0 61 CK62
Adastral Est, NW9 42 CS53
Ada St, E8 84 DV67
Adcock Wk, Orp. BR6
off Borkwood Pk 163 ET105
Adderley Gdns, SE9 125 EN91
Adderley Gro, SW11
off Culmstock Rd 120 DG85
Adderley Rd, Har. HA3 41 CF53
Adderley St, E14 85 EC72
ADDINGTON, Croy. CR0 161 DZ106
Addington Border, Croy. CR0 161 DY110
Addington Ct, SW14 98 CR83
Addington Dr, N12 44 DC51
Addington Gro, SE26 123 DY91
Addington Rd, E3 85 EA69
E16 86 EE70
N4 65 DN58
Croydon CR0 141 DN102
South Croydon CR2 160 DU111
West Wickham BR4 144 EE103
Addington Sq, SE5 102 DQ80
Addington St, SE1 200 C5
Tra Addington Village 161 EA107
Addington Village Rd,
Croy. CR0 161 EA106
Addis Cl, Enf. EN3 31 DX39
ADDISCOMBE, Croy. CR0 142 DT102
Tra Addiscombe 142 DU102
Addiscombe Av, Croy. CR0 142 DU101
Addiscombe Cl, Har. HA3 61 CJ57
Addiscombe Ct Rd,
Croy. CR0 142 DS102
Addiscombe Gro, Croy. CR0 142 DR103
Addiscombe Rd, Croy. CR0 142 DS103
Watford WD18 23 BV42
Addison Av, N14 29 DH44
W11 81 CY74
Hounslow TW3 96 CC81
Addison Br Pl, W14 99 CZ77
Addison Cl, Cat. CR3 176 DR122
Northwood HA6 39 BU53
Orpington BR5 145 EQ100
Addison Ct, Epp. CM16
off Centre Dr 18 EU31
Addison Cres, W14 99 CY76
Addison Dr, SE12
off Eltham Rd 124 EH85
Addison Gdns, W14 99 CX76
Grays RM17 off Palmers Dr 110 GC77
Surbiton KT5 138 CM98
Addison Gro, W4 98 CS76
Addison Pl, W11 81 CY74
Southall UB1
off Longford Av 78 CA73
Addison Rd, E11 68 EG58
E17 67 EB57
SE25 142 DU98
W14 99 CZ76
Bromley BR2 144 EJ99
Caterham CR3 176 DR121
Enfield EN3 30 DW39
Ilford IG6 49 EQ53
Teddington TW11 117 CH93
Woking GU21
off Chertsey Rd 167 AZ117
Addison's Cl, Croy. CR0 143 DZ103
Addison Way, NW11 63 CZ56
Hayes UB3 77 BU72
Northwood HA6 39 BT53
Addle Hill, EC4 196 G10
ADDLESTONE 152 BJ106
⇌ Addlestone 152 BK105
ADDLESTONE MOOR,
Add. KT15 134 BG103
Addlestone Moor, Add. KT15 134 BJ103
Addlestone Pk, Add. KT15 152 BH106
Addlestone Rd, Add. KT15 152 BL105
Addle St, EC2 197 J7
Adecroft Way, W.Mol. KT8 136 CC97
Adela Av, N.Mal. KT3 139 CV99
Adelaide Av, SE4 103 DZ84
Adelaide Cl, SW9
off Broughton Dr 101 DN84
Enfield EN1 30 DT38
Stanmore HA7 41 CG49
Adelaide Cotts, W7 97 CF75
Adelaide Gdns, Rom. RM6 70 EY57
Adelaide Gro, W12 81 CU74
Adelaide Pl, Wey. KT13 153 BR105
Adelaide Rd, E10 67 EB62
NW3 82 DD66
SW18 off Putney Br Rd 120 DA85
W13 79 CG74
Ashford TW15 114 BK92
Chislehurst BR7 125 EP92
Hounslow TW5 96 BY81
Ilford IG1 69 EP61
Richmond TW9 98 CM84
Southall UB2 96 BY77
Surbiton KT6 138 CL99
Teddington TW11 117 CF93
Tilbury RM18 111 GF81
Walton-on-Thames KT12 135 BU104
Adelaide St, WC2 199 P1
Adelaide Ter, Brent. TW8 97 CK78
Adela St, W10 off Kensal Rd 81 CY70
Adelina Gro, E1 84 DW71
Adelina Ms, SW12
off King's Av 121 DK88
Adeline Pl, WC1 195 N7
Adeliza Cl, Bark. IG11
off North St 87 EP66
Adelphi Ct, SE16
off Poolmans St 103 DX75
Adelphi Cres, Hayes UB4 77 BT69
Hornchurch RM12 71 FG61
Adelphi Gdns, Slou. SL1 92 AS75
Adelphi Rd, Epsom KT17 156 CR113
Adelphi Ter, WC2 200 A1
Adelphi Way, Hayes UB4 77 BT69
Adeney Cl, W6 99 CX79
Aden Gro, N16 66 DR63
Adenmore Rd, SE6 123 EA87
Aden Rd, Enf. EN3 31 DY42
Ilford IG1 69 EP59
Aden Ter, N16 66 DR63
Adie Rd, W6 99 CW76
Adine Rd, E13 86 EH70
Adler Ind Est, Hayes UB3 95 BR75
Adler St, E1 84 DU72
Adley St, E5 67 DY64
Adlington Cl, N18 46 DR50
Admaston Rd, SE18 105 EQ80
Admiral Cl, Orp. BR5 146 EX98
Admiral Ct, NW4
off Barton Cl 63 CU57
Admiral Ho, Tedd. TW11
off Twickenham Rd 117 CG91
Admiral Pl, SE16 203 L2
Admirals Cl, E18 68 EH56
Admiral Seymour Rd, SE9 105 EM84
Admirals Gate, SE10 103 EB81
Admiral Sq, SW10 100 DD81
Admiral Stirling Ct, Wey. KT13
off Weybridge Rd 152 BM105
Admiral St, SE8 103 EA82
Admirals Wk, NW3 64 DC62
Coulsdon CR5 175 DM120
Greenhithe DA9 129 FV85
Admirals Way, E14 204 A4
★ Admiralty Arch, SW1 199 N2
Admiralty Cl, SE8
off Reginald Sq 103 EA80
Admiralty Rd, Tedd. TW11 117 CF93
Admiralty Way, Tedd. TW11
off Queen's Rd 117 CF93
Admiral Wk, W9 82 DA71
Adnams Wk, Rain. RM13
off Lovell Wk 89 FF65
Adolf St, SE6 123 EB91

★ Place of interest ⇌ Railway station ⊖ London Underground station DLR Docklands Light Railway station Tra Tramlink station H Hospital Riv Pedestrian ferry landing stage

Adolphus Rd, N4 65 DP61
Adolphus St, SE8 103 DZ80
Adomar Rd, Dag. RM8 70 EX62
Adpar St, W2 82 DD70
Adrian Av, NW2
off North Circular Rd 63 CV60
Adrian Cl, Barn. EN5 27 CX44
Uxbridge (Hare.) UB9 38 BK53
Adrian Ms, SW10 100 DB79
Adrian Rd, Abb.L. WD5 7 BS31
Adrians Wk, Slou. SL2 74 AT74
Adriatic Bldg, E14
off Narrow St 85 DY73
Adrienne Av, Sthl. UB1 78 BZ70
Adstock Ms, Ger.Cr. (Chal.St.P.) SL9
off Church La 36 AX53
Adstock Way,
Grays (Bad.Dene) RM17 110 FZ77
Advance Rd, SE27 122 DQ91
Advent Ct, Wdf.Grn. IG8
off Wood La 48 EF50
Advent Way, N18 47 DX50
Advice Av, Grays RM16 110 GA75
Adys Rd, SE15 102 DT83
Aerodrome Rd, NW4 43 CT54
NW9 43 CT54
Aerodrome Way, Houns. TW5 96 BW79
Aeroville, NW9 42 CS54
Affleck St, N1 196 C1
Afghan Rd, SW11 100 DE82
★ **Africa Cen**, WC2 195 P10
Africa Ho, SE16 202 E6
Afton Dr, S.Ock. RM15 91 FV72
Agamemnon Rd, NW6 63 CZ64
Agar Cl, Surb. KT6 138 CM103
Agar Gro, NW1 83 DJ66
Agar Gro Est, NW1 83 DK66
Agar Pl, NW1 83 DJ66
Agars Plough,
Slou. (Datchet) SL3 92 AU79
Agar St, WC2 199 P1
Agate Cl, E16 86 EK72
Agate Rd, W6 99 CW76
Agates La, Ashtd. KT21 171 CK118
Agatha Cl, E1 202 E2
Agaton Rd, SE9 125 EQ89
Agave Rd, NW2 63 CW63
Agdon St, EC1 196 F4
Agincourt Rd, NW3 64 DF63
Agister Rd, Chig. IG7 50 EU50
Agnes Av, Ilf. IG1 69 EP63
Agnes Cl, E6 87 EN73
Agnesfield Cl, N12 44 DE51
Agnes Gdns, Dag. RM8 70 EX63
Agnes Rd, W3 81 CT74
Agnes Scott Ct, Wey. KT13
off Palace Dr 135 BP104
Agnes St, E14 85 DZ72
Agnew Rd, SE23 123 DX87
Agricola Ct, E3
off Parnell Rd 85 DZ67
Agricola Pl, Enf. EN1 30 DT43
Aidan Cl, Dag. RM8 70 EY63
Aileen Wk, E15 86 EF66
Ailsa Av, Twick. TW1 117 CG85
Ailsa Rd, Twick. TW1 117 CH85
Ailsa St, E14 85 EC71
AIMES GREEN, Wal.Abb. EN9 16 EF28
Ainger Ms, NW3 *off Ainger Rd* 82 DF66
Ainger Rd, NW3 82 DF66
Ainsdale Cl, Orp. BR6 145 ER102
Ainsdale Cres, Pnr. HA5 60 CA55
Ainsdale Dr, SE1 102 DU78
Ainsdale Rd, W5 79 CK70
Watford WD19 40 BW48
Ainsdale Way, Wok. GU21 166 AU118
Ainsley Av, Rom. RM7 71 FB58
Ainsley Cl, N9 46 DS46
Ainsley St, E2 84 DV69
Ainslie Wk, SW12 121 DH87
Ainslie Wd Cres, E4 47 EB50
Ainslie Wd Gdns, E4 47 EB49
Ainslie Wd Rd, E4 47 EA50
Ainsty Est, SE16 203 H5
Ainsworth Cl, NW2 63 CU62
SE15 *off Lyndhurst Gro* 102 DS82
Ainsworth Rd, E9 84 DW66
Croydon CR0 141 DP103
Ainsworth Way, NW8 82 DC67
Aintree Av, E6 86 EL67
Aintree Cl, Grav. DA12 131 GH90
Slough (Colnbr.) SL3 93 BE81
Uxbridge UB8 *off Craig Dr* 77 BP72
Aintree Cres, Ilf. IG6 49 EQ54
Aintree Est, SW6
off Dawes Rd 99 CY80
Aintree Gro, Upmin. RM14 72 FM62
Aintree Rd, Grnf. UB6 79 CH68
Aintree St, SW6 99 CY80
Aird Ct, Hmptn. TW12
off Oldfield Rd 136 BZ95
Airdrie Cl, N1 83 DM66
Hayes UB4 *off Glencoe Rd* 78 BY71
Airedale Av, W4 99 CT77
Airedale Av S, W4
off Netheravon Rd S 99 CT78
Airedale Cl, Dart. DA2 128 FQ88
Airedale Rd, SW12 120 DF87
W5 97 CJ76
Aire Dr, S.Ock. RM15 91 FV70
Airey Neave Ct, Grays RM17 110 GA75
Airfield Way, Horn. RM12 89 FH65
Watford WD25
off Ashfields 7 BU32
★ **Air Forces Mem**,
Egh. TW20 112 AX91
Airlie Gdns, W8 100 DA75
Ilford IG1 69 EP60
Air Links Ind Est, Houns. TW5 96 BW78
Air Pk Way, Felt. TW13 115 BV89
Airport Ind Est, West. TN16 162 EK114
Airport Roundabout, E16
off Connaught Br 86 EK74
Airport Way, Stai. TW19 93 BF84
Air St, W1 199 L1
Airthrie Rd, Ilf. IG3 70 EV61
Aisgill Av, W14 99 CZ78
Aisher Rd, SE28 88 EW73
Aisher Way, Sev. (Rvrhd) TN13 190 FE121
Aislibie Rd, SE12 104 EE84
Aiten Pl, W6 *off Standish Rd* 99 CU77
Aitken Cl, E8 *off Pownall Rd* 84 DU67
Mitcham CR4 140 DF101
Aitken Rd, SE6 123 EB89
Barnet EN5 27 CW43
Ajax Av, NW9 62 CS55
Ajax Rd, NW6 64 DA64
Akabusi Cl, Croy. CR0 142 DU100
Akehurst La, Sev. TN13 191 FJ125
Akehurst St, SW15 119 CU86
Akenside Rd, NW3 64 DD64
Akerman Rd, SW9 101 DP82
Surbiton KT6 137 CJ100
Akers Way, Rick. (Chorl.) WD3 21 BD44
Alabama St, SE18 105 ER80
Alacross Rd, W5 97 CJ75
Alamein Gdns, Dart. DA2 129 FR87
Alamein Rd, Swans. DA10 129 FX86
Alanbrooke, Grav. DA12 131 GJ87
Alan Cl, Dart. DA1 108 FJ84
Alandale Dr, Pnr. HA5 39 BV54
Aland Ct, SE16 203 L6
Alander Ms, E17 67 EC56
Alan Dr, Barn. EN5 27 CY44
Alan Gdns, Rom. RM7 70 FA59
Alan Hocken Way, E15 86 EE68
Alan Rd, SW19 119 CY92
Alanthus Cl, SE12 124 EF86
Alan Way, Slou. (Geo.Grn) SL3 74 AY72
Alaska St, SE1 200 D3
Alba Cl, Hayes UB4
off Ramulis Dr 78 BX70
Albacore Cres, SE13 123 EB86
Alba Gdns, NW11 63 CY58
Albain Cres, Ashf. TW15 114 BL89
Alban Cres, Borwd. WD6 26 CP39
Dartford (Fnghm) DA4 148 FN102
Alban Highwalk, EC2
off London Wall 84 DQ71
Albans Vw, Wat. WD25 7 BV33
Albany, W1 199 K1
Albany, The, Wdf.Grn. IG8 48 EF49
Albany Cl, N15 65 DP56
SW14 98 CP84
Bexley DA5 126 EW87
Bushey WD23 25 CD44
Esher KT10 154 CA109
Reigate RH2 184 DA132
Uxbridge UB10 58 BN64
Albany Ct, E4
off Chelwood Cl 31 EB44
Epping CM16 17 ET30
Albany Ctyd, W1 199 L1
Albany Cres, Edg. HA8 42 CN52
Esher (Clay.) KT10 155 CE107
Albany Mans, SW11 100 DE80
Albany Ms, N1
off Barnsbury Pk 83 DN66
SE5 *off Albany Rd* 102 DQ79
Bromley BR1 124 EG93
Kingston upon Thames KT2
off Albany Pk Rd 117 CK93
St. Albans AL2
off North Orbital Rd 8 CA27
Sutton SM1 *off Camden Rd* 158 DB106
⇌ **Albany Park** 126 EX89
Albany Pk, Slou. (Colnbr.) SL3 93 BD81
Albany Pk Av, Enf. EN3 30 DW39
Albany Pk Rd, Kings.T. KT2 118 CL93
Leatherhead KT22 171 CG119
Albany Pas, Rich. TW10 118 CM85
Albany Pl, Brent. TW8
off Albany Rd 98 CL79
Egham TW20 113 BA91
Albany Rd, E10 67 EA59
E12 68 EK63
E17 67 DY58
N4 65 DM58
N18 46 DV50
SE5 102 DR79
SW19 120 DB92
W13 79 CH73
Belvedere DA17 106 EZ79
Bexley DA5 126 EW87
Brentford TW8 97 CK79
Brentwood (Pilg.Hat.) CM15 54 FV44
Chislehurst BR7 125 EP92
Enfield EN3 31 DX37
Hornchurch RM12 71 FG60
New Malden KT3 138 CR98
Richmond TW10
off Albert Rd 118 CM85
Romford RM6 70 EZ58
Walton-on-Thames KT12 154 BX105
Windsor (Old Wind.) SL4 112 AU85
Albanys, The, Reig. RH2 184 DA131
Albany St, NW1 83 DH68
Albany Ter, NW1
off Marylebone Rd 83 DH70
Albany Vw, Buck.H. IG9 48 EG46
Alba Pl, W11
off Portobello Rd 81 CZ72
Albatross Gdns, S.Croy. CR2 161 DX111
Albatross St, SE18 105 ES80
Albatross Way, SE16 203 H5
Albemarle, SW19 119 CX89
Albemarle App, Ilf. IG2 69 EP58
Albemarle Av, Pot.B. EN6 12 DB33
Twickenham TW2 116 BZ88
Waltham Cross (Chsht) EN8 14 DW28
Albemarle Cl, Grays RM17 110 GA75
Albemarle Gdns, Ilf. IG2 69 EP58
New Malden KT3 138 CR98
Albemarle Pk, Stan. HA7
off Marsh La 41 CJ50
Albemarle Rd, Barn. EN4 44 DE45
Beckenham BR3 143 EB95
Albemarle St, W1 199 J1
Albemarle Way, EC1 196 F5
Alberon Gdns, NW11 63 CZ56
Alberta Av, Sutt. SM1 157 CY105
Alberta Est, SE17 200 G10
Alberta Rd, Enf. EN1 30 DT44
Erith DA8 107 FC81
Alberta St, SE17 200 F10
Albert Av, E4 47 EA49
SW8 101 DM80
Chertsey KT16 134 BG97
Albert Br, SW3 100 DE79
SW11 100 DE79
Albert Br Rd, SW11 100 DE80
Albert Carr Gdns, SW16 121 DL92
Albert Cl, E9
off Northiam St 84 DV67
N22 45 DK53
Grays RM16 110 GC76
Slough SL1 *off Albert St* 92 AT76
Albert Ct, SW7
off Prince Consort Rd 100 DD75
Albert Cres, E4 47 EA49
Albert Dr, SW19 119 CY89
Woking GU21 151 BD114
Albert Embk, SE1 101 DL78
Albert Gdns, E1 85 DX72
Albert Gate, SW1 198 E4
Albert Gro, SW20 139 CX95
Albert Hall Mans, SW7
off Kensington Gore 100 DD75
Albertine Cl, Epsom KT17 173 CV116
Albert Mans, SW11
off Albert Br Rd 100 DF81
★ **Albert Mem**, SW7 100 DD75
Albert Ms, E14
off Narrow St 85 DY73
N4 *off Albert Rd* 65 DM60
SE4 *off Arabin Rd* 103 DY84
W8 *off Victoria Gro* 100 DC76
Albert Murray Cl, Grav. DA12
off Armoury Dr 131 GJ87
Albert Pl, N3 44 DA53
N17 *off High Rd* 66 DT55
W8 100 DB75
Albert Rd, E10 67 EC61
E16 86 EL74
E17 67 EA57
E18 68 EH55
N4 65 DM60
N15 66 DS58
N22 45 DJ53
NW4 63 CX56
NW6 81 CZ68
NW7 43 CT50
SE9 124 EL90
SE20 123 DX94
SE25 142 DU98
W5 79 CH70
Addlestone KT15 134 BK104
Ashford TW15 114 BM92
Ashtead KT21 172 CM118
Barnet EN4 28 DC42
Belvedere DA17 106 EZ78
Bexley DA5 126 FA86
Bromley BR2 144 EK99
Buckhurst Hill IG9 48 EK47
Dagenham RM8 70 FA60
Dartford DA2 128 FJ90
Egham (Eng.Grn) TW20 112 AX93
Epsom KT17 157 CT113
Hampton (Hmptn H.) TW12 116 CC92
Harrow HA2 60 CC55
Hayes UB3 95 BS76
Hounslow TW3 96 CA84
Ilford IG1 69 EP62
Kingston upon Thames KT1 138 CM96
Mitcham CR4 140 DF97
New Malden KT3 139 CT98
Orpington (Chels.) BR6 164 EU106
Orpington (St.M.Cray) BR5 146 EV100
Redhill RH1 185 DJ129
Richmond TW10 118 CL85
Romford RM1 71 FF57
Southall UB2 96 BX76
Sutton SM1 158 DD106
Swanscombe DA10 130 FZ86
Teddington TW11 117 CF93
Twickenham TW1 117 CF88
Warlingham CR6 177 DZ117
West Drayton UB7 76 BL74
Windsor SL4 92 AS84
Albert Rd Est, Belv. DA17 106 EZ78
Albert Rd N, Reig. RH2 183 CZ133
Watford WD17 23 BV41
Albert Rd S, Wat. WD17 23 BV41
Albert Sq, E15 68 EE64
SW8 101 DM80
Albert St, N12 44 DC50
NW1 83 DH67
Brentwood (Warley) CM14 54 FW50
Slough SL1 92 AT76
Albert Ter, NW1 82 DG67
NW10 80 CR67
Buckhurst Hill IG9 48 EK47
Albert Ter Ms, NW1
off Regents Pk Rd 82 DG67
Albert Way, SE15 102 DV80
Albion Av, N10 44 DG53
SW8 101 DK82
Albion Bldgs, EC1
off Bartholomew Cl 84 DQ71
Albion Cl, W2 194 C10
Romford RM7 71 FD58
Slough SL2 74 AU74
Albion Cres, Ch.St.G. HP8 36 AV48
Albion Dr, E8 84 DT66
Albion Est, SE16 203 H5
Albion Gro, N16 66 DS63
Albion Hill, Loug. IG10 32 EJ43
Albion Ho, Slou. SL3 93 BB78
Woking GU21 167 AZ117
Albion Ms, N1 83 DN67
NW6
off Kilburn High Rd 81 CZ66
W2 194 C9
W6 *off Galena Rd* 99 CV77
Albion Par, N16
off Albion Rd 66 DR63
Gravesend DA12 131 GK86
Albion Pk, Loug. IG10 32 EK43
Albion Pl, EC1 196 F6
SE25 *off High St* 142 DU97
W6 99 CV77
Albion Rd, E17 67 EC55
N16 66 DR63
N17 66 DT54
Bexleyheath DA6 106 EZ84
Chalfont St. Giles HP8 36 AV47
Gravesend DA12 131 GJ87
Hayes UB3 77 BS72
Hounslow TW3 96 CA84
Kingston upon Thames KT2 138 CQ95
Albion Rd, Sutton SM2 158 DD107
Twickenham TW2 117 CE88
Albion Sq, E8 84 DT66
Albion St, SE16 202 G5
W2 194 C9
Croydon CR0 141 DP102
Albion Ter, E8 84 DT66
Gravesend DA12 131 GJ86
Albion Vil Rd, SE26 122 DW90
Albion Wk, N1 *off York Way* 83 DL68
Albion Way, EC1 197 H7
SE13 103 EC84
Wembley HA9
off North End Rd 62 CP62
Albion Yd, N1 *off Balfe St* 83 DL68
Albon Ho, SW18
off Neville Gill Cl 120 DB86
Albright Ind Est, Rain. RM13 89 FF71
Albrighton Rd, SE22 102 DS83
Albuhera Cl, Enf. EN2 29 DN39
Albury Av, Bexh. DA7 106 EY82
Isleworth TW7 97 CF80
Sutton SM2 157 CW109
Albury Cl, Cher. (Longcr.)
KT16 132 AU104
Epsom KT19 156 CP109
Hampton TW12 116 CA93
Albury Ct, Sutt. SM1
off Ripley Gdns 158 DC105
Albury Dr, Pnr. HA5 40 BX52
Albury Gro Rd, Wal.Cr.
(Chsht) EN8 15 DX30
Albury Ms, E12 68 EJ60
Albury Ride, Wal.Cr.
(Chsht) EN8 15 DX31
Albury Rd, Chess. KT9 156 CL106
Redhill RH1 185 DJ129
Walton-on-Thames KT12 153 BS107
Albury St, SE8 103 EA79
Albury Wk, Wal.Cr.
(Chsht) EN8 15 DX32
Albyfield, Brom. BR1 145 EM97
Albyn Rd, SE8 103 EA81
Albyns Cl, Rain. RM13 89 FG66
Albyns La, Rom. RM4 35 FC40
Alcester Cres, E5 66 DV61
Alcester Rd, Wall. SM6 159 DH105
Alcock Cl, Wall. SM6 159 DK108
Alcock Rd, Houns. TW5 96 BX80
Alcocks Cl, Tad. KT20 173 CY120
Alcocks La, Tad. (Kgswd) KT20 173 CY120
Alconbury Rd, E5 66 DU61
Alcorn Cl, Sutt. SM3 140 DA103
Alcott Cl, W7
off Westcott Cres 79 CF71
Alcuin Ct, Stan. HA7
off Old Ch La 41 CJ52
ALDBOROUGH HATCH, Ilf. IG2 69 ES55
Aldborough Rd, Dag. RM10 89 FC65
Upminster RM14 72 FM61
Aldborough Rd N, Ilf. IG2 69 ET57
Aldborough Rd S, Ilf. IG3 69 ES60
Aldborough Spur, Slou. SL1 74 AS72
Aldbourne Rd, W12 81 CT74
Aldbridge St, SE17 201 N10
Aldburgh Ms, W1 194 G8
Aldbury Av, Wem. HA9 80 CP66
Aldbury Cl, Wat. WD25 24 BX36
Aldbury Ms, N9 46 DR45
Aldbury Rd, Rick. (Mill End)
WD3 37 BF45
Aldebert Ter, SW8 101 DL80
Aldeburgh Cl, E5
off Southwold Rd 66 DV61
Aldeburgh Pl, SE10 205 N9
Woodford Green IG8 48 EG49
Aldeburgh St, SE10 205 M10
Alden Av, E15 86 EF69
ALDENHAM, Wat. WD25 24 CB38
Aldenham Av, Rad. WD7 25 CG36
★ **Aldenham Country Pk**,
Borwd. WD6 25 CH43
Aldenham Dr, Uxb. UB8 77 BP70
Aldenham Gro, Rad. WD7 9 CH34
Aldenham Rd, Borwd. (Elstree)
WD6 25 CH42
Bushey WD23 24 BZ42
Radlett WD7 25 CG35
Watford WD19 24 BX44
Watford (Let.Hth) WD25 25 CE39
Aldenham St, NW1 195 L1
Aldenholme, Wey. KT13 153 BS107
Aldensley Rd, W6 99 CV76
Alder Av, Upmin. RM14 72 FM63
Alderbourne La, Iver SL0 57 BA64
Slough (Fulmer) SL3 56 AX63
Alderbrook Rd, SW12 121 DH86
Alderbury Rd, SW13 99 CU79
Slough SL3 93 AZ75
Alderbury Rd W, Slou. SL3 93 AZ75
Alder Cl, SE15 102 DT79
Egham (Eng.Grn) TW20 112 AY92
St. Albans (Park St) AL2 8 CB28
Aldercombe La, Cat. CR3 186 DS127
Aldercroft, Couls. CR5 175 DM116
Alder Dr, S.Ock. RM15
off Laburnum Gro 91 FW70
Alder Gro, NW2 63 CV61
Aldergrove Gdns, Houns. TW3
off Bath Rd 96 BY82
Aldergrove Wk, Horn. RM12
off Airfield Way 90 FJ65
Alderholt Way, SE15
off Blakes Rd 102 DS80
Alderman Av, Bark. IG11 88 EU69
Aldermanbury, EC2 197 J8
Aldermanbury Sq, EC2 197 J7
Alderman Cl, Dart. DA1
off Lower Sta Rd 127 FE86
Alderman Judge Mall,
Kings.T. KT1 *off Eden St* 138 CL96
Aldermans Hill, N13 45 DL49
Alderman's Wk, EC2 197 M7
Aldermary Rd, Brom. BR1 144 EG95
Alder Ms, N19 *off Bredgar Rd* 65 DJ61
Aldermoor Rd, SE6 123 DZ90
Alderney Av, Houns. TW5 96 CB80
Alderney Gdns, Nthlt. UB5 78 BZ66
Alderney Ms, SE1 201 K6
Alderney Rd, E1 85 DX70
Alderney Rd, Erith DA8 107 FG80
Alderney St, SW1 199 J10
Alder Rd, SW14 98 CR83
Iver SL0 75 BC68
Sidcup DA14 125 ET90
Uxbridge (Denh.) UB9 76 BJ65
Alders, The, N21 29 DN44
Feltham TW13 116 BY91
Hounslow TW5 96 BZ79
West Byfleet KT14 152 BJ112
West Wickham BR4 143 EB102
Alders Av, Wdf.Grn. IG8 48 EE51
ALDERSBROOK, E12 68 EH61
Aldersbrook Av, Enf. EN1 30 DS40
Aldersbrook Dr, Kings.T. KT2 118 CM93
Aldersbrook La, E12 69 EM62
Aldersbrook Rd, E11 68 EH61
E12 68 EK62
Alders Cl, E11
off Aldersbrook Rd 68 EH61
W5 97 CK76
Edgware HA8 42 CQ50
Aldersey Gdns, Bark. IG11 87 ER65
Aldersford Cl, SE4 123 DX85
Aldersgate St, EC1 197 H8
Alders Gro, E.Mol. KT8
off Esher Rd 137 CD99
Aldersgrove, Wal.Abb. EN9
off Roundhills 16 EE34
Aldersgrove Av, SE9 124 EJ90
Aldershot Rd, NW6 81 CZ67
Alderside Wk, Egh. (Eng.Grn)
TW20 112 AY92
Aldersmead Av, Croy. CR0 143 DX100
Aldersmead Rd, Beck. BR3 123 DY94
Alderson Pl, Sthl. UB2 78 CC74
Alderson St, W10
off Kensal Rd 81 CY70
Alders Rd, Edg. HA8 42 CQ50
Reigate RH2 184 DB132
Alderstead Heath, Red. RH1 175 DK124
Alderstead Heath Caravan Club,
Red. RH1 175 DL123
Alderstead La, Red. RH1 185 DK126
Alderton Cl, NW10 62 CR62
Brentwood (Pilg.Hat.) CM15 54 FV43
Loughton IG10 33 EN42
Alderton Cres, NW4 63 CV57
Alderton Hall La, Loug. IG10 33 EN42
Alderton Hill, Loug. IG10 32 EL43
Alderton Ms, Loug. IG10
off Alderton Hall La 33 EN42
Alderton Ri, Loug. IG10 33 EN42
Alderton Rd, SE24 102 DQ83
Croydon CR0 142 DT101
Alderton Way, NW4 63 CV57
Loughton IG10 33 EM43
Alderville Rd, SW6 99 CZ82
Alder Wk, Ilf. IG1 69 EQ64
Watford WD25
off Aspen Pk Dr 23 BV35
Alder Way, Swan. BR8 147 FD96
Alderwick Dr, Houns. TW3 97 CD83
Alderwood Cl, Cat. CR3 186 DS125
Romford (Abridge) RM4 34 EV41
Alderwood Dr, Rom.
(Abridge) RM4 34 EV41
Alderwood Ms, Barn. EN4 28 DC38
Alderwood Rd, SE9 125 ER86
Aldford St, W1 198 F2
⊖ **Aldgate** 197 P8
Aldgate, EC3 197 P9
Aldgate Av, E1 197 P8
Aldgate Barrs Shop Cen, E1
off Whitechapel High St 84 DT72
⊖ **Aldgate East** 84 DT72
Aldgate High St, EC3 197 P9
Aldham Dr, S.Ock. RM15 91 FW71
Aldin Av N, Slou. SL1 92 AU75
Aldin Av S, Slou. SL1 92 AU75
Aldine Ct, W12
off Aldine St 81 CW74
Aldine Pl, W12
off Uxbridge Rd 81 CW74
Aldine St, W12 99 CW75
Aldingham Ct, Horn. RM12
off Easedale Dr 71 FG64
Aldingham Gdns,
Horn. RM12 71 FG64
Aldington Cl, Dag. RM8 70 EW59
Aldington Rd, SE18 104 EK76
Aldis Ms, SW17 *off Aldis St* 120 DE92
Enfield EN3
off Martini Dr 31 EA37
Aldis St, SW17 120 DE92
Aldred Rd, NW6 64 DA64
Aldren Rd, SW17 120 DC90
Aldrich Cres, Croy.
(New Adgtn) CR0 161 EC109
Aldriche Way, E4 47 EC51
Aldrich Gdns, Sutt. SM3 139 CZ104
Aldrich Ter, SW18
off Lidiard Rd 120 DC89
Aldridge Av, Edg. HA8 42 CP48
Enfield EN3 31 EA38
Ruislip HA4 60 BX61
Stanmore HA7 42 CL53
Aldridge Ri, N.Mal. KT3 138 CS101
Aldridge Rd Vil, W11 81 CZ71
Aldridge Wk, N14 45 DL45
Aldrington Rd, SW16 121 DJ92
Aldsworth Cl, W9 82 DB70
Aldwick Cl, SE9 125 ER90
Aldwick Rd, Croy. CR0 141 DM104
Aldworth Gro, SE13 123 EC86
Aldworth Rd, E15 86 EE66
Aldwych, WC2 196 B10
Aldwych Av, Ilf. IG6 69 EQ56
Aldwych Cl, Horn. RM12 71 FG61
Aldwych Underpass, WC2
off Kingsway 83 DM72
Alers Rd, Bexh. DA6 126 EX85
Alesia Cl, N22
off Nightingale Rd 45 DL52
Alestan Beck Rd, E16 86 EK71

A B C D E F G H I J K L M N O P Q R S T U V W X Y Z

★ Place of interest ⇌ Railway station ⊖ London Underground station DLR Docklands Light Railway station Tra Tramlink station H Hospital Riv Pedestrian ferry landing stage

Alexa Ct, W8
off Lexham Gdns 100 DA77
Sutton SM2
off Mulgrave Rd 158 DA107
Alexander Av, NW10 81 CV66
Alexander Cl, Barn. EN4 28 DD42
Bromley BR2 144 EG102
Sidcup DA15 125 ES85
Southall UB2 78 CC74
Twickenham TW2 117 CF89
Alexander Ct, Wal.Cr.
(Chsht) EN8 15 DX30
Alexander Cres, Cat. CR3
off Coulsdon Rd 176 DQ122
Alexander Evans Ms, SE23
off Sunderland Rd 123 DX88
★ Alexander Fleming
Laboratory Mus, W2 194 A8
Alexander Godley Cl,
Ashtd. KT21 172 CM119
Alexander Ho, Kings.T. KT2
off Kingsgate Rd 138 CL95
Alexander La, Brwd.
(Hutt.) CM13, CM15 55 GB44
Alexander Ms, W2
off Alexander St 82 DB72
Alexander Pl, SW7 198 B8
Oxted RH8
off Barrow Grn Rd 188 EE128
Alexander Rd, N19 65 DL62
Bexleyheath DA7 106 EX82
Chislehurst BR7 125 EP92
Coulsdon CR5 175 DH115
Egham TW20 113 BB92
Greenhithe DA9 129 FW85
St. Albans (Lon.Col.) AL2 9 CJ25
Alexander Sq, SW3 198 B8
Alexander St, W2 82 DA72
Alexanders Wk, Cat. CR3 186 DT126
Alexandra Av, N22 45 DK53
SW11 100 DG81
W4 98 CR80
Harrow HA2 60 BZ60
Southall UB1 78 BZ73
Sutton SM1 140 DA104
Warlingham CR6 177 DZ117
Alexandra Cl, SE8 103 DZ79
Ashford TW15
off Alexandra Rd 115 BR94
Grays RM16 111 GH75
Harrow HA2
off Alexandra Av 60 CA62
Staines TW18 114 BK93
Swanley BR8 147 FE96
Walton-on-Thames KT12 135 BU103
Alexandra Cotts, SE14 103 DZ81
Alexandra Ct, N14 29 DJ43
N16 off Belgrade Rd 66 DT63
Ashford TW15
off Alexandra Rd 115 BR93
Wembley HA9 62 CM63
Alexandra Cres, Brom. BR1 124 EF93
Alexandra Dr, SE19 122 DS92
Surbiton KT5 138 CN101
Alexandra Gdns, N10 65 DH56
W4 98 CR80
Carshalton SM5 158 DG109
Hounslow TW3 96 CB82
Alexandra Gro, N4 65 DP60
N12 44 DB50
Alexandra Ms, N2
off Fortis Grn 64 DF55
SW19 off Alexandra Rd 120 DA93
★ Alexandra Palace, N22 45 DK54
⇌ Alexandra Palace 45 DL54
Alexandra Palace Way, N22 65 DJ55
Alexandra Pk Rd, N10 45 DH54
N22 45 DK54
Alexandra Pl, NW8 82 DC67
SE25 142 DR99
Croydon CR0
off Alexandra Rd 142 DS102
Alexandra Rd, E6 87 EN69
E10 67 EC62
E17 67 DZ58
E18 68 EH55
N8 65 DN55
N9 46 DV45
N10 45 DH51
N15 66 DR57
NW4 63 CX56
NW8 82 DC66
SE26 123 DX93
SW14 98 CR83
SW19 119 CZ93
W4 98 CR75
Addlestone KT15 152 BK105
Ashford TW15 115 BR94
Borehamwood WD6 26 CR38
Brentford TW8 97 CK79
Brentwood CM14 54 FW48
Croydon CR0 142 DS102
Egham (Eng.Grn) TW20 112 AW93
Enfield EN3 31 DX42
Epsom KT17 157 CT113
Erith DA8 107 FF79
Gravesend DA12 131 GL87
Hounslow TW3 96 CB82
Kings Langley WD4 6 BN29
Kings Langley (Chipper.) WD4 6 BG30
Kingston upon Thames KT2 118 CN94
Mitcham CR4 120 DE94
Rainham RM13 89 FF67
Richmond TW9 98 CM82
Rickmansworth
(Sarratt) WD3 22 BG36
Romford RM1 71 FF58
Romford (Chad.Hth) RM6 70 EX58
Thames Ditton KT7 137 CF99
Tilbury RM18 111 GF82
Twickenham TW1 117 CJ86
Uxbridge UB8 76 BK68
Warlingham CR6 177 DY117
Watford WD17 23 BU40
Westerham (Bigg.H.) TN16 178 EH119
Alexandra Sq, Mord. SM4 140 DA99
Alexandra St, E16 86 EG71
SE14 103 DY80
Alexandra Wk, SE19 122 DS92
Dartford DA4
off Gorringe Av 149 FS96
Alexandra Way, Epsom KT19 156 CN111
Waltham Cross EN8 15 DZ34
Alexandria Rd, W13 79 CG73
Alexis St, SE16 202 B8
Alfan La, Dart. DA2 127 FD92
Alfearn Rd, E5 66 DW63
Alford Grn, Croy.
(New Adgtn) CR0 161 ED107
Alford Pl, N1 197 J1
Alford Rd, Erith DA8 107 FD78
Alfoxton Av, N15 65 DP56
Alfreda St, SW11 101 DH81
Alfred Cl, W4 off Belmont Rd 98 CR77
Alfred Gdns, Sthl. UB1 78 BY73
Alfred Ms, W1 195 M6
Alfred Pl, WC1 195 M6
Gravesend (Nthflt) DA11 131 GF88
Alfred Prior Ho, E12 69 EN63
Alfred Rd, E15 68 EF64
SE25 142 DU99
W2 82 DA71
W3 80 CQ74
Belvedere DA17 106 EZ78
Brentwood CM14 54 FX47
Buckhurst Hill IG9 48 EK47
Dartford (Hawley) DA2 128 FL91
Feltham TW13 116 BW89
Gravesend DA11 131 GH89
Kingston upon Thames
KT1 138 CL97
South Ockendon
(Aveley) RM15 90 FQ74
Sutton SM1 158 DC106
Alfred's Gdns, Bark. IG11 87 ES68
Alfred St, E3 85 DZ69
Grays RM17 110 GC79
Alfreds Way, Bark. IG11 87 EQ69
Alfreds Way Ind Est, Bark. IG11 88 EU67
Alfreton Cl, SW19 119 CX90
Alfriston Av, Croy. CR0 141 DL101
Harrow HA2 60 CA58
Alfriston Cl, Dart. DA1
off Lower Sta Rd 127 FE86
Surbiton KT5 138 CM99
Alfriston Rd, SW11 120 DF85
Algar Cl, Islw. TW7
off Algar Rd 97 CG83
Stanmore HA7 41 CF50
Algar Rd, Islw. TW7 97 CG83
Algarve Rd, SW18 120 DB88
Algernon Rd, NW4 63 CU58
NW6 82 DA67
SE13 103 EB84
Algers Cl, Loug. IG10 32 EK43
Algers Mead, Loug. IG10 32 EK43
Algers Rd, Loug. IG10 32 EK43
Algiers Rd, SE13 103 EA84
Alibon Gdns, Dag. RM10 70 FA64
Alibon Rd, Dag. RM9, RM10 70 EZ64
Alice Cl, Barn. EN5 28 DC42
Alice Ct, SW15 off Deodar Rd 99 CZ84
Alice Gilliatt Ct, W14 99 CZ79
Alice La, E3 85 DZ67
Alice Ms, Tedd. TW11
off Luther Rd 117 CF92
Alice Ruston Pl, Wok. GU22 166 AW119
Alice St, SE1 201 M7
Alice Thompson Cl, SE12 124 EJ89
Alice Walker Cl, SE24
off Shakespeare Rd 101 DP84
Alice Way, Houns. TW3 96 CB84
Alicia Av, Har. HA3 61 CH56
Alicia Cl, Har. HA3 61 CJ56
Alicia Gdns, Har. HA3 61 CH56
Alie St, E1 84 DT72
Alington Cres, NW9 62 CQ60
Alington Gro, Wall. SM6 159 DJ109
Alison Cl, E6 87 EN72
Croydon CR0
off Shirley Oaks Rd 143 DX102
Woking GU21 166 AY115
Aliwal Rd, SW11 100 DE84
Alkerden La, Green. DA9 129 FW86
Swanscombe DA10 129 FW86
Alkerden Rd, W4 98 CS78
Alkham Rd, N16 66 DT61
Allan Barclay Cl, N15
off High Rd 66 DT58
Allan Cl, N.Mal. KT3 138 CR99
Allandale Av, N3 63 CY55
Allandale Cres, Pot.B. EN6 11 CY32
Allandale Pl, Orp. BR6 146 EX104
Allandale Rd, Enf. EN3 31 DX36
Hornchurch RM11 71 FF59
Allan Way, W3 80 CQ71
Allard Cl, Orp. BR5 146 EW101
Waltham Cross
(Chsht) EN7 14 DT27
Allard Cres, Bushey
(Bushey Hth) WD23 40 CC46
Allard Gdns, SW4 121 DK85
Allardyce St, SW4 101 DM84
Allbrook Cl, Tedd. TW11 117 CE92
Allcot Cl, Felt. TW14 115 BT88
Allcroft Rd, NW5 64 DG64
Allder Way, S.Croy. CR2 159 DP108
Allenby Av, S.Croy. CR2 160 DQ109
Allenby Cl, Grnf. UB6 78 CA69
Allenby Cres, Grays RM17 110 GB78
Allenby Dr, Horn. RM11 72 FL60
Allenby Rd, SE23 123 DY90
Southall UB1 78 CA72
Westerham (Bigg.H.) TN16 178 EL117
Allen Cl, Mitch. CR4 141 DH95
Radlett (Shenley) WD7
off Russet Dr 10 CL32
Sunbury-on-Thames TW16 135 BV95
Allen Ct, Grnf. UB6 61 CF64
Allendale Av, Sthl. UB1 78 CA72
Allendale Cl, SE5
off Daneville Rd 102 DR81
SE26 123 DX92
Dartford DA2
off Princes Rd 129 FR88
Allendale Rd, Grnf. UB6 79 CH65
Allen Edwards Dr, SW8 101 DL81
Allenford Ho, SW15
off Tunworth Cres 119 CT86
Allen Ho Pk, Wok. GU22 166 AW120
Allen Pl, Twick. TW1
off Church St 117 CG88
Allen Rd, E3 85 DZ68
N16 66 DS63
Beckenham BR3 143 DX96
Croydon CR0 141 DM101
Rainham RM13 90 FJ69
Sunbury-on-Thames TW16 135 BV95
Allensbury Pl, NW1 83 DK66
Allens Rd, Enf. EN3 30 DW43
Allen St, W8 100 DA76
Allenswood Rd, SE9 104 EL83
Allerford Ct, Har. HA2 60 CB57
Allerford Rd, SE6 123 EB91
Allerton Cl, Borwd. WD6 26 CM38
Allerton Ct, NW4
off Holders Hill Rd 43 CX54
Allerton Rd, N16 66 DQ61
Borehamwood WD6 26 CL38
Allerton Wk, N7
off Durham Rd 65 DM61
Allestree Rd, SW6 99 CY80
Alleyn Cres, SE21 122 DR89
Alleyndale Rd, Dag. RM8 70 EW61
Alleyn Pk, SE21 122 DR89
Southall UB2 96 BZ77
Alleyn Rd, SE21 122 DR90
Allfarthing La, SW18 120 DB86
Allgood Cl, Mord. SM4 139 CX100
Allgood St, E2
off Hackney Rd 84 DT68
Allhallows La, EC4 201 K1
★ All Hallows-on-the-Wall
C of E Ch, EC2 197 L7
Allhallows Rd, E6 86 EL71
All Hallows Rd, N17 46 DS53
Allhusen Gdns, Slou.(Fulmer) SL3
off Alderbourne La 56 AY63
Alliance Cl, Wem. HA0 61 CK63
Alliance Ct, W3
off Alliance Rd 80 CP70
Alliance Rd, E13 86 EJ70
SE18 106 EU79
W3 80 CP70
Allied Way, W3 off Larden Rd 98 CS75
Allingham Cl, W7 79 CF73
Allingham Ms, N1
off Allingham St 84 DQ68
Allingham St, N1 84 DQ68
Allington Av, N17 46 DS51
Allington Cl, SW19
off High St Wimbledon 119 CX92
Gravesend DA12
off Farley Rd 131 GM88
Greenford UB6 78 CC66
Allington Ct, Enf. EN3 31 DX43
Slough SL2
off Myrtle Cres 74 AT73
Allington Rd, NW4 63 CV57
W10 81 CY68
Harrow HA2 60 CC57
Orpington BR6 145 ER103
Allington St, SW1 199 K7
Allison Cl, SE10
off Dartmouth Hill 103 EC81
Waltham Abbey EN9 16 EG33
Allison Gro, SE21 122 DS88
Allison Rd, N8 65 DN57
W3 80 CQ72
Allitsen Rd, NW8 194 B1
Allmains Cl, Wal.Abb. EN9 16 EH25
Allnutts Rd, Epp. CM16 18 EU33
Allnutt Way, SW4 121 DK85
Alloa Rd, SE8 203 J10
Ilford IG3 70 EU61
Allonby Dr, Ruis. HA4 59 BP59
Allonby Gdns, Wem. HA9 61 CJ60
Allotment La, Sev. TN13 191 FJ122
Allotment Way, NW2
off Midland Ter 63 CX62
Alloway Cl, Wok. GU21
off Inglewood 166 AV118
Alloway Rd, E3 85 DY69
Allports Ms, E1
off Stepney Grn 84 DW70
DLR All Saints 85 EB73
All Saints Cl, N9 46 DT47
SW8 off Lansdowne Way 101 DL81
Chigwell IG7 50 EU48
Swanscombe DA10
off High St 130 FZ85
All Saints Cres, Wat. WD25 8 BX33
All Saints Dr, SE3 104 EE82
South Croydon CR2 160 DT112
All Saints La, Rick.
(Crox.Grn) WD3 22 BN44
All Saints Ms, Har. HA3 41 CE51
All Saints Pas, SW18
off Wandsworth High St 120 DB85
All Saints Rd, SW19 120 DC94
W3 98 CQ76
W11 81 CZ71
Gravesend (Nthflt) DA11 131 GF88
Sutton SM1 140 DB104
All Saints St, N1 83 DM68
All Saints Twr, E10 67 EB59
Allsop Pl, NW1 194 E5
All Souls Av, NW10 81 CV68
All Souls Pl, W1 195 J7
Allum Cl, Borwd.
(Elstree) WD6 26 CL42
Allum Gro, Tad. KT20
off Preston La 173 CV121
Allum La, Borwd.
(Elstree) WD6 26 CM42
Allum Way, N20 44 DC46
Allwood Cl, SE26 123 DX91
Allwood Rd, Wal.Cr. EN7 14 DT27
Allyn Cl, Stai. TW18
off Penton Rd 113 BF93
Alma Av, E4 47 EC52
Hornchurch RM12 72 FL63
Almack Rd, E5 66 DW63
Alma Cl, Wok. (Knap.) GU21 166 AS118
Alma Cres, Sutt. SM1 157 CY106
Alma Gro, SE1 202 A9
Alma Pl, NW10 off Harrow Rd 81 CV69
SE19 122 DT94
Thornton Heath CR7 141 DN99
Alma Rd, N10 44 DG52
SW18 120 DC85
Carshalton SM5 158 DE106
Enfield EN3 31 DY43
Esher KT10 137 CE102
Orpington BR5 146 EX103
Reigate RH2 184 DB133
Sidcup DA14 126 EU90
Southall UB1 78 BY73
Swanscombe DA10 130 FZ85
Alma Row, Har. HA3 41 CD53
Alma Sq, NW8 82 DC69
Alma St, E15 85 ED65
NW5 83 DH65
Alma Ter, SW18 120 DD87
W8 off Allen St 100 DA76
Almeida St, N1 83 DP66
Almeric Rd, SW11 100 DF84
Almer Rd, SW20 119 CU94
Almington St, N4 65 DM60
Almners Rd, Cher.
(Lyne) KT16 133 BC100
Almond Av, W5 98 CL76
Carshalton SM5 140 DF103
Uxbridge UB10 59 BP62
West Drayton UB7 94 BN76
Woking GU22 166 AX121
Almond Cl, SE15 102 DU82
Bromley BR2 145 EN101
Egham (Eng.Grn) TW20 112 AV93
Feltham TW13
off Highfield Rd 115 BU88
Grays RM16 111 GG76
Hayes UB3 77 BS73
Ruislip HA4 off Roundways 59 BT62
Shepperton TW17 135 BQ96
Almond Dr, Swan. BR8 147 FD96
Almond Gro, Brent. TW8 97 CH80
Almond Rd, N17 46 DU52
SE16 202 E8
Dartford DA2 128 FQ87
Epsom KT19 156 CR111
Almonds Av, Buck.H. IG9 48 EG47
Almond Way, Borwd. WD6 26 CP42
Bromley BR2 145 EN101
Harrow HA2 40 CB54
Mitcham CR4 141 DK99
Almons Way, Slou. SL2 74 AV71
Almorah Rd, N1 84 DR66
Hounslow TW5 96 BX81
Alms Heath, Wok.
(Ockham) GU23 169 BP121
Almshouse La, Chess. KT9 155 CJ109
Enfield EN1 30 DV37
Alnwick Gro, Mord. SM4
off Bordesley Rd 140 DB98
Alnwick Rd, E16 86 EJ72
SE12 124 EH87
ALPERTON, Wem. HA0 80 CM67
⊖ Alperton 80 CL67
Alperton La, Grnf. UB6 79 CK69
Wembley HA0 79 CK69
Alperton St, W10 81 CZ70
Alphabet Gdns, Cars. SM5 140 DD100
Alphabet Sq, E3
off Hawgood St 85 EA71
Alpha Cl, NW1 194 C3
Alpha Ct, Whyt. CR3 176 DU118
Alpha Gro, E14 204 A5
Alpha Pl, NW6 82 DA68
SW3 100 DE79
Alpha Rd, E4 47 EB48
N18 46 DU51
SE14 103 DZ81
Brentwood (Hutt.) CM13 55 GD44
Croydon CR0 142 DS102
Enfield EN3 31 DY42
Surbiton KT5 138 CM100
Teddington TW11 117 CD92
Uxbridge UB10 77 BP70
Woking GU22 167 BB116
Woking (Chobham) GU24 150 AT110
Alpha St, SE15 102 DU82
Alpha St N, Slou. SL1 92 AU75
Alpha St S, Slou. SL1 92 AT76
Alpha Way, Egh. TW20 133 BC95
Alphea Cl, SW19
off Courtney Rd 120 DE94
Alpine Av, Surb. KT5 138 CQ103
Alpine Business Cen, E6 87 EN71
Alpine Cl, Croy. CR0 142 DS104
Alpine Copse, Brom. BR1 145 EN96
Alpine Gro, E9 84 DW66
Alpine Rd, E10 67 EB61
SE16 202 G9
Redhill RH1 184 DG131
Walton-on-Thames KT12 135 BU101
Alpine Vw, Cars. SM5 158 DE106
Alpine Wk, Stan. HA7 41 CE47
Alpine Way, E6 87 EN71
Alric Av, NW10 80 CR66
New Malden KT3 138 CS97
Alroy Rd, N4 65 DN59
Alsace Rd, SE17 201 M10
Alscot Rd, SE1 202 A8
Alscot Way, SE1 201 P8
Alsike Rd, SE2 106 EX76
Erith DA18 106 EY76
Alsom Av, Wor.Pk. KT4 157 CU105
Alsop Cl, St.Alb.
(Lon.Col.) AL2 10 CL27
Alston Cl, Surb. KT6 137 CH101
Alston Rd, N18 46 DV50
SW17 120 DD91
Barnet EN5 27 CY41
Altair Cl, N17 46 DT51
Altair Way, Nthwd. HA6 39 BT49
Altash Way, SE9 125 EM89
Altenburg Av, W13 97 CH76
Altenburg Gdns, SW11 100 DF84
Alterton Cl, Wok. GU21 166 AU117
Alt Gro, SW19
off St. George's Rd 119 CZ94
Altham Gdns, Wat. WD19 40 BX49
Altham Rd, Pnr. HA5 40 BY52
Althea St, SW6 100 DB83
Althorne Gdns, E18 68 EF56
Althorne Way, Dag. RM10 70 FA61
Althorp Cl, Barn. EN5 43 CU45
Althorpe Gro, SW11
off Westbridge Rd 100 DD81
Althorpe Ms, SW11
off Battersea High St 100 DD81
Althorpe Rd, Har. HA1 60 CC57
Althorp Rd, SW17 120 DF88
Altmore Av, E6 87 EM66
Alton Av, Stan. HA7 41 CF52
Alton Cl, Bex. DA5 126 EY88
Isleworth TW7 97 CF82
Alton Ct, Stai. TW18 133 BE95
Alton Gdns, Beck. BR3 123 EA94
Twickenham TW2 117 CD87
Alton Rd, N17 66 DR55
SW15 119 CU88
Croydon CR0 141 DN104
Richmond TW9 98 CL84
Alton St, E14 85 EB71
Altyre Cl, Beck. BR3 143 DZ99
Altyre Rd, Croy. CR0 142 DR103
Altyre Way, Beck. BR3 143 DZ99
Aluric Cl, Grays RM16 111 GH77
Alvanley Gdns, NW6 64 DB64
Alva Way, Wat. WD19 40 BX47
Alverstoke Rd, Rom. RM3 52 FL52
Alverstone Av, SW19 120 DA89
Barnet EN4 44 DE45
Alverstone Gdns, SE9 125 EQ88
Alverstone Rd, E12 69 EN63
NW2 81 CW66
New Malden KT3 139 CT98
Wembley HA9 62 CM60
Alverston Gdns, SE25 142 DS99
Alverton St, SE8 103 DZ78
Alveston Av, Har. HA3 61 CH55
Alvey Est, SE17 201 M9
Alvey St, SE17 201 M10
Alvia Gdns, Sutt. SM1 158 DC105
Alvington Cres, E8 66 DT64
Alway Av, Epsom KT19 156 CQ106
Alwen Gro, S.Ock. RM15 91 FV71
Alwold Cres, SE12 124 EH86
Alwyn Av, W4 98 CR78
Alwyn Cl, Borwd.
(Elstree) WD6 26 CM44
Croydon (New Adgtn) CR0 161 EB108
Alwyne Av, Brwd.
(Shenf.) CM15 55 GA44
Alwyne Cl, Wok. GU21 166 AY116
Alwyne La, N1 off Alwyne Vil 83 DP66
Alwyne Pl, N1 84 DQ65
Alwyne Rd, N1 84 DQ66
SW19 119 CZ93
W7 79 CE73
Alwyne Sq, N1 84 DQ65
Alwyne Vil, N1 83 DP66
Alwyn Gdns, NW4 63 CU56
W3 80 CP72
Alwyns Cl, Cher. KT16
off Alwyns La 134 BG100
Alwyns La, Cher. KT16 133 BF100
Alyth Gdns, NW11 64 DA58
Alzette Ho, E2 85 DX69
Amalgamated Dr, Brent. TW8 97 CG79
Amanda Cl, Chig. IG7 49 ER51
Amanda Ct, Slou. SL3 92 AX76
Amanda Ms, Rom. RM7 71 FC57
Amazon St, E1 off Hessel St 84 DV72
Ambassador Cl, Houns. TW3 96 BY82
Ambassador Gdns, E6 87 EM71
Ambassador's Ct, SW1 199 L3
Ambassador Sq, E14 204 B9
Amber Av, E17 47 DY53
Amber Ct, SW17
off Brudenell Rd 120 DG91
Staines TW18
off Laleham Rd 113 BF92
Ambercroft Way, Couls. CR5 175 DP119
Amberden Av, N3 64 DA55
Ambergate St, SE17 200 G10
Amber Gro, NW2
off Prayle Gro 63 CX60
Amber La, Ilf. IG6 49 EP52
Amberley Cl, Orp. BR6
off Warnford Rd 163 ET106
Pinner HA5 60 BZ55
Amberley Ct, Sid. DA14 126 EW92
Amberley Dr, Add.
(Wdhm) KT15 151 BF110
Amberley Gdns, Enf. EN1 46 DS45
Epsom KT19 157 CT105
Amberley Gro, SE26 122 DV91
Croydon CR0 142 DT101
Amberley Rd, E10 67 EB59
N13 45 DM47
SE2 106 EX79
W9 82 DA71
Buckhurst Hill IG9 48 EJ46
Enfield EN1 46 DT45
Amberley Way, Houns. TW4 116 BW85
Morden SM4 139 CZ101
Romford RM7 71 FB56
Uxbridge UB10 76 BL69
Amber Ms, N22
off Brampton Pk Rd 65 DN55
Amberside Cl, Islw. TW7 117 CD86
Amber St, E15
off Great Eastern Rd 85 ED65
Amber Wf, E2 off Nursery La 84 DT67
Amberwood Cl, Wall. SM6
off The Chase 159 DL106
Amberwood Ri, N.Mal. KT3 138 CS100
Amblecote, Cob. KT11 154 BY111
Amblecote Cl, SE12 124 EH90
Amblecote Meadows, SE12 124 EH90
Amblecote Rd, SE12 124 EH90
Ambler Rd, N4 65 DP62
Ambleside, Brom. BR1 123 ED93
Epping CM16 18 EU31
Ambleside Av, SW16 121 DK91
Beckenham BR3 143 DY99
Hornchurch RM12 71 FH64
Walton-on-Thames KT12 136 BW102
Ambleside Cl, E9
off Churchill Wk 66 DW64
E10 67 EB59
Ambleside Cres, Enf. EN3 31 DX41

★ Place of interest ⇌ Railway station ⊖ London Underground station DLR Docklands Light Railway station Tra Tramlink station H Hospital Riv Pedestrian ferry landing stage

Ambleside Dr, Felt. TW14 . . . . 115 BT88
Ambleside Gdns, SW16 . . . . . 121 DK92
　Ilford IG4. . . . . 68 EL56
　South Croydon CR2 . . . . . . 161 DX109
　Sutton SM2. . . . . 158 DC107
　Wembley HA9. . . . . 61 CK60
Ambleside Pt, SE15
　off Ilderton Rd 102 DW80
Ambleside Rd, NW10 . . . . 81 CT66
　Bexleyheath DA7 . . . . 106 FA82
Ambleside Wk, Uxb. UB8
　off High St 76 BK67
Ambleside Way, Egh. TW20 . . 113 BB94
Ambrey Way, Wall. SM6 . . . . 159 DK109
Ambrooke Rd, Belv. DA17 . . . 106 FA76
Ambrosden Av, SW1 . . . . 199 L7
Ambrose Av, NW11. . . . . 63 CY59
Ambrose CI, E6
　off Lovage App 86 EL71
　Dartford (Cray.) DA1 . . . . . 107 FF84
　Orpington BR6 . . . .
　off Stapleton Rd 145 ET104
Ambrose Ms, SW11 . . . . 100 DE82
Ambrose St, SE16 . . . . 202 D8
Ambrose Wk, E3
　off Malmesbury Rd. 85 EA68
Amelia CI, W3. . . . . 80 CP74
Amelia St, SE17 . . . . 200 G10
Amen Cor, EC4. . . . . 196 G9
　SW17. . . . . 120 DF93
Amen Ct, EC4. . . . . 196 G8
Amenity Way, Mord. SM4 . . . 139 CW100
America Sq, EC3. . . . . 197 P10
America St, SE1 . . . . 201 H3
Amerland Rd, SW18 . . . . 119 CZ86
Amersham Av, N18. . . . . 46 DR51
Amersham CI, Rom. RM3 . . . . 52 FM51
Amersham Dr, Rom. RM3 . . . . 52 FL51
Amersham Gro, SE14. . . . . . . 103 DZ81
Amersham PI, Amer. HP7 . . . . 20 AW39
Amersham Rd, SE14 . . . . 103 DZ80
　Amersham (Lt.Chal.) HP6 . . 20 AX39
　Chalfont St. Giles HP8 . . . . 20 AX39
　Croydon CR0. . . . . 142 DQ100
　Gerrards Cross SL9 . . . . 57 BB59
　Gerrards Cross
　(Chal.St.P.) SL9 . . . . 36 AX49
　Rickmansworth WD3 . . . . . 21 BB39
　Romford RM3 . . . . 52 FM51
Amersham Vale, SE14. . . . . . 103 DZ80
Amersham Wk, Rom. RM3
　off Amersham Rd. 52 FM51
Amersham Way, Amer. HP6 . . 20 AX39
Amery Gdns, NW10 . . . . 81 CV67
　Romford RM2 . . . . 72 FK55
Amery Rd, Har. HA1 . . . . 61 CG61
Amesbury, Wal.Abb. EN9 . . . . 16 EG32
Amesbury Av, SW2 . . . . 121 DL89
Amesbury CI, Epp. CM16
　off Amesbury Rd. 17 ET31
　Worcester Park KT4 . . . . . 139 CW102
Amesbury Dr, E4 . . . . 31 EB44
Amesbury Rd, Brom. BR1 . . . 144 EK97
　Dagenham RM9 . . . . 88 EX66
　Epping CM16 . . . . 17 ET31
　Feltham TW13 . . . . 116 BX89
Amesbury Twr, SW8
　off Westbury St. 101 DJ82
Ames Rd, Swans. DA10 . . . . 130 FY86
Amethyst CI, N11 . . . . 45 DK52
Amethyst Rd, E15. . . . . 67 ED63
Amey Dr, Lthd. (Bkhm) KT23 . 170 CC124
Amherst Av, W13 . . . . 79 CJ72
Amherst CI, Orp. BR5. . . . . . . 146 EU98
Amherst Dr, Orp. BR5 . . . . . . 145 ET98
Amherst Hill, Sev. TN13 . . . . 190 FE122
Amherst Rd, W13 . . . . 79 CJ72
　Sevenoaks TN13 . . . . 191 FH122
Amhurst Gdns, Islw. TW7. . . . 97 CF81
Amhurst Par, N16
　off Amhurst Pk 66 DT59
Amhurst Pk, N16 . . . . 66 DR59
Amhurst Pas, E8. . . . . 66 DU63
Amhurst Rd, E8. . . . . 66 DV64
　N16 . . . . 66 DT63
Amhurst Ter, E8 . . . . 66 DU63
Amidas Gdns, Dag. RM8 . . . . 70 EU74
　off Pitfield Cres 88 EU74
Amiel St, E1 . . . . 84 DW70
Amies St, SW11 . . . . 100 DF83
Amina Way, SE16 . . . . 202 B7
Amis Av, Add.
　(New Haw) KT15 . . . . 152 BG111
　Epsom KT19 . . . . 156 CP107
Amis Rd, Wok. GU21 . . . . 166 AS119
Amity Gro, SW20 . . . . 139 CW95
Amity Rd, E15. . . . . 86 EF67
Ammanford Gm, NW9
　off Ruthin Rd 62 CS58
Amner Rd, SW11 . . . . 120 DG86
Amor Rd, W6 . . . . 99 CW76
Amott Rd, SE15 . . . . 102 DU83
Amoy PI, E14 . . . . 85 EA72
Ⓣⓡ Ampere Way 141 DM101
Ampere Way, Croy. CR0 . . . . 141 DL101
Ampleforth Rd, SE2 . . . . 106 EV75
Ampthill Sq, NW1 . . . . 195 L1
Ampton PI, WC1 . . . . 196 B3
Ampton St, WC1 . . . . 196 B3
Amroth CI, SE23 . . . . 122 DV88
Amroth Grn, NW9
　off Fryent Gro 62 CS58
Amstel Way, Wok. GU21 . . . . 166 AT118
Amsterdam Rd, E14 . . . . 204 E7
Amundsen Ct, E14
　off Napier Av 103 EA78
Amwell CI, Enf. EN2 . . . . 30 DR43
　Watford WD25
　off Phillipers 24 BY35
Amwell Ct, Wal.Abb. EN9 . . . . 16 EF33
Amwell Ct Est, N4 . . . . 66 DQ60
Amwell St, EC1. . . . . 196 D2
Amyand Cotts, Twick. TW1
　off Amyand Pk Rd 117 CH86
Amyand La, Twick. TW1
　off Marble Hill Gdns 117 CH87
Amyand Pk Gdns, Twick. TW1
　off Amyand Pk Rd 117 CH87
Amyand Pk Rd, Twick. TW1 . . 117 CG87

Amy CI, Wall. SM6 . . . .
　off Mollison Dr 159 DL108
Amy Rd, Oxt. RH8. . . . . 188 EE129
Amyruth Rd, SE4 . . . . 123 EA85
Amy Warne CI, E6
　off Evelyn Denington Rd . . . 86 EL70
Anatola Rd, N19
　off Dartmouth Pk Hill 65 DH61
Ancaster Cres, N.Mal. KT3 . . 139 CU100
Ancaster Ms, Beck. BR3 . . . . 143 DX97
Ancaster Rd, Beck. BR3 . . . . 143 DX97
Ancaster St, SE18. . . . . 105 ES80
Anchorage CI, SW19 . . . . . . 120 DA92
Anchorage Pt, E14 . . . . 203 P4
Anchorage Pt Ind Est, SE7 . . 104 EJ76
Anchor & Hope La, SE7 . . . . 104 EH76
Anchor Bay Ind Est,
　Erith DA8. . . . . 107 FG79
Anchor Boul, Dart. DA2 . . . . 108 FQ84
Anchor CI, Bark. IG11 . . . . 88 EV69
　Waltham Cross
　(Chsht) EN8. . . . . 15 DX28
Anchor Ms, SW12
　off Hazelbourne Rd 121 DH86
Anchor Retail Pk, E1. . . . . 84 DW70
Anchor St, SE16 . . . . 202 D8
Anchor Ter, E1 off Cephas Av . 84 DW70
Anchor Wf, E3 off Watts Gro . . 85 EB71
Anchor Yd, EC1 . . . . 197 J4
Ancill CI, W6 . . . . 99 CY79
Ancona Rd, NW10 . . . . 81 CU68
　SE18 . . . . 105 ER78
Andace Pk Gdns, Brom. BR1 . 144 EJ95
Andalus Rd, SW9 . . . . 101 DL83
Ander CI, Wem. HA0 . . . . 61 CK63
Anderson CI, N21 . . . . 29 DM43
　W3. 80 CR72
　Epsom KT19 . . . . 156 CP112
　Sutton SM3. . . . . 140 DA102
　Uxbridge (Hare.) UB9 . . . . . 38 BG53
Anderson Dr, Ashf. TW15 . . . 115 BQ91
Anderson Rd, Bark. IG11
　off The Coverdales 87 ER68
Anderson PI, Houns. TW3. . . . 96 CB84
Anderson Rd, E9. . . . . 67 DX65
　Radlett (Shenley) WD7 . . . . 10 CN33
　Weybridge KT13 . . . . 135 BR104
　Woodford Green IG8 . . . . . . 68 EK55
Andersons Sq, N1
　off Gaskin St. 83 DP67
Anderson St, SW3 . . . . 198 D10
Anderson Way, Belv. DA17. . . 107 FB75
Anderton CI, SE5 . . . . 102 DR83
Andmark Ct, Sthl. UB1
　off Herbert Rd 78 BZ74
Andover Av, E16
　off King George Av. 86 EK72
Andover CI, Epsom KT19 . . . 156 CR111
　Feltham TW14 . . . . 115 BT88
　Greenford UB6
　off Ruislip Rd 78 CB70
　Uxbridge UB8 . . . . 76 BH68
Andover PI, NW6 . . . . 82 DB68
Andover Rd, N7 . . . . 65 DM61
　Orpington BR6 . . . . 145 ER102
　Twickenham TW2 . . . . 117 CD88
Andrea Av, Grays RM16 . . . . 110 GA75
Andre St, E8 . . . . 66 DU64
Andrew Borde St, WC2 . . . . 195 N8
Andrew CI, Dart. DA1 . . . . . . 127 FD85
　Ilford IG6. . . . . 49 ER51
　Radlett (Shenley) WD7 . . . . 10 CM33
Andrewes Gdns, E6 . . . . 86 EL72
Andrewes Ho, EC2 . . . . 197 J7
Andrew PI, SW8
　off Cowthorpe Rd 101 DK81
Andrew Reed Ho, SW18
　off Linstead Way 119 CY87
Andrews CI, E6
　off Linton Gdns 86 EL72
　Buckhurst Hill IG9 . . . . 48 EJ47
　Epsom KT17 . . . . 157 CT114
　Harrow HA1
　off Bessborough Rd 61 CD59
　Orpington BR5 . . . . 146 EX96
　Worcester Park KT4 . . . . . 139 CX103
Andrews Crosse, WC2 . . . . . 196 D9
Andrews La, Wal.Cr.
　(Chsht) EN7. . . . . 14 DU28
Andrews Pl, SE9 . . . . 125 EP86
　Dartford DA2
　off Old Bexley La 127 FE89
Andrew's Rd, E8 . . . . 84 DV67
Andrew St, E14. . . . . 85 EC72
Andrews Wk, SE17
　off Dale Rd 101 DP79
Andwell CI, SE2 . . . . 106 EV75
ⓇⓈ Anerley, SE20 . . . . 142 DV94
ⓇⓈ Anerley 122 DV94
Anerley Gro, SE19. . . . . 122 DT94
Anerley Hill, SE19 . . . . 122 DT93
Anerley Pk, SE20 . . . . 122 DU94
Anerley Pk Rd, SE20 . . . . 122 DU94
Anerley Rd, SE19 . . . . 122 DU94
　SE20 . . . . 122 DU94
Anerley Sta Rd, SE20 . . . . . . 122 DV95
Anerley St, SW11 . . . . 100 DF82
Anerley Vale, SE19 . . . . 122 DT94
Anfield CI, SW12
　off Belthorn Cres. 121 DJ87
Angas Ct, Wey. KT13 . . . . . . 153 BQ106
⊖ Angel. 83 DN68
Angel All, E1
　off Whitechapel Rd 84 DU72
Angel CI, N18. . . . . 46 DT49
Angel Cor Par, N18
　off Fore St. 46 DU50
Angel Ct, EC2. . . . . 197 L8
　SW1 . . . . 199 L3
　SW17 . . . . 120 DF91
Angel Edmonton, N18
　off Angel Rd. 46 DU50
Angelfield, Houns. TW3. . . . . . 96 CB84
Angel Gate, EC1 . . . . 196 G2
Angel Hill, Sutt. SM1
　off Sutton Common Rd . . . 140 DB104
Angel Hill Dr, Sutt. SM1 . . . . 140 DB104
Angelica CI, West Dr. UB7
　off Lovibonds Av. 76 BL72

Angelica Dr, E6. . . . . 87 EN71
Angelica Gdns, Croy. CR0 . . 143 DX102
Angelis Apartments, N1
　off Graham St. 83 DP68
Angell Pk Gdns, SW9 . . . . . . 101 DN83
Angell Rd, SW9. . . . . 101 DN83
Angell Town Est, SW9. . . . . . 101 DN82
Angel Ms, E1 off Cable St . . . 84 DU73
　N1 . . . . 196 E1
　SW15
　off Roehampton High St. . . 119 CU87
Angel Pas, EC4. . . . . 201 K1
Angel Rd, N18. . . . . 46 DU50
　Harrow HA1 . . . . 61 CE58
　Thames Ditton KT7 . . . . . . 137 CG101
⇌ Angel Road 46 DW50
Angel Rd, N18. . . . . 46 DV50
　Harrow HA1 . . . . 61 CE58
　Thames Ditton KT7 . . . . . . 137 CG101
Angel Rd Wks, N18. . . . . 46 DW50
Angel Sq, EC1. . . . . 196 E1
Angel St, EC1 . . . . 197 H8
Angel Wk, W6 . . . . 99 CW77
Angel Way, Rom. RM1 . . . . . . 71 FE57
Angerstein La, SE3 . . . . 104 EF80
Angle CI, Uxb. UB10. . . . . 76 BN67
Angle Grn, Dag. RM8 . . . . 70 EW60
Angle Rd, Grays RM20. . . . . . 109 FX79
Anglers CI, Rich. TW10
　off Locksmeade Rd 117 CJ91
Angler's La, NW5 . . . . 83 DH65
Anglers Reach, Surb. KT6 . . . 137 CK99
Anglesea Av, SE18 . . . . 105 EP77
Anglesea Cen, Grav. DA11
　off New Rd 131 GH86
Anglesea Ms, SE18
　off Anglesea Av. 105 EP77
Anglesea Rd, SE18 . . . . 105 EP77
　off Clive Rd. 131 GH86
Anglesea Ter, W6
　off Wellesley Av 99 CV76
Anglesey CI, Ashf. TW15 . . . . 114 BN90
Anglesey Ct Rd, Cars. SM5 . . 158 DG107
Anglesey Dr, Rain. RM13 . . . . 89 FG70
Anglesey Gdns, Cars. SM5 . . 158 DG107
Anglesey Rd, Enf. EN3 . . . . . . 30 DV42
　Watford WD19. . . . . 40 BW50
Anglesmede Cres, Pnr. HA5. . 60 CA55
Anglesmede Way, Pnr. HA5. . 60 BZ55
Angles Rd, SW16 . . . . 121 DL91
Anglia CI, N17 off Park La 46 DV52
Anglia Ct, Dag. RM8
　off Spring CI. 70 EX60
Anglia Ho, E14 . . . . 85 DY72
Anglian CI, Wat. WD24 . . . . . . 24 BW40
Anglian Rd, E11 . . . . 67 ED62
Anglia Wk, E6 . . . . 87 EM67
Anglo Rd, E3. . . . . 85 DZ68
Anglo Way, Red. RH1 . . . . . . 184 DG112
Angrave Ct, E8. . . . . 84 DT67
Angrave Pas, E8
　off Haggerston Rd 84 DT67
Angus CI, Chess. KT9 . . . . . . 156 CN106
Angus Dr, Ruis. HA4. . . . . 60 BW63
Angus Gdns, NW9 . . . . 42 CR53
Angus Home, Sev. (Cudham) TN14
　off Cudham La S. 179 ER115
Angus Rd, E13 . . . . 86 EJ69
Angus St, SE14 . . . . 103 DY80
Anhalt Rd, SW11 . . . . 100 DE80
Ankerdine Cres, SE18 . . . . . . 105 EN80
Ankerwycke Priory, Stai.
　(Wrays.) TW19. . . . . 113 AZ89
Anlaby Rd, Tedd. TW11 . . . . . 117 CE92
Anley Rd, W14 . . . . 99 CX75
Anmersh Gro, Stan. HA7 . . . . 41 CK53
Annabel CI, E14 . . . . 85 EB72
Annabel Rd, S.Ock. RM15. . . . 91 FV71
Annalee Gdns, S.Ock. RM15. . 91 FV71
Annalee Rd, S.Ock. RM15. . . . 91 FV71
Annandale Gro, Uxb. UB10
　off Thorpland Av 59 BQ62
Annandale Rd, SE10 . . . . 104 EF79
　W4. 98 CS77
　Croydon CR0. . . . . 142 DU103
　Sidcup DA15 . . . . 125 ES87
Annan Dr, Cars. SM5 . . . . . . 158 DG109
Anna Neagle CI, E7
　off Dames Rd 68 EG63
Annan Way, Rom. RM1. . . . . . 51 FD53
Anne Boleyn's Wk, Kings.T.
　KT2 . . . . 118 CL92
　Sutton SM3. . . . . 157 CX108
Anne Case Ms, N.Mal. KT3
　off Sycamore Gro. 138 CR97
Anne Compton Ms, SE12 . . . 124 EF87
　off Lancaster Rd 109 FX77
Anne of Cleves Rd, Dart. DA1. 128 FK85
Anners CI, Egh. TW20. . . . . . 133 BC97
★ Apollo Hammersmith, W6 . 99 CW78
Annesley Av, NW9 . . . . 62 CR55
Annesley CI, NW10. . . . . 62 CS62
Annesley Dr, Croy. CR0 . . . . 143 DZ104
Annesley Rd, SE3 . . . . 104 EH81
Annesley Wk, N19. . . . . 65 DJ61
Anne St, E13. . . . . 86 EG70
Anne's Wk, Cat. CR3 . . . . . . 176 DS120
Annett CI, Shep. TW17 . . . . . 135 BS98
Annette CI, Har. HA3
　off Spencer Rd. 41 CE54
Annette Cres, N1
　off Essex Rd 84 DQ66
Annette Rd, N7. . . . . 65 DM63
Anne Way, Ilf. IG6. . . . . 49 EQ51
　West Molesey KT8 . . . . . . 136 CB98
Annie Besant CI, E3 . . . . 85 DZ67
Annie Taylor Ho, E12
　off Walton Rd 69 EN63
Annifer Way, S.Ock. RM15 . . . 91 FV71
Anning St, EC2 . . . . 197 N4
Annington Rd, N2. . . . . 64 DF55
Annis Rd, E9. . . . . 85 DY65
Ann La, SW10 . . . . 100 DD80
Ann Moss Way, SE16 . . . . . . 202 F6

Angelica Gdns, Croy. CR0 . . 143 DX102
Angelis Apartments, N1 . . . . 197 P7
Ann St, SE18 . . . . 105 ER77
Annsworthy Av, Th.Hth. CR7 . 142 DR97
Annsworthy Cres, SE25
　off Grange Rd 142 DR96
Ansdell Rd, SE15 . . . . 102 DW82
Ansdell St, W8 . . . . 100 DB76
Ansdell Ter, W8
　off Ansdell St 100 DB76
Ansell Gro, Cars. SM5 . . . . . 140 DG102
Ansell Rd, SW17 . . . . 120 DE90
Anselm CI, Croy. CR0
　off Park Hill Ri. 142 DT104
Anselm Rd, SW6 . . . . 100 DA79
　Pinner HA5 . . . . 40 BZ52
Ansford Rd, Brom. BR1 . . . . 123 EC92
Ansleigh PI, W11 . . . . 81 CX73
Ansley CI, S.Croy. CR2 . . . . . 160 DV114
Anslow Gdns, Iver SL0 . . . . . . 75 BE72
Anson CI, Hem.H. (Bov.) HP3 . 5 AZ27
　Kenley CR8 . . . . 176 DR120
　Romford RM7 . . . . 51 FB54
Anson PI, SE28 . . . . 105 ER75
Anson Rd, N7 . . . . 65 DJ63
　NW2 . . . . 63 CX64
Anson Ter, Nthlt. UB5. . . . . . . 78 CB65
Anson Wk, Nthwd. HA6 . . . . . 39 BQ49
Anstead Dr, Rain. RM13 . . . . . 89 FG67
Anstey Rd, SE15 . . . . 102 DU83
Anstey Wk, N15 . . . . 65 DP56
Anstice CI, W4 . . . . 98 CS80
Anstridge Path, SE9 . . . . 125 ER86
Anstridge Rd, SE9 . . . . 125 ER86
Antelope Av, Grays RM16
　off Hogg La 110 GA76
Antelope Rd, SE18 . . . . 105 EM76
Anthony CI, NW7 . . . . 42 CS49
　Sevenoaks
　(Dunt.Grn) TN13 . . . . 190 FE121
　Watford WD19. . . . . 40 BW46
★ Anthony d'Offay Gall, W1 . 195 J9
Anthony La, Swan. BR8 . . . . 147 FG95
Anthony Rd, SE25 . . . . 142 DU100
　Borehamwood WD6 . . . . . . 26 CM40
　Greenford UB6 . . . . 79 CE68
　Welling DA16 . . . . 106 EU81
Anthonys, Wok. GU21 . . . . . 151 BB112
Anthony St, E1
　off Commercial Rd 84 DV72
Anthony Way, N18 . . . . 47 DX51
　off Salters Hill. 122 DR92
Antigua CI, SE19 . . . . 122 DR92
Antigua Wk, SE19 . . . . 122 DR92
Antill Rd, E3 . . . . 85 DY69
　N15 . . . . 66 DT56
Antill Ter, E1 . . . . 85 DX72
Antlers Hill, E4 . . . . 31 EB43
Antoinette Ct, Abb.L. WD5
　off Dairy Way 7 BT29
Anton Cres, Sutt. SM1 . . . . . 140 DA104
Antoneys CI, Pnr. HA5 . . . . . . 40 BX54
Anton PI, Wem. HA9 . . . . 62 CP62
Anton Rd, S.Ock. RM15 . . . . . 91 FV70
Anton St, E8 . . . . 66 DU64
Antrim Gro, NW3 . . . . 82 DF65
Antrim Mans, NW3 . . . . 82 DE65
Antrim Rd, NW3 . . . . 82 DF65
Antrobus CI, Sutt. SM1 . . . . . 157 CZ106
Antrobus Rd, W4 . . . . 98 CQ77
Anvil CI, SW16 . . . . 121 DJ94
　Hemel Hempstead (Bov.) HP3
　off Yew Tree Dr 5 BB28
Anvil Ct, Slou. (Langley) SL3
　off Blacksmith Row. 93 BA77
Anvil La, Cob. KT11 . . . . 153 BU114
Anvil PI, St.Alb. AL2 . . . . 8 CA26
Anvil Rd, Sun. TW16 . . . . 135 BU97
Anvil Ter, Dart. DA2
　off Old Bexley La 127 FE89
Anworth CI, Wdf.Grn. IG8 . . . . 48 EH51
Anyards Rd, Cob. KT11 . . . . . 153 BV113
Apeldoorn Dr, Wall. SM6 . . . 159 DL109
Aperdele Rd, Lthd. KT22. . . . 171 CG118
APERFIELD, West. TN16 . . . 179 EM117
Aperfield Rd, Erith DA8 . . . . . 107 FF79
　Westerham (Bigg.H.)TN16 . 178 EL117
Apers Av, Wok. GU22 . . . . . . 167 AZ121
Apex CI, Beck. BR3 . . . . 143 EB95
　Weybridge KT13 . . . . 135 BR104
Apex Cor, NW7 . . . . 42 CR49
Apex Ind Est, NW10
　off Hythe Rd 81 CU69
Apex Retail Pk, Felt. TW13 . . 116 BZ90
Apex Twr, N.Mal. KT3 . . . . . . 138 CS97
Aplin Way, Islw. TW7 . . . . 97 CE81
Apollo Av, Brom. BR1
　off Rodway Rd 144 EH95
　Northwood HA6 . . . . 39 BU50
Apollo CI, Horn. RM12 . . . . . . 71 FH61
Apollo PI, E11 . . . . 68 EE62
　SW10 . . . . 100 DD80
　Woking (St.John's) GU21
　off Church Rd 166 AU119
★ Apollo Thea, W1 . . . . 195 M10
★ Apollo Victoria Thea, SW1 . 199 K7
Apollo Way, SE28
　off Broadwater Rd 105 ER76
Apostle Way, Th.Hth. CR7 . . . 141 DP96
Apothecary St, EC4 . . . . 196 F9
Appach Rd, SW2 . . . . 121 DN86
Apple Blossom Ct, SW8
　off Pascal St. 101 DK80
Appleby CI, E4 . . . . 47 EC51
　N15 . . . . 66 DR57
　Twickenham TW2 . . . . 117 CD89
Appleby Dr, Rom. RM3 . . . . . . 52 FJ50
　Watford (Wat.) TW14 . . . . . 115 BT88
Appleby Grn, Rom. RM3
　off Appleby Dr 52 FJ50
Appleby Rd, E8 . . . . 84 DU66
　E16 . . . . 86 EF72
Appleby St, E2 . . . . 84 DT68
　Waltham Cross
　(Chsht) EN7. . . . . 14 DT26
Apple Cotts, Hem.H. (Bov.) HP3 . 5 BA27

Applecroft, St.Alb.
　(Park St) AL2 . . . . 8 CB28
Appledore Av, Bexh. DA7 . . . 107 FC81
　Ruislip HA4 . . . . 59 BV62
Appledore CI, SW17 . . . . 120 DF89
　Bromley BR2 . . . . 144 EF99
　Edgware HA8 . . . . 42 CN53
　Romford RM3 . . . . 52 FJ53
Appledore Cres, Sid. DA14. . 125 ES90
Appledore Way, NW7
　off Tavistock Av 43 CX52
Appledown Ri, Couls. CR5 . . 175 DJ115
Applefield, Amer. HP7 . . . . . . 20 AW39
Appleford Rd, W10 . . . . 81 CY70
Apple Garth, Brent. TW8 . . . . 97 CK77
Applegarth, Croy.
　(New Adgtn) CR0 . . . . 161 EB108
　Esher (Clay.) KT10. . . . . . . 155 CF106
Applegarth Dr, Dart. DA1 . . . 128 FL89
　Ilford IG2. . . . . 69 ET56
Applegarth Ho, Erith DA8. . . 107 FF82
Applegarth Rd, SE28 . . . . 88 EV74
　W14. . . . . 99 CX76
Applegate, Brwd. CM14. . . . . 54 FT43
Apple Gro, Chess. KT9 . . . . . 156 CL105
　Enfield EN1. . . . . 30 DS41
Apple Mkt, Kings.T. KT1 . . . . 137 CK96
Apple Orchard, Swan. BR8. . 147 FD98
Apple Rd, E11 . . . . 68 EE62
Appleshaw CI, Grav. DA11 . . 131 GG92
Appleton CI, Amer. HP7 . . . . . 20 AV40
　Bexleyheath DA7
　off Barnehurst Rd 107 FC82
Appleton Dr, Dart. DA2 . . . . . 127 FH90
Appleton Gdns, N.Mal. KT3 . 139 CU100
Appleton Rd, SE9 . . . . 104 EL83
　Loughton IG10 . . . . 33 EP41
Appleton Sq, Mitch. CR4
　off Silbury Av 140 DE95
Appleton Way, Horn. RM12 . . 72 FK60
Appletree Av, Uxb. UB8 . . . . . 76 BM71
　West Drayton UB7 . . . . 76 BM71
Appletree CI, SE20
　off Jasmine Gro 142 DV95
　Leatherhead KT22. . . . . . . 170 CC124
Appletree Gdns, Barn. EN4 . . 28 DE42
Appletree La, Slou. SL3 . . . . . 92 AW76
Apple Tree Roundabout,
　West Dr. UB7. . . . . 76 BM73
Appletree Wk, Wat. WD25. . . . 7 BV34
Apple Tree Yd, SW1 . . . . 199 L2
Applewood CI, N20 . . . . 44 DE46
　NW2 . . . . 63 CV62
　Uxbridge UB10
　off Burford CI 58 BL63
Applewood Dr, E13 . . . . 86 EH70
Appold St, EC2. . . . . 197 M6
　Erith DA8. . . . . 107 FF79
Apprentice Way, E5
　off Clarence Rd. 66 DV63
Approach, The, NW4 . . . . 63 CX57
　W3. 80 CR72
　Enfield EN1. . . . . 30 DV40
　Orpington BR6 . . . . 145 ET103
　Potters Bar EN6. . . . . 11 CZ32
　Upminster RM14 . . . . 72 FP62
Approach Rd, N16
　off Cowper Rd. 66 DS63
Approach Rd, E2. . . . . 84 DW68
　SW20. . . . . 139 CW96
　Ashford TW15 . . . . 115 BQ93
　Barnet EN4 . . . . 28 DD42
　Purley CR8 . . . . 159 DP112
　West Molesey KT8 . . . . . . 136 CA99
Aprey Gdns, NW4 . . . . 63 CW56
April CI, W7 . . . . 79 CE73
　Ashtead KT21 . . . . 172 CM117
　Feltham TW13 . . . . 115 BU90
　Orpington BR6
　off Briarswood Way 163 ET106
April Glen, SE23 . . . . 123 DX90
April St, E8 . . . . 66 DT63
Aprilwood CI, Add.
　(Wdhm) KT15 . . . . 151 BF111
Apsledene, Grav. DA12
　off Miskin Way 131 GK93
APSLEY, Hem.H. HP3 . . . . 6 BK25
⊖ Apsley 6 BL25
Apsley CI, Har. HA2 . . . . 60 CC57
★ Apsley Ho,
　Wellington Mus, W1 . . . . . 198 F4
Apsley Rd, SE25 . . . . 142 DV98
　New Malden KT3 . . . . 138 CQ97
Apsley Way, NW2 . . . . 63 CU61
　W1 . . . . 198 G4
★ Aquarius Experience,
　Brent. TW8 . . . . 97 CH81
Aquila CI, Lthd. KT22 . . . . . . 172 CL121
Aquila St, NW8 . . . . 82 DD68
Aquinas St, SE1 . . . . 200 E3
Arabella Dr, SW15 . . . . 98 CS84
Arabia CI, E4. . . . . 47 ED45
Arabin Rd, SE4 . . . . 103 DY84
Araglen Av, S.Ock. RM15 . . . . 91 FV71
Aragon CI, Epsom KT17. . . . . 157 CV109
　Thames Ditton KT7. . . . . . . 137 CF99
Aragon Ct, Brom. BR2 . . . . . 145 EM102
　Croydon
　(New Adgtn) CR0 . . . . 162 EE110
　Enfield EN2. . . . . 29 DM38
　Loughton IG10 . . . . 32 LA144
　Romford RM5 . . . . 51 FB51
　Sunbury-on-Thames TW16 . 115 BT94
Aragon Dr, Ilf. IG6. . . . . 49 EQ52
　Ruislip HA4 . . . . 60 BX60
Aragon Rd, Kings.T. KT2 . . . . 118 CL92
　Morden SM4. . . . . 139 CX100
Aragon Twr, SE8 . . . . 203 M9
Aragon Wk, W.Byf.
　(Byfleet) KT14 . . . . 152 BM113
Aran Ct, Wey. KT13
　off Mallards Reach 135 BR103

★ Place of interest　⇌ Railway station　⊖ London Underground station　Ⓓⓛⓡ Docklands Light Railway station　Ⓣⓡⓐ Tramlink station　Ⓗ Hospital　Ⓡⓘⓥ Pedestrian ferry landing stage

Arandora Cres, Rom. RM6 70 EV59
Aran Dr, Stan. HA7 41 CJ49
Aran Hts, Ch.St.G. HP8 36 AV49
Arbery Rd, E3 85 DY69
Arbor Cl, Beck. BR3 143 EB96
Arbor Ct, N16
off Lordship Rd 66 DR61
Arborfield Cl, SW2 121 DM88
Slough SL1 92 AS76
Arbor Rd, E4 47 ED48
Arbour Cl, Brwd. CM14 54 FW50
Leatherhead (Fetch.) KT22 171 CF123
Arbour Rd, Enf. EN3 31 DX42
Arbour Sq, E1 85 DX72
Arbour Vw, Amer. HP7 20 AV39
Arbour Way, Horn. RM12 71 FH64
Arbroath Grn, Wat. WD19 39 BU48
Arbroath Rd, SE9 104 EL83
Arbrook Chase, Esher KT10 154 CC107
Arbrook Cl, Orp. BR5 146 EU97
Arbrook La, Esher KT10 154 CC107
Arbury Ter, SE26
off Oaksford Av 122 DV90
Arbuthnot La, Bex. DA5 126 EY86
Arbuthnot Rd, SE14 103 DX82
Arbutus St, E8 84 DS67
Arcade, The, EC2 197 M7
Croydon CR0 off High St 142 DQ104
Romford RM3
off Farnham Rd 52 FK50
Arcade Pl, Rom. RM1 71 FE57
Arcadia Av, N3 44 DA53
Arcadia Caravans, Stai. TW18 134 BH95
Arcadia Cl, Cars. SM5 158 DG105
Arcadian Av, Bex. DA5 126 EY86
Arcadian Cl, Bex. DA5 126 EY86
Arcadian Gdns, N22 45 DM52
Arcadian Rd, Bex. DA5 126 EY86
Arcadia Shop Cen, W5 79 CK73
Arcadia St, E14 85 EA72
Arcany Rd, S.Ock. RM15 91 FV70
Archangel St, SE16 203 J5
Archates Av, Grays RM16 110 GA76
Archbishops Pl, SW2 121 DM86
Archdale Pl, N.Mal. KT3 138 CP97
Archdale Rd, SE22 122 DT85
Archel Rd, W14 99 CZ79
Archer Cl, Kings L. WD4 6 BM29
Kingston upon Thames KT2 118 CL94
Archer Ho, SW11
off Vicarage Cres 100 DD81
Archer Ms, Hmptn. (Hmptn H.) TW12
off Windmill Rd 116 CC93
Archer Rd, SE25 142 DV98
Orpington BR5 146 EU99
Archers Ct, S.Ock. RM15 91 FV71
Archers Dr, Enf. EN3 30 DW40
Archer Sq, SE14
off Knoyle St 103 DY79
Archer St, W1 195 M10
Archer Ter, West Dr. UB7
off Yew Av 76 BL73
Archer Way, Swan. BR8 147 FF96
Archery Cl, W2 194 C9
Harrow HA3 61 CF55
H Archery Ho, Dart. DA2 128 FP86
Archery Rd, SE9 125 EM85
Arches, The, SW6
off Munster Rd 99 CZ82
WC2 200 A2
Harrow HA2 60 CB61
Archibald Ms, W1 198 G1
Archibald Rd, N7 65 DK63
Romford RM3 52 FN53
Archibald St, E3 85 EA69
Archie Cl, West Dr. UB7 94 BN75
Archie St, SE1 201 N5
Arch Rd, Walt. KT12 136 BX104
Arch St, SE1 201 H7
⊖ Archway 65 DJ61
Archway, Rom. RM3 51 FH51
Archway Cl, N19
off St. Johns Way 65 DJ61
SW19 120 DB91
W10 81 CX71
Wallington SM6 141 DK104
Archway Mall, N19
off Magdala Av 65 DJ61
Archway Ms, SW15
off Putney Br Rd 99 CY84
Archway Rd, N6 64 DF58
N19 65 DJ60
Archway St, SW13 98 CS83
Arcola St, E8 66 DT64
Arctic St, NW5
off Gillies St 64 DG64
Arcus Rd, Brom. BR1 124 EE93
Ardbeg Rd, SE24 122 DR86
Arden Cl, SE28
off Redbourne Dr 88 EX72
Bushey (Bushey Hth) WD23 41 CF45
Harrow HA1 61 CD62
Hemel Hempstead
(Bov.) HP3 5 BA28
Arden Ct Gdns, N2 64 DD58
Arden Cres, E14 204 A8
Dagenham RM9 88 EW66
Arden Est, N1 197 M1
Arden Gro, Orp. BR6 163 EP105
Arden Ho, SW9
off Grantham Rd 101 DL82
Arden Ms, E17 67 EB57
Arden Mhor, Pnr. HA5 59 BV56
Arden Rd, N3 63 CY55
W13 79 CJ73
Ardent Cl, SE25 142 DS97
Ardesley Wd, Wey. KT13 153 BS105
Ardfern Av, SW16 141 DN97
Ardfillan Rd, SE6 123 ED88
Ardgowan Rd, SE6 124 EE87
Ardilaun Rd, N5 66 DQ63
Ardingly Cl, Croy. CR0 143 DX104
Ardleigh Cl, Horn. RM11 72 FK55
Ardleigh Ct, Brwd.
(Shenf.) CM15 55 FZ45
Ardleigh Gdns, Brwd. (Hutt.)
CM13 off Fairview Av 55 GE44
Sutton SM3 140 DA101
ARDLEIGH GREEN,
Horn. RM11 72 FJ56
Ardleigh Grn Rd, Horn. RM11 72 FK57
Ardleigh Ho, Bark. IG11
off St. Ann's 87 EQ67
Ardleigh Ms, Ilf. IG1
off Bengal Rd 69 EP62
Ardleigh Rd, E17 47 DZ53
N1 84 DR65
Ardleigh Ter, E17 47 DZ53
Ardley Cl, NW10 62 CS62
SE6 123 DY90
Ruislip HA4 59 BQ59
Ardlui Rd, SE27 122 DQ89
Ardmay Gdns, Surb. KT6 138 CL99
Ardmere Rd, SE13 123 ED86
Ardmore La, Buck.H. IG9 48 EH45
Ardmore Pl, Buck.H. IG9 48 EH45
Ardmore Rd, S.Ock. RM15 91 FV70
Ardoch Rd, SE6 123 ED89
Ardra Rd, N9 47 DX48
Ardrossan Gdns, Wor.Pk. KT4 139 CU104
Ardross Av, Nthwd. HA6 39 BS50
Ardshiel Cl, SW15
off Bemish Rd 99 CX83
Ardwell Av, Ilf. IG6 69 EQ57
Ardwell Rd, SW2 121 DL89
Ardwick Rd, NW2 64 DA63
Tra Arena 142 DW99
Arena, The, Enf. EN3 31 DZ38
Arewater Grn, Loug. IG10 33 EM39
Argali Ho, Erith DA18
off Kale Rd 106 EY76
Argall Av, E10 67 DX59
Argall Way, E10 67 DX60
Argenta Way, NW10 80 CP66
Argent Cl, Egh. TW20
off Holbrook Meadow 113 BC93
Argent St, Grays RM17 110 FY79
Argent Way, Wal.Cr.
(Chsht) EN7 14 DR26
Argles Cl, Green. DA9
off Cowley Av 129 FU85
Argon Ms, SW6 100 DA80
Argon Rd, N18 46 DW50
Argosy Gdns, Stai. TW18 113 BF93
Argosy La, Stai.
(Stanw.) TW19 114 BK87
Argus Cl, Rom. RM7 51 FB53
Argus Way, Nthlt. UB5 78 BY69
Argyle Av, Houns. TW3 116 CA86
Argyle Cl, W13 79 CG70
Argyle Gdns, Upmin. RM14 73 FR61
Argyle Pas, N17 46 DT53
Argyle Pl, W6 99 CV77
Argyle Rd, E1 85 DX70
E15 68 EE63
E16 86 EJ72
N12 44 DA50
N17 46 DU53
N18 46 DU49
W13 79 CG71
Barnet EN5 27 CW42
Greenford UB6 79 CF69
Harrow HA2 60 CB58
Hounslow TW3 116 CB85
Ilford IG1 69 EN61
Sevenoaks TN13 191 FH125
Teddington TW11 117 CE92
Argyle Sq, WC1 196 A2
Argyle St, WC1 195 P2
Argyle Wk, WC1 196 A3
Argyle Way, SE16 102 DU78
Argyll Av, Sthl. UB1 78 CB74
Argyll Cl, SW9 off Dalyell Rd 101 DM83
Argyll Gdns, Edg. HA8 42 CP54
Argyll Rd, SE18 105 EQ76
W8 100 DA75
Grays RM17 110 GA78
Argyll St, W1 195 K9
Arica Rd, SE4 103 DY84
Ariel Cl, Grav. DA12 131 GM91
Ariel Rd, NW6 82 DA65
Ariel Way, W12 81 CW74
Hounslow TW4 95 BV83
Arisdale Av, S.Ock. RM15 91 FV71
Aristotle Rd, SW4 101 DK83
Ark Av, Grays RM16 110 GA76
Arkell Gro, SE19 121 DP94
Arkindale Rd, SE6 123 EC90
ARKLEY, Barn. EN5 27 CU43
Arkley Cres, E17 67 DZ57
Arkley Dr, Barn. EN5 27 CU42
Arkley La, Barn. EN5 27 CU41
Arkley Pk, Barn. EN5 26 CR44
Arkley Rd, E17 67 DZ57
Arkley Vw, Barn. EN5 27 CV42
Arklow Ct, Rick. (Chorl.) WD3
off Station App 21 BC42
Arklow Ms, Surb. KT6
off Vale Rd S 138 CL103
Arklow Rd, SE14 103 DZ79
Arkwright Rd, NW3 64 DC64
Slough (Colnbr.) SL3 93 BE82
South Croydon CR2 160 DT110
Tilbury RM18 111 GG82
Arlesey Cl, SW15
off Lytton Gro 119 CY86
Arlesford Rd, SW9 101 DL83
Arlingford Rd, SW2 121 DN85
Arlingham Ms, Wal.Abb. EN9
off Sun St 15 EC33
Arlington, N12 44 DA48
Arlington Av, N1 84 DQ68
Arlington Cl, SE13 123 ED86
Sidcup DA15 125 ES87
Sutton SM1 140 DA103
Twickenham TW1 117 CJ86
Arlington Ct, Hayes UB3
off Shepiston La 95 BR78
Reigate RH2
off Oakfield Dr 184 DB132
Arlington Cres, Wal.Cr. EN8 15 DY34
Arlington Dr, Cars. SM5 140 DF103
Ruislip HA4 59 BR58
Arlington Gdns, W4 98 CQ78
Ilford IG1 69 EN60
Arlington Gdns, Romford RM3 52 FL53
Arlington Grn, NW7 43 CX52
Arlington Lo, SW2 101 DM84
Weybridge KT13 153 BP105
Arlington Ms, Twick. TW1
off Arlington Rd 117 CJ86
Arlington Pl, SE10
off Greenwich S St 103 EC80
Arlington Rd, N14 45 DH47
NW1 83 DH67
W13 79 CH72
Ashford TW15 114 BM92
Richmond TW10 117 CK89
Surbiton KT6 137 CK100
Teddington TW11 117 CF91
Twickenham TW1 117 CJ86
Woodford Green IG8 48 EG53
Arlington Sq, N1 84 DQ67
Arlington St, SW1 199 K2
Arlington Way, EC1 196 E2
Arliss Way, Nthlt. UB5 78 BW67
Arlow Rd, N21 45 DN46
Armada Ct, SE8
off Watergate St 103 EA79
Grays RM16 off Hogg La 110 GA76
Armadale Cl, N17 66 DV56
Armadale Rd, SW6 100 DA80
Feltham TW14 115 BU85
Woking GU21 166 AU117
Armada Way, E6 87 EP71
Armagh Rd, E3 85 DZ67
Armand Cl, Wat. WD17 23 BT38
Armfield Cl, W.Mol. KT8 136 BZ99
Armfield Cres, Mitch. CR4 140 DF96
Armfield Rd, Enf. EN2 30 DR39
Arminger Rd, W12 81 CV74
Armistice Gdns, SE25
off Penge Rd 142 DU97
Armitage Cl, Rick.
(Loud.) WD3 22 BK42
Armitage Rd, NW11 63 CZ60
SE10 205 K10
Armor Rd, Purf. RM19 109 FR77
Armour Cl, N7 off Roman Way 83 DM65
Armoury Dr, Grav. DA12 131 GJ87
Armoury Rd, SE8 103 EB82
Armoury Way, SW18 120 DA85
Armstead Wk, Dag. RM10 88 FA66
Armstrong Av, Wdf.Grn. IG8 48 EE51
Armstrong Cl, E6
off Porter Rd 87 EM72
Borehamwood WD6 26 CQ41
Dagenham RM8
off Palmer Rd 70 EX60
Pinner HA5 59 BU58
St. Albans (Lon.Col.) AL2
off Willowside 10 CL27
Sevenoaks (Halst.) TN14 181 FB115
Walton-on-Thames KT12
off Sunbury La 135 BU100
Armstrong Cres, Barn. EN4 28 DD41
Armstrong Gdns, Rad.
(Shenley) WD7 10 CL32
Armstrong Rd, SE18 105 EQ76
SW7 100 DD76
W3 81 CT74
Egham (Eng.Grn) TW20 112 AW93
Feltham TW13 116 BY92
Armstrong Way, Sthl. UB2 96 CB75
Armytage Rd, Houns. TW5 96 BX80
Arnal Cres, SW18 119 CY87
Arncliffe Cl, N11
off Kettlewell Cl 44 DG51
Arncroft Ct, Bark. IG11
off Renwick Rd 88 EV69
Arndale Wk, SW18
off Garratt La 120 DB85
Arndale Way, Egh. TW20
off Church Rd 113 BA92
Arne Gro, Orp. BR6 145 ET104
Arne St, WC2 196 A9
Arnett Cl, Rick. WD3 22 BG44
Arnett Sq, E4 47 DZ51
Arnett Way, Rick. WD3 22 BG44
Arne Wk, SE3 104 EF84
Arneways Av, Rom. RM6 70 EX55
Arneway St, SW1 199 N7
Arnewood Cl, SW15 119 CU88
Leatherhead
(Oxshott) KT22 154 CB113
Arney's La, Mitch. CR4 140 DG100
Arngask Rd, SE6 123 ED87
Arnhem Av, S.Ock.
(Aveley) RM15 90 FQ74
Arnhem Dr, Croy.
(New Adgtn) CR0 161 ED111
Arnhem Pl, E14 203 P7
Arnhem Way, SE22
off East Dulwich Gro 122 DS85
Arnhem Wf, E14
off Arnhem Pl 103 EA76
Arnison Rd, E.Mol. KT8 137 CD98
Arnold Av E, Enf. EN3 31 EA38
Arnold Av W, Enf. EN3 31 DZ38
Arnold Circ, E2 197 P3
Arnold Cl, Har. HA3 62 CM59
Arnold Cres, Islw. TW7 117 CD85
Arnold Dr, Chess. KT9 155 CK107
Arnold Est, SE1 202 A5
Arnold Gdns, N13 45 DP50
Arnold Pl, Til. RM18
off Kipling Av 111 GJ81
Arnold Rd, E3 85 EA69
N15 66 DT55
SW17 120 DF94
Dagenham RM9, RM10 88 EZ66
Gravesend DA12 131 GJ89
Northolt UB5 78 BX65
Staines TW18 114 BJ94
Waltham Abbey EN9 31 EC35
Woking GU21 167 BB116
Arnolds Av, Brwd.
(Hutt.) CM13 55 GC43
Arnolds Cl, Brwd.
(Hutt.) CM13 55 GC43
Arnolds Fm La, Brwd. (Mtnsg)
CM13 55 GE41
Arnolds La, Dart. (Sutt.H.) DA4 128 FM93
⊖ Arnos Grove 45 DJ49
Arnos Gro, N14 45 DK49
Arnos Rd, N11 45 DJ50
Arnott Cl, SE28
off Applegarth Rd 88 EW73
W4 off Fishers La 98 CR77
Arnould Av, SE5 102 DR84
Arnsberg Way, Bexh. DA7 106 FA84
Arnside Gdns, Wem. HA9 61 CK60
Arnside Rd, Bexh. DA7 106 FA81
Arnside St, SE17 102 DQ79
Arnulf St, SE6 123 EB91
Arnulls Rd, SW16 121 DN93
Arodene Rd, SW2 121 DM86
Arosa Rd, Twick. TW1 117 CK86
Arpley Sq, SE20 off High St 122 DW94
Arragon Gdns, SW16 121 DL94
West Wickham BR4 143 EB104
Arragon Rd, E6 86 EK67
SW18 120 DB88
Twickenham TW1 117 CG87
Arran Cl, Erith DA8 107 FD79
Wallington SM6 159 DH105
Arran Dr, E12 68 EK60
Arran Grn, Wat. WD19
off Prestwick Rd 40 BW46
Arran Ms, W5 80 CM74
Arranmore Ct, Bushey WD23
off Bushey Hall Rd 24 BY42
Arran Rd, SE6 123 EB89
Arran Wk, N1 84 DQ66
Arran Way, Esher KT10 136 CB103
Arras Av, Mord. SM4 140 DC99
Arreton Mead, Wok.
(Horsell) GU21 150 AY114
Arrol Rd, Beck. BR3 142 DW97
Arrow Rd, E3 85 EB69
Arrowscout Wk, Nthlt. UB5
off Argus Way 78 BY69
Arrowsmith Cl, Chig. IG7 49 ET50
Arrowsmith Path, Chig. IG7 49 ET50
Arrowsmith Rd, Chig. IG7 49 ES50
Loughton IG10 32 EL41
⊖ Arsenal 65 DN62
★ Arsenal FC, N5 65 DP62
Arsenal Rd, SE9 105 EM82
Arsenal Way, SE18 105 EQ76
Artemis Cl, Grav. DA12 131 GL87
Arterberry Rd, SW20 119 CW94
Arterial Av, Rain. RM13 89 FH70
Arterial Rd N Stifford,
Grays RM17 110 FY75
Arterial Rd Purfleet,
Purf. RM19 108 FN76
Arterial Rd W Thurrock,
Grays RM16, RM20 109 FU76
Artesian Cl, NW10 80 CR66
Hornchurch RM11 71 FF58
Artesian Gro, Barn. EN5 28 DC42
Artesian Rd, W2 82 DA72
Artesian Wk, E11 68 EE62
Arthingworth St, E15 86 EE67
Arthur Ct, W2 off Queensway 82 DB72
Arthurdon Rd, SE4 123 EA85
Arthur Gro, SE18 105 EQ77
Arthur Henderson Ho, SW6 99 CZ82
Arthur Horsley Wk, E7
off Magpie Cl 68 EF64
★ Arthur Jacob Nature Reserve,
Slou. SL3 93 BC83
Arthur Rd, E6 87 EM68
N7 65 DM63
N9 46 DT47
SW19 120 DA90
Kingston upon Thames KT2 118 CN94
New Malden KT3 139 CV99
Romford RM6 70 EW59
Westerham (Bigg.H.) TN16 178 EJ115
Arthur's Br Rd, Wok. GU21 166 AW117
Arthur St, EC4 201 L1
Bushey WD23 24 BX42
Erith DA8 107 FF80
Gravesend DA11 131 GG87
Grays RM17 110 GC79
Arthur St W, Grav. DA11 131 GG87
Arthur Toft Ho, Grays RM17
off New Rd 110 GB79
Arthur Walls Ho, E12
off Grantham Rd 69 EN62
Artichoke Dell, Rick.
(Chorl.) WD3 21 BE43
Artichoke Hill, E1 202 D1
Artichoke Pl, SE5
off Camberwell Ch St 102 DR81
Artillery Cl, Ilf. IG2
off Horns Rd 69 EQ58
Artillery La, E1 197 N7
W12 81 CU72
Artillery Pas, E1 197 N7
Artillery Pl, SE18 105 EM78
SW1 199 M7
Harrow HA3
off Chicheley Rd 40 CC52
Artillery Row, SW1 199 M7
Gravesend DA12 131 GJ87
Artington Cl, Orp. BR6 163 EQ105
Artisan Cl, E6
off Ferndale St 87 EP72
Artizan St, E1 197 N8
Arundel Av, Epsom KT17 157 CV110
Morden SM4 139 CZ98
South Croydon CR2 160 DU110
Arundel Cl, E15 68 EE63
SW11 off Chivalry Rd 120 DE85
Bexley DA5 126 EZ86
Croydon CR0 141 DP104
Hampton (Hmptn H.) TW12 116 CB92
Waltham Cross (Chsht) EN8 14 DW29
Arundel Ct, N12 44 DE51
Harrow HA2 60 CA63
Slough SL3 92 AX77
Arundel Dr, Borwd. WD6 26 CQ43
Harrow HA2 60 BZ63
Orpington BR6 164 EV106
Woodford Green IG8 48 EG52
Arundel Gdns, N21 45 DN46
W11 81 CZ73
Edgware HA8 42 CR52
Ilford IG3 70 EU61
Arundel Gt Ct, WC2 196 C10
Arundel Gro, N16 66 DS64
Arundel Pl, N1 83 DN65
Arundel Rd, Abb.L. WD5 7 BU32
Barnet EN4 28 DE41
Croydon CR0 142 DR100
Dartford DA1 108 FJ84
Hounslow TW4 96 BW83
Kingston upon Thames
KT1 138 CP96
Romford RM3 52 FM53
Sutton SM2 157 CZ108
Uxbridge UB8 76 BH68
Arundel Sq, N7 83 DN65
Arundel St, WC2 196 C10
Arundel Ter, SW13 99 CV79
Arvon Rd, N5 65 DN64
Asbaston Ter, Ilf. IG1
off Buttsbury Rd 69 EQ64
Ascalon St, SW8 101 DJ80
Ascension Rd, Rom. RM5 51 FC51
Ascham Dr, E4
off Rushcroft Rd 47 EB52
Ascham End, E17 47 DY53
Ascham St, NW5 65 DJ64
Aschurch Rd, Croy. CR0 142 DT101
Ascot Cl, Borwd.
(Elstree) WD6 26 CN43
Ilford IG6 49 ES51
Northolt UB5 60 CA64
Ascot Gdns, Enf. EN3 30 DW37
Hornchurch RM12 72 FL63
Southall UB1 78 BZ71
Ascot Ms, Wall. SM6 159 DJ109
Ascot Rd, E6 87 EM69
N15 66 DR57
N18 46 DU49
SW17 120 DG93
Feltham TW14 114 BN88
Gravesend DA12 131 GH90
Orpington BR5 145 ET98
Watford WD18 23 BS43
Ascott Av, W5 98 CL75
Ashanti Ms, E8
off Lower Clapton Rd 66 DV64
Ashbeam Cl, Brwd. CM13
off Canterbury Way 53 FW51
Ashbourne, St.Alb. AL2
off Bucknalls Dr 8 BZ31
Ashbourne Av, E18 68 EH56
N20 44 DF47
NW11 63 CZ57
Bexleyheath DA7 106 EY80
Harrow HA2 61 CD61
Ashbourne Cl, N12 44 DB49
W5 80 CN71
Coulsdon CR5 175 DJ118
Ashbourne Ct, E5
off Daubeney Rd 67 DY63
Ashbourne Gro, NW7 42 CR50
SE22 122 DT85
W4 98 CS78
Ashbourne Par, W5
off Ashbourne Rd 80 CM70
Ashbourne Ri, Orp. BR6 163 ER105
Ashbourne Rd, W5 80 CM71
Mitcham CR4 120 DG93
Romford RM3 52 FJ49
Ashbourne Sq, Nthwd. HA6 39 BS51
Ashbourne Ter, SW19 120 DA94
Ashbourne Way, NW11
off Ashbourne Av 63 CZ57
Ashbridge Rd, E11 68 EF59
Ashbridge St, NW8 194 B5
Ashbrook Rd, N19 65 DK60
Dagenham RM10 71 FB62
Windsor (Old Wind.) SL4 112 AV87
Ashburn Gdns, SW7 100 DC77
Ashburnham Av, Har. HA1 61 CF58
Ashburnham Cl, N2 64 DD55
Sevenoaks TN13
off Fiennes Way 191 FJ127
Watford WD19
off Ashburnham Dr 39 BU48
Ashburnham Dr, Wat. WD19 39 BU48
Ashburnham Gdns, Har. HA1 61 CF58
Upminster RM14 72 FP60
Ashburnham Gro, SE10 103 EB80
Ashburnham Pk, Esher KT10 154 CC105
Ashburnham Pl, SE10 103 EB80
Ashburnham Retreat, SE10 103 EB80
Ashburnham Rd, NW10 81 CW69
SW10 100 DC80
Belvedere DA17 107 FC77
Richmond TW10 117 CH90
Ashburn Pl, SW7 100 DC77
Ashburton Av, Croy. CR0 142 DV102
Ilford IG3 69 ES63
Ashburton Cl, Croy. CR0 142 DU102
Ashburton Ct, Pnr. HA5 60 BX55
Ashburton Gdns, Croy. CR0 142 DU103
Ashburton Rd, E16 86 EG72
Croydon CR0 142 DU102
Ruislip HA4 59 BU61
Ashburton Ter, E13
off Grasmere Rd 86 EG68
Ashbury Dr, Uxb. UB10 59 BP61
Ashbury Gdns, Rom. RM6 70 EX57
Ashbury Pl, SW19 120 DC93
Ashbury Rd, SW11 100 DF83
Ashby Av, Chess. KT9 156 CN107
Ashby Cl, Horn. RM11
off Holme Rd 72 FN60
Ashby Gro, N1 84 DQ66
Ashby Ms, SE4 103 DZ82
SW2 off Prague Pl 121 DL85
Ashby Rd, N15 66 DU57
SE4 103 DZ82
Watford WD24 23 BU38
Ashby St, EC1 196 G3
Ashby Wk, Croy. CR0 142 DQ100
Ashby Way, West Dr. UB7 94 BN80
Ashchurch Gro, W12 99 CU75
Ashchurch Pk Vil, W12 99 CU76
Ashchurch Ter, W12 99 CU76
Ash Cl, SE20 142 DW96
Abbots Langley WD5 7 BR32
Brentwood (Pilg.Hat.) CM15 54 FV43
Carshalton SM5 140 DF103
Edgware HA8 42 CQ49
Hatfield AL9 12 DA25
New Malden KT3 138 CR96
Orpington BR5 145 ER99

★ Place of interest ⇌ Railway station ⊖ London Underground station DLR Docklands Light Railway station Tra Tramlink station H Hospital Riv Pedestrian ferry landing stage

212

Ash Cl, Redhill RH1 . . . . 185 DJ130
Romford RM5 . . . . 51 FB52
Sidcup DA14 . . . . 126 EV90
Slough SL3 . . . . 93 BB76
Stanmore HA7 . . . . 41 CG51
Swanley BR8 . . . . 147 FC96
Uxbridge (Hare.) UB9 . . . . 38 BK53
Watford WD25 . . . . 23 BV35
Woking GU22 . . . . 166 AY120
Woking (Pyrford) GU22 . . . 168 BG115
Ashcombe Av, Surb. KT6 . . . . . 137 CK101
Ashcombe Gdns, Edg. HA8 . . . 42 CN49
Ashcombe Ho, Enf. EN3 . . . . . 31 DX41
Ashcombe Pk, NW2 . . . . 62 CS62
Ashcombe Rd, SW19 . . . . 120 DA92
Carshalton SM5 . . . . 158 DG107
Redhill RH1 . . . . 185 DJ127
Ashcombe Sq, N.Mal. KT3 . . . 138 CQ97
Ashcombe St, SW6 . . . . 100 DB82
Ashcombe Ter, Tad. KT20 . . . 173 CV120
Ash Copse, St.Alb.
(Brick.Wd) AL2 . . . . 8 BZ31
Ash Ct, Epsom KT19 . . . . 156 CQ105
Ashcroft, Pnr. HA5 . . . . 40 CA51
Ashcroft Av, Sid. DA15 . . . . . 126 EU86
Ashcroft Ct, N20
off Oakleigh Rd N 44 DD47
Ashcroft Cres, Sid. DA15 . . . . 126 EU86
Ashcroft Dr, Uxb.
(Denh.) UB9 . . . . 57 BF58
Ashcroft Pk, Cob. KT11 . . . . . 154 BY112
Ashcroft Ri, Couls. CR5 . . . . 175 DL116
Ashcroft Rd, E3 . . . . 85 DY69
Chessington KT9 . . . . 138 CM104
Ashcroft Sq, W6 *off King St* . . 99 CW77
Ashdale Cl, Stai. TW19 . . . . . . 114 BL89
Twickenham TW2 . . . . 116 CC87
Ashdale Gro, Stan. HA7 . . . . . 41 CF51
Ashdale Rd, SE12 . . . . 124 EH88
Ashdale Way, Twick. TW2
off Ashdale Cl 116 CC87
Ashdene, SE15 . . . . 102 DV81
Pinner HA5 . . . . 60 BW55
Ashdene Cl, Ashf. TW15 . . . . . 115 BQ94
Ashdon Cl, Brwd. (Hutt.) CM13
off Poplar Dr 55 GC44
South Ockendon RM15
off Afton Dr 91 FV72
Woodford Green IG8 . . . . . . 48 EH51
Ashdon Rd, NW10 . . . . 80 CS67
Bushey WD23 . . . . 24 BX41
Ashdown Cl, Beck. BR3 . . . . . 143 EB96
Bexley DA5 . . . . 127 FC87
Ashdown Cres, NW5
off Queen's Cres 64 DG64
Waltham Cross (Chsht) EN8 . 15 DY28
Ashdown Dr, Borwd. WD6 . . . . 26 CM40
Ashdown Est, E11
off High Rd Leytonstone . . 68 EE63
Ashdown Gdns, S.Croy. CR2 . 176 DV115
Ashdown Pl, T.Ditt. KT7 . . . . . 137 CG101
Ashdown Rd, Enf. EN3 . . . . . . 30 DW41
Epsom KT17 . . . . 157 CT113
Kingston upon Thames KT1 . 138 CL96
Uxbridge UB10 . . . . 76 BN68
Ashdown Wk, E14 . . . . 204 A8
Romford RM7 . . . . 51 FB54
Ashdown Way, SW17 . . . . 120 DG89
Ashen, E6 *off Downings* 87 EN72
Ashen Cross, Slou. SL3 . . . . . . 75 BB71
Ashenden Rd, E5 . . . . 67 DX64
Ashen Dr, Dart. DA1 . . . . 127 FG86
Ashen Gro, SW19 . . . . 120 DA90
Ashentree Ct, EC4 . . . . 196 E9
Ashen Vale, S.Croy. CR2 . . . . 161 DX109
Asher Loftus Way, N11 . . . . . . 44 DF51
Asher Way, E1 . . . . 202 C2
Ashfield Av, Bushey WD23 . . . . 24 CB44
Feltham TW13 . . . . 115 BV88
Ashfield Cl, Beck. BR3 . . . . . . 123 EA94
Richmond TW10 . . . . 118 CL88
Ashfield La, Chis. BR7 . . . . . . 125 EQ93
Ashfield Par, N14 . . . . 45 DK46
Ashfield Rd, N4 . . . . 66 DQ58
N14 . . . . 45 DJ48
W3 . . . . 81 CT74
Ashfields, Loug. IG10 . . . . 33 EM40
Reigate RH2 . . . . 184 DB132
Watford WD25 . . . . 23 BT35
Ashfield St, E1 . . . . 84 DV71
Ashfield Yd, E1
off Ashfield St 84 DV71
ASHFORD 114 BM92
⇌ **Ashford** 114 BL91
Ashford Av, N8 . . . . 65 DL56
Ashford TW15 . . . . 115 BP93
Brentwood CM14 . . . . 54 FV48
Hayes UB4 . . . . 78 BX72
Ashford Cl, E17 . . . . 67 DZ58
Ashford TW15 . . . . 114 BL91
Ashford Cres, Ashf. TW15 . . . . 114 BL90
Enfield EN3 . . . . 30 DW40
Ashford Gdns, Cob. KT11 . . . . 170 BX116
Ashford Grn, Wat. WD19 . . . . . 40 BX50
🅷 **Ashford Hosp**, Ashf. TW15 . 114 BL89
Ashford Ind Est, Ashf. TW15 . . 115 BQ91
Ashford Ms, N17
off Vicarage Rd 46 DU53
Ashford Rd, E6 . . . . 87 EN65
E18 . . . . 48 EH54
NW2 . . . . 63 CX63
Ashford TW15 . . . . 115 BQ94
Feltham TW13 . . . . 115 BT90
Iver SL0 . . . . 75 BC66
Staines TW18 . . . . 134 BK95
Ashford St, N1 . . . . 197 M2
Ash Grn, Uxb. (Denh.) UB9 . . . 76 BH65
Ash Gro, E8 . . . . 84 DV67
N13 . . . . 46 DQ48
NW2 . . . . 63 CX63
SE20 . . . . 142 DW96
W5 . . . . 98 CL75
Enfield EN1 . . . . 46 DS45
Feltham TW14 . . . . 115 BS88
Hayes UB3 . . . . 77 BR73
Hounslow TW5 . . . . 96 BX81
Slough (Stoke P.) SL2 . . . . . . 74 AT66
Southall UB1 . . . . 78 CA71
Staines TW18 . . . . 114 BJ93
Uxbridge (Hare.) UB9 . . . . . . 38 BK53
Ash Gro, Wembley HA0 . . . . . . 61 CG63
West Drayton UB7 . . . . 76 BM73
West Wickham BR4 . . . . 143 EC103
Ashgrove Rd, Ashf. TW15 . . . . 115 BQ92
Bromley BR1 . . . . 123 ED93
Ilford IG3 . . . . 69 ET60
Sevenoaks TN13 . . . . 190 FG127
Ash Hill Cl, Bushey WD23 . . . . 40 CB46
Ash Hill Dr, Pnr. HA5 . . . . 60 BW55
Ashingdon Cl, E4 . . . . 47 EC48
Ashington Rd, SW6 . . . . 99 CZ82
Ash Island, E.Mol. KT8 . . . . . . 137 CD97
Ashlake Rd, SW16 . . . . 121 DL91
Ashland Pl, W1 . . . . 194 F6
Ash La, Horn. RM11
off Southend Arterial Rd . . . 72 FN56
Romford RM1 . . . . 51 FG51
Ashlar Pl, SE18
off Masons Hill 105 EP77
Ashlea Rd, Ger.Cr.
(Chal.St.P.) SL9 . . . . 36 AX54
Ashleigh Av, Egh. TW20 . . . . . 113 BC94
Ashleigh Cl, Amer. HP7 . . . . . . 20 AS39
Ashleigh Ct, Wal.Abb. EN9
off Lamplighters Cl 16 EG34
Ashleigh Gdns, Sutt. SM1 . . . 140 DB103
Upminster RM14 . . . . 73 FR62
Ashleigh Pt, SE23
off Dacres Rd 123 DX90
Ashleigh Rd, SE20 . . . . 142 DV97
SW14 . . . . 98 CS83
Ashley Av, Epsom KT18 . . . . . 156 CR113
Ilford IG6 . . . . 49 EP54
Morden SM4 . . . . 140 DA99
Ashley Cen, Epsom KT18 . . . . 156 CR113
Ashley Cl, NW4 . . . . 43 CW54
Pinner HA5 . . . . 39 BV54
Sevenoaks TN13 . . . . 191 FH124
Walton-on-Thames KT12 . . 135 BT102
Ashley Ct, Epsom KT18 . . . . . 156 CR113
Woking GU21 . . . . 166 AT118
Ashley Cres, N22 . . . . 45 DN54
SW11 . . . . 100 DG83
Ashley Dr, Bans. SM7 . . . . . . 158 DA114
Borehamwood WD6 . . . . 26 CQ43
Isleworth TW7 . . . . 97 CE79
Twickenham TW2 . . . . 116 CB87
Walton-on-Thames KT12 . . 135 BU104
Ashley Gdns, N13 . . . . 46 DQ49
SW1 . . . . 199 L7
Orpington BR6 . . . . 163 ES106
Richmond TW10 . . . . 117 CK90
Wembley HA9 . . . . 62 CL61
Ashley Gro, Loug. IG10
off Staples Rd 32 EL41
Ashley La, NW4 . . . . 43 CW54
Croydon CR0 . . . . 159 DP105
ASHLEY PARK, Walt. KT12 . . . 135 BT104
Ashley Pk Av, Walt. KT12 . . . . 135 BT103
Ashley Pk Cres, Walt. KT12 . . . 135 BT102
Ashley Pk Rd, Walt. KT12 . . . . 135 BU103
Ashley Pl, SW1 . . . . 199 K7
Ashley Ri, Walt. KT12 . . . . 153 BU105
Ashley Rd, E4 . . . . 47 EA50
E7 . . . . 86 EJ66
N17 . . . . 66 DU55
N19 . . . . 65 DL60
SW19 . . . . 120 DB93
Enfield EN3 . . . . 30 DW40
Epsom KT18 . . . . 156 CR114
Hampton TW12 . . . . 136 CA95
Richmond TW9
off Jocelyn Rd 98 CL83
Sevenoaks TN13 . . . . 191 FH123
Thames Ditton KT7 . . . . 137 CF100
Thornton Heath CR7 . . . . . . 141 DM98
Uxbridge UB8 . . . . 76 BH68
Walton-on-Thames KT12 . . 135 BU102
Woking GU21 . . . . 166 AT118
Ashleys, Rick. WD3 . . . . 37 BF45
Ashley Sq, Epsom KT18 . . . . . 156 CR113
Ashley Wk, NW7 . . . . 43 CW52
Ashling Rd, Croy. CR0 . . . . . . 142 DU102
Ashlin Rd, E15 . . . . 67 ED63
Ashlone Rd, SW15 . . . . 99 CW83
Ashlyn Cl, Bushey WD23 . . . . . 24 BY42
Ashlyn Gro, Horn. RM11 . . . . . . 72 FK55
Ashlyns Pk, Cob. KT11 . . . . . . 154 BY113
Ashlyns Rd, Epp. CM16 . . . . . . 17 ET30
Ashlyns Way, Chess. KT9 . . . . 155 CK107
Ashmead, N14 . . . . 29 DJ43
Ashmead Dr, Uxb.
(Denh.) UB9 . . . . 58 BG61
Ashmead Gate, Brom. BR1 . . . 144 EJ95
Ashmead Ho, E9
off Kingsmead Way 67 DY64
Ashmead La, Uxb.
(Denh.) UB9 . . . . 58 BG61
Ashmead Rd, SE8 . . . . 103 EA82
Feltham TW14 . . . . 115 BU88
Ashmeads Ct, Rad. (Shenley) WD7
off Porters Pk Dr 9 CK33
Ashmere Av, Beck. BR3 . . . . . 143 ED96
Ashmere Cl, Sutt. SM3 . . . . . 157 CW106
Ashmere Gro, SW2 . . . . 101 DL84
Ash Ms, Epsom KT18 . . . . 156 CS113
Ashmill St, NW1 . . . . 194 B6
Ashmole Pl, SW8 . . . . 101 DM79
Ashmole St, SW8 . . . . 101 DM79
Ashmore Ct, Houns. TW5
off Wheatlands 96 CA79
Ashmore Gdns, Grav.
(Nthflt) DA11 . . . . 130 GD91
Ashmore Gro, Well. DA16 . . . . 105 ER83
Ashmore La, Kes. BR2 . . . . . . 162 EH111
Ashmore Rd, W9 . . . . 81 CZ70
Ashmount Est, N19
off Ashmount Rd 65 DK59
Ashmount Rd, N15 . . . . 66 DT57
N19 . . . . 65 DJ59
Ashmount Ter, W5
off Murray Rd 97 CK77
Ashmour Gdns, Rom. RM1 . . . . 51 FD54
Ashneal Gdns, Har. HA1 . . . . . . 61 CD62
Ashness Gdns, Grnf. UB6 . . . . . 79 CH65
Ashness Rd, SW11 . . . . 120 DF85
Ash Platt, The, Sev.
(Seal) TN14, TN15 . . . . 191 FL121
Ash Platt Rd, Sev. (Seal) TN15 191 FL121
Ash Ride, Enf. EN2 . . . . 29 DN35
Ashridge Cl, Har. HA3 . . . . 61 CJ58
Hemel Hempstead
(Bov.) HP3 . . . . 5 BA28
Ashridge Cres, SE18 . . . . 105 EQ80
Ashridge Dr, St.Alb.
(Brick.Wd) AL2 . . . . 8 BY30
Watford WD19 . . . . 40 BW50
Ashridge Gdns, N13 . . . . 45 DK50
Pinner HA5 . . . . 60 BY56
Ashridge Rd, Chesh. HP5 . . . . . . 4 AW31
Ashridge Way, Mord. SM4 . . . . 139 CZ97
Sunbury-on-Thames TW16 . 115 BU93
Ash Rd, E15 . . . . 68 EE64
Croydon CR0 . . . . 143 EA103
Dartford DA1 . . . . 128 FK88
Dartford (Hawley) DA2 . . . . 128 FM91
Gravesend DA12 . . . . 131 GJ91
Orpington BR6 . . . . 163 ET108
Shepperton TW17 . . . . 134 BN98
Sutton SM3 . . . . 139 CY101
Westerham TN16 . . . . 189 ER125
Woking GU22 . . . . 166 AX120
Ash Row, Brom. BR2 . . . . 145 EN101
ASHTEAD 172 CL118
⇌ **Ashtead** 171 CK117
Ashtead Gap, Lthd. KT22 . . . . . 171 CH116
🅷 **Ashtead Hosp**,
Ashtd. KT21 . . . . 172 CL119
ASHTEAD PARK, Ashtd. KT21 . 172 CN118
Ashtead Rd, E5 . . . . 66 DU59
Ashtead Wds Rd, Ashtd. KT21 . 171 CJ117
Ashton Cl, Sutt. SM1 . . . . 158 DA105
Walton-on-Thames KT12 . . 153 BV107
Ashton Gdns, Houns. TW4 . . . . 96 BZ84
Romford RM6 . . . . 70 EY58
Ashton Rd, E15 . . . . 67 ED64
Enfield EN3 . . . . 31 DY36
Romford RM3 . . . . 52 FK52
Woking GU21 . . . . 166 AT117
Ashton St, E14 . . . . 85 EC73
Ashtree Av, Mitch. CR4 . . . . . . 140 DE96
Ash Tree Cl, Croy. CR0 . . . . . . 143 DY100
Ashtree Cl, Orp. BR6
off Broadwater Gdns 163 EP105
Ash Tree Cl, Surb. KT6 . . . . . . 138 CL102
Ashtree Ct, Wal.Abb. EN9
off Farthingale La 16 EG34
Ash Tree Dell, NW9 . . . . 62 CQ57
Ash Tree Rd, Wat. WD24 . . . . . . 23 BV36
Ash Tree Way, Croy. CR0 . . . . 143 DY99
Ashurst Cl, SE20 . . . . 142 DV95
Dartford DA1 . . . . 107 FF83
Kenley CR8 . . . . 176 DR115
Northwood HA6 . . . . 39 BS52
Ashurst Dr, Ilf. IG2, IG6 . . . . . . 69 EP58
Shepperton TW17 . . . . 134 BL99
Tadworth (Box H.) KT20 . . . 182 CP130
Ashurst Rd, N12 . . . . 44 DE50
Barnet EN4 . . . . 28 DF43
Tadworth KT20 . . . . 173 CV121
Ashurst Wk, Croy. CR0 . . . . . . 142 DV103
Ash Vale, Rick. (Map.Cr.) WD3 . 37 BD50
Ashvale Dr, Upmin. RM14 . . . . . 73 FS61
Ashvale Gdns, Rom. RM5 . . . . . 51 FD50
Upminster RM14 . . . . 73 FS61
Ashvale Rd, SW17 . . . . 120 DF92
Ashview Cl, Ashf. TW15 . . . . . 114 BL93
Ashview Gdns, Ashf. TW15 . . . 114 BL92
Ashville Rd, E11 . . . . 67 ED61
Ash Wk, SW2 . . . . 121 DM88
South Ockendon RM15 . . . . . 91 FX69
Wembley HA0 . . . . 61 CJ63
Ashwater Rd, SE12 . . . . 124 EG88
Ashwell Cl, E6
off Northumberland Rd 86 EL72
Ashwells Rd, Brwd.
(Pilg.Hat.) CM15 . . . . 54 FS41
Ashwells Way, Ch.St.G. HP8 . . . 36 AW47
Ashwick Cl, Cat. CR3 . . . . 186 DU125
Ashwindham Ct, Wok. GU21 . 166 AS118
Ashwin St, E8 . . . . 84 DT65
Ashwood, Warl. CR6 . . . . 176 DW120
Ashwood Av, Rain. RM13 . . . . . 89 FH70
Uxbridge UB8 . . . . 76 BN72
Ashwood Gdns, Croy.
(New Adgtn) CR0 . . . . 161 EB107
Hayes UB3 *off Cranford Dr* . 95 BT77
Ashwood Pk, Lthd.
(Fetch.) KT22 . . . . 170 CC124
Woking GU22 . . . . 167 BA118
Ashwood Pl, Dart. (Bean) DA2
off Bean La 129 FV90
Ashwood Rd, E4 . . . . 47 ED48
Egham (Eng.Grn) TW20 . . . 112 AV93
Potters Bar EN6 . . . . 12 DB33
Woking GU22 . . . . 167 AZ118
Ashworth Cl, SE5
off Love Wk 102 DR82
Ashworth Rd, W9 . . . . 82 DB69
Askern Cl, Bexh. DA6 . . . . 106 EX84
Aske St, N1 . . . . 197 M2
Askew Cres, W12 . . . . 99 CT75
Askew Fm La, Grays RM17 . . . 110 FY78
Askew Rd, W12 . . . . 81 CT74
Northwood HA6 . . . . 39 BR47
Askham Ct, W12 . . . . 81 CU74
Askham Rd, W12 . . . . 81 CU74
Askill Dr, SW15
off Keswick Rd 119 CY85
Askwith Rd, Rain. RM13 . . . . . . 89 FD69
Asland Rd, E15 . . . . 86 EE67
Aslett St, SW18 . . . . 120 DB87
Asmara Rd, NW2 . . . . 63 CY64
Asmar Cl, Couls. CR5 . . . . 175 DL115
Asmuns Hill, NW11 . . . . 64 DA57
Asmuns Pl, NW11 . . . . 63 CZ57
Asolando Dr, SE17 . . . . 201 J9
Aspdin Rd, Grav.
(Nthflt) DA11 . . . . 130 GD90
Aspen Cl, N19
off Hargrave Pk 65 DJ61
W5 . . . . 98 CM75
Cobham
(Stoke D'Ab.) KT11 . . . . . . 170 BY116
Orpington BR6 . . . . 164 EU106
St. Albans (Brick.Wd) AL2 . . . 8 BY30
Staines TW18 . . . . 113 BF90
Swanley BR8 . . . . 147 FD95
West Drayton UB7 . . . . 76 BM74
Aspen Copse, Brom. BR1 . . . . 145 EM96
Aspen Ct, Brwd. CM13
off Hornbeam Cl 55 GA48
Hayes UB3 . . . . 95 BS77
Virginia Water GU25 . . . . . . 132 AY98
Aspen Dr, Wem. HA0 . . . . 61 CG63
Aspen Gdns, W6 . . . . 99 CV78
Ashford TW15 . . . . 115 BQ92
Mitcham CR4 . . . . 140 DG99
Aspen Grn, Erith DA18 . . . . . . 106 EZ76
Aspen Gro, Upmin. RM14 . . . . . 72 FN63
Aspen La, Nthlt. UB5 . . . . 78 BY69
Aspenlea Rd, W6 . . . . 99 CX79
Aspen Pk Dr, Wat. WD25 . . . . . 23 BV35
Aspen Sq, Wey. KT13
off Oatlands Dr 135 BR104
Aspen Vale, Whyt. CR3
off Whyteleafe Hill 176 DT118
Aspen Way, E14 . . . . 204 A1
Banstead SM7 . . . . 157 CX114
Enfield EN3 . . . . 31 DX35
Feltham TW13 . . . . 115 BV90
South Ockendon RM15 . . . . . 91 FX69
Aspern Gro, NW3 . . . . 64 DE64
Aspinall Rd, SE4 . . . . 103 DX83
Aspinden Rd, SE16 . . . . 202 E8
Aspley Rd, SW18 . . . . 120 DB85
Asplins Rd, N17 . . . . 46 DU53
Asprey Gro, Cat. CR3 . . . . 176 DU124
Asprey Ms, Beck. BR3
off Upper Elmers End Rd . 143 DZ99
Asprey Pl, Brom. BR1
off Chislehurst Rd 144 EK96
Asquith Cl, Dag. RM8 . . . . 70 EW60
Assam St, E1 *off White Ch La* . 84 DU72
Assata Ms, N1
off St. Paul's Rd 83 DP65
Assembly Pas, E1 . . . . 84 DW71
Assembly Wk, Cars. SM5 . . . . 140 DE101
Assher Rd, Walt. KT12 . . . . . . 136 BY104
Ass Ho La, Har. HA3 . . . . 40 CB49
Assurance Cotts, Belv. DA17
off Heron Hill 106 EZ78
Astall Cl, Har. HA3 . . . . 41 CE53
Astbury Business Pk, SE15
off Station Pas 102 DW81
Astbury Rd, SE15 . . . . 102 DW81
Astede Pl, Ashtd. KT21 . . . . . 172 CM118
Astell St, SW3 . . . . 198 C10
Asters, The, Wal.Cr. EN7 . . . . . 14 DR28
Aste St, E14 . . . . 204 D5
Asteys Row, N1 *off River Pl* . . . 83 DP66
Asthall Gdns, Ilf. IG6 . . . . 69 EQ56
Astleham Rd, Shep. TW17 . . . . 134 BL97
Astle St, SW11 . . . . 100 DG82
Astley, Grays RM17 . . . . 110 FZ79
Astley Av, NW2 . . . . 63 CW64
Aston Av, Har. HA3 . . . . 61 CJ59
Aston Cl, Ashtd. KT21 . . . . 171 CJ118
Bushey WD23 . . . . 24 CC44
Sidcup DA14 . . . . 126 EU90
Watford WD24 . . . . 24 BW40
Aston Grn, Houns. TW4 . . . . . . 96 BW82
Aston Ms, Rom. RM6 . . . . 70 EW59
Aston Pl, SW16
off Averil Gro 121 DP93
Aston Rd, SW20 . . . . 139 CW96
W5 . . . . 79 CK72
Esher (Clay.) KT10 . . . . 155 CE106
Astons Rd, Nthwd. HA6 . . . . . . 39 BQ48
Aston St, E14 . . . . 85 DY72
Aston Ter, SW12
off Cathles Rd 121 DH86
Astonville St, SW18 . . . . 120 DA88
Aston Way, Epsom KT18 . . . . . 173 CT115
Potters Bar EN6 . . . . 12 DD32
Astor Av, Rom. RM7 . . . . 71 FC58
Astor Cl, Add. KT15 . . . . 152 BK105
Kingston upon Thames KT2 . 118 CP93
Astoria Wk, SW9 . . . . 101 DN83
Astra Cl, Horn. RM12 . . . . 89 FH65
Astra Dr, Grav. DA12 . . . . 131 GL92
Astrop Ms, W6 . . . . 99 CW76
Astrop Ter, W6 . . . . 99 CW76
Astwood Ms, SW7 . . . . 100 DB77
Asylum Rd, SE15 . . . . 102 DV80
Atalanta Cl, Pur. CR8 . . . . 159 DN110
Atalanta St, SW6 . . . . 99 CX81
Atbara Ct, Tedd. TW11 . . . . . . 117 CH93
Atbara Rd, Tedd. TW11 . . . . . . 117 CH93
Atcham Rd, Houns. TW3 . . . . . . 96 CC84
Atcost Rd, Bark. IG11 . . . . 88 EU71
Atheldene Rd, SW18 . . . . 120 DB88
Athelney St, SE6 . . . . 123 EA90
Athelstan Cl, Rom. RM3
off Athelstan Rd 52 FM54
Athelstane Gro, E3 . . . . 85 DZ68
Athelstane Ms, N4
off Stroud Grn Rd 65 DN60
Athelstan Ho, E9
off Kingsmead Way 67 DZ64
Athelstan Rd, Kings.T. KT1 . . . 138 CM98
Romford RM3 . . . . 52 FM53
Athelstan Way, Orp. BR5 . . . . 146 EU95
Athelstone Rd, Har. HA3 . . . . . . 41 CD54
Athena Cl, Har. HA2
off Byron Hill Rd 61 CE61
Kingston upon Thames KT1 . 138 CM97
Athenaeum Pl, N10
off Fortis Grn Rd 65 DH55
Athenaeum Rd, N20 . . . . 44 DC46
Athena Pl, Nthwd. HA6
off The Drive 39 BT53
Athenia Cl, Wal.Cr.
(Goffs Oak) EN7 . . . . 13 DP29
Athenlay Rd, SE15 . . . . 123 DX85
Athens Gdns, W9
off Harrow Rd 82 DA70
Atherden Rd, E5 . . . . 66 DW63
Atherfold Rd, SW9 . . . . 101 DL83
Atherley Way, Houns. TW4 . . . 116 BZ87
Atherstone Ct, W2
off Delamere Ter 82 DB71
Atherstone Ms, SW7 . . . . 100 DC77
Atherton Cl, Stai.
(Stanw.) TW19 . . . . 114 BK86
Atherton Dr, SW19 . . . . 119 CX91
Atherton Gdns, Grays RM16 . 111 GJ77
Atherton Hts, Wem. HA0 . . . . . . 79 CJ65
Atherton Ms, E7 . . . . 86 EF65
Atherton Pl, Har. HA2 . . . . 61 CD55
Atherton Pl, Southall UB1
off Longford Av 78 CB73
Atherton Rd, E7 . . . . 68 EF64
SW13 . . . . 99 CU80
Ilford IG5 . . . . 48 EL54
Atherton St, SW11 . . . . 100 DE82
Athlone, Esher (Clay.) KT10 . . 155 CE107
Athlone Cl, E5
off Goulton Rd 66 DV63
Radlett WD7 . . . . 25 CH36
🅷 **Athlone Ho**, N6 . . . . 64 DF60
Athlone Rd, SW2 . . . . 121 DM87
Athlone St, NW5 . . . . 82 DG65
Athlon Rd, Wem. HA0 . . . . 79 CK68
Athol Cl, Pnr. HA5 . . . . 39 BV53
Athole Gdns, Enf. EN1 . . . . 30 DS43
Athol Gdns, Pnr. HA5 . . . . 39 BV53
Atholl Rd, Ilf. IG3 . . . . 70 EU59
Athol Rd, Erith DA8 . . . . 107 FC78
Athol Sq, E14 . . . . 85 EC72
Athol Way, Uxb. UB10 . . . . 76 BN69
Atkins Cl, Wok. GU21
off Greythorne Rd 166 AU118
Atkins Dr, W.Wick. BR4 . . . . . 143 ED103
Atkinson Cl, Orp. BR6
off Martindale Av 164 EU106
Atkinson Rd, E16 . . . . 86 EJ71
Atkins Rd, E10 . . . . 67 EB58
SW12 . . . . 121 DK87
Atlanta Boul, Rom. RM1 . . . . . 71 FE58
Atlantic Cl, Swans. DA10
off Craylands La 130 FY85
Atlantic Rd, SW9 . . . . 101 DN84
Atlantis Cl, Bark. IG11 . . . . 88 EV69
Atlas Gdns, SE7 . . . . 104 EJ77
Atlas Ms, E8 *off Tyssen St* 84 DT65
N7 . . . . 83 DM65
Atlas Rd, E13 . . . . 86 EG68
N11 . . . . 45 DH51
NW10 . . . . 80 CS69
Dartford DA1
off Cornwall Rd 108 FM83
Wembley HA9 . . . . 62 CQ63
Atley Rd, E3 . . . . 85 EA67
Atlip Rd, Wem. HA0 . . . . 80 CL67
Atney Rd, SW15 . . . . 99 CY84
Atria Rd, Nthwd. HA6 . . . . 39 BU50
Attenborough Cl, Wat. WD19
off Harrow Way 40 BY48
Atterbury Cl, West. TN16 . . . . 189 ER126
Atterbury Rd, N4 . . . . 65 DN58
Atterbury St, SW1 . . . . 199 N9
Attewood Av, NW10 . . . . 62 CS62
Attewood Rd, Nthlt. UB5 . . . . . 78 BY65
Attfield Cl, N20 . . . . 44 DD47
Attle Cl, Uxb. UB10 . . . . 76 BN68
Attlee Cl, Hayes UB4 . . . . 77 BV69
Thornton Heath CR7 . . . . . . 142 DQ100
Attlee Ct, Grays RM17 . . . . . . 110 GA76
Attlee Dr, Dart. DA1 . . . . 128 FN85
Attlee Rd, SE28 . . . . 88 EV73
Hayes UB4 . . . . 77 BU69
Attlee Ter, E17 . . . . 67 EB56
Attneave St, WC1 . . . . 196 D3
Attwood Cl, S.Croy. CR2 . . . . 160 DV114
Atwater Cl, SW2 . . . . 121 DN88
Atwell Cl, E10
off Belmont Pk Rd 67 EB58
Atwell Pl, T.Ditt. KT7 . . . . 137 CF102
Atwell Rd, SE15 *off Rye La* . . . 102 DU82
Atwood, Lthd. (Bkhm) KT23 . . 170 BY124
Atwood Av, Rich. TW9 . . . . 98 CN82
Atwood Rd, W6 . . . . 99 CV77
Atwoods All, Rich. TW9
off Leyborne Pk 98 CN81
Aubert Pk, N5 . . . . 65 DP63
Aubert Rd, N5 . . . . 65 DP63
Aubretia Cl, Rom. RM3 . . . . 52 FL53
Aubrey Av, St.Alb.
(Lon.Col.) AL2 . . . . 9 CJ26
Aubrey Pl, NW8
off Violet Hill 82 DC68
Aubrey Rd, E17 . . . . 67 EA55
N8 . . . . 65 DL57
W8 . . . . 81 CZ74
Aubrey Wk, W8 . . . . 81 CZ74
Auburn Cl, SE14 . . . . 103 DY80
Aubyn Hill, SE27 . . . . 122 DQ91
Aubyn Sq, SW15 . . . . 99 CU84
Auckland Av, Rain. RM13 . . . . . 89 FF69
Auckland Cl, SE19 . . . . 142 DT95
Enfield EN1 . . . . 30 DV37
Tilbury RM18 . . . . 111 GG82
Auckland Gdns, SE19 . . . . 142 DS95
Auckland Hill, SE27 . . . . 122 DQ91
Auckland Ri, SE19 . . . . 142 DS95
Auckland Rd, E10 . . . . 67 EB62
SE19 . . . . 142 DT95
SW11 . . . . 100 DE84
Caterham CR3 . . . . 176 DS122
Ilford IG1 . . . . 69 EP60
Kingston upon Thames KT1 . 138 CM98
Potters Bar EN6 . . . . 11 CY32
Auckland St, SE11
off Kennington La 101 DM78
Auden Pl, NW1 . . . . 82 DG67
Sutton SM3
off Wordsworth Dr 157 CW105
Audleigh Pl, Chig. IG7 . . . . 49 EN51
Audley Cl, N10 . . . . 45 DH52
SW11 . . . . 100 DG83
Addlestone KT15 . . . . 152 BH106
Borehamwood WD6 . . . . 26 CN41
Audley Ct, E18 . . . . 68 EF56
Pinner HA5
off Rickmansworth Rd 40 BW54
Audley Dr, E16 . . . . 205 P2
Warlingham CR6 . . . . 176 DW115
Audley Firs, Walt. KT12 . . . . . 154 BW105
Audley Gdns, Ilf. IG3 . . . . 69 ET61
Loughton IG10 . . . . 33 EQ40
Waltham Abbey EN9 . . . . 15 EC34
Audley Pl, Sutt. SM2 . . . . 158 DA108
Audley Rd, NW4 . . . . 63 CV58
W5 . . . . 80 CM71

★ Place of interest ⇌ Railway station ⊖ London Underground station DLR Docklands Light Railway station Tra Tramlink station 🅷 Hospital Riv Pedestrian ferry landing stage

Audley Rd, Enfield EN2 29 DP40
Richmond TW10 118 CM85
Audley Sq, W1 198 G2
Audley Wk, Orp. BR5 146 EW100
Audrey Cl, Beck. BR3 143 EB100
Audrey Gdns, Wem. HA0 61 CH61
Audrey Rd, Ilf. IG1 69 EP62
Audrey St, E2 84 DU68
Audric Cl, Kings.T. KT2 138 CN95
Audwick Cl, Wal.Cr. (Chsht) EN8 15 DX28
Augur Cl, Stai. TW18 113 BF92
Augurs La, E13 86 EH69
Augusta Cl, W.Mol. KT8 off Freeman Dr 136 BZ97
Augusta Rd, Twick. TW2 116 CC89
Augusta St, E14 85 EB72
August End, Slou. (Geo.Grn) SL3 74 AY72
Augustine Cl, Slou. (Colnbr.) SL3 93 BE83
Augustine Ct, Wal.Abb. EN9 off Beaulieu Dr 15 EB33
Augustine Rd, W14 99 CX76
Gravesend DA12 131 GJ87
Harrow HA3 40 CB53
Orpington BR5 146 EX97
Augustus Cl, W12 off Goldhawk Rd 99 CV75
Brentford TW8 97 CJ80
Augustus La, Orp. BR6 146 EU103
Augustus Rd, SW19 119 CY88
Augustus St, NW1 195 J1
Aultone Way, Cars. SM5 140 DF104
Sutton SM1 140 DB103
Aulton Pl, SE11 101 DN78
Aurelia Gdns, Croy. CR0 141 DM99
Aurelia Rd, Croy. CR0 141 DL100
Auriel Av, Dag. RM10 89 FD65
Auriga Ms, N16 66 DR64
Auriol Cl, Wor.Pk. KT4 off Auriol Pk Rd 138 CS104
Auriol Dr, Grnf. UB6 79 CD66
Uxbridge UB10 76 BN65
Auriol Pk Rd, Wor.Pk. KT4 138 CS104
Auriol Rd, W14 99 CY77
Austell Gdns, NW7 42 CS48
Austen Cl, SE28 88 EV74
Greenhithe DA9 129 FW85
Loughton IG10 33 ER41
Tilbury RM18 off Coleridge Rd 111 GJ82
Austen Gdns, Dart. DA1 108 FM84
Austen Ho, NW6 82 DA69
Austen Rd, Erith DA8 107 FB80
Harrow HA2 60 CB61
Austenway, Ger.Cr. (Chal.St.P.) SL9 56 AX55
Austen Way, Slou. SL3 off Ditton Rd 93 AZ79
Austenwood Cl, Ger.Cr. (Chal.St.P.) SL9 36 AW54
Austenwood La, Ger.Cr. (Chal.St.P.) SL9 36 AX54
Austin Av, Brom. BR2 144 EL99
Austin Cl, SE23 123 DZ87
Coulsdon CR5 175 DP118
Twickenham TW1 117 CJ85
Austin Ct, E6 off Kings Rd 86 EJ67
Austin Friars, EC2 197 L8
Austin Friars Pas, EC2 197 L8
Austin Friars Sq, EC2 197 L8
Austin Rd, SW11 100 DG81
Gravesend (Nthflt) DA11 131 GF88
Hayes UB3 95 BT75
Orpington BR5 146 EU100
Austin's La, Uxb. UB10 59 BR63
Austins Mead, Hem.H. (Bov.) HP3 5 BB28
Austin St, E2 197 P3
Austin Waye, Uxb. UB8 76 BJ67
Austral Cl, Sid. DA15 125 ET90
Austral Dr, Horn. RM11 72 FK59
Australia Rd, W12 81 CV73
Slough SL1 92 AV75
Austral St, SE11 200 F8
Austyn Gdns, Surb. KT5 138 CP102
Autumn Cl, SW19 120 DC93
Enfield EN1 30 DU39
Autumn Dr, Sutt. SM2 158 DB109
Autumn St, E3 85 EA67
Auxiliaries Way, Uxb. UB9 57 BF57
Avalon Cl, SW20 139 CY96
W13 79 CG71
Enfield EN2 29 DN40
Orpington BR6 146 EX104
Watford WD25 8 BY32
Avalon Rd, SW6 100 DB81
W13 79 CG70
Orpington BR6 146 EW103
Avard Gdns, Orp. BR6 163 EQ105
Avarn Rd, SW17 120 DF93
Avebury Ct, N1 off Poole St 84 DR67
Avebury Pk, Surb. KT6 137 CK101
Avebury Rd, E11 off Southwest Rd 67 ED60
SW19 139 CZ95
Orpington BR6 145 ER104
Avebury St, N1 off Poole St 84 DR67
AVELEY, S.Ock. RM15 91 FR73
Aveley Bypass, S.Ock. RM15 90 FQ73
Aveley Cl, Erith DA8 107 FF79
South Ockendon (Aveley) RM15 91 FR74
Aveley Rd, Rom. RM1 71 FD56
Upminster RM14 90 FP65
Aveline St, SE11 200 D10
Aveling Cl, Pur. CR8 159 DM113
Aveling Pk Rd, E17 47 EA54
Avelon Rd, Rain. RM13 89 FG67
Romford RM5 51 FD51
Ave Maria La, EC4 196 G9
Avenell Rd, N5 65 DP62
Avening Rd, SW18 off Brathway Rd 120 DA87
Avening Ter, SW18 120 DA86
Avenons Rd, E13 86 EG70
Avenue, The, E4 47 ED51
E11 (Leytonstone) 68 EF61
E11 (Wanstead) 68 EH58
N3 44 DA54
N8 65 DN55
N10 45 DJ54
N11 45 DH49
N17 46 DS54
NW6 81 CX67
SE10 103 ED80
SW4 120 DG85
SW11 120 DE87
SW18 120 DE87
W4 98 CS76
W13 79 CH73
Addlestone (New Haw) KT15 152 BG110
Barnet EN5 27 CY41
Beckenham BR3 143 EB95
Betchworth (Brock.) RH3 182 CN134
Bexley DA5 126 EX87
Brentwood CM13 53 FX51
Bromley BR1 144 EK97
Bushey WD23 24 BZ42
Carshalton SM5 158 DG108
Coulsdon CR5 175 DK115
Croydon CR0 142 DS104
Egham TW20 113 BB91
Epsom KT17 157 CV108
Esher (Clay.) KT10 155 CE107
Gravesend DA11 131 GG88
Greenhithe DA9 109 FV84
Hampton TW12 116 BZ93
Harrow HA3 41 CF53
Hornchurch RM12 72 FJ61
Hounslow TW3 116 CB85
Hounslow (Cran.) TW5 95 BU81
Isleworth TW7 97 CD79
Keston BR2 144 EK104
Leatherhead KT22 155 CF112
Loughton IG10 32 EK44
Northwood HA6 39 BQ51
Orpington BR6 145 ET103
Orpington (St.P.Cray) BR5 126 EV94
Pinner HA5 60 BZ58
Pinner (Hatch End) HA5 40 CA52
Potters Bar EN6 11 CZ30
Radlett WD7 9 CG33
Richmond TW9 98 CM82
Romford RM1 71 FD56
Slough (Datchet) SL3 92 AV81
Staines TW18 134 BH95
Staines (Wrays.) TW19 92 AX83
Sunbury-on-Thames TW16 135 BV95
Surbiton KT5 138 CM100
Sutton SM2 157 CZ109
Sutton (Cheam) SM3 157 CW108
Tadworth KT20 173 CV122
Twickenham TW1 117 CJ85
Uxbridge (Cowley) UB8 76 BK70
Uxbridge (Ickhm) UB10 58 BN63
Waltham Abbey (Nazeing) EN9 16 EJ25
Watford WD17 23 BU40
Wembley HA9 62 CM61
West Drayton UB7 94 BL76
West Wickham BR4 143 EC101
Westerham TN16 179 EM122
Whyteleafe CR3 176 DU119
Windsor (Old Wind.) SL4 112 AV85
Woking (Chobham) GU24 150 AT109
Worcester Park KT4 139 CT103
Avenue App, Kings L. WD4 6 BN30
Avenue Cl, N14 29 DJ44
NW8 82 DE67
Hounslow TW5 off The Avenue 95 BU81
Romford RM3 52 FM52
Tadworth KT20 173 CV122
West Drayton UB7 94 BK76
Avenue Ct, Tad. KT20 off The Avenue 173 CV123
Avenue Cres, W3 98 CP75
Hounslow TW5 95 BV80
Avenue Dr, Slou. SL3 75 AZ71
Avenue Elmers, Surb. KT6 138 CL99
Avenue Gdns, SE25 142 DU97
SW14 98 CS83
W3 98 CP75
Hounslow TW5 off The Avenue 95 BU80
Teddington TW11 117 CF94
Avenue Gate, Loug. IG10 32 EJ44
Avenue Ind Est, E4 47 DZ51
Romford RM3 52 FK54
Avenue Ms, N10 65 DH55
Avenue Pk Rd, SE27 121 DP89
Avenue Ri, Bushey WD23 24 CA43
Tra Avenue Road 143 DX96
Avenue Rd, E7 68 EH64
N6 65 DJ59
N12 44 DC49
N14 45 DH45
N15 66 DR57
NW3 82 DD66
NW8 82 DD66
NW10 81 CT68
SE20 142 DW95
SE25 142 DU96
SW16 141 DK96
SW20 139 CV96
W3 98 CP75
Banstead SM7 174 DB115
Beckenham BR3 142 DW95
Belvedere DA17 107 FC77
Bexleyheath DA7 106 EY83
Brentford TW8 97 CJ78
Brentwood CM14 54 FW49
Caterham CR3 176 DR122
Cobham KT11 170 BX116
Epping (They.B.) CM16 33 ER36
Epsom KT18 156 CR114
Erith DA8 107 FC80
Feltham TW13 115 BT90
Hampton TW12 136 CB95
Isleworth TW7 97 CF81
Kingston upon Thames KT1 138 CL97
New Malden KT3 138 CS98
Avenue Rd, Pinner HA5 60 BY55
Romford (Chad.Hth) RM6 70 EV59
Romford (Harold Wd) RM3 52 FM52
Sevenoaks TN13 191 FJ123
Southall UB1 96 BZ75
Staines TW18 113 BD92
Sutton SM2 158 DA110
Teddington TW11 117 CG94
Wallington SM6 159 DJ108
Westerham (Tats.) TN16 178 EL120
Woodford Green IG8 48 EJ51
Avenue S, Surb. KT5 138 CM101
Avenue Ter, N.Mal. KT3 off Kingston Rd 138 CQ97
Watford WD19 24 BY44
Averil Gro, SW16 121 DP93
Averill St, W6 99 CX79
Avern Gdns, W.Mol. KT8 136 CB98
Avern Rd, W.Mol. KT8 136 CB99
Avery Fm Row, SW1 198 G9
Avery Gdns, Ilf. IG2 69 EM57
AVERY HILL, SE9 125 EQ86
★ Avery Hill Pk, SE9 125 EQ86
Avery Hill Rd, SE9 125 ER86
Avery Row, W1 195 H10
Avey La, Loug. IG10 32 EH39
Waltham Abbey EN9 31 ED36
Aviary Cl, E16 86 EF71
Aviary Rd, Wok. GU22 168 BG116
Aviator Pk, Add. KT15 off Station Rd 134 BK104
Aviemore Cl, Beck. BR3 143 DZ99
Aviemore Way, Beck. BR3 143 DY99
Avignon Rd, SE4 103 DX83
Avington Ct, SE1 off Old Kent Rd 102 DS77
Avington Gro, SE20 122 DW94
Avington Way, SE15 off Daniel Gdns 102 DT80
Avion Cres, NW9 43 CU53
Avior Dr, Nthwd. HA6 39 BT49
Avis Gro, Croy. CR0 161 DY110
Avis Sq, E1 85 DX72
Avoca Rd, SW17 120 DG91
Avocet Ms, SE28 105 ER76
Avon Cl, Add. KT15 152 BG107
Gravesend DA12 131 GK89
Hayes UB4 78 BW70
Sutton SM1 158 DC105
Watford WD25 8 BW34
Worcester Park KT4 139 CU103
Avon Ct, Grnf. UB6 off Braund Av 78 CB70
Avondale Av, N12 44 DB50
NW2 62 CS62
Barnet EN4 44 DF46
Esher KT10 137 CG104
Staines TW18 113 BF94
Worcester Park KT4 139 CT102
Avondale Cl, Loug. IG10 49 EM45
Walton-on-Thames KT12 off Pleasant Pl 154 BW106
Avondale Ct, E11 68 EE60
E16 off Avondale Rd 86 EE71
E18 48 EH53
Avondale Cres, Enf. EN3 31 DY41
Ilford IG4 68 EK57
Avondale Dr, Hayes UB3 77 BU74
Loughton IG10 49 EM45
Avondale Gdns, Houns. TW4 116 BZ85
Avondale Ms, Brom. BR1 off Avondale Rd 124 EG93
Avondale Pk Gdns, W11 81 CY73
Avondale Pk Rd, W11 81 CY73
Avondale Pavement, SE1 off Avondale Sq 102 DU78
Avondale Ri, SE15 102 DT83
Avondale Rd, E16 86 EE71
E17 67 EA59
N3 44 DC53
N13 45 DN47
N15 65 DP57
SE9 124 EL89
SW14 98 CR83
SW19 120 DB92
Ashford TW15 114 BK90
Bromley BR1 124 EE93
Harrow HA3 61 CF55
South Croydon CR2 160 DQ107
Welling DA16 106 EW82
Avondale Sq, SE1 102 DU78
Avon Grn, S.Ock. RM15 91 FV72
Avonley Rd, SE14 102 DW80
Avonmead, Wok. GU21 off Silversmiths Way 166 AW118
Avon Ms, Pnr. HA5 40 BZ53
Avonmore Gdns, W14 off Avonmore Rd 99 CZ77
Avonmore Pl, W14 off Avonmore Rd 99 CY77
Avonmore Rd, W14 99 CZ77
Avonmouth Rd, Dart. DA1 128 FK85
Avonmouth St, SE1 201 H6
Avon Path, S.Croy. CR2 160 DQ107
Avon Pl, SE1 201 J5
Avon Rd, E17 67 ED55
SE4 103 EA83
Greenford UB6 78 CA70
Sunbury-on-Thames TW16 115 BT94
Upminster RM14 73 FR58
Avonstowe Cl, Orp. BR6 145 EQ104
Avontar Rd, S.Ock. RM15 91 FV70
Avon Way, E18 68 EG55
Avonwick Rd, Houns. TW3 96 CB82
Avril Way, E4 47 EC50
Avro Way, Wall. SM6 159 DL108
Weybridge KT13 152 BL110
Awlfield Av, N17 46 DR53
Awliscombe Rd, Well. DA16 105 ET82
Axe St, Bark. IG11 87 EQ67
Axholme Av, Edg. HA8 42 CN53
Axis Pk, Slou. (Langley) SL3 93 BB77
Axminster Cres, Well. DA16 106 EW81
Axminster Rd, N7 65 DL62
Axtaine Rd, Orp. BR5 146 EX101
Axtane, Grav. (Sthflt) DA13 130 FZ94
Axtane Cl, Dart. (Sutt.H.) DA4 148 FQ96
Axwood, Epsom KT18 172 CQ115
Aybrook St, W1 194 F7
Aycliffe Cl, Brom. BR1 145 EM98
Aycliffe Rd, W12 81 CT74
Borehamwood WD6 26 CL39
Ayebridges Av, Egh. TW20 113 BC94
Aylands Cl, Wem. HA9 off Preston Rd 62 CL61
Aylands Rd, Enf. EN3 30 DW36
Aylesbury Cl, E7 off Atherton Rd 86 EF65
Aylesbury Ct, Sutt. SM1 off Benhill Wd Rd 140 DC104
Aylesbury Est, SE17 off Villa St 102 DR78
Aylesbury Rd, SE17 102 DR78
Bromley BR2 144 EG97
Aylesbury St, EC1 196 F5
NW10 62 CR62
Aylesford Av, Beck. BR3 143 DY99
Aylesford St, SW1 199 M10
Aylesham Cen, The, SE15 102 DU81
Aylesham Cl, NW7 43 CU52
Aylesham Rd, Orp. BR6 145 ET101
Ayles Rd, Hayes UB4 77 BV69
Aylestone Av, NW6 81 CX67
Aylesworth Spur, Wind. (Old Wind.) SL4 112 AV87
Aylett Rd, SE25 142 DV98
Isleworth TW7 97 CE82
Upminster RM14 72 FQ61
Ayley Cft, Enf. EN1 30 DU43
Ayliffe Cl, Kings.T. KT1 off Cambridge Gdns 138 CN96
Aylmer Cl, Stan. HA7 41 CG49
Aylmer Dr, Stan. HA7 41 CG49
Aylmer Par, N2 64 DF57
Aylmer Rd, E11 68 EF60
N2 64 DE57
W12 98 CS75
Dagenham RM8 70 EY62
Ayloffe Rd, Dag. RM9 88 EZ65
Ayloffs Cl, Horn. RM11 72 FL57
Ayloffs Wk, Horn. RM11 72 FK57
Aylsham Dr, Uxb. UB10 59 BR62
Aylsham La, Rom. RM3 52 FJ49
Aylton Est, SE16 202 G5
Aylward Rd, SE23 123 DX89
SW20 139 CZ96
Aylwards Ri, Stan. HA7 41 CG49
Aylward St, E1 84 DW72
Aylwyn Est, SE1 201 P6
Aymer Cl, Stai. TW18 133 BE95
Aymer Dr, Stai. TW18 133 BE95
Aynhoe Rd, W14 99 CX77
Aynho St, Wat. WD18 23 BV43
Aynscombe Angle, Orp. BR6 146 EV101
Aynscombe La, SW14 98 CQ83
Aynscombe Path, SW14 off Thames Bk 98 CQ82
Ayot Path, Borwd. WD6 26 CN37
Ayr Ct, W3 off Monks Dr 80 CN71
Ayres Cl, E13 86 EG69
Ayres Cres, NW10 80 CR66
Ayres St, SE1 201 J4
Ayr Grn, Rom. RM1 51 FE52
Ayron Rd, S.Ock. RM15 91 FV70
Ayrsome Rd, N16 66 DS62
Ayrton Rd, SW7 off Wells Way 100 DD76
Ayr Way, Rom. RM1 51 FE52
Aysgarth Ct, Sutt. SM1 off Sutton Common Rd 140 DB104
Aysgarth Rd, SE21 122 DS86
Aytoun Pl, SW9 101 DM82
Aytoun Rd, SW9 101 DM82
Azalea Cl, W7 79 CF74
Ilford IG1 69 EP64
St. Albans AL2 off Shenley La 9 CH26
Azalea Ct, Wok. GU22 166 AX119
Woodford Green IG8 off The Bridle Path 48 EE52
Azalea Dr, Swan. BR8 147 FD98
Azalea Wk, Pnr. HA5 59 BV57
Southall UB2 off Navigator Dr 96 CC75
Azalea Way, Slou. (Geo.Grn) SL3 off Blinco La 74 AY72
Azania Ms, NW5 65 DH64
Azenby Rd, SE15 102 DT82
Azile Everitt Ho, SE18 off Blendon Ter 105 EQ78
Azof St, SE10 205 J9

B

Baalbec Rd, N5 65 DP64
Babbacombe Cl, Chess. KT9 155 CK106
Babbacombe Gdns, Ilf. IG4 68 EL56
Babbacombe Rd, Brom. BR1 144 EG95
Baber Dr, Felt. TW14 116 BW86
Babington Ri, Wem. HA9 80 CN65
Babington Rd, NW4 63 CV56
SW16 121 DK92
Dagenham RM8 70 EW64
Hornchurch RM12 71 FH60
Babmaes St, SW1 199 L1
Babylon La, Tad. (Lwr Kgswd) KT20 184 DA127
Bacchus Wk, N1 197 M1
Bachelor's La, Wok. GU23 168 BN124
Baches St, N1 197 L3
Back Ch La, E1 84 DU73
Back Grn, Walt. KT12 154 BW107
Back Hill, EC1 196 D5
Backhouse Pl, SE17 201 N9
Back La, N8 65 DL57
NW3 off Heath St 64 DC63
Bexley DA5 126 FA87
Brentford TW8 97 CK79
Chalfont St. Giles HP8 36 AU48
Edgware HA8 42 CQ53
Grays (N.Stfd) RM16 91 FW74
Purfleet RM19 109 FS76
Richmond TW10 117 CJ90
Rickmansworth (Chenies) WD3 21 BB38
Romford RM6 off St. Chad's Rd 70 EY59
Back La, Sevenoaks (Godden Grn) TN15 191 FN124
Sevenoaks (Ide Hill) TN14 190 FC126
Watford (Let.Hth) WD25 25 CE39
Backley Gdns, SE25 142 DU100
Back Path, Red. RH1 186 DQ133
Back Rd, Sid. DA14 126 EU91
Bacon Gro, SE1 201 P7
Bacon La, NW9 62 CP56
Edgware HA8 42 CN53
Bacon Link, Rom. RM5 51 FB51
Bacons Dr, Pot.B. (Cuffley) EN6 13 DL29
Bacons La, N6 64 DG60
Bacons Mead, Uxb. (Denh.) UB9 58 BG61
Bacon St, E1 84 DT70
E2 84 DT70
Bacon Ter, Dag. RM8 off Fitzstephen Rd 70 EV64
Bacton, NW5 64 DG64
Bacton St, E2 off Roman Rd 84 DW69
Badburgham Ct, Wal.Abb. EN9 16 EF33
Baddeley Cl, Enf. EN3 off Burton Dr 31 EA37
Baddow Cl, Dag. RM10 88 FA67
Woodford Green IG8 48 EK51
Baddow Wk, N1 84 DQ67
Baden Cl, Stai. TW18 114 BG94
Baden Pl, SE1 201 K4
Baden Powell Cl, Dag. RM9 88 EY67
Surbiton KT6 138 CM103
Baden Powell Rd, Sev. TN13 190 FE121
Baden Rd, N8 65 DK56
Ilford IG1 69 EP64
Bader Cl, Ken. CR8 176 DR115
Bader Wk, Grav. (Nthflt) DA11 130 GE90
Bader Way, Rain. RM13 89 FG65
Badger Cl, Felt. TW13 off Sycamore Cl 115 BU90
Hounslow TW4 96 BW83
Ilford IG2 69 EQ59
Badgers Cl, Ashf. TW15 off Fordbridge Rd 114 BM92
Borehamwood WD6 off Kingsley Av 26 CM40
Enfield EN2 29 DP41
Harrow HA1 61 CD58
Hayes UB3 77 BS73
Woking GU21 166 AW118
Badgers Copse, Orp. BR6 145 ET103
Worcester Park KT4 139 CT103
Badgers Cft, N20 43 CY46
SE9 125 EN90
Badgers Hill, Vir.W. GU25 132 AW99
Badgers Hole, Croy. CR0 161 DX105
Badgers La, Warl. CR6 176 DW120
BADGERS MOUNT, Sev. TN14 165 FB110
Badgers Mt, Grays (Orsett) RM16 111 GF75
Badgers Ri, Sev. (Bad.Mt) TN14 164 FA110
Badgers Rd, Sev. (Bad.Mt) TN14 165 FB110
Badgers Wk, N.Mal. KT3 138 CS96
Purley CR8 159 DK111
Rickmansworth (Chorl.) WD3 21 BF42
Whyteleafe CR3 176 DT119
Badgers Wd, Cat. CR3 186 DQ125
Badingham Dr, Lthd. (Fetch.) KT22 171 CE123
Badlis Rd, E17 47 EA54
Badlow Cl, Erith DA8 107 FE80
Badma Cl, N9 off Hudson Way 46 DW48
Badminton Cl, Borwd. WD6 26 CN40
Harrow HA1 61 CE56
Northolt UB5 78 CA65
Badminton Ms, E16 205 N2
Badminton Rd, SW12 120 DG86
Badric Ct, SW11 off Yelverton Rd 100 DD82
Badsworth Rd, SE5 102 DQ80
Baffin Way, E14 204 E1
Bagley Cl, West Dr. UB7 94 BL75
Bagley's La, SW6 100 DB81
Bagleys Spring, Rom. RM6 70 EY56
Bagot Cl, Ashtd. KT21 172 CM116
Bagshot Ct, SE18 off Prince Imperial Rd 105 EN81
Bagshot Rd, Egh. (Eng.Grn) TW20 112 AW94
Enfield EN1 46 DT45
Bagshot St, SE17 102 DS78
Bahram Rd, Epsom KT19 156 CR110
Baildon St, SE8 103 DZ80
Bailey Cl, E4 47 EC49
N11 45 DK52
Purfleet RM19 off Gabion Av 109 FR77
Bailey Cres, Chess. KT9 off Nigel Fisher Way 155 CK107
Bailey Ms, SW2 121 DN85
Bailey Pl, SE26 123 DX93
Baillie Cl, Rain. RM13 89 FH70
Baillies Wk, W5 off Liverpool Rd 97 CK75
Bainbridge Cl, Rich. (Ham) TW10 off Latchmere Cl 118 CL92
Bainbridge Rd, Dag. RM9 70 EZ63
Bainbridge St, WC1 195 N8
Baines Cl, S.Croy. CR2 off Brighton Rd 160 DQ106
Bainton Mead, Wok. GU21 166 AU117
Baird Av, Sthl. UB1 78 CB73
Baird Cl, E10 off Marconi Rd 67 EA60
NW9 62 CQ58
Bushey WD23 off Ashfield Av 24 CB44
Baird Gdns, SE19 122 DS91
Baird Rd, Enf. EN1 30 DV42
Baird St, EC1 197 J4
Bairny Wd App, Wdf.Grn. IG8 off Broadway Cl 48 EH51
Bairstow Cl, Borwd. WD6 26 CL39
Baizdon Rd, SE3 104 EE82
Bakeham La, Egh. (Eng.Grn) TW20 112 AW94
Baker Boy La, Croy. CR0 161 DZ112

★ Place of interest · Railway station · London Underground station · DLR Docklands Light Railway station · Tra Tramlink station · H Hospital · Riv Pedestrian ferry landing stage

Baker Hill Cl, Grav. (Nthflt) DA11 131 GF91
Baker La, Mitch. CR4 140 DG96
Baker Pas, NW10 off Acton La 80 CS67
Baker Rd, NW10 80 CS67
SE18 104 EL80
Bakers Av, E17 67 EB58
Bakers Cl, Ken. CR8 160 DQ114
Bakers Ct, SE25 142 DS97
Bakers End, SW20 139 CY96
Bakers Fld, N7 off Crayford Rd 65 DK63
Bakers Gdns, Cars. SM5 140 DE103
Bakers Hall Ct, EC3 201 N1
Bakers Hill, E5 66 DW60
Barnet EN5 28 DB40
Bakers La, N6 64 DF57
Epping CM16 17 ET30
Bakers Mead, Gdse. RH9 186 DW130
Baker's Ms, W1 194 F8
Bakers Ms, Orp. BR6 163 ET107
Bakers Pas, NW3 off Heath St 64 DC63
Baker's Rents, E2 197 P3
Bakers Rd, Uxb. UB8 76 BK66
Waltham Cross (Chsht) EN7 14 DV30
Bakers Row, E15 86 EE68
Baker's Row, EC1 196 D5
⊖ Baker Street 194 E6
Baker St, NW1 194 E5
W1 194 E6
Enfield EN1 30 DR41
Potters Bar EN6 27 CY35
Weybridge KT13 152 BN105
Bakers Wd, Uxb. (Denh.) UB9 57 BD60
Bakers Yd, EC1 off Baker's Row 83 DN70
Uxbridge UB8 off Bakers Rd 76 BK66
Bakery Cl, SW9 101 DM81
Bakery Path, Edg. HA8 off Station Rd 42 CP51
Bakery Pl, SW11 off Altenburg Gdns 100 DF84
Bakewell Way, N.Mal. KT3 138 CS96
Balaams La, N14 45 DK47
Balaam St, E13 86 EG69
Balaclava Rd, SE1 202 A9
Surbiton KT6 137 CJ101
Bala Grn, NW9 off Snowdon Dr 62 CS58
Balcaskie Rd, SE9 125 EM85
Balchen Rd, SE3 104 EK82
Balchier Rd, SE22 122 DV86
Balcombe Cl, Bexh. DA6 106 EX84
Balcombe St, NW1 194 D5
Balcon Ct, W5 off Boileau Rd 80 CM72
Balcon Way, Borwd. WD6 26 CQ39
Balcorne St, E9 84 DW66
Balder Ri, SE12 124 EH89
Balderton St, W1 194 G9
Baldocks Rd, Epp. (They.B.) CM16 33 ES35
Baldock St, E3 85 EB68
Baldock Way, Borwd. WD6 26 CM39
Baldry Gdns, SW16 121 DL93
Baldwin Cres, SE5 102 DQ81
Baldwin Gdns, Houns. TW3 off Chamberlain Gdns 96 CC81
Baldwin's Gdns, EC1 196 D6
Baldwins Hill, Loug. IG10 33 EM40
Baldwins La, Rick. (Crox.Grn) WD3 22 BN42
Baldwin St, EC1 197 K3
Baldwin Ter, N1 84 DQ68
Baldwyn Gdns, W3 80 CQ73
Baldwyns Pk, Bex. DA5 127 FD89
Baldwyns Rd, Bex. DA5 127 FD89
Bale Rd, E1 85 DY71
Balfern Gro, W4 98 CS78
Balfern St, SW11 100 DE81
Balfe St, N1 196 A1
Balfont Cl, S.Croy. CR2 160 DU113
Balfour Av, W7 79 CF74
Woking GU22 166 AY122
Balfour Business Cen, Sthl. UB2 96 BX76
Balfour Gro, N20 44 DF48
Balfour Ho, W10 off St. Charles Sq 81 CX71
Balfour Ms, N9 off The Broadway 46 DU48
W1 198 G2
Balfour Pl, SW15 99 CV84
W1 198 G1
Balfour Rd, N5 66 DQ63
SE25 142 DU98
SW19 120 DB94
W3 80 CQ71
W13 97 CG75
Bromley BR2 144 EK99
Carshalton SM5 158 DF108
Grays RM17 110 GC77
Harrow HA1 61 CD57
Hounslow TW3 96 CB83
Ilford IG1 69 EP61
Southall UB2 96 BX76
Weybridge KT13 152 BN105
Balfour St, SE17 201 K8
Balfron Twr, E14 off St. Leonards Rd 85 EC72
Balgonie Rd, E4 47 ED46
Balgores Cres, Rom. RM2 71 FH55
Balgores La, Rom. RM2 71 FH55
Balgores Sq, Rom. RM2 71 FH56
Balgowan Cl, N.Mal. KT3 138 CS99
Balgowan Rd, Beck. BR3 143 DY97
Balgowan St, SE18 105 ET77
BALHAM, SW12 120 DF88
⇌ Balham 121 DH88
⊖ Balham 121 DH88
Balham Continental Mkt, SW12 off Shipka Rd 121 DH88
Balham Gro, SW12 120 DG87
Balham High Rd, SW12 120 DG88
SW17 120 DG89
Balham Hill, SW12 121 DH87
Balham New Rd, SW12 121 DH87
Balham Pk Rd, SW12 120 DF88
Balham Rd, N9 46 DU47
Balham Sta Rd, SW12 121 DH88
Balkan Wk, E1 202 D1
Balladier Wk, E14 85 EB71
Ballamore Rd, Brom. BR1 124 EG90
Ballance Rd, E9 85 DX65
Ballands N, The, Lthd. KT22 171 CE122
Ballands S, The, Lthd. KT22 171 CE123
Ballantine St, SW18 100 DC84
Ballantyne Dr, Tad. (Kgswd) KT20 173 CZ121
Ballard Cl, Kings.T. KT2 118 CR94
Ballards Cl, Dag. RM10 89 FB67
Ballards Fm Rd, Croy. CR0 160 DU107
South Croydon CR2 160 DU107
Ballards Grn, Tad. KT20 173 CY119
Ballards La, N3 44 DA53
N12 44 DA53
Oxted RH8 188 EJ129
Ballards Ms, Edg. HA8 42 CN51
Ballards Ri, S.Croy. CR2 160 DU107
Ballards Rd, NW2 63 CU61
Dagenham RM10 89 FB67
Ballards Way, Croy. CR0 160 DV107
South Croydon CR2 160 DU107
Ballast Quay, SE10 204 G10
Ballater Cl, Wat. WD19 40 BW49
Ballater Rd, SW2 101 DL84
South Croydon CR2 160 DT106
Ball Ct, EC3 off Cornhill 84 DR72
Ballenger Ct, Wat. WD18 23 BV41
Ballina St, SE23 123 DX86
Ballingdon Rd, SW11 120 DG86
Ballinger Pt, E3 off Bromley High St 85 EB69
Balliol Av, E4 47 ED49
Balliol Rd, N17 46 DS53
W10 81 CW72
Welling DA16 106 EV82
Balloch Rd, SE6 123 ED88
Ballogie Av, NW10 62 CS63
Ballow Cl, SE5 off Harris St 102 DS80
Balls Pond Pl, N1 off Balls Pond Rd 84 DR65
Balls Pond Rd, N1 84 DR65
Balmain Cl, W5 79 CK74
Balmer Rd, E3 85 DZ68
Balmes Rd, N1 84 DR67
Balmoral Av, N11 44 DG50
Beckenham BR3 143 DY98
Balmoral Cl, SW15 off Westleigh Av 119 CX86
St. Albans (Park St) AL2 8 CC28
Balmoral Ct, Wor.Pk. KT4 139 CV103
Balmoral Cres, W.Mol. KT8 136 CA97
Balmoral Dr, Borwd. WD6 26 CR43
Hayes UB4 77 BT71
Southall UB1 78 BZ70
Woking GU22 167 BC116
Balmoral Gdns, W13 97 CG76
Bexley DA5 126 EZ87
Ilford IG3 69 ET60
South Croydon CR2 160 DR110
Balmoral Gro, N7 83 DM65
Balmoral Ms, W12 99 CT75
Balmoral Rd, E7 68 EJ63
E10 67 EB61
NW2 81 CV65
Abbots Langley WD5 7 BU32
Brentwood (Pilg.Hat.) CM15 54 FV44
Dartford (Sutt.H.) DA4 128 FP94
Enfield EN3 31 DX36
Harrow HA2 60 CA63
Hornchurch RM12 72 FK62
Kingston upon Thames KT1 138 CM98
Romford RM2 71 FH56
Watford WD24 24 BW38
Worcester Park KT4 139 CV104
Balmoral Way, Sutt. SM2 158 DA110
Balmore Cl, E14 85 EC72
Balmore Cres, Barn. EN4 28 DG43
Balmore St, N19 65 DH61
Balmuir Gdns, SW15 99 CW84
Balnacraig Av, NW10 62 CS63
Balniel Gate, SW1 199 N10
Balquhain Cl, Ashtd. KT21 171 CK117
Baltic Cl, SW19 120 DD94
Baltic Ct, SE16 203 J4
Baltic Pl, N1 off Kingsland Rd 84 DS67
Baltic St E, EC1 197 H5
Baltic St W, EC1 197 H5
Baltic Wf, Grav. DA11 off West St 131 GG86
Baltimore Pl, Well. DA16 105 ET82
Balvaird Pl, SW1 101 DK78
Balvernie Gro, SW18 119 CZ87
Bamber Ho, Bark. IG11 off St. Margarets 87 EQ67
Bamborough Gdns, W12 99 CW75
Bamford Av, Wem. HA0 80 CM67
Bamford Ct, E15 off Clays La 67 EB64
Bamford Rd, Bark. IG11 87 EQ65
Bromley BR1 123 EC92
Bamford Way, Rom. RM5 51 FB50
Bampfylde Cl, Wall. SM6 141 DJ104
Bampton Dr, NW7 43 CU52
Bampton Rd, SE23 123 DX90
Romford RM3 52 FL53
Bampton Way, Wok. GU21 166 AU118
Banavie Gdns, Beck. BR3 143 EC95
Banbury Cl, Enf. EN2 off Holtwhites Hill 29 DP39
Banbury Ct, WC2 195 P10
Sutton SM2 158 DA108
Banbury Enterprise Cen, Croy. CR0 off Factory La 141 DP103
Banbury Rd, E9 85 DX66
E17 47 DX52
Banbury St, SW11 100 DE82
Watford WD18 23 BU43
Banbury Vil, Grav. DA13 130 FZ94
Banbury Wk, Nthlt. UB5 off Brabazon Rd 78 CA68
Banchory Rd, SE3 104 EH80
Bancroft Av, N2 64 DE57
Buckhurst Hill IG9 48 EG47
Bancroft Chase, Horn. RM12 off Upper Rainham Rd 71 FF61
Bancroft Cl, Ashf. TW15 off Feltham Hill Rd 114 BN92
Bancroft Ct, Nthlt. UB5 78 BW67
Bancroft Ct, Reigate RH2 184 DB134
Bancroft Gdns, Har. HA3 40 CC53
Orpington BR6 145 ET102
Bancroft Rd, E1 84 DW69
Harrow HA3 40 CC54
Reigate RH2 184 DA134
Band La, Egh. TW20 113 AZ92
Bandon Cl, Uxb. UB10 76 BM67
Bandon Ri, Wall. SM6 159 DK106
Banfield Rd, SE15 102 DV84
Bangalore St, SW15 99 CW83
Bangor Cl, Nthlt. UB5 60 CB64
Bangors Cl, Iver SL0 75 BE72
Bangors Rd N, Iver SL0 75 BD67
Bangors Rd S, Iver SL0 75 BE71
Banim St, W6 99 CV76
Banister Rd, W10 81 CX69
⊖ Bank 197 K9
DLR Bank 197 K9
Bank, The, N6 off Cholmeley Pk 65 DH60
Bank Av, Mitch. CR4 140 DD96
Bank Ct, Dart. DA1 off High St 128 FL86
Bank End, SE1 201 J2
Bankfoot, Grays (Bad.Dene) RM17 110 FZ77
Bankfoot Rd, Brom. BR1 124 EE91
Bankhurst Rd, SE6 123 DZ87
Bank La, SW15 118 CS85
Kingston upon Thames KT2 118 CL94
Bank Ms, Sutt. SM1 off Sutton Ct Rd 158 DC107
★ Bank of England, EC2 197 K9
★ Bank of England Mus, EC2 197 L9
Bank Pl, Brwd. CM14 off High St 54 FW47
Banksian Wk, Islw. TW7 97 CE81
Banksia Rd, N18 46 DW50
Bankside, SE1 201 H1
Enfield EN2 29 DP39
Gravesend (Nthflt) DA11 130 GC86
Sevenoaks (Dunt.Grn) TN13 190 FE121
South Croydon CR2 160 DT107
Southall UB1 78 BX74
Woking GU21 off Wyndham Rd 166 AV118
Bankside Av, Nthlt. UB5 off Townson Av 77 BU68
Bankside Cl, Bex. DA5 127 FD91
Carshalton SM5 158 DE107
Isleworth TW7 97 CF84
Uxbridge UB8 off Summerhouse La 38 BG51
Westerham (Bigg.H.) TN16 178 EJ118
Bankside Dr, T.Ditt. KT7 137 CH102
★ Bankside Gall, SE1 200 G1
RIV Bankside Pier 201 H1
Bankside Rd, Ilf. IG1 69 EQ64
Bankside Way, SE19 off Lunham Rd 122 DS93
Banks La, Bexh. DA6 106 EZ84
Epping CM16 18 EY32
Bank's La, Lthd. (Eff.) KT24 169 BV122
Banks Rd, Borwd. WD6 26 CQ40
Bank St, E14 204 A3
Gravesend DA12 131 GH86
Sevenoaks TN13 191 FH125
Banks Way, E12 off Grantham Rd 69 EN63
Bankton Rd, SW2 101 DN84
Bankwell Rd, SE13 104 EE84
Bann Cl, S.Ock. RM15 91 FV73
Banner Cl, Purf. RM19 off Brimfield Rd 109 FR77
Bannerman Ho, SW8 101 DM79
Banner St, EC1 197 J5
Banning St, SE10 104 EE78
Bannister Cl, SW2 off Ewen Cres 121 DN88
Greenford UB6 61 CD64
Slough SL3 92 AY75
Bannister Dr, Brwd. (Hutt.) CM13 55 GC44
Bannister Gdns, Orp. BR5 off Main Rd 146 EW97
Bannister Ho, E9 off Homerton High St 67 DX64
Bannockburn Rd, SE18 105 ES77
Bannow Cl, Epsom KT19 156 CS105
★ Banqueting Ho, SW1 199 P3
BANSTEAD 174 DB115
⇌ Banstead 157 CY114
Banstead Gdns, N9 46 DS48
Banstead Pl, Bans. SM7 174 DC116
Banstead Rd, Bans. SM7 157 CX112
Carshalton SM5 158 DE107
Caterham CR3 176 DR121
Epsom KT17 157 CV110
Purley CR8 159 DN111
Banstead Rd S, Sutt. SM2 158 DD110
Banstead St, SE15 102 DW83
Banstead Way, Wall. SM6 159 DL106
Banstock Rd, Edg. HA8 42 CP51
Banting Dr, N21 29 DM43
Banton Cl, Enf. EN1 off Central Av 30 DV40
Bantry St, SE5 102 DR80
Banwell Rd, Bex. DA5 off Woodside La 126 EX86
Banyard Rd, SE16 202 E7
Banyards, Horn. RM11 72 FL56
Bapchild Pl, Orp. BR5 146 EW98
Baptist Gdns, NW5 off Queen's Cres 82 DG65
Barandon Wk, W11 81 CX73
Barbara Brosnan Ct, NW8 off Grove End Rd 82 DD68
Barbara Cl, Shep. TW17 135 BP99
Barbara Hucklesby Cl, N22 off The Sandlings 45 DP54
Barbauld Rd, N16 66 DS62
Barbel Cl, Wal.Cr. EN8 15 EA34
Barber Cl, N21 45 DN45
Barberry Cl, Rom. RM3 52 FJ52
Barber's All, E13 86 EH69
Barbers Rd, E15 85 EB68
BARBICAN, EC2 197 H7
⇌ Barbican 196 G6
⊖ Barbican 196 G6
★ Barbican Arts & Conf Cen, EC2 197 J6
Barbican Rd, Grnf. UB6 78 CB72
Barb Ms, W6 99 CW76
Barbon Cl, WC1 196 B6
Barbot Cl, N9 46 DU48
Barchard St, SW18 120 DB85
Barchester Cl, W7 79 CF74
Uxbridge UB8 76 BJ70
Barchester Rd, Har. HA3 41 CD54
Slough SL3 93 AZ75
Barchester St, E14 85 EB71
Barclay Cl, SW6 100 DA80
Leatherhead (Fetch.) KT22 170 CB123
Watford WD18 23 BU44
Barclay Oval, Wdf.Grn. IG8 48 EG49
Barclay Path, E17 67 EC57
Barclay Rd, E11 68 EE60
E13 86 EJ70
E17 67 EC57
N18 46 DR51
SW6 100 DA80
Croydon CR0 142 DR104
Barclay Way, SE22 off Lordship La 122 DU87
Grays (W.Thur.) RM20 109 FT78
Barcombe Av, SW2 121 DL89
Barcombe Cl, Orp. BR5 145 ET97
Barden Cl, Uxb. (Hare.) UB9 38 BJ52
Barden St, SE18 105 ES80
Bardeswell Cl, Brwd. CM14 54 FW47
Bardfield Av, Rom. RM6 70 EX55
Bardney Rd, Mord. SM4 140 DB98
Bardolph Av, Croy. CR0 161 DZ109
Bardolph Rd, N7 65 DL63
Richmond TW9 off St. Georges Rd 98 CM83
Bardon Wk, Wok. GU21 off Bampton Way 166 AV117
Bard Rd, W10 81 CX73
Bardsey Pl, E1 off Mile End Rd 84 DW71
Bardsey Wk, N1 off Clephane Rd 84 DQ65
Bardsley Cl, Croy. CR0 142 DT104
Bardsley La, SE10 103 EC79
Barfett St, W10 81 CZ70
Barfield, Dart. (Sutt.H.) DA4 148 FP95
Barfield Av, N20 44 DE47
Barfield Rd, E11 68 EF60
Bromley BR1 145 EN97
Barfields, Loug. IG10 33 EN42
Redhill (Bletch.) RH1 185 DP133
Barfields Gdns, Loug. IG10 off Barfields 33 EN42
Barfields Path, Loug. IG10 33 EN42
Barford Cl, NW4 43 CU53
Barford St, N1 83 DN67
Barforth Rd, SE15 102 DV83
Barfreston Way, SE20 142 DV95
Bargate Cl, SE18 105 ET78
New Malden KT3 139 CU100
Barge Ho Rd, E16 87 EP74
Barge Ho St, SE1 200 E2
Bargery Rd, SE6 123 EB88
Barge Wk, E.Mol. KT8 137 CK96
Kingston upon Thames KT1 137 CK95
Walton-on-Thames KT12 136 BX97
Bargrove Cl, SE20 122 DU94
Bargrove Cres, SE6 off Elm La 123 DZ89
Barham Av, Borwd. (Elstree) WD6 26 CM41
Barham Cl, Brom. BR2 144 EL102
Chislehurst BR7 125 EP92
Gravesend DA12 131 GM88
Romford RM7 51 FB54
Wembley HA0 79 CH65
Weybridge KT13 153 BQ105
Barham Rd, SW20 119 CU94
Chislehurst BR7 125 EP92
Dartford DA1 128 FN87
South Croydon CR2 160 DQ106
Baring Cl, SE12 124 EG89
Baring Rd, SE12 124 EG87
Barnet EN4 28 DD41
Croydon CR0 142 DU102
Baring St, N1 84 DR67
Barkantine Shop Par, The, E14 203 P5
Bark Burr Rd, Grays RM16 110 FZ75
Barker Cl, N.Mal. KT3 138 CP98
Northwood HA6 39 BT52
Barker Dr, NW1 83 DJ66
Barker Ms, SW4 101 DH84
Barker Rd, Cher. KT16 133 BE101
Barker St, SW10 100 DC79
Barker Wk, SW16 121 DK90
Barker Way, SE22 off Dulwich Common 122 DU88
Barkham Rd, N17 46 DR52
Barkham Ter, SE1 200 E6
Bark Hart Rd, Orp. BR6 146 EV102
BARKING 87 EP67
⇌ Barking 87 EQ66
⊖ Barking 87 EQ66
H Barking Hosp, Bark. IG11 87 ET66
Barking Ind Pk, Bark. IG11 87 ET67
Barking Rd, E6 86 EK68
E13 86 EH70
E16 86 EF71
BARKINGSIDE, Ilf. IG6 69 EP55
⊖ Barkingside 69 ER56
Bark Pl, W2 82 DB73
Barkston Gdns, SW5 100 DB77
Barkston Path, Borwd. WD6 26 CN37
Barkwood Cl, Rom. RM7 71 FC57
Barkworth Rd, SE16 102 DV78
Barlborough St, SE14 102 DW80
Barlby Gdns, W10 81 CX70
Barlby Rd, W10 81 CX71
Barlee Cres, Uxb. UB8 76 BJ71
Barle Gdns, S.Ock. RM15 91 FV72
Barley Brow, Wat. WD25 off High Elms La 8 BW31
Barley Cl, Bushey WD23 24 CB43
Barleycorn Way, E14 85 DZ73
Hornchurch RM11 72 FM58
Barleyfields Cl, Rom. RM6 70 EV59
Barley La, Ilf. IG3 70 EU60
Romford RM6 70 EV58
Barley Mow Ct, Bet. RH3 182 CQ134
Barley Mow Pas, EC1 196 G7
W4 98 CR78
Barley Mow Rd, Egh. (Eng.Grn) TW20 112 AW92
Barley Mow Way, Shep. TW17 134 BN98
Barley Shotts Business Pk, W10 off St. Ervans Rd 81 CZ71
Barlow Cl, Wall. SM6 159 DL108
Barlow Dr, SE18 104 EL81
Barlow Pl, W1 199 J1
Barlow Rd, NW6 81 CZ65
W3 80 CP74
Hampton TW12 116 CA94
Barlow St, SE17 201 L9
Barlow Way, Rain. RM13 89 FD71
Barmeston Rd, SE6 123 EB89
Barmor Cl, Har. HA2 40 CB54
Barmouth Av, Grnf. UB6 79 CF68
Barmouth Rd, SW18 120 DC86
Croydon CR0 143 DX103
Barnabas Ct, N21 off Cheyne Wk 29 DN43
Barnabas Rd, E9 67 DX64
Barnaby Cl, Har. HA2 60 CC61
Barnaby Pl, SW7 100 DD77
Barnaby Way, Chig. IG7 49 EP48
Barnacre Cl, Uxb. UB8 off New Peachey La 76 BK72
Barnacres Rd, Hem.H. HP3 6 BM25
Barnard Cl, SE18 105 EN77
Chislehurst BR7 145 ER95
Sunbury-on-Thames TW16 off Oak Gro 115 BV94
Wallington SM6 159 DK108
Barnard Ct, Wok. GU21 off Raglan Rd 166 AS118
Barnard Gdns, Hayes UB4 77 BV70
New Malden KT3 139 CU98
Barnard Gro, E15 off Vicarage La 86 EF66
Barnard Hill, N10 44 DG54
Barnard Ms, SW11 100 DE84
Barnardo Dr, Ilf. IG6 69 EQ56
Barnardo Gdns, E1 off Devonport St 85 DX73
Barnardo St, E1 off Devonport St 85 DX72
Barnardos Village, Ilf. IG6 69 EQ55
Barnard Rd, SW11 100 DE84
Enfield EN1 30 DV40
Mitcham CR4 140 DG97
Warlingham CR6 177 EB119
Barnard's Inn, EC1 196 E8
Barnards Pl, S.Croy. CR2 159 DP109
Barnato Cl, W.Byf. KT14 off Viscount Gdns 152 BL112
Barnby Sq, E15 off Barnby St 86 EE67
Barnby St, E15 86 EE67
NW1 195 L1
Barn Cl, Ashf. TW15 115 BP92
Banstead SM7 174 DD115
Epsom KT18 172 CQ115
Northolt UB5 78 BW68
Radlett WD7 25 CG35
Barn Cres, Pur. CR8 160 DR113
Stanmore HA7 41 CJ51
Barncroft Cl, Loug. IG10 33 EN43
Uxbridge UB8 77 BP71
Barncroft Grn, Loug. IG10 33 EN43
Barncroft Rd, Loug. IG10 33 EN43
Barneby Cl, Twick. TW2 off Rowntree Rd 117 CE88
BARNEHURST, Bexh. DA7 107 FD83
⇌ Barnehurst 107 FC82
Barnehurst Av, Bexh. DA7 107 FC81
Erith DA8 107 FC81
Barnehurst Cl, Erith DA8 107 FC81
Barnehurst Rd, Bexh. DA7 107 FC82
Barn Elms Pk, SW15 99 CW82
Barn End Dr, Dart. DA2 128 FJ90
Barn End La, Dart. DA2 128 FJ92
BARNES, SW13 99 CU82
⇌ Barnes 99 CU83
Barnes All, Hmptn. TW12 off Hampton Ct Rd 136 CC96
Barnes Av, SW13 99 CU80
Southall UB2 96 BZ77
⇌ Barnes Bridge 98 CS82
Barnes Br, SW13 98 CS82
W4 98 CS82
Barnesbury Ho, SW4 121 DK85
Barnes Cl, E12 68 EK63
★ Barnes Common, SW13 99 CU83
Barnes Ct, E16 off Ridgwell Rd 86 EJ71
Woodford Green IG8 48 EK50
BARNES CRAY, Dart. DA1 107 FH84
Barnes Cray Cotts, Dart. DA1 off Maiden La 127 FG85
Barnes Cray Rd, Dart. DA1 107 FG84
Barnesdale Cres, Orp. BR5 146 EU100
Barnes End, N.Mal. KT3 139 CU99
Barnes High St, SW13 99 CT82
H Barnes Hosp, SW14 98 CS83
Barnes Ho, Bark. IG11 off St. Marys 87 ER67
Barnes La, Kings L. WD4 6 BH27
Barnes Pikle, W5 79 CK73
Barnes Ri, Kings L. WD4 6 BM27
Barnes Rd, N18 46 DW49
Ilford IG1 69 EQ64
Barnes St, E14 85 DY72
Barnes Ter, SE8 103 DZ78
Barnes Wallis Dr, Wey. KT13 152 BL111
Barnes Way, Iver SL0 75 BF73
BARNET 27 CZ41
Barnet Bypass, Barn. EN5 26 CS41
Barnet Dr, Brom. BR2 144 EL103
BARNET GATE, Barn. EN5 27 CT44
Barnet Gate La, Barn. EN5 27 CT44
H Barnet Gen Hosp, Barn. EN5 27 CX42
Barnet Gro, E2 84 DU69
Barnet Hill, Barn. EN5 28 DA42

★ Place of interest ⇌ Railway station ⊖ London Underground station DLR Docklands Light Railway station Tra Tramlink station H Hospital Riv Pedestrian ferry landing stage

Barnet Ho, N20 44 DC47
Barnet La, N20 43 CZ46
Barnet EN5 27 CZ44
Borehamwood WD6 25 CK44
★ **Barnet Mus**, Barn. EN5 27 CY42
Barnet Rd, Barn. EN5 27 CZ43
Potters Bar EN6 28 DA35
St. Albans (Lon.Col.) AL2 10 CL27
Barnett Cl, Erith DA8 107 FF82
Leatherhead KT22 171 CH119
Barnet Trd Est, Barn. EN5 27 CZ41
Barnetts Shaw, Oxt. RH8 187 ED127
Barnett St, E1
off Cannon St Rd 84 DV72
Barnett Wd La, Ashtd. KT21 171 CJ119
Leatherhead KT22 171 CH120
Barnet Way, NW7 42 CR45
Barnet Wd Rd, Brom. BR2 144 EJ103
Barney Cl, SE7 104 EJ78
Barnfield, Bans. SM7 158 DB114
Epping CM16 18 EU28
Gravesend DA11 131 GG89
Iver SL0 75 BE72
New Malden KT3 138 CS100
Barnfield Av, Croy. CR0 142 DW103
Kingston upon Thames KT2 118 CL92
Mitcham CR4 141 DH98
Barnfield Cl, N4
off Crouch Hill 65 DL59
SW17 120 DC90
Coulsdon CR5 176 DQ119
Greenhithe DA9 129 FT86
Swanley BR8 147 FC101
Barnfield Gdns, SE18
off Plumstead Common Rd 105 EP79
Kingston upon Thames KT2 118 CL91
Barnfield Pl, E14 204 A9
Barnfield Rd, SE18 105 EP79
W5 79 CJ70
Belvedere DA17 106 EZ79
Edgware HA8 42 CQ53
Orpington BR5 146 EX97
Sevenoaks TN13 190 FD123
South Croydon CR2 160 DS109
Westerham (Tats.) TN16 178 EK120
Barnfield Way, Oxt. RH8 188 EG133
Barnfield Wd Cl, Beck. BR3 143 ED100
Barnfield Wd Rd, Beck. BR3 143 ED100
Barnham Dr, SE28 87 ET74
Barnham Rd, Grnf. UB6 78 CC69
Barnham St, SE1 201 N4
Barnhill, Pnr. HA5 60 BW57
Barn Hill, Wem. HA9 62 CP61
Barnhill Av, Brom. BR2 144 EF99
Barnhill La, Hayes UB4 77 BV69
Barnhill Rd, Hayes UB4 77 BV70
Wembley HA9 62 CQ62
Barnhurst Path, Wat. WD19 40 BW50
Barningham Way, NW9 62 CR58
Barn Lea, Rick. (Mill End) WD3 38 BG46
Barnlea Cl, Felt. TW13 116 BY89
Barn Mead, Epp.
(They.B.) CM16 33 ES36
Ongar CM5 19 FE29
Barnmead, Wok.
(Chobham) GU24 150 AT110
Barnmead Gdns, Dag. RM9 70 EZ64
Barn Meadow, Epp. CM16
off Upland Rd 17 ET25
Barn Meadow La, Lthd.
(Bkhm) KT23 170 BZ124
Barnmead Rd, Beck. BR3 143 DY95
Dagenham RM9 70 EZ64
Barnock Cl, Dart. DA1
off Lower Sta Rd 127 FE86
Barn Ri, Wem. HA9 62 CN60
BARNSBURY, N1 83 DM66
Barnsbury Cl, N.Mal. KT3 138 CQ98
Barnsbury Cres, Surb. KT5 138 CQ102
Barnsbury Est, N1
off Barnsbury Rd 83 DN67
Barnsbury Gro, N7 83 DM66
Barnsbury La, Surb. KT5 138 CP103
Barnsbury Pk, N1 83 DN66
Barnsbury Rd, N1 83 DN68
Barnsbury Sq, N1 83 DN66
Barnsbury St, N1 83 DN66
Barnsbury Ter, N1 83 DM66
Barns Ct, Wal.Abb. EN9 16 EG32
Barnscroft, SW20 139 CV97
Barnsdale Av, E14 204 A8
Barnsdale Cl, Borwd. WD6 26 CM39
Barnsdale Rd, W9 81 CZ70
Barnsfield Pl, Uxb. UB8 76 BJ66
Barnsley Rd, Rom. RM3 52 FM52
Barnsley St, E1 84 DV70
Barnstaple Path, Rom. RM3 52 FJ50
Barnstaple Rd, Rom. RM3 52 FJ50
Ruislip HA4 60 BW62
Barnston Wk, N1
off Popham St 84 DQ67
Barnston Way, Brwd.
(Hutt.) CM13 55 GC43
Barn St, N16
off Stoke Newington Ch St 66 DS62
Barnsway, Kings L. WD4 6 BL28
Barnway, Egh.
(Eng.Grn) TW20 112 AW92
Barn Way, Wem. HA9 62 CN60
Barnwell Rd, SW2 121 DN85
Dartford DA1 108 FM83
Barnwood Cl, N20 43 CZ46
W9 82 DB70
Ruislip HA4
off Lysander Rd 59 BR61
Barnyard, The, Tad. KT20 173 CU124
Baron Cl, N11
off Balmoral Av 44 DG50
Sutton SM2 158 DB110
Baroness Rd, E2 *off Diss St* 84 DT69
Baronet Gro, N17
off St. Paul's Rd 46 DU53
Baronet Rd, N17 46 DU53
Baron Gdns, Ilf. IG6 69 EQ55
Baron Gro, Mitch. CR4 140 DE98
Baron Rd, Dag. RM8 70 EX60
Barons, The, Twick. TW1 117 CH86
⊖ **Barons Court** 99 CY78
Barons Ct, Wall. SM6
off Whelan Way 141 DK104
Barons Ct Rd, W14 99 CY78
Baronsfield Rd, Twick. TW1 117 CH86
Barons Gate, Barn. EN4 28 DE44
Barons Hurst, Epsom KT18 172 CQ116
Barons Keep, W14 99 CY78
Barons Mead, Har. HA1 61 CE56
Baronsmead Rd, SW13 99 CU81
Baronsmede, W5 98 CM75
Baronsmere Rd, N2 64 DE56
Barons Pl, SE1 200 E5
Baron St, N1 83 DN68
Barons Wk, Croy. CR0 143 DY100
Barons Way, Egh. TW20 113 BD93
Baron Wk, E16 86 EF71
Mitcham CR4 140 DE98
Barque Ms, SE8
off Watergate St 103 EA79
Barrack Path, Wok. GU21 166 AT118
Barrack Rd, Houns. TW4 96 BX84
Barrack Row, Grav. DA11 131 GH86
Barracks, The, Add. KT15 134 BH104
Barracks La, Barn. EN5
off High St 27 CY41
Barra Hall Circ, Hayes UB3 77 BS72
Barra Hall Rd, Hayes UB3 77 BS73
Barrass Cl, Enf. EN3 31 EA37
Barratt Av, N22 45 DM54
Barratt Ind Pk, Sthl. UB1 96 CA75
Barratt Way, Har. HA3
off Tudor Rd 61 CD55
Barrenger Rd, N10 44 DF53
Barrens Brae, Wok. GU22 167 BA118
Barrens Cl, Wok. GU22 167 BA118
Barrens Pk, Wok. GU22 167 BA118
Barrett Cl, Rom. RM3 51 FH52
Barrett Rd, E17 67 EC56
Leatherhead (Fetch.) KT22 170 CC124
Barretts Grn Rd, NW10 80 CQ68
Barretts Gro, N16 66 DS64
Barretts Rd, Sev.
(Dunt.Grn) TN13 181 FD120
Barrett St, W1 194 G9
Barrhill Rd, SW2 121 DL89
Barricane, Wok. GU21 166 AV119
Barrie Cl, Couls. CR5 175 DJ115
Barriedale, SE14 103 DY81
Barrie Est, W2
off Craven Ter 82 DD73
Barrier App, SE7 104 EK76
Barrier Pt Rd, E16 86 EJ74
Barrier Pt Twr, E16
off Barrier Pt Rd 104 EJ75
Barringer Sq, SW17 120 DG91
Barrington Cl, NW5 64 DG64
Ilford IG5 49 EM53
Loughton IG10
off Barrington Rd 33 EQ42
Barrington Ct, Brwd.
(Hutt.) CM13 55 GC44
Barrington Dr, Uxb.
(Hare.) UB9 38 BG52
Barrington Grn, Loug. IG10 33 EQ42
Barrington Lo, Wey. KT13 153 BQ106
Barrington Pk Gdns,
Ch.St.G. HP8 36 AX46
Barrington Rd, E12 87 EN65
N8 65 DK57
SW9 101 DP83
Bexleyheath DA7 106 EX82
Loughton IG10 33 EQ41
Purley CR8 159 DJ112
Sutton SM3 140 DA102
Barrington Vil, SE18 105 EN81
Barrow Av, Cars. SM5 158 DF108
Barrow Cl, N21 45 DP48
Barrowdene Cl, Pnr. HA5
off Paines La 40 BY54
Barrowell Grn, N21 45 DP47
Barrowfield Cl, N9 46 DV48
Barrowgate Rd, W4 98 CQ78
Barrow Grn Rd, Oxt. RH8 187 EC128
Barrow Hedges Cl, Cars. SM5 158 DE108
Barrow Hedges Way,
Cars. SM5 158 DE108
Barrow Hill, Wor.Pk. KT4 138 CS103
Barrow Hill Cl, Wor.Pk. KT4
off Barrow Hill 138 CS103
Barrow Hill Est, NW8
off Barrow Hill Rd 82 DE68
Barrow Hill Rd, NW8 194 B1
Barrow La, Wal.Cr.
(Chsht) EN7 14 DT30
Barrow Pt Av, Pnr. HA5 40 BY54
Barrow Pt La, Pnr. HA5 40 BY54
Barrow Rd, SW16 121 DK93
Croydon CR0 159 DN106
Barrowsfield, S.Croy. CR2 160 DT112
Barrow Wk, Brent. TW8
off Glenhurst Rd 97 CJ78
Barr Rd, Grav. DA12 131 GM89
Potters Bar EN6 12 DC33
Barrsbrook Fm Rd, Cher. KT16
off Guildford Rd 133 BE102
Barrs Rd, NW10 80 CR66
Barry Av, N15
off Craven Pk Rd 66 DT58
Bexleyheath DA7 106 EY80
Barry Cl, Grays RM16 111 GG75
Orpington BR6 145 ES104
St. Albans AL2 8 CB25
Barry Rd, E6 86 EL72
NW10 80 CQ66
SE22 122 DU86
Barset Rd, SE15 102 DW83
Barson Cl, SE20 122 DW94
Barston Rd, SE27 122 DQ90
Barstow Cres, SW2 121 DM88
Barter St, WC1 196 A7
Barters Wk, Pnr. HA5
off High St 60 BY55
Bartholomew Cl, EC1 197 H7
SW18 100 DC84
Bartholomew Dr, Rom.
(Harold Wd) RM3 52 FK54
Bartholomew La, EC2 197 L9
Bartholomew Pl, EC1 197 H7
Bartholomew Rd, NW5 83 DJ65
Bartholomew Sq, E1
off Coventry Rd 84 DV70
EC1 197 J4
Bartholomew St, SE1 201 K7
Bartholomew Vil, NW5 83 DJ65
Bartholomew Way,
Swan. BR8 147 FE97
Barth Rd, SE18 105 ES77
Bartle Av, E6 86 EL68
Bartle Rd, W11 81 CY72
Bartlett Cl, E14 85 EA72
Bartlett Ct, EC4 196 E8
Bartlett Rd, Grav. DA11 131 GG88
Westerham TN16 189 EQ126
Bartletts Pas, EC4 196 E8
Bartlett St, S.Croy. CR2 160 DR106
Bartlow Gdns, Rom. RM5 51 FD53
Barton, The, Cob. KT11 154 BX112
Barton Av, Rom. RM7 71 FB60
Barton Cl, E6 87 EM72
E9 *off Churchill Wk* 66 DW64
NW4 63 CU57
SE15 *off Kirkwood Rd* 102 DV83
Addlestone KT15 152 BG107
Bexleyheath DA6 126 EY85
Chigwell IG7 49 EQ47
Shepperton TW17 135 BP100
Barton Grn, N.Mal. KT3 138 CR96
Barton Ho, SW6
off Wandsworth Br Rd 100 DB83
Barton Meadows, Ilf. IG6 69 EQ56
Barton Rd, W14 99 CY78
Dartford (Sutt.H.) DA4 148 FP95
Hornchurch RM12 71 FG60
Sidcup DA14 126 EY93
Slough SL3 93 AZ75
Bartons, The, Borwd.
(Elstree) WD6 25 CK44
Barton St, SW1 199 P6
Bartonway, NW8
off Queen's Ter 82 DD68
Barton Way, Borwd. WD6 26 CN40
Rickmansworth
(Crox.Grn) WD3 23 BP43
Bartram Cl, Uxb. UB8
off Lees Rd 77 BP70
Bartram Rd, SE4 123 DY85
Bartrams La, Barn. EN4 28 DC38
Bartrop Cl, Wal.Cr. EN7
off Poppy Wk 14 DR28
Barts Cl, Beck. BR3 143 EA99
Barville Cl, SE4
off St. Norbert Rd 103 DY84
Barwell Business Pk,
Chess. KT9 155 CK109
Barwick Dr, Uxb. UB8
off Harlington Rd 77 BP71
Barwick Rd, E7 68 EH63
Barwood Av, W.Wick. BR4 143 EB102
Bascombe Gro, Dart. DA1
off Lower Sta Rd 127 FE86
Bascombe St, SW2 121 DN86
Basden Gro, Felt. TW13 116 CA89
Basedale Rd, Dag. RM9 88 EV66
Baseing Cl, E6 87 EN73
Basevi Way, SE8 103 EB79
Bashley Rd, NW10 80 CR70
Basil Av, E6 86 EL68
Basildene Rd, Houns. TW4 96 BX82
Basildon Av, Ilf. IG5 49 EN53
Basildon Cl, Sutt. SM2 158 DB109
Watford WD18 23 BQ44
Basildon Rd, SE2 106 EU78
Basil Gdns, SE27 122 DQ92
Croydon CR0
off Primrose La 143 DX102
Basilon Rd, Bexh. DA7 106 EY82
Basil St, SW3 198 D6
Basin App, E14
off Commercial Rd 85 DY72
Basing Cl, T.Ditt. KT7 137 CF101
Basing Ct, SE15 102 DT81
Basingdon Way, SE5 102 DR84
Basing Dr, Bex. DA5 126 EZ86
Basingfield Rd, T.Ditt. KT7 137 CF101
Basinghall Av, EC2 197 K7
Basinghall Gdns, Sutt.
SM2 158 DB109
Basinghall St, EC2 197 K8
Basing Hill, NW11 63 CZ60
Wembley HA9 62 CM61
Basing Ho, Bark. IG11
off St. Margarets 87 ER67
Basing Ho Yd, E2 197 N2
Basing Pl, E2 197 N2
Basing Rd, Bans. SM7 157 CZ114
Rickmansworth
(Mill End) WD3 37 BF46
Basing St, W11 81 CZ72
Basing Way, N3 64 DA55
Thames Ditton KT7 137 CF101
Basire St, N1 84 DQ67
Baskerville Rd, SW18 120 DE87
Basket Gdns, SE9 124 EL85
Baslow Cl, Har. HA3 41 CD53
Baslow Wk, E5
off Overbury St 67 DX63
Basnett Rd, SW11 100 DG83
Basque Ct, SE16 203 H5
Bassano St, SE22 122 DT85
Bassant Rd, SE18 105 ET79
Bassein Pk Rd, W12 99 CT75
Basset Cl, Add.
(New Haw) KT15 152 BH110
Bassett Cl, Sutt. SM2 158 DB109
Bassett Dr, Reig. RH2 184 DA133
Bassett Flds, Epp.
(N.Wld Bas.) CM16
off High Rd 19 FD25
Bassett Gdns, Epp.
(N.Wld Bas.) CM16 19 FB26
Isleworth TW7 96 CC80
Bassett Ho, Dag. RM9 88 EV67
Bassett Rd, W10 81 CX72
Uxbridge UB8
off New Windsor St 76 BJ66
Woking GU22 167 BC116
Bassetts Cl, Orp. BR6 163 EP105
H **Bassetts Day Cen**,
Orp. BR6 163 EP105
Bassett St, NW5 82 DG65
Bassetts Way, Orp. BR6 163 EP105
Bassett Way, Grnf. UB6 78 CB72
Bassingham Rd, SW18 120 DC87
Wembley HA0 79 CK65
Bassishaw Highwalk, EC2
off London Wall 84 DQ71
Bastable Av, Bark. IG11 87 ES68
Bastion Highwalk, EC2
off London Wall 84 DQ71
Bastion Ho, EC2
off London Wall 84 DQ71
Bastion Rd, SE2 106 EU78
Baston Manor Rd, Brom. BR2 144 EH104
Baston Rd, Brom. BR2 144 EH102
Bastwick St, EC1 197 H4
Basuto Rd, SW6 100 DA81
⇌ **Bat & Ball** 191 FJ121
Bat & Ball Junct, Sev. TN14
off Bradbourne Rd 191 FJ121
Bat & Ball Rd, Sev. TN14 191 FJ121
Batavia Cl, Sun. TW16 136 BW95
Batavia Ms, SE14
off Goodwood Rd 103 DY80
Batavia Rd, SE14 103 DY80
Sunbury-on-Thames TW16 135 BV95
Batchelor St, N1 83 DN68
Batchwood Grn, Orp. BR5 146 EU97
BATCHWORTH, Rick. WD3 38 BM47
BATCHWORTH HEATH,
Rick. WD3 38 BN49
Batchworth Heath Hill,
Rick. WD3 38 BN49
Batchworth Hill, Rick. WD3 38 BM48
Batchworth La, Nthwd. HA6 39 BS50
Batchworth Roundabout,
Rick. WD3 38 BK46
Bateman Cl, Bark. IG11
off Glenny Rd 87 EQ65
Bateman Ho, SE17 *off Otto St* 101 DP79
Bateman Rd, E4 47 EA51
Rickmansworth
(Crox.Grn) WD3 22 BN44
Bateman's Bldgs, W1 195 M9
Batemans Ms, Brwd. CM14
off Warley Hill 54 FV49
Bateman's Row, EC2 197 N4
Bateman St, W1 195 M9
Bates Cl, Slou. (Geo.Grn) SL3 74 AY72
Bates Cres, SW16 121 DJ94
Croydon CR0 159 DN106
Bates Ind Est, Rom.
(Harold Wd) RM3 52 FP52
Bateson St, SE18 105 ES77
Bateson Way, Wok. GU21 151 BC114
Bates Pt, E13 *off Pelly Rd* 86 EG67
Bates Rd, Rom. RM3 52 FN52
Bate St, E14
off Three Colt St 85 DZ73
Bates Wk, Add. KT15 152 BJ108
B.A.T. Export Ho, Wok. GU21 166 AY117
Bath Cl, SE15 *off Asylum Rd* 102 DV80
Bath Ct, EC1 196 D5
Bathgate Rd, SW19 119 CX90
Bath Ho Rd, Croy. CR0 141 DL102
Bath Pas, Kings.T. KT1
off St. James Rd 137 CK96
Bath Pl, EC2 197 M3
Barnet EN5 27 CZ41
Bath Rd, E7 86 EK65
N9 46 DV47
W4 98 CS77
Dartford DA1 127 FH87
Hayes UB3 95 BQ81
Hounslow TW3, TW4,
TW5, TW6 96 BX82
Mitcham CR4 140 DD97
Romford RM6 70 EY58
Slough (Colnbr.) SL3 93 BB79
West Drayton UB7 94 BK81
Baths Rd, Brom. BR2 144 EK98
Bath St, EC1 197 J3
Gravesend DA11 131 GH86
Bath Ter, SE1 201 H7
Bathurst Av, SW19
off Brisbane Av 140 DB95
Bathurst Cl, Iver SL0 93 BF75
Bathurst Gdns, NW10 81 CV68
Bathurst Ms, W2
off Sussex Pl 82 DD73
Bathurst Rd, Ilf. IG1 69 EP60
Bathurst St, W2 82 DD73
Bathurst Wk, Iver SL0 93 BE75
Bathway, SE18 105 EN77
Batley Cl, Mitch. CR4 140 DF101
Batley Pl, N16 66 DT62
Batley Rd, N16
off Stoke Newington High St 66 DT62
Enfield EN2 30 DQ39
Batman Cl, W12 81 CV74
Baton Cl, Purf. RM19
off Brimfield Rd 109 FR77
Batoum Gdns, W6 99 CW76
Batson St, W12 99 CU75
Batsworth Rd, Mitch. CR4 140 DD97
Batten Av, Wok. GU21 166 AS119
Battenburg Wk, SE19
off Brabourne Cl 122 DS92
Batten Cl, E6 *off Savage Gdns* 87 EM72
Batten St, SW11 100 DE83
Battersby Rd, SE6 123 ED89
BATTERSEA, SW11 101 DH81
Battersea Br, SW3 100 DD80
SW11 100 DD80
Battersea Br Rd, SW11 100 DE80
Battersea Ch Rd, SW11 100 DD81
★ **Battersea Dogs Home**,
SW8 101 DH80
Battersea High St, SW11 100 DD81
★ **Battersea Park**, SW11 100 DF80
⇌ **Battersea Park** 101 DH80
Battersea Pk, SW11 100 DF80
Battersea Pk Rd, SW8 101 DH81
SW11 100 DE82
Battersea Ri, SW11 120 DE85
Battersea Sq, SW11
off Battersea High St 100 DD81
Battery Rd, SE28 105 ES75
Battis, The, Rom. RM1
off Waterloo Rd 71 FE58
Battishill Gdns, N1
off Waterloo Ter 83 DP66
Battishill St, N1
off Waterloo Ter 83 DP66
Battlebridge Ct, N1
off Wharfdale Rd 83 DL68
Battle Br La, SE1 201 M3
Battlebridge La, Red. RH1 185 DH130
Battle Br Rd, NW1 195 P1
Battle Cl, SW19 *off North Rd* 120 DC93
Battledean Rd, N5 65 DP64
Battle Rd, Belv. DA17 107 FC77
Erith DA8 107 FC77
Battlers Grn Dr, Rad. WD7 25 CE37
Batts Hill, Red. RH1 184 DE132
Reigate RH2 184 DD132
Batty St, E1 84 DU72
Baudwin Rd, SE6 124 EE89
Baugh Rd, Sid. DA14 126 EW92
Baulk, The, SW18 120 DA87
Bavant Rd, SW16 141 DL96
Bavaria Rd, N19 65 DL61
Bavdene Ms, NW4
off The Burroughs 63 CV56
Bavent Rd, SE5 102 DQ82
Bawdale Rd, SE22 122 DT85
Bawdsey Av, Ilf. IG2 69 ET56
Bawtree Cl, Sutt. SM2 158 DC110
Bawtree Rd, SE14 103 DY80
Uxbridge UB8 76 BK65
Bawtry Rd, N20 44 DF48
Baxendale, N20 44 DC47
Baxendale St, E2 84 DU69
Baxter Av, Red. RH1 184 DE134
Baxter Cl, Slou. SL1 92 AS76
Southall UB2 96 CB75
Uxbridge UB10 77 BP69
Baxter Gdns, Rom. (Noak Hill) RM3
off Cummings Hall La 52 FJ48
Baxter Rd, E16 86 EJ72
N1 84 DR65
N18 46 DV49
NW10 80 CS70
Ilford IG1 69 EP64
Bayards, Warl. CR6 176 DW118
Bay Ct, W5 *off Popes La* 98 CL76
Baycroft Cl, Pnr. HA5 60 BW55
Baydon Ct, Brom. BR2 144 EF97
Bayes Cl, SE26 122 DW92
Bayeux, Tad. KT20 173 CX122
Bayfield Rd, SE9 104 EK84
Bayford Ms, E8
off Bayford St 84 DV66
Bayford Rd, NW10 81 CX69
Bayford St, E8 84 DV66
Bayham Pl, NW1 83 DJ67
Bayham Rd, W4 98 CR76
W13 79 CH73
Morden SM4 140 DB98
Sevenoaks TN13 191 FJ123
Bayham St, NW1 83 DJ67
Bayhurst Dr, Nthwd. HA6 39 BT51
★ **Bayhurst Wood Country Pk**,
Uxb. UB9 58 BM56
Bayleys Mead, Brwd.
(Hutt.) CM13 55 GC47
Bayley St, WC1 195 M7
Bayley Wk, SE2
off Woolwich Rd 106 EY78
Baylin Rd, SW18
off Garratt La 120 DB86
Baylis Ms, Twick. TW1
off Amyand Pk Rd 117 CG87
Baylis Rd, SE1 200 D5
Bayliss Av, SE28 88 EX73
Bayliss Cl, N21 29 DL43
Southall UB1
off Whitecote Rd 78 CB72
Bayly Rd, Dart. DA1 128 FN86
Bay Manor La, Grays RM20 109 FT79
Baymans Wd, Brwd.
(Shenf.) CM15 54 FY47
Bayne Cl, E6 *off Savage Gdns* 87 EM72
Baynes Cl, Enf. EN1 30 DU40
Baynes Ms, NW3
off Belsize La 82 DD65
Baynes St, NW1 83 DJ66
Baynham Cl, Bex. DA5 126 EZ86
Bayonne Rd, W6 99 CY79
Bays Fm Ct, West Dr. UB7
off Bath Rd 94 BJ81
Bayshill Ri, Nthlt. UB5 78 CB65
Bayston Rd, N16 66 DT62
BAYSWATER, W2 82 DC72
⊖ **Bayswater** 82 DB73
Bayswater Rd, W2 194 A10
Baythorne St, E3 85 DZ71
Bay Tree Av, Lthd. KT22 171 CG120
Bay Tree Cl, Brom. BR1 144 EJ95
Ilford IG6 *off Hazel La* 49 EP52
Baytree Cl, St.Alb.
(Park St) AL2 8 CB27
Sidcup DA15 125 ET88
Waltham Cross EN7 14 DT27
Baytree Ho, E4 *off Dells Cl* 47 EB45
Baytree Rd, SW2 101 DM84
Baytree Wk, Wat. WD17 23 BT38
Baywood Sq, Chig. IG7 50 EV49
Bazalgette Cl, N.Mal. KT3 138 CR99
Bazalgette Gdns, N.Mal. KT3 138 CR99
Bazely St, E14 85 EC73
Bazile Rd, N21 29 DN44
Beacham Cl, SE7 104 EK78
Beachborough Rd,
Brom. BR1 123 EC91
Beachcroft Rd, E11 68 EE62
Beachcroft Way, N19 65 DK60
Beach Gro, Felt. TW13 116 CA89
Beachy Rd, E3 85 EA66
Beacon Cl, Bans. SM7 173 CX116
Gerrards Cross
(Chal.St.P.) SL9 36 AY52
Uxbridge UB8 58 BK64
★ **Beacon Country Pk**,
Dart. DA2 129 FV91
Beacon Dr, Dart. (Bean) DA2 129 FV90
Beaconfield Av, Epp. CM16 17 ET29
Beaconfield Rd, Epp. CM16 17 ET29

★ Place of interest ⇌ Railway station ⊖ London Underground station DLR Docklands Light Railway station Tra Tramlink station H Hospital Riv Pedestrian ferry landing stage

216

Beaconfields, Sev. TN13 . . . . 190 FF126
Beaconfield Way, Epp. CM16 . . 17 ET29
Beacon Gate, SE14 . . . . 103 DX83
Beacon Gro, Cars. SM5 . . . . . 158 DG105
Beacon Hill, N7 . . . . 65 DL84
  Purfleet RM19 . . . . 108 FP78
  Woking GU21 . . . . 166 AW118
Beacon Ri, Sev. TN13 . . . . . . 190 FG126
Beacon Rd, SE13 . . . . 123 ED86
  Erith DA8 . . . . 107 FF80
  Hounslow (Hthrw Air.) TW6 . 114 BN86
Beacon Rd Roundabout,
  Houns. (Hthrw Air.) TW6 . . 115 BP86
Beacons, The, Loug. IG10 . . . . 33 EN38
Beacons CI, E6
  off Oliver Gdns 86 EL71
Beaconsfield CI, N11 . . . . 44 DG49
  SE3 . . . . 104 EG79
  W4 . . . . 98 CQ78
Beaconsfield Gdns, Esher KT10
  off Beaconsfield Rd 155 CE108
Beaconsfield Par, SE9
  off Beaconsfield Rd 124 EL91
Beaconsfield PI,
  Epsom KT17 . . . . 156 CS112
Beaconsfield Rd, E10 . . . . 67 EC61
  E16 . . . . 86 EF70
  E17 . . . . 67 DZ58
  N9 . . . . 46 DU49
  N11 . . . . 44 DG48
  N15 . . . . 66 DS56
  NW10 . . . . 81 CT65
  SE3 . . . . 104 EF80
  SE9 . . . . 124 EL89
  SE17 . . . . 102 DR78
  W4 . . . . 98 CR76
  W5 . . . . 97 CJ75
  Bexley DA5 . . . . 127 FE88
  Bromley BR1 . . . . 144 EK97
  Croydon CR0 . . . . 142 DR100
  Enfield EN3 . . . . 31 DX37
  Epsom KT18 . . . . 172 CR119
  Esher (Clay.) KT10 . . . . . 155 CE108
  Hayes UB4 . . . . 78 BW74
  New Malden KT3 . . . . . . 138 CR96
  Southall UB1 . . . . 78 BX74
  Surbiton KT5 . . . . 138 CM101
  Twickenham TW1 . . . . . . 117 CH86
  Woking GU22 . . . . 167 AZ120
Beaconsfield Ter, Rom.
  RM6 . . . . 70 EX58
Beaconsfield Ter Rd, W14 . . . . 99 CY76
Beaconsfield Wk, E6
  off East Ham Manor Way . . 87 EN72
  SW6 . . . . 99 CZ81
Beacontree Av, E17 . . . . 47 ED53
Beacontree Rd, E11 . . . . 68 EF59
Beacon Way, Bans. SM7 . . . . 173 CX116
  Rickmansworth WD3 . . . . . 38 BG45
Beadles La, Oxt. RH8 . . . . . . 187 ED130
Beadlow CI, Cars. SM5
  off Oliverton Wk 140 DD100
Beadman PI, SE27
  off Norwood High St 121 DP91
Beadman St, SE27 . . . . 121 DP91
Beadnell Rd, SE23 . . . . 123 DX88
Beadon Rd, W6 . . . . 99 CW77
  Bromley BR2 . . . . 144 EG98
Beads Hall La, Brwd.
  (Pilg.Hat.) CM15 . . . . 54 FV42
Beaford Gro, SW20 . . . . 139 CY97
Beagle CI, Felt. TW13 . . . . . . 115 BV91
  Radlett WD7 . . . . 25 CF37
Beagles CI, Orp. BR5 . . . . . . 146 EX103
Beak St, W1 . . . . 195 L10
Beal CI, Well. DA16 . . . . 106 EU81
Beale CI, N13 . . . . 45 DP50
Beale PI, E3 . . . . 85 DZ68
Beale Rd, E3 . . . . 85 DZ67
Beales La, Wey. KT13 . . . . . 134 BN104
Beal Rd, Ilf. IG1 . . . . 69 EN61
Beam Av, Dag. RM10 . . . . 89 FB67
Beaminster Gdns, Ilf. IG6 . . . . 49 EP54
Beamish CI, Epp.
  (N.Wld Bas.) CM16 . . . . . 19 FC25
Beamish Dr, Bushey
  (Bushey Hth) WD23 . . . . . 40 CC46
Beamish Rd, N9 . . . . 46 DU46
  Orpington BR5 . . . . 146 EW101
Beam Way, Dag. RM10 . . . . . . 89 FD66
BEAN, Dart. DA2 . . . . 129 FV90
Beanacre CI, E9 . . . . 85 DZ65
Beane Cft, Grav. DA12
  off Damigos Rd 131 GM88
Bean La, Dart. (Bean) DA2 . . . 129 FV89
Bean Rd, Bexh. DA6 . . . . 106 EX84
  Greenhithe DA9 . . . . 129 FU88
Beanshaw, SE9 . . . . 125 EN91
Beansland Gro, Rom. RM6 . . . . 50 EY54
Bear All, EC4 . . . . 196 F8
Bear CI, Rom. RM7 . . . . 71 FB58
Beardell St, SE19 . . . . 122 DT93
Beardow Gro, N14 . . . . 29 DJ44
Beard Rd, Kings.T. KT2 . . . . . 118 CM92
Beardsfield, E13
  off Valetta Gro 86 EG67
Beard's Hill, Hmptn. TW12 . . . 136 CA95
Beard's Hill CI, Hmptn. TW12
  off Beard's Hill 136 CA95
Beardsley Ter, Dag. RM8
  off Fitzstephen Rd 70 EV64
Beardsley Way, W3 . . . . 98 CR75
Beards Rd, Ashf. TW15 . . . . . 115 BS93
Bearfield Rd, Kings.T. KT2 . . . 118 CL94
Bear Gdns, SE1 . . . . 201 H2
Bearing CI, Chig. IG7 . . . . 50 EU49
Bearing Way, Chig. IG7 . . . . . . 50 EU49
Bear La, SE1 . . . . 200 G2
Bear Rd, Felt. TW13 . . . . 116 BX92
Bears Den, Tad.
  (Kgswd) KT20 . . . . 173 CZ122
Bears Rails Pk, Wind.
  (Old Wind.) SL4 . . . . 112 AT87
Bearstead Ri, SE4 . . . . 123 DZ85
Bearsted Ter, Beck. BR3 . . . . 143 EA95
Bear St, WC2 . . . . 195 N10
Bearwood CI, Add. KT15
  off Ongar PI 152 BG107
  Potters Bar EN6 . . . . 12 DD31
Beasley's Ait La, Sun. TW16 . . 135 BT100

Beasleys Yd, Uxb. UB8
  off Warwick PI 76 BJ66
Beaton CI, SE15 . . . . 102 DT81
  Greenhithe DA9 . . . . 109 FV84
Beatrice Av, SW16 . . . . 141 DM97
  Wembley HA9 . . . . 62 CL64
Beatrice CI, E13
  off Chargeable La 86 EG70
  Pinner HA5 off Reid CI 59 BU56
Beatrice Ct, Buck.H. IG9 . . . . . 48 EK47
Beatrice Gdns, Grav.
  (Nthflt) DA11 . . . . 130 GE89
Beatrice PI, W8 . . . . 100 DB76
Beatrice Rd, E17 . . . . 67 EA57
  N4 . . . . 65 DN59
  N9 . . . . 46 DW45
  SE1 . . . . 202 C9
  Oxted RH8 . . . . 188 EE129
  Richmond TW10
  off Albert Rd 118 CM85
  Southall UB1 . . . . 78 BZ74
Beatson Wk, SE16 . . . . 203 K2
Beattie CI, Felt. TW14 . . . . . . 115 BQ86
  Leatherhead (Bkhm) KT23 . 170 BZ124
Beattock Ri, N10 . . . . 65 DH56
Beatty Rd, N16 . . . . 66 DS63
  Stanmore HA7 . . . . 41 CJ51
  Waltham Cross EN8 . . . . . 15 DZ34
Beatty St, NW1 . . . . 83 DJ68
Beattyville Gdns, Ilf. IG6 . . . . . 69 EN55
Beauchamp CI, W4
  off Church Path 98 CQ76
Beauchamp Ct, Stan. HA7
  off Hardwick CI 41 CJ50
Beauchamp Gdns, Rick.
  (Mill End) WD3 . . . . 38 BG46
Beauchamp PI, SW3 . . . . 198 C6
Beauchamp Rd, E7 . . . . 86 EH66
  SE19 . . . . 142 DR95
  SW11 . . . . 100 DE84
  East Molesey KT8 . . . . . 136 CB99
  Sutton SM1 . . . . 158 DA106
  Twickenham TW1 . . . . . . 117 CG87
  West Molesey KT8 . . . . . 136 CB99
Beauchamp St, EC1 . . . . 196 D7
Beauchamp Ter, SW15
  off Dryburgh Rd 99 CV83
Beauclare CI, Lthd. KT22
  off Hatherwood 171 CK121
Beauclerc Rd, W6 . . . . 99 CV76
Beauclerk CI, Felt. TW13
  off Florence Rd 115 BV88
Beaudesert Ms, West Dr. UB7 . . 94 BL75
Beaufort, E6 off Newark Knok . 87 EN71
Beaufort Av, Har. HA3 . . . . . . 61 CG56
Beaufort CI, E4
  off Higham Sta Av 47 EB51
  SW15 . . . . 119 CV87
  W5 . . . . 80 CM71
  Epping (N.Wld Bas.) CM16 . 18 FA27
  Grays (Chaff.Hun.) RM16
  off Clifford Rd 110 FZ76
  Reigate RH2 . . . . 183 CZ133
  Romford RM7 . . . . 71 FC56
  Woking GU22 . . . . 167 BC116
Beaufort Ct, Rich. TW10
  off Beaufort Rd 117 CJ91
Beaufort Dr, NW11 . . . . 64 DA56
Beaufort Gdns, NW4 . . . . 63 CW58
  SW3 . . . . 198 C6
  SW16 . . . . 121 DM94
  Hounslow TW5 . . . . 96 BY81
  Ilford IG1 . . . . 69 EN60
Beaufort Ms, SW6
  off Lillie Rd 99 CZ79
Beaufort Pk, NW11 . . . . 64 DA56
Beaufort Rd, W5 . . . . 80 CM71
  Kingston upon Thames KT1 . 138 CL98
  Reigate RH2 . . . . 183 CZ133
  Richmond TW10 . . . . 117 CJ91
  Ruislip HA4
  off Lysander Rd 59 BR61
  Twickenham TW1 . . . . . . 117 CJ87
  Woking GU22 . . . . 167 BC116
Beauforts, Egh.
  (Eng.Grn) TW20 . . . . . . 112 AW92
Beaufort St, SW3 . . . . 100 DD79
Beaufort Way, Epsom KT17 . . . 157 CU108
Beaufoy Rd, N17 . . . . 46 DS52
Beaufoy Wk, SE11 . . . . 200 C9
Beaulieu Av, E16 . . . . 205 P2
  SE26 . . . . 122 DV91
Beaulieu CI, NW9 . . . . 62 CS56
  SE5 . . . . 102 DR83
  Hounslow TW4 . . . . 116 BZ85
  Mitcham CR4 . . . . 140 DG95
  Slough (Datchet) SL3 . . . . 92 AV81
  Twickenham TW1 . . . . . . 117 CK87
  Watford WD19 . . . . 40 BW46
Beaulieu Dr, Pnr. HA5 . . . . . . 60 BX58
  Waltham Abbey EN9 . . . . . 15 EB32
Beaulieu Gdns, N21 . . . . 46 DQ45
Beaulieu PI, W4
  off Rothschild Rd 98 CQ76
Beauly Way, Rom. RM1 . . . . . 51 FE53
Beaumanor Gdns, SE9 . . . . . 125 EN91
Beaumaris Dr, Wdf.Grn. IG8 . . . 48 EK52
Beaumaris Grn, NW9
  off Goldsmith Av 62 CS58
Beaumont Av, W14 . . . . 99 CZ78
  Harrow HA2 . . . . 60 CB58
  Richmond TW9 . . . . 98 CM83
  Wembley HA0 . . . . 61 CJ64
Beaumont CI, Kings.T. KT2 . . . 118 CN94
  Romford RM2 . . . . 52 FJ54
Beaumont Cres, W14 . . . . 99 CZ78
  Rainham RM13 . . . . 89 FG65
Beaumont Dr, Ashf. TW15 . . . . 115 BR92
  Gravesend (Nthflt) DA11 . . 130 GE87
Beaumont Gdns, NW3 . . . . . . 64 DA62
  Brentwood (Hutt.) CM13
  off Bannister Dr 55 GC44
Beaumont Gate, Rad. WD7
  off Shenley Hill 25 CH35
Beaumont Gro, E1 . . . . 85 DX70
Beaumont Ms, W1 . . . . 194 G6
  Pinner HA5 . . . . 60 BY55
Beaumont PI, W1 . . . . 195 L4
  Barnet EN5 . . . . 27 CZ39
  Isleworth TW7 . . . . 117 CF85

Beaumont Ri, N19 . . . . 65 DK60
Beaumont Rd, E10 . . . . 67 EB59
  E13 . . . . 86 EH69
  SE19 . . . . 122 DQ93
  SW19 . . . . 119 CY87
  W4 . . . . 98 CQ76
  Orpington BR5 . . . . 145 ER100
  Purley CR8 . . . . 159 DN113
Beaumont Sq, E1 . . . . 85 DX70
Beaumont Vw, Wal.Cr.
  (Chsht) EN7 . . . . 14 DR26
Beaumont Wk, NW3 . . . . 82 DF66
Beauvais Ter, Nthlt. UB5 . . . . . 78 BX69
Beauval Rd, SE22 . . . . 122 DT86
Beaverbank Rd, SE9 . . . . 125 ER88
Beaverbrook Roundabout,
  Lthd. KT22 . . . . 172 CL123
Beaver CI, SE20
  off Lullington Rd 122 DU94
  Hampton TW12 . . . . 136 CB95
Beaver Gro, Nthlt. UB5
  off Jetstar Way 78 BY69
Beaver Rd, Ilf. IG6 . . . . 50 EW50
Beavers Cres, Houns. TW4 . . . 96 BW84
Beavers La, Houns. TW4 . . . . . 96 BW83
Beavers La Camp, Houns. TW4
  off Beavers La 96 BW83
Beaverwood Rd, Chis. BR7 . . . 125 ES93
Beavor Gro, W6 off Beavor La . 99 CU77
Beavor La, W6 . . . . 99 CU77
Bebbington Rd, SE18 . . . . . . 105 ES77
Bebletts CI, Orp. BR6 . . . . . . 163 ET106
Beccles CI, Dark. IG11 . . . . . . 87 ES65
Beccles St, E14 . . . . 85 DZ73
Bec CI, Ruis. HA4 . . . . 60 BX62
Beck CI, SE13 . . . . 103 EB81
Beck Ct, Beck. BR3 . . . . 143 DX97
BECKENHAM 143 EA95
Beckenham Business Cen,
  Beck. BR3 . . . . 123 DY93
Beckenham Gdns, N9 . . . . 46 DS48
Beckenham Gro, Brom. BR2 . . 143 ED96
≷ Beckenham Hill 123 EC92
Beckenham Hill Rd, SE6 . . . . 123 EB92
  Beckenham BR3 . . . . . . 123 EB92
🄷 Beckenham Hosp,
  Beck. BR3 . . . . 143 DZ96
≷ Beckenham Junction 143 EA95
🅃🄸 Beckenham Junction 143 EA95
Beckenham La, Brom. BR2 . . . 144 EE96
Beckenham PI Pk, Beck. BR3 . 123 EB94
🅃🄸 Beckenham Road 143 DY95
Beckenham Rd, Beck. BR3 . . . 143 DX95
  West Wickham BR4 . . . . . 143 EB101
Beckenshaw Gdns,
  Bans. SM7 . . . . 174 DE115
Beckers, The, N16
  off Rectory Rd 66 DU62
Becket Av, E6 . . . . 87 EN69
Becket CI, SE25 . . . . 142 DU100
  Brentwood CM13 . . . . 53 FW51
Becket Fold, Har. HA1
  off Courtfield Cres 61 CF57
Becket Rd, N18 . . . . 46 DW49
Becket St, SE1 . . . . 201 K6
Beckett Av, Ken. CR8 . . . . . . 175 DP115
Beckett Chase, Slou. SL3
  off Ditton Rd 93 AZ78
Beckett CI, NW10 . . . . 80 CR65
  SW16 . . . . 121 DK89
  Belvedere DA17
  off Tunstock Way 106 EY76
Becketts CI, Bex. DA5
  off Hill Cres 127 FC88
  Feltham TW14 . . . . 115 BV86
  Orpington BR6 . . . . 145 ET104
Becketts PI, Kings.T.
  (Hmptn W.) KT1 . . . . . . 137 CK95
Beckett Wk, Beck. BR3 . . . . . 123 DY93
Beckford Dr, Orp. BR5 . . . . . . 145 ER101
Beckford PI, SE17
  off Walworth Rd 102 DQ78
Beckford Rd, Croy. CR0 . . . . . 142 DT100
Beck La, Beck. BR3 . . . . 143 DX97
Becklow Gdns, W12
  off Becklow Rd 99 CU75
Becklow Ms, W12
  off Becklow Rd 99 CT75
Becklow Rd, W12 . . . . 99 CU75
Beckman CI, Sev.
  (Halst.) TN14 . . . . 181 FC115
Beck River Pk, Beck. BR3 . . . 143 DZ95
Beck Rd, E8 . . . . 84 DV67
Becks Rd, Sid. DA14 . . . . 126 EU90
BECKTON, E6 . . . . 87 EN71
🄳🄻🅁 Beckton 87 EN71
🄳🄻🅁 Beckton Park 87 EM73
Beckton Pk Roundabout, E16
  off Royal Albert Way 87 EM73
Beckton Retail Pk, E6 . . . . . . 87 EN71
Beckton Rd, E16 . . . . 86 EF71
Beckton Triangle Retail Pk, E6 . 87 EN70
Beck Way, Beck. BR3 . . . . . . 143 DZ97
Beckway Rd, SW16 . . . . 141 DK96
Beckway St, SE17 . . . . 201 L9
Beckwith Rd, SE24 . . . . 122 DR86
Beclands Rd, SW17 . . . . 120 DG93
Becmead Av, SW16 . . . . 121 DK91
  Harrow HA3 . . . . 61 CH57
Becondale Rd, SE19 . . . . 122 DS92
BECONTREE, Dag. RM8 . . . . . 70 EY62
🄳🄻🅁 Becontree 88 EW66
Becontree Av, Dag. RM8 . . . . . 70 EV63
BECONTREE HEATH,
  Dag. RM8 . . . . 70 FA60
Bective PI, SW15
  off Bective Rd 99 CZ84
Bective Rd, E7 . . . . 68 EG63
  SW15 . . . . 99 CZ84
Becton PI, Erith DA8 . . . . 107 FB80
Bedale Rd, Enf. EN2 . . . . 30 DQ38
  Romford RM3 . . . . 52 FN50
Bedale St, SE1 . . . . 201 K3
Bedale Wk, Dart. DA2 . . . . . . 128 FP88
BEDDINGTON, Wall. SM6 . . . 141 DK103
BEDDINGTON CORNER,
  Mitch. CR4 . . . . 140 DG101
Beddington Cross, Croy.
  CR0 . . . . 141 DK102

Beddington Fm Rd,
  Croy. CR0 . . . . 141 DL102
Beddington Gdns,
  Cars. SM5 . . . . 158 DG107
  Wallington SM6 . . . . 159 DH107
Beddington Grn, Orp. BR5 . . . 145 ET95
Beddington Gro, Wall. SM6 . . 159 DK107
🅃🄸 Beddington Lane 141 DJ100
Beddington La, Croy. CR0 . . . 141 DJ99
Beddington Path, Orp. BR5 . . . 145 ET95
Beddington Rd, Ilf. IG3 . . . . . . 69 ET59
  Orpington BR5 . . . . 145 ES96
Beddington Trd Pk W,
  Croy. CR0 . . . . 141 DL102
Beddlestead La, Warl. CR6 . . . 178 EF117
Bede CI, Pnr. HA5 . . . . 40 BX53
Bedelham Way, SE15
  off Daniel Gdns 102 DT80
Bedens Rd, Sid. DA14 . . . . . . 126 EY93
Bedevere Rd, N9 . . . . 46 DU48
Bedfont CI, Felt. TW14 . . . . . . 115 BQ86
  Mitcham CR4 . . . . 140 DG96
Bedfont Ct, Stai. TW19 . . . . . . 94 BH84
Bedfont Ct Est, Stai. TW19 . . . 94 BG83
Bedfont Grn CI, Felt. TW14 . . . 115 BS87
Bedfont La, Felt. TW13, TW14 . 115 BT87
Bedfont Rd, Felt. TW13, TW14 . 115 BS89
  Staines (Stanw.) TW19 . . . 114 BL86
Bedford Av, WC1 . . . . 195 N7
  Amersham HP6 . . . . 20 AW39
  Barnet EN5 . . . . 27 CZ43
  Hayes UB4 . . . . 77 BV72
Bedfordbury, WC2 . . . . 195 P10
Bedford CI, N10 . . . . 44 DG52
  W4 . . . . 98 CS79
  Rickmansworth
  (Chenies) WD3 . . . . 21 BB38
  Woking GU21 . . . . 166 AW115
Bedford Cor, W4
  off The Avenue 98 CS77
Bedford Ct, WC2 . . . . 199 P1
Bedford Cres, Enf. EN3 . . . . . 31 DY35
Bedford Gdns, W8 . . . . 82 DA74
  Hornchurch RM12 . . . . . . 72 FJ61
Bedford Hill, SW12 . . . . 121 DH88
  SW16 . . . . 121 DH88
Bedford Ho, SW4 . . . . 101 DL84
  off Bedford Rd 64 DE55
  SE6 off Aitken Rd 123 EB89
BEDFORD PARK, W4 . . . . 98 CR76
Bedford Pk Cor, W4
  off Bath Rd 98 CS77
Bedford Pas, SW6
  off Dawes Rd 99 CY80
Bedford PI, WC1 . . . . 195 P6
  Croydon CR0 . . . . 142 DR102
Bedford Rd, E6 . . . . 87 EN67
  E17 . . . . 47 EA54
  E18 . . . . 48 EG54
  N2 . . . . 64 DE55
  N8 . . . . 65 DK58
  N9 . . . . 46 DV45
  N15 . . . . 66 DS56
  N22 . . . . 45 DL53
  NW7 . . . . 42 CS48
  SW4 . . . . 101 DL83
  W4 . . . . 98 CR76
  W13 . . . . 79 CH73
  Dartford DA1 . . . . 128 FN87
  Gravesend (Nthflt) DA11 . . 131 GF89
  Grays RM17 . . . . 110 GB78
  Harrow HA1 . . . . 60 CC58
  Ilford IG1 . . . . 69 EP62
  Northwood HA6 . . . . 39 BQ48
  Orpington BR6 . . . . 146 EV103
  Ruislip HA4 . . . . 59 BT63
  Sidcup DA15 . . . . 125 ES90
  Twickenham TW2 . . . . . . 117 CD90
  Worcester Park KT4 . . . . 139 CW103
Bedford Row, WC1 . . . . 196 C6
Bedford Sq, WC1 . . . . 195 N7
Bedford St, WC2 . . . . 195 P10
  Watford WD24 . . . . 23 BV39
Bedford Ter, SW2
  off Lyham Rd 121 DL85
Bedford Way, WC1 . . . . 195 N5
Bedgebury Gdns, SW19 . . . . . 119 CY89
Bedgebury Rd, SE9 . . . . 104 EK84
Bedifam Ms, SE11 . . . . 200 C8
BEDMOND, Abb.L. WD5 . . . . . 7 BS27
Bedmond La, Abb.L. WD5 . . . . 7 BV25
Bedmond Rd, Abb.L. WD5 . . . . 7 BT29
  Hemel Hempstead HP3 . . . 7 BP24
Bedonwell Rd, SE2 . . . . 106 EY79
  Belvedere DA17 . . . . 106 FA79
  Bexleyheath DA7 . . . . . . 106 FA79
Bedser CI, SE11
  off Harleyford Rd 101 DM79
  Thornton Heath CR7 . . . . 142 DQ97
  Woking GU21 . . . . 167 BA116
Bedser Dr, Grnf. UB6 . . . . 61 CD64
Bedster Gdns, W.Mol. KT8 . . . 136 CB96
Bedwardine Rd, SE19 . . . . . . 122 DS94
Bedwell Gdns, Hayes UB3 . . . . 95 BS78
Bedwell Rd, N17 . . . . 46 DS53
  Belvedere DA17 . . . . 106 FA78
Beeby Rd, E16 . . . . 86 EH71
Beech Av, N20 . . . . 44 DE46
  W3 . . . . 80 CS74
  Brentford TW8 . . . . 97 CH80
  Brentwood CM13 . . . . 55 FZ48
  Buckhurst Hill IG9 . . . . . . 48 EH47
  Enfield EN2 . . . . 29 DN35
  Radlett WD7 . . . . 9 CG33
  Ruislip HA4 . . . . 59 BV60
  Sidcup DA15 . . . . 126 EU87
  South Croydon CR2 . . . . 160 DR111
  Swanley BR8 . . . . 147 FF98
  Upminster RM14 . . . . 72 FP62
  West Drayton UB7 . . . . . . 94 BN76
Beech CI, N9 . . . . 30 DU44
  SE8 off Clyde St 103 DZ79
  SW15 . . . . 119 CU87
  SW19 . . . . 119 CW93

Beech CI, Ashford TW15 . . . . . 115 BR92
  Carshalton SM5 . . . . 140 DF103
  Cobham KT11 . . . . 154 CA112
  Hornchurch RM12 . . . . . . 71 FH62
  Loughton IG10
  off Cedar Dr 33 EP40
  Staines (Stanw.) TW19 . . . 114 BK87
  Sunbury-on-Thames TW16
  off Harfield Rd 136 BX96
  Walton-on-Thames KT12 . . 154 BW105
  West Byfleet (Byfleet) KT14 152 BL112
  West Drayton UB7 . . . . . . 94 BN76
Beech CI Ct, Cob. KT11 . . . . . 154 BZ111
Beech Copse, Brom. BR1 . . . . 145 EM96
  South Croydon CR2 . . . . 160 DS106
Beech Ct, E17 . . . . 67 ED55
  SE9 . . . . 124 EL86
  Ilford IG1
  off Riverdene Rd 69 EN62
Beech Cres, Tad.
  (Box H.) KT20 . . . . 182 CQ130
Beechcroft, Ashtd. KT21 . . . . 172 CM119
  Chislehurst BR7 . . . . 25 EN94
Beechcroft Av, NW11 . . . . 63 CZ59
  Bexleyheath DA7 . . . . . . 107 FD81
  Harrow HA2 . . . . 60 CA59
  Kenley CR8 . . . . 176 DR115
  New Malden KT3 . . . . . . 138 CQ95
  Rickmansworth
  (Crox.Grn) WD3 . . . . 23 BQ44
  Southall UB1 . . . . 78 BZ74
Beechcroft CI, Houns. TW5 . . . . 96 BY80
  Orpington BR6 . . . . 163 ER105
Beechcroft Av, Wem. HA9 . . . . 62 CM62
Beechcroft Lo, Sutt. SM2
  off Devonshire Rd 158 DC108
Beechcroft Manor, Wey. KT13 . 135 BR104
Beechcroft Rd, E18 . . . . 48 EH54
  SW14 off Elm Rd 98 CQ83
  SW17 . . . . 120 DE89
  Bushey WD23 . . . . 24 BY43
  Chessington KT9 . . . . . . 138 CM104
  Orpington BR6 . . . . 163 ER105
Beechdale, N21 . . . . 45 DM47
Beechdale Rd, SW2 . . . . 121 DM86
Beechdene, Tad. KT20 . . . . . . 173 CV122
Beech Dell, Kes. BR2 . . . . . . 163 EM105
Beechdene, Tad. KT20 . . . . . . 173 CV122
Beech Dr, N2 . . . . 64 DF55
  Borehamwood WD6 . . . . . 26 CM40
  Reigate RH2 . . . . 184 DD134
  Tadworth (Kgswd) KT20 . . 173 CZ122
  Woking (Ripley) GU23 . . . 168 BG124
Beechen Cliff Way, Islw. TW7
  off Henley CI 97 CF81
Beechen Gro, Pnr. HA5 . . . . . . 60 BZ55
  Watford WD17 . . . . 24 BW42
Beechen La, Tad. KT20 . . . . . 183 CZ125
Beechenlea La, Swan. BR8 . . . 147 FH97
Beeches, The, Bans. SM7 . . . 174 DB116
  Brentwood CM14 . . . . . . 54 FV48
  Hounslow TW3 . . . . 96 CB81
  Leatherhead (Fetch.) KT22 . 171 CE124
  Rickmansworth
  (Chorl.) WD3 . . . . 21 BF43
  St. Albans (Park St) AL2 . . . 9 CE27
  Swanley BR8 off Rollo Rd . 127 FF94
  Tilbury RM18 . . . . 111 GH82
Beeches Av, Cars. SM5 . . . . . 158 DE108
  off Genoa Rd 142 DW95
  Tadworth (Kgswd) KT20 . . 174 DA123
Beeches Rd, SW17 . . . . 120 DE90
  Sutton SM3 . . . . 139 CY102
Beeches Wk, Cars. SM5 . . . . 158 DD109
Beeches Wd, Tad. KT20 . . . . 174 DA122
Beech Fm Rd, Warl. CR6 . . . . 177 EC120
Beechfield, Bans. SM7 . . . . . 158 DB113
  Kings Langley WD4 . . . . . 6 BM30
Beechfield CI, Borwd. WD6 . . . 26 CL40
Beechfield Cotts, Brom. BR1
  off Widmore Rd 144 EJ96
Beechfield Gdns, Rom. RM7 . . 71 FC59
Beechfield Rd, N4 . . . . 66 DQ58
  SE6 . . . . 123 DZ88
  Bromley BR1 . . . . 144 EJ96
  Erith DA8 . . . . 107 FE80
Beechfield Wk, Wal.Abb. EN9 . . 31 ED35
Beech Gdns, EC2
  off Aldersgate St 84 DQ71
  W5 . . . . 98 CL75
  Dagenham RM10 . . . . 89 FB66
  Woking GU21 . . . . 166 AY115
Beech Gro, Add. KT15 . . . . . . 152 BH105
  Caterham CR3 . . . . 186 DS126
  Croydon CR0 . . . . 161 DY110
  Epsom KT18 . . . . 173 CV117
  Ilford IG6 . . . . 49 ES51
  Mitcham CR4 . . . . 141 DK98
  New Malden KT3 . . . . . . 138 CR97
  South Ockendon
  (Aveley) RM15 . . . . 90 FQ74
  Woking (Mayford) GU22 . . 166 AX123
Beech Hall, Cher. (Ott.) KT16 . 151 BC108
Beech Hall Cres, E4 . . . . 47 ED52
Beech Hill, Barn. EN4 . . . . . . 28 DD38
  Woking GU22 . . . . 166 AX123
Beech Hill Av, Barn. EN4 . . . . 28 DC39
Beech Hill Gdns, Wal.Abb. EN9 . 32 EH37
Beechhill Rd, SE9 . . . . 125 EN86
Beech Holt, Lthd. KT22 . . . . . 171 CJ122
Beech Ho, Croy. CR0 . . . . . . 161 EB107
Beech Ho Rd, Croy. CR0 . . . . 142 DR104
Beech La, Beac.
  (Jordans) HP9 . . . . 36 AS52
  Buckhurst Hill IG9 . . . . . . 48 EH47
Beech Lawns, N12 . . . . 44 DD50
Beech Lo, Stai. TW18
  off Farm CI 113 BE92
Beechmeads, Cob. KT11 . . . . 154 BX113
Beechmont Av, Vir.W. GU25 . . 132 AX99
Beechmont CI, Brom. BR1 . . . 124 EE92
Beechmont Rd, Sev. TN13 . . . 191 FH129
Beechmore Gdns, Sutt. SM3 . 139 CX103

B

Beechmore Rd, SW11 100 DF81
Beechmount Av, W7 79 CD71
Beecholme, Bans. SM7 157 CY114
Beecholme Av, Mitch. CR4 141 DH95
Beecholme Est, E5
off Prout Rd 66 DV62
Beecholm Ms, Wal.Cr. EN8 15 DX28
Beech Pk, Amer. HP6 20 AV39
Beechpark Way, Wat. WD17 23 BS37
Beech Pl, Epp. CM16 17 ET31
Beech Rd, N11 45 DL51
SW16 141 DL96
Dartford DA1 128 FK88
Epsom KT17 173 CT115
Feltham TW14 115 BS87
Orpington BR6 164 EU108
Redhill RH1 185 DJ126
Reigate RH2 184 DA131
Sevenoaks TN13
off Victoria Rd 191 FH125
Slough SL3 92 AY75
Watford WD24 23 BU37
Westerham (Bigg.H.) TN16 178 EH118
Weybridge KT13
off St. Marys Rd 153 BR105
Beech Row, Rich. TW10 118 CL91
Beech St, EC2 197 H6
Romford RM7 71 FC56
Beechtree Av, Egh.
(Eng.Grn) TW20 112 AV93
Beech Tree Cl, Stan. HA7 41 CJ50
Beech Tree Glade, E4
off Forest Side 48 EF46
Beech Tree La, Stai. TW18
off Staines Rd 134 BH96
Beech Tree Pl, Sutt. SM1
off St. Nicholas Way 158 DB106
Beech Vale, Wok. GU22
off Hill Vw Rd 167 AZ118
Beechvale Cl, N12 44 DE50
Beech Wk, NW7 42 CS51
Dartford DA1 107 FG84
Epsom KT17 157 CU111
Beech Way, NW10 80 CR66
Beechway, Bex. DA5 126 EX86
Beech Way, Epsom KT17 173 CT115
South Croydon CR2 161 DX113
Twickenham TW2 116 CA90
Beech Waye, Ger.Cr. SL9 57 AZ59
Beechwood Av, N3 63 CZ55
Amersham HP6 20 AW38
Coulsdon CR5 175 DH115
Greenford UB6 78 CB69
Harrow HA2 60 CB62
Hayes UB3 77 BR73
Orpington BR6 163 ES106
Potters Bar EN6 12 DB33
Richmond TW9 98 CN81
Rickmansworth
(Chorl.) WD3 21 BB42
Ruislip HA4 59 BT61
Staines TW18 114 BH93
Sunbury-on-Thames TW16 115 BU93
Tadworth (Kgswd) KT20 174 DA121
Thornton Heath CR7 141 DP98
Uxbridge UB8 76 BN72
Weybridge KT13 153 BS105
Beechwood Circle, Har. HA2
off Beechwood Gdns 60 CB62
Beechwood Cl, NW7 42 CR50
Amersham HP6 20 AW39
Surbiton KT6 137 CJ101
Waltham Cross (Chsht) EN7 14 DS26
Weybridge KT13 153 BS105
Woking (Knap.) GU21 166 AS117
Beechwood Ct, Cars. SM5 158 DF105
Sunbury-on-Thames TW16 115 BU93
Beechwood Cres, Bexh. DA7 106 EX83
Beechwood Dr, Cob. KT11 154 CA111
Keston BR2 162 EK105
Woodford Green IG8 48 EF50
Beechwood Gdns, NW10
off St. Annes Gdns 80 CM69
Caterham CR3 176 DU122
Harrow HA2 60 CB62
Ilford IG5 69 EM57
Rainham RM13 89 FH71
Slough SL1 92 AS75
Beechwood Gro, W3
off East Acton La 80 CS73
Surbiton KT6 137 CJ101
Beechwood La, Warl. CR6 177 DX119
Beechwood Manor,
Wey. KT13 153 BS105
Beechwood Ms, N9 46 DU47
Beechwood Pk, E18 68 EG55
Leatherhead KT22 171 CJ123
Rickmansworth (Chorl.) WD3
off Rickmansworth Rd 21 BF42
Beechwood Ri, Chis. BR7 125 EP91
Watford WD24 23 BV36
Beechwood Rd, E8 84 DT65
N8 65 DK56
Caterham CR3 176 DU122
South Croydon CR2 160 DS109
Virginia Water GU25 132 AU101
Woking (Knap.) GU21 166 AS117
Beechwoods Ct, SE19
off Crystal Palace Par 122 DT92
Beechworth Cl, NW3 64 DA61
Beecot La, Walt. KT12 136 BW103
Beecroft La, SE4
off Beecroft Rd 123 DY85
Beecroft Ms, SE4
off Beecroft Rd 123 DY85
Beecroft Rd, SE4 123 DY85
Beehive Cl, E8 84 DT66
Borehamwood
(Elstree) WD6 25 CK44
Uxbridge UB10
off Honey Hill 76 BM66
Beehive Ct, Rom. RM3
off Arundel Rd 52 FM52
Beehive La, Ilf. IG1, IG4 69 EM58
Beehive Pas, EC3 197 M9
Beehive Pl, SW9 101 DN83
Beehive Rd, Stai. TW18 113 BF92
Waltham Cross (Chsht) EN7 13 DP28
Beeken Dene, Orp. BR6
off Isabella Dr 163 EQ105
Beel Cl, Amer. HP7 20 AW39
Beeleigh Rd, Mord. SM4 140 DB98
Beesfield La, Dart.
(Fnghm) DA4 148 FN101
Beeston Cl, E8
off Ferncliff Rd 66 DU64
Watford WD19 40 BX49
Beeston Dr, Wal.Cr. EN8 15 DX27
Beeston Pl, SW1 199 J7
Beeston Rd, Barn. EN4 28 DD44
Beeston Way, Felt. TW14 116 BW86
Beethoven Rd, Borwd.
(Elstree) WD6 25 CK44
Beethoven St, W10 81 CY69
Beeton Cl, Pnr. HA5 40 CA52
Begbie Rd, SE3 104 EJ81
Beggars Bush La, Wat. WD18 23 BR43
Beggars Hill, Epsom KT17 157 CT108
Beggars Hollow, Enf. EN2 30 DR37
Beggars La, West. TN16 189 ER125
Beggars Roost La, Sutt. SM1 158 DA107
Begonia Cl, E6 86 EL71
Begonia Pl, Hmptn. TW12
off Gresham Rd 116 CA93
Begonia Wk, W12
off Du Cane Rd 81 CT72
Beira St, SW12 121 DH87
Beken Ct, Wat. WD25 24 BW35
Bekesbourne St, E14
off Ratcliffe La 85 DY72
Bekesbourne Twr, Orp. BR5 146 EY102
Belcroft Cl, Brom. BR1
off Hope Pk 124 EF94
Beldam Haw, Sev.
(Halst.) TN14 164 FA112
Beldham Gdns, W.Mol. KT8 136 CB97
Belfairs Dr, Rom. RM6 70 EW59
Belfairs Grn, Wat. WD19
off Heysham Dr 40 BX50
Belfast Rd, N16 66 DT61
SE25 142 DV98
Belfield Rd, Epsom KT19 156 CR109
Belfont Wk, N7 65 DL63
Belford Gro, SE18 105 EN77
Belford Rd, Borwd. WD6 26 CM38
Belfort Rd, SE15 102 DW82
Belfour Ter, N3 44 DB54
Belfry Av, Uxb. (Hare.) UB9 38 BG53
Belfry Cl, SE16 202 E10
Belfry La, Rick. WD3 38 BJ46
Belfry Shop Cen, The,
Red. RH1 184 DF133
Belgrade Rd, N16 66 DS63
Hampton TW12 136 CB95
Belgrave Av, Rom. RM2 72 FJ55
Watford WD18 23 BT43
Belgrave Cl, N14
off Prince George Av 29 DJ43
NW7 42 CR50
W3 off Avenue Rd 98 CQ75
Orpington BR5 146 EW98
Walton-on-Thames KT12 153 BV105
Belgrave Ct, E14 203 N1
Belgrave Cres, Sun. TW16 135 BV95
Belgrave Dr, Kings L. WD4 7 BQ28
Belgrave Gdns, N14 29 DK43
NW8 82 DB67
Stanmore HA7
off Copley Rd 41 CJ50
Belgrave Hts, E11 68 EG60
Belgrave Manor, Wok. GU22 166 AY119
Belgrave Ms, Uxb. UB8 76 BK70
Belgrave Ms N, SW1 198 F5
Belgrave Ms S, SW1 198 G6
Belgrave Ms W, SW1 198 F6
Belgrave Pl, SW1 198 G6
Slough SL1 off Clifton Rd 92 AV75
Belgrave Rd, E10 67 EC60
E11 68 EG61
E13 86 EJ70
E17 67 EA57
SE25 142 DT98
SW1 199 K9
SW13 99 CT80
Hounslow TW4 96 BZ83
Ilford IG1 69 EM60
Mitcham CR4 140 DD97
Slough SL1 74 AS73
Sunbury-on-Thames TW16 135 BV95
Belgrave Sq, SW1 198 F6
Belgrave St, E1 85 DX72
Belgrave Ter, Wdf.Grn. IG8 48 EG48
Tra Belgrave Walk 140 DD97
Belgrave Wk, Mitch. CR4 140 DD97
Belgrave Yd, SW1 199 H7
BELGRAVIA, SW1 198 F7
Belgravia Cl, Barn. EN5 27 CZ41
Belgravia Gdns, Brom. BR1 124 EE93
Belgravia Ho, SW4 121 DK86
Belgravia Ms, Kings.T. KT1 137 CK98
Belgrove St, WC1 195 P2
Belham Rd, Kings L. WD4 6 BM28
Belham Wk, SE5
off D'Eynsford Rd 102 DR81
Belhaven Ct, Borwd. WD6 26 CM39
Belhus Pk, S.Ock.
(Aveley) RM15 91 FR71
Belinda Rd, SW9 101 DP83
Belitha Vil, N1 83 DM66
Bellamy Cl, E14 203 P4
W14 off Aisgill Av 99 CZ78
Edgware HA8 42 CQ48
Uxbridge UB10 58 BN62
Watford WD17 23 BU39
Bellamy Dr, Stan. HA7 41 CH53
Bellamy Rd, E4 47 EB51
Enfield EN2 30 DR40
Waltham Cross (Chsht) EN8 15 DY29
Bellamy St, SW12 121 DH87
Bellarmine Cl, SE28 105 ET75
Bellasis Av, SW2 121 DL89
Bell Av, Rom. RM3 51 FH53
West Drayton UB7 94 BM77
Bell Br Rd, Cher. KT16 133 BF102
Bell Cl, Abb.L. (Bedmond) WD5 7 BT27
Bell Cl, Greenhithe DA9 129 FT85
Pinner HA5 60 BW55
Ruislip HA4 59 BT62
Slough SL2 74 AV71
Bellclose Rd, West Dr. UB7 94 BL75
BELL COMMON, Epp. CM16 17 ER32
Bell Common, Epp. CM16 17 ES32
Bell Common Tunnel,
Epp. CM16 17 ER33
Bell Ct, Surb. KT5
off Barnsbury La 138 CP103
Bell Cres, Couls. CR5
off Maple Way 175 DH121
Bell Dr, SW18 119 CY87
Bellefield Rd, Orp. BR5 146 EV99
Bellefields Rd, SW9 101 DM83
Bellegrove Cl, Well. DA16 105 ET82
Bellegrove Par, Well. DA16
off Bellegrove Rd 105 ET83
Bellegrove Rd, Well. DA16 105 ER82
Bellenden Rd, SE15 102 DT82
Bellestaines Pleasaunce, E4 47 EA47
Belleville Rd, SW11 120 DF85
Belle Vue, Grnf. UB6 79 CD67
Belle Vue Cl, Stai. TW18 134 BG95
Belle Vue Est, NW4
off Bell La 63 CW56
Belle Vue La, Bushey
(Bushey Hth) WD23 41 CD46
Bellevue Ms, N11
off Bellevue Rd 44 DG50
Bellevue Par, SW17
off Bellevue Rd 120 DE88
Belle Vue Pk, Th.Hth. CR7 142 DQ97
Bellevue Pl, E1 84 DW70
Slough SL1 off Albert St 92 AT76
Belle Vue Rd, E17 47 ED54
Bellevue Rd, N11 44 DG49
Belle Vue Rd, NW4
off Bell La 63 CW56
Bellevue Rd, SW13 99 CU82
SW17 120 DE88
W13 79 CH70
Bexleyheath DA6 126 EZ85
Hornchurch RM11 72 FM60
Kingston upon Thames KT1 138 CL97
Belle Vue Rd, Orp. BR6
off Standard Rd 163 EN110
Bellevue Rd, Rom. RM5 51 FC51
Bellevue Ter, Uxb. (Hare.) UB9 38 BG52
Bellew St, SW17 120 DC90
Bell Fm Av, Dag. RM10 71 FC62
Bellfield, Croy. CR0 161 DY109
Bellfield Av, Har. HA3 40 CC51
Bellflower Cl, E6
off Sorrel Gdns 86 EL71
Bellflower Path, Rom. RM3 52 FJ52
Bell Gdns, E10 off Church Rd 67 EA60
E17 off Markhouse Rd 67 DZ57
Orpington BR5 146 EW99
Bellgate Ms, NW5 off York Ri 65 DH62
BELL GREEN, SE6 123 DZ90
Bell Grn, SE26 123 DZ90
Hemel Hempstead
(Bov.) HP3 5 BB27
Bell Grn La, SE26 123 DY92
Bell Hill, Croy. CR0
off Surrey St 142 DQ104
Bellhouse La, Brwd. CM14 54 FS43
Bell Ho Rd, Rom. RM7 71 FC60
BELLINGHAM, SE6 123 EB90
⇌ Bellingham 123 EB90
Bellingham Ct, Bark. IG11
off Renwick Rd 88 EV69
Bellingham Grn, SE6 123 EA90
Bellingham Rd, SE6 123 EB90
Bell Inn Yd, EC3 197 L9
Bell La, E1 197 P7
E16 205 M2
NW4 63 CX56
Abbots Langley
(Bedmond) WD5 7 BT27
Amersham HP6, HP7 20 AV39
Enfield EN3 31 DX38
Hatfield (Brook.Pk) AL9 12 DA25
Leatherhead (Fetch.) KT22 171 CD123
St. Albans (Lon.Col.) AL2 10 CL29
Twickenham TW1
off The Embankment 117 CG88
Wembley HA9
off Magnet Rd 61 CK61
Bell La Cl, Lthd. (Fetch.) KT22 171 CD123
Bellmaker Ct, E3
off St. Pauls Way 85 EA71
Bellman Av, Grav. DA12 131 GL88
Bellmarsh Rd, Add. KT15 152 BH105
Bell Meadow, SE19
off Dulwich Wd Av 122 DS91
Godstone RH9 186 DV132
Bellmount Wd Av, Wat. WD17 23 BS39
Bello Cl, SE24 121 DP87
Bellot Gdns, SE10 205 J10
Bellot St, SE10 205 J10
Bellring Cl, Belv. DA17 106 FA79
Bell Rd, E.Mol. KT8 137 CD99
Enfield EN1 30 DR39
Hounslow TW3 96 CB84
Bells All, SW6 100 DA82
Bells Gdn Est, SE15
off Buller Cl 102 DU80
Bells Hill, Barn. EN5 27 CX43
Bell's Hill, Slou. (Stoke P.) SL2 74 AU67
Bells Hill Grn, Slou.
(Stoke P.) SL2 74 AU66
Bells La, Slou. (Horton) SL3 93 BB83
Bell St, NW1 194 B6
SE18 104 EL81
Reigate RH2 184 DA134
Bellswood La, Iver SL0 75 BB71
Belltrees Gro, SW16 121 DM92
Bell Water Gate, SE18 105 EN76
Bell Weir Cl, Stai. TW19 113 BB89
Bell Wf La, EC4 197 J10
Bellwood Rd, SE15 103 DX84
Bell Yd, WC2 196 D8
Belmarsh Rd, SE28
off Western Way 105 ES75
BELMONT, Har. HA3 41 CG54
BELMONT, Sutt. SM2 158 DB111
⇌ Belmont 158 DA110
Belmont Av, N9 46 DU46
N13 45 DL50
N17 66 DQ55
Barnet EN4 28 DF43
New Malden KT3 139 CU99
Southall UB2 96 BY76
Upminster RM14 72 FM61
Welling DA16 105 ES83
Wembley HA0 80 CM67
Belmont Circle, Har. HA3 41 CH53
Belmont Cl, E4 47 ED50
N20 44 DB46
SW4 101 DJ83
Barnet EN4 28 DF42
Uxbridge UB8 76 BK65
Woodford Green IG8 48 EH49
Belmont Cotts, Slou.
(Colnbr.) SL3
off High St 93 BC80
Belmont Ct, NW11 63 CZ57
Belmont Gro, SE13 103 ED83
W4 off Belmont Rd 98 CR77
Belmont Hall Ct, SE13
off Belmont Gro 103 ED83
Belmont Hill, SE13 103 ED83
Belmont La, Chis. BR7 125 EQ92
Stanmore HA7 41 CJ52
Belmont Ms, SW19
off Chapman Sq 119 CX89
Belmont Pk, SE13 103 ED84
Belmont Pk Cl, SE13
off Belmont Pk 103 ED84
Belmont Pk Rd, E10 67 EB58
Belmont Ri, Sutt. SM2 157 CZ107
Belmont Rd, N15 66 DQ56
N17 66 DQ56
SE25 142 DV99
SW4 101 DJ83
W4 98 CR77
Beckenham BR3 143 DZ96
Bushey WD23 24 BY43
Chislehurst BR7 125 EP92
Erith DA8 106 FA80
Grays RM17 110 FZ78
Harrow HA3 61 CF55
Hornchurch RM12 72 FK62
Ilford IG1 69 EQ62
Leatherhead KT22 171 CG122
Sutton SM2 158 DA110
Twickenham TW2 117 CD89
Uxbridge UB8 76 BK66
Wallington SM6 159 DH106
Belmont St, NW1 82 DG66
Belmont Ter, W4
off Belmont Rd 98 CR77
Belmor, Borwd. (Elstree) WD6 26 CN43
Belmore Av, Hayes UB4 77 BU72
Woking GU22 167 BD116
Belmore La, N7 65 DK64
Belmore St, SW8 101 DK81
Beloe Cl, SW15 99 CU83
Belper Ct, E5 off Pedro St 67 DX63
Belsham St, E9 84 DW65
BELSIZE, Rick. WD3 5 BF33
Belsize Av, N13 45 DM51
NW3 82 DD65
W13 97 CH76
Belsize Ct, NW3
off Belsize La 64 DE64
Belsize Cres, NW3 64 DD64
Belsize Gdns, Sutt. SM1 158 DB105
Belsize Gro, NW3 82 DE65
Belsize La, NW3 82 DD65
Belsize Ms, NW3
off Belsize La 82 DD65
BELSIZE PARK, NW3 82 DE65
⊖ Belsize Park 64 DE64
Belsize Pk, NW3 82 DD65
Belsize Pk Gdns, NW3 82 DE65
Belsize Pk Ms, NW3
off Belsize La 82 DD65
Belsize Pl, NW3
off Belsize La 82 DD65
Belsize Rd, NW6 82 DB67
Harrow HA3 41 CD52
Belsize Sq, NW3 82 DD65
Belsize Ter, NW3 82 DD65
Belson Rd, SE18 105 EM77
Belswains La, Hem.H. HP3 6 BM25
Beltana Dr, Grav. DA12 131 GL91
Beltane Dr, SW19 119 CX90
Belthorn Cres, SW12 121 DJ87
Beltinge Rd, Rom. RM3 72 FM55
Beltona Gdns, Wal.Cr.
(Chsht) EN8 15 DX27
Belton Rd, E7 86 EH66
E11 68 EE63
N17 66 DS55
NW2 81 CU65
Sidcup DA14 126 EU91
Belton Way, E3 85 EA71
Beltran Rd, SW6 100 DB82
Beltwood Rd, Belv. DA17 107 FC77
BELVEDERE 107 FB77
⇌ Belvedere 106 FA76
Belvedere Av, SW19 119 CY92
Ilford IG5 49 EP54
Belvedere Bldgs, SE1 200 G5
Belvedere Cl, Esher KT10 154 CB106
Gravesend DA12 131 GJ88
Teddington TW11 117 CE92
Weybridge KT13 152 BN106
Belvedere Ct, N2 64 DD57
Belvedere Dr, SW19 119 CY92
Belvedere Gdns, St.Alb. AL2 8 CA27
West Molesey KT8 136 BZ99
Belvedere Gro, SW19 119 CY92
Belvedere Ho, Felt. TW13 115 BU88
H Belvedere Ho Day Hosp,
NW10 81 CU67
Belvedere Ind Est, Belv. DA17 107 FC76
Belvedere Ms, SE3
off Langton Way 104 EF81
SE15 102 DV83
Belvedere Pl, SE1 200 G5
SW2 off Acre La 101 DM84
Belvedere Rd, E10 67 DY60
SE1 200 C4
SE2 88 EX74
SE19 122 DT94
Belvedere Rd, W7 97 CF76
Bexleyheath DA7 106 EZ83
Brentwood CM14 54 FT48
Westerham (Bigg.H.) TN16 178 EM118
Belvedere Sq, SW19 119 CY92
Belvedere Strand, NW9 43 CT54
Belvedere Twr, The, SW10 100 DC81
Belvedere Way, Har. HA3 62 CL58
Belvoir Cl, SE9 124 EL90
Belvoir Rd, SE22 122 DU87
Belvue Cl, Nthlt. UB5 78 CA66
Belvue Rd, Nthlt. UB5 78 CA66
Bembridge Cl, NW6 81 CY66
Bembridge Ct, Slou. SL1
off Park St 92 AT76
Bembridge Gdns, Ruis. HA4 59 BR61
Bemerton Est, N1 83 DM66
Bemerton St, N1 83 DM67
Bemish Rd, SW15 99 CX83
Bempton Dr, Ruis. HA4 59 BV61
Bemsted Rd, E17 67 DZ55
Benares Rd, SE18 105 ET77
Benbow Rd, W6 99 CV76
Benbow St, SE8 103 EA79
Benbow Waye, Uxb. UB8 76 BJ71
Benbury Cl, Brom. BR1 123 EC92
Bence, The, Egh. TW20 133 BB97
Bench Fld, S.Croy. CR2 160 DT107
Bench Manor Cres, Ger.Cr.
(Chal.St.P.) SL9 36 AW54
Bencombe Rd, Pur. CR8 159 DN114
Bencroft, Wal.Cr. (Chsht) EN7 14 DU26
Bencroft Rd, SW16 121 DJ94
Bencurtis Pk, W.Wick. BR4 143 ED104
Bendall Ms, NW1 194 C6
Bendemeer Rd, SW15 99 CX83
Bendish Rd, E6 86 EL66
Bendmore Av, SE2 106 EU78
Bendon Valley, SW18 120 DB87
Bendysh Rd, Bushey WD23 24 BY41
Benedict Cl, Belv. DA17
off Tunstock Way 106 EY76
Orpington BR6 145 ES104
Benedict Dr, Felt. TW14 115 BR87
Benedictine Gate, Wal.Cr.
EN8 15 DY27
Benedict Rd, SW9 101 DM83
Mitcham CR4 140 DD97
Benedict Way, N2 64 DC55
Benenden Grn, Brom. BR2 144 EG99
Benen-Stock Rd, Stai. TW19 113 BF85
Benets Rd, Horn. RM11 72 FN60
Benett Gdns, SW16 141 DL96
Benfleet Cl, Cob. KT11 154 BY112
Sutton SM1 140 DC104
Benfleet Way, N11 44 DG47
Bengal Ct, EC3
off Birchin La 84 DR72
Bengal Rd, Ilf. IG1 69 EP63
Bengarth Dr, Har. HA3 41 CD54
Bengarth Rd, Nthlt. UB5 78 BX67
Bengeworth Rd, SE5 102 DQ83
Harrow HA1 61 CG61
Ben Hale Cl, Stan. HA7 41 CH49
Benham Cl, SW11 100 DD83
Chessington KT9
off Merritt Gdns 155 CJ107
Coulsdon CR5 175 DP118
Benham Gdns, Houns. TW4 116 BZ85
Benham Rd, W7 79 CE71
Benhams Pl, NW3
off Holly Wk 64 DC63
Benhill Av, Sutt. SM1 158 DB105
Benhill Rd, SE5 102 DR80
Sutton SM1 140 DC104
Benhill Wd Rd, Sutt. SM1 140 DC104
BENHILTON, Sutt. SM1 140 DB103
Benhilton Gdns, Sutt. SM1 140 DB104
Benhurst Av, Horn. RM12 71 FH62
Benhurst Cl, S.Croy. CR2 161 DX110
Benhurst Ct, SW16 121 DN92
Benhurst Gdns, S.Croy. CR2 160 DW110
Benhurst La, SW16 121 DN92
Benin St, SE13 123 ED87
Benison Ct, Slou. SL1
off Osborne St 92 AT76
Benjafield Cl, N18
off Brettenham Rd 46 DV49
Benjamin Cl, E8 84 DU67
Hornchurch RM11 71 FG58
Benjamin St, EC1 196 F6
Ben Jonson Rd, E1 85 DY71
Benledi St, E14 85 ED72
Benn Cl, Oxt. RH8 188 EG134
Bennelong Cl, W12 81 CV73
Bennerley Rd, SW11 120 DE85
Bennetsfield Rd, Uxb. UB11 77 BP74
Bennet's Hill, EC4 196 G10
Bennett Cl, Cob. KT11 153 BU113
Kingston upon Thames
(Hmptn W.) KT1 137 CJ95
Northwood HA6 39 BT52
Welling DA16 106 EU82
Bennett Gro, SE13 103 EB81
Bennett Pk, SE3 104 EF83
Bennett Rd, E13 86 EJ70
N16 66 DS63
Romford RM6 70 EY58
Bennetts Av, Croy. CR0 143 DY103
Greenford UB6 79 CE67
Bennetts Castle La, Dag.
RM8 70 EW63
Bennetts Cl, N17 46 DT51
Mitcham CR4 141 DH95
Bennetts Copse, Chis. BR7 124 EL93
Bennett St, SW1 199 K2
W4 98 CS79
Bennetts Way, Croy. CR0 143 DY103
Bennetts Yd, SW1 199 N7
Uxbridge UB8 off High St 76 BJ66
Bennett Way, Dart.
(Lane End) DA2 129 FR91
Benningholme Rd, Edg. HA8 42 CS51
Bennington Rd, N17 46 DS53
Woodford Green IG8 48 EE52
Bennions Cl, Horn. RM12
off Franklin Rd 90 FK65
Bennison Dr, Rom.
(Harold Wd) RM3 52 FK54
Benn St, E9 85 DY65

★ Place of interest ⇌ Railway station ⊖ London Underground station DLR Docklands Light Railway station Tra Tramlink station H Hospital Riv Pedestrian ferry landing stage

Benn's Wk, Rich. TW9
off Rosedale Rd **98** CL84
Benrek Cl, Ilf. IG6 . . . . **49** EQ53
Bensbury Cl, SW15 . . . . **119** CV87
Bensham Cl, Th.Hth. CR7 . . . . . **142** DQ98
Bensham Gro, Th.Hth. CR7 . . . **142** DQ96
Bensham La, Croy. CR0 . . . . . **141** DP101
Thornton Heath CR7 . . . . . . **141** DP98
Bensham Manor Rd,
Th.Hth. CR7 . . . . **142** DQ98
Bensington Ct, Felt. TW14 . . . **115** BR86
Benskin Rd, Wat. WD18 . . . . . . **23** BU43
Benskins La, Rom.
(Noak Hill) RM4 . . . . **52** FK46
Bensley Cl, N11 . . . . **44** DF50
Ben Smith Way, SE16 . . . . **202** C6
Benson Av, E6 . . . . **86** EJ68
Benson Cl, Houns. TW3 . . . . . . **96** CA84
Slough SL2 . . . . **74** AU74
Uxbridge UB8 . . . . **76** BL71
Benson Quay, E1 . . . . **202** F1
Benson Rd, SE23 . . . . **122** DW88
Croydon CR0 . . . . **141** DN104
Grays RM17 . . . . **110** GB79
Bentalls Cen, Kings.T. KT1 . . . **137** CK96
Bentfield Gdns, SE9
off Aldersgrove Av **124** EJ90
Benthall Gdns, Ken. CR8 . . . . **176** DQ116
Benthal Rd, N16 . . . . **66** DU61
Bentham Av, Wok. GU21 . . . . **167** BC115
Bentham Ct, N1
off Rotherfield St **84** DQ66
Bentham Rd, E9 . . . . **85** DX65
SE28 . . . . **88** EV73
Bentham Wk, NW10 . . . . **62** CQ64
Ben Tillet Cl, Bark. IG11 . . . . . . **88** EU66
Ben Tillett Cl, E16
off Newland St **87** EM74
Bentinck Cl, Ger.Cr. SL9 . . . . . . **56** AX57
Bentinck Ms, W1 . . . . **194** G8
Bentinck Rd, West Dr. UB7 . . . . **76** BK74
Bentinck St, W1 . . . . **194** G8
Bentley Ct, Rom. RM2
off Elvet Av **72** FJ55
Bentley Dr, NW2 . . . . **63** CZ62
Ilford IG2 . . . . **69** EQ58
Weybridge KT13 . . . . **152** BN109
BENTLEY HEATH, Barn. B93 . . **27** CZ35
Bentley Heath La, Barn. EN5 . . **11** CY34
Bentley Ms, Enf. EN1 . . . . **30** DR44
★ **Bentley Priory**, Stan. HA7 . . **41** CE48
Bentley Rd, N1
off Tottenham Rd **84** DS65
Bentley St, Grav. DA12 . . . . . . **131** GJ86
Bentley Way, Stan. HA7 . . . . . . **41** CG50
Woodford Green IG8 . . . . . . **48** EG48
Benton Rd, Ilf. IG1 . . . . **69** ER60
Watford WD19 . . . . **40** BX50
Bentons La, SE27 . . . . **122** DQ91
Bentons Ri, SE27 . . . . **122** DR92
Bentry Cl, Dag. RM8 . . . . **70** EY61
Bentry Rd, Dag. RM8 . . . . **70** EY61
Bentworth Rd, W12 . . . . **81** CV72
Benwell Ct, Sun. TW16 . . . . . . **135** BU95
Benwell Rd, N7 . . . . **65** DN63
Benwick Cl, SE16 . . . . **202** E8
Benworth St, E3 . . . . **85** DZ69
Benyon Path, S.Ock. RM15
off Tyssen Pl **91** FW68
Benyon Rd, N1
off Southgate Rd **84** DR67
Beomonds Row, Cher. KT16
off Heriot Rd **134** BG101
Berberis Wk, West Dr. UB7 . . . . **94** BL77
Berber Pl, E14
off Birchfield St **85** EA73
Berber Rd, SW11 . . . . **120** DF85
Berberry Cl, Edg. HA8
off Larkspur Gro **42** CQ49
Berceau Wk, Wat. WD17 . . . . . . **23** BS39
Bercta Rd, SE9 . . . . **125** EQ89
Bere Cl, Green. DA9
off London Rd **129** FW85
Beredens La, Brwd. CM13 . . . . **73** FT55
Berenger Wk, SW10
off Blantyre St **100** DD80
Berens Rd, NW10 . . . . **81** CX69
Orpington BR5 . . . . **146** EX99
Berens Way, Chis. BR7 . . . . . . **145** ET98
Beresford Av, N20 . . . . **44** DF47
W7 . . . . **79** CD71
Slough SL2 . . . . **74** AW74
Surbiton KT5 . . . . **138** CP102
Twickenham TW1 . . . . **117** CJ86
Wembley HA0 . . . . **80** CM67
Beresford Dr, Brom. BR1 . . . . **144** EK97
Woodford Green IG8 . . . . . . **48** EJ49
Beresford Gdns, Enf. EN1 . . . . . **30** DS42
Hounslow TW4 . . . . **116** BZ85
Romford RM6 . . . . **70** EY57
Beresford Rd, E4 . . . . **48** EE46
E17 . . . . **47** EB53
N2 . . . . **64** DE55
N5 . . . . **66** DQ64
N8 . . . . **65** DN57
Gravesend (Nthflt) DA11 . . . **130** GE87
Harrow HA1 . . . . **61** CD57
Kingston upon Thames KT2 . **138** CM95
New Malden KT3 . . . . **138** CQ98
Rickmansworth
(Mill End) WD3 . . . . **37** BF46
Southall UB1 . . . . **78** BX74
Sutton SM2 . . . . **157** CZ108
Beresford Sq, SE18 . . . . **105** EP77
Beresford St, SE18 . . . . **105** EP76
Beresford Ter, N5 . . . . **66** DQ64
Berestede Rd, W6 . . . . **99** CT78
Bere St, E1 *off Cranford St* . . . **85** DX73
Bergen Sq, SE16 . . . . **203** L6
Berger Cl, Orp. BR5 . . . . **145** ER100
Berger Rd, E9 . . . . **85** DX65
Berghem Ms, W14
off Blythe Rd **99** CX76
Bergholt Av, Ilf. IG4 . . . . **68** EL57
Bergholt Cres, N16 . . . . **66** DS59
Bergholt Ms, NW1
off Rossendale Way **83** DJ66
Berglen Ct, E14
off Branch Rd **85** DY72
Bering Sq, E14 *off Napier Av* . **103** EA78
Bering Wk, E16 . . . . **86** EK72
Berisford Ms, SW18 . . . . **120** DC86
Berkeley Av, Bexh. DA7 . . . . . **106** EX81
Greenford UB6 . . . . **79** CE65
Hounslow TW4 . . . . **95** BU82
Ilford IG5 . . . . **49** EN54
Romford RM5 . . . . **51** FC52
Berkeley Cl, Abb.L. WD5 . . . . **7** BT32
Borehamwood
(Elstree) WD6 . . . . **26** CN43
Hornchurch RM11 . . . . **72** FP61
Kingston upon Thames KT2 . **118** CL94
Orpington BR5 . . . . **145** ES101
Potters Bar EN6 . . . . **11** CY32
Ruislip HA4 . . . . **59** BU62
Staines TW19 . . . . **113** BD89
Berkeley Ct, N14 . . . . **29** DJ44
Rickmansworth
(Crox.Grn) WD3
off Mayfare **23** BR43
Wallington SM6 . . . . **141** DJ104
Weybridge KT13 . . . . **135** BR103
Berkeley Cres, Barn. EN4 . . . . . **28** DD43
Dartford DA1 . . . . **128** FM88
Berkeley Dr, Horn. RM11 . . . . . . **72** FN60
West Molesey KT8 . . . . **136** BZ97
Berkeley Gdns, N21 . . . . **46** DR45
W8 *off Brunswick Gdns* **82** DA74
Esher (Clay.) KT10 . . . . **155** CG107
Walton-on-Thames KT12 . . **135** BT101
West Byfleet KT14 . . . . **151** BF114
Berkeley Ho, E3 . . . . **85** EA70
Berkeley Ms, W1 . . . . **194** E8
Berkeley Pl, SW19 . . . . **119** CX93
Epsom KT18 . . . . **172** CR115
Berkeley Rd, E12 . . . . **68** EL64
N8 . . . . **65** DK57
N15 . . . . **66** DR58
NW9 . . . . **62** CN56
SW13 . . . . **99** CU81
Uxbridge UB10 . . . . **77** BQ66
Berkeleys, The, Lthd.
(Fetch.) KT22 . . . . **171** CE124
Berkeley Sq, W1 . . . . **199** J1
Berkeley St, W1 . . . . **199** J1
Berkeley Wk, N7
off Durham Rd **65** DM61
Berkeley Waye, Houns. TW5 . . . **96** BX80
Berkhampstead Rd,
Belv. DA17 . . . . **106** FA78
Berkhamsted Av, Wem. HA9 . . **80** CM65
Berkley Av, Wal.Cr. EN8 . . . . . . **15** DX34
Berkley Cres, Grav. DA12
off Milton Rd **131** GJ86
Berkley Gro, NW1
off Berkley Rd **82** DF66
Berkley Rd, NW1 . . . . **82** DF66
Gravesend DA12 . . . . **131** GH86
Berks Hill, Rick. (Chorl.) WD3 . . **21** BC43
Berkshire Cl, Cat. CR3 . . . . **176** DR122
Berkshire Gdns, N13 . . . . **45** DN51
N18 . . . . **46** DV50
Berkshire Rd, E9 . . . . **85** DZ65
Berkshire Sq, Mitch. CR4
off Berkshire Way **141** DL98
Berkshire Way, Horn. RM11 . . . **72** FN57
Mitcham CR4 . . . . **141** DL98
Bermans Cl, Brwd.
(Hutt.) CM13
off Hanging Hill La **55** GB47
Bermans Way, NW10 . . . . **62** CS63
BERMONDSEY, SE1 . . . . **201** P7
⊖ **Bermondsey** **202** C6
Bermondsey Sq, SE1 . . . . **201** N6
Bermondsey St, SE1 . . . . **201** M3
Bermondsey Wall E, SE16 . . . . **202** C5
Bermondsey Wall W, SE16 . . . **202** B4
Bermuda Rd, Til. RM18 . . . . . . **111** GG82
Bernal Cl, SE28
off Haldane Rd **88** EX73
Bernard Ashley Dr, SE7 . . . . . **104** EH78
Bernard Av, W13 . . . . **97** CH76
Bernard Cassidy St, E16 . . . . . . **86** EF71
Bernard Gdns, SW19 . . . . **119** CZ92
Bernard Gro, Wal.Abb. EN9
off Beaulieu Dr **15** EB33
Bernard Rd, N15 . . . . **66** DT57
Romford RM7 . . . . **71** FC59
Wallington SM6 . . . . **159** DH105
Bernards Cl, Ilf. IG6 . . . . **49** EQ51
Bernard St, WC1 . . . . **195** P5
Gravesend DA12 . . . . **131** GH86
Bernato Cl, W.Byf. KT14
off Viscount Gdns **152** BL112
Bernays Cl, Stan. HA7 . . . . **41** CJ51
Bernays Gro, SW9 . . . . **101** DM84
Bernel Dr, Croy. CR0 . . . . **143** DZ104
Berne Rd, Th.Hth. CR7 . . . . . . **142** DQ99
Berners Dr, W13 . . . . **79** CG72
Bernersmede, SE3
off Blackheath Pk **104** EG83
Berners Ms, W1 . . . . **195** L7
Berners Pl, W1 . . . . **195** L8
Berners Rd, N1 . . . . **83** DN68
N22 . . . . **45** DN53
Berners St, W1 . . . . **195** L7
Berney Rd, Croy. CR0 . . . . **142** DR101
Bernhardt Cres, NW8 . . . . **194** B4
Bernhart Cl, Edg. HA8 . . . . **42** CQ52
Bernice Cl, Rain. RM13 . . . . **90** FJ70
Bernville Way, Har. HA3
off Kenton Rd **62** CM57
Bernwell Rd, E4 . . . . **48** EE48
Berridge Grn, Edg. HA8 . . . . **42** CN52
Berridge Ms, NW6
off Hillfield Rd **64** DA64
Berridge Rd, SE19 . . . . **122** DR92
Berriman Rd, N7 . . . . **65** DM62
Berrington Dr, Lthd.
(E.Hors.) KT24 . . . . **169** BT124
Berriton Rd, Har. HA2 . . . . **60** BZ60
Berry Av, Wat. WD24 . . . . **23** BU36
Berrybank Cl, E4
off Greenbank Cl **47** EC47
Berry Cl, N21 . . . . **45** DP46
NW10 . . . . **80** CS66
Dagenham RM10 . . . . **70** FA64
Hornchurch RM12
off Airfield Way **72** FJ64
Rickmansworth WD3 . . . . **38** BH45
Berry Ct, Houns. TW4 . . . . **116** BZ85
Berrydale Rd, Hayes UB4 . . . . . **78** BY70
Berryfield, Slou. SL2 . . . . **74** AW72
Berryfield Cl, E17 . . . . **67** EB56
Bromley BR1 . . . . **144** EL95
Berryfield Rd, SE17 . . . . **200** G10
Berry Gro La, Wat. WD25 . . . . . **24** CA39
Berryhill, SE9 . . . . **105** EP84
Berry Hill, Stan. HA7 . . . . **41** CK49
Berryhill Gdns, SE9 . . . . **105** EP84
BERRYLANDS, Surb. KT5 . . . . **138** CM99
⇌ **Berrylands** **138** CN98
Berrylands, SW20 . . . . **139** CW97
Orpington BR6 . . . . **146** EW104
Surbiton KT5 . . . . **138** CN99
Berrylands Rd, Surb. KT5 . . . . **138** CM100
Berry La, SE21 . . . . **122** DR91
Rickmansworth WD3 . . . . . . **38** BH46
Walton-on-Thames KT12
off Burwood Rd **154** BX106
Berryman Cl, Dag. RM8
off Bennetts Castle La **70** EW62
Berrymans La, SE26 . . . . **123** DX91
Berry Meade, Ashtd. KT21 . . . **172** CM117
Berry Meade Cl, Ashtd. KT21
off Berry Meade **172** CM117
Berrymead Gdns, W3 . . . . **80** CQ74
Berrymede Rd, W4 . . . . **98** CR76
Berry Pl, EC1 . . . . **196** G3
Berryscroft Ct, Stai. TW18
off Berryscroft Rd **114** BJ94
Berryscroft Rd, Stai. TW18 . . . **114** BJ94
BERRY'S GREEN, West. TN16 . **179** EP116
Berry's Grn Rd, West.
(Berry's Grn) TN16 . . . . **179** EP116
Berry's Hill, West.
(Berry's Grn) TN16 . . . . **179** EP115
Berrys La, W.Byf.
(Byfleet) KT14 . . . . **152** BK111
Berry St, EC1 . . . . **196** G4
Berry Wk, Ashtd. KT21 . . . . . . **172** CM119
Berry Way, W5 . . . . **98** CL76
Rickmansworth WD3 . . . . **38** BH45
Bersham La, Grays
(Bad.Dene) RM17 . . . . **110** FZ77
Bertal Rd, SW17 . . . . **120** DD91
Berther Rd, Horn. RM11 . . . . . . **72** FK59
Berthold Ms, Wal.Abb. EN9 . . . **15** EB33
Berthon St, SE8 . . . . **103** EA80
Bertie Rd, NW10 . . . . **81** CU65
SE26 . . . . **123** DX93
Bertram Cotts, SW19
off Hartfield Rd **120** DA94
Bertram Rd, NW4 . . . . **63** CU58
Enfield EN1 . . . . **30** DU42
Kingston upon Thames KT2 . **118** CN94
Bertram St, N19 . . . . **65** DH61
Bertram Way, Enf. EN1 . . . . **30** DT42
Bertrand St, SE13 . . . . **103** EB83
Bertrand Way, SE28 . . . . **88** EV73
Bert Rd, Th.Hth. CR7 . . . . **142** DQ99
Berwick Av, Hayes UB4 . . . . **78** BX72
Berwick Cl, Stan. HA7
off Gordon Av **41** CF52
Twickenham TW2
off Springfield Rd **116** CA88
Waltham Cross EN8 . . . . **15** EA34
Berwick Cres, Sid. DA15 . . . . . **125** ES86
Berwick La, Ong. CM5 . . . . **19** FF36
Berwick Pond Cl, Rain. RM13 . . **90** FK68
Berwick Pond Rd, Rain. RM13 . . **90** FL68
Upminster RM14 . . . . **90** FM66
Berwick Rd, E16 . . . . **86** EH72
N22 . . . . **45** DP53
Borehamwood WD6 . . . . **26** CM38
Rainham RM13 . . . . **90** FK68
Welling DA16 . . . . **106** EV81
Berwick St, W1 . . . . **195** M9
Berwick Way, Orp. BR6 . . . . . . **146** EU102
Sevenoaks TN14 . . . . **191** FH121
Berwyn Av, Houns. TW3 . . . . **96** CB81
Berwyn Rd, SE24 . . . . **121** DP88
Richmond TW10 . . . . **98** CP84
Beryl Av, E6 . . . . **86** EL71
Beryl Ho, SE18 *off Spinel Cl* . . **105** ET78
Beryl Rd, W6 . . . . **99** CX78
Berystede, Kings.T. KT2 . . . . . **118** CP94
Besant Ct, N1
off Newington Grn Rd **66** DR64
Besant Rd, NW2 . . . . **63** CY63
Besant Wk, N7
off Newington Barrow Way . **65** DM61
Besant Way, NW10 . . . . **62** CQ64
Besley St, SW16 . . . . **121** DJ93
Bessant Dr, Rich. TW9 . . . . **98** CP81
Bessborough Gdns, SW1 . . . . **199** N10
Bessborough Pl, SW1 . . . . **199** M10
Bessborough Rd, SW15 . . . . . **119** CU88
Harrow HA1 . . . . **61** CD60
Bessborough St, SW1 . . . . **199** M10
BESSELS GREEN, Sev. TN13 . . **190** FC124
Bessels Grn Rd, Sev. TN13 . . . **190** FD123
Bessels Meadow, Sev. TN13 . . **190** FD124
Bessels Way, Sev. TN13 . . . . . **190** FC124
Bessemer Rd, SE5 . . . . **102** DQ82
Bessie Lansbury Cl, E6 . . . . **87** EN72
Bessingby Rd, Ruis. HA4 . . . . . . **59** BU61
Bessingham Wk, SE4
off Frendsbury Rd **103** DX84
Besson St, SE14 . . . . **102** DW81
Bessy St, E2 *off Roman Rd* **84** DW69
Bestwood St, SE8 . . . . **203** J9
Beswick Ms, NW6
off Lymington Rd **82** DB65
Betam Rd, Hayes UB3 . . . . **95** BR75
Beta Pl, SW4 *off Santley St* . . . **101** DL84
Beta Rd, Wok. GU22 . . . . **167** BB116
Woking (Chobham) GU24 . . **150** AT110
Beta Way, Egh. TW20 . . . . **133** BC95
BETCHWORTH **182** CR134
⇌ **Betchworth** **182** CR132
Betchworth Cl, Sutt. SM1
off Turnpike La **158** DD106
Betchworth Rd, Ilf. IG3 . . . . **69** ES61
Betchworth Way, Croy.
(New Adgtn) CR0 . . . . **161** EC109
Betenson Av, Sev. TN13 . . . . . . **190** FF122
Betham Rd, Grnf. UB6 . . . . **79** CD69
Bethany Waye, Felt. TW14 . . . . **115** BS87
Bethecar Rd, Har. HA1 . . . . **61** CE57
Bethell Av, E16 . . . . **86** EF70
Ilford IG1 . . . . **69** EN59
Bethel Rd, Sev. TN13 . . . . **191** FJ123
Welling DA16 . . . . **106** EW83
Bethersden Cl, Beck. BR3 . . . . **123** DZ94
H **Bethlem Royal Hosp**,
Beck. BR3 . . . . **143** EA101
BETHNAL GREEN, E2 . . . . **84** DU68
⇌ **Bethnal Green** **84** DV70
⊖ **Bethnal Green** **84** DW69
Bethnal Grn Est, E2 . . . . **84** DW69
★ **Bethnal Green**
Mus of Childhood, E2 . . . . . **84** DV69
Bethnal Grn Rd, E1 . . . . **197** P4
E2 . . . . **197** P4
Bethune Av, N11 . . . . **44** DF49
Bethune Rd, N16 . . . . **66** DR59
NW10 . . . . **80** CR70
Bethwin Rd, SE5 . . . . **101** DP80
Betjeman Cl, Couls. CR5 . . . . . **175** DM117
Pinner HA5 . . . . **60** CA56
Waltham Cross EN7
off Rosedale Way **14** DU28
Betley Ct, Walt. KT12 . . . . **135** BV104
Betony Cl, Croy. CR0
off Primrose La **143** DX102
Betony Rd, Rom. RM3
off Cloudberry Rd **52** FK51
Betoyne Av, E4 . . . . **48** EE49
BETSHAM, Dart. DA13 . . . . **130** FY91
BETSHAM, Dav. DA13 . . . . **130** FY91
Betsham Rd, Erith DA8 . . . . . . **107** FF80
Gravesend (Sthflt) DA13 . . . **129** FX92
Swanscombe DA10 . . . . **130** FY87
Betstyle Circ, N11 . . . . **45** DH49
Betstyle Rd, N11 . . . . **45** DH49
Betterton Dr, Sid. DA14 . . . . . . **126** EY89
Betterton Rd, Rain. RM13 . . . . . **89** FE69
Betterton St, WC2 . . . . **195** P9
Bettles Cl, Uxb. UB8
off Wescott Way **76** BJ68
Bettons Pk, E15 . . . . **86** EE67
Bettridge Rd, SW6 . . . . **99** CZ82
Betts Cl, Beck. BR3
off Kendall Rd **143** DY96
Betts Ms, E17 *off Queen's Rd* . . **67** DZ58
Betts Rd, E16
off Victoria Dock Rd **86** EH73
Betts St, E1 . . . . **202** D1
Betts Way, SE20 . . . . **142** DV95
Surbiton KT6 . . . . **137** CH102
Betula Cl, Ken. CR8 . . . . **176** DR115
Betula Wk, Rain. RM13 . . . . **90** FK69
Between Sts, Cob. KT11 . . . . . . **153** BU114
Beulah Av, Th.Hth. CR7
off Beulah Rd **142** DQ96
Beulah Cl, Edg. HA8 . . . . **42** CP48
Beulah Cres, Th.Hth. CR7 . . . . . **142** DQ96
Beulah Gro, Croy. CR0 . . . . **142** DQ100
Beulah Hill, SE19 . . . . **121** DP93
Beulah Path, E17
off Addison Rd **67** EB57
Beulah Rd, E17 . . . . **67** EB57
SW19 . . . . **119** CZ94
Epping CM16 . . . . **18** EU29
Hornchurch RM12 . . . . **72** FJ62
Sutton SM1 . . . . **158** DA105
Thornton Heath CR7 . . . . **142** DQ97
Beulah Wk, Cat. (Wold.) CR3 . . **177** DY120
Beult Rd, Dart. DA1 . . . . **107** FG83
Bevan Av, Bark. IG11 . . . . **88** EU66
Bevan Ct, Croy. CR0 . . . . **159** DN106
Bevan Ho, Grays RM16
off Laird Av **110** GD75
Bevan Pk, Epsom KT17 . . . . **157** CT110
Bevan Pl, Swan. BR8 . . . . **147** FF98
Bevan Rd, SE2 . . . . **106** EV78
Barnet EN4 . . . . **28** DF42
Bevans Cl, Green. DA9
off Johnsons Way **129** FW86
Bevan St, N1 . . . . **84** DQ67
Bevan Way, Horn. RM12 . . . . **72** FM63
Bev Callender Cl, SW8
off Daley Thompson Way . . **101** DH83
Bevenden St, N1 . . . . **197** L2
Bevercote Wk, Belv. DA17
off Osborne Rd **106** EZ79
Beveridge Rd, NW10
off Curzon Cres **80** CS66
Beverley Av, SW20 . . . . **139** CT95
Hounslow TW4 . . . . **96** BZ84
Sidcup DA15 . . . . **125** ET87
Beverley Cl, N21 . . . . **46** DQ46
SW11 *off Maysoule Rd* **100** DD84
SW13 . . . . **99** CT82
Addlestone KT15 . . . . **152** BK106
Chessington KT9 . . . . **155** CJ105
Enfield EN1 . . . . **30** DS42
Epsom KT17 . . . . **157** CW111
Hornchurch RM11 . . . . **72** FM59
Weybridge KT13 . . . . **135** BS103
Beverley Cotts, SW15
off Kingston Vale **118** CR91
Beverley Ct, N14 . . . . **45** DJ45
N20 *off Farnham Cl* **44** DC45
SE4 . . . . **103** DZ83
Slough SL1 *off Dolphin Rd* . . **92** AV75
Beverley Cres, Wdf.Grn. IG8 . . . **48** EH53
Beverley Dr, Edg. HA8 . . . . **62** CP55
Beverley Gdns, NW11 . . . . **63** CY59
SW13 . . . . **99** CT83
Hornchurch RM11 . . . . **72** FM59
Stanmore HA7 . . . . **41** CG53
Waltham Cross (Chsht) EN7 . **14** DT30
Wembley HA9 . . . . **62** CM60
Worcester Park KT4
off Green La **139** CU102
Beverley Hts, Reig. RH2 . . . . . . **184** DB132
Beverley Ho, NW8 . . . . **194** B3
Beverley La, SW15 . . . . **119** CT90
Kingston upon Thames KT2 . **118** CS94
Beverley Ms, E4
off Beverley Rd **47** ED51
Beverley Path, SW13 . . . . **99** CT82
Beverley Rd, E4 . . . . **47** ED51
E6 . . . . **86** EK69
SE20 *off Wadhurst Cl* **142** DV96
SW13 . . . . **99** CT83
W4 . . . . **99** CT78
Bexleyheath DA7 . . . . **107** FC82
Bromley BR2 . . . . **144** EL103
Dagenham RM9 . . . . **70** EY63
Kingston upon Thames KT1 . **137** CJ95
Mitcham CR4 . . . . **141** DK98
New Malden KT3 . . . . **139** CU98
Ruislip HA4 . . . . **59** BU61
Southall UB2 . . . . **96** BY76
Sunbury-on-Thames TW16 . **135** BT95
Whyteleafe CR3 . . . . **176** DS116
Worcester Park KT4 . . . . . . **139** CW103
Beverley Trd Est, Mord. SM4
off Garth Rd **139** CX101
Beverley Way, SW20 . . . . **139** CT95
New Malden KT3 . . . . **139** CT95
Beversbrook Rd, N19 . . . . **65** DK62
Beverstone Rd, SW2 . . . . **121** DM85
Thornton Heath CR7 . . . . **141** DN98
Beverston Ms, W1 . . . . **194** D7
Bevill Allen Cl, SW17 . . . . **120** DF92
Bevill Cl, SE25 . . . . **142** DU97
Bevin Cl, SE16 . . . . **203** K2
Bevin Ct, WC1 *off Holford St* . . **83** DN69
Bevington Path, SE1
off Tanner St **102** DT75
Bevington Rd, W10 . . . . **81** CY71
Beckenham BR3 . . . . **143** EB96
Bevington St, SE16 . . . . **202** C5
Bevin Rd, Hayes UB4 . . . . **77** BU69
Bevin Sq, SW17 . . . . **120** DF90
Bevin Way, WC1 . . . . **196** D2
Bevis Cl, Dart. DA2 . . . . **128** FQ87
Bevis Marks, EC3 . . . . **197** N8
Bewcastle Gdns, Enf. EN2 . . . . . **29** DL42
Bewdley St, N1 . . . . **83** DN66
Bewick Ms, SE15 . . . . **102** DV80
Bewick St, SW8 . . . . **101** DH82
Bewley Cl, Wal.Cr.
(Chsht) EN8 . . . . **15** DX31
Bewley St, E1 *off Dellow St* . . . **84** DV73
SW19 . . . . **120** DC93
Bewlys Rd, SE27 . . . . **121** DP92
Bexhill Cl, Felt. TW13 . . . . **116** BY89
Bexhill Rd, N11 . . . . **45** DK50
SE4 . . . . **123** DZ87
SW14 . . . . **98** CQ83
Bexhill Wk, E15 *off Mitre Rd* . . **86** EE68
BEXLEY **126** FA86
⇌ **Bexley** **126** FA88
Bexley Cl, Dart. DA1 . . . . **127** FE85
Bexley Gdns, N9 . . . . **46** DR48
Romford (Chad.Hth) RM6 . . **70** EV57
BEXLEYHEATH **126** EZ85
⇌ **Bexleyheath** **106** EY82
Bexley High St, Bex. DA5 . . . . . **126** FA87
Bexley La, Dart. DA1 . . . . **127** FE85
Sidcup DA14 . . . . **126** EW90
Bexley Rd, SE9 . . . . **125** EP85
Erith DA8 . . . . **107** FC80
Beynon Rd, Cars. SM5 . . . . **158** DF106
Bianca Ho, N1
off Crondall St **84** DS68
Bianca Rd, SE15 . . . . **102** DT79
Bibsworth Rd, N3 . . . . **43** CZ54
Bibury Cl, SE15 . . . . **102** DS79
Bicester Rd, Rich. TW9 . . . . **98** CN83
Bickenhall St, W1 . . . . **194** E6
Bickersteth Rd, SW17 . . . . **120** DF93
Bickerton Rd, N19 . . . . **65** DJ61
BICKLEY, Brom. BR1 . . . . **145** EM97
⇌ **Bickley** **144** EL97
Bickley Cres, Brom. BR1 . . . . . **144** EL98
Bickley Pk Rd, Brom. BR1 . . . . **144** EL97
Bickley Rd, E10 . . . . **67** EB59
Bromley BR1 . . . . **144** EK96
Bickley St, SW17 . . . . **120** DE92
Bicknell Rd, SE5 . . . . **102** DQ83
Bickney Way, Lthd.
(Fetch.) KT22 . . . . **170** CC122
Bicknoller Cl, Sutt. SM2 . . . . . . **158** DB110
Bicknoller Rd, Enf. EN1 . . . . **30** DT39
Bicknor Rd, Orp. BR6 . . . . **145** ES101
Bidborough Cl, Brom. BR2 . . . . **144** EF99
Bidborough St, WC1 . . . . **195** P3
Biddenden Way, SE9 . . . . **125** EN91
Gravesend
(Istead Rise) DA13 . . . . **130** GE94
Biddenham Turn, Wat. WD25 . . **24** BW35
Bidder St, E16 . . . . **86** EE71
Biddestone Rd, N7 . . . . **65** DM63
Biddulph Rd, W9 . . . . **82** DB69
South Croydon CR2 . . . . **160** DQ109
Bideford Av, Grnf. UB6 . . . . **79** CH68
Bideford Cl, Edg. HA8 . . . . **42** CN53
Feltham TW13 . . . . **116** BZ90
Romford RM3 . . . . **52** FJ53
Bideford Gdns, Enf. EN1 . . . . **46** DS45
Bideford Rd, Brom. BR1 . . . . . . **124** EF90
Enfield EN3 . . . . **31** DZ38
Ruislip HA4 . . . . **59** BV62
Welling DA16 . . . . **106** EV80
Bidhams Cres, Tad. KT20 . . . . **173** CW121
Bidwell Gdns, N11 . . . . **45** DJ52
Bidwell St, SE15 . . . . **102** DV81
★ **Big Ben**
(St. Stephens Tower), SW1 . **200** A5
Bigbury Cl, N17 . . . . **46** DS52
Big Common La, Red.
(Bletch.) RH1 . . . . **185** DP133
Biggerstaff Rd, E15 . . . . **85** EC67
Biggerstaff St, N4 . . . . **65** DN61
Biggin Av, Mitch. CR4 . . . . **140** DF95
BIGGIN HILL, West. TN16 . . . . . **178** EH116
Biggin Hill, SE19 . . . . **121** DP94
Biggin Hill Business Pk,
West. TN16 . . . . **178** EK115
Biggin Hill Cl, Kings.T. KT2 . . . **117** CJ92
Biggin La, Grays RM16 . . . . **111** GH79
Biggin Way, SE19 . . . . **121** DP94
Bigginwood Rd, SW16 . . . . **121** DP94
Biggs Gro Rd, Wal.Cr.
(Chsht) EN7 . . . . **14** DR27
Biggs Row, SW15
off Felsham Rd **99** CX83
Big Hill, E5 . . . . **66** DV60
Bigland St, E1 . . . . **84** DV72

★ Place of interest ⇌ Railway station ⊖ London Underground station DLR Docklands Light Railway station Tra Tramlink station H Hospital Riv Pedestrian ferry landing stage

219

Bignell Rd, SE18 105 EP78
Bignell's Cor, Pot.B.
(S.Mimms) EN6 11 CV33
Bignold Rd, E7 68 EG63
Bigwood Rd, NW11 64 DB57
Biko Cl, Uxb. UB8
off Sefton Way 76 BJ72
Billet Cl, Rom. RM6 70 EX55
Billet La, Horn. RM11 72 FK60
Iver SL0 75 BB69
Slough SL3 75 BB73
Billet Rd, E17 47 DX54
Romford RM6 70 EV55
Staines TW18
off Farnell Rd 114 BG90
Billets Hart Cl, W7 97 CE75
Billet Wks, E17 47 DZ53
Bill Hamling Cl, SE9 125 EM89
Billingford Cl, SE4 103 DX84
Billing Pl, SW10 100 DB80
Billing Rd, SW10 100 DB80
Billings Cl, Dag. RM9
off Ellerton Rd 88 EW66
★ Billingsgate Fish Mkt, E14 204 C2
Billing St, SW10 100 DB80
Billington Rd, SE14 103 DX80
Billiter Sq, EC3 197 N10
Billiter St, EC3 197 N9
Bill Nicholson Way, N17
off High Rd 46 DT52
Billockby Cl, Chess. KT9 156 CM107
Billson St, E14 204 E9
Billy Lows La, Pot.B. EN6 12 DA31
Bilsby Gro, SE9 124 EK91
Bilton Cl, Slou. (Poyle) SL3 93 BE82
Bilton Rd, Erith DA8 107 FG80
Greenford UB6 79 CH67
Bilton Way, Enf. EN3 31 DY39
Hayes UB3 95 BV75
Bina Gdns, SW5 100 DC77
Bincote Rd, Enf. EN2 29 DM41
Binden Rd, W12 99 CT76
Bindon Grn, Mord. SM4 140 DB98
Binfield Rd, SW4 101 DL81
South Croydon CR2 160 DT106
West Byfleet (Byfleet) KT14 152 BL112
Bingfield St, N1 83 DL67
Bingham Cl, S.Ock. RM15 91 FV72
Bingham Ct, N1 off Halton Rd 83 DP66
Bingham Dr, Stai. TW18 114 BK94
Woking GU21 166 AT118
Bingham Pl, W1 194 F6
Bingham Pt, SE18
off Whitworth Pl 105 EP77
Bingham Rd, Croy. CR0 142 DU102
Bingham St, N1 84 DR65
Bingley Rd, E16 86 EJ72
Greenford UB6 78 CC71
Sunbury-on-Thames TW16 115 BU94
Binley Ho, SW15
off Highcliffe Dr 119 CU86
Binney St, W1 194 G10
Binns Rd, W4 98 CS78
Binns Ter, W4 off Binns Rd 98 CS78
Binsey Wk, SE2 88 EW74
Binstead Cl, Hayes UB4
off Glencoe Rd 78 BY71
Binyon Cres, Stan. HA7 41 CF50
Birbetts Rd, SE9 125 EM89
Bircham Path, SE4
off St. Norbert Rd 103 DX84
Birchanger Rd, SE25 142 DU99
Birch Av, N13 46 DQ48
Caterham CR3 176 DR124
Leatherhead KT22 171 CF120
West Drayton UB7 76 BM72
Birch Cl, E16 86 EE71
N19 off Hargrave Pk 65 DJ61
SE15 off Bournemouth Rd 102 DU82
Addlestone
(New Haw) KT15 152 BK109
Amersham HP6 20 AS37
Brentford TW8 97 CH80
Buckhurst Hill IG9 48 EK48
Dartford (Eyns.) DA4 148 FK104
Hounslow TW3 97 CD83
Iver SL0 75 BD68
Romford RM7 71 FB55
Sevenoaks TN13 191 FH123
South Ockendon RM15 91 FX69
Teddington TW11 117 CG92
Woking GU21 166 AW119
Birch Copse, St.Alb.
(Brick.Wd) AL2 8 BY30
Birch Ct, Nthwd. HA6
off Rickmansworth Rd 39 BQ51
Birch Cres, Horn. RM11 72 FL56
South Ockendon RM15 91 FX69
Uxbridge UB10 76 BM67
Birchcroft Cl, Cat. CR3 186 DQ125
Birchdale, Ger.Cr. SL9 56 AX60
Birchdale Cl, W.Byf. KT14 152 BJ111
Birchdale Gdns, Rom. RM6 70 EX59
Birchdale Rd, E7 68 EJ64
Birchdene Dr, SE28 106 EU75
Birch Dr, Rick. (Map.Cr.) WD3 37 BD50
Birchen Cl, NW9 62 CR61
Birchend Cl, S.Croy. CR2 160 DR107
Birchen Gro, NW9 62 CR61
Birches, The, N21 29 DM44
SE7 104 EH79
Brentwood CM13 54 FY48
Bushey WD23 24 CC43
Epping (N.Wld Bas.) CM16 19 FB26
Orpington BR6 163 EN105
Swanley BR8 147 FE96
Waltham Abbey EN9
off Honey La 16 EF34
Woking GU22
off Heathside Rd 167 AZ118
Birches Cl, Epsom KT18 172 CS115
Mitcham CR4 140 DF97
Pinner HA5 60 BY57
Birchfield Cl, Add. KT15 152 BH105
Coulsdon CR5 175 DM116
Birchfield Gro, Epsom KT17 157 CW110
Birchfield Rd, Wal.Cr.
(Chsht) EN8 14 DV29
Birchfield St, E14 85 EA73
Birch Gdns, Amer. HP7 20 AS39
Dagenham RM10 71 FC62
Birchgate Ms, Tad. KT20
off Bidhams Cres 173 CW121
Birch Grn, NW9
off Clayton Fld 42 CS52
Staines TW18 114 BG91
Birch Gro, E11 68 EE62
SE12 124 EF87
W3 80 CN74
Cobham KT11 154 BW114
Potters Bar EN6 12 DA32
Shepperton TW17 135 BS96
Tadworth KT20 173 CY124
Welling DA16 106 EU84
Woking GU22 167 BD115
★ Birch Hall, Epp. CM16 33 EQ36
Birch Hill, Croy. CR0 161 DX106
Birchington Cl, Bexh. DA7 107 FB81
Orpington BR5
off Hart Dyke Rd 146 EW102
Birchington Rd, N8 65 DK58
NW6 82 DA67
Surbiton KT5 138 CM101
Birchin La, EC3 197 L9
Birchlands Av, SW12 120 DF87
Birch La, Hem.H. (Flaun.) HP3 5 BB33
Purley CR8 159 DL111
Birch Mead, Orp. BR6 145 EN103
Birchmead, Wat. WD17 23 BT38
Birchmead Av, Pnr. HA5 60 BW56
Birchmere Row, SE3 104 EF82
Birchmore Wk, N5 66 DQ62
Birch Pk, Har. HA3 40 CC52
Birch Pl, Green. DA9 129 FS86
Birch Rd, Felt. TW13 116 BX92
Romford RM7 71 FB55
Birch Row, Brom. BR2 145 EN101
Birch Tree Av, W.Wick. BR4 162 EF106
Birch Tree Gro, Chesh.
(Ley Hill) HP5 4 AV30
Birch Tree Wk, Wat. WD17 23 BT37
Birch Tree Way, Croy. CR0 142 DV103
Birch Vale, Cob. KT11 154 CA112
Birch Vw, Epp. CM16 18 EV29
Birchville Ct, Bushey
(Bushey Hth) WD23
off Heathbourne Rd 41 CE46
Birch Wk, Borwd. WD6 26 CN39
Erith DA8 107 FC79
Mitcham CR4 141 DH95
West Byfleet KT14 152 BG112
Birchway, Hayes UB3 77 BU74
Birch Way, St.Alb.
(Lon.Col.) AL2 9 CK27
Warlingham CR6 177 DY118
Birch Wd, Rad. (Shenley) WD7 10 CN34
Birchwood, Wal.Abb. EN9
off Roundhills 16 EE34
Birchwood Av, N10 64 DG55
Beckenham BR3 143 DZ98
Sidcup DA14 126 EV89
Wallington SM6 140 DG104
Birchwood Cl, Brwd. CM13
off Canterbury Way 53 FW51
Morden SM4 140 DB98
Birchwood Ct, N13 45 DP50
Edgware HA8 42 CQ54
Birchwood Dr, NW3 64 DB62
Dartford DA2 127 FE91
West Byfleet KT14 152 BG112
Birchwood Gro,
Hmptn. TW12 116 CA93
Birchwood La, Cat. CR3 185 DP125
Esher KT10 155 CD110
Leatherhead KT22 155 CD110
Sevenoaks (Knock.) TN14 180 EZ115
Birchwood Pk Av, Swan. BR8 147 FE97
Birchwood Rd, SW17 121 DH92
Dartford DA2 127 FE92
Orpington BR5 145 ER98
Swanley BR8 147 FC95
West Byfleet KT14 152 BG112
Birchwood Ter, Swan. BR8
off Birchwood Rd 147 FC95
Birchwood Way, St.Alb.
(Park St) AL2 8 CB28
Birdbrook Cl, Brwd.
(Hutt.) CM13 55 GB44
Dagenham RM10 89 FC66
Birdbrook Rd, SE3 104 EJ83
Birdcage Wk, SW1 199 L5
Birdham Cl, Brom. BR1 144 EL99
Birdhouse La, Orp. BR6 179 EN115
Birdhurst Av, S.Croy. CR2 160 DR105
Birdhurst Gdns, S.Croy. CR2 160 DR105
Birdhurst Ri, S.Croy. CR2 160 DS106
Birdhurst Rd, SW18 100 DC84
SW19 120 DE93
South Croydon CR2 160 DS106
Bird in Bush Rd, SE15 102 DU80
Bird-in-Hand La, Brom. BR1 144 EK96
Bird-in-Hand Pas, SE23
off Dartmouth Rd 122 DW89
Bird La, Brwd.
(Gt Warley) CM13 73 FX55
Upminster RM14 73 FR57
Uxbridge (Hare.) UB9 38 BJ54
Birds Fm Av, Rom. RM5 51 FB53
Birdsfield La, E3 85 DZ67
Birds Hill Dr, Lthd.
(Oxshott) KT22 155 CD113
Birds Hill Ri, Lthd.
(Oxshott) KT22 155 CD113
Birds Hill Rd, Lthd.
(Oxshott) KT22 155 CD112
Bird St, W1 194 G9
Birdswood Dr, Wok. GU21 166 AS119
Bird Wk, Twick. TW2 116 BZ88
Birdwood Cl, S.Croy. CR2 161 DX111
Teddington TW11 117 CE91
⇌ Birkbeck 142 DW97
Trm Birkbeck 142 DW97
Birkbeck Av, W3 80 CQ73
Greenford UB6 78 CC67
Birkbeck Gdns, Wdf.Grn. IG8 48 EF47
Birkbeck Gro, W3 98 CR75
Birkbeck Hill, SE21 121 DP89
Birkbeck Ms, E8
off Sandringham Rd 66 DT64
W3 off Birkbeck Rd 80 CR74
Birkbeck Pl, SE21 122 DQ88
Birkbeck Rd, E8 66 DT64
N8 65 DL56
N12 44 DC50
N17 46 DT53
NW7 43 CT50
SW19 120 DB92
W3 80 CR74
W5 97 CJ77
Beckenham BR3 142 DW96
Brentwood (Hutt.) CM13 55 GD44
Enfield EN2 30 DR39
Ilford IG2 69 ER57
Romford RM7 71 FD60
Sidcup DA14 126 EU90
Birkbeck St, E2 84 DV69
Birkbeck Way, Grnf. UB6 78 CC67
Birkdale Av, Pnr. HA5 60 CA55
Romford RM3 52 FM52
Birkdale Cl, SE16
off Masters Dr 102 DV78
SE28 off Redbourne Dr 88 EX72
Orpington BR6 145 ER101
Birkdale Gdns, Croy. CR0 161 DX105
Watford WD19 40 BX48
Birkdale Rd, SE2 106 EU77
W5 80 CL70
Birkenhead Av, Kings.T. KT2 138 CM96
Birkenhead St, WC1 196 A2
Birken Ms, Nthwd. HA6 39 BP50
Birkett Way, Ch.St.G. HP8 20 AX41
Birkhall Rd, SE6 123 ED88
Birkheads Rd, Reig. RH2 184 DA133
Birklands La, St.Alb. AL1 9 CH25
Birkwood Cl, SW12 121 DK87
Birley Rd, N20 44 DC47
Birley St, SW11 100 DG82
Birling Rd, Erith DA8 107 FD80
Birnam Rd, N4 65 DM61
Birnham Cl, Wok.
(Send M.) GU23 168 BG123
Birrell Ho, SW9
off Stockwell Rd 101 DM82
Birse Cres, NW10 62 CS63
Birstall Grn, Wat. WD19 40 BX49
Birstall Rd, N15 66 DS57
Birtley Path, Borwd. WD6 26 CL39
Biscay Rd, W6 99 CX78
Biscoe Cl, Houns. TW5 96 CA79
Biscoe Way, SE13 103 ED83
Bisenden Rd, Croy. CR0 142 DS103
Bisham Cl, Cars. SM5 140 DF102
Bisham Gdns, N6 64 DG60
Bishop Butt Cl, Orp. BR6
off Stapleton Rd 145 ET104
Bishop Cl, W4 98 CQ78
Bishop Duppa's Pk,
Shep. TW17 135 BR101
Bishop Fox Way, W.Mol. KT8 136 BZ98
Bishop Ken Rd, Har. HA3 41 CF54
Bishop Kings Rd, W14 99 CY77
Bishop Rd, N14 45 DH45
Bishop's Av, E13 86 EH67
SW6 99 CX82
Bishops Av, Borwd.
(Elstree) WD6 26 CM43
Bromley BR1 144 EJ96
Northwood HA6 39 BS49
Romford RM6 70 EW58
Bishops Av, The, N2 64 DD59
Bishops Br, W2 82 DC72
Bishops Br Rd, W2 82 DB72
Bishops Cl, E17 67 EB56
N19 off Wyndham Cres 65 DJ62
SE9 125 EQ89
Barnet EN5 27 CX44
Bishop's Cl, Couls. CR5 175 DN118
Bishops Cl, Enf. EN1
off Central Av 30 DV40
Richmond TW10 117 CK90
Bishop's Cl, Sutt. SM1 140 DA104
Bishops Cl, Uxb. UB10 76 BN68
Bishop's Ct, EC4 196 F8
WC2 196 D8
Bishops Ct, Abb.L. WD5
off Breakspeare Rd 7 BT31
Greenhithe DA9 129 FS85
Waltham Cross EN8
off Churchgate 14 DV30
Bishops Dr, Felt. TW14 115 BR86
Northolt UB5 78 BY67
Bishopsford Rd, Mord. SM4 140 DC101
Bishopsgate, EC2 197 M9
Bishopsgate Arc, EC2 197 N7
Bishopsgate Chyd, EC2 197 M7
Bishopsgate Rd, Egh.
(Eng.Grn) TW20 112 AT90
Bishops Gro, N2 64 DD58
Hampton TW12 116 BZ91
Bishop's Hall, Kings.T. KT1 137 CK96
Bishops Hall Rd, Brwd.
(Pilg.Hat.) CM15 54 FV44
Bishops Hill, Walt. KT12 135 BU101
Bishopsmead Cl,
Epsom KT19 156 CS110
Bishop's Pk, SW6 99 CX82
Bishop's Pk Rd, SW6 99 CX82
Bishops Pk Rd, SW16 141 DL95
Bishops Pl, Sutt. SM1
off Lind Rd 158 DC106
Bishops Rd, N6 64 DG58
SW6 99 CZ81
Bishop's Rd, SW11 100 DE80
Bishops Rd, W7 97 CE75
Croydon CR0 141 DP101
Hayes UB3 77 BQ71
Slough SL1 92 AU75
Bishops Ter, SE11 200 E8
Bishopsthorpe Rd, SE26 123 DX91
Bishop St, N1 84 DQ67
Bishops Wk, Chis. BR7 145 EQ95
Croydon CR0 161 DX106
Bishop's Wk, Pnr. HA5
off High St 60 BY55
Bishops Way, E2 84 DV68
Bishops Way, Egham TW20 113 BD93
Bishops Wd, Wok. GU21 166 AT117
H Bishopswood Private Hosp,
Nthwd. HA6 39 BP51
Bishopswood Rd, N6 64 DF59
Bishop Wk, Brwd.
(Shenf.) CM15 55 FZ47
Bishop Way, NW10 80 CS66
Bishop Wilfred Wd Cl, SE15
off Moncrieff St 102 DU82
Biskra, Wat. WD17 23 BU39
Bisley Cl, Wal.Cr. EN8 15 DX33
Worcester Park KT4 139 CW102
Bisley Ho, SW19 119 CX89
Bispham Rd, NW10 80 CM69
Bisson Rd, E15 85 EC68
Bisterne Av, E17 67 ED55
Bittacy Cl, NW7 43 CX51
Bittacy Hill, NW7 43 CX51
Bittacy Pk Av, NW7 43 CX51
Bittacy Ri, NW7 43 CW51
Bittacy Rd, NW7 43 CX51
Bittams La, Cher. KT16 151 BE105
Bittern Cl, Hayes UB4 78 BX71
Hemel Hempstead HP3
off Belswains La 6 BM25
Waltham Cross (Chsht) EN7 14 DQ25
Bitterne Dr, Wok. GU21 166 AT117
Bittern St, SE1 201 H5
Bittoms, The, Kings.T. KT1 137 CK97
Bixley Cl, Sthl. UB2 96 BZ77
Black Acre Cl, Amer. HP7 20 AS39
Blackacre Rd, Epp.
(They.B.) CM16 33 ES37
Blackall St, EC2 197 M4
Blackberry Cl, Shep. TW17
off Cherry Way 135 BS98
Blackberry Fm Cl, Houns. TW5 96 BY80
Blackberry Fld, Orp. BR5 146 EU95
Blackbird Hill, NW9 62 CQ61
Blackbirds La, Wat.
(Ald.) WD25 25 CD35
Blackbird Yd, E2
off Ravenscroft St 84 DT69
Blackborne Rd, Dag. RM10 88 FA65
Blackborough Cl, Reig. RH2 184 DC134
Black Boy La, N15 66 DQ57
Black Boy Wd, St.Alb.
(Brick.Wd) AL2 8 CA30
Blackbridge Rd, Wok. GU22 166 AX119
Blackbrook La, Brom.
BR1, BR2 145 EN97
Blackburn, The, Lthd. (Bkhm) KT23
off Little Bookham St 170 BZ124
Blackburne's Ms, W1 194 F10
Blackburn Rd, NW6 82 DB65
Blackburn Trd Est, Stai.
(Stanw.) TW19 114 BM86
Blackbury Cl, Pot.B. EN6 12 DC31
Blackbush Av, Rom. RM6 70 EX57
Blackbush Cl, Sutt. SM2 158 DB108
Blackdale, Wal.Cr. (Chsht) EN7 14 DU27
Blackdown Av, Wok. GU22 167 BE115
Blackdown Cl, N2 44 DC54
Woking GU22 167 BC116
Blackdown Ter, SE18
off Prince Imperial Rd 105 EN80
Black Eagle Cl, West. TN16 189 EQ127
Blackett Cl, Stai. TW18 133 BE96
Blackett St, SW15 99 CX83
Blacketts Wd Dr, Rick.
(Chorl.) WD3 21 BB43
Black Fan Cl, Enf. EN2 30 DQ39
BLACKFEN, Sid. DA15 125 ET87
Blackfen Rd, Sid. DA15 125 ES85
Blackford Cl, S.Croy. CR2 159 DP109
Blackford Rd, Wat. WD19 40 BX50
Blackford's Path, SW15
off Roehampton High St 119 CU87
⇌ Blackfriars 196 G10
⊖ Blackfriars 196 G10
Blackfriars Br, EC4 196 F10
SE1 196 F10
Blackfriars Ct, EC4 196 F10
Black Friars La, EC4 196 F10
Riv Blackfriars Millennium Pier 196 E10
Blackfriars Pas, EC4 196 F10
Blackfriars Rd, SE1 200 F5
Black Gates, Pnr. HA5
off Church La 60 BZ55
Blackhall La, Sev. TN15 191 FK123
Blackhall Pl, Sev. TN15
off Blackhall La 191 FL124
BLACKHEATH, SE3 104 EE81
★ Blackheath, SE3 103 ED81
⇌ Blackheath 104 EE83
Blackheath Av, SE10 103 ED80
Blackheath Gro, SE3 104 EF82
Blackheath Hill, SE10 103 EC81
H Blackheath Hosp, The,
SE3 104 EE83
BLACKHEATH PARK, SE3 104 EF84
Blackheath Pk, SE3 104 EF83
Blackheath Ri, SE13 103 EC82
Blackheath Rd, SE10 103 EB81
Blackheath Vale, SE3 104 EE82
Blackheath Village, SE3 104 EF82
Blackhills, Esher KT10 154 CA109
Blackhorse Cl, Amer. HP6 20 AS36
Black Horse Ct, SE1 201 L6
Blackhorse Cres, Amer. HP6 20 AS38
Trm Blackhorse Lane 142 DU101
Blackhorse La, E17 67 DX56
Croydon CR0 142 DU101
Epping (N.Wld Bas.) CM16 19 FD25
Potters Bar EN6 10 CS30
Reigate RH2 184 DB129
Blackhorse Ms, E17
off Blackhorse La 67 DX55
Black Horse Pl, Uxb. UB8
off Waterloo Rd 76 BJ67
⇌ Blackhorse Road 67 DX56
⊖ Blackhorse Road 67 DX56
Blackhorse Rd, E17 67 DX56
SE8 103 DY78
Sidcup DA14 126 EU91
Black Lake Cl, Egh. TW20 133 BA95
Blacklands Dr, Hayes UB4 77 BQ70
Blacklands Meadow, Red.
(Nutfld) RH1 185 DL133
Blacklands Rd, SE6 123 EC91
Blacklands Ter, SW3 198 D9
Blackley Cl, Wat. WD17 23 BT37
Black Lion Hill, Rad.
(Shenley) WD7 10 CL32
Black Lion La, W6 99 CU77
Black Lion Ms, W6
off Black Lion La 99 CU77
Blackmans Cl, Dart. DA1 128 FJ88
Blackmans La, Warl. CR6 162 EE114
Blackmead, Sev.
(Rvrhd) TN13 190 FE121
Blackmoor La, Wat. WD18 23 BR43
Blackmore Av, Sthl. UB1 79 CD74
Blackmore Cl, Grays RM17 110 GC78
Blackmore Ct, Wal.Abb. EN9 16 EG33
Blackmore Cres, Wok. GU21 167 BB115
Blackmore Rd, Buck.H. IG9 48 EL45
Blackmores Gro, Tedd. TW11 117 CG93
Blackmore Twr, W3 98 CQ75
Blackmore Way, Uxb. UB8 76 BK65
Blackness La, Kes. BR2 162 EK109
Woking GU22 166 AY119
★ Black Park Country Pk,
Slou. SL3 75 AZ67
Black Pk Rd, Slou. SL3 75 AZ68
Black Path, E10 67 DX59
Blackpool Gdns, Hayes UB4 77 BS70
Blackpool Rd, SE15 102 DV82
Black Prince Cl, W.Byf.
(Byfleet) KT14 152 BM114
Black Prince Rd, SE1 200 B9
SE11 200 C9
Black Rod Cl, Hayes UB3 95 BT76
Blackshaw Pl, N1
off Hertford Rd 84 DS66
Blackshaw Rd, SW17 120 DC91
Blackshots La, Grays RM16 110 GD75
Blacksmith Cl, Ashtd. KT21
off Rectory La 172 CM119
Blacksmith Row, Slou. SL3 93 BA77
Blacksmiths Cl, Rom. RM6 70 EW58
Blacksmiths Hill, S.Croy. CR2 160 DU113
Blacksmiths La, Cher. KT16 134 BG101
Orpington BR5 146 EW99
Rainham RM13 89 FF67
Staines TW18 134 BH97
Uxbridge (Denh.) UB9 57 BC61
Blacks Rd, W6
off Queen Caroline St 99 CW77
Blackstock Ms, N4
off Blackstock Rd 65 DP61
Blackstock Rd, N4 65 DP61
N5 65 DP61
Blackstone Est, E8 84 DV66
Blackstone Rd, NW2 63 CW64
Black Swan Yd, SE1 201 N4
Black's Yd, Sev. TN13
off Bank St 191 FJ125
Blackthorn Av, West Dr. UB7 94 BN77
Blackthorn Cl, Wat. WD25 7 BV32
Blackthorn Ct, Houns. TW5 96 BY80
Blackthorn Dell, Slou. SL3 92 AW76
Blackthorne Av, Croy. CR0 142 DW101
Blackthorne Cres, Slou.
(Colnbr.) SL3 93 BE83
Blackthorne Dr, E4 47 ED49
Blackthorne Rd, Slou.
(Colnbr.) SL3 93 BE83
Westerham (Bigg.H.) TN16 178 EK116
Blackthorn Gro, Bexh. DA7 106 EX83
Blackthorn St, E3 85 EA70
Blackthorn Way, Brwd. CM14 54 FX50
Blacktree Ms, SW9 101 DN83
DLR Blackwall 204 E1
Blackwall La, SE10 205 J10
Blackwall Pier, E14 205 H1
Blackwall Trd Est, E14 85 ED71
Blackwall Tunnel, E14 204 F1
Blackwall Tunnel App, SE10 205 H5
Blackwall Tunnel Northern App,
E3 85 EA68
E14 85 EA68
Blackwall Way, E14 204 E1
Blackwater Cl, E7 68 EF63
Rainham RM13 89 FD71
Blackwater Rd, Sutt. SM1
off High St 158 DB105
Blackwater St, SE22 122 DT85
Blackwell Cl, E5 67 DX63
Harrow HA3 41 CD52
Blackwell Dr, Wat. WD19 24 BW44
Blackwell Gdns, Edg. HA8 42 CN48
Blackwell Hall La, Chesh. HP5 4 AW33
Blackwell Rd, Kings L. WD4 6 BN29
Blackwood Av, N18
off Harbet Rd 47 DX50
Blackwood Cl, W.Byf. KT14 152 BJ112
Blackwood Ct, Brox. EN10
off Groom Rd 15 DZ26
Blackwood St, SE17 201 K10
Blade Ms, SW15
off Deodar Rd 99 CZ84
Bladen Cl, Wey. KT13 153 BR107
Blades Cl, Lthd. KT22 171 CK120
Blades Ct, SW15
off Deodar Rd 99 CZ84
Bladindon Dr, Bex. DA5 126 EW87
Bladon Gdns, Har. HA2 60 CB58
Blagdens Cl, N14 45 DJ47
Blagdens La, N14 45 DK47
Blagdon Rd, SE13 123 EB86
New Malden KT3 139 CT98
Blagdon Wk, Tedd. TW11 117 CJ93
Blagrove Rd, W10 81 CY71
Blair Av, NW9 62 CS59
Esher KT10 136 CC103
Blair Cl, N1 84 DQ65
Hayes UB3 95 BU77
Sidcup DA15 125 ES85
Blairderry Rd, SW2 121 DL89
Blair Dr, Sev. TN13 191 FH123
Blairhead Dr, Wat. WD19 39 BV48
Blair Rd, Slou. SL1 74 AS74
Blair St, E14 85 EC72
Blake Av, Bark. IG11 87 ES67
Blakeborough Dr, Rom.
(Harold Wd) RM3 52 FL54
Blake Cl, W10 81 CW71
Carshalton SM5 140 DE101

★ Place of interest ⇌ Railway station ⊖ London Underground station DLR Docklands Light Railway station Trm Tramlink station H Hospital Riv Pedestrian ferry landing stage

Blake Cl, Rainham RM13 89 FF67
Welling DA16 105 ES81
Blakeden Dr, Esher (Clay.) KT10 155 CF107
Blake Gdns, SW6 100 DB81
Dartford DA1 108 FM84
Blake Hall Cres, E11 68 EG60
Blake Hall Rd, E11 68 EG59
Blakehall Rd, Cars. SM5 158 DF107
Blake Hall Rd, Ong. CM5 19 FG25
Blake Ho, Beck. BR3 123 EA93
Blake Ms, Rich. TW9
off High Pk Rd 98 CN81
Blakemore Rd, SW16 121 DL90
Thornton Heath CR7 141 DM99
Blakemore Way, Belv. DA17 106 EY76
Blakeney Av, Beck. BR3 143 DZ95
Blakeney Cl, E8
off Ferncliff Rd 66 DU64
N20 44 DC46
NW1 off Rossendale Way 83 DK66
Epsom KT19 156 CR111
Blakeney Rd, Beck. BR3 123 DZ94
Blakenham Rd, SW17 120 DF91
Blaker Ct, SE7 off Fairlawn 104 EJ80
Blake Rd, E16 86 EF70
N11 45 DJ52
Croydon CR0 142 DS103
Mitcham CR4 140 DE97
Blaker Rd, E15 85 EC67
Blakes Av, N.Mal. KT3 139 CT99
Blake's Grn, W.Wick. BR4 143 EC102
Blakes La, N.Mal. KT3 139 CT99
Blakesley Av, W5 79 CJ72
Blakesley Ho, E12
off Grantham Rd 69 EN62
Blakesley Wk, SW20
off Kingston Rd 139 CZ96
Blakes Rd, SE15 102 DS80
Blakes Ter, N.Mal. KT3 139 CU99
Blake St, SE8
off Watergate St 103 EA79
Blakesware Gdns, N9 46 DR45
Blakes Way, Til. RM18
off Coleridge Rd 111 GJ82
Blakewood Cl, Felt. TW13 116 BW91
Blanchard Cl, SE9 124 EL90
Blanchard Gro, Enf. EN3 31 EA38
Blanchard Ms, Rom. RM3
off Avenue Rd 52 FK54
Blanchard Way, E8 84 DU65
Blanch Cl, SE15
off Culmore Rd 102 DW80
Blanchedowne, SE5 102 DR84
Blanche La, Pot.B. EN6 11 CT34
Blanche St, E16 86 EF70
Blanchland Rd, Mord. SM4 140 DB99
Blanchmans Rd, Warl. CR6 177 DY118
Blandfield Rd, SW12 120 DG86
Blandford Av, Beck. BR3 143 DY96
Twickenham TW2 116 CB88
Blandford Cl, N2 64 DC56
Croydon CR0 141 DL104
Romford RM7 71 FB56
Slough SL3 92 AX76
Woking GU22 167 BB117
Blandford Ct, Slou. SL3
off Blandford Rd S 92 AX76
Blandford Cres, E4 47 EC45
Blandford Rd, W4 98 CS76
W5 97 CK75
Beckenham BR3 142 DW96
Southall UB2 96 CA77
Teddington TW11 117 CD92
Blandford Rd N, Slou. SL3 92 AX76
Blandford Rd S, Slou. SL3 92 AX76
Blandford Sq, NW1 194 C5
Blandford St, W1 194 E8
Blandford Waye, Hayes UB4 78 BW72
Bland St, SE9 104 EK84
Blaney Cres, E6 87 EP69
Blanmerle Rd, SE9 125 EP88
Blann Cl, SE9 124 EK86
Blantyre St, SW10 100 DD80
Blantyre Wk, SW10
off Blantyre St 100 DD80
Blashford, NW3 82 DF66
Blashford St, SE13 123 ED87
Blasker Wk, E14 204 A10
Blattner Cl, Borwd. (Elstree) WD6 26 CL42
Blawith Rd, Har. HA1 61 CE56
Blaxland Ter, Wal.Cr. (Chsht) EN8
off Davison Dr 15 DX28
Blaydon Cl, N17 46 DV52
Ruislip HA4 59 BS59
Blaydon Wk, N17 46 DV52
Blays Cl, Egh. (Eng.Grn) TW20 112 AW93
Blays La, Egh. (Eng.Grn) TW20 112 AV94
Bleak Hill La, SE18 105 ET79
Blean Gro, SE20 122 DW94
Bleasdale Av, Grnf. UB6 79 CG68
Blechynden St, W10
off Bramley Rd 81 CX73
Bleddyn Cl, Sid. DA15 126 EW86
Bledlow Cl, SE28 88 EW73
Bledlow Ri, Grnf. UB6 78 CC68
Bleeding Heart Yd, EC1 196 E7
Blegborough Rd, SW16 121 DJ93
Blencarn Cl, Wok. GU21 166 AT116
Blendon Dr, Bex. DA5 126 EX86
Blendon Path, Brom. BR1 124 EF94
Blendon Rd, Bex. DA5 126 EX86
Blendon Ter, SE18 105 EQ78
Blendworth Pt, SW15
off Wanborough Dr 119 CV88
Blendworth Way, SE15
off Blakes Rd 102 DS80
Blenheim Av, Ilf. IG2 69 EN58
Blenheim Cl, N21
off Elm Pk Rd 46 DQ46
SE12 124 EH88
SW20 139 CW97
Dartford DA1 128 FJ86
Greenford UB6
off Leaver Gdns 79 CD68
Romford RM7 71 FC56
Slough SL3 75 AZ74
Upminster RM14 73 FS60
Blenheim Cl, Wallington SM6 159 DJ108
Watford WD19 40 BX45
West Byfleet KT14
off Madeira Rd 151 BF113
Blenheim Ct, N19
off Marlborough Rd 65 DL61
Sidcup DA14 125 ER90
Sutton SM2
off Wellesley Rd 158 DC107
Woodford Green IG8
off Navestock Cres 48 EJ52
Blenheim Cres, W11 81 CY72
Ruislip HA4 59 BR61
South Croydon CR2 160 DQ108
West Drayton UB7 94 BN77
Blenheim Dr, Well. DA16 105 ET81
Blenheim Gdns, NW2 63 CW64
SW2 121 DM86
Kingston upon Thames KT2 118 CP94
South Croydon CR2 160 DU112
South Ockendon (Aveley) RM15 90 FP74
Wallington SM6 159 DJ107
Wembley HA9 62 CL62
Woking GU22 166 AV119
Blenheim Gro, SE15 102 DU82
Blenheim Pk Rd, S.Croy. CR2 160 DQ109
Blenheim Pas, NW8
off Blenheim Ter 82 DC68
Blenheim Ri, N15
off Talbot Rd 66 DT56
Blenheim Rd, E6 86 EK69
E15 68 EE63
E17 67 DX55
NW8 82 DC68
SE20 off Maple Rd 122 DW94
SW20 139 CW97
W4 98 CS76
Abbots Langley WD5 7 BU33
Barnet EN5 27 CX41
Brentwood (Pilg.Hat.) CM15 54 FU44
Bromley BR1 144 EL98
Dartford DA1 128 FJ86
Epsom KT19 156 CR111
Harrow HA2 60 CB58
Northolt UB5 78 CB65
Orpington BR6 146 EW103
Sidcup DA15 126 EW88
Slough SL3 92 AX77
Sutton SM1 140 DA104
Blenheim Shop Cen, SE20 122 DW94
Blenheim St, W1 195 H9
Blenheim Ter, NW8 82 DC68
Blenheim Way, Epp. (N.Wld Bas.) CM16 18 FA27
Isleworth TW7 97 CG81
Blenhiem Pl, Tedd. TW11
off Teddington Pk 117 CF91
Blenkarne Rd, SW11 120 DF86
Bleriot Rd, Houns. TW5 96 BW80
Blessbury Rd, Edg. HA8 42 CQ53
Blessington Cl, SE13 103 ED83
Blessington Rd, SE13 103 ED83
Blessing Way, Bark. IG11 88 EW69
BLETCHINGLEY, Red. RH1 186 DQ132
Bletchingley Cl, Red. RH1 185 DJ129
Thornton Heath CR7 141 DP98
Bletchingley Rd, Gdse. RH9 186 DU131
Redhill (Bletch.) RH1 185 DN133
Redhill (S.Merst.) RH1 185 DJ129
Bletchley Ct, N1 197 K1
Bletchley St, N1 197 J1
Bletchmore Cl, Hayes UB3 95 BR78
Bletsoe Wk, N1
off Cropley St 84 DQ68
Blewbury Ho, SE2
off Yarnton Way 106 EX75
Bligh Rd, Grav. DA11 131 GG86
Bligh's Rd, Sev. TN13 191 FH125
Blincoe Cl, SW19 119 CX89
Blind La, Slou. (Geo.Grn) SL3 74 AY72
Blind La, Bans. SM7 174 DE115
Loughton (High Beach) IG10 32 EE40
Waltham Abbey EN9 16 EJ33
Blindman's La, Wal.Cr. (Chsht) EN8 15 DX30
Bliss Cres, SE13 103 EB82
Blissett St, SE10 103 EC81
Bliss Ms, W10 off Third Av 81 CY69
Blisworth Cl, Hayes UB4
off Braunston Dr 78 BY70
Blithbury Rd, Dag. RM9 88 EV65
Blithdale Rd, SE2 106 EU77
Blithfield St, W8 100 DB76
Blockhouse Rd, Grays RM17 110 GC79
Blockley Rd, Wem. HA0 61 CH61
Bloemfontein Av, W12 81 CV74
Bloemfontein Rd, W12 81 CV73
Blomfield Rd, W9 82 DC71
Blomfield St, EC2 197 L7
Blomfield Vil, W2 82 DB71
Blomville Rd, Dag. RM8 70 EY62
Blondell Cl, West Dr. UB7 94 BK79
Blondel St, SW11 100 DG82
Blondin Av, W5 97 CJ77
Blondin St, E3 85 EA68
Bloomburg St, SW1 199 L9
Bloomfield Cl, Wok. (Knap.) GU21 166 AS118
Bloomfield Cres, Ilf. IG2 69 EP58
Bloomfield Pl, W1 195 J10
Bloomfield Rd, N6 64 DG58
SE18 105 EP78
Bromley BR2 144 EK99
Kingston upon Thames KT1 138 CL98
Waltham Cross (Chsht) EN7 14 DQ25
Bloomfield Ter, SW1 198 G10
Westerham TN16 189 ES125
Bloom Gro, SE27 121 DP90
Bloomhall Rd, SE19 122 DR92
Bloom Pk Rd, SW6 99 CZ80
BLOOMSBURY, WC1 195 N7
Bloomsbury Cl, NW7 43 CU52
W5 80 CM73
Epsom KT19 156 CR110
Bloomsbury Ct, WC1 196 A7
Pinner HA5 60 BZ55
Bloomsbury Ho, SW4 121 DK86
Bloomsbury Pl, SW18
off Fullerton Rd 120 DC85
WC1 196 A6
Bloomsbury Sq, WC1 196 A7
Bloomsbury St, WC1 195 N7
Bloomsbury Way, WC1 195 P8
Blore Cl, SW8
off Thessaly Rd 101 DK81
Blore Ct, W1 195 M9
Blossom Cl, W5
off Almond Av 98 CL75
Dagenham RM9 88 EZ67
South Croydon CR2 160 DT106
Blossom La, Enf. EN2 30 DQ39
Blossom St, E1 197 N6
Blossom Way, Uxb. UB10 76 BM66
West Drayton UB7 94 BN77
Blossom Waye, Houns. TW5 96 BY80
Blount St, E14 85 DY72
Bloxam Gdns, SE9 124 EL85
Bloxhall Rd, E10 67 DZ60
Bloxham Cres, Hmptn. TW12 116 BZ94
Bloxworth Cl, Wall. SM6 141 DJ104
Blucher Rd, SE5 102 DQ80
Blue Anchor All, Rich. TW9
off Kew Rd 98 CL84
Blue Anchor La, SE16 202 C8
Tilbury (W.Til.) RM18 111 GL77
Blue Anchor Yd, E1 84 DU73
Blue Ball La, Egh. TW20 113 AZ92
Blue Ball Yd, SW1 199 K3
Blue Barn La, Wey. KT13 152 BN111
Bluebell Av, E12 68 EK64
Bluebell Cl, E9
off Moulins Rd 84 DW67
SE26 122 DT91
Northolt UB5
off Abbott Cl 78 BZ65
Orpington BR6 145 EQ103
Romford (Rush Grn) RM7 71 FE61
Wallington SM6 141 DH102
Bluebell Ct, Wok. GU22 166 AX119
Bluebell Dr, Abb.L. (Bedmond) WD5 7 BT27
Waltham Cross EN7 14 DR28
Bluebell Way, Ilf. IG1 87 EP65
Blueberry Cl, Wdf.Grn. IG8 48 EG51
Blueberry Gdns, Couls. CR5 175 DM116
Blueberry La, Sev. (Knock.) TN14 180 EW116
Bluebird La, Dag. RM10 88 FA66
Bluebird Way, SE28 105 ER75
St. Albans AL2 8 BY30
Bluebridge Av, Hat. AL9 11 CZ27
Bluebridge Rd, Hat. (Brook.Pk) AL9 11 CY26
Blue Cedars, Bans. SM7 157 CX114
Blue Cedars Pl, Cob. KT11 154 BX112
Bluefield Cl, Hmptn. TW12 116 CA92
Bluegates, Epsom (Ewell) KT17 157 CU108
Bluehouse Gdns, Oxt. RH8 188 EG128
Bluehouse La, Oxt. RH8 188 EG127
Bluehouse Rd, E4 48 EE48
Blue Leaves Av, Couls. CR5 175 DK121
Bluelion Pl, SE1 201 M6
Bluett Rd, St.Alb. (Lon.Col.) AL2 9 CK27
Bluewater Ho, SW18
off Smugglers Way 100 DB84
Bluewater Parkway, Green. (Bluewater) DA9 129 FS87
Bluewater Shop Cen, Green. DA9 129 FT88
Blundel La, Cob. (Stoke D'Ab.) KT11 154 CB114
Blundell Cl, E8
off Amhurst Rd 66 DU64
Blundell Rd, Edg. HA8 42 CR53
Blundell St, N7 83 DL66
Blunden Cl, Dag. RM8 70 EW60
Blunden Dr, Slou. SL3 93 BB77
Blunesfield, Pot.B. EN6 12 DD31
Blunt Rd, S.Croy. CR2 160 DR106
Blunts Av, West Dr. UB7 94 BN80
Blunts La, St.Alb. AL2 8 BW27
Blunts Rd, SE9 125 EN85
Blurton Rd, E5 66 DW63
Blyth Cl, E14 204 F8
Borehamwood WD6 26 CM39
Twickenham TW1
off Grimwood Rd 117 CF86
Blythe Cl, SE6 123 DZ87
Iver SL0 75 BF72
Blythe Hill, SE6 123 DZ87
Orpington BR5 145 ET95
Blythe Hill La, SE6 123 DZ87
Blythe Hill Pl, SE23
off Brockley Pk 123 DY87
Blythe Ms, W14
off Blythe Rd 99 CX76
Blythe Rd, W14 99 CX76
Blythe St, E2 84 DV69
Blythe Vale, SE6 123 DZ88
Blyth Rd, E17 67 DZ59
SE28 88 EW73
Bromley BR1 144 EF95
Hayes UB3 95 BS75
Blyth's Wf, E14 203 L1
Blythswood Rd, Ilf. IG3 70 EU60
Blyth Wk, Upmin. RM14 73 FS58
Blyth Wd Pk, Brom. BR1
off Blyth Rd 144 EF95
Blythwood Rd, N4 65 DL59
Pinner HA5 40 BX53
Boades Ms, NW3
off New End 64 DD63
Boadicea St, N1
off Copenhagen St 83 DM67
Boakes Cl, NW9 62 CQ56
Boakes Meadow, Sev. (Shore.) TN14 165 FF111
Boar Cl, Chig. IG7 50 EU50
Boardman Av, E4 31 EB43
Boardman Cl, Barn. EN5 27 CY43
Board Sch Rd, Wok. GU21 167 AZ116
Boar's Head Yd, Brent. TW8
off Brent Way 97 CK80
Boathouse Wk, SE15 102 DT80
Richmond TW9 98 CL81
Boat Lifter Way, SE16 203 L8
Boat Quay, E16
off Royal Albert Way 86 EJ73
Bob Anker Cl, E13
off Chesterton Rd 86 EG69
Bobbin Cl, SW4 101 DJ83
Bobby Moore Way, N10 44 DF52
Bob Marley Way, SE24
off Mayall Rd 101 DN84
Bobs La, Rom. RM1 51 FG52
Bocketts La, Lthd. KT22 171 CF124
Bockhampton Rd, Kings.T. KT2 118 CM94
Bocking St, E8 84 DV67
Boddicott Cl, SW19 119 CY89
Bodell Cl, Grays RM16 110 GB76
Bodiam Cl, Enf. EN1 30 DR40
Bodiam Rd, SW16 121 DK94
Bodicea Ms, Houns. TW4 116 BZ87
Bodle Av, Swans. DA10 130 FY87
Bodley Cl, Epp. CM16 17 ET30
New Malden KT3 138 CS99
Bodley Manor Way, SW2
off Papworth Way 121 DN87
Bodley Rd, N.Mal. KT3 138 CR100
Bodmin Cl, Har. HA2 60 BZ62
Orpington BR5 146 EW102
Bodmin Gro, Mord. SM4 140 DB99
Bodmin St, SW18 120 DA88
Bodnant Gdns, SW20 139 CU97
Bodney Rd, E8 66 DV64
Boeing Way, Sthl. UB2 95 BV76
Boevey Path, Belv. DA17 106 EZ79
Bogey La, Orp. BR6 163 EN108
Bognor Gdns, Wat. WD19
off Bowring Grn 40 BW50
Bognor Rd, Well. DA16 106 EX81
Bohemia Pl, E8 84 DV65
Bohn Rd, E1 85 DY71
Bohun Gro, Barn. EN4 28 DE44
Boileau Par, W5
off Boileau Rd 80 CM72
Boileau Rd, SW13 99 CU80
W5 80 CM72
Bois Hall Rd, Add. KT15 152 BK105
Bois Hill, Chesh. HP5 4 AS34
Bolden St, SE8 103 EB82
Bolderwood Way, W.Wick. BR4 143 EB103
Boldmere Rd, Pnr. HA5 60 BW59
Boleyn Av, Enf. EN1 30 DV39
Epsom KT17 157 CV110
Boleyn Cl, E17 67 EA56
Grays (Chaff.Hun.) RM16
off Clifford Rd 110 FZ76
Loughton IG10
off Roding Gdns 32 EL44
Staines TW18
off Chertsey La 113 BE92
Boleyn Ct, Buck.H. IG9 48 EG46
Boleyn Dr, Ruis. HA4 60 BX61
West Molesey KT8 136 BZ97
Boleyn Gdns, Brwd. CM13 55 GA48
Dagenham RM10 89 FC66
West Wickham BR4 143 EB103
Boleyn Gro, W.Wick. BR4 143 EC103
Boleyn Rd, E6 86 EK68
E7 86 EG66
N16 66 DS64
Boleyn Wk, Lthd. KT22 171 CF120
Boleyn Way, Barn. EN5 28 DC41
Ilford IG6 49 EQ51
Swanscombe DA10 130 FY87
Bolina Rd, SE16 202 G10
Bolingbroke Gro, SW11 100 DE84
H Bolingbroke Hosp, SW11 120 DE85
Bolingbroke Rd, W14 99 CX76
Bolingbroke Wk, SW11 100 DD80
Bolingbroke Way, Hayes UB3 77 BR74
Bolliger Ct, NW10
off Park Royal Rd 80 CQ70
Bollo Br Rd, W3 98 CP76
Bollo La, W3 98 CP75
W4 98 CQ77
Bolney Gate, SW7 198 B5
Bolney St, SW8 101 DM80
Bolney Way, Felt. TW13 116 BY90
Bolsover Gro, Red. RH1 185 DL129
Bolsover St, W1 195 J5
Bolstead Rd, Mitch. CR4 141 DH95
Bolt Cellar La, Epp. CM16 17 ES29
Bolt Ct, EC4 196 E9
Bolters La, Bans. SM7 157 CZ114
Boltmore Cl, NW4 63 CX55
Bolton Cl, SE20 off Selby Rd 142 DU96
Chessington KT9 155 CK107
Bolton Cres, SE5 101 DP79
Bolton Gdns, NW10 81 CX68
SW5 100 DB78
Bromley BR1 124 EF93
Teddington TW11 117 CG93
Bolton Gdns Ms, SW10 100 DB78
Bolton Rd, E15 86 EF65
N18 46 DT50
NW8 82 DB67
NW10 80 CS67
W4 98 CQ80
Chessington KT9 155 CK107
Harrow HA1 60 CC56
Boltons, The, SW10 100 DC78
Wembley HA0 61 CF63
Woodford Green IG8 48 EG49
Boltons Cl, Wok. GU22 168 BG116
Boltons La, Hayes UB3 95 BQ80
Woking GU22 168 BG116
Boltons Pl, SW5 100 DC78
Bolton St, W1 199 J2
Bolton Wk, N7
off Durham Rd 65 DM61
Bombay St, SE16 202 D8
Bombers La, West. TN16 179 ER119
Bomer Cl, West Dr. UB7 94 BN80
Bomore Rd, W11 81 CX73
Bonar Pl, Chis. BR7 124 EL94
Bonar Rd, SE15 102 DU80
Bonaventure Ct, Grav. DA12 131 GM91
Bonchester Cl, Chis. BR7 125 EN94
Bonchurch Cl, Sutt. SM2 158 DB108
Bonchurch Rd, W10 81 CY71
W13 79 CH74
Bond Cl, Sev. (Knock.) TN14 180 EX115
West Drayton UB7 76 BM72
Bond Ct, EC4 197 K9
Bondfield Av, Hayes UB4 77 BU69
Bondfield Rd, E6
off Lovage App 86 EL71
Bondfield Wk, Dart. DA1 108 FM84
Bond Gdns, Wall. SM6 159 DJ105
Bonding Yd Wk, SE16 203 L5
Bond Rd, Mitch. CR4 140 DE96
Surbiton KT6 138 CM103
Warlingham CR6 177 DX118
⊖ Bond Street 194 G9
Bond St, E15 68 EE64
W4 98 CS77
W5 79 CK73
Egham (Eng.Grn) TW20 112 AV92
Grays RM17 110 GC79
Bondway, SW8 101 DL79
Bone Mill La, Gdse. RH9
off Eastbourne Rd 187 DY134
Boneta Rd, SE18 105 EM76
Bonfield Rd, SE13 103 EC84
Bonham Gdns, Dag. RM8 70 EX61
Bonham Rd, SW2 121 DM85
Dagenham RM8 70 EX61
Bonheur Rd, W4 98 CR75
Bonhill St, EC2 197 L5
Boniface Gdns, Har. HA3 40 CB52
Boniface Rd, Uxb. UB10 59 BP62
Boniface Wk, Har. HA3 40 CB52
Bonington Ho, Enf. EN1
off Ayley Cft 30 DU43
Bonington Rd, Horn. RM12 72 FK64
Bonita Ms, SE4 103 DX83
Bon Marche Ter Ms, SE27
off Gipsy Rd 122 DS91
Bonner Hill Rd, Kings.T. KT1 138 CM97
Bonner Rd, E2 84 DW68
Bonners Cl, Wok. GU22 166 AY122
Bonnersfield Cl, Har. HA1 61 CF58
Bonnersfield La, Har. HA1 61 CG58
Bonner St, E2 84 DW68
Bonner Wk, Grays RM16
off Clifford Rd 110 FZ76
Bonnett Ms, Horn. RM11 72 FL60
Bonneville Gdns, SW4 121 DJ86
Bonney Gro, Wal.Cr. (Chsht) EN7 14 DU30
Bonney Way, Swan. BR8 147 FE96
Bonningtons, Brwd. CM13 55 GB48
Bonnington Sq, SW8 101 DM79
Bonnington Twr, Brom. BR2 144 EL100
Bonny St, NW1 83 DJ66
Bonser Rd, Twick. TW1 117 CF89
Bonsey Cl, Wok. GU22 166 AY121
Bonsey La, Wok. GU22 166 AY121
Bonseys La, Wok. (Chobham) GU24 151 AZ110
Bonsor Dr, Tad. KT20 173 CY122
Bonsor St, SE5 102 DS80
Bonville Gdns, NW4
off Handowe Cl 63 CU56
Bonville Rd, Brom. BR1 124 EF92
Bookbinders' Cotts, N20
off Manor Dr 44 DF48
Booker Cl, E14
off Wallwood St 85 DZ71
Booker Rd, N18 46 DU50
⇌ Bookham 170 BZ123
Bookham Ct, Lthd. KT23
off Church Rd 170 BZ123
Bookham Ind Est, Lthd. (Bkhm) KT23 170 BZ123
Bookham Rd, Cob. (Down.) KT11 170 BW119
Book Ms, WC2 195 N9
Boone Ct, N9 46 DW48
Boones Rd, SE13 104 EE84
Boone St, SE13 104 EE84
Boord St, SE10 205 J6
Boothby Rd, N19 65 DK61
Booth Cl, E9
off Victoria Pk Rd 84 DV67
SE28 88 EV73
Booth Dr, Stai. TW18 114 BK93
Booth Rd, NW9 42 CS54
Croydon CR0
off Waddon New Rd 141 DP103
Booth's Ct, Brwd. (Hutt.) CM13 55 GB44
Booth's Pl, W1 195 L7
Boot St, N1 197 M3
Bordars Rd, W7 79 CE71
Bordars Wk, W7 79 CE71
Borden Av, Enf. EN1 30 DR44
Border Cres, SE26 122 DV92
Border Gdns, Croy. CR0 161 EB105
Bordergate, Mitch. CR4 140 DE95
Border Rd, SE26 122 DV92
Borderside, Slou. SL2 74 AU72
Borders La, Loug. IG10 33 EN42
Bordesley Rd, Mord. SM4 140 DB98
Bordon Wk, SW15 119 CU87
Boreas Wk, N1 196 G1
Boreham Av, E16 86 EG72
Boreham Cl, E11
off Hainault Rd 67 EC60
Boreham Holt, Borwd. (Elstree) WD6 26 CM42
Boreham Rd, N22 46 DQ54
BOREHAMWOOD 26 CP41
Borehamwood Ind Pk, Borwd. WD6 26 CR40
Borgard Rd, SE18 105 EM77
Borkwood Pk, Orp. BR6 163 ET105
Borkwood Way, Orp. BR6 163 ES105
Borland Cl, Green. DA9
off Steele Av 129 FU85
Borland Rd, SE15 102 DW84
Teddington TW11 117 CH93
Bornedene, Pot.B. EN6 11 CY31
Borneo St, SW15 99 CW83
⊖ Borough 201 J5
BOROUGH, THE, SE1 201 H5
Borough High St, SE1 201 H5
Borough Hill, Croy. CR0 141 DP104
★ Borough Mkt, SE1 201 K3
Borough Rd, SE1 200 F6

★ Place of interest ⇌ Railway station ⊖ London Underground station DLR Docklands Light Railway station Tra Tramlink station H Hospital Riv Pedestrian ferry landing stage

221

Borough Rd, Isleworth TW7 . . . 97 CE81
Kingston upon Thames KT2 . 138 CN95
Mitcham CR4 . . . . 140 DE96
Westerham (Tats.) TN16 . . . 178 EK121
Borough Sq, SE1 . . . . 201 H5
Borough Way, Pot.B. EN6 . . . . . 11 CY32
Borrett Cl, SE17
off Penrose St 102 DQ78
Borrodaile Rd, SW18 . . . . 120 DB86
Borrowdale Av, Har. HA3 . . . . . 41 CG54
Borrowdale Cl, Egh. TW20
off Derwent Rd 113 BB94
Ilford IG4 . . . . 68 EL56
South Croydon CR2 . . . . . . 160 DT113
Borrowdale Ct, Enf. EN2 . . . . . 30 DQ39
Borrowdale Dr, S.Croy. CR2 . . 160 DT112
Borthwick Ms, E15
off Borthwick Rd 68 EE63
Borthwick Rd, E15 . . . . 68 EE63
NW9 *off West Hendon Bdy* . . 63 CT58
Borthwick St, SE8 . . . . 103 EA78
Borwick Av, E17 . . . . 67 DZ55
Bosanquet Cl, Uxb. UB8 . . . . . . 76 BK70
Bosbury Rd, SE6 . . . . 123 EC90
Boscastle Rd, NW5 . . . . 65 DH62
Boscobel Cl, Brom. BR1
off Woodlands Rd 145 EM96
Boscobel Pl, SW1 . . . . 198 G8
Boscobel St, NW8 . . . . 194 A5
Bosco Cl, Orp. BR6
off Strickland Way 163 ET105
Boscombe Av, E10 . . . . 67 ED59
Grays RM17 . . . . 110 GD77
Hornchurch RM11 . . . . 72 FK60
Boscombe Cl, E5 . . . . 67 DY64
Egham TW20 . . . . 133 BC95
Boscombe Gdns, SW16 . . . . . . 121 DL93
Boscombe Rd, SW17 . . . . 120 DG93
SW19 . . . . 140 DB95
W12 . . . . 81 CU74
Worcester Park KT4 . . . . . . 139 CW102
Bose Cl, N3 *off Claremont Pk* . . 43 CY53
Bosgrove, E4 . . . . 47 EC46
Boshers Gdns, Egh. TW20 . . . 113 AZ93
Boss Ho, SE1 . . . . 201 P4
Boss St, SE1 . . . . 201 P4
Bostall Heath, SE2 . . . . 106 EW78
Bostall Hill, SE2 . . . . 106 EU78
Bostall La, SE2 . . . . 106 EV78
Bostall Manorway, SE2 . . . . . . 106 EV77
Bostall Pk Av, Bexh. DA7 . . . . 106 EY80
Bostall Rd, Orp. BR5 . . . . 126 EV94
Bostal Row, Bexh. DA7
off Harlington Rd 106 EZ83
Boston Gdns, W4 . . . . 98 CS79
W7 . . . . 97 CG77
Brentford TW8 . . . . 97 CG77
Boston Gro, Ruis. HA4 . . . . 59 BQ58
★ **Boston Manor**, Brent. TW8 . 97 CH78
⊖ **Boston Manor** 97 CG77
Boston Manor Rd, Brent. TW8 . 97 CH77
Boston Pk Rd, Brent. TW8 . . . . 97 CJ78
Boston Pl, NW1 . . . . 194 D5
Boston Rd, E6 . . . . 86 EL69
E17 . . . . 67 EA58
W7 . . . . 79 CE74
Croydon CR0 . . . . 141 DM100
Edgware HA8 . . . . 42 CQ52
Boston St, E2 *off Audrey St* . . . 84 DU68
Bostonthorpe Rd, W7 . . . . 97 CE75
Boston Vale, W7 . . . . 97 CG77
Bosun Cl, E14 . . . . 204 A4
Bosville Av, Sev. TN13 . . . . . . 190 FG123
Bosville Dr, Sev. TN13 . . . . . . 190 FG123
Bosville Rd, Sev. TN13 . . . . . . 190 FG123
Boswell Cl, Orp. BR5
off Killewarren Way 146 EW100
Radlett (Shenley) WD7 . . . . . . 10 CL32
Boswell Ct, WC1 . . . . 196 A6
Boswell Path, Hayes UB3
off Croyde Av 95 BT77
Boswell Rd, Th.Hth. CR7 . . . . 142 DQ98
Boswell St, WC1 . . . . 196 A6
Bosworth Cl, E17 . . . . 47 DZ53
Bosworth Cres, Rom. RM3 . . . . 52 FJ51
Bosworth Ho, Erith DA8
off Saltford Cl 107 FE78
Bosworth Rd, N11 . . . . 45 DK51
W10 . . . . 81 CY70
Barnet EN5 . . . . 28 DA41
Dagenham RM10 . . . . 70 FA63
BOTANY BAY, Enf. EN2 . . . . . . 29 DK36
Botany Bay La, Chis. BR7 . . . . 145 EQ97
Botany Cl, Barn. EN4 . . . . 28 DE42
Botany Rd, Grav.
(Nthflt) DA11 . . . . 110 GA83
Botany Way, Purf. RM19 . . . . . 108 FP78
Boteley Cl, E4 . . . . 47 ED47
Botery's Cross, Red. RH1 . . . . 185 DP133
Botham Cl, Edg. HA8
off Pavilion Way 42 CQ52
Botham Dr, Slou. SL1 . . . . 92 AS76
Botha Rd, E13 . . . . 86 EH71
Bothwell Cl, E16 . . . . 86 EF71
Bothwell Rd, Croy.
(New Adgtn) CR0 . . . . 161 EC110
Bothwell St, W6
off Delorme St 99 CX79
BOTLEY, Chesh. HP5 . . . . 4 AV30
Botley La, Chesh. HP5 . . . . 4 AU30
Botley Rd, Chesh. HP5 . . . . 4 AT30
Botolph All, EC3 . . . . 197 M10
Botolph La, EC3 . . . . 197 M10
Botsford Rd, SW20 . . . . 139 CY96
Bottom Ho Fm La,
Ch.St.G. HP8 . . . . 36 AT45
Bottom La, Chesh. HP5 . . . . 4 AT34
Kings Langley WD4 . . . . 22 BH35
Bottrells Cl, Ch.St.G. HP8 . . . . 36 AT47
Bottrells La, Ch.St.G. HP8 . . . . 36 AT47
Bott Rd, Dart. (Hawley) DA2 . . 128 FM91
Botts Ms, W2
off Chepstow Rd 82 DA72
Botts Pas, W2
off Chepstow Rd 82 DA72
Botwell Common Rd,
Hayes UB3 . . . . 77 BR73
Botwell Cres, Hayes UB3 . . . . . 77 BS72
Botwell La, Hayes UB3 . . . . 77 BS74
Boucher Cl, Tedd. TW11 . . . . . . 117 CF92
Boucher Dr, Grav.
(Nthflt) DA11 . . . . 131 GF90
Bouchier Wk, Rain. RM13
off Deere Av 89 FG65
Boughton Av, Brom. BR2 . . . . 144 EF101
Boughton Business Pk,
Amer. HP6 . . . . 20 AV39
Boughton Hall Av, Wok.
(Send) GU23 . . . . 167 BF124
Boughton Rd, SE28 . . . . 105 ES76
Boughton Way, Amer. HP6 . . . . 20 AW38
Boulcott St, E1 . . . . 85 DX72
Boulevard, The, SW6 . . . . 100 DC81
SW17 *off Balham High Rd* . 120 DG89
SW18 *off Smugglers Way* . . 100 DB84
Greenhithe DA9
off London Rd 129 FW85
Pinner HA5 *off Pinner Rd* . . . 60 CA56
Watford WD18 . . . . 23 BR43
Woodford Green IG8 . . . . 49 EN52
Boulevard 25 Retail Pk,
Borwd. WD6 . . . . 26 CN41
Boulmer Rd, Uxb. UB8 . . . . 76 BJ69
Boulogne Rd, Croy. CR0 . . . . . 142 DQ100
Boulter Gdns, Rain. RM13 . . . . 89 FG65
Boulthurst Way, Oxt. RH8 . . . . 188 EH132
Boulton Ho, Brent. TW8
off Green Dragon La 98 CL78
Boulton Rd, Dag. RM8 . . . . 70 EY62
Boultwood Rd, E6 . . . . 86 EL72
Bounce Hill, Rom. (Nave.) RM4
off Mill La 35 FH38
Bounces La, N9 . . . . 46 DV47
Bounces Rd, N9 . . . . 46 DV46
Boundaries Rd, SW12 . . . . 120 DF89
Feltham TW13 . . . . 116 BW88
Boundary Av, E17 . . . . 67 DZ59
Boundary Cl, SE20
off Haysleigh Gdns 142 DU96
Barnet EN5 . . . . 27 CZ39
Ilford IG3 *off Loxford La* 69 ES63
Kingston upon Thames KT1 . 138 CP97
Southall UB2 . . . . 96 CA78
Boundary Ct, Epp. CM16 . . . . . 17 ER32
Boundary Dr, Brwd. (Hutt.) CM13 55 GE45
Boundary La, E13 . . . . 86 EK69
SE17 . . . . 102 DQ79
Boundary Pas, E2 . . . . 197 P4
Boundary Rd, E13 . . . . 86 EJ68
E17 . . . . 67 DZ59
N9 . . . . 30 DW44
N22 . . . . 65 DP55
NW8 . . . . 82 DB67
SW19 . . . . 120 DD93
Ashford TW15 . . . . 114 BJ92
Barking IG11 . . . . 87 EQ68
Carshalton SM5 . . . . 159 DH107
Gerrards Cross
(Chal.St.P.) SL9 . . . . 36 AX52
Pinner HA5 . . . . 60 BX58
Romford RM1 . . . . 71 FG58
Sidcup DA15 . . . . 125 ES85
Upminster RM14 . . . . 72 FN62
Wallington SM6 . . . . 159 DH107
Wembley HA9 . . . . 62 CL62
Woking GU21 . . . . 167 BA116
Boundary Row, SE1 . . . . 200 F4
Boundary St, E2 . . . . 197 P3
Erith DA8 . . . . 107 FF80
Boundary Way, Croy. CR0 . . . . 161 EA106
Watford WD25 . . . . 7 BV32
Woking GU21 . . . . 167 BA115
Boundary Yd, Wok. GU21
off Boundary Rd 167 BA116
Boundfield Rd, SE6 . . . . 124 EE90
⊖ **Bounds Green** 45 DK51
Bounds Grn Rd, N11 . . . . 45 DJ51
N22 . . . . 45 DJ51
Bourchier Cl, Sev. TN13 . . . . . 191 FH126
Bourchier St, W1 . . . . 195 M10
Bourdon Pl, W1 . . . . 195 J10
Bourdon Rd, SE20 . . . . 142 DW96
Bourdon St, W1 . . . . 195 J10
Bourke Cl, NW10
off Mayo Rd 80 CS65
SW4 . . . . 121 DL86
Bourke Hill, Couls. CR5 . . . . . . 174 DF118
Bourlet Cl, W1 . . . . 195 K7
Bourn Av, N15 . . . . 66 DR56
Barnet EN4 . . . . 28 DD43
Uxbridge UB8 . . . . 76 BN70
Bournbrook Rd, SE3 . . . . 104 EK83
Bourne, The, N14 . . . . 45 DK46
Hemel Hempstead (Bov.) HP3 . . 5 BA27
Bourne Av, N14 . . . . 45 DL47
Chertsey KT16 . . . . 134 BG97
Hayes UB3 . . . . 95 BQ76
Ruislip HA4 . . . . 60 BW64
Bournebridge Cl, Brwd.
(Hutt.) CM13 . . . . 55 GE45
Bournebridge La, Rom.
(Stap.Abb.) RM4 . . . . 50 EZ45
Bourne Cl, T.Ditt. KT7 . . . . . . 137 CF103
West Byfleet KT14 . . . . 152 BH113
Bourne Ct, Ruis. HA4 . . . . 59 BV64
Bourne Dr, Mitch. CR4 . . . . . . 140 DD96
Bourne End, Horn. RM11 . . . . . 72 FN59
Bourne End Rd, Nthwd. HA6 . . . 39 BS49
Bourne Est, EC1 . . . . 196 D6
Bournefield Rd, Whyt. CR3
off Godstone Rd 176 DT118
Bourne Gdns, E4 . . . . 47 EB49
Bourne Gro, Ashtd. KT21 . . . . . 171 CK119
Bournehall Av, Bushey WD23 . . 24 CA43
Bournehall La, Bushey WD23 . . 24 CA44
★ **Bourne Hall Mus**,
Epsom KT17 . . . . 157 CT109
Bournehall Rd, Bushey WD23 . 24 CA44
Bourne Hill, N13 . . . . 45 DL46
Bourne Hill Cl, N13
off Bourne Hill 45 DM47
Bourne Ind Pk, Dart. DA1
off Bourne Rd 127 FE85
Bourne La, Cat. CR3 . . . . 176 DR121
Bourne Mead, Bex. DA5 . . . . . . 127 FD85
Bournemead Av, Nthlt. UB5 . . . 77 BU68
Bournemead Cl, Nthlt. UB5 . . . 77 BU68
Bourne Meadow, Egh. TW20 . 133 BB98
Bournemead Way, Nthlt. UB5 . 77 BV68
Bournemouth Cl, SE15 . . . . . . 102 DU82
Bournemouth Rd, SE15 . . . . . . 102 DU82
SW19 . . . . 140 DA95
Bourne Pk Cl, Ken. CR8 . . . . . 176 DS115
Bourne Pl, W4 *off Dukes Av* . . . 98 CR78
Bourne Rd, E7 . . . . 68 EF62
N8 . . . . 65 DL58
Bexley DA5 . . . . 127 FB86
Bromley BR2 . . . . 144 EK98
Bushey WD23 . . . . 24 CA43
Dartford DA1 . . . . 127 FC86
Gravesend DA12 . . . . 131 GM89
Redhill RH1 . . . . 185 DJ130
Virginia Water GU25 . . . . . . 132 AX99
Bourneside, Vir.W. GU25 . . . . 132 AU101
Bourneside Cres, N14 . . . . 45 DK46
Bourneside Gdns, SE6 . . . . . . 123 EC92
Bourneside Rd, Add. KT15 . . . 152 BK105
Bourne St, SW1 . . . . 198 F9
Croydon CR0
off Waddon New Rd 141 DP103
Bourne Ter, W2 . . . . 82 DB71
Bourne Vale, Brom. BR2 . . . . . 144 EG101
Bournevale Rd, SW16 . . . . 121 DL91
Bourne Vw, Grnf. UB6 . . . . 79 CF65
Kenley CR8 . . . . 176 DR115
Bourne Way, Add. KT15 . . . . . 152 BJ106
Bromley BR2 . . . . 144 EF103
Epsom KT19 . . . . 156 CQ105
Sutton SM1 . . . . 157 CZ106
Swanley BR8 . . . . 147 FC97
Woking GU22 . . . . 166 AX122
Bournewood Rd, SE18 . . . . . . 106 EU80
Orpington BR5 . . . . 146 EV101
Bournville Rd, SE6 . . . . 123 EA87
Bournwell Cl, Barn. EN4 . . . . . . 28 DF41
Bourton Cl, Hayes UB3
off Avondale Dr 77 BU74
Bousfield Rd, SE14 . . . . 103 DX82
Bousley Ri, Cher. (Ott.) KT16 . 151 BD108
Boutflower Rd, SW11 . . . . 100 DE84
Bouverie Gdns, Har. HA3 . . . . . 61 CK58
Bouverie Ms, N16
off Bouverie Rd 66 DS61
Bouverie Pl, W2 . . . . 194 A8
Bouverie Rd, N16 . . . . 66 DS61
Coulsdon CR5 . . . . 174 DG118
Harrow HA1 . . . . 60 CC59
Bouverie St, EC4 . . . . 196 E9
Bouverie Way, Slou. SL3 . . . . . 92 AY78
Bouvier Rd, Enf. EN3 . . . . 30 DW38
Boveney Rd, SE23 . . . . 123 DX87
Bovey Way, S.Ock. RM15 . . . . . 91 FV71
Bovill Rd, SE23 . . . . 123 DX87
BOVINGDON, Hem.H. HP3 . . . . . . 5 BA28
Bovingdon Av, Wem. HA9 . . . . . 80 CN65
Bovingdon Cl, N19
off Brookside Rd 65 DJ61
Bovingdon Cres, Wat. WD25 . . . 8 BX34
Bovingdon La, NW9 . . . . 42 CS53
Bovingdon Rd, SW6 . . . . 100 DB81
Bovingdon Sq, Mitch. CR4
off Leicester Av 141 DL98
BOW, E3 . . . . 85 DZ68
Bow Arrow La, Dart.
DA1, DA2 . . . . 128 FN86
Bowater Cl, NW9 . . . . 62 CR57
SW2 . . . . 121 DL86
Bowater Gdns, Sun. TW16 . . . . 135 BV96
Bowater Pl, SE3 . . . . 104 EH80
Bowater Ridge, Wey. KT13 . . . . 153 BR110
Bowater Rd, SE18 . . . . 104 EK76
Bow Back Rivers Wk, E15 . . . . . 85 EB66
Bow Br Est, E3 . . . . 85 EB69
DLR **Bow Church** 85 EA69
Bow Chyd, EC4 . . . . 197 J9
Bow Common La, E3 . . . . 85 DZ70
Bowden Cl, Felt. TW14 . . . . 115 BS88
Bowden Dr, Horn. RM11 . . . . . . 72 FL60
Bowden St, SE11 . . . . 101 DN78
Bowditch, SE8 . . . . 203 M10
Bowdon Rd, E17 . . . . 67 EA59
Bowen Dr, SE21 . . . . 122 DS90
Bowen Rd, Har. HA1 . . . . 60 CC59
Bowen St, E14 . . . . 85 EB72
Bowens Wd, Croy. CR0 . . . . . . 161 DZ109
Bowen Way, Couls. CR5
off Netherne Dr 175 DK121
Bower Av, SE10 . . . . 104 EE81
Bower Cl, Nthlt. UB5 . . . . 78 BW68
Romford RM5 . . . . 51 FD52
Bower Ct, Epp. CM16 . . . . 18 EU32
Woking GU22
off Princess Rd 167 BB116
Bowerdean St, SW6 . . . . 100 DB81
Bower Fm Rd, Rom.
(Hav.at.Bow.) RM4 . . . . 51 FC48
BOWER HILL, Epp. CM16 . . . . . . 18 EU31
Bower Hill, Epp. CM16 . . . . 18 EU32
Bower Hill Ind Est, Epp. CM16 . 18 EU32
Bower La, Dart. (Eyns.) DA4 . . 148 FL103
Bowerman Av, SE14 . . . . 103 DY79
Bowerman Rd, Grays RM16 . . . 111 GG77
Bower Rd, Swan. BR8 . . . . 127 FG94
Bowers Av, Grav.
(Nthflt) DA11 . . . . 131 GF91
Bowers Rd, Sev.
(Shore.) TN14 . . . . 165 FF111
Bower St, E1 . . . . 85 DX72
Bowers Wk, E6 . . . . 86 EL72
Bower Ter, Epp. CM16
off Bower Hill 18 EU32
Bower Vale, Epp. CM16 . . . . . . 18 EU32
Bowes Cl, Sid. DA15 . . . . 126 EV86
BOWES PARK, N22 . . . . 45 DL51
⇌ **Bowes Park** 45 DL51
Bowes Rd, N11 . . . . 45 DH50
N13 . . . . 45 DL50
W3 . . . . 80 CS73
Dagenham RM8 . . . . 70 EW63
Staines TW18 . . . . 113 BE92
Walton-on-Thames KT12 . . . 135 BV103
Bowfell Rd, W6 . . . . 99 CW79
Bowford Av, Bexh. DA7 . . . . . . 106 EY81
Bowhay, Brwd. (Hutt.) CM13 . . 55 GA47
Bowhill Cl, SW9 . . . . 101 DN80
Bowie Cl, SW4 . . . . 121 DK87
Bow Ind Pk, E15 . . . . 85 EA66
Bowland Rd, SW4 . . . . 101 DK84
Woodford Green IG8 . . . . 48 EJ51
Bowland Yd, SW1 . . . . 198 E5
Bow La, EC4 . . . . 197 J9
N12 . . . . 44 DC53
Morden SM4 . . . . 139 CY100
Bowl Ct, EC2 . . . . 197 N5
Bowlers Orchard,
Ch.St.G. HP8 . . . . 36 AU48
Bowles Grn, Enf. EN1 . . . . 30 DV36
Bowles Rd, SE1
off Old Kent Rd 102 DU79
Bowley Cl, SE19 . . . . 122 DT93
Bowley La, SE19 . . . . 122 DT92
Bowling Cl, Uxb. UB10
off Birch Cres 76 BM67
Bowling Ct, Wat. WD18 . . . . 23 BU42
Bowling Grn Cl, SW15 . . . . 119 CV87
Bowling Grn La, EC1 . . . . 196 E4
Bowling Grn Pl, SE1 . . . . 201 K4
Bowling Grn Rd, Wok.
(Chobham) GU24 . . . . 150 AS109
Bowling Grn Row, SE18
off Samuel St 105 EM76
Bowling Grn St, SE11 . . . . 101 DN79
Bowling Grn Wk, N1 . . . . 197 M2
Bowls, The, Chig. IG7 . . . . 49 ES49
Bowls Cl, Stan. HA7 . . . . 41 CH50
Bowman Av, E16 . . . . 86 EF73
Bowman Ms, SW18 . . . . 119 CZ88
Bowmans Cl, W13 . . . . 79 CH74
Potters Bar EN6 . . . . 12 DD32
Bowmans Grn, Wat. WD25 . . . . 24 BX36
Bowmans Lea, SE23 . . . . 122 DW87
Bowmans Meadow, Wall.
SM6 . . . . 141 DH104
Bowmans Ms, E1
off Hooper St 84 DU72
N7 *off Seven Sisters Rd* 65 DL62
Bowmans Pl, N7
off Holloway Rd 65 DL62
Bowmans Rd, Dart. DA1 . . . . . 127 FF87
Bowman's Trd Est, NW9
off Westmoreland Rd 62 CM55
Bowmead, SE9 . . . . 125 EM89
Bowmont Cl,
Brwd. (Hutt.) CM13 . . . . 55 GB44
Bowmore Wk, NW1
off St. Paul's Cres 83 DK66
Bown Cl, Til. RM18 . . . . 111 GH82
Bowness Cl, E8
off Beechwood Rd 84 DT65
Bowness Cres, SW15 . . . . 118 CS92
Bowness Dr, Houns. TW4 . . . . . 96 BY84
Bowness Rd, SE6 . . . . 123 EB87
Bexleyheath DA7 . . . . 107 FB82
Bowness Way, Horn. RM12 . . . . 71 FG64
Bowood Rd, SW11 . . . . 100 DG84
Enfield EN3 . . . . 31 DX40
Bowring Grn, Wat. WD19 . . . . . 40 BW50
⊖ **Bow Road** 85 DZ69
Bow Rd, E3 . . . . 85 DZ69
Bowrons Av, Wem. HA0 . . . . . . 79 CK66
Bowry Dr, Stai.
(Wrays.) TW19 . . . . 113 AZ86
Bowsley Ct, Felt. TW13
off Highfield Rd 115 BU88
Bowsprit, The, Cob. KT11 . . . . 170 BW115
Bowsprit Pt, E14 . . . . 203 P6
Bow St, E15 . . . . 68 EE64
WC2 . . . . 196 A9
Bowstridge La, Ch.St.G. HP8 . . 36 AW51
Bowyer Cl, E6 . . . . 87 EM71
Bowyer Cres, Uxb.
(Denh.) UB9 . . . . 57 BF58
Bowyer Pl, SE5 . . . . 102 DR80
Bowyers Cl, Ashtd. KT21 . . . . . 172 CM118
Bowyer St, SE5 . . . . 102 DQ80
Boxall Rd, SE21 . . . . 122 DS86
Boxford Cl, S.Croy. CR2 . . . . . . 161 DX112
Boxgrove Rd, SE2 . . . . 106 EW76
BOX HILL, Tad. KT20 . . . . 182 CP131
Boxhill Dr, Grays RM20 . . . . . . 110 FY79
Boxhill Rd, Dor. RH4 . . . . 182 CL133
Tadworth (Box H.) KT20 . . . 182 CP131
Box La, Bark. IG11 . . . . 88 EV68
Boxley Rd, Mord. SM4 . . . . 140 DC98
Boxley St, E16 . . . . 205 P3
Boxmoor Rd, Har. HA3 . . . . 61 CH56
Romford RM5 . . . . 51 FC50
Boxoll Rd, Dag. RM9 . . . . 70 EZ63
Box Ridge Av, Pur. CR8 . . . . . . 159 DM112
Boxted Cl, Buck.H. IG9 . . . . 48 EL46
Boxtree La, Har. HA3 . . . . 40 CC53
Boxtree Rd, Har. HA3 . . . . 41 CD52
Boxtree Wk, Orp. BR5 . . . . 146 EX102
Boxwood Cl, West Dr. UB7
off Hawthorne Cres 94 BM75
Boxwood Way, Warl. CR6 . . . . . 177 DX117
Boxworth Cl, N12 . . . . 44 DD50
Boxworth Gro, N1
off Richmond Av 83 DM67
Boyard Rd, SE18 . . . . 105 EP78
Boyas Cres, St.Alb. AL2
off Shenley La 9 CH26
Boyce Cl, Borwd. WD6 . . . . 26 CL39
Boyce St, SE1 . . . . 200 C3
Boyce Way, E13 . . . . 86 EG70
Boycroft Av, NW9 . . . . 62 CQ58
Boyd Av, Sthl. UB1 . . . . 78 BZ74
Boyd Cl, Kings.T. KT2
off Crescent Rd 118 CN94
Boydell Ct, NW8
off St. John's Wd Pk 82 DD66
Boyd Rd, SW19 . . . . 120 DD93
Boyd St, E1 . . . . 84 DU72
Boyfield St, SE1 . . . . 200 G5
Boyland Rd, Brom. BR1 . . . . . . 124 EF92
Boyle Av, Stan. HA7 . . . . 41 CG51
Boyle Cl, Uxb. UB10 . . . . 76 BM68
Boyle Fm Island, T.Ditt. KT7 . . 137 CG100
Boyle Fm Rd, T.Ditt. KT7 . . . . . 137 CG100
Boyle St, W1 . . . . 195 K10
Boyne Av, NW4 . . . . 63 CX56
Boyne Rd, SE13 . . . . 103 EC83
Dagenham RM10 . . . . 70 FA62
Boyne Ter Ms, W11 . . . . 81 CZ74
Boyseland Ct, Edg. HA8 . . . . . . 42 CQ47
Boyson Rd, SE17 . . . . 102 DR79
Boyton Cl, E1
off Stayner's Rd 85 DX70
N8 . . . . 65 DL55
Boyton Rd, N8 . . . . 65 DL55
Brabant Ct, EC3 . . . . 197 M10
Brabant Rd, N22 . . . . 45 DM54
Brabazon Av, Wall. SM6 . . . . . . 159 DL108
Brabazon Rd, Houns. TW5 . . . . . 96 BW80
Northolt UB5 . . . . 78 CA68
Brabazon St, E14 . . . . 85 EB72
Brabourne Cl, SE19 . . . . 122 DS92
Brabourne Cres, Bexh. DA7 . . 106 EZ79
Brabourne Hts, NW7 . . . . 42 CS48
Brabourne Ri, Beck. BR3 . . . . . 143 EC99
Brabourn Gro, SE15 . . . . 102 DW82
Brace Cl, Wal.Cr. (Chsht) EN7 . . 13 DP25
Bracewell Av, Grnf. UB6 . . . . . . 61 CF64
Bracewell Rd, W10 . . . . 81 CW71
Bracewood Gdns, Croy. CR0 . . 142 DT104
Bracey Ms, N4 *off Bracey St* . . . 65 DL61
Bracey St, N4 . . . . 65 DL61
Bracken, The, E4
off Hortus Rd 47 EC47
Bracken Av, SW12 . . . . 120 DG86
Croydon CR0 . . . . 143 EB104
Brackenbridge Dr, Ruis. HA4 . . 60 BX62
Brackenbury Gdns, W6 . . . . 99 CV76
Brackenbury Rd, N2 . . . . 64 DC55
W6 . . . . 99 CV76
Bracken Cl, E6 . . . . 87 EM71
Borehamwood WD6 . . . . 26 CP39
Leatherhead (Bkhm) KT23 . 170 BZ124
Sunbury-on-Thames TW16
off Cavendish Rd 115 BT93
Twickenham TW2
off Hedley Rd 116 CA87
Woking GU22 . . . . 167 AZ118
Brackendale, N21 . . . . 45 DM47
Potters Bar EN6 . . . . 12 DA33
Brackendale Cl, Houns. TW3 . . . 96 CB81
Brackendale Gdns, Upmin.
RM14 . . . . 72 FQ63
Brackendene, Dart. DA2 . . . . . 127 FE91
St. Albans (Brick.Wd) AL2 . . . 8 BZ30
Brackendene Cl, Wok. GU21 . . 167 BA115
Bracken Dr, Chig. IG7 . . . . 49 EP51
Bracken End, Islw. TW7 . . . . . . 117 CD85
Brackenfield Cl, E5
off Tiger Way 66 DV63
Brackenforde, Slou. SL3 . . . . . . 92 AW75
Bracken Gdns, SW13 . . . . 99 CU82
Brackenhill, Cob. KT11 . . . . . . 154 CA111
Bracken Hill Cl, Brom. BR1
off Bracken Hill La 144 EF95
Bracken Hill La, Brom. BR1 . . 144 EF95
Bracken Ind Est, Ilf. IG6 . . . . . . 49 ET52
Bracken Ms, E4 *off Hortus Rd* . 47 EC47
Romford RM7 . . . . 70 FA58
Bracken Path, Epsom KT18 . . 156 CP113
Brackens, The, Enf. EN1 . . . . . . 46 DS45
Orpington BR6 . . . . 164 EU106
Brackens Dr, Brwd. CM14 . . . . . 54 FW50
Bracken Way, Wok.
(Chobham) GU24 . . . . 150 AT110
Brackenwood, Sun. TW16 . . . . 135 BU95
Brackley, Wey. KT13 . . . . 153 BR106
Brackley Cl, Wall. SM6 . . . . . . 159 DL108
Brackley Rd, W4 . . . . 98 CS78
Beckenham BR3 . . . . 123 DZ94
Brackley Sq, Wdf.Grn. IG8 . . . . 48 EK52
Brackley St, EC1 . . . . 197 H6
Brackley Ter, W4 . . . . 98 CS78
Bracklyn Cl, N1 *off Parr St* 84 DR68
Bracklyn Ct, N1
off Wimbourne St 84 DR68
Bracklyn St, N1 . . . . 84 DR68
Bracknell Cl, N22 . . . . 45 DN53
Bracknell Gdns, NW3 . . . . 64 DB63
Bracknell Gate, NW3 . . . . 64 DB64
Bracknell Way, NW3 . . . . 64 DB63
Bracondale, Esher KT10 . . . . . 154 CC107
Bracondale Rd, SE2 . . . . 106 EU77
H **Bracton Cen, The**,
Dart. DA2 . . . . 127 FF89
Bradbery, Rick. (Map.Cr.) WD3 . 37 BD50
Bradbourne Pk Rd, Sev. TN13 . 190 FG123
Bradbourne Rd, Bex. DA5 . . . . 126 FA87
Grays RM17 . . . . 110 GB79
Sevenoaks TN13 . . . . 191 FH122
Bradbourne St, SW6 . . . . 100 DA82
Bradbourne Vale Rd,
Sev. TN13 . . . . 190 FF122
Bradbury Cl, Borwd. WD6 . . . . . 26 CP39
Southall UB2 . . . . 96 BZ77
Bradbury Gdns, Slou.
(Fulmer) SL3 . . . . 56 AX63
Bradbury Ms, N16
off Bradbury St 66 DS64
Bradbury St, N16 . . . . 66 DS64
Bradd Cl, S.Ock. RM15
off Brandon Gros Av 91 FW69
Braddock Cl, Islw. TW7 . . . . 97 CF83
Romford RM5
off Hillrise Rd 51 FC51
Braddon Rd, Rich. TW9 . . . . 98 CM83
Braddyll St, SE10 . . . . 104 EE78
Bradenham Av, Well. DA16 . . . 106 EU84
Bradenham Cl, SE17 . . . . 102 DR79
Bradenham Rd, Har. HA3 . . . . . . 61 CH56
Hayes UB4 . . . . 77 BS69
Bradenhurst Cl, Cat. CR3 . . . . 186 DT126
Braden St, W9
off Shirland Rd 82 DB70
Bradfield Cl, Wok. GU22 . . . . . 166 AY118
Bradfield Dr, Bark. IG11 . . . . . . 70 EU64
Bradfield Rd, E16 . . . . 205 N4
Ruislip HA4 . . . . 60 BY64
Bradford Cl, N17
off Commercial Rd 46 DS51
SE26 *off Coombe Rd* 122 DV91
Bromley BR2 . . . . 145 EM102
Bradford Dr, Epsom KT19 . . . . 157 CT107
Bradford Rd, W3
off Warple Way 98 CS75
Ilford IG1 . . . . 69 ER60
Rickmansworth
(Herons.) WD3 . . . . 37 BC45
Bradgate, Pot.B. (Cuffley) EN6 . 13 DK27

★ Place of interest ⇌ Railway station ⊖ London Underground station DLR Docklands Light Railway station Tra Tramlink station H Hospital Riv Pedestrian ferry landing stage

222

Bradgate Cl, Pot.B. (Cuffley) EN6 . . . 13 DK28
Bradgate Rd, SE6 . . . 123 EA86
Brading Cres, E11 . . . 68 EH61
Brading Rd, SW2 . . . 121 DM87
Croydon CR0 . . . 141 DM100
Brading Ter, W12 . . . 99 CV76
Bradiston Rd, W9 . . . 81 CZ69
Bradleigh Av, Grays RM17 . . . 110 GC77
Bradley Cl, N1
off White Lion St . . . 83 DN68
N7 *off Sutterton St* . . . 83 DM65
Sutton (Belmont) SM2
off Station Rd . . . 158 DA110
Bradley Gdns, W13 . . . 79 CH72
Bradley Ms, SW17
off Bellevue Rd . . . 120 DF88
Bradley Rd, N22 . . . 45 DM54
SE19 . . . 122 DQ93
Enfield EN3 . . . 31 DY38
Waltham Abbey EN9 . . . 31 EC35
Bradley Stone Rd, E6 . . . 87 EM71
Bradman Row, Edg. HA8
off Pavilion Way . . . 42 CQ52
Bradmead, SW8 . . . 101 DH80
Bradmore Grn, Couls. CR5
off Coulsdon Rd . . . 175 DM118
Hatfield (Brook.Pk) AL9 . . . 11 CY26
Bradmore La, Hat. (Brook.Pk) AL9 . . . 11 CW27
Bradmore Pk Rd, W6 . . . 99 CV76
Bradmore Way, Couls. CR5 . . . 175 DL117
Hatfield (Brook.Pk) AL9 . . . 11 CY26
Bradshaw Cl, SW19 . . . 120 DA93
Bradshaw Dr, NW7 . . . 43 CX52
Bradshawe Waye, Uxb. UB8 . . . 76 BL71
Bradshaw Rd, Wat. WD24 . . . 24 BW39
Bradshaws Cl, SE25 . . . 142 DU97
Bradstock Rd, E9 . . . 85 DX65
Epsom KT17 . . . 157 CU106
Brad St, SE1 . . . 200 E3
Bradwell Av, Dag. RM10 . . . 70 FA61
Bradwell Cl, E18 . . . 68 EF56
Hornchurch RM12 . . . 89 FH65
Bradwell Grn, Brwd. (Hutt.) CM13 . . . 55 GC44
Bradwell Ms, N18
off Lyndhurst Rd . . . 46 DU49
Bradwell Rd, Buck.H. IG9 . . . 48 EL46
Bradwell St, E1 . . . 85 DX69
Brady Av, Loug. IG10 . . . 33 EQ40
Bradymead, E6 . . . 87 EN72
Brady St, E1 . . . 84 DV70
Braemar Av, N22 . . . 45 DL53
NW10 . . . 62 CR62
SW19 . . . 120 DA89
Bexleyheath DA7 . . . 107 FC84
South Croydon CR2 . . . 160 DQ109
Thornton Heath CR7 . . . 141 DN97
Wembley HA0 . . . 79 CK66
Braemar Cl, SE16 . . . 202 D10
Braemar Gdns, NW9 . . . 42 CR53
Hornchurch RM11 . . . 72 FN58
Sidcup DA15 . . . 125 ER90
West Wickham BR4 . . . 143 EC102
Braemar Rd, E13 . . . 86 EF70
N15 . . . 66 DS57
Brentford TW8 . . . 98 CL79
Worcester Park KT4 . . . 139 CV104
Braeside, Add. (New Haw) KT15 . . . 152 BH111
Beckenham BR3 . . . 123 EA92
Braeside Av, SW19 . . . 139 CY95
Sevenoaks TN13 . . . 190 FF124
Braeside Cl, Pnr. HA5
off The Avenue . . . 40 CA52
Sevenoaks TN13 . . . 190 FF123
Braeside Cres, Bexh. DA7 . . . 107 FC84
Braeside Rd, SW16 . . . 121 DJ94
Braes St, N1 . . . 83 DP66
Braesyde Cl, Belv. DA17 . . . 106 EZ77
Brafferton Rd, Croy. CR0 . . . 160 DQ105
Braganza St, SE17 . . . 200 F10
Bragg Cl, Dag. RM8
off Porters Av . . . 88 EV65
Bragmans La, Hem.H. (Flaun.) HP3 . . . 5 BB34
Rickmansworth (Sarratt) WD3 . . . 5 BE33
Braham St, E1 . . . 84 DT72
Braid, The, Chesh. HP5 . . . 4 AS30
Braid Av, W3 . . . 80 CS72
Braid Cl, Felt. TW13 . . . 116 BZ89
Braid Ct, W4
off Lawford Rd . . . 98 CQ80
Braidwood Pas, EC1
off Aldersgate St . . . 84 DQ71
Braidwood Rd, SE6 . . . 123 ED88
Braidwood St, SE1 . . . 201 M3
Brailsford Cl, Mitch. CR4 . . . 120 DE94
Brailsford Rd, SW2 . . . 121 DN85
Brainton Av, Felt. TW14 . . . 115 BV87
Braintree Av, Ilf. IG4 . . . 68 EL56
Braintree Ind Est, Ruis. HA4 . . . 59 BV63
Braintree Rd, Dag. RM10 . . . 70 FA62
Ruislip HA4 . . . 59 BV63
Braintree St, E2 . . . 84 DW69
Braithwaite Av, Rom. RM7 . . . 70 FA59
Braithwaite Gdns, Stan. HA7 . . . 41 CJ53
Braithwaite Rd, Enf. EN3 . . . 31 DZ41
Braithwaite Twr, W2 . . . 82 DD71
Brakefield Rd, Grav. (Sthflt) DA13 . . . 130 GB93
Brakey Hill, Red. (Bletch.) RH1 . . . 186 DS134
Bramah Grn, SW9 . . . 101 DN81
★ **Bramah Mus**, SE1 . . . 201 J3
Bramalea Cl, N6 . . . 64 DG58
Bramall Cl, E15
off Idmiston Rd . . . 68 EF64
Bramber Ct, Brent. TW8
off Sterling Pl . . . 98 CL77
Bramber Ho, Kings.T. KT2
off Kingsgate Rd . . . 138 CL95
Bramber Rd, N12 . . . 44 DE50
W14 . . . 99 CZ79
Brambleacres Cl, Sutt. SM2 . . . 158 DA108
Bramble Av, Dart. (Bean) DA2 . . . 129 FW90
Bramble Banks, Cars. SM5 . . . 158 DG109
Bramblebury Rd, SE18 . . . 105 EQ78
Bramble Cl, N15 *off Broad La* . . . 66 DU56
Beckenham BR3 . . . 143 EC99
Chigwell IG7 *off High Rd* . . . 49 EQ46
Croydon CR0 . . . 161 EA105
Shepperton TW17
off Halliford Cl . . . 135 BR98
Stanmore HA7 . . . 41 CK52
Uxbridge UB8 . . . 76 BM71
Watford WD25 . . . 7 BU34
Bramble Cft, Erith DA8 . . . 107 FC77
Brambledene Cl, Wok. GU21 . . . 166 AW118
Brambledown, Stai. TW18 . . . 134 BG95
Brambledown Cl, W.Wick. BR4 . . . 144 EE99
Brambledown Rd, Cars. SM5 . . . 158 DG108
South Croydon CR2 . . . 160 DS108
Wallington SM6 . . . 159 DH108
Bramblefield Cl, Long. DA3 . . . 149 FX97
Bramble Gdns, W12
off Wallflower St . . . 81 CT73
Bramble Hall La Mobile Home Pk, Tad. (Box H.) KT20 . . . 182 CM132
Bramble La, Amer. HP7 . . . 20 AS41
Hampton TW12 . . . 116 BZ93
Sevenoaks TN13 . . . 191 FH128
Upminster RM14 . . . 90 FQ67
Bramble Mead, Ch.St.G. HP8 . . . 36 AU48
Bramble Ri, Cob. KT11 . . . 170 BW115
Brambles, The, Chig. IG7
off Clayside . . . 49 EQ50
Waltham Cross EN8 . . . 15 DX31
West Drayton UB7 . . . 94 BL77
Brambles Cl, Cat. CR3 . . . 176 DS122
Isleworth TW7 . . . 97 CH80
Brambles Fm Dr, Uxb. UB10 . . . 76 BN69
Bramble Wk, Epsom KT18 . . . 156 CP114
Bramble Way, Wok. (Ripley) GU23 . . . 167 BF124
Bramblewood, Red. RH1 . . . 185 DH129
Bramblewood Cl, Cars. SM5 . . . 140 DE102
Brambling Cl, Bushey WD23 . . . 24 BY42
Bramblings, The, E4 . . . 47 ED49
Bramcote Av, Mitch. CR4 . . . 140 DF98
Bramcote Ct, Mitch. CR4
off Bramcote Av . . . 140 DF98
Bramcote Gro, SE16 . . . 202 F10
Bramcote Rd, SW15 . . . 99 CV84
Bramdean Cres, SE12 . . . 124 EG88
Bramdean Gdns, SE12 . . . 124 EG88
Bramerton Rd, Beck. BR3 . . . 143 DZ97
Bramerton St, SW3 . . . 100 DE79
Bramfield, Wat. WD25
off Garston La . . . 8 BY34
Bramfield Ct, N4
off Queens Dr . . . 66 DQ61
Bramfield Rd, SW11 . . . 120 DE86
Bramford Ct, N14 . . . 45 DK47
Bramford Rd, SW18 . . . 100 DC84
Bramham Gdns, SW5 . . . 100 DB78
Chessington KT9 . . . 155 CK105
Bramhope La, SE7 . . . 104 EH79
Bramlands Cl, SW11 . . . 100 DE83
Bramleas, Wat. WD18 . . . 23 BT42
Bramley Av, Couls. CR5 . . . 175 DJ115
Bramley Cl, E17 . . . 47 DY54
N14 . . . 29 DH43
Chertsey KT16 . . . 134 BH102
Gravesend (Istead Rise) DA13 . . . 131 GF94
Hayes UB3 *off Orchard Rd* . . . 77 BU73
Orpington BR6 . . . 145 EP102
Pinner HA5
off Wiltshire La . . . 59 BT55
South Croydon CR2 . . . 159 DP106
Staines TW18 . . . 114 BJ93
Swanley BR8 . . . 147 FE98
Twickenham TW2 . . . 116 CC86
Woodford Green IG8
off Orsett Ter . . . 48 EJ52
Bramley Ct, Wat. WD25
off Orchard Av . . . 7 BV31
Welling DA16 . . . 106 EV81
Bramley Cres, SW8
off Pascal St . . . 101 DK80
Ilford IG2 . . . 69 EN58
Bramley Gdns, Wat. WD19 . . . 40 BW50
Bramley Hill, S.Croy. CR2 . . . 159 DP106
Bramley Ho, SW15
off Tunworth Cres . . . 119 CT86
Bramley Ho Ct, Enf. EN2 . . . 30 DR37
Bramley Pl, Dart. DA1 . . . 107 FG84
Bramley Rd, N14 . . . 29 DH43
W5 . . . 97 CJ76
W10 . . . 81 CX73
Sutton SM1 . . . 158 DD106
Sutton (Cheam) SM2 . . . 157 CX109
Bramley Shaw, Wal.Abb. EN9 . . . 16 EF33
Bramley Way, Ashtd. KT21 . . . 172 CM117
Hounslow TW4 . . . 116 BZ85
West Wickham BR4 . . . 143 EB103
Brampton Cl, E5 . . . 66 DV61
Waltham Cross (Chsht) EN7 . . . 14 DU28
Brampton Gdns, N15
off Brampton Rd . . . 66 DQ57
Walton-on-Thames KT12 . . . 154 BW106
Brampton Gro, NW4 . . . 63 CV56
Harrow HA3 . . . 61 CG56
Wembley HA9 . . . 62 CN60
Brampton La, NW4 . . . 63 CW56
Brampton Pk Rd, N22 . . . 65 DN55
Brampton Rd, E6 . . . 86 EK69
N15 . . . 66 DQ57
NW9 . . . 62 CN56
SE2 . . . 106 EW79
Bexleyheath DA7 . . . 106 EX80
Croydon CR0 . . . 142 DT101
Uxbridge UB10 . . . 77 BP68
Watford WD19 . . . 39 BU48
Brampton Ter, Borwd. WD6 . . . 26 CN38
Bramshaw Gdns, Wat. WD19 . . . 40 BX50
Bramshaw Ri, N.Mal. KT3 . . . 138 CS100
Bramshaw Rd, E9 . . . 85 DX65
Bramshill Cl, Chig. IG7
off Tine Rd . . . 49 ES50
Bramshill Gdns, NW5 . . . 65 DH62
Bramshill Rd, NW10 . . . 81 CT68
Bramshot Av, SE7 . . . 104 EG79
Bramshot Way, Wat. WD19 . . . 39 BU47
Bramston Cl, Ilf. IG6 . . . 49 ET51
Bramston Rd, NW10 . . . 81 CU68
Bramston Rd, SW17 . . . 120 DC90
Bramwell Cl, Sun. TW16 . . . 136 BX96
Bramwell Ms, N1 . . . 83 DM67
Brancaster Dr, NW7 . . . 43 CT52
Brancaster La, Pur. CR8 . . . 160 DQ112
Brancaster Pl, Loug. IG10 . . . 33 EM41
Brancaster Rd, E12 . . . 69 EM63
SW16 . . . 121 DL90
Ilford IG2 . . . 69 ER58
Brancepeth Gdns, Buck.H. IG9 . . . 48 EG47
Branch Hill, NW3 . . . 64 DC62
Branch Pl, N1 . . . 84 DR67
Branch Rd, E14 . . . 85 DY73
Ilford IG6 . . . 50 EV50
St. Albans (Park St) AL2 . . . 9 CD27
Branch St, SE15 . . . 102 DS80
Brancker Cl, Wall. SM6
off Brown Cl . . . 159 DL108
Brancker Rd, Har. HA3 . . . 61 CK55
Brancroft Way, Enf. EN3 . . . 31 DY39
Brand Cl, N4 . . . 65 DP60
Brandesbury Sq, Wdf.Grn. IG8 . . . 49 EN52
Brandlehow Rd, SW15 . . . 99 CZ84
Brandon Cl, Grays (Chaff.Hun.) RM16 . . . 110 FZ75
Waltham Cross (Chsht) EN7 . . . 14 DS26
Brandon Est, SE17 . . . 101 DP79
Brandon Gros Av, S.Ock. RM15 . . . 91 FW69
Brandon Ms, EC2
off The Barbican . . . 84 DQ71
Brandon Rd, E17 . . . 67 EC55
N7 . . . 83 DL66
Dartford DA1 . . . 128 FN87
Southall UB2 . . . 96 BZ78
Sutton SM1 . . . 158 DB105
Brandon St, SE17 . . . 201 H9
Gravesend DA11 . . . 131 GH87
Brandram Ms, SE13
off Brandram Rd . . . 104 EE83
Brandram Rd, SE13 . . . 104 EE83
Brandreth Rd, E6 . . . 87 EM72
SW17 . . . 121 DH89
Brandries, The, Wall. SM6 . . . 141 DK104
BRANDS HILL, Slou. SL3 . . . 93 BB79
Brands Rd, Slou. SL3 . . . 93 BB79
Brand St, SE10 . . . 103 EC80
Brandville Gdns, Ilf. IG6 . . . 69 EP56
Brandville Rd, West Dr. UB7 . . . 94 BL75
Brandy Way, Sutt. SM2 . . . 158 DA108
Branfill Rd, Upmin. RM14 . . . 72 FP61
Brangbourne Rd, Brom. BR1 . . . 123 EC92
Brangton Rd, SE11 . . . 101 DM78
Brangwyn Cres, SW19 . . . 140 DD95
Branksea St, SW6 . . . 99 CY80
Branksome Av, N18 . . . 46 DT50
Branksome Cl, Tedd. TW11 . . . 117 CD91
Walton-on-Thames KT12 . . . 136 BX103
Branksome Rd, SW2 . . . 121 DL85
SW19 . . . 140 DA95
Branksome Way, Har. HA3 . . . 62 CL58
New Malden KT3 . . . 138 CQ95
Bransby Rd, Chess. KT9 . . . 156 CL107
Branscombe Gdns, N21 . . . 45 DN45
Branscombe St, SE13 . . . 103 EB83
Bransdale Cl, NW6
off West End La . . . 82 DB67
Bransell Cl, Swan. BR8 . . . 147 FC100
Bransgrove Rd, Edg. HA8 . . . 42 CM53
Branston Cres, Orp. BR5 . . . 145 ER102
Branstone Rd, Rich. TW9 . . . 98 CM81
Branton Rd, Green. DA9 . . . 129 FT86
Brants Wk, W7 . . . 79 CE70
Brantwood Av, Erith DA8 . . . 107 FC80
Isleworth TW7 . . . 97 CG84
Brantwood Cl, E17 . . . 67 EB55
West Byfleet KT14
off Brantwood Gdns . . . 152 BG113
Brantwood Ct, W.Byf. KT14
off Brantwood Dr . . . 151 BF113
Brantwood Dr, W.Byf. KT14 . . . 151 BF113
Brantwood Gdns, Enf. EN2 . . . 29 DL42
Ilford IG4 . . . 68 EL56
West Byfleet KT14 . . . 151 BF113
Brantwood Rd, N17 . . . 46 DT51
SE24 . . . 122 DQ85
Bexleyheath DA7 . . . 107 FB82
South Croydon CR2 . . . 160 DQ109
Brantwood Way, Orp. BR5 . . . 146 EW97
Brasenose Dr, SW13 . . . 99 CW79
Brasher Cl, Grnf. UB6 . . . 61 CD64
Brassett Pt, E15 . . . 86 EE67
Brassey Cl, Felt. TW14 . . . 115 BU88
Oxted RH8
off Westerham Rd . . . 188 EG129
Brassey Hill, Oxt. RH8 . . . 188 EG130
Brassey Rd, NW6 . . . 81 CZ65
Oxted RH8 . . . 188 EF130
Brassey Sq, SW11 . . . 100 DG83
Brassie Av, W3 . . . 80 CS72
Brass Tally All, SE16 . . . 203 J5
BRASTED, West. TN16 . . . 180 EW124
Brasted Cl, SE26 . . . 122 DW91
Bexleyheath DA6 . . . 126 EX85
Orpington BR6 . . . 146 EU103
Sutton SM2 . . . 158 DA110
Brasted Hill, Sev. (Knock.) TN14 . . . 180 EU120
Brasted Hill Rd, West. (Brasted) TN16 . . . 180 EV121
Brasted La, Sev. (Knock.) TN14 . . . 180 EU119
Brasted Rd, Erith DA8 . . . 107 FE80
Westerham TN16 . . . 189 ES126
Brathway Rd, SW18 . . . 120 DA87
Bratley St, E1 *off Weaver St* . . . 84 DU70
Brattle Wd, Sev. TN13 . . . 191 FH129
Braund Av, Grnf. UB6 . . . 78 CB70
Braundton Av, Sid. DA15 . . . 125 ET88
Braunston Dr, Hayes UB4 . . . 78 BY70
Bravington Cl, Shep. TW17 . . . 134 BM99
Bravington Pl, W9
off Bravington Rd . . . 81 CZ70
Bravington Rd, W9 . . . 81 CZ68
Bravingtons Wk, N1
off Pentonville Rd . . . 83 DL68
Brawlings La, Ger.Cr. (Chal.St.P.) SL9 . . . 37 BA49
Brawne Ho, SE17
off Hillingdon St . . . 101 DP79
Braxfield Rd, SE4 . . . 103 DY84
Braxted Pk, SW16 . . . 121 DM93
Bray, NW3 . . . 82 DE66
Brayards Rd, SE15 . . . 102 DV82
Braybourne Cl, Uxb. UB8 . . . 76 BJ65
Braybourne Dr, Islw. TW7 . . . 97 CF80
Braybrooke Gdns, SE19
off Fox Hill . . . 122 DT94
Braybrook St, W12 . . . 81 CT71
Brayburne Av, SW4 . . . 101 DJ82
Bray Cl, Borwd. WD6 . . . 26 CQ39
Braycourt Av, Walt. KT12 . . . 135 BV101
Bray Cres, SE16 . . . 203 H4
Braydon Rd, N16 . . . 66 DT60
Bray Dr, E16 . . . 86 EF73
Brayfield Ter, N1
off Lofting Rd . . . 83 DN66
Brayford Sq, E1
off Summercourt Rd . . . 84 DW72
Bray Gdns, Wok. GU22 . . . 167 BE116
Bray Pas, E16 . . . 86 EG73
Bray Pl, SW3 . . . 198 D9
Bray Rd, NW7 . . . 43 CX51
Cobham (Stoke D'Ab.) KT11 . . . 170 BY116
Bray Springs, Wal.Abb. EN9
off Roundhills . . . 16 EE34
Brayton Gdns, Enf. EN2 . . . 29 DK42
Braywood Av, Egh. TW20 . . . 113 AZ93
Braywood Rd, SE9 . . . 105 ER84
Brazil Cl, Croy. (Bedd.) CR0 . . . 141 DL101
Breach Barn Mobile Home Pk, Wal.Abb. EN9 . . . 16 EH29
Breach Barns La, Wal.Abb. EN9
off Galley Hill . . . 16 EF30
Breach La, Dag. RM9 . . . 88 FA69
Breach Rd, Grays RM20 . . . 109 FT79
Bread & Cheese La, Wal.Cr. (Chsht) EN7 . . . 14 DR25
Bread St, EC4 . . . 197 J9
Breakfield, Couls. CR5 . . . 175 DL116
Breakneck Hill, Green. DA9 . . . 129 FV85
Breakspear Ct, Abb.L. WD5 . . . 7 BT30
Breakspear Cl, Wat. WD24 . . . 23 BV38
Breakspeare Rd, Abb.L. WD5 . . . 7 BS31
Breakspear Path, Uxb. (Hare.) UB9 . . . 58 BJ55
Breakspear Rd, Ruis. HA4 . . . 59 BP59
Breakspear Rd N, Uxb. (Hare.) UB9 . . . 58 BN57
Breakspear Rd S, Uxb. (Ickhm) UB9, UB10 . . . 58 BM62
Breakspears Dr, Orp. BR5 . . . 146 EU95
Breakspears Ms, SE4
off Breakspears Rd . . . 103 EA82
Breakspears Rd, SE4 . . . 103 DZ83
Bream Cl, N17 . . . 66 DV56
Bream Gdns, E6 . . . 87 EN69
Breamore Cl, SW15 . . . 119 CU88
Breamore Rd, Ilf. IG3 . . . 69 ET61
Bream's Bldgs, EC4 . . . 196 D8
Bream St, E3 . . . 85 EA66
Breamwater Gdns, Rich. TW10 . . . 117 CH90
Brearley Cl, Edg. HA8
off Pavilion Way . . . 42 CQ52
Uxbridge UB8 . . . 76 BL65
Breasley Cl, SW15 . . . 99 CV84
Brechin Pl, SW7
off Rosary Gdns . . . 100 DC77
Brecknock Rd, N7 . . . 65 DJ63
N19 . . . 65 DJ63
Brecknock Rd Est, N7 . . . 65 DJ63
Breckonmead, Brom. BR1
off Wanstead Rd . . . 144 EJ96
Brecon Cl, Mitch. CR4 . . . 141 DL97
Worcester Park KT4 . . . 139 CW103
Brecon Grn, NW9
off Goldsmith Av . . . 62 CS58
Brecon Rd, W6 . . . 99 CY79
Enfield EN3 . . . 30 DW42
Brede Cl, E6 . . . 87 EN69
Bredgar, SE13 . . . 123 EC85
Bredgar Rd, N19 . . . 65 DJ61
Bredhurst Cl, SE20 . . . 122 DW93
Bredon Rd, Croy. CR0 . . . 142 DT101
Bredune, Ken. CR8 . . . 176 DR115
Breech La, Tad. KT20 . . . 173 CU124
Breer St, SW6 . . . 100 DB83
Breezers Hill, E1 . . . 202 C1
Breeze Ter, Wal.Cr. (Chsht) EN8
off Collet Cl . . . 15 DX28
Brember Rd, Har. HA2 . . . 60 CC61
Bremer Ms, E17
off Church La . . . 67 EB56
Bremer Rd, Stai. TW18 . . . 114 BG90
Bremner Cl, Swan. BR8 . . . 147 FG98
Bremner Rd, SW7 . . . 100 DC75
Brenchley Av, Grav. DA11 . . . 131 GH92
Brenchley Cl, Brom. BR2 . . . 144 EF100
Chislehurst BR7 . . . 145 EN95
Brenchley Gdns, SE23 . . . 122 DW86
Brenchley Rd, Orp. BR5 . . . 145 ET95
Bren Ct, Enf. EN3
off Colgate Pl . . . 31 EA37
Brendans Cl, Horn. RM11 . . . 72 FL60
Brenda Rd, SW17 . . . 120 DF89
Brenda Ter, Swans. DA10
off Manor Rd . . . 130 FY87
Brende Gdns, W.Mol. KT8 . . . 136 CB98
Brendon Av, NW10 . . . 62 CS63
Brendon Cl, Erith DA8 . . . 107 FE81
Esher KT10 . . . 154 CC107
Hayes UB3 . . . 95 BQ80
Brendon Ct, Rad. WD7
off The Avenue . . . 9 CH34
Brendon Dr, Esher KT10 . . . 154 CC107
Brendon Gdns, Har. HA2 . . . 60 CB63
Ilford IG2 . . . 69 ES57
Brendon Gro, N2 . . . 44 DC54
Brendon Rd, SE9 . . . 125 ER89
Dagenham RM8 . . . 70 EZ60
Brendon St, W1 . . . 194 C8
Brendon Way, Enf. EN1 . . . 46 DS45
Brenley Cl, Mitch. CR4 . . . 140 DG97
Brenley Gdns, SE9 . . . 104 EK84
Brennan Rd, Til. RM18 . . . 111 GH82
Brent, The, Dart. DA1, DA2 . . . 128 FN87
Brent Cl, Bex. DA5 . . . 126 EY88
Dartford DA2 . . . 128 FP86
Brentcot Cl, W13 . . . 79 CH70
Brent Cres, NW10 . . . 80 CM68
⊖ **Brent Cross** . . . 63 CX59
Brent Cross Gdns, NW4
off Haley Rd . . . 63 CX58
Brent Cross Shop Cen, NW4 . . . 63 CW59
Brentfield, NW10 . . . 80 CP66
Brentfield Cl, NW10
off Normans Mead . . . 80 CR65
Brentfield Gdns, NW2
off Hendon Way . . . 63 CX59
Brentfield Rd, NW10 . . . 80 CR65
Dartford DA1 . . . 128 FN86
BRENTFORD . . . 97 CK79
⇌ **Brentford** . . . 97 CJ79
Brentford Business Cen, Brent. TW8 . . . 97 CJ80
Brentford Cl, Hayes UB4 . . . 78 BX70
★ **Brentford FC**, Brent. TW8 . . . 97 CK79
Brent Grn, NW4 . . . 63 CW57
Brent Grn Wk, Wem. HA9 . . . 62 CQ62
Brentham Way, W5 . . . 79 CK70
Brenthouse Rd, E9 . . . 84 DV66
Brenthurst Rd, NW10 . . . 63 CT64
Brentlands Dr, Dart. DA1 . . . 128 FN88
Brent La, Dart. DA1 . . . 128 FM87
Brent Lea, Brent. TW8 . . . 97 CJ80
Brentmead Cl, W7 . . . 79 CE73
Brentmead Gdns, NW10 . . . 80 CM68
Brentmead Pl, NW11
off North Circular Rd . . . 63 CX58
Brenton St, E14 . . . 85 DY72
Brent Pk, NW10 . . . 62 CR64
Brent Pk Rd, NW4 . . . 63 CV59
NW9 . . . 63 CU60
Brent Pl, Barn. EN5 . . . 28 DA43
Brent Rd, E16 . . . 86 EG71
SE18 . . . 105 EP80
Brentford TW8 . . . 97 CJ79
South Croydon CR2 . . . 160 DV109
Southall UB2 . . . 96 BW76
Brent Side, Brent. TW8 . . . 97 CJ79
Brentside Cl, W13 . . . 79 CG70
Brentside Executive Cen, Brent. TW8 . . . 97 CH79
Brent St, NW4 . . . 63 CW56
Brent Ter, NW2 . . . 63 CW61
Brentvale Av, Sthl. UB1 . . . 79 CD74
Wembley HA0 . . . 80 CM67
Brent Vw Rd, NW9 . . . 63 CU59
Brent Way, N3 . . . 44 DA51
Brentford TW8 . . . 97 CK80
Dartford DA2 . . . 128 FP86
Wembley HA9 . . . 80 CP65
Brentwick Gdns, Brent. TW8 . . . 98 CL77
BRENTWOOD . . . 54 FV47
⇌ **Brentwood** . . . 54 FW48
Brentwood Bypass, Brwd. CM14, CM15 . . . 53 FR49
Brentwood Cl, SE9 . . . 125 EQ88
H **Brentwood Comm Hosp & Minor Injuries Unit**, Brwd. CM15 . . . 54 FY46
Brentwood Ct, Add. KT15 . . . 152 BH105
Brentwood Ho, SE18
off Shooter's Hill Rd . . . 104 EK80
★ **Brentwood Mus**, Brwd. CM14 . . . 54 FW49
Brentwood Pl, Brwd. CM15 . . . 54 FX46
Brentwood Rd, Brwd. CM13 . . . 55 GA49
Grays RM16 . . . 111 GH77
Romford RM1, RM2 . . . 71 FF58
Brereton Rd, N17 . . . 46 DT52
Bressenden Pl, SW1 . . . 199 J6
Bressey Av, Enf. EN1 . . . 30 DU39
Bressey Gro, E18 . . . 48 EF54
Bretlands Rd, Cher. KT16 . . . 133 BE103
Brett Cl, N16 *off Yoakley Rd* . . . 66 DS61
Northolt UB5
off Broomcroft Av . . . 78 BX69
Brett Ct, N9 . . . 46 DW47
Brett Cres, NW10 . . . 80 CR66
Brettell St, SE17
off Merrow St . . . 102 DR78
Brettenham Av, E17 . . . 47 EA53
Brettenham Rd, E17 . . . 47 EA54
N18 . . . 46 DV49
Brett Gdns, Dag. RM9 . . . 88 EY66
Brettgrave, Epsom KT19 . . . 156 CQ110
Brett Ho Cl, SW15
off Putney Heath La . . . 119 CX86
Brett Pas, E8 *off Kenmure Rd* . . . 66 DV64
Brett Pl, Wat. WD24
off The Harebreaks . . . 23 BU37
Brett Rd, E8 . . . 66 DV64
Barnet EN5 . . . 27 CW43
Brevet Cl, Purf. RM19 . . . 109 FR77
Brewer's Fld, Dart. DA2 . . . 128 FJ91
Brewer's Grn, SW1 . . . 199 M6
Brewers Hall Gdns, EC2 . . . 197 J7
Brewers La, Rich. TW9 . . . 117 CK85
Brewer St, W1 . . . 195 L10
Redhill (Bletch.) RH1 . . . 186 DQ131
★ **Brewery, The**, EC1 . . . 197 J6
Brewery, The, Rom. RM1
off Waterloo Rd . . . 71 FE57
Brewery Cl, Wem. HA0 . . . 61 CG64
Brewery La, Sev. TN13
off High St . . . 191 FJ125
Twickenham TW1 . . . 117 CF87
West Byfleet (Byfleet) KT14 . . . 152 BL113
Brewery Rd, N7 . . . 83 DL66
SE18 . . . 105 ER78
Bromley BR2 . . . 144 EL102
Woking GU21 . . . 166 AX117
Brewery Sq, EC1 . . . 196 G4
SE1 *off Horselydown La* . . . 84 DT74
Brewery Wk, Rom. RM1 . . . 71 FE57
Brewhouse La, E1 . . . 202 E3
SW15 . . . 99 CY83
Brewhouse Rd, SE18 . . . 105 EM77
Brewhouse Wk, SE16 . . . 203 K3
Brewhouse Yd, EC1 . . . 196 G4
Gravesend DA12
off Queen St . . . 131 GH86
Brewood Rd, Dag. RM8 . . . 88 EV65
Brewster Gdns, W10 . . . 81 CW71
Brewster Ho, E14 . . . 85 DZ73

★ Place of interest ⇌ Railway station ⊖ London Underground station DLR Docklands Light Railway station Tra Tramlink station H Hospital Riv Pedestrian ferry landing stage

223

Brewster Rd, E10 . . . 67 EB60
Brian Av, S.Croy. CR2 . . . 160 DS112
Brian Cl, Horn. RM12 . . . 71 FH63
Briane Rd, Epsom KT19 . . . 156 CQ110
Brian Rd, Rom. RM6 . . . 70 EW57
Briants Cl, Pnr. HA5 . . . 40 BZ54
Briant St, SE14 . . . 103 DX81
Briar Av, SW16 . . . 121 DM94
Briarbank Rd, W13 . . . 79 CG72
Briar Banks, Cars. SM5 . . . 158 DG109
Briar Cl, N2 . . . 64 DB55
N13 . . . 46 DQ48
Buckhurst Hill IG9 . . . 48 EK47
Hampton TW12 . . . 116 BZ92
Isleworth TW7 . . . 117 CF85
Waltham Cross (Chsht) EN8 . . . 14 DW29
Warlingham CR6 . . . 177 EA116
West Byfleet KT14 . . . 152 BJ111
Briar Ct, Sutt. SM3 . . . 157 CW105
Briar Cres, Nthlt. UB5 . . . 78 CB65
Briardale Gdns, NW3 . . . 64 DA62
Briarfield Av, N3 . . . 44 DB54
Briarfield Cl, Bexh. DA7
off Palmar Rd . . . 106 FA82
Briar Gdns, Brom. BR2 . . . 144 EF102
Briar Gro, S.Croy. CR2 . . . 160 DU113
Briar Hill, Pur. CR8 . . . 159 DL111
Briaris Cl, N17 . . . 46 DV52
Briar La, Cars. SM5 . . . 158 DG109
Croydon CR0 . . . 161 EB105
Briarleas Gdns, Upmin. RM14 . 73 FS59
Briar Pas, SW16 . . . 141 DL97
Briar Pl, SW16 . . . 141 DM97
Briar Rd, NW2 . . . 63 CW63
SW16 . . . 141 DL97
Bexley DA5 . . . 127 FD90
Harrow HA3 . . . 61 CJ57
Romford RM3 . . . 52 FJ52
Shepperton TW17 . . . 134 BM99
Twickenham TW2 . . . 117 CE88
Watford WD25 . . . 7 BU34
Woking (Send) GU23 . . . 167 BB123
Briars, The, Bushey (Bushey Hth) WD23 . . . 41 CE45
Rickmansworth (Sarratt) WD3 . . . 22 BH36
Slough SL3 . . . 93 AZ78
Waltham Cross (Chsht) EN8 . . . 15 DY31
Briars Ct, Lthd. KT22 . . . 155 CD114
Briars Wk, Rom. RM3 . . . 52 FL54
Briarswood, Wal.Cr. EN7 . . . 14 DS28
Briarswood Way, Orp. BR6 . . . 163 ET106
Briar Wk, SW15 . . . 99 CV84
W10 off Droop St . . . 81 CY70
Edgware HA8 . . . 42 CQ52
West Byfleet KT14 . . . 152 BG112
Briar Way, West Dr. UB7 . . . 94 BN75
Briarwood, Bans. SM7
off High St . . . 174 DA115
Briarwood Cl, NW9 . . . 62 CQ58
Feltham TW13 . . . 115 BS90
Briarwood Dr, Nthwd. HA6 . . . 39 BU54
Briarwood Rd, SW4 . . . 121 DK85
Epsom KT17 . . . 157 CU107
Briary Cl, NW3
off Fellows Rd . . . 82 DE66
Briary Ct, E16
off Turner St . . . 86 EF72
Sidcup DA14 . . . 126 EV92
Briary Gdns, Brom. BR1 . . . 124 EH92
Briary Gro, Edg. HA8 . . . 42 CP54
Briary La, N9 . . . 46 DT48
Brick Ct, EC4 . . . 196 D9
Grays RM17
off Columbia Wf Rd . . . 110 GA79
Brickcroft, Brox. EN10 . . . 15 DY26
Brickenden Ct, Wal.Abb. EN9 . . 16 EF33
Brickett Cl, Ruis. HA4 . . . 59 BQ57
BRICKET WOOD, St.Alb. AL2 . . . 8 BZ29
⇌ Bricket Wood . . . 8 CA30
Brick Fm Cl, Rich. TW9 . . . 98 CP81
Brickfield Cl, Brent. TW8 . . . 97 CJ80
Brickfield Cotts, SE18 . . . 105 ET79
Brickfield Fm Gdns, Orp. BR6 163 EQ105
Brickfield La, Barn. EN5 . . . 27 CT44
Hayes UB3 . . . 95 BR79
Brickfield Rd, SW19 . . . 120 DB91
Epping (Cooper.) CM16 . . . 18 EX29
Thornton Heath CR7 . . . 141 DP95
Brickfields, Har. HA2 . . . 61 CD61
Brickfields La, Epp. (Cooper.) CM16
off Brickfield Rd . . . 18 EX29
Brickfields Way, West Dr. UB7 . 94 BM76
Brick Kiln Cl, Wat. WD19 . . . 24 BY44
Brick Kiln La, Oxt. RH8 . . . 188 EJ131
Brick La, E1 . . . 84 DT71
E2 . . . 84 DT69
Enfield EN1, EN3 . . . 30 DV40
Stanmore HA7
off Honeypot La . . . 41 CK52
Bricklayer's Arms Distribution Cen, SE1 . . . 201 N9
Bricklayer's Arms Roundabout, SE1 . . . 201 K8
Brick St, W1 . . . 199 H3
Brickwall La, Ruis. HA4 . . . 59 BS60
Brickwood Cl, SE26 . . . 122 DV90
Brickwood Rd, Croy. CR0 . . . 142 DS103
Brideale Cl, SE15
off Colegrove Rd . . . 102 DT79
Bride Ct, EC4 . . . 196 F9
Bride La, EC4 . . . 196 F9
Bridel Ms, N1
off Colebrooke Row . . . 83 DP67
Brides Pl, N1
off De Beauvoir Rd . . . 84 DS66
Bride St, N7 . . . 83 DM65
Bridewain St, SE1 . . . 201 P6
Bridewell Pl, E1 . . . 202 E3
EC4 . . . 196 F9
Bridford Ms, W1 . . . 195 J6
Bridge, The, Har. HA3 . . . 61 CE55
Bridge App, NW1 . . . 82 DG66
Bridge Av, W6 . . . 99 CW78
W7 . . . 79 CD71
Upminster RM14 . . . 72 FN61
Bridge Barn La, Wok. GU21 . . . 166 AW117
Bridge Cl, W10
off Kingsdown Cl . . . 81 CX72
Brentwood CM13 . . . 55 FZ49
Dartford DA2 . . . 109 FR83
Enfield EN1 . . . 30 DV40
Romford RM7 . . . 71 FE58
Staines TW18 . . . 113 BE91
Teddington TW11
off Shacklegate La . . . 117 CF91
Walton-on-Thames KT12 . . . 135 BT101
West Byfleet (Byfleet) KT14 . . 152 BM112
Woking GU21 . . . 166 AW117
Bridge Cotts, Upmin. RM14 . . . 73 FU64
Bridge Ct, Wok. GU21 . . . 166 AX117
Bridge Dr, N13 . . . 45 DM49
Bridge End, E17 . . . 47 EC53
Bridgefield Cl, Bans. SM7 . . . 173 CW115
Bridgefield Rd, Sutt. SM1 . . . 158 DA107
Bridgefoot, SE1 . . . 101 DL78
Bridgefoot La, Pot.B. EN6 . . . 11 CX33
Bridge Gdns, N16
off Green Las . . . 66 DR63
Ashford TW15 . . . 115 BQ94
East Molesey KT8 . . . 137 CD98
Bridge Gate, N21
off Ridge Av . . . 46 DQ45
Bridgeham Cl, Wey. KT13
off Mayfield Rd . . . 152 BN106
Bridge Hill, Epp. CM16 . . . 17 ET33
Bridge Ho Quay, E14 . . . 204 E3
Bridgeland Rd, E16 . . . 86 EG73
Bridge La, NW11 . . . 63 CY57
SW11 . . . 100 DE81
Virginia Water GU25 . . . 132 AY99
Bridgeman Rd, N1 . . . 83 DM66
Teddington TW11 . . . 117 CG93
Bridgeman St, NW8 . . . 194 B1
Bridge Meadows, SE14 . . . 103 DX79
Bridge Ms, Wok. GU21
off Bridge Barn La . . . 166 AX117
Bridgend Rd, SW18 . . . 100 DC84
Enfield EN1 . . . 30 DW35
Bridgenhall Rd, Enf. EN1 . . . 30 DT39
Bridgen Rd, Bex. DA5 . . . 126 EY86
Bridge Pk, SW18 . . . 120 DA85
Bridge Pl, SW1 . . . 199 J8
Amersham HP6 . . . 20 AT38
Croydon CR0 . . . 142 DR101
Watford WD17 . . . 24 BX43
Bridgeport Pl, E1 . . . 202 C2
Bridger Cl, Wat. WD25 . . . 8 BX33
Bridge Rd, E6 . . . 87 EM66
E15 . . . 85 ED66
E17 . . . 67 DZ59
N9 off The Broadway . . . 46 DU48
N22 . . . 45 DL53
NW10 . . . 80 CS65
Beckenham BR3 . . . 123 DZ94
Bexleyheath DA7 . . . 106 EY82
Chertsey KT16 . . . 134 BH101
Chessington KT9 . . . 156 CL106
East Molesey KT8 . . . 137 CE98
Epsom KT17 . . . 157 CT112
Erith DA8 . . . 107 FF81
Grays RM17 . . . 110 GB78
Hounslow TW3 . . . 97 CD82
Isleworth TW7 . . . 97 CD83
Kings Langley WD4 . . . 7 BQ33
Orpington BR5 . . . 146 EV100
Rainham RM13 . . . 89 FF70
Southall UB2 . . . 96 BZ75
Sutton SM2 . . . 158 DB107
Twickenham TW1 . . . 117 CH86
Uxbridge UB8 . . . 76 BJ68
Wallington SM6 . . . 159 DJ106
Wembley HA9 . . . 62 CN62
Weybridge KT13 . . . 152 BM105
Bridge Row, Croy. CR0
off Cross Rd . . . 142 DR102
Bridges Ct, SW11 . . . 100 DD83
Bridges Dr, Dart. DA1 . . . 128 FP85
Bridges La, Croy. CR0 . . . 159 DL105
Bridges Pl, SW6 . . . 99 CZ81
Bridges Rd, SW19 . . . 120 DB93
Stanmore HA7 . . . 41 CF50
Bridges Rd Ms, SW19
off Bridges Rd . . . 120 DB93
Bridge St, SW1 . . . 199 P5
W4 . . . 98 CR77
Leatherhead KT22 . . . 171 CG122
Pinner HA5 . . . 60 BX55
Richmond TW9 . . . 117 CK85
Slough (Colnbr.) SL3 . . . 93 BD80
Staines TW18 . . . 113 BE91
Walton-on-Thames KT12 . . . 135 BT102
Bridge Ter, E15
off Bridge Rd . . . 85 ED66
SE13 off Mercator Rd . . . 103 ED84
Bridgetown Cl, SE19
off St. Kitts Ter . . . 122 DS92
Bridge Vw, W6 . . . 99 CW78
Greenhithe DA9
off London Rd . . . 129 FW85
Bridgeview Ct, Ilf. IG6 . . . 49 ER51
Bridgewater Cl, Chis. BR7 . . . 145 ES97
Bridgewater Ct, Slou. SL3 . . . 93 BA78
Bridgewater Gdns, Edg. HA8 . . . 42 CM54
Bridgewater Rd, Ruis. HA4 . . . 59 BU63
Wembley HA0 . . . 79 CJ66
Weybridge KT13 . . . 153 BR107
Bridgewater Sq, EC2 . . . 197 H6
Bridgewater St, EC2 . . . 197 H6
Bridgewater Way, Bushey WD23 . . . 24 CB44
Bridge Way, N11
off Pymmes Grn Rd . . . 45 DJ48
NW11 . . . 63 CZ57
Bridgeway, Bark. IG11 . . . 87 ET66
Bridge Way, Cob. KT11 . . . 153 BT113
Coulsdon CR5 . . . 174 DE119
Twickenham TW2 . . . 116 CC87
Uxbridge UB10 . . . 59 BP64
Bridgeway, Wem. HA0 . . . 80 CL66
Bridgeway St, NW1 . . . 195 M1
Bridge Wf, Cher. KT16 . . . 134 BJ102
Bridge Wf Rd, Islw. TW7
off Church St . . . 97 CH83
Bridgewood Cl, SE20 . . . 122 DV94
Bridgewood Rd, SW16 . . . 121 DK94
Worcester Park KT4 . . . 157 CU105
Bridge Wks, Uxb. UB8 . . . 76 BJ70
Bridge Yd, SE1 . . . 201 L2
Bridgford St, SW18 . . . 120 DC90
Bridgman Rd, W4 . . . 98 CQ76
Bridgwater Cl, Rom. RM3 . . . 52 FK50
Bridgwater Rd, E15 . . . 85 EC67
Romford RM3 . . . 52 FJ50
Bridgwater Wk, Rom. RM3 . . . 52 FK50
Bridle Cl, Enf. EN3 . . . 31 DZ37
Epsom KT19 . . . 156 CR106
Kingston upon Thames KT1 . 137 CK98
Sunbury-on-Thames TW16
off Forge La . . . 135 BU97
Bridle End, Epsom KT17 . . . 157 CT114
Bridle La, W1 . . . 195 L10
Cobham KT11 . . . 170 CB115
Leatherhead KT22 . . . 170 CB115
Rickmansworth (Loud.) WD3 . . . 22 BK41
Twickenham TW1
off Crown Rd . . . 117 CH86
Bridle Path, Croy. CR0 . . . 141 DM104
Watford WD17 . . . 23 BV40
Bridle Path, The, Epsom KT17 . 157 CV110
Woodford Green IG8 . . . 48 EE52
Bridlepath Way, Felt. TW14 . . . 115 BS88
Bridle Rd, Croy. CR0 . . . 143 EA104
Epsom KT17 . . . 157 CT113
Esher (Clay.) KT10 . . . 155 CH107
Pinner HA5 . . . 60 BW58
Bridle Rd, The, Pur. CR8 . . . 159 DL110
Bridle Way, Croy. CR0 . . . 161 EA106
Orpington BR6 . . . 163 EQ105
Bridle Way, The, Croy. CR0 . . . 161 DY110
Bridleway, The, Wall. SM6 . . . 159 DJ105
Bridleway Cl, Epsom KT17 . . . 157 CW110
Bridlington Cl, West. (Bigg.H.) TN16 . . . 178 EH119
Bridlington Rd, N9 . . . 46 DV45
Watford WD19 . . . 40 BX48
Bridport Av, Rom. RM7 . . . 71 FB58
Bridport Pl, N1 . . . 84 DR68
Bridport Rd, N18 . . . 46 DS50
Greenford UB6 . . . 78 CB67
Thornton Heath CR7 . . . 141 DN97
Bridport Ter, SW8
off Wandsworth Rd . . . 101 DK81
Bridstow Pl, W2
off Talbot Rd . . . 82 DA72
Brief St, SE5 . . . 101 DP81
Brier Lea, Tad. (Lwr Kgswd) KT20 . . . 183 CZ126
Brierley, Croy. (New Adgtn) CR0 . . . 161 EB107
Brierley Av, N9 . . . 46 DW46
Brierley Cl, SE25 . . . 142 DU98
Hornchurch RM11 . . . 72 FJ58
Brierley Rd, E11 . . . 67 ED63
SW12 . . . 121 DJ89
Brierly Gdns, E2
off Royston St . . . 84 DW68
Brier Rd, Tad. KT20 . . . 173 CV119
Briery Ct, Rick. (Chorl.) WD3 . . 22 BG42
Briery Fld, Rick. (Chorl.) WD3 . . 22 BG42
Briery Way, Amer. HP6 . . . 20 AS37
Brigade Cl, Har. HA2 . . . 61 CD61
Brigade Pl, Cat. CR3 . . . 176 DQ122
Brigade St, SE3
off Royal Par . . . 104 EF82
Brigadier Av, Enf. EN2 . . . 30 DQ39
Brigadier Hill, Enf. EN2 . . . 30 DQ38
Briggeford Cl, E5
off Geldeston Rd . . . 66 DU61
Briggs Cl, Mitch. CR4 . . . 141 DH95
Bright Cl, Belv. DA17 . . . 106 EX77
Brightfield Rd, SE12 . . . 124 EF85
Brightlands, Grav. (Nthflt) DA11 . . . 130 GE91
Brightlands Rd, Reig. RH2 . . . 184 DC132
Brightling Rd, SE4 . . . 123 DZ86
Brightlingsea Pl, E14 . . . 85 DZ73
Brightman Rd, SW18 . . . 120 DD88
Brighton Av, E17 . . . 67 DZ57
Brighton Cl, Add. KT15 . . . 152 BJ106
Uxbridge UB10 . . . 77 BP66
Brighton Dr, Nthlt. UB5 . . . 78 CA65
Brighton Gro, SE14
off Harts La . . . 103 DY81
Brighton Rd, E6 . . . 87 EN69
N2 . . . 44 DC54
N16 . . . 66 DS63
Addlestone KT15 . . . 152 BJ105
Banstead SM7 . . . 157 CZ114
Coulsdon CR5 . . . 175 DJ119
Purley CR8 . . . 160 DQ110
South Croydon CR2 . . . 160 DQ106
Surbiton KT6 . . . 137 CJ100
Sutton SM2 . . . 158 DB109
Tadworth KT20 . . . 173 CY119
Watford WD24 . . . 23 BU38
Brighton Ter, SW9 . . . 101 DM84
Brights Av, Rain. RM13 . . . 89 FH70
Brightside, The, Enf. EN3 . . . 31 DX39
Brightside Av, Stai. TW18 . . . 114 BJ94
Brightside Rd, SE13 . . . 123 ED86
Bright St, E14 . . . 85 EB72
Brightview Cl, St.Alb. (Brick.Wd) AL2 . . . 8 BY29
Brightwell Cl, Croy. CR0
off Sumner Rd . . . 141 DN102
Brightwell Cres, SW17 . . . 120 DF92
Brightwell Rd, Wat. WD18 . . . 23 BU43
Brig Ms, SE8
off Watergate St . . . 103 EA79
Brigstock Rd, Belv. DA17 . . . 107 FB77
Coulsdon CR5 . . . 175 DH115
Thornton Heath CR7 . . . 141 DN99
Brill Pl, NW1 . . . 195 N1
Brimfield Rd, Purf. RM19 . . . 109 FR77
Brim Hill, N2 . . . 64 DC56
BRIMSDOWN, Enf. EN3 . . . 31 DY41
⇌ Brimsdown . . . 31 DY41
Brimsdown Av, Enf. EN3 . . . 31 DY40
Brimsdown Ind Est, Enf. EN3 . . 31 DZ40
Brimshot La, Wok. (Chobham) GU24 . . . 150 AS109
Brimstone Cl, Orp. BR6 . . . 164 EW108
Brindle Gate, Sid. DA15 . . . 125 ES88
Brindles, Horn. RM11 . . . 72 FL56
Brindles, The, Bans. SM7 . . . 173 CZ117
Brindles Cl, Brwd. (Hutt.) CM13 . . . 55 GC47
Brindley Cl, Bexh. DA7 . . . 107 FB83
Wembley HA0 . . . 79 CJ67
Brindley Ho, SW2
off New Pk Rd . . . 121 DL87
Brindley St, SE14 . . . 103 DZ81
Brindley Way, Brom. BR1 . . . 124 EG92
Southall UB1 . . . 78 CB73
Brindwood Rd, E4 . . . 47 DZ48
Brinkburn Cl, SE2 . . . 106 EU77
Edgware HA8 . . . 42 CP54
Brinkburn Gdns, Edg. HA8 . . . 62 CN55
Brinkley, Kings.T. KT1
off Burritt Rd . . . 138 CN96
Brinkley Rd, Wor.Pk. KT4 . . . 139 CV103
Brinklow Cres, SE18 . . . 105 EP80
Brinklow Ho, W2 . . . 82 DB71
Brinkworth Rd, Ilf. IG5 . . . 68 EL55
Brinkworth Way, E9 . . . 85 DZ65
Brinley Cl, Wal.Cr. (Chsht) EN8 . 15 DX31
Brinsdale Rd, NW4 . . . 63 CX56
Brinsley Rd, Har. HA3 . . . 41 CD54
Brinsley St, E1
off Watney St . . . 84 DV72
Brinsmead, St.Alb. (Park St) AL2 . . . 9 CD27
Brinsmead Rd, Rom. RM3 . . . 52 FN54
Brinsworth Cl, Twick. TW2 . . . 117 CD89
Brinton Wk, SE1 . . . 200 F3
Brion Pl, E14 . . . 85 EC71
Brisbane Av, SW19 . . . 140 DB95
Brisbane Ct, N10
off Sydney Rd . . . 45 DH52
Brisbane Ho, Til. RM18
off Leicester Rd . . . 111 GF81
Brisbane Rd, E10 . . . 67 EB61
W13 . . . 97 CG75
Ilford IG1 . . . 69 EP59
Brisbane St, SE5 . . . 102 DR80
Briscoe Cl, E11 . . . 68 EF61
Briscoe Rd, SW19 . . . 120 DD93
Rainham RM13 . . . 90 FJ68
Briset Rd, SE9 . . . 104 EK83
Briset St, EC1 . . . 196 F6
Briset Way, N7 . . . 65 DM61
Brisson Cl, Esher KT10 . . . 154 BZ107
Bristol Cl, Stai. (Stanw.) TW19 . 114 BL86
Wallington SM6 . . . 159 DL108
Bristol Gdns, SW15
off Portsmouth Rd . . . 119 CW87
W9 . . . 82 DB70
Bristol Ms, W9
off Bristol Gdns . . . 82 DB70
Bristol Pk Rd, E17 . . . 67 DY56
Bristol Rd, E7 . . . 86 EJ65
Gravesend DA12 . . . 131 GK90
Greenford UB6 . . . 78 CB67
Morden SM4 . . . 140 DC99
Bristol Way, Slou. SL1 . . . 74 AT74
Briston Gro, N8 . . . 65 DL58
Briston Ms, NW7 . . . 43 CU52
Bristowe Cl, SW2
off Tulse Hill . . . 121 DN86
Bristow Rd, SE19 . . . 122 DS92
Bexleyheath DA7 . . . 106 EY81
Croydon CR0 . . . 159 DL105
Hounslow TW3 . . . 96 CC83
★ Britain at War Experience, SE1 . . . 201 M3
Britannia Cl, SW4
off Bowland Rd . . . 101 DK84
Erith DA8 off Manor Rd . . . 107 FF79
Northolt UB5 . . . 78 BX69
Britannia Dr, Grav. DA12 . . . 131 GM92
Britannia Gate, E16 . . . 205 N2
Britannia Ind Est, Slou. (Colnbr.) SL3 . . . 93 BE82
Britannia La, Twick. TW2 . . . 116 CC87
Britannia Rd, E14 . . . 204 A9
N12 . . . 44 DC48
SW6 . . . 100 DB80
Brentwood (Warley) CM14 . . 54 FW50
Ilford IG1 . . . 69 EP62
Surbiton KT5 . . . 138 CM101
Waltham Cross EN8 . . . 15 DZ34
Britannia Row, N1 . . . 83 DP67
Britannia St, WC1 . . . 196 B2
Britannia Wk, N1 . . . 197 K2
Britannia Way, NW10 . . . 80 CP70
SW6 off Britannia Rd . . . 100 DB81
Staines (Stanw.) TW19 . . . 114 BK87
★ British Dental Assoc Mus, W1 . . . 195 H7
British Gro, W4 . . . 99 CT78
British Gro Pas, W4 . . . 99 CT78
British Gro S, W4
off British Gro Pas . . . 99 CT78
British Legion Rd, E4 . . . 48 EF47
★ British Lib, NW1 . . . 195 N2
★ British Lib Newspaper Collection, NW9 . . . 62 CS55
★ British Med Assoc, WC1 . . 195 N4
★ British Mus, WC1 . . . 195 P7
★ British Red Cross Mus & Archives, SW1 . . . 198 F5
British St, E3 . . . 85 DZ69
Briton Cl, S.Croy. CR2 . . . 160 DS111
Briton Cres, S.Croy. CR2 . . . 160 DS111
Briton Hill Rd, S.Croy. CR2 . . . 160 DS110
Brittain Rd, Dag. RM8 . . . 70 EY62
Walton-on-Thames KT12 . . 154 BX106
Brittains La, Sev. TN13 . . . 190 FF123
Britten Cl, NW11 . . . 64 DB60
Borehamwood (Elstree) WD6
off Rodgers Cl . . . 25 CK44
Brittenden Cl, Orp. BR6 . . . 163 ES107
Brittenden Par, Orp. BR6
off Glentrammon Rd . . . 163 ET107
Britten Dr, Sthl. UB1 . . . 78 CA72
Britten St, SW3 . . . 100 DE78
Britton Cl, SE6
off Brownhill Rd . . . 123 ED87
Britton St, EC1 . . . 196 F5
Brixham Cres, Ruis. HA4 . . . 59 BU60
Brixham Gdns, Ilf. IG3 . . . 69 ES64
Brixham Rd, Well. DA16 . . . 106 EX81
Brixham St, E16 . . . 87 EM74
BRIXTON, SW2 . . . 101 DL84
⇌ Brixton . . . 101 DN84
⊖ Brixton . . . 101 DN84
★ Brixton Acad, The, SW9 . . . 101 DM83
Brixton Est, Edg. HA8 . . . 42 CP54
Brixton Hill, SW2 . . . 121 DL87
Brixton Hill Pl, SW2
off Brixton Hill . . . 121 DL87
Brixton Oval, SW2 . . . 101 DN84
Brixton Rd, SW9 . . . 101 DN82
Watford WD24 . . . 23 BV39
Brixton Sta Rd, SW9 . . . 101 DN84
Brixton Water La, SW2 . . . 121 DM85
Broad Acre, St.Alb. (Brick.Wd) AL2 . . . 8 BY30
Broadacre, Stai. TW18 . . . 114 BG92
Broadacre Cl, Uxb. UB10 . . . 59 BP62
Broadbent Cl, N6 . . . 65 DH60
Broadbent St, W1 . . . 195 H10
Broadberry Ct, N18 . . . 46 DV50
Broadbridge Cl, SE3 . . . 104 EG80
Broad Cl, Walt. KT12 . . . 136 BX104
Broadcoombe, S.Croy. CR2 . . 160 DW108
Broad Ct, WC2 . . . 196 A9
Broadcroft Av, Stan. HA7 . . . 41 CK54
Broadcroft Rd, Orp. BR5 . . . 145 ER101
Broad Ditch Rd, Grav. (Sthflt) DA13 . . . 130 GC94
Broadeaves Cl, S.Croy. CR2 . . 160 DS106
Broadfield Cl, NW2 . . . 63 CW62
Croydon CR0
off Progress Way . . . 141 DM103
Romford RM1 . . . 71 FF57
Tadworth KT20 . . . 173 CW120
Broadfield Ct, Bushey (Bushey Hth) WD23 . . . 41 CE47
Broadfield La, NW1 . . . 83 DL66
Broadfield Rd, SE6 . . . 124 EE87
Broadfields, E.Mol. KT8 . . . 137 CD100
Harrow HA2 . . . 40 CB54
Waltham Cross (Chsht) EN7 . 13 DP29
Broadfields Av, N21 . . . 45 DN45
Edgware HA8 . . . 42 CP49
Broadfields Hts, Edg. HA8 . . . 42 CP49
Broadfields La, Wat. WD19 . . . 39 BV46
Broadfield Sq, Enf. EN1 . . . 30 DV40
Broadfields Way, NW10 . . . 63 CT64
Broadfield Way, Buck.H. IG9 . . . 48 EJ48
Broadford La, Wok. (Chobham) GU24 . . . 150 AT112
BROADGATE, EC2 . . . 197 L6
Broadgate, E13 . . . 86 EJ68
EC2 off Liverpool St . . . 84 DS71
Waltham Abbey EN9 . . . 16 EF33
Broadgate Circle, EC2 . . . 197 M6
Broadgate Rd, E16 . . . 86 EK72
Broadgates Av, Barn. EN4 . . . 28 DB39
Broadgates Rd, SW18
off Ellerton Rd . . . 120 DD88
BROAD GREEN, Croy. CR0 . . . 141 DN100
Broad Grn Av, Croy. CR0 . . . 141 DP101
Broadgreen Rd, Wal.Cr. (Chsht) EN7 . . . 14 DR26
Broadham Grn Rd, Oxt. RH8 . 187 ED132
Broadham Pl, Oxt. RH8 . . . 187 ED131
Broadhead Strand, NW9 . . . 43 CT53
Broadheath Dr, Chis. BR7 . . . 125 EM92
Broad Highway, Cob. KT11 . . . 154 BX114
Broadhinton Rd, SW4 . . . 101 DH83
Broadhurst, Ashtd. KT21 . . . 172 CL116
Broadhurst Av, Edg. HA8 . . . 42 CP49
Ilford IG3 . . . 69 ET63
Broadhurst Cl, NW6
off Broadhurst Gdns . . . 82 DC65
Richmond TW10
off Lower Gro Rd . . . 118 CM85
Broadhurst Gdns, NW6 . . . 82 DB65
Chigwell IG7 . . . 49 EQ49
Ruislip HA4 . . . 60 BW61
Broadhurst Wk, Rain. RM13 . . . 89 FG65
Broadlake Cl, St.Alb. (Lon.Col.) AL2 . . . 9 CK27
Broadlands, Felt. TW13 . . . 116 BZ90
Grays (Bad.Dene) RM17
off Bankfoot . . . 110 FZ78
Broadlands Av, SW16 . . . 121 DL89
Enfield EN3 . . . 30 DV41
Shepperton TW17 . . . 135 BQ100
Broadlands Cl, N6 . . . 64 DG59
SW16 . . . 121 DL89
Enfield EN3 . . . 30 DV41
Waltham Cross EN8 . . . 15 DX34
Broadlands Dr, Warl. CR6 . . . 176 DW119
Broadlands Rd, N6 . . . 64 DF59
Bromley BR1 . . . 124 EH91
Broadlands Way, N.Mal. KT3 . 139 CT100
Broad La, EC2 . . . 197 M6
N8 off Tottenham La . . . 65 DM57
N15 . . . 66 DT56
Dartford DA2 . . . 127 FG91
Hampton TW12 . . . 116 CA93
Broad Lawn, SE9 . . . 125 EN89
Broadlawns Ct, Har. HA3 . . . 41 CF53
Broadley Gdns, Rad. (Shenley) WD7
off Queens Way . . . 10 CL32
Broadley St, NW8 . . . 194 A6
Broadley Ter, NW1 . . . 194 C5
Broadmark Rd, Slou. SL2 . . . 74 AV73
Broadmayne, SE17 . . . 201 K10
Broadmead, SE6 . . . 123 EA90
Broad Mead, Ashtd. KT21 . . . 172 CM117
Broadmead Av, Wor.Pk. KT4 . . 139 CU101
Broadmead Cl, Hmptn. TW12 . 116 CA93
Pinner HA5 . . . 40 BY52
Broadmead Rd, Hayes UB4 . . . 78 BY70
Northolt UB5 . . . 78 BY70
Woking (Send) GU22, GU23 . . . 167 BB122
Woodford Green IG8 . . . 48 EG51
Broadmeads, Wok. (Send) GU23
off Broadmead Rd . . . 167 BB122
Broad Oak, Sun. TW16 . . . 115 BT93
Woodford Green IG8 . . . 48 EH50
Broadoak Av, Enf. EN3 . . . 31 DX35
Broad Oak Cl, E4 . . . 47 EA50

★ Place of interest ⇌ Railway station ⊖ London Underground station DLR Docklands Light Railway station Tra Tramlink station H Hospital Riv Pedestrian ferry landing stage

224

Bro - Bro

Broadoak Cl, Dart. (Sutt.H.) DA4 128 FN93
Broad Oak Cl, Orp. BR5 146 EU96
Broadoak Rd, Erith DA8 107 FD80
Broadoaks, Epp. CM16 17 ET31
Surbiton KT6 138 CP102
Broadoaks Cres, W.Byf. KT14 152 BH114
Broadoaks Way, Brom. BR2 144 EF99
Broad Platts, Slou. SL3 92 AX76
Broad Ride, Egh. TW20 132 AU96
Virginia Water GU25 132 AU96
Broad Rd, Swans. DA10 130 FY86
Broad Sanctuary, SW1 199 N5
Broadstone Pl, W1 194 F7
Broadstone Rd, Horn. RM12 71 FG61
Broad St, Dag. RM10 88 FA66
Teddington TW11 117 CF93
Broad St Av, EC2 197 M7
Broad St Pl, EC2 197 L7
Broadstrood, Loug. IG10 33 EN38
Broad Vw, NW9 62 CN58
Broadview Av, Grays RM16 110 GD75
Broadview Rd, SW16 121 DK94
Broadwalk, E18 68 EF55
Broad Wk, N21 45 DM47
NW1 195 H3
SE3 104 EJ83
W1 198 F2
Caterham CR3 176 DT122
Coulsdon CR5 174 DG123
Croydon CR0 161 DY110
Epsom KT18 off Chalk La 172 CS117
Epsom (Burgh Hth) KT18 173 CX119
Broadwalk, Har. HA2 60 CA57
Broad Wk, Houns. TW5 96 BX81
Orpington BR6 146 EX104
Richmond TW9 98 CM80
Sevenoaks TN15 191 FL128
Broad Wk, The, W8 82 DB74
East Molesey KT8 137 CF97
Broadwalk, The, Nthwd. HA6 39 BQ54
Broadwalk Ct, W8 82 DA74
Broad Wk La, NW11 63 CZ59
Broad Wk N, The, Brwd. CM13 55 GA49
Broadwalk Pl, E14 204 D2
Broadwalk Shop Cen, Edg. HA8 42 CP51
Broad Wk S, The, Brwd. CM13 55 GA49
Broadwall, SE1 200 E2
Broadwater, Pot.B. EN6 12 DB30
Broadwater Cl, Stai. (Wrays.) TW19 113 AZ87
Walton-on-Thames KT12 153 BU106
Woking GU21 151 BD112
Broad Water Cres, Wey. KT13 off Churchill Dr 135 BQ104
Broadwater Fm Est, N17 46 DR54
Broadwater Gdns, Orp. BR6 163 EP105
Uxbridge (Hare.) UB9 58 BH56
Broadwater La, Uxb. (Hare.) UB9 58 BH56
Broadwater Pk, Uxb. (Denh.) UB9 58 BG58
Broadwater Pl, Wey. KT13 off Oatlands Dr 135 BS103
Broadwater Rd, N17 46 DS53
SE28 105 ER76
SW17 120 DE91
Broadwater Rd N, Walt. KT12 153 BT106
Broadwater Rd S, Walt. KT12 153 BT106
Broadway, E15 85 ED66
SW1 199 M6
Barking IG11 87 EQ66
Bexleyheath DA6 106 EY84
Grays RM17 110 GC79
Rainham RM13 89 FG70
Romford RM2 71 FG55
Staines TW18 off Kingston Rd 114 BH92
Swanley BR8 147 FC100
Tilbury RM18 111 GF82
Broadway, The, E4 47 EC51
E13 86 EH68
N8 65 DL58
N9 46 DU48
N14 off Winchmore Hill Rd 45 DK46
N22 45 DN54
NW7 42 CS50
SW13 off The Terrace 98 CS82
SW19 119 CZ93
W5 79 CK73
W7 off Cherington Rd 79 CE74
W7 (W.Ealing) 79 CG74
W13 79 CG74
Addlestone (New Haw) KT15 152 BG110
Croydon CR0 off Croydon Rd 159 DL105
Dagenham RM8 70 EZ61
Greenford UB6 78 CC70
Harrow HA2 41 CE54
Hornchurch RM12 71 FH63
Loughton IG10 33 EQ42
Pinner HA5 40 BZ52
Southall UB1 78 BX73
Staines (Laleham) TW18 134 BJ97
Stanmore HA7 41 CJ50
Sutton SM1 off Manor La 158 DC106
Sutton (Cheam) SM3 157 CY107
Thames Ditton KT7 off Hampton Ct Way 137 CE102
Watford WD17 24 BW41
Wembley HA9 off East La 62 CL62
Woking GU21 167 AZ117
Woodford Green IG8 48 EH51
Broadway Av, Croy. CR0 142 DR99
Twickenham TW1 117 CH86
Broadway Cl, S.Croy. CR2 160 DV114
Woodford Green IG8 48 EH51
Broadway Ct, SW19 off The Broadway 120 DA93
Broadway E, Uxb. (Denh.) UB9 58 BG58
Broadway Gdns, Mitch. CR4 140 DE98
Broadway Ho, Brom. BR1 off Elmfield Pk 144 EG97
Broadway Mkt, E8 84 DV67
Broadway Mkt Ms, E8 off Regents Row 84 DU67
Broadway Ms, E5 66 DT59
Broadway Ms, N13 off Elmdale Rd 45 DM50
N21 off Compton Rd 45 DP46
Broadway Par, N8 65 DL58
Hayes UB3 off Coldharbour La 77 BU74
Hornchurch RM12 off The Broadway 71 FH63
Broadway Pl, SW19 off Hartfield Rd 119 CZ93
Broadway Shop Cen, W6 off Hammersmith Bdy 99 CW77
Bexleyheath DA6 106 FA84
Broadwick St, W1 195 L10
Broadwood, Grav. DA11 131 GH92
Broadwood Av, Ruis. HA4 59 BS58
Broadwood Rd, Couls. CR5 off Netherne Dr 175 DK121
Broadwood Ter, W8 off Pembroke Rd 99 CZ77
Broad Yd, EC1 196 F5
Brocas Cl, NW3 off Fellows Rd 82 DE66
Broccoli Rd, Iver SL0 off Pinewood Rd 75 BB66
Brockbridge Ho, SW15 off Tangley Gro 119 CT86
Brockdish Av, Bark. IG11 69 ET64
Brockenhurst, W.Mol. KT8 136 BZ100
Brockenhurst Av, Wor.Pk. KT4 138 CS102
Brockenhurst Cl, Wok. GU21 151 AZ114
Brockenhurst Gdns, NW7 42 CS50
Ilford IG1 69 EQ64
Brockenhurst Ms, N18 off Lyndhurst Rd 46 DU49
Brockenhurst Rd, Croy. CR0 142 DV101
Brockenhurst Way, SW16 141 DK96
Brocket Cl, Chig. IG7 off Burrow Rd 49 ET50
Brocket Rd, Grays RM16 111 GG76
Brocket Way, Chig. IG7 49 ES50
Brock Grn, S.Ock. RM15 off Cam Grn 91 FV72
Brockham Cl, SW19 119 CZ92
Brockham Cres, Croy. (New Adgtn) CR0 161 ED108
Brockham Dr, SW2 off Fairview Pl 121 DM87
Ilford IG2 69 EP58
Brockham Hill Pk, Tad. (Box H.) KT20 182 CQ131
Brockham La, Bet. (Brock.) RH3 182 CN134
Brockham St, SE1 201 J6
Brockhurst Cl, Stan. HA7 41 CF51
Brockill Cres, SE4 103 DY84
Brocklebank Ct, Whyt. CR3 176 DU118
Brocklebank Rd, SE7 205 P9
SW18 120 DC87
Brocklehurst St, SE14 103 DX80
Brocklesbury Cl, Wat. WD24 24 BW41
Brocklesby Rd, SE25 142 DV98
BROCKLEY, SE4 123 DY85
⇌ Brockley 103 DY83
Brockley Av, Stan. HA7 42 CL48
Brockley Cl, Stan. HA7 42 CL49
Brockley Combe, Wey. KT13 153 BR105
Brockley Cres, Rom. RM5 51 FC52
Brockley Cross, SE4 off Endwell Rd 103 DY83
Brockley Footpath, SE15 102 DW84
Brockley Gdns, SE4 103 DZ82
Brockley Gro, SE4 123 DZ85
Brentwood (Hutt.) CM13 55 GA46
Brockley Hall Rd, SE4 123 DY86
Brockley Hill, Stan. HA7 41 CJ46
Brockley Ms, SE4 123 DY85
Brockley Pk, SE23 123 DY87
Brockley Ri, SE23 123 DY86
Brockley Rd, SE4 103 DZ83
Brockleyside, Stan. HA7 41 CK49
Brockley Vw, SE23 123 DY87
Brockley Way, SE4 123 DX85
Brockman Ri, Brom. BR1 123 ED91
Brock Pl, E3 85 EB70
Brock Rd, E13 86 EH71
Brocks Dr, Sutt. SM3 139 CY104
Brockshot Cl, Brent. TW8 97 CK79
Brocksparkwood, Brwd. CM13 55 GB48
Brock St, SE15 off Evelina Rd 102 DW83
Brockton Cl, Rom. RM1 71 FF56
Brock Way, Vir.W. GU25 132 AW99
Brockway Cl, E11 68 EE60
Brockway Ho, Slou. SL3 93 BB78
Brockwell Av, Beck. BR3 143 EB99
Brockwell Cl, Orp. BR5 145 ET99
★ Brockwell Park, SE24 121 DP86
Brockwell Pk Gdns, SE24 121 DN87
Brockwell Pk Row, SW2 121 DN86
Brodewater Rd, Borwd. WD6 26 CP40
Brodia Rd, N16 66 DS62
Brodie Rd, E4 47 EC46
Enfield EN2 30 DQ38
Brodie St, SE1 202 A10
Brodlove La, E1 85 DX73
Brodrick Gro, SE2 106 EV77
Brodrick Rd, SW17 120 DE89
Brograve Gdns, Beck. BR3 143 EB96
Broke Fm Dr, Orp. BR6 164 EW109
Brokengate La, Uxb. (Denh.) UB9 57 BC60
Broken Wf, EC4 197 H10
Brokes Cres, Reig. RH2 184 DA132
Brokesley St, E3 85 DZ70
Brokes Rd, Reig. RH2 184 DA132
Broke Wk, E8 84 DU67
Bromar Rd, SE5 102 DS83
Bromborough Grn, Wat. WD19 40 BW50
Bromefield, Stan. HA7 41 CJ53
Bromefield Ct, Wal.Abb. EN9 16 EG33
Bromehead Rd, E1 84 DW72
Bromehead St, E1 off Commercial Rd 84 DW72
Bromell's Rd, SW4 101 DJ84
Brome Rd, SE9 105 EM83
Bromet Cl, Wat. WD17 off Hempstead Rd 23 BT38
Bromfelde Rd, SW4 101 DK82
Bromfelde Wk, SW4 101 DK82
Bromfield St, N1 83 DN68
Bromford Cl, Oxt. RH8 188 EG133
Bromhall Rd, Dag. RM8, RM9 88 EV65
Bromhedge, SE9 125 EM90
Bromholm Rd, SE2 106 EV76
Bromleigh Cl, Wal.Cr. (Chsht) EN8 off Martins Dr 15 DY28
Bromleigh Ct, SE23 off Lapse Wd Wk 122 DV89
BROMLEY 144 EF96
BROMLEY, E3 85 EB70
Bromley, Grays RM17 110 FZ79
Bromley Av, Brom. BR1 124 EE94
⊖ Bromley-by-Bow 85 EB69
BROMLEY COMMON, Brom. BR2 145 EM101
Bromley Common, Brom. BR2 144 EJ98
Bromley Cres, Brom. BR2 144 EF97
Ruislip HA4 59 BT63
Bromley Gdns, Brom. BR2 144 EF97
Bromley Gro, Brom. BR2 143 ED96
Bromley Hall Rd, E14 85 EC71
Bromley High St, E3 85 EB69
Bromley Hill, Brom. BR1 124 EE92
Bromley La, Chis. BR7 125 EQ94
Bromley Mall, The, Brom. BR1 144 EG97
★ Bromley Mus, Orp. BR6 146 EV101
⇌ Bromley North 144 EG95
BROMLEY PARK, Brom. BR1 144 EE95
Bromley Pk, Brom. BR1 off London Rd 144 EF95
Bromley Pl, W1 195 K6
Bromley Rd, E10 67 EB58
E17 47 EA54
N17 46 DT53
N18 46 DR48
SE6 123 EB88
Beckenham BR3 143 EB95
Bromley (Downham) BR1 123 EC91
Bromley (Short.) BR2 143 EC96
Chislehurst BR7 145 EP95
⇌ Bromley South 144 EG97
Bromley St, E1 85 DX71
BROMPTON, SW3 198 B7
Brompton Arc, SW3 198 D5
Brompton Cl, SE20 off Selby Rd 142 DU96
Hounslow TW4 116 BZ85
Brompton Dr, Erith DA8 107 FH80
Brompton Gro, N2 64 DE56
★ Brompton Oratory, SW7 198 B7
Brompton Pk Cres, SW6 100 DB79
Brompton Pl, SW3 198 C6
Brompton Rd, SW1 198 C6
SW3 198 B8
SW7 198 C6
Brompton Sq, SW3 198 B6
Brompton Ter, SE18 off Prince Imperial Rd 105 EN81
Bromwich Av, N6 64 DG61
Bromyard Av, W3 80 CS74
Bromyard Ho, SE15 102 DV80
BRONDESBURY, NW2 81 CY66
⇌ Brondesbury 81 CZ66
Brondesbury Ct, NW2 81 CW65
Brondesbury Ms, NW6 off Willesden La 82 DA66
BRONDESBURY PARK, NW6 81 CW66
⇌ Brondesbury Park 81 CX67
Brondesbury Pk, NW2 81 CV65
NW6 81 CX66
Brondesbury Rd, NW6 81 CZ68
Brondesbury Vil, NW6 81 CZ68
Bronsart Rd, SW6 99 CY80
Bronsdon Way, Uxb. (Denh.) UB9 57 BF61
Bronson Rd, SW20 139 CX96
Bronte Cl, E7 off Bective Rd 68 EG63
Erith DA8 107 FB80
Ilford IG2 69 EN57
Tilbury RM18 111 GJ82
Bronte Gro, Dart. DA1 108 FM84
Bronte Ho, NW6 82 DA69
Bronte Vw, Grav. DA12 131 GJ88
Bronti Cl, SE17 102 DQ78
Bronze Age Way, Belv. DA17 107 FC76
Erith DA8 107 FC76
Bronze St, SE8 103 EA80
Brook Av, Dag. RM10 89 FB66
Edgware HA8 42 CP51
Wembley HA9 62 CN62
Brookbank Av, W7 79 CD71
Brookbank Rd, SE13 103 EA83
Brook Cl, NW7 off Frith Ct 43 CY52
SW17 120 DG89
SW20 139 CV97
W3 off West Lo Av 80 CN74
Borehamwood WD6 26 CP41
Epsom KT19 156 CS109
Romford RM2 51 FF53
Ruislip HA4 59 BS59
Staines (Stanw.) TW19 114 BM87
Brook Ct, Buck.H. IG9 48 EH46
Brook Cres, E4 47 EA49
N9 46 DV49
Brookdale, N11 45 DJ49
Brookdale Av, Upmin. RM14 72 FN62
Brookdale Cl, Upmin. RM14 72 FP62
Brookdale Rd, E17 67 EA55
SE6 123 EB86
Bexley DA5 126 EY86
Brookdene Av, Wat. WD19 39 BV45
Brookdene Dr, Nthwd. HA6 39 BT52
Brookdene Rd, SE18 105 ET77
Brook Dr, SE11 200 E7
Harrow HA1 60 CC56
Radlett WD7 9 CF33
Ruislip HA4 59 BS58
Sunbury-on-Thames TW16 off Chertsey Rd 115 BS92
Brooke Av, Har. HA2 60 CC62
Brooke Cl, Bushey WD23 40 CC45
Brookehowse Rd, SE6 123 EB90
Brookend Rd, Sid. DA15 125 ES88
Brooke Rd, E5 66 DU62
E17 67 EC56
N16 66 DT62
Brooke Rd, Grays RM17 110 GA78
Brooker Rd, Wal.Abb. EN9 15 EC34
Brookers Cl, Ashtd. KT21 171 CJ117
Brooke's Ct, EC1 196 D6
Brookes Mkt, EC1 196 E6
Brooke St, EC1 196 D7
Brooke Way, Bushey WD23 off Richfield Rd 40 CC45
Brook Fm Rd, Cob. KT11 170 BX115
Brookfield, N6 64 DG62
Epping (Thnwd) CM16 18 EW25
Woking GU21 166 AV116
Brookfield Av, E17 67 EC56
NW7 43 CV51
W5 79 CK70
Sutton SM1 158 DD105
Brookfield Cen, Wal.Cr. (Chsht) EN8 15 DX27
Brookfield Cl, NW7 43 CV51
Brentwood (Hutt.) CM13 55 GC44
Chertsey (Ott.) KT16 151 BD107
Brookfield Ct, Grnf. UB6 78 CC69
Harrow HA3 61 CK57
Brookfield Cres, NW7 43 CV51
Harrow HA3 62 CL57
Brookfield Gdns, Esher (Clay.) KT10 155 CF107
Waltham Cross (Chsht) EN8 15 DX27
Brookfield La, Wal.Cr. (Chsht) EN8 15 DX27
Brookfield La W, Wal.Cr. (Chsht) EN8 14 DV28
Brookfield Pk, NW5 65 DH62
Brookfield Path, Wdf.Grn. IG8 48 EE51
Brookfield Retail Pk, Wal.Cr. (Chsht) EN8 15 DX26
Brookfield Rd, E9 85 DY65
N9 46 DU48
W4 98 CR75
Brookfields, Enf. EN3 31 DX42
Brookfields Av, Mitch. CR4 140 DE99
Brook Gdns, E4 47 EB49
SW13 99 CT83
Kingston upon Thames KT2 138 CQ95
Brook Gate, W1 198 E1
Brook Grn, W6 99 CX77
Woking (Chobham) GU24 off Brookleys 150 AT110
Brook Hill, Oxt. RH8 187 EC130
Brookhill Cl, SE18 105 EP78
Barnet EN4 28 DE43
Brookhill Rd, SE18 105 EP78
Barnet EN4 28 DE43
Brookhouse Gdns, E4 48 EE49
Brookhurst Rd, Add. KT15 152 BH107
Brook Ind Est, Hayes UB4 78 BX74
Brooking Cl, Dag. RM8 off Campden Cres 70 EW62
Brooking Rd, E7 68 EG64
Brookland Cl, NW11 64 DA56
Brookland Garth, NW11 64 DB56
Brookland Hill, NW11 64 DA56
Brookland Ri, NW11 64 DA56
BROOKLANDS, Wey. KT13 152 BM109
Brooklands, Dart. DA1 128 FL88
Brooklands App, Rom. RM1 71 FD56
Brooklands Av, SW19 120 DB89
Sidcup DA15 125 ER89
Brooklands Business Pk, Wey. KT13 152 BN110
Brooklands Cl, Cob. KT11 170 BY115
Romford RM7 off Marshalls Rd 71 FD56
Sunbury-on-Thames TW16 135 BS95
Brooklands Ct, Add. (New Haw) KT15 152 BK110
Weybridge KT13 off Northfield Pl 153 BP108
Brooklands Dr, Grnf. UB6 79 CK67
Brooklands Gdns, Horn. RM11 72 FJ57
Potters Bar EN6 11 CY32
Brooklands Ind Pk, Wey. KT13 152 BL110
Brooklands La, Rom. RM7 71 FD56
Weybridge KT13 152 BM107
★ Brooklands Mus, Wey. KT13 152 BN109
Brooklands Pk, SE3 104 EG83
Brooklands Rd, Rom. RM7 71 FD56
Thames Ditton KT7 137 CF102
Weybridge KT13 153 BP107
Brooklands Way, Red. RH1 184 DE132
Brook La, SE3 104 EH82
Bexley DA5 126 EX86
Bromley BR1 124 EG93
Woking (Send) GU23 167 BE122
Brook La N, Brent. TW8 97 CK78
Brooklea Cl, NW9 42 CS53
Brookleys, Wok. (Chobham) GU24 150 AT110
Brooklyn Av, SE25 142 DV98
Loughton IG10 32 EL42
Brooklyn Cl, Cars. SM5 140 DE103
Woking GU22 166 AY119
Brooklyn Ct, Wok. GU22 off Brooklyn Rd 166 AY119
Brooklyn Gro, SE25 142 DV98
Brooklyn Rd, SE25 142 DV98
Bromley BR2 144 EK99
Woking GU22 166 AY118
Brooklyn Way, West Dr. UB7 94 BK76
Brookmans Av, Hat. (Brook.Pk) AL9 11 CY26
Brookmans Cl, Upmin. RM14 73 FS59
BROOKMANS PARK, Hat. AL9 11 CY26
⇌ Brookmans Park 11 CX27
Brookmarsh Ind Est, SE10 off Norman Rd 103 EB80
Brook Mead, Epsom KT19 156 CS107
Brookmead Av, Brom. BR1 145 EM99
Brookmead Cl, Orp. BR5 146 EV101
Brook Meadow, N12 44 DB49
Brook Meadow Cl, Wdf.Grn. IG8 48 EE51
Brookmeadow Way, Wal.Abb. EN9 off Breach Barn Mobile Home Pk 16 EH30
Brookmead Rd, Croy. CR0 141 DJ100
Brookmeads Est, Mitch. CR4 140 DE99
Brookmead Way, Orp. BR5 146 EV100
Brook Ms N, W2 off Craven Ter 82 DD73
Brookmill Cl, Wat. WD19 off Brookside Rd 39 BV45
Brookmill Rd, SE8 103 EA81
Brook Par, Chig. IG7 off High Rd 49 EP48
Brook Pk, Dart. DA1 off Darenth Rd 128 FN89
Brook Pk Cl, N21 29 DP44
Brook Path, Loug. IG10 32 EL42
Brook Pl, Barn. EN5 28 DA43
Brook Ri, Chig. IG7 49 EN48
Brook Rd, N8 65 DL56
N22 65 DM55
NW2 63 CU61
Borehamwood WD6 26 CN40
Brentwood CM14 54 FT48
Buckhurst Hill IG9 48 EG47
Epping CM16 18 EU33
Gravesend (Nthflt) DA11 130 GE88
Ilford IG2 69 ES58
Loughton IG10 32 EL43
Redhill (Merst.) RH1 185 DJ129
Romford RM2 51 FF53
Surbiton KT6 138 CL103
Swanley BR8 147 FD97
Thornton Heath CR7 142 DQ98
Twickenham TW1 117 CG86
Waltham Cross EN8 15 DZ34
Brook Rd S, Brent. TW8 97 CK79
Brooks Av, E6 87 EM70
Brooksbank St, E9 84 DW65
Brooksby Ms, N1 off Brooksby St 83 DN66
Brooksby St, N1 83 DN66
Brooksby's Wk, E9 67 DX64
Brooks Cl, SE9 125 EN89
Weybridge KT13 152 BN110
Brooks Ct, E15 off Clays La 67 EB64
Brookscroft, Croy. CR0 161 DY110
Brookscroft Rd, E17 47 EB53
Brookshill, Har. HA3 41 CD50
Brookshill Av, Har. HA3 41 CD50
Brookshill Dr, Har. HA3 41 CD50
Brookshill Gate, Har. (Har.Wld) HA3 41 CD50
Brookside, N21 29 DM44
Barnet EN4 28 DE44
Carshalton SM5 158 DG106
Chertsey KT16 133 BE101
Hornchurch RM11 72 FL57
Ilford IG6 49 EQ51
Orpington BR6 145 ET101
Potters Bar EN6 11 CU32
Slough (Colnbr.) SL3 93 BC80
Uxbridge UB10 76 BM66
Waltham Abbey EN9 off Broomstick Hall Rd 16 EE33
Brookside Av, Ashf. TW15 114 BJ92
Staines (Wrays.) TW19 92 AY83
Brookside Cl, Barn. EN5 27 CY44
Feltham TW13 off Sycamore Cl 115 BU90
Harrow (Kenton) HA2 61 CK57
Harrow (S.Har.) HA3 60 BY63
Brookside Cres, Pot.B. (Cuffley) EN6 13 DL27
Worcester Park KT4 off Green La 139 CU102
Brookside Gdns, Enf. EN1 30 DV37
Brookside Rd, N9 46 DV49
N19 65 DJ61
NW11 63 CY58
Gravesend (Istead Rise) DA13 131 GF94
Hayes UB4 78 BW73
Watford WD19 39 BV45
Brookside S, Barn. EN4 44 DG45
Brookside Wk, N3 43 CY54
N12 44 DA51
NW4 63 CY56
NW11 63 CY56
Brookside Way, Croy. CR0 143 DX100
Brooks La, W4 98 CN79
Brook's Ms, W1 195 H10
Brook Sq, SE18 off Shooter's Hill Rd 104 EL81
Brooks Rd, E13 86 EG67
W4 98 CN78
BROOK STREET, Brwd. CM14 54 FS49
Brook St, N17 off High Rd 46 DT54
W1 194 G10
W2 194 A10
Belvedere DA17 107 FB78
Brentwood CM14 54 FS50
Erith DA8 107 FB79
Kingston upon Thames KT1 138 CL96
Brooksville Av, NW6 81 CY67
Brooks Way, Orp. BR5 146 EW96
Brook Vale, Erith DA8 107 FB81
Brookview Rd, SW16 121 DJ92
Brookville Rd, SW6 99 CZ80
Brook Wk, N2 44 DD53
Edgware HA8 42 CR51
Brookway, SE3 104 EG83
Brook Way, Chig. IG7 49 EN48
Leatherhead KT22 171 CG118
Rainham RM13 89 FH71
Brookwood Av, SW13 99 CT83
Brookwood Cl, Brom. BR2 144 EF98
Brookwood Rd, SW18 119 CZ88
Hounslow TW3 96 CB81
Broom Av, Orp. BR5 146 EV96
Broom Cl, Brom. BR2 144 EL100
Esher KT10 154 CB106
Teddington TW11 117 CK94
Waltham Cross (Chsht) EN7 14 DU27
Broomcroft Av, Nthlt. UB5 78 BW69
Broomcroft Cl, Wok. GU22 167 BD116
Broomcroft Dr, Wok. GU22 167 BD115
Broome Cl, Epsom (Headley) KT18 182 CQ126

★ Place of interest ⇌ Railway station ⊖ London Underground station DLR Docklands Light Railway station Tra Tramlink station H Hospital Riv Pedestrian ferry landing stage

225

Broome Pl, S.Ock.
(Aveley) RM15 91 FR74
Broome Rd, Hmptn.TW12 116 BZ94
Broomer Pl, Wal.Cr. EN8 14 DW29
Broome Way, SE5 102 DQ80
Broomfield, E17 67 DZ59
St. Albans (Park St) AL2 8 CC27
Staines TW18 114 BG93
Sunbury-on-Thames TW16 135 BU95
Broomfield Av, N13 45 DM50
Broxbourne EN10 15 DY26
Loughton IG10 33 EM44
Broomfield Cl, Rom. RM5 51 FD52
Broomfield Ct, Wey. KT13 153 BP107
Broomfield La, N13 45 DM49
Broomfield Pl, W13
off Broomfield Rd 79 CH74
Broomfield Ride, Lthd.
(Oxshott) KT22 155 CD112
Broomfield Ri, Abb.L. WD5 7 BR32
Broomfield Rd, N13 45 DL50
W13 79 CH74
Addlestone
(New Haw) KT15 152 BH111
Beckenham BR3 143 DY97
Bexleyheath DA6 126 FA85
Richmond TW9 98 CM81
Romford RM6 70 EX59
Sevenoaks TN13 190 FF122
Surbiton KT5 138 CM102
Swanscombe DA10 130 FY86
Teddington TW11
off Melbourne Rd 117 CJ93
Broomfields, Esher KT10 154 CC106
Broomfield St, E14 85 EA71
Broom Gdns, Croy. CR0 143 EA104
Broom Gro, Wat. WD17 23 BU38
Broomgrove Gdns, Edg. HA8 42 CN53
Broomgrove Rd, SW9 101 DM82
Broom Hall, Lthd.
(Oxshott) KT22 155 CD114
Broomhall End, Wok. GU21
off Broomhall La 166 AY116
Broomhall La, Wok. GU21 166 AY116
Broomhall Rd, S.Croy. CR2 160 DR109
Woking GU21 166 AY116
Broom Hill, Slou.
(Stoke P.) SL2 74 AU66
Broomhill Ct, Wdf.Grn. IG8
off Broomhill Rd 48 EG51
Broomhill Ri, Bexh. DA6 126 FA85
Broomhill Rd, SW18 120 DA85
Dartford DA1 127 FH86
Ilford IG3 70 EU61
Orpington BR6 146 EU101
Woodford Green IG8 48 EG51
Broomhills, Grav. (Sthflt) DA13
off Betsham Rd 130 FY91
Broomhill Wk, Wdf.Grn. IG8 48 EF52
Broomhouse La, SW6 100 DA82
Broomhouse Rd, SW6 100 DA82
Broomlands La, Oxt. RH8 188 EJ125
Broom La, Wok.
(Chobham) GU24 150 AS109
Broomloan La, Sutt. SM1 140 DA103
Broom Lock, Tedd. TW11 117 CJ93
Broom Mead, Bexh. DA6 126 FA85
Broom Pk, Tedd. TW11 117 CK94
Broom Rd, Croy. CR0 143 EA104
Teddington TW11 117 CJ93
Broomsleigh St, NW6 63 CZ64
Broomstick Hall Rd,
Wal.Abb. EN9 16 EE33
Broomstick La, Chesh. HP5 4 AU30
Broom Water, Tedd. TW11 117 CJ93
Broom Water W, Tedd. TW11 117 CJ92
Broom Way, Wey. KT13 153 BS105
Broomwood Cl, Croy. CR0 143 DX99
Broomwood Gdns, Brwd.
(Pilg.Hat.) CM15 54 FU44
Broomwood Rd, SW11 120 DF86
Orpington BR5 146 EV96
Broseley Gdns, Rom. RM3 52 FL49
Broseley Gro, SE26 123 DY92
Broseley Rd, Rom. RM3 52 FL49
Broster Gdns, SE25 142 DT97
Brougham Rd, E8 84 DU67
W3 80 CQ72
Brougham St, SW11 100 DF82
Brough Cl, SW8
off Kenchester Cl 101 DL80
Kingston upon Thames KT2 117 CK92
Broughinge Rd, Borwd. WD6 26 CP40
Broughton Av, N3 63 CY55
Richmond TW10 117 CH90
Broughton Dr, SW9 101 DN84
Broughton Gdns, N6 65 DJ58
Broughton Rd, SW6 100 DB82
W13 79 CH73
Orpington BR6 145 ER103
Sevenoaks (Otford) TN14 181 FG116
Thornton Heath CR7 141 DN100
Broughton Rd App, SW6
off Wandsworth Br Rd 100 DB82
Broughton St, SW8 100 DG82
Broughton Way, Rick. WD3 38 BG45
Brouncker Rd, W3 98 CQ75
Brow, The, Ch.St.G. HP8 36 AX48
Watford WD25 7 BV33
Brow Cl, Orp. BR5
off Brow Cres 146 EX101
Brow Cres, Orp. BR5 146 EW102
Browells La, Felt. TW13 115 BV89
Brownacres Towpath,
Wey. KT13 135 BP102
Brown Cl, Wall. SM6 159 DL108
Browne Cl, Brwd. CM14 54 FV46
Romford RM5
off Bamford Way 51 FB50
Brownfield St, E14 85 EB72
Browngraves Rd, Hayes
UB3 95 BQ80
Brown Hart Gdns, W1 194 G10
Brownhill Rd, SE6 123 EB87
Browning Av, W7 79 CF72
Browning Av, Sutton SM1 158 DE105
Worcester Park KT4 139 CV102
Browning Cl, E17 67 EC56
W9 off Randolph Av 82 DC70
Hampton TW12 116 BZ91
Romford (Coll.Row) RM5 50 EZ52
Welling DA16 105 ES81
Browning Ho, W12
off Wood La 81 CW72
Browning Ms, W1 195 H7
Browning Rd, E11 68 EF59
E12 87 EM65
Dartford DA1 108 FM84
Enfield EN2 30 DR38
Browning St, SE17 201 J10
Browning Wk, Til. RM18
off Coleridge Rd 111 GJ82
Browning Way, Houns. TW5 96 BX81
Brownlea Gdns, Ilf. IG3 70 EU61
Brownlow Cl, Barn. EN4 28 DD43
Brownlow Ms, WC1 196 C5
Brownlow Rd, E7
off Woodford Rd 68 EH63
E8 84 DT67
N3 44 DB52
N11 45 DL51
NW10 80 CS66
W13 79 CG74
Borehamwood WD6 26 CN42
Croydon CR0 160 DS105
Redhill RH1 184 DE134
Brownlow St, WC1 196 C7
Brownrigg Rd, Ashf. TW15 114 BN91
Brown Rd, Grav. DA12 131 GL88
Brown's Bldgs, EC3 197 N9
Brownsea Wk, NW7
off Sanders La 43 CX51
Browns La, NW5 65 DH64
Brownspring Dr, SE9 125 EP91
Browns Rd, E17 67 EA55
Surbiton KT5 138 CM101
Brown St, W1 194 D8
Brownswell Rd, N2 44 DD54
Brownswood Rd, N4 65 DP62
Broxash Rd, SW11 120 DG86
Broxbourne Av, E18 68 EH56
Broxbourne Rd, E7 68 EG62
Orpington BR6 145 ET101
Broxburn Dr, S.Ock. RM15 91 FV73
Broxburn Par, S.Ock. RM15
off Broxburn Dr 91 FV73
Broxhill Rd, Rom.
(Hav.at.Bow.) RM4 51 FH48
Broxholm Rd, SE27 121 DN90
Brox La, Cher. (Ott.) KT16 151 BD109
Brox Rd, Cher. (Ott.) KT16 151 BC107
Broxted Ms, Brwd. (Hutt.) CM13
off Bannister Dr 55 GC44
Broxted Rd, SE6 123 DZ89
Broxwood Way, NW8 82 DE67
Bruce Av, Horn. RM12 72 FK61
Shepperton TW17 135 BQ100
★ **Bruce Castle Mu**, N17 46 DS53
Bruce Castle Rd, N17 46 DT53
Bruce Cl, W10
off Ladbroke Gro 81 CY71
Welling DA16 106 EV81
West Byfleet (Byfleet) KT14 152 BK113
Bruce Dr, S.Croy. CR2 161 DX109
Bruce Gdns, N20
off Balfour Gro 44 DF48
⇌ **Bruce Grove** 46 DT54
Bruce Gro, N17 46 DS53
Orpington BR6 146 EU102
Watford WD24 24 BW38
Bruce Hall Ms, SW17
off Brudenell Rd 120 DG91
Bruce Rd, E3 85 EB69
NW10 80 CR66
SE25 142 DR98
Barnet EN5
off St. Albans Rd 27 CY41
Harrow HA3 41 CE54
Mitcham CR4 120 DG94
Bruce's Wf Rd, Grays RM17 110 GA79
Bruce Way, Wal.Cr. EN8 15 DX33
Bruckner St, W10 81 CZ69
Brudenell Rd, SW17 120 DF90
Bruffs Meadow, Nthlt. UB5 78 BY65
Bruges Pl, NW1
off Randolph St 83 DJ66
Brumana Cl, Wey. KT13
off Elgin Rd 153 BP106
Brumfield Rd, Epsom KT19 156 CQ106
Brummel Cl, Bexh. DA7 107 FC83
★ **Brunei Gall**, WC1 195 N6
Brunel Cl, SE19 122 DT93
Hounslow TW5 95 BV80
Northolt UB5 78 BZ69
Romford RM1 71 FE56
Tilbury RM18 111 GH83
★ **Brunel Engine Ho**, SE16 202 F4
Brunel Est, W2 82 DA71
Brunel Pl, Sthl. UB1 78 CB72
Brunel Rd, E17 67 DY58
SE16 202 F5
W3 80 CS71
Woodford Green IG8 49 EM50
Brunel St, E16
off Victoria Dock Rd 86 EF72
Brunel Wk, N15 66 DS56
Twickenham TW2
off Stephenson Rd 116 CA87
Brunel Way, Slou. SL1 74 AT74
Brune St, E1 197 P7
Brunner Cl, NW11 64 DC57
Brunner Ct, Cher. (Ott.) KT16 151 BC106
Brunner Rd, E17 67 DZ57
W5 79 CK70
Bruno Pl, NW9 62 CQ61
Brunswick Av, N11 44 DG48
Upminster RM14 73 FS59
Brunswick Cl, Bexh. DA6 106 EX84
Pinner HA5 60 BY58
Thames Ditton KT7 137 CF102
Twickenham TW2 117 CD90
Walton-on-Thames KT12 136 BW103
Brunswick Ct, EC1
off Northampton Sq 83 DP69
SE1 201 N5
Brunswick Ct, Barnet EN4 28 DD43
Upminster RM14
off Waycross Rd 73 FS59
Brunswick Cres, N11 44 DG48
Brunswick Gdns, W5 80 CL69
W8 82 DA74
Ilford IG6 49 EQ52
Brunswick Gro, N11 44 DG48
Cobham KT11 154 BW113
Brunswick Ind Pk, N11 45 DH49
Brunswick Ms, SW16
off Potters La 121 DK93
W1 194 E8
BRUNSWICK PARK, N11 44 DF47
Brunswick Pk, SE5 102 DR81
Brunswick Pk Gdns, N11 44 DG47
Brunswick Pk Rd, N11 44 DG47
Brunswick Pl, N1 197 L3
NW1 194 G4
SE19 122 DU94
Brunswick Quay, SE16 203 J7
Brunswick Rd, E10 67 EC60
E14 off Blackwall Tunnel
Northern App 85 EC72
N15 66 DS57
W5 79 CK70
Bexleyheath DA6 106 EX84
Enfield EN3 31 EA38
Kingston upon Thames KT2 138 CN95
Sutton SM1 158 DB105
Brunswick Shop Cen, WC1 195 P4
Brunswick Sq, N17 46 DT51
WC1 196 A5
Brunswick St, E17 67 EC57
Brunswick Vil, SE5 102 DS81
Brunswick Wk, Grav. DA12 131 GK87
Brunswick Way, N11 45 DH49
Brunton Pl, E14 85 DY72
Brushfield St, E1 197 N7
Brushrise, Wat. WD24 23 BU36
Brushwood Dr, Rick.
(Chorl.) WD3 21 BC42
Brussels Rd, SW11 100 DD84
Bruton Cl, Chis. BR7 125 EM94
Bruton La, W1 199 J1
Bruton Pl, W1 199 J1
Bruton Rd, Mord. SM4 140 DC99
Bruton St, W1 199 J1
Bruton Way, W13 79 CG71
Bryan Av, NW10 81 CV66
Bryan Cl, Sun. TW16 115 BU94
Bryan Rd, SE16 203 M4
Bryan's All, SW6
off Wandsworth Br Rd 100 DB82
Bryanston Av, Twick. TW2 116 CB88
Bryanston Cl, Sthl. UB2 96 BZ77
Bryanstone Ct, Sutt. SM1
off Oakhill Rd 158 DC105
Bryanstone Rd, N8 65 DK57
Waltham Cross EN8 15 DZ34
Bryanston Ms E, W1 194 D7
Bryanston Ms W, W1 194 D7
Bryanston Pl, W1 194 D7
Bryanston Rd, Til. RM18 111 GJ82
Bryanston Sq, W1 194 D7
Bryanston St, W1 194 D9
Bryant Av, Rom. RM3 52 FK53
Bryant Cl, Barn. EN5 27 CZ43
Bryant Ct, E2 84 DT68
Bryant Rd, Nthlt. UB5 78 BW69
Bryant Row, Rom. (Noak Hill) RM3
off Cummings Hall La 52 FJ48
Bryant St, E15 85 ED66
Bryantwood Rd, N7 65 DN64
Brycedale Cres, N14 45 DK49
Bryce Rd, Dag. RM8 70 EW63
Bryden Cl, SE26 123 DY92
Brydges Pl, WC2 199 P1
Brydges Rd, E15 67 ED64
Brydon Wk, N1 off Outram Pl 83 DL67
Bryer Ct, EC2
off Aldersgate St 84 DQ71
Bryett Rd, N7 65 DL62
Brymay Cl, E3 85 EA68
Brynford Cl, Wok. GU21 166 AY115
Brynmaer Rd, SW11 100 DF81
Bryn-y-Mawr Rd, Enf. EN1 30 DT42
Bryony Cl, Loug. IG10 33 EP42
Uxbridge UB8 76 BM71
Bryony Rd, W12 81 CU73
Bryony Way, Sun. TW16 115 BT93
Bubblestone Rd, Sev.
(Otford) TN14 181 FH116
Buccleuch Rd, Slou.
(Datchet) SL3 92 AU80
Buchanan Cl, N21 29 DM43
South Ockendon
(Aveley) RM15 90 FQ74
Buchanan Ct, Borwd. WD6 26 CQ40
Buchanan Gdns, NW10 81 CV68
Buchan Cl, Uxb. UB8 76 BJ69
Buchan Rd, SE15 102 DW83
Bucharest Rd, SW18 120 DC87
Buckbean Path, Rom. RM3
off Clematis Cl 52 FJ52
Buckden Cl, N2
off Southern Rd 64 DF56
SE12 off Upwood Rd 124 EF86
Buckettsland La, Borwd. WD6 26 CR38
Buckfast Ct, W13
off Romsey Rd 79 CG73
Buckfast Rd, Mord. SM4 140 DB98
Buckfast St, E2 84 DU69
Buckham Thorns Rd,
West. TN16 189 EQ126
Buck Hill Wk, W2 198 A1
Buckhold Rd, SW18 120 DA86
Buckhurst Av, Cars. SM5 140 DE102
Sevenoaks TN13 191 FJ125
Buckhurst Cl, Red. RH1 184 DE132
BUCKHURST HILL 48 EH45
⊖ **Buckhurst Hill** 48 EK47
Buckhurst La, Sev. TN13 191 FJ125
Buckhurst Rd, West. TN16 179 EN121
Buckhurst St, E1 84 DV70
Buckhurst Way, Buck.H. IG9 48 EK49
Buckingham Arc, WC2 200 A1
Buckingham Av, N20 44 DC45
Feltham TW14 115 BV86
Greenford UB6 79 CG67
Buckingham Av,
Thornton Heath CR7 141 DN95
Welling DA16 105 ES84
West Molesey KT8 136 CB97
Buckingham Cl, W5 79 CJ71
Enfield EN1 30 DS40
Hampton TW12 116 BZ92
Hornchurch RM11 72 FK58
Orpington BR5 145 ES101
Buckingham Ct, NW4 63 CU55
Loughton IG10
off Rectory La 33 EN40
Buckingham Dr, Chis. BR7 125 EP92
Buckingham Gdns, Edg. HA8 42 CM52
Slough SL1 92 AT75
Thornton Heath CR7 141 DN96
West Molesey KT8
off Buckingham Av 136 CB96
Buckingham Gate, SW1 199 K5
Buckingham Gro, Uxb. UB10 76 BN68
Buckingham La, SE23 123 DY87
Buckingham Ms, N1
off Buckingham Rd 84 DS65
NW10 off Buckingham Rd 81 CT68
SW1 199 K6
★ **Buckingham Palace**, SW1 199 J5
Buckingham Palace Rd, SW1 199 H9
Buckingham Pl, SW1 199 K6
Buckingham Rd, E10 67 EB62
E11 68 EJ57
E15 68 EF64
E18 48 EF53
N1 84 DS65
N22 45 DL53
NW10 81 CT68
Borehamwood WD6 26 CR42
Edgware HA8 42 CM52
Gravesend DA11
off Dover Rd 130 GD87
Hampton TW12 116 BZ91
Harrow HA1 61 CD57
Ilford IG1 69 ER61
Kingston upon Thames KT1 138 CM98
Mitcham CR4 141 DL99
Richmond TW10 117 CK89
Watford WD24 24 BW37
Buckingham St, WC2 200 A1
Buckingham Way, Wall. SM6 159 DJ109
BUCKLAND, Bet. RH3 183 CU133
Buckland Av, Slou. SL3 92 AV77
Buckland Ct Gdns, Bet. RH3 183 CU133
Buckland Cres, NW3 82 DD66
Buckland Gate, Slou.
(Wexham) SL2 74 AV68
Buckland La, Bet. RH3 183 CT129
Tadworth KT20 183 CT129
Buckland Ri, Pnr. HA5 40 BW53
Buckland Rd, E10 67 EC61
Chessington KT9 156 CM106
Orpington BR6 163 ES105
Reigate RH2 183 CX133
Sutton SM2 157 CW110
Tadworth
(Lwr Kgswd) KT20 183 CZ128
Bucklands, The, Rick. WD3 38 BG45
Bucklands Rd, Tedd. TW11 117 CJ93
Buckland St, N1 197 L1
Buckland Wk, W3 98 CQ75
Morden SM4 140 DC98
Buckland Way, Wor.Pk. KT4 139 CW102
Buck La, NW9 62 CR57
Buckleigh Av, SW20 139 CY97
Buckleigh Rd, SW16 121 DK93
Buckleigh Way, SE19 142 DT95
Buckler Gdns, SE9
off Southold Ri 125 EM90
Bucklers All, SW6 99 CZ79
Bucklersbury, EC4 197 K9
Bucklersbury Pas, EC4 197 K9
Bucklers Ct, Brwd. CM14 54 FW50
Bucklers Way, Cars. SM5 140 DF104
Buckles Ct, Belv. DA17
off Fendyke Rd 106 EX76
Buckles La, S.Ock. RM15 91 FW71
Buckle St, E1 off Leman St 84 DT72
Buckles Way, Bans. SM7 173 CY116
Buckley Cl, SE23 122 DV87
Dartford DA1 107 FF82
Buckley Rd, NW6 81 CZ66
Buckley St, SE1
off Mepham St 83 DN74
Buckmaster Cl, SW9
off Stockwell Pk Rd 101 DM83
Buckmaster Rd, SW11 100 DE84
Bucknalls Cl, Wat. WD25 8 BY32
Bucknalls Dr, St.Alb.
(Brick.Wd) AL2 8 BZ31
Bucknalls La, Wat. WD25 8 BX32
Bucknall St, WC2 195 N8
Bucknall Way, Beck. BR3 143 EB98
Bucknell Cl, SW2 101 DM84
Buckner Rd, SW2 101 DM84
Bucknills Cl, Epsom KT18 156 CP114
Buckrell Rd, E4 47 ED47
Bucks Av, Wat. WD19 40 BY45
Bucks Cl, W.Byf. KT14 152 BH114
Bucks Cross Rd, Grav.
(Nthflt) DA11 131 GF90
Orpington BR6 164 EY106
BUCKS HILL, Kings L. WD4 6 BK34
Bucks Hill, Kings L. WD4 6 BK34
Buckstone Cl, SE23 122 DW86
Buckstone Rd, N18 46 DU51
Buck St, NW1 83 DH66
Buckters Rents, SE16 203 K3
Buckthorne Ho, Chig. IG7 50 EV49
Buckthorne Rd, SE4 123 DY86
Buckton Rd, Borwd. WD6 26 CM38
Buck Wk, E17 off Wood St 67 ED56
Budd Cl, N12 44 DB49
Buddings Circle, Wem. HA9 62 CQ62
Budd's All, Twick. TW1
off Arlington Cl 117 CJ85
Budebury Rd, Stai. TW18 114 BG92
Bude Cl, E17 67 DZ57
Budge La, Mitch. CR4 140 DF101
Budgen Dr, Red. RH1 184 DG131
Budge Row, EC4 197 K10
Budge's Wk, W2 82 DC73
Budgin's Hill, Orp. BR6 164 EW112
Budleigh Cres, Well. DA16 106 EW81
Budoch Ct, Ilf. IG3 70 EU61
Budoch Dr, Ilf. IG3 70 EU61
Buer Rd, SW6 99 CY82
Buff Av, Bans. SM7 158 DB114
Buffers La, Lthd. KT22
off Kingston Rd 171 CG119
Bug Hill, Cat. (Wold.) CR3 177 DX120
Bugsby's Way, SE7 205 N9
SE10 205 K8
Bulganak Rd, Th.Hth. CR7 142 DQ98
Bulinga St, SW1 199 N9
Bulkeley Cl, Egh.
(Eng.Grn) TW20 112 AW91
Bullace La, Dart. DA1
off High St 128 FL86
Bullace Row, SE5 102 DR80
Bull All, Well. DA16
off Welling High St 106 EV83
Bullards Pl, E2 85 DX69
Bullbanks Rd, Belv. DA17 107 FC77
Bullbeggars La, Gdse. RH9 186 DW132
Woking GU21 166 AV116
Bull Cl, Grays RM16 110 FZ75
Bullen St, SW11 100 DE82
Buller Cl, SE15 102 DU80
Buller Rd, N17 46 DU54
N22 45 DN54
NW10 off Chamberlayne Rd 81 CX69
Barking IG11 87 ES66
Thornton Heath CR7 142 DR96
Bullers Cl, Sid. DA14 126 EY92
Bullers Wd Dr, Chis. BR7 124 EL94
Bullescroft Rd, Edg. HA8 42 CN48
Bullfinch Cl, Sev. TN13 190 FD122
Bullfinch Dene, Sev. TN13 190 FD122
Bullfinch La, Sev. TN13 190 FD122
Bullfinch Rd, S.Croy. CR2 161 DX110
Bullhead Rd, Borwd. WD6 26 CQ41
Bull Hill, Dart. (Hort.Kir.) DA4 148 FQ98
Leatherhead KT22 171 CG121
Bullied Way, SW1 199 J9
Bull Inn Ct, WC2 200 A1
Bullivant Cl, Green. DA9 129 FU85
Bullivant St, E14 85 EC73
Bull La, N18 46 DS50
Chislehurst BR7 125 ER94
Dagenham RM10 71 FB62
Gerrards Cross
(Chal.St.P.) SL9 56 AX55
Bull Rd, E15 86 EF68
Bullrush Cl, Croy. CR0 142 DS100
Bullrush Gro, Uxb. UB8 76 BJ70
Bull's All, SW14 98 CR82
Bulls Br Ind Est, Sthl. UB2 95 BV77
Bulls Br Rd, Sthl. UB2 95 BV76
Bullsbrook Rd, Hayes UB4 78 BW74
BULLS CROSS, Enf. EN7 30 DT35
Bulls Cross, Enf. EN2 30 DU37
Bulls Cross Ride, Wal.Cr. EN7 30 DU35
Bulls Gdns, SW3 198 C8
Bull's Head Pas, EC3 197 M9
Bullsland Gdns, Rick.
(Chorl.) WD3 21 BB44
Bullsland La, Ger.Cr. SL9 37 BB45
Rickmansworth (Chorl.) WD3 21 BB44
BULLSMOOR, Enf. EN1 30 DV37
Bullsmoor Cl, Wal.Cr. EN8 30 DW35
Bullsmoor Gdns, Wal.Cr. EN8 30 DV35
Bullsmoor La, Enf. EN1, EN3 30 DW35
Waltham Cross EN7 30 DU35
Bullsmoor Ride, Wal.Cr. EN8 30 DW35
Bullsmoor Way, Wal.Cr. EN8 30 DV35
Bullwell Cres, Wal.Cr.
(Chsht) EN8 15 DY29
Bull Yd, SE15
off Peckham High St 102 DU81
Gravesend DA12
off High St 131 GH86
Bulmer Gdns, Har. HA3 61 CK59
Bulmer Ms, W11
off Ladbroke Rd 82 DA73
Bulmer Pl, W11 82 DA74
Bulmer Wk, Rain. RM13 90 FJ68
Bulow Est, SW6
off Broughton Rd 100 DB82
Bulrush Cl, Cars. SM5 140 DE103
Bulstrode Av, Houns. TW3 96 BZ82
Bulstrode Ct, Ger.Cr. SL9 56 AX58
Bulstrode Gdns, Houns. TW3 96 BZ83
Bulstrode La, Hem.H.
(Felden) HP3 6 BG27
Kings Langley (Chipper.) WD4 5 BE29
Bulstrode Pl, W1 194 G7
Slough SL1 92 AT76
Bulstrode Rd, Houns. TW3 96 CA83
Bulstrode St, W1 194 G8
Bulstrode Way, Ger.Cr. SL9 56 AX57
Bulwer Ct Rd, E11 67 ED60
Bulwer Gdns, Barn. EN5
off Bulwer Rd 28 DC42
Bulwer Rd, E11 67 ED59
N18 46 DS49
Barnet EN5 28 DB42
Bulwer St, W12 81 CW74
Bumbles Grn La, Wal.Abb. EN9 16 EH25
Bunbury Way, Epsom KT17 173 CV116
Bunby Rd, Slou. (Stoke P.) SL2 74 AT66
Bunce Dr, Cat. CR3 176 DR123
Bunces La, Wdf.Grn. IG8 48 EF52
Bundys Way, Stai. TW18 113 BF93
Bungalow Rd, SE25 142 DS98
Woking GU23 169 BQ124
Bungalows, The, SW16 121 DH94
Wallington SM6 159 DH106
Bunhill Row, EC1 197 K4
Bunhouse Pl, SW1 198 F10
Bunkers Hill, NW11 64 DC59
Belvedere DA17 106 FA77
Sidcup DA14 126 EZ90
Bunning Way, N7 83 DL66
Bunns La, NW7 43 CT51
Bunn's La, Chesh. HP5 4 AU34
Bunsen St, E3
off Kenilworth Rd 85 DY68
Buntingbridge Rd, Ilf. IG2 69 ER57
Bunting Cl, N9
off Dunnock Cl 47 DX46
Mitcham CR4 140 DF99
Bunton St, SE18 105 EN76

★ Place of interest ⇌ Railway station ⊖ London Underground station DLR Docklands Light Railway station Tra Tramlink station H Hospital Riv Pedestrian ferry landing stage

226

Bunyan Ct, EC2
off Beech St 84 DQ71
Bunyan Rd, E17 67 DY55
Bunyard Dr, Wok. GU21 151 BC114
Bunyons Cl, Brwd. CM13
off Essex Way 53 FW51
Buonaparte Ms, SW1 199 M10
H BUPA Bushey Hosp,
Bushey WD23 41 CF46
H BUPA Hartswood Hosp,
Brwd. CM13 53 FV51
H BUPA Roding Hosp, Ilf. IG4 68 EK55
Burbage Cl, SE1 201 K7
Hayes UB3 77 BR72
Waltham Cross (Chsht) EN8 15 DZ31
Burbage Rd, SE21 122 DR86
SE24 122 DQ86
Burberry Cl, N.Mal. KT3 138 CS96
Burbidge Rd, Shep. TW17 134 BN98
Burbridge Way, N17 46 DT54
Burcham St, E14 85 EB72
Burcharbro Rd, SE2 106 EX79
Burchell Ct, Bushey WD23
off Catsey La 40 CC45
Burchell Rd, E10 67 EB60
SE15 102 DV81
Burchetts Way, Shep. TW17 135 BP100
Burchett Way, Rom. RM6 70 EZ58
Burch Rd, Grav. (Nthflt) DA11 131 GF86
Burchwall Cl, Rom. RM5 51 FC52
Burcote, Wey. KT13 153 BR107
Burcote Rd, SW18 120 DD88
Burcott Gdns, Add. KT15 152 BJ107
Burcott Rd, Pur. CR8 159 DN114
Burden Cl, Brent. TW8 97 CJ78
Burdenshott Av, Rich. TW10 98 CP84
Burden Way, E11
off Brading Cres 68 EH61
Burder Cl, N1 84 DS65
Burder Rd, N1
off Balls Pond Rd 84 DS65
Burdett Av, SW20 139 CU95
Burdett Cl, W7
off Cherington Rd 97 CF75
Sidcup DA14 126 EY92
Burdett Ms, NW3
off Belsize Cres 82 DD65
W2 off Hatherley Gro 82 DB72
Burdett Rd, E3 85 DZ70
E14 85 DZ70
Croydon CR0 142 DR100
Richmond TW9 98 CM83
Burdetts Rd, Dag. RM9 88 EZ67
Burdett St, SE1 200 D6
Burdock Cl, Croy. CR0 143 DX102
Burdock Rd, N17 66 DU55
Burdon La, Sutt. SM2 157 CY108
Burdon Pk, Sutt. SM2 157 CZ109
Burfield Cl, SW17 120 DD91
Burfield Dr, Warl. CR6 176 DW119
Burfield Rd, Rick. (Chorl.) WD3 21 BB43
Windsor (Old Wind.) SL4 112 AU86
Burford Cl, Dag. RM8 70 EW62
Ilford IG6 69 EQ56
Uxbridge UB10 58 BL63
Burford Gdns, N13 45 DM48
Burford La, Epsom KT17 157 CW111
Burford Rd, E6 86 EL69
E15 85 ED66
SE6 123 DZ89
Brentford TW8 98 CL78
Bromley BR1 144 EL98
Sutton SM1 140 DA103
Worcester Park KT4 139 CT101
Burford Wk, SW6
off Cambria St 100 DB80
Burford Way, Croy.
(New Adgtn) CR0 161 EC107
Burgate Cl, Dart. DA1 107 FF83
Burges Cl, Horn. RM11 72 FM58
Burges Ct, E6 87 EN66
Burges Gro, SW13 99 CV80
Burges Rd, E6 86 EL66
Burgess Av, NW9 62 CR58
Burgess Cl, Felt. TW13 116 BY91
Waltham Cross
(Chsht) EN7 14 DQ25
Burgess Ct, Borwd. WD6
off Belford Rd 26 CM38
Burgess Hill, NW2 64 DA63
Burgess Rd, E15 68 EE63
Sutton SM1 158 DB105
Burgess St, E14 85 EA71
Burge St, SE1 201 L7
Burges Way, Stai. TW18 114 BG92
Burghfield, Epsom KT17 173 CT115
Burghfield Rd, Grav.
(Istead Rise) DA13 131 GF94
BURGH HEATH, Tad. KT20 173 CX119
Burgh Heath Rd, Epsom KT17 156 CS114
★ Burgh Ho
(Hampstead Mus), NW3 64 DD63
Burghill Rd, SE26 123 DY91
Burghley Av, Borwd. WD6 26 CQ43
New Malden KT3 138 CR95
Burghley Hall Cl, SW19 119 CY87
Burghley Ho, SW19 119 CY90
Burghley Pl, Mitch. CR4 140 DG99
Burghley Rd, E11 68 EE60
N8 65 DN55
NW5 65 DH64
SW19 119 CX91
Grays (Chaff.Hun.) RM16 109 FW76
Burghley Twr, W3 81 CT73
Burgh Mt, Bans. SM7 173 CZ115
Burgh St, N1 83 DP68
Burgh Wd, Bans. SM7 173 CY115
Burgon St, EC4 196 G9
Burgos Cl, Croy. CR0 159 DN107
Burgos Gro, SE10 103 EB81
Burgoyne Rd, N4 65 DP58
SE25 142 DT98
SW9 101 DM83
Sunbury-on-Thames TW16 115 BT93
Burham Cl, SE20
off Maple Rd 122 DW94
Burhill Gro, Pnr. HA5 40 BY54
Burhill Rd, Walt. KT12 154 BW107
Burke Cl, SW15 98 CS84
Burke St, E16 86 EF72
Burket Cl, Sthl. UB2
off Kingsbridge Rd 96 BZ77
Burland Rd, SW11 120 DF85
Brentwood CM15 54 FX46
Romford RM5 51 FC51
Burlea Cl, Walt. KT12 153 BV106
Burleigh Av, Sid. DA15 125 ET85
Wallington SM6 140 DG104
Burleigh Cl, Add. KT15 152 BH106
Burleigh Gdns, N14 45 DJ46
Ashford TW15 115 BQ92
Burleigh Ho, W10
off St. Charles Sq 81 CX71
Burleigh Pk, Cob. KT11 154 BY112
Burleigh Pl, SW15 119 CX85
Burleigh Rd, Add. KT15 152 BH105
Enfield EN1 30 DS42
Sutton SM3 139 CY102
Uxbridge UB10 77 BP67
Waltham Cross (Chsht) EN8 15 DY32
Burleigh St, WC2 196 B10
Burleigh Wk, SE6
off Muirkirk Rd 123 EC88
Burleigh Way, Enf. EN2
off Church St 30 DR41
Potters Bar (Cuffley) EN6 13 DL30
Burley Cl, E4 47 EA50
SW16 141 DK96
Burley Orchard, Cher. KT16 134 BG100
Burley Rd, E16 86 EJ72
Burlings La, Sev.
(Knock.) TN14 179 ET118
Burlington Arc, W1 199 K1
Burlington Av, Rich. TW9 98 CN81
Romford RM7 71 FB58
Slough SL1 92 AS75
Burlington Cl, E6
off Northumberland Rd 86 EL72
W9 81 CZ70
Feltham TW14 115 BR87
Orpington BR6 145 EP103
Pinner HA5 59 BV55
Burlington Gdns, W1 199 K1
W3 80 CQ74
W4 98 CQ78
Romford RM6 70 EY59
Burlington La, W4 98 CS80
Burlington Ms, SW15 119 CZ85
W3 80 CQ74
Burlington Pl, SW6
off Burlington Rd 99 CY82
Reigate RH2 184 DA134
Woodford Green IG8 48 EG48
Burlington Ri, Barn. EN4 44 DE46
Burlington Rd, N10
off Tetherdown 44 DG54
N17 46 DU53
SW6 99 CY82
W4 98 CQ78
Enfield EN2 30 DR39
Isleworth TW7 97 CD81
New Malden KT3 139 CU98
Slough SL1 92 AS75
Thornton Heath CR7 142 DQ96
Burman Cl, Dart. DA2 128 FQ87
Burma Rd, N16 66 DR63
Chertsey (Longcr.) KT16 132 AT104
Burmester Rd, SW17 120 DC90
Burnaby Cres, W4 98 CP79
Burnaby Gdns, W4 98 CQ79
Burnaby Rd, Grav.
(Nthflt) DA11 130 GE87
Burnaby St, SW10 100 DC80
Burnbrae Cl, N12 44 DB51
Burnbury Rd, SW12 121 DJ88
Burn Cl, Add. KT15 152 BK105
Leatherhead
(Oxshott) KT22 170 CC115
Burncroft Av, Enf. EN3 30 DW40
Burndell Way, Hayes UB4
off Glencoe Rd 78 BY71
Burne Jones Ho, W14 99 CZ77
Burnell Av, Rich. TW10 117 CJ92
Welling DA16 106 EU82
Burnell Gdns, Stan. HA7 41 CK53
Burnell Rd, Sutt. SM1 158 DB105
Burnell Wk, SE1 202 A10
Brentwood CM13 53 FW51
Burnels Av, E6 87 EN69
Burness Cl, N7 off Roman Way 83 DM65
Uxbridge UB8
off Whitehall Rd 76 BK68
Burne St, NW1 194 B6
Burnet Gro, Epsom KT19 156 CQ113
Burnett Cl, E9 66 DW64
Burnett Rd, Erith DA8 108 FK79
Burney Av, Surb. KT5 138 CM99
Burney Dr, Loug. IG10 33 EP40
Burney St, SE10 103 EC80
Burnfoot Av, SW6 99 CY81
Burnfoot Ct, SE22 122 DV88
Burnham, NW3 82 DE66
Burnham Av, Uxb. UB10 59 BQ63
Burnham Cl, NW7 43 CU52
SE1 202 A9
Enfield EN1 30 DS38
Harrow (Wldste) HA3 61 CG56
Burnham Ct, NW4 63 CW56
Burnham Cres, E11 68 EJ56
Dartford DA1 108 FJ84
Burnham Dr, Reig. RH2 184 DA133
Worcester Park KT4 139 CX103
Burnham Gdns, Croy. CR0 142 DT101
Hayes UB3 95 BR76
Hounslow TW4 95 BV81
Burnham Rd, E4 47 DZ50
Dagenham RM9 88 EV66
Dartford DA1 108 FJ84
Morden SM4 140 DB99
Romford RM7 71 FD55
Sidcup DA14 126 EY89
Burnhams Rd, Lthd.
(Bkhm) KT23 170 BY124
Burnham St, E2 84 DW69
Kingston upon Thames KT2 138 CN95
Burnham Way, SE26 123 DZ92
W13 97 CH77
Burnhill Cl, SE15
off Gervase St 102 DV80
Burnhill Rd, Beck. BR3 143 EA96
Burnley Cl, Wat. WD19 40 BW50
Burnley Rd, NW10 63 CU64
SW9 101 DM82
Grays RM20 109 FT81
Burnsall St, SW3 198 C10
Burns Av, Felt. TW14 115 BU86
Romford (Chad.Hth) RM6 70 EW59
Sidcup DA15 126 EV86
Southall UB1 78 CA73
Burns Cl, E17 67 EC56
SW19 120 DD93
Carshalton SM5 158 DG109
Erith DA8 107 FF81
Hayes UB4 77 BT71
Welling DA16 105 ET81
Burns Dr, Bans. SM7 157 CY114
Burnside, Ashtd. KT21 172 CM118
Burnside Av, E4 47 DZ51
Burnside Cl, SE16 203 J2
Barnet EN5 28 DA41
Twickenham TW1 117 CG86
Burnside Cres, Wem. HA0 79 CK67
Burnside Rd, Dag. RM8 70 EW61
Burns Pl, Til. RM18 111 GH81
Burns Rd, NW10 81 CT67
SW11 100 DF82
W13 97 CH75
Wembley HA0 79 CK68
Burns Way, Brwd. (Hutt.) CM13 55 GD45
Hounslow TW5 96 BX82
Burnt Ash Hill, SE12 124 EF86
Burnt Ash La, Brom. BR1 124 EG93
Burnt Ash Rd, SE12 124 EF85
Burnt Fm Ride, Enf. EN2 13 DP34
Waltham Cross EN7 13 DP31
Burnt Ho La, Dart.
(Hawley) DA2 128 FL91
Burnthwaite Rd, SW6 100 DA80
BURNT OAK, Edg. HA8 42 CQ52
⊖ Burnt Oak 42 CQ53
Burnt Oak Bdy, Edg. HA8 42 CP52
Burnt Oak Flds, Edg. HA8 42 CQ53
Burnt Oak La, Sid. DA15 126 EU86
Burntwood, Brwd. CM14 54 FW48
Burntwood Av, Horn. RM11 72 FK58
Burntwood Cl, SW18 120 DD88
Caterham CR3 176 DU121
Burntwood Gra Rd, SW18 120 DD88
Burntwood Gro, Sev. TN13 191 FH127
Burntwood La, SW17 120 DE89
Caterham CR3 176 DU121
Burntwood Rd, Sev. TN13 191 FH128
Burntwood Vw, SE19
off Bowley La 122 DT92
Burnway, Horn. RM11 72 FL59
Buross St, E1
off Commercial Rd 84 DV72
Burpham Cl, Hayes UB4
off Glencoe Rd 78 BX71
Burrage Gro, SE18 105 EQ77
Burrage Pl, SE18 105 EP78
Burrage Rd, SE18 105 EQ79
Burrard Rd, E16 86 EH72
NW6 64 DA64
Burr Cl, E1 202 B2
Bexleyheath DA7 106 EZ83
St. Albans (Lon.Col.) AL2 10 CL27
Burrell Cl, Croy. CR0 143 DY100
Edgware HA8 42 CP47
Burrell Row, Beck. BR3
off High St 143 EA96
Burrell St, SE1 200 F2
Burrells Wf Sq, E14 204 B10
Burrell Twr, E10 67 EA59
Burrfield Dr, Orp. BR5 146 EX99
Burr Hill La, Wok.
(Chobham) GU24 150 AS109
Burritt Rd, Kings.T. KT1 138 CN96
Burroughs, The, NW4 63 CV57
Burroughs Gdns, NW4 63 CV56
Burroughs Par, NW4
off The Burroughs 63 CV56
Burroway Rd, Slou. SL3 93 BB76
Burrow Cl, Chig. IG7
off Burrow Rd 49 ET50
Burrow Grn, Chig. IG7 49 ET50
BURROWHILL, Wok. GU24 150 AS108
Burrow Rd, SE22 102 DS84
Chigwell IG7 49 ET50
Burrows Chase, Wal.Abb. EN9 31 ED36
Burrows Cl, Lthd.
(Bkhm) KT23 170 BZ124
Burrows Hill Cl, Houns.
(Hthrw Air.) TW6 94 BJ84
Burrows Hill La, Houns.
(Hthrw Air.) TW6 94 BH84
Burrows Ms, SE1 200 F4
Burrows Rd, NW10 81 CW69
Burrow Wk, SE21
off Rosendale Rd 122 DQ87
Burr Rd, SW18 120 DA87
Bursdon Cl, Sid. DA15 125 ET89
Burses Way, Brwd.
(Hutt.) CM13 55 GB45
Bursland Rd, Enf. EN3 31 DX42
Burslem Av, Ilf. IG6 50 EU51
Burslem St, E1 84 DU72
Burstead Cl, Cob. KT11 154 BX113
Burstock Rd, SW15 99 CY84
Burston Dr, St.Alb.
(Park St) AL2 8 CC28
Burston Rd, SW15 119 CX85
Burston Vil, SW15
off St. John's Av 119 CX85
Burstow Rd, SW20 139 CY95
Burtenshaw Rd, T.Ditt. KT7 137 CG101
Burtley Cl, N4 66 DQ60
Burton Av, Wat. WD18 23 BU42
Burton Cl, Chess. KT9 155 CK108
Thornton Heath CR7 142 DR97
Burton Ct, SW3
off Franklin's Row 100 DF78
Burton Dr, Enf. EN3 31 EA37
Burton Gdns, Houns. TW5 96 BZ81
Burton Gro, SE17
off Portland St 102 DR78
Burtonhole Cl, NW7 43 CX49
Burtonhole La, NW7 43 CY49
Burton La, SW9 101 DN82
Waltham Cross (Chsht) EN7 14 DS29
Burton Ms, SW1 198 G9
Burton Pl, WC1 195 N3
Burton Rd, E18 68 EH55
NW6 81 CZ66
SW9 101 DP82
Kingston upon Thames KT2 118 CL94
Loughton IG10 33 EQ42
Burtons La, Ch.St.G. HP8 21 AZ43
Rickmansworth WD3 21 AZ43
Burtons Rd, Hmptn.
(Hmptn H.) TW12 116 CB91
Burton St, WC1 195 N3
Burtons Way, Ch.St.G. HP8 20 AW40
Burt Rd, E16 86 EJ74
Burtwell La, SE27 122 DR91
Burwash Ct, Orp. BR5
off Rookery Gdns 146 EW99
Burwash Ho, SE1 201 L5
Burwash Rd, SE18 105 ER78
Burway Cres, Cher. KT16 134 BG97
Burwell Av, Grnf. UB6 79 CE65
Burwell Cl, E1
off Bigland St 84 DV72
Burwell Rd, E10 67 DY60
Burwell Wk, E3 85 EA70
Burwood Av, Brom. BR2 144 EH103
Kenley CR8 159 DP114
Pinner HA5 60 BW57
Burwood Cl, Reig. RH2 184 DD134
Surbiton KT6 138 CN102
Walton-on-Thames KT12 154 BW107
Burwood Gdns, Rain. RM13 89 FF69
BURWOOD PARK, Walt. KT12 153 BT106
Burwood Pk Rd, Walt. KT12 153 BV105
Burwood Pl, W2 194 C8
Burwood Rd, Walt. KT12 153 BV107
Bury Av, Hayes UB4 77 BS68
Ruislip HA4 59 BQ58
Bury Cl, SE16 203 J2
Woking GU21 166 AX116
Bury Ct, EC3 197 N8
Burydell La, St.Alb.
(Park St) AL2 9 CD27
BURY GREEN, Wal.Cr. EN7 14 DV31
Bury Grn Rd, Wal.Cr.
(Chsht) EN7 14 DU31
Bury Gro, Mord. SM4 140 DB99
Bury La, Epp. CM16 17 ES31
Rickmansworth WD3 38 BK46
Woking GU21 166 AW116
Bury Meadows, Rick. WD3 38 BK46
Bury Pl, WC1 195 P7
Bury Ri, Hem.H. HP3 5 BD25
Bury Rd, E4 32 EE43
N22 65 DN55
Dagenham RM10 71 FB64
Epping CM16 17 ES31
Buryside Cl, Ilf. IG2 69 ET56
Bury St, EC3 197 N9
N9 46 DU46
SW1 199 K2
Ruislip HA4 59 BQ57
Bury St W, N9 46 DR45
Bury Wk, SW3 198 B9
Busbridge Ho, E14
off Brabazon St 85 EA71
Busby Pl, NW5 83 DK65
Busby St, E2
off Chilton St 84 DT70
Bushbaby Cl, SE1 201 M7
Bushbarns, Wal.Cr.
(Chsht) EN7 14 DU29
Bushberry Rd, E9 85 DY65
Bush Cl, Add. KT15 152 BJ106
Ilford IG2 69 ER57
Bush Cotts, SW18
off Putney Br Rd 120 DA85
Bush Ct, W12
off Shepherds Bush Grn 99 CX75
Bushell Cl, SW2 121 DM89
Bushell Grn, Bushey
(Bushey Hth) WD23 41 CD47
Bushell St, E1 202 C3
Bushell Way, Chis. BR7 125 EN92
Bush Elms Rd, Horn. RM11 71 FG59
Bushetts Gro, Red. RH1 185 DH129
BUSHEY 40 CA45
⇌ Bushey 24 BX44
Bushey Av, E18 68 EF55
Orpington BR5 145 ER101
Bushey Cl, E4 47 EC48
Kenley CR8 176 DS116
Uxbridge UB10 59 BP61
Bushey Ct, SW20 139 CV96
Bushey Cft, Oxt. RH8 187 EC130
Bushey Down, SW12
off Bedford Hill 121 DH89
Bushey Gro Rd, Bushey WD23 24 BX42
Bushey Hall Dr, Bushey WD23 24 BY42
Bushey Hall Rd, Bushey WD23 24 BX42
BUSHEY HEATH,
Bushey WD23 41 CE46
Bushey Hill Rd, SE5 102 DS81
Bushey La, Sutt. SM1 158 DA105
Bushey Lees, Sid. DA15
off Fen Gro 125 ET86
BUSHEY MEAD, SW20 139 CX97
Bushey Mill Cres, Wat. WD24 24 BW37
Bushey Mill La, Bushey WD23 24 BZ40
Watford WD24 24 BW37
Bushey Rd, E13 86 EJ68
N15 66 DS58
SW20 139 CV97
Croydon CR0 143 EA103
Hayes UB3 95 BS77
Sutton SM1 158 DB105
Uxbridge UB10 58 BN61
Bushey Shaw, Ashtd. KT21 171 CH117
Bushey Vw Wk, Wat. WD24 24 BX40
Bushey Way, Beck. BR3 143 ED100
Bushfield Cl, Edg. HA8 42 CP47
Bushfield Cres, Edg. HA8 42 CP47
Bushfield Rd, Hem.H.
(Bov.) HP3 5 BC25
Bushfields, Loug. IG10 33 EN43
Bushfield Wk, Swans. DA10 130 FY86
Bush Gro, NW9 62 CQ59
Stanmore HA7 41 CK53
Bushgrove Rd, Dag. RM8 70 EX63
Bush Hill, N21 46 DQ45
BUSH HILL PARK, Enf. EN1 30 DS43
⇌ Bush Hill Park 30 DT44
Bush Hill Rd, N21 30 DR44
Harrow HA3 62 CM58
Bush Ind Est, NW10 80 CR70
Bush La, EC4 197 K10
Woking (Send) GU23 167 BD124
Bushmead Cl, N15
off Copperfield Dr 66 DT56
Bushmoor Cres, SE18 105 EQ80
Bushnell Rd, SW17 121 DH89
Bush Rd, E8 84 DV67
E11 68 EF59
SE8 203 J8
Buckhurst Hill IG9 48 EK49
Richmond TW9 98 CM79
Shepperton TW17 134 BM99
Bushway, Dag. RM8 70 EX63
Bushwood, E11 68 EF60
Bushwood Dr, SE1 202 A9
Bushwood Rd, Rich. TW9 98 CN79
★ Bushy Park, Tedd. TW11 137 CF95
Bushy Pk, Hmptn.
(Hmptn H.) TW12 137 CF95
Teddington TW11 137 CF95
Bushy Pk Gdns, Tedd. TW11 117 CD92
Bushy Pk Rd, Tedd. TW11 117 CH94
Bushy Rd, Lthd.
(Fetch.) KT22 170 CB122
Teddington TW11 117 CF93
★ Business Design Cen, N1 83 DN67
Business Village, The,
Slou. SL2 74 AV74
Butcher Row, E1 85 DX73
E14 85 DX73
Butchers La, Sev. TN15 149 FX103
Butchers Rd, E16 86 EG72
Butcher Wk, Swans. DA10 130 FY87
Bute Av, Rich. TW10 118 CL89
Bute Ct, Wall. SM6
off Bute Rd 159 DJ106
Bute Gdns, W6 99 CX77
Wallington SM6 159 DJ106
Bute Gdns W, Wall. SM6 159 DJ106
Bute Ms, NW11
off Northway 64 DC56
Bute Rd, Croy. CR0 141 DN102
Ilford IG6 69 EP57
Wallington SM6 159 DJ105
Bute St, SW7 100 DD77
Bute Wk, N1
off Marquess Rd 84 DR65
Butler Av, Har. HA1 61 CD59
Butler Ct, Wem. HA0
off Harrow Rd 61 CG63
Butler Ho, Grays RM17
off Argent St 110 GB79
Butler Pl, SW1 199 M6
Butler Rd, NW10
off Curzon Cres 81 CT66
Dagenham RM8 70 EV63
Harrow HA1 60 CC59
Butlers Ct, Wal.Cr. EN8
off Trinity La 15 DY32
BUTLERS CROSS, Beac.
HP9 36 AT49
Butlers Dene Rd, Cat.
(Wold.) CR3 177 DZ120
Butlers Dr, E4 31 EC38
Butler St, E2
off Knottisford St 84 DW69
Uxbridge UB10 77 BP70
Butlers Wf, SE1 202 A3
Butler Wk, Grays RM17
off Palmers Dr 110 GD77
Buttell Cl, Grays RM17 110 GD78
Buttercross La, Epp. CM16 18 EU30
Buttercup Cl, Nthlt. UB5
off Abbott Cl 78 BZ65
Romford RM3
off Copperfields Way 52 FK53
Buttercup Sq, Stai.
(Stanw.) TW19
off Diamedes Av 114 BK88
Butterfield Cl, N17
off Devonshire Rd 46 DQ51
SE16 202 D5
Twickenham TW1
off Rugby Rd 117 CF86
Butterfields, E17 67 EC57
Butterfield Sq, E6
off Harper Rd 87 EM72
Butterfly La, SE9 125 EP86
Borehamwood
(Elstree) WD6 25 CG41
Butterfly Wk, SE5
off Denmark Hill 102 DR81
Warlingham CR6 176 DW120
Butter Hill, Cars. SM5 140 DG104
Wallington SM6 140 DG104
Butteridges Cl, Dag. RM9 88 EZ67
Butterly Av, Dart. DA1 128 FM89
Buttermere Cl, E15 67 ED63
SE1 201 P8
Feltham TW14 115 BT88
Morden SM4 139 CX100
Buttermere Dr, SW15 119 CY85
Buttermere Gdns, Pur. CR8 160 DR113
Buttermere Rd, Orp. BR5 146 EX98
Buttermere Wk, E8 84 DT65
Buttermere Way, Egh. TW20
off Keswick Rd 113 BB94
Butterwick, W6 99 CW77
Watford WD25 24 BY36
Butterworth Gdns,
Wdf.Grn. IG8 48 EG51
Buttesland St, N1 197 L2
Buttfield Cl, Dag. RM10 89 FB65
Buttlehide, Rick.
(Map.Cr.) WD3 37 BD50
Buttmarsh Cl, SE18 105 EP78
Button Rd, Grays RM17 110 FZ77
Button St, Swan. BR8 148 FJ96
Butts, The, Brent. TW8 97 CK79
Sevenoaks (Otford) TN14 181 FH116

★ Place of interest ⇌ Railway station ⊖ London Underground station DLR Docklands Light Railway station Tra Tramlink station H Hospital Riv Pedestrian ferry landing stage

227

Butts, The, Sunbury-on-Thames TW16 *off Elizabeth Gdns* 136 BW97
Buttsbury Rd, Ilf. IG1 69 EQ64
Butts Cotts, Felt. TW13 116 BZ90
Butts Cres, Felt. TW13 116 CA90
Butts Grn Rd, Horn. RM11 72 FK58
Buttsmead, Nthwd. HA6 39 BQ52
Butts Piece, Nthlt. UB5 *off Longhook Gdns* 77 BV68
Butts Rd, Brom. BR1 124 EE92
Woking GU21 166 AY117
Buxhall Cres, E9 85 DZ65
Buxted Rd, E8 84 DT66
N12 44 DE50
SE22 102 DS84
Buxton Av, Cat. CR3 176 DS121
Buxton Cl, N9 46 DW47
Woodford Green IG8 48 EK51
Buxton Ct, N1 197 J2
Buxton Cres, Sutt. SM3 157 CY105
Buxton Dr, E11 68 EE56
New Malden KT3 138 CR96
Buxton Gdns, W3 80 CP73
Buxton La, Cat. CR3 176 DR120
Buxton Path, Wat. WD19 40 BW48
Buxton Rd, E4 47 ED45
E6 86 EL69
E15 68 EE64
E17 67 DY56
N19 65 DK60
NW2 81 CV65
SW14 98 CS83
Ashford TW15 114 BK92
Epping (They.B.) CM16 33 ES36
Erith DA8 107 FD80
Grays RM16 110 GE75
Ilford IG2 69 ES58
Thornton Heath CR7 141 DP99
Waltham Abbey EN9 16 EG32
Buxton St, E1 84 DT70
Buzzard Creek Ind Est, Bark. IG11 87 ET71
Byam St, SW6 100 DC82
Byards Cft, SW16 141 DK95
Byatt Wk, Hmptn. TW12 *off Victors Dr* 116 BY93
Bychurch End, Tedd. TW11 *off Church Rd* 117 CF92
Bycliffe Ter, Grav. DA11 131 GF87
Bycroft Rd, Sthl. UB1 78 CA70
Bycroft St, SE20 *off Parish La* 123 DX94
Bycullah Av, Enf. EN2 29 DP41
Bycullah Rd, Enf. EN2 29 DP41
Bye, The, W3 80 CS72
Byegrove Rd, SW19 120 DD93
Byers Cl, Pot.B. EN6 12 DC34
Byewaters, Wat. WD18 23 BQ44
Byeway, The, SW14 98 CQ83
Bye Way, The, Har. HA3 41 CE53
Byeway, The, Rick. WD3 38 BL47
Byeways, Twick. TW2 116 CB90
Byeways, The, Ashtd. KT21 *off Skinners La* 171 CK118
Surbiton KT5 138 CN99
Byfeld Gdns, SW13 99 CU81
Byfield Cl, SE16 203 L4
Byfield Pas, Islw. TW7 97 CG83
Byfield Rd, Islw. TW7 97 CG83
BYFLEET, W.Byf. KT14 152 BM113
⇌ **Byfleet & New Haw** 152 BK110
Byfleet Rd, Add. (New Haw) KT15 152 BK108
Cobham KT11 153 BS113
West Byfleet (Byfleet) KT14 152 BN112
Byfleet Tech Cen, W.Byf. (Byfleet) KT14 152 BK111
Byford Cl, E15 86 EE66
Bygrove, Croy. (New Adgtn) CR0 161 EB107
Bygrove St, E14 85 EB72
Byland Cl, N21 45 DM45
Bylands, Wok. GU22 167 BA119
Bylands Cl, SE2 *off Finchale Rd* 106 EV76
SE16 203 J2
Byne Rd, SE26 122 DW93
Carshalton SM5 140 DE103
Bynes Rd, S.Croy. CR2 160 DR108
Byng Dr, Pot.B. EN6 12 DA31
Byng Pl, WC1 195 M5
Byng Rd, Barn. EN5 27 CX41
Byng St, E14 203 P4
Bynon Av, Bexh. DA7 106 EY83
Byre, The, N14 *off Farm La* 29 DH44
Byre Rd, N14 *off Farm La* 28 DG44
Byrne Rd, SW12 121 DH88
Byron Av, E12 86 EL65
E18 68 EF55
NW9 62 CP56
Borehamwood WD6 26 CN43
Coulsdon CR5 175 DL115
Hounslow TW4 95 BU82
New Malden KT3 139 CU99
Sutton SM1 158 DD105
Watford WD24 24 BX39
Byron Av E, Sutt. SM1 158 DD105
Byron Cl, E8 84 DU67
SE26 *off Porthcawe Rd* 123 DY91
SE28 88 EW74
Hampton TW12 116 BZ91
Waltham Cross EN7 *off Allard Cl* 14 DT27
Walton-on-Thames KT12 136 BY102
Woking (Knap.) GU21 166 AS117
Byron Ct, W9 *off Lanhill Rd* 82 DA70
Enfield EN2 *off Bycullah Rd* 29 DP40
Harrow HA1 61 CE58
Byron Dr, N2 64 DD58
Erith DA8 107 FB80
Byron Gdns, Sutt. SM1 158 DD105
Tilbury RM18 111 GJ81
Byron Hill Rd, Har. HA2 61 CD60
Byron Ho, Beck. BR3 123 EA93
Byron Ho, Slough SL3 93 BB78
Byron Ms, NW3 64 DE64
W9 *off Shirland Rd* 82 DA70
Byron Pl, Lthd. KT22 171 CH122
Byron Rd, E10 67 EB60
E17 67 EA55
NW2 63 CV61
NW7 43 CU50
W5 80 CM74
Addlestone KT15 152 BL105
Brentwood (Hutt.) CM13 55 GD45
Dartford DA1 108 FP84
Harrow HA1 61 CE58
Harrow (Wldste) HA3 41 CF54
South Croydon CR2 160 DV110
Wembley HA0 61 CJ62
Byron St, E14 *off St. Leonards Rd* 85 EC72
Byron Ter, N9 46 DW45
Byron Way, Hayes UB4 77 BT70
Northolt UB5 78 BY69
Romford RM3 52 FJ53
West Drayton UB7 94 BM77
Bysouth Cl, N15 66 DR56
Ilford IG5 49 EP53
By the Wd, Wat. WD19 40 BX47
Bythorn St, SW9 101 DM83
Byton Rd, SW17 120 DF93
Byward Av, Felt. TW14 116 BW86
Byward St, EC3 201 N1
Bywater Pl, SE16 203 L2
Bywater St, SW3 198 D10
Byway, The, Epsom KT19 157 CT105
Potters Bar EN6 12 DA33
Sutton SM2 158 DD109
Bywell Pl, W1 195 K7
Bywood Av, Croy. CR0 142 DW100
Bywood Cl, Ken. CR8 175 DP115
By-Wood End, Ger.Cr. (Chal.St.P.) SL9 37 AZ50
Byworth Wk, N19 *off Courtauld Rd* 65 DK60

C

Cabbell Pl, Add. KT15 152 BJ105
Cabbell St, NW1 194 B7
Caberfeigh Pl, Red. RH1 184 DE134
★ **Cabinet War Rooms**, SW1 199 N4
Cabinet Way, E4 47 DZ51
Cable Pl, SE10 *off Diamond Ter* 103 EC81
Cable St, E1 84 DU73
Cable Trade Pk, SE7 104 EJ77
Cabot Pl, E14 204 A2
Cabot Sq, E14 204 A2
Cabot Way, E6 *off Parr Rd* 86 EK67
Cabrera Av, Vir.W. GU25 132 AW100
Cabrera Cl, Vir.W. GU25 132 AX100
Cabul Rd, SW11 100 DE82
Cacket's Cotts, Sev. (Cudham) TN14 *off Cackets La* 179 ES115
Cackets La, Sev. (Cudham) TN14 179 ER115
Cactus Cl, SE15 *off Lyndhurst Gro* 102 DS82
Cactus Wk, W12 *off Du Cane Rd* 81 CT72
Cadbury Cl, Islw. TW7 97 CG81
Sunbury-on-Thames TW16 115 BS94
Cadbury Rd, Sun. TW16 115 BS94
Cadbury Way, SE16 202 A7
Caddington Cl, Barn. EN4 28 DE43
Caddington Rd, NW2 63 CY62
Caddis Cl, Stan. HA7 *off Daventer Dr* 41 CF52
Caddy Cl, Egh. TW20 113 BA92
Cade La, Sev. TN13 191 FJ128
Cadell Cl, E2 *off Shipton St* 84 DT69
Cade Rd, SE10 103 ED81
Cader Rd, SW18 120 DC86
Cadet Dr, SE1 202 A10
Cadet Pl, SE10 205 H10
Cadiz Ct, Dag. RM10 *off Rainham Rd S* 89 FD66
Cadiz Rd, Dag. RM10 89 FC66
Cadiz St, SE17 102 DQ78
Cadley Ter, SE23 122 DW89
Cadlocks Hill, Sev. (Halst.) TN14 164 EZ110
Cadman Cl, SW9 *off Langton Rd* 101 DP80
Cadmer Cl, N.Mal. KT3 138 CS98
Cadmore La, Wal.Cr. (Chsht) EN8 15 DX28
Cadmus Cl, SW4 *off Aristotle Rd* 101 DK83
Cadnam Pt, SW15 *off Dilton Gdns* 119 CV88
Cadogan Av, Dart. DA2 129 FR87
Cadogan Cl, E9 *off Cadogan Ter* 85 DZ66
Beckenham BR3 *off Albemarle Rd* 143 ED95
Harrow HA2 60 CB63
Teddington TW11 117 CE92
Cadogan Ct, Sutt. SM2 158 DB107
Cadogan Gdns, E18 68 EH55
N3 44 DB53
N21 29 DN43
SW3 198 E8
Cadogan Gate, SW1 198 E8
Cadogan La, SW1 198 F7
Riv **Cadogan Pier** 100 DE79
Cadogan Pl, SW1 198 E6
Cadogan Rd, SE18 105 EQ76
Surbiton KT6 137 CK99
Cadogan Sq, SW1 198 E7
Cadogan St, SW3 198 D9
Cadogan Ter, E9 85 DZ65
Cadoxton Av, N15 66 DT58
Cadwallon Rd, SE9 125 EP89
Caedmon Rd, N7 65 DM63
Caenshill Rd, Wey. KT13 152 BN108
Caenwood Cl, Wey. KT13 152 BN107
Caen Wd Rd, Ashtd. KT21 171 CJ118
Caerleon Cl, Esher (Clay.) KT10 155 CH108
Caerleon Cl, Sidcup DA14 126 EW92
Caerleon Ter, SE2 *off Blithdale Rd* 106 EV77
Caernarvon Cl, Horn. RM11 72 FN60
Mitcham CR4 141 DL97
Caernarvon Dr, Ilf. IG5 49 EN53
Caesars Wk, Mitch. CR4 140 DF99
Caesars Way, Shep. TW17 135 BR100
Cage Pond Rd, Rad. (Shenley) WD7 10 CM33
Cage Yd, Reig. RH2 *off High St* 184 DA134
Cahill St, EC1 197 J5
Cahir St, E14 204 B9
Caillard Rd, W.Byf. (Byfleet) KT14 152 BL111
Cains La, Felt. TW14 115 BS85
Caird St, W10 81 CY69
Cairn Av, W5 79 CK74
Cairndale Cl, Brom. BR1 124 EF94
Cairnes Ms, SE18 *off Shooter's Hill Rd* 104 EL81
Cairnfield Av, NW2 62 CS62
Cairngorm Cl, Tedd. TW11 *off Vicarage Rd* 117 CG92
Cairns Av, Wdf.Grn. IG8 48 EL51
Cairns Cl, Dart. DA1 128 FK85
Cairns Rd, SW11 120 DE85
Cairn Way, Stan. HA7 41 CF51
Cairo New Rd, Croy. CR0 141 DP103
Cairo Rd, E17 67 EA56
Caishowe Rd, Borwd. WD6 26 CP39
Caistor Ms, SW12 *off Caistor Rd* 121 DH87
Caistor Pk Rd, E15 86 EF67
Caistor Rd, SW12 121 DH87
Caithness Dr, Epsom KT18 156 CR114
Caithness Gdns, Sid. DA15 125 ET86
Caithness Rd, W14 99 CX77
Mitcham CR4 121 DH94
Calabria Rd, N5 83 DP65
Calais Cl, Wal.Cr. EN7 *off Argent Way* 14 DR26
Calais Gate, SE5 *off Calais St* 101 DP81
Calais St, SE5 101 DP81
Calbourne Av, Horn. RM12 71 FH64
Calbourne Rd, SW12 120 DF87
Calcott Cl, Brwd. CM14 54 FV46
Calcott Wk, SE9 124 EK91
Calcroft Av, Green. DA9 *off London Rd* 129 FW85
Calcutta Rd, Til. RM18 111 GF82
Caldbeck, Wal.Abb. EN9 15 ED34
Caldbeck Av, Wor.Pk. KT4 139 CU103
Caldecot Av, Wal.Cr. EN7 14 DT29
Caldecote Gdns, Bushey WD23 25 CE44
Caldecote La, Bushey WD23 41 CF45
Caldecot Rd, SE5 102 DQ82
Caldecott Way, E5 67 DX62
Calder Av, Grnf. UB6 79 CF68
Hatfield (Brook.Pk) AL9 12 DB26
Calder Cl, Enf. EN1 30 DS41
Calder Ct, Slou. SL3 93 AZ78
Calder Gdns, Edg. HA8 62 CN55
Calderon Pl, W10 *off St. Quintin Gdns* 81 CW71
Calderon Rd, E11 67 EC63
Calder Rd, Mord. SM4 140 DC99
Caldervale Rd, SW4 121 DK85
Calder Way, Slou. (Colnbr.) SL3 93 BF83
Calderwood, Grav. DA12 131 GL92
Calderwood St, SE18 105 EN77
Caldicot Grn, NW9 *off Snowdon Dr* 62 CS58
Caldwell Rd, Wat. WD19 40 BX49
Caldwell St, SW9 101 DM80
Caldwell Yd, EC4 *off Upper Thames St* 84 DQ73
Caldy Rd, Belv. DA17 107 FB76
Caldy Wk, N1 *off Clephane Rd* 84 DQ65
Caleb St, SE1 201 H4
Caledonian Cl, Ilf. IG3 70 EV60
⊖ **Caledonian Road** 83 DL65
Caledonian Rd, N1 196 A1
N7 65 DM64
⇌ **Caledonian Road & Barnsbury** 83 DM66
Caledonian Wf, E14 204 F9
Caledonia Rd, Stai. TW19 114 BL88
Caledonia St, N1 196 A1
Caledon Rd, E6 86 EL67
St. Albans (Lon.Col.) AL2 9 CK26
Wallington SM6 158 DG105
Cale St, SW3 198 B10
Caletock Way, SE10 205 K10
Calfstock La, Dart. (S.Darenth) DA4 148 FL98
Calico Row, SW11 *off York Pl* 100 DC83
Calidore Cl, SW2 *off Endymion Rd* 121 DM86
California Cl, Sutt. SM2 *off Station Rd* 158 DA110
California La, Bushey (Bushey Hth) WD23 41 CD46
California Rd, N.Mal. KT3 138 CQ98
Caliph Cl, Grav. DA12 131 GM90
Callaby Ter, N1 *off Wakeham St* 84 DR65
Callaghan Cl, SE13 *off Glenton Rd* 104 EE84
Callander Rd, SE6 123 EB89
Callan Gro, S.Ock. RM15 91 FV73
Callard Av, N13 45 DP50
Callcott Rd, NW6 81 CZ66
Callcott St, W8 *off Hillgate Pl* 82 DA74
Callendar Rd, SW7 100 DD76
Calley Down Cres, Croy. (New Adgtn) CR0 161 ED110
Callingham Cl, E14 *off Wallwood St* 85 DZ71
Callis Fm Cl, Stai. (Stanw.) TW19 *off Bedfont Rd* 114 BL86
Callis Rd, E17 67 DZ58
Callow Fld, Pur. CR8 159 DN113
Callow Hill, Vir.W. GU25 132 AW97
Callowland Cl, Wat. WD24 23 BV38
Callow St, SW3 100 DD79
Calluna Ct, Wok. GU22 *off Heathside Rd* 167 AZ118
Calmont Rd, Brom. BR1 123 ED93
Calmore Cl, Horn. RM12 72 FJ64
Calne Av, Ilf. IG5 49 EP53
Calonne Rd, SW19 119 CX91
Calshot Av, Grays (Chaff.Hun.) RM16 110 FZ75
Calshot Rd, Houns. (Hthrw Air.) TW6 94 BN82
Calshot St, N1 83 DM68
Calshot Way, Enf. EN2 29 DP41
Hounslow (Hthrw Air.) TW6 *off Calshot Rd* 95 BP82
Calthorpe Gdns, Edg. HA8 *off Jesmond Way* 42 CL50
Sutton SM1 140 DC104
Calthorpe St, WC1 196 C4
Calton Av, SE21 122 DS85
Calton Rd, Barn. EN5 28 DC44
Calverley Cl, Beck. BR3 123 EB93
Calverley Cres, Dag. RM10 70 FA61
Calverley Gdns, Har. HA3 61 CK59
Calverley Gro, N19 65 DK60
Calverley Rd, Epsom KT17 157 CU107
Calvert Av, E2 197 N3
Calvert Cl, Belv. DA17 106 FA77
Sidcup DA14 126 EY93
Calvert Dr, Dart. DA2 *off Old Bexley La* 127 FE89
Calverton, SE5 102 DS79
Calverton Rd, E6 87 EN67
Calvert Rd, SE10 104 EF78
Barnet EN5 27 CX40
Calvert's Bldgs, SE1 201 K3
Calvert St, NW1 *off Chalcot Rd* 82 DG67
Calvin Cl, Orp. BR5 146 EX97
Calvin St, E1 197 P5
Calydon Rd, SE7 104 EH78
Calypso Way, SE16 203 M7
Camac Rd, Twick. TW2 117 CD88
Cambalt Rd, SW15 119 CX85
Camberley Av, SW20 139 CV96
Enfield EN1 30 DS42
Camberley Cl, Sutt. SM3 139 CX104
Camberley Rd, Houns. (Hthrw Air.) TW6 94 BN83
Cambert Way, SE3 104 EH84
CAMBERWELL, SE5 102 DQ80
Camberwell Ch St, SE5 102 DR81
Camberwell Glebe, SE5 102 DR81
Camberwell Grn, SE5 102 DR81
Camberwell Gro, SE5 102 DR81
Camberwell New Rd, SE5 101 DN80
Camberwell Pas, SE5 *off Camberwell Grn* 102 DQ81
Camberwell Rd, SE5 102 DQ79
Camberwell Sta Rd, SE5 102 DQ81
Cambeys Rd, Dag. RM10 71 FB64
Camborne Av, W13 97 CH75
Romford RM3 52 FL52
Camborne Cl, Houns. (Hthrw Air.) TW6 *off Camborne Rd S* 94 BN83
Camborne Ms, W11 *off St. Marks Rd* 81 CY72
Camborne Rd, SW18 120 DA87
Croydon CR0 142 DU101
Morden SM4 139 CX99
Sidcup DA14 126 EW90
Sutton SM2 158 DA108
Welling DA16 105 ET82
Camborne Rd N, Houns. (Hthrw Air.) TW6 *off Camborne Rd S* 94 BN83
Camborne Rd S, Houns. (Hthrw Air.) TW6 94 BN83
Camborne Way, Houns. TW5 96 CA81
Hounslow (Hthrw Air.) TW6 *off Camborne Rd S* 94 BN83
Romford RM3 52 FL52
Cambourne Av, N9 47 DX45
Cambray Rd, SW12 121 DJ88
Orpington BR6 145 ET101
Cambria Cl, Houns. TW3 96 CA84
Sidcup DA15 125 ER88
Cambria Ct, Felt. TW14 *off Hounslow Rd* 115 BV87
Slough SL3 *off Turner Rd* 92 AW75
Cambria Cres, Grav. DA12 131 GL91
Cambria Gdns, Stai. TW19 114 BL87
Cambria Ho, SE26 *off High Level Dr* 122 DU91
Erith DA8 *off Larner Rd* 107 FE80
Cambrian Av, Ilf. IG2 69 ES57
Cambrian Cl, SE27 121 DP90
Cambrian Grn, NW9 *off Snowdon Dr* 62 CS57
Cambrian Gro, Grav. DA11 131 GG87
Cambrian Rd, E10 67 EA59
Richmond TW10 118 CM86
Cambria Rd, SE5 102 DQ83
Cambria St, SW6 100 DB80
Cambridge Av, NW6 82 DA68
Greenford UB6 61 CF64
New Malden KT3 139 CT96
Romford RM2 72 FJ55
Welling DA16 105 ET84
Cambridge Barracks Rd, SE18 105 EM77
Cambridge Circ, WC2 195 N9
Cambridge Cl, E17 67 DZ58
N22 *off Pellatt Gro* 45 DN53
NW10 *off Lawrence Way* 62 CQ62
SW20 139 CV95
Hounslow TW4 96 BY84
Waltham Cross (Chsht) EN8 14 DW29
West Drayton UB7 94 BK79
Woking GU21 *off Bingham Dr* 166 AT118
Cambridge Cotts, Rich. TW9 98 CN79
Cambridge Cres, E2 84 DV68
Teddington TW11 117 CG92
Cambridge Dr, SE12 124 EG85
Potters Bar EN6 11 CX31
Ruislip HA4 60 BW61
Cambridge Gdns, N10 45 DH53
N13 45 DN50
N17 *off Great Cambridge Rd* 46 DR52
Cambridge Gdns, N21 46 DR45
NW6 82 DA68
W10 81 CY72
Enfield EN1 30 DU40
Grays RM16 111 GG77
Kingston upon Thames KT1 138 CN96
Cambridge Gate, NW1 195 J3
Cambridge Gate Ms, NW1 195 J3
Cambridge Grn, SE9 125 EP88
Cambridge Gro, SE20 142 DV95
W6 99 CV77
Cambridge Gro Rd, Kings.T. KT1 138 CN96
⇌ **Cambridge Heath** 84 DV68
Cambridge Heath Rd, E1 84 DV68
E2 84 DV68
Cambridge Mans, SW11 *off Cambridge Rd* 100 DF81
Cambridge Par, Enf. EN1 *off Great Cambridge Rd* 30 DU39
Cambridge Pk, E11 68 EG59
Twickenham TW1 117 CK87
Cambridge Pk Rd, E11 *off Cambridge Pk* 68 EF59
Cambridge Pl, W8 100 DB75
Cambridge Rd, E4 47 ED46
E11 68 EF58
NW6 82 DA69
SE20 142 DV97
SW11 100 DF81
SW13 99 CT82
SW20 139 CU95
W7 97 CF75
Ashford TW15 115 BQ94
Barking IG11 87 EQ66
Bromley BR1 124 EG94
Carshalton SM5 158 DE107
Hampton TW12 116 BZ94
Harrow HA2 60 CA57
Hounslow TW4 96 BY84
Ilford IG3 69 ES60
Kingston upon Thames KT1 138 CM96
Mitcham CR4 141 DJ97
New Malden KT3 138 CS98
Richmond TW9 98 CN80
Sidcup DA14 125 ES91
Southall UB1 78 BZ74
Teddington TW11 117 CF91
Twickenham TW1 117 CK86
Uxbridge UB8 76 BK65
Walton-on-Thames KT12 135 BV100
Watford WD18 24 BW42
West Molesey KT8 136 BZ98
Cambridge Rd N, W4 98 CP78
Cambridge Rd S, W4 98 CP78
Cambridge Row, SE18 105 EP78
Cambridge Sq, W2 194 B8
Cambridge St, SW1 199 J9
Cambridge Ter, N13 45 DN50
NW1 195 J3
Cambridge Ter Ms, NW1 195 J3
Cambstone Cl, N11 44 DG47
Cambus Cl, Hayes UB4 78 BY71
Cambus Rd, E16 86 EG71
Camdale Rd, SE18 105 ET80
★ **Camden Arts Cen**, NW3 64 DC64
Camden Av, Felt. TW13 116 BW89
Hayes UB4 78 BW73
Camden Cl, Chis. BR7 125 EQ94
Gravesend DA11 130 GC88
Grays RM16 111 GH77
Camden Gdns, NW1 *off Kentish Town Rd* 83 DH66
Sutton SM1 158 DB106
Thornton Heath CR7 141 DP97
Camden Gro, Chis. BR7 125 EP93
Camden High St, NW1 83 DH67
Camden Hill Rd, SE19 122 DS93
Camdenhurst St, E14 85 DY72
Camden La, N7 *off Rowstock Gdns* 83 DK65
★ **Camden Lock Mkt & Waterbuses**, NW1 83 DH66
Camden Lock Pl, NW1 *off Chalk Fm Rd* 83 DH66
Camden Ms, NW1 83 DK65
H **Camden Ms Day Hosp**, NW1 83 DJ66
Camden Pk Rd, NW1 83 DK65
Chislehurst BR7 125 EM94
Camden Pas, N1 83 DP67
⇌ **Camden Road** 83 DJ66
Camden Rd, E11 68 EH58
E17 67 DZ58
N7 65 DK64
NW1 83 DJ67
Bexley DA5 126 EZ88
Carshalton SM5 158 DF105
Grays RM16 110 FY76
Sevenoaks TN13 191 FH122
Sutton SM1 158 DA106
Camden Row, SE3 104 EE82
Camden Sq, NW1 83 DK65
SE15 *off Watts St* 102 DT81
Camden St, NW1 83 DH66
Camden Ter, NW1 *off North Vil* 83 DK65
CAMDEN TOWN, NW1 83 DJ67
⊖ **Camden Town** 83 DH67
Camden Wk, N1 83 DP67
Camden Way, Chis. BR7 125 EM94
Thornton Heath CR7 141 DP97
Camelford Wk, W11 *off Lancaster Rd* 81 CY72
Camel Gro, Kings.T. KT2 117 CK92
Camellia Cl, Rom. RM3 *off Columbine Way* 52 FL53
Camellia Ct, Wdf.Grn. IG8 *off The Bridle Path* 48 EE52
Camellia Pl, Twick. TW2 116 CB87
Camellia St, SW8 101 DL80
Camelot Cl, SE28 105 ER75
SW19 120 DA91
Westerham (Bigg.H.) TN16 178 EJ116
Camelot St, SE15 *off Bird in Bush Rd* 102 DV80
Camel Rd, E16 86 EK74
Camera Pl, SW10 100 DD79
Cameron Cl, N18 46 DV49
N20 *off Myddelton Pk* 44 DE47

★ Place of interest ⇌ Railway station ⊖ London Underground station DLR Docklands Light Railway station Tra Tramlink station H Hospital Riv Pedestrian ferry landing stage

Cameron Cl, Bexley DA5 127 FD90
Brentwood CM14 54 FW49
Cameron Dr, Wal.Cr. EN8 15 DX34
Cameron Pl, E1 off Varden St 84 DV72
Cameron Rd, SE6 123 DZ89
Bromley BR2 144 EG98
Croydon CR0 141 DP100
Ilford IG3 69 ES60
Cameron Sq, Mitch. CR4 140 DE95
Camerton Cl, E8
off Buttermere Wk 84 DT65
Camgate Cen, Stai.
(Stanw.) TW19 114 BM86
Cam Grn, S.Ock. RM15 91 FV72
Camilla Cl, Sun. TW16 115 BS93
Camilla Rd, SE16 202 D9
Camille Cl, SE25 142 DU97
Camlan Rd, Brom. BR1 124 EF91
Camlet St, E2 197 P4
Camlet Way, Barn. EN4 28 DA40
Camley St, NW1 83 DK66
★ Camley St Natural Pk, NW1 83 DL68
Camm Gdns, Kings.T. KT1
off Church Rd 138 CM96
Thames Ditton KT7 137 CE101
Camms Ter, Dag. RM10 71 FC64
Camomile Av, Mitch. CR4 140 DF95
Camomile Rd, Rom.
(Rush Grn) RM7 71 FD61
Camomile St, EC3 197 M8
Camomile Way, West Dr. UB7 76 BL72
Campana Rd, SW6 100 DA81
Campbell Av, Ilf. IG6 69 EQ56
Woking GU22 167 AZ121
Campbell Cl, SE18
off Moordown 105 EN81
SW16 121 DK91
Romford (Hav.at.Bow.) RM1 51 FE51
Ruislip HA4 59 BU58
Twickenham TW2 117 CD89
West Byfleet KT14
off Chertsey Rd 152 BK112
Campbell Ct, N17 46 DT53
Campbell Cft, Edg. HA8 42 CN50
Campbell Gordon Way, NW2 63 CV63
Campbell Rd, E3 85 EA69
E6 86 EL67
E15 off Trevelyan Rd 68 EF63
E17 67 DZ56
N17 46 DU53
W7 79 CE73
Caterham CR3 176 DR121
Croydon CR0 141 DP101
East Molesey KT8
off Hampton Ct Rd 137 CF97
Gravesend DA11 131 GF88
Twickenham TW2 117 CD89
Weybridge KT13 152 BN108
Campbell Wk, N1
off Outram Pl 83 DL67
Campdale Rd, N7 65 DK62
Campden Cres, Dag. RM8 70 EV63
Wembley HA0 61 CH61
Campden Gro, W8 100 DA75
Campden Hill Ct, W8
off Campden Hill Rd 100 DA75
Campden Hill Gdns, W8 82 DA74
Campden Hill Gate, W8
off Duchess of Bedford's Wk 100 DA75
Campden Hill Pl, W11
off Holland Pk Av 81 CZ74
Campden Hill Rd, W8 82 DA74
Campden Hill Sq, W8 81 CZ74
Campden Hill Twrs, W11
off Notting Hill Gate 82 DA74
Campden Ho Cl, W8
off Hornton St 100 DA75
Campden Rd, S.Croy. CR2 160 DS106
Uxbridge UB10 58 BM62
Campden St, W8 82 DA74
Campen Cl, SW19 119 CY89
Camp End Rd, Wey. KT13 153 BR110
Camperdown St, E1
off Leman St 84 DT72
Campfield Rd, SE9 124 EK87
Camphill Ct, W.Byf. KT14 152 BG112
Camphill Ind Est, W.Byf. KT14 152 BH111
Camphill Rd, W.Byf. KT14 152 BG112
Campine Cl, Wal.Cr.
(Chsht) EN8
off Welsummer Way 15 DX28
Campion Cl, E6 87 EM73
Croydon CR0 160 DS105
Gravesend (Nthflt) DA11 130 GE91
Harrow HA3 62 CM58
Romford (Rush Grn) RM7 71 FD61
Uxbridge (Denh.) UB9
off Lindsey Rd 58 BG62
Uxbridge (Hlgdn) UB8 76 BM71
Watford WD25 7 BU33
Campion Ct, Grays RM17 110 GD79
Campion Dr, Tad. KT20 173 CV120
Campion Gdns, Wdf.Grn. IG8 48 EG50
Campion Pl, SE28 88 EV74
Campion Rd, SW15 99 CW84
Isleworth TW7 97 CF81
Campions, Epp. CM16 18 EU28
Loughton IG10 33 EN38
Campions, The, Borwd. WD6 26 CN38
Campions Cl, Borwd. WD6 26 CP37
Campion Ter, NW2 63 CX62
Campion Way, Edg. HA8 42 CQ49
Cample La, S.Ock. RM15 91 FU73
Camplin Rd, Har. HA3 62 CL57
Camplin St, SE14 103 DX80
Camp Rd, SW19 119 CW92
Caterham (Wold.) CR3 177 DY120
Gerrards Cross SL9 56 AX59
Campsbourne, The, N8
off High St 65 DL56
Campsbourne Rd, N8 65 DL55
Campsey Gdns, Dag. RM9 88 EV66
Campsey Rd, Dag. RM9 88 EV66
Campsfield Rd, N8
off Campsbourne Rd 65 DL55
Campshill Pl, SE13
off Campshill Rd 123 EC85
Campshill Rd, SE13 123 EC85
Campus Rd, E17 67 DZ58
Campus Way, NW4
off Greyhound Hill 63 CV55
Camp Vw, SW19 119 CV92
Cam Rd, E15 85 ED67
Camrose Av, Edg. HA8 42 CM53
Erith DA8 107 FB79
Feltham TW13 115 BV91
Camrose Cl, Croy. CR0 143 DY101
Morden SM4 140 DA98
Camrose St, SE2 106 EU78
Canada Av, N18 46 DQ51
Canada Cres, W3 80 CQ71
Canada Est, SE16 202 G6
Canada Fm Rd, Dart.
(S.Darenth) DA4 149 FU98
Longfield DA3 149 FU99
Canada Gdns, SE13 123 EC85
Canada La, Brox. EN10 15 DY25
Canada Rd, W3 80 CQ70
Cobham KT11 154 BW113
Erith DA8 107 FH80
Slough SL1 92 AV75
West Byfleet (Byfleet) KT14 152 BK111
Canadas, The, Brox. EN10 15 DY25
Canada Sq, E14 204 B2
Canada St, SE16 203 H5
⊖ Canada Water 202 G5
Canada Way, W12 81 CV73
Canadian Av, SE6 123 EB88
Canadian Mem Av, Egh. TW20 132 AT96
Canal App, SE8 103 DY79
Canal Basin, Grav. DA12 131 GK86
Canal Cl, E1 85 DY70
W10 81 CX70
Canal Est, Slou.
(Langley) SL3 93 BA75
Canal Gro, SE15 102 DU79
Canal Path, E2 84 DT67
Canal Rd, Grav. DA12 131 GJ86
Canal Side, Uxb. (Hare.) UB9
off Summerhouse La 38 BG51
Canal St, SE5 102 DR79
Canal Wk, N1 84 DR67
SE26 122 DW92
Croydon CR0 142 DS100
Canal Way, N1
off Packington Sq 84 DQ68
NW1 194 C2
NW8 194 B3
NW10 81 CT70
W10 81 CX70
Uxbridge UB8
off Summerhouse La 38 BG51
Canal Way Wk, W10 81 CX70
Canal Wf, Slou. SL3 93 BA75
⊖ Canary Wharf 204 B3
DLR Canary Wharf 204 A2
Riv Canary Wharf Pier 203 N2
Canberra Cl, NW4 63 CU55
Dagenham RM10 89 FD66
Hornchurch RM12 72 FJ63
Canberra Cres, Dag. RM10 89 FD66
Canberra Dr, Hayes UB4 78 BW69
Northolt UB5 78 BW69
Canberra Rd, E6
off Barking Rd 87 EM67
SE7 104 EJ79
W13 79 CG74
Bexleyheath DA7 106 EX79
Hounslow (Hthrw Air.) TW6 94 BN83
Canberra Sq, Til. RM18 111 GG82
Canbury Av, Kings.T. KT2 138 CM95
Canbury Ms, SE26
off Wells Pk Rd 122 DU90
Canbury Pk Rd, Kings.T. KT2 138 CL95
Canbury Pas, Kings.T. KT2 137 CK95
Canbury Path, Orp. BR5 146 EU98
Cancell Rd, SW9 101 DN81
Candahar Rd, SW11 100 DE82
Cander Way, S.Ock. RM15 91 FV73
Candle Gro, SE15 102 DV83
Candlemakers Apartments, SW18
off York Rd 100 DD83
Candler St, N15 66 DR58
Candlerush Cl, Wok. GU22 167 BB117
Candlestick La, Wal.Cr. EN7
off Park La 14 DV27
Candover Cl, West Dr. UB7 94 BK80
Candover Rd, Horn. RM12 71 FH60
Candover St, W1 195 K7
Candy St, E3 85 DZ67
Cane Hill, Rom. (Harold Wd) RM3
off Bennison Dr 52 FK54
Caneland Ct, Wal.Abb. EN9 16 EF34
Canewdon Cl, Wok. GU22
off Guildford Rd 166 AY119
Caney Ms, NW2
off Claremont Rd 63 CX61
Canfield Dr, Ruis. HA4 59 BV64
Canfield Gdns, NW6 82 DC66
Canfield Pl, NW6
off Canfield Gdns 82 DC65
Canfield Rd, Rain. RM13 89 FF67
Woodford Green IG8 48 EL52
Canford Av, Nthlt. UB5 78 BY67
Canford Cl, Enf. EN2 29 DN40
Canford Dr, Add. KT15 134 BH103
Canford Gdns, N.Mal. KT3 138 CR100
Canford Pl, Tedd. TW11 117 CH93
Canford Rd, SW11 120 DG85
Canham Rd, SE25 142 DS97
W3 98 CS75
Can Hatch, Tad. KT20 173 CY118
Canmore Gdns, SW16 121 DJ94
Cann Hall Rd, E11 68 EE63
Canning Cres, N22 45 DM53
Canning Cross, SE5 102 DS82
Canning Pas, W8 100 DC76
Canning Pl, W8 100 DC76
Canning Pl Ms, W8
off Canning Pl 100 DC76
Canning Rd, E15 86 EE68
E17 67 DY56
N5 65 DP62
Croydon CR0 142 DT103
Harrow HA3 61 CF55
Cannington Rd, Dag. RM9 88 EW65
CANNING TOWN, E16 86 EG72
⇌ Canning Town 86 EE72
⊖ Canning Town 86 EE72
DLR Canning Town 86 EE72
Cannizaro Rd, SW19 119 CW93
Cannonbury Av, Pnr. HA5 60 BX58
Cannon Cl, SW20 139 CW97
Hampton TW12
off Hanworth Rd 116 CB93
Cannon Ct, EC1
off St. John St 83 DP70
Cannon Cres, Wok.
(Chobham) GU24 150 AS111
Cannon Dr, E14 203 P1
Cannon Gro, Lthd.
(Fetch.) KT22 171 CE121
Cannon Hill, N14 45 DK48
NW6 64 DA64
Cannon Hill La, SW20 139 CY97
Cannon La, NW3 64 DD62
Pinner HA5 60 BY60
Cannon Ms, Wal.Abb. EN9 15 EB33
Cannon Pl, NW3 64 DD62
SE7 104 EL78
Cannon Rd, N14 45 DL48
Bexleyheath DA7 106 EY81
Watford WD18 24 BW43
Cannonside, Lthd.
(Fetch.) KT22 171 CE122
⇌ Cannon Street 201 K1
⊖ Cannon Street 201 K1
Cannon St, EC4 197 H9
Cannon St Rd, E1 84 DV72
Cannon Trd Est, Wem. HA9 62 CP63
Cannon Way, Lthd.
(Fetch.) KT22 171 CE121
West Molesey KT8 136 CA98
Cannon Wf Business Cen, SE8 203 K9
Cannon Workshops, E14 203 P1
Canon Av, Rom. RM6 70 EW57
Canon Beck Rd, SE16 202 G4
Canonbie Rd, SE23 122 DW87
CANONBURY, N1 84 DQ65
⇌ Canonbury 66 DQ64
Canonbury Cres, N1 84 DQ66
Canonbury Gro, N1 84 DQ66
Canonbury La, N1 83 DP66
Canonbury Pk N, N1 84 DQ65
Canonbury Pk S, N1 84 DQ65
Canonbury Pl, N1 83 DP65
Canonbury Rd, N1 83 DP65
Enfield EN1 30 DS39
Canonbury Sq, N1 83 DP66
Canonbury St, N1 84 DQ66
Canonbury Vil, N1 83 DP66
Canonbury Yd, N1
off New N Rd 84 DQ67
Canonbury Yd W, N1
off Compton Rd 83 DP65
Canon Mohan Cl, N14
off Farm La 29 DH44
Canon Rd, Brom. BR1 144 EJ97
Canon Row, SW1 199 P5
Canons Cl, N2 64 DD59
Edgware HA8 42 CM51
Radlett WD7 25 CH35
Reigate RH2 183 CZ133
Canons Cor, Edg. HA8 42 CL49
Canons Dr, Edg. HA8 42 CL51
Canons Gate, Wal.Cr.
(Chsht) EN8 15 DZ26
Canon's Hill, Couls. CR5 175 DN117
Canons La, Tad. KT20 173 CY118
Canonsleigh Rd, Dag. RM9 88 EV66
CANONS PARK, Edg. HA8 42 CL52
⊖ Canons Park 42 CL52
Canons Pk Cl, Edg. HA8
off Donnefield Av 42 CL52
Canon St, N1 84 DQ67
Canons Wk, Croy. CR0 143 DX104
Canopus Way, Nthwd. HA6 39 BU49
Staines TW19 114 BL87
Canrobert St, E2 84 DV69
Cantelowes Rd, NW1 83 DK65
Canterbury Av, Ilf. IG1 68 EL59
Sidcup DA15 126 EW89
Upminster RM14 73 FT60
Canterbury Cl, E6
off Harper Rd 87 EM72
Amersham HP7 20 AS39
Beckenham BR3 143 EB95
Chigwell IG7 49 ET48
Dartford DA1 128 FN87
Greenford UB6 78 CB72
Northwood HA6 39 BT51
Canterbury Cres, SW9 101 DN83
Canterbury Gro, SE27 121 DP90
Canterbury Ho, Borwd. WD6 26 CN40
Erith DA8 off Arthur St 107 FF80
Canterbury Ms, Lthd.
(Oxshott) KT22
off Steels La 154 CC113
Canterbury Par, S.Ock. RM15 91 FW69
Canterbury Pl, SE17 200 G9
Canterbury Rd, E10 67 EC59
NW6 82 DA68
Borehamwood WD6 26 CN40
Croydon CR0 141 DM101
Feltham TW13 116 BY90
Gravesend DA12 131 GJ89
Harrow HA1, HA2 60 CB57
Morden SM4 140 DC99
Watford WD17 23 BV40
Canterbury Ter, NW6 82 DA68
Canterbury Way, Brwd.
(Gt Warley) CM13 53 FW51
Purfleet RM19 109 FS80
Rickmansworth
(Crox.Grn) WD3 23 BQ41
Cantium Retail Pk, SE1 102 DU79
Cantley Gdns, SE19 142 DT95
Ilford IG2 69 EQ58
Cantley Rd, W7 97 CG76
Canton St, E14 85 EA72
Cantrell Rd, E3 85 DZ70
Cantwell Rd, SE18 105 EP80
Canute Gdns, SE16 203 H8
Canvey St, SE1 200 G2
Cape Cl, Bark. IG11
off North St 87 EQ65
Capel Av, Wall. SM6 159 DM106
Capel Cl, N20 44 DC48
Bromley BR2 144 EL102
Capel Ct, EC2 197 L9
SE20 off Melvin Rd 142 DW95
Capel Gdns, Ilf. IG3 69 ET63
Pinner HA5 60 BZ56
Capella Rd, Nthwd. HA6 39 BT50
Capell Av, Rick. (Chorl.) WD3 21 BC43
Capell Rd, Rick. (Chorl.) WD3 21 BC43
Capell Way, Rick. (Chorl.) WD3 21 BD43
Capel Pl, Dart. DA2 128 FJ91
Capel Pt, E7 68 EH63
Capel Rd, E7 68 EH63
E12 68 EJ63
Barnet EN4 28 DE44
Enfield EN1 30 DV36
Watford WD19 24 BY44
Capel Vere Wk, Wat. WD17 23 BS39
Capener's Cl, SW1 198 F5
Capern Rd, SW18
off Cargill Rd 120 DC88
Cape Rd, N17
off High Cross Rd 66 DU55
Cape Yd, E1 202 C2
Capibility Way, Green. DA9
off London Rd 109 FW84
Capital Business Cen,
Wem. HA0 79 CK68
Capital Ind Est, Mitch. CR4
off Willow La 140 DF99
Capital Interchange Way,
Brent. TW8 98 CN78
Capital Pk, Wok.
(Old Wok.) GU22 167 BB121
Capitol Ind Pk, NW9 62 CQ55
Capitol Way, NW9 62 CQ55
Capland St, NW8 194 A4
Caple Par, NW10
off Harley Rd 80 CS68
Caple Rd, NW10 81 CT68
Capon Cl, Brwd. CM14 54 FV46
Capper St, WC1 195 L5
Caprea Cl, Hayes UB4
off Triandra Way 78 BX71
Capri Rd, Croy. CR0 142 DT102
Capstan Cen, Til. RM18 110 GD80
Capstan Cl, Rom. RM6 70 EV58
Capstan Ct, Dart. DA2 108 FQ84
Capstan Ms, Grav. DA11
off Rosherville Way 130 GE87
Capstan Ride, Enf. EN2 29 DN40
Capstan Rd, SE8 203 M8
Capstan Sq, E14 204 E5
Capstan's Wf, Wok.
(St.John's) GU21 166 AT118
Capstan Way, SE16 203 L3
Capstone Rd, Brom. BR1 124 EF91
Captain Cook Cl,
Ch.St.G. HP8 36 AU49
Capthorne Av, Har. HA2 60 BY60
Capuchin Cl, Stan. HA7 41 CH51
Capulet Ms, E16 205 N2
Capworth St, E10 67 EA60
Caractacus Cottage Vw,
Wat. WD18 39 BU45
Caractacus Grn, Wat. WD18 23 BT44
Caradoc Cl, W2 82 DA72
Caradoc St, SE10 205 H10
Caradon Cl, E11
off Brockway Cl 68 EE61
Woking GU21 166 AV118
Caradon Way, N15 66 DR56
Caravan La, Rick. WD3 38 BL45
Caravel Cl, E14
off Tiller Rd 103 EA76
Grays RM16 110 FZ76
Caravelle Gdns, Nthlt. UB5
off Javelin Way 78 BX69
Caravel Ms, SE8
off Watergate St 103 EA79
Caraway Cl, E13 86 EH71
Caraway Pl, Wall. SM6 141 DH104
Carberry Rd, SE19 122 DS93
Carbery Av, W3 98 CM75
Carbis Cl, E4 47 ED46
Carbis Rd, E14 85 DZ72
Carbone Hill, Hert.
(Newgate St) SG13 13 DK26
Potters Bar (Cuffley) EN6 13 DJ27
Carbuncle Pas Way, N17 46 DU54
Carburton St, W1 195 J6
Carbury Cl, Horn. RM12 90 FJ65
Cardale St, E14 204 D6
Carden Rd, SE15 102 DV83
Cardiff Rd, W7 97 CG76
Enfield EN3 30 DV42
Watford WD18 23 BV44
Cardiff St, SE18 105 ES80
Cardiff Way, Abb.L. WD5 7 BU32
Cardigan Cl, Wok. GU21
off Bingham Dr 166 AS118
Cardigan Gdns, Ilf. IG3 70 EU61
Cardigan Rd, E3 85 DZ68
SW13 99 CU82
SW19 off Haydons Rd 120 DC93
Richmond TW10 118 CL86
Cardigan St, SE11 200 D10
Cardigan Wk, N1
off Ashby Gro 84 DQ66
Cardinal Av, Borwd. WD6 26 CP41
Kingston upon Thames KT2 118 CL92
Morden SM4 139 CY100
Cardinal Bourne St, SE1 201 L7
Cardinal Cl, Chis. BR7 145 ER95
Edgware HA8 off Abbots Rd 42 CR52
Morden SM4 139 CY101
South Croydon CR2 160 DU113
Waltham Cross (Chsht) EN7
off Adamsfield 14 DT26
Worcester Park KT4 157 CU105
Cardinal Ct, Borwd. WD6
off Cardinal Av 26 CP41
Cardinal Cres, N.Mal. KT3 138 CQ96
Cardinal Dr, Ilf. IG6 49 EQ51
Walton-on-Thames KT12 136 BX102
Cardinal Hinsley Cl, NW10 81 CU68
Cardinal Pl, SW15 99 CX84
Cardinal Rd, Felt. TW13 115 BV88
Ruislip HA4 60 BX60
Cardinals Wk, Hmptn. TW12 116 CC94
Sunbury-on-Thames TW16 115 BS93
Cardinals Way, N19 65 DK60
Cardinal Way, Har. HA3
off Wolseley Rd 61 CE55
Rainham RM13 90 FK68
Cardine Ms, SE15 102 DV80
Cardingham, Wok. GU21 166 AU117
Cardington Sq, Houns. TW4 96 BX84
Cardington St, NW1 195 K2
Cardinham Rd, Orp. BR6 163 ET105
Cardozo Rd, N7 65 DL64
Cardrew Av, N12 44 DD50
Cardrew Cl, N12 44 DE50
Cardross St, W6 99 CV76
Cardwell Rd, N7 65 DL63
Carew Cl, N7 65 DM61
Coulsdon CR5 175 DP119
Grays RM16
off Clockhouse La 110 FY76
Carew Ct, Sutt. SM2 158 DB109
Carew Rd, N17 46 DU54
W13 97 CJ75
Ashford TW15 115 BQ93
Mitcham CR4 140 DG96
Northwood HA6 39 BS51
Thornton Heath CR7 141 DP97
Wallington SM6 159 DJ107
Carew St, SE5 102 DQ82
Carew Way, Wat. WD19 40 BZ48
Carey Ct, Bexh. DA6 127 FB85
Carey Gdns, SW8 101 DJ81
Carey La, EC2 197 H8
Carey Pl, SW1 199 M9
Carey Rd, Dag. RM9 70 EY63
Carey's Fld, Sev.
(Dunt.Grn) TN13 181 FE120
Carey St, WC2 196 C9
Carey Way, Wem. HA9 62 CP63
Carfax Pl, SW4
off Holwood Pl 101 DK84
Carfax Rd, Hayes UB3 95 BT78
Hornchurch RM12 71 FF63
Carfree Cl, N1
off Bewdley St 83 DN66
Cargill Rd, SW18 120 DB88
Cargreen Pl, SE25
off Cargreen Rd 142 DT98
Cargreen Rd, SE25 142 DT98
Carholme Rd, SE23 123 DZ88
Carisbrooke Av, Bex. DA5 126 EX88
Watford WD24 24 BX39
Carisbrooke Cl, Enf. EN1 30 DT39
Hornchurch RM11 72 FN60
Stanmore HA7 41 CK54
Carisbrooke Ct, Slou. SL1 74 AT73
Carisbrooke Gdns, SE15
off Commercial Way 102 DT80
Carisbrooke Ho, Kings.T. KT2
off Kingsgate Rd 138 CL95
Carisbrooke Rd, E17 67 DY56
Bromley BR2 144 EJ98
Mitcham CR4 141 DK98
St. Albans AL2 8 CB26
Carisbrook Rd, Brwd.
(Pilg.Hat.) CM15 54 FV44
Carker's La, NW5 65 DH64
Carl Ekman Ho, Grav. DA11 130 GD87
Carleton Av, Wall. SM6 159 DK109
Carleton Cl, Esher KT10 137 CD102
Carleton Pl, Dart.
(Hort.Kir.) DA4 148 FQ98
Carleton Rd, N7 65 DK64
Dartford DA1 128 FN87
Waltham Cross (Chsht) EN8 15 DX28
Carleton Vil, NW5
off Leighton Gro 65 DJ64
Carlile Cl, E3 85 DZ68
Carlina Gdns, Wdf.Grn. IG8 48 EH50
Carlingford Gdns, Mitch. CR4 120 DF94
Carlingford Rd, N15 65 DP55
NW3 64 DD63
Morden SM4 139 CX100
Carlisle Av, EC3 197 N9
W3 80 CS72
Carlisle Cl, Kings.T. KT2 138 CN95
Pinner HA5 60 BY59
Carlisle Gdns, Har. HA3 61 CK59
Ilford IG1 68 EL58
Carlisle La, SE1 200 C7
Carlisle Ms, NW8 194 A6
Carlisle Pl, N11 45 DH49
SW1 199 K7
Carlisle Rd, E10 67 EA61
N4 65 DN59
NW6 81 CY67
NW9 62 CQ55
Dartford DA1 128 FN86
Hampton TW12 116 CB94
Romford RM1 71 FG57
Sutton SM1 157 CZ106
Carlisle St, W1 195 M9
Carlisle Wk, E8
off Laurel St 84 DT65
Carlisle Way, SW17 120 DG92
Carlos Pl, W1 198 G1
Carlow St, NW1
off Arlington Rd 83 DJ68
Carlton Av, N14 29 DK43
Feltham TW14 116 BW86
Greenhithe DA9 129 FS86
Harrow HA3 61 CH57
Hayes UB3 95 BS77
South Croydon CR2 160 DS108
Carlton Av E, Wem. HA9 62 CL60
Carlton Av W, Wem. HA0 61 CH61
Carlton Cl, NW3 64 DA61
Borehamwood WD6 26 CR42
Chessington KT9 155 CK107
Edgware HA8 42 CN50
Northolt UB5
off Whitton Av W 60 CC64
Upminster RM14 72 FP61
Woking GU21 151 AZ114
Carlton Ct, SW9 101 DP81
Ilford IG6 69 ER55
Uxbridge UB8 76 BK71
Carlton Cres, Sutt. SM3 157 CY105

★ Place of interest ⇌ Railway station ⊖ London Underground station DLR Docklands Light Railway station Tra Tramlink station H Hospital Riv Pedestrian ferry landing stage

229

★ Place of interest   ⇌ Railway station   ⊖ London Underground station   DLR Docklands Light Railway station   Tra Tramlink station   Ⓗ Hospital   Rtv Pedestrian ferry landing stage

230

Cavendish Cl, NW6
off Cavendish Rd 81 CZ66
NW8 194 A2
Amersham HP6 20 AV39
Hayes UB4 off Westacott 77 BS71
Sunbury-on-Thames TW16 115 BT93
Cavendish Ct, EC3 197 N8
Rickmansworth (Crox.Grn) WD3
off Mayfare 23 BR43
Sunbury-on-Thames TW16 115 BT93
Cavendish Cres, Borwd.
(Elstree) WD6 26 CN42
Hornchurch RM12 89 FH65
Cavendish Dr, E11 67 ED60
Edgware HA8 42 CM51
Esher (Clay.) KT10 155 CE106
Cavendish Gdns, Bark. IG11 69 ES64
Ilford IG1 69 EN60
Redhill RH1 184 DG133
Romford RM6 70 EY57
Cavendish Ms N, W1 195 J6
Cavendish Ms S, W1 195 J7
Cavendish Par, Houns. TW4
off Bath Rd 96 BY82
Cavendish Pl, W1 195 J8
Cavendish Rd, E4 47 EC51
N4 65 DN58
N18 46 DV50
NW6 81 CY66
SW12 121 DH86
SW19 120 DD94
W4 98 CQ81
Barnet EN5 27 CW41
Croydon CR0 141 DP102
New Malden KT3 139 CT99
Redhill RH1 184 DG134
Sunbury-on-Thames TW16 115 BT93
Sutton SM2 158 DC108
Weybridge KT13 153 BQ108
Woking GU22 166 AX119
Cavendish Sq, W1 195 J8
Longfield DA3 149 FX97
Cavendish St, N1 197 K1
Cavendish Ter, Felt. TW13
off High St 115 BU89
Cavendish Way, W.Wick. BR4 143 EB102
Cavenham Cl, Wok. GU22 166 AY119
Cavenham Gdns, Horn. RM11 72 FJ57
Ilford IG1 69 ER62
Caverleigh Way, Wor.Pk. KT4 139 CU102
Cave Rd, E13 86 EH68
Richmond TW10 117 CJ91
Caversham Av, N13 45 DN48
Sutton SM3 139 CY103
Caversham Ct, N11 44 DG48
Caversham Flats, SW3
off Caversham St 100 DF79
Caversham Rd, N15 66 DQ56
NW5 83 DJ65
Kingston upon Thames KT1 138 CM96
Caversham St, SW3 100 DF79
Caverswall St, W12 81 CW72
Caveside Cl, Chis. BR7 145 EN95
Cavill's Wk, Chig. IG7 50 EW47
Romford RM4 50 EX47
Cawdor Av, S.Ock. RM15 91 FU73
Cawdor Cres, W7 97 CG77
Cawnpore St, SE19 122 DS92
Cawsey Way, Wok. GU21 166 AY117
Caxton Av, Add. KT15 152 BG107
Caxton Dr, Uxb. UB8
off Chiltern Vw Rd 76 BK68
Caxton Gro, E3 85 EA69
Caxton La, Oxt. RH8 188 EL131
Caxton Ms, Brent. TW8
off The Butts 97 CK79
Caxton Ri, Red. RH1 184 DG133
Caxton Rd, N22 45 DM54
SW19 120 DC92
W12 99 CX75
Southall UB2 96 BX76
Caxton St, SW1 199 L6
Caxton St N, E16
off Victoria Dock Rd 86 EF73
Caxton Way, Rom. RM1 71 FE56
Watford WD18 23 BR44
Cayenne Ct, SE1 202 A3
Caygill Cl, Brom. BR2 144 EF98
Cayley Cl, Wall. SM6 159 DL108
Cayley Rd, Sthl. UB2
off McNair Rd 96 CB76
Cayton Pl, EC1 197 K3
Cayton Rd, Couls. CR5 175 DJ122
Greenford UB6 79 CE68
Cayton St, EC1 197 K3
Cazenove Rd, E17 47 EA53
N16 66 DT61
Cearns Ho, E6 86 EK67
Cearn Way, Couls. CR5 175 DM115
Cecil Av, Bark. IG11 87 ER66
Enfield EN1 30 DT42
Grays RM16 110 FZ75
Hornchurch RM11 72 FL55
Wembley HA9 62 CM64
Cecil Cl, W5 off Helena Rd 79 CK71
Ashford TW15 115 BQ93
Chessington KT9 155 CK105
Cecil Ct, WC2 199 N1
Barnet EN5 27 CX41
Cecile Pk, N8 65 DL58
Cecilia Cl, N2 64 DC55
★ Cecilia Coleman Gall, NW8 82 DD68
Cecilia Rd, E8 66 DU64
Cecil Pk, Pnr. HA5 60 BY56
Cecil Pl, Mitch. CR4 140 DF99
Cecil Rd, E11 68 EE62
E13 86 EG67
E17 47 EA53
N10 45 DH54
N14 45 DJ46
NW9 62 CS55
NW10 80 CS67
SW19 120 DB94
W3 80 CQ71
Ashford TW15 115 BQ94
Croydon CR0 141 DM100
Enfield EN2 30 DR42
Gravesend DA11 131 GF88
Harrow HA3 61 CE55
Hounslow TW3 96 CC82
Cecil Rd, Ilford IG1 69 EP63
Iver SL0 75 BE72
Potters Bar EN6 11 CU32
Romford RM6 70 EX59
Sutton SM1 157 CZ107
Waltham Cross
(Chsht) EN8 15 DX32
★ Cecil Sharp Ho, NW1 82 DG67
Cecil St, Wat. WD24 23 BV38
Cecil Way, Brom. BR2 144 EG102
Cedar Av, Barn. EN4 44 DE45
Cobham KT11 170 BW115
Enfield EN3 30 DW40
Gravesend DA12 131 GJ91
Hayes UB3 77 BU72
Romford RM6 70 EY57
Ruislip HA4 78 BW65
Sidcup DA15 126 EU87
Twickenham TW2 116 CB86
Upminster RM14 72 FN63
Waltham Cross EN8 15 DX33
West Drayton UB7 76 BM74
Cedar Cl, E3 85 DZ67
SE21 122 DQ88
SW15 118 CR91
Borehamwood WD6 26 CP42
Brentwood (Hutt.) CM13 55 GD45
Bromley BR2 144 EL104
Buckhurst Hill IG9 48 EK47
Carshalton SM5 158 DF107
East Molesey KT8
off Cedar Rd 137 CE98
Epsom KT17 157 CT114
Esher KT10 154 BZ108
Iver SL0
off Thornbridge Rd 75 BC66
Potters Bar EN6 12 DA30
Romford RM7 71 FC56
Staines TW18 134 BJ97
Swanley BR8 147 FC96
Warlingham CR6 177 DY118
Cedar Copse, Brom. BR1 145 EM96
Cedar Ct, E11
off Grosvenor Rd 68 EH57
N1 off Essex Rd 84 DQ66
SE9 124 EL86
SW19 119 CX90
Egham TW20 113 BA91
Epping CM16 18 EU31
Cedar Cres, Brom. BR2 144 EL104
Cedarcroft Rd, Chess. KT9 156 CM105
Cedar Dr, N2 64 DE56
Dartford (Sutt.H.) DA4 148 FP96
Leatherhead (Fetch.) KT22 171 CE123
Loughton IG10 33 EP40
Pinner HA5 40 CA51
Cedar Gdns, Sutt. SM2 158 DC107
Upminster RM14 72 FQ62
Woking GU21
off St. John's Rd 166 AV118
Cedar Gro, W5 98 CL76
Bexley DA5 126 EW86
Southall UB1 78 CA71
Weybridge KT13 153 BQ105
Cedar Hts, Rich. TW10 118 CL88
Cedar Hill, Epsom KT18 172 CQ116
Cedar Ho, Croy. CR0 161 EB107
Sunbury-on-Thames TW16 115 BT94
Cedarhurst, Brom. BR1
off Elstree Hill 124 EE94
Cedarhurst Dr, SE9 124 EJ85
Cedar Lawn Av, Barn. EN5 27 CY43
Cedar Mt, SE9 124 EK88
Cedarne Rd, SW6 100 DB80
Cedar Pk, Cat. CR3 176 DS121
Chigwell IG7 off High Rd 49 EP49
Cedar Pk Gdns, Rom. RM6 70 EX59
Cedar Pk Rd, Enf. EN2 30 DQ38
Cedar Pl, SE7 off Floyd Rd 104 EJ78
Northwood HA6 39 BQ51
Cedar Ri, N14 44 DG45
South Ockendon RM15
off Sycamore Way 91 FX70
Cedar Rd, N17 46 DT53
NW2 63 CW63
Brentwood (Hutt.) CM13 55 GD44
Bromley BR1 144 EJ96
Cobham KT11 153 BV114
Croydon CR0 142 DS103
Dartford DA1 128 FK88
East Molesey KT8 137 CE98
Enfield EN2 29 DP38
Erith DA8 107 FG81
Feltham TW14 115 BR88
Grays RM16 111 GG76
Hornchurch RM12 72 FJ62
Hounslow TW4 96 BW82
Romford RM7 71 FC56
Sutton SM2 158 DC107
Teddington TW11 117 CG92
Watford WD19 24 BW44
Weybridge KT13 152 BN105
Woking GU22 166 AV120
Cedars, Bans. SM7 158 DF114
Cedars, The, E15 off Portway 86 EF67
W13 off Heronsforde 79 CJ72
Buckhurst Hill IG9 48 EG46
Leatherhead KT22 172 CL121
Reigate RH2 184 DD134
Teddington TW11
off Adelaide Rd 117 CF93
West Byfleet (Byfleet) KT14 152 BM112
Cedars Av, E17 67 EA57
Mitcham CR4 140 DG98
Rickmansworth WD3 38 BJ46
Cedars Cl, NW4 63 CX55
SE13 103 ED83
Gerrards Cross
(Chal.St.P.) SL9 36 AY50
Cedars Ct, N9 off Church St 46 DS47
Cedars Dr, Uxb. UB10 76 BM68
Cedars Ms, SW4
off Cedars Rd 101 DH84
Cedars Rd, E15 86 EE65
N9 off Church St 46 DU47
N21 45 DP47
SW4 101 DH83
SW13 99 CT82
W4 98 CQ78
Beckenham BR3 143 DY96
Cedars Rd, Croydon CR0 141 DL104
Kingston upon Thames
(Hmptn W.) KT1 137 CJ95
Morden SM4 140 DA98
Cedars Wk, Rick.
(Chorl.) WD3 21 BF42
Cedar Ter, Rich. TW9 98 CL84
Cedar Ter Rd, Sev. TN13 191 FJ123
Cedar Tree Gro, SE27 121 DP92
Cedarville Gdns, SW16 121 DM93
Cedar Vista, Rich. TW9
off Kew Rd 98 CL81
Cedar Wk, Esher (Clay.) KT10 155 CF107
Kenley CR8 176 DQ116
Tadworth (Kgswd) KT20 173 CY120
Waltham Abbey EN9 15 ED34
Cedar Way, NW1 83 DK66
Slough SL3 92 AY78
Sunbury-on-Thames TW16 115 BS94
Cedar Wd Dr, Wat. WD25 23 BV35
Cedra Ct, N16 66 DU60
Cedric Av, Rom. RM1 71 FE55
Cedric Rd, SE9 125 EQ90
Celadon Cl, Enf. EN3 31 DY41
Celandine Cl, E14 85 EA71
South Ockendon RM15 91 FW70
Celandine Dr, E8 84 DT66
SE28 88 EV74
Celandine Rd, Walt. KT12 154 BY105
Celandine Way, E15 86 EE69
Celbridge Ms, W2
off Porchester Rd 82 DB72
Celedon Cl, Grays RM16 110 FY75
Celestial Gdns, SE13 103 ED84
Celia Cres, Ashf. TW15 114 BK93
Celia Rd, N19 65 DJ63
Cell Fm Av, Wind.
(Old Wind.) SL4 112 AV85
Celtic Av, Brom. BR2 144 EE97
Celtic Rd, W.Byf.
(Byfleet) KT14 152 BL114
Celtic St, E14 85 EB71
Cement Block Cotts,
Grays RM17 110 GC79
Cemetery La, SE7 104 EL79
Shepperton TW17 135 BP101
Waltham Abbey EN9 16 EF25
Cemetery Rd, E7 68 EF63
N17 46 DS52
SE2 106 EV80
Cenacle Cl, NW3 64 DA62
★ Cenotaph, The, SW1 199 P4
Centaurs Business Cen,
Islw. TW7 97 CG79
Centaur St, SE1 200 C6
Centaury Ct, Grays RM17 110 GD79
Centenary Est, Enf. EN3 31 DZ42
Centenary Rd, Enf. EN3 31 DZ42
Centenary Wk, Loug. IG10 32 EH41
Centenary Way, Amer. HP6 20 AT38
Centennial Av, Borwd.
(Elstree) WD6 41 CH45
Centennial Pk, Borwd.
(Elstree) WD6 41 CJ45
Central Av, E11 67 ED61
N2 44 DD54
N9 46 DS48
SW11 100 DF80
Enfield EN1 30 DV40
Gravesend DA12 131 GH89
Grays RM20 109 FT77
Hayes UB3 77 BU73
Hounslow TW3 96 CC84
Pinner HA5 60 BZ58
South Ockendon
(Aveley) RM15 108 FQ75
Tilbury RM18 111 GG81
Wallington SM6 159 DL106
Waltham Cross EN8 15 DY33
Welling DA16 105 ET82
West Molesey KT8 136 BZ98
Central Circ, NW4
off Hendon Way 63 CV57
★ Central Criminal Ct
(Old Bailey), EC4 196 G8
Central Dr, Horn. RM12 72 FL62
Central Gdns, Mord. SM4
off Central Rd 140 DB99
Central Hill, SE19 122 DR92
Central Ho, E15 off High St 85 EC68
H Central Middlesex Hosp,
NW10 80 CQ69
Central Par, Croy.
(New Adgtn) CR0 161 EC110
Feltham TW14 116 BW87
Greenford UB6 79 CG69
Hounslow TW5
off Heston Rd 96 CA80
Surbiton KT6
off St. Mark's Hill 138 CL100
Central Pk Av, Dag. RM10 71 FB62
Central Pk Est, Houns. TW4 116 BX85
Central Pk Rd, E6 86 EK68
Central Pl, SE25
off Portland Rd 142 DV98
Central Rd, Dart. DA1 128 FL85
Morden SM4 140 DA99
Wembley HA0 61 CH64
Worcester Park KT4 139 CU103
Central Sch Footpath, SW14 98 CQ83
Central Sq, NW11 64 DB58
Wembley HA9
off Station Gro 62 CL64
West Molesey KT8 136 BZ98
Central St, EC1 197 H3
Central Wk, Epsom KT19
off Station App 156 CR113
Central Way, NW10 80 CQ69
SE28 88 EU74
Carshalton SM5 158 DE108
Feltham TW14 115 BV85
Oxted RH8 187 ED127
Centre, The, Felt. TW13 115 BU89
Walton-on-Thames KT12 135 BT102
Centre at the Circ, W1 199 L1
Centre Av, W3 80 CR74
W10 off Harrow Rd 81 CW69
Epping CM16 17 ET32
Centre Cl, Epp. CM16
off Centre Av 17 ET32
Centre Common Rd,
Chis. BR7 125 EQ93
Centre Ct Shop Cen, SW19 119 CZ93
Centre Dr, Epp. CM16 17 ET32
Centre Grn, Epp. CM16
off Centre Av 17 ET32
Centrepoint, WC1 195 N8
Centre Rd, E7 68 EG61
E11 68 EG61
Dagenham RM10 89 FB68
Centre St, E2 84 DV68
Centre Way, E17 47 EC52
N9 46 DW47
Centreway, Ilf. IG1 69 EQ61
Centric Cl, NW1 off Oval Rd 83 DH67
Centurion Cl, N7 83 DM66
Centurion Ct, Wall. SM6
off Wandle Rd 141 DH103
Centurion La, E3
off Libra Rd 85 DZ68
Centurion Way, Erith DA18 106 FA76
Purfleet RM19 108 FM77
Century Cl, NW4 63 CX57
Century Ct, Wok. GU21 167 AZ116
Century Ms, E5
off Lower Clapton Rd 66 DW63
Century Pk, Wat. WD17 24 BW43
Century Rd, E17 67 DY55
Staines TW18 113 BC92
Century Yd, SE23 122 DW89
Cephas Av, E1 84 DW70
Cephas St, E1 84 DW70
Ceres Rd, SE18 105 ET77
Cerise Rd, SE15 102 DU81
Cerne Cl, Hayes UB4 78 BX73
Cerne Rd, Grav. DA12 131 GL91
Morden SM4 140 DC100
Cerney Ms, W2
off Gloucester Ter 82 DD73
Cerotus Pl, Cher. KT16 133 BF101
Cervantes Ct, W2
off Inverness Ter 82 DB72
Northwood HA6
off Green La 39 BT52
Cervia Way, Grav. DA12 131 GM90
Cester St, E2 off Whiston Rd 84 DU67
Ceylon Rd, W14 99 CX76
Chace Av, Pot.B. EN6 12 DD32
Chadacre Av, Ilf. IG5 69 EM55
Chadacre Rd, Epsom KT17 157 CV107
Chadbourn St, E14 85 EB71
Chad Cres, N9 46 DW48
Chadd Dr, Brom. BR1 144 EL97
Chadd Grn, E13 86 EG67
Chadfields, Til. RM18 111 GG80
Chadview Ct, Rom.
(Chad.Hth) RM6 70 EX59
Chadville Gdns, Rom. RM6 70 EX57
Chadway, Dag. RM8 70 EW60
Chadwell Av, Rom. RM6 70 EV59
Waltham Cross (Chsht) EN8 14 DW28
Chadwell Bypass,
Grays RM16 111 GF78
CHADWELL HEATH,
Rom. RM6 70 EX58
⇌ Chadwell Heath 70 EX59
H Chadwell Heath Hosp,
Rom. RM6 70 EV57
Chadwell Heath La, Rom. RM6 70 EV57
Chadwell Hill, Grays RM16 111 GH78
Chadwell Rd, Grays RM17 110 GC77
CHADWELL ST. MARY,
Grays RM16 111 GJ76
Chadwell St, EC1 196 E2
Chadwick Av, E4 47 ED49
N21 off Laidlaw Dr 29 DM43
SW19 120 DA93
Chadwick Cl, SW15 119 CT87
W7 off Westcott Cres 79 CF71
Gravesend (Nthflt) DA11 130 GE89
Teddington TW11 117 CG93
Chadwick Dr, Rom.
(Harold Wd) RM3 52 FK54
Chadwick Ms, W4
off Thames Rd 98 CP79
Chadwick Pl, Surb. KT6 137 CJ101
Chadwick Rd, E11 68 EE59
NW10 81 CT67
SE15 102 DT82
Ilford IG1 69 EP62
Chadwick St, SW1 199 N7
Chadwick Way, SE28 88 EX73
Chadwin Rd, E13 86 EH71
Chadworth Way, Esher
(Clay.) KT10 155 CD106
Chaffers Mead, Ashtd. KT21 172 CM116
Chaffinch Av, Croy. CR0 143 DX100
Chaffinch Cl, N9 47 DX46
Croydon CR0 143 DX100
Surbiton KT6 138 CN104
Chaffinch La, Wat. WD18 39 BT45
Chaffinch Rd, Beck. BR3 143 DY95
CHAFFORD HUNDRED,
Grays RM16 110 FY76
⇌ Chafford Hundred 109 FV77
Chafford Wk, Rain. RM13 90 FJ68
Chafford Way, Rom. RM6 70 EW56
Chagford St, NW1 194 D5
Chailey Av, Enf. EN1 30 DT40
Chailey Cl, Houns. TW5
off Springwell Rd 96 BX81
Chailey Pl, Walt. KT12 154 BY105
Chailey St, E5 66 DW62
Chairmans Av, Uxb.
(Denh.) UB9 57 BF58
Chalbury Wk, N1 83 DM68
Chalcombe Rd, SE2 106 EV76
Chalcot Cl, Sutt. SM2 158 DA108
Chalcot Cres, NW1 82 DF67
Chalcot Gdns, NW3 82 DF65
Chalcot Ms, SW16 121 DL90
Chalcot Rd, NW1 82 DG66
Chalcot Sq, NW1 82 DG66
Chalcott Gdns, Surb. KT6 137 CJ102
Chalcroft Rd, SE13 124 EE85
CHALDON, Cat. CR3 175 DN124
Chaldon Common Rd,
Cat. CR3 176 DQ124
Chaldon Path, Th.Hth. CR7 141 DP98
Chaldon Rd, SW6 99 CY80
Chaldon Rd, Caterham CR3 176 DR124
Chaldon Way, Couls. CR5 175 DL117
Chale Rd, SW2 121 DL86
Chalet Cl, Bex. DA5 127 FD91
Chalet Est, NW7 43 CU49
Chale Wk, Sutt. SM2
off Hulverston Cl 158 DB109
⇌ Chalfont & Latimer 20 AW39
⊖ Chalfont & Latimer 20 AW39
Chalfont Av, Amer. HP6 20 AX39
Wembley HA9 80 CP65
CHALFONT COMMON,
Ger.Cr. SL9 37 AZ49
Chalfont Ct, NW9 63 CT55
Chalfont Grn, N9 46 DS48
Chalfont Gro, Ger.Cr. SL9
off Narcot La 36 AV51
Chalfont La, Ger.Cr. SL9 37 BC51
Rickmansworth
(Chorl.) WD3 21 BB43
Rickmansworth
(Map.Cr.) WD3 37 BC51
Chalfont Pk, Ger.Cr.
(Chal.St.P.) SL9 57 AZ55
Chalfont Rd, N9 46 DS48
SE25 142 DT97
Gerrards Cross SL9 37 BB48
Hayes UB3 95 BU75
Rickmansworth
(Map.Cr.) WD3 37 BD49
CHALFONT ST. GILES 36 AV47
CHALFONT ST. PETER,
Ger.Cr. SL9 37 AZ53
H Chalfonts & Gerrards Cross Hosp,
Ger.Cr. SL9 36 AX53
Chalfont Sta Rd, Amer. HP7 20 AW40
Chalfont Wk, Pnr. HA5
off Willows Cl 40 BW54
Chalfont Way, W13 97 CH76
Chalford Cl, W.Mol. KT8 136 CA98
Chalforde Gdns, Rom. RM2 71 FH56
Chalford Rd, SE21 122 DR91
Chalford Wk, Wdf.Grn. IG8 48 EK53
Chalgrove Av, Mord. SM4 140 DA99
Chalgrove Cres, Ilf. IG5 48 EL54
Chalgrove Gdns, N3 63 CY55
Chalgrove Rd, N17 46 DV53
Sutton SM2 158 DD108
Chalice Cl, Wall. SM6
off Lavender Vale 159 DK107
Chalice Way, Green. DA9 129 FS85
Chalkenden Cl, SE20 122 DV94
⊖ Chalk Farm 82 DG66
Chalk Fm Rd, NW1 82 DG66
Chalk Hill, Wat. WD19 24 BX44
Chalk Hill Rd, W6
off Shortlands 99 CX77
Chalkhill Rd, Wem. HA9 62 CP62
Chalklands, Wem. HA9 62 CQ62
Chalk La, Ashtd. KT21 172 CM119
Barnet EN4 28 DF42
Epsom KT18 172 CR115
Chalkley Cl, Mitch. CR4 140 DF96
Chalkmill Dr, Enf. EN1 30 DV41
Chalk Paddock, Epsom KT18 172 CR115
Chalk Pit Av, Orp. BR5 146 EW97
Chalkpit La, Bet. RH3 182 CP133
Oxted RH8 187 EC125
Chalk Pit Rd, Bans. SM7 174 DA117
Epsom KT18 172 CQ119
Chalk Pit Way, Sutt. SM1 158 DC106
Chalkpit Wd, Oxt. RH8 187 ED127
Chalk Rd, E13 86 EH71
Chalkstone Cl, Well. DA16 106 EU81
Chalkwell Pk Av, Enf. EN1 30 DS42
Chalky Bk, Grav. DA11 131 GG91
Chalky La, Chess. KT9 155 CK109
Challacombe Cl, Brwd.
(Hutt.) CM13 55 GB46
Challenge Cl, Grav. DA12 131 GM91
Challenge Ct, Lthd. KT22 171 CH119
Challenge Rd, Ashf. TW15 115 BQ90
Challice Way, SW2 121 DM88
Challin St, SE20 142 DW95
Challis Rd, Brent. TW8 97 CK78
Challock Cl, West.
(Bigg.H.) TN16 178 EJ116
Challoner Cl, N2 44 DD54
Challoner Cres, W14
off Challoner St 99 CZ78
Challoners Cl, E.Mol. KT8 137 CD98
Challoner St, W14 99 CZ78
Chalmers Ct, Rick.
(Crox.Grn) WD3 22 BM44
Chalmers Rd, Ashf. TW15 115 BP91
Banstead SM7 174 DD115
Chalmers Rd E, Ashf. TW15 115 BP91
Chalmers Wk, SE17
off Hillingdon St 101 DP79
Chalmers Way, Felt. TW14 115 BU85
Chaloner Ct, SE1 201 K4
Chalsey Rd, SE4 103 DZ84
Chalton Dr, N2 64 DC58
Chalton St, NW1 195 N2
Chalvey Gdns, Slou. SL1 92 AS75
Chalvey Pk, Slou. SL1 92 AS75
Chalvey Rd E, Slou. SL1 92 AS75
Chamberlain Cl, SE28
off Broadwater Rd 105 ER76
Chamberlain Cotts, SE5
off Camberwell Gro 102 DR81
Chamberlain Cres,
W.Wick. BR4 143 EB102
Chamberlain Gdns,
Houns. TW3 96 CC81
Chamberlain La, Pnr. HA5 59 BU56
Chamberlain Pl, E17 67 DY55
Chamberlain Rd, N2 44 DC54
N9 46 DU48
W13 off Midhurst Rd 97 CG75
Chamberlain St, NW1
off Regents Pk Rd 82 DF66
Chamberlain Wk, Felt. TW13
off Burgess Cl 116 BY91
Chamberlain Way, Pnr. HA5 59 BV55

A B C D E F G H I J K L M N O P Q R S T U V W X Y Z

★ Place of interest ⇌ Railway station ⊖ London Underground station DLR Docklands Light Railway station Tra Tramlink station H Hospital Riv Pedestrian ferry landing stage

231

★ Place of interest   ⇌ Railway station   ⊖ London Underground station   Ⓓ Docklands Light Railway station   Ⓣ Tramlink station   Ⓗ Hospital   Ⓡ Pedestrian ferry landing stage

232

Chattern Rd, Ashf. TW15 . . . . . 115 BQ91
Chatterton Ms, N4
off Chatterton Rd 65 DP62
Chatterton Rd, N4 . . . . 65 DP62
Bromley BR2. . . . . 144 EK98
Chatto Rd, SW11. . . . . 120 DF85
Chaucer Av, Hayes UB4 . . . . . . 77 BU71
Hounslow TW4 . . . . 95 BX82
Richmond TW9 . . . . 98 CN82
Weybridge KT13. . . . . 152 BN108
Chaucer Cl, N11 . . . . 45 DJ50
Banstead SM7 . . . . 157 CY114
Tilbury RM18. . . . . 111 GJ82
Chaucer Ct, N16. . . . . 66 DS63
Chaucer Dr, SE1 . . . . 202 A9
Chaucer Gdns, Sutt. SM1. . . . . 140 DA104
Chaucer Grn, Croy. CR0 . . . . . 142 DV101
Chaucer Ho, Sutt. SM1. . . . . . . 140 DA104
Chaucer Pk, Dart. DA1 . . . . . . 128 FM87
Chaucer Rd, E7. . . . . 86 EG65
E11. . . . . 68 EG58
E17 . . . . 47 EC54
SE24 . . . . 121 DN85
W3. . . . . 80 CQ74
Ashford TW15 . . . . 114 BL91
Gravesend (Nthflt) DA11. . . . 130 GD90
Romford RM3. . . . . 51 FH52
Sidcup DA15. . . . . 126 EW88
Sutton SM1. . . . . 158 DA105
Welling DA16 . . . . 105 ES81
Chaucer Way, SW19 . . . . 120 DD93
Addlestone KT15 . . . . 152 BG107
Dartford DA1 . . . . 108 FN84
Slough SL1 . . . . 74 AT74
Chauncey Cl, N9. . . . . 46 DU48
Chauncy Av, Pot.B. EN6 . . . . . . 12 DC33
Chaundrye Cl, SE9 . . . . 125 EM86
Chauntler Cl, E16 . . . . 86 EH73
Chavecroft Ter, Epsom KT18. . 173 CW119
Chave Rd, Dart. DA2 . . . . 128 FL90
Chaworth Cl, Cher. KT16 . . . . 151 BC107
Chaworth Rd, Cher.
(Ott.) KT16 . . . . 151 BC107
CHEAM, Sutt. SM3 . . . . 157 CX107
⇌ **Cheam**. 157 CY108
Cheam Cl, Tad. KT20
off Waterfield. 173 CV121
Cheam Common Rd,
Wor.Pk. KT4. . . . . 139 CV103
Cheam Mans, Sutt. SM3 . . . . 157 CY108
Cheam Pk Way, Sutt. SM3 . . . 157 CY107
Cheam Rd, Epsom KT17. . . . . 157 CU109
Sutton SM1. . . . . 157 CZ107
Sutton (E.Ewell) SM2 . . . . . 157 CX110
Cheam St, SE15
off Evelina Rd 102 DV83
Cheapside, EC2. . . . . 197 J9
N13 *off Taplow Rd*. 46 DQ49
Woking GU21 . . . . 150 AX114
Cheapside La, Uxb.
(Denh.) UB9 . . . . 57 BF61
Cheddar Cl, N11
off Martock Gdns 44 DG51
Cheddar Rd, Houns.
(Hthrw Air.) TW6
off Cromer Rd. 94 BN82
Cheddar Waye, Hayes UB4. . . . 77 BV72
Cheddington Rd, N18. . . . . 46 DS48
Chedworth Cl, E16
off Hallsville Rd. 86 EF72
Cheelson Rd, S.Ock. RM15. . . . 91 FW68
Cheeseman Cl, Hmptn. TW12. 116 BY93
Cheesemans Ter, W14. . . . . . . 99 CZ78
Cheldon Av, NW7 . . . . 43 CX52
Chelford Rd, Brom. BR1 . . . . . 123 ED92
Chelmer Cres, Bark. IG11 . . . . . 88 EV68
Chelmer Dr, Brwd.
(Hutt.) CM13 . . . . 55 GE44
South Ockendon RM15 . . . . 91 FW73
Chelmer Rd, E9. . . . . 67 DX64
Grays RM16. . . . . 111 GG78
Upminster RM14 . . . . 73 FR58
Chelmsford Av, Rom. RM5. . . . 51 FD52
Chelmsford Cl, E6
off Guildford Rd 87 EM72
W6. 99 CX79
Sutton SM2. . . . . 158 DA109
Chelmsford Dr, Upmin. RM14 . 72 FM62
Chelmsford Gdns, Ilf. IG1. . . . . . 68 EL59
Chelmsford Rd, E11 . . . . 67 ED60
E17 . . . . 67 EA58
E18 . . . . 48 EF53
N14 . . . . 45 DJ45
Brentwood (Shenf.) CM15 . . 55 FZ44
Chelmsford Sq, NW10 . . . . 81 CW67
CHELSEA, SW3. . . . . 100 DD79
🅷 **Chelsea & Westminster Hosp**,
SW10. . . . . 100 DC79
★ **Chelsea Antique Mkt**,
SW3. . . . . 100 DD79
Chelsea Br, SW1 . . . . 101 DH79
SW8. . . . . 101 DH79
Chelsea Br Rd, SW1 . . . . 198 F10
Chelsea Cloisters, SW3
off Lucan Pl. 100 DE77
Chelsea Cl, NW10
off Winchelsea Rd. 80 CR67
Edgware HA8 . . . . 42 CN54
Hampton (Hmptn H.)
TW12. . . . . 116 CC92
Worcester Park KT4 . . . . . . 139 CU101
Chelsea Cres, SW10
off Harbour Av 100 DC81
Chelsea Embk, SW3. . . . . 100 DE79
★ **Chelsea FC**, SW6. . . . . 100 DB80
Chelsea Gdns, W13
off Hathaway Gdns. 79 CF71
Sutton SM3. . . . . 157 CY105
Chelsea Harbour, SW10 . . . . . 100 DC81
Chelsea Harbour Dr, SW10. . . 100 DC81
🆁 **Chelsea Harbour Pier** 100 DD81
Chelsea Manor Ct, SW3
off Chelsea Manor St 100 DE79
Chelsea Manor Gdns, SW3 . . 100 DE79
Chelsea Manor St, SW3. . . . . . 100 DE78
Chelsea Ms, Horn. RM11
off St. Leonards Way 71 FH60
Chelsea Pk Gdns, SW3. . . . . . 100 DD79
★ **Chelsea Physic Gdn**, SW3 . 100 DF79
Chelsea Sq, SW3 . . . . 198 A10
Chelsea Vista, SW6
off The Boulevard 100 DC81
Chelsea Wf, SW10. . . . . 100 DD80
CHELSFIELD, Orp. BR6. . . . . . 164 EW106
⇌ **Chelsfield** 164 EV106
Chelsfield Av, N9 . . . . 47 DX45
Chelsfield Gdns, SE26 . . . . . . 122 DW90
Chelsfield Grn, N9
off Chelsfield Av 47 DX45
Chelsfield Hill, Orp. BR6. . . . . 164 EW109
Chelsfield La, Orp. BR5, BR6 . 146 EX101
Orpington (Maypole) BR6 . 164 FA108
Sevenoaks
TN14 . . . . 165 FC109
🅷 **Chelsfield Pk Hosp**,
Orp. BR6 . . . . 164 EZ106
Chelsfield Rd, Orp. BR5 . . . . . 146 EW100
CHELSHAM, Warl. CR6 . . . . . . 177 EA117
Chelsham Cl, Warl. CR6 . . . . . 177 DY118
Chelsham Common Rd,
Warl. CR6 . . . . 177 EA117
Chelsham Ct Rd, Warl. CR6 . . 177 ED118
Chelsham Rd, SW4. . . . . 101 DK83
South Croydon CR2 . . . . . . 160 DR107
Warlingham CR6. . . . . 177 EA117
Chelston App, Ruis. HA4 . . . . . 59 BU61
Chelston Rd, Ruis. HA4 . . . . . . 59 BU60
Chelsworth Cl, Rom. RM3
off Chelsworth Dr. 52 FM53
Chelsworth Dr, SE18 . . . . 105 ER79
Romford RM3. . . . . 52 FL53
Cheltenham Av, Twick. TW1. . . 117 CG87
Cheltenham Cl, Grav. DA12 . . 131 GJ92
New Malden KT3
off Northcote Rd. 138 CQ97
Northolt UB5. . . . . 78 CB65
Cheltenham Gdns, E6 . . . . 86 EL68
Loughton IG10 . . . . 32 EL44
Cheltenham Pl, W3. . . . . 80 CP74
Harrow HA3 . . . . 62 CL56
Cheltenham Rd, E10. . . . . 67 EC58
SE15 . . . . 102 DW84
Orpington BR6 . . . . 146 EU104
Cheltenham Ter, SW3. . . . . . . 198 E10
Cheltenham Vil, Stai. TW19. . . 113 BF86
Chelverton Rd, SW15 . . . . 99 CX84
Chelwood, N20
off Oakleigh Rd N. 44 DD47
Chelwood Cl, E4. . . . . 31 EB44
Coulsdon CR5
off Starrock Rd 175 DJ119
Epsom KT17 . . . . 157 CT112
Northwood HA6 . . . . 39 BQ52
Chelwood Gdns, Rich. TW9 . . . 98 CN82
Chelwood Gdns Pas, Rich. TW9
off Chelwood Gdns. 98 CN82
Chelwood Wk, SE4. . . . . 103 DY84
Chenappa Cl, E13. . . . . 86 EG69
Chenduit Way, Stan. HA7. . . . . 41 CF50
Cheney Row, E17 . . . . 47 DZ53
Cheneys Rd, E11. . . . . 68 EE62
Cheney St, Pnr. HA5. . . . . 60 BW57
CHENIES, Rick. WD3. . . . . 21 BB38
Chenies, The, Dart. DA2 . . . . . 127 FE91
Orpington BR6 . . . . 145 ES100
Chenies Av, Amer. HP6. . . . . . . 20 AW39
Chenies Hill, Hem.H.
(Flaun.) HP3 . . . . 5 BB34
★ **Chenies Manor**, Rick. WD3 . 21 BA38
Chenies Ms, WC1 . . . . 195 M5
Chenies Par, Amer. HP7 . . . . . . 20 AW40
Chenies Pl, NW1. . . . . 83 DK68
Chenies Rd, Rick. (Chorl.) WD3 . 21 BD40
Chenies St, WC1. . . . . 195 M6
Chenies Way, Wat. WD18 . . . . . 39 BS45
Cheniston Cl, W.Byf. KT14 . . . 152 BG113
Cheniston Gdns, W8. . . . . 100 DB76
Chepstow Av, Horn. RM12. . . . 72 FL62
Chepstow Cl, SW15
off Lytton Gro 119 CY86
Chepstow Cres, W11. . . . . 82 DA73
Ilford IG3. . . . . 69 ES58
Chepstow Gdns, Sthl. UB1 . . . 78 BZ72
Chepstow Pl, W2 . . . . 82 DA72
Chepstow Ri, Croy. CR0. . . . . . 142 DS104
Chepstow Rd, W2. . . . . 82 DA72
W7. 97 CG76
Croydon CR0. . . . . 142 DS104
Chepstow Vil, W11 . . . . 81 CZ73
Chepstow Way, SE15 . . . . 102 DT80
Chequers, Buck.H. IG9
off Hills Rd 48 EH46
Chequers Cl, NW9 . . . . 62 CS55
Orpington BR5 . . . . 145 ET98
Tadworth KT20 . . . . 183 CU125
Chequers Gdns, N13 . . . . 45 DP50
Chequers La, Dag. RM9 . . . . . . 88 EZ70
Tadworth KT20 . . . . 183 CU125
Watford WD25 . . . . 8 BW30
Chequers Orchard, Iver SL0. . . 75 BF72
Chequers Par, SE9
off Eltham High St 125 EM86
Chequers Rd, Brwd. CM14. . . . 52 FM46
Loughton IG10 . . . . 33 EN43
Romford RM3. . . . . 52 FL47
Chequers Sq, Uxb. UB8
off High St. 76 BJ66
Chequer St, EC1 . . . . 197 J5
Chequers Wk, Wal.Abb. EN9 . . 16 EF33
Chequers Way, N13 . . . . 46 DQ50
Chequer Tree Cl, Wok.
(Knap.) GU21 . . . . 166 AS116
Cherbury Cl, SE28 . . . . 88 EX72
Cherbury Ct, N1 . . . . 197 L1
Cherbury St, N1 . . . . 197 L1
Cherchefelle Ms, Stan. HA7 . . . 41 CH50
Cherimoya Gdns, W.Mol. KT8
off Kelvinbrook. 136 CB97
Cherington Rd, W7 . . . . 79 CF74
Cheriton Av, Brom. BR2 . . . . . 144 EF99
Ilford IG5. . . . . 49 EM54
Cheriton Cl, W5. . . . . 79 CJ71
Barnet EN4 . . . . 28 DF41
Cheriton Ct, Walt. KT12
off St. Johns Dr. 136 BW102
Cheriton Dr, SE18 . . . . 105 ER80
Cheriton Sq, SW17 . . . . 120 DG89
Cherries, The, Slou. SL2 . . . . . 74 AV72
Cherry Acre, Ger.Cr.
(Chal.St.P.) SL9 . . . . 36 AX49
Cherry Av, Brwd. CM13 . . . . . . 55 FZ48
Slough SL3 . . . . 92 AX75
Southall UB1. . . . . 78 BX74
Swanley BR8. . . . . 147 FD97
Cherry Blossom Cl, N13 . . . . . . 45 DP50
Cherry Cl, E17 *off Eden Rd*. . . . 67 EB56
NW9 . . . . 42 CS54
SW2 *off Tulse Hill* 121 DN87
W5. 97 CK76
Banstead SM7 . . . . 157 CX114
Carshalton SM5 . . . . 140 DF103
Morden SM4. . . . . 139 CY98
Ruislip HA4
off Roundways 59 BT62
Cherrycot Hill, Orp. BR6. . . . . 163 ER105
Cherrycot Ri, Orp. BR6 . . . . . . 163 EQ105
Cherry Cres, Brent. TW8 . . . . . . 97 CH80
Cherry Cft, Rick.
(Crox.Grn) WD3. . . . . 22 BN44
Cherrycroft Gdns, Pnr. HA5
off Westfield Pk. 40 BZ52
Cherrydale, Wat. WD18. . . . . . . 23 BT42
Cherrydown Av, E4. . . . . 47 DZ48
Cherrydown Cl, E4 . . . . 47 DZ48
Cherrydown Rd, Sid. DA14. . . . 126 EX89
Cherrydown Wk, Rom. RM7. . . . 51 FB54
Cherry Gdns, Dag. RM9 . . . . . . 70 EZ64
Northolt UB5. . . . . 78 CB66
Cherry Gdn St, SE16 . . . . 202 D5
Cherry Garth, Brent. TW8 . . . . . 97 CK77
Cherry Gro, Hayes UB3 . . . . . . 77 BV74
Uxbridge UB8. . . . . 77 BP71
Cherry Hill, Barn. EN5 . . . . 28 DB44
Harrow HA3 . . . . 41 CE51
Rickmansworth
(Loud.) WD3 . . . . 22 BH41
St. Albans AL2 . . . . 8 CA25
Cherry Hill Gdns, Croy. CR0 . . 159 DM105
Cherry Hills, Wat. WD19 . . . . . . 40 BY50
Cherry Hollow, Abb.L. WD5 . . . . 7 BT31
Cherrylands Cl, NW9 . . . . 62 CQ61
Cherry La, West Dr. UB7 . . . . . 94 BM77
Cherry La Roundabout,
West Dr. UB7 . . . . 95 BP77
Cherry Laurel Wk, SW2
off Beechdale Rd. 121 DM86
Cherry Orchard, Amer. HP6 . . . 20 AS37
Ashtead KT21 . . . . 172 CP118
Slough (Stoke P.) SL2. . . . . . 74 AV66
Staines TW18. . . . . 114 BG92
West Drayton UB7 . . . . 94 BL75
Cherry Orchard Cl, Orp. BR5 . 146 EW99
Cherry Orchard Gdns, Croy. CR0
off Oval Rd 142 DR103
West Molesey KT8 . . . . 136 BZ97
Cherry Orchard Rd,
Brom. BR2. . . . . 144 EL103
Croydon CR0. . . . . 142 DR103
West Molesey KT8 . . . . 136 CA97
Cherry Ri, Ch.St.G. HP8 . . . . . . 36 AX47
Cherry Rd, Enf. EN3 . . . . 30 DW38
Cherry St, Rom. RM7 . . . . 71 FD57
Woking GU21 . . . . 166 AY118
Cherry Tree Av, St.Alb.
(Lon.Col.) AL2 . . . . 9 CK26
Staines TW18. . . . . 114 BH93
West Drayton UB7 . . . . 76 BM72
Cherry Tree Cl, E9
off Moulins Rd 84 DW67
Grays RM17. . . . . 110 GC79
Rainham RM13. . . . . 89 FG68
Wembley HA0. . . . . 61 CF63
Cherry Tree Ct, NW9. . . . . 62 CQ56
Coulsdon CR5. . . . . 175 DM117
Cherry Tree Dr, SW16 . . . . . . 121 DL90
South Ockendon RM15 . . . . 91 FX70
Cherry Tree Grn, S.Croy. CR2 . 160 DV114
Cherry Tree La, Dart. DA2 . . . 127 FF90
Epsom KT19
off Christ Ch Rd 156 CN112
Cherrytree La, Ger.Cr.
(Chal.St.P.) SL9 . . . . 36 AX54
Cherry Tree La, Iver SL0 . . . . . 76 BG67
Potters Bar EN6 . . . . 12 DB34
Rainham RM13. . . . . 89 FE69
Rickmansworth
(Herons.) WD3. . . . . 37 BC46
Slough (Fulmer) SL3 . . . . 75 AZ65
Cherry Tree Ri, Buck.H. IG9. . . 48 EJ49
Cherry Tree Rd, E15
off Wingfield Rd 68 EE63
N2 . . . . 64 DF56
Watford WD24. . . . . 23 BV36
Cherrytrees, Couls. CR5
off Netherne Dr. 175 DK121
Cherry Tree Wk, EC1 . . . . 197 J5
Beckenham BR3 . . . . 143 DZ98
West Wickham BR4. . . . . . . 162 EF105
Cherry Tree Way, Stan. HA7 . . . 41 CH51
Cherry Wk, Brom. BR2 . . . . . . 144 EG102
Grays RM16. . . . . 111 GG76
Rainham RM13. . . . . 89 FF68
Rickmansworth (Loud.) WD3 . 22 BJ40
Cherry Way, Epsom KT19. . . . 156 CR107
Shepperton TW17. . . . . 135 BR98
Slough (Horton) SL3. . . . . 93 BC83
Cherrywood Av, Egh.
(Eng.Grn) TW20. . . . . 112 AV93
Cherrywood Cl, E3 . . . . 85 DY69
Kingston upon Thames KT2 . 118 CN94
Cherrywood Dr, SW15 . . . . . . 119 CX85
Gravesend (Nthflt) DA11. . . . 130 GE90
Cherrywood La, Mord. SM4. . . 139 CY98
Cherry Wd Way, W5
off Hanger Vale La 80 CN71
Cherston Gdns, Loug. IG10
off Cherston Rd 33 EN42
Cherston Rd, Loug. IG10 . . . . . 33 EN42
CHERTSEY 134 BG102
⇌ **Chertsey** 133 BF102
Chertsey Br Rd, Cher. KT16 . . . 134 BK101
Chertsey Cl, Ken. CR8. . . . . . . 175 DP115
Chertsey Cres, Croy.
(New Adgtn) CR0 . . . . 161 EC110
Chertsey Dr, Sutt. SM3. . . . . . 139 CY103
Chertsey La, Cher. KT16. . . . . 133 BE95
Epsom KT19 . . . . 156 CN112
Staines TW18. . . . . 113 BE92
★ **Chertsey Mus**, Cher. KT16 . 134 BG100
Chertsey Rd, E11. . . . . 67 ED61
Chertsey Rd,
Addlestone KT15 . . . . 134 BH103
Ashford TW15 . . . . 115 BR94
Feltham TW13 . . . . 115 BS92
Ilford IG1. . . . . 69 ER63
Shepperton TW17 . . . . 134 BN101
Sunbury-on-Thames TW16 . 115 BR94
Twickenham TW1, TW2 . . . . 117 CF86
West Byfleet (Byfleet) KT14 . 152 BK111
Woking GU21 . . . . 151 BA113
Woking (Chobham) GU24 . . 150 AY110
Chertsey St, SW17 . . . . 120 DG92
Chervil Cl, Felt. TW13 . . . . 115 BU90
Chervil Ms, SE28 . . . . 88 EV74
Cherwell Cl, Rick.
(Crox.Grn) WD3. . . . . 22 BN43
Slough SL3 *off Tweed Rd* . . . 93 BB79
Cherwell Ct, Epsom KT19 . . . . 156 CQ105
Cherwell Gro, S.Ock. RM15 . . . . 91 FV73
Cherwell Way, Ruis. HA4 . . . . . 59 BQ58
Cheryls Cl, SW6 . . . . 100 DB81
Cheseman St, SE26 . . . . 122 DV90
Chesfield Rd, Kings.T. KT2 . . . 118 CL94
Chesham Av, Orp. BR5. . . . . . . 145 EP100
Chesham Cl, SW1. . . . . 198 F7
Romford RM7. . . . . 71 FD56
Sutton SM2. . . . . 157 CY110
Chesham Ct, Nthwd. HA6
off Frithwood Av. 39 BT51
Chesham Cres, SE20 . . . . 142 DW96
Chesham La, Ch.St.G. HP8. . . . 36 AY48
Gerrards Cross
(Chal.St.P.) SL9 . . . . 36 AY49
Chesham Ms, SW1. . . . . 198 F6
Chesham Pl, SW1. . . . . 198 F7
Chesham Rd, SE20. . . . . 142 DW96
SW19. . . . . 120 DD92
Hemel Hempstead
(Bov.) HP3 . . . . 4 AY27
Kingston upon Thames KT1 . 138 CN95
Chesham St, NW10 . . . . 62 CR62
SW1. . . . . 198 F7
Chesham Ter, W13 . . . . 97 CH75
Chesham Way, Wat. WD18 . . . . 23 BS44
Cheshire Cl, E17 . . . . 47 EB53
SE4 . . . . 103 DZ82
Chertsey (Ott.) KT16. . . . . . . 151 BC107
Hornchurch RM11. . . . . 72 FN57
Mitcham CR4 . . . . 141 DL97
Cheshire Ct, EC4. . . . . 196 E9
Slough SL1
off Clements Cl. 92 AV75
Cheshire Dr, Wat. WD25
off Ashfields 7 BT34
Cheshire Gdns, Chess. KT9 . . . 155 CK107
Cheshire Ho, N18 . . . . 46 DV49
Cheshire Rd, N22 . . . . 45 DM52
Cheshire St, E2. . . . . 84 DT70
Chesholm Rd, N16 . . . . 66 DS62
CHESHUNT, Wal.Cr. EN8 . . . . . 15 DX31
⇌ **Cheshunt** 15 DZ30
🅷 **Cheshunt Comm Hosp**,
Wal.Cr. EN8 . . . . 15 DY31
Cheshunt Pk, Wal.Cr.
(Chsht) EN7. . . . . 14 DV26
Cheshunt Rd, E7. . . . . 86 EH65
Belvedere DA17 . . . . 106 FA78
Cheshunt Wash, Wal.Cr.
(Chsht) EN8. . . . . 15 DY27
Chesil Ct, E2 . . . . 84 DW68
Chesilton Rd, SW6 . . . . 99 CZ81
Chesil Way, Hayes UB4 . . . . . . 77 BT69
Chesley Gdns, E6 . . . . 86 EK68
Cheslyn Gdns, Wat. WD17 . . . . 23 BT37
Chesney Cres, Croy.
(New Adgtn) CR0 . . . . 161 EC108
Chesney St, SW11 . . . . 100 DG81
Chesnut Est, N17 . . . . 66 DT55
Chesnut Gro, N17
off Chesnut Rd 66 DT55
Chesnut Pl, SE26
off Sydenham Hill. 122 DT91
Chesnut Rd, N17 . . . . 66 DT55
Chess Cl, Chesh. (Latimer) HP5 . 20 AX36
Rickmansworth (Loud.) WD3 . 22 BK42
Chessell Cl, Th.Hth. CR7 . . . . . 141 DP98
Chessfield Pk, Amer. HP6. . . . . 20 AY39
Chess Hill, Rick. (Loud.) WD3 . . 22 BK42
Chessholme Ct, Sun. TW16
off Scotts Av 115 BS94
Chessholme Rd, Ashf. TW15. . 115 BQ93
Chessinghams, The,
Epsom KT18. . . . . 156 CR113
CHESSINGTON. 156 CL107
Chessington Av, N3 . . . . 63 CY55
Bexleyheath DA7 . . . . 106 EY80
Chessington Cl, Epsom KT19. 156 CQ107
Chessington Ct, Pnr. HA5. . . . . 60 BZ56
Chessington Hall Gdns,
Chess. KT9 . . . . 155 CK108
Chessington Hill Pk,
Chess. KT9 . . . . 156 CN106
Chessington Lo, N3 . . . . 63 CZ55
⇌ **Chessington North** 156 CL106
Chessington Rd,
Epsom KT17, KT19 . . . . 157 CT109
⇌ **Chessington South**. 155 CK108
Chessington Way,
W.Wick. BR4. . . . . 143 EB103
★ **Chessington World of Adventure**,
Chess. KT9 . . . . 155 CJ110
Chess La, Rick. (Loud.) WD3. . . 22 BK42
Chesson Rd, W14 . . . . 99 CZ79
Chess Vale Ri, Rick.
(Crox.Grn) WD3. . . . . 22 BM44
Chess Valley Wk, Chesh. HP5 . . 20 AU35
Rickmansworth WD3 . . . . . . 22 BL44
Chess Way, Rick. (Chorl.) WD3 . 22 BG41
Chesswood Way, Pnr. HA5. . . . 40 BX54
Chester Av, Rich. TW10 . . . . . . 118 CM85
Twickenham TW2 . . . . 116 BZ88
Upminster RM14 . . . . 73 FS61
Chester Cl, SW1 . . . . 198 G5
SW13. . . . . 99 CV83
Ashford TW15 . . . . 115 BR92
Loughton IG10 . . . . 33 EQ39
Potters Bar EN6 . . . . 12 DB29
Sutton SM1. . . . . 140 DA103
Uxbridge UB8
off Dawley Av 77 BP72
Chester Cl N, NW1 . . . . 195 J2
Chester Cl S, NW1 . . . . 195 J3
Chester Cotts, SW1 . . . . 198 F9
Chester Ct, NW1. . . . . 195 J2
SE5 . . . . 102 DR80
Chester Cres, E8
off Ridley Rd. 84 DT65
Chester Dr, Har. HA2 . . . . 60 BZ58
Chesterfield Cl, Orp. BR5 . . . . 146 EX98
Chesterfield Dr, Dart. DA1 . . . . 127 FH85
Esher KT10 . . . . 137 CG103
Sevenoaks TN13 . . . . 190 FD122
Chesterfield Gdns, N4 . . . . 65 DP57
SE10 *off Crooms Hill*. 103 ED80
W1. 199 H2
Chesterfield Gro, SE22. . . . . . . 122 DT85
Chesterfield Hill, W1. . . . . 199 H1
Chesterfield Ms, N4
off Chesterfield Gdns 65 DP57
Ashford TW15
off Chesterfield Rd 114 BL91
Chesterfield Rd, E10. . . . . 67 EC58
N3 . . . . 44 DA51
W4. 98 CQ79
Ashford TW15 . . . . 114 BL91
Barnet EN5 . . . . 27 CX43
Enfield EN3. . . . . 31 DY37
Epsom KT19 . . . . 156 CR108
Chesterfield St, W1. . . . . 199 H2
Chesterfield Wk, SE10. . . . . . . 103 ED81
Chesterfield Way, SE15. . . . . . 102 DW80
Hayes UB3 . . . . 95 BU75
Chesterford Gdns, NW3. . . . . . 64 DB63
Chesterford Ho, SE18
off Shooter's Hill Rd 104 EK80
Chesterford Rd, E12 . . . . 69 EM64
Chester Gdns, W13. . . . . 79 CG72
Enfield EN3. . . . . 30 DV44
Morden SM4. . . . . 140 DC100
Chester Gate, NW1. . . . . 195 H3
Chester Gibbons Grn,
St.Alb. (Lon.Col.) AL2
off High St. 9 CK26
Chester Grn, Loug. IG10. . . . . . 33 EQ39
Chester Ms, E17
off Chingford Rd. 47 EA54
SW1. . . . . 199 H6
Chester Path, Loug. IG10 . . . . . 33 EQ39
Chester Pl, NW1 . . . . 195 H2
Chester Rd, E7 . . . . 86 EK66
E11. 68 EH58
E16 . . . . 86 EE70
E17 . . . . 67 DX57
N9. 46 DV46
N17 . . . . 66 DR55
N19 . . . . 65 DH61
NW1 . . . . 194 G3
SW19. . . . . 119 CW93
Borehamwood WD6. . . . . 26 CQ41
Chigwell IG7 . . . . 49 EN48
Hounslow TW4 . . . . 95 BV83
Hounslow (Hthrw Air.) TW6 . 94 BN83
Ilford IG3. . . . . 69 ET60
Loughton IG10 . . . . 33 EP40
Northwood HA6 . . . . 39 BS52
Sidcup DA15. . . . . 125 ES85
Watford WD18. . . . . 23 BU43
Chester Row, SW1 . . . . 198 F9
Chesters, The, N.Mal. KT3 . . . 138 CS95
Chester Sq, SW1 . . . . 199 H8
Chester Sq Ms, SW1 . . . . 199 H7
Chester St, E2. . . . . 84 DU70
SW1. . . . . 198 G6
Chester Ter, NW1 . . . . 195 H2
Chesterton Cl, SW18
off Ericcson Cl. 120 DA85
Greenford UB6. . . . . 78 CB68
Chesterton Dr, Red. RH1 . . . . . 185 DL128
Staines TW19. . . . . 114 BM88
Chesterton Ho, SW11
off Ingrave St 100 DD83
Chesterton Rd, E13. . . . . 86 EG69
W10. . . . . 81 CX71
Chesterton Sq, W8
off Pembroke Rd. 99 CZ77
Chesterton Ter, E13. . . . . 86 EG69
Kingston upon Thames KT1 . 138 CN96
Chesterton Way, Til. RM18 . . . 111 GJ82
Chester Way, SE11 . . . . 200 E9
Chesthunte Rd, N17. . . . . 46 DQ53
Chestnut All, SW6
off Lillie Rd 99 CZ79
Chestnut Av, E7 . . . . 68 EH63
N8. 65 DL57
SW14 *off Thornton Rd* 98 CR83
Brentford TW8. . . . . 97 CK77
Brentwood CM14 . . . . 54 FS45
Buckhurst Hill IG9. . . . . 48 EK48
East Molesey KT8. . . . . 137 CF97
Edgware HA8 . . . . 42 CL51
Epsom KT19 . . . . 156 CS105
Esher KT10 . . . . 137 CD101
Grays RM16. . . . . 110 GB75
Greenhithe
(Bluewater) DA9. . . . . 129 FT87
Hampton TW12 . . . . 116 CA94
Hornchurch RM12. . . . . 71 FF61
Northwood HA6 . . . . 39 BT54
Rickmansworth WD3 . . . . . . 22 BG43
Slough SL3. . . . . 92 AY75
Teddington TW11 . . . . 137 CF96
Virginia Water GU25. . . . . . . 132 AT98
Walton-on-Thames
(Whiteley Vill.) KT12 . . . . . 153 BS109
Wembley HA0. . . . . 61 CH64
West Drayton UB7 . . . . 76 BM73
West Wickham BR4. . . . . 162 EE106
Westerham TN16. . . . . 178 EK122
Weybridge KT13. . . . . 153 BQ108
Chestnut Av N, E17 . . . . 67 EC56
Chestnut Av S, E17. . . . . 67 EC56
Chestnut Cl, N14 . . . . 29 DJ43
N16 *off Lordship Gro* 66 DR61
SE6 . . . . 123 EC92
SE14 . . . . 103 DZ81

★ Place of interest ⇌ Railway station ⊖ London Underground station DLR Docklands Light Railway station Tra Tramlink station 🅷 Hospital Riv Pedestrian ferry landing stage

Chestnut Cl, SW16 121 DN91
Addlestone KT15 152 BK106
Amersham HP6 20 AS37
Ashford TW15 115 BP91
Buckhurst Hill IG9 48 EK47
Carshalton SM5 140 DF102
Egham (Eng.Grn) TW20 112 AW93
Gerrards Cross
(Chal.St.P.) SL9 37 AZ52
Gravesend (Nthflt) DA11
off Burch Rd 131 GF86
Hayes UB3 77 BS73
Hornchurch RM12
off Lancaster Dr 72 FJ63
Orpington BR6 164 EU106
Sidcup DA15 126 EU88
Sunbury-on-Thames TW16 115 BT93
Tadworth KT20 174 DA123
West Drayton UB7 95 BP80
Woking (Ripley) GU23 168 BG124
Chestnut Copse, Oxt. RH8 188 EG132
Chestnut Ct, SW6
off North End Rd 99 CZ79
Amersham HP6 20 AS37
Surbiton KT6
off Penners Gdns 138 CL101
Chestnut Cres, Walt.
(Whiteley Vill.) KT12
off Chestnut Av 153 BS109
Chestnut Dr, E11 68 EG58
Bexleyheath DA7 106 EX83
Egham (Eng.Grn) TW20 112 AX93
Harrow HA3 41 CF52
Pinner HA5 60 BX58
Chestnut Glen, Horn. RM12 71 FF61
Chestnut Gro, SE20 122 DW94
SW12 120 DG87
W5 97 CK76
Barnet EN4 28 DF43
Brentwood CM14 54 FW47
Dartford DA2 127 FD91
Ilford IG6 49 ES51
Isleworth TW7 97 CG84
Mitcham CR4 141 DK98
New Malden KT3 138 CR97
South Croydon CR2 160 DV108
Staines TW18 114 BJ93
Wembley HA0 61 CH64
Woking GU22 166 AY120
Chestnut La, N20 43 CY46
Sevenoaks TN13 191 FH124
Weybridge KT13 153 BP106
Chestnut Manor Cl,
Stai. TW18 114 BH92
Chestnut Mead, Red. RH1
off Oxford Rd 184 DE133
Chestnut Pl, Ashtd. KT21 172 CL119
Epsom KT17 157 CU111
Chestnut Ri, SE18 105 ER79
Bushey WD23 40 CB45
Chestnut Rd, SE27 121 DP90
SW20 139 CX96
Ashford TW15 115 BP91
Dartford DA1 128 FK88
Enfield EN3 31 DY36
Kingston upon Thames KT2 118 CL94
Twickenham TW2 117 CE89
Chestnut Row, N3
off Nether St 44 DA52
Chestnuts, Brwd.
(Hutt.) CM13 55 GB46
Chestnuts, The, Rom.
(Abridge) RM4 34 EV41
Walton-on-Thames KT12 135 BU102
Chestnut Wk, Ger.Cr.
(Chal.St.P.) SL9 36 AY52
Sevenoaks TN15 191 FL129
Shepperton TW17 135 BS99
Walton-on-Thames
(Whiteley Vill.) KT12
off Octagon Rd 153 BS109
Watford WD24 23 BU37
West Byfleet (Byfleet) KT14
off Royston Rd 152 BL112
Woodford Green IG8 48 EG50
Chestnut Way, Felt. TW13 115 BV90
Cheston Av, Croy. CR0 143 DY103
Chestwood Gro, Uxb. UB10 76 BM66
Cheswick Cl, Dart. DA1 107 FF84
Chesworth Cl, Erith DA8 107 FE81
Chettle Cl, SE1 201 K6
Chettle Ct, N8 65 DN58
Chetwode Dr, Epsom KT18 173 CX118
Chetwode Rd, SW17 120 DF90
Tadworth KT20 173 CW119
Chetwood Wk, E6 86 EL72
Chetwynd Av, Barn. EN4 44 DF46
Chetwynd Dr, Uxb. UB10 76 BM68
Chetwynd Rd, NW5 65 DH63
Chevalier Cl, Stan. HA7 42 CL49
Cheval Pl, SW7 198 C6
Cheval St, E14 203 P6
Cheveley Cl, Rom. RM3
off Chelsworth Dr 52 FM53
Chevely Cl, Epp.
(Cooper.) CM16 18 EX29
Cheveney Wk, Brom. BR2
off Marina Cl 144 EG97
CHEVENING, Sev. TN14 180 EZ119
Chevening Cross, Sev.
(Chev.) TN14 180 FA120
Chevening La, Sev.
(Knock.) TN14 180 EY115
Chevening Rd, NW6 81 CX68
SE10 104 EF78
SE19 122 DR93
Sevenoaks TN13, TN14 180 EZ119
Sevenoaks (Sund.) TN14 180 EY123
Chevenings, The, Sid. DA14 126 EW90
Cheverton Rd, N19 65 DK60
Chevet St, E9
off Kenworthy Rd 67 DY64
Chevington Pl, Horn. RM12
off Chevington Way 72 FK64
Chevington Way, Horn. RM12 72 FK63
Cheviot Cl, Bans. SM7 174 DB115
Bexleyheath DA7 107 FE82
Bushey WD23 24 CC44
Enfield EN1 30 DR40
Hayes UB3 95 BR80
Sutton SM2 158 DD109
Cheviot Gdns, NW2 63 CX61
SE27 121 DP91
Cheviot Gate, NW2 63 CY61
Cheviot Rd, SE27 121 DN92
Hornchurch RM11 71 FG60
Slough SL3 93 BA78
Cheviot Way, Ilf. IG2 69 ES56
Chevron Cl, E16 86 EG72
Chevy Rd, Sthl. UB2 96 CC75
Chewton Rd, E17 67 DY56
Cheyham Gdns, Sutt. SM2 157 CX110
Cheyham Way, Sutt. SM2 157 CY110
Cheyne Av, E18 68 EF55
Twickenham TW2 116 BZ88
Cheyne Cl, NW4 63 CW57
Bromley BR2
off Cedar Cres 144 EL104
Gerrards Cross SL9 56 AY60
Cheyne Ct, SW3 *off Flood St* 100 DF79
Banstead SM7 *off Park Rd* 174 DB115
Cheyne Gdns, SW3 100 DE79
Cheyne Hill, Surb. KT5 138 CM98
Cheyne Ms, SW3 100 DE79
Cheyne Path, W7 79 CF71
Cheyne Pl, SW3 100 DF79
Cheyne Rd, Ashf. TW15 115 BR93
Cheyne Row, SW3 100 DE79
Cheyne Wk, N21 29 DP43
NW4 63 CW58
SW3 100 DE79
SW10 100 DD80
Croydon CR0 142 DU103
Longfield DA3
off Cavendish Sq 149 FX97
Cheyneys Av, Edg. HA8 41 CK51
Chichele Gdns, Croy. CR0
off Brownlow Rd 160 DT105
Chichele Rd, NW2 63 CX64
Oxted RH8 188 EE128
Chicheley Gdns, Har. HA3 40 CC52
Chicheley Rd, Har. HA3 40 CC52
Chicheley St, SE1 200 C4
Chichester Av, Ruis. HA4 59 BR61
Chichester Cl, E6 86 EL72
SE3 104 EJ81
Grays RM16
off Warren La 109 FX77
Hampton TW12
off Maple Cl 116 BZ93
South Ockendon
(Aveley) RM15 90 FQ74
Chichester Ct, Epsom KT17 157 CT109
Slough SL1 92 AV75
Stanmore HA7 62 CL55
Chichester Dr, Pur. CR8 159 DM112
Sevenoaks TN13 190 FF125
Chichester Gdns, Ilf. IG1 68 EL59
Chichester Ms, SE27 121 DN91
Chichester Rents, WC2 196 D8
Chichester Ri, Grav. DA12 131 GK91
Chichester Rd, E11 68 EE62
N9 46 DU46
NW6 82 DA68
W2 82 DB71
Croydon CR0 142 DS104
Greenhithe DA9 129 FT85
Chichester St, SW1 101 DJ78
Chichester Way, E14 204 F8
Feltham TW14 115 BV87
Watford WD25 8 BY33
Chicksand St, E1 84 DT71
Chiddingfold, N12 44 DA48
Chiddingstone Av,
Bexh. DA7 106 EZ80
Chiddingstone Cl, Sutt. SM2 158 DA110
Chiddingstone St, SW6 100 DA82
Chieftan Dr, Purf. RM19 108 FM77
Chieveley Rd, Bexh. DA7 107 FB84
Chiffinch Gdns, Grav.
(Nthflt) DA11 130 GE90
Chignell Pl, W13
off The Broadway 79 CG74
CHIGWELL 49 EP48
⊖ Chigwell 49 EP49
Chigwell Hill, E1 202 D1
Chigwell Hurst Ct, Pnr. HA5 60 BX55
Chigwell La, Loug. IG10 33 EQ43
Chigwell Pk, Chig. IG7 49 EP49
Chigwell Pk Dr, Chig. IG7 49 EN48
Chigwell Ri, Chig. IG7 49 EN47
Chigwell Rd, E18 68 EH55
Woodford Green IG8 48 EJ54
CHIGWELL ROW, Chig. IG7 50 EU47
Chigwell Vw, Rom. RM5
off Lodge La 50 FA51
Chilberton Dr, Red. RH1 185 DJ130
Chilbrook Rd, Cob.
(Down.) KT11 169 BU118
Chilcombe Ho, SW15
off Fontley Way 119 CU87
Chilcot Cl, E14
off Grundy St 85 EB72
Chilcote La, Amer.
(Lt.Chal.) HP7 20 AV39
Chilcott Cl, Wem. HA0 61 CJ63
Chilcott Rd, Wat. WD24 23 BS36
Childebert Rd, SW17 121 DH89
Childeric Rd, SE14 103 DY80
Childerley, Kings.T. KT1
off Burritt Rd 138 CN97
Childerley St, SW6
off Fulham Palace Rd 99 CX81
Childers, The, Wdf.Grn. IG8 49 EM50
Childers St, SE8 103 DY79
Child La, SE10 205 L7
H Children's Trust, The,
Tad. KT20 173 CX121
Childs Av, Uxb. (Hare.) UB9 38 BJ54
Childs Cl, Horn. RM11 72 FJ58
Childs Cres, Swans. DA10 129 FX86
CHILDS HILL, NW2 64 DA61
Childs Hill Wk, NW2 63 CZ62
Childs La, SE19
off Westow St 122 DS93
Child's Ms, SW5
off Child's Pl 100 DA77
Child's Pl, SW5 100 DA77
Child's St, SW5 100 DA77
Child's Wk, SW5
off Child's St 100 DA77
Childs Way, NW11 63 CZ57
Chilham Cl, Bex. DA5 126 EZ87
Greenford UB6 79 CG68
Chilham Rd, SE9 124 EL91
Chilham Way, Brom. BR2 144 EG101
Chillerton Rd, SW17 120 DG92
Chillingworth Dr, SW11
off Wynter St 100 DC84
Chillingworth Gdns, Twick. TW1
off Tower Rd 117 CF90
Chillingworth Rd, N7 65 DM64
Chilmark Gdns, N.Mal. KT3 139 CT101
Redhill RH1 185 DL129
Chilmark Rd, SW16 141 DK96
Chilmead La, Red.
(Nutfld) RH1 185 DK132
Chilsey Grn Rd, Cher. KT16 133 BE100
Chiltern Av, Bushey WD23 24 CC44
Twickenham TW2 116 CA88
Chiltern Business Village,
Uxb. UB8 76 BH68
Chiltern Cl, Bexh. DA7
off Cumbrian Av 107 FE81
Borehamwood WD6 26 CM40
Bushey WD23 24 CB44
Croydon CR0 142 DS104
Uxbridge (Ickhm) UB10 59 BP61
Waltham Cross
(Chsht) EN7 13 DP27
Woking GU22 166 AW122
Worcester Park KT4
off Cotswold Way 139 CW103
Chiltern Dene, Enf. EN2 29 DM42
Chiltern Dr, Rick.
(Mill End) WD3 37 BF45
Surbiton KT5 138 CP99
Chiltern Gdns, NW2 63 CX62
Bromley BR2 144 EF98
Hornchurch RM12 72 FJ62
Chiltern Hts, Amer. HP7 20 AU39
Chiltern Hill, Ger.Cr.
(Chal.St.P.) SL9 36 AY53
★ Chiltern Open Air Mus,
Ch.St.G. HP8 37 AZ47
Chiltern Rd, E3 85 EA70
Gravesend (Nthflt) DA11 130 GE90
Ilford IG2 69 ES56
Pinner HA5 60 BW57
Sutton SM2 158 DB109
Chilterns, The, Sutt. SM2
off Gatton Cl 158 DB109
Chiltern St, W1 194 F6
Chiltern Vw Rd, Uxb. UB8 76 BJ68
Chiltern Way, Wdf.Grn. IG8 48 EG48
Chilthorne Cl, SE6
off Ravensbourne Pk Cres 123 DZ87
Chilton Av, W5 97 CK77
Chilton Ct, Walt. KT12 153 BU105
Chilton Gro, SE8 203 J9
Chiltonian Ind Est, SE12 124 EF86
Chilton Rd, Edg. HA8
off Manor Pk Cres 42 CN51
Grays RM16 111 GG76
Richmond TW9 98 CN83
Chiltons, The, E18
off Grove Hill 48 EG54
Chiltons Cl, Bans. SM7
off High St 174 DB115
Chilton St, E2 84 DT70
Chilver St, SE10 205 L10
Chilwell Gdns, Wat. WD19 40 BW49
Chilworth Ct, SW19
off Windlesham Gro 119 CX88
Chilworth Gdns, Sutt. SM1 140 DC104
Chilworth Ms, W2 82 DC72
Chilworth St, W2 82 DC72
Chimes Av, N13 45 DN50
Chimes Shop Cen, The,
Uxb. UB8 76 BK66
China Ms, SW2
off Craster Rd 121 DM87
★ Chinatown, W1 195 M10
Chinbrook Cres, SE12 124 EH90
Chinbrook Est, SE9 124 EK90
Chinbrook Rd, SE12 124 EH90
Chinchilla Dr, Houns. TW4 96 BW82
Chindits La, Brwd. CM14 54 FW50
Chine, The, N10 65 DJ56
N21 29 DP44
Wembley HA0 61 CH64
Ching Ct, WC2 195 P9
Chingdale Rd, E4 48 EE48
CHINGFORD, E4 47 EB46
⇌ Chingford 48 EE45
Chingford Av, E4 47 EB48
CHINGFORD GREEN, E4 48 EF46
CHINGFORD HATCH, E4 47 EC49
Chingford Ind Cen, E4 47 DY50
Chingford La, Wdf.Grn. IG8 48 EE49
Chingford Mt Rd, E4 47 EA49
Chingford Rd, E4 47 EA51
E17 47 EB53
Chingley Cl, Brom. BR1 124 EE93
Ching Way, E4 47 DZ51
Chinnery Cl, Enf. EN1
off Garnault Rd 30 DT39
Chinnor Cres, Grnf. UB6 78 CB68
Chipka St, E14 204 D5
Chipley St, SE14 103 DY79
Chipmunk Gro, Nthlt. UB5
off Argus Way 78 BY69
Chippendale All, Uxb. UB8
off Chippendale Waye 76 BK66
Chippendale St, E5 67 DX62
Chippendale Waye, Uxb. UB8 76 BK66
Chippenham Av, Wem. HA9 62 CP64
Chippenham Cl, Pnr. HA5 59 BT56
Romford RM3
off Chippenham Rd 52 FK50
Chippenham Gdns, NW6 82 DA69
Romford RM3 52 FK50
Chippenham Ms, W9 82 DA70
Chippenham Rd, W9 82 DA70
Romford RM3 52 FK51
Chippenham Wk, Rom. RM3
off Chippenham Rd 52 FK51
CHIPPERFIELD, Kings L. WD4 6 BG31
Chipperfield Cl, Upmin. RM14 73 FS60
Chipperfield Rd, Hem.H.
(Bov.) HP3 5 BB27
Kings Langley WD4 6 BK30
Orpington BR5 146 EU95
CHIPPING BARNET, Barn. EN5 27 CY42
Chipping Cl, Barn. EN5
off St. Albans Rd 27 CY41
CHIPSTEAD, Couls. CR5 174 DF118
Sev. TN13 190 FC122
⇌ Chipstead 174 DF118
Chipstead, Ger.Cr.
(Chal.St.P.) SL9 36 AW53
Chipstead Av, Th.Hth. CR7 141 DP98
CHIPSTEAD BOTTOM,
Couls. CR5 174 DE121
Chipstead Cl, SE19 122 DT94
Coulsdon CR5 174 DG116
Sutton SM2 158 DB109
Chipstead Ct, Wok. (Knap.) GU21
off Creston Av 166 AS117
Chipstead Gdns, NW2 63 CV61
Chipstead Gate, Couls. CR5
off Woodfield Cl 175 DJ119
Chipstead La, Couls. CR5 174 DB124
Sevenoaks TN13 190 FC122
Tadworth KT20 183 CZ125
Chipstead Pk, Sev. TN13 190 FD122
Chipstead Pk Cl, Sev. TN13 190 FC122
Chipstead Pl Gdns,
Sev. TN13 190 FC122
Chipstead Rd, Bans. SM7 173 CZ117
Erith DA8 107 FE80
Chipstead Sta Par, Couls.
(Chipstead) CR5
off Station App 174 DF118
Chipstead St, SW6 100 DA81
Chipstead Valley Rd,
Couls. CR5 175 DH116
Chipstead Way, Bans. SM7 174 DF115
Chip St, SW4 101 DK83
Chirk Cl, Hayes UB4
off Braunston Dr 78 BY70
Chirton Wk, Wok. GU21
off Shilburn Way 166 AU118
Chisenhale Rd, E3 85 DY68
Chisholm Rd, Croy. CR0 142 DS103
Richmond TW10 118 CM86
Chisledon Wk, E9
off Southmoor Way 85 DZ65
CHISLEHURST 125 EN94
⇌ Chislehurst 145 EN96
Chislehurst Av, N12 44 DC52
★ Chislehurst Caves,
Chis. BR7 145 EN95
Chislehurst Rd, Brom. BR1 144 EK96
Chislehurst BR7 144 EK96
Orpington BR5, BR6 145 ES98
Richmond TW10 118 CL86
Sidcup DA14 126 EU92
CHISLEHURST WEST,
Chis. BR7 125 EM92
Chislet Cl, Beck. BR3
off Abbey La 123 EA94
Chisley Rd, N15 66 DS58
Chiswell Ct, Wat. WD24 24 BW38
CHISWELL GREEN, St.Alb. AL2 8 CA26
Chiswell Grn La, St.Alb. AL2 8 BX25
Chiswell Sq, SE3
off Brook La 104 EH82
Chiswell St, EC1 197 J6
CHISWICK, W4 98 CR79
⇌ Chiswick 98 CQ80
Chiswick Br, SW14 98 CQ82
W4 98 CQ82
Chiswick Cl, Croy. CR0 141 DM104
Chiswick Common Rd, W4 98 CR77
Chiswick Ct, Pnr. HA5 60 BZ55
Chiswick Grn Studios, W4
off Evershed Wk 98 CQ77
Chiswick High Rd, W4 98 CR77
Brentford TW8 98 CM78
★ Chiswick Ho, W4 98 CS79
Chiswick Ho Grds, W4 98 CR79
Chiswick La, W4 98 CS78
Chiswick La S, W4 99 CT78
H Chiswick Lo, W4 99 CT78
Chiswick Mall, W4 99 CT79
W6 99 CT79
⊖ Chiswick Park 98 CQ77
Chiswick Pk, W4 98 CP77
Chiswick Quay, W4 98 CQ81
Chiswick Rd, N9 46 DU47
W4 98 CQ77
Chiswick Roundabout, W4
off Chiswick High Rd 98 CN78
Chiswick Sq, W4
off Hogarth Roundabout 98 CS79
Chiswick Staithe, W4 98 CQ81
Chiswick Ter, W4
off Acton La 98 CQ77
Chiswick Village, W4 98 CP78
Chiswick Wf, W4 99 CT79
Chittenden Cotts, Wok.
(Wisley) GU23 168 BL116
Chitterfield Gate, West Dr. UB7 94 BN80
Chitty's La, Dag. RM8 70 EX61
Chitty St, W1 195 L6
Chivalry Rd, SW11 120 DE85
Chivenor Gro, Kings.T. KT2 117 CK92
Chivers Rd, E4 47 EB48
Choats Manor Way, Bark. IG11 88 EW70
Dagenham RM9
off Ripple Rd 88 EY68
Choats Rd, Bark. IG11 88 EW68
Dagenham RM9 88 EW68
CHOBHAM, Wok. GU24 150 AT111
Chobham Cl, Cher.
(Ott.) KT16 151 BB107
★ Chobham Common
National Nature Reserve,
Wok. GU24 150 AS105
Chobham Gdns, SW19 119 CX89
Chobham La, Cher.
(Longcr.) KT16 132 AV102
Chobham Pk La, Wok.
(Chobham) GU24 150 AU110
Chobham Rd, E15 67 ED64
Chertsey (Ott.) KT16 151 BA108
Woking GU21 166 AY116
Woking (Horsell) GU21 150 AW113
Choir Grn, Wok. (Knap.) GU21
off Semper Cl 166 AS117
Cholmeley Cres, N6 65 DH59
Cholmeley Pk, N6 65 DH60
Cholmley Gdns, NW6
off Fortune Grn Rd 64 DA64
Cholmley Rd, T.Ditt. KT7 137 CH100
Cholmondeley Av, NW10 81 CU68
Cholmondeley Wk, Rich. TW9 117 CJ85
Choppins Ct, E1 202 E2
Chopwell Cl, E15
off Bryant St 85 ED66
CHORLEYWOOD, Rick. WD3 21 BE43
⇌ Chorleywood 21 BD42
⊖ Chorleywood 21 BD42
CHORLEYWOOD BOTTOM,
Rick. WD3 21 BD44
Chorleywood Bottom,
Rick. (Chorl.) WD3 21 BD43
Chorleywood Cl, Rick. WD3
off Nightingale Rd 38 BK45
Chorleywood Common, Rick.
(Chorl.) WD3 21 BE42
Chorleywood Cres, Orp. BR5 145 ET96
Chorleywood Ho Dr, Rick.
(Chorl.) WD3 21 BE41
Chorleywood Lo La, Rick.
(Chorl.) WD3
off Rickmansworth Rd 21 BF41
Chorleywood Rd, Rick. WD3 22 BG42
Choumert Gro, SE15 102 DU82
Choumert Ms, SE15 102 DU82
Choumert Rd, SE15 102 DT83
Choumert Sq, SE15 102 DU82
Chow Sq, E8 *off Arcola St* 66 DT64
Chrislaine Cl, Stai. (Stanw.) TW19
off High St 114 BK86
Chrisp St, E14 85 EB71
Christabel Cl, Islw. TW7
off Worton Rd 97 CE83
Christchurch Av, N12 44 DC51
NW6 81 CY66
Erith DA8 107 FD79
Harrow HA3 61 CH56
Rainham RM13 89 FF68
Teddington TW11 117 CG92
Wembley HA0 80 CL65
Christchurch Cl, N12
off Summers La 44 DD52
SW19 120 DD94
Enfield EN2 30 DQ40
Christchurch Ct, NW6 81 CY66
Christchurch Cres, Grav. DA12
off Christchurch Rd 131 GJ87
Radlett WD7 25 CG36
Christchurch Gdns,
Epsom KT19 156 CP111
Harrow HA3 61 CG56
Christchurch Grn, Wem. HA0 80 CL65
Christchurch Hill, NW3 64 DD62
Christchurch La, Barn. EN5 27 CY40
Christ Ch Mt, Epsom KT19 156 CP112
Christchurch Pk, Sutt. SM2 158 DC108
Christ Ch Pas, EC1 196 G8
Christchurch Pas, NW3 64 DC62
Barnet EN5 27 CY41
Christ Ch Path, Hayes UB3 95 BQ76
Christchurch Pl, Epsom KT19 156 CP111
Christchurch Rd, N8 65 DL58
SW2 121 DM88
SW14 118 CP85
SW19 140 DD95
Christ Ch Rd, Beck. BR3
off Fairfield Rd 143 EA96
Christchurch Rd, Dart. DA1 128 FJ87
Christ Ch Rd, Epsom KT19 156 CL112
Christchurch Rd, Grav. DA12 131 GJ88
Hounslow (Hthrw Air.) TW6
off Courtney Rd 94 BN83
Ilford IG1 69 EP60
Purley CR8 159 DP110
Sidcup DA15 125 ET91
Christ Ch Rd, Surb. KT5 138 CM100
Christchurch Rd, Til. RM18 111 GG81
Virginia Water GU25 132 AU97
Christchurch Sq, E9
off Victoria Pk Rd 84 DW67
Christchurch St, SW3 100 DF79
Christchurch Ter, SW3
off Christchurch St 100 DF79
Christchurch Way, SE10 205 J9
Woking GU21
off Church St E 167 AZ117
Christian Ct, SE16 203 M3
Christian Flds, SW16 121 DN94
Christian Flds Av,
Grav. DA12 131 GJ91
Christian St, E1 84 DU72
Christie Dr, Croy. CR0 142 DU99
Christie Gdns, Rom. RM6 70 EV58
Christie Rd, E9 85 DY65
Waltham Abbey EN9
off Deer Pk Way 31 EB36
Christies Av, Sev.
(Bad.Mt) TN14 164 FA110
Christie Wk, Cat. CR3
off Hambledon Rd 176 DR122
Christina Sq, N4
off Adolphus Rd 65 DP60
Christina St, EC2 197 M4
Christine Worsley Cl, N21
off Highfield Rd 45 DP47
Christopher Av, W7 97 CG76
Christopher Cl, SE16 203 H4
Hornchurch RM12
off Chevington Way 72 FK63
Sidcup DA15 125 ET85
Christopher Ct, Tad. KT20
off High St 173 CW123
Christopher Gdns, Dag. RM9
off Wren Rd 70 EX64
Christopher Pl, NW1 195 N3
Christopher Rd, Sthl. UB2 95 BV77
Christopher's Ms, W11
off Penzance St 81 CY74
Christopher St, EC2 197 L5

★ Place of interest ⇌ Railway station ⊖ London Underground station DLR Docklands Light Railway station Tra Tramlink station H Hospital Riv Pedestrian ferry landing stage

Christy Rd, West.(Bigg.H.) TN16 . . . . . 178 EJ115
Chryssell Rd, SW9 . . . . . 101 DN80
Chubworthy St, SE14 . . . . . 103 DY79
Chucks La, Tad. KT20 . . . . . 173 CV124
Chudleigh Cres, Ilf. IG3 . . . . . 69 ES63
Chudleigh Gdns, Sutt. SM1 . . 140 DC104
Chudleigh Rd, NW6 . . . . . 81 CX66
SE4 . . . . . 123 DZ85
Romford RM3 . . . . . 52 FL49
Twickenham TW2 . . . . . 117 CF87
Chudleigh St, E1 . . . . . 85 DX72
Chudleigh Way, Ruis. HA4 . . . 59 BU60
Chulsa Rd, SE26 . . . . . 122 DV92
Chumleigh St, SE5 . . . . . 102 DS79
Chumleigh Wk, Surb. KT5 . . . 138 CM98
Church All, Croy. CR0 . . . . . 141 DN102
Gravesend DA11 off High St 131 GH86
Watford (Ald.) WD25 . . . . . 24 CC38
Church App, SE21 . . . . . 122 DR90
Egham TW20 . . . . . 133 BC97
Sevenoaks (Cudham) TN14 off Cudham La S 179 EQ115
Staines (Stanw.) TW19 . . . . . 114 BK86
Church Av, E4 . . . . . 47 ED51
NW1 off Kentish Town Rd . . 83 DH65
SW14 . . . . . 98 CR83
Beckenham BR3 . . . . . 143 EA95
Northolt UB5 . . . . . 78 BZ66
Pinner HA5 . . . . . 60 BY58
Ruislip HA4 . . . . . 59 BR60
Sidcup DA14 . . . . . 126 EU92
Southall UB2 . . . . . 96 BY76
Churchbury Cl, Enf. EN1 . . . . . 30 DS40
Churchbury La, Enf. EN1 . . . . . 30 DR41
Churchbury Rd, SE9 . . . . . 124 EK87
Enfield EN1 . . . . . 30 DR40
Church Cl, N20 . . . . . 44 DE48
W8 off Kensington Ch St . . 100 DB75
Addlestone KT15 . . . . . 152 BH105
Edgware HA8 . . . . . 42 CQ50
Hayes UB4 . . . . . 77 BR71
Hounslow TW3 off Bath Rd 96 BZ83
Leatherhead (Fetch.) KT22 . 171 CD124
Loughton IG10 . . . . . 33 EM40
Northwood HA6 . . . . . 39 BT52
Potters Bar (Cuffley) EN6 . . 13 DL29
Radlett WD7 . . . . . 25 CG36
Staines TW18 off The Broadway 134 BJ97
Tadworth KT20 off Buckland Rd 183 CZ127
Uxbridge UB8 . . . . . 76 BH68
West Drayton UB7 . . . . . 94 BL76
Woking (Horsell) GU21 . . . . . 166 AX116
Church Ct, Reig. RH2 . . . . . 184 DB134
Richmond TW9 off George St 117 CK85
Church Cres, E9 . . . . . 85 DX66
N3 . . . . . 43 CZ53
N10 . . . . . 65 DH56
N20 . . . . . 44 DE48
South Ockendon RM15 . . . . . 91 FW69
Churchcroft Cl, SW12 off Endlesham Rd 120 DG87
Churchdown, Brom. BR1 . . . . . 124 EE91
Church Dr, NW9 . . . . . 62 CR60
Harrow HA2 . . . . . 60 BZ58
West Wickham BR4 . . . . . 144 EE104
Church Elm La, Dag. RM10 . . . 88 FA65
CHURCH END, N3 . . . . . 43 CZ53
CHURCH END, NW10 . . . . . 80 CS65
Church End, E17 . . . . . 67 EB56
NW4 . . . . . 63 CV55
Church Entry, EC4 . . . . . 196 G9
Church Fm Cl, Swan. BR8 . . . 147 FC100
★ Church Farm Ho Mus, NW4 . . . . . 63 CV55
Church Fm La, Sutt. SM3 . . . 157 CY107
Church Fm Way, Wat. (Ald.) WD25 . . . . . 24 CB38
Church Fld, Dart. DA2 . . . . . 128 FK89
Epping CM16 . . . . . 18 EU29
Radlett WD7 . . . . . 25 CG36
Sevenoaks TN13 . . . . . 190 FE122
Churchfield Av, N12 . . . . . 44 DC51
Churchfield Cl, Har. HA2 . . . . . 60 CC56
Hayes UB3 off West Av 77 BT73
Churchfield Ms, Slou. SL2 . . . 74 AU72
Churchfield Path, Wal.Cr. (Chsht) EN8 . . . . . 14 DW29
Churchfield Pl, Shep. TW17 off Chertsey Rd 135 BP101
Churchfield Rd, W3 . . . . . 80 CQ74
W7 . . . . . 97 CE75
W13 . . . . . 79 CH74
Gerrards Cross (Chal.St.P.) SL9 . . . . . 36 AX53
Reigate RH2 . . . . . 183 CZ133
Walton-on-Thames KT12 . . 135 BU102
Welling DA16 . . . . . 106 EU83
Weybridge KT13 . . . . . 152 BN105
Churchfields, E18 . . . . . 48 EG53
SE10 off Roan St 103 EC79
Loughton IG10 . . . . . 32 EL42
West Molesey KT8 . . . . . 136 CA97
Woking (Horsell) GU21 . . . . . 166 AY116
Churchfields Av, Felt. TW13 . . 116 BZ90
Weybridge KT13 . . . . . 153 BP105
Churchfields Rd, Beck. BR3 . . 143 DX96
Watford WD24 . . . . . 23 BT36
Church Gdns, W5 . . . . . 97 CK75
Wembley HA0 . . . . . 61 CG63
Church Gate, SW6 . . . . . 99 CY83
Churchgate, Wal.Cr. (Chsht) EN8 . . . . . 14 DV30
Churchgate Rd, Wal.Cr. (Chsht) EN8 . . . . . 14 DV29
Church Grn, Hayes UB3 . . . . . 77 BT72
Walton-on-Thames KT12 . . 154 BW107
Church Gro, SE13 . . . . . 103 EB84
Amersham HP6 . . . . . 20 AY39
Kingston upon Thames KT1 . 137 CJ95
Slough (Wexham) SL3 . . . . . 74 AW71
Church Hill, E17 . . . . . 67 EA56
N21 . . . . . 45 DM45
SE18 . . . . . 105 EM76
SW19 . . . . . 119 CZ92
Church Hill, Abbots Langley (Bedmond) WD5 . . . . . 7 BT26
Carshalton SM5 . . . . . 158 DF106
Caterham CR3 . . . . . 176 DT124
Dartford DA2 . . . . . 128 FK90
Dartford (Cray.) DA2 . . . . . 107 FE84
Epping CM16 . . . . . 18 EU29
Greenhithe DA9 . . . . . 129 FS85
Harrow HA1 . . . . . 61 CE60
Loughton IG10 . . . . . 32 EL41
Orpington BR6 . . . . . 146 EU101
Purley CR8 . . . . . 159 DL110
Redhill (Merst.) RH1 . . . . . 185 DH126
Redhill (Nutfld) RH1 . . . . . 185 DM133
Sevenoaks (Cudham) TN14 . 179 EQ115
Uxbridge (Hare.) UB9 . . . . . 58 BJ55
Westerham (Tats.) TN16 . . . 178 EK122
Woking (Horsell) GU21 . . . . . 166 AX116
Woking (Pyrford) GU22 . . . 167 BF117
Church Hill Rd, E17 . . . . . 67 EB56
Barnet EN4 . . . . . 44 DF45
Surbiton KT6 . . . . . 138 CL99
Sutton SM3 . . . . . 157 CX105
Church Hill Wd, Orp. BR5 . . . 145 ET99
Church Hollow, Purf. RM19 . . 108 FN78
Church Hyde, SE18 off Old Mill Rd 105 ES79
Churchill Av, Har. HA3 . . . . . 61 CH58
Uxbridge UB10 . . . . . 77 BP69
Churchill Cl, Dart. DA1 . . . . . 128 FP88
Feltham TW14 . . . . . 115 BT88
Leatherhead (Fetch.) KT22 . 171 CE123
Uxbridge UB10 . . . . . 77 BP69
Warlingham CR6 . . . . . 176 DW117
Churchill Ct, W5 . . . . . 80 CM70
Northolt UB5 . . . . . 60 CA64
Staines TW18 off Chestnut Gro 114 BJ93
Churchill Dr, Wey. KT13 . . . . . 135 BQ104
Churchill Gdns, SW1 . . . . . 101 DJ78
W3 . . . . . 80 CN72
Churchill Gdns Rd, SW1 . . . . . 101 DH78
Churchill Ms, Wdf.Grn. IG8 off High Rd Woodford Grn . 48 EF51
Churchill Pl, E14 . . . . . 204 C2
Harrow HA1 off Sandridge Cl 61 CE56
Churchill Rd, E16 . . . . . 86 EJ72
NW2 . . . . . 81 CV65
NW5 . . . . . 65 DH63
Dartford (Hort.Kir.) DA4 . . . 148 FQ98
Edgware HA8 . . . . . 42 CM51
Epsom KT19 . . . . . 156 CN111
Gravesend DA11 . . . . . 131 GF88
Grays RM17 . . . . . 110 GD79
Slough SL3 . . . . . 93 AZ77
South Croydon CR2 . . . . . 160 DQ109
Churchill Ter, E4 . . . . . 47 EA49
Churchill Wk, E9 . . . . . 66 DW64
Churchill Way, Brom. BR1 off Ethelbert Rd 144 EG97
Sunbury-on-Thames TW16 . 115 BU92
Westerham (Bigg.H.) TN16 . 162 EK113
Church Island, Stai. TW18 . . . 113 BD91
Church La, E11 . . . . . 68 EE60
E17 . . . . . 67 EB56
N2 . . . . . 64 DD55
N8 . . . . . 65 DM56
N9 . . . . . 46 DU47
N17 . . . . . 46 DS53
NW9 . . . . . 62 CQ61
SW17 . . . . . 121 DH91
SW19 . . . . . 139 CZ95
W5 . . . . . 97 CJ75
Banstead (Nork) SM7 . . . . . 173 CX117
Brentwood (Gt Warley) CM13 . 73 FW58
Brentwood (Hutt.) CM13 . . . 55 GE46
Bromley BR2 . . . . . 144 EL102
Caterham CR3 . . . . . 175 DN123
Chessington KT9 . . . . . 156 CM107
Chislehurst BR7 . . . . . 145 EQ95
Coulsdon CR5 . . . . . 174 DG122
Dagenham RM10 . . . . . 89 FB65
Enfield EN1, EN2 . . . . . 30 DR41
Epping (N.Wld Bas.) CM16 . . 19 FB26
Epsom (Headley) KT18 . . . 172 CQ124
Gerrards Cross (Chal.St.P.) SL9 . . . . . 36 AX53
Godstone RH9 . . . . . 187 DX132
Harrow HA3 . . . . . 41 CF53
Hemel Hempstead (Bov.) HP3 . 5 BB27
Kings Langley WD4 . . . . . 6 BN29
Loughton IG10 . . . . . 33 EM41
Oxted RH8 . . . . . 188 EE129
Pinner HA5 . . . . . 60 BY55
Potters Bar (Northaw) EN6 . . 12 DG30
Purfleet RM19 off London Rd Purfleet . . . 108 FN78
Rainham (Wenn.) RM13 . . . . . 90 FK72
Redhill (Bletch.) RH1 . . . . . 186 DR133
Richmond TW10 . . . . . 118 CL88
Rickmansworth (Mill End) WD3 . . . . . 38 BG46
Rickmansworth (Sarratt) WD3 . . . . . 21 BF38
Romford RM1 . . . . . 71 FE56
Romford (Abridge) RM4 . . . . . 34 EY40
Romford (Stap.Abb.) RM4 . . . 35 FC42
Slough (Stoke P.) SL2 . . . . . 74 AT69
Slough (Wexham) SL3 . . . . . 74 AW71
Teddington TW11 . . . . . 117 CF92
Thames Ditton KT7 . . . . . 137 CF100
Twickenham TW1 . . . . . 117 CG88
Upminster (N.Ock.) RM14 . . . 73 FV64
Uxbridge UB8 . . . . . 76 BH68
Wallington SM6 . . . . . 141 DK104
Waltham Cross (Chsht) EN8 . . . . . 14 DV29
Warlingham CR6 . . . . . 177 DX117
Warlingham (Chel.) CR6 . . . 177 EC116
Watford (Ald.) WD25 . . . . . 24 CB38
Westerham TN16 . . . . . 178 EK122
Weybridge KT13 . . . . . 152 BN105
Church La Av, Couls. CR5 . . . . . 175 DH122
Church La Dr, Couls. CR5 . . . . . 175 DH122
Churchley Rd, SE26 . . . . . 122 DV91
Church Manor Est, SW9 off Vassall Rd 101 DN80
Church Manorway, SE2 . . . . . 105 ET77
Erith DA8 . . . . . 107 FD76
Church Manorway Ind Est, Erith DA8 . . . . . 107 FC76
Churchmead Cl, Barn. EN4 . . . 28 DE44
Church Meadow, Surb. KT6 . . 137 CJ103
Churchmead Rd, NW10 . . . . . 81 CU65
Church Ms, Add. KT15 . . . . . 152 BJ105
Churchmore Rd, SW16 . . . . . 141 DJ95
Church Mt, N2 . . . . . 64 DD57
Church Paddock Ct, Wall. SM6 . . . . . 141 DK104
Church Pas, EC2 off Gresham St 84 DQ72
Barnet EN5 off Wood St . . . 27 CZ42
Surbiton KT6 . . . . . 138 CL99
Church Path, E11 . . . . . 68 EG57
E17 off St. Mary Rd 67 EB56
N5 . . . . . 65 DP64
N12 . . . . . 44 DC50
N17 off White Hart La 46 DS52
N20 . . . . . 44 DC49
NW10 . . . . . 80 CS66
SW14 . . . . . 98 CR83
SW19 . . . . . 140 DA96
W4 . . . . . 98 CQ76
W7 . . . . . 79 CE74
Cobham KT11 . . . . . 153 BV114
Coulsdon CR5 . . . . . 175 DN118
Gravesend (Nthflt) DA11 . . . 130 GC86
Grays RM17 . . . . . 110 GA79
Greenhithe DA9 . . . . . 129 FT85
Mitcham CR4 . . . . . 140 DE97
Southall UB1 . . . . . 78 CA74
Southall (Sthl Grn) UB2 . . . . . 96 BZ76
Woking GU21 off High St . . 167 AZ117
Church Pl, SW1 . . . . . 199 L1
W5 off Church Gdns 97 CK75
Mitcham CR4 . . . . . 140 DE97
Twickenham TW1 off Church St 117 CH88
Uxbridge (Ickhm) UB10 . . . . . 59 BQ62
Church Ri, SE23 . . . . . 123 DX88
Chessington KT9 . . . . . 156 CM107
Church Rd, E10 . . . . . 67 EB61
E12 . . . . . 68 EL64
E17 . . . . . 47 DY54
N1 . . . . . 84 DQ65
N6 . . . . . 64 DG58
N17 . . . . . 46 DS53
NW4 . . . . . 63 CV56
NW10 . . . . . 80 CS65
SE19 . . . . . 142 DS95
SW13 . . . . . 99 CT82
SW19 (Wimbledon) 119 CY91
W3 . . . . . 98 CQ75
W7 . . . . . 79 CF74
Addlestone KT15 . . . . . 152 BG106
Ashford TW15 . . . . . 114 BM90
Ashtead KT21 . . . . . 171 CK117
Barking IG11 . . . . . 87 EQ65
Bexleyheath DA7 . . . . . 106 EZ82
Bromley BR2 . . . . . 144 EG96
Bromley (Short.) BR2 . . . . . 144 EE97
Buckhurst Hill IG9 . . . . . 48 EH46
Caterham CR3 . . . . . 176 DT123
Caterham (Wold.) CR3 . . . . . 177 DX122
Croydon CR0 . . . . . 141 DP104
Dartford (Sutt.H.) DA4 . . . . . 128 FL94
East Molesey KT8 . . . . . 137 CD98
Egham TW20 . . . . . 113 BA92
Enfield EN3 . . . . . 30 DW44
Epsom KT17 . . . . . 156 CS112
Epsom (W.Ewell) KT19 . . . . . 156 CR108
Erith DA8 . . . . . 107 FD78
Esher (Clay.) KT10 . . . . . 155 CF107
Feltham TW13 . . . . . 116 BX92
Gravesend (Cobham) DA12, DA13 . . . 131 GJ94
Greenhithe DA9 . . . . . 129 FS85
Hayes UB3 . . . . . 77 BT72
Hounslow (Cran.) TW5 . . . . . 95 BV78
Hounslow (Heston) TW5 . . . . . 96 CA80
Ilford IG2 . . . . . 69 ER58
Isleworth TW7 . . . . . 97 CD81
Iver SL0 . . . . . 75 BC69
Kenley CR8 . . . . . 176 DR115
Keston BR2 . . . . . 162 EK108
Kingston upon Thames KT1 . 138 CM96
Leatherhead KT22 . . . . . 171 CH122
Leatherhead (Bkhm) KT23 . 170 BZ123
Loughton (High Beach) IG10 . 32 EH40
Mitcham CR4 . . . . . 140 DD96
Northolt UB5 . . . . . 78 BZ66
Northwood HA6 . . . . . 39 BT52
Orpington (Chels.) BR6 . . . . . 164 EY106
Orpington (Farnboro.) BR6 . 163 EQ106
Potters Bar EN6 . . . . . 12 DB30
Purley CR8 . . . . . 159 DL110
Richmond TW9, TW10 . . . . . 118 CL85
Richmond (Ham) TW10 . . . . . 118 CM92
Romford (Harold Wd) RM3 . . 52 FN53
Romford (Noak Hill) RM4 . . . 52 FK46
Sevenoaks (Halst.) TN14 . . . 164 EY111
Sevenoaks (Seal) TN15 . . . . . 191 FM121
Shepperton TW17 . . . . . 135 BP101
Sidcup DA14 . . . . . 126 EU91
Southall UB2 . . . . . 96 BZ76
Stanmore HA7 . . . . . 41 CH50
Surbiton KT6 . . . . . 137 CJ103
Sutton SM3 . . . . . 157 CY107
Swanley BR8 . . . . . 148 FK95
Swanley (Crock.) BR8 . . . . . 147 FD101
Swanscombe DA10 . . . . . 130 FZ86
Teddington TW11 . . . . . 117 CE91
Tilbury RM18 . . . . . 111 GF81
Tilbury (W.Til.) RM18 . . . . . 111 GL79
Uxbridge (Cowley) UB8 . . . . . 76 BK70
Uxbridge (Hare.) UB9 . . . . . 58 BJ55
Wallington SM6 . . . . . 141 DJ104
Warlingham CR6 . . . . . 176 DW117
Watford WD17 . . . . . 23 BU39
Welling DA16 . . . . . 106 EV82
West Byfleet (Byfleet) KT14 . 152 BM113
West Drayton UB7 . . . . . 94 BK76
Westerham (Bigg.H.) TN16 . 178 EK117
Westerham (Brasted) TN16 . 180 EV124
Whyteleafe CR3 . . . . . 176 DT118
Windsor (Old Wind.) SL4 . . . 112 AV85
Woking (Horsell) GU21 . . . . . 166 AY116
Woking (St.John's) GU21 . . . 166 AU119
Worcester Park KT4 . . . . . 138 CS102
Church Rd Merton, SW19 . . . . . 140 DD95
Church Rd Twr Block, Stan. HA7 off Church Rd 41 CJ50
Church Row, NW3 . . . . . 64 DC63
Chislehurst BR7 . . . . . 125 EQ94
Church Side, Epsom KT18 . . . 156 CP113
Churchside Cl, West. (Bigg.H.) TN16 . . . . . 178 EJ117
Church Sq, Shep. TW17 . . . . . 135 BP101
Tra Church Street 141 DP103
Church St, E15 . . . . . 86 EE67
E16 . . . . . 87 EP74
N9 . . . . . 46 DS47
NW8 . . . . . 194 A6
W2 . . . . . 194 A6
W4 . . . . . 98 CS79
Cobham KT11 . . . . . 169 BV115
Croydon CR0 . . . . . 142 DQ103
Dagenham RM10 . . . . . 89 FB65
Enfield EN2 . . . . . 30 DR41
Epsom KT17 . . . . . 156 CS113
Epsom (Ewell) KT17 . . . . . 157 CU109
Esher KT10 . . . . . 154 CB105
Gravesend DA11 . . . . . 131 GH86
Gravesend (Sthflt) DA13 . . . 130 GA92
Grays RM17 . . . . . 110 GC79
Hampton TW12 . . . . . 136 CC95
Hemel Hempstead (Bov.) HP3 . . . . . 5 BB27
Isleworth TW7 . . . . . 97 CH83
Kingston upon Thames KT1 . 137 CK96
Leatherhead KT22 . . . . . 171 CH122
Reigate RH2 . . . . . 184 DA134
Rickmansworth WD3 . . . . . 38 BL46
Sevenoaks (Seal) TN15 . . . . . 191 FN121
Sevenoaks (Shore.) TN14 . . . 165 FF111
Slough SL1 . . . . . 92 AT76
Staines TW18 . . . . . 113 BE91
Sunbury-on-Thames TW16 . 135 BV97
Sutton SM1 off High St . . . 158 DB106
Twickenham TW1 . . . . . 117 CG88
Waltham Abbey EN9 . . . . . 15 EC33
Walton-on-Thames KT12 . . 135 BU102
Watford WD18 . . . . . 24 BW42
Weybridge KT13 . . . . . 152 BN105
Woking (Old Wok.) GU22 . . . 167 BC121
Church St E, Wok. GU21 . . . . . 167 AZ117
Church St Est, NW8 . . . . . 194 A5
Church St N, E15 . . . . . 86 EE67
Church St Pas, E15 off Church St 86 EE67
Church St W, Wok. GU21 . . . . . 166 AY117
Church Stretton Rd, Houns. TW3 . . . . . 116 CC85
Church Ter, NW4 . . . . . 63 CV55
SE13 . . . . . 104 EE83
SW8 . . . . . 101 DK82
Richmond TW10 . . . . . 117 CK85
CHURCH TOWN, Gdse. RH9 . 187 DX131
Church Trd Est, The, Erith DA8 . . . . . 107 FG80
Church Vale, N2 . . . . . 64 DF55
SE23 . . . . . 122 DW89
Church Vw, S.Ock. (Aveley) RM15 . . . . . 108 FQ75
Swanley BR8 off Lime Rd . . 147 FD97
Upminster RM14 . . . . . 72 FN61
Churchview Rd, Twick. TW2 . . 117 CD88
Church Vil, Sev. TN13 off Church Fld 190 FE122
Church Wk, N6 off Swains La . . 64 DG62
N16 . . . . . 66 DR63
NW2 . . . . . 63 CZ62
NW4 . . . . . 63 CW55
NW9 . . . . . 62 CR61
SW13 . . . . . 99 CU81
SW15 . . . . . 119 CV85
SW16 . . . . . 141 DJ96
SW20 . . . . . 139 CW97
Brentford TW8 . . . . . 97 CJ79
Bushey WD23 off High St . . 24 CA44
Caterham CR3 . . . . . 176 DU124
Chertsey KT16 . . . . . 134 BG101
Dartford DA2 . . . . . 128 FK90
Dartford (Eyns.) DA4 . . . . . 148 FL104
Enfield EN2 off Church La . . 30 DR41
Gravesend DA12 . . . . . 131 GK88
Hayes UB3 . . . . . 77 BT72
Leatherhead KT22 . . . . . 171 CH122
Redhill (Bletch.) RH1 . . . . . 186 DR133
Reigate RH2 off Reigate Rd 184 DC134
Richmond TW9 off Red Lion St 117 CK85
Thames Ditton KT7 . . . . . 137 CF100
Walton-on-Thames KT12 . . 135 BU102
Weybridge KT13 off Beales La 135 BP103
Church Wk Shop Cen, Cat. CR3 off Church Wk 176 DU124
Church Way, N20 . . . . . 44 DD48
Churchway, NW1 . . . . . 195 N2
Church Way, Barn. EN4 . . . . . 28 DF42
Edgware HA8 . . . . . 42 CN51
Oxted RH8 . . . . . 188 EF132
South Croydon CR2 . . . . . 160 DT110
Churchwell Path, E9 . . . . . 66 DW64
Churchwood Gdns, Wdf.Grn. IG8 . . . . . 48 EG49
Churchyard Row, SE11 . . . . . 200 G8
Church Yd Wk, W2 off St. Marys Sq 82 DD71
Churston Av, E13 . . . . . 86 EH67
Churston Cl, SW2 off Tulse Hill 121 DP88
Churston Dr, Mord. SM4 . . . . . 139 CX99
Churston Gdns, N11 . . . . . 45 DJ51
Churton Pl, SW1 . . . . . 199 L9
Churton St, SW1 . . . . . 199 L9
Chusan Pl, E14 off Commercial Rd 85 DZ72
Chuters Cl, W.Byf. (Byfleet) KT14 . . . . . 152 BL112
Chuters Gro, Epsom KT17 . . . 157 CT112
Chyne, The, Ger.Cr. SL9 . . . . . 57 AZ57
Chyngton Cl, Sid. DA15 . . . . . 125 ET90
Cibber Rd, SE23 . . . . . 123 DX89
Cicada Rd, SW18 . . . . . 120 DC85
Cicely Rd, SE15 . . . . . 102 DU81
Cimba Wd, Grav. DA12 . . . . . 131 GL91
Cinderella Path, NW11 off North End Rd 64 DB60
Cinderford Way, Brom. BR1 . . 124 EE91
Cinder Path, Wok. GU22 . . . . . 166 AW119
Cinema Par, W5 off Ashbourne Rd 80 CM70
Cinnabar Wf, E1 . . . . . 202 C3
Cinnamon Cl, Croy. CR0 . . . . . 141 DL101
Cinnamon Row, SW11 . . . . . 100 DC83
Cinnamon St, E1 . . . . . 202 E3
Cintra Pk, SE19 . . . . . 122 DT94
Circle, The, NW2 . . . . . 62 CS62
NW7 . . . . . 42 CR50
SE1 . . . . . 201 P4
Tilbury RM18 off Toronto Rd 111 GG81
Circle Gdns, SW19 . . . . . 140 DA96
West Byfleet (Byfleet) KT14 off High Rd 152 BM112
Circle Rd, Walt. (Whiteley Vill.) KT12 . . . . . 153 BS110
Circuits, The, Pnr. HA5 . . . . . 60 BW56
Circular Rd, N17 . . . . . 66 DT55
Circular Way, SE18 . . . . . 105 EM79
Circus Ms, W1 . . . . . 194 D6
Circus Pl, EC2 . . . . . 197 L7
Circus Rd, NW8 . . . . . 82 DD69
Circus St, SE10 . . . . . 103 EC80
Cirencester St, W2 . . . . . 82 DB71
Cirrus Cl, Wall. SM6 . . . . . 159 DL108
Cirrus Cres, Grav. DA12 . . . . . 131 GL92
Cissbury Ring N, N12 . . . . . 43 CZ50
Cissbury Ring S, N12 . . . . . 43 CZ50
Cissbury Rd, N15 . . . . . 66 DR57
Citadel Pl, SE11 . . . . . 200 B10
Citizen Ho, N7 off Harvist Est 65 DN63
Citizen Rd, N7 . . . . . 65 DN63
C.I. Twr, N.Mal. KT3 . . . . . 138 CS97
Citron Ter, SE15 off Nunhead La 102 DV83
City Cross Business Pk, SE10 . 205 J8
City Forum, EC1 . . . . . 197 H2
City Gdn Row, N1 . . . . . 196 G1
City Gate Ho, Ilf. IG2 . . . . . 69 EP58
City Ho, Croy. CR0 . . . . . 141 DP101
City Mill River Towpath, E15 . . 85 EB66
★ City of Westminster Archives Cen, SW1 . . . . . 199 N6
City Pt, EC2 . . . . . 197 K6
City Rd, EC1 . . . . . 196 F1
⇌ City Thameslink 196 F9
★ City Uni, EC1 . . . . . 196 F3
Civic Sq, Til. RM18 . . . . . 111 GG82
Civic Way, Ilf. IG6 . . . . . 69 EQ56
Ruislip HA4 . . . . . 60 BX64
Clabon Ms, SW1 . . . . . 198 D7
Clacket La, West. TN16 . . . . . 178 EL124
Clack La, Ruis. HA4 . . . . . 59 BQ60
Clack St, SE16 . . . . . 202 G5
Clacton Rd, E6 . . . . . 86 EK69
E17 . . . . . 67 DY58
N17 off Sperling Rd 46 DT54
Claigmar Gdns, N3 . . . . . 44 DB53
Claire Causeway, Dart. DA2 off Crossways Boul 109 FT84
Claire Ct, N12 . . . . . 44 DC48
Bushey (Bushey Hth) WD23 . 41 CD46
Pinner HA5 off Westfield Pk 40 BZ52
Claire Gdns, Stan. HA7 . . . . . 41 CJ50
Claire Pl, E14 . . . . . 204 A6
Clairvale, Horn. RM11 . . . . . 72 FL59
Clairvale Rd, Houns. TW5 . . . . . 96 BX81
Clairview Rd, SW16 . . . . . 121 DH92
Clairville Ct, Reig. RH2 . . . . . 184 DD134
Clairville Gdns, W7 . . . . . 79 CF74
Clairville Pt, SE23 . . . . . 123 DX90
Clammas Way, Uxb. UB8 . . . . . 76 BJ71
Clamp Hill, Stan. HA7 . . . . . 41 CD49
Clancarty Rd, SW6 . . . . . 100 DA82
Clandon Av, Egh. TW20 . . . . . 113 BC94
Clandon Cl, W3 off Avenue Rd . 98 CP75
Epsom KT17 . . . . . 157 CT107
Clandon Gdns, N3 . . . . . 64 DA55
Clandon Rd, Ilf. IG3 . . . . . 69 ES61
Clandon St, SE8 . . . . . 103 EA82
Clanfield Way, SE15 off Blakes Rd 102 DS80
Clanricarde Gdns, W2 . . . . . 82 DA73
Clapgate Rd, Bushey WD23 . . 24 CB44
CLAPHAM, SW4 . . . . . 101 DH83
★ Clapham Common, SW4 . 100 DG84
⊖ Clapham Common 101 DJ84
Clapham Common N Side, SW4 . . . . . 101 DH84
Clapham Common S Side, SW4 . . . . . 121 DH86
Clapham Common W Side, SW4 . . . . . 100 DG84
Clapham Cres, SW4 . . . . . 101 DK84
Clapham Est, SW11 . . . . . 100 DE84
⇌ Clapham High Street 101 DK83
Clapham High St, SW4 . . . . . 101 DK84
⇌ Clapham Junction 100 DD84
Clapham Manor St, SW4 . . . . . 101 DJ83
⊖ Clapham North 101 DL83
CLAPHAM PARK, SW4 . . . . . 121 DK86
Clapham Pk Est, SW4 . . . . . 121 DK86
Clapham Pk Rd, SW4 . . . . . 101 DK84
Clapham Rd, SW9 . . . . . 101 DL83
Clapham Rd Est, SW4 . . . . . 101 DK83
⊖ Clapham South 121 DH86
Clap La, Dag. RM10 . . . . . 71 FB62
Claps Gate La, E6 . . . . . 87 EP70
⇌ Clapton 66 DV61
Clapton Common, E5 . . . . . 66 DT59
CLAPTON PARK, E5 . . . . . 67 DY63
Clapton Pk Est, E5 off Blackwell Cl 67 DY63
Clapton Pas, E5 . . . . . 66 DW64
Clapton Sq, E5 . . . . . 66 DW64
Clapton Ter, N16 off Oldhill St 66 DU60
Clapton Way, E5 . . . . . 66 DU63

★ Place of interest ⇌ Railway station ⊖ London Underground station DLR Docklands Light Railway station Tra Tramlink station H Hospital Riv Pedestrian ferry landing stage

235

Clara Pl, SE18 . . . 105 EN77
Clare Cl, N2
 off Thomas More Way . . . 64 DC55
 Borehamwood
 (Elstree) WD6 . . . 26 CM44
 West Byfleet KT14 . . . 152 BG113
Clare Cor, SE9 . . . 125 EP87
Clare Cotts, Red.
 (Bletch.) RH1 . . . 185 DP133
Clare Ct, Cat. (Wold.) CR3 . . . 177 EA123
 Northwood HA6 . . . 39 BS50
Clare Cres, Lthd. KT22 . . . 171 CG118
Claredale, Wok. GU22
 off Claremont Av . . . 166 AY119
Claredale St, E2 . . . 84 DU68
Clare Gdns, E7 . . . 68 EG63
 W11 off Westbourne Pk Rd . . . 81 CY72
 Barking IG11 . . . 87 ET65
 Egham TW20
 off Mowbray Cres . . . 113 BA92
Clare Hill, Esher KT10 . . . 154 CB107
Clare Ho, E3 . . . 85 DZ67
Clare La, N1 . . . 84 DQ66
Clare Lawn Av, SW14 . . . 118 CR85
Clare Mkt, WC2 . . . 196 B9
Clare Ms, SW6
 off Waterford Rd . . . 100 DB80
Claremont, St.Alb.
 (Brick.Wd) AL2 . . . 8 CA31
 Waltham Cross (Chsht) EN7 . 14 DT29
Claremont Av, Esher KT10 . . . 154 BZ107
 Harrow HA3 . . . 62 CL57
 New Malden KT3 . . . 139 CU99
 Sunbury-on-Thames TW16 . 135 BV95
 Walton-on-Thames KT12 . . 154 BX105
 Woking GU22 . . . 166 AY119
Claremont Cl, E16 . . . 87 EN74
 N1 . . . 196 E1
 SW2 off Streatham Hill . . . 121 DL88
 Grays RM16
 off Premier Av . . . 110 GC76
 Orpington BR6 . . . 163 EN105
 South Croydon CR2 . . . 176 DV115
 Walton-on-Thames KT12 . . 154 BW106
Claremont Ct, Surb. KT6
 off St. James Rd . . . 137 CK100
Claremont Cres, Dart. DA1 . . . 107 FE84
 Rickmansworth
 (Crox.Grn) WD3 . . . 23 BQ43
Claremont Dr, Esher KT10 . . . 154 CB108
 Shepperton TW17 . . . 135 BP100
 Woking GU22 . . . 166 AY119
Claremont End, Esher KT10 . . 154 CB107
Claremont Gdns, Ilf. IG3 . . . 69 ES61
 Surbiton KT6 . . . 138 CL99
 Upminster RM14 . . . 73 FR60
Claremont Gro, W4
 off Edensor Gdns . . . 98 CS80
 Woodford Green IG8 . . . 48 EJ51
★ Claremont Landscape Gdns,
 Esher KT10 . . . 154 BZ108
Claremont La, Esher KT10 . . . 154 CB105
CLAREMONT PARK,
 Esher KT10 . . . 154 CB108
Claremont Pk, N3 . . . 43 CY53
Claremont Pk Rd, Esher KT10 . 154 CB107
Claremont Pl, Grav. DA11
 off Cutmore St . . . 131 GH87
Claremont Rd, E7 . . . 68 EH64
 E17 . . . 47 DY54
 N6 . . . 65 DJ59
 NW2 . . . 63 CX62
 W9 . . . 81 CY68
 W13 . . . 79 CG71
 Barnet EN4 . . . 28 DD37
 Bromley BR1 . . . 144 EL98
 Croydon CR0 . . . 142 DU102
 Esher (Clay.) KT10 . . . 155 CE108
 Harrow HA3 . . . 41 CE54
 Hornchurch RM11 . . . 71 FG58
 Redhill RH1 . . . 184 DG131
 Staines TW18 . . . 113 BD92
 Surbiton KT6 . . . 138 CL100
 Swanley BR8 . . . 127 FE94
 Teddington TW11 . . . 117 CF92
 Twickenham TW1 . . . 117 CJ86
 West Byfleet KT14 . . . 152 BG112
Claremont Sq, N1 . . . 196 D1
Claremont St, E16 . . . 87 EN74
 N18 . . . 46 DU51
 SE10 . . . 103 EB79
Claremont Way, NW2 . . . 63 CW60
Claremount Cl, Epsom KT18 . 173 CW117
Claremount Gdns,
 Epsom KT18 . . . 173 CW117
Clarence Av, SW4 . . . 121 DK86
 Bromley BR1 . . . 144 EL98
 Ilford IG2 . . . 69 EN58
 New Malden KT3 . . . 138 CQ96
 Upminster RM14 . . . 72 FN61
Clarence Cl, Barn. EN4 . . . 28 DD43
 Bushey (Bushey Hth) WD23 . 41 CF45
 Walton-on-Thames KT12 . . 154 BW105
Clarence Ct, Egh. TW20
 off Clarence St . . . 113 AZ93
Clarence Cres, SW4 . . . 121 DK86
 Sidcup DA14 . . . 126 EV90
Clarence Dr, Egh.
 (Eng.Grn) TW20 . . . 112 AW91
Clarence Gdns, NW1 . . . 195 J3
Clarence Gate, Wdf.Grn. IG8 . 49 EN51
Clarence Gate Gdns, NW1
 off Glentworth St . . . 82 DF70
★ Clarence Ho, SW1 . . . 199 L4
Clarence La, SW15 . . . 118 CS86
Clarence Ms, E5 . . . 66 DV64
 SE16 . . . 203 H3
 SW12 . . . 121 DH87
Clarence Pl, E5 . . . 66 DV64
 Gravesend DA12 . . . 131 GH87
Clarence Rd, E5 . . . 66 DV63
 E12 . . . 68 EK64
 E16 . . . 86 EE70
 E17 . . . 47 DX54
 N15 . . . 66 DQ57
Clarence Rd, N22 . . . 45 DL52
 NW6 . . . 81 CZ66
 SE8 . . . 103 EB79
 SE9 . . . 124 EL89
 SW19 . . . 120 DB93
 W4 . . . 98 CN78
 Bexleyheath DA6 . . . 106 EY84
 Brentwood (Pilg.Hat.) CM15 . 54 FV44
 Bromley BR1 . . . 144 EK97
 Croydon CR0 . . . 142 DR101
 Enfield EN3 . . . 30 DV43
 Grays RM17 . . . 110 GA79
 Richmond TW9 . . . 98 CM81
 Sidcup DA14 . . . 126 EV90
 Sutton SM1 . . . 158 DB105
 Teddington TW11 . . . 117 CF93
 Wallington SM6 . . . 159 DH106
 Walton-on-Thames KT12 . 153 BV105
 Westerham (Bigg.H.) TN16 . 179 EM118
Clarence Row, Grav. DA12 . . . 131 GH87
Clarence St, Egh. TW20 . . . 113 AZ93
 Kingston upon Thames KT1 . 138 CL96
 Richmond TW9 . . . 98 CL84
 Southall UB2 . . . 96 BX76
 Staines TW18 . . . 113 BE91
Clarence Ter, NW1 . . . 194 E4
 Hounslow TW3 . . . 96 CB84
Clarence Wk, SW4 . . . 101 DL82
Clarence Way, NW1 . . . 83 DH66
Clarence Way Est, NW1 . . . 83 DH66
Clarenden Pl, Dart. DA2 . . . 127 FD92
Clarendon Cl, E9 . . . 84 DW66
 W2 . . . 194 B10
 Orpington BR5 . . . 146 EU97
Clarendon Ct, Slou. SL2 . . . 74 AV73
Clarendon Cres, Twick. TW2 . . 117 CD90
Clarendon Cross, W11
 off Portland Rd . . . 81 CY73
Clarendon Dr, SW15 . . . 99 CW84
Clarendon Gdns, NW4 . . . 63 CV55
 W9 . . . 82 DC70
 Dartford DA2 . . . 129 FR87
 Ilford IG1 . . . 69 EM60
 Wembley HA9 . . . 62 CL63
Clarendon Gate, Cher.
 (Ott.) KT16 . . . 151 BD107
Clarendon Grn, Orp. BR5 . . . 146 EU98
Clarendon Gro, NW1 . . . 195 M2
 Mitcham CR4 . . . 140 DF97
 Orpington BR5 . . . 146 EU97
Clarendon Ms, W2 . . . 194 B9
 Ashtead KT21 . . . 172 CL119
 Bexley DA5 . . . 127 FB88
 Borehamwood WD6
 off Clarendon Rd . . . 26 CN41
Clarendon Path, Orp. BR5 . . . 146 EU97
Clarendon Pl, W2 . . . 194 B10
 Sevenoaks TN13
 off Clarendon Rd . . . 190 FG125
Clarendon Ri, SE13 . . . 103 EC83
Clarendon Rd, E11 . . . 67 ED60
 E17 . . . 67 EB58
 E18 . . . 68 EG55
 N8 . . . 65 DM55
 N15 . . . 65 DP56
 N18 . . . 46 DU51
 N22 . . . 45 DM54
 SW19 . . . 120 DE94
 W5 . . . 80 CL70
 W11 . . . 81 CY73
 Ashford TW15 . . . 114 BM91
 Borehamwood WD6 . . . 26 CN41
 Croydon CR0 . . . 141 DP103
 Gravesend DA12 . . . 131 GJ86
 Harrow HA1 . . . 61 CE58
 Hayes UB3 . . . 95 BT75
 Redhill RH1 . . . 184 DF133
 Sevenoaks TN13 . . . 190 FG124
 Wallington SM6 . . . 159 DJ107
 Waltham Cross (Chsht) EN8 . 15 DX29
 Watford WD17 . . . 23 BV40
Clarendon St, SW1 . . . 101 DH78
Clarendon Ter, W9
 off Lanark Pl . . . 82 DC70
Clarendon Wk, W11 . . . 81 CY72
Clarendon Way, N21 . . . 30 DQ44
 Chislehurst BR7 . . . 145 ET97
 Orpington BR5 . . . 145 ET97
Clarens St, SE6 . . . 123 DZ89
Clare Pk, Amer. HP7 . . . 20 AS40
Clare Pl, SW15
 off Minstead Gdns . . . 119 CT87
Clare Pt, NW2
 off Claremont Rd . . . 63 CX60
Clare Rd, E11 . . . 67 ED58
 NW10 . . . 81 CU66
 SE14 . . . 103 DZ81
 Greenford UB6 . . . 79 CD65
 Hounslow TW4 . . . 96 BZ83
 Staines (Stanw.) TW19 . . . 114 BL87
Clare St, E2 . . . 84 DV68
Claret Gdns, SE25 . . . 142 DS98
Clareville Gro, SW7 . . . 100 DC77
Clareville Rd, Cat. CR3 . . . 176 DU124
 Orpington BR5 . . . 145 EQ103
Clareville St, SW7 . . . 100 DC77
Clare Way, Bexh. DA7 . . . 106 EY81
 Sevenoaks TN13 . . . 191 FJ127
Clare Wd, Lthd. KT22 . . . 171 CH118
Clarewood Wk, SW9 . . . 101 DP84
Clarges Ms, W1 . . . 199 H2
Clarges St, W1 . . . 199 J2
Claribel Rd, SW9 . . . 101 DP82
Clarice Way, Wall. SM6 . . . 159 DL109
Claridge Rd, Dag. RM8 . . . 70 EX60
Clarina Rd, SE20
 off Evelina Rd . . . 123 DX94
Clarissa Rd, Rom. RM6 . . . 70 EX59
Clarissa St, E8 . . . 84 DT67
Clark Cl, Erith DA8
 off Forest Rd . . . 107 FG81
Clarkebourne Dr, Grays RM17 . 110 GD79
Clarke Grn, Wat. WD25 . . . 23 BU35
Clarke Ms, N9 off Plevna Rd . . 46 DV48
Clarke Path, N16 . . . 66 DU60
Clarkes Av, Wor.Pk. KT4 . . . 139 CX102
Clarkes Dr, Uxb. UB8 . . . 76 BL71
Clarke's Ms, W1 . . . 194 G6
Clarke Way, Wat. WD25 . . . 23 BU35
Clarkfield, Rick. (Mill End) WD3 . 38 BH46
Clark Lawrence Ct, SW11
 off Winstanley Rd . . . 100 DD83
Clarks La, Epp. CM16 . . . 17 ET31
 Sevenoaks (Halst.) TN14 . . 164 EZ112
 Warlingham CR6 . . . 178 EF123
 Westerham TN16 . . . 178 EK123
Clarks Mead, Bushey WD23 . . . 40 CC45
Clarkson Rd, E16 . . . 86 EF72
Clarkson Row, NW1 . . . 195 K1
Clarksons, The, Bark. IG11 . . . 87 EQ68
Clarkson St, E2 . . . 84 DV69
Clarks Pl, EC2 . . . 197 M8
Clarks Rd, Ilf. IG1 . . . 69 ER61
Clark St, E1 . . . 84 DV71
Clark Way, Houns. TW5 . . . 96 BX80
Classon Cl, West Dr. UB7 . . . 94 BL75
Claston Cl, Dart. DA1
 off Iron Mill La . . . 107 FE84
CLATTERFORD END,
 Ong. CM5 . . . 19 FG30
Claude Rd, E10 . . . 67 EC61
 E13 . . . 86 EH67
 SE15 . . . 102 DV82
Claude St, E14 . . . 203 P8
Claudia Jones Way, SW2 . . . 121 DL86
Claudian Way, Grays RM16 . . . 111 GH76
Claudia Pl, SW19 . . . 119 CY88
Claughton Rd, E13 . . . 86 EJ68
Claughton Way, Brwd.
 (Hutt.) CM13 . . . 55 GD44
Clauson Av, Nthlt. UB5 . . . 60 CB64
Clavell St, SE10 . . . 103 EC79
Claverdale Rd, SW2 . . . 121 DM87
Claverhambury Rd,
 Wal.Abb. EN9 . . . 16 EF29
Clavering Av, SW13 . . . 99 CV79
Clavering Cl, Twick. TW1 . . . 117 CG91
Clavering Rd, E12 . . . 68 EK60
Claverings Ind Est, N9 . . . 47 DX47
Clavering Way, Brwd. (Hutt.) CM13
 off Poplar Dr . . . 55 GC44
Claverley Gro, N3 . . . 44 DA52
Claverley Vil, N3
 off Claverley Gro . . . 44 DB52
Claverton Cl, Hem.H.
 (Bov.) HP3 . . . 5 BA28
Claverton St, SW1 . . . 101 DJ78
Clave St, E1 . . . 202 F3
Claxton Gro, W6 . . . 99 CX78
Clay Av, Mitch. CR4 . . . 141 DH96
Claybank Gro, SE13
 off Algernon Rd . . . 103 EB83
Claybourne Ms, SE19
 off Church Rd . . . 122 DS94
Claybridge Rd, SE12 . . . 124 EJ91
Claybrook Cl, N2 . . . 64 DD55
Claybrook Rd, W6 . . . 99 CX79
Clayburn Gdns, S.Ock. RM15 . . 91 FV73
Claybury, Bushey WD23 . . . 40 CB45
Claybury Bdy, Ilf. IG5 . . . 68 EL55
Claybury Hall, Wdf.Grn. IG8
 off Regents Dr . . . 49 EM52
Claybury Rd, Wdf.Grn. IG8 . . . 48 EL52
Claydon Dr, Croy. CR0 . . . 159 DL105
Claydon End, Ger.Cr.
 (Chal.St.P.) SL9 . . . 56 AY55
Claydon La, Ger.Cr.
 (Chal.St.P.) SL9 . . . 56 AY55
Claydon Rd, Wok. GU21 . . . 166 AU116
Claydown Ms, SE18
 off Woolwich New Rd . . . 105 EN78
Clayfarm Rd, SE9 . . . 125 EQ89
CLAYGATE, Esher KT10 . . . 155 CE108
⇌ Claygate . . . 155 CD107
Claygate Cl, Horn. RM12 . . . 71 FG63
Claygate Cres, Croy.
 (New Adgtn) CR0 . . . 161 EC107
Claygate La, Esher KT10 . . . 137 CG103
 Thames Ditton KT7 . . . 137 CG102
 Waltham Abbey EN9 . . . 15 ED30
Claygate Lo Cl, Esher
 (Clay.) KT10 . . . 155 CE108
Claygate Rd, W13 . . . 97 CH76
CLAYHALL, Ilf. IG5 . . . 49 EM54
Clayhall Av, Ilf. IG5 . . . 68 EL55
Clayhall La, Wind.
 (Old Wind.) SL4 . . . 112 AT85
CLAY HILL, Enf. EN2 . . . 30 DQ37
Clay Hill, Enf. EN2 . . . 30 DQ37
Clayhill, Surb. KT5 . . . 138 CN99
Clayhill Cres, SE9 . . . 124 EK91
Claylands Pl, SW8 . . . 101 DN80
Claylands Rd, SW8 . . . 101 DM79
Clay La, Bushey
 (Bushey Hth) WD23 . . . 41 CE45
 Edgware HA8 . . . 42 CN46
 Epsom (Headley) KT18 . . . 172 CP124
 Staines (Stanw.) TW19 . . . 114 BM87
Claymill Ho, SE18 . . . 105 EQ78
Claymore Cl, Mord. SM4 . . . 140 DA101
Claymore Ct, E17
 off Billet Rd . . . 47 DY53
Claypit Hill, Wal.Abb. EN9 . . . 32 EJ36
Claypole Dr, Houns. TW5 . . . 96 BY81
Claypole Rd, E15 . . . 85 EC68
Clayponds Av, Brent. TW8 . . . 98 CL77
Clayponds Gdns, W5 . . . 97 CK77
H Clayponds Hosp, W5 . . . 98 CL77
Clayponds La, Brent. TW8 . . . 98 CL78
Clay Rd, The, Loug. IG10 . . . 32 EL39
Clayside, Chig. IG7 . . . 49 EQ51
Clays La, E15 . . . 67 EB64
Clay's La, Loug. IG10 . . . 33 EN39
Clays La Cl, E15 . . . 67 EB64
Clay St, W1 . . . 194 E7
Clayton Av, Upmin. RM14 . . . 72 FP64
 Wembley HA0 . . . 80 CL66
Clayton Cl, E6
 off Brandreth Rd . . . 87 EM72
Clayton Cres, N1 . . . 83 DL67
 Brentford TW8 . . . 97 CK78
Clayton Cft Rd, Dart. DA2 . . . 127 FG89
Clayton Dr, SE8 . . . 203 K10
Clayton Fld, NW9 . . . 42 CS52
Clayton Mead, Gdse. RH9 . . . 186 DV130
Clayton Ms, SE10 . . . 103 ED81
Clayton Rd, SE15 . . . 102 DU81
 Chessington KT9 . . . 155 CJ105
 Epsom KT17 . . . 156 CS113
 Hayes UB3 . . . 95 BS75
Clayton Rd, Isleworth TW7 . . . 97 CE83
 Romford RM7 . . . 71 FC60
Clayton St, SE11 . . . 101 DN79
Clayton Ter, Hayes UB4
 off Jollys La . . . 78 BX71
Clayton Wk, Amer. HP7 . . . 20 AW39
Clayton Way, Uxb. UB8 . . . 76 BK70
Clay Tye Rd, Upmin. RM14 . . . 73 FW63
Claywood Cl, Orp. BR6 . . . 145 ES101
Claywood La, Dart.
 (Bean) DA2 . . . 129 FX90
Clayworth Cl, Sid. DA15 . . . 126 EV86
Cleall Av, Wal.Abb. EN9
 off Quaker La . . . 15 EC34
Cleanthus Cl, SE18
 off Cleanthus Rd . . . 105 EP81
Cleanthus Rd, SE18 . . . 105 EP81
Clearbrook Way, E1
 off West Arbour St . . . 85 DX72
Cleardown, Wok. GU22 . . . 167 BB118
Clearmount, Wok.
 (Chobham) GU24 . . . 150 AS107
Clears, The, Reig. RH2 . . . 183 CY132
Clearwater Ter, W11
 off Lorne Gdns . . . 99 CX75
Clearwell Dr, W9 . . . 82 DB70
Cleave Av, Hayes UB3 . . . 95 BS77
 Orpington BR6 . . . 163 ES107
Cleaveland Rd, Surb. KT6 . . . 137 CK99
Cleave Prior, Couls. CR5 . . . 174 DE119
Cleaverholme Cl, SE25 . . . 142 DV100
Cleaver Sq, SE11 . . . 200 E10
Cleaver St, SE11 . . . 200 E10
Cleeve Ct, Felt. TW14
 off Kilross Rd . . . 115 BS88
Cleeve Hill, SE23 . . . 122 DV88
Cleeve Pk Gdns, Sid. DA14 . . . 126 EV89
Cleeve Rd, Lthd. KT22 . . . 171 CF120
Cleeve Way, SW15
 off Danebury Av . . . 119 CT87
Clegg Ho, SE3 off Pinto Way . 104 EH84
Clegg St, E1 . . . 202 E2
 E13 . . . 86 EG68
Cleland Path, Loug. IG10 . . . 33 EP39
Cleland Rd, Ger.Cr.
 (Chal.St.P.) SL9 . . . 36 AX54
Clematis Cl, Rom. RM3 . . . 52 FJ52
Clematis Gdns, Wdf.Grn. IG8 . . 48 EG50
Clematis St, W12 . . . 81 CT73
Clem Attlee Ct, SW6 . . . 99 CZ79
Clem Attlee Est, SW6
 off Lillie Rd . . . 99 CZ79
Clem Attlee Par, SW6
 off North End Rd . . . 99 CZ79
Clemence Rd, Dag. RM10 . . . 89 FC67
Clemence St, E14 . . . 85 DZ71
Clement Av, SW4 . . . 101 DK84
Clement Cl, NW6 . . . 81 CW66
 W4 off Acton La . . . 98 CR77
 Purley CR8
 off Croftleigh Av . . . 175 DP116
Clement Gdns, Hayes UB3 . . . 95 BS77
Clementhorpe Rd, Dag. RM9 . . 88 EW65
Clementina Rd, E10 . . . 67 DZ60
H Clementine Churchill Hosp,
 Har. HA1 . . . 61 CF62
Clementine Cl, W13
 off Balfour Rd . . . 97 CH75
Clementine Wk, Wdf.Grn. IG8
 off Salway Cl . . . 48 EG52
Clement Rd, SW19 . . . 119 CY92
 Beckenham BR3 . . . 143 DX96
 Waltham Cross (Chsht) EN8 . 15 DY27
Clements Av, E16 . . . 86 EG73
Clements Cl, Slou. SL1 . . . 92 AV75
Clements Ct, Houns. TW4 . . . 96 BX84
 Ilford IG1
 off Clements La . . . 69 EP62
Clement's Inn, WC2 . . . 196 C9
Clement's Inn Pas, WC2 . . . 196 C9
Clements La, EC4 . . . 197 L10
 Ilford IG1 . . . 69 EP62
Clements Mead, Lthd. KT22 . . 171 CG119
Clements Pl, Brent. TW8 . . . 97 CK78
Clements Rd, E6 . . . 87 EM66
 SE16 . . . 202 C7
 Ilford IG1 . . . 69 EP62
 Rickmansworth
 (Chorl.) WD3 . . . 21 BD43
 Walton-on-Thames KT12 . . 135 BV103
Clement St, Swan. BR8 . . . 128 FK93
Clement Way, Upmin. RM14 . . . 72 FM62
Clenches Fm La, Sev. TN13 . . 190 FG126
Clenches Fm Rd, Sev. TN13 . . 190 FG126
Clendon Way, SE18
 off Polthorne Gro . . . 105 ER77
Clennam St, SE1 . . . 201 J4
Clensham Ct, Sutt. SM1
 off Sutton Common Rd . . 140 DA103
Clensham La, Sutt. SM1 . . . 140 DA103
Clenston Ms, W1 . . . 194 D8
★ Cleopatra's Needle, WC2 . . 200 B2
Clephane Rd, N1 . . . 84 DQ65
Clere St, EC2 . . . 197 L4
Clerics Wk, Shep. TW17
 off Gordon Rd . . . 135 BR100
CLERKENWELL, EC1 . . . 196 F5
Clerkenwell Cl, EC1 . . . 196 E4
Clerkenwell Grn, EC1 . . . 196 E5
Clerkenwell Rd, EC1 . . . 196 D5
Clerks Cft, Red. (Bletch.) RH1 . 186 DR133
Clerks Piece, Loug. IG10 . . . 33 EM41
Clermont Rd, E9 . . . 84 DW67
Clevedon, Wey. KT13 . . . 153 BQ106
Clevedon Cl, N16
 off Smalley Cl . . . 66 DT62
Clevedon Gdns, Hayes UB3 . . 95 BR76
 Hounslow TW5 . . . 95 BV81
Clevedon Rd, SE20 . . . 143 DX95
 Kingston upon Thames KT1 . 138 CN96
 Twickenham TW1 . . . 117 CK86
Clevehurst Cl, Slou.
 (Stoke P.) SL2 . . . 74 AT65
Cleveland Av, SW20 . . . 139 CZ96
 W4 . . . 99 CT77
 Hampton TW12 . . . 116 BZ94
Cleveland Cl, Walt. KT12 . . . 135 BV104
Cleveland Cres, Borwd. WD6 . . 26 CQ43
Cleveland Dr, Stai. TW18 . . . 134 BH96
Cleveland Gdns, N4 . . . 66 DQ57
Cleveland Gdns, NW2 . . . 63 CX61
 SW13 . . . 99 CT82
 W2 . . . 82 DC72
 Worcester Park KT4 . . . 138 CS103
Cleveland Gro, E1
 off Cleveland Way . . . 84 DW70
Cleveland Ms, W1 . . . 195 K6
Cleveland Pk, Stai. TW19
 off Northumberland Cl . . . 114 BL86
Cleveland Pk Av, E17 . . . 67 EA56
Cleveland Pk Cres, E17 . . . 67 EA56
Cleveland Pl, SW1 . . . 199 L2
Cleveland Ri, Mord. SM4 . . . 139 CX101
Cleveland Rd, E18 . . . 68 EG55
 N1 . . . 84 DR66
 N9 . . . 46 DV45
 SW13 . . . 99 CT82
 W4 off Antrobus Rd . . . 98 CQ76
 W13 . . . 79 CH71
 Ilford IG1 . . . 69 EP62
 Isleworth TW7 . . . 97 CG84
 New Malden KT3 . . . 138 CS98
 Uxbridge UB8 . . . 76 BK68
 Welling DA16 . . . 105 ET82
 Worcester Park KT4 . . . 138 CS103
Cleveland Row, SW1 . . . 199 K3
Cleveland Sq, W2 . . . 82 DC72
Cleveland St, W1 . . . 195 K5
Cleveland Ter, W2 . . . 82 DC72
Cleveland Way, E1 . . . 84 DW70
Cleveley Cl, SE7 . . . 104 EK77
Cleveley Cres, W5 . . . 80 CL68
Cleveleys Rd, E5 . . . 66 DV62
Cleverly Est, W12 . . . 81 CU74
Cleve Rd, NW6 . . . 82 DA66
 Sidcup DA14 . . . 126 EX90
Cleves Av, Brwd. CM14 . . . 54 FV46
 Epsom KT17 . . . 157 CV109
Cleves Cl, Cob. KT11 . . . 153 BV114
 Loughton IG10 . . . 32 EL44
Cleves Cres, Croy.
 (New Adgtn) CR0 . . . 161 EC111
Cleves Rd, E6 . . . 86 EK67
 Richmond TW10 . . . 117 CJ90
Cleves Wk, Ilf. IG6 . . . 49 EQ52
Cleves Way, Hmptn. TW12 . . . 116 BZ94
 Ruislip HA4 . . . 60 BX60
 Sunbury-on-Thames TW16 . 115 BT93
Cleves Wd, Wey. KT13 . . . 153 BS105
Clewer Cres, Har. HA3 . . . 41 CD53
Clewer Ho, SE2
 off Wolvercote Rd . . . 106 EX75
Clichy Est, E1 . . . 84 DW71
Clifden Rd, E5 . . . 66 DW64
 Brentford TW8 . . . 97 CK79
 Twickenham TW1 . . . 117 CF88
Cliff End, Pur. CR8 . . . 159 DP112
Cliffe Rd, S.Croy. CR2 . . . 160 DR106
Cliffe Wk, Sutt. SM1
 off Turnpike La . . . 158 DC106
Clifford Av, SW14 . . . 98 CP83
 Chislehurst BR7 . . . 125 EM93
 Ilford IG5 . . . 49 EP53
 Wallington SM6 . . . 159 DJ105
Clifford Cl, Nthlt. UB5 . . . 78 BY67
Clifford Dr, SW9 . . . 101 DP84
Clifford Gdns, NW10 . . . 81 CW68
 Hayes UB3 . . . 95 BR77
Clifford Gro, Ashf. TW15 . . . 114 BN91
Clifford Rd, E16 . . . 86 EF70
 E17 . . . 47 EC54
 N9 . . . 30 DW44
 SE25 . . . 142 DU98
 Barnet EN5 . . . 28 DB41
 Grays (Chaff.Hun.) RM16 . . 110 FZ75
 Hounslow TW4 . . . 96 BX83
 Richmond TW10 . . . 117 CK89
 Wembley HA0 . . . 79 CK67
Clifford's Inn Pas, EC4 . . . 196 D9
Clifford St, W1 . . . 199 K1
Clifford Way, NW10 . . . 63 CT63
Cliff Pl, S.Ock. RM15 . . . 91 FX69
Cliff Reach, Green.
 (Bluewater) DA9 . . . 129 FS87
Cliff Rd, NW1 . . . 83 DK65
Cliff Ter, SE8 . . . 103 EA82
Cliffview Rd, SE13 . . . 103 EA83
Cliff Vil, NW1 . . . 83 DK65
Cliff Wk, E16 . . . 86 EF71
Clifton Av, E17 . . . 67 DX55
 N3 . . . 43 CZ53
 W12 . . . 81 CT74
 Feltham TW13 . . . 116 BW90
 Stanmore HA7 . . . 41 CH54
 Sutton SM2 . . . 158 DB111
 Wembley HA9 . . . 80 CM65
Clifton Cl, Add. KT15 . . . 134 BH103
 Caterham CR3 . . . 176 DR123
 Orpington BR6 . . . 163 EQ106
 Waltham Cross (Chsht) EN8 . 15 DY29
Clifton Ct, N4
 off Biggerstaff St . . . 65 DN61
 NW8 off Edgware Rd . . . 82 DD70
 Woodford Green IG8
 off Snakes La W . . . 48 EG51
Clifton Cres, SE15 . . . 102 DV80
Clifton Est, SE15
 off Consort Rd . . . 102 DV81
Clifton Gdns, N15 . . . 66 DT58
 NW11 . . . 63 CZ58
 W4 off Dolman Rd . . . 98 CR77
 W9 . . . 82 DC70
 Enfield EN2 . . . 29 DL42
 Uxbridge UB10 . . . 77 BP68
Clifton Gro, E8 . . . 84 DU65
 Gravesend DA11 . . . 131 GH87
Clifton Hill, NW8 . . . 82 DB68
Clifton Marine Par, Grav. DA11 . 131 GF86
Clifton Pk Av, SW20 . . . 139 CW96
Clifton Pl, SE16 . . . 202 G4
 W2 . . . 194 A10
 Banstead SM7 off Court Rd . 174 DA116
Clifton Ri, SE14 . . . 103 DY80
Clifton Rd, E7 . . . 86 EK65
 E16 . . . 86 EE71
 N1 . . . 84 DQ65
 N3 . . . 44 DC53
 N8 . . . 65 DK58
 N22 . . . 45 DJ53
 NW10 . . . 81 CU68

★ Place of interest ⇌ Railway station ⊖ London Underground station DLR Docklands Light Railway station Tra Tramlink station H Hospital Riv Pedestrian ferry landing stage

Clifton Rd, SE25 142 DS98
SW19 119 CX93
W9 82 DC70
Coulsdon CR5 175 DH115
Gravesend DA11 131 GG86
Greenford UB6 78 CC70
Harrow HA3 62 CM57
Hornchurch RM11 71 FG58
Hounslow (Hthrw Air.) TW6
off Inner Ring E. 95 BP83
Ilford IG2 69 ER58
Isleworth TW7 97 CD82
Kingston upon Thames KT2 118 CM94
Loughton IG10 32 EL42
Sidcup DA14 125 ES91
Slough SL1 92 AV75
Southall UB2 96 BY77
Teddington TW11 117 CE91
Wallington SM6 159 DH106
Watford WD18 23 BV43
Welling DA16 106 EW83
Cliftons La, Reig. RH2 183 CX131
Clifton St, EC2 197 M6
Clifton Ter, N4 65 DN61
Clifton Vil, W9 82 DB71
Clifton Wk, E6 86 EL72
W6 off Galena Rd 99 CV77
Dartford DA2
off Osbourne Rd 128 FP86
Clifton Way, SE15 102 DV80
Borehamwood WD6 26 CN39
Brentwood (Hutt.) CM13 55 GD46
Wembley HA0 80 CL67
Woking GU21 166 AT117
Climb, The, Rick. WD3 22 BH44
Clinch Ct, E16 86 EG71
Cline Rd, N11 45 DJ51
Clinger Ct, N1
off Pitfield St. 84 DS67
★ Clink Prison Mus, SE1 201 K2
Clink St, SE1 201 J2
Clinton Av, E.Mol. KT8 136 CC98
Welling DA16 105 ET84
Clinton Cl, Wey. KT13
off Thames St 135 BP103
Clinton Cres, Ilf. IG6 49 ES51
Clinton Rd, E3 85 DY69
E7 68 EG63
N15 66 DR56
Leatherhead KT22 171 CJ123
Clinton Ter, Sutt. SM1
off Manor La 158 DC105
Clipper Boul, Dart. DA2 109 FS83
Clipper Boul W, Dart. DA2 109 FR83
Clipper Cl, SE16 203 H4
Clipper Cres, Grav. DA12 131 GM91
Clipper Way, SE13 103 EC84
Clippesby Cl, Chess. KT9 156 CM108
Clipstone Ms, W1 195 K5
Clipstone Rd, Houns. TW3 96 CA83
Clipstone St, W1 195 J6
Clissold Cl, N2 64 DF55
Clissold Ct, N4 66 DQ61
Clissold Cres, N16 66 DR62
Clissold Rd, N16 66 DR62
Clitheroe Av, Har. HA2 60 CA60
Clitheroe Gdns, Wat. WD19 40 BX48
Clitheroe Rd, SW9 101 DL82
Romford RM5 51 FC50
Clitherow Av, W7 97 CG76
Clitherow Pas, Brent. TW8 97 CJ78
Clitherow Rd, Brent. TW8 97 CJ78
Clitterhouse Cres, NW2 63 CW60
Clitterhouse Rd, NW2 63 CW60
Clive Av, N18
off Claremont St 46 DU51
Dartford DA1 127 FF86
Clive Cl, Pot.B. EN6 11 CZ31
Clive Ct, W9 off Maida Vale 82 DC70
Cliveden Cl, N12
off Woodside Av 44 DC49
Brentwood (Shenf.) CM15 55 FZ45
Cliveden Pl, SW1 198 F8
Shepperton TW17 135 BP100
Cliveden Rd, SW19 139 CZ95
Clivedon Ct, W13 79 CH71
Clivedon Rd, E4 48 EE50
Clive Par, Nthwd. HA6
off Maxwell Rd 39 BS52
Clive Pas, SE21 off Clive Rd 122 DR90
Clive Rd, SE21 122 DR90
SW19 120 DE93
Belvedere DA17 106 FA77
Brentwood CM13 53 FW52
Enfield EN1 30 DU42
Esher KT10 154 CB105
Feltham TW14 115 BU86
Gravesend DA11 131 GH86
Romford RM2 71 FH57
Twickenham TW1 117 CF91
Clivesdale Dr, Hayes UB3 77 BV74
Clive Way, Enf. EN1 30 DU42
Watford WD24 24 BW39
Cloak La, EC4 197 J10
⇌ Clock House 143 DY96
Clockhouse Av, Bark. IG11 87 EQ67
Clockhouse Cl, SW19 119 CW90
Clock Ho Cl, W.Byf.
(Byfleet) KT14 152 BM112
Clockhouse La, Ashf. TW15 114 BN91
Feltham TW14 115 BP89
Grays RM16 91 FX74
Romford RM5 51 FB52
Clock Ho La, Sev. TN13 190 FG123
Clockhouse La E, Egh. TW20 113 BB94
Clockhouse La W, Egh. TW20 113 BA94
Clock Ho Mead, Lthd.
(Oxshott) KT22 154 CB114
Clockhouse Ms, Rick. (Chorl.) WD3
off Chorleywood Ho Dr 21 BE41
Clockhouse Pl, SW15 119 CY85
Feltham TW14 115 BQ88
Clock Ho Rd, Beck. BR3 143 DY97
Clockhouse Roundabout,
Felt. TW14 115 BP88
★ Clockmakers Company Collection,
The, Guildhall Lib, EC2 197 J8
Clock Twr Ms, N1
off Arlington Av 84 DQ67
SE28 88 EV73
Clock Twr Pl, N7 83 DL65
Clock Twr Rd, Islw. TW7 97 CF83
Cloister Cl, Rain. RM13 89 FH70
Teddington TW11 117 CH92
Cloister Gdns, SE25 142 DV100
Edgware HA8 42 CQ50
Cloister Rd, NW2 63 CZ62
W3 80 CQ71
Cloisters, The, Bushey WD23 24 CB44
Rickmansworth WD3 38 BL45
Woking GU22 167 BB121
Cloisters Av, Brom. BR2 145 EM99
Cloisters Business Cen, SW8
off Battersea Pk Rd 101 DH80
Cloisters Mall, Kings.T. KT1
off Union St 137 CK96
Clonard Way, Pnr. HA5 40 CA51
Clonbrock Rd, N16 66 DS63
Cloncurry St, SW6 99 CX82
Clonmel Cl, Har. HA2 61 CD60
Clonmell Rd, N17 66 DR55
Clonmel Rd, SW6 99 CZ80
Teddington TW11 117 CD91
Clonmore St, SW18 119 CZ88
Cloonmore Av, Orp. BR6 163 ET105
Clorane Gdns, NW3 64 DA62
Close, The, E4
off Beech Hall Rd 47 EC52
N14 45 DK47
N20 43 CZ47
SE3 off Heath La 103 ED82
Barnet EN4 28 DF44
Beckenham BR3 143 DY98
Bexley DA5 126 FA86
Brentwood CM14 54 FW48
Bushey WD23 24 CB43
Carshalton SM5 158 DE109
Dartford DA2 128 FJ90
Grays RM16 110 GC75
Harrow HA2 40 CC54
Hatfield AL9 11 CY26
Isleworth TW7 97 CD82
Iver SL0 75 BC69
Mitcham CR4 140 DF98
New Malden KT3 138 CQ96
Orpington BR5 145 ES100
Pinner (Eastcote) HA5 60 BW59
Pinner (Rayners La) HA5 60 BZ59
Potters Bar EN6 12 DA32
Purley (Pampisford Rd) CR8 159 DP110
Purley (Russ.Hill) CR8 159 DM110
Radlett WD7 9 CF33
Richmond TW9 98 CP83
Rickmansworth WD3 38 BJ46
Romford RM6 70 EY58
Sevenoaks TN13 190 FE124
Sidcup DA14 126 EV92
Sutton SM3 139 CZ101
Uxbridge UB10 76 BL66
Uxbridge (Hlgdn) UB10 76 BN67
Virginia Water GU25 132 AW99
Wembley (Barnhill Rd) HA9 62 CQ62
Wembley (Lyon Pk Av) HA0 80 CL65
West Byfleet KT14 152 BG113
Westerham
(Berry's Grn) TN16 179 EP116
Closemead Cl, Nthwd. HA6 39 BQ51
Cloth Ct, EC1 196 G7
Cloth Fair, EC1 196 G7
Clothier St, E1 197 N8
Cloth St, EC1 197 H6
Clothworkers Rd, SE18 105 ER80
Cloudberry Rd, Rom. RM3 52 FK51
Cloudesdale Rd, SW17 121 DH89
Cloudesley Pl, N1 83 DN67
Cloudesley Rd, N1 83 DN67
Bexleyheath DA7 106 EZ81
Erith DA8 107 FF81
Cloudesley Sq, N1 83 DN67
Cloudesley St, N1 83 DN67
Clouston Cl, Wall. SM6 159 DL106
Clova Rd, E7 86 EF65
Clove Cres, E14 85 ED73
Clove Hitch Quay, SW11 100 DC83
Clovelly Av, NW9 63 CT56
Uxbridge UB10 59 BQ63
Warlingham CR6 176 DV118
Clovelly Cl, Pnr. HA5 59 BV55
Uxbridge UB10 59 BQ63
Clovelly Ct, Horn. RM11 72 FN61
Clovelly Gdns, SE19 142 DT95
Enfield EN1 46 DS45
Romford RM7 51 FB53
Clovelly Rd, N8 65 DK56
W4 98 CQ75
W5 97 CJ75
Bexleyheath DA7 106 EY79
Hounslow TW3 96 CA82
Clovelly Way, E1
off Jamaica St 84 DW72
Harrow HA2 60 BZ61
Orpington BR6 145 ET100
Clover Cl, E11 off Norman Rd. 67 ED61
Clover Ct, Grays RM17
off Churchill Rd 110 GD79
Woking GU22 166 AX118
Cloverdale Gdns, Sid. DA15 125 ET86
Clover Fld, The, Bushey WD23 24 BZ44
Clover Hill, Couls. CR5 175 DH121
Clover Leas, Epp. CM16 17 ET30
Cloverleys, Loug. IG10 32 EK43
Clover Ms, SW3 off Dilke St 100 DF79
Clovers, The, Grav.
(Nthflt) DA11 130 GE91
Clover Way, Wall. SM6 140 DG102
Clove St, E13 off Barking Rd 86 EG70
Clowders Rd, SE6 123 DZ90
Clowser Cl, Sutt. SM1
off Turnpike La 158 DC106
Cloysters Grn, E1 202 B2
Cloyster Wd, Edg. HA8 41 CK52
Club Gdns Rd, Brom. BR2 144 EG101
Club Row, E1 197 P4
E2 197 P4
Clump, The, Rick. WD3 22 BG43
Clump Av, Tad. (Box H.) KT20 182 CQ131
Clumps, The, Ashf. TW15 115 BR91
Clunas Gdns, Rom. RM2 72 FK55
Clunbury Av, Sthl. UB2 96 BZ78
Clunbury St, N1 197 L1
Cluny Est, SE1 201 M6
Cluny Ms, SW5 100 DA77
Cluny Pl, SE1 201 M6
Cluse Ct, N1 off Dame St 84 DQ68
Clutterbucks, Rick.
(Sarratt) WD3 22 BG36
Clutton St, E14 85 EB71
Clydach Rd, Enf. EN1 30 DT42
Clyde Av, S.Croy. CR2 176 DV115
Clyde Circ, N15 66 DS56
Clyde Cl, Red. RH1 184 DG133
Clyde Ct, Red. RH1
off Clyde Cl 184 DG133
Clyde Cres, Upmin. RM14 73 FS58
Clyde Pl, E10 67 EB59
Clyde Rd, N15 66 DS56
N22 45 DK53
Croydon CR0 142 DT102
Staines (Stanw.) TW19 114 BK88
Sutton SM1 158 DA106
Wallington SM6 159 DJ106
Clydesdale, Enf. EN3 31 DX42
Clydesdale Av, Stan. HA7 61 CK55
Clydesdale Cl, Borwd. WD6 26 CR43
Isleworth TW7 97 CF83
Clydesdale Gdns, Rich. TW10 98 CP84
Clydesdale Ho, Erith DA18
off Kale Rd 106 EY75
Clydesdale Rd, W11 81 CZ72
Hornchurch RM11 71 FF59
Clydesdale Wk, Brox. EN10
off Tarpan Way 15 DZ25
Clyde St, SE8 103 DZ79
Clyde Ter, SE23 122 DW89
Clyde Vale, SE23 122 DW89
Clyde Way, Rom. RM1 51 FE53
Clydon Cl, Erith DA8 107 FE79
Clyfford Rd, Ruis. HA4 59 BT63
Clymping Dene, Felt. TW14 115 BV87
Clyston Rd, Wat. WD18 23 BT44
Clyston St, SW8 101 DJ82
Clyve Way, Stai. TW18 133 BE95
Coach & Horses Yd, W1 195 J10
Coach Ho La, N5
off Highbury Hill 65 DP63
SW19 119 CX91
Coach Ho Ms, SE1 201 M6
SE14 off Waller Rd 103 DX82
Coachhouse Ms, SE20 122 DV94
Coach Ho Ms, SE23 123 DX86
Coach Ho Yd, SW18
off Ebner St 100 DB84
Coachmaker Ms, SW4
off Fenwick Pl 101 DL83
Coach Rd, Bet. (Brock.) RH3 182 CL134
Chertsey (Ott.) KT16 151 BC107
Coach Yd Ms, N19
off Trinder Rd 65 DL60
Coal Ct, Grays RM17
off Columbia Wf Rd 110 GA79
Coaldale Wk, SE21
off Lairdale Cl 122 DQ87
Coalecroft Rd, SW15 99 CW84
Coal Rd, Til. RM18 111 GL77
Coal Wf Rd, W12
off Sterne St 99 CX75
Coates Av, SW18 120 DE86
Coates Dell, Wat. WD25 8 BY33
Coates Hill Rd, Brom. BR1 145 EN96
Coates Rd, Borwd.
(Elstree) WD6 41 CK45
Coate St, E2 84 DU68
Coates Wk, Brent. TW8 98 CL78
Coates Way, Wat. WD25 8 BX33
Cobb Cl, Borwd. WD6 26 CQ43
Slough (Datchet) SL3 92 AX81
Cobbett Cl, Enf. EN3 30 DW36
Cobbett Rd, SE9 104 EL83
Twickenham TW2 116 CA88
Cobbetts Av, Ilf. IG4 68 EK57
Cobbetts Cl, Wok. GU21 166 AV117
Cobbetts Hill, Wey. KT13 153 BP107
Cobbett St, SW8 101 DM80
Cobb Grn, Wat. WD25 7 BV32
Cobbins, The, Wal.Abb. EN9 16 EE33
Cobbinsend Rd, Wal.Abb. EN9 16 EK29
Cobble La, N1 off Edwards Ms 83 DP66
Cobble Ms, N5 66 DQ62
Cobblers Wk, E.Mol. KT8 137 CG95
Hampton TW12 116 CC94
Kingston upon Thames KT2 137 CG95
Teddington TW11 137 CG95
Cobbles, The, Brwd. CM15 54 FY47
Upminster RM14 73 FT59
Cobblestone Pl, Croy. CR0
off Oakfield Rd 142 DQ102
Cobbold Est, NW10 81 CT65
Cobbold Ms, W12
off Cobbold Rd 99 CT75
Cobbold Rd, E11 68 EF62
NW10 81 CT65
W12 98 CS75
Cobb's Ct, EC4
off Ludgate Hill 83 DP72
Cobb's Rd, Houns. TW4 96 BZ84
Cobb St, E1 197 P7
Cobden Cl, Uxb. UB8 76 BJ67
Cobden Hill, Rad. WD7 25 CH36
Cobden Rd, E11 68 EE62
SE25 142 DU99
Orpington BR6 163 ER105
Sevenoaks TN13 191 FJ123
COBHAM 169 BV115
Cobham, Grays RM16 110 GB75
⇌ Cobham &
Stoke D'Abernon 170 BY117
Cobham Av, N.Mal. KT3 139 CU99
★ Cobham Bus Mus,
Cob. KT11 153 BQ112
Cobham Cl, SW11 120 DE86
Bromley BR2 144 EL101
Edgware HA8 42 CP54
Enfield EN1 30 DU41
Greenhithe DA9
off Bean Rd 129 FV86
Sidcup DA15
off Park Mead 126 EV86
Wallington SM6 159 DL107
Cobham Gate, Cob. KT11 153 BV114
H Cobham Hosp, Cob. KT11 153 BV113
Cobham Ho, Bark. IG11
off St. Margarets 87 EQ67
Erith DA8 off Boundary St 107 FF80
Cobham Ms, NW1
off Agar Gro 83 DK66
Cobham Pk Rd, Cob. KT11 169 BV117
Cobham Pl, Bexh. DA6 126 EX85
Cobham Rd, E17 47 EC53
N22 65 DP55
Cobham (Stoke D'Ab.) KT11 170 CA118
Hounslow TW5 96 BW80
Ilford IG3 69 ES61
Kingston upon Thames KT1 138 CN95
Leatherhead (Fetch.) KT22 171 CE122
Cobham St, Grav. DA11 131 GG87
Cobham Ter, Green. DA9
off Bean Rd 129 FV85
Cobill Cl, Horn. RM11 72 FJ56
Cobland Rd, SE12 124 EJ91
Coborn Rd, E3 85 DZ69
Coborn St, E3 85 DZ69
Cobourg Rd, SE5 102 DT79
Cobourg St, NW1 195 L3
Cobsdene, Grav. DA12 131 GK93
Cobs Way, Add.
(New Haw) KT15 152 BJ110
Coburg Cl, SW1 199 L8
Coburg Cres, SW2 121 DM88
Coburg Gdns, Ilf. IG5 48 EK54
Coburg Rd, N22 65 DM55
Cochrane Ms, NW8 194 A1
Cochrane Rd, SW19 119 CZ94
Cochrane St, NW8 194 A1
Cockayne Way, SE8 203 L10
Cockerell Rd, E17 67 DY59
Cockerhurst Rd, Sev.
(Shore.) TN14 165 FD107
Cocker Rd, Enf. EN1 30 DV36
Cockett Rd, Slou. SL3 92 AY76
COCKFOSTERS, Barn. EN4 28 DE42
⊖ Cockfosters 28 DG42
Cockfosters Par, Barn. EN4
off Cockfosters Rd 28 DG42
Cockfosters Rd, Barn. EN4 28 DF40
Cock Hill, E1 197 N7
Cock La, EC1 196 F7
Leatherhead (Fetch.) KT22 170 CC122
Cockle Way, Rad.
(Shenley) WD7 10 CL33
Cockmannings La, Orp. BR5 146 EX102
Cockmannings Rd, Orp. BR5 146 EX101
Cockpit Steps, SW1 199 N5
Cockpit Yd, WC1 196 C6
Cocks Cres, N.Mal. KT3 139 CT98
Cocksett Av, Orp. BR6 163 ES107
Cockspur Ct, SW1 199 N2
Cockspur St, SW1 199 N2
Cocksure La, Sid. DA14 126 FA90
Cock's Yd, Uxb. UB8
off Bakers Rd 76 BJ66
Coda Cen, The, SW6 99 CY81
Code St, E1 84 DT70
Codham Hall La, Brwd.
(Gt Warley) CM13 73 FV56
Codicote Dr, Wat. WD25 8 BX34
Codicote Ter, N4
off Green Las 66 DQ61
Codling Cl, E1 202 C2
Codling Way, Wem. HA0 61 CK63
CODMORE, Chesh. HP5 4 AS29
Codmore Cres, Chesh. HP5 4 AS30
Codmore Wd Rd, Chesh. HP5 4 AW33
Codrington Ct, Wok. GU21
off Raglan Rd 166 AS118
Codrington Cres, Grav. DA12 131 GJ92
Codrington Gdns, Grav. DA12 131 GK92
Codrington Hill, SE23 123 DY87
Codrington Ms, W11
off Blenheim Cres 81 CY72
Cody Cl, Har. HA3 61 CK55
Wallington SM6
off Alcock Cl 159 DK108
Cody Rd, E16 85 ED70
Cody Rd Business Cen, E16 85 ED70
Coe Av, SE25 142 DU100
Coe's All, Barn. EN5
off Wood St 27 CY42
Coftards, Slou. SL2 74 AW72
Cogan Av, E17 47 DY53
Cohen Cl, Wal.Cr. EN8 15 DY31
Coin St, SE1 200 D2
Coity Rd, NW5 82 DG65
Cokers La, SE21
off Perifield 122 DR88
Coke's Fm La, Ch.St.G. HP8 20 AV41
Coke's La, Amer. HP7 20 AW41
Chalfont St. Giles HP8 20 AU42
Coke St, E1 84 DU72
Colas Ms, NW6
off Birchington Rd 82 DA67
Colbeck Ms, SW7 100 DB77
Colbeck Rd, Har. HA1 60 CC59
Colberg Pl, N16 66 DS59
Colborne Way, Wor.Pk. KT4 139 CW104
Colbrook Av, Hayes UB3 95 BR76
Colbrook Cl, Hayes UB3 95 BR76
Colburn Av, Cat. CR3 176 DT124
Pinner HA5 40 BY51
Colburn Way, Sutt. SM1 140 DD104
Colby Ms, SE19
off Gipsy Hill 122 DS92
Colby Rd, SE19 122 DS92
Walton-on-Thames KT12
off Winchester Rd 135 BU102
Colchester Av, E12 69 EM62
Colchester Dr, Pnr. HA5 60 BX57
Colchester Rd, E10 67 EC59
E17 67 EA58
Edgware HA8 42 CQ52
Northwood HA6 39 BU54
Romford RM3 52 FK53
Colchester St, E1
off Braham St 84 DT72
Colcokes Rd, Bans. SM7 174 DA116
Cold Arbor Rd, Sev. TN13 190 FD124
Coldbath Sq, EC1 196 D4
Coldbath St, SE13 103 EB81
COLDBLOW, Bex. DA5 127 FC89
Cold Blow Cres, Bex. DA5 127 FD88
Cold Blow La, SE14 103 DX80
Cold Blows, Mitch. CR4 140 DG97
Coldershaw Rd, W13 79 CG74
Coldfall Av, N10 44 DF54
Coldham Gro, Enf. EN3 31 DY37
Cold Harbour, E14 204 E3
Coldharbour Cl, Egh. TW20 133 BC97
Coldharbour Crest, SE9
off Great Harry Dr. 125 EN90
Coldharbour La, SE5 101 DN84
SW9 101 DN84
Bushey WD23 24 CB44
Egham TW20 133 BC97
Hayes UB3 77 BU73
Purley CR8 159 DN110
Rainham RM13 89 FE72
Redhill (Bletch.) RH1 186 DT134
Woking GU22 167 BF115
Coldharbour Pl, SE5
off Denmark Hill 102 DQ82
Coldharbour Rd, Croy. CR0 159 DN106
Gravesend (Nthflt) DA11 130 GE89
West Byfleet KT14 151 BF114
Woking GU22 167 BF115
Coldharbour Way, Croy. CR0 159 DN106
Coldshott, Oxt. RH8 188 EG133
Coldstream Gdns, SW18 119 CZ86
Coldstream Rd, Cat. CR3 176 DQ121
Cole Av, Grays RM16 111 GJ77
Colebeck Ms, N1 83 DP65
Colebert Av, E1 84 DW70
Colebrook, Cher. (Ott.) KT16 151 BD107
Colebrook Cl, NW7 43 CX52
SW15 off West Hill 119 CX87
Colebrooke Av, W13 79 CH72
Colebrooke Dr, E11 68 EH59
Colebrooke Pl, N1
off St. Peters St 83 DP67
Colebrooke Ri, Brom. BR2 144 EE96
Colebrooke Rd, Red. RH1 184 DE132
Colebrooke Row, N1 196 F1
Colebrook Gdns, Loug. IG10 33 EP40
Colebrook Ho, E14
off Brabazon St 85 EB72
Colebrook La, Loug. IG10 33 EP40
Colebrook Path, Loug. IG10 33 EP40
Colebrook Pl, Cher.
(Ott.) KT16 151 BB108
Colebrook Rd, SW16 141 DL95
Colebrook St, Erith DA8
off Erith High St 107 FF79
Colebrook Way, N11 45 DH50
Coleby Path, SE5
off Harris St 102 DR80
Cole Cl, SE28 88 EV74
Coledale Dr, Stan. HA7 41 CJ53
Coleford Rd, SW18 120 DC85
Cole Gdns, Houns. TW5 95 BU80
Colegrave Rd, E15 67 ED64
Colegrove Rd, SE15 102 DT80
Coleherne Ct, SW5 100 DB78
Coleherne Ms, SW10 100 DB78
Coleherne Rd, SW10 100 DB78
Colehill Gdns, SW6
off Fulham Palace Rd 99 CY82
Colehill La, SW6 99 CY81
Coleman Cl, SE25 142 DU96
Coleman Flds, N1 84 DQ67
Coleman Rd, SE5 102 DS80
Belvedere DA17 106 FA77
Dagenham RM9 88 EY65
Colemans Heath, SE9 125 EP90
Colemans La, Ong. CM5 19 FH30
Coleman's La, Wal.Abb. EN9 15 ED26
Coleman St, EC2 197 K8
Colenso Dr, NW7 43 CU52
Colenso Rd, E5 66 DW63
Ilford IG2 69 ES60
Cole Pk Gdns, Twick. TW1 117 CG86
Cole Pk Rd, Twick. TW1 117 CG86
Cole Pk Vw, Twick. TW1
off Hill Vw Rd 117 CG86
Colepits Wd Rd, SE9 125 EQ85
Coleraine Rd, N8 65 DN55
SE3 104 EF79
Coleridge Av, E12 86 EL65
Sutton SM1 158 DE105
Coleridge Cl, SW8 101 DH82
Waltham Cross (Chsht) EN7
off Peakes La 14 DT27
Coleridge Cres, Slou.
(Colnbr.) SL3 93 BE81
Coleridge Gdns, NW6
off Fairhazel Gdns 82 DC66
SW10 100 DB80
Coleridge La, N8
off Coleridge Rd 65 DL58
Coleridge Rd, E17 67 DZ56
N4 65 DN61
N8 65 DK58
N12 44 DC50
Ashford TW15 114 BL91
Croydon CR0 142 DW101
Dartford DA1 108 FN84
Romford RM3 51 FH52
Tilbury RM18 111 GJ82
Coleridge Sq, SW10 100 DC80
W13 off Berners Dr 79 CG72
Coleridge Wk, NW11 64 DA56
Brentwood (Hutt.) CM13 55 GC45
Coleridge Way, Hayes UB4 77 BU72
Orpington BR6 146 EU100
West Drayton UB7 94 BM77
Cole Rd, Twick. TW1 117 CG86
Watford WD17
off Stamford Rd 23 BV39
Colesburg Rd, Beck. BR3 143 DZ97
Coles Cres, Har. HA2 60 CB61
Colescroft Hill, Pur. CR8 175 DN115
Colesdale, Pot.B. (Cuffley) EN6 13 DL30
Coles Grn, Bushey
(Bushey Hth) WD23 40 CC46
Loughton IG10 33 EN39
Coles Grn Ct, NW2 63 CU61
Coles Grn Rd, NW2 63 CU60
Coleshill Rd, Tedd. TW11 117 CE93

Coningsby Dr, Wat. WD17 23 BS39
Coningham Ms, W12
off Percy Rd 81 CU74
Coningham Rd, W12 99 CV75
Coningsby Cotts, W5
off Coningsby Rd 97 CK75
Coningsby Dr, Pot.B. EN6 12 DD33
Coningsby Gdns, E4 47 EB51
Coningsby Rd, N4 65 DP59
W5 97 CJ75
South Croydon CR2 160 DQ109
Conington Rd, SE13 103 EB82
Conisbee Ct, N14 29 DJ43
Conisborough Cres, SE6 123 EC90
Coniscliffe Cl, Chis. BR7 145 EN95
Coniscliffe Rd, N13 46 DQ48
Conista Ct, Wok. GU21
off Roundthorn Way 166 AT116
Coniston Av, Bark. IG11 87 ES66
Greenford UB6 79 CH69
Upminster RM14 72 FQ63
Welling DA16 105 ES83
Coniston Cl, N20 44 DC48
SW13 off Lonsdale Rd 99 CT80
SW20 139 CX100
W4 98 CQ81
Barking IG11
off Coniston Av 87 ES66
Bexleyheath DA7 107 FC81
Dartford DA1 127 FH88
Erith DA8 107 FE80
Coniston Ct, Wey. KT13
off Hanger Hill 153 BP107
Conistone Way, N7 83 DL66
Coniston Gdns, N9 46 DW46
NW9 62 CR57
Ilford IG4 68 EL56
Pinner HA5 59 BU56
Sutton SM2 158 DD107
Wembley HA9 61 CJ60
Coniston Ho, SE5 102 DQ80
Coniston Rd, N10 45 DH54
N17 46 DU51
Bexleyheath DA7 107 FC81
Bromley BR1 124 EE93
Coulsdon CR5 175 DJ116
Croydon CR0 142 DU101
Kings Langley WD4 6 BM28
Twickenham TW2 116 CB86
Woking GU22 167 BB120
Coniston Wk, E9
off Clifden Rd 66 DW64
Coniston Way, Chess. KT9 138 CL104
Egham TW20 113 BB94
Hornchurch RM12 71 FG64
Reigate RH2 184 DE133
Conlan St, W10 81 CY70
Conley Rd, NW10 80 CS65
Conley St, SE10 205 J10
Connaught Av, E4 47 ED45
SW14 98 CQ83
Ashford TW15 114 BL91
Barnet EN4 44 DF46
Enfield EN1 30 DS40
Grays RM16 110 GB75
Hounslow TW4 116 BY85
Loughton IG10 32 EK42
Connaught Br, E16 86 EK74
Connaught Business Cen, Mitch. CR4
off Wandle Way 140 DF99
Connaught Cl, E10 67 DY61
W2 194 B9
Enfield EN1 30 DS40
Sutton SM1 140 DD103
Uxbridge UB8 off New Rd 77 BQ70
Connaught Ct, E17
off Orford Rd 67 EB56
Buckhurst Hill IG9 48 EH46
Connaught Dr, NW11 64 DA56
Weybridge KT13 152 BN111
Connaught Gdns, N10 65 DH57
N13 45 DP49
Morden SM4 140 DC98
Connaught Hts, Uxb. UB10
off Uxbridge Rd 77 BQ70
Connaught Hill, Loug. IG10 32 EK42
Connaught La, Ilf. IG1
off Connaught Rd 69 ER61
Connaught Ms, SE18 105 EN78
Ilford IG1
off Connaught Rd 69 ER61
Connaught Pl, W2 194 D10
Connaught Rd, E4 48 EE45
E11 67 ED60
E16 86 EK74
E17 67 EA57
N4 65 DN59
NW10 80 CS67
SE18 105 EN78
W13 79 CH73
Barnet EN5 27 CX44
Harrow HA3 41 CF53
Hornchurch RM12 72 FK62
Ilford IG1 69 ER61
New Malden KT3 138 CS98
Richmond TW10
off Albert Rd 118 CM85
Slough SL1 92 AV75
Sutton SM1 140 DD103
Teddington TW11 117 CD92
Connaught Roundabout, E16
off Connaught Br 86 EK73
Connaught Sq, W2 194 D9
Connaught St, W2 194 B9
Connaught Way, N13 45 DP49
Connell Cres, W5 80 CM70
Connemara Cl, Borwd. WD6
off Percheron Rd 26 CR44
Connington Cres, E4 47 ED48
Connop Rd, Enf. EN3 31 DX38
Connor Cl, E11 68 EE59
Ilford IG6 49 EP53
Connor Rd, Dag. RM9 70 EZ63
Connor St, E9
off Lauriston Rd 85 DX67
Conolly Rd, W7 79 CE74
Conquest Rd, Add. KT15 152 BG106
Conrad Cl, Grays RM16 110 GB75
Conrad Dr, Wor.Pk. KT4 139 CW102
Conrad Gdns, Grays RM16 110 GA75
Conrad Ho, N16 66 DS64
Consfield Av, N.Mal. KT3 139 CU98
Consort Cl, Brwd. CM14 54 FW50
Consort Ms, Islw. TW7 117 CD85
Consort Rd, SE15 102 DV81
Consort Way, Uxb. (Denh.) UB9
off Knowland Way 57 BF58
Cons St, SE1 200 E4
Constable Av, E16 205 P2
Constable Cl, NW11 64 DB58
Hayes UB4
off Charville La 77 BQ69
Constable Cres, N15 66 DU57
Constable Gdns, Edg. HA8 42 CN53
Isleworth TW7 117 CD85
Constable Ms, Dag. RM8
off Stonard Rd 70 EV63
Constable Rd, Grav.
(Nthflt) DA11 130 GE90
Constable Wk, SE21 122 DT90
Constance Cres, Brom. BR2 144 EF101
Constance Rd, Croy. CR0 141 DP101
Enfield EN1 30 DS44
Sutton SM1 158 DC105
Twickenham TW2 116 CB87
Constance St, E16
off Albert Rd 86 EL74
Constantine Pl, Uxb.
(Hlgdn) UB10 76 BM67
Constantine Rd, NW3 64 DE63
Constitution Hill, SW1 199 H4
Gravesend DA12 131 GJ88
Woking GU22 166 AY119
Constitution Ri, SE18 105 EN81
Consul Av, Dag. RM9 89 FC69
Consul Gdns, Swan. BR8 127 FG94
Content St, SE17 201 J9
Contessa Cl, Orp. BR6 163 ES106
Control Twr Rd, Houns.
(Hthrw Air.) TW6 94 BN83
Convair Wk, Nthlt. UB5
off Kittiwake Rd 78 BX69
Convent Cl, Beck. BR3 123 EC94
Convent Gdns, W5 97 CJ77
W11 off Kensington Pk Rd 81 CZ72
Convent Hill, SE19 122 DQ93
Convent La, Cob. KT11
off Seven Hills Rd 153 BS111
Convent Rd, Ashf. TW15 114 BN92
Convent Way, Sthl. UB2 96 BW77
Conway Cl, Rain. RM13 89 FG66
Stanmore HA7 41 CG51
Conway Cres, Grnf. UB6 79 CE68
Romford RM6 70 EW59
Conway Dr, Ashf. TW15 115 BQ93
Hayes UB3 95 BQ76
Sutton SM2 158 DB107
Conway Gdns, Enf. EN2 30 DS38
Grays RM17 110 GB80
Mitcham CR4 141 DK98
Wembley HA9 61 CJ59
Conway Gro, W3 80 CR71
Conway Ms, W1 195 K5
Conway Rd, N14 45 DL48
N15 65 DP57
NW2 63 CW61
SE18 105 ER77
SW20 139 CW95
Feltham TW13 116 BX92
Hounslow TW4 116 BZ87
Hounslow (Hthrw Air.) TW6
off Inner Ring E 95 BP83
Conway St, E13 86 EG70
W1 195 K5
Conway Wk, Hmptn. TW12
off Fearnley Cres 116 BZ93
Conybeare, NW3
off King Henry's Rd 82 DE66
Conybury Cl, Wal.Abb. EN9 16 EG32
Cony Cl, Wal.Cr. (Chsht) EN7 14 DS26
Conyers Cl, Walt. KT12 154 BX106
Woodford Green IG8 48 EE51
Conyers Rd, SW16 121 DK92
Conyer St, E3 85 DY68
Conyers Way, Loug. IG10 33 EP41
Cooden Cl, Brom. BR1
off Plaistow La 124 EH94
Cook Ct, SE16
off Rotherhithe St 84 DW74
Cooke Cl, E14 off Cabot Sq 85 EA74
Cookes Cl, E11 68 EF61
Cookes La, Sutt. SM3 157 CY107
Cookham Cl, Sthl. UB2 96 CB75
Cookham Cres, SE16 203 H4
Cookham Dene Cl, Chis. BR7 145 ER95
Cookham Hill, Orp. BR6 146 FA104
Cookham Rd, Sid. DA14 126 FA94
Swanley BR8 146 FA95
Cookhill Rd, SE2 106 EV75
Cook Rd, Dag. RM9 88 EY67
Cooks Cl, Rom. RM5 51 FC53
Cook's Hole Rd, Enf. EN2 29 DP38
Cooks Mead, Bushey WD23 24 CB44
Cookson Gro, Erith DA8 107 FB80
Cook Sq, Erith DA8 107 FF80
Cook's Rd, E15 85 EB68
Cooks Rd, SE17 101 DP79
Cooks Wf Roundabout, N18 47 DX50
Coolfin Rd, E16 86 EG72
Coolgardie Av, E4 47 EC50
Chigwell IG7 49 EN48
Coolgardie Rd, Ashf. TW15 115 BQ92
Coolhurst Rd, N8 65 DK58
Cool Oak La, NW9 62 CS59
Coomassie Rd, W9
off Bravington Rd 81 CZ70
COOMBE, Kings.T. KT2 118 CQ94
Coombe, The, Bet. RH3 182 CR131
Coombe Av, Croy. CR0 160 DS105
Sevenoaks TN14 181 FH120
Coombe Bk, Kings.T. KT2 138 CS95
Coombe Cl, Edg. HA8 42 CM54
Hounslow TW3 96 CA84
Coombe Cor, N21 45 DP46
Coombe Cres, Hmptn. TW12 116 BY94
Coombe Dr, Add. KT15 151 BF107
Kingston upon Thames KT2 118 CR94
Ruislip HA4 59 BV60
Coombe End, Kings.T. KT2 118 CR94
Coombefield Cl, N.Mal. KT3 138 CS99
Coombe Gdns, SW20 139 CU96
New Malden KT3 139 CT98
Coombe Hts, Kings.T. KT2 118 CS94
Coombe Hill Glade,
Kings.T. KT2 118 CS94
Coombe Hill Rd, Kings.T. KT2 118 CS94
Rickmansworth
(Mill End) WD3 38 BG45
Coombe Ho Chase,
N.Mal. KT3 138 CR95
Coombehurst Cl, Barn. EN4 28 DF40
Coombelands La, Add. KT15 152 BG107
Tra Coombe Lane 160 DW106
Coombe La, SW20 139 CU95
Croydon CR0 160 DV106
Coombe La W, Kings.T. KT2 118 CS94
Coombe Lea, Brom. BR1 144 EL97
Coombe Neville, Kings.T. KT2 118 CR94
Coombe Pk, Kings.T. KT2 118 CR92
Coombe Ridings, Kings.T. KT2 118 CQ92
Coombe Ri, Brwd.
(Shenf.) CM15 55 FZ46
Kingston upon Thames KT2 138 CQ95
Coombe Rd, N22 45 DN53
NW10 62 CR62
SE26 122 DV91
W4 98 CS78
W13 off Northcroft Rd 97 CH76
Bushey WD23 40 CC45
Croydon CR0 160 DR105
Gravesend DA12 131 GJ89
Hampton TW12 116 BZ93
Kingston upon Thames KT2 138 CN95
New Malden KT3 138 CS96
Romford RM3 72 FM55
Coomber Way, Croy. CR0 141 DK101
Coombes Rd, Dag. RM9 88 EZ67
St. Albans (Lon.Col.) AL2 9 CH26
Coombe Vale, Ger.Cr. SL9 56 AY60
Coombe Wk, Sutt. SM1 140 DB104
Coombe Way, W.Byf.
(Byfleet) KT14 152 BM112
Coombewood Dr, Rom. RM6 70 EZ58
Coombe Wd Hill, Pur. CR8 160 DQ112
Coombe Wd Rd, Kings.T. KT2 118 CQ92
Coombfield Dr, Dart.
(Lane End) DA2 129 FR91
Coombs St, N1 196 G1
Coomer Ms, SW6
off Coomer Pl 99 CZ79
Coomer Pl, SW6 99 CZ79
Coomer Rd, SW6
off Coomer Pl 99 CZ79
Cooms Wk, Edg. HA8
off East Rd 42 CQ53
Cooperage Cl, N17
off Brantwood Rd 46 DT51
Cooper Av, E17 47 DX53
Cooper Cl, SE1 200 E5
Greenhithe DA9 129 FT85
Cooper Ct, E15 off Clays La 67 EB64
Cooper Cres, Cars. SM5 140 DF104
Cooper Rd, NW4 63 CX58
NW10 63 CT64
Croydon CR0 159 DN105
COOPERSALE, Epp. CM16 18 EX29
Coopersale Cl, Wdf.Grn. IG8
off Navestock Cres 48 EJ52
Coopersale Common, Epp.
(Cooper.) CM16 18 EX28
Coopersale La, Epp. CM16 34 EU37
Coopersale Rd, E9 67 DX64
Coopersale St, Epp. CM16 18 EW32
Coopers Cl, E1 84 DW70
Chigwell IG7 50 EV47
Dagenham RM10 89 FB65
Dartford (S.Darenth) DA4 148 FQ95
Staines TW18 113 BE92
Coopers Ct, Rom. RM2
off Elvet Av 72 FJ55
Coopers Cres, Borwd. WD6 26 CQ39
Coopers Dr, Dart. DA2
off Old Bexley La 127 FE89
Coopers Hill La, Egh. TW20 112 AY91
Coopers Hill Rd, Red.
(Nutfld) RH1 185 DM133
Coopers La, E10 67 EB60
NW1 83 DK68
Cooper's La, SE12 124 EH89
Coopers La, Pot.B. EN6 12 DD31
Coopers La Rd, Pot.B. EN6 12 DE31
Coopers Ms, Wat. WD25
off High Elms La 8 BW31
Coopers Rd, SE1 102 DT78
Gravesend (Nthflt) DA11 130 GE88
Potters Bar EN6 12 DC30
Cooper's Row, EC3 197 P10
Coopers Row, Iver SL0 75 BC70
Coopers Shaw Rd, Til. RM18 111 GK80
Cooper St, E16
off Lawrence St 86 EF71
Coopers Wk, E15
off Maryland St 67 ED64
Waltham Cross (Chsht) EN8 15 DX28
Cooper's Yd, SE19
off Westow Hill 122 DS93
Coote Gdns, Dag. RM8 70 EZ62
Coote Rd, Bexh. DA7 106 EZ81
Dagenham RM8 70 EZ62
Copeland Dr, E14 204 A8
Copeland Rd, E17 67 EB57
SE15 102 DU82
Copeman Cl, SE26 122 DW92
Copeman Rd, Brwd.
(Hutt.) CM13 55 GD45
Copenhagen Gdns, W4 98 CQ75
Copenhagen Pl, E14 85 DZ72
Copenhagen St, N1 83 DL67
Copenhagen Way, Walt. KT12 135 BV104
Cope Pl, W8 100 DA76
Copers Cope Rd, Beck. BR3 123 DZ93
Cope St, SE16 203 H8
Copford Cl, Wdf.Grn. IG8 48 EL51
Copford Wk, N1
off Popham St 84 DQ67
Copgate Path, SW16 121 DM93
Copinger Wk, Edg. HA8
off North Rd 42 CP53
Copland Av, Wem. HA0 61 CK64
Copland Cl, Wem. HA0 61 CJ64
Copland Ms, Wem. HA0
off Copland Rd 80 CL65
Copland Rd, Wem. HA0 80 CL65
Copleigh Dr, Tad. KT20 173 CY120
Copleston Ms, SE15
off Copleston Rd 102 DT82
Copleston Pas, SE15 102 DT83
Copleston Rd, SE15 102 DT83
Copley Cl, SE17
off Hillingdon St 101 DP79
W7 79 CF71
Redhill RH1 184 DE132
Woking GU21 166 AS119
Copley Dene, Brom. BR1 144 EK95
Copley Pk, SW16 121 DM93
Copley Rd, Stan. HA7 41 CJ50
Copley St, E1 85 DX71
Copley Way, Tad. KT20 173 CX120
Copmans Wick, Rick.
(Chorl.) WD3 21 BD43
Copnor Way, SE15
off Blakes Rd 102 DS80
Coppard Gdns, Chess. KT9 155 CJ107
Copped Hall, SE21
off Glazebrook Cl 122 DR89
Coppelia Rd, SE3 104 EF84
Coppen Rd, Dag. RM8 70 EZ59
Copperas St, SE8 103 EB79
Copper Beech Cl, Grav. DA12 131 GK87
Ilford IG5 49 EN53
Orpington BR5
off Rookery Gdns 146 EW99
Woking GU22 166 AV121
Copper Beech Ct, Loug. IG10 33 EN39
Copper Beeches, Islw. TW7
off Eversley Cres 97 CD81
Copper Beech Rd,
S.Ock. RM15 91 FW69
Copper Cl, SE19
off Auckland Rd 122 DT94
Copperdale Rd, Hayes UB3 95 BU75
Copperfield, Chig. IG7 49 ER51
Copperfield App, Chig. IG7 49 ER51
Copperfield Av, Uxb. UB8 76 BN71
Copperfield Cl, S.Croy. CR2 160 DQ111
Copperfield Ct, Lthd. KT22
off Kingston Rd 171 CG121
Pinner HA5
off Copperfield Way 60 BZ56
Copperfield Dr, N15 66 DT56
Copperfield Gdns, Brwd. CM14 54 FV46
Copperfield Ms, N18 46 DS50
Copperfield Ri, Add. KT15 151 BF106
Copperfield Rd, E3 85 DY70
SE28 88 EW72
Copperfields, Dart. DA1
off Spital St 128 FL86
Leatherhead (Fetch.) KT22 170 CC122
Copperfield St, SE1 200 G4
Copperfields Way, Rom. RM3 52 FK53
Copperfield Ter, Slou. SL2
off Mirador Cres 74 AV73
Copperfield Way, Chis. BR7 125 EQ93
Pinner HA5 60 BZ56
Coppergate Cl, Brom. BR1 144 EH95
Coppergate Ct, Wal.Abb. EN9
off Farthingale La 16 EG34
Copper Mead Cl, NW2 63 CW62
Copper Mill Dr, Islw. TW7 97 CF82
Coppermill La, E17 66 DW58
Copper Mill La, SW17 120 DC91
Coppermill La, Rick. WD3 37 BE52
Uxbridge (Hare.) UB9 37 BE52
Coppermill Rd, Stai.
(Wrays.) TW19 93 BC84
Copper Ridge, Ger.Cr.
(Chal.St.P.) SL9 37 AZ50
Copper Row, SE1 201 P3
Coppetts Cl, N12 44 DE52
Coppetts Rd, N10 44 DG54
H Coppetts Wd Hosp, N10 44 DF53
Coppice, The, Ashf. TW15
off School Rd 115 BP93
Enfield EN2 29 DP42
Watford WD19 24 BW44
West Drayton UB7 76 BL72
Coppice Cl, SW20 139 CW97
Beckenham BR3 143 EB98
Ruislip HA4 59 BR58
Stanmore HA7 41 CF51
Coppice Dr, SW15 119 CV86
Staines (Wrays.) TW19 112 AX87
Coppice End, Wok. GU22 167 BE116
Coppice La, Reig. RH2 183 CZ132
Coppice Path, Chig. IG7 50 EV49
Coppice Row, Epp. CM16 33 EM36
Coppice Wk, N20 44 DA48
Coppice Way, E18 68 EF56
Coppies Gro, N11 44 DG49
Copping Cl, Croy. CR0
off Tipton Dr 160 DS105
Coppins, The, Croy.
(New Adgtn) CR0 161 EB107
Harrow HA3 41 CE51
Coppins La, Iver SL0 75 BF71
Coppock Cl, SW11 100 DE82
Coppsfield, W.Mol. KT8
off Hurst Rd 136 CA97
Copse, The, E4 48 EF46
Caterham CR3
off Tupwood La 186 DU126
Leatherhead (Fetch.) KT22 170 CB123
Copse Av, W.Wick. BR4 143 EB104
Copse Cl, SE7 104 EH79
Northwood HA6 39 BQ54
West Drayton UB7 94 BK76
Copse Edge Av, Epsom KT17 157 CT113
Copse Glade, Surb. KT6 137 CK102
COPSE HILL, SW20 119 CU94
Copse Hill, SW20 119 CV94
Purley CR8 159 DL113
Sutton SM2 158 DB108
Copse La, Beac.
(Jordans) HP9 36 AS52
Copsem Dr, Esher KT10 154 CB107
Copsem La, Esher KT10 154 CB107
Leatherhead
(Oxshott) KT22 154 CC111
Copsem Way, Esher KT10 154 CC107
Copsen Wd, Lthd. KT22 154 CC111
Copse Rd, Cob. KT11 153 BV113
Woking GU21 166 AT118
Copse Vw, S.Croy. CR2 161 DX109
Copse Wd, Iver SL0 75 BD67
Copsewood Cl, Sid. DA15 125 ES86
Copse Wd Ct, Reig. RH2
off Green La 184 DE132
Copsewood Rd, Wat. WD24 23 BV39
Copse Wd Way, Nthwd. HA6 39 BQ52
Coptefield Dr, Belv. DA17 106 EX76
Coptfold Rd, Brwd. CM14 54 FW47
Copthall Av, EC2 197 L8
Copthall Bldgs, EC2 197 K8
Copthall Cl, EC2 197 K8
Gerrards Cross
(Chal.St.P.) SL9 37 AZ52
Copthall Cor, Ger.Cr.
(Chal.St.P.) SL9 36 AY52
Copthall Ct, EC2 197 K8
Copthall Dr, NW7 43 CU52
Copthall Gdns, NW7 43 CU52
Twickenham TW1 117 CF88
COPTHALL GREEN,
Wal.Abb. EN9 16 EK33
Copthall La, Ger.Cr.
(Chal.St.P.) SL9 36 AY52
Copthall Rd E, Uxb. UB10 58 BN61
Copthall Rd W, Uxb. UB10 58 BN61
Copthall Way, Add.
(New Haw) KT15 151 BF110
Copt Hill La, Tad. KT20 173 CY120
Copthorne Av, SW12 121 DK87
Bromley BR2 145 EM103
Ilford IG6 49 EP51
Copthorne Chase, Ashf. TW15
off Ford Rd 114 BM91
Copthorne Cl, Rick.
(Crox.Grn) WD3 22 BM43
Shepperton TW17 135 BQ100
Copthorne Gdns, Horn. RM11 72 FN57
Copthorne Ms, Hayes UB3 95 BS77
Copthorne Ri, S.Croy. CR2 160 DR113
Copthorne Rd, Lthd. KT22 171 CH120
Rickmansworth
(Crox.Grn) WD3 22 BM44
Coptic St, WC1 195 P7
Copwood Cl, N12 44 DD49
Coral Cl, Rom. RM6 70 EW56
Coraline Cl, Sthl. UB1 78 BZ69
Coralline Wk, SE2 106 EW75
Coral Row, SW11
off Gartons Way 100 DC83
Coral St, SE1 200 E5
Coram Grn, Brwd.
(Hutt.) CM13 55 GD44
Coram St, WC1 195 P5
Coran Cl, N9 47 DX45
Corban Rd, Houns. TW3 96 CA83
Corbar Cl, Barn. EN4 28 DD38
Corbden Cl, SE15 102 DT81
Corbet Cl, Wall. SM6 140 DG102
Corbet Ct, EC3 197 L9
Corbet Pl, E1 197 P6
Corbet Rd, Epsom KT17 156 CS110
Corbets Av, Upmin. RM14 72 FP64
CORBETS TEY, Upmin. RM14 90 FQ65
Corbets Tey Rd, Upmin. RM14 72 FP63
Corbett Cl, Croy. CR0 161 ED112
Corbett Gro, N22 45 DL52
Corbett Ho, Wat. WD19 40 BW48
Corbett Rd, E11 68 EJ58
E17 67 EC55
Corbetts La, SE16 202 F9
Corbetts Pas, SE16 202 F9
Corbicum, E11 68 EE59
Corbidge Ct, SE8
off Glaisher St 103 EB79
Corbiere Ct, SW19
off Thornton Rd 119 CX93
Corbiere Ho, N1 84 DS67
Corbins La, Har. HA2 60 CB62
Corbridge Cres, E2 84 DV68
Corbridge Ms, Rom. RM1
off Victoria Rd 71 FF57
Corby Cl, Egh.
(Eng.Grn) TW20 112 AW93
St. Albans AL2 8 CA25
Corby Cres, Enf. EN2 29 DL42
Corby Dr, Egh.
(Eng.Grn) TW20 112 AV93
Corbylands Rd, Sid. DA15 125 ES87
Corbyn St, N4 65 DL60
Corby Rd, NW10 80 CR68
Corby Way, E3 off Knapp Rd 85 EA70
Corcorans, Brwd.
(Pilg.Hat.) CM15 54 FV44
Cordelia Cl, SE24 101 DP84
Cordelia Gdns, Stai. TW19 114 BL87
Cordelia Rd, Stai. TW19 114 BL87
Cordelia St, E14 85 EB72
Cordell Cl, Wal.Cr. (Chsht) EN8 15 DY28
Cordell Ho, N15
off Newton Rd 66 DT57
Corderoy Pl, Cher. KT16 133 BE100
Cordingley Rd, Ruis. HA4 59 BR61
Cording St, E14
off Chrisp St 85 EB71
Cordons Cl, Ger.Cr.
(Chal.St.P.) SL9 36 AX53
Cordrey Gdns, Couls. CR5 175 DL115
Cordwainers Wk, E13
off Richmond St 86 EG68
Cord Way, E14 204 A6
Cordwell Rd, SE13 124 EE85
Corefield Cl, N11
off Benfleet Way 44 DG47
Corelli Rd, SE3 104 EL82
Corfe Av, Har. HA2 60 CA63
Corfe Cl, Ashtd. KT21 171 CJ118
Borehamwood WD6
off Chester Rd 26 CR41
Hayes UB4 78 BW72
Corfe Twr, W3 98 CP75
Corfield Rd, N21 29 DM43
Corfield St, E2 84 DV69

★ Place of interest ⇌ Railway station ⊖ London Underground station DLR Docklands Light Railway station Tra Tramlink station H Hospital Riv Pedestrian ferry landing stage

Corfton Rd, W5 80 CL72
Coriander Av, E14 85 ED72
Cories Cl, Dag. RM8 70 EX61
Corinium Cl, Wem. HA9 62 CM63
Corinium Ind Est, Amer. HP6 20 AT38
Corinne Rd, N19 65 DJ63
Corinthian Manorway, Erith DA8 107 FD77
Corinthian Rd, Erith DA8 107 FD77
Corinthian Way, Stai. (Stanw.) TW19
off Clare Rd 114 BK87
Corker Wk, N7 65 DM61
Corkran Rd, Surb. KT6 137 CK101
Corkscrew Hill, W.Wick. BR4 143 ED103
Cork Sq, E1 202 D2
Cork St, W1 199 K1
Cork St Ms, W1 199 K1
Cork Tree Way, E4 47 DY50
Corlett St, NW1 194 B6
Cormongers La, Red. (Nutfld) RH1 185 DK131
Cormont Rd, SE5 101 DP81
Cormorant Cl, E17
off Banbury Rd 47 DX53
Cormorant Ho, Enf. EN3
off Alma Rd 31 DX43
Cormorant Pl, Sutt. SM1
off Sandpiper Rd 157 CZ106
Cormorant Rd, E7 68 EF63
Cormorant Wk, Horn. RM12
off Heron Flight Av 89 FH65
Cornbury Rd, Edg. HA8 41 CK52
Cornelia Dr, Hayes UB4
off Yeading La 78 BW70
Cornelia Pl, Erith DA8
off Queen St 107 FE79
Cornelia St, N7 83 DM65
Cornell Cl, Sid. DA14 126 EY93
Cornell Way, Rom. RM5 50 FA50
Corner, The, W.Byf. KT14 152 BG113
Corner Fm Cl, Tad. KT20 173 CW122
Corner Grn, SE3 104 EG83
Corner Ho St, WC2 199 P2
Corner Mead, NW9 43 CT52
Cornerside, Ashf. TW15 115 BQ94
Corney Reach Way, W4 98 CS80
Corney Rd, W4 98 CS79
Cornfield Cl, Uxb. UB8
off The Greenway 76 BK68
Cornfield Rd, Bushey WD23 24 CB42
Cornflower La, Croy. CR0 143 DX102
Cornflower Ter, SE22 122 DV86
Cornflower Way, Rom. RM3 52 FL53
Cornford Cl, Brom. BR2 144 EG99
Cornford Gro, SW12 121 DH89
Cornhill, EC3 197 L9
Cornhill Cl, Add. KT15 134 BH103
Cornhill Dr, Enf. EN3
off Ordnance Rd 31 DY37
Cornish Ct, N9 46 DV45
Cornish Gro, SE20 122 DV94
Cornish Ho, SE17 off Otto St 101 DP79
Brentford TW8
off Green Dragon La 98 CM78
Cornmill, Wal.Abb. EN9 15 EB33
Corn Mill Dr, Orp. BR6 145 ET101
Cornmill La, SE13 103 EB83
Cornmill Ms, Wal.Abb. EN9
off Highbridge St 15 EB33
Cornmow Dr, NW10 63 CT64
Cornshaw Rd, Dag. RM8 70 EX60
Cornsland, Brwd. CM14 54 FX48
Cornsland Ct, Brwd. CM14 54 FW48
Cornthwaite Rd, E5 66 DW62
Cornwall Av, E2 84 DW69
N3 44 DA52
N22 45 DL53
Esher (Clay.) KT10
off The Causeway 155 CF108
Southall UB1 78 BZ71
Welling DA16 105 ES83
West Byfleet (Byfleet) KT14 152 BM114
Cornwall Cl, Bark. IG11 87 ET65
Hornchurch RM11 72 FN56
Waltham Cross EN8 15 DY33
Cornwall Cres, W11 81 CY73
Cornwall Dr, Orp. BR5 126 EW94
Cornwall Gdns, NW10 81 CV65
SW7 100 DB76
Cornwall Gdns Wk, SW7
off Cornwall Gdns 100 DB76
Cornwall Gate, Purf. RM19
off Fanns Ri 108 FN77
Cornwall Gro, W4 98 CS78
Cornwallis Av, N9 46 DV47
SE9 125 ER89
Cornwallis Cl, Cat. CR3 176 DQ122
Erith DA8 107 FF79
Cornwallis Gro, N9 46 DV47
Cornwallis Rd, E17 67 DX56
N9 46 DV47
N19 65 DL61
Dagenham RM9 70 EX63
Cornwallis Sq, N19 65 DL61
Cornwallis Wk, SE9 105 EM83
Cornwall Ms S, SW7 100 DC76
Cornwall Ms W, SW7
off Cornwall Gdns 100 DB76
Cornwall Rd, N4 65 DN59
N15 66 DR57
N18 off Fairfield Rd 46 DU50
SE1 200 D2
Brentwood (Pilg.Hat.) CM15 54 FV43
Croydon CR0 141 DP103
Dartford DA1 108 FM83
Esher (Clay.) KT10 155 CG108
Harrow HA1 60 CC58
Pinner HA5 40 BZ52
Ruislip HA4 59 BT62
Sutton SM2 157 CZ108
Twickenham TW1 117 CG88
Uxbridge UB8 76 BK65
Windsor SL4 112 AU86
Cornwall Sq, SE11 200 F10
Cornwall St, E1
off Watney St 84 DV73
Cornwall Ter, NW1 194 E5
Cornwall Ter Ms, NW1 194 E5
Cornwall Way, Stai. TW18 113 BE93
Corn Way, E11 67 ED62
Cornwell Av, Grav. DA12 131 GJ90
Cornwood Cl, N2 64 DD57
Cornwood Dr, E1 84 DW72
Cornworthy Rd, Dag. RM8 70 EW64
Corona Rd, SE12 124 EG87
Coronation Av, N16
off Victorian Rd 66 DT62
Slough (Geo.Grn) SL3 74 AY72
Windsor SL4 92 AT81
Coronation Cl, Bex. DA5 126 EX86
Ilford IG6 69 EQ56
Coronation Dr, Horn. RM12 71 FH63
Coronation Hill, Epp. CM16 17 ET30
Coronation Rd, E13 86 EJ69
NW10 80 CM69
Hayes UB3 95 BT77
Coronation Wk, Twick. TW2 116 BZ88
Coronet St, N1 197 M3
Corporation Av, Houns. TW4 96 BY84
Corporation Row, EC1 196 E4
Corporation St, E15 86 EE68
N7 65 DL64
Corrance Rd, SW2 101 DL84
Corran Way, S.Ock. RM15 91 FV73
Corri Av, N14 45 DK49
Corrib Dr, Sutt. SM1 158 DE106
Corrie Gdns, Vir.W. GU25 132 AW101
Corrie Rd, Add. KT15 152 BK105
Woking GU22 167 BC120
Corrigan Av, Couls. CR5 158 DG114
Corrigan Cl, NW4 63 CW55
Corringham Ct, NW11
off Corringham Rd 64 DB59
Corringham Rd, NW11 64 DA59
Wembley HA9 62 CN61
Corringway, NW11 64 DB59
W5 80 CN70
Corris Grn, NW9
off Snowdon Dr 62 CS58
Corry Dr, SW9 101 DP84
Corsair Cl, Stai. TW19 114 BK87
Corsair Rd, Stai. TW19 114 BL87
Corscombe Cl, Kings.T. KT2 118 CQ92
Corsehill St, SW16 121 DJ93
Corsham St, N1 197 L3
Corsica St, N5 83 DP65
Cortayne Rd, SW6 99 CZ82
Cortina Dr, Dag. RM9
off Thames Av 89 FC69
Cortis Rd, SW15 119 CV86
Cortis Ter, SW15 119 CV86
Cortland Cl, Dart. DA1
off Lower Sta Rd 127 FE86
Corunna Rd, SW8 101 DJ81
Corunna Ter, SW8 101 DJ81
Corve La, S.Ock. RM15 91 FV73
Corvette Sq, SE10
off Feathers Pl 103 ED79
Corwell Gdns, Uxb. UB8 77 BQ72
Corwell La, Uxb. UB8 77 BQ72
Cory Dr, Brwd. (Hutt.) CM13 55 GB45
Coryton Path, W9
off Ashmore Rd 81 CZ70
Cosbycote Av, SE24 122 DQ85
Cosdach Av, Wall. SM6 159 DK108
Cosedge Cres, Croy. CR0 159 DN106
Cosgrove Cl, N21 46 DQ47
Hayes UB4 off Kingsash Dr 78 BY70
Cosmo Pl, WC1 196 A6
Cosmur Cl, W12 99 CT76
Cossall Wk, SE15 102 DV81
Cossar Ms, SW2
off Tulse Hill 121 DN86
Cosser St, SE1 200 D6
Costa St, SE15 102 DU82
Costead Manor Rd, Brwd. CM14 54 FV46
Costell's Meadow, West. TN16 189 ER126
Costons Av, Grnf. UB6 79 CD69
Costons La, Grnf. UB6 79 CD69
Coston Wk, SE4
off Hainford Cl 103 DX84
Cosway St, NW1 194 C6
Cotall St, E14 85 EA72
Coteford Cl, Loug. IG10 33 EP40
Pinner HA5 59 BU57
Coteford St, SW17 120 DF91
Cotelands, Croy. CR0 142 DS104
Cotesbach Rd, E5 66 DW62
Cotesmore Gdns, Dag. RM8 70 EW63
Cotford Rd, Th.Hth. CR7 142 DQ98
Cotham St, SE17 201 J9
Cotherstone, Epsom KT19 156 CR110
Cotherstone Rd, SW2 121 DM88
Cotlandswick, St.Alb. (Lon.Col.) AL2 9 CJ26
Cotleigh Av, Bex. DA5 126 EX89
Cotleigh Rd, NW6 82 DA66
Romford RM7 71 FD58
Cotman Cl, NW11 64 DC58
SW15 off Westleigh Av 119 CX86
Cotmandene Cres, Orp. BR5 146 EU96
Cotman Gdns, Edg. HA8 42 CN54
Cotman Ms, Dag. RM8
off Highgrove Rd 70 EW64
Cotmans Cl, Hayes UB3 77 BU74
Coton Rd, Well. DA16 106 EU83
Cotsford Av, N.Mal. KT3 138 CQ99
Cotswold Av, Bushey WD23 24 CC44
Cotswold Cl, Bexh. DA7 107 FE82
Esher KT10 137 CF104
Kingston upon Thames KT2 118 CP93
Staines TW18 114 BG92
Uxbridge UB8 76 BJ67
Cotswold Ct, EC1 197 H4
N11 44 DG49
Cotswold Gdns, E6 86 EK69
NW2 63 CX61
Brentwood (Hutt.) CM13 55 GE45
Ilford IG2 69 ER59
Cotswold Gate, NW2
off Cotswold Gdns 63 CY60
Cotswold Grn, Enf. EN2
off Cotswold Way 29 DM42
Cotswold Ms, SW11
off Battersea High St 100 DD81
Cotswold Ri, Orp. BR6 145 ET100
Cotswold Rd, Grav. (Nthflt) DA11 130 GE90
Hampton TW12 116 CA93
Romford RM3 52 FM54
Sutton SM2 158 DB110
Cotswold St, SE27
off Norwood High St 121 DP91
Cotswold Way, Enf. EN2 29 DM42
Worcester Park KT4 139 CW103
Cottage Av, Brom. BR2 144 EL102
Cottage Cl, Cher. (Ott.) KT16 151 BC107
Rickmansworth (Crox.Grn) WD3
off Scots Hill 22 BM44
Ruislip HA4 59 BR60
Watford WD17 23 BT40
Cottage Fm Way, Egh. TW20
off Green Rd 133 BC97
Cottage Fld Cl, Sid. DA14 126 EW88
Cottage Gdns, Wal.Cr. EN8 14 DW29
Cottage Grn, SE5 102 DR80
Cottage Gro, SW9 101 DL83
Surbiton KT6 137 CK100
Cottage Homes, NW7 43 CU49
Cottage Pl, SW3 198 B6
Cottage Rd, Epsom KT19 156 CR108
Cottage St, E14 85 EB73
Cottage Wk, N16
off Smalley Cl 66 DT62
Cottenham Dr, NW9 63 CT55
SW20 119 CV94
Cottenham Par, SW20
off Durham Rd 139 CV96
COTTENHAM PARK, SW20 139 CV95
Cottenham Pk Rd, SW20 119 CV94
Cottenham Pl, SW20 119 CV94
Cottenham Rd, E17 67 DZ56
Cotterill Rd, Surb. KT6 138 CL103
Cottesbrooke Cl, Slou. (Colnbr.) SL3 93 BD81
Cottesbrook St, SE14
off Nynehead St 103 DY80
Cottesloe Ms, SE1 200 E6
Cottesmore Av, Ilf. IG5 49 EN54
Cottesmore Gdns, W8 100 DB76
Cottimore Av, Walt. KT12 135 BV102
Cottimore Cres, Walt. KT12 135 BV101
Cottimore La, Walt. KT12 136 BW102
Cottimore Ter, Walt. KT12 135 BV101
Cottingham Chase, Ruis. HA4 59 BU62
Cottingham Rd, SE20 123 DX94
SW8 101 DM80
Cottington Rd, Felt. TW13 116 BX91
Cottington St, SE11 200 E10
Cottle Way, SE16 202 E5
Cotton Av, W3 80 CR72
Cotton Cl, Dag. RM9
off Flamstead Rd 88 EW66
Cottongrass Cl, Croy. CR0
off Cornflower La 143 DX102
Cotton Hill, Brom. BR1 123 ED91
Cotton La, Dart. DA2 128 FQ86
Greenhithe DA9 128 FQ85
Cotton Rd, Pot.B. EN6 12 DC31
Cotton Row, SW11 100 DC83
Cottons App, Rom. RM7 71 FD57
Cottons Ct, Rom. RM7 71 FD57
Cottons Gdns, E2 197 N2
Cottons La, SE1 201 L2
Cotton St, E14 85 EC73
Cottrell Ct, SE10
off Greenroof Way 104 EF76
Cotts Cl, W7
off Westcott Cres 79 CF71
Couchmore Av, Esher KT10 137 CE103
Ilford IG5 49 EM54
Coulgate St, SE4 103 DY83
COULSDON 175 DJ116
Coulsdon Common, Cat. CR3 176 DQ121
Coulsdon Ct Rd, Couls. CR5 175 DM116
Coulsdon La, Couls. CR5 174 DF119
Coulsdon Pl, Cat. CR3 176 DR122
Coulsdon Ri, Couls. CR5 175 DL117
Coulsdon Rd, Cat. CR3 176 DQ122
Coulsdon CR5 175 DM115
⇌ Coulsdon South 175 DK116
Coulson Cl, Dag. RM8 70 EW59
Coulson St, SW3 198 D10
Coulter Cl, Hayes UB4
off Berrydale Rd 78 BY70
Potters Bar (Cuffley) EN6 13 DK27
Coulter Rd, W6 99 CV76
Coulton Av, Grav. (Nthflt) DA11 130 GE87
Council Av, Grav. (Nthflt) DA11 130 GC86
Council Cotts, Wok. (Wisley) GU23
off Wisley La 168 BK115
Councillor St, SE5 102 DQ80
Counter Ct, SE1
off Southwark St 84 DR74
Counter St, SE1 201 M3
Countess Cl, Uxb. (Hare.) UB9 38 BJ54
Countess Rd, NW5 65 DJ64
Countisbury Av, Enf. EN1 46 DT45
Countisbury Gdns, Add. KT15
off Addlestone Pk 152 BH106
Country Way, Felt. TW13 115 BV94
Sunbury-on-Thames TW16 115 BV94
County Gate, SE9 125 EQ90
Barnet EN5 28 DB44
County Gro, SE5 102 DQ81
★ County Hall, SE1 200 B4
County Rd, E6 87 EP71
Thornton Heath CR7 141 DP96
County St, SE1 201 J7
Coupland Pl, SE18 105 EQ78
Courage Cl, Horn. RM11 72 FJ58
Courage Wk, Brwd. (Hutt.) CM13 55 GD44
Courcy Rd, N8 65 DN55
Courier Rd, Dag. RM9 89 FC70
Courland Gro, SW8 101 DK81
Courland Gro Hall, SW8 101 DK82
Courland Rd, Add. KT15 134 BH104
Courland St, SW8 101 DK81
Course, The, SE9 125 EN90
Coursers Rd, St.Alb. (Coln.Hth) AL4 10 CN27
Court, The, Ruis. HA4 60 BY63
Warlingham CR6 177 DY118
Courtauld Cl, SE28
off Pitfield Cres 88 EU74
★ Courtauld Inst of Art, WC2 196 B10
Courtauld Rd, N19 65 DK60
Courtaulds, Kings L. (Chipper.) WD4 6 BH30
Court Av, Belv. DA17 106 EZ78
Coulsdon CR5 175 DN118
Romford RM3 52 FN52
Court Bushes Rd, Whyt. CR3 176 DU120
Court Cl, Har. HA3 62 CL55
Twickenham TW2 116 CB90
Wallington SM6 159 DK108
Court Cl Av, Twick. TW2 116 CB90
Court Cres, Chess. KT9 155 CK106
Swanley BR8 147 FE98
Court Downs Rd, Beck. BR3 143 EB96
★ Court Dress Collection, Kensington Palace, W8 100 DB75
Court Dr, Croy. CR0 159 DM105
Stanmore HA7 42 CL49
Sutton SM1 158 DE105
Uxbridge UB10 76 BM67
Courtenay Av, N6 64 DE58
Harrow HA3 40 CC53
Sutton SM2 158 DA109
Courtenay Dr, Beck. BR3 143 ED96
Grays (Chaff.Hun.) RM16
off Clifford Rd 110 FZ76
Courtenay Gdns, Har. HA3 40 CC54
Upminster RM14 72 FQ60
Courtenay Ms, E17
off Cranbrook Ms 67 DY57
Courtenay Pl, E17 67 DY57
Courtenay Rd, E11 68 EF62
E17 67 DX56
SE20 123 DX94
Wembley HA9 61 CK62
Woking GU21 167 BA116
Worcester Park KT4 139 CW104
Courtenay Sq, SE11
off Courtenay St 101 DN78
Courtenay St, SE11 200 D10
Courtens Ms, Stan. HA7 41 CJ52
Court Fm Av, Epsom KT19 156 CR106
Court Fm Rd, SE9 124 EK89
Northolt UB5 78 CA66
Warlingham CR6 176 DU118
Courtfield, W5
off Castlebar Hill 79 CJ71
Courtfield Av, Har. HA1 61 CF57
Courtfield Cres, Har. HA1 61 CF57
Courtfield Gdns, SW5 100 DB77
W13 79 CG72
Ruislip HA4 59 BT61
Uxbridge (Denh.) UB9 58 BG62
Courtfield Ms, SW5
off Courtfield Gdns 100 DB77
Courtfield Ri, W.Wick. BR4 143 ED104
Courtfield Rd, SW7 100 DB77
Ashford TW15 115 BP93
Court Gdns, N7 83 DN65
Courtgate Cl, NW7 43 CT51
Court Grn Hts, Wok. GU22 166 AW120
Court Haw, Bans. SM7 174 DE115
Court Hill, Couls. CR5 174 DE117
South Croydon CR2 160 DS112
Courthill Rd, SE13 103 EC84
Courthope Rd, NW3 64 DF63
SW19 119 CY92
Greenford UB6 79 CD68
Courthope Vil, SW19 119 CY94
Court Ho Gdns, N3 44 DA51
Courthouse Rd, N12 44 DB51
Courtland Av, E4 48 EF47
NW7 42 CR48
SW16 121 DM94
Ilford IG1 69 EM61
Courtland Cl, Wdf.Grn. IG8 48 EJ53
Courtland Dr, Chig. IG7 49 EP48
Courtland Gro, SE28 88 EX73
Courtland Rd, E6
off Harrow Rd 86 EL67
Courtlands, Rich. TW10 98 CN84
Courtlands Av, SE12 124 EH85
Bromley BR2 144 EF102
Esher KT10 154 BZ107
Hampton TW12 116 BZ93
Richmond TW9 98 CP82
Slough SL3 92 AX77
Courtlands Cl, Ruis. HA4 59 BT59
South Croydon CR2 160 DT110
Watford WD24 23 BS35
Courtlands Cres, Bans. SM7 174 DA116
Courtlands Dr, Epsom KT19 156 CS107
Watford WD17, WD24 23 BS37
Courtlands Rd, Surb. KT5 138 CN101
Court La, SE21 122 DS86
Epsom KT19 156 CQ113
Iver SL0 76 BG74
Court La Gdns, SE21 122 DS87
Courtleas, Cob. KT11 154 CA113
Courtleet Dr, Erith DA8 107 FB81
Courtleigh Av, Barn. EN4 28 DD38
Courtleigh Gdns, NW11 63 CY56
Courtman Rd, N17 46 DQ52
Court Mead, Nthlt. UB5 78 BZ69
Courtmead Cl, SE24 122 DQ86
Courtnell St, W2 82 DA72
Courtney Cl, SE19 122 DS93
Courtney Cres, Cars. SM5 158 DF108
Courtney Pl, Cob. KT11 154 BZ112
Croydon CR0 141 DN104
Courtney Rd, N7
off Bryantwood Rd 65 DN64
SW19 120 DE94
Croydon CR0 141 DN104
Grays RM16 111 GJ75
Hounslow (Hthrw Air.) TW6 94 BN83
Courtney Way, Houns. (Hthrw Air.) TW6
off Courtney Rd 94 BN82
Court Par, Wem. HA0 61 CH62
Courtrai Rd, SE23 123 DY86
Court Rd, SE9 124 EL89
SE25 142 DT96
Banstead SM7 174 DA116
Caterham CR3 176 DR123
Dartford (Lane End) DA2 129 FS92
Godstone RH9 186 DW131
Orpington BR6 146 EV101
Southall UB2 96 BZ77
Uxbridge UB10 59 BP64
Courtside, N8 65 DK58
Court St, E1 off Durward St 84 DV71
Bromley BR1 144 EG96
Court Way, NW9 62 CS56
W3 80 CQ71
Ilford IG6 69 EQ55
Romford RM3 52 FL54
Twickenham TW2 117 CF87
Courtway, Wdf.Grn. IG8 48 EJ50
Courtway, The, Wat. WD19 40 BY47
Court Wd Dr, Sev. TN13 190 FG124
Court Wd Gro, Croy. CR0 161 DZ111
Court Wd La, Croy. CR0 161 DZ111
Court Yd, SE9 124 EL86
Courtyard, The, N1 83 DM66
Courtyards, The, Slou. SL3
off Waterside Dr 93 BA75
Cousin La, EC4 201 K1
Cousins Cl, West Dr. UB7 76 BL73
Couthurst Rd, SE3 104 EH79
Coutts Av, Chess. KT9 156 CL106
Coutts Cres, NW5 64 DG62
Coval Gdns, SW14 98 CP84
Coval La, SW14 98 CP84
Coval Rd, SW14 98 CP84
Coveham Cres, Cob. KT11 153 BU113
Covelees Wall, E6 87 EN72
Covell Ct, SE8
off Reginald Sq 103 EA80
Covenbrook, Brwd. CM13 55 GB48
★ Covent Garden, WC2 196 A10
⊖ Covent Garden 195 P10
Coventry Cl, E6
off Harper Rd 87 EM72
NW6 off Kilburn High Rd 82 DA67
Coventry Cross, E3
off Gillender St 85 EC70
Coventry Rd, E1 84 DV70
E2 84 DV70
SE25 142 DU98
Ilford IG1 69 EP60
Coventry St, W1 199 M1
Coverack Cl, N14 29 DJ44
Croydon CR0 143 DY101
Coverdale Cl, Stan. HA7 41 CH50
Coverdale Ct, Enf. EN3
off Raynton Rd 31 DY37
Coverdale Gdns, Croy. CR0
off Park Hill Ri 142 DT104
Coverdale Rd, N11 44 DG51
NW2 81 CX66
W12 81 CV74
Coverdales, The, Bark. IG11 87 EQ68
Covered Way, Iver SL0
off Pinewood Rd 75 BB66
Coverley Cl, E1 84 DU71
Brentwood (Gt Warley) CM13
off Wilmot Grn 53 FW51
Covert, The, Nthwd. HA6 39 BQ53
Orpington BR6 145 ES100
Coverton Rd, SW17 120 DE92
Covert Rd, Ilf. IG6 49 ET51
Coverts, The, Brwd. (Hutt.) CM13 55 GA46
Coverts Rd, Esher (Clay.) KT10 155 CF109
Covert Way, Barn. EN4 28 DC40
Covesfield, Grav. DA11
off Thames Way 131 GF86
Covet Wd Cl, Orp. BR5
off Lockesley Dr 145 ET100
Covey Cl, SW19 140 DB96
Covington Gdns, SW16 121 DP94
Covington Way, SW16 121 DM93
Cowan Cl, E6
off Oliver Gdns 86 EL71
Cowbridge La, Bark. IG11 87 EP66
Cowbridge Rd, Har. HA3 62 CM56
Cowcross St, EC1 196 F6
Cowdenbeath Path, N1 83 DM67
Cowden Rd, Orp. BR6 145 ET101
Cowden St, SE6 123 EA91
Cowdray Rd, Uxb. UB10 77 BQ67
Cowdray Way, Horn. RM12 71 FF63
Cowdrey Cl, Enf. EN1 30 DS40
Cowdrey Ct, Dart. DA1 127 FH87
Cowdrey Rd, SW19 120 DB92
Cowdry Rd, E9 off Wick Rd 85 DY65
Cowen Av, Har. HA2 60 CC61
Cowgate Rd, Grnf. UB6 79 CD68
Cowick Rd, SW17 120 DF91
Cowings Mead, Nthlt. UB5 78 BY66
Cowland Av, Enf. EN3 30 DW42
Cow La, Grnf. UB6 79 CD68
Watford WD25 24 BW36
Cow Leaze, E6 87 EN72
Cowleaze Rd, Kings.T. KT2 138 CL95
Cowles, Wal.Cr. (Chsht) EN7 14 DT27
COWLEY, Uxb. UB8 76 BJ70
Cowley Av, Cher. KT16 133 BF101
Greenhithe DA9 129 FT85
Cowley Business Pk, Uxb. UB8 76 BJ69
Cowley Cl, S.Croy. CR2 160 DW109
Cowley Cres, Uxb. UB8 76 BJ71
Walton-on-Thames KT12 154 BW105
Cowley Hill, Borwd. WD6 26 CP37
Cowley La, E11
off Cathall Rd 68 EE62
Chertsey KT16 133 BF101
Cowley Mill Rd, Uxb. UB8 76 BH68
Cowley Pl, NW4 63 CW57
Cowley Rd, E11 68 EH57
SW9 101 DN81
SW14 98 CS83
W3 81 CT74
Ilford IG1 69 EM59
Romford RM3 51 FH52
Uxbridge UB8 76 BJ68
Cowley St, SW1 199 P6

★ Place of interest ⇌ Railway station ⊖ London Underground station DLR Docklands Light Railway station Tra Tramlink station H Hospital Riv Pedestrian ferry landing stage

Cowling Cl, W11
off Wilsham St 81 CY74
Cowper Av, E6 86 EL66
Sutton SM1 158 DD105
Tilbury RM18 111 GH81
Cowper Cl, Brom. BR2 144 EK98
Chertsey KT16 133 BF100
Welling DA16 126 EU85
Cowper Ct, Wat. WD24 23 BU37
Cowper Gdns, N14 29 DJ44
Wallington SM6 159 DJ107
Cowper Rd, N14 45 DH46
N16 66 DS64
N18 46 DU50
SW19 120 DC93
W3 80 CR74
W7 79 CF73
Belvedere DA17 106 FA77
Bromley BR2 144 EK98
Kingston upon Thames KT2 118 CM92
Rainham RM13 89 FG70
Cowpers Ct, EC3
off Birchin La 84 DR72
Cowper St, EC2 197 L4
Cowper Ter, W10
off St. Marks Rd 81 CX71
Cowslip Cl, Uxb. UB10 76 BL66
Cowslip La, Wok. GU21 166 AV115
Cowslip Rd, E18 48 EH54
Cowthorpe Rd, SW8 101 DK81
Cox Cl, Rad. (Shenley) WD7 10 CM32
Coxdean, Epsom KT18 173 CW119
Coxe Pl, Har. (Wldste) HA3 61 CG56
Cox La, Chess. KT9 156 CM105
Epsom KT19 156 CP106
Coxley Ri, Pur. CR8 160 DQ113
Coxmount Rd, SE7 104 EK78
Coxson Way, SE1 201 P5
Cox's Wk, SE21 122 DU88
Coxwell Rd, SE18 105 ER78
SE19 122 DS94
Coxwold Path, Chess. KT9
off Garrison La 156 CL108
Crabbs Cft Cl, Orp. BR6
off Ladycroft Way 163 EQ106
Crab Hill, Beck. BR3 123 ED94
Crab La, Wat. (Ald.) WD25 24 CB35
Crabtree Av, Rom. RM6 70 EX56
Wembley HA0 80 CL68
Crabtree Cl, E2 197 P1
Bushey WD23 24 CB43
Crabtree Cor, Egh. TW20 133 BB95
Crabtree Ct, E15
off Clays La 67 EB64
Crabtree Dr, Lthd. KT22 171 CJ124
Crabtree Hill, Rom.
(Abridge) RM4 50 EZ45
Crabtree La, SW6 99 CX80
Crabtree Manorway Ind Est,
Belv. DA17 107 FB76
Crabtree Manorway N,
Belv. DA17 107 FC75
Crabtree Manorway S,
Belv. DA17 107 FC76
Crabtree Rd, Egh. TW20 133 BC96
Craddock Rd, Enf. EN1 30 DT41
Craddocks Av, Ashtd. KT21 172 CL117
Craddocks Par, Ashtd. KT21 172 CL117
Craddock St, NW5
off Prince of Wales Rd 82 DG65
Cradley Rd, SE9 125 ER88
★ **Crafts Council**, N1 196 E1
Cragg Av, Rad. WD7 25 CF36
Craigdale Rd, Horn. RM11 71 FF58
Craig Dr, Uxb. UB8 77 BP72
Craigen Av, Croy. CR0 142 DV102
Craigerne Rd, SE3 104 EH80
Craig Gdns, E18 48 EF54
Craigholm, SE18 105 EN82
Craigmore Twr, Wok. GU22
off Guildford Rd 166 AY119
Craig Mt, Rad. WD7 25 CH35
Craigmuir Pk, Wem. HA0 80 CM67
Craignair Rd, SW2 121 DN87
Craignish Av, SW16 141 DM96
Craig Pk Rd, N18 46 DV50
Craig Rd, Rich. TW10 117 CJ91
Craigs Ct, SW1 199 P2
Craigs Wk, Wal.Cr. (Chsht) EN8
off Davison Dr 15 DX28
Craigton Rd, SE9 105 EM84
Craigweil Av, Rad. WD7 25 CH35
Craigweil Cl, Stan. HA7 41 CK50
Craigweil Dr, Stan. HA7 41 CK50
Craigwell Av, Felt. TW13 115 BU90
Craigwell Cl, Stai. TW18 133 BE95
Craik Ct, NW6
off Carlton Vale 81 CZ68
Crail Row, SE17 201 L9
Cramer Ct, N.Mal. KT3
off Warwick Rd 138 CQ97
Cramer St, W1 194 G7
Crammerville Wk, Rain. RM13 89 FH70
Cramond Cl, W6 99 CY79
Cramond Ct, Felt. TW14
off Kilross Rd 115 BR88
Crampshaw La, Ashtd. KT21 172 CM119
Crampton Rd, SE20 122 DW93
Cramptons Rd, Sev. TN14 181 FH120
Crampton St, SE17 201 H9
Cranberry Cl, Nthlt. UB5
off Parkfield Av 78 BX68
Cranberry La, E16 86 EE70
Cranborne Av, Sthl. UB2 96 CA77
Surbiton KT6 138 CN104
Cranborne Cl, Pot.B. EN6 11 CY31
Cranborne Cres, Pot.B. EN6 11 CY31
Cranborne Gdns, Upmin. RM14 72 FP61
Cranborne Ind Est, Pot.B. EN6 11 CY30
Cranborne Rd, Bark. IG11 87 ER67
Potters Bar EN6 11 CY30
Waltham Cross (Chsht) EN8 15 DX32
Cranborne Waye, Hayes UB4 78 BW73
Cranbourn All, WC2 195 N10
Cranbourne Av, E11 68 EH56
Cranbourne Cl, SW16 141 DL97
Cranbourne Dr, Pnr. HA5 60 BX57
Cranbourne Gdns, NW11 63 CY57
Ilford IG6 69 EQ55
Cranbourne Pas, SE16 202 D5
Cranbourne Rd, E12
off High St N 68 EL64
E15 67 EC63
N10 45 DH54
Northwood HA6 59 BT55
Cranbourn St, WC2 195 N10
CRANBROOK, Ilf. IG1 69 EM60
Cranbrook Cl, Brom. BR2 144 EG100
Cranbrook Dr, Esher KT10 136 CC102
Romford RM2 71 FH56
Twickenham TW2 116 CB88
Cranbrook Ho, Erith DA8
off Boundary St 107 FF80
Cranbrook Ms, E17 67 DY57
Cranbrook Pk, N22 45 DM53
Cranbrook Ri, Ilf. IG1 69 EM59
Cranbrook Rd, SE8 103 EA81
SW19 119 CY94
W4 98 CS78
Barnet EN4 28 DD44
Bexleyheath DA7 106 EZ81
Hounslow TW4 96 BZ84
Ilford IG1, IG2, IG6 69 EN59
Thornton Heath CR7 142 DQ96
Cranbrook St, E2 *off Mace St* 85 DX68
Cranbury Rd, SW6 100 DB82
Crandon Wk, Dart. DA4
off Gorringe Av 149 FS96
Crane Av, W3 80 CQ73
Isleworth TW7 117 CG85
Cranebank Ms, Twick. TW1
off Haliburton Rd 97 CG84
Cranebrook, Twick. TW2
off Manor Rd 116 CC89
Crane Cl, Dag. RM10 88 FA65
Harrow HA2 60 CC62
Crane Ct, EC4 196 E9
Epsom KT19 156 CQ105
Cranefield Dr, Wat. WD25 8 BY32
Craneford Cl, Twick. TW2 117 CF87
Craneford Way, Twick. TW2 117 CE87
Crane Gdns, Hayes UB3 95 BT77
Crane Gro, N7 83 DN65
Cranell Grn, S.Ock. RM15 91 FV74
Crane Lo Rd, Houns. TW5 95 BV79
Crane Mead, SE16 203 H9
Crane Pk Rd, Twick. TW2 116 CB89
Crane Rd, Twick. TW2 117 CE88
Cranesbill Cl, NW9
off Colindale Av 62 CR55
Cranes Dr, Surb. KT5 138 CL98
Cranes Pk, Surb. KT5 138 CL98
Cranes Pk Av, Surb. KT5 138 CL98
Cranes Pk Cres, Surb. KT5 138 CM98
Crane St, SE10 103 ED78
SE15 102 DT81
Craneswater, Hayes UB3 95 BT80
Craneswater Pk, Sthl. UB2 96 BZ78
Cranes Way, Borwd. WD6 26 CQ43
Crane Way, Twick. TW2 116 CC87
Cranfield Cl, SE27
off Dunelm Gro 122 DQ90
Cranfield Ct, Wok. GU21
off Martindale Rd 166 AU118
Cranfield Cres,
Pot.B. (Cuffley) EN6 13 DL29
Cranfield Dr, NW9 42 CS52
Cranfield Rd, SE4 103 DZ83
Cranfield Rd E, Cars. SM5 158 DG109
Cranfield Rd W, Cars. SM5 158 DF109
Cranfield Row, SE1 200 E6
CRANFORD, Houns. TW5 95 BU80
Cranford Av, N13 45 DL50
Staines TW19 114 BL87
Cranford Cl, SW20 139 CV95
Purley CR8 160 DQ113
Staines TW19
off Canopus Way 114 BL87
Cranford Cotts, E1
off Cranford St 85 DX73
Cranford Dr, Hayes UB3 95 BT77
Cranford La, Hayes UB3 95 BR79
Hounslow (Hthrw Air.) TW6 95 BT83
Hounslow
(Hthrw Air.N.) TW6 95 BT81
Hounslow (Heston) TW5 96 BX80
Cranford Pk Rd, Hayes UB3 95 BT77
Cranford Ri, Esher KT10 154 CC106
Cranford Rd, Dart. DA1 128 FL88
Cranford St, E1 85 DX73
Cranford Way, N8 65 DM57
CRANHAM, Upmin. RM14 73 FS59
Cranham Gdns, Upmin. RM14 73 FS60
Cranham Rd, Horn. RM11 71 FH58
Cranhurst Rd, NW2 63 CW64
Cranleigh Cl, SE20 142 DV96
Bexley DA5 127 FB86
Orpington BR6 146 EU104
South Croydon CR2 160 DU112
Waltham Cross (Chsht) EN7 14 DU28
Cranleigh Dr, Swan. BR8 147 FE98
Cranleigh Gdns, N21 29 DN43
SE25 142 DS97
Barking IG11 87 ER66
Harrow HA3 62 CL57
Kingston upon Thames KT2 118 CM93
Loughton IG10 33 EM44
South Croydon CR2 160 DU112
Southall UB1 78 BZ72
Sutton SM1 140 DB103
Cranleigh Gdns Ind Est, Sthl. UB1
off Cranleigh Gdns 78 BZ72
Cranleigh Ms, SW11 100 DE82
Cranleigh Rd, N15 66 DQ57
SW19 140 DA97
Esher KT10 136 CC102
Feltham TW13 115 BT91
Cranleigh St, NW1 195 L1
Cranley Dene Ct, N10 65 DH56
Cranley Dr, Ilf. IG2 69 EQ59
Ruislip HA4 59 BT61
Cranley Gdns, N10 65 DJ56
N13 45 DM48
SW7 100 DC78
Wallington SM6 159 DJ108
Cranley Ms, SW7 100 DC78
Cranley Par, SE9
off Beaconsfield Rd 124 EL91
Cranley Pl, SW7 100 DD77
Cranley Rd, E13 86 EH71
Cranley Rd, Ilford IG2 69 EQ58
Walton-on-Thames KT12 153 BS106
Cranmer Av, W13 97 CH76
Cranmer Cl, Mord. SM4 139 CX100
Potters Bar EN6 12 DB30
Ruislip HA4 60 BX60
Stanmore HA7 41 CJ52
Warlingham CR6 177 DY117
Weybridge KT13 152 BN108
Cranmer Ct, SW3 198 C9
SW4 101 DK83
Hampton (Hmptn H.) TW12
off Cranmer Rd 116 CB92
Cranmer Fm Cl, Mitch. CR4 140 DF98
Cranmer Gdns, Dag. RM10 71 FC63
Warlingham CR6 177 DY117
Cranmer Ho, SW11
off Surrey La 100 DE81
Cranmer Rd, E7 68 EH63
SW9 101 DN80
Croydon CR0 141 DP104
Edgware HA8 42 CP48
Hampton (Hmptn H.) TW12 116 CB92
Hayes UB3 77 BR72
Kingston upon Thames KT2 118 CL92
Mitcham CR4 140 DF98
Sevenoaks TN13 190 FE123
Cranmer Ter, SW17 120 DD92
Cranmore Av, Islw. TW7 96 CC80
Cranmore Rd, Brom. BR1 124 EE90
Chislehurst BR7 125 EM92
Cranmore Way, N10 65 DJ56
Cranston Cl, Houns. TW3 96 BY82
Uxbridge UB10 59 BR61
Cranston Est, N1 197 L1
Cranston Gdns, E4 47 EB50
Cranston Pk Av, Upmin. RM14 72 FP63
Cranston Rd, SE23 123 DY88
Cranswick Rd, SE16 202 E10
Crantock Rd, SE6 123 EB89
Cranwell Cl, E3 85 EB70
Cranwell Gro, Shep. TW17 134 BM98
Cranwich Av, N21 46 DR45
Cranwich Rd, N16 66 DR59
Cranwood St, EC1 197 K3
Cranworth Cres, E4 47 ED46
Cranworth Gdns, SW9 101 DN81
Craster Rd, SW2 121 DM87
Crathie Rd, SE12 124 EH86
Cravan Av, Felt. TW13 115 BU89
Craven Av, W5 79 CJ73
Southall UB1 78 BZ71
Craven Cl, Hayes UB4 77 BU72
Craven Gdns, SW19 120 DA92
Barking IG11 87 ES68
Ilford IG6 49 ER54
Romford (Coll.Row) RM5 50 FA50
Romford (Harold Wd) RM3 52 FQ51
Craven Hill, W2 82 DC73
Craven Hill Gdns, W2 82 DC73
Craven Hill Ms, W2 82 DC73
Craven Ms, SW11
off Taybridge Rd 100 DG83
Craven Pk, NW10 80 CS67
Craven Pk Ms, NW10 80 CS67
Craven Pk Rd, N15 66 DT58
NW10 80 CS67
Craven Pas, WC2 199 P2
Craven Rd, NW10 80 CR67
W2 82 DC73
W5 79 CJ73
Croydon CR0 142 DV102
Kingston upon Thames KT2 138 CM95
Orpington BR6 146 EX104
Craven St, WC2 199 P2
Craven Ter, W2 82 DC73
Craven Wk, N16 66 DU59
Crawford Av, Wem. HA0 61 CK64
Crawford Cl, Islw. TW7 97 CE82
Crawford Compton Cl,
Horn. RM12 90 FJ65
Crawford Est, SE5 102 DQ82
Crawford Gdns, N13 45 DP48
Northolt UB5 78 BZ69
Crawford Ms, W1 194 D7
Crawford Pas, EC1 196 D5
Crawford Pl, W1 194 C8
Crawford Rd, SE5 102 DQ81
Crawfords, Swan. BR8 127 FE94
Crawford St, NW10
off Fawood Av 80 CR66
W1 194 D7
Crawley Rd, E10 67 EB60
N22 46 DQ54
Enfield EN1 46 DS45
Crawshaw Rd, Cher.
(Ott.) KT16 151 BD107
Crawshay Cl, Sev. TN13 190 FG123
Crawshay Ct, SW9
off Eythorne Rd 101 DN81
Crawthew Gro, SE22 102 DT84
Cray Av, Ashtd. KT21 172 CL116
Orpington BR5 146 EV99
Craybrooke Rd, Sid. DA14 126 EV91
Crayburne, Grav.
(Sthflt) DA13 130 FZ92
Craybury End, SE9 125 EQ89
Cray Cl, Dart. DA1 107 FG84
Craydene Rd, Erith DA8 107 FF81
Crayfield Ind Pk, Orp. BR5 146 EW96
CRAYFORD, Dart. DA1 127 FD85
⇌ **Crayford** 127 FE86
Crayford Cl, E6
off Neatscourt Rd 86 EL71
Crayford High St, Dart. DA1 107 FE84
Crayford Rd, N7 65 DK63
Dartford DA1 127 FF85
Crayford Way, Dart. DA1 127 FF85
Crayke Hill, Chess. KT9 156 CL108
Craylands, Orp. BR5 146 EW97
Craylands La, Swans. DA10 129 FX85
Craylands Sq, Swans. DA10 129 FX85
Craymill Sq, Dart. DA1 107 FF82
Crayonne Cl, Sun. TW16 135 BS95
Cray Riverway, Dart. DA1 127 FG85
Cray Rd, Belv. DA17 106 FA79
Sidcup DA14 126 EW94
Swanley BR8 147 FB100
Crayside Ind Est, Dart. DA1
off Thames Rd 107 FH84
Cray Valley Rd, Orp. BR5 146 EU99
Crealock Gro, Wdf.Grn. IG8 48 EF50
Crealock St, SW18 120 DB86
Creasey Cl, Horn. RM11 71 FH61
Creasy Cl, Abb.L. WD5 7 BT31
Creasy Est, SE1 201 M7
Crebor St, SE22 122 DU86
Credenhall Dr, Brom. BR2 145 EM102
Credenhill St, SW16 121 DJ93
Crediton Hill, NW6 64 DB64
Crediton Rd, E16
off Pacific Rd 86 EG72
NW10 81 CX67
Crediton Way, Esher
(Clay.) KT10 155 CG106
Credon Rd, E13 86 EJ68
SE16 202 E10
Credo Way, Grays RM20 109 FV79
Creechurch La, EC3 197 N9
Creechurch Pl, EC3 197 N9
Creed Ct, EC4
off Ludgate Hill 83 DP72
Creed La, EC4 196 G9
Creed's Fm Yd, Epp. CM16 17 ES31
Creek, The, Grav. DA11 130 GB85
Sunbury-on-Thames TW16 135 BU99
CREEKMOUTH, Bark. IG11 88 EU70
Creek Rd, SE8 103 EA79
SE10 103 EA79
Barking IG11 87 ET69
East Molesey KT8 137 CE98
Creekside, SE8 103 EB80
Rainham RM13 89 FE70
Creeland Gro, SE6
off Catford Hill 123 DZ88
Cree Way, Rom. RM1 51 FE52
Crefeld Cl, W6 99 CX79
Creffield Rd, W3 80 CM73
W5 80 CM73
Creighton Av, E6 86 EK68
N2 64 DE55
N10 44 DG54
Creighton Cl, W12 81 CV73
Creighton Rd, N17 46 DS52
NW6 81 CX68
W5 97 CK76
Cremer St, E2 197 P1
Cremorne Est, SW10
off Milman's St 100 DD79
Cremorne Gdns, Epsom KT19 156 CR109
Cremorne Rd, SW10 100 DC80
Gravesend (Nthflt) DA11 131 GF87
Crescent, EC3 197 P10
Crescent, The, E17 67 DY57
N11 44 DF49
NW2 63 CV62
SW13 99 CT82
SW19 120 DA90
W3 80 CS72
Abbots Langley WD5 7 BT30
Ashford TW15 114 BM92
Barnet EN5 28 DB41
Beckenham BR3 143 EA95
Bexley DA5 126 EW87
Caterham CR3 177 EA123
Chertsey KT16
off Western Av 134 BG97
Croydon CR0 142 DR99
Egham TW20 112 AY93
Epping CM16 17 ET32
Epsom KT18 156 CN114
Gravesend (Nthflt) DA11 131 GF89
Greenhithe DA9 129 FW85
Harrow HA2 61 CD60
Hayes UB3 95 BQ80
Ilford IG2 69 EN58
Leatherhead KT22 171 CH122
Loughton IG10 32 EK43
New Malden KT3 138 CQ96
Reigate RH2 *off Chartway* 184 DB134
Rickmansworth
(Crox.Grn) WD3 23 BP44
St. Albans (Brick.Wd) AL2 8 CA30
Sevenoaks TN13 191 FK121
Shepperton TW17 135 BT101
Sidcup DA14 125 ET91
Slough SL1 92 AS75
Southall UB1 96 BZ75
Surbiton KT6 138 CL99
Sutton SM1 158 DD105
Sutton (Belmont) SM2 158 DA111
Upminster RM14 73 FS59
Watford WD18 24 BW42
Watford (Ald.) WD25 24 CH37
Wembley HA0 61 CH61
West Molesey KT8 136 CA98
West Wickham BR4 144 EE100
Weybridge KT13 134 BN104
Crescent Arc, SE10
off Creek Rd 103 EC79
Crescent Av, Grays RM17 110 GD78
Hornchurch RM12 71 FF61
Crescent Cotts, Sev. TN13 181 FE120
Crescent Ct, Surb. KT6 137 CK99
Crescent Dr, Brwd.
(Shenf.) CM15 54 FY46
Orpington BR5 145 EP100
Crescent E, Barn. EN4 28 DC38
Crescent Gdns, SW19 120 DA90
Ruislip HA4 59 BV58
Swanley BR8 147 FC96
Crescent Gro, SW4 101 DJ84
Mitcham CR4 140 DE98
Crescent Ho, SE13
off Ravensbourne Pl 103 EB82
Crescent La, SW4 121 DK85
Crescent Ms, N22
off Palace Gates Rd 45 DL53
Crescent Pl, SW3 198 B8
Crescent Ri, N22 45 DK53
Barnet EN4 28 DE43
Crescent Rd, E4 48 EE45
E6 86 EJ67
E10 67 EB61
E13 86 EG67
E18 48 EJ54
N3 43 CZ53
N8 65 DK59
N9 46 DU46
N11 44 DF49
Crescent Rd, N15
off Carlingford Rd 65 DP55
N22 45 DK53
SE18 105 EP78
SW20 139 CX95
Barnet EN4 28 DE43
Beckenham BR3 143 EB96
Brentwood CM14 54 FV49
Bromley BR1 124 EG94
Caterham CR3 176 DU124
Dagenham RM10 71 FB63
Enfield EN2 29 DP41
Erith DA8 107 FF79
Kingston upon Thames KT2 118 CN94
Redhill (Bletch.) RH1 186 DQ133
Shepperton TW17 135 BQ99
Sidcup DA15 125 ET90
South Ockendon
(Aveley) RM15 108 FQ75
Crescent Row, EC1 197 H5
Crescent Stables, SW15
off Upper Richmond Rd 99 CY84
Crescent St, N1 83 DM66
Crescent Vw, Loug. IG10 32 EK44
Crescent Wk, S.Ock.
(Aveley) RM15 108 FQ75
Crescent Way, N12 44 DE51
SE4 103 EA83
SW16 121 DM94
Orpington BR6 163 ES106
South Ockendon
(Aveley) RM15 91 FR74
Crescent W, Barn. EN4 28 DC38
Crescent Wd Rd, SE26 122 DU90
Cresford Rd, SW6 100 DB81
Crespigny Rd, NW4 63 CV58
Cressage Cl, Sthl. UB1 78 CA70
Cressall Cl, Lthd. KT22 171 CH120
Cressall Mead, Lthd. KT22 171 CH120
Cress End, Rick. WD3
off Springwell Av 38 BG46
Cresset Rd, E9 84 DW65
Cresset St, SW4 101 DK83
Cressfield Cl, NW5 64 DG64
Cressida Rd, N19 65 DJ60
Cressingham Gro, Sutt. SM1 158 DC105
Cressingham Rd, SE13 103 EC83
Edgware HA8 42 CR51
Cressington Cl, N16
off Wordsworth Rd 66 DS64
Cress Ms, Brom. BR1
off Old Bromley Rd 123 ED92
Cresswell Gdns, SW5 100 DC78
Cresswell Pk, SE3 104 EF83
Cresswell Pl, SW10 100 DC78
Cresswell Rd, SE25 142 DU98
Feltham TW13 116 BY91
Twickenham TW1 117 CK86
Cresswell Way, N21 45 DN45
Cressy Ct, E1 *off Cressy Pl* 84 DW71
W6 99 CV76
Cressy Pl, E1 84 DW71
Cressy Rd, NW3 64 DF64
Crest, The, N13 45 DN49
NW4 63 CW57
Surbiton KT5 138 CN99
Waltham Cross (Chsht) EN7
off Orchard Way 13 DP27
Cresta Dr, Add. (Wdhm) KT15 151 BF110
Crest Av, Grays RM17 110 GB80
Crestbrook Av, N13 45 DP48
Crestbrook Pl, N13 45 DP48
Crest Cl, Sev. (Bad.Mt) TN14 165 FB111
Crest Dr, Enf. EN3 30 DW38
Crestfield St, WC1 196 A2
Crest Gdns, Ruis. HA4 60 BW62
Cresthill Av, Grays RM17 110 GC77
Creston Av, Wok.
(Knap.) GU21 166 AS116
Creston Way, Wor.Pk. KT4 139 CX102
Crest Rd, NW2 63 CT62
Bromley BR2 144 EF101
South Croydon CR2 160 DV108
Crest Vw, Green. DA9
off Woodland Way 109 FU84
Pinner HA5 60 BX56
Crest Vw Dr, Orp. BR5 145 EP99
Crestway, SW15 119 CV86
Crestwood Way, Houns. TW4 116 BZ85
Creswell Dr, Beck. BR3 143 EB99
Creswick Rd, W3 80 CP73
Creswick Wk, E3
off Malmesbury Rd 85 EA69
NW11 63 CZ56
Crete Hall Rd, Grav. DA11 130 GD86
Creton St, SE18 105 EN76
Crewdson Rd, SW9 101 DN80
Crewe Pl, NW10 81 CT69
Crewe's Av, Warl. CR6 176 DW116
Crewe's Cl, Warl. CR6 176 DW116
Crewe's Fm La, Warl. CR6 177 DX116
Crewe's La, Warl. CR6 177 DX116
CREWS HILL, Enf. EN2 29 DP35
⇌ **Crews Hill** 13 DM34
Crews St, E14 203 P8
Crewys Rd, NW2 63 CZ61
SE15 102 DV82
Crichton Av, Wall. SM6 159 DK106
Crichton Rd, Cars. SM5 158 DF107
Crichton St, SW8
off Westbury St 101 DJ82
Cricketers Arms Rd, Enf. EN2 30 DQ40
Cricketers Cl, N14 45 DJ45
Chessington KT9 155 CK105
Erith DA8 107 FE78
Cricketers Ct, SE11 200 F9
Cricketers Ms, SW18
off East Hill 120 DB85
Cricketers Ter, Cars. SM5
off Wrythe La 140 DE104
Cricketfield Rd, E5 66 DV63
Cricket Fld Rd, Uxb. UB8 76 BK67
Cricketfield Rd, West Dr. UB7 94 BJ77
Cricket Grn, Mitch. CR4 140 DF97
Cricket Grd Rd, Chis. BR7 145 EP95

★ Place of interest ⇌ Railway station ⊖ London Underground station DLR Docklands Light Railway station Tra Tramlink station H Hospital Riv Pedestrian ferry landing stage

241

Cricket La, Beck. BR3 123 DY93
Cricket Way, Wey. KT13 135 BS103
Cricklade Av, SW2 121 DL89
 Romford RM3 52 FK51
CRICKLEWOOD, NW2 63 CX62
⇌ Cricklewood 63 CX63
Cricklewood Bdy, NW2 63 CW62
Cricklewood La, NW2 63 CX63
Cridland St, E15
 off Church St 86 EF67
Crieff Ct, Tedd. TW11 117 CJ94
Crieff Rd, SW18 120 DC86
Criffel Av, SW2 121 DK89
Crimp Hill, Egh.
 (Eng.Grn) TW20 112 AU90
Crimp Hill Rd, Wind.
 (Old Wind.) SL4 112 AU88
Crimscott St, SE1 201 N7
Crimsworth Rd, SW8 101 DK81
Crinan St, N1 83 DL68
Cringle St, SW8 101 DJ80
Cripplegate St, EC2 197 H6
Cripps Grn, Hayes UB4
 off Stratford Rd 77 BV70
Crispe Ho, Bark. IG11
 off Dovehouse Mead 87 ER68
Crispen Rd, Felt. TW13 116 BY91
Crispian Cl, NW10 62 CS63
Crispin Cl, Ashtd. KT21 172 CM118
 Croydon CR0
 off Harrington Cl 141 DL103
Crispin Cres, Croy. CR0 141 DK104
Crispin Rd, Edg. HA8 42 CQ51
Crispin St, E1 197 P7
Crisp Rd, W6 99 CW78
Criss Cres, Ger.Cr.
 (Chal.St.P.) SL9 36 AW54
Criss Gro, Ger.Cr.
 (Chal.St.P.) SL9 36 AW54
Cristowe Rd, SW6 99 CZ82
Criterion Ms, N19 65 DK61
Crittall's Cor, Sid. DA14 126 EW94
Crockenhall Way, Grav.
 (Istead Rise) DA13 130 GE94
CROCKENHILL, Swan. BR8 147 FD101
Crockenhill La, Dart.
 (Eyns.) DA4 148 FJ102
 Swanley BR8 147 FG101
Crockenhill Rd, Orp. BR5 146 EX99
 Swanley BR8 146 EZ100
Crockerton Rd, SW17 120 DF89
Crockford Cl, Add. KT15 152 BJ105
Crockford Pk Rd, Add. KT15 152 BJ106
CROCKHAM HILL, Eden. TN8 189 EQ133
Crockham Way, SE9 125 EN91
Crocus Cl, Croy. CR0
 off Cornflower La 143 DX102
Crocus Fld, Barn. EN5 27 CZ44
Croffets, Tad. KT20 173 CX121
Croft, The, E4 48 EE47
 NW10 81 CT68
 W5 80 CL71
 Barnet EN5 27 CX42
 Hounslow TW5 96 BY79
 Loughton IG10 33 EN40
 Pinner HA5 off Rayners La 60 BZ59
 Ruislip HA4 60 BW63
 St. Albans AL2 8 CA25
 Swanley BR8 147 FC97
 Wembley HA0 61 CJ64
Croft Av, W.Wick. BR4 143 EC102
Croft Cl, NW7 42 CS48
 Belvedere DA17 106 EZ78
 Chislehurst BR7 125 EM91
 Hayes UB3 95 BQ80
 Kings Langley
 (Chipper.) WD4 6 BG30
 Uxbridge UB10 76 BN66
Croft Ct, Borwd. WD6
 off Kensington Way 26 CR41
Croftdown Rd, NW5 64 DG62
Croft End Cl, Chess. KT9
 off Ashcroft Rd 138 CM104
Croft End Rd, Kings L.
 (Chipper.) WD4 6 BG30
Crofters, The, Wind. SL4 112 AU86
Crofters Cl, Islw. TW7
 off Ploughmans End 117 CD85
Crofters Ct, SE8
 off Croft St 103 DY77
Crofters Mead, Croy. CR0 161 DZ109
Crofters Rd, Nthwd. HA6 39 BS49
Crofters Way, NW1 83 DK67
Croft Fld, Kings L.
 (Chipper.) WD4 6 BG30
Croft Gdns, W7 97 CG75
 Ruislip HA4 59 BT60
Croft La, Kings L.
 (Chipper.) WD4 6 BG30
Croftleigh Av, Pur. CR8 175 DN116
Croft Lo Cl, Wdf.Grn. IG8 48 EH51
Croft Meadow, Kings L.
 (Chipper.) WD4 6 BG30
Croft Ms, N12 44 DC48
Crofton, Ashtd. KT21 172 CL118
Crofton Av, W4 98 CR80
 Bexley DA5 126 EX87
 Orpington BR6 145 EQ103
 Walton-on-Thames KT12 136 BW104
Crofton Cl, Cher. (Ott.) KT16 151 BC108
Croftongate Way, SE4 123 DY85
Crofton Gro, E4 47 ED49
Crofton La, Orp. BR5, BR6 145 ER101
⇌ Crofton Park 123 DZ85
Crofton Pk Rd, SE4 123 DZ86
Crofton Rd, E13 86 EH70
 SE5 102 DS81
 Grays RM16 110 GE76
 Orpington BR6 145 EN104
Crofton Ter, E5
 off Studley Cl 67 DY64
 Richmond TW9 98 CM84
Crofton Way, Barn. EN5
 off Wycherley Cres 28 DB44
 Enfield EN2 29 DN40
Croft Rd, SW16 141 DN95
 SW19 120 DC94
 Bromley BR1 124 EG93
 Caterham (Wold.) CR3 177 DZ122
 Enfield EN3 31 DY39
 Gerrards Cross
 (Chal.St.P.) SL9 36 AY54
 Sutton SM1 158 DE106
 Westerham TN16 189 EP126
Crofts, The, Shep. TW17 135 BS98
Croftside, SE25 off Sunny Bk 142 DU97
Crofts La, N22
 off Glendale Av 45 DN52
Crofts Rd, Har. HA1 61 CG58
Crofts St, E1 202 B1
Croft St, SE8 203 K9
Croftway, NW3 64 DA63
 Richmond TW10 117 CH90
Croft Way, Sev. TN13 190 FF125
 Sidcup DA15 125 ES90
Crogsland Rd, NW1 82 DG66
Croham Cl, S.Croy. CR2 160 DS107
Croham Manor Rd,
 S.Croy. CR2 160 DS106
Croham Mt, S.Croy. CR2 160 DS108
Croham Pk Av, S.Croy. CR2 160 DT106
Croham Rd, S.Croy. CR2 160 DR106
Croham Valley Rd,
 S.Croy. CR2 160 DT107
Croindene Rd, SW16 141 DL95
Cromartie Rd, N19 65 DK59
Cromarty Rd, Edg. HA8 42 CP47
Crombie Cl, Ilf. IG4 69 EM57
Crombie Rd, Sid. DA15 125 ER88
Cromer Cl, Uxb. UB8
 off Dawley Av 77 BQ72
Crome Rd, NW10 80 CS65
Cromer Pl, Orp. BR6
 off Andover Rd 145 ER102
Cromer Rd, E10 off James La 67 ED58
 N17 46 DU54
 SE25 142 DV97
 SW17 120 DG93
 Barnet EN5 28 DC42
 Hornchurch RM11 72 FK59
 Hounslow (Hthrw Air.) TW6 94 BN83
 Romford RM7 71 FC58
 Romford (Chad.Hth) RM6 70 EY58
 Watford WD24 24 BW38
 Woodford Green IG8 48 EG49
Cromer Rd W, Houns.
 (Hthrw Air.) TW6 94 BN83
Cromer St, WC1 196 A3
Cromer Ter, E8
 off Ferncliff Rd 66 DU64
Cromer Vil Rd, SW18 119 CZ86
Cromford Cl, Orp. BR6 145 ES104
Cromford Path, E5
 off Overbury St 67 DX63
Cromford Rd, SW18 120 DA85
Cromford Way, N.Mal. KT3 138 CR95
Cromlix Cl, Chis. BR7 145 EP96
Crompton Pl, Enf. EN3
 off Brunswick Rd 31 EA38
Crompton St, W2 82 DD70
Cromwell Av, N6 65 DH60
 W6 99 CV78
 Bromley BR2 144 EH98
 New Malden KT3 139 CT99
 Waltham Cross (Chsht) EN7 14 DU30
Cromwell Cl, E1
 off Vaughan Way 84 DU74
 N2 64 DD56
 W3 off High St 80 CQ74
 Bromley BR2 144 EH98
 Chalfont St. Giles HP8 36 AW48
 Walton-on-Thames KT12 135 BV102
Cromwell Cres, SW5 100 DA77
Cromwell Dr, Slou. SL1 74 AS72
Cromwell Gdns, SW7 198 A7
Cromwell Gro, W6 99 CW76
 Caterham CR3 176 DQ121
Cromwell Highwalk, EC2
 off Beech St 84 DQ71
H Cromwell Hosp, The, SW5 100 DB77
Cromwell Ind Est, E10 67 DY60
Cromwell Ms, SW7 198 A8
Cromwell Pl, N6 65 DH60
 SW7 198 A8
 SW14 98 CQ83
 W3 off Grove Pl 80 CQ74
Cromwell Rd, E7 86 EJ66
 E17 67 EC57
 N3 44 DC53
 N10 44 DG52
 SW5 100 DB77
 SW7 100 DB77
 SW9 101 DP81
 SW19 120 DA92
 Beckenham BR3 143 DY96
 Borehamwood WD6 26 CL39
 Brentwood (Warley) CM14 54 FV49
 Caterham CR3 176 DQ121
 Croydon CR0 142 DR101
 Feltham TW13 115 BV88
 Grays RM17 110 GA77
 Hayes UB3 77 BR72
 Hounslow TW3 96 CA84
 Kingston upon Thames KT2 138 CL95
 Redhill RH1 184 DF133
 Teddington TW11 117 CG93
 Waltham Cross (Chsht) EN7 14 DV28
 Walton-on-Thames KT12 135 BV102
 Wembley HA0 80 CL68
 Worcester Park KT4 138 CR104
Cromwells Mere, Rom. RM1
 off Havering Rd 51 FD51
Cromwell St, Houns. TW3 96 CA84
Cromwell Twr, EC2 197 J6
Cromwell Wk, Red. RH1 184 DF134
Crondace Rd, SW6 100 DA81
Crondall Ct, N1 197 M1
Crondall Ho, SW15
 off Fontley Way 119 CU88
Crondall St, N1 197 L1
Cronin St, SE15 102 DT80
Crooked Billet, SW19
 off Woodhayes Rd 119 CW93
Crooked Billet Roundabout,
 E17 47 EA52
Crooked Billet Roundabout,
 Staines TW18 114 BG91
Crooked Billet Yd, E2
 off Kingsland Rd 84 DS69
Crooked La, Grav. DA12 131 GH86
Crooked Mile, Wal.Abb. EN9 15 EC33
Crooked Mile Roundabout,
 Wal.Abb. EN9 15 EC33
Crooked Usage, N3 63 CY55
Crooke Rd, SE8 203 K10
Crookham Rd, SW6 99 CZ81
Crook Log, Bexh. DA6 106 EX83
Crookston Rd, SE9 105 EN83
Croombs Rd, E16 86 EJ71
Crooms Hill, SE10 103 ED80
Crooms Hill Gro, SE10 103 EC80
Cropley Ct, N1
 off Cropley St 84 DR68
Cropley St, N1 84 DR68
Croppath Rd, Dag. RM10 70 FA63
Cropthorne Ct, W9
 off Maida Vale 82 DC69
Crosby Cl, Felt. TW13 116 BY91
Crosby Ct, SE1 201 K4
Crosby Rd, E7 86 EG65
 Dagenham RM10 89 FB68
Crosby Row, SE1 201 K5
Crosby Sq, EC3 197 M9
Crosby Wk, E8 off Laurel St 84 DT65
 SW2 121 DN87
Crosier Cl, SE3 104 EL81
Crosier Rd, Uxb. (Ickhm) UB10 59 BQ63
Crosier Way, Ruis. HA4 59 BS62
Crosland Pl, SW11
 off Taybridge Rd 100 DG83
Crossacres, Wok. GU22 167 BE115
Cross Av, SE10 103 ED79
Crossbow Rd, Chig. IG7 49 ET50
Crossbrook Rd, SE3 104 EL82
Crossbrook St, Wal.Cr.
 (Chsht) EN8 15 DX31
Cross Cl, SE15 off Gordon Rd 102 DV81
Cross Deep, Twick. TW1 117 CF89
Cross Deep Gdns, Twick. TW1 117 CF89
Crossfield Pl, Wey. KT13 153 BP108
Crossfield Rd, N17 66 DQ55
 NW3 82 DD66
Crossfields, Loug. IG10 33 EP43
Crossfield St, SE8 103 EA80
Crossford St, SW9 101 DM82
Crossgate, Edg. HA8 42 CN48
 Greenford UB6 79 CH65
DLR Crossharbour &
 London Arena 204 C6
Crossing Rd, Epp. CM16 18 EU32
Cross Keys Cl, N9
 off Balham Rd 46 DU47
 W1 194 G7
 Sevenoaks TN13 190 FG127
Cross Keys Sq, EC1 197 H7
Cross Lances Rd, Houns. TW3 96 CB84
Crossland Rd, Red. RH1 184 DG134
 Thornton Heath CR7 141 DP100
Crosslands, Cher. KT16 133 BE104
Crosslands Av, W5 80 CM74
 Southall UB2 96 BZ78
Crosslands Rd, Epsom KT19 156 CR107
Cross La, EC3 201 M1
 N8 65 DM55
 Bexley DA5 126 EZ87
 Chertsey (Ott.) KT16 151 BB107
Cross La E, Grav. DA12 131 GH89
Cross Las, Ger.Cr.
 (Chal.St.P.) SL9 36 AY50
Cross Las Cl, Ger.Cr. (Chal.St.P.) SL9
 off Cross Las 37 AZ50
Cross La W, Grav. DA11 131 GH89
Crosslet St, SE17 201 L8
Crosslet Vale, SE10 103 EB81
Crossley Cl, West.
 (Bigg.H.) TN16 178 EK115
Crossleys, Ch.St.G. HP8 36 AW49
Crossley St, N7 83 DN65
Crossmead, SE9 125 EM88
 Watford WD19 23 BV44
Crossmead Av, Grnf. UB6 78 CA69
Crossmount Ho, SE5 102 DQ80
Crossness La, SE28 88 EX73
★ Crossness Pumping Sta,
 SE2 88 EY72
Crossness Rd, Bark. IG11 87 ET69
Crossoaks La, Borwd. WD6 26 CR35
 Potters Bar (S.Mimms) EN6 10 CS34
Crosspath, The, Rad. WD7 25 CG35
Cross Rd, E4 48 EE46
 N11 45 DH50
 N22 45 DN52
 SE5 102 DS82
 SW19 120 DA94
 Bromley BR2 144 EL103
 Croydon CR0 142 DR102
 Dartford DA1 128 FJ86
 Dartford (Hawley) DA2 128 FM91
 Enfield EN1 30 DS42
 Feltham TW13 116 BY91
 Gravesend (Nthflt) DA11 131 GF86
 Harrow HA1 61 CD56
 Harrow (S.Har.) HA2 60 CB62
 Harrow (Wldste) HA3 41 CG54
 Kingston upon Thames KT2 118 CM94
 Orpington BR5 146 EV99
 Purley CR8 159 DP113
 Romford RM7 70 FA55
 Romford (Chad.Hth) RM6 70 EW59
 Sidcup DA14
 off Sidcup Hill 126 EV91
 Sutton SM2 158 DD106
 Sutton (Belmont) SM2 158 DA110
 Tadworth KT20 173 CW122
 Uxbridge UB8
 off New Windsor St 76 BJ66
 Waltham Cross EN8 15 DY33
 Watford WD19 24 BY44
 Weybridge KT13 135 BR104
 Woodford Green IG8 49 EM51
Cross Rds, Loug.
 (High Beach) IG10 32 EH40
Cross St, N1 83 DP67
 SW13 98 CS82
 Erith DA8 off Bexley Rd 107 FE78
Cross St, Hampton
 (Hmptn H.) TW12 116 CC92
 Uxbridge UB8 76 BJ66
 Watford WD17 24 BW41
Cross Ter, Wal.Abb. EN9
 off Stonyshotts 16 EE34
Crossthwaite Av, SE5 102 DR84
Crosswall, EC3 197 P10
Crossway, N12 44 DD51
 N16 66 DS64
 NW9 63 CT56
 SE28 88 EW72
 SW20 139 CW98
 W13 79 CG70
 Chesham HP5 4 AS30
 Dagenham RM8 70 EW62
 Enfield EN1 46 DS45
 Hayes UB3 77 BU74
 Orpington BR5 145 ER98
 Pinner HA5 39 BV54
 Ruislip HA4 60 BW63
 Walton-on-Thames KT12 135 BV103
 Woodford Green IG8 48 EJ49
Crossway, The, N22 45 DP52
 SE9 124 EK89
Cross Way, The, Har. HA3 41 CE54
Crossway, The, Uxb. UB10 76 BM68
Crossways, N21 30 DQ44
 Brentwood (Shenf.) CM15 55 GA44
 Egham TW20 113 BD93
 Romford RM2 71 FH55
 South Croydon CR2 161 DY108
 Sunbury-on-Thames TW16 115 BT94
 Sutton SM2 158 DD109
 Westerham (Tats.) TN16 178 EJ120
Crossways, The, Couls. CR5 175 DM119
 Hounslow TW5 96 BZ80
 Redhill RH1 185 DJ130
 Wembley HA9 62 CN61
Crossways Boul, Dart. DA2 108 FQ84
 Greenhithe DA9 109 FT84
Crossways Business Pk,
 Dart. DA2 108 FQ84
Crossways La, Reig. RH2 184 DC128
Crossways Rd, Beck. BR3 143 EA98
 Mitcham CR4 141 DH97
Crosswell Cl, Shep. TW17 135 BQ96
Croston St, E8 84 DU67
Crothall Cl, N13 45 DM48
Crouch Av, Bark. IG11 88 EV68
Crouch Cl, Beck. BR3
 off Abbey La 123 EA93
Crouch Cft, SE9 125 EN90
CROUCH END, N8 65 DJ58
Crouch End Hill, N8 65 DK59
Crouch Hall Rd, N8 65 DK58
⇌ Crouch Hill 65 DM59
Crouch Hill, N4 65 DL58
 N8 65 DL58
Crouch La, Wal.Cr.
 (Chsht) EN7 14 DQ28
Crouchman's Cl, SE26 122 DT90
Crouch Oak La, Add. KT15 152 BJ105
Crouch Rd, NW10 80 CR66
 Grays RM16 111 GG78
Crouch Valley, Upmin. RM14 73 FS59
Crowborough Cl, Warl. CR6 177 DY117
Crowborough Dr, Warl. CR6 177 DY118
Crowborough Path, Wat. WD19
 off Prestwick Rd 40 BX49
Crowborough Rd, SW17 120 DG93
Crowden Way, SE28 88 EW73
Crowder St, E1 84 DV73
Crow Dr, Sev. (Halst.) TN14 181 FC115
Crowfoot Cl, E9
 off Lee Conservancy Rd 67 DZ64
CROW GREEN, Brwd. CM15 54 FT41
Crow Grn La, Brwd.
 (Pilg.Hat.) CM15 54 FU43
Crow Grn Rd, Brwd.
 (Pilg.Hat.) CM15 54 FT43
Crowhurst Cl, SW9 101 DN82
Crowhurst Mead, Gdse. RH9 186 DW130
Crowhurst Way, Orp. BR5 146 EW99
Crowland Av, Hayes UB3 95 BS77
Crowland Gdns, N14 45 DL45
Crowland Rd, N15 66 DT57
 Thornton Heath CR7 142 DR98
Crowlands Av, Rom. RM7 71 FB58
Crowland Ter, N1 84 DR66
Crowland Wk, Mord. SM4 140 DB100
Crow La, Rom. RM7 70 EZ59
Crowley Cres, Croy. CR0 159 DN106
Crowline Wk, N1
 off St. Paul's Rd 84 DR65
Crowmarsh Gdns, SE23
 off Tyson Rd 122 DW87
Crown Arc, Kings.T. KT1
 off Union St 137 CK96
Crown Ash Hill, West. TN16 162 EH114
Crown Ash La, Warl. CR6 178 EG116
 Westerham TN16 178 EG116
Crown Cl, E3 85 EA67
 N22 off Winkfield Rd 45 DN53
 NW6 82 DB65
 NW7 43 CT47
 Hayes UB3 95 BT75
 Orpington BR6 164 EU105
 Slough (Colnbr.) SL3 93 BC80
 Walton-on-Thames KT12 136 BW101
Crown Ct, EC2 197 J9
 SE12 124 EH86
 WC2 196 A9
 Bromley BR2
 off Victoria Rd 144 EK99
Crown Dale, SE19 121 DP93
Crowndale Rd, NW1 83 DJ68
Crownfield Av, Ilf. IG2 69 ES57
Crownfield Rd, E15 67 ED64
Crownfields, Sev. TN13 191 FH125
Crown Hill, Croy. CR0
 off Church St 142 DQ103
 Epping CM16 17 EM33
 Waltham Abbey EN9 17 EM33
Crownhill Rd, NW10 81 CT67
 Woodford Green IG8 48 EL52
Crown Ho, Bark. IG11
 off Linton Rd 87 EQ66
Crown La, N14 45 DJ46
 SW16 121 DN92
Crown La, Bromley BR2 144 EK99
 Chislehurst BR7 145 EQ95
 Morden SM4 140 DB97
 Virginia Water GU25 132 AX100
Crown La Gdns, SW16
 off Crown La 121 DN92
Crown La Spur, Brom. BR2 144 EK100
Crown Meadow, Slou.
 (Colnbr.) SL3 93 BB80
Crownmead Way, Rom. RM7 71 FB56
Crown Ms, E13
 off Waghorn Rd 86 EJ67
 W6 99 CU77
Crown Office Row, EC4 196 D10
Crown Pas, SW1 199 L3
 Kingston upon Thames KT1
 off Church St 137 CK96
 Watford WD18
 off The Crescent 24 BW42
Crown Pl, EC2 197 M6
 NW5 off Kentish Town Rd 83 DH65
Crown Pt Par, SE19
 off Beulah Hill 121 DP93
Crown Ri, Cher. KT16 133 BF102
 Watford WD25 8 BW34
Crown Rd, N10 44 DG52
 Borehamwood WD6 26 CN39
 Enfield EN1 30 DV42
 Grays RM17 110 GA79
 Ilford IG6 69 ER56
 Morden SM4 140 DB98
 New Malden KT3 138 CQ95
 Orpington BR6 164 EU106
 Ruislip HA4 60 BX64
 Sevenoaks (Shore.) TN14 165 FF110
 Sutton SM1 158 DB105
 Twickenham TW1 117 CH86
 Virginia Water GU25 132 AW100
Crown Sq, Wok. GU21
 off Commercial Way 167 AZ117
Crownstone Rd, SW2 121 DN85
Crown St, SE5 102 DQ80
 W3 80 CP74
 Brentwood CM14 54 FW47
 Dagenham RM10 89 FC65
 Egham TW20 113 BA92
 Harrow HA2 61 CD60
Crown Ter, Rich. TW9 98 CM84
Crowntree Cl, Islw. TW7 97 CF79
Crown Wk, Uxb. UB8
 off Oxford Rd 76 BJ66
 Wembley HA9 62 CM62
Crown Way, West Dr. UB7 76 BM74
Crown Wds La, SE9 105 EP82
 SE18 105 EP82
Crown Wds Way, SE9 125 ER85
Crown Wks, E2 off Temple St 84 DV68
Crown Yd, Houns. TW3
 off High St 96 CC83
Crowshott Av, Stan. HA7 41 CJ53
Crows Rd, E15 85 ED69
 Barking IG11 87 EP65
 Epping CM16 17 ET30
Crowstone Rd, Grays RM16 110 GC75
Crowther Av, Brent. TW8 98 CL77
Crowther Rd, SE25 142 DU98
Crowthorne Cl, SW18 119 CZ88
Crowthorne Rd, W10 81 CX72
Croxdale Rd, Borwd. WD6 26 CM40
Croxden Cl, Edg. HA8 62 CM55
Croxden Wk, Mord. SM4 140 DC100
Croxford Gdns, N22 45 DP52
Croxford Way, Rom. RM7
 off Horace Av 71 FD60
⊖ Croxley 23 BP44
Croxley Business Pk,
 Wat. WD18 23 BR43
Croxley Cl, Orp. BR5 146 EV96
CROXLEY GREEN, Rick. WD3 22 BN43
⇌ Croxley Green (closed) 23 BR43
Croxley Grn, Orp. BR5 146 EV95
Croxley Rd, W9 81 CZ69
Croxley Vw, Wat. WD18 23 BS44
Croxted Cl, SE21 122 DQ87
Croxted Ms, SE24
 off Croxted Rd 122 DQ86
Croxted Rd, SE21 122 DQ87
 SE24 122 DQ87
Croyde Av, Grnf. UB6 78 CC69
 Hayes UB3 95 BS77
Croyde Cl, Sid. DA15 125 ER87
CROYDON 142 DR103
Croydon Flyover, Croy. CR0 159 DP105
Croydon Gro, Croy. CR0 141 DP102
Croydon La, Bans. SM7 158 DB114
Croydon La S, Bans. SM7 158 DB114
★ Croydon Mus, Croy. CR0 142 DQ104
Croydon Rd, E13 86 EF70
 SE20 142 DV96
 Beckenham BR3 143 DY98
 Bromley BR2 144 EF104
 Caterham CR3 176 DU122
 Croydon (Bedd.) CR0 159 DL105
 Croydon (Mitch.Com.) CR0 140 DG98
 Hounslow (Hthrw Air.) TW6 95 BP82
 Keston BR2 144 EJ104
 Mitcham CR4 140 DG98
 Reigate RH2 184 DB134
 Wallington SM6 159 DH105
 Warlingham CR6 177 ED122
 West Wickham BR4 144 EE104
 Westerham TN16 179 EM123
Croyland Rd, N9 46 DU46
Croylands Dr, Surb. KT6 138 CL101
Croysdale Av, Sun. TW16 135 BU97
Crozier Dr, S.Croy. CR2 160 DV110
Crozier Ho, SE3
 off Ebdon Way 104 EH83
Crozier Ter, E9 67 DX64
Crucible Cl, Rom. RM6 70 EV58
Crucifix La, SE1 201 M4
Cruden Ho, SE17
 off Hillingdon St 101 DP79
Cruden Rd, Grav. DA12 131 GM90
Cruden St, N1 83 DP67
Cruick Av, S.Ock. RM15 91 FW73
Cruikshank Rd, E15 68 EE63
Cruikshank St, WC1 196 D2
Crummock Gdns, NW9 62 CS57
Crumpsall St, SE2 106 EW77

★ Place of interest ⇌ Railway station ⊖ London Underground station DLR Docklands Light Railway station Tra Tramlink station H Hospital Riv Pedestrian ferry landing stage

Crundale Av, NW9 62 CN57
Crundal Twr, Orp. BR5 146 EW102
Crunden Rd, S.Croy. CR2 160 DR108
Crusader Cl, Purf. RM19
off Centurion Way 108 FN77
Crusader Gdns, Croy. CR0
off Cotelands 142 DS104
Crusader Way, Wat. WD18 23 BT44
Crushes Cl, Brwd.
(Hutt.) CM13 55 GE44
Crusoe Ms, N16 66 DR61
Crusoe Rd, Erith DA8 107 FD78
Mitcham CR4 120 DF94
Crutched Friars, EC3 197 N10
Crutches La, Beac.
(Jordans) HP9 36 AS51
Crutchfield La, Walt. KT12 135 BV103
Crutchley Rd, SE6 124 EE89
Crystal Av, Horn. RM12 72 FL63
Crystal Ct, SE19
off College Rd 122 DT92
Crystal Ho, SE18
off Spinel Cl 105 ET78
⇌ Crystal Palace 122 DU93
Crystal Palace Caravan Club, SE19
off Crystal Palace Par 122 DT92
★ Crystal Palace FC, SE25 142 DS98
★ Crystal Palace
Nat Sport Cen, SE19 122 DU93
Crystal Palace Par, SE19 122 DT93
★ Crystal Palace Pk, SE19 122 DT92
Crystal Palace Pk Rd, SE26 122 DU92
Crystal Palace Rd, SE22 102 DU84
Crystal Palace Sta Rd, SE19
off Anerley Hill 122 DU93
Crystal Ter, SE19 122 DR93
Crystal Vw Ct, Brom. BR1
off Winlaton Rd 123 ED91
Crystal Way, Dag. RM8 70 EW60
Harrow HA1 61 CF57
Cuba Dr, Enf. EN3 30 DW40
Cuba St, E14 203 P4
Cubitt Sq, Sthl. UB2
off Windmill Av 78 CC74
Cubitt Steps, E14 204 A2
Cubitt St, WC1 196 B3
Croydon CR0 159 DM106
Cubitts Yd, WC2 196 A10
Cubitt Ter, SW4 101 DJ83
CUBITT TOWN, E14 204 E6
Cuckmans Dr, St.Alb. AL2 8 CA25
Cuckoo Av, W7 79 CE70
Cuckoo Dene, W7 79 CD71
Cuckoo Hall La, N9 46 DW45
Cuckoo Hill, Pnr. HA5 60 BW55
Cuckoo Hill Dr, Pnr. HA5 60 BW55
Cuckoo Hill Rd, Pnr. HA5 60 BW56
Cuckoo La, W7 79 CE73
Cuckoo Pound, Shep. TW17 135 BS99
Cudas Cl, Epsom KT19 157 CT105
Cuddington Av, Wor.Pk. KT4 139 CT104
Cuddington Cl, Tad. KT20 173 CW120
Cuddington Glade,
Epsom KT19 156 CN112
Cuddington Pk Cl,
Bans. SM7 157 CZ113
Cuddington Way, Sutt. SM2 157 CX112
CUDHAM, Sev. TN14 179 ER115
Cudham Cl, Sutt.
(Belmont) SM2 158 DA110
Cudham Dr, Croy.
(New Adgtn) CR0 161 EC110
Cudham La N, Orp. BR6 163 ES110
Sevenoaks (Cudham) TN14 163 ER112
Cudham La S, Sev.
(Cudham) TN14 179 EQ115
Cudham Pk Rd, Sev.
(Cudham) TN14 163 ES110
Cudham Rd, Orp. BR6 163 EN111
Westerham (Tats.) TN16 178 EL120
Cudham St, SE6 123 EC87
Cudworth St, E1 84 DV70
Cuff Cres, SE9 124 EK86
CUFFLEY, Pot.B. EN6 13 DM29
⇌ Cuffley 13 DM29
Cuffley Av, Wat. WD25 8 BX34
Cuffley Hill, Wal.Cr.
(Chsht) EN7 13 DN29
Cuff Pt, E2 197 P2
Cugley Rd, Dart. DA2 128 FQ87
Culford Gdns, SW3 198 E9
Culford Gro, N1 84 DS65
Culford Ms, N1
off Culford Rd 84 DS65
Culford Rd, N1 84 DS66
Grays RM16 110 GC75
Culgaith Gdns, Enf. EN2 29 DL42
Cullen Sq, S.Ock. RM15 91 FW73
Cullen Way, NW10 80 CQ70
Cullera Cl, Nthwd. HA6 39 BT51
Cullerne Cl, Epsom
(Ewell) KT17 157 CT110
Cullesden Rd, Ken. CR8 175 DP115
Culling Rd, SE16 202 F6
Cullings Ct, Wal.Abb. EN9 16 EF33
Cullington Cl, Har. HA3 61 CG56
Cullingworth Rd, NW10 63 CU64
Culloden Cl, SE16 102 DU78
Culloden Rd, Enf. EN2 29 DP40
Culloden St, E14 85 EC72
Cullum St, EC3 197 M10
Culmington Rd, W13 97 CJ75
South Croydon CR2 160 DQ109
Culmore Rd, SE15 102 DV80
Culmstock Rd, SW11 120 DG85
Culpeper Cl, Ilf. IG6 49 EP51
Culpepper Cl, N18
off Dyson Rd 46 DV50
Culross Cl, N15 66 DQ56
Culross St, W1 198 F1
Culsac Rd, Surb. KT6 138 CL103
Culverden Rd, SW12 121 DJ89
Watford WD19 39 BW48
Culver Dr, Oxt. RH8 188 EE130
Culver Gro, Stan. HA7 41 CJ54
Culverhay, Ashtd. KT21 172 CL116
Culverhouse Gdns, SW16 121 DM90
Culverlands Cl, Stan. HA7 41 CH49
Culverley Rd, SE6 123 EB88
Culvers Av, Cars. SM5 140 DF103
Culvers Retreat, Cars. SM5 140 DF102
Culverstone Cl, Brom. BR2 144 EF100
Culvers Way, Cars. SM5 140 DF103
Culvert La, Uxb. UB8 76 BH68
Culvert Pl, SW11 100 DG82
Culvert Rd, N15 66 DS57
SW11 100 DF82
Culworth St, NW8 194 B1
Cumberland Av, NW10 80 CP69
Gravesend DA12 131 GJ87
Hornchurch RM12 72 FL62
Welling DA16 105 ES83
Cumberland Cl, E8 84 DT65
SW20 off Lansdowne Rd 119 CX94
Amersham HP7 20 AV39
Epsom KT19 156 CS110
Hornchurch RM12 72 FL62
Ilford IG6 49 EQ53
Twickenham TW1
off Westmorland Cl 117 CH86
Cumberland Cres, W14 99 CY77
Cumberland Dr, Bexh. DA7 106 EY80
Chessington KT9 138 CM104
Dartford DA1 128 FM87
Esher KT10 137 CG103
Cumberland Gdns, NW4 43 CY54
WC1 196 C2
Cumberland Gate, W1 194 D10
Cumberland Mkt, NW1 195 J2
Cumberland Mkt Est, NW1 195 J2
Cumberland Mills Sq, E14 204 F10
Cumberland Pk, NW10 81 CU69
W3 80 CQ73
Cumberland Pl, NW1 195 H2
SE6 124 EF88
Sunbury-on-Thames TW16 135 BU98
Cumberland Rd, E12 68 EK63
E13 86 EH71
E17 47 DY54
N9 46 DW46
N22 45 DM54
SE25 142 DV100
SW13 99 CT81
W3 80 CQ73
W7 97 CF75
Ashford TW15 114 BK90
Bromley BR2 144 EE98
Grays
(Chaff.Hun.) RM16 110 FY75
Harrow HA1 60 CB57
Richmond TW9 98 CN80
Stanmore HA7 62 CM55
Cumberlands, Ken. CR8 176 DR115
Cumberland St, SW1 199 J10
Staines TW18 113 BD92
Cumberland Ter, NW1 195 H1
Cumberland Ter Ms, NW1 195 H1
Cumberland Vil, W3
off Cumberland Rd 80 CQ73
Cumberlow Av, SE25 142 DT97
Cumbernauld Gdns,
Sun. TW16 115 BT92
Cumberton Rd, N17 46 DR53
Cumbrae Cl, Slou. SL2
off St. Pauls Av 74 AU74
Cumbrae Gdns, Surb. KT6 137 CK103
Cumbrian Av, Bexh. DA7 107 FE81
Cumbrian Gdns, NW2 63 CX61
Cumbrian Way, Uxb. UB8
off Chippendale Waye 76 BK66
★ Cuming Mus, SE17 201 H9
Cumley Rd, Ong. CM5 19 FE30
Cummings Hall La, Rom.
(Noak Hill) RM3 52 FJ48
Cumming St, N1 196 B1
Cumnor Gdns, Epsom KT17 157 CU107
Cumnor Ri, Ken. CR8 176 DQ117
Cumnor Rd, Sutt. SM2 158 DC107
Cunard Cres, N21 30 DR44
Cunard Pl, EC3 197 N9
Cunard Rd, NW10 80 CR69
Cunard St, SE5
off Albany Rd 102 DS79
Cunard Wk, SE16 203 J8
Cundy Rd, E16 86 EJ72
Cundy St, SW1 198 G9
Cundy St Est, SW1 198 G9
Cunliffe Cl, Epsom
(Headley) KT18 172 CP124
Cunliffe Rd, Epsom KT19 157 CT105
Cunliffe St, SW16 121 DJ93
Cunningham Av, Enf. EN3 31 DY36
Cunningham Cl, Rom. RM6 70 EW57
West Wickham BR4 143 EB103
Cunningham Pk, Har. HA1 60 CC57
Cunningham Pl, NW8 82 DD70
Cunningham Ri, Epp.
(N.Wld Bas.) CM16 19 FC25
Cunningham Rd, N15 66 DU56
Banstead SM7 174 DD115
Waltham Cross (Chsht) EN8 15 DY27
Cunnington St, W4 98 CQ76
Cupar Rd, SW11 100 DG81
Cupola Cl, Brom. BR1 124 EH92
Curates Wk, Dart. DA1 128 FK90
Cureton St, SW1 199 N9
Curfew Bell Rd, Cher. KT16 133 BF101
Curfew Ho, Bark. IG11
off St. Ann's 87 EQ67
Curie Gdns, NW9
off Pasteur Cl 42 CS54
Curlew Cl, SE28 88 EX73
South Croydon CR2 161 DX111
Curlew Ct, Surb. KT6 138 CM104
Curlew Ho, Enf. EN3
off Allington Ct 31 DX43
Curlews, The, Grav. DA12 131 GK89
Curlew St, SE1 201 P4
Curlew Ter, Ilf. IG5
off Tiptree Cres 69 EN55
Curlew Way, Hayes UB4 78 BX71
Curling Cl, Couls. CR5 175 DM120
Curling La, Grays
(Bad.Dene) RM17 110 FZ78
Curnick's La, SE27
off Chapel Rd 122 DQ91
Curnock Est, NW1
off Plender St 83 DJ67
Curran Av, Sid. DA15 125 ET85
Wallington SM6 140 DG104
Curran Cl, Uxb. UB8 76 BJ70
Currey Rd, Grnf. UB6 79 CD65
Curricle St, W3 80 CS74
Currie Hill Cl, SW19 119 CZ91
Curry Ri, NW7 43 CX51
Cursitor St, EC4 196 D8
Curtain Pl, EC2
off Curtain Rd 84 DS69
Curtain Rd, EC2 197 M5
Curthwaite Gdns, Enf. EN2 29 DK42
Curtis Cl, Rick. (Mill End) WD3 38 BG46
Curtis Dr, W3 80 CR72
Watford WD25
off Ashfields 7 BT34
Curtis Fld Rd, SW16 121 DM91
Curtis La, Wem. HA0
off Montrose Cres 80 CL65
Curtismill Cl, Orp. BR5 146 EV97
Curtis Mill Grn, Rom.
(Nave.) RM4 35 FF42
Curtis Mill La, Rom.
(Nave.) RM4 35 FF42
Curtismill Way, Orp. BR5 146 EV97
Curtis Rd, Epsom KT19 156 CQ105
Hornchurch RM11 72 FM60
Hounslow TW4 116 BZ87
Curtis St, SE1 201 P8
Curtis Way, SE1 201 P8
SE28 off Tawney Rd 88 EV73
Curvan Cl, Epsom KT17 157 CT110
Curve, The, W12 81 CU73
Curwen Av, E7
off Woodford Rd 68 EH63
Curwen Rd, W12 99 CU75
Curzon Av, Enf. EN3 31 DX43
Stanmore HA7 41 CG53
Curzon Cl, Orp. BR6 163 ER105
Weybridge KT13
off Curzon Rd 152 BN105
Curzon Cres, NW10 81 CT66
Barking IG11 87 ET68
Curzon Dr, Grays RM17 110 GC80
Curzon Gate, W1 198 G3
Curzon Mall, Slou. SL1
off High St 92 AT75
Curzon Pl, Pnr. HA5 60 BW57
Curzon Rd, N10 45 DH54
W5 79 CH70
Thornton Heath CR7 141 DN100
Weybridge KT13 152 BN105
Curzon Sq, W1 198 G3
Curzon St, W1 198 G3
Cusack Cl, Twick. TW1
off Waldegrave Rd 117 CF91
Cussons Cl, Wal.Cr.
(Chsht) EN7 14 DU29
CUSTOM HOUSE, E16 86 EK72
★ Custom Ho, EC3 201 M1
⇌ Custom House 86 EH73
DLR Custom House 86 EH73
Custom Ho Reach, SE16 203 M5
Custom Ho Wk, EC3 201 M1
Cut, The, SE1 200 E4
Cutcombe Rd, SE5 102 DQ82
Cuthberga Cl, Bark. IG11
off George St 87 EQ66
Cuthbert Gdns, SE25 142 DS97
Cuthbert Rd, E17 67 EC55
N18 off Fairfield Rd 46 DU50
Croydon CR0 141 DP103
Cuthberts Cl, Wal.Cr. EN7 14 DT29
Cuthbert St, W2 82 DD70
Cut Hills, Egh. TW20 132 AV95
Virginia Water GU25 132 AU96
Cuthill Wk, SE5 102 DR81
Cutlers Gdns, E1 197 N8
Cutlers Gdns Arc, EC2
off Cutler St 84 DS72
Cutlers Sq, E14 204 A9
Cutlers Ter, N1
off Balls Pond Rd 84 DR65
Cutler St, E1 197 N8
Cutmore St, Grav. DA11 131 GH87
Cutthroat All, Rich. TW10
off Ham St 117 CJ89
★ Cutty Sark, SE10 103 EC79
DLR Cutty Sark 103 EC79
Cutty Sark Ct, Green. DA9
off Low Cl 129 FU85
Cutty Sark Gdns, SE10
off King William Wk 103 EC79
Cuxton Cl, Bexh. DA6 126 EY85
Cyclamen Cl, Hmptn. TW12
off Gresham Rd 116 CA93
Cyclamen Rd, Swan. BR8 147 FD98
Cyclamen Way, Epsom KT19 156 CP106
Cyclops Ms, E14 203 P8
Cygnet Av, Felt. TW14 116 BW87
Cygnet Cl, NW10 62 CR64
Borehamwood WD6 26 CQ39
Northwood HA6 39 BQ52
Woking GU21 166 AV116
Cygnet Gdns, Grav.
(Nthflt) DA11 131 GF89
Cygnets, The, Felt. TW13 116 BY91
Staines TW18
off Edgell Rd 113 BF92
Cygnets Cl, Red. RH1 184 DG132
Cygnet St, E1
off Sclater St 84 DT70
Cygnet Vw, Grays RM20 109 FT77
Cygnet Way, Hayes UB4 78 BX71
Cygnus Business Cen, NW10 81 CT65
Cymbeline Ct, Har. HA1 61 CF58
Cynthia St, N1 196 C1
Cyntra Pl, E8 84 DV66
Cypress Av, Enf. EN2 29 DN35
Twickenham TW2 116 CC87
Cypress Cl, Wal.Abb. EN9 16 ED34
Cypress Ct, Vir.W. GU25 132 AY98
Cypress Gdns, SE4 123 DY85
Cypress Gro, Ilf. IG6 49 ES51
Cypress Path, Rom. RM3 52 FK52
Cypress Pl, W1 195 L5
Cypress Rd, SE25 142 DS96
Harrow HA3 41 CD54
Cypress Tree Cl, Sid. DA15
off White Oak Gdns 125 ET87
Cypress Wk, Egh.
(Eng.Grn) TW20 112 AV93
Cypress Wk, Watford WD25
off Cedar Wd Dr 23 BV35
Cypress Way, Bans. SM7 157 CX114
DLR Cyprus 87 EN73
Cyprus Av, N3 43 CY54
Cyprus Cl, N4
off Atterbury Rd 65 DP58
Cyprus Gdns, N3 43 CY54
Cyprus Pl, E2 84 DW68
E6 87 EN73
Cyprus Rd, N3 43 CZ54
N9 46 DT47
Cyprus Roundabout, E16
off Royal Albert Way 87 EN73
Cyprus St, E2 84 DW68
Cyrena Rd, SE22 122 DT86
Cyril Mans, SW11 100 DF81
Cyril Rd, Bexh. DA7 106 EY82
Orpington BR6 146 EU101
Cyrus St, EC1 196 G4
Czar St, SE8 103 EA79

D

Dabbling Cl, Erith DA8 107 FH80
Dabbs Hill La, Nthlt. UB5 60 CB64
D'Abernon Cl, Esher KT10 154 CA105
D'Abernon Dr, Cob.
(Stoke D'Ab.) KT11 170 BY116
Dabin Cres, SE10 103 EC81
Dacca St, SE8 103 DZ79
Dace Rd, E3 85 EA66
Dacre Av, Ilf. IG5 49 EN54
South Ockendon
(Aveley) RM15 91 FR74
Dacre Cl, Chig. IG7 49 EQ49
Greenford UB6 78 CB68
Dacre Cres, S.Ock.
(Aveley) RM15 91 FR74
Dacre Gdns, SE13 104 EE84
Borehamwood WD6 26 CR43
Chigwell IG7 49 EQ49
Dacre Pk, SE13 104 EE83
Dacre Pl, SE13 104 EE83
Dacre Rd, E11 68 EF60
E13 86 EH67
Croydon CR0 141 DL101
Dacres Rd, SE23 123 DX90
Dacre St, SW1 199 M6
Dade Way, Sthl. UB2 96 BZ78
Daerwood Cl, Brom. BR2 145 EM102
Daffodil Av, Brwd.
(Pilg.Hat.) CM15 54 FV43
Daffodil Cl, Croy. CR0
off Primrose La 143 DX102
Daffodil Gdns, Ilf. IG1 69 EP64
Daffodil Pl, Hmptn. TW12
off Gresham Rd 116 CA93
Daffodil St, W12 81 CT73
Dafforne Rd, SW17 120 DG90
DAGENHAM 88 FA65
Dagenham Av, Dag. RM9 88 EY67
⇌ Dagenham Dock 88 EZ68
⊖ Dagenham East 71 FC64
⊖ Dagenham Heathway 88 EZ65
Dagenham Rd, E10 67 DZ60
Dagenham RM10 71 FC63
Rainham RM13 89 FD66
Romford RM7 71 FD62
Dagger La, Borwd.
(Elstree) WD6 25 CG44
Dagmar Av, Wem. HA9 62 CM63
Dagmar Gdns, NW10 81 CX68
Dagmar Ms, Sthl. UB2
off Dagmar Rd 96 BY76
Dagmar Pas, N1 off Cross St 83 DP67
Dagmar Rd, N4 65 DN59
N15 off Cornwall Rd 66 DR56
N22 45 DK53
SE5 102 DS81
SE25 142 DS99
Dagenham RM10 89 FC66
Kingston upon Thames KT2 138 CM95
Southall UB2 96 BY76
Dagmar Ter, N1 83 DP67
Dagnall Cres, Uxb. UB8 76 BJ71
Dagnall Pk, SE25 142 DS100
Dagnall Rd, SE25 142 DS99
Dagnall St, SW11 100 DF82
Dagnam Pk Cl, Rom. RM3 52 FN50
Dagnam Pk Dr, Rom. RM3 52 FL50
Dagnam Pk Gdns, Rom. RM3 52 FN51
Dagnam Pk Sq, Rom. RM3 52 FP51
Dagnan Rd, SW12 121 DH87
Dagonet Gdns, Brom. BR1 124 EG90
Dagonet Rd, Brom. BR1 124 EG90
Dahlia Cl,
Wal.Cr. (Chsht) EN7 14 DQ25
Dahlia Dr, Swan. BR8 147 FF96
Dahlia Gdns, Ilf. IG1 87 EP65
Mitcham CR4 141 DK98
Dahlia Rd, SE2 106 EV77
Dahomey Rd, SW16 121 DJ93
Daiglen Dr, S.Ock. RM15 91 FU73
Daimler Way, Wall. SM6 159 DL108
Daines Cl, E12
off Colchester Av 69 EM62
South Ockendon RM15 91 FU70
Dainford Cl, Brom. BR1 123 ED92
Dainton Cl, Brom. BR1 144 EH95
Daintry Cl, Har. HA3 61 CG56
Daintry Lo, Nthwd. HA6 39 BT52
Daintry Way, E9
off Osborne Rd 85 DZ65
Dairsie Rd, SE9 105 EN83
Dairy Cl, NW10 81 CU67
Dartford (Sutt.H.) DA4 128 FP94
Thornton Heath CR7 142 DQ96
Dairyglen Av, Wal.Cr. EN8 15 DY31
Dairy La, SE18 105 EM77
Edenbridge (Crock.H.) TN8 189 EN134
Dairyman Cl, NW2
off Claremont Rd 63 CY62
Dairy Ms, SW9 101 DL83
Dairy Wk, SW19 119 CY91
Dairy Way, Abb.L. WD5 7 BT29
Daisy Cl, Croy. CR0
off Primrose La 143 DX102
Daisy Dobbins Wk, N19
off Hillrise Rd 65 DL59
Daisy La, SW6 100 DA83
Daisy Rd, E16
off Cranberry La 86 EE70
E18 48 EH54
Dakota Cl, Wall. SM6 159 DM108
Dakota Gdns, E6 86 EL70
Northolt UB5
off Argus Way 78 BY69
Dalberg Rd, SW2 101 DN84
Dalberg Way, SE2
off Lanridge Rd 106 EX76
Dalby Rd, SW18 100 DC84
Dalby St, NW5 83 DH65
Dalcross Rd, Houns. TW4 96 BY82
Dale, The, Kes. BR2 162 EK105
Waltham Abbey EN9 16 EE34
Dale Av, Edg. HA8 42 CM53
Hounslow TW4 96 BY83
Dalebury Rd, SW17 120 DE89
Dale Cl, SE3 104 EG83
Addlestone KT15 152 BH106
Barnet EN5 28 DB44
Dartford DA1 127 FF86
Pinner HA5 39 BV53
South Ockendon RM15 91 FU72
Dale Dr, Hayes UB4 77 BT70
Dale End, Dart. DA1
off Dale Rd 127 FF86
Dale Gdns, Wdf.Grn. IG8 48 EH49
Dalegarth Gdns, Pur. CR8 160 DR113
Dale Grn Rd, N11 45 DH48
Dale Gro, N12 44 DC50
Daleham Av, Egh. TW20 113 BA93
Daleham Dr, Uxb. UB8 77 BP72
Daleham Gdns, NW3 64 DD64
Daleham Ms, NW3 82 DD65
Dalehead, NW1 195 K1
Dalemain Ms, E16 205 N2
Dale Pk Av, Cars. SM5 140 DF103
Dale Pk Rd, SE19 142 DQ95
Dale Rd, NW5 off Grafton Rd 64 DG64
SE17 101 DP79
Dartford DA1 127 FF86
Gravesend (Sthflt) DA13 130 GA91
Greenford UB6 78 CB71
Purley CR8 159 DN112
Sunbury-on-Thames TW16 115 BT94
Sutton SM1 157 CZ105
Swanley BR8 147 FC96
Walton-on-Thames KT12 135 BT101
Dale Row, W11
off St. Marks Rd 81 CY72
Daleside, Ger.Cr. SL9 56 AY60
Orpington BR6 164 EU106
Daleside Cl, Orp. BR6 164 EU107
Daleside Dr, Pot.B. EN6 11 CZ32
Daleside Gdns, Chig. IG7 49 EQ48
Daleside Rd, SW16 121 DH92
Epsom KT19 156 CR107
Dales Path, Borwd. WD6
off Farriers Way 26 CR43
Dales Rd, Borwd. WD6 26 CR43
Dalestone Ms, Rom. RM3 51 FH51
Dale St, W4 98 CS78
Dale Vw, Epsom
(Headley) KT18 172 CP123
Erith DA8 107 FF82
Woking GU21 166 AU118
Dale Vw Av, E4 47 EC47
Dale Vw Cres, E4 47 EC47
Dale Vw Gdns, E4 47 ED48
Daleview Rd, N15 66 DS58
Dale Wk, Dart. DA2 128 FQ88
Dalewood Cl, Horn. RM11 72 FM59
Dalewood Gdns, Wor.Pk. KT4 139 CV103
Dale Wd Rd, Orp. BR6 145 ES101
Daley St, E9 85 DX65
Daley Thompson Way, SW8 101 DH82
Dalgarno Gdns, W10 81 CW71
Dalgarno Way, W10 81 CW70
Dalgleish St, E14 85 DY72
Daling Way, E3 85 DY67
Dalkeith Gro, Stan. HA7 41 CK50
Dalkeith Rd, SE21 122 DQ88
Ilford IG1 69 EQ62
Dallas Rd, NW4 63 CU59
SE26 122 DV91
W5 80 CM71
Sutton SM3 157 CY107
Dallas Ter, Hayes UB3 95 BT76
Dallega Cl, Hayes UB3
off Dawley Rd 77 BR73
Dallinger Rd, SE12 124 EF86
Dalling Rd, W6 99 CV76
Dallington Cl, Walt. KT12 154 BW107
Dallington Sq, EC1
off Dallington St 83 DP70
Dallington St, EC1 196 G4
Dallin Rd, SE18 105 EP80
Bexleyheath DA6 106 EX84
Dalmain Rd, SE23 123 DX88
Dalmally Rd, Croy. CR0 142 DT101
Dalmeny Av, N7 65 DK63
SW16 141 DN96
Dalmeny Cl, Wem. HA0 79 CJ65
Dalmeny Cres, Houns. TW3 97 CD84
Dalmeny Rd, N7 65 DK62
Barnet EN5 28 DC44
Carshalton SM5 158 DG108
Erith DA8 107 FB81
Worcester Park KT4 139 CV104
Dalmeyer Rd, NW10 81 CT65
Dalmore Av, Esher
(Clay.) KT10 155 CF107
Dalmore Rd, SE21 122 DQ89
Dalroy Cl, S.Ock. RM15 91 FU72
Dalrymple Cl, N14 45 DK45
Dalrymple Rd, SE4 103 DY84
DALSTON, E8 84 DU66
Dalston Gdns, Stan. HA7 42 CL53
⇌ Dalston Kingsland 84 DS65
Dalston La, E8 84 DT65
Dalton Av, Mitch. CR4 140 DE96

★ Place of interest ⇌ Railway station ⊖ London Underground station DLR Docklands Light Railway station Tra Tramlink station H Hospital Riv Pedestrian ferry landing stage

243

Dalton Cl, Hayes UB4 77 BR70
Orpington BR6 145 ES104
Purley CR8 160 DQ112
Dalton Grn, Slou. SL3
off Ditton Rd 93 AZ78
Dalton Rd, Har. (Har.Wld) HA3 41 CD54
Daltons Rd, Orp. BR6 147 FB104
Swanley BR8 147 FC102
Dalton St, SE27 121 DP89
Dalton Way, Wat. WD17 24 BX43
Dalwood St, SE5 102 DS81
Daly Ct, E15 off Clays La 67 EC64
Dalyell Rd, SW9 101 DM83
Damascene Wk, SE21
off Lovelace Rd 122 DQ88
Damask Cres, E16
off Cranberry La 86 EE70
Damer Ter, SW10
off Tadema Rd 100 DC80
Dames Rd, E7 68 EG62
Dame St, N1 84 DQ68
Dameswick Vw, St.Alb. AL2 8 CA27
Damien St, E1 84 DV72
Damigos Rd, Grav. DA12 131 GM88
Damon Cl, Sid. DA14 126 EV90
Damson Ct, Swan. BR8 147 FD98
Damson Dr, Hayes UB3 77 BU73
Damson Way, Cars. SM5 158 DF110
Damsonwood Rd, Sthl. UB2 96 CA76
Danbrook Rd, SW16 141 DL95
Danbury Cl, Brwd.
(Pilg.Hat.) CM15 54 FT43
Romford RM6 70 EX55
Danbury Cres, S.Ock. RM15 91 FV72
Danbury Ms, Wall. SM6 159 DH105
Danbury Rd, Loug. IG10 48 EL45
Rainham RM13 89 FF67
Danbury St, N1 83 DP68
Danbury Way, Wdf.Grn. IG8 48 EJ51
Danby St, SE15 102 DT83
Dancer Rd, SW6 99 CZ81
Richmond TW9 98 CN83
DANCERS HILL, Barn. EN5 27 CW35
Dancers Hill Rd, Barn. EN5 27 CY36
Dancers La, Barn. EN5 27 CW35
Dandelion Cl, Rom.
(Rush Grn) RM7 71 FE61
Dando Cres, SE3 104 EH83
Dandridge Cl, SE10 205 L10
Slough SL3 92 AX77
Danebury, Croy.
(New Adgtn) CR0 161 EB107
Danebury Av, SW15 118 CS86
Daneby Rd, SE6 123 EB90
Dane Cl, Amer. HP7 20 AT41
Bexley DA5 126 FA87
Orpington BR6 163 ER106
Dane Ct, Wok. GU22 167 BF115
Danecourt Gdns, Croy. CR0 142 DT104
Danecroft Rd, SE24 122 DQ85
Danehill Wk, Sid. DA14
off Hatherley Rd 126 EU90
Danehurst Cl, Egh. TW20 112 AY93
Danehurst Gdns, Ilf. IG4 68 EL57
Danehurst St, SW6 99 CY81
Daneland, Barn. EN4 28 DF44
Danemead Gro, Nthlt. UB5 60 CB64
Danemere St, SW15 99 CW83
Dane Pl, E3 off Roman Rd 85 DY68
Dane Rd, N18 46 DW48
SW19 140 DC95
W13 79 CJ74
Ashford TW15 115 BQ93
Ilford IG1 69 EQ64
Sevenoaks (Otford) TN14 181 FE117
Southall UB1 78 BY73
Warlingham CR6 177 DX117
Danes, The, St.Alb.
(Park St) AL2 8 CC28
Danesbury Rd, Felt. TW13 115 BV88
Danes Cl, Grav. (Nthflt) DA11 130 GC90
Leatherhead
(Oxshott) KT22 154 CC114
Danescombe, SE12
off Winn Rd 124 EG88
Danes Ct, Wem. HA9 62 CP62
Danescourt Cres, Sutt. SM1 140 DC103
Danescroft, NW4 63 CX57
Danescroft Av, NW4 63 CX57
Danescroft Gdns, NW4 63 CX57
Danesdale Rd, E9 85 DY65
Danesfield, SE5 102 DS79
Woking GU23
off Polesden La 167 BF123
Danesfield Cl, Walt. KT12 135 BV104
Danes Gate, Har. HA1 61 CE55
Daneshill, Red. RH1 184 DE133
Danes Hill, Wok. GU22 167 BA118
Daneshill Cl, Red. RH1 184 DE133
Danes Rd, Rom. RM7 71 FC59
Dane St, WC1 196 B7
Danes Way, Brwd.
(Pilg.Hat.) CM15 54 FU43
Leatherhead
(Oxshott) KT22 155 CD114
Daneswood Av, SE6 123 EC90
Daneswood Cl, Wey. KT13 153 BP106
Danethorpe Rd, Wem. HA0 79 CK65
Danetree Cl, Epsom KT19 156 CQ108
Danetree Rd, Epsom KT19 156 CQ108
Danette Gdns, Dag. RM10 70 EZ61
Daneville Rd, SE5 102 DR81
Dangan Rd, E11 68 EG58
Daniel Bolt Cl, E14
off Uamvar St 85 EB71
Daniel Cl, N18 46 DW49
SW17 120 DE93
Grays RM16 111 GH76
Grays (Chaff.Hun.) RM16 110 FY75
Hounslow TW4
off Harvey Rd 116 BZ87
Daniel Gdns, SE15 102 DT80
Daniell Way, Croy. CR0 141 DL102
Daniel Pl, NW4 63 CV58
Daniel Rd, W5 80 CM73

Daniels La, Warl. CR6 177 DZ116
Daniels Rd, SE15 102 DW83
Daniel Way, Bans. SM7 158 DB114
Dan Leno Wk, SW6
off Britannia Rd 100 DB80
Dan Mason Dr, W4
off Great Chertsey Rd 98 CQ82
Dansey Pl, W1 195 M10
Dansington Rd, Well. DA16 106 EU84
Danson Cres, Well. DA16 106 EV83
Danson La, Well. DA16 106 EU84
Danson Mead, Well. DA16 106 EW83
★ Danson Park, Well. DA16 106 EW84
Danson Pk, Bexh. DA6 106 EW84
Danson Rd, Bex. DA5 126 EX85
Bexleyheath DA6 126 EX85
Danson Underpass, Sid. DA15
off Danson Rd 126 EW86
Dante Pl, SE11 200 G8
Dante Rd, SE11 200 F8
Danube St, SW3 198 C10
Danvers Rd, N8 65 DK56
Danvers St, SW3 100 DD79
Danvers Way, Cat. CR3 176 DQ123
Danyon Cl, Rain. RM13 90 FJ68
Danziger Way, Borwd. WD6 26 CQ39
Daphne Gdns, E4
off Gunners Gro 47 EC48
Daphne St, SW18 120 DC86
Daplyn St, E1
off Hanbury St 84 DU71
D'Arblay St, W1 195 L9
Darby Cl, Cat. CR3 176 DQ122
Darby Cres, Sun. TW16 136 BW96
Darby Dr, Wal.Abb. EN9 15 EC33
Darby Gdns, Sun. TW16 136 BW96
Darcy Av, Wall. SM6 159 DJ105
Darcy Cl, N20 44 DD47
D'Arcy Cl, Brwd. (Hutt.) CM13 55 GB45
Darcy Cl, Couls. CR5 175 DP119
Waltham Cross (Chsht) EN8 15 DY31
D'Arcy Dr, Har. HA3 61 CK56
Darcy Gdns, Dag. RM9 88 EZ67
D'Arcy Gdns, Har. HA3 62 CL56
D'Arcy Pl, Ashtd. KT21 172 CM117
Bromley BR2 144 EG98
Darcy Rd, SW16 141 DL96
D'Arcy Rd, Ashtd. KT21 172 CM117
Darcy Rd, Islw. TW7
off London Rd 97 CG81
D'Arcy Rd, Sutt. SM3 157 CX105
Dare Gdns, Dag. RM8
off Grafton Rd 70 EY62
Darell Rd, Rich. TW9 98 CN83
DARENTH, Dart. DA2 128 FQ91
Darenth Cl, Sev. TN13 190 FC122
Darenth Gdns, West. TN16
off Quebec Av 189 ER126
Darenth Hill, Dart.
(Darenth) DA2 128 FQ92
Darenth La, Sev.
(Dunt.Grn) TN13 190 FE121
South Ockendon RM15 91 FU72
Darenth Pk Av, Dart. DA2 129 FR89
Darenth Rd, N16 66 DT59
Dartford DA1 128 FM87
Dartford (Darenth) DA2 128 FP91
Welling DA16 106 EU81
Darenth Way, Sev.
(Shore.) TN14 165 FG111
Darenth Wd Rd, Dart. DA2 129 FS89
Darent Ind Pk, Erith DA8 108 FJ79
Darent Mead, Dart.
(Sutt.H.) DA4 148 FP95
H Darent Valley Hosp,
Dart. DA2 129 FS88
Darent Valley Path,
Dart. DA1, DA2, DA4 128 FM89
Sevenoaks TN13, TN14 181 FG115
Darfield Rd, SE4 123 DZ85
Darfield Way, W10 81 CX72
Darfur St, SW15 99 CX83
Dargate Cl, SE19
off Chipstead Cl 122 DT94
Darien Rd, SW11 100 DD83
Darkes La, Pot.B. EN6 12 DA32
Dark Ho Wk, EC3
off King William St 84 DS73
Dark La, Brwd.
(Gt Warley) CM14 53 FU52
Waltham Cross (Chsht) EN7 14 DU31
Darlands Dr, Barn. EN5 27 CX43
Darlan Rd, SW6 99 CZ80
Darlaston Rd, SW19 119 CX94
Darley Cl, Add. KT15 152 BJ106
Croydon CR0 143 DY100
Darley Cft, St.Alb. AL2 8 CB28
Darley Dr, N.Mal. KT3 138 CR96
Darley Gdns, Mord. SM4 140 DB100
Darley Rd, N9 46 DT46
SW11 120 DF86
Darling Rd, SE4 103 EA83
Darling Row, E1 84 DV70
Darlington Gdns, Rom. RM3 52 FK50
Darlington Path, Rom. RM3
off Darlington Gdns 52 FK50
Darlington Rd, SE27 121 DP92
Darlton Cl, Dart. DA1 107 FF83
Darmaine Cl, S.Croy. CR2
off Churchill Rd 160 DQ108
Darnaway Pl, E14
off Abbott Rd 85 EC72
Darndale Cl, E17 47 DZ54
Darnets Fld, Sev.
(Otford) TN14 181 FF117
Darnhills, Rad. WD7 25 CG35
Darnicle Hill, Wal.Cr.
(Chsht) EN7 13 DM25
Darnley Ho, E14 85 DY72
Darnley Pk, Wey. KT13 135 BP104
Darnley Rd, E9 84 DV65
Gravesend DA11 131 GG88
Grays RM17 off Stanley Rd 110 GB79
Woodford Green IG8 48 EG53
Darnley St, Grav. DA11 131 GG87
Darnley Ter, W11
off St. James's Gdns 81 CY74
Darns Hill, Swan. BR8 147 FC101
Darrell Cl, Slou. SL3 93 AZ77
Darrell Rd, SE22 122 DU85

Darren Cl, N4 65 DM59
Darrick Wd Rd, Orp. BR6 145 ER103
Darrington Rd, Borwd. WD6 26 CL39
Darris Cl, Hayes UB4 78 BY70
Darsley Dr, SW8 101 DL81
Dart Cl, Slou. SL3 93 BB79
Upminster RM14 73 FR58
Dartfields, Rom. RM3 52 FK51
DARTFORD 128 FJ87
⇌ Dartford 128 FL86
Dartford Av, N9 30 DW44
Dartford Bypass, Dart. DA2 127 FE88
Dartford Gdns, Rom. (Chad.Hth) RM6
off Heathfield Pk Dr 70 EV58
★ Dartford Heath, Dart. DA1 127 FG88
★ Dartford Mus, Dart. DA1 128 FL87
Dartford Northern Bypass, Dart.
DA1 108 FN83
Dartford Rd, Bex. DA5 127 FC88
Dartford DA1 127 FG86
Dartford (Fnghm) DA4 148 FP95
Sevenoaks TN13 191 FJ124
Dartford St, SE17 102 DQ79
Dartford Trade Pk, Dart. DA1 128 FL89
Dartford Tunnel, Dart. DA1 109 FR83
Purfleet RM19 109 FR83
Dartford Tunnel App Rd,
Dart. DA1 128 FN86
Dart Grn, S.Ock. RM15 91 FV71
Dartmoor Wk, E14 204 A8
Dartmouth Av, Wok. GU21 151 BC114
Dartmouth Cl, W11 81 CZ72
Dartmouth Grn, Wok. GU21 151 BD114
Dartmouth Gro, SE10 103 EC81
Dartmouth Hill, SE10 103 EC81
Dartmouth Ho, Kings.T. KT2
off Kingsgate Rd 138 CL95
DARTMOUTH PARK, NW5 65 DH62
Dartmouth Pk Av, NW5 65 DH62
Dartmouth Pk Hill, N19 65 DH60
NW5 65 DH60
Dartmouth Pk Rd, NW5 65 DH63
Dartmouth Path, Wok. GU21 151 BD114
Dartmouth Pl, SE23
off Dartmouth Rd 122 DW89
W4 98 CS79
Dartmouth Rd, E16
off Fords Pk Rd 86 EG72
NW2 81 CX65
NW4 63 CU58
SE23 122 DW90
SE26 122 DW90
Bromley BR2 144 EG101
Ruislip HA4 59 BU62
Dartmouth Row, SE10 103 EC82
Dartmouth St, SW1 199 M5
Dartmouth Ter, SE10 103 ED81
Dartnell Av, W.Byf. KT14 152 BH112
Dartnell Cl, W.Byf. KT14 152 BH112
Dartnell Ct, W.Byf. KT14 152 BJ112
Dartnell Cres, W.Byf. KT14 152 BH112
DARTNELL PARK,
W.Byf. KT14 152 BJ112
Dartnell Pk Rd, W.Byf. KT14 152 BJ111
Dartnell Pl, W.Byf. KT14 152 BH112
Dartnell Rd, Croy. CR0 142 DT101
Dartrey Wk, SW10
off World's End Est 100 DD80
Dart St, W10 81 CY69
Dartview Cl, Grays RM17 110 GE77
Darvel Cl, Wok. GU21 166 AU116
Darville Rd, N16 66 DT62
Darwell Cl, E6 87 EN68
Darwin Cl, N11 45 DH48
Orpington BR6 163 ER106
Darwin Dr, Sthl. UB1 78 CB72
Darwin Gdns, Wat. WD19
off Barnhurst Path 40 BW50
Darwin Rd, N22 45 DP53
W5 97 CJ78
Slough SL3 93 AZ75
Tilbury RM18 111 GF81
Welling DA16 105 ET83
Darwin St, SE17 201 L8
Darylngton Dr, Grnf. UB6 79 CD68
Dashwood Cl, Bexh. DA6 126 FA85
Slough SL3 92 AW77
West Byfleet KT14 152 BJ112
Dashwood Rd, N8 65 DM58
Gravesend DA11 131 GG89
Dassett Rd, SE27 121 DP92
Datchelor Pl, SE5 102 DR81
DATCHET, Slou. SL3 92 AW81
⇌ Datchet 92 AV81
Datchet Pl, Slou.
(Datchet) SL3 92 AV81
Datchet Rd, SE6 123 DZ90
Slough SL3 92 AT77
Slough (Horton) SL3 93 AZ83
Windsor (Old Wind.) SL4 92 AU84
Datchworth Ct, N4
off Queens Dr 66 DQ62
Date St, SE17 102 DQ78
Daubeney Gdns, N17 46 DQ52
Daubeney Rd, E5 67 DY63
N17 46 DQ52
Daubeney Twr, SE8 203 M9
Dault Rd, SW18 120 DC86
Davall Ho, Grays RM17
off Argent St 110 GB79
Davema Cl, Chis. BR7
off Brenchley Cl 145 EN95
Davenant Rd, N19 65 DK61
Croydon CR0
off Duppas Hill Rd 159 DP105
Davenant St, E1 84 DU71
Davenham Av, Nthwd. HA6 39 BT49
Davenport Cl, Tedd. TW11 117 CG93
Davenport Rd, SE6 123 EB86
Sidcup DA14 126 EX89
Daventer Dr, Stan. HA7 41 CF52
Daventry Av, E17 67 EA57
Daventry Cl, Slou.
(Colnbr.) SL3 93 BF81
Daventry Gdns, Rom. RM3 52 FJ50
Daventry Grn, Rom. RM3
off Hailsham Rd 52 FJ50
Daventry Rd, Rom. RM3 52 FJ50
Daventry St, NW1 194 B6
Davern Cl, SE10 205 K9

Davey Cl, N7 83 DM65
Davey Rd, E9 85 EA66
Davey St, SE15 102 DT79
David Av, Grnf. UB6 79 CE69
David Cl, Hayes UB3 95 BR80
David Dr, Rom. RM3 52 FN51
Davidge St, SE1 200 F5
David Lee Pt, E15 86 EE67
David Ms, W1 194 E6
David Rd, Dag. RM8 70 EY61
Slough (Colnbr.) SL3 93 BF82
Davidson Gdns, SW8 101 DL80
Davidson La, Har. HA1
off Grove Hill 61 CF59
Davidson Rd, Croy. CR0 142 DT100
Davidson Way, Rom. RM7 71 FE58
Davids Rd, SE23 122 DW88
David St, E15 85 ED65
David's Way, Ilf. IG6 49 ES52
David Twigg Cl, Kings.T. KT2 138 CL95
Davies Cl, Croy. CR0 142 DU100
Rainham RM13 90 FJ69
Davies La, E11 68 EE61
Davies Ms, W1 195 H10
Davies St, W1 195 H10
Davington Gdns, Dag. RM8 70 EV64
Davington Rd, Dag. RM8 88 EV65
Davinia Cl, Wdf.Grn. IG8
off Deacon Way 49 EM51
Davis Av, Grav. (Nthflt) DA11 130 GE88
Davis Cl, Sev. TN13 191 FJ122
Davison Cl, Wal.Cr. EN8 15 DX28
Davison Dr, Wal.Cr.
(Chsht) EN8 15 DX28
Davison Rd, Slou. SL3
off Ditton Rd 93 AZ78
Davis Rd, W3 81 CT74
Chessington KT9 156 CN105
Grays (Chaff.Hun.) RM16 110 FZ76
South Ockendon
(Aveley) RM15 91 FR74
Weybridge KT13 152 BM110
Davis St, E13 86 EH68
Davisville Rd, W12 99 CU75
Davos Cl, Wok. GU22 166 AY119
Davys Pl, Grav. DA12 131 GL93
Dawell Dr, West.
(Bigg.H.) TN16 178 EJ117
Dawes Av, Horn. RM12 72 FK62
Isleworth TW7 117 CG85
Dawes Cl, Green. DA9 129 FT85
Dawes Ct, Esher KT10 154 CB105
Dawes Ho, SE17 201 L9
Dawes La, Rick. (Sarratt) WD3 21 BE37
Dawes Moor Cl, Slou. SL2 74 AW72
Dawes Rd, SW6 99 CY80
Uxbridge UB10 76 BL68
Dawes St, SE17 201 L10
Dawley Av, Uxb. UB8 77 BQ71
Dawley Grn, S.Ock. RM15 91 FU72
Dawley Par, Hayes UB3
off Dawley Rd 77 BQ73
Dawley Ride, Slou.
(Colnbr.) SL3 93 BE81
Dawley Rd, Hayes UB3 77 BR73
Uxbridge UB8 77 BQ73
Dawlish Av, N13 45 DL49
SW18 120 DB89
Greenford UB6 79 CG68
Dawlish Dr, Ilf. IG3 69 ES63
Pinner HA5 60 BY57
Ruislip HA4 59 BU61
Dawlish Rd, E10 67 EC61
N17 66 DU55
NW2 81 CX65
Dawlish Wk, Rom. RM3 52 FJ53
Dawnay Gdns, SW18 120 DD89
Dawnay Rd, SW18 120 DC89
Dawn Cl, Houns. TW4 96 BY83
Dawn Cres, E15 off Bridge Rd 85 ED67
Dawn Redwood Cl, Slou.
(Horton) SL3 93 BA83
Dawpool Rd, NW2 63 CT61
Daws Hill, E4 31 EC41
Daws La, NW7 43 CT50
Dawson Av, Bark. IG11 87 ES66
Orpington BR5 146 EV96
Dawson Cl, SE18 105 EQ77
Hayes UB3 77 BR71
Dawson Dr, Rain. RM13 89 FH66
Swanley BR8 127 FE94
Dawson Gdns, Bark. IG11
off Dawson Av 87 ET66
Dawson Hts Est, SE22 122 DU87
Dawson Pl, W2 82 DA73
Dawson Rd, NW2 63 CW64
Kingston upon Thames KT1 138 CM97
West Byfleet (Byfleet) KT14 152 BK111
Dawson St, E2 84 DT68
Dax Ct, Sun. TW16
off Thames St 136 BW97
Daybrook Rd, SW19 140 DB96
Daylesford Av, SW15 99 CU84
Daylop Dr, Chig. IG7 50 EV48
Daymer Gdns, Pnr. HA5 59 BV56
Daymerslea Ridge,
Lthd. KT22 171 CJ121
Days Acre, S.Croy. CR2 160 DT110
Daysbrook Rd, SW2 121 DM89
Days La, Brwd.
(Pilg.Hat.) CM15 54 FU42
Sidcup DA15 125 ES87
Dayton Dr, Erith DA8 108 FK78
Dayton Gro, SE15 102 DW81
Deacon Cl, Cob. (Down.) KT11 169 BV119
Purley CR8 159 DL109
Deacon Ms, N1 84 DR66
Deacon Pl, Cat. CR3 176 DQ123
Deacon Rd, NW2 63 CU64
Kingston upon Thames KT2 138 CM95
Deacons Cl, Borwd.
(Elstree) WD6 26 CN42
Pinner HA5 39 BV54
Deacons Hill, Wat. WD19 24 BW44
Deacon's Hill Rd, Borwd.
(Elstree) WD6 26 CM42
Deacons Leas, Orp. BR6 163 ER105
Deacons Ri, N2 64 DD57
Deacons Wk, Hmptn. TW12
off Bishops Gro 116 BZ91

Deacon Way, SE17 201 H8
Woodford Green IG8 49 EM52
Deadhearn La, Ch.St.G. HP8 36 AY46
Deadman's Ash La, Rick.
(Sarratt) WD3 22 BH36
Deakin Cl, Wat. WD18
off Chenies Way 39 BS45
Deal Ms, W5 off Darwin Rd 97 CK77
Deal Porters Way, SE16 202 G6
Deal Rd, SW17 120 DG93
Deal's Gateway, SE10
off Blackheath Rd 103 EB81
Deal St, E1 84 DU71
Dealtry Rd, SW15 99 CW84
Deal Wk, SW9 off Mandela St 101 DN80
Deanacre Cl, Ger.Cr.
(Chal.St.P.) SL9 36 AY51
DEAN BOTTOM, Dart. DA4 149 FV97
Dean Bradley St, SW1 199 P7
Dean Cl, E9 off Churchill Wk 66 DW64
SE16 203 J3
Uxbridge UB10 76 BM66
Woking GU22 167 BE115
Dean Ct, Wem. HA0 61 CH62
Deancroft Rd, Ger.Cr.
(Chal.St.P.) SL9 36 AY51
Deancross St, E1 84 DW72
Dean Dr, Stan. HA7 42 CL54
Deane Av, Ruis. HA4 60 BW64
Deane Cft Rd, Pnr. HA5 59 BV58
Deanery Cl, N2 64 DE56
Deanery Ms, W1 198 G2
Deanery Rd, E15 86 EE65
Edenbridge (Crock.H.) TN8 189 EQ134
Deanery St, W1 198 G2
Deane Way, Ruis. HA4 59 BV58
Dean Farrar St, SW1 199 M6
Dean Fld, Hem.H. (Bov.) HP3 5 BA27
Dean Gdns, E17 67 ED56
W13 off Northfield Av 79 CH74
Deanhill Rd, SW14 98 CP84
Dean La, Red. RH1 175 DH123
Dean Rd, NW2 81 CW65
SE28 88 EU73
Croydon CR0 160 DR105
Hampton TW12 116 CA92
Hounslow TW3 116 CB85
Dean Ryle St, SW1 199 P8
Deansbrook Cl, Edg. HA8 42 CQ52
Deansbrook Rd, Edg. HA8 42 CQ51
Deans Bldgs, SE17 201 K9
Deans Cl, W4 98 CP79
Abbots Langley WD5 7 BR32
Amersham HP6 20 AT37
Dean's Cl, Croy. CR0 142 DT104
Deans Cl, Edg. HA8 42 CQ51
Slough (Stoke P.) SL2 74 AV67
Tadworth KT20
off Deans La 173 CV124
Deans Ct, EC4 196 G9
Deanscroft Av, NW9 62 CQ61
Deans Dr, N13 45 DP51
Edgware HA8 42 CR50
Deansfield, Cat. CR3 186 DT125
Dean's Gate Cl, SE23 123 DX90
Deans La, W4 98 CP79
Edgware HA8 42 CQ51
Redhill (Nutfld) RH1 185 DN133
Tadworth KT20 173 CV124
Deans Ms, W1 195 J8
Deans Rd, W7 79 CF74
Brentwood CM14 54 FV49
Redhill RH1 185 DJ130
Sutton SM1 140 DB104
Dean Stanley St, SW1 199 P7
Dean St, E7 68 EG64
W1 195 M8
Deans Wk, Couls. CR5 175 DN118
Deansway, N2 64 DD56
N9 46 DS48
Deans Way, Edg. HA8 42 CQ50
Dean's Yd, SW1 199 N6
Dean Trench St, SW1 199 P7
Dean Wk, Edg. HA8
off Deansbrook Rd 42 CQ51
Deanway, Ch.St.G. HP8 36 AU48
Dean Way, Sthl. UB2 96 CB75
Dearne Cl, Stan. HA7 41 CG50
De'Arn Gdns, Mitch. CR4 140 DE97
Dearsley Ho, Rain. RM13 89 FD68
Dearsley Rd, Enf. EN1 30 DU41
Deason St, E15 off High St 85 EC67
De Barowe Ms, N5
off Leigh Rd 65 DP63
DEBDEN, Loug. IG10 33 ER41
⊖ Debden 33 EQ42
Debden Cl, Kings.T. KT2 117 CK92
Woodford Green IG8 48 EJ52
DEBDEN GREEN, Loug. IG10 33 EQ38
Debden Grn, Loug. IG10 33 EP38
Debden La, Loug. IG10 33 EP38
Debden Rd, Loug. IG10 33 EP38
Debden Wk, Horn. RM12 89 FH65
De Beauvoir Cres, N1 84 DS67
De Beauvoir Est, N1 84 DR67
De Beauvoir Rd, N1 84 DS67
De Beauvoir Sq, N1 84 DS66
DE BEAUVOIR TOWN, N1 84 DR67
Debenham Rd, Wal.Cr.
(Chsht) EN7 14 DV27
Debnams Rd, SE16 202 F9
De Bohun Av, N14 29 DH44
Deborah Cl, Islw. TW7 97 CE81
Deborah Cres, Ruis. HA4 59 BR59
Debrabant Cl, Erith DA8 107 FD79
De Brome Rd, Felt. TW13 116 BW88
De Burgh Gdns, Tad. KT20 173 CX119
De Burgh Pk, Bans. SM7 174 DB115
Deburgh Rd, SW19 120 DC94
Decies Way, Slou.
(Stoke P.) SL2 74 AU67
Decima St, SE1 201 M6
Deck Cl, SE16 203 J4
Decoy Av, NW11 63 CY57
De Crespigny Pk, SE5 102 DR82
Dee Cl, Upmin. RM14 73 FS58
Deeley Rd, SW8 101 DK81
Deena Cl, W3 80 CM72
Deepdale, SW19 119 CX91
Deepdale Av, Brom. BR2 144 EF98

★ Place of interest ⇌ Railway station ⊖ London Underground station DLR Docklands Light Railway station Tra Tramlink station H Hospital Riv Pedestrian ferry landing stage

244

Deepdale Cl, N11
off Ribblesdale Av. 44 DG51
Deepdene, W5 80 CM70
Potters Bar EN6 11 CX31
Deepdene Av, Croy. CR0 142 DT104
Deepdene Cl, E11 68 EG56
Deepdene Ct, N21 29 DP44
Deepdene Gdns, SW2 121 DM87
Deepdene Path, Loug. IG10 33 EN42
Deepdene Pt, SE23
off Dacres Rd 123 DX90
Deepdene Rd, SE5 102 DR84
Loughton IG10 33 EN42
Welling DA16 106 EU83
Deep Fld, Slou. (Datchet) SL3 92 AV80
Deepfield Way, Couls. CR5 175 DL116
Deep Pool La, Wok.
(Chobham) GU24 150 AV114
Deepwell Cl, Islw. TW7 97 CG81
Deepwood La, Grnf. UB6
off Cowgate Rd 79 CD69
Deerbrook Rd, SE24 121 DP88
Deerdale Rd, SE24 102 DQ84
Deere Av, Rain. RM13 89 FG65
Deerfield Cl, NW9
off Rookery Cl 63 CT57
Deerhurst Cl, Felt. TW13 115 BU91
Deerhurst Cres, Hmptn.
(Hmptn H.) TW12 116 CC92
Deerhurst Rd, NW2 81 CX65
SW16 121 DM92
Deerings Dr, Pnr. HA5 59 BU57
Deerings Rd, Reig. RH2 184 DB134
Deerleap Gro, E4 31 EB43
Deerleap La, Sev. TN14 164 EX113
Dee Rd, Rich. TW9 98 CM84
Deer Pk Cl, Kings.T. KT2 118 CP94
Deer Pk Gdns, Mitch. CR4 140 DD97
Deer Pk Rd, SW19 140 DB96
Deer Pk Wk, Chesh. HP5 4 AS28
Deer Pk Way, Wal.Abb. EN9 31 EC36
West Wickham BR4 144 EF103
Deers Fm Cl, Wok.
(Wisley) GU23 168 BL116
Deerswood Cl, Cat. CR3 176 DU124
Deeside Rd, SW17 120 DD90
Dee St, E14 85 EC72
Deeves Hall La, Pot.B. EN6 10 CS33
Dee Way, Epsom KT19 156 CS110
Romford RM1 51 FE53
Defiance Wk, SE18 105 EM76
Defiant Way, Wall. SM6 159 DL108
Defoe Av, Rich. TW9 98 CN80
Defoe Cl, SE16 203 M5
SW17 120 DE93
Erith DA8 *off Selkirk Dr.* 107 FE81
Defoe Ho, EC2 197 J6
Defoe Par, Grays RM16 111 GH76
Defoe Pl, EC2 *off Beech St* 84 DQ71
SW17 *off Lessingham Av* 120 DF91
Defoe Rd, N16 66 DS61
Defoe Way, Rom. RM5 51 FB51
De Frene Rd, SE26 123 DX91
De Gama Pl, E14
off Maritime Quay 103 EA78
Degema Rd, Chis. BR7 125 EP92
Dehar Cres, NW9 63 CT59
Dehavilland Cl, Nthlt. UB5 78 BX69
De Havilland Ct, Rad.
(Shenley) WD7
off Armstrong Gdns 10 CL32
De Havilland Dr, Wey. KT13 152 BL111
★ **De Havilland Mosquito Aircraft Mus**, St.Alb. AL2 10 CP29
De Havilland Rd, Edg. HA8 42 CP54
Hounslow TW5 96 BW80
De Havilland Way, Abb.L. WD5 7 BT32
Staines (Stanw.) TW19 114 BK86
Dekker Rd, SE21 122 DS86
Delabole Rd, Red. RH1 185 DL129
Delacourt Rd, SE3
off Old Dover Rd 104 EH80
Delafield Rd, SE7 104 EH78
Grays RM17 110 GD78
Delaford Cl, Iver SL0 75 BF72
Delaford Rd, SE16 202 E10
Delaford St, SW6 99 CY80
Delagarde Rd, West. TN16 189 EQ126
Delamare Cres, Croy. CR0 142 DW100
Delamare Rd, Wal.Cr.
(Chsht) EN8 15 DZ30
Delamere Gdns, NW7 42 CR51
Delamere Rd, SW20 139 CX95
W5 80 CL74
Borehamwood WD6 26 CP39
Hayes UB4 78 BX73
Delamere Ter, W2 82 DB71
Delancey Pas, NW1
off Delancey St 83 DH67
Delancey St, NW1 83 DH67
Delaporte Cl, Epsom KT17 156 CS112
De Lapre Cl, Orp. BR5 146 EX101
De Lara Way, Wok. GU21 166 AX118
Delargy Cl, Grays RM16 111 GH76
De Laune St, SE17 101 DP78
Delaware Rd, W9 82 DB70
Delawyk Cres, SE24 122 DQ86
Delcombe Av, Wor.Pk. KT4 139 CW102
Delderfield, Lthd. KT22 171 CK120
Delft Way, SE22
off East Dulwich Gro 122 DS85
Delhi Rd, Enf. EN1 46 DT45
Delhi St, N1 83 DL67
Delia St, SW18 120 DB87
Delisle Rd, SE28 87 ES74
Delius Cl, Borwd.
(Elstree) WD6 25 CJ44
Delius Gro, E15 85 ED68
Dell, The, SE2 106 EU78
SE19 142 DT95
Bexley DA5 127 FE88
Brentford TW8 97 CJ79
Brentwood
(Gt Warley) CM13 53 FV51
Feltham TW14
off Harlington Rd W 115 BV87
Gerrards Cross
(Chal.St.P.) SL9 36 AY51
Greenhithe DA9
off London Rd 129 FW85
Dell, The, Northwood HA6 39 BS47
Pinner HA5 40 BX54
Radlett WD7 25 CG36
Reigate RH2 184 DA133
Tadworth KT20 173 CW121
Waltham Abbey EN9
off Greenwich Way 31 EC36
Wembley HA0 61 CH64
Woking GU21 166 AW118
Woodford Green IG8 48 EH48
Della Path, E5
off Napoleon Rd 66 DV62
Dellbow Rd, Felt. TW14
off Central Way 115 BV85
Dell Cl, E15 85 ED67
Leatherhead (Fetch.) KT22 171 CE123
Wallington SM6 159 DK105
Woodford Green IG8 48 EH48
Dell Fm Rd, Ruis. HA4 59 BR57
Dellfield Cl, Beck. BR3
off Foxgrove Rd 123 EC94
Radlett WD7 25 CE35
Watford WD17 23 BU40
Dellfield Cres, Uxb. UB8 76 BJ70
Dellfield Par, Uxb. (Cowley) UB8
off High St 76 BJ70
Dell La, Epsom KT17 157 CU106
Dellmeadow, Abb.L. WD5 7 BS30
Dellors Cl, Barn. EN5 27 CX43
Dellow Cl, Ilf. IG2 69 ER59
Dellow St, E1 84 DV73
Dell Ri, St.Alb. (Park St) AL2 8 CB26
Dell Rd, Enf. EN3 30 DW38
Epsom KT17 157 CU107
Grays RM17 110 GB77
Watford WD24 23 BU37
West Drayton UB7 94 BM76
Dells Cl, E4 47 EB45
Teddington TW11
off Middle La 117 CF93
Dellside, Uxb. (Hare.) UB9 58 BJ57
Dell Side, Wat. WD24
off The Harebreaks 23 BU37
Dell's Ms, SW1 199 L9
Dell Wk, N.Mal. KT3 138 CS96
Dell Way, W13 79 CJ72
Dellwood, Rick. WD3 38 BH46
Dellwood Gdns, Ilf. IG5 69 EN55
Delmaire Cl, SW9
off Brighton Ter 101 DM84
Delme Cres, SE3 104 EH82
Delmey Cl, Croy. CR0
off Radcliffe Rd 142 DT104
Deloraine St, SE8 103 EA81
Delorme St, W6 99 CX79
Delta Cl, Wok.
(Chobham) GU24 150 AT110
Worcester Park KT4 139 CT104
Delta Ct, NW2 63 CU61
Delta Gain, Wat. WD19 40 BX47
Delta Gro, Nthlt. UB5 78 BX69
Delta Rd, Brwd. (Hutt.) CM13 55 GD44
Woking GU21 167 BA116
Woking (Chobham) GU24 150 AT110
Worcester Park KT4 138 CS104
Delta St, E2
off Wellington Row 84 DU69
Delta Way, Egh. TW20 133 BC95
De Luci Rd, Erith DA8 107 FC78
De Lucy St, SE2 106 EV77
Delvan Cl, SE18
off Ordnance Rd 105 EN80
Delvers Mead, Dag. RM10 71 FC63
Delverton Rd, SE17 101 DP78
Delves, Tad. KT20
off Heathcote 173 CX121
Delvino Rd, SW6 100 DA81
De Mandeville Gate, Enf. EN1
off Southbury Rd 30 DU42
De Mel Cl, Epsom KT19 156 CP112
Demesne Rd, Wall. SM6 159 DK106
Demeta Cl, Wem. HA9 62 CQ62
De Montfort Par, SW16
off Streatham High Rd 121 DL90
De Montfort Rd, SW16 121 DL90
De Morgan Rd, SW6 100 DB83
Dempster Cl, Surb. KT6 137 CJ102
Dempster Rd, SW18 120 DC85
Denbar Par, Rom. RM7
off Mawney Rd 71 FC56
Denberry Dr, Sid. DA14 126 EV90
Denbigh Cl, NW10 80 CS66
W11 81 CZ73
Chislehurst BR7 125 EM93
Hornchurch RM11 72 FN56
Ruislip HA4 59 BT61
Southall UB1 78 BZ72
Sutton SM1 157 CZ106
Denbigh Dr, Hayes UB3 95 BQ75
Denbigh Gdns, Rich. TW10 118 CM85
Denbigh Ms, SW1 199 K9
Denbigh Pl, SW1 199 K10
Denbigh Rd, E6 86 EK69
W11 81 CZ73
W13 79 CH73
Hounslow TW3 96 CB82
Southall UB1 78 BZ72
Denbigh St, SW1 199 K9
Denbigh Ter, W11 81 CZ73
Denbridge Rd, Brom. BR1 145 EM96
Denby Rd, Cob. KT11 154 BW113
Den Cl, Beck. BR3 143 ED97
Dendridge Cl, Enf. EN1 30 DV37
Dene, The, W13 79 CH71
Croydon CR0 161 DX105
Sevenoaks TN13 191 FH126
Sutton SM2 157 CZ111
Wembley HA9 62 CL63
West Molesey KT8 136 BZ99
Dene Av, Houns. TW3 96 BZ83
Sidcup DA15 126 EV87
Dene Cl, SE4 103 DY83
Bromley BR2 144 EF102
Coulsdon CR5 174 DE119
Dartford DA2 127 FE91
Worcester Park KT4 139 CT103
Dene Ct, Stan. HA7
off Marsh La 41 CJ50
Denecroft Cres, Uxb. UB10 77 BP67
Denecroft Gdns, Grays RM17 110 GD76
Dene Dr, Orp. BR6 146 EV104
Denefield Dr, Ken. CR8 176 DR115
Dene Gdns, Stan. HA7 41 CJ50
Thames Ditton KT7 137 CG103
Dene Holm Rd, Grav.
(Nthflt) DA11 130 GD90
Denehurst Gdns, NW4 63 CW58
W3 80 CP74
Richmond TW10 98 CN84
Twickenham TW2 117 CD87
Woodford Green IG8 48 EH49
Dene Path, S.Ock. RM15 91 FU72
Dene Pl, Wok. GU21 166 AV118
Dene Rd, N11 44 DF46
Ashtead KT21 172 CM119
Buckhurst Hill IG9 48 EK46
Dartford DA1 128 FM87
Northwood HA6 39 BS51
Denewood, Barn. EN5 28 DC43
Denewood Cl, Wat. WD17 23 BT37
Denewood Rd, N6 64 DF58
Denford St, SE10 205 K10
Dengie Wk, N1 *off Basire St* 84 DQ67
DENHAM, Uxb. UB9 58 BG62
⇌ **Denham** 58 BG59
★ **Denham Aerodrome**, Uxb. UB9 57 BD57
Denham Av, Uxb. (Denh.) UB9 57 BF61
Denham Cl, Uxb. (Denh.) UB9 58 BG62
Welling DA16
off Park Vw Rd 106 EW83
Denham Ct Dr, Uxb.
(Denh.) UB9 58 BH63
Denham Cres, Mitch. CR4 140 DF98
Denham Dr, Ilf. IG2 69 EQ58
Denham Gdn Village, Uxb. UB9
off Denham Grn La 57 BF58
⇌ **Denham Golf Club** 57 BD59
DENHAM GREEN, Uxb. UB9 57 BE58
Denham Grn Cl, Uxb.
(Denh.) UB9 58 BG59
Denham Grn La, Uxb.
(Denh.) UB9 57 BE57
Denham La, Ger.Cr.
(Chal.St.P.) SL9 37 BA53
Denham Lo, Uxb. UB9 76 BJ65
Denham Rd, N20 44 DF48
Egham TW20 113 BA91
Epsom KT17 157 CT112
Feltham TW14 116 BW86
Iver SL0 75 BD67
Uxbridge (Denh.) UB9 75 BE65
Denham St, SE10 205 M10
Denham Wk, Ger.Cr.
(Chal.St.P.) SL9 37 AZ51
Denham Way, Bark. IG11 87 ES67
Borehamwood WD6 26 CR39
Rickmansworth
(Map.Cr.) WD3 37 BE50
Uxbridge (Denh.) UB9 58 BG62
Denholme Rd, W9 81 CZ69
Denholme Wk, Rain. RM13
off Ryder Gdns 89 FF65
Denison Cl, N2 64 DC55
Denison Rd, SW19 120 DD93
W5 79 CJ70
Feltham TW13 115 BT91
Deniston Av, Bex. DA5 126 EY88
Denis Way, SW4
off Gauden Rd 101 DK83
Denleigh Gdns, N21 45 DN46
Thames Ditton KT7 137 CE100
Denman Dr, NW11 64 DA57
Ashford TW15 115 BP93
Esher (Clay.) KT10 155 CG106
Denman Dr N, NW11 64 DA57
Denman Dr S, NW11 64 DA57
Denman Pl, W1
off Great Windmill St 83 DK73
Denman Rd, SE15 102 DT81
Denman St, W1 199 M1
Denmark Av, SW19 119 CY94
Denmark Ct, Mord. SM4 140 DA99
Denmark Gdns, Cars. SM5 140 DF104
Denmark Gro, N1 83 DN68
⇌ **Denmark Hill** 102 DR82
Denmark Hill, SE5 102 DR81
Denmark Hill Dr, NW9 63 CT56
Denmark Hill Est, SE5 102 DR84
Denmark Pl, WC2 195 N8
Denmark Rd, N8 65 DN56
NW6 81 CZ68
SE5 102 DQ81
SE25 142 DU99
SW19 119 CX93
W13 79 CH73
Bromley BR1 144 EH95
Carshalton SM5 140 DF104
Kingston upon Thames KT1 138 CL97
Twickenham TW2 117 CD90
Denmark St, E11
off High Rd Leytonstone 68 EE62
E13 86 EH71
N17 46 DV53
WC2 195 N9
Watford WD17 23 BV40
Denmark Wk, SE27 122 DQ91
Denmead Cl, Ger.Cr. SL9 56 AY59
Denmead Ho, SW15
off Highcliffe Dr 119 CT86
Denmead Rd, Croy. CR0 141 DP102
Denmead Way, SE15
off Pentridge St 102 DT80
Dennan Rd, Surb. KT6 138 CM102
Dennard Way, Orp. BR6 163 EP105
Denner Rd, E4 47 EA47
Denne Ter, E8 84 DT67
Dennett Rd, Croy. CR0 141 DN102
Dennetts Gro, SE14
off Dennetts Rd 103 DX82
Dennettsland Rd, Eden.
(Crock.H.) TN8 189 EQ134
Dennetts Rd, SE14 102 DW81
Denning Av, Croy. CR0 159 DN105
Denning Cl, NW8 82 DC69
Hampton TW12 116 BZ93
Denning Rd, NW3 64 DD63
Dennington Cl, E5
off Detmold Rd 66 DV61
Dennington Pk Rd, NW6 82 DA65
Denningtons, The,
Wor.Pk. KT4 138 CS103
Dennis Av, Wem. HA9 62 CM64
Dennis Cl, Ashf. TW15 115 BR93
Redhill RH1 184 DE132
Dennises La, Upmin. RM14 91 FS67
Dennis Gdns, Stan. HA7 41 CJ50
Dennis La, Stan. HA7 41 CH48
Dennison Pt, E15 85 EC66
Dennis Pk Cres, SW20 139 CY95
Dennis Reeve Cl, Mitch. CR4 140 DF95
Dennis Rd, E.Mol. KT8 136 CC98
Gravesend DA11 131 GG90
South Ockendon RM15 91 FU66
Denny Av, Wal.Abb. EN9 15 ED34
Denny Cl, E6 *off Linton Gdns* 86 EL71
Denny Cres, SE11 200 E9
Denny Gdns, Dag. RM9
off Canonsleigh Rd 88 EV66
Denny Gate, Wal.Cr. EN8 15 DZ27
Denny Rd, N9 46 DV46
Slough SL3 93 AZ77
Denny St, SE11 200 E10
Den Rd, Brom. BR2 143 ED97
Densham Dr, Pur. CR8 159 DN114
Densham Rd, E15 86 EE67
Densole Cl, Beck. BR3
off Kings Hall Rd 143 DY95
Densworth Gro, N9 46 DW47
Dent Cl, S.Ock. RM15 91 FU72
DENTON, Grav. DA12 131 GL87
Denton Cl, Barn. EN5 27 CW43
Denton Ct Rd, Grav. DA12 131 GL87
Denton Gro, Walt. KT12 136 BX103
Denton Rd, N8 65 DM57
N18 46 DS49
Bexley DA5 127 FE89
Dartford DA1 127 FE88
Twickenham TW1 117 CK86
Welling DA16 106 EW80
Denton St, SW18 120 DB86
Gravesend DA12 131 GL87
Denton Ter, Bex. DA5
off Denton Rd 127 FE89
Denton Way, E5 67 DX62
Woking GU21 166 AT118
Dents Gro, Tad. KT20 183 CZ128
Dents Rd, SW11 120 DF86
Denvale Wk, Wok. GU21 166 AU118
Denver Cl, Orp. BR6 145 ES100
Denver Ind Est, Rain. RM13 89 FF71
Denver Rd, N16 66 DS59
Dartford DA1 127 FG87
Denyer St, SW3 198 C9
Denziloe Av, Uxb. UB10 77 BP69
Denzil Rd, NW10 63 CT64
Deodara Cl, N20 44 DE48
Deodar Rd, SW15 99 CY84
★ **Department for Environment, Food & Rural Affairs (D.E.F.R.A.)**, SW1 199 P2
★ **Department for Transport (D.f.T.)**, SW1 199 N8
★ **Department of Health & Dept for Work & Pensions (D.W.P.)**, SW1 199 P4
Depot App, NW2 63 CX63
Depot Rd, Epsom KT17 156 CS113
Hounslow TW3 97 CD83
DEPTFORD, SE8 103 DZ78
⇌ **Deptford** 103 DZ80
DLR **Deptford Bridge** 103 EA81
Deptford Br, SE8 103 EA81
Deptford Bdy, SE8 103 EA81
Deptford Ch St, SE8 103 EA79
Deptford Ferry Rd, E14 204 A9
Deptford Grn, SE8 103 EA79
Deptford High St, SE8 103 EA79
Deptford Strand, SE8 203 N9
Deptford Wf, SE8 203 M8
De Quincey Ms, E16 205 N2
De Quincey Rd, N17 46 DR53
Derby Arms Rd, Epsom KT18 173 CT117
Derby Av, N12 44 DC50
Harrow HA3 41 CD53
Romford RM7 71 FC58
Upminster RM14 72 FM62
Derby Cl, Epsom KT18 173 CV119
Derby Ct, E5 *off Overbury St* 67 DX63
Derby Gate, SW1 199 P4
Derby Hill, SE23 122 DW89
Derby Hill Cres, SE23 122 DW89
Derby Rd, E7 86 EJ66
E9 85 DX67
E18 48 EF53
N18 46 DW50
SW14 98 CP84
SW19 *off Russell Rd* 120 DA94
Croydon CR0 141 DP103
Enfield EN3 30 DV43
Grays RM17 110 GB78
Greenford UB6 78 CB67
Hounslow TW3 96 CB84
Surbiton KT5 138 CN102
Sutton SM1 157 CZ107
Uxbridge UB8 76 BJ68
Watford WD17 24 BW41
Derby Rd Br, Grays RM17 110 GB79
Derby Rd Ind Est, Houns. TW3
off Derby Rd 96 CB84
Derbyshire St, E2 84 DU69
Derby Sq, The, Epsom KT19
off High St 156 CR113
Derby Stables Rd,
Epsom KT18 172 CS117
Derby St, W1 198 G3
Dereham Pl, EC2 197 N3
Romford RM5 51 FB51
Dereham Rd, Bark. IG11 87 ET65
Derek Av, Epsom KT19 156 CN106
Wallington SM6 159 DH105
Wembley HA9 80 CP66
Derek Cl, Epsom
(Ewell) KT19 156 CP106
Derek Walcott Cl, SE24
off Shakespeare Rd 121 DP85
Derham Gdns,
Upmin. RM14 72 FQ62
Deri Av, Rain. RM13 89 FH70
Dericote St, E8 84 DU67
Deridene Cl, Stai. (Stanw.) TW19
off Bedfont Rd 114 BL86
Derifall Cl, E6 87 EM71
Dering Pl, Croy. CR0 160 DQ105
Dering Rd, Croy. CR0 160 DQ105
Dering St, W1 195 H9
Dering Way, Grav. DA12 131 GM88
Derinton Rd, SW17 120 DF91
Derley Rd, Sthl. UB2 96 BW76
Dermody Gdns, SE13 123 ED85
Dermody Rd, SE13 123 ED85
Deronda Rd, SE24 121 DP88
De Ros Pl, Egh. TW20 113 BA93
Deroy Cl, Cars. SM5 158 DF107
Derrick Av, S.Croy. CR2 160 DQ110
Derrick Gdns, SE7
off Anchor & Hope La 104 EJ77
Derrick Rd, Beck. BR3 143 DZ97
Derry Av, S.Ock. RM15 91 FU72
Derrydown, Wok. GU22 166 AW121
DERRY DOWNS, Orp. BR5 146 EX100
Derry Downs, Orp. BR5 146 EW100
Derry Rd, Croy. CR0 141 DL104
Derry St, W8 100 DB75
Dersingham Av, E12 69 EN64
Dersingham Rd, NW2 63 CY62
Derwent Av, N18 46 DR50
NW7 42 CR50
SW15 118 CS91
Barnet EN4 44 DF46
Pinner HA5 40 BY51
Uxbridge UB10 58 BN62
Derwent Cl, Add. KT15 152 BK106
Amersham HP7 20 AV39
Dartford DA1 127 FH88
Esher (Clay.) KT10 155 CE107
Feltham TW14 115 BT88
Watford WD25
off North Orbital Rd 8 BW34
Derwent Cres, N20 44 DC48
Bexleyheath DA7 106 FA82
Stanmore HA7 41 CJ54
Derwent Dr, NW9 62 CS57
Hayes UB4 77 BS71
Orpington BR5 145 ER101
Purley CR8 160 DR113
Derwent Gdns, Ilf. IG4 68 EL56
Wembley HA9 61 CJ59
Derwent Gro, SE22 102 DT84
Derwent Par, S.Ock. RM15 91 FV72
Derwent Ri, NW9 62 CS58
Derwent Rd, N13 45 DM49
SE20 142 DU96
SW20 139 CX100
W5 97 CJ76
Egham TW20 113 BB94
Southall UB1 78 CA72
Twickenham TW2 116 CB86
Derwent St, SE10 205 H10
Derwent Wk, Wall. SM6 159 DH108
Derwentwater Rd, W3 80 CQ74
Derwent Way, Horn. RM12 71 FH64
Derwent Yd, W5
off Northfield Av 97 CJ76
De Salis Rd, Uxb. UB10 77 BQ70
Desborough Cl, W2 82 DB71
Shepperton TW17 134 BN101
Desborough St, W2
off Cirencester St 82 DB71
Desenfans Rd, SE21 122 DS86
Desford Ct, Ashf. TW15
off Desford Way 114 BM89
Desford Ms, E16
off Desford Rd 86 EE70
Desford Rd, E16 86 EE70
Desford Way, Ashf. TW15 114 BM89
★ **Design Mus**, SE1 202 A3
Desmond Rd, Wat. WD24 23 BT36
Desmond St, SE14 103 DY79
Despard Rd, N19 65 DJ60
Detillens La, Oxt. RH8 188 EG129
Detling Cl, Horn. RM12 72 FJ64
Detling Rd, Brom. BR1 124 EG92
Erith DA8 107 FD80
Gravesend (Nthflt) DA11 130 GD88
Detmold Rd, E5 66 DW61
Devalls Cl, E6 87 EN73
Devana End, Cars. SM5 140 DF104
Devas Rd, SW20 139 CW95
Devas St, E3 85 EB70
Devenay Rd, E15 86 EF66
Devenish Rd, SE2 106 EU75
Deventer Cres, SE22 122 DS85
Deveraux Cl, Beck. BR3
off Creswell Dr 143 EB99
De Vere Cotts, W8
off Canning Pl 100 DC76
De Vere Gdns, W8 100 DC75
Ilford IG1 69 EM61
Deverell St, SE1 201 K7
De Vere Ms, W8
off Canning Pl 100 DC76
Devereux Ct, WC2 196 D9
Devereux Dr, Wat. WD17 23 BS38
Devereux La, SW13 99 CV80
Devereux Rd, SW11 120 DF86
Grays RM16 110 FZ76
De Vere Wk, Wat. WD17 23 BS40
Deverill Ct, SE20 142 DW95
Deverills Way, Slou. SL3 93 BC77
Deveron Gdns, S.Ock. RM15 91 FU71
Deveron Way, Rom. RM1 51 FE53
Devey Cl, Kings.T. KT2 118 CS94
Devils La, Egh. TW20 113 BD94
Devitt Cl, Ashtd. KT21 172 CN116
Devizes St, N1 *off Poole St* 84 DR67
Devoke Way, Walt. KT12 136 BX103
Devon Av, Twick. TW2 116 CC88
Devon Cl, N17 66 DT55
Buckhurst Hill IG9 48 EH47
Greenford UB6 79 CJ67
Kenley CR8 176 DT116
Devon Ct, Buck.H. IG9 48 EH46
Dartford (Sutt.H.) DA4 148 FP95
Devon Cres, Red. RH1 184 DD134

★ Place of interest ⇌ Railway station ⊖ London Underground station DLR Docklands Light Railway station Tra Tramlink station H Hospital Riv Pedestrian ferry landing stage

Devoncroft Gdns, Twick. TW1 . 117 CG87
Devon Gdns, N4 . 65 DP58
Devonhurst Pl, W4
off Heathfield Ter. . 98 CR78
Devonia Gdns, N18 . 46 DQ51
Devonia Rd, N1 . 83 DP68
Devonport Gdns, Ilf. IG1 . 69 EM58
Devonport Ms, W12
off Devonport Rd . 81 CV74
Devonport Rd, W12 . 99 CV75
Devonport St, E1 . 84 DW72
Devon Ri, N2 . 64 DD56
Devon Rd, Bark. IG11 . 87 ES67
Dartford (Sutt.H.) DA4 . 148 FP95
Redhill RH1 . 185 DJ130
Sutton SM2 . 157 CY109
Walton-on-Thames KT12 . 154 BW105
Watford WD24 . 24 BX39
Devons Est, E3 . 85 EB69
Devonshire Av, Dart. DA1 . 127 FH86
Sutton SM2 . 158 DC108
Tadworth (Box H.) KT20 . 182 CQ131
Woking GU21 . 151 BC114
Devonshire Cl, E15 . 68 EE63
N13 . 45 DN49
W1 . 195 H6
Devonshire Cres, NW7 . 43 CX52
Devonshire Dr, SE10 . 103 EB80
Surbiton KT6 . 137 CK102
Devonshire Gdns, N17 . 46 DQ51
N21 . 46 DQ45
W4 . 98 CQ80
Devonshire Gro, SE15 . 102 DV79
Devonshire Hill La, N17 . 46 DQ51
H Devonshire Hosp, W1 . 194 G6
Devonshire Ho, Sutt. SM2
off Devonshire Av . 158 DC108
Devonshire Ms, SW10
off Park Wk . 100 DD79
W4 off Glebe St . 98 CS78
Devonshire Ms N, W1 . 195 H6
Devonshire Ms S, W1 . 195 H6
Devonshire Ms W, W1 . 195 H5
Devonshire Pas, W4 . 98 CS78
Devonshire Pl, NW2 . 64 DA62
W1 . 194 G5
W8 off St. Mary's Pl . 100 DB76
Devonshire Pl Ms, W1 . 194 G5
Devonshire Rd, E16 . 86 EH72
E17 . 67 EA58
N9 . 46 DW46
N13 . 45 DM49
N17 . 46 DQ51
NW7 . 43 CX52
SE9 . 124 EL89
SE23 . 122 DW88
SW19 . 120 DE94
W4 . 98 CS78
W5 . 97 CJ76
Bexleyheath DA6 . 106 EY84
Carshalton SM5 . 158 DG105
Croydon CR0 . 142 DR101
Feltham TW13 . 116 BY90
Gravesend DA12 . 131 GH88
Grays RM16 . 110 FY77
Harrow HA1 . 61 CD58
Hornchurch RM12 . 72 FJ61
Ilford IG2 . 69 ER59
Orpington BR6 . 146 EU101
Pinner (Eastcote) HA5 . 60 BW58
Pinner (Hatch End) HA5 . 40 BZ53
Southall UB1 . 78 CA71
Sutton SM2 . 158 DC108
Weybridge KT13 . 152 BN105
Devonshire Row, EC2 . 197 N7
Devonshire Row Ms, W1 . 195 J5
Devonshire Sq, EC2 . 197 N8
Bromley BR2 . 144 EH98
Devonshire St, W1 . 194 G6
W4 . 98 CS78
Devonshire Ter, W2 . 82 DC72
Devonshire Way, Croy. CR0 . 143 DY103
Hayes UB4 . 77 BV72
DLR Devons Road . 85 EB70
Devons Rd, E3 . 85 EA71
Devon St, SE15 . 102 DV79
Devon Way, Chess. KT9 . 155 CJ106
Epsom KT19 . 156 CP106
Uxbridge UB10 . 76 BM68
Devon Waye, Houns. TW5 . 96 BZ80
De Walden St, W1 . 194 G7
Dewar Spur, Slou. SL3
off Ditton Rd . 93 AZ78
Dewar St, SE15 . 102 DU83
Dewberry Gdns, E6 . 86 EL71
Dewberry St, E14 . 85 EC71
Dewey Path, Horn. RM12 . 90 FJ65
Dewey Rd, N1 . 83 DN68
Dagenham RM10 . 89 FB65
Dewey St, SW17 . 120 DF92
Dewgrass Gro, Wal.Cr. EN8 . 31 DX35
Dewhurst Rd, W14 . 99 CX76
Waltham Cross (Chsht) EN8 . 14 DW29
Dewlands, Gdse. RH9 . 186 DW131
Dewlands Av, Dart. DA2 . 128 FP87
Dewlands Ct, NW4
off Holders Hill Rd . 43 CX54
Dewsbury Cl, Pnr. HA5 . 60 BZ58
Romford RM3 . 52 FL51
Dewsbury Ct, W4
off Chiswick Rd . 98 CQ77
Dewsbury Gdns, Rom. RM3 . 52 FK51
Worcester Park KT4 . 139 CU104
Dewsbury Rd, NW10 . 63 CU64
Romford RM3 . 52 FK51
Dewsbury Ter, NW1
off Camden High St . 83 DH67
Dexter Cl, Grays RM17 . 110 GA76
Dexter Ho, Erith DA18
off Kale Rd . 106 EY76
Dexter Rd, Barn. EN5 . 27 CX44
Uxbridge (Hare.) UB9 . 38 BJ54
Deyncourt Gdns,
Upmin. RM14 . 72 FQ61
Deyncourt Rd, N17 . 46 DQ53
Deynecourt Gdns, E11 . 68 EJ56
D'Eynsford Rd, SE5 . 102 DR81
Diadem Ct, W1 . 195 M9
Dial Cl, Green. DA9
off Knockhall Rd . 129 FX85
Dialmead, Pot.B. EN6
off Crossoaks La . 11 CT34
Dial Wk, The, W8 . 100 DB75
Diamedes Av, Stai.
(Stanw.) TW19 . 114 BK87
Diameter Rd, Orp. BR5 . 145 EP101
Diamond Cl, Dag. RM8 . 70 EW60
Grays RM16 . 110 FZ76
Diamond Rd, Ruis. HA4 . 60 BX63
Slough SL1 . 92 AU75
Watford WD24 . 23 BU38
Diamond St, NW10 . 80 CR66
SE15 . 102 DS80
Diamond Ter, SE10 . 103 EC81
Diamond Way, SE8
off Deptford High St . 103 EA80
Diana Cl, E18 . 48 EH53
SE8 off Staunton St . 103 DZ79
Grays (Chaff.Hun.) RM16 . 110 FZ76
Slough (Geo.Grn) SL3 . 74 AY72
Diana Gdns, Surb. KT6 . 138 CM103
Diana Ho, SW13 . 99 CT81
Diana Rd, E17 . 67 DZ55
Dianne Way, Barn. EN4 . 28 DE43
Dianthus Cl, SE2
off Carnation St . 106 EV78
Chertsey KT16 . 133 BE101
Dianthus Ct, Wok. GU22 . 166 AX118
Diban Av, Horn. RM12 . 71 FH63
Dibden Hill, Ch.St.G. HP8 . 36 AW49
Dibden La, Sev.
(Ide Hill) TN14 . 190 FE126
Dibden Row, SE1
off Gerridge St . 101 DN76
Dibden St, N1 . 83 DP67
Dibdin Cl, Sutt. SM1 . 140 DA104
Dibdin Rd, Sutt. SM1 . 140 DA104
Diceland Rd, Bans. SM7 . 173 CZ116
Dicey Av, NW2 . 63 CW64
Dickens Av, N3 . 44 DC53
Dartford DA1 . 108 FN84
Tilbury RM18 . 111 GH81
Uxbridge UB8 . 77 BP72
Dickens Cl, Erith DA8 . 107 FB80
Hayes UB3 off Croyde Av . 95 BS77
Richmond TW10 . 118 CL89
Waltham Cross EN7 . 14 DU26
Dickens Dr, Add. KT15 . 151 BF107
Chislehurst BR7 . 125 EQ93
Dickens Est, SE1 . 202 B5
SE16 . 202 B5
★ Dickens Ho, WC1 . 196 C5
Dickens La, N18 . 46 DS50
Dickenson Cl, N9
off Croyland Rd . 46 DU46
Dickenson Rd, N8 . 65 DL59
Feltham TW13 . 116 BW92
Dickensons La, SE25 . 142 DU99
Dickensons Pl, SE25 . 142 DU100
Dickenson St, NW5
off Dalby St . 83 DH65
Dickens Pl, Slou. SL3
off Bath Rd . 93 BE81
Dickens Ri, Chig. IG7 . 49 EN48
Dickens Rd, E6 . 86 EK68
Gravesend DA12 . 131 GL88
Dickens Sq, SE1 . 201 J6
Dickens St, SW8 . 101 DH82
Dickens Way, Rom. RM1 . 71 FE56
Dickenswood Cl, SE19 . 121 DP94
Dickerage La, N.Mal. KT3 . 138 CQ97
Dickerage Rd, Kings.T. KT1 . 138 CQ95
New Malden KT3 . 138 CQ95
Dickinson Av, Rick.
(Crox.Grn) WD3 . 22 BN44
Dickinson Ct, EC1
off St. John St . 83 DP70
Dickinson Sq, Rick.
(Crox.Grn) WD3 . 22 BN44
Dickson, Wal.Cr. (Chsht) EN7 . 14 DT27
Dickson Fold, Pnr. HA5 . 60 BX56
Dickson Rd, SE9 . 104 EL83
Dick Turpin Way, Felt. TW14 . 95 BT84
Didsbury Cl, E6
off Barking Rd . 87 EM67
Dieppe Cl, W14 off Gibbs Grn . 99 CZ78
Digby Cres, N4 . 66 DQ61
Digby Gdns, Dag. RM10 . 88 FA67
Digby Pl, Croy. CR0 . 142 DT104
Digby Rd, E9 . 85 DX65
Barking IG11 . 87 ET66
Digby St, E2 . 84 DW69
Digby Wk, Horn. RM12
off Pembrey Way . 90 FJ65
Digby Way, W.Byf. (Byfleet) KT14
off High Rd . 152 BM112
Dig Dag Hill, Wal.Cr.
(Chsht) EN7 . 14 DT27
Digdens Ri, Epsom KT18 . 172 CQ115
Diggon St, E1
off Stepney Way . 85 DX71
Dighton Ct, SE5 . 102 DQ79
Dighton Rd, SW18 . 120 DC85
Dignum St, N1
off Cloudesley Rd . 83 DN67
Digswell Cl, Borwd. WD6 . 26 CN38
Digswell St, N7
off Holloway Rd . 83 DN65
Dilhorne Cl, SE12 . 124 EH90
Dilke St, SW3 . 100 DF79
Dilloway Yd, Sthl. UB2
off The Green . 96 BY75
Dillwyn Cl, SE26 . 123 DY91
Dilston Cl, Nthlt. UB5
off Yeading La . 78 BW69
Dilston Gro, SE16 . 202 F8
Dilston Rd, Lthd. KT22 . 171 CG119
Dilton Gdns, SW15 . 119 CU88
Dilwyn Ct, E17
off Hillyfield . 67 DY55
Dimes Pl, W6 off King St . 99 CV77
Dimmock Dr, Grnf. UB6 . 61 CD64
Dimmocks La, Rick.
(Sarratt) WD3 . 22 BH36
Dimond Cl, E7 . 68 EG63
Dimsdale Dr, NW9 . 62 CQ60
Enfield EN1 . 30 DU44
Dimsdale Wk, E13
off Stratford Rd . 86 EG67
Dimson Cres, E3 . 85 EA70
Dingle, The, Uxb. UB10 . 77 BP68
Dingle Cl, Barn. EN5 . 27 CT44
Dingle Gdns, E14 . 204 A1
Dingle Rd, Ashf. TW15 . 115 BP92
Dingley La, SW16 . 121 DK89
Dingley Pl, EC1 . 197 J3
Dingley Rd, EC1 . 197 H3
Dingwall Av, Croy. CR0 . 142 DQ103
Dingwall Gdns, NW11 . 64 DA58
Dingwall Rd, SW18 . 120 DC87
Carshalton SM5 . 158 DF109
Croydon CR0 . 142 DR103
Dinmont St, E2 off Coate St . 84 DV68
Dinmore, Hem.H. (Bov.) HP3 . 5 AZ28
Dinsdale Cl, Wok. GU22 . 167 BA118
Dinsdale Gdns, SE25 . 142 DS99
Barnet EN5 . 28 DB43
Dinsdale Rd, SE3 . 104 EF79
Dinsmore Rd, SW12 . 121 DH87
Dinton Rd, SW19 . 120 DD93
Kingston upon Thames KT2 . 118 CM94
Diploma Av, N2 . 64 DE56
Diploma Ct, N2
off Diploma Av . 64 DE56
Dirdene Cl, Epsom KT17 . 157 CT112
Dirdene Gdns, Epsom KT17 . 157 CT112
Dirdene Gro, Epsom KT17 . 156 CS112
Dirleton Rd, E15 . 86 EF67
Disbrowe Rd, W6 . 99 CY79
Discovery Business Pk, SE16
off St. James's Rd . 102 DU76
Discovery Wk, E1 . 202 D1
Dishforth La, NW9 . 42 CS53
Disney Ms, N4
off Chesterfield Gdns . 65 DP57
Disney Pl, SE1 . 201 J4
Disney St, SE1 . 201 J4
Dison Cl, Enf. EN3 . 31 DX39
Disraeli Cl, SE28 . 88 EW74
W4 off Acton La . 98 CR77
Disraeli Ct, Slou. SL3
off Sutton Pl . 93 BB79
Disraeli Gdns, SW15
off Fawe Pk Rd . 99 CZ84
Disraeli Rd, E7 . 86 EG65
NW10 . 80 CQ68
SW15 . 99 CY84
W5 . 79 CK74
Diss St, E2 . 197 P2
Distaff La, EC4 . 197 H10
Distillery La, W6
off Fulham Palace Rd . 99 CW78
Distillery Rd, W6 . 99 CW78
Distillery Wk, Brent. TW8 . 98 CL79
Distin St, SE11 . 200 D9
District Rd, Wem. HA0 . 61 CH64
Ditch All, SE10 . 103 EB81
Ditchburn St, E14 . 204 E1
Ditches La, Cat. CR3 . 175 DM122
Coulsdon CR5 . 175 DL120
Ditches Ride, The, Loug. IG10 . 33 EN37
Ditchfield Rd, Hayes UB4 . 78 BY70
Dittisham Rd, SE9 . 124 EL91
Ditton Cl, T.Ditt. KT7 . 137 CG101
Dittoncroft Cl, Croy. CR0 . 160 DS105
Ditton Gra Cl, Surb. KT6 . 137 CK102
Ditton Gra Dr, Surb. KT6 . 137 CK102
Ditton Hill, Surb. KT6 . 137 CJ102
Ditton Hill Rd, Surb. KT6 . 137 CJ102
Ditton Lawn, T.Ditt. KT7 . 137 CG102
Ditton Pk, Slou. SL3 . 92 AX78
Ditton Pk Rd, Slou. SL3 . 92 AY79
Ditton Pl, SE20 . 142 DV95
Ditton Reach, T.Ditt. KT7 . 137 CH100
Ditton Rd, Bexh. DA6 . 126 EX85
Slough SL3 . 93 AZ79
Slough (Datchet) SL3 . 92 AX81
Southall UB2 . 96 BZ77
Surbiton KT6 . 138 CL102
Divis Way, SW15 . 119 CV86
Dixon Clark Ct, N1
off Canonbury Rd . 83 DP65
Dixon Cl, E6
off Brandreth Rd . 87 EM72
Dixon Dr, Wey. KT13 . 152 BM110
Dixon Ho, W10 . 81 CX72
Dixon Pl, W.Wick. BR4 . 143 EB102
Dixon Rd, SE14 . 103 DY81
SE25 . 142 DS97
Dixon's All, SE16 . 202 D5
Dixons Hill Cl, Hat.
(N.Mymms) AL9 . 11 CV25
Dixons Hill Rd, Hat.
(N.Mymms) AL9 . 11 CU25
Dobbin Cl, Har. HA3 . 41 CG54
Dobell Path, SE9
off Dobell Rd . 125 EM85
Dobell Rd, SE9 . 125 EM85
Dobree Av, NW10 . 81 CV66
Dobson Cl, NW6 . 82 DD66
Dobson Rd, Grav. DA12 . 131 GL92
Doby Ct, EC4 . 197 J10
Dockers Tanner Rd, E14 . 203 P7
Dockett Eddy La, Shep. TW17 . 134 BM102
Dockhead, SE1 . 202 A5
Dock Hill Av, SE16 . 203 J4
Dockland St, E16 . 87 EN74
Dockley Rd, SE16 . 202 B7
Dock Rd, E16 . 205 L1
Brentford TW8 . 97 CK80
Grays RM17 . 110 GD79
Tilbury RM18 . 111 GF82
Dockside Rd, E16 . 86 EK73
Dock St, E1 . 84 DU73
Dockwell Cl, Felt. TW14 . 95 BU84
Dockyard Ind Est, SE18
off Woolwich Ch St . 104 EL76
Doctor Johnson Av, SW17 . 121 DH90
★ Doctor Johnson's Ho, EC4 . 196 E9
Doctors Cl, SE26 . 122 DW92
Doctors La, Cat. CR3 . 175 DN123
Docwra's Bldgs, N1 . 84 DS65
Dodbrooke Rd, SE27 . 121 DN90
Doddinghurst Rd, Brwd. CM15 . 54 FW44
Doddington Gro, SE17 . 101 DP79
Doddington Pl, SE17 . 101 DP79
Dodd's Cres, W.Byf. KT14 . 152 BH114
Dodds La, Ch.St.G. HP8 . 36 AU47
Dodd's La, Wok. GU22 . 152 BG114
Dodsley Pl, N9 . 46 DV48
Dodson St, SE1 . 200 E5
Dod St, E14 . 85 DZ72
Doebury Wk, SE18
off Prestwood Cl . 106 EU79
Doel Cl, SW19 . 120 DC94
Doggets Ct, Barn. EN4 . 28 DE43
Doggett Rd, SE6 . 123 EA87
Doggetts Fm Rd, Uxb.
(Denh.) UB9 . 57 BC59
Doggetts Wd Cl, Ch.St.G. HP8 . 20 AV42
Doggetts Wd La, Ch.St.G. HP8 . 20 AV41
Doghurst Av, Hayes UB3 . 95 BP80
Doghurst Dr, West Dr. UB7 . 95 BP80
Doghurst La, Couls. CR5 . 174 DF120
Dog Kennel Hill, SE22 . 102 DS83
Dog Kennel Hill Est, SE22 . 102 DS83
Dog Kennel La, Rick.
(Chorl.) WD3 . 21 BF42
Dog La, NW10 . 62 CS63
Dogwood Cl, Grav.
(Nthflt) DA11 . 130 GE91
Doherty Rd, E13 . 86 EG70
Dokal Ind Est, Sthl. UB2
off Hartington Rd . 96 BY76
Dolben St, SE1 . 200 F3
Dolby Rd, SW6 . 99 CZ82
Dolland St, SE11 . 101 DM78
Dollis Av, N3 . 43 CZ53
Dollis Brook Wk, Barn. EN5 . 27 CY44
Dollis Cres, Ruis. HA4 . 60 BW60
DOLLIS HILL, NW2 . 63 CV62
⊖ Dollis Hill . 63 CU64
Dollis Hill Av, NW2 . 63 CV62
Dollis Hill La, NW2 . 63 CV62
Dollis Ms, N3 off Dollis Pk . 43 CZ53
Dollis Pk, N3 . 43 CZ53
Dollis Rd, N3 . 43 CY52
NW7 . 43 CY52
Dollis Valley Dr, Barn. EN5 . 27 CZ44
Dollis Valley Grn Wk, N20
off Totteridge La . 44 DC47
Barnet EN5 . 27 CY44
Dollis Valley Way, Barn. EN5 . 27 CZ44
Dolman Cl, N3
off Avondale Rd . 44 DC54
Dolman Rd, W4 . 98 CR77
Dolman St, SW4 . 101 DM84
Dolphin App, Rom. RM1 . 71 FF56
Dolphin Cl, SE16 . 203 H4
SE28 . 88 EX72
Surbiton KT6 . 137 CK100
Dolphin Ct, NW11 . 63 CY58
Slough SL1 off Dolphin Rd . 92 AV75
Staines TW18
off Bremer Rd . 114 BG90
Dolphin Ct N, Stai. TW18
off Bremer Rd . 114 BG90
Dolphin Est, Sun. TW16 . 135 BS95
Dolphin Ho, SW18
off Smugglers Way . 100 DB84
Dolphin La, E14 . 204 B1
Dolphin Rd, Nthlt. UB5 . 78 BZ68
Slough SL1 . 92 AV75
Sunbury-on-Thames TW16 . 135 BS95
Dolphin Rd N, Sun. TW16 . 135 BS95
Dolphin Rd S, Sun. TW16 . 135 BR95
Dolphin Rd W, Sun. TW16 . 135 BR95
Dolphin Sq, SW1 . 101 DJ78
W4 . 98 CS80
Dolphin St, Kings.T. KT1 . 138 CL95
Dolphin Twr, SE8
off Abinger Gro . 103 DZ79
Dolphin Way, Purf. RM19 . 109 FS78
Dombey St, WC1 . 196 B6
★ Dome, The, SE10 . 205 H3
Dome Hill, Cat. CR3 . 186 DS127
Dome Hill Pk, SE26 . 122 DT91
Dome Hill Peak, Cat. CR3 . 186 DS126
Domett Cl, SE5 . 102 DR84
Dome Way, Red. RH1 . 184 DF133
Domfe Pl, E5
off Rushmore Rd . 66 DW63
Domingo St, EC1 . 197 H4
Dominica Cl, E13 . 86 EJ68
Dominic Ct, Wal.Abb. EN9 . 15 EB33
Dominion Dr, Rom. RM5 . 51 FB51
Dominion Rd, Croy. CR0 . 142 DT101
Southall UB2 . 96 BY76
Dominion St, EC2 . 197 L6
★ Dominion Thea, W1 . 195 N8
Dominion Way, Rain. RM13 . 89 FG69
Domonic Dr, SE9 . 125 EP91
Domville Cl, N20 . 44 DD47
Donald Biggs Dr, Grav. DA12 . 131 GK87
Donald Dr, Rom. RM6 . 70 EW57
Donald Rd, E13 . 86 EH67
Croydon CR0 . 141 DM100
Donaldson Rd, NW6 . 81 CZ67
SE18 . 105 EN81
Donald Wds Gdns, Surb. KT5 . 138 CP103
Doncaster Dr, Nthlt. UB5 . 60 BZ64
Doncaster Gdns, N4
off Stanhope Gdns . 66 DQ58
Northolt UB5 . 60 BZ64
Doncaster Grn, Wat. WD19 . 40 BW50
Doncaster Rd, N9 . 46 DV45
Doncaster Way, Upmin. RM14 . 72 FM62
Doncel Ct, E4 . 47 ED45
Doncella Cl, Grays RM16
off Edmund Rd . 109 FX75
Donegal St, N1 . 196 C1
Doneraile St, SW6 . 99 CX82
Dongola Rd, E1 . 85 DY71
E13 . 86 EH69
N17 . 66 DS55
Dongola Rd W, E13
off Balaam St . 86 EH69
Donington Av, Ilf. IG6 . 69 EQ57
Donkey All, SE22 . 122 DU87
Donkey La, Dart.
(Fnghm) DA4 . 148 FP103
Enfield EN1 . 30 DU40
West Drayton UB7 . 94 BJ77
Donnay Cl, Ger.Cr. SL9 . 56 AX58
Donne Ct, SE24 . 122 DQ86
Donnefield Av, Edg. HA8 . 42 CL52
Donne Gdns, Wok. GU22 . 167 BE115
Donne Pl, SW3 . 198 C8
Mitcham CR4 . 141 DH98
Donne Rd, Dag. RM8 . 70 EW61
Donnington Rd, NW10 . 81 CV66
Harrow HA3 . 61 CK57
Sevenoaks (Dunt.Grn) TN13 . 181 FD120
Worcester Park KT4 . 139 CU103
Donnybrook Rd, SW16 . 121 DJ94
Donovan Av, N10 . 45 DH54
Donovan Cl, Epsom KT19
off Nimbus Rd . 156 CR110
Don Phelan Cl, SE5 . 102 DR81
Don Way, Rom. RM1 . 51 FE52
Doods Pk Rd, Reig. RH2 . 184 DC133
Doods Rd, Reig. RH2 . 184 DC133
Doods Way, Reig. RH2 . 184 DD133
Doone Cl, Tedd. TW11 . 117 CG93
Doon St, SE1 . 200 D3
Dorado Gdns, Orp. BR6 . 146 EX104
Doral Way, Cars. SM5 . 158 DF106
Dorando Cl, W12 . 81 CV73
Doran Dr, Red. RH1 . 184 DD134
Doran Gdns, Red. RH1 . 184 DD134
Doran Gro, SE18 . 105 ES80
Doran Wk, E15 . 85 EC66
Dora Rd, SW19 . 120 DA92
Dora St, E14 . 85 DZ72
Dorchester Av, N13 . 46 DQ49
Bexley DA5 . 126 EX88
Harrow HA2 . 60 CC58
Dorchester Cl, Dart. DA1 . 128 FM87
Northolt UB5 . 60 CB64
Orpington BR5
off Grovelands Rd . 126 EU94
Dorchester Ct, N14 . 45 DH45
SE24 . 122 DQ85
Rickmansworth (Crox.Grn) WD3
off Mayfare . 23 BR43
Woking GU22 . 167 BA116
Dorchester Dr, SE24 . 122 DQ85
Feltham TW14 . 115 BS86
Dorchester Gdns, E4 . 47 EA49
NW11 . 64 DA56
Dorchester Gro, W4 . 98 CS78
Dorchester Ms, N.Mal. KT3
off Elm Rd . 138 CR98
Twickenham TW1 . 117 CJ87
Dorchester Rd, Grav. DA12 . 131 GK90
Morden SM4 . 140 DB101
Northolt UB5 . 60 CB64
Weybridge KT13 . 135 BP104
Worcester Park KT4 . 139 CW102
Dorchester Way, Har. HA3 . 62 CM58
Dorchester Waye, Hayes UB4 . 78 BW72
Dorcis Av, Bexh. DA7 . 106 EY82
Dordrecht Rd, W3 . 80 CS74
Dore Av, E12 . 69 EN64
Doreen Av, NW9 . 62 CR60
Dore Gdns, Mord. SM4 . 140 DB101
Dorell Cl, Sthl. UB1 . 78 BZ71
Doria Dr, Grav. DA12 . 131 GL90
Dorian Rd, Horn. RM12 . 71 FG60
Doria Rd, SW6 . 99 CZ82
Doric Dr, Tad. KT20 . 173 CZ120
Doric Way, NW1 . 195 M2
Dorien Rd, SW20 . 139 CX96
Dorin Ct, Warl. CR6 . 176 DV119
Dorincourt, Wok. GU22 . 167 BE115
Doris Av, Erith DA8 . 107 FC81
Doris Rd, E7 . 86 EG66
Ashford TW15 . 115 BR93
Dorking Cl, SE8 . 103 DZ79
Worcester Park KT4 . 139 CX103
Dorking Gdns, Rom. RM3 . 52 FK50
Dorking Glen, Rom. RM3 . 52 FK49
Dorking Ri, Rom. RM3 . 52 FK49
Dorking Rd, Epsom KT18 . 172 CN116
Leatherhead KT22 . 171 CH122
Romford RM3 . 52 FK49
Tadworth KT20 . 173 CX123
Dorking Wk, Rom. RM3 . 52 FK49
Dorkins Way, Upmin. RM14 . 73 FS59
Dorlcote Rd, SW18 . 120 DD87
Dorling Dr, Epsom KT17 . 157 CT112
Dorly Cl, Shep. TW17 . 135 BS99
Dorman Pl, N9 off Balham Rd . 46 DU47
Dormans Cl, Nthwd. HA6 . 39 BR52
Dorman Wk, NW10
off Garden Way . 62 CR64
Dorman Way, NW8 . 82 DD67
Dorma Trd Pk, E10 . 67 DX60
Dormay St, SW18 . 120 DB85
Dormer Cl, E15 . 86 EF65
Barnet EN5 . 27 CX43
Dormers Av, Sthl. UB1 . 78 CA72
Dormers Ri, Sthl. UB1 . 78 CB72
DORMER'S WELLS, Sthl. UB1 . 78 CB73
Dormers Wells La, Sthl. UB1 . 78 CA72
Dormywood, Ruis. HA4 . 59 BT57
Dornberg Cl, SE3 . 104 EG80
Dornberg Rd, SE3
off Banchory Rd . 104 EH80
Dorncliffe Rd, SW6 . 99 CY82
Dornels, Slou. SL2 . 74 AW72
Dorney, NW3 . 82 DE66
Dorney Gro, Wey. KT13 . 135 BP103
Dorney Ri, Orp. BR5 . 145 ET98
Dorney Way, Houns. TW4 . 116 BY85
Dornfell St, NW6 . 63 CZ64
Dornford Gdns, Couls. CR5 . 176 DQ119
Dornton Rd, SW12 . 121 DH89
South Croydon CR2 . 160 DR106
Dorothy Av, Wem. HA0 . 80 CL66
Dorothy Evans Cl, Bexh. DA7 . 107 FB84
Dorothy Gdns, Dag. RM8 . 70 EV63
Dorothy Rd, SW11 . 100 DF83
Dorrell Pl, SW9
off Brixton Rd . 101 DN84
Dorrien Wk, SW16 . 121 DK89
Dorrington Ct, SE25 . 142 DS96
Dorrington Gdns, Horn. RM12 . 72 FK60
Dorrington Pt, E3
off Bromley High St . 85 EB69
Dorrington St, EC1 . 196 D6
Dorrington Way, Beck. BR3
off Creswell Dr . 143 EB99
Dorrit Ms, N18 . 46 DS49
Dorrit St, SE1 . 201 J4

★ Place of interest · ⇌ Railway station · ⊖ London Underground station · DLR Docklands Light Railway station · Tra Tramlink station · H Hospital · Riv Pedestrian ferry landing stage

Dorrit Way, Chis. BR7 125 EQ93
Dorrofield Cl, Rick. (Crox.Grn) WD3 23 BQ43
Dors Cl, NW9 62 CR60
Dorset Av, Hayes UB4 77 BS69
Romford RM1 71 FD55
Southall UB2 96 CA77
Welling DA16 105 ET84
Dorset Bldgs, EC4 196 F9
Dorset Cl, NW1 194 D6
Hayes UB4 77 BS69
Dorset Cres, Grav. DA12 131 GL91
Dorset Dr, Edg. HA8 42 CM51
Woking GU22 167 BB117
Dorset Est, E2 84 DT69
Dorset Gdns, Mitch. CR4 141 DM98
Dorset Ho, Enf. EN3 31 DX37
Dorset Ms, N3 44 DA53
SW1 199 H6
Dorset Pl, E15 85 ED65
Dorset Ri, EC4 196 F9
Dorset Rd, E7 86 EJ66
N15 66 DR56
N22 45 DL53
SE9 124 EL89
SW8 101 DM80
SW19 140 DA95
W5 97 CJ76
Ashford TW15 114 BK90
Beckenham BR3 143 DX97
Harrow HA1 60 CC58
Mitcham CR4 140 DE96
Sutton SM2 158 DA110
Dorset Sq, NW1 194 D5
Epsom KT19 156 CR110
Dorset St, W1 194 E7
Sevenoaks TN13
off High St 191 FH125
Dorset Way, Twick. TW2 117 CD88
Uxbridge UB10 76 BM68
West Byfleet (Byfleet) KT14 152 BK110
Dorset Waye, Houns. TW5 96 BZ80
Dorton Cl, SE15
off Chandler Way 102 DT80
Dorton Dr, Sev. TN15 191 FM122
Dorton Way, Wok. (Ripley) GU23 168 BH121
Dorville Cres, W6 99 CV76
Dorville Rd, SE12 124 EF85
Dothill Rd, SE18 105 ER80
Douai Gro, Hmptn. TW12 136 CC95
Doubleday Rd, Loug. IG10 33 EQ41
Doughty Ms, WC1 196 B5
Doughty St, WC1 196 B4
Douglas Av, E17 47 EA53
New Malden KT3 139 CV98
Romford RM3 52 FL54
Watford WD24 24 BX37
Wembley HA0 80 CL66
Douglas Cl, Grays (Chaff.Hun.) RM16 110 FY76
Stanmore HA7 41 CG50
Wallington SM6 159 DL108
Douglas Ct, Cat. CR3 176 DQ122
Westerham TN16 178 EL117
Douglas Cres, Hayes UB4 78 BW70
Douglas Dr, Croy. CR0 143 EA104
Douglas La, Stai. (Wrays.) TW19 113 AZ85
Douglas Ms, NW2 63 CY62
Banstead SM7
off North Acre 173 CZ116
Douglas Path, E14 204 E10
Douglas Rd, E4 48 EE45
E16 86 EG71
N1 84 DQ66
N22 45 DN53
NW6 81 CZ67
Addlestone KT15 134 BH104
Esher KT10 136 CB103
Hornchurch RM11 71 FF58
Hounslow TW3 96 CB83
Ilford IG3 70 EU58
Kingston upon Thames KT1 138 CP96
Reigate RH2 184 DA133
Staines (Stanw.) TW19 114 BK86
Surbiton KT6 138 CM103
Welling DA16 106 EV81
Douglas Sq, Mord. SM4 140 DA100
Douglas St, SW1 199 M9
Douglas Ter, E17
off Douglas Av 47 EA53
Douglas Way, SE8 103 DZ80
Doug Siddons Ct, Grays RM17
off Elm Rd 110 GC79
Doulton Ms, NW6
off Lymington Rd 82 DB65
Doultons, The, Stai. TW18 114 BG94
Dounesforth Gdns, SW18 120 DB88
Dounsell Ct, Brwd. (Pilg.Hat.) CM15
off Ongar Rd 54 FU44
Douro Pl, W8 100 DB76
Douro St, E3 85 EA68
Douthwaite Sq, E1 202 C2
Dove App, E6 86 EL71
Dove Cl, NW7 off Bunns La 43 CT52
Northolt UB5
off Wayfarer Rd 78 BX70
South Croydon CR2 161 DX111
Wallington SM6 159 DM108
Dovecot Cl, Pnr. HA5 59 BV57
Dovecote Av, N22 65 DN55
Dovecote Cl, Wey. KT13 135 BP104
Dovecote Gdns, SW14
off Avondale Rd 98 CR83
Dove Ct, EC2 197 K9
Dovedale Av, Har. HA3 61 CJ58
Ilford IG5 49 EN54
Dovedale Cl, Uxb. (Hare.) UB9 38 BJ54
Welling DA16 106 EU82
Dovedale Ri, Mitch. CR4 120 DF94
Dovedale Rd, SE22 122 DV85
Dartford DA2 128 FQ88
Dovedon Cl, N14 45 DL47
Dove Ho Gdns, E4 47 EA47
Dovehouse Grn, Wey. KT13
off Rosslyn Pk 153 BR105
Dovehouse Mead, Bark. IG11 87 ER68
Dovehouse St, SW3 198 B10
Dove La, Pot.B. EN6 12 DB34
Dove Ms, SW5 100 DC77
Doveney Cl, Orp. BR5 146 EW97
Dove Pk, Pnr. HA5 40 CA52
Rickmansworth (Chorl.) WD3 21 BB44
Dover Cl, NW2 off Brent Ter 63 CX61
Romford RM5 51 FC54
Dovercourt Av, Th.Hth. CR7 141 DN98
Dovercourt Est, N1 84 DR65
Dovercourt Gdns, Stan. HA7 42 CL50
Dovercourt La, Sutt. SM1 140 DC104
Dovercourt Rd, SE22 122 DS86
Doverfield, Wal.Cr. EN7 14 DQ29
Doverfield Rd, SW2 121 DL86
Dover Flats, SE1
off Old Kent Rd 102 DS77
Dover Gdns, Cars. SM5 140 DF104
Dover Ho Rd, SW15 99 CU84
Doveridge Gdns, N13 45 DP49
Dove Rd, N1 84 DR65
Dove Row, E2 84 DU67
Dover Pk Dr, SW15 119 CV86
Dover Patrol, SE3
off Kidbrooke Way 104 EH82
Dover Rd, E12 68 EJ61
N9 46 DW47
SE19 122 DR93
Gravesend (Nthflt) DA11 130 GD87
Romford RM6 70 EY58
Dover Rd E, Grav. DA11 130 GE87
Doversmead, Wok. (Knap.) GU21 166 AS116
Dover St, W1 199 J1
Dover Way, Rick. (Crox.Grn) WD3 23 BQ42
Dover Yd, W1 199 K2
Doves Cl, Brom. BR2 144 EL103
Doves Yd, N1 83 DN67
Doveton Rd, S.Croy. CR2 160 DR106
Doveton St, E1
off Malcolm Rd 84 DW70
Dove Wk, SW1 198 F10
Hornchurch RM12
off Heron Flight Av 89 FH65
Dowanhill Rd, SE6 123 ED88
Dowdeswell Cl, SW15 98 CS84
Dowding Pl, Stan. HA7 41 CG51
Dowding Rd, Uxb. UB10 76 BM66
Westerham (Bigg.H.) TN16 178 EK115
Dowding Wk, Grav. (Nthflt) DA11 130 GE90
Dowding Way, Horn. RM12 89 FH66
Watford WD25
off Ashfields 7 BT34
Dowdney Cl, NW5 65 DJ64
Dower Av, Wall. SM6 159 DH109
Dowgate Hill, EC4 197 K10
Dowland St, W10 81 CY68
Dowlas Est, SE5
off Dowlas St 102 DS80
Dowlas St, SE5 102 DS80
Dowlerville Rd, Orp. BR6 163 ET107
Dowman Cl, SW19
off Nelson Gro Rd 140 DB95
Downage, NW4 63 CW55
Downage, The, Grav. DA11 131 GG89
Downalong, Bushey (Bushey Hth) WD23 41 CD46
Downbank Av, Bexh. DA7 107 FD81
Downbarns Rd, Ruis. HA4 60 BX62
Downbury Ms, SW18
off Merton Rd 120 DA86
Down Cl, Nthlt. UB5 77 BV68
Downderry Rd, Brom. BR1 123 ED90
DOWNE, Orp. BR6 163 EM111
Downe Av, Sev. (Cudham) TN14 163 EQ112
Downe Cl, Well. DA16 106 EW80
Downend, SE18
off Moordown 105 EP80
Downer Dr, Rick. (Sarratt) WD3 22 BG36
Downe Rd, Kes. BR2 162 EK109
Mitcham CR4 140 DF96
Sevenoaks (Cudham) TN14 163 EQ114
Downers Cotts, SW4
off The Pavement 101 DJ84
Downes Cl, Twick. TW1
off St. Margarets Rd 117 CH86
Downes Ct, N21 45 DN46
Downfield, Wor.Pk. KT4 139 CT102
Downfield Cl, W9 82 DB70
Downfield Rd, Wal.Cr. (Chsht) EN8 15 DY31
Down Hall Rd, Kings.T. KT2 137 CK95
DOWNHAM, Brom. BR1 124 EF92
Downham Cl, Rom. RM5 50 FA52
Downham La, Brom. BR1
off Downham Way 123 ED92
Downham Rd, N1 84 DR66
Downham Way, Brom. BR1 123 ED92
Downhills Av, N17 66 DR55
Downhills Pk Rd, N17 66 DQ55
Downhills Way, N17 66 DQ55
★ Down Ho - Darwin Mus, Orp. BR6 163 EN112
Downhurst Av, NW7 42 CR50
Downing Cl, Har. HA2 60 CC55
Downing Dr, Grnf. UB6 79 CD67
Downing Rd, Dag. RM9 88 EZ67
Downings, E6 87 EM72
Downing St, SW1 199 P4
Downings Wd, Rick. (Map.Cr.) WD3 37 BD50
Downland Cl, N20 44 DC46
Coulsdon CR5 159 DH114
Epsom KT18 173 CV118
Downland Gdns, Epsom KT18 173 CV118
Downlands, Wal.Abb. EN9 16 EE34
Downlands Rd, Pur. CR8 159 DL113
Downland Way, Epsom KT18 173 CV118
Downleys Cl, SE9 124 EL89
Downman Rd, SE9 104 EL83
Down Pl, W6 99 CV77
Down Rd, Tedd. TW11 117 CH93
Downs, The, SW20 119 CX94
Downs Av, Chis. BR7 125 EM92
Dartford DA1 128 FN87
Epsom KT18 156 CS114
Pinner HA5 60 BZ58
Downs Br Rd, Beck. BR3 143 ED95
Downsbury Ms, SW18
off Merton Rd 120 DA85
Downs Ct, Sutt. SM2 158 DB111
Downs Ct Rd, Pur. CR8 159 DP112
Downsell Rd, E15 67 EC63
Downsfield Rd, E17 67 DY58
Downshall Av, Ilf. IG3 69 ES58
Downs Hill, Beck. BR3 123 ED94
Gravesend (Sthflt) DA13 130 GC94
Downs Hill Rd, Epsom KT18 156 CS114
Downshire Hill, NW3 64 DD63
Downs Ho Rd, Epsom KT18 173 CT118
DOWNSIDE, Cob. KT11 169 BV118
Downside, Cher. KT16 133 BF102
Epsom KT18 156 CS114
Sunbury-on-Thames TW16 135 BU95
Twickenham TW1 117 CF90
Downside Br Rd, Cob. KT11 169 BV115
Downside Cl, SW19 120 DC93
Downside Common, Cob. (Down.) KT11 169 BV118
Downside Common Rd, Cob. (Down.) KT11 169 BV118
Downside Cres, NW3 64 DE64
W13 79 CG70
Downside Orchard, Wok. GU22
off Park Rd 167 BA117
Downside Rd, Cob. (Down.) KT11 169 BV116
Sutton SM2 158 DD107
Downside Wk, Nthlt. UB5 78 BZ69
Downsland Dr, Brwd. CM14 54 FW48
Downs La, E5 off Downs Rd 66 DV63
Leatherhead KT22 171 CH123
Downs Pk Rd, E5 66 DU64
E8 66 DT64
Downs Rd, E5 66 DU63
Beckenham BR3 143 EB96
Coulsdon CR5 175 DK118
Enfield EN1 30 DS42
Epsom KT18 172 CS115
Gravesend (Istead Rise) DA13 130 GD91
Purley CR8 159 DP111
Slough SL3 92 AX75
Sutton SM2 158 DB110
Thornton Heath CR7 142 DQ95
Downs Side, Sutt. SM2 157 CZ111
Down St, W1 199 H3
West Molesey KT8 136 CA99
Down St Ms, W1 199 H3
Downs Vw, Islw. TW7 97 CF80
Tadworth KT20 173 CV121
Downsview Av, Wok. GU22 167 AZ121
Downsview Cl, Orp. BR6 164 EW110
Swanley BR8 147 FF97
Downsview Gdns, SE19 121 DP94
Downsview Rd, SE19 122 DQ94
Sevenoaks TN13 190 FF125
Downs Way, Epsom KT18 173 CT116
Downsway, Orp. BR6 163 ES106
Downs Way, Oxt. RH8 188 EE127
Downsway, S.Croy. CR2 160 DS111
Downs Way, Tad. KT20 173 CV121
Downsway, Whyt. CR3 176 DT116
Downsway, The, Sutt. SM2 158 DC109
Downs Way Cl, Tad. KT20 173 CU121
Downs Wd, Epsom KT18 173 CV117
Downswood, Reig. RH2 184 DE131
Downton Av, SW2 121 DL89
Downtown Rd, SE16 203 L4
Downview Cl, Cob. (Down.) KT11 169 BV119
Down Way, Nthlt. UB5 77 BV69
Dowrey St, N1
off Richmond Av 83 DN67
Dowry Wk, Wat. WD17 23 BT38
Dowsett Rd, N17 46 DT54
Dowson Cl, SE5 102 DR84
Doyce St, SE1 201 H4
Doyle Cl, Erith DA8 107 FE81
Doyle Gdns, NW10 81 CU67
Doyle Rd, SE25 142 DU98
Doyle Way, Til. RM18
off Coleridge Rd 111 GJ82
D'Oyley St, SW1 198 F8
D'Oyly Carte Island, Wey. KT13 135 BP102
Doynton St, N19 65 DH61
Draco St, SE17 102 DQ79
Dragonfly Cl, E13
off Hollybush St 86 EH69
Dragon La, Wey. KT13 152 BN110
Dragon Rd, SE15 102 DS79
Dragoon Rd, SE8 103 DZ78
Dragor Rd, NW10 80 CQ70
Drake Av, Cat. CR3 176 DQ122
Slough SL3 92 AX77
Staines TW18 113 BF92
Drake Cl, SE16 203 J4
Brentwood CM14 54 FX50
Drake Ct, SE19 122 DT92
W12 99 CW75
Harrow HA2 60 BZ60
Drake Cres, SE28 88 EW72
Drakefell Rd, SE4 103 DX82
SE14 103 DX82
Drakefield Rd, SW17 120 DG90
Drakeley Ct, N5
off Highbury Hill 65 DP63
Drake Ms, Horn. RM12
off Fulmar Rd 89 FG66
Drake Rd, SE4 103 EA83
Chessington KT9 156 CN106
Croydon CR0 141 DM101
Grays (Chaff.Hun.) RM16 110 FY75
Harrow HA2 60 BZ61
Mitcham CR4 140 DG100
Drakes Cl, Esher KT10 154 CA106
Waltham Cross (Chsht) EN8 15 DX28
Drakes Ctyd, NW6 81 CZ66
Drakes Dr, Nthwd. HA6 39 BP53
Drakes Rd, Amer. HP7 20 AS39
Drake St, WC1 196 B7
Enfield EN2 30 DR39
Drakes Wk, E6 87 EM67
Drakes Way, Wok. GU22 166 AX122
Drakewood Rd, SW16 121 DK94
Draper Cl, Belv. DA17 106 EZ77
Draper Cl, Isleworth TW7 97 CD82
Draper Ct, Horn. RM12
off Mavis Gro 72 FL61
Draper Pl, N1
off Dagmar Ter 83 DP67
Drapers Gdns, EC2
off Copthall Av 84 DR72
Drapers Rd, E15 67 ED63
N17 66 DT55
Enfield EN2 29 DP40
Drappers Way, SE16 202 C8
Draven Cl, Brom. BR2 144 EF101
Drawdock Rd, SE10 204 G3
Drawell Cl, SE18 105 ES78
Drax Av, SW20 119 CV94
Draxmont, SW19 119 CY93
Draycot Rd, E11 68 EH58
Surbiton KT6 138 CN102
Draycott Av, SW3 198 C8
Harrow HA3 61 CH58
Draycott Cl, NW2 63 CX62
Harrow HA3 61 CH58
Draycott Ms, SW6
off New Kings Rd 99 CZ82
Draycott Pl, SW3 198 D9
Draycott Ter, SW3 198 E8
Drayford Cl, W9 81 CZ70
Dray Gdns, SW2 121 DM85
Draymans Way, Islw. TW7 97 CF83
Drayside Ms, Sthl. UB2
off Kingston Rd 96 BZ75
Drayson Cl, Wal.Abb. EN9 16 EE32
Drayson Ms, W8 100 DA75
Drayton Av, W13 79 CG73
Loughton IG10 33 EM44
Orpington BR6 145 EP102
Potters Bar EN6 11 CY32
Drayton Br Rd, W7 79 CF73
W13 79 CF73
Drayton Cl, Houns. TW4
off Bramley Way 116 BZ85
Ilford IG1 69 ER60
Leatherhead (Fetch.) KT22 171 CE124
Drayton Ford, Rick. WD3 38 BG48
Drayton Gdns, N21 45 DP45
SW10 100 DC78
W13 79 CG73
West Drayton UB7 94 BL75
⇌ Drayton Green 79 CF72
Drayton Grn, W13 79 CG73
Drayton Grn Rd, W13 79 CH73
Drayton Gro, W13 79 CG73
⇌ Drayton Park 65 DN63
Drayton Pk, N5 65 DN64
Drayton Pk Ms, N5
off Drayton Pk 65 DN64
Drayton Rd, E11 67 ED60
N17 46 DS54
NW10 81 CT67
W13 79 CG73
Borehamwood WD6 26 CN42
Croydon CR0 141 DP103
Drayton Waye, Har. HA3 61 CH58
Drenon Sq, Hayes UB3 77 BT73
Dresden Cl, NW6 82 DB65
Dresden Rd, N19 65 DK60
Dresden Way, Wey. KT13 153 BQ106
Dressington Av, SE4 123 EA86
Drew Av, NW7 43 CY51
Drew Gdns, Grnf. UB6 79 CF65
Drew Pl, Cat. CR3 176 DR123
Drew Rd, E16 86 EL74
Drewstead Rd, SW16 121 DK89
Drey, The, Ger.Cr. (Chal.St.P.) SL9 36 AY50
Driffield Rd, E3 85 DY68
Drift, The, Brom. BR2 144 EK104
Drift La, Cob. KT11 170 BZ117
Drift Rd, Lthd. KT24 169 BT124
Drift Way, Rich. TW10 118 CM88
Slough (Colnbr.) SL3 93 BC81
Driftway, The, Bans. SM7 173 CW115
Leatherhead KT22
off Downs La 171 CH123
Mitcham CR4 140 DG95
Driftwood Av, St.Alb. AL2 8 CA26
Driftwood Dr, Ken. CR8 175 DP117
Drill Hall Rd, Cher. KT16 134 BG101
Drinkwater Rd, Har. HA2 60 CB61
Drive, The, E4 47 ED45
E17 67 EB56
E18 68 EG56
N3 44 DA52
N6 64 DF57
N11 45 DJ51
NW10 off Longstone Av 81 CT67
NW11 63 CY59
SW6 off Fulham Rd 99 CY82
SW16 141 DM97
SW20 119 CW94
W3 80 CQ72
Ashford TW15 115 BR94
Banstead SM7 173 CY117
Barking IG11 87 ET66
Barnet (High Barn.) EN5 27 CY41
Barnet (New Barn.) EN5 28 DC44
Beckenham BR3 143 EA96
Bexley DA5 126 EW86
Brentwood CM13 54 FW50
Buckhurst Hill IG9 48 EJ45
Chislehurst BR7 145 ET97
Chislehurst (Scad.Pk) BR7 145 ES95
Cobham KT11 154 BY114
Coulsdon CR5 159 DL114
Edgware HA8 42 CN50
Enfield EN2 30 DR39
Epsom KT19 157 CT107
Epsom (Headley) KT18 172 CN124
Erith DA8 107 FB80
Esher KT10 136 CC102
Feltham TW14 116 BW87
Gerrards Cross (Chal.St.P.) SL9 36 AY52
Gravesend DA12 131 GK91
Harrow HA2 60 CA59
Hatfield (Brook.Pk) AL9 12 DA25
Hounslow TW3 97 CD82
Ilford IG1 69 EM60
Isleworth TW7 97 CD82
Kingston upon Thames KT2 118 CQ94
Drive, The, Leatherhead (Fetch.) KT22 171 CE122
Leatherhead (Tyr.Wd) KT22 172 CN124
Loughton IG10 32 EL41
Morden SM4 140 DD99
Northwood HA6 39 BS54
Orpington BR6 145 ET103
Potters Bar EN6 11 CZ33
Radlett WD7 9 CG34
Rickmansworth WD3 22 BJ44
Romford (Coll.Row) RM5 51 FC53
Romford (Harold Wd) RM3 52 FL53
St. Albans (Lon.Col.) AL2 9 CG26
Sevenoaks TN13 191 FH124
Sidcup DA14 126 EV90
Slough SL3 92 AY75
Slough (Datchet) SL3 92 AV81
Staines (Wrays.) TW19 112 AX85
Surbiton KT6 138 CL101
Sutton SM2 157 CZ112
Thornton Heath CR7 142 DR98
Uxbridge UB10 58 BL63
Virginia Water GU25 133 AZ99
Wallington SM6 159 DJ110
Waltham Cross (Chsht) EN7 13 DP28
Watford WD17 23 BR37
Wembley HA9 62 CQ61
West Wickham BR4 143 ED101
Woking GU22 166 AV120
Drive Mead, Couls. CR5 159 DL114
Drive Rd, Couls. CR5 175 DM119
Drive Spur, Tad. KT20 174 DB121
Driveway, The, E17
off Hoe St 67 EB58
Potters Bar (Cuffley) EN6 13 DL28
Droitwich Cl, SE26 122 DU90
Dromey Gdns, Har. HA3 41 CF52
Dromore Rd, SW15 119 CY86
Dronfield Gdns, Dag. RM8 70 EW64
Droop St, W10 81 CY70
Drop La, St.Alb. (Brick.Wd) AL2 8 CB30
Drovers Mead, Brwd. CM14
off Warley Hill 54 FV49
Drovers Pl, SE15 102 DV80
Drovers Rd, S.Croy. CR2 160 DR106
Droveway, Loug. IG10 33 EP40
Drove Way, The, Grav. (Istead Rise) DA13 130 GE94
Druce Rd, SE21 122 DS86
Drudgeon Way, Dart. (Bean) DA2 129 FV90
Druids Cl, Ashtd. KT21 172 CM120
Druid St, SE1 201 N4
Druids Way, Brom. BR2 143 ED98
Drumaline Ridge, Wor.Pk. KT4 138 CS103
Drummond Av, Rom. RM7 71 FD56
Drummond Cen, Croy. CR0 142 DQ103
Drummond Cl, Erith DA8 107 FE81
Drummond Cres, NW1 195 M2
Drummond Dr, Stan. HA7 41 CF52
Drummond Gdns, Epsom KT19 156 CP111
Drummond Gate, SW1 199 N10
Drummond Pl, Twick. TW1 117 CH86
Drummond Rd, E11 68 EH58
SE16 202 D6
Croydon CR0 142 DQ103
Romford RM7 71 FD56
Drummonds, The, Buck.H. IG9 48 EH47
Epping CM16 18 EU30
Drummonds Pl, Rich. TW9 98 CL84
Drummond St, NW1 195 K4
Drum St, E1
off Whitechapel High St 84 DT72
Drury Cres, Croy. CR0 141 DN103
Drury La, WC2 196 A9
Drury Rd, Har. HA1 60 CC59
Drury Way, NW10 62 CR64
Drury Way Ind Est, NW10 62 CQ64
Dryad St, SW15 99 CX83
Dryburgh Gdns, NW9 62 CN55
Dryburgh Rd, SW15 99 CV83
Dryden Av, W7 79 CF72
Dryden Cl, Ilf. IG6 49 ET51
Dryden Ct, SE11 200 E9
Dryden Pl, Til. RM18
off Fielding Av 111 GH81
Dryden Rd, SW19 120 DC93
Enfield EN1 30 DS44
Harrow HA3 41 CF53
Welling DA16 105 ES81
Dryden St, WC2 196 A9
Dryden Twrs, Rom. RM3 51 FH52
Dryden Way, Orp. BR6 146 EU102
Dryfield Cl, NW10 80 CQ65
Dryfield Rd, Edg. HA8 42 CQ51
Dryfield Wk, SE8
off New King St 103 EA79
Dryhill La, Sev. (Sund.) TN14 190 FB123
Dryhill Rd, Belv. DA17 106 EZ79
Dryland Av, Orp. BR6 163 ET105
Drylands Rd, N8 65 DL58
Drynham Pk, Wey. KT13 135 BS104
Drysdale Av, E4 47 EB45
Drysdale Cl, Nthwd. HA6
off Northbrook Dr 39 BS52
Drysdale Pl, N1 197 N2
Drysdale St, N1 197 N3
Duarte Pl, Grays RM16 110 FZ76
Dublin Av, E8 84 DU67
Du Burstow Ter, W7 97 CE75
Ducal St, E2 off Brick La 84 DT69
Du Cane Cl, W12 81 CW72
Du Cane Ct, SW17 120 DG88
Du Cane Rd, W12 81 CT72
Duchess Cl, N11 45 DH50
Sutton SM1 158 DC105
Duchess Ct, Wey. KT13
off Oatlands Dr 135 BR104
Duchess Gro, Buck.H. IG9 48 EH47
Duchess Ms, W1 195 J7

★ Place of interest ⇌ Railway station ⊖ London Underground station DLR Docklands Light Railway station Tra Tramlink station H Hospital Riv Pedestrian ferry landing stage

Duchess of Bedford's Wk, W8 . 100 DA75
Duchess St, W1 . 195 J7
Duchess Wk, Sev. TN15 . 191 FL125
Duchy Rd, Barn. EN4 . 28 DD38
Duchy St, SE1 . 200 E2
Ducie St, SW4 . 101 DM84
Duckett Ms, N4
  off Duckett Rd . 65 DP58
Duckett Rd, N4 . 65 DP58
Ducketts Rd, Dart. DA1 . 127 FF85
Duckett St, E1 . 85 DX70
Ducking Stool Ct, Rom. RM1 . 71 FE56
Duck La, W1 . 195 M9
  Epping (Thnwd) CM16 . 18 EW26
Duck Lees La, Enf. EN3 . 31 DY42
Ducks Hill, Nthwd. HA6 . 39 BP54
Ducks Hill Rd, Nthwd. HA6 . 39 BP54
  Ruislip HA4 . 39 BP54
DUCKS ISLAND, Barn. EN5 . 27 CX44
Ducks Wk, Twick. TW1 . 117 CJ85
Du Cros Dr, Stan. HA7 . 41 CK51
Du Cros Rd, W3 off The Vale . 80 CS74
Dudden Hill La, NW10 . 63 CT63
Duddington Cl, SE9 . 124 EK91
Dudley Av, Har. HA3 . 61 CJ55
  Waltham Cross EN8 . 15 DX32
Dudley Cl, Add. KT15 . 134 BJ104
  Grays (Chaff.Hun.) RM16 . 110 FY75
  Hemel Hempstead
  (Bov.) HP3 . 5 BA27
Dudley Ct, NW11 . 63 CZ56
  Slough SL1 off Upton Rd . 92 AU76
Dudley Dr, Mord. SM4 . 139 CY101
  Ruislip HA4 . 59 BV64
Dudley Gdns, W13 . 97 CH75
  Harrow HA2 . 61 CD60
  Romford RM3
  off Dudley Rd . 52 FK51
Dudley Gro, Epsom KT18 . 156 CQ114
Dudley Ms, SW2
  off Bascombe St . 121 DN86
Dudley Pl, Hayes UB3
  off Pinkwell La . 95 BR77
Dudley Rd, E17 . 47 EA54
  N3 . 44 DB54
  NW6 . 81 CY68
  SW19 . 120 DA93
  Ashford TW15 . 114 BM92
  Feltham TW14 . 115 BQ88
  Gravesend (Nthflt) DA11 . 130 GE87
  Harrow HA2 . 60 CC61
  Ilford IG1 . 69 EP63
  Kingston upon Thames KT1 . 138 CM97
  Richmond TW9 . 98 CM82
  Romford RM3 . 52 FK51
  Southall UB2 . 96 BX75
  Walton-on-Thames KT12 . 135 BU100
Dudley St, W2 . 82 DD71
Dudlington Rd, E5 . 66 DW61
Dudmaston Ms, SW3 . 198 A10
Dudrich Ms, SE22
  off Melbourne Gro . 122 DT85
Dudsbury Rd, Dart. DA1 . 127 FG86
  Sidcup DA14 . 126 EV93
Dudset La, Houns. TW5 . 95 BU81
Dufferin Av, EC1 . 197 K5
Dufferin St, EC1 . 197 J5
Duffield Cl, Grays
  (Daniel Cl) RM16 . 110 FY75
  Grays (Davis Rd) RM16 . 110 FZ76
  Harrow HA1 . 61 CF57
Duffield Dr, N15
  off Copperfield Dr . 66 DT56
Duffield La, Slou.
  (Stoke P.) SL2 . 74 AT65
Duffield Pk, Slou.
  (Stoke P.) SL2 . 74 AU69
Duffield Rd, Tad. KT20 . 173 CV124
Duffins Orchard, Cher.
  (Ott.) KT16 . 151 BC108
Duff St, E14 . 85 EB72
Dufour's Pl, W1 . 195 L9
Dugard Way, SE11 . 200 F8
Dugdale Hill La, Pot.B. EN6 . 11 CY33
Dugdales, Rick.
  (Crox.Grn) WD3 . 22 BN42
Duggan Dr, Chis. BR7
  off Wood Dr . 124 EL93
Duke Gdns, Ilf. IG6
  off Duke Rd . 69 ER56
Duke Humphrey Rd, SE3 . 104 EE81
Duke of Cambridge Cl,
  Twick. TW2 . 117 CD86
Duke of Edinburgh Rd,
  Sutt. SM1 . 140 DD103
Duke of Wellington Av, SE18 . 105 EP76
Duke of Wellington Pl, SW1 . 198 G4
Duke of York Sq, SW3 . 198 E9
Duke of York St, SW1 . 199 L2
Duke Rd, W4 . 98 CR78
  Ilford IG6 . 69 ER56
Dukes Av, N3 . 44 DB53
  N10 . 65 DJ55
  W4 . 98 CR78
  Edgware HA8 . 42 CM51
  Epping (They.B.) CM16 . 33 ES35
  Grays RM17 . 110 GA75
  Harrow HA1 . 61 CE56
  Harrow (N.Har.) HA2 . 60 BZ58
  Hounslow TW4 . 96 BY84
  Kingston upon Thames KT2 . 117 CJ91
  New Malden KT3 . 139 CT97
  Northolt UB5 . 78 BY66
  Richmond TW10 . 117 CJ91
Dukes Cl, Ashf. TW15 . 115 BQ91
  Epping (N.Wld Bas.) CM16 . 19 FB27
  Gerrards Cross SL9 . 56 AX60
  Hampton TW12 . 116 BZ92
Dukes Ct, E6 . 87 EN67
  Woking GU21 . 167 AZ117
Dukes Gate, W4 off Acton La . 98 CQ77
Dukes Grn Av, Felt. TW14 . 115 BU85
Dukes Head Yd, N6
  off Highgate High St . 65 DH60
Dukes Hill, Cat. (Wold.) CR3 . 177 DY120
Duke Shore Pl, E14 . 203 M1
Duke Shore Wf, E14 . 203 M1
Dukes Kiln Dr, Ger.Cr. SL9 . 56 AW60
Dukes La, W8 . 100 DA75
  Gerrards Cross SL9 . 56 AY59
Dukes Lo, Nthwd. HA6
  off Eastbury Av . 39 BS50
Duke's Meadows, W4
  off Great Chertsey Rd . 98 CQ82
Dukes Ms, N10 off Dukes Av . 65 DH55
Duke's Ms, W1 . 194 G8
Dukes Orchard, Bex. DA5 . 127 FC88
Duke's Pas, E17 . 67 EC56
Dukes Pl, EC3 . 197 N9
Dukes Ride, Ger.Cr. SL9 . 56 AY60
  Uxbridge UB10 . 58 BL63
Dukes Rd, E6 . 87 EN67
  W3 . 80 CN71
Duke's Rd, WC1 . 195 N3
Dukes Rd, Walt. KT12 . 154 BX106
Dukesthorpe Rd, SE26 . 123 DX91
Duke St, SW1 . 199 L2
  W1 . 194 G8
  Richmond TW9 . 97 CK84
  Sutton SM1 . 158 DD105
  Watford WD17 . 24 BW41
  Woking GU21 . 167 AZ117
Duke St Hill, SE1 . 201 L2
Dukes Valley, Ger.Cr. SL9 . 56 AV61
Dukes Way, Uxb. UB8
  off Waterloo Rd . 76 BJ67
  West Wickham BR4 . 144 EE104
Dukes Wd Av, Ger.Cr. SL9 . 56 AY60
Dukes Wd Dr, Ger.Cr. SL9 . 56 AW60
Duke's Yd, W1 . 194 G10
Dulas St, N4
  off Everleigh St . 65 DM60
Dulford St, W11 . 81 CY73
Dulka Rd, SW11 . 120 DF85
Dulverton Rd, SE9 . 125 EQ89
  Romford RM3 . 52 FK51
  Ruislip HA4 . 59 BU60
  South Croydon CR2 . 160 DW110
DULWICH, SE21 . 122 DS87
★ Dulwich Coll Picture Gall,
  SE21 . 122 DS87
Dulwich Common, SE21 . 122 DS88
  SE22 . 122 DS88
Dulwich Lawn Cl, SE22
  off Colwell Rd . 122 DT85
Dulwich Oaks, The, SE21 . 122 DS90
Dulwich Rd, SE24 . 121 DN85
Dulwich Village, SE21 . 122 DS86
Dulwich Way, Rick.
  (Crox.Grn) WD3 . 22 BN43
Dulwich Wd Av, SE19 . 122 DS91
Dulwich Wd Pk, SE19 . 122 DS91
Dumbarton Av, Wal.Cr. EN8 . 15 DX34
Dumbarton Rd, SW2 . 121 DL86
Dumbleton Cl, Kings.T. KT1
  off Gloucester Rd . 138 CP95
Dumbletons, The, Rick.
  (Map.Cr.) WD3 . 37 BE49
Dumbreck Rd, SE9 . 105 EM84
Dumfries Cl, Wat. WD19 . 39 BT48
Dumont Rd, N16 . 66 DS62
Dumpton Pl, NW1
  off Gloucester Av . 82 DG66
Dumville Dr, Gdse. RH9 . 186 DV131
Dunally Pk, Shep. TW17 . 135 BR101
Dunbar Av, SW16 . 141 DN96
  Beckenham BR3 . 143 DY98
  Dagenham RM10 . 70 FA62
Dunbar Cl, Hayes UB4 . 77 BU71
  Slough SL2 . 74 AU72
Dunbar Ct, Sutt. SM1 . 158 DD106
  Walton-on-Thames KT12 . 136 BW103
Dunbar Gdns, Dag. RM10 . 70 FA64
Dunbar Rd, E7 . 86 EG65
  N22 . 45 DN53
  New Malden KT3 . 138 CQ98
Dunbar St, SE27 . 122 DQ90
Dunblane Cl, Edg. HA8
  off Tayside Dr . 42 CP47
Dunblane Rd, SE9 . 104 EL83
Dunboe Pl, Shep. TW17 . 135 BQ101
Dunboyne Rd, NW3 . 64 DF64
Dunbridge Ho, SW15
  off Highcliffe Dr . 119 CT86
Dunbridge St, E2 . 84 DU70
Duncan Cl, Barn. EN5 . 28 DC42
Duncan Gdns, Stai. TW18
  off Burges Way . 114 BG92
Duncan Gro, W3 . 80 CS72
Duncannon St, WC2 . 199 P1
Duncan Rd, E8 . 84 DV67
  Richmond TW9 . 98 CL84
  Tadworth KT20 . 173 CY119
Duncan St, N1 . 83 DP68
Duncan Ter, N1 . 196 F1
Duncan Way, Bushey WD23 . 24 BZ40
Dunch St, E1 off Watney St . 84 DV72
Duncombe Cl, Amer. HP6 . 20 AS38
Duncombe Ct, Stai. TW18 . 113 BF94
Duncombe Hill, SE23 . 123 DY87
Duncombe Rd, N19 . 65 DK60
Duncrievie Rd, SE13 . 123 ED86
Duncroft, SE18 . 105 ES80
Duncroft Cl, Reig. RH2 . 183 CZ133
Dundalk Rd, SE4 . 103 DY83
Dundas Gdns, W.Mol. KT8 . 136 CB97
Dundas Ms, Enf. EN3 . 31 EA37
Dundas Rd, SE15 . 102 DW82
Dundee Rd, E13 . 86 EH68
  SE25 . 142 DV99
Dundee St, E1 . 202 D3
Dundee Way, Enf. EN3 . 31 DY41
Dundela Gdns, Wor.Pk. KT4 . 157 CV105
Dundonald Cl, E6
  off Northumberland Rd . 86 EL72
Tra Dundonald Road . 119 CZ94
Dundonald Rd, NW10 . 81 CX67
  SW19 . 119 CY94
Dundrey Cres, Red. RH1 . 185 DL129
Dunedin Dr, Cat. CR3 . 186 DS125
Dunedin Ho, E16
  off Manwood St . 87 EM74
Dunedin Rd, E10 . 67 EB62
  Ilford IG1 . 69 EQ60
  Rainham RM13 . 89 FF69
Dunedin Way, Hayes UB4 . 78 BW70
Dunelm Gro, SE27 . 122 DQ91
Dunelm St, E1 . 85 DX72
Dunfee Way, W.Byf. KT14 . 152 BL112
Dunfield Gdns, SE6 . 123 EB91
Dunfield Rd, SE6 . 123 EB92
Dunford Rd, N7 . 65 DM63
Dungarvan Av, SW15 . 99 CU84
Dungates La, Bet.
  (Buckland) RH3 . 183 CU133
Dunheved Cl, Th.Hth. CR7 . 141 DN100
Dunheved Rd N, Th.Hth. CR7 . 141 DN100
Dunheved Rd S, Th.Hth. CR7 . 141 DN100
Dunheved Rd W, Th.Hth. CR7 . 141 DN100
Dunhill Pt, SW15
  off Dilton Gdns . 119 CV88
Dunholme Grn, N9 . 46 DT48
Dunholme La, N9
  off Dunholme Rd . 46 DT48
Dunholme Rd, N9 . 46 DT48
Dunkeld Rd, SE25 . 142 DR98
  Dagenham RM8 . 70 EV61
Dunkellin Gro, S.Ock. RM15
  off Dunkellin Way . 91 FU72
Dunkellin Way, S.Ock. RM15 . 91 FU72
Dunkery Rd, SE9 . 124 EK91
Dunkin Rd, Dart. DA1 . 108 FN84
Dunkirk Cl, Grav. DA12 . 131 GJ92
Dunkirk St, SE27
  off Waring St . 122 DQ91
Dunlace Rd, E5 . 66 DW63
Dunleary Cl, Houns. TW4 . 116 BZ87
Dunley Dr, Croy.
  (New Adgtn) CR0 . 161 EB108
Dunlin Ho, W13 . 79 CF70
Dunloe Av, N17 . 66 DR55
Dunloe St, E2 . 197 P1
Dunlop Cl, Dart. DA1
  off Joyce Grn La . 108 FL83
Dunlop Pl, SE16 . 202 A7
Dunlop Rd, Til. RM18 . 111 GF81
Dunmail Dr, Pur. CR8 . 160 DS114
Dunmore Pt, E2 . 197 P3
Dunmore Rd, NW6 . 81 CY67
  SW20 . 139 CW95
Dunmow Cl, Felt. TW13 . 116 BY91
  Loughton IG10 . 32 EL44
  Romford RM6 . 70 EW57
Dunmow Dr, Rain. RM13 . 89 FF67
Dunmow Ho, Dag. RM9 . 88 EV67
Dunmow Rd, E15 . 67 ED63
Dunmow Wk, N1
  off Popham St . 84 DQ67
Dunnage Cres, SE16 . 203 L8
Dunnets, Wok.
  (Knap.) GU21 . 166 AS117
Dunning Cl, S.Ock. RM15
  off Dent Cl . 91 FU72
Dunningford Cl, Horn. RM12 . 71 FF64
Dunn Mead, NW9
  off Field Mead . 43 CT52
Dunnock Cl, N9 . 47 DX46
  Borehamwood WD6 . 26 CN42
Dunnock Rd, E6 . 86 EL72
Dunns Pas, WC1 . 196 A8
Dunn St, E8 . 66 DT64
Dunny La, Kings L.
  (Chipper.) WD4 . 5 BE32
Dunnymans Rd, Bans. SM7 . 173 CZ115
Dunollie Pl, NW5
  off Dunollie Rd . 65 DJ64
Dunollie Rd, NW5 . 65 DJ64
Dunoon Rd, SE23 . 122 DW87
Dunraven Dr, Enf. EN2 . 29 DN40
Dunraven Rd, W12 . 81 CU74
Dunraven St, W1 . 194 E10
Dunsany Rd, W14 . 99 CX76
Dunsborough Pk, Wok.
  (Ripley) GU23 . 168 BJ120
Dunsbury Cl, Sutt. SM2
  off Nettlecombe Cl . 158 DB109
Dunsfold Ri, Couls. CR5 . 159 DK113
Dunsfold Way, Croy.
  (New Adgtn) CR0 . 161 EB108
Dunsford Way, SW15
  off Dover Pk Dr . 119 CV86
Dunsmore Cl, Bushey WD23 . 25 CD44
  Hayes UB4
  off Kingsash Dr . 78 BY70
Dunsmore Rd, Walt. KT12 . 135 BV100
Dunsmore Way,
  Bushey WD23 . 25 CD44
Dunsmure Rd, N16 . 66 DS60
Dunspring La, Ilf. IG5 . 49 EP54
Dunstable Cl, Rom. RM3
  off Dunstable Rd . 52 FK51
Dunstable Ms, W1 . 194 G6
Dunstable Rd, Rich. TW9 . 98 CL84
  Romford RM3 . 52 FK51
  West Molesey KT8 . 136 BZ98
Dunstall Grn, Wok.
  (Chobham) GU24 . 150 AW109
Dunstall Rd, SW20 . 119 CV93
Dunstall Way, W.Mol. KT8 . 136 CB97
Dunstan Cl, N2
  off Thomas More Way . 64 DC55
Dunstan Rd, NW11 . 63 CZ60
  Coulsdon CR5 . 175 DK117
Dunstans Gro, SE22 . 122 DV86
Dunstans Rd, SE22 . 122 DU87
Dunster Av, Mord. SM4 . 139 CX102
Dunster Cl, Barn. EN5 . 27 CX42
  Romford RM5 . 51 FC54
  Uxbridge (Hare.) UB9 . 38 BH53
Dunster Ct, EC3 . 197 M10
  Borehamwood WD6
  off Kensington Way . 26 CR41
Dunster Cres, Horn. RM11 . 72 FN61
Dunster Dr, NW9 . 62 CQ60
Dunster Gdns, NW6 . 81 CZ66
Dunsterville Way, SE1 . 201 L5
Dunster Way, Har. HA2 . 60 BY62
  Wallington SM6
  off Helios Rd . 140 DG102
Dunston Rd, E8 . 84 DT67
  SW11 . 100 DG82
Dunston St, E8 . 84 DT67
Dunton Cl, Surb. KT6 . 138 CL102
DUNTON GREEN, Sev. TN13 . 181 FC119
⇌ Dunton Green . 181 FF119
Dunton Rd, E10 . 67 EB59
  SE1 . 201 P10
  Romford RM1 . 71 FE56
Duntshill Rd, SW18 . 120 DB88
Dunvegan Cl, W.Mol. KT8 . 136 CB98
Dunvegan Rd, SE9 . 105 EM84
Dunwich Rd, Bexh. DA7 . 106 EZ81
Dunworth Ms, W11
  off Portobello Rd . 81 CZ72
Duplex Ride, SW1 . 198 E5
Dupont Rd, SW20 . 139 CX96
Duppas Av, Croy. CR0
  off Violet La . 159 DP105
Duppas Cl, Shep. TW17
  off Green La . 135 BR99
Duppas Hill La, Croy. CR0
  off Duppas Hill Rd . 159 DP105
Duppas Hill Rd, Croy. CR0 . 159 DP105
Duppas Hill Ter, Croy. CR0 . 141 DP104
Duppas Rd, Croy. CR0 . 141 DN104
Dupre Cl, Grays
  (Chaff.Hun.) RM16 . 110 FY76
Dupree Rd, SE7 . 205 P10
Dura Den Cl, Beck. BR3 . 123 EB94
Durand Cl, Cars. SM5 . 140 DF102
Durand Gdns, SW9 . 101 DM81
Durands Wk, SE16 . 203 L4
Durand Way, NW10 . 80 CQ66
Durant Rd, Swan. BR8 . 127 FG93
Durants Pk Av, Enf. EN3 . 31 DX42
Durants Rd, Enf. EN3 . 30 DW42
Durant St, E2 . 84 DU68
Durban Gdns, Dag. RM10 . 89 FC66
Durban Rd, E15 . 86 EE69
  E17 . 47 DZ53
  N17 . 46 DS51
  SE27 . 122 DQ91
  Beckenham BR3 . 143 DZ96
  Ilford IG2 . 69 ES60
Durban Rd E, Wat. WD18 . 23 BU42
Durban Rd W, Wat. WD18 . 23 BU42
Durbin Rd, Chess. KT9 . 156 CL105
Durdans Rd, Sthl. UB1 . 78 BZ72
Durell Gdns, Dag. RM9 . 70 EX64
Durell Rd, Dag. RM9 . 70 EX64
Durfold Dr, Reig. RH2 . 184 DC134
Durford Cres, SW15 . 119 CU88
Durham Av, Brom. BR2 . 144 EF98
  Hounslow TW5 . 96 BZ78
  Romford RM2 . 72 FJ56
  Woodford Green IG8 . 48 EK50
Durham Cl, SW20
  off Durham Rd . 139 CV96
Durham Hill, Brom. BR1 . 124 EF91
Durham Ho St, WC2 . 200 A1
Durham Pl, SW3
  off Smith St . 100 DF78
  Ilford IG1 off Eton Rd . 69 EQ63
Durham Ri, SE18 . 105 EQ78
Durham Rd, E12 . 68 EK63
  E16 . 86 EE70
  N2 . 64 DE55
  N7 . 65 DM61
  N9 . 46 DU47
  SW20 . 139 CV95
  W5 . 97 CK76
  Borehamwood WD6 . 26 CQ41
  Bromley BR2 . 144 EF97
  Dagenham RM10 . 71 FC64
  Feltham TW14 . 116 BW87
  Harrow HA1 . 60 CB57
  Sidcup DA14 . 126 EV92
Durham Row, E1 . 85 DY71
Durham St, SE11 . 101 DM78
Durham Ter, W2 . 82 DB72
Durham Wf, Brent. TW8
  off London Rd . 97 CJ80
Durham Yd, E2
  off Teesdale St . 84 DV69
Duriun Way, Erith DA8 . 107 FH80
Durley Av, Pnr. HA5 . 60 BY59
Durley Gdns, Orp. BR6 . 164 EV105
Durley Rd, N16 . 66 DS59
Durlston Rd, E5 . 66 DU61
  Kingston upon Thames KT2 . 118 CL93
Durndale La, Grav.
  (Nthflt) DA11 . 131 GF91
Durnell Way, Loug. IG10 . 33 EN41
Durnford St, N15 . 66 DS57
  SE10 off Greenwich Ch St . 103 EC79
Durning Rd, SE19 . 122 DR92
Durnsford Av, SW19 . 120 DA89
Durnsford Rd, N11 . 45 DK53
  SW19 . 120 DA89
Durrants Cl, Rain. RM13 . 90 FJ68
Durrants Dr, Rick.
  (Crox.Grn) WD3 . 23 BQ42
Durrant Way, Orp. BR6 . 163 ER106
  Swanscombe DA10 . 130 FY87
Durrell Rd, SW6 . 99 CZ81
Durrell Way, Shep. TW17 . 135 BR100
Durrington Av, SW20 . 139 CW95
Durrington Pk Rd, SW20 . 119 CW94
Durrington Rd, E5 . 67 DY63
Durrington Twr, SW8
  off Westbury St . 101 DJ82
Dursley Cl, SE3 . 104 EJ82
Dursley Gdns, SE3 . 104 EK81
Dursley Rd, SE3 . 104 EJ82
Durward St, E1 . 84 DV71
Durweston Ms, W1 . 194 E6
Durweston St, W1 . 194 E6
Dury Falls Cl, Horn. RM11 . 72 FM60
Dury Rd, Barn. EN5 . 27 CZ39
Dutch Barn Cl, Stai.
  (Stanw.) TW19 . 114 BK86
Dutch Elm Av, Wind. SL4 . 92 AT80
Dutch Gdns, Kings.T. KT2
  off Windmill Ri . 118 CP93
Dutch Yd, SW18
  off Wandsworth High St . 120 DA85
Dutton St, SE10 . 103 EC81
Dutton Way, Iver SL0 . 75 BE72
Duxberry Cl, Brom. BR2
  off Southborough La . 144 EL99
Duxford Cl, Horn. RM12 . 89 FH65
Duxford Ho, SE2
  off Wolvercote Rd . 106 EX75
Dwight Ct, SW6
  off Burlington Rd . 99 CY82
Dwight Rd, Wat. WD18 . 39 BR45
Dye Ho La, E3 . 85 EA67
Dyer's Bldgs, EC1 . 196 D7
Dyers Hall Rd, E11 . 68 EE60
Dyers La, SW15 . 99 CV84
Dyers Way, Rom. RM3 . 51 FH52
Dyke Dr, Orp. BR5 . 146 EW102
Dykes Path, Wok. GU21
  off Bentham Av . 167 BC115
Dykes Way, Brom. BR2 . 144 EF97
Dykewood Cl, Bex. DA5 . 127 FE90
Dylan Cl, Borwd. (Elstree) WD6
  off Coates Rd . 41 CK45
Dylan Rd, SE24 . 101 DP84
  Belvedere DA17 . 106 FA76
Dylways, SE5 . 102 DR84
Dymchurch Cl, Ilf. IG5 . 49 EN54
  Orpington BR6 . 163 ES105
Dymes Path, SW19
  off Queensmere Rd . 119 CX89
Dymock St, SW6 . 100 DB83
Dymoke Rd, Horn. RM11 . 71 FF59
Dymond Est, SW17
  off Glenburnie Rd . 120 DE90
Dyneley Rd, SE12 . 124 EJ91
Dyne Rd, NW6 . 81 CZ66
Dynevor Rd, N16 . 66 DS62
  Richmond TW10 . 118 CL85
Dynham Rd, NW6 . 82 DA66
Dyott St, WC1 . 195 P8
Dyrham La, Barn. EN5 . 27 CU36
Dysart Av, Kings.T. KT2 . 117 CJ92
Dysart St, EC2 . 197 M5
Dyson Rd, E11 . 68 EE58
  E15 . 86 EF65
Dysons Cl, Wal.Cr. EN8 . 15 DX33
Dysons Rd, N18 . 46 DV50

E

Eade Rd, N4 . 66 DQ59
Eagans Cl, N2 off Market Pl . 64 DE55
Eagle Av, Rom. RM6 . 70 EY58
Eagle Cl, SE16 off Varcoe Rd . 102 DW78
  Amersham HP6 . 20 AT37
  Enfield EN3 . 30 DW42
  Hornchurch RM12 . 89 FH65
  Wallington SM6 . 159 DL107
  Waltham Abbey EN9 . 16 EG34
Eagle Ct, EC1 . 196 F6
Eagle Dr, NW9 . 42 CS54
Eagle Hts, SW11
  off Bramlands Cl . 100 DE83
Eagle Hill, SE19 . 122 DR93
Eagle La, E11 . 68 EG56
Eagle Ms, N1
  off Tottenham Rd . 84 DS65
Eagle Pl, SW1 . 199 L1
  SW7 off Old Brompton Rd . 100 DC78
Eagle Rd, Wem. HA0 . 79 CK66
Eagles Dr, West. (Tats.) TN16 . 178 EK118
Eaglesfield Rd, SE18 . 105 EP80
Eagles Rd, Green. DA9 . 109 FV84
Eagle St, WC1 . 196 B7
Eagle Ter, Wdf.Grn. IG8 . 48 EH52
Eagle Trd Est, Mitch. CR4
  off Willow La . 140 DF100
Eagle Way, Brwd. CM13 . 53 FV51
  Gravesend (Nthflt) DA11 . 130 GA85
Eagle Wf, E14
  off Broomfield St . 85 EB71
Eagle Wf Rd, N1 . 84 DQ68
Ealdham Sq, SE9 . 104 EJ84
EALING, W5 . 79 CJ73
⇌ Ealing Broadway . 79 CK73
⊖ Ealing Broadway . 79 CK73
Ealing Bdy Shop Cen, W5 . 79 CK73
Ealing Cl, Borwd. WD6 . 26 CR39
★ Ealing Common, W5 . 80 CL74
⊖ Ealing Common . 80 CM74
Ealing Downs Ct, Grnf. UB6
  off Perivale La . 79 CG69
Ealing Grn, W5 . 79 CK74
H Ealing Hosp, Sthl. UB1 . 97 CD75
Ealing Pk Gdns, W5 . 97 CJ77
Ealing Rd, Brent. TW8 . 97 CK78
  Northolt UB5 . 78 CA66
  Wembley HA0 . 79 CK67
Ealing Village, W5 . 80 CL72
Eamont Cl, Ruis. HA4
  off Allonby Dr . 59 BP59
Eamont St, NW8 . 82 DE68
Eardemont Cl, Dart. DA1 . 107 FF84
Eardley Cres, SW5 . 100 DA78
Eardley Pt, SE18
  off Wilmount St . 105 EP77
Eardley Rd, SW16 . 121 DJ92
  Belvedere DA17 . 106 FA78
  Sevenoaks TN13 . 191 FH124
Earl Cl, N11 . 45 DH50
Earldom Rd, SW15 . 99 CW84
Earle Gdns, Kings.T. KT2 . 118 CL93
Earleswood, Cob. KT11 . 154 BX112
Earlham Gro, E7 . 68 EF64
  N22 . 45 DM52
Earlham St, WC2 . 195 N9
Earl Ri, SE18 . 105 ER77
Earl Rd, SW14 off Elm Rd . 98 CQ84
  Gravesend (Nthflt) DA11 . 130 GE89
EARLS COURT, SW5 . 99 CZ78
⊖ Earls Court . 100 DA78
★ Earls Court Exhib Cen,
  SW5 . 100 DA78
Earls Ct Gdns, SW5 . 100 DB78
Earls Ct Rd, SW5 . 100 DA77
  W8 . 100 DA77
Earls Ct Sq, SW5 . 100 DB78
Earls Cres, Har. HA1 . 61 CE56
Earlsdown Ho, Bark. IG11
  off Wheelers Cross . 87 ER68
Earlsferry Way, N1 . 83 DM66
EARLSFIELD, SW18 . 120 DC88
⇌ Earlsfield . 120 DC88
Earlsfield Ho, Kings.T. KT2
  off Kingsgate Rd . 138 CL95
Earlsfield Rd, SW18 . 120 DC88
Earlshall Rd, SE9 . 105 EM84
Earls La, Pot.B. EN6 . 10 CS32

★ Place of interest ⇌ Railway station ⊖ London Underground station DLR Docklands Light Railway station Tra Tramlink station H Hospital Riv Pedestrian ferry landing stage

Earlsmead, Har. HA2 60 BZ63
Earlsmead Rd, N15 66 DT57
NW10 81 CW68
Earl's Path, Loug. IG10 32 EJ40
Earls Ter, W8 99 CZ76
Earlsthorpe Ms, SW12 120 DG86
Earlsthorpe Rd, SE26 123 DX91
Earlstoke St, EC1 196 F2
Earlston Gro, E9 84 DV67
Earl St, EC2 197 M6
Watford WD17 24 BW41
Earls Wk, W8 100 DA76
Dagenham RM8 70 EV63
Earls Way, Orp. BR6
off Station Rd 145 ET103
Earlswood Av, Th.Hth. CR7 141 DN99
Earlswood Gdns, Ilf. IG5 69 EN55
Earlswood St, SE10 104 EE78
Early Ms, NW1
off Arlington Rd 83 DH67
Earnshaw St, WC2 195 N8
Earsby St, W14 99 CY77
Easby Cres, Mord. SM4 140 DB100
Easebourne Rd, Dag. RM8 70 EW64
Easedale Dr, Horn. RM12 71 FG64
Easedale Ho, Islw. TW7
off Summerwood Rd 117 CF85
Eashing Pt, SW15
off Wanborough Dr 119 CV88
Easington Way, S.Ock. RM15 91 FU71
Easley's Ms, W1 194 G8
EAST ACTON, W3 80 CR74
⊖ East Acton 81 CT72
East Acton La, W3 80 CS73
East Arbour St, E1 85 DX72
East Av, E12 86 EL66
E17 67 EB56
Hayes UB3 95 BT75
Southall UB1 78 BZ73
Wallington SM6 159 DM106
Walton-on-Thames
(Whiteley Vill.) KT12
off Octagon Rd 153 BT110
East Bk, N16 66 DS59
Eastbank Rd, Hmptn.
(Hmptn H.) TW12 116 CC92
EAST BARNET, Barn. EN4 28 DE44
East Barnet Rd, Barn. EN4 28 DE44
EAST BEDFONT, Felt. TW14 115 BS88
Eastbourne Av, W3 80 CR72
Eastbourne Gdns, SW14 98 CQ83
Eastbourne Ms, W2 82 DC72
Eastbourne Rd, E6 87 EN69
E15 86 EE67
N15 66 DS58
SW17 120 DG93
W4 98 CQ79
Brentford TW8 97 CJ78
Feltham TW13 116 BX89
Godstone RH9 186 DW132
Eastbourne Ter, W2 82 DC72
Eastbournia Av, N9 46 DV48
Eastbridge, Slou. SL2
off Victoria Rd 74 AV74
Eastbrook Av, N9 46 DW45
Dagenham RM10 71 FC63
Eastbrook Cl, Wok. GU21 167 BA116
Eastbrook Dr, Rom. RM7 71 FE62
Eastbrook Rd, SE3 104 EH80
Waltham Abbey EN9 16 EE33
EASTBURY, Nthwd. HA6 39 BS49
Eastbury Av, Bark. IG11 87 ES67
Enfield EN1 30 DS39
Northwood HA6 39 BS50
Eastbury Ct, Bark. IG11 87 ES67
Eastbury Gro, W4 98 CS78
★ Eastbury Ho, Bark. IG11 87 ET67
Eastbury Pl, Nthwd. HA6
off Eastbury Av 39 BT50
Eastbury Rd, E6 87 EN70
Kingston upon Thames KT2 118 CL94
Northwood HA6 39 BS51
Orpington BR5 145 ER100
Romford RM7 71 FD58
Watford WD19 39 BV45
Eastbury Sq, Bark. IG11 87 ET67
Eastbury Ter, E1 85 DX70
Eastcastle St, W1 195 K8
Eastcheap, EC3 197 L10
East Churchfield Rd, W3 80 CR74
Eastchurch Rd, Houns.
(Hthrw Air.) TW6 95 BS82
East Cl, W5 80 CN70
Barnet EN4 28 DG42
Greenford UB6 78 CC68
Rainham RM13 89 FH70
St. Albans AL2 8 CB25
Eastcombe Av, SE7 104 EH79
East Common, Ger.Cr. SL9 56 AY58
EASTCOTE, Pnr. HA5 60 BW58
⊖ Eastcote 60 BW59
Eastcote, Orp. BR6 145 ET102
Eastcote Av, Grnf. UB6 61 CG64
Harrow HA2 60 CB61
West Molesey KT8 136 BZ99
Eastcote La, Har. HA2 60 CA62
Northolt UB5 78 CA66
Eastcote La N, Nthlt. UB5 78 BZ65
Eastcote Pl, Pnr. HA5 59 BV58
Eastcote Rd, Har. HA2 60 CC62
Pinner HA5 60 BX57
Pinner (Eastcote Vill.) HA5 59 BU58
Ruislip HA4 59 BS59
Welling DA16 105 ER82
Eastcote St, SW9 101 DM82
Eastcote Vw, Pnr. HA5 60 BW56
EASTCOTE VILLAGE,
Pnr. HA5 59 BV57
Eastcourt, Sun. TW16 136 BW96
East Ct, Wem. HA0 61 CJ61
East Cres, N11 44 DF49
Enfield EN1 30 DT43
East Cres Rd, Grav. DA12 131 GJ86
Eastcroft Rd, Epsom KT19 156 CS108
East Cross Cen, E15 85 EA65
East Cross Route, E3 85 DZ66
E9 85 DZ66
⇌ East Croydon 142 DR103
Tra East Croydon 142 DR103
Eastdean Av, Epsom KT18 156 CP113
East Dene Dr, Rom.
(Harold Hill) RM3 52 FK50
Eastdown Pk, SE13 103 ED84
East Dr, Cars. SM5 158 DE109
Northwood HA6 39 BS47
Orpington BR5 146 EV100
Slough (Stoke P.) SL2 74 AS69
Virginia Water GU25 132 AU101
Watford WD25 23 BV35
East Duck Lees La, Enf. EN3 31 DY42
EAST DULWICH, SE22 122 DU86
⇌ East Dulwich 102 DS84
East Dulwich Gro, SE22 122 DS86
East Dulwich Rd, SE15 102 DT84
SE22 102 DT84
East End Rd, N2 64 DC55
N3 44 DA54
East End Way, Pnr. HA5 60 BY55
East Entrance, Dag. RM10 89 FB68
Eastern Av, E11 68 EJ58
Chertsey KT16 134 BG97
Grays
(W.Thur.) RM20 109 FT78
Ilford IG2, IG4 68 EL58
Pinner HA5 60 BX59
Romford RM6 70 EW56
South Ockendon
(Aveley) RM15 90 FQ74
Waltham Cross EN8 15 DY33
Eastern Av E, Rom.
RM1, RM2, RM3 71 FD55
Eastern Av W, Rom.
RM1, RM5, RM6, RM7 70 EY56
Eastern Gateway, E16 86 EJ73
Eastern Ind Est, Erith DA18 106 FA75
Eastern Pathway, Horn. RM12 90 FJ67
Eastern Perimeter Rd, Houns.
(Hthrw Air.) TW6 95 BT83
Eastern Quay Apartments, E16
off Rayleigh Rd 86 EH74
Eastern Rd, E13 86 EH68
E17 67 EC57
N2 64 DF55
N22 45 DL53
SE4 103 EA84
Grays RM17 110 GD77
Romford RM1 71 FE57
Eastern Vw, West.
(Bigg.H.) TN16 178 EJ117
Easternville Gdns, Ilf. IG2 69 EQ58
Eastern Way, SE2 88 EX74
SE28 106 EU75
Belvedere DA17 107 FB75
Erith DA18 88 EX74
Grays RM17 110 GA79
EAST EWELL, Sutt. SM2 157 CX110
East Ferry Rd, E14 204 C8
Eastfield Av, Wat. WD24 24 BX39
Eastfield Cl, Slou. SL1
off St. Laurence Way 92 AU76
Eastfield Cotts, Hayes UB3 95 BS78
Eastfield Gdns, Dag. RM10 70 FA63
Eastfield Par, Pot.B. EN6 12 DD32
Eastfield Rd, E17 67 EA56
N8 65 DL55
Brentwood CM14 54 FX47
Dagenham RM9, RM10 70 FA63
Enfield EN3 31 DX38
Waltham Cross EN8 15 DY32
Eastfields, Pnr. HA5 60 BW57
Eastfields Rd, W3 80 CQ71
Mitcham CR4 140 DG96
Eastfield St, E14 85 DY71
Eastfileds Av, SW18
off Point Pleasant 100 DA84
EAST FINCHLEY, N2 64 DD56
⊖ East Finchley 64 DE56
East Gdns, SW17 120 DE93
Woking GU22 167 BC117
Eastgate, Bans. SM7 157 CY114
Eastgate Cl, SE28 88 EX72
Eastglade, Nthwd. HA6 39 BS50
Pinner HA5 60 BY55
East Gorse, Croy. CR0 161 DY112
East Grn, Hem.H. HP3 6 BM25
East Hall La, Rain.
(Wenn.) RM13 90 FK72
East Hall Rd, Orp. BR5 146 EY101
EAST HAM, E6 86 EL68
⊖ East Ham 86 EL66
Eastham Cl, Barn. EN5 27 CY43
Eastham Cres, Brwd. CM13 55 GA49
East Ham Ind Est, E6 86 EL70
East Ham Manor Way, E6 87 EN72
H East Ham Mem Hosp, E7 86 EK66
East Ham Shop Hall, E6
off Myrtle Rd 86 EL67
East Harding St, EC4 196 E8
East Heath Rd, NW3 64 DD62
East Hill, SW18 120 DB85
Dartford DA1 128 FM87
Dartford (S.Darenth) DA4 148 FQ95
Oxted RH8 188 EE129
South Croydon CR2 160 DS110
Wembley HA9 62 CN61
Westerham (Bigg.H.) TN16 178 EH118
Woking GU22 167 BC116
East Hill Dr, Dart. DA1 128 FM87
East Hill Rd, Oxt. RH8 188 EE129
Eastholm, NW11 64 DB56
East Holme, Erith DA8 107 FD81
Eastholme, Hayes UB3 77 BU74
DLR East India 85 ED73
East India Dock Rd, E14 85 EA72
East India Way, Croy. CR0
off Lower Addiscombe Rd 142 DT102
East Kent Av, Grav.
(Nthflt) DA11 130 GC86
Eastlake Rd, SE5 101 DP82
Eastlands Cl, Oxt. RH8
off Eastlands Way 187 ED127
Eastlands Cres, SE21 122 DT86
Eastlands Way, Oxt. RH8 187 ED127
East La, SE16 202 B5
Abbots Langley WD5 7 BU29
Dartford (S.Darenth) DA4 149 FR96
Kingston upon Thames KT1
off High St 137 CK97
Wembley HA0, HA9 61 CK62
Eastlea Av, Wat. WD25 24 BY37
Eastlea Ms, E16
off Desford Rd 86 EE70
Eastleigh Av, Har. HA2 60 CB61
Eastleigh Cl, NW2 62 CS62
Sutton SM2 158 DB108
Eastleigh Rd, E17 47 DZ54
Bexleyheath DA7 107 FC82
Hounslow (Hthrw Air.) TW6
off Cranford La 95 BT83
Eastleigh Wk, SW15 119 CU87
Eastleigh Way, Felt. TW14 115 BU88
East Lo La, Enf. EN2 29 DK36
H Eastman Dental Hosp,
WC1 196 B3
Eastman Rd, W3 80 CR74
East Mascalls, SE7
off Mascalls Rd 104 EJ79
East Mead, Ruis. HA4 60 BX62
Eastmead Av, Grnf. UB6 78 CB69
Eastmead Cl, Brom. BR1 144 EL96
Eastmearn Rd, SE21 122 DQ89
East Mill, Grav. DA11 131 GF86
East Milton Rd, Grav. DA12 131 GK87
EAST MOLESEY 137 CD98
Eastmont Rd, Esher KT10 137 CE103
Eastmoor Pl, SE7
off Eastmoor St 104 EK76
Eastmoor St, SE7 104 EK76
East Mt St, E1 84 DV71
Eastney Rd, Croy. CR0 141 DP102
Eastney St, SE10 103 ED78
Eastnor, Hem.H. (Bov.) HP3 5 BA28
Eastnor Rd, SE9 125 EQ88
Easton Gdns, Borwd. WD6 26 CR42
Easton St, WC1 196 D3
East Pk Cl, Rom. RM6 70 EX57
East Parkside, SE10 205 K5
Warlingham CR6 177 EA116
East Pas, EC1 196 G6
East Pier, E1 202 D3
East Pl, SE27
off Pilgrim Hill 122 DQ91
East Poultry Av, EC1 196 F7
⊖ East Putney 119 CY85
East Ramp, Houns.
(Hthrw Air.) TW6 95 BP81
East Ridgeway, Pot.B.
(Cuffley) EN6 13 DK29
East Rd, E15 86 EG67
N1 197 K3
SW19 120 DC93
Barnet EN4 44 DG46
Edgware HA8 42 CP53
Enfield EN3 30 DW38
Feltham TW14 115 BR87
Kingston upon Thames KT2 138 CL95
Reigate RH2 183 CZ133
Romford (Chad.Hth) RM6 70 EY57
Romford (Rush Grn) RM7 71 FD59
Welling DA16 106 EV82
West Drayton UB7 94 BM77
Weybridge KT13 153 BR108
East Rochester Way, SE9 105 ES84
Bexley DA5 126 EX86
Sidcup DA15 105 ES84
East Row, E11 68 EG58
W10 81 CY70
Eastry Av, Brom. BR2 144 EF100
Eastry Rd, Erith DA8 106 FA80
EAST SHEEN, SW14 98 CR84
East Sheen Av, SW14 98 CR84
Eastside Rd, NW11 63 CZ56
East Smithfield, E1 202 A1
East St, SE17 201 J10
Barking IG11 87 EQ66
Bexleyheath DA7 106 FA84
Brentford TW8 97 CJ80
Bromley BR1 144 EG96
Chertsey KT16 134 BG101
Epsom KT17 156 CS113
Grays RM17 110 GC79
Grays (S.Stfd) RM20 110 FY79
East Surrey Gro, SE15 102 DT80
★ East Surrey Mus, Cat. CR3 176 DU124
East Tenter St, E1 84 DT72
East Ter, Grav. DA12 131 GJ86
East Thurrock Rd,
Grays RM17 110 GB79
East Twrs, Pnr. HA5 60 BX57
East Vw, E4 47 EC50
Barnet EN5 27 CZ41
Eastview Av, SE18 105 ES80
Eastville Av, NW11 63 CZ58
East Wk, Barn. EN4 44 DG45
Hayes UB3 77 BU74
Reigate RH2 184 DB134
Eastway, E9 85 DZ65
East Way, E11 68 EH57
Bromley BR2 144 EG101
Croydon CR0 143 DY103
Eastway, Epsom KT19 156 CQ112
East Way, Hayes UB3 77 BU74
Eastway, Mord. SM4 139 CX99
East Way, Ruis. HA4 59 BU60
Eastway, Wall. SM6 159 DJ105
Eastway Commercial Cen, E9 67 EA64
Eastway Cres, Har. HA2
off Eliot Dr 60 CB61
Eastwell Cl, Beck. BR3 143 DY95
Eastwick Ct, SW19
off Victoria Dr 119 CX88
Eastwick Cres, Rick.
(Mill End) WD3 37 BF47
Eastwick Dr, Lthd.
(Bkhm) KT23 170 CA123
EAST WICKHAM, Well. DA16 106 EU80
Eastwick Pk Av, Lthd.
(Bkhm) KT23 170 CB124
Eastwick Rd, Walt. KT12 153 BV106
Eastwood Cl, E18
off George La 48 EG54
N7 off Eden Gro 65 DN64
N17
off Northumberland Gro 46 DV52
Eastwood Dr, Rain. RM13 89 FH72
Eastwood Rd, E18 48 EG54
N10 44 DG54
Ilford IG3 70 EU59
West Drayton UB7 94 BN75
East Woodside, Bex. DA5 126 EY88
Eastwood St, SW16 121 DJ93
Eastworth Rd, Cher. KT16 134 BG102
Eatington Rd, E10 67 ED57
Eaton Cl, SW1 198 F9
Stanmore HA7 41 CH49
Eaton Dr, SW9 101 DP84
Kingston upon Thames KT2 118 CN94
Romford RM5 51 FB52
Eaton Gdns, Dag. RM9 88 EY66
Eaton Gate, SW1 198 F8
Northwood HA6 39 BQ51
Eaton Ho, E14
off Westferry Circ 85 EA74
Eaton La, SW1 199 J7
Eaton Ms N, SW1 198 F8
Eaton Ms S, SW1 198 G8
Eaton Ms W, SW1 198 G8
Eaton Pk, Cob. KT11 154 BY114
Eaton Pk Rd, N13 45 DN47
Cobham KT11 154 BY114
Eaton Pl, SW1 198 F7
Eaton Ri, E11 68 EJ57
W5 79 CK72
Eaton Rd, NW4 63 CW57
Enfield EN1 30 DS41
Hounslow TW3 97 CD84
Sidcup DA14 126 EX89
Sutton SM2 158 DD107
Upminster RM14 73 FS61
Eaton Row, SW1 199 H7
Eatons Mead, E4 47 EA47
Eaton Sq, SW1 199 H6
Longfield DA3
off Bramblefield Cl 149 FX97
Eaton Ter, SW1 198 F8
Eaton Ter Ms, SW1 198 F8
Eatonville Rd, SW17 120 DF89
Eatonville Vil, SW17
off Eatonville Rd 120 DF89
Ebbas Way, Epsom KT18 172 CP115
Ebbisham Cen, The,
Epsom KT19 156 CR113
Ebbisham Dr, SW8 101 DM79
Ebbisham La, Tad. KT20 173 CT121
Ebbisham Rd, Epsom KT18 156 CP114
Worcester Park KT4 139 CW103
Ebbsfleet Ind Est, Grav.
(Nthflt) DA11 130 GA85
Ebbsfleet Rd, NW2 63 CY63
Ebbsfleet Wk, Grav.
(Nthflt) DA11 130 GB86
Ebdon Way, SE3 104 EH83
Ebenezer Ho, SE11 200 E9
Ebenezer St, N1 197 K2
Ebenezer Wk, SW16 141 DJ95
Ebley Cl, SE15 102 DT79
Ebner St, SW18 120 DB85
Ebor St, E1 197 P4
Ebrington Rd, Har. HA3 61 CK58
Ebsworth St, SE23 123 DX87
Eburne Rd, N7 65 DL62
Ebury App, Rick. WD3
off Ebury Rd 38 BK46
Ebury Br, SW1 199 H10
Ebury Br Est, SW1 199 H10
Ebury Br Rd, SW1 100 DG78
Ebury Cl, Kes. BR2 144 EL104
Northwood HA6 39 BQ50
Ebury Ms, SE27 121 DP90
SW1 198 G8
Ebury Ms E, SW1 199 H8
Ebury Rd, Rick. WD3 38 BK46
Watford WD17 24 BW41
Ebury Sq, SW1 198 G9
Ebury St, SW1 199 H8
Ebury Way Cycle Path, The,
Rick. WD3 39 BP45
Watford WD18 39 BP45
Ecclesbourne Cl, N13 45 DN50
Ecclesbourne Gdns, N13 45 DN50
Ecclesbourne Rd, N1 84 DQ66
Thornton Heath CR7 142 DQ99
Eccles Rd, SW11 100 DF84
Eccleston Br, SW1 199 J8
Eccleston Cl, Barn. EN4 28 DF42
Orpington BR6 145 ER102
Eccleston Cres, Rom. RM6 70 EU59
Ecclestone Ct, Wem. HA9
off St. John's Rd 62 CL64
Ecclestone Pl, Wem. HA9 62 CM64
Eccleston Ms, SW1 198 G7
Eccleston Pl, SW1 199 H8
Eccleston Rd, W13 79 CG73
Eccleston Sq, SW1 199 J9
Eccleston Sq Ms, SW1 199 K9
Eccleston St, SW1 199 H7
Echelforde Dr, Ashf. TW15 114 BN91
Echo Hts, E4
off Mount Echo Dr 47 EB46
Echo Sq, Grav. DA12
off Old Rd E 131 GJ89
Eckersley St, E1
off Buxton St 84 DU70
Eckford St, N1 83 DN68
Eckington Ho, N15
off Fladbury Rd 66 DR58
Eckstein Rd, SW11 100 DE84
Eclipse Rd, E13 86 EH71
Ecton Rd, Add. KT15 152 BH105
Ector Rd, SE6 124 EE89
Edbrooke Rd, W9 82 DA70
Eddiscombe Rd, SW6 99 CZ82
Eddy Cl, Rom. RM7 71 FB58
Eddystone Rd, SE4 123 DY85
Eddystone Twr, SE8 203 L9
Eddystone Wk, Stai. TW19 114 BL87
Ede Cl, Houns. TW3 96 BZ83
Edenbridge Cl, SE16
off Masters Dr 102 DV78
Orpington BR5 146 EX98
Edenbridge Rd, E9 85 DX66
Enfield EN1 30 DS44
Eden Cl, NW3 64 DA61
W8 off Adam & Eve Ms 100 DA76
Addlestone
(New Haw) KT15 152 BH110
Bexley DA5 127 FD91
Enfield EN3 31 EA38
Slough SL3 93 BA78
Eden Cl, Wembley HA0 79 CK67
Edencourt Rd, SW16 121 DH93
Edendale Rd, Bexh. DA7 107 FD81
Edenfield Gdns, Wor.Pk. KT4 139 CT104
Eden Grn, S.Ock. RM15
off Bovey Way 91 FV71
Eden Gro, E17 67 EB57
N7 65 DM64
Eden Gro Rd, W.Byf.
(Byfleet) KT14 152 BL113
Edenhall Cl, Rom. RM3 52 FJ50
Edenhall Glen, Rom. RM3 52 FJ50
Edenhall Rd, Rom. RM3 52 FJ50
Edenham Way, W10
off Elkstone Rd 81 CZ71
Edenhurst Av, SW6 99 CZ83
Eden Ms, SW17
off Huntspill St 120 DC90
EDEN PARK, Beck. BR3 143 EA99
⇌ Eden Park 143 EA99
Eden Pk Av, Beck. BR3 143 DY98
Eden Pl, Grav. DA12
off Lord St 131 GH87
Eden Rd, E17 67 EB57
SE27 121 DP92
Beckenham BR3 143 DY98
Bexley DA5 127 FC91
Croydon CR0 160 DR105
Edenside Rd, Lthd.
(Bkhm) KT23 170 BZ124
Edensor Gdns, W4 98 CS80
Edensor Rd, W4 98 CS80
Eden St, Kings.T. KT1 137 CK96
Edenvale Cl, Mitch. CR4
off Edenvale Rd 120 DG94
Edenvale Rd, Mitch. CR4 120 DG94
Edenvale St, SW6 100 DB82
Eden Wk, Kings.T. KT1
off Eden St 138 CL96
Eden Wk Shop Cen,
Kings.T. KT1 138 CL96
Eden Way, Beck. BR3 143 DZ99
Warlingham CR6 177 DY118
Ederline Av, SW16 141 DM97
Edgar Cl, Swan. BR8 147 FF97
Edgar Kail Way, SE22 102 DS84
Edgarley Ter, SW6 99 CY81
Edgar Rd, E3 85 EB69
Hounslow TW4 116 BZ87
Romford RM6 70 EX59
South Croydon CR2 160 DR109
West Drayton UB7 76 BL73
Westerham (Tats.) TN16 178 EK121
Edgbaston Dr, Rad.
(Shenley) WD7 10 CL32
Edgbaston Rd, Wat. WD19 39 BV48
Edgeborough Way,
Brom. BR1 124 EK94
Edgebury, Chis. BR7 125 EP91
Edgebury Wk, Chis. BR7 125 EQ91
Edge Cl, Wey. KT13 152 BN108
Edgecombe Ho, SW19 119 CY88
Edgecoombe, S.Croy. CR2 160 DW108
Edgecoombe Cl, Kings.T. KT2 118 CR94
Edgecote Cl, W3
off Cheltenham Pl 80 CQ74
Edgecot Gro, N15
off Oulton Rd 66 DR57
Edgefield Av, Bark. IG11 87 ET66
Edgefield Cl, Dart. DA1 128 FP88
Edge Hill, SE18 105 EP79
SW19 119 CX94
Edge Hill Av, N3 64 DA55
Edge Hill Ct, SW19 119 CX94
Edgehill Ct, Walt. KT12
off St. Johns Dr 136 BW102
Edgehill Gdns, Dag. RM10 70 FA63
Edgehill Rd, W13 79 CJ71
Chislehurst BR7 125 EQ90
Mitcham CR4 141 DH95
Purley CR8 159 DN110
Edgeley, Lthd. (Bkhm) KT23 170 BY124
Edgeley La, SW4
off Edgeley Rd 101 DK83
Edgeley Rd, SW4 101 DK83
Edgell Cl, Vir.W. GU25 133 AZ97
Edgell Rd, Stai. TW18 113 BF92
Edgel St, SW18
off Ferrier St 100 DB84
Edgepoint Cl, SE27
off Knights Hill 121 DP92
Edge St, W8
off Kensington Ch St 82 DA74
Edgewood Dr, Orp. BR6 163 ET106
Edgewood Grn, Croy. CR0 143 DX102
Edgeworth Av, NW4 63 CU57
Edgeworth Cl, NW4 63 CU57
Whyteleafe CR3 176 DU118
Edgeworth Cres, NW4 63 CU57
Edgeworth Rd, SE9 104 EJ84
Barnet EN4 28 DE42
Edgington Rd, SW16 121 DK93
Edgington Way, Sid. DA14 126 EW94
EDGWARE 42 CP50
⊖ Edgware 42 CP51
Edgwarebury Gdns, Edg. HA8 42 CN50
Edgwarebury La, Borwd.
(Elstree) WD6 42 CL45
Edgware HA8 42 CN49
H Edgware Comm Hosp,
Edg. HA8 42 CP52
Edgware Ct, Edg. HA8
off Cavendish Dr 42 CN51
⊖ Edgware Road 194 B7
Edgware Rd, NW2 63 CV60
NW9 62 CR55
W2 194 C8
Edgware Rd Sub, W2
off Edgware Rd 82 DE71
Edgware Way, Edg. HA8 42 CM49
Edinburgh Av, Rick.
(Mill End) WD3 22 BG44
Edinburgh Cl, E2
off Russia La 84 DW68
Pinner HA5 60 BX59

★ Place of interest ⇌ Railway station ⊖ London Underground station DLR Docklands Light Railway station Tra Tramlink station H Hospital Riv Pedestrian ferry landing stage

Edinburgh Cl, Uxbridge UB10 59 BP63
Edinburgh Ct, SW20 139 CX99
Edinburgh Cres, Wal.Cr. EN8 15 DY33
Edinburgh Dr, Abb.L. WD5 7 BU32
Romford RM7
off Eastern Av W 71 FC56
Staines TW18 114 BK93
Uxbridge (Denh.) UB9 57 BF58
Uxbridge (Ickhm) UB10 59 BP63
Edinburgh Gate, SW1 198 D4
Edinburgh Ho, W9 82 DC69
Edinburgh Ms, Til. RM18 111 GH82
Edinburgh Rd, E13 86 EH68
E17 67 EA57
N18 46 DU50
W7 97 CF75
Sutton SM1 140 DC103
Edington Rd, SE2 106 EV76
Enfield EN3 30 DW40
Edison Av, Horn. RM12 71 FF61
Edison Cl, E17
off Exeter Rd 67 EA57
Edison Cl, Hornchurch RM12
off Edison Av 71 FF60
Edison Ct, SE10 205 L8
Edison Dr, Sthl. UB1 78 CB72
Wembley HA9 62 CL61
Edison Gro, SE18 105 ET80
Edison Rd, N8 65 DK58
Bromley BR2 144 EG96
Enfield EN3 31 DZ40
Welling DA16 105 ET81
Edis St, NW1 82 DG67
Edith Cavell Cl, N19
off Hornsey Ri Gdns 65 DK59
Edith Gdns, Surb. KT5 138 CP101
Edith Gro, SW10 100 DC79
Edithna St, SW9 101 DL83
Edith Rd, E6 86 EK66
E15 off Chandos Rd 67 ED64
N11 45 DK52
SE25 142 DR99
SW19 120 DB93
W14 99 CY77
Orpington BR6 164 EU106
Romford RM6 70 EX58
Edith Row, SW6 100 DB81
Edith St, E2 84 DU68
Edith Summerskill Ho, SW6
off Clem Attlee Ct 99 CZ80
Edith Ter, SW10 100 DC80
Edith Vil, SW15
off Bective Rd 99 CY84
W14 99 CZ77
Edith Yd, SW10
off World's End Est 100 DC80
Edmansons Cl, N17
off Bruce Gro 46 DS53
Edmeston Cl, E9 85 DY65
Edmond Halley Way, SE10 205 H5
Edmonds Ct, W.Mol. KT8
off Avern Rd 136 CB98
EDMONTON, N9 46 DU49
⇌ Edmonton Green 46 DU47
Edmonton Grn, N9
off Hertford Rd 46 DV47
Edmonton Grn Shop Cen, N9 46 DV47
Edmund Gro, Felt. TW13 116 BZ89
Edmund Hurst Dr, E6 87 EP71
Edmund Rd, Grays
(Chaff.Hun.) RM16 109 FX75
Mitcham CR4 140 DE97
Orpington BR5 146 EW100
Rainham RM13 89 FE68
Welling DA16 106 EU83
Edmunds Av, Orp. BR5 146 EX97
Edmunds Cl, Hayes UB4 78 BW71
Edmund St, SE5 102 DR80
Edmunds Wk, N2 64 DE56
Edmunds Way, Slou. SL2 74 AV71
Edna Rd, SW20 139 CX96
Edna St, SW11 100 DE81
Edrich Ho, SW4 101 DL81
Edrick Rd, Edg. HA8 42 CQ51
Edrick Wk, Edg. HA8 42 CQ51
Edric Rd, SE14 103 DX80
Edridge Cl, Bushey WD23 24 CC43
Hornchurch RM12 72 FK64
Edridge Rd, Croy. CR0 142 DQ104
Edulf Rd, Borwd. WD6 26 CP39
Edward Amey Cl, Wat. WD25 24 BW36
Edward Av, E4 47 EB51
Morden SM4 140 DD99
Edward Cl, N9 46 DT45
NW2 63 CX63
Abbots Langley WD5 7 BT32
Grays (Chaff.Hun.) RM16 109 FX76
Hampton (Hmptn H.) TW12
off Edward Rd 116 CC92
Northolt UB5 78 BW68
Romford RM2 72 FJ55
Edward Ct, E16
off Alexandra St 86 EG71
Staines TW18
off Elizabeth Av 114 BJ93
Waltham Abbey EN9 16 EF33
Edwardes Pl, W8
off Edwardes Sq 99 CZ76
Edwardes Sq, W8 100 DA76
Edward Gro, Barn. EN4 28 DD43
Edward Ms, NW1 195 J1
Edward Pauling Ho, Felt. TW14
off Westmacott Dr 115 BT87
Edward Pl, SE8 103 DZ79
Edward Rd, E17 67 DX56
SE20 123 DX94
Barnet EN4 28 DD43
Bromley BR1 124 EH94
Chislehurst BR7 125 EP92
Coulsdon CR5 175 DK115
Croydon CR0 142 DS101
Feltham TW14 115 BR85
Hampton (Hmptn H.) TW12 116 CC92
Harrow HA2 60 CC55
Northolt UB5 78 BW68
Edward Rd, Romford RM6 70 EY58
Westerham (Bigg.H.) TN16 178 EL118
Edward's Av, Ruis. HA4 77 BV65
Edwards Cl, Brwd.
(Hutt.) CM13 55 GE44
Worcester Park KT4 139 CX103
Edwards Cotts, N1
off Compton Av 83 DP65
Edwards Ct, Slou. SL1 92 AS75
Waltham Cross EN8
off Turners Hill 15 DX31
Edwards Dr, N11
off Gordon Rd 45 DK52
Edward II Av, W.Byf.
(Byfleet) KT14 152 BM114
Edwards Gdns, Swan. BR8
off Ladds Way 147 FD98
Edwards La, N16 66 DR61
Edwards Ms, N1 83 DN66
W1 194 F9
Edward Sq, N1
off Caledonian Rd 83 DM67
SE16 203 L2
Edwards Rd, Belv. DA17 106 FA77
Edward St, E16 86 EG70
SE8 103 DZ79
SE14 103 DY80
Edwards Way, Brwd.
(Hutt.) CM13 55 GE44
Edwards Yd, Wem. HA0
off Mount Pleasant 80 CL67
Edward Temme Av, E15 86 EF66
Edward Tyler Rd, SE12 124 EH89
Edward Way, Ashf. TW15 114 BM89
Edwina Gdns, Ilf. IG4 68 EL57
Edwin Av, E6 87 EN68
Edwin Cl, Bexh. DA7 106 EZ79
Rainham RM13 89 FF69
Edwin Pl, Croy. CR0
off Cross Rd 142 DR102
Edwin Rd, Dart. DA2 127 FH90
Edgware HA8 42 CR51
Twickenham TW1, TW2 117 CF88
Edwin's Mead, E9
off Lindisfarne Way 67 DY63
Edwin St, E1 84 DW70
E16 86 EG71
Gravesend DA12 131 GH87
Edwyn Cl, Barn. EN5 27 CW44
Edwyn Ho, SW18
off Neville Gill Cl 120 DB86
Eel Brook Studios, SW6
off Moore Pk Rd 100 DA80
Eel Pie Island, Twick. TW1 117 CH88
Effie Pl, SW6 100 DA80
Effie Rd, SW6 100 DA80
Effingham Cl, Sutt. SM2 158 DB108
Effingham Common, Lthd.
(Eff.) KT24 169 BU123
Effingham Common Rd, Lthd.
(Eff.) KT24 169 BU123
Effingham Ct, Wok. GU22
off Constitution Hill 166 AY118
⇌ Effingham Junction 169 BU123
Effingham Rd, N8 65 DN57
SE12 124 EE85
Croydon CR0 141 DM101
Surbiton KT6 137 CH101
Effort St, SW17 120 DE92
Effra Par, SW2 121 DN85
Effra Rd, SW2 101 DN84
SW19 120 DB93
Egan Way, Hayes UB3 77 BS73
Egbert St, NW1 82 DG67
Egbury Ho, SW15
off Tangley Gro 119 CT86
Egdean Wk, Sev. TN13 191 FJ123
Egerton Av, Swan. BR8 127 FF94
Egerton Cl, Dart. DA1 127 FH88
Pinner HA5 59 BU56
Egerton Cres, SW3 198 C8
Egerton Dr, SE10 103 EB81
Egerton Gdns, NW4 63 CV56
NW10 81 CW67
SW3 198 B7
W13 79 CH72
Ilford IG3 69 ET62
Egerton Gdns Ms, SW3 198 C7
Egerton Pl, SW3 198 C7
Weybridge KT13 153 BQ107
Egerton Rd, N16 66 DT59
SE25 142 DS97
New Malden KT3 139 CT98
Twickenham TW2 117 CE87
Wembley HA0 80 CM66
Weybridge KT13 153 BQ107
Egerton Ter, SW3 198 C7
Egerton Way, Hayes UB3 95 BP80
Eggardon Ct, Nthlt. UB5
off Lancaster Rd 78 CC65
Egg Fm La, Kings L. WD4
off Station Rd 7 BP30
Egg Hall, Epp. CM16 18 EU29
EGHAM 113 BA93
⇌ Egham 113 BA92
Egham Bypass, Egh. TW20 113 AZ92
Egham Cl, SW19
off Winterfold Cl 119 CY89
Sutton SM3 139 CY103
Egham Cres, Sutt. SM3 139 CX104
Egham Hill, Egh. TW20 112 AX93
EGHAM HYTHE, Stai. TW18 113 BE93
★ Egham Mus, Egh. TW20 113 BA92
Egham Rd, E13 86 EH71
EGHAM WICK, Egh. TW20 112 AU94
Eglantine La, Dart.
(Hort.Kir.) DA4 148 FN101
Eglantine Rd, SW18 120 DC85
Egleston Rd, Mord. SM4 140 DB100
Egley Dr, Wok. GU22 166 AX122
Egley Rd, Wok. GU22 166 AX122
Eglington Ct, SE17
off Carter St 102 DQ79
Eglington Rd, E4 47 ED45
Eglinton Hill, SE18 105 EP79
Eglinton Rd, SE18 105 EN79
Swanscombe DA10 130 FZ86
Eglise Rd, Warl. CR6 177 DY117
Egliston Ms, SW15 99 CW83
Egliston Rd, SW15 99 CW83
Eglon Ms, NW1
off Berkley Rd 82 DF66
Egmont Av, Surb. KT6 138 CM102
Egmont Pk Rd, Tad. KT20 183 CU125
Egmont Rd, N.Mal. KT3 139 CT98
Surbiton KT6 138 CM102
Sutton SM2 158 DC108
Walton-on-Thames KT12 135 BV101
Egmont St, SE14 103 DX80
Egmont Way, Tad. KT20
off Oatlands Rd 173 CY119
Egremont Ho, SE13
off Conington Rd 103 EB82
Egremont Rd, SE27 121 DN90
Egret Way, Hayes UB4 78 BX71
Eider Cl, E7 68 EF64
Hayes UB4 off Cygnet Way 78 BX71
Eighteenth Rd, Mitch. CR4 141 DL98
Eighth Av, E12 69 EM63
Hayes UB3 77 BU74
Eileen Rd, SE25 142 DR99
Eindhoven Cl, Cars. SM5 140 DG102
Eisenhower Dr, E6 86 EL71
Elaine Gro, NW5 64 DG64
Elam Cl, SE5 101 DP82
Elam St, SE5 101 DP82
Eland Pl, Croy. CR0
off Eland Rd 141 DP104
Eland Rd, SW11 100 DF83
Croydon CR0 141 DP104
Elan Rd, S.Ock. RM15 91 FU71
Elba Pl, SE17 201 J8
Elberon Av, Croy. CR0 141 DJ100
Elbe St, SW6 100 DC82
Elborough Rd, SE25 142 DU99
Elborough St, SW18 120 DA88
Elbow Meadow, Slou.
(Colnbr.) SL3 93 BF81
Elbury Dr, E16 86 EG72
Elcho St, SW11 100 DE80
Elcot Av, SE15 102 DV80
Elder Av, N8 65 DL57
Elderbek Cl, Wal.Cr. EN7 14 DU28
Elderberry Cl, Ilf. IG6
off Hazel La 49 EP52
Elderberry Gro, SE27
off Linton Gro 122 DQ92
Elderberry Rd, W5 98 CL75
Elderberry Way, E6
off Vicarage La 87 EM69
Watford WD25 23 BV35
Elder Cl, N20 44 DB47
Sidcup DA15 125 ET88
West Drayton UB7
off Yew Av 76 BL73
Elder Ct, Bushey
(Bushey Hth) WD23 41 CE47
Elderfield Pl, SW17 121 DH91
Elderfield Rd, E5 66 DW63
Slough (Stoke P.) SL2 74 AT65
Elderfield Wk, E11 68 EH57
Elderflower Way, E15 86 EE66
Elder Gdns, SE27 122 DQ91
Elder Oak Cl, SE20 142 DV95
Elder Rd, SE27 122 DQ92
Eldersley Cl, Red. RH1 184 DF132
Elderslie Cl, Beck. BR3 143 EB99
Elderslie Rd, SE9 125 EN85
Elder St, E1 197 P6
Elderton Rd, SE26 123 DY91
Eldertree Pl, Mitch. CR4
off Eldertree Way 141 DJ95
Eldertree Way, Mitch. CR4 141 DH95
Elder Wk, N1 off Essex Rd 83 DP67
Elder Way, Rain. RM13 90 FK69
Slough (Langley) SL3 93 AZ75
Elderwood Pl, SE27
off Elder Rd 122 DQ92
Eldon Av, Borwd. WD6 26 CN40
Croydon CR0 142 DW103
Hounslow TW5 96 CA80
Eldon Gro, NW3 64 DD64
Eldon Pk, SE25 142 DV98
Eldon Rd, E17 67 DZ56
N9 46 DW47
N22 45 DP53
W8 100 DB76
Caterham CR3 176 DR121
Eldon St, EC2 197 L7
Eldon Way, NW10 80 CP68
Eldred Dr, Orp. BR5 146 EW103
Eldred Gdns, Upmin. RM14 73 FS59
Eldred Rd, Bark. IG11 87 ES67
Eldrick Ct, Felt. TW14
off Kilross Rd 115 BR88
Eldridge Cl, Felt. TW14 115 BU88
Eleanor Av, Epsom KT19 156 CR110
Eleanor Cl, N15
off Arnold Rd 66 DT55
SE16 203 H4
Eleanor Cres, NW7 43 CX49
Eleanor Cross Rd, Wal.Cr. EN8 15 DY34
Eleanor Gdns, Barn. EN5 27 CX43
Dagenham RM8 70 EZ62
Eleanor Gro, SW13 98 CS83
Uxbridge (Ickhm) UB10 59 BP62
Eleanor Rd, E8 84 DV66
E15 86 EF65
N11 45 DL51
Gerrards Cross
(Chal.St.P.) SL9 36 AW53
Waltham Cross EN8 15 DY33
Eleanor St, E3 85 EA69
Eleanor Wk, SE18
off Samuel St 105 EM77
Eleanor Way, Brwd. CM14 54 FX50
Waltham Cross EN8 15 DZ34
Electric Av, SW9 101 DN84
Enfield EN3 31 DZ36
Electric La, SW9 101 DN84
Electric Par, E18
off George La 48 EG54
Surbiton KT6 137 CK100
Elektron Ho, E14
off Blackwall Way 85 ED73
⇌ Elephant & Castle 201 H8
⊖ Elephant & Castle 201 H8
Elephant & Castle, SE1 200 G7
Elephant & Castle Shop Cen, SE1
off Elephant & Castle 102 DQ77
Elephant La, SE16 202 F4
Elephant Rd, SE17 201 H8
Elers Rd, W13 97 CJ75
Hayes UB3 95 BR77
Eleven Acre Ri, Loug. IG10 33 EM41
Eley Est, N18 46 DW50
Eley Rd, N18 47 DX50
Elfindale Rd, SE24 122 DQ85
Elfin Gro, Tedd. TW11
off Broad St 117 CF92
Elford Cl, SE3 104 EH84
Elfort Rd, N5 65 DN63
Elfrida Cres, SE6 123 EA91
Elfrida Rd, Wat. WD18 24 BW43
Elf Row, E1 84 DW73
Elfwine Rd, W7 79 CE71
Elgal Cl, Orp. BR6
off Orchard Rd 163 EP106
Elgar Av, NW10
off Mitchellbrook Way 80 CR65
SW16 141 DL97
W5 98 CL75
Surbiton KT5 138 CP101
Elgar Cl, E13 off Bushey Rd 86 EJ68
SE8 off Comet St 103 EA80
Borehamwood
(Elstree) WD6 41 CK45
Buckhurst Hill IG9 48 EK47
Uxbridge UB10 58 BN61
Elgar Gdns, Til. RM18 111 GH81
Elgar St, SE16 203 L6
Elgin Av, W9 82 DB69
W12 99 CU75
Ashford TW15 115 BQ93
Harrow HA3 41 CH54
Romford RM3 52 FP52
Elgin Cl, W12 99 CV75
Elgin Cres, W11 81 CZ72
Caterham CR3 176 DU122
Hounslow (Hthrw Air.) TW6
off Eastern Perimeter Rd 95 BS82
Elgin Dr, Nthwd. HA6 39 BS52
Elgin Ms, W11
off Ladbroke Gro 81 CY72
Elgin Ms N, W9
off Randolph Av 82 DB69
Elgin Ms S, W9
off Randolph Av 82 DB69
Elgin Pl, Wey. KT13
off St. George's Av 153 BQ107
Elgin Rd, N22 45 DJ54
Croydon CR0 142 DT102
Ilford IG3 69 ES60
Sutton SM1 140 DC104
Wallington SM6 159 DJ107
Waltham Cross (Chsht) EN8 14 DW30
Weybridge KT13 152 BN106
Elgood Av, Nthwd. HA6 39 BU51
Elgood Cl, W11
off Avondale Pk Rd 81 CY73
Elham Cl, Brom. BR1 124 EK94
Elia Ms, N1 196 F1
Elias Pl, SW8 101 DN79
Elia St, N1 196 F1
Elibank Rd, SE9 105 EN84
Elim Est, SE1 201 M6
Elim Way, E13 86 EF69
Eliot Bk, SE23 122 DV89
Eliot Cotts, SE3
off Eliot Pl 104 EE82
Eliot Ct, N15
off Tynemouth Rd 66 DT56
Eliot Dr, Har. HA2 60 CB61
Eliot Gdns, SW15 99 CU84
Eliot Hill, SE13 103 EC82
Eliot Ms, NW8 82 DC68
Eliot Pk, SE13 103 EC83
Eliot Pl, SE3 104 EE82
Eliot Rd, Dag. RM9 70 EX63
Dartford DA1 128 FP85
Eliot Vale, SE3 103 ED82
Elizabethan Cl, Stai. (Stanw.) TW19
off Elizabethan Way 114 BK87
Elizabethan Way, Stai.
(Stanw.) TW19 114 BK87
Elizabeth Av, N1 84 DQ66
Amersham HP6 20 AV39
Enfield EN2 29 DP41
Ilford IG1 69 ER61
Staines TW18 114 BJ93
Elizabeth Blackwell Ho, N22
off Progress Way 45 DN53
Elizabeth Br, SW1 199 H9
Elizabeth Cl, E14
off Grundy St 85 EB72
W9 off Randolph Av 82 DC70
Barnet EN5 27 CX41
Romford RM7 51 FB53
Sutton SM1 157 CZ105
Tilbury RM18 111 GH82
Elizabeth Clyde Cl, N15 66 DS56
Elizabeth Cotts, Rich. TW9 98 CM81
Elizabeth Ct, SW1 199 N7
Gravesend DA11
off St. James's Rd 131 GG86
Watford WD17 23 BT38
Woodford Green IG8
off Navestock Cres 48 EJ52
Elizabeth Dr, Epp.
(They.B.) CM16 33 ES36
Elizabeth Est, SE17 102 DR79
Elizabeth Fry Pl, SE18 104 EL81
Elizabeth Fry Rd, E8
off Lamb La 84 DV66
Elizabeth Gdns, W3 81 CT74
Isleworth TW7
off Worple Rd 97 CG84
Stanmore HA7 41 CJ51
Sunbury-on-Thames TW16 136 BW97
Elizabeth Huggins Cotts,
Grav. DA11 131 GG89
Elizabeth Ms, NW3 82 DE65
Elizabeth Pl, N15 66 DR56
Elizabeth Ride, N9 46 DV45
Elizabeth Rd, E6 86 EK67
N15 66 DS57
Brentwood (Pilg.Hat.) CM15 54 FV44
Grays RM16 110 FZ76
Rainham RM13 89 FH71
Elizabeth Sq, SE16 203 K1
Elizabeth St, SW1 198 G8
Greenhithe DA9 129 FS85
Elizabeth Ter, SE9 125 EM86
Elizabeth Way, SE19 122 DR94
Feltham TW13 116 BW91
Orpington BR5 146 EW99
Slough (Stoke P.) SL2 74 AT67
Eliza Cook Cl, Green. DA9
off London Rd 129 FW85
Elkanette Ms, N20
off Ridgeview Rd 44 DC47
Elkington Rd, E13 86 EH70
Elkins, The, Rom. RM1 51 FE54
Elkins Rd, Slou. (Hedg.) SL2 56 AS61
Elkstone Rd, W10 81 CZ71
Ellaline Rd, W6 99 CX79
Ellanby Cres, N18 46 DV50
Elland Rd, SE15 102 DW84
Walton-on-Thames KT12 136 BX103
Ella Rd, N8 65 DL59
Ellement Cl, Pnr. HA5 60 BX57
Ellenborough Pl, SW15 99 CU84
Ellenborough Rd, N22 46 DQ53
Sidcup DA14 126 EX92
Ellenbridge Way, S.Croy. CR2 160 DS109
Ellenbrook Cl, Wat. WD24
off Hatfield Rd 23 BV39
Ellen Cl, Brom. BR1 144 EK97
Ellen Ct, N9
off Densworth Gro 46 DW47
Ellen St, E1 84 DU72
Ellen Webb Dr, Har.
(Wldste) HA3 61 CE55
Elleray Rd, Tedd. TW11 117 CF93
Ellerby St, SW6 99 CX81
Ellerdale Cl, NW3
off Ellerdale Rd 64 DC63
Ellerdale Rd, NW3 64 DC64
Ellerdale St, SE13 103 EB84
Ellerdine Rd, Houns. TW3 96 CC84
Ellerker Gdns, Rich. TW10 118 CL86
Ellerman Av, Twick. TW2 116 BZ88
Ellerman Rd, Til. RM18 111 GF82
Ellerslie, Grav. DA12 131 GK87
Ellerslie Gdns, NW10 81 CU67
Ellerslie Rd, W12 81 CV74
Ellerslie Sq Ind Est, SW2 121 DL85
Ellerton Gdns, Dag. RM9 88 EW66
Ellerton Rd, SW13 99 CU81
SW18 120 DD88
SW20 119 CU94
Dagenham RM9 88 EW66
Surbiton KT6 138 CM103
Ellery Rd, SE19 122 DR94
Ellery St, SE15 102 DV82
Ellesborough Cl, Wat. WD19 40 BW50
Ellesmere Av, NW7 42 CR48
Beckenham BR3 143 EB96
Ellesmere Cl, E11 68 EF57
Ruislip HA4 59 BQ59
Ellesmere Dr, S.Croy. CR2 160 DV114
Ellesmere Gdns, Ilf. IG4 68 EL57
Ellesmere Gro, Barn. EN5 27 CZ43
Ellesmere Pl, Walt. KT12 153 BS106
Ellesmere Rd, E3 85 DY68
NW10 63 CU64
W4 98 CR79
Greenford UB6 78 CC70
Twickenham TW1 117 CJ86
Weybridge KT13 153 BR107
Ellesmere St, E14 85 EB72
Ellice Rd, Oxt. RH8 188 EF129
Elliman Av, Slou. SL2 74 AS73
Ellingfort Rd, E8 84 DV66
Ellingham Rd, E15 67 ED63
W12 99 CU75
Chessington KT9 155 CK107
Ellington Rd, N10 65 DH56
Feltham TW13 115 BT91
Hounslow TW3 96 CB82
Ellington St, N7 83 DN65
Ellington Way, Epsom KT18 173 CV117
Elliot Cl, E15 86 EE66
Elliot Rd, NW4 63 CV58
Stanmore HA7 41 CG51
Elliott Av, Ruis. HA4 59 BV61
Elliott Cl, Wem. HA9 62 CM62
Elliott Gdns, Rom. RM3 51 FH53
Shepperton TW17 134 BN98
Elliott Rd, SW9 101 DP80
W4 98 CS77
Bromley BR2 144 EK98
Thornton Heath CR7 141 DP98
Elliotts Cl, Uxb. (Cowley) UB8 76 BJ71
Elliotts La, West.
(Brasted) TN16 180 EW124
Elliott's Pl, N1
off St. Peters St 83 DP67
Elliott Sq, NW3 82 DE66
Elliotts Row, SE11 200 F8
Elliott St, Grav. DA12 131 GK87
Ellis Av, Ger.Cr.
(Chal.St.P.) SL9 37 AZ53
Rainham RM13 89 FG71
Slough SL1 92 AS75
Ellis Cl, NW10 off High Rd 81 CV65
SE9 125 EQ89
Coulsdon CR5 175 DM120
Elliscombe Rd, SE7 104 EJ78
Ellis Ct, W7 79 CF71
Ellis Fm Cl, Wok. GU22 166 AX122
Ellisfield Dr, SW15 119 CT87
Ellison Gdns, Sthl. UB2 96 BZ77
Ellison Ho, SE13
off Lewisham Rd 103 EC82
Ellison Rd, SW13 99 CT82
SW16 121 DK94
Sidcup DA15 125 ER88
Ellis Rd, Couls. CR5 175 DM120
Mitcham CR4 140 DF100
Southall UB2 78 CC74
Ellis St, SW1 198 E8
Elliston Ho, SE18 105 EN77
Ellis Way, Dart. DA1 128 FM89
Ellmore Cl, Rom. RM3 51 FH53
Ellora Rd, SW16 121 DK92
Ellsworth St, E2 84 DV69
Ellwood Ct, W9
off Clearwell Dr 82 DB70
Ellwood Gdns, Wat. WD25 7 BV34

A B C D E F G H I J K L M N O P Q R S T U V W X Y Z

★ Place of interest ⇌ Railway station ⊖ London Underground station DLR Docklands Light Railway station Tra Tramlink station H Hospital Riv Pedestrian ferry landing stage

250

Ellwood Ri, Ch.St.G. HP8 . . . . . 36 AW47
Elmar Rd, N15. . . . . 66 DR56
Elm Av, W5 . . . . 80 CL74
Carshalton SM5 . . . . 158 DF110
Ruislip HA4. . . . . 59 BU60
Upminster RM14 . . . . 72 FP62
Watford WD19. . . . . 40 BY45
Elmbank, N14 . . . . 45 DL45
Elm Bk, Brom. BR1 . . . . 144 EK96
Elmbank Av, Barn. EN5 . . . . . . 27 CW42
Egham (Eng.Grn) TW20 . . . 112 AV93
Elmbank Gdns, SW13. . . . . 98 CS82
Elmbank Way, W7. . . . . 79 CD71
Elmbourne Dr, Belv. DA17 . . . 107 FB77
Elmbourne Rd, SW17 . . . . 120 DG90
Elmbridge Av, Surb. KT5 . . . . 138 CP99
Elmbridge Cl, Ruis. HA4 . . . . . 59 BU58
Elmbridge Dr, Ruis. HA4. . . . . 59 BT57
Elmbridge La, Wok. GU22. . . . 167 AZ119
★ Elmbridge Mus,
Wey. KT13. . . . . 152 BN105
Elmbridge Rd, Ilf. IG6 . . . . 50 EU51
Elmbridge Wk, E8
off Wilman Gro. 84 DU66
Elmbrook Cl, Sun. TW16. . . . . 135 BV95
Elmbrook Gdns, SE9 . . . . 104 EL84
Elmbrook Rd, Sutt. SM1. . . . . 157 CZ105
Elm Cl, E11 . . . . 68 EH58
N19 off Hargrave Pk 65 DJ61
NW4 . . . . 63 CX57
SW20 off Grand Dr. 139 CW98
Buckhurst Hill IG9. . . . . 48 EK47
Carshalton SM5 . . . . 140 DF102
Dartford DA1. . . . . 128 FJ88
Harrow HA2 . . . . 60 CB58
Hayes UB3 . . . . 77 BU72
Leatherhead KT22. . . . . 171 CH122
Romford RM7. . . . . 51 FB54
South Croydon CR2 . . . . . . 160 DS107
Staines (Stanw.) TW19 . . . . 114 BK88
Surbiton KT5. . . . . 138 CQ101
Tadworth (Box H.) KT20 . . 182 CQ130
Twickenham TW2 . . . . 116 CB89
Waltham Abbey EN9 . . . . . . 15 ED34
Warlingham CR6. . . . . 177 DX117
Woking GU21 . . . . 166 AX115
Woking (Send M.) GU23. . . 168 BG124
ELM CORNER, Wok. GU23. . . . 168 BN119
Elmcote Way, Rick.
(Crox.Grn) WD3. . . . . 22 BM44
Elm Ct, EC4. . . . . 196 D10
Mitcham CR4
off Armfield Cres 140 DF96
Sunbury-on-Thames TW16. 115 BT94
Elmcourt Rd, SE27 . . . . 121 DP89
Elm Cres, W5 . . . . 80 CL74
Kingston upon Thames KT2. 138 CL95
Elmcroft, N8 . . . . 65 DM57
Leatherhead KT23. . . . . 170 CA124
Elm Cft, Slou. (Datchet) SL3. . . 92 AW81
Elmcroft Av, E11 . . . . 68 EH57
N9 . . . . 30 DV44
NW11. . . . . 63 CZ59
Sidcup DA15. . . . . 125 ET86
Elmcroft Cl, E11 . . . . 68 EH56
W5. 79 CK72
Chessington KT9 . . . . 138 CL104
Feltham TW14 . . . . 115 BT86
Elmcroft Cres, NW11 . . . . 63 CY59
Harrow HA2 . . . . 60 CA55
Elmcroft Dr, Ashf. TW15 . . . . 114 BN92
Chessington KT9 . . . . 138 CL104
Elmcroft Gdns, NW9 . . . . 62 CN57
Elmcroft Rd, Orp. BR6 . . . . . . 146 EU101
Elmcroft St, E5 . . . . 66 DW63
Elmdale Rd, N13. . . . . 45 DM50
Elmdene, Surb. KT5 . . . . 138 CQ102
Elmdene Av, Horn. RM11 . . . . 72 FM57
Elmdene Cl, Beck. BR3 . . . . . . 143 DZ99
Elmdene Ct, Wok. GU22
off Constitution Hill. 166 AY118
Elmdene Rd, SE18 . . . . 105 EP78
Elmdon Rd, Houns. TW4 . . . . . 96 BX82
Hounslow (Hatt.Cr.) TW6 . . . 95 BT83
South Ockendon RM15
off Erriff Dr 91 FU71
Elm Dr, Har. HA2 . . . . 60 CB58
Leatherhead KT22. . . . . 171 CH122
Sunbury-on-Thames TW16. 136 BW96
Swanley BR8. . . . . 147 FD96
Waltham Cross
(Chsht) EN8. . . . . 15 DY28
Woking (Chobham) GU24 . 150 AT110
Elmer Av, Rom.
(Hav.at.Bow.) RM4 . . . . 51 FE48
Elmer Cl, Enf. EN2 . . . . 29 DM41
Rainham RM13. . . . . 89 FG66
Elmer Cotts, Lthd. KT22. . . . 171 CG123
Elmer Gdns, Edg. HA8 . . . . . . 42 CP52
Isleworth TW7. . . . . 97 CD83
Rainham RM13. . . . . 89 FG66
Elmer Ms, Lthd. (Fetch.) KT22 . 171 CG123
Elmer Rd, SE6. . . . . 123 EC87
Elmers Dr, Tedd. TW11
off Kingston Rd. 117 CH93
ELMERS END, Beck. BR3 . . . . 143 DY97
⇌ Elmers End 143 DX98
Tram Elmers End 143 DX98
Elmers End Rd, SE20 . . . . 142 DW96
Beckenham BR3 . . . . 142 DW96
Elmerside Rd, Beck. BR3 . . . . 143 DY98
Elmers Rd, SE25. . . . . 142 DU101
Elm Fm Caravan Pk, Cher.
(Lyne) KT16. . . . . 133 BC101
Elmfield, Lthd. (Bkhm) KT23. . 170 CA123
Elmfield Av, N8. . . . . 65 DL57
Mitcham CR4 . . . . 140 DG95
Teddington TW11. . . . . 117 CF92
Elmfield Cl, Grav. DA11 . . . . . 131 GH88
Harrow HA1 . . . . 61 CE61
Potters Bar EN6. . . . . 11 CY33
Elmfield Pk, Brom. BR1 . . . . . 144 EG97
Elmfield Rd, E4. . . . . 47 EC47
E17 . . . . 67 DX58
N2 . . . . 64 DD55
SW17. . . . . 120 DG89
Bromley BR1. . . . . 144 EG97
Potters Bar EN6. . . . . 11 CY33
Southall UB2. . . . . 96 BY76
Elmfield Way, W9 . . . . 82 DA71
Elmfield Way,
South Croydon CR2 . . . . . 160 DT109
Elm Friars Wk, NW1 . . . . 83 DK66
Elm Gdns, N2. . . . . 64 DC55
Enfield EN2. . . . . 30 DR38
Epping (N.Wld Bas.) CM16. . 19 FB26
Epsom KT18 . . . . 173 CW119
Esher (Clay.) KT10. . . . . 155 CF107
Mitcham CR4 . . . . 141 DK98
Elmgate Av, Felt. TW13 . . . . . 115 BV90
Elmgate Gdns, Edg. HA8 . . . . . 42 CR50
Elm Grn, W3 . . . . 80 CS72
Elmgreen Cl, E15
off Church St N. 86 EE67
Elm Gro, N8 . . . . 65 DL58
NW2 . . . . 63 CX63
SE15 . . . . 102 DT82
SW19. . . . . 119 CY94
Caterham CR3. . . . . 176 DS122
Epsom KT18 . . . . 156 CQ114
Erith DA8. . . . . 107 FD80
Harrow HA2 . . . . 60 CA59
Hornchurch RM11 . . . . 72 FL58
Kingston upon Thames KT2 . 138 CL95
Orpington BR6 . . . . 145 ET102
Sutton SM1. . . . . 158 DB105
Watford WD24. . . . . 23 BU37
West Drayton UB7
off Willow Av. 76 BM73
Woodford Green IG8 . . . . . . 48 EF50
Elmgrove Cres, Har. HA1 . . . . . 61 CF57
Elmgrove Gdns, Har. HA1 . . . . 61 CG57
Elm Gro Par, Wall. SM6
off Butter Hill. 140 DG104
Elm Gro Rd, SW13 . . . . 99 CU82
W5. . . . . 80 CL75
Cobham KT11 . . . . 170 BX116
Elmgrove Rd, Croy. CR0. . . . . 142 DV101
Harrow HA1 . . . . 61 CF57
Weybridge KT13. . . . . 152 BN105
Elm Hall Gdns, E11. . . . . 68 EH57
Elmhurst, Belv. DA17 . . . . 106 EY79
Elmhurst Av, N2 . . . . 64 DD55
Mitcham CR4 . . . . 121 DH94
Elmhurst Dr, E18 . . . . 48 EG54
Hornchurch RM11 . . . . 72 FJ60
Elmhurst Gdns, E18
off Elmhurst Dr. 48 EH53
Elmhurst Mans, SW4
off Edgeley Rd. 101 DK83
Elmhurst Rd, E7 . . . . 86 EH66
N17 . . . . 46 DT54
SE9 . . . . 124 EL89
Enfield EN3. . . . . 30 DW37
Slough SL3. . . . . 93 BA76
Elmhurst St, SW4. . . . . 101 DK83
Elmhurst Vil, SE15
off Cheltenham Rd 102 DW84
Elmhurst Way, Loug. IG10 . . . . 49 EM45
Elmington Cl, Bex. DA5 . . . . . 127 FB86
Elmington Est, SE5. . . . . 102 DR80
Elmington Rd, SE5 . . . . 102 DR81
Elmira St, SE13. . . . . 103 EB83
Elm La, SE6. . . . . 123 DZ89
Woking GU23 . . . . 169 BP118
Elm Lawn Cl, Uxb. UB8
off Park Rd 76 BL66
Elmlea Dr, Hayes UB3
off Grange Rd 77 BS71
Elmlee Cl, Chis. BR7. . . . . 125 EM93
Elmley Cl, E6
off Northumberland Rd . . . 86 EL71
Elmley St, SE18 . . . . 105 ER77
Elm Ms, Rich. TW10
off Grove Rd 118 CM86
Elmore Cl, Wem. HA0. . . . . 80 CL68
Elmore Rd, E11 . . . . 67 EC62
Coulsdon CR5. . . . . 174 DF121
Enfield EN3. . . . . 31 DX39
Elmores, Loug. IG10 . . . . 33 EN41
Elmore St, N1 . . . . 84 DQ66
Elm Par, Horn. RM12
off St. Nicholas Av 71 FH63
ELM PARK, Horn. RM12 . . . . . . 71 FH64
⊖ Elm Park 71 FH63
Elm Pk, SW2. . . . . 121 DM86
Stanmore HA7 . . . . 41 CH50
Elm Pk Av, N15. . . . . 66 DT57
Hornchurch RM12. . . . . 71 FG63
Elm Pk Ct, Pnr. HA5 . . . . 60 BW55
Elm Pk Gdns, NW4. . . . . 63 CX57
SW10. . . . . 100 DD78
Elmpark Gdns, S.Croy. CR2 . . 160 DW110
Elm Pk La, SW3 . . . . 100 DD78
Elm Pk Mans, SW10
off Park Wk 100 DC79
Elm Pk Rd, E10 . . . . 67 DY60
N3. . . . . 43 CZ52
N21 . . . . 46 DQ45
SE25 . . . . 142 DT97
SW3. . . . . 100 DD79
Pinner HA5 . . . . 40 BW54
Elm Pl, SW7 . . . . 100 DD78
Elm Quay Ct, SW8 . . . . 101 DK79
Elm Rd, E7 . . . . 86 EF65
E11. . . . . 67 ED61
E17 . . . . 67 EC57
N22 off Granville Rd. 45 DP53
SW14. . . . . 98 CQ83
Barnet EN5 . . . . 27 CZ42
Beckenham BR3 . . . . 143 DZ96
Chessington KT9 . . . . 156 CL105
Dartford DA1. . . . . 128 FK88
Epsom KT17 . . . . 157 CT107
Erith DA8. . . . . 107 FG81
Esher (Clay.) KT10. . . . . 155 CF107
Feltham TW14 . . . . 115 BR88
Gravesend DA12. . . . . 131 GJ90
Grays RM17. . . . . 110 GC79
Greenhithe DA9 . . . . 129 FS86
Kingston upon Thames KT2. 138 CM95
Leatherhead KT22. . . . . 171 CH122
New Malden KT3 . . . . 138 CR98
Orpington BR6 . . . . 164 EU108
Purley CR8 . . . . 159 DP113
Redhill RH1 . . . . 184 DE134
Romford RM7. . . . . 51 FB54
Sidcup DA14. . . . . 126 EU91
South Ockendon
(Aveley) RM15 . . . . 90 FQ74
Elm Rd, Thornton Heath CR7 . 142 DR98
Wallington SM6 . . . . 140 DG102
Warlingham CR6. . . . . 177 DX117
Wembley HA9. . . . . 62 CL64
Westerham TN16. . . . . 189 ES125
Woking GU21 . . . . 166 AX118
Woking (Horsell) GU21. . . . 167 AZ115
Elm Rd W, Sutt. SM3 . . . . 139 CZ101
Elm Row, NW3. . . . . 64 DC62
Elmroyd Av, Pot.B. EN6. . . . . . . 11 CZ33
Elmroyd Cl, Pot.B. EN6. . . . . . . 11 CZ33
Elms, The, SW13. . . . . 99 CT83
Elms Av, N10. . . . . 65 DH55
NW4 . . . . 63 CX57
Elmscott Gdns, N21 . . . . 30 DQ44
Elmscott Rd, Brom. BR1. . . . . 124 EF92
Elms Ct, Wem. HA0 . . . . 61 CF63
Elms Cres, SW4 . . . . 121 DJ86
Elmscroft Gdns, Pot.B. EN6 . . . 11 CY32
Elmsdale Rd, E17 . . . . 67 DZ56
Elms Fm Rd, Horn. RM12. . . . . . 72 FJ64
Elms Gdns, Dag. RM9 . . . . 70 EZ63
Wembley HA0. . . . . 61 CG63
Elmshaw Rd, SW15 . . . . 119 CU85
Elmshorn, Epsom KT17 . . . . . 173 CW116
Elmshurst Cres, N2. . . . . 64 DD56
Elmside, Croy.
(New Adgtn) CR0 . . . . 161 EB107
Elmside Rd, Wem. HA9 . . . . . . 62 CN62
Elms La, Wem. HA0 . . . . 61 CG63
Elmsleigh Av, Har. HA3 . . . . . . 61 CH56
Elmsleigh Cen, The,
Stai. TW18 . . . . 113 BF91
Elmsleigh Ct, Sutt. SM1 . . . . . 140 DB104
Elmsleigh Rd, Stai. TW18 . . . . 113 BF92
Twickenham TW2 . . . . 117 CD89
Elmslie Cl, Epsom KT18 . . . . . 156 CQ114
Woodford Green IG8 . . . . . . 49 EM51
Elmslie Pt, E3 . . . . 85 DZ71
Elms Ms, W2. . . . . 82 DD73
Elms Pk Av, Wem. HA0. . . . . . . 61 CG63
Elms Rd, SW4. . . . . 121 DJ85
Gerrards Cross
(Chal.St.P.) SL9 . . . . 36 AY52
Harrow HA3 . . . . 41 CE52
ELMSTEAD, Chis. BR7 . . . . 124 EK92
Elmstead Av, Chis. BR7 . . . . . 125 EM92
Wembley HA9. . . . . 62 CL60
Elmstead Cl, N20 . . . . 44 DA47
Epsom KT19 . . . . 156 CS106
Sevenoaks TN13 . . . . 190 FE122
Elmstead Cres, Well. DA16 . . . 106 EW79
Elmstead Gdns,
Wor.Pk. KT4. . . . . 139 CU104
Elmstead Glade, Chis. BR7. . . 125 EM93
Elmstead La, Chis. BR7 . . . . . 125 EM92
Elmstead Rd, Erith DA8 . . . . . 107 FE81
Ilford IG3. . . . . 69 ES61
West Byfleet KT14. . . . . 152 BG113
⇌ Elmstead Woods. 124 EL93
Elmstone Rd, SW6 . . . . 100 DA81
Elm St, WC1 . . . . 196 C5
Elmsway, Ashf. TW15 . . . . 114 BM92
Elmswood, Lthd.
(Bkhm) KT23 . . . . 170 BZ124
Elmsworth Av, Houns. TW3 . . . 96 CB82
Elm Ter, NW2 . . . . 64 DA62
SE9 . . . . 125 EN86
Grays RM20 . . . . 109 FV79
Harrow HA3 . . . . 41 CD52
Elmton Way, E5
off Rendlesham Rd. 66 DU62
Elm Tree Av, Esher KT10. . . . . 137 CD101
Elm Tree Cl, NW8 . . . . 82 DD69
Ashford TW15
off Convent Rd 115 BP92
Chertsey KT16. . . . . 133 BE103
Northolt UB5. . . . . 78 BZ68
Elmtree Cl, W.Byf.
(Byfleet) KT14 . . . . 152 BL113
Elm Tree Rd, NW8. . . . . 82 DD69
Elmtree Rd, Tedd. TW11. . . . . 117 CE91
Elm Tree Wk, Rick.
(Chorl.) WD3 . . . . 21 BF42
Elm Wk, NW3 . . . . 64 DA61
SW20. . . . . 139 CW98
Orpington BR6 . . . . 145 EM104
Radlett WD7 . . . . 25 CF36
Romford RM2 . . . . 71 FG55
Elm Way, N11 . . . . 44 DG51
NW10 . . . . 62 CS63
Brentwood CM14 . . . . 54 FU48
Epsom KT19 . . . . 156 CR106
Rickmansworth WD3 . . . . . . 38 BH46
Worcester Park KT4 . . . . . . 139 CW104
Elmwood Av, N13. . . . . 45 DL50
Borehamwood WD6 . . . . 26 CP42
Feltham TW13 . . . . 115 BU89
Harrow HA3 . . . . 61 CG57
Elmwood Cl, Ashtd. KT21. . . . 171 CK117
Epsom KT17 . . . . 157 CU108
Wallington SM6 . . . . 140 DG103
Elmwood Ct, SW11. . . . . 101 DH81
Ashtead KT21
off Elmwood Cl. 171 CK117
Wembley HA0. . . . . 61 CG62
Elmwood Cres, NW9 . . . . 62 CQ56
Elmwood Dr, Bex. DA5. . . . . . . 126 EY87
Epsom KT17 . . . . 157 CU107
Elmwood Gdns, W7 . . . . 79 CE72
Elmwood Pk, Ger.Cr. SL9. . . . . . 56 AY60
Elmwood Rd, SE24. . . . . 122 DR85
W4. . . . . 98 CQ79
Croydon CR0. . . . . 141 DP101
Mitcham CR4 . . . . 140 DF97
Redhill RH1 . . . . 184 DG130
Slough SL2 . . . . 74 AV73
Elmworth Gro, SE21. . . . . 122 DR89
Elnathan Ms, W9
off Shirland Rd 82 DB70
Elphinstone Rd, E17 . . . . 47 DZ54
Elphinstone St, N5
off Avenell Rd 65 DP63
Elrick Cl, Erith DA8
off Queen St 107 FE79
Elrington Rd, E8 . . . . 84 DU65
Woodford Green IG8 . . . . . . 48 EG50
Elruge Cl, West Dr. UB7 . . . . . . 94 BK76
Elsa Rd, Well. DA16. . . . . 106 EV82
Elsa St, E1. . . . . 85 DY71
Elsdale St, E9 . . . . 84 DW65
Elsden Ms, E2
off Old Ford Rd. 84 DW68
Elsden Rd, N17 . . . . 46 DT53
Elsdon Rd, Wok. GU21 . . . . . . 166 AU117
Elsenham Rd, E12 . . . . 69 EN64
Elsenham St, SW18 . . . . 119 CZ88
Elsham Rd, E11 . . . . 68 EE62
W14. 99 CY75
Elsham Ter, W14 . . . . 99 CY75
Elsiedene Rd, N21 . . . . 46 DQ45
Elsiemaud Rd, SE4 . . . . 123 DZ85
Elsie Rd, SE22. . . . . 102 DT84
Elsinge Rd, Enf. EN1. . . . . 30 DV36
Elsinore Av, Stai. TW19 . . . . . . 114 BL87
Elsinore Gdns, NW2 . . . . 63 CY62
Elsinore Rd, SE23 . . . . 123 DY88
Elsinore Way, Rich. TW9
off Lower Richmond Rd . . . 98 CP83
Elsley Rd, SW11 . . . . 100 DF83
Elspeth Rd, SW11 . . . . 100 DF84
Wembley HA0. . . . . 62 CL64
Elsrick Av, Mord. SM4 . . . . 140 DA99
Elstan Way, Croy. CR0 . . . . 143 DY101
Elstead Ct, Sutt. SM3
off Stonecot Hill 139 CY102
Elsted St, SE17 . . . . 201 L9
Elstow Cl, SE9 . . . . 125 EN85
Ruislip HA4. . . . . 60 BX59
Elstow Gdns, Dag. RM9. . . . . . . 88 EY67
Elstow Rd, Dag. RM9. . . . . 88 EY66
ELSTREE, Borwd. WD6. . . . . 25 CK43
★ Elstree Aerodrome,
Borwd. WD6 . . . . 25 CF41
⇌ Elstree & Borehamwood . . 26 CM42
Elstree Cl, Horn. RM12
off Airfield Way 89 FH65
Elstree Gdns, N9. . . . . 46 DV46
Belvedere DA17 . . . . 106 EY77
Ilford IG1 . . . . 69 EQ64
Elstree Hill, Brom. BR1 . . . . . . 124 EE94
Elstree Hill N, Borwd.
(Elstree) WD6 . . . . 25 CK44
Elstree Hill S, Borwd.
(Elstree) WD6 . . . . 41 CJ45
Elstree Pk, Borwd. WD6 . . . . . . 26 CR44
Elstree Rd, Borwd.
(Elstree) WD6 . . . . 25 CG44
Bushey (Bushey Hth) WD23 . 41 CD45
Elstree Way, Borwd. WD6. . . . . 26 CP41
Elswick Rd, SE13 . . . . 103 EB82
Elswick St, SW6 . . . . 100 DC82
Elsworth Cl, Felt. TW14. . . . . . . 115 BS88
Elsworthy, T.Ditt. KT7 . . . . 137 CE100
Elsworthy Ri, NW3. . . . . 82 DE66
Elsworthy Rd, NW3 . . . . 82 DE67
Elsworthy Ter, NW3 . . . . 82 DE66
Elsynge Rd, SW18 . . . . 120 DD85
ELTHAM, SE9 . . . . 124 EK86
⇌ Eltham. 125 EM85
Eltham Grn, SE9. . . . . 124 EJ85
Eltham Grn Rd, SE9 . . . . 104 EJ84
Eltham High St, SE9. . . . . 125 EM86
Eltham Hill, SE9 . . . . 124 EK85
★ Eltham Palace, SE9. . . . . . 124 EL87
Eltham Palace Rd, SE9. . . . . . . 124 EJ86
Eltham Pk Gdns, SE9 . . . . 105 EN84
Eltham Rd, SE9. . . . . 124 EJ85
SE12 . . . . 124 EF85
Elthiron Rd, SW6 . . . . 100 DA81
Elthorne Av, W7 . . . . 97 CF75
Elthorne Ct, Felt. TW13. . . . . . . 116 BW88
Elthorne Pk Rd, W7. . . . . 97 CF75
Elthorne Rd, N19 . . . . 65 DK61
NW9 . . . . 62 CR59
Uxbridge UB8. . . . . 76 BK68
Elthorne Way, NW9 . . . . 62 CR58
Elthruda Rd, SE13. . . . . 123 ED86
Eltisley Rd, Ilf. IG1 . . . . 69 EP63
Elton Av, Barn. EN5 . . . . 27 CZ43
Greenford UB6 . . . . 79 CF65
Wembley HA0. . . . . 61 CH64
Elton Cl, Kings.T. KT1 . . . . 117 CJ94
Elton Ho, E3 . . . . 85 DZ67
Elton Pk, Wat. WD17. . . . . 23 BV40
Elton Pl, N16. . . . . 66 DS64
Elton Rd, Kings.T. KT2 . . . . 138 CM95
Purley CR8 . . . . 159 DJ112
Elton Way, Wat. WD25 . . . . 24 CB40
Eltringham St, SW18 . . . . 100 DC84
Elvaston Ms, SW7. . . . . 100 DC76
Elvaston Pl, SW7 . . . . 100 DC76
Elveden Cl, Wok. GU22. . . . . . . 168 BH117
Elveden Pl, NW10. . . . . 80 CN68
Elveden Rd, NW10 . . . . 80 CN68
Elvedon Rd, Cob. KT11. . . . . . . 153 BV111
Feltham TW13
off Ashford Rd. 115 BT90
Elvendon Rd, N13. . . . . 45 DL51
Elver Gdns, E2
off St. Peter's Cl 84 DU68
Elverson Ms, SE8 . . . . 103 EB82
DLR Elverson Road. 103 EB82
Elverson Rd, SE8 . . . . 103 EB82
Elverton St, SW1 . . . . 199 M8
Elvet Av, Rom. RM2 . . . . 72 FJ56
Elvington Grn, Brom. BR2 . . . . 144 EF99
Elvington La, NW9. . . . . 42 CS53
Elvino Rd, SE26 . . . . 123 DY92
Elvis Rd, NW2. . . . . 81 CW65
Elwell Cl, Egh. TW20
off Mowbray Cres 113 BA92
Elwick Rd, S.Ock. RM15 . . . . 91 FW72
Elwill Way, Beck. BR3 . . . . 143 EC98
Elwin St, E2 . . . . 84 DU69
Elwood St, N5 . . . . 65 DP62
Elwyn Gdns, SE12 . . . . 124 EG87
Ely Cl, Amer. HP7 . . . . 20 AS39
Erith DA8. . . . . 107 FF82
New Malden KT3 . . . . 139 CT96
Ely Ct, EC1 . . . . 196 E7
Ely Gdns, Borwd. WD6. . . . . 26 CR43
Dagenham RM10 . . . . 71 FC62
Ilford IG1
off Canterbury Av 68 EL59
Elyne Rd, N4. . . . . 65 DN58
Ely Pl, EC1. . . . . 196 E7
Woodford Green IG8 . . . . 49 EN51
Ely Rd, E10 . . . . 67 EC58
Croydon CR0. . . . . 142 DR99
Ely Rd, Hounslow (Hthrw Air.) TW6
off Eastern Perimeter Rd . . 95 BT82
Hounslow (Houns.W.) TW4. . 96 BW83
Elysian Av, Orp. BR5. . . . . 145 ET100
Elysium Pl, SW6
off Fulham Pk Gdns 99 CZ82
Elysium St, SW6
off Fulham Pk Gdns 99 CZ82
Elystan Business Cen,
Hayes UB4 . . . . 78 BW73
Elystan Cl, Wall. SM6 . . . . 159 DH109
Elystan Pl, SW3 . . . . 198 C10
Elystan St, SW3 . . . . 198 B9
Elystan Wk, N1
off Cloudesley Rd. 83 DN67
Emanuel Av, W3 . . . . 80 CQ72
Emanuel Dr, Hmptn. TW12 . . . 116 BZ92
⊖ Embankment 200 A2
Embankment, SW15 . . . . 99 CX82
Embankment, The, Stai.
(Wrays.) TW19 . . . . 112 AW87
Twickenham TW1 . . . . 117 CG88
Embankment Gdns, SW3. . . . . 100 DF79
Riv Embankment Pier. 200 B2
Embankment Pl, WC2. . . . . 200 A2
Embassy Ct, Sid. DA14. . . . . . . 126 EV90
Welling DA16
off Welling High St 106 EV83
Embassy Gdns, Beck. BR3
off Blakeney Rd. 143 DZ95
Emba St, SE16 . . . . 202 C5
Ember Cen, Walt. KT12. . . . . . . 136 BY103
Ember Cl, Add. KT15 . . . . 152 BK106
Orpington BR5 . . . . 145 EQ101
Embercourt Rd, T.Ditt. KT7 . . . 137 CE100
Ember Fm Av, E.Mol. KT8 . . . . 137 CD100
Ember Fm Way, E.Mol. KT8 . . . 137 CD100
Ember Gdns, T.Ditt. KT7 . . . . . 137 CE101
Ember La, E.Mol. KT8. . . . . 137 CD101
Esher KT10 . . . . 137 CD101
Ember Rd, Slou. SL3 . . . . 93 BB76
Emberson Way, Epp.
(N.Wld Bas.) CM16 . . . . 19 FC26
Emberton, SE5 . . . . 102 DS79
Embleton Rd, SE13. . . . . 103 EB83
Watford WD19. . . . . 39 BU48
Embleton Wk, Hmptn. TW12
off Fearnley Cres. 116 BZ93
Embry Cl, Stan. HA7. . . . . 41 CG49
Embry Dr, Stan. HA7 . . . . 41 CG51
Embry Way, Stan. HA7 . . . . 41 CG50
Emden Cl, West Dr. UB7. . . . . . . 94 BN75
Emden St, SW6 . . . . 100 DB81
Emerald Cl, E16 . . . . 86 EL72
Emerald Ct, Slou. SL1 . . . . 92 AS75
Emerald Gdns, Dag. RM8. . . . . . 70 FA60
Emerald Sq, Sthl. UB2 . . . . 96 BX76
Emerald St, WC1. . . . . 196 B6
Emerson Dr, Horn. RM11 . . . . . . 72 FK59
Emerson Gdns, Har. HA3 . . . . . 62 CM58
EMERSON PARK, Horn. RM11 . 72 FL58
⇌ Emerson Park 72 FL59
Emerson Rd, Ilf. IG1 . . . . 69 EN59
Emersons Av, Swan. BR8. . . . . 127 FF94
Emerson St, SE1. . . . . 201 H2
Emerton Cl, Bexh. DA6. . . . . . . 106 EY84
Emerton Rd, Lthd. KT22. . . . . . 170 CC120
Emery Hill St, SW1. . . . . 199 L7
Emery St, SE1 . . . . 200 E6
Emes Rd, Erith DA8 . . . . 107 FC80
Emilia Cl, Enf. EN3 . . . . 30 DV43
Emily Davidson Dr,
Epsom KT18 . . . . 173 CV118
Emily Jackson Cl, Sev. TN13 . 191 FH124
Emley Rd, Add. KT15 . . . . 134 BG104
Emlyn Gdns, W12. . . . . 98 CS75
Emlyn La, Lthd. KT22. . . . . 171 CG122
Emlyn Rd, W12 . . . . 98 CS75
Emmanuel Lo, Wal.Cr. (Chsht) EN8
off College Rd. 14 DW30
Emmanuel Rd, SW12 . . . . 121 DJ88
Northwood HA6 . . . . 39 BT52
Emma Rd, E13 . . . . 86 EF68
Emma St, E2. . . . . 84 DV68
Emmaus Way, Chig. IG7. . . . . . . 49 EN50
Emmett Cl, Rad.
(Shenley) WD7 . . . . 10 CL33
Emmetts Cl, Wok. GU21. . . . . . 166 AW117
Emmott Av, Ilf. IG6. . . . . 69 EQ57
Emmott Cl, E1 . . . . 85 DY70
NW11. . . . . 64 DC58
Emms Pas, Kings.T. KT1
off High St. 137 CK96
Emperor's Gate, SW7. . . . . 100 DB76
Empire Av, N18. . . . . 46 DQ50
Empire Ct, Wem. HA9. . . . . 62 CP62
Empire Rd, Grnf. UB6. . . . . 79 CJ67
Empire Sq, N7 . . . . 65 DL62
SE20 off High St. 123 DX94
Empire Way, Wem. HA9 . . . . 62 CM63
Empire Wf Rd, E14 . . . . 204 F9
Empress Av, E4. . . . . 47 EA52
E12 . . . . 68 EJ61
Ilford IG1. . . . . 69 EM61
Woodford Green IG8 . . . . 48 EF52
Empress Dr, Chis. BR7 . . . . 125 EP93
Empress Ms, SE5 . . . . 102 DQ82
Empress Pl, SW6 . . . . 100 DA78
Empress Rd, Grav. DA12 . . . . . 131 GL87
Empress St, SE17. . . . . 102 DQ79
Empson St, E3 . . . . 85 EB70
Emsworth Cl, N9 . . . . 46 DW46
Emsworth Rd, Ilf. IG6. . . . . 49 EP54
Emsworth St, SW2. . . . . 121 DM89
Emu Rd, SW8 . . . . 101 DH82
Ena Rd, SW16. . . . . 141 DL97
Enborne Grn, S.Ock. RM15
off Elan Rd 91 FU71
Enbrook St, W10. . . . . 81 CY69
Endale Cl, Cars. SM5 . . . . 140 DF103
Endeavour Ho, Barn. EN5 . . . . . 28 DC42
Endeavour Rd, Wal.Cr.
(Chsht) EN8. . . . . 15 DY27
Endeavour Way, SW19 . . . . 120 DB91
Barking IG11 . . . . 88 EU68

★ Place of interest ⇌ Railway station ⊖ London Underground station DLR Docklands Light Railway station Tra Tramlink station H Hospital Riv Pedestrian ferry landing stage

Endeavour Way,
Croydon CR0 141 DK101
Endell St, WC2 195 P8
Enderby St, SE10 104 EE78
Enderley Cl, Har. HA3
off Enderley Rd 41 CE53
Enderley Rd, Har. HA3 41 CE53
Endersby Rd, Barn. EN5 27 CW43
Endersleigh Gdns, NW4 63 CU56
Endlebury Rd, E4 47 EB47
Endlesham Rd, SW12 120 DG87
Endsleigh Cl, S.Croy. CR2 160 DW110
Endsleigh Gdns, WC1 195 M4
Ilford IG1 69 EM61
Surbiton KT6 137 CJ100
Walton-on-Thames KT12 154 BW106
Endsleigh Ind Est, Sthl. UB2
off Endsleigh Rd 96 BZ77
Endsleigh Pl, WC1 195 N4
Endsleigh Rd, W13 79 CG73
Redhill RH1 185 DJ129
Southall UB2 96 BY77
Endsleigh St, WC1 195 M4
Endway, Surb. KT5 138 CN101
Endwell Rd, SE4 103 DY82
Endymion Rd, N4 65 DN59
SW2 121 DM86
Energen Cl, NW10 80 CS65
ENFIELD 30 DT41
⇌ Enfield Chase 30 DQ41
Enfield Cl, Uxb. UB8
off Villier St 76 BK68
ENFIELD HIGHWAY, Enf. EN3 30 DW41
ENFIELD LOCK, Enf. EN3 31 DZ37
⇌ Enfield Lock 31 DY37
Enfield Retail Pk, Enf. EN1 30 DV41
Enfield Rd, N1 84 DS66
W3 98 CP75
Brentford TW8 97 CK78
Enfield EN2 29 DK42
Hounslow (Hthrw Air.) TW6
off Eastern Perimeter Rd 95 BS82
ENFIELD TOWN, Enf. EN2 30 DR40
⇌ Enfield Town 30 DS42
Enfield Wk, Brent. TW8 97 CK78
ENFIELD WASH, Enf. EN3 31 DX38
Enford St, W1 194 D6
Engadine Cl, Croy. CR0 142 DT104
Engadine St, SW18 119 CZ88
Engate St, SE13 103 EC84
Engayne Gdns, Upmin. RM14 72 FP60
Engel Pk, NW7 43 CW51
Engineer Cl, SE18 105 EN79
Engineers Way, Wem. HA9 62 CN63
Englands La, NW3 82 DF65
Loughton IG10 33 EN40
England Way, N.Mal. KT3 138 CP98
Englefield Cl, Croy. CR0
off Queen's Rd 142 DQ100
Egham (Eng.Grn) TW20
off Alexandra Rd 112 AW93
Enfield EN2 29 DN40
Orpington BR5 145 ET98
Englefield Cres, Orp. BR5 145 ET98
ENGLEFIELD GREEN,
Egh. TW20 112 AV92
Englefield Grn, Egh.
(Eng.Grn) TW20 112 AW91
Englefield Path, Orp. BR5 145 ET98
Englefield Rd, N1 84 DR65
Orpington BR5 146 EU98
Engleheart Dr, Felt. TW14 115 BT86
Engleheart Rd, SE6 123 EB87
Englehurst, Egh.
(Eng.Grn) TW20 112 AW93
Englemere Pk, Lthd.
(Oxshott) KT22 154 CB114
Englewood Rd, SW12 121 DH86
Engliff La, Wok. GU22 167 BF116
English Gdns, Stai.
(Wrays.) TW19 92 AX84
English Grds, SE1 201 M3
English St, E3 85 DZ70
Enid Cl, St.Alb. (Brick.Wd) AL2 8 BZ31
Enid St, SE16 202 A6
Enmore Av, SE25 142 DU99
Enmore Gdns, SW14 118 CR85
Enmore Rd, SE25 142 DU99
SW15 99 CW84
Southall UB1 78 CA70
Ennerdale Av, Horn. RM12 71 FG64
Stanmore HA7 61 CJ55
Ennerdale Cl, Felt. TW14 115 BT88
Sutton SM1 157 CZ105
Ennerdale Dr, NW9 62 CS57
Watford WD25
off North Orbital Rd 8 BW34
Ennerdale Gdns, Wem. HA9 61 CK60
Ennerdale Ho, E3 85 DZ70
Ennerdale Rd, Bexh. DA7 106 FA81
Richmond TW9 98 CM82
Ennersdale Rd, SE13 123 ED85
Ennismore Av, W4 99 CT77
Greenford UB6 79 CE65
Ennismore Gdns, SW7 198 B5
Thames Ditton KT7 137 CE100
Ennismore Gdns Ms, SW7 198 B6
Ennismore Ms, SW7 198 B6
Ennismore St, SW7 198 B6
Ennis Rd, N4 65 DN60
SE18 105 EQ79
Ensign Cl, Pur. CR8 159 DN110
Staines (Stanw.) TW19 114 BK88
Ensign Dr, N13 46 DQ48
Ensign St, E1 84 DU73
Ensign Way, Stai.
(Stanw.) TW19 114 BK88
Wallington SM6 159 DL108
Enslin Rd, SE9 125 EN86
Ensor Ms, SW7
off Cranley Gdns 100 DD78
Enstone Rd, Enf. EN3 31 DY41
Uxbridge UB10 58 BM62
Enterdent Rd, Gdse. RH9 186 DW134
Enterprise Cl, Croy. CR0 141 DN102
Enterprise Pk, E10 67 DY60
Enterprise Way, NW10 81 CU69
SW18 100 DA84
Teddington TW11 117 CF92
Enterprize Way, SE8 203 M8
Eothen Cl, Cat. CR3 176 DU124
Eothen Hts, Cat. CR3 176 DU124
Epirus Ms, SW6 100 DA80
Epirus Rd, SW6 99 CZ80
EPPING 17 ES31
⊖ Epping 18 EU31
Epping Cl, E14 204 A8
Romford RM7 71 FB55
★ Epping Forest, Epp. & Loug. 32 EJ39
★ Epping Forest District Mus,
Wal.Abb. EN9 15 EC33
Epping Glade, E4 31 EC44
Epping La, Rom.
(Stap.Taw.) RM4 34 EV40
Epping New Rd, Buck.H. IG9 48 EH47
Loughton IG10 32 EH43
Epping Pl, N1
off Liverpool Rd 83 DN65
Epping Rd, Epp. CM16 33 EM36
Epping (Epp.Grn) CM16 17 ER27
Epping (N.Wld Bas.) CM16 18 EW28
Ongar (Toot Hill) CM5 19 FC30
Epping Way, E4 31 EB44
Epple Rd, SW6 99 CZ81
EPSOM 156 CQ114
⇌ Epsom 156 CR113
H Epsom & Ewell Comm Hosp,
Epsom KT19 156 CL111
Epsom Cl, Bexh. DA7 107 FB83
Northolt UB5 60 BZ64
⇌ Epsom Downs 173 CV115
Epsom Downs, Epsom KT18 173 CU118
Epsom Downs Metro Cen,
Tad. KT20 *off Waterfield* 173 CV120
Epsom Gap, Lthd. KT22 171 CH115
H Epsom Gen Hosp,
Epsom KT18 172 CQ115
Epsom La N, Epsom KT18 173 CV118
Tadworth KT20 173 CV118
Epsom La S, Tad. KT20 173 CW121
★ Epsom Racecourse,
Epsom KT18 173 CT118
Epsom Rd, E10 67 EC58
Ashtead KT21 172 CM118
Croydon CR0 159 DN105
Epsom KT17 157 CT110
Ilford IG3 69 ET58
Leatherhead KT22 171 CH121
Morden SM4 139 CZ101
Sutton SM3 139 CZ101
Epsom Sq, Houns. (Hthrw Air.) TW6
off Eastern Perimeter Rd 95 BT82
Epsom Way, Horn. RM12 72 FM63
Epstein Rd, SE28 88 EU74
Epworth Rd, Islw. TW7 97 CH80
Epworth St, EC2 197 L5
Equity Sq, E2
off Shacklewell St 84 DT69
Erasmus St, SW1 199 N9
Erconwald St, W12 81 CT72
Erebus Dr, SE28 105 EQ76
Eresby Dr, Beck. BR3 143 EA102
Eresby Pl, NW6 82 DA66
Erica Ct, Swan. BR8
off Azalea Dr 147 FE98
Woking GU22 166 AX118
Erica Gdns, Croy. CR0 161 EB105
Erica St, W12 81 CU73
Eric Clarke La, Bark. IG11 87 EP70
Eric Cl, E7 68 EG63
Ericcson Cl, SW18 120 DA85
Eric Rd, E7 68 EG63
NW10 *off Church Rd* 81 CT65
Romford RM6 70 EX59
Eric Steele Ho, St.Alb. AL2 8 CB27
Eric St, E3 85 DZ70
Eridge Grn Cl, Orp. BR5
off Petten Gro 146 EW102
Eridge Rd, W4 98 CR76
Erin Cl, Brom. BR1 124 EE94
Ilford IG3 70 EU58
Erindale, SE18 105 ER79
Erindale Ter, SE18 105 ER79
Eriswell Cres, Walt. KT12 153 BS107
Eriswell Rd, Walt. KT12 153 BT105
ERITH 107 FD79
⇌ Erith 107 FE78
H Erith & District Hosp,
Erith DA8 107 FD79
Erith Ct, Purf. RM19
off Thamley 108 FN77
Erith Cres, Rom. RM5 51 FC53
Erith High St, Erith DA8 107 FE78
★ Erith Lib & Mus, Erith DA8 107 FE78
Erith Rd, Belv. DA17 106 FA78
Bexleyheath DA7 107 FB84
Erith DA8 107 FB84
Erkenwald Cl, Cher. KT16 133 BE101
Erlanger Rd, SE14 103 DX81
Erlesmere Gdns, W13 97 CG76
Ermine Cl, Houns. TW4 96 BW82
Waltham Cross (Chsht) EN7 14 DV31
Ermine Ho, N17
off Moselle St 46 DT52
Ermine Rd, N15 66 DT58
SE13 103 EB83
Ermine Side, Enf. EN1 30 DU43
Ermington Rd, SE9 125 EQ89
Ermyn Cl, Lthd. KT22 171 CK121
Ermyn Way, Lthd. KT22 171 CK121
Ernald Av, E6 86 EL68
Ernan Cl, S.Ock. RM15 91 FU71
Ernan Rd, S.Ock. RM15 91 FU71
Erncroft Way, Twick. TW1 117 CF86
Ernest Av, SE27 121 DP91
Ernest Cl, Beck. BR3 143 EA99
Ernest Gdns, W4 98 CP79
Ernest Gro, Beck. BR3 143 DZ99
Ernest Rd, Horn. RM11 72 FL58
Kingston upon Thames KT1 138 CP96
Ernest Sq, Kings.T. KT1 138 CP96
Ernest St, E1 85 DX70
Ernle Rd, SW20 119 CV94
Ernshaw Pl, SW15
off Carlton Dr 119 CY85
★ Eros, W1 199 M1
Erpingham Rd, SW15 99 CW83
Erridge Rd, SW19 140 DA96
Erriff Dr, S.Ock. RM15 91 FT71
Errington Cl, Grays RM16
off Cedar Rd 111 GH76
Errington Rd, W9 81 CZ70
Errol Gdns, Hayes UB4 77 BV70
New Malden KT3 139 CU98
Erroll Rd, Rom. RM1 71 FF56
Errol St, EC1 197 J5
Erskine Cl, Sutt. SM1 140 DE104
Erskine Cres, N17 66 DV56
Erskine Hill, NW11 64 DA57
Erskine Ms, NW3
off Erskine Rd 82 DF66
Erskine Rd, E17 67 DZ56
NW3 82 DF66
Sutton SM1 158 DD105
Watford WD19 40 BW48
Erwood Rd, SE7 104 EL78
Esam Way, SW16 121 DN92
Escott Gdns, SE9 124 EL91
Escott Pl, Cher. (Ott.) KT16 151 BC107
Escot Way, Barn. EN5 27 CW43
Escreet Gro, SE18 105 EN77
Esdaile Gdns, Upmin. RM14 73 FR59
ESHER 154 CB105
⇌ Esher 137 CD103
Esher Av, Rom. RM7 71 FC58
Sutton SM3 139 CX104
Walton-on-Thames KT12 135 BU101
Esher Bypass, Chess. KT9 155 CH108
Cobham KT11 153 BU112
Esher KT10 155 CH108
Esher Cl, Bex. DA5 126 EY88
Esher KT10 154 CB106
Esher Cres, Houns. (Hthrw Air.) TW6
off Eastern Perimeter Rd 95 BS82
Esher Gdns, SW19 119 CX89
Esher Grn, Esher KT10 154 CB105
Esher Ms, Mitch. CR4 140 DF97
Esher Pk Av, Esher KT10 154 CC105
Esher Pl Av, Esher KT10 154 CB105
Esher Rd, E.Mol. KT8 137 CD100
Ilford IG3 69 ES62
Walton-on-Thames KT12 154 BX106
Eskdale, St.Alb. (Lon.Col.) AL2 10 CM27
Eskdale Av, Nthlt. UB5 78 BZ67
Eskdale Cl, Dart. DA2 128 FQ89
Wembley HA9 61 CK61
Eskdale Gdns, Pur. CR8 160 DR114
Eskdale Rd, Bexh. DA7 106 FA82
Uxbridge UB8 76 BH68
Eskley Gdns, S.Ock. RM15 91 FV70
Eskmont Ridge, SE19 122 DS94
Esk Rd, E13 86 EG70
Esk Way, Rom. RM1 51 FD52
Esmar Cres, NW9 63 CU59
Esme Ho, SW15 99 CT84
Esmeralda Rd, SE1 202 C9
Esmond Cl, Rain. RM13
off Dawson Dr 89 FH66
Esmond Rd, NW6 81 CZ67
W4 98 CR77
Esmond St, SW15 99 CY84
Esparto St, SW18 120 DB87
Essendene Cl, Cat. CR3 176 DS123
Essendene Rd, Cat. CR3 176 DS123
Essenden Rd, Belv. DA17 106 FA78
South Croydon CR2 160 DS108
Essendine Rd, W9 82 DA70
Essex Av, Islw. TW7 97 CE83
Essex Cl, E17 67 DY56
Addlestone KT15 152 BJ105
Morden SM4 139 CX101
Romford RM7 71 FB56
Ruislip HA4 60 BX60
Essex Ct, EC4 196 D9
SW13 99 CT82
Essex Gdns, N4 65 DP58
Hornchurch RM11 72 FM57
Essex Gro, SE19 122 DR93
Essex Ho, E14 *off Giraud St* 85 EB72
Essex La, Kings L. WD4 7 BS33
H Essex Nuffield Hosp,
Brwd. CM15 54 FY46
Essex Pk, N3 44 DB51
Essex Pk Ms, W3 80 CS74
Essex Pl, W4 98 CQ77
Essex Pl Sq, W4
off Chiswick High Rd 98 CR77
⇌ Essex Road 84 DQ66
Essex Rd, E4 48 EE46
E10 67 EC58
E12 68 EL64
E17 67 DY58
E18 48 EH54
N1 83 DP67
NW10 80 CS66
W3 80 CQ73
W4 *off Belmont Rd* 98 CR77
Barking IG11 87 ER66
Borehamwood WD6 26 CN41
Dagenham RM10 71 FC64
Dartford DA1 128 FK86
Enfield EN2 30 DR42
Gravesend DA11 131 GG88
Grays RM20 109 FU79
Longfield DA3 149 FX96
Romford RM7 71 FB56
Romford (Chad.Hth) RM6 70 EW59
Watford WD17 23 BU40
Essex Rd S, E11 67 ED59
Essex St, E7 68 EG64
WC2 196 D10
Essex Twr, SE20 142 DV95
Essex Vil, W8 100 DA75
Essex Way, Brwd. CM13 53 FW51
Epping CM16 18 EV32
Ongar CM5 19 FF29
Essex Wf, E5 66 DW61
Essian St, E1 85 DY71
Essoldo Way, Edg. HA8 62 CM55
Estate Way, E10 67 DZ60
Estcourt Rd, SE25 142 DV100
SW6 99 CZ80
Watford WD17 24 BW41
Estella Av, N.Mal. KT3 139 CV98
Estelle Rd, NW3 64 DF63
Esterbrooke St, SW1 199 M9
Este Rd, SW11 100 DE83
Esther Cl, N21 45 DN45
Esther Rd, E11 68 EE59
Estoria Cl, SW2 121 DN87
★ Estorick Collection of
Modern Italian Art, N1 83 DP65
Estreham Rd, SW16 121 DK93
Estridge Cl, Houns. TW3 96 CA84
Estuary Cl, Bark. IG11 88 EV69
Eswyn Rd, SW17 120 DF91
Etchingham Pk Rd, N3 44 DB52
Etchingham Rd, E15 67 EC63
Eternit Wk, SW6 99 CW81
Etfield Gro, Sid. DA14 126 EV92
Ethel Bailey Cl, Epsom KT19 156 CN112
Ethelbert Cl, Brom. BR1 144 EG97
Ethelbert Gdns, Ilf. IG2 69 EM57
Ethelbert Rd, SW20 139 CX95
Bromley BR1 144 EG97
Dartford (Hawley) DA2 128 FL91
Erith DA8 107 FC80
Orpington BR5 146 EX97
Ethelbert St, SW12
off Fernlea Rd 121 DH88
Ethelburga Rd, Rom. RM3 52 FM53
Ethelburga St, SW11 100 DE81
Etheldene Av, N10 65 DJ56
Ethelden Rd, W12 81 CV74
Ethel Rd, E16 86 EH72
Ashford TW15 114 BL92
Ethel St, SE17 201 H9
Ethel Ter, Orp. BR6 164 EW109
Ethelwine Pl, Abb.L. WD5
off The Crescent 7 BT30
Etheridge Grn, Loug. IG10
off Etheridge Rd 33 EQ41
Etheridge Rd, NW2 63 CW59
Loughton IG10 33 EP40
Etherley Rd, N15 66 DQ57
Etherow St, SE22 122 DU86
Etherstone Grn, SW16 121 DN91
Etherstone Rd, SW16 121 DN91
Ethnard Rd, SE15 102 DV79
Ethorpe Cl, Ger.Cr. SL9 56 AY57
Ethorpe Cres, Ger.Cr. SL9 56 AY57
Ethronvi Rd, Bexh. DA7 106 EY83
Etloe Rd, E10 67 EA61
Eton Av, N12 44 DC52
NW3 82 DD66
Barnet EN4 28 DE44
Hounslow TW5 96 BZ79
New Malden KT3 138 CR99
Wembley HA0 61 CH63
Eton Cl, SW18 120 DB87
Slough (Datchet) SL3 92 AU79
Eton Coll Rd, NW3 82 DF65
Eton Ct, NW3 *off Eton Av* 82 DD66
Staines TW18
off Richmond Rd 113 BF92
Wembley HA0 *off Eton Av* 61 CJ63
Eton Garages, NW3
off Lambolle Pl 82 DE65
Eton Gro, NW9 62 CN55
SE13 104 EE83
Eton Hall, NW3
off Eton Coll Rd 82 DF65
Eton Pl, NW3
off Haverstock Hill 82 DG66
Eton Ri, NW3
off Eton Coll Rd 82 DF65
Eton Rd, NW3 82 DF66
Hayes UB3 95 BT80
Ilford IG1 69 EQ64
Orpington BR6 164 EV105
Slough (Datchet) SL3 92 AT78
Eton St, Rich. TW9 118 CL85
Eton Vil, NW3 82 DF65
Eton Way, Dart. DA1 108 FJ84
Etta St, SE8 103 DY79
Etton Cl, Horn. RM12 72 FL61
Ettrick St, E14 85 EC72
Etwell Pl, Surb. KT5 138 CM100
Euclid Way, Grays RM20 109 FU78
Euesden Cl, N9 46 DV48
Eugene Cl, Rom. RM2 72 FJ56
Eugenia Rd, SE16 202 G9
Eureka Rd, Kings.T. KT1
off Washington Rd 138 CN96
Europa Pl, EC1 197 H3
Europa Trd Est, Erith DA8 107 FD78
Europe Rd, SE18 105 EM76
Eustace Rd, E6 86 EL69
SW6 100 DA80
Romford RM6 70 EX59
⇌ Euston 195 L2
⊖ Euston 195 L2
Euston Av, Wat. WD18 23 BT43
Euston Cen, NW1
off Triton Sq 83 DJ70
Euston Gro, NW1 195 M3
Euston Rd, N1 195 P2
NW1 195 J5
Croydon CR0 141 DN102
⊖ Euston Square 195 L4
Euston Sq, NW1 195 M3
Euston Sta Colonnade, NW1 195 M3
Euston St, NW1 195 L4
Euston Twr, NW1 195 K4
Evandale Rd, SW9 101 DN82
Evangelist Rd, NW5 65 DH63
Evans Av, Wat. WD25 23 BT35
Evans Business Cen, NW2 63 CU62
Evans Cl, E8
off Buttermere Wk 84 DT65
Greenhithe DA9 129 FU85
Rickmansworth (Crox.Grn) WD3
off New Rd 22 BN43
Evansdale, Rain. RM13
off New Zealand Way 89 FF69
Evans Gro, Felt. TW13 116 CA89
Evans Rd, SE6 124 EE89
Evanston Av, E4 47 EC52
Evanston Gdns, Ilf. IG4 68 EL58
Eva Rd, Rom. RM6 70 EW59
H Evelina Children's Hosp
(opening Jan 2005), SE1 200 B6
Evelina Rd, SE15 102 DW83
SE20 123 DX94
Eveline Lowe Est, SE16 202 B7
Eveline Rd, Mitch. CR4 140 DF95
Evelyn Av, NW9 62 CR56
Ruislip HA4 59 BT58
Evelyn Cl, Twick. TW2 116 CB87
Woking GU22 166 AX120
Evelyn Ct, N1 197 K1
Evelyn Cres, Sun. TW16 135 BT95
Evelyn Denington Rd, E6 86 EL70
Evelyn Dr, Pnr. HA5 40 BX52
Evelyn Fox Ct, W10 81 CW71
Evelyn Gdns, SW7 100 DD78
Godstone RH9 186 DW130
Richmond TW9 *off Kew Rd* 98 CL84
Evelyn Gro, W5 80 CM74
Southall UB1 78 BZ72
Evelyn Rd, E16 205 P2
E17 67 EC56
SW19 120 DB92
W4 98 CR76
Barnet EN4 28 DF42
Richmond TW9 98 CL83
Richmond (Ham) TW10 117 CJ90
Evelyns Cl, Uxb. UB8 76 BN72
Evelyn Sharp Cl, Rom. RM2
off Amery Gdns 72 FK55
Evelyn St, SE8 203 K9
Evelyn Ter, Rich. TW9 98 CL83
Evelyn Wk, N1 197 K1
Brentwood CM13 53 FW51
Evelyn Way, Cob.
(Stoke D'Ab.) KT11 170 BZ116
Epsom KT19 156 CN111
Sunbury-on-Thames TW16 135 BT95
Wallington SM6 159 DK105
Evelyn Yd, W1 195 M8
Evening Hill, Beck. BR3 123 EC94
Evensyde, Wat. WD18 23 BR44
Evenwood Cl, SW15 119 CY85
Everard Av, Brom. BR2 144 EG102
Slough SL1 92 AS75
Everard La, Cat. CR3
off Tillingdown Hill 176 DU122
Everard Way, Wem. HA9 62 CL62
Everatt Cl, SW18
off Amerland Rd 119 CZ86
Everdon Rd, SW13 99 CU79
Everest Cl, Grav.
(Nthflt) DA11 130 GE90
Everest Ct, Wok. GU21
off Langmans Way 166 AS116
Everest Pl, E14 85 EC71
Swanley BR8 147 FD98
Everest Rd, SE9 125 EM85
Staines (Stanw.) TW19 114 BK87
Everett Cl, Bushey
(Bushey Hth) WD23 41 CE46
Pinner HA5 59 BT55
Waltham Cross (Chsht) EN7 14 DQ25
Everett Wk, Belv. DA17
off Osborne Rd 106 EZ78
Everglade, West.
(Bigg.H.) TN16 178 EK118
Everglade Strand, NW9 43 CT53
Evergreen Ct, Stai. (Stanw.) TW19
off Evergreen Way 114 BK87
Evergreen Oak Av, Wind. SL4 92 AU83
Evergreen Sq, E8 84 DT66
Evergreen Way, Hayes UB3 77 BT73
Staines (Stanw.) TW19 114 BK87
Everilda St, N1 83 DM67
Evering Rd, E5 66 DT62
N16 66 DT62
Everington Rd, N10 44 DF54
Everington St, W6 99 CX79
Everitt Rd, NW10 80 CR69
Everlands Cl, Wok. GU22 166 AY118
Everleigh St, N4 65 DM60
Eve Rd, E11 68 EE63
E15 86 EE68
N17 66 DS55
Isleworth TW7 97 CG84
Woking GU21 167 BB115
Eversfield Gdns, NW7 42 CS52
Eversfield Rd, Reig. RH2 184 DB134
Richmond TW9 98 CM82
Evershed Wk, W4 98 CR77
Eversholt St, NW1 83 DJ68
Evershot Rd, N4 65 DM60
Eversleigh Gdns,
Upmin. RM14 73 FR60
Eversleigh Rd, E6 86 EK67
N3 43 CZ52
SW11 100 DF83
Barnet EN5 28 DC43
Eversley Av, Bexh. DA7 107 FD82
Wembley HA9 62 CN61
Eversley Cl, N21 29 DM44
Loughton IG10 33 EQ41
Eversley Cres, N21 29 DM44
Isleworth TW7 97 CD81
Ruislip HA4 59 BS61
Eversley Cross, Bexh. DA7 107 FE82
Eversley Mt, N21 29 DM44
Eversley Pk, SW19 119 CV92
Eversley Pk Rd, N21 29 DM44
Eversley Rd, SE7 104 EH79
SE19 122 DR94
Surbiton KT5 138 CM98
Eversley Way, Croy. CR0 161 EA105
Egham TW20 133 BC96
Everthorpe Rd, SE15 102 DT83
Everton Bldgs, NW1 195 K3
Everton Dr, Stan. HA7 62 CM55
Everton Rd, Croy. CR0 142 DU102
Evesham Av, E17 47 EA54
Evesham Cl, Grnf. UB6 78 CB68
Reigate RH2 183 CZ133
Sutton SM2 158 DA108
Evesham Ct, W13
off Tewkesbury Rd 79 CG74
Evesham Grn, Mord. SM4 140 DB100
Evesham Rd, E15 86 EF67
N11 45 DJ50
Gravesend DA12 131 GK89
Morden SM4 140 DB100
Reigate RH2 183 CZ134
Evesham Rd N, Reig. RH2 183 CZ133
Evesham St, W11 81 CX73
Evesham Wk, SE5
off Love Wk 102 DR82

★ Place of interest ⇌ Railway station ⊖ London Underground station DLR Docklands Light Railway station Tra Tramlink station H Hospital Riv Pedestrian ferry landing stage

Evesham Wk, SW9 101 DN82
Evesham Way, SW11 100 DG83
Ilford IG5 69 EN55
Evreham Rd, Iver SL0 75 BE72
Evry Rd, Sid. DA14 126 EW93
Ewald Rd, SW6 99 CZ82
Ewanrigg Ter, Wdf.Grn. IG8 48 EJ50
Ewan Rd, Rom.
(Harold Wd) RM3 52 FK54
Ewart Gro, N22 45 DN53
Ewart Pl, E3
off Roman Rd 85 DZ68
Ewart Rd, SE23 123 DX87
Ewe Cl, N7 83 DL65
EWELL, Epsom KT17 157 CU110
Ewell Bypass, Epsom KT17 157 CU108
Ewell Ct Av, Epsom KT19 156 CS106
Ewell Downs Rd,
Epsom KT17 157 CU111
⇌ **Ewell East** 157 CV110
Ewell Ho Gro, Epsom KT17 157 CT110
Ewellhurst Rd, Ilf. IG5 48 EL54
Ewell Pk Gdns, Epsom KT17 157 CU108
Ewell Pk Way, Epsom
(Ewell) KT17 157 CU107
Ewell Rd, Surb. KT6 138 CL100
Surbiton (Long Dit.) KT6 137 CH101
Sutton SM3 157 CY107
⇌ **Ewell West** 156 CS109
Ewelme Rd, SE23 122 DW88
Ewen Cres, SW2 121 DN87
Ewer St, SE1 201 H3
Ewhurst Av, S.Croy. CR2 160 DT109
Ewhurst Cl, E1 84 DW71
Sutton SM2 157 CW109
Ewhurst Rd, SE4 123 DZ86
Exbury Rd, SE6 123 EA89
★ **ExCeL**, E16 86 EH73
Excel Ct, WC2 199 N1
ExCeL Marina, E16
off Western Gateway 86 EH73
Excelsior Cl, Kings.T. KT1
off Washington Rd 138 CN96
Excelsior Gdns, SE13 103 EC82
ExCeL Waterfront, E16
off Western Gateway 86 EH73
Exchange Arc, EC2 197 N6
Exchange Bldgs, E1
off Cutler St 84 DS72
Exchange Cl, N11
off Benfleet Way 44 DG47
Exchange Ct, WC2 200 A1
Exchange Ho, N8
off Crouch End Hill 65 DL58
Exchange Mall, The, Ilf. IG1 69 EP61
Exchange Pl, EC2 197 M6
Exchange Rd, Wat. WD18 23 BV42
Exchange Sq, EC2 197 M6
Exchange St, Rom. RM1 71 FE57
Exchange Wk, Pnr. HA5 60 BY59
Exeforde Av, Ashf. TW15 114 BN91
Exeter Cl, E6 off Harper Rd 87 EM72
Watford WD24 24 BW40
Exeter Gdns, Ilf. IG1 68 EL60
Exeter Ho, SW15
off Putney Heath 119 CW86
Exeter Ms, NW6
off West Hampstead Ms 82 DB65
SW6 off Farm La 100 DA80
Exeter Rd, E16 86 EG71
E17 67 EA57
N9 46 DW47
N14 45 DH46
NW2 63 CY64
Croydon CR0 142 DS101
Dagenham RM10 89 FB65
Enfield EN3 31 DX41
Feltham TW13 116 BZ90
Gravesend DA12 131 GK90
Harrow HA2 60 BY61
Hounslow (Hthrw Air.) TW6 95 BS82
Welling DA16 105 ET82
Exeter St, WC2 196 A10
Exeter Way, SE14 103 DZ80
Hounslow (Hthrw Air.) TW6 95 BS83
Exford Gdns, SE12 124 EH88
Exford Rd, SE12 124 EH89
Exhibition Cl, W12 81 CW73
Exhibition Rd, SW7 198 A5
Exmoor Cl, Ilf. IG6 49 EQ53
Exmoor St, W10 81 CX70
Exmouth Mkt, EC1 196 D4
Exmouth Ms, NW1 195 L3
Exmouth Pl, E8 84 DV66
Exmouth Rd, E17 67 DZ57
Bromley BR2 144 EH97
Grays RM17 110 GB79
Hayes UB4 77 BS69
Ruislip HA4 60 BW62
Welling DA16 106 EW81
Exmouth St, E1
off Commercial Rd 84 DW72
Exning Rd, E16 86 EF70
Exon St, SE17 201 M10
Explorer Av, Stai. TW19 114 BL88
Explorer Dr, Wat. WD18 23 BT44
Express Dr, Ilf. IG3 70 EV60
Exton Cres, NW10 80 CQ66
Exton Gdns, Dag. RM8 70 EW64
Exton Rd, NW10 80 CQ66
Exton St, SE1 200 D3
Eyebright Cl, Croy. CR0
off Primrose La 143 DX102
Eyhurst Av, Horn. RM12 71 FG62
Eyhurst Cl, NW2 63 CU61
Tadworth (Kgswd) KT20 173 CZ123
Eyhurst Pk, Tad. KT20 174 DC123
Eyhurst Spur, Tad. KT20 173 CZ124
Eylewood Rd, SE27 122 DQ92
Eynella Rd, SE22 122 DT87
Eynham Rd, W12 81 CW72
EYNSFORD, Dart. DA4 148 FL103
★ **Eynsford Castle**, Dart. DA4 148 FK103
Eynsford Cl, Orp. BR5 145 EQ101
Eynsford Cres, Bex. DA5 126 EW88
Eynsford Rd, Dart.
(Fnghm) DA4 148 FM102
Greenhithe DA9 129 FW85
Ilford IG3 69 ES61
Sevenoaks TN14 165 FH108
Eynsford Rd, Swanley BR8 147 FD100
Eynsham Dr, SE2 106 EU77
Eynswood Dr, Sid. DA14 126 EV92
Eyot Gdns, W6 99 CT78
Eyot Grn, W4
off Chiswick Mall 99 CT79
Eyre Cl, Rom. RM2 71 FH56
Eyre Ct, NW8 off Finchley Rd 82 DD68
Eyre St Hill, EC1 196 D5
Eyston Dr, Wey. KT13 152 BN110
Eythorne Rd, SW9 101 DN81
Ezra St, E2 84 DT69

F

Faber Gdns, NW4 63 CU57
Fabian Rd, SW6 99 CZ80
Fabian St, E6 87 EM70
Fackenden La, Sev.
(Shore.) TN14 165 FH113
Factory La, N17 46 DT54
Croydon CR0 141 DN102
Factory Rd, E16 86 EL74
Gravesend (Nthflt) DA11 130 GC86
Factory Sq, SW16 121 DL93
Factory Yd, W7
off Uxbridge Rd 79 CE74
Faesten Way, Bex. DA5 127 FE90
Faggotts Cl, Rad. WD7 25 CJ35
Faggs Rd, Felt. TW14 115 BU85
Fagus Av, Rain. RM13 90 FK69
Faints Cl, Wal.Cr. EN7 14 DT29
Fairacre, N.Mal. KT3 138 CS97
Fairacres, SW15 99 CU84
Fair Acres, Brom. BR2 144 EG99
Fairacres, Cob. KT11 154 BX112
Croydon CR0 161 DZ109
Ruislip HA4 59 BT59
Tadworth KT20 173 CW121
Fairacres Cl, Pot.B. EN6 11 CZ33
Fairbairn Cl, Pur. CR8 159 DN113
Fairbairn Grn, SW9 101 DN81
Fairbank Av, Orp. BR6 145 EP103
Fairbank Est, N1 off East Rd 84 DR68
Fairbanks Rd, N17 66 DT55
Fairbourne, Cob. KT11 154 BX113
Fairbourne Cl, Wok. GU21
off Abercorn Way 166 AU118
Fairbourne La, Cat. CR3 176 DQ122
Fairbourne Rd, N17 66 DS55
Fairbridge Rd, N19 65 DK61
Fairbrook Cl, N13 45 DN50
Fairbrook Rd, N13 45 DN51
Fairburn Cl, Borwd. WD6 26 CN39
Fairburn Ct, SW15
off Mercier Rd 119 CY85
Fairby Rd, SE12 124 EH85
Faircharm Trd Est, SE8 103 EB80
Fairchild Cl, SW11
off Wye St 100 DD82
Fairchildes Av, Croy.
(New Adgtn) CR0 161 ED112
Fairchildes La, Warl. CR6 161 ED114
Fairchild Pl, EC2 197 N5
Fairchild St, EC2 197 N5
Fair Cl, Bushey WD23
off Claybury 40 CB45
Fairclough St, E1 84 DU72
Faircross Av, Bark. IG11 87 EQ65
Romford RM5 51 FD52
Fairdale Gdns, SW15 99 CV84
Hayes UB3 77 BU74
Fairdene Rd, Couls. CR5 175 DK117
Fairey Av, Hayes UB3 95 BT77
Fairfax Av, Epsom KT17 157 CV109
Redhill RH1 184 DE133
Fairfax Cl, Walt. KT12 135 BV102
Fairfax Gdns, SE3 104 EK81
Fairfax Ms, E16 205 P2
SW15 99 CW84
Fairfax Pl, NW6 82 DC66
W14 99 CY76
Fairfax Rd, N8 65 DN56
NW6 82 DC66
W4 98 CS76
Grays RM17 110 GB78
Teddington TW11 117 CG93
Tilbury RM18 111 GF81
Woking GU22 167 BB120
Fairfax Way, N10
off Cromwell Rd 44 DG52
Fairfield App, Stai.
(Wrays.) TW19 112 AX86
Fairfield Av, NW4 63 CV58
Edgware HA8 42 CP51
Ruislip HA4 59 BQ59
Slough (Datchet) SL3 92 AW80
Staines TW18 113 BF91
Twickenham TW2 116 CB88
Upminster RM14 72 FQ62
Watford WD19 40 BW48
Fairfield Cl, N12 44 DC49
Enfield EN3
off Scotland Grn Rd N 31 DY42
Epsom (Ewell) KT19 156 CS106
Hornchurch RM12 71 FG60
Mitcham CR4 120 DE94
Northwood HA6
off Thirlmere Gdns 39 BP50
Radlett WD7 25 CE37
Sidcup DA15 125 ET86
Slough (Datchet) SL3 92 AX80
Fairfield Ct, NW10 81 CU67
Northwood HA6
off Windsor Cl 39 BU54
Fairfield Cres, Edg. HA8 42 CP51
Fairfield Dr, SW18 120 DB85
Greenford UB6 79 CJ67
Harrow HA2 60 CC55
Fairfield E, Kings.T. KT1 138 CL96
Fairfield Gdns, N8
off Elder Av 65 DL57
Fairfield Gro, SE7 104 EK78
★ **Fairfield Halls**, Croy. CR0 142 DR104
Fairfield N, Kings.T. KT1 138 CL96
Fairfield Pk, Cob. KT11 154 BX114
Fairfield Path, Croy. CR0 142 DR104
Fairfield Pathway, Horn. RM12 90 FJ66
Fairfield Pl, Kings.T. KT1 138 CL97
Fairfield Rd, E3 85 EA68
E17 47 DY54
N8 65 DL57
N18 46 DU49
W7 97 CG76
Beckenham BR3 143 EA96
Bexleyheath DA7 106 EZ82
Brentwood CM14 54 FW48
Bromley BR1 124 EG94
Croydon CR0 142 DS104
Epping CM16 18 EV29
Ilford IG1 87 EP65
Kingston upon Thames KT1 138 CL96
Leatherhead KT22 171 CH121
Orpington BR5 145 ER100
Southall UB1 78 BZ72
Staines (Wrays.) TW19 112 AX86
Uxbridge UB8 76 BK65
West Drayton UB7 76 BL74
Woodford Green IG8 48 EG51
Fairfields, Cher. KT16 134 BG102
Gravesend DA12 131 GL92
Fairfields Cl, NW9 62 CQ57
Fairfields Cres, NW9 62 CQ56
Fairfield S, Kings.T. KT1 138 CL96
Fairfields Rd, Houns. TW3 96 CC83
Fairfield St, SW18 120 DB85
Fairfield Trade Pk,
Kings.T. KT1 138 CM97
Fairfield Wk, Lthd. KT22
off Fairfield Rd 171 CH121
Waltham Cross (Chsht) EN8 15 DY28
Fairfield Way, Barn. EN5 28 DA43
Coulsdon CR5 159 DK114
Epsom KT19 156 CS106
Fairfield W, Kings.T. KT1 138 CL96
Fairfolds, Wat. WD25 24 BY36
Fairfoot Rd, E3 85 EA70
Fairford Av, Bexh. DA7 107 FD81
Croydon CR0 143 DX99
Fairford Cl, Croy. CR0 143 DY99
Reigate RH2 184 DC132
Romford RM3
off Fairford Way 52 FP51
West Byfleet KT14 151 BF114
Fairford Ct, Sutt. SM2
off Grange Rd 158 DB108
Fairford Gdns, Wor.Pk. KT4 139 CT104
Fairford Ho, SE11 200 E9
Fairford Way, Rom. RM3 52 FP51
Fairgreen, Barn. EN4 28 DF41
Fairgreen E, Barn. EN4 28 DF41
Fairgreen Par, Mitch. CR4
off London Rd 140 DF97
Fairgreen Rd, Th.Hth. CR7 141 DP99
Fairham Av, S.Ock. RM15 91 FU73
Fairhaven, Egh. TW20 113 AZ92
Fairhaven Av, Croy. CR0 143 DX100
Fairhaven Cres, Wat. WD19 39 BU48
Fairhaven Rd, Red. RH1 184 DG130
Fairhazel Gdns, NW6 82 DB65
Fairholme, Felt. TW14 115 BR87
Fairholme Av, Rom. RM2 71 FG57
Fairholme Cl, N3 63 CY56
Fairholme Cres, Ashtd. KT21 171 CJ117
Hayes UB4 77 BT70
Fairholme Gdns, N3 63 CY55
Upminster RM14 73 FT59
Fairholme Rd, W14 99 CY78
Ashford TW15 114 BL92
Croydon CR0 141 DN101
Harrow HA1 61 CF57
Ilford IG1 69 EM59
Sutton SM1 157 CZ107
Fairholt Cl, N16 66 DS60
Fairholt Rd, N16 66 DR60
Fairholt St, SW7 198 C6
Fairkytes Av, Horn. RM11 72 FK60
Fairland Rd, E15 86 EF65
Fairlands Av, Buck.H. IG9 48 EG47
Sutton SM1 140 DA103
Thornton Heath CR7 141 DM98
Fairlands Ct, SE9
off North Pk 125 EN86
Fair La, Couls. CR5 184 DC125
Fairlawn, SE7 104 EJ79
Leatherhead (Bkhm) KT23 170 BZ124
Fairlawn Av, N2 64 DE56
W4 98 CQ77
Bexleyheath DA7 106 EX82
Fairlawn Cl, N14 29 DJ44
Esher (Clay.) KT10 155 CF107
Feltham TW13 116 BZ91
Kingston upon Thames KT2 118 CQ93
Fairlawn Dr, Wdf.Grn. IG8 48 EG52
Fairlawnes, Wall. SM6
off Maldon Rd 159 DH106
Fairlawn Gdns, Sthl. UB1 78 BZ73
Fairlawn Gro, W4 98 CQ77
Banstead SM7 158 DD113
Fairlawn Pk, SE26 123 DY92
Woking GU21 150 AY114
Fairlawn Rd, SW19 119 CZ94
Banstead SM7 158 DD112
Carshalton SM5 158 DC111
Fairlawns, Add.
(Wdhm) KT15 151 BF111
Brentwood CM14 54 FU48
Pinner HA5 40 BW54
Sunbury-on-Thames TW16 135 BU97
Twickenham TW1 117 CJ86
Watford WD17
off Langley Rd 23 BT38
Weybridge KT13 153 BS106
Fairlawns Cl, Horn. RM11 72 FM59
Staines TW18 114 BH93
Fairlea Pl, W5 79 CK70
Fairley Way, Wal.Cr.
(Chsht) EN7 14 DV28
Fairlie Gdns, SE23 122 DW87
Fairlight Av, E4 47 ED47
NW10 80 CS68
Woodford Green IG8 48 EG51
Fairlight Cl, E4 47 ED47
Worcester Park KT4 157 CW105
Fairlight Dr, Uxb. UB8 76 BK65
Fairlight Rd, SW17 120 DD91
⊖ **Fairlop** 49 ER53
Fairlop Cl, Horn. RM12 89 FH65
Fairlop Gdns, Ilf. IG6 49 EQ52
Fairlop Rd, E11 67 ED59
Ilford IG6 49 EQ54
Fairmark Dr, Uxb. UB10 76 BN65
Fairmead, Brom. BR1 145 EM98
Surbiton KT5 138 CP102
Woking GU21 166 AW118
Fairmead Cl, Brom. BR1 145 EM98
Hounslow TW5 96 BX80
New Malden KT3 138 CR97
Fairmead Cres, Edg. HA8 42 CQ48
Fairmead Gdns, Ilf. IG4 68 EL57
Fairmead Ho, E9
off Kingsmead Way 67 DY63
Fairmead Rd, N19 65 DK62
Croydon CR0 141 DM102
Loughton IG10 32 EH42
Fairmeads, Cob. KT11 154 BZ113
Loughton IG10 33 EP40
Fairmead Side, Loug. IG10 32 EJ43
FAIRMILE, Cob. KT11 154 BZ112
Fairmile Av, SW16 121 DK92
Cobham KT11 154 BY114
Fairmile Ct, Cob. KT11
off Ashcroft Pk 154 BY112
Fairmile Ho, Tedd. TW11
off Twickenham Rd 117 CG91
Fairmile La, Cob. KT11 154 BX112
Fairmile Pk Copse, Cob. KT11 154 BZ112
Fairmile Pk Rd, Cob. KT11 154 BZ113
Fairmont Av, E14
off Blackwall Way 85 ED74
Fairmont Cl, Belv. DA17
off Lullingstone Rd 106 EZ78
Fairmount Rd, SW2 121 DM86
Fairoak Cl, Ken. CR8 175 DP115
Leatherhead (Oxshott) KT22 155 CD112
Orpington BR5 145 EP101
Fairoak Dr, SE9 125 ER85
Fairoak Gdns, Rom. RM1 51 FE54
Fairoak La, Chess. KT9 155 CF111
Leatherhead
(Oxshott) KT22 155 CF111
Fairseat Cl, Bushey
(Bushey Hth) WD23
off Hive Rd 41 CE47
Fairs Rd, Lthd. KT22 171 CG119
Fairstead Wk, N1
off Popham Rd 84 DQ67
Fair St, SE1 201 N4
Hounslow TW3 off High St 96 CC83
Fairthorn Rd, SE7 205 N10
Fairtrough Rd, Orp. BR6 164 EV112
Fairview, Epsom KT17 157 CW111
Erith DA8 off Guild Rd 107 FF80
Potters Bar EN6
off Hawkshead Rd 12 DB29
Fairview Av, Brwd.
(Hutt.) CM13 55 GE45
Rainham RM13 90 FK68
Wembley HA0 79 CK65
Woking GU22 166 AY118
Fairview Cl, E17 47 DY53
Chigwell IG7 49 ES49
Woking GU22
off Fairview Av 167 AZ118
Fairview Ct, Ashf. TW15 114 BN92
Fairview Cres, Har. HA2 60 CA60
Fairview Dr, Chig. IG7 49 ES49
Orpington BR6 163 ER105
Shepperton TW17 134 BM99
Watford WD17 23 BS36
Fairview Gdns, Wdf.Grn. IG8 48 EH53
Fairview Ind Est, Oxt. RH8 188 EG133
Fairview Ind Pk, Rain. RM13 89 FD71
Fairview Pl, SW2 121 DM87
Fairview Rd, N15 66 DT57
SW16 141 DM95
Chigwell IG7 49 ES49
Enfield EN2 29 DN39
Epsom KT17 157 CT111
Gravesend
(Istead Rise) DA13 130 GD94
Sutton SM1 158 DD106
Fairview Way, Edg. HA8 42 CN49
Fairwater Av, Well. DA16 106 EU84
Fairwater Dr, Add.
(New Haw) KT15 152 BK109
Fairway, SW20 139 CW97
Bexleyheath DA6 126 EY85
Carshalton SM5 158 DC111
Chertsey KT16 134 BH102
Orpington BR5 145 ER99
Virginia Water GU25 132 AV100
Woodford Green IG8 48 EJ50
Fairway, The, N13 46 DQ48
N14 29 DH44
NW7 42 CR48
W3 80 CS72
Abbots Langley WD5 7 BR32
Barnet EN5 28 DB44
Bromley BR1 145 EM99
Gravesend DA11 131 GG89
Leatherhead KT22 171 CG118
New Malden KT3 138 CR95
Northolt UB5 78 CC65
Northwood HA6 39 BS49
Ruislip HA4 60 BX62
Upminster RM14 72 FQ59
Uxbridge UB10 76 BM68
Wembley HA0 61 CH62
West Molesey KT8 136 CB97
Weybridge KT13 152 BN111
Fairway Av, NW9 62 CP55
Borehamwood WD6 26 CP40
West Drayton UB7 76 BJ74
Fairway Cl, NW11 64 DC59
Croydon CR0 143 DY99
Epsom KT19 156 CQ105
Hounslow TW4 116 BW85
St. Albans (Park St) AL2 8 CC27
West Drayton UB7
off Fairway Av 76 BK74
Woking GU22 166 AU119
Fairway Ct, NW7
off The Fairway 42 CR48
Fairway Dr, SE28 88 EX72
Dartford DA2 128 FP87
Greenford UB6 78 CB66
Fairway Gdns, Beck. BR3 143 ED100
Fairway Gdns, Ilford IG1 69 EQ64
Fairways, Ashf. TW15 115 BP93
Kenley CR8 176 DQ117
Stanmore HA7 42 CL54
Teddington TW11 117 CK94
Waltham Abbey EN9 16 EE34
Waltham Cross (Chsht) EN8 15 DX26
Fairweather Cl, N15 66 DS56
Fairweather Rd, N16 66 DU58
Fairwyn Rd, SE26 123 DY91
Fakenham Cl, NW7 43 CU52
Northolt UB5
off Goodwood Dr 78 CA65
Fakruddin St, E1 84 DU70
Falaise, Egh. TW20 112 AY92
Falcon Av, Brom. BR1 144 EL98
Grays RM17 110 GB79
Falconberg Ct, W1 195 N8
Falconberg Ms, W1 195 M8
Falcon Cl, SE1 200 G2
W4 off Sutton La S 98 CQ79
Dartford DA1 128 FM85
Northwood HA6 39 BS52
Waltham Abbey EN9
off Kestrel Rd 16 EG34
Falcon Ct, EC4 196 D9
Woking GU21 151 BC113
Falcon Cres, Enf. EN3 31 DX43
Falcon Dr, Stai. (Stanw.) TW19 114 BK86
Falconer Rd, Bushey WD23 24 BZ44
Ilford IG6 50 EV50
Falconer Wk, N7
off Newington Barrow Way 65 DM61
Falcon Gro, SW11 100 DE83
Falcon Ho, W13 79 CF70
Falconhurst, Lthd.
(Oxshott) KT22 171 CD115
Falcon La, SW11 100 DE83
Falcon Ms, Grav. DA11 130 GE88
Falcon Pk Ind Est, NW10 63 CT64
Falcon Rd, SW11 100 DE82
Enfield EN3 31 DX43
Hampton TW12 116 BZ94
Falcons Cl, West.
(Bigg.H.) TN16 178 EK117
Falcon St, E13 86 EG70
Falcon Ter, SW11 100 DE83
Falcon Way, E11 68 EG56
E14 204 C8
NW9 42 CS54
Feltham TW14 115 BV85
Harrow HA3 62 CL57
Hornchurch RM12 89 FG66
Sunbury-on-Thames TW16 135 BS96
Watford WD25 8 BY34
FALCONWOOD, Well. DA16 105 ER83
⇌ **Falconwood** 105 EQ84
Falconwood, Egh. TW20 112 AY92
Leatherhead (E.Hors.) KT24 171 CF120
Falconwood Av, Well. DA16 105 ER82
Falconwood Par, Well. DA16 105 ES84
Falconwood Rd, Croy. CR0 161 EA108
Falcourt Cl, Sutt. SM1 158 DB106
Falkirk Cl, Horn. RM11 72 FN60
Falkirk Gdns, Wat. WD19
off Blackford Rd 40 BX50
Falkirk Ho, W9 82 DB69
Falkirk St, N1 197 N1
Falkland Av, N3 44 DA52
N11 44 DG49
Falkland Pk Av, SE25 142 DS97
Falkland Pl, NW5
off Falkland Rd 65 DJ64
Falkland Rd, N8 65 DN56
NW5 65 DJ64
Barnet EN5 27 CY40
Fallaize Av, Ilf. IG1
off Riverdene Rd 69 EP63
Falling La, West Dr. UB7 76 BL73
Falloden Way, NW11 64 DA56
Fallow Cl, Chig. IG7 49 ET50
Fallow Ct, SE16
off Argyle Way 102 DU78
Fallow Ct Av, N12 44 DC52
Fallowfield, Dart. (Bean) DA2 129 FV90
Stanmore HA7 41 CG48
Fallowfield Cl, Uxb.
(Hare.) UB9 38 BJ53
Fallowfield Ct, Stan. HA7 41 CG48
Fallow Flds, Loug. IG10 48 EJ45
Fallowfields Dr, N12 44 DE51
Fallows Cl, N2 44 DC54
Fallsbrook Rd, SW16 121 DJ94
Falman Cl, N9
off Croyland Rd 46 DU46
Falmer Rd, E17 67 EB55
N15 66 DQ57
Enfield EN1 30 DS42
Falmouth Av, E4 47 ED50
Falmouth Cl, N22
off Truro Rd 45 DM52
SE12 124 EF85
Falmouth Gdns, Ilf. IG4 68 EL57
Falmouth Ho, Kings.T. KT2
off Kingsgate Rd 138 CL95
Falmouth Rd, SE1 201 J6
Walton-on-Thames KT12 154 BW105
Falmouth St, E15 67 ED64
Falmouth Way, E17
off Gosport Rd 67 DZ57
Falstaff Cl, Dart. DA1
off Lower Sta Rd 127 FE86
Falstaff Ms, Hmptn.
(Hmptn H.) TW12
off Hampton Rd 117 CD92
Falstone, Wok. GU21 166 AV118
Fambridge Cl, SE26 123 DZ91
Fambridge Rd, Dag. RM8 70 FA60
Famet Av, Pur. CR8 160 DQ113
Famet Cl, Pur. CR8 160 DQ113
Famet Wk, Pur. CR8 160 DQ113
★ **Family Records Cen**,
Public Record Office, EC1 196 E3
Fane St, W14
off North End Rd 99 CZ79

★ Place of interest ⇌ Railway station ⊖ London Underground station DLR Docklands Light Railway station Tra Tramlink station H Hospital Riv Pedestrian ferry landing stage

Fangrove Pk, Cher. (Lyne) KT16 133 BB102
★ Fan Mus, SE10 103 EC80
Fanns Ri, Purf. RM19 108 FN77
Fann St, EC1 197 H5
EC2 197 H5
Fanshawe Av, Bark. IG11 87 EQ65
Fanshawe Cres, Dag. RM9 70 EY64
Hornchurch RM11 72 FK58
Fanshawe Rd, Grays RM16 111 GG76
Richmond TW10 117 CJ91
Fanshaw St, N1 197 M2
Fanthorpe St, SW15 99 CW83
Faraday Av, Sid. DA14 126 EU89
Faraday Cl, N7 off Bride St 83 DM65
Watford WD18 23 BR44
★ Faraday Mus, W1 199 K1
Faraday Rd, E15 86 EF65
SW19 120 DA93
W3 80 CQ73
W10 81 CY71
Southall UB1 78 CB73
Welling DA16 106 EU83
West Molesey KT8 136 CA98
Faraday Way, SE18 104 EK76
Croydon CR0 off Ampere Way 141 DM102
Orpington BR5 146 EV98
Fareham Rd, Felt. TW14 116 BW87
Fareham St, W1 195 M8
Farewell Pl, Mitch. CR4 140 DE95
Faringdon Av, Brom. BR2 145 EP100
Romford RM3 52 FJ53
Faringford Cl, Pot.B. EN6 12 DD31
Faringford Rd, E15 86 EE66
Farington Acres, Wey. KT13 135 BR104
Faris Barn Dr, Add. (Wdhm) KT15 151 BF112
Faris La, Add. (Wdhm) KT15 151 BF111
Farjeon Rd, SE3 104 EK81
FARLEIGH, Warl. CR6 161 DZ114
Farleigh Av, Brom. BR2 144 EF100
Farleigh Border, Croy. CR0 161 DY112
Farleigh Ct Rd, Warl. CR6 161 DZ114
Farleigh Dean Cres, Croy. CR0 161 EB111
Farleigh Pl, N16 off Farleigh Rd 66 DT63
Farleigh Rd, N16 66 DT63
Addlestone (New Haw) KT15 152 BG111
Warlingham CR6 177 DX118
Farleton Cl, Wey. KT13 153 BR107
Farley Common, West. TN16 189 EP126
Farleycroft, West. TN16 189 EQ126
Farley Dr, Ilf. IG3 69 ES60
Farley La, West. TN16 189 EP127
Farley Ms, SE6 123 EC87
Farley Nurs, West. TN16 189 EQ127
Farley Pk, Oxt. RH8 187 ED130
Farley Pl, SE25 142 DU98
Farley Rd, SE6 123 EB87
Gravesend DA12 131 GM88
South Croydon CR2 160 DV108
Farlington Pl, SW15 off Roehampton La 119 CV87
Farlow Cl, Grav. (Nthflt) DA11 131 GF90
Farlow Rd, SW15 99 CX83
Farlton Rd, SW18 120 DB87
Farman Gro, Nthlt. UB5 off Wayfarer Rd 78 BX69
Farm Av, NW2 63 CY62
SW16 121 DL91
Harrow HA2 60 BZ59
Swanley BR8 147 FC97
Wembley HA0 79 CJ65
Farmborough Cl, Har. HA1 off Pool Rd 61 CD59
Farm Cl, SW6 off Farm La 100 DA80
Amersham HP6 20 AX39
Barnet EN5 27 CW43
Borehamwood WD6 25 CK38
Brentwood (Hutt.) CM13 55 GC45
Buckhurst Hill IG9 48 EJ48
Chertsey (Lyne) KT16 133 BA100
Coulsdon CR5 174 DF120
Dagenham RM10 89 FC66
Leatherhead (Fetch.) KT22 171 CD124
Potters Bar (Cuffley) EN6 13 DK27
Radlett WD7 10 CL30
Shepperton TW17 134 BN101
Southall UB1 78 CB73
Staines TW18 113 BE92
Sutton SM2 158 DD108
Uxbridge UB10 59 BP61
Wallington SM6 159 DJ110
Waltham Cross (Chsht) EN8 14 DW30
West Byfleet (Byfleet) KT14 152 BM112
West Wickham BR4 144 EE104
Farmcote Rd, SE12 124 EG88
Farm Ct, NW4 63 CU55
Farm Cres, St.Alb. AL2 off Shenley La 9 CH26
Slough SL2 74 AV71
Farmcroft, Grav. DA11 131 GG89
Farmdale Rd, SE10 205 N10
Carshalton SM5 158 DE108
Farm Dr, Croy. CR0 143 DZ103
Purley CR8 159 DK112
Farm End, E4 32 EE43
Northwood HA6 off Drakes Dr 39 BP53
Farmer Rd, E10 67 EB60
Farmers Cl, Wat. WD25 7 BV33
Farmers Ct, Wal.Abb. EN9 off Winters Way 16 EG33
Farmers Rd, SE5 101 DP80
Staines TW18 113 BE92
Farmer St, W8 off Uxbridge St 82 DA74
Farm Fld, Wat. WD17 23 BS38
Farmfield Rd, Brom. BR1 124 EE92
Farm Flds, S.Croy. CR2 160 DS111
Farm Hill Rd, Wal.Abb. EN9 15 EC34
Farm Ho Cl, Brox. EN10 15 DZ25
Farmhouse Cl, Wok. GU22 167 BD115
Farmhouse Rd, SW16 121 DJ94
Farmilo Rd, E17 67 DZ59
Farmington Av, Sutt. SM1 140 DD104
Farmlands, Enf. EN2 29 DN39
Pinner HA5 59 BU56
Farmlands, The, Nthlt. UB5 78 BZ65
Farmland Wk, Chis. BR7 125 EP92
Farm La, N14 28 DG44
SW6 100 DA79
Addlestone KT15 152 BG107
Ashtead KT21 172 CN116
Carshalton SM5 158 DF110
Croydon CR0 143 DZ103
Epsom KT18 172 CP119
Purley CR8 159 DJ110
Rickmansworth (Loud.) WD3 22 BH41
Woking (Send) GU23 167 BC124
Farmleigh, N14 45 DJ45
Farmleigh Gro, Walt. KT12 153 BT106
Farm Pl, W8 off Uxbridge St 82 DA74
Dartford DA1 107 FG84
Farm Rd, N21 45 DP46
NW10 80 CR67
Edgware HA8 42 CP51
Esher KT10 136 CB102
Grays (Orsett) RM16 111 GF75
Hounslow TW4 116 BY88
Morden SM4 140 DB99
Northwood HA6 39 BQ50
Rainham RM13 90 FJ69
Rickmansworth (Chorl.) WD3 21 BA42
Sevenoaks TN14 191 FJ121
Staines TW18 114 BH93
Sutton SM2 158 DD108
Warlingham CR6 177 DY119
Woking GU22 167 BB120
Farmstead Rd, SE6 123 EB91
Harrow HA3 41 CD53
Farm St, W1 199 H1
Farm Vale, Bex. DA5 127 FB86
Farmview, Cob. KT11 170 BX116
Farm Vw, Tad. (Lwr Kgswd) KT20 183 CZ127
Farm Wk, NW11 63 CZ57
Farm Way, Buck.H. IG9 48 EJ49
Bushey WD23 24 CB42
Farmway, Dag. RM8 70 EW63
Farm Way, Horn. RM12 71 FH63
Northwood HA6 39 BS49
Staines TW19 113 BF86
Worcester Park KT4 139 CW104
Farnaby Dr, Sev. TN13 190 FF126
Farnaby Rd, SE9 104 EJ84
Bromley BR1, BR2 123 ED94
Farnan Av, E17 47 EA54
Farnan Rd, SW16 121 DL92
FARNBOROUGH, Orp. BR6 163 EP106
Farnborough Av, E17 67 DY55
South Croydon CR2 161 DX108
Farnborough Cl, Wem. HA9 off Chalkhill Rd 62 CP61
Farnborough Common, Orp. BR6 145 EM104
Farnborough Cres, Brom. BR2 off Saville Row 144 EF102
South Croydon CR2 161 DY109
Farnborough Hill, Orp. BR6 163 ER106
Farnborough Ho, SW15 off Fontley Way 119 CU88
Farnborough Way, SE15 off Blakes Rd 102 DS80
Orpington BR6 163 EQ105
Farncombe St, SE16 202 C5
Farndale Av, N13 45 DP48
Farndale Cres, Grnf. UB6 78 CC69
Farnell Ms, SW5 off Earls Ct Sq 100 DB78
Farnell Pl, W3 80 CP73
Farnell Rd, Islw. TW7 97 CD83
Staines TW18 114 BG90
Farnes Dr, Rom. RM2 52 FJ54
Farnham Cl, N20 44 DC45
Hemel Hempstead (Bov.) HP3 5 BA28
Farnham Gdns, SW20 139 CV96
Farnham Pl, SE1 200 G3
Farnham Rd, Ilf. IG3 69 ET59
Romford RM3 52 FK50
Welling DA16 106 EW82
Farnham Royal, SE11 101 DM78
FARNINGHAM, Dart. DA4 148 FN100
Farningham Cres, Cat. CR3 off Commonwealth Rd 176 DU123
Farningham Hill Rd, Dart. (Fnghm) DA4 148 FJ99
⇌ Farningham Road 148 FP96
Farningham Rd, N17 46 DU52
Caterham CR3 176 DU123
Farnley, Wok. GU21 166 AT117
Farnley Rd, E4 48 EE45
SE25 142 DR98
Farnol Rd, Dart. DA1 108 FN84
Faro Cl, Brom. BR1 145 EN96
Faroe Rd, W14 99 CX76
Farorna Wk, Enf. EN2 29 DN39
Farquhar Rd, SE19 122 DT92
SW19 120 DA90
Farquharson Rd, Croy. CR0 142 DQ102
Farraline Rd, Wat. WD18 23 BV42
Farrance Rd, Rom. RM6 70 EY58
Farrance St, E14 85 DZ72
Farrans Ct, Har. HA3 61 CH59
Farrant Av, N22 45 DN54
Farrant Cl, Orp. BR6 164 EU108
Farrant Way, Borwd. WD6 26 CL39
Farr Av, Bark. IG11 88 EU68
Farrell Ho, E1 84 DW72
Farren Rd, SE23 123 DY89
Farrer Ms, N8 off Farrer Rd 65 DJ56
Farrer Rd, N8 65 DJ56
Harrow HA3 62 CL57
Farrer's Pl, Croy. CR0 161 DX105
Farrier Cl, Sun. TW16 135 BU98
Uxbridge UB8 off Horseshoe Dr 76 BN72
Farrier Rd, Nthlt. UB5 78 CA68
Farriers Cl, Epsom KT17 156 CS111
Gravesend DA12 131 GM88
Farriers Cl, Hemel Hempstead (Bov.) HP3 off Chipperfield Rd 5 BB28
Farriers Ct, Sutt. SM3 off Forge La 157 CY108
Watford WD25 7 BV32
Farriers End, Brox. EN10 15 DZ26
Farriers Ms, SE15 off Machell Rd 102 DW83
Farriers Rd, Epsom KT17 156 CS112
Farrier St, NW1 83 DH66
Farriers Way, Borwd. WD6 26 CQ44
Farrier Wk, SW10 100 DC79
⇌ Farringdon 196 E6
⊖ Farringdon 196 E6
Farringdon La, EC1 196 E5
Farringdon Rd, EC1 196 D4
Farringdon St, EC4 196 F8
Farringford Cl, St.Alb. AL2 8 CA26
Farrington Av, Orp. BR5 146 EV97
Farrington Pl, Chis. BR7 125 ER94
Northwood HA6 39 BT49
Farrins Rents, SE16 203 K3
Farrow La, SE14 102 DW80
Farrow Pl, SE16 203 K6
Farr Rd, Enf. EN2 30 DR39
Farthingale Ct, Wal.Abb. EN9 16 EG34
Farthingale La, Wal.Abb. EN9 16 EG34
Farthingale Wk, E15 85 ED66
Farthing All, SE1 202 B5
Farthing Cl, Dart. DA1 108 FM84
Farthing Flds, E1 202 E2
Farthing Grn La, Slou. (Stoke P.) SL2 74 AU68
Farthings, Wok. (Knap.) GU21 166 AS116
Farthings, The, Kings.T. KT2 off Brunswick Rd 138 CN95
Farthings Cl, E4 48 EE48
Pinner HA5 59 BV58
Farthing St, Orp. BR6 163 EM108
Farwell Rd, Sid. DA14 126 EV90
Farwig La, Brom. BR1 144 EF95
Fashion St, E1 197 P7
Fashoda Rd, Brom. BR2 144 EK98
Fassett Rd, E8 84 DU65
Kingston upon Thames KT1 138 CL98
Fassett Sq, E8 84 DU65
Fassnidge Way, Uxb. UB8 off Oxford Rd 76 BJ66
Fauconberg Rd, W4 98 CQ79
Faulkner Cl, Dag. RM8 70 EX59
Faulkner's All, EC1 196 F6
Faulkners Rd, Walt. KT12 154 BW106
Faulkner St, SE14 102 DW81
Fauna Cl, Rom. RM6 70 EW59
Faunce St, SE17 off Harmsworth St 101 DP78
Favart Rd, SW6 100 DA81
Faverolle Grn, Wal.Cr. EN8 15 DX28
Faversham Av, E4 48 EE46
Enfield EN1 30 DR44
Faversham Cl, Chig. IG7 50 EV47
Faversham Rd, SE6 123 DZ87
Beckenham BR3 143 DZ96
Morden SM4 140 DB100
Fawcett Cl, SW11 100 DD82
SW16 121 DN91
Fawcett Est, E5 66 DU60
Fawcett Rd, NW10 81 CT67
Croydon CR0 142 DQ104
Fawcett St, SW10 100 DC79
Fawcus Cl, Esher (Clay.) KT10 off Dalmore Av 155 CF107
Fawe Pk Rd, SW15 99 CZ84
Fawe St, E14 85 EB71
Fawke Common, Sev. (Undrvr) TN15 191 FP127
Fawke Common Rd, Sev. TN15 191 FP126
Fawkes Av, Dart. DA1 128 FM89
FAWKHAM GREEN, Long. DA3 149 FV104
Fawkham Grn Rd, Long. (Fawk.Grn) DA3 149 FV104
H Fawkham Manor Hosp, Long. DA3 149 FW102
Fawkham Rd, Long. DA3 149 FX97
Fawley Rd, NW6 64 DB64
Fawnbrake Av, SE24 121 DP85
Fawn Rd, E13 86 EJ68
Chigwell IG7 49 ET50
Fawns Manor Cl, Felt. TW14 115 BQ88
Fawns Manor Rd, Felt. TW14 115 BR88
Fawood Av, NW10 80 CR66
Fawsley Cl, Slou. (Colnbr.) SL3 93 BE80
Fawters Cl, Brwd. (Hutt.) CM13 55 GD44
Fayerfield, Pot.B. EN6 12 DD31
Faygate Cres, Bexh. DA6 126 FA85
Faygate Rd, SW2 121 DM89
Fay Grn, Abb.L. WD5 7 BR33
Fayland Av, SW16 121 DJ92
Faymore Gdns, S.Ock. RM15 91 FU72
Fearney Mead, Rick. (Mill End) WD3 38 BG46
Fearnley Cres, Hmptn. TW12 116 BY92
Fearnley St, Wat. WD18 23 BV42
Fearns Mead, Brwd. CM14 off Bucklers Ct 54 FW50
Fearon St, SE10 205 M10
Featherbed La, Abb.L. (Bedmond) WD5 off Sergehill La 7 BV26
Croydon CR0 161 DZ108
Romford RM4 50 EY45
Warlingham CR6 161 ED113
Feathers La, Stai. (Wrays.) TW19 113 BA89
Feathers Pl, SE10 103 ED79
Featherstone Av, SE23 122 DV89
Featherstone Gdns, Borwd. WD6 26 CQ42
Featherstone Ind Est, Sthl. UB2 96 BY75
Featherstone Rd, NW7 43 CV51
Southall UB2 96 BY76
Featherstone St, EC1 197 K4
Featherstone Ter, Sthl. UB2 96 BY76
Featley Rd, SW9 101 DP83
Federal Rd, Grnf. UB6 79 CJ68
Federal Way, Wat. WD24 24 BW38
Federation Rd, SE2 106 EV77
Fee Fm Rd, Esher (Clay.) KT10 155 CF108
Feenan Highway, Til. RM18 111 GH80
Felbridge Av, Stan. HA7 41 CG53
Felbridge Cl, SW16 121 DN91
Sutton SM2 158 DC109
Felbrigge Rd, Ilf. IG3 69 ET61
Felcott Cl, Walt. KT12 136 BW104
Felcott Rd, Walt. KT12 136 BW104
Felday Rd, SE13 123 EB86
Felden Cl, Pnr. HA5 40 BY52
Watford WD25 8 BX34
Felden St, SW6 99 CZ81
Feldman Cl, N16 66 DU60
Felgate Ms, W6 99 CV77
Felhampton Rd, SE9 125 EP89
Felhurst Cres, Dag. RM10 71 FB63
Felicia Way, Grays RM16 111 GH77
Felipe Rd, Grays (Chaff.Hun.) RM16 109 FW76
Felix Av, N8 65 DL58
Felix La, Shep. TW17 135 BS100
Felix Rd, W13 79 CG73
Walton-on-Thames KT12 135 BU100
Felixstowe Ct, E16 off Fishguard Way 105 EP75
Felixstowe Rd, N9 46 DU49
N17 66 DT55
NW10 81 CV69
SE2 106 EV76
Fellbrigg Rd, SE22 122 DT85
Fellbrigg St, E1 off Headlam St 84 DV70
Fellbrook, Rich. TW10 117 CH90
Fellmongers Path, SE1 201 N5
Fellmongers Yd, Croy. CR0 off Surrey St 142 DQ103
Fellowes Cl, Hayes UB4 off Paddington Cl 78 BX70
Fellowes Rd, Cars. SM5 140 DE104
Fellows Ct, E2 197 P1
Fellows Rd, NW3 82 DD66
Fell Rd, Croy. CR0 142 DQ104
Felltram Way, SE7 205 N10
Fell Wk, Edg. HA8 off East Rd 42 CP53
Felmersham Cl, SW4 off Haselrigge Rd 101 DK84
Felmingham Rd, SE20 142 DW96
Felnex Trd Est, Wall. SM6 140 DG103
Felsberg Rd, SW2 121 DL86
Fels Cl, Dag. RM10 71 FB62
Fels Fm Av, Dag. RM10 71 FC62
Felsham Rd, SW15 99 CX83
Felspar Cl, SE18 105 ET78
Felstead Av, Ilf. IG5 49 EN53
Felstead Cl, Brwd. (Hutt.) CM13 55 GC44
Felstead Gdns, E14 off Ferry St 103 EC78
Felstead Rd, E11 68 EG59
Epsom KT19 156 CR111
Loughton IG10 48 EL45
Orpington BR6 146 EU103
Romford RM5 51 FC51
Waltham Cross EN8 15 DY32
Felstead St, E9 85 DZ65
Felsted Rd, E16 86 EK72
FELTHAM 115 BU89
⇌ Feltham 115 BV88
Feltham Av, E.Mol. KT8 137 CE98
Felthambrook Way, Felt. TW13 115 BV90
Feltham Business Complex, Felt. TW13 115 BV89
FELTHAMHILL, Felt. TW13 115 BT92
Feltham Hill Rd, Ashf. TW15 115 BP92
Feltham TW13 115 BU91
Feltham Rd, Ashf. TW15 115 BP91
Mitcham CR4 140 DF96
Felton Cl, Borwd. WD6 26 CL38
Broxbourne EN10 15 DZ25
Orpington BR5 145 EP100
Felton Gdns, Bark. IG11 off Sutton Rd 87 ES67
Felton Ho, SE3 off Ryan Cl 104 EH84
Felton Lea, Sid. DA14 125 ET92
Felton Rd, W13 off Camborne Av 97 CJ75
Barking IG11 off Sutton Rd 87 ES68
Felton St, N1 84 DR67
Fencepiece Rd, Chig. IG7 49 EQ50
Ilford IG6 49 EQ50
Fenchurch Av, EC3 197 M9
Fenchurch Bldgs, EC3 197 N9
Fenchurch Pl, EC3 197 N10
⇌ Fenchurch Street 197 N10
Fenchurch St, EC3 197 M10
Fen Cl, Brwd. (Shenf.) CM15 55 GC42
Fen Ct, EC3 197 M10
Fendall Rd, Epsom KT19 156 CQ106
Fendall St, SE1 201 N7
Fendt Cl, E16 off Bowman Av 86 EF73
Fendyke Rd, Belv. DA17 106 EX76
Fenelon Pl, W14 99 CZ77
Fengates Rd, Red. RH1 184 DE134
Fen Gro, Sid. DA15 125 ET86
Fenham Rd, SE15 102 DU80
Fen La, Upmin. (N.Ock.) RM14 73 FW64
Fenman Ct, N17 off Shelbourne Rd 46 DV53
Fenman Gdns, Ilf. IG3 70 EV60
Fenn Cl, Brom. BR1 124 EG93
Fennel Cl, E16 off Cranberry La 86 EE70
Croydon CR0 off Primrose La 143 DX102
Fennells Mead, Epsom KT17 157 CT109
Fennel St, SE18 105 EN79
Fenner Cl, SE16 202 E8
Fenner Ho, Walt. KT12 153 BU105
Fenner Rd, Grays RM16 109 FW77
Fenner Sq, SW11 off Thomas Baines Rd 100 DD83
Fenning St, SE1 201 M4
Fenn St, E9 66 DW64
Fenns Way, Wok. GU21 166 AY115
Fenstanton Av, N12 44 DD50
Fen St, E16 off Victoria Dock Rd 86 EF73
Fens Way, Swan. BR8 127 FG93
Fenswood Cl, Bex. DA5 126 FA85
Fentiman Rd, SW8 101 DL79
Fentiman Way, Horn. RM11 72 FL60
Fenton Av, Stai. TW18 114 BJ93
Fenton Cl, E8 off Laurel St 84 DT65
SW9 101 DM82
Chislehurst BR7 125 EM92
Redhill RH1 184 DG134
★ Fenton Ho, NW3 64 DC62
Fenton Rd, N17 46 DQ52
Grays (Chaff.Hun.) RM16 110 FY75
Redhill RH1 184 DG134
Fentons Av, E13 86 EH68
Fenwick Cl, SE18 off Ritter St 105 EN79
Woking GU21 166 AV118
Fenwick Gro, SE15 102 DU83
Fenwick Path, Borwd. WD6 26 CM38
Fenwick Pl, SW9 101 DL83
South Croydon CR2 off Columbine Av 159 DP108
Fenwick Rd, SE15 102 DU83
Ferdinand Pl, NW1 off Ferdinand St 82 DG66
Ferdinand St, NW1 82 DG65
Ferguson Av, Grav. DA12 131 GJ91
Romford RM2 52 FJ54
Surbiton KT5 138 CM99
Ferguson Cl, E14 203 P9
Bromley BR2 143 EC97
Ferguson Ct, Rom. RM2 52 FK54
Ferguson Dr, W3 80 CR72
Fergus Rd, N5 off Calabria Rd 65 DP64
Ferme Pk Rd, N4 65 DL57
N8 65 DL57
Fermor Rd, SE23 123 DY88
Fermoy Rd, W9 81 CZ70
Greenford UB6 78 CB70
Fern Av, Mitch. CR4 141 DK98
Fernbank, Buck.H. IG9 48 EH46
Fernbank Av, Horn. RM12 72 FJ63
Walton-on-Thames KT12 136 BY101
Wembley HA0 61 CF63
Fernbank Ms, SW12 121 DJ86
Fernbank Rd, Add. KT15 152 BG106
Fernbrook Av, Sid. DA15 off Blackfen Rd 125 ES85
Fernbrook Cres, SE13 124 EE86
Fernbrook Dr, Har. HA2 60 CB59
Fernbrook Rd, SE13 124 EE86
Ferncliff Rd, E8 66 DU64
Fern Cl, N1 off Ivy St 84 DS68
Erith DA8 off Hollywood Way 107 FH81
Warlingham CR6 177 DY118
Ferncroft Av, N12 44 DE51
NW3 64 DA62
Ruislip HA4 60 BW61
Ferndale, Brom. BR1 144 EJ96
Ferndale Av, E17 67 ED57
Chertsey KT16 133 BE104
Hounslow TW4 96 BY83
Ferndale Cl, Bexh. DA7 106 EY81
Ferndale Ct, SE3 104 EF80
Ferndale Cres, Uxb. UB8 76 BJ69
Ferndale Rd, E7 86 EH66
E11 68 EE61
N15 66 DT58
SE25 142 DV99
SW4 101 DL84
SW9 101 DM83
Ashford TW15 114 BK92
Banstead SM7 173 CZ116
Enfield EN3 31 DY37
Gravesend DA12 131 GH89
Romford RM5 51 FC54
Woking GU21 167 AZ116
Ferndale St, E6 87 EP73
Ferndale Ter, Har. HA1 61 CF56
Ferndale Way, Orp. BR6 163 ER106
Ferndell Av, Bex. DA5 127 FD90
Fern Dene, W13 off Templewood 79 CH71
Ferndene, St.Alb. (Brick.Wd) AL2 8 BZ31
Ferndene Rd, SE24 102 DQ84
Fernden Way, Rom. RM7 71 FB58
Ferndown, Horn. RM11 72 FM58
Northwood HA6 39 BU54
Ferndown Av, Orp. BR6 145 ER102
Ferndown Cl, Pnr. HA5 40 BY52
Sutton SM2 158 DD107
Ferndown Gdns, Cob. KT11 154 BW113
Ferndown Rd, SE9 124 EK87
Watford WD19 40 BW48
Fernery, The, Stai. TW18 113 BE92
Fernes Cl, Uxb. UB8 76 BJ72
Ferney Ct, W.Byf. (Byfleet) KT14 off Ferney Rd 152 BK112
Ferney Meade Way, Islw. TW7 97 CG82
Ferney Rd, Barn. EN4 44 DG45
Waltham Cross (Chsht) EN7 14 DR26
West Byfleet (Byfleet) KT14 152 BK112
Fern Gro, Felt. TW14 115 BV87
Ferngrove Cl, Lthd. (Fetch.) KT22 171 CE123
Fernhall Dr, Ilf. IG4 68 EK57
Fernhall La, Wal.Abb. EN9 16 EK31
Fernham Rd, Th.Hth. CR7 142 DQ97
Fernhead Rd, W9 81 CZ70
Fernheath Way, Dart. DA2 127 FD92
Fernhill, Lthd. (Oxshott) KT22 155 CD114
Fernhill Cl, Wok. GU22 166 AW120
Fernhill Ct, E17 47 ED54
Fernhill Gdns, Kings.T. KT2 117 CK92
Fernhill La, Wok. GU22 166 AW120
Fernhill Pk, Wok. GU22 166 AW120
Fernhills, Kings L. WD4 7 BR33
Fernhill St, E16 87 EM74
Fernholme Rd, SE15 123 DX85
Fernhurst Gdns, Edg. HA8 42 CN51
Fernhurst Rd, SW6 99 CY81
Ashford TW15 115 BQ91
Croydon CR0 142 DU101
Fernie Cl, Chig. IG7 50 EU50

★ Place of interest ⇌ Railway station ⊖ London Underground station DLR Docklands Light Railway station Tra Tramlink station H Hospital Riv Pedestrian ferry landing stage

Fernihough Cl, Wey. KT13 152 BN111
Fernlands Cl, Cher. KT16 133 BE104
Fern La, Houns. TW5 96 BZ78
Fernlea, Lthd. (Bkhm) KT23 170 CB124
Fernlea Rd, SW12 121 DH88
Mitcham CR4 140 DG96
Fernleigh Cl, W9 81 CZ69
Croydon CR0
off Stafford Rd 159 DN105
Walton-on-Thames KT12 135 BV104
Fernleigh Ct, Har. HA2 40 CB54
Wembley HA9 62 CL61
Fernleigh Rd, N21 45 DN47
Fernsbury St, WC1 196 D3
Ferns Cl, Enf. EN3 31 DY36
South Croydon CR2 160 DV110
Fernshaw Rd, SW10 100 DC79
Fernside, NW11
off Finchley Rd 64 DA61
Buckhurst Hill IG9 48 EH46
Fernside Av, NW7 42 CR48
Feltham TW13 115 BV91
Fernside La, Sev. TN13 191 FJ129
Fernside Rd, SW12 120 DF88
Fernsleigh Cl, Ger.Cr.
(Chal.St.P.) SL9 36 AY51
Ferns Rd, E15 86 EF65
Fern St, E3 85 EA70
Fernthorpe Rd, SW16 121 DJ93
Ferntower Rd, N5 66 DR64
Fern Twrs, Cat. CR3 186 DU125
Fern Wk, SE16 off Argyle Way 102 DU78
Ashford TW15
off Ferndale Rd 114 BK92
Fern Way, Wat. WD25 23 BU35
Fernways, Ilf. IG1
off Cecil Rd 69 EP63
Fernwood Av, SW16 121 DK91
Wembley HA0
off Bridgewater Rd 61 CJ64
Fernwood Cl, Brom. BR1 144 EJ96
Fernwood Cres, N20 44 DF48
Ferny Hill, Barn. EN4 28 DF38
Ferranti Cl, SE18 104 EK76
Ferraro Cl, Houns. TW5 96 CA79
Ferrers Av, Wall. SM6 159 DK105
West Drayton UB7 94 BK75
Ferrers Rd, SW16 121 DK92
Ferrestone Rd, N8 65 DM56
Ferrey Ms, SW9 101 DN82
Ferriby Cl, N1
off Bewdley St 83 DN66
Ferrier Pt, E16
off Forty Acre La 86 EH71
Ferrier St, SW18 100 DB84
Ferriers Way, Epsom KT18 173 CW119
Ferring Cl, Har. HA2 60 CC60
Ferrings, SE21 122 DS89
Ferris Av, Croy. CR0 143 DZ104
Ferris Rd, SE22 102 DU84
Ferron Rd, E5 66 DV62
Ferro Rd, Rain. RM13 89 FG70
Ferrour Ct, N2 64 DD55
Ferry Av, Stai. TW18 113 BE94
Ferryhills Cl, Wat. WD19 40 BW48
Ferry La, N17 66 DU56
SW13 99 CT79
Brentford TW8 98 CL79
Chertsey KT16 134 BH98
Rainham RM13 89 FE72
Richmond TW9 98 CM79
Shepperton TW17 134 BN102
Staines (Laleham) TW18 134 BJ97
Staines (Wrays.) TW19 113 BB89
Ferryman's Quay, SW6 100 DC82
Ferrymead Av, Grnf. UB6 78 CA69
Ferrymead Dr, Grnf. UB6 78 CA68
Ferrymead Gdns, Grnf. UB6 78 CC68
Ferrymoor, Rich. TW10 117 CH90
Ferry Pl, SE18
off Woolwich High St 105 EN76
Ferry Rd, SW13 99 CU80
Teddington TW11 117 CH92
Thames Ditton KT7 137 CH100
Tilbury RM18 111 GG83
Twickenham TW1 117 CH88
West Molesey KT8 136 CA97
Ferry Sq, Brent. TW8 98 CL79
Shepperton TW17 135 BP101
Ferry St, E14 204 D10
Feryby Rd, Grays RM16 111 GH76
Festing Rd, SW15 99 CX83
Festival Cl, Bex. DA5 126 EX88
Erith DA8 off Betsham Rd 107 FF80
Uxbridge UB10 77 BP67
Festival Path, Wok. GU21 166 AT119
Festival Wk, Cars. SM5 158 DF106
Festoon Way, E16 86 EK73
FETCHAM, Lthd. KT23 171 CD123
Fetcham Common La, Lthd.
(Fetch.) KT22 170 CB121
Fetcham Pk Dr, Lthd.
(Fetch.) KT22 171 CE123
Fetherstone Cl, Pot.B. EN6 12 DD32
Fetter La, EC4 196 E9
Ffinch St, SE8 103 EA80
Fiddicroft Av, Bans. SM7 158 DB114
Fiddlers Cl, Green. DA9 109 FV84
FIDDLERS HAMLET,
Epp. CM16 18 EW32
Fidler Pl, Bushey WD23
off Ashfield Av 24 CB44
Field Cl, E4 47 EB51
NW2 63 CU61
Bromley BR1 144 EJ96
Buckhurst Hill IG9 48 EJ48
Chesham HP5 4 AS28
Chessington KT9 155 CJ106
Hayes UB3 95 BQ80
Hounslow TW4 95 BV81
Romford (Abridge) RM4 34 EV41
Ruislip HA4 off Field Way 59 BQ60
South Croydon CR2 160 DV114
West Molesey KT8 136 CB99
Fieldcommon La, Walt. KT12 136 BZ101
Field Ct, WC1 196 C7
Oxted RH8 off Silkham Rd 188 EE127
Field End, Barn. EN5 27 CV42
Coulsdon CR5 159 DK114
Northolt UB5 78 BX65
Field End, Ruislip HA4 78 BW65
Twickenham TW1 117 CF91
Field End Cl, Wat. WD19 40 BY45
Field End Ms, Wat. WD19
off Field End Cl 40 BY45
Fieldend Rd, SW16 141 DJ95
Field End Rd, Pnr. HA5 59 BV58
Ruislip HA4 60 BY63
Fielders Cl, Enf. EN1
off Woodfield Cl 30 DS42
Harrow HA2 60 CC60
Fielders Way, Rad.
(Shenley) WD7 10 CL33
Fieldfare Rd, SE28 88 EW73
Fieldgate La, Mitch. CR4 140 DE97
Fieldgate St, E1 84 DU71
Fieldhouse Cl, E18 48 EG53
Fieldhouse Rd, SW12 121 DJ88
Fieldhurst, Slou. SL3 93 AZ78
Fieldhurst Cl, Add. KT15 152 BH106
Fielding Av, Til. RM18 111 GH81
Twickenham TW2 116 CC90
Fielding Gdns, Slou. SL3 92 AW75
Fielding Ho, NW6 82 DA69
Fielding Ms, SW13
off Castelnau 99 CV79
Fielding Rd, W4 98 CR76
W14 99 CX76
Fieldings, The, SE23 122 DW88
Banstead SM7 173 CZ117
Woking GU21 166 AT116
Fieldings Rd, Wal.Cr.
(Chsht) EN8 15 DZ29
Fielding St, SE17 102 DQ79
Fielding Wk, W13 97 CH76
Fielding Way, Brwd.
(Hutt.) CM13 55 GC44
Field La, Brent. TW8 97 CJ80
Teddington TW11 117 CG92
Field Mead, NW7 42 CS52
NW9 42 CS52
Field Pl, N.Mal. KT3 139 CT100
Field Rd, E7 68 EF63
N17 66 DR55
W6 99 CY78
Feltham TW14 115 BV86
South Ockendon
(Aveley) RM15 90 FQ74
Uxbridge (Denh.) UB9 57 BE63
Watford WD19 24 BY44
Fields Ct, Pot.B. EN6 12 DD33
Fieldsend Rd, Sutt. SM3 157 CY106
Fields Est, E8 84 DU66
Fieldside Cl, Orp. BR6
off State Fm Av 163 EQ105
Fieldside Rd, Brom. BR1 123 ED92
Fields Pk Cres, Rom. RM6 70 EX57
Field St, WC1 196 B2
Fieldview, SW18 120 DD88
Field Vw, Egh. TW20 113 BC92
Feltham TW13 115 BR91
Fieldview Ct, Stai. TW18
off Burges Way 114 BG93
Field Vw Ri, St.Alb.
(Brick.Wd) AL2 8 BY29
Field Vw Rd, Pot.B. EN6 12 DA33
Fieldway 161 EB108
Field Way, NW10
off Twybridge Way 80 CQ66
Croydon CR0 161 EB107
Fieldway, Dag. RM8 70 EV63
Field Way, Ger.Cr.
(Chal.St.P.) SL9 36 AX52
Greenford UB6 78 CB67
Hemel Hempstead
(Bov.) HP3 5 BA27
Fieldway, Orp. BR5 145 ER100
Field Way, Rick. WD3 38 BH46
Ruislip HA4 59 BQ60
Uxbridge UB8 76 BK70
Fieldway Cres, N5 65 DN64
Fiennes Cl, Dag. RM8 70 EW60
Fiennes Way, Sev. TN13 191 FJ127
Fiesta Dr, Dag. RM9 89 FC70
Fifehead Cl, Ashf. TW15 114 BL93
Fife Rd, E16 86 EG71
N22 45 DP52
SW14 118 CQ85
Kingston upon Thames KT1 138 CL96
Fife Ter, N1 83 DM68
Fifield Path, SE23
off Bampton Rd 123 DX90
Fifth Av, E12 69 EM63
W10 81 CY69
Grays RM20 109 FU79
Hayes UB3 77 BT74
Watford WD25 24 BX35
Fifth Cross Rd, Twick. TW2 117 CD89
Fifth Way, Wem. HA9 62 CP63
Figges Rd, Mitch. CR4 120 DG94
Figgswood, Couls. CR5
off Jennys Way 175 DJ122
Fig St, Sev. TN14 190 FF129
Fig Tree Cl, NW10
off Craven Pk 80 CS67
Filby Rd, Chess. KT9 156 CM107
Filey Av, N16 66 DU60
Filey Cl, Sutt. SM2 158 DC108
Westerham (Bigg.H.)
TN16 178 EH119
Filey Waye, Ruis. HA4 59 BU61
Filigree Ct, SE16 203 L3
Fillebrook Av, Enf. EN1 30 DS40
Fillebrook Rd, E11 67 ED60
Filmer La, Sev. TN14 191 FL121
Filmer Rd, SW6 99 CY81
Filston La, Sev. TN14 165 FE113
Filston Rd, Erith DA8
off Riverdale Rd 107 FB78
Finborough Rd, SW10 100 DB78
SW17 120 DF93
Finchale Rd, SE2 106 EU76
Fincham Cl, Uxb. UB10
off Aylsham Dr 59 BQ61
Finch Av, SE27 122 DR91
Finch Cl, NW10 62 CR64
Barnet EN5 28 DA43
Finchdean Ho, SW15
off Tangley Gro 119 CT87
Finch Dr, Felt. TW14 116 BX87
Finches Av, Rick. WD3
off Sarratt Rd 22 BL41
Finch Gdns, E4 47 EA50
Finch Grn, Rick. (Chorl.) WD3 21 BF42
Finchingfield Av, Wdf.Grn. IG8 48 EJ52
Finch La, EC3 197 L9
Amersham HP7 20 AV40
Bushey WD23 24 CA43
FINCHLEY, N3 44 DB53
Finchley Central 44 DA53
Finchley Cl, Dart. DA1 128 FN86
Finchley Ct, N3 44 DB51
Finchley La, NW4 63 CW56
Finchley Mem Hosp, N12 44 DC52
Finchley Pk, N12 44 DC49
Finchley Pl, NW8 82 DD68
Finchley Road 82 DC65
Finchley Rd, NW2 64 DA62
NW3 82 DC65
NW8 82 DD67
NW11 63 CZ58
Grays RM17 110 GB79
Finchley Road & Frognal 64 DC64
Finchley Way, N3 44 DA52
Finch Ms, SE15 102 DT80
Finden Rd, E7 68 EH64
Findhorn Av, Hayes UB4 77 BV71
Findhorn St, E14 85 EC72
Findon Cl, SW18
off Wimbledon Pk Rd 120 DA86
Harrow HA2 60 CB62
Findon Ct, Add. KT15
off Spinney Hill 151 BF106
Findon Gdns, Rain. RM13 89 FG71
Findon Rd, N9 46 DV46
W12 99 CU75
Fine Bush La, Uxb. (Hare.) UB9 59 BP58
Fingal St, SE10 205 L10
Finglesham Cl, Orp. BR5
off Westwell Cl 146 EX102
Finians Cl, Uxb. UB10 76 BM66
Finland Quay, SE16 203 L7
Finland Rd, SE4 103 DY83
Finland St, SE16 203 L6
Finlay Gdns, Add. KT15 152 BJ105
Finlays Cl, Chess. KT9 156 CN106
Finlay St, SW6 99 CX81
Finnart Cl, Wey. KT13 153 BQ105
Finnart Ho Dr, Wey. KT13
off Vaillant Rd 153 BQ105
Finney La, Islw. TW7 97 CG81
Finnis St, E2 84 DV69
Finnymore Rd, Dag. RM9 88 EY66
FINSBURY, EC1 196 E2
Finsbury Av, EC2 197 L7
Finsbury Av Sq, EC2 197 L7
Finsbury Circ, EC2 197 L7
Finsbury Cotts, N22
off Clarence Rd 45 DL52
Finsbury Ct, Wal.Cr. EN8
off Parkside 15 DY34
Finsbury Est, EC1 196 E3
Finsbury Ho, N22 45 DL53
Finsbury Mkt, EC2 197 M5
FINSBURY PARK, N4 65 DN60
★ Finsbury Park, N4 65 DP59
Finsbury Park 65 DN61
Finsbury Park 65 DN61
Finsbury Pk Av, N4 66 DQ58
Finsbury Pk Rd, N4 65 DP61
Finsbury Pavement, EC2 197 L6
Finsbury Rd, N22 45 DM53
Finsbury Sq, EC2 197 L6
Finsbury St, EC2 197 K6
Finsbury Twr, EC1 197 K5
Finsbury Way, Bex. DA5 126 EZ86
Finsen Rd, SE5 102 DQ83
Finstock Rd, W10 81 CX72
Finucane Dr, Orp. BR5 146 EW101
Finucane Gdns, Rain. RM13 89 FG65
Finucane Ri, Bushey
(Bushey Hth) WD23 40 CC47
Finway Ct, Wat. WD18
off Whippendell Rd 23 BT43
Fiona Cl, Lthd. (Bkhm) KT23 170 CA124
Firbank Cl, E16 86 EK71
Enfield EN2
off Gladbeck Way 30 DQ42
Firbank Dr, Wat. WD19 40 BY45
Woking GU21 166 AV119
Firbank La, Wok. GU21 166 AV119
Firbank Pl, Egh.
(Eng.Grn) TW20 112 AV93
Firbank Rd, SE15 102 DV82
Romford RM5 51 FB50
Fir Cl, Walt. KT12 135 BU101
Fircroft Cl, Slou. (Stoke P.) SL2 74 AU65
Woking GU22 167 AZ118
Fircroft Ct, Wok. GU22
off Fircroft Cl 167 AZ118
Fircroft Gdns, Har. HA1 61 CE62
Fircroft Rd, SW17 120 DF89
Chessington KT9 156 CM105
Fir Dene, Orp. BR6 145 EM104
Firdene, Surb. KT5 138 CQ102
Fire Bell All, Surb. KT6 138 CL100
Firecrest Dr, NW3 64 DB62
Firefly Cl, Wall. SM6 159 DL108
Firefly Gdns, E6
off Jack Dash Way 86 EL70
★ Firepower, SE18 105 EP76
Fire Sta All, Barn. EN5
off Christchurch La 27 CZ40
Firethorn Cl, Edg. HA8
off Larkspur Gro 42 CQ49
Firfield Rd, Add. KT15 152 BG105
Firfields, Wey. KT13 153 BP107
Fir Gra Av, Wey. KT13 153 BP106
Fir Gro, N.Mal. KT3 139 CT100
Woking GU21 166 AU119
Fir Gro Rd, SW9
off Marcella Rd 101 DN82
Firham Pk Av, Rom. RM3 52 FN52
Firhill Rd, SE6 123 EA91
Firlands, Wey. KT13 153 BS107
Firmingers Rd, Orp. BR6 165 FB106
Firmin Rd, Dart. DA1 128 FJ85
Fir Rd, Felt. TW13 116 BX92
Sutton SM3 139 CZ102
Firs, The, E17 off Leucha Rd 67 DY57
Firs, The, N20 44 DD46
W5 79 CK71
Bexley DA5
off Dartford Rd 127 FD88
Brentwood (Pilg.Hat.) CM15 54 FU44
Caterham CR3
off Yorke Gate Rd 176 DR122
Leatherhead (Bkhm) KT23 170 CC124
Tadworth KT20
off Brighton Rd 183 CZ126
Waltham Cross (Chsht) EN7 14 DS27
Firs Av, N10 64 DG55
N11 44 DG51
SW14 98 CQ84
Firsby Av, Croy. CR0 143 DX102
Firsby Rd, N16 66 DT60
Firs Cl, N10 off Firs Av 64 DG55
SE23 123 DX87
Esher (Clay.) KT10 155 CE107
Iver SL0
off Thornbridge Rd 75 BC67
Mitcham CR4 141 DH96
Firscroft, N13 46 DQ48
Firsdene Cl, Cher. (Ott.) KT16
off Slade Rd 151 BD107
Firs Dr, Houns. TW5 95 BV80
Loughton IG10 33 EN39
Slough SL3 75 AZ74
Firs End, Ger.Cr.
(Chal.St.P.) SL9 56 AY55
Firsgrove Cres, Brwd. CM14 54 FV49
Firsgrove Rd, Brwd. CM14 54 FV49
Firside Gro, Sid. DA15 125 ET88
Firs La, N13 46 DQ48
N21 46 DQ47
Potters Bar EN6 12 DB33
Firs Pk Av, N21 46 DR46
Firs Pk Gdns, N21 46 DQ46
Firs Rd, Ken. CR8 175 DP115
First Av, E12 68 EL63
E13 86 EG69
E17 67 EA57
N18 46 DW49
NW4 63 CW56
SW14 98 CS83
W3 81 CT74
W10 81 CZ70
Bexleyheath DA7 106 EW80
Dagenham RM10 89 FB68
Enfield EN1 30 DT44
Epsom KT19 156 CS109
Gravesend (Nthflt) DA11 130 GE88
Grays RM20 109 FU79
Greenford UB6 79 CD66
Hayes UB3 77 BT74
Romford RM6 70 EW57
Tadworth
(Lwr Kgswd) KT20 183 CY125
Waltham Abbey EN9
off Breach Barn
Mobile Home Pk 16 EH30
Walton-on-Thames KT12 135 BV100
Watford WD25 24 BW35
Wembley HA9 61 CK61
West Molesey KT8 136 BZ98
First Cl, W.Mol. KT8 136 CC97
First Cross Rd, Twick. TW2 117 CE89
First Dr, NW10 80 CQ66
First Slip, Lthd. KT22 171 CG118
First St, SW3 198 C8
Firstway, SW20 139 CW96
First Way, Wem. HA9 62 CP63
Firs Wk, Nthwd. HA6 39 BR51
Woodford Green IG8 48 EG50
Firswood Av, Epsom KT19 157 CT106
Firs Wd Cl, Pot.B. EN6 12 DF32
Firth Gdns, SW6 99 CY81
Fir Tree Av, Mitch. CR4 140 DG96
Slough (Stoke P.) SL2 74 AT70
West Drayton UB7 94 BN76
Fir Tree Cl, SW16 121 DJ92
W5 80 CL72
Epsom KT17 173 CW115
Epsom (Ewell) KT19 157 CT105
Esher KT10 154 CC106
Grays RM17 110 GD79
Leatherhead KT22 171 CJ123
Orpington BR6
off Highfield Av 163 ET106
Romford RM1 71 FD55
Firtree Ct, Borwd.
(Elstree) WD6 26 CM42
Fir Tree Gdns, Croy. CR0 161 EA105
Fir Tree Gro, Cars. SM5 158 DF108
Fir Tree Hill, Rick. WD3 22 BM38
Fir Tree Pl, Ashf. TW15
off Percy Av 114 BN92
Fir Tree Rd, Bans. SM7 157 CW114
Epsom KT17 173 CV116
Hounslow TW4 96 BY84
Leatherhead KT22 171 CJ123
Fir Trees, Rom. (Abridge) RM4 34 EV41
Fir Trees Cl, SE16 203 L3
Fir Tree Wk, Dag. RM10
off Wheel Fm Dr 71 FC62
Enfield EN1 30 DR41
Reigate RH2 184 DD134
Firwood Cl, Wok. GU21 166 AS119
Firwood Rd, Vir.W. GU25 132 AS100
Fisher Cl, Croy. CR0
off Grant Rd 142 DT102
Enfield EN3 31 EA37
Greenford UB6
off Gosling Cl 78 CA69
Kings Langley WD4 6 BN29
Walton-on-Thames KT12 153 BV105
Fisherman Cl, Rich. TW10
off Locksmeade Rd 117 CJ91
Fishermans Dr, SE16 203 J4
Fishermans Hill, Grav. DA11 130 GB85
Fisherman's Wk, E14 203 P2
Fishermans Wk, SE28
off Tugboat St 105 ES75
Fisher Rd, Har. HA3 41 CF54
Fishers Cl, SW16
off Garrad's Rd 121 DK90
Bushey WD23 24 BY41
Waltham Cross EN8 15 EA34
Fishers Ct, SE14
off Besson St 103 DX81
Fishers Ct, Brentwood CM14
off Warley Hill 54 FV50
Fishersdene, Esher
(Clay.) KT10 155 CG108
Fishers Grn La, Wal.Abb. EN9 15 EB29
Fishers La, W4 98 CR77
Epping CM16 17 ES32
Fisher St, E16 86 EG71
WC1 196 A7
Fishers Way, Belv. DA17 89 FC74
Fisherton St, NW8 82 DD70
Fishguard Spur, Slou. SL1 92 AV75
Fishguard Way, E16 105 EP75
Fishing Temple, Stai. TW18 133 BF95
Fishponds Rd, SW17 120 DE91
Keston BR2 162 EK106
Fish St Hill, EC3 197 L10
Fitzalan Rd, N3 63 CY55
Esher (Clay.) KT10 155 CE108
Fitzalan St, SE11 200 D8
Fitzgeorge Av, W14 99 CY77
New Malden KT3 138 CR95
Fitzgerald Av, SW14 98 CS83
Fitzgerald Cl, E11
off Fitzgerald Rd 68 EG57
Fitzgerald Ho, E14 85 EB72
Hayes UB3 77 BV74
Fitzgerald Rd, E11 68 EG57
SW14 98 CR83
Thames Ditton KT7 137 CG100
Fitzhardinge St, W1 194 F8
Fitzherbert Ho, Rich. TW10
off Kingsmead 118 CM86
Fitzhugh Gro, SW18 120 DD86
Fitzilian Av, Rom. RM3 52 FM53
Fitzjames Av, W14 99 CY77
Croydon CR0 142 DU103
Fitzjohn Av, Barn. EN5 27 CY43
Fitzjohn's Av, NW3 64 DC64
Fitzmaurice Pl, W1 199 J2
Fitzneal St, W12 81 CT72
Fitzrobert Pl, Egh. TW20 113 BA93
Fitzroy Cl, N6 64 DF60
Fitzroy Ct, W1 195 L5
Fitzroy Cres, W4 98 CR80
Fitzroy Gdns, SE19 122 DS94
Fitzroy Ms, W1 195 K5
Fitzroy Pk, N6 64 DF60
Fitzroy Rd, NW1 82 DG67
Fitzroy Sq, W1 195 K5
Fitzroy St, W1 195 K5
Fitzroy Yd, NW1
off Fitzroy Rd 82 DG67
Fitzstephen Rd, Dag. RM8 70 EV64
Fitzwarren Gdns, N19 65 DJ60
Fitzwilliam Av, Rich. TW9 98 CM82
Fitzwilliam Ms, E16 205 M2
Fitzwilliam Rd, SW4 101 DJ83
Fitzwygram Cl, Hmptn.
(Hmptn H.) TW12 116 CC92
Five Acre, NW9 43 CT53
Fiveacre Cl, Th.Hth. CR7 141 DN100
Five Acres, Kings L. WD4 6 BM29
St. Albans (Lon.Col.) AL2 9 CK25
Five Acres Av, St.Alb.
(Brick.Wd) AL2 8 BZ29
Fiveash Rd, Grav. DA11 131 GF87
Five Bell All, E14
off Three Colt St 85 DZ73
Five Elms Rd, Brom. BR2 144 EH104
Dagenham RM9 70 EZ62
Five Flds Cl, Wat. WD19 40 BZ48
Five Oaks, Add. KT15 151 BF107
Five Oaks La, Chig. IG7 50 EY51
Five Points, Iver SL0 75 BC69
Fives Ct, SE11 200 F8
Five Ways Cor, NW4 43 CV53
Fiveways Rd, SW9 101 DN82
Five Wents, Swan. BR8 147 FG96
Fladbury Rd, N15 66 DR58
Fladgate Rd, E11 68 EE58
Flag Cl, Croy. CR0 143 DX102
Flagstaff Cl, Wal.Abb. EN9 15 EB33
Flagstaff Rd, Wal.Abb. EN9 15 EB33
Flag Wk, Pnr. HA5
off Eastcote Rd 59 BU58
Flambard Rd, Har. HA1 61 CG58
Flamborough Cl, West.
(Bigg.H.) TN16 178 EH119
Flamborough Rd, Ruis. HA4 59 BU62
Flamborough St, E14 85 DY72
Flamborough Wk, E14
off Flamborough St 85 DY72
Flamingo Gdns, Nthlt. UB5
off Jetstar Way 78 BY69
Flamingo Wk, Horn. RM12 89 FG65
FLAMSTEAD END, Wal.Cr. EN7 14 DU28
Flamstead End Rd, Wal.Cr.
(Chsht) EN8 14 DV28
Flamstead Gdns, Dag. RM9
off Flamstead Rd 88 EW66
Flamstead Rd, Dag. RM9 88 EW66
Flamsted Av, Wem. HA9 80 CN65
★ Flamsteed Ho Mus, SE10 103 ED80
Flamsteed Rd, SE7 104 EL78
Flanchford Rd, W12 99 CT76
Reigate RH2 183 CX134
Flanders Ct, Egh. TW20 113 BC92
Flanders Cres, SW17 120 DF94
Flanders Rd, E6 87 EM68
W4 98 CS77
Flanders Way, E9 85 DX65
Flank St, E1 off Dock St 84 DU73
Flash La, Enf. EN2 29 DP37
Flask Cotts, NW3
off New End Sq 64 DD63
Flask Wk, NW3 64 DD63
Flat Iron Sq, SE1
off Union St 84 DQ74
FLAUNDEN, Hem.H. HP3 5 BB33
Flaunden Bottom, Chesh. HP5 20 AY36
Hemel Hempstead
(Flaun.) HP3 20 AY35
Flaunden Hill, Hem.H.
(Flaun.) HP3 5 AZ33

Flaunden La, Hem.H.
(Bov.) HP3 ... 5 BB32
Rickmansworth WD3 ... 5 BD33
Flaunden Pk, Hem.H.
(Flaun.) HP3 ... 5 BA32
Flavell Ms, SE10 ... 205 J10
Flaxen Cl, E4 off Flaxen Rd ... 47 EB48
Flaxen Rd, E4 ... 47 EB48
Flaxley Rd, Mord. SM4 ... 140 DB100
Flaxman Ct, W1 ... 195 M9
Flaxman Rd, SE5 ... 101 DP82
Flaxman Ter, WC1 ... 195 N3
Flaxton Rd, SE18 ... 105 ER81
Flecker Cl, Stan. HA7 ... 41 CF50
Fleece Dr, N9 ... 46 DU49
Fleece Rd, Surb. KT6 ... 137 CJ102
Fleece Wk, N7 off Manger Rd ... 83 DL65
Fleeming Cl, E17
off Pennant Ter ... 47 DZ54
Fleeming Rd, E17 ... 47 DZ54
Fleet Av, Dart. DA2 ... 128 FQ88
Upminster RM14 ... 73 FR58
Fleet Cl, Ruis. HA4 ... 59 BQ58
Upminster RM14 ... 73 FR58
West Molesey KT8 ... 136 BZ99
Fleetdale Par, Dart. DA2
off Fleet Av ... 128 FQ88
Fleet La, W.Mol. KT8 ... 136 BZ100
Fleet Pl, EC4 off Farringdon St. 83 DN72
Fleet Rd, NW3 ... 64 DE64
Dartford DA2 ... 128 FQ88
Gravesend (Nthflt) DA11 ... 130 GC90
Fleetside, W.Mol. KT8 ... 136 BZ100
Fleet Sq, WC1 ... 196 B3
Fleet St, EC4 ... 196 D9
Fleet St Hill, E1
off Weaver St ... 84 DU70
Fleetway, Egh. TW20 ... 133 BC97
Fleetway Business Pk,
Grnf. UB6 ... 79 CH68
Fleetwood Cl, E16 ... 86 EK71
Chalfont St. Giles HP8 ... 36 AU49
Chessington KT9 ... 155 CK108
Croydon CR0 ... 142 DT104
Tadworth KT20 ... 173 CW120
Fleetwood Ct, E6
off Evelyn Denington Rd ... 87 EM71
West Byfleet KT14 ... 152 BG113
Fleetwood Gro, W3
off East Acton La ... 80 CS73
Fleetwood Rd, NW10 ... 63 CU64
Kingston upon Thames KT1 ... 138 CP97
Slough SL2 ... 74 AT74
Fleetwood Sq, Kings.T. KT1 ... 138 CP97
Fleetwood St, N16
off Stoke Newington Ch St ... 66 DS61
Fleetwood Way, Wat. WD19 ... 40 BW49
Fleming Cl, W9
off Chippenham Rd ... 82 DA70
Waltham Cross (Chsht) EN7. 14 DU26
Fleming Ct, W2
off St. Marys Ter ... 82 DD71
Croydon CR0 ... 159 DN106
Fleming Dr, N21 ... 29 DM43
Fleming Gdns, Rom.
(Harold Wd) RM3
off Bartholomew Dr ... 52 FK54
Tilbury RM18
off Fielding Av ... 111 GJ81
Fleming Mead, Mitch. CR4 ... 120 DE94
Fleming Rd, SE17 ... 101 DP79
Grays (Chaff.Hun.) RM16 ... 109 FW77
Southall UB1 ... 78 CB72
Waltham Abbey EN9 ... 31 EB35
Flemings, Brwd. CM13 ... 53 FW51
Fleming Wk, NW9
off Pasteur Cl ... 42 CS54
Fleming Way, SE28 ... 88 EX73
Isleworth TW7 ... 97 CF83
Flemish Flds, Cher. KT16 ... 134 BG101
Flemming Av, Ruis. HA4 ... 59 BV60
Flempton Rd, E10 ... 67 DY59
Fletcher Cl, E6
off Trader Rd ... 87 EP72
Chertsey (Ott.) KT16 ... 151 BE107
Fletcher La, E10 ... 67 EC59
Fletcher Path, SE8
off New Butt La ... 103 EA80
Fletcher Rd, W4 ... 98 CQ76
Chertsey (Ott.) KT16 ... 151 BD107
Chigwell IG7 ... 49 ET50
Fletchers Cl, Brom. BR2 ... 144 EH98
Fletcher St, E1 off Cable St ... 84 DU73
Fletching Rd, E5 ... 66 DW62
SE7 ... 104 EJ79
Fletton Rd, N11 ... 45 DL52
Fleur de Lis St, E1 ... 197 N5
Fleur Gates, SW19
off Princes Way ... 119 CX87
Flexmere Gdns, N17
off Flexmere Rd ... 46 DR53
Flexmere Rd, N17 ... 46 DR53
Flight App, NW9 ... 43 CT54
Flimwell Cl, Brom. BR1 ... 124 EE92
Flint Cl, Bans. SM7 ... 158 DB114
Redhill RH1 ... 184 DF133
Flint Down Cl, Orp. BR5 ... 146 EU95
Flintlock Cl, Stai. TW19 ... 94 BG84
Flintmill Cres, SE3 ... 104 EL82
Flinton St, SE17 ... 201 N10
Flint St, SE17 ... 201 L9
Grays RM20 ... 109 FV79
Flitcroft St, WC2 ... 195 N8
Floathaven Cl, SE28 ... 88 EU74
Floats, The, Sev. (Rvrhd) TN13 190 FE121
Flock Mill Pl, SW18 ... 120 DB88
Flockton St, SE16 ... 202 B5
Flodden Rd, SE5 ... 102 DQ81
Flood La, Twick. TW1
off Church La ... 117 CG88
Flood Pas, SE18
off Samuel St ... 105 EM77
Flood St, SW3 ... 100 DE78
Flood Wk, SW3 ... 100 DE79
Flora Cl, E14 ... 85 EB72
Flora Gdns, W6 ... 99 CV77
Croydon CR0 ... 161 EC111
Romford RM6 ... 70 EW58
Floral Ct, Ashtd. KT21
off Rosedale ... 171 CJ118
Floral Dr, St.Alb.
(Lon.Col.) AL2 ... 9 CK26
Floral St, WC2 ... 195 P10
Flora St, Belv. DA17
off Victoria St ... 106 EZ78
Florence Av, Add.
(New Haw) KT15 ... 152 BG111
Enfield EN2 ... 30 DQ41
Morden SM4 ... 140 DC99
Florence Cantwell Wk, N19
off Hillrise Rd ... 65 DL59
Florence Cl, Grays RM20 ... 110 FY79
Hornchurch RM12 ... 72 FL61
Walton-on-Thames KT12
off Florence Rd ... 135 BV101
Watford WD25 ... 23 BU35
Florence Dr, Enf. EN2 ... 30 DQ41
Florence Elson Cl, E12
off Grantham Rd ... 69 EN63
Florence Gdns, W4 ... 98 CQ79
Romford RM6 off Roxy Av ... 70 EW59
Staines TW18 ... 114 BH94
★ Florence Nightingale Mus,
SE1 ... 200 B5
Florence Rd, E6 ... 86 EJ67
E13 ... 86 EF68
N4 ... 65 DN60
SE2 ... 106 EW76
SE14 ... 103 DZ81
SW19 ... 120 DB93
W4 ... 98 CR76
W5 ... 80 CL73
Beckenham BR3 ... 143 DX96
Bromley BR1 ... 144 EG95
Feltham TW13 ... 115 BV88
Kingston upon Thames KT2 ... 118 CM94
South Croydon CR2 ... 160 DR109
Southall UB2 ... 96 BX77
Walton-on-Thames KT12 ... 135 BV101
Florence St, E16 ... 86 EF70
N1 ... 83 DP66
NW4 ... 63 CW56
Florence Ter, SE14 ... 103 DZ81
Florence Way, SW12 ... 120 DF88
Uxbridge UB8
off Wyvern Way ... 76 BJ67
Florey Sq, N21
off Highlands Av ... 29 DM43
Florfield Pas, E8
off Reading La ... 84 DV65
Florfield Rd, E8
off Reading La ... 84 DV65
Florian Av, Sutt. SM1 ... 158 DD105
Florian Rd, SW15 ... 99 CY84
Florida Cl, Bushey
(Bushey Hth) WD23 ... 41 CD47
Florida Rd, Th.Hth. CR7 ... 141 DP95
Florida St, E2 ... 84 DU69
Florin Ct, SE1 off Tanner St ... 102 DT75
Floris Pl, SW4
off Fitzwilliam Rd ... 101 DJ83
Floriston Av, Uxb. UB10 ... 77 BQ66
Floriston Cl, Stan. HA7 ... 41 CH53
Floriston Ct, Nthlt. UB5 ... 60 CB64
Floriston Gdns, Stan. HA7 ... 41 CH53
Floss St, SW15 ... 99 CW82
Flower & Dean Wk, E1
off Thrawl St ... 84 DT71
Flower Cres, Cher.
(Ott.) KT16 ... 151 BB107
Flowerfield, Sev.
(Otford) TN14 ... 181 FF117
Flowerhill Way, Grav.
(Istead Rise) DA13 ... 130 GE94
Flower La, NW7 ... 43 CT50
Godstone RH9 ... 187 DY128
Flower Ms, NW11 ... 63 CY58
Flower Pot Cl, N15
off St. Ann's Rd ... 66 DT58
Flowers Cl, NW2 ... 63 CU62
Flowersmead, SW17 ... 120 DG89
Flowers Ms, N19
off Archway Rd ... 65 DJ61
Flower Wk, The, SW7 ... 100 DC75
Floyd Rd, SE7 ... 104 EJ78
Floyds La, Wok. GU22 ... 168 BG116
Floyer Cl, Rich. TW10
off Queens Rd ... 118 CM85
Fludyer St, SE13 ... 104 EE84
Flux's La, Epp. CM16 ... 18 EU33
Flyer's Way, The, West. TN16 ... 189 ER126
Fogerty Cl, Enf. EN3 ... 31 EB37
Foley Ms, Esher (Clay.) KT10 ... 155 CE108
Foley Rd, Esher (Clay.) KT10 ... 155 CE108
Westerham (Bigg.H.) TN16 ... 178 EK118
Foley St, W1 ... 195 K7
Folgate St, E1 ... 197 N6
Foliot St, W12 ... 81 CT72
Folkes La, Upmin. RM14 ... 73 FT57
Folkestone Ct, Slou. SL3 ... 93 BA78
Folkestone Rd, E6 ... 87 EN68
E17 ... 67 EB56
N18 ... 46 DU49
Folkingham La, NW9 ... 42 CR53
Folkington Cor, N12 ... 43 CZ50
Follet Dr, Abb.L. WD5 ... 7 BT31
Follett Cl, Wind.
(Old Wind.) SL4 ... 112 AV86
Follett St, E14 ... 85 EC72
Folly Cl, Rad. WD7 ... 25 CF36
Follyfield Rd, Bans. SM7 ... 158 DA114
Folly La, E4 ... 47 DZ52
E17 ... 47 DY53
Folly Ms, W11
off Portobello Rd ... 81 CZ72
Folly Pathway, Rad. WD7 ... 25 CF35
Folly Wall, E14 ... 204 E5
Fontaine Rd, SW16 ... 121 DM94
Fontarabia Rd, SW11 ... 100 DG84
Fontayne Av, Chig. IG7 ... 49 EQ49
Rainham RM13 ... 89 FE66
Romford RM1 ... 51 FE54
Fontenoy Rd, SW12 ... 121 DH89
Fonteyne Gdns, Wdf.Grn. IG8
off Lechmere Av ... 48 EK54
Fonthill Cl, SE20
off Selby Rd ... 142 DU96
Fonthill Ms, N4
off Lennox Rd ... 65 DN61
Fonthill Rd, N4 ... 65 DM60
Font Hills, N2 ... 44 DC54
Fontley Way, SW15 ... 119 CU87
Fontmell Cl, Ashf. TW15 ... 114 BN92
Fontmell Pk, Ashf. TW15 ... 114 BM92
Fontwell Cl, Har. HA3 ... 41 CE52
Northolt UB5 ... 78 CA65
Fontwell Dr, Brom. BR2 ... 145 EN99
Fontwell Pk Gdns, Horn. RM12. 72 FL63
Foord Cl, Dart. DA2 ... 129 FS89
Football La, Har. HA1 ... 61 CE60
Footbury Hill Rd, Orp. BR6 ... 146 EU101
Footpath, The, SW15 ... 119 CU85
FOOTS CRAY, Sid. DA14 ... 126 EV93
Foots Cray High St,
Sid. DA14 ... 126 EW93
Foots Cray La, Sid. DA14 ... 126 EW88
Footscray Rd, SE9 ... 125 EN86
Forbench Cl, Wok.
(Ripley) GU23 ... 168 BH122
Forbes Av, Pot.B. EN6 ... 12 DD33
Forbes Cl, NW2 ... 63 CU62
Hornchurch RM11
off St. Leonards Way ... 71 FH60
Forbes Ct, SE19 ... 122 DS92
Forbes St, E1 off Ellen St ... 84 DU72
Forbes Way, Ruis. HA4 ... 59 BV61
Forburg Rd, N16 ... 66 DU60
FORCE GREEN, West. TN16 ... 179 ER124
Force Grn La, West. TN16 ... 179 ER124
Fordbridge Cl, Cher. KT16 ... 134 BH102
Fordbridge Rd, Ashf. TW15 ... 114 BL93
Shepperton TW17 ... 135 BS100
Sunbury-on-Thames TW16. 135 BS100
Ford Cl, E3 off Roman Rd ... 85 DY68
Ashford TW15 ... 114 BL93
Bushey WD23 ... 24 CC42
Harrow HA1 ... 61 CD59
Rainham RM13 ... 89 FF66
Shepperton TW17 ... 134 BN98
Thornton Heath CR7 ... 141 DP100
Fordcroft Rd, Orp. BR5 ... 146 EV99
Forde Av, Brom. BR1 ... 144 EJ97
Fordel Rd, SE6 ... 123 ED88
Ford End, Uxb. (Denh.) UB9 ... 57 BF61
Woodford Green IG8 ... 48 EH51
Fordham Cl, Barn. EN4 ... 28 DE41
Hornchurch RM11 ... 72 FN59
Fordham Rd, Barn. EN4 ... 28 DD41
Fordham St, E1 ... 84 DU72
Fordhook Av, W5 ... 80 CM73
Fordingley Rd, W9 ... 81 CZ69
Fordington Ho, SE26
off Sydenham Hill ... 122 DU90
Fordington Rd, N6 ... 64 DF57
Ford La, Iver SL0 ... 76 BG72
Rainham RM13 ... 89 FF66
Fordmill Rd, SE6 ... 123 EA89
Ford Rd, E3 ... 85 DY67
Ashford TW15 ... 114 BM91
Chertsey KT16 ... 134 BH102
Dagenham RM9, RM10 ... 88 EZ66
Gravesend (Nthflt) DA11 ... 130 GB85
Woking (Old Wok.) GU22 ... 167 BB120
Fords Gro, N21 ... 46 DQ46
Fords Pk Rd, E16 ... 86 EG72
Ford Sq, E1 ... 84 DV71
Ford St, E3 ... 85 DY67
E16 ... 86 EF72
Fordwater Rd, Cher. KT16 ... 134 BH102
Fordwater Trd Est, Cher. KT16. 134 BJ102
Fordwich Cl, Orp. BR6 ... 145 ET101
Fordwych Rd, NW2 ... 63 CY63
Fordyce Cl, Horn. RM11 ... 72 FM59
Fordyce Ho, SW16
off Colson Way ... 121 DJ91
Fordyce Rd, SE13 ... 123 EC86
Fordyke Rd, Dag. RM8 ... 70 EZ61
Forefield, St.Alb. AL2 ... 8 CA27
★ Foreign & Commonwealth
Office, SW1 ... 199 P4
Foreign St, SE5 ... 101 DP82
Foreland Ct, NW4 ... 43 CY53
Foreland St, SE18
off Plumstead Rd ... 105 ER77
Foreman Ct, W6
off Hammersmith Bdy ... 99 CW77
Foremark Cl, Ilf. IG6 ... 49 ET50
Foreshore, SE8 ... 203 N9
Forest, The, E11 ... 68 EE56
Forest App, E4 ... 48 EE45
Woodford Green IG8 ... 48 EF52
Forest Av, E4 ... 48 EE45
Chigwell IG7 ... 49 EN50
Forest Business Pk, E17 ... 67 DX59
Forest Cl, E11 ... 68 EF57
Chislehurst BR7 ... 145 EN95
Waltham Abbey EN9 ... 32 EH37
Woking GU22 ... 167 BD115
Woodford Green IG8 ... 48 EH48
Forest Ct, E4 ... 48 EF46
E11 ... 68 EE56
Forest Cres, Ashtd. KT21 ... 172 CN116
Forest Cft, SE23 ... 122 DV89
FORESTDALE, Croy. CR0 ... 161 EA109
Forestdale, N14 ... 45 DK49
Forest Dr, E12 ... 68 EK62
Epping (They.B.) CM16 ... 33 ES36
Keston BR2 ... 162 EL105
Sunbury-on-Thames TW16 ... 115 BT94
Tadworth (Kgswd) KT20 ... 173 CZ121
Woodford Green IG8 ... 47 ED52
Forest Dr E, E11 ... 67 ED59
Forest Dr W, E11 ... 67 EC59
Forest Edge, Buck.H. IG9 ... 48 EJ49
Forester Rd, SE15 ... 102 DV84
Foresters Cl, Wall. SM6 ... 159 DK108
Waltham Cross EN7 ... 14 DS27
Woking GU21 ... 166 AT118
Foresters Cres, Bexh. DA7 ... 107 FB84
Foresters Dr, E17 ... 67 ED56
Wallington SM6 ... 159 DK108
Forest Gdns, N17 ... 46 DT54
FOREST GATE, E7 ... 68 EG64
⇌ Forest Gate ... 68 EG64
Forest Gate, NW9 ... 62 CS57
Forest Glade, E4 ... 48 EE49
E11 ... 68 EE58
Epping (N.Wld Bas.) CM16 ... 18 EY27
Forest Gro, E8 ... 84 DT66
Forest Hts, Buck.H. IG9 ... 48 EG47
FOREST HILL, SE23 ... 123 DX88
⇌ Forest Hill ... 122 DW89
Forest Hill Business Cen,
SE23 ... 122 DW89
Forest Hill Ind Est, SE23
off Perry Vale ... 122 DW89
Forest Hill Rd, SE22 ... 122 DV85
SE23 ... 122 DV85
Forestholme Cl, SE23 ... 122 DW89
Forest Ind Pk, Ilf. IG6 ... 49 ES53
Forest La, E7 ... 68 EE64
E15 ... 68 EE64
Chigwell IG7 ... 49 EN50
Leatherhead (E.Hors.) KT24 ... 169 BT124
Forest Mt Rd, Wdf.Grn. IG8 ... 47 ED52
Fore St, EC2 ... 197 J7
N9 ... 46 DU50
N18 ... 46 DT51
Pinner HA5 ... 59 BU57
Fore St Av, EC2 ... 197 K7
Forest Ridge, Beck. BR3 ... 143 EA97
Keston BR2 ... 162 EL105
Forest Ri, E17 ... 67 ED57
Forest Rd, E7 ... 68 EG63
E8 ... 84 DT65
E11 ... 67 ED59
E17 ... 66 DW56
N9 ... 46 DV46
N17 ... 66 DW56
Enfield EN3 ... 31 DY36
Erith DA8 ... 107 FG81
Feltham TW13 ... 116 BW89
Ilford IG6 ... 49 ES53
Leatherhead (E.Hors.) KT24 ... 169 BU123
Loughton IG10 ... 32 EK41
Richmond TW9 ... 98 CN80
Romford RM7 ... 71 FB55
Sutton SM3 ... 140 DA102
Waltham Cross (Chsht) EN8. 15 DX29
Watford WD25 ... 7 BV33
Woking GU22 ... 167 BD115
Woodford Green IG8 ... 48 EG48
Forest Side, E4 ... 48 EF45
E7 off Capel Rd ... 68 EH63
Buckhurst Hill IG9 ... 48 EJ46
Epping CM16 ... 17 ER33
Waltham Abbey EN9 ... 32 EJ36
Worcester Park KT4 ... 139 CT102
Forest St, E7 ... 68 EG64
Forest Vw, E4 ... 47 ED45
E11
off High Rd Leytonstone ... 68 EF59
Forest Vw Av, E10 ... 67 ED57
Forest Vw Rd, E12 ... 68 EL63
E17 ... 47 EC53
Loughton IG10 ... 32 EK42
Forest Wk, N10 ... 45 DH53
Bushey WD23
off Millbrook Rd ... 24 BZ39
Forest Way, N19
off Hargrave Pk ... 65 DJ61
Ashtead KT21 ... 172 CM117
Loughton IG10 ... 32 EL41
Orpington BR5 ... 145 ET99
Sidcup DA15 ... 125 ER87
Waltham Abbey EN9 ... 32 EK35
Woodford Green IG8 ... 48 EH49
Forfar Rd, N22 ... 45 DP53
SW11 ... 100 DG81
Forge, The, Pot.B.
(Northaw) EN6 ... 12 DE30
Forge Av, Couls. CR5 ... 175 DN120
Forge Br La, Couls. CR5 ... 175 DH121
Forge Cl, Brom. BR2 ... 144 EG102
Hayes UB3 off High St ... 95 BR79
Kings Langley
(Chipper.) WD4 ... 6 BG31
Forge Cotts, W5
off Ealing Grn ... 79 CK74
Forge Dr, Esher (Clay.) KT10 ... 155 CG108
Forge End, St.Alb. AL2 ... 8 CA26
Woking GU21 ... 166 AY117
Forgefield, West. (Bigg.H.) TN16
off Main Rd ... 178 EK116
Forge La, Dart. (Hort.Kir.) DA4 148 FQ98
Feltham TW13 ... 116 BY92
Gravesend DA12 ... 131 GM89
Northwood HA6 ... 39 BS52
Sunbury-on-Thames TW16 ... 135 BU97
Sutton SM3 ... 157 CY108
Forge Ms, Croy. CR0
off Addington Village Rd ... 161 EA106
Sunbury-on-Thames TW16
off Forge La ... 135 BU97
Forge Pl, NW1
off Malden Cres ... 82 DG65
Forge Way, Sev.
(Shore.) TN14 ... 165 FF111
Forlong Path, Nthlt. UB5
off Arnold Rd ... 78 BY65
Forman Pl, N16
off Farleigh Rd ... 66 DT63
Formation, The, E16
off Woolwich Manor Way ... 105 EP75
Formby Av, Stan. HA7 ... 61 CJ55
Formby Cl, Slou. SL3 ... 93 BC77
Formosa St, W9 ... 82 DB71
Formunt Cl, E16
off Vincent St ... 86 EF71
Forres Gdns, NW11 ... 64 DA58
Forrester Path, SE26 ... 123 DX91
Forrest Gdns, SW16 ... 141 DM97
Forris Av, Hayes UB3 ... 77 BT74
Forset St, W1 ... 194 C8
Forstal Cl, Brom. BR2
off Ridley Rd ... 144 EG97
Forster Cl, E17 ... 47 ED52
Forster Rd, E17 ... 67 DY58
N17 ... 66 DT55
SW2 ... 121 DL87
Beckenham BR3 ... 143 DY97
Croydon CR0
off Windmill Rd ... 142 DQ101
Forsters Cl, Rom. RM6 ... 70 EZ58
Forster's Way, SW18 ... 120 DB88
Forsters Way, Hayes UB4 ... 77 BV72
Forston St, N1
off Cropley St ... 84 DR68
Forsyte Cres, SE19 ... 142 DS95
Forsyth Gdns, SE17 ... 101 DP79
Forsythia Cl, Ilf. IG1 ... 69 EP64
Forsythia Gdns, Slou. SL3 ... 92 AY76
Forsyth Path, Wok. GU21 ... 151 BD113
Forsyth Pl, Enf. EN1 ... 30 DS43
Forsyth Rd, Wok. GU21 ... 151 BC114
Forterie Gdns, Ilf. IG3 ... 70 EU62
Fortescue Av, E8
off Mentmore Ter ... 84 DV66
Twickenham TW2 ... 116 CC90
Fortescue Rd, SW19 ... 120 DD94
Edgware HA8 ... 42 CR53
Weybridge KT13 ... 152 BM105
Fortess Gro, NW5
off Fortess Rd ... 65 DH64
Fortess Rd, NW5 ... 65 DH64
Fortess Wk, NW5
off Fortess Rd ... 65 DH64
Forthbridge Rd, SW11 ... 100 DG84
Forth Rd, Upmin. RM14 ... 73 FR58
Fortin Cl, S.Ock. RM15 ... 91 FU73
Fortin Path, S.Ock. RM15 ... 91 FU73
Fortin Way, S.Ock. RM15 ... 91 FU73
Fortis Cl, E16 ... 86 EJ72
FORTIS GREEN, N2 ... 64 DF56
Fortis Grn, N2 ... 64 DE56
N10 ... 64 DE56
Fortis Grn Av, N2 ... 64 DF55
Fortis Grn Rd, N10 ... 64 DG55
Fortismere Av, N10 ... 64 DG55
Fort La, Reig. RH2 ... 184 DB130
Fortnam Rd, N19 ... 65 DK61
★ Fortnum & Mason, W1 ... 199 K2
Fortnums Acre, Stan. HA7 ... 41 CF51
Fortress Distribution Pk,
Til. RM18 ... 111 GH84
Fort Rd, SE1 ... 202 A9
Northolt UB5 ... 78 CA66
Sevenoaks (Halst.) TN14 ... 181 FC115
Tadworth (Box H.) KT20 ... 182 CP131
Tilbury RM18 ... 111 GH84
Fortrose Gdns, SW2
off New Pk Rd ... 121 DK88
Fortrye Cl, Grav.
(Nthflt) DA11 ... 130 GE89
Fort St, E1 ... 197 N7
E16 ... 86 EH74
Fortuna Cl, N7
off Vulcan Way ... 83 DM65
Fortune Gate Rd, NW10 ... 80 CS67
Fortune Grn Rd, NW6 ... 64 DA63
Fortune La, Borwd.
(Elstree) WD6 ... 25 CK44
Fortunes Mead, Nthlt. UB5 ... 78 BY65
Fortune St, EC1 ... 197 J5
Fortune Wk, SE28
off Broadwater Rd ... 105 ER76
Fortune Way, NW10 ... 81 CU69
Forty Acre La, E16 ... 86 EG71
Forty Av, Wem. HA9 ... 62 CM62
Forty Cl, Wem. HA9 ... 62 CM61
Forty Footpath, SW14 ... 98 CQ83
Fortyfoot Rd, Lthd. KT22 ... 171 CJ121
★ Forty Hall & Mus,
Enf. EN2 ... 30 DT38
FORTY HILL, Enf. EN2 ... 30 DS37
Forty Hill, Enf. EN2 ... 30 DT38
Forty La, Wem. HA9 ... 62 CP61
Forum, The, W.Mol. KT8 ... 136 CB98
★ Forum Club, NW5 ... 65 DH64
Forum Magnum Sq, SE1 ... 200 B4
Forumside, Edg. HA8
off High St ... 42 CN51
Forum Way, Edg. HA8
off High St ... 42 CN51
Forval Cl, Mitch. CR4 ... 140 DF99
Forward Dr, Har. HA3 ... 61 CF56
Fosbury Ms, W2
off Inverness Ter ... 82 DB73
Foscote Ms, W9
off Amberley Rd ... 82 DA71
Foscote Rd, NW4 ... 63 CV58
Foskett Rd, SW6 ... 99 CZ82
Foss Av, Croy. CR0 ... 159 DN106
Fossdene Rd, SE7 ... 104 EH78
Fossdyke Cl, Hayes UB4 ... 78 BY71
Fosse Way, W13 ... 79 CG71
West Byfleet KT14
off Brantwood Dr ... 151 BF113
Fossil Rd, SE13 ... 103 EA83
Fossington Rd, Belv. DA17 ... 106 EX77
Foss Rd, SW17 ... 120 DD91
Fossway, Dag. RM8 ... 70 EW61
Foster Cl,
Wal.Cr. (Chsht) EN8 ... 15 DX30
Fosterdown, Gdse. RH9 ... 186 DV129
Foster La, EC2 ... 197 H8
Foster Rd, E13 ... 86 EG70
W3 ... 80 CS73
W4 ... 98 CR78
Fosters Cl, E18 ... 48 EH53
Chislehurst BR7 ... 125 EM92
Foster St, NW4 ... 63 CW56
Foster Wk, NW4
off New Brent St ... 63 CW56
Fothergill Cl, E13 ... 86 EG68
Fothergill Dr, N21 ... 29 DL43
Fotheringham Rd, Enf. EN1 ... 30 DT42
Fotherley Rd, Rick.
(Mill End) WD3 ... 37 BF47
Foubert's Pl, W1 ... 195 K9
Foulden Rd, N16 ... 66 DT63
Foulden Ter, N16
off Foulden Rd ... 66 DT63
Foulis Ter, SW7 ... 198 A10
Foulser Rd, SW17 ... 120 DF90
Foulsham Rd, Th.Hth. CR7 ... 142 DQ97
Founder Cl, E6 off Trader Rd ... 87 EP72
Founders Ct, EC2 ... 197 K8
Founders Dr, Uxb.
(Denh.) UB9 ... 57 BF58
Founders Gdns, SE19 ... 122 DQ94
★ Foundling Mus, WC1 ... 196 A4
Foundry Cl, SE16 ... 203 K2
Foundry Gate, Wal.Cr. EN8
off York Rd ... 15 DY34

★ Place of interest ⇌ Railway station ⊖ London Underground station DLR Docklands Light Railway station Tra Tramlink station H Hospital Riv Pedestrian ferry landing stage

Foundry La,
Slou. (Horton) SL3 . . . . 93 BB83
Foundry Ms, NW1. . . . . 195 L4
Fountain Cl, Uxb. UB8
off New Rd 77 BQ71
Fountain Ct, EC4. . . . . 196 D10
Fountain Dr, SE19. . . . . 122 DT91
Carshalton SM5 . . . . 158 DF109
Fountain Grn Sq, SE16. . . . . . 202 C4
Fountain La, Sev. TN15. . . . . . 191 FP122
Fountain Ms, N5
off Highbury Gra. 66 DQ63
NW3 . . . . 82 DF65
Fountain Pl, SW9 . . . . 101 DN81
Waltham Abbey EN9 . . . . . . 15 EC34
Fountain Rd, SW17. . . . . 120 DD92
Thornton Heath CR7. . . . . . . 142 DQ96
Fountains, The, Loug. IG10
off Fallow Flds 48 EK45
Fountains Av, Felt. TW13. . . . . 116 BZ90
Fountains Cl, Felt. TW13. . . . . 116 BZ89
Fountains Cres, N14 . . . . 45 DL45
Fountain Sq, SW1. . . . . 199 H8
Fountain St, E2
off Columbia Rd 84 DT69
Fountain Wk, Grav.
(Nthflt) DA11 . . . . 130 GE86
Fountayne Rd, N15. . . . . 66 DU56
N16 . . . . 66 DU61
Fount St, SW8. . . . . 101 DK80
Fouracres, SW12
off Little Dimocks 121 DH89
Four Acres, Cob. KT11. . . . . . . 154 BY113
Fouracres, Enf. EN3 . . . . 31 DY39
Fourland Wk, Edg. HA8 . . . . . . 42 CQ51
Fournier St, E1 . . . . 197 P6
Four Seasons Cl, E3. . . . . 85 EA68
Four Seasons Cres,
Sutt. SM3 . . . . 139 CZ103
Fourth Av, E12 . . . . 69 EM63
W10. . . . . 81 CY70
Grays RM20 . . . . 109 FU79
Hayes UB3 . . . . 77 BT74
Romford RM7 . . . . 71 FD60
Watford WD25. . . . . 24 BX35
Fourth Cross Rd, Twick. TW2. . 117 CD89
Fourth Dr, Couls. CR5. . . . . . . 175 DK116
Fourth Way, Wem. HA9. . . . . . . 62 CQ63
Four Tubs, The, Bushey WD23 . 41 CD45
Four Wents, Cob. KT11 . . . . . . 153 BV113
Four Wents, The, E4
off Kings Rd 47 ED47
Fowey Av, Ilf. IG4 . . . . 68 EK57
Fowey Cl, E1. . . . . 202 D2
Fowler Cl, SW11 . . . . 100 DD83
Fowler Rd, E7 . . . . 68 EG63
N1 off Halton Rd. 83 DP66
Ilford IG6. . . . . 50 EV51
Mitcham CR4 . . . . 140 DG96
Fowlers Cl, Sid. DA14
off Thursland Rd 126 EY92
Fowlers Mead, Wok. (Chobham)
GU24 off Windsor Rd 150 AS109
Fowlers Wk, W5 . . . . 79 CK70
Fowley Cl, Wal.Cr. EN8. . . . . . . 15 DZ34
Fowley Mead Pk, Wal.Cr. EN8 . 15 EA34
Fownes St, SW11 . . . . 100 DE83
Foxacre, Cat. CR3
off Town End Cl. 176 DS122
Fox & Knot St, EC1. . . . . 196 G6
Foxberry Rd, SE4 . . . . 103 DY83
Foxberry Wk, Grav. (Nthflt) DA11
off Rowmarsh Cl. 130 GD91
Foxborough Cl, Slou. SL3 . . . . . 93 BA78
Foxborough Gdns, SE4 . . . . . . 123 EA86
Foxbourne Rd, SW17 . . . . 120 DG89
Foxburrow Rd, Chig. IG7 . . . . . 50 EX50
Foxbury Av, Chis. BR7 . . . . . . 125 ER93
Foxbury Cl, Brom. BR1. . . . . . . 124 EH93
Orpington BR6
off Foxbury Dr. 164 EU106
Foxbury Dr, Orp. BR6. . . . . . . 164 EU107
Foxbury Rd, Brom. BR1 . . . . . . 124 EG93
Fox Cl, E1 . . . . 84 DW70
E16 . . . . 86 EG71
Borehamwood (Elstree) WD6
off Rodgers Cl. 25 CK44
Bushey WD23 . . . . 24 CB42
Orpington BR6 . . . . 164 EU106
Romford RM5. . . . . 51 FB50
Weybridge KT13. . . . . 153 BR106
Woking GU22 . . . . 167 BD115
Foxcombe,
Croy. (New Adgtn) CR0 . . 161 EB107
Foxcombe Cl, E6
off Boleyn Rd 86 EK68
Foxcombe Rd, SW15
off Alton Rd. 119 CU88
Foxcote, SE5. . . . . 102 DS78
Fox Covert, Lthd.
(Fetch.) KT22. . . . . 171 CD124
Foxcroft Rd, SE18 . . . . 105 EP81
Foxdell, Nthwd. HA6 . . . . 39 BR51
Foxdell Way, Ger.Cr.
(Chal.St.P.) SL9 . . . . 36 AY50
Foxearth Cl, West.
(Bigg.H.) TN16. . . . . 178 EL118
Foxearth Rd, S.Croy. CR2 . . . . 160 DW110
Foxearth Spur, S.Croy. CR2 . . 160 DW109
Foxes Dale, SE3 . . . . 104 EG83
Bromley BR2. . . . . 143 ED97
Foxes Dr, Wal.Cr. EN7. . . . . 14 DU29
Foxes Grn, Grays
(Orsett) RM16 . . . . 111 GG75
Foxes La, Pot.B. (Cuffley) EN6 . 13 DL28
Foxfield Cl, Nthwd. HA6. . . . . . 39 BT51
Foxfield Rd, Orp. BR6. . . . . 145 ER103
Foxglove Cl, Sid. DA15
off Wellington Av 126 EU86
Southall UB1. . . . . 78 BY73
Staines (Stanw.) TW19 . . . . 114 BK88
Foxglove Gdns, E11 . . . . 68 EJ56
Purley CR8 . . . . 159 DL111
Foxglove La, Chess. KT9 . . . . 156 CN105
Foxglove Rd, Rom.
(Rush Grn) RM7 . . . . 71 FE61
South Ockendon RM15 . . . . 91 FW71
Foxglove St, W12 . . . . 81 CT73
Foxglove Way, Wall. SM6 . . . . 141 DH102
Foxgrove, N14. . . . . 45 DL48
Fox Gro, Walt. KT12 . . . . 135 BV101
Foxgrove Av, Beck. BR3 . . . . . 123 EB94
Foxgrove Dr, Wok. GU21 . . . . . 167 BA115
Foxgrove Path, Wat. WD19 . . . . 40 BX50
Foxgrove Rd, Beck. BR3 . . . . . 123 EB94
Foxhall Rd, Upmin. RM14 . . . . . 72 FQ64
Foxham Rd, N19. . . . . 65 DK62
Foxhanger Gdns, Wok. GU22
off Oriental Rd 167 BA116
Foxherne, Slou. SL3 . . . . 92 AW75
Fox Hill, SE19 . . . . 122 DT94
Keston BR2 . . . . 162 EJ106
Foxhill, Wat. WD24 . . . . 23 BU36
Fox Hill Gdns, SE19 . . . . 122 DT94
Foxhills, Wok. GU21 . . . . 166 AW117
Foxhills Cl, Cher. (Ott.) KT16 . 151 BB107
Foxhills Ms, Cher. KT16 . . . . . 133 BB104
Foxhills Rd, Cher. (Ott.) KT16 . 151 BA105
Foxhole Rd, SE9 . . . . 124 EL85
Foxholes, Wey. KT13. . . . . 153 BR106
Fox Hollow Cl, SE18 . . . . 105 ES78
Fox Hollow Dr, Bexh. DA7 . . . . 106 EX83
Foxholt Gdns, NW10 . . . . 80 CQ66
Foxhome Cl, Chis. BR7 . . . . . . 125 EN93
Foxhounds La, Grav. DA13. . . . 130 GA90
Fox Ho Rd, Belv. DA17 . . . . . . 107 FB77
Foxlake Rd, W.Byf.
(Byfleet) KT14. . . . . 152 BM112
Foxlands Cl, Wat. WD25 . . . . . . 7 BU34
Foxlands Cres, Dag. RM10 . . . . 71 FC64
Foxlands La, Dag. RM10. . . . . . 71 FC64
Foxlands Rd, Dag. RM10 . . . . . 71 FC64
Fox La, N13. . . . . 45 DM48
W5. 80 CL70
Caterham CR3. . . . . 175 DP121
Keston BR2 . . . . 162 EH106
Leatherhead (Bkhm) KT23 . 170 BY124
Reigate RH2 . . . . 184 DB131
Fox La N, Cher. KT16 . . . . 133 BF102
Fox La S, Cher. KT16
off Guildford St. 133 BF102
Foxlees, Wem. HA0. . . . . 61 CG63
Foxley Cl, E8
off Ferncliff Rd 66 DU64
Loughton IG10 . . . . 33 EP40
Foxley Ct, Sutt. SM2 . . . . 158 DC108
Foxley Gdns, Pur. CR8 . . . . . . 159 DP113
Foxley Hill Rd, Pur. CR8 . . . . . 159 DN112
Foxley La, Pur. CR8. . . . . 159 DK111
Foxley Rd, SW9. . . . . 101 DN80
Kenley CR8 . . . . 159 DP114
Thornton Heath CR7. . . . . . . 141 DP98
Foxleys, Wat. WD19. . . . . 40 BY48
Foxley Sq, SW9
off Cancell Rd 101 DP80
Fox Manor Way, Grays RM20. 109 FV79
Foxmead Cl, Enf. EN2. . . . . 29 DM41
Foxmoor Ct, Uxb. (Denh.) UB9
off North Orbital Rd 58 BG58
Foxmore St, SW11 . . . . 100 DF81
Foxon Cl, Cat. CR3 . . . . 176 DS121
Foxon La, Cat. CR3 . . . . 176 DR121
Foxon La Gdns, Cat. CR3 . . . . 176 DS121
Fox Rd, E16. . . . . 86 EF71
Slough SL3. . . . . 92 AX77
Fox's Path, Mitch. CR4 . . . . . . 140 DE96
Foxton Gro, Mitch. CR4 . . . . . 140 DD96
Foxton Rd, Grays RM20 . . . . . 109 FX79
Foxwarren, Esher (Clay.) KT10. 155 CF109
Foxwell Ms, SE4
off Foxwell St 103 DY83
Foxwell St, SE4. . . . . 103 DY83
Foxwood Chase,
Wal.Abb. EN9 . . . . 31 ED35
Foxwood Cl, NW7. . . . . 42 CS49
Feltham TW13 . . . . 115 BV90
Foxwood Grn Cl, Enf. EN1 . . . . 30 DS44
Foxwood Gro, Grav.
(Nthflt) DA11 . . . . 130 GE88
Orpington BR6 . . . . 164 EW110
Foxwood Rd, SE3. . . . . 104 EF84
Dartford (Bean) DA2 . . . . . . 129 FV90
Foyle Dr, S.Ock. RM15 . . . . 91 FU71
Foyle Rd, N17 . . . . 46 DU53
SE3 . . . . 104 EF79
Frailey Cl, Wok. GU22. . . . . 167 BB116
Frailey Hill, Wok. GU22. . . . . . . 167 BB116
Framewood Rd,
Slou. SL2, SL3. . . . . 74 AW66
Framfield Cl, N12 . . . . 44 DA48
Framfield Ct, Enf. EN1 . . . . 30 DS44
Framfield Rd, N5. . . . . 65 DP64
W7. 79 CE72
Mitcham CR4 . . . . 120 DG94
Framlingham Cl, E5
off Detmold Rd. 66 DW61
Framlingham Cres, SE9 . . . . . . 124 EL91
Frampton Cl, Sutt. SM2 . . . . . . 158 DA108
Frampton Pk Rd, E9 . . . . 84 DW65
Frampton Rd, Epp. CM16. . . . . . 18 EU28
Hounslow TW4 . . . . 116 BY85
Potters Bar EN6 . . . . 12 DC30
Frampton St, NW8 . . . . 82 DD70
Francemary Rd, SE4. . . . . 123 EA85
Frances Av, Grays
(Chaff.Hun.) RM16. . . . . . . 109 FW77
Frances Gdns, S.Ock. RM15 . . . 91 FT72
Frances Rd, E4 . . . . 47 EA51
Frances St, SE18. . . . . 105 EM77
Franche Ct Rd, SW17 . . . . 120 DC90
Francis Av, Bexh. DA7. . . . . . . 106 FA82
Feltham TW13 . . . . 115 BU90
Ilford IG1. . . . . 69 ER61
Francis Barber Cl, SW16
off Well Cl 121 DM91
Franciscan Rd, SW17 . . . . 120 DF92
Francis Chichester Way,
SW11. . . . . 100 DG81
Francis Cl, E14 . . . . 204 F8
Epsom KT19 . . . . 156 CR105
Shepperton TW17. . . . . 134 BN98
Francisco Cl, Grays
(Chaff.Hun.) RM16. . . . . . . 109 FW76
Francis Gro, SW19 . . . . 119 CZ93
Francis Rd, E10. . . . . 67 EC60
N2 off Lynmouth Rd. 64 DF56
Caterham CR3. . . . . 176 DR122
Croydon CR0. . . . . 141 DP101
Dartford DA1. . . . . 128 FK85
Greenford UB6 . . . . 79 CJ67
Francis Rd, Harrow HA1 . . . . . . 61 CG57
Hounslow TW4 . . . . 96 BX82
Ilford IG1. . . . . 69 ER61
Orpington BR5 . . . . 146 EX97
Pinner HA5 . . . . 60 BW57
Wallington SM6 . . . . 159 DJ107
Watford WD18. . . . . 23 BV42
Francis St, E15 . . . . 68 EE64
SW1. . . . . 199 K8
Ilford IG1. . . . . 69 ER61
Francis Ter, N19
off Junction Rd. 65 DJ62
Francis Wk, N1
off Bingfield St 83 DM67
Francklyn Gdns, Edg. HA8 . . . . 42 CN48
Francombe Gdns, Rom. RM1 . . 71 FG58
Franconia Rd, SW4. . . . . 121 DJ85
Frank Bailey Wk, E12
off Gainsborough Av 69 EN64
Frank Burton Cl, SE7
off Victoria Way 104 EH78
Frank Dixon Cl, SE21 . . . . 122 DS88
Frank Dixon Way, SE21. . . . . . 122 DS88
Frankfurt Rd, SE24 . . . . 122 DQ85
Frankham St, SE8. . . . . 103 EA80
Frankland Cl, SE16 . . . . 202 E7
Rickmansworth
(Crox.Grn) WD3. . . . . 38 BN45
Woodford Green IG8 . . . . 48 EJ50
Frankland Rd, E4 . . . . 47 EA50
SW7 off Armstrong Rd 100 DD76
Rickmansworth
(Crox.Grn) WD3. . . . . 23 BP44
Franklands Dr, Add. KT15. . . . . 151 BF108
Franklin Av, Wal.Cr.
(Chsht) EN7. . . . . 14 DV30
Franklin Cl, N20 . . . . 44 DC45
SE13 . . . . 103 EB81
SE27 . . . . 121 DP90
Kingston upon Thames KT1 . 138 CN97
Franklin Cres, Mitch. CR4. . . . . 141 DJ98
Franklin Ho, NW9 . . . . 63 CT59
Franklin Pas, SE9 . . . . 104 EL83
Franklin Pl, SE13. . . . . 103 EB81
Franklin Rd, SE20 . . . . 122 DW94
Bexleyheath DA7 . . . . 106 EY81
Dartford DA2
off Old Bexley La 127 FE89
Gravesend DA12. . . . . 131 GK92
Hornchurch RM12. . . . . 90 FJ65
Watford WD17. . . . . 23 BV40
Franklins Ms, Har. HA2. . . . . . . 60 CC61
Franklin Sq, W14
off Marchbank Rd. 99 CZ78
Franklin's Row, SW3. . . . . 198 E10
Franklin St, E3
off St. Leonards St 85 EB69
N15 . . . . 66 DS58
Franklin Way, Croy. CR0 . . . . . 141 DL101
Franklyn Gdns, Ilf. IG6 . . . . 49 ER51
Franklyn Rd, NW10. . . . . 81 CT66
Walton-on-Thames KT12 . . 135 BU100
Frank Martin Ct, Wal.Cr. EN7 . . 14 DU30
Franks Av, N.Mal. KT3 . . . . . . 138 CQ98
Franks La, Dart.
(Hort.Kir.) DA4. . . . . 148 FN98
Frank St, E13 . . . . 86 EG70
Frankswood Av, Orp. BR5 . . . . 145 EP99
West Drayton UB7 . . . . 76 BM72
Frank Towell Ct, Felt. TW14. . . 115 BU88
Franlaw Cres, N13 . . . . 46 DQ49
Franmil Rd, Horn. RM12. . . . . . . 71 FG60
Fransfield Gro, SE26. . . . . 122 DV90
Frant Cl, SE20. . . . . 122 DW94
Franthorne Way, SE6 . . . . 123 EB89
Frant Rd, Th.Hth. CR7. . . . . . . 141 DP99
Fraser Cl, E6 off Linton Gdns . . 86 EL72
Bexley DA5
off Dartford Rd 127 FC88
Fraser Ho, Brent. TW8
off Green Dragon La. 98 CM78
Fraser Rd, E17. . . . . 67 EB57
N9 . . . . 46 DV48
Erith DA8. . . . . 107 FC78
Greenford UB6 . . . . 79 CH67
Waltham Cross (Chsht) EN8. 15 DY28
Fraser St, W4 . . . . 98 CS78
Frating Cres, Wdf.Grn. IG8. . . . 48 EG51
Frays Av, West Dr. UB7. . . . . . . 94 BK75
Frays Cl, West Dr. UB7 . . . . . . 94 BK76
Frays Lea, Uxb. UB8. . . . . 76 BJ68
Frays Waye, Uxb. UB8 . . . . 76 BJ67
Frazer Av, Ruis. HA4. . . . . 60 BW64
Frazer Cl, Rom. RM1. . . . . 71 FF59
Frazier St, SE1 . . . . 200 D5
Frean St, SE16 . . . . 202 B6
Freda Corbett Cl, SE15
off Bird in Bush Rd 102 DU80
Frederica Rd, E4 . . . . 47 ED45
Frederica St, N7
off Caledonian Rd. 83 DM66
Frederick Andrews Ct,
Grays RM17. . . . . 110 GD79
Frederick Cl, W2 . . . . 194 D10
Sutton SM1. . . . . 157 CZ105
Frederick Ct, NW2
off Douglas Ms 63 CY62
Frederick Cres, SW9 . . . . 101 DP80
Enfield EN3. . . . . 30 DW40
Frederick Gdns, Croy. CR0 . . . 141 DP100
Sutton SM1. . . . . 157 CZ106
Frederick Pl, SE18. . . . . 105 EP78
Frederick Rd, SE17
off Chapter Rd. 101 DP78
Rainham RM13. . . . . 89 FD68
Sutton SM1. . . . . 157 CZ106
Frederick's Pl, EC2. . . . . 197 K9
Fredericks Pl, N12. . . . . 44 DC49
Frederick Sq, SE16 . . . . 203 K1
Frederick's Row, EC1 . . . . 196 F2
Frederick St, WC1 . . . . 196 B3
Frederick Ter, E8
off Haggerston Rd 84 DT67
Frederick Vil, W7
off Lower Boston Rd. 79 CE74
Frederic Ms, SW1 . . . . 198 E5
Frederic St, E17. . . . . 67 DY57
Fredora Av, Hayes UB4. . . . . . . 77 BT70
Fred White Wk, N7
off Market Rd 83 DL65
Fred Wigg Twr, E11 . . . . 68 EF61
Freeborne Gdns, Rain. RM13
off Mungo Pk Rd. 89 FG65
Freedom Cl, E17 . . . . 67 DY56
Freedom Rd, N17 . . . . 46 DR54
Freedom St, SW11 . . . . 100 DF82
Freedown La, Sutt. SM2. . . . . 158 DC113
Freegrove Rd, N7 . . . . 65 DL64
Freeland Pk, NW4. . . . . 43 CY54
Freeland Rd, W5 . . . . 80 CM73
Freelands Av, S.Croy. CR2 . . . 161 DX109
Freelands Gro, Brom. BR1 . . . 144 EH95
Freelands Rd, Brom. BR1 . . . . 144 EH95
Cobham KT11 . . . . 153 BV114
Freeland Way, Erith DA8
off Slade Grn Rd 107 FG81
Freeling St, N1
off Caledonian Rd. 83 DM66
Freeman Cl, Nthlt. UB5. . . . . . . 78 BY66
Shepperton TW17 . . . . 135 BS98
Freeman Ct, N7
off Tollington Way 65 DL62
Freeman Dr, W.Mol. KT8 . . . . 136 BZ97
Freeman Rd, Grav. DA12 . . . . . 131 GL90
Morden SM4. . . . . 140 DD99
Freemans Cl, Slou.
(Stoke P.) SL2 . . . . 74 AT65
Freemans La, Hayes UB3 . . . . . 77 BS73
Freemantle Av, Enf. EN3. . . . . . 31 DX43
Freemantle St, SE17. . . . . 201 M10
Freeman Way, Horn. RM11 . . . . 72 FL58
★ Freemason's Hall
(United Grand Lo of England),
WC2. . . . . 196 A8
Freemasons Rd, E16. . . . . 86 EH71
Croydon CR0. . . . . 142 DS102
Free Prae Rd, Cher. KT16 . . . . 134 BG102
Freesia Cl, Orp. BR6
off Briarswood Way 163 ET106
Freethorpe Cl, SE19 . . . . 142 DR95
Free Trade Wf, E1
off The Highway 85 DX73
Freezeland Way, Uxb. UB10
off Western Av. 76 BN65
FREEZY WATER, Wal.Cr. EN8 . . 31 DY35
★ Freightliners City Fm, N7. . 83 DM65
Freightmaster Est,
Rain. RM13 . . . . 107 FG76
Freke Rd, SW11. . . . . 100 DG83
Fremantle Ho, Til. RM18
off Leicester Rd 111 GF81
Fremantle Rd, Belv. DA17. . . . 106 FA77
Ilford IG6. . . . . 49 EQ54
Fremont St, E9. . . . . 84 DW67
French Apartments, The, Pur. CR8
off Lansdowne Rd. 159 DN112
Frenchaye, Add. KT15. . . . . . . 152 BJ106
Frenches, The, Red. RH1 . . . . 184 DG132
Frenches Ct, Red. RH1
off Frenches Rd. 184 DG132
Frenches Dr, Red. RH1
off The Frenches 184 DG132
Frenches Rd, Red. RH1 . . . . . 184 DG132
French Gdns, Cob. KT11 . . . . . 154 BW114
French Ordinary Ct, EC3. . . . . 197 N10
French Pl, E1 . . . . 197 N4
French St, Sun. TW16 . . . . 136 BW96
Westerham TN16. . . . . 189 ES128
French's Wells, Wok. GU21 . . . 166 AV117
Frendsbury Rd, SE4 . . . . 103 DY84
Frensham, Wal.Cr.
(Chsht) EN7. . . . . 14 DT27
Frensham Cl, Sthl. UB1 . . . . . . 78 BZ70
Frensham Ct, Mitch. CR4
off Phipps Br Rd 140 DD97
Frensham Dr, SW15 . . . . 119 CU89
Croydon (New Adgtn) CR0. 161 EC108
Frensham Rd, SE9 . . . . 125 ER89
Kenley CR8 . . . . 159 DP114
Frensham St, SE15 . . . . 102 DU79
Frensham Way, Epsom KT17 . 173 CW116
Frere St, SW11 . . . . 100 DE82
Freshfield Av, E8. . . . . 84 DT66
Freshfield Cl, SE13
off Marischal Rd 103 ED84
Freshfield Dr, N14. . . . . 45 DH45
Freshfields, Croy. CR0 . . . . . . 143 DZ101
Freshfields Av, Upmin. RM14. . 72 FP64
Freshford St, SW18 . . . . 120 DC90
Freshmount Gdns,
Epsom KT19 . . . . 156 CP111
Freshwater Cl, SW17 . . . . 120 DG93
Freshwater Rd, SW17. . . . . . . 120 DG93
Dagenham RM8 . . . . 70 EX60
Freshwell Av, Rom. RM6 . . . . . . 70 EW56
Fresh Wf Rd, Bark. IG11 . . . . . . 87 EP67
Freshwood Cl, Beck. BR3 . . . . 143 EB95
Freshwood Way, Wall. SM6 . . 159 DH109
Freston Gdns, Barn. EN4 . . . . . 28 DG43
Freston Pk, N3 . . . . 43 CZ54
Freston Rd, W10 . . . . 81 CX73
W11. . . . . 81 CX73
Freta Rd, Bexh. DA6. . . . . 126 EZ85
★ Freud Mus, NW3. . . . . 82 DC65
Frewin Rd, SW18 . . . . 120 DD88
Friar Ms, SE27
off Prioress Rd 121 DP90
Friar Rd, Hayes UB4 . . . . 78 BX70
Orpington BR5 . . . . 146 EU99
Friars, The, Chig. IG7 . . . . 49 ES49
Friars Av, N20 . . . . 44 DE48
SW15. . . . . 119 CT90
Brentwood (Shenf.) CM15 . . 55 GA46
Friars Cl, E4. . . . . 47 EC48
N2 . . . . 64 DD56
SE1 . . . . 200 G3
Brentwood (Shenf.) CM15 . . 55 FZ45
Ilford IG1. . . . . 69 ER60
Northolt UB5
off Broomcroft Av. 78 BX69
Friars Gdns, W3
off St. Dunstans Av. 80 CR72
Friars Gate Cl, Wdf.Grn. IG8. . . 48 EG49
Friars La, Rich. TW9. . . . . 117 CK85
Friars Mead, E14. . . . . 204 D7
Friars Ms, SE9. . . . . 125 EN85
Friars Orchard, Lthd.
(Fetch.) KT22 . . . . 171 CD121
Friars Pl La, W3. . . . . 80 CR73
Friars Ri, Wok. GU22. . . . . 167 BA118
Friars Rd, E6 . . . . 86 EK67
Virginia Water GU25. . . . . . 132 AX98
Friars Stile Pl, Rich. TW10
off Friars Stile Rd 118 CL86
Friars Stile Rd, Rich. TW10 . . 118 CL86
Friar St, EC4 . . . . 196 G9
Friars Wk, N14. . . . . 45 DH46
SE2 . . . . 106 EX78
Friars Way, W3 . . . . 80 CR72
Bushey WD23 . . . . 24 BZ39
Chertsey KT16. . . . . 134 BG100
Kings Langley WD4 . . . . 6 BN30
Friars Wd, Croy. CR0. . . . . 161 DY109
Friary, The, Wind.
(Old Wind.) SL4. . . . . 112 AW86
Friary Cl, N12 . . . . 44 DE50
Friary Ct, SW1. . . . . 199 L3
Woking GU21 . . . . 166 AT118
Friary Est, SE15. . . . . 102 DU79
Friary Island, Stai.
(Wrays.) TW19 . . . . 112 AW86
Friary La, Wdf.Grn. IG8. . . . . . . 48 EG49
Friary Rd, N12. . . . . 44 DD49
SE15 . . . . 102 DU80
W3. 80 CR72
Staines (Wrays.) TW19 . . . . 112 AW86
Friary Way, N12. . . . . 44 DE49
FRIDAY HILL, E4 . . . . 47 ED47
Friday Hill, E4 . . . . 48 EE47
Friday Hill E, E4. . . . . 48 EE48
Friday Hill W, E4 . . . . 48 EE47
Friday Rd, Erith DA8 . . . . 107 FD78
Mitcham CR4 . . . . 120 DF94
Friday St, EC4 . . . . 197 H9
Frideswide Pl, NW5
off Islip St 65 DJ64
Friendly Pl, SE13
off Lewisham Rd. 103 EB81
Friendly St, SE8 . . . . 103 EA81
Friendly St Ms, SE8
off Friendly St 103 EA82
Friends Av, Wal.Cr. EN8 . . . . . . 15 DX31
Friendship Wk, Nthlt. UB5
off Wayfarer Rd. 78 BX69
Friendship Way, E15
off Carpenters Rd 85 EC67
Friends Rd, Croy. CR0. . . . . . . 142 DR104
Purley CR8 . . . . 159 DP112
Friend St, EC1. . . . . 196 F2
Friends Wk, Stai. TW18 . . . . . . 113 BF92
Uxbridge UB8
off Bakers Rd 76 BK66
FRIERN BARNET, N11. . . . . 44 DE49
Friern Barnet La, N11 . . . . 44 DE49
N20 . . . . 44 DE49
Friern Barnet Rd, N11 . . . . 44 DF50
Friern Br Retail Pk, N11. . . . . . 45 DH51
Friern Cl, Wal.Cr. EN7 . . . . 14 DS26
Friern Ct, N20 . . . . 44 DD48
Friern Mt Dr, N20 . . . . 44 DC45
Friern Pk, N12. . . . . 44 DC50
Friern Rd, SE22 . . . . 122 DU86
Friern Watch Av, N12 . . . . 44 DC49
Frigate Ms, SE8
off Watergate St 103 EA79
Frimley Av, Horn. RM11 . . . . . . 72 FN60
Wallington SM6 . . . . 159 DL106
Frimley Cl, SW19. . . . . 119 CY89
Croydon (New Adgtn) CR0. 161 EC108
Frimley Ct, Sid. DA14 . . . . 126 EV92
Frimley Cres, Croy.
(New Adgtn) CR0 . . . . 161 EC108
Frimley Gdns, Mitch. CR4. . . . 140 DE97
Frimley Rd, Chess. KT9. . . . . . 156 CL106
Ilford IG3. . . . . 69 ES62
Frimley Way, E1 . . . . 85 DX70
Fringewood Cl, Nthwd. HA6 . . 39 BP53
Frinstead Ho, W10. . . . . 81 CX73
Frinsted Cl, Orp. BR5 . . . . 146 EX98
Frinsted Rd, Erith DA8 . . . . . . 107 FD80
Frinton Cl, Wat. WD19. . . . . 39 BV47
Frinton Dr, Wdf.Grn. IG8. . . . . . 47 ED52
Frinton Ms, Ilf. IG2
off Bramley Cres. 69 EN58
Frinton Rd, E6. . . . . 86 EK69
N15 . . . . 66 DS58
SW17. . . . . 120 DG93
Romford RM5. . . . . 50 EZ52
Sidcup DA14. . . . . 126 EY89
Friston Path, Chig. IG7 . . . . 49 ES50
Friston St, SW6. . . . . 100 DB82
Friswell Pl, Bexh. DA6. . . . . . . 106 FA84
Fritham Cl, N.Mal. KT3. . . . . . . 138 CS100
Frith Ct, NW7 . . . . 43 CY52
Frithe, The, Slou. SL2 . . . . 74 AV72
Frith Knowle, Walt. KT12 . . . . 153 BV106
Frith La, NW7 . . . . 43 CY52
Frith Rd, E11 . . . . 67 EC63
Croydon CR0. . . . . 142 DQ103
Friths Dr, Reig. RH2 . . . . 184 DB131
Frith St, W1 . . . . 195 M9
Frithville Gdns, W12 . . . . 81 CW74
Frithwald Rd, Cher. KT16 . . . . 133 BF101
Frithwood Av, Nthwd. HA6 . . . . 39 BS51
Frizlands La, Dag. RM10. . . . . . 71 FB63
Frobisher Cl, Bushey WD23 . . . 24 CA44
Kenley CR8 off Hayes La . . 176 DR117
Pinner HA5 . . . . 60 BX59
Frobisher Cres, EC2
off Beech St 84 DQ71
Staines TW19. . . . . 114 BL87
Frobisher Gdns, Stai. TW19 . . 114 BL87
Frobisher Pas, E14 . . . . 204 A2
Frobisher Rd, E6. . . . . 87 EM72
N8 . . . . 65 DN56
Erith DA8. . . . . 107 FF80
Frobisher St, SE10 . . . . 104 EE79
Frobisher Way, Grav. DA12. . . . 131 GL92
Greenhithe DA9 . . . . 109 FV84
Froggy La, Uxb. (Denh.) UB9. . 57 BD62
Froghall La, Chig. IG7. . . . . 49 ER49
FROGHOLE, Eden. TN8. . . . . . . 189 ER133
Froghole La, Eden. TN8. . . . . . 189 ER132
Frogley Rd, SE22. . . . . 102 DT84
Frogmoor La, Rick. WD3. . . . . . 38 BK47

★ Place of interest ⇌ Railway station ⊖ London Underground station DLR Docklands Light Railway station Tra Tramlink station H Hospital Riv Pedestrian ferry landing stage

257

★ Place of interest   ≷ Railway station   ✈ London Underground station   DLR Docklands Light Railway station   Tra Tramlink station   Ⓗ Hospital   Riv Pedestrian ferry landing stage

258

Garrard Wk, NW10
off Garnet Rd 80 CS65
Garratt Cl, Croy. CR0 159 DL105
Garratt La, SW17 120 DD91
SW18 120 DB85
Garratt Rd, Edg. HA8 42 CN52
Garratts La, Bans. SM7 173 CZ116
Garratts Rd, Bushey WD23 40 CC45
Garratt Ter, SW17 120 DE91
Garrett Cl, W3 off Jenner Av 80 CR71
Garrett St, EC1 197 J4
Garrick Av, NW11 63 CY58
Garrick Cl, SW18 100 DC84
W5 80 CL70
Richmond TW9
off The Green 117 CK85
Staines TW18 114 BG94
Walton-on-Thames KT12 153 BV105
Garrick Cres, Croy. CR0 142 DS103
Garrick Dr, NW4 43 CW54
SE28 off Broadwater Rd 105 ER76
Garrick Gdns, W.Mol. KT8 136 CA97
Garrick Pk, NW4 43 CX54
Garrick Rd, NW9 63 CT58
Greenford UB6 78 CB70
Richmond TW9 98 CN82
Garricks Ho, Kings.T. KT1
off Wadbrook St 137 CK96
Garrick St, WC2 195 P10
Gravesend DA11
off Barrack Row 131 GH86
Garrick Way, NW4 63 CX56
Garrison Cl, SE18
off Red Lion La 105 EN80
Hounslow TW4 116 BZ85
Garrison La, Chess. KT9 155 CK108
Garrison Par, Purf. RM19
off Comet Cl 108 FN77
Garrolds Cl, Swan. BR8 147 FD96
Garron La, S.Ock. RM15 91 FT72
Garry Cl, Rom. RM1 51 FE52
Garry Way, Rom. RM1 51 FE52
Garsdale Cl, N11 44 DG51
Garside Cl, SE28
off Goosander Way 105 ER76
Hampton TW12 116 CB93
Garsington Ms, SE4 103 DZ83
Garsmouth Way, Wat. WD25 24 BX36
Garson Cl, Esher KT10
off Garson Rd 154 BZ107
Garson La, Stai.
(Wrays.) TW19 112 AX87
Garson Mead, Esher KT10 154 BZ106
Garson Rd, Esher KT10 154 BZ107
GARSTON, Wat. WD25 24 BW35
⇌ Garston 24 BX35
Garston Cres, Wat. WD25 8 BW34
Garston Dr, Wat. WD25 8 BW34
Garston Gdns, Ken. CR8
off Godstone Rd 176 DR115
Garston La, Ken. CR8 160 DR114
Watford WD25 8 BY34
Garston Pk Par, Wat. WD25 8 BX34
Garter Way, SE16 203 H5
Garth, The, N12
off Holden Rd 44 DB50
Abbots Langley WD5 7 BR33
Cobham KT11 154 BY113
Hampton (Hmptn H.) TW12
off Uxbridge Rd 116 CB93
Harrow HA3 62 CM58
Garth Cl, W4 98 CR78
Kingston upon Thames KT2 118 CM92
Morden SM4 139 CX101
Ruislip HA4 60 BX60
Garth Ct, W4 off Garth Rd 98 CR78
Garthland Dr, Barn. EN5 27 CV43
Garth Ms, W5
off Greystoke Gdns 80 CL70
Garthorne Rd, SE23 123 DX87
Garth Rd, NW2 63 CZ61
W4 98 CR79
Kingston upon Thames KT2 118 CM92
Morden SM4 139 CW100
Sevenoaks TN13 191 FJ128
South Ockendon RM15 91 FW70
Garth Rd Ind Cen,
Mord. SM4 139 CX101
Garthside, Rich. TW10 118 CL92
Garthway, N12 44 DE51
Gartlett Rd, Wat. WD17 24 BW41
Gartmoor Gdns, SW19 119 CZ88
Gartmore Rd, Ilf. IG3 69 ET60
Garton Pl, SW18 120 DC86
Gartons Cl, Enf. EN3 30 DW43
Gartons Way, SW11 100 DC83
Garvary Rd, E16 86 EH72
Garvock Dr, Sev. TN13 190 FG126
Garway Rd, W2 82 DB72
Garwood Cl, N17 46 DV53
Gascoigne Gdns, Wdf.Grn.
IG8 48 EE52
Gascoigne Pl, E2 197 P3
Gascoigne Rd, Bark. IG11 87 EQ67
Croydon (New Adgtn) CR0 161 EC110
Weybridge KT13 135 BP104
Gascony Av, NW6 82 DA66
Gascoyne Cl, Pot.B. EN6 11 CU32
Romford RM3 52 FK52
Gascoyne Dr, Dart. DA1 107 FF82
Gascoyne Rd, E9 85 DX66
Gaselee St, E14 204 E1
Gasholder Pl, SE11
off Kennington La 101 DM78
Gaskarth Rd, SW12 121 DH86
Edgware HA8 42 CQ53
Gaskell Rd, N6 64 DF58
Gaskell St, SW4 101 DL82
Gaskin St, N1 83 DP67
Gaspar Cl, SW5
off Courtfield Gdns 100 DB77
Gaspar Ms, SW5
off Courtfield Gdns 100 DB77
Gassiot Rd, SW17 120 DF91
Gassiot Way, Sutt. SM1 140 DD104
Gasson Rd, Swans. DA10 130 FY86
Gastein Rd, W6 99 CX79
Gaston Bell Cl, Rich. TW9 98 CM83
Gaston Br Rd, Shep. TW17 135 BS99
Gaston Rd, Mitch. CR4 140 DG97
Gaston Way, Shep. TW17 135 BR99
Gataker St, SE16 202 E6
Gatcombe Ms, W5 80 CM73
Gatcombe Rd, E16 205 N2
N19 65 DK62
Gatcombe Way, Barn. EN4 28 DF41
Gate Cl, Borwd. WD6 26 CQ39
Gate End, Nthwd. HA6 39 BU52
Gateforth St, NW8 194 B5
Gatehill Rd, Nthwd. HA6 39 BT52
Gatehope Dr, S.Ock. RM15 91 FT72
Gatehouse Cl, Kings.T. KT2 118 CQ94
Gatehouse Sq, SE1
off Southwark Br Rd 84 DQ74
Gateley Rd, SW9 101 DM83
Gate Ms, SW7 198 C5
Gater Dr, Enf. EN2 30 DR39
Gatesborough St, EC2 197 M4
Gatesden Cl, Lthd.
(Fetch.) KT22 170 CC123
Gatesden Rd, Lthd.
(Fetch.) KT22 170 CC123
Gates Grn Rd, Kes. BR2 162 EG105
West Wickham BR4 144 EF104
Gateshead Rd, Borwd. WD6 26 CM39
Gateside Rd, SW17 120 DF90
Gatestone Rd, SE19 122 DS93
Gate St, WC2 196 B8
Gateway, SE17 102 DQ79
Weybridge KT13
off Palace Dr 135 BP104
Gateway, The, Wok. GU21 151 BB114
Gateway Arc, N1
off Islington High St 83 DP68
Gateway Cl, Nthwd. HA6 39 BQ51
Gateway Ho, Bark. IG11
off St. Ann's 87 EQ67
Gateway Ind Est, NW10 81 CT69
Gateway Ms, E8
off Shacklewell La 66 DT64
Gateway Retail Pk, E6 87 EP70
Gateway Rd, E10 67 EB62
Gateways, The, SW3 198 C9
Waltham Cross EN7 14 DR28
Gatewick Cl, Slou. SL1 74 AS74
Gatfield Gro, Felt. TW13 116 CA89
Gathorne Rd, N22 45 DN54
Gathorne St, E2 off Mace St 85 DX68
Gatley Av, Epsom KT19 156 CP106
Gatliff Rd, SW1 100 DG78
Gatling Rd, SE2 106 EU78
Gatonby St, SE15 102 DT81
Gatting Cl, Edg. HA8
off Pavilion Way 42 CQ52
Gatting Way, Uxb. UB8 76 BL65
GATTON, Reig. RH2 184 DF128
Gatton Bottom, Red. RH1 185 DH127
Reigate RH2 184 DE128
Gatton Cl, Reig. RH2 184 DC131
Sutton SM2 158 DB109
Gatton Pk, Reig. RH2 184 DF129
Gatton Pk Rd, Red. RH1 184 DD132
Reigate RH2 184 DD132
Gatton Rd, SW17 120 DE91
Reigate RH2 184 DC131
Gattons Way, Sid. DA14 126 EZ91
Gatward Cl, N21 29 DP44
Gatward Grn, N9 46 DS47
Gatwick Rd, SW18 119 CZ87
Gravesend DA12 131 GH90
Gatwick Way, Horn. RM12
off Haydock Cl 72 FM63
Gauden Cl, SW4 101 DK83
Gauden Rd, SW4 101 DK82
Gaumont App, Wat. WD17 23 BV41
Gaumont Ter, W12
off Lime Gro 99 CW75
Gauntlet Cl, Nthlt. UB5 78 BY66
Gauntlet Cres, Ken. CR8 176 DR120
Gauntlett Ct, Wem. HA0 61 CH64
Gauntlett Rd, Sutt. SM1 158 DD106
Gaunt St, SE1 200 G6
Gaurdian Av, Grays RM16
off Clockhouse La 109 FX75
Gautrey Rd, SE15 102 DW82
Gautrey Sq, E6 87 EM72
Gavell Rd, Cob. KT11 153 BU113
Gavel St, SE17 201 L8
Gavenny Path, S.Ock. RM15 91 FT72
Gaveston Cl, W.Byf.
(Byfleet) KT14 152 BM113
Gavestone Cres, SE12 124 EH87
Gavestone Rd, SE12 124 EH87
Gaveston Rd, Lthd. KT22 171 CG120
Gaviller Pl, E5
off Clarence Rd 66 DV63
Gavina Cl, Mord. SM4 140 DE99
Gavin St, SE18 105 ES77
Gaviots Cl, Ger.Cr. SL9 57 AZ60
Gaviots Grn, Ger.Cr. SL9 56 AY60
Gaviots Way, Ger.Cr. SL9 56 AY59
Gawain Wk, N9
off Salisbury Rd 46 DU48
Gawber St, E2 84 DW69
Gawsworth Cl, E15
off Ash Rd 68 EE64
Gawthorne Av, NW7
off Lane App 43 CY50
Gawthorne Ct, E3
off Mostyn Gro 85 EA68
Gay Cl, NW2 63 CV64
Gaydon Ho, W2 82 DB71
Gaydon La, NW9 42 CS53
Gayfere Rd, Epsom KT17 157 CU106
Ilford IG5 69 EM55
Gayfere St, SW1 199 P7
Gayford Rd, W12 99 CT75
Gay Gdns, Dag. RM10 71 FC63
Gayhurst, SE17
off Hopwood Rd 102 DR79
Gayhurst Rd, E8 84 DU66
Gayler Cl, Red. (Bletch.) RH1 186 DT133
Gaylor Rd, Nthlt. UB5 60 BZ64
Tilbury RM18 110 GE81
Gaynes Ct, Upmin. RM14 72 FP63
Gaynesford Rd, SE23 123 DX89
Carshalton SM5 158 DF108
Gaynes Hill Rd, Wdf.Grn. IG8 48 EL51
Gaynes Pk, Epp.
(Cooper.) CM16 18 EY31
Gaynes Pk Rd, Upmin. RM14 72 FN63
Gaynes Rd, Upmin. RM14 72 FP61
Gay Rd, E15 85 ED68
Gaysham Av, Ilf. IG2 69 EN57
Gaysham Hall, Ilf. IG5 69 EP55
Gay St, SW15 99 CX83
Gayton Cl, Amer. HP6 20 AS35
Ashtead KT21 172 CL118
Gayton Ct, Har. HA1 61 CF58
Gayton Cres, NW3 64 DD63
Gayton Ho, E3
off Blackthorn St 85 EA70
Gayton Rd, NW3 64 DD63
SE2 off Florence Rd 106 EW76
Harrow HA1 61 CF58
Gayville Rd, SW11 120 DF86
Gaywood Av, Wal.Cr.
(Chsht) EN8 15 DX30
Gaywood Cl, SW2 121 DM88
Gaywood Est, SE1 200 G7
Gaywood Rd, E17 67 EA55
Ashtead KT21 172 CM118
Gaywood St, SE1 200 G7
Gaza St, SE17
off Braganza St 101 DP78
Gazelle Glade, Grav. DA12 131 GM92
Geariesville Gdns, Ilf. IG6 69 EP56
Geary Dr, Brwd. CM14, CM15 54 FW46
Geary Rd, NW10 63 CU64
Geary St, N7 65 DM64
G.E.C. Est, Wem. HA9 61 CK62
Geddes Pl, Bexh. DA6
off Market Pl 106 FA84
Geddes Rd, Bushey WD23 24 CC42
Gedeney Rd, N17 46 DQ53
Gedling Pl, SE1 202 A6
Geere Rd, E15 86 EF67
Gees Ct, W1 194 G9
Gee St, EC1 197 H4
Geffrye Ct, N1 197 N1
Geffrye Est, N1
off Stanway St 84 DS68
★ Geffrye Mus, E2 197 N1
Geffrye St, E2 84 DT68
Geisthorp Ct, Wal.Abb. EN9
off Winters Way 16 EG33
Geldart Rd, SE15 102 DV80
Geldeston Rd, E5 66 DU61
Gellatly Rd, SE14 102 DW82
Gell Cl, Uxb. UB10 58 BM62
Gelsthorpe Rd, Rom. RM5 51 FB52
Gemini Gro, Nthlt. UB5
off Javelin Way 78 BY69
General Gordon Pl, SE18 105 EP77
Generals Wk, The, Enf. EN3 31 DY37
General Wolfe Rd, SE10 103 ED81
Genesis Business Pk,
Wok. GU21 167 BC115
Genesis Cl, Stai.
(Stanw.) TW19 114 BM88
Genesta Rd, SE18 105 EP79
Geneva Cl, Shep. TW17 135 BS96
Geneva Dr, SW9 101 DN84
Geneva Gdns, Rom. RM6 70 EY57
Geneva Rd, Kings.T. KT1 138 CL98
Thornton Heath CR7 142 DQ99
Genever Cl, E4 47 EA50
Genista Rd, N18 46 DV50
Genoa Av, SW15 119 CW85
Genoa Rd, SE20 142 DW95
Genotin Ms, Horn. RM12
off Maybank Av 72 FJ64
Genotin Rd, Enf. EN1 30 DR41
Genotin Ter, Enf. EN1
off Genotin Rd 30 DR41
Gentian Row, SE13
off Sparta St 103 EC81
Gentlemans Row, Enf. EN2 30 DQ41
Gentry Gdns, E13
off Whitwell Rd 86 EG70
Geoffrey Av, Rom. RM3 52 FN51
Geoffrey Cl, SE5 102 DQ82
Geoffrey Gdns, E6 86 EL68
Geoffrey Rd, SE4 103 DZ83
George Avey Cft, Epp.
(N.Wld Bas.) CM16 19 FB26
George Beard Rd, SE8 203 M9
George Comberton Wk, E12
off Gainsborough Av 69 EN64
George Ct, WC2 200 A1
George Cres, N10 44 DG52
George Crook's Ho, Grays RM17
off New Rd 110 GB79
George Downing Est, N16
off Cazenove Rd 66 DT61
George V Av, Pnr. HA5 60 CA55
George V Cl, Pnr. HA5
off George V Av 60 CA55
George V Way, Grnf. UB6 79 CH67
Rickmansworth
(Sarratt) WD3 22 BG36
George Gange Way, Har.
(Wldste) HA3 61 CE55
GEORGE GREEN, Slou. SL3 74 AX72
George Grn Dr, Slou.
(Geo.Grn) SL3 75 AZ71
George Grn Rd, Slou.
(Geo.Grn) SL3 74 AX72
George Gro Rd, SE20 142 DU95
★ George Inn, SE1 201 K3
George Inn Yd, SE1 201 K3
Georgelands, Wok.
(Ripley) GU23 168 BH121
George La, E18 48 EG54
SE13 123 EC86
Bromley BR2 144 EH102
George Lansbury Ho, N22
off Progress Way 45 DN53
George Loveless Ho, E2
off Diss St 84 DT69
George Lovell Dr, Enf. EN3 31 EA37
George Lowe Ct, W2
off Bourne Ter 82 DB71
George Mathers Rd, SE11 200 F8
George Ms, NW1 195 K3
Enfield EN2 off Sydney Rd 30 DR41
George Pl, N17
off Dongola Rd 66 DS55
George Rd, E4 47 EA51
Kingston upon Thames KT2 118 CP94
George Rd,
New Malden KT3 139 CT98
George Row, SE16 202 B5
Georges Cl, Orp. BR5 146 EW97
Georges Dr, Brwd.
(Pilg.Hat.) CM15 54 FT43
Georges Mead, Borwd.
(Elstree) WD6 25 CK44
George Sq, SW19
off Mostyn Rd 139 CZ97
George's Rd, N7 65 DM64
Georges Rd, West.
(Tats.) TN16 178 EK120
Georges Sq, SW6
off North End Rd 99 CZ79
Georges Ter, Cat. CR3
off Coulsdon Rd 176 DQ122
Tramlink George Street 142 DQ103
George St, E16 86 EF72
W1 194 E8
W7 off The Broadway 79 CE74
Barking IG11 87 EQ66
Croydon CR0 142 DR103
Grays RM17 110 GA79
Hounslow TW3 96 BZ82
Richmond TW9 117 CK85
Romford RM1 71 FF58
Southall UB2 96 BY77
Staines TW18 113 BF91
Uxbridge UB8 76 BK66
Watford WD18 24 BW42
George's Wd Rd, Hat.
(Brook.Pk) AL9 12 DA26
George Tilbury Ho,
Grays RM16 111 GH75
Georgetown Cl, SE19
off St. Kitts Ter 122 DR92
Georgette Pl, SE10
off King George St 103 EC80
Georgeville Gdns, Ilf. IG6 69 EP56
Georgewood Rd, Hem.H. HP3 6 BM25
George Wyver Cl, SW19
off Beaumont Rd 119 CY87
George Yd, EC3 197 L9
W1 194 G10
Georgiana St, NW1 83 DJ67
Georgian Cl, Brom. BR2 144 EH101
Staines TW18 114 BH91
Stanmore HA7 41 CG52
Uxbridge UB10 58 BL63
Georgian Ct, SW16
off Gleneldon Rd 121 DL91
Wembley HA9 80 CN65
Georgian Way, Har. HA1 61 CE61
Georgia Rd, N.Mal. KT3 138 CQ98
Thornton Heath CR7 141 DP95
Georgina Gdns, E2
off Columbia Rd 84 DT69
Geraint Rd, Brom. BR1 124 EG91
Geraldine Rd, SW18 120 DC85
W4 98 CN79
Geraldine St, SE11 200 F7
Gerald Ms, SW1 198 G8
Gerald Rd, E16 86 EF70
SW1 198 G8
Dagenham RM8 70 EZ61
Gravesend DA12 131 GL87
Geralds Gro, Bans. SM7 157 CX114
Gerard Av, Houns. TW4
off Redfern Av 116 CA87
Gerard Gdns, Rain. RM13 89 FE68
Gerard Rd, SW13 99 CT81
Harrow HA1 61 CG58
Gerards Cl, SE16 102 DW78
Gerda Rd, SE9 125 EQ89
Gerdview Dr, Dart. DA2 128 FJ91
Germander Way, E15 86 EE69
Gernigan Ho, SW18
off Fitzhugh Gro 120 DD86
Gernon Cl, Rain. RM13
off Jordans Way 90 FK68
Gernon Rd, E3 85 DY68
Geron Way, NW2 63 CV60
Gerpins La, Upmin. RM14 90 FM68
Gerrard Cres, Brwd. CM14 54 FV48
Gerrard Gdns, Pnr. HA5 59 BU57
Gerrard Pl, W1 195 N10
Gerrard Rd, N1 83 DP68
Gerrards Cl, N14 29 DJ43
GERRARDS CROSS 56 AX58
⇌ Gerrards Cross 56 AY57
Gerrards Cross Rd, Slou.
(Stoke P.) SL2 74 AU66
Gerrards Mead, Bans. SM7
off Garratts La 173 CZ117
Gerrard St, W1 195 M10
Gerridge St, SE1 200 E5
Gerry Raffles Sq, E15
off Great Eastern Rd 85 ED65
Gertrude Rd, Belv. DA17 106 FA77
Gertrude St, SW10 100 DC79
Gervase Cl, Wem. HA9 62 CQ62
Gervase Rd, Edg. HA8 42 CQ53
Gervase St, SE15 102 DV80
Gews Cor, Wal.Cr. (Chsht) EN8 15 DX29
Ghent St, SE6 123 EA89
Ghent Way, E8 off Tyssen St 84 DT65
Giant Arches Rd, SE24 122 DQ87
Giant Tree Hill, Bushey
(Bushey Hth) WD23 41 CD46
Gibbard Ms, SW19 119 CX92
Gibbfield Cl, Rom. RM6 70 EY55
Gibbins Rd, E15 85 EC66
Gibbon Rd, SE15 102 DW82
W3 80 CS73
Kingston upon Thames KT2 138 CL95
Gibbons Cl, Borwd. WD6 26 CL39
Gibbons Rents, SE1
off Magdalen St 84 DS74
Gibbons Rd, NW10 80 CR65
Gibbon Wk, SW15
off Swinburne Rd 99 CU84
Gibbs Av, SE19 122 DR92
Gibbs Cl, SE19 122 DR92
Waltham Cross (Chsht) EN8 15 DX29
Gibbs Couch, Wat. WD19 40 BX48
Gibbs Grn, W14 99 CZ78
Edgware HA8 42 CQ50
Gibbs Rd, N18 46 DW49
Gibbs Sq, SE19 122 DR92
Gibraltar Cl, Brwd. CM13
off Essex Way 53 FW51
Gibraltar Cres, Epsom KT19 156 CS110
Gibraltar Ho, Brwd. CM13 53 FW51
Gibraltar Wk, E2 84 DT69
Gibson Cl, E1
off Colebert Av 84 DW70
N21 29 DN44
Chessington KT9 155 CJ107
Epping (N.Wld Bas.) CM16
off Beamish Cl 19 FC25
Gravesend (Nthflt) DA11 131 GF90
Isleworth TW7 97 CD83
Gibson Ct, Rom. RM1
off Regarth Av 71 FE58
Slough SL3 93 AZ78
Gibson Gdns, N16
off Northwold Rd 66 DT61
Gibson Ms, Twick. TW1
off Richmond Rd 117 CJ87
Gibson Pl, Stai. (Stanw.) TW19 114 BJ86
Gibson Rd, SE11 200 C9
Dagenham RM8 70 EW60
Sutton SM1 158 DB106
Uxbridge UB10 58 BM63
Gibson's Hill, SW16 121 DN93
Gibson Sq, N1 83 DN67
Gibson St, SE10 104 EE78
Gidd Hill, Couls. CR5 174 DG116
Gidea Av, Rom. RM2 71 FG55
Gidea Cl, Rom. RM2 71 FG55
South Ockendon RM15
off Tyssen Pl 91 FW69
GIDEA PARK, Rom. RM2 71 FG55
⇌ Gidea Park 72 FJ56
Gideon Cl, Belv. DA17 107 FB77
Gideon Ms, W5 97 CK75
Gideon Rd, SW11 100 DG83
Gidian Ct, St.Alb. AL2 9 CD27
Giesbach Rd, N19 65 DJ61
Giffard Rd, N18 46 DS50
Giffin St, SE8 103 EA80
Gifford Gdns, W7 79 CD71
Gifford Pl, Brwd. CM14
off Blackthorn Way 54 FX50
Giffordside, Grays RM16 111 GH78
Gifford St, N1 83 DL66
Gift La, E15 86 EE67
Giggs Hill, Orp. BR5 146 EU96
Giggs Hill Gdns, T.Ditt. KT7 137 CG102
Giggs Hill Rd, T.Ditt. KT7 137 CG101
Gilbert Cl, SE18 105 EM81
Swanscombe DA10 129 FX86
Gilbert Gro, Edg. HA8 42 CR53
Gilbert Ho, EC2
off The Barbican 84 DQ71
SE8 off McMillan St 103 EA79
Gilbert Pl, WC1 195 P7
Gilbert Rd, SE11 200 E9
SW19 120 DC94
Belvedere DA17 106 FA76
Bromley BR1 124 EG94
Grays (Chaff.Hun.) RM16 109 FW76
Pinner HA5 60 BX56
Romford RM1 71 FF56
Uxbridge (Hare.) UB9 38 BK54
Gilbert St, E15 68 EE63
W1 194 G9
Enfield EN3 30 DW37
Hounslow TW3 off High St 96 CC83
Gilbert Way, Croy. CR0
off Beddington Fm Rd 141 DL102
Slough SL3 off Ditton Rd 93 AZ78
Gilbey Cl, Uxb. UB10 59 BP63
Gilbey Rd, SW17 120 DE91
Gilbeys Yd, NW1 82 DG66
Gilbourne Rd, SE18 105 ET79
Gilda Av, Enf. EN3 31 DY43
Gilda Cres, N16 66 DU60
Gildea Cl, Pnr. HA5 40 CA52
Gildea St, W1 195 J7
Gilden Cres, NW5 64 DG64
Gildenhill Rd, Swan. BR8 128 FJ94
Gildersome St, SE18
off Nightingale Vale 105 EN79
Gilders Rd, Chess. KT9 156 CM107
Giles Cl, Rain. RM13 90 FK68
Giles Coppice, SE19 122 DT91
Giles Fld, Grav. DA12
off Damigos Rd 131 GM88
Giles Travers Cl, Egh. TW20 133 BC97
Gilfrid Cl, Uxb. UB8
off Craig Dr 77 BP72
Gilhams Av, Bans. SM7 157 CY112
Gilkes Cres, SE21 122 DS86
Gilkes Pl, SE21 122 DS86
Gillam Way, Rain. RM13 89 FG65
Gillan Grn, Bushey
(Bushey Hth) WD23 40 CC47
Gillards Ms, E17
off Gillards Way 67 EA56
Gillards Way, E17 67 EA56
Gill Av, E16 86 EG72
Gill Cl, Wat. WD18 23 BQ44
Gill Cres, Grav. (Nthflt) DA11 131 GF90
Gillender St, E3 85 EC70
E14 85 EC70
Gillespie Rd, N5 65 DN62
Gillett Av, E6 86 EL68
Gillette Cor, Islw. TW7 97 CG80
Gillett Pl, N16
off Gillett St 66 DS64
Gillett Rd, Th.Hth. CR7 142 DR98
Gillett St, N16 66 DS64
Gillfoot, NW1 195 K1
Gillham Ter, N17 46 DU51
Gilliam Gro, Pur. CR8 159 DN110
Gillian Cres, Rom. RM2 52 FJ54
Gillian Pk Rd, Sutt. SM3 139 CZ102
Gillian St, SE13 123 EB85
Gilliat Cl, Iver SL0
off Dutton Way 75 BE72
Gilliat Rd, Slou. SL1 74 AS73
Gilliat's Grn, Rick. (Chorl.) WD3 21 BD42
Gillies St, NW5 64 DG64

★ Place of interest ⇌ Railway station ⊖ London Underground station DLR Docklands Light Railway station Tramlink Tramlink station H Hospital Riv Pedestrian ferry landing stage

259

Gilling Ct, NW3 82 DE65
Gillingham Ms, SW1 199 K8
Gillingham Rd, NW2 63 CY62
Gillingham Row, SW1 199 K8
Gillingham St, SW1 199 J8
Gillison Wk, SE16 202 C6
Gillman Dr, E15 86 EF67
Gillmans Rd, Orp. BR5 146 EV102
Gills Hill, Rad. WD7 25 CF35
Gills Hill La, Rad. WD7 25 CF36
Gills Hollow, Rad. WD7 25 CF36
Gill's Rd, Dart.
(S.Darenth) DA2, DA4 149 FS95
Gill St, E14 85 DZ72
Gillum Cl, Barn. EN4 44 DF46
Gilmore Cl, Slou. SL3 92 AW75
Uxbridge UB10 58 BN62
Gilmore Cres, Ashf. TW15 114 BN92
Gilmore Rd, SE13 103 ED84
Gilmour Cl, Wal.Cr. EN7 30 DU35
Gilpin Av, SW14 98 CR84
Gilpin Cl, W2 off Porteus Rd 82 DC71
Mitcham CR4 140 DE96
Gilpin Cres, N18 46 DT50
Twickenham TW2 116 CB87
Gilpin Rd, E5 67 DY63
Gilpin Way, Hayes UB3 95 BR80
Gilroy Cl, Rain. RM13 89 FF65
Gilroy Way, Orp. BR5 146 EV101
Gilsland, Wal.Abb. EN9 32 EE35
Gilsland Rd, Th.Hth. CR7 142 DR98
Gilstead Ho, Bark. IG11 88 EV68
Gilstead Rd, SW6 100 DB82
Gilston Rd, SW10 100 DC78
Gilton Rd, SE6 124 EE90
Giltspur St, EC1 196 G8
Gilwell Cl, E4
off Antlers Hill 31 EB42
Gilwell La, E4 31 EC42
Gilwell Pk, E4 31 EC41
Gimcrack Hill, Lthd. KT22
off Dorking Rd 171 CH123
Gippeswyck Cl, Pnr. HA5
off Uxbridge Rd 40 BX53
⇌ Gipsy Hill 122 DS92
Gipsy Hill, SE19 122 DS91
Gipsy La, SW15 99 CU83
Grays RM17 110 GC79
★ Gipsy Moth IV, SE10 103 EC79
Gipsy Rd, SE27 122 DQ91
Welling DA16 106 EX81
Gipsy Rd Gdns, SE27 122 DQ91
Giralda Cl, E16
off Fulmer Rd 86 EK71
Giraud St, E14 85 EB72
Girdlers Rd, W14 99 CX77
Girdlestone Wk, N19 65 DJ61
Girdwood Rd, SW18 119 CY87
Girling Way, Felt. TW14 95 BU83
Girona Cl, Grays
(Chaff.Hun.) RM16 109 FW76
Gironde Rd, SW6 99 CZ80
Girtin Rd, Bushey WD23 24 CB43
Girton Av, NW9 62 CN55
Girton Cl, Nthlt. UB5 78 CC65
Girton Ct, Wal.Cr. EN8 15 DY30
Girton Gdns, Croy. CR0 143 EA104
Girton Rd, SE26 123 DX92
Northolt UB5 78 CC65
Girton Vil, W10 81 CX72
Girton Way, Rick.
(Crox.Grn) WD3 23 BQ43
Gisborne Gdns, Rain. RM13 89 FF69
Gisbourne Cl, Wall. SM6 141 DK104
Gisburne Way, Wat. WD24 23 BU37
Gisburn Rd, N8 65 DM56
Gissing Wk, N1
off Lofting Rd 83 DN66
Gittens Cl, Brom. BR1 124 EF91
Given Wilson Wk, E13 86 EF68
Glacier Way, Wem. HA0 79 CK68
Gladbeck Way, Enf. EN2 29 DP42
Gladding Rd, E12 68 EK63
Waltham Cross (Chsht) EN7 13 DP25
Glade, The, N21 29 DM44
SE7 104 EJ80
Brentwood (Hutt.) CM13 55 GA46
Bromley BR1 144 EK96
Coulsdon CR5 175 DN119
Croydon CR0 143 DX99
Enfield EN2 29 DN41
Epsom KT17 157 CU106
Gerrards Cross SL9 56 AX60
Ilford IG5 49 EM53
Leatherhead (Fetch.) KT22 170 CA122
Sevenoaks TN13 191 FH123
Staines TW18 114 BH94
Sutton SM2 157 CY109
Tadworth KT20 174 DA121
Upminster RM14 72 FQ64
West Byfleet KT14 151 BE113
West Wickham BR4 143 EB104
Woodford Green IG8 48 EH48
Glade Cl, Surb. KT6 137 CK103
Glade Ct, Ilf. IG5
off The Glade 49 EM53
Glade Gdns, Croy. CR0 143 DY101
Glade La, Sthl. UB2 96 CB75
Glades, The, Grav. DA12 131 GK93
Gladeside, N21 29 DM44
Croydon CR0 143 DX100
Gladeside Cl, Chess. KT9
off Leatherhead Rd 155 CK108
Gladeside Ct, Warl. CR6 176 DV120
Gladesmore Rd, N15 66 DT58
Glade Spur, Tad. KT20 174 DB121
Glades Shop Cen, The,
Brom. BR1 144 EG96
Gladeswood Rd, Belv. DA17 107 FB77
Gladeway, The, Wal.Abb. EN9 15 ED33
Gladiator St, SE23 123 DY86
Glading Ter, N16 66 DT62
Gladioli Cl, Hmptn. TW12
off Gresham Rd 116 CA93
Gladsdale Dr, Pnr. HA5 59 BU56
Gladsmuir Cl, Walt. KT12 136 BW103
Gladsmuir Rd, N19 65 DJ60
Barnet EN5 27 CY40
Gladstone Av, E12 86 EL66
N22 45 DN54
Feltham TW14 115 BU86
Twickenham TW2 117 CD87
Gladstone Ct, SW19
off Gladstone Rd 120 DA94
Gladstone Gdns, Houns. TW3
off Palmerston Rd 96 CC81
Gladstone Ms, N22
off Pelham Rd 45 DN54
NW6 off Cavendish Rd 81 CZ66
SE20 122 DW94
Gladstone Par, NW2
off Edgware Rd 63 CV60
Gladstone Pk Gdns, NW2 63 CV62
Gladstone Pl, E3
off Roman Rd 85 DZ68
Barnet EN5 27 CX42
Gladstone Rd, SW19 120 DA94
W4 off Acton La 98 CR76
Ashtead KT21 171 CK118
Buckhurst Hill IG9 48 EH46
Croydon CR0 142 DR101
Dartford DA1 128 FM86
Kingston upon Thames KT1 138 CN97
Orpington BR6 163 EQ106
Southall UB2 96 BY76
Surbiton KT6 137 CK103
Watford WD17 24 BW41
Gladstone St, SE1 200 F6
Gladstone Ter, SE27
off Bentons La 122 DQ91
Gladstone Way, Har.
(Wldste) HA3 61 CE55
Gladwell Rd, N8 65 DM58
Bromley BR1 124 EG93
Gladwyn Rd, SW15 99 CX83
Gladys Rd, NW6 82 DA66
Glaisher St, SE8 103 EA79
Glaisyer Way, Iver SL0 75 BC68
Glamis Cl, Wal.Cr.
(Chsht) EN7 14 DU29
Glamis Cres, Hayes UB3 95 BQ76
Glamis Dr, Horn. RM11 72 FL60
Glamis Pl, E1 84 DW73
Glamis Rd, E1 84 DW73
Glamis Way, Nthlt. UB5 78 CC65
Glamorgan Cl, Mitch. CR4 141 DL97
Glamorgan Rd, Kings.T. KT1 117 CJ94
Glanfield Rd, Beck. BR3 143 DZ98
Glanleam Rd, Stan. HA7 41 CK49
Glanmead, Brwd.
(Shenf.) CM15 54 FY46
Glanmor Rd, Slou. SL2 74 AV73
Glanthams Cl, Brwd.
(Shenf.) CM15 54 FY47
Glanthams Rd, Brwd.
(Shenf.) CM15 55 FZ47
Glanty, The, Egh. TW20 113 BB91
Glanville Dr, Horn. RM11 72 FM60
Glanville Ms, Stan. HA7 41 CG50
Glanville Rd, SW2 121 DL85
Bromley BR2 144 EH97
Glasbrook Av, Twick. TW2 116 BZ88
Glasbrook Rd, SE9 124 EK87
Glaserton Rd, N16 66 DS59
Glasford St, SW17 120 DF93
Glasgow Ho, W9 82 DB68
Glasgow Rd, E13 86 EH68
N18 off Aberdeen Rd 46 DV50
Glasgow Ter, SW1 101 DJ78
Glasse Cl, W13 79 CG73
Glasshill St, SE1 200 G4
Glasshouse Cl, Uxb. UB8
off Harlington Rd 77 BP71
Glasshouse Flds, E1 85 DX73
Glasshouse St, W1 199 L1
Glasshouse Wk, SE11 200 A10
Glasshouse Yd, EC1 197 H5
Glasslyn Rd, N8 65 DK57
Glassmill La, Brom. BR2 144 EF96
Glass St, E2 off Coventry Rd 84 DV70
Glass Yd, SE18
off Woolwich High St 105 EN76
Glastonbury Av, Wdf.Grn. IG8 48 EK52
Glastonbury Cl, Orp. BR5 146 EW102
Glastonbury Pl, E1
off Sutton St 84 DW72
Glastonbury Rd, N9 46 DU46
Morden SM4 140 DA101
Glastonbury St, NW6 63 CZ64
Glaucus St, E3 85 EB71
Glazbury Rd, W14 99 CY77
Glazebrook Cl, SE21 122 DR89
Glazebrook Rd, Tedd. TW11 117 CF94
Glebe, The, SE3 104 EE83
SW16 121 DK91
Chislehurst BR7 145 EQ95
Kings Langley WD4 6 BN29
Watford WD25 8 BW33
West Drayton UB7 94 BM77
Worcester Park KT4 139 CT102
Glebe Av, Enf. EN2 29 DP41
Harrow HA3 62 CL55
Mitcham CR4 140 DE96
Ruislip HA4 77 BV65
Uxbridge UB10 59 BQ63
Woodford Green IG8 48 EG51
Glebe Cl, W4 off Glebe St 98 CS78
Gerrards Cross
(Chal.St.P.) SL9 36 AX52
South Croydon CR2 160 DT111
Uxbridge UB10 59 BQ63
Glebe Cotts, Sutt. SM1
off Vale Rd 158 DB105
Westerham (Brasted) TN16 180 EV123
Glebe Ct, W7 79 CD73
Coulsdon CR5 175 DH115
Mitcham CR4 140 DF97
Sevenoaks TN13
off Oak La 191 FH126
Stanmore HA7 41 CJ50
Glebe Cres, NW4 63 CW56
Harrow HA3 62 CL55
Glebefield, The, Sev. TN13 190 FF123
Glebe Gdns, N.Mal. KT3 138 CS101
West Byfleet (Byfleet) KT14 152 BK114
Glebe Ho Dr, Brom. BR2 144 EH102
Glebe Hyrst, SE19
off Giles Coppice 122 DT91
South Croydon CR2 160 DT112
Glebeland Gdns, Shep. TW17 135 BQ100
Glebelands, Chig. IG7 50 EV48
Dartford DA1 107 FF84
Esher (Clay.) KT10 155 CF109
West Molesey KT8 136 CB99
Glebelands Av, E18 48 EG54
Ilford IG2 69 ER59
Glebelands Cl, SE5
off Grove Hill Rd 102 DS83
Glebelands Rd, Felt. TW14 115 BU87
Glebe La, Barn. EN5 27 CU43
Harrow HA3 62 CL56
Sevenoaks TN13 191 FH126
Glebe Path, Mitch. CR4 140 DE97
Glebe Pl, SW3 100 DE79
Dartford (Hort.Kir.) DA4 148 FQ98
Glebe Rd, E8
off Middleton Rd 84 DT66
N3 44 DC53
N8 65 DM56
NW10 81 CT65
SW13 99 CU82
Ashtead KT21 171 CK118
Bromley BR1 144 EG95
Carshalton SM5 158 DF107
Dagenham RM10 89 FB65
Egham TW20 113 BC93
Gerrards Cross
(Chal.St.P.) SL9 36 AW53
Gravesend DA11 131 GF88
Hayes UB3 77 BT74
Rainham RM13 90 FJ69
Redhill RH1 175 DH124
Staines TW18 114 BH93
Stanmore HA7 41 CJ50
Sutton SM2 157 CY109
Uxbridge UB8 76 BJ68
Warlingham CR6 177 DX117
Windsor (Old Wind.) SL4 112 AV85
Glebe Side, Twick. TW1 117 CF86
Glebe St, W4 98 CS78
Glebe Ter, E3 off Bow Rd 85 EA69
Glebe Way, Erith DA8 107 FE79
Feltham TW13 116 CA90
Hornchurch RM11 72 FL59
South Croydon CR2 160 DT111
West Wickham BR4 143 EC103
Glebeway, Wdf.Grn. IG8 48 EJ50
Gledhow Gdns, SW5 100 DC77
Gledhow Wd, Tad. KT20 174 DB121
Gledstanes Rd, W14 99 CY78
Gledwood Av, Hayes UB4 77 BT71
Gledwood Cres, Hayes UB4 77 BT71
Gledwood Dr, Hayes UB4 77 BT71
Gledwood Gdns, Hayes UB4 77 BT71
Gleed Av, Bushey
(Bushey Hth) WD23 41 CD47
Gleeson Dr, Orp. BR6 163 ET106
Gleeson Ms, Add. KT15 152 BJ105
Glegg Pl, SW15 99 CX84
Glen, The, Add. KT15 151 BF106
Bromley BR2 144 EE96
Croydon CR0 143 DX103
Enfield EN2 29 DP42
Northwood HA6 39 BR52
Orpington BR6 145 EM104
Pinner HA5 60 BY59
Pinner (Eastcote) HA5 59 BV57
Rainham RM13 90 FJ70
Slough SL3 92 AW77
Southall UB2 96 BZ78
Wembley HA9 61 CK63
Glenaffric Av, E14 204 F9
Glen Albyn Rd, SW19 119 CX89
Glenalla Rd, Ruis. HA4 59 BT59
Glenalmond Rd, Har. HA3 62 CL56
Glenalvon Way, SE18 104 EL77
Glena Mt, Sutt. SM1 158 DC105
Glenarm Rd, E5 66 DW64
Glen Av, Ashf. TW15 114 BN91
Glenavon Cl, Esher
(Clay.) KT10 155 CG108
Glenavon Gdns, Slou. SL3 92 AW77
Glenavon Rd, E15 86 EE66
Glenbarr Cl, SE9
off Dumbreck Rd 105 EP83
Glenbow Rd, Brom. BR1 124 EE93
Glenbrook N, Enf. EN2 29 DM42
Glenbrook Rd, NW6 64 DA64
Glenbrook S, Enf. EN2 29 DM42
Glenbuck Ct, Surb. KT6
off Glenbuck Rd 137 CK100
Glenbuck Rd, Surb. KT6 137 CK100
Glenburnie Rd, SW17 120 DF90
Glencairn Dr, W5 79 CH70
Glencairne Cl, E16 86 EK71
Glencairn Rd, SW16 141 DL95
Glen Cl, Shep. TW17 134 BN98
Tadworth (Kgswd) KT20 173 CY123
Glencoe Av, Ilf. IG2 69 ER59
Glencoe Dr, Dag. RM10 70 FA63
Glencoe Rd, Bushey WD23 24 CA44
Hayes UB4 78 BX71
Weybridge KT13 134 BN104
Glencorse Grn, Wat. WD19
off Caldwell Rd 40 BX49
Glen Ct, Stai. TW18
off Riverside Dr 113 BF94
Glen Cres, Wdf.Grn. IG8 48 EH51
Glendale, Swan. BR8 147 FF99
Glendale Av, N22 45 DN52
Edgware HA8 42 CM49
Romford RM6 70 EW59
Glendale Cl, SE9
off Dumbreck Rd 105 EN83
Brentwood (Shenf.) CM15 54 FY45
Woking GU21 166 AW118
Glendale Dr, SW19 119 CZ92
Glendale Gdns, Wem. HA9 61 CK60
Glendale Ms, Beck. BR3 143 EB95
Glendale Ri, Ken. CR8 175 DP115
Glendale Rd, Erith DA8 107 FC77
Gravesend (Nthflt) DA11 130 GE91
Glendale Wk, Wal.Cr.
(Chsht) EN8 15 DY30
Glendale Way, SE28 88 EW73
Glendall St, SW9 101 DM84
Glendarvon St, SW15 99 CX83
Glendevon Cl, Edg. HA8
off Tayside Dr 42 CP48
Glendish Rd, N17 46 DU53
Glendor Gdns, NW7 42 CR49
Glendower Cres, Orp. BR6 146 EU100
Glendower Gdns, SW14
off Glendower Rd 98 CR83
Glendower Pl, SW7 100 DD77
Glendower Rd, E4 47 ED46
SW14 98 CR83
Glendown Rd, SE2 106 EU78
Glendun Rd, W3 80 CS73
Gleneagle Ms, SW16
off Ambleside Av 121 DK92
Gleneagle Rd, SW16 121 DK92
Gleneagles, Stan. HA7 41 CH51
Gleneagles Cl, SE16
off Ryder Dr 102 DV78
Orpington BR6 145 ER102
Romford RM3 52 FM52
Staines (Stanw.) TW19 114 BK86
Watford WD19 40 BX49
Gleneagles Grn, Orp. BR6
off Tandridge Dr 145 ER102
Gleneagles Twr, Sthl. UB1 78 CC72
Gleneldon Ms, SW16 121 DL91
Gleneldon Rd, SW16 121 DL91
Glenelg Rd, SW2 121 DL85
Glenesk Rd, SE9 105 EN83
Glenfarg Rd, SE6 123 ED88
Glenfield Cres, Ruis. HA4 59 BR59
Glenfield Rd, SW12 121 DJ88
W13 97 CH75
Ashford TW15 115 BP93
Banstead SM7 174 DB115
Glenfield Ter, W13 97 CH75
Glenfinlas Way, SE5 101 DP80
Glenforth St, SE10 205 L10
Glengall Causeway, E14 203 P6
Glengall Gro, E14 204 D6
Glengall Rd, NW6 81 CZ67
SE15 102 DT79
Bexleyheath DA7 106 EY83
Edgware HA8 42 CP48
Woodford Green IG8 48 EG51
Glengall Ter, SE15 102 DT79
Glen Gdns, Croy. CR0 141 DN104
Glengarnock Av, E14 204 E9
Glengarry Rd, SE22 122 DS85
Glenham Dr, Ilf. IG2 69 EP57
Glenhaven Av, Borwd. WD6 26 CN41
Glenhead Cl, SE9
off Dumbreck Rd 105 EP83
Glenheadon Cl, Lthd. KT22
off Glenheadon Ri 171 CK123
Glenheadon Ri, Lthd. KT22 171 CK123
Glenhill Cl, N3 44 DA54
Glenhouse Rd, SE9 125 EN85
Glenhurst Av, NW5 64 DG63
Bexley DA5 126 EZ88
Ruislip HA4 59 BQ59
Glenhurst Ct, SE19 122 DT92
Glenhurst Ri, SE19 122 DQ94
Glenhurst Rd, N12 44 DD50
Brentford TW8 97 CJ79
Glenilla Rd, NW3 82 DE65
Glenister Ho, Hayes UB3 77 BV74
Glenister Pk Rd, SW16 121 DK94
Glenister Rd, SE10 205 K10
Glenister St, E16 87 EN74
Glenkerry Ho, E14
off Burcham St 85 EC72
Glenlea Path, SE9
off Well Hall Rd 125 EM85
Glenlea Rd, SE9 125 EM85
Glenlion Ct, Wey. KT13 135 BS104
Glenloch Rd, NW3 82 DE65
Enfield EN3 30 DW40
Glen Luce, Wal.Cr. EN8
off Turners Hill 15 DX30
Glenluce Rd, SE3 104 EG80
Glenlyon Rd, SE9 125 EN85
Glenmere Av, NW7 43 CU52
Glen Ms, E17 off Glen Rd 67 DZ57
Glenmill, Hmptn. TW12 116 BZ92
Glenmore Cl, Add. KT15 134 BH104
Glenmore Gdns, Abb.L. WD5
off Stewart Cl 7 BU32
Glenmore Rd, NW3 82 DE65
Welling DA16 105 ET81
Glenmore Way, Bark. IG11 88 EU69
Glenmount Path, SE18
off Raglan Rd 105 EQ78
Glenn Av, Pur. CR8 159 DP111
Glennie Rd, SE27 121 DN90
Glenny Rd, Bark. IG11 87 EQ65
Glenorchy Cl, Hayes UB4 78 BY71
Glenparke Rd, E7 86 EH65
Glen Ri, Wdf.Grn. IG8 48 EH51
Glen Rd, E13 86 EJ70
E17 67 DZ57
Chessington KT9 138 CL104
Glen Rd End, Wall. SM6 159 DH109
Glenrosa Gdns, Grav. DA12 131 GM92
Glenrosa St, SW6 100 DC82
Glenrose Ct, Sid. DA14 126 EV92
Glenroy St, W12 81 CW72
Glensdale Rd, SE4 103 DZ83
Glenshee Cl, Nthwd. HA6
off Rickmansworth Rd 39 BQ51
Glenshiel Rd, SE9 125 EN85
Glenside, Chig. IG7 49 EP51
Glenside Cotts, Slou. SL1 92 AT76
Glentanner Way, SW17
off Aboyne Rd 120 DD90
Glen Ter, E14 204 E4
Glentham Gdns, SW13
off Glentham Rd 99 CV79
Glentham Rd, SW13 99 CU79
Glenthorne Av, Croy. CR0 142 DV102
Glenthorne Cl, Sutt. SM3 140 DA102
Uxbridge UB10
off Uxbridge Rd 76 BN69
Glenthorne Gdns, Ilf. IG6 69 EN55
Sutton SM3 140 DA102
Glenthorne Ms, W6
off Glenthorne Rd 99 CV77
Glenthorne Rd, E17 67 DY57
Glenthorne Rd, N11 44 DF50
W6 99 CW77
Kingston upon Thames KT1 138 CM98
Glenthorpe Rd, Mord. SM4 139 CX99
Glenton Cl, Rom. RM1 51 FE51
Glenton Rd, SE13 104 EE84
Glenton Way, Rom. RM1 51 FE52
Glentrammon Av, Orp. BR6 163 ET107
Glentrammon Cl, Orp. BR6 163 ET107
Glentrammon Gdns, Orp. BR6 163 ET107
Glentrammon Rd, Orp. BR6 163 ET107
Glentworth St, NW1 194 E5
Glenure Rd, SE9 125 EN85
Glenview, SE2 106 EX79
Glen Vw, Grav. DA12 131 GJ88
Glenview Rd, Brom. BR1 144 EK96
Glenville Av, Enf. EN2 30 DQ38
Glenville Gro, SE8 103 DZ80
Glenville Ms, SW18 120 DB87
Glenville Rd, Kings.T. KT2 138 CN95
Glen Wk, Islw. TW7 117 CD85
Glen Way, Wat. WD17 23 BS38
Glenwood Av, NW9 62 CS60
Rainham RM13 89 FH70
Glenwood Cl, Har. HA1 61 CF57
Glenwood Ct, E18
off Clarendon Rd 68 EG55
Glenwood Dr, Rom. RM2 71 FG56
Glenwood Gdns, Ilf. IG2 69 EN57
Glenwood Gro, NW9 62 CQ60
Glenwood Rd, N15 65 DP57
NW7 42 CS48
SE6 123 DZ88
Epsom KT17 157 CU107
Hounslow TW3 97 CD83
Glenwood Way, Croy. CR0 143 DX100
Glenworth Av, E14 204 F9
Gliddon Dr, E5 66 DV63
Gliddon Rd, W14 99 CY78
Glimpsing Grn, Erith DA18 106 EY76
Glisson Rd, Uxb. UB10 76 BN68
Gload Cres, Orp. BR5 146 EX103
Global App, E3
off Hancock Rd 85 EB68
Globe Ind Estates,
Grays RM17 110 GC78
Globe Pond Rd, SE16 203 K3
Globe Rd, E1 84 DW69
E2 84 DW69
E15 68 EF64
Hornchurch RM11 71 FG58
Woodford Green IG8 48 EJ51
Globe Rope Wk, E14 204 D9
Globe St, SE1 201 J6
Globe Ter, E2 off Globe Rd 84 DW69
Globe Yd, W1 195 H9
Glossop Rd, S.Croy. CR2 160 DR109
Gloster Rd, N.Mal. KT3 138 CS98
Woking GU22 167 BA120
Gloucester Arc, SW7
off Gloucester Rd 100 DC77
Gloucester Av, NW1 82 DG66
Grays RM16 110 GC75
Hornchurch RM11 72 FN56
Sidcup DA15 125 ES89
Waltham Cross EN8 15 DY33
Welling DA16 105 ET84
Gloucester Circ, SE10 103 EC80
Gloucester Cl, NW10 80 CR66
Thames Ditton KT7 137 CG102
Gloucester Ct, EC3 201 N1
Richmond TW9 98 CN80
Tilbury RM18 off Dock Rd 111 GF82
Uxbridge (Denh.) UB9
off Moorfield Rd 58 BG58
Gloucester Cres, NW1 83 DH67
Staines TW18 114 BK93
Gloucester Dr, N4 65 DP61
NW11 64 DA56
Staines TW18 113 BC90
Gloucester Gdns, NW11 63 CZ59
W2 off Bishops Br Rd 82 DC72
Barnet EN4 28 DG42
Ilford IG1 68 EL59
Sutton SM1 140 DB103
Gloucester Gate, NW1 83 DH68
Gloucester Gate Ms, NW1
off Gloucester Gate 83 DH68
Gloucester Gro, Edg. HA8 42 CR53
Gloucester Gro Est, SE15 102 DS79
Gloucester Ho, NW6 82 DA68
Gloucester Ms, E10
off Gloucester Rd 67 EA59
W2 82 DC72
Gloucester Ms W, W2
off Cleveland Ter 82 DC72
Gloucester Par, Sid. DA15 126 EU85
Gloucester Pk, SW7
off Courtfield Rd 100 DC77
Gloucester Pl, NW1 194 D4
W1 194 E6
Gloucester Pl Ms, W1 194 E7
⊖ Gloucester Road 100 DC77
Gloucester Rd, E10 67 EA59
E11 68 EH57
E12 69 EM62
E17 47 DX54
N17 46 DR54
N18 46 DT50
SW7 100 DC76
W3 98 CQ75
W5 97 CJ75
Barnet EN5 28 DC43
Belvedere DA17 106 EZ78
Brentwood
(Pilg.Hat.) CM15 54 FV43
Croydon CR0 142 DR100
Dartford DA1 127 FH87
Enfield EN2 30 DQ38
Feltham TW13 116 BW88
Gravesend DA12 131 GJ91
Hampton TW12 116 CB94
Harrow HA1 60 CB57
Hounslow TW4 96 BY84
Kingston upon Thames KT1 138 CP96
Redhill RH1 184 DF133
Richmond TW9 98 CN80
Romford RM1 71 FE58
Teddington TW11 117 CE92
Twickenham TW2 116 CC88

★ Place of interest ⇌ Railway station ⊖ London Underground station DLR Docklands Light Railway station Tramlink station H Hospital Pedestrian ferry landing stage

★ Place of interest ⇌ Railway station ⊖ London Underground station DLR Docklands Light Railway station Tra Tramlink station Ⓗ Hospital Riv Pedestrian ferry landing stage

261

Grafton Rd, W3 80 CQ73
Croydon CR0 141 DN102
Dagenham RM8 70 EY61
Enfield EN2 29 DM41
Harrow HA1 60 CC57
New Malden KT3 138 CS97
Worcester Park KT4 138 CR104
Graftons, The, NW2
off Hermitage La 64 DA62
Grafton Sq, SW4 101 DJ83
Grafton St, W1 199 J1
Grafton Ter, NW5 64 DF64
Grafton Way, W1 195 K5
WC1 195 K5
West Molesey KT8 136 BZ98
Grafton Yd, NW5
off Prince of Wales Rd 83 DH65
Graham Av, W13 97 CH75
Mitcham CR4 140 DG95
Graham Cl, Brwd.
(Hutt.) CM13 55 GC43
Croydon CR0 143 EA103
Grahame Pk Est, NW9 42 CS53
Grahame Pk Way, NW7 43 CT52
NW9 43 CT54
Graham Gdns, Surb. KT6 138 CL102
Graham Rd, E8 84 DT65
E13 86 EG70
N15 65 DP55
NW4 63 CV58
SW19 119 CZ94
W4 98 CR76
Bexleyheath DA6 106 FA84
Hampton TW12 116 CA91
Harrow HA3 61 CE55
Mitcham CR4 140 DG95
Purley CR8 159 DN113
Graham St, N1 196 G1
Graham Ter, SW1 198 F9
Grainger Cl, Nthlt. UB5
off Lancaster Rd 60 CC64
Grainger Rd, N22 46 DQ53
Isleworth TW7 97 CF82
Grainge's Yd, Uxb. UB8
off Cross St 76 BJ66
Gramer Cl, E11
off Norman Rd 67 ED61
Grampian Cl, Hayes UB3 95 BR80
Orpington BR6
off Cotswold Ri 145 ET100
Sutton SM2
off Devonshire Rd 158 DC108
Grampian Gdns, NW2 63 CY60
Grampian Ho, N9
off Plevna Rd 46 DV47
Grampian Way, Slou. SL3 93 BA78
Granard Av, SW15 119 CV85
Granard Rd, SW12 120 DF87
Granaries, The, Wal.Abb. EN9 16 EE34
Granary Cl, N9 *off Turin Rd* 46 DW45
Granary Rd, E1 84 DV70
Granary St, NW1 83 DK67
Granby Pk Rd, Wal.Cr.
(Chsht) EN7 14 DT28
Granby Pl, SE1 200 D5
Granby Rd, SE9 105 EM82
Gravesend DA11 130 GC86
Granby St, E2 84 DT70
Granby Ter, NW1 195 K1
Grand Arc, N12
off Ballards La 44 DC50
Grand Av, EC1 196 G6
N10 64 DG56
Surbiton KT5 138 CP99
Wembley HA9 62 CN64
Grand Av E, Wem. HA9 62 CP64
Grand Dep Rd, SE18 105 EN78
Grand Dr, SW20 139 CW96
Southall UB2 96 CC75
Granden Rd, SW16 141 DL96
Grandfield Av, Wat. WD17 23 BT39
Grandis Cotts, Wok.
(Ripley) GU23 168 BH122
Grandison Rd, SW11 120 DF85
Worcester Park KT4 139 CW103
Grand Junct Wf, N1 197 H1
Grand Par Ms, SW15
off Upper Richmond Rd 119 CY85
Grand Stand Rd, Epsom KT18 173 CT117
Grand Union Canal Wk, W7 97 CE76
Grand Union Cl, W9
off Woodfield Rd 81 CZ71
Grand Union Cres, E8 84 DU66
Grand Union Ind Est, NW10 80 CP68
Grand Union Wk, NW1 83 DH66
Grand Vw Av, West.
(Bigg.H.) TN16 178 EJ117
Grand Wk, E1
off Solebay St 85 DY70
Granfield St, SW11 100 DD81
Grange, The, N2
off Central Av 44 DD54
N20 44 DC46
SE1 201 P6
SW19 119 CX93
Croydon CR0 143 DZ103
Dartford (S.Darenth) DA4 149 FR95
Walton-on-Thames KT12 135 BV103
Wembley HA0 80 CN66
Windsor (Old Wind.) SL4 112 AV85
Woking (Chobham) GU24 150 AS110
Worcester Park KT4 138 CR104
Grange Av, N12 44 DC50
N20 43 CY45
SE25 142 DS96
Barnet EN4 44 DE46
Stanmore HA7 41 CH54
Twickenham TW2 117 CE89
Woodford Green IG8 48 EG51
Grangecliffe Gdns, SE25 142 DS96
Grange Cl, Brwd.
(Ingrave) CM13 55 GC50
Edgware HA8 42 CQ50
Gerrards Cross
(Chal.St.P.) SL9 36 AY53
Grange Cl, Hayes UB3 77 BS71
Hounslow TW5 96 BZ79
Leatherhead KT22 171 CK120
Redhill (Bletch.) RH1 186 DR133
Redhill (Merst.) RH1 185 DH128
Sidcup DA15 126 EU90
Staines (Wrays.) TW19 112 AY86
Watford WD17 23 BU39
West Molesey KT8 136 CB98
Westerham TN16 189 EQ126
Woodford Green IG8 48 EG52
Grange Ct, WC2 196 C9
Chigwell IG7 49 EQ47
Loughton IG10 32 EK43
Northolt UB5 78 BW68
Staines TW18 114 BG92
Waltham Abbey EN9 15 EC34
Walton-on-Thames KT12 135 BU103
Grangecourt Rd, N16 66 DS60
Grange Cres, SE28 88 EW72
Chigwell IG7 49 ER50
Dartford DA2 128 FP86
Grangedale Cl, Nthwd. HA6 39 BS53
Grange Dr, Chis. BR7 124 EL93
Orpington BR6
off Rushmore Hill 164 EW109
Redhill (Merst.) RH1
off London Rd S 185 DH128
Woking GU21 150 AY114
Grange Fm Cl, Har. HA2 60 CC61
Grange Flds, Ger.Cr.
(Chal.St.P.) SL9
off Lower Rd 36 AY53
Grange Gdns, N14 45 DK46
NW3 64 DB62
SE25 142 DS96
Banstead SM7 158 DB113
Pinner HA5 60 BZ56
Grange Gro, N1 83 DP65
GRANGE HILL, Chig. IG7 49 ER51
⊖ Grange Hill 49 ER49
Grange Hill, SE25 142 DS96
Edgware HA8 42 CQ50
Grangehill Pl, SE9
off Westmount Rd 105 EM83
Grangehill Rd, SE9 105 EM83
Grange Ho, Bark. IG11
off St. Margarets 87 ER67
Erith DA8 107 FG82
Grange La, SE21 122 DT89
Watford (Let.Hth) WD25 25 CD39
Grange Mans, Epsom KT17 157 CT108
Grange Meadow, Bans. SM7 158 DB113
Grangemill Rd, SE6 123 EA90
Grangemill Way, SE6 123 EA89
Grangemount, Lthd. KT22 171 CK120
★ Grange Mus of
Comm History, NW10 62 CS63
GRANGE PARK, N21 29 DP43
⇌ Grange Park 29 DP43
Grange Pk, W5 80 CL74
Woking GU21 166 AY115
Grange Pk Av, N21 29 DP44
Grange Pk Pl, SW20 119 CV94
Grange Pk Rd, E10 67 EB60
Thornton Heath CR7 142 DR98
Grange Pl, NW6 82 DA66
Staines TW18 134 BJ96
Walton-on-Thames KT12 135 BU103
Grange Rd, E10 67 EA60
E13 86 EF69
E17 67 DY57
N6 64 DG58
N17 46 DU51
N18 46 DU51
NW10 81 CV65
SE1 201 N6
SE19 142 DR98
SE25 142 DR98
SW13 99 CU81
W4 98 CP78
W5 79 CK74
Addlestone
(New Haw) KT15 152 BG110
Borehamwood
(Elstree) WD6 26 CM43
Bushey WD23 24 BY43
Caterham CR3 186 DU125
Chessington KT9 156 CL105
Edgware HA8 42 CR51
Egham TW20 113 AZ92
Gerrards Cross
(Chal.St.P.) SL9 36 AY53
Gravesend DA11 131 GG87
Grays RM17 110 GB79
Harrow HA1 61 CG58
Harrow (S.Har.) HA2 61 CD61
Hayes UB3 77 BS72
Ilford IG1 69 EP63
Kingston upon Thames KT1 138 CL97
Leatherhead KT22 171 CK120
Orpington BR6 145 EQ103
Romford RM3 51 FH51
Sevenoaks TN13 190 FG127
South Croydon CR2 160 DQ110
South Ockendon
(Aveley) RM15 90 FQ74
Southall UB1 96 BY75
Sutton SM2 158 DA108
Thornton Heath CR7 142 DR98
Walton-on-Thames KT12 154 BY105
West Molesey KT8 136 CB98
Woking GU21 150 AY114
Granger Way, Rom. RM1 71 FG58
Grange St, N1 84 DR67
Grange Vale, Sutt. SM2 158 DB108
Grange Vw Rd, N20 44 DC46
Grange Wk, SE1 201 N6
Grangeway, N12 44 DB49
NW6 *off Messina Av* 82 DA66
Grange Way, Erith DA8 107 FH80
Iver SL0 75 BF72
Grangeway, Wdf.Grn. IG8 48 EJ49
Grangeway, The, N21 29 DP44
Grangeway Gdns, Ilf. IG4 68 EL57
Grangeways Cl, Grav.
(Nthflt) DA11 131 GF91
Grangewood, Bex. DA5
off Hurst Rd 126 EZ88
Potters Bar EN6 12 DB30
Grangewood,
Slough (Wexham) SL3 74 AW71
Grangewood Av, Grays RM16 110 GE76
Rainham RM13 90 FJ70
Grangewood Cl, Brwd. CM13
off Knight's Way 55 GA48
Pinner HA5 59 BU57
Grangewood Dr, Sun. TW16
off Forest Dr 115 BT94
Grangewood La, Beck. BR3 123 DZ93
Grangewood St, E6 86 EJ67
Grangewood Ter, SE25
off Grange Rd 142 DR97
Grange Yd, SE1 201 P7
Granham Gdns, N9 46 DT47
Granite St, SE18 105 ET78
Granleigh Rd, E11 68 EE61
Gransden Av, E8 84 DV66
Gransden Rd, W12
off Wendell Rd 99 CT75
Grant Av, Slou. SL1 74 AS72
Grantbridge St, N1 83 DP68
Grantchester Cl, Har. HA1 61 CF62
Grant Cl, N14 45 DJ45
Shepperton TW17 135 BP100
Grantham Cen, The, SW9 101 DL82
Grantham Cl, Edg. HA8 42 CL48
Grantham Gdns, Rom. RM6 70 EZ58
Grantham Grn, Borwd. WD6 26 CQ43
Grantham Pl, W1 199 H3
Grantham Rd, E12 69 EN63
SW9 101 DL82
W4 98 CS80
Grantley Pl, Esher KT10 154 CB106
Grantley Rd, Houns. TW4 96 BW82
Grantley St, E1 85 DX69
Grantock Rd, E17 47 ED53
Granton Av, Upmin. RM14 72 FM61
Granton Rd, SW16 141 DJ95
Ilford IG3 70 EU60
Sidcup DA14 126 EW93
Grant Pl, Croy. CR0 142 DT102
Grant Rd, SW11 100 DD84
Croydon CR0 142 DT102
Harrow HA3 61 CE55
Grants Cl, N17 46 DU54
NW7 43 CW52
Grants La, Oxt. RH8 188 EJ132
Grant's Quay Wf, EC3 201 L1
Grant St, E13 86 EG69
N1 *off Chapel Mkt* 83 DN68
Grantully Rd, W9 82 DB69
Grant Way, Islw. TW7 97 CG79
Granville Av, N9 46 DW48
Feltham TW13 115 BU89
Hounslow TW3 116 CA85
Granville Cl, Croy. CR0 142 DS103
West Byfleet (Byfleet) KT14
off Church Rd 152 BM113
Weybridge KT13 153 BQ107
Granville Ct, N1 84 DR67
Granville Dene, Hem.H.
(Bov.) HP3 5 BA27
Granville Gdns, SW16 141 DM95
W5 80 CM74
Granville Gro, SE13 103 EC83
Granville Ms, Sid. DA14 126 EU91
Granville Pk, SE13 103 EC83
Granville Pl, N12 (N.Finchley)
off High Rd 44 DC52
SW6 *off Maxwell Rd* 100 DB80
W1 194 F9
Pinner HA5 60 BX55
Granville Rd, E17 67 EB58
E18 48 EH54
N4 65 DM58
N12 44 DB52
N13 *off Russell Rd* 45 DM51
N22 45 DP53
NW2 63 CZ61
NW6 82 DA68
SW18 120 DA87
SW19 *off Russell Rd* 120 DA94
Barnet EN5 27 CW42
Epping CM16 18 EV29
Gravesend DA11 131 GF87
Hayes UB3 95 BT77
Ilford IG1 69 EP60
Oxted RH8 188 EF129
Sevenoaks TN13 190 FG124
Sidcup DA14 126 EU91
Uxbridge UB10 77 BP65
Watford WD18 24 BW42
Welling DA16 106 EW83
Westerham TN16 189 EQ126
Weybridge KT13 153 BQ107
Woking GU22 167 AZ120
Granville Sq, SE15 102 DS80
WC1 196 C3
Granville St, WC1 196 C3
Grape St, WC2 195 P8
Graphite Sq, SE11 200 B10
Grapsome Cl, Chess. KT9
off Nigel Fisher Way 155 CJ108
Grasdene Rd, SE18 106 EU80
Grasgarth Cl, W3
off Creswick Rd 80 CQ73
Grasholm Way, Slou. SL3 93 BC77
Grasmere Av, SW15 118 CR91
SW19 140 DA97
W3 80 CQ73
Hounslow TW3 116 CB86
Orpington BR6 145 EP104
Ruislip HA4 59 BQ59
Slough SL2 74 AU73
Wembley HA9 61 CK59
Grasmere Cl, Egh. TW20
off Keswick Rd 113 BB94
Feltham TW14 115 BT88
Loughton IG10 33 EM40
Watford WD25 7 BV32
Grasmere Ct, N22
off Palmerston Rd 45 DM51
Grasmere Gdns, Har. HA3 41 CG54
Ilford IG4 69 EM57
Orpington BR6 145 EP104
Grasmere Pt, SE15
off Ilderton Rd 102 DW80
Grasmere Rd, E13 86 EG68
N10 45 DH53
Grasmere Rd, N17 46 DU51
SE25 142 DV100
SW16 121 DM92
Bexleyheath DA7 107 FC81
Bromley BR1 144 EF95
Orpington BR6 145 EP104
Purley CR8 159 DP111
Grasmere Way, W.Byf.
(Byfleet) KT14 152 BM112
Grassfield Cl, Couls. CR5 175 DH119
Grasshaven Way, SE28 87 ET74
Grassingham End, Ger.Cr.
(Chal.St.P.) SL9 36 AY52
Grassingham Rd, Ger.Cr.
(Chal.St.P.) SL9 36 AY52
Grassington Cl, N11
off Ribblesdale Av 44 DG51
St. Albans (Brick.Wd) AL2 8 CA30
Grassington Rd, Sid. DA14 126 EU91
Grassmere Rd, Horn. RM11 72 FM56
Grassmount, SE23 122 DV89
Purley CR8 159 DJ110
Grass Pk, N3 43 CZ53
Grassway, Wall. SM6 159 DJ105
Grassy La, Sev. TN13 191 FH126
Grasvenor Av, Barn. EN5 28 DA44
Grately Way, SE15
off Daniel Gdns 102 DT80
Gratton Rd, W14 99 CY76
Gratton Ter, NW2 63 CX62
Gravel Cl, Chig. IG7 50 EU47
Graveley, Kings.T. KT1
off Willingham Way 138 CN96
Graveley Av, Borwd. WD6 26 CQ42
[Tramlink] Gravel Hill 161 DY108
Gravel Hill, N3 43 CZ54
Bexleyheath DA6 127 FB85
Croydon CR0 161 DX107
Gerrards Cross
(Chal.St.P.) SL9 36 AY53
Leatherhead KT22
off North St 171 CH121
Loughton (High Beach) IG10 32 EG38
Uxbridge UB8 58 BK64
Gravel Hill Cl, Bexh. DA6 127 FB85
Gravel La, E1 197 P8
Chigwell IG7 50 EU46
Gravelly Hill, Cat. CR3 186 DS128
Gravelly Ride, SW19 119 CV91
Gravel Pit La, SE9 125 EQ85
Gravel Pit Way, Orp. BR6 146 EU103
Gravel Rd, Brom. BR2 144 EL103
Dartford (Sutt.H.) DA4 128 FP94
Twickenham TW2 117 CE88
Gravelwood Cl, Chis. BR7 125 EQ90
Graveney Gro, SE20 122 DW94
Graveney Rd, SW17 120 DE91
GRAVESEND 131 GJ85
⇌ Gravesend 131 GG87
[H] Gravesend &
N Kent Hosp, Grav. DA11 131 GG86
Gravesend Rd, W12 81 CU73
Gravesham Ct, Grav. DA12
off Clarence Row 131 GH87
★ Gravesham Mus,
Grav. DA11 131 GH86
Gray Av, Dag. RM8 70 EZ60
Grayburn Cl, Ch.St.G. HP8 36 AU47
Gray Gdns, Rain. RM13 89 FG65
Grayham Cres, N.Mal. KT3 138 CR98
Grayham Rd, N.Mal. KT3 138 CR98
Grayland Cl, Brom. BR1 144 EK95
Graylands, Epp.
(They.B.) CM16 33 ER37
Woking GU21 166 AY116
Graylands Cl, Wok. GU21 166 AY116
Grayling Cl, E16
off Cranberry La 86 EE70
Grayling Rd, N16 66 DR61
Graylings, The, Abb.L. WD5 7 BR33
Grayling Sq, E2 84 DU69
Gray Pl, Cher. (Ott.) KT16
off Clarendon Gate 151 BD106
GRAYS 110 GA78
⇌ Grays 110 GA79
Grayscroft Rd, SW16 121 DK94
Grays End Cl, Grays RM17 110 GA76
Grays Fm Rd, Orp. BR5 146 EV95
Grayshott Rd, SW11 100 DG82
★ Gray's Inn, WC1 196 C6
Gray's Inn Pl, WC1 196 C7
Gray's Inn Rd, WC1 196 B3
Gray's Inn Sq, WC1 196 D6
Grays La, Ashf. TW15 115 BP91
Gray's La, Ashtd. KT21 172 CM119
Epsom KT18 172 CN120
Grays Pk Rd, Slou.
(Stoke P.) SL2 74 AU68
Grays Pl, Slou. SL2 74 AT74
Grays Rd, Slou. SL1 74 AT74
Uxbridge UB10 76 BL67
Westerham TN16 179 EP121
Grays Town Shop Cen, Grays RM17
off High St 110 GA79
Gray St, SE1 200 E5
Grays Wk, Brwd. (Hutt.) CM13 55 GD45
Grayswood Gdns, SW20
off Farnham Gdns 139 CV96
Grayswood Pt, SW15
off Norley Vale 119 CU88
Gray's Yd, W1 194 G9
Graywood Ct, N12 44 DC52
Grazebrook Rd, N16 66 DR61
Grazeley Cl, Bexh. DA6 127 FC85
Grazeley Ct, SE19
off Gipsy Hill 122 DS91
Great Acre Ct, SW4
off St. Alphonsus Rd 101 DK84
Great Bell All, EC2 197 K8
Great Benty, West Dr. UB7 94 BL77
★ Great Bookham Common,
Lthd. KT23 170 BZ121
Great Brownings, SE21 122 DT91
Great Bushey Dr, N20 44 DB46
Great Cambridge Junct, N18
off North Circular Rd 46 DR49
Great Cambridge Rd, N9 46 DS46
N17 46 DR50
N18 46 DR50
Broxbourne (Turnf.) EN10 15 DY26
Great Cambridge Rd,
Enfield EN1 30 DU42
Waltham Cross (Chsht) EN8 14 DW34
Great Castle St, W1 195 J8
Great Cen Av, Ruis. HA4 60 BW64
Great Cen St, NW1 194 D6
Great Cen Way, NW10 62 CS64
Wembley HA9 62 CQ63
Great Chapel St, W1 195 M8
Great Chart St, SW11
off Wynter St 100 DC84
Great Chertsey Rd, W4 98 CQ82
Feltham TW13 116 CA90
Great Ch La, W6 99 CX78
Great Coll St, SW1 199 P6
Great Cross Av, SE10 104 EE80
Great Cullings, Rom. RM7 71 FE61
Great Cumberland Ms, W1 194 D9
Great Cumberland Pl, W1 194 D8
Great Dover St, SE1 201 J5
Greatdown Rd, W7 79 CF70
Great Eastern Rd, E15 85 ED66
Brentwood CM14 54 FW49
Great Eastern St, EC2 197 M3
Great Eastern Wk, EC2 197 N7
Great Ellshams, Bans. SM7 174 DA116
Great Elms Rd, Brom. BR2 144 EJ98
Great Fld, NW9 42 CS53
Greatfield Av, E6 87 EM70
Greatfield Cl, N19
off Warrender Rd 65 DJ63
SE4 103 EA84
Greatfields Dr, Uxb. UB8 76 BN71
Greatfields Rd, Bark. IG11 87 ER67
Great Fleete Way, Bark. IG11
off Choats Rd 88 EW68
Great Galley Cl, Bark. IG11 88 EV69
Great Gdns Rd, Horn. RM11 71 FH58
Great Gatton Cl, Croy. CR0 143 DY101
Great George St, SW1 199 N5
Great Gregories La, Epp. CM16 17 ES33
Great Gro, Bushey WD23 24 CB42
Great Gros, Wal.Cr. EN7 14 DS28
Great Guildford St, SE1 201 H2
Greatham Rd, Bushey WD23 24 BX41
Greatham Wk, SW15 119 CU88
Great Harry Dr, SE9 125 EN90
Greathurst End, Lthd.
(Bkhm) KT23 170 BZ124
Great James St, WC1 196 B5
Great Julians, Rick. WD3
off Grove Cres 22 BN42
Great Marlborough St, W1 195 K9
Great Maze Pond, SE1 201 L4
Great Nelmes Chase,
Horn. RM11 72 FM57
Greatness La, Sev. TN14 191 FJ121
Greatness Rd, Sev. TN14 191 FJ121
Great Newport St, WC2
off Cranbourn St 83 DK73
Great New St, EC4 196 E8
Great N Leisure Pk, N12 44 DD52
Great N Rd, N2 64 DE56
N6 64 DE56
Barnet EN5 27 CZ38
Barnet (New Barn.) EN5 28 DA43
Hatfield AL9, AL10 12 DB27
Potters Bar EN6 12 DB27
Great N Way, NW4 43 CW54
Great Oaks, Brwd.
(Hutt.) CM13 55 GB44
Chigwell IG7 49 EQ49
Greatorex St, E1 84 DU71
Great Ormond St, WC1 196 A6
[H] Great Ormond St Hosp for
Children, The, WC1 196 A5
Great Owl Rd, Chig. IG7 49 EN48
Great Pk, Kings L. WD4 6 BM30
Great Percy St, WC1 196 C2
Great Peter St, SW1 199 M7
Great Pettits Ct, Rom. RM1 51 FE54
⊖ Great Portland Street 195 J5
Great Portland St, W1 195 J6
Great Pulteney St, W1 195 L10
Great Queen St, WC2 196 A9
Dartford DA1 128 FM87
Great Ropers La, Brwd. CM13 53 FU51
Great Russell St, WC1 195 N8
Great St. Helens, EC3 197 M8
Great St. Thomas Apostle,
EC4 197 J10
Great Scotland Yd, SW1 199 P3
Great Slades, Pot.B. EN6 11 CZ33
Great Smith St, SW1 199 N6
Great South-West Rd,
Felt. TW14 115 BQ87
Hounslow TW4 95 BT84
Great Spilmans, SE22 122 DS85
Great Stockwood Rd, Wal.Cr.
(Chsht) EN7 14 DR26
Great Strand, NW9 43 CT53
Great Suffolk St, SE1 200 G3
Great Sutton St, EC1 196 G5
Great Swan All, EC2 197 K8
Great Tattenhams,
Epsom KT18 173 CV118
Great Thrift, Orp. BR5 145 EQ98
Great Till Cl,
Sev.(Otford) TN14 181 FE116
Great Titchfield St, W1 195 K8
Great Twr St, EC3 197 M10
Great Trinity La, EC4 197 J10
Great Turnstile, WC1 196 C7
GREAT WARLEY,
Brwd. CM14 53 FV53
Great Warley St, Brwd.
(Gt Warley) CM13 53 FU53
Great Western Rd, W2 81 CZ71
W9 81 CZ71
W11 81 CZ71
Great W Rd, W4 98 CP78
W6 99 CT78
Brentford TW8 98 CP78
Hounslow TW5 96 BX82
Isleworth TW7 97 CE80
Great Wf Rd, E14
off Churchill Pl 85 EB74
Great Winchester St, EC2 197 L8
Great Windmill St, W1 195 M10
Greatwood, Chis. BR7 125 EN94

★ Place of interest ⇌ Railway station ⊖ London Underground station DLR Docklands Light Railway station Tra Tramlink station H Hospital Riv Pedestrian ferry landing stage

Greatwood Cl, Cher. (Ott.) KT16 ... 151 BC109
Great Woodcote Dr, Pur. CR8 . 159 DK110
Great Woodcote Pk, Pur. CR8 . 159 DK110
Great Yd, SE1 ... 201 N4
Greaves Cl, Bark. IG11 off Norfolk Rd ... 87 ES66
Greaves Pl, SW17 ... 120 DE91
Grebe Av, Hayes UB4 off Cygnet Way ... 78 BX72
Grebe Cl, E7 off Cormorant Rd ... 68 EF64
E17 ... 47 DY52
Barking IG11 ... 88 EU70
Grebe Ct, Sutt. SM1 ... 157 CZ106
Grebe Crest, Grays RM20 ... 109 FU77
Grecian Cres, SE19 ... 121 DP93
Greding Wk, Brwd. (Hutt.) CM13 ... 55 GB47
Gredo Ho, Bark. IG11 ... 88 EV69
Greek Ct, W1 ... 195 N9
★ Greek Orthodox Cath of the Divine Wisdom (St. Sophia), W2 ... 82 DB73
Greek St, W1 ... 195 N9
Greek Yd, WC2 ... 195 P10
Green, The, E4 ... 47 EC46
E11 ... 68 EH58
E15 ... 86 EE65
N9 ... 46 DU47
N14 ... 45 DK48
N21 ... 45 DN45
SW14 ... 98 CQ83
SW19 ... 119 CX92
W3 ... 80 CS72
W5 off High St ... 79 CK74
Bexleyheath DA7 ... 106 FA81
Bromley BR1 off Downham Way ... 124 EG90
Bromley (Hayes) BR2 ... 144 EG101
Carshalton SM5 ... 158 DG105
Caterham (Wold.) CR3 ... 177 EA123
Chalfont St. Giles HP8 off High St. ... 36 AW47
Croydon CR0 ... 161 DZ109
Dartford DA2 ... 129 FR89
Epping (They.B.) CM16 ... 33 ES37
Epsom KT17 ... 157 CU111
Esher (Clay.) KT10 ... 155 CF107
Feltham TW13 ... 115 BV89
Hayes UB3 off Wood End ... 77 BS72
Hemel Hempstead (Bov.) HP3 ... 5 BA29
Hounslow TW5 off Heston Rd ... 96 CA79
Leatherhead (Fetch.) KT22 . 171 CD124
Morden SM4 ... 139 CY98
New Malden KT3 ... 138 CQ97
Orpington (Pr.Bot.) BR6 off Rushmore Hill ... 164 EW110
Orpington (St.P.Cray) BR5 off The Avenue ... 126 EV94
Rainham (Wenn.) RM13 ... 90 FL73
Richmond TW9 ... 117 CK85
Rickmansworth (Crox.Grn) WD3 ... 22 BN44
Rickmansworth (Sarratt) WD3 ... 22 BG35
Romford (Hav.at.Bow.) RM4 . 51 FE48
Sevenoaks TN13 ... 191 FK122
Shepperton TW17 ... 135 BS98
Sidcup DA14 ... 126 EU91
Slough (Datchet) SL3 ... 92 AV80
South Ockendon RM15 ... 91 FW69
Southall UB2 ... 96 BY76
Staines (Wrays.) TW19 ... 112 AY86
Sutton SM1 ... 140 DB104
Tadworth (Burgh Hth) KT20 . 173 CY119
Tilbury (W.Til.) RM18 ... 111 GL79
Twickenham TW2 ... 117 CE88
Uxbridge (Hare.) UB9 ... 38 BJ53
Uxbridge (Ickhm) UB10 ... 59 BQ61
Waltham Abbey EN9 off Sewardstone Rd ... 15 EC34
Waltham Cross (Chsht) EN8 . 14 DW28
Walton-on-Thames (Whiteley Vill.) KT12 off Octagon Rd ... 153 BS110
Warlingham CR6 ... 177 DX117
Watford (Let.Hth) WD25 ... 25 CE39
Welling DA16 ... 105 ES84
Wembley HA0 ... 61 CG61
West Drayton UB7 ... 94 BK76
Westerham TN16 ... 189 ER126
Woking (Ripley) GU23 ... 168 BH121
Woodford Green IG8 ... 48 EG50
Greenacre, Dart. DA1 off Oakfield La ... 128 FL89
Woking (Knap.) GU21 off Mead Ct ... 166 AS116
Greenacre Cl, Barn. EN5 ... 27 CZ38
Northolt UB5 ... 60 BZ64
Swanley BR8 ... 147 FE98
Greenacre Ct, Egh. (Eng.Grn) TW20 ... 112 AW93
Greenacre Gdns, E17 ... 67 EC56
Greenacre Pl, Wall. (Hackbr.) SM6 off Park Rd ... 141 DH103
Greenacres, N3 ... 43 CY54
SE9 ... 125 EN86
Bushey (Bushey Hth) WD23 . 41 CD47
Green Acres, Croy. CR0 ... 142 DT104
Greenacres, Epp. CM16 ... 17 ET29
Leatherhead (Bkhm) KT23 . 170 CB124
Oxted RH8 ... 188 EE127
Greenacres Av, Uxb. UB10 ... 58 BM62
Greenacres Cl, Orp. BR6 ... 163 EQ105
Rainham RM13 ... 90 FL69
Greenacres Dr, Stan. HA7 ... 41 CH52
Greenacre Sq, SE16 ... 203 J4
Greenacre Wk, N14 ... 45 DL48
Greenall Cl, Wal.Cr. (Chsht) EN8 ... 15 DY30
Green Arbour Ct, EC1 ... 196 F8
Green Av, NW7 ... 42 CR49
W13 ... 97 CH76
Greenaway Av, N18 ... 47 DX51
Greenaway Gdns, NW3 ... 64 DB63
Green Bk, E1 ... 202 D3
N12 ... 44 DB49
Greenbank, Wal.Cr. (Chsht) EN8 ... 14 DV28
Greenbank Av, Wem. HA0 ... 61 CG64
Greenbank Cl, E4 ... 47 EC47
Romford RM3 ... 52 FK48
Greenbank Cres, NW4 ... 63 CY56
Greenbank Rd, Wat. WD17 ... 23 BR36
Greenbanks, Dart. DA1 ... 128 FL89
Upminster RM14 ... 73 FS60
Greenbay Rd, SE7 ... 104 EK80
Greenberry St, NW8 ... 194 B1
Greenbrook Av, Barn. EN4 ... 28 DC39
Greenbury Cl, Rick. (Chorl.) WD3 ... 21 BC42
Green Cl, NW9 ... 62 CQ58
NW11 ... 64 DC59
Bromley BR2 ... 144 EE97
Carshalton SM5 ... 140 DF103
Feltham TW13 ... 116 BY92
Hatfield AL9 off Station Rd ... 11 CY26
Waltham Cross (Chsht) EN8 . 15 DY32
Greencoat Pl, SW1 ... 199 L8
Greencoat Row, SW1 ... 199 L7
Greencourt Av, Croy. CR0 ... 142 DV103
Edgware HA8 ... 42 CP53
Greencourt Gdns, Croy. CR0 . 142 DV102
Greencourt Rd, Orp. BR5 ... 145 ER99
Green Ct Rd, Swan. BR8 ... 147 FD99
Greencrest Pl, NW2 off Dollis Hill La ... 63 CU62
Green Cft, Edg. HA8 off Deans La ... 42 CQ50
Greencroft Av, Ruis. HA4 ... 60 BW61
Greencroft Cl, E6 off Neatscourt Rd ... 86 EL71
Greencroft Gdns, NW6 ... 82 DB66
Enfield EN1 ... 30 DS41
Greencroft Rd, Houns. TW5 ... 96 BZ81
Green Curve, Bans. SM7 ... 157 CZ114
Green Dale, SE5 ... 102 DR84
SE22 ... 122 DS85
Green Dale Cl, SE22 off Green Dale ... 122 DS85
Greendale Ms, Slou. SL2 ... 74 AU73
Greendale Wk, Grav. (Nthflt) DA11 ... 130 GE90
Green Dragon Ct, SE1 ... 201 K2
Green Dragon La, N21 ... 29 DP44
Brentford TW8 ... 98 CL78
Green Dragon Yd, E1 off Old Montague St ... 84 DU71
Green Dr, Slou. SL3 ... 92 AY77
Southall UB1 ... 78 CA74
Woking (Ripley) GU23 ... 167 BF123
Green E Rd, Beac. (Jordans) HP9 ... 36 AS52
Green Edge, Wat. WD25 off Clarke Grn ... 23 BU35
Greene Fielde End, Stai. TW18 . 114 BK94
Green End, N21 ... 45 DP47
Chessington KT9 ... 156 CL105
Green End Business Cen, Rick. WD3 off Church La ... 22 BG37
Greenend Rd, W4 ... 98 CS75
Greenfarm Cl, Orp. BR6 ... 163 ET106
Greenfell Mans, SE8 off Glaisher St ... 103 EB79
Greenfield Av, Surb. KT5 ... 138 CP101
Watford WD19 ... 40 BX47
Greenfield Dr, N2 ... 64 DF56
Greenfield End, Ger.Cr. (Chal.St.P.) SL9 ... 36 AY51
Greenfield Gdns, NW2 ... 63 CY61
Dagenham RM9 ... 88 EX67
Orpington BR5 ... 145 ER101
Greenfield Link, Couls. CR5 . 175 DL115
Greenfield Rd, E1 ... 84 DU71
N15 ... 66 DS57
Dagenham RM9 ... 88 EW67
Dartford DA2 ... 127 FD92
Greenfields, Loug. IG10 ... 33 EN42
Potters Bar (Cuffley) EN6 off South Dr ... 13 DL30
Greenfields Cl, Brwd. CM13 off Essex Way ... 53 FW51
Loughton IG10 ... 33 EN42
Greenfield St, Wal.Abb. EN9 . 15 EC34
Greenfield Way, Har. HA2 ... 60 CB55
GREENFORD ... 78 CB69
⇌ Greenford ... 79 CD67
⊖ Greenford ... 79 CD67
Greenford Av, W7 ... 79 CE70
Southall UB1 ... 78 BZ73
Greenford Gdns, Grnf. UB6 ... 78 CB69
Greenford Rd, Grnf. UB6 ... 78 CC71
Harrow HA1 ... 61 CE64
Southall UB1 ... 78 CC74
Sutton SM1 ... 158 DB105
Green Gdns, Orp. BR6 ... 163 EQ106
Greengate, Grnf. UB6 ... 79 CH65
Greengate St, E13 ... 86 EH68
Green Glade, Epp. (They.B.) CM16 ... 33 ES37
Green Glades, Horn. RM11 ... 72 FM58
Greenhalgh Wk, N2 ... 64 DC56
Greenham Cl, SE1 ... 200 D5
Greenham Cres, E4 ... 47 DZ51
Greenham Rd, N10 ... 44 DG54
Greenham Wk, Wok. GU21 ... 166 AW118
Greenhaven Dr, SE28 ... 88 EV72
Greenhayes Av, Bans. SM7 ... 158 DA114
Greenhayes Cl, Reig. RH2 ... 184 DC134
Greenhayes Gdns, Bans. SM7 . 174 DA115
Greenheys Cl, Nthwd. HA6 ... 39 BS53
Greenheys Dr, E18 ... 68 EF55
Greenheys Pl, Wok. GU22 off White Rose La ... 167 AZ118
Greenhill, NW3 off Hampstead High St ... 64 DD63
SE18 ... 105 EM78
Green Hill, Buck.H. IG9 ... 48 EJ46
Orpington BR6 ... 162 EL112
Greenhill, Sutt. SM1 ... 140 DC103
Wembley HA9 ... 62 CP61
Greenhill Av, Cat. CR3 ... 176 DV121
Greenhill Cres, Wat. WD18 ... 23 BS44
Greenhill Gdns, Nthlt. UB5 ... 78 BZ68
Greenhill Gro, E12 ... 68 EL63
Green Hill La, Warl. CR6 ... 177 DY117
Greenhill Pk, NW10 ... 80 CS67
Barnet EN5 ... 28 DB43
Greenhill Rd, NW10 ... 80 CS67
Gravesend (Nthflt) DA11 ... 131 GF89
Harrow HA1 ... 61 CE58
Greenhills Cl, Rick. WD3 ... 22 BH43
Greenhill's Rents, EC1 ... 196 G6
Greenhills Ter, N1 off Baxter Rd ... 84 DR65
Greenhill Ter, SE18 ... 105 EM78
Northolt UB5 ... 78 BZ68
Greenhill Way, Croy. CR0 ... 161 DX111
Harrow HA1 ... 61 CE58
Wembley HA9 ... 62 CP61
GREENHITHE ... 129 FV85
⇌ Greenhithe ... 129 FU85
Greenhithe Cl, Sid. DA15 ... 125 ES87
Greenholm Rd, SE9 ... 125 EP85
Green Hundred Rd, SE15 ... 102 DU79
Greenhurst La, Oxt. RH8 ... 188 EG132
Greenhurst Rd, SE27 ... 121 DN92
Greening St, SE2 ... 106 EW77
Greenlake Ter, Stai. TW18 ... 113 BF94
Greenland Cres, Sthl. UB2 ... 96 BW76
Greenland Ms, SE8 off Trundleys Rd ... 103 DX78
Greenland Pier ... 203 M7
Greenland Pl, NW1 off Greenland Rd ... 83 DH67
Greenland Quay, SE16 ... 203 J8
Greenland Rd, NW1 ... 83 DJ67
Barnet EN5 ... 27 CW44
Greenlands, Cher. KT16 ... 133 BC104
Greenlands Rd, Stai. TW18 ... 114 BG91
Weybridge KT13 ... 135 BP104
Greenland St, NW1 off Camden High St ... 83 DH67
Green La, E4 ... 32 EE41
NW4 ... 63 CX57
SE9 ... 125 EN89
SE20 ... 123 DX94
SW16 ... 121 DM94
W7 ... 97 CE75
Addlestone KT15 ... 134 BG104
Amersham HP6 ... 20 AS38
Ashtead KT21 ... 171 CJ117
Brentwood (Pilg.Hat.) CM15 . 54 FV43
Brentwood (Warley) CM14 ... 53 FU52
Caterham CR3 ... 176 DQ122
Chertsey KT16 ... 133 BE103
Chesham HP5 ... 4 AV33
Chessington KT9 ... 156 CL109
Chigwell IG7 ... 49 ER47
Chislehurst BR7 ... 125 EP91
Cobham KT11 ... 154 BY112
Coulsdon CR5 ... 184 DA125
Dagenham RM8 ... 70 EU60
Edgware HA8 ... 42 CN50
Egham TW20 ... 113 BB91
Egham (Thorpe) TW20 ... 133 BD95
Feltham TW13 ... 116 BY92
Harrow HA1 ... 61 CE62
Hemel Hempstead (Bov.) HP3 . 5 AZ28
Hounslow TW4 ... 95 BV83
Ilford IG1, IG3 ... 69 EQ61
Leatherhead KT22 ... 171 CK121
Morden SM4 ... 140 DB100
New Malden KT3 ... 138 CQ99
Northwood HA6 ... 39 BT52
Purley CR8 ... 159 DJ111
Redhill RH1 ... 184 DE132
Redhill (Bletch.) RH1 ... 186 DS131
Reigate RH2 ... 183 CZ134
Rickmansworth (Crox.Grn) WD3 ... 22 BM43
Shepperton TW17 ... 135 BQ100
Slough (Datchet) SL3 ... 92 AV81
South Ockendon RM15 ... 91 FR69
Staines TW18 ... 133 BE95
Stanmore HA7 ... 41 CH49
Sunbury-on-Thames TW16 . 115 BT94
Tadworth KT20 ... 183 CZ126
Thornton Heath CR7 ... 141 DN95
Upminster RM14 ... 91 FR68
Uxbridge UB8 ... 77 BQ71
Waltham Abbey EN9 ... 16 EJ34
Walton-on-Thames KT12 ... 153 BV107
Warlingham CR6 ... 177 DY116
Watford WD19 ... 40 BW46
West Byfleet (Byfleet) KT14 . 152 BM112
West Molesey KT8 ... 136 CB99
Woking (Chobham) GU24 ... 150 AT110
Woking (Mayford) GU24 off Copper Beech Cl ... 166 AV121
Woking (Ockham) GU23 ... 169 BP124
Worcester Park KT4 ... 139 CU102
Green La Av, Walt. KT12 ... 154 BW106
Green La Cl, Cher. KT16 ... 133 BE103
West Byfleet (Byfleet) KT14 . 152 BM112
Green La Gdns, Th.Hth. CR7 . 142 DQ96
Green Las, N4 ... 66 DQ60
N8 ... 65 DP55
N13 ... 45 DM51
N15 ... 65 DP55
N16 ... 66 DQ62
N21 ... 45 DP46
Epsom KT19 ... 156 CS109
Greenlaw Gdns, N.Mal. KT3 . 139 CT101
Greenlawn La, Brent. TW8 off Ealing Rd ... 97 CK77
Green Lawns, Ruis. HA4 ... 60 BW60
Greenlaw St, SE18 ... 105 EN76
Green Leaf Av, Wall. SM6 ... 159 DK105
Greenleaf Cl, SW2 off Tulse Hill ... 121 DN87
Greenleafe Dr, Ilf. IG6 ... 69 EP56
Greenleaf Rd, E6 off Redclyffe Rd ... 86 EJ67
E17 ... 67 DZ55
Greenlea Pk, SW19 ... 140 DD95
Green Leas, Sun. TW16 ... 115 BT93
Waltham Abbey EN9 off Roundhills ... 15 ED34
Green Leas Cl, Sun. TW16 off Green Leas ... 115 BT93
Greenleaves Ct, Ashf. TW15 off Redleaves Av ... 115 BP93
Greenleigh Av, Orp. BR5 ... 146 EV98
Green Man Gdns, W13 ... 79 CG73
Green Man La, W13 ... 79 CG74
Green Man La, Feltham TW14 . 95 BU84
Green Manor Way, Grav. DA11 . 110 FZ84
Green Man Pas, W13 ... 79 CG73
Green Man Roundabout, E11 . 68 EF59
Greenman St, N1 ... 84 DQ66
Green Mead, Esher KT10 off Winterdown Gdns ... 154 BZ107
Greenmead Cl, SE25 ... 142 DU99
Green Meadow, Pot.B. EN6 ... 12 DA30
Greenmeads, Wok. GU22 ... 166 AY122
Green Moor Link, N21 ... 45 DP45
Greenmoor Rd, Enf. EN3 ... 30 DW40
Green N Rd, Beac. (Jordans) HP9 ... 36 AS51
Greenoak Pl, Barn. EN4 ... 28 DF40
Greenoak Ri, West. (Bigg.H.) TN16 ... 178 EJ118
Greenoak Way, SW19 ... 119 CX91
Greenock Rd, SW16 ... 141 DK95
W3 ... 98 CP76
Greenock Way, Rom. RM1 ... 51 FE51
Greeno Cres, Shep. TW17 ... 134 BN99
★ Green Park, SW1 ... 199 J4
⊖ Green Park ... 199 K3
Green Pk, Stai. TW18 ... 113 BE90
Greenpark Ct, Wem. HA0 ... 79 CJ66
Green Pk Way, Grnf. UB6 ... 79 CE67
Green Pl, Dart. DA1 ... 127 FE85
Green Pt, E15 ... 86 EE65
Green Pond Cl, E17 ... 67 DZ55
Green Pond Rd, E17 ... 67 DY55
Green Ride, Epp. CM16 ... 33 EP35
Loughton IG10 ... 32 EG43
Green Rd, N14 ... 29 DH44
N20 ... 44 DC48
Egham (Thorpe) TW20 ... 133 BB98
Greenroof Way, SE10 ... 205 L7
Greensand Cl, Red. (S.Merst.) RH1 ... 185 DK128
Green Sand Rd, Red. RH1 ... 184 DG133
Greensand Way, Gdse. RH9 . 186 DV134
Greens Cl, The, Loug. IG10 ... 33 EN40
Green's Ct, W1 ... 195 M10
Green's End, SE18 ... 105 EP77
Greenshank Cl, E17 off Banbury Rd ... 47 DY52
Greenshaw, Brwd. CM14 ... 54 FV46
Greenshields Ind Est, E16 ... 205 P3
Greenside, Bex. DA5 ... 126 EY88
Borehamwood WD6 ... 26 CN38
Dagenham RM8 ... 70 EW60
Swanley BR8 ... 147 FD96
Greenside Cl, N20 ... 44 DD47
SE6 ... 123 ED89
Greenside Dr, Ashtd. KT21 ... 171 CH118
Greenside Rd, W12 ... 99 CU76
Croydon CR0 ... 141 DN101
Weybridge KT13 ... 135 BP104
Greenside Wk, West. (Bigg.H.) TN16 off Kings Rd ... 178 EH118
Greenslade Av, Ashtd. KT21 . 172 CP119
Greenslade Rd, Bark. IG11 ... 87 ER66
Greensleeves Dr, Brwd. CM14 off Mascalls La ... 54 FV50
Green Slip Rd, Barn. EN5 ... 27 CZ40
Greenstead Av, Wdf.Grn. IG8 . 48 EJ52
Greenstead Cl, Brwd. (Hutt.) CM13 ... 55 GE45
Woodford Green IG8 off Greenstead Gdns ... 48 EJ51
Greenstead Gdns, SW15 ... 119 CU85
Woodford Green IG8 ... 48 EJ51
GREENSTED GREEN, Ong. CM5 ... 19 FH28
Greensted Rd, Loug. IG10 ... 48 EL45
Ongar CM5 ... 19 FG28
Greenstone Ms, E11 ... 68 EG58
GREEN STREET, Borwd. WD6 . 26 CP37
Green St, E7 ... 86 EH65
E13 ... 86 EJ67
W1 ... 194 E10
Borehamwood WD6 ... 26 CN36
Enfield EN3 ... 30 DW40
Radlett (Shenley) WD7 ... 26 CN36
Rickmansworth (Chorl.) WD3 . 21 BC40
Sunbury-on-Thames TW16 . 135 BU95
GREEN STREET GREEN, Dart. DA2 ... 129 FU93
GREEN STREET GREEN, Orp. BR6 ... 163 ES107
Green St Grn Rd, Dart. DA1, DA2 ... 128 FP88
Greensward, Bushey WD23 ... 24 CB44
Green Ter, EC1 ... 196 E3
Green Tiles La, Uxb. (Denh.) UB9 ... 57 BF58
Greentrees, Epp. CM16 ... 18 EU31
Green Vale, W5 ... 80 CM72
Bexleyheath DA6 ... 126 EX85
Greenvale Rd, SE9 ... 105 EM84
Green Verges, Stan. HA7 ... 41 CK52
Green Vw, Chess. KT9 ... 156 CM108
Greenview Av, Beck. BR3 ... 143 DY100
Croydon CR0 ... 143 DY100
Greenview Cl, W3 ... 80 CS74
Green Vw Cl, Hem.H. (Bov.) HP3 . 5 BA29
Greenview Ct, Ashf. TW15 off Village Way ... 114 BM91
Green Wk, NW4 ... 63 CX57
SE1 ... 201 M7
Buckhurst Hill IG9 ... 48 EL45
Dartford DA1 ... 107 FF84
Hampton TW12 off Orpwood Cl ... 116 BZ93
Ruislip HA4 ... 59 BT60
Southall UB2 ... 96 CA78
Woodford Green IG8 ... 48 EL51
Green Wk, The, E4 ... 47 EC46
Greenway, N14 ... 45 DL47
N20 ... 44 DA47
Green Way, SE9 ... 124 EK85
Greenway, SW20 ... 139 CW98
Brentwood (Hutt.) CM13 ... 55 GA45
Green Way, Brom. BR2 ... 144 EL100
Greenway, Chis. BR7 ... 125 EN92
Dagenham RM8 ... 70 EW61
Harrow HA3 ... 62 CL57
Hayes UB4 ... 77 BV70
Leatherhead (Bkhm) KT23 . 170 CB123
Greenway, Pinner HA5 ... 39 BV54
Green Way, Red. RH1 ... 184 DE132
Greenway, Rom. RM3 ... 52 FP51
Green Way, Sun. TW16 ... 135 BU98
Greenway, Wall. SM6 ... 159 DJ105
Westerham (Tats.) TN16 ... 178 EJ120
Woodford Green IG8 ... 48 EJ50
Greenway, The, NW9 ... 42 CR54
Enfield EN3 ... 31 DX35
Epsom KT18 ... 172 CN115
Gerrards Cross (Chal.St.P.) SL9 ... 56 AX55
Harrow HA3 ... 41 CE53
Hounslow TW4 ... 96 BZ84
Orpington BR5 ... 146 EV100
Oxted RH8 ... 188 EH133
Pinner HA5 ... 60 BZ58
Potters Bar EN6 ... 12 DA33
Rickmansworth (Mill End) WD3 ... 38 BG45
Uxbridge UB8 ... 76 BJ68
Uxbridge (Ickhm) UB10 ... 59 BQ61
Greenway Av, E17 ... 67 ED56
Greenway Cl, N4 ... 66 DQ61
N11 ... 44 DG51
N15 off Copperfield Dr ... 66 DT56
N20 ... 44 DA47
NW9 ... 42 CR54
West Byfleet KT14 ... 152 BG113
Greenway Dr, Stai. TW18 ... 134 BK95
Greenway Gdns, NW9 ... 42 CR54
Croydon CR0 ... 143 DZ104
Greenford UB6 ... 78 CA69
Harrow HA3 ... 41 CE54
Greenways, Abb.L. WD5 ... 7 BS32
Beckenham BR3 ... 143 EA96
Egham TW20 ... 112 AY92
Esher KT10 ... 155 CE105
Tadworth KT20 ... 183 CV125
Waltham Cross (Chsht) EN7 . 13 DP29
Woking GU22 off Pembroke Rd ... 167 BA117
Greenways, The, Twick. TW1 off South Western Rd ... 117 CG86
Greenwell Cl, Gdse. RH9 ... 186 DV130
Greenwell St, W1 ... 195 J5
Green W Rd, Beac. (Jordans) HP9 ... 36 AS52
GREENWICH, SE10 ... 103 ED79
⇌ Greenwich ... 103 EB80
DLR Greenwich ... 103 EB80
Greenwich Ch St, SE10 ... 103 EC79
Greenwich Ct, Wal.Cr. EN8 off Parkside ... 15 DY34
Greenwich Cres, E6 off Swan App ... 86 EL71
Greenwich Foot Tunnel, E14 . 103 EC78
SE10 ... 103 EC78
Greenwich High Rd, SE10 ... 103 EB81
Greenwich Ind Est, SE7 ... 205 P9
Greenwich Mkt, SE10 off King William Wk ... 103 EC79
★ Greenwich Park, SE10 ... 103 ED80
Greenwich Pk, SE10 ... 104 EE80
Greenwich Pk St, SE10 ... 103 ED78
★ Greenwich Pier, SE10 ... 103 EC79
Greenwich Quay, SE8 ... 103 EB79
Greenwich S St, SE10 ... 103 EB81
Greenwich Vw Pl, E14 ... 204 B7
Greenwich Way, Wal.Abb. EN9 . 31 EC36
Greenwood Av, Dag. RM10 ... 71 FB63
Enfield EN3 ... 31 DY40
Waltham Cross (Chsht) EN7 . 14 DV31
Greenwood Cl, Add. (Wdhm) KT15 ... 151 BF111
Amersham HP6 ... 20 AS37
Bushey (Bushey Hth) WD23 off Langmead Dr ... 41 CE45
Morden SM4 ... 139 CY98
Orpington BR5 ... 145 ES100
Sidcup DA15 off Hurst Rd ... 126 EU89
Thames Ditton KT7 ... 137 CG102
Waltham Cross (Chsht) EN7 off Greenwood Av ... 14 DV31
Greenwood Ct, SW1 ... 199 K10
Greenwood Dr, E4 off Avril Way ... 47 EC50
Watford WD25 ... 7 BV34
Greenwood Gdns, N13 ... 45 DP48
Caterham CR3 ... 186 DU125
Ilford IG6 ... 49 EQ52
Oxted RH8 ... 188 EG134
Radlett (Shenley) WD7 ... 10 CL33
Greenwood Ho, Grays RM17 off Argent St ... 110 GB79
Greenwood La, Hmptn. (Hmptn H.) TW12 ... 116 CB92
Greenwood Pk, Kings.T. KT2 ... 118 CS94
Greenwood Pl, NW5 off Highgate Rd ... 65 DH64
Greenwood Rd, E8 ... 84 DU65
E13 off Valetta Gro ... 86 EF68
Bexley DA5 ... 127 FD91
Chigwell IG7 ... 50 EV49
Croydon CR0 ... 141 DP101
Isleworth TW7 ... 97 CE83
Mitcham CR4 ... 141 DK97
Thames Ditton KT7 ... 137 CG102
Woking GU21 ... 166 AS120
Greenwoods, The, Har. (S.Har.) HA2 ... 60 CC61
Greenwood Ter, NW10 ... 80 CR67
Greenwood Way, Sev. TN13 ... 190 FF125
Green Wrythe Cres, Cars. SM5 ... 140 DE102
Green Wrythe La, Cars. SM5 . 140 DD100
Greenyard, Wal.Abb. EN9 ... 15 EC33
Greer Rd, Har. HA3 ... 40 CC53
Greet St, SE1 ... 200 E3
Greg Cl, E10 ... 67 EC58
Gregor Ms, SE3 ... 104 EG80
Gregory Av, Pot.B. EN6 ... 12 DC33
Gregory Cl, Wok. GU21 ... 166 AW117
Gregory Cres, SE9 ... 124 EK87

★ Place of interest ⇌ Railway station ⊖ London Underground station DLR Docklands Light Railway station Tra Tramlink station H Hospital Riv Pedestrian ferry landing stage

Gregory Dr, Wind. (Old Wind.) SL4 112 AV86
Gregory Ms, Wal.Abb. EN9
off Beaulieu Dr 15 EB33
Gregory Pl, W8 100 DB75
Gregory Rd, Rom. RM6 70 EX56
Southall UB2 96 CA76
Gregson Cl, Borwd. WD6 26 CQ39
Gregson's Ride, Loug. IG10 33 EN38
Greig Cl, N8 65 DL57
Greig Ter, SE17
off Lorrimore Sq 101 DP79
Grenaby Av, Croy. CR0 142 DR101
Grenaby Rd, Croy. CR0 142 DR101
Grenada Rd, SE7 104 EJ80
Grenade St, E14 85 DZ73
Grenadier Pl, Cat. CR3 176 DQ122
Grenadier St, E16 87 EN74
Grenadine Cl, Wal.Cr. EN7
off Allwood Rd 14 DT27
Grena Gdns, Rich. TW9 98 CM84
Grena Rd, Rich. TW9 98 CM84
Grendon Gdns, Wem. HA9 62 CN61
Grendon St, NW8 194 B4
Grenfell Av, Horn. RM12 71 FF60
Grenfell Cl, Borwd. WD6 26 CQ39
Grenfell Gdns, Har. HA3 62 CL59
Grenfell Rd, W11 81 CX73
Mitcham CR4 120 DF93
Grenfell Twr, W11 81 CX73
Grenfell Wk, W11 81 CX73
Grennell Cl, Sutt. SM1 140 DD103
Grennell Rd, Sutt. SM1 140 DC103
Grenoble Gdns, N13 45 DN51
Grenville Cl, N3 43 CZ53
Cobham KT11 154 BX113
Surbiton KT5 138 CQ102
Waltham Cross EN8 15 DX32
Grenville Ct, SE19
off Lymer Av 122 DT92
Grenville Gdns, Wdf.Grn. IG8 48 EJ53
Grenville Ms, SW7 100 DC77
Hampton TW12 116 CB92
Grenville Pl, NW7 42 CR50
SW7 100 DC76
Grenville Rd, N19 65 DL60
Croydon (New Adgtn) CR0 161 EC109
Grays (Chaff.Hun.) RM16 109 FV78
Grenville St, WC1 196 A5
Gresham Av, N20 44 DF49
Warlingham CR6 177 DY118
Gresham Cl, Bex. DA5 126 EY86
Brentwood CM14 54 FW48
Enfield EN2 30 DQ41
Oxted RH8 188 EF128
Gresham Dr, Rom. RM6 70 EV57
Gresham Gdns, NW11 63 CY60
Gresham Pl, N19 65 DK61
Gresham Rd, E6 87 EM68
E16 86 EH72
NW10 62 CR64
SE25 142 DU98
SW9 101 DN83
Beckenham BR3 143 DY96
Brentwood CM14 54 FW48
Edgware HA8 42 CM51
Hampton TW12 116 CA93
Hounslow TW3 96 CC81
Oxted RH8 188 EF128
Staines TW18 113 BF92
Uxbridge UB10 76 BN68
Gresham St, EC2 197 H8
Gresham Way, SW19 120 DA90
Gresley Cl, E17 67 DY58
N15 off Clinton Rd 66 DR56
Gresley Ct, Pot.B. EN6 12 DC29
Gresley Rd, N19 65 DJ60
Gressenhall Rd, SW18 119 CZ86
Gresse St, W1 195 M7
Gresswell Cl, Sid. DA14 126 EU90
Greswell St, SW6 99 CX81
Gretton Rd, N17 46 DS52
Greville Av, S.Croy. CR2 161 DX110
Greville Cl, Ashtd. KT21 172 CL119
Twickenham TW1 117 CH87
Greville Hall, NW6 82 DB68
Greville Ms, NW6
off Greville Rd 82 DB68
Greville Pk Av, Ashtd. KT21 172 CL118
Greville Pk Rd, Ashtd. KT21 172 CL118
Greville Pl, NW6 82 DB68
Greville Rd, E17 67 EC56
NW6 82 DB67
Richmond TW10 118 CM86
Greville St, EC1 196 E7
Grey Alders, Bans. SM7
off High Beeches 157 CW114
Greycaine Rd, Wat. WD24 24 BX37
Grey Cl, NW11 64 DC58
Greycoat Pl, SW1 199 M7
Greycoat St, SW1 199 M7
Greycot Rd, Beck. BR3 123 EA92
Grey Eagle St, E1 197 P6
Greyfell Cl, Stan. HA7
off Coverdale Cl 41 CH50
Greyfields Cl, Pur. CR8 159 DP113
Greyfriars, Brwd. (Hutt.) CM13 55 GB45
Greyfriars Pas, EC1 196 G8
Greyfriars Rd, Wok. (Ripley) GU23 168 BG124
Greyhound Hill, NW4 63 CU55
Greyhound La, SW16 121 DK93
Grays (Orsett) RM16 111 GG75
Potters Bar EN6 11 CU33
Greyhound Rd, N17 66 DS55
NW10 81 CV69
W6 99 CX79
W14 99 CY79
Sutton SM1 158 DC106
Greyhound Ter, SW16 141 DJ95
Greyhound Way, Dart. DA1 127 FE86
Greys Pk Cl, Kes. BR2 162 EJ106
Greystead Rd, SE23 122 DW87
Greystoke Av, Pnr. HA5 60 CA55
Greystoke Dr, Ruis. HA4 59 BP58
Greystoke Gdns, W5 80 CL70
Enfield EN2 29 DK42
Greystoke Pk Ter, W5 79 CK69
Greystoke Pl, EC4 196 D8
Greystone Cl, S.Croy. CR2 160 DW111
Greystone Gdns, Har. HA3 61 CJ58
Ilford IG6 49 EQ54
Greystone Path, E11
off Grove Rd 68 EF59
Greystones Dr, Reig. RH2 184 DC132
Greyswood Av, N18 47 DX51
Greyswood St, SW16 121 DH93
Greythorne Rd, Wok. GU21 166 AU118
Grey Twrs Av, Horn. RM11 72 FK60
Grey Twrs Gdns, Horn. RM11
off Grey Twrs Av 72 FK60
Grice Av, West. (Bigg.H.) TN16 162 EH113
Gridiron Pl, Upmin. RM14 72 FP62
Grierson Rd, SE23 123 DX87
Grieves Rd, Grav. (Nthflt) DA11 131 GF90
Griffin Av, Upmin. RM14 73 FS58
Griffin Cen, The, Felt. TW14 115 BV85
Griffin Cl, NW10 63 CV64
Griffin Manor Way, SE28 105 ER76
Griffin Rd, N17 46 DS54
SE18 105 ER78
Griffins, The, Grays RM16 110 GB75
Griffins Cl, N21 46 DR45
Griffin Wk, Green. DA9
off Church Rd 129 FT85
Griffin Way, Sun. TW16 135 BU96
Griffith Cl, Dag. RM8
off Gibson Rd 70 EW60
Griffiths Cl, Wor.Pk. KT4 139 CV103
Griffiths Rd, SW19 120 DA94
Griffon Way, Wat. WD25
off Ashfields 7 BT34
Grifon Rd, Grays (Chaff.Hun.) RM16 109 FW76
Griggs App, Ilf. IG1 69 EQ61
Griggs Gdns, Horn. RM12
off Tylers Cres 72 FJ64
Griggs Pl, SE1 201 N7
Griggs Rd, E10 67 EC58
Grilse Cl, N9 46 DV49
Grimsby Gro, E16 87 EP74
Grimsby St, E2
off Cheshire St 84 DU70
Grimsdyke Cres, Barn. EN5 27 CW41
Grimsdyke Rd, Pnr. HA5 40 BY52
Grimsel Path, SE5
off Laxley Cl 101 DP80
Grimshaw Cl, N6 64 DG59
Grimshaw Way, Rom. RM1 71 FF57
Grimstone Cl, Rom. RM5 51 FB51
Grimston Rd, SW6 99 CZ82
Grimwade Av, Croy. CR0 142 DU104
Grimwade Cl, SE15 102 DW83
Grimwood Rd, Twick. TW1 117 CF87
Grindall Cl, Croy. CR0
off Hillside Rd 159 DP105
Grindal St, SE1 200 D5
Grindleford Av, N11 44 DG47
Grindley Gdns, Croy. CR0 142 DT100
Grinling Pl, SE8 103 EA79
Grinstead Rd, SE8 103 DY78
Grisedale Cl, Pur. CR8 160 DS114
Grisedale Gdns, Pur. CR8 160 DS114
Grittleton Av, Wem. HA9 80 CP65
Grittleton Rd, W9 82 DA70
Grizedale Ter, SE23 122 DV89
Grobars Av, Wok. GU21 166 AW115
Grocer's Hall Ct, EC2 197 K9
Grogan Cl, Hmptn. TW12 116 BZ93
Groombridge Cl, Walt. KT12 153 BV106
Welling DA16 126 EU85
Groombridge Rd, E9 85 DX66
Groom Cl, Brom. BR2 144 EH98
Groom Cres, SW18 120 DD87
Groomfield Cl, SW17 120 DG91
Groom Pl, SW1 198 G6
Groom Rd, Brox. EN10 15 DZ26
Grooms Cotts, Chesh. HP5 4 AV30
Grooms Dr, Pnr. HA5 59 BU57
Grosmont Rd, SE18 105 ET78
Grosse Way, SW15 119 CV86
Grosvenor Av, N5 66 DQ64
SW14 98 CS83
Carshalton SM5 158 DF107
Harrow HA2 60 CB58
Hayes UB4 77 BS68
Kings Langley WD4 7 BQ28
Richmond TW10
off Grosvenor Rd 118 CL85
Grosvenor Cl, Iver SL0 75 BD69
Loughton IG10 33 EP39
Grosvenor Cotts, SW1 198 F8
Grosvenor Ct, N14 45 DJ45
NW6 81 CX67
Rickmansworth (Crox.Grn) WD3
off Mayfare 23 BR43
Slough SL1
off Stoke Poges La 74 AS72
Grosvenor Cres, NW9 62 CN56
SW1 198 G5
Dartford DA1 128 FK85
Uxbridge UB10 77 BP66
Grosvenor Cres Ms, SW1 198 F5
Grosvenor Dr, Horn. RM11 72 FJ60
Loughton IG10 33 EP39
Grosvenor Est, SW1 199 N8
Grosvenor Gdns, E6 86 EK69
N10 65 DJ55
N14 29 DK43
NW2 63 CW64
NW11 63 CZ58
SW1 199 H6
SW14 98 CS83
Kingston upon Thames KT2 117 CK93
Upminster RM14 73 FR60
Wallington SM6 159 DJ108
Woodford Green IG8 48 EG51
Grosvenor Gdns Ms E, SW1 199 J6
Grosvenor Gdns Ms N, SW1 199 H7
Grosvenor Gdns Ms S, SW1 199 J7
Grosvenor Gate, W1 198 E1
Grosvenor Hill, SW19 119 CY93
W1 195 H10
Grosvenor Pk, SE5 102 DQ79
Grosvenor Pk Rd, E17 67 EA57
Grosvenor Path, Loug. IG10 33 EP39
Grosvenor Pl, SW1 198 G5
Weybridge KT13
off Vale Rd 135 BR104
Grosvenor Ri E, E17 67 EB57
Grosvenor Rd, E6 86 EK67
E7 86 EH65
E10 67 EC60
E11 68 EG57
N3 43 CZ52
N9 46 DV46
N10 45 DH53
SE25 142 DU98
SW1 101 DH79
W4 98 CP78
W7 79 CG74
Belvedere DA17 106 FA79
Bexleyheath DA6 126 EX85
Borehamwood WD6 26 CN41
Brentford TW8 97 CK79
Dagenham RM8 70 EZ60
Epsom KT18 172 CR119
Hounslow TW3 96 BZ83
Ilford IG1 69 EQ62
Northwood HA6 39 BT50
Orpington BR5 145 ES100
Richmond TW10 118 CL85
Romford RM7 71 FD59
Southall UB2 96 BZ76
Staines TW18 114 BG94
Twickenham TW1 117 CG87
Wallington SM6 159 DH107
Watford WD17 24 BW42
West Wickham BR4 143 EB102
Grosvenor Sq, W1 194 G10
Kings Langley WD4
off Grosvenor Av 7 BQ28
Grosvenor St, W1 195 H10
Grosvenor Ter, SE5 101 DP80
Grosvenor Vale, Ruis. HA4 59 BT61
Grosvenor Way, E5 66 DW61
Grosvenor Wf Rd, E14 204 F9
Grote's Bldgs, SE3 104 EE82
Grote's Pl, SE3 104 EE82
Groton Rd, SW18 120 DB89
Grotto Pas, W1 194 G6
Grotto Rd, Twick. TW1 117 CF89
Weybridge KT13 135 BP104
Grove, The, E15 86 EE65
N3 44 DA53
N4 65 DM59
N6 64 DG60
N8 65 DK57
N13 45 DN50
N14 29 DJ43
NW9 62 CR57
NW11 63 CY59
W5 79 CK74
Addlestone KT15 152 BH106
Bexleyheath DA6 106 EX84
Brentwood CM14 54 FT49
Caterham CR3 175 DP121
Chesham HP5 20 AX36
Coulsdon CR5 175 DK115
Edgware HA8 42 CP49
Egham TW20 113 BA92
Enfield EN2 29 DN40
Epsom KT17 156 CS113
Epsom (Ewell) KT17 157 CT110
Esher KT10 136 CB102
Gravesend DA12 131 GH87
Greenford UB6 78 CC72
Hatfield (Brook.Pk) AL9 12 DA27
Isleworth TW7 97 CE81
Potters Bar EN6 12 DC32
Radlett WD7 9 CG34
Sidcup DA14 126 EY91
Slough SL1 92 AU75
Stanmore HA7 41 CG47
Swanley BR8 147 FF97
Swanscombe DA10 130 FZ85
Teddington TW11 117 CG91
Twickenham TW1
off Bridge Rd 117 CH86
Upminster RM14 72 FP63
Uxbridge UB10 58 BN64
Walton-on-Thames KT12 135 BV101
Watford WD17 23 BQ37
West Wickham BR4 143 EB104
Westerham (Bigg.H.) TN16 178 EK118
Woking GU21 167 AZ116
Grove Av, N3 44 DA52
N10 45 DJ54
W7 79 CE72
Epsom KT17 156 CS113
Pinner HA5 60 BY56
Sutton SM1 158 DA107
Twickenham TW1 117 CF88
Grove Bk, Wat. WD19 40 BX46
Grovebarns, Stai. TW18 114 BG93
Grovebury Cl, Erith DA8 107 FD79
Grovebury Gdns, St.Alb. (Park St) AL2 8 CC27
Grovebury Rd, SE2 106 EV75
Grove Cl, N14 off Avenue Rd 45 DH45
SE23 123 DX88
Bromley BR2 144 EG103
Epsom KT19 156 CN110
Feltham TW13 116 BY91
Gerrards Cross (Chal.St.P.) SL9
off Grove La 36 AW53
Kingston upon Thames KT1 138 CM98
Slough SL1 off Alpha St S 92 AU76
Uxbridge UB10 58 BN64
Windsor (Old Wind.) SL4 112 AV87
Grove Cotts, SW3 100 DE79
Grove Ct, SE3 104 EG81
Barnet EN5 off High St 27 CZ41
East Molesey KT8
off Walton Rd 137 CD99
Waltham Abbey EN9
off Highbridge St 15 EB33
Grove Cres, E18 48 EF54
NW9 62 CQ56
Feltham TW13 116 BY91
Kingston upon Thames KT1 138 CL97
Rickmansworth (Crox.Grn) WD3 22 BN42
Grove Cres, Walton-on-Thames KT12 135 BV101
Grove Cres Rd, E15 85 ED65
Grovedale Cl, Wal.Cr. (Chsht) EN7 14 DT30
Grovedale Rd, N19 65 DK61
Grove End, E18
off Grove Hill 48 EF54
NW5 off Chetwynd Rd 65 DH63
Gerrards Cross (Chal.St.P.) SL9 36 AW53
Grove End Gdns, NW8
off Grove End Rd 82 DD68
Grove End La, Esher KT10 137 CD102
Grove End Rd, NW8 82 DD69
Grove Fm Ct, Mitch. CR4
off Brookfields Av 140 DF98
Grove Fm Pk, Nthwd. HA6 39 BR50
Grove Footpath, Surb. KT5 138 CL98
Grove Gdns, NW4 63 CU56
NW8 194 C3
Dagenham RM10 71 FC62
Enfield EN3 31 DX39
Teddington TW11 117 CG91
Grove Grn Rd, E11 67 EC62
Grove Hall Ct, NW8
off Hall Rd 82 DC69
Grove Hall Rd, Bushey WD23 24 BY42
Grove Heath, Wok. (Ripley) GU23 168 BJ124
Grove Heath Ct, Wok. (Ripley) GU23 168 BJ124
Grove Heath N, Wok. (Ripley) GU23 168 BH122
Grove Heath Rd, Wok. (Ripley) GU23 168 BJ123
Groveherst Rd, Dart. DA1 108 FM83
Grove Hill, E18 48 EF54
Gerrards Cross (Chal.St.P.) SL9 36 AW52
Harrow HA1 61 CE59
Grove Hill Rd, SE5 102 DS83
Harrow HA1 61 CE59
Grovehill Rd, Red. RH1 184 DE134
Grove Ho Rd, N8 65 DL56
Groveland Av, SW16 121 DM94
Groveland Ct, EC4 197 J9
Groveland Rd, Beck. BR3 143 DZ97
Grovelands, St.Alb. (Park St) AL2 8 CB27
West Molesey KT8 136 CA98
Grovelands Cl, SE5 102 DS82
Harrow HA2 60 CB62
Grovelands Ct, N14 45 DK45
Grovelands Rd, N13 45 DM49
N15 66 DU58
Orpington BR5 126 EU94
Purley CR8 159 DL112
Grovelands Way, Grays RM17 110 FZ78
Groveland Way, N.Mal. KT3 138 CQ99
Grove La, SE5 102 DR81
Chesham HP5 4 AV27
Chigwell IG7 49 ET48
Coulsdon CR5 158 DG113
Epping CM16
off High St 18 EU30
Gerrards Cross (Chal.St.P.) SL9 36 AW53
Kingston upon Thames KT1 138 CL98
Uxbridge UB8 76 BM70
Grove La Ter, SE5
off Grove La 102 DS83
Groveley Rd, Sun. TW16 115 BT92
Grove Mkt Pl, SE9 125 EM86
Grove Ms, W6 99 CW76
W11 off Portobello Rd 81 CZ72
Grove Mill La, Wat. WD17 23 BP37
Grove Mill Pl, Cars. SM5 140 DG104
GROVE PARK, SE12 124 EG89
GROVE PARK, W4 98 CP80
⇌ Grove Park 124 EG90
Grove Pk, E11 68 EH58
NW9 62 CQ56
SE5 102 DS82
Grove Pk Av, E4 47 EB52
Grove Pk Br, W4 98 CQ80
Grove Pk Gdns, W4 98 CP79
Grove Pk Ms, W4 98 CQ80
Grove Pk Rd, N15 66 DS56
SE9 124 EJ90
W4 98 CP80
Rainham RM13 89 FG67
Grove Pk Ter, W4 98 CP79
Grove Pas, E2 84 DV68
Teddington TW11 117 CG92
Grove Path, Wal.Cr. (Chsht) EN7 14 DU31
Grove Pl, NW3
off Christchurch Hill 64 DD63
SW12 off Cathles Rd 121 DH86
W3 80 CQ74
W5 off The Grove 79 CK74
Banstead SM7 158 DF112
Barking IG11
off Clockhouse Av 87 EQ67
Watford WD25 24 CB39
Weybridge KT13
off Princes Rd 153 BQ106
Grove Rd, E3 85 DX67
E4 47 EB49
E11 68 EF59
E17 67 EB58
E18 48 EF54
N11 45 DH50
N12 44 DD50
N15 66 DS57
NW2 81 CW65
SW13 99 CT82
SW19 120 DC94
W3 80 CQ74
W5 79 CK73
Amersham HP6 20 AT37
Ashtead KT21 172 CM118
Barnet EN4 28 DE41
Belvedere DA17 106 EZ79
Bexleyheath DA7 107 FC84
Borehamwood WD6 26 CN39
Brentford TW8 97 CJ78
Chertsey KT16 133 BF100
East Molesey KT8 137 CD98
Grove Rd, Edgware HA8 42 CN51
Epsom KT17 156 CS113
Gravesend (Nthflt) DA11 130 GB85
Grays RM17 110 GC79
Hounslow TW3 96 CB84
Isleworth TW7 97 CE81
Mitcham CR4 141 DH96
Northwood HA6 39 BR50
Oxted RH8
off Southlands La 187 EC134
Pinner HA5 60 BZ57
Richmond TW10 118 CM86
Rickmansworth (Mill End) WD3 38 BG47
Romford RM6 70 EV59
Sevenoaks TN14 191 FJ121
Sevenoaks (Seal) TN15 191 FN122
Shepperton TW17 135 BQ100
Surbiton KT6 137 CK99
Sutton SM1 158 DB107
Thornton Heath CR7 141 DN98
Twickenham TW2 117 CD90
Uxbridge UB8 76 BK66
Westerham (Tats.) TN16 178 EJ120
Woking GU21 167 AZ116
Grove Rd W, Enf. EN3 30 DW37
Grover Rd, Wat. WD19 40 BX45
Grove Shaw, Tad. (Kgswd) KT20 173 CY124
Groveside Cl, W3 80 CN72
Carshalton SM5 140 DE103
Groveside Rd, E4 48 EE47
Grovestile Waye, Felt. TW14 115 BR87
Grove St, N18 46 DT51
SE8 203 M8
Grove Ter, NW5 65 DH62
Teddington TW11 117 CG91
Grove Ter Ms, NW5
off Grove Ter 65 DH62
Grove Vale, SE22 102 DS84
Chislehurst BR7 125 EN93
Grove Vil, E14 85 EB73
Groveway, SW9 101 DM81
Dagenham RM8 70 EX63
Grove Way, Esher KT10 136 CC101
Rickmansworth (Chorl.) WD3 21 BB42
Uxbridge UB8 76 BK66
Wembley HA9 62 CP64
Grovewood, Rich. TW9
off Sandycombe Rd 98 CN81
Grovewood Cl, Rick. (Chorl.) WD3 21 BB43
Grove Wd Hill, Couls. CR5 159 DK114
Grovewood Pl, Wdf.Grn. IG8 49 EM51
Grubb St, Oxt. RH8 188 EJ128
Grummant Rd, SE15 102 DT81
Grundy St, E14 85 EB72
Gruneisen Rd, N3 44 DB52
Guardian Cl, Horn. RM11 71 FH60
Guards Av, Cat. CR3 176 DQ122
Guardsman Cl, Brwd. CM14 54 FX50
★ Guards Mus, SW1 199 L5
Gubbins La, Rom. RM3 52 FM52
Gubyon Av, SE24 121 DP85
Guerin Sq, E3 85 DZ69
Guernsey Cl, Houns. TW5 96 CA81
Guernsey Fm Dr, Wok. GU21 166 AX115
Guernsey Gro, SE24 122 DQ87
Guernsey Ho, Enf. EN3
off Eastfield Rd 31 DX38
Guernsey Rd, E11 67 ED60
Guibal Rd, SE12 124 EH87
Guildersfield Rd, SW16 121 DL94
Guildford Av, Felt. TW13 115 BT89
Guildford Gdns, Rom. RM3 52 FL51
Guildford Gro, SE10 103 EB81
Guildford La, Wok. GU22 166 AX120
Guildford Rd, E6 86 EL72
E17 47 EC53
SW8 101 DL81
Chertsey KT16 133 BE102
Croydon CR0 142 DR100
Ilford IG3 69 ES61
Leatherhead (Fetch.) KT22 171 CG122
Romford RM3 52 FL51
Woking GU22 166 AY119
Woking (Mayford) GU22 166 AX122
Guildford St, Cher. KT16 134 BG101
Staines TW18 114 BG93
Guildford Way, Wall. SM6 159 DL106
★ Guildhall, The, EC2 197 K8
★ Guildhall Art Gall, Guildhall Lib, EC2 197 J8
Guildhall Bldgs, EC2
off Basinghall St 84 DR72
Guildhall Yd, EC2 197 K8
Guildhouse St, SW1 199 K8
Guildown Av, N12 44 DB49
Guild Rd, SE7 104 EK78
Erith DA8 107 FF80
Guildsway, E17 47 DZ53
Guileshill La, Wok. (Ockham) GU23 168 BL123
Guilford Av, Surb. KT5 138 CM99
Guilford Pl, WC1 196 B5
Guilford St, WC1 196 A5
Guilford Vil, Surb. KT5
off Alpha Rd 138 CM100
Guilsborough Cl, NW10 80 CS66
Guinevere Gdns, Wal.Cr. EN8 15 DY31
Guinness Cl, E9 85 DY66
Hayes UB3 95 BR76
Guinness Ct, Wok. GU21
off Iveagh Rd 166 AT118
Guinness Sq, SE1 201 M8
Guinness Trust Bldgs, SE1
off Snowsfields 102 DS75
SE11 200 G10
SW3 198 D9
SW9 101 DP84
Guinness Trust Est, N16
off Holmleigh Rd 66 DS60
Guion Rd, SW6 99 CZ82
Gulland Cl, Bushey WD23 24 CC43
Gulland Wk, N1
off Clephane Rd 84 DQ65
Gull Cl, Wall. SM6 159 DL108
Gullet Wd Rd, Wat. WD25 23 BU35
Gulliver Cl, Nthlt. UB5 78 BZ67
Gulliver Rd, Sid. DA15 125 ES89

★ Place of interest ⇌ Railway station ⊖ London Underground station DLR Docklands Light Railway station Tm Tramlink station H Hospital Riv Pedestrian ferry landing stage

Gulliver St, SE16 203 M6
Gull Wk, Horn. RM12
off Heron Flight Av 89 FH66
Gulston Wk, SW3 198 E9
Gumleigh Rd, W5 97 CJ77
Gumley Gdns, Islw. TW7 97 CG83
Gumley Rd, Grays RM20 109 FX79
Gumping Rd, Orp. BR5 145 EQ103
Gundulph Rd, Brom. BR2 144 EJ97
Gunfleet Cl, Grav. DA12 131 GL87
Gun Hill, Til. (W.Til.) RM18 111 GK79
Gunmakers La, E3 85 DY67
Gunnell Cl, SE26 122 DU92
Croydon CR0 142 DU100
Gunner Dr, Enf. EN3 31 EA37
Gunner La, SE18 105 EN78
GUNNERSBURY, W4 98 CP77
⇌ **Gunnersbury** 98 CP78
⊖ **Gunnersbury** 98 CP78
Gunnersbury Av, W3 98 CN76
W4 98 CN76
W5 80 CM74
Gunnersbury Cl, W4
off Grange Rd 98 CP78
Gunnersbury Ct, W3
off Bollo La 98 CP75
Gunnersbury Cres, W3 98 CN75
Gunnersbury Dr, W5 98 CM75
Gunnersbury Gdns, W3 98 CN75
Gunnersbury La, W3 98 CN76
Gunnersbury Ms, W4
off Chiswick High Rd 98 CP78
★ **Gunnersbury Park**, W3 98 CM77
Gunnersbury Pk, W3 98 CM77
W5 98 CM77
★ **Gunnersbury Park Mus & Art Cen**, W3 98 CN76
Gunners Gro, E4 47 EC48
Gunners Rd, SW18 120 DD89
Gunnery Ter, SE18 105 EQ77
Gunning Rd, Grays RM17 110 GD78
Gunning St, SE18 105 ES77
Gunn Rd, Swans. DA10 130 FY86
Gunpowder Sq, EC4 196 E8
Gunstor Rd, N16 66 DS63
Gun St, E1 197 P7
Gunter Gro, SW10 100 DC79
Edgware HA8 42 CR53
Gunters Mead, Lthd. KT22
off Queens Dr 154 CC111
Gunterstone Rd, W14 99 CY77
Gunthorpe St, E1 84 DT71
Gunton Rd, E5 66 DV62
SW17 120 DG93
Gunwhale Cl, SE16 203 J3
Gurdon Rd, SE7 104 EG78
Gurnard Cl, West Dr. UB7
off Trout Rd 76 BK73
Gurnell Gro, W13 79 CF70
Gurney Cl, E15 *off Gurney Rd* 68 EE64
E17 47 DX53
Barking IG11 87 EP65
Gurney Cres, Croy. CR0 141 DM102
Gurney Dr, N2 64 DC57
Gurney Rd, E15 68 EE64
SW6 100 DC83
Carshalton SM5 158 DG105
Northolt UB5 77 BV69
Guthrie St, SW3 198 B10
Gutteridge La, Rom. (Stap.Abb.) RM4 35 FC44
Gutter La, EC2 197 J8
Guyatt Gdns, Mitch. CR4
off Ormerod Gdns 140 DG96
Guy Barnett Gro, SE3
off Casterbridge Rd 104 EG83
Guy Rd, Wall. SM6 141 DK104
Guyscliff Rd, SE13 123 EC85
Guysfield Cl, Rain. RM13 89 FG67
Guysfield Dr, Rain. RM13 89 FG67
H **Guy's Hosp**, SE1 201 L4
Guy St, SE1 201 L4
Gwalior Rd, SW15
off Felsham Rd 99 CX83
Gwendolen Av, SW15 119 CX85
Gwendolen Cl, SW15 119 CX85
Gwendoline Av, E13 86 EH67
Gwendwr Rd, W14 99 CY78
Gwent Cl, Wat. WD25 8 BX34
Gwillim Cl, Sid. DA15 126 EU85
Gwydor Rd, Beck. BR3 143 DX98
Gwydyr Rd, Brom. BR2 144 EF97
Gwyn Cl, SW6 100 DC80
Gwynne Av, Croy. CR0 143 DX101
Gwynne Cl, W4
off Pumping Sta Rd 99 CT79
Gwynne Pk Av, Wdf.Grn. IG8 49 EM51
Gwynne Pl, WC1 196 C3
Gwynne Rd, SW11 100 DD82
Caterham CR3 176 DR123
Gwynn Rd, Grav. (Nthflt) DA11 130 GC89
Gyfford Wk, Wal.Cr. EN7 14 DV31
Gylcote Cl, SE5 102 DR84
Gyles Pk, Stan. HA7 41 CJ53
Gyllyngdune Gdns, Ilf. IG3 69 ET61
Gypsy Cor, W3 80 CR71
Gypsy La, Kings L. WD4 23 BR35
Slough (Stoke P.) SL2 56 AS63

H

Haarlem Rd, W14 99 CX76
Haberdasher Est, N1
off Haberdasher St 84 DR69
Haberdasher Pl, N1 197 L2
Haberdasher St, N1 197 L2
Habgood Rd, Loug. IG10 32 EL41
Haccombe Rd, SW19
off Haydons Rd 120 DC93
HACKBRIDGE, Wall. SM6 141 DH103
⇌ **Hackbridge** 141 DH103
Hackbridge Grn, Wall. SM6 140 DG103
Hackbridge Pk Gdns, Cars. SM5 140 DG103
Hackbridge Rd, Wall. SM6 140 DG103
Hacketts La, Wok. GU22 151 BF114
Hackford Rd, SW9 101 DM81
Hackford Wk, SW9 101 DM81
Hackforth Cl, Barn. EN5 27 CV43
Hackington Cres, Beck. BR3 123 EA93
HACKNEY, E8 84 DV65
⇌ **Hackney Central** 84 DV65
★ **Hackney City Fm**, E2 84 DU68
Hackney Cl, Borwd. WD6 26 CR43
⇌ **Hackney Downs** 66 DV64
Hackney Gro, E8
off Reading La 84 DV65
★ **Hackney Marsh**, E9 67 DY62
★ **Hackney Mus**, E8 84 DV65
Hackney Rd, E2 197 P3
HACKNEY WICK, E9 67 EA64
⇌ **Hackney Wick** 85 EA65
Hackworth Pt, E3
off Rainhill Way 85 EB69
HACTON, Rain. RM13 72 FM64
Hacton Dr, Horn. RM12 72 FK63
Hacton La, Horn. RM12 72 FM62
Upminster RM14 72 FM64
Hadar Cl, N20 44 DB46
Hadden Rd, SE28 105 ES76
Hadden Way, Grnf. UB6 79 CD65
Haddestoke Gate, Wal.Cr. (Chsht) EN8 15 DZ26
Haddington Rd, Brom. BR1 123 ED90
Haddon Cl, Borwd. WD6 26 CN41
Enfield EN1 30 DU44
New Malden KT3 139 CT99
Weybridge KT13 135 BR104
Haddonfield, SE8 203 J9
Haddon Gro, Sid. DA15 126 EU87
Haddon Rd, Orp. BR5 146 EW99
Rickmansworth (Chorl.) WD3 21 BC43
Sutton SM1 158 DB105
Haddo St, SE10 103 EB79
Hadfield Cl, Sthl. UB1
off Adrienne Av 78 BZ69
Hadfield Rd, Stai. (Stanw.) TW19 114 BK86
Hadlands Cl, Hem.H. (Bov.) HP3 5 AZ26
Hadleigh Cl, E1
off Mantus Rd 84 DW70
SW20 139 CZ96
Hadleigh Dr, Sutt. SM2 158 DA109
Hadleigh Rd, N9 46 DV45
Hadleigh St, E2 84 DW70
Hadleigh Wk, E6 86 EL72
HADLEY, Barn. EN5 27 CZ40
Hadley Cl, N21 29 DN44
Borehamwood (Elstree) WD6 26 CM44
Hadley Common, Barn. EN5 28 DA40
Hadley Gdns, W4 98 CR78
Southall UB2 96 BZ78
Hadley Grn, Barn. EN5 27 CZ40
Hadley Grn Rd, Barn. EN5 27 CZ40
Hadley Grn W, Barn. EN5 27 CZ40
Hadley Gro, Barn. EN5 27 CY40
Hadley Highstone, Barn. EN5 27 CZ39
Hadley Pl, Wey. KT13 152 BN108
Hadley Ridge, Barn. EN5 27 CZ41
Hadley Rd, Barn. (Had.Wd) EN4 29 DH38
Barnet (New Barn.) EN5 28 DB42
Belvedere DA17 106 EZ77
Enfield EN2 29 DL38
Mitcham CR4 141 DK98
Hadley St, NW1 83 DH65
Hadley Way, N21 29 DN44
HADLEY WOOD, Barn. EN4 28 DD38
⇌ **Hadley Wood** 28 DC38
Hadley Wd Ri, Ken. CR8 175 DP115
Hadlow Pl, SE19 122 DU94
Hadlow Rd, Sid. DA14 125 EU91
Welling DA16 106 EW80
Hadlow Way, Grav. (Istead Rise) DA13 130 GE94
Hadrian Cl, Stai. TW19
off Hadrian Way 114 BL88
Hadrian Ct, Sutt. SM2
off Stanley Rd 158 DB108
Hadrian Est, E2 84 DU68
Hadrian Ms, N7 *off Roman Way* 83 DM66
Hadrians Ride, Enf. EN1 30 DT43
Hadrian St, SE10 104 EE78
Hadrian Way, Stai. (Stanw.) TW19 114 BL87
Hadyn Pk Rd, W12 99 CU75
Hafer Rd, SW11 100 DF84
Hafton Rd, SE6 124 EE88
Hagden La, Wat. WD18 23 BT43
Haggard Rd, Twick. TW1 117 CH87
HAGGERSTON, E2 84 DT68
Haggerston Rd, E8 84 DT66
Borehamwood WD6 26 CL38
Hague St, E2
off Derbyshire St 84 DU69
Ha-Ha Rd, SE18 105 EM79
Haig Gdns, Grav. DA12 131 GJ87
Haig Pl, Mord. SM4
off Green La 140 DA100
Haig Rd, Grays RM16 111 GG76
Stanmore HA7 41 CJ50
Uxbridge UB8 77 BP71
Westerham (Bigg.H.) TN16 178 EL117
Haig Rd E, E13 86 EJ69
Haig Rd W, E13 86 EJ69
Haigville Gdns, Ilf. IG6 69 EP56
Hailes Cl, SW19 *off North Rd* 120 DC93
Haileybury Av, Enf. EN1 30 DT44
Haileybury Rd, Orp. BR6 164 EU105
Hailey Rd, Erith DA18 106 FA75
Hailsham Av, SW2 121 DM89
Hailsham Cl, Rom. RM3 52 FJ50
Surbiton KT6 137 CK101
Hailsham Dr, Har. HA1 61 CD55
Hailsham Gdns, Rom. RM3 52 FJ50
Hailsham Rd, SW17 120 DG93
Romford RM3 52 FJ50
Hailsham Ter, N18 46 DQ50
Haimo Rd, SE9 124 EK85
HAINAULT, Ilf. IG6 49 ES52
⊖ **Hainault** 49 ES52
Hainault Ct, E17 67 ED56
★ **Hainault Forest Country Pk**, Chig. IG7 50 EW47
Hainault Gore, Rom. RM6 70 EY57
Hainault Gro, Chig. IG7 49 EQ49
Hainault Ind Est, Ilf. IG6 50 EW50
Hainault Rd, E11 67 EC60
Chigwell IG7 49 EP48
Romford RM5 51 FC54
Romford (Chad.Hth) RM6 70 EZ58
Romford (Lt.Hth) RM6 70 EV55
Hainault St, SE9 125 EP88
Ilford IG1 69 EP61
Haines Ct, Wey. KT13
off St. George's Lo 153 BR106
Haines Wk, Mord. SM4
off Dorchester Rd 140 DB101
Haines Way, Wat. WD25 7 BU34
Hainford Cl, SE4 103 DX84
Haining Cl, W4
off Wellesley Rd 98 CN78
Hainthorpe Rd, SE27 121 DP90
Hainton Cl, E1 84 DV72
Halberd Ms, E5
off Knightland Rd 66 DV61
Halbutt Gdns, Dag. RM9 70 EZ62
Halbutt St, Dag. RM9 70 EZ63
Halcomb St, N1 84 DS67
Halcot Av, Bexh. DA6 127 FB85
Halcrow St, E1 *off Newark St* 84 DV71
Halcyon Way, Horn. RM11 72 FM60
Haldane Cl, N10 45 DH52
Enfield EN3 31 EB38
Haldane Gdns, Grav. DA11 130 GC88
Haldane Pl, SW18 120 DB88
Haldane Rd, E6 86 EK69
SE28 88 EX73
SW6 99 CZ80
Southall UB1 78 CC72
Haldan Rd, E4 47 EC51
Haldon Cl, Chig. IG7
off Arrowsmith Rd 49 ES50
Haldon Rd, SW18 119 CZ85
Hale, The, E4 47 ED52
N17 66 DU55
Hale Cl, E4 47 EC48
Edgware HA8 42 CQ50
Orpington BR6 163 EQ105
Hale Dr, NW7 42 CQ51
HALE END, E4 47 ED51
Hale End, Rom. RM3 51 FH51
Woking GU22 166 AV121
Hale End Cl, Ruis. HA4 59 BU58
Hale End Rd, E4 47 ED51
E17 47 ED53
Woodford Green IG8 47 ED52
Halefield Rd, N17 46 DU53
Hale Gdns, N17 66 DU55
W3 80 CN74
Hale Gro Gdns, NW7 42 CR50
Hale La, NW7 42 CR50
Edgware HA8 42 CP50
Sevenoaks (Otford) TN14 181 FE117
Hale Path, SE27 121 DP91
Hale Rd, E6 86 EL70
N17 66 DU55
Halesowen Rd, Mord. SM4 140 DB101
Hales St, SE8
off Deptford High St 103 EA80
Hale St, E14 85 EB73
Staines TW18 113 BE91
Haleswood, Cob. KT11 153 BV114
Halesworth Cl, E5
off Theydon Rd 66 DW61
Romford RM3 52 FL52
Halesworth Rd, SE13 103 EB83
Romford RM3 52 FL51
Hale Wk, W7 79 CE71
Haley Rd, NW4 63 CW58
Half Acre, Brent. TW8 97 CK79
Halfacre Hill, Ger.Cr. (Chal.St.P.) SL9 36 AY53
Half Acre Rd, W7 79 CE74
Halfhide La, Brox. (Turnf.) EN10 15 DY26
Waltham Cross (Chsht) EN8 15 DX27
Halfhides, Wal.Abb. EN9 15 ED33
Half Moon Ct, EC1 197 H7
Half Moon Cres, N1 83 DM68
Half Moon La, SE24 122 DQ86
Epping CM16 17 ET31
Half Moon Pas, E1
off Braham St 84 DT72
Half Moon St, W1 199 J2
Halford Cl, Edg. HA8 42 CP54
Halford Rd, E10 67 ED57
SW6 100 DA79
Richmond TW10 118 CL85
Uxbridge UB10 58 BN64
Halfway Ct, Purf. RM19
off Thamley 108 FN77
Halfway Grn, Walt. KT12 135 BV104
Halfway St, Sid. DA15 125 ER87
Haliburton Rd, Twick. TW1 117 CG85
Haliday Wk, N1
off Balls Pond Rd 84 DR65
Halidon Cl, E9
off Urswick Rd 66 DW64
Halidon Ri, Rom. RM3 52 FP51
Halifax Cl, St.Alb. AL2 8 BZ30
Watford WD25
off Ashfields 7 BT34
Halifax Rd, Enf. EN2 30 DQ40
Greenford UB6 78 CB67
Rickmansworth (Herons.) WD3 37 BC45
Halifax St, SE26 122 DV91
Halifield Dr, Belv. DA17 106 EY76
Haling Down Pas, S.Croy. CR2 160 DQ109
Haling Gro, S.Croy. CR2 160 DQ108
Haling Pk, S.Croy. CR2 160 DQ107
Haling Pk Gdns, S.Croy. CR2 159 DP107
Haling Pk Rd, S.Croy. CR2 159 DP106
Haling Rd, S.Croy. CR2 160 DR107
Halings La, Uxb. (Denh.) UB9 57 BE56
Halkin Arc, SW1 198 F6
Halkingcroft, Slou. SL3 92 AW75
Halkin Ms, SW1 198 F6
Halkin Pl, SW1 198 F6
Halkin St, SW1 198 G5
Hall, The, SE3 104 EG83
Hallam Cl, Chis. BR7 125 EM92
Watford WD24 24 BW40
Hallam Gdns, Pnr. HA5 40 BY52
Hallam Ms, W1 195 J6
Hallam Rd, N15 65 DP56
Hallam Rd, SW13 99 CV83
Hallam St, W1 195 J5
Halland Way, Nthwd. HA6 39 BR51
Hall Av, N18
off Weir Hall Av 46 DR51
South Ockendon (Aveley) RM15 90 FQ74
Hall Cl, W5 80 CL71
Rickmansworth (Mill End) WD3 38 BG46
Hall Ct, Slou. (Datchet) SL3 92 AV80
Teddington TW11
off Teddington Pk 117 CF92
Hall Cres, S.Ock. (Aveley) RM15 108 FQ75
Hall Dr, SE26 122 DW92
W7 79 CE72
Uxbridge (Hare.) UB9 38 BJ53
Halley Gdns, SE13 103 ED84
Halley Rd, E7 86 EJ65
E12 86 EK65
Waltham Abbey EN9 31 EB36
Halleys App, Wok. GU21 166 AU118
Halleys Ct, Wok. GU21
off Halleys App 166 AU118
Halley St, E14 85 DY71
Halleys Wk, Add. KT15 152 BJ108
Hall Fm Cl, Stan. HA7 41 CH49
Hall Fm Dr, Twick. TW2 117 CD87
Hallfield Est, W2 82 DC72
Hallford Way, Dart. DA1 128 FJ85
Hall Gdns, E4 47 DZ49
Hall Gate, NW8 *off Hall Rd* 82 DC69
Hall Grn La, Brwd. (Hutt.) CM13 55 GC45
Hall Hill, Oxt. RH8 187 ED131
Sevenoaks (Seal) TN15 191 FP123
Halliards, The, Walt. KT12
off Felix Rd 135 BU100
Halliday Cl, Rad. (Shenley) WD7 10 CL32
Halliday Sq, Sthl. UB2 79 CD74
Halliford Cl, Shep. TW17 135 BR98
Halliford Rd, Shep. TW17 135 BS99
Sunbury-on-Thames TW16 135 BS99
Halliford St, N1 84 DQ66
Halliloo Valley Rd, Cat. (Wold.) CR3 177 DZ119
Hallingbury Ct, E17 67 EB55
Hallington Cl, Wok. GU21 166 AV117
Halliwell Rd, SW2 121 DM86
Halliwick Rd, N10 44 DG53
Hall La, E4 47 DY50
E4 (Junct) 47 DY50
NW4 43 CU53
Brentwood (Shenf.) CM15 55 FZ44
Hayes UB3 95 BR80
South Ockendon RM15 91 FX68
Upminster RM14 72 FQ60
Hallmark Trd Est, NW10
off Great Cen Way 62 CQ63
Hallmead Rd, Sutt. SM1 140 DB104
Hall Oak Wk, NW6
off Barlow Rd 81 CZ65
Hallowell Av, Croy. CR0 159 DL105
Hallowell Cl, Mitch. CR4 140 DG97
Hallowell Rd, Nthwd. HA6 39 BS52
Hallowes Cres, Wat. WD19
off Hayling Rd 39 BU48
Hallowfield Way, Mitch. CR4 140 DD98
Hallows Gro, Sun. TW16
off Groveley Rd 115 BT92
Hall Pk Rd, Upmin. RM14 72 FQ64
★ **Hall Pl**, Bex. DA5 127 FC86
Hall Pl, W2 82 DD70
Woking GU21 167 BA116
Hall Pl Cres, Bex. DA5 127 FC85
Hall Pl Dr, Wey. KT13 153 BS106
Hall Rd, E6 87 EM67
E15 67 ED63
NW8 82 DC69
Dartford DA1 108 FM84
Gravesend (Nthflt) DA11 130 GC90
Isleworth TW7 117 CD85
Romford (Chad.Hth) RM6 70 EW58
Romford (Gidea Pk) RM2 71 FH55
South Ockendon (Aveley) RM15 108 FQ75
Wallington SM6 159 DH109
Hallside Rd, Enf. EN1 30 DT38
Hallsland Way, Oxt. RH8 188 EF133
Hall St, EC1 196 G2
N12 44 DC50
Hallsville Rd, E16 86 EF72
Hallswelle Rd, NW11 63 CZ57
Hall Ter, Rom. RM3 52 FN52
South Ockendon (Aveley) RM15 109 FR75
Hall Twr, W2 194 A6
Hall Vw, SE9 124 EK89
Hall Way, Pur. CR8 159 DP113
Hallwood Cres, Brwd. (Shenf.) CM15 54 FY45
Hallywell Cres, E6 87 EM71
Halons Rd, SE9 125 EN87
Halpin Pl, SE17 201 L9
Halsbrook Rd, SE3 104 EK83
Halsbury Cl, Stan. HA7 41 CH49
Halsbury Rd, W12 81 CV74
Halsbury Rd E, Nthlt. UB5 60 CC63
Halsbury Rd W, Nthlt. UB5 60 CB64
Halsend, Hayes UB3 77 BV74
Halsey Ms, SW3 198 D8
Halsey Pk, St.Alb. (Lon.Col.) AL2 10 CM27
Halsey Pl, Wat. WD24 23 BV38
Halsey Rd, Wat. WD18 23 BV41
Halsey St, SW3 198 D8
Halsham Cres, Bark. IG11 87 ET65
Halsmere Rd, SE5 101 DP81
HALSTEAD, Sev. TN14 164 EZ113
Halstead Cl, Croy. CR0
off Charles St 142 DQ104
Halstead Ct, N1 197 L1
Halstead Gdns, N21 46 DR46
Halstead Hill, Wal.Cr. (Chsht) EN7 14 DS29
Halstead La, Sev. (Knock.) TN14 164 EZ114
Halstead Rd, E11 68 EG57
Halstead Rd, N21 46 DQ46
Enfield EN1 30 DS42
Erith DA8 107 FE81
Halstead Way, Brwd. (Hutt.) CM13 55 GC44
Halston Cl, SW11 120 DF86
Halstow Rd, NW10 81 CX69
SE10 205 M10
Halsway, Hayes UB3 77 BU74
Halter Cl, Borwd. WD6
off Clydesdale Cl 26 CR43
Halton Cl, N11
off Colney Hatch La 44 DF51
Halton Cross St, N1 83 DP67
Halton Pl, N1 *off Dibden St* 84 DQ67
Halton Rd, N1 83 DP66
Grays RM16 111 GJ76
Halt Robin La, Belv. DA17
off Halt Robin Rd 107 FB77
Halt Robin Rd, Belv. DA17 106 FA77
HAM, Rich. TW10 117 CK90
Ham, The, Brent. TW8 97 CJ80
Hambalt Rd, SW4 121 DJ85
Hamble Cl, Ruis. HA4
off Chichester Av 59 BS61
Woking GU21 166 AU117
Hamble Ct, Tedd. TW11 117 CK94
Hambledon Cl, Uxb. UB8
off Aldenham Dr 77 BP71
Hambledon Gdns, SE25 142 DT97
Hambledon Hill, Epsom KT18 172 CQ116
Hambledon Pl, SE21 122 DS88
Hambledon Rd, SW18 119 CZ87
Caterham CR3 176 DR123
Hambledon Vale, Epsom KT18 172 CQ116
Hambledown Rd, Sid. DA15 125 ER87
Hamble La, S.Ock. RM15 91 FT71
Hamble St, SW6 100 DB83
Hambleton Cl, Wor.Pk. KT4
off Cotswold Way 139 CW103
Hamble Wk, Nthlt. UB5
off Brabazon Rd 78 CA68
Woking GU21 166 AU118
Hamblings Cl, Rad. (Shenley) WD7 9 CK33
Hambridge Way, SW2 121 DN87
Hambro Av, Brom. BR2 144 EG102
Hambrook Rd, SE25 142 DV97
Hambro Rd, SW16 121 DK93
Brentwood CM14 54 FX47
Hambrough Rd, Sthl. UB1 78 BY74
Hamburgh Ct, Wal.Cr. EN8 15 DX28
Ham Cl, Rich. TW10 117 CJ90
Ham Common, Rich. TW10 118 CM91
Ham Cft Cl, Felt. TW13
off Harvest Rd 115 BU90
Hamden Cres, Dag. RM10 71 FB62
Hamel Cl, Har. HA3 61 CK55
Hamelin St, E14
off St. Leonards Rd 85 EC72
Hamer Cl, Hem.H. (Bov.) HP3 5 BA28
Hamerton Rd, Grav. (Nthflt) DA11 130 GB85
Hameway, E6 87 EN70
Ham Fm Rd, Rich. TW10 117 CK91
Hamfield Cl, Oxt. RH8 187 EC127
Hamfrith Rd, E15 86 EF65
Ham Gate Av, Rich. TW10 117 CK90
Hamhaugh Island, Shep. TW17 134 BN103
★ **Ham Ho**, Rich. TW10 117 CJ88
Hamilton Av, N9 46 DU45
Cobham KT11 153 BU113
Ilford IG6 69 EP56
Romford RM1 51 FD54
Surbiton KT6 138 CP102
Sutton SM3 139 CY103
Woking GU22 167 BE115
Hamilton Cl, N17 66 DT55
NW8 82 DD69
SE16 203 L5
Barnet EN4 28 DE42
Chertsey KT16 133 BF102
Epsom KT19 156 CQ112
Feltham TW13 115 BT92
Potters Bar EN6 11 CU33
Purley CR8 159 DP112
St. Albans (Brick.Wd) AL2 8 CA30
Stanmore HA7 41 CF47
Hamilton Ct, W5 80 CM73
W9 *off Maida Vale* 82 DC69
Hamilton Cres, N13 45 DN49
Brentwood CM14 54 FW49
Harrow HA2 60 BZ62
Hounslow TW3 116 CB85
Hamilton Dr, Rom. RM3 52 FL54
Hamilton Gdns, NW8 82 DC69
Hamilton La, N5
off Hamilton Pk 65 DP63
Hamilton Mead, Hem.H. (Bov.) HP3 5 BA27
Hamilton Ms, SW18
off Merton Rd 120 DA88
W1 199 H4
Hamilton Pk, N5 65 DP63
Hamilton Pk W, N5 65 DP63
Hamilton Pl, N19
off Wedmore St 65 DK62
W1 198 G3
Sunbury-on-Thames TW16 115 BV94
Tadworth (Kgswd) KT20 173 CZ122
Hamilton Rd, E15 86 EE69
E17 47 DY54
N2 64 DC55
N9 46 DU45
NW10 63 CU64
NW11 63 CX59
SE27 122 DR91
SW19 120 DB94
W4 98 CS75
W5 80 CL73
Barnet EN4 28 DE42
Bexleyheath DA7 106 EY82
Brentford TW8 97 CK79

★ Place of interest ⇌ Railway station ⊖ London Underground station DLR Docklands Light Railway station Tra Tramlink station H Hospital Riv Pedestrian ferry landing stage

265

Hamilton Rd, Feltham TW13 115 BT91
Harrow HA1 61 CE57
Hayes UB3 77 BV73
Ilford IG1 69 EP63
Kings Langley WD4 7 BQ33
Romford RM2 71 FH57
Sidcup DA15 126 EU91
Southall UB1 78 BZ74
Thornton Heath CR7 142 DR97
Twickenham TW2 117 CE88
Uxbridge UB8 76 BK71
Watford WD19 39 BV48
Hamilton Rd Ind Est, SE27 122 DR91
Hamilton Sq, N12
off Sandringham Gdns 44 DD51
SE1 201 L4
Hamilton St, SE8
off Deptford High St 103 EA79
Watford WD18 24 BW43
Hamilton Ter, NW8 82 DB68
Hamilton Wk, Erith DA8 107 FF80
Hamilton Way, N3 44 DA51
N13 45 DP49
Wallington SM6 159 DK109
Ham Island, Wind.
(Old Wind.) SL4 92 AX84
Ham La, Egh. (Eng.Grn) TW20 112 AV91
Windsor (Old Wind.) SL4 92 AX84
Hamlea Cl, SE12 124 EF85
Hamlet, The, SE5 102 DR83
Hamlet Cl, SE13
off Old Rd 104 EE84
Romford RM5 50 FA52
St. Albans AL2 8 BZ30
Hamlet Gdns, W6 99 CU77
Hamlet Ho, Erith DA8
off Waterhead Cl 107 FE80
Hamleton Ter, Dag. RM9
off Flamstead Rd 88 EW66
Hamlet Rd, SE19 122 DT94
Romford RM5 50 FA52
Hamlet Sq, NW2 63 CY62
Hamlets Way, E3 85 DZ70
Hamlet Way, SE1 201 L4
★ Hamleys, W1 195 K10
Hamlin Cres, Pnr. HA5 60 BW57
Hamlin Rd, Sev. TN13 190 FE121
Hamlyn Cl, Edg. HA8 42 CL48
Hamlyn Gdns, SE19 122 DS94
Hamm Ct, Wey. KT13 134 BL103
Hammelton Grn, SW9
off Cromwell Rd 101 DP81
Hammelton Rd, Brom. BR1 144 EF95
Hammer Par, Wat. WD25 7 BU33
Hammers Gate, St.Alb. AL2 8 CA25
Hammers La, NW7 43 CU50
HAMMERSMITH, W6 99 CW78
⊖ Hammersmith 99 CW77
Hammersmith Br, SW13 99 CV79
W6 99 CV79
Hammersmith Br Rd, W6 99 CW78
Hammersmith Bdy, W6 99 CW77
Hammersmith Flyover, W6 99 CW78
Hammersmith Gro, W6 99 CW76
H Hammersmith Hosp, W12 81 CT72
Hammersmith Rd, W6 99 CX77
W14 99 CX77
Hammersmith Ter, W6 99 CU78
Hammet Cl, Hayes UB4
off Willow Tree La 78 BX71
Hammett St, EC3 197 P10
Hamm Moor La, Add. KT15 152 BL106
Hammond Av, Mitch. CR4 141 DH96
Hammond Cl, Barn. EN5 27 CY43
Greenford UB6
off Lilian Board Way 61 CD64
Hampton TW12 136 CA95
Waltham Cross (Chsht) EN7 14 DS26
Woking GU21 166 AW115
Hammond Rd, Enf. EN1 30 DV40
Southall UB2 96 BY76
Woking GU21 166 AW115
Hammonds Cl, Dag. RM8 70 EW62
Hammonds La, Brwd. CM13 53 FV51
HAMMOND STREET,
Wal.Cr. EN7 14 DR26
Hammond St, NW5 83 DJ65
Hammondstreet Rd, Wal.Cr.
(Chsht) EN7 14 DR26
Hammond Way, SE28
off Oriole Way 88 EV73
Hamond Cl, S.Croy. CR2 159 DP109
Hamonde Cl, Edg. HA8 42 CP47
Ham Pk Rd, E7 86 EF66
E15 86 EF66
Hampden Av, Beck. BR3 143 DY96
Hampden Cl, NW1 195 N1
Epping (N.Wld Bas.) CM16 18 FA27
Slough (Stoke P.) SL2 74 AU69
Hampden Cres, Brwd. CM14 54 FW49
Waltham Cross (Chsht) EN7 14 DV31
Hampden Gurney St, W1 194 D9
Hampden La, N17 46 DT53
Hampden Pl, St.Alb. (Frog.) AL2 9 CE29
Hampden Rd, N8 65 DN56
N10 44 DG52
N17 46 DU53
N19 off Holloway Rd 65 DK61
Beckenham BR3 143 DY96
Gerrards Cross
(Chal.St.P.) SL9 36 AX53
Grays RM17 110 GB78
Harrow HA3 40 CC53
Kingston upon Thames KT1 138 CN97
Romford RM5 51 FB52
Slough SL3 93 AZ76
Hampden Sq, N14
off Osidge La 45 DH46
Hampden Way, N14 45 DH47
Watford WD17 23 BS36
Hampermill La, Wat. WD19 39 BT47
Hampshire Cl, N18
off Berkshire Gdns 46 DV50
Hampshire Hog La, W6
off King St 99 CV77
Hampshire Rd, N22 45 DM52
Hornchurch RM11 72 FN56
Hampshire St, NW5
off Torriano Av 83 DK65
Hampson Way, SW8 101 DM81
HAMPSTEAD, NW3 64 DD63
⊖ Hampstead 64 DC63
Hampstead Av, Wdf.Grn. IG8 49 EN52
Hampstead Cl, SE28 88 EV74
St. Albans AL2
off Bucknalls Dr 8 BZ31
Hampstead Gdns, NW11 64 DA58
Romford (Chad.Hth) RM6 70 EV57
HAMPSTEAD GARDEN SUBURB,
N2 64 DC57
Hampstead Grn, NW3 64 DE64
Hampstead Gro, NW3 64 DC62
★ Hampstead Heath, NW3 64 DD61
⇌ Hampstead Heath 64 DE63
Hampstead Hts, N2 64 DC56
Hampstead High St, NW3 64 DC63
Hampstead Hill Gdns, NW3 64 DD63
Hampstead La, N6 64 DD59
NW3 64 DD59
Hampstead Rd, NW1 83 DJ68
Hampstead Sq, NW3 64 DC62
Hampstead Wk, E3
off Waterside Cl 85 DZ67
Hampstead Way, NW11 64 DC60
HAMPTON 136 CB95
⇌ Hampton 136 CA95
Hampton Cl, N11
off Balmoral Av 45 DH50
NW6 82 DA69
SW20 119 CW94
⇌ Hampton Court 137 CE98
Hampton Ct, N1 off Upper St 83 DP65
Hampton Ct Av, E.Mol. KT8 137 CD99
Hampton Ct Cres, E.Mol. KT8 137 CD97
★ Hampton Court Palace & Pk,
E.Mol. KT8 137 CE97
Hampton Ct Par, E.Mol. KT8
off Creek Rd 137 CE98
Hampton Ct Rd, E.Mol. KT8 137 CF97
Hampton TW12 136 CC96
Kingston upon Thames KT1 137 CF97
Hampton Ct Way, E.Mol. KT8 137 CE100
Thames Ditton KT7 137 CE103
Hampton Cres, Grav. DA12 131 GL89
Hampton Fm Ind Est,
Felt. TW13 116 BZ90
Hampton Gro, Epsom KT17 157 CT111
HAMPTON HILL,
Hmptn. TW12 116 CC93
Hampton Hill Business Pk,
Hmptn. TW12
off Wellington Rd 116 CC92
Hampton La, Felt. TW13 116 BY91
Hampton Mead, Loug. IG10 33 EP41
Hampton Ms, NW10
off Minerva Rd 80 CR69
Hampton Ri, Har. HA3 62 CL58
Hampton Rd, E4 47 DZ50
E7 68 EH64
E11 67 ED60
Croydon CR0 142 DQ100
Hampton (Hmptn H.) TW12 117 CD92
Ilford IG1 69 EP63
Teddington TW11 117 CD92
Twickenham TW2 117 CD90
Worcester Park KT4 139 CU103
Hampton Rd E, Felt. TW13 116 BZ90
Hampton Rd W, Felt. TW13 116 BY89
Hampton St, SE1 200 G9
SE17 200 G9
HAMPTON WICK,
Kings.T. KT1 137 CH95
⇌ Hampton Wick 137 CJ95
Ham Ridings, Rich. TW10 118 CM92
HAMSEY GREEN, Warl. CR6 176 DW116
Hamsey Grn Gdns, Warl. CR6 176 DV116
Hamsey Way, S.Croy. CR2 176 DV115
Hamshades Cl, Sid. DA15 125 ET90
Ham St, Rich. TW10 117 CJ89
Ham Vw, Croy. CR0 143 DY100
Ham Yd, W1 195 M10
Hanah Ct, SW19 119 CX94
Hanameel St, E16 205 N2
Hana Ms, E5 off Goulton Rd 66 DW63
Hanbury Cl, NW4 63 CW55
Waltham Cross (Chsht) EN8 15 DX29
Hanbury Dr, E11
off High Rd Leytonstone 68 EF59
N21 29 DM43
Westerham (Bigg.H.) TN16 162 EH113
Hanbury Ms, N1 off Mary St 84 DQ67
Hanbury Path, Wok. GU21 151 BD114
Hanbury Rd, N17 46 DV54
W3 98 CP75
Hanbury St, E1 197 P6
Hanbury Wk, Bex. DA5 127 FE90
Hancock Ct, Borwd. WD6 26 CQ39
Hancock Rd, E3 85 EC69
SE19 122 DR93
Handa Wk, N1
off Clephane Rd 84 DR65
Hand Ct, WC1 196 C7
Handcroft Rd, Croy. CR0 141 DP101
Handel Cl, Edg. HA8 42 CM51
Handel Cres, Til. RM18 111 GG80
Handel Pl, NW10
off Mitchellbrook Way 80 CR65
Handel St, WC1 195 P4
Handel Way, Edg. HA8 42 CN52
Handen Rd, SE12 124 EE85
Handforth Rd, SW9 101 DN80
Ilford IG1 off Winston Way 69 EP62
Handley Gro, NW2 63 CX62
Handley Page Rd, Wall. SM6 159 DM108
Handley Rd, E9 84 DW66
Handowe Cl, NW4 63 CU56
Handpost Hill, Pot.B.
(Northaw) EN6 13 DH28
Handside Cl, Wor.Pk. KT4
off Carters Cl 139 CX102
Hands Wk, E16 86 EG72
Handsworth Av, E4 47 ED51
Handsworth Rd, N17 66 DR55
Handsworth Way, Wat. WD19
off Hayling Rd 39 BU48
Handtrough Way, Bark. IG11
off Fresh Wf Rd 87 EP68
Hanford Cl, SW18 120 DA88
Hanford Rd, S.Ock.
(Aveley) RM15 90 FQ74
Hanford Row, SW19 119 CW93
Hangar Ruding, Wat. WD19 40 BZ48
Hanger Grn, W5 80 CN70
Hanger Hill, Wey. KT13 153 BP107
⊖ Hanger Lane 80 CM69
Hanger La, W5 80 CM70
Hanger Vale La, W5 80 CM72
Hanger Vw Way, W3 80 CN72
Hanging Hill La, Brwd. CM13 55 GB48
Hanging Sword All, EC4 196 E9
Hangrove Hill, Orp. BR6 163 EP113
Hankey Pl, SE1 201 L5
Hankins La, NW7 42 CS48
Hanley Gdns, N4 65 DM60
Hanley Pl, Beck. BR3 123 EA94
Hanley Rd, N4 65 DL60
Hanmer Wk, N7
off Newington Barrow Way 65 DM62
Hannah Cl, NW10 62 CQ63
Beckenham BR3 143 EC97
Hannah Ct, N13 45 DM47
Hannah Mary Way, SE1 202 C9
Hannah Ms, Wall. SM6 159 DJ108
Hannards Way, Ilf. IG6 50 EV50
Hannay La, N8 65 DK59
Hannay Wk, SW16 121 DK89
Hannell Rd, SW6 99 CY80
Hannen Rd, SE27
off Norwood High St 121 DP90
Hannibal Rd, E1 84 DW71
Staines (Stanw.) TW19 114 BK87
Hannibal Way, Croy. CR0 159 DM106
Hannington Rd, SW4 101 DH83
Hanover Av, E16 205 M2
Feltham TW13 115 BU88
Hanover Circle, Hayes UB3 77 BQ72
Hanover Cl, Egh.
(Eng.Grn) TW20 112 AV93
Redhill RH1 185 DJ128
Richmond TW9 98 CN80
Slough SL1 92 AU76
Sutton SM3 157 CZ105
Hanover Ct, SE19
off Anerley Rd 122 DU94
W12 off Uxbridge Rd 81 CU74
Woking GU22
off Midhope Rd 166 AY119
Hanover Dr, Chis. BR7 125 EQ91
Hanover Gdns, SE11 101 DN79
Abbots Langley WD5 7 BT30
Ilford IG6 49 EQ52
Hanover Gate, NW1 194 C3
Hanover Gate Mans, NW1 194 C4
Hanover Ho, Surb. KT6
off Lenelby Rd 138 CN102
Hanover Pk, SE15 102 DU81
Hanover Pl, E3
off Brokesley St 85 DZ69
WC2 196 A9
Brentwood CM14
off Mascalls La 54 FV50
Hanover Rd, N15 66 DT56
NW10 81 CW66
SW19 120 DC94
Hanover Sq, W1 195 J9
Hanover St, W1 195 J9
Croydon CR0 off Abbey Rd 141 DP104
Hanover Ter, NW1 194 C3
Hanover Ter Ms, NW1 194 C3
Hanover Wk, Wey. KT13 135 BS104
Hanover Way, Bexh. DA6 106 EX83
Hanover W Ind Est, NW10 80 CR68
Hanover Yd, N1 off Noel Rd 83 DP68
Hansard Ms, W14
off Holland Rd 99 CX75
Hansart Way, Enf. EN2
off The Ridgeway 29 DN39
Hanscomb Ms, SW4
off Bromell's Rd 101 DJ84
Hans Cres, SW1 198 D6
Hanselin Cl, Stan. HA7 41 CF50
Hansen Dr, N21 29 DM43
Hanshaw Dr, Edg. HA8 42 CR53
Hansler Gro, E.Mol. KT8 137 CD98
Hansler Rd, SE22 122 DT85
Hansol Rd, Bexh. DA6 126 EY85
Hanson Cl, SW12 121 DH87
SW14 98 CQ83
Beckenham BR3 123 EB93
Loughton IG10
off Hanson Dr 33 EQ40
West Drayton UB7 94 BM76
Hanson Dr, Loug. IG10 33 EQ40
Hanson Gdns, Sthl. UB1 96 BY75
Hanson Grn, Loug. IG10
off Hanson Dr 33 EQ40
Hanson St, W1 195 K6
Hans Pl, SW1 198 E6
Hans Rd, SW3 198 D6
Hans St, SW1 198 E7
Hanway Pl, W1 195 M8
Hanway Rd, W7 79 CD72
Hanway St, W1 195 M8
HANWELL, W7 79 CF74
⇌ Hanwell 79 CE73
HANWORTH, Felt. TW13 116 BX91
Hanworth La, Cher. KT16 133 BF102
Hanworth Rd, Felt. TW13 115 BV88
Hampton TW12 116 CB93
Hounslow TW3, TW4 96 CB83
Sunbury-on-Thames TW16 115 BU94
Hanworth Ter, Houns. TW3 96 CB84
Hanworth Trd Est, Felt. TW13 116 BY90
Hanyards End, Pot.B.
(Cuffley) EN6 13 DL28
Hanyards La, Pot.B.
(Cuffley) EN6 13 DK28
Hapgood Cl, Grnf. UB6 61 CD64
Harads Pl, E1 202 C1
Harben Rd, NW6 82 DC66
Harberson Rd, E15 86 EF67
SW12 121 DH88
Harberton Rd, N19 65 DJ60
Harbet Rd, E4 47 DX50
N18 47 DX50
Harbet Rd, W2 194 A7
Harbex Cl, Bex. DA5 127 FB87
Harbinger Rd, E14 204 B9
Harbledown Pl, Orp. BR5 146 EW98
Harbledown Rd, SW6 100 DA81
South Croydon CR2 160 DU111
Harbord Cl, SE5
off De Crespigny Pk 102 DR82
Harbord St, SW6 99 CX81
Harborne Cl, Wat. WD19 40 BW50
Harborough Av, Sid. DA15 125 ES87
Harborough Rd, SW16 121 DM91
Harbour Av, SW10 100 DC81
Harbourer Cl, Ilf. IG6 50 EV50
Harbourer Rd, Ilf. IG6 50 EV50
Harbour Ex Sq, E14 204 C5
Harbourfield Rd, Bans. SM7 174 DB115
Harbour Reach, SW6
off The Boulevard 100 DC81
Harbour Rd, SE5 102 DQ83
Harbour Yd, SW10
off Harbour Av 100 DC81
Harbridge Av, SW15 119 CT87
Harbury Rd, Cars. SM5 158 DE109
Harbut Rd, SW11 100 DD84
Harcombe Rd, N16 66 DS62
Harcourt, Stai. (Wrays.) TW19 112 AY86
Harcourt Av, E12 69 EM63
Edgware HA8 42 CQ48
Sidcup DA15 126 EW86
Wallington SM6 159 DH105
Harcourt Cl, Egh. TW20 113 BC93
Isleworth TW7 97 CG83
Harcourt Fld, Wall. SM6 159 DH105
Harcourt Lo, Wall. SM6
off Croydon Rd 159 DH105
Harcourt Ms, Rom. RM2 71 FF57
Harcourt Rd, E15 86 EF68
N22 45 DK53
SE4 103 DY84
SW19 off Russell Rd 120 DA94
Bexleyheath DA6 106 EY84
Bushey WD23 24 CC43
Thornton Heath CR7 141 DM100
Wallington SM6 159 DH105
Harcourt St, W1 194 C7
Harcourt Ter, SW10 100 DB78
Hardcastle Cl, Croy. CR0 142 DU100
Hardcourts Cl, W.Wick. BR4 143 EB104
Hardell Cl, Egh. TW20 113 BA92
Hardel Ri, SW2 121 DP89
Hardel Wk, SW2
off Papworth Way 121 DN87
Harden Fm Cl, Couls. CR5 175 DJ121
Harden Rd, Grav.
(Nthflt) DA11 131 GF90
Hardens Manorway, SE7 104 EK76
Harders Rd, SE15 102 DV82
Hardess St, SE24
off Herne Hill Rd 102 DQ83
Hardie Cl, NW10 62 CR64
Hardie Rd, Dag. RM10 71 FC62
Harding Cl, SE17
off Hillingdon St 102 DQ79
Croydon CR0 142 DT104
Watford WD25 8 BW33
Hardinge Cl, Uxb. UB8
off Dawley Av 77 BP72
Hardinge Rd, N18 46 DS50
NW10 81 CV67
Hardinge St, E1 84 DW72
Harding Ho, Hayes UB3 77 BV72
Harding Rd, Bexh. DA7 106 EZ82
Epsom KT18 172 CS119
Grays RM16 111 GG76
Hardings Cl, Iver SL0 75 BD69
Harding's Cl, Kings.T. KT2 138 CM95
Hardings La, SE20 123 DX93
Harding Spur, Slou. SL3
off Ditton Rd 93 AZ78
Hardings Row, Iver SL0 75 BC69
Hardley Cres, Horn. RM11 72 FK56
Hardman Rd, SE7 205 P10
Kingston upon Thames KT2 138 CL96
Hardwick Cl, Lthd.
(Oxshott) KT22 170 CC115
Stanmore HA7 41 CJ50
Hardwick Cres, Dart. DA2 128 FP86
Hardwicke Av, Houns. TW5 96 CA81
Hardwicke Gdns, Amer. HP6 20 AS38
Hardwicke Ms, WC1 196 C3
Hardwicke Pl, St.Alb.
(Lon.Col.) AL2 9 CK27
Hardwicke Rd, N13 45 DL51
W4 98 CR77
Reigate RH2 184 DA133
Richmond TW10 117 CJ91
Hardwicke St, Bark. IG11 87 EQ67
Hardwick Grn, W13 79 CH71
Hardwick La, Cher.
(Lyne) KT16 133 BC101
Hardwick St, EC1 196 E3
Hardwicks Way, SW18
off Buckhold Rd 120 DA85
Hardwidge St, SE1 201 M4
Hardy Av, E16 205 N2
Gravesend (Nthflt) DA11 130 GE89
Ruislip HA4 59 BV64
Hardy Cl, SE16 203 J5
Barnet EN5 27 CY44
Pinner HA5 60 BX59
Hardy Gro, Dart. DA1 108 FN84
Hardy Rd, E4 47 DZ51
SE3 104 EF80
SW19 120 DB94
Hardys Cl, E.Mol. KT8
off Feltham Av 137 CE98
Hardy Way, Enf. EN2 29 DN39
Hare & Billet Rd, SE3 103 ED81
Harebell Dr, E6 87 EN71
Harebell Hill, Cob. KT11 154 BX114
Harebell Way, Rom. RM3 52 FK52
Harebreaks, The, Wat. WD24 23 BV38
Harecastle Cl, Hayes UB4
off Braunston Dr 78 BY70
Hare Ct, EC4 196 D9
Harecourt Rd, N1 84 DQ65
Hare Cres, Wat. WD25 7 BU32
Harecroft, Lthd. (Fetch.) KT22 170 CB123
Haredale Rd, SE24 102 DQ84
Haredon Cl, SE23 122 DW87
HAREFIELD, Uxb. UB9 38 BL53
Harefield, Esher KT10 155 CE105
Harefield Av, Sutt. SM2 157 CY109
Harefield Cl, Enf. EN2 29 DN39
H Harefield Hosp, Uxb. UB9 38 BJ53
Harefield Ms, SE4 103 DZ83
Harefield Rd, N8 65 DK57
SE4 103 DZ83
SW16 121 DM94
Rickmansworth WD3 38 BK50
Sidcup DA14 126 EX89
Uxbridge UB8 76 BK65
Harefield Rd Ind Est,
Rick. WD3 38 BL49
Hare Hall La, Rom. RM2 71 FH56
Hare Hill, Add. KT15 151 BF107
Hare Hill Cl, Wok.
(Pyrford) GU22 168 BG115
Harelands Cl, Wok. GU21 166 AW117
Harelands La, Wok. GU21 166 AW117
Hare La, Esher (Clay.) KT10 155 CE107
Hare Marsh, E2
off Cheshire St 84 DU70
Harendon, Tad. KT20 173 CW121
Hare Pl, EC4 196 E9
Hare Row, E2 84 DV68
Hares Bk, Croy.
(New Adgtn) CR0 161 ED110
Haresfield Rd, Dag. RM10 88 FA65
Harestone Dr, Cat. CR3 176 DT124
Harestone Hill, Cat. CR3 186 DT126
Harestone La, Cat. CR3 186 DS125
H Harestone Marie Curie Cen,
Cat. CR3 186 DT125
Harestone Valley Rd, Cat. CR3 186 DT126
Hare St, SE18 105 EN76
Hare Ter, Grays RM20
off Mill La 109 FX78
Hare Wk, N1 197 N1
Harewood, Rick. WD3 22 BH43
Harewood Av, NW1 194 C5
Northolt UB5 78 BY66
Harewood Cl, Nthlt. UB5 78 BZ66
Reigate RH2 184 DC132
Harewood Dr, Ilf. IG5 49 EM54
Harewood Gdns,
S.Croy. CR2 176 DV115
Harewood Hill, Epp.
(They.B.) CM16 33 ES35
Harewood Pl, W1 195 J9
Slough SL1 92 AU76
Harewood Rd, SW19 120 DE93
Brentwood (Pilg.Hat.) CM15 54 FV44
Chalfont St. Giles HP8 20 AW41
Isleworth TW7 97 CF80
South Croydon CR2 160 DS107
Watford WD19 39 BV48
Harewood Row, NW1 194 C6
Harewood Ter, Sthl. UB2 96 BZ77
Harfield Gdns, SE5 102 DS83
Harfield Rd, Sun. TW16 136 BX96
Harford Cl, E4 47 EB45
Harford Dr, Wat. WD17 23 BS38
Harford Ms, N19
off Wedmore St 65 DK62
Harford Rd, E4 47 EB45
Harford St, E1 85 DY70
Harford Wk, N2 64 DD57
Harfst Way, Swan. BR8 147 FC95
Hargood Cl, Har. HA3 62 CL58
Hargood Rd, SE3 104 EJ81
Hargrave Pk, N19 65 DJ61
Hargrave Pl, N7
off Brecknock Rd 65 DK64
Hargrave Rd, N19 65 DJ61
Hargreaves Av, Wal.Cr.
(Chsht) EN7 14 DV30
Hargreaves Cl, Wal.Cr.
(Chsht) EN7 14 DV31
Hargwyne St, SW9 101 DM83
Haringey Pk, N8 65 DL58
Haringey Pas, N4 65 DP58
N8 65 DN56
Haringey Rd, N8 65 DL56
Harington Ter, N9 46 DR48
N18 46 DR48
Harkett Cl, Har. HA3
off Byron Rd 41 CF54
Harkett Ct, Har. HA3 41 CF54
Harkness, Wal.Cr. (Chsht) EN7 14 DU29
Harkness Cl, Epsom KT17 173 CW116
Romford RM3 52 FM50
Harland Av, Croy. CR0 142 DT104
Sidcup DA15 125 ER90
Harland Cl, SW19 140 DB97
Harland Rd, SE12 124 EG88
Harlands Gro, Orp. BR6
off Pinecrest Gdns 163 EP105
Harlech Gdns, Houns. TW5 96 BW79
Pinner HA5 60 BX59
Harlech Rd, N14 45 DL48
Abbots Langley WD5 7 BU31
Harlech Twr, W3 98 CP75
Harlequin Av, Brent. TW8 97 CG79
Harlequin Cen, Wat. WD17 24 BW42
Harlequin Cl, Hayes UB4
off Cygnet Way 78 BX71
Isleworth TW7 117 CE85
Harlequin Ho, Erith DA18
off Kale Rd 106 EY76
Harlequin Rd, Tedd. TW11 117 CH94
★ Harlequins F.C. (Rugby),
Twick. TW2 117 CE87
Harlescott Rd, SE15 103 DX84
HARLESDEN, NW10 80 CS68
⇌ Harlesden 80 CR68
⊖ Harlesden 80 CR68
Harlesden Cl, Rom. RM3 52 FM52
Harlesden Gdns, NW10 81 CT67
Harlesden La, NW10 81 CU67
Harlesden Rd, NW10 81 CU67
Romford RM3 52 FM51
Harlesden Wk, Rom. RM3
off Harlesden Rd 52 FM52
Harleston Cl, E5
off Theydon Rd 66 DW61
Harley Cl, Wem. HA0 79 CK65
Harley Ct, E11
off Blake Hall Rd 68 EG59

★ Place of interest ⇌ Railway station ⊖ London Underground station DLR Docklands Light Railway station Tra Tramlink station H Hospital Riv Pedestrian ferry landing stage

266

Har - Hau

Harley Cres, Har. HA1 61 CD56
Harleyford, Brom. BR1 144 EH95
Harleyford Rd, SE11 101 DM79
Harleyford St, SE11 101 DN79
Harley Gdns, SW10 100 DC78
Orpington BR6 163 ES105
Harley Gro, E3 85 DZ69
Harley Pl, W1 195 H7
Harley Rd, NW3 82 DD66
NW10 80 CS68
Harrow HA1 61 CD56
Harley St, W1 195 H7
Harling Ct, SW11
off Latchmere Rd 100 DF82
Harlinger St, SE18 104 EL76
HARLINGTON, Hayes UB3 95 BQ79
Harlington Cl, Hayes UB3
off New Rd 95 BQ80
Harlington Rd, Bexh. DA7 106 EY83
Hounslow (Hthrw Air.) TW6 95 BT84
Uxbridge UB8 77 BP71
Harlington Rd E,
Felt. TW13, TW14 115 BV87
Harlington Rd W, Felt. TW14 115 BV86
Harlow Gdns, Rom. RM5 51 FC51
Harlow Rd, N13 46 DR48
Rainham RM13 89 FF67
Harlton Ct, Wal.Abb. EN9 16 EF34
Harlyn Dr, Pnr. HA5 59 BV55
Harman Av, Grav. DA11 131 GH92
Woodford Green IG8 48 EF52
Harman Cl, E4 47 ED49
NW2 63 CY62
Harman Dr, NW2 63 CY62
Sidcup DA15 125 ET86
Harman Pl, Pur. CR8 159 DP111
Harman Rd, Enf. EN1 30 DT43
Harmer Rd, Swans. DA10 130 FZ86
Harmer St, Grav. DA12 131 GJ86
HARMONDSWORTH,
West Dr. UB7 94 BK79
Harmondsworth La,
West Dr. UB7 94 BL79
Harmondsworth Rd,
West Dr. UB7 94 BL78
Harmony Cl, NW11 63 CY57
Wallington SM6 159 DL109
Harmony Ter, Har. HA2
off Goldsmith Cl 60 CB60
Harmony Way, NW4
off Victoria Rd 63 CW56
Harmood Gro, NW1
off Clarence Way 83 DH66
Harmood Pl, NW1
off Harmood St 83 DH66
Harmood St, NW1 83 DH66
Harmsworth Ms, SE11 200 F7
Harmsworth St, SE17 101 DP78
Harmsworth Way, N20 43 CZ46
Harness Rd, SE28 106 EU75
Harnetts Cl, Swan. BR8 147 FD100
Harold Av, Belv. DA17 106 EZ78
Hayes UB3 95 BT76
Harold Ct Rd, Rom. RM3 52 FP51
Harold Cres, Wal.Abb. EN9 15 EC32
Harold Est, SE1 201 N7
Harold Gibbons Ct, SE7 104 EJ79
HAROLD HILL, Rom. RM3 52 FL50
Harold Hill Ind Est, Rom. RM3 52 FK52
Harold Laski Ho, EC1 196 F3
HAROLD PARK, Rom. RM3 52 FN51
Harold Pl, SE11 101 DN78
Harold Rd, E4 47 EC49
E11 68 EE60
E13 86 EH67
N8 65 DM57
N15 66 DT57
NW10 80 CR69
SE19 122 DS93
Dartford (Hawley) DA2 128 FM91
Sutton SM1 158 DD105
Woodford Green IG8 48 EG53
Haroldstone Rd, E17 67 DX57
Harold Vw, Rom. RM3 52 FM54
HAROLD WOOD, Rom. RM3 52 FL54
⇌ Harold Wood 52 FM53
H Harold Wd Hosp,
Rom. RM3 52 FL54
Harp All, EC4 196 F8
Harpenden Rd, E12 68 EJ61
SE27 121 DP90
Harpenmead Pt, NW2
off Granville Rd 63 CZ61
H Harperbury Hosp,
Rad. WD7 9 CJ31
Harper Cl, N14
off Alexandra Ct 29 DJ43
Grays RM16
off Hedingham Rd 109 FW78
Harper La, Rad. WD7 9 CG32
Harper Ms, SW17 120 DC90
Harper Rd, E6 87 EM72
SE1 201 H6
Harpers Yd, N17
off Ruskin Rd 46 DT53
Harpesford Av, Vir.W. GU25 132 AV99
Harp Island Cl, NW10 62 CR61
Harp La, EC3 201 M1
Harpley Sq, E1 84 DW69
Harpour Rd, Bark. IG11 87 EQ65
Harp Rd, W7 79 CF70
Harpsden St, SW11 100 DG81
Harps Oak La, Red. RH1 184 DF125
Harpswood, Couls. CR5
off Jennys Way 175 DJ122
Harpur Ms, WC1 196 B6
Harpurs, Tad. KT20 173 CX122
Harpur St, WC1 196 B6
Harraden Rd, SE3 104 EJ81
Harrap Chase, Grays
(Bad.Dene) RM17 110 FZ78
Harrap St, E14 85 EC73
Harrier Av, E11
off Eastern Av 68 EH58
Harrier Cl, Horn. RM12 89 FH65
Harrier Ms, SE28 105 ER76
Harrier Rd, NW9 42 CS54
Harriers Cl, W5 80 CL73
Harrier Way, E6 87 EM70
Waltham Abbey EN9 16 EG34
Harriescourt, Wal.Abb. EN9 16 EG32
Harries Rd, Hayes UB4 78 BW70
Harriet Cl, E8 84 DU67
Harriet Gdns, Croy. CR0 142 DU103
Harriet St, SW1 198 E5
Harriet Tubman Cl, SW2 121 DN87
Harriet Wk, SW1 198 E5
Harriet Walker Way, Rick. WD3
off Thellusson Way 37 BF45
Harriet Way, Bushey WD23 41 CD45
HARRINGAY, N8 65 DN57
⇌ Harringay 65 DN58
Harringay Gdns, N8 65 DP56
⇌ Harringay Green Lanes 65 DP58
Harringay Rd, N15 65 DP57
Harrington Cl, NW10 62 CR62
Croydon CR0 141 DL103
Harrington Ct, W10
off Dart St 81 CZ69
Harrington Gdns, SW7 100 DB77
Harrington Hill, E5 66 DV60
Tra Harrington Road 142 DW97
Harrington Rd, E11 68 EE60
SE25 142 DU98
SW7 100 DD77
Harrington Sq, NW1 195 K1
Harrington St, NW1 195 K2
Harrington Way, SE18 104 EK76
Harriott Cl, SE10 205 K9
Harriotts Cl, Ashtd. KT21
off Harriotts La 171 CJ120
Harriotts La, Ashtd. KT21 171 CJ119
Harris Cl, Enf. EN2 29 DP39
Gravesend (Nthflt) DA11 130 GE90
Hounslow TW3 96 CA81
Romford RM3 52 FL52
Harris La, Rad. (Shenley) WD7 10 CN34
Harrison Cl, N20 44 DE46
Brentwood (Hutt.) CM13 55 GD43
Northwood HA6 39 BQ51
Harrison Ct, Shep. TW17
off Greeno Cres 135 BP99
Harrison Dr, Epp.
(N.Wld Bas.) CM16 19 FB26
Harrison Rd, Dag. RM10 89 FB65
Harrisons Ri, Croy. CR0 141 DP104
Harrison St, WC1 196 A3
Harrisons Wf, Purf. RM19 108 FN78
Harrison Wk, Wal.Cr.
(Chsht) EN8 15 DX30
Harrison Way, Sev. TN13 190 FG122
Waltham Abbey EN9
off Greenwich Way 31 EC36
Harris Rd, Bexh. DA7 106 EY81
Dagenham RM9 70 EZ64
Watford WD25 23 BU35
Harris St, E17 67 DZ59
SE5 102 DR80
Harris Way, Sun. TW16 135 BS95
★ Harrods, SW1 198 D6
Harrogate Ct, N11
off Coverdale Rd 44 DG51
Slough SL3 93 BA78
Harrogate Rd, Wat. WD19 40 BW48
Harrold Rd, Dag. RM8 70 EV64
HARROW 61 CD59
⇌ Harrow & Wealdstone 61 CE56
⊖ Harrow & Wealdstone 61 CE56
★ Harrow Arts Cen, Pnr. HA5 40 CB52
Harrow Av, Enf. EN1 30 DT44
Harroway Rd, SW11 100 DD82
Harrow Bottom Rd,
Vir.W. GU25 133 AZ100
Harrowby Gdns, Grav.
(Nthflt) DA11 130 GE89
Harrowby St, W1 194 C8
Harrow Cl, Add. KT15 134 BH103
Chessington KT9 155 CK108
Harrow Cres, Rom. RM3 51 FH52
Harrowdene Cl, Wem. HA0 61 CK63
Harrowdene Gdns,
Tedd. TW11 117 CG93
Harrowdene Rd, Wem. HA0 61 CK62
Harrow Dr, N9 46 DT46
Hornchurch RM11 71 FH60
Harrowes Meade, Edg. HA8 42 CN48
Harrow Flds Gdns, Har. HA1 61 CE62
Harrow Gdns, Orp. BR6 164 EV105
Warlingham CR6 177 DZ115
Harrowgate Rd, E9 85 DY65
Harrow Grn, E11
off Harrow Rd 68 EE62
Harrow La, E14 204 D1
Harrow Manorway, SE2 88 EW74
Harrow Mkt, Slou. SL3 93 BA76
★ Harrow Mus & Heritage Cen,
Har. HA2 60 CC55
HARROW ON THE HILL,
Har. HA1 61 CE61
⇌ Harrow on the Hill 61 CE58
⊖ Harrow on the Hill 61 CE58
Harrow Pk, Har. HA1 61 CE61
Harrow Pas, Kings.T. KT1
off Market Pl 137 CK96
Harrow Pl, E1 197 N8
Harrow Rd, E6 86 EL67
E11 68 EE62
NW10 81 CV69
W2 81 CZ70
W9 81 CZ70
W10 81 CX70
Barking IG11 87 ES67
Carshalton SM5 158 DE106
Feltham TW14 114 BN88
Ilford IG1 69 EQ63
Sevenoaks (Knock.) TN14 180 EY115
Slough SL3 93 AZ76
Warlingham CR6 177 DZ115
Wembley HA0 61 CJ64
Wembley (Tkgtn) HA9 62 CM64
★ Harrow Sch, Har. HA1 61 CE60
Harrow Vw, Har. HA1, HA2 61 CD56
Hayes UB3 77 BU72
Uxbridge UB10 77 BQ69
Harrow Vw Rd, W5 79 CH70
Harrow Way, Shep. TW17 135 BQ96
Watford WD19 40 BY48
HARROW WEALD, Har. HA3 41 CD53
Harrow Weald Pk, Har. HA3 41 CD51
Harston Dr, Enf. EN3 31 EA38
Hart Cl, Red. (Bletch.) RH1 186 DT134
Hart Cor, Grays RM20 109 FX78
Hart Cres, Chig. IG7 49 ET50
Hart Dyke Cres, Swan. BR8
off Hart Dyke Rd 147 FD97
Hart Dyke Rd, Orp. BR5 146 EW102
Swanley BR8 147 FD97
Harte Rd, Houns. TW3 96 BZ82
Hartfield Av, Borwd.
(Elstree) WD6 26 CN43
Northolt UB5 77 BV68
Hartfield Cl, Borwd.
(Elstree) WD6 26 CN43
Hartfield Cres, SW19 119 CZ94
West Wickham BR4 144 EG104
Hartfield Gro, SE20 142 DV95
Hartfield Pl, Grav.
(Nthflt) DA11 130 GD87
Hartfield Rd, SW19 119 CZ94
Chessington KT9 155 CK106
West Wickham BR4 162 EG105
Hartfield Ter, E3 85 EA68
Hartford Av, Har. HA3 61 CG55
Hartforde Rd, Borwd. WD6 26 CN40
Hartford Rd, Bex. DA5 126 FA86
Epsom KT19 156 CN107
Hart Gro, W5 80 CN74
Southall UB1 78 CA71
Harthall La, Hem.H. HP3 7 BS26
Kings Langley WD4 7 BP28
Hartham Cl, N7 65 DL64
Isleworth TW7 97 CG81
Hartham Rd, N7 65 DL64
N17 46 DT54
Isleworth TW7 97 CF81
Harting Rd, SE9 124 EL91
Hartington Cl, Har. HA1 61 CE63
Hartington Ct, W4 98 CP80
Hartington Pl, Reig. RH2 184 DA132
Hartington Rd, E16 86 EH72
E17 67 DY58
SW8 101 DL81
W4 98 CP80
W13 79 CH73
Southall UB2 96 BY75
Twickenham TW1 117 CH87
Hartismere Rd, SW6 99 CZ80
Hartlake Rd, E9 85 DX65
Hartland Cl, N21
off Elmscott Gdns 30 DQ44
Addlestone
(New Haw) KT15 152 BJ110
Edgware HA8 42 CN47
Hartland Dr, Edg. HA8 42 CN47
Ruislip HA4 59 BV62
Hartland Rd, E15 86 EF66
N11 44 DF50
NW1 83 DH66
NW6 81 CZ68
Addlestone KT15 152 BG108
Epping CM16 18 EU31
Hampton (Hmptn H.) TW12 116 CB91
Hornchurch RM12 71 FG61
Isleworth TW7 97 CG83
Morden SM4 140 DA101
Waltham Cross (Chsht) EN8 15 DX30
Hartlands Cl, Bex. DA5 126 EZ86
Hartland Way, Croy. CR0 143 DY103
Morden SM4 139 CZ101
Hartlepool Ct, E16
off Fishguard Way 105 EP75
Hartley Av, E6 86 EL67
NW7 43 CT50
Hartley Cl, NW7 43 CT50
Bromley BR1 145 EM96
Slough (Stoke P.) SL3 74 AW67
Hartley Copse, Wind.
(Old Wind.) SL4 112 AU86
Hartley Down, Pur. CR8 159 DM113
Hartley Fm Est, Pur. CR8 175 DM115
HARTLEY GREEN, Long. DA3 149 FX99
Hartley Hill, Pur. CR8 175 DM115
Hartley Old Rd, Pur. CR8 159 DM114
Hartley Rd, E11 68 EF60
Croydon CR0 141 DP101
Welling DA16 106 EW80
Westerham TN16 189 ER125
Hartley St, E2 84 DW69
Hartley Way, Pur. CR8 175 DM115
Hartmann Rd, E16 86 EK74
Hartmoor Ms, Enf. EN3 31 DX37
Hartnoll St, N7 off Eden Gro 65 DM64
Harton Cl, Brom. BR1 144 EK95
Harton Rd, N9 46 DV47
Harton St, SE8 103 EA81
Hart Rd,
W.Byf. (Byfleet) KT14 152 BL113
Hartsbourne Av, Bushey
(Bushey Hth) WD23 40 CC47
Hartsbourne Cl, Bushey
(Bushey Hth) WD23 41 CD47
Hartsbourne Rd, Bushey
(Bushey Hth) WD23 41 CD47
Harts Cl, Bushey WD23 24 CA40
Hartscroft, Croy. CR0 161 DY109
Harts Gro, Wdf.Grn. IG8 48 EG50
Hartshill Cl, Uxb. UB10 76 BN65
Hartshill Rd, Grav.
(Nthflt) DA11 131 GF89
Hartshill Wk, Wok. GU21 166 AV116
Hartshorn All, EC3 197 N9
Hartshorn Gdns, E6 87 EN70
Hartslands Rd, Sev. TN13 191 FJ123
Harts La, SE14 103 DY80
Barking IG11 87 EP65
Hartslock Dr, SE2 106 EX75
Hartsmead Rd, SE9 125 EM89
Hartspring La, Bushey WD23 24 CA39
Watford WD25 24 CA39
Hart St, EC3 197 N10
Brentwood CM14 54 FW47
Hartsway, Enf. EN3 30 DW42
Hartswood Cl, Brwd. CM14 54 FY49
Hartswood Gdns, W12 99 CT76
Hartswood Grn, Bushey
(Bushey Hth) WD23 41 CD47
Hartswood Rd, W12 99 CT75
Brentwood CM14 54 FY49
Hartsworth Cl, E13 86 EF68
Hartville Rd, SE18 105 ES77
Hartwell Dr, E4 47 EC51
Hartwell St, E8
off Dalston La 84 DT65
Harvard Hill, W4 98 CP79
Harvard La, W4 98 CP78
Harvard Rd, SE13 123 EC85
W4 98 CP78
Isleworth TW7 97 CE81
Harvard Wk, Horn. RM12 71 FG63
Harvel Cl, Orp. BR5 146 EU97
Harvel Cres, SE2 106 EX78
Harvest Bk Rd, W.Wick. BR4 144 EF104
Harvest Ct, Shep. TW17 134 BN98
Harvest End, Wat. WD25 24 BX36
Harvester Rd, Epsom KT19 156 CR110
Harvesters Cl, Islw. TW7 117 CD85
Harvest La, Loug. IG10 48 EK45
Thames Ditton KT7 137 CG100
Harvest Rd, Bushey WD23 24 CB42
Egham (Eng.Grn) TW20 112 AX92
Feltham TW13 115 BU91
Harvest Way, Swan. BR8 147 FD101
Harvey, Grays RM16 110 GB75
Harvey Dr, Hmptn. TW12 136 CB95
Harveyfields, Wal.Abb. EN9 15 EC34
Harvey Gdns, E11
off Harvey Rd 68 EF60
SE7 104 EJ78
Loughton IG10 33 EP41
Harvey Ho, Brent. TW8
off Green Dragon La 98 CL78
Harvey Pt, E16 off Fife Rd 86 EH71
Harvey Rd, E11 68 EE60
N8 65 DM57
SE5 102 DR81
Hounslow TW4 116 BZ87
Ilford IG1 69 EP64
Northolt UB5 78 BW66
Rickmansworth
(Crox.Grn) WD3 22 BN44
St. Albans (Lon.Col.) AL2 9 CJ26
Slough SL3 93 BB76
Uxbridge UB10 76 BN68
Walton-on-Thames KT12 135 BU101
Harveys La, Rom. RM7 71 FD61
Harvey St, N1 84 DR67
Harvill Rd, Sid. DA14 126 EX92
Harvil Rd, Uxb. (Hare.) UB9 58 BK58
Uxbridge (Ickhm) UB10 58 BL60
Harvington Wk, E8
off Wilman Gro 84 DU66
Harvist Est, N7 65 DN63
Harvist Rd, NW6 81 CX69
Harwater Dr, Loug. IG10 33 EM40
Harwell Cl, Ruis. HA4 59 BR60
Harwell Pas, N2 64 DF56
Harwood Av, Brom. BR1 144 EH96
Hornchurch RM11 72 FL55
Mitcham CR4 140 DE97
Harwood Cl, N12
off Summerfields Av 44 DE51
Wembley HA0
off Harrowdene Rd 61 CK63
Harwood Dr, Uxb. UB10 76 BM67
Harwood Gdns, Wind.
(Old Wind.) SL4 112 AV87
Harwood Hall La,
Upmin. RM14 90 FP65
Harwood Rd, SW6 100 DA80
Harwoods Rd, Wat. WD18 23 BU42
Harwoods Yd, N21
off Wades Hill 45 DN45
Harwood Ter, SW6 100 DB81
Hascombe Ter, SE5
off Love Wk 102 DR82
Haselbury Rd, N9 46 DS49
N18 46 DS49
Haseldine Rd, St.Alb.
(Lon.Col.) AL2 9 CK26
Haseley End, SE23
off Tyson Rd 122 DW87
Haselrigge Rd, SW4 101 DK84
Haseltine Rd, SE26 123 DZ91
Haselwood Dr, Enf. EN2 29 DP42
Haskard Rd, Dag. RM9 70 EX63
Hasker St, SW3 198 C8
Haslam Av, Sutt. SM3 139 CY102
Haslam Cl, N1 83 DN66
Uxbridge UB10 59 BQ61
Haslam St, SE15 102 DT80
Haslemere Av, NW4 63 CX58
SW18 120 DB89
W7 97 CG76
W13 97 CG76
Barnet EN4 44 DF46
Hounslow TW5 96 BW82
Mitcham CR4 140 DD96
Haslemere Cl, Hmptn. TW12 116 BZ92
Wallington SM6
off Stafford Rd 159 DL106
Haslemere Gdns, N3 63 CZ55
Haslemere Heathrow Est,
Houns. TW4 95 BV82
Haslemere Rd, N8 65 DK59
N21 45 DP47
Bexleyheath DA7 106 EZ82
Ilford IG3 69 ET61
Thornton Heath CR7 141 DP99
Hasler Cl, SE28 88 EV73
Haslett Rd, Shep. TW17 135 BS96
Hasluck Gdns, Barn. EN5 28 DC44
Hassard St, E2
off Hackney Rd 84 DT68
Hassendean Rd, SE3 104 EH79
Hassett Rd, E9 85 DX65
Hassocks Cl, SE26 122 DV90
Hassocks Rd, SW16 141 DK95
Hassock Wd, Kes. BR2 162 EK105
Hassop Rd, NW2 63 CX63
Hassop Wk, SE9 124 EL91
Hasted Cl, Green. DA9 129 FW86
Hasted Rd, SE7 104 EK78
Hastings Av, Ilf. IG6 69 EQ56
Hastings Cl, SE15 102 DU80
Barnet EN5
off Leicester Rd 28 DC42
Grays RM17 110 FY79
Wembley HA0 61 CJ63
Hastings Dr, Surb. KT6 137 CJ100
Hastings Ho, SE18 105 EM77
Hastings Rd, N11 45 DJ50
N17 66 DR55
W13 79 CH73
Bromley BR2 144 EL102
Croydon CR0 142 DT102
Romford RM2 71 FH57
Hastings St, SE18 105 EQ76
WC1 195 P3
Hastings Way, Bushey WD23 24 BY42
Rickmansworth
(Crox.Grn) WD3 23 BP42
Hastingwood Trd Est, N18 47 DX51
Hastoe Cl, Hayes UB4
off Kingsash Dr 78 BY70
Hat & Mitre Ct, EC1 196 G5
Hatch, The, Enf. EN3 31 DX39
Hatcham Pk Ms, SE14
off Hatcham Pk Rd 103 DX81
Hatcham Pk Rd, SE14 103 DX81
Hatcham Rd, SE15 102 DW79
Hatchard Rd, N19 65 DK61
Hatch Cl, Add. KT15 134 BH104
Hatchcroft, NW4 63 CV55
HATCH END, Pnr. HA5 40 BY51
⇌ Hatch End 40 BZ52
Hatchers Ms, SE1 201 N5
Hatchett Rd, Felt. TW14 115 BQ88
Hatch Gdns, Tad. KT20 173 CX120
Hatch Gro, Rom. RM6 70 EY56
Hatchlands Rd, Red. RH1 184 DE134
Hatch La, E4 47 ED49
Cobham KT11 169 BP119
Coulsdon CR5 174 DG115
West Drayton UB7 94 BK80
Woking (Ockham) GU23 169 BP120
Hatch Pl, Kings.T. KT2 118 CM92
Hatch Rd, SW16 141 DL96
Brentwood (Pilg.Hat.) CM15 54 FU43
Hatch Side, Chig. IG7 49 EN50
Hatchwood Cl, Wdf.Grn. IG8
off Sunset Av 48 EF49
Hatcliffe Cl, SE3 104 EF83
Hatcliffe St, SE10 205 K10
Hatfield Cl, SE14
off Reaston St 103 DX80
Brentwood (Hutt.) CM13 55 GD45
Hornchurch RM12 72 FK64
Ilford IG6 69 EP55
Mitcham CR4 140 DD98
Sutton SM2 158 DA109
West Byfleet KT14 152 BH112
Hatfield Mead, Mord. SM4
off Central Rd 140 DA99
Hatfield Rd, E15 68 EE64
W4 98 CR75
W13 79 CG74
Ashtead KT21 172 CM119
Dagenham RM9 88 EY65
Grays (Chaff.Hun.) RM16 109 FX77
Potters Bar EN6 12 DC30
Slough SL1 92 AU75
Watford WD24 23 BV39
Hatfields, SE1 200 E2
Loughton IG10 33 EP41
Hathaway Cl, Brom. BR2 145 EM102
Ruislip HA4
off Stafford Rd 59 BT63
Stanmore HA7 41 CG50
Hathaway Cres, E12 87 EM65
Hathaway Gdns, W13 79 CF71
Grays RM17
off Hathaway Rd 110 GB76
Romford RM6 70 EX57
Hathaway Rd, Croy. CR0 141 DP101
Grays RM17 110 GB77
Hatherleigh Cl, NW7 43 CX52
Chessington KT9 155 CK106
Morden SM4 140 DA98
Hatherleigh Gdns, Pot.B. EN6 12 DD32
Hatherleigh Rd, Ruis. HA4 59 BU61
Hatherleigh Way, Rom. RM3 52 FK53
Hatherley Cres, Sid. DA14 126 EU89
Hatherley Gdns, E6 86 EK68
N8 65 DL58
Hatherley Gro, W2 82 DB72
Hatherley Ms, E17 67 EA56
Hatherley Rd, E17 67 DZ56
Richmond TW9 98 CM82
Sidcup DA14 126 EU91
Hatherley St, SW1 199 L8
Hathern Gdns, SE9 125 EN91
Hatherop Rd, Hmptn. TW12 116 BZ94
Hatherwood, Lthd. KT22 171 CK121
Hathorne Cl, SE15 102 DV82
Hathway St, SE15
off Gibbon Rd 102 DW82
Hathway Ter, SE14
off Kitto Rd 102 DW82
Hatley Av, Ilf. IG6 69 EQ56
Hatley Cl, N11 44 DF50
Hatley Rd, N4 65 DM61
Hatteraick St, SE16 202 G4
Hattersfield Cl, Belv. DA17 106 EZ77
Hatters La, Wat. WD18 23 BR44
HATTON, Felt. TW14 95 BT84
Hatton Cl, SE18 105 ER80
Gravesend (Nthflt) DA11 130 GE90
Grays (Chaff.Hun.) RM16 109 FX76
Hatton Ct, E5 off Gilpin Rd 67 DY63
⊖ Hatton Cross 95 BT84
Hatton Gdn, EC1 196 E6
Hatton Gdns, Mitch. CR4 140 DF99
Hatton Grn, Felt. TW14 95 BU84
Hatton Gro, West Dr. UB7 94 BK75
Hatton Ho, E1
off Cable St 84 DU73
Hatton Pl, EC1 196 E5
Hatton Rd, Croy. CR0 141 DN102
Feltham TW14 115 BS85
Waltham Cross
(Chsht) EN8 15 DX29
Hatton Row, NW8 194 A5
Hatton St, NW8 194 A5
Hatton Wall, EC1 196 D6
Haul Rd, NW1 83 DL68

A B C D E F G H I J K L M N O P Q R S T U V W X Y Z

Haunch of Venison Yd, W1 . . . . 195 H9
Havana Cl, Rom. RM1
  off Exchange St. 71 FE57
Havana Rd, SW19 . . . . 120 DA89
Havannah St, E14 . . . . 204 A5
Havant Rd, E17 . . . . 67 EC55
Havant Way, SE15
  off Daniel Gdns. 102 DT80
Havelock Pl, Har. HA1 . . . . 61 CE58
Havelock Rd, N17 . . . . 46 DU54
  SW19 . . . . 120 DC92
  Belvedere DA17 . . . . 106 EZ77
  Bromley BR2 . . . . 144 EJ98
  Croydon CR0 . . . . 142 DT102
  Dartford DA1 . . . . 127 FH87
  Gravesend DA11 . . . . 131 GF88
  Harrow HA3 . . . . 61 CE55
  Kings Langley WD4 . . . . 6 BN28
  Southall UB2 . . . . 96 BZ76
Havelock St, N1 . . . . 83 DL67
  Ilford IG1 . . . . 69 EP61
Havelock Ter, SW8 . . . . 101 DH80
Havelock Wk, SE23 . . . . 122 DW88
Haven, The, SE26
  off Springfield Rd 122 DV92
  Grays RM16. . . . . 111 GF78
  Richmond TW9 . . . . 98 CN83
  Sunbury-on-Thames TW16. 115 BU94
Haven Cl, SE9 . . . . 125 EM90
  SW19 . . . . 119 CX90
  Gravesend
  (Istead Rise) DA13 . . . . . 131 GF94
  Hayes UB4 . . . . 77 BS71
  Sidcup DA14. . . . . 126 EW93
  Swanley BR8. . . . . 147 FF96
Haven Ct, Esher KT10
  off Portsmouth Rd 137 CE103
Havengore Av, Grav. DA12 . . . 131 GL87
Haven Grn, W5 . . . . 79 CK72
Haven Grn Ct, W5
  off Haven Grn. 79 CK72
Havenhurst Ri, Enf. EN2 . . . . . . 29 DN40
Haven La, W5 . . . . 80 CL72
Haven Ms, E3
  off St. Pauls Way. 85 DZ71
Haven Pl, W5
  off The Broadway 79 CK73
  Grays RM16. . . . . 110 GC75
Haven Rd, Ashf. TW15. . . . . . . 115 BP91
Havensfield, Kings L.
  (Chipper.) WD4 . . . . 6 BH31
Haven St, NW1
  off Castlehaven Rd 83 DH66
Haven Ter, W5
  off The Broadway 79 CK73
Havenwood, Wem. HA9 . . . . . . 62 CP62
Havenwood Cl, Brwd. CM13
  off Wilmot Grn 53 FW51
Haverfield Gdns, Rich. TW9 . . 98 CN80
Haverfield Rd, E3 . . . . 85 DY69
Haverford Way, Edg. HA8 . . . . 42 CM53
Haverhill Rd, E4 . . . . 47 EC46
  SW12. . . . . 121 DJ88
HAVERING-ATTE-BOWER,
  Rom. RM4. . . . . 51 FE48
Havering Dr, Rom. RM1 . . . . . . 71 FE56
Havering Gdns, Rom. RM6. . . . 70 EW57
HAVERING PARK, Rom. RM5. 50 FA50
Havering Rd, Rom. RM1 . . . . . . 71 FD55
Havering St, E1
  off Devonport St. 85 DX72
Havering Way, Bark. IG11 . . . . 88 EV69
Havers Av, Walt. KT12. . . . . . 154 BX106
Haversfield Est, Brent. TW8 . . 98 CL78
Haversham Cl, Twick. TW1 . . . 117 CK86
Haversham Pl, N6. . . . . 64 DF61
Haverstock Ct, Orp. BR5. . . . . 146 EU96
Haverstock Hill, NW3 . . . . 64 DE64
Haverstock Pl, N1
  off Haverstock St 83 DP68
Haverstock Rd, NW5 . . . . 64 DG64
Haverstock St, N1. . . . . 196 G1
Haverthwaite Rd, Orp. BR6 . . 145 ER103
Havil St, SE5 . . . . 102 DS80
Havisham Pl, SE19 . . . . 121 DP93
Hawarden Gro, SE24 . . . . 122 DQ87
Hawarden Hill, NW2 . . . . 63 CU62
Hawarden Rd, E17 . . . . 67 DX56
  Caterham CR3. . . . . 176 DQ121
Hawbridge Rd, E11 . . . . 67 ED60
Hawes Cl, Nthwd. HA6. . . . . . . 39 BT52
Hawes La, E4 . . . . 31 EC38
  West Wickham BR4. . . . . . 143 ED102
Hawes Rd, N18. . . . . 46 DV51
  Bromley BR1. . . . . 144 EH95
  Tadworth KT20
  off Hatch Gdns 173 CX120
Hawes St, N1 . . . . 83 DP66
Haweswater Dr, Wat. WD25 . . . 8 BW33
Haweswater Ho, Islw. TW7
  off Summerwood Rd 117 CF85
Hawfield Bk, Orp. BR6 . . . . . . 146 EX104
Hawfield Gdns, St.Alb.
  (Park St) AL2 . . . . 9 CD26
Hawgood St, E3 . . . . 85 EA71
Hawk Cl, Wal.Abb. EN9 . . . . . . 16 EG34
Hawkdene, E4. . . . . 31 EB44
Hawke Pk Rd, N22 . . . . 65 DP55
Hawke Pl, SE16. . . . . 203 J4
Hawke Rd, SE19 . . . . 122 DS93
Hawkesbury Rd, SW15 . . . . . . 119 CV85
Hawkes Cl, Grays RM17
  off New Rd. 110 GB79
Hawkesfield Rd, SE23 . . . . . . 123 DY89
Hawkesley Cl, Twick. TW1 . . . 117 CG91
Hawke's Pl, Sev. TN13 . . . . . . 190 FG127
Hawkes Rd, Felt. TW14 . . . . . . 115 BU87
  Mitcham CR4. . . . . 140 DE95
Hawkesworth Cl,
  Nthwd. HA6 . . . . 39 BS52
Hawke Twr, SE14
  off Nynehead St 103 DY79
Hawkewood Rd, Sun. TW16. . 135 BU97
Hawkhirst Rd, Ken. CR8 . . . . . 176 DR115
Hawkhurst, Cob. KT11 . . . . . . 154 CA114

Hawkhurst Gdns,
  Chess. KT9 . . . . 156 CL105
  Romford RM5 . . . . 51 FD51
Hawkhurst Rd, SW16 . . . . 141 DK95
Hawkhurst Way, N.Mal. KT3 . 138 CR99
  West Wickham BR4. . . . . . . 143 EB103
Hawkinge Wk, Orp. BR5. . . . . 146 EV97
Hawkinge Way, Horn. RM12. . . 90 FJ65
Hawkins Av, Grav. DA12. . . . . 131 GJ91
Hawkins Cl, NW7 off Hale La. . 42 CR50
  Borehamwood WD6
  off Banks Rd 26 CQ40
  Harrow HA1 . . . . 61 CD59
Hawkins Dr, Grays
  (Chaff.Hun.) RM16. . . . . . 109 FX75
Hawkins Rd, Tedd. TW11 . . . . 117 CH93
Hawkins Way, SE6 . . . . 123 EA92
  Hemel Hempstead
  (Bov.) HP3 . . . . 5 BA26
Hawkley Gdns, SE27 . . . . 121 DP89
Hawkridge Cl, Rom. RM6 . . . . 70 EW59
Hawkridge Dr, Grays RM17 . . 110 GD78
Hawksbrook La, Beck. BR3. . . 143 EB100
Hawkshaw Cl, SW2
  off Tierney Rd 121 DL87
Hawkshead Cl, Brom. BR1. . . 124 EE94
Hawkshead La, Hat.
  (N.Mymms) AL9 . . . . 11 CW28
Hawkshead Rd, NW10 . . . . . . 81 CT66
  W4. . . . . 98 CS75
  Potters Bar EN6 . . . . 12 DB29
Hawks Hill, Epp.
  (N.Wld Bas.) CM16. . . . . . 18 FA27
Hawk's Hill, Lthd. KT22. . . . . . 171 CF123
Hawkshill Cl, Esher KT10 . . . . 154 CA107
Hawkshill Way, Esher KT10 . . 154 BZ107
Hawkslade Rd, SE15 . . . . 123 DX85
Hawksley Rd, N16 . . . . 66 DS62
Hawksmead Cl, Enf. EN3 . . . . . 31 DX35
Hawks Ms, SE10 off Luton Pl. 103 EC80
Hawksmoor, Rad.
  (Shenley) WD7 . . . . 10 CN33
Hawksmoor Cl, E6
  off Allhallows Rd 86 EL72
  SE18 . . . . 105 ES78
Hawksmoor Grn, Brwd.
  (Hutt.) CM13 . . . . 55 GD43
Hawksmoor Ms, E1
  off Cable St. 84 DV73
Hawksmoor St, W6 . . . . 99 CX79
Hawksmouth, E4 . . . . 47 EB45
Hawks Rd, Kings.T. KT1 . . . . . 138 CM96
Hawkstone Rd, SE16 . . . . 202 G9
Hawksview, Cob. KT11. . . . . . 154 BZ113
Hawksway, Stai. TW18 . . . . . . 113 BF90
Hawkswell Cl, Wok. GU21 . . . 166 AT117
Hawkswell Wk, Wok. GU21
  off Lockfield Dr 166 AS117
Hawkswood Gro, Slou.
  (Fulmer) SL3 . . . . 75 AZ65
Hawkswood La, Ger.Cr. SL9 . . 57 AZ64
Hawk Ter, Ilf. IG5
  off Tiptree Cres 69 EN55
Hawkwell Ct, E4
  off Colvin Gdns. 47 EC48
Hawkwell Ho, Dag. RM8 . . . . . 70 FA60
Hawkwell Wk, N1
  off Basire St 84 DQ67
Hawkwood Cres, E4 . . . . 31 EB44
Hawkwood La, Chis. BR7 . . . . 145 EQ95
Hawkwood Mt, E5 . . . . 66 DV60
Hawlands Dr, Pnr. HA5. . . . . . . 60 BY59
HAWLEY, Dart. DA2 . . . . 128 FM92
Hawley Cl, Hmptn. TW12 . . . . 116 BZ93
Hawley Cres, NW1 . . . . 83 DH66
Hawley Ms, NW1
  off Hawley St 83 DH66
Hawley Mill, Dart. DA2 . . . . . . 128 FN91
Hawley Rd, N18 . . . . 47 DX50
  NW1 . . . . 83 DH66
  Dartford DA1, DA2 . . . . 128 FL89
HAWLEY'S CORNER,
  West. TN16 . . . . 179 EN121
Hawley St, NW1 . . . . 83 DH66
Hawley Ter, Dart. DA2
  off Hawley Rd 128 FN92
Hawley Vale, Dart. DA2. . . . . . 128 FN92
Hawley Way, Ashf. TW15. . . . . 114 BN92
Haws La, Stai. TW19 . . . . 114 BG86
Hawstead La, Orp. BR6 . . . . . 164 EZ106
Hawstead Rd, SE6 . . . . 123 EB86
Hawsted, Buck.H. IG9. . . . . . . 48 EH45
Hawthorn Av, E3. . . . . 85 DZ67
  N13 . . . . 45 DL50
  Brentwood CM13 . . . . 55 FZ48
  Carshalton SM5 . . . . 158 DG108
  Rainham RM13. . . . . 89 FH70
  Richmond TW9 off Kew Rd. 98 CL82
  Thornton Heath CR7. . . . . . 141 DP95
Hawthorn Cen, Har. HA1 . . . . . 61 CF56
Hawthorn Cl, Abb.L WD5 . . . . . 7 BU32
  Banstead SM7 . . . . 157 CY114
  Gravesend DA12. . . . . 131 GH91
  Hampton TW12 . . . . 116 CA92
  Hounslow TW5 . . . . 96 BV80
  Iver SL0. . . . . 75 BD68
  Orpington BR5 . . . . 145 ER100
  Watford WD17. . . . . 23 BT38
  Woking GU22 . . . . 166 AY120
Hawthorn Cotts, Well. DA16
  off Hook La. 106 EU83
Hawthorn Ct, Rich. TW9
  off West Hall Rd 98 CP81
Hawthorn Cres, SW17 . . . . . . 120 DG92
  South Croydon CR2 . . . . . . 160 DW111
Hawthornden Cl, N12
  off Fallowfields Dr 44 DE51
Hawthornden Cl,
  Brom. BR2. . . . . 144 EF103
Hawthornden Rd,
  Brom. BR2. . . . . 144 EF103
Hawthorn Dr, Har. HA2 . . . . . . 60 BZ58
  Uxbridge (Denh.) UB9 . . . . 58 BJ65
  West Wickham BR4. . . . . . 162 EE105
Hawthorne Av, Har. HA3 . . . . . 61 CG58
  Mitcham CR4 . . . . 140 DD96
  Ruislip HA4. . . . . 59 BV58
  Waltham Cross (Chsht) EN7. 14 DV31

Hawthorne Av, Westerham
  (Bigg.H.) TN16 . . . . 178 EK115
Hawthorne Cl, N1. . . . . 84 DS65
  Bromley BR1. . . . . 145 EM97
  Sutton SM1
  off Aultone Way 140 DB103
  Waltham Cross (Chsht) EN7. 14 DV31
Hawthorne Ct, Nthwd. HA6
  off Ryefield Cres 39 BU54
  Walton-on-Thames KT12
  off Ambleside Av 136 BX103
Hawthorne Cres, Slou. SL1 . . 74 AU74
  West Drayton UB7 . . . . 94 BM75
Hawthorne Fm Av, Nthlt. UB5. 78 BY67
Hawthorne Ms, Grnf. UB6
  off Greenford Rd. 78 CC72
Hawthorne Pl, Epsom KT17. . 156 CS112
Hawthorne Rd, E17 . . . . 67 EA55
  Bromley BR1. . . . . 144 EL97
  Radlett WD7 . . . . 9 CG34
  Staines TW18. . . . . 113 BC92
Hawthorne Way, N9 . . . . 46 DS47
  Staines (Stanw.) TW19 . . . 114 BK87
Hawthorn Gdns, W5. . . . . 97 CK76
Hawthorn Gro, SE20 . . . . 122 DV94
  Barnet EN5 . . . . 27 CT44
  Enfield EN2. . . . . 30 DR38
Hawthorn Hatch, Brent. TW8 . 97 CH80
Hawthorn La, Sev. TN13 . . . . 190 FF122
Hawthorn Ms, NW7
  off Holders Hill Rd 43 CY53
Hawthorn Pl, Erith DA8 . . . . . 107 FC78
Hawthorn Rd, N8 . . . . 65 DK55
  N18 . . . . 46 DT50
  NW10 . . . . 81 CU66
  Bexleyheath DA6 . . . . 106 EZ84
  Brentford TW8. . . . . 97 CH80
  Buckhurst Hill IG9. . . . . 48 EK49
  Dartford DA1. . . . . 128 FK88
  Sutton SM1. . . . . 158 DE107
  Wallington SM6 . . . . 159 DH108
  Woking GU22 . . . . 166 AX120
  Woking (Send M.) GU23. . . 168 BG124
Hawthorns, Wdf.Grn. IG8 . . . . 48 EG48
Hawthorns, The, Ch.St.G. HP8 . 20 AW40
  Epsom KT17
  off Ewell Bypass 157 CT107
  Loughton IG10 . . . . 33 EN42
  Oxted RH8. . . . . 188 EG133
  Rickmansworth
  (Map.Cr.) WD3. . . . . 37 BD50
  Slough (Colnbr.) SL3 . . . . . 93 BF81
Hawthorn Wk, W10
  off Droop St 81 CY70
Hawthorn Way, Add.
  (New Haw) KT15. . . . . 152 BJ110
  Shepperton TW17 . . . . 135 BR98
Hawtrees, Rad. WD7. . . . . 25 CF35
Hawtrey Av, Nthlt. UB5 . . . . . . 78 BX68
Hawtrey Cl, Slou. SL1 . . . . 92 AV75
Hawtrey Dr, Ruis. HA4 . . . . 59 BU59
Hawtrey Rd, NW3 . . . . 82 DE66
Haxted Rd, Brom. BR1
  off North Rd 144 EH95
Hayburn Way, Horn. RM12 . . . 71 FF60
Hay Cl, E15. . . . . 86 EE66
  Borehamwood WD6 . . . . . . 26 CQ40
Haycroft Cl, Couls. CR5
  off Caterham Dr 175 DP118
Haycroft Gdns, NW10 . . . . 81 CU67
Haycroft Rd, SW2 . . . . 121 DL85
  Surbiton KT6. . . . . 138 CL104
Hay Currie St, E14. . . . . 85 EB72
Hayday Rd, E16 . . . . 86 EG71
Hayden Ct, Add.
  (New Haw) KT15. . . . . 152 BH111
Hayden Rd, Wal.Abb. EN9 . . . 31 EC35
Haydens Cl, Orp. BR5 . . . . . . 146 EV100
Haydens Pl, W11
  off Portobello Rd. 81 CZ72
Hayden Way, Rom. RM5. . . . . . 51 FC54
Haydn Av, Pur. CR8 . . . . 159 DN114
Haydns Ms, W3
  off Emanuel Av 80 CQ72
Haydock Av, Nthlt. UB5 . . . . . . 78 CA65
Haydock Cl, Horn. RM12 . . . . . 72 FM63
Haydock Grn, Nthlt. UB5
  off Haydock Av 78 CA65
Haydon Cl, NW9 . . . . 62 CQ56
  Enfield EN1
  off Mortimer Dr. 30 DS44
  Romford RM3 off Heaton Av. 51 FH52
Haydon Dr, Pnr. HA5 . . . . 59 BU56
Haydon Pk Rd, SW19 . . . . 120 DB92
Haydon Rd, Dag. RM8 . . . . 70 EW61
  Watford WD19. . . . . 24 BY44
Haydon St, EC3. . . . . 197 P10
Haydon Wk, E1 off Mansell St. 84 DT73
Haydon Way, SW11 . . . . 100 DD84
HAYES. 77 BS72
HAYES, Brom. BR2. . . . . 144 EG103
≷ Hayes 144 EF102
Hayes, The, Epsom KT18 . . . . 172 CR119
≷ Hayes & Harlington 95 BT76
Hayes Barton, Wok. GU22 . . . 167 BD116
Hayes Bypass, Hayes
  UB3, UB4 . . . . 78 BX70
Hayes Chase, W.Wick. BR4 . . 144 EE99
Hayes Cl, Brom. BR2 . . . . 144 EG103
  Grays RM20. . . . . 109 FW79
Hayes Ct, SW2 . . . . 121 DL86
Hayes Cres, NW11 . . . . 63 CZ57
  Sutton SM3. . . . . 157 CX105
Hayes Dr, Rain. RM13. . . . . . . 89 FH66
HAYES END, Hayes UB3 . . . . 77 BQ71
Hayes End Cl, Hayes UB4. . . . 77 BR70
Hayes End Dr, Hayes UB4. . . . 77 BR70
Hayes End Rd, Hayes UB4 . . . 77 BR70
Hayesford Pk Dr, Brom. BR2 . 144 EF99
Hayes Gdn, Brom. BR2 . . . . . 144 EG103
Hayes Gro, SE15 . . . . 102 DT84
⊞ Hayes Gro Priory Hosp,
  Brom. BR2. . . . . 144 EG103
Hayes Hill, Brom. BR2. . . . . . . 144 EE102
Hayes Hill Rd, Brom. BR2 . . . 144 EF102
Hayes La, Beck. BR3 . . . . 143 EC97

Hayes La, Bromley BR2 . . . . . 144 EG99
  Kenley CR8 . . . . 160 DQ114
Hayes Mead Rd, Brom. BR2. . 144 EE102
Hayes Metro Cen, Hayes UB4 . 77 BW73
Hayes Pk, Hayes UB4. . . . . 77 BS70
Hayes Pl, NW1 . . . . 194 C5
Hayes Rd, Brom. BR2 . . . . 144 EG98
  Greenhithe DA9 . . . . 129 FS87
  Southall UB2. . . . . 95 BV77
Hayes St, Brom. BR2 . . . . 144 EH102
HAYES TOWN, Hayes UB3. . . 95 BU75
Hayes Wk, Brox. EN10
  off Landau Way. 15 DZ25
  Potters Bar EN6
  off Hyde Av 12 DB33
Hayes Way, Beck. BR3. . . . . . 143 EC98
Hayes Wd Av, Brom. BR2 . . . . 144 EH102
Hayfield Cl, Bushey WD23 . . . 24 CB42
Hayfield Pas, E1
  off Stepney Grn 84 DW70
Hayfield Rd, Orp. BR5. . . . . . . 146 EU99
Hayfield Yd, E1
  off Mile End Rd. 84 DW70
Haygarth Pl, SW19 . . . . 119 CX92
Haygreen Cl, Kings.T. KT2. . . 118 CP93
Hay Hill, W1 . . . . 199 J1
Hayland Cl, NW9 . . . . 62 CR56
Hay La, NW9. . . . . 62 CR56
  Slough (Fulmer) SL3 . . . . . 56 AX63
Hayles St, SE11. . . . . 200 F8
Haylett Gdns, Kings.T. KT1
  off Anglesea Rd 137 CK98
Hayling Av, Felt. TW13 . . . . . . 115 BU90
Hayling Cl, N16
  off Boleyn Rd 66 DS64
Hayling Rd, Wat. WD19. . . . . . 39 BV47
Haymaker Cl, Uxb. UB10
  off Honey Hill 76 BM66
Hayman Cres, Hayes UB4 . . . . 77 BR68
Hayman St, N1 off Cross St. . . 83 DP66
Haymarket, SW1. . . . . 199 M1
Haymarket Arc, SW1. . . . . 199 M1
Haymeads Dr, Esher KT10 . . . 154 CC107
Haymer Gdns, Wor.Pk. KT4 . . 139 CU104
Haymerle Rd, SE15 . . . . 102 DU79
Haymill Cl, Grnf. UB6 . . . . 79 CF69
Hayne Rd, Beck. BR3 . . . . 143 DZ96
Haynes Cl, N11 . . . . 44 DG48
  N17 . . . . 46 DV52
  SE3 . . . . 104 EE83
  Slough SL3. . . . . 93 AZ78
  Woking (Ripley) GU23 . . . . 168 BH122
Haynes Dr, N9. . . . . 46 DV48
Haynes La, SE19 . . . . 122 DS93
Haynes Pk Ct, Horn. RM11
  off Slewins Cl 72 FJ57
Haynes Rd, Grav.
  (Nthflt) DA11 . . . . 131 GF90
  Hornchurch RM11 . . . . 72 FK57
  Wembley HA0. . . . . 80 CL66
Hayne St, EC1 . . . . 196 G6
Haynt Wk, SW20 . . . . 139 CY97
★ Hay's Galleria, SE1 . . . . . . 201 M2
Hay's La, SE1 . . . . 201 M3
Hay's Ms, W1 . . . . 199 H1
Haysleigh Gdns, SE20 . . . . . . 142 DU96
Haysoms Cl, Rom. RM1 . . . . . 71 FE56
Haystall Cl, Hayes UB4. . . . . . . 77 BS68
Hay St, E2 . . . . 84 DU67
Hays Wk, Sutt. SM2 . . . . 157 CX110
Hayter Ct, E11 . . . . 68 EH61
Hayter Rd, SW2 . . . . 121 DL85
Hayton Cl, E8
  off Buttermere Wk. 84 DT65
Haywain, Oxt. RH8 . . . . 187 ED130
Hayward Cl, SW19 . . . . 140 DB95
  Dartford DA1. . . . . 127 FD85
Hayward Dr, Dart. DA1 . . . . . . 128 FM89
★ Hayward Gall, SE1 . . . . 200 C2
Hayward Gdns, SW15 . . . . . . 119 CW86
Hayward Rd, N20. . . . . 44 DC47
  Thames Ditton KT7 . . . . . . 137 CG102
Haywards, Brwd.
  (Hutt.) CM13 . . . . 55 GE44
  Romford (Chad.Hth) RM6. . 70 EV57
Hayward's Pl, EC1. . . . . 196 F5
Haywood Cl, Pnr. HA5 . . . . 60 BX54
Haywood Ct, Wal.Abb. EN9 . . 16 EF34
Haywood Dr, Rick. WD3
  off Haywood Pk 21 BF43
Haywood Pk, Rick.
  (Chorl.) WD3 . . . . 21 BF43
Haywood Ri, Orp. BR6 . . . . . . 163 ES105
Haywood Rd, Brom. BR2 . . . . 144 EK98
Hayworth Cl, Enf. EN3
  off Green St 31 DY40
Hazon Way, Epsom KT19 . . . . 156 CR112
Heacham Av, Uxb. UB10 . . . . . 59 BQ62
Headcorn Pl, Th.Hth. CR7
  off Headcorn Rd 141 DM98
Headcorn Rd, N17. . . . . 46 DT52
  Bromley BR1. . . . . 124 EF92
  Thornton Heath CR7. . . . . . 141 DM98
Headfort Pl, SW1 . . . . 198 G5
Headingley Cl, Ilf. IG6. . . . . 49 ET51
  Radlett (Shenley) WD7 . . . 10 CL32
  Waltham Cross (Chsht) EN7. 14 DT26
Headington Rd, SW18 . . . . . . 120 DC89
Headlam Rd, SW4 . . . . 121 DK86
Headlam St, E1. . . . . 84 DV70
HEADLEY, Epsom KT18 . . . . 182 CQ125
Headley App, Ilf. IG2. . . . . 69 EN57
Headley Av, Wall. SM6 . . . . . . 159 DM106
Headley Chase, Brwd. CM14 . 54 FW49
Headley Cl, Epsom KT19 . . . . 156 CN107
Headley Common, Brwd. CM13
  off Warley Gap 53 FV52
Headley Common Rd, Epsom
  (Headley) KT18 . . . . 182 CR127
  Tadworth KT20 . . . . 182 CR127
Headley Ct, SE26 . . . . 122 DV92
Headley Dr,
  Croy. (New Adgtn) CR0 . . 161 EB108
  Epsom KT18 . . . . 173 CV119
  Ilford IG2. . . . . 69 EP58
Headley Gro, Tad. KT20. . . . . 173 CV120

Hazel Dr, Erith DA8 . . . . 107 FH81
  South Ockendon RM15 . . . 91 FW69
Hazeleigh, Brwd. CM13 . . . . . 55 GB48
Hazeleigh Gdns, Wdf.Grn. IG8. 48 EL50
Hazel End, Swan. BR8 . . . . . . 147 FE99
Hazel Gdns, Edg. HA8 . . . . . . 42 CP49
  Grays RM16. . . . . 110 GE76
Hazelgreen Cl, N21 . . . . 45 DP46
Hazel Gro, SE26 . . . . 123 DX91
  Enfield EN3
  off Dimsdale Dr. 30 DU44
  Orpington BR6 . . . . 145 EP103
  Romford RM6. . . . . 70 EY55
  Staines TW18. . . . . 114 BH93
  Watford WD25
  off Cedar Wd Dr 23 BV35
  Wembley HA0
  off Carlyon Rd. 80 CL67
Hazel Gro Est, SE26 . . . . 123 DX91
Hazelhurst, Beck. BR3. . . . . . 143 ED95
Hazelhurst Rd, SW17 . . . . 120 DC91
Hazel La, Ilf. IG6 . . . . 49 EP52
  Richmond TW10 . . . . 118 CL89
Hazell Cres, Rom. RM5. . . . . . 51 FB53
Hazells Rd, Grav. DA13. . . . . 130 GD92
Hazellville Rd, N19 . . . . 65 DK59
Hazell Way, Slou.
  (Stoke P.) SL2 . . . . 74 AT65
Hazel Mead, Barn. EN5 . . . . . 27 CV43
  Epsom KT17 . . . . 157 CU110
Hazelmere Cl, Felt. TW14 . . . . 115 BR86
  Leatherhead KT22. . . . . . . 171 CH119
  Northolt UB5. . . . . 78 BZ68
Hazelmere Dr, Nthlt. UB5. . . . . 78 BZ68
Hazelmere Gdns, Horn. RM11 . 71 FH55
Hazelmere Rd, NW6 . . . . 82 DA67
  Northolt UB5. . . . . 78 BZ68
  Orpington BR5 . . . . 145 EQ98
Hazelmere Wk, Nthlt. UB5 . . . 78 BZ68
Hazelmere Way, Brom. BR2 . . 144 EG100
Hazel Ms, N22
  off Alexandra Rd. 65 DN55
Hazel Ri, Horn. RM11 . . . . 72 FJ58
Hazel Rd, E15
  off Wingfield Rd 68 EE64
  NW10 . . . . 81 CW69
  Dartford DA1. . . . . 128 FK89
  Erith DA8. . . . . 107 FG81
  St. Albans (Park St) AL2 . . . 8 CB28
  West Byfleet KT14 . . . . . . 152 BG114
Hazeltree La, Nthlt. UB5. . . . . . 78 BY69
Hazel Tree Rd, Wat. WD24. . . . 23 BV37
Hazel Wk, Brom. BR2 . . . . 145 EN100
Hazel Way, E4 . . . . 47 DZ51
  SE1 . . . . 201 P8
  Coulsdon CR5 . . . . 174 DF119
  Leatherhead (Fetch.) KT22 170 CC122
HAZELWOOD, Sev. TN14 . . . 163 ER111
Hazelwood, Loug. IG10 . . . . . . 32 EK43
Hazelwood Av, Mord. SM4 . . . 140 DB98
Hazelwood Cl, W5 . . . . 98 CL75
  Harrow HA2 . . . . 60 CB56
Hazelwood Ct, NW10
  off Neasden La N 62 CS62
Hazelwood Cres, N13 . . . . 45 DN49
Hazelwood Cft, Surb. KT6 . . . 138 CL100
Hazelwood Dr, Pnr. HA5. . . . . . 39 BV54
Hazelwood Gdns, Brwd.
  (Pilg.Hat.) CM15 . . . . 54 FU44
Hazelwood Gro, S.Croy. CR2 . 160 DV113
Hazelwood Hts, Oxt. RH8. . . . 188 EG131
Hazelwood La, N13 . . . . 45 DN49
  Abbots Langley WD5 . . . . . 8 BQ32
  Coulsdon CR5 . . . . 174 DF119
Hazelwood Pk Cl, Chig. IG7 . . 49 ES50
Hazelwood Rd, E17 . . . . 67 DY57
  Enfield EN1. . . . . 30 DT44
  Oxted RH8. . . . . 188 EH132
  Rickmansworth
  (Crox.Grn) WD3 . . . . 23 BQ44
  Sevenoaks (Cudham) TN14. 163 ER112
  Woking (Knap.) GU21. . . . 166 AS118
Hazlebury Rd, SW6. . . . . 100 DB82
Hazledean Rd, Croy. CR0 . . . 142 DR103
Hazledene Rd, W4 . . . . 98 CQ79
Hazlemere Gdns, Wor.Pk. KT4. 139 CV102
Hazlemere Rd, Slou. SL2 . . . . 74 AW74
Hazlewell Rd, SW15 . . . . 119 CV85
Hazlewood Cl, E5
  off Mandeville St. 67 DY62
Hazlewood Cres, W10 . . . . 81 CY70
Hazlitt Cl, Felt. TW13 . . . . 116 BY91
Hazlitt Ms, W14
  off Hazlitt Rd 99 CY76
Hazlitt Rd, W14 . . . . 99 CY76
Headley Gro, Tad. KT20. . . . . 173 CV120

Headley Rd, Epsom
(Tyr.Wd) KT18 ... 172 CN123
Epsom (Woodcote) KT18 ... 172 CP118
Leatherhead KT22 ... 171 CK123
Head's Ms, W11
off Artesian Rd ... 82 DA72
HEADSTONE, Har. HA2 ... 60 CC56
Headstone Dr, Har. HA1, HA3 ... 61 CE55
Headstone Gdns, Har. HA2 ... 60 CC56
⇌ **Headstone Lane** ... 40 CB53
Headstone La, Har. HA2, HA3 ... 60 CB56
Headstone Rd, Har. HA1 ... 61 CE57
Head St, E1 ... 85 DX72
Headway, The, Epsom KT17 ... 157 CT109
Headway Cl, Rich. TW10
off Locksmeade Rd ... 117 CJ91
Heald St, SE14 ... 103 DZ81
Healey Dr, Orp. BR6 ... 163 ET105
Healey Rd, Wat. WD18 ... 23 BT44
Healey St, NW1 ... 83 DH65
Heanor Ct, E5 *off Pedro St* ... 67 DX62
Heards La, Brwd.
(Shenf.) CM15 ... 55 FZ41
Hearne Ct, Ch.St.G. HP8
off Gordon Way ... 36 AV48
Hearne Rd, W4 ... 98 CN79
Hearn Ri, Nthlt. UB5 ... 78 BX67
Hearn Rd, Rom. RM1 ... 71 FF58
Hearn's Bldgs, SE17 ... 201 L9
Hearn's Rd, Orp. BR5 ... 146 EW98
Hearn St, EC2 ... 197 N5
Hearnville Rd, SW12 ... 120 DG88
H **Heart Hosp, The**, W1 ... 194 G7
Heath, The, W7
off Lower Boston Rd ... 79 CE74
Caterham CR3 ... 176 DQ124
Radlett WD7 ... 9 CG33
Heathacre, Slou. (Colnbr.) SL3
off Park St ... 93 BE81
Heatham Pk, Twick. TW2 ... 117 CF87
Heath Av, Bexh. DA7 ... 106 EX79
Heathbourne Rd, Bushey
(Bushey Hth) WD23 ... 41 CE47
Stanmore HA7 ... 41 CE47
Heathbridge, Wey. KT13 ... 152 BN108
Heath Brow, NW3
off North End Way ... 64 DC62
Heath Cl, NW11 ... 64 DB59
W5 ... 80 CM70
Banstead SM7 ... 158 DB114
Hayes UB3 ... 95 BR80
Orpington BR5
off Sussex Rd ... 146 EW100
Potters Bar EN6 ... 12 DB30
Romford RM2 ... 71 FG55
Staines (Stanw.) TW19 ... 114 BJ86
Heathclose, Swan. BR8
off Bonney Way ... 147 FE96
Heath Cl, Vir.W. GU25 ... 132 AX98
Heathclose Av, Dart. DA1 ... 127 FH87
Heathclose Rd, Dart. DA1 ... 127 FG88
Heathcock Ct, WC2 *off Strand* ... 83 DL73
Heathcote, Tad. KT20 ... 173 CX121
Heathcote Av, Ilf. IG5 ... 49 EM54
Heathcote Ct, Ilf. IG5
off Heathcote Av ... 49 EM54
Heathcote Gro, E4 ... 47 EC48
Heathcote Pt, E9 *off Wick Rd* ... 85 DX65
Heathcote Rd, Epsom KT18 ... 156 CR114
Twickenham TW1 ... 117 CH86
Heathcote St, WC1 ... 196 B4
Heathcote Way, West Dr. UB7
off Tavistock Rd ... 76 BK74
Heath Cotts, Pot.B. EN6
off Heath Rd ... 12 DB30
Heath Ct, Houns. TW4 ... 96 BZ84
Uxbridge UB8 ... 76 BL66
Heathcroft, NW11 ... 64 DB60
W5 ... 80 CM70
Heathcroft Av, Sun. TW16 ... 115 BT94
Heathcroft Gdns, E17 ... 47 ED53
Heathdale Av, Houns. TW4 ... 96 BY83
Heathdene, Tad. KT20
off Canons La ... 173 CY119
Heathdene Dr, Belv. DA17 ... 107 FB77
Heathdene Rd, SW16 ... 121 DM94
Wallington SM6 ... 159 DH108
Heathdown Rd, Wok. GU22 ... 167 BD115
Heath Dr, NW3 ... 64 DB63
SW20 ... 139 CW98
Epping (They.B.) CM16 ... 33 ES35
Potters Bar EN6 ... 12 DA30
Romford RM2 ... 51 FG53
Sutton SM2 ... 158 DC109
Tadworth KT20 ... 183 CU125
Woking (Send) GU23 ... 167 BB122
Heathedge, SE26 ... 122 DV89
Heath End Rd, Bex. DA5 ... 127 FE88
Heather Av, Rom. RM1 ... 51 FD54
Heatherbank, SE9 ... 105 EM82
Chislehurst BR7 ... 145 EN96
Heatherbank Cl, Cob. KT11
off Nightingale Cl ... 154 BX111
Dartford DA1 ... 127 FE86
Heather Cl, E6 ... 87 EP72
N7
off Newington Barrow Way ... 65 DM62
SE13 ... 123 ED86
SW8 ... 101 DH83
Abbots Langley WD5 ... 7 BU32
Addlestone
(New Haw) KT15 ... 152 BH110
Brentwood (Pilg.Hat.) CM15 ... 54 FV43
Hampton TW12 ... 136 BZ95
Isleworth TW7
off Harvesters Cl ... 117 CD85
Redhill RH1 ... 185 DH130
Romford RM1 ... 51 FD53
Tadworth KT20 ... 173 CY122
Uxbridge UB8
off Violet Av ... 76 BM71
Woking GU21 ... 166 AW115
Heatherdale Cl, Kings.T. KT2 ... 118 CN93
Heatherdene Cl, N12
off Bow La ... 44 DC53
Mitcham CR4 ... 140 DE98
Heatherden Grn, Iver SL0 ... 75 BC67
Heatherden La, Iver SL0
off Pinewood Rd ... 75 BB66
Heather Dr, Dart. DA1 ... 127 FG87
Heather Dr, Enfield EN2
off Chasewood Av ... 29 DP40
Romford RM1 ... 51 FD54
Heather End, Swan. BR8 ... 147 FD98
Heatherfields, Add.
(New Haw) KT15 ... 152 BH110
Heatherfold Way, Pnr. HA5 ... 59 BT55
Heather Gdns, NW11 ... 63 CY58
Romford RM1 ... 51 FD54
Sutton SM2 ... 158 DA107
Waltham Abbey EN9 ... 31 EC36
Heather Glen, Rom. RM1 ... 51 FD54
Heatherlands, Sun. TW16 ... 115 BU93
Heather La, Wat. WD24 ... 23 BT35
West Drayton UB7 ... 76 BL72
Heatherley Dr, Ilf. IG5 ... 68 EL55
Heather Pk Dr, Wem. HA0 ... 80 CN66
Heather Pl, Esher KT10
off Park Rd ... 154 CB105
Heather Ri, Bushey WD23 ... 24 BZ40
Heather Rd, E4 ... 47 DZ51
NW2 ... 63 CT61
SE12 ... 124 EG89
Heathers, The, Stai. TW19 ... 114 BM87
Heatherset Cl, Esher KT10 ... 154 CC106
Heatherset Gdns, SW16 ... 121 DM94
Heatherside Dr, Vir.W. GU25 ... 132 AU100
Heatherside Rd,
Epsom KT19 ... 156 CR108
Sidcup DA14 *off Wren Rd* ... 126 EX90
Heatherton Ter, N3 ... 44 DB54
Heathervale Caravan Pk, Add.
(New Haw) KT15 ... 152 BJ110
Heathervale Rd, Add.
(New Haw) KT15 ... 152 BH110
Heather Wk, W10 *off Droop St* ... 81 CY70
Edgware HA8 ... 42 CP50
Twickenham TW2
off Stephenson Rd ... 116 CA87
Walton-on-Thames
(Whiteley Vill.) KT12
off Octagon Rd ... 153 BT110
Heather Way, Pot.B. EN6 ... 11 CZ32
Romford RM1 ... 51 FD54
South Croydon CR2 ... 161 DX109
Stanmore HA7 ... 41 CF51
Woking (Chobham) GU24 ... 150 AS108
Heatherwood Cl, E12 ... 68 EJ61
Heatherwood Dr, Hayes UB4
off Charville La ... 77 BR68
Heath Fm Ct, Wat. WD17
off Grove Mill La ... 23 BR37
Heathfield, E4 ... 47 EC48
Chislehurst BR7 ... 125 EQ93
Cobham KT11 ... 154 CA114
Heathfield Av, SW18
off Heathfield Rd ... 120 DD87
South Croydon CR2 ... 161 DY109
Heathfield Cl, E16 ... 86 EK71
Keston BR2 ... 162 EJ106
Potters Bar EN6 ... 12 DB30
Watford WD19 ... 40 BW45
Woking GU22 ... 167 BA118
Heathfield Dr, Mitch. CR4 ... 140 DE95
Heathfield Gdns, NW11 ... 63 CX58
SE3 ... 104 EE82
SW18 *off Heathfield Rd* ... 120 DD86
W4 ... 98 CQ78
Croydon CR0
off Coombe Rd ... 160 DR105
Heathfield La, Chis. BR7 ... 125 EP93
Heathfield N, Twick. TW2 ... 117 CF87
Heathfield Pk, NW2 ... 81 CW65
Heathfield Pk Dr, Rom.
(Chad.Hth) RM6 ... 70 EV57
Heathfield Ri, Ruis. HA4 ... 59 BQ59
Heathfield Rd, SW18 ... 120 DC86
W3 ... 98 CP75
Bexleyheath DA6 ... 106 EZ84
Bromley BR1 ... 124 EF94
Bushey WD23 ... 24 BY42
Croydon CR0 ... 160 DR105
Keston BR2 ... 162 EJ106
Sevenoaks TN13 ... 190 FF122
Walton-on-Thames KT12 ... 154 BY105
Woking GU22 ... 167 BA118
Heathfields Cl, Ashtd. KT21 ... 171 CJ118
Heathfields Ct, Houns. TW4
off Frampton Rd ... 116 BY85
Heathfield S, Twick. TW2 ... 117 CF87
Heathfield Sq, SW18 ... 120 DD87
Heathfield St, W11
off Portland Rd ... 81 CY73
Heathfield Ter, SE18 ... 105 ET79
W4 ... 98 CQ78
Heathfield Vale, S.Croy. CR2 ... 161 DX109
Heath Gdns, Twick. TW1 ... 117 CF88
Heathgate, NW11 ... 64 DB58
Heathgate Pl, NW3
off Agincourt Rd ... 64 DF64
Heath Gro, SE20
off Maple Rd ... 122 DW94
Sunbury-on-Thames TW16 ... 115 BT94
Heath Hurst Rd, NW3 ... 64 DE63
Heathhurst Rd, S.Croy. CR2 ... 160 DS109
Heathland Rd, N16 ... 66 DS60
Heathlands, Tad. KT20 ... 173 CX122
Heathlands Cl, Sun. TW16 ... 135 BU96
Twickenham TW1 ... 117 CF89
Woking GU21 ... 150 AY114
Heathlands Ri, Dart. DA1 ... 127 FH86
Heathlands Way, Houns. TW4 ... 116 BY85
Heath La, SE3 ... 103 ED82
Dartford (Lower) DA1 ... 128 FJ88
Dartford (Upper) DA1 ... 127 FG89
Heathlee Rd, SE3 ... 104 EF84
Dartford DA1 ... 127 FE86
Heathley End, Chis. BR7 ... 125 EQ93
Heathmans Rd, SW6 ... 99 CZ81
Heath Mead, SW19 ... 119 CX90
Heath Pk Ct, Rom. RM2
off Heath Pk Rd ... 71 FG57
Heath Pk Dr, Brom. BR1 ... 144 EL97
Heath Pk Rd, Rom. RM2 ... 71 FG57
Heath Pas, NW3 ... 64 DB61
Heath Ridge Grn, Cob. KT11 ... 154 CA113
Heath Ri, SW15 ... 119 CX86
Bromley BR2 ... 144 EF100
Virginia Water GU25 ... 132 AX98
Woking (Ripley) GU23 ... 168 BH123
Heath Rd, SW8 ... 101 DH82
Bexley DA5 ... 127 FC88
Caterham CR3 ... 176 DR123
Dartford DA1 ... 127 FF86
Grays RM16 ... 111 GG75
Harrow HA1 ... 60 CC59
Hounslow TW3 ... 96 CB84
Leatherhead
(Oxshott) KT22 ... 154 CC112
Potters Bar EN6 ... 12 DA30
Romford RM6 ... 70 EX59
Thornton Heath CR7 ... 142 DQ97
Twickenham TW1, TW2 ... 117 CF88
Uxbridge UB10 ... 77 BQ70
Watford WD19 ... 40 BX45
Weybridge KT13 ... 152 BN106
Woking GU21 ... 167 AZ115
★ **Heathrow Airport (London)**,
Houns. TW6 ... 95 BP81
Heathrow Cl, West Dr. UB7 ... 94 BH81
Heathrow Ho, Houns. TW5
off Bath Rd ... 95 BU81
Heathrow Interchange,
Hayes UB4 ... 78 BW74
Heathrow Int Trd Est,
Houns. TW4 ... 95 BV83
⇌ **Heathrow Terminal 4** ... 115 BP85
⊖ **Heathrow Terminal 4** ... 115 BP85
⇌ **Heathrow Terminals 1,2,3** ... 95 BP83
⊖ **Heathrow Terminals 1,2,3** ... 95 BP83
Heathrow Tunnel App, Houns.
(Hthrw Air.) TW6 ... 95 BP83
Heathrow Vehicle Tunnel, Houns.
(Hthrw Air.) TW6 ... 95 BP81
Heaths Cl, Enf. EN1 ... 30 DS40
Heath Side, NW3 ... 64 DD63
Heathside, Esher KT10 ... 137 CE104
Hounslow TW4 ... 116 BZ87
Heath Side, Orp. BR5 ... 145 EQ102
Heathside, Wey. KT13 ... 153 BP106
Heathside Av, Bexh. DA7 ... 106 EY81
Heathside Cl, Esher KT10 ... 137 CE104
Ilford IG2 ... 69 ER57
Northwood HA6 ... 39 BR50
Heathside Ct, Tad. KT20 ... 173 CV123
Heathside Cres, Wok. GU22 ... 167 AZ117
Heathside Gdns, Wok. GU22 ... 167 BA117
Heathside Pk Rd, Wok. GU22 ... 167 AZ118
Heathside Pl, Epsom KT18 ... 173 CX118
Heathside Rd, Nthwd. HA6 ... 39 BR49
Woking GU22 ... 167 AZ118
Heathstan Rd, W12 ... 81 CU72
Heath St, NW3 ... 64 DC63
Dartford DA1 ... 128 FK87
Heath Vw, N2 ... 64 DC56
Heathview Av, Dart. DA1 ... 127 FE86
Heath Vw Cl, N2 ... 64 DC56
Heathview Ct, SW19 ... 119 CX89
Heathview Cres, Dart. DA1 ... 127 FG88
Heathview Dr, SE2 ... 106 EX79
Heathview Gdns, SW15 ... 119 CW87
Heath Vw Gdns, Grays RM16 ... 110 GC75
Heath Vw Rd, Grays RM16 ... 110 GC75
Heathview Rd, Th.Hth. CR7 ... 141 DN98
Heath Vil, SE18 ... 105 ET78
SW18 *off Cargill Rd* ... 120 DC88
Heathville Rd, N19 ... 65 DL59
Heathwall St, SW11 ... 100 DF83
Heathway, SE3 ... 104 EF80
Caterham CR3 ... 186 DQ125
Croydon CR0 ... 143 DZ104
Dagenham RM9, RM10 ... 88 FA66
Heath Way, Erith DA8 ... 107 FC81
Heathway, Iver SL0 ... 75 BD68
Leatherhead (E.Hors.) KT24 ... 169 BT124
Woodford Green IG8 ... 48 EJ49
Heathway Ind Est, Dag. RM10
off Manchester Way ... 71 FB63
Heathwood Gdns, SE7 ... 104 EL77
Swanley BR8 ... 147 FC96
Heathwood Pt, SE23
off Dacres Rd ... 123 DX90
Heathwood Wk, Bex. DA5 ... 127 FE88
Heaton Av, Rom. RM3 ... 51 FH52
Heaton Cl, E4 ... 47 EC48
Romford RM3 ... 52 FJ52
Heaton Ct, Wal.Cr. (Chsht) EN8 ... 15 DX29
Heaton Gra Rd, Rom. RM2 ... 51 FF54
Heaton Rd, SE15 ... 102 DU83
Mitcham CR4 ... 120 DG94
Heaton Way, Rom. RM3 ... 52 FJ52
Heaven Tree Cl, N1 ... 66 DQ64
Heaver Rd, SW11 *off Wye St* ... 100 DD83
Heavitree Cl, SE18 ... 105 ER78
Heavitree Rd, SE18 ... 105 ER78
Hebden Ct, E2
off Laburnum St ... 84 DT67
Hebden Ter, N17
off Commercial Rd ... 46 DS51
Hebdon Rd, SW17 ... 120 DE90
Heber Rd, NW2 ... 63 CX64
SE22 ... 122 DT86
Hebron Rd, W6 ... 99 CV76
Hecham Cl, E17 ... 47 DY54
Heckets Ct, Esher KT10
off Copsem La ... 154 CC110
Heckfield Pl, SW6
off Fulham Rd ... 100 DA80
Heckford Cl, Wat. WD18 ... 23 BQ44
Heckford St, E1
off The Highway ... 85 DX73
Hector St, SE18 ... 105 ES77
Heddington Gro, N7 ... 65 DM64
Heddon Cl, Islw. TW7 ... 97 CG84
Heddon Ct Av, Barn. EN4 ... 28 DF43
Heddon Ct Par, Barn. EN4
off Cockfosters Rd ... 28 DG43
Heddon Rd, Barn. EN4 ... 28 DF43
Heddon St, W1 ... 195 K10
Hedge Hill, Enf. EN2 ... 29 DP39
Hedge La, N13 ... 45 DP48
Hedgeley, Ilf. IG4 ... 69 EM56
Hedgemans Rd, Dag. RM9 ... 88 EX66
Hedgemans Way, Dag. RM9 ... 88 EY65
Hedge Pl Rd, Green. DA9 ... 129 FT86
Hedgerley Ct, Wok. GU21 ... 166 AW117
Hedgerley Gdns, Grnf. UB6 ... 78 CC68
Hedgerley Grn, Slou.
(Hedg.) SL2 ... 56 AT58
Hedgerley La, Ger.Cr. SL9 ... 56 AV59
Hedgerley La, Slough SL2 ... 56 AS58
Hedgerow, Ger.Cr.
(Chal.St.P.) SL9 ... 36 AY51
Hedgerow La, Barn. EN5 ... 27 CV43
Hedgerows, The, Grav.
(Nthflt) DA11 ... 130 GE89
Hedgerow Wk, Wal.Cr. EN8 ... 15 DX30
Hedgers Cl, Loug. IG10
off Newmans La ... 33 EN42
Hedgers Gro, E9 ... 85 DY65
Hedger St, SE11 ... 200 F8
Hedgeside Rd, Nthwd. HA6 ... 39 BQ50
Hedge Wk, SE6 ... 123 EB91
Hedgewood Gdns, Ilf. IG5 ... 69 EN57
Hedgley St, SE12 ... 124 EF85
Hedingham Cl, N1
off Popham Rd ... 84 DQ66
Hedingham Ho, Kings.T. KT2
off Kingsgate Rd ... 138 CL95
Hedingham Rd, Dag. RM8 ... 70 EV64
Grays (Chaff.Hun.) RM16 ... 109 FW78
Hornchurch RM11 ... 72 FN60
Hedley Av, Grays RM20 ... 109 FW80
Hedley Cl, Rom. RM1
off High St ... 71 FE57
Hedley Rd, Twick. TW2 ... 116 CA87
Hedley Row, N5 *off Poets Rd* ... 66 DR64
Hedworth Av, Wal.Cr. EN8 ... 15 DX33
Heenan Cl, Bark. IG11
off Glenny Rd ... 87 EQ65
Heene Rd, Enf. EN2 ... 30 DR39
Heideck Gdns, Brwd. (Hutt.) CM13
off Victors Cres ... 55 GB47
Heidegger Cres, SW13
off Trinity Ch Rd ... 99 CV79
Heigham Rd, E6 ... 86 EK66
Heighton Gdns, Croy. CR0 ... 159 DP106
Heights, The, SE7 ... 104 EJ78
Beckenham BR3 ... 123 EC94
Loughton IG10 ... 33 EM40
Northolt UB5 ... 60 BZ64
Waltham Abbey
(Nazeing) EN9 ... 16 EH25
Weybridge KT13 ... 152 BN110
Heights Cl, SW20 ... 119 CV94
Banstead SM7 ... 173 CY116
★ **Heinz Gall, R.I.B.A.**, W1 ... 194 F8
Heiron St, SE17 ... 101 DP79
Helby Rd, SW4 ... 121 DK86
Helder Gro, SE12 ... 124 EF87
Helder St, S.Croy. CR2 ... 160 DR107
Heldmann Cl, Houns. TW3 ... 97 CD84
Helegon Cl, Orp. BR6 ... 163 ET105
Helena Cl, Barn. EN4 ... 28 DD38
Helena Pl, E9 *off Fremont St* ... 84 DW67
Helena Rd, E13 ... 86 EF68
E17 ... 67 EA57
NW10 ... 63 CV64
W5 ... 79 CK71
Helena Sq, SE16 ... 203 K1
Helen Av, Felt. TW14 ... 115 BV87
Helen Cl, N2
off Thomas More Way ... 64 DC55
Dartford DA1 ... 127 FH87
West Molesey KT8 ... 136 CB98
Helen Rd, Horn. RM11 ... 72 FK55
Helens Gate, Wal.Cr. EN8 ... 15 DZ26
Helenslea Av, NW11 ... 63 CZ60
Helen's Pl, E2
off Roman Rd ... 84 DW69
Helen St, SE18
off Wilmount St ... 105 EP77
Helford Cl, Ruis. HA4
off Chichester Av ... 59 BS61
Helford Wk, Wok. GU21 ... 166 AU118
Helford Way, Upmin. RM14 ... 73 FR58
Helgiford Gdns, Sun. TW16 ... 115 BS94
Helios Rd, Wall. SM6 ... 140 DG102
Helix Gdns, SW2
off Helix Rd ... 121 DM86
Helix Rd, SW2 ... 121 DM86
Helleborine, Grays
(Bad.Dene) RM17 ... 110 FZ78
Hellen Way, Wat. WD19 ... 40 BX49
Hellings St, E1 ... 202 C3
Helm Cl, Epsom KT19 ... 156 CN112
Helme Cl, SW19 ... 119 CZ92
Helmet Row, EC1 ... 197 J4
Helmore Rd, Bark. IG11 ... 87 ET66
Helmsdale, Wok. GU21
off Winnington Way ... 166 AV118
Helmsdale Cl, Hayes UB4 ... 78 BY70
Romford RM1 ... 51 FE52
Helmsdale Rd, SW16 ... 141 DJ95
Romford RM1 ... 51 FE52
Helmsley Pl, E8 ... 84 DV66
Helperby Rd, NW10
off Mayo Rd ... 80 CS65
Helsinki Sq, SE16 ... 203 L6
Helston Cl, Pnr. HA5 ... 40 BZ52
Helston Pl, Abb.L. WD5
off Shirley Rd ... 7 BT32
Helvellyn Cl, Egh. TW20 ... 113 BB94
Helvetia St, SE6 ... 123 DZ89
Hemans St, SW8 ... 101 DK80
Hemberton Rd, SW9 ... 101 DL83
Hemery Rd, Grnf. UB6 ... 61 CD64
Hemingford Cl, N12 ... 44 DD50
Hemingford Rd, N1 ... 83 DM67
Sutton SM3 ... 157 CW105
Watford WD17 ... 23 BS36
Heming Rd, Edg. HA8 ... 42 CP52
Hemington Av, N11 ... 44 DF50
Hemlock Cl, Tad.
(Kgswd) KT20 ... 173 CY123
Hemlock Rd, W12 ... 81 CT73
Hemmen La, Hayes UB3 ... 77 BT72
Hemming Cl, Hmptn. TW12
off Chandler Cl ... 136 CA95
Hemmings Cl, Sid. DA14 ... 126 EV89
Hemming St, E1 ... 84 DU70
Hemming Way, Wat. WD25 ... 23 BU35
Hemnall St, Epp. CM16 ... 17 ET31
Hempshaw Av, Bans. SM7 ... 174 DF116
Hempson Av, Slou. SL3 ... 92 AW76
Hempstead Cl, Buck.H. IG9 ... 48 EG47
Hempstead Rd, E17 ... 47 ED54
Hemel Hempstead HP3 ... 5 BA27
Kings Langley WD4 ... 6 BM26
Watford WD17 ... 23 BT39
Hemp Wk, SE17 ... 201 L8
Hemsby Rd, Chess. KT9 ... 156 CM107
Hemstal Rd, NW6 ... 82 DA66
Hemsted Rd, Erith DA8 ... 107 FE80
Hemswell Dr, NW9 ... 42 CS53
Hemsworth Ct, N1
off Hemsworth St ... 84 DS68
Hemsworth St, N1 ... 84 DS68
Hemus Pl, SW3
off Chelsea Manor St ... 100 DE78
Hen & Chicken Ct, EC4
off Fleet St ... 83 DN72
Henbane Path, Rom. RM3
off Clematis Cl ... 52 FK52
Henbit Cl, Tad. KT20 ... 173 CV119
Henbury Way, Wat. WD19 ... 40 BX48
Henchman St, W12 ... 81 CT72
Hencroft St N, Slou. SL1 ... 92 AT75
Hencroft St S, Slou. SL1 ... 92 AT76
Hendale Av, NW4 ... 63 CU55
Henderson Cl, NW10 ... 80 CQ65
Hornchurch RM11 ... 71 FH61
Henderson Dr, NW8
off Cunningham Pl ... 82 DD70
Dartford DA1 ... 108 FM84
H **Henderson Hosp**,
Sutt. SM2 ... 158 DB109
Henderson Pl, Abb.L.
(Bedmond) WD5 ... 7 BT27
Henderson Rd, E7 ... 86 EJ65
N9 ... 46 DV46
SW18 ... 120 DE87
Croydon CR0 ... 142 DR100
Hayes UB4 ... 77 BU69
Westerham (Bigg.H.) TN16 ... 162 EJ112
Hendham Rd, SW17 ... 120 DE89
HENDON, NW4 ... 63 CV56
⇌ **Hendon** ... 63 CU58
Hendon Av, N3 ... 43 CY53
⊖ **Hendon Central** ... 63 CW57
Hendon Gdns, Rom. RM5 ... 51 FC51
Hendon Gro, Epsom KT19 ... 156 CN109
Hendon Hall Ct, NW4
off Parson St ... 63 CX55
Hendon La, N3 ... 63 CY55
Hendon Pk Row, NW11 ... 63 CZ58
Hendon Rd, N9 ... 46 DU47
Hendon Way, NW2 ... 63 CZ62
NW4 ... 63 CV58
Staines (Stanw.) TW19 ... 114 BK86
Hendon Wd La, NW7 ... 27 CT44
Hendren Cl, Grnf. UB6
off Dimmock Dr ... 61 CD64
Hendre Rd, SE1 ... 201 N9
Hendrick Av, SW12 ... 120 DF86
Heneage Cres, Croy.
(New Adgtn) CR0 ... 161 EC110
Heneage La, EC3 ... 197 N9
Heneage St, E1 ... 84 DT71
Henfield Cl, N19 ... 65 DJ60
Bexley DA5 ... 126 FA86
Henfield Rd, SW19 ... 139 CZ95
Hengelo Gdns, Mitch. CR4 ... 140 DD98
Hengist Rd, SE12 ... 124 EH87
Erith DA8 ... 107 FB80
Hengist Way, Brom. BR2 ... 144 EE98
Hengrave Rd, SE23 ... 123 DX87
Hengrove Ct, Bex. DA5
off Hurst Rd ... 126 EY88
Hengrove Cres, Ashf. TW15 ... 114 BK90
Henhurst Rd, Grav.
(Cobham) DA12 ... 131 GK94
Henley Av, Sutt. SM3 ... 139 CY104
Henley Cl, Grnf. UB6 ... 78 CC68
Isleworth TW7 ... 97 CF81
Henley Ct, N14 ... 45 DJ45
Woking GU22 ... 167 BB120
Henley Cross, SE3 ... 104 EH83
Henley Deane, Grav.
(Nthflt) DA11 ... 130 GE91
Henley Dr, SE1 ... 202 A8
Kingston upon Thames KT2 ... 119 CT94
Henley Gdns, Pnr. HA5 ... 59 BV55
Romford RM6 ... 70 EY57
Henley Rd, E16 ... 105 EM75
N18 ... 46 DS49
NW10 ... 81 CW67
Ilford IG1 ... 69 EQ63
Henley St, SW11 ... 100 DG82
Henley Way, Felt. TW13 ... 116 BX92
Henlow Pl, Rich. TW10
off Sandpits Rd ... 117 CK89
Hennel Cl, SE23 ... 122 DW90
Hennessy Ct, Wok. GU21 ... 151 BC113
Hennessy Rd, N9 ... 46 DW47
Henniker Gdns, E6 ... 86 EK69
Henniker Ms, SW3
off Callow St ... 100 DD79
Henniker Pt, E15 ... 68 EE64
Henniker Rd, E15 ... 67 ED64
Henningham Rd, N17 ... 46 DR53
Henning St, SW11 ... 100 DE81
Henrietta Cl, SE8 ... 103 EA79
Henrietta Ms, WC1 ... 196 A4
Henrietta Pl, W1 ... 195 H9
Henrietta St, E15 ... 67 EC64
WC2 ... 196 A10
Henriques St, E1 ... 84 DU72
Henry Addlington Cl, E6 ... 87 EP71
Henry Cl, Enf. EN2 ... 30 DS38
Henry Cooper Way, SE9 ... 124 EK90
Henry Darlot Dr, NW7 ... 43 CX50
Henry De Gray Cl,
Grays RM17 ... 110 FZ77
Henry Dent Cl, SE5 ... 102 DR83
Henry Dickens Ct, W11 ... 81 CX74
Henry Doulton Dr, SW17 ... 121 DH91
Henry Jackson Rd, SW15 ... 99 CX83
Henry Macaulay Av,
Kings.T. KT2 ... 137 CK95
Henry Rd, E6 ... 86 EL68
N4 ... 66 DQ60
Barnet EN4 ... 28 DD43
Henry's Av, Wdf.Grn. IG8 ... 48 EF50
Henryson Rd, SE4 ... 123 EA85

★ Place of interest ⇌ Railway station ⊖ London Underground station DLR Docklands Light Railway station Tra Tramlink station H Hospital Riv Pedestrian ferry landing stage

Henry St, Brom. BR1 144 EH95
Grays RM17
off East Thurrock Rd 110 GC79
Henry's Wk, Ilf. IG6 49 ER52
Henry Tate Ms, SW16 121 DN92
Hensford Gdns, SE26
off Wells Pk Rd 122 DV91
Henshall Pt, E3
off Bromley High St 85 EB69
Henshall St, N1 84 DR65
Henshawe Rd, Dag. RM8 70 EX62
Henshaw St, SE17 201 K8
Hensley Pt, E9 off Wick Rd 85 DX65
Henslowe Rd, SE22 122 DU85
Henslow Way, Wok. GU21 151 BD114
Henson Av, NW2 63 CW64
Henson Cl, Orp. BR6 145 EP103
Henson Path, Har. HA3 61 CK55
Henson Pl, Nthlt. UB5 78 BW67
Henstridge Pl, NW8 82 DE68
Hensworth Rd, Ashf. TW15 114 BK93
Henty Cl, SW11 100 DE80
Henty Wk, SW15 119 CV85
Henville Rd, Brom. BR1 144 EH95
Henwick Rd, SE9 104 EK83
Henwood Side, Wdf.Grn. IG8
off Love La 49 EM51
Hepburn Cl, Grays
(Chaff.Hun.) RM16 109 FX77
Hepburn Gdns, Brom. BR2 144 EE102
Hepburn Ms, SW11
off Webbs Rd 120 DF85
Hepple Cl, Islw. TW7 97 CH82
Hepplestone Cl, SW15
off Dover Pk Dr 119 CV86
Hepscott Rd, E9 85 EA66
Hepworth Ct, Bark. IG11 70 EU64
Hepworth Gdns, Bark. IG11 70 EU64
Hepworth Rd, SW16 121 DL94
Hepworth Wk, NW3
off Haverstock Hill 64 DE64
Hepworth Way, Walt. KT12 135 BT102
Heracles Cl, Wall. SM6 159 DL108
Herald Gdns, Wall. SM6 141 DH104
Herald's Pl, SE11 200 F8
Herald St, E2
off Three Colts La 84 DV70
Herald Wk, Dart. DA1
off Temple Hill Sq 128 FM85
Herbal Hill, EC1 196 E5
Herbert Cres, SW1 198 E6
Woking (Knap.) GU21 166 AS117
Herbert Gdns, NW10 81 CV68
W4
off Magnolia Rd 98 CP79
Romford RM6 70 EX59
St. Albans AL2 8 CB29
Herbert Ms, SW2
off Bascombe St 121 DN86
Herbert Morrison Ho, SW6
off Clem Attlee Ct 99 CZ79
Herbert Pl, SE18
off Plumstead Common Rd 105 EP79
Herbert Rd, E12 68 EL63
E17 67 DZ59
N11 45 DL52
N15 66 DT57
NW9 63 CU58
SE18 105 EN80
SW19 119 CZ94
Bexleyheath DA7 106 EY82
Bromley BR2 144 EK99
Hornchurch RM11 72 FL59
Ilford IG3 69 ES61
Kingston upon Thames KT1 138 CM97
Southall UB1 78 BZ74
Swanley BR8 127 FH93
Swanscombe DA10 130 FZ86
Herbert St, E13 86 EG68
NW5 82 DG65
Herbert Ter, SE18
off Herbert Rd 105 EP79
Herbrand St, WC1 195 P4
Hercies Rd, Uxb. UB10 76 BM66
Hercules Pl, N7
off Hercules St 65 DL62
Hercules Rd, SE1 200 C7
Hercules St, N7 65 DL62
Hereford Av, Barn. EN4 44 DF46
Hereford Cl, Epsom KT18 156 CR113
Staines TW18 134 BH95
Hereford Copse, Wok. GU22 166 AV119
Hereford Ct, Sutt. SM2
off Worcester Rd 158 DA108
Hereford Gdns, SE13
off Longhurst Rd 124 EE85
Ilford IG1 68 EL59
Pinner HA5 60 BY57
Twickenham TW2 116 CC88
Hereford Ho, NW6 82 DA68
Hereford Ms, W2
off Hereford Rd 82 DA72
Hereford Pl, SE14
off Royal Naval Pl 103 DZ80
Hereford Retreat, SE15
off Bird in Bush Rd 102 DU80
Hereford Rd, E11 68 EH57
W2 82 DA72
W3 80 CP73
W5 97 CJ76
Feltham TW13 116 BW88
Hereford Sq, SW7 100 DC77
Hereford St, E2 84 DU70
Hereford Way, Chess. KT9 155 CJ106
Herent Dr, Ilf. IG5 68 EL56
Hereward Av, Pur. CR8 159 DN111
Hereward Cl, Wal.Abb. EN9 15 ED32
Hereward Gdns, N13 45 DN50
Hereward Grn, Loug. IG10 33 EQ39
Hereward Rd, SW17 120 DF91
Herga Ct, Har. HA1 61 CE62
Watford WD17 23 BU40
Herga Rd, Har. HA3 61 CF56
Herington Gro, Brwd.
(Hutt.) CM13 55 GA45
Heriot Av, E4 47 EA47
Heriot Rd, NW4 63 CW57
Chertsey KT16 134 BG101
Heriots Cl, Stan. HA7 41 CG49
Heritage Cl, SW9 101 DP83
Uxbridge UB8 76 BJ70
Heritage Hill, Kes. BR2 162 EJ106
Heritage Pl, SW18
off Earlsfield Rd 120 DC88
Heritage Vw, Har. HA1 61 CF62
Heritage Wk, Rick. (Chorl.) WD3
off Chenies Rd 21 BE41
Herkomer Cl, Bushey WD23 24 CB44
Herkomer Rd, Bushey WD23 24 CA43
Herlwyn Av, Ruis. HA4 59 BS62
Herlwyn Gdns, SW17 120 DF91
Hermes Cl, W9
off Chippenham Rd 82 DA70
Hermes St, N1 196 D1
Hermes Wk, Nthlt. UB5
off Hotspur Rd 78 CA68
Hermes Way, Wall. SM6 159 DK108
Herm Ho, Enf. EN3
off Eastfield Rd 31 DX38
Hermiston Av, N8 65 DL57
Hermitage, The, SE23 122 DW88
SW13 99 CT81
Feltham TW13 115 BT90
Richmond TW10 117 CK85
Uxbridge UB8 76 BL65
Hermitage Cl, E18 68 EF56
SE2 off Felixstowe Rd 106 EW76
Enfield EN2 29 DP40
Esher (Clay.) KT10 155 CG107
Shepperton TW17 134 BN98
Slough SL3 92 AW76
Hermitage Ct, E18 68 EG56
NW2 off Hermitage La 64 DA62
Potters Bar EN6
off Southgate Rd 12 DC33
Hermitage Gdns, NW2 64 DA62
SE19 122 DQ93
Hermitage La, N18 46 DR50
NW2 64 DA62
SE25 142 DU100
SW16 121 DM94
Croydon CR0 142 DU100
Hermitage Path, SW16 141 DL95
Hermitage Rd, N4 65 DP59
N15 65 DP59
SE19 122 DQ94
Kenley CR8 176 DQ116
Woking GU21 166 AT119
Hermitage Row, E8 66 DU64
Hermitage St, W2 82 DD71
Hermitage Wk, E18 68 EF56
Hermitage Wall, E1 202 C3
Hermitage Waterside, E1 202 B2
Hermitage Way, Stan. HA7 41 CG53
Hermitage Wds Cres,
Wok. GU21 166 AS119
Hermit Pl, NW6
off Belsize Rd 82 DB67
Hermit Rd, E16 86 EF71
Hermit St, EC1 196 F2
Hermon Gro, Hayes UB3 77 BU74
Hermon Hill, E11 68 EG57
E18 68 EG57
Herndon Cl, Egh. TW20 113 BA91
Herndon Rd, SW18 120 DC85
Herne Cl, NW10
off North Circular Rd 62 CR64
HERNE HILL, SE24 122 DQ85
⇌ Herne Hill 121 DP86
Herne Hill, SE24 122 DQ86
Herne Hill Ho, SE24
off Railton Rd 121 DP86
Herne Hill Rd, SE24 102 DQ83
Herne Ms, N18
off Lyndhurst Rd 46 DU49
Herne Pl, SE24 121 DP85
Herne Rd, Bushey WD23 24 CB44
Surbiton KT6 137 CK103
Hernes Cl, Stai. TW18
off Staines Rd 134 BH95
Heron Cl, E17 47 DZ54
NW10 80 CS65
Buckhurst Hill IG9 48 EG46
Hemel Hempstead HP3
off Belswains La 6 BM25
Rickmansworth WD3 38 BK47
Sutton SM1
off Sandpiper Rd 157 CZ106
Uxbridge UB8 76 BK65
Heron Ct, Brom. BR2 144 EJ98
Heron Cres, Sid. DA14 125 ES90
Heron Dale, Add. KT15 152 BK106
Herondale, S.Croy. CR2 161 DX109
Herondale Av, SW18 120 DD88
Heron Dr, N4 66 DQ61
Slough SL3 93 BB77
Heronfield, Egh.
(Eng.Grn) TW20 112 AV93
Potters Bar EN6 12 DC30
Heron Flight Av, Horn. RM12 89 FG66
Herongate Rd, E12 68 EJ61
Swanley BR8 127 FE93
Waltham Cross (Chsht) EN8 15 DY27
Heron Hill, Belv. DA17 106 EZ77
Heron Ms, Ilf. IG1
off Balfour Rd 69 EP61
Heron Pl, SE16 203 L2
Uxbridge UB8
off Summerhouse La 38 BG51
Heron Quay, E14 203 P3
DLR Heron Quays 204 A3
Heron Rd, SE24 102 DQ84
Croydon CR0
off Tunstall Rd 142 DS103
Twickenham TW1 97 CG84
Heronry, The, Walt. KT12 153 BU107
Herons, The, E11 68 EF58
Herons Cft, Wey. KT13 153 BR107
Heronsforde, W13 79 CJ72
HERONSGATE, Rick. WD3 37 BD45
Heronsgate, Edg. HA8 42 CN50
Heronsgate Rd, Rick.
(Chorl.) WD3 21 BB44
Heronslea, Wat. WD25 24 BW36
Heronslea Dr, Stan. HA7 42 CL50
Heron's Pl, Islw. TW7 97 CH83
Heron Sq, Rich. TW9
off Bridge St 117 CK85
Herons Ri, Barn. EN4 28 DE42
Heronswood, Wal.Abb. EN9
off Roundhills 16 EE34
Heron Trd Est, W3
off Alliance Rd 80 CP70
Heron Wk, Nthwd. HA6 39 BS49
Woking GU21
off Blackmore Cres 151 BC114
Heronway, Brwd. (Hutt.) CM13 55 GA46
Heron Way, Felt. TW14
off The Causeway 95 BU84
Grays RM20 109 FV78
Upminster RM14 73 FS60
Heronway, Wdf.Grn. IG8 48 EJ49
Herrick Rd, N5 66 DQ62
Herrick St, SW1 199 N8
Herries St, W10 81 CY68
Herringham Rd, SE7 104 EJ76
Herrings La, Cher. KT16 134 BG100
Herrongate Cl, Enf. EN1 30 DT40
Hersant Cl, NW10 81 CU67
Herschell Ms, SE5
off Bicknell Rd 102 DQ83
Herschell Rd, SE23 123 DY87
Herschel Pk Dr, Slou. SL1 92 AT75
Herschel St, Slou. SL1 92 AT75
HERSHAM, Walt. KT12 154 BX107
⇌ Hersham 136 BY104
Hersham Bypass, Walt. KT12 153 BV106
Hersham Cl, SW15 119 CU87
Hersham Gdns, Walt. KT12 154 BW105
Hersham Rd, Walt. KT12 154 BW105
Hertford Av, SW14 118 CR85
Hertford Cl, Barn. EN4 28 DD41
Hertford Pl, W1 195 K5
Hertford Rd, N1 84 DS67
N2 64 DE55
N9 46 DV47
Barking IG11 87 EP66
Barnet EN4 28 DC41
Enfield EN3 30 DW41
Ilford IG2 69 ES58
Waltham Cross EN8 31 DX37
Hertford Sq, Mitch. CR4
off Hertford Way 141 DL98
Hertford St, W1 199 H2
Hertford Wk, Belv. DA17
off Hoddesdon Rd 106 FA78
Hertford Way, Mitch. CR4 141 DL98
Hertslet Rd, N7 65 DM62
Hertsmere Rd, E14 203 P1
Hervey Cl, N3 44 DA53
Hervey Pk Rd, E17 67 DY56
Hervey Rd, SE3 104 EH81
Hesa Rd, Hayes UB3 77 BU72
Hesewall Cl, SW4
off Brayburne Av 101 DJ82
Hesiers Hill, Warl. CR6 178 EE117
Hesiers Rd, Warl. CR6 178 EE117
Hesketh Av, Dart. DA2 128 FP88
Hesketh Pl, W11 81 CY73
Hesketh Rd, E7 68 EG62
Heslop Rd, SW12 120 DF88
Hesper Ms, SW5 100 DB78
Hesperus Cres, E14 204 B9
Hessel Rd, W13 97 CG75
Hessel St, E1 84 DV72
Hesselyn Dr, Rain. RM13 89 FH66
Hessle Gro, Epsom KT17 157 CT111
Hestercombe Av, SW6 99 CY82
Hesterman Way, Croy. CR0 141 DL102
Hester Rd, N18 46 DU50
SW11 100 DE80
Hester Ter, Rich. TW9
off Chilton Rd 98 CN83
HESTON, Houns. TW5 96 BZ80
Heston Av, Houns. TW5 96 BY80
Heston Gra La, Houns. TW5 96 BZ79
Heston Ind Mall, Houns. TW5 96 BZ80
Heston Rd, Houns. TW5 96 CA80
Heston St, SE14 103 DZ81
Heswell Grn, Wat. WD19
off Fairhaven Cres 39 BU48
Hetherington Rd, SW4 101 DL84
Shepperton TW17 135 BQ96
Hetherington Way, Uxb. UB10 58 BL63
Hethersett Cl, Reig. RH2 184 DC131
Hetley Gdns, SE19
off Fox Hill 122 DT94
Hetley Rd, W12 81 CV74
Heton Gdns, NW4 63 CU56
Heusden Way, Ger.Cr. SL9 57 AZ60
Hevelius Cl, SE10 205 K10
Hever Ct Rd, Grav. DA12 131 GK93
Hever Cft, SE9 125 EN91
Hever Gdns, Brom. BR1 145 EN97
Heverham Rd, SE18 105 ES77
Heversham Rd, Bexh. DA7 106 FA82
Hewens Rd, Hayes UB4 77 BQ70
Uxbridge UB10 77 BQ70
Hewer St, W10 81 CX71
Hewers Way, Tad. KT20 173 CV120
Hewett Cl, Stan. HA7 41 CH49
Hewett Pl, Swan. BR8 147 FD98
Hewett Rd, Dag. RM8 70 EX64
Hewett St, EC2 197 N5
Hewins Cl, Wal.Abb. EN9
off Broomstick Hall Rd 16 EE33
Hewish Rd, N18 46 DS49
Hewison St, E3 85 DZ68
Hewitt Av, N22 45 DP54
Hewitt Cl, Croy. CR0 143 EA104
Hewitt Rd, N8 65 DN57
Hewitts Rd, Orp. BR6 164 EZ108
Hewlett Rd, E3 85 DY68
Hexagon, The, N6 64 DF60
Hexal Rd, SE6 124 EE90
Hexham Gdns, Islw. TW7 97 CG80
Hexham Rd, SE27 122 DQ89
Barnet EN5 28 DB42
Morden SM4 140 DB102
HEXTABLE, Swan. BR8 127 FG94
Hextalls La, Red. (Bletch.) RH1 186 DR128
Heybourne Rd, N17 46 DV52
Heybridge Av, SW16 121 DL94
Heybridge Dr, Ilf. IG6 49 ER54
Heybridge Way, E10 67 DY59
Heyford Av, SW8 101 DL80
SW20 139 CZ97
Heyford Rd, Mitch. CR4 140 DE96
Radlett WD7 25 CF37
Heyford Ter, SW8
off Heyford Av 101 DL80
Heygate St, SE17 201 H9
Heylyn Sq, E3
off Malmesbury Rd 85 DZ69
Heymede, Lthd. KT22 171 CJ123
Heynes Rd, Dag. RM8 70 EW63
Heysham Dr, Wat. WD19 40 BW50
Heysham La, NW3 64 DB62
Heysham Rd, N15 66 DR58
Heythorp Cl, Wok. GU21 166 AT117
Heythorp St, SW18 119 CZ88
Heythrop Dr, Uxb.
(Ickhm) UB10 58 BM63
Heywood Av, NW9 42 CS53
Heyworth Rd, E5 66 DV63
E15 68 EF64
Hibbert Av, Wat. WD24 24 BX38
Hibbert Lo, Ger.Cr. (Chal.St.P.) SL9
off Gold Hill E 36 AX54
Hibbert Rd, E17 67 DZ59
Harrow HA3 41 CF54
Hibbert St, SW11 100 DC83
Hibberts Way, Ger.Cr. SL9
off North Pk 56 AY56
Hibbs Cl, Swan. BR8 147 FD96
Hibernia Dr, Grav. DA12 131 GM90
Hibernia Gdns, Houns. TW3 96 CA84
Hibernia Pt, SE2
off Wolvercote Rd 106 EX75
Hibernia Rd, Houns. TW3 96 CA84
Hibiscus Cl, Edg. HA8
off Campion Way 42 CQ49
Hichisson Rd, SE15 122 DW85
Hickin Cl, SE7 104 EK77
Hickin St, E14 204 D6
Hickling Rd, Ilf. IG1 69 EP64
Hickman Av, E4 47 EC51
Hickman Cl, E16 86 EK71
Hickman Rd, Rom. RM6 70 EW59
Hickmans Cl, Gdse. RH9 186 DW132
Hickmore Wk, SW4 101 DJ83
Hickory Cl, N9 46 DU45
Hicks Av, Grnf. UB6 79 CD68
Hicks Cl, SW11 100 DE83
Hicks St, SE8 203 K10
Hidcote Cl, Wok. GU22 167 BB116
Hidcote Gdns, SW20 139 CV97
Hide, E6 off Downings 87 EN72
Hideaway, The, Abb.L. WD5 7 BU31
Hide Pl, SW1 199 M9
Hide Rd, Har. HA1 61 CD56
Hides St, N7
off Sheringham Rd 83 DM65
Hide Twr, SW1 199 M9
Higgins Rd, Wal.Cr. (Chsht) EN7 14 DR27
Higgins Wk, Hmptn. TW12
off Abbott Cl 116 BY93
High Acres, Abb.L. WD5 7 BR32
HIGHAM HILL, E17 47 DY54
Higham Hill Rd, E17 47 DY54
Higham Pl, E17 67 DY55
Higham Rd, N17 66 DR55
Woodford Green IG8 48 EG51
Highams Ct, E4 off Friars Cl 47 ED48
Highams Lo Business Cen,
E17 67 DY55
HIGHAMS PARK, E4 47 ED50
⇌ Highams Park 47 ED51
Highams Pk Ind Est, E4 47 EC51
Higham Sta Av, E4 47 EB51
Higham St, E17 67 DY55
Higham Vw, Epp.
(N.Wld Bas.) CM16 19 FB26
Highbanks Cl, Well. DA16 106 EV80
Highbanks Rd, Pnr. HA5 40 CB50
Highbank Way, N8 65 DN58
HIGH BARNET, Barn. EN5 27 CX40
⊖ High Barnet 28 DA42
Highbarns, Hem.H. HP3 6 BN25
Highbarrow Rd, Croy. CR0 142 DU101
HIGH BEACH, Loug. IG10 32 EG39
High Beech, S.Croy. CR2 160 DS108
High Beeches, Bans. SM7 157 CX114
Gerrards Cross SL9 56 AX60
Orpington BR6 164 EU107
Sidcup DA14 126 EY92
High Beeches Cl, Pur. CR8 159 DK110
High Beech Rd, Loug. IG10 32 EK42
High Br, SE10 103 ED78
Highbridge Ind Est, Uxb. UB8 76 BJ66
Highbridge Rd, Bark. IG11 87 EP67
Highbridge St, Wal.Abb. EN9 15 EA33
High Br Wf, SE10 103 ED78
Highbrook Rd, SE3 104 EK83
High Broom Cres,
W.Wick. BR4 143 EB101
HIGHBURY, N5 65 DP64
⇌ Highbury & Islington 83 DP65
⊖ Highbury & Islington 83 DP65
Highbury Av, Th.Hth. CR7 141 DN96
Highbury Cl, N.Mal. KT3 138 CQ98
West Wickham BR4 143 EB103
Highbury Cor, N5 83 DN65
Highbury Cres, N5 65 DN64
Highbury Est, N5 66 DQ64
Highbury Gdns, Ilf. IG3 69 ES61
Highbury Gra, N5 65 DP63
Highbury Gro, N5 65 DP65
Highbury Hill, N5 65 DN62
Highbury Ms, N7
off Holloway Rd 83 DN65
Highbury New Pk, N5 66 DQ64
Highbury Pk, N5 65 DP62
Highbury Pk Ms, N5
off Highbury Gra 66 DQ63
Highbury Pl, N5 83 DP65
Highbury Quad, N5 66 DQ62
Highbury Rd, SW19 119 CY92
Highbury Sta Rd, N1 83 DN65
Highbury Ter, N5 65 DP64
Highbury Ter Ms, N5 65 DP64
High Canons, Borwd. WD6 26 CQ37
High Cedar Dr, SW20 119 CV94
Highclere Cl, Ken. CR8 176 DQ115
Highclere Rd, N.Mal. KT3 138 CR97
Highclere St, SE26 123 DY91
Highcliffe Dr, SW15 119 CT86
Highcliffe Gdns, Ilf. IG4 68 EL57
High Cl, Rick. WD3 22 BJ43
Highcombe, SE7 104 EH79
Highcombe Cl, SE9 124 EK88
High Coombe Pl, Kings.T.
KT2 118 CR94
Highcroft, NW9 62 CR57
Highcroft Av, Wem. HA0 80 CN67
Highcroft Ct, Lthd.
(Bkhm) KT23 170 CA123
Highcroft Gdns, NW11 63 CZ58
Highcroft Rd, N19 65 DL59
Hemel Hempstead
(Felden) HP3 6 BG25
High Cross, Wat. (Ald.) WD25 25 CD37
High Cross Cen, N15 66 DU56
High Cross Rd, N17 66 DU55
Highcross Rd, Grav.
(Sthflt) DA13 129 FX92
Highcross Way, SW15 119 CU88
Highdaun Dr, SW16 141 DM98
Highdown, Wor.Pk. KT4 138 CS103
Highdown La, Sutt. SM2 158 DB111
Highdown Rd, SW15 119 CV86
High Dr, Cat. (Wold.) CR3 177 DZ122
Leatherhead (Oxshott) KT22 155 CD114
New Malden KT3 138 CQ95
High Elms, Chig. IG7 49 ES49
Upminster RM14 73 FS60
Woodford Green IG8 48 EG50
High Elms Cl, Nthwd. HA6 39 BR51
High Elms La, Wat. WD25 7 BV31
High Elms Rd, Orp. BR6 163 EP110
HIGHER DENHAM, Uxb. UB9 57 BB59
Higher Dr, Bans. SM7 157 CX112
Purley CR8 159 DN113
Higher Grn, Epsom KT17 157 CU113
Highfield, Bans. SM7 174 DE117
Bushey (Bushey Hth) WD23 41 CE47
Chalfont St. Giles HP8 36 AX47
Feltham TW13 115 BU88
Kings Langley WD4 6 BL28
Watford WD19 40 BZ48
Highfield Av, NW9 62 CQ57
NW11 63 CX59
Erith DA8 107 FB79
Greenford UB6 61 CE64
Orpington BR6 163 ET106
Pinner HA5 60 BZ57
Wembley HA9 62 CM62
Highfield Cl, N22 45 DN53
NW9 62 CQ57
SE13 123 ED86
Egham (Eng.Grn) TW20 112 AW93
Leatherhead (Oxshott) KT22 155 CD111
Northwood HA6 39 BS53
Romford RM5 51 FC51
Surbiton KT6 137 CJ102
West Byfleet KT14 152 BG113
Highfield Ct, N14 29 DJ44
Highfield Cres, Horn. RM12 72 FM61
Northwood HA6 39 BS53
Highfield Dr, Brom. BR2 144 EE98
Caterham CR3 176 DU122
Epsom KT19 157 CT108
Uxbridge (Ickhm) UB10 58 BL63
West Wickham BR4 143 EB103
Highfield Gdns, NW11 63 CY58
Grays RM16 110 GD75
Highfield Grn, Epp. CM16 17 ES31
Highfield Hill, SE19 122 DR94
Highfield Link, Rom. RM5 51 FC51
Highfield Ms, NW6
off Compayne Gdns 82 DB66
Highfield Pl, Epp. CM16 17 ES31
Highfield Rd, N21 45 DP47
NW11 63 CY58
W3 80 CP71
Bexleyheath DA6 126 EZ85
Bromley BR1 145 EM98
Bushey WD23 24 BY43
Caterham CR3 176 DU122
Chertsey KT16 134 BG102
Chislehurst BR7 145 ET97
Dartford DA1 128 FK87
Feltham TW13 115 BU89
Hornchurch RM12 72 FM61
Isleworth TW7 97 CF81
Northwood HA6 39 BS53
Purley CR8 159 DM110
Romford RM5 51 FC52
Sunbury-on-Thames TW16 135 BT98
Surbiton KT5 138 CQ101
Sutton SM1 158 DE106
Waltham Cross
(Chsht) EN7 14 DS26
Walton-on-Thames KT12 135 BU102
West Byfleet KT14 152 BG113
Westerham (Bigg.H.) TN16 178 EJ117
Woodford Green IG8 48 EL52
Highfield Rd S, Dart. DA1 128 FK87
Highfields, Ashtd. KT21 171 CK119
Leatherhead (Fetch.) KT22 171 CD124
Potters Bar (Cuffley) EN6 13 DL28
Radlett WD7 25 CF35
Highfields Gro, N6 64 DF60
Highfield Twr, Rom. RM5 51 FD50
Highfield Way, Horn. RM12 72 FM61
Potters Bar EN6 12 DB32
Rickmansworth WD3 22 BH44
High Firs, Rad. WD7 25 CF35
Swanley BR8 147 FE98
High Foleys, Esher
(Clay.) KT10 155 CH108
High Gables, Loug. IG10 32 EK43
High Garth, Esher KT10 154 CC107
HIGHGATE, N6 64 DG61
⊖ Highgate 65 DH58
Highgate Av, N6 65 DH58
★ Highgate Cem, N6 64 DG60
Highgate Cl, N6 64 DG59
Highgate High St, N6 64 DG60
Highgate Hill, N6 65 DH60
N19 65 DH60
Highgate Ho, SE26
off Sydenham Hill 122 DU90
Highgate Rd, NW5 65 DH63

★ Place of interest ⇌ Railway station ⊖ London Underground station DLR Docklands Light Railway station Tra Tramlink station H Hospital Riv Pedestrian ferry landing stage

270

Highgate Wk, SE23 122 DW89
Highgate W Hill, N6 64 DG61
High Gro, SE18 105 ER80
Highgrove, Brwd.
(Pilg.Hat.) CM15 54 FV44
High Gro, Brom. BR1 144 EJ95
Highgrove Cl, N11
off Balmoral Av 44 DG50
Chislehurst BR7 144 EL95
Highgrove Ms, Cars. SM5 140 DF104
Grays RM17 110 GC78
Highgrove Rd, Dag. RM8 70 EW64
Highgrove Way, Ruis. HA4 59 BU58
High Hill Est, E5
off Mount Pleasant La 66 DV60
High Hill Ferry, E5 66 DV60
High Hill Rd, Warl. CR6 177 EC115
High Holborn, WC1 196 A8
High Ho La, Grays
(Orsett) RM16 111 GJ75
Tilbury (W.Til.) RM18 111 GK77
Highland Av, W7 79 CE72
Brentwood CM15 54 FW46
Dagenham RM10 71 FC62
Loughton IG10 32 EL44
Highland Cotts, Wall. SM6 159 DH105
Highland Ct, E18 48 EH53
Highland Cft, Beck. BR3 123 EB92
Highland Dr, Bushey WD23 40 CC45
Highland Pk, Felt. TW13 115 BT91
Highland Rd, SE19 122 DS93
Bexleyheath DA6 126 FA85
Bromley BR1, BR2 144 EF95
Northwood HA6 39 BT54
Purley CR8 159 DN114
Sevenoaks (Bad.Mt) TN14 165 FB111
Highlands, Ashtd. KT21 171 CJ119
Watford WD19 40 BW46
Highlands, The, Edg. HA8 42 CP54
Potters Bar EN6 28 DB43
Rickmansworth WD3 38 BH45
Highlands Av, N21 29 DM43
W3 80 CQ73
Leatherhead KT22 171 CJ122
Highlands Cl, N4
off Mount Vw Rd 65 DL59
Gerrards Cross
(Chal.St.P.) SL9 37 AZ52
Hounslow TW3 96 CB81
Leatherhead KT22 171 CH122
Highlands End, Ger.Cr.
(Chal.St.P.) SL9 36 AY52
Highlands Gdns, Ilf. IG1 69 EM60
Highlands Heath, SW15 119 CW87
Highlands Hill, Swan. BR8 147 FG96
Highlands La, Ger.Cr.
(Chal.St.P.) SL9 37 AZ51
Woking GU22 166 AY122
Highlands Pk, Lthd. KT22 171 CK123
Sevenoaks (Seal) TN15 191 FL121
Highlands Rd, Barn. EN5 28 DA43
Leatherhead KT22 171 CH122
Orpington BR5 146 EV101
Reigate RH2 184 DD133
High La, W7 79 CD72
Caterham CR3 177 DZ119
Warlingham CR6 177 DZ118
High Lawns, Har. HA1 61 CE62
Highlea Cl, NW9 42 CS53
High Level Dr, SE26 122 DU91
Highlever Rd, W10 81 CW71
Highmead, SE18 105 ET80
High Mead, Chig. IG7 49 EQ47
Harrow HA1 61 CE57
West Wickham BR4 143 ED103
Highmead Cres, Wem. HA0 80 CM66
High Meadow Cl, Pnr. HA5
off Daymer Gdns 59 BV56
High Meadow Cres, NW9 62 CR57
High Meadow Pl, Cher. KT16 133 BF100
High Meadows, Chig. IG7 49 ER50
High Meads Rd, E16 86 EK72
Highmore Rd, SE3 104 EE80
High Mt, NW4 63 CU58
High Oaks, Enf. EN2 29 DM38
High Pk Av, Rich. TW9 98 CN81
High Pk Rd, Rich. TW9 98 CN81
High Path, SW19 140 DB95
High Pine Cl, Wey. KT13 153 BQ106
High Pines, Warl. CR6 176 DW119
High Pt, N6 64 DG59
SE9 125 EP90
Weybridge KT13 152 BN106
High Ridge, Pot.B.
(Cuffley) EN6 13 DL27
Highridge Cl, Epsom KT18 172 CS115
High Ridge Cl, Hem.H. HP3 6 BK25
High Ridge Rd, Hem.H. HP3 6 BK25
High Rd, N2 44 DD53
N11 45 DH50
N12 44 DC51
N15 66 DT58
N17 46 DT53
N20 44 DC45
N22 65 DN55
NW10 (Willesden) 81 CV65
Buckhurst Hill IG9 48 EH47
Bushey (Bushey Hth) WD23 41 CD46
Chigwell IG7 49 EM50
Coulsdon CR5 174 DF121
Dartford (Wilm.) DA2 128 FJ90
Epping CM16 17 ER32
Epping (N.Wld Bas.) CM16 19 FB27
Epping (Thnwd) CM16 18 EV28
Harrow (Har.Wld) HA3 41 CE52
Ilford IG1 69 EP62
Ilford (Seven Kings) IG3 69 ET60
Loughton IG10 48 EJ45
Pinner HA5 59 BV56
Reigate RH2 184 DD126
Romford (Chad.Hth) RM6 70 EV60
Uxbridge UB8 76 BJ71
Watford WD25 23 BT35
Wembley HA0, HA9 61 CK64
West Byfleet (Byfleet) KT14 152 BM112
High Rd Ickenham, Uxb. UB10 59 BP62
High Rd Leyton, E10 67 EB60
E15 67 EC62
High Rd Leytonstone, E11 68 EE63
E15 68 EE63
High Rd Turnford, Brox. EN10 15 DY25
High Rd Woodford Grn, E18 48 EF52
Woodford Green IG8 48 EF52
Highshore Rd, SE15 102 DT82
High Silver, Loug. IG10 32 EK42
High Standing, Cat. CR3 186 DQ125
Highstead Cres, Erith DA8 107 FE81
Highstone Av, E11 68 EG58
High St, E11 68 EG57
E13 86 EG68
E15 85 EC68
E17 67 DZ57
N8 65 DL56
N14 45 DK46
NW7 43 CV49
NW10 (Harlesden) 81 CT68
SE20 122 DV93
SE25 (S.Norwood) 142 DT98
W3 80 CP74
W5 79 CK73
Abbots Langley WD5 6 BN29
Abbots Langley
(Bedmond) WD5 7 BS31
Addlestone KT15 152 BH105
Banstead SM7 174 DA115
Barnet EN5 27 CY41
Beckenham BR3 143 EA96
Borehamwood (Elstree) WD6 25 CK44
Brentford TW8 97 CK79
Brentwood CM14 54 FV47
Bromley BR1 144 EG96
Bushey WD23 24 CA44
Carshalton SM5 158 DG105
Caterham CR3 176 DS123
Chalfont St. Giles HP8 36 AW48
Chislehurst BR7 125 EP93
Cobham KT11 153 BV114
Croydon CR0 142 DQ103
Dartford DA1 128 FL86
Dartford (Bean) DA2 129 FV90
Dartford (Eyns.) DA4 148 FL103
Dartford (Fnghm) DA4 148 FM100
Edgware HA8 42 CN51
Egham TW20 113 BA92
Epping CM16 17 ET31
Epsom KT19 156 CR113
Epsom (Ewell) KT17 157 CT109
Esher KT10 154 CB105
Esher (Clay.) KT10 155 CF107
Feltham TW13 115 BT90
Gerrards Cross
(Chal.St.P.) SL9 36 AY53
Godstone RH9 186 DV131
Gravesend DA11 131 GH86
Gravesend (Nthflt) DA11 130 GB86
Grays RM17 110 GA79
Greenhithe DA9 109 FV84
Hampton TW12 116 CC93
Harrow HA1, HA2 61 CE60
Harrow (Wldste) HA3 61 CE55
Hayes UB3 95 BS78
Hemel Hempstead (Bov.) HP3 5 BA27
Hornchurch RM11, RM12 72 FK60
Hounslow TW3 96 CC83
Hounslow (Cran.) TW5 95 BV80
Ilford (Barkingside) IG6 49 EQ54
Iver SL0 75 BE72
Kings Langley WD4 7 BT27
Kingston upon Thames KT1 137 CK96
Kingston upon Thames
(Hmptn W.) KT1 137 CJ95
Leatherhead KT22 171 CH122
Leatherhead (Oxshott) KT22 155 CD113
New Malden KT3 138 CS97
Northwood HA6 39 BT53
Orpington BR6 146 EU102
Orpington (Downe) BR6 163 EN111
Orpington (Farnboro.) BR6 163 EP106
Orpington
(Grn St Grn) BR6 163 ET108
Orpington (St.M.Cray) BR5 146 EW98
Oxted RH8 187 ED130
Oxted (Lmpfld) RH8 188 EG128
Pinner HA5 60 BY55
Potters Bar EN6 12 DC33
Purfleet RM19
off London Rd Purfleet 108 FN78
Purley CR8 159 DN111
Redhill RH1 184 DF134
Redhill (Bletch.) RH1 186 DQ133
Redhill (Merst.) RH1 185 DH128
Redhill (Nutfld) RH1 185 DM133
Reigate RH2 184 DA134
Rickmansworth WD3 38 BK46
Romford RM1 71 FE57
Ruislip HA4 59 BS59
St. Albans (Lon.Col.) AL2 9 CJ25
Sevenoaks TN13 191 FJ125
Sevenoaks
(Chipstead) TN13 190 FC122
Sevenoaks (Otford) TN14 181 FF116
Sevenoaks (Seal) TN15 191 FL121
Sevenoaks (Shore.) TN14 165 FF110
Shepperton TW17 135 BP100
Slough SL1 92 AU75
Slough (Colnbr.) SL3 93 BC80
Slough (Datchet) SL3 92 AV81
Slough (Langley) SL3 93 AZ78
South Ockendon
(Aveley) RM15 91 FR74
Southall UB1 78 BZ74
Staines TW18 113 BF91
Staines (Stanw.) TW19 114 BK86
Staines (Wrays.) TW19 112 AY86
Sutton SM1 158 DB105
Sutton (Cheam) SM3 157 CY107
Swanley BR8 147 FF98
Swanscombe DA10 130 FZ85
Tadworth KT20 173 CW123
Teddington TW11 117 CG92
Thames Ditton KT7 137 CG101
Thornton Heath CR7 142 DQ98
Twickenham (Whitton) TW2 116 CC87
Uxbridge UB8 76 BK67
Uxbridge (Cowley) UB8 76 BJ70
Uxbridge (Hare.) UB9 38 BJ54
Waltham Cross EN8 15 DY34
Waltham Cross (Chsht) EN8 15 DX29
Walton-on-Thames KT12 135 BU102
Watford WD17 23 BV41
High St, Wembley HA9 62 CM63
West Drayton (Harm.) UB7 94 BK79
West Drayton (Yiew.) UB7 76 BK74
West Molesey KT8 136 CA98
West Wickham BR4 143 EB102
Westerham TN16 189 EQ127
Westerham (Brasted) TN16 180 EV124
Weybridge KT13 152 BN105
Woking GU21 166 AY117
Woking (Chobham) GU24 150 AS111
Woking (Horsell) GU21 166 AV115
Woking (Old Wok.) GU22 167 BB121
Woking (Ripley) GU23 168 BJ121
High St Colliers Wd, SW19 120 DD94
⊖ **High Street Kensington** 100 DB75
High St Ms, SW19 119 CY92
High St N, E6 86 EL67
E12 68 EL64
High St Ponders End,
Enf. EN3 30 DW42
High St S, E6 87 EM68
High St Wimbledon, SW19 119 CX92
High Timber St, EC4 197 H10
High Tor Cl, Brom. BR1
off Babbacombe Rd 124 EH94
High Tree Cl, Add. KT15 151 BF106
High Tree Ct, W7 79 CE73
High Trees, SW2 121 DN88
Barnet EN4 28 DE43
Croydon CR0 143 DY102
Dartford DA2
off Bow Arrow La 128 FP86
High Trees Cl, Cat. CR3 176 DT123
High Trees Ct, Brwd. CM14
off Warley Mt 54 FW49
Highview, Cat. CR3 176 DS124
High Vw, Ch.St.G. HP8 36 AX47
Highview, Nthlt. UB5 78 BY69
High Vw, Pnr. HA5 60 BW56
Rickmansworth (Chorl.) WD3 22 BG42
Sutton SM2 157 CZ111
Watford WD18 23 BT44
Highview, Wok. (Knap.) GU21
off Mulgrave Way 166 AS117
Highview Av, Edg. HA8 42 CQ49
High Vw Av, Grays RM17 110 GC78
Highview Av, Wall. SM6 159 DM106
High Vw Caravan Pk,
Kings L. WD4 7 BR28
High Vw Cl, SE19 142 DT96
Loughton IG10 32 EJ43
Highview Cl, Pot.B. EN6 12 DC33
Highview Cres, Brwd.
(Hutt.) CM13 55 GC44
Highview Gdns, N3 63 CY55
N11 45 DJ50
Edgware HA8 42 CQ49
High Vw Gdns, Grays RM17 110 GC78
Highview Gdns, Pot.B. EN6 12 DC33
Upminster RM14 72 FP61
Highview Ho, Rom. RM6 70 EY56
Highview Path, Bans. SM7 174 DA115
High Vw Rd, E18 68 EF55
Highview Rd, SE19 122 DR93
W13 79 CG71
Sidcup DA14 126 EV91
Highway, The, E1 202 C1
E14 202 C1
Orpington BR6 164 EW106
Stanmore HA7 41 CF53
Sutton SM2 158 DC109
Highwold, Couls. CR5 174 DG118
Highwood, Brom. BR2 144 EE97
Highwood Av, N12 44 DC49
Bushey WD23 24 BZ39
Highwood Cl, Brwd. CM14 54 FV45
Kenley CR8 176 DQ117
Orpington BR6 145 EQ103
Highwood Dr, Orp. BR6 145 EQ103
Highwood Gdns, Ilf. IG5 69 EM57
Highwood Gro, NW7 42 CR50
Highwood Hall La, Hem.H. HP3 7 BQ25
HIGHWOOD HILL, NW7 43 CU47
Highwood Hill, NW7 43 CT47
H **Highwood Hosp**,
Brwd. CM15 54 FW45
Highwood La, Loug. IG10 33 EN43
Highwood Rd, N19 65 DL62
Highwoods, Cat. CR3 186 DS125
Leatherhead KT22 171 CJ121
High Worple, Har. HA2 60 BZ59
Highworth Rd, N11 45 DK51
Hilary Av, Mitch. CR4 140 DG97
Hilary Cl, SW6 100 DB80
Erith DA8 107 FC81
Hornchurch RM12 72 FK64
Hilary Rd, W12 81 CT72
Slough SL3 92 AY75
Hilbert Rd, Sutt. SM3 139 CX104
Hilborough Way, Orp. BR6 163 ER106
Hilda May Av, Swan. BR8 147 FE97
Hilda Rd, E6 86 EK66
E16 86 EE70
Hilda Ter, SW9 101 DN82
Hilda Vale Cl, Orp. BR6 163 EP105
Hilda Vale Rd, Orp. BR6 163 EN105
Hildenborough Gdns,
Brom. BR1 124 EE93
Hilden Dr, Erith DA8 107 FH80
Hildenlea Pl, Brom. BR2 144 EE96
Hildenley Cl, Red. RH1
off Malmstone Av 185 DK128
Hilders, The, Ashtd. KT21 172 CP117
Hildreth St, SW12 121 DH88
Hildyard Rd, SW6 100 DA79
Hiley Rd, NW10 81 CW69
Hilfield La, Wat. (Ald.) WD25 25 CD41
Hilfield La S, Bushey WD23 25 CF44
Hilgrove Rd, NW6 82 DC66
Hiliary Gdns, Stan. HA7 41 CJ54
Hiljon Cres, Ger.Cr.
(Chal.St.P.) SL9 36 AY53
Hill, The, Cat. CR3 176 DT124
Gravesend (Nthflt) DA11 130 GC86
Hillars Heath Rd, Couls. CR5 175 DL115
Hillary Av, Grav. (Nthflt) DA11 130 GE90
Hillary Cres, Walt. KT12 136 BW102
Hillary Dr, Islw. TW7 97 CF84
Hillary Ri, Barn. EN5 28 DA42
Hillary Rd, Sthl. UB2 96 CA76
Hill Barn, S.Croy. CR2 160 DS111
Hillbeck Cl, SE15 102 DW80
Hillbeck Way, Grnf. UB6 79 CD67
Hillborne Cl, Hayes UB3 95 BU78
Hillborough Av, Sev. TN13 191 FK122
Hillborough Cl, SW19 120 DC94
Hillbrook Gdns, Wey. KT13 152 BN108
Hillbrook Rd, SW17 120 DF90
Hill Brow, Brom. BR1 144 EK95
Dartford DA1 127 FF86
Hillbrow, N.Mal. KT3 139 CT97
Hillbrow Cl, Bex. DA5 127 FD91
Hillbrow Cotts, Gdse. RH9 186 DW132
Hillbrow Ct, Gdse. RH9 186 DW132
Hillbrow Rd, Brom. BR1 124 EE94
Esher KT10 154 CC105
Hillbury Av, Har. HA3 61 CH57
Hillbury Cl, Warl. CR6 176 DV118
Hillbury Gdns, Warl. CR6 176 DW118
Hillbury Rd, SW17 121 DH90
Warlingham CR6 176 DU117
Whyteleafe CR3 176 DU117
Hill Cl, NW2 63 CV62
NW11 64 DA58
Barnet EN5 27 CW43
Chislehurst BR7 125 EP92
Cobham KT11 154 CA112
Gravesend
(Istead Rise) DA13 130 GE94
Harrow HA1 61 CE62
Purley CR8 160 DQ113
Stanmore HA7 41 CH49
Woking GU21 166 AX115
Hillcote Av, SW16 121 DN94
Hill Ct, Nthlt. UB5 60 CA64
Hillcourt Av, N12 44 DB51
Hillcourt Est, N16 66 DR60
Hillcourt Rd, SE22 122 DV86
Hill Cres, N20 44 DB47
Bexley DA5 127 FC88
Harrow HA1 61 CG57
Hornchurch RM11 72 FJ58
Surbiton KT5 138 CM99
Worcester Park KT4 139 CW103
Hillcrest, N6 64 DG59
N21 45 DP45
Hill Crest, Pot.B. EN6 12 DC34
Sevenoaks TN13 190 FG122
Sidcup DA15 126 EU87
Hillcrest, Wey. KT13 153 BP105
Hillcrest Av, NW11 63 CY57
Chertsey KT16 151 BE105
Edgware HA8 42 CP49
Grays RM20 109 FU79
Pinner HA5 60 BX56
Hillcrest Caravan Pk, Tad.
(Box H.) KT20 182 CP131
Hillcrest Cl, SE26 122 DU91
Beckenham BR3 143 DZ99
Epsom KT18 173 CT115
Waltham Cross
(Goffs Oak) EN7 14 DQ29
Hillcrest Ct, Sutt. SM2
off Eaton Rd 158 DD107
Hillcrest Dr, Green. DA9
off Riverview Rd 129 FV85
Hillcrest Gdns, N3 63 CY56
NW2 63 CU62
Esher KT10 137 CF104
Hillcrest Par, Couls. CR5 159 DH114
Hillcrest Rd, E17 47 ED54
E18 48 EF54
W3 80 CN74
W5 80 CL71
Bromley BR1 124 EG92
Dartford DA1 127 FF87
Hornchurch RM11 71 FG59
Loughton IG10 32 EK44
Ongar CM5 19 FE30
Orpington BR6 146 EU103
Purley CR8 159 DM110
Radlett (Shenley) WD7 10 CN33
Westerham (Bigg.H.) TN16 178 EK116
Whyteleafe CR3 176 DT117
Hillcrest Vw, Beck. BR3 143 DZ100
Hillcrest Way, Epp. CM16 18 EU31
Hillcrest Waye, Ger.Cr. SL9 57 AZ59
Hillcroft, Loug. IG10 33 EN40
Hillcroft Av, Pnr. HA5 60 BZ58
Purley CR8 159 DJ113
Hillcroft Cres, W5 80 CL72
Ruislip HA4 60 BX62
Watford WD19 39 BV46
Wembley HA9 62 CM63
Hillcroft Rd, E6 87 EP71
Hillcroome Rd, Sutt. SM2 158 DD107
Hillcross Av, Mord. SM4 139 CZ99
Hilldale Rd, Sutt. SM1 157 CZ105
Hilldeane Rd, Pur. CR8 159 DN109
Hilldene Av, Rom. RM3 52 FJ51
Hilldene Cl, Rom. RM3 52 FK50
Hilldown Rd, SW16 121 DL94
Bromley BR2 144 EE102
Hill Dr, NW9 62 CQ60
SW16 141 DM97
Hilldrop Cres, N7 65 DK64
Hilldrop Est, N7 65 DK64
Hilldrop La, N7 65 DK64
Hilldrop Rd, N7 65 DK64
Bromley BR1 124 EG93
HILL END, Uxb. UB9 38 BH51
Hillend, SE18 105 EN81
Hill End, Orp. BR6
off The Approach 145 ET103
Hill End Rd, Uxb. (Hare.) UB9 38 BH51
Hillersdon, Slou. SL2 74 AV71
Hillersdon Av, SW13 99 CU82
Edgware HA8 42 CM50
Hillery Cl, SE17 201 L9
Hilley Fld La, Lthd.
(Fetch.) KT22 170 CC122
Hill Fm Av, Wat. WD25 7 BU33
Hill Fm Cl, Wat. WD25 7 BU33
Hill Fm Ind Est, Wat. WD25 7 BT33
Hill Fm La, Ch.St.G. HP8 36 AT46
Hill Fm Rd, W10 81 CW71
Gerrards Cross
(Chal.St.P.) SL9 36 AY52
Uxbridge UB10
off Austin's La 59 BR63
Hillfield Av, N8 65 DL57
NW9 62 CS57
Wembley HA0 80 CL66
Hillfield Cl, Har. HA2 60 CC56
Redhill RH1 184 DG134
Hillfield Ct, NW3 64 DE64
Hillfield Par, Mord. SM4 140 DE100
Hillfield Pk, N10 65 DH56
N21 45 DN47
Hillfield Pk Ms, N10 65 DH56
Hillfield Rd, NW6 63 CZ64
Gerrards Cross
(Chal.St.P.) SL9 36 AY52
Hampton TW12 116 BZ94
Redhill RH1 184 DG134
Sevenoaks (Dunt.Grn) TN13 181 FE120
Hillfield Sq, Ger.Cr.
(Chal.St.P.) SL9 36 AY52
Hillfoot Av, Rom. RM5 51 FC53
Hillfoot Rd, Rom. RM5 51 FC53
Hillgate Pl, SW12 121 DH87
W8 82 DA74
Hillgate St, W8 82 DA74
Hill Gate Wk, N6 65 DJ58
Hill Gro, Felt. TW13
off Watermill Way 116 BZ89
Hillgrove, Ger.Cr.
(Chal.St.P.) SL9 37 AZ53
Hill Gro, Rom. RM1 71 FE55
Hill Hall, Epp. CM16 34 EZ35
Hillhouse, Wal.Abb. EN9 16 EF33
Hill Ho Av, Stan. HA7 41 CF52
Hill Ho Cl, N21 45 DN45
Gerrards Cross (Chal.St.P.) SL9
off Rickmansworth La 36 AY52
Hill Ho Dr, Hmptn. TW12 136 CA95
Weybridge KT13 152 BN111
Hill Ho Rd, SW16 121 DM92
Hillhouse Rd, Dart. DA2 128 FQ87
Hillhurst Gdns, Cat. CR3 176 DS120
Hilliard Rd, Nthwd. HA6 39 BT53
Hilliards Ct, E1 202 E2
Hilliards Rd, Uxb. UB8 76 BK72
Hillier Cl, Barn. EN5 28 DB44
Hillier Gdns, Croy. CR0
off Crowley Cres 159 DN106
Hillier Pl, Chess. KT9 155 CJ107
Hillier Rd, SW11 120 DF86
Hilliers Av, Uxb. UB8
off Harlington Rd 76 BN69
Hilliers La, Croy. CR0 141 DL104
Hillingdale, West.
(Bigg.H.) TN16 178 EH118
HILLINGDON, Uxb. UB 76 BN69
⊖ **Hillingdon** 58 BN64
Hillingdon Av, Sev. TN13 191 FJ121
Staines TW19 114 BL88
Hillingdon Hill, Uxb. UB10 76 BL69
H **Hillingdon Hosp**,
Uxb. UB8 76 BM71
Hillingdon Ri, Sev. TN13 191 FK122
Hillingdon Rd, Bexh. DA7 107 FC82
Gravesend DA11 131 GG89
Uxbridge UB10 76 BL67
Watford WD25 7 BU34
Hillingdon St, SE5 101 DP80
SE17 101 DP80
Hillington Gdns, Wdf.Grn. IG8 48 EK54
Hill La, Ruis. HA4 59 BQ60
Tadworth (Kgswd) KT20 173 CY121
Hill Leys, Pot.B. (Cuffley) EN6 13 DL28
Hillman Cl, Horn. RM11 72 FK55
Uxbridge UB8 58 BL64
Hillman Dr, W10 81 CW70
Hillman St, E8 84 DV65
Hillmarton Rd, N7 65 DL64
Hillmead Dr, SW9 101 DP84
Hillmont Rd, Esher KT10 137 CE104
Hillmore Gro, SE26 123 DX92
Hillmount, Wok. GU22
off Constitution Hill 166 AY119
Hill Pk Dr, Lthd. KT22 171 CF119
Hill Path, SW16
off Valley Rd 121 DM92
Hillpoint, Rick. (Loud.) WD3 22 BJ43
Hillreach, SE18 105 EM78
Hill Ri, N9 30 DV44
NW11 64 DB56
SE23 *off London Rd* 122 DV88
Dartford (Lane End) DA2 129 FR92
Esher KT10 137 CH103
Gerrards Cross
(Chal.St.P.) SL9 36 AX54
Greenford UB6 78 CC66
Potters Bar EN6 12 DC34
Potters Bar (Cuffley) EN6 13 DK27
Richmond TW10 117 CK85
Rickmansworth WD3 22 BH44
Ruislip HA4 59 BQ60
Slough SL3 93 BA79
Upminster RM14 72 FN61
Hillrise, Walt. KT12 135 BT101
Hillrise Av, Wat. WD24 24 BX38
Hill Ri Cres, Ger.Cr.
(Chal.St.P.) SL9 36 AY54
Hillrise Rd, N19 65 DL59
Romford RM5 51 FC51
Hill Rd, N10 44 DF53
NW8 82 DC68
Brentwood CM14 54 FU48
Carshalton SM5 158 DE107
Dartford DA2 128 FL89
Epping (They.B.) CM16 33 ES37
Harrow HA1 61 CG57
Leatherhead (Fetch.) KT22 170 CB122
Mitcham CR4 141 DH95
Northwood HA6 39 BR51
Pinner HA5 60 BY57
Purley CR8 159 DM112
Sutton SM1 158 DB106
Wembley HA0 61 CH62
Hillsborough Grn, Wat. WD19
off Ashburnham Dr 39 BU48
Hillsborough Rd, SE22 122 DS85
Hills Chace, Brwd. CM14 54 FW49

★ Place of interest ⇌ Railway station ⊖ London Underground station DLR Docklands Light Railway station Tra Tramlink station H Hospital Riv Pedestrian ferry landing stage

★ Place of interest   ≈ Railway station   ● London Underground station   DLR Docklands Light Railway station   Tra Tramlink station   H Hospital   Riv Pedestrian ferry landing stage

Holly Dr, E4 47 EB45
Brentford TW8 97 CG79
Potters Bar EN6 12 DB33
South Ockendon RM15 91 FX70
Windsor SL4 112 AS85
Holly Fm Rd, Sthl. UB2 96 BY78
Hollyfield Av, N11 44 DF50
Hollyfield Rd, Surb. KT5 138 CM101
Hollyfields, Brox. EN10 15 DY26
Holly Gdns, Bexh. DA7
off Stephen Rd 107 FC84
West Drayton UB7 94 BM75
Holly Grn, Wey. KT13 135 BR104
Holly Gro, NW9 62 CQ59
SE15 102 DT82
Bushey WD23 41 CD45
Pinner HA5 40 BY53
Hollyhedge Rd, Cob. KT11 153 BV114
Holly Hedges La, Hem.H.
(Bov.) HP3 5 BC30
Rickmansworth WD3 5 BC30
Holly Hedge Ter, SE13 123 ED85
Holly Hill, N21 29 DM44
NW3 64 DC63
Holly Hill Dr, Bans. SM7 174 DA116
Holly Hill Pk, Bans. SM7 174 DA117
Holly Hill Rd, Belv. DA17 107 FB78
Erith DA8 107 FB78
Holly Ho, Brwd. CM15
off Sawyers Hall La 54 FX46
H Holly Ho Hosp, Buck.H. IG9 48 EH47
Holly La, Bans. SM7 174 DA116
Holly La E, Bans. SM7 174 DA116
Holly La W, Bans. SM7 174 DA117
Holly Lo Gdns, N6 64 DG61
Holly Lo Mobile Home Pk,
Tad. KT20 183 CY126
Hollymead, Cars. SM5 140 DF104
Hollymead Rd, Couls. CR5 174 DG118
Hollymeoak Rd, Couls. CR5 175 DH119
Holly Ms, SW10
off Drayton Gdns 100 DC78
Hollymoor La, Epsom KT19 156 CR110
Holly Mt, NW3
off Holly Bush Hill 64 DC63
Hollymount Cl, SE10 103 EC81
Holly Pk, N3 63 CZ55
N4 65 DM59
Holly Pk Est, N4
off Blythwood Rd 65 DM59
Holly Pk Gdns, N3 64 DA55
Holly Pk Rd, N11 44 DG50
W7 79 CF74
Holly Pl, NW3 off Holly Wk 64 DC63
Holly Rd, E11 68 EF59
W4 off Dolman Rd 98 CR77
Dartford DA1 128 FK88
Enfield EN3 31 DX36
Hampton (Hmptn H.) TW12 116 CC93
Hounslow TW3 96 CB84
Orpington BR6 164 EU108
Twickenham TW1 117 CG88
Holly St, E8 84 DT65
Holly Ter, N6
off Highgate W Hill 64 DG60
N20 off Swan La 44 DC47
Holly Tree Av, Swan. BR8 147 FE96
Hollytree Cl, SW19 119 CX88
Holly Tree Cl, Chesh.
(Ley Hill) HP5 4 AV31
Hollytree Cl, Ger.Cr.
(Chal.St.P.) SL9 36 AY50
Holly Tree Rd, Cat. CR3
off Elm Gro 176 DS122
Holly Vw Cl, NW4 63 CU58
Holly Village, N6
off Swains La 65 DH61
Holly Wk, NW3 64 DC63
Enfield EN2 30 DQ41
Richmond TW9 98 CL82
Holly Way, Mitch. CR4 141 DK98
Hollywood Ct, Borwd. (Elstree) WD6
off Deacon's Hill Rd 26 CM42
Hollywood Gdns, Hayes UB4 77 BV72
Hollywood Ms, SW10
off Hollywood Rd 100 DC79
Hollywood Rd, E4 47 DY50
SW10 100 DC79
Hollywoods, Croy. CR0 161 DZ109
Hollywood Way, Erith DA8 107 FH81
Woodford Green IG8 47 ED52
Holman Rd, SW11 100 DD82
Epsom KT19 156 CQ106
Holmbank Dr, Shep. TW17 135 BS98
Holmbridge Gdns, Enf. EN3 31 DX42
Holmbrook Dr, NW4 63 CX57
Holmbury Ct, SW17 120 DF90
SW19 off Cavendish Rd 120 DE94
Holmbury Gdns, Hayes UB3
off Church Rd 77 BT74
Holmbury Gro, Croy. CR0 161 DZ108
Holmbury Pk, Brom. BR1 124 EL94
Holmbury Vw, E5 66 DV60
Holmbush Rd, SW15 119 CY86
Holm Cl, Add. (Wdhm) KT15 151 BE112
Holmcote Gdns, N5 66 DQ64
Holmcroft, Tad. KT20 183 CV125
Holmcroft Way, Brom. BR2 145 EM99
Holmdale Cl, Borwd. WD6 26 CM40
Holmdale Gdns, NW4 63 CX57
Holmdale Rd, NW6 64 DA64
Chislehurst BR7 125 EQ92
Holmdale Ter, N15 66 DS59
Holmdene Av, NW7 43 CU51
SE24 122 DQ85
Harrow HA2 60 CB55
Holmdene Cl, Beck. BR3 143 EC96
Holmead Rd, SW6 100 DB80
Holmebury Cl, Bushey
(Bushey Hth) WD23 41 CE47
Holme Chase, Wey. KT13 153 BQ107
Holme Cl, Wal.Cr. (Chsht) EN8 15 DY31
Holme Ct, Islw. TW7
off Twickenham Rd 97 CG83
Holmedale, Slou. SL2 74 AW73
Holmefield Ct, NW3 82 DE65
Holme Lacey Rd, SE12 124 EF86
Holme Lea, Wat. WD25
off Kingsway 8 BW34
Holme Pk, Borwd. WD6 26 CM40
Holme Rd, E6 86 EL67
Hornchurch RM11 72 FN60
Holmes Av, E17 67 DZ55
NW7 43 CY50
Holmes Cl, Wok. GU22 167 AZ121
Holmesdale, Wal.Cr. EN8 31 DX35
Holmesdale Av, SW14 98 CP83
Holmesdale Cl, SE25 142 DT97
Holmesdale Hill, Dart.
(S.Darenth) DA4 148 FQ95
Holmesdale Rd, N6 65 DH59
SE25 142 DR99
Bexleyheath DA7 106 EX82
Croydon CR0 142 DR99
Dartford (S.Darenth) DA4 148 FQ95
Reigate RH2 184 DA133
Richmond TW9 98 CM81
Sevenoaks TN13 191 FJ123
Teddington TW11 117 CJ93
Holmesley Rd, SE23 123 DY86
Holmes Pl, SW10
off Fulham Rd 100 DC79
Holmes Rd, NW5 65 DH64
SW19 120 DC94
Twickenham TW1 117 CF89
Holmes Ter, SE1 200 D4
HOLMETHORPE, Red. RH1 185 DH132
Holmethorpe Av, Red. RH1 185 DH131
Holmethorpe Ind Est,
Red. RH1 185 DH131
Holme Way, Stan. HA7 41 CF51
Holmewood Gdns, SW2 121 DM87
Holmewood Rd, SE25 142 DS97
SW2 121 DL87
Holmfield Av, NW4 63 CX57
Holm Gro, Uxb. UB10 76 BN66
Holmhurst Rd, Belv. DA17 107 FB78
Holmlea Rd, Slou.
(Datchet) SL3 92 AX81
Holmlea Wk, Slou.
(Datchet) SL3 92 AW81
Holmleigh Av, Dart. DA1 108 FJ84
Holmleigh Rd, N16 66 DS60
Holmleigh Rd Est, N16
off Holmleigh Rd 66 DT60
Holm Oak Cl, SW15
off West Hill 119 CZ86
Holm Oak Ms, SW4
off King's Av 121 DL85
Holmsdale Cl, Iver SL0 75 BF72
Holmsdale Gro, Bexh. DA7 107 FE82
Holmshaw Cl, SE26 123 DY91
Holmshill La, Borwd. WD6 26 CS36
Holmside Ri, Wat. WD19 39 BV48
Holmside Rd, SW12 120 DG86
Holmsley Cl, N.Mal. KT3 139 CT100
Holmsley Ho, SW15
off Tangley Gro 119 CT87
Holms St, E2 84 DU68
Holmstall Av, Edg. HA8 62 CQ55
Holm Wk, SE3
off Blackheath Pk 104 EG82
Holmwood Av, Brwd.
(Shenf.) CM15 55 GA44
South Croydon CR2 160 DT113
Holmwood Cl, Add. KT15 152 BG106
Harrow HA2 60 CC55
Northolt UB5 78 CB65
Sutton SM2 157 CX109
Holmwood Gdns, N3 44 DA54
Wallington SM6 159 DH107
Holmwood Gro, NW7 42 CR50
Holmwood Rd, Chess. KT9 155 CK106
Enfield EN3 31 DX36
Ilford IG3 69 ES61
Sutton SM2 157 CW110
Holmwood Vil, SE7 205 N10
Holne Chase, N2 64 DC58
Morden SM4 139 CZ100
Holness Rd, E15 86 EF65
Holroyd Cl, Esher (Clay.) KT10 155 CF109
Holroyd Rd, SW15 99 CW84
Esher (Clay.) KT10 155 CF109
Holsart Cl, Tad. KT20 173 CV122
Holstein Av, Wey. KT13 152 BN105
Holstein Way, Erith DA18 106 EY76
Holstock Rd, Ilf. IG1 69 EQ62
Holsworth Cl, Har. HA2 60 CC57
Holsworthy Sq, WC1 196 C5
Holsworthy Way, Chess. KT9 155 CJ106
Holt, The, Ilf. IG6 49 EQ51
Wallington SM6 159 DJ105
Holt Cl, N10 64 DG56
SE28 88 EV73
Borehamwood (Elstree) WD6 26 CM42
Chigwell IG7 49 ET50
Holt Ct, E15 off Clays La 67 EC64
Holton St, E1 85 DX70
Holt Rd, E16 86 EL74
Romford RM3 52 FL52
Wembley HA0 61 CH62
Holtsmere Cl, Wat. WD25 24 BW35
Holt Way, Chig. IG7 49 ET50
Holtwhite Av, Enf. EN2 30 DQ40
Holtwhites Hill, Enf. EN2 29 DP39
Holtwood Rd, Lthd.
(Oxshott) KT22 154 CC113
Holwell Pl, Pnr. HA5 60 BY56
Holwood Cl, Walt. KT12 136 BW103
Holwood Pk Av, Orp. BR6 163 EM105
Holwood Pl, SW4 101 DK84
Holybourne Av, SW15 119 CU87
HOLYFIELD, Wal.Abb. EN9 15 ED28
Holyfield Rd, Wal.Abb. EN9 15 EC29
Holyhead Cl, E3 85 EA69
E6 off Valiant Way 87 EM71
Holyoake Av, Wok. GU21 166 AW117
Holyoake Ct, SE16 203 L4
Holyoake Cres, Wok. GU21 166 AW117
Holyoake Ter, Sev. TN13 190 FG124
Holyoake Wk, N2 64 DC55
W5 79 CJ70
Holyoak Rd, SE11 200 F8
Holyport Rd, SW6 99 CW80
Holyrood Av, Har. HA2 60 BY63
Holyrood Gdns, Edg. HA8 62 CP55
Grays RM16 111 GJ77
Holyrood Ms, E16 205 N2
Holyrood Rd, Barn. EN5 28 DC44
Holyrood St, SE1 201 M3
HOLYWELL, Wat. WD18 23 BS44
Holywell Cl, SE3 104 EG79
SE16 202 E10
Orpington BR6 164 EU105
Staines TW19 114 BL88
Holywell Ind Est, Wat. WD18 23 BR44
Holywell La, EC2 197 N4
Holywell Rd, Wat. WD18 23 BU43
Holywell Row, EC2 197 M5
Holywell Way, Stai. TW19 114 BL88
Home Cl, Cars. SM5 140 DF103
Leatherhead (Fetch.) KT22 171 CD121
Northolt UB5 78 BZ69
Virginia Water GU25 132 AX100
Home Ct, Felt. TW13 115 BU88
Homecroft Gdns, Loug. IG10 33 EP42
Homecroft Rd, N22 46 DQ53
SE26 122 DW92
Homedean Rd, Sev.
(Chipstead) TN13 190 FC122
Home Fm, Orp. BR6
off Hawstead La 164 FA106
Home Fm Cl, Cher.
(Ott.) KT16 151 BA108
Esher KT10 154 CB107
Shepperton TW17 135 BS98
Tadworth KT20 173 CX117
Thames Ditton KT7 137 CF101
Home Fm Gdns, Walt. KT12 136 BW103
Homefarm Rd, W7 79 CE72
Home Fm Rd, Rick. WD3 38 BN49
Home Fm Way, Slou.
(Stoke P.) SL3 74 AW67
Homefield, Hem.H. (Bov.) HP3 5 BB28
Waltham Abbey EN9 16 EG32
Walton-on-Thames KT12 154 BX105
Homefield Av, Ilf. IG2 69 ES57
Homefield Cl, NW10 80 CQ65
Addlestone (Wdhm) KT15 151 BE112
Epping CM16 18 EU30
Hayes UB4 78 BW70
Leatherhead KT22 171 CJ121
Orpington BR5 146 EV98
Swanley BR8 147 FF97
Homefield Fm Rd, Dart.
(Sutt.H.) DA4 148 FM96
Homefield Gdns, N2 64 DD55
Mitcham CR4 140 DC96
Tadworth KT20 173 CW120
Homefield Ms, Beck. BR3 143 EA95
Homefield Pk, Sutt. SM1 158 DB107
Homefield Ri, Orp. BR6 164 EU102
Homefield Rd, SW19 119 CX93
W4 99 CT77
Bromley BR1 144 EJ95
Bushey WD23 24 CA43
Coulsdon CR5 175 DP119
Edgware HA8 42 CR51
Radlett WD7 25 CF37
Rickmansworth
(Chorl.) WD3 21 BD42
Sevenoaks TN13 190 FE122
Walton-on-Thames KT12 136 BY101
Warlingham CR6 176 DW119
Wembley HA0 61 CG63
Homefield St, N1 197 M1
Home Gdns, Dag. RM10 71 FC62
Dartford DA1 128 FL86
Home Hill, Swan. BR8 127 FF94
Homeland Dr, Sutt. SM2 158 DB109
Homelands, Lthd. KT22 171 CJ121
Homelands Dr, SE19 122 DS94
Home Lea, Orp. BR6 163 ET106
Homeleigh Ct, Wal.Cr. EN8 14 DV29
Homeleigh Rd, SE15 123 DX85
Homemead, SW12 121 DJ89
Gravesend DA12
off Home Mead Cl 131 GH87
Home Mead, Stan. HA7 41 CJ53
Home Mead Cl, Grav. DA12 131 GH87
Home Meadow, Bans. SM7 174 DA116
Homemead Rd, Brom. BR2 145 EM99
Croydon CR0 141 DJ100
★ Home Office, SW1 199 M5
Home Orchard, Dart. DA1 128 FL86
Home Pk, Oxt. RH8 188 EG131
Home Pk Mill Link Rd,
Kings L. WD4 7 BP31
Home Pk Rd, SW19 120 DA90
Home Pk Wk, Kings.T. KT1 137 CK98
Homer Cl, Bexh. DA7 107 FC81
Homer Dr, E14 203 P8
Home Rd, SW11 100 DE82
Homer Rd, E9 85 DY65
Croydon CR0 143 DX100
Homer Row, W1 194 C7
Homersham Rd,
Kings.T. KT1 138 CN96
Homer St, W1 194 C7
HOMERTON, E9 67 DY64
⇌ Homerton 85 DX65
Homerton Gro, E9 67 DX64
Homerton High St, E9 66 DW64
H Homerton Hosp, E9 67 DX64
Homerton Rd, E9 67 DY64
Homerton Row, E9 66 DW64
Homerton Ter, E9
off Morning La 84 DW65
Homesdale Cl, E11 68 EG57
Homesdale Rd,
Brom. BR1, BR2 144 EJ98
Caterham CR3 176 DR123
Orpington BR5 145 ES101
Homesfield, NW11 64 DA57
Homestall Rd, SE22 122 DW85
Homestead, The, N11 45 DH49
Dartford DA1 128 FJ86
Homestead Cl, St.Alb.
(Park St) AL2 8 CC27
Homestead Gdns, Esher
(Clay.) KT10 155 CE106
Homestead Paddock, N14 29 DH43
Homestead Pk, NW2 63 CT62
Homestead Rd, SW6 99 CZ80
Caterham CR3 176 DR123
Dagenham RM8 70 EZ61
Orpington BR6 164 EV108
Rickmansworth WD3
off Park Rd 38 BK45
Staines TW18 114 BH93
Homestead Way, Croy.
(New Adgtn) CR0 161 EC111
Homewaters Av, Sun. TW16 135 BT95
Home Way, Rick.
(Mill End) WD3 37 BF46
Homeway, Rom. RM3 52 FP51
Homewillow Cl, N21 29 DP44
Homewood, Slou.
(Geo.Grn) SL3 74 AX72
Homewood Av, Pot.B.
(Cuffley) EN6 13 DL27
Homewood Cl, Hmptn. TW12
off Fearnley Cres 116 BZ93
Homewood Cres, Chis. BR7 125 ES93
Homewood La, Pot.B. EN6 13 DJ27
Homildon Ho, SE26
off Sydenham Hill 122 DU90
Honduras St, EC1 197 H4
Honeybourne Rd, NW6 64 DB64
Honeybourne Way, Orp. BR5 145 ER102
Honey Brook, Wal.Abb. EN9 16 EE33
Honeybrook Rd, SW12 121 DJ87
Honey Cl, Dag. RM10 89 FB65
Honeycroft, Loug. IG10 33 EN42
Honeycroft Hill, Uxb. UB10 76 BL66
Honeyden Rd, Sid. DA14 126 EY93
Honey Hill, Uxb. UB10 76 BM66
Honey La, EC2 197 J9
Waltham Abbey EN9 32 EG35
Honeyman Cl, NW6 81 CX66
Honeypot Cl, NW9 62 CM56
Honeypot La, NW9 62 CM55
Brentwood CM14 54 FU48
Stanmore HA7 62 CM55
Honeypots Rd, Wok. GU22 166 AX122
Honeysett Rd, N17
off Reform Row 46 DT54
Honeysuckle Cl, Brwd.
(Pilg.Hat.) CM15 54 FV43
Iver SL0 75 BC72
Romford RM3
off Cloudberry Rd 52 FK51
Southall UB1 78 BY73
Honeysuckle Gdns, Croy. CR0
off Primrose La 143 DX102
Honeywell Rd, SW11 120 DF86
Honeywood Cl, Pot.B. EN6 12 DE33
Honeywood Rd, NW10 81 CT68
Isleworth TW7 97 CG84
Honeywood Wk, Cars. SM5 158 DF105
Honister Cl, Stan. HA7 41 CH53
Honister Gdns, Stan. HA7 41 CH52
Honister Hts, Pur. CR8 160 DR114
Honister Pl, Stan. HA7 41 CH53
Honiton Gdns, NW7 43 CX52
Honiton Ho, Enf. EN3
off Exeter Rd 31 DX41
Honiton Rd, NW6 81 CZ68
Romford RM7 71 FD58
Welling DA16 105 ET82
Honley Rd, SE6 123 EB87
Honnor Gdns, Islw. TW7 97 CD82
Honnor Rd, Stai. TW18 114 BK94
HONOR OAK, SE23 122 DW86
HONOR OAK PARK, SE4 123 DY86
⇌ Honor Oak Park 123 DX86
Honor Oak Pk, SE23 122 DW86
Honor Oak Ri, SE23 122 DW86
Honor Oak Rd, SE23 122 DW88
Hood Av, N14 29 DH44
SW14 118 CQ85
Orpington BR5 146 EV99
Hood Cl, Croy. CR0
off Parson's Mead 141 DP102
Hoodcote Gdns, N21 45 DP45
Hood Ct, EC4 196 E9
Hood Rd, SW20 119 CT94
Rainham RM13 89 FE67
Hood Wk, Rom. RM7 51 FB53
HOOK, Chess. KT9 156 CL105
Hook, The, Barn. EN5 28 DD44
Hookers Rd, E17 67 DX55
Hook Fm Rd, Brom. BR2 144 EK99
Hookfield, Epsom KT19 156 CQ113
Hookfields, Grav.
(Nthflt) DA11 130 GE90
Hook Gate, Enf. EN1 30 DV36
HOOK GREEN, Dart. DA2 127 FG91
HOOK GREEN, Grav. DA13 130 FZ93
Hook Grn La, Dart. DA2 127 FF90
Hook Grn Rd, Grav.
(Sthflt) DA13 130 FY94
HOOK HEATH, Wok. GU22 166 AV120
Hook Heath Av, Wok. GU22 166 AV119
Hook Heath Gdns,
Wok. GU22 166 AT121
Hook Heath Rd, Wok. GU22 166 AW121
Hook Hill, S.Croy. CR2 160 DS110
Hook Hill La, Wok. GU22 166 AV121
Hook Hill Pk, Wok. GU22 166 AV121
Hooking Grn, Har. HA2 60 CB57
Hook La, Pot.B. EN6 12 DF32
Romford RM4 34 EZ44
Welling DA16 125 ET85
Hook Ri N, Surb. KT6 138 CN104
Hook Ri S, Surb. KT6 138 CN104
Hook Ri S Ind Pk, Surb. KT6 138 CN104
Hook Rd, Chess. KT9 155 CK106
Epsom KT19 156 CR111
Surbiton KT6 138 CL104
Hooks Cl, SE15
off Woods Rd 102 DV81
Hooks Hall Dr, Dag. RM10 71 FC62
Hookstone Way, Wdf.Grn. IG8 48 EK52
Hooks Way, SE22
off Dulwich Common 122 DU88
Hook Wk, Edg. HA8 42 CQ51
Hookwood Cor, Oxt. RH8
off Hookwood La 188 EH128
Hookwood La, Oxt. RH8 188 EH128
Hookwood Rd, Orp. BR6 164 EW111
HOOLEY, Couls. CR5 174 DG122
Hooper Dr, Uxb. UB8
off Barncroft Cl 77 BP71
Hooper Rd, E16 86 EG72
Hooper's Ct, SW3 198 D5
Hooper's Ms, Bushey WD23 40 CB46
Hooper St, E1 84 DU72
Hoopers Yd, Sev. TN13 191 FJ126
Hoop La, NW11 63 CZ59
Hope Cl, N1 off Wallace Rd 84 DQ65
SE12 124 EH90
Brentford TW8
off Burford Rd 98 CL78
Romford (Chad.Hth) RM6 70 EW56
Sutton SM1 158 DC106
Woodford Green IG8
off West Gro 48 EJ51
Hopedale Rd, SE7 104 EH79
Hopefield Av, NW6 81 CY68
Hope Grn, Wat. WD25 7 BU33
Hope Pk, Brom. BR1 124 EF94
Hope Rd, Swans. DA10 130 FZ86
Hopes Cl, Houns. TW5
off Old Cote Dr 96 CA79
Hope St, SW11 100 DD83
Hope Ter, Grays RM20 109 FX78
Hopetown St, E1 off Brick La 84 DT71
Hopewell Cl, Grays RM16
off Hatfield Rd 109 FX78
Hopewell Dr, Grav. DA12 131 GM92
Hopewell St, SE5 102 DR80
Hopewell Yd, SE5
off Hopewell St 102 DR80
Hope Wf, SE16
off St. Marychurch St 102 DW75
Hopfield, Wok. (Horsell) GU21 166 AY116
Hopfield Av, W.Byf.
(Byfleet) KT14 152 BL112
Hopgarden La, Sev. TN13 190 FG128
Hop Gdns, WC2 199 P1
Hop Gdn Way, Wat. WD25
off High Elms La 8 BW31
Hopgood St, W12
off Macfarlane Rd 81 CW74
Hopkins Cl, N10 44 DG52
Romford RM2 72 FJ55
Hopkins Ms, E15
off West Rd 86 EF67
Hopkinsons Pl, NW1
off Fitzroy Rd 82 DG67
Hopkins St, W1 195 L9
Hoppers Rd, N13 45 DN47
N21 45 DN47
Hoppett Rd, E4 48 EE48
Hoppety, The, Tad. KT20 173 CX122
Hopping La, N1
off St. Mary's Gro 83 DP65
Hoppingwood Av, N.Mal. KT3 138 CS97
Hoppit Rd, Wal.Abb. EN9 15 EB32
Hoppner Rd, Hayes UB4 77 BQ68
Hop St, SE10 205 L8
Hopton Gdns, SE1 200 G2
New Malden KT3 139 CU100
Hopton Rd, SW16 121 DL92
Hopton St, SE1 200 G2
Hoptree Cl, N12
off Woodside Pk Rd 44 DB49
Hopwood Cl, SW17 120 DC90
Watford WD17 23 BR36
Hopwood Rd, SE17 102 DR79
Hopwood Wk, E8
off Wilman Gro 84 DU66
Horace Av, Rom. RM7 71 FC60
Horace Rd, E7 68 EH63
Ilford IG6 69 EQ55
Kingston upon Thames KT1 138 CM97
Horatio Ct, SE16
off Rotherhithe St 84 DW74
Horatio Pl, E14 204 E4
SW19 off Kingston Rd 120 DA94
Horatio St, E2 84 DT68
Horatius Way, Croy. CR0 159 DM106
Horbury Cres, W11 82 DA73
Horbury Ms, W11
off Ladbroke Rd 81 CZ73
Horder Rd, SW6 99 CY81
Hordle Prom E, SE15
off Daniel Gdns 102 DT80
Hordle Prom N, SE15
off Blakes Rd 102 DT80
Hordle Prom S, SE15
off Blakes Rd 102 DT80
Hordle Prom W, SE15
off Blakes Rd 102 DS80
Horizon Way, SE7 104 EH77
Horksley Gdns, Brwd. (Hutt.)
CM13 off Bannister Dr 55 GC44
Horle Wk, SE5 101 DP82
Horley Cl, Bexh. DA6 126 FA85
Horley Rd, SE9 124 EL91
Hormead Rd, W9 81 CZ70
Hornbeam Av, Upmin. RM14 72 FN63
Hornbeam Chase,
S.Ock. RM15 91 FX69
Hornbeam Cl, NW7 43 CT48
SE11 200 D8
Borehamwood WD6 26 CN39
Brentwood CM13 55 GB48
Buckhurst Hill IG9
off Hornbeam Rd 48 EK48
Epping (They.B.) CM16 33 ES37
Ilford IG1 69 ER64
Northolt UB5 60 BZ64
Hornbeam Cres, Brent. TW8 97 CH80
Hornbeam Gdns, Slou. SL1
off Upton Rd 92 AU76
Hornbeam Gro, E4 48 EE48
Hornbeam La, E4 32 EE43
Bexleyheath DA7 107 FC82
Hornbeam Rd, Buck.H. IG9 48 EK48
Epping (They.B.) CM16 33 ER37
Hayes UB4 78 BW71
Hornbeams, St.Alb.
(Brick.Wd) AL2 8 BZ30
Hornbeams Av, Enf. EN1 30 DW35
Hornbeam Sq, E3
off Hawthorn Av 85 DZ67
Hornbeams Ri, N11 44 DG51
Hornbeam Ter, Cars. SM5 140 DE102
Hornbeam Wk, Rich. TW10 118 CM90
Walton-on-Thames
(Whiteley Vill.) KT12
off Octagon Rd 153 BT109
Hornbeam Way, Brom. BR2 145 EN100

★ Place of interest ⇌ Railway station ⊖ London Underground station DLR Docklands Light Railway station Tra Tramlink station H Hospital Riv Pedestrian ferry landing stage

Hornbeam Way, Waltham Cross EN7 14 DT29
Hornbill Cl, Uxb. UB8 76 BK72
Hornblower Cl, SE16 203 K8
Hornbuckle Cl, Har. HA2 61 CD61
Hornby Cl, NW3 82 DD66
Horncastle Cl, SE12 124 EG87
Horncastle Rd, SE12 124 EG87
HORNCHURCH 72 FJ61
⊖ Hornchurch 72 FK62
Hornchurch Cl, Kings.T. KT2 117 CK91
Hornchurch Hill, Whyt. CR3 176 DT117
Hornchurch Rd, Horn. RM11, RM12 71 FG60
Horndean Cl, SW15 off Bessborough Rd 119 CU88
Horndon Cl, Rom. RM5 51 FC53
Horndon Grn, Rom. RM5 51 FC53
Horndon Rd, Rom. RM5 51 FC53
Horner La, Mitch. CR4 140 DD96
Horne Rd, Shep. TW17 134 BN98
Hornets, The, Wat. WD18 23 BV42
Horne Way, SW15 99 CW82
Hornfair Rd, SE7 104 EJ79
Hornford Way, Rom. RM7 71 FE59
Hornhill Rd, Ger.Cr. SL9 37 BB50
Rickmansworth (Map.Cr.) WD3 37 BD50
Horniman Dr, SE23 122 DV88
★ Horniman Mus, SE23 122 DV88
Horning Cl, SE9 124 EL91
Horn La, SE10 205 M9
W3 80 CQ73
Woodford Green IG8 48 EG51
Horn Link Way, SE10 205 M8
Hornminster Glen, Horn. RM11 72 FN61
Horn Pk Cl, SE12 124 EH85
Horn Pk La, SE12 124 EH85
Hornsby La, Grays (Orsett) RM16 111 GG75
Horns Cft Cl, Bark. IG11 off Thornhill Gdns 87 ES66
Horns End Pl, Pnr. HA5 60 BW56
HORNSEY, N8 65 DM55
⇌ Hornsey 65 DM56
Hornsey La, N6 65 DH60
N19 65 DJ60
Hornsey La Est, N19 off Hornsey La 65 DK59
Hornsey La Gdns, N6 65 DJ59
Hornsey Pk Rd, N8 65 DM55
Hornsey Ri, N19 65 DK59
Hornsey Ri Gdns, N19 65 DK59
Hornsey Rd, N7 65 DM61
N19 65 DL60
Hornsey St, N7 65 DM64
HORNS GREEN, Sev. TN14 179 ES117
Hornshay St, SE15 102 DW79
Horns Rd, Ilf. IG2, IG6 69 EQ57
Hornton Pl, W8 100 DA75
Hornton St, W8 82 DA74
Horsa Rd, SE12 124 EJ87
Erith DA8 107 FC80
Horse & Dolphin Yd, W1 195 N10
Horsebridge Cl, Dag. RM9 88 EY67
Horsecroft, Bans. SM7 off Lyme Regis Rd 173 CZ117
Horsecroft Cl, Orp. BR6 146 EV102
Horsecroft Rd, Edg. HA8 42 CR52
Horse Fair, Kings.T. KT1 137 CK96
Horseferry Pl, SE10 103 EC79
Horseferry Rd, E14 85 DY73
SW1 199 M7
Horse Guards Av, SW1 199 P3
★ Horse Guards Par, SW1 199 N3
Horse Guards Rd, SW1 199 N3
Horse Hill, Chesh. HP5 4 AX32
Horse Leaze, E6 87 EN72
HORSELL, Wok. GU21 166 AY116
Horsell Birch, Wok. GU21 166 AV115
Horsell Common, Wok. GU21 150 AX114
Horsell Common Rd, Wok. GU21 150 AW114
Horsell Ct, Cher. KT16 off Stepgates 134 BH101
Horsell Moor, Wok. GU21 166 AX117
Horsell Pk, Wok. GU21 166 AX116
Horsell Pk Cl, Wok. GU21 166 AX116
Horsell Ri, Wok. GU21 166 AX115
Horsell Ri Cl, Wok. GU21 166 AX115
Horsell Rd, N5 65 DN64
Orpington BR5 146 EV95
Horsell Vale, Wok. GU21 166 AY115
Horsell Way, Wok. GU21 166 AW116
Horselydown La, SE1 201 P4
Horseman Side, Brwd. (Nave.S.) CM14 51 FH45
Horsemans Ride, St.Alb. AL2 8 CA26
Horsemongers Ms, SE1 201 J5
Horsemoor Cl, Slou. SL3 off Parlaunt Rd 93 BA77
Horsenden Av, Grnf. UB6 61 CE64
Horsenden Cres, Grnf. UB6 61 CF64
Horsenden La N, Grnf. UB6 79 CF65
Horsenden La S, Grnf. UB6 79 CG67
Horse Ride, SW1 199 L3
Tadworth KT20 183 CY125
Horse Rd, E7 off Centre Rd 68 EH62
Horseshoe, The, Bans. SM7 173 CZ115
Coulsdon CR5 159 DK113
Horseshoe Business Pk, St.Alb. AL2 off Lye La 8 CA30
Horseshoe Cl, E14 204 D10
NW2 63 CV61
Waltham Abbey EN9 16 EG34
Horse Shoe Ct, EC1 off St. John St 83 DP70
Horse Shoe Cres, Nthlt. UB5 78 CA68
Horseshoe Dr, Uxb. UB8 76 BN72
Horse Shoe Grn, Sutt. SM1 off Aultone Way 140 DB103
Horseshoe Hill, Wal.Abb. EN9 16 EJ33
Horseshoe La, N20 43 CX46
Horseshoe La, Enfield EN2 off Chase Side 30 DQ41
Watford WD25 7 BV32
Horseshoe Ridge, Wey. KT13 153 BQ111
Horse Yd, N1 off Essex Rd 83 DP67
Horsfeld Gdns, SE9 124 EL85
Horsfeld Rd, SE9 124 EK85
Horsfield Cl, Dart. DA2 128 FQ87
Horsford Rd, SW2 121 DM85
Horsham Av, N12 44 DE50
Horsham Rd, Bexh. DA6 126 FA85
Feltham TW14 115 BQ86
Horsley Cl, Epsom KT19 156 CR113
Horsleydown Old Stairs, SE1 201 P3
Horsley Dr, Croy. (New Adgtn) CR0 161 EC108
Kingston upon Thames KT2 117 CK92
Horsley Rd, E4 47 EC47
Bromley BR1 off Palace Rd 144 EH95
Cobham KT11 169 BV119
Horsleys, Rick. (Map.Cr.) WD3 37 BD50
Horsley St, SE17 102 DR79
Horsmonden Cl, Orp. BR6 145 ES101
Horsmonden Rd, SE4 123 DZ85
Hortensia Rd, SW10 100 DC80
Horticultural Pl, W4 off Heathfield Ter 98 CR78
HORTON, Epsom KT19 156 CP110
HORTON, Slou. SL3 93 BA83
Horton Av, NW2 63 CY63
Horton Br Rd, West Dr. UB7 76 BM74
Horton Cl, West Dr. UB7 76 BM74
★ Horton Country Pk, Epsom KT19 156 CM110
Horton Footpath, Epsom KT19 156 CQ111
Horton Gdns, Epsom KT19 156 CQ111
Horton Hill, Epsom KT19 156 CQ111
Horton Ind Pk, West Dr. UB7 76 BM74
HORTON KIRBY, Dart. DA4 149 FR98
Horton La, Epsom KT19 156 CP110
★ Horton Park Children's Fm, Epsom KT19 156 CN110
Horton Rd, E8 84 DV65
Dartford (Hort.Kir.) DA4 148 FQ97
Slough (Colnbr.) SL3 93 BA81
Slough (Datchet) SL3 92 AV80
Slough (Poyle) SL3 93 BE83
Staines TW19 114 BG85
West Drayton UB7 76 BN74
Horton St, SE13 103 EB83
Hortons Way, West. TN16 189 ER126
Horton Way, Croy. CR0 143 DX99
Dartford (Fnghm) DA4 148 FM101
Hortus Rd, E4 47 EC47
Southall UB2 96 BZ75
Horvath Cl, Wey. KT13 153 BR105
Horwood Cl, Rick. WD3 off Thellusson Way 38 BG45
Horwood Ct, Wat. WD24 24 BX37
Hosack Rd, SW17 120 DF89
Hoser Av, SE12 124 EG89
Hosey Common La, West. TN16 189 ES130
Hosey Common Rd, Eden. TN8 189 EQ133
Westerham TN16 189 ER130
HOSEY HILL, West. TN16 189 ES127
Hosey Hill, West. TN16 189 ER127
Hosier La, EC1 196 F7
Hoskins Cl, E16 86 EJ72
Hayes UB3 off Cranford Dr 95 BT78
Hoskins Rd, Oxt. RH8 188 EE129
Hoskins St, SE10 103 ED78
Hoskins Wk, Oxt. RH8 188 EE129
Hospital Br Rd, Twick. TW2 116 CB87
H Hospital for Tropical Diseases, NW1 83 DK67
H Hospital of St. John & St. Elizabeth, NW8 82 DD68
Hospital Rd, E9 off Homerton Row 67 DX64
Hounslow TW3 96 CA83
Sevenoaks TN13 191 FJ121
Hospital Way, SE13 123 ED86
Hotham Cl, Dart. (Sutt.H.) DA4 128 FP94
Swanley BR8 147 FH95
West Molesey KT8 off Garrick Gdns 136 CA97
Hotham Rd, SW15 99 CW83
SW19 120 DC94
Hotham Rd Ms, SW19 off Haydons Rd 120 DC94
Hotham St, E15 86 EE67
Hothfield Pl, SE16 202 G7
Hotspur Rd, Nthlt. UB5 78 CA68
Hotspur St, SE11 200 D10
Houblon Rd, Rich. TW10 118 CL85
Houblons Hill, Epp. (Cooper.) CM16 18 EW31
Houghton Cl, E8 off Buttermere Wk 84 DT65
Hampton TW12 116 BY93
Houghton Rd, N15 off West Grn Rd 66 DT57
Houghton St, WC2 196 C9
Houlder Cres, Croy. CR0 159 DP107
Houndsden Rd, N21 29 DM44
Houndsditch, EC3 197 N8
Houndsfield Rd, N9 46 DV45
HOUNSLOW 96 BZ84
⇌ Hounslow 116 CB85
Hounslow Av, Houns. TW3 116 CB85
Hounslow Business Pk, Houns. TW3 96 CA84
⊖ Hounslow Central 96 CA83
⊖ Hounslow East 96 CC82
Hounslow Gdns, Houns. TW3 116 CB85
★ Hounslow Heath, Houns. TW4 116 BY86
Hounslow Rd, Felt. (Feltham) TW14 115 BV88
Feltham (Han.) TW13 116 BX91
Twickenham TW2 116 CC86
HOUNSLOW WEST, Houns. TW4 96 BX83
⊖ Hounslow West 96 BY82
Houseman Way, SE5 off Hopewell St 102 DR80
★ Houses of Parliament, SW1 200 A5
Houston Pl, Esher KT10 off Lime Tree Av 137 CE102
Houston Rd, SE23 123 DY89
Surbiton KT6 137 CH100
Hove Av, E17 67 DZ57
Hove Cl, Brwd. (Hutt.) CM13 55 GC47
Grays RM17 off Argent St 110 GA79
Hoveden Rd, NW2 63 CY64
Hove Gdns, Sutt. SM1 140 DB102
Hoveton Rd, SE28 88 EW72
Hoveton Way, Ilf. IG6 49 EP52
Howard Agne Cl, Hem.H. (Bov.) HP3 5 BA27
Howard Av, Bex. DA5 126 EW88
Epsom KT17 157 CU110
Howard Business Pk, Wal.Abb. EN9 off Howard Cl 15 ED33
Howard Cl, N11 44 DG47
NW2 63 CY63
W3 80 CP72
Ashtead KT21 172 CM118
Bushey (Bushey Hth) WD23 41 CE45
Hampton TW12 116 CC93
Leatherhead KT22 171 CJ123
Loughton IG10 32 EL44
Sunbury-on-Thames TW16 off Catherine Dr 115 BT93
Tadworth KT20 183 CT125
Waltham Abbey EN9 15 ED34
Watford WD24 23 BU37
Howard Ct, Reig. RH2 184 DC133
Howard Dr, Borwd. WD6 26 CR42
Howard Ms, N5 off Hamilton Pk 65 DP63
Slough SL3 off Laburnum Gro 93 BB79
Howard Pl, Reig. RH2 184 DA132
Howard Rd, E6 87 EM68
E11 68 EE62
E17 67 EA55
N15 66 DS58
N16 66 DR63
NW2 63 CX63
SE20 142 DW95
SE25 142 DU99
Barking IG11 87 ER67
Bromley BR1 124 EG94
Coulsdon CR5 175 DJ115
Dartford DA1 128 FN86
Grays (Chaff.Hun.) RM16 109 FW76
Ilford IG1 69 EP63
Isleworth TW7 97 CF83
Leatherhead (Eff.Junct.) KT24 169 BU122
New Malden KT3 138 CS97
Southall UB1 78 CB72
Surbiton KT5 138 CM100
Upminster RM14 72 FQ61
Woking GU22 167 BA120
Howards Cl, Pnr. HA5 39 BV54
Woking GU22 167 BA120
Howards Crest Cl, Beck. BR3 143 EC96
Howards La, SW15 119 CV85
Addlestone KT15 151 BE107
Howards Rd, E13 86 EG69
Woking GU22 167 AZ120
Howards Thicket, Ger.Cr. SL9 56 AW61
Howard St, T.Ditt. KT7 137 CH101
Howards Wd Dr, Ger.Cr. SL9 56 AX61
Howard Wk, N2 64 DC56
Howard Way, Barn. EN5 27 CX43
Howarth Ct, E15 off Clays La 67 EC64
Howarth Rd, SE2 106 EU78
Howberry Cl, Edg. HA8 41 CK51
Howberry Rd, Edg. HA8 41 CK51
Stanmore HA7 41 CK51
Thornton Heath CR7 142 DR95
Howbury La, Erith DA8 107 FG82
Howbury Rd, SE15 102 DW83
Howcroft Cres, N3 44 DA52
Howcroft La, Grnf. UB6 off Cowgate Rd 79 CD69
Howden Cl, SE28 88 EX73
Howden Rd, SE25 142 DT96
Howden St, SE15 102 DU83
Howe Cl, Rad. (Shenley) WD7 10 CL32
Romford RM7 50 FA53
Howe Dr, Cat. CR3 176 DR122
Howell Cl, Rom. RM6 70 EX57
Howell Hill Cl, Epsom KT17 157 CW111
Howell Hill Gro, Epsom KT17 157 CW110
Howell Wk, SE1 200 G9
Howes Cl, N3 64 DA55
Howfield Pl, N17 66 DT55
Howgate Rd, SW14 98 CR83
Howick Pl, SW1 199 L7
Howie St, SW11 100 DE80
Howitt Cl, N16 off Allen Rd 66 DS63
NW3 off Howitt Rd 82 DE65
Howitt Rd, NW3 82 DE65
Howitts Cl, Esher KT10 154 CA107
Howland Est, SE16 202 G6
Howland Ms E, W1 195 L6
Howland St, W1 195 K6
Howland Way, SE16 203 L5
How La, Couls. CR5 174 DG117
Howletts La, Ruis. HA4 59 BQ57
Howletts Rd, SE24 122 DQ86
Howley Pl, W2 82 DC71
Howley Rd, Croy. CR0 141 DP104
Hows Cl, Uxb. UB8 off Hows Rd 76 BJ67
Howse Rd, Wal.Abb. EN9 off Deer Pk Way 31 EB35
Howsman Rd, SW13 99 CU79
Howson Rd, SE4 103 DY84
Howson Ter, Rich. TW10 118 CL86
Hows Rd, Uxb. UB8 76 BJ67
Hows St, E2 84 DT68
Howton Pl, Bushey (Bushey Hth) WD23 41 CD46
HOW WOOD, St.Alb. AL2 8 CC27
⇌ How Wood 8 CC28
How Wd, St.Alb. (Park St) AL2 8 CB28
HOXTON, N1 197 M1
Hoxton Mkt, N1 197 M3
Hoxton Sq, N1 197 M3
Hoxton St, N1 197 N3
Hoylake Cres, Uxb. (Ickhm) UB10 58 BN60
Hoylake Gdns, Mitch. CR4 141 DJ97
Romford RM3 52 FN53
Ruislip HA4 59 BV60
Watford WD19 40 BX49
Hoylake Rd, W3 80 CS72
Hoyland Cl, SE15 off Commercial Way 102 DV80
Hoyle Rd, SW17 120 DE92
Hoy St, E16 86 EF72
Hoy Ter, Grays RM20 109 FX78
★ H.Q.S. Wellington, Master Mariners' Hall, WC2 196 D10
Hubbard Dr, Chess. KT9 155 CJ107
Hubbard Rd, SE27 122 DQ91
Hubbards Chase, Horn. RM11 72 FN57
Hubbards Cl, Horn. RM11 72 FN57
Uxbridge UB8 77 BP72
Hubbards Rd, Rick. (Chorl.) WD3 21 BD43
Hubbard St, E15 86 EE67
Hubbinet Ind Est, Rom. RM7 71 FC55
Hubert Gro, SW9 101 DL83
Hubert Rd, E6 86 EK69
Brentwood CM14 54 FV48
Rainham RM13 89 FF69
Slough SL3 92 AX76
Hucknall Cl, Rom. RM3 52 FM51
Huddart St, E3 85 DZ71
Huddleston Cl, E2 84 DW68
Huddlestone Cres, Red. RH1 185 DK128
Huddlestone Rd, E7 68 EF63
NW2 81 CV65
Huddleston Rd, N7 65 DK63
Hudons Cl, Grays RM20 109 FT78
Hudson Av, Uxb. (Denh.) UB9 57 BF58
Hudson Cl, Wat. WD24 23 BT36
Hudson Ct, E14 off Maritime Quay 103 EA78
SW19 120 DB94
Hudson Gdns, Orp. BR6 off Superior Dr 163 ET107
Hudson Palce, Slou. SL3 off Ditton Rd 93 AZ78
Hudson Pl, SE18 105 EQ78
Hudson Rd, Bexh. DA7 106 EZ82
Hayes UB3 95 BR79
Hudsons, Tad. KT20 173 CX121
Hudson's Pl, SW1 199 J8
Hudson Way, N9 46 DW48
NW2 off Gratton Ter 63 CX62
Huggin Ct, EC4 197 J10
Huggin Hill, EC4 197 J10
Huggins Pl, SW2 off Roupell Rd 121 DM88
Hughan Rd, E15 67 ED64
Hugh Dalton Av, SW6 99 CZ79
Hughenden Av, Har. HA3 61 CH57
Hughenden Gdns, Nthlt. UB5 78 BW69
Hughenden Rd, Wor.Pk. KT4 139 CU101
Hughendon Ter, E15 off Westdown Rd 67 EC63
Hughes Cl, N12 off Coleridge Rd 44 DC50
Hughes Rd, Ashf. TW15 115 BQ94
Grays RM16 111 GG76
Hayes UB3 77 BV73
Hughes Wk, Croy. CR0 off St. Saviours Rd 142 DQ101
Hugh Gaitskell Cl, SW6 99 CZ79
Hugh Ms, SW1 199 J9
Hugh St, SW1 199 J9
Hugo Gdns, Rain. RM13 89 FF65
Hugo Gryn Way, Rad. (Shenley) WD7 off Farm Cl 10 CL31
Hugon Rd, SW6 100 DB83
Hugo Rd, N19 65 DJ63
Huguenot Pl, E1 84 DT71
SW18 120 DC85
Huguenot Sq, SE15 off Scylla Rd 102 DV83
HULBERRY, Swan. BR8 147 FG103
Hullbridge Ms, N1 off Sherborne St 84 DR67
Hull Cl, SE16 203 J4
Sutton SM2 off Yarbridge Cl 158 DB110
Waltham Cross (Chsht) EN7 14 DR26
Hulletts La, Brwd. (Pilg.Hat.) CM15 54 FT43
Hull Pl, E16 off Fishguard Way 105 EP75
Hull St, EC1 197 H3
Hulme Pl, SE1 201 J5
Hulse Av, Bark. IG11 87 ER65
Romford RM7 51 FB53
Hulse Ter, Ilf. IG1 off Buttsbury Rd 69 EQ64
Hulsewood Cl, Dart. DA2 127 FH90
Hulton Cl, Lthd. KT22 171 CJ123
Hulverston Cl, Sutt. SM2 158 DB110
Humber Av, S.Ock. RM15 91 FT72
Humber Cl, West Dr. UB7 76 BK74
Humber Dr, W10 81 CX70
Upminster RM14 73 FR58
Humber Rd, NW2 63 CV61
SE3 104 EF79
Dartford DA1 128 FK85
Humberstone Rd, E13 86 EJ69
Humberton Cl, E9 off Marsh Hill 67 DY64
Humber Way, Slou. SL3 93 BA77
Humbolt Rd, W6 99 CY79
Hume Av, Til. RM18 111 GG83
Hume Cl, Til. RM18 off Hume Av 111 GG83
Humes Av, W7 97 CE76
Hume Ter, E16 off Prince Regent La 86 EJ72
Hume Way, Ruis. HA4 59 BU58
Hummer Rd, Egh. TW20 113 BA91
Humphrey Cl, Ilf. IG5 49 EM53
Leatherhead (Fetch.) KT22 170 CC122
Humphrey St, SE1 201 P10
Humphries Cl, Dag. RM9 70 EZ63
Hundred Acre, NW9 43 CT54
Hungerdown, E4 47 EC46
Hungerford Av, Slou. SL2 74 AS71
Hungerford Br, SE1 200 A2
WC2 200 A2
Hungerford La, WC2 199 P2
Hungerford Rd, N7 65 DK64
Hungerford Sq, Wey. KT13 off Rosslyn Pk 153 BR105
Hungerford St, E1 off Commercial Rd 84 DV72
Hungry Hill, Wok. (Ripley) GU23 off Hungry Hill La 168 BK124
Hungry Hill La, Wok. (Send) GU23 168 BK124
Hunsdon Cl, Dag. RM9 88 EY65
Hunsdon Dr, Sev. TN13 191 FH123
Hunsdon Rd, SE14 103 DX79
Hunslett St, E2 off Royston St 84 DW68
Hunstanton Cl, Slou. (Colnbr.) SL3 93 BC80
Hunston Rd, Mord. SM4 140 DB102
Hunt Cl, W11 81 CX74
Hunter Av, Brwd. (Shenf.) CM15 55 GA44
Hunter Cl, SE1 201 L7
SW12 off Balham Pk Rd 120 DG88
Borehamwood WD6 26 CQ43
Potters Bar EN6 12 DB33
Wallington SM6 159 DL108
Huntercrombe Gdns, Wat. WD19 40 BW50
Hunter Dr, Horn. RM12 72 FJ63
Hunter Ho, Felt. TW13 115 BU88
Hunter Rd, SW20 139 CW95
Ilford IG1 69 EP64
Thornton Heath CR7 142 DR97
Hunters, The, Beck. BR3 143 EC95
Hunters Cl, Bex. DA5 127 FE90
Epsom KT19 off Marshalls Cl 156 CQ113
Hemel Hempstead (Bov.) HP3 5 BA29
Hunters Ct, Rich. TW9 off Friars La 117 CK85
Huntersfield Cl, Reig. RH2 184 DB131
Hunters Gate, Wat. WD25 off Hunters La 7 BU33
Hunters Gro, Har. HA3 61 CJ56
Hayes UB3 77 BU74
Orpington BR6 163 EP105
Romford RM5 51 FB50
Hunters Hall Rd, Dag. RM10 70 FA63
Hunters Hill, Ruis. HA4 60 BW62
Hunters La, Wat. WD25 7 BT33
Hunters Meadow, SE19 off Dulwich Wd Av 122 DS91
Hunters Reach, Wal.Cr. EN7 14 DT29
Hunters Ride, St.Alb. (Brick.Wd) AL2 8 CA31
Hunters Rd, Chess. KT9 138 CL104
Hunters Sq, Dag. RM10 70 FA63
Hunter St, WC1 196 A4
Hunters Wk, Sev. (Knock.) TN14 164 EY114
Hunters Way, Croy. CR0 off Brownlow Rd 160 DS105
Enfield EN2 29 DN39
Hunter Wk, E13 86 EG68
Borehamwood WD6 off Hunter Cl 26 CQ43
Hunting Cl, Esher KT10 154 CA105
Huntingdon Cl, Mitch. CR4 141 DL97
Huntingdon Gdns, W4 98 CQ80
Worcester Park KT4 139 CW104
Huntingdon Rd, N2 64 DE55
N9 46 DW46
Redhill RH1 184 DF134
Woking GU21 166 AT117
Huntingdon St, E16 86 EF72
N1 83 DM66
Huntingfield, Croy. CR0 161 DZ108
Huntingfield Rd, SW15 99 CU84
Huntingfield Way, Egh. TW20 113 BD94
Hunting Gate Cl, Enf. EN2 29 DN41
Hunting Gate Dr, Chess. KT9 156 CL108
Hunting Gate Ms, Sutt. SM1 140 DB104
Twickenham TW2 off Colne Rd 117 CE88
Huntings Rd, Dag. RM10 88 FA65
Huntland Cl, Rain. RM13 89 FH71
Huntley Av, Grav. (Nthflt) DA11 130 GB86
H Huntley Cen, WC1 195 M5
Huntley Cl, Stai. (Stanw.) TW19 off Cambria Gdns 114 BL87
Huntley Dr, N3 44 DA51
Huntley St, WC1 195 L5
Huntley Way, SW20 139 CU96
Huntly Rd, SE25 142 DS98
HUNTON BRIDGE, Kings L. WD4 7 BP33
Hunton Br Hill, Kings L. WD4 7 BQ33
Hunton St, E1 84 DU70
Hunt Rd, Grav. (Nthflt) DA11 130 GE90
Southall UB2 96 CA76
Hunt's Cl, SE3 104 EG82
Hunt's Ct, WC2 199 N1
Hunts La, E15 85 EC68
Huntsman Cl, Warl. CR6 176 DW119
Huntsman Rd, Ilf. IG6 50 EU51
Huntsmans Cl, Felt. TW13 115 BV91
Leatherhead (Fetch.) KT22 off The Green 171 CD124
Huntsmans Dr, Upmin. RM14 72 FQ64
Huntsman St, SE17 201 L9
Hunts Mead, Enf. EN3 31 DX41
Hunts Mead Cl, Chis. BR7 125 EM94
Huntsmoor Rd, Epsom KT19 156 CR106
Huntspill St, SW17 120 DC90
Hunts Slip Rd, SE21 122 DS90
Huntsworth Ms, NW1 194 D5
Hunt Way, SE22 off Dulwich Common 122 DU88
Hurcules Way, Wat. WD25 off Ashfields 7 BT33
Hurdwick Pl, NW1 off Harrington Sq 83 DJ68
Hurley Cl, Walt. KT12 135 BV103
Hurley Cres, SE16 203 J4

★ Place of interest ⇌ Railway station ⊖ London Underground station DLR Docklands Light Railway station Tram Tramlink station H Hospital Riv Pedestrian ferry landing stage

Hurley Ho, SE11 200 E9
Hurley Rd, Grnf. UB6 78 CB72
Hurlfield, Dart. DA2 128 FJ90
Hurlford, Wok. GU21 166 AU117
Hurlingham Business Pk, SW6 100 DA83
Hurlingham Ct, SW6 99 CZ83
Hurlingham Gdns, SW6 99 CZ83
★ Hurlingham Ho, SW6 100 DA83
★ Hurlingham Park, SW6 99 CZ82
Hurlingham Retail Pk, SW6
off Carnwath Rd 100 DB83
Hurlingham Rd, SW6 99 CZ82
Bexleyheath DA7 106 EZ80
Hurlingham Sq, SW6 100 DB83
Hurlock St, N5 65 DP62
Hurlstone Rd, SE25 142 DR99
Hurn Ct Rd, Houns. TW4
off Renfrew Rd 96 BX82
Hurnford Cl, S.Croy. CR2 160 DS110
Huron Cl, Orp. BR6
off Winnipeg Dr 163 ET107
Huron Rd, SW17 120 DG89
Hurren Cl, SE3 104 EE83
Hurricane Rd, Wall. SM6 159 DL108
Hurricane Way, Abb.L. WD5
off Abbey Dr 7 BU32
Epping (N.Wld Bas.) CM16 18 EZ27
Slough SL3 93 BB78
Hurry Cl, E15 86 EE66
Hursley Rd, Chig. IG7
off Tufter Rd 49 ET50
Hurst Av, E4 47 EA49
N6 65 DJ58
Hurstbourne, Esher
(Clay.) KT10 155 CF107
Hurstbourne Gdns, Bark. IG11 87 ES65
Hurstbourne Ho, SW15
off Tangley Gro 119 CT86
Hurstbourne Rd, SE23 123 DY88
Hurst Cl, E4 47 EA48
NW11 64 DB58
Bromley BR2 144 EF102
Chessington KT9 156 CN106
Northolt UB5 78 BZ65
Woking GU22 166 AW120
Hurstcourt Rd, Sutt. SM1 140 DB103
Hurstdene Av, Brom. BR2 144 EF102
Staines TW18 114 BH93
Hurstdene Gdns, N15 66 DS59
Hurst Dr, Tad. KT20 183 CU126
Waltham Cross EN8 15 DX34
Hurst Est, SE2 106 EX78
Hurstfield, Brom. BR2 144 EG99
Hurstfield Cres, Hayes UB4 77 BS70
Hurstfield Rd, W.Mol. KT8 136 CA97
HURST GREEN, Oxt. RH8 188 EG132
⇌ Hurst Green 188 EF132
Hurst Grn Cl, Oxt. RH8 188 EG132
Hurst Grn Rd, Oxt. RH8 188 EF132
Hurst Gro, Walt. KT12 135 BT102
Hurstlands, Oxt. RH8 188 EG132
Hurstlands Cl, Horn. RM11 72 FJ59
Hurst La, SE2 106 EX78
East Molesey KT8 136 CC98
Egham TW20 133 BA96
Epsom (Headley) KT18 172 CQ124
Hurstleigh Cl, Red. RH1 184 DF132
Hurstleigh Dr, Red. RH1 184 DF132
Hurstleigh Gdns, Ilf. IG5 49 EM53
Hurstmead Ct, Edg. HA8 42 CP49
Hurst Pk Av, Horn. RM12
off Newmarket Way 72 FL63
Hurst Pl, Nthwd. HA6 39 BP53
Hurst Ri, Barn. EN5 28 DA41
Hurst Rd, E17 67 EB55
N21 45 DN46
Bexley DA5 126 EX88
Buckhurst Hill IG9 48 EK46
Croydon CR0 160 DR106
East Molesey KT8 136 CA97
Epsom KT19 156 CR111
Epsom (Headley) KT18 172 CR123
Erith DA8 107 FC80
Sidcup DA15 126 EU89
Tadworth KT20 172 CR123
Walton-on-Thames KT12 136 BW99
West Molesey KT8 136 BY97
Hurst Springs, Bex. DA5 126 EY88
Hurst St, SE24 121 DP86
Hurst Vw Rd, S.Croy. CR2 160 DS108
Hurst Way, Sev. TN13 191 FJ127
South Croydon CR2 160 DS107
Woking (Pyrford) GU22 151 BE114
Hurstway Wk, W11 81 CX73
Hurstwood Av, E18 68 EH56
Bexley DA5 126 EY88
Bexleyheath DA7 107 FE81
Brentwood CM15
off Ongar Rd 54 FV45
Erith DA8 107 FE81
Hurstwood Ct, Upmin. RM14 72 FQ60
Hurstwood Dr, Brom. BR1 145 EM97
Hurstwood Rd, NW11 63 CY56
Hurtwood Rd, Walt. KT12 136 BZ101
Hurworth Av, Slou. SL3 92 AW76
Huson Cl, NW3 82 DE66
Hussain Cl, Har. HA1 61 CF63
Hussars Cl, Houns. TW4 96 BY83
Husseywell Cres, Brom. BR2 144 EG102
Hutchingsons Rd, Croy.
(New Adgtn) CR0 161 EC111
Hutchings St, E14 203 P5
Hutchings Wk, NW11 64 DB56
Hutchins Cl, E15
off Gibbins Rd 85 EC66
Hornchurch RM12 72 FL62
Hutchinson Ter, Wem. HA9 61 CK62
Hutchins Rd, SE28 88 EU73
Hutson Ter, Purf. RM19
off London Rd Purfleet 109 FR79
HUTTON, Brwd. CM13 55 GD44
Hutton Cl, Grnf. UB6
off Mary Peters Dr 61 CD64
Woodford Green IG8 48 EH51
Hutton Dr, Brwd. (Hutt.) CM13 55 GD45
Hutton Gdns, Har. HA3 40 CC52
Hutton Gate, Brwd.
(Hutt.) CM13 55 GB45
Hutton Gro, N12 44 DB50
Hutton La, Har. HA3 40 CC52
HUTTON MOUNT, Brwd. CM13 55 GB46
Hutton Rd, Brwd.
(Shenf.) CM15 55 FZ45
Hutton Row, Edg. HA8
off Pavilion Way 42 CQ52
Hutton St, EC4 196 E9
Hutton Village, Brwd.
(Hutt.) CM13 55 GE45
Hutton Wk, Har. HA3 40 CC52
Huxbear St, SE4 123 DZ85
Huxley Cl, Nthlt. UB5 78 BY67
Uxbridge UB8 76 BK70
Huxley Dr, Rom. RM6 70 EV59
Huxley Gdns, NW10 80 CM69
Huxley Par, N18 46 DR50
Huxley Pl, N13 45 DP49
Huxley Rd, E10 67 EC61
N18 46 DR49
Welling DA16 105 ET83
Huxley Sayze, N18 46 DR50
Huxley St, W10 81 CY69
Hyacinth Cl, Hmptn. TW12
off Gresham Rd 116 CA93
Ilford IG1 87 EP65
Hyacinth Ct, Pnr. HA5
off Tulip Ct 60 BW55
Hyacinth Dr, Uxb. UB10 76 BL66
Hyacinth Rd, SW15 119 CU88
Hyburn Cl, St.Alb.
(Brick.Wd) AL2 8 BZ30
Hycliffe Gdns, Chig. IG7 49 EQ49
HYDE, THE, NW9 63 CT56
Hyde, The, NW9 62 CS57
Hyde Av, Pot.B. EN6 12 DB33
Hyde Cl, E13 86 EG68
Ashford TW15
off Hyde Ter 115 BS93
Barnet EN5 27 CZ41
Grays (Chaff.Hun.) RM16 109 FX76
Hyde Ct, N20 44 DD48
Waltham Cross EN8
off Parkside 15 DY34
Hyde Cres, NW9 62 CS57
Hyde Dr, Orp. BR5 146 EV98
Hyde Est Rd, NW9 63 CT57
Hyde Fm Ms, SW12
off Telferscot Rd 121 DK88
Hydefield Cl, N21 46 DR46
Hydefield Ct, N9 46 DS47
Hyde Ho, NW9 62 CS57
Hyde La, SW11
off Battersea Br Rd 100 DE81
Hemel Hempstead HP3 7 BR26
Hemel Hempstead
(Bov.) HP3 5 BA27
St. Albans (Frog.) AL2 9 CE28
Woking (Ockham) GU23 168 BN120
Hyde Meadows, Hem.H.
(Bov.) HP3 5 BA28
★ Hyde Park, W2 198 B2
Hyde Pk, SW7 198 B2
W1 198 B2
Hyde Pk Av, N21 46 DQ47
⊖ Hyde Park Corner 198 F4
Hyde Pk Cor, W1 198 G4
Hyde Pk Cres, W2 194 B9
Hyde Pk Gdns, N21 46 DQ46
W2 194 A10
Hyde Pk Gdns Ms, W2 194 A10
Hyde Pk Gate, SW7 100 DC75
Hyde Pk Gate Ms, SW7
off Hyde Pk Gate 100 DC75
Hyde Pk Pl, W2 194 C10
Hyde Pk Sq, W2 194 B9
Hyde Pk Sq Ms, W2 194 B9
Hyde Pk St, W2 194 B9
Hyderabad Way, E15 86 EE66
Hyde Rd, N1 84 DR67
Bexleyheath DA7 106 EZ82
Richmond TW10
off Albert Rd 118 CM85
South Croydon CR2 160 DS113
Watford WD17 23 BU40
Hyder Rd, Grays RM16 111 GJ76
Hydeside Gdns, N9 46 DT47
Hydes Pl, N1
off Compton Av 83 DP66
Hyde St, SE8
off Deptford High St 103 EA79
Hyde Ter, Ashf. TW15 115 BS93
Hydethorpe Av, N9 46 DT47
Hydethorpe Rd, SW12 121 DJ88
Hyde Vale, SE10 103 EC80
Hyde Wk, Mord. SM4 140 DA101
Hyde Way, N9 46 DT47
Hayes UB3 95 BT77
Hyland Cl, Horn. RM11 71 FH59
Hylands Cl, Epsom KT18 172 CQ115
Hylands Ms, Epsom KT18 172 CQ115
Hylands Rd, E17 47 ED54
Epsom KT18 172 CQ115
Hyland Way, Horn. RM11 71 FH59
Hylton St, SE18 105 ET77
Hyndewood, SE23 123 DX90
Hyndford Cres, Green. DA9
off London Rd 129 FW85
Hyndman St, SE15 102 DV79
Hynton Rd, Dag. RM8 70 EW61
Hyperion Pl, Epsom KT19 156 CR109
Hyrons Cl, Amer. HP6 20 AS38
Hyrstdene, S.Croy. CR2 159 DP105
Hyson Rd, SE16 202 E10
Hythe, The, Stai. TW18 113 BE92
Hythe Av, Bexh. DA7 106 EZ80
Hythe Cl, N18 46 DU49
Orpington BR5
off Sandway Rd 146 EW98
HYTHE END, Stai. TW19 113 BB90
Hythe End Rd, Stai.
(Wrays.) TW19 113 BA89
Hythe Fld Av, Egh. TW20 113 BD93
Hythe Pk Rd, Egh. TW20 113 BC92
Hythe Path, Th.Hth. CR7 142 DR97
Hythe Rd, NW10 81 CU70
Staines TW18 113 BD92
Thornton Heath CR7 142 DR96
Hythe Rd Ind Est, NW10 81 CU69
Hythe St, Dart. DA1 128 FL86
Hythe St Lwr, Dart. DA1 128 FL85
Hyver Hill, NW7 26 CR44

I

Ian Sq, Enf. EN3
off Lansbury Rd 31 DX39
Ibbetson Path, Loug. IG10 33 EP41
Ibbotson Av, E16 86 EF72
Ibbott St, E1 off Mantus Rd 84 DW70
Iberian Av, Wall. SM6 159 DK105
Ibis La, W4 98 CQ81
Ibis Way, Hayes UB4
off Cygnet Way 78 BX72
Ibscott Cl, Dag. RM10 89 FC65
Ibsley Gdns, SW15 119 CU88
Ibsley Way, Barn. EN4 28 DE43
★ Ice Ho, Holland Pk, W8 99 CZ75
Icehouse Wd, Oxt. RH8 188 EE131
Iceland Rd, E3 85 EA67
Iceni Ct, E3 off Roman Rd 85 DZ67
Ice Wf, N1 off New Wf Rd 83 DL68
Ice Wf Marina, N1
off New Wf Rd 83 DL68
Ickburgh Est, E5
off Ickburgh Rd 66 DV62
Ickburgh Rd, E5 66 DV62
ICKENHAM, Uxb. UB10 59 BQ62
⊖ Ickenham 59 BQ63
Ickenham Cl, Ruis. HA4 59 BR61
Ickenham Rd, Ruis. HA4 59 BR60
Uxbridge (Ickhm) UB10 59 BQ61
Ickleton Rd, SE9 124 EL91
Icklingham Gate, Cob. KT11 154 BW112
Icklingham Rd, Cob. KT11 154 BW112
Icknield Dr, Ilf. IG2 69 EP57
Ickworth Pk Rd, E17 67 DY56
Ida Rd, N15 66 DR57
Ida St, E14 85 EC72
Iden Cl, Brom. BR2 144 EE97
Idlecombe Rd, SW17 120 DG93
Idmiston Rd, E15 68 EF64
SE27 122 DQ90
Worcester Park KT4 139 CT101
Idmiston Sq, Wor.Pk. KT4 139 CT101
Idol La, EC3 201 M1
Idonia St, SE8 103 DZ80
Iffley Cl, Uxb. UB8 76 BK66
Iffley Rd, W6 99 CV76
Ifield Rd, SW10 100 DB79
Ifield Way, Grav. DA12 131 GK93
Ifor Evans Pl, E1
off Mile End Rd 85 DX70
Ightham Rd, Erith DA8 106 FA80
Ikea Twr, NW10 62 CR64
Ilbert St, W10 81 CX69
Ilchester Gdns, W2 82 DB73
Ilchester Pl, W14 99 CZ76
Ilchester Rd, Dag. RM8 70 EV64
Ildersly Gro, SE21 122 DR89
Ilderton Rd, SE15 102 DW80
SE16 202 E10
Ilex Cl, Egh. (Eng.Grn) TW20 112 AV94
Sunbury-on-Thames TW16
off Oakington Dr 136 BW96
Ilex Ho, N4 65 DM59
Ilex Rd, NW10 81 CT65
Ilex Way, SW16 121 DN92
ILFORD 69 EQ62
⇌ Ilford 69 EN62
Ilford Hill, Ilf. IG1 69 EN62
Ilford La, Ilf. IG1 69 EP62
Ilfracombe Cres, Horn. RM12 72 FJ63
Ilfracombe Gdns, Rom. RM6 70 EV59
Ilfracombe Rd, Brom. BR1 124 EF90
Iliffe St, SE17 200 G10
Iliffe Yd, SE17 200 G10
Ilkeston Ct, E5
off Overbury St 67 DX63
Ilkley Cl, SE19 122 DR93
Ilkley Rd, E16 86 EJ71
Watford WD19 40 BX50
Illingworth Cl, Mitch. CR4 140 DD97
Illingworth Way, Enf. EN1 30 DS42
Ilmington Rd, Har. HA3 61 CK58
Ilminster Gdns, SW11 100 DE84
Imber Cl, N14 45 DJ45
Esher KT10 off Ember La 137 CD102
Imber Ct Trd Est,
E.Mol. KT8 137 CD100
Imber Gro, Esher KT10 137 CD101
Imber Pk Rd, Esher KT10 137 CD102
Imber St, N1 84 DR67
Imer Pl, T.Ditt. KT7 137 CF101
Imperial Av, N16
off Victorian Rd 66 DT62
Imperial Business Est,
Grav. DA11 131 GF86
Imperial Cl, Har. HA2 60 CA58
★ Imperial Coll, Uni of London,
SW7 100 DD76
Imperial Coll Rd, SW7 100 DD76
Imperial Cres, SW6
off William Morris Way 100 DC82
Weybridge KT13
off Churchill Dr 135 BQ104
Imperial Dr, Grav. DA12 131 GM92
Harrow HA2 60 CA59
Imperial Gdns, Mitch. CR4 141 DH97
Imperial Ms, E6
off Central Pk Rd 86 EJ68
Imperial Pk, Wat. WD24 24 BW39
Imperial Retail Pk, Grav. DA11 131 GG86
Imperial Rd, N22 45 DL53
SW6 100 DB81
Feltham TW14 115 BS87
Imperial Sq, SW6 100 DB81
Imperial St, E3 85 EC69
Imperial Trd Est, Rain. RM13
off Lambs La N 90 FJ70
★ Imperial War Mus, SE1 200 E7
Imperial Way, Chis. BR7 125 EQ90
Croydon CR0 159 DM107
Harrow HA3 62 CL58
Watford WD24 24 BW39
Imperial Wf, SW6 100 DC82
Imprimo Pk, Loug. IG10 33 ER42
Imre Cl, W12
off Ellerslie Rd 81 CV74
Inca Dr, SE9 125 EP87
Ince Rd, Walt. KT12 153 BS107
Inchmery Rd, SE6 123 EB89
Inchwood, Croy. CR0 161 EB105
Independent Pl, E8
off Downs Pk Rd 66 DT64
Independents Rd, SE3
off Blackheath Village 104 EF83
Inderwick Rd, N8 65 DM57
Indescon Ct, E14 204 A5
India Pl, WC2 196 B10
India Rd, Slou. SL1 92 AV75
India St, EC3 197 P9
India Way, W12 81 CV73
Indigo Ms, E14 off Ashton St 85 EC73
N16 66 DR62
Indus Rd, SE7 104 EJ80
Industry Ter, SW9
off Canterbury Cres 101 DN83
Ingal Rd, E13 86 EG70
Ingate Pl, SW8 101 DH81
Ingatestone Rd, E12 68 EJ60
SE25 142 DV98
Woodford Green IG8 48 EG52
Ingelow Rd, SW8 101 DH82
Ingels Mead, Epp. CM16 17 ET29
Ingersoll Rd, W12 81 CV74
Enfield EN3 30 DW38
Ingestre Pl, W1 195 L9
Ingestre Rd, E7 68 EG63
NW5 65 DH63
Ingham Cl, S.Croy. CR2 161 DX109
Ingham Rd, NW6 64 DA63
South Croydon CR2 160 DW109
Inglebert St, EC1 196 D2
Ingleboro Dr, Pur. CR8 160 DR113
Ingleborough St, SW9 101 DN82
Ingleby Dr, Har. HA1 61 CD62
Ingleby Gdns, Chig. IG7 50 EV48
Ingleby Rd, N7
off Bryett Rd 65 DL62
Dagenham RM10 89 FB65
Grays RM16 111 GH76
Ilford IG1 69 EP60
Ingleby Way, Chis. BR7 125 EN92
Wallington SM6 159 DK109
Ingle Cl, Pnr. HA5 60 BY55
Ingledew Rd, SE18 105 ER78
Inglefield, Pot.B. EN6 12 DA30
Ingleglen, Horn. RM11 72 FN59
Inglehurst, Add.
(New Haw) KT15 152 BH110
Inglehurst Gdns, Ilf. IG4 69 EM57
Inglemere Rd, SE23 123 DX90
Mitcham CR4 120 DF94
Inglesham Wk, E9 85 DZ65
Ingleside, Slou. (Colnbr.) SL3 93 BE81
Ingleside Cl, Beck. BR3 123 EA94
Ingleside Gro, SE3 104 EF79
Inglethorpe St, SW6 99 CX81
Ingleton Av, Well. DA16 126 EU85
Ingleton Rd, N18 46 DU51
Carshalton SM5 158 DE109
Ingleton St, SW9 101 DN82
Ingleway, N12 44 DD51
Inglewood, Cher. KT16 133 BF104
Croydon CR0 161 DY109
Woking GU21 166 AV118
Inglewood Cl, E14 204 A8
Hornchurch RM12 72 FK63
Ilford IG6 49 ET51
Inglewood Copse, Brom. BR1 144 EL96
Inglewood Gdns, St.Alb. AL2
off North Orbital Rd 9 CE25
Inglewood Rd, NW6 64 DA64
Bexleyheath DA7 107 FD84
Inglis Barracks, NW7 43 CX50
Inglis Rd, W5 80 CM73
Croydon CR0 142 DT102
Inglis St, SE5 101 DP81
Ingoldsby Rd, Grav. DA12 131 GL88
Ingram Av, NW11 64 DC59
Ingram Cl, SE11 200 C8
Stanmore HA7 41 CJ50
Ingram Rd, N2 64 DE56
Dartford DA1 128 FL88
Grays RM17 110 GD77
Thornton Heath CR7 142 DQ95
Ingrams Cl, Walt. KT12 154 BW106
Ingram Way, Grnf. UB6 79 CD67
Ingrave Ho, Dag. RM9 88 EV67
Ingrave Rd,
Brwd. CM13, CM15 54 FX47
Romford RM1 71 FD56
Ingrave St, SW11 100 DD83
Ingrebourne Gdns,
Upmin. RM14 72 FQ60
Ingrebourne Rd, Rain. RM13 89 FH70
Ingrebourne Valley Grn Way,
Horn. RM12 72 FK64
Ingress Gdns, Green. DA9 129 FX85
Ingress Pk Av, Green. DA9
off London Rd 129 FW85
Ingress St, W4
off Devonshire Rd 98 CS78
Ingreway, Rom. RM3 52 FP52
Inigo Jones Rd, SE7 104 EL80
Inigo Pl, WC2 195 P10
Inkerman Rd, NW5 83 DH65
Woking (Knap.) GU21 166 AS118
Inkerman Ter, W8
off Allen St 100 DA76
Inkerman Way, Wok. GU21 166 AS118
Inks Grn, E4 47 EC50
Inkster Ho, SW11
off Ingrave St 100 DE83
Inman Rd, NW10 80 CS67
SW18 120 DC87
Inmans Row, Wdf.Grn. IG8 48 EG49
Inner Circle, NW1 194 F3
Inner Pk Rd, SW19 119 CX88
Inner Ring E, Houns.
(Hthrw Air.) TW6 95 BP83
Inner Ring W, Houns.
(Hthrw Air.) TW6 94 BN83
Inner Temple La, EC4 196 D9
Innes Cl, SW20 139 CY96
Innes Gdns, SW15 119 CV86
Innes Yd, Croy. CR0
off Whitgift St 142 DQ104
Inniskilling Rd, E13 86 EJ68
Innova Business Pk, Enf. EN3 31 DZ36
Innovation Cl, Wem. HA0 80 CL67
Innova Way, Enf. EN3 31 DZ36
Inskip Cl, E10 67 EB61
Inskip Dr, Horn. RM11 72 FL60
Inskip Rd, Dag. RM8 70 EX60
★ Institute of Contemporary Arts
(I.C.A.), SW1 199 N2
Institute Pl, E8 66 DV64
Institute Rd, Epp.
(Cooper.) CM16 18 EX29
Instone Rd, Dart. DA1 128 FK87
Integer Gdns, E11 67 ED59
Interchange E Ind Est, E5
off Grosvenor Way 66 DW61
International Av, Houns. TW5 96 BW78
International Trd Est, Sthl. UB2 95 BV76
Inveraray Pl, SE18
off Old Mill Rd 105 ER79
Inver Cl, E5 off Theydon Rd 66 DW61
Inverclyde Gdns, Rom. RM6 70 EX56
Inver Ct, W2
off Inverness Ter 82 DB72
Inveresk Gdns, Wor.Pk. KT4 139 CT104
Inverforth Cl, NW3
off North End Way 64 DC61
Inverforth Rd, N11 45 DH50
Inverine Rd, SE7 104 EH78
Invermore Pl, SE18 105 EQ77
Inverness Av, Enf. EN1 30 DS39
Inverness Dr, Ilf. IG6 49 ES51
Inverness Gdns, W8
off Vicarage Gate 82 DB74
Inverness Ms, E16 87 EQ74
W2 off Inverness Ter 82 DB73
Inverness Pl, W2 82 DB73
Inverness Rd, N18
off Aberdeen Rd 46 DV50
Hounslow TW3 96 BZ84
Southall UB2 96 BY77
Worcester Park KT4 139 CX102
Inverness St, NW1 83 DH67
Inverness Ter, W2 82 DB73
Inverton Rd, SE15 103 DX84
Invicta Cl, Chis. BR7 125 EN92
Feltham TW14
off Westmacott Dr 115 BT88
Invicta Gro, Nthlt. UB5 78 BZ69
Invicta Plaza, SE1 200 F2
Invicta Rd, SE3 104 EG80
Dartford DA2 128 FP86
Inville Rd, SE17 102 DR78
Inwen Ct, SE8 103 DY78
Inwood Av, Couls. CR5 175 DN120
Hounslow TW3 96 CC83
Inwood Cl, Croy. CR0 143 DY103
Inwood Ct, Walt. KT12 136 BW103
Inwood Rd, Houns. TW3 96 CB84
Inworth St, SW11 100 DE82
Inworth Wk, N1
off Popham St 84 DQ67
Iona Cl, SE6 123 EA87
Morden SM4 140 DB101
Ionian Bldg, E14
off Narrow St 85 DY73
Ionia Wk, Grav. DA12
off Cervia Way 131 GM90
Ion Sq, E2 off Hackney Rd 84 DU68
Ipswich Rd, SW17 120 DG93
Ireland Cl, E6
off Bradley Stone Rd 87 EM71
Ireland Pl, N22
off Whittington Rd 45 DL52
Ireland Yd, EC4 196 G9
Irene Rd, SW6 100 DA81
Cobham (Stoke D'Ab.) KT11 154 CA114
Orpington BR6 145 ET101
Ireton Av, Walt. KT12 135 BS103
Ireton Cl, N10 44 DG52
Ireton Pl, Grays RM17
off Russell Rd 110 GA77
Ireton St, E3
off Tidworth Rd 85 EA70
Iris Av, Bex. DA5 126 EY85
Iris Cl, E6 86 EL70
Brentwood (Pilg.Hat.) CM15 54 FV43
Croydon CR0 143 DX102
Surbiton KT6 138 CM101
Iris Ct, Pnr. HA5 60 BW55
Iris Cres, Bexh. DA7 106 EZ79
Iris Path, Rom. RM3
off Clematis Cl 52 FJ52
Iris Rd, Epsom
(W.Ewell) KT19 156 CP106
Iris Wk, Edg. HA8 off Ash Cl 42 CQ49
Iris Way, E4 47 DZ51
Irkdale Av, Enf. EN1 30 DT39
Iron Br Cl, NW10 62 CS64
Southall UB2 78 CC74
Iron Br Rd, Uxb. UB11 94 BN75
West Drayton UB7 94 BN75
Iron Mill La, Dart. DA1 107 FE84
Iron Mill Pl, SW18
off Garratt La 120 DB86
Dartford DA1 107 FF84
Iron Mill Rd, SW18 120 DB86
Ironmonger La, EC2 197 K9
Ironmonger Pas, EC1 197 J4
Ironmonger Row, EC1 197 J3
Ironmongers Pl, E14 204 A9
Ironside Cl, SE16 203 H4
Irons Way, Rom. RM5 51 FC52
Irvine Av, Har. HA3 61 CG55
Irvine Cl, N20 44 DE47
Irvine Gdns, S.Ock. RM15 91 FT72
Irvine Pl, Vir.W. GU25 132 AY99
Irvine Way, Orp. BR6 145 ET101
Irving Av, Nthlt. UB5 78 BX67
Irving Gro, SW9 101 DM82
Irving Ms, N1 off Alwyne Rd 84 DQ65
Irving Rd, W14 99 CX76
Irving St, WC2 199 N1

★ Place of interest ⇌ Railway station ⊖ London Underground station DLR Docklands Light Railway station Tra Tramlink station H Hospital Riv Pedestrian ferry landing stage

Irving Wk, Swans. DA10 130 FY87
Irving Way, NW9 63 CT57
Swanley BR8 147 FD96
Irwin Av, SE18 105 ES80
Irwin Cl, Uxb. UB10 58 BN62
Irwin Gdns, NW10 81 CV67
Isabel Gate, Wal.Cr. (Chsht) EN8 15 DZ26
Isabel Hill Cl, Hmptn. TW12 off Upper Sunbury Rd 136 CB95
Isabella Cl, N14 45 DJ45
Isabella Ct, Rich. TW10 off Grove Rd 118 CM86
Isabella Dr, Orp. BR6 163 EQ105
Isabella Rd, E9 66 DW64
Isabella St, SE1 200 F3
Isabelle Cl, Wal.Cr. (Goffs Oak) EN7 14 DQ29
Isabel St, SW9 101 DM81
Isambard Cl, Uxb. UB8 76 BK69
Isambard Ms, E14 204 E7
Isambard Pl, SE16 202 G3
Isbell Gdns, Rom. RM1 51 FE52
Isel Way, SE22 off East Dulwich Gro 122 DS85
Isham Rd, SW16 141 DL96
Isis Cl, SW15 99 CW84
Ruislip HA4 59 BQ58
Isis Dr, Upmin. RM14 73 FS58
Isis St, SW18 120 DC89
Island, The, Stai. (Wrays.) TW19 113 BA90
West Drayton UB7 94 BH81
Island Cl, Stai. TW18 113 BE91
Island Fm Av, W.Mol. KT8 136 BZ99
Island Fm Rd, W.Mol. KT8 136 BZ99
DLR Island Gardens 204 D9
Island Rd, Mitch. CR4 120 DF94
Island Row, E14 85 DZ72
Isla Rd, SE18 105 EQ79
Islay Gdns, Houns. TW4 116 BX85
Islay Wk, N1 off Douglas Rd 84 DQ66
Isledon Rd, N7 65 DN62
Islehurst Cl, Chis. BR7 145 EN95
ISLEWORTH 97 CF83
⇌ Isleworth 97 CF82
Isleworth Business Complex, Islw. TW7 off St. John's Rd 97 CF82
Isleworth Prom, Twick. TW1 97 CH84
ISLINGTON, N1 83 DM67
Islington Grn, N1 83 DP67
Islington High St, N1 196 E1
Islington Pk Ms, N1 off Islington Pk St 83 DN66
Islington Pk St, N1 83 DN66
Islip Gdns, Edg. HA8 42 CR52
Northolt UB5 78 BY66
Islip Manor Rd, Nthlt. UB5 78 BY66
Islip St, NW5 65 DJ64
Ismailia Rd, E7 86 EH66
★ Ismaili Cen & Zamana Gall, SW7 198 A8
Ismay Ct, Slou. SL2 off Elliman Av 74 AS73
Isom Cl, E13 off Belgrave Rd 86 EJ70
ISTEAD RISE, Grav. DA13 130 GE94
Istead Ri, Grav. DA13 131 GF94
Itchingwood Common Rd, Oxt. RH8 188 EJ133
Ivanhoe Cl, Uxb. UB8 76 BK71
Ivanhoe Dr, Har. HA3 61 CG55
Ivanhoe Rd, SE5 102 DT83
Hounslow TW4 96 BX83
Ivatt Pl, W14 99 CZ78
Ivatt Way, N17 65 DP55
Iveagh Av, NW10 80 CN68
Iveagh Cl, E9 85 DX67
NW10 80 CN68
Northwood HA6 39 BP53
Iveagh Rd, Wok. GU21 166 AT118
Iveagh Ter, NW10 off Iveagh Av 80 CN68
Ivedon Rd, Well. DA16 106 EW82
Ive Fm Cl, E10 67 EA61
Ive Fm La, E10 67 EA61
Iveley Rd, SW4 101 DJ82
IVER 75 BF72
⇌ Iver 93 BF75
Iverdale Cl, Iver SL0 75 BC73
Ivere Dr, Barn. EN5 28 DB44
IVER HEATH, Iver SL0 75 BD69
Iverhurst Cl, Bexh. DA6 126 EX85
Iver La, Iver SL0 76 BH71
Uxbridge UB8 76 BH71
Iverna Ct, W8 100 DA76
Iverna Gdns, W8 100 DA76
Feltham TW14 115 BR85
Iver Rd, Brwd. (Pilg.Hat.) CM15 54 FV44
Iver SL0 76 BG72
Iverson Rd, NW6 81 CZ65
Ivers Way, Croy. (New Adgtn) CR0 161 EB108
Ives Gdns, Rom. RM1 off Sims Cl 71 FF56
Ives Rd, E16 86 EE71
Slough SL3 93 AZ76
Ives St, SW3 198 C8
Ivestor Ter, SE23 122 DW87
Ivimey St, E2 84 DU69
Ivinghoe Cl, Enf. EN1 30 DS40
Watford WD25 24 BX35
Ivinghoe Rd, Bushey WD23 41 CD45
Dagenham RM8 70 EV64
Rickmansworth (Mill End) WD3 38 BG45
Ivor Gro, SE9 125 EP88
Ivor Pl, NW1 194 D5
Ivor St, NW1 83 DJ66
Ivorydown, Brom. BR1 124 EG91
Ivory Sq, SW11 off Gartons Way 100 DC83
Ivy Bower Cl, Green. DA9 off Riverview Rd 129 FV85
Ivybridge Cl, Twick. TW1 117 CG86
Ivybridge Cl, Uxbridge UB8 76 BL69
Ivybridge Est, Islw. TW7 117 CF85
Ivybridge La, WC2 200 A1
IVY CHIMNEYS, Epp. CM16 17 ES32
Ivy Chimneys Rd, Epp. CM16 17 ES32
Ivychurch Cl, SE20 122 DW94
Ivychurch La, SE17 201 P10
Ivy Cl, Dart. DA1 128 FN87
Gravesend DA12 131 GJ90
Harrow HA2 60 BZ63
Pinner HA5 60 BW59
Sunbury-on-Thames TW16 136 BW96
Ivy Cotts, E14 off Grove Vil 85 EB73
Ivy Ct, SE16 off Argyle Way 102 DU78
Ivy Cres, W4 98 CQ77
Ivydale Rd, SE15 103 DX83
Carshalton SM5 140 DF103
Ivyday Gro, SW16 121 DM90
Ivydene, W.Mol. KT8 136 BZ99
Ivydene Cl, Sutt. SM1 158 DC105
Ivy Gdns, N8 65 DL58
Mitcham CR4 141 DK97
Ivy Ho La, Sev. TN14 181 FD118
Ivyhouse Rd, Dag. RM9 88 EX65
Ivy Ho Rd, Uxb. UB10 59 BP62
Ivy La, Houns. TW4 96 BZ84
Sevenoaks (Knock.) TN14 180 EY116
Woking GU22 167 BB118
Ivy Lea, Rick. WD3 off Springwell Av 38 BG46
Ivy Lo La, Rom. RM3 52 FP53
Ivy Mill Cl, Gdse. RH9 186 DV132
Ivy Mill La, Gdse. RH9 186 DU132
Ivymount Rd, SE27 121 DN90
Ivy Pl, Surb. KT5 off Alpha Rd 138 CM100
Ivy Rd, E16 off Pacific Rd 86 EG72
E17 67 EA58
N14 45 DJ45
NW2 63 CW63
SE4 103 DZ84
SW17 off Tooting High St 120 DE92
Hounslow TW3 96 CB84
Surbiton KT6 138 CN102
Ivy St, N1 84 DS68
Ivy Wk, Dag. RM9 88 EY65
Ixworth Pl, SW3 198 B10
Izane Rd, Bexh. DA6 106 EZ84

J

Jacaranda Cl, N.Mal. KT3 138 CS97
Jacaranda Gro, E8 84 DT66
Jackass La, Kes. BR2 162 EH107
Oxted (Tand.) RH8 187 DZ131
Jack Barnett Way, N22 45 DM54
Jack Clow Rd, E15 86 EE68
Jack Cornwell St, E12 69 EN63
Jack Dash Way, E6 86 EL70
Jackets La, Nthwd. HA6 39 BP53
Uxbridge (Hare.) UB9 38 BN52
Jacketts Fld, Abb.L. WD5 7 BT31
Jack Goodchild Way, Kings.T. KT1 off Kingston Rd 138 CP97
Jacklin Grn, Wdf.Grn. IG8 48 EG49
Jackman Ms, NW10 62 CS62
Jackmans La, Wok. GU21 166 AU119
Jackman St, E8 84 DV67
Jacks La, Uxb. (Hare.) UB9 38 BG53
Jackson Cl, E9 84 DW66
Epsom KT18 156 CR114
Greenhithe DA9 off Cowley Av 129 FU85
Hornchurch RM11 72 FM56
Uxbridge UB10 off Jackson Rd 76 BL66
Jackson Ct, E11 off Brading Cres 68 EH60
Jackson Rd, N7 65 DM63
Barking IG11 87 ER67
Barnet EN4 28 DE44
Bromley BR2 144 EL103
Uxbridge UB10 76 BL66
Jacksons Dr, Wal.Cr. EN7 14 DU28
Jacksons La, N6 64 DG59
Jacksons Pl, Croy. CR0 off Cross Rd 142 DR102
Jackson St, SE18 105 EN79
Jacksons Way, Croy. CR0 143 EA104
Jackson Way, Epsom KT19 off Lady Harewood Way 156 CN109
Southall UB2 96 CB75
Jack Walker Ct, N5 65 DP63
Jacob Ho, Erith DA18 off Kale Rd 106 EX75
Jacobs Av, Rom. (Harold Wd) RM3 52 FL54
Jacobs Cl, Dag. RM10 71 FB63
Jacobs Ho, E13 86 EJ69
Jacobs La, Dart. (Hort.Kir.) DA4 148 FQ97
Jacob St, SE1 202 A4
Jacob's Well Ms, W1 194 G8
Jacqueline Cl, Nthlt. UB5 off Canford Av 78 BZ67
Jade Cl, E16 86 EK72
NW2 off Marble Dr 63 CX59
Dagenham RM8 70 EW60
Jaffe Rd, Ilf. IG1 69 EQ60
Jaffray Pl, SE27 off Chapel Rd 121 DP91
Jaffray Rd, Brom. BR2 144 EK98
Jaggard Way, SW12 120 DF87
Jagger Cl, Dart. DA2 128 FQ87
Jago Cl, SE18 105 EQ79
Jago Wk, SE5 102 DR80
Jail La, West. (Bigg.H.) TN16 178 EK116
Jamaica Rd, SE1 202 A5
SE16 202 D6
Thornton Heath CR7 141 DP100
Jamaica St, E1 84 DW72
James Av, NW2 63 CW64
Dagenham RM8 70 EZ60
James Bedford Cl, Pnr. HA5 40 BW54
James Boswell Cl, SW16 off Curtis Fld Rd 121 DN91
James Cl, E13 off Richmond St 86 EG68
James Cl, NW11 off Woodlands 63 CY58
Bushey WD23 off Aldenham Rd 24 BY43
Romford RM2 71 FG57
James Collins Cl, W9 off Fermoy Rd 81 CZ70
James Ct, N1 off Morton Rd 84 DQ66
James Dudson Ct, NW10 80 CQ66
James Gdns, N22 45 DP52
James Hammett Ho, E2 off Ravenscroft St 84 DT69
James Joyce Wk, SE24 off Shakespeare Rd 101 DP84
James La, E10 67 ED59
E11 67 ED58
James Lee Sq, Enf. EN3 31 EA38
James Martin Cl, Uxb. (Denh.) UB9 58 BG58
James Meadow, Slou. SL3 off Ditton Rd 93 AZ79
James Newman Ct, SE9 off Great Harry Dr 125 EN90
Jameson Cl, W3 off Acton La 98 CQ75
Jameson Ct, E2 84 DW68
Jameson St, W8 82 DA74
James Pl, N17 46 DT53
James Rd, Dart. DA1 127 FG87
James's Cotts, Rich. TW9 off Kew Rd 98 CN80
James Sinclair Pt, E13 86 EJ67
James St, W1 194 G8
WC2 196 A10
Barking IG11 87 EQ66
Enfield EN1 30 DT43
Epping CM16 17 ET28
Hounslow TW3 97 CD83
James Ter, SW14 off Mullins Path 98 CR83
Jamestown Rd, NW1 83 DH67
Jamestown Way, E14 204 G1
James Watt Way, Erith DA8 107 FF79
James Way, Wat. WD19 40 BX49
James Yd, E4 47 ED51
Jamieson Ho, Houns. TW4 116 BZ87
Jamnagar Cl, Stai. TW18 113 BF93
Jamuna Cl, E14 85 DY71
Jane St, E1 off Commercial Rd 84 DV72
Janet St, E14 204 A6
Janeway Pl, SE16 202 D5
Janeway St, SE16 202 C5
Janice Ms, Ilf. IG1 off Oakfield Rd 69 EP62
Janmead, Brwd. (Hutt.) CM13 55 GB45
Janoway Hill La, Wok. GU21 166 AW119
Jansen Wk, SW11 off Hope St 100 DD84
Janson Cl, E15 off Janson Rd 68 EE64
NW10 62 CR62
Janson Rd, E15 68 EE64
Jansons Rd, N15 66 DS55
Japan Cres, N4 65 DM60
Japan Rd, Rom. RM6 70 EX58
Japonica Cl, Wok. GU21 166 AW118
Jardine Rd, E1 85 DX73
Jarrah Cotts, Purf. RM19 off London Rd Purfleet 109 FR79
Jarrett Cl, SW2 121 DP88
Jarrow Cl, Mord. SM4 140 DB99
Jarrow Rd, N17 66 DV56
SE16 202 F9
Romford RM6 70 EW58
Jarrow Way, E9 67 DY63
Jarvis Cleys, Wal.Cr. (Chsht) EN7 14 DT26
Jarvis Cl, Bark. IG11 off Westbury Rd 87 ER67
Barnet EN5 27 CX43
Jarvis Rd, SE22 off Melbourne Gro 102 DS84
South Croydon CR2 160 DR107
Jarvis Way, Rom. (Harold Wd) RM3 52 FL54
Jasmin Cl, Nthwd. HA6 39 BT53
Jasmine Cl, Ilf. IG1 69 EP64
Orpington BR6 145 EP103
Southall UB1 78 BY73
Woking GU21 166 AT116
Jasmine Gdns, Croy. CR0 143 EB104
Harrow HA2 60 CA61
Jasmine Gro, SE20 142 DV95
Jasmine Rd, Rom. (Rush Grn) RM7 71 FE61
Jasmine Ter, West Dr. UB7 94 BN75
Jasmine Way, E.Mol. KT8 off Hampton Ct Way 137 CE98
Jasmin Rd, Epsom KT19 156 CP106
Jason Cl, Brwd. CM14 54 FT49
Weybridge KT13 153 BQ106
Jason Ct, W1 off Marylebone La 82 DG72
Jasons Hill, Chesh. HP5 4 AV30
Jason Wk, SE9 125 EN91
Jasper Cl, Enf. EN3 30 DW38
Jasper Pas, SE19 122 DT93
Jasper Rd, E16 86 EK72
SE19 122 DT92
Jasper Wk, N1 197 K2
Javelin Way, Nthlt. UB5 78 BX69
Jaycroft, Enf. EN2 off The Ridgeway 29 DN39
Jay Gdns, Chis. BR7 125 EM91
Jay Ms, SW7 100 DC75
Jays Covert, Couls. CR5 174 DG119
Jazzfern Ter, Wem. HA0 off Maybank Av 61 CG64
Jean Batten Cl, Wall. SM6 159 DM108
Jebb Av, SW2 121 DL86
Jebb St, E3 85 EA68
Jedburgh Rd, E13 86 EJ69
Jedburgh St, SW11 100 DG84
Jeddo Rd, W12 99 CT75
Jefferson Cl, W13 97 CH76
Ilford IG2 69 EP57
Slough SL3 93 BA77
Jefferson Wk, SE18 off Kempt St 105 EN79
Jeffreys Pl, NW1 off Jeffreys St 83 DJ66
Jeffreys Rd, SW4 101 DL82
Enfield EN3 31 DZ41
Jeffreys St, NW1 83 DH66
Jeffreys Wk, SW4 101 DL82
Jeffries Ho, NW10 80 CR67
Jeffs Cl, Hmptn. TW12 off Uxbridge Rd 116 CB93
Jeffs Rd, Sutt. SM1 157 CZ105
Jeger Av, E2 84 DT67
Jeken Rd, SE9 104 EJ84
Jelf Rd, SW2 121 DN85
Jellicoe Av, Grav. DA12 131 GJ90
Jellicoe Av W, Grav. DA12 off Kitchener Av 131 GJ90
Jellicoe Gdns, Stan. HA7 41 CF51
Jellicoe Rd, E13 off Jutland Rd 86 EG70
N17 46 DR52
Watford WD18 23 BU44
Jemma Knowles Cl, SW2 off Neil Wates Cres 121 DN88
Jemmett Cl, Kings.T. KT2 138 CP95
Jengar Cl, Sutt. SM1 158 DB105
Jenkins Av, St.Alb. (Brick.Wd) AL2 8 BY30
Jenkins La, E6 87 EN68
Barking IG11 87 EP68
Jenkins Rd, E13 86 EH70
Jenner Av, W3 80 CR71
Jenner Cl, Sid. DA14 off Elm Rd 126 EU91
Jenner Ho, SE3 104 EE79
Jenner Pl, SW13 99 CV79
Jenner Rd, N16 66 DT61
Jenner Way, Epsom KT19 off Monro Pl 156 CN109
Jennett Rd, Croy. CR0 141 DN104
Jennifer Rd, Brom. BR1 124 EF90
Jennings Cl, Add. (New Haw) KT15 off Woodham La 152 BJ109
Surbiton KT6 137 CJ101
Jennings Rd, SE22 122 DT86
Jennings Way, Barn. EN5 27 CW41
Jenningtree Rd, Erith DA8 107 FH80
Jenningtree Way, Belv. DA17 107 FC75
Jenny Hammond Cl, E11 off Newcomen Rd 68 EF62
Jenny Path, Rom. RM3 52 FK52
Jennys Way, Couls. CR5 175 DJ122
Jenson Way, SE19 122 DT94
Jenton Av, Bexh. DA7 106 EY81
Jephson Rd, E7 86 EJ66
Jephson St, SE5 off Grove La 102 DR81
Jephtha Rd, SW18 120 DA86
Jeppos La, Mitch. CR4 140 DF98
Jepps Cl, Wal.Cr. EN7 off Little Gro Av 14 DS27
Jepson Ho, SW6 off Pearscroft Rd 100 DB81
Jerdan Pl, SW6 100 DA80
Jeremiah St, E14 85 EB72
Jeremys Grn, N18 46 DV49
Jermyn St, SW1 199 K2
Jerningham Av, Ilf. IG5 49 EP54
Jerningham Rd, SE14 103 DY82
Jerome Cres, NW8 194 B4
Jerome Pl, Kings.T. KT1 off Wadbrook St 137 CK96
Jerome St, E1 197 P6
Jerome Twr, W3 98 CP75
Jerrard St, N1 197 N1
SE13 103 EB83
Jersey Av, Stan. HA7 41 CH54
Jersey Cl, Cher. KT16 133 BF104
Jersey Dr, Orp. BR5 145 ER100
Jersey Ho, Enf. EN3 off Eastfield Rd 31 DX38
Jersey Par, Houns. TW5 96 CB81
Jersey Rd, E11 67 ED60
E16 off Prince Regent La 86 EJ72
SW17 121 DH93
W7 97 CG75
Hounslow TW3, TW5 96 CB81
Ilford IG1 69 EP63
Isleworth TW7 97 CE79
Rainham RM13 89 FG66
Jersey St, E2 off Bethnal Grn Rd 84 DV69
Jerusalem Pas, EC1 196 F5
Jervis Av, Enf. EN3 31 DY35
Jervis Ct, W1 195 J9
Jerviston Gdns, SW16 121 DN93
Jesmond Av, Wem. HA9 80 CM65
Jesmond Cl, Mitch. CR4 141 DH97
Jesmond Rd, Croy. CR0 142 DT101
Jesmond Way, Stan. HA7 42 CL50
Jessam Av, E5 66 DV60
Jessamine Pl, Dart. DA2 128 FQ87
Jessamine Rd, W7 79 CE74
Jessamine Ter, Swan. BR8 off Birchwood Rd 147 FC95
Jessamy Rd, Wey. KT13 135 BP103
Jessel Dr, Loug. IG10 33 EQ39
Jesse Rd, E10 67 EC60
Jessett Cl, Erith DA8 off West St 107 FD77
Jessica Rd, SW18 120 DC86
Jessie Blythe La, N19 65 DL59
Jessiman Ter, Shep. TW17 134 BN99
Jessop Av, Sthl. UB2 96 BZ77
Jessop Rd, SE24 off Milkwood Rd 101 DP84
Jessop Sq, E14 off Heron Quay 85 EA74
Jessops Way, Croy. CR0 141 DJ100
Jessup Cl, SE18 105 EQ77
Jetstar Way, Nthlt. UB5 78 BY69
Jetty Wk, Grays RM17 110 GA79
Jevington Way, SE12 124 EH89
Jewel Rd, E17 67 EA55
Jewels Hill, West. (Bigg.H.) TN16 162 EG112
★ Jewel Twr, Hos of Parliament, SW1 199 P6
★ Jewish Mus, NW1 83 DH67
Jewry St, EC3 197 P9
Jew's Row, SW18 100 DB84
Jews Wk, SE26 122 DV91
Jeymer Av, NW2 63 CV64
Jeymer Dr, Grnf. UB6 78 CC67
Jeypore Pas, SW18 off Jeypore Rd 120 DC86
Jeypore Rd, SW18 120 DC87
Jillian Cl, Hmptn. TW12 116 CA94
Jim Bradley Cl, SE18 off John Wilson St 105 EN77
Jim Griffiths Ho, SW6 off Clem Attlee Ct 99 CZ79
Joan Cres, SE9 124 EK87
Joan Gdns, Dag. RM8 70 EY61
Joan Rd, Dag. RM8 70 EY61
Joan St, SE1 200 F3
Jocelyn Rd, Rich. TW9 98 CL83
Jocelyn St, SE15 102 DU81
Jockey's Flds, WC1 196 C6
Jodane St, SE8 203 M9
Jodrell Cl, Islw. TW7 97 CG81
Jodrell Rd, E3 85 DZ67
Jodrell Way, Grays (W.Thur.) RM20 109 FT78
Joel St, Nthwd. HA6 59 BU55
Pinner HA5 59 BU55
Johanna St, SE1 200 D5
John Adam St, WC2 200 A1
John Aird Ct, W2 82 DC71
John Archer Way, SW18 120 DD86
John Ashby Cl, SW2 121 DL86
John Austin Cl, Kings.T. KT2 off Queen Elizabeth Rd 138 CM95
John Barnes Wk, E15 86 EF65
John Bradshaw Rd, N14 off High St 45 DK46
John Burns Dr, Bark. IG11 87 ES66
Johnby Cl, Enf. EN3 off Manly Dixon Dr 31 DY37
John Campbell Rd, N16 66 DS64
John Carpenter St, EC4 196 F10
John Cobb Rd, Wey. KT13 152 BN108
John Cornwell VC Ho, E12 69 EN63
John Drinkwater Cl, E11 off Browning Rd 68 EF59
John Felton Rd, SE16 202 B5
John Fisher St, E1 84 DU73
John Gooch Dr, Enf. EN2 29 DP39
John Harrison Way, SE10 205 K7
John Horner Ms, N1 off Frome St 84 DQ68
H John Howard Cen, E9 85 DY65
John Islip St, SW1 199 P9
John Keats Ho, N22 45 DM52
John Maurice Cl, SE17 201 K8
John McKenna Wk, SE16 202 C6
John Newton Ct, Well. DA16 off Danson La 106 EV83
John Parker Cl, Dag. RM10 89 FB66
John Parker Sq, SW11 off Thomas Baines Rd 100 DD83
John Penn St, SE13 103 EB81
John Perrin Pl, Har. HA3 62 CL59
John Princes St, W1 195 J8
John Rennie Wk, E1 202 E2
John Roll Way, SE16 202 C6
John Ruskin St, SE5 101 DP80
Johns Av, NW4 63 CW56
Johns Cl, Ashf. TW15 115 BQ91
Johns Ct, Sutt. SM2 off Mulgrave Rd 158 DB107
Johnsdale, Oxt. RH8 188 EF129
John Silkin La, SE8 203 J9
Johns La, Mord. SM4 140 DC99
John's Ms, WC1 196 C5
John Smith Av, SW6 99 CZ80
John Smith Ms, E14 204 F1
Johnson Cl, E8 84 DU67
Gravesend (Nthflt) DA11 130 GD90
Johnson Rd, NW10 80 CR67
Bromley BR2 144 EK99
Croydon CR0 142 DR101
Hounslow TW5 96 BW80
Johnsons Av, Sev. (Bad.Mt) TN14 165 FB110
Johnsons Cl, Cars. SM5 140 DF104
Johnson's Ct, EC4 off Fleet St 83 DN72
Johnsons Ct, Sev. (Seal) TN15 off School La 191 FM121
Johnsons Dr, Hmptn. TW12 136 CC95
Johnson's Pl, SW1 101 DJ78
Johnson St, E1 off Cable St 84 DW73
Southall UB2 96 BW76
Johnsons Way, NW10 80 CP70
Greenhithe DA9 129 FW86
Johnsons Yd, Uxb. UB8 off Redford Way 76 BJ66
John Spencer Sq, N1 83 DP65
John's Pl, E1 off Damien St 84 DV72
Johns Rd, West. (Tats.) TN16 178 EK120
John's Ter, Croy. CR0 142 DR102
Romford RM3 52 FP51
Johnston Cl, SW9 off Hackford Rd 101 DM81
Johnstone Rd, E6 87 EM69
Johnston Rd, Wdf.Grn. IG8 48 EG50
Johnston Ter, NW2 off Kara Way 63 CX62
John St, E15 86 EF67
SE25 142 DU98
WC1 196 C5
Enfield EN1 30 DT43
Grays RM17 110 GC79
Hounslow TW3 96 BY82
Johns Wk, Whyt. CR3 176 DU119
John Trundle Ct, EC2 off The Barbican 84 DQ71
John Walsh Twr, E11 68 EF61
John Watkin Cl, Epsom KT19 156 CP109
John William Cl, Grays RM16 off Lancaster Rd 109 FX78
John Williams Cl, SE14 103 DX79
Kingston upon Thames KT2 off Henry Macaulay Av 137 CK95
John Wilson St, SE18 105 EN76
John Woolley Cl, SE13 104 EE84
Joiner's Arms Yd, SE5 off Denmark Hill 102 DR81
Joiners Cl, Chesh. (Ley Hill) HP5 4 AV30
Gerrards Cross (Chal.St.P.) SL9 37 AZ52

★ Place of interest ⇌ Railway station ⊖ London Underground station DLR Docklands Light Railway station Tra Tramlink station H Hospital Riv Pedestrian ferry landing stage

Joiners La, Ger.Cr.
(Chal.St.P.) SL9 36 AY53
Joiners Pl, N5
off Leconfield Rd 66 DR63
Joiner St, SE1 201 L3
Joiners Way, Ger.Cr.
(Chal.St.P.) SL9 36 AY52
Joiners Yd, N1
off Caledonia St 83 DL68
Joinville Pl, Add. KT15 152 BK105
Jolliffe Rd, Red. RH1 185 DJ126
Jollys La, Har. HA2 61 CD60
Hayes UB4 78 BX71
Jonathan Ct, W4
off Windmill Rd 98 CS77
Jonathan St, SE11 200 B10
Jones Rd, E13
off Holborn Rd 86 EH70
Waltham Cross
(Chsht) EN7 13 DP30
Jones St, W1 199 H1
Jones Wk, Rich. TW10
off Pyrland Rd 118 CM86
Jonquil Gdns, Hmptn. TW12
off Partridge Rd 116 BZ93
Jonson Cl, Hayes UB4 77 BU71
Mitcham CR4 141 DH98
Jordan Cl, Dag. RM10
off Muggeridge Rd 71 FB63
Harrow HA2
off Hamilton Cres 60 BZ62
South Croydon CR2 160 DT111
Watford WD25 23 BT35
Jordan Ct, SW15
off Charlwood Rd 99 CX84
Jordan Rd, Grnf. UB6 79 CH67
JORDANS, Beac. HP9 36 AT52
Jordans Cl, Islw. TW7 97 CE81
Staines (Stanw.) TW19 114 BJ87
Jordans La, Beac.
(Jordans) HP9 36 AS53
Jordans Rd, Rick. WD3 38 BG45
Jordans Way, Beac.
(Jordans) HP9 36 AT51
Rainham RM13 90 FK68
St. Albans (Brick.Wd) AL2 8 BZ30
Joseph Av, W3 80 CR72
Joseph Hardcastle Cl, SE14 103 DX80
Josephine Av, SW2 121 DM85
Tadworth KT20 183 CZ126
Josephine Cl, Tad. KT20 183 CZ127
Joseph Locke Way, Esher KT10
off Mill Rd 136 CA103
Joseph Powell Cl, SW12
off Hazelbourne Rd 121 DH86
Joseph Ray Rd, E11 68 EE61
Joseph St, E3 85 DZ70
Joseph Trotter Cl, EC1
off Myddelton St 83 DN69
Joshua Cl, N10 45 DH52
South Croydon CR2 159 DP108
Joshua St, E14
off St. Leonards Rd 85 EC72
Joshua Wk, Wal.Cr. EN8
off Longcroft Dr 15 EA34
Josling Cl, Grays RM17 110 FZ79
Joslin Rd, Purf. RM19 108 FQ78
Joslyn Cl, Enf. EN3 31 EA38
Joubert St, SW11 100 DF82
Journeys End, Slou.
(Stoke P.) SL2 74 AS71
Jowett St, SE15 102 DT80
Joyce Av, N18 46 DT50
Joyce Ct, Wal.Abb. EN9 15 ED34
Joyce Dawson Way, SE28
off Thamesmere Dr 88 EU73
Joyce Dawson Way Shop Arc, SE28
off Thamesmere Dr 88 EU73
Joyce Grn La, Dart. DA1 108 FL81
Joyce Grn Wk, Dart. DA1 108 FM84
Joyce Page Cl, SE7
off Lansdowne La 104 EK79
Joyce Wk, SW2 121 DN86
JOYDENS WOOD, Bex. DA5 127 FC92
Joydens Wd Rd, Bex. DA5 127 FD91
Joydon Dr, Rom. RM6 70 EV58
Joyes Cl, Rom. RM3 52 FK49
Joyners Cl, Dag. RM9 70 EZ63
Joy Rd, Grav. DA12 131 GJ88
Jubb Powell Ho, N15 66 DS58
Jubilee Av, E4 47 EC51
Romford RM7 71 FB57
St. Albans (Lon.Col.) AL2 9 CK26
Twickenham TW2 116 CC88
Jubilee Cl, NW9 62 CR58
Greenhithe DA9 129 FW86
Pinner HA5 40 BW54
Romford RM7 71 FB57
Staines (Stanw.) TW19 114 BJ87
Jubilee Ct, Stai. TW18
off Leacroft 114 BG92
Waltham Abbey EN9 16 EF33
Jubilee Cres, E14 204 E7
N9 46 DU46
Addlestone KT15 152 BK106
Gravesend DA12 131 GL89
Jubilee Dr, Ruis. HA4 60 BX63
★ Jubilee Gdns, SE1 200 B3
Jubilee Gdns, Sthl. UB1 78 CA72
Jubilee Pl, SW3 198 C10
Jubilee Ri, Sev. (Seal) TN15 191 FM121
Jubilee Rd, Grays RM20 109 FV79
Greenford UB6 79 CH67
Orpington BR6 164 FA107
Sutton SM3 157 CX108
Watford WD24 23 BU38
Jubilee St, E1 84 DW72
Jubilee Wk, Wat. WD19 39 BV49
Jubilee Way, SW19 140 DB95
Chessington KT9 156 CN105
Feltham TW14 115 BT88
Sidcup DA14 126 EU89
Judd St, WC1 195 P3
Jude St, E16 86 EF72
Judeth Gdns, Grav. DA12 131 GL92
Judge Heath La, Hayes UB3 77 BQ72
Uxbridge UB8 77 BQ72
Judges Hill, Pot.B. EN6 12 DE29
Judge St, Wat. WD24 23 BV38
Judge Wk, Esher (Clay.) KT10 155 CE107
Judith Av, Rom. RM5 51 FB51
Juer St, SW11 100 DE80
Jug Hill, West. (Bigg.H.) TN16
off Hillcrest Rd 178 EK116
Juglans Rd, Orp. BR6 146 EU102
Jules Thorn Av, Enf. EN1 30 DT41
Julia Gdns, Bark. IG11 88 EX68
Julia Garfield Ms, E16
off Wesley Av 86 EH74
Juliana Cl, N2 64 DC55
Julian Av, W3 80 CP73
Julian Cl, Barn. EN5 28 DB41
Woking GU21 166 AW118
Julian Hill, Har. HA1 61 CE61
Weybridge KT13 152 BN108
Julian Pl, E14 204 C10
Julian Rd, Orp. BR6 164 EU107
Julians Cl, Sev. TN13 190 FG127
Julians Way, Sev. TN13 190 FG127
Julia St, NW5
off Oak Village 64 DG63
Julien Rd, W5 97 CJ76
Coulsdon CR5 175 DK115
Juliette Rd, E13 86 EF68
Juliette Way, S.Ock. RM15 108 FM75
Julius Nyerere Cl, N1
off Copenhagen St 83 DN70
Junction App, SE13 103 EC83
SW11 100 DE83
Junction Av, W10
off Harrow Rd 81 CW69
Junction Ms, W2 194 B8
Junction Pk, Kings L. WD4 7 BQ33
Junction Pl, W2 194 B8
Junction Rd, E13 86 EH68
N9 46 DU46
N17 66 DU55
N19 65 DJ63
W5 97 CK77
Ashford TW15 115 BQ92
Brentford TW8 97 CK77
Brentwood CM14 54 FW49
Dartford DA1 128 FK86
Harrow HA1 61 CE58
Romford RM1 71 FF56
South Croydon CR2 160 DR106
Junction Rd E, Rom. RM6
off Kenneth Rd 70 EY59
Junction Rd W, Rom. RM6 70 EY59
Junction Shop Cen, The, SW11
off St. John's Hill 100 DE84
June Cl, Couls. CR5 159 DH114
Junewood Cl, Add.
(Wdhm) KT15 151 BF111
Juniper Av, St.Alb.
(Brick.Wd) AL2 8 CA31
Juniper Cl, Barn. EN5 27 CX43
Broxbourne EN10 15 DZ25
Chessington KT9 156 CM107
Rickmansworth WD3 38 BK48
Wembley HA9 62 CM64
Westerham (Bigg.H.)
TN16 178 EL117
Juniper Ct, Slou. SL1
off Nixey Cl 92 AU75
Juniper Cres, NW1 82 DG66
Juniper Gdns, SW16
off Leonard Rd 141 DJ95
Radlett (Shenley) WD7 10 CL33
Sunbury-on-Thames TW16 115 BT93
Juniper Gate, Rick. WD3 38 BK47
Juniper Gro, Wat. WD17 23 BU38
Juniper La, E6 86 EL71
Juniper Rd, Ilf. IG1 69 EN63
Juniper St, E1 84 DW73
Juniper Wk, Swan. BR8 147 FD96
Juniper Way, Hayes UB3 77 BR73
Romford RM3 52 FL53
Juno Way, SE14 103 DX79
Jupiter Way, N7 83 DM65
Jupp Rd, E15 85 ED66
Jupp Rd W, E15 85 EC67
Jurgens Rd, Purf. RM19
off London Rd Purfleet 109 FR79
Jury St, Grav. DA11
off Princes St 131 GH86
Justice Wk, SW3
off Lawrence St 100 DE79
Justin Cl, Brent. TW8 97 CK80
Justin Rd, E4 47 DZ51
Jute La, Enf. EN3 31 DY40
Jutland Cl, N19
off Sussex Way 65 DL60
Jutland Gdns, Couls. CR5 175 DM120
Jutland Pl, Egh. TW20
off Mullens Rd 113 BC92
Jutland Rd, E13 86 EG70
SE6 123 EC87
Jutsums Av, Rom. RM7 71 FB58
Jutsums La, Rom. RM7 71 FB58
Juxon Cl, Har. HA3
off Augustine Rd 40 CB53
Juxon St, SE11 200 C8

K

Kaduna Cl, Pnr. HA5 59 BU57
Kale Rd, Erith DA18 106 EY75
Kambala Rd, SW11 100 DD82
Kandlewood,
Brwd. (Hutt.) CM13 55 GB45
Kangley Br Rd, SE26 123 DZ92
Kaplan Dr, N21 29 DL43
Kara Way, NW2 63 CX63
Karen Cl, Brwd. CM15 54 FW45
Rainham RM13 89 FE68
Karen Ct, SE4
off Wickham Rd 103 DZ82
Bromley BR1 off Blyth Rd 144 EF95
Karen Ter, E11
off Montague Rd 68 EF61
Karenza Ct, Wem. HA9
off Lulworth Av 61 CJ59
Kariba Cl, N9 46 DW48
Karina Cl, Chig. IG7 49 ES50
Karoline Gdns, Grnf. UB6
off Oldfield La N 79 CD68
Kashgar Rd, SE18 105 ET78
Kashmir Cl, Add.
(New Haw) KT15 152 BK109
Kashmir Rd, SE7 104 EK80
Kassala Rd, SW11 100 DF81
Katella Trd Est, Bark. IG11 87 ES69
Kates Cl, Barn. EN5 27 CU43
Katharine St, Croy. CR0 142 DQ104
Katherine Cl, SE16 203 H3
Addlestone KT15 152 BG107
Katherine Gdns, SE9 104 EK84
Ilford IG6 49 EQ52
Katherine Ms, Whyt. CR3 176 DT117
Katherine Pl, Abb.L. WD5
off Arundel Rd 7 BU31
Katherine Rd, E6 86 EK66
E7 68 EJ64
Twickenham TW1
off London Rd 117 CG88
Katherine Sq, W11
off Wilsham St 81 CY74
Kathleen Av, W3 80 CQ71
Wembley HA0 80 CL66
Kathleen Rd, SW11 100 DF83
Kavanaghs Rd, Brwd. CM14 54 FU48
Kavanaghs Ter, Brwd. CM14
off Kavanaghs Rd 54 FV48
Kaye Don Way, Wey. KT13 152 BN111
Kayemoor Rd, Sutt. SM2 158 DE108
Kay Rd, SW9 101 DL82
Kays Ter, E18
off Walpole Rd 48 EF53
Kay St, E2 84 DU68
Welling DA16 106 EV81
Kay Way, SE10
off Greenwich High Rd 103 EB80
Kaywood Cl, Slou. SL3 92 AW76
Kean St, WC2 196 B9
Kearton Cl, Ken. CR8 176 DQ117
Keary Rd, Swans. DA10 130 FY87
Keatley Grn, E4 47 DZ51
Keats Av, E16 205 P2
Redhill RH1 184 DG132
Romford RM3 51 FH52
Keats Cl, E11
off Nightingale La 68 EH57
NW3 off Keats Gro 64 DE63
SE1 201 P9
SW19 off North Rd 120 DD93
Chigwell IG7 49 EQ51
Enfield EN3 31 DX43
Hayes UB4 77 BU71
Keats Gdns, Til. RM18 111 GH82
Keats Gro, NW3 64 DD63
★ Keats Ho, NW3 64 DE63
Keats Ho, Beck. BR3 123 EA93
Keats Pl, EC2 197 K7
Keats Rd, Belv. DA17 107 FC76
Welling DA16 105 ES81
Keats Wk, Brwd. (Hutt.) CM13
off Byron Rd 55 GD45
Keats Way, Croy. CR0 142 DW100
Greenford UB6 78 CB71
West Drayton UB7 94 BM77
Keble Cl, Nthlt. UB5 60 CC64
Worcester Park KT4 139 CT102
Keble Pl, SW13
off Somerville Av 99 CV79
Keble St, SW17 120 DC91
Keble Ter, Abb.L. WD5 7 BT32
Kechill Gdns, Brom. BR2 144 EG101
Kedelston Ct, E5
off Redwald Rd 67 DX63
Kedeston Ct, Sutt. SM1
off Hurstcourt Rd 140 DB102
Kedleston Dr, Orp. BR5 145 ET100
Kedleston Wk, E2
off Middleton St 84 DV69
Keedonwood Rd, Brom. BR1 124 EE92
Keel Cl, SE16 203 J3
Barking IG11 88 EW68
Keele Cl, Wat. WD24 24 BW40
Keeley Rd, Croy. CR0 142 DQ103
Keeley St, WC2 196 B9
Keeling Rd, SE9 124 EK85
Keely Cl, Barn. EN4 28 DE43
Keemor Cl, SE18
off Llanover Rd 105 EN80
Keensacre, Iver SL0 75 BD68
Keens Cl, SW16 121 DK92
Keens Rd, Croy. CR0 160 DQ105
Keens Yd, N1
off St. Paul's Rd 83 DP65
Keep, The, SE3 104 EG82
Kingston upon Thames KT2 118 CM93
Keepers Ms, Tedd. TW11 117 CJ93
Keepers Wk, Vir.W. GU25 132 AX99
Keep La, N11
off Gardeners Cl 44 DG47
Keetons Rd, SE16 202 D6
Keevil Dr, SW19 119 CX87
Keighley Cl, N7 off Penn Rd 65 DL64
Keighley Rd, Rom. RM3 52 FL52
Keightley Dr, SE9 125 EQ88
Keilder Cl, Uxb. UB10
off Charnwood Rd 76 BN68
Keildon Rd, SW11 100 DF84
Keir, The, SW19
off West Side Common 119 CW92
Keir Hardie Est, E5
off Springfield 66 DV60
Keir Hardie Ho, W6
off Lochaline St 99 CW79
Keir Hardie Way, Bark. IG11 88 EU66
Hayes UB4 77 BU69
Keith Av, Dart. (Sutt.H.) DA4 128 FP93
Keith Connor Cl, SW8
off Daley Thompson Way 101 DH83
Keith Gro, W12 99 CU75
Keith Pk Cres, West.
(Bigg.H.) TN16 162 EH112
Keith Pk Rd, Uxb. UB10 76 BM66
Keith Rd, E17 47 DZ53
Barking IG11 87 ER68
Hayes UB3 95 BS76
Keith Way, Horn. RM11 72 FL59
Kelbrook Rd, SE3 104 EL83
Kelburn Way, Rain. RM13
off Dominion Way 89 FG69
Kelby Path, SE9 125 EP90
Kelceda Cl, NW2 63 CU61
Kelf Gro, Hayes UB3 77 BT72
Kelfield Gdns, W10 81 CW72
Kelfield Ms, W10
off Kelfield Gdns 81 CX72
Kelland Cl, N8 off Palace Rd 65 DK57
Kelland Rd, E13 86 EG70
Kellaway Rd, SE3 104 EJ82
Keller Cres, E12 68 EK63
Kellerton Rd, SE13 124 EE85
Kellett Rd, SW2 101 DN84
Kelling Gdns, Croy. CR0 141 DP101
Kellino St, SW17 120 DF91
Kellner Rd, SE28 105 ET76
Kell St, SE1 200 G6
Kelly Av, SE15 102 DT80
Kelly Cl, NW10 62 CR62
Shepperton TW17 135 BS96
Kelly Ct, Borwd. WD6 26 CQ40
Kelly Ms, W9
off Woodfield Rd 81 CZ71
Kelly Rd, NW7 43 CY51
Kelly St, NW1 83 DH65
Kelly Way, Rom. RM6 70 EY57
Kelman Cl, SW4 101 DK82
Waltham Cross EN8 15 DX31
Kelmore Gro, SE22 102 DU84
Kelmscott Cl, E17 47 DZ54
Watford WD18 23 BU43
Kelmscott Cres, Wat. WD18 23 BU43
Kelmscott Gdns, W12 99 CU76
Kelmscott Rd, SW11 120 DE85
Kelross Pas, N5
off Kelross Rd 66 DQ63
Kelross Rd, N5 65 DP63
Kelsall Cl, SE3 104 EH82
Kelsall Ms, Rich. TW9
off Melliss Av 98 CP81
Kelsey Gate, Beck. BR3 143 EB96
Kelsey La, Beck. BR3 143 EA96
Kelsey Pk Av, Beck. BR3 143 EB96
Kelsey Pk Rd, Beck. BR3 143 EA96
Kelsey Rd, Orp. BR5 146 EV96
Kelsey Sq, Beck. BR3 143 EA96
Kelsey St, E2 84 DV70
Kelsey Way, Beck. BR3 143 EA97
Kelshall, Wat. WD25 24 BY36
Kelshall Ct, N4
off Brownswood Rd 66 DQ61
Kelsie Way, Ilf. IG6 49 ES52
Kelso Dr, Grav. DA12 131 GM91
Kelson Ho, E14 204 E6
Kelso Pl, W8 100 DB76
Kelso Rd, Cars. SM5 140 DC101
Kelston Rd, Ilf. IG6 49 EP54
Kelvedon Av, Walt. KT12 153 BS108
Kelvedon Cl, Brwd.
(Hutt.) CM13 55 GE44
Kingston upon Thames KT2 118 CM93
Kelvedon Ho, SW8 101 DL81
Kelvedon Rd, SW6 99 CZ80
Kelvedon Wk, Rain. RM13
off Ongar Way 89 FE67
Kelvedon Way, Wdf.Grn. IG8 49 EM51
Kelvin Av, N13 45 DM51
Leatherhead KT22 171 CF119
Teddington TW11 117 CE93
Kelvinbrook, W.Mol. KT8 136 CB97
Kelvin Cl, Epsom KT19 156 CN107
Kelvin Cres, Har. HA3 41 CE52
Kelvin Dr, Twick. TW1 117 CH86
Kelvin Gdns, Croy. CR0 141 DL101
Southall UB1 78 CA72
Kelvin Gro, SE26 122 DV90
Chessington KT9 138 CL104
Kelvington Cl, Croy. CR0 143 DY101
Kelvington Rd, SE15 123 DX85
Kelvin Ind Est, Grnf. UB6 78 CB66
Kelvin Par, Orp. BR6 145 ES102
Kelvin Rd, N5 65 DP63
Tilbury RM18 111 GG82
Welling DA16 106 EU83
Kember St, N1
off Carnoustie Dr 83 DM66
Kemble Cl, Pot.B. EN6 12 DD33
Weybridge KT13 153 BR105
Kemble Cotts, Add. KT15
off Emley Rd 134 BG104
Kemble Dr, Brom. BR2 144 EL104
Kemble Par, Pot.B. EN6
off High St 12 DC32
Kemble Rd, N17 46 DU53
SE23 123 DX88
Croydon CR0 141 DN104
Kembleside Rd, West.
(Bigg.H.) TN16 178 EJ118
Kemble St, WC2 196 B9
Kemerton Rd, SE5 102 DQ83
Beckenham BR3 143 EB96
Croydon CR0 142 DT101
Kemeys St, E9 67 DY64
Kemishford, Wok. GU22 166 AU123
Kemnal Rd, Chis. BR7 125 ER91
Kempe Cl, Slou. SL3 93 BC77
Kempe Rd, NW6 81 CX68
Enfield EN1 30 DV36
Kemp Gdns, Croy. CR0
off St. Saviours Rd 142 DQ100
Kempis Way, SE22
off East Dulwich Gro 122 DS85
Kemplay Rd, NW3 64 DD63
Kemp Pl, Bushey WD23 24 CA44
Kemp Rd, Dag. RM8 70 EX60
Kemprow, Wat. (Ald.) WD25 25 CD36
Kemp's Ct, W1 195 L9
Kemps Dr, E14 off Morant St 85 EA73
Northwood HA6 39 BT52
Kempsford Gdns, SW5 100 DA78
Kempsford Rd, SE11 200 E9
Kemps Gdns, SE13
off Thornford Rd 123 EC85
Kempshott Rd, SW16 121 DK94
Kempson Rd, SW6 100 DA81
Kempthorne Rd, SE8 203 L8
Kempton Av, Horn. RM12 72 FM63
Northolt UB5 78 CA65
Sunbury-on-Thames TW16 135 BV95
Kempton Cl, Erith DA8 107 FC79
Uxbridge UB10 59 BQ63
Kempton Ct, E1
off Durward St 84 DV71
Kempton Ct, Sunbury-on-Thames
TW16 135 BV95
⇌ Kempton Park
(Race days only) 115 BV94
★ Kempton Park Racecourse,
Sun. TW16 116 BW94
Kempton Rd, E6 87 EM67
Hampton TW12 136 BZ96
Kempton Wk, Croy. CR0 143 DY100
Kempt St, SE18 105 EN79
Kemsing Cl, Bex. DA5 126 EY87
Bromley BR2 144 EF103
Thornton Heath CR7 142 DQ98
Kemsing Rd, SE10 205 M10
Kemsley, SE13 123 EC85
Kemsley Cl, Grav.
(Nthflt) DA11 131 GF91
Greenhithe DA9 129 FV86
Kemsley Rd, West.
(Tats.) TN16 178 EK119
Kenbury Cl, Uxb. UB10 58 BN62
Kenbury Gdns, SE5
off Kenbury St 102 DQ82
Kenbury St, SE5 102 DQ82
Kenchester Cl, SW8 101 DL80
Kencot Cl, Erith DA18 106 EZ75
Kendal Av, N18 46 DR49
W3 80 CN70
Barking IG11 87 ES66
Epping CM16 18 EU31
Kendal Cl, SW9 101 DP80
Feltham TW14
off Ambleside Dr 115 BT88
Hayes UB4 77 BS68
Reigate RH2 184 DD133
Slough SL2 74 AU73
Woodford Green IG8 48 EF47
Kendal Cft, Horn. RM12 71 FG64
Kendal Dr, Slou. SL2 74 AU73
Kendale, Grays RM16 111 GH76
Kendale Rd, Brom. BR1 124 EE92
Kendal Gdns, N18 46 DR49
Gravesend DA11
off Thames Way 131 GF86
Sutton SM1 140 DC103
Kendall Av, Beck. BR3 143 DY96
South Croydon CR2 160 DR109
Kendall Av S, S.Croy. CR2 160 DQ110
Kendall Ct, SW19
off Byegrove Rd 120 DD93
Borehamwood WD6
off Gregson Cl 26 CQ39
Kendall Pl, W1 194 F7
Kendall Rd, SE18 104 EL81
Beckenham BR3 143 DY96
Isleworth TW7 97 CG82
Kendalmere Cl, N10 45 DH53
Kendal Par, N18
off Great Cambridge Rd 46 DR49
Kendal Pl, SW15 119 CZ85
Kendal Rd, NW10 63 CU63
Waltham Abbey EN9
off Deer Pk Way 31 EC36
Kendals Cl, Rad. WD7 25 CE36
Kendal St, W2 194 C9
Kender St, SE14 102 DW80
Kendoa Rd, SW4 101 DK84
Kendon Cl, E11
off The Avenue 68 EH57
Kendor Av, Epsom KT19 156 CQ111
Kendra Hall Rd, S.Croy. CR2 159 DP108
Kendrey Gdns, Twick. TW2 117 CE86
Kendrick Ms, SW7
off Reece Ms 100 DD77
Kendrick Pl, SW7 100 DD77
Kendrick Rd, Slou. SL3 92 AV76
Kenelm Cl, Har. HA1 61 CG62
Keneme Dr, Barn. EN5 27 CY43
Kenford Cl, Wat. WD25 7 BV32
Kenia Wk, Grav. DA12 131 GM90
Kenilford Rd, SW12 121 DH87
Kenilworth Av, E17 47 EA54
SW19 120 DA92
Cobham (Stoke D'Ab.) KT11 154 CB114
Harrow HA2 60 BZ63
Romford RM3 52 FP50
Kenilworth Cl, Bans. SM7 174 DB116
Borehamwood WD6 26 CQ41
Slough SL1 92 AT76
Kenilworth Ct, SW15
off Lower Richmond Rd 99 CX83
Watford WD17
off Hempstead Rd 23 BU39
Kenilworth Cres, Enf. EN1 30 DS39
Kenilworth Dr, Borwd. WD6 26 CQ41
Rickmansworth
(Crox.Grn) WD3 23 BP42
Walton-on-Thames KT12 136 BX104
Kenilworth Gdns, SE18 105 EP82
Hayes UB4 77 BT71
Hornchurch RM12 72 FJ62
Ilford IG3 69 ET61
Loughton IG10 33 EM44
Southall UB1 78 BZ69
Staines TW18 114 BJ92
Watford WD19 40 BW50
Kenilworth Rd, E3 85 DY68
NW6 81 CZ67
SE20 143 DX95
W5 80 CL74
Ashford TW15 114 BK90
Edgware HA8 42 CQ48
Epsom KT17 157 CU107
Orpington BR5 145 EQ100
KENLEY 176 DQ116
⇌ Kenley 160 DQ114
Kenley Av, NW9 42 CS53
Kenley Cl, Barn. EN4 28 DE42
Bexley DA5 126 FA87
Caterham CR3 176 DR120
Chislehurst BR7 145 ES97
Kenley Gdns, Horn. RM12 72 FM61
Thornton Heath CR7 141 DP98
Kenley La, Ken. CR8 160 DQ114
Kenley Rd, SW19 139 CZ96

★ Place of interest ⇌ Railway station ⊖ London Underground station DLR Docklands Light Railway station Tra Tramlink station H Hospital Riv Pedestrian ferry landing stage

Kenley Rd, Kingston upon Thames
KT1 138 CP96
Twickenham TW1 117 CG86
Kenley Wk, W11 81 CY73
Sutton SM3 157 CX105
Kenlor Rd, SW17 120 DD92
Kenmare Dr, N17 46 DT54
Mitcham CR4 120 DF94
Kenmare Gdns, N13 45 DP49
Kenmare Rd, Th.Hth. CR7 141 DN100
Kenmere Gdns, Wem. HA0 80 CN67
Kenmere Rd, Well. DA16 106 EW82
Kenmont Gdns, NW10 81 CV69
Kenmore Av, Har. HA3 61 CG56
Kenmore Cl, Rich. TW9
off Kent Rd 98 CN80
Kenmore Cres, Hayes UB4 77 BT69
Kenmore Gdns, Edg. HA8 42 CP54
Kenmore Rd, Har. HA3 61 CK55
Kenley CR8 159 DP114
Kenmure Rd, E8 66 DV64
Kenmure Yd, E8
off Kenmure Rd 66 DV64
Kennacraig Cl, E16 205 N3
Kennard Rd, E15 85 ED66
N11 44 DF50
Kennard St, E16 87 EM74
SW11 100 DG82
Kennedy Av, Enf. EN3 30 DW44
Kennedy Cl, E13 86 EG68
Mitcham CR4 140 DG96
Orpington BR5 145 ER102
Pinner HA5 40 BZ51
Waltham Cross
(Chsht) EN8 15 DX28
Kennedy Gdns, Sev. TN13 191 FJ123
Kennedy Path, W7
off Harp Rd 79 CF70
Kennedy Rd, W7 79 CE71
Barking IG11 87 ES67
Kennedy Wk, SE17
off Flint St 102 DR77
Kennel Cl, Lthd. (Fetch.) KT22 170 CC124
Kennel La, Lthd. (Fetch.) KT22 170 CC122
Kennelwood Cres, Croy.
(New Adgtn) CR0 161 ED111
Kennet Cl, SW11
off Maysoule Rd 100 DD84
Upminster RM14 73 FS58
Kennet Grn, S.Ock. RM15 91 FV73
Kenneth Av, Ilf. IG1 69 EP63
Kenneth Cres, NW2 63 CV64
Kenneth Gdns, Stan. HA7 41 CG51
Kenneth More Rd, Ilf. IG1
off Oakfield Rd 69 EP62
Kenneth Rd, Bans. SM7 174 DD115
Romford RM6 70 EX59
Kenneth Robbins Ho, N17 46 DV52
Kennet Rd, W9 81 CZ70
Dartford DA1 107 FG83
Isleworth TW7 97 CF83
Kennet Sq, Mitch. CR4 140 DE95
Kennet St, E1 202 C2
Kennett Ct, Swan. BR8 147 FE97
Kennett Dr, Hayes UB4 78 BY71
Kennett Rd, Slou. SL3 93 BB76
Kennet Wf La, EC4 197 J10
Kenninghall, N18 46 DV50
Kenninghall Rd, E5 66 DU62
N18 46 DW50
Kenning St, SE16 202 G4
Kennings Way, SE11 200 F10
Kenning Ter, N1 84 DS67
KENNINGTON, SE11 101 DN79
⊖ Kennington 200 F10
Kennington Grn, SE11
off Montford Pl 101 DN78
Kennington Gro, SE11
off Oval Way 101 DM79
Kennington La, SE11 200 E10
Kennington Oval, SE11 101 DM79
Kennington Pk, SW9 101 DN80
Kennington Pk Est, SE11
off Harleyford St 101 DN79
Kennington Pk Gdns, SE11 101 DP79
Kennington Pk Pl, SE11 101 DN79
Kennington Pk Rd, SE11 101 DN79
Kennington Rd, SE1 200 D6
SE11 200 D7
Kenny Dr, Cars. SM5 158 DF109
Kenny Rd, NW7 43 CY50
Kenrick Pl, W1 194 F6
Kenrick Sq, Red. (Bletch.) RH1 186 DS133
KENSAL GREEN, NW10 81 CW69
⇌ Kensal Green 81 CW69
⊖ Kensal Green 81 CW69
★ Kensal Green Cem, W10 81 CW69
KENSAL RISE, NW6 81 CX68
⇌ Kensal Rise 81 CW68
Kensal Rd, W10 81 CY70
KENSAL TOWN, W10 81 CX70
Kensal Wf, W10
off Ladbroke Gro 81 CX70
KENSINGTON, W8 99 CZ75
Kensington Av, E12 86 EL65
Thornton Heath CR7 141 DN95
Watford WD18 23 BT42
Kensington Ch Ct, W8 100 DB75
Kensington Ch St, W8 82 DA74
Kensington Ch Wk, W8 100 DB75
Kensington Cl, N11 44 DG51
Kensington Ct, NW7
off Grenville Pl 42 CR50
W8 100 DB75
Kensington Ct Gdns, W8
off Kensington Ct Pl 100 DB76
Kensington Ct Ms, W8
off Kensington Ct Pl 100 DB75
Kensington Ct Pl, W8 100 DB75
Kensington Dr, Wdf.Grn. IG8 48 EK53
★ Kensington Gdns, W2 82 DC74
Kensington Gdns, Ilf. IG1 69 EM61
Kingston upon Thames KT1
off Portsmouth Rd 137 CK97
Kensington Gdns Sq, W2 82 DB72
Kensington Gate, W8 100 DC76
Kensington Gore, SW7 100 DD75
Kensington Hall Gdns, W14
off Beaumont Av 99 CZ78
Kensington High St, W8 100 DA76
W14 99 CY77
Kensington Mall, W8 82 DA74
⇌ Kensington (Olympia) 99 CY76
⊖ Kensington (Olympia) 99 CY76
★ Kensington Palace, W8 100 DB75
Kensington Palace Gdns, W8 82 DB74
Kensington Pk Gdns, W11 81 CZ73
Kensington Pk Ms, W11
off Kensington Pk Rd 81 CZ72
Kensington Pk Rd, W11 81 CZ73
Kensington Pl, W8 82 DA74
Kensington Rd, SW7 198 A5
W8 100 DB75
Brentwood (Pilg.Hat.) CM15 54 FU44
Northolt UB5 78 CA69
Romford RM7 71 FC58
Kensington Sq, W8 100 DB75
Kensington Ter, S.Croy. CR2
off Sanderstead Rd 160 DR108
Kensington Village, W14
off Avonmore Rd 99 CZ77
Kensington Way, Borwd. WD6 26 CR41
Kent Av, W13 79 CH71
Dagenham RM9 88 FA70
Welling DA16 125 ET85
Kent Cl, Borwd. WD6 26 CR38
Mitcham CR4 141 DL98
Orpington BR6 163 ES107
Staines TW18 114 BK93
Uxbridge UB8 76 BJ65
Kent Dr, Barn. EN4 28 DG42
Hornchurch RM12 72 FK63
Teddington TW11 117 CE92
Kentford Way, Nthlt. UB5 78 BY67
Kent Gdns, W13 79 CH71
Ruislip HA4 59 BV58
Kent Gate Way, Croy. CR0 161 EA106
KENT HATCH, Eden. TN8 189 EP131
Kent Hatch Rd, Eden.
(Crock.H.) TN8 189 EM131
Oxted RH8 188 EJ129
⇌ Kent House 143 DY95
Kent Ho La, Beck. BR3 123 DY92
Kent Ho Rd, SE26 143 DX95
Beckenham BR3 123 DY92
Kentish Bldgs, SE1 201 K3
Kentish La, Hat. AL9 12 DC25
Kentish Rd, Belv. DA17 106 FA77
KENTISH TOWN, NW5 83 DJ65
⇌ Kentish Town 65 DJ64
⊖ Kentish Town 65 DJ64
Kentish Town Rd, NW1 83 DH66
NW5 83 DH66
⇌ Kentish Town West 82 DG65
Kentish Way, Brom. BR1 144 EG96
Kentlea Rd, SE28 105 ES75
Kentmere Rd, SE18 105 ES77
KENTON, Har. HA3 61 CH57
⇌ Kenton 61 CH58
⊖ Kenton 61 CH58
Kenton Av, Har. HA1 61 CF59
Southall UB1 78 CA73
Sunbury-on-Thames TW16 136 BY96
Kenton Ct, W14
off Kensington High St 99 CZ76
Kenton Gdns, Har. HA3 61 CJ57
Kenton La, Har. HA3 61 CJ55
Kenton Pk Av, Har. HA3 61 CK56
Kenton Pk Cl, Har. HA3 61 CJ56
Kenton Pk Cres, Har. HA3 61 CK56
Kenton Pk Rd, Har. HA3 61 CJ56
Kenton Rd, E9 85 DX65
Harrow HA1, HA3 61 CK57
Kenton St, WC1 195 P4
Kenton Way, Hayes UB4
off Exmouth Rd 77 BS69
Woking GU21 166 AT117
Kent Pas, NW1 194 D4
Kent Rd, N21 46 DR46
W4 98 CQ76
Dagenham RM10 71 FB64
Dartford DA1 128 FK86
East Molesey KT8 136 CC98
Gravesend DA11 131 GG88
Grays RM17 110 GC79
Kingston upon Thames KT1
off The Bittoms 137 CK97
Longfield DA3 149 FX96
Orpington BR5 146 EV100
Richmond TW9 98 CN80
West Wickham BR4 143 EB102
Woking GU22 167 BB116
Kents Pas, Hmptn. TW12 136 BZ95
Kent St, E2 84 DT68
E13 86 EJ69
Kent Ter, NW1 194 C3
Kent Twr, SE20 122 DV94
Kent Vw, S.Ock.
(Aveley) RM15 108 FQ75
Kent Vw Gdns, Ilf. IG3 69 ES61
Kent Way, Surb. KT6 138 CL104
Kentwell Cl, SE4 103 DY84
Kentwode Grn, SW13 99 CU80
Kent Yd, SW7 198 C5
Kenver Av, N12 44 DD51
Kenward Rd, SE9 124 EJ85
Kenway, Rain. RM13 90 FJ69
Romford RM5 51 FC54
Ken Way, Wem. HA9 62 CQ61
Kenway Cl, Rain. RM13
off Kenway 90 FJ69
Kenway Dr, Amer. HP7 20 AV39
Kenway Rd, SW5 100 DB77
Kenway Wk, Rain. RM13
off Kenway 90 FK69
Kenwood Av, N14 29 DK43
SE14 off Besson St 103 DX81
Kenwood Cl, NW3 64 DD60
West Drayton UB7 94 BN79
Kenwood Dr, Beck. BR3 143 EC97
Rickmansworth
(Mill End) WD3 37 BF47
Walton-on-Thames KT12 153 BV107
Kenwood Gdns, E18 68 EH55
Ilford IG2 69 EN56
★ Kenwood Ho
(The Iveagh Bequest), NW3 64 DE60
Kenwood Pk, Wey. KT13 153 BR107
Kenwood Ridge, Ken. CR8 175 DP117
Kenwood Rd, N6 64 DF58
N9 46 DU46
Kenworth Cl, Wal.Cr. EN8 15 DX33
Kenworthy Rd, E9 67 DY64
Kenwyn Dr, NW2 62 CS62
Kenwyn Rd, SW4 101 DK84
SW20 139 CW95
Dartford DA1 128 FK85
Kenya Rd, SE7 104 EK80
Kenyngton Dr, Sun. TW16 115 BU92
Kenyngton Pl, Har. HA3 61 CJ57
Kenyon St, SW6 99 CX81
Keogh Rd, E15 86 EE65
Kepler Rd, SW4 101 DL84
Keppel Rd, E6 87 EM66
Dagenham RM9 70 EY63
Keppel Row, SE1 201 H3
Keppel Spur, Wind.
(Old Wind.) SL4 112 AV87
Keppel St, WC1 195 N6
Kerbela St, E2
off Cheshire St 84 DU70
Kerbey St, E14 85 EB72
Kerdistone Cl, Pot.B. EN6 12 DB30
Kerfield Cres, SE5 102 DR81
Kerfield Pl, SE5 102 DR81
Kernow Cl, Horn. RM12 72 FL61
Kerri Cl, Barn. EN5 27 CW42
Kerridge Ct, N1 84 DS65
Kerrill Av, Couls. CR5 175 DN119
Kerrison Pl, W5 79 CK74
Kerrison Rd, E15 85 ED67
SW11 100 DE83
W5 79 CK74
Kerrison Vil, W5
off Kerrison Pl 79 CK74
Kerry Av, S.Ock.
(Aveley) RM15 108 FM75
Stanmore HA7 41 CK49
Kerry Cl, E16 86 EH72
N13 45 DM47
Upminster RM14 73 FT59
Kerry Ct, Stan. HA7 41 CK49
Kerry Dr, Upmin. RM14 73 FT59
Kerry Path, SE14 103 DZ79
Kerry Rd, SE14 103 DZ79
Kerry Ter, Wok. GU21 167 BB116
Kersey Dr, S.Croy. CR2 160 DW112
Kersey Gdns, SE9 124 EL91
Romford RM3 52 FL53
Kersfield Rd, SW15 119 CX86
Kershaw Cl, SW18
off Westover Rd 120 DD86
Grays (Chaff.Hun.) RM16 109 FW77
Hornchurch RM11 72 FL59
Kershaw Rd, Dag. RM10 70 FA62
Kersley Ms, SW11 100 DF82
Kersley Rd, N16 66 DS62
Kersley St, SW11 100 DF82
Kerstin Cl, Hayes UB3
off St. Mary's Rd 77 BT73
Kerswell Cl, N15 66 DS57
Kerwick Cl, N7
off Sutterton St 83 DM66
Keslake Rd, NW6 81 CX68
Kessock Cl, N17 66 DV57
Kesteven Cl, Ilf. IG6 49 ET51
Kestlake Rd, Bex. DA5
off East Rochester Way 126 EW86
KESTON 162 EJ106
Keston Av, Add.
(New Haw) KT15 152 BG111
Coulsdon CR5 175 DN119
Keston BR2 162 EJ106
Keston Cl, N18 46 DR48
Welling DA16 106 EW80
Keston Gdns, Kes. BR2 162 EJ105
Keston Ms, Wat. WD17
off Nascot Rd 23 BV40
Keston Pk Cl, Kes. BR2 145 EM104
Keston Rd, N17 66 DR55
SE15 102 DU83
Thornton Heath CR7 141 DN100
Kestral Ct, Wall. SM6
off Carew Rd 159 DJ106
Kestrel Av, E6 off Swan App 86 EL71
SE24 121 DP85
Staines TW18 113 BF90
Kestrel Cl, NW9 42 CS54
NW10 62 CR64
Epsom KT19 156 CN111
Hornchurch RM12 89 FH66
Ilford IG6 50 EW49
Kingston upon Thames KT2 117 CK91
Watford WD25 8 BY34
Kestrel Ho, EC1 197 H2
W13 79 CF70
Enfield EN3 off Alma Rd 31 DX43
Kestrel Pl, SE14
off Milton Ct Rd 103 DY79
Kestrel Rd, Wal.Abb. EN9 16 EG34
Kestrels, The, St.Alb.
(Brick.Wd) AL2
off Bucknalls Dr 8 BZ31
Kestrel Way, Croy.
(New Adgtn) CR0 161 ED109
Hayes UB3 off Betam Rd 95 BR75
Keswick Av, SW15 118 CS92
SW19 140 DA96
Hornchurch RM11 72 FK60
Keswick Bdy, SW15
off Upper Richmond Rd 119 CY85
Keswick Cl, Sutt. SM1 158 DC105
Keswick Ct, Slou. SL2
off Stoke Rd 74 AT73
Keswick Dr, Enf. EN3 30 DW36
Keswick Gdns, Ilf. IG4 68 EL57
Purfleet RM19
off London Rd Purfleet 108 FQ79
Ruislip HA4 59 BR58
Wembley HA9 62 CL63
Keswick Ms, W5 80 CL74
Keswick Rd, SW15 119 CY85
Bexleyheath DA7 106 FA82
Egham TW20 113 BB94
Orpington BR6 145 ET102
Keswick Rd,
Twickenham TW2 116 CC86
West Wickham BR4 144 EE103
Kettering Rd, Enf. EN3
off Beaconsfield Rd 31 DX37
Romford RM3 52 FL52
Kettering St, SW16 121 DJ93
Kett Gdns, SW2 121 DM85
Kettlebaston Rd, E10 67 DZ60
Kettlewell Cl, N11 44 DG51
Woking GU21 150 AX114
Kettlewell Ct, Swan. BR8 147 FF96
Kettlewell Dr, Wok. GU21 150 AY114
Kettlewell Hill, Wok. GU21 150 AY114
Ketton Grn, Red. RH1
off Malmstone Av 185 DK128
Kevan Dr, Wok. (Send) GU23 167 BE124
Kevan Ho, SE5 102 DQ80
Kevelioc Rd, N17 46 DQ53
Kevin Cl, Houns. TW4 96 BX82
Kevington Cl, Orp. BR5 145 ET98
Kevington Dr, Chis. BR7 145 ET98
Orpington BR5 145 ET98
KEW, Rich. TW9 98 CN79
⇌ Kew Bridge 98 CM78
Kew Br, Brent. TW8 98 CM79
Richmond TW9 98 CM79
Kew Br Arches, Rich. TW9
off Kew Br 98 CM79
Kew Br Ct, W4 98 CN78
Kew Br Rd, Brent. TW8 98 CM79
★ Kew Bridge Steam Mus,
Brent. TW8 98 CM78
Kew Cres, Sutt. SM3 139 CY104
Kewferry Dr, Nthwd. HA6 39 BP50
Kewferry Rd, Nthwd. HA6 39 BQ51
Kew Foot Rd, Rich. TW9 98 CL84
⇌ Kew Gardens 98 CM81
⊖ Kew Gardens 98 CM81
Kew Gdns Rd, Rich. TW9 98 CM80
Kew Grn, Rich. TW9 98 CN80
Kew Meadow Path,
Rich. TW9 98 CN81
★ Kew Observatory,
Rich. TW9 97 CH83
★ Kew Palace, Royal Botanic Gdns,
Rich. TW9 98 CL80
Kew Rd, Rich. TW9 98 CN79
Keybridge Ho, SW8 101 DL79
Key Cl, E1 84 DV70
Keyes Rd, NW2 63 CX64
Dartford DA1 108 FM84
Keymer Cl, West.
(Bigg.H.) TN16 178 EK116
Keymer Rd, SW2 121 DM89
Keynes Cl, N2 64 DF55
Keynsham Av, Wdf.Grn. IG8 48 EE49
Keynsham Gdns, SE9 124 EL85
Keynsham Rd, SE9 124 EK85
Morden SM4 140 DB102
Keynsham Wk, Mord. SM4 140 DB102
Keys, The, Brwd. CM13
off Eagle Way 53 FW51
Keyse Rd, SE1 201 P7
Keysham Av, Houns. TW5
off The Avenue 95 BU81
Keys Ho, Enf. EN3
off Beaconsfield Rd 31 DX37
Keystone Cres, N1 196 A1
Keywood Dr, Sun. TW16 115 BU93
Keyworth Cl, E5 67 DY63
Keyworth St, SE1 200 G6
Kezia St, SE8
off Trundleys Rd 103 DY78
Khalsa Av, Grav. DA12 131 GJ87
Khalsa Ct, N22 off Acacia Rd 45 DP53
Khama Rd, SW17 120 DE91
Khartoum Pl, Grav. DA12 131 GJ86
Khartoum Rd, E13 86 EH69
SW17 120 DD91
Ilford IG1 69 EP64
Khyber Rd, SW11 100 DE82
Kibworth St, SW8 101 DM80
KIDBROOKE, SE3 104 EH83
⇌ Kidbrooke 104 EH83
Kidbrooke Gdns, SE3 104 EG82
Kidbrooke Gro, SE3 104 EG81
Kidbrooke La, SE9 104 EL84
Kidbrooke Pk Cl, SE3 104 EH81
Kidbrooke Pk Rd, SE3 104 EH81
Kidbrooke Way, SE3 104 EH82
Kidderminster Pl, Croy. CR0
off Kidderminster Rd 141 DP102
Kidderminster Rd, Croy. CR0 141 DP102
Kidderpore Av, NW3 64 DA63
Kidderpore Gdns, NW3 64 DA63
Kidd Pl, SE7 104 EL78
Kidlington Way, NW9 42 CS54
Kidman Cl, Rom. RM2
off Elvet Av 72 FJ55
Kielder Cl, Ilf. IG6 49 ET51
Kiffen St, EC2 197 L4
Kilberry Cl, Islw. TW7 97 CD81
KILBURN, NW6 82 DA68
⊖ Kilburn 81 CZ65
Kilburn Br, NW6
off Kilburn High Rd 82 DA67
Kilburn Gate, NW6
off Kilburn Priory 82 DB68
⇌ Kilburn High Road 82 DA67
Kilburn High Rd, NW6 81 CZ66
Kilburn La, W9 81 CX69
W10 81 CX69
⊖ Kilburn Park 82 DA68
Kilburn Pk Rd, NW6 82 DA69
Kilburn Pl, NW6 82 DA67
Kilburn Priory, NW6 82 DB67
Kilburn Sq, NW6 82 DA67
Kilburn Vale, NW6
off Belsize Rd 82 DB67
Kilby Cl, Wat. WD25 24 BX35
Kilcorral Cl, Epsom KT17 157 CU114
Kildare Cl, Ruis. HA4 60 BW60
Kildare Gdns, W2 82 DA72
Kildare Rd, E16 86 EG71
Kildare Ter, W2 82 DA72
Kildare Wk, E14
off Farrance St 85 EA72
Kildonan Cl, Wat. WD17 23 BT39
Kildoran Rd, SW2 121 DL85
Kildowan Rd, Ilf. IG3 70 EU60
Kilgour Rd, SE23 123 DY86
Kilkie St, SW6 100 DC82
Killarney Rd, SW18 120 DC86
Killasser Ct, Tad. KT20 173 CW123
Killburns Mill Cl, Wall. SM6
off London Rd 159 DH105
Killearn Rd, SE6 123 ED88
Killester Gdns, Wor.Pk. KT4 157 CV105
Killewarren Way, Orp. BR5 146 EW100
Killick Cl, Sev.
(Dunt.Grn) TN13 190 FE121
Killick St, N1 83 DM68
Killieser Av, SW2 121 DL89
Killip Cl, E16 86 EF72
Killowen Av, Nthlt. UB5 60 CC64
Killowen Rd, E9 85 DX65
Killy Hill, Wok.
(Chobham) GU24 150 AS108
Killyon Rd, SW8 101 DJ82
Killyon Ter, SW8 101 DJ82
Kilmaine Rd, SW6 99 CY80
Kilmarnock Gdns, Dag. RM8
off Lindsey Rd 70 EW62
Kilmarnock Pk, Reig. RH2 184 DB133
Kilmarnock Rd, Wat. WD19 40 BX49
Kilmarsh Rd, W6 99 CW77
Kilmartin Av, SW16 141 DM97
Kilmartin Rd, Ilf. IG3 70 EU61
Kilmartin Way, Horn. RM12 71 FH64
Kilmeston Way, SE15
off Daniel Gdns 102 DT80
Kilmington Cl, Brwd.
(Hutt.) CM13 55 GB47
Kilmington Rd, SW13 99 CU79
Kilmiston Av, Shep. TW17 135 BQ100
Kilmorey Gdns, Twick. TW1 117 CH85
Kilmorey Rd, Twick. TW1 97 CH84
Kilmorie Rd, SE23 123 DY88
Kiln Av, Amer. HP6 20 AW38
Kiln Cl, Hayes UB3
off Brickfield La 95 BR79
Kilndown, Grav. DA12 131 GK93
Kilner St, E14 85 EA71
Kiln La, Bet. (Brock.) RH3 182 CQ134
Chesham (Ley Hill) HP5 4 AV31
Epsom KT17 156 CS111
Woking (Ripley) GU23 168 BH124
Kiln Ms, SW17 120 DD92
Kiln Pl, NW5 64 DG64
Kiln Rd, Epp.
(N.Wld Bas.) CM16 18 FA27
Kilnside, Esher (Clay.) KT10 155 CG108
Kiln Way, Grays
(Bad.Dene) RM17 110 FZ78
Northwood HA6 39 BS51
Kilnwood, Sev. (Halst.) TN14 164 EZ113
Kiln Wd La, Rom.
(Hav.at.Bow.) RM4 51 FD50
Kilpatrick Way, Hayes UB4 78 BY71
Kilravock St, W10 81 CY69
Kilross Rd, Felt. TW14 115 BR88
Kilrue La, Walt. KT12 153 BT105
Kilrush Ter, Wok. GU21 167 BA116
Kilsby Wk, Dag. RM9
off Rugby Rd 88 EV65
Kilsha Rd, Walt. KT12 135 BV100
Kilsmore La, Wal.Cr.
(Chsht) EN8 15 DX28
Kilvinton Dr, Enf. EN2 30 DR38
Kilworth Av, Brwd.
(Shenf.) CM15 55 GA44
Kimbell Gdns, SW6 99 CY81
Kimbell Pl, SE3
off Tudway Rd 104 EJ84
Kimberley Av, E6 86 EL68
SE15 102 DV82
Ilford IG2 69 ER59
Romford RM7 71 FC58
Kimberley Cl, Slou. SL3 93 AZ77
Kimberley Dr, Sid. DA14 126 EX89
Kimberley Gdns, N4 65 DP57
Enfield EN1 30 DT41
Kimberley Gate, Brom. BR1
off Oaklands Rd 124 EF94
Kimberley Ind Est, E17 47 DZ53
Kimberley Pl, Pur. CR8
off Brighton Rd 159 DN111
Kimberley Ride, Cob. KT11 154 CB113
Kimberley Rd, E4 48 EE46
E11 67 ED61
E16 86 EF70
E17 47 DZ53
N17 46 DU54
N18 46 DV51
NW6 81 CY67
SW9 101 DL82
Beckenham BR3 143 DX96
Croydon CR0 141 DP100
Kimberley Way, E4 48 EE46
Kimber Rd, SW18 120 DA87
Kimble Cl, Wat. WD18 23 BS44
Kimble Cres, Bushey WD23 40 CC45
Kimble Rd, SW19 120 DD93
Kimbolton Cl, SE12 124 EF86
Kimbolton Grn, Borwd. WD6 26 CQ42
Kimbolton Row, SW3 198 B9
Kimmeridge Gdns, SE9 124 EL91
Kimmeridge Rd, SE9 124 EL91
Kimpton Av, Brwd. CM15 54 FV45
Kimpton Ho, SW15
off Fontley Way 119 CU87
Kimpton Link Business Cen,
Sutt. SM3
off Kimpton Rd 139 CZ103
Kimpton Pl, Wat. WD25 8 BX34
Kimpton Rd, SE5 102 DR81
Sutton SM3 139 CZ103
Kimptons Cl, Pot.B. EN6 11 CX33
Kimptons Mead, Pot.B. EN6 11 CX32
Kimpton Trade & Business Cen,
Sutt. SM3 139 CZ103
Kinburn Dr, Egh. TW20 112 AY92
Kinburn St, SE16 203 H4
Kincaid Rd, SE15 102 DV80
Kincardine Gdns, W9
off Harrow Rd 81 CZ70
Kinch Gro, Wem. HA9 62 CM59
Kincraig Dr, Sev. TN13 190 FG124
Kinder Cl, SE28 88 EX73

★ Place of interest ⇌ Railway station ⊖ London Underground station DLR Docklands Light Railway station Tra Tramlink station H Hospital Riv Pedestrian ferry landing stage

Kindersley Way, Abb.L. WD5 7 BQ31
Kinder St, E1
off Cannon St Rd 84 DV72
Kinetic Cres, Enf. EN3 31 DZ36
Kinfauns Av, Horn. RM11 72 FJ58
Kinfauns Rd, SW2 121 DN89
Ilford IG3 70 EU60
Kingaby Gdns, Rain. RM13 89 FG66
King Acre Ct, Stai. TW18
off Moor La 113 BE90
King Alfred Av, SE6 123 EA90
King Alfred Rd, Rom. RM3 52 FM54
King & Queen Cl, SE9
off St. Keverne Rd 124 EL91
King & Queen St, SE17 201 J9
King Arthur Cl, SE15 102 DW80
King Arthur Ct, Wal.Cr. EN8 15 DX31
King Charles Cres, Surb. KT5 138 CM101
King Charles Rd, Rad.
(Shenley) WD7 10 CL32
Surbiton KT5 138 CM99
King Charles St, SW1 199 N4
King Charles Ter, E1 202 E1
King Charles Wk, SW19
off Princes Way 119 CY88
Kingcup Cl, Croy. CR0
off Primrose La 143 DX102
King David La, E1 84 DW73
Kingdon Rd, NW6 82 DA65
King Edward Av, Dart. DA1 128 FK86
Rainham RM13 90 FK68
King Edward Dr, Chess. KT9
off Kelvin Gro 138 CL104
Grays RM16 110 GE75
King Edward Ms, SW13 99 CU81
King Edward Rd, E10 67 EC60
E17 67 DY55
Barnet EN5 28 DA42
Brentwood CM14 54 FW48
Greenhithe DA9 129 FU85
Radlett (Shenley) WD7 10 CM33
Romford RM1 71 FF58
Waltham Cross EN8 15 DY33
Watford WD19 24 BY44
King Edward VII Av,
Wind. SL4 92 AS80
H **King Edward Seventh 's Hosp for Officers**, W1 194 G6
King Edward's Gdns, W3 80 CN74
King Edwards Gro,
Tedd. TW11 117 CH93
King Edward's Pl, W3
off King Edward's Gdns 80 CN74
King Edwards Rd, E9 84 DV67
N9 46 DV45
Barking IG11 87 ER67
King Edward's Rd, Enf. EN3 31 DX42
King Edwards Rd, Ruis. HA4 59 BR60
King Edward St, EC1 197 H8
King Edward III Ms, SE16 202 E5
King Edward Wk, SE1 200 E6
Kingfield Cl, Wok. GU22 167 AZ120
Kingfield Dr, Wok. GU22 167 AZ120
Kingfield Gdns, Wok. GU22 167 AZ120
Kingfield Grn, Wok. GU22 167 AZ120
Kingfield Rd, W5 79 CK70
Woking GU22 166 AY120
Kingfield St, E14 204 E9
Kingfisher Av, E11
off Eastern Av 68 EH58
Kingfisher Cl, SE28 88 EW73
Brentwood (Hutt.) CM13 55 GA45
Harrow (Har.Wld) HA3 41 CF52
Northwood HA6 39 BP53
Orpington BR5 146 EX98
Walton-on-Thames KT12
off Old Esher Rd 154 BY106
Kingfisher Ct, SW19
off Queensmere Rd 119 CY89
Enfield EN2
off Mount Vw 29 DM38
Surbiton KT6
off Ewell Rd 138 CM101
Sutton SM1
off Sandpiper Rd 157 CZ106
Woking GU21
off Vale Fm Rd 166 AY117
Woking (Sheer.) GU21
off Blackmore Cres 151 BC114
Kingfisher Dr, Green. DA9
off London Rd 129 FU85
Hemel Hempstead HP3
off Belswains La 6 BM25
Redhill RH1 184 DG131
Richmond TW10 117 CH91
Staines TW18 113 BF91
Kingfisher Gdns, S.Croy. CR2 161 DX111
Kingfisher Lure, Kings L. WD4 7 BP29
Rickmansworth (Loud.) WD3 22 BH42
Kingfisher Ms, SE13 103 EB84
Kingfisher Rd, Upmin. RM14 73 FT60
Kingfisher Sq, SE8 103 DZ79
Kingfisher St, E6 86 EL71
Kingfisher Wk, NW9
off Eagle Dr 42 CS54
Kingfisher Way, NW10 62 CR64
Beckenham BR3 143 DX99
King Frederik IX Twr, SE16 203 M6
King Gdns, Croy. CR0 159 DP106
King George Av, E16 86 EK72
Bushey WD23 24 CB44
Ilford IG2 69 ER57
Walton-on-Thames KT12 136 BX102
King George Cl, Rom. RM7 71 FC55
Sunbury-on-Thames TW16 115 BS92
H **King George Hosp**,
Ilf. IG3 70 EV57
King George Rd, Wal.Abb. EN9 15 EC34
King George Av, Wat. WD18 23 BS43
King Georges Dr, Add.
(New Haw) KT15 152 BG110
Southall UB1 78 BZ71
King George VI Av,
Mitch. CR4 140 DF98
Westerham TN16 178 EK116
King George Sq, Rich. TW10 118 CM86
King Georges Rd, Brwd.
(Pilg.Hat.) CM15 54 FV44
King George's Trd Est,
Chess. KT9 156 CN105
King George St, SE10 103 EC80
Kingham Cl, SW18 120 DC87
W11 99 CY75
King Harolds Way,
Bexh. DA7 106 EX80
King Henry Ms, Orp. BR6
off Osgood Av 163 ET106
King Henry's Ct, Wal.Abb. EN9
off Deer Pk Way 31 EC36
Tra **King Henry's Drive** 161 EB109
King Henry's Dr, Croy.
(New Adgtn) CR0 161 EC109
King Henry's Ms, Enf. EN3 31 EA37
King Henry's Reach, W6 99 CW79
King Henry's Rd, NW3 82 DE66
Kingston upon Thames KT1 138 CP97
King Henry St, N16 66 DS64
King Henry's Wk, N1 84 DS65
King Henry Ter, E1 202 E1
Kinghorn St, EC1 197 H7
King James Av, Pot.B.
(Cuffley) EN6 13 DL29
King James Ct, SE1 200 G5
King James St, SE1 200 G5
King John Ct, EC2 197 N4
King John's Cl, Stai.
(Wrays.) TW19 112 AW86
King John St, E1 85 DX71
King Johns Wk, SE9 124 EK88
Kinglake Ct, Wok. GU21
off Raglan Rd 166 AS118
Kinglake Est, SE17 201 N10
Kinglake St, SE17 102 DS78
Kingly Ct, W1 195 K10
Kingly St, W1 195 K9
Kingsand Rd, SE12 124 EG89
Kings Arbour, Sthl. UB2 96 BY78
Kings Arms Ct, E1
off Old Montague St 84 DU71
Kings Arms Yd, EC2 197 K8
Kingsash Dr, Hayes UB4 78 BY70
Kings Av, N10 64 DG55
N21 45 DP46
King's Av, SW4 121 DK87
SW12 121 DK88
Kings Av, W5 79 CK72
Bromley BR1 124 EF93
Buckhurst Hill IG9 48 EK47
Carshalton SM5 158 DE108
Greenford UB6 78 CB72
Hounslow TW3 96 CB81
New Malden KT3 138 CS98
Romford RM6 70 EZ58
Sunbury-on-Thames TW16 115 BT92
Watford WD18 23 BT42
West Byfleet (Byfleet) KT14 152 BK112
Woodford Green IG8 48 EH51
Kings Bench St, SE1 200 G4
Kings Bench Wk, EC4 196 E9
Kingsbridge Av, W3 98 CM75
Kingsbridge Circ, Rom. RM3 52 FL51
Kingsbridge Cl, Rom. RM3 52 FL51
Kingsbridge Ct, E14
off Dockers Tanner Rd 103 EA77
Kingsbridge Cres, Sthl. UB1 78 BZ71
Kingsbridge Dr, NW7 43 CX52
Kingsbridge Rd, W10 81 CW72
Barking IG11 87 ER68
Morden SM4 139 CX101
Romford RM3 52 FL51
Southall UB2 96 BZ77
Walton-on-Thames KT12 135 BV101
Kingsbridge Way, Hayes UB4 77 BS69
Kingsbrook, Lthd. KT22
off Ryebrook Rd 171 CG118
KINGSBURY, NW9 62 CP58
⊖ **Kingsbury** 62 CN57
Kingsbury Circle, NW9 62 CN57
H **Kingsbury Comm Hosp**,
NW9 62 CN56
Kingsbury Cres, Stai. TW18 113 BD91
Kingsbury Dr, Wind.
(Old Wind.) SL4 112 AV86
Kingsbury Rd, N1 84 DS65
NW9 62 CP57
Kingsbury Ter, N1 84 DS65
Kingsbury Trd Est, NW9 62 CR58
Kings Butts, SE9
off Strongbow Cres 125 EM85
Kings Chace Vw, Enf. EN2
off Crofton Way 29 DN40
Kings Chase, Brwd. CM14 54 FW48
East Molesey KT8 136 CC97
Kingsclere Cl, SW15 119 CU87
Kingsclere Ct, Barn. EN5
off Gloucester Rd 28 DC43
Kingsclere Pl, Enf. EN2
off Chase Side 30 DQ40
Kingscliffe Gdns, SW19 119 CZ88
Kings Cl, E10 67 EB59
NW4 63 CX56
Chalfont St. Giles HP8 36 AX47
Dartford DA1 107 FE84
Kings Langley
(Chipper.) WD4 6 BH31
Northwood HA6 39 BT51
Staines TW18 114 BK94
Thames Ditton KT7 137 CG100
Walton-on-Thames KT12 135 BV102
King's Cl, Wat. WD18
off Lady's Cl 23 BV42
H **King's Coll Hosp**, SE5 102 DR82
H **King's Coll Hospital, Dulwich**,
SE22 102 DS84
Kings Coll Rd, NW3 82 DE66
Ruislip HA4 59 BT58
Kingscote Rd, W4 98 CR76
Croydon CR0 142 DV101
New Malden KT3 138 CR97
Kingscote St, EC4 196 F10
Kings Ct, E13 86 EH67
W6 off King St 99 CU77
Tadworth KT20 173 CW122
Wembley HA9 62 CP61
Kingscourt Rd, SW16 121 DK90
Kings Ct S, SW3
off Chelsea Manor Gdns 100 DE78
Kings Cres, N4 66 DQ62
Kings Cres Est, N4 66 DQ61
Kingscroft Rd, NW2 81 CZ65
Kingscroft Rd, Banstead SM7 174 DD115
Leatherhead KT22 171 CH120
KING'S CROSS, N1 83 DK67
⇌ **King's Cross** 195 P1
King's Cross Br, N1 196 A2
King's Cross Rd, WC1 196 C2
⊖ **King's Cross St. Pancras** 195 P1
⇌ **King's Cross Thameslink** 196 A1
Kingsdale Ct, Wal.Abb. EN9
off Lamplighters Cl 16 EG34
Kingsdale Gdns, W11 81 CX74
Kingsdale Rd, SE18 105 ET80
SE20 123 DX94
Kingsdene, Tad. KT20 173 CV121
Kingsdown Av, W3 80 CS73
W13 97 CH75
South Croydon CR2 159 DP109
Kingsdown Cl, SE16
off Masters Dr 102 DV78
W10 81 CX72
Gravesend DA12
off Farley Rd 131 GM88
Kingsdowne Rd, Surb. KT6 138 CL101
Kingsdown Rd, E11 68 EE62
N19 65 DL61
Epsom KT17 157 CU113
Sutton SM3 157 CY106
Kingsdown Way, Brom. BR2 144 EG101
Kings Dr, Edg. HA8 42 CM49
Gravesend DA12 131 GH90
Surbiton KT5 138 CN101
Teddington TW11 117 CD92
Thames Ditton KT7 137 CH100
Wembley HA9 62 CP61
Kings Dr, The, Walt. KT12 153 BT110
Kingsend, Ruis. HA4 59 BR60
KINGS FARM, Grav. DA12 131 GJ90
Kings Fm Av, Rich. TW10 98 CN84
Kings Fm Rd, Rick.
(Chorl.) WD3 21 BD44
Kingsfield Av, Har. HA2 60 CB56
Kingsfield Ct, Wat. WD19 40 BX45
Kingsfield Dr, Enf. EN3 31 DX35
Kingsfield Ho, SE9 124 EK90
Kingsfield Rd, Har. HA1 61 CD59
Watford WD19 40 BX45
Kingsfield Ter, Dart. DA1
off Priory Rd S 128 FK86
Kingsfield Way, Enf. EN3 31 DX35
Kingsford St, NW5 64 DF64
Kingsford Way, E6 87 EM71
Kings Gdns, NW6
off West End La 82 DA66
Ilford IG1 69 ER60
Upminster RM14 73 FS59
King's Garth Ms, SE23
off London Rd 122 DW89
Kingsgate, Wem. HA9 62 CQ62
Kingsgate Av, N3 64 DA55
Kingsgate Cl, Bexh. DA7 106 EY81
Orpington BR5
off Main Rd 146 EW97
Kingsgate Pl, NW6 82 DA66
Kingsgate Rd, NW6 82 DA66
Kingston upon Thames KT2 138 CL95
Kings Grn, Loug. IG10 32 EL41
Kingsground, SE9 124 EL87
Kings Gro, SE15 102 DV80
Romford RM1 71 FG57
Kingshall Ms, SE13
off Lewisham Rd 103 EC83
Kings Hall Rd, Beck. BR3 123 DY94
Kings Head Hill, E4 47 EB45
Kings Head La, W.Byf.
(Byfleet) KT14 152 BK111
Kings Head Yd, SE1 201 K3
Kings Highway, SE18 105 ES79
Kings Hill, Loug. IG10 32 EL40
Kingshill Av, Har. HA3 61 CH56
Hayes UB4 77 BS69
Northolt UB5 77 BU69
Romford RM5 51 FC51
Worcester Park KT4 139 CU101
Kingshill Cl, Hayes UB4
off Kingshill Av 77 BU69
Kingshill Dr, Har. HA3 61 CH55
Kingshold Est, E9
off Victoria Pk Rd 84 DW67
Kingshold Rd, E9 84 DW66
Kingsholm Gdns, SE9 104 EK84
Kingshurst Rd, SE12 124 EG87
Kingside Business Pk, SE18
off Woolwich Ch St 104 EL76
Kings Keep, Kings.T. KT1
off Beaufort Rd 138 CL98
KINGSLAND, N1 84 DS65
Kingsland, NW8
off Broxwood Way 82 DE67
Potters Bar EN6 11 CZ33
Kingsland Grn, E8 84 DS65
Kingsland High St, E8 66 DT64
Kingsland Pas, E8
off Kingsland Grn 84 DS65
Kingsland Rd, E2 197 N2
E8 84 DS68
E13 86 EJ69
Kingsland Shop Cen, E8 84 DT65
Kings La, Egh.
(Eng.Grn) TW20 112 AU92
Kings Langley
(Chipper.) WD4 6 BG31
Sutton SM1 158 DD107
KINGS LANGLEY 6 BM30
⇌ **Kings Langley** 7 BQ30
Kings Langley Bypass, Kings L.
WD4 6 BK28
Kingslawn Cl, SW15 119 CV85
off Howards La
Kingslea, Lthd. KT22 171 CG120
Kingsleigh Pl, Mitch. CR4
off Chatsworth Pl 140 DF97
Kingsleigh Wk, Brom. BR2
off Stamford Dr 144 EF98
Kingsley Av, W13 79 CG72
Banstead SM7 174 DA115
Borehamwood WD6 26 CM40
Dartford DA1 128 FN85
Egham (Eng.Grn) TW20 112 AV93
Hounslow TW3 96 CC82
Southall UB1 78 CA73
Kingsley Av, Sutton SM1 158 DD105
Waltham Cross
(Chsht) EN8 14 DV29
Kingsley Cl, N2 64 DC57
Dagenham RM10 71 FB63
Kingsley Ct, Edg. HA8 42 CP47
Kingsley Dr, Wor.Pk. KT4
off Badgers Copse 139 CT103
Kingsley Flats, SE1
off Old Kent Rd 102 DS77
Kingsley Gdns, E4 47 EA50
Hornchurch RM11 72 FK56
Kingsley Ms, E1 202 E1
W8 off Stanford Rd 100 DB76
Chislehurst BR7 125 EP93
Kingsley Pl, N6 64 DG59
Kingsley Rd, E7 86 EG66
E17 47 EC54
N13 45 DN49
NW6 81 CZ67
SW19 120 DB92
Brentwood (Hutt.) CM13 55 GD45
Croydon CR0 141 DN102
Harrow HA2 60 CC63
Hounslow TW3 96 CC82
Ilford IG6 49 EQ53
Loughton IG10 33 ER41
Orpington BR6 163 ET108
Pinner HA5 60 BZ56
Kingsley St, SW11 100 DF83
Kingsley Wk, Grays RM16 111 GG77
Kingsley Way, N2 64 DC58
Kingsley Wd Dr, SE9 125 EM90
Kingslyn Cres, SE19 142 DS95
Kings Lynn Cl, Rom. RM3
off Kings Lynn Dr 52 FK51
Kings Lynn Dr, Rom. RM3 52 FK51
Kings Lynn Path, Rom. RM3
off Kings Lynn Dr 52 FK51
Kings Mall, W6 99 CW77
Kingsman Par, SE18
off Woolwich Ch St 105 EM76
Kingsman St, SE18 105 EM76
Kingsmead, Barn. EN5 28 DA42
Potters Bar (Cuffley) EN6 13 DL28
Richmond TW10 118 CM86
Waltham Cross EN8 15 DX28
Westerham (Bigg.H.) TN16 178 EK116
Kingsmead Av, N9 46 DV46
NW9 62 CR59
Mitcham CR4 141 DJ97
Romford RM1 71 FE58
Sunbury-on-Thames TW16 136 BW97
Surbiton KT6 138 CN103
Worcester Park KT4 139 CV104
Kingsmead Cl, Epsom KT19 156 CR108
Sidcup DA15 126 EU89
Teddington TW11 117 CG93
Kingsmead Dr, Nthlt. UB5 78 BZ66
Kingsmead Est, E9 67 DY64
Kingsmead Ho, E9
off Kingsmead Way 67 DY63
Kings Meadow, Kings L. WD4 6 BN28
Kings Mead Pk, Esher
(Clay.) KT10 155 CE108
Kingsmead Rd, SW2 121 DN89
Kingsmead Way, E9 67 DY63
Kingsmere Cl, SW15
off Felsham Rd 99 CY83
Kingsmere Pk, NW9 62 CP60
Kingsmere Pl, N16 66 DR60
Kingsmere Rd, SW19 119 CX89
Kings Ms, SW4 off King's Av 121 DL85
King's Ms, WC1 196 C5
Kings Ms, Chig. IG7 49 EQ47
Kingsmill Gdns, Dag. RM9 70 EZ64
Kingsmill Rd, Dag. RM9 70 EZ64
Kingsmill Ter, NW8 82 DD68
Kingsnympton Pk,
Kings.T. KT2 118 CP93
Kings Oak, Rom. RM7 70 FA55
H **King's Oak Private Hosp**,
Enf. EN2 29 DN38
King's Orchard, SE9 124 EL86
Kings Paddock, Hmptn. TW12 136 CC95
Kings Par, Cars. SM5
off Wrythe La 140 DE104
Kingspark Ct, E18 68 EG55
King's Pas, E11 68 EE59
Kings Pas, Kings.T. KT1 137 CK96
Kings Pl, SE1 201 H5
W4 98 CQ78
Buckhurst Hill IG9 48 EJ47
Loughton IG10 48 EK45
King Sq, EC1 197 H3
King's Reach Twr, SE1 200 E2
Kings Ride Gate, Rich. TW10 98 CN84
Kingsridge, SW19 119 CY89
Kingsridge Gdns, Dart. DA1 128 FK86
Kings Rd, E4 47 ED46
E6 86 EJ67
E11 68 EE59
King's Rd, N17 46 DT53
Kings Rd, N18 46 DU50
N22 45 DM53
NW10 81 CV66
SE25 142 DU97
King's Rd, SW1 198 C10
SW3 198 C10
SW6 100 DB81
SW10 100 DB81
Kings Rd, SW14 98 CR83
SW19 120 DA93
W5 79 CK71
Addlestone
(New Haw) KT15 152 BH110
Barking IG11 off North St 87 EQ66
Barnet EN5 27 CW41
Brentwood CM14 54 FW48
Chalfont St. Giles HP8 36 AX47
Egham TW20 113 BA91
Feltham TW13 116 BW88
Harrow HA2 60 BZ61
Kingston upon Thames KT2 118 CL94
Mitcham CR4 140 DG97
Orpington BR6 163 ET105
Richmond TW10 118 CM85
Romford RM1 71 FG57
St. Albans (Lon.Col.) AL2 9 CJ26
Slough SL1 92 AS76
Kings Rd, Surbiton KT6 137 CJ102
Sutton SM2 158 DA110
Teddington TW11 117 CD92
Twickenham TW1 117 CH86
King's Rd, Uxb. UB8 76 BK68
Kings Rd, Wal.Cr. EN8 15 DY34
Walton-on-Thames KT12 135 BV103
West Drayton UB7 94 BM75
Westerham (Bigg.H.) TN16 178 EJ116
Woking GU21 167 BA116
Kings Rd Bungalows, Har. HA2
off Kings Rd 60 BZ62
King's Scholars' Pas, SW1 199 K8
King Stairs Cl, SE16 202 E4
King's Ter, NW1
off Plender St 83 DJ67
Kings Ter, Islw. TW7
off Worple Rd 97 CG83
Kingsthorpe Rd, SE26 123 DX91
⇌ **Kingston** 138 CL95
Kingston Av, Felt. TW14 115 BS86
Leatherhead KT22 171 CH121
Sutton SM3 139 CY104
West Drayton UB7 76 BM73
Kingston Br, Kings.T. KT1 137 CK96
Kingston Bypass, SW15 118 CS91
SW20 118 CS91
Esher KT10 137 CG104
New Malden KT3 139 CT95
Surbiton KT5, KT6 138 CL104
Kingston Cl, Nthlt. UB5 78 BZ67
Romford RM6 70 EY55
Teddington TW11 117 CH93
Kingston Ct, N4
off Wiltshire Gdns 66 DQ58
Gravesend (Nthflt) DA11 130 GB85
Kingston Cres, Ashf. TW15 114 BJ92
Beckenham BR3 143 DZ95
Kingston Gdns, Croy. CR0
off Wandle Rd 141 DL104
Kingston Hall Rd,
Kings.T. KT1 137 CK97
Kingston Hill, Kings.T. KT2 118 CQ93
Kingston Hill Av, Rom. RM6 70 EY55
Kingston Hill Pl,
Kings.T. KT2 118 CQ91
H **Kingston Hosp**,
Kings.T. KT2 138 CP95
Kingston Ho Gdns, Lthd. KT22
off Upper Fairfield Rd 171 CG121
Kingston La, Tedd. TW11 117 CG92
Uxbridge UB8 76 BL69
West Drayton UB7 94 BM75
★ **Kingston Mus & Heritage Cen**,
Kings.T. KT1 138 CL96
Kingston Pk Est, Kings.T. KT2 118 CP93
Kingston Pl, Har. HA3
off Richmond Gdns 41 CF52
Kingston Ri,
Add. (New Haw) KT15 152 BG110
Kingston Rd, N9 46 DU47
SW15 119 CU88
SW19 139 CZ95
SW20 139 CW96
Ashford TW15 114 BL93
Barnet EN4 28 DD43
Epsom KT17, KT19 156 CS106
Ilford IG1 69 EP63
Kingston upon Thames KT1 138 CP97
Leatherhead KT22 171 CG117
New Malden KT3 138 CR98
Romford RM1 71 FF56
Southall UB2 96 BZ75
Staines TW18 114 BH93
Surbiton KT5 138 CP103
Teddington TW11 117 CH92
Worcester Park KT4 138 CP103
Kingston Sq, SE19 122 DR92
KINGSTON UPON THAMES 138 CL96
KINGSTON VALE, SW15 118 CS91
Kingston Vale, SW15 118 CR91
Kingstown St, NW1 82 DG67
King St, E13 86 EG70
EC2 197 J9
N2 64 DD55
N17 46 DT53
SW1 199 L3
W3 80 CP74
W6 99 CU77
WC2 195 P10
Chertsey KT16 134 BG102
Gravesend DA12 131 GH86
Richmond TW9 117 CK85
Southall UB2 96 BY76
Twickenham TW1 117 CG88
Watford WD18 24 BW42
Kings Wk, Grays RM17 110 GA79
King's Wk, Kings.T. KT2 137 CK95
Kings Wk, S.Croy. CR2 160 DV114
Kings Wk Shop Mall, SW3
off King's Rd 100 DF78
Kings Warren, Lthd.
(Oxshott) KT22 154 CC111
Kingswater Pl, SW11
off Battersea Ch Rd 100 DE80
Kingsway, N12 44 DC51
SW14 98 CP83
WC2 196 B8
Croydon CR0 159 DM106
Enfield EN3 30 DV43
Gerrards Cross
(Chal.St.P.) SL9 56 AY55
Kings Way, Har. HA1 61 CE56
Kingsway, Hayes UB3 77 BQ71
Iver SL0 off High St 75 BE72
New Malden KT3 139 CW98
Orpington BR5 145 ES99
Potters Bar (Cuffley) EN6 13 DL30
Staines TW19 114 BK88
Watford WD25 8 BW34
Wembley HA9 62 CL63
West Wickham BR4 144 EE104
Woking GU21 166 AX118
Woodford Green IG8 48 EJ50
Kingsway, The, Epsom KT17 157 CT111

★ Place of interest ⇌ Railway station ⊖ London Underground station DLR Docklands Light Railway station Tra Tramlink station H Hospital Riv Pedestrian ferry landing stage

Kingsway Av, S.Croy. CR2 160 DW109
Woking GU21 166 AX118
Kingsway Business Pk, Hmptn. TW12 136 BZ95
Kingsway Cres, Har. HA2 60 CC56
Kingsway Pl, EC1 196 E4
Kingsway Rd, Sutt. SM3 157 CY108
Kingsway Shop Cen, NW3 off Hampstead High St 64 DC63
Kingswear Rd, NW5 65 DH62
Ruislip HA4 59 BU61
Kingswell Ride, Pot.B. (Cuffley) EN6 13 DL30
Kingsway Business Pk, Wok. GU21 151 BC114
Kings Wf, E8 off Kingsland Rd 84 DS67
KINGSWOOD, Tad. KT20 173 CY123
KINGSWOOD, Wat. WD25 7 BV34
⇌ Kingswood 173 CZ121
Kingswood Av, NW6 81 CY67
Belvedere DA17 106 EZ77
Bromley BR2 144 EE97
Hampton TW12 116 CB93
Hounslow TW3 96 BZ81
South Croydon CR2 176 DV115
Swanley BR8 147 FF98
Thornton Heath CR7 141 DN99
Kingswood Cl, N20 28 DC44
SW8 101 DL80
Dartford DA1 128 FJ86
Egham (Eng.Grn) TW20 112 AX91
Enfield EN1 30 DS43
New Malden KT3 139 CT100
Orpington BR6 145 ER101
Surbiton KT6 138 CL101
Weybridge KT13 153 BP108
Kingswood Creek, Stai. (Wrays.) TW19 112 AX85
Kingswood Dr, SE19 122 DS91
Carshalton SM5 140 DF102
Sutton SM2 158 DB109
Kingswood Est, SE21 off Bowen Dr 122 DS91
Kingswood La, S.Croy. CR2 160 DW113
Warlingham CR6 176 DW115
Kingswood Ms, N15 off Harringay Rd 65 DP57
Kingswood Pk, N3 43 CZ54
Kingswood Pl, SE13 104 EE84
Kingswood Ri, Egh. (Eng.Grn) TW20 112 AX92
Kingswood Rd, E11 68 EE59
SE20 122 DW93
SW2 121 DL86
SW19 119 CZ94
W4 98 CQ76
Bromley BR2 143 ED98
Ilford IG3 70 EU60
Sevenoaks (Dunt.Grn) TN13 181 FE120
Tadworth KT20 173 CV121
Watford WD25 7 BV34
Wembley HA9 62 CN62
Kingswood Ter, W4 off Kingswood Rd 98 CQ76
Kingswood Way, S.Croy. CR2 160 DW113
Wallington SM6 159 DL106
Kingsworth Cl, Beck. BR3 143 DY99
Kingsworthy Cl, Kings.T. KT1 138 CM97
King's Yd, SW15 off Stanbridge Rd 99 CW83
Kingthorpe Rd, NW10 80 CR66
Kingthorpe Ter, NW10 80 CR65
Kingwell Rd, Barn. EN4 28 DD38
Kingweston Cl, NW2 off Windmill Dr 63 CY62
King William IV Gdns, SE20 off St. John's Rd 122 DW93
King William La, SE10 off Orlop St 104 EE78
King William St, EC4 201 L1
King William Wk, SE10 103 EC79
Kingwood Rd, SW6 99 CX81
Kinlet Rd, SE18 105 EQ81
Kinloch Dr, NW9 62 CS59
Kinloch St, N7 off Hornsey Rd 65 DM62
Kinloss Ct, N3 off Haslemere Gdns 63 CZ56
Kinloss Gdns, N3 63 CZ56
Kinloss Rd, Cars. SM5 140 DC101
Kinnaird Av, W4 98 CQ80
Bromley BR1 124 EF93
Kinnaird Cl, Brom. BR1 124 EF93
Kinnaird Way, Wdf.Grn. IG8 49 EM51
Kinnear Rd, W12 99 CT75
Kinnerton Pl N, SW1 198 E5
Kinnerton Pl S, SW1 198 E5
Kinnerton St, SW1 198 F5
Kinnerton Yd, SW1 198 E5
Kinnoul Rd, W6 99 CY79
Kinross Av, Wor.Pk. KT4 139 CU103
Kinross Cl, Edg. HA8 off Tayside Dr 42 CP47
Harrow HA3 62 CM57
Sunbury-on-Thames TW16 115 BT92
Kinross Dr, Sun. TW16 115 BT92
Kinross Ter, E17 47 DZ54
Kinsale Rd, SE15 102 DU83
Kintore Way, SE1 201 P8
Kintyre Cl, SW16 141 DM97
Kinveachy Gdns, SE7 104 EL78
Kinver Rd, SE26 122 DW91
Kipings, Tad. KT20 173 CX122
Kipling Av, Til. RM18 111 GH81
Kipling Dr, SW19 120 DD93
Kipling Est, SE1 201 L5
Kipling Pl, Stan. HA7 off Uxbridge Rd 41 CF51
Kipling Rd, Bexh. DA7 106 EY81
Dartford DA1 128 FP85
Kipling St, SE1 201 L5
Kipling Ter, N9 46 DR48
Kipling Twrs, Rom. RM3 51 FH52
KIPPINGTON, Sev. TN13 190 FG126
Kippington Cl, Sev. TN13 190 FF124
Kippington Dr, SE9 124 EK88
Kippington Ho, Sev. TN13 off Kippington Rd 190 FG126
Kippington Rd, Sev. TN13 190 FG124
Kirby Cl, Epsom KT19 157 CT106
Ilford IG6 49 ES51
Loughton IG10 48 EL45
Northwood HA6 39 BT51
Romford RM3 52 FN50
Kirby Est, SE16 202 D6
Kirby Gro, SE1 201 M4
Kirby Rd, Dart. DA2 128 FQ87
Woking GU21 166 AW117
Kirby St, EC1 196 E6
Kirby Way, Walt. KT12 136 BW100
Kirchen Rd, W13 79 CH73
Kirkby Cl, N11 off Coverdale Rd 44 DG51
Kirkcaldy Grn, Wat. WD19 off Trevose Way 40 BW48
Kirk Ct, Sev. TN13 190 FG123
Kirkdale, SE26 122 DV89
Kirkdale Rd, E11 68 EE60
Kirkfield Cl, W13 off Broomfield Rd 79 CH74
Kirkham Rd, E6 86 EL72
Kirkham St, SE18 105 ES79
Kirkland Av, Ilf. IG5 49 EN54
Woking GU21 166 AS116
Kirkland Cl, Sid. DA15 125 ES86
Kirkland Dr, Enf. EN2 29 DP39
Kirkland Wk, E8 84 DT65
Kirk La, SE18 105 EQ79
Kirkleas Rd, Surb. KT6 138 CL102
Kirklees Rd, Dag. RM8 70 EW64
Thornton Heath CR7 141 DN99
Kirkley Rd, SW19 140 DA95
Kirkly Cl, S.Croy. CR2 160 DS109
Kirkman Pl, W1 195 M7
Kirkmichael Rd, E14 off Dee St 85 EC72
Kirk Ri, Sutt. SM1 140 DB104
Kirk Rd, E17 67 DZ58
Kirkside Rd, SE3 104 EG79
Kirkstall Av, N17 66 DR56
Kirkstall Gdns, SW2 121 DK88
Kirkstall Rd, SW2 121 DK88
Kirkstead Ct, E5 off Mandeville St 67 DY62
Kirksted Rd, Mord. SM4 140 DB102
Kirkstone Way, Brom. BR1 124 EE94
Kirk St, WC1 196 B5
Kirkton Rd, N15 66 DS56
Kirkwall Pl, E2 84 DW69
Kirkwall Spur, Slou. SL1 74 AS71
Kirkwood Rd, SE15 102 DV82
Kirn Rd, W13 off Kirchen Rd 79 CH73
Kirrane Cl, N.Mal. KT3 139 CT99
Kirtley Rd, SE26 123 DY91
Kirtling St, SW8 101 DJ80
Kirton Cl, W4 off Dolman Rd 98 CR77
Hornchurch RM12 90 FJ65
Kirton Gdns, E2 off Chambord St 84 DT69
Kirton Rd, E13 86 EJ68
Kirton Wk, Edg. HA8 42 CQ52
Kirwyn Way, SE5 101 DP80
Kitcat Ter, E3 85 EA69
Kitchener Av, Grav. DA12 131 GJ90
Kitchener Rd, E7 86 EH65
E17 47 EB53
N2 64 DE55
N17 66 DR55
Dagenham RM10 89 FB65
Thornton Heath CR7 142 DR97
Kitchenride Cor, Cher. KT16 151 BA105
Kite Pl, E2 off Nelson Gdns 84 DU69
Kite Yd, SW11 off Cambridge Rd 100 DF81
Kitley Gdns, SE19 142 DT95
Kitsmead La, Cher. (Longcr.) KT16 132 AX103
Kitson Rd, SE5 102 DR80
SW13 99 CU81
Kitswell Way, Rad. WD7 9 CF33
Kitters Grn, Abb.L. WD5 off High St 7 BS31
Kittiwake Cl, S.Croy. CR2 161 DY110
Kittiwake Pl, Sutt. SM1 off Sandpiper Rd 157 CZ106
Kittiwake Rd, Nthlt. UB5 78 BX69
Kittiwake Way, Hayes UB4 78 BX71
Kitto Rd, SE14 103 DX82
KITT'S END, Barn. EN5 27 CY37
Kitt's End Rd, Barn. EN5 27 CX36
Kiver Rd, N19 65 DK61
Kiwi Cl, Twick. TW1 off Crown Rd 117 CH86
Klea Av, SW4 121 DJ86
Knapdale Cl, SE23 122 DV89
Knapmill Rd, SE6 123 EA89
Knapmill Way, SE6 123 EB89
Knapp Cl, NW10 80 CS65
Knapp Rd, E3 85 EA70
Ashford TW15 114 BM91
Knapton Ms, SW17 off Seely Rd 120 DG93
Knaresborough Dr, SW18 120 DB88
Knaresborough Pl, SW5 100 DB77
Knatchbull Rd, NW10 80 CR67
SE5 102 DQ81
Knebworth Av, E17 47 EA53
Knebworth Path, Borwd. WD6 26 CR42
Knebworth Rd, N16 off Nevill Rd 66 DS63
Knee Hill, SE2 106 EW77
Knee Hill Cres, SE2 106 EW77
Kneller Gdns, Islw. TW7 117 CD85
Kneller Rd, SE4 103 DY84
New Malden KT3 138 CS101
Twickenham TW2 116 CC86
Knight Cl, Dag. RM8 off Burnside Rd 70 EW61
Knighten St, E1 202 C3
Knighthead Pt, E14 203 P6
Knightland Rd, E5 66 DV61
Knighton Cl, Rom. RM7 71 FD58
South Croydon CR2 159 DP108
Woodford Green IG8 48 EH49
Knighton Dr, Wdf.Grn. IG8 48 EG49
Knighton Grn, Buck.H. IG9 off High Rd 48 EH47
Knighton La, Buck.H. IG9 48 EH47
Knighton Pk Rd, SE26 123 DX92
Knighton Rd, E7 68 EG62
Romford RM7 71 FC58
Sevenoaks (Otford) TN14 181 FF116
Knighton Way La, Uxb. (Denh.) UB9 76 BH65
Knightrider Ct, EC4 off Godliman St 84 DQ73
Knightrider St, EC4 197 H10
Knights Arc, SW1 198 D5
Knights Av, W5 98 CL75
⊖ Knightsbridge 198 D5
Knightsbridge, SW1 198 E5
SW7 198 C5
Knightsbridge Ct, Slou. (Langley) SL3 off High St 93 BA77
Knightsbridge Cres, Stai. TW18 114 BH93
Knightsbridge Gdns, Rom. RM7 71 FD57
Knightsbridge Grn, SW1 198 D5
Knights Cl, E9 off Churchill Wk 66 DW64
Egham TW20 113 BD93
Knights Ct, Kings.T. KT1 138 CL97
Romford RM6 70 EY58
Knights Hill, SE27 121 DP92
Knights Hill Sq, SE27 off Knights Hill 121 DP91
Knights La, N9 46 DU48
Knights Manor Way, Dart. DA1 128 FM86
Knights Ms, Sutt. SM2 off York Rd 158 DA108
Knights Pk, Kings.T. KT1 138 CL97
Knights Pl, Red. RH1 off Noke Dr 184 DG133
Knight's Pl, Twick. TW2 off May Rd 117 CE88
Knights Ridge, Orp. BR6 off Stirling Dr 164 EV106
Knights Rd, E16 205 N4
Stanmore HA7 41 CJ49
Knights Wk, SE11 200 F9
Romford (Abridge) RM4 34 EV41
Knight's Way, Brwd. CM13 55 GA48
Knights Way, Ilf. IG6 49 EQ51
Knightswood, Wok. GU21 166 AT118
Knightswood Cl, Edg. HA8 42 CQ47
Knightswood Rd, Rain. RM13 off Rainham Rd 89 FG68
Knightwood Cres, N.Mal. KT3 138 CS100
Knipp Hill, Cob. KT11 154 BZ113
Knivet Rd, SW6 100 DA79
Knobs Hill Rd, E15 85 EB67
KNOCKHALL, Green. DA9 129 FW85
Knockhall Chase, Green. DA9 129 FV85
Knockhall Rd, Green. DA9 129 FW86
KNOCKHOLT, Sev. TN14 180 EU116
⇌ Knockholt 164 EY109
Knockholt Cl, Sutt. SM2 158 DB110
Knockholt Main Rd, Sev. (Knock.) TN14 180 EY115
KNOCKHOLT POUND, Sev. TN14 180 EX115
Knockholt Rd, SE9 124 EK85
Sevenoaks (Halst.) TN14 164 EZ113
Knole, The, SE9 125 EN91
Gravesend (Istead Rise) DA13 130 GE94
Knole Cl, Croy. CR0 off Stockbury Rd 142 DW100
Knole Gate, Sid. DA15 off Woodside Cres 125 ES90
★ Knole Ho & Pk, Sev. TN15 191 FL126
Knole La, Sev. TN13, TN15 191 FJ126
Knole Rd, Dart. DA1 127 FG87
Sevenoaks TN13 191 FK123
Knole Way, Sev. TN13 191 FJ125
Knoll, The, W13 79 CJ71
Beckenham BR3 143 EB95
Bromley BR2 144 EG103
Chertsey KT16 133 BF102
Cobham KT11 154 CA113
Leatherhead KT22 171 CJ120
Knoll Ct, SE19 122 DT92
Knoll Cres, Nthwd. HA6 39 BS53
Knoll Dr, N14 44 DG45
Knollmead, Surb. KT5 138 CQ102
Knoll Pk Rd, Cher. KT16 133 BF102
Knoll Ri, Orp. BR6 145 ET102
Knoll Rd, SW18 120 DC85
Bexley DA5 126 FA87
Sidcup DA14 126 EV92
Knolls, The, Epsom KT17 173 CW116
Knolls Cl, Wor.Pk. KT4 139 CV104
Knollys Cl, SW16 121 DN90
Knollys Rd, SW16 121 DN90
Knolton Way, Slou. SL2 74 AW72
Knottisford St, E2 84 DW69
Knotts Grn Ms, E10 67 EB58
Knotts Grn Rd, E10 67 EB58
Knotts Pl, Sev. TN13 190 FG124
Knowland Way, Uxb. (Denh.) UB9 57 BF58
Knowle, The, Tad. KT20 173 CW121
Knowle Av, Bexh. DA7 106 EY80
Knowle Cl, SW9 101 DN83
Knowle Gdns, W.Byf. KT14 off Madeira Rd 151 BF113
Knowle Grn, Stai. TW18 114 BG92
Knowle Gro, Vir.W. GU25 132 AW101
Knowle Gro Cl, Vir.W. GU25 132 AW101
Knowle Hill, Vir.W. GU25 132 AV101
Knowle Pk, Cob. KT11 170 BY115
Knowle Pk Av, Stai. TW18 114 BH93
Knowle Rd, Brom. BR2 144 EL103
Twickenham TW2 117 CE88
Knowles Cl, West Dr. UB7 76 BL74
Knowles Hill Cres, SE13 123 ED85
Knowles Ho, SW18 off Neville Gill Cl 120 DB86
Knowles Wk, SW4 101 DJ83
Knowl Hill, Wok. GU22 167 BB119
Knowl Pk, Borwd. (Elstree) WD6 26 CL43
Knowlton Grn, Brom. BR2 144 EF99
Knowl Way, Borwd. (Elstree) WD6 26 CL42
Knowsley Av, Sthl. UB1 78 CA74
Knowsley Rd, SW11 100 DF82
Knoxfield Caravan Pk, Dart. DA2 129 FS90
Knox Rd, E7 86 EF65
Knox St, W1 194 D6
Knoyle St, SE14 103 DY79
Knutsford Av, Wat. WD24 24 BX38
Kohat Rd, SW19 120 DB92
Koh-i-noor Av, Bushey WD23 24 CA44
Koonowla Cl, West. (Bigg.H.) TN16 178 EK115
Kooringa, Warl. CR6 176 DV119
Korda Cl, Shep. TW17 134 BM97
Kossuth St, SE10 205 H10
Kotree Way, SE1 202 C9
Kramer Ms, SW5 off Kempsford Gdns 100 DA78
Kreedman Wk, E8 66 DU64
Kreisel Wk, Rich. TW9 98 CM79
Kuala Gdns, SW16 141 DM95
Kuhn Way, E7 off Forest La 68 EG64
Kydbrook Cl, Orp. BR5 145 ER101
Kylemore Cl, E6 off Parr Rd 86 EK68
Kylemore Rd, NW6 82 DA66
Kymberley Rd, Har. HA1 61 CE58
Kyme Rd, Horn. RM11 71 FF58
Kynance Cl, Rom. RM3 52 FJ48
Kynance Gdns, Stan. HA7 41 CJ53
Kynance Ms, SW7 100 DB76
Kynance Pl, SW7 100 DC76
Kynaston Av, N16 off Dynevor Rd 66 DT62
Thornton Heath CR7 142 DQ99
Kynaston Cl, Har. HA3 41 CD52
Kynaston Cres, Th.Hth. CR7 142 DQ99
Kynaston Rd, N16 66 DS62
Bromley BR1 124 EG92
Enfield EN2 30 DR39
Orpington BR5 146 EV101
Thornton Heath CR7 142 DQ99
Kynaston Wd, Har. HA3 41 CD52
Kynersley Cl, Cars. SM5 off William St 140 DF104
Kynock Rd, N18 46 DW49
Kyrle Rd, SW11 120 DG85
Kytes Dr, Wat. WD25 8 BX33
Kytes Est, Wat. WD25 8 BX33
Kyverdale Rd, N16 66 DT61

L

Laburnham Cl, Upmin. RM14 73 FU59
Wembley HA0 off Highcroft Av 80 CN67
Laburnham Gdns, Upmin. RM14 73 FT59
Laburnum Av, N9 46 DS47
N17 46 DR52
Dartford DA1 128 FJ88
Hornchurch RM12 71 FF62
Sutton SM1 140 DE104
Swanley BR8 147 FC97
West Drayton UB7 76 BM73
Laburnum Cl, E4 47 DZ51
N11 44 DG51
SE15 off Clifton Way 102 DW80
Waltham Cross (Chsht) EN8 15 DX31
Laburnum Ct, E2 off Laburnum St 84 DT67
Stanmore HA7 41 CJ49
Laburnum Cres, Sun. TW16 off Batavia Rd 135 BV95
Laburnum Gdns, N21 46 DQ47
Croydon CR0 143 DX101
Laburnum Gro, N21 46 DQ47
NW9 62 CQ59
Gravesend (Nthflt) DA11 130 GD87
Hounslow TW3 96 BZ84
New Malden KT3 138 CR96
Ruislip HA4 59 BR58
St. Albans AL2 8 CB25
Slough SL3 93 BB79
South Ockendon RM15 91 FW69
Southall UB1 78 BZ70
Laburnum Ho, Dag. RM10 off Bradwell Av 70 FA61
Laburnum Pl, Egh. (Eng.Grn) TW20 112 AV93
Laburnum Rd, SW19 120 DC94
Chertsey KT16 134 BG102
Epping (Cooper.) CM16 18 EW29
Epsom KT18 156 CS113
Hayes UB3 95 BT77
Mitcham CR4 140 DG96
Woking GU22 166 AX120
Laburnum St, E2 84 DT67
Laburnum Wk, Horn. RM12 72 FJ64
Laburnum Way, Brom. BR2 145 EN101
Staines TW19 114 BM88
Waltham Cross (Chsht) EN7 off Millcrest Rd 13 DP28
Lacebark Cl, Sid. DA15 125 ET87
Lacey Av, Couls. CR5 175 DN120
Lacey Cl, N9 46 DU47
Egham TW20 113 BD94
Lacey Dr, Couls. CR5 175 DN120
Dagenham RM8 70 EV63
Edgware HA8 42 CL49
Hampton TW12 136 BZ95
Lacey Grn, Couls. CR5 175 DN120
Lacey Wk, E3 85 EA68
Lackford Rd, Couls. CR5 174 DF118
Lackington St, EC2 197 L6
Lackmore Rd, Enf. EN1 30 DW35
Lacock Cl, SW19 120 DC93
Lacock Ct, W13 off Singapore Rd 79 CG74
Lacon Rd, SE22 102 DU84
Lacy Rd, SW15 99 CX84
Ladas Rd, SE27 122 DQ91
Ladbroke Ct, Red. RH1 184 DG132
Ladbroke Cres, W11 off Ladbroke Gro 81 CY72
Ladbroke Gdns, W11 81 CZ73
⊖ Ladbroke Grove 81 CY72
Ladbroke Gro, W10 81 CX70
W11 81 CY72
Redhill RH1 184 DG133
Ladbroke Ms, W11 off Ladbroke Rd 81 CY74
Ladbroke Rd, W11 81 CZ74
Enfield EN1 30 DT44
Epsom KT18 156 CR114
Redhill RH1 184 DG133
Ladbroke Sq, W11 81 CZ73
Ladbroke Ter, W11 81 CZ73
Ladbroke Wk, W11 81 CZ74
Ladbrook Cl, Pnr. HA5 60 BZ57
Ladbrooke Cl, Pot.B. EN6 off Strafford Gate 12 DA32
Ladbrooke Cres, Sid. DA14 126 EX90
Ladbrooke Dr, Pot.B. EN6 12 DA32
Ladbrook Rd, SE25 142 DR97
Ladderstile Ride, Kings.T. KT2 118 CP92
Ladderswood Way, N11 45 DJ50
Ladds Way, Swan. BR8 147 FD98
Lady Aylesford Av, Stan. HA7 41 CH50
Lady Booth Rd, Kings.T. KT1 138 CL96
Ladybower Ct, E5 off Gilpin Rd 67 DY63
Ladycroft Gdns, Orp. BR6 163 EQ106
Ladycroft Rd, SE13 103 EB83
Ladycroft Wk, Stan. HA7 41 CK53
Ladycroft Way, Orp. BR6 163 EQ106
Lady Dock Path, SE16 203 K5
Ladyfield Cl, Loug. IG10 33 EP42
Ladyfields, Grav. (Nthflt) DA11 131 GF91
Loughton IG10 33 EP42
Lady Forsdyke Way, Epsom KT19 156 CN109
Ladygate La, Ruis. HA4 59 BP58
Ladygrove, Croy. CR0 161 DY109
Lady Harewood Way, Epsom KT19 156 CN109
Lady Hay, Wor.Pk. KT4 139 CT103
Lady Margaret Rd, N19 65 DJ63
NW5 65 DJ64
Southall UB1 78 BZ71
Ladymeadow, Kings L. WD4 6 BK27
Lady's Cl, Wat. WD18 23 BV42
Ladysmith Av, E6 86 EL68
Ilford IG2 69 ER59
Ladysmith Cl, NW7 off Colenso Dr 43 CU52
Ladysmith Rd, E16 86 EF69
N17 46 DU54
N18 46 DV50
SE9 125 EN86
Enfield EN1 30 DS41
Harrow HA3 41 CE54
Lady Somerset Rd, NW5 65 DH63
Ladythorpe Cl, Add. KT15 off Church Rd 152 BH105
Ladywalk, Rick. (Map.Cr.) WD3 37 BE50
LADYWELL, SE13 123 EA85
⇌ Ladywell 123 EB85
H Ladywell Cen, SE4 123 EA86
Ladywell Cl, SE4 off Adelaide Av 103 DZ84
Ladywell Hts, SE4 123 DZ86
Ladywell Rd, SE13 123 EA85
Ladywell St, E15 off Plaistow Gro 86 EF67
Ladywood Av, Orp. BR5 145 ES99
Ladywood Cl, Rick. WD3 22 BH41
Ladywood Rd, Dart. (Lane End) DA2 129 FS92
Surbiton KT6 138 CN103
Lady Yorke Pk, Iver SL0 75 BD65
Lafone Av, Felt. TW13 off Alfred Rd 116 BW88
Lafone St, SE1 201 P4
Lagado Ms, SE16 203 J3
Lagger, The, Ch.St.G. HP8 36 AV48
Lagger Cl, Ch.St.G. HP8 36 AV48
Laglands Cl, Reig. RH2 184 DC132
Lagonda Av, Ilf. IG6 49 ET51
Lagonda Way, Dart. DA1 108 FJ84
Lagoon Rd, Orp. BR5 146 EV99
Laidlaw Dr, N21 29 DM42
Laing Cl, Ilf. IG6 49 ER51
Laing Dean, Nthlt. UB5 78 BW67
Laings Av, Mitch. CR4 140 DF96
Lainlock Pl, Houns. TW3 off Spring Gro Rd 96 CB81
Lainson St, SW18 120 DA87
Lairdale Cl, SE21 122 DQ88
Laird Av, Grays RM16 110 GD75
Laird Ho, SE5 102 DQ80
Lairs Cl, N7 off Manger Rd 83 DL65
Laitwood Rd, SW12 121 DH88
Lake, The, Bushey (Bushey Hth) WD23 40 CC46
Lake Av, Brom. BR1 124 EG93
Rainham RM13 90 FK68
Lake Cl, SW19 off Lake Rd 119 CZ92
Dagenham RM8 off Winding Way 70 EX62
West Byfleet (Byfleet) KT14 152 BK112
Lakedale Rd, SE18 105 ES79
Lake Dr, Bushey (Bushey Hth) WD23 40 CC47
Lakefield Cl, SE20 off Limes Av 122 DV94
Lakefield Rd, N22 45 DP54
Lakefields Cl, Rain. RM13 90 FK68
Lake Gdns, Dag. RM10 70 FA64
Richmond TW10 117 CH89
Wallington SM6 141 DH104
Lakehall Gdns, Th.Hth. CR7 141 DP99
Lakehall Rd, Th.Hth. CR7 141 DP99
Lake Ho Rd, E11 68 EG62
Lakehurst Rd, Epsom KT19 156 CS106
Lakeland Cl, Chig. IG7 50 EV49
Harrow HA3 41 CD51
Lakenheath, N14 29 DK44
Lake Ri, Grays RM20 109 FU77
Romford RM1 71 FF55
Lake Rd, SW19 119 CZ92

★ Place of interest ⇌ Railway station ⊖ London Underground station DLR Docklands Light Railway station Tra Tramlink station H Hospital Riv Pedestrian ferry landing stage

Lake Rd, Croydon CR0 143 DZ103
Romford RM6 70 EX56
Virginia Water GU25 132 AV98
Laker Pl, SW15 119 CZ86
Lakers Ri, Bans. SM7 174 DE116
Lakeside, N3 44 DB54
W13 off Edgehill Rd 79 CJ72
Beckenham BR3 143 EB97
Enfield EN2 29 DK42
Rainham RM13 90 FL68
Redhill RH1 184 DG132
Wallington SM6
off Derek Av 141 DH104
Weybridge KT13 135 BS103
Woking GU21 166 AS119
Lakeside Av, SE28 88 EU74
Ilford IG4 68 EK56
Lakeside Cl, SE25 142 DU96
Chigwell IG7 49 ET49
Ruislip HA4 59 BR56
Sidcup DA15 126 EW85
Woking GU21 166 AS119
Lakeside Ct, N4 65 DP61
Borehamwood (Elstree) WD6
off Cavendish Cres 26 CN43
Lakeside Cres, Barn. EN4 28 DF43
Brentwood CM14 54 FX48
Weybridge KT13
off Churchill Dr 135 BQ104
Lakeside Dr, Brom. BR2 144 EL104
Esher KT10 154 CC107
Slough (Stoke P.) SL2 74 AS67
Lakeside Gra, Wey. KT13 135 BQ104
Lakeside Pl, St.Alb.
(Lon.Col.) AL2 9 CK27
Lakeside Rd, N13 45 DM49
W14 99 CX76
Slough SL3 93 BF80
Waltham Cross
(Chsht) EN8 14 DW28
Lakeside Way, Wem. HA9 62 CN63
Lakes Rd, Kes. BR2 162 EJ106
Lakeswood Rd, Orp. BR5 145 EP100
Lake Vw, Edg. HA8 42 CM50
Potters Bar EN6 12 DC33
Lakeview Ct, SW19
off Victoria Dr 119 CY89
Lakeview Rd, SE27 121 DN92
Lake Vw Rd, Sev. TN13 190 FG122
Lakeview Rd, Well. DA16 106 EV84
Lakis Cl, NW3 off Flask Wk 64 DC63
LALEHAM, Stai. TW18 134 BJ97
Laleham Av, NW7 42 CR48
Laleham Cl, Stai. TW18
off Worple Rd 134 BH95
Laleham Ct, Wok. GU21 166 AY116
★ Laleham Heritage Cen,
Stai. TW18 134 BJ97
Laleham Pk, Stai. TW18 134 BJ98
Laleham Reach, Cher. KT16 134 BH96
Laleham Rd, SE6 123 EC86
Shepperton TW17 134 BM98
Staines TW18 113 BF92
Lalor St, SW6 99 CY82
Lambarde Av, SE9 125 EN91
Lambarde Dr, Sev. TN13 190 FG123
Lambarde Rd, Sev. TN13 190 FG122
Lambardes Cl, Orp. BR6 164 EW110
Lamb Cl, Nthlt. UB5
off Ruislip Rd 78 BY69
Tilbury RM18
off Coleridge Rd 111 GJ82
Watford WD25 8 BW34
Lamberhurst Cl, Orp. BR5 146 EX102
Lamberhurst Rd, SE27 121 DN91
Dagenham RM8 70 EZ60
Lambert Av, Rich. TW9 98 CP83
Slough SL3 92 AY75
Lambert Cl, West.
(Bigg.H.) TN16 178 EK116
Lambert Ct, Bushey WD23 24 BX42
Lambert Jones Ms, EC2
off The Barbican 84 DQ71
Lambert Rd, E16 86 EH72
N12 44 DD50
SW2 121 DL85
Banstead SM7 158 DA114
Lamberts Pl, Croy. CR0 142 DR102
Lamberts Rd, Surb. KT5 138 CL99
Lambert St, N1 83 DN66
Lambert Wk, Wem. HA9 61 CK62
Lambert Way, N12
off Woodhouse Rd 44 DC50
LAMBETH, SE1 200 B6
Lambeth Br, SE1 200 A8
SW1 200 A8
Lambeth High St, SE1 200 B9
Lambeth Hill, EC4 197 H10
⊖ Lambeth North 200 D5
★ Lambeth Palace, SE1 200 B7
Lambeth Palace Rd, SE1 200 B7
Lambeth Rd, SE1 200 C7
SE11 200 C7
Croydon CR0 141 DN101
Lambeth Wk, SE11 200 C8
Lamb La, E8 84 DV66
Lamble St, NW5 64 DG64
Lambley Rd, Dag. RM9 88 EV65
Lambly Hill, Vir.W. GU25 132 AY97
Lambolle Pl, NW3 82 DE65
Lambolle Rd, NW3 82 DE65
Lambourn Chase, Rad. WD7 25 CF36
Lambourn Cl, W7 97 CF75
South Croydon CR2 159 DP109
Lambourne Av, SW19 119 CZ91
Lambourne Cl, Chig. IG7 50 EV48
Lambourne Ct, Wdf.Grn. IG8
off Navestock Cres 48 EJ52
Lambourne Cres, Chig. IG7 50 EV47
Woking GU21 151 BD113
Lambourne Dr, Brwd.
(Hutt.) CM13 55 GE45
Cobham KT11 170 BX115
LAMBOURNE END,
Rom. RM4 34 EX44
Lambourne Gdns, E4 47 EA47
Barking IG11
off Lambourne Rd 87 ET66
Enfield EN1 30 DT40
Hornchurch RM12 72 FK61
Lambourne Gro, Kings.T. KT1
off Kenley Rd 138 CP96
Lambourne Pl, SE3
off Shooter's Hill Rd 104 EH81
Lambourne Rd, E11 67 EC59
Barking IG11 87 ES66
Chigwell IG7 49 ES49
Ilford IG3 69 ES61
Lambourn Rd, SW4 101 DH83
Lambrook Ter, SW6 99 CY81
Lamb's Bldgs, EC1 197 K5
Lambs Cl, Pot.B.
(Cuffley) EN6 13 DM29
Lambs Conduit Pas, WC1 196 B6
Lamb's Conduit St, WC1 196 B5
Lambscroft Av, SE9 124 EJ90
Lambscroft Way, Ger.Cr.
(Chal.St.P.) SL9 36 AY54
Lambs La N, Rain. RM13 90 FJ70
Lambs La S, Rain. RM13 89 FH71
Lambs Meadow,
Wdf.Grn. IG8 48 EK54
Lambs Ms, N1
off Colebrooke Row 83 DP67
Lamb's Pas, EC1 197 K6
Lambs Ter, N9 46 DR47
Lamb St, E1 197 P6
Lambs Wk, Enf. EN2 30 DQ40
Lambton Av, Wal.Cr. EN8 15 DX32
Lambton Ms, N19
off Lambton Rd 65 DL60
Lambton Pl, W11
off Westbourne Gro 81 CZ72
Lambton Rd, N19 65 DL60
SW20 139 CW95
Lamb Wk, SE1 201 M5
Lamb Yd, Wat. WD17 24 BX43
Lamerock Rd, Brom. BR1 124 EF91
Lamerton Rd, Ilf. IG6 49 EP54
Lamerton St, SE8 103 EA79
Lamford Cl, N17 46 DR52
Lamington St, W6 99 CV77
Lamlash St, SE11 200 F8
Lammas Av, Mitch. CR4 140 DG96
Lammas Cl, Stai. TW18 113 BE90
Lammas Ct, Stai. TW19 113 BD89
Lammas Dr, Stai. TW18 113 BD90
Lammas Grn, SE26 122 DV90
Lammas La, Esher KT10 154 CA106
Lammas Pk, W5 97 CJ75
Lammas Pk Gdns, W5 97 CJ75
Lammas Pk Rd, W5 79 CJ74
Lammas Rd, E9 85 DX66
E10 67 DY61
Richmond TW10 117 CJ91
Watford WD18 24 BW43
Lammermoor Rd, SW12 121 DH87
Lamont Rd, SW10 100 DC79
Lamont Rd Pas, SW10
off Lamont Rd 100 DD79
LAMORBEY, Sid. DA15 125 ET88
Lamorbey Cl, Sid. DA15 125 ET88
Lamorna Av, Grav. DA12 131 GJ90
Lamorna Cl, E17 47 EC53
Orpington BR6 146 EU101
Radlett WD7 9 CH34
Lamorna Gro, Stan. HA7 41 CK53
Lampard Gro, N16 66 DT60
Lampern Sq, E2
off Nelson Gdns 84 DU69
Lampeter Cl, NW9 62 CS58
Woking GU22 166 AY118
Lampeter Sq, W6
off Humbolt Rd 99 CY79
Lamplighter Cl, E1
off Cleveland Way 84 DW70
Lamplighters Cl, Dart. DA1 128 FM86
Waltham Abbey EN9 16 EG34
Lampmead Rd, SE12 124 EE85
Lamp Office Ct, WC1 196 B5
Lamport Cl, SE18 105 EM77
LAMPTON, Houns. TW3 96 CB81
Lampton Av, Houns. TW3 96 CB81
Lampton Ho Cl, SW19 119 CX91
Lampton Pk Rd, Houns. TW3 96 CB82
Lampton Rd, Houns. TW3 96 CB82
Lamson Rd, Rain. RM13 89 FF70
Lanacre Av, NW9 43 CT53
Lanark Cl, W5 79 CJ71
Lanark Ms, W9 off Lanark Rd 82 DC69
Lanark Pl, W9 82 DC70
Lanark Rd, W9 82 DB68
Lanark Sq, E14 204 C6
Lanata Wk, Hayes UB4
off Ramulis Dr 78 BX70
Lanbury Rd, SE15 103 DX84
Lancashire Ct, W1 195 J10
Lancaster Av, E18 68 EH56
SE27 121 DP89
SW19 119 CX92
Barking IG11 87 ES66
Barnet EN4 28 DD38
Mitcham CR4 141 DL99
Lancaster Cl, N1
off Hertford Rd 84 DS66
N17 off Park La 46 DU52
NW9 43 CT52
Ashford TW15
off Station Cres 114 BL91
Brentwood (Pilg.Hat.) CM15 54 FU43
Bromley BR2 144 EF98
Egham TW20 112 AX92
Kingston upon Thames KT2 117 CK92
Staines (Stanw.) TW19 114 BL86
Woking GU21 167 BA116
Lancaster Cotts, Rich. TW10
off Lancaster Pk 118 CL86
Lancaster Ct, SE27 121 DP89
SW6 99 CZ80
W2 off Lancaster Gate 82 DC73
Banstead SM7 157 CZ114
Walton-on-Thames KT12 135 BU101
Lancaster Dr, E14 204 E3
NW3 82 DE65
Hemel Hempstead
(Bov.) HP3 5 AZ27
Hornchurch RM12 71 FH64
Loughton IG10 32 EL44
Lancaster Gdns, SW19 119 CY92
W13 97 CH75
Lancaster Gdns, Bromley BR1
off Southborough Rd 144 EL99
Kingston upon Thames KT2 117 CK92
⊖ Lancaster Gate 82 DD73
Lancaster Gate, W2 82 DC73
Lancaster Gro, NW3 82 DD65
★ Lancaster Ho, SW1 199 K4
Lancaster Ms, SW18
off East Hill 120 DB85
W2 82 DC73
Richmond TW10
off Richmond Hill 118 CL86
Lancaster Pk, Rich. TW10 118 CL85
Lancaster Pl, SW19
off Lancaster Rd 119 CX92
WC2 196 B10
Hounslow TW4 96 BW82
Ilford IG1 off Staines Rd 69 EQ64
Twickenham TW1 117 CG86
Lancaster Rd, E7 86 EG66
E11 68 EE61
E17 47 DX54
N4 65 DN59
N11 45 DK51
N18 46 DT50
NW10 63 CT64
SE25 142 DT96
SW19 119 CX92
W11 81 CY72
Barnet EN4 28 DD43
Enfield EN2 30 DR39
Epping (N.Wld Bas.) CM16 18 FA26
Grays (Chaff.Hun.) RM16 109 FX78
Harrow HA2 60 CA57
Northolt UB5 78 CC65
Southall UB1 78 BY73
Uxbridge UB8 76 BK65
Lancaster St, SE1 200 G5
Lancaster Ter, W2 82 DD73
Lancaster Wk, W2 82 DC74
Hayes UB3 77 BQ72
Lancaster Way, Abb.L. WD5 7 BT31
Worcester Park KT4 139 CV101
Lancaster W, W11
off Grenfell Rd 81 CX73
Lancastrian Rd, Wall. SM6 159 DL108
Lancefield St, W10 81 CZ69
Lancell St, N16
off Stoke Newington Ch St 66 DS61
Lancelot Av, Wem. HA0 61 CK63
Lancelot Cres, Wem. HA0 61 CK63
Lancelot Gdns, Barn. EN4 44 DG45
Lancelot Pl, SW7 198 D5
Lancelot Rd, Ilf. IG6 49 ES51
Welling DA16 106 EU84
Wembley HA0 61 CK64
Lance Rd, Har. HA1 60 CC59
Lancer Sq, W8 off Old Ct Pl 100 DB75
Lancey Cl, SE7
off Cleveley Cl 104 EK77
Lanchester Rd, N6 64 DF57
Lanchester Way, SE14 102 DW81
Lancing Gdns, N9 46 DT46
Lancing Rd, W13
off Drayton Grn Rd 79 CH73
Croydon CR0 141 DM100
Feltham TW13 115 BT89
Ilford IG2 69 ER58
Orpington BR6 146 EU103
Romford RM3 52 FL52
Lancing St, NW1 195 M3
Lancing Way, Rick.
(Crox.Grn) WD3 23 BP43
Lancresse Cl, Uxb. UB8 76 BK65
Lancresse Ct, N1 84 DS67
Landale Gdns, Dart. DA1 128 FJ87
Landau Way, Brox. EN10 15 DZ26
Erith DA8 108 FK78
Landcroft Rd, SE22 122 DT86
Landells Rd, SE22 122 DT86
Lander Rd, Grays RM17 110 GD78
Landford Cl, Rick. WD3 38 BL47
Landford Rd, SW15 99 CW83
Landgrove Rd, SW19 120 DA92
Landmann Way, SE14 103 DX79
Landmark Hts, E5 67 DY63
Landmead Rd, Wal.Cr.
(Chsht) EN8 15 DY29
Landon Pl, SW1 198 D6
Landons Cl, E14 204 E2
Landon Wk, E14
off Cottage St 85 EB73
Landon Way, Ashf. TW15
off Courtfield Rd 115 BP93
Landor Rd, SW9 101 DL83
Landor Wk, W12 99 CU75
Landport Way, SE15
off Daniel Gdns 102 DT80
Landra Gdns, N21 29 DP44
Landridge Dr, Enf. EN1 30 DV38
Landridge Rd, SW6 99 CZ82
Landrock Rd, N8 65 DL58
Landscape Rd, Warl. CR6 176 DV119
Woodford Green IG8 48 EH52
Landseer Av, E12 69 EN64
Gravesend (Nthflt) DA11 130 GD90
Landseer Cl, SW19
off Brangwyn Cres 140 DC95
Edgware HA8 42 CN54
Hornchurch RM11 71 FH60
Landseer Rd, N19 65 DL62
Enfield EN1 30 DU43
New Malden KT3 138 CR101
Sutton SM1 158 DA107
Lands End, Borwd.
(Elstree) WD6 25 CK44
Landstead Rd, SE18 105 ER80
Landway, The, Orp. BR5 146 EW97
Lane, The, NW8
off Marlborough Pl 82 DC68
SE3 104 EG83
Chertsey KT16 134 BG97
Virginia Water GU25 132 AY97
Lane App, NW7 43 CY50
Lane Av, Green. DA9 129 FW86
Lane Cl, NW2 63 CV62
Addlestone KT15 152 BG106
LANE END, Dart. DA2 129 FR92
Lane End, Bexh. DA7 107 FB83
Epsom KT18 156 CP114
Lane Gdns, Bushey
(Bushey Hth) WD23 41 CE45
Esher KT10 off Vale Rd 155 CF108
Lane Ms, E12
off Colchester Av 69 EM62
Lanercost Cl, SW2 121 DN89
Lanercost Gdns, N14 45 DL45
Lanercost Rd, SW2 121 DN89
Lanes Av, Grav. (Nthflt) DA11 131 GG90
Lanesborough Pl, SW1 198 G4
Laneside, Chis. BR7 125 EP92
Edgware HA8 42 CQ50
Laneside Av, Dag. RM8 70 EZ59
Laneway, SW15 119 CV85
Lane Wd Cl, Amer. HP7 20 AT39
Lanfranc Rd, E3 85 DY68
Lanfrey Pl, W14
off North End Rd 99 CZ78
Langaller La, Lthd. KT22 170 CB122
Langbourne Av, N6 64 DG61
Langbourne Pl, E14 204 B10
Langbourne Way, Esher
(Clay.) KT10 155 CG107
Langbrook Rd, SE3 104 EK83
Lang Cl, Lthd. (Fetch.) KT22 170 CB123
Langcroft Cl, Cars. SM5 140 DF104
Langdale Av, Mitch. CR4 140 DF97
Langdale Cl, SE17 102 DQ79
SW14 98 CP84
Dagenham RM8 70 EW60
Orpington BR6
off Grasmere Rd 145 EP104
Woking GU21 166 AW116
Langdale Cres, Bexh. DA7 106 FA80
Langdale Dr, Hayes UB4 77 BS68
Langdale Gdns, Grnf. UB6 79 CH69
Hornchurch RM12 71 FG64
Waltham Cross EN8 31 DX35
Langdale Rd, SE10 103 EC80
Thornton Heath CR7 141 DN98
Langdale St, E1
off Burslem St 84 DV72
Langdale Wk, Grav. (Nthflt) DA11
off Landseer Av 130 GE90
Langdon Ct, NW10 80 CS67
Langdon Cres, E6 87 EN68
Langdon Dr, NW9 62 CQ60
Langdon Pk, Tedd. TW11 117 CJ94
Langdon Pk Rd, N6 65 DJ59
Langdon Pl, SW14
off Rosemary La 98 CQ83
Langdon Rd, E6 87 EN67
Bromley BR2 144 EH97
Morden SM4 140 DC99
Langdons Ct, Sthl. UB2 96 CA76
Langdon Shaw, Sid. DA14 125 ET92
Langdon Wk, Mord. SM4 140 DC99
Langdon Way, SE1 202 C9
Langford Cl, E8 66 DU64
N15 66 DS58
NW8 off Langford Pl 82 DC68
W3 98 CP75
Langford Ct, NW8 82 DC68
Langford Cres, Barn. EN4 28 DF42
Langford Grn, SE5 102 DS83
Brentwood (Hutt.) CM13 55 GC44
Langford Pl, NW8 82 DC68
Sidcup DA14 126 EU90
Langford Rd, SW6 100 DB82
Barnet EN4 28 DE42
Woodford Green IG8 48 EJ51
Langfords, Buck.H. IG9 48 EK47
Langfords Way, Croy. CR0 161 DY111
Langham Cl, N15
off Langham Rd 65 DP55
Langham Ct, Horn. RM11 72 FK59
Langham Dene, Ken. CR8 175 DP115
Langham Dr, Rom. RM6 70 EV58
Langham Gdns, N21 29 DN43
W13 79 CH73
Edgware HA8 42 CQ52
Richmond TW10 117 CJ91
Wembley HA0 61 CJ61
Langham Ho Cl, Rich. TW10 117 CK91
Langham Pk Pl, Brom. BR2 144 EF98
Langham Pl, N15 65 DP55
W1 195 J7
W4 off Hogarth Roundabout 98 CS79
Egham TW20 113 AZ92
Langham Rd, N15 65 DP55
SW20 139 CW95
Edgware HA8 42 CQ51
Teddington TW11 117 CH92
Langham St, W1 195 J7
Langhedge Cl, N18
off Langhedge La 46 DT51
Langhedge La, N18 46 DT50
Langhedge La Ind Est, N18 46 DT51
Langholm Cl, SW12
off King's Av 121 DK87
Langholme, Bushey WD23 40 CC46
Langhorn Dr, Twick. TW2 117 CE87
Langhorne Rd, Dag. RM10 88 FA66
Langland Ct, Nthwd. HA6 39 BQ52
Langland Cres, Stan. HA7 62 CL55
Langland Dr, Pnr. HA5 40 BY52
Langland Gdns, NW3 64 DB64
Croydon CR0 143 DZ103
Langlands Dr, Dart.
(Lane End) DA2 129 FS92
Langlands Ri, Epsom KT19
off Burnet Gro 156 CQ113
Langler Rd, NW10 81 CW68
LANGLEY, Slou. SL3 93 BA76
⇌ Langley 93 BA75
Langley Av, Ruis. HA4 59 BV60
Surbiton KT6 137 CK102
Worcester Park KT4 139 CX103
Langley Broom, Slou. SL3 93 AZ78
LANGLEYBURY, Kings L. WD4 7 BP34
Langleybury La, Kings L. WD4 23 BP37
Langley Business Cen, Slou.
(Langley) SL3 93 BA75
Langley Cl, Epsom KT18 172 CR119
Romford RM3 52 FK52
Langley Cor, Slou.
(Fulmer) SL3 75 AZ65
Langley Ct, WC2 195 P10
Beckenham BR3 143 EB99
Langley Cres, E11 68 EJ59
Langley Cres, Dagenham RM9 88 EW66
Edgware HA8 42 CQ48
Hayes UB3 95 BT80
Kings Langley WD4 6 BN30
Langley Dr, E11 68 EH59
W3 80 CP74
Brentwood CM14 54 FU48
Langley Gdns, Brom. BR2 144 EJ98
Dagenham RM9 88 EW66
Orpington BR5 145 EP100
Langley Gro, N.Mal. KT3 138 CS96
Langley Hill, Kings L. WD4 6 BM29
Langley Hill Cl, Kings L. WD4 6 BN29
Langley La, SW8 101 DM79
Abbots Langley WD5 7 BT31
Epsom (Headley) KT18 182 CP125
Langley Lo La, Kings L. WD4 6 BN31
Langley Meadow, Loug. IG10 33 ER40
Langley Oaks Av, S.Croy.
CR2 160 DU110
Langley Pk, NW7 42 CS51
★ Langley Park Country Pk,
Slou. SL3 75 BA70
Langley Pk Rd, Iver SL0 75 BC72
Slough SL3 93 BA75
Sutton SM1, SM2 158 DC106
Langley Quay, Slou.
(Langley) SL3 93 BA75
Langley Rd, SW19 139 CZ95
Abbots Langley WD5 7 BS31
Beckenham BR3 143 DY98
Isleworth TW7 97 CF82
Kings Langley
(Chipper.) WD4 6 BH30
Slough SL3 92 AW75
South Croydon CR2 161 DX109
Staines TW18 113 BF93
Surbiton KT6 138 CL101
Watford WD17 23 BU39
Welling DA16 106 EW79
Langley Row, Barn. EN5 27 CZ39
Langley St, WC2 195 P9
LANGLEY VALE, Epsom KT18 172 CR120
Langley Vale Rd, Epsom KT18 172 CR118
Langley Wk, Wok. GU22
off Midhope Rd 166 AY119
Langley Way, Wat. WD17 23 BS40
West Wickham BR4 143 ED102
Langmans La, Wok. GU21 166 AV118
Langmans Way, Wok. GU21 166 AS116
Langmead Dr, Bushey
(Bushey Hth) WD23 41 CD46
Langmead St, SE27
off Beadman St 121 DP91
Langmore Ct, Bexh. DA6
off Regency Way 106 EX83
Langport Ct, Walt. KT12 136 BW102
Langridge Ms, Hmptn. TW12
off Oak Av 116 BZ93
Langroyd Rd, SW17 120 DF89
Langshott Cl, Add.
(Wdhm) KT15 151 BE111
Langside Av, SW15 99 CU84
Langside Cres, N14 45 DK48
Langston Hughes Cl, SE24
off Shakespeare Rd 101 DP84
Langston Rd, Loug. IG10 33 EQ43
Lang St, E1 84 DW70
Langthorn Ct, EC2 197 K8
Langthorne Cres,
Grays RM17 110 GC77
Langthorne Rd, E11 67 ED62
Langthorne St, SW6 99 CX80
Langton Av, E6 87 EN69
N20 44 DC45
Epsom KT17 157 CT111
Langton Cl, WC1 196 C3
Addlestone KT15 134 BH104
Woking GU21 166 AT117
Langton Gro, Nthwd. HA6 39 BQ50
Langton Ho, SW16
off Colson Way 121 DJ91
Langton Pl, SW18
off Merton Rd 120 DA88
Langton Ri, SE23 122 DV87
Langton Rd, NW2 63 CW62
SW9 101 DP80
Harrow HA3 40 CC52
West Molesey KT8 136 CC98
Langton St, SW10 100 DC79
Langton Way, SE3 104 EF81
Croydon CR0 160 DS105
Egham TW20 113 BC93
Grays RM16 111 GJ77
Langtry Pl, SW6
off Seagrave Rd 100 DA79
Langtry Rd, NW8 82 DB67
Northolt UB5 78 BX68
Langtry Wk, NW8
off Alexandra Pl 82 DC66
Langwood Chase, Tedd. TW11 117 CJ93
Langwood Cl, Ashtd. KT21 172 CN117
Langwood Gdns, Wat. WD17 23 BU39
Langworth Cl, Dart. DA2 128 FK90
Langworth Dr, Hayes UB4 77 BU72
Lanhill Rd, W9 82 DA70
Lanier Rd, SE13 123 EC86
Lanigan Dr, Houns. TW3 116 CB85
Lankaster Gdns, N2 44 DD53
Lankers Dr, Har. HA2 60 BZ58
Lankton Cl, Beck. BR3 143 EC95
Lannock Rd, Hayes UB3 77 BS74
Lannoy Rd, SE9 125 EQ88
Lanrick Rd, E14 85 ED72
Lanridge Rd, SE2 106 EX76
Lansbury Av, N18 46 DR50
Barking IG11 88 EU66
Feltham TW14 115 BV86
Romford RM6 70 EY57
Lansbury Cl, NW10 62 CQ64
Lansbury Cres, Dart. DA1 128 FN85
Lansbury Dr, Hayes UB4 77 BT71
Lansbury Est, E14 85 EB72
Lansbury Gdns, E14 85 ED72
Tilbury RM18 111 GG81

★ Place of interest ⇌ Railway station ⊖ London Underground station DLR Docklands Light Railway station Tram Tramlink station H Hospital Riv Pedestrian ferry landing stage

Lansbury Rd, Enf. EN3 31 DX39
Lansbury Way, N18 46 DS50
Lanscombe Wk, SW8 101 DL81
Lansdell Rd, Mitch. CR4 140 DG96
Lansdown Cl, Walt. KT12
 off St. Johns Dr 136 BW102
 Woking GU21 166 AT119
Lansdowne Av, Bexh. DA7 106 EX80
 Orpington BR6 145 EP102
 Slough SL1 74 AS74
Lansdowne Cl, SW20 119 CX94
 Surbiton KT5
 off Kingston Rd 138 CP103
 Twickenham TW1
 off Lion Rd 117 CF88
 Watford WD25 8 BX34
Lansdowne Copse, Wor.Pk. KT4
 off The Avenue 139 CU103
Lansdowne Ct, Pur. CR8 159 DP110
 Slough SL1 74 AS74
 Worcester Park KT4
 off The Avenue 139 CU103
Lansdowne Cres, W11 81 CY73
Lansdowne Dr, E8 84 DU65
Lansdowne Gdns, SW8 101 DL81
Lansdowne Grn, SW8
 off Hartington Rd 101 DL81
Lansdowne Gro, NW10 62 CS63
Lansdowne Hill, SE27 121 DP90
Lansdowne La, SE7 104 EK79
Lansdowne Ms, SE7 104 EK78
 W11 off Lansdowne Rd 81 CZ74
Lansdowne Pl, SE1 201 L7
 SE19 122 DT94
Lansdowne Ri, W11 81 CY73
Lansdowne Rd, E4 47 EA47
 E11 68 EF61
 E17 67 EA57
 E18 68 EG55
 N3 43 CZ52
 N10 45 DJ54
 N17 46 DT53
 SW20 119 CW94
 W11 81 CY73
 Bromley BR1 124 EG94
 Croydon CR0 142 DR103
Lansdowne Rd,
 Epsom KT19 156 CQ108
 Harrow HA1 61 CE59
 Hounslow TW3 96 CB83
 Ilford IG3 69 ET60
 Purley CR8 159 DN112
 Sevenoaks TN13 191 FK122
 Staines TW18 114 BH94
 Stanmore HA7 41 CJ51
 Tilbury RM18 111 GF82
 Uxbridge UB8 77 BP72
Lansdowne Row, W1 199 J2
Lansdowne Sq, Grav.
 (Nthflt) DA11 131 GF86
Lansdowne Ter, WC1 196 A5
Lansdowne Wk, W11 81 CY74
Lansdowne Way, SW8 101 DK81
Lansdowne Wd Cl, SE27 121 DP90
Lansdown Pl, Grav.
 (Nthflt) DA11 131 GF88
Lansdown Rd, E7 86 EJ66
 Gerrards Cross
 (Chal.St.P.) SL9 36 AX53
 Sidcup DA14 126 EV90
Lansfield Av, N18 46 DU49
Lantern Cl, SW15 99 CU84
 Wembley HA0 61 CK64
Lanterns Ct, E14 204 A5
Lantern Way, West Dr. UB7 94 BL75
Lant St, SE1 201 H4
Lanvanor Rd, SE15 102 DW82
Lapford Cl, W9 81 CZ70
La Plata Gro, Brwd. CM14 54 FV48
Lapponum Wk, Hayes UB4
 off Lochan Cl 78 BX71
Lapse Wd Wk, SE23 122 DV88
Lapstone Gdns, Har. HA3 61 CJ58
Lapwing Cl, Erith DA8 107 FH80
 South Croydon CR2 161 DY110
Lapwing Ct, Surb. KT6
 off Chaffinch Cl 138 CN104
Lapwings, The, Grav. DA12 131 GK89
Lapwing Twr, SE8
 off Abinger Gro 103 DZ79
Lapwing Way, Abb.L. WD5 7 BU31
 Hayes UB4 78 BX72
Lapworth Cl, Orp. BR6 146 EW103
Lara Cl, SE13 123 EC86
 Chessington KT9 156 CL108
Larbert Rd, SW16 141 DJ95
Larby Pl, Epsom KT17 156 CS110
Larch Av, W3 80 CS74
 St. Albans (Brick.Wd) AL2 8 BY30
Larch Cl, E13 86 EH70
 N11 44 DG52
 N19 off Bredgar Rd 65 DJ61
 SE8 off Clyde St 103 DZ79
 SW12 121 DH89
 Tadworth KT20 174 DC121
 Waltham Cross EN7
 off The Firs 14 DS27
 Warlingham CR6 177 DY119
Larch Cres, Epsom KT19 156 CP107
 Hayes UB4 78 BW70
Larchdene, Orp. BR6 145 EN103
Larch Dr, W4
 off Gunnersbury Av 98 CN78
Larches, The, N13 46 DQ48
 Amersham HP6 20 AV38
 Bushey WD23 24 BY43
 Northwood HA6
 off Rickmansworth Rd 39 BQ51
 Uxbridge UB10 77 BP69
 Woking GU21 166 AY116
Larches Av, SW14 98 CR84
 Enfield EN1 30 DW35
Larch Grn, NW9
 off Clayton Fld 42 CS53
Larch Gro, Sid. DA15 125 ET88
Larch Rd, E10 off Walnut Rd 67 EA61
 NW2 63 CW63
 Dartford DA1 128 FK87
Larch Tree Way, Croy. CR0 143 EA104
Larch Wk, Swan. BR8 147 FD96
Larch Way, Brom. BR2 145 EN101
Larchwood Av, Rom. RM5 51 FB51
Larchwood Cl, Bans. SM7 173 CY116
 Romford RM5 51 FC51
Larchwood Dr, Egh.
 (Eng.Grn) TW20 112 AV93
Larchwood Gdns, Brwd.
 (Pilg.Hat.) CM15 54 FU44
Larchwood Rd, SE9 125 EP89
Larcombe Cl, Croy. CR0 160 DT105
Larcom St, SE17 201 J9
Larden Rd, W3 80 CS74
Largewood Av, Surb. KT6 138 CN103
Largo Wk, Erith DA8
 off Selkirk Dr 107 FE81
Larissa St, SE17 201 L10
Lark Av, Stai. TW18
 off Kestrel Av 113 BF90
Larkbere Rd, SE26 123 DY91
Lark Cl, Brwd. CM14
 off Warley Hill 54 FV49
Larken Cl, Bushey WD23
 off Larken Dr 40 CC46
Larken Dr, Bushey WD23 40 CC46
Larkfield, Cob. KT11 153 BU113
Larkfield Av, Har. HA3 61 CH55
Larkfield Cl, Brom. BR2 144 EF103
Larkfield Rd, Rich. TW9 98 CL84
 Sevenoaks TN13 190 FC123
 Sidcup DA14 125 ET90
Larkfields, Grav. (Nthflt) DA11 130 GE90
Larkhall Cl, Walt. KT12 154 BW107
Larkhall La, SW4 101 DK82
Larkhall Ri, SW4 101 DJ83
Larkham Cl, Felt. TW13 115 BS90
Larkhill Ter, SE18 105 EN81
Larkin Cl, Brwd. (Hutt.) CM13 55 GC45
 Coulsdon CR5 175 DM117
Larkings La, Slou.
 (Stoke P.) SL2 74 AV67
Lark Row, E2 84 DW67
Larksfield, Egh.
 (Eng.Grn) TW20 112 AW94
Larksfield Gro, Enf. EN1 30 DV39
Larks Gro, Bark. IG11
 off Thornhill Gdns 87 ES66
Larkshall Ct, Rom. RM7 51 FC54
Larkshall Cres, E4 47 EC49
Larkshall Rd, E4 47 EC50
Larkspur Cl, E6 86 EL71
 N17 off Fryatt Rd 46 DR52
 NW9 62 CP57
 Orpington BR6 146 EW103
 Ruislip HA4 59 BQ59
 South Ockendon RM15 91 FW69
Larkspur Gro, Edg. HA8 42 CQ49
Larkspur Way, Epsom KT19 156 CQ106
Larkswood Cl, Erith DA8 107 FG81
Larkswood Ct, E4 47 ED50
Larkswood Leisure Pk, E4 47 EC49
Larkswood Ri, Pnr. HA5 60 BW56
Larkswood Rd, E4 47 EA49
Lark Way, Cars. SM5 140 DE101
Larkway Cl, NW9 62 CR56
Larmans Rd, Enf. EN3 30 DW36
Larnach Rd, W6 99 CX79
Larne Rd, Ruis. HA4 59 BT59
Larner Rd, Erith DA8 107 FE80
La Roche Cl, Slou. SL3 92 AW76
Larpent Av, SW15 119 CW85
Larsen Dr, Wal.Abb. EN9 15 ED34
Larwood Cl, Grnf. UB6 61 CD64
Lascelles Av, Har. HA1 61 CD59
Lascelles Cl, E11 67 ED61
 Brentwood (Pilg.Hat.) CM15 54 FU43
Lascelles Rd, Slou. SL3 92 AV76
Lascotts Rd, N22 45 DM51
Las Palmas Est, Shep. TW17 135 BQ101
Lassa Rd, SE9 124 EL85
Lassell St, SE10 103 ED78
Lasseter Pl, SE3
 off Vanbrugh Hill 104 EF79
Lasswade Rd, Cher. KT16 133 BF101
Latchett Rd, E18 48 EH53
Latchford Pl, Chig. IG7
 off Manford Way 50 EV49
Latching Cl, Rom. RM3
 off Troopers Dr 52 FK49
Latchingdon Ct, E17 67 DX56
Latchingdon Gdns,
 Wdf.Grn. IG8 48 EL51
Latchmere Cl, Rich. TW10 118 CL92
Latchmere La, Kings.T. KT2 118 CM93
Latchmere Pas, SW11
 off Cabul Rd 100 DE82
Latchmere Rd, SW11 100 DF82
 Kingston upon Thames KT2 118 CL94
Latchmere St, SW11 100 DF82
Latchmoor Av, Ger.Cr.
 (Chal.St.P.) SL9 56 AX56
Latchmoor Gro, Ger.Cr.
 (Chal.St.P.) SL9 56 AX56
Latchmoor Way, Ger.Cr.
 (Chal.St.P.) SL9 56 AX56
Lateward Rd, Brent. TW8 97 CK79
Latham Cl, E6
 off Oliver Gdns 86 EL72
 Dartford DA2 129 FS89
 Twickenham TW1 117 CG87
 Westerham (Bigg.H.) TN16 178 EJ116
Latham Ho, E1 85 DX72
Latham Rd, Bexh. DA6 126 FA85
 Twickenham TW1 117 CF87
Lathams Way, Croy. CR0 141 DM102
Lathkill Cl, Enf. EN1 46 DU45
Lathom Rd, E6 87 EM66
LATIMER, Chesh. HP5 20 AY36
Latimer, SE17
 off Beaconsfield Rd 102 DS78
Latimer Av, E6 87 EM67
Latimer Cl, Amer. HP6 20 AW39
 Pinner HA5 40 BW53
 Watford WD18 39 BS45
 Woking GU22 167 BB116
 Worcester Park KT4 157 CV105
Latimer Dr, Horn. RM12 72 FK62
Latimer Gdns, Pnr. HA5 40 BW53
H Latimer Ho Day Hosp, W1 195 K6
Latimer Pl, W10 81 CW72
⊖ Latimer Road 81 CX73
Latimer Rd, E7 68 EH63
 N15 66 DS58
 SW19 120 DB93
 W10 81 CW72
 Barnet EN5 28 DB41
 Chesham HP5 20 AU36
 Croydon CR0 off Abbey Rd 141 DP104
 Rickmansworth
 (Chenies) WD3 21 BB38
 Teddington TW11 117 CF92
Latona Dr, Grav. DA12 131 GM92
Latona Rd, SE15 102 DU79
La Tourne Gdns, Orp. BR6 145 EQ104
Lattimer Pl, W4 98 CS79
Latton Cl, Esher KT10 154 CB105
 Walton-on-Thames KT12 136 BY101
Latymer Cl, Wey. KT13 153 BQ105
Latymer Ct, W6 99 CX77
Latymer Rd, N9 46 DT46
Latymer Way, N9 46 DR47
Lauder Cl, Nthlt. UB5 78 BX68
Lauderdale Dr, Rich. TW10 117 CK90
Lauderdale Pl, EC2
 off Beech St 84 DQ71
Lauderdale Rd, W9 82 DB69
 Kings Langley WD4 7 BQ33
Lauderdale Twr, EC2 197 H6
Laud St, SE11 200 B10
 Croydon CR0 142 DQ104
Laughton Ct, Borwd. WD6
 off Banks Rd 26 CR40
Laughton Rd, Nthlt. UB5 78 BX67
Launcelot Rd, Brom. BR1 124 EG91
Launcelot St, SE1 200 D5
Launceston Cl, Rom. RM3 52 FJ53
Launceston Gdns, Grnf. UB6 79 CJ67
Launceston Pl, W8 100 DC76
Launceston Rd, Grnf. UB6 79 CJ67
Launch St, E14 204 D6
Launders La, Rain. RM13 90 FM69
Laundress La, N16 66 DU62
Laundry La, N1
 off Greenman St 84 DQ67
 Waltham Abbey EN9 16 EE25
Laundry Ms, SE23 123 DY87
Laundry Rd, W6 99 CY79
Launton Dr, Bexh. DA6
 off Danson Rd 106 EX84
Laura Cl, E11 68 EJ57
 Enfield EN1 30 DS43
Lauradale Rd, N2 64 DF56
Laura Dr, Swan. BR8 127 FG94
Laura Pl, E5 66 DW63
Laurel Av, Egh.
 (Eng.Grn) TW20 112 AV92
 Gravesend DA12 131 GJ89
 Potters Bar EN6 11 CZ32
 Slough SL3 92 AY75
 Twickenham TW1 117 CF88
Laurel Bk Gdns, SW6
 off New Kings Rd 99 CZ82
Laurel Bk Rd, Enf. EN2 30 DQ39
Laurel Bk Vil, W7
 off Lower Boston Rd 79 CE74
Laurel Cl, N19
 off Hargrave Pk 65 DJ61
 SW17 120 DE92
 Brentwood (Hutt.) CM13 55 GB43
 Dartford DA1
 off Willow Rd 128 FJ88
 Ilford IG6 49 EQ51
 Sidcup DA14 126 EU90
 Slough (Colnbr.) SL3 93 BE80
 Watford WD19 40 BX45
 Woking GU21 151 BD113
Laurel Ct, Pot.B. (Cuffley) EN6
 off Station Rd 13 DM29
Laurel Cres, Croy. CR0 143 EA104
 Romford RM7 71 FE60
 Woking GU21 151 BC113
Laurel Dr, N21 45 DN45
 Oxted RH8 188 EF131
 South Ockendon RM15 91 FX70
Laurel Flds, Pot.B. EN6 11 CZ31
Laurel Gdns, E4 47 EB45
 NW7 42 CR48
 W7 79 CE74
 Addlestone
 (New Haw) KT15 152 BH110
 Bromley BR1
 off Southborough Rd 144 EL98
 Hounslow TW4 96 BY84
Laurel Gro, SE20 122 DV94
 SE26 123 DX91
Laurel La, Horn. RM12
 off Station La 72 FL61
 West Drayton UB7 94 BL77
Laurel Lo La, Barn. EN5 27 CW36
Laurel Manor, Sutt. SM2
 off Devonshire Rd 158 DC108
Laurel Pk, Har. HA3 41 CF52
Laurel Rd, SW13 99 CU82
 SW20 139 CV95
 Gerrards Cross
 (Chal.St.P.) SL9 36 AX53
 Hampton (Hmptn H.) TW12 117 CD92
Laurels, The, Bans. SM7 173 CZ117
 Cobham KT11 170 BY115
 Dartford DA2 128 FJ90
 Waltham Cross EN7 14 DS27
 Weybridge KT13 135 BR104
Laurels Rd, Iver SL0 75 BD68
Laurel St, E8 84 DT65
Laurel Vw, N12 44 DB48
Laurel Way, E18 68 EF56
 N20 44 DA48
Laurence Ms, W12
 off Askew Rd 99 CU75
Laurence Pountney Hill, EC4 197 K10
Laurence Pountney La, EC4 197 K10
Laurie Gro, SE14 103 DY81
Laurie Rd, W7 79 CE71
Laurier Rd, NW5 65 DH62
 Croydon CR0 142 DT101
Laurie Wk, Rom. RM1 71 FE57
Laurimel Cl, Stan. HA7
 off September Way 41 CH51
Laurino Pl, Bushey
 (Bushey Hth) WD23 40 CC47
Lauriston Rd, E9 85 DX67
 SW19 119 CX93
Lausanne Rd, N8 65 DN56
 SE15 102 DW81
Lauser Rd, Stai.
 (Stanw.) TW19 114 BJ87
Lavell St, N16 66 DR63
Lavender Av, NW9 62 CQ60
 Brentwood (Pilg.Hat.) CM15 54 FV43
 Mitcham CR4 140 DE95
 Worcester Park KT4 139 CW104
Lavender Cl, SW3
 off Danvers St 100 DD79
 Bromley BR2 144 EL100
 Carshalton SM5 158 DG105
 Caterham CR3 186 DQ125
 Coulsdon CR5 175 DJ119
 Leatherhead KT22 171 CJ123
 Romford RM3 52 FK52
 Waltham Cross (Chsht) EN7 14 DT27
Lavender Ct, W.Mol. KT8
 off Molesham Way 136 CB97
Lavender Dr, Uxb. UB8 76 BM71
Lavender Gdns, SW11 100 DF84
 Enfield EN2 29 DP39
 Harrow HA3
 off Uxbridge Rd 41 CE51
Lavender Gate, Lthd. KT22 154 CB113
Lavender Gro, E8 84 DT66
 Mitcham CR4 140 DE95
Lavender Hill, SW11 100 DE84
 Enfield EN2 29 DN39
 Swanley BR8 147 FD97
Lavender Pk Rd, W.Byf. KT14 152 BG112
Lavender Pl, Ilf. IG1 69 EP64
Lavender Ri, West Dr. UB7 94 BN75
Lavender Rd, SE16 203 K2
 SW11 100 DD83
 Carshalton SM5 158 DG105
 Croydon CR0 141 DM100
 Enfield EN2 30 DR39
 Epsom KT19 156 CP106
 Sutton SM1 158 DD105
 Uxbridge UB8 76 BM71
 Woking GU22 167 BB116
Lavender St, E15
 off Manbey Gro 86 EE65
Lavender Sweep, SW11 100 DF84
Lavender Ter, SW11
 off Falcon Rd 100 DE83
Lavender Vale, Wall. SM6 159 DK107
Lavender Wk, SW11 100 DF84
 Mitcham CR4 140 DG97
Lavender Way, Croy. CR0 143 DX100
Lavengro Rd, SE27 122 DQ89
Lavenham Rd, SW18 119 CZ89
Lavernock Rd, Bexh. DA7 106 FA82
Lavers Rd, N16 66 DS62
Laverstoke Gdns, SW15 119 CU87
Laverton Ms, SW5
 off Laverton Pl 100 DB77
Laverton Pl, SW5 100 DB77
Lavidge Rd, SE9 124 EL89
Lavina Gro, N1
 off Wharfdale Rd 83 DM68
Lavington Cl, E9
 off Beanacre Cl 85 DZ65
Lavington Rd, W13 79 CH74
 Croydon CR0 141 DM104
Lavington St, SE1 200 G3
Lavinia Av, Wat. WD25 8 BX34
Lavinia Rd, Dart. DA1 128 FM86
Lavrock La, Rick. WD3 38 BM45
Lawdons Gdns, Croy. CR0 159 DP105
Lawford Av, Rick.
 (Chorl.) WD3 21 BC44
Lawford Cl, Horn. RM12 72 FJ63
 Rickmansworth
 (Chorl.) WD3 21 BC44
 Wallington SM6 159 DL109
Lawford Gdns, Dart. DA1 128 FJ85
 Kenley CR8 176 DQ116
Lawford Rd, N1 84 DS66
 NW5 83 DJ65
 W4 98 CQ80
Law Ho, Bark. IG11 88 EU68
Lawless St, E14 85 EB73
Lawley Rd, N14 45 DH45
Lawley St, E5 66 DW63
Lawn, The, Sthl. UB2 96 CA78
Lawn Av, West Dr. UB7 94 BJ75
Lawn Cl, N9 46 DT45
 Bromley BR1 124 EH93
 New Malden KT3 138 CS96
 Ruislip HA4 59 BT62
 Slough (Datchet) SL3 92 AW80
 Swanley BR8 147 FC96
Lawn Cres, Rich. TW9 98 CN82
Lawn Fm Gro, Rom. RM6 70 EY56
Lawnfield, NW2
 off Coverdale Rd 81 CX66
Lawn Gdns, W7 79 CE74
Lawn Ho Cl, E14 204 D4
Lawn La, SW8 101 DL79
Lawn Pk, Sev. TN13 191 FH127
Lawn Rd, NW3 64 DF64
 Beckenham BR3 123 DZ94
 Gravesend DA11 130 GC86
 Uxbridge UB8
 off New Windsor St 76 BJ66
Lawns, The, E4 47 EA50
 SE3 off Lee Ter 104 EE83
 SE19 142 DR95
 Pinner HA5 40 CB52
 Radlett (Shenley) WD7 10 CL33
 Sidcup DA14 126 EV91
 Sutton SM2 157 CY108
Lawns Ct, Wem. HA9
 off The Avenue 62 CM61
Lawns Cres, Grays RM17 110 GD79
Lawnside, SE3 104 EF84
Lawns Way, Rom. RM5 51 FC52
Lawn Ter, SE3 104 EE83
Lawn Vale, Pnr. HA5 40 BX54
Lawrance Gdns, Wal.Cr.
 (Chsht) EN8 15 DX28
Lawrence Av, E12 69 EN63
 E17 47 DX53
 N13 45 DP49
 NW7 42 CS49
 NW10 80 CR67
 New Malden KT3 138 CR100
Lawrence Bldgs, N16 66 DT62
Lawrence Campe Cl, N20
 off Friern Barnet La 44 DD48
Lawrence Cl, E3 85 EA68
 N15 off Lawrence Rd 66 DS56
Lawrence Ct, NW7 42 CS50
Lawrence Cres, Dag. RM10 71 FB62
 Edgware HA8 42 CN54
Lawrence Dr, Uxb. UB10 59 BQ63
Lawrence Gdns, NW7 43 CT48
 Tilbury RM18 111 GH80
Lawrence Hill, E4 47 EA47
Lawrence Hill Gdns,
 Dart. DA1 128 FJ86
Lawrence Hill Rd, Dart. DA1 128 FJ86
Lawrence La, EC2 197 J9
 Betchworth
 (Buckland) RH3 183 CV131
Lawrence Orchard, Rick.
 (Chorl.) WD3 21 BD43
Lawrence Pl, N1
 off Outram Pl 83 DL67
Lawrence Rd, E6 86 EK67
 E13 86 EH67
 N15 66 DS56
 N18 46 DV49
 SE25 142 DT98
 W5 97 CK77
 Erith DA8 107 FB80
 Hampton TW12 116 BZ94
 Hayes UB4 77 BQ68
 Hounslow TW4 96 BW84
 Pinner HA5 60 BX57
 Richmond TW10 117 CJ91
 Romford RM2 71 FH57
 West Wickham BR4 162 EG105
Lawrence Sq, Grav. DA11
 off Haynes Rd 131 GF90
Lawrence St, E16 86 EF71
 NW7 43 CT49
 SW3 100 DE79
Lawrence Way, NW10 62 CQ62
Lawrence Weaver Cl, Mord. SM4
 off Green La 140 DA100
Lawrie Pk Av, SE26 122 DV92
Lawrie Pk Cres, SE26 122 DV92
Lawrie Pk Gdns, SE26 122 DV91
Lawrie Pk Rd, SE26 122 DV93
Laws Cl, SE25 off Farnley Rd 142 DR98
Lawson Cl, E16 86 EJ71
 SW19 119 CX90
Lawson Est, SE1 201 K7
Lawson Gdns, Dart. DA1 128 FK85
 Pinner HA5 59 BV55
Lawson Rd, Dart. DA1 108 FK84
 Enfield EN3 30 DW39
 Southall UB1 78 BZ70
Lawson Wk, Cars. SM5 158 DF110
Law St, SE1 201 L6
Lawton Rd, E3 85 DY69
 E10 67 EC60
 Barnet EN4 28 DD41
 Loughton IG10 33 EP41
Laxcon Cl, NW10 62 CQ64
Laxey Rd, Orp. BR6 163 ET107
Laxley Cl, SE5 101 DP80
Laxton Gdns, Rad. (Shenley) WD7
 off Porters Pk Dr 10 CL32
 Redhill RH1 185 DK128
Laxton Pl, NW1 195 J4
Layard Rd, SE16 202 E8
 Enfield EN1 30 DT39
 Thornton Heath CR7 142 DR96
Layard Sq, SE16 202 E8
Layborne Av, Rom. RM3
 off Cummings Hall La 52 FJ48
Layburn Cres, Slou. SL3 93 BB79
Laycock St, N1 83 DN65
Layer Gdns, W3 80 CN73
Layfield Cl, NW4 63 CV59
Layfield Cres, NW4 63 CV59
Layfield Rd, NW4 63 CV59
Layhams Rd, Kes. BR2 162 EF106
 West Wickham BR4 143 ED104
Laymarsh Cl, Belv. DA17 106 EZ76
Laymead Cl, Nthlt. UB5 78 BY65
Laystall St, EC1 196 D5
Layters Av, Ger.Cr.
 (Chal.St.P.) SL9 36 AW54
Layters Av S, Ger.Cr.
 (Chal.St.P.) SL9 36 AW54
Layters Cl, Ger.Cr.
 (Chal.St.P.) SL9 36 AW54
Layters End, Ger.Cr.
 (Chal.St.P.) SL9 36 AW54
LAYTER'S GREEN, Ger.Cr. SL9 36 AV54
Layters Grn La, Ger.Cr.
 (Chal.St.P.) SL9 56 AU55
Layter's Grn Mobile Home Pk,
 Ger.Cr. (Chal.St.P.) SL9
 off Layters Grn La 36 AV54
Layters Way, Ger.Cr. SL9 56 AX56
Layton Ct, Wey. KT13
 off Castle Vw Rd 153 BP105
Layton Cres, Croy. CR0 159 DN106
Layton Pl, Rich. TW9
 off Station Av 98 CN81
Layton Rd, Brent. TW8 97 CK78
 Hounslow TW3 96 CB84
Laytons Bldgs, SE1 201 J4
Laytons La, Sun. TW16 135 BT96
Layzell Wk, SE9
 off Mottingham La 124 EK88
Lazar Wk, N7 off Briset Way 65 DM61
Lea, The, Egh. TW20 133 BB95
Leabank Cl, Har. HA1 61 CE62
Leabank Sq, E9 85 EA65
Leabank Vw, N15 66 DU58
Leabourne Rd, N16 66 DU58
LEA BRIDGE, E5 67 DX62
Lea Br Business Cen, E10
 off Burwell Rd 67 DY60
Lea Br Rd, E5 66 DW62
 E10 67 DY60

★ Place of interest ⇌ Railway station ⊖ London Underground station DLR Docklands Light Railway station Tra Tramlink station H Hospital Riv Pedestrian ferry landing stage

Lea Br Rd, E17 67 ED56
Lea Bushes, Wat. WD25 24 BY35
Leachcroft, Ger.Cr.
(Chal.St.P.) SL9 36 AV53
Leach Gro, Lthd. KT22 171 CJ122
Lea Cl, Bushey WD23 24 CB43
Twickenham TW2 116 BZ87
Lea Cres, Ruis. HA4 59 BT63
Leacroft, Stai. TW18 114 BH91
Leacroft Av, SW12 120 DF87
Leacroft Cl, Ken. CR8 176 DQ116
Staines TW18 114 BH91
West Drayton UB7 76 BL72
Leacroft Rd, Iver SL0 75 BD72
Leadale Av, E4 47 EA47
Leadale Rd, N15 66 DU58
N16 66 DU58
Leadbeaters Cl, N11
off Goldsmith Rd 44 DF50
Leadbetter Dr, Wat. WD25
off Greenbank Rd 23 BR36
★ **Leadenhall Mkt**, EC3 197 M9
Leadenhall Pl, EC3 197 M9
Leadenhall St, EC3 197 M9
Leadenham Ct, E3
off Spanby Rd 85 EA70
Leader Av, E12 69 EN64
Leadings, The, Wem. HA9 62 CQ62
Leaf Cl, Nthwd. HA6 39 BR52
Thames Ditton KT7 137 CE99
Leaf Gro, SE27 121 DN92
Leafield Cl, SW16 121 DP93
Woking GU21
off Winnington Way 166 AV118
Leafield La, Sid. DA14 126 EZ91
Leafield Rd, SW20 139 CZ97
Sutton SM1 140 DA103
Leaford Cres, Wat. WD24 23 BT37
Leaforis Rd, Wal.Cr. EN7 14 DU28
Leafy Gro, Croy. CR0 161 DY111
Keston BR2 162 EJ106
Leafy Oak Rd, SE12 124 EJ90
Leafy Way, Brwd. (Hutt.) CM13 55 GD46
Croydon CR0 142 DT103
Lea Gdns, Wem. HA9 62 CL63
Leagrave St, E5 66 DW62
Lea Hall Rd, E10 67 EA60
Leaholme Way, Ruis. HA4 59 BP58
Leahurst Rd, SE13 123 ED85
Leake St, SE1 200 C4
Lealand Rd, N15 66 DT58
Leamington Av, E17 67 EA57
Bromley BR1 124 EJ92
Morden SM4 139 CZ98
Orpington BR6 163 ES105
Leamington Cl, E12 68 EL64
Bromley BR1 124 EJ92
Hounslow TW3 116 CC85
Romford RM3 52 FM51
Leamington Cres, Har. HA2 60 BY62
Leamington Gdns, Ilf. IG3 69 ET61
Leamington Pk, W3 80 CR71
Leamington Pl, Hayes UB4 77 BT70
Leamington Rd, Rom. RM3 52 FN50
Southall UB2 96 BX77
Leamington Rd Vil, W11 81 CZ71
Leamore St, W6 99 CV77
Lea Mt, Wal.Cr. EN7 14 DS28
Leamouth Rd, E6
off Remington Rd 86 EL72
E14 85 ED72
Leander Ct, SE8 103 EA81
Leander Dr, Grav. DA12 131 GM91
Leander Gdns, Wat. WD25 24 BY37
Leander Rd, SW2 121 DM86
Northolt UB5 78 CA68
Thornton Heath CR7 141 DM98
Learner Dr, Har. HA2 60 CA61
Lea Rd, Beck. BR3
off Fairfield Rd 143 EA96
Enfield EN2 30 DR39
Grays RM16 111 GG78
Sevenoaks TN13 191 FJ127
Southall UB2 96 BY77
Waltham Abbey EN9 15 EA34
Learoyd Gdns, E6 87 EN73
Leas, The, Bushey WD23 24 BZ39
Staines TW18
off Raleigh Ct 114 BG91
Upminster RM14 73 FR59
Leas Cl, Chess. KT9 156 CM108
Leas Dale, SE9 125 EN90
Leas Dr, Iver SL0 75 BE72
Leas Grn, Chis. BR7 125 ET93
Leaside, Lthd. (Bkhm) KT23 170 CA123
Leaside Av, N10 64 DG55
Leaside Ct, Uxb. UB10
off The Larches 77 BP69
Leaside Rd, E5 66 DW60
Leas La, Warl. CR6 177 DX118
Leasowes Rd, E10 67 EA60
Lea Sq, E3 *off Lefevre Wk* 85 DZ67
Leas Rd, Warl. CR6 177 DX118
Leasway, Brwd. CM14 54 FX48
Upminster RM14 72 FQ62
Leathart Cl, Horn. RM12
off Dowding Way 89 FH66
Leatherbottle Grn, Erith DA18 106 EZ76
Leather Bottle La, Belv. DA17 106 EY77
Leather Cl, Mitch. CR4 140 DG96
Leatherdale St, E1
off Portelet Rd 85 DX70
Leather Gdns, E15
off Abbey Rd 86 EE67
LEATHERHEAD 171 CF121
⇌ **Leatherhead** 171 CG121
Leatherhead Bypass Rd,
Lthd. KT22 171 CH120
Leatherhead Cl, N16 66 DT60
LEATHERHEAD COMMON,
Lthd. KT22 171 CF119
H **Leatherhead Hosp**,
Lthd. KT22 171 CJ122
★ **Leatherhead Mus of Local History**, Lthd. KT22 171 CH122
Leatherhead Rd, Ashtd. KT21 171 CK121
Chessington KT9 155 CJ111
Leatherhead KT22 171 CK121
Leatherhead
(Oxshott) KT22 155 CD114
Leather La, EC1 196 E7
Hornchurch RM11
off North St 72 FK60
★ **Leather Mkt Bermondsey**,
SE1 201 M5
Leathermarket Ct, SE1 201 M5
Leathermarket St, SE1 201 M5
Leathersellers Cl, Barn. EN5
off The Avenue 27 CY42
Leathsail Rd, Har. HA2 60 CB62
Leathwaite Rd, SW11 100 DF84
Leathwell Rd, SE8 103 EB82
Lea Vale, Dart. DA1 107 FD84
Lea Valley Rd, E4 31 DX43
Enfield EN3 31 DX43
Lea Valley Trd Est, N18 47 DX50
Lea Valley Viaduct, E4 47 DX50
N18 47 DX50
Lea Valley Wk, E3 85 EC70
E5 67 DY62
E9 67 DY62
E10 67 DY62
E14 85 EB71
E15 85 EC69
E17 46 DW53
N9 47 DY46
N15 66 DU58
N16 66 DU58
N17 46 DW53
N18 46 DW53
Enfield EN3 31 DZ41
Waltham Abbey EN9 15 DZ30
Waltham Cross EN8 15 DZ30
Leaveland Cl, Beck. BR3 143 EA98
Leaver Gdns, Grnf. UB6 79 CD68
Leavesden Ct, Abb.L. WD5
off Mallard Rd 7 BU31
LEAVESDEN GREEN,
Wat. WD25 7 BT34
Leavesden Rd, Stan. HA7 41 CG51
Watford WD24 23 BV38
Weybridge KT13 153 BP106
LEAVES GREEN, Kes. BR2 162 EK109
Leaves Grn Cres, Kes. BR2 162 EJ111
Leaves Grn Rd, Kes. BR2 162 EK111
Leaview, Wal.Abb. EN9 15 EB33
Lea Vw Hos, E5
off Springfield 66 DV60
Leaway, E10 66 DX60
Leazes Av, Cat. CR3 175 DN123
Leazes La, Cat. CR3 175 DN123
Lebanon Av, Felt. TW13 116 BX92
Lebanon Cl, Wat. WD17 23 BR36
Lebanon Ct, Twick. TW1 117 CH87
Lebanon Dr, Cob. KT11 154 CA113
Lebanon Gdns, SW18 120 DA86
Westerham (Bigg.H.) TN16 178 EK117
Lebanon Pk, Twick. TW1 117 CH87
Trm **Lebanon Road** 142 DS103
Lebanon Rd, SW18 120 DA85
Croydon CR0 142 DS102
Lebrun Sq, SE3 104 EH83
Lechmere App, Wdf.Grn. IG8 48 EJ54
Lechmere Av, Chig. IG7 49 EQ49
Woodford Green IG8 48 EK54
Lechmere Rd, NW2 81 CV65
Leckford Rd, SW18 120 DC89
Leckwith Av, Bexh. DA7 106 EY79
Lecky St, SW7 100 DD78
Leclair Ho, SE3
off Gallus Sq 104 EH83
Leconfield Av, SW13 99 CT83
Leconfield Rd, N5 66 DR63
Leconfield Wk, Horn. RM12
off Airfield Way 90 FJ65
Le Corte Cl, Kings L. WD4 6 BM29
Leda Av, Enf. EN3 31 DX39
Leda Rd, SE18 105 EM76
Ledbury Est, SE15 102 DV80
Ledbury Ms N, W11
off Ledbury Rd 82 DA73
Ledbury Ms W, W11
off Ledbury Rd 82 DA73
Ledbury Pl, Croy. CR0
off Ledbury Rd 160 DQ105
Ledbury Rd, W11 81 CZ72
Croydon CR0 160 DQ105
Reigate RH2 183 CZ133
Ledbury St, SE15 102 DU80
Ledger Dr, Add. KT15 151 BF106
Ledgers Rd, Slou. SL1 92 AS75
Warlingham CR6 177 EA116
Ledrington Rd, SE19
off Anerley Hill 122 DU93
Ledway Dr, Wem. HA9 62 CM59
LEE, SE12 104 EE84
⇌ **Lee** 124 EG86
Lee, The, Nthwd. HA6 39 BT50
Lee Av, Rom. RM6 70 EY58
Lee Br, SE13 103 EC83
Leechcroft Av, Sid. DA15 125 ET85
Swanley BR8 147 FF97
Leechcroft Rd, Wall. SM6 140 DG104
Leech La, Epsom
(Headley) KT18 182 CQ126
Leatherhead KT22 182 CQ126
Lee Ch St, SE13 104 EE84
Lee Cl, E17 47 DX53
Barnet EN5 28 DC42
Lee Conservancy Rd, E9 67 DZ64
Leecroft Rd, Barn. EN5 27 CY43
Leeds Cl, Orp. BR6 146 EX103
Leeds Pl, N4
off Tollington Pk 65 DM61
Leeds Rd, Ilf. IG1 69 ER60
Slough SL1 74 AS73
Leeds St, N18 46 DU50
Lee Fm Cl, Chesh. HP5 4 AU30
Leefern Rd, W12 99 CU75
Leefe Way, Pot.B. EN6 13 DK28
Lee Gdns Av, Horn. RM11 72 FN60
Leegate, SE12 124 EF85
Leegate Cl, Wok. GU21
off Sythwood 166 AV116
Lee Grn, SE12
off Lee High Rd 124 EF85
Orpington BR5 146 EU99
Lee Grn La, Epsom KT18 172 CP124
Lee Gro, Chig. IG7 49 EN47
Lee High Rd, SE12 103 ED83
Lee High Rd, SE13 103 ED83
Leeke St, WC1 196 B2
Leeland Rd, W13 79 CG74
Leeland Ter, W13 79 CG74
Leeland Way, NW10 63 CT63
Leeming Rd, Borwd. WD6 26 CM39
Lee Pk, SE3 104 EF84
Lee Pk Way, N9 47 DX49
N18 47 DX49
Leerdam Dr, E14 204 E7
Lee Rd, NW7 43 CX52
SE3 104 EF83
SW19 140 DB95
Enfield EN1 30 DU44
Greenford UB6 79 CJ67
Lees, The, Croy. CR0 143 DZ103
Lees Av, Nthwd. HA6 39 BT53
Leeside, Barn. EN5 27 CY43
Potters Bar EN6
off Wayside 12 DD31
Leeside Ct, SE16 203 H2
Leeside Cres, NW11 63 CZ58
Leeside Rd, N17 46 DV51
Leeson Rd, SE24 101 DN84
Leesons Hill, Chis. BR7 145 ES97
Orpington BR5 146 EU97
Leesons Way, Orp. BR5 145 ET96
Lees Pl, W1 194 F10
Lees Rd, Uxb. UB8 77 BP70
Lee St, E8 84 DT67
Lee Ter, SE3 104 EE83
SE13 104 EE83
★ **Lee Valley Pk**, E10 15 DZ31
Lee Valley Pathway, E9 67 DZ62
E10 66 DW59
E17 66 DW59
Waltham Abbey EN9 15 EA31
Lee Valley Technopark, N17 66 DU55
Lee Vw, Enf. EN2 29 DP39
Leeward Gdns, SW19 119 CZ93
Leeway, SE8 203 M10
Leeway Cl, Pnr. HA5 40 BZ52
Leewood Cl, SE12
off Upwood Rd 124 EF86
Leewood Pl, Swan. BR8 147 FD98
Lefevre Wk, E3 85 DZ67
Lefroy Rd, W12 99 CT75
Legard Rd, N5 65 DP62
Legatt Rd, SE9 124 EK85
Leggatt Rd, E15 85 EC68
Leggatts Cl, Wat. WD24 23 BT36
Leggatts Ri, Wat. WD25 23 BU35
Leggatts Way, Wat. WD24 23 BT36
Leggatts Wd Av, Wat. WD24 23 BV36
Legge St, SE13 123 EC85
Leghorn Rd, NW10 81 CT68
SE18 105 ER78
Legion Cl, N1 83 DN65
Legion Ct, Mord. SM4 140 DA100
Legion Rd, Grnf. UB6 78 CC67
Legion Ter, E3
off Lefevre Wk 85 DZ67
Legion Way, N12 44 DE52
Legon Av, Rom. RM7 71 FC60
Legrace Av, Houns. TW4 96 BX82
Leicester Av, Mitch. CR4 141 DL98
Leicester Cl, Wor.Pk. KT4 157 CW105
Leicester Ct, WC2 195 N10
Leicester Gdns, Ilf. IG3 69 ES59
Leicester Ms, N2
off Leicester Rd 64 DE55
Leicester Pl, WC2 195 N10
Leicester Rd, E11 68 EH57
N2 64 DE55
Barnet EN5 28 DB43
Croydon CR0 142 DS101
Tilbury RM18 111 GF81
⊖ **Leicester Square** 195 N10
Leicester Sq, WC2 199 N1
Leicester St, WC2 195 N10
Leigh, The, Kings.T. KT2 118 CS93
Leigham Av, SW16 121 DL90
Leigham Cl, Wall. SM6
off Stafford Rd 159 DJ107
Leigham Ct Rd, SW16 121 DL89
Leigham Dr, Islw. TW7 97 CE80
Leigham Vale, SW2 121 DM90
SW16 121 DM90
Leigh Av, Ilf. IG4 68 EK56
Leigh Cl, Add. KT15 151 BF108
New Malden KT3 138 CR98
Leigh Cor, Cob. KT11
off Leigh Hill Rd 154 BW114
Leigh Ct, SE4
off Lewisham Way 103 EA82
Borehamwood WD6
off Banks Rd 26 CR40
Harrow HA2 61 CE60
Leigh Ct Cl, Cob. KT11 154 BW114
Leigh Cres, Croy.
(New Adgtn) CR0 161 EB108
Leigh Dr, Rom. RM3 52 FK49
Leigh Gdns, NW10 81 CW68
Leigh Hill Rd, Cob. KT11 154 BW114
Leigh Hunt Dr, N14 45 DK46
Leigh Hunt St, SE1 201 H4
Leigh Orchard Cl, SW16 121 DM90
Leigh Pk,
Slou. (Datchet) SL3 92 AV80
Leigh Pl, EC1 196 D6
Cobham KT11 170 BW115
Dartford DA2
off Hawley Rd 128 FN92
Feltham TW13
off Hanworth Rd 116 BW88
Welling DA16 106 EU82
Leigh Pl La, Gdse. RH9 187 DY132
Leigh Rd, E6 87 EN65
E10 67 EC59
N5 65 DP63
Cobham KT11 153 BV113
Gravesend DA11 131 GH89
Hounslow TW3 97 CD84
Leigh Rodd, Wat. WD19 40 BZ48
Leigh St, WC1 195 P4
Leigh Ter, Orp. BR5
off Saxville Rd 146 EV97
Leighton Av, E12 69 EN64
Pinner HA5 60 BY55
Leighton Cl, Edg. HA8 42 CN54
Leighton Cres, NW5
off Leighton Gro 65 DJ64
Leighton Gdns, NW10 81 CV68
South Croydon CR2 160 DV113
Tilbury RM18 111 GG80
Leighton Gro, NW5 65 DJ64
★ **Leighton Ho Mus**, W14 99 CZ76
Leighton Pl, NW5 65 DJ64
Leighton Rd, NW5 65 DK64
W13 97 CG75
Enfield EN1 30 DT43
Harrow (Har.Wld) HA3 41 CD54
Leighton St, Croy. CR0 141 DP102
Leighton Way, Epsom KT18 156 CR114
Leila Parnell Pl, SE7 104 EJ79
Leinster Av, SW14 98 CQ83
Leinster Gdns, W2 82 DC72
Leinster Ms, W2 82 DC73
Leinster Pl, W2 82 DC72
Leinster Rd, N10 65 DH56
Leinster Sq, W2 82 DA72
Leinster Ter, W2 82 DC73
Leiston Spur, Slou. SL1 74 AS72
Leisure La, W.Byf. KT14 152 BH112
Leisure Way, N12 44 DD52
Leith Cl, NW9 62 CR60
Slough SL1 74 AU74
Leithcote Gdns, SW16 121 DM91
Leithcote Path, SW16 121 DM90
Leith Hill, Orp. BR5 146 EU95
Leith Hill Grn, Orp. BR5
off Leith Hill 146 EU95
Leith Pk Rd, Grav. DA12 131 GH88
Leith Rd, N22 45 DP53
Epsom KT17 156 CS112
Leith Yd, NW6 *off Quex Rd* 82 DA67
Lela Av, Houns. TW4 96 BW82
Lelitia Cl, E8
off Pownall Rd 84 DU67
Leman St, E1 84 DT72
Lemark Cl, Stan. HA7 41 CJ50
Le May Av, SE12 124 EH90
Lemmon Rd, SE10 104 EE79
Lemna Rd, E11 68 EE59
Lemonfield Dr, Wat. WD25 8 BY32
Lemonwell Ct, SE9
off Lemonwell Dr 125 EQ85
Lemonwell Dr, SE9 125 EQ85
Lemsford Cl, N15 66 DU57
Lemsford Ct, N4
off Brownswood Rd 66 DQ61
Borehamwood WD6 26 CQ42
Lemuel St, SW18 120 DB86
Lena Cres, N9 46 DW47
Lena Gdns, W6 99 CW76
Lena Kennedy Cl, E4 47 EB51
Lenanton Steps, E14 204 A4
Lendal Ter, SW4 101 DK83
Lenelby Rd, Surb. KT6 138 CN102
Len Freeman Pl, SW6
off John Smith Av 99 CZ80
Lenham Rd, SE12 104 EF84
Bexleyheath DA7 106 EZ79
Sutton SM1 158 DB105
Thornton Heath CR7 142 DR96
Lenmore Av, Grays RM17 110 GC76
Lennard Av, W.Wick. BR4 144 EE103
Lennard Cl, W.Wick. BR4 144 EE103
Lennard Rd, SE20 122 DW93
Beckenham BR3 123 DX93
Bromley BR2 145 EM102
Croydon CR0 142 DQ102
Sevenoaks
(Dunt.Grn) TN13 181 FE120
Lennard Row, S.Ock.
(Aveley) RM15 91 FR74
Lennon Rd, NW2 63 CW64
Lennox Av, Grav. DA11 131 GF86
Lennox Cl, Grays
(Chaff.Hun.) RM16 109 FW77
Romford RM1 71 FF58
Lennox Gdns, NW10 63 CT63
SW1 198 D7
Croydon CR0 159 DP105
Ilford IG1 69 EM60
Lennox Gdns Ms, SW1 198 D7
Lennox Rd, E17 67 DZ58
N4 65 DM61
Gravesend DA11 131 GF86
Lennox Rd E, Grav. DA11 131 GG87
Lenor Cl, Bexh. DA6 106 EY84
Lensbury Cl, Wal.Cr. (Chsht) EN8
off Ashdown Cres 15 DY28
Lensbury Way, SE2 106 EW76
Lens Rd, E7 86 EJ66
Lenthall Av, Grays RM17 110 GA75
Lenthall Rd, E8 84 DU66
Loughton IG10 33 ER42
Lenthorp Rd, SE10 205 K10
Lentmead Rd, Brom. BR1 124 EF90
Lenton Path, SE18 105 ER79
Lenton Ri, Rich. TW9
off Evelyn Ter 98 CL83
Lenton St, SE18 105 ER77
Leof Cres, SE6 123 EB92
Leominster Rd, Mord. SM4 140 DC100
Leominster Wk, Mord. SM4 140 DC100
Leonard Av, Mord. SM4 140 DC99
Romford RM7 71 FD60
Sevenoaks (Otford) TN14 181 FH116
Swanscombe DA10 130 FY87
Leonard Pl, N16 *off Allen Rd* 66 DS63
Leonard Rd, E4 47 EA51
E7 68 EG63
N9 46 DT48
SW16 141 DJ95
Southall UB2 96 BX76
Leonard Robbins Path, SE28
off Tawney Rd 88 EV73
Leonard St, E16 86 EL74
EC2 197 L4
Leonard Way, Brwd. CM14 54 FS49
Leontine Cl, SE15 102 DU80
Leopards Ct, EC1 196 D6
Leopold Av, SW19 119 CZ92
Leopold Ms, E9
off Fremont St 84 DW67
Leopold Rd, E17 67 EA57
N2 64 DD55
N18 46 DV50
Leopold Rd, NW10 80 CS66
SW19 119 CZ91
W5 80 CM74
Leopold St, E3 85 DZ71
Leopold Ter, SW19
off Dora Rd 120 DA92
Leo St, SE15 102 DV80
Leo Yd, EC1 196 G5
Le Personne Rd, Cat. CR3 176 DR122
Leppoc Rd, SW4 121 DK85
Leret Way, Lthd. KT22 171 CH121
Leroy St, SE1 201 M8
Lerwick Dr, Slou. SL1 74 AS71
Lescombe Cl, SE23 123 DY90
Lescombe Rd, SE23 123 DY90
Lesley Cl, Bex. DA5 127 FB87
Gravesend
(Istead Rise) DA13 131 GF94
Swanley BR8 147 FD97
Leslie Gdns, Sutt. SM2 158 DA108
Leslie Gro, Croy. CR0 142 DS102
Leslie Gro Pl, Croy. CR0
off Leslie Gro 142 DR102
Leslie Pk Rd, Croy. CR0 142 DS102
Leslie Rd, E11 67 EC63
E16 86 EH72
N2 64 DD55
Woking (Chobham) GU24 150 AS110
Leslie Smith Sq, SE18
off Nightingale Vale 105 EN79
★ **Lesnes Abbey (ruins)**,
Erith DA18 106 EX77
Lesney Fm Est, Erith DA8 107 FD80
Lesney Pk, Erith DA8 107 FD79
Lesney Pk Rd, Erith DA8 107 FD79
Lessar Av, SW4 121 DJ85
Lessingham Av, SW17 120 DF91
Ilford IG5 69 EN55
Lessing St, SE23 123 DY87
Lessington Av, Rom. RM7 71 FC58
Lessness Av, Bexh. DA7 106 EX80
LESSNESS HEATH,
Belv. DA17 107 FB78
Lessness Pk, Belv. DA17 106 EZ78
Lessness Rd, Belv. DA17
off Stapley Rd 106 FA78
Morden SM4 140 DC100
Lester Av, E15 86 EE69
Leston Cl, Rain. RM13 89 FG69
Leswin Pl, N16
off Leswin Rd 66 DT62
Leswin Rd, N16 66 DT62
Letchfield, Chesh.
(Ley Hill) HP5 4 AV31
Letchford Gdns, NW10 81 CU69
Letchford Ms, NW10
off Letchford Gdns 81 CU69
Letchford Ter, Har. HA3 40 CB53
LETCHMORE HEATH,
Wat. WD25 25 CD38
Letchmore Rd, Rad. WD7 25 CG36
Letchworth Av, Felt. TW14 115 BT87
Letchworth Cl, Brom. BR2 144 EG99
Watford WD19 40 BX50
Letchworth Dr, Brom. BR2 144 EG99
Letchworth St, SW17 120 DF91
Lethbridge Cl, SE13 103 EC81
Letter Box La, Sev. TN13 191 FJ129
Letterstone Rd, SW6
off Varna Rd 99 CZ80
Lettice St, SW6 99 CZ81
Lett Rd, E15 85 ED66
Lettsom St, SE5 102 DS82
Lettsom Wk, E13 86 EG68
Leucha Rd, E17 67 DY57
Levana Cl, SW19 119 CY88
Levehurst Way, SW4 101 DL82
Leven Cl, Wal.Cr. EN8 15 DX33
Watford WD19 40 BX50
Levendale Rd, SE23 123 DY89
Leven Dr, Wal.Cr. EN8 15 DX33
Leven Rd, E14 85 EC71
Leven Way, Hayes UB3 77 BS72
Leveret Cl, Croy.
(New Adgtn) CR0 161 ED111
Watford WD25 7 BU34
Leverett St, SW3 198 C8
Leverholme Gdns, SE9 125 EN90
Leverson St, SW16 121 DJ93
Lever Sq, Grays RM16 111 GG77
Lever St, EC1 196 G3
Leverton Pl, NW5
off Leverton St 65 DJ64
Leverton St, NW5 65 DJ64
Leverton Way, Wal.Abb. EN9 15 EC33
Leveson Rd, Grays RM16 111 GH76
Levett Gdns, Ilf. IG3 69 ET63
Levett Rd, Bark. IG11 87 ES65
Leatherhead KT22 171 CH120
Levine Gdns, Bark. IG11 88 EX68
Levison Way, N19
off Grovedale Rd 65 DK61
Lewes Cl, Grays RM17 110 GA79
Northolt UB5 78 CA65
Lewesdon Cl, SW19 119 CX88
Lewes Rd, N12 44 DE50
Bromley BR1 144 EK96
Romford RM3 52 FJ49
Leweston Pl, N16 66 DT59
Lewes Way, Rick.
(Crox.Grn) WD3 23 BQ42
Lewey Ho, E3 85 DZ70
Lewgars Av, NW9 62 CQ58
Lewin Rd, SW14 98 CR83
SW16 121 DK93
Bexleyheath DA6 106 EY84
Lewins Rd, Epsom KT18 156 CP114
Gerrards Cross
(Chal.St.P.) SL9 56 AX55
Lewis Av, E17 47 EA53
Lewis Cl, N14 *off Orchid Rd* 45 DJ45
Addlestone KT15 152 BJ105
Brentwood (Shenf.) CM15 55 FZ45
Uxbridge (Hare.) UB9 38 BJ54
Lewis Cres, NW10 62 CQ64

★ Place of interest ⇌ Railway station ⊖ London Underground station DLR Docklands Light Railway station Trm Tramlink station H Hospital RIv Pedestrian ferry landing stage

Lewis Gdns, N2 44 DD54
Lewis Gro, SE13 103 EC83
LEWISHAM, SE13 103 EB84
⇌ Lewisham 103 EC83
DLR Lewisham 103 EC83
Lewisham Cen, SE13 103 EC83
Lewisham High St, SE13 103 EC83
Lewisham Hill, SE13 103 EC82
Lewisham Pk, SE13 123 EB86
Lewisham Rd, SE13 103 EB81
Lewisham St, SW1 199 N5
Lewisham Way, SE4 103 DZ81
SE14 103 DZ81
Lewis La, Ger.Cr.
(Chal.St.P.) SL9 36 AY53
Lewis Pl, E8 66 DU64
Lewis Rd, Horn. RM11 72 FJ58
Mitcham CR4 140 DD96
Richmond TW10
off Red Lion St 117 CK85
Sidcup DA14 126 EW90
Southall UB1 96 BY75
Sutton SM1 158 DB105
Swanscombe DA10 130 FY86
Welling DA16 106 EW83
Lewis St, NW1 83 DH65
Lewiston Cl, Wor.Pk. KT4 139 CV101
Lewis Way, Dag. RM10 89 FB65
Lexden Dr, Rom. RM6 70 EV58
Lexden Rd, W3 80 CP73
Mitcham CR4 141 DK98
Lexham Ct, Grnf. UB6 79 CD67
Lexham Gdns, W8 100 DB76
Lexham Gdns Ms, W8 100 DB76
Lexham Ho, Bark. IG11
off St. Margarets 87 ER67
Lexham Ms, W8 100 DA77
Lexham Wk, W8
off Lexham Gdns 100 DB76
Lexington, The, EC1 197 K4
Lexington Cl, Borwd. WD6 26 CM41
Lexington Ct, Pur. CR8 160 DQ110
Lexington St, W1 195 L9
Lexington Way, Barn. EN5 27 CX42
Upminster RM14 73 FT58
Lexton Gdns, SW12 121 DK88
Leyborne Av, W13 97 CH75
Leyborne Pk, Rich. TW9 98 CN81
Leybourne Av, W.Byf.
(Byfleet) KT14 152 BM113
Leybourne Cl, Brom. BR2 144 EG100
West Byfleet (Byfleet) KT14
off Leybourne Av 152 BM113
Leybourne Rd, E11 68 EF60
NW1 83 DH66
NW9 62 CN57
Uxbridge UB10 77 BQ67
Leybourne St, NW1
off Hawley St 83 DH66
Leybridge Ct, SE12 124 EG85
Leyburn Cl, E17
off Church La 67 EB56
Leyburn Cres, Rom. RM3 52 FL52
Leyburn Gdns, Croy. CR0 142 DS103
Leyburn Gro, N18 46 DU51
Leyburn Rd, N18 46 DU51
Romford RM3 52 FL52
Leycroft Cl, Loug. IG10 33 EN43
Leycroft Gdns, Erith DA8 107 FH81
Leydenhatch La, Swan. BR8 147 FC95
Leyden St, E1 197 P7
Leydon Cl, SE16 203 J3
Leyfield, Wor.Pk. KT4 138 CS102
Leyhill Cl, Swan. BR8 147 FE99
Ley Hill Rd, Hem.H.
(Bov.) HP3 4 AX30
Leyland Av, Enf. EN3 31 DY40
Leyland Cl, Wal.Cr.
(Chsht) EN8 14 DW28
Leyland Gdns, Wdf.Grn. IG8 48 EJ50
Leyland Rd, SE12 124 EG85
Leylands La, Stai. TW19 113 BF85
Leylang Rd, SE14 103 DX80
Leys, The, N2 64 DC56
Harrow HA3 62 CM58
Leys Av, Dag. RM10 89 FC66
Leys Cl, Dag. RM10 89 FC66
Harrow HA1 61 CD57
Uxbridge (Hare.) UB9 38 BK53
Leysdown Av, Bexh. DA7 107 FC84
Leysdown Rd, SE9 124 EL89
Leysfield Rd, W12 99 CU75
Leys Gdns, Barn. EN4 28 DG43
Leyspring Rd, E11 68 EF60
Leys Rd, Lthd.
(Oxshott) KT22 155 CD112
Leys Rd E, Enf. EN3 31 DZ39
Leys Rd W, Enf. EN3 31 DY39
Ley St, Ilf. IG1, IG2 69 EP61
Leyswood Dr, Ilf. IG2 69 ES57
Leythe Rd, W3 98 CQ75
LEYTON, E11 67 EB60
⊖ Leyton 67 EC62
Leyton Business Cen, E10 67 EA61
Leyton Cross Rd, Dart. DA2 127 FF90
Leyton Gra, E10
off Goldsmith Rd 67 EB60
Leyton Gra Est, E10 67 EB60
Leyton Grn Rd, E10 67 EC58
Leyton Ind Village, E10 67 DX59
⇌ Leyton Midland Road 67 EC60
★ Leyton Orient FC, E10 67 EB62
Leyton Pk Rd, E10 67 EC62
Leyton Rd, E15 67 ED64
SW19 120 DC94
LEYTONSTONE, E11 67 ED59
⊖ Leytonstone 68 EE60
⇌ Leytonstone High Road 68 EE61
Leytonstone Rd, E15 68 EE64
Leywick St, E15 86 EE68
Lezayre Rd, Orp. BR6 163 ET107
Liardet St, SE14 103 DY79
Liberia Rd, N5 83 DP65
★ Liberty, W1 195 K9
Liberty, The, Rom. RM1 71 FE57
Liberty 2 Shop Cen, Rom. RM1
off Mercury Gdns 71 FF57
Liberty Av, SW19 140 DD95
Liberty Hall Rd, Add. KT15 152 BG106
Liberty La, Add. KT15 152 BG106
Liberty Ms, SW12 121 DH86
Liberty Ri, Add. KT15 152 BG107
Liberty Shop Cen, Rom. RM1
off Market Pl 71 FE57
Liberty St, SW9 101 DM81
Libra Rd, E3 85 DZ67
E13 86 EG68
Library Hill, Brwd. CM14
off Coptfold Rd 54 FX47
Library Pl, E1 off Cable St 84 DV73
Library St, SE1 200 F5
Library Way, Twick. TW2
off Nelson Rd 116 CC87
Licenced Victuallers Nat Homes,
Uxb. (Denh.) UB9
off Denham Grn La 57 BF58
Lichfield Cl, Barn. EN4 28 DF41
Lichfield Ct, Rich. TW9
off Sheen Rd 98 CL84
Lichfield Gdns, Rich. TW9 98 CL84
Lichfield Gro, N3 44 DA53
Lichfield Rd, E3 85 DY69
E6 86 EK69
N9 off Winchester Rd 46 DU47
NW2 63 CY63
Dagenham RM8 70 EV63
Hounslow TW4 96 BW83
Northwood HA6 59 BU55
Richmond TW9 98 CM81
Woodford Green IG8 48 EE49
Lichfield Ter, Upmin. RM14 73 FS61
Lichfield Way, S.Croy. CR2 161 DX110
Lichlade Cl, Orp. BR6 163 ET105
Lidbury Rd, NW7 43 CY51
Lidcote Gdns, SW9 101 DN82
Liddall Way, West Dr. UB7 76 BM74
Liddell Cl, Har. HA3 61 CK55
Liddell Gdns, NW10 81 CW68
Liddell Rd, NW6 82 DA65
Lidding Rd, Har. HA3 61 CK57
Liddington Rd, E15 86 EF67
Liddon Rd, E13 86 EH69
Bromley BR1 144 EJ97
Liden Cl, E17
off Hitcham Rd 67 DZ60
Lidfield Rd, N16 66 DR63
Lidgate Rd, SE15
off Chandler Way 102 DT80
Lidiard Rd, SW18 120 DC89
Lidlington Pl, NW1 195 K1
Lido Sq, N17 46 DR54
Lidstone Cl, Wok. GU21 166 AV117
Lidyard Rd, N19 65 DJ60
Lieutenant Ellis Way,
Wal.Cr. EN7, EN8 14 DT31
★ Lifetimes Mus, Croy. CR0 142 DQ104
Liffler Rd, SE18 105 ES78
Liffords Pl, SW13 99 CT82
Lifford St, SW15 99 CX84
Lightcliffe Rd, N13 45 DN49
Lighter Cl, SE16 203 L8
Lighterman Ms, E1 85 DX72
Lighterman's Ms, Grav. DA11
off Rosherville Way 130 GE87
Lightermans Rd, E14 204 A5
Lightermans Way, Green. DA9
off London Rd 109 FW84
Lightfoot Rd, N8 65 DL57
Lightley Cl, Wem. HA0
off Stanley Av 80 CM66
Lightswood Cl, Wal.Cr.
(Chsht) EN7 14 DR27
Ligonier St, E2 197 P4
Lilac Av, Enf. EN1 30 DW36
Woking GU22 166 AX120
Lilac Cl, E4 47 DZ51
Brentwood (Pilg.Hat.) CM15
off Magnolia Way 54 FV43
Waltham Cross (Chsht) EN7
off Greenwood Av 14 DV31
Lilac Gdns, W5 97 CK76
Croydon CR0 143 EA104
Hayes UB3 77 BS72
Romford RM7 71 FE60
Swanley BR8 147 FD97
Lilac Ms, N8 off Courcy Rd 65 DN55
Lilac Pl, SE11 200 B9
West Drayton UB7
off Cedar Av 76 BM73
Lilac St, W12 81 CU73
Lila Pl, Swan. BR8 147 FE98
Lilburne Gdns, SE9 124 EL85
Lilburne Rd, SE9 124 EL85
Lilburne Wk, NW10 80 CQ65
Lile Cres, W7 79 CE71
Lilestone Est, NW8
off Fisherton St 82 DD70
Lilestone St, NW8 194 B4
Lilford Rd, SE5 101 DP82
Lilian Barker Cl, SE12 124 EG85
Lilian Board Way, Grnf. UB6 61 CD64
Lilian Cl, N16
off Barbauld Rd 66 DS62
Lilian Cres, Brwd. (Hutt.) CM13 55 GC47
Lilian Gdns, Wdf.Grn. IG8 48 EH53
Lilian Rd, SW16 141 DJ95
Lillechurch Rd, Dag. RM8 88 EV65
Lilleshall Rd, Mord. SM4 140 DD100
Lilley Cl, E1 202 C3
Brentwood CM14 54 FT49
Lilley Dr, Tad. (Kgswd) KT20 174 DB122
Lilley La, NW7 42 CR50
Lillian Av, W3 98 CN75
Lillian Rd, SW13 99 CU79
Lillie Rd, SW6 99 CY80
Westerham (Bigg.H.) TN16 178 EK118
Lillieshall Rd, SW4 101 DH83
Lillie Yd, SW6 100 DA79
Lillington Ho, N7
off Harvist Est 65 DN63
Lillington Gdns Est, SW1 199 L9
Lilliots La, Lthd. KT22
off Kingston Rd 171 CG119
Lilliput Av, Nthlt. UB5 78 BZ67
Lilliput Rd, Rom. RM7 71 FD59
Lily Cl, W14 99 CY77
Lily Dr, West Dr. UB7 94 BK77
Lily Gdns, Wem. HA0 79 CJ68
Lily Pl, EC1 196 E6
Lily Rd, E17 67 EA58
Lilyville Rd, SW6 99 CZ81
Limbourne Av, Dag. RM8 70 EZ59
Limburg Rd, SW11 100 DF84
Lime Av, Brwd. CM13 55 FZ48
Gravesend (Nthflt) DA11 130 GD87
Upminster RM14 72 FN63
West Drayton UB7 76 BM73
Windsor SL4 92 AT80
Limeburner La, EC4 196 F9
Limebush Cl, Add.
(New Haw) KT15 152 BJ109
Lime Cl, E1 202 C2
Bromley BR1 144 EL98
Buckhurst Hill IG9 48 EK48
Carshalton SM5 140 DF103
Harrow HA3 41 CF54
Pinner HA5 59 BT55
Romford RM7 71 FC56
South Ockendon RM15 91 FW69
Watford WD19 40 BX45
Lime Ct, Mitch. CR4
off Lewis Rd 140 DD96
Lime Cres, Sun. TW16 136 BW96
Limecroft Cl, Epsom KT19 156 CR108
Limedene Cl, Pnr. HA5 40 BX53
Lime Gro, E4 47 DZ51
N20 43 CZ46
W12 99 CW75
Addlestone KT15 152 BG105
Hayes UB3 77 BR73
Ilford IG6 49 ET51
New Malden KT3 138 CR97
Orpington BR6 145 EP103
Ruislip HA4 59 BV59
Sidcup DA15 125 ET86
Twickenham TW1 117 CF86
Warlingham CR6 177 DY118
Woking GU22 166 AY121
Limeharbour, E14 204 C5
LIMEHOUSE, E14 85 DY73
⇌ Limehouse 85 DY72
DLR Limehouse 85 DY72
Limehouse Causeway, E14 85 DZ73
Limehouse Flds Est, E14 85 DY71
Limehouse Link, E14 203 N1
Limekiln Dr, SE7 104 EH79
Limekiln Pl, SE19 122 DT94
Lime Meadow Av,
S.Croy. CR2 160 DU113
Lime Pit La, Sev. TN14 181 FC117
Limerick Cl, SW12 121 DJ87
Limerick Gdns, Upmin. RM14 73 FT59
Lime Rd, Epp. CM16 17 ET31
Richmond TW9
off St. Mary's Gro 98 CM84
Swanley BR8 147 FD97
Lime Row, Erith DA18
off Northwood Pl 106 EZ76
Limerston St, SW10 100 DC79
Limes, The, W2
off Linden Gdns 82 DA73
Brentwood CM13 55 FZ48
Bromley BR2 144 EL103
Hornchurch RM11
off Ashlyn Gro 72 FK55
Purfleet RM19
off Tank Hill Rd 108 FN78
Woking GU21 166 AX115
Limes Av, E11 68 EH56
N12 44 DC49
NW7 42 CS51
NW11 63 CY59
SE20 122 DV94
SW13 99 CT82
Carshalton SM5 140 DF102
Chigwell IG7 49 ER51
Croydon CR0 141 DN104
Limes Av, The, N11 45 DH50
Limes Cl, Ashf. TW15 114 BN92
Limes Ct, Brwd. CM15
off Sawyers Hall La 54 FX46
Limesdale Gdns, Edg. HA8 42 CQ54
Limes Fld Rd, SW14
off White Hart La 98 CS83
Limesford Rd, SE15 103 DX84
Limes Gdns, SW18 120 DA86
Limes Gro, SE13 103 EC84
Limes Pl, Croy. CR0 142 DR101
Limes Rd, Beck. BR3 143 EB96
Croydon CR0 142 DR100
Egham TW20 113 AZ92
Waltham Cross (Chsht) EN8 15 DX32
Weybridge KT13 152 BN105
Limes Row, Orp. BR6
off Orchard Rd 163 EP106
Limestone Wk, Erith DA18 106 EX76
Lime St, E17 67 DY56
EC3 197 M10
Lime St Pas, EC3 197 M9
Limes Wk, SE15 102 DV84
W5 off Chestnut Gro 97 CK75
Lime Ter, W7 off Manor Ct Rd 79 CE73
Lime Tree Av, Esher KT10 137 CD102
Greenhithe
(Bluewater) DA9 129 FU88
Thames Ditton KT7 137 CD102
Limetree Cl, SW2 121 DM88
Lime Tree Cl, Lthd.
(Bkhm) KT23 170 CA124
Lime Tree Gro, Croy. CR0 143 DZ104
Lime Tree Pl, Mitch. CR4 141 DH95
Lime Tree Rd, Houns. TW5 96 CB81
Limetree Ter, Well. DA16
off Hook La 106 EU83
Limetree Wk, SW17
off Church La 120 DG92
Lime Tree Wk, Amer. HP7 20 AT39
Bushey (Bushey Hth) WD23 41 CE46
Enfield EN2 30 DQ38
Rickmansworth WD3 22 BH43
Sevenoaks TN13 191 FH125
Virginia Water GU25 132 AY98
West Wickham BR4 162 EF105
Lime Wk, E15 off Church St N 86 EE67
Uxbridge (Denh.) UB9 58 BJ64
Limewood Cl, E17 67 DZ56
W13 off St. Stephens Rd 79 CH72
Beckenham BR3 143 EC99
Limewood Ct, Ilf. IG4 69 EM57
Limewood Rd, Erith DA8 107 FC80
Lime Wks Rd, Red.
(Merst.) RH1 185 DJ126
LIMPSFIELD, Oxt. RH8 188 EG128
Limpsfield Av, SW19 119 CX89
Thornton Heath CR7 141 DM99
LIMPSFIELD CHART,
Oxt. RH8 188 EL130
Limpsfield Rd, S.Croy. CR2 160 DU112
Warlingham CR6 176 DW116
Linacre Cl, SE15 102 DV83
Linacre Ct, W6 99 CX78
Linacre Rd, NW2 81 CV65
Linberry Wk, SE8 203 M9
Linchfield Rd, Slou.
(Datchet) SL3 92 AW81
Linchmere Rd, SE12 124 EF87
Lincoln Av, N14 45 DJ48
SW19 119 CX90
Romford RM7 71 FD60
Twickenham TW2 116 CB89
Lincoln Cl, SE25
off Woodside Grn 142 DU100
Erith DA8 107 FF82
Greenford UB6 78 CC67
Harrow HA2 60 BZ57
Hornchurch RM11 72 FN57
Lincoln Ct, N16 66 DR59
Borehamwood WD6 26 CR43
Lincoln Cres, Enf. EN1 30 DS43
Lincoln Dr, Rick.
(Crox.Grn) WD3 23 BP42
Watford WD19 40 BW48
Woking GU22 167 BE115
Lincoln Gdns, Ilf. IG1 68 EL59
Lincoln Grn Rd, Orp. BR5 145 ET99
Lincoln Ms, NW6
off Willesden La 81 CZ67
SE21 122 DR88
Lincoln Pk, Amer. HP7 20 AS39
Lincoln Rd, E7 86 EK65
E13 86 EH70
E18 off Grove Rd 48 EG53
N2 64 DE55
SE25 142 DV97
Enfield EN1, EN3 30 DU43
Erith DA8 107 FF82
Feltham TW13 116 BZ90
Gerrards Cross
(Chal.St.P.) SL9 36 AY53
Harrow HA2 60 BZ57
Mitcham CR4 141 DL99
New Malden KT3 138 CQ97
Northwood HA6 59 BT55
Sidcup DA14 126 EV92
Wembley HA0 79 CK65
Worcester Park KT4 139 CV102
Lincolns, The, NW7 43 CT48
Lincolns Flds, Epp. CM16 17 ET29
Lincolnshott, Grav.
(Sthflt) DA13 130 GB92
★ Lincoln's Inn, WC2 196 C8
Lincoln's Inn Flds, WC2 196 B8
Lincoln St, E11 68 EE61
SW3 198 D9
Lincoln Wk, Epsom KT19
off Hollymoor La 156 CR110
Lincoln Way, Enf. EN1 30 DV43
Rickmansworth
(Crox.Grn) WD3 23 BP42
Sunbury-on-Thames
TW16 135 BS95
Lincombe Rd, Brom. BR1 124 EF90
Lindal Cres, Enf. EN2 29 DL42
Lindale Cl, Vir.W. GU25 132 AT98
Lindales, The, N17
off Brantwood Rd 46 DT51
Lindal Rd, SE4 123 DZ85
Lindbergh Rd, Wall. SM6 159 DL109
Linden Av, NW10 81 CX68
Coulsdon CR5 175 DH116
Dartford DA1 128 FJ88
Enfield EN1 30 DU39
Hounslow TW3 116 CB85
Ruislip HA4 59 BU60
Thornton Heath CR7 141 DP98
Wembley HA9 62 CM64
Linden Chase Rd, Sev. TN13 191 FH122
Linden Cl, N14 29 DJ44
Addlestone
(New Haw) KT15 152 BG111
Orpington BR6 164 EU106
Purfleet RM19 108 FQ79
Ruislip HA4 59 BU60
Stanmore HA7 41 CH50
Tadworth KT20 173 CX120
Thames Ditton KT7 137 CF101
Waltham Cross EN7 14 DV30
Linden Ct, W12 81 CW74
Egham (Eng.Grn) TW20 112 AV93
Leatherhead KT22 171 CH121
Linden Cres, Grnf. UB6 79 CF65
Kingston upon Thames KT1 138 CM96
Woodford Green IG8 48 EH51
Linden Dr, Cat. CR3 176 DQ124
Gerrards Cross (Chal.St.P.) SL9
off Woodside Hill 36 AY54
Lindenfield, Chis. BR7 145 EP96
Linden Gdns, W2 82 DA73
W4 98 CR78
Enfield EN1 30 DU39
Leatherhead KT22 171 CJ121
Linden Gro, SE15 102 DV83
SE26 122 DW93
New Malden KT3 138 CS97
Teddington TW11
off Waldegrave Rd 117 CF92
Walton-on-Thames KT12 135 BT103
Warlingham CR6 177 DY118
Linden Ho, Slou. SL3 93 BB78
Linden Lawns, Wem. HA9 62 CM63
Linden Lea, N2 64 DC57
Watford WD25 7 BU33
Linden Leas, W.Wick. BR4 143 ED103
Linden Ms, N1 66 DR64
W2 off Linden Gdns 82 DA73
Linden Pas, W4
off Linden Gdns 98 CR78
Linden Pit Path, Lthd. KT22 171 CH121
Linden Pl, Epsom KT17
off East St 156 CS112
Mitcham CR4 140 DE98
Linden Ri, Brwd. CM14 54 FX50
Linden Rd, E17 off High St 67 DZ57
N10 65 DH56
N11 44 DF47
N15 66 DQ56
Hampton TW12 116 CA94
Leatherhead KT22 171 CH121
Weybridge KT13 153 BQ109
Lindens, The, N12 44 DD50
W4 off Hartington Rd 98 CQ81
Croydon (New Adgtn) CR0 161 EC107
Loughton IG10 33 EM43
Linden Sq, Sev. TN13
off London Rd 190 FE122
Uxbridge UB8
off Summerhouse La 38 BG51
Linden St, Rom. RM7 71 FD56
Linden Wk, N19
off Hargrave Pk 65 DJ61
Linden Way, N14 29 DJ44
Purley CR8 159 DJ110
Shepperton TW17 135 BQ99
Woking GU22 167 AZ121
Woking (Send M.) GU23 167 BF124
Lindeth Cl, Stan. HA7 41 CH51
Lindfield Gdns, NW3 64 DB64
Lindfield Rd, W5 79 CJ70
Croydon CR0 142 DT100
Romford RM3 52 FL50
Lindfield St, E14 85 EA72
Lindhill Cl, Enf. EN3 31 DX39
Lindisfarne Cl, Grav. DA12
off St. Benedict's Av 131 GL89
Lindisfarne Rd, SW20 119 CU94
Dagenham RM8 70 EW62
Lindisfarne Way, E9 67 DY63
Lindley Est, SE15
off Bird in Bush Rd 102 DU80
Lindley Pl, Rich. TW9 98 CN81
Lindley Rd, E10 67 EB61
Godstone RH9 186 DW130
Walton-on-Thames KT12 136 BX104
Lindley St, E1 84 DW71
Lindore Rd, SW11 100 DF84
Lindores Rd, Cars. SM5 140 DC101
Lindo St, SE15
off Selden Rd 102 DW82
Lind Rd, Sutt. SM1 158 DC106
Lindrop St, SW6 100 DC82
Lindsay Cl, Chess. KT9 156 CL108
Epsom KT19 156 CQ113
Staines (Stanw.) TW19 114 BK85
Lindsay Dr, Har. HA3 62 CL58
Shepperton TW17 135 BR100
Lindsay Pl, Wal.Cr. EN7 14 DV30
Lindsay Rd, Add.
(New Haw) KT15 152 BG110
Hampton (Hmptn H.) TW12 116 CB91
Worcester Park KT4 139 CV103
Lindsay Sq, SW1 199 N10
Lindsell St, SE10 103 EC81
Lindsey Cl, Brwd. CM14 54 FU49
Bromley BR1 144 EK97
Mitcham CR4 141 DL98
Lindsey Gdns, Felt. TW14 115 BR87
Lindsey Ms, N1 84 DQ66
Lindsey Rd, Dag. RM8 70 EW63
Uxbridge (Denh.) UB9 58 BG62
Lindsey St, EC1 196 G6
Epping CM16 17 ER28
Lindsey Way, Horn. RM11 72 FJ57
Lind St, SE8 103 EB82
Lindum Rd, Tedd. TW11 117 CJ94
Lindvale, Wok. GU21 166 AY115
Lindway, SE27 121 DP92
Lindwood Cl, E6
off Northumberland Rd 86 EL71
Linfield Cl, NW4 63 CW55
Walton-on-Thames KT12 153 BV106
Linfields, Amer. HP7 20 AW40
LINFORD, S.le H. SS17 111 GM75
Linford Rd, E17 67 EC55
Grays RM16 111 GH78
Tilbury (W.Til.) RM18 111 GJ78
Linford St, SW8 101 DJ81
Lingards Rd, SE13 103 EC84
Lingey Cl, Sid. DA15 125 ET89
Lingfield Av, Dart. DA2 128 FP87
Kingston upon Thames KT1 138 CL98
Upminster RM14 72 FM62
Lingfield Cl, Enf. EN1 30 DS44
Northwood HA6 39 BS52
Lingfield Cres, SE9 105 ER84
Lingfield Gdns, N9 46 DV45
Coulsdon CR5 175 DP119
Lingfield Rd, SW19 119 CX92
Gravesend DA12 131 GH89
Worcester Park KT4 139 CW104
Lingfield Way, Wat. WD17 23 BT38
Lingham St, SW9 101 DL82
Lingholm Way, Barn. EN5 27 CX43
Lingmere Cl, Chig. IG7 49 EQ47
Lingmoor Dr, Wat. WD25 8 BW33
Ling Rd, E16 86 EG71
Erith DA8 107 FC79
Lingrove Gdns, Buck.H. IG9
off Beech La 48 EH47
Lings Coppice, SE21 122 DR89
Lingwell Rd, SW17 120 DE90
Lingwood Gdns, Islw. TW7 97 CE80
Lingwood Rd, E5 66 DU59
Linhope St, NW1 194 D4
Linington Av, Chesh. HP5 4 AU30
Link, The, SE9 125 EN90
W3 80 CP72
Enfield EN3 31 DY39
Northolt UB5
off Eastcote La 60 BZ64
Pinner HA5 60 BW59
Slough SL2 74 AV72
Wembley HA0
off Nathans Rd 61 CJ60
Link Av, Wok. GU22 167 BD115
Linkfield, Brom. BR2 144 EG100

★ Place of interest ⇌ Railway station ⊖ London Underground station DLR Docklands Light Railway station Tra Tramlink station H Hospital Riv Pedestrian ferry landing stage

★ Place of interest　　⇌ Railway station　　⊖ London Underground station　　DLR Docklands Light Railway station　　Tra Tramlink station　　Ⓗ Hospital　　Riv Pedestrian ferry landing stage

285

★ Place of interest   ≠ Railway station   ➔ London Underground station   DLR Docklands Light Railway station   Tra Tramlink station   H Hospital   Riv Pedestrian ferry landing stage

286

Loudwater La, Rick. WD3 22 BK42
Loudwater Ridge, Rick.
(Loud.) WD3 22 BJ42
Loudwater Rd, Sun. TW16 135 BU98
Loughborough Est, SW9
off Loughborough Rd 101 DP82
⇌ Loughborough Junction 101 DP83
Loughborough Pk, SW9 101 DP84
Loughborough Rd, SW9 101 DN82
Loughborough St, SE11 200 C10
Lough Rd, N7 83 DM65
LOUGHTON 33 EM43
⊖ Loughton 32 EL43
Loughton Ct, Wal.Abb. EN9 16 EH33
Loughton La, Epp.
(They.B.) CM16 33 ER38
Loughton Way, Buck.H. IG9 48 EK46
Louisa Cl, E9
off Wetherell Rd 85 DX67
Louisa Gdns, E1
off Louisa St 85 DX70
Louisa Ho, SW15 98 CS84
Louisa St, E1 85 DX70
Louise Aumonier Wk, N19
off Hillrise Rd 65 DL59
Louise Bennett Cl, SE24
off Shakespeare Rd 101 DP84
Louise Ct, E11
off Grosvenor Rd 68 EH57
Louise Gdns, Rain. RM13 89 FE69
Louise Rd, E15 86 EE65
Louise Wk, Hem.H. (Bov.) HP3 5 BA28
Louis Gdns, Chis. BR7
off Walden Av 125 EM91
Louis Ms, N10 45 DH53
Louisville Rd, SW17 120 DG90
Louvaine Rd, SW11 100 DD84
Louvain Rd, Green. DA9 129 FS87
Louvain Way, Wat. WD25 7 BV32
Lovage App, E6 86 EL71
Lovat Cl, NW2 63 CT62
Lovat La, EC3 201 M1
Lovatt Cl, Edg. HA8 42 CP51
Lovatt Dr, Ruis. HA4 59 BU57
Lovatts, Rick. (Crox.Grn) WD3 22 BN42
Lovat Wk, Houns. TW5
off Cranford La 96 BY80
Loveday Rd, W13 79 CH74
Love Grn La, Iver SL0 75 BD71
Lovegrove St, SE1 102 DU78
Lovegrove Wk, E14 204 D3
Love Hill La, Slou. SL3 75 BA73
Lovekyn Cl, Kings.T. KT2
off Queen Elizabeth Rd 138 CM96
Lovelace Av, Brom. BR2 145 EN100
Lovelace Cl, Lthd.
(Eff.Junct.) KT24 169 BU123
Lovelace Dr, Wok. GU22 167 BF115
Lovelace Gdns, Bark. IG11 70 EU63
Surbiton KT6 137 CK101
Walton-on-Thames KT12 154 BW106
Lovelace Grn, SE9 105 EM83
Lovelace Rd, SE21 122 DQ89
Barnet EN4 44 DE45
Surbiton KT6 137 CJ101
Lovelands La, Tad. KT20 184 DB127
Love La, EC2 197 J8
N17 46 DT52
SE18 105 EP77
SE25 142 DV97
Abbots Langley WD5 7 BT30
Bexley DA5 126 EZ86
Godstone RH9 186 DW132
Gravesend DA12 131 GJ87
Iver SL0 75 BD72
Kings Langley WD4 6 BL29
Mitcham CR4 140 DE97
Morden SM4 140 DA101
Pinner HA5 60 BY55
South Ockendon
(Aveley) RM15 108 FQ75
Surbiton KT6 137 CK103
Sutton SM3 157 CY106
Tadworth KT20 183 CT126
Woodford Green IG8 49 EM51
Lovel Av, Well. DA16 106 EU82
Lovel End, Ger.Cr.
(Chal.St.P.) SL9 36 AW52
Lovelinch Cl, SE15 102 DW79
Lovell Ho, E8 84 DU67
Lovell Pl, SE16 203 L6
Lovell Rd, Enf. EN1 30 DV35
Richmond TW10 117 CJ90
Southall UB1 78 CB72
Lovell Wk, Rain. RM13 89 FG65
Lovel Mead, Ger.Cr.
(Chal.St.P.) SL9 36 AW52
Lovelock Cl, Ken. CR8 176 DQ117
Lovel Rd, Ger.Cr.
(Chal.St.P.) SL9 36 AW52
Loveridge Ms, NW6
off Loveridge Rd 81 CZ65
Loveridge Rd, NW6 81 CZ65
Lovering Rd, Wal.Cr.
(Chsht) EN7 14 DQ26
Lovers La, Green. DA9 109 FX84
Lovers Wk, N3 44 DA52
NW7 43 CZ51
SE10 104 EE79
Lover's Wk, W1 198 F2
Lovett Dr, Cars. SM5 140 DC101
Lovett Rd, St.Alb. AL2
off Shenley La 9 CH26
Staines TW18 113 BB91
Uxbridge (Hare.) UB9 58 BJ55
Lovett's Pl, SW18
off Old York Rd 100 DB84
Lovett Way, NW10 62 CQ64
Love Wk, SE5 102 DR82
Lovibonds Av, Orp. BR6 163 EP105
West Drayton UB7 76 BM72
Lowbell La, St.Alb.
(Lon.Col.) AL2 10 CL27
Lowbrook Rd, Ilf. IG1 69 EP64
Low Cl, Green. DA9 129 FU85
Low Cross Wd La, SE21 122 DT90
Lowdell Cl, West Dr. UB7 76 BL72
Lowden Rd, N9 46 DV46
SE24 101 DP84
Southall UB1 78 BY73
Lowe, The, Chig. IG7 50 EU50
Lowe Av, E16 86 EG71
Lowe Cl, Chig. IG7 50 EU50
Lowell St, E14 85 DY72
Lowen Rd, Rain. RM13 89 FD68
Lower Addiscombe Rd,
Croy. CR0 142 DS102
Lower Addison Gdns, W14 99 CY75
Lower Alderton Hall La,
Loug. IG10 33 EN43
LOWER ASHTEAD,
Ashtd. KT21 171 CJ119
Lower Barn Rd, Pur. CR8 160 DR112
Lower Bedfords Rd,
Rom. RM1 51 FE51
Lower Belgrave St, SW1 199 H7
Lower Boston Rd, W7 79 CE74
Lower Br Rd, Red. RH1 184 DF134
Lower Broad St, Dag. RM10 88 FA67
Lower Bury La, Epp. CM16 17 ES31
Lower Camden, Chis. BR7 125 EM94
Lower Ch Hill, Green. DA9 129 FS85
Lower Ch St, Croy. CR0
off Waddon New Rd 141 DP103
LOWER CLAPTON, E5 67 DX63
Lower Clapton Rd, E5 66 DV64
Lower Clarendon Wk, W11
off Lancaster Rd 81 CY72
Lower Common S, SW15 99 CV83
Lower Coombe St,
Croy. CR0 160 DQ105
Lower Ct Rd, Epsom KT19 156 CQ111
Lower Cft, Swan. BR8 147 FF98
Lower Downs Rd, SW20 139 CX95
Lower Drayton Pl, Croy. CR0
off Drayton Rd 141 DP103
Lower Dunnymans, Bans. SM7
off Basing Rd 157 CZ114
LOWER EDMONTON, N9 46 DT46
Lower Fm Rd, Lthd.
(Eff.) KT24 169 BV124
LOWER FELTHAM, Felt. TW13 115 BS90
Lower George St, Rich. TW9
off George St 117 CK85
Lower Gravel Rd, Brom. BR2 144 EL102
LOWER GREEN, Esher KT10 136 CA103
Lower Grn Gdns,
Wor.Pk. KT4 139 CU102
Lower Grn Rd, Esher KT10 136 CB103
Lower Grn W, Mitch. CR4 140 DE97
Lower Grosvenor Pl, SW1 199 H6
Lower Gro Rd, Rich. TW10 118 CM86
Lower Guild Hall, Green.
(Bluewater) DA9
off Bluewater Parkway 129 FU88
Lower Hall La, E4 47 DY50
Lower Hampton Rd,
Sun. TW16 136 BW97
Lower Ham Rd, Kings.T. KT2 117 CK93
Lower Higham Rd,
Grav. DA12 131 GM88
Lower High St, Wat. WD17 24 BX44
Lower Hill Rd, Epsom KT19 156 CP112
LOWER HOLLOWAY, N7 65 DM64
Lower James St, W1 195 L10
Lower John St, W1 195 L10
Lower Kenwood Av, Enf. EN2 29 DK43
Lower Kings Rd, Kings.T. KT2 118 CL94
LOWER KINGSWOOD,
Tad. KT20 184 DA127
Lower Lea Crossing, E14 86 EE73
E16 86 EE73
Lower Maidstone Rd, N11
off Telford Rd 45 DJ51
Lower Mall, W6 99 CV78
Lower Mardyke Av,
Rain. RM13 89 FC68
Lower Marsh, SE1 200 D5
Lower Marsh La, Kings.T. KT1 138 CM98
Lower Mead, Iver SL0 75 BD69
Lower Meadow, Wal.Cr. EN8 15 DX27
Lower Merton Ri, NW3 82 DE66
Lower Morden La,
Mord. SM4 139 CW100
Lower Mortlake Rd,
Rich. TW9 98 CL84
Lower Noke Cl, Brwd. CM14 52 FL47
Lower Northfield, Bans. SM7 157 CZ114
Lower Paddock Rd,
Wat. WD19 24 BY44
Lower Pk Rd, N11 45 DJ50
Belvedere DA17 106 FA76
Coulsdon CR5 174 DE118
Loughton IG10 32 EK43
Lower Pillory Down,
Cars. SM5 158 DG113
Lower Plantation, Rick.
(Loud.) WD3 22 BJ41
Lower Queens Rd, Buck.H.
IG9 48 EK47
Lower Range Rd, Grav. DA12 131 GL87
Lower Richmond Rd, SW14 98 CP83
SW15 99 CW83
Richmond TW9 98 CN83
Lower Rd, SE8 202 F6
SE16 203 H8
Belvedere DA17 106 FA76
Brentwood
(Mtnsg) CM13, CM15 55 GD41
Erith DA8 107 FD77
Gerrards Cross SL9 36 AY53
Gravesend (Nthflt) DA11 110 FY84
Harrow HA2 61 CD61
Hemel Hempstead HP3 6 BN25
Kenley CR8 159 DP113
Leatherhead
(Fetch.) KT22, KT23, KT24 171 CD123
Loughton IG10 33 EN40
Orpington BR5 146 EV101
Rickmansworth
(Chorl.) WD3 21 BC42
Sutton SM1 158 DC105
Swanley BR8 127 FF94
Tilbury RM18 111 GG84
Uxbridge (Denh.) UB9 57 BC59
Lower Robert St, WC2
off John Adam St 83 DL73
Lower Rose Gall, Green.
(Bluewater) DA9
off Bluewater Parkway 129 FU88
Lower Sandfields, Wok.
(Send) GU23 167 BD124
Lower Sand Hills, T.Ditt. KT7 137 CJ101
Lower Sawley Wd, Bans. SM7
off Upper Sawley Wd 157 CZ114
Lower Shott, Wal.Cr.
(Chsht) EN7 14 DT26
Lower Sloane St, SW1 198 F9
Lower Sq, Islw. TW7 97 CH83
Lower Sta Rd, Dart.
(Cray.) DA1 127 FE86
Lower Strand, NW9 43 CT54
Lower Sunbury Rd,
Hmptn. TW12 136 BZ96
Lower Swaines, Epp. CM16 17 ES30
LOWER SYDENHAM, SE26 123 DX91
⇌ Lower Sydenham 123 DZ92
Lower Sydenham Ind Est,
SE26 123 DZ92
Lower Tail, Wat. WD19 40 BY48
Lower Talbot Wk, W11
off Lancaster Rd 81 CY72
Lower Teddington Rd, Kings.T.
KT1 137 CK95
Lower Ter, NW3 64 DC62
Lower Thames St, EC3 201 L1
Lower Thames Wk, Green.
(Bluewater) DA9
off Bluewater Parkway 129 FU88
Lower Tub, Bushey WD23 41 CD45
Lower Wd Rd, Esher
(Clay.) KT10 155 CG107
Lowestoft Cl, E5
off Theydon Rd 66 DW61
Lowestoft Ms, E16 105 EP75
Lowestoft Rd, Wat. WD24 23 BV39
Loweswater Cl, Wat. WD25 8 BW33
Wembley HA9 61 CK61
Lowfield Rd, NW6 82 DA66
W3 80 CQ72
Lowfield St, Dart. DA1 128 FL89
Low Hall Cl, E4 47 EA45
Low Hall La, E17 67 DY58
Lowick Rd, Har. HA1 61 CE56
Lowlands Dr, Stai.
(Stanw.) TW19 114 BK85
Lowlands Gdns, Rom. RM7 71 FB58
Lowlands Rd, Har. HA1 61 CE59
Pinner HA5 60 BW59
South Ockendon
(Aveley) RM15 90 FP74
Lowman Rd, N7 65 DM63
Lowndes Cl, SW1 198 G7
Lowndes Ct, W1 195 K9
Bromley BR1
off Queens Rd 144 EG96
Lowndes Pl, SW1 198 F7
Lowndes Sq, SW1 198 E5
Lowndes St, SW1 198 E6
Lowood Ct, SE19 122 DT92
Lowood St, E1 off Dellow St 84 DV73
Lowry Cl, Erith DA8 107 FD77
Lowry Cres, Mitch. CR4 140 DE96
Lowry Rd, Dag. RM8 70 EV63
Lowshoe La, Rom. RM5 51 FB53
Lowson Gro, Wat. WD19 40 BY45
LOW STREET, Til. RM18 111 GM79
Low St La, Til. (E.Til.) RM18 111 GM78
Lowswood Cl, Nthwd. HA6 39 BQ53
Lowther Cl, Borwd.
(Elstree) WD6 26 CM43
Lowther Dr, Enf. EN2 29 DL42
Lowther Gdns, SW7 198 A5
Lowther Hill, SE23 123 DY87
Lowther Rd, E17 47 DY54
N7 off Mackenzie Rd 65 DN64
SW13 99 CT81
Kingston upon Thames KT2 138 CM95
Stanmore HA7 62 CM55
Lowthorpe, Wok. GU21
off Shilburn Way 166 AU118
Lowth Rd, SE5 102 DQ82
LOXFORD, Ilf. IG1 69 EQ64
Loxford Av, E6 86 EK68
Loxford La, Ilf. IG1, IG3 69 EQ64
Loxford Rd, Bark. IG11 87 EP65
Caterham CR3 186 DT125
Loxford Ter, Bark. IG11
off Fanshawe Av 87 EQ65
Loxford Way, Cat. CR3 186 DT125
Loxham Rd, E4 47 EA52
Loxham St, WC1 196 A3
Loxley Cl, SE26 123 DX92
Loxley Rd, SW18 120 DD88
Hampton TW12 116 BZ91
Loxton Rd, SE23 123 DX88
Loxwood Cl, Felt. TW14 115 BR88
Orpington BR5 146 EX103
Loxwood Rd, N17 66 DS55
Lubbock Rd, Chis. BR7 125 EM94
Lubbock St, SE14 102 DW80
Lucan Dr, Stai. TW18 114 BK94
Lucan Pl, SW3 198 B9
Lucan Rd, Barn. EN5 27 CY41
Lucas Av, E13 86 EH67
Harrow HA2 60 CA61
Lucas Cl, NW10
off Pound La 81 CU66
Lucas Ct, Har. HA2 60 CA60
Waltham Abbey EN9 16 EF33
Lucas Cres, Green. DA9
off London Rd 129 FW85
Lucas Gdns, N2 44 DC54
Lucas Rd, SE20 122 DW93
Grays RM17 110 GA76
Lucas Sq, NW11
off Hampstead Way 64 DA58
Lucas St, SE8 103 EA81
Lucern Cl, Wal.Cr. (Chsht) EN7 14 DS27
Lucerne Cl, N13 45 DL49
Woking GU22
off Claremont Av 166 AY119
Lucerne Ct, Erith DA18
off Middle Way 106 EY76
Lucerne Gro, E17 67 ED56
Lucerne Ms, W8
off Kensington Mall 82 DA74
Lucerne Rd, N5 65 DP63
Orpington BR6 145 ET102
Thornton Heath CR7 141 DP99
Lucerne Way, Rom. RM3 52 FK51
Lucey Rd, SE16 202 B7
Lucey Way, SE16 202 C7
Lucie Av, Ashf. TW15 115 BP93
Lucien Rd, SW17 120 DG91
SW19 120 DB89
Lucknow St, SE18 105 ES80
Lucorn Cl, SE12 124 EF86
Lucton Ms, Loug. IG10 33 EP42
Luctons Av, Buck.H. IG9 48 EJ46
Lucy Cres, W3 80 CQ71
Lucy Gdns, Dag. RM8
off Grafton Rd 70 EY62
Luddesdon Rd, Erith DA8 106 FA80
Luddington Av, Vir.W. GU25 133 AZ96
Ludford Cl, NW9 42 CS54
Croydon CR0
off Warrington Rd 159 DP105
Ludgate Bdy, EC4 196 F9
Ludgate Circ, EC4 196 F9
Ludgate Hill, EC4 196 F9
Ludgate Sq, EC4 196 G9
Ludham Cl, SE28
off Rollesby Way 88 EW72
Ilford IG6 49 EP53
Ludlow Cl, Brom. BR2
off Aylesbury Rd 144 EG97
Harrow HA2 60 BZ63
Ludlow Mead, Wat. WD19 39 BV48
Ludlow Pl, Grays RM17 110 GB76
Ludlow Rd, W5 79 CJ70
Feltham TW13 115 BU91
Ludlow St, EC1 197 H4
Ludlow Way, N2 64 DC56
Rickmansworth
(Crox.Grn) WD3 23 BQ42
Ludovick Wk, SW15 98 CS84
Ludwick Ms, SE14 103 DY80
Luffield Rd, SE2 106 EV76
Luffman Rd, SE12 124 EH90
Lugard Rd, SE15 102 DV82
Lugg App, E12 69 EN62
Luke Ho, E1 84 DV72
Luke St, EC2 197 M4
Lukin Cres, E4 47 ED48
Lukin St, E1 84 DW72
Lukintone Cl, Loug. IG10 32 EL44
Lullarook Cl, West.
(Bigg.H.) TN16 178 EJ116
Lullingstone Av, Swan. BR8 147 FF97
Lullingstone Cl, Orp. BR5
off Lullingstone Cres 126 EV94
Lullingstone Cres, Orp. BR5 126 EU94
Lullingstone La, SE13 123 ED87
Dartford (Eyns.) DA4 148 FJ104
★ Lullingstone Park
Visitor Cen, Dart. DA4 165 FG107
Lullingstone Rd, Belv. DA17 106 EZ79
★ Lullingstone Roman Vil,
Dart. DA4 147 FH104
Lullington Garth, N12 43 CZ50
Borehamwood WD6 26 CP43
Bromley BR1 144 EE94
Lullington Rd, SE20 122 DU94
Dagenham RM9 88 EY66
Lulot Gdns, N19 65 DH61
Lulworth, SE17 201 K10
Lulworth Av, Houns. TW5 96 CB80
Waltham Cross (Chsht) EN7 13 DP29
Wembley HA9 61 CJ59
Lulworth Cl, Har. HA2 60 BZ62
Lulworth Cres, Mitch. CR4 140 DE96
Lulworth Dr, Pnr. HA5 60 BX59
Romford RM5 51 FB50
Lulworth Gdns, Har. HA2 60 BY61
Lulworth Rd, SE9 124 EL89
SE15 102 DV82
Welling DA16 105 ET82
Lulworth Waye, Hayes UB4 78 BW72
Lumen Rd, Wem. HA9 61 CK61
Lumiere Ct, SW17 120 DG89
Lumley Cl, Belv. DA17 106 FA79
Lumley Ct, WC2 200 A1
Lumley Gdns, Sutt. SM3 157 CY106
Lumley Rd, Sutt. SM3 157 CY107
Lumley St, W1 194 G9
Lunar Cl, West.
(Bigg.H.) TN16 178 EK116
Luna Rd, Th.Hth. CR7 142 DQ97
Lundin Wk, Wat. WD19
off Woodhall La 40 BX49
Lundy Dr, Hayes UB3 95 BS77
Lundy Wk, N1
off Clephane Rd 84 DQ65
Lunedale Rd, Dart. DA2 128 FQ88
Lunedale Wk, Dart. DA2
off Lunedale Rd 128 FP88
Lunghurst Rd, Cat.
(Wold.) CR3 177 DZ120
Lunham Rd, SE19 122 DS93
Lupin Cl, SW2 off Palace Rd 121 DP89
Croydon CR0
off Primrose La 143 DX102
Romford (Rush Grn) RM7 71 FD61
West Drayton UB7
off Magnolia St 94 BK78
Lupin Cres, Ilf. IG1
off Bluebell Way 69 EP64
Lupino Ct, SE11 200 C9
Luppit Cl, Brwd. (Hutt.) CM13 55 GA46
Lupton Cl, SE12 124 EH90
Lupton St, NW5 65 DJ63
Lupus St, SW1 101 DH79
Luralda Gdns, E14 204 E10
Lurgan Av, W6 99 CX79
Lurline Gdns, SW11 100 DG81
Luscombe Ct, Brom. BR2 144 EE96
Luscombe Way, SW8 101 DL80
Lushes Ct, Loug. IG10
off Lushes Rd 33 EP43
Lushes Rd, Loug. IG10 33 EP43
Lushington Dr, Cob. KT11 153 BV114
Lushington Rd, NW10 81 CV68
SE6 123 EB92
Lushington Ter, E8
off Wayland Av 66 DU64
Lusted Hall La, West.
(Tats.) TN16 178 EJ120
Lusted Rd, Sev. TN13 181 FE120
Luther Cl, Edg. HA8 42 CQ47
Luther King Cl, E17 67 DY58
Luther Ms, Tedd. TW11
off Luther Rd 117 CF92
Luther Rd, Tedd. TW11 117 CF92
Luton Pl, SE10 103 EC80
Luton Rd, E17 67 DZ55
Sidcup DA14 126 EW90
Luton St, NW8 194 A5
Lutton Ter, NW3 off Flask Wk 64 DD63
Luttrell Av, SW15 119 CV85
Lutwyche Rd, SE6 123 DZ89
Luxborough La, Chig. IG7 48 EL48
Luxborough St, W1 194 F6
Luxembourg Ms, E15
off Leytonstone Rd 68 EE64
Luxemburg Gdns, W6 99 CX77
Luxfield Rd, SE9 124 EL88
Luxford St, SE16 203 H9
Luxmore St, SE4 103 DZ81
Luxor St, SE5 102 DQ83
Luxted Rd, Orp. BR6 163 EN112
Lyall Av, SE21 122 DS90
Lyall Ms, SW1 198 F7
Lyall Ms W, SW1 198 F7
Lyall St, SW1 198 F7
Lyal Rd, E3 85 DY68
Lycett Pl, W12
off Becklow Rd 99 CU75
Lych Gate, Wat. WD25 8 BX33
Lych Gate Rd, Orp. BR6 146 EU102
Lych Gate Wk, Hayes UB3 77 BT73
Lych Way, Wok. GU21 166 AX116
Lyconby Gdns, Croy. CR0 143 DY101
Lycrome Rd, Chesh. HP5 4 AS28
Lydd Cl, Sid. DA14 125 ES90
Lydden Ct, SE9 125 ES86
Lydden Gro, SW18 120 DB87
Lydden Rd, SW18 120 DB87
Lydd Rd, Bexh. DA7 106 EZ80
Lydeard Rd, E6 87 EM66
Lydele Cl, Wok. GU21 167 AZ115
Lydford Cl, N16
off Pellerin Rd 66 DS64
Lydford Rd, N15 66 DR57
NW2 81 CX65
W9 81 CZ70
Lydhurst Av, SW2 121 DM89
Lydia Rd, Erith DA8 107 FF79
Lydney Cl, SE15 102 DS80
SW19 off Princes Way 119 CY89
Lydon Rd, SW4 101 DJ83
Lydstep Rd, Chis. BR7 125 EN91
Lye, The, Tad. KT20 173 CW122
LYE GREEN, Chesh. HP5 4 AT27
Lye La, St.Alb. (Brick.Wd) AL2 8 CA30
Lyfield, Lthd. (Oxshott) KT22 154 CB114
Lyford Rd, SW18 120 DD87
Lygon Pl, SW1 199 H7
Lyham Cl, SW2 121 DL86
Lyham Rd, SW2 121 DL85
Lyle Cl, Mitch. CR4 140 DG101
Lyle Pk, Sev. TN13 191 FH123
Lymbourne Cl, Sutt. SM2 158 DA110
Lyme Fm Rd, SE12 104 EG84
Lyme Gro, E9
off St. Thomas's Sq 84 DW66
Lymer Av, SE19 122 DT92
Lyme Regis Rd, Bans. SM7 173 CZ117
Lyme Rd, Well. DA16 106 EV81
Lymescote Gdns, Sutt. SM1 140 DA103
Lyme St, NW1 83 DJ66
Lyme Ter, NW1
off Royal Coll St 83 DJ66
Lyminge Cl, Sid. DA14 125 ET91
Lyminge Gdns, SW18 120 DE88
Lymington Av, N22 45 DN54
Lymington Cl, E6
off Valiant Way 87 EM71
SW16 141 DK96
Lymington Dr, Ruis. HA4 59 BR61
Lymington Gdns,
Epsom KT19 157 CT106
Lymington Rd, NW6 82 DB65
Dagenham RM8 70 EX60
Lyminster Cl, Hayes UB4
off West Quay Dr 78 BY71
Lympstone Gdns, SE15 102 DU80
Lynbridge Gdns, N13 45 DP49
Lynbrook Cl, SE15
off Blakes Rd 102 DS80
Rainham RM13 89 FD68
Lynceley Gra, Epp. CM16 18 EU29
Lynch, The, Uxb. UB8
off New Windsor St 76 BJ67
Lynch Cl, Uxb. UB8
off New Windsor St 76 BJ66
Lynchen Cl, Houns. TW5
off The Avenue 95 BU81
Lynch Wk, SE8 off Prince St 103 DZ79
Lyncott Cres, SW4 101 DH84
Lyncroft Av, Pnr. HA5 60 BY57
Lyncroft Gdns, NW6 64 DA64
W13 97 CJ75
Epsom KT17 157 CT109
Hounslow TW3 96 CC84
Lyndale, NW2 63 CZ63
Lyndale Av, NW2 63 CZ62
Lyndale Cl, SE3 104 EF79
Lyndale Ct, W.Byf. KT14
off Parvis Rd 152 BG113
Lyndale Est, Grays RM20 109 FV79
Lyndale Rd, Red. RH1 184 DF131
Lynden Way, Swan. BR8 147 FC97
Lyndhurst Av, N12 44 DF51
NW7 43 CS51
SW16 141 DK96
Pinner HA5 39 BV53
Southall UB1 78 CB74
Sunbury-on-Thames TW16 135 BU97
Surbiton KT5 138 CP102
Twickenham TW2 116 BZ88
Lyndhurst Cl, NW10 62 CR62
Bexleyheath DA7 107 FB83
Croydon CR0 142 DT104
Orpington BR6 163 EP105

★ Place of interest ⇌ Railway station ⊖ London Underground station DLR Docklands Light Railway station Tra Tramlink station H Hospital Riv Pedestrian ferry landing stage

Lyn - Mal

Lyndhurst Cl, Woking GU21 166 AX115
Lyndhurst Ct, E18
off Churchfields 48 EG53
Sutton SM2
off Overton Rd 158 DA108
Lyndhurst Dr, E10 67 EC59
Hornchurch RM11 72 FJ60
New Malden KT3 138 CS100
Sevenoaks TN13 190 FE124
Lyndhurst Gdns, N3 43 CY53
NW3 64 DD64
Barking IG11 87 ES65
Enfield EN1 30 DS42
Ilford IG2 69 ER58
Pinner HA5 39 BV53
Lyndhurst Gro, SE15 102 DS82
Lyndhurst Ho, SW15
off Ellisfield Dr 119 CU87
Lyndhurst Ri, Chig. IG7 49 EN49
Lyndhurst Rd, E4 47 EC52
N18 46 DU49
N22 45 DM51
NW3 64 DD64
Bexleyheath DA7 107 FB83
Coulsdon CR5 174 DG116
Greenford UB6 78 CB70
Thornton Heath CR7 141 DN98
Lyndhurst Sq, SE15 102 DT81
Lyndhurst Ter, NW3 64 DD64
Lyndhurst Way, SE15 102 DT81
Brentwood (Hutt.) CM13 55 GC45
Chertsey KT16 133 BE104
Sutton SM2 158 DA108
Lyndon Av, Pnr. HA5 40 BY51
Sidcup DA15 125 ET85
Wallington SM6 140 DG104
Lyndon Rd, Belv. DA17 106 FA77
Lyndon Yd, SW17
off Riverside Rd 120 DC91
Lyndwood Dr, Wind.
(Old Wind.) SL4 112 AU86
LYNE, Cher. KT16 133 BA102
Lyne Cl, Vir.W. GU25 133 AZ100
Lyne Cres, E17 47 DZ53
Lyne Crossing Rd, Cher.
(Lyne) KT16 133 BA100
Lynegrove Av, Ashf. TW15 115 BQ92
Lyneham Wk, E5 67 DY64
Pinner HA5 59 BT55
Lyne La, Cher. (Lyne) KT16 133 BA100
Egham TW20 133 BA99
Virginia Water GU25 133 BA100
Lyne Rd, Vir.W. GU25 132 AX100
Lynette Av, SW4 121 DH86
Lynett Rd, Dag. RM8 70 EX61
Lynford Cl, Barn. EN5
off Rowley La 27 CT43
Edgware HA8 42 CQ52
Lynford Gdns, Edg. HA8 42 CP48
Ilford IG3 69 ET61
Lynhurst Cres, Uxb. UB10 77 BQ66
Lynhurst Rd, Uxb. UB10 77 BQ66
Lynmere Rd, Well. DA16 106 EV82
Lyn Ms, E3 off Tredegar Sq 85 DZ69
N16 66 DS63
Lynmouth Av, Enf. EN1 30 DT44
Morden SM4 139 CX101
Lynmouth Dr, Ruis. HA4 59 BV61
Lynmouth Gdns, Grnf. UB6 79 CH67
Hounslow TW5 96 BX81
Lynmouth Ri, Orp. BR5 146 EV98
Lynmouth Rd, E17 67 DY58
N2 64 DF55
N16 66 DT60
Greenford UB6 79 CH67
Lynn Cl, Ashf. TW15
off Goffs Rd 115 BR92
Harrow HA3 41 CD54
Lynne Cl, Orp. BR6 163 ET107
South Croydon CR2 160 DW111
Lynne Wk, Esher KT10 154 CC106
Lynne Way, NW10 80 CS65
Northolt UB5 78 BX68
Lynn Ms, E11 off Lynn Rd 68 EE61
Lynn Rd, E11 68 EE61
SW12 121 DH87
Ilford IG2 69 ER59
Lynn St, Enf. EN2 30 DR39
Lynross Cl, Rom. RM3 52 FM54
Lynscott Way, S.Croy. CR2 159 DP109
Lynsted Cl, Bexh. DA6 127 FB85
Bromley BR1 144 EJ96
Lynsted Ct, Beck. BR3
off Churchfields Rd 143 DY96
Lynsted Gdns, SE9 104 EK83
Lynton Av, N12 44 DD49
NW9 63 CT56
W13 79 CG72
Orpington BR5 146 EV98
Romford RM7 50 FA53
Lynton Cl, NW10 62 CS64
Chessington KT9 156 CL105
Isleworth TW7 97 CF84
Lynton Cres, Ilf. IG2 69 EP58
Lynton Crest, Pot.B. EN6
off Strafford Gate 12 DA32
Lynton Est, SE1 202 B9
Lynton Gdns, N11 45 DK51
Enfield EN1 46 DS45
Lynton Mead, N20 44 DA48
Lynton Par, Wal.Cr. EN8
off Turners Hill 15 DX30
Lynton Rd, E4 47 EB50
N8 65 DK57
NW6 81 CZ67
SE1 202 A9
W3 80 CN73
Croydon CR0 141 DN100
Gravesend DA11 131 GG88
Harrow HA2 60 BY61
New Malden KT3 138 CR99
Lynton Rd S, Grav. DA11 131 GG88
Lynton Ter, W3 off Lynton Rd 80 CQ72
Lynton Wk, Hayes UB4 77 BS69
Lynwood Av, Couls. CR5 175 DH115
Lynwood Av, Egham TW20 112 AY93
Epsom KT17 157 CT114
Slough SL3 92 AX76
Lynwood Cl, E18 48 EJ53
Harrow HA2 60 BY62
Romford RM5 51 FB51
Woking GU21 151 BD113
Lynwood Dr, Nthwd. HA6 39 BT53
Romford RM5 51 FB51
Worcester Park KT4 139 CU103
Lynwood Gdns, Croy. CR0 159 DM105
Southall UB1 78 BZ72
Lynwood Gro, N21 45 DN46
Orpington BR6 145 ES101
Lynwood Hts, Rick. WD3 22 BH43
Lynwood Rd, SW17 120 DF90
W5 80 CL70
Epsom KT17 157 CT114
Redhill RH1 184 DG132
Thames Ditton KT7 137 CF103
Lynx Way, E16
off Festoon Way 86 EK73
Lyon Business Pk, Bark. IG11 87 ES68
Lyon Meade, Stan. HA7 41 CJ53
Lyon Pk Av, Wem. HA0 80 CL65
Lyon Rd, SW19 140 DC95
Harrow HA1 61 CF58
Romford RM1 71 FF59
Walton-on-Thames KT12 136 BY103
Lyonsdene, Tad. KT20 183 CZ127
Lyonsdown Av, Barn. EN5 28 DC44
Lyonsdown Rd, Barn. EN5 28 DC44
Lyons Pl, NW8 82 DD70
Lyon St, N1
off Caledonian Rd 83 DM66
Lyons Wk, W14 99 CY77
Lyon Way, Grnf. UB6 79 CE67
Lyoth Rd, Orp. BR5 145 EQ103
Lyric Dr, Grnf. UB6 78 CB70
Lyric Ms, SE26 122 DW91
Lyric Rd, SW13 99 CT81
★ Lyric Thea, W6 99 CW77
Lysander Cl, Hem.H.
(Bov.) HP3 5 AZ27
Lysander Gdns, Surb. KT6
off Ewell Rd 138 CM100
Lysander Gro, N19 65 DK60
Lysander Ms, N19
off Lysander Gro 65 DJ60
Lysander Rd, Croy. CR0 159 DM107
Ruislip HA4 59 BR61
Lysander Way, Abb.L. WD5 7 BU32
Orpington BR6 145 EQ104
Lysias Rd, SW12 120 DG86
Lysia St, SW6 99 CX80
Lysley Pl, Hat. AL9 12 DC27
Lysons Wk, SW15
off Swinburne Rd 119 CU85
Lyster Ms, Cob. KT11 153 BV113
Lytchet Rd, Brom. BR1 124 EH94
Lytchet Way, Enf. EN3 30 DW39
Lytchgate Cl, S.Croy. CR2 160 DS108
Lytcott Dr, W.Mol. KT8
off Freeman Dr 136 BZ97
Lytcott Gro, SE22 122 DT85
Lyte St, E2 off Bishops Way 84 DW68
Lytham Av, Wat. WD19 40 BX50
Lytham Cl, SE28 88 EY72
Lytham Gro, W5 80 CM69
Lytham St, SE17 102 DR78
Lyttelton Cl, NW3 82 DE66
Lyttelton Rd, E10 67 EB62
N2 64 DC57
Lyttleton Rd, N8 65 DN55
Lytton Av, N13 45 DN47
Enfield EN3 31 DY38
Lytton Cl, N2 64 DD57
Loughton IG10 33 ER41
Northolt UB5 78 BZ66
Lytton Gdns, Wall. SM6 159 DK105
Lytton Gro, SW15 119 CX85
Lytton Pk, Cob. KT11 154 BZ112
Lytton Rd, E11 68 EE59
Barnet EN5 28 DC42
Grays RM16 111 GG77
Pinner HA5 40 BY52
Romford RM2 71 FH57
Woking GU22 167 BB116
Lytton Strachey Path, SE28
off Titmuss Av 88 EV73
Lyveden Rd, SE3 104 EH80
SW17 120 DE93
Lywood Cl, Tad. KT20 173 CW122

M

Mabbotts, Tad. KT20 173 CX121
Mabbutt Cl, St.Alb.
(Brick.Wd) AL2 8 BY30
Mabel Rd, Swan. BR8 127 FG93
Mabel St, Wok. GU21 166 AX117
Maberley Cres, SE19 122 DU94
Maberley Rd, SE19 142 DT95
Beckenham BR3 143 DX97
Mabledon Pl, WC1 195 N3
Mablethorpe Rd, SW6 99 CY80
Mabley St, E9 85 DY65
McAdam Dr, Enf. EN2
off Rowantree Rd 29 DP40
Macaret Cl, N20 44 DB45
MacArthur Cl, E7 86 EG65
Erith DA8 off West St 107 FE78
MacArthur Ter, SE7 104 EL79
Macaulay Av, Esher KT10 137 CE103
Macaulay Ct, SW4 101 DH83
Macaulay Rd, E6 86 EK68
SW4 101 DH83
Caterham CR3 176 DS122
Macaulay Sq, SW4 101 DH84
Macaulay Way, SE28
off Booth Cl 88 EV73
McAuley Cl, SE1 200 D6
SE9 125 EP85
Macauley Ms, SE13 103 EC82
Macbean St, SE18 105 EN76
Macbeth St, W6 99 CV78
McCall Cl, SW4
off Jeffreys Rd 101 DL82
McCall Cres, SE7 104 EL78
McCarthy Rd, Felt. TW13 116 BX92
Macclesfield Br, NW1 82 DE68
Macclesfield Rd, EC1 197 H2
SE25 142 DV99
Macclesfield St, W1 195 N10
McClintock Pl, Enf. EN3 31 EB38
McCoid Way, SE1 201 H5
McCrone Ms, NW3
off Belsize La 82 DD65
McCudden Rd, Dart. DA1
off Cornwall Rd 108 FM83
McCullum Rd, E3 85 DZ67
McDermott Cl, SW11 100 DE83
McDermott Rd, SE15 102 DU83
Macdonald Av, Dag. RM10 71 FB62
Hornchurch RM11 72 FL56
Macdonald Rd, E7 68 EG63
E17 47 EC54
N11 44 DF50
N19 65 DJ61
Macdonald Way, Horn. RM11 72 FL56
Macdonnell Gdns, Wat. WD25
off High Rd 23 BT35
McDonough Cl, Chess. KT9 156 CL105
McDowall Cl, E16 86 EF71
McDowall Rd, SE5 102 DQ81
Macduff Rd, SW11 100 DG81
Mace Cl, E1 202 D2
Mace Ct, Grays RM17 110 GE79
Mace La, Sev.
(Cudham) TN14 163 ER113
McEntee Av, E17 47 DY53
Mace St, E2 85 DX68
McEwen Way, E15 85 ED67
Macey Ho, SW11
off Surrey La 100 DE81
MacFarlane La, Islw. TW7 97 CF79
Macfarlane Rd, W12 81 CW74
Macfarren Pl, NW1 194 G5
McGrath Rd, E15 68 EF64
McGredy, Wal.Cr. (Chsht) EN7 14 DV29
Macgregor Rd, E16 86 EJ71
McGregor Rd, W11 81 CZ72
Machell Rd, SE15 102 DW83
McIntosh Cl, Rom. RM1 71 FE55
Wallington SM6 159 DL108
Macintosh Cl, Wal.Cr. EN7 14 DR26
McIntosh Rd, Rom. RM1 71 FE55
Mackay Rd, SW4 101 DH83
McKay Rd, SW20 119 CV94
McKay Trd Est, Slou.
(Colnbr.) SL3 93 BE82
McKellar Cl, Bushey
(Bushey Hth) WD23 40 CC47
Mackennal St, NW8 194 C1
Mackenzie Mall, Slou. SL1
off High St 92 AT75
Mackenzie Rd, N7 83 DM65
Beckenham BR3 142 DW96
Mackenzie St, Slou. SL1 74 AT74
Mackenzie Wk, E14 204 A3
McKenzie Way, Epsom KT19 156 CN110
Mackenzie Way, Grav. DA12 131 GK93
McKerrell Rd, SE15 102 DU81
Mackeson Rd, NW3 64 DF63
Mackie Rd, SW2 121 DN87
Mackintosh La, E9
off Homerton High St 67 DX64
Macklin St, WC2 196 A8
Mackrow Wk, E14
off Robin Hood La 85 EC73
Macks Rd, SE16 202 C8
Mackworth St, NW1 195 K2
Maclaren Ms, SW15
off Clarendon Dr 99 CW84
Maclean Rd, SE23 123 DY86
Maclennan Av, Rain. RM13 90 FK69
Macleod Cl, Grays RM17 110 GD77
Macleod Rd, N21 29 DL43
McLeod Rd, SE2 106 EV77
McLeod's Ms, SW7
off Emperor's Gate 100 DB76
Macleod St, SE17 102 DQ78
Maclise Rd, W14 99 CY76
McMillan Cl, Grav. DA12 131 GJ91
Macmillan Gdns, Dart. DA1 108 FN84
McMillan St, SE8 103 EA79
Macmillan Way, SW17 121 DH91
McNair Rd, Sthl. UB2 96 CB75
McNeil Rd, SE5 102 DS82
McNicol Dr, NW10 80 CQ68
Macoma Rd, SE18 105 ER79
Macoma Ter, SE18 105 ER79
Maconochies Rd, E14 204 B10
Macon Way, Upmin. RM14 73 FT59
Macquarie Way, E14 204 C9
McRae La, Mitch. CR4 140 DF101
Macroom Rd, W9 81 CZ69
Mac's Pl, EC4 196 D8
★ Madame Tussaud's, NW1 194 F5
Madan Rd, West. TN16 189 ER125
Madans Wk, Epsom KT18 156 CR114
Mada Rd, Orp. BR6 145 EP104
Maddams St, E3 85 EB70
Madden Cl, Swans. DA10 129 FX86
Maddison Cl, Tedd. TW11 117 CF93
Maddocks Cl, Sid. DA14 126 EY92
Maddock Way, SE17 101 DP79
Maddox La, Lthd.
(Bkhm) KT23 170 BY123
Maddox Pk, Lthd.
(Bkhm) KT23 170 BY123
Maddox St, W1 195 J10
Madeira Av, Brom. BR1 124 EE94
Madeira Cl, W.Byf. KT14
off Brantwood Gdns 152 BG113
Madeira Cres, W.Byf. KT14
off Brantwood Gdns 152 BG113
Madeira Gro, Wdf.Grn. IG8 48 EJ51
Madeira Rd, E11 67 ED60
N13 45 DP49
SW16 121 DL92
Mitcham CR4 140 DF98
West Byfleet KT14 151 BF113
Madeira Wk, Brwd. CM15 54 FY48
Reigate RH2 184 DD133
Madeley Rd, W5 80 CL72
Madeline Gro, Ilf. IG1 69 ER64
Madeline Rd, SE20 142 DU95
Madells, Epp. CM16 17 ET31
Madge Gill Way, E6
off Ron Leighton Way 86 EL67
Madinah Rd, E8 84 DU65
Madingley, Kings.T. KT1
off St. Peters Rd 138 CN96
Madison Cres, Bexh. DA7 106 EW80
Madison Gdns, Bexh. DA7 106 EW80
Bromley BR2 144 EF97
Madison Way, Sev. TN13 190 FF123
Madras Pl, N7 83 DN65
Madras Rd, Ilf. IG1 69 EP63
Madresfield Ct, Rad. (Shenley)
WD7 off Russet Dr 10 CL32
Madrid Rd, SW13 99 CU81
Madrigal La, SE5 101 DP80
Madron St, SE17 201 N10
Maesmaur Rd, West.
(Tats.) TN16 178 EK121
Mafeking Av, E6 86 EK68
Brentford TW8 98 CL79
Ilford IG2 69 ER59
Mafeking Rd, E16 86 EF70
N17 46 DU54
Enfield EN1 30 DT41
Staines (Wrays.) TW19 113 BB89
Magazine Pl, Lthd. KT22 171 CH122
Magazine Rd, Cat. CR3 175 DP122
Magdala Av, N19 65 DH61
Magdala Rd, Islw. TW7 97 CG83
South Croydon CR2
off Napier Rd 160 DR108
Magdalen Cl, W.Byf.
(Byfleet) KT14 152 BL114
Magdalen Cres, W.Byf.
(Byfleet) KT14 152 BL114
Magdalene Cl, SE15
off Pilkington Rd 102 DV82
Magdalene Gdns, E6 87 EN70
Magdalene Rd, Shep. TW17 134 BM98
Magdalen Gdns, Brwd.
(Hutt.) CM13 55 GE44
Magdalen Gro, Orp. BR6 164 EV105
Magdalen Pas, E1
off Prescot St 84 DT73
Magdalen Rd, SW18 120 DC88
Magdalen St, SE1 201 M3
Magee St, SE11 101 DN79
Magellan Pl, E14
off Maritime Quay 103 EA78
Maggie Blakes Causeway, SE1
off Shad Thames 84 DT74
Magna Carta La, Stai.
(Wrays.) TW19 112 AX88
★ Magna Carta Monument,
Egh. TW20 112 AX89
Magna Rd, Egh.
(Eng.Grn) TW20 112 AV93
Magnaville Rd, Bushey
(Bushey Hth) WD23 41 CE45
Magnet Est, Grays RM20 109 FW78
Magnet Rd, Grays RM20 109 FW79
Wembley HA9 61 CK61
Magnin Cl, E8 off Wilde Cl 84 DU67
Magnolia Av, Abb.L. WD5 7 BU32
Magnolia Cl, E10 67 EA61
Kingston upon Thames KT2 118 CQ93
St. Albans (Park St) AL2 9 CD27
Magnolia Ct, Har. HA3 62 CM59
Richmond TW9
off West Hall Rd 98 CP81
Wallington SM6
off Parkgate Rd 159 DH106
Magnolia Dr, West.
(Bigg.H.) TN16 178 EK116
Magnolia Gdns, Edg. HA8 42 CQ49
Slough SL3 92 AW76
Magnolia Pl, SW4 121 DL85
W5 off Montpelier Rd 80 CL71
Magnolia Rd, W4 98 CP79
Magnolia St, West Dr. UB7 94 BK77
Magnolia Way, Brwd.
(Pilg.Hat.) CM15 54 FV43
Epsom KT19 156 CQ106
Magnum Cl, Rain. RM13 90 FJ70
Magpie All, EC4 196 E9
Magpie Cl, E7 68 EF64
NW9 off Eagle Dr 42 CS54
Coulsdon CR5
off Ashbourne Cl 175 DJ118
Enfield EN1 30 DU39
Magpie Hall Cl, Brom. BR2 144 EL100
Magpie Hall La, Brom. BR2 145 EM99
Magpie Hall Rd, Bushey
(Bushey Hth) WD23 41 CE47
Magpie La, Brwd. CM13 53 FW54
Magpie Pl, SE14
off Milton Ct Rd 103 DY79
Magri Wk, E1 off Ashfield St 84 DW71
Maguire Dr, Rich. TW10 117 CJ91
Maguire St, SE1 202 A4
Mahlon Av, Ruis. HA4 59 BV64
Mahogany Cl, SE16 203 L3
Mahon Cl, Enf. EN1 30 DT39
Maida Av, E4 47 EB45
W2 82 DC71
MAIDA HILL, W9 81 CZ70
Maida Rd, Belv. DA17 106 FA76
MAIDA VALE, W9 82 DB70
⊖ Maida Vale 82 DC69
Maida Vale, W9 82 DB68
Maida Vale Rd, Dart. DA1 127 FG85
Maida Way, E4 47 EB45
Maiden Erlegh Av, Bex. DA5 126 EY88
Maiden La, NW1 83 DK66
SE1 201 J2
WC2 200 A1
Dartford DA1 107 FG83
Maiden Rd, E15 86 EE66
Maidenshaw Rd,
Epsom KT19 156 CR112
Maidenstone Hill, SE10 103 EC81
Maids of Honour Row, Rich. TW9
off The Green 117 CK85
Maidstone Av, Rom. RM5 51 FC54
Maidstone Bldgs Ms, SE1 201 J3
Maidstone Ho, E14
off Carmen St 85 EB72
Maidstone Rd, N11 45 DJ51
Grays RM17 110 GA79
Maidstone Rd,
Sevenoaks TN13 190 FE122
Sevenoaks (Seal) TN15 191 FN121
Sidcup DA14 126 EX93
Swanley BR8 147 FB95
Maidstone St, E2
off Audrey St 84 DU68
Main Av, Enf. EN1 30 DT43
Northwood HA6 39 BQ48
Main Dr, Ger.Cr. SL9 56 AW57
Iver SL0 93 BE77
Wembley HA9 61 CK62
Main Par, Rick. (Chorl.) WD3
off Whitelands Av 21 BC42
Main Par Flats, Rick. (Chorl.) WD3
off Whitelands Av 21 BC42
Main Ride, Egh. TW20 112 AS93
Mainridge Rd, Chis. BR7 125 EN91
Main Rd, Dart. (Fnghm) DA4 148 FL100
Dartford (Sutt.H.) DA4 128 FP93
Edenbridge (Crock.H.) TN8 189 EQ134
Iver SL0
off Pinewood Rd 75 BB66
Longfield DA3 149 FX96
Orpington BR5 146 EW95
Romford RM1, RM2 71 FF56
Sevenoaks (Knock.) TN14 180 EV117
Sevenoaks (Sund.) TN14 180 EX124
Sidcup DA14 125 ES90
Swanley (Crock.) BR8 147 FD100
Swanley (Hext.) BR8 127 FF94
Westerham TN16 162 EJ113
Main St, Felt. TW13 116 BX92
Maisemore St, SE15
off Peckham Pk Rd 102 DU80
Maisie Webster Cl, Stai.
(Stanw.) TW19
off Lauser Rd 114 BK87
Maitland Cl, Houns. TW4 96 BZ83
Walton-on-Thames KT12 136 BY103
West Byfleet KT14 152 BG113
Maitland Cl Est, SE10
off Greenwich High Rd 103 EB80
Maitland Pk Est, NW3 82 DF65
Maitland Pk Rd, NW3 82 DF65
Maitland Pk Vil, NW3 82 DF65
Maitland Pl, E5
off Clarence Rd 66 DV63
Maitland Rd, E15 86 EF65
SE26 123 DX93
Maizey Ct, Brwd. (Pilg.Hat.) CM15
off Danes Way 54 FU43
Majendie Rd, SE18 105 ER78
Majestic Way, Mitch. CR4 140 DF96
Major Rd, E15 67 EC64
SE16 202 C6
Majors Fm Rd, Slou. SL3 92 AX80
Makepeace Av, N6 64 DG61
Makepeace Rd, E11 68 EG56
Northolt UB5 78 BY68
Makins St, SW3 198 C9
Malabar St, E14 203 P5
Malam Gdns, E14
off Wades Pl 85 EB73
Malan Cl, West.
(Bigg.H.) TN16 178 EL117
Malan Sq, Rain. RM13 89 FH65
Malbrook Rd, SW15 99 CV84
Malcolm Ct, Stan. HA7 41 CJ50
Malcolm Cres, NW4 63 CU58
Malcolm Dr, Surb. KT6 138 CL102
Malcolm Pl, E2 84 DW70
Malcolm Rd, E1 84 DW70
SE20 122 DW94
SE25 142 DU100
SW19 119 CY93
Coulsdon CR5 175 DK115
Uxbridge UB10 58 BM63
Malcolms Way, N14 29 DJ43
Malcolm Way, E11 68 EG57
Malden Av, SE25 142 DV98
Greenford UB6 61 CE64
Malden Cl, Amer. HP6 20 AT38
Malden Ct, N.Mal. KT3
off West Barnes La 139 CV97
Malden Cres, NW1 82 DG65
Malden Flds, Bushey WD23
off Aldenham Rd 24 BX43
Malden Grn Av, Wor.Pk. KT4 139 CT102
Malden Hill, N.Mal. KT3 139 CT97
Malden Hill Gdns,
N.Mal. KT3 139 CT97
⇌ Malden Manor 138 CS101
Malden Pk, N.Mal. KT3 139 CT100
Malden Pl, NW5
off Grafton Ter 64 DG64
Malden Rd, NW5 64 DG64
Borehamwood WD6 26 CN41
New Malden KT3 138 CS99
Sutton SM3 157 CX105
Watford WD17 23 BU40
Worcester Park KT4 139 CT101
MALDEN RUSHETT,
Chess. KT9 155 CH111
Malden Way, N.Mal. KT3 139 CT99
Maldon Cl, E15 off David St 67 ED64
N1 off Popham Rd 84 DQ67
SE5 102 DS83
Maldon Ct, Wall. SM6
off Maldon Rd 159 DJ106
Maldon Rd, N9 46 DT48
W3 80 CQ73
Romford RM7 71 FC59
Wallington SM6 159 DH106
Maldon Wk, Wdf.Grn. IG8 48 EJ51
Malet Cl, Egh. TW20 113 BD93
Malet Pl, WC1 195 M5
Malet St, WC1 195 M5
Maley Av, SE27 121 DP89
Malford Ct, E18 48 EG54
Malford Gro, E18 68 EF56
Malfort Rd, SE5 102 DS83
Malham Cl, N11
off Catterick Cl 44 DG51
Malham Rd, SE23 123 DX88
Malins Cl, Barn. EN5 27 CV43
Mall, The, E15 85 ED66
N14 45 DL48
SW1 199 L4
SW14 118 CQ85

★ Place of interest ⇌ Railway station ⊖ London Underground station DLR Docklands Light Railway station Tra Tramlink station H Hospital Riv Pedestrian ferry landing stage

Mal - Map

Mall, The, W5 80 CL73
Croydon CR0 142 DQ103
Harrow HA3 62 CM58
Hornchurch RM11 71 FH60
St. Albans (Park St) AL2 8 CC27
Surbiton KT6 137 CK99
Mallams Ms, SW9
off St. James's Cres 101 DP83
Mallard Cl, E9
off Berkshire Rd 85 DZ65
NW6 82 DA68
W7 97 CE75
Barnet EN5 off The Hook 28 DD44
Dartford DA1 128 FM85
Redhill RH1 184 DG131
Twickenham TW2
off Stephenson Rd 116 CA87
Upminster RM14 73 FT59
Mallard Path, SE28 105 ER76
Mallard Pl, Twick. TW1 117 CG90
Mallard Pt, E3
off Rainhill Way 85 EB69
Mallard Rd, Abb.L. WD5 7 BU31
South Croydon CR2 161 DX110
Mallards, The, Hem.H. HP3
off Belswains La 6 BM25
Staines TW18
off Thames Side 134 BH96
Mallards Reach, Wey. KT13 135 BR103
Mallards Rd, Bark. IG11 88 EU70
Woodford Green IG8 48 EH52
Mallard Wk, Beck. BR3 143 DX99
Sidcup DA14 126 EW92
Mallard Way, NW9 62 CQ59
Brentwood (Hutt.) CM13 55 GB45
Northwood HA6 39 BQ52
Wallington SM6 159 DJ109
Watford WD25 24 BY37
Mallet Dr, Nthlt. UB5 60 BZ64
Mallet Rd, SE13 123 ED86
★ Mall Galleries, SW1 199 N2
Malling, SE13 123 EC85
Malling Cl, Croy. CR0 142 DW100
Malling Gdns, Mord. SM4 140 DC100
Malling Way, Brom. BR2 144 EF101
Mallinson Cl, Horn. RM12 72 FJ64
Mallinson Rd, SW11 120 DE85
Croydon CR0 141 DK104
Mallion Ct, Wal.Abb. EN9 16 EF33
Mallord St, SW3 100 DD79
Mallory Cl, SE4 103 DY84
Mallory Gdns, Barn. EN4 44 DG45
Mallory St, NW8 194 C4
Mallow Cl, Croy. CR0
off Marigold Way 143 DX102
Gravesend (Nthflt) DA11 130 GE91
Tadworth KT20 173 CV119
Mallow Ct, Grays RM17 110 GD79
Mallow Mead, NW7 43 CY52
Mallows, The, Uxb. UB10 59 BP62
Mallow St, EC1 197 K4
Mallow Wk, Wal.Cr. EN7 14 DR28
Mall Rd, W6 99 CV78
Mallys Pl, Dart.
(S.Darenth) DA4 148 FQ95
Malmains Cl, Beck. BR3 143 ED99
Malmains Way, Beck. BR3 143 EC98
Malm Cl, Rick. WD3 38 BK47
Malmesbury Cl, Pnr. HA5 59 BT56
Malmesbury Rd, E3 85 DZ69
E16 86 EE71
E18 48 EF53
Morden SM4 140 DC101
Malmesbury Ter, E16 86 EF71
Malmsmead Ho, E9
off Kingsmead Way 67 DY64
Malmstone Av, Red. RH1 185 DJ128
Malpas Dr, Pnr. HA5 60 BX57
Malpas Rd, E8 84 DV65
SE4 103 DZ82
Dagenham RM9 88 EX65
Grays RM16 111 GJ76
Slough SL2 74 AV73
Malta Rd, E10 67 EA60
Tilbury RM18 111 GF82
Malta St, EC1 196 G4
Maltby Cl, Orp. BR6
off Vinson Cl 146 EU102
Maltby Dr, Enf. EN1 30 DV38
Maltby Rd, Chess. KT9 156 CN107
Maltby St, SE1 201 P5
Malt Hill, Egh. TW20 112 AY92
Malt Ho Cl, Wind.
(Old Wind.) SL4 112 AV87
Malthouse Dr, W4 98 CS79
Feltham TW13 116 BX92
Malthouse Pas, SW13
off The Terrace 98 CS82
Malthouse Pl, Rad. WD7 9 CG34
Malthus Path, SE28
off Owen Cl 88 EW74
Malting Ho, E14 85 DZ73
Maltings, The, Kings L. WD4 7 BQ33
Orpington BR6 145 ET102
Oxted RH8 188 EF131
Romford RM1 71 FF59
Staines TW18
off Church St 113 BE91
West Byfleet
(Byfleet) KT14 152 BM113
Maltings Cl, SW13
off Cleveland Gdns 98 CS82
Maltings Dr, Epp. CM16
off Palmers Hill 18 EU29
Maltings La, Epp. CM16 18 EU29
Maltings Ms, Sid. DA15
off Station Rd 126 EU90
Maltings Pl, SW6 100 DB81
Malting Way, Islw. TW7 97 CF83
Malt La, Rad. WD7 25 CG35
Maltmans La, Ger.Cr.
(Chal.St.P.) SL9 56 AW55
Malton Ms, SE18
off Malton St 105 ES79
W10 off Cambridge Gdns 81 CY72
Malton Rd, W10
off St. Marks Rd 81 CY72
Malton St, SE18 105 ES79
Maltravers St, WC2 196 C10
Malt St, SE1 102 DU79
Malus Cl, Add. KT15 151 BF108
Malus Dr, Add. KT15 151 BF107
Malva Cl, SW18
off St. Ann's Hill 120 DB85
Malvern Av, E4 47 ED52
Bexleyheath DA7 106 EY80
Harrow HA2 60 BY62
Malvern Cl, SE20
off Derwent Rd 142 DU96
W10 81 CZ71
Bushey WD23 24 CC44
Chertsey (Ott.) KT16 151 BC107
Mitcham CR4 141 DJ97
Surbiton KT6 138 CL102
Uxbridge UB10 59 BP61
Malvern Ct, SE14
off Avonley Rd 102 DW80
SW7 198 A9
Slough SL3
off Hill Ri 93 BA79
Sutton SM2
off Overton Rd 158 DA108
Malvern Dr, Felt. TW13 116 BX92
Ilford IG3 69 ET63
Woodford Green IG8 48 EJ50
Malvern Gdns, NW2 63 CY61
NW6 off Carlton Vale 81 CZ68
Harrow HA3 62 CL55
Loughton IG10 33 EM44
Malvern Ms, NW6
off Malvern Rd 82 DA69
Malvern Pl, NW6 81 CZ69
Malvern Rd, E6 86 EL67
E8 84 DU66
E11 68 EE61
N8 65 DM55
N17 66 DU55
NW6 82 DA69
Enfield EN3 31 DY37
Grays RM17 110 GD77
Hampton TW12 116 CA94
Hayes UB3 95 BS80
Hornchurch RM11 71 FG58
Orpington BR6 164 EV105
Surbiton KT6 138 CL103
Thornton Heath CR7 141 DN98
Malvern Ter, N1 83 DN67
N9 off Latymer Rd 46 DT46
Malvern Way, W13
off Templewood 79 CH71
Rickmansworth
(Crox.Grn) WD3 23 BP43
Malvina Av, Grav. DA12 131 GH89
Malwood Rd, SW12 121 DH86
Malyons, The, Shep. TW17
off Gordon Rd 135 BR100
Malyons Rd, SE13 123 EB85
Swanley BR8 127 FF94
Malyons Ter, SE13 123 EB85
Managers St, E14 204 E3
Manatee Pl, Wall. SM6
off Croydon Rd 141 DK104
Manaton Cl, SE15 102 DV83
Manaton Cres, Sthl. UB1 78 CA72
Manbey Gro, E15 86 EE65
Manbey Pk Rd, E15 86 EE65
Manbey Rd, E15 86 EE65
Manbey St, E15 86 EE65
Manbre Rd, W6 99 CW79
Manbrough Av, E6 87 EM69
Manchester Ct, E16 86 EH72
Manchester Dr, W10 81 CY70
Manchester Gro, E14 204 D10
Manchester Ms, W1 194 F7
Manchester Rd, E14 204 D10
N15 66 DR58
Thornton Heath CR7 142 DQ97
Manchester Sq, W1 194 F8
Manchester St, W1 194 F7
Manchester Way,
Dag. RM10 71 FB63
Manchuria Rd, SW11 120 DG86
Manciple St, SE1 201 K5
Mandalay Rd, SW4 121 DJ85
Mandarin St, E14
off Salter St 85 EA73
Mandarin Way,
Hayes UB4 78 BX71
Mandela Cl, NW10 80 CQ66
Mandela Rd, E16 86 EG72
Mandela St, NW1 83 DJ67
SW9 101 DN80
Mandela Way, SE1 201 N8
Mandeville Cl, SE3
off Vanbrugh Pk 104 EF80
SW20 139 CY95
Watford WD17 23 BT38
Mandeville Ct, E4 47 DY49
Egham TW20 113 BA91
Mandeville Dr, Surb. KT6 137 CK102
Mandeville Ms, SW4
off Clapham Pk Rd 101 DL84
Mandeville Pl, W1 194 G8
Mandeville Rd, N14 45 DH47
Enfield EN3 31 DX36
Isleworth TW7 97 CG82
Northolt UB5 78 CA66
Potters Bar EN6 12 DC32
Shepperton TW17 134 BN99
Mandeville St, E5 67 DY62
Mandeville Wk, Brwd.
(Hutt.) CM13 55 GE44
Mandrake Rd, SW17 120 DF90
Mandrake Way, E15 86 EE66
Mandrell Rd, SW2 121 DL85
Manette St, W1 195 N9
Manford Cl, Chig. IG7 50 EU49
Manford Cross, Chig. IG7 50 EU50
Manford Ind Est, Erith DA8 107 FG79
Manford Way, Chig. IG7 49 ES49
Manfred Rd, SW15 119 CZ85
Manger Rd, N7 83 DL65
Mangold Way, Erith DA18 106 EY76
Manhattan Wf, E16 205 M4
Manilla St, E14 203 P4
Manister Rd, SE2 106 EU76
Manitoba Ct, SE16
off Renforth St 102 DW75
Manitoba Gdns, Orp. BR6
off Superior Dr 163 ET107
Manley Ct, N16 off Stoke
Newington High St 66 DT62
Manley St, NW1 82 DG67
Manly Dixon Dr, Enf. EN3 31 DY37
Mannamead, Epsom KT18 172 CS119
Mannamead Cl, Epsom KT18
off Mannamead 172 CS119
Mann Cl, Croy. CR0
off Salem Pl 142 DQ104
Manningford Cl, EC1 196 F2
Manning Gdns, Har. HA3 61 CK59
Manning Pl, Rich. TW10
off Grove Rd 118 CM86
Manning Rd, E17
off Southcote Rd 67 DY57
Dagenham RM10 88 FA65
Orpington BR5 146 EX99
Manning St, S.Ock.
(Aveley) RM15 90 FQ74
Manningtree Cl, SW19 119 CY88
Manningtree Rd, Ruis. HA4 59 BV63
Manningtree St, E1
off White Ch La 84 DU72
Mannin Rd, Rom. RM6 70 EV59
Mannock Dr, Loug. IG10 33 EQ40
Mannock Ms, E18 48 EH53
Mannock Rd, N22 65 DP55
Dartford DA1
off Barnwell Rd 108 FM83
Manns Cl, Islw. TW7 117 CF85
Manns Rd, Edg. HA8 42 CN51
Manoel Rd, Twick. TW2 116 CC89
Manor Av, SE4 103 DZ82
Caterham CR3 176 DS124
Hornchurch RM11 72 FJ57
Hounslow TW4 96 BX83
Northolt UB5 78 BZ66
Manorbrook, SE3 104 EG84
Manor Chase, Wey. KT13 153 BP106
Manor Cl, E17 off Manor Rd 47 DY54
NW7 off Manor Dr 42 CR50
NW9 62 CP57
SE28 88 EW72
Barnet EN5 27 CY42
Dagenham RM10 89 FD65
Dartford (Cray.) DA1 107 FD84
Dartford (Wilm.) DA2 127 FG90
Romford RM1
off Manor Rd 71 FG57
Ruislip HA4 59 BT60
South Ockendon
(Aveley) RM15 90 FQ74
Warlingham CR6 177 DY117
Woking GU22 167 BF116
Worcester Park KT4 138 CS102
Manor Cl S, S.Ock. (Aveley) RM15
off Manor Cl 90 FQ74
Manor Cotts, Nthwd. HA6 39 BT53
Manor Cotts App, N2 44 DC54
Manor Ct, E10
off Grange Pk Rd 67 EB60
N2 64 DF57
SW6 off Bagley's La 100 DB81
Enfield EN1 30 DV36
Radlett WD7 25 CF38
Twickenham TW2 116 CC89
Wembley HA9 62 CL64
Weybridge KT13 153 BP105
Manor Ct Rd, W7 79 CE73
Manor Cres, Epsom KT19 156 CN112
Hornchurch RM11 72 FJ57
Surbiton KT5 138 CN100
West Byfleet (Byfleet) KT14 152 BM113
Manorcrofts Rd, Egh. TW20 113 BA93
Manordene Cl, T.Ditt. KT7 137 CG102
Manordene Rd, SE28 88 EW72
Manor Dr, N14 45 DH45
N20 44 DE48
NW7 42 CR50
Addlestone
(New Haw) KT15 152 BG110
Epsom KT19 156 CS107
Esher KT10 137 CF103
Feltham TW13
off Lebanon Av 116 BX92
St. Albans AL2 8 CA27
Sunbury-on-Thames TW16 135 BU96
Surbiton KT5 138 CM100
Wembley HA9 62 CM63
Manor Dr, The, Wor.Pk. KT4 138 CS102
Manor Dr N, N.Mal. KT3 138 CR101
Worcester Park KT4 138 CS102
Manor Est, SE16 202 D9
Manor Fm, Dart.
(Fnghm) DA4 148 FM101
Manor Fm Av, Shep. TW17 135 BP100
Manor Fm Cl, Wor.Pk. KT4 138 CS102
Manor Fm Dr, E4 48 EE48
Manor Fm Est, Stai.
(Wrays.) TW19 112 AW86
Manor Fm La, Egh. TW20 113 BA92
Manor Fm Rd, Enf. EN1 30 DV35
Thornton Heath CR7 141 DN96
Wembley HA0 79 CK68
Manorfield Cl, N19
off Junction Rd 65 DJ63
Manor Flds, SW15 119 CX86
Manorfields Cl, Chis. BR7 145 ET97
Manor Gdns, N7 65 DL62
SW20 139 CZ96
W3 98 CN77
W4 off Devonshire Rd 98 CS78
Hampton TW12 116 CB94
Richmond TW9 98 CM84
Ruislip HA4 60 BW64
South Croydon CR2 160 DT107
Sunbury-on-Thames TW16 135 BU96
Manor Gate, Nthlt. UB5 78 BY66
Manorgate Rd, Kings.T. KT2 138 CN95
Manor Grn Rd, Epsom KT19 156 CP113
Manor Gro, SE15 102 DW79
Beckenham BR3 143 EB96
Richmond TW9 98 CN84
Manor Hall Av, NW4 43 CW54
Manor Hall Dr, NW4 43 CX54
Manorhall Gdns, E10 67 EA60
⊖ Manor House 65 DP59
Manor Ho Ct, Epsom KT18 156 CQ113
Shepperton TW17 135 BP101
Manor Ho Dr, NW6 81 CX66
Manor Ho Dr, Northwood HA6 39 BP52
Walton-on-Thames KT12 153 BT107
Manor Ho Est, Stan. HA7
off Old Ch La 41 CH51
Manor Ho Gdns, Abb.L. WD5 7 BR31
Manor Ho La, Slou.
(Datchet) SL3 92 AV80
Manor Ho Way, Islw. TW7 97 CH83
Manor La, SE12 124 EE86
SE13 104 EE84
Feltham TW13 115 BU89
Gerrards Cross SL9 56 AX59
Hayes UB3 95 BR79
Longfield (Fawk.Grn) DA3 149 FW101
Sevenoaks TN15 149 FW103
Sunbury-on-Thames
TW16 135 BU96
Sutton SM1 158 DC106
Tadworth KT20 184 DA129
Manor La Ter, SE13 104 EE84
Manor Leaze, Egh. TW20 113 BB92
Manor Ms, NW6
off Cambridge Av 82 DA68
SE4 103 DZ82
Manor Mt, SE23 122 DW88
Manor Par, NW10
off Station Rd 81 CT68
MANOR PARK, E12 68 EL63
⇌ Manor Park 68 EK63
Manor Pk, SE13 103 ED84
Chislehurst BR7 145 ER96
Richmond TW9 98 CM84
Staines TW18 113 BD90
Manor Pk Cl, W.Wick. BR4 143 EB102
Manor Pk Cres, Edg. HA8 42 CN51
Manor Pk Dr, Har. HA2 60 CB55
Manor Pk Gdns, Edg. HA8 42 CN50
Manor Pk Par, SE13
off Lee High Rd 103 ED84
Manor Pk Rd, E12 68 EK63
N2 64 DD55
NW10 81 CT67
Chislehurst BR7 145 EQ95
Sutton SM1 158 DC106
West Wickham BR4 143 EB102
Manor Pl, SE17 101 DP78
Chislehurst BR7 145 ER95
Dartford DA1
off Highfield Rd S 128 FL88
Feltham TW14 115 BU88
Mitcham CR4 141 DJ97
Staines TW18 114 BH92
Sutton SM1 158 DB105
Walton-on-Thames KT12
off Manor Rd 135 BT101
Manor Rd, E10 67 EA59
E15 86 EE69
E16 86 EE69
E17 47 DY54
N16 66 DR61
N17 46 DU53
N22 45 DL51
SE25 142 DU98
SW20 139 CZ96
W13 79 CG73
Ashford TW15 114 BM92
Barking IG11 87 ET65
Barnet EN5 27 CY43
Beckenham BR3 143 EB96
Bexley DA5 127 FB88
Chigwell IG7 49 EP50
Dagenham RM10 89 FC65
Dartford DA1 107 FE84
East Molesey KT8 137 CD98
Enfield EN2 30 DR40
Erith DA8 107 FF79
Gravesend DA12 131 GH86
Grays RM17 110 GC79
Grays (W.Thur.) RM20 109 FW79
Harrow HA1 61 CG58
Hayes UB3 77 BU72
Loughton IG10 32 EH44
Loughton (High Beach) IG10 32 EH38
Mitcham CR4 141 DJ98
Potters Bar EN6 11 CZ31
Redhill RH1 185 DJ129
Reigate RH2 183 CZ132
Richmond TW9 98 CM83
Romford RM1 71 FG57
Romford (Chad.Hth) RM6 70 EX58
Romford (Lamb.End) RM4 50 EW47
Ruislip HA4 59 BR60
St. Albans (Lon.Col.) AL2 9 CJ26
Sevenoaks (Sund.) TN14 180 EX124
Sidcup DA15 125 ET90
Sutton SM2 157 CZ108
Swanscombe DA10 129 FX86
Teddington TW11 117 CH92
Tilbury RM18 111 GG82
Twickenham TW2 116 CC89
Wallington SM6 159 DH105
Waltham Abbey EN9 15 ED33
Walton-on-Thames KT12 135 BT101
Watford WD17 23 BV39
West Wickham BR4 143 EB103
Westerham (Tats.) TN16 178 EL120
Woking GU21 166 AW116
Woking (Send M.) GU23 167 BF123
Woodford Green IG8 49 EM51
Manor Rd N, Esher KT10 137 CF104
Thames Ditton KT7 137 CG103
Wallington SM6 159 DH105
Manor Rd S, Esher KT10 155 CE105
Manorside, Barn. EN5 27 CY42
Manorside Cl, SE2 106 EW77
Manor Sq, Dag. RM8 70 EX61
Manor Vale, Brent. TW8 97 CJ78
Manor Vw, N3 44 DB54
Manor Wk, Wey. KT13 153 BP106
Manor Way, E4 47 ED49
NW9 62 CS55
SE3 104 EF84
SE23 122 DW87
SE28 88 EW74
Banstead SM7 174 DF116
Beckenham BR3 143 EA96
Bexley DA5 126 FA88
Bexleyheath DA7 107 FD83
Borehamwood WD6 26 CQ42
Brentwood CM14 54 FU48
Manor Way, Bromley BR2 144 EL100
Egham TW20 113 AZ93
Manorway, Enf. EN1 46 DS45
Manor Way, Grays RM17 110 GB80
Harrow HA2 60 CB56
Leatherhead
(Oxshott) KT22 170 CC115
Mitcham CR4 141 DJ97
Orpington BR5 145 EQ98
Potters Bar EN6 12 DA30
Purley CR8 159 DL112
Rainham RM13 89 FE71
Rickmansworth
(Crox.Grn) WD3 22 BN42
Ruislip HA4 59 BS59
South Croydon CR2 160 DS107
Southall UB2 96 BX77
Swanscombe DA10 109 FX84
Waltham Cross (Chsht) EN8
off Russells Ride 15 DY31
Woking GU22 167 BB121
Manorway, Wdf.Grn. IG8 48 EJ50
Manor Way, Wor.Pk. KT4 138 CS102
Manor Way, The, Wall. SM6 159 DH105
Manor Waye, Uxb. UB8 76 BK67
Manor Way Ind Est,
Grays RM17 110 GC80
Manor Wd Rd, Pur. CR8 159 DL113
Manpreet Ct, E12
off Morris Av 69 EM64
Manresa Rd, SW3 100 DE78
Mansard Beeches, SW17 120 DG92
Mansard Cl, Horn. RM12 71 FG61
Pinner HA5 60 BX55
Mansbridge Way, NW7 43 CY52
Manse Cl, Hayes UB3 95 BR79
Mansel Cl, Slou. SL2 74 AV71
Mansel Gro, E17 47 EA53
Mansell Rd, W3 98 CR75
Greenford UB6 78 CB71
Mansell St, E1 202 A1
Mansell Way, Cat. CR3 176 DR122
Mansel Rd, SW19 119 CY93
Mansergh Cl, SE18 104 EL80
Manse Rd, N16 66 DT62
Manser Rd, Rain. RM13 89 FE69
Manse Way, Swan. BR8 147 FG98
Mansfield Av, N15 66 DR56
Barnet EN4 28 DF44
Ruislip HA4 59 BV60
Mansfield Cl, N9 30 DU44
Orpington BR5 146 EX101
Weybridge KT13 153 BP106
Mansfield Dr, Hayes UB4 77 BS70
Redhill RH1 185 DK128
Mansfield Gdns, Horn. RM12 72 FK61
Mansfield Hill, E4 47 EB46
Mansfield Ms, W1 195 H7
Mansfield Pl, NW3
off New End 64 DC63
Mansfield Rd, E11 68 EH58
E17 67 DZ56
NW3 64 DF64
W3 80 CP70
Chessington KT9 155 CJ106
Ilford IG1 69 EN61
South Croydon CR2 160 DR107
Swanley BR8 127 FE93
Mansfield St, W1 195 H7
Mansford St, E2 84 DU68
Manship Rd, Mitch. CR4 120 DG94
Mansion Cl, SW9
off Cowley Rd 101 DN81
Mansion Gdns, NW3 64 DB62
★ Mansion Ho, EC4 197 K9
⊖ Mansion House 197 J10
Mansion Ho Pl, EC4 197 K9
Mansion Ho St, EC4 197 K9
Mansion La, Iver SL0 75 BC74
Manson Ms, SW7 100 DC77
Manson Pl, SW7 100 DD77
Manstead Gdns, Rain. RM13 89 FH72
Mansted Gdns, Rom. RM6 70 EW59
Manston Av, Sthl. UB2 96 CA77
Manston Cl, SE20
off Garden Rd 142 DW95
Waltham Cross
(Chsht) EN8 14 DW30
Manstone Rd, NW2 63 CY64
Manston Gro, Kings.T. KT2 117 CK92
Manston Way, Horn. RM12 89 FH65
Manthorp Rd, SE18 105 EQ78
Mantilla Rd, SW17 120 DG91
Mantle Rd, SE4 103 DY83
Mantlet Cl, SW16 121 DJ94
Mantle Way, E15
off Romford Rd 86 EE66
Manton Av, W7 97 CF75
Manton Cl, Hayes UB3 77 BS73
Manton Rd, SE2 106 EU77
Enfield EN3 31 EA37
Mantua St, SW11 100 DD83
Mantus Cl, E1 off Mantus Rd 84 DW70
Mantus Rd, E1 84 DW70
Manus Way, N20
off Blakeney Cl 44 DC47
Manville Gdns, SW17 121 DH89
Manville Rd, SW17 120 DG89
Manwood Rd, SE4 123 DZ85
Manwood St, E16 87 EM74
Manygate La, Shep. TW17 135 BQ101
Manygates, SW12 121 DH89
Mapesbury Ms, NW4
off Station Rd 63 CU58
Mapesbury Rd, NW2 81 CY65
Mapeshill Pl, NW2 81 CW65
Mape St, E2 84 DV70
Maple Av, E4 47 DZ50
W3 80 CS74
Harrow HA2 60 CB61
Upminster RM14 72 FP62
West Drayton UB7 76 BL73
Maple Cl, N3 44 DA51
N16 66 DU58
SW4 121 DK86

★ Place of interest ⇌ Railway station ⊖ London Underground station DLR Docklands Light Railway station Tra Tramlink station H Hospital Riv Pedestrian ferry landing stage

Maple Cl, Brentwood CM13
off Cherry Av 55 FZ48
Buckhurst Hill IG9 48 EK48
Bushey WD23 24 BY40
Epping (They.B.) CM16
off Loughton La 33 ER37
Hampton TW12 116 BZ93
Hayes UB4 78 BX69
Hornchurch RM12 71 FH62
Ilford IG6 49 ES50
Mitcham CR4 141 DH95
Orpington BR5 145 ER99
Ruislip HA4 59 BV58
Swanley BR8 147 FE96
Whyteleafe CR3 176 DT117
Maple Ct, Egh. (Eng.Grn) TW20
off Ashwood Rd 112 AV93
New Malden KT3 138 CS97
Maple Cres, Sid. DA15 126 EU86
Slough SL2 74 AV73
Maplecroft Cl, E6
off Allhallows Rd 86 EL72
MAPLE CROSS, Rick. WD3 37 BD49
Maple Cross Ind Est, Rick.
(Map.Cr.) WD3 37 BF49
Mapledale Av, Croy. CR0 142 DU103
Mapledene, Chis. BR7
off Kemnal Rd 125 EQ92
Mapledene Rd, E8 84 DT66
Maple Dr, S.Ock. RM15 91 FX70
Maplefield, St.Alb.
(Park St) AL2 8 CB29
Maplefield La, Ch.St.G. HP8 20 AV41
Maple Gdns, Edg. HA8 42 CS52
Staines TW19 114 BL89
Maple Gate, Loug. IG10 33 EN40
Maple Gro, NW9 62 CQ59
W5 97 CK76
Brentford TW8 97 CH80
Southall UB1 78 BZ71
Watford WD17 23 BU39
Woking GU22 166 AY121
Maple Hill, Hem.H. (Bov.) HP3
off Ley Hill Rd 4 AX30
Maplehurst, Lthd. KT22 171 CD123
Maplehurst Cl, Kings.T. KT1 138 CL98
Maplehust Cl, Dart. DA2
off Old Bexley La 127 FE89
Maple Ind Est, Felt. TW13
off Maple Way 115 BU90
Maple Leaf Cl, Abb.L. WD5 7 BU32
Mapleleaf Cl, S.Croy. CR2 161 DX111
Maple Leaf Cl, West. (Bigg.H.) TN16
off Main Rd 178 EK116
Maple Leaf Dr, Sid. DA15 125 ET88
Mapleleafe Gdns, Ilf. IG6 69 EP55
Maple Leaf Sq, SE16 203 J4
Maple Lo Cl, Rick.
(Map.Cr.) WD3 37 BE49
Maple Ms, NW6
off Kilburn Pk Rd 82 DB68
SW16 121 DM92
Maple Pl, W1 195 L5
Banstead SM7 157 CX114
West Drayton UB7
off Maple Av 76 BM73
Maple Rd, E11 68 EE58
SE20 142 DV95
Ashtead KT21 171 CK119
Dartford DA1 128 FJ88
Gravesend DA12 131 GJ91
Grays RM17 110 GC79
Hayes UB4 78 BW69
Surbiton KT6 138 CL99
Whyteleafe CR3 176 DT117
Woking (Ripley) GU23 168 BG124
Maples, The, Bans. SM7 158 DB114
Chertsey (Ott.) KT16 151 BB107
Esher (Clay.) KT10 155 CG108
Waltham Cross
(Goffs Oak) EN7 14 DS28
Maplescombe La, Dart.
(Fnghm) DA4 148 FN104
Maples Pl, E1 off Raven Row 84 DV71
Maple Springs, Wal.Abb. EN9 16 EG33
Maplestead Rd, SW2 121 DM87
Dagenham RM9 88 EV67
Maple St, W1 195 K6
Romford RM7 71 FC56
Maplethorpe Rd, Th.Hth. CR7 141 DP98
Mapleton Cl, Brom. BR2 144 EG100
Mapleton Cres, SW18 120 DB86
Enfield EN3 30 DW38
Mapleton Rd, E4 47 EC48
SW18 120 DB86
Edenbridge TN8 189 ET133
Enfield EN1 30 DV40
Westerham TN16 189 ES130
Maple Wk, W10
off Droop St 81 CX70
Sutton SM2 158 DB110
Maple Way, Couls. CR5 175 DH121
Feltham TW13 115 BU90
Waltham Abbey EN9 off Breach
Barn Mobile Home Pk 16 EH30
Maplin Cl, N21 29 DM44
Maplin Ho, SE2
off Wolvercote Rd 106 EX75
Maplin Pk, Slou. SL3 93 BC75
Maplin Rd, E16 86 EG72
Maplin St, E3 85 DZ69
Mapperley Dr, Wdf.Grn. IG8
off Forest Dr 48 EE52
Maran Way, Erith DA18 106 EX75
Marathon Way, SE28 105 ET75
Marban Rd, W9 81 CZ69
★ Marble Arch, W1 194 E10
⊖ Marble Arch 194 E10
Marble Cl, W3 80 CP74
Marble Dr, NW2 63 CX60
Marble Hill Cl, Twick. TW1 117 CH87
Marble Hill Gdns, Twick. TW1 117 CH87
★ Marble Hill Ho, Twick. TW1 117 CJ87
Marble Ho, SE18
off Felspar Cl 105 ET78
Marble Quay, E1 202 B2
Marbles Way, Tad. KT20 173 CX119
Marbrook Ct, SE12 124 EJ90
Marcella Rd, SW9 101 DN82
Marcellina Way, Orp. BR6 145 ES104
Marcet Rd, Dart. DA1 128 FJ85
Marchant Rd, E11 67 ED61
Marchant St, SE14 103 DY79
Marchbank Rd, W14 99 CZ79
Marchmant Cl, Horn. RM12 72 FJ62
Marchmont Gdns, Rich. TW10
off Marchmont Rd 118 CM85
Marchmont Rd, Rich. TW10 118 CM85
Wallington SM6 159 DJ108
Marchmont St, WC1 195 P4
March Rd, Twick. TW1 117 CG87
Weybridge KT13 152 BN106
Marchside Cl, Houns. TW5
off Springwell Rd 96 BX81
Marchwood Cl, SE5 102 DS80
Marchwood Cres, W5 79 CJ72
Marcia Rd, SE1 201 N9
Marcilly Rd, SW18 120 DD85
Marconi Gdns, Brwd. CM15
off Hatch Rd 54 FW43
Marconi Rd, E10 67 EA60
Gravesend (Nthflt) DA11 130 GD90
Marconi Way, Sthl. UB1 78 CB72
Marcon Pl, E8 84 DV65
Marco Rd, W6 99 CW76
Marcourt Lawns, W5 80 CL70
Marcus Ct, E15 86 EE67
Marcuse Rd, Cat. CR3 176 DR123
Marcus Garvey Ms, SE22
off St. Aidan's Rd 122 DV85
Marcus Garvey Way, SE24 101 DN84
Marcus Rd, Dart. DA1 127 FG87
Marcus St, E15 86 EF67
SW18 120 DB86
Marcus Ter, SW18 120 DB86
Mardale Dr, NW9 62 CR57
Mardell Rd, Croy. CR0 143 DX99
Marden Av, Brom. BR2 144 EG100
Marden Cl, Chig. IG7 50 EV47
Marden Cres, Bex. DA5 127 FC85
Croydon CR0 141 DM100
Marden Pk, Cat. (Wold.) CR3 187 DZ125
Marden Rd, N17 66 DS55
Croydon CR0 141 DM100
Romford RM1 71 FE58
Marden Sq, SE16 202 D7
Marder Rd, W13 97 CG75
Mardyke Cl, Rain. RM13
off Lower Mardyke Av 89 FC68
Mardyke Ho, Rain. RM13
off Lower Mardyke Av 89 FD68
Marechal Niel Av, Sid. DA15 125 ER90
Maresfield, Croy. CR0 142 DS104
Maresfield Gdns, NW3 64 DC64
Mare St, E8 84 DV67
Marfleet Cl, Cars. SM5 140 DE103
Margaret Av, E4 31 EB44
Brentwood (Shenf.) CM15 55 FZ45
Margaret Bondfield Av,
Bark. IG11 88 EU66
Margaret Bldgs, N16
off Margaret Rd 66 DT60
Margaret Cl, Abb.L. WD5 7 BT32
Epping CM16
off Margaret Rd 18 EU29
Potters Bar EN6 12 DC33
Romford RM2
off Margaret Rd 71 FH57
Staines TW18
off Charles Rd 114 BK93
Waltham Abbey EN9 15 ED33
Margaret Ct, W1 195 K8
Margaret Dr, Horn. RM11 72 FM60
Margaret Gardner Dr, SE9 125 EM89
Margaret Ingram Cl, SW6
off John Smith Av 99 CZ80
Margaret Lockwood Cl,
Kings.T. KT1 138 CM98
Margaret Rd, N16 66 DT60
Barnet EN4 28 DD42
Bexley DA5 126 EX86
Epping CM16 18 EU29
Romford RM2 71 FH57
Margaret Sq, Uxb. UB8 76 BJ67
Margaret St, W1 195 J8
Margaretta Ter, SW3 100 DE79
Margaretting Rd, E12 68 EJ61
Margaret Way, Couls. CR5 175 DP118
Ilford IG4 68 EL58
Margate Rd, SW2 121 DL85
Margeholes, Wat. WD19 40 BY47
MARGERY, Tad. KT20 184 DA129
Margery Gro, Tad. KT20 183 CY129
Margery La, Tad. KT20 183 CZ129
Margery Pk Rd, E7 86 EG65
Margery Rd, Dag. RM8 70 EX62
Margery St, WC1 196 D3
Margery Wd La, Tad. KT20 183 CZ129
Margherita Pl, Wal.Abb. EN9 16 EF34
Margherita Rd, Wal.Abb. EN9 16 EG34
Margin Dr, SW19 119 CX92
Margravine Gdns, W6 99 CX78
Margravine Rd, W6 99 CX78
Marham Gdns, SW18 120 DE88
Morden SM4 140 DC100
Maria Cl, SE1 202 D8
Mariam Gdns, Horn. RM12 72 FM61
Marian Cl, Hayes UB4 78 BX70
Marian Ct, Sutt. SM1 158 DB106
Marian Pl, E2 84 DV68
Marian Rd, SW16 141 DJ95
Marian Sq, E2
off Pritchard's Rd 84 DU68
Marian St, E2 off Hackney Rd 84 DV68
Marian Way, NW10 81 CT66
Maria Ter, E1 85 DX71
Maria Theresa Cl, N.Mal. KT3 138 CR99
Maricas Av, Har. HA3 41 CD53
Marie Lloyd Gdns, N19
off Hornsey Ri Gdns 65 DL59
Marie Lloyd Wk, E8
off Forest Rd 84 DU65
Marie Manor Way, Dart. DA2
off Crossways Boul 109 FS84
Mariette Way, Wall. SM6 159 DL109
Marigold All, SE1 200 F1
Marigold Cl, Sthl. UB1
off Lancaster Rd 78 BY73
Marigold Rd, N17 46 DW52
Marigold St, SE16 202 D5
Marigold Way, E4
off Silver Birch Av 47 DZ51
Croydon CR0 143 DX102
H Marillac Hosp, Brwd. CM13 53 FX51
Marina App, Hayes UB4 78 BY71
Marina Av, N.Mal. KT3 139 CV99
Marina Cl, Brom. BR2 144 EG97
Chertsey KT16 134 BH102
Marina Dr, Dart. DA1 128 FN88
Gravesend (Nthflt) DA11 131 GF87
Welling DA16 105 ES82
Marina Gdns, Rom. RM7 71 FC58
Waltham Cross (Chsht) EN8 14 DW30
Marina Way, Iver SL0 75 BF73
Teddington TW11
off Fairways 117 CK94
Marine Dr, SE18 105 EM77
Barking IG11 88 EV70
Marinefield Rd, SW6 100 DB82
Mariner Gdns, Rich. TW10 117 CJ90
Mariner Rd, E12
off Dersingham Av 69 EM63
Mariners Ct, Green. DA9
off High St 109 FV84
Mariners Ms, E14 204 F8
Mariners Wk, Erith DA8
off Frobisher Rd 107 FF79
Mariner's Way, Grav. DA11
off Rosherville Way 130 GE87
Marine St, SE16 202 B6
Marine Twr, SE8
off Abinger Gro 103 DZ79
Marion Av, Shep. TW17 135 BP99
Marion Cl, Bushey WD23 24 BZ39
Ilford IG6 49 ER52
Marion Cres, Orp. BR5 146 EU99
Marion Gro, Wdf.Grn. IG8 48 EE50
Marion Rd, NW7 43 CU50
Thornton Heath CR7 142 DQ99
Marischal Rd, SE13 103 ED83
Marisco Cl, Grays RM16 111 GH77
Marish La, Uxb. (Denh.) UB9 57 BC56
Marish Wf, Slou. (Mdgrn) SL3 92 AY75
Maritime Cl, Green. DA9 129 FV85
Maritime Gate, Grav. DA11
off Rosherville Way 130 GE87
Maritime Ho, Bark. IG11
off Linton Rd 87 EQ66
Maritime Quay, E14 204 A10
Maritime St, E3 85 DZ70
Marius Pas, SW17
off Marius Rd 120 DG89
Marius Rd, SW17 120 DG89
Marjorams Av, Loug. IG10 33 EM40
Marjorie Gro, SW11 100 DF84
Marjorie Ms, E1
off Arbour Sq 85 DX72
Markab Rd, Nthwd. HA6 39 BT50
Mark Av, E4 31 EB44
Mark Cl, Bexh. DA7 106 EY81
Southall UB1
off Longford Av 78 CB74
Mark Dr, Ger.Cr.
(Chal.St.P.) SL9 36 AX49
Marke Cl, Kes. BR2 162 EL105
Markedge La, Couls. CR5 174 DE124
Redhill RH1 184 DF126
Markeston Grn, Wat. WD19 40 BX49
Market Ct, W1 195 K8
Market Est, N7 83 DL65
Marketfield Rd, Red. RH1 184 DF134
Marketfield Way, Red. RH1 184 DF134
Market Hill, SE18 105 EN76
Market La, Edg. HA8 42 CQ53
Iver SL0 93 BC75
Slough SL3 93 BC76
Market Link, Rom. RM1 71 FE56
Market Meadow, Orp. BR5 146 EW98
Market Ms, W1 199 H3
Market Pl, N2 64 DE55
NW11 64 DC56
SE16 202 C8
W1 195 K8
W3 80 CQ74
Bexleyheath DA6 106 FA84
Brentford TW8 97 CJ80
Dartford DA1
off Market St 128 FL87
Enfield EN2 off The Town 30 DR41
Gerrards Cross
(Chal.St.P.) SL9 36 AX53
Kingston upon Thames KT1 137 CK96
Romford RM1 71 FE57
Romford (Abridge) RM4 34 EV41
Tilbury RM18 111 GF82
Market Rd, N7 83 DL65
Richmond TW9 98 CN83
Market Row, SW9
off Atlantic Rd 101 DN84
Market Sq, E14 off Chrisp St 85 EB72
N9 off New Rd 46 DU47
Bromley BR1 144 EG96
Staines TW18
off Clarence St 113 BE91
Uxbridge UB8 off High St 76 BJ66
Waltham Abbey EN9
off Leverton Way 15 EC33
Westerham TN16 189 EQ127
Woking GU21
off Cawsey Way 166 AY117
Market St, E6 87 EM68
SE18 105 EN77
Dartford DA1 128 FL87
Watford WD18 23 BV42
Market Way, E14
off Kerbey St 85 EB72
Wembley HA0 off Turton Rd 62 CL64
Westerham TN16
off Costell's Meadow 189 ER126
Market Yd Ms, SE1 201 N6
Markfield, Croy. CR0 161 DZ110
Markfield Gdns, E4 47 EB45
Markfield Rd, N15 66 DU56
Caterham CR3 186 DV126
Markham Pl, SW3 198 D10
Markham Rd,
Wal.Cr. (Chsht) EN7 14 DQ26
Markham Sq, SW3 198 D10
Markham St, SW3 198 C10
Markhole Cl, Hmptn. TW12
off Priory Rd 116 BZ94
Markhouse Av, E17 67 DY58
Markhouse Rd, E17 67 DZ57
Markland Ho, W10 81 CX73
Mark La, EC3 201 N1
Gravesend DA12 131 GL86
Markmanor Av, E17 67 DY59
Mark Oak La, Lthd. KT22 170 CA122
Mark Rd, N22 45 DP54
Marksbury Av, Rich. TW9 98 CN83
MARK'S GATE, Rom. RM6 50 EY54
Mark Sq, EC2 197 M4
Marks Rd, Rom. RM7 71 FC57
Warlingham CR6 177 DY118
Marks Sq, Grav. (Nthflt) DA11 131 GF91
Mark St, E15 86 EE66
EC2 197 M4
Reigate RH2 184 DB133
Markville Gdns, Cat. CR3 186 DU125
Markway, Sun. TW16 136 BW96
Mark Way, Swan. BR8 147 FG99
Markwell Cl, SE26
off Longton Gro 122 DV91
Markyate Rd, Dag. RM8 70 EV64
Marlands Rd, Ilf. IG5 68 EL55
Marlborough, SW3 198 C8
Marlborough Av, E8 84 DU67
N14 45 DJ48
Edgware HA8 42 CP48
Ruislip HA4 59 BQ58
Marlborough Cl, N20
off Marlborough Gdns 44 DF48
SE17 200 G9
SW19 120 DE93
Grays RM16 110 GC75
Orpington BR6
off Aylesham Rd 145 ET101
Upminster RM14 73 FS60
Walton-on-Thames KT12
off Arch Rd 136 BX104
Marlborough Ct, W1 195 K9
W8 100 DA77
Wallington SM6
off Cranley Gdns 159 DJ108
Marlborough Cres, W4 98 CR76
Hayes UB3 off High St 95 BR80
Sevenoaks TN13 190 FE124
Marlborough Dr, Ilf. IG5 68 EL55
Weybridge KT13 135 BQ104
Marlborough Gdns, N20 44 DF48
Upminster RM14 73 FR60
Marlborough Gate Ho, W2
off Elms Ms 82 DD73
Marlborough Gro, SE1 102 DU78
Marlborough Hill, NW8 82 DC67
Harrow HA1 61 CF56
★ Marlborough Ho, SW1 199 L3
Marlborough La, SE7 104 EJ79
Marlborough Ms, Bans. SM7 174 DA115
Marlborough Pk Av,
Sid. DA15 126 EU87
Marlborough Pl, NW8 82 DC68
Marlborough Rd, E4 47 EA51
E7 86 EJ66
E15 off Borthwick Rd 68 EE63
E18 68 EG55
N9 46 DT46
N19 65 DK61
N22 45 DL52
SW1 199 L3
SW19 120 DD93
W4 98 CQ78
W5 97 CK75
Ashford TW15 114 BK92
Bexleyheath DA7 106 EX83
Brentwood (Pilg.Hat.) CM15 54 FU44
Bromley BR2 144 EJ98
Dagenham RM8 70 EV63
Dartford DA1 128 FJ86
Feltham TW13 116 BX89
Hampton TW12 116 CA93
Isleworth TW7 97 CH81
Richmond TW10 118 CL86
Romford RM7 70 FA56
Slough SL3 92 AX77
South Croydon CR2 160 DQ108
Southall UB2 96 BW76
Sutton SM1 140 DA104
Uxbridge UB10 77 BP70
Watford WD18 23 BV42
Woking GU21 167 BA116
Marlborough St, SW3 198 B9
Marlborough Yd, N19 65 DK61
Marld, The, Ashtd. KT21 172 CM118
Marle Gdns, Wal.Abb. EN9 15 EC32
Marler Rd, SE23 123 DY88
Marlescroft Way, Loug. IG10 33 EP43
Marley Av, Bexh. DA7 106 EX79
Marley Cl, N15
off Stanmore Rd 65 DP56
Addlestone KT15 151 BF107
Greenford UB6 78 CA69
Marley Wk, NW2
off Lennon Rd 63 CW64
Marl Fld Cl, Wor.Pk. KT4 139 CU102
Marlin Cl, Sun. TW16 115 BT93
Marlingdene Cl, Hmptn. TW12 116 CA93
Marlings Cl, Chis. BR7 145 ES98
Whyteleafe CR3 176 DS117
Marlings Pk Av, Chis. BR7 145 ES98
Marling Way, Grav. DA12 131 GL92
Marlins, The, Nthwd. HA6 39 BT51
Marlins Cl, Rick. (Chorl.) WD3 21 BE40
Sutton SM1
off Turnpike La 158 DC106
Marlins Meadow, Wat. WD18 23 BR44
Marlin Sq, Abb.L. WD5 7 BT31
Marloes Cl, Wem. HA0 61 CK63
Marloes Rd, W8 100 DB76
Marlow Av, Purf. RM19 108 FN77
Marlow Cl, SE20 142 DV97
Marlow Ct, NW6 81 CX66
NW9 63 CT55
Marlow Cres, Twick. TW1 117 CF86
Marlow Dr, Sutt. SM3 139 CX103
Marlowe Cl, Chis. BR7 125 ER93
Ilford IG6 49 EQ53
Marlowe Ct, SE19
off Lymer Av 122 DT92
Marlowe Gdns, SE9 125 EN86
Romford RM3
off Shenstone Gdns 52 FJ53
Marlowe Rd, E17 67 EC56
Marlowes, The, NW8 82 DD67
Dartford DA1 107 FD84
Marlowe Sq, Mitch. CR4 141 DJ98
Marlowe Way, Croy. CR0 141 DL103
Marlow Gdns, Hayes UB3 95 BR76
Marlow Rd, E6 87 EM69
SE20 142 DV97
Southall UB2 96 BZ76
Marlow Way, SE16 203 H4
Marlpit Av, Couls. CR5 175 DL117
Marlpit La, Couls. CR5 175 DK116
Marl Rd, SW18 100 DB84
Marl St, SW18
off Marl Rd 100 DC84
Marlton St, SE10 205 L10
Marlwood Cl, Sid. DA15 125 ES89
Marlyon Rd, Ilf. IG6 50 EV50
Marmadon Rd, SE18 105 ET77
Marmion App, E4 47 EA49
Marmion Av, E4 47 DZ49
Marmion Cl, E4 47 DZ49
Marmion Ms, SW11
off Taybridge Rd 100 DG83
Marmion Rd, SW11 100 DG84
Marmont Rd, SE15 102 DU81
Marmora Rd, SE22 122 DW86
Marmot Rd, Houns. TW4 96 BX83
Marne Av, N11 45 DH49
Welling DA16 106 EU83
Marnell Way, Houns. TW4 96 BX83
Marne St, W10 81 CY69
Marney Rd, SW11 100 DG84
Marneys Cl, Epsom KT18 172 CN115
Marnfield Cres, SW2 121 DM88
Marnham Av, NW2 63 CY63
Marnham Cres, Grnf. UB6 78 CB69
Marnock Rd, SE4 123 DY85
Maroon St, E14 85 DY71
Maroons Way, SE6 123 EA92
Marquess Rd, N1 84 DR65
Marquis Cl, Wem. HA0 80 CM66
Marquis Rd, N4 65 DM60
N22 45 DM51
NW1 83 DK65
Marrabon Cl, Sid. DA15 126 EU88
Marram Ct, Grays RM17
off Medlar Rd 110 GE79
Marrick Cl, SW15 99 CU84
Marrilyne Av, Enf. EN3 31 DZ38
Marriott Cl, Felt. TW14 115 BR86
Marriot Ter, Rick. (Chorl.) WD3 21 BF42
Marriott Lo Cl, Add. KT15 152 BJ105
Marriott Rd, E15 86 EE67
N4 65 DM60
N10 44 DF53
Barnet EN5 27 CX41
Dartford DA1 128 FN87
Marriotts Cl, NW9 63 CT58
Mar Rd, S.Ock. RM15 91 FW70
Marrowells, Wey. KT13 135 BS104
Marryat Cl, Houns. TW4
off Wellington Rd S 96 BZ84
Marryat Pl, SW19 119 CY91
Marryat Rd, SW19 119 CX92
Enfield EN1 30 DV35
Marryat Sq, SW6 99 CY81
Marsala Rd, SE13 103 EB84
Marsden Rd, N9 46 DV47
SE15 102 DT83
Marsden St, NW5 82 DG65
Marsden Way, Orp. BR6 163 ET105
Marshall Cl, SW18
off Allfarthing La 120 DC86
Harrow HA1 off Bowen Rd 61 CD59
Hounslow TW4 116 BZ85
South Croydon CR2 160 DU113
Marshall Dr, Hayes UB4 77 BT71
Marshall Path, SE28
off Attlee Rd 88 EV73
Marshall Pl, Add.
(New Haw) KT15 152 BJ109
Marshall Rd, E10 67 EB62
N17 46 DR53
Marshalls Cl, N11 45 DH49
Epsom KT19 156 CQ113
Marshalls Dr, Rom. RM1 71 FE55
Marshall's Gro, SE18 104 EL77
Marshalls Pl, SE16 202 A7
Marshalls Rd, Rom. RM7 71 FD56
Marshall's Rd, Sutt. SM1 158 DB105
Marshall St, W1 195 L9
Marshalsea Rd, SE1 201 J4
Marsham Cl, Chis. BR7 125 EP92
Marsham La, Ger.Cr. SL9 56 AY58
Marsham Lo, Ger.Cr. SL9 56 AY58
Marsham St, SW1 199 N7
Marsham Way, Ger.Cr. SL9 56 AY57
Marsh Av, Epsom KT19 156 CS110
Mitcham CR4 140 DG96
Marshbrook Cl, SE3 104 EK83
Marsh Cl, NW7 43 CT48
Waltham Cross EN8 15 DZ33
Marsh Ct, SW19 140 DC95
Marshcroft Dr, Wal.Cr.
(Chsht) EN8 15 DY30
Marsh Dr, NW9 63 CT58
Marshe Cl, Pot.B. EN6 12 DD32
Marsh Fm Rd, Twick. TW2 117 CF88
Marshfield, Slou.
(Datchet) SL3 92 AW81
Marshfield St, E14 204 D6
Marshfoot Rd,
Grays RM16, RM17 110 GE78
Marshgate La, E15 85 EB67
Marshgate Path, SE28
off Tom Cribb Rd 105 EQ77
Marshgate Sidings, E15 85 EB67
Marsh Grn Rd, Dag. RM10 88 FA67
Marsh Hill, E9 67 DY64
Marsh La, E10 67 EA61
N17 46 DV52
NW7 42 CS49

★ Place of interest ⇌ Railway station ⊖ London Underground station DLR Docklands Light Railway station Tra Tramlink station H Hospital Riv Pedestrian ferry landing stage

Marsh La, Addlestone KT15 . . 152 BH105
Stanmore HA7 . . . . 41 CJ50
Marsh Rd, Pnr. HA5 . . . . 60 BY56
Wembley HA0 . . . . 79 CK68
Marshside Cl, N9 . . . . 46 DW46
Marsh St, E14 . . . . 204 B9
Dartford DA1 . . . . 108 FN82
Marsh Ter, Orp. BR5
off Buttermere Rd 146 EX98
Marsh Vw, Grav. DA12
off Damigos Rd 131 GM88
Marsh Wall, E14 . . . . 203 P3
Marsh Way, Rain. RM13 . . . . . 89 FD70
Marsland Cl, SE17 . . . . 101 DP78
Marston, Epsom KT19 . . . . . . 156 CQ111
Marston Av, Chess. KT9 . . . . . 156 CL107
Dagenham RM10 . . . . 70 FA61
Marston Cl, NW6 . . . . 82 DC66
Dagenham RM10 . . . . 70 FA62
Marston Ct, Walt. KT12
off St. Johns Dr 136 BW102
Marston Dr, Warl. CR6 . . . . . . 177 DY118
Marston Ho, Grays RM17 . . . . 110 GA79
Marston Rd, Ilf. IG5 . . . . 48 EL53
Teddington TW11 . . . . 117 CH92
Woking GU21 . . . . 166 AV117
Marston Way, SE19 . . . . 121 DP94
Marsworth Av, Pnr. HA5 . . . . . . 40 BX53
Marsworth Cl, Hayes UB4 . . . . 78 BY71
Watford WD18 . . . . 23 BS44
Martaban Rd, N16 . . . . 66 DS61
Martara Ms, SE17
off Penrose St 102 DQ78
Martello St, E8 . . . . 84 DV66
Martello Ter, E8 . . . . 84 DV66
Martell Rd, SE21 . . . . 122 DR90
Martel Pl, E8 off Dalston La . . . 84 DT65
Marten Rd, E17 . . . . 47 EA54
Martens Av, Bexh. DA7 . . . . . . 107 FC84
Martens Cl, Bexh. DA7 . . . . . . 107 FC84
Martha Ct, E2 . . . . 84 DV68
Martham Cl, SE28 . . . . 88 EX73
Ilford IG6 . . . . 49 EP53
Martha Rd, E15 . . . . 86 EE65
Martha's Bldgs, EC1 . . . . 197 K4
Martha St, E1 . . . . 84 DV72
Marthorne Cres, Har. HA3 . . . . 41 CD54
Martina Ter, Chig. IG7
off Manford Way 49 ET50
Martin Bowes Rd, SE9 . . . . . . 105 EM83
Martinbridge Trd Est, Enf. EN1 . 30 DU43
Martin Cl, N9 . . . . 47 DX46
South Croydon CR2 . . . . 161 DX111
Uxbridge UB10
off Valley Rd 76 BL68
Warlingham CR6 . . . . 176 DV116
Martin Cres, Croy. CR0 . . . . . 141 DN102
Martindale, SW14 . . . . 118 CQ85
Iver SL0 . . . . 75 BD70
Martindale Av, E16 . . . . 86 EG73
Orpington BR6 . . . . 164 EU106
Martindale Rd, SW12 . . . . 121 DH87
Hounslow TW4 . . . . 96 BY83
Woking GU21 . . . . 166 AT118
Martin Dene, Bexh. DA6 . . . . . 126 EZ85
Martin Dr, Dart.
(Stone) DA2 . . . . 128 FQ86
Northolt UB5 . . . . 60 BZ64
Rainham RM13 . . . . 89 FH70
Martineau Cl, Esher KT10 . . . . 155 CD105
Martineau Ms, N5
off Martineau Rd 65 DP63
Martineau Rd, N5 . . . . 65 DP63
Martineau St, E1 . . . . 84 DW73
Martingale Cl, Sun. TW16 . . . . 135 BU98
Martingales Cl, Rich. TW10 . . . 117 CK90
Martin Gdns, Dag. RM8 . . . . . . 70 EW63
Martin Gro, Mord. SM4 . . . . . 140 DA97
Martini Dr, Enf. EN3 . . . . 31 EA37
Martin La, EC4 . . . . 197 L10
Martin Ri, Bexh. DA6 . . . . 126 EZ85
Martin Rd, Dag. RM8 . . . . 70 EW63
Dartford DA2 . . . . 128 FJ90
Slough SL1 . . . . 92 AS76
South Ockendon
(Aveley) RM15 . . . . 91 FR73
Martins Cl, Orp. BR5 . . . . 146 EX97
Radlett WD7 . . . . 25 CE36
West Wickham BR4 . . . . 143 ED102
Martins Dr, Wal.Cr.
(Chsht) EN8 . . . . 15 DY28
Martinsfield Cl, Chig. IG7 . . . . 49 ES49
Martins Mt, Barn. EN5 . . . . 28 DA42
Martins Pl, SE28
off Martin St 87 ES74
Martin's Plain, Slou.
(Stoke P.) SL2 . . . . 74 AT69
Martins Rd, Brom. BR2 . . . . . . 144 EE96
Martins Shaw, Sev.
(Chipstead) TN13 . . . . 190 FC122
Martinstown Cl, Horn. RM11 . . 72 FN58
Martin St, SE28 . . . . 87 ES74
Martins Wk, N10 . . . . 44 DG53
SE28 . . . . 87 ES74
Borehamwood WD6
off Siskin Cl 26 CN42
Martinsyde, Wok. GU22 . . . . . 167 BC117
Martin Way, SW20 . . . . 139 CY97
Morden SM4 . . . . 139 CY97
Woking GU21 . . . . 166 AU118
Martlands Ind Est, Wok. GU22
off Smarts Heath La 166 AU123
Martlesham Cl, Horn. RM12 . . . 72 FJ64
Martlet Gro, Nthlt. UB5
off Javelin Way 78 BX69
Martlett Ct, WC2 . . . . 196 A9
Martley Dr, Ilf. IG2 . . . . 69 EP57
Martock Cl, Har. HA3 . . . . 61 CG56
Martock Gdns, N11 . . . . 44 DF50
Marton Cl, SE6 . . . . 123 EA90
Marton Rd, N16 . . . . 66 DS61
MARTYR'S GREEN,
Wok. KT11 . . . . 169 BR120
Martyrs La, Wok. GU21 . . . . . 151 BB112
Martys Yd, NW3
off Hampstead High St 64 DD63
Marvell Av, Hayes UB4 . . . . . . 77 BU71
Marvels Cl, SE12 . . . . 124 EH89
Marvels La, SE12 . . . . 124 EH89
Marville Rd, SW6 . . . . 99 CZ80
Marvin St, E8
off Sylvester Rd 84 DV65
Marwell, West. TN16 . . . . 189 EP126
Marwell Cl, Rom. RM1 . . . . 71 FG57
West Wickham BR4
off Deer Pk Way 144 EF103
Marwood Cl, Kings L. WD4 . . . . 6 BN29
Welling DA16 . . . . 106 EV83
Marwood Dr, NW7 . . . . 43 CX52
Mary Adelaide Cl, SW15 . . . . . 118 CS91
Mary Ann Gdns, SE8 . . . . 103 EA79
Maryatt Av, Har. HA2 . . . . 60 CB61
Marybank, SE18 . . . . 105 EM77
Mary Cl, Stan. HA7 . . . . 62 CM56
Mary Datchelor Cl, SE5 . . . . . 102 DR81
Maryfield Cl, Bex. DA5 . . . . . . 127 FE90
Marygold Wk, Amer. HP6 . . . . . 20 AV39
Mary Grn, NW8 . . . . 82 DB67
Maryhill Cl, Ken. CR8 . . . . . . 176 DQ117
⇌ Maryland 86 EE65
Maryland Ind Est, E15
off Maryland Rd 67 ED64
Maryland Pk, E15 . . . . 68 EE64
Maryland Pt, E15
off Leytonstone Rd 86 EE65
Maryland Rd, E15 . . . . 67 ED64
N22 . . . . 45 DM51
Thornton Heath CR7 . . . . 141 DP95
Maryland Sq, E15 . . . . 68 EE64
Marylands Rd, W9 . . . . 82 DA70
Maryland St, E15 . . . . 67 ED64
Maryland Wk, N1
off Popham St 84 DQ67
Maryland Way, Sun. TW16 . . . 135 BU96
Mary Lawrenson Pl, SE3 . . . . 104 EF80
MARYLEBONE, NW1 . . . . 194 D8
⇌ Marylebone 194 D5
⊖ Marylebone 194 D5
Marylebone Flyover, NW1 . . . 194 A7
W2 . . . . 194 A7
Marylebone High St, W1 . . . . 194 G6
Marylebone La, W1 . . . . 195 H9
Marylebone Ms, W1 . . . . 195 H7
Marylebone Pas, W1 . . . . 195 L8
Marylebone Rd, NW1 . . . . 194 C6
Marylebone St, W1 . . . . 194 G7
Marylee Way, SE11 . . . . 200 C10
Mary Macarthur Ho, W6
off Field Rd 99 CY79
Maryon Gro, SE7 . . . . 104 EL77
Maryon Ms, NW3
off South End Rd 64 DE63
Maryon Rd, SE7 . . . . 104 EL77
SE18 . . . . 104 EL77
Mary Peters Dr, Grnf. UB6 . . . . 61 CD64
Mary Pl, W11 . . . . 81 CY73
Mary Rose Cl, Grays
(Chaff.Hun.) RM16 . . . . 109 FW77
Hampton TW12
off Ashley Rd 136 CA95
Mary Rose Mall, E6
off Frobisher Rd 87 EN71
Maryrose Way, N20 . . . . 44 DD46
Mary Seacole Cl, E8
off Clarissa St 84 DT67
Maryside, Slou. SL3 . . . . 92 AY75
Mary's Ter, Twick. TW1 . . . . . . 117 CG87
Mary St, E16 off Barking Rd . . . 86 EF71
N1 . . . . 84 DQ67
Mary Ter, NW1 . . . . 83 DH67
Mary Way, Wat. WD19 . . . . 40 BX49
Masbro Rd, W14 . . . . 99 CX76
Mascalls Ct, SE7
off Victoria Way 104 EJ79
Mascalls Gdns, Brwd. CM14 . . 54 FT49
Mascalls La, Brwd. CM14 . . . . 54 FT49
H Mascalls Pk, Brwd. CM14 . . 54 FV51
Mascalls Rd, SE7 . . . . 104 EJ79
Mascotte Rd, SW15 . . . . 99 CX84
Mascotts Cl, NW2 . . . . 63 CV62
Masefield Av, Borwd. WD6 . . . . 26 CP43
Southall UB1 . . . . 78 CA73
Stanmore HA7 . . . . 41 CF50
Masefield Cl, Erith DA8 . . . . . 107 FF81
Romford RM3 . . . . 52 FJ53
Masefield Ct, Brwd. CM14 . . . . 54 FW49
Masefield Cres, N14 . . . . 29 DJ44
Romford RM3 . . . . 52 FJ53
Masefield Dr, Upmin. RM14 . . . 72 FQ59
Masefield Gdns, E6 . . . . 87 EN70
Masefield La, Hayes UB4 . . . . . 77 BV70
Masefield Rd, Dart. DA1 . . . . . 128 FP85
Gravesend (Nthflt) DA11 . . . 130 GD90
Grays RM16 . . . . 110 GE75
Hampton TW12
off Wordsworth Rd 116 BZ91
Masefield Vw, Orp. BR6 . . . . . 145 EQ104
Masefield Way, Stai. TW19 . . . 114 BM88
Masham Ho, Erith DA18
off Kale Rd 106 EX75
Mashie Rd, W3 . . . . 80 CS72
Mashiters Hill, Rom. RM1 . . . . 51 FD53
Mashiters Wk, Rom. RM1 . . . . . 71 FE55
Maskall Cl, SW2 . . . . 121 DN88
Maskani Wk, SW16
off Bates Cres 121 DJ94
Maskell Rd, SW17 . . . . 120 DC90
Maskelyne Cl, SW11 . . . . 100 DE81
Mason Bradbear Ct, N1
off St. Paul's Rd 84 DR65
Mason Cl, E16 . . . . 86 EG73
SE16 . . . . 202 C10
SW20 . . . . 139 CX95
Bexleyheath DA7 . . . . 107 FB83
Borehamwood WD6 . . . . 26 CQ40
Hampton TW12 . . . . 136 BZ95
Mason Dr, Rom. (Harold Wd) RM3
off Whitmore Av 52 FL54
Masonic Hall Rd, Cher. KT16 . 133 BF100
Mason Rd, Sutt. SM1
off Manor Pl 158 DB106
Woodford Green IG8 . . . . 48 EE49
Masons Arms Ms, W1 . . . . 195 J9
Masons Av, EC2 . . . . 197 K8
Croydon CR0 . . . . 142 DQ104
Harrow HA3 . . . . 61 CF56
Masons Ct, Wem. HA9
off Mayfields 62 CN61
Masons Grn La, W3 . . . . 80 CN71
Masons Hill, SE18 . . . . 105 EP77
Masons Hill,
Bromley BR1, BR2 . . . . 144 EG97
Mason's Pl, EC1 . . . . 196 G2
Masons Pl, Mitch. CR4 . . . . . . 140 DF95
Masons Rd, Enf. EN1 . . . . 30 DW36
Mason St, SE17 . . . . 201 L9
Mason's Yd, SW1 . . . . 199 L2
SW19
off High St Wimbledon 119 CX92
Mason Way, Wal.Abb. EN9 . . . 16 EF34
Massey Cl, N11 off Grove Rd . . 45 DH50
Massey Ct, E6 . . . . 86 EJ67
Massie Rd, E8 off Graham Rd . 84 DU65
Massingberd Way, SW17 . . . . 121 DH91
Massinger St, SE17 . . . . 201 M9
Massingham St, E1 . . . . 85 DX70
Masson Av, Ruis. HA4 . . . . 78 BW65
Master Cl, Oxt. RH8
off Church La 188 EE129
Master Gunner Pl, SE18 . . . . . 104 EL80
Masterman Ho, SE5 . . . . 102 DR80
Masterman Rd, E6 . . . . 86 EL69
Masters Cl, SW16
off Blegborough Rd 121 DJ93
Masters Dr, SE16 . . . . 102 DV78
Masters St, E1 . . . . 85 DX71
Masthead Cl, Dart. DA2 . . . . . 108 FQ84
Riv Masthouse Terrace 204 A10
Masthouse Ter, E14 . . . . 204 A9
Mast Leisure Pk, SE16 . . . . . . 203 J7
Mastmaker Rd, E14 . . . . 204 A5
Maswell Pk Cres, Houns. TW3 . 116 CC85
Maswell Pk Rd, Houns. TW3 . . 116 CB85
Matcham Rd, E11 . . . . 68 EE62
Matchless Dr, SE18 . . . . 105 EN80
Matfield Cl, Brom. BR2 . . . . . . 144 EG99
Matfield Rd, Belv. DA17 . . . . . 106 FA79
Matham Gro, SE22 . . . . 102 DT84
Matham Rd, E.Mol. KT8 . . . . . 137 CD99
Matheson Rd, W14 . . . . 99 CZ77
Mathews Av, E6 . . . . 87 EN68
Mathews Pk Av, E15 . . . . 86 EF65
Mathias Cl, Epsom KT18 . . . . . 156 CQ113
Mathisen Way, Slou.
(Colnbr.) SL3 . . . . 93 BE81
Matilda Cl, SE19
off Elizabeth Way 122 DR94
Matilda St, N1 . . . . 83 DM67
Matlock Cl, SE24 . . . . 102 DQ84
Barnet EN5 . . . . 27 CX43
Matlock Ct, SE5
off Denmark Hill Est 102 DR84
Matlock Cres, Sutt. SM3 . . . . . 157 CY105
Watford WD19 . . . . 40 BW48
Matlock Gdns, Horn. RM12 . . . 72 FL62
Sutton SM3 . . . . 157 CY105
Matlock Pl, Sutt. SM3 . . . . . . 157 CY105
Matlock Rd, E10 . . . . 67 EC58
Caterham CR3 . . . . 176 DS121
Matlock St, E14 . . . . 85 DY72
Matlock Way, N.Mal. KT3 . . . . 138 CR95
Matrimony Pl, SW8 . . . . 101 DJ82
Matson Ct, Wdf.Grn. IG8
off The Bridle Path 48 EE52
Matthew Arnold Cl,
Cob. KT11 . . . . 153 BU114
Staines TW18
off Elizabeth Av 114 BJ93
Matthew Cl, W10 . . . . 81 CX70
Matthew Ct, Mitch. CR4 . . . . . 141 DK99
Matthew Parker St, SW1 . . . . . 199 N5
Matthews Cl, Rom.
(Hav.at.Bow.) RM3
off Oak Rd 52 FM53
Matthews Gdns, Croy.
(New Adgtn) CR0 . . . . 161 ED111
Matthews Rd, Grnf. UB6 . . . . . . 61 CD64
Matthews St, SW11 . . . . 100 DF82
Matthews Yd, WC2 . . . . 195 P9
Matthias Rd, N16 . . . . 66 DR64
Mattingley Way, SE15
off Daniel Gdns 102 DT80
Mattison Rd, N4 . . . . 65 DN58
Mattock La, W5 . . . . 79 CH74
W13 . . . . 79 CH74
Maud Cashmore Way, SE18 . . 105 EM76
Maude Cres, Wat. WD24 . . . . . 23 BV37
Maude Rd, E17 . . . . 67 DY57
SE5 . . . . 102 DS81
Swanley BR8 . . . . 127 FG93
Maudesville Cotts, W7
off The Broadway 79 CE74
Maude Ter, E17 . . . . 67 DY56
Maud Gdns, E13 . . . . 86 EF67
Barking IG11 . . . . 87 ET68
Maudlin's Grn, E1 . . . . 202 B2
Maud Rd, E10 . . . . 67 EC62
E13 . . . . 86 EF68
Maudslay Rd, SE9 . . . . 105 EM83
H Maudsley Hosp, The, SE5 . 102 DR82
Maudsley Ho, Brent. TW8
off Green Dragon La 98 CL78
Maud St, E16 . . . . 86 EF71
Maud Wilkes Cl, NW5 . . . . 65 DJ64
Mauleverer Rd, SW2 . . . . 121 DL85
Maundeby Wk, NW10
off Neasden La 80 CS65
Maunder Cl, Grays RM16
off Lancaster Rd 109 FX77
Maunder Rd, W7 . . . . 79 CF74
Maunsel St, SW1 . . . . 199 M8
Maurice Av, N22 . . . . 45 DP54
Caterham CR3 . . . . 176 DR122
Maurice Brown Cl, NW7 . . . . . . 43 CX50
Maurice St, W12 . . . . 81 CV72
Maurice Wk, NW11 . . . . 64 DC56
Maurier Cl, Nthlt. UB5 . . . . 78 BW67
Mauritius Rd, SE10 . . . . 205 J9
Maury Rd, N16 . . . . 66 DU61
Mauveine Gdns, Houns. TW3
off Hibernia Rd 96 CA84
Mavelstone Cl, Brom. BR1 . . . 144 EL95
Mavelstone Rd, Brom. BR1 . . . 144 EL95
Maverton Rd, E3 . . . . 85 EA67
Mavis Av, Epsom KT19 . . . . . . 156 CS106
Mavis Cl, Epsom KT19 . . . . . . 156 CS106
Mavis Gro, Horn. RM12 . . . . . . 72 FL61
Mavis Wk, E6 . . . . 86 EL71
Mawbey Est, SE1 . . . . 102 DU78
Mawbey Pl, SE1 . . . . 102 DT78
Mawbey Rd, SE1
off Old Kent Rd 102 DT78
Chertsey (Ott.) KT16 . . . . . . 151 BD107
Mawbey St, SW8 . . . . 101 DL80
Mawney Cl, Rom. RM7 . . . . 51 FB54
Mawney Rd, Rom. RM7 . . . . 71 FC56
Mawson Cl, SW20 . . . . 139 CY96
Mawson La, W4
off Great W Rd 99 CT79
Maxey Gdns, Dag. RM9 . . . . . . 70 EY63
Maxey Rd, SE18 . . . . 105 EQ77
Dagenham RM9 . . . . 70 EY63
Maxfield Cl, N20 . . . . 44 DC45
Maxilla Gdns, W10
off Cambridge Gdns 81 CX72
Maxilla Wk, W10
off Kingsdown Cl 81 CX72
Maximfeldt Rd, Erith DA8 . . . . 107 FE78
Maxim Rd, N21 . . . . 29 DN44
Dartford DA1 . . . . 127 FE85
Erith DA8 . . . . 107 FE77
Maxted Pk, Har. HA1 . . . . 61 CE59
Maxted Rd, SE15 . . . . 102 DT83
Maxwell Cl, Croy. CR0 . . . . . . 141 DL102
Hayes UB3 . . . . 77 BU73
Rickmansworth
(Mill End) WD3 . . . . 38 BG47
Maxwell Dr, W.Byf. KT14 . . . . . 152 BJ111
Maxwell Gdns, Orp. BR6 . . . . . 145 ET104
Maxwell Ri, Wat. WD19 . . . . . . 40 BY45
Maxwell Rd, SW6 . . . . 100 DB80
Ashford TW15 . . . . 115 BQ93
Borehamwood WD6 . . . . 26 CP41
Northwood HA6 . . . . 39 BR52
Welling DA16 . . . . 106 EU84
West Drayton UB7 . . . . 94 BM77
Maxwelton Av, NW7 . . . . 42 CR50
Maxwelton Cl, NW7 . . . . 42 CR50
Maya Angelou Ct, E4
off Bailey Cl 47 EC49
Maya Cl, SE15 . . . . 102 DV82
Mayall Rd, SE24 . . . . 121 DP85
Maya Pl, N11 . . . . 45 DK52
Maya Rd, N2 . . . . 64 DC56
May Av, Grav. (Nthflt) DA11 . . 131 GF88
Orpington BR5 . . . . 146 EV99
May Av Ind Est, Grav. (Nthflt) DA11
off May Av 131 GF88
Maybank Av, E18 . . . . 48 EH54
Hornchurch RM12 . . . . 71 FH64
Wembley HA0 . . . . 61 CF64
Maybank Gdns, Pnr. HA5 . . . . . 59 BU57
Maybank Lo, Horn. RM12 . . . . . 72 FJ64
Maybank Rd, E18 . . . . 48 EH53
May Bate Av, Kings.T. KT2 . . . 137 CK95
Maybells Commercial Est,
Bark. IG11 . . . . 88 EX68
Mayberry Pl, Surb. KT5 . . . . . 138 CM101
Maybourne Cl, SE26 . . . . 122 DV92
Maybourne Ri, Wok. GU22 . . . 166 AX124
Maybrick Rd, Horn. RM11 . . . . 72 FJ58
Maybrook Meadow Est,
Bark. IG11 . . . . 88 EU66
MAYBURY, Wok. GU22 . . . . . . 167 BB117
Maybury Av, Dart. DA2 . . . . . . 128 FQ88
Waltham Cross (Chsht) EN8 . 14 DV28
Maybury Cl, Enf. EN1 . . . . 30 DV38
Loughton IG10 . . . . 33 EP42
Orpington BR5 . . . . 145 EP99
Tadworth KT20
off Ballards Grn 173 CY119
Maybury Gdns, NW10 . . . . 81 CV65
Maybury Hill, Wok. GU22 . . . . 167 BB116
Maybury Ms, N6 . . . . 65 DJ59
Maybury Rd, E13 . . . . 86 EJ70
Barking IG11 . . . . 87 ET68
Woking GU21 . . . . 167 AZ117
Maybury St, SW17 . . . . 120 DE92
Maybush Rd, Horn. RM11 . . . . . 72 FL59
Maychurch Cl, Stan. HA7 . . . . . 41 CK52
May Cl, Chess. KT9 . . . . 156 CM107
Maycock Gro, Nthwd. HA6 . . . . 39 BT51
May Cotts, Wat. WD18 . . . . 24 BW43
May Ct, SW19 . . . . 140 DC95
Grays RM17 off Medlar Rd . . 110 GE79
Maycroft, Pnr. HA5 . . . . 39 BV54
Maycroft Av, Grays RM17 . . . . 110 GD78
Maycroft Gdns, Grays RM17 . . 110 GD78
Maycroft Rd, Wal.Cr.
(Chsht) EN7 . . . . 14 DS26
Maycross Av, Mord. SM4 . . . . 139 CZ97
Mayday Gdns, SE3 . . . . 104 EL82
H Mayday Hosp,
Th.Hth. CR7 . . . . 141 DP100
Mayday Rd, Th.Hth. CR7 . . . . 141 DP100
Maydwell Lo, Borwd. WD6 . . . . 26 CM40
Mayell Cl, Lthd. KT22 . . . . 171 CJ123
Mayerne Rd, SE9 . . . . 124 EK85
Mayer Rd, Wal.Abb. EN9
off Deer Pk Way 31 EB36
Mayesbrook Rd, Bark. IG11 . . . 87 ET67
Dagenham RM8 . . . . 70 EU62
Ilford IG3 . . . . 70 EU62
Mayes Cl, Swan. BR8 . . . . 147 FG98
Warlingham CR6 . . . . 177 DX118
Mayesford Rd, Rom. RM6 . . . . . 70 EW59
Mayes Rd, N22 . . . . 45 DN54
Mayeswood Rd, SE12 . . . . 124 EJ90
MAYFAIR, W1 . . . . 199 H1
Mayfair Av, Bexh. DA7 . . . . . . 106 EX81
Ilford IG1 . . . . 69 EM61
Romford RM6 . . . . 70 EX58
Twickenham TW2 . . . . 116 CC87
Worcester Park KT4 . . . . 139 CU102
Mayfair Cl, Beck. BR3 . . . . . . 143 EB95
Surbiton KT6 . . . . 138 CL102
Mayfair Gdns, N17 . . . . 46 DR51
Woodford Green IG8 . . . . 48 EG52
Mayfair Ms, NW1
off Regents Pk Rd 82 DF66
Mayfair Pl, W1 . . . . 199 J2
Mayfair Rd, Dart. DA1 . . . . 128 FK85
Mayfair Ter, N14 . . . . 45 DK45
Mayfare, Rick. (Crox.Grn) WD3 . 23 BR43
Mayfield, Bexh. DA7 . . . . 106 EZ83
Leatherhead KT22 . . . . 171 CJ121
Waltham Abbey EN9 . . . . 15 ED34
Mayfield Av, N12 . . . . 44 DC49
N14 . . . . 45 DK47
W4 . . . . 98 CS77
Mayfield Av, W13 . . . . 97 CH76
Addlestone
(New Haw) KT15 . . . . 152 BH110
Gerrards Cross SL9 . . . . 56 AX56
Harrow HA3 . . . . 61 CH57
Orpington BR6 . . . . 145 ET102
Woodford Green IG8 . . . . 48 EG52
Mayfield Cl, E8 off Forest Rd . . 84 DT65
SW4 . . . . 121 DK85
Addlestone
(New Haw) KT15 . . . . 152 BJ110
Ashford TW15 . . . . 115 BP93
Thames Ditton KT7 . . . . 137 CH102
Uxbridge UB10 . . . . 77 BP69
Walton-on-Thames KT12 . . 153 BU105
Mayfield Cres, N9 . . . . 30 DV44
Thornton Heath CR7 . . . . 141 DM98
Mayfield Dr, Pnr. HA5 . . . . 60 BZ56
Mayfield Gdns, NW4 . . . . 63 CX58
W7 . . . . 79 CD72
Brentwood CM14 . . . . 54 FV46
Staines TW18 . . . . 113 BF93
Walton-on-Thames KT12 . . 153 BU105
Mayfield Mans, SW15
off West Hill 119 CX87
Mayfield Pk, West Dr. UB7 . . . . 94 BJ76
Mayfield Rd, E4 . . . . 47 EC47
E8 . . . . 84 DT66
E13 . . . . 86 EF70
E17 . . . . 47 DY54
N8 . . . . 65 DM58
SW19 . . . . 139 CZ95
W3 . . . . 80 CP73
W12 . . . . 98 CS75
Belvedere DA17 . . . . 107 FC77
Bromley BR1 . . . . 144 EL99
Dagenham RM8 . . . . 70 EW60
Enfield EN3 . . . . 31 DX40
Gravesend DA11 . . . . 131 GF87
South Croydon CR2 . . . . 160 DR109
Sutton SM2 . . . . 158 DD107
Thornton Heath CR7 . . . . 141 DM98
Walton-on-Thames KT12 . . 153 BU105
Weybridge KT13 . . . . 152 BM106
Mayfields, Grays RM16 . . . . . 110 GC75
Swanscombe DA10
off Madden Cl 130 FY86
Wembley HA9 . . . . 62 CN61
Mayfields Cl, Wem. HA9 . . . . . 62 CN61
Mayflower Cl, SE16 . . . . 203 J8
Ruislip HA4
off Leaholme Way 59 BQ58
South Ockendon RM15 . . . . . 91 FW70
Mayflower Ct, SE16
off St. Marychurch St 102 DW75
Mayflower Rd, SW9 . . . . 101 DL83
Grays (Chaff.Hun.) RM16 . . 109 FW78
St. Albans (Park St) AL2 . . . . . 8 CB27
Mayflower St, SE16 . . . . 202 F5
Mayfly Cl, Orp. BR5 . . . . 146 EX98
Pinner HA5 . . . . 60 BW59
Mayfly Gdns, Nthlt. UB5
off Ruislip Rd 78 BX69
MAYFORD, Wok. GU22 . . . . . . 166 AW122
Mayford Cl, SW12 . . . . 120 DF87
Beckenham BR3 . . . . 143 DX97
Woking GU22 . . . . 166 AX122
Mayford Grn, Wok. GU22
off Smarts Heath Rd 166 AW122
Mayford Rd, SW12 . . . . 120 DF87
May Gdns, Borwd.
(Elstree) WD6 . . . . 25 CK44
Wembley HA0 . . . . 79 CJ68
Maygoods Cl, Uxb. UB8 . . . . . . 76 BK71
Maygoods Grn, Uxb. UB8
off Worcester Rd 76 BK71
Maygoods La, Uxb. UB8 . . . . . 76 BK71
Maygood St, N1 . . . . 83 DM68
Maygoods Vw, Uxb. UB8
off Benbow Waye 76 BJ71
Maygreen Cres, Horn. RM11 . . 71 FG59
Maygrove Rd, NW6 . . . . 81 CZ65
Mayhew Cl, E4 . . . . 47 EA48
Mayhill Rd, SE7 . . . . 104 EH79
Barnet EN5 . . . . 27 CY44
Mayhurst Av, Wok. GU22 . . . . 167 BC116
Mayhurst Cl, Wok. GU22 . . . . 167 BC116
Mayhurst Cres, Wok. GU22 . . 167 BC116
Maylands Av, Horn. RM12 . . . . 71 FH63
Maylands Dr, Sid. DA14 . . . . . 126 EX90
Uxbridge UB8 . . . . 76 BK65
Maylands Rd, Wat. WD19 . . . . . 40 BW49
Maylands Way, Rom. RM3 . . . . 52 FQ51
Maynard Cl, N15
off Brunswick Rd 66 DS56
SW6 off Cambria St 100 DB80
Erith DA8 . . . . 107 FF80
Maynard Ct, Enf. EN3
off Harston Dr 31 EA38
Waltham Abbey EN9 . . . . 16 EF34
Maynard Path, E17 . . . . 67 EC57
Maynard Pl, Pot.B. EN6 . . . . . . 13 DL29
Maynard Rd, E17 . . . . 67 EC57
Maynards, Horn. RM11 . . . . 72 FL59
Maynards Quay, E1 . . . . 202 F1
Maynooth Gdns, Cars. SM5 . . 140 DF101
Mayo Cl, Wal.Cr. (Chsht) EN8 . . 14 DW28
Mayola Rd, E5 . . . . 66 DW63
Mayo Rd, NW10 . . . . 80 CS65
Croydon CR0 . . . . 142 DR99
Walton-on-Thames KT12 . . 135 BT101
Mayor's La, Dart. DA2 . . . . 128 FJ92
Mayow Rd, SE23 . . . . 123 DX90
SE26 . . . . 123 DX91
Mayplace Av, Dart. DA1 . . . . . 107 FG84
Mayplace Cl, Bexh. DA7 . . . . . 107 FB83
Mayplace La, SE18 . . . . 105 EP80
Mayplace Rd E, Bexh. DA7 . . . 107 FB83
Dartford DA1 . . . . 107 FC83
Mayplace Rd W, Bexh. DA7 . . . 106 FA84
MAYPOLE, Orp. BR6 . . . . 164 EZ106
Maypole Cres, Erith DA8 . . . . 108 FK79
Ilford IG6 . . . . 49 ER52
Maypole Dr, Chig. IG7 . . . . 50 EU48
Maypole Rd, Grav. DA12 . . . . 131 GM88

★ Place of interest ⇌ Railway station ⊖ London Underground station DLR Docklands Light Railway station Tra Tramlink station H Hospital Riv Pedestrian ferry landing stage

Maypole Rd, Orpington BR6 164 EZ106
May Rd, E4 47 EA51
E13 86 EG68
Dartford (Hawley) DA2 128 FM91
Twickenham TW2 117 CE88
Mayroyd Av, Surb. KT6 138 CN103
May's Bldgs Ms, SE10
off Crooms Hill 103 ED80
Mays Cl, Wey. KT13 152 BM110
Mays Ct, WC2 199 P1
Maysfield Rd, Wok.
(Send) GU23 167 BD123
MAY'S GREEN, Cob. KT11 169 BT121
Mays Gro, Wok. (Send) GU23 167 BD123
Mays Hill Rd, Brom. BR2 144 EE96
Mays La, E4 47 ED47
Barnet EN5 27 CY43
Maysoule Rd, SW11 100 DD84
Mays Rd, Tedd. TW11 117 CD92
Mayston Ms, SE10
off Westcombe Hill 104 EG78
May St, W14
off North End Rd 99 CZ78
Mayswood Gdns, Dag. RM10 89 FC65
Maythorne Cl, Wat. WD18 23 BS42
Mayton St, N7 65 DM62
Maytree Cl, Edg. HA8 42 CQ48
Rainham RM13 89 FE68
Maytree Cres, Wat. WD24 23 BT35
Maytree Gdns, W5
off South Ealing Rd 97 CK75
May Tree La, Stan. HA7 41 CF52
Maytrees, Rad. WD7 25 CG37
Maytree Wk, SW2 121 DN89
Mayville Est, N16
off King Henry St 66 DS64
Mayville Rd, E11 68 EE61
Ilford IG1 69 EP64
May Wk, E13 86 EH68
Maywater Cl, S.Croy. CR2 160 DR111
Maywin Dr, Horn. RM11 72 FM60
Maywood Cl, Beck. BR3 123 EB94
⇌ Maze Hill 104 EE79
Maze Hill, SE3 104 EE79
SE10 104 EE79
Mazenod Av, NW6 82 DA66
Maze Rd, Rich. TW9 98 CN80
Mead, The, N2 44 DC54
W13 79 CH71
Ashtead KT21 172 CL119
Beckenham BR3 143 EC95
Uxbridge UB10 58 BN61
Wallington SM6 159 DK107
Waltham Cross (Chsht) EN8 14 DW29
Watford WD19 40 BY48
West Wickham BR4 143 ED102
Mead Av, Slou. SL3 93 BB75
Mead Cl, Egh. TW20 113 BB93
Grays RM16 110 GB75
Harrow HA3 41 CD53
Loughton IG10 33 EP40
Redhill RH1 184 DG131
Romford RM2 51 FG54
Slough SL3 93 BB75
Swanley BR8 147 FG99
Uxbridge (Denh.) UB9 58 BG61
Mead Ct, NW9 62 CQ57
Egham TW20
off Holbrook Meadow 113 BC93
Waltham Abbey EN9 15 EB34
Woking (Knap.) GU21 166 AS116
Mead Cres, E4 47 EC49
Dartford DA1
off Beech Rd 128 FK88
Sutton SM1 158 DE105
Meadcroft Rd, SE11 101 DP79
Meade Cl, W4 98 CN79
Meade Ct, Tad. KT20 173 CU124
Mead End, Ashtd. KT21 172 CM116
Meades, The, Wey. KT13 153 BQ107
Meadfield, Edg. HA8 42 CP47
Mead Fld, Har. HA2
off Kings Rd 60 BZ62
Meadfield Av, Slou. SL3 93 BA76
Meadfield Grn, Edg. HA8 42 CP47
Meadfield Rd, Slou. SL3 93 BA76
Meadfoot Rd, SW16 121 DJ94
Meadgate Av, Wdf.Grn. IG8 48 EL50
Mead Gro, Rom. RM6 70 EY55
Mead Ho La, Hayes UB4 77 BR70
Meadhurst Rd, Cher. KT16 134 BH102
Meadlands Dr, Rich. TW10 117 CK89
Mead La, Cher. KT16 134 BH102
Mead La Caravan Pk,
Cher. KT16 134 BJ102
Meadow, The, Chis. BR7 125 EQ93
Meadow Av, Croy. CR0 143 DX100
Meadow Bk, N21 29 DM44
Meadowbank, NW3 82 DF66
SE3 104 EF83
Kings Langley WD4 6 BN30
Surbiton KT5 138 CM100
Watford WD19 40 BW45
Meadowbank Cl, SW6 99 CW80
Meadowbank Gdns,
Houns. TW5 95 BU82
Meadowbank Rd, NW9 62 CR59
Meadowbanks, Barn. EN5 27 CT43
Meadowbrook, Oxt. RH8 187 EC130
Meadowbrook Cl, Slou.
(Colnbr.) SL3 93 BF82
Meadow Cl, E4
off Mount Echo Av 47 EB46
E9 67 DZ64
SE6 123 EA92
SW20 139 CW98
Barnet EN5 27 CZ44
Bexleyheath DA6 126 EZ85
Chislehurst BR7 125 EP92
Enfield EN3 31 DY38
Esher KT10 137 CF104
Hounslow TW4 116 CA86
Northolt UB5 78 CA68
Purley CR8 159 DK113
Richmond TW10 118 CL88
Meadow Cl, Ruislip HA4 59 BT58
St. Albans (Brick.Wd) AL2 8 CA29
St. Albans (Lon.Col.) AL2 9 CK27
Sevenoaks TN13 190 FG123
Sutton SM1
off Aultone Way 140 DB103
Walton-on-Thames KT12 154 BZ105
Windsor (Old Wind.) SL4 112 AV86
Meadow Ct, Epsom KT18 156 CQ113
Redhill RH1 185 DK130
Staines TW18 113 BE90
Meadowcourt Rd, SE3 104 EF84
Meadowcroft, Brom. BR1 145 EM97
Bushey WD23 24 CB44
Gerrards Cross
(Chal.St.P.) SL9 36 AX54
Meadowcroft Rd, N13 45 DN47
Meadowcross, Wal.Abb. EN9 16 EE34
Meadow Dr, N10 65 DH55
NW4 43 CW54
Amersham HP6 20 AS37
Woking (Ripley) GU23 167 BF123
Meadow Gdns, Edg. HA8 42 CP51
Staines TW18 113 BD92
Meadow Garth, NW10 80 CQ65
Meadowgate Cl, NW7
off Stanhope Gdns 43 CT50
Meadow Hill, Couls. CR5 159 DJ113
New Malden KT3 138 CS100
Purley CR8 159 DJ113
Meadowlands, Cob. KT11 153 BU113
Hornchurch RM11 72 FL59
Oxted RH8 188 EG134
Meadowlands Pk, Add. KT15 134 BL104
Meadow La, SE12 124 EH90
Leatherhead (Fetch.) KT22 170 CC121
Meadowlea Cl, West Dr. UB7 94 BK79
Meadow Ms, SW8 101 DM79
Meadow Pl, SW8 101 DL80
W4 off Edensor Rd 98 CS80
Meadow Ri, Couls. CR5 159 DK113
Meadow Rd, SW8 101 DM79
SW19 120 DC94
Ashford TW15 115 BR92
Ashtead KT21 172 CL117
Barking IG11 87 ET66
Borehamwood WD6 26 CP40
Bromley BR2 144 EE95
Bushey WD23 24 CB43
Dagenham RM9 88 EZ65
Epping CM16 17 ET29
Esher (Clay.) KT10 155 CE107
Feltham TW13 116 BY89
Gravesend DA11 131 GG89
Loughton IG10 32 EL43
Pinner HA5 60 BX57
Romford RM7 71 FC60
Slough SL3 92 AY76
Southall UB1 78 BZ73
Sutton SM1 158 DE106
Virginia Water GU25 132 AS99
Watford WD25 7 BU34
Meadow Row, SE1 201 H7
Meadows, The, Amer. HP7 20 AS39
Orpington BR6 164 EW107
Sevenoaks (Halst.) TN14 164 EZ113
Warlingham CR6 177 DX117
Meadows Cl, E10 67 EA61
Meadows End, Sun. TW16 135 BU95
Meadowside, SE9 104 EJ84
Beaconsfield (Jordans) HP9 36 AT52
Dartford DA1 128 FK88
Leatherhead (Bkhm) KT23 170 CA123
Walton-on-Thames KT12 136 BW103
Meadow Side, Wat. WD25 7 BV31
Meadowside Rd, Sutt. SM2 157 CY109
Upminster RM14 72 FQ64
Meadows Leigh Cl,
Wey. KT13 135 BQ104
Meadow Stile, Croy. CR0
off High St 142 DQ104
Meadowsweet Cl, E16
off Monarch Dr 86 EK71
SW20 139 CW99
Meadow Vw, Ch.St.G. HP8 36 AU48
Chertsey KT16 off Mead La 134 BJ102
Harrow HA1 61 CE60
Meadowview, Orp. BR5 146 EW97
Meadow Vw, Sid. DA15 126 EV87
Staines TW19 113 BF85
Meadowview Rd, SE6 123 DZ92
Bexley DA5 126 EY86
Epsom KT19 156 CS109
Meadow Vw Rd, Hayes UB4 77 BQ70
Thornton Heath CR7 141 DP99
Meadow Wk, E18 68 EG56
Dagenham RM9 88 EZ65
Dartford DA2 128 FJ91
Epsom KT17, KT19 156 CS107
Tadworth KT20 173 CV124
Wallington SM6 141 DH104
Meadow Way, NW9 62 CR57
Abbots Langley
(Bedmond) WD5 7 BT27
Addlestone KT15 152 BH105
Chessington KT9 156 CL106
Chigwell IG7 49 EQ48
Dartford DA2 128 FQ87
Kings Langley WD4 6 BN30
Leatherhead (Bkhm) KT23 170 CB123
Orpington BR6 145 EN104
Potters Bar EN6 12 DA34
Rickmansworth WD3 38 BJ45
Ruislip HA4 59 BV58
Tadworth KT20 173 CY118
Upminster RM14 72 FQ62
Wembley HA9 61 CK63
Windsor (Old Wind.) SL4 112 AV86
Meadow Way, The, Har. HA3 41 CE53
Meadow Waye, Houns. TW5 96 BY79
Mead Path, SW17 120 DC92
Mead Pl, E9 84 DW65
Croydon CR0 141 DP102
Rickmansworth WD3 38 BH46
Mead Plat, NW10 80 CQ65
Mead Rd, Cat. CR3 176 DT123
Chislehurst BR7 125 EQ93
Dartford DA1 128 FK88
Edgware HA8 42 CN51
Gravesend DA11 131 GH89
Mead Rd,
Radlett (Shenley) WD7 10 CM33
Richmond TW10 117 CJ90
Uxbridge UB8 76 BK66
Walton-on-Thames KT12 154 BY105
Mead Row, SE1 200 D6
Meads, The, Edg. HA8 42 CR51
St. Albans (Brick.Wd) AL2 8 BZ29
Sutton SM3 139 CY104
Upminster RM14 73 FS61
Uxbridge UB8 76 BL70
Meads La, Ilf. IG3 69 ES59
Meads Rd, N22 45 DP54
Enfield EN3 31 DY39
Meadsway, Brwd. CM13 53 FV51
Mead Ter, Wem. HA9
off Meadow Way 61 CK63
Meadvale Rd, W5 79 CH70
Croydon CR0 142 DT101
Mead Wk, Slou. SL3 93 BB75
Meadway, N14 45 DK47
NW11 64 DB58
SW20 139 CW98
Ashford TW15 114 BN91
Barnet EN5 28 DA42
Beckenham BR3 143 EC95
Mead Way, Brom. BR2 144 EF100
Bushey WD23 24 BY40
Coulsdon CR5 175 DL118
Croydon CR0 143 DY103
Meadway, Enf. EN3 30 DW36
Epsom KT19 156 CQ112
Esher KT10 154 CB109
Grays RM17 110 GD77
Ilford IG3 69 ES63
Leatherhead
(Oxshott) KT22 155 CD114
Romford RM2 51 FG54
Ruislip HA4 59 BR58
Sevenoaks (Halst.) TN14 164 EZ113
Staines TW18 114 BG94
Surbiton KT5 138 CQ102
Twickenham TW2 117 CD88
Warlingham CR6 176 DW115
Woodford Green IG8 48 EJ50
Meadway, The, SE3
off Heath La 103 ED82
Buckhurst Hill IG9 48 EK46
Loughton IG10 33 EM44
Orpington BR6 164 EV106
Potters Bar (Cuffley) EN6 13 DM28
Sevenoaks TN13 190 FF122
Meadway Cl, NW11 64 DB58
Barnet EN5 28 DA42
Pinner HA5
off Highbanks Rd 40 CB51
Staines TW18 113 BF94
Meadway Ct, NW11 64 DB58
Meadway Dr, Add. KT15 152 BJ108
Woking GU21 166 AW116
Meadway Gdns, Ruis. HA4 59 BR58
Meadway Gate, NW11 64 DA58
Meadway Pk, Ger.Cr. SL9 56 AX60
Meaford Way, SE20 122 DV94
Meakin Est, SE1 201 M6
Meanley Rd, E12 68 EL63
Meard St, W1 195 M9
Meare Cl, Tad. KT20 173 CW123
Meath Cl, Orp. BR5 146 EV99
Meath Rd, E15 86 EF68
Ilford IG1 69 EQ62
Meath St, SW11 101 DH81
Mecklenburgh Pl, WC1 196 B4
Mecklenburgh Sq, WC1 196 B4
Mecklenburgh St, WC1 196 B4
Medburn St, NW1 83 DK68
Medbury Rd, Grav. DA12 131 GM88
Medcalf Rd, Enf. EN3 31 DZ37
Medcroft Gdns, SW14 98 CQ84
Medebourne Cl, SE3 104 EG83
Mede Cl, Stai. (Wrays.) TW19 112 AX88
Mede Fld, Lthd. KT22 171 CD124
Medesenge Way, N13 45 DP51
Medfield St, SW15 119 CV87
Medhurst Cl, E3
off Arbery Rd 85 DY68
Woking (Chobham) GU24 150 AT109
Medhurst Cres, Grav. DA12 131 GM90
Medhurst Gdns, Grav. DA12 131 GM90
Medhurst Rd, E3
off Arbery Rd 85 DY68
Median Rd, E5 66 DW64
★ Medici Galleries, W1 199 J1
Medick Ct, Grays RM17 110 GE79
Medina Av, Esher KT10 137 CE104
Medina Gro, N7
off Medina Rd 65 DN62
Medina Ho, Erith DA8
off Waterhead Cl 107 FE80
Medina Rd, N7 65 DN62
Grays RM17 110 GD77
Medina Sq, Epsom KT19 156 CN109
Medlake Rd, Egh. TW20 113 BC93
Medland Cl, Wall. SM6 140 DG102
Medland Ho, E14
off Branch Rd 85 DY73
Medlar Cl, Nthlt. UB5
off Parkfield Av 78 BY68
Medlar Ct, Slou. SL2 74 AW74
Medlar Rd, Grays RM17 110 GD79
Medlar St, SE5 102 DQ81
Medley Rd, NW6 82 DA65
Medman Cl, Uxb. UB8
off Chiltern Vw Rd 76 BJ68
Medora Rd, SW2 121 DM87
Romford RM7 71 FD56
Medow Mead, Rad. WD7 9 CF33
Medusa Rd, SE6 123 EB86
Medway Bldgs, E3
off Medway Rd 85 DY68
Medway Cl, Croy. CR0 142 DW100
Ilford IG1 69 EQ64
Watford WD25 8 BW34
Medway Dr, Grnf. UB6 79 CF68
Medway Gdns, Wem. HA0 61 CG63
Medway Ms, E3
off Medway Rd 85 DY68
Medway Par, Grnf. UB6 79 CF68
Medway Rd, E3 85 DY68
Dartford DA1 107 FG83
Medway St, SW1 199 N7
Medwin St, SW4 101 DM84
Meerbrook Rd, SE3 104 EJ83
Meeson Rd, E15 86 EF67
Meesons La, Grays RM17 110 FZ77
Meeson St, E5 67 DY63
Meeting Fld Path, E9
off Chatham Pl 84 DW65
Meeting Ho All, E1 202 E2
Meeting Ho La, SE15 102 DV81
Megg La, Kings L.
(Chipper.) WD4 6 BH29
Mehetabel Rd, E9 84 DW65
Meister Cl, Ilf. IG1 69 ER60
Melancholy Wk, Rich. TW10 117 CJ89
Melanda Cl, Chis. BR7 125 EM92
Melanie Cl, Bexh. DA7 106 EY81
Melba Gdns, Til. RM18 111 GG80
Melba Way, SE13 103 EB81
Melbourne Av, N13 45 DM51
W13 79 CG74
Pinner HA5 60 CB55
Melbourne Cl, Orp. BR6 145 ES101
Uxbridge UB10 58 BN63
Wallington SM6
off Melbourne Rd 159 DJ106
Melbourne Ct, E5
off Daubeney Rd 67 DY63
N10 off Sydney Rd 45 DH52
SE20 122 DU94
Melbourne Gdns, Rom. RM6 70 EY57
Melbourne Gro, SE22 102 DS84
Melbourne Ho, Hayes UB4 78 BW70
Melbourne Ms, SE6 123 EC87
SW9 101 DN81
Melbourne Pl, WC2 196 C10
Melbourne Rd, E6 87 EM67
E10 67 EB59
E17 67 DY56
SW19 140 DA95
Bushey WD23 24 CB44
Ilford IG1 69 EP60
Teddington TW11 117 CJ93
Tilbury RM18 110 GE81
Wallington SM6 159 DH106
Melbourne Sq, SW9
off Melbourne Ms 101 DN81
Melbourne Ter, SW6
off Waterford Rd 100 DB80
Melbourne Way, Enf. EN1 30 DT44
Melbury Av, Sthl. UB2 96 CB76
Melbury Cl, Cher. KT16 134 BG101
Chislehurst BR7 125 EM93
Esher (Clay.) KT10 155 CH107
West Byfleet KT14 152 BG114
Melbury Ct, W8 99 CZ76
Melbury Dr, SE5
off Sedgmoor Pl 102 DS80
Melbury Gdns, SW20 139 CV95
Melbury Rd, W14 99 CZ76
Harrow HA3 62 CM57
Melcombe Gdns, Har. HA3 62 CM58
Melcombe Pl, NW1 194 D6
Melcombe St, NW1 194 E5
Meldex Cl, NW7 43 CW51
Meldon Cl, SW6
off Bagley's La 100 DB81
Meldone Cl, Surb. KT5 138 CP100
Meldrum Cl, Orp. BR5
off Killewarren Way 146 EW100
Oxted RH8 188 EF132
Meldrum Rd, Ilf. IG3 70 EU61
Melfield Gdns, SE6 123 EB91
Melford Av, Bark. IG11 87 ES65
Melford Cl, Chess. KT9 156 CM106
Melford Rd, E6 87 EM70
E11 68 EE61
E17 67 DY56
SE22 122 DU87
Ilford IG1 69 ER61
Melfort Av, Th.Hth. CR7 141 DP97
Melfort Rd, Th.Hth. CR7 141 DP97
Melgund Rd, N5 65 DN64
Melina Cl, Hayes UB3
off Middleton Rd 77 BR71
Melina Pl, NW8 82 DD69
Melina Rd, W12 99 CV75
Melior Pl, SE1 201 M4
Melior St, SE1 201 L4
Meliot Rd, SE6 123 ED89
Melksham Cl, Rom. RM3 52 FL52
Melksham Dr, Rom. RM3
off Melksham Gdns 52 FM52
Melksham Gdns, Rom. RM3 52 FL52
Melksham Grn, Rom. RM3
off Melksham Gdns 52 FM52
Meller Cl, Croy. CR0 141 DL104
Melling Dr, Enf. EN1 30 DU39
Melling St, SE18 105 ES79
Mellish Cl, Bark. IG11 87 ET67
Mellish Gdns, Wdf.Grn. IG8 48 EG50
Mellish Ind Est, SE18 104 EL76
Mellish St, E14 203 P6
Mellish Way, Horn. RM11
off Slewins Cl 72 FJ57
Mellison Rd, SW17 120 DE92
Melliss Av, Rich. TW9 98 CP81
Mellitus St, W12 81 CT72
Mellor Cl, Walt. KT12 136 BZ101
Mellow Cl, Bans. SM7 158 DB114
Mellow La E, Hayes UB4 77 BQ69
Mellow La W, Uxb. UB10 77 BQ69
Mellows Rd, Ilf. IG5 69 EM55
Wallington SM6 159 DK106
Mells Cres, SE9 125 EM91
Mell St, SE10
off Trafalgar Rd 104 EE78
Melody La, N5 65 DP64
Melody Rd, SW18 120 DC85
Westerham
(Bigg.H.) TN16 178 EJ118
Melon Pl, W8
off Kensington Ch St 100 DA75
Melon Rd, E11 68 EE62
SE15 102 DU81
Melrose Av, N22 45 DP53
NW2 63 CV64
SW16 141 DM97
SW19 120 DA89
Borehamwood WD6 26 CP43
Melrose Av, Dartford DA1
off Lower Sta Rd 127 FE86
Greenford UB6 78 CB68
Mitcham CR4 121 DH94
Potters Bar EN6 12 DB32
Twickenham TW2 116 CB87
Melrose Cl, SE12 124 EG88
Greenford UB6 78 CB68
Hayes UB4 77 BU71
Melrose Ct, W13
off Williams Rd 79 CG74
Melrose Cres, Orp. BR6 163 ER105
Melrose Dr, Sthl. UB1 78 CA74
Melrose Gdns, W6 99 CW76
Edgware HA8 42 CP54
New Malden KT3 138 CR97
Walton-on-Thames KT12 154 BW106
Melrose Pl, Wat. WD17
off Wentworth Cl 23 BT38
Melrose Rd, SW13 99 CT82
SW18 119 CZ86
SW19 140 DA96
W3 off Stanley Rd 98 CQ76
Coulsdon CR5 175 DH115
Pinner HA5 60 BZ56
Westerham (Bigg.H.) TN16 178 EJ116
Weybridge KT13 152 BN106
Melrose Ter, W6 99 CW75
Melsa Rd, Mord. SM4 140 DC100
Melstock Av, Upmin. RM14 72 FQ63
Melthorne Dr, Ruis. HA4 60 BW62
Melthorpe Gdns, SE3 104 EL81
Melton Cl, Ruis. HA4 60 BW60
Melton Ct, SW7 198 A9
Sutton SM2 158 DC108
Melton Flds, Epsom KT19 156 CR109
Melton Gdns, Rom. RM1 71 FF59
Melton Pl, Epsom KT19 156 CR109
Melton Rd, Red. RH1 185 DJ130
Melton St, NW1 195 L3
Melville Av, SW20 119 CU94
Greenford UB6 61 CF64
South Croydon CR2 160 DT106
Melville Cl, Uxb. UB10 59 BR62
Melville Gdns, N13 45 DP50
Melville Pl, N1 off Essex Rd 83 DP67
Melville Rd, E17 67 DZ55
NW10 80 CR66
SW13 99 CU81
Rainham RM13 89 FG70
Romford RM5 51 FB52
Sidcup DA14 126 EW89
Melville Vil Rd, W3
off High St 80 CR74
Melvin Rd, SE20 142 DW95
Melvinshaw, Lthd. KT22 171 CJ121
Melvyn Cl, Wal.Cr.
(Chsht) EN7 13 DP28
Melyn Cl, N7 off Anson Rd 65 DJ63
Memel Ct, EC1 197 H5
Memel St, EC1 197 H5
Memess Path, SE18 105 EN79
Memorial Av, E15 86 EE69
Memorial Cl, Houns. TW5 96 BZ79
H Memorial Hosp, SE18 105 EN82
Mendip Cl, SE26 122 DW91
Hayes UB3 95 BR80
Slough SL3 93 BA78
Worcester Park KT4 139 CW102
Mendip Dr, NW2 63 CX61
Mendip Ho, N9 off New Rd 46 DU48
Mendip Rd, SW11 100 DC83
Bexleyheath DA7 107 FE81
Bushey WD23 24 CC44
Hornchurch RM11 71 FG59
Ilford IG2 69 ES57
Mendora Rd, SW6 99 CY80
Mendoza Cl, Horn. RM11 72 FL57
Menelik Rd, NW2 63 CY63
Menlo Gdns, SE19 122 DR94
Menon Dr, N9 46 DV48
Menotti St, E2
off Dunbridge St 84 DU70
Menthone Pl, Horn. RM11 72 FK59
Mentmore Cl, Har. HA3 61 CJ58
Mentmore Ter, E8 84 DV66
Meon Cl, Tad. KT20 173 CV122
Meon Ct, Islw. TW7 97 CE82
Meon Rd, W3 98 CQ75
Meopham Rd, Mitch. CR4 141 DJ95
Mepham Cres, Har. HA3 40 CC52
Mepham Gdns, Har. HA3 40 CC52
Mepham St, SE1 200 C3
Mera Dr, Bexh. DA7 106 FA84
Merantun Way, SW19 140 DB95
Merbury Cl, SE13 123 EC85
Merbury Rd, SE28 105 ES75
Mercator Pl, E14 204 A10
Mercator Rd, SE13 103 ED84
Mercer Cl, T.Ditt. KT7 137 CF101
Merceron St, E1 84 DV70
Mercer Pl, Pnr. HA5
off Crossway 40 BW54
Mercers Cl, SE10 205 K9
Mercers Pl, W6 99 CW77
Mercers Rd, N19 65 DK62
Mercer St, WC2 195 P9
Mercer Wk, Uxb. UB8
off High St 76 BJ66
Merchants Cl, SE25
off Clifford Rd 142 DU98
Merchants Ho, SE10
off Hoskins St 103 ED78
Merchant St, E3 85 DZ69
Merchiston Rd, SE6 123 ED89
Merchland Rd, SE9 125 EQ88
Mercia Gro, SE13 103 EC84
Mercia Wk, Wok. GU21
off Church St W 167 AZ117
Mercier Rd, SW15 119 CY85
Mercury Cen, Felt. TW14 115 BV85
Mercury Gdns, Rom. RM1 71 FE56
Mercury Way, SE14 103 DX79
Mercy Ter, SE13 103 EB84
Merebank La, Croy. CR0 159 DM106
Mere Cl, SW15 119 CX87
Orpington BR6 145 EP103
Meredith Av, NW2 63 CW64
Meredith Cl, Pnr. HA5 40 BX52
Meredith Ms, SE4 103 DZ84

★ Place of interest ⇌ Railway station ⊖ London Underground station DLR Docklands Light Railway station Tra Tramlink station H Hospital Riv Pedestrian ferry landing stage

292

Meredith Rd, Grays RM16 111 GG77
Meredith St, E13 86 EG69
EC1 196 F3
Meredyth Rd, SW13 99 CU82
Mere End, Croy. CR0 143 DX101
Merefield Gdns, Tad. KT20 173 CX119
Mere Rd, Shep. TW17 135 BP100
Slough SL1 92 AT76
Tadworth KT20 173 CV124
Weybridge KT13 135 BR104
Mere Side, Orp. BR6 145 EN103
Mereside Pl, Vir.W. GU25 132 AX100
Meretone Cl, SE4 103 DY84
Merevale Cres, Mord. SM4 140 DC100
Mereway Rd, Twick. TW2 117 CD88
Merewood Cl, Brom. BR1 145 EN96
Merewood Rd, Bexh. DA7 107 FC82
Mereworth Cl, Brom. BR2 144 EF99
Mereworth Dr, SE18 105 EP80
Merganser Gdns, SE28
off Avocet Ms 105 ER76
MERIDEN, Wat. WD25 24 BY35
Meriden Cl, Brom. BR1 124 EK94
Ilford IG6 49 EQ53
Meriden Way, Wat. WD25 24 BY36
Meridian Gate, E14 204 D4
Meridian Pl, E14 204 D4
Meridian Rd, SE7 104 EK80
Meridian Sq, E15 85 ED66
Meridian Trd Est, SE7 104 EH77
Meridian Wk, N17
off Commercial Rd 46 DS51
Meridian Way, N9 46 DW50
N18 46 DW51
Enfield EN3 31 DX44
Meriel Wk, Green. DA9
off London Rd 129 FW85
Merifield Rd, SE9 104 EJ84
Merino Cl, E11 68 EJ56
Merino Pl, Sid. DA15
off Blackfen Rd 126 EU86
Merivale Rd, SW15 99 CY84
Harrow HA1 60 CC59
Merland Cl, Tad. KT20 173 CW120
Merland Grn, Tad. KT20
off Merland Ri 173 CW120
Merland Ri, Epsom KT18 173 CW119
Tadworth KT20 173 CW119
Merle Av, Uxb. (Hare.) UB9 38 BH54
Merlewood, Sev. TN13 191 FH123
Merlewood Cl, Cat. CR3 176 DR120
Merlewood Dr, Chis. BR7 145 EM95
Merley Ct, NW9 62 CQ60
Merlin Cl, Croy. CR0
off Minster Dr 160 DS105
Grays (Chaff.Hun.) RM16 110 FY76
Ilford IG6 50 EW50
Mitcham CR4 140 DE97
Northolt UB5 78 BW69
Romford RM5 51 FD51
Slough SL3 93 BB79
Wallington SM6 159 DM107
Waltham Abbey EN9 16 EG34
Merlin Ct, Wok. GU21
off Blackmore Cres 151 BC114
Merlin Cres, Edg. HA8 42 CM53
Merlin Gdns, Brom. BR1 124 EG90
Romford RM5 51 FD51
Merling Cl, Chess. KT9
off Coppard Gdns 155 CK106
Merlin Gro, Beck. BR3 143 DZ98
Ilford IG6 49 EP52
Merlin Ho, Enf. EN3
off Allington Ct 31 DX43
Merlin Rd, E12 68 EJ61
Romford RM5 51 FD51
Welling DA16 106 EU84
Merlin Rd N, Well. DA16 106 EU84
Merlins Av, Har. HA2 60 BZ62
Merlin St, WC1 196 D3
Merlin Way, Epp.
(N.Wld Bas.) CM16 18 FA27
Watford WD25
off Ashfields 7 BT34
Mermagen Dr, Rain. RM13 89 FH66
Mermaid Cl, Grav. DA11
off Rosherville Way 130 GE87
Mermaid Ct, SE1 201 K4
SE16 203 M3
Mermaid Twr, SE8
off Abinger Gro 103 DZ79
Mermerus Gdns,
Grav. DA12 131 GM91
Merredene St, SW2 121 DM86
Merriam Av, E9 85 DZ65
Merriam Cl, E4 47 EC50
Merrick Rd, Sthl. UB2 96 BZ75
Merrick Sq, SE1 201 J6
Merridale, SE12 124 EG85
Merridene, N21 29 DP44
Merrielands Cres, Dag. RM9 88 EZ67
Merrilands Rd, Wor.Pk. KT4 139 CW102
Merrilees Rd, Sid. DA15 125 ES88
Merrilyn Cl, Esher
(Clay.) KT10 155 CG107
Merriman Rd, SE3 104 EJ81
Merrington Rd, SW6 100 DA79
Merrin Hill, S.Croy. CR2 160 DS111
Merrion Av, Stan. HA7 41 CK50
Merrion Wk, SE17
off Dawes St 102 DR78
Merritt Gdns, Chess. KT9 155 CJ107
Merritt Rd, SE4 123 DZ85
Merrivale, N14 29 DK44
Merrivale Av, Ilf. IG4 68 EK56
Merrivale Gdns, Wok. GU21 166 AW117
Merrow Rd, Sutt. SM2 157 CX109
Merrows Cl, Nthwd. HA6
off Rickmansworth Rd 39 BQ51
Merrow St, SE17 102 DQ79
Merrow Wk, SE17 201 L10
Merrow Way, Croy.
(New Adgtn) CR0 161 EC107
Merrydown Way, Chis. BR7 144 EL95
Merryfield, SE3 104 EF82
Merryfield Gdns, Stan. HA7 41 CJ50
Merryfield Ho, SE9
off Grove Pk Rd 124 EJ90
Merryfields, Uxb. UB8
off The Greenway 76 BL68
Merryfields Way, SE6 123 EB87
MERRY HILL, Bushey WD23 40 CA46
Merryhill Cl, E4 47 EB45
Merry Hill Mt, Bushey WD23 40 CB46
Merry Hill Rd, Bushey WD23 40 CB46
Merryhills Cl, West.
(Bigg.H.) TN16 178 EK116
Merryhills Ct, N14 29 DJ43
Merryhills Dr, Enf. EN2 29 DK42
Merrylands, Cher. KT16 133 BE104
Merrylands Rd, Lthd.
(Bkhm) KT23 170 BZ123
Merrymeet, Bans. SM7 158 DF114
Merryweather Cl, Dart. DA1 128 FM86
Merrywood Gro, Tad. KT20 183 CX130
Merrywood Pk, Reig. RH2 184 DB132
Tadworth (Box H.) KT20 182 CP130
Mersea Ho, Bark. IG11 87 EP65
Mersey Av, Upmin. RM14 73 FR58
Mersey Rd, E17 67 DZ55
Mersey Wk, Nthlt. UB5
off Brabazon Rd 78 CA68
Mersham Dr, NW9 62 CN57
Mersham Pl, SE20 142 DV95
Mersham Rd, Th.Hth. CR7 142 DR97
MERSTHAM, Red. RH1 185 DJ128
⇌ Merstham 185 DJ128
Merstham Rd, Red. RH1 185 DN129
Merten Rd, Rom. RM6 70 EY59
Merthyr Ter, SW13 99 CV79
MERTON, SW19 140 DA95
Merton Av, W4 99 CT77
Northolt UB5 60 CC64
Uxbridge UB10 77 BP66
Merton Gdns, Orp. BR5 145 EP99
Tadworth KT20
off Marbles Way 173 CX120
Merton Hall Gdns, SW20 139 CY95
Merton Hall Rd, SW19 139 CY95
Merton High St, SW19 120 DB94
Merton Ind Pk, SW19 140 DC95
Merton La, N6 64 DF61
Merton Mans, SW20 139 CX96
MERTON PARK, SW19 140 DA96
Tra Merton Park 140 DA95
Merton Pk Par, SW19
off Kingston Rd 139 CZ95
Merton Pl, Grays RM16 111 GG77
Merton Ri, NW3 82 DE66
Merton Rd, E17 67 EC57
SE25 142 DU99
SW18 120 DA85
SW19 120 DB94
Barking IG11 87 ET66
Enfield EN2 30 DR38
Harrow HA2 60 CC60
Ilford IG3 69 ET59
Slough SL1 92 AU76
Watford WD18 23 BV42
Merton Wk, Lthd. KT22 171 CG118
Merton Way, Lthd. KT22 171 CG119
Uxbridge UB10 77 BP66
West Molesey KT8 136 CB98
Merttins Rd, SE15 123 DX85
Meru Cl, NW5 64 DG63
Mervan Rd, SW2 101 DN84
Mervyn Av, SE9 125 EQ90
Mervyn Rd, W13 97 CG76
Shepperton TW17 135 BQ101
Meryfield Cl, Borwd. WD6 26 CM40
Mesne Way, Sev.
(Shore.) TN14 165 FF112
Messaline Av, W3 80 CQ72
Messant Cl, Rom.
(Harold Wd) RM3 52 FK54
Messent Rd, SE9 124 EJ85
Messeter Pl, SE9 125 EN86
Messina Av, NW6 82 DA66
Metcalf Rd, Ashf. TW15 115 BP92
Metcalf Wk, Felt. TW13
off Gabriel Cl 116 BY91
Meteor St, SW11 100 DG84
Meteor Way, Wall. SM6 159 DL108
Metford Cres, Enf. EN3 31 EA38
Metheringham Way, NW9 42 CS53
Methley St, SE11 101 DN78
★ Methodist Cen Hall, SW1 199 N5
Methuen Cl, Edg. HA8 42 CN52
Methuen Pk, N10 45 DH54
Methuen Rd, Belv. DA17 107 FB77
Bexleyheath DA6 106 EZ84
Edgware HA8 42 CN52
Methwold Rd, W10 81 CX71
Metro Cen, The, Islw. TW7 97 CE82
Metropolis Cen, Borwd. WD6 26 CN41
Metropolitan Cen, The,
Grnf. UB6 78 CB67
Metropolitan Cl, E14
off Broomfield St 85 EA71
Metropolitan Ho, Pot.B. EN6 12 DA32
Meux Cl, Wal.Cr. (Chsht) EN7 14 DU31
Mews, The, N1
off St. Paul St 84 DQ67
N8 off Turnpike La 65 DN55
Grays RM17 110 GC77
Ilford IG4 68 EK57
Romford RM1
off Market Link 71 FE56
Sevenoaks TN13 190 FG123
Twickenham TW1
off Bridge Rd 117 CH86
Mews Deck, E1 202 E1
Mews End, West.
(Bigg.H.) TN16 178 EK118
Mews Pl, Wdf.Grn. IG8 48 EG49
Mews St, E1 202 B2
Mexfield Rd, SW15 119 CZ85
Meyer Grn, Enf. EN1 30 DU38
Meyer Rd, Erith DA8 107 FC79
Meymott St, SE1 200 F3
Meynell Cres, E9 85 DX66
Meynell Gdns, E9 85 DX66
Meynell Rd, E9 85 DX66
Romford RM3 51 FH52
Meyrick Cl, Wok. (Knap.) GU21 166 AS116
Meyrick Rd, NW10 81 CU65
SW11 100 DD83
Mezen Cl, Nthwd. HA6 39 BR50
Miah Ter, E1
off Wapping High St 84 DU74
Miall Wk, SE26 123 DY91
Micawber Av, Uxb. UB8 76 BN70
Micawber St, N1 197 J2
Michael Faraday Ho, SE17
off Beaconsfield Rd 102 DS78
Michael Gdns, Grav. DA12 131 GL92
Hornchurch RM11 72 FK56
Michael Gaynor Cl, W7 79 CF74
Michaelmas Cl, SW20 139 CW97
Michael Rd, E11 68 EE60
SE25 142 DS97
SW6 100 DB81
Michaels Cl, SE13 104 EE84
Michaels La, Long.
(Fawk.Grn) DA3 149 FV103
Sevenoaks TN15 149 FV103
Micheldever Rd, SE12 124 EE86
Michelham Gdns, Tad. KT20
off Waterfield 173 CW121
Twickenham TW1 117 CF90
Michels Row, Rich. TW9
off Kew Foot Rd 98 CL84
Michigan Av, E12 68 EL63
Michleham Down, N12 43 CZ49
Micholls Av, Ger.Cr. SL9 36 AY49
Micklefield Way,
Borwd. WD6 26 CL38
Mickleham Cl, Orp. BR5 145 ET96
Mickleham Gdns, Sutt. SM3 157 CY107
Mickleham Rd, Orp. BR5 145 ET95
Mickleham Way, Croy.
(New Adgtn) CR0 161 ED108
Micklethwaite Rd, SW6 100 DA79
Midas Ind Est, Uxb. UB8 76 BH68
Midas Met Ind Est, The, Mord. SM4
off Garth Rd 139 CX102
Midcroft, Ruis. HA4 59 BS60
Mid Cross La, Ger.Cr.
(Chal.St.P.) SL9 36 AY50
Middle Boy, Rom.
(Abridge) RM4 34 EW41
Middle Cl, Amer. HP6 20 AT37
Coulsdon CR5 175 DN120
Epsom KT17 off Middle La 156 CS112
Middle Cres, Uxb.
(Denh.) UB9 57 BD59
Middle Dene, NW7 42 CR48
Middle Fld, NW8 82 DD67
Middlefielde, W13 79 CH71
Middlefield Gdns, Ilf. IG2 69 EP58
Middlefields, Croy. CR0 161 DY109
Middle Furlong, Bushey WD23 24 CB42
Middle Gorse, Croy. CR0 161 DY112
MIDDLE GREEN, Slou. SL3 74 AY73
Middle Grn, Slou. SL3 74 AY74
Staines TW18 114 BK94
Middle Grn Cl, Surb. KT5
off Alpha Rd 138 CM100
Middlegreen Rd, Slou. SL3 74 AX74
Middleham Gdns, N18 46 DU51
Middleham Rd, N18 46 DU51
Middle Hill, Egh. TW20 112 AW91
Middle La, N8 65 DL57
Epsom KT17 156 CS112
Hemel Hempstead (Bov.) HP3 5 BA29
Sevenoaks (Seal) TN15
off Church Rd 191 FM121
Teddington TW11 117 CF93
Middle La Ms, N8
off Middle La 65 DL57
Middle Meadow, Ch.St.G. HP8 36 AW48
Middle Ope, Wat. WD24 23 BV37
Middle Pk Av, SE9 124 EK86
Middle Path, Har. HA2
off Middle Rd 61 CD60
Middle Rd, E13 off London Rd 86 EG68
SW16 141 DK96
Barnet EN4 28 DE44
Brentwood (Ingrave) CM13 55 GC50
Harrow HA2 61 CD61
Leatherhead KT22 171 CH121
Uxbridge (Denh.) UB9 57 BC59
Waltham Abbey EN9 15 EB32
Middle Row, W10 81 CY70
Middlesborough Rd, N18 46 DU51
Middlesex Business Cen,
Sthl. UB2 96 CA75
Middlesex Cl, Sthl. UB1
off Allenby Rd 78 CB70
Middlesex Ct, W4
off British Gro 99 CT77
★ Middlesex Guildhall, SW1 199 P5
H Middlesex Hosp, W1 195 L7
Middlesex Ho, Wem. HA0 79 CK67
Middlesex Pas, EC1 196 G7
Middlesex Rd, Mitch. CR4 141 DL99
Middlesex St, E1 197 N7
Middlesex Wf, E5 66 DW61
Middle St, EC1 197 H6
Croydon CR0 off Surrey St 142 DQ104
Middle Temple, EC4 196 D10
Middle Temple La, EC4 196 D9
Middleton Av, E4 47 DZ49
Greenford UB6 79 CD68
Sidcup DA14 126 EW93
Middleton Cl, E4 47 DZ48
Middleton Dr, SE16 203 J5
Pinner HA5 59 BU55
Middleton Gdns, Ilf. IG2 69 EP58
Middleton Gro, N7 65 DL64
Middleton Hall La,
Brwd. CM15 54 FY47
Middleton Ms, N7
off Middleton Gro 65 DL64
Middleton Pl, W1 195 K7
Middleton Rd, E8 84 DT66
NW11 64 DA59
Brentwood (Shenf.) CM15 54 FY46
Carshalton SM5 140 DE101
Cobham (Down.) KT11 169 BV119
Epsom KT19 156 CR110
Hayes UB3 77 BR71
Morden SM4 140 DC100
Rickmansworth
(Mill End) WD3 38 BG46
Middleton St, E2 84 DV69
Middleton Way, SE13 103 ED84
Middle Wk, Wok. GU21
off Commercial Way 166 AY117
Middleway, NW11 64 DB57
Middle Way, SW16 141 DK96
Erith DA18 106 EY76
Hayes UB4 78 BW70
Watford WD24 23 BV37
Middle Way, The, Har. HA3 41 CF54
Middle Yd, SE1 201 L2
Middlings, The, Sev. TN13 190 FF125
Middlings Ri, Sev. TN13 190 FF126
Middlings Wd, Sev. TN13 190 FF125
Midfield Av, Bexh. DA7 107 FC83
Swanley BR8 127 FH93
Midfield Par, Bexh. DA7 107 FC83
Midfield Way, Orp. BR5 146 EU95
Midford Pl, W1 195 L5
Midgarth Cl, Lthd.
(Oxshott) KT22 154 CC114
Midholm, NW11 64 DB56
Wembley HA9 62 CN60
Midholm Cl, NW11 64 DB56
Midholm Rd, Croy. CR0 143 DY103
Midhope Cl, Wok. GU22 166 AY119
Midhope Gdns, Wok. GU22
off Midhope Rd 166 AY119
Midhope Rd, Wok. GU22 166 AY119
Midhope St, WC1 196 A3
Midhurst Av, N10 64 DG55
Croydon CR0 141 DN101
Midhurst Cl, Horn. RM12 71 FG63
Midhurst Gdns, Uxb. UB10 77 BQ66
Midhurst Hill, Bexh. DA6 126 FA86
Midhurst Rd, W13 97 CG75
Midhurst Way, E5 66 DU63
Midland Cres, NW3
off Finchley Rd 82 DC65
Midland Pl, E14 204 D10
Midland Rd, E10 67 EC59
NW1 195 N1
Midland Ter, NW2 63 CX62
NW10 80 CS70
Midleton Rd, N.Mal. KT3 138 CQ97
Midlothian Rd, E3
off Burdett Rd 85 DZ71
Midmoor Rd, SW12 121 DJ88
SW19 139 CX95
Midship Cl, SE16 203 J3
Midship Pt, E14 203 P5
Midstrath Rd, NW10 62 CS63
Mid St, Red. (S.Nutfld) RH1 185 DM134
Midsummer Av, Houns. TW4 96 BZ84
Midway, Sutt. SM3 139 CZ101
Walton-on-Thames KT12 135 BV103
Midway Av, Cher. KT16 134 BG97
Egham TW20 133 BB97
Midway Cl, Stai. TW18 114 BH90
Midwinter Cl, Well. DA16
off Hook La 106 EU83
Midwood Cl, NW2 63 CV62
Miena Way, Ashtd. KT21 171 CK117
Miers Cl, E6 87 EN67
Mighell Av, Ilf. IG4 68 EK57
Mike Spring Ct, Grav. DA12 131 GK91
Milan Rd, Sthl. UB1 96 BZ75
Milborne Gro, SW10 100 DC78
Milborne St, E9 84 DW65
Milborough Cres, SE12 124 EE86
Milbourne La, Esher KT10 154 CC107
Milbrook, Esher KT10 154 CC107
Milburn Dr, West Dr. UB7 76 BL73
Milburn Wk, Epsom KT18 172 CS115
Milcombe Cl, Wok. GU21
off Inglewood 166 AV118
Milcote St, SE1 200 F5
Mildenhall Rd, E5 66 DW63
Slough SL1 74 AS72
Mildmay Av, N1 84 DR65
Mildmay Gro N, N1 66 DR64
Mildmay Gro S, N1 66 DR64
Mildmay Pk, N1 66 DR64
Mildmay Pl, N16
off Boleyn Rd 66 DS64
Sevenoaks (Shore.) TN14 165 FF111
Mildmay Rd, N1 66 DS64
Ilford IG1
off Winston Way 69 EP62
Romford RM7 71 FC57
Mildmay St, N1 84 DR65
Mildred Av, Borwd. WD6 26 CN42
Hayes UB3 95 BR77
Northolt UB5 60 CB64
Watford WD18 23 BT42
Mildred Cl, Dart. DA1 128 FN86
Mildred Rd, Erith DA8 107 FE78
Mile Cl, Wal.Abb. EN9 15 EC33
MILE END, E1 85 DX69
⊖ Mile End 85 DY69
Mile End, The, E17 47 DX53
MILE END GREEN, Dart. DA2 149 FW96
Mile End Pl, E1 85 DX70
Mile End Rd, E1 84 DW71
E3 84 DW71
Mile Path, Wok. GU22 166 AV120
Mile Rd, Wall. SM6 141 DJ102
Miles Dr, SE28 87 ER74
Miles La, Cob. KT11 154 BY113
Milespit Hill, NW7 43 CV50
Miles Pl, NW1 194 A6
Surbiton KT5
off Villiers Av 138 CM98
Miles Rd, N8 65 DL55
Epsom KT19 156 CR112
Mitcham CR4 140 DE97
Miles St, SW8 101 DL79
Milestone Cl, N9
off Chichester Rd 46 DU47
Sutton SM2 158 DD107
Woking (Ripley) GU23 168 BG122
Milestone Rd, SE19 122 DT93
Dartford DA2 128 FP86
Miles Way, N20 44 DE47
Milfoil St, W12 81 CU73
Milford Cl, SE2 106 EY79
Milford Gdns, Croy. CR0
off Tannery Cl 143 DX99
Edgware HA8 42 CN52
Wembley HA0 61 CK64
Milford Gro, Sutt. SM1 158 DC105
Milford La, WC2 196 C10
Milford Ms, SW16 121 DM90
Milford Rd, W13 79 CH74
Southall UB1 78 CA73
Milford Twrs, SE6
off Thomas La 123 EB87
Milking La, Kes. BR2 162 EK111
Orpington BR6 162 EL112
Milk St, E16 87 EP74
EC2 197 J9
Bromley BR1 124 EH93
Milkwell Gdns, Wdf.Grn. IG8 48 EH52
Milkwell Yd, SE5 102 DQ81
Milkwood Rd, SE24 121 DP85
Milk Yd, E1 202 F1
Millais Av, E12 69 EN64
Millais Cres, Epsom KT19 156 CS106
Millais Gdns, Edg. HA8 42 CN54
Millais Pl, Til. RM18 111 GG80
Millais Rd, E11 67 EC63
Enfield EN1 30 DT43
New Malden KT3 138 CS100
Millais Way, Epsom KT19 156 CQ105
Millan Cl, Add.
(New Haw) KT15 152 BH110
Milland Ct, Borwd. WD6 26 CR39
Millard Cl, N16
off Boleyn Rd 66 DS64
Millard Ter, Dag. RM10
off Church Elm La 88 FA65
Mill Av, Uxb. UB8 76 BJ68
Millbank, SW1 199 P7
Staines TW18 114 BH92
Riv Millbank
Millennium Pier 200 A9
Millbank Twr, SW1 199 P9
Millbank Way, SE12 124 EG85
Millbourne Rd, Felt. TW13 116 BY91
Mill Br Pl, Uxb. UB8 76 BH68
Millbro, Swan. BR8 127 FG94
Millbrook, Wey. KT13 153 BS105
Millbrook Av, Well. DA16 105 ER84
Millbrook Gdns, Rom.
(Chad.Hth) RM6 70 EZ58
Romford (Gidea Pk) RM2 51 FE54
Millbrook Pl, NW1
off Hampstead Rd 83 DJ68
Millbrook Rd, N9 46 DV46
SW9 101 DP83
Bushey WD23 24 BZ39
Mill Brook Rd, Orp. BR5 146 EW98
Millbrook Way, Slou.
(Colnbr.) SL3 93 BE82
Mill Cl, Cars. SM5 140 DG103
Chesham HP5 4 AS34
Hemel Hempstead HP3 6 BN25
Leatherhead (Bkhm) KT23 170 CA124
West Drayton UB7 94 BK76
Mill Cor, Barn. EN5 27 CZ39
Mill Ct, E10 67 EC62
Millcrest Rd, Wal.Cr.
(Chsht) EN7 13 DP28
Millcroft Ho, SE6 123 EC91
Millen Ct, Dart. DA4
off The Street 148 FQ98
MILL END, Rick. WD3 37 BF46
Millender Wk, SE16 202 G9
Millennium Br, EC4 197 H10
SE1 197 H10
Millennium Cl, E16
off Russell Rd 86 EG72
Uxbridge UB8 76 BH68
Millennium Dr, E14 204 F8
Millennium Harbour, E14 203 N4
Millennium Pl, E2 84 DV68
Millennium Sq, SE1 202 A4
Millennium Way, SE10 205 H4
Millennium Wf, Rick. WD3
off Wharf La 38 BL45
Miller Av, Enf. EN3 31 EA38
Miller Cl, Mitch. CR4 140 DF101
Pinner HA5 40 BW54
Miller Pl, Ger.Cr. SL9 56 AX57
Miller Rd, SW19 120 DD93
Croydon CR0 141 DM102
Miller's Av, E8 66 DT64
Millers Cl, NW7 43 CU49
Chigwell IG7 50 EV47
Rickmansworth
(Chorl.) WD3 21 BE41
Staines TW18 114 BH92
Millers Copse, Epsom KT18 172 CR119
Millers Ct, W4
off Chiswick Mall 99 CT78
Millers Grn Cl, Enf. EN2 29 DP41
Millers La, Chig. IG7 50 EV46
Millers La, Wind. SL4 112 AT86
Millers Meadow Cl, SE3
off Meadowcourt Rd 124 EF85
Miller's Ter, E8 66 DT64
Miller St, NW1 83 DJ68
Millers Way, W6 99 CW75
Miller Wk, SE1 200 E3
Millet Rd, Grnf. UB6 78 CB69
Mill Fm Av, Sun. TW16 115 BS94
Mill Fm Cl, Pnr. HA5 40 BW54
Mill Fm Cres, Houns. TW4 116 BY88
Millfield, Sun. TW16 135 BR95
Millfield Av, E17 47 DY53
Millfield Dr, Grav.
(Nthflt) DA11 130 GE89
Millfield La, N6 64 DF61
Tadworth KT20 183 CZ125
Millfield Pl, N6 64 DG61
Millfield Rd, Edg. HA8 42 CQ54
Hounslow TW4 116 BY88
Millfields Cl, Orp. BR5 146 EV97
Millfields Cotts, Orp. BR5
off Millfields Cl 146 EV98
Millfields Est, E5
off Denton Way 67 DX62
Millfields Rd, E5 66 DW63
Millford, Wok. GU21 166 AV117
Mill Gdns, SE26 122 DV91
Mill Grn, Mitch. CR4
off London Rd 140 DG101
Mill Grn Business Pk, Mitch. CR4
off Mill Grn Rd 140 DG101
Mill Grn Rd, Mitch. CR4 140 DF101

★ Place of interest ⇌ Railway station ⊖ London Underground station DLR Docklands Light Railway station Tra Tramlink station H Hospital Riv Pedestrian ferry landing stage

293

Millgrove St, SW11 100 DG82
Millharbour, E14 204 B6
Millhaven Cl, Rom. RM6 70 EV58
Millhedge Cl, Cob. KT11 170 BY116
MILL HILL, NW7 43 CU50
Mill Hill, SW13
off Mill Hill Rd 99 CU82
Brentwood (Shenf.) CM15 54 FY45
≠ Mill Hill Broadway 42 CS51
Mill Hill Circ, NW7
off Watford Way 43 CT50
⊖ Mill Hill East 43 CX52
Mill Hill Gro, W3
off Mill Hill Rd 80 CP74
Mill Hill La, Bet. (Brock.) RH3 182 CP134
Mill Hill Rd, SW13 99 CU82
W3 98 CP75
Millhoo Ct, Wal.Abb. EN9 16 EF34
Mill Ho Cl, Dart. (Eyns.) DA4
off Mill La 148 FL102
Millhouse La, Abb.L.
(Bedmond) WD5 7 BT27
Mill Ho La, Cher. KT16 133 BB98
Egham TW20 133 BB98
Millhouse Pl, SE27 121 DP91
Millicent Rd, E10 67 DZ60
Milligan St, E14 203 N1
Milliners Ct, Loug. IG10
off The Croft 33 EN40
Milliners Ho, SW18
off Point Pleasant 100 DA84
Milling Rd, Edg. HA8 42 CR52
Millington Rd, Hayes UB3 95 BS76
Mill La, E4 31 EB41
NW6 63 CZ64
SE18 105 EN78
Carshalton SM5 158 DF105
Chalfont St. Giles HP8 36 AU47
Croydon CR0 141 DM104
Dartford (Eyns.) DA4 148 FL102
Egham TW20 133 BC98
Epsom KT17 157 CT109
Gerrards Cross SL9 57 AZ58
Grays RM20 109 FX78
Grays (Chaff.Hun.) RM16
off Warren La 109 FX77
Kings Langley WD4 6 BN29
Leatherhead (Fetch.) KT22 171 CG122
Ongar (Toot Hill) CM5 19 FE29
Orpington (Downe) BR6 163 EN110
Oxted RH8 188 EF132
Oxted (Lmpfld Cht.) RH8 189 EM131
Redhill RH1 185 DJ131
Rickmansworth
(Crox.Grn) WD3 23 BQ44
Romford (Chad.Hth) RM6 70 EY58
Romford (Nave.) RM4 35 FH40
Sevenoaks TN14 191 FJ121
Sevenoaks (Shore.) TN14 165 FF110
Slough (Horton) SL3 93 BB83
Waltham Cross EN8 15 DY28
West Byfleet (Byfleet) KT14 152 BM113
Westerham TN16 189 EQ127
Woking (Ripley) GU23 168 BK119
Woodford Green IG8 48 EF50
Mill La Trd Est, Croy. CR0 141 DM104
Millman Ms, WC1 196 B5
Millman Pl, WC1
off Millman St 83 DM70
Millman St, WC1 196 B5
Millmark Gro, SE14 103 DY82
Millmarsh La, Enf. EN3 31 DY40
Mill Mead, Stai. TW18 113 BF91
Millmead, W.Byf.
(Byfleet) KT14 152 BM112
Mill Mead Rd, N17 66 DV56
Mill Pk Av, Horn. RM12 72 FL61
Mill Pl, E14
off Commercial Rd 85 DY72
Chislehurst BR7 145 EP95
Dartford DA1 107 FG84
Kingston upon Thames KT1 138 CM97
Slough (Datchet) SL3 92 AX82
Mill Pl Caravan Pk, Slou.
(Datchet) SL3 92 AW82
Mill Plat, Islw. TW7 97 CG82
Mill Plat Av, Islw. TW7 97 CG82
Mill Pond Cl, SW8
off Crimsworth Rd 101 DK80
Sevenoaks TN14 191 FK121
Millpond Ct, Add. KT15 152 BL106
Millpond Est, SE16 202 D5
Millpond Pl, Cars. SM5 140 DG104
Mill Pond Rd, Dart. DA1 128 FL86
Mill Ridge, Edg. HA8 42 CM50
Mill Rd, E16 86 EH74
SW19 120 DC94
Cobham KT11 170 BW115
Dartford (Hawley) DA2 128 FM91
Epsom KT17 157 CT112
Erith DA8 107 FC80
Esher KT10 136 CA103
Gravesend (Nthflt) DA11 130 GE87
Ilford IG1 69 EN62
Purfleet RM19 108 FP79
Sevenoaks (Dunt.Grn) TN13 190 FE121
South Ockendon
(Aveley) RM15 90 FQ73
Tadworth KT20 173 CX123
Twickenham TW2 116 CC89
West Drayton UB7 94 BJ76
Mill Row, N1 84 DS67
Mills Cl, Uxb. UB10 76 BN68
Mills Ct, EC2 197 N3
Mills Gro, E14
off Dewberry St 85 EC71
NW4 63 CX55
Mill Shaw, Oxt. RH8 188 EF132
Mill Shot Cl, SW6 99 CW80
Millside, Cars. SM5 140 DF103
Millside Ct, Iver SL0 94 BH75
Millside Ind Est, Dart. DA1 108 FK84
Millside Pl, Islw. TW7 97 CH82
Millsmead Way, Loug. IG10 33 EM40
Millson Cl, N20 44 DD47
Mills Rd, Walt. KT12 154 BW106
Mills Row, W4 98 CR77
Mills Spur, Wind.
(Old Wind.) SL4 112 AV87
Millstead Cl, Tad. KT20 173 CV122
Millstone Cl, Dart.
(S.Darenth) DA4 148 FQ96
Millstone Ms, Dart.
(S.Darenth) DA4 148 FQ95
Millstream Cl, N13 45 DN50
Millstream Rd, SE1 201 P5
Mill St, SE1 202 A5
W1 195 J10
Kingston upon Thames KT1 138 CL97
Slough SL2 74 AT74
Slough (Colnbr.) SL3 93 BD80
Westerham TN16 189 ER127
Mills Way, Brwd. (Hutt.) CM13 55 GC46
Millthorne Cl, Rick.
(Crox.Grn) WD3 22 BM43
Mill Vale, Brom. BR2 144 EF96
Mill Vw, St.Alb. (Park St) AL2
off Park St 9 CD27
Mill Vw Cl, Epsom
(Ewell) KT17 157 CT108
Millview Cl, Reig. RH2 184 DD132
Mill Vw Gdns, Croy. CR0 143 DX104
MILLWALL, E14 204 B8
Millwall Dock Rd, E14 203 P6
★ Millwall FC, SE16 102 DW78
Millway, NW7 42 CS50
Mill Way, Bushey WD23 24 BY40
Feltham TW14 115 BV85
Leatherhead KT22 172 CM124
Millway, Reig. RH2 184 DD134
Mill Way, Rick. (Mill End) WD3 37 BF46
Millway Gdns, Nthlt. UB5 78 BZ65
Millwell Cres, Chig. IG7 49 ER50
Millwood Rd, Houns. TW3 116 CC85
Orpington BR5 146 EW97
Millwood St, W10
off St. Charles Sq 81 CY71
Mill Yd, E1 off Cable St 84 DU73
Milman Cl, Pnr. HA5 60 BX55
Milman Rd, NW6 81 CY68
Milman's St, SW10 100 DD79
Milmead Ind Cen, N17 46 DV54
Milne Ct, E18
off Churchfields 48 EG53
Milne Feild, Pnr. HA5 40 CA52
Milne Gdns, SE9 124 EL85
Milne Pk E, Croy.
(New Adgtn) CR0 161 ED111
Milne Pk W, Croy.
(New Adgtn) CR0 161 ED111
Milner App, Cat. CR3 176 DU121
Milner Cl, Cat. CR3 176 DT121
Watford WD25 7 BV34
Milner Ct, Bushey WD23 24 CB44
Milner Dr, Cob. KT11 154 BZ112
Twickenham TW2 117 CD87
Milner Pl, N1 83 DN67
Carshalton SM5
off High St 158 DG105
Milner Rd, E15 86 EE69
SW19 140 DB95
Caterham CR3 176 DU122
Dagenham RM8 70 EW61
Kingston upon Thames KT1 137 CK97
Morden SM4 140 DD99
Thornton Heath CR7 142 DR97
Milner Sq, N1 83 DP66
Milner St, SW3 198 D8
Milner Wk, SE9 125 ER89
Milne Way, Uxb.
(Hare.) UB9 38 BH53
Milnthorpe Rd, W4 98 CR79
Milo Rd, SE22 122 DT86
Milroy Av, Grav.
(Nthflt) DA11 130 GE89
Milroy Wk, SE1 200 F2
Milson Rd, W14 99 CY76
MILTON, Grav. DA12 131 GK86
Milton Av, E6 86 EK66
N6 65 DJ59
NW9 62 CQ55
NW10 80 CQ67
Barnet EN5 27 CZ43
Croydon CR0 142 DR101
Gerrards Cross
(Chal.St.P.) SL9 56 AX56
Gravesend DA12 131 GJ88
Hornchurch RM12 71 FF61
Sevenoaks
(Bad.Mt) TN14 165 FB110
Sutton SM1 140 DD104
Milton Cl, N2 64 DC57
SE1 201 P9
Hayes UB4 77 BU72
Slough (Horton) SL3 93 BA83
Sutton SM1 140 DD104
Milton Ct, EC2 197 K6
Romford (Chad.Hth) RM6
off Cross Rd 70 EW59
Uxbridge UB10 59 BP62
Waltham Abbey EN9 15 EC34
Milton Ct Rd, SE14 103 DY79
Milton Cres, Ilf. IG2 69 EQ59
Milton Dr, Borwd. WD6 26 CP43
Shepperton TW17 134 BL98
Milton Flds, Ch.St.G. HP8 36 AV48
Milton Gdn Est, N16
off Milton Gro 66 DS63
Milton Gdns, Epsom KT18 156 CS114
Staines TW19
off Chesterton Dr 114 BM88
Tilbury RM18 111 GH81
Milton Gro, N11 45 DJ50
N16 66 DR63
Milton Hall Rd, Grav. DA12 131 GK88
Milton Hill, Ch.St.G. HP8 36 AV48
Milton Pk, N6 65 DJ59
Milton Pl, N7
off George's Rd 65 DN64
Gravesend DA12 131 GJ86
Milton Rd, E17 67 EA56
N6 65 DJ59
N15 65 DP56
NW7 43 CU50
NW9 off West Hendon Bdy 63 CU59
Milton Rd, SE24 121 DP86
SW14 98 CR83
SW19 120 DC93
W3 80 CR74
W7 79 CF73
Addlestone KT15 152 BG107
Belvedere DA17 106 FA77
Brentwood CM14 54 FV49
Caterham CR3 176 DR121
Croydon CR0 142 DR102
Egham TW20 113 AZ92
Gravesend DA12 131 GJ86
Grays RM17 110 GB78
Hampton TW12 116 CA94
Harrow HA1 61 CE56
Mitcham CR4 120 DG94
Romford RM1 71 FG58
Sevenoaks (Dunt.Grn) TN13 190 FE121
Sutton SM1 140 DA104
Swanscombe DA10 130 FY86
Uxbridge UB10 58 BN63
Wallington SM6 159 DJ107
Walton-on-Thames KT12 136 BX104
Welling DA16 105 ET81
★ Milton's Cottage,
Ch.St.G. HP8 36 AV48
Milton St, EC2 197 K6
Swanscombe DA10 129 FX86
Waltham Abbey EN9 15 EC34
Watford WD24 23 BV38
Milton Way, West Dr. UB7 94 BM77
Milverton Dr, Uxb. UB10 59 BQ63
Milverton Gdns, Ilf. IG3 69 ET61
Milverton Ho, SE23 123 DY90
Milverton Rd, NW6 81 CW66
Milverton St, SE11 101 DN78
Milverton Way, SE9 125 EN91
Milward St, E1
off Stepney Way 84 DV71
Milward Wk, SE18
off Spearman St 105 EN79
MIMBRIDGE, Wok. GU24 150 AV113
Mimms Hall Rd, Pot.B. EN6 11 CX31
Mimms La, Pot.B.
(S.Mimms) EN6 10 CQ33
Radlett (Shenley) WD7 10 CN33
Mimosa Cl, Brwd.
(Pilg.Hat.) CM15 54 FV43
Orpington BR6
off Berrylands 146 EW104
Romford RM3 52 FJ52
Mimosa Rd, Hayes UB4 78 BW71
Mimosa St, SW6 99 CZ81
Mina Av, Slou. SL3 92 AX75
Minard Rd, SE6 124 EE87
Mina Rd, SE17 102 DS78
SW19 140 DA95
Minchenden Cres, N14 45 DJ48
Minchin Cl, Lthd. KT22 171 CG122
Mincing La, EC3 197 M10
Woking (Chobham) GU24 150 AT108
Minden Rd, SE20 142 DV95
Sutton SM3 139 CZ103
Minehead Rd, SW16 121 DM92
Harrow HA2 60 CA62
Mineral St, SE18 105 ES77
Minera Ms, SW1 198 G8
Minerva Cl, SW9 101 DN80
Sidcup DA14 125 ES90
Staines TW19 114 BG85
Minerva Dr, Wat. WD24 23 BS36
Minerva Rd, E4 47 EB52
NW10 80 CQ70
Kingston upon Thames KT1 138 CM96
Minerva St, E2 84 DV68
Minet Av, NW10 80 CS68
Minet Dr, Hayes UB3 77 BU74
Minet Gdns, NW10 80 CS68
Hayes UB3 77 BU74
Minet Rd, SW9 101 DP82
Minford Gdns, W14 99 CX75
Mingard Wk, N7
off Hornsey Rd 65 DM61
Ming St, E14 85 EA73
Ministers Gdns, St.Alb. AL2
off Frogmore 9 CE28
★ Ministry of Defence, SW1 199 P3
Ministry Way, SE9 125 EM89
Miniver Pl, EC4
off Garlick Hill 84 DQ73
Mink Ct, Houns. TW4 96 BW83
Minniedale, Surb. KT5 138 CM99
Minnow St, SE17 off East St 102 DS77
Minnow Wk, SE17 201 N9
Minorca Rd, Wey. KT13 152 BN105
Minories, EC3 197 P10
Minshull Pl, Beck. BR3 123 EA94
Minshull St, SW8
off Wandsworth Rd 101 DK81
Minson Rd, E9 85 DX67
Minstead Gdns, SW15 119 CT87
Minstead Way, N.Mal. KT3 138 CS100
Minster Av, Sutt. SM1
off Leafield Rd 140 DA103
Minster Ct, EC3
off Mincing La 84 DR73
Hornchurch RM11 72 FN61
St. Albans (Frog.) AL2 9 CE28
Minster Dr, Croy. CR0 160 DS105
Minster Gdns, W.Mol. KT8
off Molesey Av 136 BZ99
Minsterley Av, Shep. TW17 135 BS98
Minster Pavement, EC3
off Mincing La 84 DR73
Minster Rd, NW2 63 CY64
Bromley BR1 124 EH94
Minster Wk, N8
off Lightfoot Rd 65 DL56
Minster Way, Horn. RM11 72 FM60
Slough SL3 93 AZ75
Minstrel Gdns, Surb. KT5 138 CM98
Mint Business Pk, E16 86 EG71
Mint Cl, Uxb. (Hlgdn) UB10 77 BP69
Mintern Cl, N13 45 DP48
Minterne Av, Sthl. UB2 96 CA77
Minterne Rd, Har. HA3 62 CM57
Minterne Waye, Hayes UB4 78 BW72
Mintern St, N1 84 DR68
Mint La, Tad.
(Lwr Kgswd) KT20 184 DA129
Minton Ms, NW6
off Lymington Rd 82 DB65
Mint Rd, Bans. SM7 174 DC116
Wallington SM6 159 DH105
Mint St, SE1 201 H4
Mint Wk, Croy. CR0
off High St 142 DQ104
Warlingham CR6 177 DX118
Woking (Knap.) GU21 166 AS117
Mirabel Rd, SW6 99 CZ80
Mirador Cres, Slou. SL2 74 AV73
Miramar Way, Horn. RM12 72 FK64
Miranda Cl, E1 off Sidney St 84 DW71
Miranda Ct, W3 off Queens Dr 80 CM72
Miranda Rd, N19 65 DJ60
Mirfield St, SE7 104 EK77
Miriam Rd, SE18 105 ES78
Mirravale Trd Est, Dag. RM8 70 EZ59
Mirren Cl, Har. HA2 60 BZ63
Mirrie La, Uxb. (Denh.) UB9 57 BC57
Mirror Path, SE9
off Lambscroft Av 124 EJ90
Misbourne Av, Ger.Cr.
(Chal.St.P.) SL9 36 AY50
Misbourne Cl, Ger.Cr.
(Chal.St.P.) SL9 36 AY50
Misbourne Ct, Slou. SL3
off High St 93 BA77
Misbourne Meadows, Uxb.
(Denh.) UB9 57 BC60
Misbourne Rd, Uxb. UB10 76 BN67
Misbourne Vale, Ger.Cr.
(Chal.St.P.) SL9 36 AX50
Miskin Rd, Dart. DA1 128 FJ87
Miskin Way, Grav. DA12 131 GK93
Missenden Cl, Felt. TW14 115 BT88
Missenden Gdns,
Mord. SM4 140 DC100
Mission Gro, E17 67 DY57
Mission Pl, SE15 102 DU81
Mission Sq, Brent. TW8 98 CL79
Mistletoe Cl, Croy. CR0
off Marigold Way 143 DX102
Misty's Fld, Walt. KT12 136 BW102
Mitali Pas, E1
off Back Ch La 84 DU72
MITCHAM 140 DG97
Tra Mitcham 140 DE98
Mitcham Gdn Village,
Mitch. CR4 140 DG99
Mitcham Ind Est, Mitch. CR4 140 DG95
≠ Mitcham Junction 140 DG99
Tra Mitcham Junction 140 DG99
Mitcham La, SW16 121 DJ93
Mitcham Pk, Mitch. CR4 140 DF98
Mitcham Rd, E6 86 EL69
SW17 120 DF92
Croydon CR0 141 DL100
Ilford IG3 69 ET59
Mitchell Av, Grav.
(Nthflt) DA11 130 GD89
Mitchellbrook Way, NW10 80 CR65
Mitchell Cl, SE2 106 EW77
Abbots Langley WD5 7 BU32
Belvedere DA17 107 FC76
Dartford DA1 128 FL89
Hemel Hempstead
(Bov.) HP3 5 AZ27
Rainham RM13 90 FJ68
Mitchell Rd, N13 45 DP50
Orpington BR6 163 ET105
Mitchell's Pl, SE21
off Dulwich Village 122 DS87
Mitchell St, EC1 197 H4
Mitchell Wk, E6 86 EL71
Amersham HP6 20 AS38
Swanscombe DA10 130 FY87
Mitchell Way, NW10 80 CQ65
Bromley BR1 144 EG95
Mitchison Rd, N1 84 DR65
Mitchley Av, Pur. CR8 160 DQ113
South Croydon CR2 160 DQ113
Mitchley Gro, S.Croy. CR2 160 DU113
Mitchley Hill, S.Croy. CR2 160 DT113
Mitchley Rd, N17 66 DU55
Mitchley Vw, S.Croy. CR2 160 DU113
Mitford Cl, Chess. KT9
off Merritt Gdns 155 CJ107
Mitford Rd, N19 65 DL61
Mitre, The, E14
off Three Colt St 85 DZ73
Mitre Av, E17
off Greenleaf Rd 67 DZ55
Mitre Cl, Brom. BR2
off Beckenham La 144 EF96
Shepperton TW17
off Gordon Dr 135 BR100
Sutton SM2 158 DC108
Mitre Ct, EC2 197 J8
EC4 196 E9
Mitre Rd, E15 86 EE68
SE1 200 E4
Mitre Sq, EC3 197 N9
Mitre St, EC3 197 N9
Mitre Way, W10 81 CV70
Mixbury Gro, Wey. KT13 153 BR107
Mixnams La, Cher. KT16 134 BG97
Mizen Cl, Cob. KT11 154 BX114
Mizen Way, Cob. KT11 170 BW115
Moat, The, N.Mal. KT3 138 CS95
Ongar CM5 19 FF29
Moat Cl, Bushey WD23 24 CB43
Orpington BR6 163 ET107
Sevenoaks
(Chipstead) TN13 190 FB123
Moat Ct, Ashtd. KT21 172 CL117
Moat Cres, N3 64 DB55
Moat Cft, Well. DA16 106 EW83
Moat Dr, E13 off Boundary Rd 86 EJ68
Harrow HA1 60 CC56
Ruislip HA4 59 BS59
Slough SL2 74 AW71
Moated Fm Dr, Add. KT15 152 BJ108
Moat Fm Rd, Nthlt. UB5 78 BZ65
Moatfield Rd, Bushey WD23 24 CB43
Moat La, Erith DA8 107 FG81
Moat Pl, SW9 101 DM83
W3 80 CP72
Uxbridge (Denh.) UB9 58 BH63
Moatside, Enf. EN3 31 DX42
Moatside, Feltham TW13 116 BW91
Moatview Ct, Bushey WD23 24 CB43
Moberley Rd, SW4 121 DK87
Modbury Gdns, NW5
off Queen's Cres 82 DG65
Modder Pl, SW15 99 CX84
Model Cotts, SW14
off Upper Richmond Rd W 98 CQ84
Model Fm Cl, SE9 124 EL90
Modling Ho, E2 85 DX68
Moelwyn Hughes Ct, N7
off Hilldrop Cres 65 DK64
Moelyn Ms, Har. HA1 61 CG57
Moffat Rd, N13 45 DL51
SW17 120 DE91
Thornton Heath CR7 142 DQ96
Moffats Cl, Hat. AL9 12 DA26
Moffats La, Hat. AL9 11 CZ26
MOGADOR, Tad. KT20 183 CY129
Mogador Cotts, Tad. KT20
off Mogador Rd 183 CX128
Mogador Rd, Tad.
(Lwr Kgswd) KT20 183 CX128
Mogden La, Islw. TW7 117 CE85
Mohmmad Khan Rd, E11
off Harvey Rd 68 EF60
Moira Cl, N17 46 DS54
Moira Rd, SE9 105 EM84
Moir Cl, S.Croy. CR2 160 DU109
Moland Mead, SE16 203 H10
Molash Rd, Orp. BR5 146 EX98
Molasses Row, SW11
off Cinnamon Row 100 DC83
Mole Abbey Gdns, W.Mol. KT8
off New Rd 136 CA97
Mole Business Pk,
Lthd. KT22 171 CG121
Mole Ct, Epsom KT19 156 CQ105
Molember Ct, E.Mol. KT8 137 CE99
Molember Rd, E.Mol. KT8 137 CE99
Mole Rd, Lthd. (Fetch.) KT22 171 CD121
Walton-on-Thames KT12 154 BX106
Molescroft, SE9 125 EQ90
Molesey Av, W.Mol. KT8 136 BZ98
Molesey Cl, Walt. KT12 154 BY105
Molesey Dr, Sutt. SM3 139 CY103
Molesey Pk Av, W.Mol. KT8 136 CB99
Molesey Pk Cl, E.Mol. KT8 136 CC99
Molesey Pk Rd, E.Mol. KT8 137 CD99
West Molesey KT8 136 CB99
Molesey Rd, Walt. KT12 154 BX106
West Molesey KT8 136 BY99
Molesford Rd, SW6 100 DA81
Molesham Cl, W.Mol. KT8 136 CB97
Molesham Way, W.Mol. KT8 136 CB97
Moles Hill, Lthd.
(Oxshott) KT22 155 CD111
Molesworth Rd, Cob. KT11 153 BU113
Molesworth St, SE13 103 EC83
Mole Valley Pl, Ashtd. KT21 171 CK119
Mollands La, S.Ock. RM15 91 FW70
Mollison Av, Enf. EN3 31 DY43
Mollison Dr, Wall. SM6 159 DL107
Mollison Ri, Grav. DA12 131 GL92
Mollison Sq, Wall. SM6
off Mollison Dr 159 DL108
Mollison Way, Edg. HA8 42 CN54
Molloy Ct, Wok. GU21
off Courtenay Rd 167 BA116
Molly Huggins Cl, SW12 121 DJ87
Molteno Rd, Wat. WD17 23 BU39
Molyneaux Av, Hem.H.
(Bov.) HP3 5 AZ27
Molyneux Dr, SW17 121 DH91
Molyneux Rd, Wey. KT13 152 BN106
Molyneux St, W1 194 C7
Monahan Av, Pur. CR8 159 DM112
Monarch Cl, Felt. TW14 115 BS87
Rainham RM13
off Rainham Rd 89 FG68
Tilbury RM18 111 GH82
West Wickham BR4 162 EF105
Monarch Dr, E16 86 EK71
Monarch Ms, E17 67 EB57
SW16 121 DN92
Monarch Par, Mitch. CR4
off London Rd 140 DF96
Monarch Pl, Buck.H. IG9 48 EJ47
Monarch Rd, Belv. DA17 106 FA76
Monarchs Ct, NW7
off Grenville Pl 42 CR50
Monarchs Way, Ruis. HA4 59 BR60
Waltham Cross EN8 15 DY34
Mona Rd, SE15 102 DW82
Monastery Gdns, Enf. EN2 30 DR40
Mona St, E16 86 EF71
Monaveen Gdns, W.Mol. KT8 136 CA97
Monck St, SW1 199 N7
Monclar Rd, SE5 102 DR84
Moncorvo Cl, SW7 198 B5
Moncrieff Cl, E6
off Linton Gdns 86 EL72
Moncrieff Pl, SE15
off Rye La 102 DU82
Moncrieff St, SE15 102 DU82
Mondial Way, Hayes UB3 95 BQ80
Monega Rd, E7 86 EJ65
E12 86 EK65
Money Av, Cat. CR3 176 DR122
MONEYHILL, Rick. WD3 38 BH46
Moneyhill Par, Rick. WD3
off Uxbridge Rd 38 BH46
Money Hill Rd, Rick. WD3 38 BJ46
Money La, West Dr. UB7 94 BK76
Money Rd, Cat. CR3 176 DR122
Mongers La, Epsom KT17 157 CT110
Monica Cl, Wat. WD24 24 BW40
Monier Rd, E3 85 EA66
Monivea Rd, Beck. BR3 123 DZ94
Monkchester Cl, Loug. IG10 33 EN39
Monk Dr, E16 86 EG72
MONKEN HADLEY, Barn. EN5 27 CZ39
Monkfrith Av, N14 29 DH44
Monkfrith Cl, N14 45 DH45
Monkfrith Way, N14 44 DG45
Monkhams Av, Wdf.Grn. IG8 48 EG50
Monkhams Dr, Wdf.Grn. IG8 48 EH49
Monkhams La, Buck.H. IG9 48 EH48
Woodford Green IG8 48 EG50
Monkleigh Rd, Mord. SM4 139 CY97

★ Place of interest | ≠ Railway station | ⊖ London Underground station | DLR Docklands Light Railway station | Tra Tramlink station | H Hospital | Riv Pedestrian ferry landing stage

294

Monk Pas, E16 *off Monk Dr* 86 EG73
Monks Av, Barn. EN5 28 DC44
West Molesey KT8 136 BZ99
Monks Chase, Brwd. (Ingrave) CM13 55 GC50
Monks Cl, SE2 106 EX77
Enfield EN2 30 DQ40
Harrow HA2 60 CB61
Ruislip HA4 60 BX63
Monks Cres, Add. KT15 152 BH106
Walton-on-Thames KT12 135 BV102
Monksdene Gdns, Sutt. SM1 140 DB104
Monks Dr, W3 80 CN71
Monks Grn, Lthd. (Fetch.) KT22 170 CC121
Monksgrove, Loug. IG10 33 EN43
Monksmead, Borwd. WD6 26 CQ42
MONKS ORCHARD, Croy. CR0 143 DZ101
Monks Orchard, Dart. DA1 128 FJ89
Monks Orchard Rd, Beck. BR3 143 EA102
Monks Pk, Wem. HA9 80 CQ65
Monks Pk Gdns, Wem. HA9 80 CP65
Monks Pl, Cat. CR3 *off Tillingdown Hill* 176 DU122
Monk's Ridge, N20 43 CV46
Monks Rd, Bans. SM7 174 DA116
Enfield EN2 30 DQ40
Virginia Water GU25 132 AX98
Monk St, SE18 105 EN77
Monks Wk, Cher. KT16 133 BE98
Gravesend (Sthflt) DA13 130 GA93
Monk's Wk, Reig. RH2 184 DB134
Monks Way, NW11 *off Hurstwood Rd* 63 CZ56
Beckenham BR3 143 EA99
Orpington BR5 145 EQ102
Staines TW18 114 BK94
West Drayton UB7 *off Harmondsworth La* 94 BL79
Monks Well, Green. DA9 *off London Rd* 129 FW85
Monkswell Ct, N10 *off Pembroke Rd* 44 DG53
Monkswell La, Couls. CR5 174 DB124
Monkswood Av, Wal.Abb. EN9 15 ED33
Monkswood Gdns, Borwd. WD6 26 CR42
Ilford IG5 69 EN55
Monkton Rd, Well. DA16 105 ET82
Monkton St, SE11 200 E8
Monkville Av, NW11 63 CZ56
Monkwell Sq, EC2 197 J7
Monkwood Cl, Rom. RM1 71 FG57
Monmouth Av, E18 68 EH56
Kingston upon Thames KT1 117 CJ94
Monmouth Cl, W4 *off Beaumont Rd* 98 CR76
Mitcham CR4 *off Recreation Way* 141 DL98
Welling DA16 106 EU84
Monmouth Gro, Brent. TW8 *off Sterling Pl* 98 CL77
Monmouth Pl, W2 *off Monmouth Rd* 82 DA72
Monmouth Rd, E6 87 EM69
N9 46 DV47
W2 82 DB72
Dagenham RM9 70 EZ64
Hayes UB3 95 BS77
Watford WD17 23 BV41
Monmouth St, WC2 195 P9
Monnery Rd, N19 65 DJ62
Monnow Grn, S.Ock. (Aveley) RM15 *off Monnow Rd* 90 FQ73
Monnow Rd, SE1 202 B10
South Ockendon (Aveley) RM15 90 FQ73
Mono La, Felt. TW13 115 BV89
Monoux Gro, E17 47 EA53
Monroe Cres, Enf. EN1 30 DV39
Monroe Dr, SW14 118 CP85
Monro Gdns, Har. HA3 41 CE52
Monro Pl, Epsom KT19 156 CN109
Monro Way, E5 66 DV63
Monsal Ct, E5 *off Redwald Rd* 67 DX63
Monsell Ct, N4 *off Monsell Rd* 65 DP62
Monsell Gdns, Stai. TW18 113 BE92
Monsell Rd, N4 65 DP62
Monson Rd, NW10 81 CU68
SE14 103 DX80
Redhill RH1 184 DF130
Mons Wk, Egh. TW20 113 BC92
Mons Way, Brom. BR2 144 EL100
Montacute Rd, SE6 123 DZ87
Bushey (Bushey Hth) WD23 41 CE45
Croydon (New Adgtn) CR0 161 EC109
Morden SM4 140 DD100
Montagu Cres, N18 46 DV49
Montague Av, SE4 103 DZ84
W7 79 CF74
South Croydon CR2 160 DS112
Montague Cl, SE1 201 K2
Walton-on-Thames KT12 135 BU101
Montague Dr, Cat. CR3 *off Drake Av* 176 DQ122
Montague Gdns, W3 80 CN73
Montague Hall Pl, Bushey WD23 24 CA44
Montague Pl, WC1 195 N6
Montague Rd, E8 66 DU64
E11 68 EF61
N8 65 DM57
N15 66 DU56
SW19 120 DB94
W7 79 CF74
W13 79 CH72
Croydon CR0 141 DP102
Hounslow TW3 96 CB83
Richmond TW10 118 CL86
Slough SL1 74 AT73
Slough (Datchet) SL3 92 AV81
Southall UB2 96 BY77
Uxbridge UB8 76 BK66
Montague Sq, SE15 *off Clifton Way* 102 DW80
Montague St, EC1 197 H7
Montague St, WC1 195 P6
Montague Waye, Sthl. UB2 96 BY76
Montagu Gdns, N18 46 DV49
Wallington SM6 159 DJ105
Montagu Mans, W1 194 E6
Montagu Ms N, W1 194 E7
Montagu Ms S, W1 194 E8
Montagu Ms W, W1 194 E8
Montagu Pl, W1 194 D7
Montagu Rd, N9 46 DW49
N18 46 DV50
NW4 63 CU58
Montagu Rd Ind Est, N18 46 DW49
Montagu Row, W1 194 E7
Montagu Sq, W1 194 E7
Montagu St, W1 194 E8
Montaigne Cl, SW1 199 N8
Montalt Rd, Wdf.Grn. IG8 48 EF50
Montana Cl, S.Croy. CR2 160 DR110
Montana Gdns, SE26 123 DZ92
Sutton SM1 *off Lind Rd* 158 DC106
Montana Rd, SW17 120 DG91
SW20 139 CW95
Montayne Rd, Wal.Cr. (Chsht) EN8 15 DX32
Montbelle Rd, SE9 125 EP90
Montbretia Cl, Orp. BR5 146 EW98
Montcalm Cl, Brom. BR2 144 EG100
Hayes UB4 *off Ayles Rd* 77 BV69
Montcalm Rd, SE7 104 EK80
Montclare St, E2 197 P3
Monteagle Av, Bark. IG11 87 EQ65
Monteagle Way, E5 *off Rendlesham Rd* 66 DU62
SE15 102 DV83
Montefiore St, SW8 101 DH82
Montego Cl, SE24 *off Railton Rd* 101 DN84
Montem Rd, SE23 123 DZ87
New Malden KT3 138 CS98
Montem St, N4 *off Thorpedale Rd* 65 DM60
Montenotte Rd, N8 65 DJ57
Monterey Cl, Bex. DA5 127 FC89
Montesole Ct, Pnr. HA5 40 BW54
Montevetro, SW11 100 DD81
Montford Pl, SE11 101 DN78
Montford Rd, Sun. TW16 135 BU98
Montfort Gdns, Ilf. IG6 49 EQ51
Montfort Pl, SW19 119 CX88
Montgolfier Wk, Nthlt. UB5 *off Jetstar Way* 78 BY69
Montgomery Av, Esher KT10 137 CE104
Montgomery Cl, Grays RM16 110 GC75
Mitcham CR4 141 DL98
Sidcup DA15 125 ET86
Montgomery Ct, W4 *off St. Thomas' Rd* 98 CQ79
Montgomery Cres, Rom. RM3 52 FJ50
Montgomery Dr, Wal.Cr. (Chsht) EN8 15 DY28
Montgomery Pl, Slou. SL2 74 AW72
Montgomery Rd, W4 98 CQ77
Dartford (S.Darenth) DA4 149 FR95
Edgware HA8 42 CM51
Woking GU22 166 AY118
Montgomery St, E14 204 C3
Montholme Rd, SW11 120 DF86
Monthope Rd, E1 *off Casson St* 84 DU71
Montolieu Gdns, SW15 119 CV85
Montpelier Av, W5 79 CJ71
Bexley DA5 126 EX87
Montpelier Cl, Uxb. UB10 76 BN67
Montpelier Gdns, E6 86 EK69
Romford RM6 70 EW59
Montpelier Gro, NW5 65 DJ64
Montpelier Ms, SW7 198 C6
Montpelier Pl, E1 84 DW72
SW7 198 C6
Montpelier Ri, NW11 63 CY59
Wembley HA9 61 CK60
Montpelier Rd, N3 44 DC53
SE15 102 DV81
W5 79 CK71
Purley CR8 159 DP110
Sutton SM1 158 DC105
Montpelier Row, SE3 104 EF82
Twickenham TW1 117 CH87
Montpelier Sq, SW7 198 C5
Montpelier St, SW7 198 C5
Montpelier Ter, SW7 198 C5
Montpelier Vale, SE3 104 EF82
Montpelier Wk, SW7 198 C6
Montpelier Way, NW11 63 CY59
Montrave Rd, SE20 122 DW93
Montreal Pl, WC2 196 B10
Montreal Rd, Ilf. IG1 69 EQ59
Sevenoaks TN13 190 FE123
Tilbury RM18 111 GG82
Montrell Rd, SW2 121 DL88
Montrose Av, NW6 81 CY68
Edgware HA8 42 CQ54
Romford RM2 52 FJ54
Sidcup DA15 126 EU87
Slough (Datchet) SL3 92 AW80
Twickenham TW2 116 CB87
Welling DA16 105 ER83
Montrose Cl, Ashf. TW15 115 BQ93
Welling DA16 105 ET83
Woodford Green IG8 48 EG49
Montrose Ct, SW7 198 A5
Montrose Cres, N12 44 DC51
Wembley HA0 80 CL65
Montrose Gdns, Lthd. (Oxshott) KT22 155 CD112
Mitcham CR4 140 DF97
Sutton SM1 140 DB103
Montrose Pl, SW1 198 G5
Montrose Rd, Felt. TW14 115 BR86
Harrow HA3 41 CE54
Montrose Wk, Wey. KT13 135 BP104
Montrose Way, SE23 123 DX88
Slough (Datchet) SL3 92 AX81
Montrouge Cres, Epsom KT17 173 CW116
Montserrat Av, Wdf.Grn. IG8 47 ED52
Montserrat Cl, SE19 122 DR92
Montserrat Rd, SW15 99 CY84
⊖ Monument 197 L10
★ Monument, The, EC3 201 L1
Monument Gdns, SE13 123 EC85
Monument Grn, Wey. KT13 135 BP104
Monument Hill, Wey. KT13 153 BP105
Monument La, Ger.Cr. (Chal.St.P.) SL9 36 AY51
Monument Rd, Wey. KT13 153 BP105
Woking GU21 151 BA114
Monument St, EC3 197 L10
Monument Way, N17 66 DT55
Monument Way E, Wok. GU21 167 BB115
Monument Way W, Wok. GU21 167 BA115
Monza St, E1 202 F1
Moodkee St, SE16 202 F6
Moody Rd, SE15 102 DT80
Moody St, E1 85 DX69
Moon La, Barn. EN5 27 CZ41
Moon St, N1 83 DP67
Moorcroft Gdns, Brom. BR2 *off Southborough Rd* 144 EL99
Moorcroft La, Uxb. UB8 76 BN71
Moorcroft Rd, SW16 121 DL90
Moorcroft Way, Pnr. HA5 60 BY57
Moordown, SE18 105 EN81
Moore Av, Grays RM20 110 FY78
Tilbury RM18 111 GH82
Moore Cl, SW14 *off Little St. Leonards* 98 CQ83
Addlestone KT15 152 BH106
Dartford DA2 129 FR89
Mitcham CR4 141 DH96
Wallington SM6 *off Brabazon Av* 159 DL109
Moore Cres, Dag. RM9 88 EV67
Moorefield Rd, N17 46 DT54
Moore Gro Cres, Egh. TW20 112 AY94
Moorehead Way, SE3 104 EH83
Mooreland Rd, Brom. BR1 124 EF94
Moore Pk Rd, SW6 100 DB80
Moore Rd, SE19 122 DQ93
Swanscombe DA10 130 FY86
Moores Pl, Brwd. CM14 54 FX47
Moore St, SW3 198 D8
Moore Wk, E7 *off Stracey Rd* 68 EG63
Moore Way, SE22 *off Lordship La* 122 DU88
Sutton SM2 158 DA109
Moorey Cl, E15 *off Stephen's Rd* 86 EF67
Moorfield Av, W5 79 CK70
Moorfield Rd, Chess. KT9 156 CL106
Enfield EN3 30 DW39
Orpington BR6 146 EU101
Uxbridge UB8 76 BK72
Uxbridge (Hare.) UB9 58 BG59
Moorfields, EC2 197 K7
Moorfields Cl, Stai. TW18 133 BE95
H Moorfields Eye Hosp, EC1 197 K3
Moorfields Highwalk, EC2 *off Fore St* 84 DR71
⇌ Moorgate 197 K7
⊖ Moorgate 197 K7
Moorgate, EC2 197 K8
Moorgate Pl, EC2 197 K8
Moorhall Rd, Uxb. (Hare.) UB9 58 BH58
Moorhayes Dr, Stai. TW18 134 BJ97
Moorhen Cl, Erith DA8 107 FH80
Moorholme, Wok. GU22 *off Oakbank* 166 AY119
MOORHOUSE BANK, West. TN16 189 EM128
Moorhouse Rd, W2 82 DA72
Harrow HA3 61 CK55
Oxted RH8 189 EM131
Westerham TN16 189 EM128
Moorhurst Av, Wal.Cr. (Chsht) EN7 13 DN29
Moorings, SE28 88 EV73
Moorings, The, Wind. SL4 *off Straight Rd* 112 AW87
Moorland Cl, Rom. RM5 51 FB52
Twickenham TW2 *off Telford Rd* 116 CA87
Moorland Rd, SW9 101 DP84
West Drayton UB7 94 BJ79
Moorlands, St.Alb. (Frog.) AL2 *off Frogmore* 9 CE28
Moorlands, The, Wok. GU22 167 AZ121
Moorlands Av, NW7 43 CV51
Moorlands Est, SW9 101 DN84
Moor La, EC2 197 K7
Chessington KT9 156 CL105
Rickmansworth WD3 38 BM47
Rickmansworth (Sarratt) WD3 21 BE36
Staines TW18, TW19 113 BE90
Upminster RM14 73 FS60
West Drayton UB7 94 BJ79
Woking GU22 166 AY122
Moor La Crossing, Wat. WD18 39 BQ46
Moormead Dr, Epsom KT19 156 CS106
Moor Mead Rd, Twick. TW1 117 CG86
Moormede Cres, Stai. TW18 113 BF91
Moor Mill La, St.Alb. (Coln.St) AL2 9 CE29
MOOR PARK, Nthwd. HA6 39 BQ49
⊖ Moor Park 39 BR48
Moor Pk Est, Nthwd. HA6 39 BQ49
Moor Pk Gdns, Kings.T. KT2 118 CS94
Moor Pk Ind Est, Wat. WD18 39 BQ45
★ Moor Park Mansion, Rick. WD3 38 BN48
Moor Pk Rd, Nthwd. HA6 39 BR50
Moor Pl, EC2 197 K7
Moor Rd, The, Sev. TN14 181 FH120
Moorside Rd, Brom. BR1 124 EE90
Moorsom Way, Couls. CR5 175 DK117
Moorstown Ct, Slou. SL1 92 AS75
Moor St, W1 195 N9
Moortown Rd, Wat. WD19 40 BW49
Moor Vw, Wat. WD18 39 BU45
Moot Ct, NW9 62 CN57
Moran Cl, St.Alb. (Brick.Wd) AL2 8 BZ31
Morant Gdns, Rom. RM5 51 FB50
Morant Pl, N22 *off Commerce Rd* 45 DM53
Morant Rd, Grays RM16 111 GH76
Morants Ct Cross, Sev. (Dunt.Grn) TN14 181 FB118
Morants Ct Rd, Sev. (Dunt.Grn) TN13 181 FC118
Morant St, E14 85 EA73
Mora Rd, NW2 63 CW63
Mora St, EC1 197 J3
Morat St, SW9 101 DM81
Moravian Pl, SW10 *off Milman's St* 100 DD79
Moravian St, E2 84 DW69
Moray Av, Hayes UB3 77 BT74
Moray Cl, Edg. HA8 *off Pentland Av* 42 CP47
Romford RM1 51 FE52
Moray Dr, Slou. SL2 74 AU72
Moray Ms, N7 *off Durham Rd* 65 DM61
Moray Rd, N4 65 DM61
Moray Way, Rom. RM1 51 FD52
Mordaunt Gdns, Dag. RM9 88 EY66
Mordaunt Ho, NW10 80 CR67
Mordaunt Rd, NW10 80 CR67
Mordaunt St, SW9 101 DM83
MORDEN 140 DA97
⊖ Morden 140 DB97
Morden Cl, Tad. KT20 *off Marbles Way* 173 CX120
Morden Ct, Mord. SM4 140 DB98
Morden Gdns, Grnf. UB6 61 CF64
Mitcham CR4 140 DD98
★ Morden Hall Pk N.T., Mord. SM4 140 DB97
Morden Hall Rd, Mord. SM4 140 DB97
Morden Hill, SE13 103 EC82
Morden La, SE13 103 EC81
MORDEN PARK, Mord. SM4 139 CY99
Tra Morden Road 140 DB96
Morden Rd, SE3 104 EG82
SW19 140 DB95
Mitcham CR4 140 DC98
Romford RM6 70 EY59
Morden Rd Ms, SE3 104 EG82
⇌ Morden South 140 DA99
Morden St, SE13 103 EB81
Morden Way, Sutt. SM3 140 DA101
Morden Wf Rd, SE10 205 H7
Mordon Rd, Ilf. IG3 69 ET59
Mordred Rd, SE6 124 EE89
Moreau Wk, Slou. (Geo.Grn) SL3 *off Alan Way* 74 AY72
Morecambe Cl, E1 85 DX71
Hornchurch RM12 71 FH64
Morecambe Gdns, Stan. HA7 41 CK49
Morecambe St, SE17 201 J9
Morecambe Ter, N18 46 DR49
More Cl, E16 86 EF72
W14 99 CY77
Purley CR8 159 DN111
Morecoombe Cl, Kings.T. KT2 118 CP94
Moree Way, N18 46 DU49
Moreland Av, Grays RM16 110 GC75
Slough (Colnbr.) SL3 93 BC80
Moreland Cl, Slou. (Colnbr.) SL3 *off Moreland Av* 93 BC80
Moreland Dr, Ger.Cr. SL9 57 AZ59
Moreland St, EC1 196 G2
Moreland Way, E4 47 EB48
More La, Esher KT10 136 CB103
Morel Ct, Sev. TN13 191 FH122
Morella Cl, Vir.W. GU25 132 AW98
Morella Rd, SW12 120 DF87
Morell Cl, Barn. EN5 *off Galdana Av* 28 DC41
Morello Av, Uxb. UB8 77 BP71
Morello Cl, Swan. BR8 147 FD98
Morello Dr, Slou. SL3 75 AZ74
Moremead, Wal.Abb. EN9 15 ED33
Moremead Rd, SE6 123 DZ91
Morena St, SE6 123 EB87
Moresby Av, Surb. KT5 138 CP101
Moresby Rd, E5 66 DV60
Moresby Wk, SW8 101 DH82
Moretaine Rd, Ashf. TW15 *off Hengrove Cres* 114 BK90
Moreton Av, Islw. TW7 97 CE81
Moreton Cl, E5 66 DW61
N15 66 DR58
NW7 43 CW51
SW1 199 L10
Swanley BR8 *off Bonney Way* 147 FE96
Waltham Cross (Chsht) EN7 14 DV27
Moreton Gdns, Wdf.Grn. IG8 48 EL50
Moreton Ind Est, Swan. BR8 147 FH98
Moreton Pl, SW1 199 L10
Moreton Rd, N15 66 DR58
South Croydon CR2 160 DR106
Worcester Park KT4 139 CU103
Moreton St, SW1 199 L10
Moreton Ter, SW1 199 L10
Moreton Ter Ms N, SW1 199 L10
Moreton Ter Ms S, SW1 199 L10
Moreton Twr, W3 80 CP74
Morewood Cl, Sev. TN13 190 FF123
Morewood Cl Ind Pk, Sev. TN13 *off Morewood Cl* 190 FF123
Morford Cl, Ruis. HA4 59 BV59
Morford Way, Ruis. HA4 59 BV59
Morgan Av, E17 67 ED56
Morgan Cl, Dag. RM10 88 FA66
Northwood HA6 39 BT51
Morgan Cres, Epp. (They.B.) CM16 33 ER36
Morgan Dr, Green. DA9 129 FS87
Morgan Gdns, Wat. (Ald.) WD25 24 CB38
Morgan Rd, N7 65 DN64
W10 81 CZ71
Bromley BR1 124 EG94
Morgans La, SE1 201 M3
Hayes UB3 77 BR71
Morgan St, E3 85 DY69
E16 86 EF71
Morgan Way, Rain. RM13 90 FJ69
Woodford Green IG8 48 EL51
Moriatry Cl, N7 65 DL63
Morie St, SW18 120 DB85
Morieux Rd, E10 67 DZ60
Moring Rd, SW17 120 DG91
Morkyns Wk, SE21 122 DS90
Morland Av, Croy. CR0 142 DS102
Dartford DA1 127 FH85
Morland Cl, NW11 64 DB60
Hampton TW12 116 BZ92
Mitcham CR4 140 DE97
Morland Gdns, NW10 80 CR66
Southall UB1 78 CB74
Morland Ms, N1 *off Lofting Rd* 83 DN66
Morland Rd, E17 67 DX57
SE20 123 DX93
Croydon CR0 142 DS102
Dagenham RM10 88 FA66
Harrow HA3 62 CL57
Ilford IG1 69 EP61
Sutton SM1 158 DC106
H Morland Rd Day Hosp, Dag. RM10 88 FA66
Morland Way, Wal.Cr. (Chsht) EN8 15 DY28
Morley Av, E4 47 ED52
N18 46 DU49
N22 45 DN54
Morley Cl, Orp. BR6 145 EP103
Slough SL3 93 AZ75
Morley Cres, Edg. HA8 42 CQ47
Ruislip HA4 60 BW61
Morley Cres E, Stan. HA7 41 CJ54
Morley Cres W, Stan. HA7 41 CJ54
Morley Hill, Enf. EN2 30 DR38
Morley Rd, E10 67 EC60
E15 86 EF68
SE13 103 EC84
Barking IG11 87 ER67
Chislehurst BR7 145 EQ95
Romford RM6 70 EY57
South Croydon CR2 160 DT110
Sutton SM3 139 CZ102
Twickenham TW1 117 CK86
Morley Sq, Grays RM16 111 GG77
Morley St, SE1 200 E6
Morna Rd, SE5 102 DQ82
Morning La, E9 84 DW65
Morning Ri, Rick. (Loud.) WD3 22 BK41
Morningside Rd, Wor.Pk. KT4 139 CV103
Mornington Av, W14 99 CZ77
Bromley BR1 144 EJ97
Ilford IG1 69 EN59
Mornington Cl, West. (Bigg.H.) TN16 178 EK117
Woodford Green IG8 48 EG49
Mornington Ct, Bex. DA5 127 FC88
⊖ Mornington Crescent 83 DH68
Mornington Cres, NW1 83 DJ68
Hounslow TW5 95 BV81
Mornington Gro, E3 85 EA69
Mornington Ms, SE5 102 DQ81
Mornington Pl, NW1 *off Mornington Ter* 83 DH68
Mornington Rd, E4 47 ED45
E11 68 EF60
SE8 103 DZ80
Ashford TW15 115 BQ92
Greenford UB6 78 CB71
Loughton IG10 33 EQ41
Radlett WD7 9 CG34
Woodford Green IG8 48 EF49
Mornington St, NW1 83 DH68
Mornington Ter, NW1 83 DH67
Mornington Wk, Rich. TW10 117 CK91
Morocco St, SE1 201 M5
Morpeth Av, Borwd. WD6 26 CM38
Morpeth Gro, E9 85 DX67
Morpeth Rd, E9 84 DW67
Morpeth St, E2 85 DX69
Morpeth Ter, SW1 199 K7
Morpeth Wk, N17 *off West Rd* 46 DV52
Morrab Gdns, Ilf. IG3 69 ET62
Morrice Cl, Slou. SL3 93 AZ77
Morris Av, E12 69 EM64
Morris Cl, Croy. CR0 143 DY100
Gerrards Cross (Chal.St.P.) SL9 37 AZ53
Orpington BR6 145 ES104
Morris Ct, E4 47 EB48
Enfield EN3 *off Martini Dr* 31 EA37
Waltham Abbey EN9 16 EF34
Morris Gdns, SW18 120 DA87
Dartford DA1 128 FN85
Morrish Rd, SW2 121 DL87
Morrison Av, E4 47 EA51
N17 66 DS55
Morrison Rd, Bark. IG11 88 EY68
Hayes UB4 77 BV69
Morrison St, SW11 100 DG83
Morris Pl, N4 65 DN61
Morris Rd, E14 85 EB71
E15 68 EE63
Dagenham RM8 70 EZ61
Isleworth TW7 97 CF83
Romford RM3 51 FH52
Morris St, E1 84 DV72
Morriston Cl, Wat. WD19 40 BW50
Morris Way, St.Alb. (Lon.Col.) AL2 10 CL26
Morse Cl, E13 86 EG69
Uxbridge (Hare.) UB9 38 BJ54
Morshead Rd, W9 82 DA69
Morson Rd, Enf. EN3 31 DY44
Morston Cl, Tad. KT20 *off Waterfield* 173 CV120
Morston Gdns, SE9 125 EM91
Morten Cl, SW4 121 DK86
Morten Gdns, Uxb. (Denh.) UB9 58 BG59
Morteyne Rd, N17 46 DR53
Mortgramit Sq, SE18 *off Powis St* 105 EN76
Mortham St, E15 85 ED67
Mortimer Cl, NW2 63 CZ62

★ Place of interest ⇌ Railway station ⊖ London Underground station DLR Docklands Light Railway station Tra Tramlink station H Hospital Riv Pedestrian ferry landing stage

Mortimer Cl, SW16 . . . . . 121 DK89
Bushey WD23 . . . . . 24 CB44
Mortimer Cres, NW6 . . . . . 82 DB67
Worcester Park KT4 . . . . . 138 CR104
Mortimer Dr, Enf. EN1 . . . . . 30 DR43
Mortimer Est, NW6 . . . . . 82 DB67
Mortimer Gate, Wal.Cr. EN8 . . 15 DZ27
Mortimer Ho, W11
off St. Anns Rd 81 CX74
Mortimer Mkt, WC1 . . . . . 195 L5
Mortimer Pl, NW6 . . . . . 82 DB67
Mortimer Rd, E6 . . . . . 87 EM69
N1 . . . . . 84 DS66
NW10 . . . . . 81 CW69
W13 . . . . . 79 CJ72
Erith DA8 . . . . . 107 FD79
Mitcham CR4 . . . . . 140 DF95
Orpington BR6 . . . . . 146 EU103
Slough SL3 . . . . . 92 AX76
Westerham (Bigg.H.) TN16 . 162 EJ112
Mortimer Sq, W11
off St. Anns Rd 81 CX73
Mortimer St, W1 . . . . . 195 K8
Mortimer Ter, NW5
off Gordon Ho Rd 65 DH63
MORTLAKE, SW14 . . . . . 98 CQ83
⇌ Mortlake 98 CQ83
Mortlake Cl, Croy. CR0
off Richmond Rd 141 DL104
Mortlake Dr, Mitch. CR4 . . . . . 140 DE95
Mortlake High St, SW14 . . . . . 98 CR83
Mortlake Rd, E16 . . . . . 86 EH72
Ilford IG1 . . . . . 69 EQ63
Richmond TW9 . . . . . 98 CN80
Mortlake Ter, Rich. TW9
off Kew Rd 98 CN80
Mortlock Cl, SE15
off Cossall Wk 102 DV81
Morton, Tad. KT20
off Hudsons 173 CX121
Morton Cl, Wall. SM6 . . . . . 159 DM108
Woking GU21 . . . . . 166 AW115
Morton Ct, Nthlt. UB5 . . . . . 60 CC64
Morton Cres, N14 . . . . . 45 DK49
Morton Gdns, Wall. SM6 . . . . . 159 DJ106
Morton Ms, SW5
off Earls Ct Gdns 100 DB77
Morton Pl, SE1 . . . . . 200 D7
Morton Rd, E15 . . . . . 86 EF66
N1 . . . . . 84 DQ66
Morden SM4 . . . . . 140 DD99
Woking GU21 . . . . . 166 AW115
Morton Way, N14 . . . . . 45 DJ48
Morvale Cl, Belv. DA17 . . . . . 106 EZ77
Morval Rd, SW2 . . . . . 121 DN85
Morven Cl, Pot.B. EN6 . . . . . 12 DC31
Morven Rd, SW17 . . . . . 120 DF90
Morville Ho, SW18
off Fitzhugh Gro 120 DD86
Morville St, E3 . . . . . 85 EA68
Morwell St, WC1 . . . . . 195 N7
Mosbach Gdns, Brwd.
(Hutt.) CM13 . . . . . 55 GB47
Moscow Pl, W2
off Moscow Rd 82 DB73
Moscow Rd, W2 . . . . . 82 DA73
Moseley Row, SE10 . . . . . 205 L8
Moselle Av, N22 . . . . . 45 DN54
Moselle Cl, N8
off Miles Rd 65 DM55
Moselle Ho, N17
off William St 46 DT52
Moselle Pl, N17
off High Rd 46 DT52
Moselle Rd, West.
(Bigg.H.) TN16 . . . . . 178 EL118
Moselle St, N17 . . . . . 46 DT52
Mospey Cres, Epsom KT17 . . . 173 CT115
Moss Bk, Grays RM17 . . . . . 110 FZ78
Mossborough Cl, N12 . . . . . 44 DB51
Mossbury Rd, SW11 . . . . . 100 DE83
Moss Cl, E1
off Old Montague St 84 DU71
Pinner HA5 . . . . . 40 BZ54
Rickmansworth WD3 . . . . . 38 BK47
Mossdown Cl, Belv. DA17 . . . . . 106 FA77
Mossendew Cl, Uxb.
(Hare.) UB9 . . . . . 38 BK53
Mossfield, Cob. KT11 . . . . . 153 BU113
Mossford Ct, Ilf. IG6 . . . . . 69 EP55
Mossford Grn, Ilf. IG6 . . . . . 69 EP55
Mossford La, Ilf. IG6 . . . . . 49 EP54
Mossford St, E3 . . . . . 85 DZ70
Moss Gdns, Felt. TW13 . . . . . 115 BU89
South Croydon CR2
off Warren Av 161 DX108
Moss Hall Ct, N12 . . . . . 44 DB51
Moss Hall Cres, N12 . . . . . 44 DB51
Moss Hall Gro, N12 . . . . . 44 DB51
Mossington Gdns, SE16 . . . . . 202 F9
Moss La, Pnr. HA5 . . . . . 60 BZ55
Romford RM1
off Wheatsheaf Rd 71 FF58
Mosslea Rd, SE20 . . . . . 122 DW93
Bromley BR2 . . . . . 144 EK99
Orpington BR6 . . . . . 145 EQ104
Whyteleafe CR3 . . . . . 176 DT116
Mossop St, SW3 . . . . . 198 C8
Moss Rd, Dag. RM10 . . . . . 88 FA66
South Ockendon RM15 . . . . . 91 FW71
Watford WD25 . . . . . 7 BV34
Moss Side, St.Alb.
(Brick.Wd) AL2 . . . . . 8 BZ30
Mossville Gdns, Mord. SM4 . . 139 CZ97
Moss Way, Dart.
(Lane End) DA2 . . . . . 129 FR91
Moston Cl, Hayes UB3
off Fuller Way 95 BT78
Mostyn Av, Wem. HA9 . . . . . 62 CM64
Mostyn Gdns, NW10 . . . . . 81 CX68
Mostyn Gro, E3 . . . . . 85 DZ68
Mostyn Rd, SW9 . . . . . 101 DN81
SW19 . . . . . 139 CZ95
Bushey WD23 . . . . . 24 CC43
Edgware HA8 . . . . . 42 CR52
Mosul Way, Brom. BR2 . . . . . 144 EL100
Mosyer Dr, Orp. BR5 . . . . . 146 EX103
Motcomb St, SW1 . . . . . 198 E6
Moth Cl, Wall. SM6 . . . . . 159 DL108
Mothers' Sq, E5 . . . . . 66 DV63
Motherwell Way, Grays
RM20 . . . . . 109 FU78
Motley Av, EC2 . . . . . 197 M4
Motley St, SW8
off St. Rule St 101 DJ82
MOTSPUR PARK, N.Mal.
KT3 . . . . . 139 CU100
⇌ Motspur Park 139 CV99
Motspur Pk, N.Mal. KT3 . . . . . 139 CT100
MOTTINGHAM, SE9 . . . . . 124 EJ89
⇌ Mottingham 124 EL88
Mottingham Gdns, SE9 . . . . . 124 EK88
Mottingham La, SE9 . . . . . 124 EJ88
SE12 . . . . . 124 EJ88
Mottingham Rd, N9 . . . . . 31 DX44
SE9 . . . . . 124 EL89
Mottisfont Rd, SE2 . . . . . 106 EU76
Motts Hill La, Tad. KT20 . . . . . 173 CU123
Mott St, E4 . . . . . 31 ED38
Loughton (High Beach) IG10 . . 32 EF39
Mouchotte Cl, West.
(Bigg.H.) TN16 . . . . . 162 EH112
Moulins Rd, E9 . . . . . 84 DW67
Moulsford Ho, N7 . . . . . 65 DK64
Moultain Hill, Swan. BR8 . . . . . 147 FG98
Moulton Av, Houns. TW3 . . . . . 96 BY82
Moultrie Way, Upmin. RM14 . . 73 FS59
Mound, The, SE9 . . . . . 125 EN90
Moundfield Rd, N16 . . . . . 66 DU58
Mount, The, N20 . . . . . 44 DC47
NW3 off Heath St 64 DC63
W3 . . . . . 80 CP74
Brentwood CM14 . . . . . 54 FW48
Coulsdon CR5 . . . . . 174 DG115
Epsom (Ewell) KT17 . . . . . 157 CT110
Esher KT10 . . . . . 154 CA107
Leatherhead (Fetch.) KT22 . 171 CE123
New Malden KT3 . . . . . 139 CT97
Potters Bar EN6 . . . . . 12 DB30
Rickmansworth WD3 . . . . . 22 BJ44
Romford RM3 . . . . . 52 FJ48
Tadworth KT20 . . . . . 183 CZ126
Virginia Water GU25 . . . . . 132 AX100
Waltham Cross (Chsht) EN7 . 14 DR26
Warlingham CR6 . . . . . 176 DU119
Wembley HA9 . . . . . 62 CP61
Weybridge KT13 . . . . . 135 BS103
Woking GU21 . . . . . 166 AX118
Woking (St.John's) GU21 . . 166 AU119
Worcester Park KT4 . . . . . 157 CV105
Mountacre Cl, SE26 . . . . . 122 DT91
Mount Adon Pk, SE22 . . . . . 122 DU87
Mountague Pl, E14 . . . . . 85 EC73
Mountain Ct, Dart. (Eyns.) DA4
off Pollyhaugh 148 FL103
Mount Angelus Rd, SW15 . . . . . 119 CT87
Mount Ararat Rd, Rich. TW10 . 118 CL85
Mount Ash Rd, SE26 . . . . . 122 DV90
Mount Av, E4 . . . . . 47 EA48
W5 . . . . . 79 CK71
Brentwood CM13 . . . . . 55 GA44
Caterham CR3 . . . . . 176 DQ124
Romford RM3 . . . . . 52 FQ51
Southall UB1 . . . . . 78 CA72
Mountbatten Cl, SE18 . . . . . 105 ES79
SE19 . . . . . 122 DS92
Slough SL1 . . . . . 92 AU76
Mountbatten Ct, SE16
off Rotherhithe St 84 DW74
Buckhurst Hill IG9 . . . . . 48 EK47
Mountbatten Gdns, Beck. BR3
off Balmoral Av 143 DY98
Mountbatten Ms, SW18
off Inman Rd 120 DC88
Mountbel Rd, Stan. HA7 . . . . . 41 CG53
Mount Cl, W5 . . . . . 79 CJ71
Barnet EN4 . . . . . 28 DG42
Bromley BR1 . . . . . 144 EL95
Carshalton SM5 . . . . . 158 DG109
Kenley CR8 . . . . . 176 DQ116
Leatherhead (Fetch.) KT22 . 171 CE123
Sevenoaks TN13 . . . . . 190 FF123
Woking GU22 . . . . . 166 AV121
Mount Cl, The, Vir.W. GU25 . . 132 AX100
Mountcombe Cl, Surb. KT6 . . 138 CL101
Mount Cor, Felt. TW13 . . . . . 116 BX89
Mount Ct, SW15
off Weimar St 99 CY83
West Wickham BR4 . . . . . 144 EE103
Mount Cres, Brwd. CM14 . . . . . 54 FX49
Mount Culver Av, Sid. DA14 . . 126 EX93
Mount Dr, Bexh. DA6 . . . . . 126 EY85
Harrow HA2 . . . . . 60 BZ57
St. Albans (Park St) AL2 . . . . . 9 CD25
Wembley HA9 . . . . . 62 CQ61
Mount Dr, The, Reig. RH2 . . . . . 184 DC132
Mountearl Gdns, SW16 . . . . . 121 DM90
Mount Echo Av, E4 . . . . . 47 EB47
Mount Echo Dr, E4 . . . . . 47 EB46
MOUNT END, Epp. CM16 . . . . . 18 EZ32
Mount Ephraim La, SW16 . . . . . 121 DK90
Mount Ephraim Rd, SW16 . . . 121 DK90
Mount Est, The, E5
off Mount Pleasant La 66 DV61
Mount Felix, Walt. KT12 . . . . . 135 BT102
Mountfield Cl, SE6 . . . . . 123 ED87
Mountfield Rd, E6 . . . . . 87 EN68
N3 . . . . . 64 DA55
W5 . . . . . 79 CK72
Mountfield Way, Orp. BR5 . . . 146 EW98
Mountford St, E1
off Adler St 84 DU72
Mountfort Cres, N1
off Barnsbury Sq 83 DN66
Mountfort Ter, N1
off Barnsbury Sq 83 DN66
Mount Gdns, SE26 . . . . . 122 DV90
Mount Grace Rd, Pot.B. EN6 . . 12 DA31
Mount Gro, Edg. HA8 . . . . . 42 CQ48
Mountgrove Rd, N5 . . . . . 65 DP62
Mount Harry Rd, Sev. TN13 . . 190 FG123
MOUNT HERMON,
Wok. GU22 . . . . . 166 AX118
Mount Hermon Cl,
Wok. GU22 . . . . . 166 AX118
Mount Hermon Rd,
Wok. GU22 . . . . . 166 AX119
Mount Hill La, Ger.Cr. SL9 . . . . . 56 AV60
Mounthurst Rd, Brom. BR2 . . 144 EF101
Mountington Pk Cl, Har. HA3 . . 61 CK58
Mountjoy Cl, SE2 . . . . . 106 EV75
Mountjoy Ho, EC2
off The Barbican 84 DQ71
Mount La, Uxb. (Denh.) UB9 . . 57 BD61
Mount Lee, Egh. TW20 . . . . . 112 AY92
Mount Ms, Hmptn. TW12 . . . . . 136 CB95
Mount Mills, EC1 . . . . . 196 G3
Mountnessing Bypass,
Brwd. CM15 . . . . . 55 GD41
Mount Nod Rd, SW16 . . . . . 121 DM90
Mount Pk, Cars. SM5 . . . . . 158 DG109
Mount Pk Av, Har. HA1 . . . . . 61 CD61
South Croydon CR2 . . . . . 159 DP109
Mount Pk Cres, W5 . . . . . 79 CK72
Mount Pk Rd, W5 . . . . . 79 CK71
Harrow HA1 . . . . . 61 CD62
Pinner HA5 . . . . . 59 BU57
Mount Pl, W3 off High St 80 CP74
Mount Pleasant, SE27 . . . . . 122 DQ91
WC1 . . . . . 196 C5
Barnet EN4 . . . . . 28 DE42
Epsom KT17 . . . . . 157 CT110
Ruislip HA4 . . . . . 60 BW61
Uxbridge (Hare.) UB9 . . . . . 38 BG53
Wembley HA0 . . . . . 80 CL67
Westerham (Bigg.H.) TN16 . 178 EK117
Weybridge KT13 . . . . . 134 BN104
Mount Pleasant Av, Brwd.
(Hutt.) CM13 . . . . . 55 GE44
Mount Pleasant Cres, N4 . . . . . 65 DM59
Mount Pleasant Hill, E5 . . . . . 66 DV61
Mount Pleasant La, E5 . . . . . 66 DV61
St. Albans (Brick.Wd) AL2 . . . . 8 BY30
Mount Pleasant Pl, SE18
off Orchard Rd 105 ER77
Mount Pleasant Rd, E17 . . . . . 47 DY54
N17 . . . . . 46 DS54
NW10 . . . . . 81 CW66
SE13 . . . . . 123 EB86
W5 . . . . . 79 CJ70
Caterham CR3 . . . . . 176 DU123
Chigwell IG7 . . . . . 49 ER49
Dartford DA1 . . . . . 128 FM86
New Malden KT3 . . . . . 138 CQ97
Romford RM5 . . . . . 51 FD51
Mount Pleasant Vil, N4 . . . . . 65 DM59
Mount Pleasant Wk,
Bex. DA5 . . . . . 127 FC85
Mount Rd, NW2 . . . . . 63 CV62
NW4 . . . . . 63 CU58
SE19 . . . . . 122 DR93
SW19 . . . . . 120 DA89
Barnet EN4 . . . . . 28 DE43
Bexleyheath DA6 . . . . . 126 EX85
Chessington KT9 . . . . . 156 CM106
Dagenham RM8 . . . . . 70 EZ60
Dartford DA1 . . . . . 127 FF86
Epping CM16 . . . . . 18 EW32
Feltham TW13 . . . . . 116 BY90
Hayes UB3 . . . . . 95 BT75
Ilford IG1 . . . . . 69 EP64
Mitcham CR4 . . . . . 140 DE96
New Malden KT3 . . . . . 138 CR97
Woking GU22 . . . . . 166 AV121
Woking (Chobham) GU24 . 150 AV112
Mount Row, W1 . . . . . 199 H1
Mountsfield Cl, Stai. TW19 . . . 114 BG86
Mountsfield Ct, SE13 . . . . . 123 ED86
Mountside, Felt. TW13 . . . . . 116 BY90
Stanmore HA7 . . . . . 41 CF53
Mounts Pond Rd, SE3 . . . . . 103 ED82
Mount Sq, The, NW3
off Heath St 64 DC62
Mounts Rd, Green. DA9 . . . . . 129 FV85
Mount Stewart Av, Har. HA3 . . 61 CK58
Mount St, W1 . . . . . 198 G1
Mount Ter, E1 off New Rd 84 DV71
Mount Vernon, NW3 . . . . . 64 DC63
H Mount Vernon Hosp,
Nthwd. HA6 . . . . . 39 BP51
Mount Vw, NW7 . . . . . 42 CR48
W5 . . . . . 79 CK70
Enfield EN2 . . . . . 29 DM38
Mountview, Nthwd. HA6 . . . . . 39 BT51
Mount Vw, Rick. WD3 . . . . . 38 BH46
St. Albans (Lon.Col.) AL2 . . . 10 CL27
Mountview Cl, NW11 . . . . . 64 DB60
Mountview Ct, N8
off Green Las 65 DP56
Mount Vw Rd, E4 . . . . . 47 EC45
N4 . . . . . 65 DL59
NW9 . . . . . 62 CR56
Mountview Rd, Esher
(Clay.) KT10 . . . . . 155 CH108
Orpington BR6 . . . . . 146 EU101
Waltham Cross (Chsht) EN7 . 14 DS26
Mount Vil, SE27 . . . . . 121 DP90
Mount Way, Cars. SM5 . . . . . 158 DG109
Mountway, Pot.B. EN6 . . . . . 12 DA30
Mountwood, W.Mol. KT8 . . . . . 136 CA97
Mountwood Cl, S.Croy. CR2 . . 160 DV110
Movers La, Bark. IG11 . . . . . 87 ER67
Mowat Ind Est, Wat. WD24 . . . . 24 BW38
Mowatt Cl, N19 . . . . . 65 DK60
Mowbray Av, W.Byf.
(Byfleet) KT14 . . . . . 152 BL113
Mowbray Cres, Egh. TW20 . . . 113 BA92
Mowbray Rd, NW6 . . . . . 81 CY66
SE19 . . . . . 142 DT95
Barnet EN5 . . . . . 28 DC42
Edgware HA8 . . . . . 42 CN49
Richmond TW10 . . . . . 117 CJ90
Mowbrays Cl, Rom. RM5 . . . . . 51 FC53
Mowbrays Rd, Rom. RM5 . . . . . 51 FC54
Mowbrey Gdns, Loug. IG10 . . . 33 EQ40
Mowlem St, E2 . . . . . 84 DV68
Mowlem Trd Est, N17 . . . . . 46 DW52
Mowll St, SW9 . . . . . 101 DN80
Moxom Av, Wal.Cr.
(Chsht) EN8 . . . . . 15 DY30
Moxon Cl, E13
off Whitelegg Rd 86 EF68
Moxon St, W1 . . . . . 194 F7
Barnet EN5 . . . . . 27 CZ41
Moye Cl, E2 off Dove Row 84 DU67
Moyers Rd, E10 . . . . . 67 EC59
Moylan Rd, W6 . . . . . 99 CY79
Moyne Ct, Wok. GU21
off Iveagh Rd 166 AT118
Moyne Pl, NW10 . . . . . 80 CN68
Moynihan Dr, N21 . . . . . 29 DL43
Moys Cl, Croy. CR0 . . . . . 141 DL100
Moyser Rd, SW16 . . . . . 121 DH92
Mozart St, W10 . . . . . 81 CZ69
Mozart Ter, SW1 . . . . . 198 G9
Muchelney Rd, Mord. SM4 . . 140 DC100
Muckhatch La, Egh. TW20 . . . 133 BB97
MUCKINGFORD,
S.le H. SS17 . . . . . 111 GM76
Muckingford Rd, S.le H.
(Linford) SS17 . . . . . 111 GM77
Tilbury (W.Til.) RM18 . . . . . 111 GL77
DLR Mudchute 204 C8
Muddy La, Slou. SL2 . . . . . 74 AS71
Mudlands Ind Est, Rain. RM13
off Manor Way 89 FE69
Mud La, W5 . . . . . 79 CK71
Muggeridge Cl, S.Croy. CR2 . . 160 DR106
Muggeridge Rd, Dag. RM10 . . . 71 FB63
MUGSWELL, Couls. CR5 . . . . . 184 DB125
Muirdown Av, SW14 . . . . . 98 CQ84
Muir Dr, SW18 . . . . . 120 DD86
Muirfield, W3 . . . . . 80 CS72
Muirfield Cl, SE16
off Ryder Dr 102 DV78
Watford WD19 . . . . . 40 BW49
Muirfield Cres, E14 . . . . . 204 B6
Muirfield Grn, Wat. WD19 . . . . 40 BW49
Muirfield Rd, Wat. WD19 . . . . . 40 BX49
Woking GU21 . . . . . 166 AU118
Muirkirk Rd, SE6 . . . . . 123 EC88
Muir Rd, E5 . . . . . 66 DU63
Muir St, E16
off Newland St 87 EM74
Mukberry Cl, Wat. WD25
off Greenbank Rd 23 BS36
Mulberry Av, Stai. TW19 . . . . . 114 BL88
Windsor SL4 . . . . . 92 AT82
Mulberry Business Cen, SE16 . 203 J5
Mulberry Cl, E4 . . . . . 47 EA47
N8 . . . . . 65 DL57
NW3
off Hampstead High St 64 DD63
NW4 . . . . . 63 CW55
SE7 off Charlton Pk Rd 104 EK79
SE22 . . . . . 122 DU85
SW3 off Beaufort St 100 DD79
SW16 . . . . . 121 DJ91
Amersham HP7 . . . . . 20 AT39
Barnet EN4 . . . . . 28 DD42
Northolt UB5
off Parkfield Av 78 BY68
Romford RM2 . . . . . 71 FH56
St. Albans (Park St) AL2 . . . . . 8 CB28
Weybridge KT13 . . . . . 135 BP104
Woking GU21 . . . . . 150 AY114
Mulberry Ct, Bark. IG11
off Westrow Dr 87 ET66
Mulberry Cres, Brent. TW8 . . . 97 CH80
West Drayton UB7 . . . . . 94 BN75
Mulberry Dr, Purf. RM19 . . . . . 108 FM77
Slough SL3 . . . . . 92 AY78
Mulberry Gdns, Rad.
(Shenley) WD7 . . . . . 10 CL33
Mulberry Gate, Bans. SM7 . . . 173 CZ116
Mulberry Hill, Brwd.
(Shenf.) CM15 . . . . . 55 FZ45
Mulberry La, Croy. CR0 . . . . . 142 DT102
Mulberry Ms, SE14
off Lewisham Way 103 DZ81
Wallington SM6
off Ross Rd 159 DJ107
Mulberry Par, West Dr. UB7 . . . 94 BN76
Mulberry Pl, W6
off Chiswick Mall 99 CU78
Mulberry Rd, E8 . . . . . 84 DT66
Gravesend (Nthflt) DA11 . . 130 GE90
Mulberry St, E1 off Adler St . . . 84 DU72
Mulberry Trees, Shep. TW17 . . 135 BQ101
Mulberry Wk, SW3 . . . . . 100 DD79
Mulberry Way, E18 . . . . . 48 EH54
Belvedere DA17 . . . . . 107 FC75
Ilford IG6 . . . . . 69 EQ56
Mulgrave Rd, NW10 . . . . . 63 CT63
SE18 . . . . . 105 EM77
SW6 . . . . . 99 CZ79
W5 . . . . . 79 CK69
Croydon CR0 . . . . . 142 DR104
Harrow HA1 . . . . . 61 CG61
Sutton SM2 . . . . . 158 DA107
Mulgrave Way, Wok.
(Knap.) GU21 . . . . . 166 AS118
Mulholland Cl, Mitch. CR4 . . . 141 DH96
Mulkern Rd, N19 . . . . . 65 DK60
Mullards Cl, Mitch. CR4 . . . . . 140 DF102
Mullein Ct, Grays RM17 . . . . . 110 GD79
Mullens Rd, Egh. TW20 . . . . . 113 BB92
Muller Rd, SW4 . . . . . 121 DK86
Mullet Gdns, E2
off St. Peter's Cl 84 DU68
Mullins Path, SW14 . . . . . 98 CR83
Mullion Cl, Har. HA3 . . . . . 40 CB53
Mullion Wk, Wat. WD19
off Ormskirk Rd 40 BX49
Mull Wk, N1 off Clephane Rd . . 84 DQ65
Mulready St, NW8 . . . . . 194 B5
Multi-way, W3 off Valetta Rd . . 98 CS75
Multon Rd, SW18 . . . . . 120 DD87
Mulvaney Way, SE1 . . . . . 201 L5
Mumford Ct, EC2 . . . . . 197 J8
Mumford Rd, SE24
off Railton Rd 121 DP85
Mumfords La, Ger.Cr.
(Chal.St.P.) SL9 . . . . . 56 AU55
Muncaster Cl, Ashf. TW15 . . . . 114 BN91
Muncaster Rd, SW11 . . . . . 120 DF85
Ashford TW15 . . . . . 115 BP92
Muncies Ms, SE6 . . . . . 123 EC89
Mundania Rd, SE22 . . . . . 122 DV86
Munday Rd, E16 . . . . . 86 EG72
Mundells, Wal.Cr. EN7 . . . . . 14 DU27
Munden Dr, Wat. WD25 . . . . . 24 BY37
Munden Gro, Wat. WD24 . . . . . 24 BW38
Munden St, W14 . . . . . 99 CY77
Munden Vw, Wat. WD25 . . . . . 24 BX36
Mundesley Cl, Wat. WD19 . . . . 40 BW49
Mundesley Spur, Slou. SL1 . . . 74 AS72
Mundford Rd, E5 . . . . . 66 DW61
Mundon Gdns, Ilf. IG1 . . . . . 69 ER60
Mund St, W14 . . . . . 99 CZ78
Mundy St, N1 . . . . . 197 M2
Munford Dr, Swans. DA10 . . . . 130 FY87
Mungo Pk Cl, Bushey
(Bushey Hth) WD23 . . . . . 40 CC47
Mungo Pk Rd, Grav. DA12 . . . . 131 GK92
Rainham RM13 . . . . . 89 FG65
Mungo Pk Way, Orp. BR5 . . . . 146 EW101
Munnery Way, Orp. BR6 . . . . . 145 EN104
Munnings Gdns, Islw. TW7 . . . 117 CD85
Munro Dr, N11 . . . . . 45 DJ51
Munro Ms, W10 . . . . . 81 CY71
Munro Rd, Bushey WD23 . . . . . 24 CB43
Munro Ter, SW10 . . . . . 100 DD80
Munslow Gdns, Sutt. SM1 . . . 158 DD105
Munster Av, Houns. TW4 . . . . . 96 BZ84
Munster Ct, Tedd. TW11 . . . . . 117 CJ93
Munster Gdns, N13 . . . . . 45 DP49
Munster Ms, SW6
off Lillie Rd 99 CY80
Munster Rd, SW6 . . . . . 99 CZ81
Teddington TW11 . . . . . 117 CH93
Munster Sq, NW1 . . . . . 195 J3
Munton Rd, SE17 . . . . . 201 J8
Murchison Av, Bex. DA5 . . . . . 126 EX88
Murchison Rd, E10 . . . . . 67 EC61
Murdoch Cl, Stai. TW18 . . . . . 114 BG92
Murdock Cl, E16
off Rogers Rd 86 EF72
Murdock St, SE15 . . . . . 102 DV79
Murfett Cl, SW19 . . . . . 119 CY89
Murfitt Way, Upmin. RM14 . . . 72 FN63
Muriel Av, Wat. WD18 . . . . . 24 BW43
Muriel St, N1 . . . . . 83 DM68
Murillo Rd, SE13 . . . . . 103 ED84
Murphy St, SE1 . . . . . 200 D5
Murray Av, Brom. BR1 . . . . . 144 EH96
Hounslow TW3 . . . . . 116 CB85
Murray Business Cen,
Orp. BR5 . . . . . 146 EV97
Murray Cres, Pnr. HA5 . . . . . 40 BX53
Murray Grn, Wok. GU21
off Bunyard Dr 151 BC114
Murray Gro, N1 . . . . . 197 J1
Murray Ms, NW1 . . . . . 83 DK66
Murray Rd, SW19 . . . . . 119 CX93
W5 . . . . . 97 CJ77
Chertsey (Ott.) KT16 . . . . . 151 BC107
Northwood HA6 . . . . . 39 BS53
Orpington BR5 . . . . . 146 EV97
Richmond TW10 . . . . . 117 CH89
Murrays La, W.Byf.
(Byfleet) KT14 . . . . . 152 BK114
Murray Sq, E16 . . . . . 86 EG72
Murray St, NW1 . . . . . 83 DK66
Murrays Yd, SE18 . . . . . 105 EP77
Murray Ter, NW3 off Flask Wk . . 64 DD63
W5 off Murray Rd 97 CK77
Murrells Wk, Lthd.
(Bkhm) KT23 . . . . . 170 CA123
Murreys, The, Ashtd. KT21 . . . 171 CK118
Mursell Est, SW8 . . . . . 101 DM81
Murthering La, Rom. RM4 . . . . 35 FG43
Murtwell Dr, Chig. IG7 . . . . . 49 EQ51
Musard Rd, W6 . . . . . 99 CY79
W14 . . . . . 99 CY79
Musbury St, E1 . . . . . 84 DW72
Muscal, W6 . . . . . 99 CY79
Muscatel Pl, SE5
off Dalwood St 102 DS81
Muschamp Rd, SE15 . . . . . 102 DT83
Carshalton SM5 . . . . . 140 DE103
Muscovy Ho, Erith DA18
off Kale Rd 106 EY75
Muscovy St, EC3 . . . . . 201 N1
★ Museum in Docklands,
E14 . . . . . 204 A1
★ Museum Interpretative Cen,
E6 . . . . . 87 EM70
Museum La, SW7
off Exhibition Rd 100 DD76
★ Museum of Artillery,
The Rotunda, SE18 . . . . . 105 EM78
★ Museum of Gdn History,
SE1 . . . . . 200 B7
★ Museum of Instruments,
Royal Coll of Music, SW7 . 100 DD76
★ Museum of London, EC2 . 197 H7
★ Museum of Richmond,
Rich. TW9 . . . . . 117 CK85
Museum Pas, E2
off Victoria Pk Sq 84 DV69
Museum St, WC1 . . . . . 195 P7
Musgrave Cl, Barn. EN4 . . . . . 28 DC39
Waltham Cross EN7
off Allwood Rd 14 DT27
Musgrave Cres, SW6 . . . . . 100 DA81
Musgrave Rd, Islw. TW7 . . . . . 97 CF81
Musgrove Rd, SE14 . . . . . 103 DX81
Musjid Rd, SW11
off Kambala Rd 100 DD82
Muskalls Cl, Wal.Cr.
(Chsht) EN7 . . . . . 14 DU27
Musket Cl, Barn. EN4
off East Barnet Rd 28 DD43
Musquash Way, Houns. TW4 . . 96 BW82
Mussenden La, Dart.
(Hort.Kir.) DA4 . . . . . 148 FQ99
Longfield (Fawk.Grn) DA3 . 149 FS101
Mustard Mill Rd, Stai. TW18
off High St 113 BE91
Muston Rd, E5 . . . . . 66 DV61
Mustow Pl, SW6
off Munster Rd 99 CZ82
Muswell Av, N10 . . . . . 45 DH54
MUSWELL HILL, N10 . . . . . 65 DH55
Muswell Hill, N10 . . . . . 65 DH55
Muswell Hill Bdy, N10 . . . . . 65 DH55
Muswell Hill Pl, N10 . . . . . 65 DH56
Muswell Hill Rd, N6 . . . . . 64 DG58
N10 . . . . . 64 DG56
Muswell Ms, N10
off Muswell Rd 65 DH55
Muswell Rd, N10 . . . . . 65 DH55
Mutchetts Cl, Wat. WD25 . . . . . 8 BY33
Mutrix Rd, NW6 . . . . . 82 DA67

★ Place of interest ⇌ Railway station ⊖ London Underground station DLR Docklands Light Railway station Tra Tramlink station H Hospital Riv Pedestrian ferry landing stage

Mutton La, Pot.B. EN6 11 CY31
Mutton Pl, NW1
off Harmood St. 83 DH65
Muybridge Rd, N.Mal. KT3 138 CQ96
Myatt Rd, SW9 101 DP81
Myatt's Flds N, SW9
off Eythorne Rd. 101 DN81
Mycenae Rd, SE3 104 EG80
Myddelton Av, Enf. EN1 30 DS38
Myddelton Cl, Enf. EN1 30 DT39
Myddelton Gdns, N21 45 DP45
Myddelton Pk, N20 44 DD48
Myddelton Pas, EC1 196 E2
Myddelton Rd, N8 65 DL56
Myddelton Sq, EC1 196 E2
Myddelton St, EC1 196 E3
Myddleton Av, N4 66 DQ61
Myddleton Ms, N22 45 DL52
Myddleton Path, Wal.Cr.
(Chsht) EN7 14 DV31
Myddleton Rd, N22 45 DL52
Uxbridge UB8 76 BJ67
Myers La, SE14 103 DX79
Mygrove Cl, Rain. RM13 90 FK68
Mygrove Gdns, Rain. RM13 90 FK68
Mygrove Rd, Rain. RM13 90 FK68
Myles Ct, Wal.Cr. EN7 14 DQ29
Mylis Cl, SE26 122 DV91
Mylius Cl, SE14
off Kender St. 102 DW81
Mylne Cl, Wal.Cr. EN8 14 DW27
Mylne St, EC1 196 D1
Mylor Cl, Wok. GU21 150 AY114
Mymms Dr, Hat. AL9 12 DA26
Mynns Cl, Epsom KT18 156 CP114
Mynterne Ct, SW19
off Swanton Gdns 119 CX88
Myra St, SE2 106 EU78
Myrdle St, E1 84 DU71
Myrke, The, Slou.
(Datchet) SL3 92 AT77
Myrna Cl, SW19 120 DE94
Myron Pl, SE13 103 EC83
Myrtle Av, Felt.TW14 95 BS84
Ruislip HA4 59 BU59
Myrtleberry Cl, E8
off Beechwood Rd 84 DT65
Myrtle Cl, Barn. EN4 44 DF46
Erith DA8 107 FE81
Slough (Colnbr.) SL3 93 BE81
Uxbridge UB8
off Violet Av. 76 BM71
West Drayton UB7 94 BM76
Myrtle Cres, Slou. SL2 74 AT73
Myrtledene Rd, SE2 106 EU78
Myrtle Gdns, W7 79 CE74
Myrtle Gro, Enf. EN2 30 DR38
New Malden KT3 138 CQ96
South Ockendon
(Aveley) RM15 108 FQ75
Myrtle Pl, Dart. DA2 129 FR87
Myrtle Rd, E6 86 EL67
E17 67 DY58
N13 46 DQ48
W3 80 CQ74
Brentwood CM14 54 FW49
Croydon CR0 143 EA104
Dartford DA1 128 FK88
Hampton (Hmptn H.) TW12 116 CC93
Hounslow TW3 96 CC82
Ilford IG1 69 EP61
Romford RM3 52 FJ51
Sutton SM1 158 DC106
Myrtleside Cl, Nthwd. HA6 39 BR52
Myrtle Wk, N1 197 M1
Mysore Rd, SW11 100 DF83
Myton Rd, SE21 122 DR90

N

N1 Shop Cen, N1 83 DN68
Nadine Ct, Wall. SM6
off Woodcote Rd. 159 DJ109
Nadine St, SE7 104 EJ78
Nafferton Ri, Loug. IG10 32 EK43
Nagle Cl, E17 47 ED54
Nag's Head Ct, EC1 197 H5
Nags Head La, Brwd. CM14 53 FR51
Upminster RM14 52 FQ53
Welling DA16 106 EV83
Nags Head Rd, Enf. EN3 30 DW42
Nags Head Shop Cen, N7 65 DM63
Nailsworth Cres, Red. RH1 185 DK129
Nailzee Cl, Ger.Cr. SL9 56 AY59
Nairn Ct, Til. RM18
off Dock Rd 111 GF82
Nairne Gro, SE24 122 DR85
Nairn Grn, Wat. WD19 39 BU48
Nairn Rd, Ruis. HA4 78 BW65
Nairn St, E14 85 EC71
Nallhead Rd, Felt.TW13 116 BW92
Namba Roy Cl, SW16 121 DM91
Namton Dr, Th.Hth. CR7 141 DM98
Nan Clark's La, NW7 43 CT47
Nancy Downs, Wat. WD19 40 BW45
Nankin St, E14 85 EA72
Nansen Rd, SW11 100 DG84
Gravesend DA12 131 GK91
Nansen Village, N12 44 DB49
Nantes Cl, SW18 100 DC84
Nantes Pas, E1 197 P6
Nant Rd, NW2 63 CZ61
Nant St, E2
off Cambridge Heath Rd. 84 DV69
Naoroji St, WC1 196 D3
Nap, The, Kings L. WD4 6 BN29
Napier Av, E14 204 A10
SW6 99 CZ83
Napier Cl, SE8
off Amersham Vale 103 DZ80
W14 off Napier Rd 99 CZ76
Hornchurch RM11 71 FH60
St. Albans (Lon.Col.) AL2 9 CK25
West Drayton UB7 94 BM76
Napier Ct, SW6
off Ranelagh Gdns 99 CZ83
Waltham Cross (Chsht) EN8
off Flamstead End Rd 14 DV28
Napier Dr, Bushey WD23 24 BY42
Napier Gro, N1 197 J1
Napier Ho, Rain. RM13 89 FF69
Napier Pl, W14 99 CZ76
Napier Rd, E6 87 EN67
E11 68 EE63
E15 86 EE68
N17 66 DS55
NW10 81 CV69
SE25 142 DV98
W14 99 CZ76
Ashford TW15 115 BR94
Belvedere DA17 106 EZ77
Bromley BR2 144 EH98
Enfield EN3 31 DX43
Gravesend (Nthflt) DA11 131 GF88
Hounslow (Hthrw Air.) TW6 94 BK81
Isleworth TW7 97 CG84
South Croydon CR2 160 DR108
Wembley HA0 61 CK64
Napier Ter, N1 83 DP66
Napier Wk, Ashf. TW15
off Napier Rd 115 BR94
Napoleon Rd, E5 66 DV62
Twickenham TW1 117 CH87
Napsbury Av, St.Alb.
(Lon.Col.) AL2 9 CJ26
Napton Cl, Hayes UB4
off Kingsash Dr. 78 BY70
Narbonne Av, SW4 121 DJ85
Narboro Ct, Rom. RM1
off Manor Rd. 71 FG57
Narborough Cl, Uxb. UB10
off Aylsham Dr 59 BQ61
Narborough St, SW6 100 DB82
Narcissus Rd, NW6 64 DA64
Narcot La, Ch.St.G. HP8 36 AU48
Gerrards Cross
(Chal.St.P.) SL9 36 AV52
Narcot Rd, Ch.St.G. HP8 36 AU48
Narcot Way, Ch.St.G. HP8 36 AU49
Nare Rd, S.Ock. (Aveley) RM15 90 FQ73
Naresby Fold, Stan. HA7 41 CJ51
Narford Rd, E5 66 DU62
Narrow Boat Cl, SE28
off Ridge Cl 105 ER75
Narrow La, Warl. CR6 176 DV119
Narrow St, E14 85 DY73
Narrow Way, Brom. BR2 144 EL100
Nascot Pl, Wat. WD17 23 BV39
Nascot Rd, Wat. WD17 23 BV40
Nascot St, W12 81 CW72
Watford WD17 23 BV40
Nascot Wd Rd, Wat. WD17 23 BT37
Naseberry Ct, E4
off Merriam Cl. 47 EC50
Naseby Cl, NW6 82 DC66
Isleworth TW7 97 CE81
Naseby Ct, Walt. KT12
off Clements Rd 136 BW103
Naseby Rd, SE19 122 DR93
Dagenham RM10 70 FA62
Ilford IG5 49 EM53
Nash Cl, Borwd. (Elstree) WD6 26 CM42
Sutton SM1 140 DD104
Nash Ct, E14 204 B3
Nash Cft, Grav. (Nthflt) DA11 130 GE91
Nash Dr, Red. RH1 184 DF132
Nash Gdns, Red. RH1 184 DF132
Nash Grn, Brom. BR1 124 EG93
Hemel Hempstead HP3 6 BM25
Nash La, Kes. BR2 162 EG106
Nash Mills La, Hem.H. HP3 6 BM26
Nash Rd, N9 46 DW47
SE4 103 DX84
Romford RM6 70 EX56
Slough SL3 93 AZ77
Nash St, NW1 195 J3
Nash's Yd, Uxb. UB8
off Bakers Rd 76 BK66
Nash Way, Har. HA3 61 CH58
Nasmyth St, W6 99 CV76
Nassau Path, SE28
off Disraeli Cl 88 EW74
Nassau Rd, SW13 99 CT81
Nassau St, W1 195 K7
Nassington Rd, NW3 64 DE63
Natalie Cl, Felt. TW14 115 BR87
Natalie Ms, Twick. TW2
off Sixth Cross Rd 117 CD90
Natal Rd, N11 45 DL51
SW16 121 DK93
Ilford IG1 69 EP63
Thornton Heath CR7 142 DR97
Nathan Cl, Upmin. RM14 73 FS60
Nathaniel Cl, E1
off Thrawl St 84 DT71
Nathans Rd, Wem. HA0 61 CJ60
Nathan Way, SE28 105 ES77
★ National Army Mus, SW3 100 DF79
H National Blood Service/
Brentwood Transfusion Cen,
Brwd. CM15 55 FZ46
★ National Gall, WC2 199 N1
H National Hosp for Neurology &
Neurosurgery, The, WC1 196 A5
★ National Maritime Mus,
SE10 103 ED79
★ National Portrait Gall,
WC2 199 N1
National Ter, SE16
off Bermondsey Wall E 102 DV75
Nation Way, E4 47 EC46
★ Natural History Mus,
SW7 100 DD76
Naunton Way, Horn. RM12 72 FK62
Naval Row, E14 85 EC73
Naval Wk, Brom. BR1
off High St. 144 EG97
Navarino Gro, E8 84 DU65
Navarino Rd, E8 84 DU65
Navarre Gdns, Rom. RM5 51 FB51
Navarre Rd, E6 86 EL68
Navarre St, E2 197 P4
Navenby Wk, E3
off Rounton Rd 85 EA70
Navestock Cl, E4
off Mapleton Rd 47 EC48
Navestock Cres, Wdf.Grn. IG8 48 EJ53
Navestock Ho, Bark. IG11 88 EV68
Navigator Dr, Sthl. UB2 96 CC75
Navigator Pk, Sthl. UB2
off Southall La 96 BW77
Navy St, SW4 101 DK83
Naxos Bldg, E14
off Hutchings St 103 EA75
Nayim Pl, E8 off Amhurst Rd 66 DV64
Naylor Gro, Enf. EN3
off South St. 31 DX43
Naylor Rd, N20 44 DC47
SE15 102 DV80
Naylor Ter, Slou. (Colnbr.) SL3
off Vicarage Way 93 BC80
Nazareth Gdns, SE15 102 DV82
NAZEING GATE, Wal.Abb. EN9 16 EJ25
Nazeing Wk, Rain. RM13
off Ongar Way 89 FE67
Nazrul St, E2 197 P2
Neagle Cl, Borwd. WD6
off Balcon Way 26 CQ39
Neal Av, Sthl. UB1 78 BZ70
Neal Cl, Ger.Cr. SL9 57 BB60
Northwood HA6 39 BU53
Neal Ct, Wal.Abb. EN9 16 EF33
Nealden St, SW9 101 DM83
Neale Cl, N2 64 DC55
Neal St, WC2 195 P9
Watford WD18 24 BW43
Neal's Yd, WC2 195 P9
Near Acre, NW9 43 CT53
NEASDEN, NW2 62 CS62
⊖ Neasden 62 CS64
Neasden Cl, NW10 62 CS64
Neasden La, NW10 62 CS63
Neasden La N, NW10 62 CR62
Neasham Rd, Dag. RM8 70 EV64
Neate St, SE5 102 DT79
Neath Gdns, Mord. SM4 140 DC100
Neathouse Pl, SW1 199 K8
Neats Acre, Ruis. HA4 59 BR59
Neatscourt Rd, E6 86 EK71
Neave Cres, Rom. RM3 52 FJ53
Neb La, Oxt. RH8 187 EC131
Nebraska St, SE1 201 K5
Neckinger, SE16 202 A6
Neckinger Est, SE16 202 A6
Neckinger St, SE1 202 A5
Nectarine Way, SE13 103 EB82
Needham Rd, W11
off Westbourne Gro 82 DA72
Needham Ter, NW2
off Kara Way 63 CX62
Needleman St, SE16 203 H5
Needles Bk, Gdse. RH9 186 DV131
Neela Cl, Uxb. UB10 59 BP63
Neeld Cres, NW4 63 CV57
Wembley HA9 62 CN64
Neeld Par, Wem. HA9
off Harrow Rd 62 CN64
Neil Cl, Ashf. TW15 115 BQ92
Neil Wates Cres, SW2 121 DN88
Nelgarde Rd, SE6 123 EA87
Nella Rd, W6 99 CX79
Nelldale Rd, SE16 202 F8
Nellgrove Rd, Uxb. UB10 77 BP70
Nell Gwynn Cl, Rad.
(Shenley) WD7 10 CL32
Nell Gwynne Av, Shep. TW17 135 BR100
Nell Gwynne Cl, Epsom KT19 156 CN111
Nello James Gdns, SE27 122 DR91
Nelmes Cl, Horn. RM11 72 FM57
Nelmes Cres, Horn. RM11 72 FL57
Nelmes Rd, Horn. RM11 72 FL59
Nelmes Way, Horn. RM11 72 FL56
Nelson Cl, NW6 82 DA68
Brentwood (Warley) CM14 54 FX50
Croydon CR0 141 DP102
Feltham TW14 115 BT88
Romford RM7 51 FB53
Slough SL3 92 AX77
Uxbridge UB10 77 BP69
Walton-on-Thames KT12 135 BV102
Westerham (Bigg.H.) TN16 178 EL117
Nelson Ct, SE16
off Brunel Rd 84 DW74
Nelson Gdns, E2 84 DU69
Hounslow TW3 116 CA86
Nelson Gro Rd, SW19 140 DB95
H Nelson Hosp, SW20 139 CZ96
Nelson La, Uxb. UB10
off Nelson Rd 77 BP69
Nelson Mandela Cl, N10 44 DG54
Nelson Mandela Rd, SE3 104 EJ83
Nelson Pas, EC1 197 J3
Nelson Pl, N1 196 G1
Sidcup DA14 126 EU91
Nelson Rd, E4 47 EB51
E11 68 EG56
N8 65 DM57
N9 46 DV47
N15 66 DS56
SE10 103 EC79
SW19 120 DB94
Ashford TW15 114 BL92
Belvedere DA17 106 EZ78
Bromley BR2 144 EJ98
Caterham CR3 176 DR123
Dartford DA1 128 FJ86
Enfield EN3 31 DX44
Gravesend (Nthflt) DA11 131 GF89
Harrow HA1 61 CD60
Hounslow TW3, TW4 116 CA86
Hounslow (Hthrw Air.) TW6 94 BM81
New Malden KT3 138 CR99
Rainham RM13 89 FF68
Sidcup DA14 126 EU91
South Ockendon RM15 91 FW68
Stanmore HA7 41 CJ51
Twickenham TW2 116 CC86
Uxbridge UB10 77 BP69
★ Nelson's Column, WC2 199 P2
Nelson Sq, SE1 200 F4
Nelson's Row, SW4 101 DK84
Nelson St, E1 84 DV72
E6 87 EM68
E16 off Huntingdon St 86 EF73
Nelsons Yd, NW1
off Mornington Cres 83 DJ68
Nelson Ter, N1 196 G1
Nelson Trd Est, SW19 140 DB95
Nelson Wk, SE16 203 L3
Epsom KT19 156 CN109
Nelwyn Av, Horn. RM11 72 FM57
Nemoure Rd, W3 80 CQ73
Nene Gdns, Felt. TW13 116 BZ89
Nene Rd, Houns.
(Hthrw Air.) TW6 95 BP81
Nepaul Rd, SW11 100 DE82
Nepean St, SW15 119 CU86
Neptune Cl, Rain. RM13
off Rainham Rd 89 FF68
Neptune Ct, Borwd. WD6
off Clarendon Rd 26 CN41
Neptune Rd, Har. HA1 61 CD58
Hounslow
(Hthrw Air.) TW6 95 BR81
Neptune St, SE16 202 F6
Neptune Wk, Erith DA8 107 FD77
Nero Ct, Brent. TW8
off Justin Cl 97 CK80
Nesbit Rd, SE9 104 EK84
Nesbitt Cl, SE3
off Hurren Cl 104 EE83
Nesbitts All, Barn. EN5
off Bath Pl 27 CZ41
Nesbitt Sq, SE19
off Coxwell Rd 122 DS94
Nesham St, E1 202 B2
Ness Rd, Erith DA8 108 FK79
Ness St, SE16 202 B6
Nesta Rd, Wdf.Grn. IG8 48 EE51
Nestles Av, Hayes UB3 95 BT76
Neston Rd, Wat. WD24 24 BW37
Nestor Av, N21 29 DP44
Nethan Dr, S.Ock.
(Aveley) RM15 90 FQ73
Netheravon Rd, W4 99 CT77
W7 79 CF74
Netheravon Rd S, W4 99 CT78
Netherbury Rd, W5 97 CK76
Netherby Gdns, Enf. EN2 29 DL42
Netherby Pk, Wey. KT13 153 BS106
Netherby Rd, SE23 122 DW87
Nether Cl, N3 44 DA52
Nethercote Av, Wok. GU21 166 AT117
Nethercourt Av, N3 44 DA51
Netherfield Gdns, Bark. IG11 87 ER65
Netherfield Rd, N12 44 DB50
SW17 120 DG90
Netherford Rd, SW4 101 DJ82
Netherhall Gdns, NW3 82 DC65
Netherhall Way, NW3
off Netherhall Gdns 64 DC64
Netherlands, The, Couls. CR5 175 DJ119
Netherlands Rd, Barn. EN5 28 DD44
Netherleigh Cl, N6 65 DH60
Nethern Ct Rd, Cat.
(Wold.) CR3 177 EA123
Netherne Dr, Couls. CR5 175 DH121
Netherne La, Couls. CR5 175 DK121
Redhill RH1 175 DJ123
Netherpark Dr, Rom. RM2 51 FF54
Nether St, N3 44 DA53
N12 44 DA50
Netherton Gro, SW10 100 DC79
Netherton Rd, N15 66 DR58
Twickenham TW1 117 CH85
Netherwood, N2 44 DD54
Netherwood Pl, W14
off Netherwood Rd 99 CX76
Netherwood Rd, W14 99 CX76
Netherwood St, NW6 81 CZ66
Netley Cl, Croy.
(New Adgtn) CR0 161 EC108
Sutton SM3 157 CX106
Netley Dr, Walt. KT12 136 BZ101
Netley Gdns, Mord. SM4 140 DC101
Netley Rd, E17 67 DZ57
Brentford TW8 98 CL79
Hounslow
(Hthrw Air.) TW6 95 BR81
Ilford IG2 69 ER57
Morden SM4 140 DC101
Netley St, NW1 195 K3
Nettlecombe Cl, Sutt. SM2 158 DB109
Nettleden Av, Wem. HA9 80 CN65
Nettlefold Pl, SE27 121 DP90
Nettlestead Cl, Beck. BR3
off Copers Cope Rd 123 DZ94
Nettleton Rd, SE14 103 DX81
Hounslow
(Hthrw Air.) TW6 95 BP81
Uxbridge UB10 58 BM63
Nettlewood Rd, SW16 121 DK94
Neuchatel Rd, SE6 123 DZ89
Nevada Cl, N.Mal. KT3
off Georgia Rd 138 CQ98
Nevada St, SE10 103 EC79
Nevell Rd, Grays RM16 111 GH76
Nevern Pl, SW5 100 DA77
Nevern Rd, SW5 100 DA77
Nevern Sq, SW5 100 DA77
Nevil Cl, Nthwd. HA6 39 BQ50
Neville Av, N.Mal. KT3 138 CR95
Neville Cl, E11 68 EF62
NW1 195 N1
NW6 81 CZ68
SE15 102 DU80
W3 off Acton La 98 CQ75
Banstead SM7 158 DB114
Esher KT10 154 BZ107
Hounslow TW3 96 CB82
Potters Bar EN6 11 CZ31
Sidcup DA15 125 ET91
Slough (Stoke P.) SL2 74 AT65
Neville Dr, N2 64 DC58
Neville Gdns, Dag. RM8 70 EX62
Neville Gill Cl, SW18 120 DA86
Neville Pl, N22 45 DM53
Neville Rd, E7 86 EG66
NW6 81 CZ68
W5 79 CK70
Croydon CR0 142 DR101
Dagenham RM8 70 EX61
Ilford IG6 49 EQ53
Kingston upon Thames KT1 138 CN96
Richmond TW10 117 CJ90
Nevilles Ct, NW2 63 CU62
Neville St, SW7 100 DD78
Neville Ter, SW7 100 DD78
Neville Wk, Cars. SM5
off Green Wrythe La 140 DE101
Nevill Gro, Wat. WD24 23 BV39
Nevill Rd, N16 66 DS63
Nevill Way, Loug. IG10
off Valley Hill 48 EL45
Nevin Dr, E4 47 EB46
Nevinson Cl, SW18 120 DD86
Nevis Cl, Rom. RM1 51 FE51
Nevis Rd, SW17 120 DG89
New Acres Rd, SE28 105 ES75
NEW ADDINGTON,
Croy. CR0 161 ED109
Tra New Addington 161 EC110
Newall Rd, Houns.
(Hthrw Air.) TW6 95 BQ81
New Arc, Uxb. UB8
off High St. 76 BK67
Newark Cl, Wok.
(Ripley) GU23 168 BG121
Newark Cotts, Wok.
(Ripley) GU23 168 BG121
Newark Ct, Walt. KT12
off St. Johns Dr. 136 BW102
Newark Cres, NW10 80 CR69
Newark Grn, Borwd. WD6 26 CR41
Newark Knok, E6 87 EN72
Newark La, Wok.
(Ripley) GU23 167 BF118
Newark Par, NW4
off Greyhound Hill 63 CU55
Newark Rd, S.Croy. CR2 160 DR107
Newark St, E1 84 DV71
Newark Way, NW4 63 CU56
New Ash Cl, N2
off Oakridge Dr 64 DD55
NEW ASH GREEN, Long. DA3 149 FX103
New Atlas Wf, E14 203 N7
New Barn Cl, Wall. SM6 159 DM107
NEW BARNET, Barn. EN5 28 DB42
⇌ New Barnet 28 DD43
New Barn La, Beac. HP9 36 AS49
Sevenoaks (Cudham) TN14 179 EQ116
Westerham TN16 179 EQ118
Whyteleafe CR3 176 DS117
New Barn Rd, Grav.
(Sthflt) DA13 130 GC90
Swanley BR8 147 FE95
New Barns Av, Mitch. CR4 141 DK98
New Barn St, E13 86 EG70
New Barns Way, Chig. IG7 49 EP48
New Battlebridge La,
Red. RH1 185 DH130
NEW BECKENHAM,
Beck. BR3 123 DZ93
⇌ New Beckenham 123 DZ94
Newberries Av, Rad. WD7 25 CJ35
New Berry La, Walt. KT12 154 BX106
Newbery Rd, Erith DA8 107 FF81
Newbiggin Path, Wat. WD19 40 BW49
Newbolt Av, Sutt. SM3 157 CW106
Newbolt Rd, Stan. HA7 41 CF51
New Bond St, W1 195 H9
Newborough Grn, N.Mal. KT3 138 CR98
New Brent St, NW4 63 CW57
Newbridge Pt, SE23
off Windrush La 123 DX90
New Br St, EC4 196 F9
New Broad St, EC2 197 M7
New Bdy, W5 79 CJ73
Hampton (Hmptn H.) TW12
off Hampton Rd 117 CD92
New Bdy Bldgs, W5
off New Bdy 79 CK73
Newburgh Rd, W3 80 CQ74
Grays RM17 110 GD78
Newburgh St, W1 195 K9
New Burlington Ms, W1 195 K10
New Burlington Pl, W1 195 K10
New Burlington St, W1 195 K10
Newburn St, SE11 101 DM78
Newbury Av, Enf. EN3 31 DZ38
Newbury Cl, Dart. DA2
off Lingfield Av 128 FP87
Northolt UB5 78 BZ65
Romford RM3 52 FK51
Newbury Gdns, Epsom KT19 157 CT105
Romford RM3 52 FK51
Upminster RM14 72 FM62
Newbury Ho, N22 45 DL53
Newbury Ms, NW5
off Malden Rd 82 DG65
NEWBURY PARK, Ilf. IG2 69 ER57
⊖ Newbury Park 69 ER58
Newbury Rd, E4 47 EC51
Bromley BR2 144 EG97
Hounslow
(Hthrw Air.) TW6 94 BM81
Ilford IG2 69 ER58
Romford RM3 52 FK50
Newbury St, EC1 197 H7
Newbury Wk, Rom. RM3 52 FK50
Newbury Way, Nthlt. UB5 78 BY65
New Butt La, SE8 103 EA80
New Butt La N, SE8
off Reginald Rd 103 EA80
Newby Cl, Enf. EN1 30 DS40
Newby Pl, E14 85 EC73
Newby St, SW8 101 DH83
New Caledonian Wf, SE16 203 M6
Newcastle Av, Ilf. IG6 50 EU51
Newcastle Cl, EC4 196 F8
Newcastle Pl, W2 194 A7
Newcastle Row, EC1 196 E4
New Cavendish St, W1 195 J6
New Change, EC4 197 H9
New Chapel Sq, Felt. TW13 115 BV88
New Charles St, EC1 196 G2
NEW CHARLTON, SE7 104 EJ77
New Ch Ct, SE19
off Waldegrave Rd 122 DU94
New Ch Rd, SE5 102 DQ80
New City Rd, E13 86 EJ69
New Cl, SW19 140 DC97
Feltham TW13 116 BY92

★ Place of interest ⇌ Railway station ⊖ London Underground station DLR Docklands Light Railway station Tra Tramlink station H Hospital Riv Pedestrian ferry landing stage

297

New Coll Ct, NW3
off Finchley Rd 82 DC65
New Coll Ms, N1
off Islington Pk St 83 DN66
New Coll Par, NW3
off Finchley Rd 82 DD65
Newcombe Gdns, SW16 121 DL91
Hounslow TW4
off Wellington Rd S 96 BZ84
Newcombe Pk, NW7 42 CS50
Wembley HA0 80 CM67
Newcombe Ri, West Dr. UB7 76 BL72
Newcombe St, W8
off Kensington Pl 82 DA74
Newcomen Rd, E11 68 EF62
SW11 100 DD83
Newcomen St, SE1 201 K4
Newcome Path, Rad. (Shenley) WD7
off Newcome Rd 10 CN34
Newcome Rd, Rad. (Shenley)
WD7 10 CN34
New Compton St, WC2 195 N9
New Concordia Wf, SE1 202 B4
New Coppice, Wok. GU21 166 AS119
New Cotts, Rain.
(Wenn.) RM13 90 FJ72
New Ct, EC4 196 D10
Addlestone KT15 134 BJ104
Newcourt, Uxb. UB8 76 BJ71
Newcourt St, NW8 194 B1
★ New Covent Garden
Flower Mkt, SW8 101 DK79
★ New Covent Garden Mkt,
SW8 101 DK80
New Crane Pl, E1 202 F2
Newcroft Cl, Uxb. UB8 76 BM71
NEW CROSS, SE14 103 DY81
⇌ New Cross 103 DZ80
⊖ New Cross 103 DZ80
NEW CROSS GATE, SE14 103 DX81
⇌ New Cross Gate 103 DY81
⊖ New Cross Gate 103 DY81
New Cross Rd, SE14 102 DW80
Newdales Cl, N9
off Balham Rd 46 DU47
Newdene Av, Nthlt. UB5 78 BX68
Newdigate Grn, Uxb.
(Hare.) UB9 38 BK53
Newdigate Rd, Uxb.
(Hare.) UB9 38 BJ53
Newdigate Rd E, Uxb.
(Hare.) UB9 38 BK53
Newell St, E14 85 DZ72
NEW ELTHAM, SE9 125 EN89
⇌ New Eltham 125 EP88
New End, NW3 64 DC63
New End Sq, NW3 64 DD63
Newent Cl, SE15 102 DS80
Carshalton SM5 140 DF102
New Fm Av, Brom. BR2 144 EG98
New Fm Cl, Stai. TW18
off Ashford Rd 134 BK95
New Fm Dr, Rom.
(Abridge) RM4 34 EV41
New Fm La, Nthwd. HA6 39 BS53
New Ferry App, SE18 105 EN76
New Fetter La, EC4 196 E8
Newfield Cl, Hmptn. TW12
off Percy Rd 136 CA95
Newfield Ri, NW2 63 CV62
New Ford Rd, Wal.Cr. EN8 15 DZ34
New Forest La, Chig. IG7 49 EN51
Newgale Gdns, Edg. HA8 42 CM53
New Gdn Dr, West Dr. UB7
off Drayton Gdns 94 BL75
Newgate, Croy. CR0 142 DQ102
Newgate Cl, Felt. TW13 116 BY89
Newgate St, E4 48 EF48
EC1 196 G8
Newgatestreet Rd, Wal.Cr.
(Chsht) EN7 13 DP27
Newgate St Village,
Hert. SG13 13 DL25
New Globe Wk, SE1 201 H2
New Goulston St, E1 197 P8
New Grn Pl, SE19
off Hawke Rd 122 DS93
New Hall Cl, Hem.H. (Bov.) HP3 5 BA27
Newhall Ct, Wal.Abb. EN9 16 EF33
New Hall Dr, Rom. RM3 52 FL53
Newhall Gdns, Walt. KT12
off Rodney Rd 136 BW103
H Newham Gen Hosp, E13 86 EJ70
Newhams Row, SE1 201 N5
Newham Way, E6 86 EJ71
E16 86 EF71
Newhaven Cl, Hayes UB3 95 BT77
Newhaven Cres, Ashf. TW15 115 BR92
Newhaven Gdns, SE9 104 EK84
Newhaven La, E16 86 EF70
Newhaven Rd, SE25 142 DR99
NEW HAW, Add. KT15 152 BK108
New Haw Rd, Add. KT15 152 BJ106
New Heston Rd, Houns. TW5 96 BZ80
New Horizons Ct, Brent. TW8
off Shield Dr 97 CG79
Newhouse Av, Rom. RM6 70 EX55
Newhouse Cl, N.Mal. KT3 138 CS101
Newhouse Cres, Wat. WD25 7 BV32
New Ho La, Grav. DA11 131 GF90
Newhouse Rd, Hem.H.
(Bov.) HP3 5 BA26
Newhouse Wk, Mord. SM4 140 DC101
Newick Cl, Bex. DA5 127 FB86
Newick Rd, E5 66 DV62
Newing Grn, Brom. BR1 124 EK94
NEWINGTON, SE1 201 H8
Newington Barrow Way, N7 65 DM62
Newington Butts, SE1 200 G9
SE11 200 G9
Newington Causeway, SE1 200 G7
Newington Grn, N1 66 DR64
N16 66 DR64
Newington Grn Rd, N1 84 DR65
New Inn Bdy, EC2 197 N4
New Inn Pas, WC2 196 C9
New Inn Sq, EC2 197 N4
New Inn St, EC2 197 N4
New Inn Yd, EC2 197 N4
New James Ct, SE15
off Nunhead La 102 DV83
New Jersey Ter, SE15
off Nunhead La 102 DV83
New Jubilee Ct, Wdf.Grn. IG8
off Grange Av 48 EG52
New Kent Rd, SE1 201 H7
New Kings Rd, SW6 99 CZ82
New King St, SE8 103 EA79
Newland Cl, Pnr. HA5 40 BY51
Newland Ct, Wem. HA9
off Forty Av 62 CN61
Newland Dr, Enf. EN1 30 DV39
Newland Gdns, W13 97 CG75
Newland Rd, N8 65 DL55
Newlands, Abb.L.
(Bedmond) WD5 7 BT26
Newlands, The, Wall. SM6 159 DJ108
Newlands Av, Rad. WD7 9 CF34
Thames Ditton KT7 137 CE102
Woking GU22 167 AZ121
Newlands Cl, Brwd.
(Hutt.) CM13 55 GD45
Edgware HA8 42 CL48
Southall UB2 96 BY78
Walton-on-Thames KT12 154 BY105
Wembley HA0 79 CJ65
Newlands Ct, SE9 125 EN86
Newlands Dr, Slou.
(Colnbr.) SL3 93 BE83
Newlands Pk, SE26 123 DX92
Newlands Pl, Barn. EN5 27 CX43
Newlands Quay, E1 202 F1
Newlands Rd, SW16 141 DL96
Woodford Green IG8 48 EF47
Newland St, E16 86 EL74
Newlands Wk, Wat. WD25
off Trevellance Way 8 BX33
Newlands Way, Chess. KT9 155 CJ106
Potters Bar EN6 12 DB30
Newlands Wd, Croy. CR0 161 DZ109
New La, Guil. (Sutt.Grn) GU4 166 AY122
Newling Cl, E6 off Porter Rd 87 EM72
New Lo Dr, Oxt. RH8 188 EF128
New London St, EC3 197 N10
New Lydenburg St, SE7 104 EJ76
Newlyn Cl, Orp. BR6 163 ET105
St. Albans (Brick.Wd) AL2 8 BY30
Uxbridge UB8 76 BN71
Newlyn Gdns, Har. HA2 60 BZ59
Newlyn Rd, N17 46 DT53
NW2 off Tilling Rd 63 CW60
Barnet EN5 27 CZ42
Welling DA16 105 ET82
NEW MALDEN 138 CR97
⇌ New Malden 138 CS97
Newman Cl, Horn. RM11 72 FL57
Newman Pas, W1 195 L7
Newman Rd, E13 86 EH69
E17 off Southcote Rd 67 DX57
Bromley BR1 144 EG95
Croydon CR0 141 DM102
Hayes UB3 77 BV73
Newmans Cl, Loug. IG10 33 EP41
Newman's Ct, EC3 197 L9
Newmans Dr, Brwd.
(Hutt.) CM13 55 GC45
Newmans La, Loug. IG10 33 EN41
Surbiton KT6 137 CK100
Newmans Rd, Grav.
(Nthflt) DA11 131 GF89
Newman's Row, WC2 196 C7
Newman St, W1 195 L7
Newmans Way, Barn. EN4 28 DC39
Newman Yd, W1 195 M8
Newmarket Av, Nthlt. UB5 60 CA64
Newmarket Grn, SE9
off Middle Pk Av 124 EK87
Newmarket Way, Horn. RM12 72 FL63
Newmarsh Rd, SE28 87 ET74
New Mill Rd, Orp. BR5 146 EW95
Newminster Rd, Mord. SM4 140 DC100
New Mt St, E15 85 ED66
Newnes Path, SW15
off Putney Pk La 99 CV84
Newnham Av, Ruis. HA4 60 BW60
Newnham Cl, Loug. IG10 32 EK44
Northolt UB5 60 CC64
Slough SL2 74 AU74
Thornton Heath CR7 142 DQ96
Newnham Gdns, Nthlt. UB5 60 CC64
Newnham Ms, N22
off Newnham Rd 45 DM53
Newnham Pl, Grays RM16 111 GG77
Newnham Rd, N22 45 DM53
Newnhams Cl, Brom. BR1 145 EM97
Newnham Ter, SE1 200 D6
Newnham Way, Har. HA3 62 CL57
New N Pl, EC2 197 M5
New N Rd, N1 197 L1
Ilford IG6 49 ER52
New N St, WC1 196 B6
Newnton Cl, N4 66 DR59
New Oak Rd, N2 44 DC54
New Orleans Wk, N19 65 DK59
New Oxford St, WC1 195 N8
New Par, Ashf. TW15
off Church Rd 114 BM91
Rickmansworth WD3
off The Green 22 BM44
Rickmansworth (Chorl.) WD3
off Whitelands Av 21 BC42
New Par Flats, Rick. (Chorl.) WD3
off Whitelands Av 21 BC42
New Pk Av, N13 46 DQ48
New Pk Cl, Nthlt. UB5 78 BY65
New Pk Ct, SW2 121 DL87
New Pk Par, SW2
off Doverfield Rd 121 DL86
New Pk Rd, SW2 121 DK88
Ashford TW15 115 BQ92
Uxbridge (Hare.) UB9 38 BJ53
New Peachey La, Uxb. UB8 76 BK72
Newpiece, Loug. IG10 33 EP41
New Pl Gdns, Upmin. RM14 73 FR61
New Pl Sq, SE16 202 D6
New Plaistow Rd, E15 86 EE67
New Plymouth Ho,
Rain. RM13 89 FF69
Newport Av, E13 86 EH70
E14 85 ED73
Newport Cl, Enf. EN3 31 DY37
Newport Ct, WC2 195 N10
Newport Mead, Wat. WD19
off Kilmarnock Rd 40 BX49
Newport Pl, WC2 195 N10
Newport Rd, E10 67 EC61
E17 67 DY56
SW13 99 CU81
Hayes UB4 77 BR71
Hounslow (Hthrw Air.) TW6 94 BN81
Newports, Swan. BR8 147 FD101
Newport St, SE11 200 B9
New Printing Ho Sq, WC1
off Gray's Inn Rd 83 DM70
New Priory Ct, NW6
off Mazenod Av 82 DA66
New Providence Wf, E14
off Blackwall Way 85 ED74
Newquay Cres, Har. HA2 60 BY61
Newquay Gdns, Wat. WD19
off Fulford Gro 39 BV47
Newquay Rd, SE6 123 EB89
New Quebec St, W1 194 E9
New Ride, SW7 198 D4
New River Ct, N5 66 DR63
Waltham Cross (Chsht) EN7
off Pengelly Cl 14 DV30
New River Cres, N13 45 DP49
New River Head, EC1 196 E2
New River Trd Est, Wal.Cr.
(Chsht) EN8 15 DX26
New River Wk, N1 66 DQ65
New River Way, N4 66 DR59
New Rd, E1 84 DV71
E4 47 EB49
N8 65 DL57
N9 46 DU48
N17 46 DT53
N22 46 DQ53
NW7 43 CY52
NW7 (Barnet Gate) 43 CT45
SE2 106 EX77
Amersham HP6 20 AS37
Borehamwood
(Elstree) WD6 25 CK44
Brentford TW8 97 CK79
Brentwood CM14 54 FX47
Chalfont St. Giles HP8 20 AY41
Chertsey KT16 133 BF101
Dagenham RM9, RM10 88 FA67
Dartford (S.Darenth) DA4 148 FQ96
Epping CM16 18 FA32
Esher KT10 136 CC104
Esher (Clay.) KT10 155 CF110
Feltham TW14 115 BV88
Feltham (E.Bed.) TW14 115 BR86
Feltham (Han.) TW13 116 BY92
Gravesend DA11 131 GH86
Grays RM17 110 GA79
Grays (Manor Way) RM17 110 GB79
Harrow HA1 61 CF63
Hayes UB3 95 BQ80
Hounslow TW3
off Station Rd 96 CB84
Ilford IG3 69 ES61
Kings Langley
(Chipper.) WD4 5 BF30
Kingston upon Thames KT2 118 CN94
Leatherhead KT22 155 CF110
Mitcham CR4 140 DF102
Orpington BR6 146 EU101
Oxted (Lmpfld) RH8 188 EH130
Potters Bar (S.Mimms) EN6 11 CU33
Radlett WD7 25 CE36
Radlett (Shenley) WD7 10 CN34
Rainham RM13 89 FG69
Richmond TW10 117 CJ91
Rickmansworth
(Ch.End) WD3 21 BF39
Rickmansworth
(Crox.Grn) WD3 22 BN43
Romford (Abridge) RM4 34 EX44
Sevenoaks (Sund.) TN14 180 EX124
Shepperton TW17 135 BP97
Slough (Datchet) SL3 92 AX81
Slough (Langley) SL3 93 BA76
Staines TW18 113 BC92
Swanley BR8 147 FF97
Swanley (Hext.) BR8 127 FF94
Tadworth KT20 173 CW123
Uxbridge UB8 77 BQ70
Watford WD17 24 BW42
Watford (Let.Hth) WD25 25 CE39
Welling DA16 106 EV82
West Molesey KT8 136 CA97
Weybridge KT13 153 BQ106
New Rd Hill, Kes. BR2 162 EL109
Orpington BR6 162 EL109
New Row, WC2 195 P10
Newry Rd, Twick. TW1 97 CG84
Newsam Av, N15 66 DR57
★ New Scotland Yd, SW1 199 M6
Newsham Rd, Wok. GU21 166 AT117
Newsholme Dr, N21 29 DM43
NEW SOUTHGATE, N11 45 DK49
⇌ New Southgate 45 DH50
New Spring Gdns Wk, SE11
off Goding St 101 DL78
New Sq, WC2 196 C8
Feltham TW14 115 BQ88
Slough SL1 92 AT75
New Sq Pas, WC2 off New Sq 83 DM72
Newstead Av, Orp. BR6 145 ER104
Newstead Ri, Cat. CR3 186 DV126
Newstead Rd, SE12 124 EE87
Newstead Wk, Cars. SM5 140 DC101
Newstead Way, SW19 119 CX91
New St, EC2 197 N7
Staines TW18 114 BG91
Watford WD18 24 BW42
Westerham TN16 189 EQ127
New St Hill, Brom. BR1 124 EH92
New St Sq, EC4 196 E8
New Swan Yd, Grav. DA12
off Bank St 131 GH86
Newteswell Dr,
Wal.Abb. EN9 15 ED32
Newton Abbot Rd, Grav.
(Nthflt) DA11 131 GF89
Newton Av, N10 44 DG53
W3 98 CQ75
Newton Cl, E17 67 DY58
Harrow HA2 60 CA61
Slough SL3 93 AZ75
Newton Ct, Wind.
(Old Wind.) SL4 112 AU86
Newton Cres, Borwd. WD6 26 CQ42
Newton Gro, W4 98 CS77
Newton Ho, Enf. EN3
off Exeter Rd 31 DX41
Newton La, Wind.
(Old Wind.) SL4 112 AV86
Newton Pl, E14 203 P8
Newton Rd, E15 67 ED64
N15 66 DT57
NW2 63 CW62
SW19 119 CY94
W2 82 DA72
Chigwell IG7 50 EV50
Harrow HA3 41 CE54
Isleworth TW7 97 CF82
Purley CR8 159 DJ112
Tilbury RM18 111 GG82
Welling DA16 106 EU83
Wembley HA0 80 CM66
Newtons Cl, Rain. RM13 89 FF66
Newtons Ct, Dart. DA2 109 FR84
Newtonside Orchard,
Wind. SL4 112 AU86
Newton St, WC2 196 A8
Newtons Yd, SW18
off Wandsworth High St 120 DB85
Newton Wk, Edg. HA8
off North Rd 42 CP53
Newton Way, N18 46 DQ50
Newton Wd, Ashtd. KT21 156 CL114
Newton Wd Rd, Ashtd. KT21 172 CM116
NEW TOWN, Dart. DA1 128 FN86
Newtown Rd, Uxb.
(Denh.) UB9 76 BH65
Newtown St, SW11
off Strasburg Rd 101 DH81
New Trinity Rd, N2 64 DD55
New Turnstile, WC1 196 B7
New Union Cl, E14 204 E6
New Union St, EC2 197 K7
H New Victoria Hosp,
Kings.T. KT2 138 CS95
New Wanstead, E11 68 EF58
New Way Rd, NW9 62 CS56
New Wf Rd, N1 83 DL68
New Wickham La, Egh. TW20 113 BA94
New Windsor St, Uxb. UB8 76 BJ67
NEWYEARS GREEN,
Uxb. UB9 58 BN59
New Years Grn La,
Uxb. (Hare.) UB9 58 BL58
New Years La, Orp. BR6 164 EU114
Sevenoaks (Knock.) TN14 179 ET116
New Zealand Av, Walt. KT12 135 BT102
New Zealand Way, W12 81 CV73
Rainham RM13 89 FF69
Niagara Av, W5 97 CJ77
Niagara Cl, N1
off Cropley St 84 DR68
Waltham Cross (Chsht) EN8 15 DX29
Nibthwaite Rd, Har. HA1 61 CE57
Nicholas Cl, Grnf. UB6 78 CB68
South Ockendon RM15 91 FW69
Watford WD24 23 BV37
Nicholas Ct, E13
off Tunmarsh La 86 EH69
Nicholas Gdns, W5 97 CK75
Woking GU22 167 BE116
Nicholas La, EC4 197 L10
Nicholas Ms, W4
off Short Rd 98 CS79
Nicholas Pas, EC4 197 L10
Nicholas Rd, E1 84 DW70
Borehamwood
(Elstree) WD6 26 CM44
Croydon CR0 159 DL105
Dagenham RM8 70 EZ61
Nicholas Wk, Grays RM16
off Godman Rd 111 GH75
Nicholas Way, Nthwd. HA6 39 BQ53
Nicholay Rd, N19 65 DK60
Nichol Cl, N14 45 DK46
Nicholes Rd, Houns. TW3 96 CA84
Nichol La, Brom. BR1 124 EG94
Nicholl Rd, Epp. CM16 17 ET31
Nicholls Av, Uxb. UB8 76 BN70
Nichollsfield Wk, N7
off Hillmarton Rd 65 DM64
Nicholls Pt, E15
off Park Gro 86 EG67
Nicholl St, E2 84 DU67
Nichols Cl, N4
off Osborne Rd 65 DN60
Chessington KT9
off Merritt Gdns 155 CJ107
Nichols Ct, E2 197 P1
Nichols Grn, W5
off Montpelier Rd 80 CL71
Nicholson Ms, Egh. TW20
off Nicholson Wk 113 BA92
Nicholson Rd, Croy. CR0 142 DT102
Nicholson St, SE1 200 F3
Nicholson Wk, Egh. TW20 113 BA92
Nicholson Way, Sev. TN13 191 FK122
Nickelby Cl, SE28 88 EW72
Uxbridge UB8
off Dickens Av 77 BP72
Nickols Wk, SW18
off Jew's Row 100 DB84
Nicola Cl, Har. HA3 41 CD54
South Croydon CR2 160 DQ107
Nicola Ms, Ilf. IG6 49 EP52
Nicol Cl, Ger.Cr.
(Chal.St.P.) SL9 36 AX53
Twickenham TW1
off Cassilis Rd 117 CH86
Nicol End, Ger.Cr.
(Chal.St.P.) SL9 36 AW53
Nicoll Pl, NW4 63 CV58
Nicoll Rd, NW10 80 CS67
Nicoll Way, Borwd. WD6 26 CR43
Nicol Rd, Ger.Cr.
(Chal.St.P.) SL9 36 AW53
Nicolson Dr, Bushey
(Bushey Hth) WD23 40 CC46
Nicolson Rd, Orp. BR5 146 EX101
Nicosia Rd, SW18 120 DE87
Niederwald Rd, SE26 123 DY91
Nield Rd, Hayes UB3 95 BT75
Nield Way, Rick. WD3
off Thellusson Way 37 BF45
Nigel Cl, Nthlt. UB5
off Church Rd 78 BY67
Nigel Fisher Way, Chess. KT9 155 CJ108
Nigel Ms, Ilf. IG1 69 EP63
Nigel Playfair Av, W6
off King St 99 CV77
Nigel Rd, E7 68 EJ64
SE15 102 DU83
Nigeria Rd, SE7 104 EJ80
Nightingale Av, E4 48 EE50
Harrow HA1 61 CH59
Leatherhead
(W.Hors.) KT24 169 BR124
Upminster RM14 73 FT60
Nightingale Cl, E4 48 EE49
W4 off Grove Pk Ter 98 CQ79
Abbots Langley WD5 7 BU31
Carshalton SM5 140 DG103
Cobham KT11 154 BX111
Epsom KT19 156 CN112
Gravesend (Nthflt) DA11 130 GE91
Pinner HA5 60 BW57
Radlett WD7 25 CF36
Nightingale Ct, E11
off Nightingale La 68 EH57
Slough SL1
off St. Laurence Way 92 AU76
Nightingale Cres, Lthd.
(W.Hors.) KT24 169 BQ124
Romford RM3 off Lister Av 52 FL54
Nightingale Dr, Epsom KT19 156 CP107
Nightingale Est, E5 66 DU62
Nightingale Gro, SE13 123 ED85
Dartford DA1 108 FN84
Nightingale La, E11 68 EG57
N6 64 DE60
N8 65 DL56
SW4 120 DF87
SW12 120 DF87
Bromley BR1 144 EJ96
Richmond TW10 118 CL87
Sevenoaks (Ide Hill) TN14 190 FB130
Nightingale Ms, E3
off Chisenhale Rd 85 DY68
E11 68 EG57
SE11 200 E8
Kingston upon Thames KT1
off South La 137 CK97
Nightingale Pl, SE18 105 EN79
SW10 off Fulham Rd 100 DC79
Rickmansworth WD3
off Nightingale Rd 38 BK45
Nightingale Rd, E5 66 DV62
N1 84 DQ65
N9 30 DW44
N22 45 DL53
NW10 81 CT68
W7 79 CF74
Bushey WD23 24 CA43
Carshalton SM5 140 DF104
Esher KT10 154 BZ106
Hampton TW12 116 CA92
Orpington BR5 145 EQ100
Rickmansworth WD3 38 BJ46
South Croydon CR2 161 DX111
Waltham Cross (Chsht) EN7 14 DQ25
Walton-on-Thames KT12 135 BV101
West Molesey KT8 136 CB99
Nightingales, Wal.Abb. EN9
off Roundhills 16 EE34
Nightingales, The, Stai. TW19 114 BM87
Nightingales Cor, Amer. HP7
off Chalfont Sta Rd 20 AW40
Nightingale Shott,
Egh. TW20 113 AZ93
Nightingales La, Ch.St.G. HP8 36 AX46
Nightingale Sq, SW12 120 DG87
Nightingale Vale, SE18 105 EN79
Nightingale Wk, SW4 121 DH86
Nightingale Way, E6 86 EL71
Redhill (Bletch.) RH1 186 DS134
Swanley BR8 147 FE97
Uxbridge (Denh.) UB9 57 BF59
Nile Cl, N16 off Evering Rd 66 DT62
Nile Dr, N9 46 DW47
Nile Path, SE18
off Jackson St 105 EN79
Nile Rd, E13 86 EJ68
Nile St, N1 197 J2
Nile Ter, SE15 102 DT78
Nimbus Rd, Epsom KT19 156 CR110
Nimegen Way, SE22 122 DS85
Nimmo Dr, Bushey
(Bushey Hth) WD23 41 CD45
Nimrod Cl, Nthlt. UB5
off Britannia Cl 78 BX69
Nimrod Pas, N1
off Tottenham Rd 84 DS65
Nimrod Rd, SW16 121 DH93
Nina Mackay Cl, E15
off Arthingworth St 86 EE67
Nine Acres Cl, E12 68 EL64
Nineacres Way, Couls. CR5 175 DL116
NINE ELMS, SW8 101 DH80
Nine Elms Av, Uxb. UB8 76 BK71
Nine Elms Cl, Felt. TW14 115 BT88
Uxbridge UB8 76 BK72
Nine Elms Gro, Grav. DA11 131 GG87
Nine Elms La, SW8 101 DJ80
Ninefields, Wal.Abb. EN9 16 EF33
Ninehams Cl, Cat. CR3 176 DR120
Ninehams Gdns, Cat. CR3 176 DR120
Ninehams Rd, Cat. CR3 176 DR121
Westerham (Tats.) TN16 178 EJ121
Nine Stiles Cl, Uxb.
(Denh.) UB9 76 BH65
Nineteenth Rd, Mitch. CR4 141 DL98
Ninhams Wd, Orp. BR6 163 EN105

★ Place of interest | ⇌ Railway station | ⊖ London Underground station | DLR Docklands Light Railway station | Tra Tramlink station | H Hospital | Riv Pedestrian ferry landing stage

Ninnings Rd, Ger.Cr. (Chal.St.P.) SL9 37 AZ52
Ninnings Way, Ger.Cr. (Chal.St.P.) SL9 37 AZ52
Ninth Av, Hayes UB3 77 BU73
Nisbet Ho, E9 off Homerton High St 67 DX64
Nita Rd, Brwd. CM14 54 FW50
Nithdale Rd, SE18 105 EP80
Nithsdale Gro, Uxb. UB10 off Tweeddale Gro 59 BQ62
Niton Cl, Barn. EN5 27 CX44
Niton Rd, Rich. TW9 98 CN83
Niton St, SW6 99 CX80
Niven Cl, Borwd. WD6 26 CQ39
Nixey Cl, Slou. SL1 92 AU75
N.L.A. Twr, Croy. CR0 142 DR103
NOAK HILL, Rom. RM4 52 FK47
Noak Hill Rd, Rom. RM3 52 FJ49
Nobel Dr, Hayes UB3 95 BR80
Nobel Rd, N18 46 DW50
Noble St, EC2 197 H8
Walton-on-Thames KT12 135 BV104
Nobles Way, Egh. TW20 112 AY93
NOEL PARK, N22 45 DN54
Noel Pk Rd, N22 45 DN54
Noel Rd, E6 86 EL70
N1 83 DP68
W3 80 CP72
Noel Sq, Dag. RM8 70 EW63
Noel St, W1 195 L9
Noel Ter, SE23 off Dartmouth Rd 122 DW89
Noke Dr, Red. RH1 184 DG133
Noke Fm Barns, Couls. CR5 174 DF122
Noke La, St.Alb. AL2 8 BY26
Noke Side, St.Alb. AL2 8 CA27
Nolan Way, E5 66 DU63
Nolton Pl, Edg. HA8 42 CM53
Nonsuch Cl, Ilf. IG6 49 EP51
Nonsuch Ct Av, Epsom KT17 157 CV110
Nonsuch Ind Est, Epsom KT17 156 CS111
★ Nonsuch Mansion Ho, Sutt. SM3 157 CW107
Nonsuch Wk, Sutt. SM2 157 CW110
Nora Gdns, NW4 63 CX56
NORBITON, Kings.T. KT2 138 CP96
⇌ Norbiton 138 CN95
Norbiton Av, Kings.T. KT1 138 CN96
Norbiton Common Rd, Kings.T. KT1 138 CP97
Norbiton Rd, E14 85 DZ72
Norbreck Gdns, NW10 off Lytham Gro 80 CM69
Norbreck Par, NW10 off Lytham Gro 80 CM69
Norbroke St, W12 81 CT73
Norburn St, W10 off Chesterton Rd 81 CY71
NORBURY, SW16 141 DN95
⇌ Norbury 141 DM95
Norbury Av, SW16 141 DM95
Hounslow TW3 117 CD85
Thornton Heath CR7 141 DN96
Watford WD24 24 BW39
Norbury Cl, SW16 141 DN95
Norbury Ct Rd, SW16 141 DL97
Norbury Cres, SW16 141 DM95
Norbury Cross, SW16 141 DL97
Norbury Gdns, Rom. RM6 70 EX57
Norbury Gro, NW7 42 CS48
Norbury Hill, SW16 121 DN94
Norbury Ri, SW16 141 DL97
Norbury Rd, E4 47 EA50
Feltham TW13 off Bedfont Rd 115 BT90
Reigate RH2 183 CZ134
Thornton Heath CR7 142 DQ96
Norcombe Gdns, Har. HA3 61 CJ58
Norcott Cl, Hayes UB4 off Willow Tree La 78 BW70
Norcott Rd, N16 66 DU61
Norcroft Gdns, SE22 122 DU87
Norcutt Rd, Twick. TW2 117 CE88
Nordenfeldt Rd, Erith DA8 107 FD78
Nordmann Pl, S.Ock. RM15 91 FX70
Norfield Rd, Dart. DA2 127 FC91
Norfolk Av, N13 45 DP51
N15 66 DT58
South Croydon CR2 160 DU110
Watford WD24 24 BW38
Norfolk Cl, N2 off Park Rd 64 DE55
N13 45 DP51
Barnet EN4 28 DG42
Dartford DA1 128 FN86
Twickenham TW1 off Cassilis Rd 117 CH86
Norfolk Cres, W2 194 C8
Sidcup DA15 125 ES87
Norfolk Fm Cl, Wok. GU22 167 BD116
Norfolk Fm Rd, Wok. GU22 167 BD115
Norfolk Gdns, Bexh. DA7 106 EZ81
Borehamwood WD6 26 CR42
Norfolk Ho, SE3 104 EE79
Norfolk Ho Rd, SW16 121 DK90
Norfolk Ms, W10 off Blagrove Rd 81 CZ71
Norfolk Pl, W2 194 A8
Grays RM16 off Mayflower Rd 109 FW78
Welling DA16 106 EU82
Norfolk Rd, E6 87 EM67
E17 47 DX54
NW8 82 DD67
NW10 80 CS66
SW19 120 DE94
Barking IG11 87 ES66
Barnet EN5 28 DA41
Dagenham RM10 71 FB64
Enfield EN3 30 DV44
Esher (Clay.) KT10 155 CE106
Feltham TW13 116 BW88
Gravesend DA12 131 GK86
Harrow HA1 60 CB57
Ilford IG3 69 ES60
Rickmansworth WD3 38 BL46
Romford RM7 71 FC58
Thornton Heath CR7 142 DQ97
Upminster RM14 72 FN62
Norfolk Rd, Uxbridge UB8 76 BK65
Norfolk Row, SE1 200 B8
Norfolk Sq, W2 194 A9
Norfolk Sq Ms, W2 194 A9
Norfolk St, E7 68 EG63
Norfolk Ter, W6 off Field Rd 99 CY78
Norgrove Pk, Ger.Cr. SL9 56 AY56
Norgrove St, SW12 120 DG87
Norheads La, Warl. CR6 178 EG119
Westerham (Bigg.H.) TN16 178 EJ116
Norhyrst Av, SE25 142 DT97
NORK, Bans. SM7 173 CY115
Nork Gdns, Bans. SM7 157 CY114
Nork Ri, Bans. SM7 173 CX116
Nork Way, Bans. SM7 173 CY115
Norland Ho, W11 81 CX74
Norland Pl, W11 81 CY74
Norland Rd, W11 81 CX74
Norlands Cres, Chis. BR7 145 EP95
Norlands Gate, Chis. BR7 145 EP95
Norlands La, Egh. TW20 133 BE97
Norland Sq, W11 81 CY74
Norley Vale, SW15 119 CU88
Norlington Rd, E10 67 EC60
E11 67 EC60
Norman Av, N22 45 DP53
Epsom KT17 157 CT112
Feltham TW13 116 BY89
South Croydon CR2 160 DQ110
Southall UB1 78 BY73
Twickenham TW1 117 CH87
Normanby Cl, SW15 off Manfred Rd 119 CZ85
Normanby Rd, NW10 63 CT63
Norman Cl, Epsom KT18 173 CV119
Orpington BR6 145 EQ104
Romford RM5 51 FB54
Waltham Abbey EN9 15 ED33
Norman Ct, Ilf. IG2 69 ER59
Potters Bar EN6 12 DC30
Woodford Green IG8 off Monkhams Av 48 EH50
Norman Cres, Brwd. CM13 55 GA48
Hounslow TW5 96 BX81
Pinner HA5 40 BW53
Normand Gdns, W14 off Greyhound Rd 99 CY79
Normand Ms, W14 off Normand Rd 99 CY79
Normand Rd, W14 99 CZ79
Normandy Av, Barn. EN5 27 CZ43
Normandy Cl, SE26 123 DY90
Normandy Dr, Hayes UB3 77 BQ72
Normandy Rd, SW9 101 DN81
Normandy Ter, E16 86 EH72
Normandy Wk, Egh. TW20 off Mullens Rd 113 BC92
Normandy Way, Erith DA8 107 FE81
Norman Gro, E3 85 DY68
Normanhurst, Ashf. TW15 114 BN92
Brentwood (Hutt.) CM13 55 GC44
Normanhurst Av, Bexh. DA7 106 EX81
Normanhurst Dr, Twick. TW1 off St. Margarets Rd 117 CH85
Normanhurst Rd, SW2 121 DM89
Orpington BR5 146 EV96
Walton-on-Thames KT12 136 BX103
Norman Rd, E6 87 EM70
E11 67 ED61
N15 66 DT57
SE10 103 EB80
SW19 120 DC94
Ashford TW15 115 BR93
Belvedere DA17 107 FB76
Dartford DA1 128 FL88
Hornchurch RM11 71 FG59
Ilford IG1 69 EP64
Sutton SM1 158 DA106
Thornton Heath CR7 141 DP99
Normans, The, Slou. SL2 74 AV72
Norman's Bldgs, EC1 off Ironmonger Row 84 DQ69
Normans Cl, NW10 80 CR65
Gravesend DA11 131 GG87
Uxbridge UB8 76 BL71
Normansfield Av, Tedd. TW11 117 CJ94
Normansfield Cl, Bushey WD23 40 CB45
Normanshire Av, E4 47 EC49
Normanshire Dr, E4 47 EA49
Normans Mead, NW10 80 CR65
Norman St, EC1 197 H3
Normanton Av, SW19 120 DA89
Normanton Pk, E4 48 EE48
Normanton Rd, S.Croy. CR2 160 DS107
Normanton St, SE23 123 DX89
Norman Way, N14 45 DL47
W3 80 CP71
Normington Cl, SW16 121 DN92
Norrice Lea, N2 64 DD57
Norris Rd, Stai. TW18 113 BF91
Norris St, SW1 199 M1
Norris Way, Dart. DA1 107 FF83
Norroy Rd, SW15 99 CX84
Norrys Cl, Barn. EN4 28 DF43
Norrys Rd, Barn. EN4 28 DF42
Norseman Cl, Ilf. IG3 70 EV60
Norseman Way, Grnf. UB6 off Olympic Way 78 CB67
Norstead Pl, SW15 119 CU89
Norsted La, Orp. BR6 164 EU110
North Access Rd, E17 67 DX58
North Acre, NW9 42 CS53
Banstead SM7 173 CZ116
NORTH ACTON, W3 80 CR70
⊖ North Acton 80 CR70
North Acton Rd, NW10 80 CR69
Northallerton Way, Rom. RM3 52 FK50
Northall Rd, Bexh. DA7 107 FC82
Northampton Gro, N1 66 DR64
Northampton Pk, N1 84 DQ65
Northampton Rd, EC1 196 E4
Croydon CR0 142 DU103
Enfield EN3 31 DY42
Northampton Row, EC1 196 E3
Northampton Sq, EC1 196 F3
Northampton St, N1 84 DQ66
Northanger Rd, SW16 121 DL93
North App, Nthwd. HA6 39 BQ47
Watford WD25 23 BT35
North Arc, Croy. CR0 off North End 142 DQ103
North Audley St, W1 194 F9
North Av, N18 46 DU49
W13 79 CH72
Brentwood CM14 53 FR45
Carshalton SM5 158 DF108
Harrow HA2 60 CB58
Hayes UB3 77 BU73
Radlett (Shenley) WD7 10 CL32
Richmond TW9 off Sandycombe Rd 98 CN81
Southall UB1 78 BZ73
Walton-on-Thames (Whiteley Vill.) KT12 153 BS109
NORTHAW, Pot.B. EN6 12 DF30
Northaw Pl, Pot.B. EN6 12 DD30
Northaw Rd E, Pot.B. (Cuffley) EN6 13 DK31
Northaw Rd W, Pot.B. EN6 12 DG30
North Bk, NW8 194 A3
Northbank Rd, E17 47 EC54
NORTH BECKTON, E6 86 EL70
North Birkbeck Rd, E11 67 ED62
Northborough Rd, SW16 141 DK97
Northbourne, Brom. BR2 144 EG101
Northbourne Rd, SW4 101 DK84
North Branch Av, W10 off Harrow Rd 81 CW69
Northbrook Dr, Nthwd. HA6 39 BS53
Northbrook Rd, N22 45 DL52
SE13 123 ED85
Barnet EN5 27 CY44
Croydon CR0 142 DR99
Ilford IG1 69 EN61
Northburgh St, EC1 196 G4
North Carriage Dr, W2 194 B10
NORTH CHEAM, Sutt. SM3 139 CW104
Northchurch, SE17 201 L10
Northchurch Rd, N1 84 DR66
Wembley HA9 80 CM65
Northchurch Ter, N1 84 DS66
North Circular Rd, E4 (A406) 47 DZ52
E6 (A406) 87 EP68
E11 (A406) 48 EJ54
E12 (A406) 69 EN64
E17 (A406) 47 DZ52
E18 (A406) 48 EJ54
N3 (A406) 64 DB55
N11 (A406) 44 DD53
N12 (A406) 44 DD53
N13 (A406) 45 DN50
N18 (A406) 46 DS50
NW2 (A406) 62 CS62
NW10 (A406) 80 CP66
NW11 (A406) 63 CY56
W3 (A406) 98 CM75
W4 (A406) 98 CM75
W5 (A406) 98 CM75
Barking (A406) IG11 87 EP68
Ilford (A406) IG1, IG4 68 EL60
Northcliffe Cl, Wor.Pk. KT4 138 CS104
Northcliffe Dr, N20 43 CZ46
North Cl, Barn. EN5 27 CW43
Bexleyheath DA6 106 EX84
Chigwell IG7 50 EU50
Dagenham RM10 88 FA67
Feltham TW14 off North Rd 115 BR86
Morden SM4 139 CY98
St. Albans AL2 8 CB25
North Colonnade, E14 204 A2
North Common, Wey. KT13 153 BP105
North Common Rd, W5 80 CL73
Uxbridge UB8 58 BK64
Northcote, Add. KT15 152 BK105
Leatherhead (Oxshott) KT22 154 CC114
Pinner HA5 40 BW54
Northcote Av, W5 80 CL73
Isleworth TW7 117 CG85
Southall UB1 78 BY73
Surbiton KT5 138 CN101
Northcote Ms, SW11 off Northcote Rd 100 DE84
Northcote Rd, E17 67 DY56
NW10 80 CS66
SW11 100 DE84
Croydon CR0 142 DR100
Gravesend DA11 131 GF88
New Malden KT3 138 CQ97
Sidcup DA14 125 ES91
Twickenham TW1 117 CG85
North Cotts, St.Alb. (Lon.Col.) AL2 9 CG25
Northcott Av, N22 45 DL53
Northcotts, Abb.L. WD5 off Long Elms 7 BR33
North Countess Rd, E17 47 DZ54
Northcourt, Rick. (Mill End) WD3 off Springwell Av 38 BG46
NORTH CRAY, Sid. DA14 126 FA90
North Cray Rd, Bex. DA5 126 EZ90
Sidcup DA14 126 EY93
North Cres, E16 85 ED70
N3 43 CZ54
WC1 195 M6
Northcroft Cl, Egh. (Eng.Grn) TW20 112 AV92
Northcroft Gdns, Egh. (Eng.Grn) TW20 112 AV92
Northcroft Rd, W13 97 CH75
Egham (Eng.Grn) TW20 112 AV92
Epsom KT19 156 CR108
Northcroft Ter, W13 off Northcroft Rd 97 CH75
Northcroft Vil, Egh. (Eng.Grn) TW20 112 AV92
North Cross Rd, SE22 122 DT85
Ilford IG6 69 EQ56
North Dene, NW7 42 CR48
Northdene, Chig. IG7 49 ER50
North Dene, Houns. TW3 96 CB81
Northdene Gdns, N15 66 DT58
North Down, S.Croy. CR2 160 DS111
Northdown Cl, Ruis. HA4 59 BT62
Northdown Gdns, Ilf. IG2 69 ES57
Northdown Rd, Cat. (Wold.) CR3 177 EA123
Gerrards Cross (Chal.St.P.) SL9 36 AY51
Hornchurch RM11 71 FH59
Longfield DA3 149 FX96
Sutton SM2 158 DA110
Welling DA16 106 EV82
North Downs Cres, Croy. (New Adgtn) CR0 161 EB110
H North Downs Private Hosp, The, Cat. CR3 186 DT125
North Downs Rd, Croy. (New Adgtn) CR0 161 EB110
Northdown St, N1 83 DM68
North Downs Way, Bet. RH3 183 CU130
Caterham CR3 185 DN126
Godstone RH9 187 DY128
Oxted RH8 188 EE126
Redhill RH1 184 DG128
Reigate RH2 184 DD130
Sevenoaks TN13, TN14 181 FD118
Tadworth KT20 183 CX130
Westerham TN16 179 ER121
North Dr, SW16 121 DJ91
Hounslow TW3 96 CC82
Orpington BR6 163 ES105
Romford RM2 72 FJ55
Ruislip HA4 59 BS59
Slough SL2 74 AS69
Virginia Water GU25 132 AS100
⇌ North Dulwich 122 DR85
⊖ North Ealing 80 CM72
North End, NW3 64 DC61
Northend, Brwd. CM14 54 FW50
North End, Buck.H. IG9 48 EJ45
Croydon CR0 142 DQ103
Romford (Noak Hill) RM3 52 FJ47
North End Av, NW3 64 DC61
North End Cres, W14 99 CZ77
North End Ho, W14 99 CY77
North End La, Orp. BR6 163 EN110
North End Par, W14 off North End Rd 99 CY77
North End Rd, NW11 64 DA60
SW6 99 CZ79
W14 99 CY77
Northend Rd, Dart. DA1 107 FF80
Erith DA8 107 FF80
North End Rd, Wem. HA9 62 CN62
Northend Trd Est, Erith DA8 107 FE81
North End Way, NW3 64 DC61
Northern Av, N9 46 DT47
Northernhay Wk, Mord. SM4 139 CY98
Northern Perimeter Rd, Houns. (Hthrw Air.) TW6 95 BQ81
Northern Perimeter Rd W, Houns. (Hthrw Air.) TW6 94 BK81
Northern Relief Rd, Bark. IG11 87 EP66
Northern Rd, E13 86 EH67
Northern Service Rd, Barn. EN5 27 CY41
Northey Av, Sutt. SM2 157 CZ110
North Eyot Gdns, W6 99 CU78
Northey St, E14 85 DY73
Northfield, Loug. IG10 32 EK42
Northfield Av, W5 97 CH75
W13 97 CH75
Orpington BR5 146 EW100
Pinner HA5 60 BX56
Northfield Cl, Brom. BR1 144 EL95
Hayes UB3 95 BT76
Northfield Ct, Stai. TW18 134 BH95
Northfield Cres, Sutt. SM3 157 CY105
Northfield Fm Ms, Cob. KT11 off Portsmouth Rd 153 BU114
Northfield Gdns, Dag. RM9 off Northfield Rd 70 EZ63
Watford WD24 24 BW37
Northfield Ind Est, NW10 80 CN69
Northfield Pk, Hayes UB3 95 BT76
Northfield Path, Dag. RM9 70 EZ62
Northfield Pl, Wey. KT13 153 BP108
Northfield Rd, E6 87 EM66
N16 66 DS59
W13 97 CH75
Barnet EN4 28 DE41
Borehamwood WD6 26 CP39
Cobham KT11 153 BU113
Dagenham RM9 70 EZ63
Enfield EN3 30 DV43
Hounslow TW5 96 BX79
Staines TW18 134 BH95
Waltham Cross EN8 15 DY32
⊖ Northfields 97 CH76
Northfields, SW18 100 DA84
Ashtead KT21 172 CL119
Grays RM17 110 GC77
Northfields Ind Est, Wem. HA0 80 CN67
Northfields Rd, W3 80 CP71
NORTH FINCHLEY, N12 44 DD50
NORTHFLEET, Grav. DA10 130 GD86
⇌ Northfleet 130 GA86
NORTHFLEET GREEN, Grav. DA13 130 GC92
Northfleet Grn Rd, Grav. DA13 130 GC93
Northfleet Ind Est, Grav. DA11 110 FZ84
North Flockton St, SE16 202 B4
North Gdn, E14 off Westferry Circ 85 DZ74
North Gdns, SW19 120 DD94
Northgate, Nthwd. HA6 39 BQ52
Northgate Dr, NW9 62 CS58
Northgate Ind Pk, Rom. RM5 50 EZ54
Northgate Path, Borwd. WD6 26 CM39
North Glade, The, Bex. DA5 126 EZ87
North Gower St, NW1 195 L3
North Grn, NW9 off Clayton Fld 42 CS52
Slough SL1 74 AS73
⊖ North Greenwich 205 H4
North Gro, N6 64 DG59
N15 66 DR57
Chertsey KT16 133 BF100
NORTH HARROW, Har. HA2 60 CA58
⊖ North Harrow 60 CA57
North Hatton Rd, Houns. (Hthrw Air.) TW6 95 BR81
North Hill, N6 64 DF58
Rickmansworth WD3 21 BE40
North Hill Av, N6 64 DG58
North Hill Dr, Rom. RM3 52 FK48
North Hill Grn, Rom. RM3 52 FK49
NORTH HILLINGDON, Uxb. UB10 77 BQ66
NORTH HYDE, Sthl. UB2 96 BY77
North Hyde Gdns, Hayes UB3 95 BU77
North Hyde La, Houns. TW5 96 BY78
Southall UB2 96 BY78
North Hyde Rd, Hayes UB3 95 BT76
Northiam, N12 44 DA48
Northiam St, E9 84 DV67
Northington St, WC1 196 B5
NORTH KENSINGTON, W10 81 CW72
North Kent Av, Grav. (Nthflt) DA11 130 GC86
Northlands, Pot.B. EN6 12 DD31
Northlands Av, Orp. BR6 163 ES105
Northlands St, SE5 102 DQ82
North La, Tedd. TW11 117 CF93
North Lo Cl, SW15 off Westleigh Av 119 CX85
H North London Blood Transfusion Cen, NW9 42 CR54
H North London Nuffield Hosp, Enf. EN2 29 DN40
NORTH LOOE, Epsom KT17 157 CW113
North Mall, N9 off St. Martins Rd 46 DV47
North Mead, Red. RH1 184 DF131
North Ms, WC1 196 C5
H North Middlesex Hosp, N18 46 DS50
North Mymms Pk, Hat. AL9 11 CT25
NORTH OCKENDON, Upmin. RM14 73 FV64
Northolm, Edg. HA8 42 CR49
Northolme Cl, Grays RM16 off Premier Av 110 GC76
Northolme Gdns, Edg. HA8 42 CN53
Northolme Ri, Orp. BR6 145 ES103
Northolme Rd, N5 66 DQ63
NORTHOLT 78 BZ66
⊖ Northolt 78 CA66
★ Northolt Aerodrome, Ruis. HA4 77 BT65
Northolt Av, Ruis. HA4 59 BV64
Northolt Gdns, Grnf. UB6 61 CF64
⇌ Northolt Park 60 CB63
Northolt Rd, Har. HA2 60 CB63
Hounslow (Hthrw Air.) TW6 94 BK81
Northolt Way, Horn. RM12 90 FJ65
North Orbital Rd, Rick. WD3 37 BE52
St. Albans AL1, AL2, AL4 9 CK25
Uxbridge (Denh.) UB9 57 BF60
Watford WD25 7 BU34
Northover, Brom. BR1 124 EF90
North Par, Chess. KT9 156 CL106
North Pk, SE9 125 EM86
Gerrards Cross SL9 56 AY56
Iver SL0 93 BC76
North Pk La, Gdse. RH9 186 DU129
North Pas, SW18 100 DA84
North Peckham Est, SE15 102 DT80
North Perimeter Rd, Uxb. UB8 off Kingston La 76 BL69
North Pl, Mitch. CR4 120 DF94
Teddington TW11 117 CF93
Waltham Abbey EN9 off Highbridge St 15 EB33
Northpoint, Brom. BR1 off Sherman Rd 144 EG95
North Pole La, Kes. BR2 162 EF107
North Pole Rd, W10 81 CW71
Northport St, N1 84 DR67
North Ride, W2 198 B1
Northridge Rd, Grav. DA12 131 GJ90
North Riding, St.Alb. (Brick.Wd) AL2 8 CA30
North Rd, N6 64 DG59
N7 83 DL65
N9 46 DV46
SE18 105 ES77
SW19 120 DC93
W5 97 CK76
Belvedere DA17 107 FB76
Brentford TW8 98 CL79
Brentwood CM14 54 FW46
Bromley BR1 144 EH95
Dartford DA1 127 FF86
Edgware HA8 42 CP53
Feltham TW14 115 BR86
Hayes UB3 77 BR71
Ilford IG3 69 ES61
Purfleet RM19 109 FR77
Richmond TW9 98 CN83
Rickmansworth (Chorl.) WD3 21 BD43
Romford (Chad.Hth) RM6 70 EY57
Romford (Hav.at.Bow.) RM4 51 FE48
South Ockendon RM15 91 FW68
Southall UB1 78 CA73
Surbiton KT6 137 CK100
Waltham Cross EN8 15 DY33
Walton-on-Thames KT12 154 BW106
West Drayton UB7 94 BM76
West Wickham BR4 143 EB102
Woking GU21 167 BA116
North Rd Av, Brwd. CM14 54 FW46
Northrop Rd, Houns. (Hthrw Air.) TW6 95 BS81
North Row, W1 194 E10
North Service Rd, Brwd. CM14 54 FW47
North Several, SE3 off Orchard Rd 103 ED82
NORTH SHEEN, Rich. TW9 98 CN82
⇌ North Sheen 98 CN84

★ Place of interest ⇌ Railway station ⊖ London Underground station DLR Docklands Light Railway station Tra Tramlink station H Hospital Riv Pedestrian ferry landing stage

Northside Rd, Brom. BR1
off Mitchell Way 144 EG95
North Side Wandsworth Common,
SW18 120 DC85
Northspur Rd, Sutt. SM1 140 DA104
North Sq, N9
off St. Martins Rd 46 DV47
NW11 64 DA57
Northstead Rd, SW2 121 DN89
North St, E13 86 EG68
NW4 63 CW57
SW4 101 DJ83
Barking IG11 87 EP65
Bexleyheath DA7 106 FA84
Bromley BR1 144 EG95
Carshalton SM5 140 DF104
Dartford DA1 128 FK87
Egham TW20 113 AZ92
Gravesend DA12
off South St 131 GH87
Hornchurch RM11 72 FK59
Isleworth TW7 97 CG83
Leatherhead KT22 171 CG121
Redhill RH1 184 DF133
Romford RM1, RM5 71 FD55
North St Pas, E13 86 EH68
North Tenter St, E1 84 DT72
North Ter, SW3 198 B7
Northumberland All, EC3 197 N9
Northumberland Av, E12 68 EJ60
WC2 199 P2
Enfield EN1 30 DV39
Hornchurch RM11 72 FJ57
Isleworth TW7 97 CF81
Welling DA16 105 ER84
Northumberland Cl,
Erith DA8 107 FC80
Staines (Stanw.) TW19 114 BL86
Northumberland Cres,
Felt. TW14 115 BS86
Northumberland Gdns, N9 46 DT48
Bromley BR1 145 EN98
Isleworth TW7 97 CG80
Mitcham CR4 141 DK99
Northumberland Gro, N17 46 DV52
NORTHUMBERLAND HEATH,
Erith DA8 107 FC80
⇌ **Northumberland Park** 46 DV53
Northumberland Pk, N17 46 DT52
Erith DA8 107 FC80
Northumberland Pl, W2 82 DA72
Richmond TW10 117 CK85
Northumberland Rd, E6 86 EL72
E17 67 EA59
Barnet EN5 28 DC44
Gravesend
(Istead Rise) DA13 131 GF94
Harrow HA2 60 BZ57
Northumberland Row, Twick. TW2
off Colne Rd 117 CE88
Northumberland St, WC2 199 P2
Northumberland Way,
Erith DA8 107 FC81
Northumbria St, E14 85 EA72
North Verbena Gdns, W6
off St. Peter's Sq 99 CU78
Northview, N7 65 DL62
North Vw, SW19 119 CV92
W5 79 CJ70
Ilford IG6 50 EU52
Pinner HA5 60 BW59
Northview, Swan. BR8 147 FE96
North Vw Av, Til. RM18 111 GG81
Northview Cres, NW10 63 CT63
North Vw Cres, Epsom KT18 173 CV117
North Vw Dr, Wdf.Grn. IG8 48 EK54
North Vw Rd, N8 65 DK55
Sevenoaks TN14
off Seal Rd 191 FJ121
North Vil, NW1 83 DK65
North Wk, W2
off Bayswater Rd 82 DC73
Croydon (New Adgtn) CR0 161 EB106
NORTH WATFORD, Wat. WD24 23 BV37
North Way, N9 46 DW47
N11 45 DJ51
NW9 62 CP55
Northway, NW11 64 DB57
Morden SM4 139 CY97
North Way, Pnr. HA5 60 BW55
Northway, Rick. WD3 38 BK45
North Way, Uxb. UB10 76 BL66
Northway, Wall. SM6 159 DJ105
Northway Circ, NW7 42 CR49
Northway Cres, NW7 42 CR49
Northway Ho, N20 44 DC46
Northway Rd, SE5 102 DQ83
Croydon CR0 142 DT100
Northways Par, NW3
off Finchley Rd 82 DD66
North Weald Airfield, Epp.
(N.Wld Bas.) CM16 18 EZ26
NORTH WEALD BASSETT,
Epp. CM16 19 FB27
North Weald Cl, Horn. RM12
off Airfield Way 89 FH65
Northweald La, Kings.T. KT2 117 CK92
NORTH WEMBLEY,
Wem. HA0 61 CH61
⇌ **North Wembley** 61 CK62
⊖ **North Wembley** 61 CK62
North Western Av, Wat.
WD24, WD25 24 BW36
Northwest Pl, N1
off Chapel Mkt 83 DN68
North Wf Rd, W2 82 DD71
Northwick Av, Har. HA3 61 CG58
Northwick Circle, Har. HA3 61 CJ58
Northwick Cl, NW8
off Northwick Ter 82 DD70
Harrow HA1
off Nightingale Av 61 CH59
⊖ **Northwick Park** 61 CG59
H **Northwick Pk Hosp**,
Har. HA1 61 CH59
Northwick Pk Rd, Har. HA1 61 CF58
Northwick Rd, Wat. WD19 40 BW49
Wembley HA0 79 CK67
Northwick Ter, NW8 82 DD70
Northwick Wk, Har. HA1 61 CF59
Northwold Dr, Pnr. HA5
off Cuckoo Hill 60 BW55
Northwold Est, E5 66 DU61
Northwold Rd, E5 66 DT61
N16 66 DT61
NORTHWOOD 39 BR51
⊖ **Northwood** 39 BS52
Northwood, Grays RM16 111 GH75
H **Northwood & Pinner**
Comm Hosp, Nthwd. HA6 39 BU53
Northwood Av, Horn. RM12 71 FG63
Purley CR8 159 DN113
Northwood Cl, Wal.Cr. EN7 14 DT27
North Wd Ct, SE25
off Regina Rd 142 DU97
Northwood Gdns, N12 44 DD50
Greenford UB6 61 CF64
Ilford IG5 69 EN56
Northwood Hall, N6 65 DJ59
NORTHWOOD HILLS,
Nthwd. HA6 39 BT54
⊖ **Northwood Hills** 39 BU54
Northwood Ho, SE27 122 DR91
Northwood Pl, Erith DA18 106 EZ76
Northwood Rd, N6 65 DH59
SE23 123 DZ88
Carshalton SM5 158 DG107
Hounslow
(Hthrw Air.) TW6 94 BK81
Thornton Heath CR7 141 DP96
Uxbridge (Hare.) UB9 38 BJ53
Northwood Twr, E17 67 EC56
Northwood Way, SE19
off Roman Ri 122 DR93
Northwood HA6 39 BU52
Uxbridge (Hare.) UB9 38 BK53
NORTH WOOLWICH, E16 104 EL75
⇌ **North Woolwich** 105 EN75
North Woolwich Rd, E16 205 L2
North Woolwich Roundabout, E16
off North Woolwich Rd 86 EK74
★ **North Woolwich Sta Mus**,
E16 105 EN75
North Worple Way, SW14 98 CR83
Nortoft Rd, Ger.Cr.
(Chal.St.P.) SL9 37 AZ51
Norton Av, Surb. KT5 138 CP101
Norton Cl, E4 47 EA50
Borehamwood WD6 26 CN39
Enfield EN1 *off Brick La* 30 DV40
Norton Folgate, E1 197 N6
Norton Gdns, SW16 141 DL96
Norton La, Cob. KT11 169 BT119
Norton Rd, E10 67 DZ60
Dagenham RM10 89 FD65
Uxbridge UB8 76 BK69
Wembley HA0 79 CK65
Norval Rd, Wem. HA0 61 CH61
Norvic Ho, Erith DA8
off Waterhead Cl 107 FF80
Norway Dr, Slou. SL2 74 AV71
Norway Gate, SE16 203 L6
Norway Pl, E14
off Commercial Rd 85 DZ72
Norway St, SE10 103 EB79
Norway Wk, Rain. RM13
off The Glen 90 FJ70
Norwich Ho, E14
off Cordelia St 85 EB72
Norwich Ms, Ilf. IG3
off Ashgrove Rd 70 EU60
Norwich Pl, Bexh. DA6 106 FA84
Norwich Rd, E7 68 EG64
Dagenham RM9 88 FA68
Greenford UB6 78 CB67
Northwood HA6 59 BT55
Thornton Heath CR7 142 DQ97
Norwich St, EC4 196 D8
Norwich Wk, Edg. HA8 42 CQ52
Norwich Way, Rick.
(Crox.Grn) WD3 23 BP41
NORWOOD, SE19 122 DS93
Norwood Av, Rom. RM7 71 FE59
Wembley HA0 80 CM67
Norwood Cl, NW2 63 CY62
Southall UB2 96 CA77
Twickenham TW2
off Fourth Cross Rd 117 CD89
Norwood Cres, Houns.
(Hthrw Air.) TW6 95 BQ81
Norwood Dr, Har. HA2 60 BZ58
Norwood Fm La, Cob. KT11 153 BU111
Norwood Gdns, Hayes UB4 78 BW70
Southall UB2 96 BZ77
NORWOOD GREEN,
Sthl. UB2 96 CA77
Norwood Grn Rd, Sthl. UB2 96 CA77
Norwood High St, SE27 121 DP90
⇌ **Norwood Junction** 142 DT98
Norwood La, Iver SL0 75 BD70
NORWOOD NEW TOWN,
SE19 122 DQ93
Norwood Pk Rd, SE27 122 DQ92
Norwood Rd, SE24 121 DP88
SE27 121 DP89
Southall UB2 96 BZ77
Waltham Cross
(Chsht) EN8 15 DY30
Norwood Ter, Sthl. UB2
off Tentelow La 96 CB77
Notley End, Egh.
(Eng.Grn) TW20 112 AW93
Notley St, SE5 102 DR80
Notre Dame Est, SW4 101 DJ84
Notson Rd, SE25 142 DV98
Notting Barn Rd, W10 81 CX70
Nottingdale Sq, W11
off Wilsham St 81 CY74
Nottingham Av, E16 86 EJ71
Nottingham Cl, Wat. WD25 7 BU33
Woking GU21 166 AT118
Nottingham Ct, WC2 195 P9
Woking GU21
off Nottingham Cl 166 AT118
Nottingham Pl, W1 194 F5
Nottingham Rd, E10 67 EC58
SW17 120 DF88
Isleworth TW7 97 CF82
Rickmansworth
(Herons.) WD3 37 BC45
South Croydon CR2 160 DQ105
Nottingham St, W1 194 F6
Nottingham Ter, NW1 194 F5
NOTTING HILL, W11 81 CY73
⊖ **Notting Hill Gate** 82 DA73
Notting Hill Gate, W11 82 DA74
Nova Ms, Sutt. SM3 139 CY102
Novar Cl, Orp. BR6 145 ET101
Nova Rd, Croy. CR0 141 DP101
Novar Rd, SE9 125 EQ88
Novello St, SW6 100 DA81
Novello Way, Borwd. WD6 26 CR39
Nowell Rd, SW13 99 CU79
Nower, The, Sev. TN14 179 ET119
Nower Hill, Pnr. HA5 60 BZ56
Noyna Rd, SW17 120 DF90
Nuding Cl, SE13 103 EA83
Nuffield Rd, Swan. BR8 127 FG93
H **Nuffield Speech &**
Language Unit, W5 79 CJ71
Nugent Ind Pk, Orp. BR5 146 EW99
Nugent Rd, N19 65 DL60
SE25 142 DT97
Nugents Ct, Pnr. HA5
off St. Thomas' Dr 40 BY53
Nugents Pk, Pnr. HA5 40 BY53
Nugent Ter, NW8 82 DC68
Numa Ct, Brent. TW8
off Justin Cl 97 CK80
★ **No. 2 Willow Rd**, NW3 64 DE63
Nunappleton Way, Oxt. RH8 188 EG132
Nun Ct, EC2 197 K8
Nuneaton Rd, Dag. RM9 88 EX66
Nunfield, Kings L.
(Chipper.) WD4 6 BH31
NUNHEAD, SE15 102 DW83
⇌ **Nunhead** 102 DW82
Nunhead Cres, SE15 102 DV83
Nunhead Est, SE15 102 DV84
Nunhead Grn, SE15 102 DV83
Uxbridge (Denh.) UB9 57 BF58
Nunhead Gro, SE15 102 DV83
Nunhead La, SE15 102 DV83
Nunhead Pas, SE15
off Peckham Rye 102 DU83
Nunnington Cl, SE9 124 EL90
Nunns Rd, Enf. EN2 30 DQ40
Nunns Way, Grays RM17 110 GD77
Nunsbury Dr, Brox. EN10 15 DY25
Nuns Wk, Vir.W. GU25 132 AX99
NUPER'S HATCH,
Rom. RM4 51 FE45
Nupton Dr, Barn. EN5 27 CW44
Nursery, The, Erith DA8 107 FF80
Nursery Av, N3 44 DC54
Bexleyheath DA7 106 EZ83
Croydon CR0 143 DX103
Nursery Cl, SE4 103 DZ82
SW15 99 CX84
Addlestone (Wdhm) KT15 151 BF110
Amersham HP7 20 AS39
Croydon CR0 143 DX103
Dartford DA2 128 FQ87
Enfield EN3 31 DX39
Epsom KT17 156 CS110
Feltham TW14 115 BV87
Orpington BR6 146 EU101
Romford RM6 70 EX58
Sevenoaks TN13 191 FJ122
South Ockendon RM15 91 FW70
Swanley BR8 147 FC96
Tadworth KT20 183 CU125
Woking GU21 166 AW116
Woodford Green IG8 48 EH50
Nursery Ct, N17
off Nursery St 46 DT52
Nursery Gdns, Chis. BR7 125 EP93
Enfield EN3 31 DX39
Hounslow TW4 116 BZ85
Staines TW18 114 BH94
Sunbury-on-Thames TW16 135 BT96
Waltham Cross EN7 14 DR28
Nursery La, E2 84 DT67
E7 86 EG65
W10 81 CW71
Slough SL3 74 AW74
Uxbridge UB8 76 BK70
Nurserymans Rd, N11 44 DG47
Nursery Pl, Sev. TN13 190 FD122
Nursery Rd, E9 *off Morning La* 84 DW65
N2 44 DD53
N14 45 DJ45
SW9 101 DM84
Broxbourne EN10 15 DY25
Loughton IG10 32 EJ43
Loughton
(High Beach) IG10 32 EH39
Pinner HA5 60 BW55
Sunbury-on-Thames TW16 135 BS96
Sutton SM1 158 DC105
Tadworth KT20 183 CU125
Thornton Heath CR7 142 DR98
Nursery Rd Merton, SW19 140 DB96
Nursery Rd Mitcham,
Mitch. CR4 140 DE97
Nursery Rd Wimbledon, SW19
off Worple Rd 119 CY94
Nursery Row, SE17 201 K9
Barnet EN5
off St. Albans Rd 27 CY41
Nursery St, N17 46 DT52
Nursery Wk, NW4 63 CV55
Romford RM7 71 FD59
Nursery Way, Stai.
(Wrays.) TW19 112 AX86
Nursery Waye, Uxb. UB8 76 BK67
Nurstead Rd, Erith DA8 106 FA80
Nutberry Av, Grays RM16 110 GA75
Nutberry Cl, Grays RM16
off Long La 110 GA75
Nutbourne St, W10 81 CY69
Nutbrook St, SE15 102 DU83
Nutbrowne Rd, Dag. RM9 88 EZ67
Nutcroft Gro, Lthd.
(Fetch.) KT22 171 CE121
Nutcroft Rd, SE15 102 DV80
NUTFIELD, Red. RH1 185 DM133
Nutfield Cl, N18 46 DU51
Carshalton SM5 140 DE104
Nutfield Gdns, Ilf. IG3 69 ET61
Northolt UB5 78 BW68
Nutfield Marsh Rd, Red.
(Nutfld) RH1 185 DJ130
Nutfield Rd, E15 67 EC63
NW2 63 CU61
SE22 122 DT85
Coulsdon CR5 174 DG116
Redhill RH1 184 DG134
Redhill (S.Merst.) RH1 185 DJ129
Thornton Heath CR7 141 DP98
Nutfield Way, Orp. BR6 145 EN103
Nutford Pl, W1 194 C8
Nuthatch Cl, Stai. TW19 114 BM88
Nuthatch Gdns, SE28 105 ER75
Nuthurst Av, SW2 121 DM89
Nutkin Wk, Uxb. UB8
off Park Rd 76 BL66
Nutley Cl, Swan. BR8 147 FF95
Nutley Ct, Reig. RH2
off Nutley La 183 CZ134
Nutley La, Reig. RH2 183 CZ133
Nutley Ter, NW3 82 DC65
Nutmead Cl, Bex. DA5 127 FC88
Nutmeg Cl, E16
off Cranberry La 86 EE70
Nutmeg La, E14 85 ED72
Nuttall St, N1 84 DS68
Nutter La, E11 68 EJ58
Nuttfield Cl, Rick.
(Crox.Grn) WD3 23 BP44
Nutt Gro, Edg. HA8 41 CK47
Nut Tree Cl, Orp. BR6 146 EX104
Nutt St, SE15 102 DT80
Nutty La, Shep. TW17 135 BQ98
Nutwell St, SW17 120 DE92
Nutwood Gdns, Wal.Cr. (Chsht) EN7
off Great Stockwood Rd 14 DS26
Nuxley Rd, Belv. DA17 106 EZ79
Nyall Ct, Rom. RM2
off Elvet Av 72 FJ55
Nyanza St, SE18 105 ER79
Nye Bevan Est, E5 67 DX62
Nyefield Pk, Tad. KT20 183 CU126
Nye Way, Hem.H. (Bov.) HP3 5 BA28
Nylands Av, Rich. TW9 98 CN81
Nymans Gdns, SW20
off Hidcote Gdns 139 CV97
Nynehead St, SE14 103 DY80
Nyon Gro, SE6 123 DZ89
Nyssa Cl, Wdf.Grn. IG8
off Gwynne Pk Av 49 EM51
Nyth Cl, Upmin. RM14 73 FR58
Nyton Cl, N19
off Courtauld Rd 65 DL60

O

O2 Shop Cen, NW3
off Finchley Rd 82 DC65
Oakapple Cl, S.Croy. CR2 160 DV114
Oak Apple Ct, SE12 124 EG89
Oak Av, N8 65 DL56
N10 45 DH52
N17 46 DR52
Croydon CR0 143 EA103
Egham TW20 113 BC94
Enfield EN2 29 DM38
Hampton TW12 116 BY92
Hounslow TW5 96 BX80
St. Albans (Brick.Wd) AL2 8 CA30
Sevenoaks TN13 191 FH128
Upminster RM14 72 FP62
Uxbridge UB10 59 BP61
West Drayton UB7 94 BN76
Oakbank, Brwd.
(Hutt.) CM13 55 GE43
Oak Bk, Croy.
(New Adgtn) CR0 161 EC107
Oakbank, Lthd.
(Fetch.) KT22 170 CC123
Woking GU22 166 AY119
Oakbank Av, Walt. KT12 136 BZ101
Oakbank Gro, SE24 102 DQ84
Oakbrook Cl, Brom. BR1 124 EH91
Oakbury Rd, SW6 100 DB82
Oak Cl, N14 45 DH45
Dartford DA1 107 FE84
Sutton SM1 140 DC103
Tadworth (Box H.) KT20 182 CP130
Waltham Abbey EN9 15 ED34
Oakcombe Cl, N.Mal. KT3
off Traps La 138 CS95
Oak Cottage Cl, SE6 124 EF88
Oak Cres, E16 86 EE71
Oakcroft Cl, Pnr. HA5 39 BV54
West Byfleet KT14 151 BF114
Oakcroft Rd, SE13 103 ED82
Chessington KT9 156 CM105
West Byfleet KT14 151 BF114
Oakcroft Vil, Chess. KT9 156 CM105
Oakdale, N14 45 DH46
Oakdale Av, Har. HA3 62 CL57
Northwood HA6 39 BU54
Oakdale Cl, Wat. WD19 40 BW49
Oakdale Gdns, E4 47 EC50
Oakdale La, Eden.
(Crock.H.) TN8 189 EP133
Oakdale Rd, E7 86 EH66
E11 67 ED61
E18 48 EH54
N4 66 DQ58
SE15 102 DW83
SW16 121 DL92
Epsom KT19 156 CR109
Watford WD19 40 BW48
Weybridge KT13 134 BN104
Oakdale Way, Mitch. CR4
off Wolseley Rd 140 DG101
Oakdene, SE15
off Carlton Gro 102 DV81
Oak Dene, W13
off The Dene 79 CH71
Oakdene, Rom. RM3 52 FM54
Oakdene, Tadworth KT20 173 CY120
Waltham Cross
(Chsht) EN8 15 DY30
Woking (Chobham) GU24 150 AT110
Oakdene Av, Chis. BR7 125 EN92
Erith DA8 107 FC79
Thames Ditton KT7 137 CG102
Oakdene Cl, Horn. RM11 71 FH58
Pinner HA5 40 BZ52
Oakdene Dr, Surb. KT5 138 CQ101
Oakdene Ms, Sutt. SM3 139 CZ102
Oakdene Par, Cob. KT11
off Anyards Rd 153 BV114
Oakdene Pk, N3 43 CZ52
Oakdene Rd, Cob. KT11 153 BV114
Leatherhead (Bkhm) KT23 170 BZ124
Orpington BR5 145 ET99
Redhill RH1 184 DE134
Sevenoaks TN13 190 FG122
Uxbridge UB10 77 BP68
Watford WD24 23 BV36
Oakden St, SE11 200 E8
Oak Dr, Tad. (Box H.) KT20 182 CP130
Oake Ct, SW15 119 CY85
Oaken Coppice,
Ashtd. KT21 172 CN119
Oak End Dr, Iver SL0 75 BC68
Oaken Dr, Esher
(Clay.) KT10 155 CF107
Oak End Way, Add.
(Wdhm) KT15 151 BE112
Gerrards Cross SL9 57 AZ57
Oakenholt Ho, SE2
off Hartslock Dr 106 EX75
Oaken La, Esher (Clay.) KT10 155 CE106
Oakenshaw Cl, Surb. KT6 138 CL101
Oakes Cl, E6
off Savage Gdns 87 EM72
Oakeshott Av, N6 64 DG61
Oakey La, SE1 200 D6
Oak Fm, Borwd. WD6 26 CQ43
Oakfield, E4 47 EB50
Rickmansworth
(Mill End) WD3 37 BF45
Woking GU21 166 AS116
Oakfield Av, Har. HA3 61 CH55
Oakfield Cl, N.Mal. KT3
off Blakes La 139 CT99
Potters Bar EN6 11 CZ31
Ruislip HA4 59 BT58
Weybridge KT13 153 BQ105
Oakfield Ct, N8 65 DL59
NW2 *off Hendon Way* 63 CX59
Borehamwood WD6 26 CP41
Oakfield Dr, Reig. RH2 184 DA132
Oakfield Gdns, N18 46 DS49
SE19 122 DS92
Beckenham BR3 143 EA99
Carshalton SM5 140 DE102
Greenford UB6 79 CD70
Oakfield Glade, Wey. KT13 153 BQ105
Oakfield La, Bex. DA5 127 FE89
Dartford DA1, DA2 127 FG89
Keston BR2 162 EJ105
Oakfield Pk Rd, Dart. DA1 128 FK89
Oakfield Pl, Dart. DA1 128 FK89
Oakfield Rd, E6 86 EL67
E17 47 DY54
N3 44 DB53
N4 65 DN58
N14 45 DL48
SE20 122 DV94
SW19 119 CX90
Ashford TW15 115 BP92
Ashtead KT21 171 CK117
Cobham KT11 153 BV113
Croydon CR0 142 DQ102
Ilford IG1 69 EP61
Orpington BR6
off Goodmead Rd 146 EU101
Oakfields, Sev. TN13 191 FH126
Walton-on-Thames KT12 135 BU102
West Byfleet KT14 152 BH114
Oakfields Rd, NW11 63 CY58
Oakfield St, SW10 100 DC79
Oakford Rd, NW5 65 DJ63
Oak Gdns, Croy. CR0 143 EA103
Edgware HA8 42 CQ54
Oak Glade, Epp. (Cooper.) CM16
off Coopersale Common 18 EX29
Epsom KT19
off Christ Ch Rd 156 CN112
Northwood HA6 39 BP53
Oak Glen, Horn. RM11 72 FL55
Oak Grn, Abb.L. WD5 7 BS32
Oak Grn Way, Abb.L. WD5 7 BS32
Oak Gro, NW2 63 CY63
Ruislip HA4 59 BV59
Sunbury-on-Thames
TW16 115 BV94
West Wickham BR4 143 EC103
Oak Gro Rd, SE20 142 DW95
Oakhall Ct, E11 68 EH58
Oakhall Dr, Sun. TW16 115 BT92
Oak Hall Rd, E11 68 EH58
Oakham Cl, SE6
off Rutland Wk 123 DZ89
Barnet EN4 28 DF41
Oakham Dr, Brom. BR2 144 EF98
Oakhampton Rd, NW7 43 CX52
Oak Hill, Epsom KT18 172 CR116
Oakhill, Esher (Clay.) KT10 155 CG107
Oak Hill, Surb. KT6 138 CL101
Woodford Green IG8 47 ED52
Oakhill Av, NW3 64 DB63
Pinner HA5 40 BY54
Oakhill Cl, Ashtd. KT21 171 CJ118
Rickmansworth
(Map.Cr.) WD3 37 BE49
Oak Hill Cl, Wdf.Grn. IG8 47 ED52
Oakhill Ct, SW19 119 CX94
Oak Hill Cres, Surb. KT6 138 CL101
Woodford Green IG8 47 ED52
Oakhill Dr, Surb. KT6 138 CL101
Oakhill Gdns, Wey. KT13 135 BS103
Oak Hill Gdns, Wdf.Grn. IG8 48 EE53
Oak Hill Gro, Surb. KT6 138 CL101
Oak Hill Pk, NW3 64 DB63
Oak Hill Pk Ms, NW3 64 DC63
Oakhill Path, Surb. KT6 138 CL100

★ Place of interest ⇌ Railway station ⊖ London Underground station DLR Docklands Light Railway station Tra Tramlink station H Hospital Riv Pedestrian ferry landing stage

300

Oakhill Pl, SW15
off Oakhill Rd 120 DA85
Oakhill Rd, SW15 119 CZ85
SW16 141 DL95
Addlestone KT15 151 BF107
Ashtead KT21 171 CJ118
Beckenham BR3 143 EC96
Orpington BR6 145 ET102
Purfleet RM19 108 FP78
Rickmansworth (Map.Cr.) WD3 37 BD49
Oak Hill Rd, Rom. (Stap.Abb.) RM4 51 FD45
Sevenoaks TN13 190 FG124
Surbiton KT6 138 CL100
Oakhill Rd, Sutt. SM1 140 DB104
Oak Hill Way, NW3 64 DC63
Oakhouse Rd, Bexh. DA6 126 FA85
Oakhurst, Wok. (Chobham) GU24 150 AS109
Oakhurst Av, Barn. EN4 44 DE45
Bexleyheath DA7 106 EY80
Oakhurst Cl, E17 68 EE56
Chislehurst BR7 145 EM95
Ilford IG6 49 EQ53
Teddington TW11 117 CE92
Oakhurst Gdns, E4 48 EF46
E17 68 EE56
Bexleyheath DA7 106 EY80
Oakhurst Gro, SE22 102 DU84
Oakhurst Pl, Wat. WD18
off Cherrydale 23 BT42
Oakhurst Ri, Cars. SM5 158 DE110
Oakhurst Rd, Enf. EN3 31 DX36
Epsom KT19 156 CQ107
Oakington Av, Amer. HP6 20 AY39
Harrow HA2 60 CA59
Hayes UB3 95 BR77
Wembley HA9 62 CM62
Oakington Dr, Sun. TW16 136 BW96
Oakington Manor Dr, Wem. HA9 62 CN64
Oakington Rd, W9 82 DA70
Oakington Way, N8 65 DL58
Oakland Gdns, Brwd. (Hutt.) CM13 55 GC43
Oakland Pl, Buck.H. IG9 48 EG47
Oakland Rd, E15 67 ED63
Oaklands, N21 45 DM47
Kenley CR8 160 DQ114
Leatherhead (Fetch.) KT22 171 CD124
Twickenham TW2 116 CC87
Oaklands Av, N9 30 DV44
Esher KT10 137 CD102
Hatfield AL9 11 CY27
Isleworth TW7 97 CF79
Romford RM1 71 FE55
Sidcup DA15 125 ET87
Thornton Heath CR7 141 DN98
Watford WD19 39 BV46
West Wickham BR4 143 EB104
Oaklands Cl, Bexh. DA6 126 EZ85
Chessington KT9 155 CJ105
Orpington BR5 145 ES100
Oaklands Ct, Add. KT15 134 BH104
Watford WD17 23 BU39
Wembley HA0 61 CK64
Oaklands Dr, S.Ock. RM15 91 FW71
Oaklands Est, SW4 121 DJ86
Oaklands Gdns, Ken. CR8 160 DQ114
Oaklands Gate, Nthwd. HA6
off Green La 39 BS51
Oaklands Gro, W12 81 CU74
Oaklands La, Barn. EN5 27 CV42
Westerham (Bigg.H.) TN16 162 EH113
Oaklands Pk Av, Ilf. IG1
off High Rd 69 ER61
Oaklands Pl, SW4
off St. Alphonsus Rd 101 DJ84
Oaklands Rd, N20 43 CZ45
NW2 63 CX63
SW14 98 CR83
W7 97 CF75
Bexleyheath DA6 106 EZ84
Bromley BR1 124 EE94
Dartford DA2 128 FP88
Gravesend (Nthflt) DA11 131 GF91
Waltham Cross (Chsht) EN7 14 DS26
Oaklands Way, Tad. KT20 173 CW122
Wallington SM6 159 DK108
Oakland Way, Epsom KT19 156 CR107
Oak La, E14 85 DZ73
N2 44 DD54
N11 45 DK51
Egham (Eng.Grn) TW20 112 AW90
Isleworth TW7 97 CE84
Potters Bar (Cuffley) EN6 13 DM28
Sevenoaks TN13 190 FG127
Twickenham TW1 117 CG87
Woking GU22
off Beaufort Rd 167 BC116
Woodford Green IG8 48 EF49
Oaklawn Rd, Lthd. KT22 171 CE118
Oak Leaf Cl, Epsom KT19 156 CQ112
Oakleafe Gdns, Ilf. IG6 69 EP55
Oaklea Pas, Kings.T. KT1 137 CK97
Oakleigh Av, N20 44 DD47
Edgware HA8 42 CP54
Surbiton KT6 138 CN102
Oakleigh Cl, N20 44 DF48
Swanley BR8 147 FE97
Oakleigh Ct, Barn. EN4
off Church Hill Rd 28 DE44
Edgware HA8 42 CQ54
Oakleigh Cres, N20 44 DE47
Oakleigh Dr, Rick. (Crox.Grn) WD3 23 BQ44
Oakleigh Gdns, N20 44 DC46
Edgware HA8 42 CM50
Orpington BR6 163 ES105
Oakleigh Ms, N20
off Oakleigh Rd N 44 DC47
OAKLEIGH PARK, N20 44 DD46
⇌ **Oakleigh Park** 44 DD45
Oakleigh Pk Av, Chis. BR7 145 EN95
Oakleigh Pk N, N20 44 DD46
Oakleigh Pk S, N20 44 DE47
Oakleigh Ri, Epp. CM16
off Bower Hill 18 EU32
Oakleigh Rd, Pnr. HA5 40 BZ51
Uxbridge UB10 77 BQ66
Oakleigh Rd N, N20 44 DD47
Oakleigh Rd S, N11 44 DG48
Oakleigh Way, Mitch. CR4 141 DH95
Surbiton KT6 138 CN102
Oakley Av, W5 80 CN73
Barking IG11 87 ET66
Croydon CR0 159 DL105
Oakley Cl, E4 47 EC48
E6 *off Northumberland Rd* 86 EL72
W7 79 CE73
Addlestone KT15 152 BK105
Grays RM20 109 FW79
Isleworth TW7 97 CD81
Oakley Ct, Loug. IG10
off Hillyfields 33 EN40
Mitcham CR4
off London Rd 140 DG102
Oakley Cres, EC1 196 G1
Slough SL1 74 AS73
Oakley Dr, SE9 125 ER88
SE13 123 ED86
Bromley BR2 144 EL104
Romford RM3 52 FN50
Oakley Gdns, N8 65 DM57
SW3 100 DE79
Banstead SM7 174 DB115
Oakley Pk, Bex. DA5 126 EW87
Oakley Pl, SE1 102 DT78
Oakley Rd, N1 84 DR66
SE25 142 DV99
Bromley BR2 144 EL104
Harrow HA1 61 CE58
Warlingham CR6 176 DU118
Oakley Sq, NW1 195 L1
Oakley St, SW3 100 DE79
Oakley Wk, W6 99 CX79
Oakley Yd, E2
off Bacon St 84 DT70
Oak Lo Av, Chig. IG7 49 ER50
Oak Lo Cl, Stan. HA7
off Dennis La 41 CJ50
Walton-on-Thames KT12 154 BW106
Oak Lo Dr, W.Wick. BR4 143 EB101
Oak Lo La, West. TN16 189 ER125
Oak Manor Dr, Wem. HA9
off Oakington Manor Dr 62 CM64
Oakmead Av, Brom. BR2 144 EG100
Oakmeade, Pnr. HA5 40 CA51
Oakmead Gdns, Edg. HA8 42 CR49
Oakmead Grn, Epsom KT18 172 CP115
Oakmead Pl, Mitch. CR4 140 DE95
Oakmead Rd, SW12 120 DG88
Croydon CR0 141 DK100
Oakmere Av, Pot.B. EN6 12 DC33
Oakmere Cl, Pot.B. EN6 12 DD31
Oakmere La, Pot.B. EN6 12 DC32
Oakmere Rd, SE2 106 EU79
Oakmoor Way, Chig. IG7 49 ES50
Oakmount Pl, Orp. BR6 145 ER102
Oak Pk, W.Byf. KT14 151 BE113
Oak Pk Gdns, SW19 119 CX87
Oak Pk Ms, E5 *off Brooke Rd* 66 DT62
Oak Path, Bushey WD23
off Ashfield Av 24 CB44
Oak Piece, Epp. (N.Wld Bas.) CM16 19 FC25
Oak Pl, SW18
off East Hill 120 DB85
Oakridge, St.Alb. (Brick.Wd) AL2 8 BZ29
Oakridge Av, Rad. WD7 9 CF34
Oakridge Dr, N2 64 DD55
Oakridge La, Brom. BR1
off Downham Way 123 ED92
Radlett WD7 9 CF33
Watford (Ald.) WD25 25 CD35
Oakridge Rd, Brom. BR1 123 ED91
Oak Ri, Buck.H. IG9 48 EK48
Oak Rd, W5
off The Broadway 79 CK73
Caterham CR3 176 DS122
Cobham KT11 170 BX115
Epping CM16 17 ET30
Erith (Northumb.Hth) DA8 107 FC80
Erith (Slade Grn) DA8 107 FG81
Gravesend DA12 131 GJ90
Grays RM17 110 GC79
Greenhithe DA9 129 FS86
Leatherhead KT22 171 CG118
New Malden KT3 138 CR96
Orpington BR6 164 EU108
Reigate RH2 184 DB133
Romford RM3 52 FM53
Westerham TN16 189 ER125
Oak Row, SW16 141 DJ96
Oakroyd Av, Pot.B. EN6 11 CZ33
Oakroyd Cl, Pot.B. EN6 11 CZ34
Oaks, The, N12 44 DB49
SE18 105 EQ78
Dartford DA2
off Bow Arrow La 128 FP86
Epsom KT18 157 CT114
Hayes UB4
off Charville La 77 BQ68
Ruislip HA4 59 BS59
Staines TW18
off Moormede Cres 113 BF91
Swanley BR8 147 FE96
Tadworth KT20 173 CW123
Watford WD19 40 BW46
West Byfleet KT14 152 BG113
Woodford Green IG8 48 EE51
Oaks Av, SE19 122 DS92
Feltham TW13 116 BY89
Romford RM5 51 FC54
Worcester Park KT4 139 CV104
Oaks Cl, Lthd. KT22 171 CG121
Radlett WD7 25 CF35
Oaksford Av, SE26 122 DV90
Oaks Gro, E4 48 EE47
Oakshade Rd, Brom. BR1 123 ED91
Leatherhead (Oxshott) KT22 154 CC114
Oakshaw, Oxt. RH8 187 ED127
Oakshaw Rd, SW18 120 DB87
Oakside, Uxb. (Denh.) UB9 76 BH65
Oaks La, Croy. CR0 142 DW104
Ilford IG2 69 ES57
Oak Sq, Sev. TN13
off High St 191 FJ126
Oaks Rd, Croy. CR0 160 DV106
Kenley CR8 159 DP114
Reigate RH2 184 DC133
Staines (Stanw.) TW19 114 BK86
Woking GU21 166 AY117
Oaks Track, Cars. SM5 158 DF111
Wallington SM6 159 DH110
Oak St, Rom. RM7 71 FC57
Oaks Way, Cars. SM5 158 DF108
Epsom KT18
off Epsom La N 173 CV119
Kenley CR8 160 DQ114
Surbiton KT6 137 CK103
Oakthorpe Rd, N13 45 DN50
Oaktree Av, N13 45 DP48
Oak Tree Av, Green. (Bluewater) DA9 129 FT87
Oak Tree Cl, W5
off Pinewood Gro 79 CJ72
Abbots Langley WD5 7 BR32
Oaktree Cl, Brwd. CM13
off Hawthorn Av 55 FZ49
Oak Tree Cl, Loug. IG10 33 EQ39
Stanmore HA7 41 CJ52
Virginia Water GU25 132 AX101
Oaktree Cl, Wal.Cr. EN7 13 DP28
Oak Tree Ct, Borwd. (Elstree) WD6
off Barnet La 25 CK44
Oak Tree Dell, NW9 62 CQ57
Oak Tree Dr, N20 44 DB46
Egham (Eng.Grn) TW20 112 AW92
Slough SL3
off Tamar Way 93 BB78
Oak Tree Gdns, Brom. BR1 124 EH92
Oaktree Gro, Ilf. IG1 69 ER64
Oak Tree Rd, NW8 194 A3
Oak Vw, Wat. WD18
off Gade Av 23 BS41
Oakview Cl, Wal.Cr. EN7 14 DV28
Watford WD19
off Parkside 24 BW44
Oakview Gdns, N2 64 DD56
Oakview Gro, Croy. CR0 143 DY102
Oakview Rd, SE6 123 EB92
Oak Village, NW5 64 DG63
Oak Wk, Wall. SM6
off Helios Rd 140 DG102
Oak Way, N14 45 DH45
Oakway, SW20 139 CW98
Oak Way, W3 80 CS74
Ashtead KT21 172 CN116
Oakway, Brom. BR2 143 ED96
Oak Way, Croy. CR0 143 DX100
Feltham TW14 115 BS88
Oakway, Wok. GU21 166 AS119
Oakway Cl, Bex. DA5 126 EY86
Oakway Pl, Rad. WD7
off Watling St 9 CG34
Oakways, SE9 125 EP86
Oakwell Dr, Pot.B. EN6 13 DH32
OAKWOOD, N14 29 DK44
⊖ **Oakwood** 29 DJ43
Oakwood, Wall. SM6 159 DH109
Waltham Abbey EN9
off Roundhills 31 ED35
Oakwood Av, N14 45 DK45
Beckenham BR3 143 EC96
Borehamwood WD6 26 CP42
Brentwood (Hutt.) CM13 55 GE44
Bromley BR2 144 EH97
Epsom KT19 156 CP109
Mitcham CR4 140 DD96
Purley CR8 159 DP112
Southall UB1 78 CA73
Oakwood Chase, Horn. RM11 72 FM58
Oakwood Cl, N14 29 DJ44
Chislehurst BR7 125 EM93
Dartford DA1 128 FP88
Redhill RH1 184 DG134
Woodford Green IG8
off Green Wk 48 EL51
Oakwood Ct, W14 99 CZ76
Oakwood Cres, N21 29 DL44
Greenford UB6 79 CG65
Oakwood Dr, SE19 122 DR93
Bexleyheath DA7 107 FD84
Edgware HA8 42 CQ51
Sevenoaks TN13 191 FH123
Oakwood Gdns, Ilf. IG3 69 ET61
Orpington BR6 145 EQ103
Sutton SM1 140 DA103
Oakwood Hill, Loug. IG10 33 EM44
Oakwood Hill Ind Est, Loug. IG10 33 EQ43
Oakwood La, W14 99 CZ76
Oakwood Pk Rd, N14 45 DK45
Oakwood Pl, Croy. CR0 141 DN100
Oakwood Ri, Cat. CR3 186 DS125
Oakwood Rd, NW11 64 DB57
SW20 139 CU95
Croydon CR0 141 DN100
Orpington BR6 145 EQ103
Pinner HA5 39 BV54
Redhill (Merst.) RH1 185 DN129
St. Albans (Brick.Wd) AL2 8 BY29
Virginia Water GU25 132 AW99
Woking GU21 166 AS119
Oakwood Vw, N14 29 DK44
Oakworth Rd, W10 81 CW71
Oarsman Pl, E.Mol. KT8 137 CE98
Oast Ho Cl, Stai. (Wrays.) TW19 112 AY87
Oasthouse Way, Orp. BR5 146 EV98
Oast Rd, Oxt. RH8 188 EF131
Oates Cl, Brom. BR2 143 ED97
Oates Rd, Rom. RM5 51 FB50
Oatfield Ho, N15
off Bushey Rd 66 DS58
Oatfield Rd, Orp. BR6 145 ET102
Tadworth KT20 173 CV120
Oatland Ri, E17 47 DY54
Oatlands Av, Wey. KT13 153 BR106
Oatlands Chase, Wey. KT13 135 BS104
Oatlands Cl, Wey. KT13 153 BQ105
Oatlands Dr, Wey. KT13 135 BR104
Oatlands Grn, Wey. KT13
off Oatlands Dr 135 BR104
Oatlands Mere, Wey. KT13 135 BR104
OATLANDS PARK, Wey. KT13 153 BR105
Oatlands Rd, Enf. EN3 30 DW39
Tadworth KT20 173 CY119
Oat La, EC2 197 H8
Oban Cl, E13 86 EJ70
Oban Ho, Bark. IG11
off Wheelers Cross 87 ER68
Oban Rd, E13 86 EJ69
SE25 142 DR98
Oban St, E14 85 ED72
Obelisk Ride, Egh. TW20 112 AS93
Oberon Cl, Borwd. WD6 26 CQ39
Oberon Way, Shep. TW17 134 BL97
Oberstein Rd, SW11 100 DD84
Oborne Cl, SE24 121 DP85
Observatory Gdns, W8 100 DA75
Observatory Ms, E14 204 F8
Observatory Rd, SW14 98 CQ84
Observatory Shop Cen, Slou. SL1 92 AU75
Observatory Wk, Red. RH1
off Lower Br Rd 184 DF134
Occupation La, SE18 105 EP81
W5 97 CK77
Occupation Rd, SE17 201 H10
W13 97 CH75
Watford WD18 23 BV43
Ocean Est, E1 85 DX70
Ocean St, E1 85 DX71
Ocean Wf, E14 203 P5
Ockenden Cl, Wok. GU22
off Ockenden Rd 167 AZ118
Ockenden Gdns, Wok. GU22
off Ockenden Rd 167 AZ118
Ockenden Rd, Wok. GU22 167 AZ118
⇌ **Ockendon** 91 FX69
Ockendon Ms, N1
off Ockendon Rd 84 DR65
Ockendon Rd, N1 84 DR65
Upminster RM14 72 FQ64
OCKHAM, Wok. GU23 168 BN121
Ockham Dr, Lthd. (W.Hors.) KT24 169 BR124
Orpington BR5 126 EU94
Ockham La, Cob. KT11 169 BT118
Woking (Ockham) GU23 169 BP120
Ockham Rd N, Lthd. KT24 169 BQ124
Woking (Ockham) GU23 168 BN121
Ockley Ct, Sutt. SM1
off Oakhill Rd 158 DC105
Ockley Rd, SW16 121 DL90
Croydon CR0 141 DM101
Ockleys Mead, Gdse. RH9 186 DW129
Octagon Arc, EC2 197 M7
Octagon Rd, Walt. (Whiteley Vill.) KT12 153 BS109
Octavia Cl, Mitch. CR4 140 DE99
Octavia Ms, W9
off Bravington Rd 81 CZ70
Octavia Rd, Islw. TW7 97 CF82
Octavia St, SW11 100 DE81
Octavia Way, SE28
off Booth Cl 88 EV73
Staines TW18 114 BG93
Octavius St, SE8 103 EA80
Odard Rd, W.Mol. KT8
off Down St 136 CA98
Oddesey Rd, Borwd. WD6 26 CP39
Odell Cl, Bark. IG11 87 ET66
Odeon, The, Bark. IG11
off Longbridge Rd 87 ER66
Odessa Rd, E7 68 EF62
NW10 81 CU68
Odessa St, SE16 203 M5
Odger St, SW11 100 DF82
Odhams Wk, WC2 196 A9
Odyssey Business Pk, Ruis. HA4 59 BV64
Offa's Mead, E9
off Lindisfarne Way 67 DY63
Offenbach Ho, E2 85 DX68
Offenham Rd, SE9 125 EM91
Offers Ct, Kings.T. KT1
off Winery La 138 CM97
Offerton Rd, SW4 101 DJ83
Offham Slope, N12 43 CZ50
Offley Pl, Islw. TW7 97 CD82
Offley Rd, SW9 101 DN80
Offord Cl, N17 46 DU52
Offord Rd, N1 83 DM66
Offord St, N1 83 DM66
Ogilby St, SE18 105 EM77
Oglander Rd, SE15 102 DT84
Ogle St, W1 195 K6
Oglethorpe Rd, Dag. RM10 70 EZ62
Ohio Rd, E13 86 EF70
Oil Mill La, W6 99 CU78
Okeburn Rd, SW17 120 DG92
Okehampton Cl, N12 44 DD50
Okehampton Cres, Well. DA16 106 EV81
Okehampton Rd, NW10 81 CW67
Romford RM3 52 FJ51
Okehampton Sq, Rom. RM3 52 FJ51
Okemore Gdns, Orp. BR5 146 EW98
Olaf St, W11 81 CX73
Old Acre, Wok. GU22 152 BG114
Oldacre Ms, SW12
off Balham Gro 121 DH87
★ **Old Admiralty Bldgs (M.o.D.)**, SW1 199 N3
Old Amersham Rd, Ger.Cr. SL9 57 BB60
Old Av, W.Byf. KT14 151 BE113
Weybridge KT13 153 BR107
Old Av Cl, W.Byf. KT14 151 BE113
Old Bailey, EC4 196 G9
Old Barge Ho All, SE1
off Upper Grd 83 DN74
Old Barn Cl, Sutt. SM2 157 CY108
Old Barn La, Ken. CR8 176 DT116
Rickmansworth (Crox.Grn) WD3 22 BM43
Old Barn Ms, Rick. WD3
off Old Barn La 22 BM43
Old Barn Rd, Epsom KT18 172 CQ117
Old Barn Way, Bexh. DA7 107 FD83
Old Barrack Yd, SW1 198 F4
Old Barrowfield, E15
off New Plaistow Rd 86 EE67
Old Bath Rd, Slou. (Colnbr.) SL3 93 BE81
Old Bellgate Pl, E14 203 P7
Oldberry Rd, Edg. HA8 42 CR51
Old Bethnal Grn Rd, E2 84 DU69
OLD BEXLEY, Bex. DA5 127 FB87
Old Bexley La, Bex. DA5 127 FD89
Dartford DA1 127 FF88
Old Billingsgate Wk, EC3
off Lower Thames St 84 DS72
Old Bond St, W1 199 K1
Oldborough Rd, Wem. HA0 61 CJ61
Old Brewers Yd, WC2 195 P9
Old Brewery Ms, NW3
off Hampstead High St 64 DD63
Old Br Cl, Nthlt. UB5 78 CA68
Old Br St, Kings.T. (Hmptn W.) KT1 137 CK96
Old Broad St, EC2 197 L9
Old Bromley Rd, Brom. BR1 123 ED92
Old Brompton Rd, SW5 100 DA78
SW7 100 DA78
Old Bldgs, WC2 196 D8
Old Burlington St, W1 195 K10
Oldbury Cl, Cher. KT16
off Oldbury Rd 133 BE101
Orpington BR5 146 EX98
Oldbury Pl, W1 194 G6
Oldbury Rd, Cher. KT16 133 BE101
Enfield EN1 30 DU40
Old Canal Ms, SE15
off Nile Ter 102 DT78
Old Carriageway, The, Sev. TN13 190 FC123
Old Castle St, E1 197 P7
Old Cavendish St, W1 195 H8
Old Change Ct, EC4
off Carter La 84 DQ72
Old Chapel Rd, Swan. BR8 147 FC101
Old Charlton Rd, Shep. TW17 135 BQ99
Old Chelsea Ms, SW3
off Danvers St 100 DD79
Old Chertsey Rd, Wok. (Chobham) GU24 150 AV110
Old Chestnut Av, Esher KT10 154 CA107
Old Chorleywood Rd, Rick. WD3
off Chorleywood Rd 22 BK44
Oldchurch Gdns, Rom. RM7 71 FD59
H **Oldchurch Hosp**, Rom. RM7 71 FE58
Old Ch La, NW9 62 CQ61
Brentwood (Mtnsg) CM13 55 GE42
Greenford UB6
off Perivale La 79 CG69
Stanmore HA7 41 CJ52
Old Ch Path, Esher KT10
off High St 154 CB105
Oldchurch Ri, Rom. RM7 71 FD59
Old Ch Rd, E1 85 DX72
E4 47 EA49
Oldchurch Rd, Rom. RM7 71 FD59
Old Ch St, SW3 100 DD78
Old Claygate La, Esher (Clay.) KT10 155 CG107
Old Clem Sq, SE18
off Kempt St 105 EN79
Old Coach Rd, Cher. KT16 133 BD99
Old Coal Yd, SE28
off Pettman Cres 105 ER77
Old Common Rd, Cob. KT11 153 BU112
Old Compton St, W1 195 M10
Old Cote Dr, Houns. TW5 96 CA79
OLD COULSDON, Couls. CR5 175 DN119
Old Ct, Ashtd. KT21 172 CL119
Old Ct Pl, W8 100 DB75
★ **Old Curiosity Shop**, WC2 196 B8
Old Dairy Ms, SW12
off Chestnut Gro 120 DG87
Old Dartford Rd, Dart. (Fnghm) DA4 148 FM100
Old Dean, Hem.H. (Bov.) HP3 5 BA27
Old Deer Pk Gdns, Rich. TW9 98 CL83
Old Devonshire Rd, SW12 121 DH87
Old Dock App Rd, Grays RM17 110 GE77
Old Dock Cl, Rich. TW9
off Watcombe Cotts 98 CN79
Old Dover Rd, SE3 104 EG80
Olden La, Pur. CR8 159 DN112
Old Esher Cl, Walt. KT12
off Old Esher Rd 154 BX106
Old Esher Rd, Walt. KT12 154 BX106
Old Farleigh Rd, S.Croy. CR2 160 DW110
Warlingham CR6 161 DY113
Old Fm Av, N14 45 DJ45
Sidcup DA15 125 ER88
Old Fm Cl, Houns. TW4 96 BZ84
Old Fm Gdns, Swan. BR8 147 FF97
Old Farmhouse Dr, Lthd. (Oxshott) KT22 171 CD115
Old Fm Pas, Hmptn. TW12 136 CC95
Old Fm Rd, N2 44 DD53
Hampton TW12 116 BZ93
West Drayton UB7 94 BK75
Old Fm Rd E, Sid. DA15 126 EU89
Old Fm Rd W, Sid. DA15 125 ET89
Old Ferry Dr, Stai. (Wrays.) TW19 112 AW86
Old Fld Cl, Amer. HP6 20 AY39
Oldfield Cl, Brom. BR1 145 EM98
Greenford UB6 61 CE64
Stanmore HA7 41 CG50
Waltham Cross (Chsht) EN8 15 DY28
Oldfield Dr, Wal.Cr. (Chsht) EN8 15 DY28
Oldfield Fm Gdns, Grnf. UB6 79 CD67
Oldfield Gdns, Ashtd. KT21 171 CK119
Oldfield Gro, SE16 203 H9
Oldfield La N, Grnf. UB6 79 CE65
Oldfield La S, Grnf. UB6 78 CC70
Oldfield Ms, N6 65 DJ59
Oldfield Rd, N16 66 DS62

★ Place of interest ⇌ Railway station ⊖ London Underground station DLR Docklands Light Railway station Tra Tramlink station H Hospital Riv Pedestrian ferry landing stage

Old - Orc

Oldfield Rd, NW10 81 CT66
SW19 119 CY93
W3 *off Valetta Rd* 99 CT75
Bexleyheath DA7 106 EY82
Bromley BR1 145 EM98
Hampton TW12 136 BZ95
St. Albans (Lon.Col.) AL2 9 CK25
Oldfields Circ, Nthlt. UB5 78 CC65
Oldfields Rd, Sutt. SM1 139 CZ104
Oldfields Trd Est, Sutt. SM1 140 DA104
Oldfield Wd, Wok. GU22
off Maybury Hill 167 BB117
Old Fish St Hill, EC4 197 H10
Old Fleet La, EC4 196 F8
Old Fold Cl, Barn. EN5
off Old Fold La 27 CZ39
Old Fold La, Barn. EN5 27 CZ39
Old Fold Vw, Barn. EN5 27 CW41
OLD FORD, E3 85 DZ66
Old Ford Rd, E2 84 DW68
E3 85 DY68
Old Forge Cl, Stan. HA7 41 CG49
Watford WD25 7 BU33
Old Forge Cres, Shep. TW17 135 BP100
Old Forge Ms, W12
off Goodwin Rd 99 CV75
Old Forge Rd, Enf. EN1 30 DT38
Old Forge Way, Sid. DA14 126 EV91
Old Fox Cl, Cat. CR3 175 DP121
Old Fox Footpath, S.Croy. CR2
off Essenden Rd 160 DS108
Old Gannon Cl, Nthwd. HA6 39 BQ50
Old Gdn, The, Sev. TN13 190 FD123
Old Gloucester St, WC1 196 A6
Old Gro Cl, Wal.Cr.
(Chsht) EN7 14 DR26
Old Hall Cl, Pnr. HA5 40 BY53
Old Hall Dr, Pnr. HA5 40 BY53
Oldham Ter, W3 80 CQ74
Old Harrow La, West. TN16 179 EQ119
Old Hatch Manor, Ruis. HA4 59 BT59
Old Hill, Chis. BR7 145 EN95
Orpington BR6 163 ER107
Woking GU22 166 AX120
Oldhill St, N16 66 DU60
Old Homesdale Rd,
Brom. BR2 144 EJ98
Old Hosp Cl, SW12 120 DF88
Old Ho Cl, SW19 119 CY92
Epsom KT17 157 CT110
Old Ho Gdns, Twick. TW1 117 CJ85
Old Ho La, Kings L. WD4 22 BL35
Old Howlett's La, Ruis. HA4 59 BQ58
Old Jamaica Rd, SE16 202 B6
Old James St, SE15 102 DV83
Old Jewry, EC2 197 K9
Old Kenton La, NW9 62 CP57
Old Kent Rd, SE1 201 L7
SE15 102 DS77
Old Kingston Rd,
Wor.Pk. KT4 138 CQ104
Old La, Cob. KT11 169 BP117
Westerham (Tats.) TN16 178 EK121
Old La Gdns, Cob. KT11 169 BT122
Old Lo La, Ken. CR8 159 DM114
Purley CR8 159 DM114
Old Lo Pl, Twick. TW1
off St. Margarets Rd 117 CH86
Old Lo Way, Stan. HA7 41 CG50
Old London Rd,
Epsom KT18 173 CU118
Kingston upon Thames KT2 138 CL96
Sevenoaks (Bad.Mt) TN14 164 FA110
Sevenoaks (Knock.P.) TN14 180 EY115
Old Maidstone Rd, Sid. DA14 126 EZ94
OLD MALDEN, Wor.Pk. KT4 138 CR102
Old Malden La, Wor.Pk. KT4 138 CR103
Old Malt Way, Wok. GU21 166 AX117
Old Manor Dr, Grav. DA12 131 GJ88
Isleworth TW7 116 CC86
Old Manor Ho Ms, Shep. TW17
off Squires Br Rd 134 BN97
Old Manor Rd, Sthl. UB2 96 BX77
Old Manor Way, Bexh. DA7 107 FD82
Chislehurst BR7 125 EM92
Old Manor Yd, SW5
off Earls Ct Rd 100 DB77
Old Mkt Sq, E2 197 P2
Old Marylebone Rd, NW1 194 C7
Old Mead, Ger.Cr.
(Chal.St.P.) SL9 36 AY51
Old Ms, Har. HA1
off Hindes Rd 61 CE57
Old Mill Cl, Dart.
(Eyns.) DA4 148 FL102
Old Mill Ct, E18 68 EJ55
Old Mill La, Red. RH1 185 DH128
Uxbridge UB8 76 BH72
Old Mill Pl, Rom. RM7 71 FD58
Old Mill Rd, SE18 105 ER79
Kings Langley WD4 7 BQ33
Uxbridge (Denh.) UB9 58 BG62
Old Mitre Ct, EC4 *off Fleet St* 83 DN72
Old Montague St, E1 84 DU71
Old Nichol St, E2 197 P4
Old N St, WC1 196 B6
Old Nursery Pl, Ashf. TW15
off Park Rd 115 BP92
Old Oak Av, Couls. CR5 174 DE119
Old Oak Cl, Chess. KT9 156 CM105
Cobham KT11
off Copse Rd 153 BV113
OLD OAK COMMON, NW10 81 CT71
Old Oak Common La, NW10 80 CS71
W3 80 CS71
Old Oak La, NW10 80 CS69
Old Oak Rd, W3 81 CT73
Old Oaks, Wal.Abb. EN9 16 EE32
★ Old Operating Thea Mus &
Herb Garret, SE1 201 L3
Old Orchard,
St.Alb.(Park St) AL2 8 CC26
Sunbury-on-Thames TW16 136 BW96
West Byfleet
(Byfleet) KT14 152 BM112
Old Orchard, The, NW3
off Nassington Rd 64 DF63
Old Orchard Cl, Barn. EN4 28 DD38
Uxbridge UB8 76 BN72
Old Otford Rd, Sev. TN14 181 FH117
Old Palace La, Rich. TW9 117 CJ85
Old Palace Rd, Croy. CR0 141 DP104
Weybridge KT13 135 BP104
Old Palace Ter, Rich. TW9
off King St 117 CK85
Old Palace Yd, SW1 199 P6
Richmond TW9 117 CJ85
Old Paradise St, SE11 200 B8
Old Pk Av, SW12 120 DG86
Enfield EN2 30 DQ42
Old Parkbury La, St.Alb.
(Coln.St) AL2 9 CF30
Old Pk Gro, Enf. EN2 30 DQ42
Old Pk La, W1 198 G3
Old Pk Ms, Houns. TW5 96 BZ80
Old Pk Ride, Wal.Cr. EN7 14 DT33
Old Pk Ridings, N21 29 DP44
Old Pk Rd, N13 45 DM49
SE2 106 EU78
Enfield EN2 29 DP41
Old Pk Rd S, Enf. EN2 29 DP42
Old Pk Vw, Enf. EN2 29 DN41
Old Parvis Rd, W.Byf. KT14 152 BK112
Old Perry St, Chis. BR7 125 ES94
Gravesend (Nthflt) DA11 130 GE89
Old Polhill, Sev. TN14 181 FD115
Old Pound Cl, Islw. TW7 97 CG81
Old Priory, Uxb. (Hare.) UB9 59 BP59
Old Pye St, SW1 199 M6
Old Quebec St, W1 194 E9
Old Queen St, SW1 199 N5
Old Rectory Cl, Tad. KT20 173 CU124
Old Rectory Gdns, Edg. HA8 42 CN51
Old Rectory La, Uxb.
(Denh.) UB9 57 BE59
Old Redding, Har. HA3 40 CC49
Old Reigate Rd, Bet. RH3 182 CP134
Dorking RH4 182 CL134
Oldridge Rd, SW12 120 DG87
Old River Lea Towpath, E15
off City Mill River Towpath 85 EB66
Old Rd, SE13 104 EE84
Addlestone KT15 151 BF108
Betchworth
(Buckland) RH3 182 CR134
Dartford DA1 107 FD84
Enfield EN3 30 DW39
Old Rd E, Grav. DA12 131 GH88
Old Rd W, Grav. DA11 131 GF88
Old Rope Wk, Sun. TW16
off The Avenue 135 BV97
Old Royal Free Pl, N1
off Liverpool Rd 83 DN67
Old Royal Free Sq, N1 83 DN67
Old Ruislip Rd, Nthlt. UB5 78 BX68
Olds App, Wat. WD18 39 BP46
Old Savill's Cotts, Chig. IG7
off The Chase 49 EQ49
Old Sch Cl, SE10 205 J7
SW19 140 DA96
Beckenham BR3 143 DX96
Old Sch Ct, Stai.
(Wrays.) TW19 112 AY87
Old Sch Cres, E7 86 EF65
Old Sch Ms, Egh. TW20 113 BD92
Weybridge KT13 153 BR105
Old Sch Pl, Croy. CR0 159 DN105
Woking GU22 166 AY121
Old Sch Rd, Uxb. UB8 76 BM70
Old Schs La, Epsom KT17 157 CT109
Old Sch Sq, E14
off Pelling St 85 EA72
Thames Ditton KT7 137 CF100
Olds Cl, Wat. WD18 39 BP46
Old Seacoal La, EC4 196 F8
Old Shire La, Ger.Cr. SL9 37 BA46
Rickmansworth
(Chorl.) WD3 21 BB44
Waltham Abbey EN9 32 EG35
Old Slade La, Iver SL0 93 BE76
Old Solesbridge La, Rick.
(Chorl.) WD3 22 BG41
Old S Cl, Pnr. HA5 40 BX53
Old S Lambeth Rd, SW8 101 DL80
★ Old Spitalfields Mkt, E1 197 P6
Old Sq, WC2 196 C8
Old Sta App, Lthd. KT22 171 CG121
Old Sta Rd, Hayes UB3 95 BT76
Loughton IG10 32 EL43
Old Sta Yd, Brom. BR2
off Bourne Way 144 EF102
Oldstead Rd, Brom. BR1 123 ED91
Old Stockley Rd,
West Dr. UB7 95 BP75
⇌ Old Street 197 K3
⊖ Old Street 197 K3
Old St, E13 86 EH68
EC1 197 H4
Old Swan Yd, Cars. SM5 158 DF105
Old Tilburstow Rd,
Gdse. RH9 186 DW134
Old Town, SW4 101 DJ83
Croydon CR0 141 DP104
Old Tram Yd, SE18
off Lakedale Rd 105 ES77
Old Tye Av, West.
(Bigg.H.) TN16 178 EL116
Old Uxbridge Rd, Rick.
(Map.Cr.) WD3 37 BE53
Old Wk, The, Sev.
(Otford) TN14 181 FH117
Old Watford Rd, St.Alb.
(Brick.Wd) AL2 8 BY30
Old Watling St, Grav. DA11 131 GG92
Old Westhall Cl, Warl. CR6 176 DW119
Old Wf Way, Wey. KT13
off Weybridge Rd 152 BM105
OLD WINDSOR, Wind. SL4 112 AU86
Old Windsor Lock, Wind.
(Old Wind.) SL4 112 AW85
OLD WOKING, Wok. GU22 167 BA121
Old Woking Rd,
W.Byf. KT14 151 BF113
Woking GU22 167 BE116
Old Woolwich Rd, SE10 103 ED79
Old Yd, The, West. TN16 180 EW124
Old York Rd, SW18 120 DB85
Oleander Cl, Orp. BR6 163 ER106
O'Leary Sq, E1 84 DW71
Olga St, E3 85 DY68
Olinda Rd, N16 66 DT58
Oliphant St, W10 81 CX69
Oliver Av, SE25 142 DT97
Oliver Cl, W4 98 CP79
Addlestone KT15 152 BG105
Grays RM20 109 FT80
St. Albans (Park St) AL2 9 CD27
Oliver Cres, Dart.
(Fnghm) DA4 148 FM101
Oliver Gdns, E6 86 EL72
Oliver-Goldsmith Est, SE15 102 DU81
Oliver Gro, SE25 142 DT98
Oliver Ms, SE15 102 DU82
Olive Rd, E13 86 EJ69
NW2 63 CW63
SW19 *off Norman Rd* 120 DC94
W5 97 CK76
Dartford DA1 128 FK88
Oliver Rd, E10 67 EB61
E17 67 EC57
NW10 80 CQ68
Brentwood
(Shenf.) CM15 55 GA43
Grays RM20 109 FT81
New Malden KT3 138 CQ96
Rainham RM13 89 FF67
Sutton SM1 158 DD105
Swanley BR8 147 FD97
Olivers Yd, EC1 197 L4
Olive St, Rom. RM7 71 FD57
Olivette St, SW15 99 CX83
Olivia Dr, Slou. SL3
off Ditton Rd 93 AZ78
Olivia Gdns, Uxb.
(Hare.) UB9 38 BJ53
Ollards Gro, Loug. IG10 32 EK42
Olleberrie La, Rick.
(Sarratt) WD3 5 BD32
Ollerton Grn, E3 85 DZ67
Ollerton Rd, N11 45 DK50
Olley Cl, Wall. SM6 159 DL108
Ollgar Cl, W12 81 CT74
Olliffe St, E14 204 E7
Olmar St, SE1 102 DU79
Olney Rd, SE17 101 DP79
Olron Cres, Bexh. DA6 126 EX85
Olven Rd, SE18 105 EQ80
Olveston Wk, Cars. SM5 140 DD100
Olwen Ms, Pnr. HA5 40 BX54
Olyffe Av, Well. DA16 106 EU82
Olyffe Dr, Beck. BR3 143 EC95
★ Olympia, W14 99 CY76
Olympia Ms, W2
off Queensway 82 DB73
Olympia Way, W14 99 CY76
Olympic Way, Grnf. UB6 78 CB67
Wembley HA9 62 CN63
Olympus Sq, E5
off Nolan Way 66 DU63
Oman Av, NW2 63 CW63
O'Meara St, SE1 201 J3
Omega Cl, E14 204 B6
Omega Pl, N1 196 A1
Omega Rd, Wok. GU21 167 BA115
Omega St, SE14 103 EA81
Ommaney Rd, SE14 103 DX81
Omnibus Way, E17 47 EA54
Ondine Rd, SE15 102 DT84
Onega Gate, SE16 203 K6
O'Neill Path, SE18
off Kempt St 105 EN79
One Tree Cl, SE23 122 DW86
Ongar Cl, Add. KT15 151 BF107
Romford RM6 70 EW57
Ongar Hill, Add. KT15 152 BG107
Ongar Pl, Add. KT15 152 BG107
Ongar Rd, SW6 100 DA79
Addlestone KT15 152 BG106
Brentwood CM15 54 FV45
Romford RM4 34 EW40
Ongar Way, Rain. RM13 89 FE67
Onra Rd, E17 67 EA59
Onslow Av, Rich. TW10 118 CL85
Sutton SM2 157 CZ110
Onslow Cl, E4 47 EC47
Thames Ditton KT7 137 CE102
Woking GU22 167 BA117
Onslow Cres, Chis. BR7 145 EP95
Woking GU22 167 BA117
Onslow Dr, Sid. DA14 126 EX89
Onslow Gdns, E18 68 EH55
N10 65 DH57
N21 29 DN43
SW7 100 DD78
South Croydon CR2 160 DU112
Thames Ditton KT7 137 CE102
Wallington SM6 159 DJ107
Onslow Ms, Cher. KT16 134 BG100
Onslow Ms E, SW7
off Cranley Pl 100 DD77
Onslow Ms W, SW7
off Cranley Pl 100 DD77
Onslow Rd, Croy. CR0 141 DM101
New Malden KT3 139 CU98
Richmond TW10 118 CL85
Walton-on-Thames KT12 153 BT105
Onslow Sq, SW7 198 A8
Onslow St, EC1 196 E5
Onslow Way, T.Ditt. KT7 137 CE102
Woking GU22 167 BF115
Ontario Cl, Brox. EN10 15 DY25
Ontario St, SE1 200 G7
Ontario Way, E14 203 P1
On The Hill, Wat. WD19 40 BY47
Opal Cl, E16 86 EK72
Opal Ct, Slou. (Wexham) SL3
off Wexham St 74 AV70
Opal Ms, NW6
off Priory Pk Rd 81 CZ67
Ilford IG1 *off Ley St* 69 EP61
Opal St, SE11 200 F9
Opecks Cl, Slou. SL2
off Church La 74 AV70
Openshaw Rd, SE2 106 EV77
Openview, SW18 120 DC88
Ophelia Gdns, NW2
off Hamlet Sq 63 CY62
Ophir Ter, SE15 102 DU81
Opossum Way, Houns. TW4 96 BW82
Oppenheim Rd, SE13 103 EC82
Oppidans Ms, NW3
off Meadowbank 82 DF66
Oppidans Rd, NW3 82 DF66
Orange Ct, E1 202 C3
Orange Ct La, Orp. BR6 163 EN109
Orange Gro, E11 68 EE62
Chigwell IG7 49 EQ51
Orange Hill Rd, Edg. HA8 42 CQ52
Orange Pl, SE16 202 G7
Orangery, The, Rich. TW10 117 CJ89
Orangery La, SE9 125 EM85
Orange Sq, SW1 198 G9
Orange St, WC2 199 M1
Orange Tree Hill, Rom.
(Hav.at.Bow.) RM4 51 FD50
Orange Yd, W1 195 N9
Oransay Rd, N1 84 DQ65
Oransay Wk, N1
off Clephane Rd 84 DQ65
Oratory La, SW3 198 A10
Orbain Rd, SW6 99 CY80
Orbel St, SW11 100 DE81
Orbital Cres, Wat. WD25 23 BT35
Orbital One, Dart. DA1 128 FP89
Orb St, SE17 201 K9
Orchard, The, N14 29 DH43
N21 30 DR44
NW11 64 DA57
SE3 103 ED82
W4 98 CR77
W5 79 CK71
Banstead SM7 174 DA115
Epsom KT17 157 CT108
Epsom (Ewell) KT17
off Tayles Hill Dr 157 CT110
Hounslow TW3 96 CC82
Kings Langley WD4 6 BN29
Rickmansworth (Crox.Grn) WD3
off Green La 22 BM43
Sevenoaks
(Dunt.Grn) TN13 181 FE120
Swanley BR8 147 FD96
Virginia Water GU25 132 AY99
Weybridge KT13 153 BP105
Woking GU22 166 AY122
Orchard Av, N3 64 DA55
N14 29 DJ44
N20 44 DD47
Addlestone (Wdhm) KT15 151 BF111
Ashford TW15 115 BQ93
Belvedere DA17 106 EY79
Brentwood CM13 55 FZ48
Croydon CR0 143 DY101
Dartford DA1 127 FH87
Feltham TW14 115 BR85
Gravesend DA11 131 GH92
Hounslow TW5 96 BY80
Mitcham CR4 140 DG102
New Malden KT3 138 CS96
Rainham RM13 90 FJ70
Southall UB1 78 BY74
Thames Ditton KT7 137 CG102
Watford WD25 7 BV32
Orchard Cl, E4
off Chingford Mt Rd 47 EA49
E11 68 EH56
N1 *off Morton Rd* 84 DQ66
NW2 63 CU62
SE23 *off Brenchley Gdns* 122 DW86
SW20 *off Grand Dr* 139 CW98
W10 81 CY71
Ashford TW15 115 BQ93
Banstead SM7 158 DB114
Bexleyheath DA7 106 EY81
Borehamwood
(Elstree) WD6 26 CM42
Bushey (Bushey Hth) WD23 41 CD46
Edgware HA8 42 CL51
Egham TW20 113 BB92
Epsom (W.Ewell) KT19 156 CP107
Leatherhead KT22 171 CF119
Leatherhead
(E.Hors.) KT24 169 BT124
Leatherhead (Fetch.) KT22 171 CD122
Northolt UB5 60 CC64
Potters Bar (Cuffley) EN6 13 DL28
Radlett WD7 25 CE37
Rickmansworth
(Chorl.) WD3 21 BD42
Ruislip HA4 59 BQ59
South Ockendon RM15 91 FW70
Surbiton KT6 137 CH101
Uxbridge (Denh.) UB9 76 BH65
Walton-on-Thames KT12
off Garden Rd 135 BV101
Watford WD17 23 BT40
Wembley HA0 80 CL67
Woking GU22 167 BB116
Orchard Ct, Hem.H. (Bov.) HP3 5 BA27
Isleworth TW7
off Thornbury Av 97 CD81
Twickenham TW2 117 CD89
Wallington SM6
off Parkgate Rd 159 DH106
Worcester Park KT4 139 CU102
Orchard Cres, Edg. HA8 42 CQ50
Enfield EN1 30 DT39
Orchard Dr, SE3
off Orchard Rd 104 EE82
Ashtead KT21 171 CK120
Edgware HA8 42 CM50
Epping (They.B.) CM16 33 ES36
Grays RM17 110 GA75
Rickmansworth
(Chorl.) WD3 21 BC41
St. Albans (Park St) AL2 8 CB27
Uxbridge UB8 76 BK70
Watford WD17 23 BT39
Woking GU21 167 AZ115
Orchard End, Cat. CR3 176 DS122
Leatherhead (Fetch.) KT22 170 CC124
Weybridge KT13 135 BS103
Orchard End Av, Amer. HP7 20 AT39
Orchard Est, Wdf.Grn. IG8 48 EJ52
Orchard Gdns, Chess. KT9 156 CL105
Orchard Gdns, Epsom KT18 156 CQ114
Sutton SM1 158 DA106
Waltham Abbey EN9 15 EC34
Orchard Gate, NW9 62 CS56
Esher KT10 137 CD102
Greenford UB6 79 CH65
Orchard Grn, Orp. BR6 145 ES103
Orchard Gro, SE20 122 DU94
Croydon CR0 143 DY101
Edgware HA8 42 CN53
Gerrards Cross
(Chal.St.P.) SL9 36 AW53
Harrow HA3 62 CM57
Orpington BR6 145 ET103
Orchard Hill, SE13
off Coldbath St 103 EB82
Carshalton SM5 158 DF106
Dartford DA1 127 FE85
Orchard Ho, Erith DA8
off Northend Rd 107 FF81
Orchard La, SW20 139 CV95
Brentwood
(Pilg.Hat.) CM15 54 FT43
East Molesey KT8 137 CD100
Woodford Green IG8 48 EJ49
Orchard Lea Cl, Wok. GU22 167 BE115
ORCHARD LEIGH, Chesh. HP5 4 AV28
Orchard Leigh, Chesh. HP5 4 AU28
Orchardleigh, Lthd. KT22 171 CH122
Orchardleigh Av, Enf. EN3 30 DW40
Orchard Mains, Wok. GU22 166 AW119
Orchardmede, N21 30 DR44
Orchard Ms, N1
off Southgate Gro 84 DR66
Orchard Path, Slou. SL3 75 BA72
Orchard Pl, E5 66 DV64
E14 86 EE73
N17 46 DT52
Keston BR2 162 EJ109
Sevenoaks (Sund.) TN14 180 EY124
Waltham Cross (Chsht) EN8
off Turners Hill 15 DX30
Orchard Ri, Croy. CR0 143 DY102
Kingston upon Thames KT2 138 CQ95
Pinner HA5 59 BT55
Richmond TW10 98 CP84
Orchard Ri E, Sid. DA15 125 ET85
Orchard Ri W, Sid. DA15 125 ES85
Orchard Rd, N6 65 DH59
SE3 104 EE82
SE18 105 ER77
Barnet EN5 27 CZ42
Belvedere DA17 106 FA77
Brentford TW8 97 CJ79
Bromley BR1 144 EJ95
Chalfont St. Giles HP8 36 AW47
Chessington KT9 156 CL105
Dagenham RM10 88 FA67
Enfield EN3 30 DW43
Gravesend (Nthflt) DA11 130 GC89
Hampton TW12 116 BZ94
Hayes UB3 77 BT73
Hounslow TW4 116 BZ85
Kingston upon Thames KT1 138 CL96
Mitcham CR4 140 DG102
Orpington (Farnboro.) BR6 163 EP106
Orpington (Pr.Bot.) BR6 164 EW110
Reigate RH2 184 DB134
Richmond TW9 98 CN83
Romford RM7 51 FB53
Sevenoaks (Otford) TN14 181 FF116
Sevenoaks (Rvrhd) TN13 190 FE122
Sidcup DA14 125 ES91
South Croydon CR2 160 DV114
South Ockendon RM15 91 FW70
Sunbury-on-Thames TW16
off Hanworth Rd 115 BV94
Sutton SM1 158 DA106
Swanscombe DA10 130 FY85
Twickenham TW1 117 CG85
Welling DA16 106 EV83
Windsor (Old Wind.) SL4 112 AV86
Orchards, The, Epp. CM16 18 EU32
Orchards Cl, W.Byf. KT14 152 BG114
Orchardson St, NW8 82 DD70
Orchard Sq, W14 *off Sun Rd* 99 CZ78
Orchards Residential Pk, The,
Slou. SL3 75 AZ74
Orchards Shop Cen,
Dart. DA1 128 FL86
Orchard St, E17 67 DY56
W1 194 F9
Dartford DA1 128 FL86
Orchard Ter, Enf. EN1
off Great Cambridge Rd 30 DU44
Orchard Vw, Cher. KT16
off Colonels La 134 BG100
Uxbridge UB8 76 BK70
Orchard Vil, Sid. DA14 126 EW93
Orchard Way, Add. KT15 152 BH106
Ashford TW15 114 BM89
Beckenham BR3 143 DY99
Chigwell IG7 50 EU48
Croydon CR0 143 DY102
Dartford DA2 128 FK90
Enfield EN1 30 DS41
Esher KT10 154 CC107
Hemel Hempstead
(Bov.) HP3 5 BA28
Oxted RH8 188 EG133
Potters Bar EN6 12 DB28
Rickmansworth
(Mill End) WD3 38 BG45
Slough SL3 74 AY74
Sutton SM1 158 DD105
Tadworth KT20 183 CZ126
Waltham Cross
(Chsht) EN7 13 DP27
Orchard Waye, Uxb. UB8 76 BK68
Orchehill Av, Ger.Cr. SL9 56 AX56
Orchehill Ct, Ger.Cr. SL9 56 AY57
Orchehill Ri, Ger.Cr. SL9 56 AY57
Orchid Cl, E6 86 EL71
Chessington KT9 155 CJ108
Romford (Abridge) RM4 34 EV41
Southall UB1 78 BY72
Waltham Cross
(Goffs Oak) EN7 14 DQ30
Orchid Ct, Egh. TW20 113 BB91
Romford RM7 71 FE61

★ Place of interest ⇌ Railway station ⊖ London Underground station DLR Docklands Light Railway station Tra Tramlink station H Hospital Riv Pedestrian ferry landing stage

Orchid Rd, N14 45 DJ45
Orchid St, W12 81 CU73
Orchis Gro, Grays
(Bad.Dene) RM17 110 FZ78
Orchis Way, Rom. RM3 52 FM51
Orde Hall St, WC1 196 B5
Ordell Rd, E3 85 DZ68
Ordnance Cl, Felt. TW13 115 BU90
Ordnance Cres, SE10 204 G4
Ordnance Hill, NW8 82 DD67
Ordnance Ms, NW8
off St. Ann's Ter 82 DD68
Ordnance Rd, E16 86 EF71
SE18 105 EN79
Enfield EN3 31 DX37
Gravesend DA12 131 GJ86
Oregano Cl, West Dr. UB7
off Camomile Way 76 BM72
Oregano Dr, E14 85 ED72
Oregon Av, E12 69 EM63
Oregon Cl, N.Mal. KT3
off Georgia Rd 138 CQ98
Oregon Sq, Orp. BR6 145 ER102
Orestes Ms, NW6
off Aldred Rd 64 DA64
Oreston Rd, Rain. RM13 90 FK69
Orford Ct, SE27 121 DP89
Orford Gdns, Twick. TW1 117 CF89
Orford Rd, E17 67 EA57
E18 68 EH55
SE6 123 EB90
Organ Hall Rd, Borwd. WD6 26 CL39
Organ La, E4 47 EC47
Oriel Cl, Mitch. CR4 141 DK98
Oriel Ct, NW3 off Heath St 64 DC63
Oriel Dr, SW13 99 CV79
Oriel Gdns, Ilf. IG5 69 EM55
Oriel Pl, NW3 off Heath St 64 DC63
Oriel Rd, E9 85 DX65
Oriel Way, Nthlt. UB5 78 CB66
Oriental Cl, Wok. GU22
off Oriental Rd 167 BA117
Oriental Rd, E16 86 EK74
Woking GU22 167 BA117
Oriental St, E14
off Morant St 85 EA73
Orient Ind Pk, E10 67 EA61
Orient St, SE11 200 F8
Orient Way, E5 67 DX62
E10 67 DY61
Oriole Cl, Abb.L. WD5 7 BU31
Oriole Way, SE28 88 EV73
Orion Rd, N11 45 DH51
Orion Way, Nthwd. HA6 39 BT49
Orissa Rd, SE18 105 ES78
Orkney St, SW11 100 DG82
Orlando Gdns, Epsom KT19 156 CR110
Orlando Rd, SW4 101 DJ83
Orleans Cl, Esher KT10 137 CD103
★ Orleans Ho Gall,
Twick. TW1 117 CH88
Orleans Rd, SE19 122 DR93
Twickenham TW1 117 CH87
Orlestone Gdns, Orp. BR6 164 EY106
Orleston Ms, N7 83 DN65
Orleston Rd, N7 83 DN65
Orley Fm Rd, Har. HA1 61 CE62
Orlop St, SE10 104 EE78
Ormanton Rd, SE26 122 DU91
Orme Ct, W2 82 DB73
Orme Ct Ms, W2
off Orme La 82 DB73
Orme La, W2 82 DB73
Ormeley Rd, SW12 121 DH88
Orme Rd, Kings.T. KT1 138 CP96
Sutton SM1
off Grove Rd 158 DB107
Ormerod Gdns, Mitch. CR4 140 DG96
Ormesby Cl, SE28
off Wroxham Rd 88 EX73
Ormesby Dr, Pot.B. EN6 11 CX32
Ormesby Way, Har. HA3 62 CM58
Orme Sq, W2
off Bayswater Rd 82 DB73
Ormiston Gro, W12 81 CV74
Ormiston Rd, SE10 104 EG78
Ormond Av, Hmptn. TW12 136 CB95
Richmond TW10
off Ormond Rd 117 CK85
Ormond Cl, WC1 196 A6
Romford (Harold Wd) RM3
off Chadwick Dr 52 FK54
Ormond Cres, Hmptn. TW12 136 CB95
Ormond Dr, Hmptn. TW12 116 CB94
Ormonde Av, Epsom KT19 156 CR109
Orpington BR6 145 EQ103
Ormonde Gate, SW3 100 DF78
Ormonde Pl, SW1 198 F9
Ormonde Ri, Buck.H. IG9 48 EJ46
Ormonde Rd, SW14 98 CP83
Northwood HA6 39 BR49
Woking GU21 166 AW116
Ormonde Ter, NW8 82 DF67
Ormond Ms, WC1 196 A5
Ormond Rd, N19 65 DL60
Richmond TW10 117 CK85
Ormond Yd, SW1 199 L2
Ormsby, Sutt. SM2
off Grange Rd 158 DB108
Ormsby Gdns, Grnf. UB6 78 CC68
Ormsby Pl, N16
off Victorian Gro 66 DT62
Ormsby Pt, SE18
off Troy Ct 105 EP77
Ormsby St, E2 84 DT68
Ormside St, SE15 102 DW79
Ormside Way, Red. RH1 185 DH130
Ormskirk Rd, Wat. WD19 40 BX49
Ornan Rd, NW3 64 DE64
Orpen Wk, N16 66 DS62
Orphanage Rd, Wat.
WD17, WD24 24 BW40
Orpheus St, SE5 102 DR81
ORPINGTON 145 ES102
⇌ Orpington 145 ET103
Orpington Bypass, Orp. BR6 146 EV103
Sevenoaks TN14 164 FA109
Orpington Gdns, N18 46 DS48
H Orpington Hosp,
Orp. BR6 163 ET105
Orpington Rd, N21 45 DP46
Chislehurst BR7 145 ES97
Orpin Rd, Red. RH1 185 DH130
Orpwood Cl, Hmptn. TW12 116 BZ92
ORSETT HEATH,
Grays RM16 111 GG75
Orsett Heath Cres,
Grays RM16 111 GG76
Orsett Rd, Grays RM17 110 GA78
Orsett St, SE11 200 C10
Orsett Ter, W2 82 DC72
Woodford Green IG8 48 EJ53
Orsman Rd, N1 84 DS67
Orton St, E1 202 B3
Orville Rd, SW11 100 DD82
Orwell Cl, Hayes UB3 77 BS73
Rainham RM13 89 FD71
Orwell Ct, N5 66 DQ63
Orwell Rd, E13 86 EJ68
Osbaldeston Rd, N16 66 DU61
Osberton Rd, SE12 124 EG85
Osbert St, SW1 199 M9
Osborn Cl, E8 84 DU67
Osborne Av, Stai. TW19 114 BL88
Osborne Cl, Barn. EN4 28 DF41
Beckenham BR3 143 DY98
Feltham TW13 116 BX92
Hornchurch RM11 71 FH58
Osborne Ct, Pot.B. EN6 12 DB29
Osborne Gdns, Pot.B. EN6 12 DB30
Thornton Heath CR7 142 DQ96
Osborne Gro, E17 67 DZ56
N4 65 DN60
Osborne Ms, E17
off Osborne Gro 67 DZ56
Osborne Pl, Sutt. SM1 158 DD106
Osborne Rd, E7 68 EH64
E9 85 DZ65
E10 67 EB62
N4 65 DM60
N13 45 DN48
NW2 81 CV65
W3 98 CP76
Belvedere DA17 106 EZ78
Brentwood (Pilg.Hat.) CM15 54 FU44
Buckhurst Hill IG9 48 EH46
Dagenham RM9 70 EZ64
Egham TW20 113 AZ93
Enfield EN3 31 DY40
Hornchurch RM11 71 FH58
Hounslow TW3 96 BZ83
Kingston upon Thames KT2 118 CL94
Potters Bar EN6 12 DB30
Redhill RH1 184 DG131
Southall UB1 78 CC72
Thornton Heath CR7 142 DQ96
Uxbridge UB8
off Oxford Rd 76 BJ66
Waltham Cross (Chsht) EN8 15 DY27
Walton-on-Thames KT12 135 BU102
Watford WD24 24 BW38
Osborne Sq, Dag. RM9 70 EZ63
Osborne St, Slou. SL1 92 AT75
Osborne Ter, SW17
off Church La 120 DG92
Osborne Way, Chess. KT9
off Bridge Rd 156 CM106
Osborn Gdns, NW7 43 CX52
Osborn La, SE23 123 DY87
Osborn St, E1 84 DT71
Osborn Ter, SE3 off Lee Rd 104 EF84
Osbourne Av, NW7 43 CX52
Kings Langley WD4 6 BM28
Osbourne Hts, Brwd. CM14
off Warley Hill 54 FV49
Osbourne Rd, Dart. DA2 128 FP86
Oscar Faber Pl, N1
off St. Peter's Way 84 DS66
Oscar St, SE8 103 EA81
Oseney Cres, NW5 83 DJ65
Osgood Av, Orp. BR6 163 ET106
Osgood Gdns, Orp. BR6 163 ET106
OSIDGE, N14 45 DH46
Osidge La, N14 44 DG46
Osier Cres, N10 44 DF53
Osier La, SE10 205 L7
Osier Ms, W4 99 CT79
Osier Pl, Egh. TW20 113 BC93
Osiers Rd, SW18 100 DA84
Osier St, E1 84 DW70
Osier Way, E10 67 EB62
Banstead SM7 157 CY114
Mitcham CR4 140 DE99
Oslac Rd, SE6 123 EB92
Oslo Ct, NW8 194 B1
Oslo Sq, SE16 203 L6
Osman Cl, N15
off Tewkesbury Rd 66 DR58
Osman Rd, N9 46 DU48
W6 off Batoum Gdns 99 CW76
Osmond Cl, Har. HA2 60 CC61
Osmond Gdns, Wall. SM6 159 DJ106
Osmund St, W12
off Braybrook St 81 CT72
Osnaburgh St, NW1 195 J5
NW1 (north section) 195 J3
Osnaburgh Ter, NW1 195 J4
Osney Ho, SE2
off Hartslock Dr 106 EX75
Osney Wk, Cars. SM5 140 DD100
Osney Way, Grav. DA12 131 GM89
Osprey Cl, E6
off Dove App 86 EL71
E11 68 EG56
E17 47 DY52
Leatherhead (Fetch.) KT22 170 CC122
Sutton SM1
off Sandpiper Rd 157 CZ106
Watford WD25 8 BY34
West Drayton UB7 94 BK75
Osprey Ct, Wal.Abb. EN9 16 EG34
Osprey Gdns, S.Croy. CR2 161 DX110
Osprey Hts, SW11
off Bramlands Cl 100 DE83
Osprey Ms, Enf. EN3 30 DV43
Osprey Rd, Wal.Abb. EN9 16 EG34
Ospringe Cl, SE20 122 DW94
Ospringe Ct, SE9
off Alderwood Rd 125 ER86
Ospringe Rd, NW5 65 DJ63
Osram Ct, W6 off Lena Gdns 99 CW76
Osram Rd, Wem. HA9 61 CK62
Osric Path, N1 197 M1
Ossian Ms, N4 65 DM59
Ossian Rd, N4 65 DM59
Ossington Bldgs, W1 194 F6
Ossington Cl, W2
off Ossington St 82 DB73
Ossington St, W2 82 DA73
Ossory Rd, SE1 102 DU78
Ossulston St, NW1 195 M1
Ossulton Pl, N2
off East End Rd 64 DC55
Ossulton Way, N2 64 DC56
Ostade Rd, SW2 121 DM87
Ostell Cres, Enf. EN3 31 EA38
Osten Ms, SW7
off Emperor's Gate 100 DB76
Osterberg Rd, Dart. DA1 108 FM84
OSTERLEY, Islw. TW7 96 CC80
⊖ Osterley 97 CD80
Osterley Av, Islw. TW7 97 CD80
Osterley Cl, Orp. BR5
off Leith Hill 146 EU95
Osterley Ct, Islw. TW7 97 CD81
Osterley Cres, Islw. TW7 97 CE81
Osterley Gdns, Th.Hth. CR7 142 DQ96
Osterley Ho, E14
off Giraud St 85 EB72
Osterley La, Islw. TW7 97 CE78
Southall UB2 96 CA78
Osterley Pk, Islw. TW7 97 CD78
★ Osterley Park Ho,
Islw. TW7 96 CC78
Osterley Pk Rd, Sthl. UB2 96 BZ76
Osterley Pk Vw Rd, W7 97 CE75
Osterley Rd, N16 66 DS63
Isleworth TW7 97 CE80
Osterley Views, Sthl. UB2
off West Pk Rd 78 CC74
Oster Ter, E17
off Southcote Rd 67 DX57
Ostlers Dr, Ashf. TW15
off New Pk Rd 115 BQ92
Ostliffe Rd, N13 46 DQ50
Oswald Cl, Lthd.
(Fetch.) KT22 170 CC122
Oswald Rd, Lthd.
(Fetch.) KT22 170 CC122
Southall UB1 78 BY74
Oswald's Mead, E9
off Lindisfarne Way 67 DY63
Oswald St, E5 67 DX62
Oswald Ter, NW2
off Temple Rd 63 CW62
Osward, Croy. CR0 161 DZ109
Osward Pl, N9 46 DV47
Osward Rd, SW17 120 DF89
Oswell Ho, E1 202 E2
Oswin St, SE11 200 G8
Oswyth Rd, SE5 102 DS82
OTFORD, Sev. TN14 181 FG116
Otford Cl, SE20 142 DW95
Bexley DA5
off Southwold Rd 127 FB86
Bromley BR1 145 EN97
Otford Cres, SE4 123 DZ86
Otford La, Sev. (Halst.) TN14 164 EZ112
Otford Rd, Sev. TN14 181 FH118
Othello Cl, SE11 200 F10
Otho Ct, Brent. TW8 97 CK80
Otis St, E3 85 EC69
Otley App, Ilf. IG2 69 EP58
Otley Dr, Ilf. IG2 69 EP57
Otley Rd, E16 86 EJ72
Otley Ter, E5 67 DX61
Otley Way, Wat. WD19 40 BW48
Otlinge Cl, Orp. BR5 146 EX98
Ottawa Ct, Brox. EN10 15 DY25
Ottawa Gdns, Dag. RM10 89 FD66
Ottawa Rd, Til. RM18 111 GG82
Ottaway St, E5
off Stellman Cl 66 DU62
Ottenden Cl, Orp. BR6
off Southfleet Rd 163 ES105
Otterbourne Rd, E4 47 ED48
Croydon CR0 142 DQ103
Otterburn Gdns, Islw. TW7 97 CG80
Otterburn Ho, SE5 102 DQ80
Otterburn St, SW17 120 DF93
Otter Cl, E15 85 EC67
Chertsey (Ott.) KT16 151 BB107
Otterden St, SE6 123 EA91
Otterfield Rd, West Dr. UB7 76 BL73
Ottermead La, Cher.
(Ott.) KT16 151 BC107
Otter Meadow, Lthd. KT22 171 CF119
Otter Rd, Grnf. UB6 78 CC70
Otters Cl, Orp. BR5 146 EX98
OTTERSHAW, Cher. KT16 151 BC106
Otterspool La, Wat. WD25 24 BY38
Otterspool Service Rd, Wat.
WD25 24 BZ39
Otterspool Way, Wat. WD25 24 BY37
Otto Cl, SE26 122 DV90
Ottoman Ter, Wat. WD17
off Ebury Rd 24 BW41
Otto St, SE17 101 DP79
Ottways Av, Ashtd. KT21 171 CK119
Ottways La, Ashtd. KT21 171 CK120
Otway Gdns, Bushey WD23 41 CE45
Otways Cl, Pot.B. EN6 12 DB32
Oulton Cl, E5
off Mundford Rd 66 DW61
SE28 off Rollesby Way 88 EW72
Oulton Cres, Bark. IG11 87 ET65
Potters Bar EN6 11 CX32
Oulton Rd, N15 66 DR57
Oulton Way, Wat. WD19 40 BY49
Oundle Av, Bushey WD23 24 CC44
Ousden Cl, Wal.Cr.
(Chsht) EN8 15 DY30
Ousden Dr, Wal.Cr.
(Chsht) EN8 15 DY30
Ouseley Rd, SW12 120 DF88
Staines (Wrays.) TW19 112 AW87
Windsor (Old Wind.) SL4 112 AW87
Outer Circle, NW1 194 F5
Outfield Rd, Ger.Cr.
(Chal.St.P.) SL9 36 AX52
Outgate Rd, NW10 81 CT66
Outlook Dr, Ch.St.G. HP8 36 AX48
Outram Pl, N1 83 DL67
Weybridge KT13 153 BQ106
Outram Rd, E6 86 EL67
N22 45 DK53
Croydon CR0 142 DT102
Outwich St, EC3 197 N8
Outwood La, Couls. CR5 174 DF118
Tadworth (Kgswd) KT20 174 DB122
★ Oval, The,
Surrey County Cricket Club,
SE11 101 DM79
⊖ Oval 101 DN79
Oval, The, E2 84 DV68
Banstead SM7 158 DA114
Broxbourne EN10 15 DY25
Sidcup DA15 126 EU87
Oval Gdns, Grays RM17 110 GC76
Oval Pl, SW8 101 DM80
Oval Rd, NW1 83 DH67
Croydon CR0 142 DS102
Oval Rd N, Dag. RM10 89 FB67
Oval Rd S, Dag. RM10 89 FB68
Oval Way, SE11 101 DM78
Gerrards Cross SL9 56 AY56
Ovenden Rd, Sev.
(Sund.) TN14 180 EX120
Overbrae, Beck. BR3 123 EA93
Overbrook Wk, Edg. HA8 42 CN52
Overbury Av, Beck. BR3 143 EB97
Overbury Cres, Croy.
(New Adgtn) CR0 161 EC110
Overbury Rd, N15 66 DR58
Overbury St, E5 67 DX63
Overcliffe, Grav. DA11 131 GG86
Overcliff Rd, SE13 103 EA83
Grays RM17 110 GD78
Overcourt Cl, Sid. DA15 126 EV86
Overdale, Ashtd. KT21 172 CL115
Redhill (Bletch.) RH1 186 DQ133
Overdale Av, N.Mal. KT3 138 CQ96
Overdale Rd, W5 97 CJ76
Overdown Rd, SE6 123 EA91
Overhill, Warl. CR6 176 DW119
Overhill Rd, SE22 122 DU87
Purley CR8 159 DN109
Overhill Way, Beck. BR3 143 ED99
Overlea Rd, E5 66 DU59
Overmead, Sid. DA15 125 ER87
Swanley BR8 147 FE99
Oversley Ho, W2 82 DA71
Overstand Cl, Beck. BR3 143 EA99
Overstone Gdns, Croy. CR0 143 DZ101
Overstone Rd, W6 99 CW76
Overstrand Ho, Horn. RM12
off Sunrise Av 71 FH61
Overstream, Rick.
(Loud.) WD3 22 BH42
Over The Misbourne,
Ger.Cr. SL9 57 BA58
Uxbridge (Denh.) UB9 57 BC58
Overthorpe Cl, Wok.
(Knap.) GU21 166 AS117
Overton Cl, NW10 80 CQ65
Isleworth TW7
off Avenue Rd 97 CF81
Overton Ct, E11 68 EG59
Overton Dr, E11 68 EH59
Romford RM6 70 EW59
Overton Ho, SW15
off Tangley Gro 119 CT87
Overton Rd, E10 67 DY60
N14 29 DL43
SE2 106 EW76
SW9 101 DN82
Sutton SM2 158 DA107
Overton Rd E, SE2 106 EX76
Overtons Yd, Croy. CR0 142 DQ104
Overy St, Dart. DA1 128 FL86
Ovesdon Av, Har. HA2 60 BZ60
Ovett Cl, SE19 122 DS93
Ovex Cl, E14 204 E5
Ovington Ct, Wok. GU21
off Roundthorn Way 166 AT116
Ovington Gdns, SW3 198 C7
Ovington Ms, SW3 198 C7
Ovington Sq, SW3 198 C7
Ovington St, SW3 198 C7
Owen Cl, SE28 88 EW74
Croydon CR0 142 DR100
Hayes UB4 77 BV69
Romford RM5 51 FB51
Slough SL3
off Ditton Rd 93 AZ78
Owen Gdns, Wdf.Grn. IG8 48 EL51
Owenite St, SE2 106 EV77
Owen Pl, Lthd. KT22
off Church Rd 171 CH122
Owen Rd, N13 46 DQ50
Hayes UB4 77 BV69
Owen's Ct, EC1 196 F2
Owen's Row, EC1 196 F2
Owen St, EC1 196 F1
Owens Way, SE23 123 DY87
Rickmansworth
(Crox.Grn) WD3 22 BN43
Owen Wk, SE20
off Sycamore Gro 122 DU94
Owen Waters Ho, Ilf. IG5 49 EM53
Owen Way, NW10 80 CQ65
Owgan Cl, SE5
off Benhill Rd 102 DR80
Owl Cl, S.Croy. CR2 161 DX110
Owlets Hall Cl, Horn. RM11
off Prospect Rd 72 FM55
Owl Pk, Loug.
(High Beach) IG10 32 EF40
Ownstead Gdns,
S.Croy. CR2 160 DT111
Ownsted Hill, Croy.
(New Adgtn) CR0 161 EC110
Oxberry Av, SW6 99 CY82
Oxdowne Cl, Cob.
(Stoke D'Ab.) KT11 154 CB114
Oxenden Wd Rd, Orp. BR6 164 EV107
Oxendon St, SW1 199 M1
Oxenford St, SE15 102 DT83
Oxenholme, NW1 195 L1
Oxenpark Av, Wem. HA9 62 CL59
Oxestalls Rd, SE8 203 L10
Oxford Av, SW20 139 CY96
Grays RM16 111 GG77
Hayes UB3 95 BT80
Hornchurch RM11 72 FN56
Hounslow TW5 96 CA78
★ Oxford Circ, W1 195 K8
⊖ Oxford Circus 195 K8
Oxford Circ Av, W1 195 K9
Oxford Cl, N9 46 DV47
Ashford TW15 115 BQ94
Gravesend DA12 131 GM89
Mitcham CR4 141 DJ97
Northwood HA6 39 BQ49
Waltham Cross
(Chsht) EN8 15 DX29
Oxford Ct, EC4 197 K10
W3 80 CN72
Brentwood (Warley) CM14 54 FX49
Feltham TW13
off Oxford Way 116 BX91
Oxford Cres, N.Mal. KT3 138 CR100
Oxford Dr, SE1 201 M3
Ruislip HA4 60 BW61
Oxford Gdns, N20 44 DD46
N21 46 DQ45
W4 98 CN78
W10 81 CY72
Uxbridge (Denh.) UB9 57 BF62
Oxford Gate, W6 99 CX77
Oxford Ms, Bex. DA5
off Bexley High St 126 FA87
Oxford Pl, NW10
off Neasden La N 62 CR62
Oxford Rd, E15 85 ED65
N4 65 DN60
N9 46 DV47
NW6 82 DA68
SE19 122 DR93
SW15 99 CY84
W5 79 CK73
Carshalton SM5 158 DE107
Enfield EN3 30 DV43
Gerrards Cross SL9 57 BA60
Harrow HA1 60 CC58
Harrow (Wldste) HA3 61 CF55
Ilford IG1 69 EQ63
Redhill RH1 184 DE133
Romford RM3 52 FM51
Sidcup DA14 126 EV92
Teddington TW11 117 CD92
Uxbridge UB8, UB9 76 BJ65
Wallington SM6 159 DJ106
Woodford Green IG8 48 EJ50
Oxford Rd N, W4 98 CP78
Oxford Rd S, W4 98 CN78
Oxford Sq, W2 194 C9
Oxford St, W1 195 L8
Watford WD18 23 BV43
Oxford Wk, Sthl. UB1 78 BZ74
Oxford Way, Felt. TW13 116 BX91
Oxgate Gdns, NW2 63 CV62
Oxgate La, NW2 63 CV61
Oxhawth Cres, Brom. BR2 145 EN99
OXHEY, Wat. WD19 24 BW44
Oxhey Av, Wat. WD19 40 BX45
Oxhey Dr, Nthwd. HA6 39 BV50
Watford WD19 40 BW48
Oxhey Dr S, Nthwd. HA6 39 BV50
Oxhey La, Har. HA3 40 CA50
Pinner HA5 40 CA50
Watford WD19 40 BZ47
Oxhey Ridge Cl, Nthwd.
HA6 39 BU50
Oxhey Rd, Wat. WD19 24 BW44
Ox La, Epsom KT17
off Church St 157 CU109
Oxleas, E6 87 EP72
Oxleas Cl, Well. DA16 105 ER82
Oxleay Ct, Har. HA2 60 CA60
Oxleay Rd, Har. HA2 60 CA60
Oxleigh Cl, N.Mal. KT3 138 CS99
Oxley Cl, SE1 202 A10
Romford RM2 52 FJ54
Oxleys Rd, NW2 63 CV62
Waltham Abbey EN9 16 EG32
Oxlip Cl, Croy. CR0
off Marigold Way 143 DX102
Oxlow La, Dag. RM9, RM10 70 FA63
Oxonian St, SE22 102 DT84
Oxo Twr Wf, SE1 200 E1
OXSHOTT, Lthd. KT22 155 CD113
⇌ Oxshott 154 CC113
Oxshott Ri, Cob. KT11 154 BX113
Oxshott Rd, Lthd. KT22 171 CE115
Oxshott Way, Cob. KT11 170 BY115
OXTED 187 ED129
⇌ Oxted 188 EE129
Oxted Cl, Mitch. CR4 140 DD97
Oxted Rd, Gdse. RH9 186 DW130
Oxtoby Way, SW16 141 DK96
Oyster Catchers Cl, E16
off Freemasons Rd 86 EH72
Oyster Catcher Ter, Ilf. IG5
off Tiptree Cres 69 EN55
Oyster La, W.Byf.
(Byfleet) KT14 152 BK110
Oyster Row, E1
off Lukin St 84 DW72
Ozolins Way, E16 86 EG72

P

Pablo Neruda Cl, SE24
off Shakespeare Rd 101 DP84
Paceheath Cl, Rom. RM5 51 FD51
Pace Pl, E1 off Bigland St 84 DV72
PACHESHAM PARK,
Lthd. KT22 171 CG116
Pachesham Pk, Lthd. KT22 171 CG117
Pacific Cl, Felt. TW14 115 BT88
Swanscombe DA10
off Craylands La 130 FY85

★ Place of interest ⇌ Railway station ⊖ London Underground station DLR Docklands Light Railway station Tra Tramlink station H Hospital Riv Pedestrian ferry landing stage

Pacific Rd, E16 86 EG72
Packet Boat La, Uxb. UB8 76 BH72
Packham Cl, Orp. BR6
off Berrylands 146 EW104
Packham Ct, Wor.Pk. KT4
off Lavender Av 139 CW104
Packham Rd, Grav.
(Nthflt) DA11 131 GF90
Packhorse La, Borwd. WD6 26 CS37
Potters Bar (Ridge) EN6 10 CR31
Packhorse Rd, Ger.Cr.
(Chal.St.P.) SL9 56 AY58
Sevenoaks TN13 190 FC123
Packington Rd, W3 98 CQ76
Packington Sq, N1 84 DQ67
Packington St, N1 83 DP67
Packmores Rd, SE9 125 ER85
Padbrook, Oxt. RH8 188 EG129
Padbrook Cl, Oxt. RH8 188 EH128
Padbury, SE17 102 DS78
Padbury Cl, Felt. TW14 115 BR88
Padbury Ct, E2 84 DT69
Padcroft Rd, West Dr. UB7 76 BK74
Padden Ct, NW7
off Bittacy Hill 43 CY52
Paddenswick Rd, W6 99 CU76
PADDINGTON, W2 82 DB71
≠ Paddington 82 DC72
⊖ Paddington 82 DC72
Paddington Cl, Hayes UB4 78 BX70
Paddington Grn, W2 194 A6
Paddington St, W1 194 F6
Paddock, The, Ger.Cr.
(Chal.St.P.) SL9 36 AY50
Slough (Datchet) SL3 92 AV81
Uxbridge (Ickhm) UB10 59 BP63
Westerham TN16 189 EQ126
Paddock Cl, SE3 104 EG82
SE26 123 DX91
Dartford (S.Darenth) DA4 148 FQ95
Northolt UB5 78 CA68
Orpington BR6
off State Fm Av 163 EP105
Oxted RH8 188 EF131
Watford WD19 24 BY44
Worcester Park KT4 138 CS102
Paddock Gdns, SE19
off Westow St 122 DS93
Paddock La, Iver SL0
off Pinewood Rd 75 BB66
Paddock Rd, NW2 63 CU62
Bexleyheath DA6 106 EY84
Ruislip HA4 60 BX62
Paddocks, The, NW7 43 CY51
Addlestone
(New Haw) KT15 152 BH110
Barnet EN4 28 DF41
Rickmansworth
(Chorl.) WD3 21 BF42
Romford (Stap.Abb.) RM4 35 FF44
Sevenoaks TN13 191 FK124
Virginia Water GU25 132 AY100
Wembley HA9 62 CP61
Weybridge KT13 135 BS104
Paddocks Cl, Ashtd. KT21 172 CL118
Cobham KT11 154 BW114
Harrow HA2 60 CB63
Orpington BR5 146 EX103
Paddocks Mead, Wok. GU21 166 AS116
Paddocks Retail Pk,
Wey. KT13 152 BL111
Paddocks Way, Ashtd. KT21 172 CL118
Chertsey KT16 134 BH102
Paddock Wk, Warl. CR6 176 DV119
Paddock Way, SW15 119 CW87
Chislehurst BR7 125 ER94
Oxted RH8 188 EF131
Woking GU21 151 BB114
Padfield Ct, Wem. HA9
off Forty Av 62 CM62
Padfield Rd, SE5 102 DQ83
Padgets, The, Wal.Abb. EN9 15 ED34
Padley Cl, Chess. KT9 156 CM106
Padnall Ct, Rom. RM6
off Padnall Rd 70 EX55
Padnall Rd, Rom. RM6 70 EX56
Padstow Cl, Orp. BR6 163 ET105
Slough SL3 92 AY76
Padstow Rd, Enf. EN2 29 DP40
Padstow Wk, Felt. TW14 115 BT88
Padua Rd, SE20 142 DW95
Pagden St, SW8 101 DH81
Pageant Av, NW9 42 CR53
Pageant Cl, Til. RM18 111 GJ81
Pageant Cres, SE16 203 L2
Pageantmaster Ct, EC4 196 F9
Pageant Wk, Croy. CR0 142 DS104
Page Av, Wem. HA9 62 CQ62
Page Cl, Dag. RM9 70 EY64
Dartford (Bean) DA2 129 FW90
Hampton TW12 116 BY93
Harrow HA3 62 CM58
Page Cres, Croy. CR0 159 DN106
Erith DA8 107 FF80
Page Grn Rd, N15 66 DU57
Page Grn Ter, N15 66 DT57
Page Heath La, Brom. BR1 144 EK97
Page Heath Vil, Brom. BR1 144 EK97
Pagehurst Rd, Croy. CR0 142 DV101
Page Meadow, NW7 43 CU52
Page Rd, Felt. TW14 115 BR86
Pages Hill, N10 44 DG54
Pages La, N10 44 DG54
Romford RM3 52 FP54
Uxbridge UB8 76 BJ65
Page St, NW7 43 CU53
SW1 199 N8
Pages Wk, SE1 201 M8
Pages Yd, W4
off Church St 98 CS79
Paget Av, Sutt. SM1 140 DD104
Paget Cl, Hmptn. TW12 117 CD91
Paget Gdns, Chis. BR7 145 EP95
Paget La, Islw. TW7 97 CD83
Paget Pl, Kings.T. KT2 118 CQ93
Paget Pl, Thames Ditton KT7
off Brooklands Rd 137 CG102
Paget Ri, SE18 105 EN80
Paget Rd, N16 66 DR60
Ilford IG1 69 EP63
Slough SL3 93 AZ77
Uxbridge UB10 77 BQ70
Paget St, EC1 196 F2
Paget Ter, SE18 105 EN79
Pagette Way, Grays
(Bad.Dene) RM17 110 GA77
Pagitts Gro, Barn. EN4 28 DB39
Paglesfield, Brwd.
(Hutt.) CM13 55 GC44
Pagnell St, SE14 103 DZ80
Pagoda Av, Rich. TW9 98 CM83
Pagoda Gdns, SE3 103 ED82
Pagoda Vista, Rich. TW9 98 CM82
Paignton Rd, N15 66 DS58
Ruislip HA4 59 BU62
Paines Brook Rd, Rom. RM3
off Paines Brook Way 52 FM51
Paines Brook Way,
Rom. RM3 52 FM51
Paines Cl, Pnr. HA5 60 BY55
Paines La, Pnr. HA5 40 BY53
Pains Cl, Mitch. CR4 141 DH96
Pains Hill, Oxt. RH8 188 EJ132
★ Painshill Park,
Cob. KT11 153 BS114
Painsthorpe Rd, N16
off Oldfield Rd 66 DS62
Painters Ash La, Grav.
(Nthflt) DA11 130 GD90
Painters La, Enf. EN3 31 DY35
Painters Ms, SE16
off Macks Rd 102 DU77
Painters Rd, Ilf. IG2 69 ET55
Paisley Rd, N22 45 DP53
Carshalton SM5 140 DD102
Pakeman St, N7 65 DM62
Pakenham Cl, SW12
off Balham Pk Rd 120 DG88
Pakenham St, WC1 196 C3
Pakes Way, Epp.
(They.B.) CM16 33 ES37
Palace Av, W8 82 DB74
Palace Cl, Kings L. WD4 6 BM30
Palace Ct, NW3 64 DB64
W2 82 DB73
Bromley BR1
off Palace Gro 144 EH95
Harrow HA3 62 CL58
Palace Ct Gdns, N10 65 DJ55
Palace Dr, Wey. KT13 135 BP104
Palace Gdns, Buck.H. IG9 48 EK46
Palace Gdns Ms, W8 82 DA74
Palace Gdns Prec, Enf. EN2
off Sydney Rd 30 DR41
Palace Gdns Ter, W8 82 DA74
Palace Gate, W8 100 DC75
Palace Gates Rd, N22 45 DK53
Palace Grn, W8 100 DB75
Croydon CR0 161 DZ108
Palace Gro, SE19 122 DT94
Bromley BR1 144 EH95
Palace Ms, E17 67 DZ56
SW1 198 G9
SW6 off Hartismere Rd 99 CZ80
Palace of Industry, Wem. HA9 62 CN63
Palace Par, E17 67 EA56
Palace Pl, SW1 199 K6
Palace Rd, N8 65 DK57
N11 45 DL52
SE19 122 DT94
SW2 121 DM88
Bromley BR1 144 EH95
East Molesey KT8 137 CD97
Kingston upon Thames KT1 137 CK98
Ruislip HA4 60 BY63
Westerham TN16 179 EN121
Palace Rd Est, SW2 121 DM88
Palace Sq, SE19 122 DT94
Palace St, SW1 199 K6
Palace Vw, SE12 124 EG89
Bromley BR1 144 EG97
Croydon CR0 161 DZ105
Palace Vw Rd, E4 47 EB50
Palace Way, Wey. KT13
off Palace Dr 135 BP104
Palamos Rd, E10 67 EA60
Palatine Av, N16
off Stoke Newington Rd 66 DT63
Palatine Rd, N16 66 DS63
Palermo Rd, NW10 81 CU68
Palestine Gro, SW19 140 DD95
Palewell Cl, Orp. BR5 146 EV96
Palewell Common Dr, SW14 118 CR85
Palewell Pk, SW14 118 CR85
Paley Gdns, Loug. IG10 33 EP41
Palfrey Pl, SW8 101 DM80
Palgrave Av, Sthl. UB1 78 CA73
Palgrave Gdns, NW1 194 C4
Palgrave Rd, W12 99 CT76
Palissy St, E2 197 P3
Palladino Ho, SW17
off Laurel Cl 120 DE92
Pallant Way, Orp. BR6 145 EN104
Pallet Way, SE18 104 EL81
Palliser Dr, Rain. RM13 89 FG71
Palliser Rd, W14 99 CY78
Chalfont St. Giles HP8 36 AU48
Pallister Ter, SW15
off Roehampton Vale 119 CT90
Pall Mall, SW1 199 L3
Pall Mall E, SW1 199 N2
Palmar Cres, Bexh. DA7 106 FA83
Palmar Rd, Bexh. DA7 106 FA82
Palmarsh Cl, Orp. BR5
off Wotton Grn 146 EX98
Palm Av, Sid. DA14 126 EX93
Palm Cl, E10 67 EB62
Palmeira Rd, Bexh. DA7 106 EX83
Palmer Av, Bushey WD23 24 CB43
Gravesend DA12 131 GK91
Sutton SM3 157 CW105
Palmer Cl, Houns. TW5 96 CA81
West Wickham BR4 143 ED104
Palmer Cres, Cher.
(Ott.) KT16 151 BD107
Palmer Cres,
Kingston upon Thames KT1 138 CL97
Palmer Gdns, Barn. EN5 27 CX43
Palmer Pl, N7 65 DN64
Palmer Rd, E13 86 EH70
Dagenham RM8 70 EX60
Palmers Av, Grays RM17 110 GC78
Palmers Dr, Grays RM17 110 GC77
Palmersfield Rd, Bans. SM7 158 DA114
PALMERS GREEN, N13 45 DN48
≠ Palmers Green 45 DM49
Palmers Gro, W.Mol. KT8 136 CA98
Palmers Hill, Epp. CM16 18 EU29
Palmers La, Enf. EN1, EN3 30 DV39
Palmers Moor La, Iver SL0 76 BG70
Palmers Orchard, Sev.
(Shore.) TN14 165 FF111
Palmers Pas, SW14
off Palmers Rd 98 CQ83
Palmers Rd, E2 85 DX68
N11 45 DJ50
SW14 98 CQ83
SW16 141 DM96
Borehamwood WD6 26 CP39
Palmerston Av, Slou. SL3 92 AV76
Palmerston Cl, Wok. GU21 151 AZ114
Palmerston Cres, N13 45 DM50
SE18 105 EQ79
Palmerstone Ct, Vir.W. GU25
off Sandhills La 132 AY99
Palmerston Gdns,
Grays RM20 109 FX78
Palmerston Gro, SW19 120 DA94
Palmerston Rd, E7 68 EH64
E17 67 DZ56
N22 45 DM52
NW6 82 DA66
SW14 98 CQ84
SW19 120 DA94
W3 98 CQ76
Buckhurst Hill IG9 48 EH47
Carshalton SM5 158 DF105
Croydon CR0 142 DR99
Grays RM20 109 FX78
Harrow HA3 61 CF55
Hounslow TW3 96 CC81
Orpington BR6 163 EQ105
Rainham RM13 90 FJ68
Sutton SM1
off Vernon Rd 158 DC106
Twickenham TW2 117 CF86
Palmerston Way, SW8
off Bradmead 101 DH80
Palmer St, SW1 199 M5
Palmers Way, Wal.Cr.
(Chsht) EN8 15 DY29
Palm Gro, W5 98 CL76
Palm Rd, Rom. RM7 71 FC57
Pamela Gdns, Pnr. HA5 59 BV57
Pamela Wk, E8
off Marlborough Av 84 DU67
Pampisford Rd, Pur. CR8 159 DN111
South Croydon CR2 159 DP108
Pams Way, Epsom KT19 156 CR106
Pancras La, EC4 197 J9
Pancras Rd, NW1 83 DK68
Pancroft, Rom. (Abridge) RM4 34 EV41
Pandora Rd, NW6 82 DA65
Panfield Ms, Ilf. IG2
off Cranbrook Rd 69 EN58
Panfield Rd, SE2 106 EU76
Pangbourne Av, W10 81 CW71
Pangbourne Dr, Stan. HA7 41 CK50
Pangbourne Ho, N7 65 DL64
Panhard Pl, Sthl. UB1 78 CB73
Pank Av, Barn. EN5 28 DC43
Pankhurst Av, E16
off Wesley Av 86 EH74
Pankhurst Cl, SE14
off Briant St 103 DX80
Isleworth TW7 97 CF83
Pankhurst Rd, Walt. KT12 136 BW101
Panmuir Rd, SW20 139 CV95
Panmure Cl, N5 65 DP63
Panmure Rd, SE26 122 DV90
Pannells Cl, Cher. KT16 133 BF102
Pansy Gdns, W12 81 CU73
Panters, Swan. BR8 127 FF94
Panther Dr, NW10 62 CR64
Pantile Rd, Wey. KT13 153 BR105
Pantile Row, Slou. SL3 93 BA77
Pantiles, The, NW11
off Willifield Way 63 CZ57
Bexleyheath DA7 106 EZ80
Bromley BR1 144 EL97
Bushey
(Bushey Hth) WD23 41 CD45
Pantiles Cl, N13 45 DP50
Woking GU21 166 AV118
Pantile Wk, Uxb. UB8
off High St 76 BJ66
Panton St, SW1 199 M1
Panyer All, EC4 197 H9
Papercourt La, Wok.
(Ripley) GU23 167 BF122
Papermill Cl, Cars. SM5 158 DG105
Papillons Wk, SE3 104 EG82
Papworth Gdns, N7
off Liverpool Rd 65 DM64
Papworth Way, SW2 121 DN87
Parade, The, SW11 100 DF80
Brentwood CM14
off Kings Rd 54 FW48
Dartford DA1
off Crayford Way 127 FF85
Epsom KT18 156 CR113
Epsom (Epsom Com.) KT18
off Spa Dr 156 CN114
Esher (Clay.) KT10 155 CE107
Hampton TW12
off Hampton Rd 117 CD92
Romford RM3 52 FP51
South Ockendon
(Aveley) RM15 108 FQ75
Sunbury-on-Thames TW16 115 BT94
Virginia Water GU25 132 AX100
Watford WD17 23 BV41
Watford (Carp.Pk) WD19 40 BY48
Watford (S.Oxhey) WD19
off Prestwick Rd 40 BX48
Parade Ms, SE27
off Norwood Rd 121 DP89
Paradise Cl, Wal.Cr.
(Chsht) EN7 14 DV28
Paradise Pas, N7 65 DN64
Paradise Path, SE28
off Birchdene Dr 88 EU74
Paradise Pl, SE18
off Woodhill 104 EL77
Paradise Rd, SW4 101 DL82
Richmond TW9 117 CK85
Waltham Abbey EN9 15 EC34
Paradise Row, E2
off Bethnal Grn Rd 84 DV69
Paradise St, SE16 202 D5
Paradise Wk, SW3 100 DF79
Paragon, The, SE3 104 EF82
Paragon Cl, E16 86 EG72
Paragon Gro, Surb. KT5 138 CM100
Paragon Ms, SE1 201 L8
Paragon Pl, SE3 104 EF82
Surbiton KT5
off Berrylands Rd 138 CM100
Paragon Rd, E9 84 DW65
Parbury Ri, Chess. KT9 156 CL107
Parbury Rd, SE23 123 DY86
Parchment Cl, Amer. HP6 20 AS37
Parchmore Rd, Th.Hth. CR7 141 DP96
Parchmore Way, Th.Hth. CR7 141 DP96
Pardoner St, SE1 201 L6
Pardon St, EC1 196 G4
Pares Cl, Wok. GU21 166 AX116
Parfett St, E1 84 DU71
Parfitt Cl, NW3
off North End 64 DC61
Parfour Dr, Ken. CR8 176 DQ116
Parfrey St, W6 99 CW79
Parham Dr, Ilf. IG2 69 EP58
Parham Way, N10 45 DJ54
Paris Gdn, SE1 200 F2
Parish Cl, Horn. RM11 71 FH61
Watford WD25 off Crown Ri 8 BX34
Parish Gate Dr, Sid. DA15 125 ES86
Parish La, SE20 123 DX93
Parish Ms, SE20 123 DX94
Parish Wf, SE18
off Woodhill 104 EL77
Park, The, N6 64 DG58
NW11 64 DB60
SE19 122 DS94
SE23 off Park Hill 122 DV88
W5 79 CK74
Carshalton SM5 158 DF106
Leatherhead (Bkhm) KT23 170 CA123
Sidcup DA14 125 ET92
Park App, Well. DA16 106 EV84
Park Av, E6 87 EN67
E15 86 EE65
N3 44 DB53
N13 45 DN48
N18 46 DU49
N22 45 DL54
NW2 81 CV65
NW10 80 CM69
NW11 64 DB60
SW14 98 CR84
Barking IG11 87 EQ65
Brentwood (Hutt.) CM13 55 GC46
Bromley BR1 124 EF93
Bushey WD23 24 BZ40
Carshalton SM5 158 DG107
Caterham CR3 176 DS124
Egham TW20 113 BC93
Enfield EN1 30 DS44
Gravesend DA12 131 GJ88
Gravesend (Perry St) DA11 130 GE88
Grays RM20 109 FU79
Hounslow TW3 116 CB86
Ilford IG1 69 EN61
Mitcham CR4 121 DH94
Orpington BR6 146 EU103
Orpington (Farnboro.) BR6 145 EM104
Potters Bar EN6 12 DC34
Radlett WD7 9 CH33
Rickmansworth
(Chorl.) WD3 22 BG43
Ruislip HA4 59 BR58
Southall UB1 78 CA74
Staines TW18 113 BF93
Staines (Wrays.) TW19 112 AX85
Upminster RM14 73 FS59
Watford WD18 23 BU42
West Wickham BR4 143 EC103
Woodford Green IG8 48 EH50
Park Av E, Epsom KT17 157 CU107
Park Av Ms, Mitch. CR4
off Park Av 121 DH94
Park Av N, N8 65 DK55
NW10 63 CV64
Park Av Rd, N17 46 DV52
Park Av S, N8 65 DK56
Park Av W, Epsom KT17 157 CU107
Park Boul, Rom. RM2 51 FF53
Park Chase, Wem. HA9 62 CM63
Park Cl, E9 84 DW67
NW2 63 CV62
NW10 80 CM69
SW1 198 D5
W4 98 CR78
W14 99 CZ76
Addlestone
(New Haw) KT15 152 BH110
Bushey WD23 24 BX41
Carshalton SM5 158 DF107
Epping (N.Wld Bas.) CM16 18 FA27
Esher KT10 154 BZ107
Hampton TW12 136 CC95
Harrow HA3 41 CE53
Hatfield (Brook.Pk) AL9 11 CZ26
Hounslow TW3 116 CC85
Kingston upon Thames KT2 138 CN95
Leatherhead (Fetch.) KT22 171 CD124
Oxted RH8 188 EF128
Rickmansworth WD3 39 BP49
Walton-on-Thames KT12 135 BT103
Park Cor Rd, Grav.
(Sthflt) DA13 130 FZ91
Park Ct, SE26 122 DV93
Kingston upon Thames
(Hmptn W.) KT1 137 CJ95
Park Ct, New Malden KT3 138 CR98
Wembley HA9 62 CL64
West Byfleet KT14 152 BG113
Woking GU22
off Park Dr 167 AZ118
Park Cres, N3 44 DB52
W1 195 H5
Borehamwood
(Elstree) WD6 26 CM41
Enfield EN2 30 DR42
Erith DA8 107 FC79
Harrow HA3 41 CE53
Hornchurch RM11 71 FG59
Twickenham TW2 117 CD88
Park Cres Ms E, W1 195 J5
Park Cres Ms W, W1 195 H6
Park Cres Rd, Erith DA8 107 FD79
Park Cft, Edg. HA8 42 CQ53
Parkcroft Rd, SE12 124 EF87
Park Dale, N11 45 DK51
Parkdale Cres, Wor.Pk. KT4 138 CR104
Parkdale Rd, SE18 105 ES78
Park Dr, N21 30 DQ44
NW11 64 DB60
SE7 104 EL79
SW14 98 CR84
W3 98 CN76
Ashtead KT21 172 CN118
Dagenham RM10 71 FC62
Harrow (Har.Wld) HA3 41 CE51
Harrow (N.Har.) HA2 60 CA59
Potters Bar EN6 12 DA31
Romford RM1 71 FD56
Upminster RM14 72 FQ63
Weybridge KT13 153 BP106
Woking GU22 167 AZ118
Park Dr Cl, SE7 104 EL78
Park End, NW3
off South Hill Pk 64 DE63
Bromley BR1 144 EF95
Park End Rd, Rom. RM1 71 FE56
Parker Av, Til. RM18 111 GJ81
Parker Cl, E16 86 EL74
Carshalton SM5 158 DF107
Parker Ms, WC2 196 A8
Parke Rd, SW13 99 CU81
Sunbury-on-Thames TW16 135 BU98
Parker Rd, Croy. CR0 160 DQ105
Grays RM17 110 FZ78
Parkers Cl, Ashtd. KT21 172 CL119
Parkers Hill, Ashtd. KT21 172 CL119
Parkers La, Ashtd. KT21 172 CL119
Parkers Row, SE1 202 A5
Parker St, E16 86 EL74
WC2 196 A8
Watford WD24 23 BV39
Parkes Rd, Chig. IG7 49 ES50
Park Fm Cl, N2 64 DC55
Pinner HA5
off Field End Rd 59 BV57
Park Fm Rd, Brom. BR1 144 EK95
Kingston upon Thames KT2 118 CL94
Upminster RM14 72 FM64
Parkfield, Rick. (Chorl.) WD3 21 BF42
Sevenoaks TN15 191 FM123
Parkfield Av, SW14 98 CS84
Feltham TW13 115 BU90
Harrow HA2 40 CC54
Northolt UB5 78 BX68
Uxbridge (Hlgdn) UB10 77 BP69
Parkfield Cl, Edg. HA8 42 CP51
Northolt UB5 78 BY68
Parkfield Cres, Felt. TW13 115 BU90
Harrow HA2 40 CC54
Ruislip HA4 60 BY62
Parkfield Dr, Nthlt. UB5 78 BX68
Parkfield Gdns, Har. HA2 60 CB55
Parkfield Rd, NW10 81 CU66
SE14 103 DZ81
Feltham TW13 115 BU90
Harrow HA2 60 CC62
Northolt UB5 78 BY68
Uxbridge (Ickhm) UB10 59 BP61
Parkfields, SW15 99 CW84
Croydon CR0 143 DZ102
Leatherhead
(Oxshott) KT22 155 CD111
Parkfields Av, NW9 62 CR60
SW20 139 CV95
Parkfields Cl, Cars. SM5
off Devonshire Rd 158 DG105
Parkfields Rd, Kings.T. KT2 118 CM92
Parkfield St, N1
off Berners Rd 83 DN68
Parkfield Vw, Pot.B. EN6 12 DB32
Parkfield Way, Brom. BR2 145 EM100
Park Gdns, NW9 62 CP55
Erith DA8 off Valley Rd 107 FD77
Kingston upon Thames KT2 118 CM92
Park Gate, N2 64 DD55
N21 45 DM45
Parkgate, SE3 104 EF83
Park Gate, W5
off Mount Av 79 CK71
Parkgate Av, Barn. EN4 28 DC39
Parkgate Cl, Kings.T. KT2
off Warboys App 118 CP93
Parkgate Cres, Barn. EN4 28 DC40
Parkgate Gdns, SW14 118 CR85
Parkgate Ms, N6
off Stanhope Rd 65 DJ59
Parkgate Rd, SW11 100 DE80
Orpington BR6 165 FB105
Wallington SM6 158 DG106
Watford WD24 24 BW37
Park Gates, Har. HA2 60 CA63
Park Gra Gdns, Sev. TN13
off Solefields Rd 191 FJ127
Park Grn, Lthd.
(Bkhm) KT23 170 CA124
Park Gro, E15 86 EG67
N11 45 DK52
Bexleyheath DA7 107 FC84
Bromley BR1 144 EH95
Chalfont St. Giles HP8 20 AX41
Edgware HA8 42 CM50
Park Gro Rd, E11 68 EE61
Park Hall Rd, N2 64 DE56
SE21 122 DQ90
Reigate RH2 184 DA132

★ Place of interest ≠ Railway station ⊖ London Underground station DLR Docklands Light Railway station Tra Tramlink station H Hospital Riv Pedestrian ferry landing stage

Parkham Ct, Brom. BR2 144 EE96
Parkham St, SW11 100 DE81
Park Hill, SE23 122 DV89
SW4 121 DK85
W5 79 CK71
Bromley BR1 144 EL98
Carshalton SM5 158 DE107
Loughton IG10 32 EK43
Richmond TW10 118 CM86
Park Hill Cl, Cars. SM5 158 DE106
Parkhill Cl, Horn. RM12 72 FJ62
Park Hill Ct, SW17
off Beeches Rd 120 DF90
Park Hill Ri, Croy. CR0 142 DS103
Parkhill Rd, E4 47 EC46
NW3 64 DF64
Bexley DA5 126 EZ87
Park Hill Rd, Brom. BR2 144 EE96
Croydon CR0 142 DS103
Epsom KT17 157 CT111
Parkhill Rd, Sid. DA15 125 ER90
Park Hill Rd, Wall. SM6 159 DH108
Parkhill Wk, NW3 64 DF64
Parkholme Rd, E8 84 DT65
Park Ho, N21 45 DM45
Park Ho Gdns, Twick. TW1 117 CJ86
Parkhouse St, SE5 102 DR80
Parkhurst, Epsom KT19 156 CQ110
Parkhurst Gdns, Bex. DA5 126 FA87
Parkhurst Rd, E12 69 EN63
E17 67 DY56
N7 65 DL63
N11 44 DG49
N17 46 DU54
N22 45 DM52
Bexley DA5 126 FA87
Sutton SM1 158 DD105
Park Ind Est, St.Alb.
(Frog.) AL2 9 CE27
Parkland Av, Rom. RM1 71 FE55
Slough SL3 92 AX77
Upminster RM14 72 FP64
Parkland Cl, Chig. IG7 49 EQ48
Sevenoaks TN13 191 FJ129
Parkland Gdns, SW19 119 CX88
Parkland Gro, Ashf. TW15 114 BN91
Parkland Rd, N22 45 DM54
Ashford TW15 114 BN91
Woodford Green IG8 48 EG52
Parklands, N6 65 DH59
Addlestone KT15 152 BJ106
Chigwell IG7 49 EQ48
Epping (Cooper.) CM16 18 EX29
Leatherhead (Bkhm) KT23 170 CA123
Oxted RH8 188 EE131
Surbiton KT5 138 CM99
Waltham Abbey EN9 15 ED32
Parklands Cl, SW14 118 CQ85
Barnet EN4 28 DD38
Ilford IG2 69 EQ59
Parklands Ct, Houns. TW5 96 BX82
Parklands Dr, N3 63 CY55
Parklands Rd, SW16 121 DH92
Parklands Way, Wor.Pk. KT4 138 CS104
Parkland Wk, N4 65 DM59
N6 65 DK59
N10 65 DH56
Park La, E15 *off High St* 85 ED67
N9 46 DT48
N17 46 DU52
W1 198 G3
Ashtead KT21 172 CM118
Banstead SM7 174 DD118
Carshalton SM5 158 DG105
Coulsdon CR5 175 DK121
Croydon CR0 142 DR104
Harrow HA2 60 CB62
Hayes UB4 77 BS71
Hornchurch RM11 71 FG58
Hornchurch (Elm Pk) RM12 89 FH65
Hounslow TW5 95 BU80
Richmond TW9 97 CK84
Romford (Chad.Hth) RM6 70 EX58
Sevenoaks TN13 191 FJ124
Sevenoaks (Seal) TN15 191 FN121
Slough SL3 92 AV76
Slough (Horton) SL3 93 BA83
South Ockendon
(Aveley) RM15 91 FR74
Stanmore HA7 41 CG48
Sutton SM3 157 CY107
Swanley BR8 148 FJ96
Teddington TW11 117 CF93
Uxbridge (Hare.) UB9 38 BG53
Wallington SM6 158 DG105
Waltham Cross EN8 14 DW33
Waltham Cross (Chsht) EN7 14 DU26
Wembley HA9 62 CL64
Park La Cl, N17 46 DU52
PARK LANGLEY, Beck. BR3 143 EC99
Parklawn Av, Epsom KT18 156 CP113
Park Lawn Rd, Wey. KT13 153 BQ105
Park Lawns, Wem. HA9 62 CM63
Parklea Cl, NW9 42 CS53
Parkleigh Rd, SW19 140 DB96
Park Ley Rd, Cat.
(Wold.) CR3 177 DX120
Parkleys, Rich. TW10 117 CK91
Parkmead, SW15 119 CV86
Park Mead, Har. HA2 60 CB62
Parkmead, Loug. IG10 33 EN43
Park Mead, Sid. DA15 126 EV85
Parkmead Gdns, NW7 43 CT51
Park Ms, SE24
off Croxted Rd 122 DQ86
Chislehurst BR7 125 EP93
East Molesey KT8 136 CC98
Hampton (Hmptn H.) TW12
off Park Rd 116 CC92
Rainham RM13
off Sowrey Av 89 FG65
Parkmore Cl, Wdf.Grn. IG8 48 EG49
Park Nook Gdns, Enf. EN2 30 DR37
Park Par, NW10 81 CT68
Park Pl, E14 203 P2
SW1 199 K3
W3 98 CN77
W5 79 CK74
Amersham HP6 20 AT38
Gravesend DA12 131 GJ86
Park Pl, Hampton (Hmptn H.)
TW12 116 CC93
St. Albans (Park St) AL2 9 CD27
Sevenoaks TN13 190 FD123
Wembley HA9 62 CM63
Woking GU22
off Park Dr 167 AZ118
Park Pl Vil, W2 82 DC71
Park Ridings, N8 65 DN55
Park Ri, SE23 123 DY88
Harrow HA3 41 CE53
Leatherhead KT22 171 CH121
Park Ri Cl, Lthd. KT22 171 CH121
Park Ri Rd, SE23 123 DY88
Park Rd, E6 86 EJ67
E10 67 EA60
E12 68 EH60
E15 86 EG67
E17 67 DZ57
N2 64 DD55
N8 65 DJ56
N11 45 DK52
N14 45 DK45
N15 65 DP56
N18 46 DT49
NW1 194 B2
NW4 63 CU59
NW8 194 B2
NW9 62 CR59
NW10 80 CS67
SE25 142 DS98
SW19 120 DD93
W4 98 CQ80
W7 79 CF73
Amersham HP6 20 AT37
Ashford TW15 115 BP92
Ashtead KT21 172 CL118
Banstead SM7 174 DB115
Barnet EN5 27 CZ42
Barnet (New Barn.) EN4 28 DE42
Beckenham BR3 123 DZ94
Brentwood CM14 54 FV46
Bromley BR1 144 EH95
Bushey WD23 24 CA44
Caterham CR3 176 DS123
Chislehurst BR7 125 EP93
Dartford DA1 128 FN87
East Molesey KT8 136 CC98
Egham TW20 113 BA91
Enfield EN3 31 DY36
Esher KT10 154 CB105
Feltham TW13 116 BX91
Gravesend DA11 131 GH88
Grays RM17 110 GB78
Hampton (Hmptn H.) TW12 116 CB91
Hayes UB4 77 BS71
Hounslow TW3 96 CC84
Ilford IG1 69 ER62
Isleworth TW7 97 CH81
Kenley CR8 175 DP115
Kingston upon Thames KT2 118 CM92
Kingston upon Thames
(Hmptn W.) KT1 137 CJ95
New Malden KT3 138 CR98
Orpington BR5 146 EW99
Oxted RH8 188 EF128
Potters Bar EN6 12 DG30
Radlett WD7 25 CG35
Redhill RH1 184 DF132
Richmond TW10 118 CM86
Rickmansworth WD3 38 BK45
Shepperton TW17 134 BN102
Staines (Stanw.) TW19 114 BH86
Sunbury-on-Thames TW16 115 BV94
Surbiton KT5 138 CM99
Sutton SM3 157 CY107
Swanley BR8 147 FF97
Swanscombe DA10 130 FY86
Teddington TW11 117 CF93
Twickenham TW1 117 CJ86
Uxbridge UB8 76 BL66
Wallington SM6 159 DH106
Wallington (Hackbr.) SM6 141 DH103
Waltham Cross EN8 15 DX33
Warlingham CR6 162 EE114
Watford WD17 23 BU39
Wembley HA0 80 CL65
Woking GU22 167 BA117
Park Rd E, W3 98 CP75
Uxbridge UB10
off Hillingdon Rd 76 BK68
Park Rd N, W3 98 CP75
W4 98 CR78
Park Row, SE10 103 ED79
PARK ROYAL, NW10 80 CN69
⊖ **Park Royal** 80 CN70
H **Park Royal Cen for**
Mental Health, NW10 80 CQ68
Park Royal Rd, NW10 80 CQ69
W3 80 CQ69
Parkshot, Rich. TW9 98 CL84
Parkside, N3 44 DB53
NW2 63 CU62
NW7 43 CU51
SE3 104 EF80
SW19 119 CX91
Addlestone
(New Haw) KT15 152 BH110
Buckhurst Hill IG9 48 EH47
Gerrards Cross (Chal.St.P.) SL9
off Lower Rd 57 AZ56
Grays RM16 110 GE76
Hampton
(Hmptn H.) TW12 117 CD92
Potters Bar EN6
off High St 12 DC32
Sevenoaks (Halst.) TN14 164 EZ113
Sidcup DA14 126 EV89
Sutton SM3 157 CY107
Waltham Cross EN8 15 DY34
Watford WD19 24 BW44
Parkside Av, SW19 119 CX92
Bexleyheath DA7 107 FD82
Bromley BR1 144 EL98
Romford RM1 71 FD55
Tilbury RM18 111 GH82
Parkside Business Est, SE8
off Rolt St 103 DY79
Parkside Cl, SE20 122 DW94
Parkside Ct, Wey. KT13 152 BN105
Parkside Cres, N7 65 DN62
Surbiton KT5 138 CQ100
Parkside Cross, Bexh. DA7 107 FE82
Parkside Dr, Edg. HA8 42 CN48
Watford WD17 23 BS40
Parkside Est, E9
off Rutland Rd 84 DW67
Parkside Gdns, SW19 119 CX91
Barnet EN4 44 DF46
Coulsdon CR5 175 DH117
H **Parkside Hosp**, SW19 119 CX90
Parkside Ho, Dag. RM10 71 FC62
Parkside Pl, Stai. TW18
off Commercial Rd 114 BG93
Parkside Rd, SW11 100 DG81
Belvedere DA17 107 FC77
Hounslow TW3 116 CB85
Northwood HA6 39 BT50
Warlingham CR6 177 EA116
Parkside Ter, N18
off Great Cambridge Rd 46 DR49
Orpington BR6
off Willow Wk 145 EP104
Parkside Wk, SE10 205 H7
Slough SL1 92 AU76
Parkside Way, Har. HA2 60 CB56
Park S, SW11 *off Austin Rd* 100 DG81
Park Sq, Esher KT10
off Park Rd 154 CB105
Romford (Abridge) RM4
off New Rd 34 EY44
Park Sq E, NW1 195 H4
Park Sq Ms, NW1 195 H5
Park Sq W, NW1 195 H4
Parkstead Rd, SW15 119 CU85
Parkstone Av, N18 46 DT50
Hornchurch RM11 72 FK58
Parkstone Rd, E17 67 EC55
SE15 *off Rye La* 102 DU82
PARK STREET, St.Alb. AL2 9 CD26
≠ **Park Street** 9 CD26
Park St, SE1 201 H2
W1 194 F10
Croydon CR0 142 DQ103
St. Albans AL2 9 CD26
Slough SL1 92 AT76
Slough (Colnbr.) SL3 93 BD80
Teddington TW11 117 CE93
Park St La, St.Alb.
(Park St) AL2 8 CB30
Park Ter, Green. DA9 129 FV85
Sevenoaks (Sund.) TN14
off Main Rd 180 EX124
Worcester Park KT4 139 CU102
Parkthorne Cl, Har. HA2 60 CB58
Parkthorne Dr, Har. HA2 60 CA58
Parkthorne Rd, SW12 121 DK87
Park Vw, N21 45 DM45
W3 80 CQ71
New Malden KT3 139 CT97
Pinner HA5 40 BZ53
Potters Bar EN6 12 DC33
South Ockendon
(Aveley) RM15 91 FR74
Wembley HA9 62 CP64
Parkview Ct, SW18
off Broomhill Rd 120 DA86
Park Vw Ct, Ilf. IG2
off Brancaster Rd 69 ES58
Woking GU22 166 AY119
Park Vw Cres, N11 45 DH49
Parkview Dr, Mitch. CR4 140 DD96
Park Vw Est, E2 85 DX68
N5 66 DQ63
Park Vw Gdns, NW4 63 CW57
Grays RM17 110 GB78
Ilford IG4 69 EM56
Park Vw Ho, SE24
off Hurst St 121 DP86
Parkview Ho, Horn. RM12
off Sunrise Av 71 FH61
Park Vw Ms, SW9 101 DM82
Park Vw Rd, N3 44 DB53
N17 66 DU55
NW10 63 CT63
Parkview Rd, SE9 125 EP89
Park Vw Rd, W5 80 CL71
Caterham (Wold.) CR3 177 DY122
Parkview Rd, Croy. CR0 142 DU102
Park Vw Rd, Pnr. HA5 39 BV52
Southall UB1 78 CA74
Uxbridge UB8 76 BN72
Welling DA16 106 EW83
Park Vw Rd Est, N17 46 DV54
Park Village E, NW1 83 DH68
Park Village W, NW1 83 DH68
Park Vil, Rom. RM6 70 EX58
Parkville Rd, SW6 99 CZ80
Park Vista, SE10 103 ED79
Park Wk, N6 *off North Rd* 64 DG59
SE10 *off Crooms Hill* 103 ED80
SW10 100 DC79
Ashtead KT21
off Rectory La 172 CM119
Parkway, N14 45 DL47
Park Way, N20 44 DF49
Parkway, NW1 83 DH67
Park Way, NW11 63 CY57
Parkway, SW20 139 CX98
Park Way, Bex. DA5 127 FE90
Brentwood (Shenf.) CM15 55 FZ46
Parkway, Croy.
(New Adgtn) CR0 161 EC109
Park Way, Edg. HA8 42 CP53
Enfield EN2 29 DN40
Parkway, Erith DA18 106 EY76
Park Way, Felt. TW14 115 BV87
Parkway, Ilf. IG3 69 ET62
Park Way, Lthd. (Bkhm) KT23 170 CA123
Parkway, Rain. RM13
off Upminster Rd S 89 FG70
Park Way, Rick. WD3 38 BJ46
Parkway, Rom. RM2 71 FF55
Park Way, Ruis. HA4 59 BU60
Parkway, Uxb. UB10 76 BN66
Park Way, W.Mol. KT8 136 CB97
Parkway, Wey. KT13 153 BR105
Woodford Green IG8 48 EJ50
Parkway, The, Hayes
UB3, UB4 78 BW72
Parkway, The, Hounslow
(Cran.) TW4, TW5 95 BV82
Iver SL0 75 BC68
Northolt UB5 78 BX69
Southall UB2 95 BU78
Parkway Trd Est, Houns. TW5 96 BW79
Park W, W2 194 C9
Park W Pl, W2 194 C8
Parkwood, N20 44 DF48
Beckenham BR3 143 EA95
Parkwood Av, Esher KT10 136 CC102
Parkwood Cl, Bans. SM7 173 CX115
Parkwood Gro, Sun. TW16 135 BU97
Parkwood Ms, N6 65 DH58
Parkwood Rd, SW19 119 CZ92
Banstead SM7 173 CX115
Bexley DA5 126 EZ87
Isleworth TW7 97 CF81
Redhill (Nutfld) RH1 185 DL133
Westerham (Tats.) TN16 178 EL121
Parkwood Vw, Bans. SM7 173 CW116
Park Wks Rd, Red. RH1 185 DM133
Parlaunt Rd, Slou. SL3 93 BA77
Parley Dr, Wok. GU21 166 AW117
Parliament Ct, E1
off Sandy's Row 84 DS71
Parliament Hill, NW3 64 DE63
Parliament Ms, SW14
off Thames Bk 98 CQ82
Parliament Sq, SW1 199 P5
Parliament St, SW1 199 P5
Parliament Vw Apartments,
SE1 200 B8
Parma Cres, SW11 100 DF84
Parmiter St, E2 84 DV68
Parmoor Ct, EC1 197 H4
Parnell Cl, W12 99 CV76
Abbots Langley WD5 7 BT30
Edgware HA8 42 CP49
Grays (Chaff.Hun.) RM16 109 FW78
Parnell Gdns, Wey. KT13 152 BN111
Parnell Rd, E3 85 DZ67
Parnham St, E14
off Blount St 85 DY72
Parolles Rd, N19 65 DJ60
Paroma Rd, Belv. DA17 106 FA76
Parr Av, Epsom KT17 157 CV109
Parr Cl, N9 46 DV49
N18 46 DV49
Grays (Chaff.Hun.) RM16 109 FW77
Leatherhead KT22 171 CF120
Parr Ct, N1 *off New N Rd* 84 DR68
Feltham TW13 116 BW91
Parrock, The, Grav. DA12 131 GJ88
Parrock Av, Grav. DA12 131 GJ88
PARROCK FARM,
Grav. DA12 131 GK91
Parrock Rd, Grav. DA12 131 GJ88
Parrock St, Grav. DA12 131 GH87
Parrotts Cl, Rick.
(Crox.Grn) WD3 22 BN42
Parr Pl, W4
off Chiswick High Rd 99 CT77
Parr Rd, E6 86 EK67
Stanmore HA7 41 CK53
Parrs Cl, S.Croy. CR2
off Florence Rd 160 DR109
Parrs Pl, Hmptn. TW12 116 CA94
Parr St, N1 84 DR68
Parry Av, E6 87 EM72
Parry Cl, Epsom KT17 157 CU108
Parry Dr, Wey. KT13 152 BN110
Parry Grn N, Slou. SL3 93 AZ77
Parry Grn S, Slou. SL3 93 AZ77
Parry Pl, SE18 105 EP77
Parry Rd, SE25 142 DS97
W10 81 CY69
Parry St, SW8 101 DL79
Parsifal Rd, NW6 64 DA64
Parsley Gdns, Croy. CR0
off Primrose La 143 DX102
Parsloes Av, Dag. RM9 70 EX63
Parsonage Cl, Abb.L. WD5 7 BS30
Hayes UB3 77 BT72
Warlingham CR6 177 DY116
Parsonage Gdns, Enf. EN2 30 DQ40
Parsonage La, Dart.
(Sutt.H.) DA4 128 FP93
Enfield EN1, EN2 30 DR40
Sidcup DA14 126 EZ91
Parsonage Manorway,
Belv. DA17 106 FA79
Parsonage Rd, Ch.St.G. HP8 36 AV48
Egham (Eng.Grn) TW20 112 AX92
Grays RM20 109 FW79
Rainham RM13 90 FJ69
Rickmansworth WD3 38 BK45
Parsonage St, E14 204 E9
Parsons Cl, Sutt. SM1 140 DB104
Parsons Cres, Edg. HA8 42 CN48
Parsonsfield Cl, Bans. SM7 173 CX115
Parsonsfield Rd, Bans. SM7 173 CX116
PARSONS GREEN, SW6 100 DA81
⊖ **Parsons Green** 99 CZ81
Parsons Grn, SW6 100 DA81
Parsons Grn La, SW6 100 DA81
Parsons Gro, Edg. HA8 42 CN48
Parsons Ho, SW2
off New Pk Rd 121 DL87
Parson's Ho, W2 82 DD70
Parsons La, Dart. DA2 127 FH90
Parson's Mead, Croy. CR0 141 DP102
Parsons Mead, E.Mol. KT8 136 CC97
Parsons Pightle, Couls. CR5 175 DN120
Parsons Rd, E13 *off Old St* 86 EJ68
Slough SL3 *off Ditton Rd* 93 AZ78
Parson St, NW4 63 CW56
Parthenia Rd, SW6 100 DA81
Parthia Cl, Tad. KT20 173 CV119
Partingdale La, NW7 43 CX50
Partington Cl, N19 65 DK60
Partridge Cl, E16
off Fulmer Rd 86 EK71
Barnet EN5 27 CW44
Bushey WD23 40 CB46
Chesham HP5 4 AS28
Stanmore HA7 42 CL49
Partridge Ct, EC1
off Percival St 83 DP70
Partridge Dr, Orp. BR6 145 EQ104
Partridge Grn, SE9 125 EN90
Partridge Knoll, Pur. CR8 159 DP112
Partridge Mead, Bans. SM7 173 CW116
Partridge Rd, Hmptn. TW12 116 BZ93
Sidcup DA14 125 ES90
Partridge Sq, E6
off Nightingale Way 86 EL71
Partridge Way, N22 45 DL53
Parvills, Wal.Abb. EN9 15 ED32
Parvin St, SW8 101 DK81
Parvis Rd, W.Byf. KT14 152 BG113
Pasadena Cl, Hayes UB3 95 BV75
Pasadena Cl Trd Est, Hayes UB3
off Pasadena Cl 95 BV75
Pascal St, SW8 101 DK80
Pascoe Rd, SE13 123 ED85
Pasfield, Wal.Abb. EN9 15 ED33
Pasley Cl, SE17
off Penrose St 102 DQ78
Pasquier Rd, E17 67 DY55
Passey Pl, SE9 125 EM86
Passfield Dr, E14
off Uamvar St 85 EB71
Passfield Path, SE28
off Booth Cl 88 EV73
Passing All, EC1 196 G5
Passmore Gdns, N11 45 DK51
Passmore St, SW1 198 F9
★ **Passport Office**, SW1 199 J8
Pastens Rd, Oxt. RH8 188 EJ131
Pasteur Cl, NW9 42 CS54
Pasteur Dr, Rom.
(Harold Wd) RM3 52 FK54
Pasteur Gdns, N18 45 DP50
Paston Cl, E5
off Caldecott Way 67 DX62
Wallington SM6 141 DJ104
Paston Cres, SE12 124 EH87
Pastoral Way, Brwd. CM14
off Warley Hill 54 FV50
Pastor St, SE11 200 G8
Pasture Cl, Bushey WD23 40 CC45
Wembley HA0 61 CH62
Pasture Rd, SE6 124 EF88
Dagenham RM9 70 EZ63
Wembley HA0 61 CH61
Pastures, The, N20 43 CZ46
Watford WD19 40 BW45
Pastures Mead, Uxb. UB10 76 BN65
Patch, The, Sev. TN13 190 FE122
Patcham Ct, Sutt. SM2 158 DC109
Patcham Ter, SW8 101 DH81
Patch Cl, Uxb. UB10 76 BM67
PATCHETTS GREEN,
Wat. WD25 24 CC39
Patching Way, Hayes UB4
off Glencoe Rd 78 BY71
Paternoster Cl, Wal.Abb. EN9 16 EF33
Paternoster Hill,
Wal.Abb. EN9 16 EF32
Paternoster Row, EC4 197 H9
Romford (Noak Hill) RM4 52 FJ47
Paternoster Sq, EC4 196 G9
Paterson Rd, Ashf. TW15 114 BK92
Pater St, W8 100 DA76
Pates Manor Dr, Felt. TW14 115 BR87
Path, The, SW19 140 DB95
Pathfield Rd, SW16 121 DK93
Pathway, The, Rad. WD7 25 CF36
Watford WD19
off Anthony Cl 40 BX46
Patience Rd, SW11 100 DE82
Patio Cl, SW4 121 DK86
Patmore Est, SW8 101 DJ81
Patmore La, Walt. KT12 153 BT107
Patmore Rd, Wal.Abb. EN9 16 EE34
Patmore St, SW8 101 DJ81
Patmore Way, Rom. RM5 51 FB50
Patmos Rd, SW9 101 DP80
Paton Cl, E3 85 EA69
Paton St, EC1 197 H3
Patricia Ct, Chis. BR7
off Manor Pk Rd 145 ER95
Welling DA16 106 EV80
Patricia Dr, Horn. RM11 72 FL60
Patricia Gdns, Sutt. SM2
off The Crescent 158 DA111
Patrick Connolly Gdns, E3
off Talwin St 85 EB69
Patrick Gro, Wal.Abb. EN9
off Beaulieu Dr 15 EB33
Patrick Rd, E13 86 EJ69
Patrington Cl, Uxb. UB8
off Boulmer Rd 76 BJ69
Patriot Sq, E2 84 DV68
Patrol Pl, SE6 123 EB86
Patrons Dr, Uxb.
(Denh.) UB9 57 BF58
Patshull Pl, NW5
off Patshull Rd 83 DJ65
Patshull Rd, NW5 83 DJ65
Patten All, Rich. TW10
off The Hermitage 117 CK85
Pattenden Rd, SE6 123 DZ88
Patten Rd, SW18 120 DE87
Patterdale Cl, Brom. BR1 124 EF93
Patterdale Rd, SE15 102 DW80
Dartford DA2 129 FR88
Patterson Ct, SE19 122 DT94
Dartford DA1 128 FN85
Patterson Rd, SE19 122 DT93
Pattina Wk, SE16 203 L3
Pattison Pt, E16 *off Fife Rd* 86 EG71
Pattison Rd, NW2 64 DA62
Pattison Wk, SE18 105 EQ78
Paul Cl, E15 86 EE66
Paulet Rd, SE5 101 DP82
Paul Gdns, Croy. CR0 142 DT103
Paulhan Rd, Har. HA3 61 CK56
Paulin Dr, N21 45 DN45
Pauline Cres, Twick. TW2 116 CC88
Paulinus Cl, Orp. BR5 146 EW96
Paul Julius Cl, E14 204 F1
Paul Robeson Cl, E6
off Eastbourne Rd 87 EN69

★ Place of interest ≠ Railway station ⊖ London Underground station DLR Docklands Light Railway station Tra Tramlink station H Hospital Riv Pedestrian ferry landing stage

305

Pauls Grn, Wal.Cr. EN8
off Eleanor Rd 15 DY33
Paul's Pl, Ashtd. KT21 172 CP119
Paul St, E15 85 ED67
EC2 197 L5
Paul's Wk, EC4 196 G10
Paultons Sq, SW3 100 DD79
Paultons St, SW3 100 DD79
Pauntley St, N19 65 DJ60
Paved Ct, Rich. TW9 117 CK85
Paveley Dr, SW11 100 DE80
Paveley St, NW8 194 C4
Pavement, The, SW4 101 DJ84
W5 *off Popes La* 98 CL76
Pavement Ms, Rom. RM6
off Clarissa Rd 70 EX59
Pavement Sq, Croy. CR0 142 DU102
Pavet Cl, Dag. RM10 89 FB65
Pavilion Gdns, Stai. TW18 114 BH94
Pavilion La, Beck. BR3
off Lennard Rd 123 DZ93
Pavilion Ms, N3
off Windermere Av 44 DA54
Pavilion Rd, SW1 198 E7
Ilford IG1 69 EM59
Pavilions, The, Epp.
(N.Wld Bas.) CM16 19 FC25
Uxbridge UB8 76 BJ66
Pavilion Shop Cen, The,
Wal.Cr. EN8 15 DX34
Pavilion Sq, SW17 120 DF90
Pavilion St, SW1 198 E7
Pavilion Ter, E.Mol. KT8 137 CF98
Ilford IG2
off Southdown Cres 69 ES57
Pavilion Way, Amer. HP6 20 AW39
Edgware HA8 42 CP52
Ruislip HA4 60 BW61
Pawleyne Cl, SE20 122 DW94
Pawsey Cl, E13
off Plashet Rd 86 EG67
Pawson's Rd, Croy. CR0 142 DQ100
Paxford Rd, Wem. HA0 61 CH61
Paxton Cl, Rich. TW9 98 CM82
Walton-on-Thames KT12 136 BW101
Paxton Gdns, Wok. GU21 151 BE112
Paxton Pl, SE27 122 DS91
Paxton Rd, N17 46 DT52
SE23 123 DY90
W4 98 CS79
Bromley BR1 124 EG94
Paxton Ter, SW1 101 DH79
Payne Cl, Bark. IG11 87 ES66
Paynell Ct, SE3
off Lawn Ter 104 EE83
Payne Rd, E3 85 EB68
Paynesfield Av, SW14 98 CR83
Paynesfield Rd, Bushey
(Bushey Hth) WD23 41 CF45
Westerham (Tats.) TN16 178 EK119
Payne St, SE8 103 DZ79
Paynes Wk, W6 99 CY79
Peabody Av, SW1 199 H10
Peabody Cl, SE10
off Devonshire Dr 103 EB81
SW1 *off Lupus St* 101 DH79
Croydon CR0
off Shirley Rd 142 DW102
Peabody Ct, Enf. EN3
off Martini Dr 31 EA37
Peabody Dws, WC1 195 P4
Peabody Est, EC1 197 J5
N1 (Islington)
off Greenman St 84 DQ66
N17 46 DS53
SE1 200 E3
SE24 122 DQ87
SW3 *off Margaretta Ter* 100 DE79
W6 *off The Square* 99 CW78
W10 81 CW71
Peabody Hill, SE21 121 DP88
Peabody Hill Est, SE21 121 DP87
Peabody Sq, SE1 200 F5
Peabody Twr, EC1
off Golden La 84 DQ70
Peabody Trust, SE1 201 H3
Peabody Yd, N1
off Greenman St 84 DQ67
Peace Cl, N14 29 DH43
SE25 142 DS98
Waltham Cross EN7
off Goffs La 14 DU29
Peace Dr, Wat. WD17 23 BU41
Peace Gro, Wem. HA9 62 CP62
Peace Prospect, Wat. WD17 23 BU41
Peace Rd, Iver SL0 75 AZ69
Slough SL3 75 BA68
Peace St, SE18
off Nightingale Vale 105 EP79
Peach Cft, Grav.
(Nthflt) DA11 130 GE90
Peaches Cl, Sutt. SM2 157 CY108
Peachey Cl, Uxb. UB8 76 BK72
Peachey La, Uxb. UB8 76 BK71
Peach Rd, W10 81 CX69
Peach Tree Av, West Dr. UB7
off Pear Tree Av 76 BM72
Peachum Rd, SE3 104 EF79
Peachwalk Ms, E3
off Grove Rd 85 DX68
Peacock Av, Felt. TW14 115 BR88
Peacock Cl, Horn. RM11 72 FL56
Peacock Gdns, S.Croy. CR2 161 DY110
Peacocks Cen, The,
Wok. GU21 166 AY117
Peacock St, SE17 200 G9
Gravesend DA12 131 GJ87
Peacock Wk, E16 86 EH72
Abbots Langley WD5 7 BU31
Peacock Yd, SE17 200 G9
Peak, The, SE26 122 DW90
Peakes La, Wal.Cr.
(Chsht) EN7 14 DT27
Peakes Way, Wal.Cr.
(Chsht) EN7 14 DT27
Peaketon Av, Ilf. IG4 68 EK56
Peak Hill, SE26 122 DW91
Peak Hill Av, SE26 122 DW91
Peak Hill Gdns, SE26 122 DW91
Peaks Hill, Pur. CR8 159 DK110
Peaks Hill Ri, Pur. CR8 159 DL110
Pea La, Upmin. RM14 91 FU66
Peal Gdns, W13
off Ruislip Rd E 79 CG70
Peall Rd, Croy. CR0 141 DM100
Pearce Cl, Mitch. CR4 140 DG96
Pearcefield Av, SE23 122 DW88
Pearce Rd, W.Mol. KT8 136 CB97
Pear Cl, NW9 62 CR56
SE14
off Southerngate Way 103 DY80
Pearcroft Rd, E11 67 ED61
Pearcy Cl, Rom.
(Harold Hill) RM3 52 FL52
Peardon St, SW8 101 DH82
Peareswood Gdns,
Stan. HA7 41 CK53
Peareswood Rd, Erith DA8 107 FF81
Pearfield Rd, SE23 123 DY90
Pearl Cl, E6 87 EN72
NW2 *off Marble Dr* 63 CX59
Pearl Ct, Wok. GU21
off Langmans Way 166 AS116
Pearl Rd, E17 67 EA55
Pearl St, E1 202 E2
Pearmain Cl, Shep. TW17 135 BP99
Pearman St, SE1 200 E6
Pear Pl, SE1 200 D4
Pear Rd, E11 67 ED62
Pearscroft Ct, SW6 100 DB81
Pearscroft Rd, SW6 100 DB81
Pearse St, SE15
off Dragon Rd 102 DS79
Pearson Cl, SE5
off Medlar St 102 DQ81
Purley CR8 159 DP111
Pearson Ms, SW4
off Edgeley Rd 101 DK83
Pearsons Av, SE14
off Tanners Hill 103 EA81
Pearson St, E2 84 DS68
Pearson Way, Dart. DA1 128 FM89
Pears Rd, Houns. TW3 96 CC83
Peartree Av, SW17 120 DC90
Pear Tree Av, West Dr. UB7 76 BM72
Pear Tree Cl, E2 84 DT67
Addlestone KT15
off Pear Tree Rd 152 BG106
Amersham HP7
off Orchard End Av 20 AT39
Chessington KT9 156 CN106
Peartree Cl, Erith DA8 107 FD81
Pear Tree Cl, Mitch. CR4 140 DE96
Peartree Cl, S.Croy. CR2 160 DV114
South Ockendon RM15 91 FW68
Pear Tree Cl, Swan. BR8 147 FD96
Peartree Ct, E18
off Churchfields 48 EH53
Pear Tree Ct, EC1 196 E5
Peartree Gdns, Dag. RM8 70 EV63
Romford RM7 51 FB54
Peartree La, E1 202 G1
Pear Tree Rd, Add. KT15 152 BG106
Ashford TW15 115 BQ92
Peartree Rd, Enf. EN1 30 DS41
Pear Tree St, EC1 196 G4
Pear Tree Wk, Wal.Cr.
(Chsht) EN7 14 DR26
Peartree Way, SE10 205 M8
Peary Pl, E2
off Kirkwall Pl 84 DW69
Pease Cl, Horn. RM12
off Dowding Way 89 FH66
Peatfield Cl, Sid. DA15
off Woodside Rd 125 ES90
Peatmore Av, Wok. GU22 168 BG116
Peatmore Cl, Wok. GU22 168 BG116
Pebble Cl, Tad. KT20 182 CS128
PEBBLE COOMBE,
Tad. KT20 182 CS128
Pebble Hill Rd, Bet. RH3 182 CS131
Tadworth KT20 182 CS131
Pebble La, Epsom KT18 172 CN121
Leatherhead KT22 182 CL125
Pebble Way, W3 80 CP74
Pebworth Rd, Har. HA1 61 CG61
Peckarmans Wd, SE26 122 DU90
Peckett Sq, N5
off Highbury Gra 66 DQ63
Peckford Pl, SW9 101 DN82
PECKHAM, SE15 102 DU81
Peckham Gro, SE15 102 DS80
Peckham High St, SE15 102 DU81
Peckham Hill St, SE15 102 DU80
Peckham Pk Rd, SE15 102 DU80
Peckham Rd, SE5 102 DS81
SE15 102 DS81
⇌ **Peckham Rye** 102 DU82
Peckham Rye, SE15 102 DU83
SE22 102 DU84
Pecks Yd, E1 197 P6
Peckwater St, NW5 65 DJ64
Pedham Pl Ind Est,
Swan. BR8 147 FG99
Pedlars Wk, N7 83 DL65
Pedley Rd, Dag. RM8 70 EW60
Pedley St, E1 84 DT70
Pedro St, E5 67 DX62
Pedworth Gdns, SE16 202 F9
Peek Cres, SW19 119 CX92
Peel Cl, E4 47 EB47
N9 *off Plevna Rd* 46 DU48
Peel Dr, NW9 63 CT55
Ilford IG5 68 EL55
Peel Gro, E2 84 DW68
Peel Pas, W8
off Peel St 82 DA74
Peel Pl, Ilf. IG5 48 EL54
Peel Prec, NW6 82 DA68
Peel Rd, E18 48 EF53
NW6 81 CZ69
Harrow (Wldste) HA3 61 CF55
Orpington BR6 163 EQ106
Wembley HA9 61 CK62
Peel St, W8 82 DA74
Peel Way, Rom. RM3 52 FM54
Uxbridge UB8 76 BL71
Peerage Way, Horn. RM11 72 FL59
Peerless Dr, Uxb.
(Hare.) UB9 58 BJ57
Peerless St, EC1 197 K3
Pegamoid Rd, N18 46 DW48
Pegasus Cl, N16
off Green Las 66 DR63
Pegasus Ct, Abb.L. WD5
off Furtherfield 7 BT32
Gravesend DA12 131 GJ90
Pegasus Pl, SE11
off Clayton St 101 DN79
SW6 *off Ackmar Rd* 100 DA81
Pegasus Rd, Croy. CR0 159 DN107
Pegasus Way, N11 45 DH51
Pegelm Gdns, Horn. RM11 72 FM59
Peggotty Way, Uxb. UB8
off Dickens Av 77 BP72
Pegg Rd, Houns. TW5 96 BX80
Pegley Gdns, SE12 124 EG89
Pegmire La, Wat. (Ald.) WD25 24 CC39
Pegrum Dr, St.Alb. AL2
off Shenley La 9 CH26
Pegwell St, SE18 105 ES80
Peket Cl, Stai. TW18 133 BE95
Pekin Cl, E14
off Pekin St 85 EA72
Pekin St, E14 85 EA72
Peldon Ct, Rich. TW9 98 CM84
Peldon Pas, Rich. TW10
off Worple Way 98 CM84
Peldon Wk, N1
off Britannia Row 83 DP67
Pelham Av, Bark. IG11 87 ET67
Pelham Cl, SE5 102 DS82
Pelham Cres, SW7 198 B9
Pelham Pl, SW7 198 B9
W13 *off Ruislip Rd E* 79 CF70
Pelham Rd, E18 68 EH55
N15 66 DT56
N22 45 DN54
SW19 120 DA94
Beckenham BR3 142 DW96
Bexleyheath DA7 106 FA83
Gravesend DA11 131 GF87
Ilford IG1 69 ER61
Pelham Rd S, Grav. DA11 131 GF88
Pelhams, The, Wat. WD25 24 BX35
Pelhams Cl, Esher KT10 154 CA105
Pelham St, SW7 198 A8
Pelhams Wk, Esher KT10 136 CA104
Pelham Ter, Grav. DA11
off Campbell Rd 131 GF87
Pelican Est, SE15 102 DT81
Pelican Pas, E1
off Cambridge Heath Rd 84 DW70
Pelier St, SE17
off Langdale Cl 102 DQ79
Pelinore Rd, SE6 124 EE89
Pellant Rd, SW6 99 CY80
Pellatt Gro, N22 45 DN53
Pellatt Rd, SE22 122 DT85
Wembley HA9 61 CK61
Pellerin Rd, N16 66 DS64
Pelling Hill, Wind.
(Old Wind.) SL4 112 AV87
Pelling St, E14 85 EA72
Pellipar Cl, N13 45 DN48
Pellipar Gdns, SE18 105 EM78
Pelly Ct, Epp. CM16 17 ET31
Pelly Rd, E13 86 EG68
Pelter St, E2 197 P2
Pelton Av, Sutt. SM2 158 DB110
Pelton Rd, SE10 205 H10
Pembar Av, E17 67 DY55
Pemberley Chase, Epsom
(W.Ewell) KT19 156 CP106
Pemberley Cl, Epsom
(W.Ewell) KT19 156 CP106
Pember Rd, NW10 81 CX69
Pemberton Av, Rom. RM2 71 FH55
Pemberton Gdns, N19 65 DJ62
Romford RM6 70 EY57
Swanley BR8 147 FE97
Pemberton Ho, SE26
off High Level Dr 122 DU91
Pemberton Pl, E8
off Mare St 84 DV66
Esher KT10
off Carrick Gate 136 CC104
Pemberton Rd, N4 65 DN57
East Molesey KT8 136 CC98
Pemberton Row, EC4 196 E8
Pemberton Ter, N19 65 DJ62
Pembrey Way, Horn. RM12 90 FJ65
Pembridge Av, Twick. TW2 116 BZ88
Pembridge Chase, Hem.H.
(Bov.) HP3
off Pembridge Cl 5 BA28
Pembridge Cl, Hem.H.
(Bov.) HP3 5 AZ28
Pembridge Cres, W11 82 DA73
Pembridge Gdns, W2 82 DA73
Pembridge Ms, W11 82 DA73
Pembridge Pl, SW15 120 DA85
W2 82 DA73
Pembridge Rd, W11 82 DA73
Hemel Hempstead
(Bov.) HP3 5 BA28
Pembridge Sq, W2 82 DA73
Pembridge Vil, W2 82 DA73
W11 82 DA73
Pembroke Av, N1 83 DL67
Enfield EN1 30 DV38
Harrow HA3 61 CG55
Pinner HA5 60 BX60
Surbiton KT5 138 CP99
Walton-on-Thames KT12 154 BX105
Pembroke Cl, SW1 198 G5
Banstead SM7 174 DB117
Erith DA8
off Pembroke Rd 107 FD77
Hornchurch RM11 72 FM56
Pembroke Cotts, W8
off Pembroke Sq 100 DA76
Pembroke Dr, Wal.Cr.
(Chsht) EN7 13 DP29
Pembroke Gdns, W8 99 CZ77
Pembroke Gdns,
Dagenham RM10 71 FB62
Woking GU22 167 BA118
Pembroke Gdns Cl, W8 100 DA76
Pembroke Ms, E3
off Morgan St 85 DY69
N10 *off Pembroke Rd* 44 DG53
W8 *off Earls Wk* 100 DA76
Sevenoaks TN13
off Pembroke Rd 191 FH125
Pembroke Pl, W8 100 DA76
Dartford (Sutt.H.) DA4 148 FP95
Edgware HA8 42 CN52
Isleworth TW7
off Thornbury Rd 97 CE82
Pembroke Rd, E6 87 EM71
E17 67 EB57
N8 65 DL56
N10 44 DG53
N13 46 DQ48
N15 66 DT57
SE25 142 DS98
W8 100 DA77
Bromley BR1 144 EJ96
Erith DA8 107 FC78
Greenford UB6 78 CB70
Ilford IG3 69 ET60
Mitcham CR4 140 DG96
Northwood HA6 39 BQ48
Ruislip HA4 59 BS60
Sevenoaks TN13 191 FH125
Wembley HA9 61 CK62
Woking GU22 167 BA118
Pembroke Sq, W8 100 DA76
Pembroke St, N1 83 DL66
Pembroke Studios, W8 99 CZ76
Pembroke Vil, W8 100 DA77
Richmond TW9 97 CK84
Pembroke Wk, W8 100 DA77
Pembroke Way, Hayes UB3 95 BQ76
Pembry Cl, SW9 101 DN81
Pembury Av, Wor.Pk. KT4 139 CU101
Pembury Cl, Brom. BR2 144 EF101
Coulsdon CR5 158 DG114
Pembury Ct, Hayes UB3 95 BR79
Pembury Cres, Sid. DA14 126 EY89
Pembury Pl, E5 66 DV64
Pembury Rd, E5 66 DV64
N17 46 DT54
SE25 142 DU98
Bexleyheath DA7 106 EY80
Pemdevon Rd, Croy. CR0 141 DN101
Pemell Cl, E1
off Colebert Av 84 DW70
Pemerich Cl, Hayes UB3 95 BT78
Pempath Pl, Wem. HA9 61 CK61
Penally Pl, N1
off Shepperton Rd 84 DR67
Penang St, E1 202 E2
Penard Rd, Sthl. UB2 96 CA76
Penarth St, SE15 102 DW79
Penates, Esher KT10 155 CD105
Penberth Rd, SE6 123 EC89
Penbury Rd, Sthl. UB2 96 BZ77
Pencombe Ms, W11
off Denbigh Rd 81 CZ73
Pencraig Way, SE15 102 DV79
Pencroft Dr, Dart. DA1
off Shepherds La 128 FJ87
Pendall Cl, Barn. EN4 28 DE42
Penda Rd, Erith DA8 107 FB80
Pendarves Rd, SW20 139 CW95
Penda's Mead, E9
off Lindisfarne Way 67 DY63
Pendell Av, Hayes UB3 95 BT80
Pendell Ct, Red.
(Bletch.) RH1 185 DP131
Pendell Rd, Red.
(Bletch.) RH1 185 DP131
Pendennis Cl, W.Byf. KT14 152 BG114
Pendennis Rd, N17 66 DR55
SW16 121 DL91
Orpington BR6 146 EW103
Sevenoaks TN13 191 FH123
Penderel Rd, Houns. TW3 116 CA85
Penderry Ri, SE6 123 ED89
Penderyn Way, N7 65 DK63
Pendle Rd, SW16 121 DH93
Pendlestone Rd, E17 67 EA57
Pendragon Rd, Brom. BR1 124 EF90
Pendragon Wk, NW9 62 CS58
Pendrell Rd, SE4 103 DY82
Pendrell St, SE18 105 ER80
Pendula Dr, Hayes UB4 78 BX70
Pendulum Ms, E8
off Birkbeck Rd 66 DT64
Penerley Rd, SE6 123 EB88
Rainham RM13 89 FH71
Penfold Cl, Croy. CR0
off Epsom Rd 141 DN104
Penfold La, Bex. DA5 126 EX89
Penfold Pl, NW1 194 A6
Penfold Rd, N9 47 DX46
Penfold St, NW1 194 A5
NW8 194 A5
Penford Gdns, SE9 104 EK83
Penford St, SE5 101 DP82
Pengarth Rd, Bex. DA5 126 EX85
PENGE, SE20 122 DW94
⇌ **Penge East** 122 DW93
Penge Ho, SW11 *off Wye St* 100 DD83
Penge La, SE20 122 DW94
Pengelly Cl, Wal.Cr.
(Chsht) EN7 14 DV30
Penge Rd, E13 86 EJ66
SE20 142 DU97
SE25 142 DU97
⇌ **Penge West** 122 DV93
Penhale Cl, Orp. BR6 164 EU105
Penhall Rd, SE7 104 EK77
Penhill Rd, Bex. DA5 126 EW87
Penhurst, Wok. GU21 151 AZ114
Penhurst Pl, SE1 200 C7
Penhurst Rd, Ilf. IG6 49 EP52
Penifather La, Grnf. UB6 79 CD69
Peninsular Cl, Felt. TW14 115 BR86
Peninsular Pk Rd, SE7 205 N9
Penistone Rd, SW16 121 DL94
Penistone Wk, Rom. RM3
off Okehampton Rd 52 FJ51
Penketh Dr, Har. HA1 61 CD62
Penman Cl, St.Alb. AL2 8 CA27
Penman's Grn, Kings L.
WD4 5 BF32
Penmon Rd, SE2 106 EU76
Pennack Rd, SE15 102 DT79
Pennant Ms, W8 100 DB77
Pennant Ter, E17 47 DZ54
Pennard Rd, W12 99 CW75
Pennards, The, Sun. TW16 136 BW96
Penn Cl, Grnf. UB6 78 CB68
Harrow HA3 61 CJ56
Rickmansworth
(Chorl.) WD3 21 BD44
Uxbridge UB8 76 BK70
Penn Dr, Uxb.
(Denh.) UB9 57 BF58
Penne Cl, Rad. WD7 9 CF34
Penner Cl, SW19 119 CY89
Penners Gdns, Surb. KT6 138 CL101
Pennethorne Cl, E9
off Victoria Pk Rd 84 DW67
Pennethorne Ho, SW11
off Wye St 100 DD83
Pennethorne Rd, SE15 102 DV80
Penney Cl, Dart. DA1 128 FK87
Penn Gdns, Chis. BR7 145 EP96
Romford RM5 50 FA52
Penn Gaskell La, Ger.Cr.
(Chal.St.P.) SL9 37 AZ50
Pennine Dr, NW2 63 CY61
Pennine Ho, N9
off Plevna Rd 46 DU48
Pennine La, NW2
off Pennine Dr 63 CY61
Pennine Way, Bexh. DA7 107 FE81
Gravesend (Nthflt) DA11 130 GE90
Hayes UB3 95 BR80
Pennington Cl, SE27
off Hamilton Rd 122 DR91
Romford RM5 50 FA50
Pennington Dr, N21 29 DL43
Weybridge KT13 135 BS104
Pennington Rd, Ger.Cr.
(Chal.St.P.) SL9 36 AX52
Penningtons, The,
Amer. HP6 20 AS37
Pennington St, E1 202 C1
Pennington Way, SE12 124 EH89
Pennis La, Long.
(Fawk.Grn) DA3 149 FX100
Penniston Cl, N17 46 DQ54
Penn La, Bex. DA5 126 EX85
Penn Meadow, Slou.
(Stoke P.) SL2 74 AT67
Penn Pl, Rick. WD3
off Northway 38 BK45
Penn Rd, N7 65 DL64
Gerrards Cross
(Chal.St.P.) SL9 36 AX53
Rickmansworth
(Mill End) WD3 37 BF46
St. Albans (Park St) AL2 8 CC27
Slough (Datchet) SL3 92 AX81
Watford WD24 23 BV39
Penn St, N1 84 DR67
Penn Way, Rick. (Chorl.) WD3 21 BD44
Penny Cl, Rain. RM13 89 FH69
Pennycroft, Croy. CR0 161 DY109
Pennyfather La, Enf. EN2 30 DQ40
Pennyfield, Cob. KT11 153 BU113
Pennyfields, E14 85 EA73
Brentwood CM14 54 FW49
Penny La, Shep. TW17 135 BS101
Pennylets Grn, Slou.
(Stoke P.) SL2 74 AT66
Penny Ms, SW12
off Caistor Rd 121 DH87
Pennymoor Wk, W9
off Ashmore Rd 81 CZ69
Penny Rd, NW10 80 CP69
Pennyroyal Av, E6 87 EN72
Penpoll Rd, E8 84 DV65
Penpool La, Well. DA16 106 EV83
Penrhyn Av, E17 47 DZ53
Penrhyn Cl, Cat. CR3
off Buxton La 176 DR120
Penrhyn Cres, E17 47 EA53
SW14 98 CQ84
Penrhyn Gdns, Kings.T. KT1
off Surbiton Rd 137 CK98
Penrhyn Gro, E17 47 EA53
Penrhyn Rd, Kings.T. KT1 138 CL97
Penrith Cl, SW15 119 CY85
Beckenham BR3
off Albemarle Rd 143 EB95
Reigate RH2 184 DE133
Uxbridge UB8
off Chippendale Waye 76 BK66
Penrith Cres, Rain. RM13 71 FG64
Penrith Pl, SE27
off Harpenden Rd 121 DP89
Penrith Rd, N15 66 DR57
Ilford IG6 49 ET51
New Malden KT3 138 CR98
Romford RM3 52 FN51
Thornton Heath CR7 142 DQ96
Penrith St, SW16 121 DJ93
Penrose Av, Wat. WD19 40 BX47
Penrose Dr, Epsom KT19 156 CN111
Penrose Gro, SE17 102 DQ78
Penrose Ho, SE17 102 DQ78
Penrose Rd, Lthd.
(Fetch.) KT22 170 CC122
Penrose St, SE17 102 DQ78
Penryn St, NW1 83 DK68
Penry St, SE1 201 N9
Pensbury Pl, SW8 101 DJ82
Pensbury St, SW8 101 DJ82
Penscroft Gdns, Borwd. WD6 26 CR42
Pensford Av, Rich. TW9 98 CN82
Penshurst Av, Sid. DA15 126 EU86
Penshurst Cl, Ger.Cr.
(Chal.St.P.) SL9 36 AX54
Penshurst Gdns, Edg. HA8 42 CP50
Penshurst Grn, Brom. BR2 144 EF99
Penshurst Rd, E9 85 DX66
N17 46 DT52
Bexleyheath DA7 106 EZ81
Potters Bar EN6 12 DD31

★ Place of interest ⇌ Railway station ⊖ London Underground station DLR Docklands Light Railway station Tra Tramlink station H Hospital Riv Pedestrian ferry landing stage

306

Penshurst Rd,
Thornton Heath CR7 141 DP99
Penshurst Wk, Brom. BR2
off Hayesford Pk Dr 144 EF99
Penshurst Way, Orp. BR5
off Star La 146 EW98
Sutton SM2 158 DA108
Pensilver Cl, Barn. EN4 28 DE42
Pensons La, Ong. CM5 19 FG28
Penstemon Cl, N3 44 DA52
Penstemon Dr, Swans. DA10
off Craylands La 129 FX85
Penstock Footpath, N22 65 DL55
Pentavia Retail Pk, NW7
off Bunns La 43 CT52
Pentelow Gdns, Felt. TW14 115 BU86
Pentire Cl, Upmin. RM14 73 FS58
Pentire Rd, E17 47 ED53
Pentland Av, Edg. HA8 42 CP47
Shepperton TW17 134 BN99
Pentland Cl, N9 46 DW47
NW11 63 CY61
Pentland Gdns, SW18
off St. Ann's Hill 120 DC86
Pentland Pl, Nthlt. UB5 78 BY67
Pentland Rd, Bushey WD23 24 CC44
Pentlands Cl, Mitch. CR4 141 DH97
Pentland St, SW18 120 DC86
Pentland Way, Uxb. UB10 59 BQ62
Pentlow St, SW15 99 CW83
Pentlow Way, Buck.H. IG9 48 EL45
Pentney Rd, E4 47 ED46
SW12 121 DJ88
SW19
off Midmoor Rd 139 CY95
Penton Av, Stai. TW18 113 BF94
Penton Dr, Wal.Cr.
(Chsht) EN8 15 DX29
Penton Gro, N1 196 D1
Penton Hall Dr, Stai. TW18 134 BG95
Penton Hook Rd, Stai. TW18 114 BG94
Penton Ho, SE2
off Hartslock Dr 106 EX75
Penton Pk, Cher. KT16 134 BG97
Penton Pl, SE17 200 G10
Penton Ri, WC1 196 C2
Penton Rd, Stai. TW18 113 BF94
Penton St, N1 83 DN68
PENTONVILLE, N1 196 D1
Pentonville Rd, N1 196 B1
Pentrich Av, Enf. EN1 30 DU38
Pentridge St, SE15 102 DT80
Pentyre Av, N18 46 DR50
Penwerris Av, Islw. TW7 96 CC80
Penwith Rd, SW18 120 DB89
Penwith Wk, Wok. GU22
off Wych Hill Pk 166 AX119
Penwood End, Wok. GU22 166 AV121
Penwood Ho, SW15
off Tunworth Cres 119 CT86
Penwortham Rd, SW16 121 DH93
South Croydon CR2 160 DQ110
Penylan Pl, Edg. HA8 42 CN52
Penywern Rd, SW5 100 DA78
Penzance Cl, Uxb. (Hare.) UB9 38 BK53
Penzance Gdns, Rom. RM3 52 FN51
Penzance Pl, W11 81 CY74
Penzance Rd, Rom. RM3 52 FN51
Penzance St, W11 81 CY74
Peony Cl, Brwd.
(Pilg.Hat.) CM15 54 FV44
Peony Ct, Wdf.Grn. IG8
off The Bridle Path 48 EE52
Peony Gdns, W12 81 CU73
Pepler Ms, SE5
off Cobourg Rd 102 DT79
Peplins Cl, Hat. AL9 11 CY26
Peplins Way, Hat. AL9 11 CY25
Peploe Rd, NW6 81 CX68
Peplow Cl, West Dr. UB7
off Tavistock Rd 76 BK74
Pepper All, Loug.
(High Beach) IG10 32 EG39
Pepper Cl, E6 87 EM71
Caterham CR3 186 DS125
Peppercorn Cl, Th.Hth. CR7 142 DR96
Pepper Hill, Grav.
(Nthflt) DA11 130 GC90
Pepperhill La, Grav.
(Nthflt) DA11 130 GC90
Peppermead Sq, SE13 123 EA85
Peppermint Cl, Croy. CR0 141 DL101
Peppermint Pl, E11
off Birch Gro 68 EE62
Pepper St, E14 204 B6
SE1 201 H4
Peppie Cl, N16
off Bouverie Rd 66 DS61
Pepys Cl, Ashtd. KT21 172 CN117
Dartford DA1 108 FN84
Gravesend (Nthflt) DA11 130 GD90
Slough SL3 93 BB79
Tilbury RM18 111 GJ81
Uxbridge UB10 59 BP63
Pepys Cres, E16 205 N2
Barnet EN5 27 CW43
Pepys Ri, Orp. BR6 145 ET102
Pepys Rd, SE14 103 DX81
SW20 139 CW95
Pepys St, EC3 197 N10
Perceval Av, NW3 64 DE64
Percheron Cl, Islw. TW7 97 CG83
Percheron Rd, Borwd. WD6 26 CR44
Perch St, E8 66 DT63
Percival Cl, Lthd. KT22 154 CB111
Percival Ct, N17 off High Rd 46 DT52
Northolt UB5 60 CA64
★ Percival David Foundation of
Chinese Art, WC1 195 N4
Percival Gdns, Rom. RM6 70 EW58
Percival Rd, SW14 98 CQ84
Enfield EN1 30 DT42
Feltham TW13 115 BT89
Hornchurch RM11 72 FJ58
Orpington BR6 145 EP103
Percival St, EC1 196 F4
Percival Way, Epsom KT19 156 CQ105
Percy Av, Ashf. TW15 114 BN92
Percy Bryant Rd, Sun. TW16 115 BS94
Percy Bush Rd, West Dr. UB7 94 BM76
Percy Circ, WC1 196 C2
Percy Gdns, Enf. EN3 31 DX43
Hayes UB4 77 BS69
Isleworth TW7 97 CG82
Worcester Park KT4 138 CR102
Percy Ms, W1 195 M7
Percy Pas, W1 195 L7
Percy Pl, Slou. (Datchet) SL3 92 AV81
Percy Rd, E11 68 EE59
E16 86 EE71
N12 44 DC50
N21 46 DQ45
SE20 143 DX95
SE25 142 DU99
W12 99 CU75
Bexleyheath DA7 106 EY82
Hampton TW12 116 CA94
Ilford IG3 70 EU59
Isleworth TW7 97 CG84
Mitcham CR4 140 DG101
Romford RM7 71 FB55
Twickenham TW2 116 CB88
Watford WD18 23 BV42
Percy St, W1 195 M7
Grays RM17 110 GC79
Percy Way, Twick. TW2 116 CC88
Percy Yd, WC1 196 C2
Peregrine Cl, NW10 62 CR64
Watford WD25 8 BY34
Peregrine Ct, SW16
off Leithcote Gdns 121 DM91
Welling DA16 105 ET81
Peregrine Gdns, Croy. CR0 143 DY103
Peregrine Ho, EC1 196 G2
Peregrine Rd, Ilf. IG6 50 EV50
Sunbury-on-Thames TW16 135 BT96
Waltham Abbey EN9 16 EG34
Peregrine Wk, Horn. RM12
off Heron Flight Av 89 FH65
Peregrine Way, SW19 119 CW94
Perham Rd, W14 99 CY78
Perham Way, St.Alb.
(Lon.Col.) AL2 9 CK26
Peridot St, E6 86 EL71
Perifield, SE21 122 DQ88
Perimeade Rd, Grnf. UB6 79 CJ68
Periton Rd, SE9 104 EK84
PERIVALE, Grnf. UB6 79 CJ67
⊖ Perivale 79 CG68
Perivale Gdns, W13
off Bellevue Rd 79 CH70
Watford WD25 7 BV34
Perivale Gra, Grnf. UB6 79 CG69
Perivale Ind Pk, Grnf. UB6 79 CH68
Perivale La, Grnf. UB6 79 CG69
Perivale New Business Cen,
Grnf. UB6 79 CH68
Perkin Cl, Houns. TW3
off Hibernia Rd 96 CB84
Wembley HA0 61 CH64
Perkins Cl, Green. DA9 129 FT85
Perkins Ct, Ashf. TW15 114 BM92
Perkin's Rents, SW1 199 M6
Perkins Rd, Ilf. IG2 69 ER57
Perkins Sq, SE1 201 J2
Perks Cl, SE3
off Hurren Cl 104 EE83
Perleybrooke La, Wok. GU21
off Bampton Way 166 AU117
Permain Cl, Rad.
(Shenley) WD7 9 CK33
Perpins Rd, SE9 125 ES86
Perram Cl, Brox. EN10 15 DY26
Perran Rd, SW2
off Christchurch Rd 121 DP89
Perran Wk, Brent. TW8 98 CL78
Perren St, NW5
off Ryland Rd 83 DH65
Perrers Rd, W6 99 CV77
Perrin Cl, Ashf. TW15
off Fordbridge Rd 114 BM92
Perrin Ct, Wok. GU21
off Blackmore Cres 167 BB115
Perrin Rd, Wem. HA0 61 CG63
Perrins Ct, NW3
off Hampstead High St 64 DC63
Perrins La, NW3 64 DC63
Perrin's Wk, NW3 64 DC63
Perriors Cl, Wal.Cr.
(Chsht) EN7 14 DU27
Perrott St, SE18 105 EQ77
Perry Av, W3 80 CR72
Perry Cl, Rain. RM13
off Lowen Rd 89 FD68
Uxbridge UB8
off Harlington Rd 77 BQ72
Perry Ct, E14
off Napier Av 103 EA78
N15 off Albert Rd 66 DS58
Perryfield Way, NW9 63 CT58
Richmond TW10 117 CH89
Perry Gdns, N9
off Deansway 46 DS48
Perry Garth, Nthlt. UB5 78 BW67
Perry Gro, Dart. DA1 108 FN84
Perry Hall Cl, Orp. BR6 146 EU101
Perry Hall Rd, Orp. BR6 145 ET100
Perry Hill, SE6 123 DZ90
Perry Ho, SW2
off Tierney Rd 121 DL87
Rainham RM13
off Lowen Rd 89 FD68
Perry How, Wor.Pk. KT4 139 CT102
Perryman Ho, Bark. IG11 87 EQ67
Perrymans Fm Rd, Ilf. IG2 69 ER58
Perry Mead, Bushey WD23 40 CB45
Enfield EN2 29 DP40
Perrymead St, SW6 100 DA81
Perryn Rd, SE16 202 D6
W3 80 CR73
Perry Oaks Dr, Houns.
(Hthrw Air.) TW6 94 BH82
Perry Ri, SE23 123 DY90
Perry Rd, Dag. RM9 88 EZ70
Perrysfield Rd, Wal.Cr.
(Chsht) EN8 15 DY27
Perrys La, Sev.
(Knock.) TN14 164 EV113
Perrys Pl, W1 195 M8
PERRY STREET, Grav. DA11 130 GE88
Perry St, Chis. BR7 125 ER93
Dartford DA1 107 FE84
Gravesend (Nthflt) DA11 130 GE88
Perry St Gdns, Chis. BR7
off Old Perry St 125 ES93
Perry Vale, SE23 122 DW89
Perry Way, S.Ock.
(Aveley) RM15 90 FQ73
Persant Rd, SE6 124 EE89
Perseverance Cotts, Wok.
(Ripley) GU23 168 BJ121
Perseverance Pl, SW9 101 DN80
Richmond TW9
off Shaftesbury Rd 98 CL83
Persfield Cl, Epsom KT17 157 CU110
Pershore Cl, Ilf. IG2 69 EP57
Pershore Gro, Cars. SM5 140 DD100
Pert Cl, N10 45 DH52
Perth Av, NW9 62 CR59
Hayes UB4 78 BW70
Perth Cl, SW20
off Huntley Way 139 CU96
Perth Rd, E10 67 DY60
E13 86 EH68
N4 65 DN60
N22 45 DP53
Barking IG11 87 ER68
Beckenham BR3 143 EC96
Ilford IG2 69 EN58
Perth Ter, Ilf. IG2 69 EQ59
Perwell Av, Har. HA2 60 BZ60
Perwell Ct, Har. HA2 60 BZ60
Peter Av, NW10 81 CV66
Oxted RH8 187 ED129
Peterboat Cl, SE10 205 J8
Peterborough Av,
Upmin. RM14 73 FS60
Peterborough Gdns, Ilf. IG1 68 EL59
Peterborough Ms, SW6 100 DA82
Peterborough Rd, E10 67 EC57
SW6 100 DA82
Carshalton SM5 140 DE100
Harrow HA1 61 CE60
Peterborough Vil, SW6 100 DB81
Peterchurch Ho, SE15
off Commercial Way 102 DV79
Petergate, SW11 100 DC84
Peterhead Ms, Slou. SL3
off Grampian Way 93 BA78
Peter Heathfield Ho, E15
off High St 85 ED67
Peterhill Cl, Ger.Cr.
(Chal.St.P.) SL9 36 AY50
Peterhouse Gdns, SW6
off Bagley's La 100 DB81
Peter James Business Cen,
Hayes UB3 95 BU75
Peterley Business Cen, E2
off Hackney Rd 84 DV68
★ Peter Pan Statue, W2 82 DD74
Peter Rogers Way, Iver SL0
off Pinewood Rd 75 BB66
Peters Av, St.Alb.
(Lon.Col.) AL2 9 CJ26
Peters Cl, Dag. RM8 70 EX60
Stanmore HA7 41 CK51
Welling DA16 105 ES82
Petersfield Av, Rom. RM3 52 FL51
Slough SL2 74 AU74
Staines TW18 114 BJ92
Petersfield Cl, N18 46 DQ50
Romford RM3 52 FN51
Petersfield Cres, Couls. CR5 175 DL115
Petersfield Ri, SW15 119 CV88
Petersfield Rd, W3 98 CQ75
Staines TW18 114 BJ92
PETERSHAM, Rich. TW10 118 CL88
Petersham Av, W.Byf.
(Byfleet) KT14 152 BL112
Petersham Cl, Rich. TW10 117 CK89
Sutton SM1 158 DA106
West Byfleet
(Byfleet) KT14 152 BL112
Petersham Dr, Orp. BR5 145 ET96
Petersham Gdns, Orp. BR5 145 ET96
Petersham La, SW7 100 DC76
Petersham Ms, SW7 100 DC76
Petersham Pl, SW7 100 DC76
Petersham Rd, Rich. TW10 118 CL86
Petersham Ter, Croy. CR0
off Richmond Grn 141 DL104
Peters Hill, EC4 197 H10
Peter's La, EC1 196 G6
Peterslea, Kings L. WD4 7 BP29
Petersmead Cl, Tad. KT20 173 CW123
Peters Path, SE26 122 DV91
Peterstone Rd, SE2 106 EV76
Peterstow Cl, SW19 119 CY89
Peter St, W1 195 L10
Gravesend DA12 131 GH87
Peterwood Way, Croy. CR0 141 DM103
Petherton Rd, N5 66 DQ64
Petley Rd, W6 99 CW79
Peto Pl, NW1 195 J4
Peto St N, E16
off Victoria Dock Rd 86 EF73
Petrie Cl, NW2 81 CY65
★ Petrie Mus of
Egyptian Archaeology,
WC1 195 M5
Pett Cl, Horn. RM11 71 FH61
Petten Cl, Orp. BR5 146 EX102
Petten Gro, Orp. BR5 146 EW102
Petters Rd, Ashtd. KT21 172 CM116
★ Petticoat La (Market), E1 197 N7
Petticoat Sq, E1 197 P8
Pettits Boul, Rom. RM1 51 FE53
Pettits Cl, Rom. RM1 51 FE54
Pettits La, Rom. RM1 51 FE54
Pettits La N, Rom. RM1 51 FD53
Pettits Pl, Dag. RM10 70 FA64
Pettits Rd, Dag. RM10 70 FA64
Pettiward Cl, SW15 99 CW84
Pettley Gdns, Rom. RM7 71 FD57
Pettman Cres, SE28 105 ER76
Pettsgrove Av, Wem. HA0 61 CJ64
Petts Hill, Nthlt. UB5 60 CB64
Petts La, Shep. TW17 134 BN98
Pett St, SE18 104 EL77
PETTS WOOD, Orp. BR5 145 ER99
⇌ Petts Wood 145 EQ99
Petts Wd Rd, Orp. BR5 145 EQ99
Petty France, SW1 199 L6
Pettys Cl, Wal.Cr. (Chsht) EN8 15 DX28
Petworth Cl, Couls. CR5 175 DJ119
Northolt UB5 78 BZ66
Petworth Gdns, SW20
off Hidcote Gdns 139 CV97
Uxbridge UB10 77 BQ67
Petworth Rd, N12 44 DE50
Bexleyheath DA6 126 FA85
Petworth St, SW11 100 DE81
Petworth Way, Horn. RM12 71 FF63
Petyt Pl, SW3
off Old Ch St 100 DE79
Petyward, SW3 198 C9
Pevensey Av, N11 45 DK50
Enfield EN1 30 DR40
Pevensey Cl, Islw. TW7 96 CC80
Pevensey Rd, E7 68 EF63
SW17 120 DD91
Feltham TW13 116 BY88
Peverel, E6
off Downings 87 EN72
Peverel Ho, Dag. RM10 70 FA61
Peveret Cl, N11
off Woodland Rd 45 DH50
Peveril Dr, Tedd. TW11 117 CD92
Pewsey Cl, E4 47 EA50
Peyton Pl, SE10 103 EC80
Peyton's Cotts, Red. RH1 185 DM132
Pharaoh Cl, Mitch. CR4 140 DF101
Pharaoh's Island,
Shep. TW17 134 BM103
Pheasant Cl, E16
off Maplin Rd 86 EG72
Purley CR8
off Partridge Knoll 159 DP113
Pheasant Hill, Ch.St.G. HP8 36 AW47
Pheasants Way, Rick. WD3 38 BH45
Pheasant Wk, Ger.Cr.
(Chal.St.P.) SL9 36 AX49
Phelp St, SE17 102 DR79
Phelps Way, Hayes UB3 95 BT77
Phene St, SW3 100 DE79
Philan Way, Rom. RM5 51 FD51
Philbeach Gdns, SW5 100 DA78
Phil Brown Pl, SW8
off Daley Thompson Way 101 DH82
Philchurch Pl, E1
off Ellen St 84 DU72
Philimore Cl, SE18 105 ES78
Philip Av, Rom. RM7 71 FD60
Swanley BR8 147 FD98
Philip Cl, Brwd. CM15 54 FV44
Romford RM7
off Philip Av 71 FD60
Philip Gdns, Croy. CR0 143 DZ103
Philip La, N15 66 DR56
Philipot Path, SE9 125 EM86
Philippa Gdns, SE9 124 EK85
Philippa Way, Grays RM16 111 GH77
Philip Rd, Rain. RM13 89 FE69
Staines TW18 114 BK93
Philips Cl, Cars. SM5 140 DG102
Philip St, E13 86 EG70
Philip Sydney Rd,
Grays RM16 109 FX78
Philip Wk, SE15 102 DU83
Phillida Rd, Rom. RM3 52 FN54
Phillimore Gdns, NW10 81 CW67
W8 100 DA75
Phillimore Gdns Cl, W8
off Phillimore Gdns 100 DA76
Phillimore Pl, W8 100 DA75
Radlett WD7 25 CE36
Phillimore Wk, W8 100 DA76
Phillipers, Wat. WD25 24 BY35
Phillipp St, N1 84 DS67
Phillips Cl, Dart. DA1 127 FH86
Philpot La, EC3 197 M10
Woking (Chobham) GU24 150 AV113
Philpot Path, Ilf. IG1
off Sunnyside Rd 69 EQ62
Philpots Cl, West Dr. UB7 76 BK73
Philpot Sq, SW6
off Peterborough Rd 100 DB83
Philpot St, E1 84 DV72
Phineas Pett Rd, SE9 104 EL83
Tra Phipps Bridge 140 DC97
Phipps Br Rd, SW19 140 DC96
Mitcham CR4 140 DC96
Phipps Hatch La, Enf. EN2 30 DQ38
Phipp's Ms, SW1 199 J7
Phipp St, EC2 197 M4
Phoebeth Rd, SE4 123 EA85
Phoenix Cl, E8
off Stean St 84 DT67
E17 47 DZ54
Epsom KT19 156 CN112
Northwood HA6 39 BT49
West Wickham BR4 144 EE103
Phoenix Dr, Kes. BR2 144 EK104
Phoenix Pk, Brent. TW8 97 CK78
Phoenix Pl, WC1 196 C4
Dartford DA1 128 FK87
Phoenix Rd, NW1 195 M2
SE20 122 DW93
Phoenix St, WC2 195 N9
Phoenix Way, Houns. TW5 96 BW79
Phoenix Wf, SE10 205 K4
Phoenix Wf Rd, SE1 202 A5
Phoenix Yd, WC1 196 C3
★ Photographers' Gall,
WC2 195 N10
Phygtle, The, Ger.Cr.
(Chal.St.P.) SL9 36 AY51
Phyllis Av, N.Mal. KT3 139 CV99
★ Physical Energy Statue,
W2 82 DC74
Physic Pl, SW3
off Royal Hosp Rd 100 DF79
Piazza, The, WC2
off Covent Gdn 83 DL73
Picardy Manorway,
Belv. DA17 107 FB76
Picardy Rd, Belv. DA17 106 FA77
Picardy St, Belv. DA17 106 FA76
Piccadilly, W1 199 J3
Piccadilly Arc, SW1 199 K2
⊖ Piccadilly Circus 199 L1
Piccadilly Circ, W1 199 M1
Piccadilly Pl, W1 199 L1
Pickard St, EC1 196 G2
Pickering Av, E6 87 EN68
Pickering Cl, E9
off Cassland Rd 85 DX66
Pickering Gdns, N11 44 DG51
Croydon CR0 142 DT100
Pickering Ms, W2
off Bishops Br Rd 82 DB72
Pickering Pl, SW1 199 L3
Pickering St, N1
off Essex Rd 83 DP67
Pickets Cl, Bushey
(Bushey Hth) WD23 41 CD46
Pickets St, SW12 121 DH87
Pickett Cft, Stan. HA7 41 CK53
Picketts Lock La, N9 46 DW47
Pickford Cl, Bexh. DA7 106 EY82
Pickford Dr, Slou. SL3 75 AZ74
Pickford Gdn, Slou. SL1
off Stoke Poges La 74 AS74
Pickford La, Bexh. DA7 106 EY82
Pickford Rd, Bexh. DA7 106 EY83
Pickfords Wf, N1 197 H1
Pick Hill, Wal.Abb. EN9 16 EF32
Pickhurst Grn, Brom. BR2 144 EF101
Pickhurst La, Brom. BR2 144 EF102
West Wickham BR4 144 EE100
Pickhurst Mead, Brom. BR2 144 EF101
Pickhurst Pk, Brom. BR2 144 EE99
Pickhurst Ri, W.Wick. BR4 143 EC101
Pickins Piece, Slou.
(Horton) SL3 93 BA82
Pickle Herring St, SE1
off Tooley St 84 DS74
Pickmoss La, Sev.
(Otford) TN14 181 FH116
Pickwick Cl, Houns. TW4
off Dorney Way 116 BY85
Pickwick Ct, SE9
off West Pk 124 EL88
Pickwick Gdns, Grav.
(Nthflt) DA11 130 GD90
Pickwick Ms, N18 46 DS50
Pickwick Pl, Har. HA1 61 CE59
Pickwick Rd, SE21 122 DR87
Pickwick St, SE1 201 H5
Pickwick Ter, Slou. SL2
off Maple Cres 74 AV73
Pickwick Way, Chis. BR7 125 EQ93
Pickworth Cl, SW8
off Kenchester Cl 101 DL80
Picquets Way, Bans. SM7 173 CY116
Picton Pl, W1 194 G9
Surbiton KT6 138 CN102
Picton St, SE5 102 DR80
Piedmont Rd, SE18 105 ER78
Pield Heath Av, Uxb. UB8 76 BN70
Pield Heath Rd, Uxb. UB8 76 BM71
Piercing Hill, Epp.
(They.B.) CM16 33 ER35
Pier Head, E1 202 D3
Piermont Grn, SE22 122 DV85
Piermont Pl, Brom. BR1 144 EL96
Piermont Rd, SE22 122 DV85
Pier Par, E16
off Pier Rd 87 EN74
Pierrepoint Arc, N1
off Islington High St 83 DP68
Pierrepoint Rd, W3 80 CP73
Pierrepoint Row, N1
off Islington High St 83 DP68
Pier Rd, E16 105 EM75
Erith DA8 107 FE79
Feltham TW14 115 BV85
Gravesend (Nthflt) DA11 131 GF86
Greenhithe DA9 109 FV84
Pier St, E14 204 E8
Pier Ter, SW18
off Jew's Row 100 DC84
Pier Wk, Grays RM17 110 GA80
Pier Way, SE28 105 ER76
Pigeonhouse La, Couls. CR5 184 DC125
Pigeon La, Hmptn. TW12 116 CA91
Piggs Cor, Grays RM17 110 GC76
Piggy La, Rick. (Chorl.) WD3 21 BB44
Pigott St, E14 85 EA72
Pike Cl, Brom. BR1 124 EH92
Uxbridge UB10 76 BM67
Pike La, Upmin. RM14 73 FT64
Pike Rd, NW7
off Ellesmere Av 42 CR49
Pikes End, Pnr. HA5 59 BV56
Pikes Hill, Epsom KT17 156 CS113
Pikestone Cl, Hayes UB4
off Berrydale Rd 78 BY70
Pike Way, Epp.
(N.Wld Bas.) CM16 18 FA27
Pilgrimage St, SE1 201 K5
Pilgrim Cl, Mord. SM4 140 DB101
St. Albans (Park St) AL2 8 CC27
Pilgrim Hill, SE27 122 DQ91
Orpington BR5 146 EY96
Pilgrims Cl, N13 45 DM49
Brentwood
(Pilg.Hat.) CM15 54 FT43
Northolt UB5 60 CC64
Watford WD25
off Kytes Dr 8 BX33
Pilgrims Ct, SE3 104 EG81
Dartford DA1 128 FN85
PILGRIM'S HATCH,
Brwd. CM15 54 FU42
Pilgrim's La, NW3 64 DD63
Pilgrims La, Cat. CR3 185 DM125
Grays (N.Stfd) RM16 91 FW74
Oxted (Titsey) RH8 188 EH125
Westerham TN16 178 EL123
Pilgrims Ms, E14
off Blackwall Way 85 EC73
Pilgrims Pl, NW3
off Hampstead High St 64 DD63
Reigate RH2 184 DA132

A B C D E F G H I J K L M N O P Q R S T U V W X Y Z

★ Place of interest ⇌ Railway station ⊖ London Underground station DLR Docklands Light Railway station Tra Tramlink station H Hospital Riv Pedestrian ferry landing stage

Pilgrims Ri, Barn. EN4 . . . . **28** DE43
Pilgrims Rd, Swans. DA10 . . . . **110** FY84
Pilgrim St, EC4 . . . . **196** F9
Pilgrims Vw, Green. DA9 . . . . **129** FW86
Pilgrims Way, E6
off High St N **86** EL67
N19 . . . . **65** DK60
Pilgrims' Way, Bet. RH3 . . . . . . **183** CY131
Caterham CR3 . . . . **185** DN126
Pilgrims Way, Dart. DA1 . . . . . **128** FN88
Pilgrims' Way, Red. RH1 . . . . . **185** DJ127
Pilgrims Way, Reig. RH2 . . . . . **184** DA131
Sevenoaks (Chev.) TN14 . . . **180** EV121
South Croydon CR2 . . . . **160** DT106
Pilgrim's Way, Wem. HA9 . . . . . **62** CP60
Pilgrims Way, West. TN16 . . . . **179** EM123
Pilgrims Way W, Sev.
(Otford) TN14 . . . . **181** FD116
Pilkington Rd, SE15 . . . . **102** DV82
Orpington BR6 . . . . **145** EQ103
Pillions La, Hayes UB4 . . . . **77** BR70
Pilot Cl, SE8 . . . . **103** DZ79
Pilots Pl, Grav. DA12 . . . . **131** GJ86
Pilsdon Cl, SW19
off Inner Pk Rd **119** CX88
Piltdown Rd, Wat. WD19 . . . . . . **40** BX49
Pilton Est, The, Croy. (Pitlake) CR0
off Pitlake **141** DP103
Pilton Pl, SE17 . . . . **201** J10
Pimento Ct, W5
off Olive Rd **97** CK76
PIMLICO, SW1 . . . . **199** K10
⊖ **Pimlico** **199** M10
Pimlico Rd, SW1 . . . . **198** F10
Pimlico Wk, N1 . . . . **197** M2
Pimpernel Way, Rom. RM3 . . . . **52** FK51
Pinchbeck Rd, Orp. BR6 . . . . . . **163** ET107
Pinchfield, Rick.
(Map.Cr.) WD3 . . . . **37** BE50
Pinchin St, E1 . . . . **84** DU73
Pincott Pl, SE4 . . . . **103** DX84
Pincott Rd, SW19 . . . . **120** DC94
Bexleyheath DA6 . . . . **126** FA85
Pindar St, EC2 . . . . **197** M6
PINDEN, Dart. DA2 . . . . **149** FW96
Pindock Ms, W9
off Warwick Av **82** DB70
Pineapple Ct, SW1 . . . . **199** K6
Pineapple Rd, Amer. HP7 . . . . . **20** AT39
Pine Av, E15 . . . . **67** EE64
Gravesend DA12 . . . . **131** GK88
West Wickham BR4 . . . . **143** EB102
Pine Cl, E10
off Walnut Rd **67** EB61
N14 . . . . **45** DJ45
N19 *off Hargrave Pk* **65** DJ61
SE20 . . . . **142** DW95
Addlestone
(New Haw) KT15 . . . . **152** BH111
Kenley CR8 . . . . **176** DR117
Stanmore HA7 . . . . **41** CH49
Swanley BR8 . . . . **147** FF98
Waltham Cross
(Chsht) EN8 . . . . **15** DX28
Woking GU21 . . . . **166** AW117
Pine Coombe, Croy. CR0 . . . . . **161** DX105
Pine Ct, Upmin. RM14 . . . . **72** FN63
Pine Cres, Brwd.
(Hutt.) CM13 . . . . **55** GD43
Carshalton SM5 . . . . **158** DD111
Pinecrest Gdns, Orp. BR6 . . . . **163** EP105
Pinecroft, Brwd.
(Hutt.) CM13 . . . . **55** GB45
Romford (Gidea Pk) RM2 . . . **72** FJ56
Pinecroft Cres, Barn. EN5
off Hillside Gdns **27** CY42
Pinedene, SE15
off Meeting Ho La **102** DV81
Pinefield Cl, E14 . . . . **85** EA73
Pine Gdns, Ruis. HA4 . . . . **59** BV60
Surbiton KT5 . . . . **138** CN100
Pine Glade, Orp. BR6 . . . . **163** EM105
Pine Gro, N4 . . . . **65** DL61
N20 . . . . **43** CZ46
SW19 . . . . **119** CZ92
Bushey WD23 . . . . **24** BZ40
Hatfield (Brook.Pk) AL9 . . . . . **12** DB25
St. Albans (Brick.Wd) AL2 . . . . **8** BZ30
Weybridge KT13 . . . . **153** BP106
Pine Gro Ms, Wey. KT13 . . . . . **153** BQ106
Pine Hill, Epsom KT18 . . . . **172** CR115
Pinehurst, Sev. TN14 . . . . **191** FL121
Pinehurst Cl, Abb.L. WD5 . . . . . . **7** BS32
Tadworth (Kgswd) KT20 . . . **174** DA122
Pinehurst Wk, Orp. BR6 . . . . . . **145** ES102
Pinelands Cl, SE3
off St. John's Pk **104** EF80
Pinel Cl, Vir.W. GU25 . . . . **132** AY98
Pinemartin Cl, NW2 . . . . **63** CW62
Pine Ms, NW10
off Clifford Gdns **81** CX68
Pineneedle La, Sev. TN13 . . . . **191** FH123
Pine Pl, Bans. SM7 . . . . **157** CX114
Hayes UB4 . . . . **77** BT70
Pine Ridge, Cars. SM5 . . . . . . **158** DG109
Pine Rd, N11 . . . . **44** DG47
NW2 . . . . **63** CW63
Woking GU22 . . . . **166** AW120
Pines, The, N14 . . . . **29** DJ43
Borehamwood WD6
off Anthony Rd **26** CM40
Coulsdon CR5 . . . . **175** DH118
Purley CR8 . . . . **159** DP113
Sunbury-on-Thames TW16 . **135** BU97
Woking GU21 . . . . **151** AZ114
Woodford Green IG8 . . . . **48** EG48
Pines Av, Enf. EN1 . . . . **30** DV36
Pines Cl, Nthwd. HA6 . . . . **39** BS51
Pines Rd, Brom. BR1 . . . . **144** EL96
Pine St, EC1 . . . . **196** D4
Pinetree Cl, Ger.Cr.
(Chal.St.P.) SL9 . . . . **36** AW52
Pine Tree Cl, Houns. TW5 . . . . . **95** BV81
Pine Tree Hill, Wok. GU22 . . . . **167** BD116
Pine Trees Dr, Uxb. UB10 . . . . . **58** BL63
Pine Vw Manor, Epp. CM16 . . . **18** EU30
Pine Wk, Bans. SM7 . . . . **174** DF117
Bromley BR1 . . . . **144** EJ95
Carshalton SM5 . . . . **158** DD110
Caterham CR3 . . . . **176** DT122
Cobham KT11 . . . . **154** BX114
Surbiton KT5 . . . . **138** CN100
Pine Way, Egh. (Eng.Grn) TW20
off Ashwood Rd **112** AV93
Pine Wd, Sun. TW16 . . . . **135** BU95
Pinewood Av, Add.
(New Haw) KT15 . . . . **152** BJ109
Pinner HA5 . . . . **40** CB51
Rainham RM13 . . . . **89** FH70
Sevenoaks TN14 . . . . **191** FK121
Sidcup DA15 . . . . **125** ES88
Uxbridge UB8 . . . . **76** BM72
Pinewood Cl, Borwd. WD6 . . . . . **26** CR39
Croydon CR0 . . . . **143** DY104
Gerrards Cross SL9
off Dukes Wd Av **56** AY59
Iver SL0 . . . . **75** BC66
Northwood HA6 . . . . **39** BV50
Orpington BR6 . . . . **145** ER102
Pinner HA5 . . . . **40** CB51
Watford WD17 . . . . **23** BU39
Woking GU21 . . . . **151** BA114
Pinewood Dr, Orp. BR6 . . . . . . **163** ES106
Potters Bar EN6 . . . . **11** CZ31
Staines TW18
off Cotswold Cl **114** BG92
Pinewood Grn, Iver SL0 . . . . **75** BC66
Pinewood Gro, W5 . . . . **79** CJ72
Addlestone
(New Haw) KT15 . . . . **152** BH110
Pinewood Ms, Stai. (Stanw.) TW19
off Oaks Rd **114** BK86
Pinewood Pk, Add.
(New Haw) KT15 . . . . **152** BH111
Pinewood Pl, Dart. DA2
off Old Bexley La **127** FE89
Pinewood Ride, Iver SL0 . . . . . . **75** BA68
Slough SL3 . . . . **75** BA68
Pinewood Rd, SE2 . . . . **106** EX79
Bromley BR2 . . . . **144** EG98
Feltham TW13 . . . . **115** BV90
Iver SL0 . . . . **75** BB67
Romford
(Hav.at.Bow.) RM4 . . . . **51** FC49
Virginia Water GU25 . . . . **132** AU98
Pinewood Way, Brwd.
(Hutt.) CM13 . . . . **55** GD43
Pinfold Rd, SW16 . . . . **121** DL91
Bushey WD23 . . . . **24** BZ40
Pinglestone Cl, West Dr. UB7 . . **94** BL80
Pinkcoat Cl, Felt. TW13
off Tanglewood Way **115** BV90
Pinkerton Pl, SW16
off Riggindale Rd **121** DK91
Pinkham Way, N11 . . . . **44** DG52
Pinks Hill, Swan. BR8 . . . . **147** FE99
Pinkwell Av, Hayes UB3 . . . . **95** BR77
Pinkwell La, Hayes UB3 . . . . **95** BQ77
Pinley Gdns, Dag. RM9
off Stamford Rd **88** EV67
Pinnacle Hill, Bexh. DA7 . . . . . **107** FB84
Pinnacle Hill N, Bexh. DA7 . . . . **107** FB83
Pinnacles, Wal.Abb. EN9 . . . . . . **16** EE34
Pinn Cl, Uxb. UB8
off High Rd **76** BK72
Pinnell Rd, SE9 . . . . **104** EK84
PINNER, ... **60** BY56
⊖ **Pinner** **60** BY56
Pinner Ct, Pnr. HA5 . . . . **60** CA56
PINNER GREEN, Pnr. HA5 . . . . . **40** BW53
Pinner Grn, Pnr. HA5 . . . . **40** BW54
Pinner Gro, Pnr. HA5 . . . . **60** BY56
Pinner Hill, Pnr. HA5 . . . . **40** BW53
Pinner Hill Rd, Pnr. HA5 . . . . . . **40** BW54
Pinner Pk, Pnr. HA5 . . . . **40** CA53
Pinner Pk Av, Har. HA2 . . . . **60** CB55
Pinner Pk Gdns, Har. HA2 . . . . . . **60** CC54
Pinner Rd, Har. HA1, HA2 . . . . . . **60** CB57
Northwood HA6 . . . . **39** BT53
Pinner HA5 . . . . **60** BZ56
Watford WD19 . . . . **24** BX44
Pinner Vw, Har. HA1, HA2 . . . . . **60** CC58
PINNERWOOD PARK, Pnr.
HA5 . . . . **40** BW52
Pinnocks Av, Grav. DA11 . . . . . **131** GH88
Pinn Way, Ruis. HA4 . . . . **59** BS59
Pinstone Way, Ger.Cr. SL9 . . . . **57** BB61
Pintail Cl, E6 *off Swan App* **86** EL71
Pintail Rd, Wdf.Grn. IG8 . . . . . . **48** EH52
Pintail Way, Hayes UB4 . . . . **78** BX71
Pinter Ho, SW9
off Grantham Rd **101** DL82
Pinto Cl, Borwd. WD6
off Percheron Rd **26** CR44
Pinto Way, SE3 . . . . **104** EH84
Pioneer Pl, Croy. CR0 . . . . **161** EA109
Pioneers Ind Pk, Croy. CR0 . . . **141** DL102
Pioneer St, SE15 . . . . **102** DU81
Pioneer Way, W12
off Du Cane Rd **81** CV72
Swanley BR8 . . . . **147** FE97
Watford WD18 . . . . **23** BT44
Piper Cl, N7 . . . . **83** DM65
Piper Rd, Kings.T. KT1 . . . . **138** CN97
Pipers Cl, Cob. KT11 . . . . **170** BX115
Pipers End, Vir.W. GU25 . . . . . **132** AX97
Piper's Gdns, Croy. CR0 . . . . . **143** DY101
Pipers Grn, NW9 . . . . **62** CQ57
Pipers Grn La, Edg. HA8 . . . . . . **42** CL48
Pipewell Rd, Cars. SM5 . . . . . **140** DE100
Pippin Cl, NW2 . . . . **63** CV62
Croydon CR0 . . . . **143** DZ102
Radlett (Shenley) WD7 . . . . **9** CK33
Pippins, The, Slou. SL3
off Pickford Dr **75** AZ74
Watford WD25
off Garston Dr **8** BW34
Pippins Cl, West Dr. UB7 . . . . . . **94** BK76
Pippins Ct, Ashf. TW15 . . . . . . **115** BP93
Piquet Rd, SE20 . . . . **142** DW96
Pirbright Cres, Croy.
(New Adgtn) CR0 . . . . **161** EC107
Pirbright Rd, SW18 . . . . **119** CZ88
Pirie Cl, SE5
off Denmark Hill **102** DR83
Pirie St, E16 . . . . **86** EH74
Pirrip Cl, Grav. DA12 . . . . **131** GM89
Pitcairn Cl, Rom. RM7 . . . . **70** FA56
Pitcairn Rd, Mitch. CR4 . . . . . . **120** DF94
Pitcairn's Path, Har. HA2
off Eastcote Rd **60** CC62
Pitchfont La, Oxt. RH8 . . . . **178** EF124
Pitchford St, E15 . . . . **85** ED66
Pitfield Cres, SE28 . . . . **88** EU74
Pitfield Est, N1 . . . . **197** L2
Pitfield St, N1 . . . . **197** M3
Pitfield Way, NW10 . . . . **80** CQ65
Enfield EN3 . . . . **30** DW39
Pitfold Cl, SE12 . . . . **124** EG86
Pitfold Rd, SE12 . . . . **124** EG86
Pitlake, Croy. CR0 . . . . **141** DP103
Pitman Ho, SE8
off Tanners Hill **103** EA81
Pitman St, SE5 . . . . **102** DQ80
Pitmaston Ho, SE13
off Lewisham Rd **103** EC82
Pitmaston Rd, SE13
off Morden Hill **103** EC82
Pitsea Pl, E1 *off Pitsea St* **85** DX72
Pitsea St, E1 . . . . **85** DX72
Pitshanger La, W5 . . . . **79** CH70
★ **Pitshanger Manor & Gall**,
W5 . . . . **79** CJ74
Pitshanger Pk, W13 . . . . **79** CJ69
Pitson Cl, Add. KT15 . . . . **152** BK105
Pitt Cres, SW19 . . . . **120** DB91
Pittman Cl, Brwd.
(Ingrave) CM13 . . . . **55** GC50
Pittman Gdns, Ilf. IG1 . . . . **69** EQ64
Pitt Pl, Epsom KT17 . . . . **156** CS114
Pitt Rd, Croy. CR0 . . . . **142** DQ99
Epsom KT17 . . . . **156** CS114
Orpington BR6 . . . . **163** EQ105
Thornton Heath CR7 . . . . **142** DQ99
Pitt's Head Ms, W1 . . . . **198** G3
Pittsmead Av, Brom. BR2 . . . . . **144** EG101
Pitt St, W8 . . . . **100** DA75
Pittville Gdns, SE25 . . . . **142** DU97
Pittwood, Brwd.
(Shenf.) CM15 . . . . **55** GA46
Pitwood Grn, Tad. KT20 . . . . . **173** CW120
Pitwood Pk Ind Est, Tad. KT20
off Waterfield **173** CV120
Pixfield Ct, Brom. BR2
off Beckenham La **144** EF96
Pixley St, E14 . . . . **85** DZ72
Pixton Way, Croy. CR0 . . . . **161** DY109
Place Fm Av, Orp. BR6 . . . . **145** ER102
Place Fm Rd, Red.
(Bletch.) RH1 . . . . **186** DR130
Placehouse La, Couls. CR5 . . . **175** DM119
Plain, The, Epp. CM16 . . . . **18** EV29
PLAISTOW, E13 . . . . **86** EF69
PLAISTOW, Brom. BR1 . . . . **124** EF93
⊖ **Plaistow** **86** EF68
Plaistow Gro, E15 . . . . **86** EF67
Bromley BR1 . . . . **124** EH94
H **Plaistow Hosp**, E13 . . . . **86** EJ68
Plaistow La, Brom. BR1 . . . . . . **124** EH94
Plaistow Pk Rd, E13 . . . . **86** EH68
Plaistow Rd, E13 . . . . **86** EF67
E15 . . . . **86** EF67
Plaitford Cl, Rick. WD3 . . . . **38** BL47
Plane Av, Grav. (Nthflt) DA11 . **130** GD87
Planes, The, Cher. KT16 . . . . . . **134** BJ101
Plane St, SE26 . . . . **122** DV90
★ **Planetarium**, NW1 . . . . **194** E5
Plane Tree Cres, Felt. TW13 . . . . **115** BV90
Plane Tree Wk, N2 . . . . **64** DD55
SE19 *off Central Hill* **122** DS93
Plantaganet Pl, Wal.Abb. EN9 . . **15** EB33
Plantagenet Cl, Wor.Pk. KT4 . . **156** CR105
Plantagenet Gdns,
Rom. RM6 . . . . **70** EX59
Plantagenet Pl, Rom. RM6
off Broomfield Rd **70** EX59
Plantagenet Rd, Barn. EN5 . . . . . **28** DC42
Plantain Gdns, E11
off Hollydown Way **67** ED62
Plantain Pl, SE1 . . . . **201** K4
Plantation, The, SE3 . . . . **104** EG82
Plantation Cl, Green. DA9 . . . . . **129** FT86
Plantation Dr, Orp. BR5 . . . . . . **146** EX102
Plantation La, Warl. CR6 . . . . . **177** DY119
Plantation Rd, Amer. HP6 . . . . . . **20** AS37
Erith DA8 . . . . **107** FG81
Swanley BR8 . . . . **127** FG94
Plantation Way, Amer. HP6 . . . . **20** AS37
Plantation Wf, SW11 . . . . **100** DC83
Plasel Ct, E13
off Plashet Rd **86** EG67
Plashet Gdns, Brwd. CM13 . . . . . **55** GA49
Plashet Gro, E6 . . . . **86** EJ67
Plashet Rd, E13 . . . . **86** EG67
Plassy Rd, SE6 . . . . **123** EB87
Platford Grn, Horn. RM11 . . . . . . **72** FL56
Platina St, EC2 . . . . **197** L4
Plato Rd, SW2 . . . . **101** DL84
Platt, The, SW15 . . . . **99** CX83
Platts Av, Wat. WD17 . . . . **23** BV41
Platt's Eyot, Hmptn. TW12 . . . . **136** CA96
Platt's La, NW3 . . . . **64** DA63
Platts Rd, Enf. EN3 . . . . **30** DW39
Platt St, NW1 . . . . **83** DK68
Plawsfield Rd, Beck. BR3 . . . . . **143** DX95
Plaxtol Cl, Brom. BR1 . . . . **144** EJ95
Plaxtol Rd, Erith DA8 . . . . **106** FA80
Plaxton Ct, E11
off Woodhouse Rd **68** EF62
Playfair St, W6
off Winslow Rd **99** CW78
Playfield Av, Rom. RM5 . . . . **51** FC53
Playfield Cres, SE22 . . . . **122** DT85
Playfield Rd, Edg. HA8 . . . . **42** CQ54
Playford Rd, N4 . . . . **65** DM61
Playgreen Way, SE6 . . . . **123** EA91
Playground Cl, Beck. BR3
off Churchfields Rd **143** DX96
Playhouse Ct, SE1
off Southwark Br Rd **102** DQ75
Playhouse Yd, EC4 . . . . **196** F9
Plaza Par, NW6
off Kilburn High Rd **82** DB68
Plaza Shop Cen, The, W1 . . . . . **195** L8
Plaza W, Houns. TW3 . . . . **96** CB81
Pleasance, The, SW15 . . . . **99** CV84
Pleasance Rd, SW15 . . . . **119** CV85
Orpington BR5 . . . . **146** EV96
Pleasant Gro, Croy. CR0 . . . . . **143** DZ104
Pleasant Pl, N1 . . . . **83** DP66
Rickmansworth
(Map.Cr.) WD3 . . . . **37** BE52
Walton-on-Thames KT12 . . **154** BW107
Pleasant Row, NW1 . . . . **83** DH67
Pleasant Vw, Erith DA8 . . . . **107** FE78
Pleasant Vw Pl, Orp. BR6
off High St **163** EP106
Pleasant Way, Wem. HA0 . . . . . . **79** CJ68
Pleasure Pit Rd, Ashtd. KT21 . **172** CP118
Plender St, NW1 . . . . **83** DJ67
Pleshey Rd, N7 . . . . **65** DK63
Plesman Way, Wall. SM6 . . . . . . **159** DL109
Plevna Cres, N15 . . . . **66** DS58
Plevna Rd, N9 . . . . **46** DU48
Hampton TW12 . . . . **136** CB95
Plevna St, E14 . . . . **204** D6
Pleydell Av, SE19 . . . . **122** DT94
W6 . . . . **99** CT77
Pleydell Ct, EC4 . . . . **196** E9
Pleydell Est, EC1
off Radnor St **84** DQ69
Pleydell St, EC4 . . . . **196** E9
Plimsoll Cl, E14
off Grundy St **85** EB72
Plimsoll Rd, N4 . . . . **65** DN62
Plough Ct, EC3 . . . . **197** L10
Plough Fm Cl, Ruis. HA4 . . . . . . **59** BR58
Plough Hill, Pot.B.
(Cuffley) EN6 . . . . **13** DL28
Plough Ind Est, Lthd. KT22 . . **171** CG120
Plough La, SE22 . . . . **122** DT86
SW17 . . . . **120** DB92
SW19 . . . . **120** DB92
Cobham (Down.) KT11 . . . . . **169** BU116
Purley CR8 . . . . **159** DL109
Rickmansworth
(Sarratt) WD3 . . . . **5** BF33
Slough (Stoke P.) SL2 . . . . . . **74** AV67
Teddington TW11 . . . . **117** CG92
Uxbridge (Hare.) UB9 . . . . **38** BJ51
Wallington SM6 . . . . **159** DL105
Plough La Cl, Wall. SM6 . . . . . **159** DL106
Ploughlees La, Slou. SL1 . . . . . . **74** AS73
Ploughmans Cl, NW1
off Crofters Way **83** DK67
Ploughmans End, Islw. TW7 . . **117** CD85
Ploughmans Wk, N2
off Long La **44** DC54
Plough Ms, SW11
off Plough Ter **100** DD84
Plough Pl, EC4 . . . . **196** E8
Plough Ri, Upmin. RM14 . . . . **73** FS59
Plough Rd, SW11 . . . . **100** DD83
Epsom KT19 . . . . **156** CR109
Plough St, E1
off Leman St **84** DT72
Plough Ter, SW11 . . . . **100** DD84
Plough Way, SE16 . . . . **203** J8
Plough Yd, EC2 . . . . **197** N5
Plover Cl, Stai. TW18
off Waters Dr **113** BF90
Plover Gdns, Upmin. RM14 . . . . . **73** FT60
Plover Way, SE16 . . . . **203** K6
Hayes UB4 . . . . **78** BX72
Plowden Bldgs, EC4
off Middle Temple La **83** DN72
Plowman Cl, N18 . . . . **46** DR50
Plowman Way, Dag. RM8 . . . . . . **70** EW60
Plumbers Row, E1 . . . . **84** DU71
Plumbridge St, SE10
off Blackheath Hill **103** EC81
Plum Cl, Felt. TW13
off Highfield Rd **115** BU88
Plum Garth, Brent. TW8 . . . . **97** CK77
Plum La, SE18 . . . . **105** EP80
Plummer La, Mitch. CR4 . . . . . . **140** DF96
Plummer Rd, SW4 . . . . **121** DK87
Plummers Cft, Sev.
(Dunt.Grn) TN13 . . . . **190** FE121
Plumpton Av, Horn. RM12 . . . . . **72** FL63
Plumpton Cl, Nthlt. UB5 . . . . **78** CA65
Plumpton Way, Cars. SM5 . . . . **140** DE104
PLUMSTEAD, SE18 . . . . **105** ES78
⇌ **Plumstead** **105** ER77
Plumstead Common Rd, SE18 **105** EP79
Plumstead High St, SE18 . . . . . **105** ES77
Plumstead Rd, SE18 . . . . **105** EP77
Plumtree Cl, Dag. RM10 . . . . **89** FB65
Wallington SM6 . . . . **159** DK108
Plumtree Ct, EC4 . . . . **196** E8
Plumtree Mead, Loug. IG10 . . . . **33** EN41
Plymouth Dr, Sev. TN13 . . . . . . **191** FJ124
Plymouth Pk, Sev. TN13 . . . . . . **191** FJ124
Plymouth Rd, E16 . . . . **86** EG71
Bromley BR1 . . . . **144** EH95
Grays (Chaff.Hun.) RM16 . . . **109** FW77
Plymouth Wf, E14 . . . . **204** F8
Plympton Av, NW6 . . . . **81** CZ66
Plympton Cl, Belv. DA17
off Halifield Dr **106** EY76
Plympton Pl, NW8 . . . . **194** B5
Plympton Rd, NW6 . . . . **81** CZ66
Plympton St, NW8 . . . . **194** B5
Plymstock Rd, Well. DA16 . . . . **106** EW80
Pocketsdell La, Hem.H.
(Bov.) HP3 . . . . **4** AX28
Pocklington Cl, NW9 . . . . **42** CS54
Pocock Av, West Dr. UB7 . . . . . . **94** BM76
Pococks La, Wind. (Eton) SL4 . . **92** AS78
Pocock St, SE1 . . . . **200** F4
Podmore Rd, SW18 . . . . **100** DC84
Poets Gate, Wal.Cr. EN7 . . . . **14** DS28
Poets Rd, N5 . . . . **66** DR64
Poets Way, Har. HA1
off Blawith Rd **61** CE56
Point, The, Ruis. HA4
off Bedford Rd **59** BU63
Pointalls Cl, N3 . . . . **44** DC54
Point Cl, SE10
off Point Hill **103** EC81
Pointer Cl, SE28 . . . . **88** EX72
Pointers, The, Ashtd. KT21 . . . **172** CL120
Pointers Cl, E14 . . . . **204** B10
Pointers Rd, Cob. KT11 . . . . . . **169** BQ116
Point Hill, SE10 . . . . **103** EC80
Point of Thomas Path, E1 . . . . **202** G1
Point Pl, Wem. HA9 . . . . **80** CP66
Point Pleasant, SW18 . . . . **100** DA84
Point Wf La, Brent. TW8
off High St **98** CL79
Poland Ho, E15 . . . . **85** ED67
Poland St, W1 . . . . **195** L9
Polebrook Rd, SE3 . . . . **104** EJ83
Pole Cat All, Brom. BR2 . . . . . . **144** EF103
Polecroft La, SE6 . . . . **123** DZ89
Polehamptons, The, Hmptn.
TW12 *off High St* **116** CC94
Pole Hill Rd, E4 . . . . **47** EC45
Hayes UB4 . . . . **77** BQ69
Uxbridge UB10 . . . . **77** BQ69
Polesden Gdns, SW20 . . . . **139** CV96
Polesden La, Wok.
(Send M.) GU23 . . . . **167** BF122
Poles Hill, Rick. (Sarratt) WD3 . . . **5** BE33
Polesteeple Hill, West.
(Bigg.H.) TN16 . . . . **178** EK117
Polesworth Ho, W2 . . . . **82** DA71
Polesworth Rd, Dag. RM9 . . . . . . **88** EX66
Polhill, Sev. (Halst.) TN14 . . . . **181** FC115
Police Sta La, Bushey WD23
off Sparrows Herne **40** CB45
Police Sta Rd, Walt. KT12 . . . . **154** BW107
★ **Polish Inst & Sikorski Mus**,
SW7 . . . . **198** A5
Pollard Av, Uxb. (Denh.) UB9 . . **57** BF58
Pollard Cl, E16 . . . . **86** EG73
N7 . . . . **65** DM64
Chigwell IG7 . . . . **50** EU50
Windsor (Old Wind.) SL4 . . **112** AV85
Pollard Rd, N20 . . . . **44** DE47
Morden SM4 . . . . **140** DD99
Woking GU22 . . . . **167** BB116
Pollard Row, E2 . . . . **84** DU69
Pollards, Rick. (Map.Cr.) WD3 . . **37** BD50
Pollards Cl, Loug. IG10 . . . . **32** EJ43
Waltham Cross
(Chsht) EN7 . . . . **14** DQ29
Pollards Cres, SW16 . . . . **141** DL97
Pollards Hill E, SW16 . . . . **141** DM97
Pollards Hill N, SW16 . . . . **141** DL97
Pollards Hill S, SW16 . . . . **141** DL97
Pollards Hill W, SW16 . . . . **141** DL97
Pollards Oak Cres, Oxt. RH8 . . **188** EG132
Pollards Oak Rd, Oxt. RH8 . . . **188** EG132
Pollard St, E2 . . . . **84** DU69
Pollards Wd Hill, Oxt. RH8 . . . **188** EH130
Pollards Wd Rd, SW16 . . . . **141** DL96
Oxted RH8 . . . . **188** EH131
Pollard Wk, Sid. DA14 . . . . **126** EW93
Pollen St, W1 . . . . **195** J9
Pollitt Dr, NW8
off Cunningham Pl **82** DD70
★ **Pollock's Toy Mus**, W1 . . . . . **195** L6
Pollyhaugh, Dart.
(Eyns.) DA4 . . . . **148** FL104
Polperro Cl, Orp. BR6
off Cotswold Ri **145** ET100
Polperro Ms, SE11 . . . . **200** E8
Polsted Rd, SE6 . . . . **123** DZ87
Polsten Ms, Enf. EN3
off Martini Dr **31** EA37
Polthorne Est, SE18 . . . . **105** ER77
Polthorne Gro, SE18 . . . . **105** EQ77
Polworth Rd, SW16 . . . . **121** DL92
Polygon, The, SW4
off Old Town **101** DJ84
Polygon Rd, NW1 . . . . **195** M1
Polytechnic St, SE18 . . . . **105** EN77
Pomell Way, E1
off Commercial St **84** DT72
Pomeroy Cres, Wat. WD24 . . . . . **23** BV36
Pomeroy St, SE14 . . . . **102** DW81
Pomfret Rd, SE5
off Flaxman Rd **101** DP83
Pomoja La, N19 . . . . **65** DK61
Pompadour Cl, Brwd. CM14
off Queen St **54** FW50
Pond Cl, N12
off Summerfields Av **44** DE51
SE3 . . . . **104** EF82
Ashtead KT21 . . . . **172** CL117
Uxbridge (Hare.) UB9 . . . . **38** BJ54
Walton-on-Thames KT12 . . **153** BU107
Pond Cottage La, W.Wick.
BR4 . . . . **143** EA102
Pond Cotts, SE21 . . . . **122** DS88
PONDERS END, Enf. EN3 . . . . . . **30** DW43
⇌ **Ponders End** **31** DX43
Ponders End Ind Est, Enf. EN3 . **31** DZ42
Pond Fm Cl, Tad. KT20 . . . . . . **173** CU124
Pond Fld End, Loug. IG10 . . . . . **48** EJ45
Pondfield La, Brwd. CM13 . . . . . **55** GA49
Pondfield Rd, Brom. BR2 . . . . . **144** EE102
Dagenham RM10 . . . . **71** FB64
Kenley CR8 . . . . **175** DP116
Orpington BR6 . . . . **145** EP104
Pond Grn, Ruis. HA4 . . . . **59** BS61
Pond Hill Gdns, Sutt. SM3 . . . . **157** CY107
Pond La, Ger.Cr.
(Chal.St.P.) SL9 . . . . **36** AV53
Pond Lees Cl, Dag. RM10
off Leys Av **89** FD66
Pond Mead, SE21 . . . . **122** DR86
Pond Path, Chis. BR7
off Heathfield La **125** EP93
Pond Piece, Lthd.
(Oxshott) KT22 . . . . **154** CB114
Pond Pl, SW3 . . . . **198** B9
Pond Rd, E15 . . . . **86** EE68
SE3 . . . . **104** EF82
Egham TW20 . . . . **113** BC93
Hemel Hempstead HP3 . . . . **6** BN25
Woking GU22 . . . . **166** AU120
Ponds, The, Wey. KT13
off Ellesmere Rd **153** BS107
Pondside Cl, Hayes UB3
off Providence La **95** BR80
Pond Sq, N6
off South Gro **64** DG60
Pond St, NW3 . . . . **64** DE64
Pond Wk, Upmin. RM14 . . . . **73** FS61
Pond Way, Tedd. TW11
off Holmesdale Rd **117** CJ93
Pondwood Ri, Orp. BR6 . . . . . . **145** ES101
Ponler St, E1 . . . . **84** DV72

★ Place of interest ⇌ Railway station ⊖ London Underground station DLR Docklands Light Railway station Tra Tramlink station H Hospital Riv Pedestrian ferry landing stage

308

Ponsard Rd, NW10 . . . 81 CV69
Ponsford St, E9 . . . 84 DW65
Ponsonby Pl, SW1 . . . 199 N10
Ponsonby Rd, SW15 . . . 119 CV87
Ponsonby Ter, SW1 . . . 199 N10
Pontefract Rd, Brom. BR1 . . . 124 EF92
Pontoise Cl, Sev. TN13 . . . 190 FF122
Ponton Rd, SW8 . . . 101 DK79
Pont St, SW1 . . . 198 D7
Pont St Ms, SW1 . . . 198 D7
Pontypool Pl, SE1 . . . 200 F4
Pontypool Wk, Rom. RM3
off Saddleworth Rd . . . 52 FJ51
Pony Chase, Cob. KT11 . . . 154 BZ113
Pool Cl, Beck. BR3 . . . 123 EA92
West Molesey KT8 . . . 136 BZ99
Pool Ct, SE6 . . . 123 EA89
Poole Cl, Ruis. HA4
off Chichester Av . . . 59 BS61
Poole Ct Rd, Houns. TW4
off Vicarage Fm Rd . . . 96 BY82
Poole Ho, Grays RM16 . . . 111 GJ75
Pool End Cl, Shep. TW17 . . . 134 BN99
Poole Rd, E9 . . . 85 DX65
Epsom KT19 . . . 156 CR107
Hornchurch RM11 . . . 72 FM59
Woking GU21 . . . 166 AY117
Pooles Bldgs, EC1 . . . 196 D5
Pooles La, SW10
off Lots Rd . . . 100 DC80
Dagenham RM9 . . . 88 EY68
Pooles Pk, N4
off Seven Sisters Rd . . . 65 DN61
Poole St, N1 . . . 84 DR67
Poole Way, Hayes UB4 . . . 77 BR69
Pooley Av, Egh. TW20 . . . 113 BB92
POOLEY GREEN, Egh. TW20 . . . 113 BC92
Pooley Grn Cl, Egh. TW20 . . . 113 BB92
Pooley Grn Rd, Egh. TW20 . . . 113 BB92
Pool Gro, Croy. CR0 . . . 161 DY112
Pool La, Slou. SL1 . . . 74 AS73
Poolmans St, SE16 . . . 203 H4
Pool Rd, Har. HA1 . . . 61 CD59
West Molesey KT8 . . . 136 BZ100
Poolsford Rd, NW9 . . . 62 CS56
Poonah St, E1
off Hardinge St . . . 84 DW72
Pootings Rd, Eden.
(Crock.H.) TN8 . . . 189 ER134
Pope Cl, SW19 . . . 120 DD93
Feltham TW14 . . . 115 BT88
Pope Rd, Brom. BR2 . . . 144 EK99
Popes Av, Twick. TW2 . . . 117 CE89
Popes Cl, Amer. HP6 . . . 20 AT37
Slough (Colnbr.) SL3 . . . 93 BB80
Popes Dr, N3 . . . 44 DA53
Popes Gro, Croy. CR0 . . . 143 DZ104
Twickenham TW1, TW2 . . . 117 CF89
Pope's Head All, EC3
off Cornhill . . . 84 DR72
Popes La, W5 . . . 97 CK76
Oxted RH8 . . . 188 EE134
Watford WD24 . . . 23 BV37
Popes Rd, SW9 . . . 101 DN83
Abbots Langley WD5 . . . 7 BS31
Pope St, SE1 . . . 201 N5
Popham Cl, Felt. TW13 . . . 116 BZ90
Popham Gdns, Rich. TW9
off Lower Richmond Rd . . . 98 CN83
Popham Rd, N1 . . . 84 DQ67
Popham St, N1 . . . 83 DP67
POPLAR, E14 . . . 204 B2
DLR **Poplar** . . . 204 B1
Poplar Av, Amer. HP7 . . . 20 AT39
Gravesend DA12 . . . 131 GJ91
Leatherhead KT22 . . . 171 CH122
Mitcham CR4 . . . 140 DF95
Orpington BR6 . . . 145 EP103
Southall UB2 . . . 96 CB76
West Drayton UB7 . . . 76 BM73
Poplar Bath St, E14
off Lawless St . . . 85 EB73
Poplar Business Pk, E14 . . . 204 D1
Poplar Cl, E9
off Lee Conservancy Rd . . . 67 DZ64
Pinner HA5 . . . 40 BX53
Slough (Colnbr.) SL3 . . . 93 BE81
South Ockendon RM15 . . . 91 FX70
Poplar Ct, SW19 . . . 120 DA92
Poplar Cres, Epsom KT19 . . . 156 CQ107
Poplar Dr, Bans. SM7 . . . 157 CX114
Brentwood (Hutt.) CM13 . . . 55 GC44
Poplar Fm Cl, Epsom KT19 . . . 156 CQ107
Poplar Gdns, N.Mal. KT3 . . . 138 CR96
Poplar Gro, N11 . . . 44 DG51
W6 . . . 99 CW75
New Malden KT3 . . . 138 CR97
Wembley HA9 . . . 62 CQ62
Woking GU22 . . . 166 AY119
Poplar High St, E14 . . . 85 EA73
Poplar Mt, Belv. DA17 . . . 107 FB77
Poplar Pl, SE28 . . . 88 EW73
W2 . . . 82 DB73
Hayes UB3
off Central Av . . . 77 BU73
Poplar Rd, SE24 . . . 102 DQ84
SW19 . . . 140 DA96
Ashford TW15 . . . 115 BQ92
Leatherhead KT22 . . . 171 CH122
Sutton SM3 . . . 139 CZ102
Uxbridge (Denh.) UB9 . . . 58 BJ64
Poplar Rd S, SW19 . . . 140 DA97
Poplar Row, Epp.
(They.B.) CM16 . . . 33 ES37
Poplars, The, N14 . . . 29 DH43
Gravesend DA12 . . . 131 GL87
Romford (Abridge) RM4
off Hoe La . . . 34 EV41
Waltham Cross
(Chsht) EN7 . . . 14 DS26
Poplars Av, NW10 . . . 81 CW65
Poplars Cl, Ruis. HA4 . . . 59 BS60
Watford WD25 . . . 7 BV32
Poplar Shaw, Wal.Abb. EN9 . . . 16 EF33
Poplars Rd, E17 . . . 67 EB58
Poplar St, Rom. RM7 . . . 71 FC56
Poplar Vw, Wem. HA9
off Magnet Rd . . . 61 CK61
Poplar Wk, SE24 . . . 102 DQ84
Caterham CR3 . . . 176 DS123
Poplar Wk, Croydon CR0 . . . 142 DQ103
Poplar Way, Felt. TW13 . . . 115 BU90
Ilford IG6 . . . 69 EQ56
Poppins Ct, EC4 . . . 196 F9
Poppleton Rd, E11 . . . 68 EE58
Poppy Cl, Belv. DA17
off Picardy Manorway . . . 107 FB76
Brentwood
(Pilg.Hat.) CM15 . . . 54 FV43
Northolt UB5
off Abbott Cl . . . 78 BZ65
Wallington SM6 . . . 140 DG102
★ **Poppy Factory Mus, The**,
Rich. TW10 . . . 117 CK86
Poppy La, Croy. CR0 . . . 142 DW101
Poppy Wk, Wal.Cr. EN7 . . . 14 DR28
Porchester Cl, SE5 . . . 102 DQ84
Hornchurch RM11 . . . 72 FL58
Porchester Gdns, W2 . . . 82 DB73
Porchester Gdns Ms, W2
off Porchester Gdns . . . 82 DB72
Porchester Mead, Beck. BR3 . . . 123 EB93
Porchester Ms, W2 . . . 82 DB72
Porchester Pl, W2 . . . 194 C9
Porchester Rd, W2 . . . 82 DB71
Kingston upon Thames KT1 . . . 138 CP96
Porchester Sq, W2 . . . 82 DB72
Porchester Ter, W2 . . . 82 DC73
Porchester Ter N, W2 . . . 82 DB72
Porchfield Cl, Grav. DA12 . . . 131 GJ89
Sutton SM2 . . . 158 DB110
Porch Way, N20 . . . 44 DF48
Porcupine Cl, SE9 . . . 124 EL89
Porden Rd, SW2 . . . 101 DM84
Porlock Av, Har. HA2 . . . 60 CC60
Porlock Rd, W10
off Ladbroke Gro . . . 81 CX70
Enfield EN1 . . . 46 DT45
Porlock St, SE1 . . . 201 K4
Porrington Cl, Chis. BR7 . . . 145 EM95
Portal Cl, SE27 . . . 121 DN90
Ruislip HA4 . . . 59 BU63
Uxbridge UB10 . . . 76 BL66
Port Av, Green. DA9 . . . 129 FV86
Portbury Cl, SE15
off Clayton Rd . . . 102 DU81
Port Cres, E13
off Jenkins Rd . . . 86 EH70
★ **Portcullis Ho**, SW1 . . . 199 P4
Portcullis Lo Rd, Enf. EN2 . . . 30 DR41
Portelet Ct, N1
off De Beauvoir Est . . . 84 DS67
Portelet Rd, E1 . . . 85 DX69
Porten Rd, W14 . . . 99 CY76
Porter Cl, Grays RM20 . . . 109 FW79
Porter Rd, E6 . . . 87 EM72
Porters Av, Dag. RM8, RM9 . . . 88 EV65
Porters Cl, Brwd. CM14 . . . 54 FU46
Portersfield Rd, Enf. EN1 . . . 30 DS42
Porters Pk Dr, Rad.
(Shenley) WD7 . . . 9 CK33
Porter Sq, N19
off Hornsey Rd . . . 65 DL60
Porter St, SE1 . . . 201 J2
W1 . . . 194 E6
Porters Wk, E1 . . . 202 E1
Porters Way, West Dr. UB7 . . . 94 BM76
Porteus Rd, W2 . . . 82 DC71
Portgate Cl, W9 . . . 81 CZ70
Porthallow Cl, Orp. BR6
off Sevenoaks Rd . . . 163 ET105
Porthcawe Rd, SE26 . . . 123 DY91
Port Hill, Orp. BR6 . . . 164 EV112
Porthkerry Av, Well. DA16 . . . 106 EU84
Portia Way, E3 . . . 85 DZ70
Portinscale Rd, SW15 . . . 119 CY85
Portland Av, N16 . . . 66 DT59
Gravesend DA12 . . . 131 GH89
New Malden KT3 . . . 139 CT101
Sidcup DA15 . . . 126 EU86
Portland Cl, Rom. RM6 . . . 70 EY57
Worcester Park KT4 . . . 139 CV101
Portland Cres, SE9 . . . 124 EL89
Feltham TW13 . . . 115 BR91
Greenford UB6 . . . 78 CB70
Stanmore HA7 . . . 41 CK54
Portland Dr, Enf. EN2 . . . 30 DS38
Redhill RH1 . . . 185 DK129
Waltham Cross
(Chsht) EN7 . . . 14 DU31
Portland Gdns, N4 . . . 65 DP58
Romford RM6 . . . 70 EX57
Portland Gro, SW8 . . . 101 DM81
Portland Hts, Nthwd. HA6 . . . 39 BT49
H **Portland Hosp for Women &**
Children, The, W1 . . . 195 J5
Portland Ho, Red. RH1 . . . 185 DK129
Portland Ms, W1 . . . 195 L9
Portland Pk, Ger.Cr. SL9 . . . 56 AX58
Portland Pl, W1 . . . 195 J7
Epsom KT17 . . . 156 CS112
Portland Ri, N4 . . . 65 DP60
Portland Ri Est, N4 . . . 66 DQ60
Portland Rd, N15 . . . 66 DT56
SE9 . . . 124 EL89
SE25 . . . 142 DU98
W11 . . . 81 CY73
Ashford TW15 . . . 114 BL90
Bromley BR1 . . . 124 EJ91
Gravesend DA12 . . . 131 GH88
Hayes UB4 . . . 77 BS69
Kingston upon Thames KT1 . . . 138 CL97
Mitcham CR4 . . . 140 DE96
Southall UB2 . . . 96 BZ76
Portland Sq, E1 . . . 202 D2
Portland St, SE17 . . . 201 K10
Portland Ter, Rich. TW9 . . . 97 CK84
Portland Wk, SE17
off Portland St . . . 102 DR79
Portley La, Cat. CR3 . . . 176 DS121
Portley Wd Rd, Whyt. CR3 . . . 176 DT120
Portman Av, SW14 . . . 98 CR83
Portman Cl, W1 . . . 194 E8
Bexley DA5 . . . 127 FE88
Bexleyheath DA7
off Queen Anne's Gate . . . 106 EX83
Portman Dr, Wdf.Grn. IG8 . . . 48 EK54
Portman Gdns, NW9 . . . 42 CR54
Uxbridge UB10 . . . 76 BN66
Portman Gate, NW1 . . . 194 C5
Portman Hall, Har. HA3 . . . 41 CD49
Portman Ms S, W1 . . . 194 F9
Portman Pl, E2 . . . 84 DW69
Portman Rd, Kings.T. KT1 . . . 138 CM96
Portman Sq, W1 . . . 194 E8
Portman St, W1 . . . 194 F9
Portmeadow Wk, SE2 . . . 106 EX75
Portmeers Cl, E17
off Lennox Rd . . . 67 DZ58
Portmore Gdns, Rom. RM5 . . . 50 FA50
Portmore Pk Rd, Wey. KT13 . . . 152 BN105
Portmore Quays, Wey. KT13
off Weybridge Rd . . . 152 BM105
Portmore Way, Wey. KT13 . . . 134 BN104
Portnall Dr, Vir.W. GU25 . . . 132 AT99
Portnall Ri, Vir.W. GU25 . . . 132 AT99
Portnall Rd, W9 . . . 81 CZ68
Virginia Water GU25 . . . 132 AT99
Portnalls Cl, Couls. CR5 . . . 175 DH116
Portnalls Ri, Couls. CR5 . . . 175 DH116
Portnalls Rd, Couls. CR5 . . . 175 DH118
Portnoi Cl, Rom. RM1 . . . 51 FD54
Portobello Ct, W11
off Westbourne Gro . . . 81 CZ73
Portobello Ms, W11
off Portobello Rd . . . 82 DA73
Portobello Rd, W10 . . . 81 CZ72
W11 . . . 81 CZ72
Porton Ct, Surb. KT6 . . . 137 CJ100
Portpool La, EC1 . . . 196 D6
Portree Cl, N22
off Nightingale Rd . . . 45 DM52
Portree St, E14 . . . 85 ED72
Portsdown, Edg. HA8
off Rectory La . . . 42 CN50
Portsdown Av, NW11 . . . 63 CZ58
Portsdown Ms, NW11 . . . 63 CZ58
Portsea Ms, W2 . . . 194 C9
Portsea Pl, W2 . . . 194 C9
Portsea Rd, Til. RM18 . . . 111 GJ81
Portslade Rd, SW8 . . . 101 DJ82
Portsmouth Av, T.Ditt. KT7 . . . 137 CG101
Portsmouth Ct, Slou. SL1 . . . 74 AS73
Portsmouth Ms, E16
off Wesley Av . . . 86 EH74
Portsmouth Rd, SW15 . . . 119 CV87
Cobham KT11 . . . 153 BU114
Esher KT10 . . . 154 CC105
Kingston upon Thames KT1 . . . 137 CJ99
Surbiton KT6 . . . 137 CJ99
Thames Ditton KT7 . . . 137 CE103
Woking (Ripley) GU23 . . . 168 BM119
Portsmouth St, WC2 . . . 196 B9
Portsoken St, E1 . . . 197 P10
Portugal Gdns, Twick. TW2
off Fulwell Pk Av . . . 116 CC89
Portugal Rd, Wok. GU21 . . . 167 BA116
Portugal St, WC2 . . . 196 B9
Portway, E15 . . . 86 EF67
Epsom KT17 . . . 157 CU110
Rainham RM13
off Avelon Rd . . . 89 FG67
Portway Cres, Epsom KT17 . . . 157 CU109
Portway Gdns, SE18
off Shooter's Hill Rd . . . 104 EK80
Postern Grn, Enf. EN2 . . . 29 DN40
Post La, Twick. TW2 . . . 117 CD88
Post Meadow, Iver SL0 . . . 75 BD69
Postmill Cl, Croy. CR0 . . . 143 DX104
Post Office App, E7 . . . 68 EH64
Post Office Ct, EC3 . . . 197 L9
Post Office La, Slou.
(Geo.Grn) SL3 . . . 74 AX72
Post Office Row, Oxt. RH8 . . . 188 EL131
Post Office Way, SW8 . . . 101 DK80
Post Rd, Sthl. UB2 . . . 96 CB76
Postway Ms, Ilf. IG1
off Clements Rd . . . 69 EP62
Potier St, SE1 . . . 201 L7
Potter Cl, Mitch. CR4 . . . 141 DH96
Potterells, Hat.
(N.Mymms) AL9 . . . 11 CX25
Potteries, The, Cher. KT16 . . . 151 BE107
Potterne Cl, SW19 . . . 119 CX87
POTTERS BAR . . . 12 DA32
⇌ **Potters Bar** . . . 12 DA32
H **Potters Bar Comm Hosp**,
Pot.B. EN6 . . . 12 DC34
★ **Potters Bar Mus,**
The Wyllyotts Cen,
Pot.B. EN6 . . . 11 CZ32
Potters Cl, Croy. CR0 . . . 143 DY102
Loughton IG10 . . . 32 EL40
Potters Ct, Pot.B. EN6 . . . 12 DA32
Potters Cross, Iver SL0 . . . 75 BE69
POTTERS CROUCH,
St.Alb. AL2 . . . 8 BX25
Potters Flds, SE1 . . . 201 N3
Potters Gro, N.Mal. KT3 . . . 138 CQ98
Potters Hts Cl, Pnr. HA5 . . . 39 BV52
Potters La, SW16 . . . 121 DK93
Barnet EN5 . . . 28 DA42
Borehamwood WD6 . . . 26 CQ39
Woking (Send) GU23 . . . 167 BB123
Potters Ms, Borwd. (Elstree) WD6
off Elstree Hill N . . . 25 CK44
Potters Rd, SW6 . . . 100 DC82
Barnet EN5 . . . 28 DB42
Potter St, Nthwd. HA6 . . . 39 BU53
Pinner HA5 . . . 39 BV53
Potter St Hill, Pnr. HA5 . . . 39 BV51
Pottery La, W11
off Portland Rd . . . 81 CY73
Pottery Rd, Bex. DA5 . . . 127 FC89
Brentford TW8 . . . 98 CL79
Pottery St, SE16 . . . 202 D5
Pottipher Pl, Brwd. CM14
off Warley Hill . . . 54 FV49
Pott St, E2 . . . 84 DV69
Poulcott, Stai. (Wrays.) TW19 . . . 112 AY86
Poulett Gdns, Twick. TW1 . . . 117 CG88
Poulett Rd, E6 . . . 87 EM68
Poulner Way, SE15
off Daniel Gdns . . . 102 DT80
Poulters Wd, Kes. BR2 . . . 162 EK106
Poultney Cl, Rad.
(Shenley) WD7 . . . 10 CM32
Poulton Av, Sutt. SM1 . . . 140 DD104
Poulton Cl, E8
off Spurstowe Ter . . . 66 DV64
Poultry, EC2 . . . 197 K9
Pound Cl, Orp. BR6 . . . 145 ER103
Surbiton KT6 . . . 137 CJ102
Pound Ct, Ashtd. KT21 . . . 172 CM118
Pound Ct Dr, Orp. BR6 . . . 145 ER103
Pound Cres, Lthd.
(Fetch.) KT22 . . . 171 CD121
Pound Fm Cl, Esher KT10
off Ember La . . . 137 CD102
Poundfield, Wat. WD25
off Ashfields . . . 23 BT35
Poundfield Ct, Wok. GU22
off High St . . . 167 BC121
Poundfield Gdns, Wok. GU22 . . . 167 BC120
Poundfield Rd, Loug. IG10 . . . 33 EN43
Pound La, NW10 . . . 81 CU65
Epsom KT19 . . . 156 CR112
Radlett (Shenley) WD7 . . . 10 CM33
Sevenoaks TN13 . . . 180 EX115
Sevenoaks (Knock.P.) TN14 . . . 191 FH124
Pound Pk Rd, SE7 . . . 104 EK77
Pound Pl, SE9 . . . 125 EN86
Pound Rd, Bans. SM7 . . . 173 CZ117
Chertsey KT16 . . . 134 BH101
Pound St, Cars. SM5 . . . 158 DF106
Pound Way, Chis. BR7
off Royal Par . . . 125 EQ94
Pounsley Rd, Sev.
(Dunt.Grn) TN13 . . . 190 FE121
Pountney Rd, SW11 . . . 100 DG83
POVEREST, Orp. BR5 . . . 145 ET99
Poverest Rd, Orp. BR5 . . . 145 ET99
Powder Mill La, Dart. DA1 . . . 128 FL89
Twickenham TW2 . . . 116 BZ88
Powdermill La, Wal.Abb. EN9 . . . 15 EB33
Powdermill Ms, Wal.Abb. EN9
off Powdermill La . . . 15 EB33
Powdermill Way, Wal.Abb.
EN9 . . . 15 EB32
Powell Cl, Chess. KT9
off Coppard Gdns . . . 155 CK106
Dartford DA2 . . . 129 FS89
Edgware HA8 . . . 42 CM51
Wallington SM6 . . . 159 DK108
Powell Gdns, Dag. RM10 . . . 70 FA63
Powell Rd, E5 . . . 66 DV62
Buckhurst Hill IG9 . . . 48 EJ45
Powell's Wk, W4 . . . 98 CS79
Power Dr, Enf. EN3 . . . 31 DZ36
Powergate Business Pk,
NW10 . . . 80 CR69
Power Ind Est, Erith DA8 . . . 107 FG81
Power Rd, W4 . . . 98 CN77
Powers Ct, Twick. TW1 . . . 117 CK87
Powerscroft Rd, E5 . . . 66 DW63
Sidcup DA14 . . . 126 EW93
Powis Ct, Pot.B. EN6 . . . 12 DC34
Powis Gdns, NW11 . . . 63 CZ59
W11 . . . 81 CZ72
Powis Ms, W11
off Westbourne Pk Rd . . . 81 CZ72
Powis Pl, WC1 . . . 196 A5
Powis Rd, E3 . . . 85 EB69
Powis Sq, W11 . . . 81 CZ72
Powis St, SE18 . . . 105 EN76
Powis Ter, W11 . . . 81 CZ72
Powle Ter, Ilf. IG1
off Oaktree Gro . . . 69 EQ64
Powlett Pl, NW1
off Harmood St . . . 83 DH65
Pownall Gdns, Houns. TW3 . . . 96 CB84
Pownall Rd, E8 . . . 84 DT67
Hounslow TW3 . . . 96 CB84
Pownsett Ter, Ilf. IG1
off Buttsbury Rd . . . 69 EQ64
Powster Rd, Brom. BR1 . . . 124 EH92
Powys Cl, Bexh. DA7 . . . 106 EX79
Powys Ct, Borwd. WD6
off Kensington Way . . . 26 CR41
Powys La, N13 . . . 45 DL50
N14 . . . 45 DL49
POYLE, Slou. SL3 . . . 93 BE81
Poyle Pk, Slou. (Colnbr.) SL3 . . . 93 BE83
Poyle Rd, Slou. (Colnbr.) SL3 . . . 93 BE83
Poyle Tech Cen, Slou. SL3 . . . 93 BE82
Poynder Rd, Til. RM18 . . . 111 GH81
Poynders Ct, SW4
off Poynders Rd . . . 121 DJ86
Poynders Gdns, SW4 . . . 121 DJ87
Poynders Rd, SW4 . . . 121 DJ86
Poynings, The, Iver SL0 . . . 93 BF77
Poynings Cl, Orp. BR6 . . . 146 EW103
Poynings Rd, N19 . . . 65 DJ62
Poynings Way, N12 . . . 44 DA50
Romford RM3
off Arlington Gdns . . . 52 FL53
Poyntell Cres, Chis. BR7 . . . 145 ER95
Poynter Ho, W11 . . . 81 CX74
Poynter Rd, Enf. EN1 . . . 30 DU43
Poynton Rd, N17 . . . 46 DU54
Poyntz Rd, SW11 . . . 100 DF82
Poyser St, E2 . . . 84 DV68
Prae, The, Wok. GU22 . . . 167 BF118
Praed Ms, W2 . . . 194 A8
Praed St, W2 . . . 194 B7
Pragel St, E13 . . . 86 EH68
Pragnell Rd, SE12 . . . 124 EH89
Prague Pl, SW2 . . . 121 DL85
Prah Rd, N4 . . . 65 DN61
Prairie Cl, Add. KT15 . . . 134 BH104
Prairie Rd, Add. KT15 . . . 134 BH104
Prairie St, SW8 . . . 100 DG82
Pratt Ms, NW1
off Pratt St . . . 83 DJ67
PRATT'S BOTTOM, Orp. BR6 . . . 164 EV110
Pratts La, Walt. KT12
off Molesey Rd . . . 154 BX105
Pratts Pas, Kings.T. KT1
off Eden St . . . 138 CL96
Pratt St, NW1 . . . 83 DJ67
Pratt Wk, SE11 . . . 200 C8
Prayle Gro, NW2 . . . 63 CX60
Prebend Gdns, W4 . . . 99 CT76
W6 . . . 99 CT76
Prebend St, N1 . . . 84 DQ67
Precinct, The, Egh. TW20
off High St . . . 113 BA92
West Molesey KT8
off Victoria Av . . . 136 CB97
Precinct Rd, Hayes UB3 . . . 77 BU73
Precincts, The, Mord. SM4
off Green La . . . 140 DA100
Premier Av, Grays RM16 . . . 110 GC75
Premier Cor, W9
off Kilburn La . . . 81 CZ68
Premiere Pl, E14 . . . 203 P1
Premier Pk, NW10 . . . 80 CP67
Premier Pk Rd, NW10 . . . 80 CP68
Premier Pl, SW15
off Putney High St . . . 99 CY84
Prendergast Rd, SE3 . . . 104 EE83
Prentis Rd, SW16 . . . 121 DK91
Prentiss Ct, SE7 . . . 104 EK77
Presburg Rd, N.Mal. KT3 . . . 138 CS99
Presburg St, E5
off Glyn Rd . . . 67 DX62
Prescelly Pl, Edg. HA8 . . . 42 CM53
Prescot St, E1 . . . 84 DT73
Prescott Av, Orp. BR5 . . . 145 EP100
Prescott Cl, SW16 . . . 121 DL94
Hornchurch RM11 . . . 71 FH60
Prescott Grn, Loug. IG10 . . . 33 EQ41
Prescott Ho, SE17
off Hillingdon St . . . 101 DP79
Prescott Pl, SW4 . . . 101 DK83
Prescott Rd, Slou.
(Colnbr.) SL3 . . . 93 BE82
Waltham Cross
(Chsht) EN8 . . . 15 DY27
Presentation Ms, SW2
off Palace Rd . . . 121 DM88
President Dr, E1 . . . 202 D2
President St, EC1 . . . 197 H2
Prespa Cl, N9
off Hudson Way . . . 46 DW47
Press Rd, NW10 . . . 62 CR62
Uxbridge UB8 . . . 76 BK65
Prestage Way, E14 . . . 85 EC73
Prestbury Ct, Wok. GU21
off Muirfield Rd . . . 166 AU118
Prestbury Cres, Bans. SM7 . . . 174 DF116
Prestbury Rd, E7 . . . 86 EJ66
Prestbury Sq, SE9 . . . 125 EM91
Prested Rd, SW11
off St. John's Hill . . . 100 DE84
Prestige Way, NW4
off Heriot Rd . . . 63 CW57
PRESTON, Wem. HA9 . . . 61 CK59
Preston Av, E4 . . . 47 ED51
Preston Cl, SE1 . . . 201 M8
Twickenham TW2 . . . 117 CE90
Preston Ct, Walt. KT12
off St. Johns Dr . . . 136 BW102
Preston Dr, E11 . . . 68 EJ57
Bexleyheath DA7 . . . 106 EX81
Epsom KT19 . . . 156 CS107
Preston Gdns, NW10
off Church Rd . . . 80 CS65
Enfield EN3 . . . 31 DY37
Ilford IG1 . . . 68 EL58
Preston Gro, Ashtd. KT21 . . . 171 CJ117
Preston Hill, Har. HA3 . . . 62 CM58
Preston La, Tad. KT20 . . . 173 CV121
Preston Pl, NW2 . . . 81 CU65
Richmond TW10 . . . 118 CL85
⊖ **Preston Road** . . . 62 CL60
Preston Rd, E11 . . . 68 EE58
SE19 . . . 121 DP93
SW20 . . . 119 CT94
Gravesend (Nthflt) DA11 . . . 130 GE88
Harrow HA3 . . . 62 CL59
Romford RM3 . . . 52 FK49
Shepperton TW17 . . . 134 BN99
Slough SL2 . . . 74 AW73
Wembley HA9 . . . 62 CL61
Prestons Rd, E14 . . . 204 E4
Bromley BR2 . . . 144 EG104
Preston Waye, Har. HA3 . . . 62 CL60
Prestwick Cl, Sthl. UB2
off Ringway . . . 96 BY78
Prestwick Rd, Wat. WD19 . . . 40 BX50
Prestwood, Slou. SL2 . . . 74 AV72
Prestwood Av, Har. HA3 . . . 61 CH56
Prestwood Cl, SE18 . . . 106 EU80
Harrow HA3 . . . 61 CJ56
Prestwood Dr, Rom. RM5 . . . 51 FC50
Prestwood Gdns, Croy. CR0 . . . 142 DQ101
Prestwood St, N1 . . . 197 J1
Pretoria Av, E17 . . . 67 DY56
Pretoria Cl, N17
off Pretoria Rd . . . 46 DT52
Pretoria Cres, E4 . . . 47 EC46
Pretoria Ho, Erith DA8
off Waterhead Cl . . . 107 FE80
Pretoria Rd, E4 . . . 47 EC46
E11 . . . 67 ED60
E16 . . . 86 EF69
N17 . . . 46 DT52
SW16 . . . 121 DH93
Chertsey KT16 . . . 133 BF102
Ilford IG1 . . . 69 EP64
Romford RM7 . . . 71 FC56
Watford WD18 . . . 23 BU42
Pretoria Rd N, N18 . . . 46 DT51
Pretty La, Couls. CR5 . . . 175 DJ121
Prevost Rd, N11 . . . 44 DG47
Prey Heath, Wok. GU22 . . . 166 AV123
Prey Heath Cl, Wok. GU22 . . . 166 AW124
Prey Heath Rd, Wok. GU22 . . . 166 AV124
Price Cl, NW7 . . . 43 CY51
SW17 . . . 120 DF90
Price Rd, Croy. CR0 . . . 159 DP106
Price's Ct, SW11 . . . 100 DD83
Price's St, SE1 . . . 200 G3
Price's Yd, N1 . . . 83 DM67
Price Way, Hmptn. TW12
off Victors Dr . . . 116 BY93
Pricklers Hill, Barn. EN5 . . . 28 DB44
Prickley Wd, Brom. BR2 . . . 144 EF102
Priddy's Yd, Croy. CR0
off Church St . . . 142 DQ103
Prideaux Pl, W3
off Friars Pl La . . . 80 CR73
WC1 . . . 196 C2
Prideaux Rd, SW9 . . . 101 DL83

★ Place of interest ⇌ Railway station ⊖ London Underground station DLR Docklands Light Railway station Tra Tramlink station H Hospital Riv Pedestrian ferry landing stage

Pridham Rd, Th.Hth. CR7 142 DR98
Priest Ct, EC2 197 H8
Priestfield Rd, SE23 123 DY90
Priest Hill, Egh. TW20 112 AW90
Windsor (Old Wind.) SL4 112 AW90
Priestlands Pk Rd, Sid. DA15 125 ET90
Priestley Cl, N16
off Ravensdale Rd 66 DT59
Priestley Gdns, Rom. RM6 70 EV58
Priestley Rd, Mitch. CR4 140 DG96
Priestley Way, E17 67 DX55
NW2 63 CU60
Priestly Gdns, Wok. GU22 167 BA120
Priestman Pt, E3
off Rainhill Way 85 EB69
Priest Pk Av, Har. HA2 60 CA61
Priests Av, Rom. RM1 51 FD54
Priests Br, SW14 98 CS84
SW15 98 CS84
Priests Fld, Brwd.
(Ingrave) CM13 55 GC50
Priests La, Brwd. CM15 54 FY47
Prima Rd, SW9 101 DN80
Primrose Av, Enf. EN2 30 DR39
Romford RM6 70 EV59
Primrose Cl, SE6 123 EC92
Harrow HA2 60 BZ63
Wallington SM6 141 DH102
Primrose Dr, West Dr. UB7 94 BK77
Primrose Gdns, NW3 82 DE65
Bushey WD23 40 CB45
Ruislip HA4 60 BW64
Primrose Glen, Horn. RM11 72 FL56
PRIMROSE HILL, NW8 82 DF67
Primrose Hill, EC4 196 E9
Brentwood CM14 54 FW48
Kings Langley WD4 7 BP28
Primrose Hill Ct, NW3 82 DF66
Primrose Hill Rd, NW3 82 DE66
Primrose Hill Studios, NW1
off Fitzroy Rd 82 DG67
Primrose La, Croy. CR0 143 DX102
Primrose Ms, NW1
off Sharpleshall St 82 DF66
SE3 104 EH80
W5 off St. Mary's Rd 97 CK75
Primrose Path, Wal.Cr.
(Chsht) EN7 14 DU31
Primrose Rd, E10 67 EB60
E18 48 EH54
Walton-on-Thames KT12 154 BW106
Primrose Sq, E9 84 DW66
Primrose St, EC2 197 M6
Primrose Wk, SE14
off Alexandra St 103 DY80
Epsom KT17 157 CT108
Primrose Way, Wem. HA0 79 CK68
Primula St, W12 81 CU72
Prince Albert Rd, NW1 194 C1
NW8 194 C1
Prince Alberts Wk, Wind. SL4 92 AU81
Prince Arthur Ms, NW3
off Perrins La 64 DC63
Prince Arthur Rd, NW3 64 DC64
Prince Charles Av, Dart.
(S.Darenth) DA4 149 FR96
Prince Charles Dr, NW4 63 CW59
Prince Charles Rd, SE3 104 EF81
Prince Charles Way, Wall. SM6 141 DH104
Prince Consort Dr, Chis. BR7 145 ER95
Prince Consort Rd, SW7 100 DC76
Princedale Rd, W11 81 CY74
Prince Edwards Rd, E9 85 DZ65
Prince George Av, N14 29 DJ42
Prince George Duke of Kent Ct,
Chis. BR7
off Holbrook La 125 ER94
Prince George Rd, N16 66 DS63
Prince George's Av, SW20 139 CW96
Prince George's Rd, SW19 140 DD95
Prince Henry Rd, SE7 104 EK80
★ Prince Henry's Room,
EC4 196 D9
Prince Imperial Rd, SE18 105 EM81
Chislehurst BR7 125 EP94
Prince John Rd, SE9 124 EL85
Princelet St, E1 84 DT71
Prince of Orange La, SE10
off Greenwich High Rd 103 EC80
Prince of Wales Cl, NW4
off Church Ter 63 CV56
Prince of Wales Dr, SW8 101 DH80
SW11 100 DF81
Prince of Wales Footpath, Enf.
EN3 31 DY38
Prince of Wales Gate, SW7 198 B4
Prince of Wales Pas, NW1 195 K3
Prince of Wales Rd, NW5 82 DG65
SE3 104 EF81
Sutton SM1 140 DD103
Prince of Wales Ter, W4 98 CS78
W8 off Kensington Rd 100 DB75
DLR Prince Regent 86 EJ73
Prince Regent La, E13 86 EH69
E16 86 EJ71
Prince Regent Ms, NW1 195 K3
Prince Regent Rd, Houns.
TW3 96 CC83
Prince Rd, SE25 142 DS99
Prince Rupert Rd, SE9 105 EM84
Prince's Arc, SW1 199 L2
Princes Av, N3 44 DA53
N10 64 DG55
N13 45 DN50
N22 45 DK53
NW9 62 CP56
W3 98 CN76
Carshalton SM5 158 DF108
Dartford DA2 128 FP88
Enfield EN3 31 DY36
Greenford UB6 78 CB72
Orpington BR5 145 ES99
South Croydon CR2 176 DV115
Surbiton KT6 138 CN102
Watford WD18 23 BT43
Princes Av,
Woodford Green IG8 48 EH49
Princes Cl, N4 65 DP60
NW9 62 CN56
SW4 off Old Town 101 DJ83
Edgware HA8 42 CN50
Epping (N.Wld Bas.) CM16 19 FC25
Sidcup DA14 126 EX90
South Croydon CR2 176 DV115
Teddington TW11 117 CD91
Princes Ct, E1 202 E1
SE16 203 M7
Wembley HA9 62 CL64
Princes Dr, Har. HA1 61 CE55
Prince's Dr, Lthd.
(Oxshott) KT22 155 CE112
Princesfield Rd, Wal.Abb.
EN9 16 EH33
Princes Gdns, SW7 198 A6
W3 80 CN71
W5 79 CJ70
Princes Gate, SW7 198 B5
Princes Gate Ct, SW7 198 A5
Princes Gate Ms, SW7 198 A6
Princes La, N10 65 DH55
Princes Ms, W2
off Hereford Rd 82 DA73
Princes Par, Pot.B. EN6
off High St 12 DC32
Princes Pk, Rain. RM13 89 FG66
Princes Pk Av, NW11 63 CY58
Hayes UB3 77 BR73
Princes Pk Circle, Hayes UB3 77 BR73
Princes Pk Cl, Hayes UB3 77 BR73
Princes Pk La, Hayes UB3 77 BR73
Princes Pk Par, Hayes UB3 77 BR73
Princes Pl, SW1 199 L2
W11 81 CY74
Princes Plain, Brom. BR2 144 EL101
Princes Ri, SE13 103 EC82
Princes Riverside Rd, SE16 203 H2
Princes Rd, N18 46 DW49
SE20 123 DX93
SW14 98 CR83
SW19 120 DA93
W13
off Broomfield Rd 79 CH74
Ashford TW15 114 BM92
Buckhurst Hill IG9 48 EJ47
Dartford DA1, DA2 127 FG86
Egham TW20 113 AZ93
Feltham TW13 115 BT89
Gravesend DA12 131 GJ90
Ilford IG6 69 ER56
Kingston upon Thames KT2 118 CN94
Richmond TW10 118 CM85
Richmond (Kew) TW9 98 CM80
Romford RM1 71 FG57
Swanley BR8 127 FG93
Teddington TW11 117 CD91
Weybridge KT13 153 BP106
Princess Alice Way, SE28 105 ER75
Princess Av, Wem. HA9 62 CL61
Princess Cl, SE28
off Redbourne Dr 88 EX72
Princess Cres, N4 65 DP61
Princesses Wk, Rich. TW9
off Kew Rd 98 CL80
Princess Gdns, Wok. GU22 167 BB116
H Princess Grace Hosp, The,
W1 194 F5
Princess La, Ruis. HA4 59 BS60
Princess Louise Cl, W2 194 A6
H Princess Louise Hosp,
W10 81 CX71
Princess Mary's Rd, Add.
KT15 152 BJ105
Princess May Rd, N16 66 DS63
Princess Ms, NW3
off Belsize Cres 82 DD65
Kingston upon Thames KT1 138 CM97
Princess Par, Orp. BR6
off Crofton Rd 145 EN104
Princess Pk Manor, N11 44 DG50
Princes Sq, W2 82 DB73
Princess Rd, NW1 82 DG67
NW6 82 DA68
Croydon CR0 142 DQ100
Woking GU22 167 BB116
H Princess Royal Uni Hosp, The,
Orp. BR6 145 EN104
Princess St, SE1 200 G7
Princes St, EC2 197 K8
N17 off Queen St 46 DS51
W1 195 J9
Bexleyheath DA7 106 EZ84
Gravesend DA11 131 GH86
Richmond TW9
off Sheen Rd 118 CL85
Slough SL1 92 AV75
Sutton SM1 158 DD105
Princess Way, Red. RH1 184 DG133
Princes Ter, E13 86 EH67
Prince St, SE8 103 DZ79
Watford WD17 24 BW41
Princes Vw, Dart. DA1 128 FN88
Princes Way, SW19 119 CX87
Brentwood (Hutt.) CM13 55 GA46
Buckhurst Hill IG9 48 EJ47
Croydon CR0 159 DM106
Ruislip HA4 60 BY63
West Wickham BR4 162 EF105
Princes Yd, W11
off Princedale Rd 81 CY74
Princethorpe Ho, W2 82 DB71
Princethorpe Rd, SE26 123 DX91
Princeton Ct, SW15
off Felsham Rd 99 CX83
Princeton St, WC1 196 B6
Principal Sq, E9
off Chelmer Rd 67 DX64
Pringle Gdns, SW16 121 DJ91
Purley CR8 159 DM110
Printers Inn Ct, EC4 196 D8
Printers Ms, E3 85 DY67
Printer St, EC4 196 E8
Printing Ho La, Hayes UB3 95 BS75
Printing Ho Yd, E2 197 N2
Print Village, SE15
off Chadwick Rd 102 DT82
Priolo Rd, SE7 104 EJ78
Prior Av, Sutt. SM2 158 DE108
Prior Bolton St, N1 83 DP65
Prior Chase, Grays
(Bad.Dene) RM17 110 FZ77
Prioress Cres, Green. DA9
off London Rd 129 FW85
Prioress Rd, SE27 121 DP90
Prioress St, SE1 201 L7
Prior Rd, Ilf. IG1 69 EN62
Priors, The, Ashtd. KT21 171 CK119
Priors Cl, Slou. SL1 92 AU76
Priors Ct, Wok. GU21 166 AU118
Priors Cft, E17 47 DY54
Woking GU22 167 BA120
Priors Fm La, Nthlt. UB5
off Abbott Cl 78 BZ65
Priors Fld, Nthlt. UB5
off Arnold Rd 78 BY65
Priorsford Av, Orp. BR5 146 EU98
Priors Gdns, Ruis. HA4 60 BW64
Priors Mead, Enf. EN1 30 DS39
Priors Pk, Horn. RM12 72 FJ62
Priors Shop Cen, The, N12
off High Rd 44 DC50
Prior St, SE10 103 EC80
Priory, The, SE3 104 EF84
Godstone RH9 186 DV131
Priory Av, E4 47 DZ48
E17 67 EA57
N8 65 DK56
W4 98 CS77
Orpington BR5 145 ER100
Sutton SM3 157 CX105
Uxbridge
(Hare.) UB9 58 BJ56
Wembley HA0 61 CF63
Priory Cl, E4 47 DZ48
E18 48 EG53
N3 off Church Cres 43 CZ53
N14 29 DH43
N20 43 CZ45
SW19 off High Path 140 DB95
Beckenham BR3 143 DY97
Brentwood
(Pilg.Hat.) CM15 54 FU43
Chislehurst BR7 145 EM95
Dartford DA1 128 FJ85
Hampton TW12
off Priory Gdns 136 BZ95
Hayes UB3 77 BV73
Ruislip HA4 59 BT60
Stanmore HA7 41 CF48
Sunbury-on-Thames TW16
off Staines Rd E 115 BU94
Uxbridge (Denh.) UB9 58 BG62
Uxbridge (Hare.) UB9 58 BH56
Walton-on-Thames KT12 135 BU104
Wembley (Sudbury) HA0 61 CF63
Woking GU21 151 BD113
Priory Ct, E17 67 DZ55
EC4 off Carter La 83 DP72
SW8 101 DK81
Bushey WD23
off Sparrows Herne 40 CC46
Epsom KT17
off Old Schs La 157 CT109
Priory Ct Est, E17
off Priory Ct 47 DZ54
Priory Cres, SE19 122 DQ94
Sutton SM3 157 CX105
Wembley HA0 61 CG62
Priory Dr, SE2 106 EX78
Stanmore HA7 41 CF48
Priory Fld Dr, Edg. HA8 42 CP49
Priory Flds, Dart.
(Fnghm) DA4 148 FM103
Priory Gdns, N6 65 DH58
SE25 142 DT98
SW13 99 CT83
W4 98 CS77
W5 off Hanger La 80 CL69
Ashford TW15 115 BR92
Dartford DA1 128 FK85
Hampton TW12 116 BZ94
Uxbridge (Hare.) UB9 58 BJ56
Wembley HA0 61 CG63
Priory Gate, Wal.Cr. EN8 15 DZ27
Priory Grn, Stai. TW18 114 BH92
Priory Grn Est, N1 83 DM68
Priory Gro, SW8 101 DL81
Barnet EN5 28 DA43
Romford RM3 52 FL48
Priory Hill, Dart. DA1 128 FK85
Wembley HA0 61 CG63
H Priory Hosp, The, N14 45 DL46
Priory La, SW15 118 CS86
Dartford (Fnghm) DA4 148 FM102
Richmond TW9
off Forest Rd 98 CN80
West Molesey KT8 136 CA98
Priory Ms, SW8 101 DK81
Hornchurch RM11 71 FH60
Staines TW18
off Chestnut Manor Cl 114 BH92
Priory Pk, SE3 104 EF83
Priory Pk Rd, NW6 81 CZ67
Wembley HA0 61 CG63
Priory Path, Rom. RM3 52 FL48
Priory Pl, Dart. DA1 128 FK86
Walton-on-Thames KT12 135 BU104
Priory Rd, E6 86 EK67
N8 65 DK56
NW6 82 DB67
SW19 120 DD94
W4 98 CR76
Barking IG11 87 ER66
Chessington KT9 138 CL104
Croydon CR0 141 DN101
Gerrards Cross
(Chal.St.P.) SL9 56 AX55
Hampton TW12 116 BZ94
Hounslow TW3 116 CC85
Loughton IG10 32 EL42
Richmond TW9 98 CN79
Romford RM3 52 FL48
Sutton SM3 157 CX105
Priory Rd N, Dart. DA1 108 FK84
Priory Rd S, Dart. DA1 128 FK85
Priory Shop Cen, Dart. DA1 128 FL86
Priory St, E3
off St. Leonards St 85 EB69
Priory Ter, NW6 82 DB67
Sunbury-on-Thames TW16
off Staines Rd E 115 BU94
Priory Vw, Bushey
(Bushey Hth) WD23 41 CE45
Priory Wk, SW10 100 DC78
Priory Way, Ger.Cr.
(Chal.St.P.) SL9 56 AX55
Harrow HA2 60 CB56
Slough (Datchet) SL3 92 AV80
Southall UB2 96 BX76
West Drayton UB7 94 BL79
Priscilla Cl, N15
off Conway Rd 66 DQ57
Pritchard's Rd, E2 84 DU67
Pritchett Cl, Enf. EN3 31 EA37
Priter Rd, SE16 202 C7
Priter Way, SE16
off Dockley Rd 102 DU76
Private Rd, Enf. EN1 30 DS43
Probert Rd, SW2 121 DN85
Probyn Rd, SW2 121 DP89
Procter St, WC1 196 B7
Proctor Cl, Mitch. CR4 140 DG95
Proctors Cl, Felt. TW14 115 BU88
Profumo Rd, Walt. KT12 154 BX106
Progress Business Pk, Croy.
CR0 141 DM103
Progress Way, N22 45 DN53
Croydon CR0 141 DM103
Enfield EN1 30 DU43
Promenade, The, W4 98 CS81
Promenade App Rd, W4 98 CS80
Promenade de Verdun, Pur.
CR8 159 DK111
Promenade Mans, Edg. HA8
off Hale La 42 CP50
Prospect Business Pk, Loug.
IG10 33 EQ42
Prospect Cl, SE26 122 DV91
Belvedere DA17 106 FA77
Hounslow TW3 96 BZ81
Ruislip HA4 60 BX59
Prospect Cotts, SW18
off Point Pleasant 100 DA84
Prospect Cres, Twick. TW2 116 CC86
Prospect Gro, Grav. DA12 131 GK87
Prospect Hill, E17 67 EB56
Prospect La, Egh.
(Eng.Grn) TW20 112 AT92
Prospect Pl, E1 202 F2
N2 64 DD56
N7 off Parkhurst Rd 65 DL63
N17 46 DS53
NW2 off Ridge Rd 63 CZ62
NW3 off Holly Wk 64 DC63
W4 off Chiswick High Rd 98 CR78
Bromley BR2 144 EH97
Dartford DA1 128 FL86
Epsom KT17
off Clayton Rd 156 CS113
Gravesend DA12 131 GK87
Grays RM17 110 GB79
Romford RM5 51 FC54
Staines TW18 113 BF92
Prospect Pl Shop Pk, Dart. DA1
off Westgate Rd 128 FL86
Prospect Quay, SW18 100 DA84
Prospect Ring, N2 64 DD55
Prospect Rd, NW2 63 CZ62
Barnet EN5 28 DA43
Hornchurch RM11 72 FM55
Sevenoaks TN13 191 FJ123
Surbiton KT6 137 CJ100
Waltham Cross
(Chsht) EN8 14 DW29
Woodford Green IG8 48 EJ50
Prospect St, SE16 202 E6
Prospect Vale, SE18 104 EL77
Prospect Way, Brwd.
(Hutt.) CM13 55 GE42
Prospero Rd, N19 65 DJ60
Prossers, Tad. KT20
off Croffets 173 CX121
Protea Cl, E16
off Hermit Rd 86 EF70
Prothero Gdns, NW4 63 CV57
Prothero Ho, NW10 80 CR66
Prothero Rd, SW6 99 CY80
Prout Gro, NW10 62 CS63
Prout Rd, E5 66 DV62
Provence St, N1
off St. Peters St 84 DQ68
Providence Cl, E9
off Wetherell Rd 85 DX67
Providence Ct, W1 194 G10
Providence La, Hayes UB3 95 BR80
Providence Pl, N1
off Upper St 83 DP67
Epsom KT17 156 CS112
Romford RM5 50 EZ54
Woking GU22 152 BG114
Providence Rd, West Dr. UB7 76 BL74
Providence Row, N1
off Pentonville Rd 83 DM68
Providence Row Cl, E2
off Ainsley St 84 DV69
Providence Sq, SE1
off Jacob St 102 DT75
Providence St, N1
off St. Peters St 84 DQ68
Greenhithe DA9 129 FU85
Providence Yd, E2
off Ezra St 84 DU69
Provident Ind Est, Hayes
UB3 95 BU75
Provost Est, N1 197 K2
Provost Rd, NW3 82 DF66
Provost St, N1 197 K3
Prowse Av, Bushey
(Bushey Hth) WD23 40 CC47
Prowse Pl, NW1
off Bonny St 83 DH66
Pruden Cl, N14 45 DJ47
Prudent Pas, EC2 197 J8
Prune Hill, Egh.
(Eng.Grn) TW20 112 AX94
Prusom St, E1 202 E3
Pryor Cl, Abb.L. WD5 7 BT32
Pryors, The, NW3 64 DD62
★ P.S. Tattershall Castle,
SW1 200 A3
H Public Health
Laboratory Service HQ,
NW9 62 CS55
★ Public Record Office, Rich.
TW9 98 CP80
Puck La, Wal.Abb. EN9 15 ED29
Pucknells Cl, Swan. BR8
off Birchwood Rd 147 FC95
Puddenhole Cotts, Bet. RH3 182 CN133
Pudding La, EC3 201 L1
Chigwell IG7 49 ET46
Sevenoaks (Seal) TN15
off Church St 191 FN121
DLR Pudding Mill Lane 85 EB67
Pudding Mill La, E15 85 EB67
Puddle Dock, EC4 196 G10
Puddledock La, Dart. DA2 127 FE92
Westerham TN16 189 ET133
Puers La, Beac.
(Jordans) HP9 36 AS51
Puffin Cl, Bark. IG11 88 EV69
Beckenham BR3 143 DX99
Puffin Ter, Ilf. IG5
off Tiptree Cres 69 EN55
Pulborough Rd, SW18 119 CZ87
Pulborough Way, Houns.
TW4 96 BW84
Pulford Rd, N15 66 DR58
Pulham Av, N2 64 DC56
Puller Rd, Barn. EN5 27 CY40
Pulleyns Av, E6 86 EL69
Pullman Ct, SW2 121 DL88
Pullman Gdns, SW15 119 CW86
Pullman Pl, SE9 124 EL85
Pullmans Pl, Stai. TW18 114 BG92
Pulross Rd, SW9 101 DM83
Pulteney Cl, E3 85 DZ67
Isleworth TW7
off Gumley Gdns 97 CG83
Pulteney Gdns, E18
off Pulteney Rd 68 EH55
Pulteney Rd, E18 68 EH55
Pulteney Ter, N1 83 DM67
Pulton Pl, SW6 100 DA80
Puma Ct, E1 197 P6
Pump All, Brent. TW8 97 CK80
Pump Cl, Nthlt. UB5
off Union Rd 78 CA68
Pump Ct, EC4 196 D9
Pumphandle Path, N2
off Tarling Rd 44 DC54
Pump Hill, Loug. IG10 33 EM40
Pump Ho Cl, SE16 202 G5
Bromley BR2 144 EF96
Pump Ho Ms, E1
off Hooper St 84 DU73
Pumping Sta Rd, W4 98 CS80
Pump La, SE14 102 DW80
Chesham HP5 4 AS32
Hayes UB3 95 BV75
Orpington BR6 165 FB106
Pump Pail N, Croy. CR0
off Old Town 142 DQ104
Pump Pail S, Croy. CR0
off Southbridge Rd 142 DQ104
Pundersons Gdns, E2 84 DV69
Punjab La, Sthl. UB1
off Herbert Rd 78 BZ74
Purbeck Av, N.Mal. KT3 139 CT100
Purbeck Cl, Red. RH1 185 DK128
Purbeck Dr, NW2 63 CY61
Woking GU21 151 AZ114
Purbeck Rd, Horn. RM11 71 FG60
Purberry Gro, Epsom KT17 157 CT110
Purbrock Av, Wat. WD25 24 BW36
Purbrook Est, SE1 201 N5
Purbrook St, SE1 201 N6
Purcell Cl, Borwd. WD6 25 CK39
Kenley CR8 160 DR114
Purcell Cres, SW6 99 CY80
Purcell Ms, NW10
off Suffolk Rd 80 CS66
Purcell Rd, Grnf. UB6 78 CB71
Purcells Av, Edg. HA8 42 CN50
Purcells Cl, Ashtd. KT21
off Albert Rd 172 CM118
Purcell St, N1 84 DS68
Purchese St, NW1 83 DK68
Purdy St, E3 85 EB70
Purelake Ms, SE13 103 ED83
PURFLEET 108 FP77
⇌ Purfleet 108 FN78
Purfleet Bypass, Purf. RM19 108 FP77
Purfleet Ind Pk, S.Ock.
(Aveley) RM15 108 FM75
Purfleet Rd, S.Ock.
(Aveley) RM15 108 FN75
Purfleet Thames Terminal, Purf.
RM19 108 FQ80
Purkis Cl, Uxb. UB8
off Dawley Rd 77 BQ72
Purland Cl, Dag. RM8 70 EZ60
Purland Rd, SE28 105 ET75
Purleigh Av, Wdf.Grn. IG8 48 EL51
PURLEY 159 DM111
⇌ Purley 159 DP112
H Purley & District
War Mem Hosp, Pur. CR8 159 DN111
Purley Av, NW2 63 CY62
Purley Bury Av, Pur. CR8 160 DQ110
Purley Bury Cl, Pur. CR8 160 DQ110
Purley Cl, Ilf. IG5 49 EN54
Purley Downs Rd, Pur. CR8 160 DQ110
South Croydon CR2 160 DR111
Purley Hill, Pur. CR8 159 DP112
Purley Knoll, Pur. CR8 159 DM111
⇌ Purley Oaks 160 DQ109
Purley Oaks Rd, S.Croy. CR2 160 DR109
Purley Par, Pur. CR8
off High St 159 DN111
Purley Pk Rd, Pur. CR8 159 DP110
Purley Pl, N1
off Islington Pk St 83 DP66
Purley Ri, Pur. CR8 159 DM112
Purley Rd, N9 46 DR48
Purley CR8 159 DN111

★ Place of interest | ⇌ Railway station | ⊖ London Underground station | DLR Docklands Light Railway station | Tra Tramlink station | H Hospital | Riv Pedestrian ferry landing stage

Purley Rd,
South Croydon CR2 160 DR108
Purley Vale, Pur. CR8 159 DP113
Purley Way, Croy. CR0 141 DM101
Purley CR8 159 DN108
Purley Way Cres, Croy. CR0
off Purley Way 141 DM101
Purlieu Way, Epp.
(They.B.) CM16 33 ES35
Purlings Rd, Bushey WD23 24 CB43
Purneys Rd, SE9 104 EK84
Purrett Rd, SE18 105 ET78
Purser's Cross Rd, SW6 99 CZ81
Pursewardens Cl, W13 79 CJ74
Pursley Gdns, Borwd. WD6 26 CN38
Pursley Rd, NW7 43 CV52
Purves Rd, NW10 81 CW68
Puteaux Ho, E2 85 DX68
PUTNEY, SW15 99 CY84
⇌ **Putney** 99 CY84
⊖ **Putney Bridge** 99 CY83
Putney Br, SW6 99 CY83
SW15 99 CY83
Putney Br App, SW6 99 CY83
Putney Br Rd, SW15 99 CY84
SW18 99 CY84
Putney Common, SW15 99 CW83
Putney Ex Shop Cen, SW15 99 CX84
Putney Gdns, Rom. (Chad.Hth) RM6
off Heathfield Pk Dr 70 EV58
PUTNEY HEATH, SW15 119 CW86
Putney Heath, SW15 119 CW86
Putney Heath La, SW15 119 CX86
Putney High St, SW15 99 CX84
Putney Hill, SW15 119 CX86
H **Putney Hosp**, SW15 99 CW82
Putney Pk Av, SW15 99 CU84
Putney Pk La, SW15 99 CV84
Putney Rd, Enf. EN3 31 DX36
PUTNEY VALE, SW15 119 CT90
Putney Wf Twr, SW15 99 CY83
Puttenham Cl, Wat. WD19 40 BW48
Pycroft Way, N9 46 DU49
Pye Cl, Cat. CR3
off St. Lawrence Way 176 DR123
Pyecombe Cor, N12 43 CZ49
Pyghtle, The, Uxb.
(Denh.) UB9 58 BG60
Pylbrook Rd, Sutt. SM1 140 DA104
Pyle Hill, Wok. GU22 166 AX124
Pylon Way, Croy. CR0 141 DL102
Pym Cl, Barn. EN4 28 DD43
Pymers Mead, SE21 122 DQ88
Pymmes Cl, N13 45 DM50
N17 46 DV53
Pymmes Gdns N, N9 46 DT48
Pymmes Gdns S, N9 46 DT48
Pymmes Grn Rd, N11 45 DH49
Pymmes Rd, N13 45 DL51
Pymms Brook Dr, Barn.
EN4 28 DE42
Pym Orchard, West.
(Brasted) TN16 180 EW124
Pym Pl, Grays RM17 110 GA77
Pynchester Cl, Uxb. UB10 58 BN61
Pyne Rd, Surb. KT6 138 CN102
Pynest Grn La, Wal.Abb.
EN9 32 EG38
Pyne Ter, SW19
off Windlesham Gro 119 CX88
Pynfolds, SE16 202 E5
Pynham Cl, SE2 106 EU76
Pynnacles Cl, Stan. HA7 41 CH50
Pyrcroft La, Wey. KT13 153 BP106
Pyrcroft Rd, Cher. KT16 133 BF101
PYRFORD, Wok. GU22 167 BE115
Pyrford Common Rd, Wok.
GU22 167 BD116
★ **Pyrford Ct**, Wok. GU22 167 BE117
PYRFORD GREEN, Wok.
GU22 168 BH117
Pyrford Heath, Wok. GU22 167 BF116
Pyrford Lock, Wok.
(Wisley) GU23 168 BJ116
Pyrford Rd, W.Byf. KT14 152 BG113
Woking GU22 152 BG114
PYRFORD VILLAGE, Wok.
GU22 168 BG118
Pyrford Wds Cl, Wok. GU22 167 BF115
Pyrford Wds Rd, Wok. GU22 167 BE115
Pyrland Rd, N5 66 DR64
Richmond TW10 118 CM86
Pyrles Grn, Loug. IG10 33 EP39
Pyrles La, Loug. IG10 33 EP40
Pyrmont Gro, SE27 121 DP90
Pyrmont Rd, W4 98 CN79
Ilford IG1
off High Rd 69 EQ61
Pytchley Cres, SE19 122 DQ93
Pytchley Rd, SE22 102 DS83

Q

Quadrangle, The, W2 194 B8
Quadrangle Cl, SE1 201 M8
Quadrangle Ms, Stan. HA7 41 CJ52
Quadrant, The, SE24
off Herne Hill 122 DQ85
SW20 139 CY95
Bexleyheath DA7 106 EX80
Epsom KT17 156 CS113
Purfleet RM19 108 FQ77
Richmond TW9 98 CL84
Sutton SM2 158 DC107
Quadrant Arc, W1 199 L1
Romford RM1 71 FE57
Quadrant Cl, NW4
off The Burroughs 63 CV57
Quadrant Gro, NW5 64 DF64
Quadrant Ho, Sutt. SM2 158 DC107
Quadrant Rd, Rich. TW9 97 CK84
Thornton Heath CR7 141 DP98
Quadrant Way, Wey. KT13
off Weybridge Rd 152 BM105
Quad Rd, Wem. HA9
off Courtenay Rd 61 CK62
Quaggy Wk, SE3 104 EG84
Quail Gdns, S.Croy. CR2 161 DY110
Quainton St, NW10 62 CR62
Quaker Cl, Sev. TN13 191 FK123
Quaker Ct, E1 197 P5
Quaker La, Sthl. UB2 96 CA76
Waltham Abbey EN9 15 EC34
Quakers Course, NW9 43 CT53
Quakers Hall La, Sev. TN13 191 FJ122
Quakers La, Islw. TW7 97 CG81
Potters Bar EN6 12 DB30
Quaker's Pl, E7 68 EK64
Quaker St, E1 197 P5
Quakers Wk, N21 30 DR44
Quality Ct, WC2 196 D8
Quality St, Red. RH1 185 DH128
Quantock Cl, Hayes UB3 95 BR80
Slough SL3 93 BA78
Quantock Dr, Wor.Pk. KT4 139 CW103
Quantock Gdns, NW2 63 CX61
Quantock Rd, Bexh. DA7
off Cumbrian Av 107 FE82
Quarles Cl, Rom. RM5 50 FA52
Quarley Way, SE15
off Daniel Gdns 102 DT80
Quarrendon St, SW6 100 DA82
Quarr Rd, Cars. SM5 140 DD100
Quarry, The, Bet. RH3
off Station Rd 182 CS132
Quarry Cl, Lthd. KT22 171 CK121
Oxted RH8 188 EE130
Quarry Cotts, Sev. TN13 190 FG123
Quarry Gdns, Lthd. KT22 171 CK121
Quarry Hill, Grays RM17 110 GA78
Sevenoaks TN15 191 FK123
Quarry Hill Pk, Reig. RH2 184 DC131
Quarry Ms, Purf. RM19
off Fanns Ri 108 FN77
Quarry Pk Rd, Sutt. SM1 157 CZ107
Quarry Ri, Sutt. SM1 157 CZ107
Quarry Rd, SW18 120 DC86
Godstone RH9 186 DW128
Oxted RH8 188 EE130
Quarryside Business Pk, Red.
RH1 185 DH130
Quarterdeck, The, E14 203 P5
Quartermaine Av, Wok.
GU22 167 AZ122
Quarter Mile La, E10 67 EB63
Quaves Rd, Slou. SL3 92 AV76
Quay La, Green. DA9 109 FV84
Quayside Wk, Kings.T. KT1
off Bishop's Hall 137 CK96
Quay W, Tedd. TW11 117 CH92
Quebec Av, West. TN16 189 ER126
★ **Quebec Ho (Wolfe's Ho)**,
West. TN16 189 ER126
Quebec Ms, W1 194 E9
Quebec Rd, Hayes UB4 78 BW73
Ilford IG1, IG2 69 EP59
Tilbury RM18 111 GG82
Quebec Sq, West. TN16 189 ER126
Quebec Way, SE16 203 J5
Queen Adelaide Rd, SE20 122 DW93
Queen Alexandra's Ct, SW19 119 CZ92
Queen Alexandra's Way, Epsom
KT19 156 CN112
Queen Anne Av, N15
off Suffield Rd 66 DT57
Bromley BR2 144 EF97
Queen Anne Dr, Esher
(Clay.) KT10 155 CE108
Queen Anne Ms, W1 195 J7
Queen Anne Rd, E9 85 DX65
Queen Anne's Cl,
Twick. TW2 117 CD90
Queen Anne's Gdns, W4 98 CS76
Queen Annes Gdns, W5 98 CL75
Enfield EN1 30 DS44
Leatherhead KT22
off Upper Fairfield Rd 171 CH121
Queen Anne's Gdns, Mitch.
CR4 140 DF97
Queen Anne's Gate, SW1 199 M5
Bexleyheath DA7 106 EX83
Queen Anne's Gro, W4 98 CS76
Queen Annes Gro, W5 98 CL75
Enfield EN1 46 DR45
Queen Anne's Ms, Lthd. KT22
off Fairfield Rd 171 CH121
Queen Annes Pl, Enf. EN1 30 DS44
Queen Annes Ter, Lthd. KT22
off Upper Fairfield Rd 171 CH121
Queen Anne St, W1 195 H8
Queen Anne's Wk, WC1
off Guilford St 83 DL70
Queen Anne Ter, E1 202 E1
Queenborough Gdns, Chis.
BR7 125 ER93
Ilford IG2 69 EN56
Queen Caroline Est, W6 99 CW78
Queen Caroline St, W6 99 CW77
H **Queen Charlotte's &**
Chelsea Hosp, W12 81 CU72
Queendale Ct, Wok. GU21
off Roundthorn Way 166 AT116
Queen Elizabeth Ct, Brox. EN10
off Groom Rd 15 DZ26
Waltham Abbey EN9
off Greenwich Way 31 EC36
Queen Elizabeth Gdns, Mord.
SM4 140 DA98
★ **Queen Elizabeth Hall &**
Purcell Room, SE1 200 B2
H **Queen Elizabeth Hosp**,
SE18 104 EL80
Queen Elizabeth Pl, Til.
RM18 111 GG84
Queen Elizabeth Rd, E17 67 DY55
Kingston upon Thames KT2 138 CM95
Queen Elizabeths Cl, N16 66 DR61
Queen Elizabeths Dr, N14 45 DL46
Queen Elizabeth's Dr, Croy.
(New Adgtn) CR0 161 ED110
Queen Elizabeth II Br, Dart.
DA1 109 FR82
Purfleet RM19 109 FR82
★ **Queen Elizabeth II Conf Cen**,
SW1 199 N5
Queen Elizabeth's Gdns, Croy.
(New Adgtn) CR0
off Queen Elizabeth's Dr 161 ED110
★ **Queen Elizabeth's Hunting Lo**,
Epping Forest, E4 48 EF45
Queen Elizabeth St, SE1 201 N4
Queen Elizabeths Wk, N16 66 DR61
Queen Elizabeth's Wk, Wall.
SM6 159 DK105
Queen Elizabeth Wk, SW13 99 CV81
Windsor SL4 92 AS82
Queen Elizabeth Way, Wok.
GU22 167 AZ119
Queenhill Rd, S.Croy. CR2 160 DV110
Queenhithe, EC4 197 J10
Queen Margaret's Gro, N1 66 DS64
Queen Mary Av, Mord. SM4 139 CX99
Queen Mary Cl, Rom. RM1 71 FF58
Surbiton KT6 138 CN104
Woking GU22 167 BC116
Queen Mary Ct, Stai. TW19
off Long La 114 BL88
Queen Mary Rd, SE19 121 DP93
Shepperton TW17 135 BQ96
Queen Mary's Av, Cars. SM5 158 DF108
Queen Marys Av, Wat. WD18 23 BS42
Queen Marys Ct, Wal.Abb. EN9
off Greenwich Way 31 EC35
Queen Marys Dr, Add.
(New Haw) KT15 151 BF110
★ **Queen Mary's Gdns**, NW1 194 F3
H **Queen Mary's Hosp**, NW3 64 DC62
Sidcup DA14 126 EU93
H **Queen Mary's Hosp for Children**,
Cars. SM5 140 DC102
H **Queen Mary's Uni Hosp**
(Roehampton), SW15 119 CU86
Queen Mother's Dr, Uxb.
(Denh.) UB9 57 BF58
Queen of Denmark Ct, SE16 203 M6
Queens Acre, Sutt. SM3 157 CX108
Queens All, Epp. CM16 17 ET31
Queens Av, N3 44 DC52
N10 64 DG55
N20 44 DD47
Queen's Av, N21 45 DP46
Queens Av, Felt. TW13 116 BW91
Greenford UB6 78 CB72
Stanmore HA7 61 CJ55
Watford WD18 23 BT42
West Byfleet (Byfleet) KT14 152 BK112
Woodford Green IG8 48 EH50
Queensberry Ms W, SW7
off Queen's Gate 100 DD77
Queensberry Pl, E12 68 EK64
SW7 100 DD77
Richmond TW9
off Friars La 117 CK85
Queensberry Way, SW7
off Harrington Rd 100 DD77
Queensborough Ms, W2
off Porchester Ter 82 DC73
Queensborough Pas, W2
off Porchester Ter 82 DC73
Queensborough S Bldgs, W2
off Porchester Ter 82 DC73
Queensborough Studios, W2
off Porchester Ter 82 DC73
Queensborough Ter, W2 82 DB73
Queensbridge Pk, Islw. TW7 117 CE85
Queensbridge Rd, E2 84 DT67
E8 84 DT66
QUEENSBURY, Har. HA3 61 CK55
⊖ **Queensbury** 62 CM55
Queensbury Circle Par, Har. HA3
off Streatfield Rd 62 CL55
Stanmore HA7
off Streatfield Rd 62 CL55
Queensbury Rd, NW9 62 CR59
Wembley HA0 80 CM68
Queensbury Sta Par, Edg.
HA8 62 CM55
Queensbury St, N1 84 DQ66
Queen's Circ, SW8
off Queenstown Rd 101 DH80
SW11
off Queenstown Rd 101 DH80
Queens Cl, Edg. HA8 42 CN50
Tadworth KT20 173 CU124
Wallington SM6
off Queens Rd 159 DH106
Windsor (Old Wind.) SL4 112 AU85
★ **Queens Club (Tennis Cen)**,
W14 99 CY78
Queens Club Gdns, W14 99 CY79
Queens Ct, SE23 122 DW88
Richmond TW10 118 CM86
Slough SL1 74 AT73
Queenscourt, Wem. HA9 62 CL63
Queens Ct, Wey. KT13 153 BR106
Woking GU22
off Hill Vw Rd 167 AZ118
Queens Ct Ride, Cob. KT11 153 BU113
Queen's Cres, NW5 82 DG65
Queens Cres, Rich. TW10 118 CM85
Queenscroft Rd, SE9 124 EK85
Queensdale Cres, W11 81 CX74
Queensdale Pl, W11 81 CY74
Queensdale Rd, W11 81 CX74
Queensdale Wk, W11 81 CY74
Queensdown Rd, E5 66 DV63
Queens Dr, E10 67 EA59
N4 65 DP61
W3 80 CM72
W5 80 CM72
Abbots Langley WD5 7 BT32
Leatherhead
(Oxshott) KT22 154 CC111
Queen's Dr, Slou. SL3 75 AZ66
Queens Dr, Surb. KT5 138 CN101
Thames Ditton KT7 137 CG101
Waltham Cross EN8 15 EA34
Queens Dr, The, Rick.
(Mill End) WD3 37 BF45
Queens Elm Par, SW3
off Old Ch St 100 DD78
Queen's Elm Sq, SW3
off Old Ch St 100 DD78
Queensferry Wk, N17
off Jarrow Rd 66 DV56
★ **Queen's Gall, The**, SW1 199 J5
Queens Gdns, NW4 63 CW57
W2 82 DC73
Queens Gdns, W5 79 CJ70
Dartford DA2 128 FP88
Queen's Gdns, Houns. TW5 96 BY81
Queens Gdns, Rain. RM13 89 FD68
Upminster RM14 73 FT58
Queen's Gate, SW7 100 DD77
Queensgate, Cob. KT11 154 BX112
Waltham Cross EN8 15 DZ34
Queen's Gate Gdns, SW7 100 DC76
Queens Gate Gdns, SW15
off Upper Richmond Rd 99 CV84
Queensgate Gdns, Chis. BR7 145 ER95
Queen's Gate Ms, SW7 100 DC75
Queensgate Pl, NW6 82 DA66
Queen's Gate Pl, SW7 100 DC76
Queen's Gate Pl Ms, SW7 100 DC76
Queen's Gate Ter, SW7 100 DC76
Queen's Gro, NW8 82 DD67
Queen's Gro Ms, NW8 82 DD67
Queens Gro Rd, E4 47 ED46
Queen's Head Pas, EC4 197 H8
Queen's Head St, N1 83 DP67
Queens Head Yd, SE1 201 K3
Queens Ho, Tedd. TW11 117 CF93
★ **Queen's Ice Rink**, W2 82 DB73
Queenside Ms, Horn. RM12
off Station La 72 FL61
Queensland Av, N18 46 DQ51
SW19 140 DB95
Queensland Cl, E17 47 DZ54
Queensland Ho, E16
off Rymill St 87 EN74
Queens La, N10 65 DH55
Ashford TW15
off Clarendon Rd 114 BM91
Queens Mkt, E13
off Green St 86 EJ67
Queensmead, NW8 82 DD67
Leatherhead KT22 154 CC111
Slough (Datchet) SL3 92 AV81
Queensmead Av, Epsom
KT17 157 CV110
Queensmead Rd, Brom. BR2 144 EF96
Queensmere Cl, SW19 119 CX89
Queensmere Rd, SW19 119 CX89
Slough SL1
off Wellington St 92 AU75
Queensmere Shop Cen, Slou.
SL1 92 AT75
Queens Ms, W2 82 DB73
Queensmill Rd, SW6 99 CX80
Queens Par, N11
off Colney Hatch La 44 DF50
W5 80 CM72
Queens Par Cl, N11
off Colney Hatch La 44 DF50
⇌ **Queen's Park** 81 CY68
⊖ **Queen's Park** 81 CY68
Queens Pk Ct, W10 81 CX69
Queens Pk Gdns, Felt. TW13
off Vernon Rd 115 BU90
★ **Queens Park Rangers FC**,
W12 81 CV74
Queens Pk Rd, Cat. CR3 176 DS123
Romford RM3 52 FM53
Queens Pas, Chis. BR7
off High St 125 EP93
Queens Pl, Mord. SM4 140 DA98
Watford WD17 24 BW41
Queen's Prom, Kings.T. KT1
off Portsmouth Rd 137 CK97
Queen Sq, WC1 196 A5
Queen Sq Pl, WC1 196 A5
Queens Reach, E.Mol. KT8 137 CE98
Queens Ride, SW13 99 CU83
SW15 99 CU83
Queen's Ride, Rich. TW10 118 CP88
Queens Ri, Rich. TW10 118 CM86
Queens Rd, E11 67 ED59
E13 86 EH67
Queen's Rd, E17 67 DZ58
Queens Rd, N3 44 DC53
N9 46 DV48
Queen's Rd, N11 45 DL52
Queens Rd, NW4 63 CW57
SE14 102 DV81
SE15 102 DV81
SW14 98 CR83
SW19 119 CZ93
W5 80 CL72
Barking IG11 87 EQ66
Barnet EN5 27 CX41
Beckenham BR3 143 DY96
Brentwood CM14 54 FW48
Bromley BR1 144 EG96
Buckhurst Hill IG9 48 EH47
Chislehurst BR7 125 EP93
Queen's Rd, Croy. CR0 141 DP100
Queens Rd, Egh. TW20 113 AZ93
Enfield EN1 30 DS42
Epping (N.Wld Bas.) CM16 19 FB26
Queen's Rd, Erith DA8 107 FE79
Queens Rd, Felt. TW13 115 BV88
Gravesend DA12 131 GJ90
Hampton (Hmptn H.) TW12 116 CB91
Hayes UB3 77 BS72
Queen's Rd, Houns. TW3 96 CB83
Queens Rd, Kings.T. KT2 118 CN94
Loughton IG10 32 EL41
Mitcham CR4 140 DD97
Morden SM4 140 DA98
New Malden KT3 139 CT98
Richmond TW10 118 CM85
Queen's Rd, Slou. SL1 74 AT73
Queens Rd, Slou.
(Datchet) SL3 92 AU81
Southall UB2 96 BX75
Sutton SM2 158 DA110
Queen's Rd, Tedd. TW11 117 CE93
Thames Ditton KT7 137 CF99
Queens Rd, Twick. TW1 117 CF88
Queen's Rd, Uxb. UB8 76 BJ69
Queens Rd, Wall. SM6 159 DH106
Waltham Cross EN8 15 DY34
Walton-on-Thames KT12 153 BV106
Watford WD17 24 BW42
Queen's Rd, Well. DA16 106 EV82
Queens Rd, West Dr. UB7 94 BM75
Weybridge KT13 153 BQ105
⇌ **Queens Road Peckham** 102 DW81
Queens Rd W, E13 86 EG68
Queen's Row, SE17 102 DR79
Queens Ter, E13 86 EH67
Queen's Ter, NW8 82 DD68
Queens Ter, Islw. TW7 97 CG84
Queens Ter Cotts, W7
off Boston Rd 97 CE75
Queensthorpe Rd, SE26 123 DX91
★ **Queen's Twr**, SW7 100 DD76
Queenstown Gdns, Rain.
RM13 89 FF69
Queenstown Ms, SW8
off Queenstown Rd 101 DH82
Queenstown Rd, SW8 101 DH79
⇌ **Queenstown Road**
(Battersea) 101 DH81
Queen St, EC4 197 J10
N17 46 DS51
W1 199 H2
Bexleyheath DA7 106 EZ83
Brentwood (Warley) CM14 54 FW50
Chertsey KT16 134 BG102
Croydon CR0
off Church Rd 142 DQ104
Erith DA8 107 FE79
Gravesend DA12 131 GH86
Kings Langley
(Chipper.) WD4 6 BG32
Romford RM7 71 FD58
Queen St Pl, EC4 201 J1
Queensville Rd, SW12 121 DK87
Queens Wk, E4
off The Green Wk 47 ED46
NW9 62 CQ61
SE1 200 B3
SW1 199 K3
Queens Wk, W5 79 CJ70
Ashford TW15 114 BK91
Queen's Wk, Har. HA1 61 CE56
Queens Wk, Ruis. HA4 60 BX62
⊖ **Queensway** 82 DB73
Queens Way, NW4 63 CW57
Queensway, W2 82 DB72
Queens Way, Croy. CR0 159 DM107
Queensway, Enf. EN3 30 DV42
Queens Way, Felt. TW13 116 BW91
Queensway, Orp. BR5 145 EQ99
Queens Way, Rad.
(Shenley) WD7 10 CL32
Queensway, Red. RH1 184 DF133
Sunbury-on-Thames TW16 135 BV96
Queens Way, Wal.Cr. EN8 15 DZ34
Queensway, W.Wick. BR4 144 EE104
Queensway, The, Ger.Cr.
(Chal.St.P.) SL9 56 AX55
Queensway N, Walt. KT12
off Robinsway 154 BW105
Queensway S, Walt. KT12
off Trenchard Cl 154 BW106
Queenswell Av, N20 44 DE48
Queenswood Av, E17 47 EC53
Brentwood (Hutt.) CM13 55 GD43
Hampton TW12 116 CB93
Hounslow TW3 96 BZ82
Thornton Heath CR7 141 DN99
Wallington SM6 159 DK105
Queenswood Cres, Wat. WD25 7 BU33
Queenswood Gdns, E11 68 EG60
Queenswood Pk, N3 43 CY54
Queen's Wd Rd, N10 65 DH58
Queenswood Rd, SE23 123 DX90
Sidcup DA15 125 ET85
Queens Yd, WC1 195 L5
Queen Victoria Av, Wem. HA0 79 CK66
★ **Queen Victoria Mem**,
SW1 199 K4
Queen Victoria St, EC4 196 G10
Queen Victoria's Wk, Wind.
SL4 92 AS81
Queen Victoria Ter, E1 202 E1
Quemerford Rd, N7 65 DM64
Quendon Dr, Wal.Abb. EN9 15 ED33
Quennell Cl, Ashtd. KT21
off Parkers La 172 CL119
Quennel Way, Brwd.
(Hutt.) CM13 55 GC45
Quentin Pl, SE13 104 EE83
Quentin Rd, SE13 104 EE83
Quentins Dr, West.
(Berry's Grn) TN16 179 EP116
Quentins Wk, West.
(Berry's Grn) TN16
off St. Anns Way 179 EP116
Quentin Way, Vir.W. GU25 132 AV98
Quernmore Cl, Brom. BR1 124 EG93
Quernmore Rd, N4 65 DN58
Bromley BR1 124 EG93
Querrin St, SW6 100 DC82
Quex Ms, NW6
off Quex Rd 82 DA67
Quex Rd, NW6 82 DA67
Quickley La, Rick.
(Chorl.) WD3 21 BB44
Quickley Ri, Rick.
(Chorl.) WD3 21 BC44
Quickmoor La, Kings L. WD4 6 BH33
Quick Rd, W4 98 CS78
Quicks Rd, SW19 120 DB94
Quick St, N1 196 G1
Quick St Ms, N1 196 F1
Quickswood, NW3
off King Henry's Rd 82 DE66
Quickwood Cl, Rick. WD3 22 BG44
Quiet Cl, Add. KT15 152 BG105
Quiet Nook, Brom. BR2
off Croydon Rd 144 EK104
Quill Hall La, Amer. HP6 20 AT37
Quill La, SW15 99 CX84
Quillot, The, Walt. KT12 153 BT106
Quill St, N4 65 DN62
W5 80 CL69
Quilp St, SE1 201 H4
Quilter Gdns, Orp. BR5 146 EW102
Quilter Rd, Orp. BR5 146 EW102
Quilter St, E2 84 DU69

★ Place of interest ⇌ Railway station ⊖ London Underground station DLR Docklands Light Railway station Tra Tramlink station H Hospital Riv Pedestrian ferry landing stage

Quilter St, SE18 105 ET78
Quilting Ct, SE16
off Poolmans St 103 DX75
Quinbrookes, Slou. SL2 74 AW72
Quince Rd, SE13 103 EB82
Quince Tree Cl, S.Ock. RM15 91 FW70
Quincy Rd, Egh. TW20 113 BA92
Quinta Dr, Barn. EN5 27 CV43
Quintin Av, SW20 139 CZ95
Quintin Cl, Pnr. HA5
off High Rd 59 BV57
Quinton Cl, Beck. BR3 143 EC97
Hounslow TW5 95 BV80
Wallington SM6 159 DH105
Quinton Rd, T.Ditt. KT7 137 CG102
Quinton St, SW18 120 DC89
Quintrell Cl, Wok. GU21 166 AV117
Quixley St, E14 85 ED73
Quorn Rd, SE22 102 DS84

R

Raans Rd, Amer. HP6 20 AT38
Rabbit La, Walt. KT12 153 BU108
Rabbit Row, W8
off Kensington Mall 82 DA74
Rabbits Rd, E12 68 EL63
Dartford (S.Darenth) DA4 149 FR96
Rabbs Mill Ho, Uxb. UB8 76 BK68
Rabies Heath Rd, Gdse. RH9 186 DU134
Redhill (Bletch.) RH1 186 DS133
Rabournmead Dr, Nthlt. UB5 60 BY64
Raby Rd, N.Mal. KT3 138 CR98
Raby St, E14 off Salmon La 85 DY72
Raccoon Way, Houns. TW4 96 BW82
Rachel Cl, Ilf. IG6 69 ER55
Rachel Pt, E5 off Muir Rd 66 DU63
Rackham Cl, Well. DA16 106 EV82
Rackham Ms, SW16
off Westcote Rd 121 DJ93
Racton Rd, SW6 100 DA79
Radbourne Av, W5 97 CJ77
Radbourne Cl, E5
off Overbury St 67 DX63
Radbourne Cres, E17 47 ED54
Radbourne Rd, SW12 121 DJ87
Radcliffe Av, NW10 81 CU68
Enfield EN2 30 DQ39
Radcliffe Gdns, Cars. SM5 158 DE108
Radcliffe Ms, Hmptn. (Hmptn H.)
TW12 off Taylor Cl 116 CC92
Radcliffe Path, SW8
off Robertson St 101 DH82
Radcliffe Rd, N21 45 DP46
SE1 201 N6
Croydon CR0 142 DT103
Harrow HA3 41 CG54
Radcliffe Sq, SW15 119 CX86
Radcliffe Way, Nthlt. UB5 78 BX69
Radcot Av, Slou. SL3 93 BB76
Radcot Pt, SE23 123 DX90
Radcot St, SE11 101 DN78
Raddington Rd, W10 81 CY71
Radfield Way, Sid. DA15 125 ER87
Radford Rd, SE13 123 EC86
Radford Way, Bark. IG11 87 ET69
Radipole Rd, SW6 99 CZ81
Radius Pk, Felt. TW14 95 BT84
Radland Rd, E16 86 EF72
Radlet Av, SE26 122 DV90
RADLETT 25 CH35
⇌ Radlett 25 CG35
Radlett Cl, E7 86 EF65
Radlett La, Rad.
(Shenley) WD7 25 CK35
Radlett Pk Rd, Rad. WD7 9 CG34
Radlett Pl, NW8 82 DE67
Radlett Rd, St.Alb. AL2 9 CE28
Watford WD17, WD24 24 BW41
Watford (Ald.) WD25 24 CB39
Radley Av, Ilf. IG3 69 ET63
Radley Cl, Felt. TW14 115 BT88
Radley Ct, SE16 203 J4
Radley Gdns, Har. HA3 62 CL56
Radley Ho, SE2
off Wolvercote Rd 106 EX75
Radley Ms, W8 100 DA76
Radley Rd, N17 46 DS54
Radley's La, E18 48 EG54
Radleys Mead, Dag. RM10 89 FB65
Radley Sq, E5
off Dudlington Rd 66 DW61
Radlix Rd, E10 67 EA60
Radnor Av, Har. HA1 61 CE57
Welling DA16 126 EV85
Radnor Cl, Chis. BR7
off Homewood Cres 125 ES93
Mitcham CR4 141 DL98
Radnor Cres, SE18 106 EU79
Ilford IG4 69 EM57
Radnor Gdns, Enf. EN1 30 DS39
Twickenham TW1 117 CF89
Radnor Gro, Uxb. UB10
off Charnwood Rd 76 BN68
Radnor Ms, W2 194 A9
Radnor Pl, W2 194 B9
Radnor Rd, NW6 81 CY67
SE15 102 DU80
Harrow HA1 61 CD57
Twickenham TW1 117 CF89
Weybridge KT13 134 BN104
Radnor St, EC1 197 J3
Radnor Ter, W14 99 CZ77
Radnor Wk, E14 204 A8
SW3 100 DE78
Croydon CR0 143 DZ100
Radnor Way, NW10 80 CP70
Slough SL3 92 AY77
Radolphs, Tad. KT20
off Heathcote 173 CX122
Radstock Av, Har. HA3 61 CG55
Radstock Cl, N11
off Martock Gdns 44 DG51
Radstock St, SW11 100 DE80
Radstock Way, Red. RH1 185 DK128
Radstone Ct, Wok. GU22 167 AZ118
Radwell Path, Borwd. WD6
off Cromwell Rd 26 CL39
Radzan Cl, Dart. DA2
off Old Bexley La 127 FE89
Raeburn Gdns, Barn. EN5 27 CV43
Raeburn Av, Dart. DA1 127 FH85
Surbiton KT5 138 CP100
Raeburn Cl, NW11 64 DC58
Kingston upon Thames KT1 117 CK94
Raeburn Ct, Wok. GU21
off Martin Way 166 AU118
Raeburn Rd, Edg. HA8 42 CN54
Hayes UB4 77 BR68
Sidcup DA15 125 ES86
Raeburn St, SW2 101 DL84
Rafford Way, Brom. BR1 144 EH96
Raft Rd, SW18 off North Pas 100 DA84
★ Ragged Sch Mus, E3 85 DY71
Raggleswood, Chis. BR7 145 EN95
Rag Hill Cl, West.
(Tats.) TN16 178 EL121
Rag Hill Rd, West.
(Tats.) TN16 178 EK121
Raglan Av, Wal.Cr. EN8 15 DX34
Raglan Cl, Houns. TW4
off Vickers Way 116 BY85
Reigate RH2 184 DC132
Raglan Ct, SE12 124 EG85
South Croydon CR2 159 DP106
Wembley HA9 62 CM63
Raglan Gdns, Wat. WD19 39 BV46
Raglan Prec, Cat. CR3 176 DS122
Raglan Rd, E17 67 EC57
SE18 105 EQ78
Belvedere DA17 106 EZ77
Bromley BR2 144 EJ98
Enfield EN1 46 DS45
Reigate RH2 184 DB131
Woking (Knap.) GU21 166 AS118
Raglan St, NW5 83 DH65
Raglan Ter, Har. HA2 60 CB63
Raglan Way, Nthlt. UB5 78 CC65
Ragley Cl, W3 off Church Rd 98 CQ75
Rags La, Wal.Cr. (Chsht) EN7 14 DS27
Ragwort Ct, SE26
off Lawrie Pk Gdns 122 DV92
Rahn Rd, Epp. CM16 18 EU31
Raider Cl, Rom. RM7 50 FA53
Railey Ms, NW5 65 DJ64
Railpit La, Warl. CR6 178 EE115
Railshead Rd, Islw. TW7 97 CH84
Railton Rd, SE24 101 DN84
Railway App, N4
off Wightman Rd 65 DN58
SE1 201 L2
Harrow HA3 61 CF56
Twickenham TW1 117 CG87
Wallington SM6 159 DH107
Railway Av, SE16 202 G4
Railway Children Wk, SE12
off Baring Rd 124 EG89
Bromley BR1
off Reigate Rd 124 EG89
Railway Cotts, Rad. WD7
off Shenley Hill 25 CH35
Watford WD24 23 BV39
Railway Ms, E3
off Wellington Way 85 EA69
W10 off Ladbroke Gro 81 CY72
Railway Pas, Tedd. TW11
off Victoria Rd 117 CG93
Railway Pl, SW19
off Hartfield Rd 119 CZ93
Belvedere DA17 106 FA76
Gravesend DA12
off Windmill St 131 GH87
Railway Ri, SE22
off Grove Vale 102 DS84
Railway Rd, Tedd. TW11 117 CF91
Waltham Cross EN8 15 DY33
Railway Side, SW13 98 CS83
Railway Sq, Brwd. CM14
off Fairfield Rd 54 FW48
Railway St, N1 196 A1
Gravesend (Nthflt) DA11 130 GA85
Romford RM6 70 EW60
Railway Ter, SE13
off Ladywell Rd 123 EB85
Feltham TW13 115 BU88
Kings Langley WD4 6 BN27
Slough SL2 74 AT74
Staines TW18 113 BD92
Westerham TN16 189 ER125
Rainborough Cl, NW10 80 CQ65
Rainbow Av, E14 204 B10
Rainbow Ct, Wat. WD19
off Oxhey Rd 24 BW44
Woking GU21
off Langmans Way 166 AS116
Rainbow Ind Est, West Dr.
UB7 76 BK73
Rainbow Quay, SE16 203 L7
Rainbow Rd, Grays
(Chaff.Hun.) RM16 109 FW77
Rainbow St, SE5 102 DS80
Rainer Cl, Wal.Cr.
(Chsht) EN8 15 DX29
Raines Ct, N16
off Northwold Rd 66 DT61
Raine St, E1 202 E2
RAINHAM 89 FG69
⇌ Rainham 89 FF70
Rainham Cl, SE9 125 ER86
SW11 120 DE86
★ Rainham Hall, Rain.
RM13 89 FG70
Rainham Rd, NW10 81 CW69
Rainham RM13 89 FE66
Rainham Rd N, Dag. RM10 71 FB61
Rainham Rd S, Dag. RM10 71 FB63
Rainhill Way, E3 85 EA69
Rainsborough Av, SE8 203 K9
Rainsford Cl, Stan. HA7
off Coverdale Cl 41 CJ50
Rainsford Rd, NW10 80 CP69
Rainsford St, W2 194 B8
Rainsford Way, Horn. RM12 71 FG60
Rainton Rd, SE7 205 N10
Rainville Rd, W6 99 CW79
Raisins Hill, Pnr. HA5 60 BW55
Raith Av, N14 45 DK48
Raleana Rd, E14 204 E2
Raleigh Av, Hayes UB4 77 BV71
Wallington SM6 159 DK105
Raleigh Cl, NW4 63 CW57
Erith DA8 107 FF79
Pinner HA5 60 BX59
Ruislip HA4 59 BT61
Raleigh Ct, SE16
off Rotherhithe St 85 DX74
SE19 off Lymer Av 122 DT92
Beckenham BR3 143 EB95
Staines TW18 114 BG91
Wallington SM6 159 DH107
Raleigh Dr, N20 44 DE48
Esher (Clay.) KT10 155 CD106
Surbiton KT5 138 CQ102
Raleigh Gdns, SW2
off Brixton Hill 121 DM86
Mitcham CR4 140 DF96
Raleigh Ms, N1
off Queen's Head St 83 DP67
Orpington BR6
off Osgood Av 163 ET106
Raleigh Rd, N8 65 DN56
SE20 123 DX94
Enfield EN2 30 DR42
Feltham TW13 115 BT90
Richmond TW9 98 CM83
Southall UB2 96 BY78
Raleigh St, N1 83 DP67
Raleigh Way, N14 45 DK46
Feltham TW13 116 BW92
Ralliwood Rd, Ashtd. KT21 172 CN119
Ralph Ct, W2
off Queensway 82 DB72
Ralph Perring Ct, Beck. BR3 143 EA98
Ralston St, SW3
off Tedworth Sq 100 DF78
Ralston Way, Wat. WD19 40 BX47
Rama Ct, SW16 121 DK94
Rama Ct, Har. HA1 61 CE61
Ramac Way, SE7 205 P9
Rama La, SE19 122 DT94
Rambler Cl, SW16 121 DJ91
Rambler La, Slou. SL3 92 AW76
Rame Cl, SW17 120 DG92
Ramilles Cl, SW2 121 DL86
Ramillies Pl, W1 195 K9
Ramillies Rd, NW7 42 CS47
W4 98 CR77
Sidcup DA15 126 EV86
Ramillies St, W1 195 K9
Ramney Dr, Enf. EN3 31 DY37
Ramornie Cl, Walt. KT12 154 BZ106
Rampart St, E1
off Commercial Rd 84 DV72
Ram Pas, Kings.T. KT1
off High St 137 CK96
Rampayne St, SW1 199 M10
Ram Pl, E9 off Chatham Pl 84 DW65
Rampton Cl, E4 47 EA48
Ramsay Gdns, Rom. RM3 52 FJ53
Ramsay Ms, SW3
off King's Rd 100 DE79
Ramsay Pl, Har. HA1 61 CE60
Ramsay Rd, E7 68 EE63
W3 98 CQ76
Ramscroft Cl, N9 46 DS45
Ramsdale Rd, SW17 120 DG92
RAMSDEN, Orp. BR5 146 EW102
Ramsden Cl, Orp. BR5 146 EW102
Ramsden Dr, Rom. RM5 50 FA52
Ramsden Rd, N11 44 DF50
SW12 120 DG86
Erith DA8 107 FD80
Orpington BR5, BR6 146 EV101
Ramsey Cl, NW9 63 CT58
Greenford UB6 60 CC64
Hatfield (Brook.Pk) AL9 12 DD27
Ramsey Ho, Wem. HA9 80 CL65
Ramsey Ms, N4
off Monsell Rd 65 DP62
Ramsey Rd, Th.Hth. CR7 141 DM100
Ramsey St, E2 84 DU70
Ramsey Wk, N1 84 DR65
Ramsey Way, N14 45 DJ45
Ramsgate Cl, E16 205 P3
Ramsgate St, E8
off Dalston La 84 DT65
Ramsgill App, Ilf. IG2 69 ET56
Ramsgill Dr, Ilf. IG2 69 ET57
Rams Gro, Rom. RM6 70 EY56
Ram St, SW18 120 DB85
Ramulis Dr, Hayes UB4 78 BX70
Ramus Wd Av, Orp. BR6 163 ES106
Rancliffe Gdns, SE9 104 EL84
Rancliffe Rd, E6 86 EL68
Randall Av, NW2 63 CT62
Randall Cl, SW11 100 DE81
Erith DA8 107 FC79
Slough SL3 93 AZ78
Randall Ct, NW7
off Page St 43 CU52
Randall Dr, Horn. RM12 72 FJ63
Randall Pl, SE10 103 EC80
Randall Rd, SE11 200 B10
Randall Row, SE11 200 B9
Randalls Cres, Lthd. KT22 171 CG120
Randalls Dr, Brwd.
(Hutt.) CM13 55 GE44
Randalls Pk Av, Lthd. KT22 171 CG120
Randalls Pk Dr, Lthd. KT22
off Randalls Rd 171 CG121
Randalls Rd, Lthd. KT22 171 CE119
Randall's Wk, St.Alb. AL2 8 BZ30
Randalls Way, Lthd. KT22 171 CG121
Randell's Rd, N1 83 DL67
Randle Rd, Rich. TW10 117 CJ91
Randlesdown Rd, SE6 123 EA91
Randles La, Sev.
(Knock.) TN14 180 EX115
Randolph App, E16 86 EK72
Randolph Av, W9 82 DC70
Randolph Cl, Bexh. DA7 107 FC83
Cobham
(Stoke D'Ab.) KT11 170 CA115
Randolph Cl,
Kingston upon Thames KT2 118 CQ92
Woking (Knap.) GU21
off Creston Av 166 AS117
Randolph Cres, W9 82 DC70
Randolph Gdns, NW6 82 DB68
Randolph Gro, Rom. RM6
off Donald Dr 70 EW57
Randolph Ho, Croy. CR0 142 DQ102
Randolph Ms, W9 82 DC70
Randolph Rd, E17 67 EB57
W9 82 DC70
Bromley BR2 145 EM102
Epsom KT17 157 CT114
Slough SL3 92 AY76
Southall UB1 96 BZ75
Randolph's La, West. TN16 189 EP126
Randolph St, NW1 83 DJ66
Randon Cl, Har. HA2 40 CB54
Ranelagh Av, SW6 99 CZ83
SW13 99 CU82
Ranelagh Br, W2
off Gloucester Ter 82 DB71
Ranelagh Cl, Edg. HA8 42 CN49
Ranelagh Dr, Edg. HA8 42 CN49
Twickenham TW1 117 CH85
★ Ranelagh Gdns, SW3 100 DG78
Ranelagh Gdns, E11 68 EJ57
SW6 99 CZ83
W4 off Grove Pk Gdns 98 CQ80
W6 99 CT76
Gravesend (Nthflt) DA11 131 GF87
Ilford IG1 69 EN60
Ranelagh Gdns Mans, SW6
off Ranelagh Gdns 99 CY83
Ranelagh Gro, SW1 198 G10
Ranelagh Ms, W5
off Ranelagh Rd 97 CK75
Ranelagh Pl, N.Mal. KT3 138 CS99
Ranelagh Rd, E6 87 EN67
E11 68 EE63
E15 86 EE67
N17 66 DS55
N22 45 DM53
NW10 81 CT68
SW1 off Lupus St 101 DJ78
W5 97 CK75
Redhill RH1 184 DE134
Southall UB1 78 BX74
Wembley HA0 61 CK64
Ranfurly Rd, Sutt. SM1 140 DA103
Rangefield Rd, Brom. BR1 124 EE92
Rangemoor Rd, N15 66 DT57
Range Rd, Grav. DA12 131 GL87
Rangers Rd, E4 48 EE45
Loughton IG10 48 EE45
Rangers Sq, SE10 103 ED81
Range Wk, Add. KT15
off Monks Cres 152 BH106
Range Way, Shep. TW17 134 BN101
Rangeworth Pl, Sid. DA15
off Priestlands Pk Rd 125 ET90
Rangoon St, EC3 197 P9
Rankin Cl, NW9 62 CS55
Ranleigh Gdns, Bexh. DA7 106 EZ80
Ranmere St, SW12
off Ormeley Rd 121 DH88
Ranmoor Cl, Har. HA1 61 CD56
Ranmoor Gdns, Har. HA1 61 CD56
Ranmore Av, Croy. CR0 142 DT104
Ranmore Cl, Red. RH1 184 DG131
Ranmore Path, Orp. BR5 146 EU98
Ranmore Rd, Sutt. SM2 157 CX109
Rannoch Cl, Edg. HA8 42 CP47
Rannoch Rd, W6 99 CW79
Rannock Av, NW9 62 CS59
Ranskill Rd, Borwd. WD6 26 CN39
Ransom Cl, Wat. WD19 40 BW45
Ransome's Dock Business Cen, SW11
off Parkgate Rd 100 DE80
Ransom Rd, SE7
off Floyd Rd 104 EJ78
Ransom Wk, SE7
off Woolwich Rd 104 EJ78
Ranston Cl, Uxb. (Denh.) UB9
off Nightingale Way 57 BF58
Ranston St, NW1 194 B6
Ranulf Rd, NW2 63 CZ63
Ranwell Cl, E3
off Beale Rd 85 DZ67
Ranwell St, E3 85 DZ67
Ranworth Cl, Erith DA8 107 FE82
Ranworth Rd, N9 46 DW47
Ranyard Cl, Chess. KT9 138 CM104
Raphael Av, Rom. RM1 71 FF55
Tilbury RM18 111 GG80
Raphael Cl, Rad.
(Shenley) WD7 10 CL32
Raphael Dr, T.Ditt. KT7 137 CF101
Watford WD24 24 BX40
Raphael Rd, Grav. DA12 131 GK87
Raphael St, SW7 198 D5
Rapier Cl, Purf. RM19 108 FN77
Rasehill Cl, Rick. WD3 22 BJ43
Rashleigh St, SW8
off Peardon St 101 DH82
Rashleigh Way, Dart.
(Hort.Kir.) DA4 148 FQ98
Rasper Rd, N20 44 DC47
Rastell Av, SW2 121 DK89
Ratcliffe Cl, SE12 124 EG87
Uxbridge UB8 76 BK69
Ratcliffe Cross St, E1 85 DX72
Ratcliffe La, E14 85 DY72
Ratcliffe Orchard, E1 85 DX73
Ratcliff Rd, E7 68 EJ64
Rathbone Mkt, E16
off Barking Rd 86 EF71
Rathbone Pl, W1 195 M8
Rathbone Pt, E5
off Nolan Way 66 DU63
Rathbone St, E16 86 EF71
W1 195 L7
Rathcoole Av, N8 65 DM56
Rathcoole Gdns, N8 65 DM57
Rathfern Rd, SE6 123 DZ88
Rathgar Av, W13 79 CH74
Rathgar Cl, N3 43 CZ54
Rathgar Rd, SW9
off Coldharbour La 101 DP83
Rathmell Dr, SW4 121 DK86
Rathmore Rd, SE7 104 EH78
Gravesend DA11 131 GH87
Rathwell Path, Borwd. WD6 26 CL39
Rats La, Loug.
(High Beach) IG10 32 EH38
Rattray Rd, SW2 101 DN84
Raul Rd, SE15 102 DU81
Raveley St, NW5 65 DJ63
Ravel Gdns, S.Ock.
(Aveley) RM15 90 FQ72
Ravel Rd, S.Ock.
(Aveley) RM15 90 FQ72
Raven Cl, NW9
off Eagle Dr 42 CS54
Rickmansworth WD3 38 BJ45
Raven Ct, E5
off Stellman Cl 66 DU62
Ravencroft, Grays RM16
off Alexandra Cl 111 GH75
Ravendale Rd, Sun. TW16 135 BT96
Ravenet St, SW11
off Strasburg Rd 101 DH81
Ravenfield, Egh.
(Eng.Grn) TW20 112 AW93
Ravenfield Rd, SW17 120 DF90
Ravenhill Rd, E13 86 EJ68
Ravenna Rd, SW15 119 CX85
Ravenoak Way, Chig. IG7 49 ES50
Ravenor Pk Rd, Grnf. UB6 78 CB69
Raven Rd, E18 48 EJ54
Raven Row, E1 84 DV71
⇌ Ravensbourne 123 ED94
Ravensbourne Av, Beck. BR3 123 ED94
Bromley BR2 123 ED94
Staines TW19 114 BL88
Ravensbourne Cres, Rom.
RM3 72 FM55
Ravensbourne Gdns, W13 79 CH71
Ilford IG5 49 EN53
Ravensbourne Pk, SE6 123 EA87
Ravensbourne Pk Cres, SE6 123 DZ87
Ravensbourne Pl, SE13 103 EB82
Ravensbourne Rd, SE6 123 DZ87
Bromley BR1 144 EG97
Dartford DA1 107 FG83
Twickenham TW1 117 CJ86
Ravensbury Av, Mord. SM4 140 DC99
Ravensbury Ct, Mitch. CR4
off Ravensbury Gro 140 DD98
Ravensbury Gro, Mitch. CR4 140 DD98
Ravensbury La, Mitch. CR4 140 DD98
Ravensbury Path, Mitch. CR4 140 DD98
Ravensbury Rd, SW18 120 DA89
Orpington BR5 145 ET98
Ravensbury Ter, SW18 120 DB89
Ravenscar Rd, Brom. BR1 124 EE91
Surbiton KT6 138 CM103
Ravens Cl, Brom. BR2 144 EF96
Chessington KT9 137 CK100
Enfield EN1 30 DS40
Redhill RH1 184 DF132
Ravenscourt, Sun. TW16 135 BT95
Ravenscourt Av, W6 99 CU77
Ravenscourt Cl, Horn. RM12
off Ravenscourt Dr 72 FL62
Ruislip HA4 59 BQ59
Ravenscourt Dr, Horn. RM12 72 FL62
Ravenscourt Gdns, W6 99 CU77
Ravenscourt Gro, Horn. RM12 72 FL61
⊖ Ravenscourt Park 99 CU77
Ravenscourt Pk, W6 99 CU76
Ravenscourt Pl, W6 99 CV77
Ravenscourt Rd, W6 99 CV77
Orpington BR5 146 EU97
Ravenscourt Sq, W6 99 CU76
Ravenscraig Rd, N11 45 DH49
Ravenscroft, Wat. WD25 8 BY34
Ravenscroft Av, NW11 63 CZ59
Wembley HA9 62 CM60
Ravenscroft Cl, E16 86 EG71
Ravenscroft Cres, SE9 125 EM90
Ravenscroft Pk, Barn. EN5 27 CX42
Ravenscroft Pt, E9
off Kenton Rd 85 DX65
Ravenscroft Rd, E16 86 EG71
W4 98 CQ77
Beckenham BR3 142 DW96
Weybridge KT13 153 BQ111
Ravenscroft St, E2 84 DT68
Ravensdale Av, N12 44 DC49
Ravensdale Gdns, SE19 122 DR94
Hounslow TW4 96 BY83
Ravensdale Ms, Stai. TW18
off Worple Rd 114 BH93
Ravensdale Rd, N16 66 DT59
Hounslow TW4 96 BY83
Ravensdon St, SE11 101 DN78
Ravensfield, Slou. SL3 92 AX75
Ravensfield Cl, Dag. RM9 70 EX63
Ravensfield Gdns, Epsom
KT19 156 CS106
Ravenshaw St, NW6 63 CZ64
Ravenshead Cl, S.Croy. CR2 160 DW111
Ravenshill, Chis. BR7 145 EP95
Ravenshurst Av, NW4 63 CW56
Ravenside Cl, N18 47 DX51
Ravenside Retail Pk, N18 47 DX50
Ravenslea Rd, SW12 120 DF87
Ravensmead, Ger.Cr.
(Chal.St.P.) SL9 37 AZ50
Ravensmead Rd, Brom. BR2 123 ED94
Ravensmede Way, W4 99 CT77
Ravensmere, Epp. CM16 18 EU31
Ravens Ms, SE12
off Ravens Way 124 EG85
Ravenstone, SE17 102 DS78
Ravenstone Rd, N8 65 DN55
NW9 off West Hendon Bdy. 63 CT58
Ravenstone St, SW12 120 DG88
Ravens Way, SE12 124 EG85
Ravenswold, Ken. CR8 176 DQ115
Ravenswood, Bex. DA5 126 EY88
Ravenswood Av, Surb. KT6 138 CM103
West Wickham BR4 143 EC102
Ravenswood Cl, Cob. KT11 170 BX115
Romford RM5 51 FB50
Ravenswood Ct, Kings.T.
KT2 118 CP93
Woking GU22 167 AZ118

★ Place of interest ⇌ Railway station ⊖ London Underground station DLR Docklands Light Railway station Tra Tramlink station H Hospital Riv Pedestrian ferry landing stage

Ravenswood Cres, Har. HA2 60 BZ61
West Wickham BR4 143 EC102
Ravenswood Gdns, Islw. TW7 97 CE81
Ravenswood Pk, Nthwd. HA6 39 BU51
Ravenswood Rd, E17 67 EB56
SW12 121 DH87
Croydon CR0 141 DP104
Ravensworth Rd, NW10 81 CV69
SE9 125 EM91
Ravey St, EC2 197 M4
Ravine Gro, SE18 105 ES79
Rav Pinter Cl, N16 66 DS59
Rawlings Cl, Beck. BR3
off Creswell Dr 143 EB99
Orpington BR6 163 ET106
Rawlings Cres, Wem. HA9 62 CP62
Rawlings St, SW3 198 D8
Rawlins Cl, N3 63 CY55
South Croydon CR2 161 DY108
Rawlyn Cl, Grays RM16
off Hedingham Rd 109 FW78
Rawnsley Av, Mitch. CR4 140 DD99
Rawreth Wk, N1
off Basire St 84 DQ67
Rawson St, SW11
off Strasburg Rd 100 DG81
Rawsthorne Cl, E16
off Kennard St 87 EM74
Rawstone Wk, E13 86 EG68
Rawstorne Pl, EC1 196 F2
Rawstorne St, EC1 196 F2
Rayburn Rd, Horn. RM11 72 FN59
Ray Cl, Chess. KT9
off Merritt Gdns 155 CJ107
Raydean Rd, Barn. EN5 28 DB43
Raydon Rd, Wal.Cr.
(Chsht) EN8 15 DX32
Raydons Gdns, Dag. RM9 70 EY64
Raydons Rd, Dag. RM9 70 EY64
Raydon St, N19 65 DH61
Rayfield, Epp. CM16 18 EU30
Rayfield Cl, Brom. BR2 144 EL100
Rayford Av, SE12 124 EF87
Rayford Cl, Dart. DA1 128 FJ85
Ray Gdns, Bark. IG11 88 EU68
Stanmore HA7 41 CH50
Ray Lamb Way, Erith DA8 107 FH79
Raylands Mead, Ger.Cr. SL9
off Bull La 56 AW57
Rayleas Cl, SE18 105 EP81
Rayleigh Av, Tedd. TW11 117 CE93
Rayleigh Cl, N13
off Rayleigh Rd 46 DR48
Brentwood (Hutt.) CM13 55 GC44
Rayleigh Ct, Kings.T. KT1 138 CM96
Rayleigh Ri, S.Croy. CR2 160 DS107
Rayleigh Rd, E16 86 EH74
N13 46 DQ48
SW19 139 CZ95
Brentwood (Hutt.) CM13 55 GB44
Woodford Green IG8 48 EJ51
Ray Lo Rd, Wdf.Grn. IG8 48 EJ51
Ray Massey Way, E6
off Ron Leighton Way 86 EL67
Raymead, NW4
off Tenterden Gro 63 CW56
Raymead Av, Th.Hth. CR7 141 DN99
Raymead Cl, Lthd.
(Fetch.) KT22 171 CE122
Raymead Pas, Th.Hth. CR7
off Raymead Av 141 DN99
Raymead Way, Lthd.
(Fetch.) KT22 171 CE122
Raymere Gdns, SE18 105 ER80
Raymond Av, E18 68 EF55
W13 97 CG76
Raymond Bldgs, WC1 196 C6
Raymond Cl, SE26 122 DW92
Abbots Langley WD5 7 BR32
Slough (Colnbr.) SL3 93 BE81
Raymond Ct, N10
off Pembroke Rd 44 DG52
Potters Bar EN6
off St. Francis Cl 12 DC34
Sutton SM2
off Mulgrave Rd 158 DB107
Raymond Gdns, Chig. IG7 50 EV48
Raymond Rd, E13 86 EJ66
SW19 119 CY93
Beckenham BR3 143 DY98
Ilford IG2 69 ER59
Slough SL3 93 BA76
Raymond Way, Esher
(Clay.) KT10 155 CG107
Raymouth Rd, SE16 202 E8
Rayne Ct, E18 68 EF56
Rayners Cl, Slou.
(Colnbr.) SL3 93 BC80
Wembley HA0 61 CK64
Rayners Ct, Grav. DA11 130 GB86
Harrow HA2 60 CA60
Rayners Cres, Nthlt. UB5 77 BV69
Rayners Gdns, Nthlt. UB5 77 BV68
RAYNERS LANE, Har. HA2 60 BZ60
⊖ Rayners Lane 60 BZ59
Rayners La, Har. HA2 60 CB61
Pinner HA5 60 BZ58
Rayners Rd, SW15 119 CY85
Rayner Twr, E10 67 EA59
Raynes Av, E11 68 EJ59
RAYNES PARK, SW20 139 CV97
⇌ Raynes Park 139 CW96
Raynham Av, N18 46 DU51
Raynham Rd, N18 46 DU50
W6 99 CV77
Raynham Ter, N18 46 DU50
Raynor Cl, Sthl. UB1 78 BZ74
Raynor Pl, N1
off Elizabeth Av 84 DQ67
Raynton Cl, Har. HA2 60 BY60
Hayes UB4 77 BT70
Raynton Dr, Hayes UB4 77 BT70
Raynton Rd, Enf. EN3 31 DX37
Ray Rd, Rom. RM5 51 FB50
West Molesey KT8 136 CB99
Rays Av, N18 46 DW49
Rays Hill, Dart.
(Hort.Kir.) DA4 148 FQ98
Rays Rd, N18 46 DW49
West Wickham BR4 143 EC101
Ray St, EC1 196 E5
Ray St Br, EC1 196 E5
Ray Wk, N7 off Andover Rd 65 DM61
Raywood Cl, Hayes UB3 95 BQ80
Reachview Cl, NW1
off Baynes St 83 DJ66
Read Cl, T.Ditt. KT7 137 CG101
Read Ct, Wal.Abb. EN9 16 EG33
Readens, The, Bans. SM7 174 DF116
Reade Wk, NW10
off Denbigh Cl 80 CS66
Reading Arch Rd, Red. RH1 184 DF134
Reading La, E8 84 DV65
Reading Rd, Nthlt. UB5 60 CB64
Sutton SM1 158 DC106
Readings, The, Rick.
(Chorl.) WD3 21 BF41
Reading Way, NW7 43 CX50
Read Rd, Ashtd. KT21 171 CK117
Reads Cl, Ilf. IG1
off Chapel Rd 69 EP62
Reads Rest La, Tad. KT20 173 CZ119
Read Way, Grav. DA12 131 GK92
Reapers Cl, NW1
off Crofters Way 83 DK67
Reapers Way, Islw. TW7
off Hall Rd 117 CD85
Reardon Ct, N21
off Cosgrove Cl 46 DQ47
Reardon Path, E1 202 E3
Reardon St, E1 202 D2
Reaston St, SE14 102 DW80
Reckitt Rd, W4 98 CS78
Record St, SE15 102 DW79
Recovery St, SW17 120 DE92
Recreation Av, Rom. RM7 71 FC57
Romford
(Harold Wd) RM3 52 FM54
Recreation Rd, SE26 123 DX91
Bromley BR2 144 EF96
Sidcup DA15
off Woodside Rd 125 ES90
Southall UB2 96 BY77
Recreation Way, Mitch. CR4 141 DK97
Rector St, N1 84 DQ67
Rectory Chase, Brwd.
(Lt.Warley) CM13 73 FX56
Rectory Cl, E4 47 EA48
N3 43 CZ53
SW20 139 CW97
Ashtead KT21 172 CM119
Dartford DA1 107 FE84
Shepperton TW17 134 BN97
Sidcup DA14 126 EV91
Stanmore HA7 41 CH51
Surbiton KT6 137 CJ102
West Byfleet
(Byfleet) KT14 152 BL113
Rectory Cres, E11 68 EJ58
Rectory Fm Rd, Enf. EN2 29 DM38
Rectory Fld Cres, SE7 104 EJ80
Rectory Gdns, N8 65 DL56
SW4 off Fitzwilliam Rd 101 DJ83
Chalfont St. Giles HP8 36 AV48
Northolt UB5 78 BZ67
Upminster RM14 73 FR61
Rectory Grn, Beck. BR3 143 DZ95
Rectory Gro, SW4 101 DJ83
Croydon CR0 141 DP103
Hampton TW12 116 BZ91
Rectory La, SW17 120 DG93
Ashtead KT21 172 CM118
Banstead SM7 158 DF114
Betchworth
(Buckland) RH3 183 CT131
Edgware HA8 42 CN51
Kings Langley WD4 6 BN28
Loughton IG10 33 EN40
Radlett (Shenley) WD7 10 CN33
Rickmansworth WD3 38 BK46
Sevenoaks TN13 191 FJ126
Sidcup DA14 126 EW91
Stanmore HA7 41 CH50
Surbiton KT6 137 CH102
Wallington SM6 159 DJ105
West Byfleet
(Byfleet) KT14 152 BL113
Westerham TN16 178 EL123
Westerham
(Brasted) TN16 180 EW123
Rectory Meadow, Grav.
(Sthflt) DA13 130 GA93
Rectory Orchard, SW19 119 CY91
Rectory Pk, S.Croy. CR2 160 DS113
Rectory Pk Av, Nthlt. UB5 78 BZ69
Rectory Pl, SE18 105 EN77
⇌ Rectory Road 66 DT62
Rectory Rd, E12 69 EM64
E17 67 EB55
N16 66 DT62
SW13 99 CU82
W3 80 CP74
Beckenham BR3 143 EA95
Coulsdon CR5 184 DD125
Dagenham RM10 88 FA66
Grays RM17 110 GD76
Hayes UB3 77 BU72
Hounslow TW4 95 BV81
Keston BR2 162 EK108
Rickmansworth WD3 38 BK46
Southall UB2 96 BZ76
Sutton SM1 140 DA104
Swanscombe DA10 130 FY87
Tilbury (W.Til.) RM18 111 GK79
Rectory Sq, E1 85 DX71
Rectory Way, Uxb. UB10 59 BP62
Reculver Ms, N18
off Lyndhurst Rd 46 DU49
Reculver Rd, SE16 203 H10
Red Anchor Cl, SW3
off Old Ch St 100 DE79
Redan Pl, W2 82 DB72
Redan St, W14 99 CX76
Redan Ter, SE5
off Flaxman Rd 102 DQ82
Redbarn Cl, Pur. CR8
off Whytecliffe Rd S 159 DP111
Red Barracks Rd, SE18 105 EM77
Redberry Gro, SE26 122 DW90
Redbourne Av, N3 44 DA53
Redbourne Dr, SE28 88 EX72
REDBRIDGE, Ilf. IG 69 EM58
⊖ Redbridge 68 EK58
Redbridge Enterprise Cen, Ilf.
IG1 69 EQ61
Redbridge Gdns, SE5 102 DS80
Redbridge La E, Ilf. IG4 68 EK58
Redbridge La W, E11 68 EH58
Redburn St, SW3 100 DF79
Redbury Cl, Rain. RM13
off Deri Av 89 FH70
Redcar Cl, Nthlt. UB5 60 CB64
Redcar Rd, Rom. RM3 52 FM50
Redcar St, SE5 102 DQ80
Redcastle Cl, E1 84 DW73
Red Cedars Rd, Orp. BR6 145 ES101
Redchurch St, E2 197 P4
Redcliffe Cl, SW5
off Warwick Rd 100 DB78
Redcliffe Gdns, SW5 100 DB78
SW10 100 DB78
W4 98 CP80
Ilford IG1 69 EN60
Redcliffe Ms, SW10 100 DB78
Redcliffe Pl, SW10 100 DC79
Redcliffe Rd, SW10 100 DC78
Redcliffe Sq, SW10 100 DB78
Redcliffe St, SW10 100 DB79
Redclose Av, Mord. SM4 140 DA99
Redclyffe Rd, E6 86 EJ67
Red Cottage Ms, Slou. SL3 92 AW76
Red Ct, Slou. SL1 74 AS74
Redcourt, Wok. GU22 167 BD115
Redcroft Rd, Sthl. UB1 78 CC73
Redcross Way, SE1 201 J4
Redden Ct Rd, Rom. RM3 72 FL55
Redding Cl, Dart. DA2 129 FS89
Reddings, The, NW7 43 CT48
Borehamwood WD6 26 CM41
Reddings Av, Bushey WD23 24 CB43
Reddings Cl, NW7 43 CT49
Reddington Cl, S.Croy. CR2 160 DR109
Reddington Dr, Slou. SL3 92 AY76
Reddins Rd, SE15 102 DU79
Reddons Rd, Beck. BR3 123 DY94
Reddown Rd, Couls. CR5 175 DK118
Reddy Rd, Erith DA8 107 FF79
Rede Ct, Wey. KT13
off Old Palace Rd 135 BP104
Redenham Ho, SW15
off Tangley Gro 119 CT87
Rede Pl, W2
off Chepstow Pl 82 DA72
Redesdale Gdns, Islw. TW7 97 CG80
Redesdale St, SW3 100 DF79
Redfern Av, Houns. TW4 116 CA87
Redfern Cl, Uxb. UB8 76 BJ67
Redfern Gdns, Rom. RM2 52 FK54
Redfern Rd, NW10 80 CS66
SE6 123 EC87
Redfield La, SW5 100 DA77
Redfield Ms, SW5
off Redfield La 100 DA77
Redford Av, Couls. CR5 159 DH114
Thornton Heath CR7 141 DM98
Wallington SM6 159 DL107
Redford Cl, Felt. TW13 115 BT89
H Redford Lo Psychiatric Hosp,
N9 46 DU47
Redford Wk, N1
off Britannia Row 83 DP67
Redford Way, Uxb. UB8 76 BJ66
Redgate Dr, Brom. BR2 144 EH103
Redgate Ter, SW15
off Lytton Gro 119 CX86
Redgrave Cl, Croy. CR0 142 DT100
Redgrave Rd, SW15 99 CX83
Redhall Ct, Cat. CR3 176 DR123
Redhall La, Rick. WD3 22 BL39
Redheath Cl, Wat. WD25 23 BT35
REDHILL 184 DG134
⇌ Redhill 184 DG133
Red Hill, Chis. BR7 125 EN92
Uxbridge (Denh.) UB9 57 BD61
Redhill Dr, Edg. HA8 42 CQ54
Redhill Rd, Cob. KT11 153 BP113
Redhill St, NW1 195 J2
Red Ho La, Bexh. DA6 106 EX84
Walton-on-Thames KT12 135 BU103
Redhouse Rd, Croy. CR0 141 DK100
Westerham (Tats.) TN16 178 EJ120
Red Ho Sq, N1
off Ashby Gro 84 DQ65
★ Red Ho, The (William Morris Ho),
Bexh. DA6 106 EY84
Redington Gdns, NW3 64 DB63
Redington Rd, NW3 64 DB63
Redland Gdns, W.Mol. KT8
off Dunstable Rd 136 BZ98
Redlands, Couls. CR5 175 DL116
Redlands Ct, Brom. BR1 124 EF94
Redlands Rd, Enf. EN3 31 DY39
Sevenoaks TN13 190 FF124
Redlands Way, SW2 121 DM87
Red La, Esher (Clay.) KT10 155 CG107
Oxted RH8 188 EH133
Redleaf Cl, Belv. DA17 106 FA79
Red Leaf Cl, Slou. SL3
off Pickford Dr 75 AZ74
Redleaves Av, Ashf. TW15 115 BP93
Redlees Cl, Islw. TW7 97 CG84
Red Leys, Uxb. UB8
off Park Rd 76 BL66
Red Lion Cl, SE17
off Red Lion Row 102 DQ79
Orpington BR5 146 EW100
Red Lion Ct, EC4 196 E8
Red Lion Hill, N2 44 DD54
Red Lion La, SE18 105 EN80
Hemel Hempstead HP3 6 BM26
Rickmansworth
(Sarratt) WD3 22 BG35
Woking (Chobham) GU24 150 AS109
Red Lion Pl, SE18
off Shooter's Hill Rd 105 EN81
Red Lion Rd, Surb. KT6 138 CM103
Woking (Chobham) GU24 150 AS109
Red Lion Row, SE17 102 DQ79
Red Lion Sq, SW18
off Wandsworth High St 120 DA85
Red Lion Sq, WC1 196 B7
Red Lion St, WC1 196 B6
Richmond TW9 117 CK85
Red Lion Yd, W1 198 G2
Watford WD17
off High St 24 BW42
Red Lo Cres, Bex. DA5 127 FD90
Red Lo Rd, Beck. BR3 143 ED100
Bexley DA5 127 FD90
West Wickham BR4 143 EC102
Redman Cl, Nthlt. UB5 78 BW68
Redmans La, Sev.
(Shore.) TN14 165 FE107
Redman's Rd, E1 84 DW71
Redmead La, E1 202 B3
Redmead Rd, Hayes UB3 95 BS77
Redmore Rd, W6 99 CV77
Red Oak Cl, Orp. BR6 145 EP104
Red Oaks Mead, Epp.
(They.B.) CM16 33 ER37
Red Path, E9 85 DZ65
Red Pl, W1 194 F10
Redpoll Way, Erith DA18 106 EX76
Red Post Hill, SE21 122 DR85
SE24 102 DR84
Redriffe Rd, E13 86 EF67
Redriff Est, SE16 203 M6
Redriff Rd, SE16 203 J7
Romford RM7 51 FB54
Red Rd, Borwd. WD6 26 CM41
Brentwood CM14 54 FV49
Redroofs Cl, Beck. BR3 143 EB95
Redruth Cl, N22
off Palmerston Rd 45 DM52
Redruth Gdns, Rom. RM3 52 FM50
Redruth Rd, E9 85 DX67
Romford RM3 52 FM50
Redruth Wk, Rom. RM3 52 FN50
Red Sq, N16 66 DR62
Redstart Cl, E6
off Columbine Av 86 EL71
SE14
off Southerngate Way 103 DY80
Croydon
(New Adgtn) CR0 161 ED110
Redstone Hill, Red. RH1 184 DG134
Redstone Manor, Red. RH1 184 DG134
Redstone Pk, Red. RH1 184 DG134
Redston Rd, N8 65 DK56
REDSTREET, Grav. DA13 130 GB93
Red St, Grav. (Sthflt) DA13 130 GA93
Redvers Rd, N22 45 DN54
Warlingham CR6 176 DW118
Redvers St, N1 197 N2
Redwald Rd, E5 67 DX63
Redway Dr, Twick. TW2 116 CC87
Redwing Cl, S.Croy. CR2 161 DX111
Redwing Gdns, W.Byf. KT14 152 BH112
Redwing Gro, Abb.L. WD5 7 BU31
Redwing Path, SE28 105 ER75
Redwing Rd, Wall. SM6 159 DL108
Redwood, Egh. TW20 133 BE96
Redwood Chase, S.Ock.
RM15 91 FW70
Redwood Cl, E3 85 EA68
N14 off The Vale 45 DK45
SE16 203 L3
Buckhurst Hill IG9
off Beech La 48 EH47
Kenley CR8 160 DQ114
Sidcup DA15 126 EU87
Uxbridge UB10
off The Larches 77 BP68
Watford WD19 40 BW49
Redwood Ct, NW6
off The Avenue 81 CY66
Redwood Est, Houns. TW5 95 BV79
Redwood Gdns, E4 31 EB44
Chigwell IG7 50 EU50
Redwood Ms, SW4
off Hannington Rd 101 DH83
Ashford TW15
off Napier Rd 115 BR94
Redwood Mt, Reig. RH2 184 DA131
Redwood Ri, Borwd. WD6 26 CN37
Redwoods, SW15 119 CU88
Addlestone KT15 152 BG107
Redwood Wk, Surb. KT6 137 CK102
Redwood Way, Barn. EN5 27 CX43
Reece Ms, SW7 100 DD77
Reed Av, Orp. BR6 145 ES104
Reed Cl, E16 86 EG71
SE12 124 EG85
Iver SL0 75 BE72
St. Albans (Lon.Col.) AL2 9 CK27
Reede Gdns, Dag. RM10 71 FB64
Reede Rd, Dag. RM10 88 FA65
Reede Way, Dag. RM10 89 FB65
⇌ Reedham 159 DM113
Reedham Cl, N17 66 DV56
St. Albans (Brick.Wd) AL2 8 CA29
Reedham Dr, Pur. CR8 159 DN113
Reedham Pk Av, Pur. CR8 175 DN116
Reedham St, SE15 102 DU82
Reedholm Vil, N16
off Winston Rd 66 DR63
Reed Pl, Shep. TW17 134 BM102
West Byfleet KT14 151 BE113
Reed Pond Wk, Rom. RM2 51 FF54
Reed Rd, N17 46 DT54
Reeds Cres, Wat. WD24 24 BW40
Reedsfield Cl, Ashf. TW15
off The Yews 115 BP91
Reedsfield Rd, Ashf. TW15 115 BP91
Reeds Pl, NW1
off Royal Coll St 83 DJ66
Reeds Wk, Wat. WD24 24 BW40
Reedworth St, SE11 200 E9
Ree La Cotts, Loug. IG10
off Englands La 33 EN40
Reenglass Rd, Stan. HA7 41 CK49
Rees Dr, Stan. HA7 42 CL49
Rees Gdns, Croy. CR0 142 DT100
Reesland Cl, E12 87 EN65
Rees St, N1 84 DQ67
Reets Fm Cl, NW9 62 CS58
Reeves Av, NW9 62 CR59
Tra Reeves Corner 141 DP103
Reeves Cor, Croy. CR0
off Roman Way 141 DP103
Reeves Cres, Swan. BR8 147 FD97
Reeves Ms, W1 198 F1
Reeves Rd, E3 85 EB70
SE18 105 EP79
Reflection, The, E16
off Woolwich Manor Way 105 EP75
Reform Row, N17 46 DT54
Reform St, SW11 100 DF82
Regal Cl, E1
off Old Montague St 84 DU71
W5 79 CK71
Regal Ct, N18
off College Cl 46 DT50
Regal Cres, Wall. SM6 141 DH104
Regal Dr, N11 45 DH50
Regal La, NW1
off Regents Pk Rd 82 DG67
Regal Pl, E3
off Coborn St 85 DZ69
SW6 off Maxwell Rd 100 DB80
Regal Row, SE15
off Astbury Rd 102 DW81
Regal Way, Har. HA3 62 CL58
Watford WD24 24 BW38
Regan Way, N1 197 M1
Regarder Rd, Chig. IG7 50 EU50
Regarth Av, Rom. RM1 71 FE58
Regatta Ho, Tedd. TW11
off Twickenham Rd 117 CG91
Regency Cl, W5 80 CL72
Chigwell IG7 49 EQ50
Hampton TW12 116 BZ92
Regency Ct, Brwd. CM14 54 FW47
Sutton SM1
off Brunswick Rd 158 DB105
Regency Cres, NW4 43 CX54
Regency Dr, Ruis. HA4 59 BS60
West Byfleet KT14 151 BF113
Regency Gdns, Horn. RM11 72 FJ59
Walton-on-Thames KT12 136 BW102
Regency Ho, SW6
off The Boulevard 100 DC81
Regency Lo, Buck.H. IG9 48 EK47
Regency Ms, NW10
off High Rd 81 CU65
SW9 off Lothian Rd 101 DP80
Beckenham BR3 143 EC95
Isleworth TW7
off Queensbridge Pk 117 CE85
Regency Pl, SW1 199 N8
Regency St, SW1 199 M8
Regency Ter, SW7
off Fulham Rd 100 DD78
Regency Wk, Croy. CR0 143 DY100
Richmond TW10
off Grosvenor Rd 118 CL85
Regency Way, Bexh. DA6 106 EX83
Woking GU22 167 BD115
Regent Av, Uxb. UB10 77 BP66
Regent Cl, N12
off Nether St 44 DC50
Addlestone
(New Haw) KT15 152 BK109
Grays RM16 110 GC75
Harrow HA3 62 CL58
Hounslow TW4 95 BV81
Redhill RH1 185 DJ129
Regent Ct, Slou. SL1
off Stoke Poges La 74 AS72
Regent Cres, Red. RH1 184 DF132
Regent Gdns, Ilf. IG3 70 EU58
Regent Gate, Wal.Cr. EN8 15 DY34
Regent Pk, Lthd. KT22 171 CG118
Regent Pl, SW19
off Haydons Rd 120 DB92
W1 195 L10
Croydon CR0
off Grant Rd 142 DT102
Regent Rd, SE24 121 DP86
Epping CM16 17 ET30
Surbiton KT5 138 CM99
Regents Av, N13 45 DM50
Regents Br Gdns, SW8 101 DL80
Regents Cl, Hayes UB4
off Park Rd 77 BS71
Radlett WD7 9 CG34
South Croydon CR2 160 DS107
Whyteleafe CR3 176 DS118
Regents Dr, Kes. BR2 162 EK106
Woodford Green IG8 49 EN52
Regents Ms, NW8
off Langford Pl 82 DC68
REGENT'S PARK, NW1 194 G1
★ Regent's Park, NW1 194 D1
⊖ Regent's Park 195 H5
Regent's Pk Est, NW1 195 K3
Regents Pk Rd, N3 63 CZ55
NW1 82 DF67
Regents Pk Ter, NW1
off Oval Rd 83 DH67
Regent's Pl, SE3 104 EG82
Regents Pl, Loug. IG10 48 EK45
Regent Sq, E3 85 EB69
WC1 196 A3
Belvedere DA17 107 FB77
Regents Row, E8 84 DU67
Regent St, NW10
off Wellington Rd 81 CX69
SW1 199 M1
W1 195 J8
W4 98 CN78
Watford WD24 23 BV38
Regents Wf, N1
off All Saints St 83 DM68
Regina Cl, Barn. EN5 27 CX41
Reginald Rd, E7 86 EG66
SE8 103 EA80
Northwood HA6 39 BT53
Romford RM3 52 FN53
Reginald Sq, SE8 103 EA80
Regina Pt, SE16 202 G6
Regina Rd, N4 65 DM60
SE25 142 DU97
W13 79 CG74
Southall UB2 96 BY77

★ Place of interest ⇌ Railway station ⊖ London Underground station DLR Docklands Light Railway station Tra Tramlink station H Hospital Riv Pedestrian ferry landing stage

Regina Ter, W13 . . . . **79** CG74
Regis PI, SW2 . . . . **101** DM84
Regis Rd, NW5 . . . . **65** DH64
Regnart Bldgs, NW1 . . . . **195** L4
Reid Av, Cat. CR3 . . . . **176** DR121
Reid CI, Couls. CR5 . . . . **175** DH116
   Pinner HA5 . . . . **59** BU56
Reidhaven Rd, SE18 . . . . **105** ES77
REIGATE **184** DA134
   ⇌ Reigate **184** DA133
Reigate Av, Sutt. SM1 . . . . . . **140** DA102
Reigate Business Ms, Reig. RH2
   off Albert Rd N. **183** CZ133
Reigate Hill, Reig. RH2 . . . . . **184** DB130
Reigate Hill CI, Reig. RH2 . . . . **184** DA131
Reigate Rd, Bet. RH3 . . . . **182** CS132
   Bromley BR1 . . . . **124** EF90
   Epsom KT17, KT18 . . . . . . **157** CT110
   Ilford IG3 . . . . **69** ET61
   Leatherhead KT22 . . . . . . **171** CJ123
   Redhill RH1 . . . . **184** DB134
   Reigate RH2 . . . . **184** DB134
   Tadworth KT20 . . . . **173** CX117
Reigate Way, Wall. SM6 . . . . . **159** DL106
Reighton Rd, E5 . . . . **66** DU62
Reinickendorf Av, SE9 . . . . . . **125** EQ85
Reizel CI, N16 . . . . **66** DT60
Relay Rd, W12 . . . . **81** CW73
Relf Rd, SE15 . . . . **102** DU83
Reliance Sq, EC2 . . . . **197** N4
Relko Ct, Epsom KT19 . . . . . . **156** CR110
Relko Gdns, Sutt. SM1 . . . . . . **158** DD106
Relton Ms, SW7 . . . . **198** C6
Rembrandt CI, E14 . . . . **204** F7
   SW1 . . . . **198** F9
Rembrandt Ct, Epsom KT19 . . **157** CT107
Rembrandt Dr, Grav.
   (Nthflt) DA11 . . . . **130** GD90
Rembrandt Rd, SE13 . . . . **104** EE84
   Edgware HA8 . . . . **42** CN54
Rembrandt Way, Walt. KT12 . . **135** BV104
Remington Rd, E6 . . . . **86** EL72
   N15 . . . . **66** DR58
Remington St, N1 . . . . **196** G1
Remnant St, WC2 . . . . **196** B8
Remus Rd, E3
   off Monier Rd **85** EA66
Renaissance Wk, SE10 . . . . . . **205** L6
Rendle CI, Croy. CR0 . . . . **142** DT99
Rendlesham Av, Rad. WD7 . . . **25** CF37
Rendlesham Rd, E5 . . . . **66** DU63
   Enfield EN2 . . . . **29** DP39
Rendlesham Way, Rick.
   (Chorl.) WD3 . . . . **21** BC44
Renforth St, SE16 . . . . **202** G5
Renfree Way, Shep. TW17 . . . . **134** BM101
Renfrew CI, E6 . . . . **87** EN73
Renfrew Rd, SE11 . . . . **200** F8
   Hounslow TW4 . . . . **96** BX82
   Kingston upon Thames KT2 . **118** CP94
Renmans, The, Ashtd. KT21 . . **172** CM116
Renmuir St, SW17 . . . . **120** DF93
Rennell St, SE13 . . . . **103** EC83
Rennels Way, Islw. TW7
   off St. John's Rd **97** CE82
Renness Rd, E17 . . . . **67** DY55
Rennets CI, SE9 . . . . **125** ES85
Rennets Wd Rd, SE9 . . . . **125** ER85
Rennie CI, Ashf. TW15 . . . . . . **114** BK90
Rennie Est, SE16 . . . . **202** E9
Rennie St, SE1 . . . . **200** F2
Rennison CI, Wal.Cr. EN7
   off Allwood Rd **14** DT27
Renovation, The, E16
   off Woolwich Manor Way . . **105** EP75
Renown CI, Croy. CR0 . . . . **141** DP102
   Romford RM7 . . . . **50** FA53
Rensburg Rd, E17 . . . . **67** DX57
Renshaw CI, Belv. DA17
   off Grove Rd **106** EZ79
Renters Av, NW4 . . . . **63** CW58
Renton CI, Orp. BR5 . . . . **146** EX101
Renwick Ind Est, Bark. IG11 . . **88** EV67
Renwick Rd, Bark. IG11 . . . . . **88** EV70
Repens Way, Hayes UB4
   off Stipularis Dr **78** BX70
Rephidim St, SE1 . . . . **201** M7
Replingham Rd, SW18 . . . . . . **119** CZ88
Reporton Rd, SW6 . . . . **99** CY81
Repository Rd, SE18 . . . . **105** EM79
Repton Av, Hayes UB3 . . . . . . **95** BR77
   Romford RM2 . . . . **71** FG55
   Wembley HA0 . . . . **61** CJ63
Repton CI, Cars. SM5 . . . . **158** DE106
Repton Ct, Beck. BR3 . . . . **143** EB95
   Ilford IG5 off Repton Gro . . **49** EM53
Repton Dr, Rom. RM2 . . . . **71** FG56
Repton Gdns, Rom. RM2 . . . . . **71** FG55
Repton Gro, Ilf. IG5 . . . . **49** EM53
Repton PI, Amer. HP7 . . . . **20** AU39
Repton Rd, Har. HA3 . . . . **62** CM56
   Orpington BR6 . . . . **146** EU104
Repton St, E14 . . . . **85** DY72
Repton Way, Rick.
   (Crox.Grn) WD3 . . . . **22** BN43
Repulse CI, Rom. RM5 . . . . . . **51** FB53
Reservoir CI, Green. DA9
   off Knockhall Rd **129** FW86
   Thornton Heath CR7 . . . . . **142** DR98
Reservoir Rd, N14 . . . . **29** DJ43
   SE4 . . . . **103** DY82
   Ruislip HA4 . . . . **59** BQ57
Resham CI, Sthl. UB2
   off Scotts Rd **96** BW76
Resolution Wk, SE18 . . . . **105** EM76
Resolution Way, SE8
   off Deptford High St **103** EA80
Restavon Pk, West.
   (Berry's Grn) TN16 . . . . . . **179** EP116
Restell CI, SE3 . . . . **104** EE79
Restmor Way, Wall. SM6 . . . . . **140** DG103
Reston CI, Borwd. WD6 . . . . . . **26** CN38
Reston Path, Borwd. WD6 . . . . **26** CN38
Reston PI, SW7
   off Hyde Pk Gate **100** DC75

Restons Cres, SE9 . . . . **125** ER86
Restormel CI, Houns. TW3 . . . . **116** CA85
Retcar CI, N19
   off Dartmouth Pk Hill **65** DH61
Retcar PI, N19 . . . . **65** DH61
Retford CI, Borwd. WD6
   off The Campions **26** CN38
   Romford RM3 . . . . **52** FN51
Retford Rd, Rom. RM3 . . . . . . **52** FM51
Retford St, N1 . . . . **197** N1
Retingham Way, E4 . . . . **47** EB48
Retreat, The, NW9 . . . . **62** CR57
   SW14
   off South Worple Way **98** CS83
   Addlestone KT15 . . . . **152** BK106
   Amersham HP6 . . . . **20** AY39
   Brentwood CM14
   off Costead Manor Rd. . . . **54** FV46
   Brentwood (Hutt.) CM13 . . **55** GB44
   Egham TW20 . . . . **112** AX92
   Grays RM17 . . . . **110** GB79
   Harrow HA2 . . . . **60** CA59
   Kings Langley WD4 . . . . . . **7** BQ31
   Orpington BR6 . . . . **164** EV107
   Surbiton KT5 . . . . **138** CM100
   Thornton Heath CR7 . . . . . **142** DR98
   Worcester Park KT4 . . . . . . **139** CV103
Retreat CI, Har. HA3 . . . . **61** CJ57
Retreat PI, E9 . . . . **84** DW65
Retreat Rd, Rich. TW9 . . . . . . **117** CK85
Retreat Way, Chig. IG7 . . . . . . **50** EV48
Reubens Rd, Brwd.
   (Hutt.) CM13 . . . . **55** GB44
Reunion Row, E1 . . . . **202** E1
Reveley Sq, SE16 . . . . **203** L5
Revell CI, Lthd.
   (Fetch.) KT22 . . . . **170** CB122
Revell Dr, Lthd. (Fetch.) KT22 . **170** CB122
Revell Ri, SE18 . . . . **105** ET79
Revell Rd, Kings.T. KT1 . . . . . . **138** CP95
   Sutton SM1 . . . . **157** CZ107
Revelon Rd, SE4 . . . . **103** DY84
Revelstoke Rd, SW18 . . . . **119** CZ89
Reventlow Rd, SE9 . . . . **125** EQ88
Reverdy Rd, SE1 . . . . **202** B9
Reverend CI, Har. HA2 . . . . . . **60** CB62
Revesby Rd, Cars. SM5 . . . . . . **140** DD100
Review Rd, NW2 . . . . **63** CT61
   Dagenham RM10 . . . . **89** FB67
Rewell St, SW6 . . . . **100** DC80
Rewley Rd, Cars. SM5 . . . . **140** DD100
Rex Av, Ashf. TW15 . . . . **114** BN93
Rex CI, Rom. RM5 . . . . **51** FB52
Rex PI, W1 . . . . **198** G1
Reydon Av, E11 . . . . **68** EJ58
Reynard CI, SE4
   off Foxwell St **103** DY83
   Bromley BR1 . . . . **145** EM97
Reynard Dr, SE19 . . . . **122** DT94
Reynard PI, SE14
   off Milton Ct Rd **103** DY79
Reynardson Rd, N17 . . . . **46** DQ52
Reynolah Gdns, SE7
   off Rathmore Rd **104** EH78
Reynolds Av, E12 . . . . **69** EN64
   Chessington KT9 . . . . **156** CL108
   Romford RM6 . . . . **70** EW59
Reynolds CI, NW11 . . . . **64** DB59
   SW19 . . . . **140** DD95
   Carshalton SM5 . . . . **140** DF102
Reynolds Ct, E11
   off Cobbold Rd. **68** EF62
   Romford RM6 . . . . **70** EX55
Reynolds Dr, Edg. HA8 . . . . . . **62** CM55
Reynolds PI, SE3 . . . . **104** EH80
   Richmond TW10
   off Cambrian Rd **118** CM86
Reynolds Rd, SE15 . . . . **122** DW85
   W4 . . . . **98** CQ76
   Hayes UB4 . . . . **78** BW70
   New Malden KT3 . . . . **138** CR101
Reynolds Way, Croy. CR0 . . . . **160** DS105
Rheidol Ms, N1
   off Rheidol Ter **84** DQ68
Rheidol Ter, N1 . . . . **83** DP68
Rheingold Way, Wall. SM6 . . . **159** DL109
Rheola CI, N17 . . . . **46** DT53
Rhoda St, E2 off Brick La **84** DT70
Rhodes Av, N22 . . . . **45** DJ53
Rhodes CI, Egh. TW20
   off Mullens Rd **113** BC92
Rhodesia Rd, E11 . . . . **67** ED61
   SW9 . . . . **101** DL82
Rhodes Moorhouse Ct, Mord.
   SM4 . . . . **140** DA100
Rhodes St, N7
   off Mackenzie Rd **65** DM64
Rhodes Way, Wat. WD24 . . . . . **24** BX40
Rhodeswell Rd, E14 . . . . **85** DY71
Rhododendron Ride, Egh.
   TW20 . . . . **112** AT94
   Slough SL3 . . . . **75** AZ69
Rhodrons Av, Chess. KT9 . . . . **156** CL106
Rhondda Gro, E3 . . . . **85** DY69
Rhyl Rd, Grnf. UB6 . . . . **79** CF68
Rhyl St, NW5 . . . . **82** DG65
Rhys Av, N11 . . . . **45** DK52
Rialto Rd, Mitch. CR4 . . . . **140** DG96
Ribble CI, Wdf.Grn. IG8
   off Prospect Rd **48** EJ51
Ribbledale, St.Alb.
   (Lon.Col.) AL2 . . . . **10** CM27
Ribblesdale Av, N11 . . . . **44** DG51
   Northolt UB5 . . . . **78** CB65
Ribblesdale Rd, N8 . . . . **65** DM56
   SW16 . . . . **121** DH93
   Dartford DA2 . . . . **128** FQ88
Ribbon Dance Ms, SE5
   off Camberwell Gro. **102** DR81
Ribchester Av, Grnf. UB6 . . . . **79** CF69
Ribston CI, Brom. BR2 . . . . . . **145** EM102
   Radlett (Shenley) WD7
   off Wayside. **9** CK33
Ricardo Path, SE28
   off Byron CI **88** EW74
Ricardo Rd, Wind.
   (Old Wind.) SL4 . . . . **112** AV86

Ricardo St, E14 . . . . **85** EB72
Ricards Rd, SW19 . . . . **119** CZ92
Ricardo St, SE18 . . . . **104** EL77
Richard Fell Ho, E12
   off Walton Rd **69** EN63
Richard Foster CI, E17 . . . . . . **67** DZ59
Richard Ho Dr, E16 . . . . **86** EK72
Richards CI, Bushey WD23 . . . **41** CD45
   Harrow HA1 . . . . **61** CG57
   Hayes UB3 . . . . **95** BR79
   Uxbridge UB10 . . . . **76** BN67
Richardson CI, E8
   off Clarissa St. **84** DT67
   Greenhithe DA9
   St. Albans (Lon.Col.) AL2 . . **10** CL27
Richardson Cres, Wal.Cr.
   (Chsht) EN7 . . . . **13** DP25
Richardson Rd, E15 . . . . **86** EE68
Richardson's Ms, W1 . . . . **195** K5
Richards PI, E17 . . . . **67** EA55
   SW3 . . . . **198** C8
Richards Rd, Cob.
   (Stoke D'Ab.) KT11 . . . . . **154** CB114
Richard St, E1
   off Commercial Rd **84** DV72
Richbell CI, Ashtd. KT21 . . . . . **171** CK118
Richbell PI, WC1 . . . . **196** B6
Richborne Ter, SW8 . . . . **101** DM80
Richborough CI, Orp. BR5 . . . . **146** EX98
Richborough Rd, NW2 . . . . . . **63** CX63
Richens CI, Houns. TW3 . . . . . **97** CD82
Riches Rd, Ilf. IG1 . . . . **69** EQ61
Richfield Rd, Bushey WD23 . . . **40** CC45
Richford Rd, E15 . . . . **86** EF67
Richford St, W6 . . . . **99** CW75
RICHINGS PARK, Iver SL0 . . . . **93** BE75
Richings Way, Iver SL0 . . . . . . **93** BF76
Richlands Av, Epsom KT17 . . . **157** CU105
Rich La, SW5
   off Warwick Rd **100** DB78
Richmead Gdns, Erith DA8 . . . **107** FG80
RICHMOND **118** CL86
   ⇌ Richmond **98** CL84
   ⊖ Richmond **98** CL84
Richmond Av, E4 . . . . **47** ED50
   N1 . . . . **83** DM67
   NW10 . . . . **81** CW65
   SW20 . . . . **139** CY95
   Feltham TW14 . . . . **115** BS86
   Uxbridge UB10 . . . . **77** BP65
Richmond Br, Rich. TW9 . . . . . **117** CK86
   Twickenham TW1 . . . . **117** CK86
Richmond Bldgs, W1 . . . . **195** M9
Richmond CI, E17 . . . . **67** DZ58
   Amersham HP6 . . . . **20** AT38
   Borehamwood WD6 . . . . . **26** CR43
   Epsom KT18 . . . . **156** CS114
   Leatherhead
   (Fetch.) KT22 . . . . **170** CC124
   Waltham Cross
   (Chsht) EN8 . . . . **14** DW29
   Westerham
   (Bigg.H.) TN16 . . . . **178** EH119
Richmond Ct, Pot.B. EN6 . . . . **12** DC31
Richmond Cres, E4 . . . . **47** ED50
   N1 . . . . **83** DM67
   N9 . . . . **46** DU46
   Slough SL1 . . . . **74** AU74
   Staines TW18 . . . . **113** BF92
Richmond Dr, Grav. DA12 . . . . **131** GL89
   Shepperton TW17 . . . . **135** BQ100
   Watford WD17 . . . . **23** BS39
   Woodford Green IG8 . . . . . **49** EN52
Richmond Gdns, NW4 . . . . . . **63** CU57
   Harrow HA3 . . . . **41** CF51
Richmond Grn, Croy. CR0 . . . . **141** DL104
Richmond Gro, N1 . . . . **83** DP66
   Surbiton KT5 . . . . **138** CM100
Richmond Hill, Rich. TW10 . . . **118** CL86
Richmond Hill Ct, Rich. TW10 . **118** CL86
Richmond Ms, W1 . . . . **195** M9
   Teddington TW11
   off Broad St **117** CF93
★ Richmond Palace (remains),
   Rich. TW9 . . . . **117** CJ85
★ Richmond Park, Rich. TW10 **118** CN88
Richmond Pk, Kings.T. KT2 . . . **118** CN88
   Loughton IG10
   off Fallow Flds **48** EJ45
   Richmond TW10 . . . . **118** CN88
Richmond Pk Rd, SW14 . . . . . **118** CQ85
   Kingston upon Thames KT2 . **118** CL94
Richmond PI, SE18 . . . . **105** EQ77
Richmond Rd, E4 . . . . **47** ED46
   E7 . . . . **68** EH64
   E8 . . . . **84** DT66
   E11 . . . . **67** ED61
   N2 . . . . **44** DC54
   N11 . . . . **45** DL51
   N15 . . . . **66** DS58
   SW20 . . . . **139** CV95
   W5 . . . . **98** CL75
   Barnet EN5 . . . . **28** DB43
   Coulsdon CR5 . . . . **175** DH115
   Croydon CR0 . . . . **141** DL104
   Grays RM17 . . . . **110** GC79
   Ilford IG1 . . . . **69** EQ62
   Isleworth TW7 . . . . **97** CG83
   Kingston upon Thames KT2 . **117** CK92
   Potters Bar EN6 . . . . **12** DC31
   Romford RM1 . . . . **71** FF58
   Staines TW18 . . . . **113** BF92
   Thornton Heath CR7 . . . . . **141** DP97
   Twickenham TW1 . . . . **117** CJ86
Richmond St, E13 . . . . **86** EG68
Richmond Ter, SW1 . . . . **199** P4
Richmond Ter Ms, SW1 . . . . . **199** P4
Richmond Way, E11 . . . . **68** EG61
   W12 . . . . **99** CX75
   W14 . . . . **99** CX76
   Leatherhead (Fetch.) KT22 . **170** CB123
   Rickmansworth
   (Crox.Grn) WD3 . . . . **23** BQ42
Richmount Gdns, SE3 . . . . . . **104** EG83
Rich St, E14 . . . . **85** DZ73

Rickard CI, NW4 . . . . **63** CV56
   SW2 . . . . **121** DM88
   West Drayton UB7 . . . . . . **94** BK76
Rickards CI, Surb. KT6 . . . . . . **138** CL102
Ricketts Hill Rd, West.
   (Tats.) TN16 . . . . **178** EK118
Rickett St, SW6 . . . . **100** DA79
Rickman Cres, Add. KT15 . . . . **134** BH104
Rickman Hill, Couls. CR5 . . . . **175** DH118
Rickman Hill Rd, Couls. CR5 . . **175** DH118
Rickmans La, Slou.
   (Stoke P.) SL2 . . . . **56** AS64
Rickman St, E1 . . . . **84** DW69
RICKMANSWORTH **38** BL45
   ⇌ Rickmansworth **38** BK45
   ⊖ Rickmansworth **38** BK45
Rickmansworth La, Ger.Cr.
   (Chal.St.P.) SL9 . . . . **37** AZ50
Rickmansworth Pk, Rick.
   WD3 . . . . **38** BK45
Rickmansworth Rd, Nthwd.
   HA6 . . . . **39** BR52
   Pinner HA5 . . . . **39** BV54
   Rickmansworth
   (Chorl.) WD3 . . . . **21** BE41
   Uxbridge (Hare.) UB9 . . . . **38** BJ53
   Watford WD17, WD18 . . . . **23** BS42
Rick Roberts Way, E15 . . . . . . **85** EC67
Rickthorne Rd, N19
   off Landseer Rd **65** DL61
Rickyard Path, SE9 . . . . **104** EL84
Ridding La, Grnf. UB6 . . . . **61** CF64
Riddings, The, Cat. CR3 . . . . . **186** DT125
   ⇌ Riddlesdown **160** DR113
Riddlesdown Av, Pur. CR8 . . . . **160** DQ112
Riddlesdown Rd, Pur. CR8 . . . **160** DQ111
Riddons Rd, SE12 . . . . **124** EJ90
Ride, The, Brent. TW8 . . . . **97** CH78
   Enfield EN3 . . . . **30** DW41
Rideout St, SE18 . . . . **105** EM77
Rider CI, Sid. DA15 . . . . **125** ES86
Riders Way, Gdse. RH9 . . . . . **186** DW131
Ridgdale St, E3 . . . . **85** EB68
RIDGE, Pot.B. EN6 . . . . **10** CS34
Ridge, The, Bex. DA5 . . . . **126** EZ87
   Caterham (Wold.) CR3 . . . **187** EB126
   Coulsdon CR5 . . . . **159** DL114
   Epsom KT18 . . . . **172** CP117
   Leatherhead (Fetch.) KT22 . **171** CD124
   Orpington BR6 . . . . **145** ER103
   Purley CR8 . . . . **159** DJ110
   Surbiton KT5 . . . . **138** CN99
   Twickenham TW2 . . . . **117** CD87
   Woking GU22 . . . . **167** BB117
Ridge Av, N21 . . . . **46** DQ45
   Dartford DA1 . . . . **127** FF86
Ridgebrook Rd, SE3 . . . . **104** EJ84
Ridge CI, NW4 . . . . **43** CX54
   NW9 . . . . **62** CR56
   SE28 . . . . **105** ER75
   Woking GU22 . . . . **166** AV121
Ridge Crest, Enf. EN2 . . . . **29** DM39
Ridgecroft CI, Bex. DA5 . . . . . **127** FC88
Ridgefield, Wat. WD17 . . . . . . **23** BS37
Ridgegate CI, Reig. RH2 . . . . . **184** DD132
RIDGEHILL, Rad. WD7 . . . . . . **10** CQ30
Ridge Hill, NW11 . . . . **63** CY60
Ridgehurst Av, Wat. WD25 . . . **7** BT34
Ridgelands, Lthd.
   (Fetch.) KT22 . . . . **171** CD124
Ridge La, Wat. WD17 . . . . **23** SB38
Ridge Langley, S.Croy. CR2 . . . **160** DU109
Ridgemead Rd, Egh.
   (Eng.Grn) TW20 . . . . **112** AU90
Ridgemont Gdns, Edg. HA8 . . . **42** CQ49
Ridgemount, Wey. KT13
   off Oatlands Dr **135** BS103
Ridgemount Av, Couls. CR5 . . **175** DH117
   Croydon CR0 . . . . **143** DX102
Ridgemount CI, SE20
   off Anerley Pk. **122** DV94
Ridgemount End, Ger.Cr.
   (Chal.St.P.) SL9 . . . . **36** AY50
Ridgemount Gdns, Enf. EN2 . . **29** DP40
Ridge Pk, Pur. CR8 . . . . **159** DK110
Ridge Rd, N8 . . . . **65** DM58
   N21 . . . . **46** DQ46
   NW2 . . . . **63** CZ62
   Mitcham CR4 . . . . **121** DH94
   Sutton SM3 . . . . **139** CY102
Ridge St, Wat. WD24 . . . . **23** BV38
Ridgeview CI, Barn. EN5 . . . . . **27** CX44
Ridgeview Lo, St.Alb.
   (Lon.Col.) AL2 . . . . **10** CM28
Ridgeview Rd, N20 . . . . **44** DB48
Ridge Way, SE19
   off Central Hill **122** DS93
Ridgeway, SE28
   off Pettman Cres **105** ER77
   Brentwood (Hutt.) CM13 . . **55** GB46
   Bromley BR2 . . . . **144** EG103
Ridge Way, Dart. (Cray.) DA1 . **127** FF86
Ridgeway, Dart.
   (Lane End) DA2 . . . . **129** FS92
   Epsom KT19 . . . . **156** CQ112
Ridge Way, Felt. TW13 . . . . . . **116** BY90
Ridgeway, Grays RM17 . . . . . . **110** GE77
Ridge Way, Iver SL0 . . . . **75** BE74
Ridgeway, Rick. WD3 . . . . **38** BH45
   Virginia Water GU25 . . . . . **132** AY99
   Woking (Horsell) GU21 . . . **166** AX115
   Woodford Green IG8 . . . . . **48** EJ49
Ridgeway, The, E4 . . . . **47** EB47
   N3 . . . . **44** DB52
   N11 . . . . **44** DF49
   N14 . . . . **45** DL47
   NW7 . . . . **43** CU49
   NW9 . . . . **62** CS56
   NW11 . . . . **63** CY60
   W3 . . . . **98** CN76
   Croydon CR0 . . . . **141** DM104
   Enfield EN2 . . . . **29** DN39
   Gerrards Cross
   (Chal.St.P.) SL9 . . . . **56** AY55
   Harrow (Kenton) HA3 . . . . **61** CJ58
   Harrow (N.Har.) HA2 . . . . . **60** CA58
   Leatherhead (Fetch.) KT22 . **171** CD123
   Leatherhead
   (Oxshott) KT22 . . . . **154** CC114

Ridgeway, The,
   Potters Bar EN6 . . . . **12** DD34
   Potters Bar (Cuffley) EN6 . . **12** DE28
   Radlett WD7 . . . . **25** CF37
   Romford (Gidea Pk) RM2 . . **71** FG56
   Romford (Harold Wd) RM3 . **52** FL53
   Ruislip HA4 . . . . **59** BU59
   South Croydon CR2 . . . . . **160** DS110
   Stanmore HA7 . . . . **41** CJ51
   Walton-on-Thames KT12 . . **135** BT102
   Watford WD17 . . . . **23** BS37
Ridgeway Av, Barn. EN4 . . . . . **28** DF44
   Gravesend DA12 . . . . **131** GH90
Ridgeway CI, Lthd.
   (Oxshott) KT22 . . . . **154** CC114
   Woking GU21 . . . . **166** AX116
Ridgeway Cres, Orp. BR6 . . . . **145** ES104
Ridgeway Cres Gdns, Orp.
   BR6 . . . . **145** ES103
Ridgeway Dr, Brom. BR1 . . . . . **124** EH91
Ridgeway E, Sid. DA15 . . . . . . **125** CT85
Ridgeway Est, The, Iver SL0 . . **75** BF74
Ridgeway Gdns, N6 . . . . **65** DJ59
   Ilford IG4 . . . . **68** EL57
   Woking GU21 . . . . **166** AX115
Ridgeway Rd, SW9 . . . . **101** DP83
   Isleworth TW7 . . . . **97** CE80
   Redhill RH1 . . . . **184** DE134
Ridgeway Rd N, Islw. TW7 . . . **97** CE79
Ridgeway Wk, Nthlt. UB5
   off Fortunes Mead **78** BY65
Ridgeway W, Sid. DA15 . . . . . . **125** ES84
Ridgewell CI, N1 off Basire St . **84** DQ67
   SE26 . . . . **123** DZ91
   Dagenham RM10 . . . . **89** FB67
Ridgewell Gro, Horn. RM12
   off Airfield Way **89** FH65
Ridgmount Gdns, WC1 . . . . . . **195** M5
Ridgmount PI, WC1 . . . . **195** M6
Ridgmount Rd, SW18 . . . . **120** DB85
Ridgmount St, WC1 . . . . **195** M6
Ridgway, SW19 . . . . **119** CX93
   Woking (Pyrford) GU22 . . . **167** BF115
Ridgway, The, Sutt. SM2 . . . . . **158** DD108
Ridgway Gdns, SW19 . . . . **119** CX94
Ridgway PI, SW19 . . . . **119** CY93
Ridgway Rd,
   (Pyrford) GU22 . . . . **167** BF115
Riding, The, NW11
   off Golders Grn Rd **63** CZ59
   Woking GU21 . . . . **151** BB114
Riding Ct Rd, Slou.
   (Datchet) SL3 . . . . **92** AW80
Riding Hill, S.Croy. CR2 . . . . . **160** DU113
Riding Ho St, W1 . . . . **195** K7
Ridings, The, E11
   off Malcolm Way **68** EG57
   W5 . . . . **80** CM70
   Addlestone KT15 . . . . **151** BF107
   Ashtead KT21 . . . . **171** CK117
   Chesham HP5 . . . . **20** AX36
   Chigwell IG7
   off Manford Way **50** EV49
   Cobham KT11 . . . . **154** CA112
   Epsom KT18 . . . . **172** CS115
   Epsom (Ewell) KT17 . . . . . **157** CT109
   Iver SL0 . . . . **93** BF77
   Reigate RH2 . . . . **184** DD131
   Sunbury-on-Thames TW16 . **135** BU95
   Surbiton KT5 . . . . **138** CN99
   Tadworth KT20 . . . . **173** CZ120
   Westerham (Bigg.H.) TN16 . **178** EL117
   Woking (Ripley) GU23 . . . . **168** BG123
Ridings Av, N21 . . . . **29** DP42
Ridings CI, N6
   off Hornsey La Gdns **65** DJ59
Ridings La, Wok. GU23 . . . . . . **168** BN123
Ridlands Gro, Oxt. RH8 . . . . . **188** EL130
Ridlands La, Oxt. RH8 . . . . . . **188** EK130
Ridlands Ri, Oxt. RH8 . . . . **188** EL130
Ridler Rd, Enf. EN1 . . . . **30** DS38
Ridley Av, W13 . . . . **97** CH76
Ridley CI, Bark. IG11 . . . . **87** ET66
   Romford RM3 . . . . **51** FH53
Ridley Rd, E7 . . . . **68** EJ63
   E8 . . . . **66** DT64
   NW10 . . . . **81** CU68
   SW19 . . . . **120** DB94
   Bromley BR2 . . . . **144** EF97
   Warlingham CR6 . . . . **176** DW118
   Welling DA16 . . . . **106** EV81
Ridsdale Rd, SE20 . . . . **142** DV95
   Woking GU21 . . . . **166** AV117
Riefield Rd, SE9 . . . . **105** EQ84
Riesco Dr, Croy. CR0 . . . . **160** DW107
Riffel Rd, NW2 . . . . **63** CW64
Riffhams, Brwd. CM13 . . . . . . **55** GB48
Rifle Butts All, Epsom KT18 . . **173** CT115
Rifle PI, SE11 . . . . **101** DN79
Rifle St, E14 . . . . **85** EB71
Rigault Rd, SW6 . . . . **99** CY82
Rigby CI, Croy. CR0 . . . . **141** DN104
Rigby Gdns, Grays RM16 . . . . **111** GH77
Rigby La, Hayes UB3 . . . . **95** BR75
Rigby Ms, Ilf. IG1
   off Cranbrook Rd **69** EP61
Rigby PI, Enf. EN3 . . . . **31** EA37
Rigden St, E14 . . . . **85** EB72
Rigeley Rd, NW10 . . . . **81** CU69
Rigg App, E10 . . . . **67** DX60
Rigge PI, SW4 . . . . **101** DK84
Riggindale Rd, SW16 . . . . **121** DK92
Riley Rd, SE1 . . . . **201** N6
   Enfield EN3 . . . . **30** DW38
Riley St, SW10 . . . . **100** DD79
Rinaldo Rd, SW12 . . . . **121** DH87
Ring, The, W2 . . . . **194** B10
Ring CI, Brom. BR1
   off Garden Rd **124** EH94
Ringcroft St, N7 . . . . **65** DN64
Ringers Rd, Brom. BR1 . . . . . . **144** EG97
Ringford Rd, SW18 . . . . **119** CZ85
Ringlet CI, E16 . . . . **86** EH71
Ringlewell CI, Enf. EN1
   off Central Av. **30** DV40
Ringley Pk Rd, Reig. RH2 . . . . **184** DC134
Ringmer Av, SW6 . . . . **99** CY81
Ringmer Gdns, N19
   off Sussex Way **65** DL61

★ Place of interest   ⇌ Railway station   ⊖ London Underground station   **DLR** Docklands Light Railway station   **Tra** Tramlink station   **H** Hospital   **Riv** Pedestrian ferry landing stage

314

Ringmer Pl, N21 30 DR43
Ringmer Way, Brom. BR1 145 EM99
Ringmore Ri, SE23 122 DV87
Ringmore Rd, Walt. KT12 136 BW104
Ring Rd, W12 81 CW73
Ringshall Rd, Orp. BR5 146 EU97
Ringslade Rd, N22 45 DM54
Ringstead Rd, SE6 123 EB87
Sutton SM1 158 DD105
Ringway, N11 45 DJ51
Southall UB2 96 BY78
Ringway Rd, St.Alb. (Park St) AL2 8 CB27
Ringwold Cl, Beck. BR3 123 DY94
Ringwood Av, N2 44 DF54
Croydon CR0 141 DL101
Hornchurch RM12 72 FK61
Orpington BR6 164 EW110
Redhill RH1 184 DF131
Ringwood Cl, Pnr. HA5 60 BW55
Ringwood Gdns, E14 204 A8
SW15 119 CU89
Ringwood Rd, E17 67 DZ58
Ringwood Way, N21 45 DP46
Hampton (Hmptn H.) TW12 116 CA91
RIPLEY, Wok. GU23 168 BJ122
Ripley Av, Egh. TW20 112 AY93
Ripley Bypass, Wok. GU23 168 BK122
Ripley Cl, Brom. BR1
off Ringmer Way 145 EM99
Croydon (New Adgtn) CR0 161 EC107
Slough SL3 92 AY77
Ripley Gdns, SW14 98 CR83
Sutton SM1 158 DC105
Ripley La, Wok. GU23 168 BL123
Ripley Ms, E11
off Wadley Rd 68 EE59
Ripley Rd, E16 86 EJ72
Belvedere DA17 106 FA77
Enfield EN2 30 DQ39
Hampton TW12 116 CA94
Ilford IG3 69 ET61
RIPLEY SPRINGS, Egh. TW20 112 AY93
Ripley Vw, Loug. IG10 33 EP38
Ripley Vil, W5
off Castlebar Rd 79 CJ72
Ripley Way, Epsom KT19 156 CN111
Waltham Cross (Chsht) EN7 14 DV30
Riplington Ct, SW15
off Longwood Dr 119 CU87
Ripon Cl, Nthlt. UB5 60 CA64
Ripon Gdns, Chess. KT9 155 CK106
Ilford IG1 68 EL58
Ripon Rd, N9 46 DV45
N17 66 DR55
SE18 105 EP79
Ripon Way, Borwd. WD6 26 CQ43
Rippersley Rd, Well. DA16 106 EU81
Ripple Rd, Bark. IG11 87 EQ66
Dagenham RM9 88 EV67
Rippleside Commercial Est, Bark. IG11 88 EW68
Ripplevale Gro, N1 83 DM66
Rippolson Rd, SE18 105 ET78
Ripston Rd, Ashf. TW15 115 BR92
Risborough Dr, Wor.Pk. KT4 139 CU101
Risborough St, SE1 200 G4
Risdon St, SE16 202 G5
Rise, The, E11 68 EG57
N13 45 DN49
NW7 43 CT51
NW10 62 CR63
Bexley DA5 126 EW87
Borehamwood (Elstree) WD6 26 CM43
Buckhurst Hill IG9 48 EK45
Dartford DA1 107 FF84
Edgware HA8 42 CP50
Epsom KT17 157 CT110
Gravesend DA12 131 GL91
Greenford UB6 61 CG64
St. Albans (Park St) AL2 9 CD25
Sevenoaks TN13 191 FJ129
South Croydon CR2 160 DW109
Tadworth KT20 173 CW121
Uxbridge UB10 76 BM68
Waltham Abbey EN9
off Breach Barn Mobile Home Pk 16 EH30
Risebridge Chase, Rom. RM1 51 FF52
Risebridge Rd, Rom. RM2 51 FF54
Risedale Rd, Bexh. DA7 107 FB83
Riseldine Rd, SE23 123 DY86
Rise Pk Boul, Rom. RM1 51 FF53
Rise Pk Par, Rom. RM1 51 FE54
Riseway, Brwd. CM15 54 FY48
Rising Hill Cl, Nthwd. HA6
off Ducks Hill Rd 39 BQ51
Risinghill St, N1 83 DM68
Risingholme Cl, Bushey WD23 40 CB45
Harrow HA3 41 CE53
Risingholme Rd, Har. HA3 41 CE54
Risings, The, E17 67 ED56
Rising Sun Ct, EC1 196 G7
Risley Av, N17 46 DQ53
Rita Rd, SW8 101 DM80
Ritches Rd, N15 66 DQ57
Ritchie Rd, Croy. CR0 142 DV100
Ritchie St, N1 83 DN68
Ritchings Av, E17 67 DY56
Ritherdon Rd, SW17 120 DG89
Ritson Rd, E8 84 DU65
Ritter St, SE18 105 EN79
Ritz Ct, Pot.B. EN6 12 DA31
Ritz Par, W5
off Connell Cres 80 CM70
Rivaz Pl, E9 84 DW65
Rivenhall Gdns, E18 68 EF56
River Ash Est, Shep. TW17 135 BT101
River Av, N13 45 DP48
Thames Ditton KT7 137 CG101
River Bk, N21 46 DQ45
East Molesey KT8 137 CE97
Riverbank, Stai. TW18 113 BF93
River Bk, T.Ditt. KT7 137 CF99
West Molesey KT8 136 BZ97
Riverbank Way, Brent. TW8 97 CJ79
River Barge Cl, E14 204 E5
River Brent Business Pk, W7 97 CE76
River Cl, E11 68 EJ58
Rainham RM13 89 FH71
Ruislip HA4 59 BT58
Southall UB2 96 CC75
Surbiton KT6
off Catherine Rd 137 CK99
Waltham Cross EN8 15 EA34
River Ct, Shep. TW17 135 BQ101
Woking GU21 167 BC115
Rivercourt Rd, W6 99 CV77
River Crane Wk, Felt. TW13 116 BX88
Hounslow TW4 116 BX88
River Crane Way, Felt. TW13
off Watermill Way 116 BZ89
Riverdale, SE13
off Lewisham High St 103 EC83
Riverdale Cl, Bark. IG11 88 EV70
Riverdale Dr, SW18
off Strathville Rd 120 DB88
Woking GU22 167 AZ121
Riverdale Gdns, Twick. TW1 117 CJ86
Riverdale Rd, SE18 105 ET78
Bexley DA5 126 EZ87
Erith DA8 107 FB78
Feltham TW13 116 BY91
Twickenham TW1 117 CJ86
Riverdene, Edg. HA8 42 CQ48
Riverdene Rd, Ilf. IG1 69 EN62
River Dr, Upmin. RM14 72 FQ58
Riverfield Rd, Stai. TW18 113 BF93
River Front, Enf. EN1 30 DR41
River Gdns, Cars. SM5 140 DG103
Feltham TW14 115 BV85
River Gro Pk, Beck. BR3 143 DZ95
RIVERHEAD, Sev. TN13 190 FD122
Riverhead Cl, E17 47 DX54
Riverhead Dr, Sutt. SM2 158 DA110
River Hill, Cob. KT11 169 BV115
Riverhill, Sev. TN15 191 FL130
Riverholme Dr, Epsom KT19 156 CR109
River Island Cl, Lthd. (Fetch.) KT22 171 CD121
River La, Lthd. KT22 171 CD120
Richmond TW10 117 CK88
Rivermead, E.Mol. KT8 136 CC97
West Byfleet (Byfleet) KT14 152 BM113
Rivermead Cl, Add. KT15 152 BJ108
Teddington TW11 117 CH92
Rivermead Ct, SW6 99 CZ83
Rivermead Ho, E9
off Kingsmead Way 67 DY64
Rivermead Rd, N18 47 DX51
Rivermeads Av, Twick. TW2 116 CA90
Rivermount, Walt. KT12 135 BT101
Rivernook Cl, Walt. KT12 136 BW99
River Pk Av, Stai. TW18 113 BD91
River Pk Gdns, Brom. BR2 123 ED94
River Pk Rd, N22 45 DM54
River Pl, N1 84 DQ66
River Reach, Tedd. TW11 117 CJ92
River Rd, Bark. IG11 87 ES68
Brentwood CM14 54 FS49
Buckhurst Hill IG9 48 EL46
Staines TW18 133 BF95
River Rd Business Pk, Bark. IG11 87 ET69
Riversdale, Grav. (Nthflt) DA11 130 GE89
Riversdale Rd, N5 65 DP62
Romford RM5 51 FB52
Thames Ditton KT7 137 CG99
Riversdell Cl, Cher. KT16 133 BF101
Riversfield Rd, Enf. EN1 30 DS41
Riverside, NW4 63 CV59
SE7 205 P7
Chertsey KT16 134 BG97
Dartford (Eyns.) DA4 148 FK103
Egham (Runny.) TW20 113 BA90
St. Albans (Lon.Col.) AL2 10 CL27
Shepperton TW17 135 BS101
Staines TW18 133 BF95
Staines (Wrays.) TW19 112 AW87
Twickenham TW1 117 CH88
Riverside, The, E.Mol. KT8 137 CD97
Riverside Av, E.Mol. KT8 137 CD99
Riverside Business Cen, SW18 120 DB88
Riverside Cl, E5 66 DW60
W7 79 CE70
Kings Langley WD4 7 BP29
Kingston upon Thames KT1 137 CK98
Orpington BR5 146 EW96
Staines TW18 133 BF95
Wallington SM6 141 DH104
Riverside Ct, E4
off Chelwood Cl 31 EB44
SW8 101 DK79
Riverside Dr, NW11 63 CY58
W4 98 CR80
Esher KT10 154 CA105
Mitcham CR4 140 DE99
Richmond TW10 117 CH89
Rickmansworth WD3 38 BK46
Staines TW18 133 BF95
Staines (Egh.H.) TW18 113 BE92
Riverside Gdns, N3 63 CY55
W6 99 CV78
Enfield EN2 30 DQ40
Wembley HA0 80 CL68
Woking (Old Wok.) GU22 167 BB121
Riverside Ind Est, Bark. IG11 88 EU69
Dartford DA1 128 FL85
Enfield EN3 31 DY44
Riverside Mans, E1 202 F1
Riverside Ms, Croy. CR0
off Wandle Rd 141 DL104
Riverside Pk, Wey. KT13
off Wey Meadows 152 BL106
Riverside Path, Wal.Cr. (Chsht) EN8
off Dewhurst Rd 15 DY29
Riverside Pl, Stai. (Stanw.) TW19 114 BK86
Riverside Retail Pk, Sev. TN14 181 FH119
Riverside Rd, E15 85 EC68
N15 66 DU58
SW17 120 DB91
Riverside Rd, Sidcup DA14 126 EY90
Staines TW18 113 BF94
Staines (Stanw.) TW19 114 BK85
Walton-on-Thames KT12 154 BX105
Watford WD19 23 BV44
Riverside Twr, SW6 100 DC82
Riverside Wk, Bex. DA5 126 EW87
Isleworth TW7 97 CE83
Kingston upon Thames KT1
off High St 137 CK96
Loughton IG10 33 EP44
West Wickham BR4
off The Alders 143 EB102
Riverside Way, Dart. DA1 128 FL85
St. Albans AL2 9 CD32
Uxbridge UB8 76 BH67
Riverside W, SW18
off Smugglers Way 100 DB84
Riverside Yd, SW17
off Riverside Rd 120 DC91
River St, EC1 196 D2
River Ter, W6
off Crisp Rd 99 CW78
Riverton Cl, W9 81 CZ69
River Vw, Enf. EN2
off Chase Side 30 DQ41
Grays RM16 111 GG77
Riverview Gdns, SW13 99 CV79
Cobham KT11 153 BU113
Twickenham TW1 117 CF89
Riverview Gro, W4 98 CP79
River Vw Hts, SE16 202 B4
RIVERVIEW PARK, Grav. DA12 131 GK92
Riverview Pk, SE6 123 EA89
Riverview Rd, W4 98 CP79
Epsom KT19 156 CQ105
Greenhithe DA9 129 FU85
River Wk, Uxb. (Denh.) UB9 58 BJ64
Walton-on-Thames KT12 135 BU100
Riverway, N13 45 DN50
River Way, Epsom KT19 156 CR106
Loughton IG10 33 EN44
Riverway, Stai. TW18 134 BH95
River Way, Twick. TW2 116 CB89
River Wey Navigation, Wok. GU23 167 BB122
Riverwood La, Chis. BR7 145 ER95
Rivey Cl, W.Byf. KT14 151 BF114
Rivington Av, Wdf.Grn. IG8 48 EK54
Rivington Ct, NW10 81 CU67
Rivington Cres, NW7 43 CT52
Rivington Pl, EC2 197 N3
Rivington St, EC2 197 M3
Rivington Wk, E8
off Wilde Cl 84 DU67
Rivulet Rd, N17 46 DQ52
Rixon Cl, Slou. (Geo.Grn) SL3 74 AY72
Rixon Ho, SE18
off Barnfield Rd 105 EP79
Rixon St, N7 65 DN62
Rixsen Rd, E12 68 EL64
Roach Rd, E3 85 EA66
Roads Pl, N19
off Hornsey Rd 65 DL61
Roakes Av, Add. KT15 134 BH103
Roan St, SE10 103 EC79
Robarts Cl, Pnr. HA5
off Field End Rd 59 BV57
Robb Rd, Stan. HA7 41 CG51
Robert Adam St, W1 194 F8
Roberta St, E2 84 DU69
Robert Burns Ms, SE24
off Mayall Rd 121 DP85
Robert Cl, W9
off Randolph Av 82 DC70
Chigwell IG7 49 ET50
Potters Bar EN6 11 CY33
Walton-on-Thames KT12 153 BV106
Robert Dashwood Way, SE17 201 H9
Robert Keen Cl, SE15
off Cicely Rd 102 DU81
Robert Lowe Cl, SE14 103 DX80
Roberton Dr, Brom. BR1 144 EJ95
Robert Owen Ho, SW6 99 CX81
Robertsbridge Rd, Cars. SM5 140 DC102
Roberts Cl, SE9 125 ER88
SE16 203 J5
Orpington BR5 146 EW99
Romford RM3 51 FH53
Staines (Stanw.) TW19 114 BJ86
Sutton SM3 157 CX108
Thornton Heath CR7
off Kitchener Rd 142 DR97
Waltham Cross (Chsht) EN8
off Norwood Rd 15 DY30
West Drayton UB7 76 BL74
Roberts La, Ger.Cr. (Chal.St.P.) SL9 37 BA50
Roberts Ms, SW1 198 F7
Orpington BR6 146 EU102
Robertson Cl, Brox. EN10 15 DY26
Robertson Ct, Wok. GU21
off Raglan Rd 166 AS118
Robertson Rd, E15 85 EC67
Robertson St, SW8 101 DH83
Robert's Pl, EC1 196 E4
Roberts Rd, E17 47 EB53
NW7 43 CY51
Belvedere DA17 106 FA78
Watford WD18
off Tucker St 24 BW43
Robert St, E16 87 EP74
NW1 195 J3
SE18 105 ER77
WC2 200 A1
Croydon CR0
off High St 142 DQ104
Roberts Way, Egh. (Eng.Grn) TW20 112 AW94
Roberts Wd Dr, Ger.Cr. (Chal.St.P.) SL9 37 AZ50
Robeson St, E3
off Ackroyd Dr 85 DZ71
Robeson Way, Borwd. WD6 26 CQ39
Robina Cl, Bexh. DA6 106 EX84
Northwood HA6 39 BT53
Robin Cl, NW7 42 CS48
Robin Cl, Addlestone KT15 152 BK106
Hampton TW12 116 BY92
Romford RM5 51 FD52
Robin Ct, SE16 202 B8
Wallington SM6
off Carew Rd 159 DJ107
Robin Cres, E6 86 EK71
Robin Gdns, Red. RH1 184 DG131
Robin Gro, N6 64 DG61
Brentford TW8 97 CJ79
Harrow HA3 62 CM58
Robin Hill Dr, Chis. BR7 124 EL93
Robinhood Cl, Mitch. CR4 141 DJ97
Robin Hood Cl, Wok. GU21 166 AT118
Robin Hood Cres, Wok. (Knap.) GU21 166 AS117
Robin Hood Dr, Bushey WD23 24 BZ39
Harrow HA3 41 CF52
Robin Hood Gdns, E14
off Woolmore St 85 EC73
Robin Hood Grn, Orp. BR5 146 EU99
Robin Hood La, E14 85 EC73
SW15 118 CS91
Bexleyheath DA6 126 EY85
Guildford (Sutt.Grn) GU4 167 AZ124
Robinhood La, Mitch. CR4 141 DJ97
Robin Hood La, Sutt. SM1 158 DA106
Robin Hood Rd, SW19 119 CV92
Brentwood CM15 54 FV45
Woking GU21 166 AT118
Robin Hood Way, SW15 118 CS91
SW20 118 CS91
Greenford UB6 79 CF65
Robinia Av, Grav. (Nthflt) DA11 130 GD87
Robinia Cl, SE20
off Sycamore Gro 142 DU95
Ilford IG6 49 ES51
Robinia Cres, E10 67 EB61
Robins Cl, St.Alb. (Lon.Col.) AL2
off High St 10 CL27
Uxbridge UB8
off Newcourt 76 BJ71
Robins Ct, SE12 124 EJ90
Robinscroft Ms, SE10
off Sparta St 103 EB81
Robins Gro, W.Wick. BR4 144 EG104
Robins La, Epp. (They.B.) CM16 33 EQ36
Robinson Av, Wal.Cr. (Chsht) EN7 13 DP28
Robinson Cl, E11 68 EE62
Hornchurch RM12 89 FH66
Robinson Cres, Bushey (Bushey Hth) WD23 40 CC46
Robinson Rd, E2 84 DW68
SW17 120 DE93
Dagenham RM10 70 FA63
Robinsons Cl, W13 79 CG71
Robinson St, SW3
off Christchurch St 100 DF79
Robins Orchard, Ger.Cr. (Chal.St.P.) SL9 36 AY51
Robinsway, Wal.Abb. EN9
off Roundhills 16 EE34
Walton-on-Thames KT12 154 BW105
Robin Way, Orp. BR5 146 EV97
Potters Bar (Cuffley) EN6 13 DL28
Staines TW18 113 BF90
Robin Willis Way, Wind. (Old Wind.) SL4 112 AU86
Robinwood Gro, Uxb. UB8 76 BM70
Robinwood Pl, SW15 118 CR91
Roborough Wk, Horn. RM12 90 FJ65
Robsart St, SW9 101 DM82
Robson Av, NW10 81 CU67
Robson Cl, E6
off Linton Gdns 86 EL72
Enfield EN2 29 DP40
Gerrards Cross (Chal.St.P.) SL9 36 AY50
Robson Rd, SE27 121 DP90
Robsons Cl, Wal.Cr. EN8 14 DW29
Robyns Cft, Grav. (Nthflt) DA11 130 GE90
Robyns Way, Sev. TN13 190 FF122
Roch Av, Edg. HA8 42 CM54
Rochdale Rd, E17 67 EA59
SE2 106 EV78
Rochdale Way, SE8
off Octavius St 103 EA80
Rochelle Cl, SW11 100 DD84
Rochelle St, E2 197 P3
Rochemont Wk, E8
off Pownall Rd 84 DT67
Roche Rd, SW16 141 DM95
Rochester Av, E13 86 EJ67
Bromley BR1 144 EH96
Feltham TW13 115 BT89
Rochester Cl, SW16 121 DL94
Enfield EN1 30 DS39
Sidcup DA15 126 EV86
Rochester Dr, Bex. DA5 126 EZ86
Pinner HA5 60 BX57
Watford WD25 8 BW34
Rochester Gdns, Cat. CR3 176 DS122
Croydon CR0 142 DS104
Ilford IG1 69 EM59
Rochester Ms, NW1 83 DJ66
Rochester Pl, NW1 83 DJ65
Rochester Rd, NW1 83 DJ65
Carshalton SM5 158 DF105
Dartford DA1 128 FN87
Gravesend DA12 131 GL87
Hornchurch RM12
off Airfield Way 89 FH65
Northwood HA6 59 BT55
Staines TW18 113 BD92
Rochester Row, SW1 199 L8
Rochester Sq, NW1 83 DJ66
Rochester St, SW1 199 M7
Rochester Ter, NW1 83 DJ65
Rochester Wk, SE1 201 K2
Rochester Way, SE3 104 EH81
SE9 105 EM83
Dartford DA1 127 FD87
Rickmansworth (Crox.Grn) WD3 23 BP42
Rochester Way Relief Rd, SE3 104 EH81
Rochester Way Relief Rd, SE9 104 EL84
Roche Wk, Cars. SM5 140 DD100
Rochford Av, Brwd. (Shenf.) CM15 55 GA43
Loughton IG10 33 EQ41
Romford RM6 70 EW57
Waltham Abbey EN9 15 ED33
Rochford Cl, E6
off Boleyn Rd 86 EK68
Broxbourne EN10 15 DY26
Hornchurch RM12 89 FH65
Rochford Grn, Loug. IG10 33 EQ41
Rochfords Gdns, Slou. SL2 74 AW74
Rochford St, NW5 64 DF64
Rochford Wk, E8
off Wilman Gro 84 DU66
Rochford Way, Croy. CR0 141 DL100
Rockall Ct, Slou. SL3 93 BB76
Rock Av, SW14
off South Worple Way 98 CR83
Rockbourne Rd, SE23 123 DX88
Rockchase Gdns, Horn. RM11 72 FL58
★ **Rock Circ**, W1 199 M1
Rockdale Rd, Sev. TN13 191 FH125
Rockells Pl, SE22 122 DV86
Rockfield Cl, Oxt. RH8 188 EF131
Rockfield Rd, Oxt. RH8 188 EF129
Rockford Av, Grnf. UB6 79 CG68
Rock Gdns, Dag. RM10 71 FB64
Rock Gro Way, SE16 202 C8
Rockhall Rd, NW2 63 CX63
Rockhall Way, NW2
off Midland Ter 63 CX62
Rockhampton Cl, SE27
off Rockhampton Rd 121 DN91
Rockhampton Rd, SE27 121 DN91
South Croydon CR2 160 DS107
Rock Hill, SE26 122 DT91
Orpington BR6 164 FA107
Rockingham Av, Horn. RM11 71 FH58
Rockingham Cl, SW15 99 CT84
Uxbridge UB8 76 BJ67
Rockingham Est, SE1 201 H7
Rockingham Par, Uxb. UB8 76 BJ66
Rockingham Rd, Uxb. UB8 76 BH67
Rockingham St, SE1 201 H7
Rockland Rd, SW15 99 CY84
Rocklands Dr, Stan. HA7 41 CH54
Rockleigh Ct, Brwd. (Shenf.) CM15
off Hutton Rd 55 GA45
Rockley Rd, W14 99 CX75
Rockliffe Av, Kings L. WD4 6 BN30
Rockmount Rd, SE18 105 ET78
SE19 122 DR93
Rockshaw Rd, Red. RH1 185 DM127
Rocks La, SW13 99 CU81
Rock St, N4 65 DN61
Rockware Av, Grnf. UB6 79 CD67
Rockways, Barn. EN5 27 CT44
Rockwell Gdns, SE19 122 DS92
Rockwell Rd, Dag. RM10 71 FB64
Rockwood Pl, W12 99 CW75
Rocky La, Reig. RH2 184 DF128
Rocliffe St, N1 196 G1
Rocombe Cres, SE23 122 DW87
Rocque La, SE3 104 EF83
Rodborough Rd, NW11 64 DA60
Roden Ct, N6
off Hornsey La 65 DK59
Roden Gdns, Croy. CR0 142 DS100
Rodenhurst Rd, SW4 121 DJ86
Roden St, N7 65 DM62
Ilford IG1 69 EN62
Rodeo Cl, Erith DA8 107 FH81
Roderick Rd, NW3 64 DF63
Rodgers Cl, Borwd. (Elstree) WD6 25 CK44
Roding Av, Wdf.Grn. IG8 48 EL51
Roding Gdns, Loug. IG10 32 EL44
Roding La, Buck.H. IG9 48 EL46
Chigwell IG7 49 EN46
Roding La N, Wdf.Grn. IG8 48 EK54
Roding La S, Ilf. IG4 68 EK56
Woodford Green IG8 68 EK56
Roding Ms, E1 202 C2
Roding Rd, E5 67 DX63
E6 87 EP71
Loughton IG10 32 EL43
Rodings, The, Upmin. RM14 73 FR58
Woodford Green IG8 48 EJ51
Rodings Row, Barn. EN5
off Leecroft Rd 27 CY43
Roding Trd Est, Bark. IG11 87 EP66
⊖ **Roding Valley** 48 EK49
Roding Vw, Buck.H. IG9 48 EK46
Roding Way, Rain. RM13 90 FK68
Rodmarton St, W1 194 E7
Rodmell Cl, Hayes UB4 78 BY70
Rodmell Slope, N12 43 CZ50
Rodmere St, SE10
off Trafalgar Rd 104 EE78
Rodmill La, SW2 121 DL87
Rodney Cl, Croy. CR0 141 DP102
New Malden KT3 138 CS99
Pinner HA5 60 BY59
Walton-on-Thames KT12
off Rodney Rd 136 BW102
Rodney Ct, W9
off Maida Vale 82 DC70
Rodney Gdns, Pnr. HA5 59 BV57
West Wickham BR4 162 EG105
Rodney Grn, Walt. KT12 136 BW103
Rodney Pl, E17 47 DY54
SE17 201 J8
SW19 140 DC95
Rodney Rd, E11 68 EH56
SE17 201 J8
Mitcham CR4 140 DE96
New Malden KT3 138 CS99
Twickenham TW2 116 CA86
Walton-on-Thames KT12 136 BW103
Rodney St, N1 83 DM68
Rodney Way, Rom. RM7 50 FA53
Slough (Colnbr.) SL3 93 BE81
Rodona Rd, Wey. KT13 153 BR111

★ Place of interest ⇌ Railway station ⊖ London Underground station DLR Docklands Light Railway station Tra Tramlink station H Hospital Riv Pedestrian ferry landing stage

Rodway Rd, SW15 119 CU87
Bromley BR1 144 EH95
Rodwell Cl, Ruis. HA4 60 BW60
Rodwell Ct, Add. KT15
off Garfield Rd 152 BJ105
Rodwell Pl, Edg. HA8
off Whitchurch La. 42 CN51
Rodwell Rd, SE22 122 DT86
Roebourne Way, E16 105 EN75
Roebuck Cl, Ashtd. KT21 172 CL120
Feltham TW13 115 BV91
Reigate RH2 184 DB134
Roebuck La, N17
off High Rd. 46 DT51
Buckhurst Hill IG9 48 EJ45
Roebuck Rd, Chess. KT9 156 CN106
Ilford IG6 50 EV50
Roedean Av, Enf. EN3 30 DW39
Roedean Cl, Enf. EN3 30 DW39
Orpington BR6 164 EV105
Roedean Cres, SW15 118 CS86
Roedean Dr, Rom. RM1 71 FE56
Roe End, NW9 62 CQ56
Roe Grn, NW9 62 CQ57
ROEHAMPTON, SW15 119 CU85
Roehampton Cl, SW15 99 CU84
Gravesend DA12 131 GL87
Roehampton Dr, Chis. BR7 125 EQ93
Roehampton Gate, SW15 118 CS86
Roehampton High St, SW15 119 CV87
Roehampton La, SW15 99 CU84
H Roehampton Priory Hosp, The, SW15 99 CT84
Roehampton Vale, SW15 118 CS90
Roe La, NW9 62 CP56
Roe Way, Wall. SM6 159 DL107
Rofant Rd, Nthwd. HA6 39 BS51
Roffes La, Cat. CR3 176 DR124
Roffey Cl, Pur. CR8 175 DP116
Roffey St, E14 204 D5
Roffords, Wok. GU21 166 AV117
Rogate Ho, E5
off Muir Rd 66 DU62
Roger Dowley Ct, E2 84 DW68
Rogers Cl, Cat. CR3
off Tillingdown Hill 176 DV122
Coulsdon CR5 175 DP118
Waltham Cross (Chsht) EN7 14 DR26
Rogers Ct, Swan. BR8 147 FG98
Rogers Gdns, Dag. RM10 70 FA64
Rogers La, Slou.
(Stoke P.) SL2 74 AT67
Warlingham CR6 177 DZ118
Rogers Mead, Gdse. RH9
off Ivy Mill La 186 DV132
Rogers Rd, E16 86 EF72
SW17 120 DD91
Dagenham RM10 70 FA64
Grays RM17 110 GC77
Rogers Ruff, Nthwd. HA6 39 BQ53
Roger St, WC1 196 C5
Rogers Wk, N12
off Brook Meadow 44 DB48
Rojack Rd, SE23 123 DX88
Rokeby Ct, Wok. GU21 166 AT117
Rokeby Gdns, Wdf.Grn. IG8 48 EG53
Rokeby Pl, SW20 119 CV94
Rokeby Rd, SE4 103 DZ82
Rokeby St, E15 86 EE67
Roke Cl, Ken. CR8 160 DQ114
Roke Lo Rd, Ken. CR8 159 DP113
Roke Rd, Ken. CR8 176 DQ115
Roker Pk Av, Uxb. UB10 58 BL63
Rokesby Cl, Well. DA16 105 ER82
Rokesby Pl, Wem. HA0 61 CK64
Rokesly Av, N8 65 DL57
Roland Gdns, SW7 100 DC78
Feltham TW13 116 BY90
Roland Ms, E1
off Stepney Grn 85 DX71
Roland Rd, E17 67 ED56
Roland Way, SE17 102 DR78
SW7 off Roland Gdns 100 DC78
Worcester Park KT4 139 CT103
Roles Gro, Rom. RM6 70 EX56
Rolfe Cl, Barn. EN4 28 DE42
Rolinsden Way, Kes. BR2 162 EK105
Rollesby Rd, Chess. KT9 156 CN107
Rollesby Way, SE28 88 EW73
Rolleston Av, Orp. BR5 145 EP100
Rolleston Cl, Orp. BR5 145 EP101
Rolleston Rd, S.Croy. CR2 160 DR108
Roll Gdns, Ilf. IG2 69 EN57
Rollins St, SE15 102 DW79
Rollit Cres, Houns. TW3 116 CA85
Rollit St, N7
off Hornsey Rd 65 DM64
Rollo Rd, Swan. BR8 127 FF94
Rolls Bldgs, EC4 196 D8
Rollscourt Av, SE24 122 DQ85
Rolls Pk Av, E4 47 EA51
Rolls Pk Rd, E4 47 EB50
Rolls Pas, EC4 196 D8
Rolls Rd, SE1 202 A10
Rolt St, SE8 103 DY79
Rolvenden Gdns, Brom.
BR1 124 EK94
Rolvenden Pl, N17
off Manor Rd 46 DU53
★ Roman Bath, WC2 196 C10
Roman Cl, W3
off Avenue Gdns 98 CP75
Feltham TW14 116 BW85
Rainham RM13 89 FD68
Uxbridge (Hare.) UB9 38 BH53
Romanfield Rd, SW2 121 DM87
Roman Gdns, Kings L. WD4 7 BP30
Roman Ho, Rain. RM13
off Roman Cl 89 FD68
Romanhurst Av, Brom. BR2 144 EE98
Romanhurst Gdns, Brom.
BR2 144 EE98
Roman Ind Est, Croy. CR0 142 DS101
Roman Ri, SE19 122 DR93
Roman Rd, E2 84 DW69
Roman Rd, E3 85 DY68
E6 86 EL70
N10 45 DH52
NW2 63 CW62
W4 98 CS77
Brentwood CM15 55 GC41
Gravesend (Nthflt) DA11 130 GC90
Ilford IG1 87 EP65
Roman Sq, SE28 88 EU74
Romans Way, Wok. GU22 168 BG115
Roman Vil Rd, Dart.
(S.Darenth) DA2, DA4 128 FQ92
Roman Way, N7 83 DM65
SE15 off Clifton Way 102 DW80
Carshalton SM5 158 DF109
Croydon CR0 141 DP103
Dartford DA1 127 FE85
Enfield EN1 30 DT43
Waltham Abbey EN9 31 EB35
Roman Way Ind Est, N1
off Offord St 83 DM66
Romany Gdns, E17
off McEntee Av 47 DY53
Sutton SM3 140 DA101
Romany Ri, Orp. BR5 145 EQ102
Roma Read Cl, SW15
off Bessborough Rd 119 CV87
Roma Rd, E17 67 DY55
Romberg Rd, SW17 120 DG90
Romborough Gdns, SE13 123 EC85
Romborough Way, SE13 123 EC85
Rom Cres, Rom. RM7 71 FF59
Romeland, Borwd.
(Elstree) WD6 25 CK44
Waltham Abbey EN9 15 EC33
Romero Cl, SW9
off Stockwell Rd 101 DM83
Romero Sq, SE3 104 EJ84
Romeyn Rd, SW16 121 DM90
ROMFORD 71 FF57
⇌ Romford 71 FE58
Romford Rd, E7 68 EH64
E12 68 EL63
E15 86 EE66
Chigwell IG7 50 EU48
Romford RM5 50 EY52
South Ockendon
(Aveley) RM15 90 FQ73
Romford St, E1 84 DU71
Romilly Dr, Wat. WD19 40 BY49
Romilly Rd, N4 65 DP61
Romilly St, W1 195 M10
Rommany Rd, SE27 122 DR91
Romney Chase, Horn. RM11 72 FM58
Romney Cl, N17 46 DV53
NW11 64 DC60
SE14 off Kender St 102 DW80
Ashford TW15 115 BQ92
Chessington KT9 156 CL105
Harrow HA2 60 CA59
Romney Dr, Brom. BR1 124 EK94
Harrow HA2 60 CA59
Romney Gdns, Bexh. DA7 106 EZ81
Romney Lock, Wind. SL4 92 AS79
Romney Ms, W1 194 F6
Romney Par, Hayes UB4
off Romney Rd 77 BR68
Romney Rd, SE10 103 EC79
Gravesend (Nthflt) DA11 130 GE90
Hayes UB4 77 BR68
New Malden KT3 138 CR100
Romney Row, NW2
off Brent Ter 63 CX61
Romney St, SW1 199 N7
Romola Rd, SE24 121 DP88
Romsey Cl, Orp. BR6 163 EP105
Slough SL3 93 AZ76
Romsey Gdns, Dag. RM9 88 EX67
Romsey Rd, W13 79 CG73
Dagenham RM9 88 EX67
Romside Pl, Rom. RM7
off Brooklands La 71 FD56
Romulus Ct, Brent. TW8
off Justin Cl 97 CK80
Rom Valley Way, Rom. RM7 71 FE59
Ronald Av, E15 86 EE69
Ronald Cl, Beck. BR3 143 DZ98
Ronald Ct, St.Alb. AL2 8 BY29
Ronald Ho, SE3
off Cambert Way 104 EJ84
Ronald Rd, Rom. RM3 52 FN53
Ronaldsay Spur, Slou. SL1 74 AS71
Ronalds Rd, N5 65 DN64
Bromley BR1 144 EG95
Ronaldstone Rd, Sid. DA15 125 ES86
Ronald St, E1
off Devonport St 84 DW72
Rona Rd, NW3 64 DG63
Ronart St, Har. (Wldste) HA3
off Stuart Rd 61 CF55
Rona Wk, N1
off Ramsey Wk 84 DR65
Rondu Rd, NW2 63 CY64
Ronelean Rd, Surb. KT6 138 CM104
Roneo Cor, Horn. RM12 71 FF60
Roneo Link, Horn. RM12 71 FF60
Ronfearn Av, Orp. BR5 146 EX99
Ron Leighton Way, E6 86 EL67
Ronneby Cl, Wey. KT13 135 BS104
Ronnie La, E12
off Walton Rd 69 EN63
Ronson Way, Lthd. KT22 171 CG121
Ronver Rd, SE12 124 EF87
Rood La, EC3 197 M10
Roof of the World Caravan Pk, Tad.
(Box H.) KT20 182 CP132
Rookby Ct, N21
off Carpenter Gdns 45 DP47
Rook Cl, Horn. RM12 89 FG66
Wembley HA9 62 CP62
Rookdean, Sev.
(Chipstead) TN13 190 FC122
Rookeries Cl, Felt. TW13 115 BV90
Rookery, The, Grays RM20 109 FU79
Rookery Cl, NW9 63 CT57
Leatherhead (Fetch.) KT22 171 CE124
Rookery Ct, Grays RM20 109 FU79
Rookery Cres, Dag. RM10 89 FB66
Rookery Dr, Chis. BR7 145 EN95
Rookery Gdns, Orp. BR5 146 EW99
Rookery Hill, Ashtd. KT21 172 CN118
Rookery La, Brom. BR2 144 EK100
Grays RM17 110 GD78
Rookery Mead, Couls. CR5
off Netherne Dr 175 DK122
Rookery Rd, SW4 101 DJ84
Orpington BR6 163 EM110
Staines TW18 114 BH92
Rookery Vw, Grays RM17 110 GD78
Rookery Way, NW9 63 CT57
Tadworth
(Lwr Kgswd) KT20 183 CZ127
Rookesley Rd, Orp. BR5 146 EX101
Rooke Way, SE10 205 K10
Rookfield Av, N10 65 DJ56
Rookfield Cl, N10
off Cranmore Way 65 DJ56
Rook La, Cat. CR3 175 DM124
Rookley Cl, Sutt. SM2 158 DB110
Rooks Hill, Rick. (Loud.) WD3 22 BK42
Rooksmead Rd, Sun. TW16 135 BT96
Rookstone Rd, SW17 120 DF92
Rook Wk, E6
off Allhallows Rd 86 EL72
Rookwood Av, Loug. IG10 33 EQ41
New Malden KT3 139 CU98
Wallington SM6 159 DK105
Rookwood Cl, Grays RM17 110 GB77
Redhill RH1 185 DH129
Rookwood Gdns, E4
off Whitehall Rd 48 EF46
Loughton IG10 33 EQ41
Rookwood Ho, Bark. IG11
off St. Marys 87 ER68
Rookwood Rd, N16 66 DT59
★ Roosevelt Mem, W1 194 G10
Roosevelt Way, Dag. RM10 89 FD65
Rootes Dr, W10 81 CX70
Ropemaker Rd, SE16 203 K5
Ropemakers Flds, E14 203 M1
Ropemaker St, EC2 197 K6
Roper La, SE1 201 N5
Ropers Av, E4 47 EC50
Ropers Orchard, SW3
off Danvers St 100 DE79
Roper St, SE9 125 EM86
Ropers Wk, SW2
off Brockwell Pk Gdns 121 DN87
Roper Way, Mitch. CR4 140 DG96
Ropery St, E3 85 DZ70
Rope St, SE16 203 L7
Rope Wk, Sun. TW16 136 BW97
Rope Wk Gdns, E1
off Commercial Rd 84 DU72
Ropewalk Ms, E8
off Middleton Rd 84 DT66
Rope Yd Rails, SE18 105 EP76
Ropley St, E2 84 DU68
Rosa Alba Ms, N5
off Kelross Rd 66 DQ63
Rosa Av, Ashf. TW15 114 BN91
Rosaline Rd, SW6 99 CY80
Rosamond St, SE26 122 DV90
Rosamund Cl, S.Croy. CR2 160 DR105
Rosamun St, Sthl. UB2 96 BY77
Rosary, The, Egh. TW20 133 BD96
Rosary Cl, Houns. TW3 96 BY82
Rosary Ct, Pot.B. EN6 12 DB30
Rosary Gdns, SW7 100 DC77
Ashford TW15 115 BP91
Bushey WD23 41 CE45
Rosaville Rd, SW6 99 CZ80
Roscoe St, EC1 197 J5
Roscoff Cl, Edg. HA8 42 CQ53
Roseacre, Oxt. RH8 188 EG134
Roseacre Cl, W13
off Middlefielde 79 CH71
Hornchurch RM11 72 FM60
Shepperton TW17 134 BN99
Roseacre Rd, Well. DA16 106 EV83
Rose All, EC2
off Bishopsgate 84 DS71
SE1 201 J2
Rose & Crown Ct, EC2 197 H8
Rose & Crown Yd, SW1 199 L2
Roseary Cl, West Dr. UB7 94 BK77
Rose Av, E18 48 EH54
Gravesend DA12 131 GL88
Mitcham CR4 140 DF95
Morden SM4 140 DC99
Rosebank, SE20 122 DV94
Rose Bk, Brwd. CM14 54 FX48
Rosebank, Epsom KT18 156 CQ114
Waltham Abbey EN9 16 EE33
Rosebank Av, Horn. RM12 72 FJ64
Wembley HA0 61 CF63
Rosebank Cl, N12 44 DE50
Teddington TW11 117 CG93
Rose Bk Cotts, Wok. GU22 166 AY122
Rosebank Gdns, E3 85 DZ68
Gravesend (Nthflt) DA11 130 GE88
Rosebank Gro, E17 67 DZ55
Rosebank Rd, E17 67 EB58
W7 97 CE75
Rosebank Vil, E17 67 EA56
Rosebank Wk, NW1
off Maiden La 83 DK66
SE18 off Woodhill 104 EL77
Rosebank Way, W3 80 CR72
Rose Bates Dr, NW9 62 CN56
Roseberry Cl, Upmin. RM14 73 FT58
Roseberry Ct, Wat. WD17
off Grandfield Av 23 BU39
Roseberry Gdns, N4 65 DP58
Dartford DA1 128 FJ87
Orpington BR6 145 ES104
Upminster RM14 73 FT59
Roseberry Pl, E8 84 DT65
Roseberry St, SE16 202 D9
Rosebery Av, E12 86 EL65
EC1 196 D5
N17 46 DU54
Epsom KT17 156 CS114
Harrow HA2 60 BZ63
New Malden KT3 139 CT96
Sidcup DA15 125 ES87
Thornton Heath CR7 142 DQ96
Rosebery Cl, Mord. SM4 139 CX100
Rosebery Ct, EC1
off Rosebery Av 83 DN70
Rosebery Ct,
Gravesend (Nthflt) DA11 131 GF88
Rosebery Cres, Wok. GU22 167 AZ121
Rosebery Gdns, N8 65 DL57
W13 79 CG72
Sutton SM1 158 DB105
Rosebery Ms, N10 45 DJ54
SW2 off Rosebery Rd 121 DL86
Rosebery Rd, N9 46 DU48
N10 45 DJ54
SW2 121 DL86
Bushey WD23 40 CB45
Epsom KT18 172 CR119
Grays RM17 110 FY79
Hounslow TW3 116 CC85
Kingston upon Thames KT1 138 CP96
Sutton SM1 157 CZ107
Rosebery Sq, EC1 196 D5
Kingston upon Thames KT1 138 CN96
Rosebine Av, Twick. TW2 117 CD87
Rosebriar Cl, Wok. GU22 168 BG116
Rosebriars, Cat. CR3 176 DS120
Esher KT10 154 CC106
Rosebriar Wk, Wat. WD24 23 BT36
Rosebury Rd, SW6 100 DB82
Rosebury Sq, Wdf.Grn. IG8 49 EN52
Rosebury Vale, Ruis. HA4 59 BT60
Rose Bushes, Epsom KT17 173 CV116
Rose Ct, E1 197 P7
SE26 122 DV89
Pinner HA5
off Nursery Rd 60 BW55
Waltham Cross EN7 14 DU27
Rosecourt Rd, Croy. CR0 141 DM100
Rosecroft Av, NW3 64 DA62
Rosecroft Cl, Orp. BR5 146 EW100
Westerham (Bigg.H.) TN16
off Lotus Rd 179 EM118
Rosecroft Dr, Wat. WD17 23 BS36
Rosecroft Gdns, NW2 63 CU62
Twickenham TW2 117 CD88
Rosecroft Rd, Sthl. UB1 78 CA70
Rosecroft Wk, Pnr. HA5 60 BX57
Wembley HA0 61 CK64
Rosedale, Ashtd. KT21 171 CJ118
Caterham CR3 176 DS123
Rose Dale, Orp. BR6 145 EP103
Rosedale Av, Hayes UB3 77 BR71
Waltham Cross (Chsht) EN7 14 DT29
Rosedale Cl, SE2
off Finchale Rd 106 EV76
W7 off Boston Rd 97 CF75
Dartford DA2 128 FP87
St. Albans (Brick.Wd) AL2 8 BY30
Stanmore HA7 41 CH51
Rosedale Ct, N5 65 DP63
Rosedale Gdns, Dag. RM9 88 EV66
Rosedale Pl, Croy. CR0 143 DX101
Rosedale Rd, E7 68 EJ64
Dagenham RM9 88 EV66
Epsom KT17 157 CU106
Grays RM17 110 GD78
Richmond TW9 98 CL84
Romford RM1 51 FC54
Rosedale Ter, W6
off Dalling Rd 99 CV76
Rosedale Way, Wal.Cr.
(Chsht) EN7 14 DU29
Rosedene, NW6 81 CX67
Rosedene Av, SW16 121 DM90
Croydon CR0 141 DM101
Greenford UB6 78 CA69
Morden SM4 140 DA99
Rosedene Ct, Dart. DA1
off Shepherds La 128 FJ87
Ruislip HA4 59 BS60
Rosedene Gdns, Ilf. IG2 69 EN56
Rosedene Ter, E10 67 EB61
Rosedew Rd, W6 99 CX79
Rose Dr, Chesh. HP5 4 AS32
Rose End, Wor.Pk. KT4 139 CX102
Rosefield, Sev. TN13 190 FG124
Rosefield Cl, Cars. SM5 158 DE106
Rosefield Gdns, E14 85 EA73
Chertsey (Ott.) KT16 151 BD107
Rosefield Rd, Stai. TW18 114 BG91
Roseford Ct, W12 99 CX75
Rose Gdn Cl, Edg. HA8 42 CL51
Rose Gdns, W5 97 CK76
Feltham TW13 115 BU89
Southall UB1 78 CA70
Staines (Stanw.) TW19
off Diamedes Av 114 BK87
Watford WD18 23 BU43
Rose Glen, NW9 62 CR56
Romford RM7 71 FE60
Rosehart Ms, W11
off Westbourne Gro 82 DA72
Rosehatch Av, Rom. RM6 70 EX55
Roseheath Rd, Houns. TW4 116 BZ85
ROSEHILL, Sutt. SM1 140 DB102
Rosehill, Esher (Clay.) KT10 155 CG107
Hampton TW12 136 CA95
Rose Hill, Sutt. SM1 140 DB104
Rosehill Av, Sutt. SM1 140 DC102
Woking GU21 166 AW116
Rosehill Ct, Slou. SL1
off Yew Tree Rd 92 AU76
Rosehill Fm Meadow, Bans. SM7
off The Tracery 174 DB115
Rosehill Gdns, Abb.L. WD5 7 BQ32
Greenford UB6 61 CF64
Sutton SM1 140 DB103
Rosehill Pk W, Sutt. SM1 140 DC102
Rosehill Rd, SW18 120 DC86
Westerham (Bigg.H.) TN16 178 EJ117
Roseland Cl, N17
off Cavell Rd 46 DR52
Rose La, Rom. RM6 70 EX55
Woking (Ripley) GU23 168 BJ121
Rose Lawn, Bushey
(Bushey Hth) WD23 40 CC46
Roseleigh Av, N5 65 DP63
Roseleigh Cl, Twick. TW1 117 CK86
Rosemary Av, N3 44 DB54
N9 46 DV46
Enfield EN2 30 DR39
Hounslow TW4 96 BX82
Romford RM1 71 FF55
West Molesey KT8 136 CA97
Rosemary Cl, Croy. CR0 141 DL100
Oxted RH8 188 EG133
South Ockendon RM15 91 FW69
Uxbridge UB8 76 BN71
Rosemary Dr, E14 85 ED72
Ilford IG4 68 EK57
Rosemary Gdns, SW14
off Rosemary La 98 CQ83
Chessington KT9 156 CL105
Dagenham RM8 70 EZ60
Rosemary La, SW14 98 CQ83
Egham TW20 133 BB97
Rosemary Rd, SE15 102 DT80
SW17 120 DC90
Welling DA16 105 ET81
Rosemary St, N1
off Shepperton Rd 84 DR67
Rosemead, NW9 63 CT59
Chertsey KT16 134 BH101
Potters Bar EN6 12 DC30
Rosemead Av, Felt. TW13 115 BT89
Mitcham CR4 141 DJ96
Wembley HA9 62 CL64
Rosemead Gdns, Brwd.
(Hutt.) CM13 55 GD42
Rosemont Av, N12 44 DC51
Rosemont Rd, NW3 82 DC65
W3 80 CP73
New Malden KT3 138 CQ97
Richmond TW10 118 CL86
Wembley HA0 80 CL67
Rosemoor St, SW3 198 D9
Rosemount Av, W.Byf. KT14 152 BG113
Rosemount Cl, Wdf.Grn. IG8
off Chapelmount Rd 49 EM51
Rosemount Dr, Brom. BR1 145 EM98
Rosemount Pt, SE23
off Dacres Rd 123 DX90
Rosemount Rd, W13 79 CG72
Rosenau Cres, SW11 100 DE81
Rosenau Rd, SW11 100 DE81
Rosendale Rd, SE21 122 DQ87
SE24 122 DQ87
Roseneath Av, N21 45 DP46
Roseneath Cl, Orp. BR6 164 EW108
Roseneath Rd, SW11 120 DG86
Roseneath Wk, Enf. EN1 30 DS42
Rosens Wk, Edg. HA8 42 CP48
Rosenthal Rd, SE6 123 EB86
Rosenthorpe Rd, SE15 123 DX85
Rose Pk Cl, Hayes UB4 78 BW70
Rosepark Ct, Ilf. IG5 49 EM54
Roserton St, E14 204 D5
Rosery, The, Croy. CR0 143 DX100
Roses, The, Wdf.Grn. IG8 48 EF52
Rose Sq, SW3 198 A10
Rose St, EC4 196 G8
WC2 195 P10
Gravesend (Nthflt) DA11 130 GB86
Rosethorn Cl, SW12 121 DJ87
Rosetta Cl, SW8 101 DL80
Rosetti Ter, Dag. RM8
off Marlborough Rd 70 EV63
Rose Valley, Brwd. CM14 54 FW48
Roseveare Rd, SE12 124 EJ91
Rose Vil, Dart. DA1 128 FP87
Roseville Av, Houns. TW3 116 CA85
Roseville Rd, Hayes UB3 95 BU78
Rosevine Rd, SW20 139 CW95
Rose Wk, Pur. CR8 159 DK111
Surbiton KT5 138 CP99
West Wickham BR4 143 ED103
Rose Wk, The, Rad. WD7 25 CH37
Rosewarne Cl, Wok. GU21
off Muirfield Rd 166 AU118
Rose Way, SE12 124 EG85
Roseway, SE21 122 DR86
Rose Way, Edg. HA8 42 CQ49
Rosewell Cl, SE20 122 DV94
Rosewood, Dart. DA2 127 FE91
Esher KT10 137 CG103
Sutton SM2 158 DC110
Woking GU22 167 BA119
Rosewood Av, Grnf. UB6 61 CG64
Hornchurch RM12 71 FG64
Rosewood Cl, Sid. DA14 126 EW90
Rosewood Ct, Brom. BR1 144 EJ95
Romford RM6 70 EW57
Rosewood Dr, Enf. EN2 29 DN35
Shepperton TW17 134 BM99
Rosewood Gdns, SE13
off Morden Hill 103 EC82
Rosewood Gro, Sutt. SM1 140 DC103
Rosewood Sq, W12
off Primula St 81 CU72
Rosewood Ter, SE20
off Laurel Gro 122 DW94
Rosher Cl, E15 85 ED66
ROSHERVILLE, Grav. DA11 131 GF85
Rosherville Way, Grav. DA11 130 GE87
Rosina St, E9 67 DX64
Roskell Rd, SW15 99 CX83
Roslin Rd, W3 98 CP76
Roslin Sq, W3 98 CP76
Roslin Way, Brom. BR1 124 EG92
Roslyn Cl, Mitch. CR4 140 DD96
Roslyn Ct, Wok. GU21
off St. John's Rd 166 AU118
Roslyn Gdns, Rom. RM2 51 FF54
Roslyn Rd, N15 66 DR57
Rosmead Rd, W11 81 CY73
Rosoman Pl, EC1 196 E4
Rosoman St, EC1 196 E3
Rossall Cl, Horn. RM11 71 FG58
Rossall Cres, NW10 80 CM69
Ross Av, NW7 43 CY50
Dagenham RM8 70 EZ61
Ross Cl, Har. HA3 40 CC52
Hayes UB3 95 BR77
Northolt UB5 61 CD63
Ross Ct, SW15 119 CX87
Ross Cres, Wat. WD25 23 BU35
Rossdale, Sutt. SM1 158 DE106
Rossdale Dr, N9 30 DW44
NW9 62 CQ60
Rossdale Rd, SW15 99 CW84
Rosse Ms, SE3 104 EH81
Rossendale St, E5 66 DV61
Rossendale Way, NW1 83 DJ66
Rossetti Gdns, Couls. CR5 175 DM118

★ Place of interest ⇌ Railway station ⊖ London Underground station DLR Docklands Light Railway station Tra Tramlink station H Hospital Riv Pedestrian ferry landing stage

316

★ Place of interest ⇌ Railway station ⊖ London Underground station DLR Docklands Light Railway station Tra Tramlink station H Hospital Riv Pedestrian ferry landing stage

317

Ruislip Rd, Grnf. UB6 78 CA69
Northolt UB5 78 BX68
Southall UB1 78 CA69
Ruislip Rd E, W7 79 CD70
W13 79 CD70
Greenford UB6 79 CD70
Ruislip St, SW17 120 DF91
Rumania Wk, Grav. DA12 131 GM90
Rumbold Rd, SW6 100 DB80
Rum Cl, E1 202 F1
Rumsey Cl, Hmptn. TW12 116 BZ93
Rumsey Ms, N4
off Monsell Rd 65 DP62
Rumsey Rd, SW9 101 DM83
Rumsley, Wal.Cr. EN7 14 DU27
Runbury Circle, NW9 62 CR61
Runciman Cl, Orp. BR6 164 EW110
Runcorn Cl, N17 66 DV56
Runcorn Pl, W11 81 CY73
Rundell Cres, NW4 63 CV57
Runes Cl, Mitch. CR4 140 DD98
Runnel Fld, Har. HA1 61 CE62
Runnemede Rd, Egh. TW20 113 BA91
Running Horse Yd, Brent. TW8
off Pottery Rd 98 CL79
Running Waters, Brwd. CM13 55 GA49
Runnymede, SW19 140 DD95
Runnymede Cl, Twick. TW2 116 CB86
Runnymede Ct, Croy. CR0 142 DT103
Egham TW20 113 BA91
Runnymede Cres, SW16 141 DK95
Runnymede Gdns, Grnf.
UB6 79 CD68
Twickenham TW2 116 CB86
H Runnymede Hosp, Cher.
KT16 133 BD104
Runnymede Ho, E9
off Kingsmead Way 67 DY63
Runnymede Rd, Twick. TW2 116 CB86
Runrig Hill, Amer. HP6 20 AS35
Runway, The, Ruis. HA4 59 BV64
Rupack St, SE16 202 F5
Rupert Av, Wem. HA9 62 CL64
Rupert Ct, W1 195 M10
West Molesey KT8
off St. Peter's Rd 136 CA98
Rupert Gdns, SW9 101 DP82
Rupert Rd, N19
off Holloway Rd 65 DK62
NW6 81 CZ68
W4 98 CS76
Rupert St, W1 195 M10
Rural Cl, Horn. RM11 71 FH60
Rural Vale, Grav.
(Nthflt) DA11 130 GE87
Rural Way, SW16 121 DH94
Redhill RH1 184 DG134
Rusbridge Cl, E8
off Amhurst Rd 66 DU64
Ruscoe Dr, Wok. GU22
off Pembroke Rd 167 BA117
Ruscoe Rd, E16 86 EF72
Ruscombe Dr, St.Alb.
(Park St) AL2 8 CB26
Ruscombe Gdns, Slou.
(Datchet) SL3 92 AU80
Ruscombe Way, Felt. TW14 115 BT87
Rush, The, SW19
off Kingston Rd 139 CZ95
Rusham Pk Av, Egh. TW20 113 AZ93
Rusham Rd, SW12 120 DF86
Egham TW20 113 AZ93
Rushbrook Cres, E17 47 DZ53
Rushbrook Rd, SE9 125 EQ89
Rush Common Ms, SW2 121 DM87
Rushcroft Rd, E4 47 EA52
SW2 101 DN84
Rushden Cl, SE19 122 DR94
Rushdene, SE2 106 EX76
Rushdene Av, Barn. EN4 44 DE45
Rushdene Cl, Nthlt. UB5 78 BW69
Rushdene Cres, Nthlt. UB5 78 BW68
Rushdene Rd, Brwd. CM15 54 FW45
Pinner HA5 60 BX58
Rushdene Wk, West.
(Bigg.H.) TN16 178 EK117
Rushden Gdns, NW7 43 CW51
Ilford IG5 69 EN55
Rushdon Cl, Grays RM17 110 GA76
Romford RM1 71 FG57
Rush Dr, Wal.Abb. EN9 31 EC36
Rushen Wk, Cars. SM5
off Paisley Rd 140 DD102
Rushes Mead, Uxb. UB8
off Frays Waye 76 BJ67
Rushet Rd, Orp. BR5 146 EU96
Rushett Cl, T.Ditt. KT7 137 CH102
Rushett La, Chess. KT9 155 CJ111
Epsom KT18 155 CJ111
Rushett Rd, T.Ditt. KT7 137 CH101
Rushey Cl, N.Mal. KT3 138 CR98
Rushey Grn, SE6 123 EB87
Rushey Hill, Enf. EN2 29 DM42
Rushey Mead, SE4 123 EA85
Rushfield, Pot.B. EN6 11 CX33
Rushford Rd, SE4 123 DZ86
RUSH GREEN, Rom. RM7 71 FC59
Rush Grn Gdns, Rom. RM7 71 FC60
Rush Grn Rd, Rom. RM7 71 FC60
Rushgrove Av, NW9 63 CT57
Rush Gro St, SE18 105 EM77
Rush Hill Ms, SW11
off Rush Hill Rd 100 DG83
Rush Hill Rd, SW11 100 DG83
Rushleigh Av, Wal.Cr.
(Chsht) EN8 15 DX31
Rushley Cl, Kes. BR2 162 EK105
Rushmead, E2
off Florida St 84 DV69
Richmond TW10 117 CH90
Rushmead Cl, Croy. CR0 160 DT105
Rushmere Av, Upmin.
RM14 72 FQ62
Rushmere Ct, Wor.Pk. KT4
off The Avenue 139 CU103
Rushmere Ho, SW15
off Fontley Way 119 CU88
Rushmere La, Chesh.
(Orch.L.) HP5 4 AU28
Rushmere Pl, SW19 119 CX92
Egham TW20 112 AY92
Rushmoor Cl, Pnr. HA5 59 BV56
Rickmansworth WD3 38 BK47
Rushmore Cl, Brom. BR1 144 EL97
Rushmore Cres, E5
off Rushmore Rd 67 DX63
Rushmore Hill, Orp. BR6 164 EW110
Sevenoaks (Knock.) TN14 164 EX112
Rushmore Rd, E5 66 DW63
Rusholme Av, Dag. RM10 70 FA62
Rusholme Gro, SE19 122 DS92
Rusholme Rd, SW15 119 CX86
Rushout Av, Har. HA3 61 CH58
Rushton Av, Wat. WD25 23 BU35
Rushton St, N1 84 DR68
Rushworth Av, NW4
off Rushworth Gdns 63 CU55
Rushworth Gdns, NW4 63 CU56
Rushworth Rd, Reig. RH2 184 DA133
Rushworth St, SE1 200 G4
Rushy Meadow La, Cars.
SM5 140 DE103
Ruskin Av, E12 86 EL65
Feltham TW14 115 BT86
Richmond TW9 98 CN80
Upminster RM14 72 FQ59
Waltham Abbey EN9 16 EE34
Welling DA16 106 EU83
Ruskin Cl, NW11 64 DB58
Waltham Cross
(Chsht) EN7 14 DS26
Ruskin Dr, Orp. BR6 145 ES104
Welling DA16 106 EU83
Worcester Park KT4 139 CV103
Ruskin Gdns, W5 79 CK70
Harrow HA3 62 CM56
Romford RM3 51 FH52
Ruskin Gro, Dart. DA1 128 FN85
Welling DA16 106 EU82
Ruskin Pk Ho, SE5 102 DR83
Ruskin Rd, N17 46 DT53
Belvedere DA17 106 FA77
Carshalton SM5 158 DF106
Croydon CR0 141 DP103
Grays RM16 111 GG77
Isleworth TW7 97 CF83
Southall UB1 78 BY73
Staines TW18 113 BF94
Ruskin Wk, N9
off Durham Rd 46 DU47
SE24 122 DQ85
Bromley BR2 145 EM100
Ruskin Way, SW19 140 DD95
Rusland Av, Orp. BR6 145 ER104
Rusland Hts, Har. HA1
off Rusland Pk Rd 61 CE56
Rusland Pk Rd, Har. HA1 61 CE56
Rusper Cl, NW2 63 CW62
Stanmore HA7 41 CJ49
Rusper Rd, N22 46 DQ54
Dagenham RM9 88 EW65
Russell Av, N22 45 DP54
Russell Cl, NW10 80 CQ66
SE7 104 EJ80
W4 99 CT79
Amersham HP6 20 AX39
Beckenham BR3 143 EB97
Bexleyheath DA7 106 FA84
Brentwood CM15 54 FV45
Dartford DA1 107 FG83
Northwood HA6 39 BQ50
Ruislip HA4 60 BW61
Tadworth KT20 183 CU125
Woking GU21 166 AW115
Russell Ct, SW1 199 L3
Leatherhead KT22 171 CH122
St. Albans AL2 8 CA30
Russell Cres, Wat. WD25
off High Rd 23 BT35
Russell Dr, Stai.
(Stanw.) TW19 114 BK86
Russell Gdns, N20 44 DE47
NW11 63 CY58
W14 99 CY76
Richmond TW10 117 CJ89
West Drayton UB7 94 BN78
Russell Gdns Ms, W14 99 CY76
Russell Grn Cl, Pur. CR8 159 DN110
Russell Gro, NW7 42 CS50
SW9 101 DN80
Russell Hill, Pur. CR8 159 DM110
Russell Hill Pl, Pur. CR8 159 DN111
Russell Hill Rd, Pur. CR8 159 DN110
Russell Kerr Cl, W4
off Burlington La 98 CQ80
Russell La, N20 44 DE47
Watford WD17 23 BR36
Russell Mead, Har.
(Har.Wld) HA3 41 CF53
Russell Par, NW11
off Golders Grn Rd 63 CY58
Russell Pl, NW3
off Aspern Gro 64 DE64
SE16 203 K7
Dartford (Sutt.H.) DA4 148 FN95
Russell Rd, E4 47 DZ49
E10 67 EB58
E16 86 EG72
E17 67 DZ55
N8 65 DK58
N13 45 DM51
N15 66 DS57
N20 44 DE47
NW9 63 CT58
SW19 120 DA94
W14 99 CY76
Buckhurst Hill IG9 48 EH46
Enfield EN1 30 DT38
Gravesend DA12 131 GK86
Grays RM17 110 GA77
Mitcham CR4 140 DE97
Northolt UB5 60 CC64
Northwood HA6 39 BQ49
Shepperton TW17 135 BQ101
Tilbury RM18 110 GE81
Russell Rd, Twickenham TW2 117 CF86
Walton-on-Thames KT12 135 BU100
Woking GU21 166 AW115
Russells, Tad. KT20 173 CX122
Russell's Footpath, SW16 121 DL92
⊖ Russell Square 195 P5
Russell Sq, WC1 195 P5
Longfield DA3
off Cavendish Sq 149 FX97
Russells Ride, Wal.Cr.
(Chsht) EN8 15 DX31
Russell St, WC2 196 A10
Russell Wk, Rich. TW10
off Park Hill 118 CM86
Russell Way, Sutt. SM1 158 DA106
Watford WD19 39 BV45
Russet Cl, Stai. TW19 113 BF86
Uxbridge UB10
off Uxbridge Rd 77 BQ70
Walton-on-Thames KT12 136 BX104
Russet Cres, N7
off Stock Orchard Cres 65 DM64
Russet Dr, Croy. CR0 143 DY102
Radlett (Shenley) WD7 10 CL32
Russets, The, Ger.Cr.
(Chal.St.P.) SL9
off Austenwood Cl 36 AX54
Russets Cl, E4
off Larkshall Rd 47 ED49
Russett Cl, Orp. BR6 164 EV106
Waltham Cross EN7 14 DS26
Russett Ct, Cat. CR3 186 DU125
Russett Hill, Ger.Cr.
(Chal.St.P.) SL9 56 AY55
Russetts, Horn. RM11 72 FL56
Russetts Cl, Wok. GU21 167 AZ115
Russett Way, SE13 103 EB82
Swanley BR8 147 FD96
Russia Ct, EC2 197 J8
Russia Dock Rd, SE16 203 L3
Russia La, E2 84 DW68
Russia Row, EC2 197 J9
Russia Wk, SE16 203 K5
Russington Rd, Shep. TW17 135 BR100
Rusthall Av, W4 98 CR77
Rusthall Cl, Croy. CR0 142 DW100
Rustic Av, SW16 121 DH94
Rustic Cl, Upmin. RM14 73 FS60
Rustic Pl, Wem. HA0 61 CK63
Rustic Wk, E16
off Lambert Rd 86 EH72
Rustington Wk, Mord. SM4 139 CZ101
Ruston Av, Surb. KT5 138 CP101
Ruston Gdns, N14
off Farm La 28 DG44
Ruston Ms, W11
off St. Marks Rd 81 CY72
Ruston Rd, SE18 104 EL76
Ruston St, E3 85 DZ67
Rust Sq, SE5 102 DR80
Rutford Rd, SW16 121 DL92
Ruth Cl, Stan. HA7 62 CM56
Ruthen Cl, Epsom KT18 156 CP114
Rutherford Cl, Borwd. WD6 26 CQ40
Sutton SM2 158 DD107
Uxbridge UB8 76 BM70
Rutherford St, SW1 199 M8
Rutherford Twr, Sthl. UB1 78 CB72
Rutherford Way, Bushey
(Bushey Hth) WD23 41 CD46
Wembley HA9 62 CN63
Rutherglen Rd, SE2 106 EU79
Rutherwick Ri, Couls. CR5 175 DL117
Rutherwyke Cl,
Epsom KT17 157 CU107
Rutherwyk Rd, Cher. KT16 133 BE101
Ruthin Cl, NW9 62 CS58
Ruthin Rd, SE3 104 EG79
Ruthven Av, Wal.Cr. EN8 15 DX33
Ruthven St, E9
off Lauriston Rd 85 DX67
Rutland App, Horn. RM11 72 FN57
Rutland Av, Sid. DA15 126 EU87
Rutland Cl, SW14 98 CQ83
SW19
off Rutland Rd 120 DE94
Ashtead KT21 172 CL117
Bexley DA5 126 EX88
Chessington KT9 156 CM107
Dartford DA1 128 FK87
Epsom KT19 156 CR110
Redhill RH1 184 DF133
Rutland Ct, Enf. EN3 30 DW43
Rutland Dr, Horn. RM11 72 FN57
Morden SM4 139 CZ100
Richmond TW10 117 CK88
Rutland Gdns, N4 65 DP58
SW7 198 C5
W13 79 CG71
Croydon CR0 160 DS105
Dagenham RM8 70 EW64
Rutland Gdns Ms, SW7 198 C5
Rutland Gate, SW7 198 C5
Belvedere DA17 107 FB78
Bromley BR2 144 EF98
Rutland Gate Ms, SW7 198 B5
Rutland Gro, W6 99 CV78
Rutland Ms, NW8
off Boundary Rd 82 DB67
Rutland Ms E, SW7 198 B6
Rutland Ms S, SW7 198 B6
Rutland Ms W, SW7
off Ennismore St 100 DE76
Rutland Pk, NW2 81 CW65
SE6 123 DZ89
Rutland Pk Gdns, NW2
off Rutland Pk 81 CW65
Rutland Pk Mans, NW2
off Walm La 81 CW65
Rutland Pl, EC1 197 H5
Bushey (Bushey Hth) WD23
off The Rutts 41 CD46
Rutland Rd, E7 86 EK66
E9 84 DW67
E11 68 EH57
E17 67 EA58
SW19 120 DE94
Harrow HA1 60 CC58
Hayes UB3 95 BR77
Ilford IG1 69 EP63
Rutland Rd, Southall UB1 78 CA71
Twickenham TW2 117 CD89
Rutland St, SW7 198 C6
Rutland Wk, SE6 123 DZ89
Rutland Way, Orp. BR5 146 EW100
Rutley Cl, SE17 off Royal Rd 101 DP79
Romford (Harold Wd) RM3
off Pasteur Dr 52 FK54
Rutlish Rd, SW19 140 DA95
Rutson Rd, W.Byf.
(Byfleet) KT14 152 BM114
Rutter Gdns, Mitch. CR4 140 DC98
Rutters Cl, West Dr. UB7 94 BN75
Rutts, The, Bushey
(Bushey Hth) WD23 41 CD46
Rutts Ter, SE14 103 DX81
Ruvigny Gdns, SW15 99 CX83
Ruxbury Rd, Cher. KT16 133 BC100
Ruxley Cl, Epsom KT19 156 CP106
Sidcup DA14 126 EX93
Ruxley Cor Ind Est, Sid.
DA14 126 EX93
Ruxley Cres, Esher
(Clay.) KT10 155 CH107
Ruxley Gdns, Shep. TW17 135 BQ99
Ruxley La, Epsom KT19 156 CR106
Ruxley Ms, Epsom KT19 156 CP106
Ruxley Ridge, Esher
(Clay.) KT10 155 CG108
Ruxton Cl, Swan. BR8 147 FE97
Ryall Cl, St.Alb.
(Brick.Wd) AL2 8 BY29
Ryalls Ct, N20 44 DF48
Ryan Cl, SE3 104 EJ84
Ruislip HA4 59 BV60
Ryan Dr, Brent. TW8 97 CG79
Ryan Way, Wat. WD24 24 BW39
Ryarsh Cres, Orp. BR6 163 ES105
Rybrook Dr, Walt. KT12 136 BW103
Rycott Path, SE22
off Lordship La 122 DU87
Rycroft La, Sev. TN14 190 FE130
Rycroft Way, N17 66 DT55
Ryculff Sq, SE3 104 EF82
Rydal Cl, NW4 43 CY53
Purley CR8 160 DR113
Rydal Ct, Wat. WD25
off Grasmere Cl 7 BV32
Rydal Cres, Grnf. UB6 79 CH69
Rydal Dr, Bexh. DA7 106 FA81
West Wickham BR4 144 EE103
Rydal Gdns, NW9 62 CS57
SW15 118 CS92
Hounslow TW3 116 CB86
Wembley HA9 61 CJ60
Rydal Rd, SW16 121 DK91
Rydal Way, Egh. TW20 113 BB94
Enfield EN3 30 DW44
Ruislip HA4 60 BW63
Ryde, The, Stai. TW18 134 BH95
Ryde Cl, Wok.
(Ripley) GU23 168 BJ121
Ryde Heron, Wok. (Knap.) GU21
off Robin Hood Rd 166 AS117
RYDENS, Walt. KT12 136 BW103
Rydens Av, Walt. KT12 135 BV103
Rydens Cl, Walt. KT12 136 BW103
Rydens Gro, Walt. KT12 154 BX105
Rydens Pk, Walt. KT12
off Rydens Rd 136 BX103
Rydens Rd, Walt. KT12 136 BX103
Rydens Way, Wok. GU22 167 BA120
Ryde Pl, Twick. TW1 117 CJ86
Ryder Cl, Brom. BR1 124 EH92
Bushey WD23 24 CB44
Hemel Hempstead
(Bov.) HP3 5 BA28
Ryder Ct, SW1 199 L2
Ryder Dr, SE16 102 DV78
Ryder Gdns, Rain. RM13 89 FF65
Ryder Ms, E9
off Homerton High St 66 DW64
Ryders Ter, NW8
off Blenheim Ter 82 DC68
Ryder St, SW1 199 L2
Ryder Yd, SW1 199 L2
Rydes Cl, Wok. GU22 167 BC120
Ryde Vale Rd, SW12 121 DH89
Rydon Business Cen, Lthd.
KT22 171 CH119
Rydons Cl, SE9 104 EL83
Rydon's La, Couls. CR5 176 DQ120
Rydon St, N1
off St. Paul St 84 DQ67
Rydon's Wd Cl, Couls. CR5 176 DQ120
Rydston Cl, N7
off Sutterton St 83 DM66
Rye, The, N14 45 DJ45
Ryebridge Cl, Lthd. KT22 171 CG118
Ryebrook Rd, Lthd. KT22 171 CG118
Rye Cl, Bex. DA5 127 FB86
Hornchurch RM12 72 FJ64
Ryecotes Mead, SE21 122 DS88
Rye Ct, Slou. SL1
off Alpha St S 92 AU76
Rye Cres, Orp. BR5 146 EW102
Ryecroft, Grav. DA12 131 GL92
Ryecroft Av, Ilf. IG5 49 EP54
Twickenham TW2 116 CB87
Ryecroft Cres, Barn. EN5 27 CV43
Ryecroft Rd, SE13 123 EC85
SW16 121 DN93
Orpington BR5 145 ER100
Sevenoaks (Otford) TN14 181 FG116
Ryecroft St, SW6 100 DB81
Ryedale, SE22 122 DV86
Ryedale Ct, Sev. TN13
off London Rd 190 FE121
Rye Fld, Ashtd. KT21 171 CK117
Orpington BR5 146 EX102
Ryefield Av, Uxb. UB10 77 BP66
Ryefield Ct, Nthwd. HA6
off Ryefield Cres 39 BU54
Ryefield Cres, Nthwd. HA6 39 BU54
Ryefield Par, Nthwd. HA6
off Ryefield Cres 39 BU54
Ryefield Path, SW15 119 CU88
Ryefield Rd, SE19 122 DQ93
Ryegates, SE15
off Caulfield Rd 102 DV82
Rye Hill Pk, SE15 102 DW84
Ryeland Cl, West Dr. UB7 76 BL72
Ryelands Cl, Cat. CR3 176 DS121
Ryelands Ct, Lthd. KT22 171 CG118
Ryelands Cres, SE12 124 EJ86
Ryelands Pl, Wey. KT13 135 BS104
Rye La, SE15 102 DU81
Sevenoaks TN14 181 FG117
Rye Pas, SE15 102 DU83
Rye Rd, SE15 103 DX84
Rye Wk, SW15
off Chartfield Av 119 CX85
Rye Way, Edg. HA8
off Canons Dr 42 CM51
Ryfold Rd, SW19 120 DA90
Ryhope Rd, N11 45 DH49
Rykhill, Grays RM16 111 GH76
Ryland Cl, Felt. TW13 115 BT91
Rylandes Rd, NW2 63 CU62
South Croydon CR2 160 DV109
Ryland Ho, Croy. CR0 142 DQ104
Ryland Rd, NW5 83 DH65
Rylett Cres, W12 99 CT76
Rylett Rd, W12 99 CT75
Rylston Rd, N13 46 DR48
SW6 99 CZ79
Rymer Rd, Croy. CR0 142 DS101
Rymer St, SE24 121 DP86
Rymill Cl, Hem.H.
(Bov.) HP3 5 BA28
Rymill St, E16 87 EN74
Rysbrack St, SW3 198 D6
Rysted La, West. TN16 189 EQ126
Rythe Cl, Chess. KT9
off Nigel Fisher Way 155 CJ108
Rythe Ct, T.Ditt. KT7 137 CG101
Rythe Rd, Esher
(Clay.) KT10 155 CD106
Ryvers Rd, Slou. SL3 93 AZ76
★ Saatchi Gall, SE1 200 B5

S

Sabah Ct, Ashf. TW15 114 BN91
Sabbarton St, E16
off Victoria Dock Rd 86 EF72
Sabella Ct, E3 85 DZ68
Sabina Rd, Grays RM16 111 GJ77
Sabine Rd, SW11 100 DF83
Sable Cl, Houns. TW4 96 BW83
Sable St, N1 83 DP66
Sach Rd, E5 66 DV61
Sackville Av, Brom. BR2 144 EG102
Sackville Cl, Har. HA2 61 CD62
Sevenoaks TN13 191 FH122
Sackville Ct, Rom. RM3
off Sackville Cres 52 FL53
Sackville Cres, Rom. RM3 52 FL53
Sackville Est, SW16 121 DL90
Sackville Gdns, Ilf. IG1 69 EM60
Sackville Rd, Dart. DA2 128 FK89
Sutton SM2 158 DA108
Sackville St, W1 199 L1
Sackville Way, SE22
off Dulwich Common 122 DU88
Saddington St, Grav. DA12 131 GH87
Saddlebrook Pk, Sun. TW16 115 BS94
Saddlers Cl, Barn. (Arkley) EN5 27 CV43
Borehamwood WD6
off Farriers Way 26 CR44
Pinner HA5 40 CA51
Saddlers Ms, SW8
off Portland Gro 101 DM81
Kingston upon Thames
(Hmptn W.) KT1 137 CJ95
Wembley HA0
off The Boltons 61 CF63
Saddler's Pk,
Dart. (Eyns.) DA4 148 FK104
Saddlers Path, Borwd. WD6 26 CR43
Saddlers Way, Epsom KT18 172 CR119
Saddlescombe Way, N12 44 DA50
Saddleworth Rd, Rom. RM3 52 FJ51
Saddleworth Sq, Rom. RM3 52 FJ51
Saddle Yd, W1 199 H2
Sadler Cl, Mitch. CR4 140 DF96
Waltham Cross (Chsht) EN7
off Markham Rd 14 DQ25
Sadlers Ride, W.Mol. KT8 136 CC96
★ Sadler's Wells Thea, EC1 196 F2
Saffron Av, E14 85 ED73
Saffron Cl, NW11 63 CZ57
Croydon CR0 141 DL100
Slough (Datchet) SL3 92 AV81
Saffron Ct, Felt. TW14
off Staines Rd 115 BQ87
Saffron Hill, EC1 196 E5
Saffron Rd, Grays
(Chaff.Hun.) RM16 109 FW77
Romford RM5 51 FC54
Saffron St, EC1 196 E6
Saffron Way, Surb. KT6 137 CK102
Sage Cl, E6
off Bradley Stone Rd 87 EM71
Sage Ms, SE22
off Lordship La 122 DT85
Sage St, E1 off Cable St 84 DW73
Sage Way, WC1 196 B3
Saigasso Cl, E16
off Royal Rd 86 EK72
Sailmakers Ct, SW6
off William Morris Way 100 DC83
Sail St, SE11 200 C8
Sainfoin Rd, SW17 120 DG89
Sainsbury Rd, SE19 122 DS92
St. Agatha's Dr, Kings.T. KT2 118 CM93
St. Agathas Gro, Cars. SM5 140 DF102
St. Agnes Cl, E9
off Gore Rd 84 DW67
St. Agnes Pl, SE11 101 DN79
St. Agnes Well, EC1
off Old St 84 DR70
St. Aidans Ct, W13
off St. Aidans Rd 97 CH75
Barking IG11
off Choats Rd 88 EV69
St. Aidan's Rd, SE22 122 DV86
St. Aidans Rd, W13 97 CH75

St. Aidan's Way, Grav. DA12 131 GL90
St. Albans Av, E6 87 EM69
St. Alban's Av, W4 98 CR77
St. Albans Av, Felt. TW13 116 BX92
Upminster RM14 73 FS60
Weybridge KT13 134 BN104
St. Albans Cl, NW11 64 DA60
Gravesend DA12 131 GK90
St. Albans Ct, EC2 197 J8
St. Albans Cres, N22 45 DN53
St. Alban's Cres, Wdf.Grn. IG8 48 EG52
St. Albans Gdns, Grav. DA12 131 GK90
St. Alban's Gdns, Tedd. TW11 117 CG92
St. Albans Gro, W8 100 DB76
St. Alban's Gro, Cars. SM5 140 DE101
St. Albans La, NW11
off West Heath Dr 64 DA60
Abbots Langley (Bedmond) WD5 7 BT26
St. Alban's Pl, N1 83 DP67
St. Albans Rd, NW5 64 DG62
NW10 80 CS67
Barnet EN5 27 CX39
Dartford DA1 128 FM87
Epping (Cooper.) CM16 18 EX29
Ilford IG3 69 ET60
St. Alban's Rd, Kings.T. KT2 118 CL93
St. Albans Rd, Pot.B. (Dance.H.) EN6 27 CV35
Potters Bar (S.Mimms) EN6 11 CV34
Radlett (Shenley) WD7 10 CQ30
Reigate RH2 184 DA133
St. Albans (Lon.Col.) AL2 10 CN28
St. Alban's Rd, Sutt. SM1 157 CZ105
St. Albans Rd, Wat. WD17, WD24, WD25 23 BV40
St. Alban's Rd, Wdf.Grn. IG8 48 EG52
St. Albans St, SW1 199 M1
St. Albans Ter, W6
off Margravine Rd 99 CY79
St. Alban's Vil, NW5
off Highgate Rd 64 DG62
St. Alfege Pas, SE10 103 EC79
St. Alfege Rd, SE7 104 EK79
St. Alphage Gdns, EC2 197 J7
St. Alphage Highwalk, EC2 197 K7
St. Alphage Wk, Edg. HA8 42 CQ54
St. Alphege Rd, N9 46 DW45
St. Alphonsus Rd, SW4 101 DJ84
St. Amunds Cl, SE6 123 EA91
H **St. Andrew's at Harrow**, Har. HA1 61 CE61
St. Andrews Av, Horn. RM12 71 FG64
Wembley HA0 61 CG63
St. Andrew's Cl, N12
off Woodside Av 44 DC49
St. Andrews Cl, NW2 63 CV62
SE16 *off Ryder Dr* 102 DV78
SE28 88 EX72
St. Andrew's Cl, Islw. TW7 97 CD81
St. Andrews Cl, Ruis. HA4 60 BX61
St. Andrew's Cl, Shep. TW17 135 BR98
Staines (Wrays.) TW19 112 AY87
St. Andrews Cl, Stan. HA7 41 CJ54
Thames Ditton KT7 137 CH102
St. Andrew's Cl, Wind. (Old Wind.) SL4 112 AU86
St. Andrews Cl, Wok. GU21
off St. Mary's Rd 166 AW117
St. Andrew's Ct, SW18
off Waynflete St 120 DC89
St. Andrews Ct, Slou. (Colnbr.) SL3
off High St 93 BD80
Watford WD17 23 BV39
St. Andrews Dr, Orp. BR5 146 EV100
Stanmore HA7 41 CJ53
St. Andrews Gdns, Cob. KT11 154 BW113
St. Andrew's Gro, N16 66 DR60
St. Andrew's Hill, EC4 196 G10
H **St. Andrew's Hosp**, E3 85 EB70
St. Andrew's Ms, N16 66 DS60
St. Andrews Ms, SE3
off Mycenae Rd 104 EG80
St. Andrews Pl, NW1 195 J4
Brentwood (Shenf.) CM15 55 FZ47
St. Andrews Rd, E11 68 EE58
E13 86 EH69
E17 47 DX54
N9 46 DW45
NW9 62 CR60
NW10 81 CV65
NW11 63 CZ58
W3 80 CS73
W7 *off Churchfield Rd* 97 CE75
W14 99 CY79
Carshalton SM5 140 DE104
Coulsdon CR5 174 DG116
Croydon CR0
off Lower Coombe St 160 DQ105
Enfield EN1 30 DR41
St. Andrew's Rd, Grav. DA12 131 GJ87
St. Andrews Rd, Ilf. IG1 69 EM59
Romford RM7 71 FD58
Sidcup DA14 126 EX90
St. Andrew's Rd, Surb. KT6 137 CK100
St. Andrews Rd, Til. RM18 110 GE81
Uxbridge UB10 76 BM66
Watford WD19 40 BX48
St. Andrews Sq, W11
off St. Marks Rd 81 CY72
St. Andrew's Sq, Surb. KT6 137 CK100
St. Andrews Twr, Sthl. UB1 78 CC73
St. Andrew St, EC4 196 E7
St. Andrews Wk, Cob. KT11 169 BV115
St. Andrews Way, E3 85 EB70
Oxted RH8 188 EL130
St. Anna Rd, Barn. EN5
off Sampson Av 27 CX43
St. Annes Av, Stai. (Stanw.) TW19 114 BK87
St. Annes Boul, Red. RH1 185 DH132
St. Anne's Cl, N6
off Highgate W Hill 64 DG62
St. Annes Cl, Wal.Cr. (Chsht) EN7 14 DU28
St. Anne's Cl, Wat. WD19 40 BW49
St. Anne's Ct, W1 195 M9
St. Anne's Dr, Red. RH1 184 DG133
St. Annes Dr N, Red. RH1 184 DG132
St. Annes Gdns, NW10 80 CM69
St. Anne's Mt, Red. RH1 184 DG133
St. Annes Pas, E14
off Newell St 85 DZ72
St. Annes Ri, Red. RH1 184 DG133
St. Annes Rd, E11 67 ED61
St. Anne's Rd, St.Alb. (Lon.Col.) AL2 9 CK27
Uxbridge (Hare.) UB9 58 BJ55
Wembley HA0 61 CK64
St. Anne's Row, E14
off Commercial Rd 85 DZ72
St. Anne St, E14
off Commercial Rd 85 DZ72
St. Anne's Way, Red. RH1
off St. Anne's Dr 184 DG133
St. Ann's, Bark. IG11 87 EQ67
St. Anns Cl, Cher. KT16 133 BF100
St. Ann's Cres, SW18 120 DC86
St. Ann's Gdns, NW5
off Queen's Cres 82 DG65
St. Ann's Hill, SW18 120 DB85
St. Anns Hill Rd, Cher. KT16 133 BC100
H **St. Ann's Hosp**, N15 66 DQ57
St. Ann's La, SW1 199 N6
St. Ann's Pk Rd, SW18 120 DC86
St. Ann's Pas, SW13 98 CS83
St. Anns Rd, N9 46 DT47
St. Ann's Rd, N15 65 DP57
SW13 99 CT82
St. Anns Rd, W11 81 CX73
St. Ann's Rd, Bark. IG11
off Axe St 87 EQ67
St. Anns Rd, Cher. KT16 133 BF100
St. Ann's Rd, Har. HA1 61 CE58
St. Ann's Shop Cen, Har. HA1 61 CE58
St. Ann's St, SW1 199 N6
St. Ann's Ter, NW8 82 DD68
St. Anns Vil, W11 81 CX74
St. Anns Way, S.Croy. CR2 159 DP107
Westerham (Berry's Grn) TN16 179 EP116
St. Anselm's Pl, W1 195 H9
St. Anselms Rd, Hayes UB3 95 BT75
St. Anthonys Av, Wdf.Grn. IG8 48 EJ51
St. Anthonys Cl, E1 202 B2
SW17 *off College Gdns* 120 DE89
H **St. Anthony's Hosp**, Sutt. SM3 139 CX102
St. Anthony's Way, Felt. TW14 95 BT84
St. Antony's Rd, E7 86 EH66
St. Arvans Cl, Croy. CR0 142 DS104
St. Asaph Rd, SE4 103 DX83
St. Aubyn's Av, SW19 119 CZ92
St. Aubyns Av, Houns. TW3 116 CA85
St. Aubyns Cl, Orp. BR6 145 ET104
St. Aubyns Gdns, Orp. BR6 145 ET103
St. Aubyn's Rd, SE19 122 DT93
St. Audrey Av, Bexh. DA7 106 FA82
St. Augustine Rd, Grays RM16 111 GH77
St. Augustine's Av, W5 80 CL68
St. Augustines Av, Brom. BR2 144 EL99
St. Augustine's Av, S.Croy. CR2 160 DQ107
St. Augustines Av, Wem. HA9 62 CL62
St. Augustine's Path, N5
off Highbury New Pk 66 DQ63
St. Augustines Rd, NW1 83 DK66
St. Augustine's Rd, Belv. DA17 106 EZ77
St. Austell Cl, Edg. HA8 42 CM54
St. Austell Rd, SE13 103 EC82
St. Awdry's Rd, Bark. IG11 87 ER66
St. Awdry's Wk, Bark. IG11
off Station Par 87 EQ66
St. Barnabas Cl, SE22
off East Dulwich Gro 122 DS85
Beckenham BR3 143 EC96
St. Barnabas Ct, Har. HA3 40 CC53
St. Barnabas Gdns, W.Mol. KT8 136 CA99
St. Barnabas Rd, E17 67 EA58
Mitcham CR4 120 DG94
Sutton SM1 158 DD106
Woodford Green IG8 48 EH53
St. Barnabas St, SW1 198 G10
St. Barnabas Ter, E9 67 DX64
St. Barnabas Vil, SW8 101 DL81
St. Bartholomews Cl, SE26 122 DW91
H **St. Bartholomew's Hosp**, EC1 196 G7
St. Bartholomews Rd, E6 86 EL67
★ **St. Bartholomew-the-Great Ch**, EC1 196 G7
St. Benedict's Av, Grav. DA12 131 GK89
St. Benedict's Cl, SW17
off Church La 120 DG92
St. Benet's Cl, SW17
off College Gdns 120 DE89
St. Benet's Gro, Cars. SM5 140 DC101
St. Benet's Pl, EC3 197 L10
St. Benjamins Dr, Orp. BR6 164 EW109
St. Bernards, Croy. CR0 142 DS104
St. Bernard's Cl, SE27
off St. Gothard Rd 122 DR91
H **St. Bernard's Hosp**, Sthl. UB1 97 CD75
St. Bernard's Rd, E6 86 EK67
St. Bernards Rd, Slou. SL3 92 AW76
St. Blaise Av, Brom. BR1 144 EH96
St. Botolph Rd, Grav. DA11 130 GC90
St. Botolph Row, EC3 197 P9
St. Botolph's Av, Sev. TN13 190 FG124
St. Botolph's Rd, Sev. TN13 190 FG124
St. Botolph St, EC3 197 P9
St. Brides Av, EC4 196 F9
Edgware HA8 42 CM53
★ **St. Bride's Ch & Crypt Mus**, EC4 196 F9
St. Brides Cl, Erith DA18
off St. Katherines Rd 106 EX75
St. Bride's Pas, EC4 196 F9
St. Bride St, EC4 196 F8
St. Catherines, Wok. GU22 166 AW119
St. Catherines Cl, SW17
off College Gdns 120 DE89
St. Catherines Cross, Red. (Bletch.) RH1 186 DS134
St. Catherines Dr, SE14
off Kitto Rd 103 DX82
St. Catherines Fm Ct, Ruis. HA4 59 BQ58
St. Catherine's Ms, SW3 198 D8
St. Catherines Rd, E4 47 EA47
Ruislip HA4 59 BR57
St. Catherines Twr, E10
off Kings Cl 67 EB59
St. Cecilia Rd, Grays RM16 111 GH77
St. Cecilia's Cl, Sutt. SM3 139 CY102
St. Chads Cl, Surb. KT6 137 CJ101
St. Chad's Dr, Grav. DA12 131 GL90
St. Chad's Gdns, Rom. RM6 70 EY59
St. Chad's Pl, WC1 196 A2
St. Chad's Rd, Rom. RM6 70 EY58
Tilbury RM18 111 GG80
St. Chad's St, WC1 196 A2
St. Charles Ct, Wey. KT13 152 BN106
H **St. Charles Hosp**, W10 81 CX71
St. Charles Pl, W10
off Chesterton Rd 81 CY71
Weybridge KT13 152 BN106
St. Charles Rd, Brwd. CM14 54 FW46
St. Charles Sq, W10 81 CY71
St. Christopher Rd, Uxb. UB8 76 BK71
St. Christopher's Cl, Islw. TW7 97 CE81
St. Christopher's Dr, Hayes UB3 77 BV73
St. Christophers Gdns, Th.Hth. CR7 141 DN97
St. Christophers Ms, Wall. SM6 159 DJ106
St. Christopher's Pl, W1 194 G8
St. Clair Cl, Oxt. RH8 187 EC130
Reigate RH2 184 DC134
St. Clair Dr, Wor.Pk. KT4 139 CV104
St. Clair Rd, E13 86 EH68
St. Clair's Rd, Croy. CR0 142 DS103
St. Clare Business Pk, Hmptn. TW12 116 CC93
St. Clare Cl, Ilf. IG5 49 EM54
St. Clare St, EC3 197 P9
St. Clement Cl, Uxb. UB8 76 BK72
★ **St. Clement Danes Ch**, WC2 196 C9
St. Clements Av, Grays RM20 109 FU79
St. Clement's Cl, Grav. (Nthflt) DA11
off Coldharbour Rd 131 GF90
St. Clements Ct, EC4
off Clements La 84 DR73
N7 *off Arundel Sq* 83 DN65
Purfleet RM19
off Thamley 108 FN77
St. Clements Hts, SE26 122 DU90
St. Clement's La, WC2 196 C9
St. Clements Rd, Grays RM20 109 FW80
St. Clements St, N7 83 DN65
St. Clements Way, Grays RM20
off London Rd 109 FT79
Greenhithe DA9
off London Rd 129 FU85
St. Clements Yd, SE22
off Archdale Rd 122 DT85
St. Cloud Rd, SE27 122 DQ91
St. Columba's Cl, Grav. DA12 131 GL90
St. Crispins Cl, NW3 64 DE63
Southall UB1 78 BZ72
St. Crispins Way, Cher. (Ott.) KT16 151 BC109
St. Cross St, EC1 196 E6
St. Cuthberts Cl, Egh. TW20 112 AX92
St. Cuthberts Gdns, Pnr. HA5
off Westfield Pk 40 BZ52
St. Cuthberts Rd, N13 45 DN51
NW2 81 CZ65
St. Cyprian's St, SW17 120 DF91
St. David Cl, Uxb. UB8 76 BK71
St. Davids, Couls. CR5 175 DM117
St. Davids Cl, SE16
off Masters Dr 102 DV78
Iver SL0 75 BD67
St. David's Cl, Reig. RH2 184 DC133
St. Davids Cl, Wem. HA9 62 CQ62
St. David's Cl, W.Wick. BR4 143 EB101
St. David's Ct, E17 67 EC55
St. David's Cres, Grav. DA12 131 GK91
St. Davids Dr, Edg. HA8 42 CM53
St. David's Dr, Egh. (Eng.Grn) TW20 112 AW94
St. Davids Ms, E3
off Morgan St 85 DY69
St. Davids Pl, NW4 63 CV59
St. Davids Rd, Swan. BR8 127 FF93
St. Davids Sq, E14 204 C10
St. Denis Rd, SE27 122 DR91
St. Dionis Rd, SW6 99 CZ82
St. Donatts Rd, SE14 103 DZ81
St. Dunstan's All, EC3 197 M10
St. Dunstans Av, W3 80 CR73
St. Dunstans Cl, Hayes UB3 95 BT77
St. Dunstan's Ct, EC4
off Fleet St 83 DN72
St. Dunstan's Dr, Grav. DA12 131 GL91
St. Dunstans Gdns, W3
off St. Dunstans Av 80 CR73
St. Dunstan's Hill, EC3 201 M1
Sutton SM1 157 CY106
St. Dunstan's La, EC3 201 M1
Beckenham BR3 143 EC100
St. Dunstan's Rd, E7 86 EJ65
St. Dunstans Rd, SE25 142 DT98
W6 99 CX78
W7 97 CE75
St. Dunstan's Rd, Felt. TW13 115 BT90
St. Dunstans Rd, Houns. TW4 96 BW82
H **St. Ebba's Hosp**, Epsom KT19 156 CQ109
St. Edith Cl, Epsom KT18
off St. Elizabeth Dr 156 CQ114
St. Edmunds Av, Ruis. HA4 59 BR58
St. Edmunds Cl, NW8
off St. Edmunds Ter 82 DF67
St. Edmunds Cl, SW17
off College Gdns 120 DE89
Erith DA18
off St. Katherines Rd 106 EX75
St. Edmunds Dr, Stan. HA7 41 CG53
St. Edmund's La, Twick. TW2 116 CB87
St. Edmunds Rd, N9 46 DU45
Dartford DA1 108 FM84
Ilford IG1 69 EM58
St. Edmunds Sq, SW13 99 CW79
St. Edmunds Ter, NW8 82 DE67
St. Edwards Cl, NW11 64 DA58
Croydon (New Adgtn) CR0 161 ED111
St. Edwards Way, Rom. RM1 71 FD57
St. Egberts Way, E4 47 EC46
St. Elizabeth Dr, Epsom KT18 156 CQ114
St. Elmo Rd, W12 81 CT74
St. Elmos Rd, SE16 203 K4
St. Erkenwald Ms, Bark. IG11
off St. Erkenwald Rd 87 ER67
St. Erkenwald Rd, Bark. IG11 87 ER67
St. Ermin's Hill, SW1 199 M6
St. Ervans Rd, W10 81 CY71
St. Faiths Cl, Enf. EN2 30 DQ39
St. Faith's Rd, SE21 121 DP88
St. Fidelis Rd, Erith DA8 107 FD77
St. Fillans Rd, SE6 123 EC88
St. Francis Av, Grav. DA12 131 GL91
St. Francis Cl, Orp. BR5 145 ES100
Potters Bar EN6 12 DC33
Watford WD19 39 BV46
St. Francis Rd, SE22 102 DS84
Erith DA8 *off West St* 107 FD77
Uxbridge (Denh.) UB9 57 BF58
St. Francis Way, Grays RM16 111 GJ77
Ilford IG1 69 ES63
St. Frideswides Ms, E14
off Lodore St 85 EC72
St. Gabriel's Cl, E11 68 EH61
St. Gabriels Rd, NW2 63 CX64
St. Georges Av, E7 86 EH66
N7 65 DK63
NW9 62 CQ56
St. George's Av, W5 97 CK75
St. Georges Av, Grays RM17 110 GC77
Hornchurch RM11 72 FM59
Southall UB1 78 BZ73
St. George's Av, Wey. KT13 153 BP107
St. George's Cen, Grav. DA11 131 GH86
St. Georges Cen, Har. HA1
off St. Ann's Rd 61 CE58
St. Georges Circ, SE1 200 F6
St. Georges Cl, NW11 63 CZ58
SE28 *off Redbourne Dr* 88 EX72
St. George's Cl, SW8
off Patmore St 101 DJ81
St. Georges Cl, Wem. HA0 61 CG62
St. George's Cl, Wey. KT13 153 BR106
St. Georges Ct, E6 87 EM70
EC4 196 F8
SW7 *off Gloucester Rd* 100 DC76
St. Georges Cres, Grav. DA12 131 GK91
St. George's Dr, SW1 199 K10
St. Georges Dr, Uxb. UB10 58 BM62
Watford WD19 40 BY48
St. Georges Flds, W2 194 C9
St. Georges Gdns, Epsom KT17 157 CT114
St. George's Gdns, Surb. KT6
off Hamilton Av 138 CP103
St. Georges Gro, SW17 120 DD90
St. Georges Gro Est, SW17 120 DD90
ST. GEORGE'S HILL, Wey. KT13 153 BQ110
H **St. George's Hosp**, SW17 120 DD92
Hornchurch RM12 72 FK63
St. Georges Ind Est, Kings.T. KT2
off Richmond Rd 117 CK92
St. Georges La, EC3 197 M10
St. George's Lo, Wey. KT13 153 BR106
St. Georges Ms, NW1
off Regents Pk Rd 82 DF66
SE1 200 E6
St. Georges Pl, Twick. TW1
off Church St 117 CG88
St. Georges Rd, E7 86 EH65
E10 67 EC62
N9 46 DU48
N13 45 DM48
NW11 63 CZ58
SE1 200 E6
St. George's Rd, SW19 119 CZ93
St. Georges Rd, W4 98 CS75
W7 79 CF74
Addlestone KT15 152 BJ105
St. George's Rd, Beck. BR3 143 EB95
St. Georges Rd, Brom. BR1 145 EM96
Dagenham RM9 70 EY64
Enfield EN1 30 DT38
St. George's Rd, Felt. TW13 116 BX91
St. Georges Rd, Ilf. IG1 69 EM59
St. George's Rd, Kings.T. KT2 118 CN94
Mitcham CR4 141 DH97
Orpington BR5 145 ER100
St. Georges Rd, Rich. TW9 98 CM83
St. George's Rd, Sev. TN13 191 FH122
Sidcup DA14 126 EX93
St. Georges Rd, Swan. BR8 147 FF98
Twickenham TW1 117 CH85
Wallington SM6 159 DH106
Watford WD24 23 BV38
St. George's Rd, Wey. KT13 153 BR107
St. Georges Rd W, Brom. BR1 144 EL95
St. Georges Sq, E7 86 EH66
E14 *off Narrow St* 85 DY73
SE8 203 M8
St. George's Sq, SW1 199 M10
New Malden KT3
off High St 138 CS97
St. George's Sq Ms, SW1 101 DK78
St. Georges Ter, NW1
off Regents Pk Rd 82 DF66
St. George St, W1 195 J9
St. Georges Wk, Croy. CR0 142 DQ104
St. Georges Way, SE15 102 DS79
St. Georges Wf, SW8 101 DL78
St. Gerards Cl, SW4 121 DJ85
St. German's Pl, SE3 104 EG81
St. Germans Rd, SE23 123 DY88
St. Giles Av, Dag. RM10 89 FB66
Potters Bar EN6 11 CV32
Uxbridge UB10 59 BQ63
St. Giles Cl, Dag. RM10
off St. Giles Av 89 FB66
Orpington BR6 163 ER106
St. Giles Ct, WC2
off St. Giles High St 83 DL72
St. Giles High St, WC2 195 N8
St. Giles Pas, WC2 195 N9
St. Giles Rd, SE5 102 DS80
St. Gilles Ho, E2 85 DX68
St. Gothard Rd, SE27 122 DR91
St. Gregory Cl, Ruis. HA4 60 BW63
St. Gregorys Cres, Grav. DA12 131 GL89
St. Helena Rd, SE16 203 H9
St. Helena St, WC1 196 D3
St. Helens Cl, Uxb. UB8 76 BK72
St. Helens Ct, Epp. CM16
off Hemnall St 18 EU30
Rainham RM13 89 FG70
St. Helens Cres, SW16
off St. Helens Rd 141 DM95
St. Helens Gdns, W10 81 CX72
St. Helens Pl, EC3 197 M8
St. Helens Rd, SW16 141 DM95
St. Helen's Rd, W13
off Dane Rd 79 CH74
St. Helens Rd, Erith DA18 106 EX75
Ilford IG1 69 EM58
ST. HELIER, Cars. SM5 140 DD101
⇌ **St. Helier** 140 DA100
St. Helier Av, Mord. SM4 140 DC101
H **St. Helier Hosp**, Cars. SM5 140 DC102
St. Heliers Av, Houns. TW3 116 CA85
St. Heliers Rd, E10 67 EC58
St. Hildas Av, Ashf. TW15 114 BL92
St. Hildas Cl, NW6 81 CX66
SW17 120 DE89
St. Hilda's Rd, SW13 99 CV79
St. Hilda's Way, Grav. DA12 131 GK91
St. Huberts Cl, Ger.Cr. SL9 56 AY60
St. Huberts La, Ger.Cr. SL9 57 AZ61
St. Hughe's Cl, SW17
off College Gdns 120 DE89
St. Hughs Rd, SE20
off Ridsdale Rd 142 DV95
St. Ives Cl, Rom. RM3 52 FM52
St. Ivians Dr, Rom. RM2 71 FG55
St. James Av, N20 44 DE48
W13 79 CG74
Epsom KT17 157 CT111
Sutton SM1 158 DA106
St. James Cl, N20 44 DE48
SE18 *off Congleton Gro* 105 EQ78
Barnet EN4 28 DD42
Epsom KT18 156 CS114
New Malden KT3 139 CT99
Ruislip HA4 60 BW61
Woking GU21 166 AU118
St. James Ct, Green. DA9 129 FT86
St. James Gdns, Rom. (Lt.Hth) RM6 70 EV56
Wembley HA0 79 CK66
St. James Gate, NW1
off St. Paul's Cres 83 DK66
St. James Gro, SW11
off Reform St 100 DF82
St. James La, Green. DA9 129 FS88
St. James Ms, E14 204 E7
E17 *off St. James's St* 67 DY57
Weybridge KT13 153 BP105
St. James Oaks, Grav. DA11
off Trafalgar Rd 131 GG87
St. James Pl, Dart. DA1
off Spital St 128 FK86
St. James Rd, E15 68 EF64
N9 *off Queens Rd* 46 DV47
Brentwood CM14 54 FW48
Carshalton SM5 140 DE104
Kingston upon Thames KT1 138 CL96
Mitcham CR4 120 DG94
Purley CR8 159 DP113
Sevenoaks TN13 191 FH122
Surbiton KT6 137 CK100
Sutton SM1 158 DA106
Waltham Cross (Chsht) EN7 14 DQ28
Watford WD18 23 BV43
ST. JAMES'S, SW1 199 L3
St. James's, SE14 103 DY81
St. James's Av, E2 84 DW68
Beckenham BR3 143 DY97
Gravesend DA11 131 GG87
Hampton (Hmptn H.) TW12 116 CC92
St. James's Cl, SW17
off St. James's Dr 120 DF89
St. James's Cotts, Rich. TW9
off Paradise Rd 117 CK85
St. James's Ct, SW1 199 L6
St. James's Cres, SW9 101 DN83
St. James's Dr, SW12 120 DF88
SW17 120 DF88
St. James's Gdns, W11 81 CY74
St. James's La, N10 65 DH56
St. James's Mkt, SW1 199 M1
★ **St. James's Palace**, SW1 199 L4
★ **St. James's Park**, SW1 199 M4
⊖ **St. James's Park** 199 M6
St. James's Pk, Croy. CR0 142 DQ101
St. James's Pas, EC3 197 N9
St. James's Pl, SW1 199 K3
St. James's Rd, SE1 202 C10
SE16 202 C6
Croydon CR0 141 DP101
Gravesend DA11 131 GG86
Hampton (Hmptn H.) TW12 116 CB92
St. James's Sq, SW1 199 L2

★ Place of interest ⇌ Railway station ⊖ London Underground station DLR Docklands Light Railway station Tra Tramlink station H Hospital Riv Pedestrian ferry landing stage

St. James's St, E17 67 DY57
SW1 199 K2
Gravesend DA11 131 GG86
St. James's Ter, NW8
off Prince Albert Rd 82 DF68
St. James's Ter Ms, NW8 82 DF67
⇌ St. James Street 67 DY57
St. James St, W6 99 CW78
St. James's Wk, EC1 196 F4
St. James Wk, Iver SL0 93 BE75
St. James Way, Sid. DA14 126 EY92
St. Jeromes Gro, Hayes UB3 77 BQ72
St. Joans Rd, N9 46 DT46
St. John Fisher Rd, Erith
DA18 106 EX76
ST. JOHN'S, SE8 103 EA82
ST. JOHN'S, Wok. GU21 166 AV118
⇌ St. John's 103 EA82
St. Johns Av, N11 44 DF50
St. John's Av, NW10 81 CT67
SW15 119 CX85
St. Johns Av, Brwd. CM14 54 FX49
St. John's Av, Epsom KT17 157 CT112
St. Johns Av, Lthd. KT22 171 CH121
St. John's Ch Rd, E9 66 DW64
St. Johns Cl, N14
off Chase Rd 29 DJ44
St. John's Cl, SW6
off Dawes Rd 100 DA80
St. Johns Cl, Lthd. KT22 171 CJ120
St. John's Cl, Pot.B. EN6 12 DC33
St. Johns Cl, Rain. RM13 89 FG66
St. John's Cl, Uxb. UB8 76 BH67
Wembley HA9 62 CL64
St. Johns Cl, West.
(Berry's Grn) TN16
off St. Johns Ri 179 EP116
St. John's Cotts, SE20
off Maple Rd 122 DW94
Rich. TW9
off Kew Foot Rd 98 CL84
St. Johns Ct, Buck.H. IG9 48 EH46
St. John's Ct, Egh. TW20 113 BA92
Isleworth TW7 97 CF82
St. Johns Ct, Nthwd. HA6
off Murray Rd 39 BS53
St. John's Ct, Wok. GU21
off St. Johns Hill Rd 166 AU119
St. John's Cres, SW9 101 DN83
St. Johns Dr, SW18 120 DB88
Walton-on-Thames KT12 136 BW102
St. John's Est, N1 197 L1
SE1 201 P4
St. John's Gdns, W11 81 CZ73
★ St. John's Gate & Mus of the
Order of St. John, EC1 196 F5
St. Johns Gro, N19 65 DJ61
SW13 off Terrace Gdns 99 CT82
Richmond TW9
off Kew Foot Rd 98 CL84
St. John's Hill, SW11 100 DD84
Coulsdon CR5 175 DN117
Purley CR8 175 DN116
Sevenoaks TN13 191 FJ123
St. John's Hill Gro, SW11 100 DD84
St. Johns Hill Rd, Wok. GU21 166 AU119
★ St. John's Jerusalem, Dart.
DA4 128 FP94
St. John's La, EC1 196 F5
St. John's Lye, Wok. GU21 166 AT119
St. John's Ms, W11
off Ledbury Rd 82 DA72
Woking GU21 166 AU119
St. Johns Par, Sid. DA14 126 EU91
St. John's Pk, SE3 104 EF80
St. John's Pas, SW19
off Ridgway Pl 119 CY93
St. John's Path, EC1 196 F5
St. Johns Pathway, SE23
off Devonshire Rd 122 DW88
St. John's Pl, EC1 196 F5
St. Johns Ri, West.
(Berry's Grn) TN16 179 EP116
Woking GU21 166 AV119
St. John's Rd, E4 47 EB48
E6 off Ron Leighton Way 86 EL67
St. Johns Rd, E16 86 EG72
St. John's Rd, E17 47 EB54
N15 66 DS58
St. Johns Rd, NW11 63 CZ58
St. John's Rd, SE20 122 DW94
SW11 100 DE84
SW19 119 CY94
Barking IG11 87 ES67
Carshalton SM5 140 DE104
St. Johns Rd, Croy. CR0
off Sylverdale Rd 141 DP104
St. John's Rd, Dart. DA2 128 FQ87
St. Johns Rd, E.Mol. KT8 137 CD98
St. John's Rd, Epp. CM16 17 ET30
St. Johns Rd, Erith DA8 107 FD78
St. John's Rd, Felt. TW13 116 BY91
St. Johns Rd, Grav. DA12 131 GK87
Grays RM16 111 GH78
St. John's Rd, Har. HA1 61 CF58
St. Johns Rd, Ilf. IG2 69 ER59
St. John's Rd, Islw. TW7 97 CE82
Kingston upon Thames
(Hmptn W.) KT1 137 CJ96
St. Johns Rd, Lthd. KT22 171 CJ121
Loughton IG10 33 EM40
New Malden KT3 138 CQ97
St. John's Rd, Orp. BR5 145 ER100
Richmond TW9 98 CL84
St. Johns Rd, Rom. RM5 51 FC50
St. John's Rd, Sev. TN13 191 FH121
St. Johns Rd, Sid. DA14 126 EV91
Slough SL2 74 AU74
Southall UB2 96 BY76
Sutton SM1 140 DA103
Uxbridge UB8 76 BH67
Watford WD17 23 BV40
St. John's Rd, Well. DA16 106 EV83
Wembley HA9 61 CK63
Woking GU21 166 AV118
St. John's Sq, EC1 196 F5
St. Johns Ter, E7 86 EH65
SE18 105 EQ79
SW15 off Kingston Vale 118 CR91
W10 off Harrow Rd 81 CX70
St. John's Ter, Enf. EN2 30 DR37
St. John St, EC1 196 G5
St. Johns Vale, SE8 103 EA82
St. Johns Vil, N19 65 DK61
St. John's Vil, W8
off St. Mary's Pl 100 DB76
St. John's Waterside, Wok. GU21
off Copse Rd 166 AU118
St. Johns Way, N19 65 DK60
ST. JOHN'S WOOD, NW8 82 DC69
⊖ St. John's Wood 82 DD68
St. John's Wd Ct, NW8 194 A3
St. John's Wd High St, NW8 194 A1
St. John's Wd Pk, NW8 82 DD67
St. John's Wd Rd, NW8 82 DD70
St. John's Wd Ter, NW8 82 DD68
St. Josephs Cl, W10
off Bevington Rd 81 CY71
St. Joseph's Cl, Orp. BR6 163 ET105
St. Joseph's Ct, SE7 104 EH79
St. Josephs Dr, Sthl. UB1 78 BY74
St. Joseph's Gro, NW4 63 CV56
St. Josephs Rd, N9 46 DV45
St. Joseph's Rd, Wal.Cr. EN8 15 DY33
St. Josephs St, SW8
off Battersea Pk Rd 101 DH81
St. Joseph's Vale, SE3 103 ED82
St. Judes Cl, Egh. TW20 112 AW92
St. Jude's Rd, E2 84 DV68
Egham TW20 112 AW90
St. Jude St, N16 66 DS64
St. Julians, Sev. TN15 191 FN128
St. Julian's Cl, SW16 121 DN91
St. Julian's Fm Rd, SE27 121 DN91
St. Julian's Rd, NW6 81 CZ66
St. Justin Cl, Orp. BR5 146 EX97
★ St. Katharine's Dock, E1 202 A1
Riv St. Katharine's Pier 201 P2
St. Katharines Prec, NW1
off Outer Circle 83 DH68
St. Katharine's Way, E1 202 A2
St. Katherines Rd, Cat. CR3 186 DU125
Erith DA18 106 EX75
St. Katherine's Row, EC3 197 N9
St. Katherine's Wk, W11
off Freston Rd 81 CX73
St. Keverne Rd, SE9 124 EL91
St. Kilda Rd, W13 79 CG74
Orpington BR6 145 ET102
St. Kilda's Rd, N16 66 DR60
Brentwood CM15 54 FV45
Harrow HA1 61 CE58
St. Kitts Ter, SE19 122 DS92
St. Laurence Cl, NW6 81 CX67
Orpington BR5 146 EX97
Uxbridge UB8 76 BJ71
St. Laurence Way, Slou. SL1 92 AU76
St. Lawrence Cl, Abb.L. WD5 7 BS30
Edgware HA8 42 CM52
Hemel Hempstead
(Bov.) HP3 5 BA27
St. Lawrence Dr, Pnr. HA5 59 BV58
★ St. Lawrence Jewry Ch,
EC2 197 J8
St. Lawrence Rd, Upmin.
RM14 72 FQ61
St. Lawrence St, E14 204 E2
St. Lawrence's Way, Reig. RH2
off Church St 184 DA134
St. Lawrence Ter, W10 81 CY71
St. Lawrence Way, SW9 101 DN81
Caterham CR3 176 DQ123
St. Albans (Brick.Wd) AL2 8 BZ30
St. Leonards Av, E4 47 ED51
Harrow HA3 61 CJ56
St. Leonards Cl, Bushey
WD23 24 BY42
Grays RM17 110 FZ79
St. Leonard's Cl, Well. DA16
off Hook La 106 EU83
St. Leonards Ct, N1 197 J2
St. Leonard's Gdns, Houns.
TW5 96 BY80
St. Leonards Gdns, Ilf. IG1 69 EQ64
St. Leonards Ri, Orp. BR6 163 ES105
St. Leonards Rd, E14 85 EB71
NW10 80 CR70
St. Leonard's Rd, SW14 98 CP83
St. Leonards Rd, W13 79 CJ73
Amersham HP6 20 AS35
Croydon CR0 141 DP104
Epsom KT18 173 CW119
Esher (Clay.) KT10 155 CF107
St. Leonard's Rd, Surb. KT6 137 CK99
St. Leonards Rd, T.Ditt. KT7 137 CG100
Waltham Abbey EN9 16 EE25
St. Leonards Sq, NW5 82 DG65
St. Leonard's Sq, Surb. KT6
off St. Leonard's Rd 137 CK99
St. Leonards St, E3 85 EB69
St. Leonard's Ter, SW3 100 DF78
St. Leonards Wk, SW16 121 DM94
Iver SL0 93 BF76
St. Leonards Way, Horn.
RM11 71 FH61
St. Loo Av, SW3 100 DE79
St. Louis Rd, SE27 122 DQ91
St. Loy's Rd, N17 46 DS54
St. Lucia Dr, E15 86 EF67
St. Luke Cl, Uxb. UB8 76 BK72
ST. LUKE'S, EC1 197 J4
St. Luke's Av, SW4 101 DK84
St. Lukes Av, Enf. EN2 30 DR38
St. Luke's Av, Ilf. IG1 69 EP64
St. Luke's Cl, EC1 197 J4
SE25 142 DV100
St. Lukes Cl, Dart.
(Lane End) DA2 129 FS92
Swanley BR8 147 FD96
St. Luke's Est, EC1 197 K3
H St. Luke's Hosp for the Clergy,
W1 195 K5
St. Lukes Ms, W11
off Basing St 81 CZ72
St. Lukes Rd, W11 81 CZ71
St. Lukes Rd, Uxbridge UB10 76 BL66
Whyteleafe CR3
off Whyteleafe Hill 176 DT118
Windsor (Old Wind.) SL4 112 AU86
St. Lukes Sq, E16 86 EF72
St. Luke's St, SW3 198 B10
H St. Luke's Woodside Hosp,
N10 64 DG56
St. Luke's Yd, W9 81 CZ68
St. Malo Av, N9 46 DW48
St. Margaret Dr, Epsom
KT18 156 CR114
ST. MARGARETS, Twick. TW1 117 CG85
St. Margarets, Bark. IG11 87 ER67
St. Margarets Av, N15 65 DP56
N20 44 DC47
Ashford TW15 115 BP92
Harrow HA2 60 CC62
Sidcup DA15 125 ER90
St. Margaret's Av, Sutt.
SM3 139 CY104
St. Margarets Av, Uxb. UB8 76 BN70
Westerham (Berry's Grn) TN16
off Berry's Grn Rd 179 EP116
St. Margarets Cl, EC2
off Lothbury 84 DR72
Dartford DA2 129 FR89
Iver SL0
off St. Margarets Gate 75 BD68
Orpington BR6 164 EV105
St. Margaret's Ct, SE1 201 J3
St. Margaret's Cres, SW15 119 CV85
Gravesend DA12 131 GL90
St. Margaret's Dr, Twick. TW1 117 CH85
St. Margarets Gate, Iver SL0 75 BD68
St. Margaret's Gro, E11 68 EF62
SE18 105 EQ79
St. Margarets Gro, Twick.
TW1 117 CG86
H St. Margaret's Hosp, Epp.
CM16 18 EV29
St. Margarets La, W8 100 DB76
St. Margarets Pas, SE13
off Church Ter 104 EE83
St. Margarets Path, SE18 105 EQ78
St. Margarets Rd, E12 68 EJ61
St. Margaret's Rd, N17 66 DS55
NW10 81 CW69
St. Margarets Rd, SE4 103 DZ84
W7 97 CE75
Coulsdon CR5 175 DH121
Dartford
(S.Darenth) DA2, DA4 129 FS93
Edgware HA8 42 CP50
St. Margaret's Rd, Grav.
(Nthflt) DA11 130 GE89
St. Margarets Rd, Islw. TW7 97 CH84
St. Margarets Rd, Ruis. HA4 59 BR58
St. Margarets Rd, Twick. TW1 97 CH84
St. Margarets Sq, SE4
off Adelaide Av 103 DZ84
St. Margaret's St, SW1 199 P5
St. Margaret's Ter, SE18 105 EQ78
⇌ St. Margarets 117 CH86
St. Marks Av, Grav.
(Nthflt) DA11 131 GF87
St. Marks Cl, SE10
off Ashburnham Gro 103 EC80
SW6 off Ackmar Rd 100 DA81
W11 off Lancaster Rd 81 CY72
St. Mark's Cl, Barn. EN5 28 DB41
St. Marks Cl, Har. HA1
off Nightingale Av 61 CH59
St. Marks Cres, NW1 82 DG67
St. Mark's Gate, E9
off Cadogan Ter 85 DZ66
St. Mark's Gro, SW10 100 DB79
St. Mark's Hill, Surb. KT6 138 CL100
St. Mark's Pl, SW19
off Wimbledon Hill Rd 119 CZ93
St. Marks Pl, W11 81 CY72
St. Marks Ri, E8 66 DT64
St. Marks Rd, SE25
off Coventry Rd 142 DU98
St. Mark's Rd, W5
off The Common 80 CL74
St. Marks Rd, W7 97 CE75
W10 81 CX72
W11 81 CY72
Bromley BR2 144 EH97
Enfield EN1 30 DT44
St. Mark's Rd, Epsom KT18 173 CW118
St. Marks Rd, Mitch. CR4 140 DF96
St. Mark's Rd, Tedd. TW11 117 CH94
St. Marks Sq, NW1 82 DG67
St. Mark St, E1 84 DT72
St. Martha's Av, Wok. GU22 167 AZ121
St. Martin Cl, Uxb. UB8 76 BK72
★ St. Martin-in-the-Fields Ch,
WC2 199 P1
St. Martins, Nthwd. HA6
off Batchworth La 39 BR50
St. Martins App, Ruis. HA4 59 BS59
St. Martins Av, E6 86 EK68
Epsom KT18 156 CS114
St. Martins Cl, NW1 83 DJ67
Enfield EN1 30 DV39
Epsom KT17
off Church Rd 156 CS113
Erith DA18
off St. Helens Rd 106 EX75
St. Martin's Cl, Wat. WD19
off Muirfield Rd 40 BW49
West Drayton UB7
off St. Martin's Rd 94 BK76
St. Martin's Ct, WC2
off St. Martin's La 83 DK73
Ashford TW15 114 BJ92
St. Martins Dr, Walt. KT12 136 BW104
St. Martins Est, SW2 121 DN88
St. Martin's La, WC2 195 P10
St. Martins La, Beck. BR3 143 EB99
St. Martin's-le-Grand, EC1 197 H8
St. Martins Meadow, West.
(Brasted) TN16 180 EW123
St. Martin's Ms, WC2 199 P1
St. Martins Ms, Wok.
(Pyrford) GU22 168 BG116
St. Martin's Pl, WC2 199 P1
St. Martins Rd, N9 46 DV47
St. Martin's Rd, SW9 101 DM82
St. Martins Rd, Dart. DA1 128 FM86
St. Martin's Rd, West Dr. UB7 94 BJ76
St. Martin's St, WC2 199 N1
St. Martins Ter, N10
off Pages La 44 DG54
St. Martins Way, SW17 120 DC90
St. Mary Abbots Pl, W8 99 CZ76
St. Mary Abbots Ter, W14
off Holland Pk Rd 99 CZ76
St. Mary at Hill, EC3 201 M1
★ St. Mary at Hill Ch, EC3 201 M1
St. Mary Av, Wall. SM6 140 DG104
St. Mary Axe, EC3 197 M9
St. Marychurch St, SE16 202 F5
ST. MARY CRAY, Orp. BR5 146 EW99
⇌ St. Mary Cray 146 EU98
★ St. Mary-le-Bow Ch, EC2 197 J9
St. Mary Rd, E17 67 EA56
St. Marys, Bark. IG11 87 ER67
St. Marys App, E12 69 EM64
St. Marys Av, E11 68 EH58
St. Mary's Av, N3 43 CY54
St. Marys Av, Brwd.
(Shenf.) CM15 55 GA43
St. Mary's Av, Brom. BR2 144 EE97
Northwood HA6 39 BS50
Staines (Stanw.) TW19 114 BK87
Teddington TW11 117 CF93
St. Mary's Av Cen, Sthl. UB2 96 CB77
St. Mary's Av N, Sthl. UB2 96 CB77
St. Mary's Av S, Sthl. UB2 96 CB77
St. Mary's Cl, N17
off Kemble Rd 46 DT53
St. Marys Cl, Chess. KT9 156 CM108
Epsom KT17 157 CU108
St. Mary's Cl, Grav. DA12 131 GJ89
St. Marys Cl, Grays RM17
off Dock Rd 110 GD79
St. Mary's Cl, Lthd.
(Fetch.) KT22 171 CD123
St. Marys Cl, Orp. BR5 146 EV96
St. Mary's Cl, Oxt. RH8 188 EE129
Staines (Stanw.) TW19 114 BK87
Sunbury-on-Thames TW16
off Green Way 135 BU98
Uxbridge (Hare.) UB9 58 BH55
St. Marys Cl, Wat. WD18
off King St 23 BV42
St. Mary's Copse, Wor.Pk.
KT4 138 CS103
St. Marys Ct, E6 87 EM70
St. Mary's Ct, SE7 104 EK80
W5 off St. Mary's Rd 97 CK75
St. Mary's Cres, NW4 63 CV55
Hayes UB3 77 BT73
St. Marys Cres, Islw. TW7 97 CD80
St. Mary's Cres, Stai.
(Stanw.) TW19 114 BK87
St. Marys Dr, Felt. TW14 115 BQ87
St. Mary's Dr, Sev. TN13 190 FE123
St. Mary's Gdns, SE11 200 E8
St. Mary's Gate, W8 100 DB76
St. Marys Grn, N2
off Thomas More Way 64 DC55
Westerham (Bigg.H.) TN16 178 EJ118
St. Mary's Gro, N1 83 DP65
SW13 99 CV83
W4 98 CP79
Richmond TW9 98 CM84
St. Marys Gro, West.
(Bigg.H.) TN16 178 EJ118
H St. Mary's Hosp, W2 194 A8
St. Mary's La, Upmin. RM14 72 FN61
St. Marys Mans, W2 82 DC71
St. Mary's Ms, NW6
off Priory Rd 82 DB66
Richmond TW10 117 CJ89
St. Mary's Mt, Cat. CR3 176 DT124
St. Marys Path, N1 83 DP67
St. Mary's Pl, SE9
off Eltham High St 125 EN86
W5 off St. Mary's Rd 97 CK75
W8 100 DB76
St. Marys Rd, E10 67 EC62
E13 86 EH68
N8 off High St 65 DL56
N9 46 DW46
St. Mary's Rd, NW10 80 CS67
St. Marys Rd, NW11 63 CY59
St. Mary's Rd, SE15 102 DW81
SE25 142 DS97
SW19 (Wimbledon) 119 CY92
W5 97 CK75
Barnet EN4 44 DF45
Bexley DA5 127 FC88
St. Marys Rd, E.Mol. KT8 137 CD99
St. Mary's Rd, Grays RM16 111 GH77
Greenhithe DA9 129 FS85
Hayes UB3 77 BT73
St. Marys Rd, Ilf. IG1 69 EQ61
Leatherhead KT22 171 CH122
St. Mary's Rd, Slou. SL3 74 AY74
South Croydon CR2 160 DR110
St. Marys Rd, Surb. KT6 137 CK100
Surbiton (Long Dit.) KT6 137 CJ101
Swanley BR8 147 FD98
St. Mary's Rd, Uxb. (Denh.)
UB9 57 BF58
Uxbridge (Hare.) UB9 58 BH56
Waltham Cross (Chsht) EN8 14 DW29
Watford WD18 23 BV42
St. Marys Rd, Wey. KT13 153 BR105
St. Mary's Rd, Wok. GU21 166 AW117
Worcester Park KT4 138 CS103
St. Marys Sq, W2 82 DD71
St. Mary's Sq, W5
off St. Mary's Rd 97 CK75
St. Marys Ter, W2 82 DD71
St. Mary's Twr, EC1
off Fortune St 84 DQ70
St. Mary St, SE18 105 EM77
St. Marys Vw, Har. HA3 61 CJ57
St. Mary's Vw, Wat. WD18
off King St 24 BW42
St. Mary's Wk, SE11 200 E8
Hayes UB3
off St. Mary's Rd 77 BT73
Redhill (Bletch.) RH1 186 DR133
St. Mary's Way, Chig. IG7 49 EN50
St. Mary's Way, Gerrards Cross
(Chal.St.P.) SL9 36 AX54
St. Matthew Cl, Uxb. UB8 76 BK72
St. Matthew's Av, Surb. KT6 138 CL102
St. Matthews Cl, Rain. RM13 89 FG66
Watford WD19 24 BX44
St. Matthew's Dr, Brom. BR1 145 EM97
St. Matthew's Rd, SW2 101 DM84
St. Matthews Rd, W5
off The Common 80 CL74
St. Matthew's Rd, Red. RH1 184 DF133
St. Matthew's Row, E2 84 DU69
St. Matthew St, SW1 199 M7
St. Matthias Cl, NW9 63 CT57
St. Maur Rd, SW6 99 CZ81
St. Mellion Cl, SE28
off Redbourne Dr 88 EX72
St. Merryn Cl, SE18 105 ER80
St. Michael's All, EC3 197 L9
St. Michaels Av, N9 46 DW45
St. Michael's Av, Wem. HA9 80 CN65
St. Michaels Cl, E16
off Fulmer Rd 86 EK71
St. Michael's Cl, N3 43 CZ54
St. Michaels Cl, N12 44 DE50
Bromley BR1 144 EL97
Erith DA18
off St. Helens Rd 106 EX75
South Ockendon
(Aveley) RM15 90 FQ73
Walton-on-Thames KT12 136 BW103
Worcester Park KT4 139 CT103
St. Michaels Cres, Pnr. HA5 60 BY58
St. Michaels Dr, Wat. WD25 7 BV33
St. Michaels Gdns, W10
off St. Lawrence Ter 81 CY71
St. Michaels Rd, NW2 63 CW63
St. Michael's Rd, SW9 101 DM82
Ashford TW15 114 BN92
St. Michaels Rd, Cat. CR3 176 DR122
Croydon CR0 142 DQ102
Grays RM16 111 GH78
Wallington SM6 159 DJ107
Welling DA16 106 EV83
St. Michael's Rd, Wok. GU21 151 BD114
St. Michaels St, W2 194 A8
St. Michaels Ter, N22 45 DL54
St. Michaels Way, Pot.B. EN6 12 DB30
St. Mildred's Ct, EC2
off Poultry 84 DR72
St. Mildreds Rd, SE12 124 EE87
St. Monica's Rd, Tad. KT20 173 CZ121
St. Nazaire Cl, Egh. TW20
off Mullens Rd 113 BC92
St. Neots Cl, Borwd. WD6 26 CN38
St. Neots Rd, Rom. RM3 52 FM52
St. Nicholas Av, Horn. RM12 71 FG62
St. Nicholas Cen, Sutt. SM1
off St. Nicholas Way 158 DB105
St. Nicholas Cl, Amer. HP7 20 AV39
Borehamwood
(Elstree) WD6 25 CK44
Uxbridge UB8 76 BK72
St. Nicholas Cres, Wok.
(Pyrford) GU22 168 BG116
St. Nicholas Dr, Sev. TN13 191 FH126
Shepperton TW17 134 BN101
St. Nicholas Glebe, SW17 120 DG93
St. Nicholas Gro,
Brwd. (Ingrave) CM13 55 GC50
St. Nicholas Hill, Lthd. KT22 171 CH122
St. Nicholas Pl, Loug. IG10 33 EN42
St. Nicholas Rd, SE18 105 ET78
Sutton SM1 158 DB106
Thames Ditton KT7 137 CF100
St. Nicholas St, SE8
off Lucas St 103 EA81
St. Nicholas Way, Sutt. SM1 158 DB105
St. Nicolas La, Chis. BR7 144 EL95
St. Ninian's Ct, N20 44 DF48
St. Norbert Grn, SE4 103 DY84
St. Norbert Rd, SE4 103 DY84
St. Normans Way,
Epsom KT17 157 CU110
St. Olaf's Rd, SW6 99 CY80
St. Olaves Cl, Stai. TW18 113 BF94
St. Olaves Ct, EC2 197 K9
St. Olave's Est, SE1 201 N4
St. Olaves Gdns, SE11 200 D8
St. Olaves Rd, E6 87 EN67
St. Olave's Wk, SW16 141 DJ96
St. Olav's Sq, SE16 202 F6
St. Oswald's Pl, SE11 101 DM78
St. Oswald's Rd, SW16 141 DP95
St. Oswulf St, SW1 199 N9
ST. PANCRAS, WC1 195 P3
⇌ St. Pancras 195 P2
H St. Pancras Hosp, NW1 83 DK67
St. Pancras Way, NW1 83 DJ66
St. Patrick's Ct, Wdf.Grn. IG8 48 EE52
St. Patrick's Gdns, Grav.
DA12 131 GK90
St. Patricks Pl, Grays RM16 111 GJ77
St. Paul Cl, Uxb. UB8 76 BK71
⊖ St. Paul's 197 H8
St. Paul's All, EC4
off St. Paul's Chyd 83 DP72
St. Paul's Av, NW2 81 CV65
SE16 203 J2
St. Pauls Av, Har. HA3 62 CM57
Slough SL2 74 AT73
★ St. Paul's Cath, EC4 197 H9
St. Paul's Chyd, EC4 196 G9
St. Paul's Cl, SE7 104 EK78
W5 98 CM75
St. Pauls Cl, Add. KT15 152 BG106
St. Paul's Cl, Ashf. TW15 115 BQ92
Carshalton SM5 140 DE102
St. Pauls Cl, Chess. KT9 155 CK105
Hayes UB3 95 BR78
St. Paul's Cl, Houns. TW3 96 BY82
St. Pauls Cl, S.Ock.
(Aveley) RM15 90 FQ73
Swanscombe DA10
off Swanscombe St 130 FY87
St. Paul's Ct, W14
off Colet Gdns 99 CX77
St. Pauls Ctyd, SE8
off Deptford High St 103 EA80
ST. PAUL'S CRAY, Orp. BR5 146 EU96

★ Place of interest ⇌ Railway station ⊖ London Underground station DLR Docklands Light Railway station Tra Tramlink station H Hospital Riv Pedestrian ferry landing stage

St. Pauls Cray Rd, Chis. BR7 . 145 ER95
St. Paul's Cres, NW1 . . . . . 83 DK66
St. Pauls Dr, E15 . . . . . 67 ED64
St. Paul's Ms, NW1
off St. Paul's Cres 83 DK66
St. Paul's Pl, N1 . . . . . 84 DR65
St. Pauls Pl, S.Ock.
(Aveley) RM15 . . . . . 90 FQ73
St. Pauls Ri, N13 . . . . . 45 DP51
St. Paul's Rd, N1 . . . . . 83 DP65
N17 . . . . . 46 DU52
Barking IG11 . . . . . 87 EQ67
Brentford TW8 . . . . . 97 CK79
Erith DA8 . . . . . 107 FC80
Richmond TW9 . . . . . 98 CM83
Staines TW18 . . . . . 113 BD92
Thornton Heath CR7 . . . . . 142 DQ97
St. Pauls Rd, Wok. GU22 . . . . 167 BA117
St. Paul's Shrubbery, N1 . . . . 84 DR65
St. Pauls Sq, Brom. BR2 . . . . 144 EG96
St. Paul's Ter, SE17
off Westcott Rd 101 DP79
St. Pauls Twr, E10 . . . . . 67 EB59
St. Paul St, N1 . . . . . 84 DQ67
St. Pauls Wk, Kings.T. KT2
off Alexandra Rd 118 CN94
St. Pauls Way, E3 . . . . . 85 DZ71
E14 . . . . . 85 DZ71
St. Paul's Way, N3 . . . . . 44 DB52
St. Pauls Way, Wal.Abb. EN9
off Rochford Av 15 ED33
Watford WD24 . . . . . 24 BW40
St. Pauls Wd Hill, Orp. BR5 . . 145 ES96
St. Peter's All, EC3 . . . . . 197 L9
St. Peter's Av, E2
off St. Peter's Cl 84 DU68
E17 . . . . . 68 EE56
St. Peters Av, N18 . . . . . 46 DU49
Westerham
(Berry's Grn) TN16 . . . . . 179 EP116
St. Petersburgh Ms, W2 . . . . 82 DB73
St. Petersburgh Pl, W2 . . . . 82 DB73
St. Peter's Cl, E2 . . . . . 84 DU68
St. Peters Cl, SW17
off College Gdns 120 DE89
St. Peter's Cl, Barn. EN5 . . . . 27 CV43
St. Peters Cl, Bushey
(Bushey Hth) WD23 . . . . . 41 CD46
Chislehurst BR7 . . . . . 125 ER94
Gerrards Cross (Chal.St.P.) SL9
off Lewis La 36 AY53
Ilford IG2 . . . . . 69 ES56
Rickmansworth
(Mill End) WD3 . . . . . 38 BH46
St. Peter's Cl, Ruis. HA4 . . . . 60 BX61
St. Peters Cl, Stai. TW18 . . . . 113 BF93
Swanscombe DA10 . . . . . 130 FZ87
Windsor (Old Wind.) SL4
off Church Rd 112 AU85
Woking GU22 . . . . . 167 BC120
St. Peter's Ct, NW4 . . . . . 63 CW57
St. Peters Ct, SE3
off Eltham Rd 104 EF84
SE4 off Wickham Rd 103 DZ82
Gerrards Cross (Chal.St.P.) SL9
off High St 36 AY53
West Molesey KT8 . . . . . 136 CA98
St. Peter's Gdns, SE27 . . . . . 121 DN90
St. Peter's Gro, W6 . . . . . 99 CU77
H St. Peter's Hosp, Cher.
KT16 . . . . . 133 BD104
St. Peters La, Orp. BR5 . . . . 146 EU96
St. Peter's Pl, W9
off Shirland Rd 82 DB70
St. Peters Rd, N9 . . . . . 46 DW46
St. Peter's Rd, W6 . . . . . 99 CU78
St. Peters Rd, Brwd. CM14
off Crescent Rd 54 FV49
St. Peter's Rd, Croy. CR0 . . . . 160 DR105
Grays RM16 . . . . . 111 GH77
St. Peters Rd, Kings.T. KT1 . . . 138 CN96
Southall UB1 . . . . . 78 CA71
Twickenham TW1 . . . . . 117 CH85
Uxbridge UB8 . . . . . 76 BK71
St. Peter's Rd, W.Mol. KT8 . . . 136 CA98
St. Peters Rd, Wok. GU22 . . . . 167 BB121
St. Peter's Sq, E2
off St. Peter's Cl 84 DU68
W6 . . . . . 99 CU78
St. Peters St, N1 . . . . . 83 DP67
St. Peter's St, S.Croy. CR2 . . . 160 DR106
St. Peters Ter, SW6 . . . . . 99 CY80
St. Peter's Vil, W6 . . . . . 99 CU77
St. Peter's Way, N1 . . . . . 84 DS66
St. Peters Way, W5 . . . . . 79 CK71
St. Peter's Way, Add. KT15 . . . 134 BG104
Chertsey KT16 . . . . . 151 BD105
St. Peters Way, Hayes UB3 . . . 95 BR78
Rickmansworth
(Chorl.) WD3 . . . . . 21 BB43
St. Philip's Av, Wor.Pk. KT4 . . . 139 CV103
St. Philips Gate, Wor.Pk. KT4 . . 139 CV103
St. Philip Sq, SW8 . . . . . 101 DH82
St. Philip's Rd, E8 . . . . . 84 DU65
St. Philips Rd, Surb. KT6 . . . . 137 CK100
St. Philip St, SW8 . . . . . 101 DH82
St. Philip's Way, N1
off Linton St 84 DQ67
St. Pinnock Av, Stai. TW18 . . . 134 BG95
St. Quentin Ho, SW18
off Fitzhugh Gro 120 DD86
St. Quentin Rd, Well. DA16 . . . 105 ET83
St. Quintin Av, W10 . . . . . 81 CW71
St. Quintin Gdns, W10 . . . . . 81 CW71
St. Quintin Rd, E13 . . . . . 86 EH68
St. Raphael's Way, NW10 . . . . 62 CQ64
St. Regis Cl, N10 . . . . . 45 DH54
St. Ronan's Cl, Barn. EN4 . . . . 28 DD38
St. Ronans Cres, Wdf.Grn.
IG8 . . . . . 48 EG52
St. Rule St, SW8 . . . . . 101 DJ82
St. Saviour's Est, SE1 . . . . . 201 P6
St. Saviour's Rd, SW2 . . . . . 121 DM85
St. Saviours Rd, Croy. CR0 . . . 142 DQ100
Saints Cl, SE27
off Wolfington Rd 121 DP91
Saints Dr, E7 . . . . . 68 EK64
St. Silas Pl, NW5 . . . . . 82 DG65
St. Silas St Est, NW5 . . . . . 82 DG65
St. Simon's Av, SW15 . . . . . 119 CW85
St. Stephens Av, E17 . . . . . 67 EC57
W12 . . . . . 99 CV75
W13 . . . . . 79 CH72
St. Stephen's Av, Ashtd.
KT21 . . . . . 172 CL116
St. Stephens Cl, E17 . . . . . 67 EB57
NW8 off Avenue Cl 82 DE67
Southall UB1 . . . . . 78 CA71
St. Stephens Cres, W2 . . . . . 82 DA72
Brentwood CM13 . . . . . 55 GA49
Thornton Heath CR7 . . . . . 141 DN97
St. Stephens Gdn Est, W2
off Shrewsbury Rd 82 DA72
St. Stephens Gdns, SW15
off Manfred Rd 119 CZ85
W2 . . . . . 82 DA72
Twickenham TW1 . . . . . 117 CJ86
St. Stephens Gro, SE13 . . . . . 103 EC83
St. Stephens Ms, W2
off Chepstow Rd 82 DA71
St. Stephen's Par, E7
off Green St 86 EJ66
St. Stephen's Pas, Twick. TW1
off Richmond Rd 117 CJ86
St. Stephens Rd, E3 . . . . . 85 DZ68
St. Stephens Rd, E6 . . . . . 86 EJ66
St. Stephen's Rd, E17
off Grove Rd 67 EB57
St. Stephens Rd, W13 . . . . . 79 CH72
St. Stephen's Rd, Barn. EN5 . . . 27 CX43
St. Stephens Rd, Enf. EN3 . . . . 31 DX37
Hounslow TW3 . . . . . 116 CA86
St. Stephen's Rd, West Dr.
UB7 . . . . . 76 BK74
St. Stephens Row, EC4 . . . . . 197 K9
St. Stephens Ter, SW8 . . . . . 101 DM80
St. Stephen's Wk, SW7 . . . . . 100 DC77
Saints Wk, Grays RM16 . . . . . 111 GJ77
St. Swithin's La, EC4 . . . . . 197 K10
St. Swithun's Rd, SE13 . . . . . 123 ED85
St. Teresa Wk, Grays RM16 . . . 111 GH76
St. Theresa Cl, Epsom KT18 . . 156 CQ114
St. Theresa's Rd, Felt. TW14 . . . 95 BT84
St. Thomas' Cl, Surb. KT6 . . . 138 CM102
St. Thomas Cl, Wok. GU21
off St. Mary's Rd 166 AW117
St. Thomas Ct, Bex. DA5 . . . . . 126 FA87
St. Thomas Dr, Orp. BR5 . . . . 145 EQ102
St. Thomas' Dr, Pnr. HA5 . . . . 40 BY53
St. Thomas Gdns, Ilf. IG1 . . . . 87 EQ65
H St. Thomas' Hosp, SE1 . . . 200 B6
St. Thomas Pl, NW1
off Maiden La 83 DK66
St. Thomas Rd, E16 . . . . . 86 EG72
N14 . . . . . 45 DK45
St. Thomas' Rd, W4 . . . . . 98 CQ79
St. Thomas Rd, Belv. DA17 . . . 107 FC75
Brentwood CM14 . . . . . 54 FX47
Gravesend (Nthflt) DA11
off St. Margaret's Rd 130 GE89
St. Thomas's Av, Grav. DA11 . 131 GH88
St. Thomas's Cl, Wal.Abb.
EN9 . . . . . 16 EH33
St. Thomas's Gdns, NW5
off Queen's Cres 82 DG65
St. Thomas's Pl, E9 . . . . . 84 DW66
St. Thomas's Rd, N4 . . . . . 65 DN61
NW10 . . . . . 80 CS67
St. Thomas's Sq, E9 . . . . . 84 DV66
St. Thomas St, SE1 . . . . . 201 K3
St. Thomas's Way, SW6 . . . . . 99 CZ80
St. Thomas Wk, Slou.
(Colnbr.) SL3 . . . . . 93 BD80
St. Timothy's Ms, Brom. BR1
off Wharton Rd 144 EH95
St. Ursula Gro, Pnr. HA5 . . . . 60 BX57
St. Ursula Rd, Sthl. UB1 . . . . 78 CA72
St. Vincent Cl, SE27 . . . . . 121 DP92
St. Vincent Rd, Twick. TW2 . . . 116 CC86
Walton-on-Thames KT12 . . . 135 BV104
St. Vincents Av, Dart. DA1 . . . 128 FN85
ST. VINCENT'S HAMLET, Brwd.
CM14 . . . . . 52 FP46
St. Vincents Rd, Dart. DA1 . . . 128 FN86
St. Vincent St, W1 . . . . . 194 G7
St. Vincents Way, Pot.B. EN6 . . 12 DC33
St. Wilfrids Cl, Barn. EN4 . . . . 28 DE43
St. Wilfrids Rd, Barn. EN4 . . . . 28 DD43
St. Winefride's Av, E12 . . . . . 69 EM64
St. Winifreds, Ken. CR8 . . . . . 176 DQ115
St. Winifreds Cl, Chig. IG7 . . . 49 EQ50
St. Winifred's Rd, Tedd. TW11 . 117 CH93
Westerham (Bigg.H.) TN16 . 179 EM118
Saladin Dr, Purf. RM19 . . . . . 108 FN77
Sala Ho, SE3 off Pinto Way . . . 104 EH84
Salamanca Pl, SE1 . . . . . 200 B9
Salamanca St, SE1 . . . . . 200 A9
Salamander Cl, Kings.T. KT2 . 117 CJ92
Salamander Quay, Uxb. (Hare.) UB9
off Coppermill La 38 BG52
Salamons Way, Rain. RM13 . . . 89 FE72
Salcombe Dr, Mord. SM4 . . . . 139 CX102
Romford RM6 . . . . . 70 EZ58
Salcombe Gdns, NW7 . . . . . 43 CW51
Salcombe Pk, Loug. IG10 . . . . 32 EK43
Salcombe Rd, E17 . . . . . 67 DZ59
N16 . . . . . 66 DS64
Ashford TW15 . . . . . 114 BL91
Salcombe Way, Hayes UB4
off Portland Rd 77 BS69
Ruislip HA4 . . . . . 59 BU61
Salcot Cres, Croy.
(New Adgtn) CR0 . . . . . 161 EC110
Salcote Rd, Grav. DA12 . . . . . 131 GL92
Salcott Rd, SW11 . . . . . 120 DE85
Croydon CR0 . . . . . 141 DL104
Salehurst Cl, Har. HA3 . . . . . 62 CL57
Salehurst Rd, SE4 . . . . . 123 DZ86
Salem Pl, Croy. CR0 . . . . . 142 DQ104
Gravesend (Nthflt) DA11 . . . 130 GD87
Salem Rd, W2 . . . . . 82 DB73
Sale Pl, W2 . . . . . 194 B7
Salesian Gdns, Cher. KT16 . . . 134 BG102
Sale St, E2 off Hereford St . . . 84 DU70
Salford Rd, SW2 . . . . . 121 DK88
Salhouse Cl, SE28
off Rollesby Way 88 EW72
Salisbury Av, N3 . . . . . 63 CZ55
Barking IG11 . . . . . 87 ES66
Sutton SM1 . . . . . 157 CZ107
Salisbury Av, Swanley BR8 . . 147 FG98
Salisbury Cl, SE17 . . . . . 201 K8
Amersham HP7 . . . . . 20 AS39
Potters Bar EN6 . . . . . 12 DC32
Upminster RM14
off Canterbury Av 73 FT61
Worcester Park KT4 . . . . . 139 CT104
Salisbury Ct, EC4 . . . . . 196 F9
Salisbury Cres, Wal.Cr.
(Chsht) EN8 . . . . . 15 DX32
Salisbury Gdns, SW19 . . . . . 119 CY94
Buckhurst Hill IG9 . . . . . 48 EK47
Salisbury Hall Gdns, E4 . . . . 47 EA51
Salisbury Ho, E14
off Hobday St 85 EB72
Salisbury Ms, SW6
off Dawes Rd 99 CZ80
Bromley BR2
off Salisbury Rd 144 EL99
Salisbury Pl, SW9 . . . . . 101 DP80
W1 . . . . . 194 D6
West Byfleet KT14 . . . . . 152 BJ111
Salisbury Rd, E4 . . . . . 47 EA48
E7 . . . . . 86 EG65
E10 . . . . . 67 EC61
E12 . . . . . 68 EK64
E17 . . . . . 67 EC57
N4 . . . . . 65 DP57
N9 . . . . . 46 DU48
N22 . . . . . 65 DP53
SE25 . . . . . 142 DU100
SW19 . . . . . 119 CY94
W13 . . . . . 97 CG75
Banstead SM7 . . . . . 158 DB114
Barnet EN5 . . . . . 27 CY41
Bexley DA5 . . . . . 126 FA88
Bromley BR2 . . . . . 144 EL99
Carshalton SM5 . . . . . 158 DF107
Dagenham RM10 . . . . . 89 FB65
Dartford DA2 . . . . . 128 FQ88
Enfield EN3 . . . . . 31 DZ37
Feltham TW13 . . . . . 116 BW88
Godstone RH9 . . . . . 186 DW131
Gravesend DA11 . . . . . 131 GF88
Grays RM17 . . . . . 110 GC79
Harrow HA1 . . . . . 61 CD57
Hounslow TW4 . . . . . 96 BW83
Hounslow
(Hthrw Air.) TW6 . . . . . 115 BQ85
Ilford IG3 . . . . . 69 ES61
New Malden KT3 . . . . . 138 CR97
Pinner HA5 . . . . . 59 BU56
Richmond TW9 . . . . . 98 CL84
Romford RM2 . . . . . 71 FH57
Southall UB2 . . . . . 96 BY77
Uxbridge UB8 . . . . . 76 BH68
Watford WD24 . . . . . 23 BV38
Woking GU22 . . . . . 166 AY119
Worcester Park KT4 . . . . . 139 CT104
Salisbury Sq, EC4 . . . . . 196 E9
Salisbury St, NW8 . . . . . 194 A5
W3 . . . . . 98 CQ75
Salisbury Ter, SE15 . . . . . 102 DW83
Salisbury Wk, N19 . . . . . 65 DJ61
Salix Cl, Lthd. (Fetch.) KT22 . . 170 CB123
Sunbury-on-Thames TW16
off Oak Gro 115 BV94
Salix Rd, Grays RM17 . . . . . 110 GD79
Salliesfield, Twick. TW2 . . . . . 117 CD86
Sally Murrey Cl, E12
off Grantham Rd 69 EN63
Salmen Rd, E13 . . . . . 86 EF68
Salmond Cl, Stan. HA7
off Robb Rd 41 CG51
Salmonds Gro, Brwd.
(Ingrave) CM13 . . . . . 55 GC50
Salmon La, E14 . . . . . 85 DY72
Salmon Rd, Belv. DA17 . . . . . 106 FA78
Dartford DA1 . . . . . 108 FM83
Salmons La, Whyt. CR3 . . . . . 176 DU119
Salmons La W, Cat. CR3 . . . . 176 DS120
Salmons Rd, N9 . . . . . 46 DU46
Chessington KT9 . . . . . 155 CK107
Salmon St, E14
off Salmon La 85 DZ72
NW9 . . . . . 62 CP60
Salomons Rd, E13
off Chalk Rd 86 EJ71
Salop Rd, E17 . . . . . 67 DX58
Saltash Cl, Sutt. SM1 . . . . . 157 CZ105
Saltash Rd, Ilf. IG6 . . . . . 49 ER52
Welling DA16 . . . . . 106 EW81
Salt Box Hill, West. TN16 . . . 162 EH113
Saltcoats Rd, W4 . . . . . 98 CS75
Saltcote Cl, Dart. DA1
off Lower Sta Rd 127 FE86
Saltcroft Cl, Wem. HA9 . . . . . 62 CP60
Salter Cl, Har. HA2 . . . . . 60 BZ62
Salterford Rd, SW17 . . . . . 120 DG93
Salter Rd, SE16 . . . . . 203 H3
Salters Cl, Rick. WD3 . . . . . 38 BL46
Salters Gdns, Wat. WD17 . . . . 23 BU39
Salters Hall Ct, EC4 . . . . . 197 K10
Salters Hill, SE19 . . . . . 122 DR92
Salters Rd, E17 . . . . . 67 ED56
W10 . . . . . 81 CX70
Salter St, E14 . . . . . 85 EA73
NW10 . . . . . 81 CU69
Salterton Rd, N7 . . . . . 65 DL62
Saltford Cl, Erith DA8 . . . . . 107 FE78
Salthill Cl, Uxb. UB8 . . . . . 58 BL64
Saltley Cl, E6
off Dunnock Rd 86 EL72
Saltoun Rd, SW2 . . . . . 101 DN84
Saltram Cl, N15 . . . . . 66 DT56
Saltram Cres, W9 . . . . . 81 CZ69
Saltwell St, E14 . . . . . 85 EA73
Saltwood Cl, Orp. BR6 . . . . . 164 EW105
Saltwood Gro, SE17
off Merrow St 102 DR78
Salusbury Rd, NW6 . . . . . 81 CY67
Salutation Rd, SE10 . . . . . 205 J8
Salvia Gdns, Grnf. UB6
off Selborne Gdns 79 CG68
Salvin Rd, SW15 . . . . . 99 CX83
Salway Cl, Wdf.Grn. IG8 . . . . 48 EF52
Salway Pl, E15
off Broadway 86 EE65
Salway Rd, E15
off Great Eastern Rd 85 ED65
Samantha Cl, E17 . . . . . 67 DZ59
Samantha Ms, Rom.
(Hav.at.Bow.) RM4 . . . . . 51 FE48
Sam Bartram Cl, SE7 . . . . . 104 EJ78
Sambruck Ms, SE6 . . . . . 123 EB88
Samels Ct, W6
off South Black Lion La . . . 99 CU78
Samford St, NW8 . . . . . 194 A5
Samira Cl, E17
off Colchester Rd 67 EA58
Samos Rd, SE20 . . . . . 142 DV96
Samphire Ct, Grays RM17
off Salix Rd 110 GE80
Sampson Av, Barn. EN5 . . . . . 27 CX43
Sampson Cl, Belv. DA17
off Carrill Way 106 EX76
Sampsons Ct, Shep. TW17
off Linden Way 135 BQ99
Sampson St, E1 . . . . . 202 C3
Samson St, E13 . . . . . 86 EJ68
Samuel Cl, E8
off Pownall Rd 84 DT67
SE14 . . . . . 103 DX79
SE18 . . . . . 104 EL77
Samuel Gray Gdns, Kings.T.
KT2 . . . . . 137 CK95
Samuel Johnson Cl, SW16
off Curtis Fld Rd 121 DN91
Samuel Lewis Trust Dws, E8
off Amhurst Rd 66 DU63
N1 off Liverpool Rd 83 DN66
SW3 . . . . . 198 B9
SW6 . . . . . 100 DA80
Samuels Cl, W6
off South Black Lion La . . . 99 CU78
Samuel St, SE15 . . . . . 102 DT80
SE18 . . . . . 105 EM77
Sancroft Cl, NW2 . . . . . 63 CV62
Sancroft Rd, Har. HA3 . . . . . 41 CF54
Sancroft St, SE11 . . . . . 200 C10
Sanctuary, The, SW1 . . . . . 199 N5
Bexley DA5 . . . . . 126 EX86
Morden SM4 . . . . . 140 DA100
Sanctuary Cl, Dart. DA1 . . . . 128 FJ86
Uxbridge (Hare.) UB9 . . . . . 38 BJ52
Sanctuary Rd, Houns.
(Hthrw Air.) TW6 . . . . . 114 BN86
Sanctuary St, SE1 . . . . . 201 J5
Sandale Cl, N16
off Stoke Newington Ch St . . 66 DR62
Sandall Cl, W5 . . . . . 80 CL70
Sandall Rd, NW5 . . . . . 83 DJ65
W5 . . . . . 80 CL70
Sandal Rd, N18 . . . . . 46 DU50
New Malden KT3 . . . . . 138 CR99
Sandal St, E15 . . . . . 86 EE67
Sandalwood Av, Cher. KT16 . . 133 BD104
Sandalwood Cl, E1
off Solebay St 85 DY70
Sandalwood Dr, Ruis. HA4 . . . . 59 BQ59
Sandalwood Rd, Felt. TW13 . . . 115 BV90
Sandbach Pl, SE18 . . . . . 105 EQ77
Sandbanks, Felt. TW14 . . . . . 115 BT88
Sandbanks Hill, Dart.
(Bean) DA2 . . . . . 129 FV93
Sandbourne Av, SW19 . . . . . 140 DB97
Sandbourne Rd, SE4 . . . . . 103 DY82
Sandbrook Cl, NW7 . . . . . 42 CR51
Sandbrook Rd, N16 . . . . . 66 DS62
Sandby Grn, SE9 . . . . . 104 EL83
Sandcliff Rd, Erith DA8 . . . . . 107 FD77
Sandcroft Cl, N13 . . . . . 45 DP51
Sandells Av, Ashf. TW15 . . . . 115 BQ91
Sandell St, SE1 . . . . . 200 D4
Sanderling Way, Green. DA9
off London Rd 129 FU85
Sanders Cl, Hmptn.
(Hmptn H.) TW12 . . . . . 116 CC92
St. Albans (Lon.Col.) AL2 . . . 9 CK27
Sandersfield Gdns, Bans.
SM7 . . . . . 174 DA115
Sandersfield Rd, Bans. SM7 . . 174 DB115
Sanders La, NW7 . . . . . 43 CX52
Sanderson Av, Sev.
(Bad.Mt) TN14 . . . . . 164 FA110
Sanderson Cl, NW5 . . . . . 65 DH63
Sanderson Rd, Uxb. UB8 . . . . 76 BJ65
SANDERSTEAD, S.Croy.
CR2 . . . . . 160 DT111
⇌ Sanderstead 160 DR109
Sanderstead Av, NW2 . . . . . 63 CY61
Sanderstead Cl, SW12
off Atkins Rd 121 DJ87
Sanderstead Ct Av, S.Croy.
CR2 . . . . . 160 DU113
Sanderstead Hill, S.Croy.
CR2 . . . . . 160 DS111
Sanderstead Rd, E10 . . . . . 67 DY60
Orpington BR5 . . . . . 146 EV100
South Croydon CR2 . . . . . 160 DR108
Sanders Way, N19
off Sussex Way 65 DK60
Sandes Pl, Lthd. KT22 . . . . . 171 CG118
Sandfield Gdns, Th.Hth. CR7 . 141 DP97
Sandfield Pas, Th.Hth. CR7 . . 142 DQ97
Sandfield Rd, Th.Hth. CR7 . . . 141 DP97
Sandfields, Wok.
(Send) GU23 . . . . . 167 BD124
Sandford Av, N22 . . . . . 46 DQ52
Loughton IG10 . . . . . 33 EQ41
Sandford Cl, E6 . . . . . 87 EM70
Sandford Ct, N16 . . . . . 66 DS60
Sandford Rd, E6 . . . . . 86 EL70
Bexleyheath DA7 . . . . . 106 EY84
Bromley BR2 . . . . . 144 EG98
Sandford St, SW6
off King's Rd 100 DB80
Sandgate Cl, Rom. RM7 . . . . . 71 FD59
Sandgate La, SW18 . . . . . 120 DE88
Sandgate Rd, Well. DA16 . . . . 106 EW80
Sandgate St, SE15 . . . . . 102 DV79
Sandham Pt, SE18
off Troy Ct 105 EP77
Sandhills, Wall. SM6 . . . . . 159 DK105
Sandhills La, Vir.W. GU25 . . . 132 AY99
Sandhills Meadow, Shep.
TW17 . . . . . 135 BQ101
Sandhurst Av, Har. HA2 . . . . . 60 CB58
Surbiton KT5 . . . . . 138 CP101
Sandhurst Cl, NW9 . . . . . 62 CN55
Sandhurst Cl,
South Croydon CR2 . . . . . 160 DS109
Sandhurst Dr, Ilf. IG3 . . . . . 69 ET63
Sandhurst Rd, N9 . . . . . 30 DW44
NW9 . . . . . 62 CN55
SE6 . . . . . 123 ED88
Bexley DA5 . . . . . 126 EX85
Orpington BR6 . . . . . 146 EU104
Sidcup DA15 . . . . . 125 ET90
Tilbury RM18 . . . . . 111 GJ82
Sandhurst Way, S.Croy. CR2 . 160 DS108
Sandifer Dr, NW2 . . . . . 63 CX62
Sandiford Rd, Sutt. SM3 . . . . 139 CZ103
Sandiland Cres, Brom. BR2 . . 144 EF103
Tra Sandilands 142 DT103
Sandilands, Croy. CR0 . . . . . 142 DU103
Sevenoaks TN13 . . . . . 190 FD122
Sandilands Rd, SW6 . . . . . 100 DB81
Sandison St, SE15 . . . . . 102 DT83
Sandlands Gro, Tad. KT20 . . . 173 CU123
Sandlands Rd, Tad. KT20 . . . . 173 CU123
Sandland St, WC1 . . . . . 196 C7
Sandling Ri, SE9 . . . . . 125 EN90
Sandlings, The, N22 . . . . . 45 DN54
Sandlings Cl, SE15
off Pilkington Rd 102 DV82
Sandmartin Way, Wall. SM6 . . 140 DG102
Sandmere Rd, SW4 . . . . . 101 DL84
Sandon Cl, Esher KT10 . . . . . 137 CD101
Sandon Rd, Wal.Cr.
(Chsht) EN8 . . . . . 14 DW30
Sandow Cres, Hayes UB3 . . . . 95 BT76
Sandown Av, Dag. RM10 . . . . 89 FC65
Esher KT10 . . . . . 154 CC106
Hornchurch RM12 . . . . . 72 FK61
Sandown Cl, Houns. TW5 . . . . 95 BU81
Sandown Ct, Sutt. SM2
off Grange Rd 158 DB108
Sandown Dr, Cars. SM5 . . . . . 158 DG109
Sandown Gate, Esher KT10 . . 136 CC104
Sandown Ind Pk, Esher KT10 . 136 CA103
★ Sandown Park Racecourse,
Esher KT10 . . . . . 136 CB104
Sandown Rd, SE25 . . . . . 142 DV99
Coulsdon CR5 . . . . . 174 DG116
Esher KT10 . . . . . 154 CC105
Gravesend DA12 . . . . . 131 GJ93
Watford WD24 . . . . . 24 BW38
Sandown Way, Nthlt. UB5 . . . . 78 BY65
Sandpiper Cl, E17 . . . . . 47 DX53
SE16 . . . . . 203 M4
Greenhithe DA9
off London Rd 129 FU86
Sandpiper Dr, Erith DA8 . . . . 107 FH80
Sandpiper Rd, S.Croy. CR2 . . 161 DX111
Sutton SM1 . . . . . 157 CZ106
Sandpipers, The, Grav. DA12 . 131 GK89
Sandpiper Way, Orp. BR5 . . . . 146 EX98
Sandpit Hall Rd, Wok.
(Chobham) GU24 . . . . . 150 AU112
Sandpit La, Brwd.
(Pilg.Hat.) CM14, CM15 . . . . 54 FT46
Sandpit Pl, SE7 . . . . . 104 EL78
Sandpit Rd, Brom. BR1 . . . . . 124 EE92
Dartford DA1 . . . . . 108 FJ84
Sandpits Rd, Croy. CR0 . . . . . 161 DX105
Richmond TW10 . . . . . 117 CK89
Sandra Cl, N22 off New Rd . . . 46 DQ53
Hounslow TW3 . . . . . 116 CB85
Sandridge Cl, Har. HA1 . . . . . 61 CE56
Sandridge St, N19 . . . . . 65 DJ61
Sandringham Av, SW20 . . . . . 139 CY96
Sandringham Cl, SW19 . . . . . 119 CX88
Enfield EN1 . . . . . 30 DS40
Ilford IG6 . . . . . 69 EQ55
Woking GU22 . . . . . 168 BG116
Sandringham Ct, W9
off Maida Vale 82 DC69
Sandringham Cres, Har. HA2 . . 60 CA61
Sandringham Dr, Ashf. TW15 . 114 BK91
Dartford DA2
off Old Bexley La 127 FE89
Welling DA16 . . . . . 105 ES82
Sandringham Gdns, N8 . . . . . 65 DL58
N12 . . . . . 44 DC51
Hounslow TW5 . . . . . 95 BU81
Ilford IG6 . . . . . 69 EQ55
West Molesey KT8
off Rosemary Av 136 CA98
Sandringham Ms, W5
off High St 79 CK73
Hampton TW12
off Oldfield Rd 136 BZ95
Sandringham Pk, Cob. KT11 . . 154 BZ112
Sandringham Rd, E7 . . . . . 68 EJ64
E8 . . . . . 66 DT64
E10 . . . . . 67 ED58
N22 . . . . . 66 DQ55
NW2 . . . . . 81 CV65
NW11 . . . . . 63 CY59
Barking IG11 . . . . . 87 ET65
Brentwood
(Pilg.Hat.) CM15 . . . . . 54 FV43
Bromley BR1 . . . . . 124 EG92
Hounslow
(Hthrw Air.) TW6 . . . . . 114 BL85
Northolt UB5 . . . . . 78 CA66
Potters Bar EN6 . . . . . 12 DB30
Thornton Heath CR7 . . . . . 142 DQ99
Watford WD24 . . . . . 24 BW37
Worcester Park KT4 . . . . . 139 CU104
Sandringham Way, Wal.Cr.
EN8 . . . . . 15 DX34
Sandrock Pl, Croy. CR0 . . . . . 161 DX105
Sandrock Rd, SE13 . . . . . 103 EA83
Sandroyd Way, Cob. KT11 . . . 154 CA113
SANDS END, SW6 . . . . . 100 DC81
Sand's End La, SW6 . . . . . 100 DB81
Sandstone La, E16 . . . . . 86 EH73
Sandstone Pl, N19 . . . . . 65 DH61
Sandstone Rd, SE12 . . . . . 124 EH89
Sands Way, Wdf.Grn. IG8 . . . . 48 EL51
Sandtoft Rd, SE7 . . . . . 104 EH79
Sandway Path, Orp. BR5
off Okemore Gdns 146 EW98

★ Place of interest ⇌ Railway station ⊖ London Underground station DLR Docklands Light Railway station Tra Tramlink station H Hospital Riv Pedestrian ferry landing stage

321

Sandway Rd, Orp. BR5 146 EW98
Sandwell Cres, NW6 82 DA65
Sandwich St, WC1 195 P3
Sandwick Cl, NW7
off Sebergham Gro 43 CU52
Sandy Bk Rd, Grav. DA12 131 GH88
Sandy Bury, Orp. BR6 145 ER104
Sandy Cl, Wok. GU22
off Sandy La 167 BB117
Sandycombe Rd, Felt. TW14 115 BU88
Richmond TW9 98 CN83
Sandycoombe Rd, Twick. TW1 117 CJ86
Sandycroft, SE2 106 EU79
Epsom KT17 157 CW110
Sandycroft Rd, Amer. HP6 20 AV39
Sandy Dr, Cob. KT11 154 CA111
Feltham TW14 115 BS88
Sandy Hill Av, SE18 105 EP78
Sandy Hill Rd, SE18 105 EP78
Sandyhill Rd, Ilf. IG1 69 EP63
Sandy Hill Rd, Wall. SM6 159 DJ109
Sandy La, Bushey WD23 24 CC41
Cobham KT11 154 CA112
Dartford (Bean) DA2 129 FW89
Grays (Chad.St.M.) RM16 111 GH79
Grays (W.Thur.) RM20
off London Rd W Thurrock 109 FV79
Harrow HA3 62 CM58
Kingston upon Thames KT1 117 CG94
Leatherhead KT22 154 CA112
Mitcham CR4 140 DG95
Northwood HA6 39 BU50
Orpington BR6 146 EU101
Orpington
(St.P.Cray) BR5 146 EX95
Oxted RH8 187 EC129
Oxted (Lmpfld) RH8 188 EH127
Redhill (Bletch.) RH1 185 DP132
Richmond TW10 117 CJ89
Sevenoaks TN13 191 FJ123
Sidcup DA14 126 EX94
South Ockendon
(Aveley) RM15 90 FM73
Sutton SM2 157 CY108
Tadworth (Kgswd) KT20 173 CZ124
Teddington TW11 117 CG94
Virginia Water GU25 132 AY98
Walton-on-Thames KT12 135 BV100
Watford WD25 24 CC41
Westerham TN16 189 ER125
Woking GU22 167 BC116
Woking
(Chobham) GU24 150 AS109
Woking (Pyrford) GU22 167 BF117
Woking (Send) GU23 167 BC123
Sandy La Est, Rich. TW10 117 CK89
Sandy La N, Wall. SM6 159 DK107
Sandy La S, Wall. SM6 159 DK107
Sandy Lo La, Nthwd. HA6 39 BR47
Sandy Lo Rd, Rick. WD3 39 BP47
Sandy Lo Way, Nthwd. HA6 39 BS50
Sandy Mead, Epsom KT19 156 CN109
Sandymount Av, Stan. HA7 41 CJ50
Sandy Ridge, Chis. BR7 125 EN93
Sandy Ri, Ger.Cr.
(Chal.St.P.) SL9 36 AY53
Sandy Rd, NW3 64 DB62
Addlestone KT15 152 BG107
Sandy's Row, E1 197 N7
Sandy Way, Cob. KT11 154 CA112
Croydon CR0 143 DZ104
Walton-on-Thames KT12 135 BT102
Woking GU22 167 BC117
Sanford La, N16
off Lawrence Bldgs 66 DT61
Sanford St, SE14 103 DY79
Sanford Ter, N16 66 DT62
Sanford Wk, N16
off Sanford Ter 66 DT61
SE14
off Cold Blow La 103 DY79
Sanger Av, Chess. KT9 156 CL106
Sanger Dr, Wok.
(Send) GU23 167 BC123
Sangley Rd, SE6 123 EB87
SE25 142 DS98
Sangora Rd, SW11 100 DD84
San Juan Dr, Grays RM16
off Hatfield Rd 109 FW77
San Luis Dr, Grays RM16
off Hatfield Rd 109 FW77
San Marcos Dr, Grays RM16
off Hatfield Rd 109 FW77
Sansom Rd, E11 68 EE61
Sansom St, SE5 102 DR80
Sans Wk, EC1 196 E4
Santers La, Pot.B. EN6 11 CY33
Santiago Way, Grays RM16
off Mayflower Rd 109 FX78
Santley St, SW4 101 DM84
Santos Rd, SW18 120 DA85
Santway, The, Stan. HA7 41 CE50
Sanway Cl, W.Byf.
(Byfleet) KT14 152 BL114
Sanway Rd, W.Byf.
(Byfleet) KT14 152 BL114
Sapcote Trd Cen, NW10 63 CT64
Saperton Wk, SE11 200 C8
Sapho Pk, Grav. DA12 131 GM91
Saphora Cl, Orp. BR6
off Oleander Cl 163 ER106
Sapperton Ct, EC1 197 H4
Sapphire Cl, E6 87 EN72
Dagenham RM8 70 EW60
Sapphire Rd, SE8 203 L9
Sappho Ct, Wok. GU21
off Langmans Way 166 AS116
Saracen Cl, Croy. CR0 142 DR100
Saracen's Head Yd, EC3 197 N9
★ **Saracens R.F.C. (share Vicarage Rd with Watford F.C.)**, Wat.
WD18 23 BV43
Saracen St, E14 85 EA72
Sara Ct, Beck. BR3
off Albemarle Rd 143 EB95
Sara Cres, Green. DA9 109 FU84
Sarah Ho, SW15 99 CT84
Sara Ho, Erith DA8
off Larner Rd 107 FE80
Sara Pk, Grav. DA12 131 GL91
Saratoga Rd, E5 66 DW63
Sardinia St, WC2 196 B9
Sargeant Cl, Uxb. UB8
off Ratcliffe Cl 76 BK69
Sarita Cl, Har. HA3 41 CD54
Sarjant Path, SW19
off Queensmere Rd 119 CX89
Sark Cl, Houns. TW5 96 CA80
Sark Ho, Enf. EN3
off Eastfield Rd 31 DX38
Sark Wk, E16 86 EH72
Sarnesfield Ho, SE15
off Pencraig Way 102 DV79
Sarnesfield Rd, Enf. EN2
off Church St 30 DR41
SARRATT, Rick. WD3 22 BG35
Sarratt Bottom, Rick.
(Sarratt) WD3 21 BE36
Sarratt La, Rick. WD3 22 BH40
Sarratt Rd, Rick. WD3 22 BM41
Sarre Av, Horn. RM12 90 FJ65
Sarre Rd, NW2 63 CZ64
Orpington BR5 146 EW99
Sarsby Dr, Stai. TW19 113 BA89
Sarsen Av, Houns. TW3 96 BZ82
Sarsfeld Rd, SW12 120 DF88
Sarsfield Rd, Grnf. UB6 79 CH68
Sartor Rd, SE15 103 DX84
Sarum Complex, Uxb. UB8 76 BH68
Sarum Grn, Wey. KT13 135 BS104
Sarum Ter, E3
off Bow Common La 85 DY70
Satanita Cl, E16
off Fulmer Rd 86 EK72
Satchell Mead, NW9 43 CT53
Satchwell Rd, E2 84 DU69
Satis Ct, Epsom KT17
off Windmill Av 157 CT111
Sattar Ms, N16
off Clissold Rd 66 DR62
Sauls Grn, E11
off Napier Rd 68 EE62
Saunder Cl, Wal.Cr. EN8
off Welsummer Way 15 DX27
Saunders Cl, E14 203 N1
Gravesend (Nthflt) DA11 130 GE89
Saunders Copse, Wok.
GU22 166 AV122
Saunders La, Wok. GU22 166 AS122
Saunders Ness Rd, E14 204 E10
Saunders Rd, SE18 105 ET78
Uxbridge UB10 76 BM66
Saunders St, SE11 200 D8
Saunders Way, SE28
off Oriole Way 88 EV73
Dartford DA1 128 FM89
Saunderton Rd, Wem. HA0 61 CH64
Saunton Av, Hayes UB3 95 BT80
Saunton Rd, Horn. RM12 71 FG61
Savage Gdns, E6 87 EM72
EC3 197 N10
Savay Cl, Uxb. (Denh.) UB9 58 BG59
Savay La, Uxb. (Denh.) UB9 58 BG58
Savernake Rd, N9 30 DU44
NW3 64 DF63
Savery Dr, Surb. KT6 137 CJ101
Savile Cl, N.Mal. KT3 138 CS99
Thames Ditton KT7 137 CF102
Savile Gdns, Croy. CR0 142 DT103
Savile Row, W1 195 K10
Savill Cl, Wal.Cr. (Chsht) EN7
off Markham Rd 14 DQ25
Saville Cres, Ashf. TW15 115 BR93
Saville Rd, E16 86 EL74
W4 98 CR76
Romford RM6 70 EZ58
Twickenham TW1 117 CF88
Saville Row, Brom. BR2 144 EF102
Enfield EN3 31 DX40
Savill Gdns, SW20
off Bodnant Gdns 139 CU97
Savill Ms, Egh. TW20
off Armstrong Rd 112 AX93
Savill Row, Wdf.Grn. IG8 48 EF51
Savona Cl, SW19 119 CY94
Savona Est, SW8 101 DJ80
Savona St, SW8 101 DJ80
Savoy Av, Hayes UB3 95 BS78
Savoy Bldgs, WC2 200 B1
Savoy Cl, E15
off Arthingworth St 86 EE67
Edgware HA8 42 CN50
Uxbridge (Hare.) UB9 38 BK54
Savoy Ct, WC2 200 A1
Savoy Hill, WC2 200 B1
Riv **Savoy Pier** 200 B1
Savoy Pl, WC2 200 A1
Savoy Rd, Dart. DA1 128 FK85
Savoy Row, WC2 196 B10
Savoy Steps, WC2
off Savoy St 83 DM73
Savoy St, WC2 196 B10
Savoy Way, WC2 200 B1
Sawbill Cl, Hayes UB4 78 BX71
Sawkins Cl, SW19 119 CY89
Sawley Rd, W12 81 CT74
Sawmill Yd, E3 85 DY67
Sawtry Cl, Cars. SM5 140 DE101
Sawtry Way, Borwd. WD6 26 CN38
Sawyer Cl, N9 *off Lion Rd* 46 DU47
Sawyers Chase, Rom.
(Abridge) RM4 34 EV41
Sawyers Cl, Dag. RM10 89 FC65
Sawyers Gro, Brwd. CM15
off Sawyers Hall La 54 FX46
Sawyers Hall La, Brwd. CM15 54 FW45
Sawyer's Hill, Rich. TW10 118 CP87
Sawyers La, Borwd.
(Elstree) WD6 25 CH40
Potters Bar EN6 11 CX34
Sawyers Lawn, W13 79 CF72
Sawyer St, SE1 201 H4
Saxby Rd, SW2 121 DL87
Saxham Rd, Bark. IG11 87 ES68
Saxlingham Rd, E4 47 ED48
Saxon Av, Felt. TW13 116 BZ89
Saxonbury Av, Sun. TW16 135 BV97
Saxonbury Cl, Mitch. CR4 140 DD97
Saxonbury Gdns, Surb. KT6 137 CJ102
Saxon Cl, E17 67 EA59
Amersham HP6 20 AS38
Brentwood CM13 55 GA48
Gravesend (Nthflt) DA11 130 GC90
Romford RM3 52 FM54
Sevenoaks (Otford) TN14 181 FF117
Slough SL3 93 AZ75
Surbiton KT6 137 CK100
Uxbridge UB8 76 BM71
Saxon Ct, Borwd. WD6 26 CL40
Saxon Dr, W3 80 CP72
Saxonfield Cl, SW2 121 DM87
Saxon Gdns, Sthl. UB1
off Saxon Rd 78 BY73
Saxon Pl, Dart.
(Hort.Kir.) DA4 148 FQ99
Saxon Rd, E3 85 DZ68
E6 87 EM70
N22 45 DP53
SE25 142 DR99
Ashford TW15 115 BR93
Bromley BR1 124 EF94
Dartford (Hawley) DA2 128 FL91
Ilford IG1 87 EP65
Kingston upon Thames KT2 138 CL95
Southall UB1 78 BY74
Walton-on-Thames KT12 136 BX104
Wembley HA9 62 CQ62
Saxons, Tad. KT20 173 CX121
Saxon Shore Way, Grav.
DA12 131 GM86
Saxon Wk, Sid. DA14 126 EW93
Saxon Way, N14 29 DK44
Reigate RH2 183 CZ133
Waltham Abbey EN9 15 EC33
West Drayton UB7 94 BJ79
Windsor (Old Wind.) SL4 112 AV86
Saxony Par, Hayes UB3 77 BQ71
Saxton Cl, SE13 103 ED83
Saxton Ms, Wat. WD17
off Dellfield Cl 23 BU40
Saxville Rd, Orp. BR5 146 EV97
Sayer Cl, Green. DA9 129 FU85
Sayers Cl, Lthd. (Fetch.) KT22 170 CC124
Sayers Wk, Rich. TW10
off Stafford Pl 118 CM87
Sayesbury La, N18 46 DU50
Sayes Ct, SE8
off Sayes Ct St 103 DZ78
Addlestone KT15 152 BJ106
Sayes Ct Fm Dr, Add. KT15 152 BH106
Sayes Ct Rd, Orp. BR5 146 EU98
Sayes Ct St, SE8 103 DZ79
Scadbury Pk, Chis. BR7 125 ET93
Scads Hill Cl, Orp. BR6 145 ET100
Scala St, W1 195 L6
Scales Rd, N17 66 DT55
Scammel Way, Wat. WD18 23 BT44
Scampston Ms, W10 81 CX72
Scampton Rd, Houns.
(Hthrw Air.) TW6
off Southampton Rd 114 BM86
Scandrett St, E1 202 D3
Scarba Wk, N1
off Marquess Rd 84 DR65
Scarborough Cl, Sutt. SM2 157 CZ111
Westerham (Bigg.H.) TN16 178 EJ118
Scarborough Rd, E11 67 ED60
N4 65 DN59
N9 46 DW45
Hounslow (Hthrw Air.) TW6
off Southern Perimeter Rd 115 BQ86
Scarborough St, E1
off West Tenter St 84 DT72
Scarbrook Rd, Croy. CR0 142 DQ104
Scarle Rd, Wem. HA0 79 CK65
Scarlet Cl, Orp. BR5 146 EV98
Scarlet Rd, SE6 124 EE90
Scarlett Cl, Wok. GU21
off Bingham Dr 166 AT118
Scarlette Manor Way, SW2
off Papworth Way 121 DN87
Scarsbrook Rd, SE3 104 EK83
Scarsdale Pl, W8
off Wrights La 100 DB76
Scarsdale Rd, Har. HA2 60 CC62
Scarsdale Vil, W8 100 DA76
Scarth Rd, SW13 99 CT83
Scatterdells La, Kings L.
(Chipper.) WD4 5 BF30
Scawen Cl, Cars. SM5 158 DG105
Scawen Rd, SE8 103 DY78
Scawfell St, E2 84 DT68
Scaynes Link, N12 44 DA50
Sceaux Est, SE5 102 DS81
Sceptre Rd, E2 84 DW69
Schofield Wk, SE3
off Dornberg Cl 104 EH80
Scholars Pl, N16
off Oldfield Rd 66 DS62
Scholars Rd, E4 47 EC46
SW12 121 DJ88
Scholars Wk, Ger.Cr.
(Chal.St.P.) SL9 36 AY51
Slough SL3
off Station Rd 93 BA75
Scholars Way, Amer. HP6 20 AT38
Scholefield Rd, N19 65 DK60
Schonfeld Sq, N16 66 DR61
Schoolbank Rd, SE10 205 K8
Schoolbell Ms, E3
off Arbery Rd 85 DY68
School Cres, Dart.
(Cray.) DA1 107 FF84
Schoolfield Rd, Grays
RM20 109 FU79
School Grn La, Epp.
(N.Wld Bas.) CM16 19 FC25
School Hill, Red. RH1 185 DJ128
Schoolhouse Gdns, Loug.
IG10 33 EP42
Schoolhouse La, E1 85 DX73
School Ho La, Tedd. TW11 117 CH94
School La, SE23 122 DV89
Addlestone KT15 152 BG105
Bushey WD23 40 CB45
School La, Caterham CR3 186 DT126
Chalfont St. Giles HP8 36 AV47
Chigwell IG7 49 ET49
Dartford (Bean) DA2 129 FW90
Dartford (Hort.Kir.) DA4 148 FQ98
Egham TW20 113 BA92
Gerrards Cross
(Chal.St.P.) SL9 36 AX54
Kingston upon Thames KT1
off School Rd 137 CJ95
Leatherhead (Fetch.) KT22 171 CD122
Longfield DA3 149 FT100
Pinner HA5 60 BY56
St. Albans
(Brick.Wd) AL2 8 CA31
Sevenoaks (Seal) TN15 191 FM121
Shepperton TW17 135 BP100
Slough SL2 74 AT73
Slough (Stoke P.) SL2 74 AV67
Surbiton KT6 138 CN102
Swanley BR8 147 FH95
Tadworth KT20
off Chequers La 183 CU125
Welling DA16 106 EV83
Woking (Ockham) GU23 169 BP122
School Mead, Abb.L. WD5 7 BS32
School Pas, Kings.T. KT1 138 CM96
Southall UB1 78 BZ74
School Rd, E12 *off Sixth Av* 69 EM63
NW10 80 CR70
Ashford TW15 115 BP93
Chislehurst BR7 145 EQ95
Dagenham RM10 88 FA67
East Molesey KT8 137 CD98
Hampton
(Hmptn H.) TW12 116 CC93
Hounslow TW3 96 CC83
Kingston upon Thames KT1 137 CJ95
Ongar CM5 19 FG32
Potters Bar EN6 12 DC30
West Drayton UB7 94 BK79
School Rd Av, Hmptn.
(Hmptn H.) TW12 116 CC93
School Wk, Slou. SL2
off Grasmere Av 74 AV73
Sunbury-on-Thames TW16 135 BT98
School Way, N12 *off High Rd* 44 DC49
Schoolway, N12
(Woodhouse Rd) 44 DD51
School Way, Dag. RM8 70 EW62
Schooner Cl, E14 204 F7
SE16 203 H4
Barking IG11 88 EV69
Schooner Ct, Dart. DA2 108 FQ84
Schroder Ct, Egh.
(Eng.Grn) TW20 112 AV92
Schubert Rd, SW15 119 CZ85
Borehamwood
(Elstree) WD6 25 CK44
★ **Science Mus**, SW7 198 A7
Scilla Ct, Grays RM17 110 GD79
Sclater St, E1 197 P4
Scoble Pl, N16
off Amhurst Rd 66 DT63
Scoles Cres, SW2 121 DN88
Scope Way, Kings.T. KT1 138 CL98
Scoresby St, SE1 200 F3
Scorton Av, Grnf. UB6 79 CG68
Scotch Common, W13 79 CG71
Scoter Cl, Wdf.Grn. IG8
off Mallards Rd 48 EH52
Scot Gro, Pnr. HA5 40 BX52
Scotia Rd, SW2 121 DN87
Scotland Br Rd, Add.
(New Haw) KT15 152 BG111
Scotland Grn, N17 46 DT54
Scotland Grn Rd, Enf. EN3 31 DX43
Scotland Grn Rd N, Enf. EN3 31 DX42
Scotland Pl, SW1 199 P2
Scotland Rd, Buck.H. IG9 48 EJ46
Scotney Cl, Orp. BR6 163 EN105
Scotney Wk, Horn. RM12
off Bonington Rd 72 FK64
Scotscraig, Rad. WD7 25 CF35
Scotsdale Cl, Orp. BR5 145 ES98
Sutton SM3 157 CY108
Scotsdale Rd, SE12 124 EH85
Scotshall La, Warl. CR6 161 EC114
Scots Hill, Rick.
(Crox.Grn) WD3 22 BM44
Scots Hill Cl, Rick. WD3
off Scots Hill 22 BM44
Scotsmill La, Rick.
(Crox.Grn) WD3 22 BM44
Scotswood St, EC1 196 E4
Scotswood Wk, N17 46 DU52
Scott Cl, SW16 141 DM95
Epsom KT19 156 CQ106
West Drayton UB7 94 BM77
Scott Ct, W3
off Petersfield Rd 98 CQ75
Scott Cres, Erith DA8
off Cloudesley Rd 107 FF81
Harrow HA2 60 CB60
Scott Ellis Gdns, NW8 82 DD69
Scottes La, Dag. RM8
off Valence Av 70 EX60
Scott Fm Cl, T.Ditt. KT7 137 CH102
Scott Gdns, Houns. TW5 96 BX80
Scott Ho, E13
off Queens Rd W 86 EG68
N18 46 DU50
Scott Lidgett Cres, SE16 202 B5
Scott Rd, Grav. DA12 131 GK92
Grays RM16 111 GG77
Scott Russell Pl, E14 204 B10
Scotts Av, Brom. BR2 143 ED96
Sunbury-on-Thames TW16 115 BS94
Scotts Cl, Horn. RM12
off Rye Cl 72 FJ64
Staines TW19 114 BK88
Scotts Dr, Hmptn. TW12 116 CB94
Scotts Fm Rd, Epsom KT19 156 CQ107
Scotts La, Brom. BR2 143 ED97
Walton-on-Thames KT12 154 BX105
Scotts Rd, E10 67 EC60
W12 99 CV75
Bromley BR1 124 EG94
Southall UB2 96 BW76
Scott St, E1 84 DV70
Scotts Way, Sev. TN13 190 FE122
Sunbury-on-Thames TW16 115 BS93
Scottswood Cl, Bushey WD23
off Scottswood Rd 24 BY40
Scottswood Rd, Bushey
WD23 24 BY40
Scott Trimmer Way, Houns.
TW3 96 BY82
Scottwell Dr, NW9 63 CT57
Scoulding Rd, E16 86 EF72
Scouler St, E14 204 F1
Scout App, NW10 62 CS63
Scout La, SW4
off Old Town 101 DJ83
Scout Way, NW7 42 CR49
Scovell Cres, SE1 201 H5
Scovell Rd, SE1 201 H5
Scratchers La, Long.
(Fawk.Grn) DA3 149 FR103
Scrattons Ter, Bark. IG11 88 EX68
Scriven St, E8 84 DT67
Scrooby St, SE6 123 EB86
Scrubbitts Pk Rd, Rad. WD7 25 CG35
Scrubbitts Sq, Rad. WD7
off The Dell 25 CG36
Scrubs La, NW10 81 CU69
W10 81 CU69
Scrutton Cl, SW12 121 DK87
Scrutton St, EC2 197 M5
Scudamore La, NW9 62 CQ55
Scudders Hill, Long.
(Fawk.Grn) DA3 149 FV100
Scutari Rd, SE22 122 DW85
Scylla Cres, Houns.
(Hthrw Air.) TW6 115 BP87
Scylla Pl, Wok. (St.John's) GU21
off Church Rd 166 AU119
Scylla Rd, SE15 102 DV83
Hounslow
(Hthrw Air.) TW6 115 BP86
Seaborough Rd, Grays RM16 111 GJ76
Seabright St, E2
off Bethnal Grn Rd 84 DV69
Seabrook Dr, W.Wick. BR4 144 EE103
Seabrooke Ri, Grays RM17 110 GB79
Seabrook Gdns, Rom. RM7 70 FA59
Seabrook Rd, Dag. RM8 70 EX62
Kings Langley WD4 7 BR27
Seaburn Cl, Rain. RM13 89 FE68
Seacole Cl, W3 80 CR71
Seacon Twr, E14
off Hutchings St 103 EA75
Seacourt Rd, SE2 106 EX75
Slough SL3 93 BB77
Seacroft Gdns, Wat. WD19 40 BX48
Seafield Rd, N11 45 DK49
Seaford Cl, Ruis. HA4 59 BR61
Seaford Rd, E17 67 EB55
N15 66 DR57
W13 79 CH74
Enfield EN1 30 DS42
Hounslow
(Hthrw Air.) TW6 114 BK85
Seaford St, WC1 196 A3
Seaforth Av, N.Mal. KT3 139 CV99
Seaforth Cl, Rom. RM1 51 FE52
Seaforth Cres, N5 66 DQ64
Seaforth Dr, Wal.Cr. EN8 15 DX34
Seaforth Gdns, N21 45 DM45
Epsom KT19 157 CT105
Woodford Green IG8 48 EJ50
Seaforth Pl, SW1
off Buckingham Gate 101 DJ76
Seagrave Rd, SW6 100 DA79
Seagry Rd, E11 68 EG58
Seagull Cl, Bark. IG11 88 EU69
Seagull La, E16 86 EG73
SEAL, Sev. TN15 191 FN121
Sealand Rd, Houns.
(Hthrw Air.) TW6 114 BN86
Sealand Wk, Nthlt. UB5
off Wayfarer Rd 78 BY69
Seal Dr, Sev. (Seal) TN15 191 FM121
Seal Hollow Rd, Sev.
TN13, TN15 191 FJ124
Seal Rd, Sev. TN14, TN15 191 FJ121
Seal St, E8 66 DT63
Seaman Cl, St.Alb.
(Park St) AL2 9 CD25
Searches La, Abb.L.
(Bedmond) WD5 7 BV28
Searchwood Rd, Warl. CR6 176 DV118
Searle Pl, N4
off Evershot Rd 65 DM60
Searles Cl, SW11 100 DE80
Searles Dr, E6 87 EP71
Searles Rd, SE1 201 L8
Sears St, SE5 102 DR80
Seasprite Cl, Nthlt. UB5 78 BX69
Seaton Av, Ilf. IG3 69 ES64
Seaton Cl, E13
off New Barn St 86 EH70
SE11 200 E10
SW15 119 CV88
Twickenham TW2 117 CD86
Seaton Dr, Ashf. TW15 114 BL89
Seaton Gdns, Ruis. HA4 59 BU62
Seaton Pt, E5 *off Nolan Way* 66 DV63
Seaton Rd, Dart. DA1 127 FG87
Hayes UB3 95 BR77
Mitcham CR4 140 DE96
St. Albans (Lon.Col.) AL2 9 CK26
Twickenham TW2 116 CC86
Welling DA16 106 EW80
Wembley HA0 80 CL68
Seaton Sq, NW7
off Tavistock Av 43 CX52
Seaton St, N18 46 DU50
Sebastian Av, Brwd.
(Shenf.) CM15 55 GA44
Sebastian St, EC1 196 G3
Sebastopol Rd, N9 46 DU49
Sebbon St, N1 83 DP66
Sebergham Gro, NW7 43 CU52
Sebert Rd, E7 68 EH64
Sebright Pas, E2
off Hackney Rd 84 DU68
Sebright Rd, Barn. EN5 27 CX40
Secker Cres, Har. HA3 40 CC53
Secker St, SE1 200 D3

★ Place of interest · Railway station · London Underground station · DLR Docklands Light Railway station · Tra Tramlink station · H Hospital · Riv Pedestrian ferry landing stage

322

Second Av, E12 68 EL63
E13 86 EG69
E17 67 EA57
N18 46 DW49
NW4 63 CX56
SW14 98 CS83
W3 81 CT74
W10 81 CY70
Dagenham RM10 89 FB67
Enfield EN1 30 DT43
Grays RM20 109 FU79
Hayes UB3 77 BT74
Romford RM6 70 EW57
Waltham Abbey EN9
off Breach Barn
Mobile Home Pk 16 EH30
Walton-on-Thames KT12 135 BV100
Watford WD25 24 BX35
Wembley HA9 61 CK61
Second Cl, W.Mol. KT8 136 CC98
Second Cross Rd, Twick. TW2 117 CE89
Second Way, Wem. HA9 62 CP63
Sedan Way, SE17 201 M10
Sedcombe Cl, Sid. DA14
off Knoll Rd 126 EV91
Sedcote Rd, Enf. EN3 30 DW43
Sedding St, SW1 198 F8
Seddon Highwalk, EC2
off Beech St 84 DQ71
Seddon Ho, EC2
off The Barbican 84 DQ71
Seddon Rd, Mord. SM4 140 DD99
Seddon St, WC1 196 C3
Sedgebrook Rd, SE3 104 EK82
Sedgecombe Av, Har. HA3 61 CJ57
Sedge Ct, Grays RM17 110 GE80
Sedgefield Cl, Rom. RM3 52 FM49
Sedgefield Cres, Rom. RM3 52 FM49
Sedgeford Rd, W12 81 CT74
Sedgehill Rd, SE6 123 EA91
Sedgemere Av, N2 64 DC55
Sedgemere Rd, SE2 106 EW76
Sedgemoor Dr, Dag. RM10 70 FA63
Sedge Rd, N17 46 DW52
Sedgeway, SE6 124 EF88
Sedgewick Av, Uxb. UB10 77 BP66
Sedgewood Cl, Brom. BR2 144 EF101
Sedgmoor Pl, SE5 102 DS80
Sedgwick Rd, E10 67 EC61
Sedgwick St, E9 67 DX64
Sedleigh Rd, SW18 119 CZ86
Sedlescombe Rd, SW6 99 CZ79
Sedley, Grav. (Sthflt) DA13 130 GA93
Sedley Cl, Enf. EN1 30 DV38
Sedley Gro, Uxb. (Hare.) UB9 58 BJ56
Sedley Pl, W1 195 H9
Sedley Ri, Loug. IG10 33 EM40
Sedum Cl, NW9 62 CP57
Seeley Dr, SE21 122 DS91
Seelig Av, NW9 63 CU59
Seely Rd, SW17 120 DG93
Seer Grn La, Beac.
(Jordans) HP9 36 AS52
Seething La, EC3 201 N1
Seething Wells La, Surb.
KT6 137 CJ100
Sefton Av, NW7 42 CR50
Harrow HA3 41 CD53
Sefton Cl, Orp. BR5 145 ET98
Slough (Stoke P.) SL2 74 AT66
Sefton Paddock, Slou.
(Stoke P.) SL2 74 AU66
Sefton Pk, Slou.
(Stoke P.) SL2 74 AU66
Sefton Rd, Croy. CR0 142 DU102
Epsom KT19 156 CR110
Orpington BR5 145 ET98
Sefton St, SW15 99 CW82
Sefton Way, Uxb. UB8 76 BJ72
Segal Cl, SE23 123 DY87
Segrave Cl, Wey. KT13 152 BN108
Sekforde St, EC1 196 F5
Sekhon Ter, Felt. TW13 116 CA90
Selah Dr, Swan. BR8 147 FC95
Selan Gdns, Hayes UB4 77 BV71
Selbie Av, NW10 63 CT64
Selborne Av, E12
off Walton Rd 69 EN63
Bexley DA5 126 EY88
Selborne Gdns, NW4 63 CU56
Greenford UB6 79 CG67
Selborne Rd, E17 67 DZ57
N14 45 DL48
N22 45 DM53
SE5 off Denmark Hill 102 DR82
Croydon CR0 142 DS104
Ilford IG1 69 EN61
New Malden KT3 138 CS96
Sidcup DA14 126 EV91
Selbourne Av, E17 67 DZ56
Addlestone
(New Haw) KT15 152 BH110
Surbiton KT6 138 CM103
Selbourne Cl, Add.
(New Haw) KT15 152 BH109
Selbourne Sq, Gdse. RH9 186 DW130
Selbourne Wk, E17
off Selbourne Wk
Shop Cen 67 DZ56
Selbourne Wk Shop Cen, E17 67 DZ56
Selby Chase, Ruis. HA4 59 BV61
Selby Cl, E6 off Linton Gdns 86 EL71
Chessington KT9 156 CL108
Chislehurst BR7 125 EN93
Selby Gdns, Sthl. UB1 78 CA70
Selby Grn, Cars. SM5 140 DE101
Selby Rd, E11 68 EE62
E13 86 EH71
N17 46 DS51
SE20 142 DU96
W5 79 CH70
Ashford TW15 115 BQ93
Carshalton SM5 140 DE101
Selby St, E1 84 DU70
Selby Wk, Wok. GU21
off Wyndham Rd 166 AV118
Selcroft Rd, Pur. CR8 159 DP112
Selden Rd, SE15 102 DW82
Selden Wk, N7
off Durham Rd 65 DM61
★ Selfridges, W1 194 G9
SELHURST, SE25 142 DS100
⇌ Selhurst 142 DS99
Selhurst Cl, SW19 119 CX88
Woking GU21 167 AZ115
Selhurst New Rd, SE25 142 DS100
Selhurst Pl, SE25 142 DS100
Selhurst Rd, N9 46 DR48
SE25 142 DS99
Selinas La, Dag. RM8 70 EY59
Selkirk Dr, Erith DA8 107 FE81
Selkirk Rd, SW17 120 DE91
Twickenham TW2 116 CC89
Sell Cl, Wal.Cr. (Chsht) EN7
off Gladding Rd 13 DP26
Sellers Cl, Borwd. WD6 26 CQ39
Sellers Hall Cl, N3 44 DA52
Sellincourt Rd, SW17 120 DE92
Sellindge Cl, Beck. BR3 123 DZ94
Sellons Av, NW10 81 CT67
Sellwood Dr, Barn. EN5 27 CX43
Sellwood St, SW2
off Tulse Hill 121 DN87
SELSDON, S.Croy. CR2 160 DW110
Selsdon Av, S.Croy. CR2
off Selsdon Rd 160 DR107
Selsdon Cl, Rom. RM5 51 FC53
Surbiton KT6 138 CL99
Selsdon Cres, S.Croy. CR2 160 DW109
Selsdon Pk Rd, S.Croy. CR2 161 DX109
Selsdon Rd, E11 68 EG59
E13 86 EJ67
NW2 63 CT61
SE27 121 DP90
Addlestone
(New Haw) KT15 152 BG111
South Croydon CR2 160 DR106
Selsdon Rd Ind Est, S.Croy. CR2
off Selsdon Rd 160 DR107
Selsdon Way, E14 204 C7
Selsea Pl, N16
off Crossway 66 DS64
Selsey Cres, Well. DA16 106 EX81
Selsey St, E14 85 EA71
Selvage La, NW7 42 CR50
Selway Cl, Pnr. HA5 59 BV56
Selwood Cl, Stai.
(Stanw.) TW19 114 BJ86
Selwood Gdns, Stai.
(Stanw.) TW19 114 BJ86
Selwood Pl, SW7 100 DD78
Selwood Rd, Brwd. CM14 54 FT48
Chessington KT9 155 CK105
Croydon CR0 142 DV103
Sutton SM3 139 CZ102
Woking GU22 167 BB120
Selwood Ter, SW7
off Onslow Gdns 100 DD78
Selworthy Cl, E11 68 EG57
Selworthy Ho, SW11 100 DD81
Selworthy Rd, SE6 123 DZ90
Selwyn Av, E4 47 EC51
Ilford IG3 69 ES58
Richmond TW9 98 CL83
Selwyn Cl, Houns. TW4 96 BY84
Selwyn Ct, SE3 104 EE83
Edgware HA8
off Camrose Av 42 CP52
Selwyn Cres, Well. DA16 106 EV84
Selwyn Pl, Orp. BR5 146 EV97
Selwyn Rd, E3 85 DZ68
E13 86 EH67
NW10 80 CR66
New Malden KT3 138 CR99
Tilbury RM18
off Dock Rd 111 GF82
Semley Pl, SW1 198 G9
Semley Rd, SW16 141 DL96
Semper Cl, Wok.
(Knap.) GU21 166 AS117
Semper Rd, Grays RM16 111 GJ75
Senate St, SE15 102 DW82
Senator Wk, SE28
off Broadwater Rd 105 ER76
SEND, Wok. GU23 167 BC124
Sendall Ct, SW11 100 DD83
Send Barns La, Wok.
(Send) GU23 167 BD124
Send Cl, Wok. (Send) GU23 167 BC123
SEND MARSH, Wok. GU23 167 BF124
Send Marsh Rd, Wok.
(Ripley) GU23 167 BF123
Send Par Cl, Wok. (Send) GU23
off Send Rd 167 BC123
Send Rd, Wok.
(Send) GU23 167 BB122
Seneca Rd, Th.Hth. CR7 142 DQ98
Senga Rd, Wall. SM6 140 DG102
Senhouse Rd, Sutt. SM3 139 CX104
Senior St, W2 82 DB71
Senlac Rd, SE12 124 EH88
Sennen Rd, Enf. EN1 46 DT45
Sennen Wk, SE9 124 EL90
Senrab St, E1 85 DX72
Sentinel Cl, Nthlt. UB5 78 BY70
Sentinel Sq, NW4 63 CW56
Sentis Ct, Nthwd. HA6
off Carew Rd 39 BS51
September Way, Stan. HA7 41 CH51
Sequoia Cl, Bushey
(Bushey Hth) WD23
off Giant Tree Hill 41 CD46
Sequoia Gdns, Orp. BR6 145 ET101
Sequoia Pk, Pnr. HA5 40 CB51
Serbin Cl, E10 67 EC59
Serenaders Rd, SW9 101 DN82
Sergeants Grn La, Wal.Abb.
EN9 16 EJ33
Sergeants Pl, Cat. CR3
off Coulsdon Rd 176 DQ122
Sergehill La, Abb.L.
(Bedmond) WD5 7 BT27
Serjeants Inn, EC4 196 E9
Serle St, WC2 196 C8
Sermed Ct, Slou. SL2 74 AW74
Sermon Dr, Swan. BR8 147 FC97
Sermon La, EC4 197 H9
★ Serpentine, The, W2 198 B3
Serpentine Ct, Sev. TN13 191 FK122
★ Serpentine Gall, W2 198 A3
Serpentine Grn, Red. RH1
off Malmstone Av 185 DK129
Serpentine Rd, W2 198 D3
Sevenoaks TN13 191 FJ123
Service Rd, The, Pot.B. EN6 12 DA32
Services Way, Iver SL0
off Pinewood Rd 75 BB66
Servidan Dr, Brom. BR1 144 EK95
Setchell Rd, SE1 201 P8
Setchell Way, SE1 201 P8
Seth St, SE16 202 G5
Seton Gdns, Dag. RM9 88 EW66
Settle Pt, E13
off London Rd 86 EG68
Settle Rd, E13
off London Rd 86 EG68
Romford RM3 52 FN49
Settles St, E1 84 DU71
Settrington Rd, SW6 100 DB82
Seven Acres, Cars. SM5 140 DE103
Northwood HA6 39 BU51
Swanley BR8 147 FD100
Seven Arches App, Wey.
KT13 152 BM108
Seven Arches Rd, Brwd.
CM14 54 FX48
Seven Hills Cl, Walt. KT12 153 BS109
Seven Hills Rd, Cob. KT11 153 BS111
Iver SL0 75 BC65
Walton-on-Thames KT12 153 BS109
Seven Hills Rd S, Cob. KT11 153 BS113
SEVEN KINGS, Ilf. IG3 69 ES59
⇌ Seven Kings 69 ES60
Seven Kings Rd, Ilf. IG3 69 ET61
Seven Kings Way, Kings.T.
KT2 138 CL95
SEVENOAKS 191 FJ125
⇌ Sevenoaks 190 FG124
Sevenoaks Business Cen, Sev.
TN14 191 FJ121
Sevenoaks Bypass, Sev.
TN14 190 FC123
Sevenoaks Cl, Bexh. DA7 107 FC84
Romford RM3 52 FJ49
Sutton SM2 158 DA110
SEVENOAKS COMMON, Sev.
TN13 191 FH129
Sevenoaks Ct, Nthwd. HA6 39 BQ52
H Sevenoaks Hosp, Sev.
TN13 191 FJ121
Sevenoaks Ho, SE25 142 DU97
★ Sevenoaks Mus, Sev.
TN13 191 FJ125
Sevenoaks Rd, SE4 123 DY86
Orpington BR6 163 ET106
Orpington
(Grn St Grn) BR6 163 ET108
Sevenoaks (Otford) TN14 181 FH116
Sevenoaks Way, Orp. BR5 126 EW94
Sidcup DA14 126 EW94
⇌ Seven Sisters 66 DS57
⊖ Seven Sisters 66 DS57
Seven Sisters Rd, N4 65 DM62
N7 65 DM62
N15 66 DQ59
Seven Stars Cor, W12
off Goldhawk Rd 99 CU76
Seven Stars Yd, E1
off Brick La 84 DT71
Seventh Av, E12 69 EM63
Hayes UB3 77 BU74
Severnake Cl, E14 204 A8
Severn Av, Rom. RM2 71 FH55
Severn Cres, Slou. SL3 93 BB78
Severn Dr, Enf. EN1 30 DU38
Esher KT10 137 CG103
Upminster RM14 73 FR58
Walton-on-Thames KT12 136 BX103
Severn Rd, S.Ock.
(Aveley) RM15 90 FQ72
Severns Fld, Epp. CM16 18 EU29
Severnvale, St.Alb. (Lon.Col.) AL2
off Thamesdale 10 CM27
Severn Way, NW10 63 CT64
Watford WD25 8 BW34
Severus Rd, SW11 100 DE84
Seville Ms, N1 84 DS66
Seville St, SW1 198 E5
Sevington Rd, NW4 63 CV58
Sevington St, W9 82 DB70
Seward Rd, W7 97 CG75
Beckenham BR3 143 DX96
SEWARDSTONE, E4 31 EC39
SEWARDSTONEBURY, E4 32 EE42
Sewardstone Gdns, E4 31 EB43
Sewardstone Grn, E4 32 EE42
Sewardstone Rd, E2 84 DW68
E4 47 EB45
Waltham Abbey EN9 31 EC38
Sewardstone Roundabout,
Wal.Abb. EN9 31 EC35
Sewardstone St, Wal.Abb.
EN9 15 EC34
Seward St, EC1 196 G4
Sewdley St, E5 67 DX62
Sewell Cl, Grays
(Chaff.Hun.) RM16 109 FW78
Sewell Rd, SE2 106 EU76
Sewell St, E13 86 EG69
Sextant Av, E14 204 F8
Sexton Cl, Rain. RM13
off Blake Cl 89 FF67
Waltham Cross (Chsht) EN7
off Shambrook Rd 14 DQ25
Sexton Rd, Til. RM18 111 GF81
Seymer Rd, Rom. RM1 71 FD55
Seymour Av, N17 46 DU54
Caterham CR3 176 DQ123
Epsom KT17 157 CV109
Morden SM4 139 CX101
Seymour Cl, E.Mol. KT8 136 CC99
Loughton IG10 32 EL44
Pinner HA5 40 BZ53
Seymour Ct, E4 48 EF47
Seymour Dr, Brom. BR2 145 EM102
Seymour Gdns, SE4 103 DY83
Feltham TW13 116 BW91
Ilford IG1 69 EM60
Ruislip HA4 60 BX60
Surbiton KT5 138 CM99
Seymour Gdns,
Twickenham TW1 117 CH87
Seymour Ms, W1 194 F8
Seymour Pl, SE25 142 DV98
W1 194 D7
Hornchurch RM11
off North St 72 FK59
Seymour Rd, E4 47 EB46
E6 86 EK68
E10 67 DZ60
N3 44 DB52
N8 65 DN57
N9 46 DV47
SW18 119 CZ87
SW19 119 CX89
W4 98 CQ77
Carshalton SM5 158 DG106
Chalfont St. Giles HP8 36 AW49
East Molesey KT8 136 CC99
Gravesend (Nthflt) DA11 131 GF88
Hampton
(Hmptn H.) TW12 116 CC92
Kingston upon Thames KT1 137 CK95
Mitcham CR4 140 DG101
Tilbury RM18 111 GF81
Seymours, The, Loug. IG10 33 EN39
Seymour St, SE18 105 EQ76
W1 194 D9
W2 194 D9
Seymour Ter, SE20 142 DV95
Seymour Vil, SE20 142 DV95
Seymour Wk, SW10 100 DC79
Swanscombe DA10 130 FY87
Seymour Way, Sun. TW16 115 BS93
Seyssel St, E14 204 E8
Shaa Rd, W3 80 CR73
Shacklands Rd, Sev.
(Bad.Mt) TN14 165 FB111
Shackleford Rd, Wok.
GU22 167 BA121
Shacklegate La, Tedd. TW11 117 CE91
Shackleton Cl, SE23
off Featherstone Av 122 DV89
Shackleton Ct, E14
off Maritime Quay 103 EA78
W12 99 CV75
Shackleton Rd, Slou. SL1 74 AT73
Southall UB1 78 BZ73
Shackleton Way, Abb.L. WD5
off Lysander Way 7 BU32
SHACKLEWELL, N16 66 DT63
Shacklewell Grn, E8 66 DT63
Shacklewell La, E8 66 DT64
Shacklewell Rd, N16 66 DT63
Shacklewell Row, E8 66 DT63
Shacklewell St, E2 84 DT70
Shadbolt Av, E4 47 DY50
Shadbolt Cl, Wor.Pk. KT4 139 CT103
Shad Thames, SE1 201 P3
SHADWELL, E1 202 F1
⊖ Shadwell 84 DW73
DLR Shadwell 84 DW73
Shadwell Ct, Nthlt. UB5
off Shadwell Dr 78 BZ68
Shadwell Dr, Nthlt. UB5 78 BZ69
Shadwell Gdns Est, E1
off Martha St 84 DW72
Shadwell Pierhead, E1 202 G1
Shadwell Pl, E1
off Sutton St 84 DW73
Shady Bush Cl, Bushey WD23 40 CC45
Shady La, Wat. WD17 23 BV40
Shaef Way, Tedd. TW11 117 CG94
Shafter Rd, Dag. RM10 89 FC65
Shaftesbury, Loug. IG10 32 EK41
Shaftesbury Av, W1 195 M10
WC2 195 M10
Barnet EN5 28 DC42
Enfield EN3 31 DX40
Feltham TW14 115 BU86
Harrow HA2 60 CB60
Harrow (Kenton) HA3 61 CK58
Southall UB2 96 CA77
Shaftesbury Circle, Har. HA2
off Shaftesbury Av 60 CC60
Shaftesbury Ct, N1
off Shaftesbury St 84 DR68
Shaftesbury Cres, Stai. TW18 114 BK94
Shaftesbury Gdns, NW10 80 CS70
Shaftesbury La, Dart. DA1 108 FP84
Shaftesbury Ms, SW4
off Clapham Common
S Side 121 DJ85
W8 off Stratford Rd 100 DA76
Shaftesbury Pl, W14
off Warwick Rd 99 CZ77
Shaftesbury Pt, E13
off High St 86 EH68
Shaftesbury Rd, E4 47 ED46
E7 86 EJ66
E10 67 EA60
E17 67 EB58
N18 46 DS51
N19 65 DL60
Beckenham BR3 143 DZ96
Carshalton SM5 140 DD101
Epping CM16 17 ET29
Richmond TW9 98 CL83
Romford RM1 71 FF58
Watford WD17 24 BW41
Woking GU22 167 BA117
Shaftesburys, The, Bark. IG11 87 EQ67
Shaftesbury St, N1 197 J1
Shaftesbury Way, Kings L.
WD4 7 BQ28
Twickenham TW2 117 CD90
Shaftesbury Waye, Hayes
UB4 77 BV71
Shafto Ms, SW1 198 D7
Shafton Rd, E9 85 DX67
Shaggy Calf La, Slou. SL2 74 AU73
Shakespeare Av, N11 45 DJ50
NW10 80 CR67
Feltham TW14 115 BU86
Hayes UB4 77 BV70
Tilbury RM18 111 GH82
Shakespeare Cres, E12 87 EM65
NW10 80 CR67
Shakespeare Dr, Har. HA3 62 CM58
Shakespeare Gdns, N2 64 DF56
Shakespeare Ho, N14
off High St 45 DK47
Shakespeare Rd, E17 47 DX54
N3 off Popes Dr 44 DA53
NW7 43 CT49
SE24 121 DP85
W3 80 CQ74
W7 79 CF73
Addlestone KT15 152 BK105
Bexleyheath DA7 106 EY81
Dartford DA1 108 FN84
Romford RM1 71 FF58
★ Shakespeare's Globe Thea,
SE1 201 H1
Shakespeare Sq, Ilf. IG6 49 EQ51
Shakespeare St, Wat. WD24 23 BV38
Shakespeare Twr, EC2 197 J6
Shakespeare Way, Felt. TW13 116 BW91
Shakspeare Ms, N16
off Shakspeare Wk 66 DS63
Shakspeare Wk, N16 66 DS63
Shalbourne Sq, E9 85 DZ65
Shalcomb St, SW10 100 DC79
Shalcross Dr, Wal.Cr.
(Chsht) EN8 15 DZ30
Shalden Ho, SW15
off Tunworth Cres 119 CT86
Shaldon Dr, Mord. SM4 139 CY99
Ruislip HA4 60 BW62
Shaldon Rd, Edg. HA8 42 CM53
Shaldon Way, Walt. KT12 136 BW104
Shale Grn, Red. RH1
off Bletchingley Rd 185 DK129
Shalfleet Dr, W10 81 CX73
Shalford Cl, Orp. BR6 163 EQ105
Shalimar Gdns, W3 80 CQ73
Shalimar Rd, W3
off Hereford Rd 80 CQ73
Shallons Rd, SE9 125 EP91
Shalstone Rd, SW14 98 CP83
Shalston Vil, Surb. KT6 138 CM100
Shambrook Rd, Wal.Cr.
(Chsht) EN7 13 DP25
Shamrock Cl, Lthd.
(Fetch.) KT22 171 CD121
Shamrock Ho, SE26
off Talisman Sq 122 DU91
Shamrock Rd, Croy. CR0 141 DM100
Gravesend DA12 131 GL87
Shamrock St, SW4 101 DK83
Shamrock Way, N14 45 DH46
Shandon Rd, SW4 121 DJ86
Shand St, SE1 201 M4
Shandy St, E1 85 DX71
Shanklin Cl, Wal.Cr. EN7
off Hornbeam Way 14 DT29
Shanklin Gdns, Wat. WD19 40 BW49
Shanklin Rd, N8 65 DK57
N15 66 DU56
Shanklin Way, SE15
off Pentridge St 102 DT80
Shannon Cl, NW2 63 CX62
Southall UB2 96 BX78
Shannon Gro, SW9 101 DM84
Shannon Pl, NW8
off Allitsen Rd 82 DE68
Shannon Way, Beck. BR3 123 EB93
South Ockendon
(Aveley) RM15 90 FQ73
Shantock Hall La, Hem.H.
(Bov.) HP3 4 AY29
Shantock La, Hem.H.
(Bov.) HP3 4 AX30
Shap Cres, Cars. SM5 140 DF102
Shapland Way, N13 45 DM50
Shapwick Cl, N11
off Friern Barnet Rd 44 DF50
Shardcroft Av, SE24 121 DP85
Shardeloes Rd, SE4 103 DZ83
SE14 103 DZ83
Sharland Cl, Th.Hth. CR7
off Dunheved Rd N 141 DN100
Sharland Rd, Grav. DA12 131 GJ89
Sharman Ct, Sid. DA14 126 EU91
Sharman Row, Slou. SL3
off Ditton Rd 93 AZ78
Sharnbrooke Cl, Well. DA16 106 EW83
Sharney Av, Slou. SL3 93 BB76
Sharon Cl, Epsom KT19 156 CQ113
Leatherhead (Bkhm) KT23 170 CA124
Surbiton KT6 137 CK102
Sharon Gdns, E9 84 DW67
Sharon Rd, W4 98 CR78
Enfield EN3 31 DY40
Sharpe Cl, W7
off Templeman Rd 79 CF71
Sharpleshall St, NW1 82 DF66
Sharpness Cl, Hayes UB4 78 BY71
Sharps La, Ruis. HA4 59 BR60
Sharp Way, Dart. DA1 108 FM83
Sharratt St, SE15 102 DW79
Sharsted St, SE17 101 DP78
Sharvel La, Nthlt. UB5 77 BU67
Shavers Pl, SW1 199 M1
Shaw Av, Bark. IG11 88 EY68
Shawbrooke Rd, SE9 124 EJ85
Shawbury Rd, SE22 122 DT85
Shaw Cl, SE28 88 EV74
Bushey (Bushey Hth) WD23 41 CE47
Chertsey (Ott.) KT16 151 BC107
Epsom KT17 157 CT111
Hornchurch RM11 71 FH60
South Croydon CR2 160 DT112
Waltham Cross
(Chsht) EN8 14 DW28
Shaw Ct, SW11 100 DD83
Windsor SL4 112 AU85
Shaw Cres, Brwd.
(Hutt.) CM13 55 GD43
South Croydon CR2 160 DT112
Tilbury RM18 111 GH81
Shaw Dr, Walt. KT12 136 BW101
Shawfield Ct, West Dr. UB7 94 BL76
Shawfield Pk, Brom. BR1 144 EK96
Shawfield St, SW3 100 DE78

★ Place of interest ⇌ Railway station ⊖ London Underground station DLR Docklands Light Railway station Tra Tramlink station H Hospital Riv Pedestrian ferry landing stage

323

★ Place of interest　　⇌ Railway station　　⊖ London Underground station　　DLR Docklands Light Railway station　　Tra Tramlink station　　Ⓗ Hospital　　Riv Pedestrian ferry landing stage

324

Short La,
St. Albans (Brick.Wd) AL2 8 BZ30
Staines TW19 114 BM88
Shortmead Dr, Wal.Cr.
(Chsht) EN8 15 DY31
Short Path, SE18
off Westdale Rd 105 EP79
Short Rd, E11 68 EE61
E15 85 ED67
W4 98 CS79
Hounslow
(Hthrw Air.) TW6 114 BL86
Shorts Cft, NW9 62 CP56
Shorts Gdns, WC2 195 P9
Shorts Rd, Cars. SM5 158 DE105
Short St, NW4
off New Brent St 63 CW56
SE1 200 E4
Short Wall, E15 85 EC69
Shortway, N12 44 DE51
Short Way, SE9 104 EL83
Twickenham TW2 116 CC87
Shortwood Av, Stai. TW18 114 BH90
Shortwood Common, Stai.
TW18 114 BH91
Shotfield, Wall. SM6 159 DH107
Shothanger Way, Hem.H.
(Bov.) HP3 5 BC26
Shott Cl, Sutt. SM1
off Turnpike La 158 DC106
Shottendane Rd, SW6 100 DA81
Shottery Cl, SE9 124 EL90
Shottfield Av, SW14 98 CS84
Shoulder of Mutton All, E14
off Narrow St 85 DY73
Shouldham St, W1 194 C7
Showers Way, Hayes UB3 77 BU74
Shrapnel Cl, SE18 104 EL80
Shrapnel Rd, SE9 105 EM83
SHREDING GREEN, Iver SL0 75 BB72
Shrewsbury Av, SW14 98 CQ84
Harrow HA3 62 CL56
Shrewsbury Cl, Surb. KT6 138 CL103
Shrewsbury Ct, EC1
off Whitecross St 84 DQ70
Shrewsbury Cres, NW10 80 CR67
Shrewsbury La, SE18 105 EP81
Shrewsbury Ms, W2
off Chepstow Rd 82 DA71
Shrewsbury Rd, E7 68 EK64
N11 45 DJ51
W2 82 DA72
Beckenham BR3 143 DY97
Carshalton SM5 140 DE100
Hounslow
(Hthrw Air.) TW6 115 BQ86
Redhill RH1 184 DE134
Shrewsbury St, W10 81 CW70
Shrewsbury Wk, Islw. TW7
off South St 97 CG83
Shrewton Rd, SW17 120 DF94
Shroffold Rd, Brom. BR1 124 EE91
Shropshire Cl, Mitch.
CR4 141 DL98
Shropshire Ho, N18
off Cavendish Rd 46 DV50
Shropshire Pl, WC1 195 L5
Shropshire Rd, N22 45 DM52
Shroton St, NW1 194 B6
Shrubberies, The, E18 48 EG54
Chigwell IG7 49 EQ50
Shrubbery, The, E11 68 EH57
Upminster RM14 72 FQ62
Shrubbery Cl, N1
off St. Paul St 84 DQ67
Shrubbery Gdns, N21 45 DP45
Shrubbery Rd, N9 46 DU48
SW16 121 DL91
Dartford (S.Darenth) DA4 149 FR95
Gravesend DA12 131 GH88
Southall UB1 78 BZ74
Shrubland Gro, Wor.Pk. KT4 139 CW104
Shrubland Rd, E8 84 DU67
E10 67 EA59
E17 67 EA57
Banstead SM7 173 CZ116
Shrublands, Hat. AL9 12 DB26
Shrublands, The, Pot.B.
EN6 11 CY33
Shrublands Av, Croy. CR0 161 EA105
Shrublands Cl, N20 44 DD46
SE26 122 DW90
Chigwell IG7 49 EQ51
Shrubsall Cl, SE9 124 EL88
Shrubs Rd, Rick. WD3 38 BM51
Shuna Wk, N1
off St. Paul's Rd 84 DR65
Shurland Av, Barn. EN4 28 DD44
Shurland Gdns, SE15
off Rosemary Rd 102 DT80
Shurlock Av, Swan. BR8 147 FD96
Shurlock Dr, Orp. BR6 163 EQ105
Shuters Sq, W14
off Sun Rd 99 CZ78
Shuttle Cl, Sid. DA15 125 ET87
Shuttlemead, Bex. DA5 126 EZ87
Shuttle Rd, Dart. DA1 107 FG83
Shuttle St, E1
off Buxton St 84 DU70
Shuttleworth Rd, SW11 100 DE82
Siamese Ms, N3
off Station Rd 44 DA53
Sibella Rd, SW4 101 DK82
Sibley Cl, Bexh. DA6 126 EY85
Bromley BR1
off Southborough Rd 144 EL99
Sibley Gro, E12 86 EL66
Sibthorpe Rd, SE12 124 EH86
Sibton Rd, Cars. SM5 140 DE101
Sicilian Av, WC1 196 A7
Sicklefield Cl, Wal.Cr.
(Chsht) EN7 14 DT26
Sidbury St, SW6 99 CY81
SIDCUP 125 ET91
⇌ Sidcup 126 EU89
Sidcup Bypass, Chis. BR7 125 ES91
Orpington BR5 126 EX94
Sidcup DA14 125 ES91
Sidcup High St, Sid. DA14 126 EU91
Sidcup Hill, Sid. DA14 126 EV91
Sidcup Hill Gdns, Sid. DA14
off Sidcup Hill 126 EW92
Sidcup Pl, Sid. DA14 126 EU92
Sidcup Rd, SE9 124 EK87
SE12 124 EH85
Sidcup Tech Cen, Sid. DA14 126 EX92
Siddeley Dr, Houns. TW4 96 BY83
Siddons La, NW1 194 E5
Siddons Rd, N17 46 DU53
SE23 123 DY89
Croydon CR0 141 DN104
Side Rd, E17 67 DZ57
Uxbridge (Denh.) UB9 57 BD59
Sidewood Rd, SE9 125 ER88
Sidford Pl, SE1 200 C7
Sidings, The, E11 67 EC60
Loughton IG10 32 EL44
Staines TW18
off Leacroft 114 BH91
Sidings Ms, N7 65 DN62
Siding Way, St.Alb. AL2
off Shenley La 9 CH26
Sidmouth Av, Islw. TW7 97 CE82
Sidmouth Cl, Wat. WD19 39 BV47
Sidmouth Dr, Ruis. HA4 59 BU62
Sidmouth Par, NW2
off Sidmouth Rd 81 CW66
Sidmouth Rd, E10 67 EC62
NW2 81 CW66
Orpington BR5 146 EV99
Welling DA16 106 EW80
Sidmouth St, WC1 196 A3
Sidney Av, N13 45 DM50
Sidney Cl, Uxb. UB8
off Barnfield Pl 76 BJ67
Sidney Elson Way, E6
off Edwin Av 87 EN68
Sidney Gdns, Brent. TW8 97 CJ79
Sidney Gro, EC1 196 F1
Sidney Rd, E7 68 EG62
N22 45 DM52
SE25 142 DU99
SW9 101 DM82
Beckenham BR3 143 DY96
Epping (They.B.) CM16 33 ER36
Harrow HA2 60 CC55
Staines TW18 114 BG91
Twickenham TW1 117 CG86
Walton-on-Thames KT12 135 BU101
Sidney Sq, E1 84 DW72
Sidney St, E1 84 DV71
Sidworth St, E8 84 DV66
Siebert Rd, SE3 104 EG79
Siemens Rd, SE18 104 EK76
Sigdon Rd, E8 66 DU64
Sigers, The, Pnr. HA5 59 BV58
Signmakers Yd, NW1
off Delancey St 83 DH67
Sigrist Sq, Kings.T. KT2 138 CL95
Silbury Av, Mitch. CR4 140 DE95
Silbury Ho, SE26
off Sydenham Hill 122 DU90
Silbury St, N1 197 K2
Silchester Rd, W10 81 CX72
Silecroft Rd, Bexh. DA7 106 FA81
Silesia Bldgs, E8
off London La 84 DV66
Silex St, SE1 200 G5
Silk Cl, SE12 124 EG85
Silkfield Rd, NW9 62 CS57
Silkham Rd, Oxt. RH8 187 ED127
Silkin Ho, Wat. WD19 40 BW48
Silk Mill Ct, Wat. WD19
off Silk Mill Rd 39 BV45
Silk Mill Rd, Wat. WD19 39 BV45
Silk Mills Cl, Sev. TN14 191 FJ121
Silk Mills Pas, SE13
off Russett Way 103 EB82
Silk Mills Path, SE13
off Lewisham Rd 103 EC82
Silk Mills Sq, E9 85 DZ65
Silkstream Rd, Edg. HA8 42 CQ53
Silk St, EC2 197 J6
Silsden Cres, Ch.St.G. HP8
off London Rd 36 AX48
Silsoe Rd, N22 45 DM54
Silver Birch Av, E4 47 DZ51
Epping (N.Wld Bas.) CM16 18 EY27
Silver Birch Cl, N11 44 DG51
SE6 off Selworthy Rd 123 DZ90
SE28 88 EU74
Addlestone (Wdhm) KT15 151 BE112
Dartford DA2 127 FE91
Uxbridge UB10 58 BL63
Silver Birch Ct, Wal.Cr.
(Chsht) EN8 15 DX31
Silver Birches, Brwd.
(Hutt.) CM13 55 GA46
Silver Birch Gdns, E6 87 EM70
Silver Birch Ms, Ilf. IG6
off Fencepiece Rd 49 EQ51
Silverbirch Wk, NW3
off Queen's Cres 82 DG65
Silvercliffe Gdns, Barn. EN4 28 DE42
Silver Cl, SE14
off Southerngate Way 103 DY80
Harrow HA3 41 CD52
Tadworth (Kgswd) KT20 173 CY124
Silver Cres, W4 98 CP77
Silverdale, SE26 122 DW91
Enfield EN2 29 DL42
Silverdale Av, Ilf. IG3 69 ES57
Leatherhead
(Oxshott) KT22 154 CC114
Walton-on-Thames KT12 135 BT104
Silverdale Cl, W7 79 CE74
Northolt UB5 60 BZ64
Sutton SM1 157 CZ105
Silverdale Ct, Stai. TW18 114 BH92
Silverdale Dr, SE9 124 EL89
Hornchurch RM12 71 FH64
Sunbury-on-Thames TW16 135 BV96
Silverdale Gdns, Hayes UB3 95 BU75
Silverdale Rd, E4 47 ED51
Bexleyheath DA7 107 FB82
Bushey WD23 24 BY43
Hayes UB3 95 BU75
Orpington (Petts Wd) BR5 145 EQ98
Orpington (St.P.Cray) BR5 146 EU97
Silver Dell, Wat. WD24 23 BT35
Silvergate, Epsom KT19 156 CQ106
Silverglade Business Pk, Chess.
KT9 155 CJ112
Silverhall St, Islw. TW7 97 CG83
Silver Hill, Ch.St.G. HP8 36 AV47
Silverholme Cl, Har. HA3 61 CK59
Silver Jubilee Way, Houns.
TW4 95 BV82
Silverland St, E16 87 EM74
Silver La, Pur. CR8 159 DK112
West Wickham BR4 143 ED103
Silverleigh Rd, Th.Hth. CR7 141 DM98
Silverlocke Rd, Grays RM17 110 GD79
Silvermead, E18
off Churchfields 48 EG52
Silvermere Av, Rom. RM5 51 FB51
Silvermere Dr, N18 47 DX51
Silvermere Rd, SE6 123 EB86
Silver Pl, W1 195 L10
Silver Rd, SE13 103 EB83
W12 81 CX73
Gravesend DA12 131 GL89
Silversmiths Way,
Wok. GU21 166 AW118
Silver Spring Cl, Erith DA8 107 FB79
Silverstead La, West. TN16 179 ER121
Silverstone Cl, Red. RH1
off Goodwood Rd 184 DF132
Silverston Way, Stan. HA7 41 CJ51
⇌ Silver Street 46 DT50
Silver St, N18 46 DS49
Enfield EN1 30 DR41
Romford (Abridge) RM4 34 EV41
Waltham Abbey EN9 15 EC34
Waltham Cross
(Goffs Oak) EN7 14 DR30
Silverthorne Rd, SW8 101 DH82
Silverthorn Gdns, E4 47 EA47
Silverton Rd, W6 99 CX79
SILVERTOWN, E16 104 EJ75
⇌ Silvertown &
London City Airport 86 EK74
Silvertown Way, E16 86 EF72
Silver Tree Cl, Walt. KT12 135 BU104
Silvertree La, Grnf. UB6
off Cowgate Rd 79 CD69
Silvertrees, St.Alb. (Brick.Wd) AL2
off West Riding 8 BZ30
Silver Wk, SE16 203 M3
Silver Way, Rom. RM7 71 FB55
Uxbridge UB10
off Oakdene Rd 77 BP68
Silverwood Cl, Beck. BR3 123 EA94
Croydon CR0 161 DZ109
Northwood HA6 39 BQ53
Silvester Rd, SE22 122 DT85
Silvester St, SE1 201 J5
Silvocea Way, E14 85 ED72
Silwood Est, SE16 202 G9
Silwood St, SE16 202 G9
Simla Ho, SE1 201 L5
Simmil Rd, Esher
(Clay.) KT10 155 CE106
Simmons Cl, N20 44 DE46
Chessington KT9 155 CJ108
Slough SL3
off Common Rd 93 BA77
Simmons Gate, Esher KT10
off Claremont La 154 CC106
Simmons La, E4 47 ED47
Simmons Pl, Stai. TW18
off Chertsey La 113 BE92
Simmons Rd, SE18 105 EP78
Simmons Way, N20 44 DE47
Simms Cl, Cars. SM5 140 DE103
Simms Gdns, N2 44 DC54
Simms Rd, SE1 202 B9
Simnel Rd, SE12 124 EH87
Simon Cl, W11
off Portobello Rd 81 CZ73
Simon Dean, Hem.H.
(Bov.) HP3 5 BA27
Simonds Rd, E10 67 EA61
Simone Cl, Brom. BR1 144 EK95
Simone Dr, Ken. CR8 176 DQ116
Simons Cl, Cher. (Ott.) KT16 151 BC107
Simons Wk, E15
off Waddington Rd 67 ED64
Egham (Eng.Grn) TW20 112 AW94
Simplemarsh Ct, Add. KT15
off Simplemarsh Rd 152 BH105
Simplemarsh Rd, Add. KT15 152 BG105
Simpson Cl, N21
off Macleod Rd 29 DL43
Simpson Dr, W3 80 CR72
Simpson Rd, Houns. TW4 116 BZ86
Rainham RM13 89 FF65
Richmond TW10 117 CJ91
Simpsons Rd, E14 204 C1
Bromley BR2 144 EG97
Simpson St, SW11 100 DE82
Simpsons Way, Slou. SL1
off Stoke Poges La 74 AS74
Simrose Ct, SW18
off Wandsworth High St 120 DA85
Sims Cl, Rom. RM1 71 FF56
Sims Wk, SE3 104 EF84
Sinclair Ct, Beck. BR3 123 EA94
Sinclair Dr, Sutt. SM2 158 DB109
Sinclair Gdns, W14 99 CX75
Sinclair Gro, NW11 63 CX58
Sinclair Pl, SE4 123 EA86
Sinclair Rd, E4 47 DZ50
W14 99 CX75
Sinclair Way, Dart.
(Lane End) DA2 129 FR91
Sinclare Cl, Enf. EN1 30 DT39
Sincots Rd, Red. RH1
off Lower Br Rd 184 DF134
Sinderby Cl, Borwd. WD6 26 CL39
Singapore Rd, W13 79 CG74
Singer St, EC2 197 L3
Singles Cross La, Sev.
(Knock.) TN14 164 EW114
SINGLE STREET, West. TN16 179 EN115
Single St, West.
(Berry's Grn) TN16 179 EP115
Singleton Cl, SW17 120 DF94
Croydon CR0
off St. Saviours Rd 142 DQ101
Singleton Cl, Hornchurch RM12
off Carfax Rd 71 FF63
Singleton Rd, Dag. RM9 70 EZ64
Singleton Scarp, N12 44 DA50
SINGLEWELL, Grav. DA12 131 GK93
Singlewell Rd, Grav. DA11 131 GH89
Singret Pl, Uxb. (Cowley) UB8
off High St 76 BJ70
Sinnott Rd, E17 47 DX53
Sion Rd, Twick. TW1 117 CH88
SIPSON, West Dr. UB7 94 BN79
Sipson Cl, West Dr. UB7 94 BN79
Sipson La, Hayes UB3 94 BN79
West Drayton UB7 94 BN79
Sipson Rd, West Dr. UB7 94 BN78
Sipson Way, West Dr. UB7 94 BN80
Sir Alexander Cl, W3 81 CT74
Sir Alexander Rd, W3 81 CT74
Sir Cyril Black Way, SW19 120 DA94
Sirdar Rd, N22 65 DP55
W11 81 CX73
Mitcham CR4
off Grenfell Rd 120 DG93
Sirdar Strand, Grav. DA12 131 GM92
Sir Francis Way, Brwd. CM14 54 FV47
Sirinham Pt, SW8 101 DM79
Sirius Rd, Nthwd. HA6 39 BU50
Sir John Kirk Cl, SE5
off Bethwin Rd 102 DQ80
★ Sir John Soane's Mus,
WC2 196 B8
Sir Thomas More Est, SW3
off Beaufort St 100 DD79
Sise La, EC4 197 K9
Siskin Cl, Borwd. WD6 26 CN42
Bushey WD23 24 BY42
Sisley Rd, Bark. IG11 87 ES67
Sispara Gdns, SW18 119 CZ86
Sissinghurst Rd, Croy. CR0 142 DU101
Sissulu Ct, E6 86 EJ67
Sister Mabel's Way, SE15
off Radnor Rd 102 DU80
Sisters Av, SW11 100 DF84
Sistova Rd, SW12 121 DH88
Sisulu Pl, SW9 101 DN83
Sittingbourne Av, Enf. EN1 30 DR44
Sitwell Gro, Stan. HA7 41 CF50
Siverst Cl, Nthlt. UB5 78 CB65
Sivill Ho, E2 84 DT69
Siviter Way, Dag. RM10 89 FB66
Siward Rd, N17 46 DR53
SW17 120 DC90
Bromley BR2 144 EH97
Six Acres Est, N4 65 DN61
Six Bells La, Sev. TN13 191 FJ126
Six Bridges Trd Est, SE1 102 DU78
Sixth Av, E12 69 EM63
W10 81 CY69
Hayes UB3 77 BT74
Watford WD25 24 BX35
Sixth Cross Rd, Twick. TW2 116 CC90
Skardu Rd, NW2 63 CY64
Skarnings Ct, Wal.Abb. EN9 16 EG33
Skeena Hill, SW18 119 CY87
Skeet Hill La, Orp.
BR5, BR6 146 EY103
Skeffington Rd, E6 86 EL67
Skeffington St, SE18 105 EQ76
Skelbrook St, SW18 120 DB89
Skelgill Rd, SW15 99 CZ84
Skelley Rd, E15 86 EF66
Skelton Cl, E8
off Buttermere Wk 84 DT65
Skelton Rd, E7 86 EG65
Skeltons La, E10 67 EB59
Skelwith Rd, W6 99 CW79
Skenfrith Ho, SE15
off Commercial Way 102 DV79
Skerne Rd, Kings.T. KT2 137 CK95
Skerne Wk, Kings.T. KT2 137 CK95
Skerries Ct, Slou. (Langley) SL3
off Blacksmith Row 93 BA77
Sketchley Gdns, SE16 203 H10
Sketty Rd, Enf. EN1 30 DS41
Skibbs La, Orp. BR5, BR6 146 EZ103
Skid Hill La, Warl. CR6 162 EF113
Skidmore Way, Rick. WD3 38 BL46
Skiers St, E15 86 EE67
Skiffington Cl, SW2 121 DN88
Skillet Hill, Wal.Abb. EN9 32 EH35
Skinner Ct, E2
off Parmiter St 84 DV68
Skinner Pl, SW1 198 F9
★ Skinners' Hall, EC4 197 K10
Skinners La, EC4 197 J10
Ashtead KT21 171 CK118
Hounslow TW5 96 CB81
Skinner St, EC1 196 E3
Skinney La, Dart.
(Hort.Kir.) DA4 148 FQ97
Skip La, Uxb. (Hare.) UB9 58 BL60
Skippers Cl, Green. DA9 129 FV85
Skips Cor, Epp.
(N.Wld Bas.) CM16 19 FD25
Skipsea Ho, SW18
off Fitzhugh Gro 120 DD86
Skipsey Av, E6 87 EM69
Skipton Cl, N11
off Ribblesdale Av 44 DG51
Skipton Dr, Hayes UB3 95 BQ76
Skipworth Rd, E9 84 DW67
Skomer Wk, N1
off Ashby Gro 84 DQ65
Skylark Rd, Uxb.
(Denh.) UB9 57 BC60
Skylines Village, E14 204 D5
Sky Peals Rd, Wdf.Grn. IG8 47 ED53
Skyport Dr, West Dr. UB7 94 BK80
Slade, The, SE18 105 ES79
Sladebrook Rd, SE3 104 EK83
Slade Ct, Cher. (Ott.) KT16 151 BD107
Radlett WD7 25 CG35
Sladedale Rd, SE18 105 ES78
Slade End, Epp.
(They.B.) CM16 33 ES36
Slade Gdns, Erith DA8 107 FF81
⇌ Slade Green 107 FG81
Slade Grn Rd, Erith DA8 107 FG80
Slade Ho, Houns. TW4 116 BZ86
Slade Oak La, Ger.Cr. SL9 57 BB55
Slade Oak La,
Uxbridge (Denh.) UB9 57 BD59
Slade Rd, Cher. (Ott.) KT16 151 BD107
Slades Cl, Enf. EN2 29 DN41
Slades Dr, Chis. BR7 125 EQ90
Slades Gdns, Enf. EN2 29 DN40
Slades Hill, Enf. EN2 29 DN41
Slades Ri, Enf. EN2 29 DN41
Slade Twr, E10 67 EB61
Slade Wk, SE17
off Heiron St 101 DP79
Slagrove Pl, SE13 123 EA85
Slaidburn St, SW10 100 DC79
Slaithwaite Rd, SE13 103 EC84
Slaney Pl, N7
off Hornsey Rd 65 DN64
Slaney Rd, Rom. RM1 71 FE57
Slapleys, Wok. GU22 166 AX120
Slater Cl, SE18
off Woolwich New Rd 105 EN78
Slattery Rd, Felt. TW13 116 BW88
Sleaford Grn, Wat. WD19 40 BX48
Sleaford Ho, E3
off Chiltern Rd 85 EA70
Sleaford St, SW8 101 DJ80
Sledmere Ct, Felt. TW14
off Kilross Rd 115 BS88
Sleepers Fm Rd, Grays
RM16 111 GH75
Slewins Cl, Horn. RM11 72 FJ57
Slewins La, Horn. RM11 72 FJ57
Slievemore Cl, SW4
off Voltaire Rd 101 DK83
Slines Oak Rd, Cat.
(Wold.) CR3 177 EA123
Warlingham CR6 177 EA119
Slingsby Pl, WC2 195 P10
Slip, The, West. TN16 189 EQ126
Slippers Pl, SE16 202 E6
Slipshoe St, Reig. RH2
off West St 183 CZ134
Sloane Av, SW3 198 B8
Sloane Ct E, SW3 198 F10
Sloane Ct W, SW3 198 F10
Sloane Gdns, SW1 198 F9
Orpington BR6 145 EQ104
H Sloane Hosp, Beck. BR3 143 ED95
⊖ Sloane Square 198 F9
Sloane Sq, SW1 198 F9
Sloane St, SW1 198 E6
Sloane Ter, SW1 198 E8
Sloane Wk, Croy. CR0 143 DZ100
Slocock Hill, Wok. GU21 166 AW117
Slocum Cl, SE28 88 EW73
SLOUGH 74 AS74
⇌ Slough 74 AT74
Slough La, NW9 62 CQ58
Betchworth
(Buckland) RH3 183 CU133
Epsom (Headley) KT18 182 CQ125
★ Slough Mus, Slou. SL1 92 AU75
Slough Rd, Iver SL0 75 BE68
Slough (Datchet) SL3 92 AU78
Slowmans Cl, St.Alb.
(Park St) AL2 8 CC28
Sly St, E1
off Cannon St Rd 84 DV72
Smaldon Cl, West Dr. UB7
off Walnut Av 94 BN76
Smallberry Av, Islw. TW7 97 CF82
Smallbrook Ms, W2
off Craven Rd 82 DD72
Smalley Cl, N16 66 DT62
Smalley Rd Est, N16
off Smalley Cl 66 DT62
Small Grains, Long.
(Fawk.Grn) DA3 149 FV104
Smallholdings Rd,
Epsom KT17 157 CW114
Smallwood Rd, SW17 120 DD91
Smardale Rd, SW18
off Alma Rd 120 DC85
Smarden Cl, Belv. DA17
off Essenden Rd 106 FA78
Smarden Gro, SE9 125 EM91
Smart Cl, Rom. RM3 51 FH53
Smarts Grn, Wal.Cr.
(Chsht) EN7 14 DT27
Smarts Heath La, Wok.
GU22 166 AU123
Smarts Heath Rd, Wok.
GU22 166 AT123
Smarts La, Loug. IG10 32 EK42
Smarts Pl, N18
off Fore St 46 DU50
Smart's Pl, WC2 196 A8
Smarts Rd, Grav. DA12 131 GH89
Smart St, E2 85 DX69
Smeaton Cl, Chess. KT9
off Merritt Gdns 155 CK107
Waltham Abbey EN9 16 EE32
Smeaton Rd, SW18 120 DA87
Enfield EN3 31 EA37
Woodford Green IG8 49 EM50
Smeaton St, E1 202 D2
Smedley St, SW4 101 DK82
SW8 101 DK82
Smeed Rd, E3 85 EA66
Smiles Pl, SE13 103 EC82
⇌ Smitham 175 DL115
Smitham Bottom La, Pur.
CR8 159 DJ111
Smitham Downs Rd, Pur.
CR8 159 DK113
Smith Cl, SE16 203 H3
★ Smithfield Cen Mkt, EC1 196 G7
Smithfield St, EC1 196 F7
Smithies Ct, E15 67 EC64
Smithies Rd, SE2 106 EV77
Smiths Caravan Site, Iver
SL0 75 BC74
Smith's Ct, W1 195 L10
Smiths Ct, Epp. CM16
off High Rd 18 EW25
Smiths Fm Est, Nthlt. UB5 78 CA68

★ Place of interest ⇌ Railway station ⊖ London Underground station DLR Docklands Light Railway station Tra Tramlink station H Hospital Riv Pedestrian ferry landing stage

325

Smiths La, Eden.
(Crock.H.) TN8 189 EQ133
Waltham Cross
(Chsht) EN7 14 DR26
Smithson Rd, N17 46 DR53
Smiths Pt, E13
off Brooks Rd 86 EG67
Smith Sq, SW1 199 P7
Smith St, SW3 198 D10
Surbiton KT5 138 CM100
Watford WD18 24 BW42
Smiths Yd, SW18
off Summerley St 120 DC89
Smith's Yd, Croy. CR0
off St. Georges Wk 142 DQ104
Smith Ter, SW3 100 DF78
Smithwood Cl, SW19 119 CY88
Smithy Cl, Tad.
(Lwr Kgswd) KT20 183 CZ126
Smithy La, Tad.
(Lwr Kgswd) KT20 183 CZ127
Smithy St, E1 84 DW71
Smock Wk, Croy. CR0 142 DQ100
Smokehouse Yd, EC1 196 G6
Smugglers Wk, Green. DA9 129 FV85
Smugglers Way, SW18 100 DB84
Smug Oak Grn Business Cen,
St.Alb. AL2 8 CB30
Smug Oak La, St.Alb.
(Brick.Wd) AL2 8 CB30
Smyrks Rd, SE17 102 DS78
Smyrna Rd, NW6 82 DA66
Smythe Rd, Dart.
(Sutt.H.) DA4 148 FN95
Smythe St, E14 85 EB73
Snag La, Sev.
(Cudham) TN14 163 ES109
Snakes La, Barn. EN4 29 DH41
Snakes La E, Wdf.Grn. IG8 48 EJ51
Snakes La W, Wdf.Grn. IG8 48 EG51
Snape Spur, Slou. SL1 74 AS72
SNARESBROOK, E11 68 EE57
⊖ Snaresbrook 68 EG57
Snaresbrook Dr, Stan. HA7 41 CK49
Snaresbrook Rd, E11 68 EE56
Snarsgate St, W10 81 CW71
Snatts Hill, Oxt. RH8 188 EF129
Sneath Av, NW11 63 CZ59
Snelling Av, Grav.
(Nthflt) DA11 130 GE89
Snellings Rd, Walt. KT12 154 BW106
Snells La, Amer. HP7 20 AV39
Snells Pk, N18 46 DT51
Snells Wd Ct, Amer. HP7 20 AW40
Sneyd Rd, NW2 63 CW63
Snipe Cl, Erith DA8 107 FH80
Snodland Cl, Orp. BR6
off Mill La 163 EN110
Snowberry Cl, E15 67 ED63
Snowbury Rd, SW6 100 DB82
Snowden Av, Uxb. UB10 77 BP68
Snowden St, EC2 197 M5
Snowdon Cres, Hayes UB3 95 BQ76
Snowdon Dr, NW9 62 CS58
Snowdon Rd, Houns. (Hthrw Air.)
TW6 off Southern
Perimeter Rd 115 BQ85
Snowdown Cl, SE20 143 DX95
Snowdrop Cl, Hmptn. TW12
off Gresham Rd 116 CA93
Snowdrop Path, Rom. RM3 52 FK52
Snow Hill, EC1 196 F7
Snow Hill Ct, EC1 196 G8
Snowman Ho, NW6 82 DB67
Snowsfields, SE1 201 L4
Snowshill Rd, E12 68 EL64
Snowy Fielder Waye, Islw.
TW7 97 CH82
Soames St, SE15 102 DT83
Soames Wk, N.Mal. KT3 138 CS95
Soane Cl, W5 97 CK75
Soap Ho La, Brent. TW8 98 CL80
Socket La, Brom. BR2 144 EH100
SOCKETT'S HEATH, Grays
RM16 110 GD76
Soham Rd, Enf. EN3 31 DZ37
SOHO, W1 195 M10
Soho Sq, W1 195 M8
Soho St, W1 195 M8
Sojourner Truth Cl, E8
off Richmond Rd 84 DV65
Solander Gdns, E1
off Dellow St 84 DV73
Solar Way, Enf. EN3 31 DZ36
Solebay St, E1 85 DY70
Sole Fm Cl, Lthd.
(Bkhm) KT23 170 BZ124
Solefields Rd, Sev. TN13 191 FH128
Solent Ri, E13 86 EG69
Solent Rd, NW6 64 DA64
Hounslow
(Hthrw Air.) TW6 114 BM86
Soleoak Dr, Sev. TN13 191 FH127
Solesbridge Cl, Rick. (Chorl.) WD3
off Solesbridge La 21 BF41
Solesbridge La, Rick. WD3 22 BG40
Soley Ms, WC1 196 D2
Solna Av, SW15 119 CW85
Solna Rd, N21 46 DR46
Solomon Av, N9 46 DU49
Solomons Hill, Rick. WD3
off Northway 38 BK45
Solomon's Pas, SE15 102 DV84
Solom's Ct Rd, Bans. SM7 174 DE117
Solon New Rd, SW4 101 DL84
Solon New Rd Est, SW4
off Solon New Rd 101 DL84
Solon Rd, SW2 101 DL84
Solway Cl, E8
off Buttermere Wk 84 DT65
Hounslow TW4 96 BY83
Solway Rd, N22 45 DP53
SE22 102 DU84
Somaford Gro, Barn. EN4 28 DD44
Somali Rd, NW2 63 CZ63
Somborne Ho, SW15
off Fontley Way 119 CU87
Somerby Rd, Bark. IG11 87 ER66
Somercoates Cl, Barn. EN4 28 DE41
Somerden Rd, Orp. BR5 146 EX101
Somerfield Cl, Tad. KT20 173 CY119
Somerfield Rd, N4 65 DP61
Somerford Cl, Pnr. HA5 59 BU56
Somerford Gro, N16 66 DT63
N17 46 DU52
Somerford Gro Est, N16
off Somerford Gro 66 DT63
Somerford St, E1 84 DV70
Somerford Way, SE16 203 K5
Somerhill Av, Sid. DA15 126 EV87
Somerhill Rd, Well. DA16 106 EV82
Somerleyton Pas, SW9 101 DP84
Somerleyton Rd, SW9 101 DN84
Somersby Gdns, Ilf. IG4 69 EM57
Somers Cl, NW1
off Platt St 83 DK68
Reigate RH2 184 DA133
Somers Cres, W2 194 B9
Somerset Av, SW20 139 CV96
Chessington KT9 155 CK105
Welling DA16 125 ET85
Somerset Cl, N17 46 DR54
Epsom KT19 156 CS109
New Malden KT3 138 CS100
Walton-on-Thames KT12
off Queens Rd 153 BV106
Woodford Green IG8 48 EG53
Somerset Est, SW11 100 DD81
Somerset Gdns, N6 64 DG59
N17 46 DS52
SE13 103 EB82
SW16 141 DM97
Hornchurch RM11 72 FN60
Teddington TW11 117 CE92
★ Somerset Ho, WC2 196 B10
Somerset Ho, SW19 119 CX90
Somerset Rd, E17 67 EA57
N17 66 DT55
N18 46 DT50
NW4 63 CW56
SW19 119 CY91
W4 98 CR76
W13 79 CH74
Barnet EN5 28 DB43
Brentford TW8 97 CJ79
Dartford DA1 127 FH86
Enfield EN3 31 EA38
Harrow HA1 60 CC57
Kingston upon Thames KT1 138 CM96
Orpington BR6 146 EU101
Southall UB1 78 BZ71
Teddington TW11 117 CE92
Somerset Sq, W14 99 CY75
Somerset Way, Iver SL0 93 BF75
Somerset Waye, Houns. TW5 96 BY79
Somersham Rd, Bexh. DA7 106 EY82
Somers Ms, W2 194 B9
Somers Pl, SW2 121 DM87
Reigate RH2 184 DA133
Somers Rd, E17 67 DZ56
SW2 121 DM86
Reigate RH2 183 CZ133
SOMERS TOWN, NW1 195 N2
Somers Way, Bushey WD23 40 CC45
Somerton Av, Rich. TW9 98 CP83
Somerton Cl, Pur. CR8 175 DN115
Somerton Rd, NW2 63 CY62
SE15 102 DV84
Somertrees Av, SE12 124 EH89
Somervell Rd, Har. HA2 60 BZ64
Somerville Av, SW13 99 CV79
Somerville Rd, SE20 123 DX94
Cobham KT11 154 CA114
Dartford DA1 128 FM86
Romford RM6 70 EW58
Sonderburg Rd, N7 65 DM61
Sondes St, SE17 102 DR79
Sonia Cl, Wat. WD19 40 BW45
Sonia Ct, Har. HA1 61 CF58
Sonia Gdns, N12
off Woodside Av 44 DC49
NW10 63 CT63
Hounslow TW5 96 CA80
Sonnet Wk, West. (Bigg.H.) TN16
off Kings Rd 178 EH118
Sonning Gdns, Hmptn.
TW12 116 BY93
Sonning Rd, SE25 142 DU100
Soper Cl, E4 47 DZ50
SE23 123 DX88
Soper Dr, Cat. CR3
off Hambledon Rd 176 DR123
Soper Ms, Enf. EN3
off Harston Dr 31 EA38
Sopers Rd, Pot.B.
(Cuffley) EN6 13 DM29
Sophia Cl, N7
off Mackenzie Rd 83 DM65
Sophia Rd, E10 67 EB60
E16 86 EH72
Sophia Sq, SE16 203 K1
Sopwith Av, Chess. KT9 156 CL106
Sopwith Cl, Kings.T. KT2 118 CM92
Westerham (Bigg.H.) TN16 178 EK116
Sopwith Dr, W.Byf. KT14 152 BL111
Weybridge KT13 152 BL111
Sopwith Rd, Houns. TW5 96 BW80
Sopwith Way, SW8 101 DH80
Kingston upon Thames KT2 138 CL95
Sorbie Cl, Wey. KT13 153 BR107
Sorrel Bk, Croy. CR0 161 DY110
Sorrel Cl, SE28 88 EU74
Sorrel Ct, Grays RM17
off Salix Rd 110 GD79
Sorrel Gdns, E6 86 EL71
Sorrel La, E14 85 ED72
Sorrell Cl, SE14
off Southerngate Way 103 DY80
Sorrel Wk, Rom. RM1 71 FF55
Sorrel Way, Grav.
(Nthflt) DA11 130 GE91
Sorrento Rd, Sutt. SM1 140 DB104
Sotheby Rd, N5 65 DP62
Sotheran Cl, E8 84 DU67
Sotheron Rd, SW6 100 DB80
Sotheron Rd, Watford WD17 24 BW40
Soudan Rd, SW11 100 DF81
Souldern Rd, W14 99 CX76
Souldern St, Wat. WD18 23 BU43
Sounds Lo, Swan. BR8 147 FC100
South Access Rd, E17 67 DY59
Southacre Way, Pnr. HA5 40 BW53
SOUTH ACTON, W3 98 CN76
⇌ South Acton 98 CQ76
South Acton Est, W3 98 CP75
South Africa Rd, W12 81 CV74
South Albert Rd, Reig. RH2 183 CZ133
SOUTHALL 78 BX74
⇌ Southall 96 BZ75
Southall La, Houns. TW5 95 BV79
Southall UB2 95 BV79
Southall Pl, SE1 201 K5
Southall Way, Brwd. CM14 54 FT49
Southampton Bldgs, WC2 196 D8
Southampton Gdns,
Mitch. CR4 141 DL99
Southampton Ms, E16 205 P2
Southampton Pl, WC1 196 A7
Southampton Rd, NW5 64 DF64
Hounslow
(Hthrw Air.) TW6 114 BN86
Southampton Row, WC1 196 A6
Southampton St, WC2 196 A10
Southampton Way, SE5 102 DR80
Southam St, W10 81 CY70
South App, Nthwd. HA6 39 BR48
South Audley St, W1 198 G1
South Av, E4 47 EB45
Carshalton SM5 158 DF108
Egham TW20 113 BC93
Richmond TW9
off Sandycombe Rd 98 CN82
Southall UB1 78 BZ73
Walton-on-Thames
(Whiteley Vill.) KT12 153 BS110
South Av Gdns, Sthl. UB1 78 BZ73
South Bk, Chis. BR7 125 EQ91
Surbiton KT6 138 CL100
Southbank, T.Ditt. KT7 137 CH101
South Bk, West. TN16 189 ER126
Southbank Business Cen,
SW8 101 DK79
South Bk Ter, Surb. KT6 138 CL100
SOUTH BEDDINGTON, Wall.
SM6 159 DK107
⇌ South Bermondsey 202 F10
South Birkbeck Rd, E11 67 ED62
South Black Lion La, W6 99 CU78
South Bolton Gdns, SW5 100 DB78
South Border, The, Pur. CR8 159 DK111
SOUTHBOROUGH, Brom.
BR2 145 EM100
Southborough Cl, Surb. KT6 137 CK102
Southborough La, Brom.
BR2 144 EL99
Southborough Rd, E9 84 DW67
Bromley BR1 144 EL97
Surbiton KT6 138 CL102
Southbourne, Brom. BR2 144 EG101
Southbourne Av, NW9 42 CQ54
Southbourne Cl, Pnr. HA5 60 BY59
Southbourne Cres, NW4 63 CY56
Southbourne Gdns, SE12 124 EH85
Ilford IG1 69 EQ64
Ruislip HA4 59 BV60
Southbridge Pl, Croy. CR0 160 DQ105
Southbridge Rd, Croy. CR0 160 DQ105
Southbridge Way, Sthl. UB2 96 BY75
Southbrook Dr, Wal.Cr.
(Chsht) EN8 15 DX28
Southbrook Ms, SE12 124 EF86
Southbrook Rd, SE12 124 EF86
SW16 141 DL95
⇌ Southbury 30 DV42
Southbury Av, Enf. EN1 30 DU43
Southbury Cl, Horn. RM12 72 FK64
Southbury Rd, Enf. EN1, EN3 30 DR41
South Carriage Dr, SW1 198 D4
SW7 198 A5
SOUTH CHINGFORD, E4 47 DZ50
Southchurch Rd, E6 87 EM68
South Circular Rd,
SE6 (A205) 123 ED87
SE9 (A205) 105 EM83
SE12 (A205) 124 EH86
SE18 (A205) 105 EN79
SE21 (A205) 122 DS88
SE22 (A205) 122 DV88
SE23 (A205) 123 DZ88
SW2 (A205) 121 DN88
SW4 (A205) 120 DG85
SW11 (A3) 120 DE85
SW12 (A205) 121 DN88
SW14 (A205) 98 CS84
SW15 (A205) 99 CW84
SW18 (A3) 120 DE85
W4 (A205) 98 CN78
Brentford (A205) TW8 98 CN78
Richmond (A205) TW9 98 CP82
Southcliffe Dr, Ger.Cr.
(Chal.St.P.) SL9 36 AY50
South Cl, N6 65 DH58
Barnet EN5 27 CZ41
Bexleyheath DA6 106 EX84
Dagenham RM10 88 FA67
Morden SM4 140 DA100
Pinner HA5 60 BZ59
St. Albans AL2 8 CB25
Twickenham TW2 116 CA90
West Drayton UB7 94 BM76
Woking GU21 166 AW116
South Cl Grn, Red. RH1 185 DH129
South Colonnade, E14 204 A2
Southcombe St, W14 99 CY77
South Common Rd, Uxb.
UB8 76 BL65
Southcote, Wok. GU21 166 AX115
Southcote Av, Felt. TW13 115 BT89
Surbiton KT5 138 CP101
Southcote Ri, Ruis. HA4 59 BR59
Southcote Rd, E17 67 DX57
N19 65 DJ63
SE25 142 DV100
Redhill RH1 185 DJ129
South Croydon CR2 160 DS110
South Cottage Dr, Rick.
(Chorl.) WD3 21 BF43
South Cottage Gdns, Rick.
(Chorl.) WD3 21 BF43
Southcott Ms, NW8 194 B1
South Countess Rd, E17 67 DZ55
South Cres, E16 85 ED70
WC1 195 M7
South Cft, Egh.
(Eng.Grn) TW20 112 AV92
Southcroft Av, Well. DA16 105 ES83
West Wickham BR4 143 EC103
Southcroft Rd, SW16 120 DG93
SW17 120 DG93
Orpington BR6 145 ES104
South Cross Rd, Ilf. IG6 69 EQ57
South Croxted Rd, SE21 122 DR90
SOUTH CROYDON 160 DQ107
⇌ South Croydon 160 DR106
Southdale, Chig. IG7 49 ER51
SOUTH DARENTH, Dart. DA4 149 FR95
Southdean Gdns, SW19 119 CZ89
South Dene, NW7 42 CR48
Southdene,
Sev. (Halst.) TN14 164 EY113
Southdown Av, W7 97 CG76
Southdown Cres, Har. HA2 60 CB60
Ilford IG2 69 ES57
Southdown Dr, SW20
off Crescent Rd 119 CX94
Southdown Rd, SW20 139 CX95
Carshalton SM5 158 DG109
Caterham (Wold.) CR3 177 DZ122
Hornchurch RM11 71 FH59
Walton-on-Thames KT12 154 BY105
Southdowns, Dart.
(S.Darenth) DA4 149 FR96
South Dr, Bans. SM7 158 DE113
Brentwood CM14 54 FX49
Coulsdon CR5 175 DK115
Orpington BR6 163 ES106
Potters Bar (Cuffley) EN6 13 DL30
Romford RM2 72 FJ55
Ruislip HA4 59 BS60
Sutton SM2 157 CY110
Virginia Water GU25 132 AU102
⊖ South Ealing 97 CJ76
South Ealing Rd, W5 97 CK75
South Eastern Av, N9 46 DT48
South Eaton Pl, SW1 198 G8
South Eden Pk Rd, Beck. BR3 143 EB100
South Edwardes Sq, W8 99 CZ76
SOUTHEND, SE6 123 EB91
South End, W8
off St. Albans Gro 100 DB76
Croydon CR0 160 DQ105
Southend Arterial Rd, Brwd.
CM13 73 FV57
Hornchurch RM11 52 FK54
Romford RM2, RM3 52 FK54
Upminster RM14 73 FR57
South End Cl, NW3 64 DE63
Southend Cl, SE9 125 EP86
Southend Cres, SE9 125 EN86
South End Grn, NW3
off South End Rd 64 DE63
Southend La, SE6 123 DZ91
SE26 123 DZ91
Waltham Abbey EN9 16 EH34
Southend Rd, E4 47 DY50
E6 87 EM66
E17 47 EB53
E18 48 EG53
South End Rd, NW3 64 DE63
Southend Rd, Beck. BR3 123 EA94
Grays RM17 110 GC77
South End Rd, Horn. RM12 89 FH65
Rainham RM13 89 FG67
Southend Rd, Wdf.Grn. IG8 48 EJ54
South End Row, W8 100 DB76
Southerland Cl, Wey. KT13 153 BQ105
Southern Av, SE25 142 DT97
Feltham TW14 115 BU88
Southern Dr, Loug. IG10 33 EM44
Southerngate Way, SE14 103 DY80
Southern Gro, E3 85 DZ69
Southernhay, Loug. IG10 32 EK43
Southern Perimeter Rd, Houns.
(Hthrw Air.) TW6 115 BR85
Southern Pl, Swan. BR8 147 FD98
Southern Rd, E13 86 EH68
N2 64 DF56
Southern Row, W10 81 CY70
Southerns La, Couls. CR5 184 DC125
Southern St, N1 83 DM68
Southern Way, SE10 205 L8
Romford RM7 70 FA58
Southerton Rd, W6 99 CW76
Southerton Way, Rad.
(Shenley) WD7 10 CL33
South Esk Rd, E7 86 EJ65
Southey Ms, E16 205 N2
Southey Rd, N15 66 DS57
SW9 101 DN81
SW19 120 DA94
Southey St, SE20 123 DX94
Southey Wk, Til. RM18 111 GH81
Southfield, Barn. EN5 27 CX44
Southfield Av, Wat. WD24 24 BW38
Southfield Cl, Uxb. UB8 76 BN69
Southfield Cotts, W7
off Oaklands Rd 97 CF75
Southfield Gdns, Twick. TW1 117 CF91
Southfield Pk, Har. HA2 60 CB56
Southfield Pl, Wey. KT13 153 BP108
Southfield Rd, N17
off The Avenue 46 DS54
W4 98 CS76
Chislehurst BR7 145 ET97
Enfield EN3 30 DV44
Waltham Cross EN8 15 DY32
SOUTHFIELDS, SW18 120 DA88
⊖ Southfields 119 CZ88
Southfields, NW4 63 CU55
East Molesey KT8 137 CE100
Swanley BR8 127 FE94
Southfields Av, Ashf. TW15 115 BP93
Southfields Ct, SW19 119 CY88
Sutton SM1
off Sutton Common Rd 140 DA103
Southfields Ms, SW18
off Southfields Rd 120 DA86
Southfields Pas, SW18 120 DA86
Southfields Rd, SW18 120 DA86
Caterham (Wold.) CR3 177 EB123
SOUTHFLEET, Grav. DA13 130 GB93
Southfleet Rd, Dart.
(Bean) DA2 129 FW91
Gravesend (Nthflt) DA11 131 GF89
Orpington BR6 145 ES104
Swanscombe DA10 130 FZ87
South Gdns, SW19 120 DD94
SOUTHGATE, N14 45 DJ47
⊖ Southgate 45 DJ46
Southgate, Purf. RM19 108 FQ77
Southgate Av, Felt. TW13 115 BR91
Southgate Circ, N14
off The Bourne 45 DK46
Southgate Gro, N1 84 DR66
Southgate Rd, N1 84 DR67
Potters Bar EN6 12 DC33
South Gipsy Rd, Well. DA16 106 EX83
South Glade, The, Bex. DA5 126 EZ88
South Grn, NW9
off Clayton Fld 42 CS53
Slough SL1 74 AS73
⇌ South Greenford 79 CE69
South Gro, E17 67 DZ57
N6 64 DG60
N15 66 DR57
Chertsey KT16 133 BF100
South Gro Ho, N6
off Highgate W Hill 64 DG60
SOUTH HACKNEY, E9 84 DW66
South Hall Cl, Dart.
(Fnghm) DA4 148 FM101
South Hall Dr, Rain. RM13 89 FH71
SOUTH HAMPSTEAD, NW6 82 DB66
⇌ South Hampstead 82 DC66
SOUTH HAREFIELD,
Uxb. UB9 58 BJ56
SOUTH HARROW, Har. HA2 60 CB62
⊖ South Harrow 60 CC62
South Hill, Chis. BR7 125 EM93
South Hill Av, Har. HA1, HA2 60 CC62
South Hill Gro, Har. HA1 61 CE63
South Hill Pk, NW3 64 DE63
South Hill Pk Gdns, NW3 64 DE63
South Hill Rd, Brom. BR2 144 EE97
Gravesend DA12 131 GH88
Southholme Cl, SE19 142 DS95
SOUTH HORNCHURCH, Rain.
RM13 89 FE67
South Huxley, N18 46 DR50
Southill La, Pnr. HA5 59 BU56
Southill Rd, Chis. BR7 124 EL94
Southill St, E14
off Chrisp St 85 EB72
South Island Pl, SW9 101 DM80
SOUTH KENSINGTON, SW7 100 DB76
⊖ South Kensington 198 A8
South Kensington Sta Arc, SW7
off Pelham St 100 DD77
South Kent Av, Grav.
(Nthflt) DA11 130 GC86
⇌ South Kenton 61 CJ60
⊖ South Kenton 61 CJ60
SOUTH LAMBETH, SW8 101 DL81
South Lambeth Pl, SW8 101 DL79
South Lambeth Rd, SW8 101 DL79
Southland Rd, SE18 105 ET80
Southlands Av, Orp. BR6 163 ER105
Southlands Cl, Couls. CR5 175 DM117
Southlands Dr, SW19 119 CX89
Southlands Gro, Brom. BR1 144 EL97
Southlands La, Oxt.
(Tand.) RH8 187 EB134
Southlands Rd, Brom.
BR1, BR2 144 EJ99
Iver SL0 57 BF64
Uxbridge (Denh.) UB9 57 BF63
Southland Way, Houns. TW3 117 CD85
South La, Kings.T. KT1 137 CK97
New Malden KT3 138 CR98
South La W, N.Mal. KT3 138 CR98
SOUTHLEA, Slou. SL3 92 AV82
Southlea Rd, Slou.
(Datchet) SL3 92 AV81
Windsor SL4 92 AU84
South Lo Av, Mitch. CR4 141 DL98
South Lo Cres, Enf. EN2 29 DK42
South Lo Dr, N14 29 DL43
Iver SL0 off Pinewood Rd 75 BB67
South Lo Rd, Walt. KT12 153 BU109
H South London & Maudsley
NHS Trust - Landor Rd Unit,
SW9 101 DL83
★ South London Art Gall,
SE5 102 DS81
Southly Cl, Sutt. SM1 140 DA104
South Mall, N9
off Edmonton Grn
Shop Cen 46 DU48
South Mead, NW9 43 CT53
Epsom KT19 156 CS108
Redhill RH1 184 DF131
Southmead Cres, Wal.Cr.
(Chsht) EN8 15 DY30
South Meadows, Wem. HA9 62 CM64
Southmead Rd, SW19 119 CY88
SOUTH MERSTHAM, Red.
RH1 185 DJ130
⇌ South Merton 139 CZ97
SOUTH MIMMS, Pot.B. EN6 11 CT32
South Molton La, W1 195 H9
South Molton Rd, E16 86 EG72
South Molton St, W1 195 H9
Southmont Rd, Esher KT10 137 CE103
Southmoor Way, E9 85 DZ65
SOUTH NORWOOD, SE25 142 DT97
South Norwood Hill, SE25 142 DS96
South Oak Rd, SW16 121 DM91
SOUTH OCKENDON 91 FW70
Southold Ri, SE9 125 EM90
Southolm St, SW11 101 DH81
South Ordnance Rd, Enf. EN3 31 EA37
Southover, N12 44 DA49
Bromley BR1 124 EG92
SOUTH OXHEY, Wat. WD19 40 BW48
South Par, SW3 198 A10

★ Place of interest ⇌ Railway station ⊖ London Underground station DLR Docklands Light Railway station Tra Tramlink station H Hospital Riv Pedestrian ferry landing stage

326

South Par, W4 98 CR77
Waltham Abbey EN9
off Sun St 15 EC33
South Pk, SW6 100 DA82
Gerrards Cross SL9 57 AZ57
Sevenoaks TN13 191 FH125
South Pk Av, Rick. (Chorl.) WD3 21 BF43
South Pk Cres, SE6 124 EF88
Gerrards Cross SL9 56 AY56
Ilford IG1 69 ER62
South Pk Dr, Bark. IG11 69 ES63
Gerrards Cross SL9 56 AY56
Ilford IG3 69 ES63
South Pk Gro, N.Mal. KT3 138 CQ98
South Pk Hill Rd, S.Croy. CR2 160 DR106
South Pk Ms, SW6 100 DB83
South Pk Rd, SW19 120 DA93
Ilford IG1 69 ER62
South Pk Ter, Ilf. IG1 69 ER62
South Pk Vw, Ger.Cr. SL9 57 AZ56
South Pk Way, Ruis. HA4 78 BW65
South Penge Pk Est, SE20 142 DV96
South Perimeter Rd, Uxb. UB8
off Kingston La 76 BL69
South Pl, EC2 197 L6
Enfield EN3 30 DW43
Surbiton KT5 138 CM101
South Pl Ms, EC2 197 L7
South Pt, Sutt. SM1 158 DC107
Southport Rd, SE18 105 ER77
DLR **South Quay** 204 B4
South Ridge, Wey. KT13 153 BP110
Southridge Pl, SW20 119 CX94
South Riding, St.Alb. (Brick.Wd) AL2 8 CA30
South Ri, Cars. SM5 158 DE109
South Ri Way, SE18 105 ER78
South Rd, N9 46 DU46
SE23 123 DX89
SW19 120 DC93
W5 97 CK77
Edgware HA8 42 CP53
Egham (Eng.Grn) TW20 112 AW93
Erith DA8 107 FF79
Feltham TW13 116 BX92
Hampton TW12 116 BY93
Rickmansworth (Chorl.) WD3 21 BC43
Romford (Chad.Hth) RM6 70 EY58
Romford (Lt.Hth) RM6 70 EW57
South Ockendon RM15 91 FW72
Southall UB1 96 BZ75
Twickenham TW2 117 CD90
West Drayton UB7 94 BM76
Weybridge KT13 153 BQ106
Weybridge (St.Geo.H.) KT13 153 BP109
Woking GU21 150 AX114
South Row, SE3 104 EF82
SOUTH RUISLIP, Ruis. HA4 60 BW63
⇌ **South Ruislip** 60 BW63
⊖ **South Ruislip** 60 BW63
Southsea Av, Wat. WD18 23 BU42
Southsea Rd, Kings.T. KT1 138 CL98
South Sea St, SE16 203 M6
South Side, W6 99 CT76
Southside, Ger.Cr. (Chal.St.P.) SL9 56 AX55
Southside Common, SW19 119 CW93
Southspring, Sid. DA15 125 ER87
South Sq, NW11 64 DB58
WC1 196 D7
SOUTH STIFFORD, Grays RM20 109 FW78
SOUTH STREET, West. TN16 179 EM119
South St, W1 198 G2
Brentwood CM14 54 FW47
Bromley BR1 144 EG96
Enfield EN3 31 DX43
Epsom KT18 156 CR113
Gravesend DA12 131 GH87
Isleworth TW7 97 CG83
Rainham RM13 89 FC68
Romford RM1 71 FF58
Staines TW18 113 BF92
South Tenter St, E1 84 DT73
South Ter, SW7 198 B8
Surbiton KT6 138 CL100
SOUTH TOTTENHAM, N15 66 DS57
⇌ **South Tottenham** 66 DT57
South Vale, SE19 122 DS93
Harrow HA1 61 CE63
Southvale Rd, SE3 104 EE82
South Vw, Brom. BR1 144 EH96
Epsom KT19 156 CN109
Southview Av, NW10 63 CT64
South Vw Av, Til. RM18 111 GG81
Southview Cl, SW17 120 DG92
Bexley DA5 126 EZ86
Swanley BR8 147 FF98
Waltham Cross (Chsht) EN7 14 DS26
South Vw Cl, Wok. GU22
off Constitution Hill 166 AY118
Southview Cres, Ilf. IG2 69 EP58
South Vw Dr, E18 68 EH55
Upminster RM14 72 FN62
Southview Gdns, Wall. SM6 159 DJ108
South Vw Rd, N8 65 DK55
Ashtead KT21 171 CK119
Southview Rd, Brom. BR1 123 ED91
Caterham (Wold.) CR3 177 EB124
South Vw Rd, Dart. DA2 128 FK90
Gerrards Cross SL9 56 AX56
Grays RM20 109 FW79
Loughton IG10 33 EM44
Pinner HA5 39 BV51
Southview Rd, Warl. CR6 176 DU119
Southviews, S.Croy. CR2 161 DX109
South Vil, NW1 83 DK65
Southville, SW8 101 DK81
Southville Cl, Epsom KT19 156 CR109
Feltham TW14 115 BS88
Southville Cres, Felt. TW14 115 BS88
Southville Rd, Felt. TW14 115 BS88
Thames Ditton KT7 137 CH101
South Wk, Hayes UB3
off Middleton Rd 77 BR71
South Wk, Reigate RH2
off Church St 184 DB134
West Wickham BR4 144 EE104
SOUTHWARK, SE1 200 G3
⊖ **Southwark** 200 F3
Southwark Br, EC4 201 J2
SE1 201 J2
Southwark Br Rd, SE1 200 G6
★ **Southwark Cath**, SE1 201 K2
Southwark Pk Est, SE16 202 E8
Southwark Pk Rd, SE16 202 A8
Southwark Pl, Brom. BR1
off St. Georges Rd 145 EM97
Southwark St, SE1 200 G2
Southwater Cl, E14 85 DZ72
Beckenham BR3 123 EB94
South Way, N9 46 DW47
N11 *off Ringway* 45 DJ51
Southway, N20 44 DA47
NW11 64 DB58
SW20 139 CW98
South Way, Abb.L. WD5 7 BT33
Bromley BR2 144 EG101
Southway, Cars. SM5 158 DD110
South Way, Croy. CR0 143 DY104
Harrow HA2 60 CA56
Purfleet RM19 109 FS76
Southway, Wall. SM6 159 DJ105
South Way, Wem. HA9 62 CN64
SOUTH WEALD, Brwd. CM14 54 FS47
South Weald Dr, Wal.Abb. EN9 15 ED33
South Weald Rd, Brwd. CM14 54 FU48
Southwell Av, Nthlt. UB5 78 CA65
Southwell Cl, Grays RM16
off Hedingham Rd 109 FW78
Southwell Gdns, SW7 100 DC77
Southwell Gro Rd, E11 68 EE61
Southwell Rd, SE5 102 DQ83
Croydon CR0 141 DN100
Harrow HA3 61 CK58
South Western Rd, Twick. TW1 117 CG86
Southwest Rd, E11 67 ED60
South Wf Rd, W2 82 DD72
Southwick Ms, W2 194 A8
Southwick Pl, W2 194 B9
Southwick St, W2 194 B8
SOUTH WIMBLEDON, SW19 120 DB94
⊖ **South Wimbledon** 120 DB94
Southwold Dr, Bark. IG11 70 EU64
Southwold Rd, E5 66 DV61
Bexley DA5 127 FB86
Watford WD24 24 BW38
Southwold Spur, Slou. SL3 93 BC75
Southwood Av, N6 65 DH59
Chertsey (Ott.) KT16 151 BC108
Coulsdon CR5 175 DJ115
Kingston upon Thames KT2 138 CQ95
Southwood Cl, Brom. BR1 145 EM98
Worcester Park KT4 139 CX102
Southwood Dr, Surb. KT5 138 CQ101
SOUTH WOODFORD, E18 48 EF54
⊖ **South Woodford** 48 EG54
South Woodford to Barking Relief Rd, E11 68 EJ56
E12 69 EN62
E18 68 EJ56
Barking IG11 69 EN62
Ilford IG1, IG4 69 EN62
Southwood Gdns, Esher KT10 137 CG104
Ilford IG2 69 EP56
H **Southwood Hosp**, N6 64 DG59
Southwood La, N6 64 DG59
Southwood Lawn Rd, N6 64 DG59
Southwood Rd, SE9 125 EP89
SE28 88 EV74
Southwood Smith St, N1
off Old Royal Free Sq 83 DN67
South Worple Av, SW14 98 CS83
South Worple Way, SW14 98 CR83
Soval Ct, Nthwd. HA6
off Maxwell Rd 39 BR52
Sovereign Cl, E1 202 E1
W5 79 CJ71
Barnet EN4 28 DF41
Purley CR8 159 DM110
Ruislip HA4 59 BS60
Sovereign Ct, Brom. BR2 145 EM99
West Molesey KT8 136 BZ98
Sovereign Cres, SE16 203 K1
Sovereign Gro, Wem. HA0 61 CK62
Sovereign Ms, E2
off Pearson St 84 DT68
Barnet EN4
off Bournwell Cl 28 DF41
Sovereign Pk, NW10 80 CP70
Sovereign Pl, Har. HA1 61 CF57
Kings Langley WD4 6 BN29
Sovereign Rd, Bark. IG11 88 EW69
Sowerby Cl, SE9 124 EL85
Sowrey Av, Rain. RM13 89 FF65
Soyer Ct, Wok. GU21
off Raglan Rd 166 AS118
Space Way, Felt. TW14 115 BU85
Spa Cl, SE25 142 DS95
Spa Dr, Epsom KT18 156 CN114
Spafield St, EC1 196 D4
Spa Grn Est, EC1 196 E2
Spa Hill, SE19 142 DR95
Spalding Cl, Edg. HA8
off Blundell Rd 42 CS52
Spalding Rd, NW4 63 CW58
SW17 121 DH92
Spalt Cl, Brwd. (Hutt.) CM13 55 GB47
Spanby Rd, E3 85 EA70
Spaniards Cl, NW11 64 DD60
Spaniards End, NW3 64 DC60
Spaniards Rd, NW3 64 DC61
Spanish Pl, W1 194 G8
Spanish Rd, SW18 120 DC85
Spareleaze Hill, Loug. IG10 33 EM43
Sparepenny La, Dart. (Eyns.) DA4 148 FL102
Sparkbridge Rd, Har. HA1 61 CE56
Sparkford Gdns, N11
off Friern Barnet Rd 44 DG50
Sparkford Ho, SW11 100 DD81
Sparks Cl, W3 *off Joseph Av* 80 CR72
Dagenham RM8 70 EX61
Hampton TW12
off Victors Dr 116 BY93
Spa Rd, SE16 201 P7
Sparrow Cl, Hmptn. TW12 116 BY93
Sparrow Dr, Orp. BR5 145 EQ102
Sparrow Fm Dr, Felt. TW14 116 BX87
Sparrow Fm Rd, Epsom KT17 157 CU105
Sparrow Grn, Dag. RM10 71 FB62
Sparrows Herne, Bushey WD23 40 CB45
Sparrows La, SE9 125 EQ87
Sparrows Mead, Red. RH1 184 DG131
Sparrows Way, Bushey WD23
off Sparrows Herne 40 CC46
Sparsholt Rd, N19 65 DM60
Barking IG11 87 ES67
Sparta St, SE10 103 EB81
★ **Speaker's Cor**, W2 194 E10
Speaker's Ct, Croy. CR0
off St. James's Rd 142 DR102
Spearman St, SE18 105 EN79
Spear Ms, SW5 100 DA78
Spearpoint Gdns, Ilf. IG2 69 ET56
Spears Rd, N19 65 DL60
Speart La, Houns. TW5 96 BY80
Spedan Cl, NW3 64 DB62
Speechly Ms, E8
off Alvington Cres 66 DT64
Speedbird Way, West Dr. UB7 94 BH80
Speedgate Hill, Long. (Fawk.Grn) DA3 149 FU103
Speed Highwalk, EC2
off Beech St 84 DQ71
Speed Ho, EC2 197 K6
Speedwell Ct, Grays RM17 110 GE80
Speedwell St, SE8
off Comet St 103 EA80
Speedy Pl, WC1 195 P3
Speer Rd, T.Ditt. KT7 137 CF99
Speirs Cl, N.Mal. KT3 139 CT100
Spekehill, SE9 125 EM90
Speke Ho, SE5 102 DQ80
Speke Rd, Th.Hth. CR7 142 DR96
Speldhurst Cl, Brom. BR2 144 EF99
Speldhurst Rd, E9 85 DX66
W4 98 CR76
Spellbrook Wk, N1
off Basire St 84 DQ67
Spelman St, E1 84 DU71
Spelthorne Gro, Sun. TW16 115 BT94
Spelthorne La, Ashf. TW15 135 BQ95
Spence Av, W.Byf. (Byfleet) KT14 152 BL114
Spence Cl, SE16 203 M5
Spencer Av, N13 45 DM51
Hayes UB4 77 BU71
Waltham Cross (Chsht) EN7 14 DS26
Spencer Cl, N3 43 CZ54
NW10 80 CM69
Epsom KT18 172 CS119
Orpington BR6 145 ES103
Uxbridge UB8 76 BJ69
Woking GU21 151 BC113
Woodford Green IG8 48 EJ50
H **Spencer Cl Mental Hosp**, Epp. CM16 18 EV29
Spencer Ct, NW8
off Marlborough Pl 82 DC68
Spencer Dr, N2 64 DC58
Spencer Gdns, SE9 125 EM85
SW14 118 CQ85
Egham (Eng.Grn) TW20 112 AX92
Spencer Hill, SW19 119 CY93
Spencer Hill Rd, SW19 119 CY94
★ **Spencer Ho**, SW1 199 K3
Spencer Ms, SW8
off Lansdowne Way 101 DM81
W6 *off Greyhound Rd* 99 CY79
Spencer Pk, SW18 120 DD85
Spencer Pas, E2
off Pritchard's Rd 84 DV68
Spencer Pl, N1
off Canonbury La 83 DP66
Croydon CR0
off Gloucester Rd 142 DR101
Spencer Ri, NW5 65 DH63
Spencer Rd, E6 86 EK67
E17 47 EC53
N8 65 DM57
N11 45 DH49
N17 46 DU53
SW18 100 DD84
SW20 139 CV95
W3 80 CQ74
W4 98 CQ80
Bromley BR1 124 EE94
Caterham CR3 176 DR121
Cobham KT11 169 BV115
East Molesey KT8 136 CC99
Harrow HA3 41 CE54
Ilford IG3 69 ET60
Isleworth TW7 97 CD81
Mitcham CR4 140 DG97
Mitcham (Bedd.Cor.) CR4 140 DG101
Rainham RM13 89 FD69
Slough SL3 93 AZ76
South Croydon CR2 160 DS106
Twickenham TW2 117 CE90
Wembley HA0 61 CJ61
Spencer St, EC1 196 F3
Gravesend DA11 131 GG87
Southall UB2 96 BX75
Spencer Wk, NW3 64 DD63
SW15 99 CX84
Rickmansworth WD3 22 BJ43
Tilbury RM18 111 GG82
Spencer Yd, SE3
off Blackheath Village 104 EF82
Spenser Av, Wey. KT13 152 BN108
Spenser Cres, Upmin. RM14 72 FQ59
Spenser Gro, N16 66 DS63
Spenser Ms, SE21
off Croxted Rd 122 DR88
Spenser Rd, SE24 121 DN85
Spenser St, SW1 199 L6
Spensley Wk, N16
off Clissold Rd 66 DR62
Speranza St, SE18 105 ET78
Sperling Rd, N17 46 DS54
Spert St, E14 85 DY73
Speyhawk Pl, Pot.B. EN6 12 DB30
Speyside, N14 29 DJ44
Spey St, E14 85 EC71
Spey Way, Rom. RM1 51 FE52
Spezia Rd, NW10 81 CU68
Spice Quay Hts, SE1 202 A3
Spicer Cl, SW9 101 DP82
Walton-on-Thames KT12 136 BW100
Spicers Fld, Lthd. (Oxshott) KT22 155 CD113
Spicersfield, Wal.Cr. (Chsht) EN7 14 DU27
Spice's Yd, Croy. CR0 160 DQ105
Spielman Rd, Dart. DA1 108 FM84
Spigurnell Rd, N17 46 DR53
Spikes Br Moorings, Hayes UB4
off Berwick Av 78 BY72
Spikes Br Rd, Sthl. UB1 78 BY72
Spilsby Cl, NW9
off Kenley Av 42 CS54
Spilsby Rd, Rom. RM3 52 FK52
Spindle Cl, SE18 104 EL76
Spindles, Til. RM18 111 GG80
Spindlewood Gdns, Croy. CR0 160 DS105
Spindlewoods, Tad. KT20 173 CV122
Spindrift Av, E14 204 B8
Spinel Cl, SE18 105 ET78
Spingate Cl, Horn. RM12 72 FK64
Spinnaker Cl, Bark. IG11 88 EV69
Spinnells Rd, Har. HA2 60 BZ60
Spinney, The, N21 45 DN45
SW16 121 DK90
Barnet EN5 28 DB40
Brentwood (Hutt.) CM13 55 GC44
Epsom KT18 173 CV119
Leatherhead (Bkhm) KT23 170 CB124
Leatherhead (Oxshott) KT22 154 CC112
Potters Bar EN6 12 DD31
Purley CR8 159 DP111
Sidcup DA14 126 EY92
Stanmore HA7 42 CL49
Sunbury-on-Thames TW16 135 BU95
Sutton SM3 157 CW105
Swanley BR8 147 FE96
Watford WD17 23 BU39
Wembley HA0 61 CG62
Spinney Cl, Beck. BR3 143 EB98
Cobham KT11 154 CA111
New Malden KT3 138 CS99
Rainham RM13 89 FE68
West Drayton UB7
off Yew Av 76 BL73
Worcester Park KT4 139 CT104
Spinneycroft, Lthd. KT22 171 CD115
Spinney Dr, Felt. TW14 115 BQ87
Spinney Gdns, SE19 122 DT92
Dagenham RM9 70 EY64
Spinney Hill, Add. KT15 151 BE106
Spinney Oak, Brom. BR1 144 EL96
Chertsey (Ott.) KT16 151 BD107
Spinneys, The, Brom. BR1 145 EM96
Spinney Way, Sev. (Cudham) TN14 163 ER111
Spire Cl, Grav. DA12 131 GH88
Spires, The, Dart. DA1 128 FK89
Spires Shop Cen, The, Barn. EN5 27 CY41
Spirit Quay, E1 202 C2
★ **Spitalfields Comm Fm**, E1 84 DU70
Spital La, Brwd. CM14 54 FT48
Spital Sq, E1 197 N6
Spital St, E1 84 DU70
Dartford DA1 128 FK86
Spital Yd, E1 197 N6
Spitfire Est, Houns. TW5 96 BW78
Spitfire Rd, Wall. SM6 159 DL108
Spitfire Way, Houns. TW5 96 BW78
Spode Wk, NW6
off Lymington Rd 82 DB65
Spondon Rd, N15 66 DU56
Spoonbill Way, Hayes UB4 78 BX71
Spooners Dr, St.Alb. (Park St) AL2 8 CC27
Spooners Ms, W3
off Churchfield Rd 80 CR74
Spooner Wk, Wall. SM6 159 DK106
Sporle Ct, SW11 100 DD83
Sportsbank St, SE6 123 EC87
Spotted Dog Path, E7
off Upton La 86 EG65
Spottons Gro, N17
off Gospatrick Rd 46 DQ53
Spout Hill, Croy. CR0 161 EA106
Spout La, Eden. (Crock.H.) TN8 189 EQ134
Staines TW19 114 BG85
Spout La N, Stai. TW19 94 BH84
Spratt Hall Rd, E11 68 EG58
Spratts All, Cher. (Ott.) KT16 151 BE107
Spratts La, Cher. (Ott.) KT16 151 BE107
Spray La, Twick. TW2 117 CE86
Spray St, SE18 105 EP77
Spread Eagle Wk Shop Cen, Epsom KT19
off High St 156 CR113
Spreighton Rd, W.Mol. KT8 136 CB98
Spriggs Oak, Epp. CM16
off Palmers Hill 18 EU29
Sprimont Pl, SW3 198 D10
Springall St, SE15 102 DV80
Springate Fld, Slou. SL3 92 AY75
Spring Av, Egh. TW20 112 AY93
Springbank, N21 29 DM44
Springbank Av, Horn. RM12 72 FJ64
Springbank Rd, SE13 123 ED86
Springbank Wk, NW1
off St. Paul's Cres 83 DK66
Spring Bottom La, Red. (Bletch.) RH1 185 DN127
Springbourne Ct, Beck. BR3 143 EC95
Spring Br Ms, W5
off Spring Br Rd 79 CK73
Spring Br Rd, W5 79 CK73
Spring Cl, Barn. EN5 27 CX43
Borehamwood WD6 26 CN39
Chesham (Latimer) HP5 20 AX36
Dagenham RM8 70 EX60
Uxbridge (Hare.) UB9 38 BK53
Springclose La, Sutt. SM3 157 CY107
Spring Cotts, Surb. KT6
off St. Leonard's Rd 137 CK99
Spring Ct, Sid. DA15
off Station Rd 126 EU90
Spring Ct Rd, Enf. EN2 29 DN38
Springcroft Av, N2 64 DF56
Spring Cfts, Bushey WD23 24 CA43
Springdale Ms, N16
off Springdale Rd 66 DR63
Springdale Rd, N16 66 DR63
Spring Dr, Pnr. HA5
off Eastcote Rd 59 BU58
Spring Fm Cl, Rain. RM13 90 FK69
Springfield, E5 66 DV60
Bushey (Bushey Hth) WD23 41 CD46
Epping CM16 17 ET32
Oxted RH8 187 ED130
Springfield Av, N10 65 DJ55
SW20 139 CZ97
Brentwood (Hutt.) CM13 55 GE45
Hampton TW12 116 CB93
Swanley BR8 147 FF98
Springfield Cl, N12 44 DB50
Potters Bar EN6 12 DD31
Rickmansworth (Crox.Grn) WD3 23 BP43
Stanmore HA7 41 CG48
Woking (Knap.) GU21 166 AS118
Springfield Ct, Wall. SM6
off Springfield Rd 159 DH106
Springfield Dr, Ilf. IG2 69 EQ58
Leatherhead KT22 171 CE119
Springfield Gdns, E5 66 DV60
NW9 62 CR57
Bromley BR1 145 EM98
Ruislip HA4 59 BV60
Upminster RM14 72 FQ62
West Wickham BR4 143 EB103
Woodford Green IG8 48 EJ52
Springfield Gro, SE7 104 EJ79
Sunbury-on-Thames TW16 135 BT95
Springfield La, NW6 82 DB67
Weybridge KT13 153 BP105
Springfield Meadows, Wey. KT13 153 BP105
Springfield Mt, NW9 62 CS57
Springfield Pl, N.Mal. KT3 138 CQ98
Springfield Ri, SE26 122 DV90
Springfield Rd, E4 48 EE46
E6 87 EM66
E15 86 EE69
E17 67 DZ58
N11 45 DH50
N15 66 DU56
NW8 82 DC67
SE26 122 DV92
SW19 119 CZ92
W7 79 CE74
Ashford TW15 114 BM92
Bexleyheath DA7 107 FB83
Bromley BR1 145 EM98
Epsom KT17 157 CW110
Grays RM16 110 GD75
Harrow HA1 61 CE58
Hayes UB4 78 BW74
Kingston upon Thames KT1 138 CL97
Slough SL3 93 BB80
Teddington TW11 117 CG92
Thornton Heath CR7 142 DQ95
Twickenham TW2 116 CA88
Wallington SM6 159 DH106
Waltham Cross (Chsht) EN8 15 DY32
Watford WD25
off Haines Way 7 BV33
Welling DA16 106 EV83
Springfields, Wal.Abb. EN9 16 EE34
Springfields Cl, Cher. KT16 134 BH102
H **Springfield Uni Hosp**, SW17 120 DE89
Springfield Wk, NW6 82 DB67
Orpington BR6
off Place Fm Av 145 ER102
Spring Gdns, N5
off Grosvenor Av 66 DQ64
SW1 199 N2
Hornchurch RM12 71 FH63
Orpington BR6 164 EV107
Romford RM7 71 FC57
Wallington SM6 159 DJ106
Watford WD25 24 BW35
West Molesey KT8 136 CC99
Westerham (Bigg.H.) TN16 178 EJ118
Woodford Green IG8 48 EJ52
Spring Gdns Ind Est, Rom. RM7 71 FC57
SPRING GROVE, Islw. TW7 97 CF81
Spring Gro, SE19
off Alma Pl 122 DT94
W4 98 CN78
Gravesend DA12 131 GH88
Hampton TW12
off Plevna Rd 136 CB95
Leatherhead (Fetch.) KT22 170 CB123
Loughton IG10 32 EK44
Mitcham CR4 140 DG95
Spring Gro Cres, Houns. TW3 96 CC81
Spring Gro Rd, Houns. TW3 96 CB81
Isleworth TW7 96 CB81
Richmond TW10 118 CM85
Springhead Enterprise Pk, Grav. DA11 130 GC88
Springhead Rd, Erith DA8 107 FF79
Gravesend (Nthflt) DA11 130 GC87
Spring Hill, E5 66 DU59

★ Place of interest ⇌ Railway station ⊖ London Underground station DLR Docklands Light Railway station Tra Tramlink station H Hospital Riv Pedestrian ferry landing stage

Spring Hill, SE26 122 DW91
Springhill Cl, SE5 102 DR83
Springholm Cl, West.
(Bigg.H.) TN16 178 EJ118
Springhurst Cl, Croy. CR0 161 DZ105
Spring Lake, Stan. HA7 41 CH49
Spring La, E5 66 DV60
N10 64 DG55
SE25 142 DV100
Oxted RH8 187 ED131
Spring Ms, W1 194 E6
Epsom KT17
off Old Schs La 157 CT109
Richmond TW9
off Rosedale Rd 98 CL84
Spring Pk Av, Croy. CR0 143 DX103
Spring Pk Dr, N4 66 DQ60
Springpark Dr, Beck. BR3 143 EC97
Spring Pk Rd, Croy. CR0 143 DX103
Spring Pas, SW15
off Embankment 99 CX83
Spring Path, NW3 64 DD64
Spring Pl, N3
off Windermere Av 44 DA54
NW5 65 DH64
Springpond Rd, Dag. RM9 70 EY64
Springrice Rd, SE13 123 EC86
Spring Ri, Egh. TW20 112 AY93
Spring Rd, Felt. TW13 115 BT90
Springs, The, Brox. EN10 15 DY25
Springshaw Cl, Sev. TN13 190 FD123
Spring Shaw Rd, Orp. BR5 146 EU95
Spring St, W2 82 DD72
Epsom KT17 157 CT109
Spring Ter, Rich. TW9 118 CL85
Springtide Cl, SE15
off Staffordshire St 102 DU81
Spring Vale, Bexh. DA7 107 FB84
Greenhithe DA9 129 FW86
Springvale Av, Brent. TW8 97 CK78
Spring Vale Cl, Swan. BR8 147 FF95
Springvale Est, W14
off Blythe Rd 99 CY76
Spring Vale N, Dart. DA1 128 FK87
Springvale Retail Pk, Orp.
BR5 146 EW97
Spring Vale S, Dart. DA1 128 FK87
Springvale Ter, W14 99 CX76
Springvale Way, Orp. BR5 146 EW97
Spring Vil Rd, Edg. HA8 42 CN52
Spring Wk, E1
off Old Montague St 84 DU71
Springwater Cl, SE18 105 EN81
Springway, Har. HA1 61 CD59
Springwell Av, NW10 81 CT67
Rickmansworth
(Mill End) WD3 38 BG47
Springwell Cl, SW16
off Etherstone Rd 121 DN91
Springwell Ct, Houns. TW4 96 BX82
Springwell Hill, Uxb.
(Hare.) UB9 38 BH51
Springwell La, Rick. WD3 38 BG49
Uxbridge (Hare.) UB9 38 BG49
Springwell Rd, SW16 121 DN91
Hounslow TW4, TW5 96 BX81
Springwood, Wal.Cr.
(Chsht) EN7 14 DU26
Springwood Cl, Uxb.
(Hare.) UB9 38 BK53
Springwood Cres, Edg. HA8 42 CP47
Springwood Pl, Wey. KT13
off Cobbetts Hill 153 BP108
Spring Wds, Vir.W. GU25 132 AV98
Springwood Way, Rom. RM1 71 FG57
Sprowston Ms, E7 86 EG65
Sprowston Rd, E7 68 EG64
Spruce Cl, Red. RH1 184 DF133
Spruce Ct, W5
off Elderberry Rd 98 CL76
Sprucedale Cl, Swan. BR8 147 FE96
Sprucedale Gdns, Croy. CR0 161 DX105
Wallington SM6 159 DK109
Spruce Hills Rd, E17 47 EC54
Spruce Pk, Brom. BR2
off Cumberland Rd 144 EF98
Spruce Rd, West.
(Bigg.H.) TN16 178 EK116
Spruce Way, St.Alb.
(Park St) AL2 8 CB27
Sprules Rd, SE4 103 DY82
Spur, The, Wal.Cr. (Chsht) EN8
off Welsummer Way 15 DX28
Spur Cl, Abb.L. WD5 7 BR33
Romford (Abridge) RM4 34 EV41
Spurfield, W.Mol. KT8 136 CB97
Spurgate, Brwd. (Hutt.) CM13 55 GA47
Spurgeon Av, SE19 142 DR95
Spurgeon Rd, SE19 142 DR95
Spurgeon St, SE1 201 K7
Spurling Rd, SE22 102 DT84
Dagenham RM9 88 EZ65
Spurrell Av, Bex. DA5 127 FD91
Spur Rd, N15
off Philip La 66 DR56
SE1 200 D4
SW1 199 K5
Barking IG11 87 EQ68
Edgware HA8 42 CL49
Feltham TW14 115 BV85
Isleworth TW7 97 CH80
Orpington BR6 146 EU103
Spur Rd Est, Edg. HA8 42 CM49
Spurstowe Rd, E8
off Marcon Pl 84 DV65
Spurstowe Ter, E8 66 DV64
Squadrons App, Horn. RM12 90 FJ65
Square, The, W6 99 CW78
Carshalton SM5 158 DG106
Hayes UB3 77 BR74
Ilford IG1 69 EN59
Richmond TW9 117 CK85
Sevenoaks TN13
off Amherst Hill 190 FE122
Swanley BR8 147 FD97
Square, The, Watford WD24
off The Harebreaks 23 BV37
West Drayton UB7 94 BH81
Westerham (Tats.) TN16 178 EJ120
Weybridge KT13 153 BQ105
Woking (Wisley) GU23 168 BL116
Woodford Green IG8 48 EG50
Square Rigger Row, SW11
off York Pl 100 DC83
Squarey St, SW17 120 DC90
★ **Squerryes Ct**, West. TN16 189 EQ128
Squerryes Mede, West. TN16 189 EQ127
Squire Gdns, NW8
off St. John's Wd Rd 82 DD69
Squires, The, Rom. RM7 71 FC58
Squires Br Rd, Shep. TW17 134 BM98
Squires Ct, SW19 120 DA91
Chertsey KT16
off Springfields Cl 134 BH102
Squires Fld, Swan. BR8 147 FF95
Squires La, N3 44 DB54
Squires Mt, NW3
off East Heath Rd 64 DD62
Squires Rd, Shep. TW17 134 BM98
Squires Wk, Ashf. TW15
off Napier Rd 115 BR94
Squires Way, Dart. DA2 127 FD91
Squires Wd Dr, Chis. BR7 124 EL94
Squirrel Cl, Houns. TW4 96 BW82
Squirrel Keep, W.Byf. KT14 152 BH112
Squirrel Ms, W13 79 CG73
Squirrels, The, SE13
off Belmont Hill 103 ED83
Bushey WD23 25 CD44
Pinner HA5 60 BZ55
Squirrels Chase, Grays
(Orsett) RM16
off Hornsby La 111 GG75
Squirrels Cl, N12
off Woodside Av 44 DC49
Uxbridge UB10 76 BN66
Squirrels Grn, Lthd.
(Bkhm) KT23 170 CA123
Worcester Park KT4 139 CT102
Squirrels Heath Av, Rom.
RM2 71 FH55
Squirrels Heath La, Horn.
RM11 72 FJ56
Romford RM2 72 FJ56
Squirrels Heath Rd, Rom.
RM3 72 FL55
Squirrels La, Buck.H. IG9 48 EK48
Squirrels Trd Est, The, Hayes
UB3 95 BU76
Squirrels Way, Epsom KT18 172 CR115
Squirrel Wd, W.Byf. KT14 152 BH112
Squirries St, E2 84 DU69
Stable Cl, Nthlt. UB5 78 CA68
Stable Ms, Twick. TW1
off Grove Av 117 CF88
Stables, The, Buck.H. IG9 48 EJ45
Cobham KT11 154 BZ114
Swanley BR8 147 FH95
Stables End, Orp. BR6 145 EQ104
Stables Ms, SE27 122 DQ92
Stables Way, SE11 200 D10
Stable Wk, N1
off Wharfdale Rd 83 DL68
N2 *off Old Fm Rd* 44 DD53
Stable Way, W10
off Latimer Rd 81 CW72
Stable Yd, SW1 199 K4
SW9 *off Broomgrove Rd* 101 DM82
SW15 *off Danemere St* 99 CW83
Stable Yd Rd, SW1 199 K3
Stacey Av, N18 46 DW49
Stacey Cl, E10
off Halford Rd 67 ED57
Gravesend DA12 131 GL92
Stacey St, N7 65 DN62
WC2 195 N9
Stackhouse St, SW3 198 D6
Stack Rd, Dart.
(Hort.Kir.) DA4 149 FR97
Stacy Path, SE5
off Harris St 102 DS80
Stadium Business Cen, Wem.
HA9 62 CP62
Stadium Retail Pk, Wem. HA9
off Wembley Pk Dr 62 CN62
Stadium Rd, NW2 63 CV59
SE18 104 EL80
Stadium Rd E, NW2 63 CW59
Stadium St, SW10 100 DC80
Stadium Way, Dart. DA1 127 FE85
Wembley HA9 62 CM63
Staffa Rd, E10 67 DY60
Stafford Av, Horn. RM11 72 FK55
Stafford Cl, E17 67 DZ58
N14 29 DJ43
NW6 82 DA69
Caterham CR3 176 DT123
Grays (Chaff.Hun.) RM16 109 FW77
Greenhithe DA9 129 FT85
Sutton SM3 157 CY107
Waltham Cross
(Chsht) EN8 14 DV29
Stafford Ct, W8 100 DA76
Stafford Cross, Croy. CR0 159 DM106
Stafford Gdns, Croy. CR0 159 DM106
Stafford Pl, SW1 199 K6
Richmond TW10 118 CM87
Stafford Rd, E3 85 DZ68
E7 86 EJ66
NW6 82 DA69
Caterham CR3 176 DT122
Croydon CR0 159 DN105
Harrow HA3 40 CC52
New Malden KT3 138 CQ97
Ruislip HA4 59 BT63
Sidcup DA14 125 ES91
Wallington SM6 159 DJ107
Staffordshire St, SE15 102 DU81
Stafford Sq, Wey. KT13
off Rosslyn Pk 153 BR105
Stafford St, W1 199 K2
Stafford Ter, W8 100 DA76
Stafford Way, Sev. TN13 191 FJ127
Staff St, EC1 197 L3
Stagbury Av, Couls. CR5 174 DE118
Stagbury Cl, Couls. CR5 174 DE119
Stag Cl, Edg. HA8 42 CP54
Staggart Grn, Chig. IG7 49 ET51
Stagg Hill, Barn. EN4 28 DD35
Potters Bar EN6 28 DD35
Stag La, NW9 62 CQ55
SW15 119 CT89
Buckhurst Hill IG9 48 EH47
Edgware HA8 42 CP54
Rickmansworth
(Chorl.) WD3 21 BC44
Stag Leys, Ashtd. KT21 172 CL120
Stag Leys Cl, Bans. SM7 174 DD115
Stag Pl, SW1 199 K6
Stag Ride, SW19 119 CT90
Stags Way, Islw. TW7 97 CF79
Stainash Cres, Stai. TW18 114 BH92
Stainash Par, Stai. TW18
off Kingston Rd 114 BH92
Stainbank Rd, Mitch. CR4 141 DH97
Stainby Cl, West Dr. UB7 94 BL76
Stainby Rd, N15 66 DT56
Stainer Ho, SE3 *off Ryan Cl* 104 EJ84
Stainer Rd, Borwd. WD6 25 CK39
Stainer St, SE1 201 L3
STAINES 114 BG91
⇌ **Staines** 114 BG92
Staines Av, Sutt. SM3 139 CX103
Staines Br, Stai. TW18 113 BE92
Staines Bypass, Ashf. TW15 114 BH91
Staines TW18, TW19 114 BH91
Staines La, Cher. KT16 133 BF99
Staines La Cl, Cher. KT16 133 BF100
Staines Rd, Cher. KT16 133 BF97
Feltham TW14 115 BR87
Hounslow TW3, TW4 96 CB83
Ilford IG1 69 EQ63
Staines TW18 134 BH95
Staines (Wrays.) TW19 112 AY87
Twickenham TW2 116 CA90
Staines Rd E, Sun. TW16 115 BU94
Staines Rd W, Ashf. TW15 115 BP93
Sunbury-on-Thames TW16 115 BP93
Staines Wk, Sid. DA14
off Evry Rd 126 EW93
Stainford Cl, Ashf. TW15 115 BR92
Stainforth Rd, E17 67 EA56
Ilford IG2 69 ER59
Staining La, EC2 197 J8
Stainmore Cl, Chis. BR7 145 ER95
Stainsbury St, E2
off Royston St 84 DW68
Stainsby Pl, E14
off Stainsby Rd 85 EA72
Stainsby Rd, E14 85 EA72
Stains Cl, Wal.Cr.
(Chsht) EN8 15 DY28
Stainton Rd, SE6 123 ED86
Enfield EN3 30 DW39
Stainton Wk, Wok. GU21
off Inglewood 166 AW118
Stairfoot La, Sev.
(Chipstead) TN13 190 FC122
Staithes Way, Tad. KT20 173 CV120
Stalbridge St, NW1 194 C6
Stalham St, SE16 202 E7
Stalham Way, Ilf. IG6 49 EP53
Stalisfield Pl, Orp. BR6
off Mill La 163 EN110
Stambourne Way, SE19 122 DS94
West Wickham BR4 143 EC104
⊖ **Stamford Brook** 99 CT77
Stamford Brook Av, W6 99 CT76
Stamford Brook Gdns, W6
off Stamford Brook Rd 99 CT76
Stamford Brook Rd, W6 99 CT76
Stamford Cl, N15 66 DU56
Harrow HA3 41 CE52
Potters Bar EN6 12 DD32
Southall UB1 78 CA73
Stamford Cotts, SW10
off Billing St 100 DB80
Stamford Ct, W6
off Goldhawk Rd 99 CT77
Stamford Dr, Brom. BR2 144 EF98
Stamford Gdns, Dag. RM9 88 EW66
Stamford Grn Rd, Epsom
KT18 156 CP113
Stamford Gro E, N16
off Oldhill St 66 DU60
Stamford Gro W, N16
off Oldhill St 66 DU60
STAMFORD HILL, N16 66 DS60
⇌ **Stamford Hill** 66 DS59
Stamford Hill, N16 66 DT61
Stamford Hill Est, N16 66 DT60
🅗 **Stamford Hosp**, W6 99 CU77
Stamford Rd, E6 86 EL67
N1 84 DS66
N15 66 DU57
Dagenham RM9 88 EV67
Walton-on-Thames KT12
off Kenilworth Dr 136 BX104
Watford WD17 23 BV40
Stamford St, SE1 200 D3
Stamp Pl, E2 197 P2
Stanard Cl, N16 66 DS59
Stanborough Av, Borwd.
WD6 26 CN37
Stanborough Cl, Borwd.
WD6 26 CN38
Hampton TW12 116 BZ93
Stanborough Pk, Wat. WD25 23 BV35
Stanborough Pas, E8
off Abbot St 84 DT65
Stanborough Rd, Houns.
TW3 97 CD83
Stanbridge Pl, N21 45 DP47
Stanbridge Rd, SW15 99 CW83
Stanbrook Rd, SE2 106 EV75
Gravesend DA11 131 GF88
Stanbury Av, Wat. WD17 23 BS37
Stanbury Rd, SE15 102 DV81
Stancroft, NW9 62 CS56
Standale Gro, Ruis. HA4 59 BQ57
Standard Ind Est, E16 105 EM75
Standard Pl, EC2 197 N3
Standard Rd, NW10 80 CQ70
Belvedere DA17 106 FA78
Bexleyheath DA6 106 EY84
Standard Rd, Enfield EN3 31 DY38
Hounslow TW4 96 BY83
Orpington BR6 163 EN110
Standen Av, Horn. RM12 72 FK62
Standen Rd, SW18 119 CZ87
Standfield, Abb.L. WD5 7 BS31
Standfield Gdns, Dag. RM10
off Standfield Rd 88 FA65
Standfield Rd, Dag. RM10 70 FA64
Standish Ho, SE3
off Elford Cl 104 EJ84
Standish Rd, W6 99 CU77
Standlake Pt, SE23 123 DX90
Stane Cl, SW19
off Hayward Cl 140 DB95
Stane St, Lthd. KT22 182 CL126
Stane Way, SE18 104 EK80
Epsom KT17 157 CU110
Stanfield Rd, E3 85 DY68
Stanford Cl, Hmptn. TW12 116 BZ93
Romford RM7 71 FB58
Ruislip HA4 59 BQ58
Woodford Green IG8 48 EL50
Stanford Ct, SW6
off Bagley's La 100 DB81
Waltham Abbey EN9 16 EG33
Stanford Gdns, S.Ock.
(Aveley) RM15 91 FR74
Stanford Ho, Bark. IG11 88 EV68
Stanford Pl, SE17 201 M9
Stanford Rd, N11 44 DF50
SW16 141 DK96
W8 100 DB76
Grays RM16 110 GD76
Stanford St, SW1 199 M9
Stanford Way, SW16 141 DK96
Stangate Cres, Borwd. WD6 26 CS43
Stangate Gdns, Stan. HA7 41 CH49
Stanger Rd, SE25 142 DU98
Stanham Pl, Dart. DA1
off Crayford Way 107 FG84
Stanham Rd, Dart. DA1 128 FJ85
Stanhope Av, N3 63 CZ55
Bromley BR2 144 EF102
Harrow HA3 41 CD53
Stanhope Cl, SE16 203 J4
Stanhope Gdns, N4 65 DP58
N6 65 DH58
NW7 43 CT50
SW7 100 DC77
Dagenham RM8 70 EZ62
Ilford IG1 69 EM60
Stanhope Gate, W1 198 G2
Stanhope Gro, Beck. BR3 143 DZ99
Stanhope Heath, Stai.
(Stanw.) TW19 114 BJ86
Stanhope Ms E, SW7 100 DC77
Stanhope Ms S, SW7
off Gloucester Rd 100 DC77
Stanhope Ms W, SW7 100 DC77
Stanhope Par, NW1 195 K2
Stanhope Pk Rd, Grnf. UB6 78 CC70
Stanhope Pl, W2 194 D9
Stanhope Rd, E17 67 EB57
N6 65 DJ58
N12 44 DC50
Barnet EN5 27 CW44
Bexleyheath DA7 106 EY82
Carshalton SM5 158 DG108
Croydon CR0 142 DS104
Dagenham RM8 70 EZ61
Greenford UB6 78 CC71
Rainham RM13 89 FG68
Sidcup DA15 126 EU91
Swanscombe DA10 130 FZ85
Waltham Cross EN8 15 DY33
Stanhope Row, W1 199 H3
Stanhopes, Oxt. RH8 188 EH128
Stanhope St, NW1 195 K3
Stanhope Ter, W2 194 A10
Stanhope Way, Sev. TN13 190 FD122
Staines (Stanw.) TW19 114 BJ86
Stanier Cl, W14
off Aisgill Av 99 CZ78
Staniland Dr, Wey. KT13 152 BM110
Stanlake Ms, W12 81 CW74
Stanlake Rd, W12 81 CV74
Stanlake Vil, W12 81 CV74
Stanley Av, Bark. IG11 87 ET68
Beckenham BR3 143 EC96
Dagenham RM8 70 EZ60
Greenford UB6 78 CC67
New Malden KT3 139 CU99
Romford RM2 71 FG56
St. Albans AL2 8 CA25
Wembley HA0 80 CL66
Stanley Cl, SW8 101 DM79
Coulsdon CR5 175 DM117
Greenhithe DA9 129 FS85
Hornchurch RM12
off Stanley Rd 72 FJ61
Romford RM2 71 FG56
Uxbridge UB8 76 BK67
Wembley HA0 80 CL66
Stanley Cotts, Slou. SL2 74 AT74
Stanley Ct, Cars. SM5
off Stanley Pk Rd 158 DG108
Stanley Cres, W11 81 CZ73
Gravesend DA12 131 GK92
Stanleycroft Cl, Islw. TW7 97 CE81
Stanley Gdns, NW2 63 CW64
W3 80 CS74
W11 81 CZ73
Borehamwood WD6 26 CL39
Mitcham CR4
off Ashbourne Rd 120 DG93
South Croydon CR2 160 DU112
Wallington SM6 159 DJ107
Walton-on-Thames KT12 154 BW107
Stanley Gdns Ms, W11
off Stanley Cres 81 CZ73
Stanley Gdns Rd, Tedd. TW11 117 CE92
Stanley Grn E, Slou. SL3 93 AZ77
Stanley Grn W, Slou. SL3 93 AZ77
Stanley Gro, SW8 100 DG82
Croydon CR0 141 DN100
Stanley Pk Dr, Wem. HA0 80 CM66
Stanley Pk Rd, Cars. SM5 158 DF108
Wallington SM6 159 DH107
Stanley Rd, E4 47 ED46
Stanley Rd, E10 67 EB58
E12 68 EL64
E15 85 ED67
E18 48 EF53
N2 64 DD55
N9 46 DT46
N10 45 DH52
N11 45 DK51
N15 65 DP56
NW9 *off West Hendon Bdy* 63 CU59
SW14 98 CP84
SW19 120 DA94
W3 98 CQ76
Ashford TW15 114 BL92
Bromley BR2 144 EH98
Carshalton SM5 158 DG108
Croydon CR0 141 DN101
Enfield EN1 30 DS41
Gravesend (Nthflt) DA11 130 GE88
Grays RM17 110 GB78
Harrow HA2 60 CC61
Hornchurch RM12 72 FJ61
Hounslow TW3 96 CC84
Ilford IG1 69 ER61
Mitcham CR4 120 DG94
Morden SM4 140 DA98
Northwood HA6 39 BU53
Orpington BR6 146 EU102
Sidcup DA14 126 EU90
Southall UB1 78 BY73
Sutton SM2 158 DB107
Swanscombe DA10 130 FZ86
Teddington TW11 117 CE91
Twickenham TW2 117 CD90
Watford WD17 24 BW41
Wembley HA9 80 CM65
Woking GU21 167 AZ116
Stanley Rd N, Rain. RM13 89 FE67
Stanley Rd S, Rain. RM13 89 FF68
Stanley Sq, Cars. SM5 158 DF109
Stanley St, SE8 103 DZ80
Caterham CR3
off Coulsdon Rd 176 DQ122
Stanley Ter, N19 65 DL61
Stanley Way, Orp. BR5 146 EV99
Stanmer St, SW11 100 DE81
STANMORE 41 CG50
⊖ **Stanmore** 41 CK50
Stanmore Gdns, Rich. TW9 98 CM83
Sutton SM1 140 DC104
Stanmore Hall, Stan. HA7 41 CH48
Stanmore Hill, Stan. HA7 41 CG48
Stanmore Pl, NW1
off Arlington Rd 83 DH67
Stanmore Rd, E11 68 EF60
N15 65 DP56
Belvedere DA17 107 FC77
Richmond TW9 98 CM83
Watford WD24 23 BV39
Stanmore St, N1
off Caledonian Rd 83 DM67
Stanmore Ter, Beck. BR3 143 EA96
Stanmore Way, Loug. IG10 33 EN39
Stanmount Rd, St.Alb. AL2 8 CA25
Stannard Ms, E8 84 DU65
Stannard Rd, E8 84 DU65
Stannary Pl, SE11 101 DN78
Stannary St, SE11 101 DN79
Stannet Way, Wall. SM6 159 DJ105
Stannington Path, Borwd.
WD6 26 CN39
Stansfeld Rd, E6 86 EK71
Stansfield Rd, SW9 101 DM83
Hounslow TW4 95 BV82
Stansgate Rd, Dag. RM10 70 FA61
Stanstead Cl, Brom. BR2 144 EF99
Stanstead Gro, SE6
off Stanstead Rd 123 DZ88
Stanstead Manor, Sutt. SM1 158 DA107
Stanstead Rd, E11 68 EH57
SE6 123 DX88
SE23 123 DX88
Caterham CR3 186 DR125
Hounslow
(Hthrw Air.) TW6 114 BM86
Stansted Cl, Horn. RM12 89 FH65
Stansted Cres, Bex. DA5 126 EX88
Stanswood Gdns, SE5 102 DS80
Stanthorpe Cl, SW16 121 DL92
Stanthorpe Rd, SW16 121 DL92
Stanton Av, Tedd. TW11 117 CE92
Stanton Cl, Epsom KT19 156 CP106
Orpington BR5 146 EW101
Worcester Park KT4 139 CX102
Stanton Ho, SE16 203 M4
Stanton Rd, SE26
off Stanton Way 123 DZ91
SW13 99 CT82
SW20 139 CX96
Croydon CR0 142 DQ101
Stanton Sq, SE26
off Stanton Way 123 DZ91
Stanton Way, SE26 123 DZ91
Slough SL3 92 AY77
Stanway Cl, Chig. IG7 49 ES50
Stanway Ct, N1 197 N1
Stanway Gdns, W3 80 CN74
Edgware HA8 42 CQ50
Stanway Rd, Wal.Abb. EN9 16 EG33
Stanway St, N1 84 DS68
STANWELL, Stai. TW19 114 BL87
Stanwell Cl, Stai.
(Stanw.) TW19 114 BK86
Stanwell Gdns, Stai.
(Stanw.) TW19 114 BK86
STANWELL MOOR, Stai.
TW19 114 BG85
Stanwell Moor Rd, Stai.
TW19 114 BH85
West Drayton UB7 94 BH81
Stanwell New Rd, Stai.
TW18 114 BH90
Stanwell Rd, Ashf. TW15 114 BL89
Feltham TW14 115 BQ87
Slough (Horton) SL3 93 BA83
Stanwick Rd, W14 99 CZ77
Stanworth St, SE1 201 P5
Stanwyck Dr, Chig. IG7 49 EQ50
Stanwyck Gdns, Rom. RM3 51 FH50
Stapenhill Rd, Wem. HA0 61 CH62

★ Place of interest ⇌ Railway station ⊖ London Underground station DLR Docklands Light Railway station Tra Tramlink station H Hospital Riv Pedestrian ferry landing stage

Staple Cl, Bex. DA5 . . . 127 FD90
Staplefield Cl, SW2 . . . 121 DL88
Pinner HA5 . . . 40 BY52
STAPLEFORD ABBOTTS, Rom. RM4 . . . 35 FC43
★ Stapleford Airfield, Rom. RM4 . . . 34 EZ40
Stapleford Av, Ilf. IG2 . . . 69 ES57
Stapleford Cl, E4 . . . 47 EC48
SW19 . . . 119 CY87
Kingston upon Thames KT1 . . . 138 CN97
Stapleford Ct, Sev. TN13 . . . 190 FF123
Stapleford Gdns, Rom. RM5 . . . 50 FA51
Stapleford Rd, Rom. RM4 . . . 35 FB42
Wembley HA0 . . . 79 CK66
STAPLEFORD TAWNEY, Rom. RM4 . . . 35 FC37
Stapleford Tawney, Ong. CM5 . . . 19 FC32
Romford RM4 . . . 35 FD35
Stapleford Way, Bark. IG11 . . . 88 EV69
Staple Hill Rd, Wok. (Chob.Com.) GU24 . . . 150 AS105
Staplehurst Rd, SE13 . . . 124 EE85
Carshalton SM5 . . . 158 DE108
Staple Inn, WC1 . . . 196 D7
Staple Inn Bldgs, WC1 . . . 196 D7
Staples Cl, SE16 . . . 203 K2
Staples Cor, NW2 . . . 63 CV60
Staples Cor Business Pk, NW2 . . . 63 CV60
Staples Rd, Loug. IG10 . . . 32 EL41
Staple St, SE1 . . . 201 L5
Stapleton Cl, Pot.B. EN6 . . . 12 DD31
Stapleton Cres, Rain. RM13 . . . 89 FG65
Stapleton Gdns, Croy. CR0 . . . 159 DN106
Stapleton Hall Rd, N4 . . . 65 DM59
Stapleton Rd, SW17 . . . 120 DG90
Bexleyheath DA7 . . . 106 EZ80
Borehamwood WD6 . . . 26 CN38
Orpington BR6 . . . 145 ET104
Stapley Rd, Belv. DA17 . . . 106 FA78
Stapylton Rd, Barn. EN5 . . . 27 CY41
Star All, EC3 . . . 197 N10
Star & Garter Hill, Rich. TW10 . . . 118 CL88
Starboard Av, Green. DA9 . . . 129 FV86
Starboard Way, E14 . . . 204 A6
Starch Ho La, Ilf. IG6 . . . 49 ER54
Starcross St, NW1 . . . 195 L3
Starfield Rd, W12 . . . 99 CU75
Star Hill, Dart. DA1 . . . 127 FE85
Woking GU22 . . . 166 AW119
Star Hill Rd, Sev. (Dunt.Grn) TN14 . . . 180 EZ116
Starkey Cl, Wal.Cr. (Chsht) EN7 off Shambrook Rd . . . 14 DQ25
Star La, E16 . . . 86 EE70
Coulsdon CR5 . . . 174 DG122
Epping CM16 . . . 18 EU30
Orpington BR5 . . . 146 EW98
Starling Cl, Buck.H. IG9 . . . 48 EG46
Pinner HA5 . . . 60 BW55
Starling La, Pot.B. (Cuffley) EN6 . . . 13 DM28
Starlings, The, Lthd. (Oxshott) KT22 . . . 154 CC113
Starling Wk, Hmptn. TW12 off Oak Av . . . 116 BY93
Starmans Cl, Dag. RM9 . . . 88 EY67
Star Path, Nthlt. UB5 off Brabazon Rd . . . 78 CA68
Star Pl, E1 . . . 202 A1
Star Rd, W14 . . . 99 CZ79
Isleworth TW7 . . . 97 CD82
Uxbridge UB10 . . . 77 BQ70
Starrock La, Couls. (Chipstead) CR5 . . . 174 DF120
Starrock Rd, Couls. CR5 . . . 175 DH119
Star St, E16 . . . 86 EF71
W2 . . . 194 A8
Starts Cl, Orp. BR6 . . . 145 EN104
Starts Hill Av, Orp. BR6 . . . 163 EP105
Starts Hill Rd, Orp. BR6 . . . 145 EN104
Starveall Cl, West Dr. UB7 . . . 94 BM76
Starwood Cl, W.Byf. KT14 . . . 152 BJ111
Starwood Ct, Slou. SL3 off London Rd . . . 92 AW76
Star Yd, WC2 . . . 196 D8
State Fm Av, Orp. BR6 . . . 163 EP105
Staten Gdns, Twick. TW1 . . . 117 CF88
Statham Gro, N16 off Green Las . . . 66 DQ63
N18 . . . 46 DS50
Station App, E4 (Highams Pk) off The Avenue . . . 47 ED51
E7 off Woodford Rd . . . 68 EH63
E11 (Snaresbrook) off High St . . . 68 EG57
N11 off Friern Barnet Rd . . . 45 DH50
N12 (Woodside Pk) . . . 44 DB49
N16 (Stoke Newington) off Stamford Hill . . . 66 DT61
NW10 off Station Rd . . . 81 CT69
SE1 . . . 200 C3
SE3 off Kidbrooke Pk Rd . . . 104 EH83
SE9 (Mottingham) . . . 125 EM88
SE26 (Lwr Sydenham) off Worsley Br Rd . . . 123 DZ92
SE26 (Sydenham) off Sydenham Rd . . . 122 DW91
SW6 . . . 99 CY83
SW16 . . . 121 DK92
W7 . . . 79 CE74
Amersham (Lt.Chal.) HP7 off Chalfont Sta Rd . . . 20 AX39
Ashford TW15 . . . 114 BL91
Barnet EN5 . . . 28 DC42
Bexley DA5 off Bexley High St . . . 126 FA87
Bexleyheath DA7 off Avenue Rd . . . 106 EY82
Bexleyheath (Barne.) DA7 . . . 107 FC82
Bromley (Hayes) BR2 . . . 144 EG102
Buckhurst Hill IG9 off Cherry Tree Ri . . . 48 EK49
Chislehurst BR7 . . . 145 EN95
Chislehurst (Elm.Wds) BR7 . . . 124 EL93
Coulsdon CR5 . . . 175 DK116
Coulsdon (Chipstead) CR5 . . . 174 DF118
Station App, Dartford DA1 . . . 128 FL86
Dartford (Cray.) DA1 . . . 127 FF86
Epping (They.B.) CM16 off Coppice Row . . . 33 ES36
Epsom KT18 . . . 156 CR113
Epsom (Ewell E.) KT17 . . . 157 CV110
Epsom (Ewell W.) KT19 off Chessington Rd . . . 157 CT109
Epsom (Stoneleigh) KT19 . . . 157 CU106
Esher (Hinch.Wd) KT10 . . . 137 CF104
Gerrards Cross SL9 . . . 56 AY57
Grays RM17 . . . 110 GA79
Greenford UB6 . . . 79 CD66
Hampton TW12 off Milton Rd . . . 136 CA95
Harrow HA1 . . . 61 CE59
Hayes UB3 . . . 95 BT75
Kenley CR8 off Hayes La . . . 160 DQ114
Kingston upon Thames KT1 . . . 138 CN95
Leatherhead KT22 . . . 171 CG121
Leatherhead (Oxshott) KT22 . . . 154 CC113
Loughton IG10 . . . 32 EL43
Loughton (Debden) IG10 . . . 33 EQ42
Northwood HA6 . . . 39 BS52
Orpington BR6 . . . 145 ET103
Orpington (Chels.) BR6 . . . 164 EV106
Orpington (St.M.Cray) BR5 . . . 146 EV98
Oxted RH8 . . . 188 EE128
Pinner HA5 . . . 60 BY55
Pinner (Hatch End) HA5 off Uxbridge Rd . . . 40 CA52
Purley CR8 off Whytecliffe Rd S . . . 159 DN111
Radlett WD7 off Shenley Hill . . . 25 CG35
Richmond TW9 . . . 98 CN81
Rickmansworth (Chorl.) WD3 . . . 21 BC42
Ruislip HA4 off Pembroke Rd . . . 59 BS60
Ruislip (S.Ruis.) HA4 . . . 59 BV64
Shepperton TW17 . . . 135 BQ100
South Croydon CR2 off Sanderstead Rd . . . 160 DR109
Staines TW18 . . . 114 BG92
Sunbury-on-Thames TW16 . . . 135 BU95
Sutton (Belmont) SM2 off Brighton Rd . . . 158 DB110
Sutton (Cheam) SM2 . . . 157 CY108
Swanley BR8 . . . 147 FE98
Upminster RM14 . . . 72 FQ61
Uxbridge (Denh.) UB9 off Middle Rd . . . 57 BD59
Virginia Water GU25 . . . 132 AX98
Waltham Cross EN8 . . . 15 DY34
Waltham Cross (Chsht) EN8 . . . 15 DZ30
Watford WD18 off Cassiobury Pk Av . . . 23 BT41
Watford (Carp.Pk) WD19 off Prestwick Rd . . . 40 BX48
Welling DA16 . . . 105 ET82
Wembley HA0 . . . 79 CH65
West Byfleet KT14 . . . 152 BG112
West Drayton UB7 . . . 76 BL74
Weybridge KT13 . . . 152 BN107
Whyteleafe CR3 . . . 176 DU117
Woking GU22 . . . 167 AZ117
Worcester Park KT4 . . . 139 CU102
Station App N, Sid. DA15 . . . 126 EU89
Station App Path, SE9 off Glenlea Rd . . . 125 EM85
Station App Rd, W4 . . . 98 CQ80
Coulsdon CR5 . . . 175 DK115
Tadworth KT20 . . . 173 CW122
Tilbury RM18 . . . 111 GG84
Station Av, SW9 off Coldharbour La . . . 101 DP83
Caterham CR3 . . . 176 DU124
Epsom KT19 . . . 156 CS109
New Malden KT3 . . . 138 CS97
Richmond TW9 . . . 98 CN81
Walton-on-Thames KT12 . . . 153 BU105
Station Cl, N3 . . . 44 DA53
N12 (Woodside Pk) . . . 44 DB49
Hampton TW12 . . . 136 CB95
Hatfield AL9 off Station Rd . . . 11 CY26
Potters Bar EN6 . . . 11 CZ31
Station Ct, SW6 off Townmead Rd . . . 100 DC81
Station Cres, N15 . . . 66 DR56
SE3 . . . 104 EG78
Ashford TW15 . . . 114 BK90
Wembley HA0 . . . 79 CH65
Stationers Hall Ct, EC4 off Ludgate Hill . . . 83 DP72
Station Est, Beck. BR3 off Elmers End Rd . . . 143 DX98
Station Est Rd, Felt. TW14 . . . 115 BV88
Station Footpath, Kings L. WD4 . . . 7 BP31
Station Gar Ms, SW16 off Estreham Rd . . . 121 DK93
Station Gdns, W4 . . . 98 CQ80
Station Gro, Wem. HA0 . . . 80 CL65
Station Hill, Brom. BR2 . . . 144 EG103
Station Ho Ms, N9 off Fore St . . . 46 DU49
Station La, Horn. RM12 . . . 72 FK62
Station Par, E11 . . . 68 EG57
N14 off High St . . . 45 DK46
NW2 . . . 81 CW65
SW12 off Balham High Rd . . . 120 DG88
W3 . . . 80 CN72
Ashford TW15 off Woodthorpe Rd . . . 114 BM91
Barking IG11 . . . 87 EQ66
Barnet EN4 off Cockfosters Rd . . . 28 DG42
Feltham TW14 . . . 115 BV87
Hornchurch RM12 off Rosewood Av . . . 71 FH63
Richmond TW9 . . . 98 CN81
Sevenoaks TN13 off London Rd . . . 190 FG124
Uxbridge (Denh.) UB9 . . . 58 BG59
Virginia Water GU25 . . . 132 AX98
Station Pas, E18 off Maybank Rd . . . 48 EH54
SE15 . . . 102 DW81
Station Path, E8 off Amhurst Rd . . . 84 DV65
Staines TW18 . . . 113 BF91
Station Pl, N4 off Seven Sisters Rd . . . 65 DN61
Station Ri, SE27 off Norwood Rd . . . 121 DP89
Station Rd, E4 (Chingford) . . . 47 ED46
E7 . . . 68 EG63
E12 . . . 68 EK63
E17 . . . 67 DY58
N3 . . . 44 DA53
N11 . . . 45 DH50
N17 . . . 66 DU55
N19 . . . 65 DJ62
N21 . . . 45 DP46
N22 . . . 45 DM54
NW4 . . . 63 CU58
NW7 . . . 42 CS50
NW10 . . . 81 CT68
SE13 . . . 103 EC83
SE20 . . . 122 DW93
SE25 (Norwood Junct.) . . . 142 DT98
SW13 . . . 99 CU83
SW19 . . . 140 DC95
W5 . . . 80 CM72
W7 (Hanwell) . . . 79 CE74
Addlestone KT15 . . . 152 BJ105
Ashford TW15 . . . 114 BM91
Barnet EN5 . . . 28 DB43
Belvedere DA17 . . . 106 FA76
Betchworth RH3 . . . 182 CS131
Bexleyheath DA7 . . . 106 EY83
Borehamwood WD6 . . . 26 CN42
Brentford TW8 . . . 97 CJ79
Bromley BR1 . . . 144 EG95
Bromley (Short.) BR2 . . . 144 EE96
Carshalton SM5 . . . 158 DF105
Caterham (Wold.) CR3 . . . 177 DZ123
Chertsey KT16 . . . 133 BF102
Chessington KT9 . . . 156 CL106
Chigwell IG7 . . . 49 EP48
Cobham (Stoke D'Ab.) KT11 . . . 170 BY117
Croydon (E.Croy.) CR0 . . . 142 DR103
Croydon (W.Croy.) CR0 . . . 142 DQ102
Dartford (Cray.) DA1 . . . 127 FF86
Dartford (Eyns.) DA4 . . . 148 FK104
Dartford (S.Darenth) DA4 . . . 148 FP96
Edgware HA8 . . . 42 CN51
Egham TW20 . . . 113 BA92
Epping CM16 . . . 18 EU31
Epping (N.Wld Bas.) CM16 . . . 19 FB27
Esher KT10 . . . 137 CD103
Esher (Clay.) KT10 . . . 155 CD106
Gerrards Cross SL9 . . . 56 AY57
Gravesend (Betsham) DA13 . . . 130 GA91
Gravesend (Nthflt) DA11 . . . 130 GB86
Greenhithe DA9 . . . 129 FU85
Hampton TW12 . . . 136 CA95
Harrow HA1 . . . 61 CF59
Harrow (N.Har.) HA2 . . . 60 CB57
Hatfield (Brook.Pk) AL9 . . . 11 CX25
Hayes UB3 . . . 95 BT76
Hounslow TW3 . . . 96 CB84
Ilford IG1 . . . 69 EP62
Ilford (Barkingside) IG6 . . . 69 ER55
Kenley CR8 . . . 160 DQ114
Kings Langley WD4 . . . 7 BP29
Kingston upon Thames KT2 . . . 138 CN95
Kingston upon Thames (Hmptn W.) KT1 . . . 137 CJ95
Leatherhead KT22 . . . 171 CG121
Loughton IG10 . . . 32 EL42
New Malden (Mots.Pk) KT3 . . . 139 CV99
Orpington BR6 . . . 145 ET103
Orpington (St.P.Cray) BR5 . . . 146 EW98
Potters Bar (Cuffley) EN6 . . . 13 DM29
Radlett WD7 . . . 25 CG35
Redhill RH1 . . . 184 DG133
Redhill (Merst.) RH1 . . . 185 DJ128
Rickmansworth WD3 . . . 38 BK45
Romford (Chad.Hth) RM6 . . . 70 EX59
Romford (Gidea Pk) RM2 . . . 71 FH56
Romford (Harold Wd) RM3 . . . 52 FM53
St. Albans (Brick.Wd) AL2 . . . 8 CA31
Sevenoaks (Dunt.Grn) TN13 . . . 181 FE120
Sevenoaks (Halst.) TN14 . . . 164 EZ111
Sevenoaks (Otford) TN14 . . . 181 FH116
Sevenoaks (Shore.) TN14 . . . 165 FG111
Shepperton TW17 . . . 135 BQ99
Sidcup DA15 . . . 126 EU91
Slough (Langley) SL3 . . . 93 BA76
Staines (Wrays.) TW19 . . . 113 AZ86
Sunbury-on-Thames TW16 . . . 115 BU94
Sutton (Belmont) SM2 . . . 158 DA110
Swanley BR8 . . . 147 FE98
Teddington TW11 . . . 117 CF92
Thames Ditton KT7 . . . 137 CF101
Twickenham TW1 . . . 117 CF88
Upminster RM14 . . . 72 FQ61
Uxbridge UB8 . . . 76 BJ70
Waltham Cross EN8 . . . 15 EA34
Watford WD17 . . . 23 BV40
West Byfleet KT14 . . . 152 BG112
West Drayton UB7 . . . 76 BK74
West Wickham BR4 . . . 143 EC102
Westerham (Brasted) TN16 . . . 180 EV123
Whyteleafe CR3 . . . 176 DT118
Woking (Chobham) GU24 . . . 150 AT111
Station Rd E, Oxt. RH8 . . . 188 EE128
Station Rd N, Belv. DA17 . . . 107 FB76
Egham TW20 . . . 113 BA92
Redhill (Merst.) RH1 . . . 185 DJ128
Station Rd S, Red. (Merst.) RH1 . . . 185 DJ128
Station Rd W, Oxt. RH8 . . . 188 EE129
Station Sq, Orp. (Petts Wd) BR5 . . . 145 EQ99
Romford RM2 . . . 71 FH56
Station St, E15 . . . 85 ED66
E16 . . . 87 EP74
Station Ter, NW10 . . . 81 CX68
Station Ter, SE5 . . . 102 DQ81
St. Albans (Park St) AL2 off Park St . . . 9 CD26
Station Vw, Grnf. UB6 . . . 79 CD67
Station Way, Buck.H. (Rod.Val.) IG9 . . . 48 EJ49
Epsom (Epsom) KT19 . . . 156 CR113
Esher (Clay.) KT10 . . . 155 CE107
Sutton (Cheam) SM3 . . . 157 CY107
Station Yd, Twick. TW1 . . . 117 CG87
Staunton Rd, Kings.T. KT2 . . . 118 CL93
Staunton St, SE8 . . . 103 DZ79
★ Stave Hill Ecological Pk, SE16 . . . 203 K4
Staveley Cl, E9 off Churchill Wk . . . 66 DW64
N7 off Penn Rd . . . 65 DL63
SE15 off Asylum Rd . . . 102 DV81
Staveley Gdns, W4 . . . 98 CR81
Staveley Rd, W4 . . . 98 CR80
Ashford TW15 . . . 115 BR93
Staveley Way, Wok. (Knap.) GU21 . . . 166 AS117
Staverton Rd, NW2 . . . 81 CW66
Hornchurch RM11 . . . 72 FK58
Stave Yd Rd, SE16 . . . 203 K3
Stavordale Rd, N5 . . . 65 DP63
Carshalton SM5 . . . 140 DC101
Stayne End, Vir.W. GU25 . . . 132 AU98
Stayner's Rd, E1 . . . 85 DX70
Stayton Rd, Sutt. SM1 . . . 140 DA104
Steadfast Rd, Kings.T. KT1 . . . 137 CK95
Stead St, SE17 . . . 201 K9
Steam Fm La, Felt. TW14 . . . 95 BT84
Stean St, E8 . . . 84 DT67
Stebbing Ho, W11 . . . 81 CX74
Stebbing Way, Bark. IG11 . . . 88 EU68
Stebondale St, E14 . . . 204 E9
Stedham Pl, WC1 . . . 195 P8
Stedman Cl, Bex. DA5 . . . 127 FE90
Uxbridge UB10 . . . 58 BN62
Steed Cl, Horn. RM11 . . . 71 FH61
Steedman St, SE17 . . . 201 H9
Steeds Rd, N10 . . . 44 DF53
Steeds Way, Loug. IG10 . . . 32 EL41
Steele Av, Green. DA9 . . . 129 FT85
Steele Rd, E11 . . . 68 EE63
N17 . . . 66 DS55
NW10 . . . 80 CQ68
W4 . . . 98 CQ76
Isleworth TW7 . . . 97 CG84
Steeles Ms N, NW3 off Steeles Rd . . . 82 DF65
Steeles Ms S, NW3 off Steeles Rd . . . 82 DF65
Steeles Rd, NW3 . . . 82 DF65
Steele Wk, Erith DA8 . . . 107 FB79
Steel's La, E1 off Devonport St . . . 84 DW72
Steels La, Lthd. (Oxshott) KT22 . . . 154 CB114
Steelyard Pas, EC4 off Upper Thames St . . . 84 DR73
Steen Way, SE22 off East Dulwich Gro . . . 122 DS85
Steep Cl, Orp. BR6 . . . 163 ET107
Steep Hill, SW16 . . . 121 DK90
Croydon CR0 . . . 160 DS105
Steeplands, Bushey WD23 . . . 40 CB45
Steeple Cl, SW6 . . . 99 CY82
SW19 . . . 119 CY92
Steeple Ct, E1 off Coventry Rd . . . 84 DV70
Steeple Gdns, Add. KT15 off Weatherall Cl . . . 152 BH106
Steeple Hts Dr, West. (Bigg.H.) TN16 . . . 178 EK117
Steeplestone Cl, N18 . . . 46 DQ50
Steeple Wk, N1 off Basire St . . . 84 DQ67
Steerforth St, SW18 . . . 120 DB89
Steers Mead, Mitch. CR4 . . . 140 DF95
Steers Way, SE16 . . . 203 L5
Stella Cl, Uxb. UB8 off Morello Av . . . 77 BP71
Stellar Ho, N17 . . . 46 DT51
Stella Rd, SW17 . . . 120 DF93
Stelling Rd, Erith DA8 . . . 107 FD80
Stellman Cl, E5 . . . 66 DU62
Stembridge Rd, SE20 . . . 142 DV96
Sten Cl, Enf. EN3 . . . 31 EA37
Stents La, Cob. KT11 . . . 170 BZ120
Stepbridge Path, Wok. GU21 off Goldsworth Rd . . . 166 AX117
Stepgates, Cher. KT16 . . . 134 BH101
Stepgates Cl, Cher. KT16 . . . 134 BH101
Stephan Cl, E8 . . . 84 DU67
Stephen Av, Rain. RM13 . . . 89 FG65
Stephen Cl, Egh. TW20 . . . 113 BC93
Orpington BR6 . . . 145 ET104
Stephendale Rd, SW6 . . . 100 DB82
Stephen Ms, W1 . . . 195 M7
Stephen Pl, SW4 off Rectory Gro . . . 101 DJ83
Stephen Rd, Bexh. DA7 . . . 107 FC83
Stephens Cl, Rom. RM3 . . . 52 FJ50
Stephenson Av, Til. RM18 . . . 111 GG81
Stephenson Rd, E17 . . . 67 DY57
W7 . . . 79 CF72
Twickenham TW2 . . . 116 CA87
Stephenson St, E16 . . . 86 EE70
NW10 . . . 80 CS69
Stephenson Way, NW1 . . . 195 L4
Watford WD24 . . . 24 BX41
Stephen's Rd, E15 . . . 86 EE67
Stephen St, W1 . . . 195 M7
STEPNEY, E1 . . . 84 DW71
Stepney Causeway, E1 . . . 85 DX72
⊖ Stepney Green . . . 85 DX70
Stepney Grn, E1 . . . 84 DW71
Stepney High St, E1 . . . 85 DX71
Stepney Way, E1 . . . 84 DV71
Sterling Av, Edg. HA8 . . . 42 CM49
Waltham Cross EN8 . . . 15 DX34
Sterling Cl, NW10 . . . 81 CU65
Sterling Gdns, SE14 . . . 103 DY79
Sterling Ho, SE3 off Cambert Way . . . 104 EH84
Sterling Ind Est, Dag. RM10 . . . 71 FB63
Sterling Pl, W5 . . . 98 CL77
Weybridge KT13 off Oatlands Av . . . 153 BS105
Sterling Rd, Enf. EN2 . . . 30 DR38
Sterling St, SW7 . . . 198 C6
Sterling Way, N18 . . . 46 DR50
★ Sternberg Cen, N3 . . . 44 DB54
Stern Cl, Bark. IG11 . . . 88 EW68
Sterndale Rd, W14 . . . 99 CX76
Dartford DA1 . . . 128 FM87
Sterne St, W12 . . . 99 CX75
Sternhall La, SE15 . . . 102 DU83
Sternhold Av, SW2 . . . 121 DK89
Sterry Cres, Dag. RM10 off Alibon Rd . . . 70 FA64
Sterry Dr, Epsom KT19 . . . 156 CS105
Thames Ditton KT7 . . . 137 CE100
Sterry Gdns, Dag. RM10 . . . 88 FA65
Sterry Rd, Bark. IG11 . . . 87 ET67
Dagenham RM10 . . . 70 FA63
Sterry St, SE1 . . . 201 K5
Steucers La, SE23 . . . 123 DY87
Steve Biko La, SE6 . . . 123 EA91
Steve Biko Rd, N7 . . . 65 DN62
Steve Biko Way, Houns. TW3 . . . 96 CA83
Stevedale Rd, Well. DA16 . . . 106 EW82
Stevedore St, E1 . . . 202 D2
Stevenage Cres, Borwd. WD6 . . . 26 CL39
Stevenage Rd, E6 . . . 87 EN65
SW6 . . . 99 CX80
Stevens Av, E9 . . . 84 DW65
Stevens Cl, Beck. BR3 . . . 123 EA93
Bexley DA5 . . . 127 FD91
Steven's Cl, Dart. (Lane End) DA2 . . . 129 FS92
Stevens Cl, Epsom KT17 off Upper High St . . . 156 CS113
Hampton TW12 . . . 116 BY93
Pinner HA5 off Bridle Rd . . . 60 BW57
Stevens Grn, Bushey (Bushey Hth) WD23 . . . 40 CC46
Stevens La, Esher (Clay.) KT10 . . . 155 CG108
Stevenson Cl, Barn. EN5 . . . 28 DD44
Erith DA8 . . . 107 FH80
Stevenson Cres, SE16 . . . 202 C10
Stevens Pl, Pur. CR8 . . . 159 DP113
Stevens Rd, Dag. RM8 . . . 70 EV62
Stevens St, SE1 . . . 201 N6
Steven's Wk, Croy. CR0 . . . 161 DY111
Stevens Way, Chig. IG7 . . . 49 ES49
Steventon Rd, W12 . . . 81 CT73
Steward Cl, Wal.Cr. (Chsht) EN8 . . . 15 DY30
Stewards Cl, Epp. CM16 . . . 18 EU33
Stewards Grn La, Epp. CM16 . . . 18 EV32
Stewards Grn Rd, Epp. CM16 . . . 18 EU33
Stewards Holte Wk, N11 off Coppies Gro . . . 45 DH49
Steward St, E1 . . . 197 N7
Stewards Wk, Rom. RM1 . . . 71 FE57
Stewart, Tad. KT20 . . . 173 CX121
Stewart Av, Shep. TW17 . . . 134 BN98
Slough SL1 . . . 74 AT71
Upminster RM14 . . . 72 FP62
Stewart Cl, NW9 . . . 62 CQ58
Abbots Langley WD5 . . . 7 BT32
Chislehurst BR7 . . . 125 EP92
Hampton TW12 . . . 116 BY92
Woking GU21 off Nethercote Av . . . 166 AT117
Stewart Rainbird Ho, E12 . . . 69 EN64
Stewart Rd, E15 . . . 67 EC63
Stewartsby Cl, N18 . . . 46 DQ50
Stewart's Gro, SW3 . . . 198 A10
Stewart's Rd, SW8 . . . 101 DJ80
Stewart St, E14 . . . 204 E5
Stew La, EC4 . . . 197 H10
Steyne Rd, W3 . . . 80 CQ74
Steyning Cl, Ken. CR8 . . . 175 DP116
Steyning Gro, SE9 . . . 125 EM91
Steynings Way, N12 . . . 44 DA50
Steyning Way, Houns. TW4 . . . 96 BW84
Steynton Av, Bex. DA5 . . . 126 EX89
Stickland Rd, Belv. DA17 off Picardy Rd . . . 106 FA77
Stickleton Cl, Grnf. UB6 . . . 78 CB69
Stifford Hill, Grays (N.Stfd) RM16 . . . 91 FX74
South Ockendon RM15 . . . 91 FW73
Stifford Rd, S.Ock. RM15 . . . 91 FR74
Stilecroft Gdns, Wem. HA0 . . . 61 CH62
Stile Hall Gdns, W4 . . . 98 CN78
Stile Hall Par, W4 off Chiswick High Rd . . . 98 CN78
Stile Path, Sun. TW16 . . . 135 BU98
Stile Rd, Slou. SL3 . . . 92 AX76
Stiles Cl, Brom. BR2 . . . 145 EM100
Erith DA8 off Riverdale Rd . . . 107 FB78
Stillingfleet Rd, SW13 . . . 99 CU79
Stillington St, SW1 . . . 199 L8
Stillis Rd, Iver SL0 off Pinewood Rd . . . 75 BB66
Stillness Rd, SE23 . . . 123 DY86
Stilton Path, Borwd. WD6 . . . 26 CN38
Stilwell Dr, Uxb. UB8 . . . 76 BM70
Stilwell Roundabout, Uxb. UB8 . . . 76 BN73
Stipularis Dr, Hayes UB4 . . . 78 BX70
Stirling Av, Pnr. HA5 . . . 60 BY59
Wallington SM6 . . . 159 DL108
Stirling Cl, SW16 . . . 141 DJ95
Banstead SM7 . . . 173 CZ117
Rainham RM13 . . . 89 FH69
Uxbridge UB8 off Ferndale Cres . . . 76 BJ69
Stirling Cor, Barn. EN5 . . . 26 CR44
Borehamwood WD6 . . . 26 CR44
Stirling Dr, Orp. BR6 . . . 164 EV106
Stirling Gro, Houns. TW3 . . . 96 CC82

★ Place of interest ⇌ Railway station ⊖ London Underground station DLR Docklands Light Railway station Tra Tramlink station H Hospital Riv Pedestrian ferry landing stage

Stirling Rd, E13 86 EH68
E17 67 DY55
N17 46 DU53
N22 45 DP53
SW9 101 DL82
W3 98 CP76
Harrow HA3 61 CF55
Hayes UB3 77 BV73
Hounslow (Hthrw Air.) TW6 114 BM86
Twickenham TW2 116 CA87
Stirling Rd Path, E17 67 DY55
Stirling Wk, N.Mal. KT3 138 CQ99
Surbiton KT5 138 CP100
Stirling Way, Abb.L. WD5 7 BU32
Borehamwood WD6 26 CR44
Croydon CR0 141 DL101
Stites Hill Rd, Couls. CR5 175 DP120
Stiven Cres, Har. HA2 60 BZ62
Stoats Nest Rd, Couls. CR5 159 DL114
Stoats Nest Village, Couls. CR5 175 DL115
Stockbury Rd, Croy. CR0 142 DW100
Stockdale Rd, Dag. RM8 70 EZ61
Stockdove Way, Grnf. UB6 79 CF69
Stocker Gdns, Dag. RM9 88 EW66
Stockers Fm Rd, Rick. WD3 38 BK48
Stockers La, Wok. GU22 167 AZ120
★ Stock Exchange, EC2 196 G8
Stockfield Rd, SW16 121 DM90
Esher (Clay.) KT10 155 CE106
Stockham's Cl, S.Croy. CR2 160 DR111
Stock Hill, West. (Bigg.H.) TN16 178 EK116
Stockholm Ho, E1 84 DU73
Stockholm Rd, SE16 102 DW78
Stockholm Way, E1 202 B2
Stockhurst Cl, SW15 99 CW82
Stockingswater La, Enf. EN3 31 DY41
Stockland Rd, Rom. RM7 71 FD58
Stock La, Dart. DA2 128 FJ91
Stockley Cl, West Dr. UB7 95 BP75
Stockley Fm Rd, West Dr. UB7
off Stockley Rd 95 BP76
Stockley Pk, Uxb. UB11 77 BP74
Stockley Pk Roundabout, Uxb. UB11 77 BP74
Stockley Rd, Uxb. UB8 77 BP73
West Drayton UB7 95 BP77
Stock Orchard Cres, N7 65 DM64
Stock Orchard St, N7 65 DM64
Stockport Rd, SW16 141 DK95
Rickmansworth (Herons.) WD3 37 BC45
Stocksfield Rd, E17 67 EC55
Stocks Pl, E14
off Grenade St 85 DZ73
Stock St, E13 86 EG68
Stockton Cl, Barn. EN5 28 DC42
Stockton Gdns, N17
off Stockton Rd 46 DQ52
NW7 42 CS48
Stockton Rd, N17 46 DQ52
N18 46 DU51
STOCKWELL, SW9 101 DM81
⊖ Stockwell 101 DL81
Stockwell Av, SW9 101 DM83
Stockwell Cl, Brom. BR1 144 EH96
Waltham Cross (Chsht) EN7 14 DU28
Stockwell Gdns, SW9 101 DM82
Stockwell Gdns Est, SW9 101 DL82
Stockwell Grn, SW9 101 DM82
Stockwell La, SW9 101 DM82
Waltham Cross (Chsht) EN7 14 DU28
Stockwell Ms, SW9
off Stockwell Rd 101 DM82
Stockwell Pk Cres, SW9 101 DM82
Stockwell Pk Est, SW9 101 DN82
Stockwell Pk Rd, SW9 101 DM81
Stockwell Pk Wk, SW9 101 DM83
Stockwell Rd, SW9 101 DM82
Stockwell St, SE10 103 EC79
Stockwell Ter, SW9 101 DM81
Stodart Rd, SE20 142 DW95
Stofield Gdns, SE9
off Aldersgrove Av 124 EK90
Stoford Cl, SW19 119 CY87
Stoke Av, Ilf. IG6 50 EU51
Stoke Cl, Cob. (Stoke D'Ab.) KT11 170 BZ116
Stoke Common Rd, Slou. (Fulmer) SL3 56 AU63
Stoke Ct Dr, Slou. (Stoke P.) SL2 74 AS67
STOKE D'ABERNON, Cob. KT11 170 BZ116
Stoke Gdns, Slou. SL1 74 AS74
STOKE GREEN, Slou. SL2 74 AU70
Stoke Grn, Slou. (Stoke P.) SL2 74 AU70
Stokenchurch St, SW6 100 DB81
STOKE NEWINGTON, N16 66 DS61
⇌ Stoke Newington 66 DT61
Stoke Newington Ch St, N16 66 DR62
Stoke Newington Common, N16 66 DT62
Stoke Newington High St, N16 66 DT62
Stoke Newington Rd, N16 66 DT64
Stoke Pl, NW10 81 CT69
STOKE POGES, Slou. SL2 74 AT66
Stoke Poges La, Slou. SL1, SL2 74 AS72
Stoke Rd, Cob. KT11 170 BW115
Kingston upon Thames KT2 118 CQ94
Rainham RM13 90 FK68
Slough SL2 74 AT71
Walton-on-Thames KT12 136 BW104
Stokesay, Slou. SL2 74 AT73
Stokesby Rd, Chess. KT9 156 CM107
Stokesheath Rd, Lthd. (Oxshott) KT22 154 CC111
Stokesley St, W12 81 CT72
Stokes Ridings, Tad. KT20 173 CX123
Stokes Rd, E6 86 EL70
Croydon CR0 143 DX100
Stoke Wd, Slou. (Stoke P.) SL2 56 AT63
Stoll Cl, NW2 63 CW62
Stompond La, Walt. KT12 135 BU103
Stonard Rd, N13 45 DN48
Dagenham RM8 70 EV64
Stonards Hill, Epp. CM16 18 EW31
Loughton IG10 33 EM44
Stondon Pk, SE23 123 DY87
Stondon Wk, E6 86 EK68
STONE, Green. DA9 129 FT85
Stonebanks, Walt. KT12 135 BU101
STONEBRIDGE, NW10 80 CP67
Stonebridge Common, E8
off Mayfield Rd 84 DT66
⇌ Stonebridge Park 80 CN66
⊖ Stonebridge Park 80 CN66
Stonebridge Pk, NW10 80 CR66
Stonebridge Rd, N15 66 DS57
Gravesend (Nthflt) DA11 130 GA85
Stonebridge Way, Wem. HA9 80 CP65
Stone Bldgs, WC2 196 C7
Stonechat Sq, E6
off Peridot St 86 EL71
Stone Cl, SW4
off Larkhall Ri 101 DJ82
Dagenham RM8 70 EZ61
West Drayton UB7 76 BM74
Stonecot Cl, Sutt. SM3 139 CY102
Stonecot Hill, Sutt. SM3 139 CY102
Stone Cres, Felt. TW14 115 BT87
Stonecroft Av, Iver SL0 75 BE72
Stonecroft Cl, Barn. EN5 27 CV42
Stonecroft Rd, Erith DA8 107 FC80
Stonecroft Way, Croy. CR0 141 DL101
Stonecrop Cl, NW9 62 CR55
⇌ Stone Crossing 129 FS85
Stonecutter Ct, EC4
off Stonecutter St 83 DP72
Stonecutter St, EC4 196 F8
Stonefield Cl, Bexh. DA7 106 FA83
Ruislip HA4 60 BY64
Stonefield St, N1 83 DN67
Stonefield Way, SE7
off Greenbay Rd 104 EK80
Ruislip HA4 60 BY63
Stonegate Cl, Orp. BR5
off Main Rd 146 EW97
Stonegrove, Edg. HA8 42 CL49
Stonegrove Est, Edg. HA8 42 CM49
Stonegrove Gdns, Edg. HA8 42 CM50
Stonehall Av, Ilf. IG1 68 EL58
Stone Hall Gdns, W8
off St. Mary's Gate 100 DB76
Stone Hall Pl, W8
off St. Mary's Gate 100 DB76
Stone Hall Rd, N21 45 DM45
Stoneham Rd, N11 45 DJ51
STONEHILL, Cher. KT16 150 AY107
Stonehill Cl, SW14 118 CR85
Stonehill Cres, Cher. (Ott.) KT16 150 AY107
Stonehill Grn, Dart. DA2 127 FC94
Stonehill Rd, SW14 118 CQ85
W4 *off Wellesley Rd* 98 CN78
Chertsey (Ott.) KT16 151 BA105
Woking (Chobham) GU24 150 AW108
Stonehills Business Pk, N18
off Silvermere Dr 47 DX51
Stonehills Ct, SE21 122 DS90
Stonehill Wds Pk, Sid. DA14 127 FB93
Stonehorse Rd, Enf. EN3 30 DW43
Stone Ho Ct, EC3 197 M8
Stonehouse Gdns, Cat. CR3 186 DS125
H Stone Ho Hosp, Dart. DA2 128 FQ86
Stonehouse La, Purf. RM19 109 FS79
Sevenoaks (Halst.) TN14 164 EX109
Stonehouse Rd, Sev. (Halst.) TN14 164 EW110
Stoneings La, Sev. (Knock.) TN14 179 ET118
Stone Lake Retail Pk, SE7 104 EH77
STONELEIGH, Epsom KT17 157 CU106
⇌ Stoneleigh 157 CU106
Stoneleigh Av, Enf. EN1 30 DV39
Worcester Park KT4 157 CU105
Stoneleigh Bdy, Epsom KT17 157 CU106
Stoneleigh Cl, Wal.Cr. EN8 15 DX33
Stoneleigh Cres, Epsom KT19 157 CT106
Stoneleigh Ms, E3
off Stanfield Rd 85 DY68
Stoneleigh Pk, Wey. KT13 153 BQ106
Stoneleigh Pk Av, Croy. CR0 143 DX100
Stoneleigh Pk Rd, Epsom KT19 157 CT107
Stoneleigh Pl, W11 81 CX73
Stoneleigh Rd, N17 66 DT55
Carshalton SM5 140 DE101
Ilford IG5 68 EL55
Oxted RH8 188 EL130
Stoneleigh St, W11 81 CX73
Stoneleigh Ter, N19 65 DH61
Stonells Rd, SW11
off Chatham Rd 120 DF85
Stonemasons Cl, N15 66 DR56
Stone Ness Rd, Grays RM20 109 FV79
Stonenest St, N4 65 DM60
Stone Pk Av, Beck. BR3 143 EA98
Stone Pl, Wor.Pk. KT4 139 CU103
Stone Pl Rd, Green. DA9 129 FS85
Stone Rd, Brom. BR2 144 EF99
Stones All, Wat. WD18 23 BV42
Stones Cross Rd, Swan. BR8 147 FC99
Stones End St, SE1 201 H5
Stones Rd, Epsom KT17 156 CS112
Stone St, Croy. CR0 159 DN106
Gravesend DA11 131 GH86
Stoneswood Rd, Oxt. RH8 188 EH130
Stonewall, E6 87 EN71
Stonewood, Dart. (Bean) DA2 129 FW90
Stonewood Rd, Erith DA8 107 FE78
Stoney All, SE18 105 EN82
Stoneyard La, E14 204 B1
Stoney Br Rd, Wal.Abb. EN9 16 EG34
Stoney Cft, Couls. CR5 175 DJ122
Stoneycroft Cl, SE12 124 EF87
Stoneycroft Rd, Wdf.Grn. IG8 48 EL51
Stoneydeep, Tedd. TW11
off Twickenham Rd 117 CG91
Stoneydown, E17 67 DY56
Stoneydown Av, E17 67 DY56
Stoneyfield Rd, Couls. CR5 175 DM117
Stoneyfields Gdns, Edg. HA8 42 CQ49
Stoneyfields La, Edg. HA8 42 CQ50
Stoneylands Ct, Egh. TW20 113 AZ92
Stoneylands Rd, Egh. TW20 113 AZ92
Stoney La, E1 197 N8
SE19 *off Church Rd* 122 DT93
Hemel Hempstead (Bov.) HP3 5 BB27
Kings Langley (Chipper.) WD4 5 BE30
Stoney St, SE1 201 K2
Stonhouse St, SW4 101 DK83
Stonny Cft, Ashtd. KT21 172 CM117
Stonor Rd, W14 99 CZ77
Stonycroft Cl, Enf. EN3
off Brimsdown Av 31 DY40
Stony La, Amer. HP6 20 AY38
Stony Path, Loug. IG10 33 EM40
Stonyshotts, Wal.Abb. EN9 16 EE34
Stoop Ct, W.Byf. KT14 152 BH112
Stopes St, SE15 102 DT80
Stopford Rd, E13 86 EG67
SE17 101 DP78
Store Rd, E16 105 EN75
Storers Quay, E14 204 F9
Store St, E15 67 ED64
WC1 195 M7
Storey Rd, E17 67 DZ56
N6 64 DF58
Storey's Gate, SW1 199 N5
Storey St, E16 87 EN74
Stories Ms, SE5 102 DS82
Stories Rd, SE5 102 DS83
Stork Rd, E7 86 EF65
Storksmead Rd, Edg. HA8 42 CS52
Storks Rd, SE16 202 C7
Stormont Rd, N6 64 DF59
SW11 100 DG83
Stormont Way, Chess. KT9 155 CJ106
Stormount Dr, Hayes UB3 95 BQ75
Stornaway Rd, Slou. SL3 93 BC77
Stornaway Strand, Grav. DA12 131 GM91
Storr Gdns, Brwd. (Hutt.) CM13 55 GD43
Storrington Rd, Croy. CR0 142 DT102
Story St, N1
off Carnoustie Dr 83 DM66
Stothard Pl, EC2
off Bishopsgate 84 DS71
Stothard St, E1
off Colebert Av 84 DW70
Stott Cl, SW18 120 DD86
Stoughton Av, Sutt. SM3 157 CX106
Stoughton Cl, SE11 200 C9
SW15 *off Bessborough Rd* 119 CU88
Stour Av, Sthl. UB2 96 CA76
Stourcliffe St, W1 194 D9
Stour Cl, Kes. BR2 162 EJ105
Stourhead Cl, SW19
off Castlecombe Dr 119 CX87
Stourhead Gdns, SW20 139 CU97
Stour Rd, E3 85 EA66
Dagenham RM10 70 FA61
Dartford DA1 107 FG83
Grays RM16 111 GG78
Stourton Av, Felt. TW13 116 BZ91
Stour Way, Upmin. RM14 73 FS58
Stowage, SE8 103 EA79
Stow Cres, E17 47 DY52
Stowe Ct, Dart. DA2 128 FQ87
Stowe Cres, Ruis. HA4 59 BP58
Stowe Gdns, N9 46 DT46
Stowell Av, Croy. (New Adgtn) CR0 161 ED110
Stowe Pl, N15 66 DS55
Stowe Rd, W12 99 CV75
Orpington BR6 164 EV105
Stowting Rd, Orp. BR6 163 ES105
Stox Mead, Har. HA3 41 CD53
Stracey Rd, E7 68 EG63
NW10 80 CR67
Strachan Pl, SW19
off Woodhayes Rd 119 CW93
Stradbroke Dr, Chig. IG7 49 EN51
Stradbroke Gro, Buck.H. IG9 48 EK46
Ilford IG5 68 EL55
Stradbroke Pk, Chig. IG7 49 EP51
Stradbroke Rd, N5 66 DQ63
Stradbrook Cl, Har. HA2
off Stiven Cres 60 BZ62
Stradella Rd, SE24 122 DQ86
Strafford Av, Ilf. IG5 49 EN54
Strafford Cl, Pot.B. EN6
off Strafford Gate 12 DA32
Strafford Gate, Pot.B. EN6 12 DA32
Strafford Rd, W3 98 CQ75
Barnet EN5 27 CY41
Hounslow TW3 96 BZ83
Twickenham TW1 117 CG87
Strafford St, E14 203 P4
Strahan Rd, E3 85 DY69
Straight, The, Sthl. UB1 96 BX75
Straight Rd, Rom. RM3 52 FJ52
Windsor (Old Wind.) SL4 112 AU85
Straightsmouth, SE10 103 EC80
Strait Rd, E6 86 EL73
Straker's Rd, SE22 102 DV84
STRAND, WC2 195 P10
Strand, WC2 199 P1
Strand Cl, Epsom KT18 172 CR119
Strand Ct, SE18
off Strandfield Cl 105 ES78
Strand Dr, Rich. TW9
off Bessant Dr 98 CP80
Strandfield Cl, SE18 105 ES78
Strand La, WC2 196 C10
Strand on the Grn, W4 98 CN79
Strand Pl, N18 46 DR49
Strand Sch App, W4
off Thames Rd 98 CN79
Strangeways, Wat. WD17 23 BS36
Strangways Ter, W14
off Melbury Rd 99 CZ76
Stranraer Gdns, Slou. SL1 74 AS74
Stranraer Rd, Houns. (Hthrw Air.) TW6 114 BL86
Stranraer Way, N1 83 DL66
Strasburg Rd, SW11 101 DH81
Stratfield Pk Cl, N21 45 DP45
Stratfield Rd, Borwd. WD6 26 CN41
Slough SL1 92 AU75
STRATFORD, E15 85 EC65
⇌ Stratford 85 EC65
⊖ Stratford 85 EC66
DLR Stratford 85 EC66
Stratford Av, W8
off Stratford Rd 100 DA76
Uxbridge UB10 76 BM68
Stratford Cen, The, E15 85 ED66
Stratford Cl, Bark. IG11 88 EU66
Dagenham RM10 89 FC66
Stratford Ct, N.Mal. KT3
off Kingston Rd 138 CR98
Stratford Gro, SW15 99 CX84
Stratford Ho Av, Brom. BR1 144 EL97
Stratford Pl, W1 195 H9
Stratford Rd, E13 86 EF67
NW4 63 CX56
W8 100 DA76
Hayes UB4 77 BV70
Hounslow (Hthrw Air.) TW6 115 BP86
Southall UB2 96 BY77
Thornton Heath CR7 141 DN98
Watford WD17 23 BU40
Stratford Vil, NW1 83 DJ66
Stratford Way, St.Alb. (Brick.Wd) AL2 8 BZ29
Watford WD17 23 BT40
Strathan Cl, SW18 119 CY86
Strathaven Rd, SE12 124 EH86
Strathblaine Rd, SW11 100 DD84
Strathbrook Rd, SW16 121 DM94
Strathcona Rd, Wem. HA9 61 CK61
Strathdale, SW16 121 DM92
Strathdon Dr, SW17 120 DD90
Strathearn Av, Hayes UB3 95 BT80
Twickenham TW2 116 CB88
Strathearn Pl, W2 194 A10
Strathearn Rd, SW19 120 DA92
Sutton SM1 158 DA106
Stratheden Par, SE3
off Stratheden Rd 104 EG80
Stratheden Rd, SE3 104 EG81
Strathfield Gdns, Bark. IG11 87 ER65
Strathleven Rd, SW2 121 DL85
Strathmore Cl, Cat. CR3 176 DS121
Strathmore Gdns, N3 44 DB53
W8 *off Palace Gdns Ter* 82 DA74
Edgware HA8 42 CP54
Hornchurch RM12 71 FF60
Strathmore Rd, SW19 120 DA90
Croydon CR0 142 DQ101
Teddington TW11 117 CE91
Strathnairn St, SE1 202 C9
Strathray Gdns, NW3 82 DE65
Strath Ter, SW11 100 DE84
Strathville Rd, SW18 120 DB89
Strathyre Av, SW16 141 DN97
Stratton Av, Enf. EN2 30 DR37
Wallington SM6 159 DK109
Stratton Chase Dr, Ch.St.G. HP8 36 AU47
Stratton Cl, SW19 140 DA96
Bexleyheath DA7 106 EY83
Edgware HA8 42 CM51
Hounslow TW3 96 BZ81
Walton-on-Thames KT12
off St. Johns Dr 136 BW102
Strattondale St, E14 204 D6
Stratton Dr, Bark. IG11 69 ET64
Stratton Gdns, Sthl. UB1 78 BZ72
Stratton Rd, SW19 140 DA96
Bexleyheath DA7 106 EY83
Romford RM3 52 FN50
Sunbury-on-Thames TW16 135 BT96
Stratton St, W1 199 J2
Stratton Ter, West. TN16
off High St 189 EQ127
Stratton Wk, Rom. RM3 52 FN50
Strauss Rd, W4 98 CR75
Strawberry Flds, Swan. BR8 147 FE95
STRAWBERRY HILL, Twick. TW1 117 CE90
⇌ Strawberry Hill 117 CE90
Strawberry Hill, Twick. TW1 117 CF90
Strawberry Hill Cl, Twick. TW1 117 CF90
Strawberry Hill Rd, Twick. TW1 117 CF90
Strawberry La, Cars. SM5 140 DF104
Strawberry Vale, N2 44 DD53
Twickenham TW1 117 CG90
Straw Cl, Cat. CR3 176 DQ123
Strayfield Rd, Enf. EN2 29 DP37
Streakes Fld Rd, NW2 63 CU61
Stream Cl, W.Byf. (Byfleet) KT14 152 BK112
Streamdale, SE2 106 EU79
Stream La, Edg. HA8 42 CP50
Streamline Ms, SE22 122 DU88
Streamside Cl, N9 46 DT46
Bromley BR2 144 EG98
Streamway, Belv. DA17 106 FA79
Streatfield Av, E6 87 EM67
Streatfield Rd, Har. HA3 61 CK55
STREATHAM, SW16 121 DL91
⇌ Streatham 121 DL92
Streatham Cl, SW16 121 DL89
⇌ Streatham Common 121 DK94
Streatham Common N, SW16 121 DL92
Streatham Common S, SW16 121 DL93
Streatham Ct, SW16 121 DL90
Streatham High Rd, SW16 121 DL92
STREATHAM HILL, SW2 121 DM87
⇌ Streatham Hill 121 DL89
Streatham Hill, SW2 121 DL89
STREATHAM PARK, SW16 121 DJ91
Streatham Pl, SW2 121 DL87
Streatham Rd, SW16 140 DG95
Mitcham CR4 140 DG95
Streatham St, WC1 195 N8
STREATHAM VALE, SW16 121 DK94
Streatham Vale, SW16 121 DJ94
Streathbourne Rd, SW17 120 DG89
Streatley Pl, NW3
off New End Sq 64 DC63
Streatley Rd, NW6 81 CZ66
Street, The, Ashtd. KT21 172 CL119
Dartford (Hort.Kir.) DA4 148 FP98
Kings Langley (Chipper.) WD4 6 BG31
Leatherhead (Fetch.) KT22 171 CD122
Streeters La, Wall. SM6 141 DK104
Streetfield Ms, SE3 104 EG83
Streimer Rd, E15 85 EC68
Strelley Way, W3 80 CS73
Stretton Mans, SE8
off Glaisher St 103 EA79
Stretton Pl, Amer. HP6 20 AT38
Stretton Rd, Croy. CR0 142 DS101
Richmond TW10 117 CJ89
Stretton Way, Borwd. WD6 26 CL38
Strickland Av, Dart. DA1 108 FL83
Strickland Row, SW18 120 DD87
Strickland St, SE8 103 EA82
Strickland Way, Orp. BR6 163 ET105
Stride Rd, E13 86 EF68
Strides Ct, Cher. KT16
off Brox Rd 151 BC107
Strimon Cl, N9 46 DW47
Stringhams Copse, Wok. (Ripley) GU23 167 BF124
Stripling Way, Wat. WD18 23 BU44
Strode Cl, N10
off Pembroke Rd 44 DG52
Strode Rd, E7 68 EG63
N17 46 DS54
NW10 81 CU65
SW6 99 CX80
Strodes Coll La, Egh. TW20 113 AZ92
Strodes Cres, Stai. TW18 114 BJ92
Strode St, Egh. TW20 113 BA91
Strone Rd, E7 86 EJ65
E12 86 EK65
Strone Way, Hayes UB4 78 BY70
Strongbow Cres, SE9 125 EM85
Strongbow Rd, SE9 125 EM85
Strongbridge Cl, Har. HA2 60 CA60
Stronsa Rd, W12 99 CT75
Strood Av, Rom. RM7 71 FD60
Stroud Cres, SW15 119 CU90
STROUDE, Vir.W. GU25 133 AZ96
Stroude Rd, Egh. TW20 113 BA93
Virginia Water GU25 132 AY98
Stroudes Cl, Wor.Pk. KT4 138 CS101
Stroud Fld, Nthlt. UB5 78 BY65
Stroud Gate, Har. HA2 60 CB63
STROUD GREEN, N4 65 DM58
Stroud Grn Gdns, Croy. CR0 142 DW101
Stroud Grn Rd, N4 65 DM60
Stroud Grn Way, Croy. CR0 142 DV101
Stroudley Wk, E3 85 EB69
Stroud Rd, SE25 142 DU100
SW19 120 DA90
Strouds Cl, Rom. (Chad.Hth) RM6 70 EV57
Stroudwater Pk, Wey. KT13 153 BP107
Stroud Way, Ashf. TW15
off Courtfield Rd 115 BP93
Strouts Pl, E2 197 P2
Struan Gdns, Wok. GU21 166 AY115
Strutton Grd, SW1 199 M6
Struttons Av, Grav. (Nthflt) DA11 131 GF89
Strype St, E1 197 P7
Stuart Av, NW9 63 CU59
W5 80 CM74
Bromley BR2 144 EG102
Harrow HA2 60 BZ62
Walton-on-Thames KT12 135 BV102
Stuart Cl, Brwd. (Pilg.Hat.) CM15 54 FV43
Swanley BR8 127 FF94
Uxbridge UB10 76 BN65
Stuart Ct, Borwd. (Elstree) WD6
off High St 25 CK44
Stuart Cres, N22 45 DM53
Croydon CR0 143 DZ104
Hayes UB3 77 BQ72
Stuart Evans Cl, Well. DA16 106 EW83
Stuart Gro, Tedd. TW11 117 CE92
Stuart Mantle Way, Erith DA8 107 FD80
Stuart Pl, Mitch. CR4 140 DF95
Stuart Rd, NW6 82 DA69
SE15 102 DW84
SW19 120 DA90
W3 80 CQ74
Barking IG11 87 ET66
Barnet EN4 44 DE45
Gravesend DA11 131 GG86
Grays RM17 110 GB78
Harrow HA3 41 CF54
Richmond TW10 117 CH89
Thornton Heath CR7 142 DQ98
Warlingham CR6 176 DV120
Welling DA16 106 EV81
Stuart Twr, W9 82 DC69
Stuart Way, Stai. TW18 114 BH93
Virginia Water GU25 132 AU97
Waltham Cross (Chsht) EN7 14 DV31
Stubbers La, Upmin. RM14 91 FR65
Stubbins Hall La, Wal.Abb. EN9 15 EB28
Stubbs Cl, NW9 62 CQ57
Stubbs Dr, SE16 202 D10
Stubbs End Cl, Amer. HP6 20 AS37
Stubbs Hill, Sev. (Knock.) TN14 164 EW113
Stubbs La, Tad. (Lwr Kgswd) KT20 183 CZ128
Stubbs Ms, Dag. RM8
off Marlborough Rd 70 EV63
Stubbs Pt, E13 86 EH70

★ Place of interest ⇌ Railway station ⊖ London Underground station DLR Docklands Light Railway station Tra Tramlink station H Hospital Riv Pedestrian ferry landing stage

Stubbs Way, SW19
off Brangwyn Cres . . . 140 DD95
Stubbs Wd, Amer. HP6 . . . 20 AS36
Stucley Pl, NW1
off Hawley Cres . . . 83 DH66
Stucley Rd, Houns. TW5 . . . 96 CC80
Studdridge St, SW6 . . . 100 DA82
Studd St, N1 . . . 83 DP67
Stud Grn, Wat. WD25 . . . 7 BV32
Studholme Ct, NW3 . . . 64 DA63
Studholme St, SE15 . . . 102 DV80
Studio Dr, Iver SL0
off Pinewood Rd . . . 75 BB66
Studio Pl, SW1 . . . 198 E5
Studios, The, Bushey WD23 . . . 24 CA44
Studios Rd, Shep. TW17 . . . 134 BM97
Studio Way, Borwd. WD6 . . . 26 CQ40
Studland, SE17 . . . 201 K10
Studland Cl, Sid. DA15 . . . 125 ET90
Studland Rd, SE26 . . . 123 DX92
W7 . . . 79 CD72
Kingston upon Thames KT2 . 118 CL93
West Byfleet
(Byfleet) KT14 . . . 152 BM113
Studland St, W6 . . . 99 CV77
Studley Av, E4 . . . 47 ED52
Studley Cl, E5 . . . 67 DY64
Studley Ct, Sid. DA14 . . . 126 EV92
Studley Dr, Ilf. IG4 . . . 68 EK58
Studley Est, SW4 . . . 101 DL81
Studley Gra Rd, W7 . . . 97 CE75
Studley Rd, E7 . . . 86 EH65
SW4 . . . 101 DL81
Dagenham RM9 . . . 88 EX66
Stukeley Rd, E7 . . . 86 EH66
Stukeley St, WC2 . . . 196 A8
Stump Rd, Epp. CM16 . . . 18 EW27
Stumps Hill La, Beck. BR3 . . . 123 EA93
Stumps La, Whyt. CR3 . . . 176 DS117
Sturdy Rd, SE15 . . . 102 DV82
Sturge Av, E17 . . . 47 EB54
Sturgeon Rd, SE17 . . . 102 DQ78
Sturges Fld, Chis. BR7 . . . 125 ER93
Sturgess Av, NW4 . . . 63 CV59
Sturge St, SE1 . . . 201 H4
Sturlas Way, Wal.Cr. EN8 . . . 15 DX33
Sturmer Way, N7 . . . 65 DM64
Sturminster Cl, Hayes UB4 . . . 78 BW72
Sturrock Cl, N15 . . . 66 DR56
Sturry St, E14 . . . 85 EB72
Sturts La, Tad. KT20 . . . 183 CT127
Sturt St, N1 . . . 197 J1
Stutfield St, E1 . . . 84 DU72
Stychens Cl, Red.
(Bletch.) RH1 . . . 186 DQ133
Stychens La, Red.
(Bletch.) RH1 . . . 186 DQ132
Stylecroft Rd, Ch.St.G. HP8 . . . 36 AX47
Styles Gdns, SW9 . . . 101 DP83
Styles Way, Beck. BR3 . . . 143 EC98
Styventon Pl, Cher. KT16 . . . 133 BF101
Subrosa Dr, Red. RH1 . . . 185 DH130
Succombs Hill, Warl. CR6 . . . 176 DV120
Whyteleafe CR3 . . . 176 DV120
Succombs Pl, Warl. CR6 . . . 176 DV120
Sudbourne Rd, SW2 . . . 121 DL85
Sudbrooke Rd, SW12 . . . 120 DF86
Sudbrook Gdns, Rich. TW10 . . . 117 CK90
Sudbrook La, Rich. TW10 . . . 118 CL88
SUDBURY, Wem. HA0 . . . 61 CG64
Sudbury, E6
off Newark Knok . . . 87 EN72
⇌ Sudbury & Harrow Road . . . 61 CH64
Sudbury Av, Wem. HA0 . . . 61 CK62
Sudbury Ct Dr, Har. HA1 . . . 61 CF62
Sudbury Ct Rd, Har. HA1 . . . 61 CF62
Sudbury Cres, Brom. BR1 . . . 124 EG93
Wembley HA0 . . . 61 CH64
Sudbury Cft, Wem. HA0 . . . 61 CF63
Sudbury Gdns, Croy. CR0
off Langton Way . . . 160 DS105
Sudbury Hts Av, Grnf. UB6 . . . 61 CF64
⊖ Sudbury Hill . . . 61 CE63
Sudbury Hill, Har. HA1 . . . 61 CE61
Sudbury Hill Cl, Wem. HA0 . . . 61 CF63
⇌ Sudbury Hill Harrow . . . 61 CE63
Sudbury Ho, SW18
off Wandsworth High St . . . 120 DB85
Sudbury Rd, Bark. IG11 . . . 69 ET64
⊖ Sudbury Town . . . 79 CH65
Sudeley St, N1 . . . 196 G1
Sudicamps Ct, Wal.Abb.
EN9 . . . 16 EG33
Sudlow Rd, SW18 . . . 100 DA84
Sudrey St, SE1 . . . 201 H5
Suez Av, Grnf. UB6 . . . 79 CF68
Suez Rd, Enf. EN3 . . . 31 DY42
Suffield Cl, S.Croy. CR2 . . . 161 DX112
Suffield Rd, E4 . . . 47 EB48
N15 . . . 66 DT57
SE20 . . . 142 DW96
Suffolk Cl, Borwd. WD6
off Clydesdale Cl . . . 26 CR43
St. Albans (Lon.Col.) AL2 . . . 9 CJ25
Suffolk Ct, E10 . . . 67 EA59
Ilford IG3 . . . 69 ES58
Suffolk La, EC4 . . . 197 K10
Suffolk Pk Rd, E17 . . . 67 DY56
Suffolk Pl, SW1 . . . 199 N2
Suffolk Rd, E13 . . . 86 EF69
N15 . . . 66 DR58
NW10 . . . 80 CS66
SE25 . . . 142 DT98
SW13 . . . 99 CT80
Barking IG11 . . . 87 ER66
Dagenham RM10 . . . 71 FC64
Dartford DA1 . . . 128 FL86
Enfield EN3 . . . 30 DV43
Gravesend DA12 . . . 131 GK86
Harrow HA2 . . . 60 BZ58
Ilford IG3 . . . 69 ES58
Potters Bar EN6 . . . 11 CY32
Sidcup DA14 . . . 126 EW93
Worcester Park KT4 . . . 139 CT103
Suffolk St, E7 . . . 68 EG64
SW1 . . . 199 N2
Suffolk Way, Horn. RM11 . . . 72 FN56
Sevenoaks TN13 . . . 191 FJ125
Sugar Bakers Ct, EC3
off Creechurch La . . . 84 DS72
Sugar Ho La, E15 . . . 85 EC68
Sugar Loaf Wk, E2
off Victoria Pk Sq . . . 84 DW69
Sugar Quay Wk, EC3 . . . 201 N1
Sugden Rd, SW11 . . . 100 DG83
Thames Ditton KT7 . . . 137 CH102
Sugden Way, Bark. IG11 . . . 87 ET68
Sulgrave Gdns, W6
off Sulgrave Rd . . . 99 CW75
Sulgrave Rd, W6 . . . 99 CW75
Sulina Rd, SW2 . . . 121 DL87
Sulivan Ct, SW6 . . . 100 DA83
Sulivan Rd, SW6 . . . 100 DA83
Sullivan Av, E16 . . . 86 EK71
Sullivan Cl, SW11 . . . 100 DE83
Dartford DA1 . . . 127 FH86
Hayes UB4 . . . 78 BW71
West Molesey KT8
off Victoria Av . . . 136 CA97
Sullivan Cres, Uxb.
(Hare.) UB9 . . . 38 BK54
Sullivan Rd, SE11 . . . 200 E8
Tilbury RM18 . . . 111 GG81
Sullivans Reach, Walt. KT12 . . . 135 BT101
Sullivan Way, Borwd.
(Elstree) WD6 . . . 25 CJ44
Sultan Rd, E11 . . . 68 EH56
Sultan St, SE5 . . . 102 DQ80
Beckenham BR3 . . . 143 DX96
Sultan Ter, N22
off Vincent Rd . . . 45 DN54
Sumatra Rd, NW6 . . . 64 DA64
Sumburgh Rd, SW12 . . . 120 DG86
Sumburgh Way, Slou. SL1 . . . 74 AS71
Summer Av, E.Mol. KT8 . . . 137 CE99
Summercourt Rd, E1 . . . 84 DW72
Summerene Cl, SW16 . . . 121 DJ94
Summerfield, Ashtd. KT21 . . . 171 CK119
Summerfield Av, NW6 . . . 81 CY68
Summerfield Cl, Add. KT15
off Spinney Hill . . . 151 BF106
St. Albans (Lon.Col.) AL2 . . . 9 CJ26
Summerfield La, Surb. KT6 . . . 137 CK103
Summerfield Pl, Cher.
(Ott.) KT16
off Crawshaw Rd . . . 151 BD107
Summerfield Rd, W5 . . . 79 CH70
Loughton IG10 . . . 32 EK44
Watford WD25 . . . 23 BU35
Summerfields Av, N12 . . . 44 DE51
Summerfield St, SE12 . . . 124 EF87
Summer Gdns, E.Mol. KT8 . . . 137 CE99
Summer Gro, Borwd.
(Elstree) WD6 . . . 25 CK44
Summerhayes Cl,
Wok. GU21 . . . 150 AY114
Summerhays, Cob. KT11 . . . 154 BX113
Summer Hill, Borwd.
(Elstree) WD6 . . . 26 CN43
Chislehurst BR7 . . . 145 EN96
Summerhill Cl, Orp. BR6 . . . 145 ES104
Summerhill Gro, Enf. EN1 . . . 30 DS44
Summerhill Rd, N15 . . . 66 DR56
Dartford DA1 . . . 128 FK87
Summer Hill Vil, Chis. BR7 . . . 145 EN95
Summerhill Way, Mitch. CR4 . . . 140 DG95
Summerhouse Av, Houns.
TW5 . . . 96 BY81
Summerhouse Dr, Bex. DA5 . . . 127 FD91
Dartford DA2 . . . 127 FD91
Summerhouse La, Uxb.
(Hare.) UB9 . . . 38 BG52
Watford (Ald.) WD25 . . . 24 CC40
West Drayton UB7 . . . 94 BK79
Summerhouse Rd, N16 . . . 66 DS61
Summerhouse Way, Abb.L.
WD5 . . . 7 BT30
Summerland Gdns, N10 . . . 65 DH55
Summerlands Av, W3 . . . 80 CQ73
Summerlay Cl, Tad. KT20 . . . 173 CY120
Summerlee Av, N2 . . . 64 DF56
Summerlee Gdns, N2 . . . 64 DF56
Summerley St, SW18 . . . 120 DB89
Summerly Av, Reig. RH2
off Burnham Dr . . . 184 DA133
Summer Rd, E.Mol. KT8 . . . 137 CE99
Thames Ditton KT7 . . . 137 CF99
Summersby Rd, N6 . . . 65 DH58
Summers Cl, Sutt. SM2
off Overton Rd . . . 158 DA108
Wembley HA9 . . . 62 CP60
Weybridge KT13 . . . 152 BN111
Summerskille Cl, N9
off Plevna Rd . . . 46 DV47
Summers La, N12 . . . 44 DD52
Summers Row, N12 . . . 44 DE51
SUMMERSTOWN, SW17 . . . 120 DB90
Summerstown, SW17 . . . 120 DC90
Summer St, EC1 . . . 196 D5
Summerswood Cl, Ken. CR8
off Longwood Rd . . . 176 DR116
Summerswood La, Borwd.
WD6 . . . 10 CS34
Summerton Way, SE28 . . . 88 EX72
Summer Trees, Sun. TW16
off The Avenue . . . 135 BV95
Summerville Gdns, Sutt.
SM1 . . . 157 CZ107
Summerwood Rd, Islw.
TW7 . . . 117 CF85
Summit, The, Loug. IG10 . . . 33 EM39
Summit Av, NW9 . . . 62 CR57
Summit Cl, N14 . . . 45 DJ47
NW9 . . . 62 CR56
Edgware HA8 . . . 42 CN52
Summit Ct, NW2 . . . 63 CY64
Summit Dr, Wdf.Grn. IG8 . . . 48 EK54
Summit Est, N16 . . . 66 DU59
Summit Pl, Wey. KT13
off Caenshill Rd . . . 152 BN108
Summit Rd, E17 . . . 67 EB56
Northolt UB5 . . . 78 CA66
Potters Bar EN6 . . . 11 CY30
Summit Way, N14 . . . 45 DH47
SE19 . . . 122 DS94
Sumner Av, SE15
off Peckham Rd . . . 102 DT81
Sumner Cl, Lthd.
(Fetch.) KT22 . . . 171 CD124
Orpington BR6 . . . 163 EQ105
Sumner Est, SE15 . . . 102 DT80
Sumner Gdns, Croy. CR0 . . . 141 DN102
Sumner Pl, SW7 . . . 198 A9
Addlestone KT15 . . . 152 BG106
Sumner Pl Ms, SW7 . . . 198 A9
Sumner Rd, SE15 . . . 102 DT80
Croydon CR0 . . . 141 DN102
Harrow HA1 . . . 60 CC59
Sumner Rd S, Croy. CR0 . . . 141 DN102
Sumner St, SE1 . . . 200 G2
Sumpter Cl, NW3 . . . 82 DC65
Sun All, Rich. TW9
off Kew Rd . . . 98 CL84
Sunbeam Cres, W10 . . . 81 CW70
Sunbeam Rd, NW10 . . . 80 CQ70
SUNBURY, Sun. TW16 . . . 153 BV107
⇌ Sunbury . . . 135 BT95
Sunbury Av, NW7 . . . 42 CR50
SW14 . . . 98 CR84
Sunbury Cl, Walt. KT12
off Sunbury La . . . 135 BU100
Sunbury Ct, Sun. TW16 . . . 136 BX96
Sunbury Ct Island, Sun.
TW16 . . . 136 BX97
Sunbury Ct Ms, Sun. TW16
off Lower Hampton Rd . . . 136 BX96
Sunbury Ct Rd, Sun. TW16 . . . 136 BW96
Sunbury Cres, Felt. TW13
off Ryland Cl . . . 115 BT91
Sunbury Cross Cen, Sun.
TW16 . . . 115 BT94
Sunbury Gdns, NW7 . . . 42 CR50
Sunbury La, SW11 . . . 100 DD81
Walton-on-Thames KT12 . . . 135 BU100
Sunbury Lock Ait, Walt.
KT12 . . . 135 BV98
Sunbury Rd, Felt. TW13 . . . 115 BT90
Sutton SM3 . . . 139 CX104
Sunbury St, SE18 . . . 105 EM76
Sunbury Way, Felt. TW13 . . . 116 BW92
Sun Ct, EC3 . . . 197 L9
Erith DA8 . . . 107 FF82
Suncroft Pl, SE26 . . . 122 DW90
Sundale Av, S.Croy. CR2 . . . 160 DW110
Sunderland Ct, SE22 . . . 122 DU87
Sunderland Gro, Wat. WD25
off Ashfields . . . 7 BT34
Sunderland Mt, SE23
off Sunderland Rd . . . 123 DX89
Sunderland Rd, SE23 . . . 123 DX88
W5 . . . 97 CK76
Sunderland Ter, W2 . . . 82 DB72
Sunderland Way, E12 . . . 68 EK61
Sundew Av, W12 . . . 81 CU73
Sundew Ct, Grays RM17
off Salix Rd . . . 110 GD79
Sundial Av, SE25 . . . 142 DT97
Sundon Cres, Vir.W. GU25 . . . 132 AV99
Sundorne Rd, SE7 . . . 104 EH78
Sundown Av, S.Croy. CR2 . . . 160 DT111
Sundown Rd, Ashf. TW15 . . . 115 BQ92
Sundra Wk, E1
off Beaumont Gro . . . 85 DX70
SUNDRIDGE, Brom. BR1 . . . 124 EJ93
SUNDRIDGE, Sev. TN14 . . . 180 EZ124
Sundridge Av, Brom. BR1 . . . 144 EK95
Chislehurst BR7 . . . 124 EK94
Welling DA16 . . . 105 ER82
Sundridge Cl, Dart. DA1 . . . 128 FN86
Sundridge Ho, Brom. BR1
off Burnt Ash La . . . 124 EH92
Sundridge La, Sev.
(Knock.) TN14 . . . 180 EV117
⇌ Sundridge Park . . . 124 EH94
Sundridge Pl, Croy. CR0
off Inglis Rd . . . 142 DU102
Sundridge Rd, Croy. CR0 . . . 142 DT101
Sevenoaks
(Dunt.Grn) TN14 . . . 180 FA120
Woking GU22 . . . 167 BA119
Sunfields Pl, SE3 . . . 104 EH80
Sunflower Way, Rom. RM3 . . . 52 FK53
Sun Hill, Long.
(Fawk.Grn) DA3 . . . 149 FU104
Woking GU22 . . . 166 AU121
Sunken Rd, Croy. CR0
off Coombe La . . . 160 DW106
Sunkist Way, Wall. SM6 . . . 159 DL109
Sunland Av, Bexh. DA6 . . . 106 EY84
Sun La, SE3 . . . 104 EH80
Gravesend DA12 . . . 131 GJ89
Sunleigh Rd, Wem. HA0 . . . 80 CL67
Sunley Gdns, Grnf. UB6 . . . 79 CG67
Sunlight Cl, SW19 . . . 120 DC93
Sunlight Sq, E2 . . . 84 DV69
Sunmead Cl, Lthd.
(Fetch.) KT22 . . . 171 CF122
Sunmead Rd, Sun. TW16 . . . 135 BU97
Sunna Gdns, Sun. TW16 . . . 135 BV96
Sunningdale, N14
off Wilmer Way . . . 45 DK50
Sunningdale Av, W3 . . . 80 CS73
Barking IG11 . . . 87 ER67
Feltham TW13 . . . 116 BY89
Rainham RM13 . . . 89 FH70
Ruislip HA4 . . . 60 BW60
Sunningdale Cl, E6 . . . 87 EM69
SE16 off Ryder Dr . . . 102 DV78
SE28 . . . 88 EY72
Stanmore HA7 . . . 41 CG52
Surbiton KT6
off Culsac Rd . . . 138 CL103
Sunningdale Gdns, NW9 . . . 62 CQ57
W8 off Lexham Ms . . . 100 DA76
Sunningdale Rd, Brom. BR1 . . . 144 EL98
Rainham RM13 . . . 89 FG66
Sutton SM1 . . . 157 CZ105
Sunningfields Cres, NW4 . . . 43 CV54
Sunningfields Rd, NW4 . . . 43 CV54
Sunning Hill, Grav.
(Nthflt) DA11 . . . 130 GE89
Sunninghill Rd, SE13 . . . 103 EB82
Sunnings La, Upmin.
RM14 . . . 90 FQ65
Sunningvale Av, West.
(Bigg.H.) TN16 . . . 178 EJ115
Sunningvale Cl, West.
(Bigg.H.) TN16 . . . 178 EK116
Sunny Bk, SE25 . . . 142 DU97
Sunnybank, Epsom KT18 . . . 172 CQ116
Sunny Bk, Warl. CR6 . . . 177 DY117
Sunnybank Rd, Pot.B. EN6 . . . 12 DA33
Sunnybank Vil, Red. RH1 . . . 186 DT132
Sunny Cres, NW10 . . . 80 CQ66
Sunnycroft Gdns, Upmin.
RM14 . . . 73 FT59
Sunnycroft Rd, SE25 . . . 142 DU97
Hounslow TW3 . . . 96 CB82
Southall UB1 . . . 78 CA71
Sunnydale, Orp. BR6 . . . 145 EN103
Sunnydale Gdns, NW7 . . . 42 CR51
Sunnydale Rd, SE12 . . . 124 EH85
Sunnydell, St.Alb. AL2 . . . 8 CB26
Sunnydene Av, E4 . . . 47 ED50
Ruislip HA4 . . . 59 BU61
Sunnydene Cl, Rom. RM3 . . . 52 FM52
Sunnydene Gdns, Wem. HA0 . . . 79 CJ65
Sunnydene Rd, Pur. CR8 . . . 159 DP113
Sunnydene St, SE26 . . . 123 DY91
Sunnyfield, NW7 . . . 43 CT49
Sunnyfield Rd, Chis. BR7 . . . 146 EU97
Sunny Gdns Par, NW4
off Great N Way . . . 43 CW54
Sunny Gdns Rd, NW4 . . . 43 CV54
Sunny Hill, NW4 . . . 63 CV55
Sunnyhill Cl, E5 . . . 67 DY63
Sunnyhill Rd, SW16 . . . 121 DL91
Rickmansworth
(Map.Cr.) WD3 . . . 37 BD51
Sunnyhurst Cl, Sutt. SM1 . . . 140 DA104
Sunnymead Av, Mitch. CR4 . . . 141 DJ97
Sunnymead Rd, NW9 . . . 62 CR59
SW15 . . . 119 CV85
SUNNYMEADS, Stai. TW19 . . . 92 AY84
⇌ Sunnymeads . . . 92 AY83
Sunnymede, Chig. IG7 . . . 50 EV48
Sunnymede Av, Cars. SM5 . . . 158 DD111
Chesham HP5 . . . 4 AS28
Epsom KT19 . . . 156 CS109
Sunnymede Dr, Ilf. IG6 . . . 69 EP56
Sunny Ms, Rom. RM5
off Chase Cross Rd . . . 51 FC52
Sunny Nook Gdns, S.Croy. CR2
off Selsdon Rd . . . 160 DR107
Sunny Ri, Cat. CR3 . . . 176 DR124
Sunny Rd, The, Enf. EN3 . . . 31 DX39
Sunnyside, NW2 . . . 63 CZ62
SW19 . . . 119 CY93
Walton-on-Thames KT12 . . . 136 BW99
Sunnyside Cotts, Chesh. HP5 . . . 4 AU26
Sunnyside Dr, E4 . . . 47 EC45
Sunnyside Gdns, Upmin.
RM14 . . . 72 FQ61
Sunnyside Pas, SW19 . . . 119 CY93
Sunnyside Pl, SW19
off Sunnyside . . . 119 CY93
Sunnyside Rd, E10 . . . 67 EA60
N19 . . . 65 DK59
W5 . . . 79 CK74
Epping CM16 . . . 17 ET32
Ilford IG1 . . . 69 EQ62
Teddington TW11 . . . 117 CD91
Sunnyside Rd E, N9 . . . 46 DU48
Sunnyside Rd N, N9 . . . 46 DT48
Sunnyside Rd S, N9 . . . 46 DT48
Sunnyside Ter, NW9
off Edgware Rd . . . 62 CR55
Sunny Vw, NW9 . . . 62 CR57
Sunny Way, N12 . . . 44 DE52
Sun Pas, SE16 . . . 202 B6
Sunray Av, SE24 . . . 102 DR84
Brentwood (Hutt.) CM13 . . . 55 GE44
Bromley BR2 . . . 144 EL100
Surbiton KT5 . . . 138 CP103
West Drayton UB7 . . . 94 BK75
Sunrise Av, Horn. RM12 . . . 72 FJ62
Sunrise Cl, Felt. TW13
off Exeter Rd . . . 116 BZ90
Sun Rd, W14 . . . 99 CZ78
Swanscombe DA10 . . . 130 FZ86
Sunset Av, E4 . . . 47 EB46
Woodford Green IG8 . . . 48 EF49
Sunset Cl, Erith DA8 . . . 107 FH81
Sunset Ct, Wdf.Grn. IG8
off Navestock Cres . . . 48 EJ52
Sunset Dr, Rom.
(Hav.at.Bow.) RM4 . . . 51 FH50
Sunset Gdns, SE25 . . . 142 DT96
Sunset Ms, Rom. RM5
off Highfield Rd . . . 51 FC51
Sunset Rd, SE5 . . . 102 DQ84
SE28 . . . 106 EU75
Sunset Vw, Barn. EN5 . . . 27 CY40
Sunshine Way, Mitch. CR4 . . . 140 DF96
Sunstone Gro, Red. RH1 . . . 185 DL129
Sun St, EC2 . . . 197 M7
Waltham Abbey EN9 . . . 15 EC33
Sun St Pas, EC2 . . . 197 M7
Sun Wk, E1 . . . 202 B1
Sunwell Cl, SE15
off Cossall Wk . . . 102 DV81
Superior Dr, Orp. BR6 . . . 163 ET107
SURBITON . . . 138 CM101
⇌ Surbiton . . . 137 CK100
Surbiton Ct, Surb. KT6 . . . 137 CJ100
Surbiton Cres, Kings.T. KT1 . . . 138 CL98
H Surbiton Gen Hosp, Surb.
KT6 . . . 138 CL100
Surbiton Hall Cl, Kings.T.
KT1 . . . 138 CL98
Surbiton Hill Pk, Surb. KT5 . . . 138 CN99
Surbiton Hill Rd, Surb. KT6 . . . 138 CL98
Surbiton Par, Surb. KT6
off St. Mark's Hill . . . 138 CL100
Surbiton Rd, Kings.T. KT1 . . . 138 CL98
Surlingham Cl, SE28 . . . 88 EX73
Surma Cl, E1 . . . 84 DV70
Surman Cres, Brwd.
(Hutt.) CM13 . . . 55 GC45
Surmans Cl, Dag. RM9
off Goresbrook Rd . . . 88 EV67
Surrendale Pl, W9 . . . 82 DA70
Surrey Canal Rd, SE14 . . . 102 DW79
SE15 . . . 102 DW79
Surrey Cres, W4 . . . 98 CN78
★ Surrey Docks City Fm,
SE16 . . . 203 M5
Surrey Dr, Horn. RM11 . . . 72 FN56
Surrey Gdns, N4
off Finsbury Pk Av . . . 66 DQ58
Surrey Gdns, Leatherhead
(Eff.Junct.) KT24 . . . 169 BT123
Surrey Gro, SE17
off Surrey Sq . . . 102 DS78
Sutton SM1 . . . 140 DD104
Surrey Hills, Tad.
(Box H.) KT20 . . . 182 CP130
Surrey Hills Av, Tad.
(Box H.) KT20 . . . 182 CQ130
Surrey La, SW11 . . . 100 DE81
Surrey La Est, SW11 . . . 100 DE81
Surrey Lo, SE1 . . . 200 D7
Surrey Ms, SE27
off Hamilton Rd . . . 122 DS91
Surrey Mt, SE23 . . . 122 DV88
⊖ Surrey Quays . . . 203 H8
Surrey Quays Retail Cen,
SE16 . . . 203 H7
Surrey Quays Rd, SE16 . . . 202 G6
Surrey Rd, SE15 . . . 123 DX85
Barking IG11 . . . 87 ES67
Dagenham RM10 . . . 71 FB64
Harrow HA1 . . . 60 CC57
West Wickham BR4 . . . 143 EB102
Surrey Row, SE1 . . . 200 F4
Surrey Sq, SE17 . . . 201 M10
Surrey St, E13 . . . 86 EH69
WC2 . . . 196 C10
Croydon CR0 . . . 142 DQ104
Surrey Ter, SE17 . . . 201 N10
Surrey Twr, SE20 . . . 122 DW94
Surrey Twrs, Add. KT15
off Garfield Rd . . . 152 BJ106
Surrey Water Rd, SE16 . . . 203 J3
Surridge Cl, Rain. RM13 . . . 90 FJ69
Surridge Gdns, SE19
off Hancock Rd . . . 122 DR93
Surr St, N7 . . . 65 DL64
Sury Basin, Kings.T. KT2 . . . 138 CL95
Susan Cl, Rom. RM7 . . . 71 FC55
Susan Lawrence Ho, E12
off Walton Rd . . . 69 EN63
Susannah St, E14 . . . 85 EB72
Susan Rd, SE3 . . . 104 EH82
Susan Wd, Chis. BR7 . . . 145 EN95
Sussex Av, Islw. TW7 . . . 97 CE83
Romford RM3 . . . 52 FM52
Sussex Cl, N19
off Cornwallis Rd . . . 65 DL61
Chalfont St. Giles HP8 . . . 36 AV47
Ilford IG4 . . . 69 EM58
New Malden KT3 . . . 138 CS98
Slough SL1 . . . 92 AV75
Twickenham TW1
off Westmorland Cl . . . 117 CH86
Sussex Cres, Nthlt. UB5 . . . 78 CA65
Sussex Gdns, N4 . . . 66 DQ57
N6 off Great N Rd . . . 64 DF57
W2 . . . 82 DD72
Chessington KT9 . . . 155 CK107
Sussex Keep, Slou. SL1
off Sussex Cl . . . 92 AV75
Sussex Ms, SE6
off Ravensbourne Pk . . . 123 EA87
Sussex Ms E, W2 . . . 194 A9
Sussex Ms W, W2 . . . 194 A10
Sussex Pl, NW1 . . . 194 D3
W2 . . . 194 A9
W6 . . . 99 CW78
Erith DA8 . . . 107 FB80
New Malden KT3 . . . 138 CS98
Slough SL1 . . . 92 AV75
Sussex Ring, N12 . . . 44 DA50
Sussex Rd, E6 . . . 87 EN67
Brentwood CM14 . . . 54 FV49
Carshalton SM5 . . . 158 DF107
Dartford DA1 . . . 128 FN87
Erith DA8 . . . 107 FB80
Harrow HA1 . . . 60 CC57
Mitcham CR4
off Lincoln Rd . . . 141 DL99
New Malden KT3 . . . 138 CS98
Orpington BR5 . . . 146 EW100
Sidcup DA14 . . . 126 EV92
South Croydon CR2 . . . 160 DR107
Southall UB2 . . . 96 BX76
Uxbridge UB10 . . . 59 BQ63
Watford WD24 . . . 23 BU38
West Wickham BR4 . . . 143 EB102
Sussex Sq, W2 . . . 194 A10
Sussex St, E13 . . . 86 EH69
SW1 . . . 101 DH78
Sussex Way, N7 . . . 65 DL61
N19 . . . 65 DL60
Barnet EN4 . . . 28 DG43
Uxbridge (Denh.) UB9 . . . 57 BF57
Sutcliffe Cl, NW11 . . . 64 DB57
Bushey WD23 . . . 24 CC42
Sutcliffe Ho, Hayes UB3 . . . 77 BU72
Sutcliffe Rd, SE18 . . . 105 ES79
Welling DA16 . . . 106 EW82
Sutherland Av, W9 . . . 82 DC69
W13 . . . 79 CH72
Hayes UB3 . . . 95 BU77
Orpington BR5 . . . 145 ET100
Potters Bar (Cuffley) EN6 . . . 13 DK28
Sunbury-on-Thames TW16 . . . 135 BT96
Welling DA16 . . . 105 ES84
Westerham (Bigg.H.) TN16 . . . 178 EK117
Sutherland Cl, Barn. EN5 . . . 27 CY42
Greenhithe DA9 . . . 129 FT85
Sutherland Ct, NW9 . . . 62 CP57
Sutherland Dr, SW19 . . . 140 DD95
Sutherland Gdns, SW14 . . . 98 CS83
Sunbury-on-Thames TW16
off Sutherland Av . . . 135 BT96
Worcester Park KT4 . . . 139 CV102
Sutherland Gro, SW18 . . . 119 CY86
Teddington TW11 . . . 117 CE92
Sutherland Pl, W2 . . . 82 DA72
Sutherland Rd, E17 . . . 47 DX54
N9 . . . 46 DU46
N17 . . . 46 DU52
W4 . . . 98 CS79
W13 . . . 79 CG72

★ Place of interest   ⇌ Railway station   ⊖ London Underground station   DLR Docklands Light Railway station   Tra Tramlink station   H Hospital   Riv Pedestrian ferry landing stage

Sutherland Rd,
Belvedere DA17 106 FA76
Croydon CR0 141 DN101
Enfield EN3 31 DX43
Southall UB1 78 BZ72
Sutherland Rd Path, E17 67 DX55
Sutherland Row, SW1 199 J10
Sutherland Sq, SE17 102 DQ78
Sutherland St, SW1 199 H10
Sutherland Wk, SE17 102 DQ78
Sutherland Way, Pot.B.
(Cuffley) EN6 13 DK28
Sutlej Rd, SE7 104 EJ80
Sutterton St, N7 83 DM65
SUTTON 158 DB107
⇌ Sutton 158 DC107
SUTTON AT HONE, Dart.
DA4 148 FN95
Sutton Av, Slou. SL3 92 AW75
Woking GU21 166 AS119
Sutton Cl, Beck. BR3
off Albemarle Rd 143 EB95
Loughton IG10 48 EL45
Pinner HA5 59 BU57
⇌ Sutton Common 140 DB103
Sutton Common Rd, Sutt.
SM1, SM3 139 CZ101
Sutton Ct, W4 98 CQ79
Sutton SM2 158 DC107
Sutton Ct Rd, E13 86 EJ69
W4 98 CQ80
Sutton SM1 158 DC107
Uxbridge UB10 77 BP67
Sutton Cres, Barn. EN5 27 CX43
Sutton Dene, Houns. TW3 96 CB81
Sutton Est, SW3 198 C10
W10 81 CW71
Sutton Est, The, N1 83 DP66
Sutton Gdns, Bark. IG11
off Sutton Rd 87 ES67
Croydon CR0 142 DT99
Redhill RH1 185 DK129
Sutton Grn, Bark. IG11
off Sutton Rd 87 ES67
Sutton Gro, Sutt. SM1 158 DD105
Sutton Hall Rd, Houns. TW5 96 CA80
★ Sutton Heritage Cen, Cars.
SM5 158 DF105
H Sutton Hosp, Sutt. SM2 158 DB110
★ Sutton Ho, E9 66 DW64
Sutton La, EC1 196 G5
Banstead SM7 174 DB115
Hounslow TW3 96 BZ83
Slough SL3 93 BC78
Sutton SM2 158 DB111
Sutton La N, W4 98 CQ78
Sutton La S, W4 98 CQ79
Sutton Par, NW4
off Church Rd 63 CW56
Sutton Pk Rd, Sutt. SM1 158 DB107
Sutton Path, Borwd. WD6
off Stratfield Rd 26 CN40
Sutton Pl, E9 66 DW64
Dartford DA4 128 FN92
Slough SL3 93 BB79
Sutton Rd, E13 86 EF70
E17 47 DX53
N10 44 DG54
Barking IG11 87 ES68
Hounslow TW5 96 CA81
Watford WD17 24 BW41
Sutton Row, W1 195 N8
Suttons Av, Horn. RM12 72 FJ62
Suttons Gdns, Horn. RM12 72 FK62
Suttons La, Horn. RM12 72 FK64
Sutton Sq, E9
off Urswick Rd 66 DW64
Hounslow TW5 96 BZ81
Sutton St, E1 84 DW72
Sutton's Way, EC1 197 J5
Sutton Wk, SE1 200 C3
Sutton Way, W10 81 CW71
Hounslow TW5 96 BZ81
Swabey Rd, Slou. SL3 93 BA77
Swaby Rd, SW18 120 DC88
Swaffham Way, N22
off White Hart La 45 DP52
Swaffield Rd, SW18 120 DB87
Sevenoaks TN13 191 FJ122
Swain Cl, SW16 121 DH93
Swain Rd, Th.Hth. CR7 142 DQ99
Swains Cl, West Dr. UB7 94 BL75
Swains La, N6 64 DG62
Swainson Rd, W3 99 CT75
Swains Rd, SW17 120 DF94
Swain St, NW8 194 B4
Swaisland Dr, Dart.
(Cray.) DA1 127 FF85
Swaisland Rd, Dart. DA1 127 FH85
Swakeleys Dr, Uxb. UB10 58 BM63
Swakeleys Rd, Uxb.
(Ickhm) UB10 58 BM62
Swale Cl, S.Ock.
(Aveley) RM15 90 FQ72
Swaledale Cl, N11
off Ribblesdale Av 44 DG51
Swaledale Rd, Dart. DA2 128 FQ88
Swale Rd, Dart. DA1 107 FG83
Swallands Rd, SE6 123 EA90
Swallow Cl, SE14 102 DW81
Bushey WD23 40 CC46
Erith DA8 107 FE81
Grays
(Chaff.Hun.) RM16 109 FW77
Greenhithe DA9 129 FT85
Rickmansworth WD3 38 BJ45
Staines TW18 113 BF91
Swallowdale, Iver SL0 75 BD69
South Croydon CR2 161 DX109
Swallow Dr, NW10
off Kingfisher Way 80 CR65
Northolt UB5 78 CA68
Swallowfield, Egh. (Eng.Grn) TW20
off Heronfield 112 AV93
Swallowfield Rd, SE7 104 EH78
Swallowfields, Grav. (Nthflt) DA11
off Hillary Av 130 GE90
Swallowfield Way, Hayes
UB3 95 BR75
Swallow Gdns, SW16 121 DK92
Swallow Oaks, Abb.L. WD5 7 BT31
Swallow Pas, W1 195 J9
Swallow Pl, W1 195 J9
Swallow St, E6 86 EL71
W1 199 L1
Iver SL0 75 BD69
Swallowtail Cl, Orp. BR5 146 EX98
Swallow Wk, Horn. RM12
off Heron Flight Av 89 FH65
Swanage Rd, E4 47 EC52
SW18 120 DC86
Swanage Waye, Hayes UB4 78 BW72
Swan & Pike Rd, Enf. EN3 31 EA38
Swan App, E6 86 EL71
Swan Av, Upmin. RM14 73 FT60
Swanbourne Dr, Horn.
RM12 72 FJ64
Swanbridge Rd, Bexh. DA7 106 FA81
Swan Business Pk, Dart.
DA1 108 FK84
Swan Cl, E17 47 DY53
Croydon CR0 142 DS101
Feltham TW13 116 BY91
Orpington BR5 146 EU97
Rickmansworth WD3
off Parsonage Rd 38 BK45
Swan Ct, SW3
off Flood St 100 DE78
Swandon Way, SW18 100 DB84
Swan Dr, NW9 42 CS54
Swanfield Rd, Wal.Cr. EN8 15 DY33
Swanfield St, E2 197 P3
Swanland Rd, Hat.
(N.Mymms) AL9 11 CV28
Potters Bar
(S.Mimms) EN6 11 CV33
Swan La, EC4 201 K1
N20 44 DC48
Dartford DA1 127 FF87
Loughton IG10 48 EJ45
SWANLEY 147 FE98
⇌ Swanley 147 FD98
Swanley Bar La, Pot.B. EN6 12 DB28
Swanley Bypass, Sid. DA14 147 FC97
Swanley BR8 147 FC97
Swanley Cen, Swan. BR8 147 FE97
Swanley Cres, Pot.B. EN6 12 DB29
Swanley La, Swan. BR8 147 FF97
Swanley Rd, Well. DA16 106 EW81
SWANLEY VILLAGE, Swan.
BR8 148 FJ95
Swanley Village Rd, Swan.
BR8 147 FH95
Swan Mead, SE1 201 M7
Hemel Hempstead HP3
off Belswains La 6 BM25
Swan Pas, E1
off Cartwright St 84 DT73
Swan Path, E10
off Jesse Rd 67 EC60
Swan Pl, SW13 99 CT82
Swan Rd, SE16 202 G4
SE18 104 EK76
Feltham TW13 116 BY92
Iver SL0 75 BF72
Southall UB1 78 CB72
West Drayton UB7 94 BK75
SWANSCOMBE 130 FZ86
⇌ Swanscombe 130 FZ85
Swanscombe Ho, W11
off St. Anns Rd 81 CX74
Swanscombe Rd, W4 98 CS78
W11 81 CX74
Swanscombe St, Swans.
DA10 130 FY87
Swansea Ct, E16
off Fishguard Way 87 EP74
Swansea Rd, Enf. EN3 30 DW42
Hounslow (Hthrw Air.) TW6
off Southern Perimeter Rd 115 BQ86
Swanshope, Loug. IG10 33 EP40
Swansland Gdns, E17
off McEntee Av 47 DY53
Swanston Path, Wat. WD19 40 BW48
Swan St, SE1 201 J6
Isleworth TW7 97 CH83
Swanton Gdns, SW19 119 CX88
Swanton Rd, Erith DA8 107 FB80
Swan Wk, SW3 100 DF79
Romford RM1 71 FE57
Shepperton TW17 135 BS101
Swan Way, Enf. EN3 31 DX40
Swanwick Cl, SW15 119 CT87
Swan Yd, N1
off Highbury Sta Rd 83 DP65
Sward Rd, Orp. BR5 146 EU100
Swaton Rd, E3 85 EA70
Swaylands Rd, Belv. DA17 106 FA79
Swaynesland Rd, Eden.
(Crock.H.) TN8 189 EM134
Swaythling Cl, N18 46 DV49
Swaythling Ho, SW15
off Tunworth Cres 119 CT86
Swedenborg Gdns, E1 84 DU73
Sweden Gate, SE16 203 K7
Sweeney Cres, SE1 202 A5
Sweeps Ditch Cl, Stai. TW18 134 BG95
Sweeps La, Egh. TW20 113 AZ92
Orpington BR5 146 EX99
Sweet Briar Grn, N9 46 DT48
Sweet Briar Gro, N9 46 DT48
Sweet Briar La, Epsom
KT18 156 CR114
Sweet Briar Wk, N18 46 DT49
Sweetcroft La, Uxb. UB10 76 BN66
Sweetmans Av, Pnr. HA5 60 BX55
Sweets Way, N20 44 DD47
Swetenham Wk, SE18
off Sandbach Pl 105 EQ78
Swete St, E13 86 EG68
Sweyne Rd, Swans. DA10 130 FY86
Sweyn Pl, SE3 104 EG82
Swievelands Rd, West.
(Bigg.H.) TN16 178 EH119
Swift Cl, E17 47 DY52
Swift Cl, Harrow HA2 60 CB61
Hayes UB3 off Church Rd 77 BT72
Upminster RM14 73 FS60
Swift Rd, Felt. TW13 116 BY90
Southall UB2 96 BZ76
Swiftsden Way, Brom. BR1 124 EE93
Swift St, SW6 99 CZ81
Swiftsure Rd, Grays
(Chaff.Hun.) RM16 109 FW77
SWILLET, THE, Rick. WD3 21 BB44
Swinbrook Rd, W10 81 CY71
Swinburne Ct, SE5
off Basingdon Way 102 DR84
Swinburne Cres, Croy. CR0 142 DW100
Swinburne Gdns, Til. RM18 111 GH82
Swinburne Rd, SW15 99 CU84
Swinderby Rd, Wem. HA0 80 CL65
Swindon Cl, Ilf. IG3
off Salisbury Rd 69 ES61
Romford RM3 52 FM50
Swindon Gdns, Rom. RM3 52 FM50
Swindon La, Rom. RM3 52 FM50
Swindon Rd, Houns.
(Hthrw Air.) TW6 115 BQ85
Swindon St, W12 81 CV74
Swinfield Cl, Felt. TW13 116 BY91
Swinford Gdns, SW9 101 DP83
Swingate La, SE18 105 ES79
Swinnerton St, E9 67 DY64
Swinton Cl, Wem. HA9 62 CP60
Swinton Pl, WC1 196 B2
Swinton St, WC1 196 B2
Swires Shaw, Kes. BR2 162 EK105
Swiss Av, Wat. WD18 23 BS42
Swiss Cl, Wat. WD18 23 BS41
⊖ Swiss Cottage 82 DD66
Swiss Ct, W1 199 N1
Swiss Ter, NW6 82 DD66
Switch Ho, E14
off Blackwall Way 85 ED73
Swithland Gdns, SE9 125 EN91
Swyncombe Av, W5 97 CH77
Swynford Gdns, NW4
off Handowe Cl 63 CU56
Sybil Ms, N4
off Lothair Rd N 65 DP58
Sybil Phoenix Cl, SE8 203 J10
Sybourn St, E17 67 DZ59
Sycamore App, Rick.
(Crox.Grn) WD3 23 BQ43
Sycamore Av, E3 85 DZ67
W5 97 CK76
Hayes UB3 77 BS73
Sidcup DA15 125 ET86
Upminster RM14 72 FN62
Sycamore Cl, E16
off Clarence Rd 86 EE70
N9 off Pycroft Way 46 DU49
SE9 124 EL89
W3 off Bromyard Av 80 CS74
Barnet EN4 28 DD44
Bushey WD23 24 BY40
Carshalton SM5 158 DF105
Chalfont St. Giles HP8 36 AU48
Edgware HA8 off Ash Cl 42 CQ49
Feltham TW13 115 BU90
Gravesend DA12 131 GK87
Leatherhead (Fetch.) KT22 171 CE123
Loughton IG10
off Cedar Dr 33 EP40
Northolt UB5 78 BY67
South Croydon CR2 160 DS106
Waltham Cross EN7 14 DT27
Watford WD25 23 BV35
West Drayton UB7
off Whitethorn Av 76 BM73
Sycamore Ct, Surb. KT6
off Penners Gdns 138 CL101
Sycamore Dr, Brwd. CM14
off Copperfield Gdns 54 FW46
St. Albans (Park St) AL2 9 CD27
Swanley BR8 147 FE97
Sycamore Gdns, W6 99 CV75
Mitcham CR4 140 DD96
Sycamore Gro, NW9 62 CQ59
SE6 123 EC86
SE20 122 DU94
New Malden KT3 138 CR97
Sycamore Hill, N11 44 DG51
Sycamore Ms, SW4 101 DJ83
Sycamore Ri, Bans. SM7 157 CX114
Chalfont St. Giles HP8 36 AU48
Sycamore Rd, SW19 119 CW93
Chalfont St. Giles HP8 36 AU48
Dartford DA1 128 FK88
Rickmansworth
(Crox.Grn) WD3 23 BQ43
Sycamores, The, Rad. WD7
off The Avenue 9 CH34
South Ockendon (Aveley) RM15
off Dacre Av 91 FR74
Sycamore St, EC1 197 H5
Sycamore Wk, W10
off Fifth Av 81 CY70
Egham (Eng.Grn) TW20 112 AV93
Ilford IG6 off Civic Way 69 EQ56
Slough (Geo.Grn) SL3 74 AY72
Sycamore Way, S.Ock.
RM15 91 FX70
Teddington TW11 117 CJ93
Thornton Heath CR7 141 DN99
SYDENHAM, SE26 122 DW92
⇌ Sydenham 122 DW91
Sydenham Av, N21
off Fleming Dr 29 DM43
SE26 122 DV92
Sydenham Cl, Rom. RM1 71 FF56
Sydenham Cotts, SE12 124 EJ89
⇌ Sydenham Hill 122 DT90
Sydenham Hill, SE23 122 DV88
SE26 122 DU90
Sydenham Hill Est, SE26 122 DU90
Sydenham Pk, SE26 122 DW90
Sydenham Pk Rd, SE26 122 DW90
Sydenham Ri, SE23 122 DV89
Sydenham Rd, SE26 122 DW92
Croydon CR0 142 DR101
Sydmons Ct, SE23 122 DW87
Sydner Ms, N16
off Sydner Rd 66 DT63
Sydner Rd, N16 66 DT63
Sydney Av, Pur. CR8 159 DM112
Sydney Cl, SW3 198 A9
Sydney Cres, Ashf. TW15 115 BP93
Sydney Gro, NW4 63 CW57
Sydney Ms, SW3 198 A9
Sydney Pl, SW7 198 A9
Sydney Rd, E11
off Mansfield Rd 68 EH58
N8 65 DN56
N10 44 DG53
SE2 106 EW76
SW20 139 CX96
W13 79 CG74
Bexleyheath DA6 106 EX84
Enfield EN2 30 DR42
Feltham TW14 115 BU88
Ilford IG6 49 EQ54
Richmond TW9 98 CL84
Sidcup DA14 125 ES91
Sutton SM1 158 DA105
Teddington TW11 117 CF92
Tilbury RM18 111 GG82
Watford WD18 23 BS43
Woodford Green IG8 48 EG49
Sydney St, SW3 198 B10
Syke Cluan, Iver SL0 93 BE75
Syke Ings, Iver SL0 93 BE76
Sykes Dr, Stai. TW18 114 BH92
Sylvana Cl, Uxb. UB10 76 BM67
Sylvan Av, N3 44 DA54
N22 45 DM52
NW7 43 CT51
Hornchurch RM11 72 FL58
Romford RM6 70 EZ58
Sylvan Cl, Grays (Chaff.Hun.) RM16
off Warren La 110 FY77
Oxted RH8 188 EH129
South Croydon CR2 160 DV110
Woking GU22 167 BB117
Sylvan Ct, N12
off Holden Rd 44 DB49
Sylvan Est, SE19 142 DT95
Sylvan Gdns, Surb. KT6 137 CK101
Sylvan Gro, NW2 63 CX63
SE15 102 DV80
Sylvan Hill, SE19 142 DS95
Sylvan Ms, Green. DA9
off London Rd 129 FW85
Sylvan Rd, E7 86 EG65
E11 68 EG57
E17 67 EA57
SE19 142 DT95
Ilford IG1
off Hainault St 69 EQ61
Sylvan Wk, Brom. BR1 145 EM97
Sylvan Way, Chig. IG7 50 EV48
Dagenham RM8 70 EV62
West Wickham BR4 162 EE105
Sylverdale Rd, Croy. CR0 141 DP104
Purley CR8 159 DP113
Sylvester Av, Chis. BR7 125 EM93
Sylvester Gdns, Ilf. IG6 50 EV50
Sylvester Path, E8
off Sylvester Rd 84 DV65
Sylvester Rd, E8 84 DV65
E17 67 DZ59
N2 44 DC54
Wembley HA0 61 CJ64
Sylvestres, Sev.
(Rvrhd) TN13 190 FD121
Sylvestrus Cl, Kings.T. KT1 138 CN95
Sylvia Av, Brwd. (Hutt.) CM13 55 GC47
Pinner HA5 40 BZ51
Sylvia Ct, Wem. HA9
off Harrow Rd 80 CP66
Sylvia Gdns, Wem. HA9 80 CP66
Symes Ms, NW1
off Camden High St 83 DJ68
Symington Ms, E9
off Coopersale Rd 67 DX64
Symister Ms, N1 197 M3
Symonds Ct, Wal.Cr. (Chsht) EN8
off High St 15 DX28
Symons St, SW3 198 E9
Symphony Ms, W10
off Third Av 81 CY69
Syon Gate Way, Brent. TW8 97 CG80
★ Syon Ho & Pk, Brent. TW8 97 CJ81
⇌ Syon Lane 97 CG80
Syon La, Islw. TW7 97 CH80
Syon Pk Gdns, Islw. TW7 97 CF80
Syon Vista, Rich. TW9 97 CK81
Syracuse Av, Rain. RM13 90 FL69
Syringa Ct, Grays RM17 110 GD80
Sythwood, Wok. GU21 166 AV117

T

Tabard Cen, SE1
off Prioress St 102 DR76
Tabard Gdn Est, SE1 201 L5
Tabard St, SE1 201 K5
Tabarin Way, Epsom KT17 173 CW116
Tabernacle Av, E13
off Barking Rd 86 EG70
Tabernacle St, EC2 197 L5
Tableer Av, SW4 121 DK85
Tabley Rd, N7 65 DL63
Tabor Gdns, Sutt. SM3 157 CZ107
Tabor Gro, SW19 119 CY94
Tabor Rd, W6 99 CV76
Tabors Ct, Brwd. (Shenf.) CM15
off Shenfield Rd 55 FZ45
Tabrums Way, Upmin. RM14 73 FS59
Tachbrook Est, SW1 101 DK78
Tachbrook Ms, SW1 199 K8
Tachbrook Rd, Felt. TW14 115 BT87
Southall UB2 96 BX77
Uxbridge UB8 76 BJ68
Tachbrook St, SW1 199 L9
Tack Ms, SE4 103 EA83
Tadema Rd, SW10 100 DC80
Tadlows Cl, Upmin. RM14 72 FP64
Tadmor Cl, Sun. TW16 135 BT98
Tadmor St, W12 81 CX74
Tadorne Rd, Tad. KT20 173 CW121
TADWORTH 173 CV121
⇌ Tadworth 173 CW122
Tadworth Av, N.Mal. KT3 139 CT99
Tadworth Cl, Tad. KT20 173 CX122
Tadworth Par, Horn. RM12
off Maylands Av 71 FH63
Tadworth Rd, NW2 63 CU61
Tadworth St, Tad. KT20 173 CW123
Taeping St, E14 204 B8
Taffy's How, Mitch. CR4 140 DE97
Taft Way, E3
off St. Leonards St 85 EB69
Tagalie Pl, Rad. (Shenley) WD7
off Porters Pk Dr 10 CL32
Tagg's Island, Hmptn. TW12 137 CD96
Tailworth St, E1
off Chicksand St 84 DU71
Tait Rd, Croy. CR0 142 DS101
Takeley Cl, Rom. RM5 51 FD54
Waltham Abbey EN9 15 ED33
Takhar Ms, SW11
off Cabul Rd 100 DE82
Talacre Rd, NW5 82 DG65
Talbot Av, N2 64 DD55
Slough SL3 93 AZ76
Watford WD19 40 BY45
Talbot Cl, N15 66 DT56
Talbot Ct, EC3 197 L10
Talbot Cres, NW4 63 CU57
Talbot Gdns, Ilf. IG3 70 EU61
Talbot Ho, E14
off Giraud St 85 EB72
N7 off Harvist Est 65 DN62
Talbot Pl, SE3 104 EE82
Slough (Datchet) SL3 92 AW81
Talbot Rd, E6 87 EN68
E7 68 EG63
N6 64 DG58
N15 66 DT56
N22 45 DJ54
SE22 102 DS84
W2 81 CZ72
W11 81 CZ72
W13 79 CG73
Ashford TW15 114 BK92
Bromley BR2
off Masons Hill 144 EH98
Carshalton SM5 158 DG106
Dagenham RM9 88 EZ65
Harrow HA3 41 CF54
Isleworth TW7 97 CG84
Rickmansworth WD3 38 BL46
Southall UB2 96 BY77
Thornton Heath CR7 142 DR98
Twickenham TW2 117 CE88
Wembley HA0 61 CK64
Talbot Roundabout, Epp.
(N.Wld Bas.) CM16 19 FD25
Talbot Sq, W2 194 A9
Talbot Wk, NW10
off Garnet Rd 80 CS65
W11 81 CY72
Talbot Yd, SE1 201 K3
Talbrook, Brwd. CM14 54 FT48
Taleworth Cl, Ashtd. KT21 171 CK120
Taleworth Pk, Ashtd. KT21 171 CK120
Taleworth Rd, Ashtd. KT21 171 CK119
Talfourd Pl, SE15 102 DT81
Talfourd Rd, SE15 102 DT81
Talgarth Rd, W6 99 CY78
W14 99 CY78
Talgarth Wk, NW9 62 CS57
Talisman Cl, Ilf. IG3 70 EV60
Talisman Sq, SE26 122 DU91
Talisman Way, Epsom KT17 173 CW116
Wembley HA9 62 CM62
Tallack Cl, Har. HA3
off College Hill Rd 41 CE52
Tallack Rd, E10 67 DZ60
Tall Elms Cl, Brom. BR2 144 EF99
Tallents Cl, Dart.
(Sutt.H.) DA4 128 FP94
Tallis Cl, E16 86 EH72
Tallis Ct, Rom. RM2
off Elvet Av 72 FJ55
Tallis Gro, SE7 104 EH79
Tallis St, EC4 196 E10
Tallis Vw, NW10 80 CR65
Tallis Way, Borwd. WD6 25 CK39
Brentwood CM14
off Mascalls La 54 FV50
Tallon Rd, Brwd. (Hutt.) CM13 55 GE43
Tall Trees, SW16 141 DM97
Slough (Colnbr.) SL3 93 BE81
Tall Trees Cl, Horn. RM11 72 FK58
Tally Ho Cor, N12 44 DC50
Tally Rd, Oxt. RH8 188 EL131
Talma Gdns, Twick. TW2 117 CE86
Talmage Cl, SE23
off Tyson Rd 122 DW87
Talman Gro, Stan. HA7 41 CK51
Talma Rd, SW2 101 DN84
Talus Cl, Purf. RM19
off Brimfield Rd 109 FR77
Talwin St, E3 85 EB69
Tamar Cl, E3 off Lefevre Wk 85 DZ67
Upminster RM14 73 FS58
Tamar Dr, S.Ock.
(Aveley) RM15 90 FQ72
Tamarind Yd, E1 202 C2
Tamarisk Cl, S.Ock. RM15 91 FW70
Tamarisk Rd, S.Ock. RM15 91 FW69
Tamarisk Sq, W12 81 CT73
Tamar Sq, Wdf.Grn. IG8 48 EH51
Tamar St, SE7
off Woolwich Rd 104 EL76
Tamar Way, N17 66 DU55
Slough SL3 93 BB78
Tamerton Sq, Wok. GU22 166 AY119
Tamesis Gdns, Wor.Pk. KT4 138 CS102
Tamesis Strand, Grav. DA12 131 GL92
Tamian Way, Houns. TW4 96 BW84
Tamworth Av, Wdf.Grn. IG8 48 EE51
Tamworth La, Mitch. CR4 141 DH96
Tamworth Pk, Mitch. CR4 141 DH98
Tamworth Pl, Croy. CR0 142 DQ103
Tamworth Rd, Croy. CR0 141 DP103
Tamworth St, SW6 100 DA79
Tancred Rd, N4 65 DP58
Tandem Cen, SW19
off Prince George's Rd 140 DD95

★ Place of interest ⇌ Railway station ⊖ London Underground station DLR Docklands Light Railway station Tra Tramlink station H Hospital Riv Pedestrian ferry landing stage

Tandem Way, SW19 140 DD95
TANDRIDGE, Oxt. RH8 187 EA133
Tandridge Ct, Cat. CR3 176 DU122
Tandridge Dr, Orp. BR6 145 ER102
Tandridge Gdns, S.Croy. CR2 187 DT113
Tandridge Hill La, Gdse. RH9 187 DZ128
Tandridge La,
Oxt. (Tand.) RH8 187 EA131
Tandridge Pl, Orp. BR6
off Tandridge Dr 145 ER101
Tandridge Rd, Warl. CR6 177 DX119
Tanfield Av, NW2 63 CT63
Tanfield Cl, Wal.Cr. EN7 14 DU27
Tanfield Rd, Croy. CR0 160 DQ105
Tangent Link, Rom.
(Harold Hill) RM3 52 FK53
Tangent Rd, Rom. RM3
off Ashton Rd 52 FK53
Tangier Rd, Rich. TW10 98 CP83
Tangier Way, Tad. KT20 173 CY117
Tangier Wd, Tad. KT20 173 CY118
Tanglebury Cl, Brom. BR1 145 EM98
Tangle Tree Cl, N3 44 DB54
Tanglewood Cl, Cher.
(Longcr.) KT16 132 AV104
Croydon CR0 142 DW104
Stanmore HA7 41 CE47
Uxbridge UB10 76 BN69
Woking GU22 167 BD116
Tanglewood Way, Felt. TW13 115 BV90
Tangley Gro, SW15 119 CT87
Tangley Pk Rd, Hmptn. TW12 116 BZ93
Tanglyn Av, Shep. TW17 135 BP99
Tangmere Cres, Horn. RM12 89 FH65
Tangmere Gdns, Nthlt. UB5 78 BW68
Tangmere Gro, Kings.T. KT2 117 CK92
Tangmere Way, NW9 42 CS54
Tanhouse Rd, Oxt. RH8 187 ED132
Tanhurst Wk, SE2
off Alsike Rd 106 EX76
Tankerton Rd, Surb. KT6 138 CM103
Tankerton St, WC1 196 A3
Tankerville Rd, SW16 121 DK93
Tank Hill Rd, Purf. RM19 108 FN78
Tank La, Purf. RM19 108 FN77
Tankridge Rd, NW2 63 CV61
Tanner Pt, E13 off Pelly Rd 86 EG67
Tanners Cl, Walt. KT12 135 BV100
Tanners Dean, Lthd. KT22 171 CJ122
Tanners End La, N18 46 DS49
Tanners Hill, SE8 103 DZ81
Abbots Langley WD5 7 BT31
Tanners La, Ilf. IG6 69 EQ55
Tanner St, SE1 201 N5
Barking IG11 87 EQ65
Tanners Wd Cl, Abb.L. WD5
off Tanners Wd La 7 BS32
Tanners Wd La, Abb.L.
WD5 7 BS32
Tannery, The, Red. RH1
off Oakdene Rd 184 DE134
Tannery Cl, Beck. BR3 143 DX99
Dagenham RM10 71 FB62
Tannery La, Wok.
(Send) GU23 167 BF122
Tannington Ter, N5 65 DN62
Tannsfeld Rd, SE26 123 DX92
Tansley Cl, N7
off Hilldrop Rd 65 DK64
Tanswell Est, SE1 200 E5
Tanswell St, SE1 200 D5
Tansy Cl, E6 87 EN72
Romford RM3 52 FL51
Tantallon Rd, SW12 120 DG88
Tant Av, E16 86 EF72
Tantony Gro, Rom. RM6 70 EX55
Tanworth Cl, Nthwd. HA6 39 BQ51
Tanworth Gdns, Pnr. HA5 39 BV54
Tanyard La, Bex. DA5
off Bexley High St 126 FA87
Tanza Rd, NW3 64 DF63
Tapestry Cl, Sutt. SM2 158 DB108
Taplow, NW3 82 DD66
SE17 off Thurlow St 102 DS78
Taplow Rd, N13 46 DQ49
Taplow St, N1 197 J1
Tappesfield Rd, SE15 102 DW83
Tapp St, E1 84 DV70
Tapster St, Barn. EN5 27 CZ42
Tara Ms, N8
off Edison Rd 65 DK58
Taransay Wk, N1
off Essex Rd 84 DR65
Tarbert Ms, N15
off Roslyn Rd 66 DS57
Tarbert Rd, SE22 122 DS85
Tarbert Wk, E1
off Juniper St 84 DW73
Target Cl, Felt. TW14 115 BS86
Tariff Cres, SE8 203 M8
Tariff Rd, N17 46 DU51
Tarleton Gdns, SE23 122 DV88
Tarling Cl, Sid. DA14 126 EV90
Tarling Rd, E16 86 EF72
N2 44 DC54
Tarling St, E1 84 DV72
Tarling St Est, E1 84 DW72
Tarmac Way, West Dr. UB7 94 BH80
Tarnbank, Enf. EN2 29 DL43
Tarn St, SE1 201 H7
Tarnwood Pk, SE9 125 EM88
Tarnworth Rd, Rom. RM3 52 FN50
Tarpan Way, Brox. EN10 15 DZ26
Tarquin Ho, SE26 122 DU91
Tarragon Cl, SE14 103 DY80
Tarragon Gro, SE26 123 DX93
Tarrant Pl, W1 194 D7
Tarrington Cl, SW16 121 DK90
Tartar Rd, Cob. KT11 154 BW113
Tarver Rd, SE17 101 DP78
Tarves Way, SE10 103 EB80
Tash Pl, N11
off Woodland Rd 45 DH50
Tasker Cl, Hayes UB3 95 BQ80
Tasker Ho, Bark. IG11
off Dovehouse Mead 87 ER68
Tasker Rd, NW3 64 DF64
Grays RM16 111 GH76
Tasman Ct, E14
off Westferry Rd 103 EB77
Tasman Ct,
Sunbury-on-Thames TW16 115 BS94
Tasmania Ho, Til. RM18
off Hobart Rd 111 GG81
Tasmania Ter, N18 46 DQ51
Tasman Rd, SW9 101 DL83
Tasman Wk, E16
off Royal Rd 86 EK72
Tasso Rd, W6 99 CY79
Tatam Rd, NW10 80 CQ66
Tatchbury Ho, SW15
off Tunworth Cres 119 CT86
Tate & Lyle Jetty, E16 104 EL75
★ Tate Britain, SW1 199 P9
Tate Cl, Lthd. KT22 171 CJ123
Tate Gdns, Bushey WD23 41 CE45
★ Tate Modern, SE1 200 G2
Tate Rd, E16
off Newland St 87 EM74
Gerrards Cross
(Chal.St.P.) SL9 37 AZ50
Sutton SM1 158 DA106
TATLING END, Ger.Cr. SL9 57 BB61
Tatnell Rd, SE23 123 DY86
TATSFIELD, West. TN16 178 EL120
Tatsfield App Rd, West.
(Tats.) TN16 178 EH123
Tatsfield La, West.
(Tats.) TN16 179 EM121
TATTENHAM CORNER, Epsom
KT18 173 CV118
⇌ Tattenham Corner 173 CV118
Tattenham Cor Rd, Epsom
KT18 173 CT117
Tattenham Cres, Epsom
KT18 173 CU118
Tattenham Gro, Epsom
KT18 173 CV118
Tattenham Way, Tad. KT20 173 CX118
Tattersall Cl, SE9 124 EL85
Tatton Cres, N16
off Clapton Common 66 DT59
Tatum St, SE17 201 L9
Tauber Cl, Borwd.
(Elstree) WD6 26 CM42
Tauheed Cl, N4 66 DQ61
Taunton Av, SW20 139 CV96
Caterham CR3 176 DT123
Hounslow TW3 96 CC82
Taunton Cl, Bexh. DA7 107 FD82
Ilford IG6 49 ET51
Sutton SM3 140 DA102
Taunton Dr, N2 44 DC54
Enfield EN2 29 DN41
Taunton La, Couls. CR5 175 DN119
Taunton Ms, NW1 194 D5
Taunton Pl, NW1 194 D4
Taunton Rd, SE12 124 EE85
Gravesend (Nthflt) DA11 130 GA85
Greenford UB6 78 CB67
Romford RM3 52 FJ49
Taunton Vale, Grav. DA12 131 GK90
Taunton Way, Stan. HA7 62 CL55
Tavern Cl, Cars. SM5 140 DE101
Taverners Cl, W11
off Addison Av 81 CY74
Taverner Sq, N5
off Highbury Gra 66 DQ63
Taverners Way, E4
off Douglas Rd 48 EE46
Tavern La, SW9 101 DN82
Tavistock Av, E17 67 DY55
NW7 43 CX52
Greenford UB6 79 CG68
Tavistock Cl, N16
off Crossway 66 DS64
Potters Bar EN6 12 DD31
Romford RM3 52 FK53
Staines TW18 114 BK94
Tavistock Ct, WC2
off Tavistock St 83 DL73
Tavistock Cres, W11 81 CZ71
Mitcham CR4 141 DL98
Tavistock Gdns, Ilf. IG3 69 ES63
Tavistock Gate, Croy. CR0 142 DR102
Tavistock Gro, Croy. CR0 142 DR101
Tavistock Ms, E18
off Avon Way 68 EG56
W11 off Lancaster Rd 81 CZ72
Tavistock Pl, E18 off Avon Way 68 EG55
N14 off Chase Side 45 DH45
WC1 195 N4
Tavistock Rd, E7 68 EF63
E15 86 EF65
E18 68 EG55
N4 66 DR58
NW10 81 CT68
W11 81 CZ72
Bromley BR2 144 EF98
Carshalton SM5 140 DD102
Croydon CR0 142 DR102
Edgware HA8 42 CN53
Uxbridge UB10 59 BQ64
Watford WD24 24 BX39
Welling DA16 106 EW81
West Drayton UB7 76 BK74
Tavistock Sq, WC1 195 N4
Tavistock St, WC2 196 A10
Tavistock Ter, N19 65 DK62
Tavistock Twr, SE16 203 K7
Tavistock Wk, Cars. SM5
off Tavistock Rd 140 DD102
Taviton St, WC1 195 M4
Tavy Cl, SE11 200 E10
Tawney Common, Epp.
(They.Mt) CM16 18 FA32
Tawney Rd, SE28 88 EV73
Tawny Av, Upmin. RM14 72 FP64
Tawny Cl, W13 79 CH74
Feltham TW13
off Chervil Cl 115 BU90
Tawny Way, SE16 203 J8
Tayben Av, Twick. TW2 117 CE86
Taybridge Rd, SW11 100 DG83
Tayburn Cl, E14 85 EC72
Tayfield Cl, Uxb. UB10 59 BQ62
Tayler Cotts, Pot.B. EN6
off Crossoaks La 11 CT34
Tayles Hill, Epsom KT17
off Tayles Hill Dr 157 CT110
Tayles Hill Dr, Epsom KT17 157 CT110
Taylor Av, Rich. TW9 98 CP82
Taylor Cl, N17 46 DU52
SE8 103 DZ79
Epsom KT19 156 CN111
Hampton
(Hmptn H.) TW12 116 CC92
Hounslow TW3 96 CC81
Orpington BR6 163 ET105
Romford RM5 50 FA52
Uxbridge (Hare.) UB9
off High St 38 BJ53
Taylor Ct, E15 off Clays La 67 EC64
Taylor Rd, Ashtd. KT21 171 CK117
Mitcham CR4 120 DE94
Wallington SM6 159 DH106
Taylor Row, Dart. DA2 128 FJ90
Romford (Noak Hill) RM3
off Cummings Hall La 52 FJ48
Taylors Bldgs, SE18
off Spray St 105 EP77
Taylors Cl, Sid. DA14 125 ET91
Taylors Grn, W3
off Long Dr 80 CS72
Taylors La, NW10 80 CS66
SE26 122 DV91
Barnet EN5 27 CZ39
Taymount Ri, SE23 122 DW89
Taynton Dr, Red. RH1 185 DK129
Tayport Cl, N1 83 DL66
Tayside Dr, Edg. HA8 42 CP48
Tay Way, Rom. RM1 51 FF53
Taywood Rd, Nthlt. UB5 78 BZ69
Teak Cl, SE16 203 L3
Teal Av, Orp. BR5 146 EX98
Teal Cl, E16
off Fulmer Rd 86 EK71
South Croydon CR2 161 DX111
Teal Ct, Wall. SM6
off Carew Rd 159 DJ107
Teal Dr, Nthwd. HA6 39 BQ52
Teale St, E2 84 DU68
Tealing Dr, Epsom KT19 156 CR105
Teal Pl, Sutt. SM1
off Sandpiper Rd 157 CZ106
Teal St, SE10 205 L6
Teal Way, Hem.H. HP3
off Belswains La 6 BM25
Teardrop Ind Est, Swan. BR8 147 FH99
Teasel Cl, Croy. CR0 143 DX102
Teasel Cres, SE28 87 ES74
Teasel Way, E15 86 EE69
Teazle Meade, Epp. (Thnwd) CM16
off Carpenters Arms La 18 EV25
Teazle Wd Hill, Lthd. KT22 171 CE117
Teazlewood Pk, Lthd. KT22 171 CG117
Tebworth Rd, N17 46 DT52
Teck Cl, Islw. TW7 97 CG82
Tedder Cl, Chess. KT9 155 CJ106
Ruislip HA4
off West End Rd 59 BV64
Uxbridge UB10 76 BM66
Tedder Rd, S.Croy. CR2 160 DW108
TEDDINGTON 117 CG93
⇌ Teddington 117 CG93
Teddington Cl, Epsom KT19 156 CR110
Teddington Lock, Tedd. TW11 117 CH91
H Teddington Mem Hosp, Tedd.
TW11 117 CE93
Teddington Pk, Tedd. TW11 117 CF92
Teddington Pk Rd, Tedd. TW11 117 CF91
Tedworth Gdns, SW3
off Tedworth Sq 100 DF78
Tedworth Sq, SW3 100 DF78
Tee, The, W3 80 CS72
Tees Av, Grnf. UB6 79 CE68
Tees Cl, Upmin. RM14 73 FR59
Teesdale Av, Islw. TW7 97 CG81
Teesdale Cl, E2 84 DV68
Teesdale Gdns, SE25 142 DS96
Isleworth TW7 97 CG81
Teesdale Rd, E11 68 EF58
Dartford DA2 128 FQ88
Teesdale St, E2 84 DV68
Teesdale Yd, E2
off Teesdale St 84 DV68
Tees Dr, Rom. RM3 52 FK48
Teeswater Ct, Erith DA18
off Middle Way 106 EX76
Teevan Cl, Croy. CR0 142 DU101
Teevan Rd, Croy. CR0 142 DU101
Teggs La, Wok. GU22 167 BF116
Teignmouth Cl, SW4 101 DK84
Edgware HA8 42 CM54
Teignmouth Gdns, Grnf. UB6 79 CF68
Teignmouth Rd, NW2 63 CX64
Welling DA16 106 EW82
Telcote Way, Ruis. HA4
off Woodlands Av 60 BW59
★ Telecom Twr, W1 195 K6
Telegraph Hill, NW3 64 DB62
Telegraph La, Esher
(Clay.) KT10 155 CF107
Telegraph Ms, Ilf. IG3 70 EU60
Telegraph Path, Chis. BR7 125 EP92
Telegraph Pl, E14 204 B8
Telegraph Rd, SW15 119 CV87
Telegraph St, EC2 197 K8
Telegraph Track, Cars. SM5 158 DG110
Telemann Sq, SE3 104 EH83
Telephone Pl, SW6
off Lillie Rd 99 CZ79
Telfer Cl, W3
off Church Rd 98 CQ75
Telferscot Rd, SW12 121 DK88
Telford Av, SW2 121 DL88
Telford Cl, E17 67 DY59
SE19
off St. Aubyn's Rd 122 DT93
Watford WD25 24 BX35
Telford Dr, Walt. KT12 136 BW101
Telford Rd, N11 45 DJ51
NW9
off West Hendon Bdy 63 CU58
SE9 125 ER89
W10 81 CY71
St. Albans (Lon.Col.) AL2 9 CJ27
Southall UB1 78 CB73
Twickenham TW2 116 CA87
Telfords Yd, E1 202 C1
Telford Ter, SW1 101 DJ79
Telford Way, W3 80 CS71
Hayes UB4 78 BY71
Telham Rd, E6 87 EN68
Tell Gro, SE22 102 DT84
Tellisford, Esher KT10 154 CB105
Tellson Av, SE18 104 EL81
Telscombe Cl, Orp. BR6 145 ES103
Telston La, Sev.
(Otford) TN14 181 FF117
Temeraire St, SE16 202 G5
Temperley Rd, SW12 120 DG87
Tempest Av, Pot.B. EN6 12 DC32
Tempest Mead, Epp.
(N.Wld Bas.) CM16 19 FB27
Tempest Rd, Egh. TW20 113 BC93
Tempest Way, Rain. RM13 89 FG65
Templar Dr, SE28 88 EX72
Gravesend DA11 131 GG92
Templar Ho, NW2
off Shoot Up Hill 81 CZ65
Rainham RM13
off Chantry Way 89 FD68
Templar Pl, Hmptn. TW12 116 CA94
Templars Av, NW11 63 CZ58
Templars Cres, N3 44 DA54
Templars Dr, Har. HA3 41 CD51
Templar St, SE5 101 DP82
⊖ Temple 196 C10
Temple, EC4 83 DN73
★ Temple, The, EC4 196 D10
Temple Av, EC4 196 E10
N20 44 DD45
Croydon CR0 143 DZ103
Dagenham RM8 70 FA60
★ Temple Bar, EC4 196 D9
Temple Bar Rd, Wok. GU21 166 AT119
Temple Cl, E11
off Wadley Rd 68 EE59
N3 off Cyprus Rd 43 CZ54
SE28 105 EQ76
Epsom KT19 156 CR112
Waltham Cross
(Chsht) EN7 14 DU31
Watford WD17 23 BT40
Templecombe Ms, Wok. GU22
off Dorchester Ct 167 BA116
Templecombe Rd, E9 84 DW67
Templecombe Way, Mord.
SM4 139 CY99
Temple Ct, E1
off Rectory Sq 85 DX71
Potters Bar EN6 11 CY31
Templecroft, Ashf. TW15 115 BR93
Templedene Av, Stai. TW18 114 BH94
Templefield Cl, Add. KT15 152 BH107
Temple Fortune Hill, NW11 64 DA57
Temple Fortune La, NW11 64 DA58
Temple Fortune Par, NW11
off Finchley Rd 63 CZ57
Temple Gdns, N21
off Barrowell Grn 45 DP47
NW11 63 CZ58
Dagenham RM8 70 EX62
Rickmansworth WD3 39 BP49
Staines TW18 133 BF95
Temple Gro, NW11 64 DA58
Enfield EN2 29 DP41
Temple Hill, Dart. DA1 128 FM86
Temple Hill Sq, Dart. DA1 128 FM85
Templehof Av, NW2 63 CW59
Temple La, EC4 196 E9
Templeman Cl, Pur. CR8
off Croftleigh Av 175 DP116
Templeman Rd, W7 79 CF71
Templemead Cl, W3 80 CS72
Temple Mead Cl, Stan. HA7 41 CH51
Templemead Ho, E9
off Kingsmead Way 67 DY63
Templemere, Wey. KT13 135 BR104
Temple Mill La, E15 67 EB63
★ Temple of Mithras, EC4 197 K9
Templepan La, Rick. WD3 22 BL37
Temple Pk, Uxb. UB8 76 BN69
Temple Pl, WC2 196 C10
Templer Av, Grays RM16 111 GG77
Temple Rd, E6 86 EL67
N8 65 DM56
NW2 63 CW63
W4 98 CQ76
W5 97 CK76
Croydon CR0 160 DR105
Epsom KT19 156 CR112
Hounslow TW3 96 CB84
Richmond TW9 98 CM83
Westerham (Bigg.H.) TN16 178 EK117
Temple Sheen, SW14 118 CQ85
Temple Sheen Rd, SW14 98 CP84
Temple St, E2 84 DV68
Templeton Av, E4 47 EA49
Templeton Cl, N16
off Boleyn Rd 66 DS64
SE19 142 DR95
Templeton Ct, NW7
off Kingsbridge Dr 43 CX52
Templeton Pl, SW5 100 DA77
Templeton Rd, N15 66 DR58
Temple Way, Sutt. SM1 140 DD104
Temple W Ms, SE11 200 F7
Templewood, W13 79 CH71
Templewood Av, NW3 64 DB62
Temple Wd Dr, Red. RH1 184 DF130
Templewood Gdns, NW3 64 DB62
Templewood La, Slou. SL2 56 AS63
Templewood Pk, Slou. SL2 56 AT63
Templewood Pt, NW2
off Granville Rd 63 CZ61
Tempsford Av, Borwd. WD6 26 CR42
Tempsford Cl, Enf. EN2
off Gladbeck Way 30 DQ41
Temsford Cl, Har. HA2 40 CC54
Ten Acre, Wok. GU21
off Abercorn Way 166 AU118
Ten Acre La, Egh. TW20 133 BC96
Ten Acres, Lthd.
(Fetch.) KT22 171 CD124
Ten Acres Cl, Lthd.
(Fetch.) KT22 171 CD124
Tenbury Cl, E7
off Romford Rd 68 EK64
Tenbury Ct, SW2 121 DK88
Tenby Av, Har. HA3 41 CH54
Tenby Cl, N15
off Hanover Rd 66 DT56
Romford RM6 70 EY58
Tenby Gdns, Nthlt. UB5 78 CA65
Tenby Rd, E17 67 DY57
Edgware HA8 42 CM53
Enfield EN3 30 DW41
Romford RM6 70 EY58
Welling DA16 106 EX81
Tenchleys La, Oxt. RH8 188 EK131
Tench St, E1 202 D3
Tenda Rd, SE16 202 D9
Tendring Way, Rom. RM6 70 EW57
Tenham Av, SW2 121 DK88
Tenison Ct, W1 195 K10
Tenison Way, SE1 200 D3
Tennand Cl, Wal.Cr.
(Chsht) EN7 14 DT26
Tenniel Cl, W2
off Porchester Gdns 82 DC72
Tennis Ct La, E.Mol. KT8
off Hampton Ct Way 137 CF97
Tennison Av, Borwd. WD6 26 CP43
Tennison Cl, Couls. CR5 175 DP120
Tennison Rd, SE25 142 DT98
Tennis St, SE1 201 K4
Tenniswood Rd, Enf. EN1 30 DT39
Tennyson Av, E11 68 EG59
E12 86 EL66
NW9 62 CQ55
Grays RM17 110 GB76
New Malden KT3 139 CV99
Twickenham TW1 117 CF88
Waltham Abbey EN9 16 EE34
Tennyson Cl, Enf. EN3 31 DX43
Feltham TW14 115 BT86
Welling DA16 105 ES81
Tennyson Rd, E10 67 EB61
E15 86 EE66
E17 67 DZ58
NW6 81 CZ67
NW7 43 CU50
SE20 123 DX94
SW19 120 DC93
W7 79 CF73
Addlestone KT15 152 BL105
Ashford TW15 114 BL92
Brentwood (Hutt.) CM13 55 GC45
Dartford DA1 128 FN85
Hounslow TW3 96 CC82
Romford RM3 52 FJ52
St. Albans AL2 8 CA26
Tennyson St, SW8 101 DH82
Tennyson Wk, Grav.
(Nthflt) DA11 130 GD90
Tilbury RM18 111 GH82
Tennyson Way, Horn. RM12 71 FF61
Tensing Av, Grav.
(Nthflt) DA11 130 GE90
Tensing Rd, Sthl. UB2 96 CA76
Tentelow La, Sthl. UB2 96 CA78
Tenterden Cl, NW4 63 CX55
SE9 125 EM91
Tenterden Dr, NW4 63 CX55
Tenterden Gdns, NW4 63 CX55
Croydon CR0 142 DU101
Tenterden Gro, NW4 63 CX56
Tenterden Rd, N17 46 DT52
Croydon CR0 142 DU101
Dagenham RM8 70 EZ61
Tenterden St, W1 195 J9
Tenter Grd, E1 197 P7
Tenter Pas, E1
off Mansell St 84 DT72
Tent Peg La, Orp. BR5 145 EQ99
Tent St, E1 84 DV70
Terborch Way, SE22
off East Dulwich Gro 122 DS85
Tercel Path, Chig. IG7 50 EV49
Teredo St, SE16 203 J7
Terence Cl, Grav. DA12 131 GM88
Terence Ct, Belv. DA17
off Nuxley Rd 106 EZ79
Teresa Gdns, Wal.Cr. EN8 14 DW34
Teresa Ms, E17 67 EA56
Teresa Wk, N10
off Connaught Gdns 65 DH57
Terling Cl, E11 68 EF62
Terling Rd, Dag. RM8 70 FA61
Terlings, The, Brwd. CM14 54 FU48
Terling Wk, N1
off Britannia Row 84 DQ67
Terminus Pl, SW1 199 J7
Tern Gdns, Upmin. RM14 73 FS60
Tern Way, Brwd. CM14 54 FS49
Terrace, The, E4
off Chingdale Rd 48 EE48
N3 off Hendon La 43 CZ54
NW6 82 DA67
SW13 98 CS82
Addlestone KT15 152 BL106
Gravesend DA12 131 GH86
Sevenoaks TN13 190 FD122
Woodford Green IG8
off Broadmead Rd 48 EG51
Terrace Gdns, SW13 99 CT82
Watford WD17 23 BV40
Terrace La, Rich. TW10 118 CL86
Terrace Rd, E9 84 DW66
E13 86 EG67
Walton-on-Thames KT12 135 BU101
Terraces, The, Dart. DA2 128 FQ87
Terrace St, Grav. DA12 131 GH86
Terrace Wk, Dag. RM9 70 EY64
Terrapin Rd, SW17 121 DH90
Terretts Pl, N1
off Upper St 83 DP66
Terrick Rd, N22 45 DL53
Terrick St, W12 81 CV72
Terrilands, Pnr. HA5 60 BZ55
Terront Rd, N15 66 DQ57
Tersha St, Rich. TW9 98 CM84
Tessa Sanderson Pl, SW8 101 DH83

★ Place of interest ⇌ Railway station ⊖ London Underground station DLR Docklands Light Railway station Tra Tramlink station H Hospital Riv Pedestrian ferry landing stage

Tessa Sanderson Way, Grnf. UB6
off Lilian Board Way 61 CD64
Testers Cl, Oxt. RH8 188 EH131
Testerton Wk, W11 81 CX73
Tetbury Pl, N1
off Upper St 83 DP67
Tetcott Rd, SW10 100 DC80
Tetherdown, N10 64 DG55
Tetty Way, Brom. BR2 144 EG96
Teversham La, SW8 101 DL81
Teviot Av, S.Ock.
(Aveley) RM15 90 FQ72
Teviot Cl, Well. DA16 106 EV81
Teviot St, E14 85 EC71
Tewkesbury Av, SE23 122 DV88
Pinner HA5 60 BY57
Tewkesbury Cl, N15
off Tewkesbury Rd 66 DR58
Barnet EN4
off Approach Rd 28 DD42
Loughton IG10 32 EL44
West Byfleet
(Byfleet) KT14 152 BK111
Tewkesbury Gdns, NW9 62 CP55
Tewkesbury Rd, N15 66 DR58
W13 79 CG73
Carshalton SM5 140 DD102
Tewkesbury Ter, N11 45 DJ51
Tewson Rd, SE18 105 ES78
Teynham Av, Enf. EN1 30 DR44
Teynham Grn, Brom. BR2 144 EG99
Teynton Ter, N17 46 DQ53
Thackeray Av, N17 46 DU54
Tilbury RM18 111 GH81
Thackeray Cl, SW19 119 CX94
Harrow HA2 60 CA60
Isleworth TW7 97 CG82
Uxbridge UB8
off Dickens Av 77 BP72
Thackeray Dr, Rom. RM6 70 EU59
Thackeray Rd, E6 86 EK68
SW8 101 DH82
Thackeray St, W8 100 DB75
Thakeham Cl, SE26 122 DV92
Thalia Cl, SE10 103 ED79
Thalmassing Cl, Brwd.
(Hutt.) CM13 55 GB47
Thame Rd, SE16 203 J4
Thames Av, SW10 100 DC81
Chertsey KT16 134 BG97
Dagenham RM9 89 FB70
Greenford UB6 79 CF68
Thames Bk, SW14 98 CQ82
Thamesbank Pl, SE28 88 EW72
Thames Circle, E14 204 A8
Thames Cl, Cher. KT16 134 BH101
Hampton TW12 136 CB96
Rainham RM13 89 FH72
Thames Ct, W.Mol. KT8 136 CB96
Thames Cres, W4
off Corney Rd 98 CS80
Thamesdale, St.Alb.
(Lon.Col.) AL2 10 CM27
THAMES DITTON 137 CF100
⇌ Thames Ditton 137 CF101
Thames Ditton Island, T.Ditt.
KT7 137 CG99
Thames Dr, Grays RM16 111 GG78
Ruislip HA4 59 BQ58
Thames Edge Ct, Stai. TW18
off Clarence St 113 BE91
Thames Europort, Dart. DA2 109 FS84
Thamesfield Ct, Shep. TW17 135 BQ101
★ Thames Flood Barrier &
Visitors Cen, SE18 104 EK75
Thames Gate, Dart. DA1
off St. Edmunds Rd 108 FN84
Thamesgate Cl, Rich. TW10
off Locksmeade Rd 117 CH91
Thames Gateway, Dag. RM9 88 EZ68
Rainham RM13 89 FG72
South Ockendon RM15 108 FP75
Thameshill Av, Rom. RM5 51 FC54
★ Thames Ho, SW1 199 P8
Thameside, Tedd. TW11 117 CK94
Thameside Ind Est, E16 104 EL75
Thameside Wk, SE28 87 ET72
THAMESMEAD, SE28 87 ET74
Thamesmead, Walt.
KT12 135 BU101
THAMESMEAD NORTH,
SE28 88 EW72
Thames Meadow, Shep.
TW17 135 BR102
West Molesey KT8 136 CA96
Thamesmead Spine Rd, Belv.
DA17 107 FB75
THAMESMEAD WEST,
SE18 105 EP76
Thamesmere Dr, SE28 88 EU73
Thames Pl, SW15 99 CX83
Thames Pt, SW6
off The Boulevard 100 DC81
Thames Quay, SW10
off Harbour Av 100 DC81
Thames Rd, E16 86 EK74
W4 98 CN79
Barking IG11 87 ET69
Dartford DA1 107 FF82
Grays RM17 110 GB80
Slough SL3 93 BA77
Thames Side, Cher. KT16 134 BJ100
Kingston upon Thames KT1 137 CK95
Staines TW18 134 BH96
Thames St, SE10 103 EB79
Hampton TW12 136 CB95
Kingston upon Thames KT1 137 CK96
Staines TW18 113 BE91
Sunbury-on-Thames TW16 135 BV98
Walton-on-Thames KT12 135 BT101
Weybridge KT13 135 BP103
Thamesvale Cl, Houns. TW3 96 CA83
H Thames Valley Nuffield Hosp,
Slou. SL2 74 AW67
Thames Vw, Grays RM16 111 GG78
Thames Village, W4 98 CQ81
Thames Way, Grav. DA11 130 GD88
Thames Wf, E16 205 K2
Thamley, Purf. RM19 108 FN77
Thanescroft Gdns, Croy. CR0 142 DS104
Thanet Dr, Kes. BR2
off Phoenix Dr 144 EK104
Thanet Pl, Croy. CR0 160 DQ105
Thanet Rd, Bex. DA5 126 FA87
Erith DA8 107 FE80
Thanet St, WC1 195 P3
Thane Vil, N7 65 DM62
Thane Wks, N7 65 DM62
Thanington Ct, SE9 125 ES86
Thant Cl, E10 67 EB62
Tharp Rd, Wall. SM6 159 DK106
Thatcham Gdns, N20 44 DC45
Thatcher Cl, West Dr. UB7
off Classon Cl 94 BL75
Thatcher Ct, Dart. DA1
off Heath St 128 FK87
Thatchers Cl, Loug. IG10 33 EQ40
Thatchers Way, Islw. TW7 117 CD85
Thatches Gro, Rom. RM6 70 EY56
Thavies Inn, EC1 196 E8
Thaxted Ct, N1 197 K1
Thaxted Grn, Brwd.
(Hutt.) CM13 55 GC43
Thaxted Ho, Dag. RM10 89 FB66
Thaxted Pl, SW20 119 CX94
Thaxted Rd, SE9 125 EQ89
Buckhurst Hill IG9 48 EL45
Thaxted Wk, Rain. RM13
off Ongar Way 89 FF67
Thaxted Way, Wal.Abb. EN9 15 ED33
Thaxton Rd, W14 99 CZ79
Thayers Fm Rd, Beck. BR3 143 DY95
Thayer St, W1 194 G7
Thaynesfield, Pot.B. EN6 12 DD31
★ Theatre Mus, WC2 196 A10
★ Theatre Royal, WC2 196 A9
Theatre Sq, E15
off Great Eastern Rd 85 ED65
Theatre St, SW11 100 DF83
Theberton St, N1 83 DN67
Theed St, SE1 200 D3
Thellusson Way, Rick. WD3 37 BF45
Thelma Cl, Grav. DA12 131 GM92
Thelma Gdns, SE3 104 EK81
Feltham TW13 116 BY90
Thelma Gro, Tedd. TW11 117 CG93
Theobald Cres, Har. HA3 40 CB53
Theobald Rd, E17 67 DZ59
Croydon CR0 141 DP103
Theobalds Av, N12 44 DC49
Grays RM17 110 GC78
Theobalds Cl, Pot.B.
(Cuffley) EN6 13 DM30
Theobalds Ct, N4
off Queens Dr 66 DQ61
⇌ Theobalds Grove 15 DX32
Theobalds La, Wal.Cr.
(Chsht) EN8 14 DV32
Theobalds Pk Rd, Enf. EN2 29 DP35
Theobald's Rd, WC1 196 B6
Theobalds Rd, Pot.B.
(Cuffley) EN6 13 DL30
Theobald St, SE1 201 K7
Borehamwood WD6 26 CM40
Radlett WD7 25 CH36
Theodora Way, Pnr. HA5 59 BT55
Theodore Rd, SE13 123 EC86
Tra Therapia Lane 141 DL101
Therapia La, Croy. CR0 141 DL100
Therapia Rd, SE22 122 DW86
Theresa Rd, W6 99 CU77
Theresas Wk, S.Croy. CR2
off Sanderstead Rd 160 DR110
Therfield Ct, N4
off Brownswood Rd 66 DQ61
Thermopylae Gate, E14 204 C9
Theseus Wk, N1 196 G1
Thesiger Rd, SE20 123 DX94
Thessaly Rd, SW8 101 DJ80
Thetford Cl, N13 45 DP51
Thetford Gdns, Dag. RM9 88 EX66
Thetford Rd, Ashf. TW15 114 BL91
Dagenham RM9 88 EX67
New Malden KT3 138 CR100
Thetis Ter, Rich. TW9
off Kew Grn 98 CN79
THEYDON BOIS, Epp. CM16 33 ET37
⊖ Theydon Bois 33 ET36
Theydon Bower, Epp. CM16 18 EU31
Theydon Ct, Wal.Abb. EN9 16 EG33
Theydon Gdns, Rain. RM13 89 FE66
THEYDON GARNON, Epp.
CM16 34 EW35
Theydon Gate, Epp.
(They.B.) CM16
off Coppice Row 33 ES37
Theydon Gro, Epp. CM16 18 EU30
Woodford Green IG8 48 EJ51
THEYDON MOUNT, Epp.
CM16 18 FA34
Theydon Pk Rd, Epp.
(They.B.) CM16 33 ES39
Theydon Pl, Epp. CM16 17 ET31
Theydon Rd, E5 66 DW61
Epping CM16 17 ER34
Theydon St, E17 67 DZ59
Thicket, The, West Dr. UB7 76 BL72
Thicket Cres, Sutt. SM1 158 DC105
Thicket Gro, SE20
off Anerley Rd 122 DU94
Dagenham RM9 88 EW65
Thicket Rd, SE20 122 DU94
Sutton SM1 158 DC105
Thicketts, Sev. TN13 191 FJ123
Thickthorne La, Stai. TW18 114 BJ94
Third Av, E12 68 EL63
E13 86 EG69
E17 67 EA57
W3 81 CT74
W10 81 CY69
Dagenham RM10 89 FB67
Enfield EN1 30 DT43
Grays RM20 109 FU79
Hayes UB3 77 BT74
Romford RM6 70 EW58
Third Av, Waltham Abbey EN9
off Breach Barn
Mobile Home Pk 16 EH30
Watford WD25 24 BX35
Wembley HA9 61 CK61
Third Cl, W.Mol. KT8 136 CB98
Third Cross Rd, Twick. TW2 117 CD89
Third Way, Wem. HA9 62 CP63
Thirleby Rd, SW1 199 L7
Edgware HA8 42 CR53
Thirlmere Av, Grnf. UB6 79 CJ69
Thirlmere Cl, Egh. TW20
off Keswick Rd 113 BB94
Thirlmere Gdns, Nthwd. HA6 39 BQ51
Wembley HA9 61 CJ60
Thirlmere Ho, Islw. TW7
off Summerwood Rd 117 CF85
Thirlmere Ri, Brom. BR1 124 EF93
Thirlmere Rd, N10 45 DH53
SW16 121 DK91
Bexleyheath DA7 107 FC82
Thirsk Cl, Nthlt. UB5 78 CA65
Thirsk Rd, SE25 142 DR98
SW11 100 DG83
Borehamwood WD6 26 CN37
Mitcham CR4 120 DG94
Thirston Path, Borwd. WD6 26 CN40
Thirza Rd, Dart. DA1 128 FM86
Thistlebrook, SE2 106 EW76
Thistlebrook Ind Est, SE2 106 EW75
Thistlecroft Gdns, Stan. HA7 41 CK53
Thistlecroft Rd, Walt. KT12 154 BW105
Thistledene, T.Ditt. KT7 137 CE100
West Byfleet KT14 151 BF113
Thistledene Av, Har. HA2 60 BY62
Romford RM5 51 FB50
Thistledown, Grav. DA12 131 GK93
Thistlefield Cl, Bex. DA5
off Murchison Av 126 EX88
Thistle Gro, SW10 100 DC78
Thistlemead, Chis. BR7 145 EP96
Thistle Mead, Loug. IG10 33 EN41
Thistle Rd, Grav. DA12 131 GL87
Thistlewaite Rd, E5 66 DV62
Thistlewood Cl, N7 65 DM61
Thistlewood Cres, Croy.
(New Adgtn) CR0 161 ED112
Thistleworth Cl, Islw. TW7 97 CD80
Thistley Cl, N12
off Summerfields Av 44 DE51
Thistley Ct, SE8
off Glaisher St 103 EB79
Thomas a'Beckett Cl, Wem.
HA0 61 CF63
Thomas Av, Cat. CR3 176 DQ121
Thomas Baines Rd, SW11 100 DD83
Thomas Cl, Brwd. CM15 54 FY48
Thomas Cribb Ms, E6 87 EM72
Thomas Darby Ct, W11 81 CY72
Thomas Dean Rd, SE26
off Kangley Br Rd 123 DZ91
Thomas Dinwiddy Rd, SE12 124 EH89
Thomas Doyle St, SE1 200 F6
Thomas Dr, Grav. DA12 131 GK89
Thomas Hardy Ho, N22 45 DM52
Thomas La, SE6 123 EA87
Thomas More Ho, EC2
off The Barbican 84 DQ71
Thomas More St, E1 202 B1
Thomas More Way, N2 64 DC55
Thomas Pl, W8
off St. Mary's Pl 100 DB76
Thomas Rd, E14 85 DZ72
Thomas Rochford Way, Wal.Cr.
EN8 15 DZ27
Thomas Sims Ct, Horn.
RM12 71 FH64
Thomas St, SE18 105 EN77
Thomas Wall Cl, Sutt. SM1
off Clarence Rd 158 DB106
Thompson Av, Rich. TW9 98 CN83
Thompson Cl, Ilf. IG1
off High Rd 69 EQ61
Slough SL3 93 BA77
Sutton SM3
off Barrington Rd 140 DA102
Thompson Rd, SE22 122 DT86
Dagenham RM9 70 EZ62
Hounslow TW3 96 CB84
Uxbridge UB10 76 BL66
Thompson's Av, SE5 102 DQ80
Thompsons Cl, Wal.Cr. EN7 14 DT29
Thompson's La, Loug.
(High Beach) IG10 32 EF39
Thompson Way, Rick. WD3 38 BG45
Thomson Cres, Croy. CR0 141 DN102
Thomson Rd, Har. HA3 61 CE55
Thong La, Grav. DA12 131 GM90
Thorburn Sq, SE1 202 B9
Thorburn Way, SW19 140 DC95
Thoresby St, N1 197 J2
Thorkhill Gdns, T.Ditt. KT7 137 CG102
Thorkhill Rd, T.Ditt. KT7 137 CH101
Thorley Cl, W.Byf. KT14 152 BG114
Thorley Gdns, Wok. GU22 152 BG114
Thornaby Gdns, N18 46 DU51
Thornash Cl, Wok. GU21 166 AW115
Thornash Rd, Wok. GU21 166 AW115
Thornash Way, Wok. GU21 166 AW115
Thorn Av, Bushey
(Bushey Hth) WD23 40 CC46
Thornbank Cl, Stai. TW19 114 BG85
Thornbridge Rd, Iver SL0 75 BC67
Thornbrook, Epp.
(Thnwd) CM16 18 EX25
Thornbury Av, Islw. TW7 97 CD80
Thornbury Cl, N16
off Boleyn Rd 66 DS64
NW7 off Kingsbridge Dr 43 CX52
Thornbury Gdns, Borwd.
WD6 26 CQ42
Thornbury Rd, SW2 121 DL86
Isleworth TW7 97 CD81
Thornbury Sq, N6 65 DJ60
Thornby Rd, E5 66 DW62
Thorncliffe Rd, SW2 121 DL86
Southall UB2 96 BZ78
Thorn Cl, Brom. BR2 145 EN100
Northolt UB5 78 BZ69
Thorncombe Rd, SE22 122 DS85
Thorncroft, Egh.
(Eng.Grn) TW20 112 AW94
Hornchurch RM11 71 FH58
Thorncroft Cl, Couls. CR5
off Waddington Av 175 DN120
Thorncroft Dr, Lthd. KT22 171 CH123
Thorncroft Rd, Sutt. SM1 158 DB105
Thorncroft St, SW8 101 DL80
Thorndales, Brwd. CM14 54 FX49
Thorndean St, SW18 120 DC89
Thorndene Av, N11 44 DG46
Thorndike Av, Nthlt. UB5 78 BX67
Thorndike Cl, SW10 100 DC80
Thorndike Rd, N1 84 DQ65
Thorndike St, SW1 199 M10
Thorndon Cl, Orp. BR5 145 ET96
Thorndon Ct, Brwd.
(Gt Warley) CM13 53 FW51
Thorndon Gdns, Epsom
KT19 156 CS105
Thorndon Gate, Brwd.
(Ingrave) CM13 55 GC50
Thorndon Rd, Orp. BR5 145 ET96
Thorn Dr, Slou.
(Geo.Grn) SL3 74 AY72
Thorndyke Ct, Pnr. HA5
off Westfield Pk 40 BZ52
Thorne Cl, E11 68 EE63
E16 86 EG72
Ashford TW15 115 BQ94
Erith DA8 107 FC79
Thorneloe Gdns, Croy. CR0 159 DN106
Thorne Pas, SW13 98 CS82
Thorne Rd, SW8 101 DL80
Thornes Cl, Beck. BR3 143 EC97
Thorne St, E16 86 EF72
SW13 98 CS83
Thornet Wd Rd, Brom. BR1 145 EN97
THORNEY, Iver SL0 94 BH76
Thorney Cres, SW11 100 DD80
Thorneycroft Cl, Walt. KT12 136 BW100
Thorneycroft Dr, Enf. EN3 31 EA37
Thorney Hedge Rd, W4 98 CP77
Thorney La N, Iver SL0 75 BF74
Thorney La S, Iver SL0 93 BF75
Thorney Mill Rd, Iver SL0 94 BG76
West Drayton UB7 94 BG76
Thorney St, SW1 199 P8
Thornfield Av, NW7 43 CY53
Thornfield Rd, W12 99 CV75
Banstead SM7 174 DA117
Thornford Rd, SE13 123 EC85
Thorngate Rd, W9 82 DA70
Thorngrove Rd, E13 86 EH67
Thornham Gro, E15 67 ED64
Thornham St, SE10 103 EB79
Thornhaugh Ms, WC1 195 N5
Thornhaugh St, WC1 195 N6
Thornhill, Epp.
(N.Wld Bas.) CM16 19 FC26
Thornhill Av, SE18 105 ES80
Surbiton KT6 138 CL103
Thornhill Br Wf, N1
off Caledonian Rd 83 DM67
Thornhill Cres, N1 83 DM66
Thornhill Gdns, E10 67 EB61
Barking IG11 87 ES66
Thornhill Gro, N1
off Lofting Rd 83 DM66
Thornhill Rd, E10 67 EB61
N1 83 DN66
Croydon CR0 142 DQ101
Northwood HA6 39 BQ49
Surbiton KT6 138 CL103
Uxbridge UB10 58 BM63
Thornhill Sq, N1 83 DM66
Thornhill Way, Shep. TW17 134 BN99
Thorn Ho, Beck. BR3 143 DY95
Thorn La, Rain. RM13 90 FK68
Thornlaw Rd, SE27 121 DN91
Thornley Cl, N17 46 DU52
Thornley Dr, Har. HA2 60 CB61
Thornley Pl, SE10
off Caradoc St 104 EE78
Thornridge, Brwd. CM14 54 FV45
Thornsbeach Rd, SE6 123 EC88
Thornsett Pl, SE20 142 DV96
Thornsett Rd, SE20 142 DV96
SW18 120 DB89
Thornside, Edg. HA8
off High St 42 CN51
Thorns Meadow, West.
(Brasted) TN16 180 EW123
Thorn Ter, SE15
off Nunhead Gro 102 DW83
Thornton Av, SW2 121 DK88
W4 98 CS77
Croydon CR0 141 DM100
West Drayton UB7 94 BM76
Thornton Cl, West Dr. UB7 94 BM76
Thornton Ct, SW20 139 CX99
Thornton Cres, Couls. CR5 175 DN119
Thornton Dene, Beck. BR3 143 EA96
Thornton Gdns, SW12 121 DK88
Thornton Gro, Pnr. HA5 40 CA51
THORNTON HEATH 141 DP98
⇌ Thornton Heath 142 DQ98
Thornton Hill, SW19 119 CY94
Thornton Pl, W1 194 E6
Thornton Rd, E11 67 ED61
N18 46 DW48
SW12 121 DK87
SW14 98 CR83
SW19 119 CX93
Barnet EN5 27 CY41
Belvedere DA17 107 FB77
Bromley BR1 124 EG92
Carshalton SM5 140 DD102
Croydon CR0 141 DM101
Ilford IG1 69 EP63
Potters Bar EN6 12 DC30
Thornton Heath CR7 141 DM101
Thornton Rd E, SW19
off Thornton Rd 119 CX93
Thornton Rd Retail Pk, Croy.
CR0 141 DM100
Thornton Row, Th.Hth. CR7
off London Rd 141 DN99
Thorntons Fm Av, Rom. RM7 71 FD60
Thornton St, SW9 101 DN82
Thornton Way, NW11 64 DB57
Thorntree Rd, SE7 104 EK78
Thornville Gro, Mitch. CR4 140 DC96
Thornville St, SE8 103 EA81
THORNWOOD, Epp. CM16 18 EW25
Thornwood Cl, E18 48 EH54
Thornwood Rd, SE13 124 EE85
Epping CM16 18 EV29
Thorogood Gdns, E15 68 EE64
Thorogood Way, Rain. RM13 89 FE67
Thorold Cl, S.Croy. CR2 161 DX110
Thorold Rd, N22 45 DL52
Ilford IG1 69 EP61
Thoroughfare, The, Tad. KT20 183 CU125
Thorparch Rd, SW8 101 DK81
THORPE, Egh. TW20 133 BC97
Thorpebank Rd, W12 81 CU74
Thorpe Bypass, Egh. TW20 133 BB96
Thorpe Cl, W10
off Cambridge Gdns 81 CY72
Croydon (New Adgtn)
CR0 161 EC111
Orpington BR6 145 ES103
H Thorpe Coombe Hosp,
E17 67 EC55
Thorpe Cres, E17 47 DZ54
Watford WD19 40 BW45
Thorpedale Gdns, Ilf. IG2, IG6 69 EN56
Thorpedale Rd, N4 65 DL60
THORPE GREEN, Egh. TW20 133 BA98
Thorpe Hall Rd, E17 47 EC53
Thorpe Ind Est, Egh. TW20 133 BC96
THORPE LEA, Egh. TW20 113 BB93
Thorpe Lea Rd, Egh. TW20 113 BB93
Thorpe Lo, Horn. RM11 72 FL59
★ Thorpe Park, Cher. KT16 133 BE98
Thorpe Rd, E6 87 EM67
E7 68 EF63
E17 47 EC54
N15 66 DS58
Barking IG11 87 ER66
Chertsey KT16 133 BD99
Kingston upon Thames KT2 118 CL94
Staines TW18 113 BD93
Thorpeside Cl, Stai. TW18 133 BE96
Thorpe Wk, Grnf. UB6
off Conway Cres 79 CE68
Thorpewood Av, SE26 122 DV89
Thorpland Av, Uxb. UB10 59 BQ62
Thorsden Cl, Wok. GU22 166 AY118
Thorsden Ct, Wok. GU22
off Guildford Rd 166 AY118
Thorsden Way, SE19
off Oaks Av 122 DS91
Thorverton Rd, NW2 63 CY62
Thoydon Rd, E3 85 DY68
Thrale Rd, SW16 121 DJ92
Thrale St, SE1 201 J3
Thrasher Cl, E8
off Stean St 84 DT67
Thrawl St, E1 84 DT71
Threadneedle St, EC2 197 L9
Three Barrels Wk, EC4 197 J10
Three Colts Cor, E2
off Weaver St 84 DU70
Three Colts La, E2 84 DV70
Three Colt St, E14 85 DZ73
Three Cors, Bexh. DA7 107 FB82
Three Cups Yd, WC1 196 C7
Three Forests Way, Chig. IG7 50 EW48
Loughton IG10 32 EK38
Romford RM4 50 EW48
Waltham Abbey EN9 32 EK36
Three Gates Rd, Long.
(Fawk.Grn) DA3 149 FU102
Three Households, Ch.St.G.
HP8 36 AT49
Three Kings Rd, Mitch. CR4 140 DG97
Three Kings Yd, W1 195 H10
Three Mill La, E3 85 EC69
Three Oak La, SE1 201 P4
Three Oaks Cl, Uxb. UB10 58 BM62
Three Quays Wk, EC3 201 N1
Three Valleys Way, Bushey WD23
off Aldenham Rd 24 BY43
Threshers Pl, W11 81 CY73
Thriffwood, SE26 122 DW90
Thrift, The, Dart.
(Bean) DA2 129 FW90
Thrift Fm La, Borwd. WD6 26 CP40
Thrift Grn, Brwd. CM13
off Knight's Way 55 GA48
Thrift La, Sev.
(Cudham) TN14 179 ER117
Thrifts Hall Fm Ms, Epp.
(They.B.) CM16 33 ET37
Thrifts Mead, Epp.
(They.B.) CM16 33 ES37
Thrigby Rd, Chess. KT9 156 CM107
Throckmorten Rd, E16 86 EH72
Throgmorton Av, EC2 197 L8
Throgmorton St, EC2 197 L8
Throwley Cl, SE2 106 EW76
Throwley Rd, Sutt. SM1 158 DB106
Throwley Way, Sutt. SM1 158 DB105
Thrums, The, Wat. WD24 23 BV37
Thrupp Cl, Mitch. CR4 141 DH96
Thrupps Av, Walt. KT12 154 BX106
Thrupps La, Walt. KT12 154 BX106
Thrush Grn, Har. HA2 60 CA56
Rickmansworth WD3 38 BJ45
Thrush La, Pot.B.
(Cuffley) EN6 13 DL28
Thrush St, SE17 201 H10
Thruxton Way, SE15
off Daniel Gdns 102 DT80
Thunderer Rd, Dag. RM9 88 EY70
Thurbarn Rd, SE6 123 EB92
Thurland Rd, SE16 202 B6
Thurlby Cl, Har. HA1
off Gayton Rd 61 CG58
Woodford Green IG8 49 EM50
Thurlby Rd, SE27 121 DN91
Wembley HA0 79 CK65
Thurleigh Av, SW12 120 DG86
Thurleigh Rd, SW12 120 DG86
Thurleston Av, Mord. SM4 139 CY99
Thurlestone Av, N12 44 DF51
Ilford IG3 69 ET63
Thurlestone Cl, Shep. TW17 135 BQ100

★ Place of interest ⇌ Railway station ⊖ London Underground station DLR Docklands Light Railway station Tra Tramlink station H Hospital Riv Pedestrian ferry landing stage

Thurlestone Rd, SE27 121 DN90
Thurloe Cl, SW7 198 B8
Thurloe Gdns, Rom. RM1 71 FF58
Thurloe Pl, SW7 198 A8
Thurloe Pl Ms, SW7 198 A8
Thurloe Sq, SW7 198 B8
Thurloe St, SW7 198 A8
Thurloe Wk, Grays RM17 110 GA76
Thurlow Cl, E4
off Higham Sta Av 47 EB51
Thurlow Gdns, Ilf. IG6 49 ER51
Wembley HA0 61 CK64
Thurlow Hill, SE21 122 DQ88
Thurlow Pk Rd, SE21 121 DP88
Thurlow Rd, NW3 64 DD64
W7 97 CG75
Thurlow St, SE17 201 L10
Thurlow Ter, NW5 64 DG64
Thurlstone Rd, Ruis. HA4 59 BU62
Thurlton Ct, Wok. GU21
off Chobham Rd 166 AY116
Thurnby Ct, Twick. TW2 117 CE90
Thurnham Way, Tad. KT20 173 CW120
Thurrock Lakeside, Grays
RM20 109 FV77
Thurrock Pk Way, Til. RM18 110 GD80
Thursby Rd, Wok. GU21 166 AU118
Thursland Rd, Sid. DA14 126 EY92
Thursley Cres, Croy.
(New Adgtn) CR0 161 ED108
Thursley Gdns, SW19 119 CX89
Thursley Rd, SE9 125 EM90
Thurso Cl, Rom. RM3 52 FP51
Thurso St, SW17 120 DD91
Thurstan Rd, SW20 119 CV94
Thurston Rd, SE13 103 EB82
Slough SL1 74 AS72
Southall UB1 78 BZ72
Thurston Rd Ind Est, SE13
off Jerrard St 103 EB83
Thurtle Rd, E2 84 DT67
Thwaite Cl, Erith DA8 107 FC79
Thyer Cl, Orp. BR6
off Isabella Dr 163 EQ105
Thyme Cl, SE3
off Nelson Mandela Rd 104 EJ83
Thyra Gro, N12 44 DB51
Tibbatts Rd, E3 85 EB70
Tibbenham Pl, SE6
off Fordmill Rd 123 EA89
Tibbenham Wk, E13 86 EF68
Tibberton Sq, N1
off Popham Rd 84 DQ66
Tibbets Cl, SW19 119 CX88
Tibbet's Cor, SW15 119 CX87
Tibbet's Cor Underpass, SW15
off West Hill 119 CX87
Tibbet's Ride, SW15 119 CX87
Tibbles Cl, Wat. WD25 24 BY35
Tibbs Hill Rd, Abb.L. WD5 7 BT30
Tiber Gdns, N1
off Copenhagen St 83 DM67
Ticehurst Cl, Orp. BR5
off Grovelands Rd 126 EU94
Ticehurst Rd, SE23 123 DY89
Tichborne, Rick.
(Map.Cr.) WD3 37 BD50
Tichmarsh, Epsom KT19 156 CQ110
Tickford Cl, SE2
off Ampleforth Rd 106 EW75
Tidal Basin Rd, E16 205 L1
Tidenham Gdns, Croy. CR0 142 DS104
Tideswell Rd, SW15 119 CW85
Croydon CR0 143 EA104
Tideway Cl, Rich. TW10
off Locksmeade Rd 117 CH91
Tideway Ind Est, SW8 101 DJ79
Tideway Wk, SW8
off Cringle St 101 DJ80
Tidey St, E3 85 EA71
Tidford Rd, Well. DA16 105 ET82
Tidworth Rd, E3 85 EA70
Tidy's La, Epp. CM16 18 EV29
Tiepigs La, Brom. BR2 144 EE103
West Wickham BR4 144 EE103
Tierney Rd, SW2 121 DL88
Tiger La, Brom. BR2 144 EH98
Tiger Way, E5 66 DV63
Tigris Cl, N9 46 DW47
Tilbrook Rd, SE3 104 EJ83
Tilburstow Hill Rd, Gdse.
RH9 186 DW132
TILBURY 111 GG81
Tilbury Cl, SE15
off Sumner Rd 102 DT80
Orpington BR5 146 EV96
Tilbury Docks, Til. RM18 110 GE84
★ Tilbury Fort, Til. RM18 111 GJ84
Tilbury Gdns, Til. RM18 111 GG84
Tilbury Hotel Rd, Til. RM18 111 GG84
Tilbury Rd, E6 87 EM68
E10 67 EC59
⇌ Tilbury Town 110 GE82
Tilbury Wk, Slou. SL3 93 BB76
Tildesley Rd, SW15 119 CW86
Tile Fm Rd, Orp. BR6 145 ER104
Tilehouse Cl, Borwd. WD6 26 CM41
Tilehouse La, Ger.Cr. SL9 37 BE53
Rickmansworth
(Map.Cr.) WD3 37 BE53
Uxbridge (Denh.) UB9 57 BE58
Tilehouse Way, Uxb.
(Denh.) UB9 57 BF59
Tilehurst Pt, SE2
off Yarnton Way 106 EW75
Tilehurst Rd, SW18 120 DD88
Sutton SM3 157 CY106
Tilekiln Cl, Wal.Cr. EN7 14 DT29
Tile Kiln La, N6
off Winchester Rd 65 DH60
N13 46 DQ50
Bexley DA5 127 FC89
Uxbridge (Hare.) UB9 59 BP59
Tilers Cl, Red. RH1
off Nutfield Rd 185 DJ131
Tile Yd, E14
off Commercial Rd 85 DZ72
Tileyard Rd, N7 83 DL66
Tilford Av, Croy.
(New Adgtn) CR0 161 EC109
Tilford Gdns, SW19 119 CX89
Tilia Cl, Sutt. SM1 157 CZ106
Tilia Rd, E5
off Clarence Rd 66 DV63
Tilia Wk, SW9
off Moorland Rd 101 DP84
Till Av, Dart. (Fnghm) DA4 148 FM102
Tiller Rd, E14 203 P6
Tillett Cl, NW10 80 CQ65
Tillett Sq, SE16 203 L5
Tillett Way, E2
off Gosset St 84 DU69
Tilley La, Epsom
(Headley) KT18 172 CQ123
Tillgate Common, Red. RH1 186 DQ133
Tillingbourne Gdns, N3 63 CZ55
Tillingbourne Grn, Orp. BR5 146 EU98
Tillingbourne Way, N3
off Tillingbourne Gdns 63 CZ55
Tillingdown Hill, Cat. CR3 176 DU122
Tillingdown La, Cat. CR3 176 DV124
Tillingham Ct, Wal.Abb. EN9 16 EG33
Tillingham Way, N12 44 DA49
Tilling Rd, NW2 63 CW60
Tilling Way, Wem. HA9 61 CK61
Tillman St, E1
off Bigland St 84 DV72
Tilloch St, N1
off Carnoustie Dr 83 DM66
Tillotson Rd, N9 46 DT47
Harrow HA3 40 CB52
Ilford IG1 69 EN59
Tilly's La, Stai. TW18 113 BF91
Tilmans Mead, Dart.
(Fnghm) DA4 148 FM101
Tilney Ct, EC1 197 J4
Tilney Dr, Buck.H. IG9 48 EG47
Tilney Gdns, N1 84 DR65
Tilney Rd, Dag. RM9 88 EZ65
Southall UB2 96 BW77
Tilney St, W1 198 G2
Tilson Gdns, SW2 121 DL87
Tilson Ho, SW2
off Tilson Gdns 121 DL87
Tilson Rd, N17 46 DU53
Tilston Cl, E11
off Matcham Rd 68 EF62
Tilt Cl, Cob. KT11 170 BY116
Tilt Meadow, Cob. KT11 170 BY116
Tilton St, SW6 99 CY79
Tilt Rd, Cob. KT11 170 BW115
Tiltwood, The, W3
off Acacia Rd 80 CQ73
Tilt Yd App, SE9 125 EM86
Timber Cl, Chis. BR7 145 EN96
Woking GU22
off Hacketts La 151 BF114
Timber Ct, Grays RM17
off Columbia Wf Rd 110 GA79
Timbercroft, Epsom KT19 156 CS105
Timbercroft La, SE18 105 ES79
Timberdene, NW4 43 CX54
Timberdene Av, Ilf. IG6 49 EP53
Timberhill, Ashtd. KT21
off Ottways La 172 CL119
Timber Hill Cl, Cher. KT16 151 BC108
Timber Hill Rd, Cat. CR3 176 DU124
Timberland Cl, SE15
off Peckham Hill St 102 DU80
Timberland Rd, E1 84 DV72
Timber La, Cat. CR3
off Timber Hill Rd 176 DU124
Timberling Gdns, S.Croy. CR2
off Sanderstead Rd 160 DR109
Timber Mill Way, SW4 101 DK83
Timber Pond Rd, SE16 203 J3
Timber Ridge, Rick.
(Loud.) WD3 22 BK42
Timberslip Dr, Wall. SM6 159 DK109
Timber St, EC1 197 H4
Timbertop Rd, West.
(Bigg.H.) TN16 178 EJ118
Timberwharf Rd, N16 66 DU58
Timbrell Pl, SE16 203 M3
Time Sq, E8 66 DT64
Times Sq, Sutt. SM1 158 DB106
Times Sq Shop Cen, Sutt. SM1
off High St 158 DB106
Timothy Cl, SW4
off Elms Rd 121 DJ85
Bexleyheath DA6 126 EY85
Timothy Ho, Erith DA18
off Kale Rd 106 EY75
Timothy Rd, E3 85 DZ71
Timperley Gdns, Red. RH1 184 DE132
Timsbury Wk, SW15 119 CU88
Timsway, Stai. TW18 113 BF92
Tindale Cl, S.Croy. CR2 160 DR111
Tindall Cl, Rom. RM3 52 FM54
Tindal St, SW9 101 DP81
Tinderbox All, SW14 98 CR83
Tine Rd, Chig. IG7 49 ES50
Tingeys Top La, Enf. EN2 29 DN36
Tinniswood Cl, N5
off Drayton Pk 65 DN64
Tinsey Cl, Egh. TW20 113 BB92
Tinsley Rd, E1 84 DW71
Tintagel Cl, Epsom KT17 157 CT114
Tintagel Cres, SE22 102 DT84
Tintagel Dr, Stan. HA7 41 CK49
Tintagel Gdns, SE22
off Oxonian St 102 DT84
Tintagel Rd, Orp. BR5 146 EW103
Tintagel Way, Wok. GU22 167 BA116
Tintern Av, NW9 62 CP55
Tintern Cl, SW15 119 CY85
SW19 120 DC94
Tintern Ct, W13
off Green Man La 79 CG73
Tintern Gdns, N14 45 DL45
Tintern Path, NW9
off Ruthin Cl 62 CS58
Tintern Rd, N22 46 DQ53
Carshalton SM5 140 DD102
Tintern St, SW4 101 DL84
Tintern Way, Har. HA2 60 CB60
Tinto Rd, E16 86 EG70
Tinwell Ms, Borwd. WD6
off Cranes Way 26 CQ43
Tinworth St, SE11 200 A10
Tippendell La, St.Alb.
(Park St) AL2 8 CB26
Tippetts Cl, Enf. EN2 30 DQ39
Tipthorpe Rd, SW11 100 DG83
Tipton Cotts, Add. KT15
off Oliver Cl 152 BG105
Tipton Dr, Croy. CR0 160 DS105
Tiptree Cl, E4
off Mapleton Rd 47 EC48
Hornchurch RM11 72 FN60
Tiptree Cres, Ilf. IG5 69 EN55
Tiptree Dr, Enf. EN2 30 DR42
Tiptree Est, Ilf. IG5 69 EN55
Tiptree Rd, Ruis. HA4 59 BV63
Tirlemont Rd, S.Croy. CR2 160 DQ108
Tirrell Rd, Croy. CR0 142 DQ100
Tisbury Ct, W1 off Rupert St 83 DK73
Tisbury Rd, SW16 141 DL96
Tisdall Pl, SE17 201 L9
Titan Rd, Grays RM17 110 GA78
Titchborne Row, W2 194 C9
Titchfield Rd, NW8 82 DF67
Carshalton SM5 140 DD102
Enfield EN3 31 DY37
Titchfield Wk, Cars. SM5
off Titchfield Rd 140 DD101
Titchwell Rd, SW18 120 DD87
Tite Hill, Egh. TW20 112 AX92
Tite St, SW3 100 DF78
★ Tithe Barn Agricultural &
Folk Mus, The, Upmin.
RM14 73 FR59
Tithe Barn Cl, Kings.T. KT2 138 CM95
Tithe Barn Ct, Abb.L. WD5
off Dairy Way 7 BT29
Tithe Barn Way, Nthlt. UB5 77 BV69
Tithe Cl, NW7 43 CU53
Hayes UB4
off Gledwood Dr 77 BT71
Virginia Water GU25 132 AX100
Walton-on-Thames KT12 135 BV100
Tithe Ct, Slou. SL3 93 BA77
Tithe Fm Av, Har. HA2 60 CA62
Tithe Fm Cl, Har. HA2 60 CA62
Tithe La, Stai. (Wrays.) TW19 113 BA86
Tithe Meadow, Wat. WD18 23 BR44
Tithe Meadows, Vir.W. GU25 132 AW100
Tithepit Shaw La, Warl. CR6 176 DV115
Tithe Wk, NW7 43 CU53
Titian Av, Bushey
(Bushey Hth) WD23 41 CE45
Titley Cl, E4 47 EA50
Titmus Cl, Uxb. UB8 77 BQ72
Titmuss Av, SE28 88 EV73
Titmuss St, W12
off Goldhawk Rd 99 CW75
TITSEY, Oxt. RH8 188 EH125
Titsey Hill, Oxt. (Titsey) RH8 178 EF123
Titsey Rd, Oxt. RH8 188 EH125
Tiverton Av, Ilf. IG5 69 EN55
Tiverton Cl, Croy. CR0
off Exeter Rd 142 DT101
Tiverton Dr, SE9 125 EQ88
Tiverton Gro, Rom. RM3 52 FN50
Tiverton Ho, Enf. EN3 31 DX41
Tiverton Rd, N15 66 DR58
N18 46 DS50
NW10 81 CX67
Edgware HA8 42 CM54
Hounslow TW3 96 CC82
Potters Bar EN6 12 DD31
Ruislip HA4 59 BU62
Thornton Heath CR7
off Willett Rd 141 DN99
Wembley HA0 80 CL68
Tiverton St, SE1 201 H7
Tiverton Way, NW7 43 CX52
Chessington KT9 155 CJ106
Tivoli Ct, SE16 203 M4
Tivoli Gdns, SE18 104 EL77
Tivoli Rd, N8 65 DK57
SE27 122 DQ92
Hounslow TW4 96 BY84
Toad La, Houns. TW4 96 BZ84
Tobacco Dock, E1 202 D1
Tobacco Quay, E1 202 D1
Tobago St, E14 203 P4
Tobin Cl, NW3 82 DE66
Toby La, E1 85 DY70
Toby Way, Surb. KT5 138 CP103
Todd Cl, Rain. RM13 90 FK70
Todds Wk, N7
off Andover Rd 65 DM61
Toft Av, Grays RM17 110 GD77
Tokenhouse Yd, EC2 197 K8
Token Yd, SW15
off Montserrat Rd 99 CY84
TOKYNGTON, Wem. HA9 80 CP65
Tokyngton Av, Wem. HA9 80 CN65
Toland Sq, SW15 119 CU85
Tolcarne Dr, Pnr. HA5 59 BV55
Toldene Ct, Couls. CR5 175 DM120
Toley Av, Wem. HA9 62 CL59
Toll Bar Ct, Sutt. SM2 158 DB109
Tollbridge Cl, W10
off Kensal Rd 81 CY70
Tolldene Cl, Wok. (Knap.) GU21
off Robin Hood Rd 166 AS117
Tollers La, Couls. CR5 175 DM119
Tollesbury Gdns, Ilf. IG6 69 ER55
Tollet St, E1 85 DX70
Tollgate Cl, Rick.
(Chorl.) WD3 21 BF41
Tollgate Dr, SE21 122 DS89
Hayes UB4 78 BX73
Tollgate Gdns, NW6 82 DB68
Tollgate Rd, E6 86 EK71
E16 86 EJ71
Dartford DA2 129 FR87
Waltham Cross EN8 31 DX35
Tollhouse La, Wall. SM6 159 DJ109
Tollhouse Way, N19 65 DJ61
Tollington Pk, N4 65 DM61
Tollington Pl, N4 65 DM61
Tollington Rd, N7 65 DM63
Tollington Way, N7 65 DL62
Tolmers Av, Pot.B.
(Cuffley) EN6 13 DL28
Tolmers Gdns, Pot.B.
(Cuffley) EN6 13 DL29
Tolmers Ms, Hert.
(Newgate St) SG13 13 DL25
Tolmers Pk, Hert.
(Newgate St) SG13 13 DL25
Tolmers Rd, Pot.B.
(Cuffley) EN6 13 DL27
Tolmers Sq, NW1 195 L4
Tolpits Cl, Wat. WD18 23 BT43
Tolpits La, Wat. WD18 23 BT44
Tolpuddle Av, E13
off Rochester Av 86 EJ67
Tolpuddle St, N1 83 DN68
Tolsford Rd, E5 66 DV64
Tolson Rd, Islw. TW7 97 CG83
Tolvaddon, Wok. GU21
off Cardingham 166 AU117
Tolverne Rd, SW20 139 CW95
TOLWORTH, Surb. KT6 138 CN103
⇌ Tolworth 138 CP103
Tolworth Bdy, Surb. KT6 138 CP102
Tolworth Cl, Surb. KT6 138 CP102
Tolworth Gdns, Rom. RM6 70 EX57
H Tolworth Hosp, Surb.
KT6 138 CN103
Tolworth Pk Rd, Surb. KT6 138 CM103
Tolworth Ri N, Surb. KT5
off Elmbridge Av 138 CQ101
Tolworth Ri S, Surb. KT5
off Warren Dr S 138 CQ102
Tolworth Rd, Surb. KT6 138 CL103
Tolworth Twr, Surb. KT6 138 CP103
Tomahawk Gdns, Nthlt. UB5
off Javelin Way 78 BX69
Tom Coombs Cl, SE9
off Well Hall Rd 104 EL84
Tom Cribb Rd, SE28 105 EQ76
Tom Gros Cl, E15
off Maryland St 67 ED64
Tom Hood Cl, E15
off Maryland St 67 ED64
Tom Jenkinson Rd, E16 205 N2
Tomkins Cl, Borwd. WD6
off Tallis Way 26 CL39
Tomkyns La, Upmin. RM14 73 FR56
Tomlin Cl, Epsom KT19 156 CR111
Tomlins Gro, E3 85 EA69
Tomlinson Cl, E2 84 DT69
W4 98 CP78
Tomlins Orchard, Bark. IG11 87 EQ67
Tomlins Ter, E14
off Rhodeswell Rd 85 DZ71
Tomlins Wk, N7
off Briset Way 65 DM61
Tomlyns Cl, Brwd.
(Hutt.) CM13 55 GE44
Tom Mann Cl, Bark. IG11 87 ES67
Tom Nolan Cl, E15 86 EE68
Tomo Ind Est, Uxb. UB8 76 BJ72
Tompion St, EC1 196 F3
Toms Hill, Kings L. WD4
off Bucks Hill 6 BJ33
Rickmansworth WD3 22 BL36
Toms La, Abb.L.
(Bedmond) WD5 7 BR28
Kings Langley WD4 7 BP29
Tom Smith Cl, SE10
off Maze Hill 104 EE79
Tomswood Ct, Ilf. IG6 49 EQ53
Tomswood Hill, Ilf. IG6 49 EP52
Tomswood Rd, Chig. IG7 49 EN51
Tom Thumbs Arch, E3
off Malmesbury Rd 85 EA68
Tom Williams Ho, SW6
off Clem Attlee Ct 99 CZ79
Tonbridge Cl, Bans. SM7 158 DF114
Tonbridge Cres, Har. HA3 62 CL56
Tonbridge Ho, SE25 142 DU97
Tonbridge Rd, Rom. RM3 52 FK52
Sevenoaks TN13 191 FJ127
West Molesey KT8 136 BY98
Tonbridge St, WC1 195 P2
Tonbridge Wk, WC1
off Tonbridge St 83 DL69
Tonfield Rd, Sutt. SM3 139 CZ102
Tonge Cl, Beck. BR3 143 EA99
Tonsley Hill, SW18 120 DB85
Tonsley Pl, SW18 120 DB85
Tonsley Rd, SW18 120 DB85
Tonsley St, SW18 120 DB85
Tonstall Rd, Epsom KT19 156 CR110
Mitcham CR4 140 DG96
Tony Cannell Ms, E3
off Maplin St 85 DZ69
Tooke Cl, Pnr. HA5 40 BY53
Tookey Cl, Har. HA3 62 CM59
Took's Ct, EC4 196 D8
Tooley St, SE1 201 L2
Gravesend (Nthflt) DA11 130 GD87
Toorack Rd, Har. HA3 41 CD54
TOOT HILL, Ong. CM5 19 FF30
Toot Hill Rd, Ong. CM5 19 FF29
⇌ Tooting 120 DG93
⊖ Tooting Bec 120 DF90
Tooting Bec Gdns, SW16 121 DK91
Tooting Bec Rd, SW16 120 DG90
SW17 120 DG90
⊖ Tooting Broadway 120 DE92
TOOTING GRAVENEY,
SW17 120 DE93
Tooting Gro, SW17 120 DE92
Tooting High St, SW17 120 DE93
Tootswood Rd, Brom. BR2 144 EE99
Tooveys Mill Cl, Kings L. WD4 6 BN28
Topaz Wk, NW2
off Marble Dr 63 CX59
Topcliffe Dr, Orp. BR6 163 ER105
Top Dartford Rd, Dart. DA2 127 FF94
Swanley BR8 127 FF94
Topham Sq, N17 46 DQ53
Topham St, EC1 196 D4
Top Ho Ri, E4
off Parkhill Rd 47 EC45
Topiary, The, Ashtd. KT21 172 CL120
Topiary Sq, Rich. TW9 98 CM83
Topland Rd, Ger.Cr.
(Chal.St.P.) SL9 36 AX52
Toplands Av, S.Ock.
(Aveley) RM15 90 FP74
Topley St, SE9 104 EK84
Topmast Pt, E14 203 P5
Top Pk, Beck. BR3 144 EE99
Gerrards Cross SL9 56 AW58
Topping La, Uxb. UB8 76 BK69
Topp Wk, NW2 63 CW61
Topsfield Cl, N8
off Wolseley Rd 65 DK57
Topsfield Par, N8
off Tottenham La 65 DL57
Topsfield Rd, N8 65 DL57
Topsham Rd, SW17 120 DF90
Torbay Rd, NW6 81 CZ66
Harrow HA2 60 BY61
Torbay St, NW1
off Hawley Rd 83 DH66
Torbitt Way, Ilf. IG2 69 ET57
Torbridge Cl, Edg. HA8 42 CL52
Torbrook Cl, Bex. DA5 126 EY86
Torcross Dr, SE23 122 DW89
Torcross Rd, Ruis. HA4 59 BV62
Tor Gdns, W8 100 DA75
Tor Gro, SE28 87 ES74
Torin Ct, Egh.
(Eng.Grn) TW20 112 AW92
Torland Dr, Lthd.
(Oxshott) KT22 155 CD114
Tor La, Wey. KT13 153 BQ111
Tormead Cl, Sutt. SM1 158 DA107
Tormount Rd, SE18 105 ES79
Toronto Av, E12 69 EM63
Toronto Rd, E11 67 ED63
Ilford IG1 69 EP60
Tilbury RM18 111 GG82
Torquay Gdns, Ilf. IG4 68 EK56
Torquay St, W2
off Harrow Rd 82 DB71
Torrance Cl, SE7 104 EK79
Hornchurch RM11 71 FH60
Torrens Rd, E15 86 EF65
SW2 121 DM85
Torrens Sq, E15 86 EE65
Torrens St, EC1 196 E1
Torrens Wk, Grav. DA12 131 GL92
Torres Sq, E14
off Maritime Quay 103 EA78
Torre Wk, Cars. SM5 140 DE102
Torrey Dr, SW9
off Overton Rd 101 DN82
Torriano Av, NW5 65 DK64
Torriano Cotts, NW5
off Torriano Av 65 DJ64
Torriano Ms, NW5
off Torriano Av 65 DK64
Torridge Gdns, SE15 102 DW84
Torridge Rd, Slou. SL3 93 BB79
Thornton Heath CR7 141 DP99
Torridon Cl, Wok. GU21 166 AV117
Torridon Rd, SE6 123 ED88
SE13 123 ED87
Torrington Av, N12 44 DD50
Torrington Cl, N12 44 DD49
Esher (Clay.) KT10 155 CE107
Torrington Dr, Har. HA2 60 CB63
Loughton IG10 33 EQ42
Potters Bar EN6 12 DD32
Torrington Gdns, N11 45 DJ51
Greenford UB6 79 CJ66
Loughton IG10 33 EQ42
Torrington Gro, N12 44 DE50
Torrington Pk, N12 44 DC50
Torrington Pl, E1 202 C2
WC1 195 L6
Torrington Rd, E18 68 EG55
Dagenham RM8 70 EZ60
Esher (Clay.) KT10 155 CE107
Greenford UB6 79 CJ67
Ruislip HA4 59 BT62
Torrington Sq, WC1 195 N5
Croydon CR0
off Tavistock Gro 142 DR101
Torrington Way, Mord. SM4 140 DA100
Tor Rd, Well. DA16 106 EW81
Torr Rd, SE20 123 DX94
Torver Rd, Har. HA1 61 CE56
Torver Way, Orp. BR6 145 ER104
Torwood La, Whyt. CR3 176 DT120
Torwood Rd, SW15 119 CU85
Torworth Rd, Borwd. WD6 26 CM39
Tothill St, SW1 199 M5
Totnes Rd, Well. DA16 106 EV80
Totnes Wk, N2 64 DD56
Tottan Ter, E1 85 DX72
Tottenhall Rd, N13 45 DN51
TOTTENHAM, N17 46 DS53
⊖ Tottenham Court Road 195 M8
Tottenham Ct Rd, W1 195 L5
Tottenham Grn E, N15 66 DT56
TOTTENHAM HALE, N17 66 DV55
⇌ Tottenham Hale 66 DV55
⊖ Tottenham Hale 66 DV55
Tottenham Hale Retail Pk,
N15 66 DU56
★ Tottenham Hotspur FC,
N17 46 DT52
Tottenham La, N8 65 DL57
Tottenham Ms, W1 195 L6
Tottenham Rd, N1 84 DS65
Tottenham St, W1 195 L7
Totterdown St, SW17 120 DF91
TOTTERIDGE, N20 43 CY46
⊖ Totteridge & Whetstone 44 DB47
Totteridge Common, N20 43 CU47
Totteridge Grn, N20 44 DA47
Totteridge Ho, SW11 100 DD82
Totteridge La, N20 44 DA47
Totteridge Rd, Enf. EN3 31 DX37
Totteridge Village, N20 43 CY46
Totternhoe Cl, Har. HA3 61 CJ57
Totton Rd, Th.Hth. CR7 141 DN97
Toulmin St, SE1 201 H5
Toulon St, SE5 102 DQ80
Tournay Rd, SW6 99 CZ80
Tours Pas, SW11 100 DD84
Toussaint Wk, SE16 202 C6
Tovey Cl, St.Alb.
(Lon.Col.) AL2 9 CK26

★ Place of interest ⇌ Railway station ⊖ London Underground station DLR Docklands Light Railway station Tra Tramlink station H Hospital Riv Pedestrian ferry landing stage

335

Tovil Cl, SE20 142 DU96
Towcester Rd, E3 85 EB70
Tower, The, Couls. CR5 175 DK122
Tower 42, EC2 197 M8
Tower Br, E1 201 P3
SE1 201 P3
Tower Br App, E1 201 P2
★ **Tower Br Experience**,
SE1 201 P3
Tower Br Piazza, SE1 201 P3
Tower Br Rd, SE1 201 M7
Tower Br Wf, E1 202 B3
Tower Cl, NW3
off Lyndhurst Rd 64 DD64
SE20 122 DV94
Gravesend DA12 131 GL92
Ilford IG6 49 EP51
Orpington BR6 145 ET103
Woking GU21 166 AX117
Tower Ct, WC2 195 P9
Brentwood CM14 54 FV47
Tower Cft, Dart. (Eyns.) DA4
off High St 148 FL103
Tower Gdns,
Esher (Clay.) KT10 155 CG108
Tower Gdns Rd, N17 46 DQ53
Towergate Cl, Uxb. UB8
off Harefield Rd 58 BL64
DLR **Tower Gateway** 84 DT73
Tower Gro, Wey. KT13 135 BS103
Tower Hamlets Rd, E7 68 EF63
E17 67 EA55
⊖ **Tower Hill** 197 P10
Tower Hill, EC3 201 N1
Brentwood CM14 54 FW47
Kings Langley
(Chipper.) WD4 5 BE29
Tower Hill Ter, EC3
off Tower Hill 84 DS73
Tower La, Wem. HA9
off Main Dr 61 CK62
Tower Ms, E17 67 EA56
★ **Tower Millennium Pier**,
EC3 201 N2
Tower Mill Rd, SE15
off Wells Way 102 DS79
★ **Tower of London**, EC3 201 P1
Tower Pk Rd, Dart. DA1 127 FF85
Tower Pl, EC3 201 N1
Warlingham CR6 177 EA115
Tower Pt, Enf. EN2 30 DR42
Tower Retail Pk, Dart. DA1 127 FF85
Tower Ri, Rich. TW9
off Jocelyn Rd 98 CL83
Tower Rd, NW10 81 CU66
Belvedere DA17 107 FC77
Bexleyheath DA7 107 FB84
Dartford DA1 128 FJ86
Epping CM16 17 ES30
Orpington BR6 145 ET103
Tadworth KT20 173 CW123
Twickenham TW1 117 CF90
Tower Royal, EC4 197 J10
Towers, The, Ken. CR8 176 DQ115
Towers Av, Uxb.
(Hlgdn) UB10 77 BQ69
Towers Pl, Rich. TW9
off Eton St 118 CL85
Towers Rd, Grays RM17 110 GC78
Pinner HA5 40 BY53
Southall UB1 78 CA70
Tower St, WC2 195 N9
Towers Wk, Wey. KT13 153 BP107
(S.Darenth) DA4 149 FR95
Tower Ter, N22
off Mayes Rd 45 DM54
SE4 *off Foxberry Rd* 103 DY84
Tower Vw, Croy. CR0 143 DX101
Towfield Rd, Felt. TW13 116 BZ89
Towing Path Wk, N1
off York Way 83 DL67
Town, The, Enf. EN2 30 DR41
Towncourt Cres, Orp. BR5 145 EQ99
Towncourt La, Orp. BR5 145 ER100
Town Ct Path, N4 66 DQ60
Town End, Cat. CR3 176 DS122
Town End Cl, Cat. CR3 176 DS122
Towney Mead, Nthlt. UB5 78 BZ68
Towney Mead Ct, Nthlt. UB5
off Towney Mead 78 BZ68
Town Fm Way, Stai. (Stanw.) TW19
off Town La 114 BK87
Townfield, Rick. WD3 38 BJ45
Townfield Cor, Grav. DA12 131 GJ88
Town Fld La, Ch.St.G. HP8 36 AW48
Townfield Rd, Hayes UB3 77 BT74
Townfield Sq, Hayes UB3 77 BT74
Town Fld Way, Islw. TW7 97 CG82
Towngate, Cob. KT11 170 BY115
Town Hall App, N16
off Milton Gro 66 DS63
Town Hall App Rd, N15 66 DT56
Town Hall Av, W4 98 CR78
Town Hall Rd, SW11 100 DF83
Townholm Cres, W7 97 CF76
Town La, Stai.
(Stanw.) TW19 114 BK86
Townley Ct, E15 86 EF65
Townley Rd, SE22 122 DS85
Bexleyheath DA6 126 EZ85
Townley St, SE17 201 K10
Townmead, Red. RH1 186 DR133
Townmead Business Cen, SW6
off William Morris Way 100 DC83
Town Meadow, Brent. TW8 97 CK80
Townmead Rd, SW6 100 DC82
Richmond TW9 98 CP82
Waltham Abbey EN9 15 EC34
Town Path, Egh. TW20 113 BA92
Town Pier, Grav. DA11
off West St 131 GH86
Town Quay, Bark. IG11 87 EP67
Town Rd, N9 46 DV47
Townsend Av, N14 45 DK49
Townsend Ind Est, NW10 80 CR68
Townsend La, NW9 62 CR59
Woking GU22
off St. Peters Rd 167 BB121
Townsend Rd, N15 66 DT57
Ashford TW15 114 BL92
Southall UB1 78 BY74
Townsend St, SE17 201 L9
Townsend Way, Nthwd. HA6 39 BT52
Townsend Yd, N6 65 DH60
Townshend Cl, Sid. DA14 126 EV93
Townshend Est, NW8 82 DE68
Townshend Rd, NW8 82 DE67
Chislehurst BR7 125 EP92
Richmond TW9 98 CM84
Townshend Ter, Rich. TW9 98 CM84
Townslow La, Wok.
(Wisley) GU23 168 BJ116
Townson Av, Nthlt. UB5 77 BU69
Townson Way, Nthlt. UB5
off Townson Av 77 BU68
Town Sq, Erith DA8
off Pier Rd 107 FE79
Woking GU21
off Church St E 167 AZ117
Town Sq Cres, Green.
(Bluewater) DA9 129 FT87
Town Tree Rd, Ashf. TW15 114 BN92
Towpath, Shep. TW17 134 BM103
Towpath Rd, N18 47 DX51
Towpath Wk, E9 67 DZ64
Towpath Way, Croy. CR0 142 DT100
Towton Rd, SE27 122 DQ89
Toynbec Cl, Chis. BR7
off Beechwood Ri 125 EP91
★ **Toynbee Hall**, E1 84 DT71
Toynbee Rd, SW20 139 CY95
Toynbee St, E1 197 P7
Toyne Way, N6
off Gaskell Rd 64 DF58
Tracery, The, Bans. SM7 174 DB115
Tracey Av, NW2 63 CW64
Tracious Cl, Wok. GU21
off Sythwood 166 AV116
Tracious La, Wok. GU21 166 AV116
Tracy Av, Slou. SL3
off Ditton Rd 93 AZ79
Tracy Ct, Stan. HA7 41 CJ52
Trade Cl, N13 45 DN49
Trader Rd, E6 87 EP72
Tradescant Rd, SW8 101 DL80
Trading Est Rd, NW10 80 CQ70
Trafalgar Av, N17 46 DS51
SE15 102 DT78
Worcester Park KT4 139 CX102
Trafalgar Business Cen,
Bark. IG11 87 ET70
Trafalgar Cl, SE16 203 K8
Trafalgar Ct, E1 202 G1
Cobham KT11 153 BU113
Trafalgar Dr, Walt. KT12 135 BU104
Trafalgar Gdns, E1 85 DX71
W8 *off South End Row* 100 DB76
Trafalgar Gro, SE10 103 ED79
Trafalgar Ms, E9 85 DZ65
Trafalgar Pl, E11 68 EG56
N18 46 DU50
Trafalgar Rd, SE10 103 ED79
SW19 120 DB94
Dartford DA1 128 FL89
Gravesend DA11 131 GG87
Rainham RM13 89 FF68
Twickenham TW2 117 CD89
Trafalgar Sq, SW1 199 N2
WC2 199 N2
Trafalgar St, SE17 201 K10
Trafalgar Ter, Har. HA1
off Nelson Rd 61 CE60
Trafalgar Way, E14 204 D2
Croydon CR0 141 DM103
Trafford Cl, E15 67 EB64
Ilford IG6 49 ET51
Radlett (Shenley) WD7 10 CL32
Trafford Rd, Th.Hth. CR7 141 DM99
Tralee Ct, SE16 202 E10
Tramsheds Ind Est, Croy.
CR0 141 DK101
Tramway Av, E15 86 EE66
N9 46 DV45
Tramway Cl, SE20
off Oak Gro Rd 142 DW96
Tramway Path, Mitch. CR4 140 DF99
Tranby Pl, E9
off Homerton High St 67 DX64
Tranley Ms, NW3
off Fleet Rd 64 DE64
Tranmere Rd, N9 46 DT45
SW18 120 DC89
Twickenham TW2 116 CB87
Tranquil Dale, Bet.
(Buckland) RH3 183 CT132
Tranquil Pas, SE3
off Tranquil Vale 104 EF82
Tranquil Ri, Erith DA8
off West St 107 FE78
Tranquil Vale, SE3 104 EE82
Transept St, NW1 194 B7
Transmere Cl, Orp. BR5 145 EQ100
Transmere Rd, Orp. BR5 145 EQ100
Transom Cl, SE16 203 L8
Transom Sq, E14 204 B9
Transport Av, Brent. TW8 97 CG78
Tranton Rd, SE16 202 C6
Traps Hill, Loug. IG10 33 EM41
Traps La, N.Mal. KT3 138 CS95
Travellers Way, Houns. TW4 96 BW82
Travers Cl, E17 47 DX53
Travers Rd, N7 65 DN62
Treacy Cl, Bushey
(Bushey Hth) WD23 40 CC47
Treadgold St, W11 81 CX73
Treadway St, E2 84 DV68
Treadwell Rd, Epsom KT18 172 CS115
Treasury Cl, Wall. SM6 159 DK106
Treaty Cen, Houns. TW3 96 CB83
Treaty Rd, Houns. TW3
off Hanworth Rd 96 CB83
Treaty St, N1 83 DM67
Trebble Rd, Swans. DA10 130 FY86
Trebeck St, W1 199 H2
Trebovir Rd, SW5 100 DA78
Treby St, E3 85 DZ70
Trecastle Way, N7
off Carleton Rd 65 DK63
Tredegar Ms, E3
off Tredegar Ter 85 DZ69
Tredegar Rd, E3 85 DZ68
N11 45 DK52
Dartford DA2 127 FG89
Tredegar Sq, E3 85 DZ69
Tredegar Ter, E3 85 DZ69
Trederwen Rd, E8 84 DU67
Tredown Rd, SE26 122 DW92
Tredwell Cl, SW2
off Hillside Rd 121 DM89
Bromley BR2 144 EL98
Tredwell Rd, SE27 121 DP91
Treebourne Rd, West.
(Bigg.H.) TN16 178 EJ117
Tree Cl, Rich. TW10 117 CK88
Treemount Ct, Epsom KT17 156 CS113
Treen Av, SW13 99 CT83
Tree Rd, E16 86 EJ72
Treeside Cl, West Dr. UB7 94 BK77
Tree Tops, Brwd. CM15 54 FW46
Treetops, Grav. DA12 131 GH92
Whyteleafe CR3 176 DU118
Treetops Cl, SE2 106 EY78
Northwood HA6 39 BR50
Treetops Vw, Loug. IG10 48 EK45
Treeview Cl, SE19 142 DS95
Treewall Gdns, Brom. BR1 124 EH91
Tree Way, Reig. RH2 184 DB131
Trefgarne Rd, Dag. RM10 70 FA61
Trefil Wk, N7 65 DL63
Trefoil Ho, Erith DA18
off Kale Rd 106 EY75
Trefoil Rd, SW18 120 DC85
Trefusis Wk, Wat. WD17 23 BS39
Tregaron Av, N8 65 DL58
Tregaron Gdns, N.Mal. KT3
off Avenue Rd 138 CS98
Tregarthen Pl, Lthd. KT22 171 CJ121
Tregarth Pl, Wok. GU21 166 AT117
Tregarvon Rd, SW11 100 DG84
Tregenna Av, Har. HA2 60 BZ63
Tregenna Cl, N14 29 DJ43
Tregenna Ct, Har. HA2 60 CA63
Trego Rd, E9 85 EA66
Tregothnan Rd, SW9 101 DL83
Tregunter Rd, SW10 100 DC79
Trehearn Rd, Ilf. IG6 49 ER52
Treherne Ct, SW9
off Eythorne Rd 101 DN81
SW17 120 DG91
Trehern Rd, SW14 98 CR83
Trehurst St, E5 67 DY64
Trelawn Cl, Cher. (Ott.) KT16 151 BC108
Trelawney Av, Slou. SL3 92 AX76
Trelawney Cl, E17
off Orford Rd 67 EB56
Trelawney Est, E9 84 DW65
Trelawney Gro, Wey. KT13 152 BN107
Trelawney Rd, Ilf. IG6 49 ER52
Trelawn Rd, E10 67 EC62
SW2 121 DN85
Trellick Twr, W10 81 CZ70
Trellis Sq, E3
off Malmesbury Rd 85 DZ69
Treloar Gdns, SE19
off Hancock Rd 122 DR93
Tremadoc Rd, SW4 101 DK84
Tremaine Cl, SE4 103 EA82
Tremaine Rd, SE20 142 DV96
Trematon Pl, Tedd. TW11 117 CJ94
Tremlett Gro, N19 65 DJ62
Tremlett Ms, N19 65 DJ62
Trenance, Wok. GU21
off Cardingham 166 AU117
Trenance Gdns, Ilf. IG3 70 EU62
Trenchard Av, Ruis. HA4 59 BV63
Trenchard Cl, NW9
off Fulbeck Dr 42 CS53
Stanmore HA7 41 CG51
Walton-on-Thames KT12 154 BW106
Trenchard Ct, Mord. SM4
off Green La 140 DA100
Trenchard St, SE10 103 ED78
Trenches La, Slou. SL3 75 BA73
Trenchold St, SW8 101 DL79
Trenear Cl, Orp. BR6 164 EU105
Trenham Dr, Warl. CR6 176 DW116
Trenholme Cl, SE20 122 DV94
Trenholme Ct, Cat. CR3 176 DU122
Trenholme Rd, SE20 122 DV94
Trenholme Ter, SE20 122 DV94
Trenmar Gdns, NW10 81 CV69
Trent Av, W5 97 CJ76
Upminster RM14 73 FR58
Trentbridge Cl, Ilf. IG6 49 ET51
Trent Cl, Rad. (Shenley) WD7
off Edgbaston Dr 10 CL32
Trent Gdns, N14 29 DH44
Trentham Cres, Wok. GU22 167 BA121
Trentham Dr, Orp. BR5 146 EU98
Trentham St, SW18 120 DA88
★ **Trent Park Country Pk**,
Barn. EN4 29 DH40
Trent Rd, SW2 121 DM85
Buckhurst Hill IG9 48 EH46
Slough SL3 93 BB79
Trent Way, Hayes UB4 77 BS68
Worcester Park KT4 139 CW104
Trentwood Side, Enf. EN2 29 DM41
Treport St, SW18 120 DB87
Tresco Cl, Brom. BR1 124 EE93
Trescoe Gdns, Har. HA2 60 BY59
Romford RM5 51 FC50
Tresco Gdns, Ilf. IG3 70 EU61
Tresco Rd, SE15 102 DV84
Tresham Cres, NW8 194 B4
Tresham Rd, Bark. IG11 87 ET66
Tresham Wk, E9
off Churchill Wk 66 DW64
Tresilian Av, N21 29 DM43
Tresillian Way, Wok. GU21 166 AU116
Tressell Cl, N1
off Sebbon St 83 DP66
Tressillian Cres, SE4 103 EA83
Tressillian Rd, SE4 103 DZ84
Tresta Wk, Wok. GU21 166 AU115
Trestis Cl, Hayes UB4
off Jollys La 78 BY71
Treston Ct, Stai. TW18 113 BF92
Treswell Rd, Dag. RM9 88 EY67
Tretawn Gdns, NW7 42 CS49
Tretawn Pk, NW7 42 CS49
Trevanion Rd, W14 99 CY78
Treve Av, Har. HA1 60 CC59
Trevellance Way, Wat. WD25 8 BW33
Trevelyan Av, E12 69 EM63
Trevelyan Cl, Dart. DA1 108 FM84
Trevelyan Cres, Har. HA3 61 CK59
Trevelyan Gdns, NW10 81 CW67
Trevelyan Rd, E15 68 EE63
SW17 120 DE92
Trevera Ct, Wal.Cr. EN8
off Eleanor Rd 15 DY33
Trevereux Hill, Oxt. RH8 189 EM131
Treveris St, SE1 200 F3
Treverton St, W10 81 CX70
Treves Cl, N21 29 DM43
Treville St, SW15 119 CV87
Treviso Rd, SE23
off Farren Rd 123 DX89
Trevithick Cl, Felt. TW14 115 BT88
Trevithick Dr, Dart. DA1 108 FM84
Trevithick St, SE8 103 EA78
Trevone Gdns, Pnr. HA5 60 BY58
Trevor Cl, Barn. EN4 28 DD43
Bromley BR2 144 EF101
Harrow HA3
off Kenton La 41 CF52
Isleworth TW7 117 CF85
Northolt UB5 78 BW68
Trevor Cres, Ruis. HA4 59 BT63
Trevor Gdns, Edg. HA8 42 CR53
Northolt UB5 78 BW68
Ruislip HA4
off Clyfford Rd 59 BU63
Trevor Pl, SW7 198 C5
Trevor Rd, SW19 119 CY94
Edgware HA8 42 CR53
Hayes UB3 95 BS75
Woodford Green IG8 48 EG52
Trevor Sq, SW7 198 D5
Trevor St, SW7 198 C5
Trevor Wk, SW7
off Trevor Sq 100 DF75
Trevose Av, W.Byf. KT14 151 BF114
Trevose Rd, E17 47 ED53
Trevose Way, Wat. WD19 40 BW48
Trewarden Av, Iver SL0 75 BD68
Trewenna Dr, Chess. KT9 155 CK106
Potters Bar EN6 12 DD32
Trewince Rd, SW20 139 CW95
Trewint St, SW18 120 DC89
Trewsbury Ho, SE2
off Hartslock Dr 106 EX75
Trewsbury Rd, SE26 123 DX92
Triandra Way, Hayes UB4 78 BX71
Triangle, The, EC1 196 G4
N13 *off Lodge Dr* 45 DN49
Barking IG11
off Tanner St 87 EQ65
Hampton TW12
off High St 136 CC95
Kingston upon Thames KT1
off Kenley Rd 138 CQ96
Woking GU21 166 AW118
Triangle Business Cen, NW10
off Enterprise Way 81 CU69
Triangle Ct, E16
off Tollgate Rd 86 EK71
Triangle Est, SE11
off Kennington La 101 DM78
Triangle Pas, Barn. EN4
off Station App 28 DC42
Triangle Pl, SW4 101 DK84
Triangle Rd, E8 84 DV67
Trident Cen, Wat. WD24 24 BW39
Trident Gdns, Nthlt. UB5
off Jetstar Way 78 BX69
Trident Ind Est, Slou.
(Colnbr.) SL3 93 BE83
Trident Rd, Wat. WD25 7 BT34
Trident St, SE16 203 J8
Trident Way, Sthl. UB2 95 BV76
Trigg's Cl, Wok. GU22 166 AX119
Trigg's La, Wok.
GU21, GU22 166 AW118
Trig La, EC4 197 H10
Trigo Ct, Epsom KT19
off Blakeney Cl 156 CR111
Trigon Rd, SW8 101 DM80
Trilby Rd, SE23 123 DX89
Trimmer Wk, Brent. TW8 98 CL79
Trim St, SE14 103 DZ79
Trinder Gdns, N19
off Trinder Rd 65 DL60
Trinder Ms, Tedd. TW11 117 CG92
Trinder Rd, N19 65 DL60
Barnet EN5 27 CW43
Tring Av, W5 80 CM74
Southall UB1 78 BZ72
Wembley HA9 80 CN65
Tring Cl, Ilf. IG2 69 EQ57
Romford RM3 52 FM49
Tring Gdns, Rom. RM3 52 FL49
Tring Grn, Rom. RM3 52 FM49
Tringham Cl, Cher.
(Ott.) KT16 151 BC107
Tring Wk, Rom. RM3
off Tring Gdns 52 FL49
Trinidad Gdns, Dag. RM10 89 FD66
Trinidad St, E14 85 DZ73
Trinity Av, N2 64 DD55
Enfield EN1 30 DT44
Trinity Buoy Wf, E14 205 K1
Trinity Ch Pas, SW13 99 CV79
Trinity Ch Rd, SW13 99 CV79
Trinity Ch Sq, SE1 201 J6
Trinity Cl, E8 84 DT65
E11 68 EE61
NW3
off Hampstead High St 64 DD63
SE13 *off Wisteria Rd* 103 ED84
SW4 *off The Pavement* 101 DJ84
Bromley BR2 144 EL102
Hounslow TW4 96 BY84
Trinity Cl, Northwood HA6 39 BS51
South Croydon CR2 160 DS109
Staines (Stanw.) TW19 114 BJ86
Trinity Cotts, Rich. TW9
off Trinity Rd 98 CM83
Trinity Ct, N1
off Downham Rd 84 DS66
NW2 *off Anson Rd* 63 CW64
SE7 *off Charlton La* 104 EK77
Trinity Cres, SW17 120 DF89
Trinity Dr, Uxb. UB8
off Titmus Cl 77 BQ72
Trinity Gdns, E16
off Cliff Wk 86 EF70
SW9 101 DM84
Dartford DA1
off Summerhill Rd 128 FK86
Trinity Gro, SE10 103 EC81
Trinity Hall Cl, Wat. WD24 24 BW41
★ **Trinity Ho**, EC3 197 N10
Trinity La, Wal.Cr. EN8 15 DY32
Trinity Ms, SE20 142 DV95
W10
off Cambridge Gdns 81 CX72
Trinity Path, SE26 122 DW90
Trinity Pl, EC3 201 P1
Bexleyheath DA6 106 EZ84
Trinity Ri, SW2 121 DN88
Trinity Rd, N2 64 DD55
N22 45 DL53
SW17 120 DF89
SW18 120 DD85
SW19 120 DA93
Gravesend DA12 131 GJ87
Ilford IG6 69 EQ55
Richmond TW9 98 CM83
Southall UB1 78 BY74
Trinity Sq, EC3 201 N1
Trinity St, E16
off Vincent St 86 EG71
SE1 201 J5
Enfield EN2 30 DQ40
Trinity Wk, NW3 82 DC65
Trinity Way, E4 47 DZ51
W3 80 CS73
Trio Pl, SE1 201 J5
Tripps Hill, Ch.St.G. HP8 36 AU48
Tripps Hill Cl, Ch.St.G. HP8 36 AU48
Tristan Sq, SE3 104 EE83
Tristram Cl, E17 67 ED55
Tristram Dr, N9
off Barbot Cl 46 DU48
Tristram Rd, Brom. BR1 124 EF91
Triton Sq, NW1 195 K4
Tritton Av, Croy. CR0 159 DL105
Tritton Rd, SE21 122 DR90
Trittons, Tad. KT20 173 CW121
Triumph Cl, Grays
(Chaff.Hun.) RM16 109 FW77
Hayes UB3 95 BQ80
Triumph Ho, Bark. IG11 88 EV69
Triumph Rd, E6 87 EM72
Trivett Cl, Green. DA9 129 FU85
★ **Trocadero Cen**, W1 199 M1
Trojan Ct, NW6
off Willesden La 81 CY66
Trojan Way, Croy. CR0 141 DM104
Trolling Down Hill, Dart.
DA2 128 FP89
Troon Cl, SE16 202 E10
SE28 *off Fairway Dr* 88 EX72
Troon St, E1
off White Horse Rd 85 DY72
Troopers Dr, Rom. RM3 52 FK49
Trosley Av, Grav. DA11 131 GH89
Trosley Rd, Belv. DA17 106 FA79
Trossachs Rd, SE22 122 DS85
Trothy Rd, SE1 202 C8
Trotsworth Av, Vir.W. GU25 132 AX98
Trotsworth Ct, Vir.W. GU25 132 AY98
Trotters Bottom, Barn. EN5 27 CU37
Trotters La, Wok.
(Mimbr.) GU24 150 AV112
Trotter Way, Epsom KT19 156 CP112
Trott Rd, N10 44 DF52
Trotts La, West. TN16 189 EQ127
Trott St, SW11 100 DE81
Trotwood, Chig. IG7 49 ER51
Trotwood Cl, Brwd. (Shenf.) CM15
off Middleton Rd 54 FY46
Troughton Rd, SE7 205 P10
Troutbeck Cl, Slou. SL2 74 AU73
Troutbeck Rd, SE14 103 DY81
Trout La, West Dr. UB7 76 BJ73
Trout Ri, Rick. (Loud.) WD3 22 BH41
Trout Rd, West Dr. UB7 76 BK74
Troutstream Way, Rick.
(Loud.) WD3 22 BH42
Trouville Rd, SW4 121 DJ86
Trowbridge Est, E9
off Osborne Rd 85 DZ65
Trowbridge Rd, E9 85 DZ65
Romford RM3 52 FK51
Trowers Way, Red. RH1 185 DH131
Trowley Ri, Abb.L. WD5 7 BS31
Trowlock Av, Tedd. TW11 117 CJ93
Trowlock Island, Tedd. TW11 117 CK92
Trowlock Way, Tedd. TW11 117 CK93
Troy Cl, Tad. KT20 173 CV120
Troy Ct, SE18 105 EP77
Troy Rd, SE19 122 DR93
Troy Town, SE15 102 DU83
Trubshaw Rd, Sthl. UB2
off Havelock Rd 96 CB76
Truesdale Dr, Uxb.
(Hare.) UB9 58 BJ57
Truesdale Rd, E6 87 EM72
Trulock Ct, N17 46 DU52
Trulock Rd, N17 46 DU52
Truman Cl, Edg. HA8
off Pavilion Way 42 CP52
Truman's Rd, N16 66 DS64
Trumpers Way, W7 97 CE76
Trumper Way, Uxb. UB8 76 BJ67
Trumpington Rd, E7 68 EF63
Trumps Grn Av, Vir.W. GU25 132 AX100
Trumps Grn Cl, Vir.W. GU25
off Trumps Grn Rd 132 AY99
Trumps Grn Rd, Vir.W. GU25 132 AX100
Trumps Mill La, Vir.W. GU25 133 AZ100

★ Place of interest ⇌ Railway station ⊖ London Underground station DLR Docklands Light Railway station Tra Tramlink station H Hospital Riv Pedestrian ferry landing stage

Trump St, EC2 197 J9
Trundlers Way, Bushey
(Bushey Hth) WD23 41 CE46
Trundle St, SE1 201 H4
Trundleys Rd, SE8 203 J10
Trundleys Ter, SE8 203 J9
Trunks All, Swan. BR8 147 FB96
Truro Gdns, Ilf. IG1 68 EL59
Truro Rd, E17 67 DZ56
N22 45 DL52
Gravesend DA12 131 GK90
Truro St, NW5 82 DG65
Truro Wk, Rom. RM3
off Saddleworth Rd. 52 FJ51
Truro Way, Hayes UB4
off Portland Rd 77 BS69
Truslove Rd, SE27 121 DN92
Trussley Rd, W6 99 CW76
Trustees Way, Uxb.
(Denh.) UB9 57 BF57
Trustons Gdns, Horn. RM11 71 FG59
Trust Rd, Wal.Cr. EN8 15 DY34
Trust Wk, SE21
off Peabody Hill 121 DP88
Tryfan Cl, Ilf. IG4 68 EK57
Tryon Cres, E9 84 DW67
Tryon St, SW3 198 D10
Trys Hill, Cher. (Lyne) KT16 133 AZ103
Trystings Cl, Esher
(Clay.) KT10 155 CG107
Tuam Rd, SE18 105 ER79
Tubbenden Cl, Orp. BR6 145 ES103
Tubbenden Dr, Orp. BR6 163 ER105
Tubbenden La, Orp. BR6 145 ES104
Tubbenden La S, Orp. BR6 163 ER106
Tubbs Rd, NW10 81 CT68
Tubs Hill Par, Sev. TN13 190 FG124
Tubwell Rd, Slou.
(Stoke P.) SL2 74 AV67
Tucker Rd, Cher.
(Ott.) KT16 151 BD107
Tucker St, Wat. WD18 24 BW43
Tuckey Gro, Wok.
(Ripley) GU23 167 BF124
Tuck Rd, Rain. RM13 89 FG65
Tudor Av, Hmptn. TW12 116 CA93
Romford RM2 71 FG55
Waltham Cross
(Chsht) EN7 14 DU31
Watford WD24 24 BX38
Worcester Park KT4 139 CV104
Tudor Cl, N6 65 DJ59
NW3 64 DE64
NW7 43 CU51
NW9 62 CQ61
SW2 *off Elm Pk.* 121 DM86
Ashford TW15 114 BL91
Banstead SM7 173 CY115
Brentwood (Shenf.) CM15 55 FZ44
Chessington KT9 156 CL106
Chigwell IG7 49 EN49
Chislehurst BR7 145 EM95
Cobham KT11 154 BZ113
Coulsdon CR5 175 DN118
Dartford DA1 127 FH86
Epsom KT17 157 CT110
Gravesend (Nthflt) DA11 130 GE88
Leatherhead
(Bkhm) KT23 170 CA124
Pinner HA5 59 BU57
South Croydon CR2 176 DV115
Sutton SM3 157 CX106
Wallington SM6 159 DJ108
Waltham Cross
(Chsht) EN7 14 DV31
Woking GU22 167 BA117
Woodford Green IG8 48 EH50
Tudor Ct, E17 67 DY59
Borehamwood WD6 26 CL40
Feltham TW13 116 BW91
Swanley BR8 147 FC101
Tudor Ct N, Wem. HA9 62 CN64
Tudor Ct S, Wem. HA9 62 CN64
Tudor Cres, Enf. EN2 29 DP39
Ilford IG6 49 EP51
Tudor Dr, Kings.T. KT2 118 CL92
Morden SM4 139 CX100
Romford RM2 71 FG56
Walton-on-Thames KT12 136 BX102
Watford WD24 24 BX38
Tudor Est, NW10 80 CP68
Tudor Gdns, NW9 62 CQ61
SW13 *off Treen Av.* 98 CS83
W3 80 CN72
Harrow HA3
off Tudor Rd 41 CD54
Romford RM2 71 FG56
Twickenham TW1 117 CF88
Upminster RM14 72 FQ61
West Wickham BR4 143 EC104
Tudor Gro, E9 84 DW66
N20 *off Church Cres.* 44 DE48
Tudor Ho, Surb. KT6
off Lenelby Rd. 138 CN102
Tudor La, Wind.
(Old Wind.) SL4 112 AW87
Tudor Manor Gdns, Wat.
WD25 8 BX32
Tudor Ms, Rom. RM1
off Eastern Rd. 71 FF57
Tudor Par, Rick. WD3
off Berry La. 38 BG45
Tudor Pl, Mitch. CR4 120 DE94
Tudor Rd, E4 47 EB51
E6 86 EJ67
E9 84 DV67
N9 46 DV45
SE19 122 DT94
SE25 142 DV99
Ashford TW15 115 BR93
Barking IG11 87 ET67
Barnet EN5 28 DA41
Beckenham BR3 143 EB97
Hampton TW12 116 CA94
Harrow HA3 41 CD54
Hayes UB3 77 BR72
Hounslow TW3 97 CD84
Kingston upon Thames KT2 118 CN94
Pinner HA5 40 BW54
Southall UB1 78 BY73
Tudors, The, Reig. RH2 184 DC131
Tudor Sq, Hayes UB3 77 BR71
Tudor St, EC4 196 E10
Tudor Wk, Bex. DA5 126 EY86
Tudorwalk, Grays RM17
off Thurloe Wk 110 GA76
Tudor Wk, Lthd. KT22 171 CF120
Watford WD24 24 BX37
Weybridge KT13
off West Palace Gdns 135 BP104
Tudor Way, N14 45 DK46
W3 98 CN75
Orpington BR5 145 ER100
Rickmansworth
(Mill End) WD3 38 BG46
Uxbridge UB10 76 BN65
Waltham Abbey EN9 15 ED33
Tudor Well Cl, Stan. HA7 41 CH50
Tudway Rd, SE3 104 EH83
Tufnail Rd, Dart. DA1 128 FM86
TUFNELL PARK, N7 65 DK63
⊖ **Tufnell Park** 65 DJ63
Tufnell Pk Rd, N7 65 DJ63
N19 65 DJ63
Tufter Rd, Chig. IG7 49 ET50
Tufton Gdns, W.Mol. KT8 136 CB96
Tufton Rd, E4 47 EA49
Tufton St, SW1 199 N6
Tugboat St, SE28 105 ES75
Tugela Rd, Croy. CR0 142 DR100
Tugela St, SE6 123 DZ89
Tugmutton Cl, Orp. BR6
off Acorn Way 163 EP105
Tugwood Cl, Couls. CR5
off Netherne Dr. 175 DK121
Tuilerie St, E2 84 DU68
Tulip Cl, E6
off Bradley Stone Rd 87 EM71
Brentwood (Pilg.Hat.) CM15
off Poppy Cl 54 FV43
Croydon CR0 143 DX102
Hampton TW12
off Partridge Rd 116 BZ93
Romford RM3
off Cloudberry Rd 52 FK51
Southall UB2
off Chevy Rd 96 CC75
Tulip Ct, Pnr. HA5 60 BW55
Tulip Gdns, Ilf. IG1 87 EP65
Tulip Tree Ct, Sutt. SM2
off The Crescent 158 DA111
Tulip Way, West Dr. UB7 94 BK77
Tull St, Mitch. CR4 140 DF101
Tulse Cl, Beck. BR3 143 EC97
TULSE HILL, SE21 122 DQ88
⇌ **Tulse Hill** 121 DP89
Tulse Hill, SW2 121 DN86
Tulse Hill Est, SW2 121 DN86
Tulsemere Rd, SE27 122 DQ89
Tulyar Cl, Tad. KT20 173 CV120
Tumber St, Epsom
(Headley) KT18 182 CQ125
Tumblewood Rd, Bans.
SM7 173 CY116
Tumbling Bay, Walt. KT12 135 BU100
Tummons Gdns, SE25 142 DS96
Tuncombe Rd, N18 46 DS49
Tunis Rd, W12 81 CV74
Tunley Grn, E14
off Burdett Rd 85 DZ71
Tunley Rd, NW10 80 CS67
SW17 120 DG88
Tunmarsh La, E13 86 EJ69
Tunmers End, Ger.Cr.
(Chal.St.P.) SL9 36 AW53
Tunnan Leys, E6 87 EN72
Tunnel Av, SE10 204 G4
Tunnel Est, Grays RM20 109 FT77
Tunnel Gdns, N11 45 DJ52
Tunnel Rd, SE16 202 F4
Reigate RH2
off Church St 184 DA133
Tunnel Wd Cl, Wat. WD17 23 BT37
Tunnel Wd Rd, Wat. WD17 23 BT37
Tunstall Av, Ilf. IG6 50 EU51
Tunstall Cl, Orp. BR5 163 ES105
Tunstall Rd, SW9 101 DM84
Croydon CR0 142 DS102
Tunstall Wk, Brent. TW8 98 CL79
Tunstock Way, Belv. DA17 106 EY76
Tunworth Cl, NW9 62 CQ58
Tunworth Cres, SW15 119 CT86
Tun Yd, SW8 *off Peardon St* 101 DH82
Tupelo Rd, E10 67 EB61
Tuppy St, SE28 105 EQ76
Tupwood Ct, Cat. CR3 186 DU125
Tupwood La, Cat. CR3 186 DU125
Tupwood Scrubbs Rd, Cat.
CR3 186 DU128
Turenne Cl, SW18 100 DC84
Turfhouse La, Wok.
(Chobham) GU24 150 AS109
Turin Rd, N9 46 DW45
Turin St, E2 84 DU69
Turkey Oak Cl, SE19 142 DS95
⇌ **Turkey Street** 30 DW37
Turkey St, Enf. EN1, EN3 30 DV37
Turks Cl, Uxb. UB8
off Harlington Rd 76 BN69
Turk's Head Yd, EC1 196 F6
Turks Row, SW3 198 E10
Turle Rd, N4 65 DM60
SW16 141 DL96
Turlewray Cl, N4 65 DM60
Turley Cl, E15 86 EE67
Turnagain La, EC4 196 F8
Dartford DA2 127 FG90
Turnage Rd, Dag. RM8 70 EY60
Turnberry Cl, NW4 43 CX54
SE16 *off Ryder Dr.* 102 DV78
Turnberry Ct, Wat. WD19 40 BW48
Turnberry Dr, St.Alb.
(Brick.Wd) AL2 8 BY30
Turnberry Quay, E14 204 C6
Turnberry Way, Orp. BR6 145 ER102
Turnbull Cl, Green. DA9 129 FS87
Turnbury Cl, SE28 88 EX72
Turnchapel Ms, SW4
off Cedars Rd 101 DH83
Turner Av, N15 66 DS56
Turner Av, Mitcham CR4 140 DF95
Twickenham TW2 116 CC90
Turner Cl, NW11 64 DB58
SW9 101 DP81
Hayes UB4
off Charville La 77 BQ68
Wembley HA0 61 CK64
Turner Ct, Dart. DA1 128 FJ85
Turner Dr, NW11 64 DB58
Turner Pl, SW11
off Cairns Rd 120 DE85
Turner Rd, E17 67 EC55
Bushey WD23 24 CC42
Dartford (Bean) DA2 129 FV90
Edgware HA8 62 CM55
Hornchurch RM12
off Upper Rainham Rd 71 FF61
New Malden KT3 138 CR101
Slough SL3 92 AW75
Westerham
(Bigg.H.) TN16 162 EJ112
Turners Cl, Stai. TW18 114 BH92
Turners Ct, Rom. (Abridge) RM4
off Ongar Rd 34 EV41
Turners Gdns, Sev. TN13 191 FJ128
Turners Hill, Wal.Cr.
(Chsht) EN8 15 DX30
Turners La, Walt. KT12 153 BV107
Turners Meadow Way, Beck.
BR3 143 DZ95
Turners Rd, E3 85 DZ71
Turner St, E1 84 DV71
E16 86 EF72
Turners Way, Croy. CR0 141 DN103
Turners Wd, NW11 64 DC59
Turners Wd Dr, Ch.St.G. HP8 36 AX48
Turneville Rd, W14 99 CZ79
Turney Grn, E14
off Wallwood St 85 DZ71
Turney Rd, SE21 122 DR87
Turneys Orchard, Rick.
(Chorl.) WD3 21 BD43
TURNFORD, Brox. EN10 15 DZ26
⊖ **Turnham Green** 98 CS77
Turnham Grn Ter, W4 98 CS77
Turnham Grn Ter Ms, W4
off Turnham Grn Ter 98 CS77
Turnham Rd, SE4 123 DY85
Turnmill St, EC1 196 E5
Turnoak Av, Wok. GU22 166 AY120
Turnoak La, Wok. GU22
off Wych Hill La 166 AY119
Turnpike Cl, SE8
off Amersham Vale 103 DZ80
Turnpike Dr, Orp. BR6 164 EW109
Turnpike Ho, EC1 196 G3
⊖ **Turnpike Lane** 65 DN55
Turnpike La, N8 65 DM56
Sutton SM1 158 DC106
Tilbury (W.Til.) RM18 111 GK78
Uxbridge UB10 76 BL69
Turnpike Link, Croy. CR0 142 DS103
Turnpike Way, Islw. TW7 97 CG81
Turnpin La, SE10 103 EC79
Turnstone Cl, E13 86 EG69
NW9 *off Kestrel Cl* 42 CS54
South Croydon CR2 161 DY110
Uxbridge (Ickhm) UB10 59 BP64
Turnstones, The, Grav. DA12 131 GK89
Watford WD25 24 BY36
Turp Av, Grays RM16 110 GC75
Turpentine La, SW1 199 J10
Turpin Av, Rom. RM5 50 FA52
Turpin Cl, Enf. EN3
off Burton Dr 31 EA37
Turpington Cl, Brom. BR2 144 EL100
Turpington La, Brom. BR2 144 EL101
Turpin La, Erith DA8 107 FG80
Turpin Rd, Felt. TW14
off Staines Rd 115 BT86
Turpins La, Wdf.Grn. IG8 49 EM50
Turpin Way, N19
off Elthorne Rd 65 DK61
Wallington SM6 159 DH108
Turquand St, SE17 201 J9
Turret Gro, SW4 101 DJ83
Turton Rd, Wem. HA0 62 CL64
Turville St, E2 197 P4
Tuscan Rd, SE18 105 ER78
Tuskar St, SE10 104 EE78
Tussauds Cl, Rick. WD3
off New Rd 22 BN43
Tustin Est, SE15 102 DW79
Tuttlebee La, Buck.H. IG9 48 EG47
Tuxford Cl, Borwd. WD6 26 CL38
Twankhams All, Epp. CM16
off Hemnall St 18 EU30
Tweedale Ct, E15 67 EC64
Tweeddale Gro, Uxb. UB10 59 BQ62
Tweeddale Rd, Cars. SM5 140 DD102
Tweed Glen, Rom. RM1 51 FD52
Tweed Grn, Rom. RM1 51 FE52
Tweedmouth Rd, E13 86 EH68
Tweed Rd, Slou. SL3 93 BA79
Tweed Way, Rom. RM1 51 FD52
Tweedy Cl, Enf. EN1 30 DT43
Tweedy Rd, Brom. BR1 144 EF95
Tweezer's All, WC2 196 D10
Twelve Acre Cl, Lthd.
(Bkhm) KT23 170 BZ124
Twelve Acre Ho, E12
off Grantham Rd 69 EN62
Twelvetrees Cres, E3 85 EC70
Twentyman Cl, Wdf.Grn. IG8 48 EG50
TWICKENHAM 117 CG89
⇌ **Twickenham** 117 CF87
Twickenham Br, Rich. TW9 117 CJ85
Twickenham TW1 117 CJ85
Twickenham Cl, Croy. CR0 141 DM104
Twickenham Gdns, Grnf. UB6 61 CG64
Harrow HA3 41 CE52
Twickenham Rd, E11 67 ED61
Feltham TW13 116 BZ90
Isleworth TW7 97 CG83
Richmond TW9 97 CJ84
Teddington TW11 117 CG92
Twickenham Trd Est, Twick.
TW1 117 CF86
Twig Folly Cl, E2
off Roman Rd 85 DX68
Twigg Cl, Erith DA8 107 FE80
Twilley St, SW18 120 DB87
Twine Cl, Bark. IG11
off Thames Rd 88 EV69
Twine Ct, E1 84 DW73
Twineham Grn, N12
off Tillingham Way 44 DA49
Twine Ter, E3
off Ropery St 85 DZ70
Twining Av, Twick. TW2 116 CC90
Twinn Rd, NW7 43 CY51
Twinoaks, Cob. KT11 154 CA113
Twin Tumps Way, SE28 88 EU73
Twisden Rd, NW5 65 DH63
Twisleton Ct, Dart. DA1
off Priory Hill 128 FK86
Twitchells La, Beac.
(Jordans) HP9 36 AT51
TWITTON, Sev. TN14 181 FF116
Twitton La, Sev.
(Otford) TN14 181 FD115
Twitton Meadows, Sev.
(Otford) TN14 181 FE116
Two Rivers Retail Pk, Stai.
TW18 113 BE91
Twybridge Way, NW10 80 CQ66
Twycross Ms, SE10 205 J9
Twyford Abbey Rd, NW10 80 CM69
Twyford Av, N2 64 DF55
W3 80 CN73
Twyford Cres, W3 80 CN74
Twyford Ho, N15
off Chisley Rd 66 DS58
Twyford Pl, WC2 196 B8
Twyford Rd, Cars. SM5 140 DD102
Harrow HA2 60 CB60
Ilford IG1 69 EQ64
Twyford St, N1 83 DM67
Tyas Rd, E16 86 EF70
Tybenham Rd, SW19 140 DA97
Tyberry Rd, Enf. EN3 30 DV41
Tyburn La, Har. HA1 61 CE59
Tyburns, The, Brwd.
(Hutt.) CM13 55 GC47
Tyburn Way, W1 194 E10
Tycehurst Hill, Loug. IG10 33 EM42
Tydcombe Rd, Warl. CR6 176 DW119
Tye La, Epsom
(Headley) KT18 182 CR127
Orpington BR6 163 EQ106
Tadworth KT20
off Dorking Rd 183 CT128
Tyers Est, SE1 201 M4
Tyers Gate, SE1 201 M4
Tyers St, SE11 200 B10
Tyers Ter, SE11 101 DM78
Tyeshurst Cl, SE2 106 EY78
Tyfield Cl, Wal.Cr.
(Chsht) EN8 14 DW30
Tykeswater La, Borwd.
(Elstree) WD6 25 CJ39
Tylecroft Rd, SW16 141 DL96
Tyle Grn, Horn. RM11 72 FL56
Tylehurst Gdns, Ilf. IG1 69 EQ64
Tyle Pl, Wind.
(Old Wind.) SL4 112 AU85
Tyler Cl, E2 84 DT68
Erith DA8
off Brook St 107 FB80
Tyler Gdns, Add. KT15 152 BJ105
Tyler Gro, Dart. DA1
off Spielman Rd 108 FM84
Tyler Rd, Sthl. UB2
off McNair Rd 96 CB76
Tylers Cl, Gdse. RH9 186 DV130
Kings Langley WD4 6 BL28
Loughton IG10 48 EL45
Tyler's Ct, W1 195 M9
Tylers Cres, Horn. RM12 72 FJ64
Tylersfield, Abb.L. WD5 7 BT31
Tylers Gate, Har. HA3 62 CL58
Tylers Grn Rd, Swan. BR8 147 FC100
Tylers Hill Rd, Chesh. HP5 4 AT30
Tylers Path, Cars. SM5
off Rochester Rd 158 DF105
Tyler St, SE10 104 EE78
Tylers Way, Wat. WD25 25 CD42
Tyler Wk, Slou. SL3
off Ditton Rd 93 AZ78
Tyler Way, Brwd. CM14 54 FV46
Tylney Av, SE19 122 DT92
Tylney Rd, E7 68 EJ63
Bromley BR1 144 EK96
Tymperley Ct, SW19
off Windlesham Gro 119 CY88
Tynan Cl, Felt. TW14
off Sandycombe Rd 115 BU88
Tyndale Ct, E14 204 B10
Tyndale La, N1
off Upper St 83 DP66
Tyndale Ter, N1
off Canonbury La 83 DP66
Tyndall Rd, E10 67 EC61
Welling DA16 105 ET83
Tyne Cl, Upmin. RM14 73 FR58
Tynedale, St.Alb. (Lon.Col.) AL2
off Thamesdale 10 CM27
Tynedale Cl, Dart. DA2 129 FR88
Tyne Gdns, S.Ock.
(Aveley) RM15 90 FQ73
Tyneham Cl, SW11
off Shirley Gro 100 DG83
Tyneham Rd, SW11 100 DG82
Tynemouth Cl, E6
off Covelees Wall 87 EP72
Tynemouth Dr, Enf. EN1 30 DU38
Tynemouth Rd, N15 66 DT56
SE18 105 ET78
Mitcham CR4 120 DG94
Tynemouth St, SW6 100 DC82
Tyne St, E1
off Old Castle St 84 DT72
Tynsdale Rd, NW10
off Mayo Rd 80 CS65
Tynwald Ho, SE26
off Sydenham Hill 122 DU90
Type St, E2 85 DX68
Tyrawley Rd, SW6 100 DB81
Tyre La, NW9
off Sheaveshill Av 62 CS56
Tyrell Cl, Har. HA1 61 CE63
Tyrell Ct, Cars. SM5 158 DF105
Tyrell Ri, Brwd. CM14 54 FW50
Tyrells Cl, Upmin. RM14 72 FN61
Tyrols Rd, SE23
off Wastdale Rd 123 DX88
Tyrone Rd, E6 87 EM68
Tyron Way, Sid. DA14 125 ES91
Tyrrell Av, Well. DA16 126 EU85
Tyrrell Rd, SE22 102 DU84
Tyrrells Hall Cl, Grays RM17 110 GD79
Tyrrell Sq, Mitch. CR4 140 DE95
TYRRELL'S WOOD, Lthd.
KT22 172 CM123
Tyrrel Way, NW9 63 CT59
Tyrwhitt Rd, SE4 103 EA83
Tysea Hill, Rom.
(Stap.Abb.) RM4 51 FF45
Tysoe Av, Enf. EN3 31 DZ36
Tysoe St, EC1 196 D3
Tyson Rd, SE23 122 DW87
Tyssen Pas, E8 84 DT65
Tyssen Pl, S.Ock. RM15 91 FW69
Tyssen Rd, N16 66 DT62
Tyssen St, E8 84 DT65
N1 *off Hoxton St* 84 DS68
Tytherton Rd, N19 65 DK62

U

Uamvar St, E14 85 EB71
Uckfield Gro, Mitch. CR4 140 DG95
Uckfield Rd, Enf. EN3 31 DX37
Udall Gdns, Rom. RM5 50 FA51
Udall St, SW1 199 L9
Udney Pk Rd, Tedd. TW11 117 CG92
Uffington Rd, NW10 81 CU67
SE27 121 DN91
Ufford Cl, Har. HA3
off Ufford Rd 40 CB52
Ufford Rd, Har. HA3 40 CB52
Ufford St, SE1 200 E4
Ufton Gro, N1 84 DR66
Ufton Rd, N1 84 DR66
Uhura Sq, N16 66 DS62
Ujima Ct, SW16
off Sunnyhill Rd 121 DL91
Ullathorne Rd, SW16 121 DJ91
Ulleswater Rd, N14 45 DL49
Ullin St, E14
off St. Leonards Rd 85 EC71
Ullswater Business Pk, Couls.
CR5 175 DL116
Ullswater Cl, SW15 118 CR91
Bromley BR1 124 EE93
Hayes UB4 77 BS68
Ullswater Ct, Har. HA2
off Oakington Av 60 CA59
Ullswater Cres, SW15 118 CR91
Coulsdon CR5 175 DL116
Ullswater Rd, SE27 121 DP89
SW13 99 CU80
Ullswater Way, Horn. RM12 71 FG64
Ulstan Cl, Cat. (Wold.) CR3 177 EA123
Ulster Gdns, N13 46 DQ49
Ulster Pl, NW1 195 H5
Ulster Ter, NW1 195 H4
Ulundi Rd, SE3 104 EE79
Ulva Rd, SW15
off Ravenna Rd 119 CX85
Ulverscroft Rd, SE22 122 DT85
Ulverstone Rd, SE27 121 DP89
Ulverston Rd, E17 47 ED54
Ulwin Av, W.Byf.
(Byfleet) KT14 152 BL113
Ulysses Rd, NW6 63 CZ64
Umberston St, E1
off Hessel St 84 DV72
Umbria St, SW15 119 CU86
Umfreville Rd, N4 65 DP58
Undercliff Rd, SE13 103 EA83
UNDERHILL, Barn. EN5 28 DA43
Underhill, Barn. EN5 28 DA43
Underhill Pk Rd, Reig. RH2 184 DA131
Underhill Pas, NW1
off Camden High St 83 DH67
Underhill Rd, SE22 122 DV86
Underhill St, NW1
off Camden High St 83 DH67
Underne Av, N14 45 DH47
UNDERRIVER, Sev. TN15 191 FN130
Underriver Ho Rd, Sev.
(Undrvr) TN15 191 FP130
Undershaft, EC3 197 M9
Undershaw Rd, Brom. BR1 124 EE90
Underwood, Croy.
(New Adgtn) CR0 161 EC106
Underwood, The, SE9 125 EM89
Underwood Rd, E1 84 DU70
E4 47 EB50
Caterham CR3 186 DS126
Woodford Green IG8 48 EK52
Underwood Row, N1 197 J2
Underwood St, N1 197 J2
Undine Rd, E14 204 C8
Undine St, SW17 120 DF92
Uneeda Dr, Grnf. UB6 79 CD67
Unicorn Ho, Brom. BR1
off Elmfield Rd 144 EG97
Unicorn Wk, Green. DA9 129 FT85
Union Cl, E11 67 ED63
Union Cotts, E15
off Welfare Rd 86 EE66
Union Ct, EC2 197 M8
Richmond TW9
off Eton St 118 CL85
Union Dr, E1
off Canal Cl 85 DY70
Union Gro, SW8 101 DK82
Union Rd, N11 45 DK51
SW4 101 DK82
SW8 101 DK82
Bromley BR2 144 EK99

★ Place of interest ⇌ Railway station ⊖ London Underground station DLR Docklands Light Railway station Tra Tramlink station H Hospital Riv Pedestrian ferry landing stage

337

Union Rd, Croydon CR0 . . . . . **142** DQ101
Northolt UB5 . . . . **78** CA68
Wembley HA0 . . . . **80** CL65
Union Sq, N1 . . . . **84** DQ67
Union St, E15 . . . . **85** EC67
SE1 . . . . **200** G3
Barnet EN5 . . . . **27** CY42
Kingston upon Thames KT1 . **137** CK96
Union Wk, E2 . . . . **197** N2
Union Wf, N1 . . . . **197** H1
H **United Elizabeth Garrett Anderson Hosp & Hosp for Women, The**, NW1 . . . . **195** N3
Unity Cl, NW10 . . . . **81** CU65
SE19
off Crown Dale **122** DQ92
Croydon
(New Adgtn) CR0 . . . . **161** EB109
Unity Rd, Enf. EN3 . . . . **30** DW37
Unity Ter, Har. HA2
off Scott Cres **60** CB61
Unity Trd Est, Wdf.Grn. IG8 . . . . **68** EK55
Unity Way, SE18 . . . . **104** EK76
Unity Wf, SE1 . . . . **202** A4
University Cl, NW7 . . . . **43** CT52
Bushey WD23 . . . . **24** CA42
H **University Coll Hosp**, WC1 . . . . **195** L5
Obstetric Hosp, WC1 . . . . **195** L5
Out-Patients, W1 . . . . **195** L4
Private Wing, WC1 . . . . **195** L5
★ **University Coll London**, WC1 . . . . **195** M4
H **University Coll London - Maternity Wing**, WC1 . . . . **195** L5
H **University Coll London - The Maxillofacial Unit (Acute Out-Patients only)**, WC1 . . . . **195** L5
University Gdns, Bex. DA5 . . . **126** EZ87
H **University Hosp Lewisham**, SE13 . . . . **123** EB85
★ **University of London**, WC1 . . . . **195** N5
University Pl, Erith DA8
off Belmont Rd **107** FB80
University Rd, SW19 . . . . **120** DD93
University St, WC1 . . . . **195** L5
University Way, E16 . . . . **87** EN73
Dartford DA1 . . . . **108** FJ84
Unwin Av, Felt. TW14 . . . . **115** BS85
Unwin Cl, SE15 . . . . **102** DU79
Unwin Rd, SW7 . . . . **198** A6
Isleworth TW7 . . . . **97** CE83
Upbrook Ms, W2
off Chilworth St **82** DC72
Upcerne Rd, SW10 . . . . **100** DC80
Upchurch Cl, SE20 . . . . **122** DV94
Up Cor, Ch.St.G. HP8 . . . . **36** AW47
Up Cor Cl, Ch.St.G. HP8 . . . . . . **36** AV47
Upcroft Av, Edg. HA8 . . . . **42** CQ50
Updale Cl, Pot.B. EN6 . . . . **11** CY33
Updale Rd, Sid. DA14 . . . . **125** ET91
Upfield, Croy. CR0 . . . . **142** DV103
Upfield Rd, W7 . . . . **79** CF70
Upgrove Manor Way, SW2
off Trinity Ri **121** DN87
Uphall Rd, Ilf. IG1 . . . . **69** EP64
Upham Pk Rd, W4 . . . . **98** CS77
Uphavering Ho, Horn. RM12
off Parkhill Cl **72** FJ61
Uphill Dr, NW7 . . . . **42** CS50
NW9 . . . . **62** CQ57
Uphill Gro, NW7 . . . . **42** CS49
Uphill Rd, NW7 . . . . **42** CS49
Upland Ct Rd, Rom. RM3 . . . . . . **52** FM54
Upland Dr, Hat. AL9 . . . . **12** DB25
Upland Ms, SE22
off Upland Rd **122** DU85
Upland Rd, E13
off Sutton Rd **86** EF70
SE22 . . . . **122** DU85
Bexleyheath DA7 . . . . **106** EZ83
Caterham CR3 . . . . **177** EB120
Epping CM16 . . . . **17** ET25
South Croydon CR2 . . . . **160** DR106
Sutton SM2 . . . . **158** DD108
Uplands, Ashtd. KT21 . . . . **171** CK120
Beckenham BR3 . . . . **143** EA96
Rickmansworth
(Crox.Grn) WD3 . . . . **22** BM44
Uplands, The, Ger.Cr. SL9 . . . . . **56** AY60
Loughton IG10 . . . . **33** EM41
Ruislip HA4 . . . . **59** BU60
St. Albans
(Brick.Wd) AL2 . . . . **8** BY30
Uplands Av, E17
off Blackhorse La **47** DX54
Uplands Business Pk, E17 . . . . **47** DX54
Uplands Cl, SW14
off Monroe Dr **118** CP85
Gerrards Cross SL9 . . . . **56** AY60
Sevenoaks TN13 . . . . **190** FF123
Uplands Dr, Lthd.
(Oxshott) KT22 . . . . **155** CD113
Uplands End, Wdf.Grn. IG8 . . . **48** EL52
Uplands Pk Rd, Enf. EN2 . . . . . **29** DN41
Uplands Rd, N8 . . . . **65** DM57
Barnet EN4 . . . . **44** DG46
Brentwood
(Warley) CM14 . . . . **54** FY50
Kenley CR8 . . . . **176** DQ116
Orpington BR6 . . . . **146** EV102
Romford RM6 . . . . **70** EX55
Woodford Green IG8 . . . . **48** EL52
Uplands Way, N21 . . . . **29** DN43
Sevenoaks TN13 . . . . **190** FF123
Upland Way, Epsom KT18 . . . **173** CW118
UPMINSTER **72** FQ62
⇌ **Upminster** **72** FQ61
⊖ **Upminster** **72** FQ61
⊖ **Upminster Bridge** **72** FN61
Upminster Rd, Horn.
RM11, RM12 . . . . **72** FM61
Upminster RM14 . . . . **72** FM61
Upminster Rd N, Rain.
RM13 . . . . **90** FJ69
Upminster Rd S, Rain.
RM13 . . . . **89** FG70
Upminster Trd Pk, Upmin.
RM14 . . . . **73** FX59
⊖ **Upney** **87** ET66
Upney Cl, Horn. RM12
off Tylers Cres **72** FJ64
Upney La, Bark. IG11 . . . . **87** ES65
Upnor Way, SE17 . . . . **201** N10
Uppark Dr, Ilf. IG2 . . . . **69** EQ58
Upper Abbey Rd, Belv.
DA17 . . . . **106** EZ77
Upper Addison Gdns, W14 . . . . **99** CY75
Upper Bk St, E14 . . . . **204** B3
Upper Bardsey Wk, N1
off Clephane Rd **84** DQ65
Upper Belgrave St, SW1 . . . . . **198** G6
Upper Berkeley St, W1 . . . . . . **194** D9
Upper Beulah Hill, SE19 . . . . . **142** DS95
Upper Bourne End La, Hem.H.
HP1 . . . . **5** BA25
Upper Brentwood Rd, Rom.
RM2 . . . . **72** FJ56
Upper Br Rd, Red. RH1 . . . . . . **184** DE134
Upper Brighton Rd, Surb.
KT6 . . . . **137** CK100
Upper Brockley Rd, SE4 . . . . . **103** DZ82
Upper Brook St, W1 . . . . **198** F1
Upper Butts, Brent. TW8 . . . . . . **97** CJ79
Upper Caldy Wk, N1
off Clephane Rd **84** DQ65
Upper Camelford Wk, W11
off Lancaster Rd **81** CY72
Upper Cavendish Av, N3 . . . . . . **64** DA55
Upper Cheyne Row, SW3 . . . . **100** DE79
Upper Ch Hill, Green. DA9 . . . . **129** FS85
UPPER CLAPTON, E5 . . . . **66** DV60
Upper Clapton Rd, E5 . . . . **66** DV60
Upper Clarendon Wk, W11
off Lancaster Rd **81** CY72
Upper Cornsland, Brwd.
CM14 . . . . **54** FX48
Upper Ct Rd,
Cat. (Wold.) CR3 . . . . **177** EA123
Epsom KT19 . . . . **156** CQ111
Upper Dengie Wk, N1
off Popham Rd **84** DQ67
Upper Dr, West.
(Bigg.H.) TN16 . . . . **178** EJ118
Upper Dunnymans, Bans. SM7
off Basing Rd **157** CZ114
UPPER EDMONTON, N18 . . . . . **46** DU51
UPPER ELMERS END, Beck.
BR3 . . . . **143** DZ100
Upper Elmers End Rd, Beck.
BR3 . . . . **143** DY98
Upper Fairfield Rd, Lthd.
KT22 . . . . **171** CH121
Upper Fm Rd, W.Mol. KT8 . . . **136** BZ98
Upper Fosters, NW4
off New Brent St **63** CW57
Upper Grn E, Mitch. CR4 . . . . . **140** DF97
Upper Grn W, Mitch. CR4
off London Rd **140** DF97
Upper Grenfell Wk, W11
off Whitchurch Rd **81** CX73
Upper Grosvenor St, W1 . . . . . **198** F1
Upper Grotto Rd, Twick.
TW1 . . . . **117** CF89
Upper Grd, SE1 . . . . **200** D2
Upper Gro, SE25 . . . . **142** DS98
Upper Gro Rd, Belv. DA17 . . . . **106** EZ79
Upper Guild Hall, Green.
(Bluewater) DA9
off Bluewater Parkway **129** FU88
Upper Gulland Wk, N1
off Clephane Rd **84** DQ65
UPPER HALLIFORD, Shep.
TW17 . . . . **135** BS97
⇌ **Upper Halliford** **135** BS96
Upper Halliford Bypass, Shep.
TW17 . . . . **135** BS99
Upper Halliford Grn, Shep. TW17
off Holmbank Dr **135** BS98
Upper Halliford Rd, Shep.
TW17 . . . . **135** BS96
Upper Ham Rd, Kings.T.
KT2 . . . . **117** CK91
Richmond TW10 . . . . **117** CK91
Upper Handa Wk, N1
off Clephane Rd **84** DR65
Upper Hawkwell Wk, N1
off Popham Rd **84** DQ67
Upper High St, Epsom
KT17 . . . . **156** CS113
Upper Highway, Abb.L.
WD5 . . . . **7** BR33
Kings Langley WD4 . . . . **7** BQ32
Upper Hill Ri, Rick. WD3 . . . . . . **22** BH44
Upper Hitch, Wat. WD19 . . . . . . **40** BY46
UPPER HOLLOWAY, N19 . . . . . . **65** DJ62
⇌ **Upper Holloway** **65** DK61
Upper Holly Hill Rd, Belv.
DA17 . . . . **107** FB78
Upper James St, W1 . . . . **195** L10
Upper John St, W1 . . . . **195** L10
Upper Lismore Wk, N1
off Clephane Rd **84** DQ65
Upper Lo Way, Couls. CR5
off Netherne Dr **175** DK122
Upper Mall, W6 . . . . **99** CU78
Upper Marsh, SE1 . . . . **200** C6
Upper Montagu St, W1 . . . . . . **194** D6
Upper Mulgrave Rd, Sutt.
SM2 . . . . **157** CY108
Upper N St, E14 . . . . **85** EA71
UPPER NORWOOD,
SE19 . . . . **122** DR94
Upper Paddock Rd, Wat.
WD19 . . . . **24** BY44
Upper Palace Rd, E.Mol.
KT8 . . . . **136** CC97
Upper Pk, Loug. IG10 . . . . **32** EK42
Upper Pk Rd, N11 . . . . **45** DH50
NW3 . . . . **64** DF64
Belvedere DA17 . . . . **107** FB77
Bromley BR1 . . . . **144** EH95
Kingston upon Thames KT2 . **118** CN93
Upper Phillimore Gdns, W8 . . **100** DA75
Upper Pillory Down, Cars.
SM5 . . . . **158** DG113
Upper Pines, Bans. SM7 . . . . . **174** DF117
Upper Rainham Rd, Horn.
RM12 . . . . **71** FF63
Upper Ramsey Wk, N1
off Clephane Rd **84** DR65
Upper Rawreth Wk, N1
off Popham Rd **84** DQ67
Upper Richmond Rd, SW15 . . . **99** CY84
Upper Richmond Rd W,
SW14 . . . . **98** CP84
Richmond TW10 . . . . **98** CN84
Upper Rd, E13 . . . . **86** EG69
Uxbridge (Denh.) UB9 . . . . . . **57** BD59
Wallington SM6 . . . . **159** DK106
Upper Rose Gall, Green.
(Bluewater) DA9
off Bluewater Parkway **129** FU88
Upper Ryle, Brwd. CM14 . . . . . **54** FV45
Upper St. Martin's La, WC2 . . **195** P10
Upper Sawley Wd, Bans.
SM7 . . . . **157** CZ114
Upper Selsdon Rd, S.Croy.
CR2 . . . . **160** DT108
Upper Sheppey Wk, N1
off Clephane Rd **84** DQ66
Upper Sheridan Rd, Belv. DA17
off Coleman Rd **106** FA77
Upper Shirley Rd, Croy.
CR0 . . . . **142** DW103
Upper Shott, Wal.Cr.
(Chsht) EN7 . . . . **14** DT26
Upper Sq, Islw. TW7 . . . . **97** CG83
Upper Sta Rd, Rad. WD7 . . . . . . **25** CG35
Upper St, N1 . . . . **83** DN68
Upper Sunbury Rd, Hmptn.
TW12 . . . . **136** BY95
Upper Sutton La, Houns.
TW5 . . . . **96** CA80
Upper Swaines, Epp. CM16 . . . **17** ET30
UPPER SYDENHAM,
SE26 . . . . **122** DU91
Upper Tachbrook St, SW1 . . . **199** K8
Upper Tail, Wat. WD19 . . . . **40** BY48
Upper Talbot Wk, W11
off Lancaster Rd **81** CY72
Upper Teddington Rd, Kings.T.
KT1 . . . . **137** CJ95
Upper Ter, NW3 . . . . **64** DC62
Upper Thames St, EC4 . . . . . . **196** G10
Upper Thames Wk, Green.
(Bluewater) DA9
off Bluewater Parkway **129** FU88
Upper Tollington Pk, N4 . . . . . . **65** DN60
Upperton Rd, Sid. DA14 . . . . . **125** ET92
Upperton Rd E, E13
off Inniskilling Rd **86** EJ69
Upperton Rd W, E13 . . . . **86** EJ69
UPPER TOOTING, SW17 . . . . . **120** DE90
Upper Tooting Pk, SW17 . . . . . **120** DF89
Upper Tooting Rd, SW17 . . . . . **120** DF91
Upper Town Rd, Grnf. UB6 . . . . **78** CB70
Upper Tulse Hill, SW2 . . . . . . **121** DM87
Upper Vernon Rd, Sutt.
SM1 . . . . **158** DD106
Upper Wk, Vir.W. GU25 . . . . . . **132** AY98
UPPER WALTHAMSTOW,
E17 . . . . **67** EB56
Upper Walthamstow Rd,
E17 . . . . **67** ED56
⇌ **Upper Warlingham** **176** DU118
Upper W St, Reig. RH2 . . . . . . **183** CZ134
Upper Wickham La, Well.
DA16 . . . . **106** EV80
Upper Wimpole St, W1 . . . . . . **195** H6
Upper Woburn Pl, WC1 . . . . . . **195** N3
Upper Woodcote Village, Pur.
CR8 . . . . **159** DK112
Uppingham Av, Stan. HA7 . . . . **41** CH53
Upsdell Av, N13 . . . . **45** DN51
UPSHIRE, Wal.Abb. EN9 . . . . . . **16** EJ32
Upshirebury Grn, Wal.Abb. EN9
off Horseshoe Hill **16** EK33
Upshire Rd, Wal.Abb. EN9 . . . . . **16** EF32
Upshott La, Wok. GU22 . . . . . . **167** BF117
Upstall St, SE5 . . . . **101** DP81
UPTON, E7 . . . . **86** EH66
UPTON, Slou. SL1 . . . . **92** AU76
Upton, Wok. GU21 . . . . **166** AV117
Upton Av, E7 . . . . **86** EG66
Upton Cl, NW2
off Somerton Rd **63** CY62
Bexley DA5 . . . . **126** EZ86
St. Albans (Park St) AL2 . . . . . **9** CD25
Slough SL1 . . . . **92** AT76
Upton Ct, SE20
off Blean Gro **122** DW94
Upton Ct Rd, Slou. SL3 . . . . . . **92** AU76
Upton Dene, Sutt. SM2 . . . . . . **158** DB108
Upton Gdns, Har. HA3 . . . . **61** CH57
H **Upton Hosp**, Slou. SL1 . . . . . **92** AT76
Upton La, E7 . . . . **86** EG66
Upton Lo Cl, Bushey WD23 . . . . **40** CC45
UPTON PARK, E6 . . . . **86** EJ67
UPTON PARK, Slou. SL1 . . . . . . **92** AT76
⊖ **Upton Park** **86** EH67
Upton Pk, Slou. SL1 . . . . **92** AT76
Upton Pk Rd, E7 . . . . **86** EH66
Upton Rd, N18 . . . . **46** DU50
SE18 . . . . **105** EQ79
Bexley DA5 . . . . **126** EZ86
Bexleyheath DA6 . . . . **106** EY84
Hounslow TW3 . . . . **96** CA83
Slough SL1 . . . . **92** AU76
Thornton Heath CR7 . . . . **142** DR96
Watford WD18 . . . . **23** BV42
Upton Rd S, Bex. DA5 . . . . **126** EZ86
Upway, N12 . . . . **44** DE52
Gerrards Cross
(Chal.St.P.) SL9 . . . . **37** AZ53
Upwood Rd, SE12 . . . . **124** EF86
SW16 . . . . **141** DL95
Urban Av, Horn. RM12 . . . . **72** FJ62
Urlwin St, SE5 . . . . **102** DQ79
Urlwin Wk, SW9 . . . . **101** DN82
Urmston Dr, SW19 . . . . **119** CY88
Ursula Ms, N4
off Portland Ri **66** DQ60
Ursula St, SW11 . . . . **100** DE81
Urswick Gdns, Dag. RM9
off Urswick Rd **88** EY66
Urswick Rd, E9 . . . . **66** DW64
Dagenham RM9 . . . . **88** EX66
Usborne Ms, SW8 . . . . **101** DM80
Usher Rd, E3 . . . . **85** DZ68
Usherwood Cl, Tad.
(Box H.) KT20 . . . . **182** CP131
Usk Rd, SW11 . . . . **100** DC84
South Ockendon (Aveley)
RM15 . . . . **90** FQ72
Usk St, E2 . . . . **85** DX69
Utopia Village, NW1
off Chalcot Rd **82** DG67
Uvedale Cl, Croy. (New Adgtn) CR0
off Uvedale Cres **161** ED111
Uvedale Cres, Croy.
(New Adgtn) CR0 . . . . **161** ED111
Uvedale Rd, Dag. RM10 . . . . . . **70** FA62
Enfield EN2 . . . . **30** DR43
Oxted RH8 . . . . **188** EF129
Uverdale Rd, SW10 . . . . **100** DC80
UXBRIDGE **76** BK66
⊖ **Uxbridge** **76** BK66
Uxbridge Gdns, Felt. TW13
off Marlborough Rd **116** BX89
UXBRIDGE MOOR, Iver SL0 . . . **76** BG67
UXBRIDGE MOOR, Uxb. UB8 . . **76** BG67
Uxbridge Rd, W3 . . . . **80** CL73
W5 . . . . **79** CJ73
W5 (Ealing Com.) **80** CL73
W7 . . . . **79** CF74
W12 . . . . **81** CU74
W13 . . . . **79** CF74
Feltham TW13 . . . . **116** BW89
Hampton
(Hmptn H.) TW12 . . . . **116** CA91
Harrow HA3 . . . . **40** CC52
Hayes UB4 . . . . **78** BW73
Iver SL0 . . . . **74** AY71
Kingston upon Thames KT1 . **137** CK98
Pinner HA5 . . . . **40** CB52
Rickmansworth WD3 . . . . **37** BF47
Slough SL1, SL2, SL3 . . . . **92** AU75
Southall UB1 . . . . **78** CA74
Stanmore HA7 . . . . **41** CF51
Uxbridge UB10 . . . . **76** BN69
Uxbridge St, W8 . . . . **82** DA74
Uxendon Cres, Wem. HA9 . . . . **62** CL60
Uxendon Hill, Wem. HA9 . . . . . **62** CM60

V

Vache La, Ch.St.G. HP8 . . . . . . **36** AW47
Vache Ms, Ch.St.G. HP8 . . . . . . **36** AX46
Vaillant Rd, Wey. KT13 . . . . . **153** BQ105
Valance Av, E4 . . . . **48** EF46
Valan Leas, Brom. BR2 . . . . . . **144** EE97
Vale, The, N10 . . . . **44** DG53
N14 . . . . **45** DK45
NW11 . . . . **63** CX62
SW3 . . . . **100** DD79
W3 . . . . **80** CR74
Brentwood CM14 . . . . **54** FW46
Coulsdon CR5 . . . . **159** DK114
Croydon CR0 . . . . **143** DX103
Feltham TW14 . . . . **115** BV86
Gerrards Cross
(Chal.St.P.) SL9 . . . . **36** AX53
Hounslow TW5 . . . . **96** BY79
Ruislip HA4 . . . . **60** BW63
Sunbury-on-Thames TW16
off Ashridge Way **115** BU93
Woodford Green IG8 . . . . **48** EG52
Vale Av, Borwd. WD6 . . . . **26** CP43
Vale Border, Croy. CR0 . . . . . . **161** DX111
Vale Cl, N2 *off Church Vale* **64** DF55
W9 *off Maida Vale* **82** DC69
Brentwood
(Pilg.Hat.) CM15 . . . . **54** FT43
Gerrards Cross
(Chal.St.P.) SL9 . . . . **36** AX53
Orpington BR6 . . . . **163** EN105
Weybridge KT13 . . . . **135** BR104
Woking GU21 . . . . **166** AY116
Vale Cotts, SW15
off Kingston Vale **118** CR91
Vale Ct, W9
off Maida Vale **82** DC69
Weybridge KT13 . . . . **135** BR104
Vale Cres, SW15 . . . . **118** CS90
Vale Cft, Esher (Clay.) KT10 . . **155** CE108
Pinner HA5 . . . . **60** BY57
Vale Dr, Barn. EN5 . . . . **27** CZ42
Vale End, SE22
off Grove Vale **102** DS84
Vale Fm Rd, Wok. GU21 . . . . . **166** AX117
Vale Gro, N4 . . . . **66** DQ59
W3 *off The Vale* **80** CR74
Slough SL1 . . . . **92** AS76
Vale Ind Est, Wat. WD18 . . . . . . **39** BQ46
Vale La, W3 . . . . **80** CN71
Valence Av, Dag. RM8 . . . . **70** EX62
Valence Circ, Dag. RM8 . . . . **70** EX62
Valence Dr, Wal.Cr.
(Chsht) EN7 . . . . **14** DU28
★ **Valence Ho Mus**, Dag.
RM8 . . . . **70** EY61
Valence Rd, Erith DA8 . . . . **107** FD80
Valence Wd Rd, Dag. RM8 . . . . **70** EX62
Valencia Rd, Stan. HA7 . . . . **41** CJ49
Valency Cl, Nthwd. HA6 . . . . . . **39** BT49
Valentia Pl, SW9
off Brixton Sta Rd **101** DN84
Valentine Av, Bex. DA5 . . . . . . **126** EY89
Valentine Ct, SE23 . . . . **123** DX89
Valentine Pl, SE1 . . . . **200** F4
Valentine Rd, E9 . . . . **85** DX65
Harrow HA2 . . . . **60** CC62
Valentine Row, SE1 . . . . **200** F5
Valentines Rd, Ilf. IG1 . . . . **69** EP60
Valentines Way, Rom. RM7 . . . . **71** FE61
Valentine Way, Ch.St.G. HP8 . . **36** AX48
Valentyne Cl, Croy.
(New Adgtn) CR0 . . . . **162** EE111
Vale of Health, NW3
off East Heath Rd **64** DD62
Vale Par, SW15
off Kingston Vale **118** CR91
Valerian Way, E15 . . . . **86** EE69
Valerie Ct, Bushey WD23 . . . . . **40** CC45
Sutton SM2
off Stanley Rd **158** DB108
Vale Ri, NW11 . . . . **63** CZ60
Vale Rd, E7 . . . . **86** EH65
N4 . . . . **66** DQ59
Bromley BR1 . . . . **145** EN96
Bushey WD23 . . . . **24** BY43
Dartford DA1 . . . . **127** FH88
Epsom KT19 . . . . **157** CT105
Esher (Clay.) KT10 . . . . **155** CE109
Gravesend (Nthflt) DA11 . . . **130** GD87
Mitcham CR4 . . . . **141** DK97
Sutton SM1 . . . . **158** DB105
Weybridge KT13 . . . . **135** BR104
Worcester Park KT4 . . . . **157** CT105
Vale Rd N, Surb. KT6 . . . . **138** CL103
Vale Rd S, Surb. KT6 . . . . **138** CL103
Vale Row, N5
off Gillespie Rd **65** DP62
Vale Royal, N7 . . . . **83** DL66
Valery Pl, Hmptn. TW12
off Priory Rd **116** CA94
Vale St, SE27 . . . . **122** DR90
Valeswood Rd, Brom. BR1 . . . **124** EF92
Vale Ter, N4 . . . . **66** DQ58
Valetta Gro, E13 . . . . **86** EG68
Valetta Rd, W3 . . . . **98** CS75
Valette St, E9 . . . . **84** DV65
Valiant Cl, Nthlt. UB5
off Ruislip Rd **78** BX69
Romford RM7 . . . . **50** FA54
Valiant Ho, SE7 . . . . **104** EJ78
Valiant Path, NW9
off Blundell Rd **42** CS52
Valiant Way, E6 . . . . **87** EM71
Vallance Rd, E1 . . . . **84** DU70
E2 . . . . **84** DU69
N22 . . . . **45** DJ54
Vallentin Rd, E17 . . . . **67** EC56
Valley Av, N12 . . . . **44** DD49
Valley Cl, Dart. DA1 . . . . **127** FF86
Loughton IG10 . . . . **33** EM44
Pinner HA5
off Alandale Dr **39** BV54
Waltham Abbey EN9 . . . . **15** EC32
Valley Ct, Cat. CR3
off Beechwood Gdns **176** DU122
Kenley CR8
off Hayes La **160** DQ114
Valley Dr, NW9 . . . . **62** CN58
Gravesend DA12 . . . . **131** GK91
Sevenoaks TN13 . . . . **191** FH125
Valleyfield Rd, SW16 . . . . **121** DM92
Valley Flds Cres, Enf. EN2 . . . . **29** DN40
Valley Gdns, SW19 . . . . **120** DD94
Wembley HA0 . . . . **80** CM66
★ **Valley Gdns, The**, Egh.
TW20 . . . . **132** AS96
Valley Gro, SE7 . . . . **104** EJ78
Valley Hill, Loug. IG10 . . . . **48** EL45
Valley Link Ind Est, Enf. EN3 . . **31** DY44
Valley Ms, Twick. TW1
off Cross Deep **117** CG89
Valley Ri, Wat. WD25 . . . . **7** BV33
Valley Rd, SW16 . . . . **121** DM91
Belvedere DA17 . . . . **107** FB77
Bromley BR2 . . . . **144** EE96
Dartford DA1 . . . . **127** FF86
Erith DA8 . . . . **107** FD77
Kenley CR8 . . . . **176** DR115
Longfield
(Fawk.Grn) DA3 . . . . **149** FV102
Orpington BR5 . . . . **146** EV95
Rickmansworth WD3 . . . . **22** BG43
Uxbridge UB10 . . . . **76** BL68
Valley Side, E4 . . . . **47** EA47
Valley Side Par, E4
off Valley Side **47** EA47
Valley Vw, Barn. EN5 . . . . **27** CY44
Greenhithe DA9 . . . . **129** FV86
Waltham Cross
(Chsht) EN7 . . . . **14** DQ28
Westerham
(Bigg.H.) TN16 . . . . **178** EJ118
Valley Vw Gdns, Ken. CR8
off Godstone Rd **176** DS115
Valley Wk, Croy. CR0 . . . . . . **142** DW103
Rickmansworth
(Crox.Grn) WD3 . . . . **23** BQ43
Valley Way, Ger.Cr. SL9 . . . . . . **56** AW58
Valliere Rd, NW10 . . . . **81** CV69
Valliers Wd Rd, Sid. DA15 . . . . **125** ER88
Vallis Way, W13 . . . . **79** CG71
Chessington KT9 . . . . **155** CK105
Valmar Rd, SE5 . . . . **102** DQ81
Val McKenzie Av, N7
off Parkside Cres **65** DN62
Valnay St, SW17 . . . . **120** DF92
Valognes Av, E17 . . . . **47** DY53
Valonia Gdns, SW18 . . . . **119** CZ86
Vambery Rd, SE18 . . . . **105** EQ79
Vanbrough Cres, Nthlt.
UB5 . . . . **78** BW67
Vanbrugh Cl, E16
off Fulmer Rd **86** EK71
Vanbrugh Dr, Walt. KT12 . . . . **136** BW101
Vanbrugh Flds, SE3 . . . . **104** EF80
Vanbrugh Hill, SE3 . . . . **104** EF78
SE10 . . . . **104** EF78
Vanbrugh Pk, SE3 . . . . **104** EF80
Vanbrugh Pk Rd, SE3 . . . . **104** EF80
Vanbrugh Pk Rd W, SE3 . . . . . **104** EF80
Vanbrugh Rd, W4 . . . . **98** CR76
Vanbrugh Ter, SE3 . . . . **104** EF81
Vanburgh Cl, Orp. BR6 . . . . . . **145** ES102
Vancouver Cl, Epsom KT19 . . **156** CQ111
Orpington BR6 . . . . **163** ET105
Vancouver Rd, SE23 . . . . **123** DY89
Broxbourne EN10 . . . . **15** DY25
Edgware HA8 . . . . **42** CP53
Hayes UB4 . . . . **77** BV70
Richmond TW10 . . . . **117** CJ91
Vanderbilt Rd, SW18 . . . . **120** DC88
Vanderville Gdns, N2
off Tarling Rd **44** DC54
Vandome Cl, E16 . . . . **86** EH72

Vandon Pas, SW1 199 L6
Vandon St, SW1 199 L6
Van Dyck Av, N.Mal. KT3 138 CR101
Vandyke Cl, SW15 119 CX87
Redhill RH1 184 DF131
Vandyke Cross, SE9 124 EL85
Vandy St, EC2 197 M5
Vane Cl, NW3 64 DD63
Harrow HA3 62 CM58
Vanessa Cl, Belv. DA17 106 FA78
Vanessa Wk, Grav. DA12 131 GM92
Vanessa Way, Bex. DA5 127 FD90
Vane St, SW1 199 L8
Van Gogh Cl, Islw. TW7
off Twickenham Rd 97 CG83
Vanguard Cl, E16 86 EG71
Croydon CR0 141 DP102
Romford RM7 51 FB54
Vanguard St, SE8 103 EA81
Vanguard Way, Cat. CR3
off Slines Oak Rd 177 EB121
Wallington SM6 159 DL108
Warlingham CR6 177 EB121
Vanneck Sq, SW15 119 CU85
Vanner Pt, E9 off Wick Rd 85 DX65
Vanners Par, W.Byf. (Byfleet) KT14
off Brewery La 152 BL113
Vanoc Gdns, Brom. BR1 124 EG90
Vanquisher Wk, Grav. DA12 131 GM90
Vansittart Rd, E7 68 EF63
Vansittart St, SE14 103 DY80
Vanston Pl, SW6 100 DA80
Vantage Ms, E14 204 E3
Vantage Pl, W8
off Abingdon Rd 100 DA76
Vant Rd, SW17 120 DF92
Varcoe Rd, SE16 102 DV78
Vardens Rd, SW11 100 DD84
Varden St, E1 84 DV72
Vardon Cl, W3 80 CR72
Varley Par, NW9 62 CS56
Varley Rd, E16 86 EH72
Varley Way, Mitch. CR4 140 DD96
Varna Rd, SW6 99 CY80
Hampton TW12 136 CB95
Varndell St, NW1 195 K2
Varney Cl, Wal.Cr.
(Chsht) EN7 14 DU27
Varnishers Yd, N1
off Caledonian Rd 83 DL68
Varsity Dr, Twick. TW1 117 CE85
Varsity Row, SW14
off William's La 98 CQ82
Vartry Rd, N15 66 DR58
Vassall Rd, SW9 101 DN80
Vauban Est, SE16 202 A7
Vauban St, SE16 202 A7
Vaughan Av, NW4 63 CU57
W6 99 CT77
Hornchurch RM12 72 FK63
Vaughan Cl, Hmptn. TW12
off Oak Av 116 BY93
Vaughan Gdns, Ilf. IG1 69 EM59
Vaughan Rd, E15 86 EF65
SE5 102 DQ83
Harrow HA1 60 CC59
Thames Ditton KT7 137 CH101
Welling DA16 105 ET82
Vaughan St, SE16 203 M5
Vaughan Way, E1 202 B1
Vaughan Williams Cl, SE8
off Watson's St 103 EA80
Vaughan Williams Way, Brwd. CM14
off Mascalls La 53 FU51
Vaux Cres, Walt. KT12 153 BV107
VAUXHALL, SE11 101 DL78
⇌ Vauxhall 101 DL79
⊖ Vauxhall 101 DL79
Vauxhall Br, SE1 101 DL78
SW1 101 DL78
Vauxhall Br Rd, SW1 199 L8
Vauxhall Cl, Grav.
(Nthflt) DA11 131 GF87
Vauxhall Gdns, S.Croy. CR2 160 DQ107
Vauxhall Gdns Est, SE11 101 DM78
Vauxhall Gro, SW8 101 DL79
Vauxhall Pl, Dart. DA1 128 FL87
Vauxhall St, SE11 101 DM78
Vauxhall Wk, SE11 200 B10
Vawdrey Cl, E1 84 DW70
Veals Mead, Mitch. CR4 140 DE95
Vectis Gdns, SW17
off Vectis Rd 121 DH93
Vectis Rd, SW17 121 DH93
Veda Rd, SE13 103 EA84
Vega Cres, Nthwd. HA6 39 BT50
Vegal Cres, Egh.
(Eng.Grn) TW20 112 AW92
Vega Rd, Bushey WD23 40 CC45
Veldene Way, Har. HA2 60 BZ62
Velde Way, SE22
off East Dulwich Gro 122 DS85
Velletri Ho, E2 85 DX68
Vellum Dr, Cars. SM5 140 DG104
Venables Cl, Dag. RM10 71 FB63
Venables St, NW8 194 A6
Vencourt Pl, W6 99 CU78
Venetian Rd, SE5 102 DQ82
Venetia Rd, N4 65 DP58
W5 97 CK75
Venette Cl, Rain. RM13 89 FH71
Venner Rd, SE26 122 DW93
Venners Cl, Bexh. DA7 107 FE82
Venn St, SW4 101 DJ84
Ventnor Av, Stan. HA7 41 CH53
Ventnor Dr, N20 44 DB48
Ventnor Gdns, Bark. IG11 87 ES65
Ventnor Rd, SE14 103 DX80
Sutton SM2 158 DB108
Venton Cl, Wok. GU21 166 AV117
Ventura Pk, St.Alb. AL2 9 CF29
Venture Cl, Bex. DA5 126 EY87
Venue St, E14 85 EC71
Venus Hill, Hem.H. (Bov.) HP3 5 BA31
Venus Rd, SE18 105 EM76
Veny Cres, Horn. RM12 72 FK64
Vera Av, N21 29 DN43
Vera Ct, Wat. WD19 40 BX45
Vera Lynn Cl, E7
off Dames Rd 68 EG63
Vera Rd, SW6 99 CY81
Verbena Cl, E16
off Pretoria Rd 86 EF70
South Ockendon RM15 91 FW72
West Drayton UB7
off Magnolia St 94 BK78
Verbena Gdns, W6 99 CU78
Verdant La, SE6 124 EE88
Verdayne Av, Croy. CR0 143 DX102
Verdayne Gdns, Warl. CR6 176 DW116
Verderers Rd, Chig. IG7 50 EU50
Verdun Rd, SE18 106 EU79
SW13 99 CU79
Verdure Cl, Wat. WD25 8 BY32
Vereker Dr, Sun. TW16 135 BU97
Vereker Rd, W14 99 CY78
Vere Rd, Loug. IG10 33 EQ42
Vere St, W1 195 H9
Verity Cl, W11 81 CY72
Vermeer Gdns, SE15
off Elland Rd 102 DW84
Vermont Cl, Enf. EN2 29 DP42
Vermont Rd, SE19 122 DR93
SW18 120 DB86
Sutton SM1 140 DB104
Verney Gdns, Dag. RM9 70 EY63
Verney Rd, SE16 102 DU79
Dagenham RM9 70 EY64
Slough SL3 93 BA77
Verney St, NW10 62 CR62
Verney Way, SE16 102 DV78
Vernham Rd, SE18 105 EQ79
Vernon Av, E12 69 EM63
SW20 139 CX96
Enfield EN3 31 DY36
Woodford Green IG8 48 EH52
Vernon Cl, Cher. (Ott.) KT16 151 BD107
Epsom KT19 156 CQ107
Orpington BR5 146 EV97
Staines TW19
off Long La 114 BL88
Vernon Ct, Stan. HA7
off Vernon Dr 41 CH53
Vernon Cres, Barn. EN4 28 DG44
Brentwood CM13 55 GA48
Vernon Dr, Cat. CR3 176 DQ122
Stanmore HA7 41 CG53
Uxbridge
(Hare.) UB9 38 BJ53
Vernon Ms, E17
off Vernon Rd 67 DZ56
W14 off Vernon St 99 CY77
Vernon Pl, WC1 196 A7
Vernon Ri, WC1 196 C2
Greenford UB6 61 CD64
Vernon Rd, E3 85 DZ68
E11 68 EE60
E15 86 EE66
E17 67 DZ57
N8 65 DN55
SW14 98 CR83
Bushey WD23 24 BY43
Feltham TW13 115 BT89
Ilford IG3 69 ET60
Romford RM5 51 FC50
Sutton SM1 158 DC106
Swanscombe DA10 130 FZ86
Vernon Sq, WC1 196 C2
Vernon St, W14 99 CY77
Vernon Wk, Tad. KT20 173 CX120
Vernon Yd, W11
off Portobello Rd 81 CZ73
Veroan Rd, Bexh. DA7 106 EY82
Verona Cl, Uxb. UB8 76 BJ72
Verona Ct, W4
off Chiswick La 98 CS78
Verona Dr, Surb. KT6 138 CL103
Verona Gdns, Grav. DA12 131 GL91
Verona Ho, Erith DA8
off Waterhead Cl 107 FF80
Verona Rd, E7
off Upton La 86 EG66
Veronica Cl, Rom. RM3 52 FJ52
Veronica Gdns, SW16 141 DJ95
Veronica Rd, SW17 121 DH90
Veronique Gdns, Ilf. IG6 69 EP57
Verralls, Wok. GU22 167 BB117
Verran Rd, SW12
off Balham Gro 121 DH87
Versailles Rd, SE20 122 DU94
Verulam Av, E17 67 DZ58
Purley CR8 159 DJ112
Verulam Bldgs, WC1 196 C6
Verulam Pas, Wat. WD17 23 BV40
Verulam Rd, Grnf. UB6 78 CA70
Verulam St, WC1 196 D6
Verwood Dr, Barn. EN4 28 DF41
Verwood Rd, Har. HA2 40 CC54
Veryan, Wok. GU21 166 AU117
Veryan Cl, Orp. BR5 146 EW98
Vesey Path, E14
off East India Dock Rd 85 EB72
Vespan Rd, W12 99 CU75
Vesta Rd, SE4 103 DY82
Vestris Rd, SE23 123 DX89
Vestry Ms, SE5 102 DS81
Vestry Rd, E17 67 EB56
SE5 102 DS81
Sevenoaks TN14 181 FH119
Vestry St, N1 197 K2
Vetch Cl, Felt. TW14 115 BT88
Vevey St, SE6 123 DZ89
Vexil Cl, Purf. RM19 109 FR77
Veysey Gdns, Dag. RM10 70 FA62
Viaduct Pl, E2
off Viaduct St 84 DV69
Viaduct St, E2 84 DV69
Vian Av, Enf. EN3 31 DY35
Vian St, SE13 103 EB83
Vibart Gdns, SW2 121 DM87
Vibart Wk, N1
off Outram Pl 83 DL67
Vicarage Av, SE3 104 EG81
Egham TW20 113 BB93
Vicarage Cl, Brwd. CM14 54 FS49
Erith DA8 107 FC79
Northolt UB5 78 BZ66
Potters Bar EN6 12 DF30
Ruislip HA4 59 BR59
Tadworth KT20 173 CY124
Vicarage Cl,
Worcester Park KT4 138 CS102
Vicarage Ct, W8
off Vicarage Gate 100 DB75
Egham TW20 113 BB93
Feltham TW14 115 BQ87
Vicarage Cres, SW11 100 DD81
Egham TW20 113 BB92
Vicarage Dr, SW14 118 CR85
Barking IG11 87 EQ66
Beckenham BR3 143 EA95
Gravesend (Nthflt) DA11 130 GC86
Vicarage Fm Rd, Houns.
TW3, TW5 96 BY82
Vicarage Flds, Walt. KT12 136 BW100
Vicarage Fld Shop Cen, Bark.
IG11 87 EQ66
Vicarage Gdns, SW14
off Vicarage Rd 118 CQ85
W8 82 DA74
Mitcham CR4 140 DE97
Vicarage Gate, W8 100 DB75
Vicarage Gate Ms, Tad. KT20 173 CY124
Vicarage Gro, SE5 102 DR81
Vicarage Hill, West. TN16 189 ER126
Vicarage La, E6 87 EM69
E15 86 EE66
Chigwell IG7 49 EQ47
Epsom KT17 157 CU109
Hemel Hempstead
(Bov.) HP3 5 BB26
Ilford IG1 69 ER60
Kings Langley WD4 6 BM29
Leatherhead KT22 171 CH122
Sevenoaks (Dunt.Grn) TN13
off London Rd 181 FD119
Staines (Laleham) TW18 134 BH97
Staines (Wrays.) TW19 112 AY88
Vicarage Pk, SE18 105 EQ78
Vicarage Path, N8 65 DL59
Vicarage Pl, Slou. SL1 92 AU76
Vicarage Rd, E10 67 EB60
E15 86 EF66
N17 46 DU52
NW4 63 CU58
SE18 105 EQ78
SW14 118 CQ85
Bexley DA5 127 FB88
Croydon CR0 141 DN104
Dagenham RM10 89 FB65
Egham TW20 113 BB93
Epping (Cooper.) CM16 18 EW29
Hornchurch RM12 71 FG60
Kingston upon Thames KT1 137 CK96
Kingston upon Thames
(Hmptn W.) KT1 137 CJ95
Staines TW18 113 BE91
Sunbury-on-Thames
TW16 115 BT92
Sutton SM1 158 DB105
Teddington TW11 117 CG92
Twickenham TW2 117 CE89
Twickenham
(Whitton) TW2 116 CC86
Watford WD18 23 BU44
Woking GU22 167 AZ121
Woodford Green IG8 48 EL52
Vicarage Sq, Grays RM17 110 GA79
Vicarage Wk, SW11
off Battersea Ch Rd 100 DD81
Reigate RH2
off Chartway 184 DB134
Vicarage Way, NW10 62 CR62
Gerrards Cross SL9 57 AZ58
Harrow HA2 60 CA59
Slough (Colnbr.) SL3 93 BC80
Vicars Br Cl, Wem. HA0 80 CL68
Vicars Cl, E9
off Northiam St 84 DW67
E15 86 EG67
Enfield EN1 30 DS40
Vicars Hill, SE13 103 EB84
Vicars Moor La, N21 45 DN45
Vicars Oak Rd, SE19 122 DS93
Vicars Rd, NW5 64 DG64
Vicars Wk, Dag. RM8 70 EV62
Viceroy Cl, N2
off Market Pl 64 DE56
Viceroy Ct, NW8
off Prince Albert Rd 82 DE68
Viceroy Par, N2 off High Rd 64 DE55
Viceroy Rd, SW8 101 DL81
Vickers Cl, Wall. SM6 159 DM108
Vickers Dr N, Wey. KT13 152 BL110
Vickers Dr S, Wey. KT13 152 BL111
Vickers Rd, Erith DA8 107 FD78
Vickers Way, Houns. TW4 116 BY85
Victor App, Horn. RM12
off Abbs Cross Gdns 72 FK60
Victor Cl, Horn. RM12 72 FK60
Victor Ct, Horn. RM12 72 FK60
Rainham RM13
off Askwith Rd 89 FD68
Victor Gdns, Horn. RM12 72 FK60
Victor Gro, Wem. HA0 80 CL66
⇌ Victoria 199 J8
⊖ Victoria 199 J8
★ Victoria & Albert Mus,
SW7 198 A7
Victoria Arc, SW1
off Terminus Pl 101 DH76
Victoria Av, E6 86 EK67
EC2 197 N7
N3 43 CZ53
Barnet EN4 28 DD42
Gravesend DA12
off Sheppy Pl 131 GH87
Grays RM16 110 GC75
Hounslow TW3 116 BZ85
Romford RM5 51 FB51
South Croydon CR2 160 DQ110
Surbiton KT6 137 CK101
Uxbridge UB10 77 BP66
Wallington SM6 140 DG104
Wembley HA9 80 CP65
West Molesey KT8 136 CA97
Victoria Cl, Barn. EN4 28 DD42
Grays RM16 110 GC75
Hayes UB3
off Commonwealth Av 77 BR72
Victoria Cl, Rickmansworth WD3
off Nightingale Rd 38 BK45
Waltham Cross EN8 15 DX30
West Molesey KT8
off Victoria Av 136 CA97
Weybridge KT13 135 BR104
★ Victoria Coach Sta, SW1 199 H9
Victoria Cotts, Rich. TW9 98 CM81
Victoria Ct, Wem. HA9 80 CN65
Victoria Cres, N15 66 DS57
SE19 122 DS93
SW19 119 CZ94
Iver SL0 76 BG73
Victoria Dock Rd, E16 86 EF72
Victoria Dr, SW19 119 CX87
Dartford (S.Darenth) DA4 149 FR96
Victoria Embk, EC4 200 B1
SW1 200 A4
WC2 200 B1
★ Victoria Embankment Gdns,
WC2 200 A1
Victoria Gdns, W11 82 DA74
Hounslow TW5 96 BY81
Westerham (Bigg.H.) TN16 178 EJ115
Victoria Gro, N12 44 DC50
W8 100 DC76
Victoria Gro Ms, W2
off Ossington St 82 DB73
Victoria Hill Rd, Swan. BR8 147 FF95
H Victoria Hosp, Rom.
RM1 71 FF56
Victoria Ind Est, NW10 80 CS69
Victoria Ind Pk, Dart. DA1 128 FL85
Victoria La, Barn. EN5 27 CZ42
Hayes UB3 95 BQ78
Victoria Ms, E8
off Dalston La 66 DU64
NW6 82 DA67
SW4 off Victoria Ri 101 DH84
SW18 120 DC88
Victorian Gro, N16 66 DS62
Victorian Rd, N16 66 DS62
★ Victoria Park, E9 85 DY66
Victoria Pk Rd, E9 84 DW67
Victoria Pk Sq, E2 84 DW69
Victoria Pas, NW8
off Cunningham Pl 82 DD70
Watford WD18 23 BV42
Victoria Pl, SE22
off Underhill Rd 122 DU85
SW1 199 J8
Epsom KT17 156 CS112
Richmond TW9 117 CK85
Victoria Pt, E13
off Victoria Rd 86 EG68
Victoria Retail Pk, Ruis. HA4 60 BY64
Victoria Ri, SW4 101 DH83
Victoria Rd, E4 48 EE46
E11 68 EE63
E13 86 EG68
E17 47 EC54
E18 48 EH54
N4 65 DM59
N9 46 DT49
N15 66 DU56
N18 46 DT49
N22 45 DJ53
NW4 63 CW56
NW6 81 CZ67
NW7 43 CT50
NW10 80 CR71
SW14 98 CR83
W3 80 CR71
W5 79 CH71
W8 100 DC76
Addlestone KT15 152 BK105
Barking IG11 87 EP65
Barnet EN4 28 DD42
Bexleyheath DA6 106 FA84
Brentwood (Warley) CM14 54 FW49
Bromley BR2 144 EK99
Buckhurst Hill IG9 48 EK47
Bushey WD23 40 CB46
Chislehurst BR7 125 EN92
Coulsdon CR5 175 DK115
Dagenham RM10 71 FB64
Dartford DA1 128 FK85
Erith DA8 107 FE79
Feltham TW13 115 BV88
Gravesend (Nthflt) DA11 131 GF88
Kingston upon Thames KT1 138 CM96
Mitcham CR4 120 DE94
Romford RM1 71 FE58
Ruislip HA4 60 BW64
Sevenoaks TN13 191 FH125
Sidcup DA15 125 ET90
Slough SL2 74 AV74
Southall UB2 96 BZ76
Staines TW18 113 BE90
Surbiton KT6 137 CK100
Sutton SM1 158 DD106
Teddington TW11 117 CG93
Twickenham TW1 117 CG87
Uxbridge UB8
off New Windsor St 76 BJ66
Waltham Abbey EN9 15 EC34
Watford WD24 23 BV38
Weybridge KT13 135 BR104
Woking GU22 166 AY117
Victoria Scott Ct, Dart. DA1 107 FE83
Victoria Sq, SW1 199 J6
Victoria Steps, Brent. TW8
off Kew Br Rd 98 CM79
Victoria St, E15 86 EE66
SW1 199 K7
Belvedere DA17 106 EZ78
Egham (Eng.Grn) TW20 112 AW93
Slough SL1 92 AT75
Victoria Ter, N4 65 DN60
NW10
off Old Oak La 80 CS69
Harrow HA1 61 CE60
★ Victoria Twr, SW1 199 P6
Victoria Vil, Rich. TW9 98 CM83
Victoria Way, SE7 205 P10
Weybridge KT13 135 BR104
Woking GU21 166 AY117
Victoria Wf, E14 203 L1
Victoria Yd, E1
off Fairclough St 84 DU72
Victor Rd, NW10 81 CV69
SE20 123 DX94
Harrow HA2 60 CC55
Teddington TW11 117 CE91
Victors Cres, Brwd.
(Hutt.) CM13 55 GB47
Victors Dr, Hmptn. TW12 116 BY93
Victor Smith Ct, St.Alb.
(Brick.Wd) AL2 8 CA31
Victors Way, Barn. EN5 27 CZ41
Victor Vil, N9 46 DR48
Victor Wk, NW9 42 CS53
Hornchurch RM12
off Abbs Cross Gdns 72 FK60
Victory Av, Mord. SM4 140 DC99
Victory Business Cen, Islw.
TW7 97 CF83
Victory Cl, Grays
(Chaff.Hun.) RM16 109 FW77
Staines TW19
off Long La 114 BL88
Victory Pk Rd, Add. KT15 152 BJ105
Victory Pl, E14
off Northey St 85 DY73
SE17 201 J8
SE19
off Westow St 122 DS93
Victory Rd, E11 68 EH56
SW19 120 DC94
Chertsey KT16 134 BG102
Rainham RM13 89 FG68
Victory Rd Ms, SW19
off Victory Rd 120 DC94
Victory Wk, SE8
off Ship St 103 EA81
Victory Way, SE16 203 L5
Dartford DA2 108 FQ84
Hounslow TW5 96 BW78
Romford RM7 51 FB54
Vidler Cl, Chess. KT9
off Merritt Gdns 155 CJ107
Vienna Cl, Ilf. IG5 68 EK55
View, The, SE2 106 EY78
View Cl, N6 64 DF59
Chigwell IG7 49 ER50
Harrow HA1 61 CD56
Westerham
(Bigg.H.) TN16 178 EJ116
Viewfield Cl, Har. HA3 62 CL59
Viewfield Rd, SW18 119 CZ86
Bexley DA5 126 EW88
Viewland Rd, SE18 105 ET78
Viewlands Av, West. TN16 179 ES120
View Rd, N6 64 DF59
Potters Bar EN6 12 DC32
Viga Rd, N21 29 DN44
Vigerons Way, Grays RM16 111 GH77
Viggory La, Wok. GU21 166 AW115
Vigilant Cl, SE26 122 DU91
Vigilant Way, Grav. DA12 131 GL92
Vignoles Rd, Rom. RM7 70 FA59
Vigo St, W1 199 K1
Viking Cl, E3
off Selwyn Rd 85 DY68
Viking Ct, SW6 100 DA79
Viking Gdns, E6
off Jack Dash Way 86 EL70
Viking Pl, E10 67 DZ60
Viking Rd, Grav.
(Nthflt) DA11 130 GC90
Southall UB1 78 BY73
Viking Way, Brwd.
(Pilg.Hat.) CM15 54 FV45
Erith DA8 107 FC76
Rainham RM13 89 FG70
Villa Ct, Dart. DA1
off Greenbanks 128 FL89
Villacourt Rd, SE18 106 EU80
Village, The, SE7 104 EJ79
Greenhithe
(Bluewater) DA9 129 FT87
Village Arc, E4
off Station Rd 47 ED46
Village Cl, E4 47 EC50
NW3
off Belsize La 64 DD64
Weybridge KT13
off Oatlands Dr 135 BR104
Village Ct, E17
off Eden Rd 67 EB57
Village Gdns, Epsom KT17 157 CT110
Village Grn Av, West.
(Bigg.H.) TN16 178 EL117
Village Grn Rd, Dart. DA1 107 FG84
Village Grn Way, West.
(Bigg.H.) TN16
off Main Rd 178 EL117
Village Hts, Wdf.Grn. IG8 48 EF50
Village Ms, NW9 62 CR61
Village Pk Cl, Enf. EN1 30 DS44
Village Rd, N3 43 CY53
Egham TW20 133 BC97
Enfield EN1 30 DS44
Uxbridge (Denh.) UB9 57 BF61
Village Row, Sutt. SM2 158 DA108
Village Sq, The, Couls. CR5
off Netherne Dr 175 DK122
Village Way, NW10 62 CR63
SE21 122 DR86
Amersham HP7 20 AX40
Ashford TW15 114 BM91
Beckenham BR3 143 EA96
Pinner HA5 60 BY59
South Croydon CR2 160 DU113
Village Way E, Har. HA2 60 BZ59
Villa Rd, SW9 101 DN83
Villas Rd, SE18 105 EQ77
Villa St, SE17 102 DR78
Villier Ct, Uxb. UB8
off Villier St 76 BK68
Villiers, The, Wey. KT13 153 BR107
Villiers Av, Surb. KT5 138 CM99
Twickenham TW2 116 BZ88
Villiers Cl, E10 67 EA61
Surbiton KT5 138 CM98

★ Place of interest ⇌ Railway station ⊖ London Underground station DLR Docklands Light Railway station Tra Tramlink station H Hospital Riv Pedestrian ferry landing stage

Villiers Ct, N20
off Buckingham Av 44 DC45
Villiers Gro, Sutt. SM2 ....157 CX109
Villiers Path, Surb. KT5....138 CL99
Villiers Rd, NW2.........81 CU65
Beckenham BR3.......143 DX96
Isleworth TW7.........97 CE82
Kingston upon Thames KT1.138 CM97
Southall UB1.........78 BZ74
Watford WD19........24 BY44
Villiers St, WC2.........199 P1
Villier St, E10..........76 BK68
Vincam Cl, Twick. TW2....116 CA87
Vincent Av, Cars. SM5....158 DD111
Croydon CR0.........161 DY111
Surbiton KT5.........138 CP102
Vincent Cl, SE16.........203 K5
Barnet EN5..........28 DA41
Bromley BR2.........144 EH98
Chertsey KT16........133 BE101
Esher KT10..........136 CB104
Ilford IG6...........49 EQ51
Leatherhead (Fetch.) KT22 CB123
Sidcup DA15.........125 ES88
Waltham Cross
(Chsht) EN8.........15 DY28
West Drayton UB7.....94 BN79
Vincent Dr, Shep. TW17...135 BS97
Uxbridge UB10
off Birch Cres 76 BM67
Vincent Gdns, NW2.......63 CT62
Vincent Grn, Couls. CR5...174 DF120
off High Rd........174 DF120
Vincent Ms, E3.........85 EA68
Vincent Rd, E4.........47 ED51
N15.............66 DQ56
N22.............45 DN54
SE18............105 EP77
W3.............98 CQ76
Chertsey KT16.......133 BE101
Cobham
(Stoke D'Ab.) KT11...170 BY116
Coulsdon CR5........175 DJ116
Croydon CR0........142 DS101
Dagenham RM9.......88 EY66
Hounslow TW4........96 BX82
Isleworth TW7.......97 CD81
Kingston upon Thames KT1.138 CN97
Rainham RM13........90 FJ70
Wembley HA0........80 CM66
Vincent Row,
(Hmptn H.) TW12......116 CC93
Vincent's Cl, Couls. CR5...174 DF120
Vincents La, NW7.......43 CW49
Vincents Path, Nthlt. UB5
off Arnold Rd........78 BY65
Vincent Sq, SW1........199 L8
Westerham
(Bigg.H.) TN16......162 EJ113
Vincent St, E16.........86 EF71
SW1.............199 M8
Vincent Ter, N1........83 DP68
Vince St, EC1.........197 L3
Vine, The, Sev. TN13.....191 FH124
Vine Av, Sev. TN13......191 FH124
Vine Cl, Stai. TW19......114 BG85
Surbiton KT5.........138 CM100
Sutton SM1..........140 DC104
West Drayton UB7......94 BN77
Vine Ct, E1
off Whitechapel Rd.....84 DU71
Harrow HA3.........62 CL58
Vine Ct Rd, Sev. TN13....191 FJ124
Vinegar All, E17.........67 EB56
Vine Gdns, Ilf. IG1......69 EQ64
Vinegar St, E1.........202 D2
Vinegar Yd, SE1........201 M4
Vine Gro, Uxb. UB10.....76 BN66
Vine Hill, EC1.........196 D5
Vine La, SE1..........201 N3
Uxbridge UB10.......76 BM67
Vine Pl, W5
off The Common.......80 CL74
Hounslow TW3........96 CB84
Viner Cl, Walt. KT12.....136 BW100
Vineries, The, N14......29 DJ44
Enfield EN1.........30 DS41
Vineries Bk, NW7.......43 CV50
Vineries Cl, Dag. RM9
off Heathway........88 FA65
West Drayton UB7.....94 BN79
Vine Rd, E15.........86 EF66
SW13............99 CT83
East Molesey KT8.....136 CC98
Orpington BR6.......163 ET107
Slough (Stoke P.) SL2...74 AT65
Vines Av, N3..........44 DB53
Vine Sq, W14..........99 CZ78
Vine St, EC3.........197 P10
W1.............199 L1
Romford RM7........71 FC57
Uxbridge UB8.......76 BK67
Vine St Br, EC1.......196 E5
Vine Way, Brwd. CM14....54 FW46
Vine Yd, SE1.........201 J4
Vineyard Av, NW7.......43 CY52
Vineyard Cl, SE6.......123 EA88
Kingston upon Thames KT1.138 CM97
Vineyard Gro, N3.......44 DB53
Vineyard Hill, Pot.B.
(Northaw) EN6........12 DG29
Vineyard Hill Rd, SW19...120 DA91
Vineyard Pas, Rich. TW9
off Paradise Rd......118 CL85
Vineyard Path, SW14.....98 CR83
Vineyard Rd, Felt. TW13...115 BU90
Vineyard Row, Kings.T.
(Hmptn W.) KT1.......137 CJ95
Vineyards Rd, Pot.B. EN6..12 DF30
Vineyard Wk, EC1......196 D4
Viney Bk, Croy. CR0.....161 DZ109
Viney Rd, SE13........103 EB83
Vining St, SW9.........101 DN84
Vinlake Av, Uxb. UB10....58 BM62

★ Vinopolis, SE1.........201 J2
Vinson Cl, Orp. BR6......146 EU102
Vintners Ct, EC4........197 J10
Vintry Ms, E17
off Cleveland Pk Cres...67 EA56
Viola Av, SE2.........106 EV77
Feltham TW14........116 BW86
Staines TW19........114 BK88
Viola Cl, S.Ock. RM15....91 FW69
Viola Sq, W12.........81 CT73
Violet Av, Enf. EN2......30 DR38
Uxbridge UB8.......76 BM71
Violet Cl, E16.........86 EE70
SE8 off Dorking Cl....103 DZ79
Sutton SM3.........139 CY102
Wallington SM6......141 DH102
Violet Gdns, Croy. CR0...159 DN106
Violet Hill, NW8.......82 DC68
Violet La, Croy. CR0.....159 DN106
Violet Rd, E3.........85 EB70
E17.............67 EA58
E18.............48 EH54
Violet St, E2
off Three Colts La.....84 DV70
Violet Way, Rick.
(Loud.) WD3.........22 BJ42
Virgil Pl, W1.........194 D7
Virgil St, SE1.........200 C6
Virginia Av, Vir.W. GU25..132 AW99
Virginia Beeches, Vir.W.
GU25............132 AW97
Virginia Cl, Ashtd. KT21
off Skinners La......171 CK118
New Malden KT3
off Willow Rd.......138 CQ98
Romford RM5........51 FC52
Staines TW18
off Blacksmiths La....134 BJ97
Weybridge KT13......153 BQ107
Virginia Dr, Vir.W. GU25..132 AW99
Virginia Gdns, Ilf. IG6....49 EQ54
Virginia Pl, Cob. KT11....153 BU114
Virginia Rd, E2.........197 P3
Thornton Heath CR7....141 DP95
Virginia St, E1........202 C1
Virginia Wk, SW2.......121 DM86
Gravesend DA12......131 GK93
VIRGINIA WATER......132 AX99
⇌ Virginia Water........132 AY99
Viscount Cl, N11.......45 DH50
Viscount Dr, E6........87 EM71
Viscount Gdns, W.Byf. KT14.152 BL112
Viscount Gro, Nthlt. UB5
off Wayfarer Rd......78 BX69
Viscount Rd, Stai.
(Stanw.) TW19.......114 BK88
Viscount St, EC1.......197 H5
Viscount Way, Houns.
(Hthrw Air.) TW6......95 BS84
Vista, The, SE9........124 EK86
Sidcup DA14
off Langdon Shaw.....125 ET92
Vista Av, Enf. EN3......31 DX40
Vista Dr, Ilf. IG4.......68 EK57
Vista Way, Har. HA3......62 CL58
Viveash Cl, Hayes UB3....95 BT76
Vivian Av, NW4........63 CV57
Wembley HA9........62 CN64
Vivian Cl, Wat. WD19....39 BU46
Vivian Comma Cl, N4
off Blackstock Rd.....65 DP62
Vivian Gdns, Wat. WD19...39 BU46
Wembley HA9........62 CN64
Vivian Rd, E3.........85 DY68
Vivian Sq, SE15
off Scylla Rd.........102 DV83
Vivian Way, N2........64 DD57
Vivien Cl, Chess. KT9....156 CL108
Vivienne Cl, Twick. TW1...97 CJ86
Voce Rd, SE18.........105 ER80
Voewood Cl, N.Mal. KT3...139 CT100
Volta Cl, N9
off Hudson Way......46 DW48
Voltaire Rd, SW4......101 DK83
Voltaire Way, Hayes UB3
off Judge Heath La....77 BS73
Volt Av, NW10........80 CR69
Volta Way, Croy. CR0....141 DM102
Voluntary Pl, E11......68 EG58
Vorley Rd, N19........65 DJ61
Voss Ct, SW16.........121 DL93
Voss St, E2..........84 DU69
Voyagers Cl, SE28......88 EW72
Voysey Cl, N3.........63 CY55
Vulcan Cl, E6.........87 EN72
SE28............103 DZ82
Vulcan Gate, Enf. EN2....29 DN40
Vulcan Rd, SE4........103 DZ82
Vulcan Ter, SE4........103 DZ82
Vulcan Way, N7........83 DM65
Croydon
(New Adgtn) CR0.....162 EE110
Vyne, The, Bexh. DA7....107 FB83
Vyner Rd, W3.........80 CR73
Vyner St, E2..........84 DV67
Vyners Way, Uxb. UB10...58 BN64
Vyse Cl, Barn. EN5......27 CW42

W

Wacketts, Wal.Cr. (Chsht) EN7
off Spicersfield......14 DU27
Wadbrook St, Kings.T. KT1..137 CK96
Wadding St, SE17.......201 K9
Waddington Av, Couls. CR5..175 DN120
Waddington Cl, Couls. CR5..175 DP119
Enfield EN1.........30 DS42
Waddington Rd, E15.....67 ED64
Waddington St, E15.....85 ED65
Waddington Way, SE19....121 DP94
WADDON, Croy. CR0......141 DN103
⇌ Waddon...........159 DN105
Waddon Cl, Croy. CR0....141 DN104
Waddon Ct Rd, Croy. CR0..159 DN105
Ⓣ Waddon Marsh.......141 DM102
Waddon Marsh Way, Croy.
CR0............141 DM102
Waddon New Rd, Croy. CR0.141 DP104

Waddon Pk Av, Croy. CR0..159 DN105
Waddon Rd, Croy. CR0....141 DN104
Waddon Way, Croy. CR0...159 DP107
Wade Av, Orp. BR5......146 EX101
Wades Gro, N21........45 DN45
Wades Hill, N21........29 DN44
Wades La, Tedd. TW11
off High St.........117 CG92
Wadeson St, E2........84 DV68
Wades Pl, E14........85 EB73
Wadeville Av, Rom. RM6...70 EZ59
Wadeville Cl, Belv. DA17..106 FA79
Wadham Av, E17.......47 EB52
Wadham Cl, Shep. TW17...135 BQ101
Wadham Gdns, NW3.....82 DE67
Greenford UB6.......79 CD65
Wadham Rd, E17.......47 EB53
SW15............99 CY84
Abbots Langley WD5....7 BT31
Wadhurst Cl, SE20......142 DV96
Wadhurst Rd, SW8......101 DJ81
W4.............98 CR76
Wadley Rd, E11........68 EE59
Wadsworth Business Cen, Grnf.
UB6............79 CJ68
Wadsworth Cl, Enf. EN3...31 DX43
Greenford UB6.......79 CJ68
Wadsworth Rd, Grnf. UB6..79 CH68
Wager St, E3.........85 DZ70
Waggon Ms, N14
off Chase Side......45 DJ46
Waggon Rd, Barn. EN4....28 DC37
Waghorn Rd, E13.......86 EJ67
Harrow HA3.........61 CK55
Waghorn St, SE15......102 DU83
Wagner St, SE15.......102 DW80
Wagon Rd, Barn. EN4....28 DB36
Wagon Way, Rick.
(Loud.) WD3.........22 BJ41
Wagstaff Gdns, Dag. RM9..88 EW66
Wagtail Cl, NW9
off Swan Dr.........42 CS54
Wagtail Gdns, S.Croy. CR2.161 DY110
Wagtail Wk, Beck. BR3....143 EC99
Wagtail Way, Orp. BR5....146 EX98
Waid Cl, Dart. DA1......128 FM86
Waights Ct, Kings.T. KT2..138 CL95
Wain Cl, Pot.B. EN6......12 DB29
Wainfleet Av, Rom. RM5...51 FC54
Wainford Cl, SW19
off Windlesham Gro....119 CX88
Wainwright Av, Brwd.
(Hutt.) CM13.........55 GD44
Wainwright Gro, Islw. TW7.97 CD84
Waite Davies Rd, SE12...124 EF87
Waite St, SE15........102 DT79
Waithman St, EC4......196 F9
Wakefield Av, W.Byf.
(Byfleet) KT14.......152 BL112
Wakefield Cres, Slou.
(Stoke P.) SL2.......74 AT66
Wakefield Gdns, SE19....122 DS94
Ilford IG1..........68 EL58
Wakefield Ms, WC1......196 A3
Wakefield Rd, N11......45 DK50
N15.............66 DT57
Greenhithe DA9......129 FW85
Richmond TW10......117 CK85
Wakefield St, E6.......86 EK67
N18.............46 DU50
WC1............196 A4
Wakefield Wk, Wal.Cr.
(Chsht) EN8.........15 DY31
Wakeford Cl, SW4
off Clapham Common
S Side...........121 DJ85
Wakehams Hill, Pnr. HA5..60 BZ55
Wakeham St, N1.......84 DR65
Wakehurst Path, Wok. GU21.151 BC114
Wakehurst Rd, SW11....120 DE85
Wakeling Rd, W7.......79 CF71
Wakeling St, E14.......85 DY72
Wakelin Rd, E15.......86 EE68
Wakely Cl, West.
(Bigg.H.) TN16......178 EJ118
Wakeman Rd, NW10.....81 CW69
Wakemans Hill Av, NW9...62 CR57
Wakerfield Cl, Horn. RM11..72 FM57
Wakering Rd, Bark. IG11...87 EQ65
Wakerley Cl, E6
off Truesdale Rd......87 EM72
Wake Rd, Loug.
(High Beach) IG10....32 EJ38
Wakley St, EC1........196 F2
Walberswick St, SW8....101 DL80
Walbrook, EC4........197 K10
Walbrook Ho, N9......46 DW46
Walbrook Wf, EC4
off Upper Thames St...84 DQ73
Walburgh St, E1
off Bigland St.......84 DV72
Walburton Rd, Pur. CR8...159 DJ113
Walcorde Av, SE17......201 J9
Walcot Rd, Enf. EN3.....31 DZ40
Walcot Sq, SE11.......200 E8
Walcott St, SW1.......199 L8
Waldair Ct, E16
off Barge Ho Rd......105 EP75
Waldair Wf, E16.......105 EP75
Waldeck Gro, SE27.....121 DP90
Waldeck Rd, N15.......65 DP56
SW14
off Lower Richmond Rd.98 CQ83
W4.............98 CN79
W13............79 CH72
Dartford DA1........128 FM86
Waldeck Ter, SW14
off Lower Richmond Rd.98 CQ83
Waldegrave Av, Tedd. TW11
off Waldegrave Rd.....117 CF92
Waldegrave Ct, Upmin.
RM14............72 FP60
Waldegrave Gdns, Twick. TW1.117 CF89
Upminster RM14......72 FP60
Waldegrave Pk, Twick. TW1.117 CF91
Waldegrave Rd, N8.....65 DN55
SE19............122 DT94
W5.............80 CM72

Waldegrave Rd,
Bromley BR1........144 EL98
Dagenham RM8.......70 EW61
Teddington TW11......117 CF91
Twickenham TW1......117 CF91
Waldegrove, Croy. CR0...142 DT104
Waldemar Av, SW6......99 CY81
W13............79 CJ74
Waldemar Rd, SW19....120 DA92
Walden Av, N13........46 DQ49
Chislehurst BR7......125 EM91
Rainham RM13.......89 FD68
Walden Cl, Belv. DA17....106 EZ78
Walden Gdns, Th.Hth. CR7..141 DM97
Waldenhurst Rd, Orp. BR5.146 EX101
Walden Par, Chis. BR7
off Walden Rd.......125 EM93
Walden Rd, N17.......46 DR53
Chislehurst BR7......125 EM93
Hornchurch RM11.....72 FK58
Waldens Cl, Orp. BR5....146 EX101
Waldenshaw Rd, SE23....122 DW88
Waldens Pk Rd, Wok. GU21.166 AW116
Waldens Rd, Orp. BR5....146 EY101
Woking GU21........166 AX117
Walden St, E1........84 DV72
Walden Way, NW7......43 CX51
Hornchurch RM11.....72 FK58
Ilford IG6..........49 ES52
Waldo Cl, SW4........121 DJ85
Waldo Pl, Mitch. CR4....120 DE94
Waldorf Cl, S.Croy. CR2...159 DP109
Waldo Rd, NW10.......81 CU69
Bromley BR1........144 EK97
Waldram Cres, SE23.....122 DW88
Waldram Pk Rd, SE23....123 DX88
Waldram Pl, SE23
off Waldram Cres.....122 DW88
Waldrist Way, Erith DA18..106 EZ75
Waldron Gdns, Brom. BR2.143 ED97
Waldronhyrst, S.Croy.
CR2............159 DP105
Waldron Ms, SW3
off Old Ch St........100 DD79
Waldron Rd, SW18......120 DC90
Harrow HA1, HA2.....61 CE60
Waldrons, The, Croy. CR0..159 DP105
Oxted RH8.........188 EF131
Waldrons Path, S.Croy. CR2.160 DQ105
Waldstock Rd, SE28.....88 EU73
Waleran Cl, Stan. HA7....41 CF51
Walerand Rd, SE13......103 EC82
Waleran Flats, SE1
off Old Kent Rd......102 DS77
Wales Av, Cars. SM5.....158 DF106
Wales Cl, SE15........102 DV80
Wales Fm Rd, W3.......80 CR71
Waleton Acres, Wall. SM6..159 DJ107
Waley St, E1.........85 DX71
Walfield Av, N20.......44 DB45
Walford Rd, N16.......66 DS63
Uxbridge UB8.......76 BJ68
Walfrey Gdns, Dag. RM9...88 EY66
WALHAM GREEN, SW6....100 DB80
Walham Grn Ct, SW6
off Waterford Rd......100 DB80
Walham Gro, SW6......100 DA80
Walham Ri, SW19......119 CY93
Walham Yd, SW6
off Walham Gro......100 DA80
Walk, The, Horn. RM11....72 FM61
Oxted (Tand.) RH8....187 EA133
Potters Bar EN6......12 DA32
Sunbury-on-Thames
TW16............115 BT94
Walkden Rd, Chis. BR7....125 EN92
Walker Cl, N11........45 DJ49
SE18............105 EQ77
W7.............79 CE74
Dartford DA1........107 FF83
Feltham TW14
off Westmacott Dr....115 BT87
Hampton TW12
off Fearnley Cres.....116 BZ93
Walker Cres, Slou. SL3
off Ditton Rd........93 AZ78
Walker Ms, SW2
off Effra Rd.........121 DN85
Walkers Ct, E8
off Wilton Way.......84 DU65
W1.............195 M10
Walkerscroft Mead, SE21..122 DQ88
Walkers Pl, SW15
off Felsham Rd......99 CY83
Walkfield Dr, Epsom KT18..173 CV117
Walkford Way, SE15
off Daniel Gdns......102 DT80
Walkley Rd, Dart. DA1....127 FH85
Walks, The, N2........64 DD55
Walkynscroft, SE15
off Firbank Rd......102 DV82
Wallace Cl, SE28
off Haldane Rd......88 EX73
Shepperton TW17.....135 BR98
Uxbridge UB10
off Grays Rd........76 BL68
Wallace Cres, Cars. SM5..158 DF106
Wallace Flds, Epsom KT17..157 CT112
Wallace Gdns, Swans. DA10
off Milton St.......130 FY86
Wallace Rd, N1........84 DQ65
Grays RM17.........110 GA76
Wallace Sq, Couls. CR5
off Cayton Rd.......175 DK122
Wallace Wk, Add. KT15...152 BJ105
Wallace Way, N19
off Giesbach Rd......65 DK61
Romford RM1
off Havering Rd......51 FD53
Wallasey Cres, Uxb. UB10..58 BN61
Wallbutton Rd, SE4......103 DY83
Wall End Rd, E6.......87 EM66
Wallenger Av, Rom. RM2...71 FH55
Waller Dr, Nthwd. HA6....39 BU54
Waller La, Cat. CR3.....176 DT123
Waller Rd, SE14.......103 DX81

Wallers Cl, Dag. RM9.....88 EY67
Woodford Green IG8....49 EM51
Wallers Hoppit, Loug. IG10..32 EL40
Waller Way, SE10
off Greenwich High Rd..103 EB80
Wallflower St, W12......81 CT73
Wallgrave Rd, SW5......100 DB77
Wallhouse Rd, Erith DA8...107 FH80
Wallingford Av, W10.....81 CX71
Wallingford Rd, Uxb. UB8..76 BH68
WALLINGTON........159 DJ106
⇌ Wallington........159 DH107
Wallington Cl, Ruis. HA4...59 BQ58
Wallington Cor, Wall. SM6
off Manor Rd N......159 DH105
Wallington Rd, Ilf. IG3....69 ET59
Wallington Sq, Wall. SM6
off Woodcote Rd.....159 DH107
Wallis All, SE1........201 J4
Wallis Cl, SW11.......100 DD83
Dartford DA2........127 FF90
Hornchurch RM11.....71 FH60
Wallis Ct, Slou. SL1
off Nixey Cl.........92 AU76
Wallis Ms, N22
off Brampton Pk Rd....65 DN55
Leatherhead
(Fetch.) KT22.......171 CG122
Wallis Pk, Grav.
(Nthflt) DA11........130 GB85
Wallis Rd, E9.........85 DZ65
Southall UB1........78 CB72
Wallis's Cotts, SW2......121 DL87
Wallman Pl, N22
off Bounds Grn Rd....45 DM53
Wallorton Gdns, SW14....98 CR84
Wallside, EC2.........197 J7
Wall St, N1..........84 DR65
Wallwood Rd, E11......67 ED60
Wallwood St, E14......85 DZ71
Walmar Cl, Barn. EN4....28 DD39
Walmer Cl, E4.........47 EB47
Orpington BR6
off Tubbenden La S....163 ER105
Romford RM7........51 FB54
Walmer Gdns, W13.....97 CG75
Walmer Ho, N9........46 DT45
Walmer Pl, W1........194 D6
Walmer Rd, W10
off Latimer Rd......81 CW72
W11............81 CY73
Walmer St, W1........194 D6
Walmer Ter, SE18......105 EQ77
Walmgate Rd, Grnf. UB6..79 CH67
Walmington Fold, N12....44 DA51
Walm La, NW2........63 CX64
Walmsley Ho, SW16
off Colson Way......121 DJ91
Walney Wk, N1
off St. Paul's Rd.....84 DQ65
Walnut Av, West Dr. UB7...94 BN76
Walnut Cl, SE8
off Clyde St.........103 DZ79
Carshalton SM5......158 DF106
Dartford (Eyns.) DA4...148 FK104
Epsom KT18........173 CT115
Hayes UB3.........77 BS73
Ilford IG6
off Civic Way.......69 EQ56
St. Albans (Park St) AL2..8 CB27
Walnut Ct, W5.........98 CL75
Walnut Dr, Tad. (Kgswd) KT20
off Warren Lo Dr.....173 CY124
Walnut Gdns, E15
off Burgess Rd......68 EE63
Walnut Grn, Bushey WD23..24 BZ40
Walnut Gro, Bans. SM7...157 CX114
Enfield EN1.........30 DR43
Hornchurch RM12
off High St.........72 FK60
Walnut Ms, Sutt. SM2....158 DC108
Walnut Rd, E10........67 EA61
Walnuts, The, Orp. BR6...146 EU102
Walnut Shop Cen, Orp. BR6.146 EU102
Walnuts Rd, Orp. BR6....146 EU102
Walnut Tree Av, Dart. DA1..128 FL89
Mitcham CR4
off De'Arn Gdns.....140 DE97
Walnut Tree Cl, SW13....99 CT81
Banstead SM7.......157 CY112
Chislehurst BR7......145 EQ95
Waltham Cross
(Chsht) EN8.........15 DX31
Walnut Tree Cotts, SW19
off Church Rd......119 CY91
Walnut Tree La, W.Byf.
(Byfleet) KT14.......152 BK112
Walnut Tree Rd, SE10....104 EE78
Brentford TW8.......98 CL79
Dagenham RM8.......70 EX61
Erith DA8.........107 FE78
Hounslow TW5.......96 BZ79
Shepperton TW17.....135 BQ96
Walnut Tree Wk, SE11....200 D8
Walnut Way, Buck.H. IG9..48 EK48
Ruislip HA4.........78 BW65
Swanley BR8.......147 FD96
Walpole Av, Couls. CR5...174 DF118
Richmond TW9.......98 CM82
Walpole Cl, W13.......97 CJ75
Grays RM17
off Palmers Dr......110 GC77
Pinner HA5.........40 CA51
Walpole Cres, Tedd. TW11..117 CF92
Walpole Gdns, W4......98 CQ78
Twickenham TW2.....117 CE89
Walpole Ms, NW8
off Queen's Gro.....82 DD67
SW19 off Walpole Rd...120 DD93
Walpole Pk, W5.......79 CJ74
Weybridge KT13......152 BN108
Walpole Pl, SE18
off Brookhill Rd......105 EP77
Teddington TW11......117 CF92
Walpole Rd, E6.........86 EJ66
E17.............67 DY56
E18.............48 EF53
N17 (Downhills Way)...66 DQ55
N17 (Lordship La)....46 DQ54

★ Place of interest ⇌ Railway station ⊖ London Underground station DLR Docklands Light Railway station Tra Tramlink station H Hospital Riv Pedestrian ferry landing stage

Walpole Rd, SW19 120 DD93
Bromley BR2 144 EK99
Croydon CR0 142 DR103
Surbiton KT6 138 CL100
Teddington TW11 117 CF92
Twickenham TW2 117 CE89
Windsor (Old Wind.) SL4 112 AV87
Walpole St, SW3 198 D10
Walrond Av, Wem. HA9 62 CL64
Walsham Cl, N16
off Braydon Rd 66 DU59
SE28 88 EX73
Walsham Rd, SE14 103 DX82
Feltham TW14 115 BV87
Walsh Cres, Croy.
(New Adgtn) CR0 162 EE112
Walshford Way, Borwd. WD6 26 CN38
Walsingham Gdns, Epsom
KT19 156 CS105
Walsingham Pk, Chis. BR7 145 ER96
Walsingham Pl, SW4
off Clapham Common
W Side 100 DF84
SW11 120 DG86
Walsingham Rd, E5 66 DU62
W13 79 CG74
Croydon
(New Adgtn) CR0 161 EC110
Enfield EN2 30 DR42
Mitcham CR4 140 DF99
Orpington BR5 146 EV95
Walsingham Wk, Belv. DA17 106 FA79
Walsingham Way, St.Alb.
(Lon.Col.) AL2 9 CJ27
Walter Hurford Par, E12
off Walton Rd 69 EN63
Walter Rodney Cl, E6
off Stevenage Rd 87 EM65
Walters Cl, SE17 201 J9
Hayes UB3
off St. Anselms Rd 95 BT75
Waltham Cross
(Chsht) EN7 13 DP25
Walters Ho, SE17
off Otto St 101 DP79
Walters Mead, Ashtd. KT21 172 CL117
Walters Rd, SE25 142 DS98
Enfield EN3 30 DW43
Walter St, E2 85 DX69
Kingston upon Thames KT2
off Sopwith Way 138 CL95
Walters Way, SE23 123 DX86
Walters Yd, Brom. BR1 144 EG96
Walter Ter, E1 85 DX72
Walterton Rd, W9 81 CZ70
Walter Wk, Edg. HA8 42 CQ51
WALTHAM ABBEY 32 EF35
★ Waltham Abbey (ruins),
Wal.Abb. EN9 15 EC33
Waltham Av, NW9 62 CN58
Hayes UB3 95 BQ76
Waltham Cl, Brwd. (Hutt.) CM13
off Bannister Dr 55 GC44
Dartford DA1 127 FG86
Orpington BR5 146 EX102
WALTHAM CROSS 15 DZ33
⇌ Waltham Cross 15 DY34
Waltham Dr, Edg. HA8 42 CN54
Waltham Gdns, Enf. EN3 30 DW36
Waltham Gate, Wal.Cr. EN8 15 DZ26
Waltham Pk Way, E17 47 EA53
Waltham Rd, Cars. SM5 140 DD101
Caterham CR3 176 DV122
Southall UB2 96 BY76
Waltham Abbey EN9 16 EF26
Woodford Green IG8 48 EL51
WALTHAMSTOW, E17 47 EB54
Walthamstow Av, E4 47 EA52
Walthamstow Business Cen,
E17 47 EC54
⇌ Walthamstow Central 67 EA56
⊖ Walthamstow Central 67 EA56
⇌ Walthamstow
Queens Road 67 DZ57
Waltham Way, E4 47 DZ49
Waltheof Av, N17 46 DR53
Waltheof Gdns, N17 46 DR53
Walton Av, Har. HA2 60 BZ64
New Malden KT3 139 CT98
Sutton SM3 139 CZ104
Wembley HA9 62 CP62
Walton Br, Shep. TW17 135 BS101
Walton-on-Thames KT12
off Bridge St 135 BS101
Walton Br Rd, Shep. TW17 135 BS101
Walton Cl, E5 off Orient Way 67 DX62
NW2 63 CV61
SW8 101 DL80
Harrow HA1 61 CD56
H Walton Comm Hosp, Walt.
KT12 135 BV103
Walton Ct, Wok. GU21 167 BA116
Walton Cres, Har. HA2 60 BZ63
Walton Dr, NW10
off Mitchellbrook Way 80 CR65
Harrow HA1 61 CD56
Walton Gdns, W3 80 CP71
Brentwood (Hutt.) CM13 55 GC43
Feltham TW13 115 BT91
Waltham Abbey EN9 15 EB33
Wembley HA9 62 CL61
Walton Grn, Croy.
(New Adgtn) CR0 161 EC108
Walton La, Shep. TW17 135 BR101
Walton-on-Thames KT12 135 BQ102
Weybridge KT13 135 BP103
WALTON-ON-THAMES 135 BT103
⇌ Walton-on-Thames 153 BU105
WALTON ON THE HILL,
Tad. KT20 183 CT125
Walton Pk, Walt. KT12 136 BX103
Walton Pk La, Walt. KT12 136 BX103
Walton Pl, SW3 198 D6
Walton Rd, E12 69 EN63
E13 86 EJ68
N15 66 DT57
Bushey WD23 24 BX42
East Molesey KT8 136 CA98
Epsom
(Epsom Downs) KT18 173 CT117
Walton Rd,
Epsom (Headley) KT18 172 CQ121
Harrow HA1 61 CD56
Romford RM5 50 EZ52
Sidcup DA14 126 EW89
Walton-on-Thames KT12 136 BW99
West Molesey KT8 136 BY99
Woking GU21 167 AZ116
Walton St, SW3 198 C8
Enfield EN2 30 DR39
Tadworth KT20 173 CU124
Walton Ter, Wok. GU21 167 BB115
Walton Way, W3 80 CP71
Mitcham CR4 141 DJ98
Walt Whitman Cl, SE24
off Shakespeare Rd 101 DP84
Walverns Cl, Wat. WD19 24 BW44
WALWORTH, SE17 201 H10
★ Walworth Garden Fm -
Horticultural Training Cen,
SE17 101 DP78
Walworth Pl, SE17 102 DQ78
Walworth Rd, SE1 201 H8
SE17 201 H8
Walwyn Av, Brom. BR1 144 EK97
Wambrook Cl, Brwd.
(Hutt.) CM13 55 GC46
Wanborough Dr, SW15 119 CV88
Wanderer Dr, Bark. IG11 88 EV69
Wandle Bk, SW19 120 DD93
Croydon CR0 141 DL104
Wandle Ct, Epsom KT19 156 CQ105
Wandle Ct Gdns, Croy.
CR0 159 DL105
Tra Wandle Park 141 DN103
Wandle Rd, SW17 120 DE89
Croydon CR0 142 DQ104
Croydon (Waddon) CR0 141 DL104
Morden SM4 140 DC98
Wallington SM6 141 DH103
Wandle Side, Croy. CR0 141 DM104
Wallington SM6 141 DH104
Wandle Tech Pk, Mitch. CR4
off Goat Rd 140 DF101
Wandle Trd Est, Mitch. CR4
off Budge La 140 DF101
Wandle Way, SW18 120 DB88
Mitcham CR4 140 DF99
Wandon Rd, SW6 100 DB80
WANDSWORTH, SW18 119 CZ85
Wandsworth Br, SW6 100 DB83
SW18 100 DB83
Wandsworth Br Rd, SW6 100 DB81
⇌ Wandsworth Common 120 DF88
Wandsworth Common,
SW12 120 DE86
Wandsworth Common W Side,
SW18 120 DC85
Wandsworth High St, SW18 120 DA85
★ Wandsworth Mus, SW18 120 DB85
Wandsworth Plain, SW18 120 DB85
⇌ Wandsworth Road 101 DJ82
Wandsworth Rd, SW8 101 DK80
Wandsworth Shop Cen,
SW18 120 DB86
⇌ Wandsworth Town 100 DB84
Wangey Rd, Rom. RM6 70 EX59
Wang Ho, Brent. TW8 97 CJ78
Wanless Rd, SE24 102 DQ83
Wanley Rd, SE5 102 DR84
Wanlip Rd, E13 86 EH70
Wanmer Ct, Reig. RH2
off Birkheads Rd 184 DA133
Wannions Cl, Chesh. HP5 4 AU30
Wannock Gdns, Ilf. IG6 49 EP52
Wansbeck Rd, E3 85 DZ66
E9 85 DZ66
Wansbury Way, Swan. BR8 147 FG99
Wansdown Pl, SW6
off Fulham Rd 100 DB80
Wansey St, SE17 201 H9
Wansford Cl, Brwd. CM14 54 FT48
Wansford Grn, Wok. GU21
off Kenton Way 166 AT117
Wansford Pk, Borwd. WD6 26 CS42
Wansford Rd, Wdf.Grn. IG8 48 EJ53
WANSTEAD, E11 68 EH59
⊖ Wanstead 68 EH58
Wanstead Cl, Brom. BR1 144 EJ96
Wanstead La, Ilf. IG1 68 EK58
⇌ Wanstead Park 68 EH63
Wanstead Pk, E11 68 EK59
Wanstead Pk Av, E12 68 EK61
Wanstead Pk Rd, Ilf. IG1 69 EM60
Wanstead Pl, E11 68 EG58
Wanstead Rd, Brom. BR1 144 EJ96
Wansunt Rd, Bex. DA5 127 FC88
Wantage Rd, SE12 124 EF85
Wantz La, Rain. RM13 89 FH70
Wantz Rd, Dag. RM10 71 FB63
Waplings, The, Tad. KT20 173 CV124
WAPPING, E1 202 C2
⊖ Wapping 202 F3
Wapping Dock St, E1 202 E3
Wapping High St, E1 202 B3
Wapping La, E1 202 E1
Wapping Wall, E1 202 F2
Wapseys La, Slou.
(Hedg.) SL2 56 AS58
Wapshott Rd, Stai. TW18 113 BE93
Warbank Cl, Croy.
(New Adgtn) CR0 162 EE111
Warbank Cres, Croy.
(New Adgtn) CR0 162 EE110
Warbank La, Kings.T. KT2 119 CT94
Warbeck Rd, W12 81 CV74
Warberry Rd, N22 45 DM54
Warblers Grn, Cob. KT11 154 BZ114
Warboys App, Kings.T. KT2 118 CP93
Warboys Cres, E4 47 EC50
Warboys Rd, Kings.T. KT2 118 CP93
Warburton Cl, N1
off Culford Rd 84 DS65
Harrow HA3 41 CD51
Warburton Rd, E8 84 DV66
Twickenham TW2 116 CB88
Warburton St, E8
off Warburton Rd 84 DV67
Warburton Ter, E17 47 EB54
War Coppice Rd, Cat. CR3 186 DR127
Wardalls Gro, SE14 102 DW80
Ward Av, Grays RM17 110 GA77
Ward Cl, Erith DA8 107 FD79
Iver SL0 75 BF72
South Croydon CR2 160 DS106
Waltham Cross (Chsht) EN7
off Spicersfield 14 DU27
Wardell Cl, NW7 42 CS52
Wardell Fld, NW9 42 CS53
Warden Av, Har. HA2 60 BZ60
Romford RM5 51 FC50
Warden Rd, NW5 82 DG65
Wardens Fld Cl, Orp. BR6 163 ES107
Wardens Gro, SE1 201 H3
Ward Gdns, Rom. (Harold Wd) RM3
off Whitmore Av 52 FK54
Ward La, Warl. CR6 176 DW116
Wardle St, E9 67 DX64
Wardley St, SW18
off Garratt La 120 DB87
Wardo Av, SW6 99 CY81
Wardour Ms, W1 195 L9
Wardour St, W1 195 M10
Ward Rd, E15 85 ED67
N19 65 DJ62
Wardrobe Pl, EC4
off Carter La 83 DP72
Wardrobe Ter, EC4 196 G9
Wards La, Borwd.
(Elstree) WD6 25 CG40
Ward's Pl, Egh. TW20 113 BC93
Wards Rd, Ilf. IG2 69 ER59
Wards Wf App, E16 104 EK75
Wareham Cl, Houns. TW3 96 CB84
Waremead Rd, Ilf. IG2 69 EP57
Warenford Way, Borwd. WD6 26 CN39
Warenne Rd, Lthd. (Fetch.)
KT22 170 CC122
Ware Pt Dr, SE28 105 ER75
Warescot Cl, Brwd. CM15 54 FV45
Warescot Rd, Brwd. CM15 54 FV45
Warfield Rd, NW10 81 CX69
Feltham TW14 115 BS87
Hampton TW12 136 CB95
Warfield Yd, NW10
off Warfield Rd 81 CX69
Wargrave Av, N15 66 DT58
Wargrave Rd, Har. HA2 60 CC62
Warham Rd, N4 65 DN57
Harrow HA3 41 CF54
Sevenoaks (Otford) TN14 181 FH116
South Croydon CR2 160 DQ106
Warham St, SE5 101 DP80
Waring Cl, Orp. BR6 163 ET107
Waring Dr, Orp. BR6 163 ET107
Waring Rd, Sid. DA14 126 EW93
Waring St, SE27 122 DQ91
Warkworth Gdns, Islw. TW7 97 CG80
Warkworth Rd, N17 46 DR52
Warland Rd, SE18 105 ER80
WARLEY, Brwd. CM14 54 FV50
Warley Av, Dag. RM8 70 EZ59
Hayes UB4 77 BU71
Warley Cl, E10
off Millicent Rd 67 DZ60
Warley Gap, Brwd.
(Lt.Warley) CM13 53 FV52
Warley Hill, Brwd.
CM13, CM14 53 FV51
Warley Mt, Brwd. CM14 54 FW49
Warley Rd, N9 46 DW47
Brentwood CM13 53 FT54
Hayes UB4 77 BU72
Ilford IG5 49 EN53
Upminster RM14 52 FQ54
Woodford Green IG8 48 EH52
Warley St, E2 85 DX69
Brentwood
(Gt Warley) CM13 73 FW58
Upminster RM14 73 FW58
Warley St Flyover, Brwd.
CM13 73 FX57
Warley Wds Cres, Brwd.
CM14 54 FV49
WARLINGHAM 177 DX118
Warlingham Rd, Th.Hth. CR7 141 DP98
Warlock Rd, W9 82 DA70
Warlow Cl, Enf. EN3 31 EA37
Warlters Cl, N7
off Warlters Rd 65 DL63
Warlters Rd, N7 65 DL63
Warltersville Rd, N19 65 DL59
Warmington Cl, E5
off Orient Way 67 DX62
Warmington Rd, SE24 122 DQ86
Warmington St, E13
off Barking Rd 86 EG70
Warminster Gdns, SE25 142 DU96
Warminster Rd, SE25 142 DT96
Warminster Sq, SE25 142 DU96
Warminster Way, Mitch. CR4 141 DH95
Warndon St, SE16 202 G9
Warneford Pl, Wat. WD19 24 BY44
Warneford Rd, Har. HA3 61 CK55
Warneford St, E9 84 DV67
Warne Pl, Sid. DA15
off Westerham Dr 126 EV86
Warner Av, Sutt. SM3 139 CY103
Warner Cl, E15 68 EE64
NW9 63 CT59
Hampton TW12
off Tangley Pk Rd 116 BZ92
Hayes UB3 95 BR80
Warner Ho, SE13
off Conington Rd 103 EB82
Warner Par, Hayes UB3 95 BR80
Warner Pl, E2 84 DU68
Warner Rd, E17 67 DY56
N8 65 DK56
SE5 102 DQ81
Bromley BR1 124 EF94
Warners Cl, Wdf.Grn. IG8 48 EG50
Warners La, Kings.T. KT2 117 CK91
Warners Path, Wdf.Grn. IG8 48 EG50
Warner St, EC1 196 D5
Warner Ter, E14
off Broomfield St 85 EA71
Warner Yd, EC1 196 D5
Warnford Ho, SW15
off Tunworth Cres 119 CT86
Warnford Ind Est, Hayes
UB3 95 BS75
Warnford Rd, Orp. BR6 163 ET106
Warnham Ct Rd, Cars. SM5 158 DF108
Warnham Rd, N12 44 DE50
Warple Ms, W3
off Warple Way 98 CS75
Warple Way, W3 80 CS74
Warren, The, E12 68 EL63
Ashtead KT21 172 CL119
Carshalton SM5 158 DD109
Gerrards Cross
(Chal.St.P.) SL9 37 AZ52
Gravesend DA12 131 GK91
Hayes UB4 77 BU72
Hounslow TW5 96 BZ80
Leatherhead
(Oxshott) KT22 154 CC112
Radlett WD7 9 CG33
Tadworth (Kgswd) KT20 173 CY123
Worcester Park KT4 156 CR105
Warren Av, E10 67 EC62
Bromley BR1 124 EE94
Orpington BR6 163 ET106
Richmond TW10 98 CP84
South Croydon CR2 161 DX108
Sutton SM2 157 CZ110
Warren Cl, N9 47 DX45
SE21 off Lairdale Cl 122 DQ87
Bexleyheath DA6 126 FA85
Esher KT10 154 CB105
Hayes UB4 78 BW71
Slough SL3 92 AY76
Wembley HA9 61 CK61
Warren Ct, Chig. IG7 49 ER49
Sevenoaks TN13 191 FJ125
Weybridge KT13 152 BN106
Warren Cres, N9 46 DT45
Warren Cutting, Kings.T.
KT2 118 CR94
Warrender Rd, N19 65 DJ62
Chesham HP5 4 AS29
Warrender Way, Ruis. HA4 59 BU59
Warren Dr, Grnf. UB6 78 CB70
Hornchurch RM12 71 FG62
Orpington BR6 164 EV106
Ruislip HA4 60 BX59
Tadworth (Kgswd) KT20 173 CZ122
Warren Dr, The, E11 68 EJ59
Warren Dr N, Surb. KT5 138 CP102
Warren Dr S, Surb. KT5 138 CQ102
Warreners La, Wey. KT13 153 BR109
Warren Fld, Epp. CM16 18 EU32
Iver SL0 75 BC68
Warrenfield Cl, Wal.Cr. (Chsht) EN7
off Portland Dr 14 DU31
Warren Flds, Stan. HA7
off Valencia Rd 41 CJ49
Warren Footpath, Twick. TW1 117 CJ88
Warren Gdns, E15
off Ashton Rd 67 ED64
Orpington BR6 164 EU106
Warrengate La, Pot.B. EN6 11 CW31
Warrengate Rd, Hat.
(N.Mymms) AL9 11 CW28
Warren Gro, Borwd. WD6 26 CR42
Warren Hastings Ct, Grav. DA11
off Pier Rd 131 GF86
Warren Hts, Grays
(Chaff.Hun.) RM16 110 FY77
Loughton IG10 32 EJ43
Warren Hill, Epsom KT18 172 CR116
Loughton IG10 32 EJ44
Warren Ho, E3
off Bromley High St 85 EB69
Warren La, SE18 105 EP76
Grays RM16 109 FW77
Leatherhead
(Oxshott) KT22 154 CC111
Oxted RH8 188 EF134
Stanmore HA7 41 CF48
Woking GU22 168 BH118
Warren La Gate, SE18 105 EP76
Warren Lo Dr, Tad.
(Kgswd) KT20 173 CY124
Warren Mead, Bans. SM7 173 CW115
Warren Ms, W1 195 K5
Warrenne Way, Reig. RH2 184 DA134
Warren Pk, Kings.T. KT2 118 CQ93
Tadworth (Box H.) KT20 182 CQ131
Warlingham CR6 177 DX118
Warren Pk Rd, Sutt. SM1 158 DD107
Warren Pond Rd, E4 48 EF46
Warren Ri, N.Mal. KT3 138 CR95
Warren Rd, E4 47 EC47
E10 67 EC62
E11 68 EJ60
NW2 63 CT61
SW19 120 DE93
Addlestone
(New Haw) KT15 152 BG110
Ashford TW15 115 BS94
Banstead SM7 157 CW114
Bexleyheath DA6 126 FA85
Bromley BR2 144 EG103
Bushey
(Bushey Hth) WD23 40 CC46
Croydon CR0 142 DS102
Dartford DA1 128 FK90
Gravesend (Sthflt) DA13 130 GB92
Ilford IG6 69 ER57
Kingston upon Thames KT2 118 CQ93
Orpington BR6 163 ET106
Purley CR8 159 DP112
Reigate RH2 184 DB133
Sidcup DA14 126 EW90
Twickenham TW2 116 CC86
Uxbridge UB10 58 BL63
Warrens Shawe La, Edg.
HA8 42 CP46
⊖ Warren Street 195 L4
Warren St, W1 195 J5
Warren Ter, Grays RM16
off Arterial Rd W Thurrock 109 FX75
Romford RM6 70 EX56
Warren Wk, SE7 104 EJ79
Warren Way, NW7 43 CY51
Weybridge KT13 153 BQ106
Warren Wd Cl, Brom. BR2 144 EF103
Warriner Av, Horn. RM12 72 FK61
Warriner Dr, N9 46 DU48
Warriner Gdns, SW11 100 DF81
Warrington Cres, W9 82 DC70
Warrington Gdns, W9
off Warwick Av 82 DC70
Hornchurch RM11 72 FJ58
Warrington Pl, E14 204 E2
Warrington Rd, Croy. CR0 141 DP104
Dagenham RM8 70 EX61
Harrow HA1 61 CE57
Richmond TW10 117 CK85
Warrington Spur, Wind.
(Old Wind.) SL4 112 AV87
Warrington Sq, Dag. RM8 70 EX61
Warrior Av, Grav. DA12 131 GJ91
Warrior Sq, E12 69 EN63
Warsaw Cl, Ruis. HA4
off Glebe Av 77 BV65
Warsdale Dr, NW9
off Mardale Dr 62 CR57
Warspite Rd, SE18 104 EL76
Warton Rd, E15 85 EC66
Warwall, E6 87 EP72
⊖ Warwick Avenue 82 DC70
Warwick Av, W2 82 DC70
W9 82 DC70
Edgware HA8 42 CP48
Egham TW20 133 BC95
Harrow HA2 60 BZ63
Potters Bar (Cuffley) EN6 13 DK27
Staines TW18 114 BJ93
Warwick Cl, Barn. EN4 28 DD43
Bexley DA5 126 EZ87
Bushey (Bushey Hth) WD23
off Magnaville Rd 41 CE45
Hampton TW12 116 CC94
Hornchurch RM11
off Wiltshire Av 72 FM56
Orpington BR6 146 EU104
Potters Bar (Cuffley) EN6 13 DK27
Warwick Ct, SE15 102 DU82
WC1 196 C7
Rickmansworth
(Chorl.) WD3 21 BF41
Surbiton KT6 off Hook Rd 138 CL103
Warwick Cres, W2 82 DC71
Hayes UB4 77 BT70
Warwick Deeping, Cher.
(Ott.) KT16 151 BC106
Warwick Dene, W5 80 CL74
Warwick Dr, SW15 99 CV83
Waltham Cross
(Chsht) EN8 15 DX28
Warwick Est, W2 82 DB71
Warwick Gdns, N4 66 DQ57
W14 99 CZ76
Ashtead KT21 171 CJ117
Barnet EN5
off Great N Rd 27 CZ38
Ilford IG1 69 EP60
Romford RM2 72 FJ55
Thames Ditton KT7 137 CF99
Warwick Gro, E5 66 DV60
Surbiton KT5 138 CM101
Warwick Ho St, SW1 199 N2
Warwick La, EC4 196 G9
Rainham RM13 90 FM68
Upminster RM14 90 FP68
Woking GU21 166 AU119
Warwick Ms, Rick. WD3
off New Rd 22 BN43
Warwick Pas, EC4 196 G8
Warwick Pl, W5
off Warwick Rd 97 CK75
W9 82 DC71
Gravesend (Nthflt) DA11 130 GB85
Uxbridge UB8 76 BJ66
Warwick Pl N, SW1 199 K9
Warwick Quad Shop Mall, Red.
RH1 off London Rd 184 DG133
Warwick Rd, E4 47 EA50
E11 68 EH57
E12 68 EL64
E15 86 EF65
E17 47 DZ53
N11 45 DK51
N18 46 DS49
SE20 142 DV97
SW5 99 CZ77
W5 97 CK75
W14 99 CZ77
Ashford TW15 114 BL92
Barnet EN5 28 DB42
Borehamwood WD6 26 CR41
Coulsdon CR5 159 DJ114
Enfield EN3 31 DZ37
Hounslow TW4 95 BV83
Kingston upon Thames KT1 137 CJ95
New Malden KT3 138 CQ97
Rainham RM13 90 FJ70
Redhill RH1 184 DF133
Sidcup DA14 126 EV92
Southall UB2 96 BZ76
Sutton SM1 158 DC105
Thames Ditton KT7 137 CF99
Thornton Heath CR7 141 DN97
Twickenham TW2 117 CE88
Welling DA16 106 EW83
West Drayton UB7 94 BL75
Warwick Row, SW1 199 J6
Warwickshire Path, SE8 103 DZ80
Warwick Sq, EC4 196 G8
SW1 199 K10
Warwick Sq Ms, SW1 199 K9
Warwick St, W1 195 L10
Warwick Ter, SE18 105 ER79
Warwick Way, SW1 199 K9
Dartford DA1
off Hawley Rd 128 FL89
Rickmansworth
(Crox.Grn) WD3 23 BQ42
WARWICK WOLD, Red. RH1 185 DN129
Warwick Wold Rd, Red. RH1 185 DN128
Warwick Yd, EC1 197 J5
Washington Av, E12 68 EL63

★ Place of interest ⇌ Railway station ⊖ London Underground station DLR Docklands Light Railway station Tra Tramlink station H Hospital Riv Pedestrian ferry landing stage

Washington Cl, Reig. RH2 184 DA131
Washington Rd, E6
off St. Stephens Rd 86 EJ66
E18 48 EF54
SW13 99 CU80
Kingston upon Thames KT1 138 CN96
Worcester Park KT4 139 CV103
Wash La, Pot.B. EN6 11 CV33
Washneys Rd, Orp. BR6 164 EV113
Washpond La, Warl. CR6 177 EC118
Wash Rd, Brwd. (Hutt.) CM13 55 GD44
Wastdale Rd, SE23 123 DX88
Watchfield Ct, W4 98 CQ78
Watchgate, Dart.
(Lane End) DA2 129 FR91
Watcombe Cotts, Rich. TW9 98 CN79
Watcombe Pl, SE25
off Albert Rd 142 DV99
Watcombe Rd, SE25 142 DV99
Waterbank Rd, SE6 123 EB90
Waterbeach Rd, Dag. RM9 88 EW65
Waterbrook La, NW4 63 CW57
Water Circ, Green.
(Bluewater) DA9 129 FT88
Watercress Pl, N1
off Hertford Rd 84 DS66
Watercress Rd, Wal.Cr.
(Chsht) EN7 14 DR26
Watercress Way, Wok. GU21 166 AV117
Watercroft Rd, Sev.
(Halst.) TN14 164 EZ110
Waterdale Rd, SE2 106 EU79
Waterdales, Grav.
(Nthflt) DA11 130 GD88
Waterdell Pl, Rick. WD3
off Uxbridge Rd 38 BG47
Waterden Rd, E15 67 EA64
WATER END, Hat. AL9 11 CV26
Waterer Gdns, Tad. KT20 173 CX118
Waterer Ri, Wall. SM6 159 DK107
Waterfall Cl, N14 45 DJ48
Virginia Water GU25 132 AU97
Waterfall Cotts, SW19 120 DD93
Waterfall Rd, N11 45 DH49
N14 45 DJ48
SW19 120 DD93
Waterfall Ter, SW17 120 DE93
Waterfield, Rick.
(Herons.) WD3 37 BC45
Tadworth KT20 173 CV119
Waterfield Cl, SE28 88 EV74
Belvedere DA17 106 FA76
Waterfield Dr, Warl. CR6 176 DW119
Waterfield Gdns, SE25 142 DS99
Waterfield Grn, Tad. KT20 173 CW120
Waterfields, Lthd. KT22 171 CH119
Waterfields Shop Pk, Wat. WD17
off New Rd 24 BX42
Waterfields Way, Wat. WD17 24 BX42
Waterford Cl, Cob. KT11 154 BY111
Waterford Rd, SW6 100 DB81
Waterfront Studios Business Cen, E16
off Dock Rd 86 EF74
Water Gdns, Stan. HA7 41 CH51
Water Gdns, The, W2 194 C8
Watergardens, The, Kings.T.
KT2 118 CQ93
Watergate, EC4 196 F10
Watergate, The, Wat. WD19 40 BX47
Watergate St, SE8 103 EA79
Watergate Wk, WC2 200 A2
Waterglade Ind Pk, Grays
RM20 109 FT78
Waterhall Av, E4 48 EE49
Waterhall Cl, E17 47 DX53
Waterhead Cl, Erith DA8 107 FE80
Waterhouse Cl, E16 86 EK71
NW3
off Lyndhurst Rd 64 DD64
W6
off Great Ch La 99 CX77
Waterhouse La, Ken. CR8 176 DQ119
Redhill (Bletch.) RH1 186 DT132
Tadworth (Kgswd) KT20 173 CY121
Waterhouse Sq, EC1 196 D7
Wateridge Cl, E14 203 P7
Wateringbury Cl, Orp. BR5 146 EV97
Water La, E15 86 EE65
EC3 201 M1
N9 46 DV46
NW1
off Kentish Town Rd 83 DH66
SE14 102 DW80
Cobham KT11 170 BY115
Hemel Hempstead
(Bov.) HP3 5 BA29
Ilford IG3 69 ES62
Kings Langley WD4 7 BP29
Kingston upon Thames KT1 137 CK95
Oxted (Titsey) RH8 188 EG126
Purfleet RM19 108 FN77
Redhill RH1 185 DP130
Richmond TW9 117 CK85
Sevenoaks (Shore.) TN14 165 FF112
Sidcup DA14 126 EZ89
Twickenham TW1
off The Embankment 117 CG88
Watford WD17 24 BW42
Westerham TN16 189 ER127
Water Lily Cl, Sthl. UB2
off Navigator Dr 96 CC75
⇌ **Waterloo** 200 D4
⊖ **Waterloo** 200 D4
Waterloo Br, SE1 200 B1
WC2 200 B1
Waterloo Cl, E9
off Churchill Wk 66 DW64
Feltham TW14 115 BT88
⇌ **Waterloo East** 200 D3
Waterloo Est, E2 84 DW68
Waterloo Gdns, E2 84 DW68
N1 *off Barnsbury St* 83 DP66
Romford RM7 71 FD58
⇌ **Waterloo International** 200 C4
Riv **Waterloo Millennium Pier** 200 B4
Waterloo Pas, NW6 81 CZ66
Waterloo Pl, SW1 199 M2
Richmond TW9
off Sheen Rd 118 CL85
Richmond (Kew) TW9 98 CN79
Waterloo Rd, E6 86 EJ66
E7
off Wellington Rd 68 EF64
E10 67 EA59
NW2 63 CU60
SE1 200 D4
Brentwood CM14 54 FW46
Epsom KT19 156 CR112
Ilford IG6 49 EQ54
Romford RM7 71 FE57
Sutton SM1 158 DD106
Uxbridge UB8 76 BJ67
Waterloo St, Grav. DA12 131 GJ87
Waterloo Ter, N1 83 DP66
Waterlow Ct, NW11
off Heath Cl 64 DB59
Waterlow Rd, N19 65 DJ60
Waterman Cl, Wat. WD19 23 BV44
★ **Watermans Art Cen**,
Brent. TW8 98 CL79
Waterman's Cl, Kings.T. KT2
off Woodside Rd 118 CL94
Waterman St, SW15 99 CX83
Watermans Wk, SE16 203 K6
Watermans Way, Epp.
(N.Wld Bas.) CM16 18 FA27
Greenhithe DA9
off London Rd 129 FW85
Waterman Way, E1 202 D2
Watermead, Felt. TW14 115 BS88
Tadworth KT20 173 CV120
Woking GU21 166 AT116
Watermead Ho, E9
off Kingsmead Way 67 DY64
Watermead La, Cars. SM5
off Middleton Rd 140 DF101
Watermeadow Cl, Erith DA8 107 FH81
Watermeadow La, SW6 100 DC82
Watermead Rd, SE6 123 EC91
Watermead Way, N17 66 DV55
Watermen's Sq, SE20 122 DW94
Water Ms, SE15 102 DW84
Watermill Cl, Rich. TW10 117 CJ90
Watermill La, N18 46 DS50
Watermill Way, SW19 140 DC95
Water Mill Way, Dart.
(S.Darenth) DA4 148 FP96
Watermill Way, Felt. TW13 116 BZ89
Watermint Cl, Orp. BR5
off Wagtail Way 146 EX98
Watermint Quay, N16 66 DU59
Waterperry La, Wok.
(Chobham) GU24 150 AT110
Water Rd, Wem. HA0 80 CM67
Waters Dr, Rick. WD3 38 BL46
Staines TW18 113 BF90
Watersedge, Epsom KT19 156 CQ105
Waters Edge Ct, Erith DA8
off Erith High St 107 FF79
Watersfield Way, Edg. HA8 41 CK52
Waters Gdns, Dag. RM10 70 FA64
Waterside, Beck. BR3 143 EA95
Dartford DA1 127 FE85
Gravesend DA11
off Rosherville Way 130 GE87
Water Side, Kings L. WD4 6 BN29
Waterside, Rad. WD7 9 CH34
St. Albans (Lon.Col.) AL2 10 CL27
Uxbridge UB8 76 BJ71
Waterside Av, Beck. BR3
off Creswell Dr 143 EB99
Waterside Cl, E3 85 DZ67
SE16 202 C5
Barking IG11 70 EU63
Northolt UB5 78 BZ69
Romford
(Harold Wd) RM3 52 FN52
Surbiton KT6
off Culsac Rd 138 CL103
Waterside Ct, SE13
off Weardale Rd 103 ED84
Kings Langley WD4
off Water Side 7 BP29
Waterside Dr, Slou.
(Langley) SL3 93 AZ75
Walton-on-Thames KT12 135 BU99
Waterside Ms, Uxb. UB8
off Summerhouse La 38 BG51
Waterside Path, SW18
off Smugglers Way 100 DB84
Waterside Pl, NW1
off Princess Rd 82 DG67
Waterside Pt, SW11 100 DE80
Waterside Rd, Sthl. UB2 96 CA76
Waterside Twr, SW6 100 DC81
Waterside Trd Cen, W7 97 CE76
Waterside Way, SW17 120 DC91
Woking GU21
off Winnington Way 166 AV118
Watersmeet Way, SE28 88 EW72
Waterson Rd, Grays RM16 111 GH77
Waterson St, E2 197 N2
Waters Pl, SW15
off Danemere St 99 CW82
Watersplash Cl, Kings.T.
KT1 138 CL97
Watersplash La, Hayes UB3 95 BU77
Hounslow TW5 95 BV78
Watersplash Rd, Shep.
TW17 134 BN98
Waters Rd, SE6 124 EE90
Kingston upon Thames KT1 138 CP96
Waters Sq, Kings.T. KT1 138 CP97
Water St, WC2 196 C10
Waterton Av, Grav. DA12 131 GL87
Water Twr Cl, Uxb. UB8 58 BL64
Water Twr Hill, Croy. CR0 160 DR105
Water Twr Pl, N1
off Old Royal Free Sq 83 DN67
Water Twr Rd, Brwd. CM14
off Warley Hill 54 FV50
Waterview Ho, E14 85 DY71
Waterway Rd, Lthd. KT22 171 CG122
Waterworks Cor, E18 48 EE54
Waterworks La, E5 67 DX61
Waterworks Rd, SW2 121 DM86
Waterworks Yd, Croy. CR0
off Surrey St 142 DQ104
Watery La, SW20 139 CZ96
Chertsey (Lyne) KT16 133 BD101
Northolt UB5 78 BW68
St. Albans (Flam.) AL3 9 CK28
Sidcup DA14 126 EV93
Wates Way, Brwd. CM15 54 FX46
Mitcham CR4 140 DF100
Wates Way Ind Est, Mitch. CR4
off Wates Way 140 DF100
Wateville Rd, N17 46 DQ53
WATFORD 23 BT41
⊖ **Watford** 23 BT41
Watford Arches Retail Pk, Wat.
WD17
off Lower High St 24 BX43
Watford Business Pk, Wat. WD18 23 BS44
Watford Bypass, Borwd. WD6 41 CG45
Watford Cl, SW11
off Petworth St 100 DE81
Watford Fld Rd, Wat. WD18 24 BW43
★ **Watford FC**, Wat. WD18 23 BV43
H **Watford Gen Hosp**, Wat.
WD18 23 BV43
WATFORD HEATH, Wat.
WD19 40 BY46
Watford Heath, Wat. WD19 40 BX45
⇌ **Watford High Street** 24 BW42
⇌ **Watford Junction** 24 BW40
★ **Watford Mus**, Wat. WD17 24 BW43
⇌ **Watford North** 24 BW37
Watford Rd, E16 86 EG71
Borehamwood
(Elstree) WD6 25 CJ44
Harrow HA1 61 CG61
Kings Langley WD4 7 BP32
Northwood HA6 39 BT52
Radlett WD7 25 CE36
Rickmansworth
(Crox.Grn) WD3 23 BQ43
St. Albans AL2 8 CA27
Wembley HA0 61 CG61
⇌ **Watford Stadium Halt**
(closed) 23 BU44
Watford Way, NW4 63 CU56
NW7 63 CU56
⇌ **Watford West (closed)** 23 BT43
Watkin Rd, Wem. HA9 62 CP62
Watkins Cl, Nthwd. HA6
off Chestnut Av 39 BT53
Watkinson Rd, N7 83 DM65
Watkins Ri, Pot.B. EN6
off The Walk 12 DB32
Watling Av, Edg. HA8 42 CR52
Watling Ct, EC4 197 J9
Borehamwood WD6 25 CK44
Watling Fm Cl, Stan. HA7 41 CJ46
Watling Gdns, NW2 81 CY65
Watling Knoll, Rad. WD7 9 CF33
Watlings Cl, Croy. CR0 143 DY100
Watling St, EC4 197 H9
SE15 *off Dragon Rd* 102 DS79
Bexleyheath DA6 107 FB84
Borehamwood
(Elstree) WD6 25 CJ40
Dartford DA1, DA2 128 FP87
Gravesend DA11,
DA12, DA13 130 GC90
Radlett WD7 9 CF32
St. Albans AL2 8 CC25
Watling St Caravan Site
(Travellers), St.Alb.
(Park St) AL2 8 CC25
Watlington Gro, SE26 123 DY92
Watney Mkt, E1
off Commercial Rd 84 DV72
Watney Rd, SW14 98 CQ83
Watneys Rd, Mitch. CR4 141 DK99
Watney St, E1 84 DV72
Watson Av, E6 87 EN66
Sutton SM3 139 CY103
Watson Cl, N16
off Matthias Rd 66 DR64
SW19 120 DE93
Grays RM20 109 FU81
Watson Gdns, Rom.
(Harold Wd) RM3 52 FK54
Watson's Ms, W1 194 C7
Watsons Rd, N22 45 DM53
Watson's St, SE8 103 EA80
Watson St, E13 86 EH68
Watsons Yd, NW2
off North Circular Rd 63 CT61
Wattendon Rd, Ken. CR8 175 DP116
Wattisfield Rd, E5 66 DW62
Watts Cl, N15
off Seaford Rd 66 DS57
Tadworth KT20 173 CX122
Watts Cres, Purf. RM19 108 FQ77
Watts Fm Par, Wok.
(Chobham) GU24
off Barnmead 150 AT110
Watts Gro, E3 85 EB71
Watts La, Chis. BR7 145 EP95
Tadworth KT20 173 CX122
Teddington TW11 117 CG92
Watts Mead, Tad. KT20 173 CX122
Watts Rd, T.Ditt. KT7 137 CG101
Watts St, E1 202 E2
SE15 102 DT81
Watts Way, SW7 198 A6
Wat Tyler Rd, SE3 103 EC82
SE10 103 EC82
Wauthier Cl, N13 45 DP50
Wavell Cl, Wal.Cr.
(Chsht) EN8 15 DY27
Wavell Dr, Sid. DA15 125 ES86
Wavel Ms, N8 65 DK56
NW6 *off Acol Rd* 82 DB66
Wavel Pl, SE26
off Sydenham Hill 122 DT91
Wavendene Av, Egh. TW20 113 BB94
Wavendon Av, W4 98 CR78
Waveney Av, SE15 102 DV84
Waveney Cl, E1 202 C2
Waverley Av, E4 47 DZ49
E17 67 ED55
Waverley Av, Kenley CR8 176 DS116
Surbiton KT5 138 CP100
Sutton SM1 140 DB103
Twickenham TW2 116 BZ88
Wembley HA9 62 CM64
Waverley Cl, E18 48 EJ53
Bromley BR2 144 EK99
Hayes UB3 95 BR77
West Molesey KT8 136 CA99
Waverley Ct, Wok. GU22 166 AY118
Waverley Cres, SE18 105 ER78
Romford RM3 52 FJ52
Waverley Dr, Cher. KT16 133 BD104
Virginia Water GU25 132 AU97
Waverley Gdns, E6
off Oliver Gdns 86 EL71
NW10 80 CM69
Barking IG11 87 ES68
Grays RM16 110 GA75
Ilford IG6 49 EQ54
Northwood HA6 39 BU53
Waverley Gro, N3 63 CY55
Waverley Ind Est, Har. HA1 61 CD55
Waverley Pl, N4
off Adolphus Rd 65 DP61
NW8 82 DD68
Leatherhead KT22
off Church Rd 171 CH122
Waverley Rd, E17 67 EC55
E18 48 EJ53
N8 65 DK58
N17 46 DV52
SE18 105 EQ78
SE25 142 DV98
Cobham
(Stoke D'Ab.) KT11 154 CB114
Enfield EN2 29 DP42
Epsom KT17 157 CV106
Harrow HA2 60 BZ60
Leatherhead
(Oxshott) KT22 154 CB114
Rainham RM13 89 FH69
Southall UB1 78 CA73
Weybridge KT13 152 BN106
Waverley Vil, N17 46 DT54
Waverley Wk, W2 82 DA71
Waverley Way, Cars. SM5 158 DE107
Waverton Ho, E3 85 DZ67
Waverton Rd, SW18 120 DC87
Waverton St, W1 198 G2
Wavertree Ct, SW2
off Streatham Hill 121 DM88
Wavertree Rd, E18 48 EG54
SW2 121 DL88
Waxlow Cres, Sthl. UB1 78 CA72
Waxlow Rd, NW10 80 CQ68
Waxwell Cl, Pnr. HA5 40 BX54
Waxwell La, Pnr. HA5 40 BX54
Way, The, Reig. RH2 184 DD133
Waybourne Gro, Ruis. HA4 59 BQ58
Waycross Rd, Upmin.
RM14 73 FS58
Waye Av, Houns. TW5 95 BU81
Wayfarer Rd, Nthlt. UB5 78 BX70
Wayfaring Grn, Grays
(Bad.Dene) RM17
off Curling La 110 FZ78
Wayfield Link, SE9 125 ER86
Wayford St, SW11 100 DE82
Wayland Av, E8 66 DU64
Waylands, Hayes UB3 77 BR71
Staines (Wrays.) TW19 112 AY86
Swanley BR8 147 FF98
Waylands Cl, Sev.
(Knock.) TN14 180 EY115
Waylands Mead, Beck. BR3 143 EB95
Wayleave, The, SE28 88 EV73
Waylett Pl, SE27 121 DP90
Wembley HA0 61 CK63
Wayman Ct, E8 84 DV65
Wayne Cl, Orp. BR6 145 ET104
Wayneflete Twr Av, Esher
KT10 136 CA104
Waynflete Av, Croy. CR0 141 DP104
Waynflete Sq, W10 81 CX73
Waynflete St, SW18 120 DC89
Wayside, NW11 63 CY60
SW14 118 CQ85
Croydon CR0
off Field Way 161 EB107
Kings Langley
(Chipper.) WD4 6 BH30
Potters Bar EN6 12 DD33
Radlett (Shenley) WD7 9 CK33
Wayside Av, Bushey WD23 25 CD44
Hornchurch RM12 72 FK61
Wayside Cl, N14 29 DJ44
Romford RM1 71 FF55
Wayside Commercial Est, Bark.
IG11 88 EU67
Wayside Ct, Twick. TW1 117 CJ86
Wembley HA9
off Oakington Av 62 CN62
Woking GU21
off Langmans Way 166 AS116
Wayside Gdns, SE9
off Wayside Gro 125 EM91
Dagenham RM10 70 FA64
Gerrards Cross SL9 56 AX59
Wayside Gro, SE9 125 EM91
Wayside Ms, Ilf. IG2
off Gaysham Av 69 EN57
Wayville Rd, Dart. DA1 128 FP87
Way Volante, Grav. DA12 131 GL91
Weald, The, Chis. BR7 125 EM93
Weald Cl, SE16 202 D10
Brentwood CM14 54 FU48
Bromley BR2 144 EL103
Gravesend
(Istead Rise) DA13 130 GE94
★ **Weald Country Pk**, Brwd.
CM14 54 FS45
Weald Hall La, Epp.
(Thnwd) CM16 18 EW25
Weald La, Har. HA3 41 CD54
Weald Pk Way, Brwd.
(S.Wld) CM14 54 FS48
Weald Ri, Har. HA3 41 CF52
Weald Rd, Brwd. CM14 53 FR46
Sevenoaks TN13 191 FH129
Weald Rd, Uxbridge UB10 76 BN68
Weald Sq, E5
off Rossington St 66 DV61
WEALDSTONE, Har. HA3 61 CF55
Wealdstone Rd, Sutt. SM3 139 CZ103
Weald Way, Cat. CR3 186 DS128
Wealdway, Grav. DA13 131 GH93
Weald Way, Hayes UB4 77 BS69
Romford RM7 71 FB58
Wealdwood Gdns, Pnr. HA5
off Highbanks Rd 40 CB51
Weale Rd, E4 47 ED48
Weall Cl, Pur. CR8 159 DM112
Weall Grn, Wat. WD25 7 BV32
Weardale Av, Dart. DA2 128 FQ89
Weardale Gdns, Enf. EN2 30 DR39
Weardale Rd, SE13 103 ED84
Wear Pl, E2 84 DV69
Wearside Rd, SE13 103 EB84
Weasdale Ct, Wok. GU21
off Roundthorn Way 166 AT116
Weatherall Cl, Add. KT15 152 BH106
Weatherley Cl, E3 85 DZ71
Weaver Cl, E6
off Trader Rd 87 EP73
Croydon CR0 160 DT105
Weavers Cl, Grav. DA11 131 GG88
Isleworth TW7 97 CE84
Weavers La, Sev. TN14 191 FJ121
Weavers Orchard, Grav.
(Sthflt) DA13 130 GA93
Weavers Ter, SW6 100 DA79
Weaver St, E1 84 DU70
Weavers Way, NW1 83 DK67
Weaver Wk, SE27 121 DP91
Webb Cl, W10 81 CW70
Slough SL3 92 AX77
Webber Cl, Borwd. (Elstree) WD6
off Rodgers Cl 25 CK44
Erith DA8 107 FH80
Webber Row, SE1 200 E6
Webber St, SE1 200 E4
Webb Est, E5 66 DU59
Webb Gdns, E13
off Kelland Rd 86 EG70
Webb Pl, NW10
off Old Oak La 81 CT69
Webb Rd, SE3 104 EF79
Webb's All, Sev. TN13, TN15 191 FJ125
Webbscroft Rd, Dag. RM10 71 FB63
Webbs Rd, SW11 120 DF85
Hayes UB4 77 BV69
Webb St, SE1 201 M7
Webheath Est, NW6 81 CZ66
Webley Ct, Enf. EN3
off Sten Cl 31 EA37
Webster Cl, Horn. RM12 72 FK62
Leatherhead
(Oxshott) KT22 154 CB114
Waltham Abbey EN9 16 EG33
Webster Gdns, W5 79 CK74
Webster Rd, E11 67 EC62
SE16 202 C7
Websters Cl, Wok. GU22 166 AU120
Wedderburn Rd, NW3 64 DD64
Barking IG11 87 ER67
Wedgewood Cl, Epp. CM16
off Theydon Gro 18 EU30
Northwood HA6 39 BQ51
Wedgewoods, West. (Tats.) TN16
off Westmore Rd 178 EJ121
Wedgewood Wk, NW6
off Lymington Rd 64 DB64
Wedgwood Ms, W1 195 N9
Wedgwood Pl, Cob. KT11
off Portsmouth Rd 153 BU114
Wedgwood Way, SE19 122 DQ94
Wedlake Cl, Horn. RM11 72 FL60
Wedlake St, W10
off Kensal Rd 81 CY70
Wedmore Av, Ilf. IG5 49 EN53
Wedmore Gdns, N19 65 DK61
Wedmore Ms, N19
off Wedmore St 65 DK62
Wedmore Rd, Grnf. UB6 79 CD69
Wedmore St, N19 65 DK62
Wednesbury Gdns, Rom.
RM3 52 FM52
Wednesbury Grn, Rom. RM3
off Wednesbury Gdns 52 FM52
Wednesbury Rd, Rom. RM3 52 FM52
Weech Rd, NW6 64 DA63
Weedington Rd, NW5 64 DG64
Weedon Cl, Ger.Cr.
(Chal.St.P.) SL9 36 AV53
Weekley Sq, SW11
off Thomas Baines Rd 100 DD83
Weigall Rd, SE12 104 EG84
Weighhouse St, W1 194 G9
Weighton Rd, SE20 142 DV96
Harrow HA3 41 CD53
Weihurst Gdns, Sutt. SM1 158 DD106
Weimar St, SW15 99 CY83
Weind, The, Epp.
(They.B.) CM16 33 ES36
Weirdale Av, N20 44 DF47
Weir Est, SW12 121 DJ87
Weir Hall Av, N18 46 DR51
Weir Hall Gdns, N18 46 DR50
Weir Hall Rd, N17 46 DR50
N18 46 DR50
Weir Pl, Stai. TW18 133 BE95
Weir Rd, SW12 121 DJ87
SW19 120 DB90
Bexley DA5 127 FB87
Chertsey KT16 134 BH101
Walton-on-Thames KT12 135 BU100
Weirside Gdns, West Dr. UB7 76 BK74
Weir's Pas, NW1 195 N2
Weiss Rd, SW15 99 CX83
Welbeck Av, Brom. BR1 124 EG91
Hayes UB4 77 BV70
Sidcup DA15 126 EU88
Welbeck Cl, N12
off Torrington Pk 44 DD50
Borehamwood WD6 26 CN41
Epsom KT17 157 CU108
New Malden KT3 139 CT99
Welbeck Rd, E6 86 EK69
Barnet EN4 28 DD44

★ Place of interest ⇌ Railway station ⊖ London Underground station DLR Docklands Light Railway station Tra Tramlink station H Hospital Riv Pedestrian ferry landing stage

Welbeck Rd,
Carshalton SM5 ... 140 DE102
Harrow HA2 ... 60 CB60
Sutton SM1 ... 140 DD103
Welbeck St, W1 ... 195 H8
Welbeck Wk, Cars. SM5
off Welbeck Rd ... 140 DE102
Welbeck Way, W1 ... 195 H8
Welby St, SE5 ... 101 DP81
Welch Ho, Enf. EN3
off Beaconsfield Rd ... 31 DX37
Welch Pl, Pnr. HA5 ... 40 BW53
Welcomes Rd, Ken. CR8 ... 176 DQ116
Welcote Dr, Nthwd. HA6 ... 39 BR51
Welden, Slou. SL2 ... 74 AW72
Welders La, Beac.
(Jordans) HP9 ... 36 AT52
Gerrards Cross
(Chal.St.P.) SL9 ... 36 AT52
Weldon Cl, Ruis. HA4 ... 77 BV65
Weldon Dr, W.Mol. KT8 ... 136 BZ98
Weldon Way, Red. RH1 ... 185 DK129
Weld Pl, N11 ... 45 DH50
Welfare Rd, E15 ... 86 EE66
Welford Cl, E5
off Denton Way ... 67 DX62
Welford Pl, SW19 ... 119 CY91
Welham Rd, SW16 ... 120 DG92
SW17 ... 120 DG92
Welhouse Rd, Cars. SM5 ... 140 DE102
Wellacre Rd, Har. HA3 ... 61 CH58
Wellan Cl, Sid. DA15 ... 126 EV85
Welland Cl, Slou. SL3 ... 93 BA79
Welland Gdns, Grnf. UB6 ... 79 CF68
Welland Ms, E1 ... 202 C2
Wellands Cl, Brom. BR1 ... 145 EM96
Welland St, SE10 ... 103 EC79
Well App, Barn. EN5 ... 27 CW43
Wellbrook Rd, Orp. BR6 ... 163 EN105
Well Cl, SW16 ... 121 DM91
Ruislip HA4
off Parkfield Cres ... 60 BY62
Woking GU21 ... 166 AW117
Wellclose Sq, E1 ... 84 DU73
Wellclose St, E1 ... 202 C1
Wellcome Av, Dart. DA1 ... 108 FM84
★ **Wellcome Trust**, NW1 ... 195 L4
Well Cottage Cl, E11 ... 68 EJ59
Well Ct, EC4 ... 197 J9
SW16 ... 121 DM91
Welldon Cres, Har. HA1 ... 61 CE58
WELL END, Borwd. WD6 ... 26 CR38
Well End Rd, Borwd. WD6 ... 26 CQ37
Weller Cl, Amer. HP6 ... 20 AS37
Weller Rd, Amer. HP6 ... 20 AS37
Wellers Cl, West. TN16 ... 189 EQ127
Wellers Gro, Wal.Cr.
(Chsht) EN7 ... 14 DU28
Weller St, SE1 ... 201 H4
Wellesford Cl, Bans. SM7 ... 173 CZ117
Wellesley Av, W6 ... 99 CV76
Iver SL0 ... 93 BF76
Northwood HA6 ... 39 BT50
Wellesley Cl, SE7
off Wellington Gdns ... 104 EJ78
Wellesley Ct, W9
off Maida Vale ... 82 DC69
Wellesley Ct Rd, Croy. CR0 ... 142 DR103
Wellesley Cres, Pot.B. EN6 ... 11 CY33
Twickenham TW2 ... 117 CE89
Wellesley Gro, Croy. CR0 ... 142 DR103
Wellesley Pk Ms, Enf. EN2 ... 29 DP40
Wellesley Pas, Croy. CR0
off Wellesley Rd ... 142 DQ103
Wellesley Path, Slou. SL1
off Wellesley Rd ... 92 AU75
Wellesley Pl, NW1 ... 195 M3
Tra **Wellesley Road** ... 142 DQ103
Wellesley Rd, E11 ... 68 EG57
E17 ... 67 EA58
N22 ... 45 DN54
NW5 ... 64 DG64
W4 ... 98 CN78
Brentwood CM14 ... 54 FW46
Croydon CR0 ... 142 DQ102
Harrow HA1 ... 61 CE57
Ilford IG1 ... 69 EP61
Slough SL1 ... 92 AU75
Sutton SM2 ... 158 DC107
Twickenham TW2 ... 117 CD90
Wellesley St, E1 ... 85 DX71
Wellesley Ter, N1 ... 197 J2
Welley Av, Stai.
(Wrays.) TW19 ... 92 AY84
Welley Rd, Slou.
(Horton) SL3 ... 92 AY84
Staines (Wrays.) TW19 ... 112 AX85
Well Fm Rd, Warl. CR6 ... 176 DU119
Wellfield Av, N10 ... 65 DH55
Wellfield Gdns, Cars. SM5 ... 158 DE109
Wellfield Rd, SW16 ... 121 DL91
Wellfields, Loug. IG10 ... 33 EN41
Wellfield Wk, SW16 ... 121 DM92
Wellfit St, SE24
off Hinton Rd ... 101 DP83
Wellgarth, Grnf. UB6 ... 79 CH65
Wellgarth Rd, NW11 ... 64 DB60
Well Gro, N20 ... 44 DC45
Well Hall Par, SE9
off Well Hall Rd ... 105 EM84
Well Hall Rd, SE9 ... 105 EM83
WELL HILL, Orp. BR6 ... 165 FB107
Well Hill, Orp. BR6 ... 165 FB107
Well Hill La, Orp. BR6 ... 165 FB108
Well Hill Rd, Sev. TN14 ... 165 FC107
Wellhouse La, Barn. EN5 ... 27 CW42
Wellhouse Rd, Beck. BR3 ... 143 DZ98
WELLING ... 106 EU83
⇌ **Welling** ... 106 EU82
Welling High St, Well. DA16 ... 106 EV83
Wellings Ho, Hayes UB3 ... 77 BV74
★ **Wellington Arch**, W1 ... 198 G4
Wellington Av, E4 ... 47 EA47
N9 ... 46 DV48
N15 ... 66 DT58
Hounslow TW3 ... 116 CA85
Pinner HA5 ... 40 BZ53
Sidcup DA15 ... 126 EU86
Virginia Water GU25 ... 132 AV99
Worcester Park KT4 ... 157 CW105
Wellington Bldgs, SW1
off Ebury Br Rd ... 101 DH78
Wellington Cl, SE14
off Rutts Ter ... 103 DX81
W11 *off Ledbury Rd* ... 82 DA72
Dagenham RM10 ... 89 FC66
Walton-on-Thames KT12
off Hepworth Way ... 135 BT102
Watford WD19
off Highfield ... 40 BZ48
Wellington Ct, NW8
off Wellington Rd ... 82 DD68
Ashford TW15
off Wellington Rd ... 114 BL92
Staines TW19
off Clare Rd ... 114 BL87
Wellington Cres, N.Mal. KT3 ... 138 CQ97
Wellington Dr, Dag. RM10 ... 89 FC66
Purley CR8 ... 159 DM110
Wellington Gdns, SE7 ... 104 EJ79
Twickenham TW2 ... 117 CD91
Wellington Gro, SE10
off Crooms Hill ... 103 ED80
Wellington Hill, Loug.
(High Beach) IG10 ... 32 EG37
H **Wellington Hosp**, NW8 ... 194 A1
Wellington Ho, Rom. RM2
off Elvet Av ... 72 FJ55
Wellingtonia Av, Rom.
(Hav.at.Bow.) RM4 ... 51 FE48
Wellington Ms, SE7 ... 104 EJ79
SE22
off Peckham Rye ... 102 DU84
SW16
off Woodbourne Av ... 121 DK90
Wellington Pk Est, NW2 ... 63 CU61
Wellington Pas, E11
off Wellington Rd ... 68 EG57
Wellington Pl, N2
off Great N Rd ... 64 DE57
NW8 ... 194 A2
Brentwood CM14 ... 54 FW50
Cobham KT11 ... 154 BZ112
Wellington Rd, E6 ... 87 EM68
E7 ... 68 EF63
E10 ... 67 DY60
E11 ... 68 EG57
E17 ... 67 DY55
NW8 ... 82 DD68
NW10 ... 81 CX69
SW19 ... 120 DA89
W5 ... 97 CJ76
Ashford TW15 ... 114 BL92
Belvedere DA17 ... 106 EZ78
Bexley DA5 ... 126 EX85
Bromley BR2 ... 144 EJ98
Caterham CR3 ... 176 DQ122
Croydon CR0 ... 141 DP101
Dartford DA1 ... 128 FJ86
Enfield EN1 ... 30 DS42
Epping (N.Wld Bas.) CM16 ... 18 FA27
Feltham TW14 ... 115 BS85
Hampton TW12 ... 117 CD92
Harrow HA3 ... 61 CE55
Orpington BR5 ... 146 EV100
Pinner HA5 ... 40 BZ53
St. Albans (Lon.Col.) AL2 ... 9 CK26
Tilbury RM18 ... 111 GG83
Twickenham TW2 ... 117 CD92
Uxbridge UB8 ... 76 BJ67
Watford WD17 ... 23 BV40
Wellington Rd N, Houns. TW4 ... 96 BZ83
Wellington Rd S, Houns. TW4 ... 96 BZ84
Wellington Row, E2 ... 84 DT69
Wellington Sq, SW3 ... 198 D10
Wellington St, SE18 ... 105 EN77
WC2 ... 196 A10
Barking IG11
off Axe St ... 87 EQ67
Gravesend DA12 ... 131 GJ87
Slough SL1 ... 92 AT75
Wellington Ter, E1 ... 202 D2
W2
off Notting Hill Gate ... 82 DB73
Harrow HA1
off West St ... 61 CD60
Woking (Knap.) GU21
off Victoria Rd ... 166 AS118
Wellington Way, E3 ... 85 EA69
Weybridge KT13 ... 152 BN110
Welling Way, SE9 ... 105 ER83
Welling DA16 ... 105 ER83
Well La, SW14 ... 118 CQ85
Brentwood
(Pilg.Hat.) CM15 ... 54 FT41
Woking GU21 ... 166 AW117
Wellmeade Dr, Sev. TN13 ... 191 FH127
Wellmeadow Rd, SE6 ... 124 EE87
SE13 ... 124 EE86
W7 ... 97 CG77
Wellow Wk, Cars. SM5 ... 140 DD102
Well Pas, NW3 ... 64 DD62
Well Path, Wok. GU21
off Well La ... 166 AW117
Well Rd, NW3 ... 64 DD62
Barnet EN5 ... 27 CW43
Potters Bar (Northaw) EN6 ... 12 DE28
Wells, The, N14 ... 45 DK45
Wells Cl, Lthd. KT23 ... 170 CB124
Northolt UB5
off Yeading La ... 78 BW69
South Croydon CR2 ... 160 DS106
Waltham Cross (Chsht) EN7
off Bloomfield Rd ... 14 DQ25
Wells Ct, Rom. RM1
off Regarth Av ... 71 FE58
Wells Dr, NW9 ... 62 CR60
Wells Gdns, Dag. RM10 ... 71 FB64
Ilford IG1 ... 68 EL59
Rainham RM13 ... 89 FF65
Wells Ho Rd, NW10 ... 80 CS71
Wellside Cl, Barn. EN5 ... 27 CW42
Wellside Gdns, SW14
off Well La ... 118 CQ85
Wells Ms, W1 ... 195 L7
Wellsmoor Gdns, Brom. BR1 ... 145 EN97
Wells Pk Rd, SE26 ... 122 DU90
Wells Path, Hayes UB4 ... 77 BS69
Wells Pl, SW18 ... 120 DC87
Redhill RH1 ... 185 DH130
Wells Ri, NW8 ... 82 DF67
Wells Rd, W12 ... 99 CW75
Bromley BR1 ... 145 EM96
Epsom KT18 ... 156 CN114
Wells Sq, WC1 ... 196 B3
Wells St, W1 ... 195 K7
Wellstead Av, N9 ... 46 DW45
Wellstead Rd, E6 ... 87 EN68
Wells Ter, N4 ... 65 DN61
Wellstones, Wat. WD17 ... 23 BV41
Wellstones Yd, Wat. WD17
off Wellstones ... 23 BV41
Well St, E9 ... 84 DV66
E15 ... 86 EE65
Wells Way, SE5 ... 102 DR79
SW7 ... 100 DD76
Wells Yd S, N7
off George's Rd ... 65 DN64
Well Wk, NW3 ... 64 DD63
Well Way, Epsom KT18 ... 172 CN115
Wellwood Cl, Couls. CR5
off The Vale ... 159 DL114
Wellwood Rd, Ilf. IG3 ... 70 EU60
Welsford St, SE1 ... 202 B10
Welsh Cl, E13 ... 86 EG69
Welshpool Ho, E8
off Benjamin Cl ... 84 DU67
Welshpool St, E8
off Broadway Mkt ... 84 DV67
Welshside Wk, NW9
off Fryent Gro ... 62 CS58
Welstead Way, W4 ... 99 CT77
Welsummer Way, Wal.Cr. EN8 ... 15 DX27
Weltje Rd, W6 ... 99 CU78
Welton Rd, SE18 ... 105 ES80
Welwyn Av, Felt. TW14 ... 115 BT86
Welwyn St, E2
off Globe Rd ... 84 DW69
Welwyn Way, Hayes UB4 ... 77 BS70
WEMBLEY ... 62 CL64
⇌ **Wembley Central** ... 62 CL64
⊖ **Wembley Central** ... 62 CL64
Wembley Commercial Cen, Wem.
HA9 ... 61 CK61
★ **Wembley Conf Cen**, Wem.
HA9 ... 62 CM63
Wembley Hill Rd, Wem. HA9 ... 62 CM64
WEMBLEY PARK, Wem. HA9 ... 62 CM61
⊖ **Wembley Park** ... 62 CN62
Wembley Pk Business Cen, Wem.
HA9 ... 62 CP62
Wembley Pk Dr, Wem. HA9 ... 62 CM62
Wembley Pt, Wem. HA9 ... 80 CP66
Wembley Rd, Hmptn. TW12 ... 116 CA94
★ **Wembley Stadium**
(under redevelopment),
Wem. HA9 ... 62 CN63
⇌ **Wembley Stadium** ... 62 CM64
Wembley Way, Wem. HA9 ... 80 CP65
Wemborough Rd, Stan. HA7 ... 41 CJ52
Wembury Ms, N6
off Wembury Rd ... 65 DH59
Wembury Rd, N6 ... 65 DH59
Wemyss Rd, SE3 ... 104 EF82
Wend, The, Couls. CR5 ... 159 DK114
Croydon CR0 ... 161 DZ111
Wendela Cl, Wok. GU22 ... 167 AZ118
Wendela Ct, Har. HA1 ... 61 CE62
Wendell Rd, W12 ... 99 CT75
Wendle Ct, SW8 ... 101 DL79
Wendley Dr, Add.
(New Haw) KT15 ... 151 BF110
Wendling Rd, Sutt. SM1 ... 140 DD102
Wendon St, E3 ... 85 DZ67
Wendover, SE17 ... 102 DS78
Wendover Cl, Hayes UB4
off Kingsash Dr ... 78 BY70
Wendover Dr, N.Mal. KT3 ... 139 CT100
Wendover Gdns, Brwd. CM13 ... 55 GB47
Wendover Pl, Stai. TW18 ... 113 BD92
Wendover Rd, NW10 ... 81 CT68
SE9 ... 104 EK83
Bromley BR2 ... 144 EH97
Staines TW18 ... 113 BC92
Wendover Way, Bushey WD23 ... 24 CC44
Hornchurch RM12 ... 72 FJ64
Orpington BR6
off Glendower Cres ... 146 EU100
Welling DA16 ... 126 EU85
Wendron Cl, Wok. GU21
off Shilburn Way ... 166 AU118
Wendy Cl, Enf. EN1 ... 30 DT44
Wendy Way, Wem. HA0 ... 80 CL67
Wenham Gdns, Brwd. (Hutt.) CM13
off Bannister Dr ... 55 GC44
Wenlack Cl, Uxb. (Denh.) UB9
off Lindsey Rd ... 58 BG62
Wenlock Ct, N1 ... 197 L1
Wenlock Gdns, NW4
off Rickard Cl ... 63 CU56
Wenlock Rd, N1 ... 84 DQ68
Edgware HA8 ... 42 CP52
Wenlock St, N1 ... 197 J1
WENNINGTON, Rain. RM13 ... 90 FK73
Wennington Rd, E3 ... 85 DX68
Rainham RM13 ... 89 FG70
Wensley Av, Wdf.Grn. IG8 ... 48 EF52
Wensley Cl, N11
off Pickering Gdns ... 44 DG51
SE9 ... 125 EM86
Romford RM5 ... 50 FA50
Wensleydale Av, Ilf. IG5 ... 48 EL54
Wensleydale Gdns, Hmptn.
TW12 ... 116 CB94
Wensleydale Pas, Hmptn.
TW12 ... 136 CA95
Wensleydale Rd, Hmptn.
TW12 ... 116 CA93
Wensley Rd, N18 ... 46 DV51
Wensum Way, Rick. WD3 ... 38 BK46
Wentbridge Path, Borwd.
WD6 ... 26 CN38
Wentland Cl, SE6 ... 123 ED89
Wentland Rd, SE6 ... 123 ED89
WENTWORTH, Vir.W. GU25 ... 132 AS100
Wentworth Av, N3 ... 44 DA52
Borehamwood
(Elstree) WD6 ... 26 CM43
Wentworth Cl, N3 ... 44 DB52
SE28 ... 88 EX72
Wentworth Cl, Ashford TW15
off Reedsfield Rd ... 115 BP91
Bromley BR2
off Hillside La ... 144 EG103
Gravesend DA11 ... 131 GG92
Morden SM4 ... 140 DA101
Orpington BR6 ... 163 ES106
Potters Bar EN6
off Strafford Gate ... 12 DA31
Surbiton KT6 ... 137 CK103
Watford WD17 ... 23 BT38
Woking (Ripley) GU23 ... 168 BH121
Wentworth Ct, Surb. KT6
off Culsac Rd ... 138 CL103
Wentworth Cres, SE15 ... 102 DU80
Hayes UB3 ... 95 BR76
Wentworth Dene, Wey. KT13
off Pine Gro ... 153 BP106
Wentworth Dr, Dart. DA1 ... 127 FG86
Pinner HA5 ... 59 BU57
Virginia Water GU25 ... 132 AT98
Wentworth Gdns, N13 ... 45 DP49
★ **Wentworth Golf Course**, Vir.W.
GU25 ... 132 AT100
Wentworth Hill, Wem. HA9 ... 62 CM60
Wentworth Ms, E3
off Eric St ... 85 DZ70
Wentworth Pk, N3 ... 44 DA52
Wentworth Pl, Grays RM16 ... 110 GD76
Stanmore HA7
off Greenacres Dr ... 41 CH51
Wentworth Rd, E12 ... 68 EK63
NW11 ... 63 CZ58
Barnet EN5 ... 27 CX41
Croydon CR0 ... 141 DN101
Southall UB2 ... 96 BW77
Wentworth St, E1 ... 197 P8
Wentworth Way, Pnr. HA5 ... 60 BX56
Rainham RM13 ... 89 FH69
South Croydon CR2 ... 160 DU114
Wenvoe Av, Bexh. DA7 ... 107 FB82
Wepham Cl, Hayes UB4
off Glencoe Rd ... 78 BX71
Wernbrook St, SE18 ... 105 EQ79
Werndee Rd, SE25 ... 142 DU98
Werneth Hall Rd, Ilf. IG5 ... 69 EM55
Werrington St, NW1 ... 195 L1
Werter Rd, SW15 ... 99 CY84
Wescott Way, Uxb. UB8 ... 76 BJ68
Wesleyan Pl, NW5
off Gordon Ho Rd ... 65 DH63
Wesley Av, E16 ... 205 P2
NW10 ... 80 CR69
Hounslow TW3 ... 96 BY82
Wesley Cl, N7 ... 65 DM61
SE17 ... 200 G9
Harrow HA2 ... 60 CC61
Orpington BR5 ... 146 EW97
Waltham Cross
(Chsht) EN7 ... 14 DQ28
Wesley Dr, Egh. TW20 ... 113 BA93
Wesley Rd, E10 ... 67 EC59
NW10 ... 80 CQ67
Hayes UB3 ... 77 BU73
★ **Wesley's Ho**, EC1 ... 197 L4
Wesley Sq, W11
off Bartle Rd ... 81 CY72
Wesley St, W1 ... 194 G7
Wessels, Tad. KT20 ... 173 CX121
Wessex Av, SW19 ... 140 DA96
Wessex Cl, Ilf. IG3 ... 69 ES58
Kingston upon Thames KT1
off Gloucester Rd ... 138 CP95
Thames Ditton KT7 ... 137 CF103
Wessex Dr, Erith DA8 ... 107 FE81
Pinner HA5 ... 40 BY52
Wessex Gdns, NW11 ... 63 CY60
Wessex La, Grnf. UB6 ... 79 CD68
Wessex Rd, Houns.
(Hthrw Air.) TW6 ... 94 BK82
Wessex St, E2 ... 84 DW69
Wessex Wk, Dart. DA2
off Old Bexley La ... 127 FE89
Wessex Way, NW11 ... 63 CY59
West 12 Shop Cen, W12
off Shepherds Bush Grn ... 99 CX75
Westacott, Hayes UB4 ... 77 BS71
Westacott Cl, N19 ... 65 DK60
Westacres, Esher KT10 ... 154 BZ108
WEST ACTON, W3 ... 80 CN72
⊖ **West Acton** ... 80 CN72
Westall Rd, Loug. IG10 ... 33 EP41
West App, Orp. BR5 ... 145 EQ99
West Arbour St, E1 ... 85 DX72
West Av, E17 ... 67 EB56
N3 ... 44 DA51
NW4 ... 63 CX57
Hayes UB3 ... 77 BT73
Pinner HA5 ... 60 BZ58
St. Albans AL2 ... 8 CB25
Southall UB1 ... 78 BZ73
Wallington SM6 ... 159 DL106
Walton-on-Thames
(Whiteley Vill.) KT12 ... 153 BS109
West Av Rd, E17 ... 67 EA56
West Bk, N16 ... 66 DS59
Barking IG11
off Highbridge Rd ... 87 EP67
Enfield EN2 ... 30 DQ40
Westbank Rd, Hmptn.
(Hmptn H.) TW12 ... 116 CC93
WEST BARNES, N.Mal. KT3 ... 139 CU99
West Barnes La, SW20 ... 139 CV97
New Malden KT3 ... 139 CV97
Westbeech Rd, N22 ... 65 DN55
Westbere Dr, Stan. HA7 ... 41 CK49
Westbere Rd, NW2 ... 63 CY63
Westbourne Av, W3 ... 80 CR72
Sutton SM3 ... 139 CY103
Westbourne Br, W2 ... 82 DC71
Westbourne Cl, Hayes UB4 ... 77 BV70
Westbourne Cres, W2 ... 82 DD73
Westbourne Cres Ms, W2
off Westbourne Cres ... 82 DD73
Westbourne Dr, SE23 ... 123 DX89
Brentwood CM14 ... 54 FT49
Westbourne Gdns, W2 ... 82 DB72
WESTBOURNE GREEN, W2 ... 82 DA71
Westbourne Gro, W2 ... 82 DA72
W11 ... 81 CZ73
Westbourne Gro Ms, W11
off Westbourne Gro ... 82 DA72
Westbourne Gro Ter, W2 ... 82 DB72
⊖ **Westbourne Park** ... 81 CZ71
Westbourne Pk Ms, W2
off Westbourne Gdns ... 82 DB72
Westbourne Pk Pas, W2
off Westbourne Pk Vil ... 82 DA71
Westbourne Pk Rd, W2 ... 82 DA71
W11 ... 81 CY72
Westbourne Pk Vil, W2 ... 82 DA71
Westbourne Pl, N9
off Eastbournia Av ... 46 DV48
Westbourne Rd, N7 ... 83 DN65
SE26 ... 123 DX93
Bexleyheath DA7 ... 106 EY80
Croydon CR0 ... 142 DT100
Feltham TW13 ... 115 BT90
Staines TW18 ... 114 BH94
Uxbridge UB8 ... 77 BP70
Westbourne St, W2 ... 82 DD73
Westbourne Ter, SE23
off Westbourne Dr ... 123 DX89
W2 ... 82 DD72
Westbourne Ter Ms, W2 ... 82 DC72
Westbourne Ter Rd, W2 ... 82 DC71
Westbridge Rd, SW11 ... 100 DD81
WEST BROMPTON, SW10 ... 100 DB79
⇌ **West Brompton** ... 100 DA78
⊖ **West Brompton** ... 100 DA78
Westbrook Av, Hmptn. TW12 ... 116 BZ94
Westbrook Cl, Barn. EN4 ... 28 DD41
Westbrook Cres, Barn. EN4 ... 28 DD41
Westbrook Dr, Orp. BR5 ... 146 EW102
Westbrooke Cres, Well. DA16 ... 106 EW83
Westbrooke Rd, Sid. DA15 ... 125 ER89
Welling DA16 ... 106 EV83
Westbrook Rd, SE3 ... 104 EH81
Hounslow TW5 ... 96 BZ80
Staines TW18
off South St ... 113 BF92
Thornton Heath CR7 ... 142 DR95
Westbrook Sq, Barn. EN4
off Westbrook Cres ... 28 DD41
Westbury Av, N22 ... 65 DP55
Esher (Clay.) KT10 ... 155 CF107
Southall UB1 ... 78 CA70
Wembley HA0 ... 80 CL66
Westbury Cl, Ruis. HA4 ... 59 BU59
Shepperton TW17
off Burchetts Way ... 135 BP100
Whyteleafe CR3
off Beverley Rd ... 176 DS116
Westbury Dr, Brwd. CM14 ... 54 FV47
Westbury Gro, N12 ... 44 DA51
Westbury La, Buck.H. IG9 ... 48 EJ47
Westbury Lo Cl, Pnr. HA5 ... 60 BX55
Westbury Par, SW12
off Balham Hill ... 121 DH86
Westbury Pl, Brent. TW8 ... 97 CK79
Westbury Rd, E7 ... 68 EH64
E17 ... 67 EA56
N11 ... 45 DL51
N12 ... 44 DA51
SE20 ... 143 DX95
W5 ... 80 CL72
Barking IG11 ... 87 ER67
Beckenham BR3 ... 143 DY97
Brentwood CM14 ... 54 FW47
Bromley BR1 ... 144 EK95
Buckhurst Hill IG9 ... 48 EJ47
Croydon CR0 ... 142 DR100
Feltham TW13 ... 116 BX88
Ilford IG1 ... 69 EM61
New Malden KT3 ... 138 CR98
Northwood HA6 ... 39 BS49
Waltham Cross (Chsht) EN8
off Turners Hill ... 15 DX30
Watford WD18 ... 23 BV43
Wembley HA0 ... 80 CL66
Westbury St, SW8 ... 101 DJ82
Westbury Ter, E7 ... 86 EH65
Upminster RM14 ... 73 FS61
Westerham TN16 ... 189 EQ127
WEST BYFLEET ... 152 BH113
⇌ **West Byfleet** ... 152 BG112
Westcar La, Walt. KT12 ... 153 BV107
West Carriage Dr, W2 ... 198 A3
West Cen St, WC1 ... 195 P8
West Cen Av, W10
off Harrow Rd ... 81 CV69
West Chantry, Har. HA3
off Chantry Rd ... 40 CB53
Westchester Dr, NW4 ... 63 CX55
West Cl, N9 ... 46 DT48
Ashford TW15 ... 114 BL91
Barnet EN5 ... 27 CV43
Barnet (Cockfos.) EN4 ... 28 DG42
Greenford UB6 ... 78 CC68
Hampton TW12 *off Oak Av* ... 116 BY93
Rainham RM13 ... 89 FH70
Wembley HA9 ... 62 CM60
Westcombe Av, Croy. CR0 ... 141 DL100
Westcombe Ct, SE3
off Westcombe Pk Rd ... 104 EF80
Westcombe Dr, Barn. EN5 ... 28 DA43
Westcombe Hill, SE3 ... 104 EG78
SE10 ... 104 EG78
Westcombe Lo Dr, Hayes
UB4 ... 77 BR71
⇌ **Westcombe Park** ... 104 EG78
Westcombe Pk Rd, SE3 ... 104 EE79
West Common, Ger.Cr. SL9 ... 56 AX57
West Common Cl, Ger.Cr.
SL9 ... 56 AY57
West Common Rd, Brom.
BR2 ... 144 EG103
Keston BR2 ... 162 EH105
Uxbridge UB8 ... 58 BK64
Westcoombe Av, SW20 ... 139 CT95
Westcote Ri, Ruis. HA4 ... 59 BQ59
Westcote Rd, SW16 ... 121 DJ92
West Cotts, NW6 ... 64 DA64
Westcott Av, Grav.
Nthflt) DA11 ... 131 GG90

★ Place of interest ⇌ Railway station ⊖ London Underground station DLR Docklands Light Railway station Tra Tramlink station H Hospital Riv Pedestrian ferry landing stage

Westcott Cl, N15
off Ermine Rd 66 DT58
Bromley BR1
off Ringmer Way 144 EL99
Croydon (New Adgtn) CR0
off Castle Hill Av 161 EB109
Westcott Cres, W7 79 CE72
Westcott Rd, SE17 101 DP79
Westcott Way, Sutt. SM2 157 CW110
WESTCOURT, Grav. DA12 131 GL89
West Ct, SE18
off Prince Imperial Rd 105 EM81
Westcourt, Sun. TW16 135 BV96
West Ct, Wem. HA0 61 CJ61
West Cres Rd, Grav. DA12 131 GH86
Westcroft Cl, NW2 63 CY63
Enfield EN3 30 DW38
Westcroft Gdns, Mord. SM4 139 CZ97
Westcroft Rd, Cars. SM5 158 DG105
Wallington SM6 158 DG105
Westcroft Sq, W6 99 CU77
Westcroft Way, NW2 63 CY63
West Cromwell Rd, SW5 99 CZ77
W14 99 CZ77
West Cross Cen, Brent. TW8 97 CG79
West Cross Route, W10 81 CX73
W11 81 CX73
West Cross Way, Brent.
TW8 97 CH79
⇌ West Croydon 142 DQ102
Tra West Croydon 142 DQ102
Westdale Pas, SE18 105 EP79
Westdale Rd, SE18 105 EP79
Westdean Av, SE12 124 EH88
Westdean Cl, SW18 120 DB86
West Dene, Sutt. SM3
off Park La 157 CY107
West Dene Dr, Rom. RM3 52 FK50
Westdene Way, Wey. KT13 135 BS104
Westdown Rd, E15 67 EC63
SE6 123 EA87
WEST DRAYTON 94 BK76
⇌ West Drayton 76 BL74
West Drayton Pk Av, West Dr.
UB7 94 BL76
West Drayton Rd, Uxb. UB8 76 BM72
Uxbridge (Hayes End) UB8 77 BP71
West Dr, SW16 121 DJ91
Carshalton SM5 158 DD110
Harrow HA3 41 CD51
Sutton (Cheam) SM2 157 CX109
Tadworth KT20 173 CX118
Virginia Water GU25 132 AT101
Watford WD25 23 BV36
West Dr Gdns, Har. HA3 41 CD51
WEST DULWICH, SE21 122 DR90
⇌ West Dulwich 122 DR88
⇌ West Ealing 79 CH73
West Eaton Pl, SW1 198 F8
West Eaton Pl Ms, SW1 198 F8
Wested La, Swan. BR8 147 FG101
West Ella Rd, NW10 80 CS66
WEST END, Esher KT10 154 BZ107
West End Av, E10 67 EC57
Pinner HA5 60 BX56
West End Cl, NW10 80 CQ66
West End Ct, Pnr. HA5 60 BX56
Slough (Stoke P.) SL2 74 AT67
West End Gdns, Esher KT10 154 BZ106
Northolt UB5
off Edward Cl 78 BW68
West End La, NW6 82 DA66
Barnet EN5 27 CX42
Esher KT10 154 BZ107
Hayes UB3 95 BQ80
Pinner HA5 60 BX55
Slough (Stoke P.) SL2 74 AS67
West End Rd, Nthlt. UB5 78 BW66
Ruislip HA4 59 BV64
Southall UB1 78 BY74
Westerdale Rd, SE10 104 EG78
Westerfield Rd, N15 66 DT57
Westerfolds Cl, Wok. GU22 167 BC116
Westergate Rd, SE2 106 EY78
WESTERHAM 189 EQ126
Westerham Av, N9 46 DR48
Westerham Cl, Add. KT15 152 BJ107
Sutton SM2 158 DA110
Westerham Dr, Sid. DA15 126 EV86
Westerham Hill, West. TN16 179 EN121
Westerham Rd, E10 67 EB59
Keston BR2 162 EK107
Oxted RH8 188 EF129
Sevenoaks TN13 190 FC123
Westerham TN16 189 EM128
Westerham
(Brasted) TN16 189 ET125
Westerley Cres, SE26 123 DZ92
Westerley Ware, Rich. TW9
off Kew Grn 98 CN79
Westermain, Add.
(New Haw) KT15 152 BJ110
Western Av, NW11 63 CX58
W3 80 CR71
W5 80 CM69
Brentwood CM14 54 FW46
Chertsey KT16 134 BG97
Dagenham RM10 89 FC65
Egham TW20 133 BB97
Epping CM16 17 ET32
Grays RM20 109 FT78
Greenford UB6 79 CF69
Northolt UB5 78 BZ67
Romford RM2 52 FJ54
Ruislip HA4 77 BP65
Uxbridge (Denh.) UB9 58 BJ63
Uxbridge (Ickhm) UB10 77 BP65
Western Av Business Pk, W3
off Mansfield Rd 80 CP70
Western Av Underpass, W5
off Western Av 80 CM69
Western Beach Apartments,
E16 205 M2
Western Cl, Cher. KT16
off Western Av 134 BG97
Western Ct, N3
off Huntley Dr 44 DA51
Western Cross Cl, Green. DA9
off Johnsons Way 129 FW86
Western Dr, Shep. TW17 135 BR100
H Western Eye Hosp, NW1 194 D6
Western Gdns, W5 80 CN73
Brentwood CM14 54 FW47
Western Gateway, E16 205 M1
Western La, SW12 120 DG87
Western Ms, W9
off Great Western Rd 81 CZ70
Western Par, Barn. EN5
off Great N Rd 28 DA43
Western Pathway, Horn.
RM12 90 FJ65
Western Perimeter Rd, Houns.
(Hthrw Air.) TW6 94 BH83
Western Pl, SE16 202 G4
Western Rd, E13 86 EJ67
E17 67 EC57
N2 64 DF56
N22 45 DM54
NW10 80 CQ70
SW9 101 DN83
SW19 140 DD95
W5 79 CK73
Brentwood CM14 54 FW47
Epping CM16 17 ET32
Mitcham CR4 140 DD95
Romford RM1 71 FE57
Southall UB2 96 BX76
Sutton SM1 158 DA106
Western Ter, W6
off Chiswick Mall 99 CU78
Western Trd Est, NW10 80 CQ70
Western Vw, Hayes UB3 95 BT75
Westernville Gdns, Ilf. IG2 69 EQ59
Western Way, SE28 105 ER76
Barnet EN5 28 DA44
WEST EWELL, Epsom KT19 156 CS108
West Fm Av, Ashtd. KT21 171 CJ118
West Fm Cl, Ashtd. KT21 171 CJ119
West Fm Dr, Ashtd. KT21 171 CK119
DLR Westferry 85 EA73
Westferry Circ, E14 203 P2
Westferry Rd, E14 203 N2
WESTFIELD, Wok. GU22 167 AZ122
Westfield, Ashtd. KT21 172 CM118
Loughton IG10 32 EJ43
Reigate RH2 184 DB131
Sevenoaks TN13 191 FJ122
Westfield Av, S.Croy. CR2 160 DR113
Watford WD24 24 BW37
Woking GU22 166 AY121
Westfield Cl, NW9 62 CQ55
SW10 100 DC80
Enfield EN3 31 DY41
Gravesend DA12 131 GJ93
Sutton SM1 157 CZ105
Waltham Cross EN8 15 DZ31
Westfield Common, Wok.
GU22 166 AY122
Westfield Dr, Har. HA3 61 CK57
Leatherhead (Bkhm) KT23 170 CA122
Westfield Gdns, Har. HA3 61 CK56
Westfield Gro, Wok. GU22 167 AZ120
Westfield La, Har. HA3 61 CK56
Slough (Geo.Grn) SL3 74 AX73
Westfield Par, Add.
(New Haw) KT15 152 BK110
Westfield Pk, Pnr. HA5 40 BZ52
Westfield Pk Dr, Wdf.Grn.
IG8 48 EL51
Westfield Rd, NW7 42 CR48
W13 79 CG74
Beckenham BR3 143 DZ96
Bexleyheath DA7 107 FC82
Croydon CR0 141 DP103
Dagenham RM9 70 EY63
Mitcham CR4 140 DF96
Surbiton KT6 137 CK99
Sutton SM1 157 CZ105
Walton-on-Thames KT12 136 BY101
Woking GU22 166 AX122
Westfields, SW13 99 CT83
Westfields Av, SW13 98 CS83
Westfields Rd, W3 80 CP71
Westfield St, SE18 104 EK76
Westfield Wk, Wal.Cr. EN8
off Westfield Cl 15 DZ31
Westfield Way, E1 85 DY69
Ruislip HA4 59 BS62
Woking GU22 166 AY122
⊖ West Finchley 44 DB51
West Gdn Pl, W2 194 C9
West Gdns, E1 202 E1
SW17 120 DE93
Epsom KT17 156 CS110
West Gate, W5 80 CL69
Westgate Cl, Epsom KT18
off Chalk La 172 CR115
Westgate Ct, Wal.Cr. EN8
off Holmesdale 31 DX35
Westgate Ho, Brent. TW8 97 CK78
Westgate Rd, SE25 142 DV98
Beckenham BR3 143 EB96
Dartford DA1 128 FK86
Westgate St, E8 84 DV67
Westgate Ter, SW10 100 DB78
Westglade Ct, Har. HA3 61 CK57
West Gorse, Croy. CR0 161 DY112
WEST GREEN, N15 66 DQ55
West Grn Pl, Grnf. UB6
off Uneeda Dr 79 CD67
West Grn Rd, N15 65 DP56
West Gro, SE10 103 EC81
Walton-on-Thames KT12 153 BV105
Woodford Green IG8 48 EJ51
Westgrove La, SE10 103 EC81
West Halkin St, SW1 198 F6
West Hallowes, SE9 124 EK88
Westhall Pk, Warl. CR6 176 DW119
West Hall Rd, Rich. TW9 98 CP81
Westhall Rd, Warl. CR6 176 DV119
WEST HAM, E15 86 EE66
⇌ West Ham 86 EE69
⊖ West Ham 86 EE69
West Ham La, E15 86 EE66
West Ham Pk, E7 86 EG66
WEST HAMPSTEAD, NW6 64 DB64
⇌ West Hampstead 82 DA65
⊖ West Hampstead 82 DA65
West Hampstead Ms, NW6 82 DB65
⇌ West Hampstead
(Thameslink) 82 DA65
★ West Ham United FC, E13 86 EJ68
West Harding St, EC4 196 E8
West Harold, Swan. BR8 147 FD97
WEST HARROW, Har. HA1 60 CC59
⊖ West Harrow 60 CC58
West Hatch Manor, Ruis.
HA4 59 BT60
Westhay Gdns, SW14 118 CP85
WEST HEATH, SE2 106 EX79
West Heath, Oxt. RH8 188 EG130
West Heath Av, NW11 64 DA60
West Heath Cl, NW3 64 DA62
Dartford DA1
off West Heath Rd 127 FF86
West Heath Dr, NW11 64 DA60
West Heath Gdns, NW3 64 DA62
West Heath La, Sev. TN13 191 FH128
West Heath Rd, NW3 64 DA61
SE2 106 EX79
Dartford DA1 127 FF86
WEST HENDON, NW9 62 CS59
West Hendon Bdy, NW9 63 CT58
West Hill, SW15 119 CX87
SW18 120 DA85
Dartford DA1 128 FK86
Epsom KT19 156 CQ113
Harrow HA2 61 CE61
Orpington BR6 163 EM112
Oxted RH8 187 ED130
South Croydon CR2 160 DS110
Wembley HA9 62 CM60
West Hill Av, Epsom KT19 156 CQ112
West Hill Bk, Oxt. RH8 187 ED130
Westhill Cl, Grav. DA12
off Leith Pk Rd 131 GH88
West Hill Ct, N6 64 DG62
West Hill Dr, Dart. DA1 128 FJ86
West Hill Pk, N6
off Merton La 64 DF61
West Hill Ri, Dart. DA1 128 FK86
West Hill Rd, SW18 120 DA86
Woking GU22 166 AX119
West Hill Way, N20 44 DB46
Westholm, NW11 64 DB56
West Holme, Erith DA8 107 FC81
Westholme, Orp. BR6 145 ES101
Westholme Gdns, Ruis. HA4 59 BU60
Westhorne Av, SE9 124 EJ86
SE12 124 EG87
Westhorpe Gdns, NW4 63 CW55
Westhorpe Rd, SW15 99 CW83
West Ho Cl, SW19 119 CY88
Westhurst Dr, Chis. BR7 125 EP92
West Hyde La, Ger.Cr.
(Chal.St.P.) SL9 37 AZ52
West India Av, E14 203 P2
West India Dock Rd, E14 85 DZ72
DLR West India Quay 204 B1
⊖ West Kensington 99 CZ78
West Kent Av, Grav.
(Nthflt) DA11 130 GC86
West Kent Cold Storage, Sev.
(Dunt.Grn) TN14 181 FF120
WEST KILBURN, W9 81 CZ69
Westlake Cl, N13 45 DN48
Hayes UB4
off Lochan Cl 78 BY70
Westlake Rd, Wem. HA9 61 CK61
Westland Av, Horn. RM11 72 FL60
Westland Cl, Stai.
(Stanw.) TW19 114 BL86
Watford WD25
off Ashfields 7 BT34
Westland Dr, Brom. BR2 144 EF103
Hatfield AL9 11 CY27
Westland Ho, E16
off Rymill St 87 EN74
Westland Pl, N1 197 K2
Westland Rd, Wat. WD17 23 BV40
Westlands Cl, Hayes UB3
off Granville Rd 95 BU77
Westlands Ct, Epsom KT18 172 CQ115
Westlands Ter, SW12
off Gaskarth Rd 121 DJ86
Westlands Way, Oxt. RH8 187 ED127
West La, SE16 202 D5
Westlea Av, Wat. WD25 24 BY37
Westlea Rd, W7 97 CG76
Westleigh Av, SW15 119 CV85
Coulsdon CR5 174 DG116
Westleigh Dr, Brom. BR1 144 EL95
Westleigh Gdns, Edg. HA8 42 CN53
Westlinks, Wem. HA0
off Alperton La 79 CK69
Westlinton Cl, NW7 43 CY51
West Lo Av, W3 80 CN74
Westlyn Cl, Rain. RM13 90 FJ69
Westmacott Dr, Felt. TW14 115 BT88
West Mall, W8
off Palace Gdns Ter 82 DA74
West Malling Way, Horn.
RM12 72 FJ64
Westmark Pt, SW15
off Norley Vale 119 CV88
Westmead, SW15 119 CV86
West Mead, Epsom KT19 156 CS107
Ruislip HA4 60 BW63
Westmead, Wok. GU21 166 AV117
Westmead Cor, Cars. SM5
off Colston Av 158 DE105
Westmeade Cl, Wal.Cr.
(Chsht) EN7 14 DV29
Westmead Rd, Sutt. SM1 158 DD105
Westmede, Chig. IG7 49 EQ51
Westmere Dr, NW7 42 CR48
West Mersea Cl, E16 205 P3
West Ms, N17 46 DV51
SW1 199 J9
H West Middlesex Uni Hosp, Islw.
TW7 97 CG82
West Mill, Grav. DA11 131 GF86
Westmill Ct, N4
off Brownswood Rd 66 DQ61
WESTMINSTER, SW1 199 K6
⊖ Westminster 200 A5
★ Westminster Abbey, SW1 199 P6
★ Westminster Abbey Mus,
SW1 199 P6
Westminster Av, Th.Hth. CR7 141 DP96
Westminster Br, SE1 200 A5
SW1 200 A5
Westminster Br Rd, SE1 200 C5
★ Westminster Cath, SW1 199 K7
★ Westminster City Hall,
SW1 199 L6
Westminster Cl, Felt. TW14 115 BU88
Ilford IG6 49 ER54
Teddington TW11 117 CG92
Westminster Dr, N13 45 DL50
Westminster Gdns, E4 48 EE46
SW1 199 P8
Barking IG11 87 ES68
Ilford IG6 49 EQ54
★ Westminster Millennium Pier,
SW1 200 A4
Riv Westminster
Millennium Pier 200 A4
Westminster Rd, N9 46 DV46
W7 79 CE74
Sutton SM1 140 DD103
Westmoat Cl, Beck. BR3 123 EC94
WEST MOLESEY 136 BZ99
H West Molesey Hosp, W.Mol.
KT8 136 CA99
Westmont Rd, Esher KT10 137 CE103
Westmoor Gdns, Enf. EN3 31 DX40
Westmoor Rd, Enf. EN3 31 DX40
Westmoor St, SE7 104 EJ76
Westmore Grn, West. (Tats.)
TN16 178 EJ121
Westmoreland Av, Horn.
RM11 72 FJ57
Welling DA16 105 ES83
Westmoreland Bldgs, EC1
off Bartholomew Cl 84 DQ71
Westmoreland Dr, Sutt. SM2 158 DB109
Westmoreland Pl, SW1 101 DH78
W5 off Mount Av 79 CK71
Bromley BR1 144 EG97
Westmoreland Rd, NW9 62 CN56
SE17 102 DQ79
SW13 99 CT81
Bromley BR1, BR2 144 EE99
Westmoreland St, W1 194 G7
Westmoreland Ter, SW1 101 DH78
Westmoreland Wk, SE17 102 DR79
Westmore Rd,
West. (Tats.) TN16 178 EJ121
Westmorland Cl, E12 68 EK61
Epsom KT19 156 CS110
Twickenham TW1 117 CH86
Westmorland Rd, E17 67 EA58
Harrow HA1 60 CB57
Westmorland Sq, Mitch. CR4
off Westmorland Way 141 DL99
Westmorland Ter, SE20 122 DV94
Westmorland Way, Mitch.
CR4 141 DK98
Westmount Rd, SE9 105 EM82
WEST NORWOOD, SE27 122 DQ90
⇌ West Norwood 121 DP90
West Oak, Beck. BR3 143 ED95
Westoe Rd, N9 46 DV47
Weston Av, Add. KT15 152 BG105
Grays RM20 109 FT77
Thames Ditton KT7 137 CE101
West Molesey KT8 136 BY97
Weston Cl, Brwd.
(Hutt.) CM13 55 GC45
Coulsdon CR5 175 DM120
Potters Bar EN6 11 CZ32
Weston Ct, N4
off Queens Dr 66 DQ62
N20 off Farnham Cl 44 DC45
Weston Dr, Cat. CR3
off Coulsdon Rd 176 DQ122
Stanmore HA7 41 CH53
West One Shop Cen, W1 194 G9
Weston Gdns, Islw. TW7 97 CD81
Woking GU22 167 BE116
WESTON GREEN, T.Ditt. KT7 137 CF102
Weston Grn, Dag. RM9 70 EZ63
Thames Ditton KT7 137 CE102
Weston Grn Rd, Esher KT10 137 CD102
Thames Ditton KT7 137 CE102
Weston Gro, Brom. BR1 144 EF95
Weston Pk, N8 65 DL58
Kingston upon Thames KT1
off Fairfield W 138 CL96
Thames Ditton KT7 137 CE102
Weston Pk Cl, T.Ditt. KT7
off Weston Pk 137 CE102
Weston Ri, WC1 196 C1
Weston Rd, W4 98 CQ76
Bromley BR1 124 EF94
Dagenham RM9 70 EY63
Enfield EN2 30 DR39
Epsom KT17 156 CS111
Thames Ditton KT7 137 CE102
Weston St, SE1 201 L6
Weston Wk, E8 off Mare St 84 DV66
Weston Way, Wok. GU22 167 BE116
Westover Cl, Sutt. SM2 158 DB109
Westover Hill, NW3 64 DA61
Westover Rd, SW18 120 DC86
Westow Hill, SE19 122 DS93
Westow St, SE19 122 DS93
West Palace Gdns, Wey. KT13 135 BP104
West Pk, SE9 124 EL89
West Pk Av, Rich. TW9 98 CN81
West Pk Cl, Houns. TW5
off Heston Gra La 96 BZ79
Romford RM6 70 EX57
West Pk Hill, Brwd. CM14 54 FU48
H West Pk Hosp, Epsom
KT19 156 CM112
West Pk Rd, Epsom KT19 156 CM112
Richmond TW9 98 CN81
Southall UB2 78 CC74
West Parkside, SE10 205 L7
Warlingham CR6 177 EA115
West Pier, E1 202 D3
West Pl, SW19 119 CW92
Westpoint Trd Est, W3 80 CP71
Westpole Av, Barn. EN4 28 DG42
Westport Rd, E13 86 EH70
Westport St, E1 85 DX72
West Poultry Av, EC1 196 F7
West Quarters, W12 81 CU72
West Quay Dr, Hayes UB4 78 BY71
West Ramp, Houns.
(Hthrw Air.) TW6 94 BN81
West Ridge Gdns, Grnf. UB6 78 CC68
West Riding, St.Alb.
(Brick.Wd) AL2 8 BZ30
West Rd, E15 86 EF67
N17 46 DV51
SW3 100 DF79
SW4 121 DK85
W5 80 CL71
Barnet EN4 44 DG46
Chessington KT9 155 CJ112
Feltham TW14 115 BR86
Kingston upon Thames KT2 138 CQ95
Romford (Chad.Hth) RM6 70 EX58
Romford (Rush Grn) RM7 71 FD59
South Ockendon RM15 91 FV69
West Drayton UB7 94 BM76
Weybridge KT13 153 BP109
Westrow, SW15 119 CW85
West Row, W10 81 CY70
Westrow Dr, Bark. IG11 87 ET65
Westrow Gdns, Ilf. IG3 69 ET61
⇌ West Ruislip 59 BQ61
⊖ West Ruislip 59 BQ61
West Shaw, Long. DA3 149 FX96
West Sheen Vale, Rich. TW9 98 CM84
Westside, NW4 43 CV54
West Side, Brox. EN10
off High Rd Turnford 15 DY25
West Side Common, SW19 119 CW92
West Smithfield, EC1 196 F7
West Spur Rd, Uxb. UB8 76 BK69
West Sq, SE11 200 F7
Iver SL0 off High St 75 BF72
West St, E2 84 DV68
E11 68 EE62
E17 off Grove Rd 67 EB57
WC2 195 N9
Bexleyheath DA7 106 EZ84
Brentford TW8 97 CJ79
Bromley BR1 144 EG95
Carshalton SM5 140 DF104
Croydon CR0 160 DQ105
Epsom KT18 156 CR113
Epsom (Ewell) KT17 156 CS110
Erith DA8 107 FD77
Gravesend DA11 131 GG86
Grays RM17 110 GA79
Harrow HA1 61 CD60
Reigate RH2 183 CY133
Sutton SM1 158 DB106
Watford WD17 23 BV40
Woking GU21
off Church St E 167 AZ117
West St La, Cars. SM5 158 DF105
⇌ West Sutton 158 DA105
West Temple Sheen, SW14 98 CP84
West Tenter St, E1 84 DT72
West Thamesmead Business Pk,
SE28 105 ET76
WEST THURROCK, Grays
RM20 109 FU78
West Thurrock Way, Grays
RM20 109 FT77
WEST TILBURY, Til. RM18 111 GL79
West Twrs, Pnr. HA5 60 BX58
Westvale Ms, W3 80 CS74
West Valley Rd, Hem.H. HP3 6 BJ25
West Vw, NW4 63 CW56
Feltham TW14 115 BQ87
Loughton IG10 33 EM41
West Vw Av, Whyt. CR3
off Station Rd 176 DU118
Westview Cl, NW10 63 CT64
W7 79 CE72
W10 81 CW72
Rainham RM13 90 FJ69
West Vw Ct, Borwd. (Elstree) WD6
off High St 25 CK44
Westview Cres, N9 46 DS45
Westview Dr, Wdf.Grn. IG8 48 EK54
West Vw Gdns, Borwd. (Elstree) WD6
off High St 25 CK44
West Vw Rd, Dart. DA1 128 FM86
Swanley BR8 147 FG98
Swanley (Crock.) BR8 147 FD100
Westview Rd, Warl. CR6 176 DV119
Westville Rd, W12 99 CU75
Thames Ditton KT7 137 CG102
West Wk, W5 80 CL71
Barnet EN4 44 DG45
Hayes UB3 77 BU74
West Walkway, The, Sutt. SM1
off Cheam Rd 158 DB106
Westward Rd, E4 47 DZ50
Westward Way, Har. HA3 62 CL58
West Warwick Pl, SW1 199 K9
WEST WATFORD, Wat. WD18 23 BU42
West Way, N18 46 DR49
NW10 62 CR62
Westway, SW20 139 CV97
W2 82 DA71
W9 82 DA71
W10 81 CY72
W12 81 CU73
West Way, Brwd. CM14 54 FU48
Carshalton SM5 158 DD110
Westway, Cat. CR3 176 DR122
West Way, Croy. CR0 143 DY103
Edgware HA8 42 CP51
Hounslow TW5 96 BZ81
Westway, Orp. BR5 145 ER99
West Way, Pnr. HA5 60 BX56
Rickmansworth WD3 38 BH46
Ruislip HA4 59 BT60
Shepperton TW17 135 BR100
West Wickham BR4 143 ED100
Westway Cl, SW20 139 CV97
Westway Cross Shop Pk, Grnf.
UB6 79 CE67
West Way Gdns, Croy. CR0 143 DX103
Westway Gdns, Red. RH1 184 DG131
Westways, Epsom KT19 157 CT105

★ Place of interest ⇌ Railway station ⊖ London Underground station DLR Docklands Light Railway station Tra Tramlink station H Hospital Riv Pedestrian ferry landing stage

Westways, Westerham TN16 . **189** EQ126
Westwell CI, Orp. BR5 . . . . . . **146** EX102
Westwell Rd, SW16 . . . . **121** DL93
Westwell Rd App, SW16
  off Westwell Rd **121** DL93
Westwick Gdns, W14 . . . . . . **99** CX75
  Hounslow TW4 . . . . **95** WB82
WEST WICKHAM **143** EC103
⇌ West Wickham **143** EC101
Westwick PI, Wat. WD25 . . . . **8** BW34
Westwood Av, SE19 . . . . . . **142** DQ95
  Addlestone (Wdhm) KT15 . **151** BF117
  Brentwood CM14 . . . . . . **54** FU49
  Harrow HA2 . . . . **60** CB63
Westwood CI, Amer. HP6 . . . **20** AX39
  Bromley BR1 . . . . **144** EK97
  Esher KT10 . . . . **136** CC104
  Potters Bar EN6 . . . . . . **12** DA30
  Ruislip HA4 . . . . **59** BP58
Westwood Dr, Amer. HP6 . . . **20** AX39
Westwood Gdns, SW13 . . . . . **99** CT83
Westwood Hill, SE26 . . . . . **122** DU92
Westwood La, Sid. DA15 . . . **126** EU85
  Welling DA16 . . . . **105** ET83
Westwood Pk, SE23 . . . . . . **122** DV87
Westwood PI, SE26 . . . . . . **122** DU91
Westwood Rd, E16 . . . . . . **205** P3
  SW13 . . . . **99** CT83
  Coulsdon CR5 . . . . **175** DK118
  Gravesend (Sthflt) DA13. . **131** FY93
  Ilford IG3 . . . . **69** ET60
West Woodside, Bex. DA5 . . **126** EY87
Westwood Way, Sev. TN13. . **190** FF122
West World, SW13 . . . . **80** CL69
West Yoke, Sev. (Ash) TN15 . **149** FX103
Wetheral Dr, Stan. HA7 . . . . **41** CH53
Wetherby CI, Nthlt. UB5. . . . . **78** CB65
Wetherby Gdns, SW5 . . . . . **100** DC77
Wetherby Ms, SW5
  off Bolton Gdns. **100** DB78
Wetherby PI, SW7 . . . . **100** DC77
Wetherby Rd, Borwd. WD6 . . **26** CL39
  Enfield EN2 . . . . **30** DQ39
Wetherby Way, Chess. KT9 . **156** CL108
Wetherden St, E17 . . . . **67** DZ59
Wetheredl Rd, E9. . . . . **85** DX67
Wetherill Rd, N10 . . . . **44** DG53
★ Wetland Cen,The, SW13 . . **99** CV80
Wettern CI, S.Croy. CR2
  off Purley Oaks Rd **160** DS110
Wetton PI, Egh. TW20 . . . . . **113** AZ92
Wexfenne Gdns, Wok. GU22 . **168** BH116
Wexford Rd, SW12 . . . . . . **120** DF87
Ⓗ Wexham Pk Hosp, Slou.
  SL2 . . . . **74** AW70
Wexham PK La, Slou.
  (Wexham) SL3 . . . . **74** AW70
Wexham PI, Slou.
  (Wexham) SL2 . . . . **74** AX65
Wexham Rd, Slou. SL1, SL2. . **74** AV71
WEXHAM STREET, Slou. SL3 . **74** AW67
Wexham St, Slou.
  (Wexham) SL2, SL3 . . . . **74** AW67
Wexham Wds, Slou.
  (Wexham) SL3 . . . . **74** AW71
Wey Av, Cher. KT16 . . . . . **134** BG97
Weybank, Wok.
  (Wisley) GU23 . . . . **168** BL116
Wey Barton,
  W.Byf. (Byfleet) KT14 . . **152** BM113
Weybourne PI, S.Croy. CR2 . **160** DR110
Weybourne St, SW18 . . . . . **120** DC89
WEYBRIDGE **152** BN105
⇌ Weybridge. **152** BN107
Weybridge Business Pk, Add.
  KT15 . . . . **152** BL105
Weybridge Ct, SE16
  off Argyle Way. **102** DU78
Ⓗ Weybridge Hosp, Wey.
  KT13. . . . . **152** BN105
Weybridge Pk, Wey. KT13. . **153** BP106
Weybridge Pt, SW11 . . . . . **100** DG82
Weybridge Rd, Add. KT15 . . **134** BK104
  Thornton Heath CR7. . . . **141** DN98
  Weybridge KT13 . . . . . . **134** BL104
Weybridge Trd Est, Add. KT15 **152** BL105
Wey CI, W.Byf. KT14
  off Broadoaks Cres **152** BH113
Wey Ct, Add.
  (New Haw) KT15. . . . . . **152** BK109
  Epsom KT19 . . . . **156** CQ105
Weydown CI, SW19 . . . . . . **119** CY88
Weyhill Rd, E1
  off Commercial Rd **84** DU72
Weylands CI, Walt. KT12. . . **136** BZ102
Weylands Pk, Wey. KT13 . . . **153** BR107
Weylond Rd, Dag. RM8 . . . . **70** EZ62
Wey Manor Rd, Add.
  (New Haw) KT15. . . . . . **152** BK109
Weyman Rd, SE3 . . . . **104** EJ81
Weymead CI, Cher. KT16 . . . **134** BJ102
Wey Meadows, Wey. KT13 . . **152** BL106
Weymede, W.Byf.
  (Byfleet) KT14 . . . . . . **152** BM112
Weymouth Av, NW7 . . . . . . **42** CS50
  W5. . . . . **97** CJ76
Weymouth Ct, Sutt.
  off Coveleees Wall **87** EP72
Weymouth Ct, Sutt. SM2 . . **158** DA108
Weymouth Ms, W1. . . . . . . **195** H6
Weymouth Rd, Hayes UB4. . . **77** BS69
Weymouth St, W1 . . . . . . **194** G7
Weymouth Ter, E2 . . . . **84** DT68
Weymouth Wk, Stan. HA7 . . **41** CG51
Wey Rd, Wey. KT13. . . . . . **134** BM104
Weyside CI, W.Byf.
  (Byfleet) KT14 . . . . . . **152** BM112
Weystone Rd, Add. KT15
  off Weybridge Rd **152** BM105
Whadcote St, N4
  off Seven Sisters Rd **65** DN61
Whalebone Av, Rom. RM6 . . **70** EZ58
Whalebone Ct, EC2. . . . . . **197** L8
Whalebone Gro, Rom. RM6 . . **70** EZ58
Whalebone La, E15
  off West Ham La **86** EE66
Whalebone La N, Rom. RM6. . **70** EY57
Whalebone La S, Dag. RM8. . **70** EZ59
  Romford RM6. . . . . **70** EZ59
Whaley Rd, Pot.B. EN6 . . . . **12** DC33

Wharfdale CI, N11
  off Ribblesdale Av. **44** DG51
Wharfdale Ct, E5
  off Rushmore Rd **67** DX63
Wharfdale Gdns, Th.Hth.
  CR7 . . . . **141** DM98
Wharfedale Gdns, Th.Hth. . . **141** DM98
Wharfedale Rd, N1. . . . . . . **83** DL68
Wharfedale St, SW10 . . . . **100** DB78
Wharf La, Rick. WD3 . . . . . **38** BL46
  Twickenham TW1 . . . . . **117** CG88
  Woking (Ripley) GU23 . . **168** BJ118
  Woking (Send) GU23 . . . **167** BC123
Wharf PI, E2 . . . . **84** DU67
Wharf Rd, E15. . . . . **85** ED67
  N1 . . . . **84** DQ68
  Brentwood CM14 . . . . . . **54** FW48
  Enfield EN3 . . . . **31** DY44
  Gravesend DA12. . . . . . **131** GL86
  Grays RM17. . . . . **110** FZ79
  Staines (Wrays.) TW19 . . **112** AW87
Wharf Rd S, Grays RM17 . . **110** FZ79
Wharfside CI, Erith DA8
  off Erith High St **107** FF79
Wharfside Rd, E16 . . . . **86** EE71
Wharf St, E16 . . . . **86** EE71
Wharncliffe Dr, Sthl. UB1. . . **79** CD74
Wharncliffe Gdns, SE25 . . **142** DS96
Wharncliffe Rd, SE25 . . . . **142** DS96
Wharton CI, NW10 . . . . **80** CS65
Wharton Cotts, WC1
  off Wharton St **83** DM69
Wharton Rd, Brom. BR1. . . . **144** EH95
Wharton St, WC1 . . . . **196** C3
Whateley Rd, SE20 . . . . . . **123** DX94
  SE22 . . . . **122** DT85
Whatley Av, SW20 . . . . . . **139** CY97
Whatman Rd, SE23 . . . . . . **123** DX87
Whatmore CI, Stai. TW19 . . **114** BG86
Wheatash Rd, Add. KT15 . . **134** BH103
Wheatcroft, Wal.Cr.
  (Chsht) EN7 . . . . **14** DV28
Wheatfields, E6
  off Oxleas **87** EP72
  Enfield EN3 . . . . **31** DY40
Wheatfield Way, Kings.T. KT1. **138** CL96
Wheathill Rd, SE20. . . . . . **142** DV97
Wheat Knoll, Ken. CR8 . . . **176** DQ116
Wheatlands, Houns. TW5. . . **96** CA79
Wheatlands Rd, SW17
  off Stapleton Rd **120** DG90
Wheatley CI, NW4 . . . . **43** CU54
  Greenhithe DA9
  off Steele Av **129** FU85
  Hornchurch RM11 . . . . . **72** FK57
Wheatley Cres, Hayes UB3 . . **77** BU73
Wheatley Gdns, N9 . . . . . . **46** DS47
Wheatley Ho, SW15
  off Tangley Gro **119** CU87
Wheatley Rd, Islw. TW7 . . . **97** CF83
Wheatley's Ait, Sun. TW16 . . **135** BU99
Wheatley St, W1 . . . . **194** G7
Wheatley Ter Rd, Erith DA8 . **107** FF79
Wheatley Way, Ger.Cr.
  (Chal.St.P.) SL9 . . . . **36** AY51
Wheat Sheaf CI, E14. . . . . **204** B8
Wheatsheaf CI, Cher.
  (Ott.) KT16 . . . . **151** BD107
  Northolt UB5. . . . . **60** BY64
  Woking GU21 . . . . **166** AY116
Wheatsheaf Hill, Sev.
  (Halst.) TN14 . . . . **164** EZ109
Wheatsheaf La, SW6 . . . . . **99** CW80
  SW8. . . . . **101** DL80
  Staines TW18. . . . . . . **113** BF94
Wheatsheaf Rd, Rom. RM1 . . **71** FF58
Wheatsheaf Ter, SW6 . . . . . **99** CZ80
Wheatstone CI, Mitch. CR4 . **140** DE95
  Slough SL3
  off Upton Ct Rd. **92** AU76
Wheatstone Rd, W10 . . . . . . **81** CY71
Wheeler Av, Oxt. RH8 . . . . **187** ED129
Wheeler CI, Wdf.Grn. IG8
  off Chigwell Rd **49** EM50
Wheeler Gdns, N1
  off Outram PI **83** DL67
Wheelers, Epp. CM16 . . . . . **17** ET29
Wheelers Cross, Bark. IG11 . . **87** ER68
Wheelers Dr, Ruis. HA4
  off Wallington CI **59** BQ58
Wheelers Fm Gdns, Epp.
  (N.Wld Bas.) CM16 . . . . . **19** FB26
Wheelers La, Epsom KT18 . . **156** CP113
Wheelers Orchard, Ger.Cr.
  (Chal.St.P.) SL9 . . . . **36** AY51
Wheel Fm Dr, Dag. RM10 . . . **71** FC62
Wheellock CI, Erith DA8
  off Ashfield Av **24** CB44
Wheelwright CI, Bushey WD23
  off Ashfield Av **24** CB44
Wheelwright St, N7 . . . . . . **83** DM66
Whelan Way, Wall. SM6 . . . **141** DK104
Wheler St, E1 . . . . **197** P5
Whellock Rd, W4 . . . . **98** CS76
WHELPLEY HILL, Chesh. HP5 . . **4** AX26
Whelpley Hill Pk, Chesh.
  (Whel.Hill) HP5 . . . . **4** AX26
Whenman Av, Bex. DA5 . . . **127** FC89
Whernside CI, SE28 . . . . . . **88** EW73
WHETSTONE, N20 . . . . **44** DB47
Whetstone CI, N20
  off Oakleigh Rd N. **44** DD47
Whetstone Pk, WC2 . . . . . **196** B8
Whetstone Rd, SE3. . . . . . **104** EJ82
Whewell Rd, N19 . . . . **65** DL61
Whichcote St, SE1 . . . . . . **200** D3
Whidborne CI, SE8
  off Cliff Ter **103** EA82
Whidborne St, WC1 . . . . . **196** A3
Whiffins Orchard, Epp.
  (Cooper.) CM16 . . . . **18** EX29
Whimbrel CI, SE28 . . . . **88** EW73
  South Croydon CR2 . . . . **160** DR111
Whimbrel Way, Hayes UB4 . . **78** BX72
Whinchat Rd, SE28. . . . . . **105** ER76
Whinfell CI, SW16. . . . . . . **121** DK92
Whinfell Way, Grav. DA12 . . **131** GM91
Whinyates Rd, SE9 . . . . . . **104** EL83

Whippendell CI, Orp. BR5 . . **146** EV95
Whippendell Hill, Kings L. WD4 . **6** BJ30
Whippendell Rd, Wat. WD18 . . **23** BU43
Whippendell Way, Orp. BR5 . . **146** EV95
Ⓗ Whipps Cross Hosp, E11 . **67** ED58
Whipps Cross Rd, E11 . . . . . **67** ED57
Whiskin St, EC1 . . . . **196** F3
Whisperwood, Rick.
  (Loud.) WD3 . . . . **22** BH41
Whisperwood CI, Har. HA3 . . **41** CE52
Whistler Gdns, Edg. HA8 . . . **42** CM54
Whistler Ms, SE15
  off Kelly Av **102** DT80
  Dagenham RM8 . . . . **70** EV64
Whistlers Av, SW11. . . . . . **100** DD80
Whistler St, N5 . . . . **65** DP63
Whiston Rd, E2. . . . . **84** DT68
Whitacre Ms, SE11
  off Stannary St **101** DN78
Whitakers Way, Loug. IG10 . . **33** EM39
Whitbread CI, N17 . . . . **46** DU53
Whitbread Rd, SE4 . . . . . . **103** DY84
Whitburn Rd, SE13 . . . . . . **103** EB84
Whitby Av, NW10 . . . . **80** CP69
Whitby CI, Green. DA9. . . . **129** FU85
  Westerham
  (Bigg.H.) TN16 . . . . . . **178** EH119
Whitby Gdns, NW9 . . . . **62** CN55
  Sutton SM1. . . . . **140** DD103
Whitby Rd, SE18. . . . . . . **105** EM77
  Harrow HA2 . . . . **60** CC62
  Ruislip HA4 . . . . **59** BV62
  Sutton SM1 . . . . **140** DD103
Whitby St, E1 . . . . **197** P4
Whitcher CI, SE14. . . . . . . **103** DY79
Whitcher PI, NW1
  off Rochester Rd **83** DJ66
Whitchurch Av, Edg. HA8 . . . **42** CM52
Whitchurch CI, Edg. HA8 . . . **42** CM51
Whitchurch Gdns, Edg. HA8 . . **42** CM51
Whitchurch La, Edg. HA8 . . . **41** CK52
Whitchurch Rd, W11 . . . . . . **81** CX73
  Romford RM3. . . . . **52** FK49
Whitcomb St, WC2
  off Whitcomb St **83** DK73
Whitcombe Ms, Rich. TW9 . . **98** CP81
Whitcomb St, WC2 . . . . . . **199** N1
Whiteadder Way, E14 . . . . **204** C8
Whitear Wk, E15. . . . . **85** ED65
White Av, Grav. (Nthflt) DA11. **131** GF90
Whitebarn La, Dag. RM10 . . . **88** FA67
Whitebeam Av, Brom. BR2. . **145** EN100
Whitebeam CI, SW9
  off Clapham Rd **101** DM80
  Radlett (Shenley) WD7
  off Mulberry Gdns **10** CM33
  Waltham Cross EN7
  off The Laurels **14** DS26
Whitebeam Dr, S.Ock. RM15 . **91** FW69
Whitebeams, Hat. AL10 . . . . **95** BS76
White Beams, St.Alb.
  (Park St) AL2 . . . . **8** CC28
White Beam Way, Tad. KT20 . **173** CU121
White Bear PI, NW3
  off New End Sq **64** DD63
White Br Av, Mitch. CR4 . . . **140** DD98
Whitebridge CI, Felt. TW14 . **115** BT86
White Butts Rd, Ruis. HA4 . . **60** BX62
WHITECHAPEL, E1 . . . . **84** DU72
Ⓣ Whitechapel **84** DU72
★ Whitechapel Art Gall, E1 . **84** DT72
Whitechapel High St, E1 . . . **84** DT72
Whitechapel Rd, E1 . . . . . . **84** DU72
White Ch La, E1 . . . . **84** DU72
White Ch Pas, E1
  off White Ch La **84** DU72
Ⓣ White City. **81** CW73
White City CI, W12 . . . . **81** CW73
White City Est, W12 . . . . . . **81** CV73
White City Rd, W12 . . . . . . **81** CV73
White Conduit St, N1
  off Chapel Mkt **83** DN68
Whitecote Rd, Sthl. UB1 . . . . **78** CB72
White Craig CI, Pnr. HA5 . . . **40** CA50
Whitecroft, Swan. BR8 . . . . **147** FE96
Whitecroft CI, Beck. BR3. . . **143** ED98
Whitecroft Way, Beck. BR3 . **143** EC99
Whitecross PI, EC2 . . . . . . **197** L6
Whitecross St, EC1. . . . . . **197** J4
Whitefield Av, NW2 . . . . **63** CW59
  Purley CR8 . . . . **175** DN116
Whitefield CI, SW15 . . . . . **119** CY86
  Orpington BR5 . . . . **146** EW97
Whitefields Rd, Wal.Cr.
  (Chsht) EN8. . . . . **14** DW28
Whitefoot La, Brom. BR1 . . **123** EC91
Whitefoot Ter, Brom. BR1 . . **124** EE90
Whiteford Rd, Slou. SL2. . . . **74** AS71
White Friars, Sev. TN13. . . . **190** FG127
Whitefriars Av, Har. HA3. . . . **41** CE54
Whitefriars Dr, Har. HA3. . . . **41** CD54
Whitefriars St, EC4. . . . . . **196** E9
White Gdns, Dag. RM10 . . . . **88** FA65
Whitegate Gdns, Har. HA3. . . **41** CF52
White Gates, Horn. RM12 . . . **72** FJ61
Whitegates, Whyt. CR3
  off Court Bushes Rd **176** DU119
  Woking GU22
  off Loop Rd. **167** AZ120
Whitegates CI, Rick.
  (Crox.Grn) WD3. . . . . . . **22** BN42
Whitegate Way, Tad. KT20 . . **173** CV120
Whitehall, SW1. . . . . **199** P2
White Hall, Rom. (Abridge) RM4
  off Market PI. **34** EV41
Whitehall CI, Chig. IG7. . . . . **50** EU48
  Uxbridge UB8. . . . . **76** BJ67
Whitehall Ct, SW1 . . . . . . **199** P3
Whitehall Cres, Chess. KT9 . **155** CK106
Whitehall Fm La, Vir.W. GU25 **132** AY96
Whitehall Gdns, E4. . . . . . . **48** EE46
  SW1 . . . . **199** P3
  W3. . . . . **80** CN74
  W4. . . . . **98** CP79
Whitehall La, Buck.H. IG9. . . **48** EG47
  Egham TW20. . . . . **113** AZ94
  Erith DA8. . . . . **107** FF82

Whitehall La, Grays RM17 . . **110** GC78
  Staines (Wrays.) TW19 . . **113** BA86
Whitehall Pk, N19. . . . . **65** DJ60
Whitehall Pk Rd, W4. . . . . . **98** CP79
Whitehall PI, E7
  off Station Rd **68** EG64
  SW1 . . . . **199** P3
  Wallington SM6
  off Bernard Rd **159** DH105
Whitehall Rd, E4. . . . . **48** EE47
  W7. . . . . **97** CG75
  Bromley BR2. . . . . **144** EK99
  Grays RM17. . . . . **110** GC77
  Harrow HA1 . . . . **61** CE59
  Thornton Heath CR7. . . . **141** DN99
  Uxbridge UB8. . . . . **76** BK67
  Woodford Green IG8 . . . . **48** EE47
Whitehall St, N17 . . . . **46** DT52
White Hart Ct, Ch.St.G. HP8 . **36** AU48
  Sevenoaks TN13 . . . . . **191** FJ128
White Hart Ct, EC2
  off Bishopsgate **84** DS72
  Woking (Ripley) GU23 . . **168** BJ121
⇌ White Hart Lane **46** DT52
White Hart La, N17 . . . . **46** DR53
  N22 . . . . **45** DN53
  NW10 off Church Rd **81** CT65
  SW13 . . . . **98** CS80
  Romford RM7 . . . . **50** FA53
White Hart Meadows, Wok.
  (Ripley) GU23 . . . . . . **168** BJ121
White Hart Rd, SE18. . . . . **105** ES77
  Orpington BR6 . . . . **146** EU101
White Hart Row, Cher. KT16
  off Heriot Rd **134** BG101
White Hart Slip, Brom. BR1
  off Market Sq **144** EG96
White Hart St, EC4 . . . . . . **196** G8
  SE11 . . . . **200** E10
White Hart Wd, Sev. TN13 . . **191** FJ129
White Hart Yd, SE1 . . . . . . **201** K3
Whitehaven, Slou. SL1 . . . . **74** AT73
Whitehaven CI, Brom. BR2. . **144** EG98
  Waltham Cross
  (Goffs Oak) EN7 . . . . **14** DS28
Whitehaven St, NW8 . . . . . **194** B5
Whitehead CI, N18 . . . . **46** DR50
  SW18. . . . . **120** DC87
  Dartford DA2. . . . . **128** FJ90
Whitehead's Gro, SW3 . . . . **198** C10
Whiteheart Av, Uxb. UB8 . . . **77** BQ71
Whitehead Rd, Ruis. HA4 . . . **59** BQ59
White Heron Ms, Tedd. TW11 . **117** CF93
White Hill, Couls.
  (Chipstead) CR5. . . . . . **174** DC124
  Northwood HA6 . . . . **38** BN51
  Rickmansworth WD3 . . . . **38** BN51
  South Croydon CR2
  off St. Mary's Rd. **160** DR109
Whitehill La, Grav. DA12 . . . **131** GK90
  Redhill (Bletch.) RH1. . . . **186** DR127
  Woking (Ockham) GU23 . . **169** BQ123
Whitehill Par, Grav. DA12. . **131** GJ90
Whitehill PI, Vir.W. GU25 . . . **132** AY99
  White Hill Rd, Chesh. HP5 . . . **4** AX26
Whitehill Rd, Dart. DA1 . . . **127** FG85
  Gravesend DA12. . . . . . **131** GJ89
Whitehills Rd, Loug. IG10. . . . **33** EN41
White Horse All, EC1 . . . . . **196** F6
White Horse Dr, Epsom
  KT18 . . . . **156** CQ114
Whitehorse Hill, Chis. BR7 . . **125** EN91
White Horse La, E1. . . . . **85** DX70
Whitehorse La, SE25 . . . . . **142** DR98
White Horse La, St.Alb.
  (Lon.Col.) AL2 . . . . **10** CL25
  Woking (Ripley) GU23 . . **168** BJ121
White Horse Ms, SE1 . . . . **200** E6
White Horse Rd, E1 . . . . **85** DY72
  E6 . . . . **87** EM69
Whitehorse Rd, Croy. CR0 . . **142** DR100
  Thornton Heath CR7. . . . **142** DR100
White Horse St, W1 . . . . . . **199** H3
White Horse Yd, EC2. . . . . **197** K8
Whitehouse Av, Borwd. WD6 . **26** CP41
White Ho CI, Ger.Cr.
  (Chal.St.P) SL9 . . . . **36** AY52
White Ho Dr, Stan. HA7 . . . . **41** CJ49
White Ho La, Abb.L.
  (Bedmond) WD5 . . . . **7** BV26
  Enfield EN2
  off Brigadier Hill **30** DQ39
White Ho La, Sev. TN14 . . . **190** FF130
White Ho Rd, Sev. TN14 . . . **190** FF130
Whitehouse Way, N14 . . . . . **45** DH47
  Iver SL0. . . . . **75** BD69
  Slough SL3. . . . . **92** AW76
Whitehurst Dr, N18 . . . . **47** DX50
White Kennett St, E1 . . . . . **197** N8
White Knights Rd,
  Wey. KT13 . . . . **153** BQ108
White Knobs Way, Cat. CR3 . **186** DU125
Whitelands Av, Rick.
  (Chorl.) WD3 . . . . **21** BC42
Whitelands Way, Rom. RM3. . **52** FK54
White La, Oxt. RH8. . . . . . . **178** EH123
  Warlingham CR6. . . . . . **178** EH123
Whitelegges, W13. . . . . **79** CJ72
Whitelegg Rd, E13 . . . . **86** EF68
Whiteley Rd, SE19 . . . . **122** DR92
Whiteleys Shop Cen, W2 . . . **82** DB72
Whiteleys Way, Felt. TW13 . . **116** CA90
WHITELEY VILLAGE, Walt.
  KT12 . . . . **153** BS110
White Lion CI, Amer. HP7. . . **20** AU39
White Lion Ct, EC3 . . . . . . **197** M9
White Lion Gate, Cob. KT11
  off Virginia PI. **153** BU114
White Lion Hill, EC4 . . . . . **196** G10
White Lion Rd, Amer. HP7 . . **20** AT38
White Lion St, N1. . . . . . . **196** C1
White Lo, SE19 . . . . **121** DP94
White Lo CI, N2 . . . . **64** DD58
  Isleworth TW7
  off Twickenham Rd **97** CG82
  Sevenoaks TN13 . . . . . **191** FH123
  Sutton SM2. . . . . **158** DC108

White Lyon Ct, EC2
  off Fann St **84** DQ70
White Lyons Rd, Brwd. CM14 . **54** FW47
White Oak Business Pk, Swan.
  BR8 off London Rd **147** FE97
White Oak Dr, Beck. BR3 . . **143** EC96
White Oak Gdns, Sid. DA15 . **125** ET87
White Oaks, Bans. SM7 . . . **158** DB113
Whiteoaks La, Grnf. UB6 . . . **79** CD68
White Orchards, N20 . . . . . . **43** CZ45
  Stanmore HA7 . . . . **41** CG50
White Post, Dart.
  (Fngham) DA4 . . . . **148** FN101
Whitepost Hill, Red. RH1 . . **184** DE134
White Post La, E9. . . . . **85** DZ66
  SE13 . . . . **103** EA83
White Post St, SE15 . . . . . **102** DW80
White Rd, E15. . . . . **86** EE66
  Betchworth RH3 . . . . . . **182** CN133
  Tadworth (Box H.) KT20 . **182** CN133
White Rose La, Wok. GU22 . **167** AZ117
Whites Av, Ilf. IG2 . . . . **69** ES58
Whites CI, Green. DA9 . . . . **129** FW86
Whites Grds, SE1 . . . . **201** N5
Whites Grds Est, SE1 . . . . **201** N4
White Shack La, Rick. WD3 . . **22** BM37
Whites La, Slou. (Datchet)
  SL3 . . . . **92** AV79
White's Row, E1 . . . . **197** P7
White's Sq, SW4
  off Nelson's Row **101** DK84
Whitestile Rd, Brent. TW8 . . **97** CJ78
Whitestone La, NW3
  off Heath St. **64** DC63
Whitestone Wk, NW3
  off North End Way **64** DC62
White St, Sthl. UB1 . . . . **96** BX75
White Swan Ms, W4
  off Bennett St **98** CS79
Whitethorn Av, Couls. CR5. . **174** DG115
  West Drayton UB7 . . . . . **76** BL73
Whitethorn Gdns, Croy. CR0 . **142** DV103
  Enfield EN2 . . . . **30** DR43
  Hornchurch RM11 . . . . . **72** FJ58
Whitethorn PI, West Dr. UB7
  off Whitethorn Av **76** BM74
Whitethorn St, E3 . . . . **85** EA70
Whiteways Ct, Stai. TW18
  off Pavilion Gdns. **114** BH94
Whitewebbs La, Enf. EN2. . . **30** DS35
Whitewebbs Pk, Enf. EN2 . . **30** DQ35
Whitewebbs Rd, Enf. EN2 . . **29** DP35
Whitewebbs Way, Orp. BR5 . **145** ET95
Whitewood Cotts, West.
  (Tats.) TN16 . . . . **178** EJ120
Whitfield CI, W1 . . . . **195** K5
Whitfield Rd, E6 . . . . **86** EJ66
  SE3 . . . . **103** ED81
  Bexleyheath DA7 . . . . . **106** EZ80
Whitfield St, W1 . . . . **195** M7
Whitfield Way, Rick.
  (Mill End) WD3 . . . . **37** BF46
Whitford Gdns, Mitch. CR4 . **140** DF97
Whitgift Av, S.Croy. CR2 . . **160** DQ106
Whitgift Cen, Croy. CR0 . . **142** DQ103
Whitgift Ho, SW11
  off Westbridge Rd **100** DE81
Whitgift St, SE11 . . . . **200** B8
  Croydon CR0. . . . . **142** DQ104
Whit Hern Ct, Wal.Cr. EN8
  off College Rd. **14** DW30
Whiting Av, Bark. IG11 . . . . **87** EP66
Whitings, Ilf. IG2. . . . . **69** ER57
Whitings Rd, Barn. EN5 . . . . **27** CW43
Whitings Way, E6 . . . . **87** EN71
Whitland Rd, Cars. SM5. . . **140** DD102
Whitlars Dr, Kings L. WD4 . . . **6** BM28
Whitley CI, Abb.L. WD5 . . . . . **7** BU32
  Staines (Stanw.) TW19 . . **114** BL86
Whitley Rd, N17. . . . . **46** DS54
Whitlock Dr, SW19 . . . . . . **119** CY87
Whitman Rd, E3
  off Mile End Rd **85** DY70
Whitmead CI, S.Croy. CR2 . . **160** DS107
Whitmore Av, Rom.
  (Harold Wd) RM3 . . . . . . **52** FL54
Whitmore CI, N11 . . . . **45** DH50
Whitmore Est, N1. . . . . **84** DS67
Whitmore Gdns, NW10 . . . . **81** CW68
Whitmore Rd, N1 . . . . **84** DS67
  Beckenham BR3 . . . . . . **143** DZ97
  Harrow HA1 . . . . **60** CC59
Whitmores CI, Epsom KT18 . **172** CQ115
Whitnell Way, SW15 . . . . . **119** CX85
Whitney Av, Ilf. IG4 . . . . **68** EK56
Whitney Rd, E10. . . . . **67** EB59
Whitney Wk, Sid. DA14 . . . **126** EY93
Whitstable CI, Beck. BR3 . . **143** DZ95
  Ruislip HA4
  off Chichester Av. **59** BS61
Whitstable Ho, W10 . . . . . . **81** CX72
Whitstable PI, Croy. CR0 . . **160** DQ105
Whitstone La, Beck. BR3 . . **143** EB99
Whittaker Av, Rich. TW9
  off Hill St **117** CK85
Whittaker Rd, E6 . . . . **86** EJ66
  Sutton SM3. . . . . **139** CZ104
Whittaker St, SW1 . . . . . . **198** F9
Whittaker Way, SE1 . . . . . **202** C9
Whitta Rd, E12 . . . . **68** EK63
Whittell Gdns, SE26 . . . . . **122** DW90
Whittenham CI, Slou. SL2 . . **74** AU74
Whittingstall Rd, SW6 . . . . **99** CZ81
Whittington Av, EC3. . . . . **197** M9
  Hayes UB4 . . . . **77** BT71
Whittington Ct, N2 . . . . **64** DF57
Ⓗ Whittington Hosp, N19 . . **65** DJ61
Whittington Ms, N12
  off Fredericks PI **44** DC49
Whittington Rd, N22 . . . . . **45** DL52
  Brentwood (Hutt.) CM13. . **55** GC44
Whittington Way, Pnr. HA5 . . **60** BY57
Whittlebury CI, Cars. SM5 . . **158** DF108
Whittle CI, E17 . . . . **67** DY58
  Southall UB1. . . . . **78** CB72

★ Place of interest   ⇌ Railway station   Ⓣ London Underground station   ⒹⓁⓇ Docklands Light Railway station   Ⓣⓡⓐ Tramlink station   Ⓗ Hospital   Ⓡⓘⓥ Pedestrian ferry landing stage

Whittle Cl, Watford WD25 off Ashfields 7 BT34
Whittle Rd, Houns. TW5 96 BW80
Southall UB2 off Post Rd 96 CB75
Whittlesea Cl, Har. HA3 40 CC52
Whittlesea Path, Har. HA3 40 CC53
Whittlesea Rd, Har. HA3 40 CC53
Whittlesey St, SE1 200 D3
WHITTON, Twick. TW2 116 CB87
≠ Whitton 116 CC87
Whitton Av E, Grnf. UB6 61 CE64
Whitton Av W, Grnf. UB6 60 CC64
Northolt UB5 60 CC64
Whitton Cl, Grnf. UB6 79 CH65
Whitton Dene, Houns. TW3 116 CB85
Isleworth TW7 117 CD85
Whitton Dr, Grnf. UB6 79 CG65
Whitton Manor Rd, Islw. TW7 116 CC85
Whitton Rd, Houns. TW3 96 CB84
Twickenham TW1, TW2 117 CF86
Whitton Wk, E3 85 EA68
Whitton Waye, Houns. TW3 116 CA86
Whitwell Rd, E13 86 EG69
Watford WD25 24 BX35
Whitworth Cresent, Enf. EN3 off Martini Dr 31 EA37
Whitworth Pl, SE18 105 EP77
Whitworth Rd, SE18 105 EN80
SE25 142 DS97
Whitworth St, SE10 205 J10
Whopshott Av, Wok. GU21 166 AW116
Whopshott Cl, Wok. GU21 166 AW116
Whopshott Dr, Wok. GU21 166 AW116
Whorlton Rd, SE15 102 DV83
Whybridge Cl, Rain. RM13 89 FE67
Whychcote Pt, NW2 off Claremont Rd 63 CW59
Whymark Av, N22 65 DN55
Whymark Cl, Rain. RM13 off Rainham Rd 89 FG68
Whytebeam Vw, Whyt. CR3 176 DT118
Whytecliffe Rd N, Pur. CR8 159 DP111
Whytecliffe Rd S, Pur. CR8 159 DN111
Whytecroft, Houns. TW5 96 BX80
WHYTELEAFE, Cat. CR3 176 DS118
≠ Whyteleafe 176 DT117
Whyteleafe Business Village, Whyt. CR3 off Whyteleafe Hill 176 DT118
Whyteleafe Hill, Whyt. CR3 176 DT118
Whyteleafe Rd, Cat. CR3 176 DS120
≠ Whyteleafe South 176 DU119
Whyteville Rd, E7 86 EH65
Wichling Cl, Orp. BR5 146 EX102
Wickenden Rd, Sev. TN13 191 FJ122
Wicken's Meadow, Sev. (Dunt.Grn) TN14 181 FF119
Wickersley Rd, SW11 100 DG82
Wickers Oake, SE19 122 DT91
Wicker St, E1 off Burslem St 84 DV72
Wicket, The, Croy. CR0 161 EA106
Wicket Rd, Grnf. UB6 79 CG69
Wickets, The, Ashf. TW15 114 BL91
Wickets End, Rad. (Shenley) WD7 10 CL33
Wickets Way, Ilf. IG6 49 ET51
Wickford Cl, Rom. RM3 off Wickford Dr 52 FM50
Wickford Dr, Rom. RM3 52 FM50
Wickford St, E1 84 DW70
Wickford Way, E17 67 DX56
Wickham Av, Croy. CR0 143 DY103
Sutton SM3 157 CW106
Wickham Chase, W.Wick. BR4 143 ED101
Wickham Cl, E1 84 DW71
Enfield EN3 30 DV41
New Malden KT3 139 CT99
Uxbridge (Hare.) UB9 38 BK53
Wickham Ct Rd, W.Wick. BR4 143 EC103
Wickham Cres, W.Wick. BR4 143 EC103
Wickham Fld, Sev. (Otford) TN14 181 FF116
Wickham Gdns, SE4 103 DZ83
Wickham La, SE2 106 EU78
Egham TW20 113 BA94
Welling DA16 106 EU78
Wickham Ms, SE4 103 DZ82
Wickham Rd, E4 47 EC52
SE4 103 DZ84
Beckenham BR3 143 EB96
Croydon CR0 143 DX103
Grays RM16 111 GJ75
Harrow HA3 41 CD54
Wickham St, SE11 200 B10
Welling DA16 105 ES82
Wickham Way, Beck. BR3 143 EC98
Wick La, E3 85 EA68
Egham (Eng.Grn) TW20 112 AT92
Wickliffe Av, N3 43 CY54
Wickliffe Gdns, Wem. HA9 62 CP61
Wicklow St, WC1 196 B2
Wick Rd, E9 85 DX65
Egham (Eng.Grn) TW20 112 AV94
Teddington TW11 117 CH94
Wicks Cl, SE9 124 EK91
Wicksteed Cl, Bex. DA5 127 FD90
Wicksteed Ho, Brent. TW8 off Green Dragon La 98 CM78
Wickwood St, SE5 101 DP82
Wid Cl, Brwd. (Hutt.) CM13 55 GD43
Widdecombe Av, Har. HA2 60 BY61
Widdenham Rd, N7 65 DM63
Widdin St, E15 85 ED66
Widecombe Cl, Rom. RM3 52 FK53
Widecombe Gdns, Ilf. IG4 68 EL56
Widecombe Rd, SE9 124 EL90
Widecombe Way, N2 64 DD57
Widecroft Rd, Iver SL0 75 BE72
Widegate St, E1 197 N7
Widenham Cl, Pnr. HA5 off Bridle Rd 60 BW57
Wide Way, Mitch. CR4 141 DK97
Widewing Cl, Tedd. TW11 117 CH94
Widgeon Cl, E16 off Maplin Rd 86 EH72
Widgeon Rd, Erith DA8 107 FH80
Widgeon Way, Wat. WD25 24 BY36
Widley Rd, W9 82 DA69
WIDMORE, Brom. BR1 144 EH97
WIDMORE GREEN, Brom. BR1 144 EJ95
Widmore Lo Rd, Brom. BR1 144 EK96
Widmore Rd, Brom. BR1 144 EG96
Uxbridge UB8 77 BP70
Widworthy Hayes, Brwd. (Hutt.) CM13 55 GB46
Wieland Rd, Nthwd. HA6 39 BU52
Wigan Ho, E5 off Warwick Gro 66 DV60
Wigeon Path, SE28 105 ER76
Wigeon Way, Hayes UB4 78 BX72
Wiggenhall Rd, Wat. WD18 23 BV43
Wiggie La, Red. RH1 184 DG132
Wiggins La, Rich. TW10 117 CJ89
Wiggins Mead, NW9 43 CT52
Wigginton Av, Wem. HA9 80 CP65
Wigham Ho, Bark. IG11 87 EQ66
Wightman Rd, N4 65 DN57
N8 65 DN56
Wigley Bush La, Brwd. (S.Wld) CM14 54 FS47
Wigley Rd, Felt. TW13 116 BX88
Wigmore Ct, W13 off Singapore Rd 79 CG74
Wigmore Pl, W1 195 H8
Wigmore Rd, Cars. SM5 140 DD103
Wigmore St, W1 194 F9
Wigmore Wk, Cars. SM5 140 DD103
Wigram Rd, E11 68 EJ58
Wigram Sq, E17 47 EC54
Wigston Cl, N18 46 DS50
Wigston Rd, E13 86 EH70
Wigton Gdns, Stan. HA7 42 CL53
Wigton Pl, SE11 off Milverton St 101 DN78
Wigton Rd, E17 47 DZ53
Romford RM3 52 FL49
Wigton Way, Rom. RM3 52 FL49
Wilberforce Rd, N4 65 DP61
NW9 63 CU58
Wilberforce Way, SW19 119 CX93
Gravesend DA12 131 GK92
Wilbraham Pl, SW1 198 E8
Wilbury Av, Sutt. SM2 157 CZ110
Wilbury Rd, Wok. GU21 166 AX117
Wilbury Way, N18 46 DR50
Wilby Ms, W11 81 CZ74
Wilcon Way, Wat. WD25 8 BX34
Wilcot Av, Wat. WD19 40 BY45
Wilcot Cl, Wat. WD19 off Wilcot Av 40 BY45
Wilcox Cl, SW8 101 DL80
Borehamwood WD6 26 CQ39
Wilcox Gdns, Shep. TW17 134 BM97
Wilcox Pl, SW1 199 L7
Wilcox Rd, SW8 101 DL80
Sutton SM1 158 DB105
Teddington TW11 117 CD91
Wildacres, Nthwd. HA6 39 BT49
West Byfleet KT14 152 BJ111
Wildbank Ct, Wok. GU22 off White Rose La 167 AZ118
Wild Ct, WC2 196 B8
Wildcroft Gdns, Edg. HA8 41 CK51
Wildcroft Rd, SW15 119 CW87
Wilde Cl, E8 84 DU67
Tilbury RM18 off Coleridge Rd 111 GJ82
Wilde Pl, N13 off Medesenge Way 45 DP51
SW18 off Heathfield Rd 120 DD87
Wilder Cl, Ruis. HA4 59 BV60
Wilderness, The, E.Mol. KT8 136 CC99
Hampton (Hmptn H.) TW12 off Park Rd 116 CB91
WILDERNESSE, Sev. TN15 191 FL122
Wildernesse Av, Sev. (Seal) TN15 191 FL122
Wildernesse Mt, Sev. TN13 191 FK122
Wilderness Ms, SW4 off The Chase 101 DH84
Wilderness Rd, Chis. BR7 125 EP94
Oxted RH8 188 EE130
Wilde Rd, Erith DA8 107 FB80
Wilders Cl, Wok. GU21 166 AW118
Wilderton Rd, N16 66 DS59
Wildfell Rd, SE6 123 EB87
Wild Goose Dr, SE14 102 DW81
Wild Grn N, Slou. SL3 off Verney Rd 93 BA77
Wild Grn S, Slou. SL3 off Swabey Rd 93 BA77
Wild Hatch, NW11 64 DA58
Wild Oaks Cl, Nthwd. HA6 39 BT51
Wild's Rents, SE1 201 M6
Wild St, WC2 196 A9
Wildwood, Nthwd. HA6 39 BR51
Wildwood Av, St.Alb. (Brick.Wd) AL2 8 BZ30
Wildwood Cl, SE12 124 EF87
Woking GU22 167 BF115
Wildwood Ct, Ken. CR8 176 DR115
Wildwood Gro, NW3 off North End Way 64 DC60
Wildwood Ri, NW11 64 DC60
Wildwood Rd, NW11 64 DC59
Wildwood Ter, NW3 64 DC60
Wilford Cl, Enf. EN2 30 DR41
Northwood HA6 39 BR52
Wilford Rd, Slou. SL3 93 AZ77
Wilfred Av, Rain. RM13 89 FG71
Wilfred Owen Cl, SW19 off Tennyson Rd 120 DC93
Wilfred St, SW1 199 K6
Gravesend DA12 131 GH86
Woking GU21 166 AX118
Wilfred Turney Est, W6 off Hammersmith Gro 99 CW76
Wilfrid Gdns, W3 80 CQ71
Wilhelmina Av, Couls. CR5 175 DJ119
Wilkes Rd, Brent. TW8 98 CL79
Brentwood (Hutt.) CM13 55 GD43
Wilkes St, E1 84 DT71
Wilkie Way, SE22 off Lordship La 122 DU88
Wilkins Cl, Hayes UB3 95 BT78
Mitcham CR4 140 DE95
Wilkinson Cl, Dart. DA1 108 FM84
Uxbridge UB10 77 BP67
Waltham Cross (Chsht) EN7 14 DQ26
Wilkinson Rd, E16 86 EJ72
Wilkinson St, SW8 101 DM80
Wilkinson Way, W4 98 CR75
Wilkin St, NW5 83 DH65
Wilkin St Ms, NW5 off Wilkin St 83 DH65
Wilkins Way, West. (Brasted) TN16 180 EV124
Wilks Av, Dart. DA1 128 FM89
Wilks Gdns, Croy. CR0 143 DY102
Wilks Pl, N1 197 N1
Willan Rd, N17 46 DR54
Willan Wall, E16 off Victoria Dock Rd 86 EF73
Willard St, SW8 101 DH83
Willats Cl, Cher. KT16 off Alwyns La 133 BF100
Willcocks Cl, Chess. KT9 138 CL104
Willcott Rd, W3 80 CP74
Will Crooks Gdns, SE9 104 EJ84
Willen Fld Rd, NW10 80 CQ68
Willenhall Av, Barn. EN5 28 DC44
Willenhall Dr, Hayes UB3 77 BS73
Willenhall Rd, SE18 105 EP78
Willersley Av, Orp. BR6 145 ER104
Sidcup DA15 125 ET88
Willersley Cl, Sid. DA15 125 ET88
WILLESDEN, NW10 81 CT65
H Willesden Comm Hosp, NW10 81 CU66
WILLESDEN GREEN, NW10 81 CV66
⊖ Willesden Green 81 CW65
≠ Willesden Junction 81 CT69
⊖ Willesden Junction 81 CT69
Willesden La, NW2 81 CX65
NW6 81 CX65
Willes Rd, NW5 83 DH65
Willett Cl, Nthlt. UB5 off Broomcroft Av 78 BW69
Orpington BR5 145 ES100
Willett Ho, E13 off Queens Rd W 86 EG68
Willett Pl, Th.Hth. CR7 off Willett Rd 141 DN99
Willett Rd, Th.Hth. CR7 141 DN99
Willetts La, Uxb. (Denh.) UB9 57 BF63
Willett Way, Orp. BR5 145 ER99
Willey Broom La, Cat. CR3 185 DN125
Willey Fm La, Cat. CR3 186 DQ126
Willey La, Cat. CR3 186 DR125
William Barefoot Dr, SE9 125 EN91
William Bonney Est, SW4 101 DK84
William Booth Rd, SE20 142 DU95
William Carey Way, Har. HA1 61 CE59
William Cl, N2 off King St 64 DD55
SE13 103 EC82
Romford RM5 51 FC53
Southall UB2 off Windmill Av 96 CC75
William Cory Prom, Erith DA8 107 FE78
William Covell Cl, Enf. EN2 29 DM38
William Dr, Stan. HA7 41 CH50
William Dunbar Ho, NW6 81 CZ68
William Dyce Ms, SW16 off Babington Rd 121 DK91
William Ellis Cl, Wind. (Old Wind.) SL4 112 AU85
William Ellis Way, SE16 202 C7
William Evans Rd, Epsom KT19 156 CN111
William IV St, WC2 199 P1
William Gdns, SW15 119 CV85
William Guy Gdns, E3 off Talwin St 85 EB69
William Harvey Ho, SW19 off Whitlock Dr 119 CY88
William Henry Wk, SW8 off Nine Elms La 101 DK79
William Margrie Cl, SE15 off Moncrieff St 102 DU82
William Ms, SW1 198 E5
William Morley Cl, E6 86 EK67
William Morris Cl, E17 67 DZ55
★ William Morris Gall, Lloyd Pk, E17 67 EA55
William Morris Way, SW6 100 DC83
William Nash Ct, Orp. BR5 off Brantwood Way 146 EW97
William Perkin Ct, Grnf. UB6 off Greenford Rd 79 CE65
William Pl, E3 off Roman Rd 85 DZ68
William Rd, NW1 195 J3
SW19 119 CY94
Caterham CR3 176 DR122
Sutton SM1 158 DC106
William Russell Ct, Wok. GU21 off Raglan Rd 166 AS118
Williams Av, E17 47 DZ53
William Saville Ho, NW6 81 CZ68
Williams Bldgs, E2 84 DW70
Williams Cl, N8 off Coolhurst Rd 65 DK58
SW6 off Pellant Rd 99 CY80
Addlestone KT15 off Monks Cres 152 BH106
Williams Dr, Houns. TW3 off Hibernia Rd 96 CA84
Williams Gro, N22 45 DN53
Surbiton KT6 137 CJ100
William's La, SW14 98 CQ83
Williams La, Mord. SM4 140 DC99
Williamson Cl, SE10 205 K10
Williamson Rd, N4 65 DP58
Williamson St, N7 65 DL63
Williamson Way, NW7 43 CY51
Rickmansworth WD3 38 BG46
William Sq, SE16 203 L1
Williams Rd, W13 79 CG73
Southall UB2 96 BY77
Williams Ter, Croy. CR0 159 DN107
William St, E10 67 EB58
N17 46 DT52
William St, SW1 198 E5
Barking IG11 87 EQ66
Bushey WD23 24 BX41
Carshalton SM5 140 DE104
Gravesend DA12 131 GH87
Grays RM17 110 GB79
Slough SL1 74 AT74
Williams Way, Dart. DA2 off Old Bexley La 127 FE89
Radlett WD7 25 CJ35
Willifield Way, NW11 63 CZ56
Willingale Cl, Brwd. (Hutt.) CM13 off Fairview Av 55 GE44
Loughton IG10 off Willingale Rd 33 EQ40
Woodford Green IG8 48 EK51
Willingale Rd, Loug. IG10 33 EQ41
Willingdon Rd, N22 45 DP54
Willinghall Cl, Wal.Abb. EN9 15 ED32
Willingham Cl, NW5 off Leighton Rd 65 DJ64
Willingham Ter, NW5 off Leighton Rd 65 DJ64
Willingham Way, Kings.T. KT1 138 CN97
Willington Ct, E5 off Mandeville St 67 DY62
Willington Rd, SW9 101 DL83
Willis Av, Sutt. SM2 158 DE107
Willis Cl, Epsom KT18 156 CP113
Willis Ho, E12 off Grantham Rd 69 EN62
Willis Rd, E15 86 EF67
Croydon CR0 142 DQ101
Erith DA8 107 FC77
Willis St, E14 85 EB72
Willmore End, SW19 140 DB95
Willoughby Av, Croy. CR0 159 DM105
Willoughby Ct, St.Alb. (Lon.Col.) AL2 9 CK26
Willoughby Dr, Rain. RM13 89 FE66
Willoughby Gro, N17 46 DV52
Willoughby Ho, EC2 off The Barbican 84 DQ71
Willoughby La, N17 46 DV52
Willoughby Ms, SW4 off Wixs La 101 DH84
Willoughby Pk Rd, N17 46 DV52
Willoughby Pas, E14 203 P2
Willoughby Rd, N8 65 DN55
NW3 64 DD63
Kingston upon Thames KT2 138 CM95
Slough SL3 93 BA76
Twickenham TW1 117 CK86
Willoughbys, The, SW14 off Upper Richmond Rd W 98 CS84
Willoughby St, WC1 195 P7
Willoughby Way, SE7 205 P8
Willow Av, SW13 99 CT82
Sidcup DA15 126 EU86
Swanley BR8 147 FF97
Uxbridge (Denh.) UB9 58 BJ64
West Drayton UB7 76 BM73
Willow Bk, SW6 99 CY83
Richmond TW10 117 CH90
Woking GU22 166 AY122
Willowbank Gdns, Tad. KT20 173 CV122
Willowbank Pl, Pur. CR8 off Kingsdown Av 159 DP109
Willowbay Cl, Barn. EN5 off Chesterfield Rd 27 CX44
Willow Br Rd, N1 84 DQ65
Willowbrook Est, SE15 off Sumner Rd 102 DT80
Willowbrook Rd, SE15 102 DT79
Southall UB2 96 CA76
Staines TW19 114 BL89
Willow Business Cen, Mitch. CR4 off Willow La 140 DF99
Willow Cl, Add. (Wdhm) KT15 151 BF111
Bexley DA5 126 EZ86
Brentford TW8 97 CJ79
Brentwood (Hutt.) CM13 55 GB44
Bromley BR2 145 EM99
Buckhurst Hill IG9 48 EK48
Erith DA8 off Willow Rd 107 FG81
Hornchurch RM12 71 FH62
Orpington BR5 146 EV101
Slough (Colnbr.) SL3 93 BC80
Thornton Heath CR7 141 DP100
Waltham Cross (Chsht) EN7 14 DS26
Willow Cotts, Mitch. CR4 141 DJ97
Richmond TW9 off Kew Grn 98 CN79
Willow Ct, EC2 197 M4
Edgware HA8 42 CL49
Willowcourt Av, Har. HA3 61 CH57
Willow Cres E, Uxb. (Denh.) UB9 58 BJ64
Willow Cres W, Uxb. (Denh.) UB9 58 BJ64
Willowdene, N6 off Denewood Rd 64 DF59
Brentwood (Pilg.Hat.) CM15 54 FT43
Willow Dene, Bushey (Bushey Hth) WD23 41 CE45
Pinner HA5 40 BX54
Willowdene, Wal.Cr. EN8 15 DY27
Willowdene Cl, Twick. TW2 116 CC87
Willowdene Ct, Brwd. CM14 54 FW49
Willow Dr, Barn. EN5 27 CY42
Woking (Ripley) GU23 168 BG124
Willow Edge, Kings L. WD4 6 BN29
Willow End, N20 44 DA47
Northwood HA6 39 BU51
Surbiton KT6 138 CL102
Willow Fm La, SW15 off Queens Ride 99 CV83
Willowfield Cl, SE18 105 ES78
Willow Gdns, Houns. TW3 96 CA81
Ruislip HA4 59 BT61
Willow Grn, NW9 off Clayton Fld 42 CS53
Borehamwood WD6 26 CR43
Willow Gro, E13 off Libra Rd 86 EG68
Chislehurst BR7 125 EN93
Ruislip HA4 59 BT61
Willowhayne Dr, Walt. KT12 135 BV101
Willowhayne Gdns, Wor.Pk. KT4 139 CW104
Willowherb Wk, Rom. RM3 off Clematis Cl 52 FJ52
Willow La, SE18 105 EM77
Amersham HP7 20 AT41
Mitcham CR4 140 DF99
Watford WD18 23 BU43
Willow Mead, Chig. IG7 50 EU48
Willowmead, Stai. TW18 off Northfield Rd 134 BH95
Willowmead Cl, W5 79 CK71
Woking GU21 166 AU116
Willowmere, Esher KT10 154 CC105
Willow Mt, Croy. CR0 off Langton Way 142 DS104
Willow Pk, Sev. (Otford) TN14 181 FF117
Slough (Stoke P.) SL2 74 AU66
Willow Path, Wal.Abb. EN9 16 EE34
Willow Pl, SW1 199 L8
Willow Rd, NW3 64 DD63
W5 98 CL75
Dartford DA1 128 FJ88
Enfield EN1 30 DS41
Erith DA8 107 FG81
New Malden KT3 138 CQ98
Romford RM6 70 EY58
Slough (Colnbr.) SL3 93 BE82
Wallington SM6 159 DH108
Willows, The, Buck.H. IG9 48 EK48
Esher (Clay.) KT10 off Albany Cres 155 CE107
Grays RM17 110 GE79
Rickmansworth (Mill End) WD3 off Uxbridge Rd 38 BG47
Watford WD19 off Brookside Rd 39 BV45
West Byfleet (Byfleet) KT14 152 BL113
Weybridge KT13 134 BN104
Willows Av, Mord. SM4 140 DB99
Willows Cl, Pnr. HA5 40 BW54
Willowside, St.Alb. (Lon.Col.) AL2 10 CL27
Willows Path, Epsom KT18 156 CP114
Willow St, E4 47 ED45
EC2 197 M4
Romford RM7 71 FC56
Willow Tree Cl, E3 off Birdsfield La 85 DZ67
SW18 off Cargill Rd 120 DB88
Hayes UB4 78 BW70
Romford (Abridge) RM4 34 EV41
Uxbridge UB10 59 BQ62
Willow Tree La, Hayes UB4 78 BW70
Willowtree Marina, Hayes UB4 78 BY72
Willow Tree Wk, Brom. BR1 144 EH95
Willowtree Way, Th.Hth. CR7 off Kensington Av 141 DN95
Willow Vale, W12 81 CU74
Chislehurst BR7 125 EP93
Leatherhead (Fetch.) KT22 170 CB123
Willow Vw, SW19 140 DD95
Willow Wk, E17 67 DZ57
N2 44 DD54
N15 65 DP56
N21 29 DM44
SE1 201 N8
Chertsey KT16 134 BG101
Dartford DA1 128 FJ85
Egham (Eng.Grn) TW20 112 AW92
Orpington BR6 145 EP104
Sutton SM3 139 CZ104
Tadworth (Box H.) KT20 off Oak Dr 182 CQ130
Upminster RM14 73 FS60
Willow Way, N3 44 DB52
SE26 122 DV90
W11 off Freston Rd 81 CX74
Epsom KT19 156 CR107
Godstone RH9 186 DV132
Potters Bar EN6 12 DB33
Radlett WD7 25 CE36
Romford RM3 52 FP51
St. Albans AL2 8 CA27
Sunbury-on-Thames TW16 135 BU98
Tadworth (Box H.) KT20 off Oak Dr 182 CP130
Twickenham TW2 116 CB89
Wembley HA0 61 CG62
West Byfleet KT14 152 BJ111
Woking GU22 166 AX121
Willow Wd Cres, SE25 142 DS100
Willrose Cres, SE2 106 EW78
Wills Cres, Houns. TW3 116 CB86
Wills Gro, NW7 43 CU50
Willson Rd, Egh. (Eng.Grn) TW20 112 AV92
Wilman Gro, E8 84 DU66
Wilmar Cl, Hayes UB4 77 BR70
Uxbridge UB8 76 BK66
Wilmar Gdns, W.Wick. BR4 143 EB102
Wilmcote Ho, W2 82 DB71
Wilmer Cl, Kings.T. KT2 118 CM92
Wilmer Cres, Kings.T. KT2 118 CM92
Wilmer Gdns, N1 84 DS67
Wilmerhatch La, Epsom KT18 172 CP118
Wilmer Lea Cl, E15 85 EC66
Wilmer Pl, N16 off Stoke Newington Ch St 66 DT61
Wilmer Way, N14 45 DK50
WILMINGTON, Dart. DA2 128 FK91
Wilmington Av, W4 98 CR80
Orpington BR6 146 EW103
Wilmington Ct Rd, Dart. DA2 127 FG90
Wilmington Gdns, Bark. IG11 87 ER65
Wilmington Sq, WC1 196 D3
Wilmington St, WC1 196 D3
Wilmot Cl, N2 44 DC54
SE15 102 DU80
Wilmot Grn, Brwd. (Gt Warley) CM13 53 FW51
Wilmot Pl, NW1 83 DJ66
W7 off Boston Rd 79 CE74
Wilmot Rd, E10 67 EB61
N17 66 DR55
Carshalton SM5 158 DF106
Dartford DA1 127 FH85
Purley CR8 159 DN112

★ Place of interest ≠ Railway station ⊖ London Underground station DLR Docklands Light Railway station Tra Tramlink station H Hospital Riv Pedestrian ferry landing stage

346

Wilmots Cl, Reig. RH2 184 DC133
Wilmot St, E2 84 DV70
Wilmot Way, Bans. SM7 158 DA114
Wilmount St, SE18 105 EP77
Wilna Rd, SW18 120 DC87
Wilsham St, W11 81 CX74
Wilshaw Cl, NW4 63 CU55
Wilshaw St, SE14 103 EA81
Wilsman Rd, S.Ock. RM15 91 FW68
Wilsmere Dr, Har. HA3 41 CF52
Northolt UB5 78 BY65
Wilson Av, Mitch. CR4 120 DE94
Wilson Cl, S.Croy. CR2
off Bartlett St 160 DR106
Wembley HA9 62 CM59
Wilson Dr, Cher. (Ott.) KT16 151 BB106
Wembley HA9 62 CM59
Wilson Gdns, Har. HA1 60 CC59
Wilson Gro, SE16 202 D5
Wilson La, Dart. DA4 149 FT96
Wilson Rd, E6 86 EK69
SE5 102 DS81
Chessington KT9 156 CM107
Ilford IG1 69 EM59
Wilsons, Tad. KT20
off Heathcote 173 CX121
Wilsons Pl, E14
off Salmon La 85 DZ72
Wilsons Rd, W6 99 CX78
Wilson St, E17 67 EC57
EC2 197 L6
N21 45 DN45
Wilson Way, Wok. GU21 166 AX116
Wilstone Cl, Hayes UB4
off Kingsash Dr 78 BY70
Wilthorne Gdns, Dag. RM10
off Acre Rd 89 FB66
Wilton Av, W4 98 CS78
Wilton Cl, West Dr. UB7 94 BK79
Wilton Cres, SW1 198 F5
SW19 139 CZ95
Wilton Dr, Rom. RM5 51 FC52
Wilton Gdns, Walt. KT12 136 BX102
West Molesey KT8 136 CA97
Wilton Gro, SW19 139 CZ95
New Malden KT3 139 CT100
Wilton Ms, SW1 198 G6
Wilton Par, Felt. TW13
off Highfield Rd 115 BU89
Wilton Pk Ct, SE18
off Prince Imperial Rd 105 EN81
Wilton Pl, SW1 198 F5
Addlestone
(New Haw) KT15 152 BK109
Wilton Rd, N10 44 DG54
SE2 106 EW76
SW1 199 J7
SW19 120 DE94
Barnet (Cockfos.) EN4 28 DF42
Hounslow TW4 96 BX83
Ilford IG1 *off Ilford La* 69 EP62
Wilton Row, SW1 198 F5
Wilton Sq, N1 84 DR67
Wilton St, SW1 199 H6
Wilton Ter, SW1 198 F6
Wilton Vil, N1 84 DR67
Wilton Way, E8 84 DU65
Wiltshire Av, Horn. RM11 72 FM56
Wiltshire Cl, NW7 43 CT50
SW3 198 D8
Dartford DA2 129 FR87
Wiltshire Gdns, N4 66 DQ58
Twickenham TW2 116 CC88
Wiltshire La, Pnr. HA5 59 BT55
Wiltshire Rd, SW9 101 DN83
Orpington BR6 146 EU101
Thornton Heath CR7 141 DN97
Wiltshire Row, N1 84 DR67
Wilverley Cres, N.Mal. KT3 138 CS100
Wimbart Rd, SW2 121 DM87
WIMBLEDON, SW19 119 CY93
⇌ **Wimbledon** 119 CZ93
⊖ **Wimbledon** 119 CZ93
Tram **Wimbledon** 119 CZ93
★ **Wimbledon (All England Tenn & Croquet Club)**, SW19 119 CY91
Wimbledon Br, SW19 119 CZ93
⇌ **Wimbledon Chase** 139 CY96
★ **Wimbledon Common**, SW19 119 CT91
Wimbledon Common, SW19 119 CU91
Wimbledon Hill Rd, SW19 119 CY93
WIMBLEDON PARK, SW19 119 CZ90
⊖ **Wimbledon Park** 120 DA90
Wimbledon Pk, SW19 119 CZ89
Wimbledon Pk Est, SW19 119 CY88
Wimbledon Pk Rd, SW18 119 CZ87
SW19 119 CZ88
Wimbledon Pk Side, SW19 119 CX89
Wimbledon Rd, SW17 120 DC91
Wimbledon Stadium Business Cen, SW17
off Riverside Rd 120 DB90
★ **Wimbledon Windmill Mus**, SW19 119 CV89
Wimbolt St, E2 84 DU69
Wimborne Av, Hayes UB4 77 BV72
Southall UB2 96 CA77
Wimborne Cl, SE12 124 EF85
Buckhurst Hill IG9 48 EH47
Epsom KT17 156 CS113
Worcester Park KT4 139 CW102
Wimborne Dr, NW9 62 CN55
Pinner HA5 60 BX59
Wimborne Gdns, W13 79 CH72
Wimborne Gro, Wat. WD17 23 BS37
Wimborne Rd, N9 46 DU47
N17 46 DS54
Wimborne Way, Beck. BR3 143 DX97
Wimbourne Av, Chis. BR7 145 ET98
Orpington BR5 145 ET98
Wimbourne Ct, N1
off Wimbourne St 84 DR68
Wimbourne St, N1 84 DR68
Wimpole Cl, Brom. BR2 144 EJ98
Kingston upon Thames KT1 138 CM96
Wimpole Ms, W1 195 H6
Wimpole Rd, West Dr. UB7 76 BK74
Wimpole St, W1 195 H8
Wimshurst Cl, Croy. CR0 141 DL102
Winans Wk, SW9 101 DN82
Wincanton Cres, Nthlt. UB5 60 CA64
Wincanton Gdns, Ilf. IG6 69 EP55
Wincanton Rd, SW18 119 CZ87
Romford RM3 52 FK48
Winchcombe Rd, Cars. SM5 140 DD101
Winchcomb Gdns, SE9 104 EK83
Winchelsea Av, Bexh. DA7 106 EZ80
Winchelsea Cl, SW15 119 CX85
Winchelsea Rd, E7 68 EG62
N17 66 DS55
NW10 80 CR67
Winchelsey Ri, S.Croy. CR2 160 DT107
Winchendon Rd, SW6 99 CZ80
Teddington TW11 117 CD91
Winchester Av, NW6 81 CY67
NW9 62 CN55
Hounslow TW5 96 BZ79
Upminster RM14 73 FT60
Winchester Cl, E6
off Boultwood Rd 86 EL72
SE17 200 G9
Amersham HP7 20 AS39
Bromley BR2 144 EF97
Enfield EN1 30 DS43
Esher KT10 154 CA105
Kingston upon Thames KT2 118 CP94
Slough (Colnbr.) SL3 93 BE81
Winchester Ct, E17
off Billet Rd 47 DY53
Winchester Cres, Grav. DA12 131 GK90
Winchester Dr, Pnr. HA5 60 BX57
Winchester Gro, Sev. TN13 191 FH123
Winchester Ho, SE18
off Shooter's Hill Rd 104 EK80
Winchester Ms, NW3
off Winchester Rd 82 DD66
Winchester Pk, Brom. BR2 144 EF97
Winchester Pl, E8
off Kingsland High St 66 DT64
N6 65 DH60
W3 *off Avenue Rd* 98 CQ75
Winchester Rd, E4 47 EC52
N6 65 DH60
N9 46 DU46
NW3 82 DD66
Bexleyheath DA7 106 EX82
Bromley BR2 144 EF97
Feltham TW13 116 BZ90
Harrow HA3 62 CL56
Hayes UB3 95 BS80
Ilford IG1 69 ER62
Northwood HA6 59 BT55
Orpington BR6 164 EW105
Twickenham TW1 117 CH86
Walton-on-Thames KT12 135 BU102
Winchester Sq, SE1 201 K2
Winchester St, SW1 199 J10
W3 80 CQ74
Winchester Wk, SE1 201 K2
Winchester Way, Rick. (Crox.Grn) WD3 23 BP43
Winchet Wk, Croy. CR0 142 DW100
Winchfield Cl, Har. HA3 61 CJ58
Winchfield Ho, SW15
off Highcliffe Dr 119 CT86
Winchfield Rd, SE26 123 DY92
Winchfield Way, Rick. WD3 38 BJ45
Winchilsea Cres, W.Mol. KT8 136 CC96
WINCHMORE HILL, N21 45 DM45
⇌ **Winchmore Hill** 45 DN46
Winchmore Hill Rd, N14 45 DK46
N21 45 DK46
Winchstone Cl, Shep. TW17 134 BM98
Winckley Cl, Har. HA3 62 CM57
Wincott St, SE11 200 E8
Wincrofts Dr, SE9 105 ER84
Windall Cl, SE19 142 DU95
Windborough Rd, Cars. SM5 158 DG108
Windermere Av, N3 64 DA55
NW6 81 CY67
SW19 140 DB97
Harrow HA3 61 CJ59
Hornchurch RM12 71 FG64
Ruislip HA4 60 BW59
Wembley HA9 61 CJ59
Windermere Cl, Dart. DA1 127 FH88
Egham TW20
off Derwent Rd 113 BB94
Feltham TW14 115 BT88
Orpington BR6 145 EP104
Rickmansworth (Chorl.) WD3 21 BC43
Staines TW19 *off Viola Av* 114 BL88
Windermere Ct, SW13 99 CT79
Kenley CR8 175 DP115
Wembley HA9
off Windermere Av 61 CJ59
Windermere Gdns, Ilf. IG4 68 EL57
Windermere Gro, Wem. HA9
off Windermere Av 61 CJ60
Windermere Ho, Islw. TW7
off Summerwood Rd 117 CF85
Windermere Pt, SE15
off Ilderton Rd 102 DW80
Windermere Rd, N10 45 DH53
N19 *off Holloway Rd* 65 DJ61
SW15 118 CS91
SW16 141 DJ95
W5 97 CJ76
Bexleyheath DA7 107 FC82
Coulsdon CR5 175 DL115
Croydon CR0 142 DT102
Southall UB1 78 BZ71
West Wickham BR4 144 EE103
Windermere Way, Reig. RH2 184 DD133
West Drayton UB7
off Providence Rd 76 BM74
Winders Rd, SW11 100 DE82
Windfield, Lthd. KT22 171 CH121
Windfield Cl, SE26 123 DX91
Windham Av, Croy. (New Adgtn) CR0 161 ED110
Windham Rd, Rich. TW9 98 CM83
Windhover Way, Grav. DA12 131 GL91
Windings, The, S.Croy. CR2 160 DT111
Winding Way, Dag. RM8 70 EW62
Harrow HA1 61 CE63
Windlass Pl, SE8 203 L9
Windlesham Gro, SW19 119 CX88
Windley Cl, SE23 122 DW89
Windmill All, W4
off Windmill Rd 98 CS77
Windmill Av, Epsom KT17 157 CT111
Southall UB2 96 CC75
Windmill Br Ho, Croy. CR0 142 DS102
Windmill Cl, SE1 202 C8
SE13 103 EC82
Caterham CR3 176 DQ121
Epsom KT17 157 CT112
Sunbury-on-Thames TW16 115 BS94
Surbiton KT6 137 CH102
Upminster RM14 72 FN61
Waltham Abbey EN9 16 EE34
Windmill Ct, NW2 81 CY65
Windmill Dr, NW2 63 CY62
SW4 121 DJ85
Keston BR2 162 EJ105
Leatherhead KT22 171 CJ123
Reigate RH2 184 DD132
Rickmansworth (Crox.Grn) WD3 22 BM44
Windmill End, Epsom KT17 157 CT112
Windmill Gdns, Enf. EN2 29 DN41
Windmill Grn, Shep. TW17 135 BS101
Windmill Gro, Croy. CR0 142 DQ101
WINDMILL HILL, Grav. DA11 131 GG88
Windmill Hill, NW3 64 DC62
Enfield EN2 29 DP41
Kings Langley (Chipper.) WD4 5 BF32
Ruislip HA4 59 BT59
Windmill Ho, E14 203 P8
Windmill La, E15 85 ED65
Barnet EN5 27 CT44
Bushey (Bushey Hth) WD23 41 CE46
Epsom KT17 157 CT112
Greenford UB6 78 CC71
Isleworth TW7 97 CE77
Southall UB2 96 CC76
Surbiton KT6 137 CH100
Waltham Cross (Chsht) EN8 15 DX30
Windmill Ms, W4
off Windmill Rd 98 CS77
Windmill Pas, W4 98 CS77
Windmill Ri, Kings.T. KT2 118 CP94
Windmill Rd, N18 46 DR49
SW18 120 DD86
SW19 119 CV88
W4 98 CS77
W5 97 CJ77
Brentford TW8 97 CK78
Croydon CR0 142 DQ101
Gerrards Cross (Chal.St.P.) SL9 36 AX52
Hampton (Hmptn H.) TW12 116 CB92
Mitcham CR4 141 DJ99
Sevenoaks TN13 191 FH130
Slough (Fulmer) SL3 56 AX64
Sunbury-on-Thames TW16 135 BS95
Windmill Rd W, Sun. TW16 135 BS96
Windmill Row, SE11 101 DN78
Windmill Shott, Egh. TW20
off Rusham Rd 113 AZ93
Windmill St, W1 195 M7
Bushey (Bushey Hth) WD23 41 CE46
Gravesend DA12 131 GH86
Windmill Wk, SE1 200 E3
Windmill Way, Reig. RH2 184 DD132
Ruislip HA4 59 BT60
Windmore Av, Pot.B. EN6 11 CW31
Windmore Cl, Wem. HA0 61 CG64
Windover Av, NW9 62 CR56
Windrose Cl, SE16 203 H4
Windrush, N.Mal. KT3 138 CP98
Windrush Av, Slou. SL3 93 BB76
Windrush Cl, SW11
off Maysoule Rd 100 DD84
W4 98 CQ81
Uxbridge UB10 58 BM63
Windrush La, SE23 123 DX90
Windrush Rd, NW10 80 CR67
Windrush Sq, SW2
off Rushcroft Rd 101 DN84
Windsock Cl, SE16 203 M8
WINDSOR 92 AS82
Windsor Av, E17 47 DY54
SW19 140 DC95
Edgware HA8 42 CP49
Grays RM16 110 GB75
New Malden KT3 138 CQ99
Sutton SM3 139 CY104
Uxbridge UB10 77 BP67
West Molesey KT8 136 CA97
★ **Windsor Castle**, Wind. SL4 92 AS81
Windsor Cen, The, SE27
off Advance Rd 122 DQ91
Windsor Cl, N3 43 CY54
SE27 122 DQ91
Borehamwood WD6 26 CN39
Brentford TW8 97 CH79
Chislehurst BR7 125 EP92
Harrow HA2 60 CA62
Hemel Hempstead (Bov.) HP3 5 BA28
Northwood HA6 39 BU54
Waltham Cross (Chsht) EN7 14 DU30
Windsor Ct, N14 45 DJ45
Sunbury-on-Thames TW16
off Windsor Rd 115 BU93
Windsor Ct Rd, Wok. (Chobham) GU24 150 AS109
Windsor Cres, Har. HA2 60 CA63
Wembley HA9 62 CP62
Windsor Dr, Ashf. TW15 114 BK91
Barnet EN4 28 DF44
Dartford DA1 127 FG86
Orpington BR6 164 EU107
Windsor Gdns, W9 82 DA71
Croydon CR0
off Richmond Rd 141 DL104
Hayes UB3 95 BR76
★ **Windsor Great Pk**, Egh. & Wind. 112 AS93
Windsor Gt Pk, Ascot SL5 112 AS93
Egham TW20 112 AS93
Windsor Gro, SE27 122 DQ91
Windsor Ms, SE6 123 EC88
SE23 123 DY88
Windsor Pk Rd, Hayes UB3 95 BT80
Windsor Pl, SW1 199 L7
Chertsey KT16
off Windsor St 134 BG100
Windsor Rd, E4
off Chivers Rd 47 EB49
E7 68 EH64
E10 67 EB61
E11 68 EG60
N3 43 CY54
N7 65 DL62
N13 45 DN48
N17 46 DU54
NW2 81 CV65
W5 80 CL73
Barnet EN5 27 CY44
Bexleyheath DA6 106 EY84
Brentwood (Pilg.Hat.) CM15 54 FV44
Dagenham RM8 70 EY62
Egham (Eng.Grn) TW20 113 AZ90
Enfield EN3 31 DX36
Gerrards Cross SL9 56 AW60
Gravesend DA12 131 GH90
Harrow HA3 41 CD53
Hornchurch RM11 72 FJ59
Hounslow TW4 95 BV82
Ilford IG1 69 EP63
Kingston upon Thames KT2 118 CL94
Richmond TW9 98 CM82
Slough SL1 92 AS76
Slough (Datchet) SL3 92 AT80
Slough (Stoke P.) SL2 56 AU63
Southall UB2 96 BZ76
Staines (Wrays.) TW19 112 AY86
Sunbury-on-Thames TW16 115 BU93
Teddington TW11 117 CD92
Thornton Heath CR7 141 DP96
Watford WD24 24 BW38
Woking (Chobham) GU24 150 AS109
Worcester Park KT4 139 CU103
Windsors, The, Buck.H. IG9 48 EL47
Windsor St, N1 83 DP67
Chertsey KT16 134 BG100
Uxbridge UB8 76 BJ66
Windsor Ter, N1 197 J2
Windsor Wk, SE5 102 DR82
Walton-on-Thames KT12
off King George Av 136 BX102
Weybridge KT13 153 BP106
Windsor Way, W14 99 CX77
Rickmansworth WD3 38 BG46
Woking GU22 167 BC116
Windsor Wf, E9 67 DZ64
Windsor Wd, Wal.Abb. EN9
off Monkswood Av 16 EE33
Windspoint Dr, SE15
off Ethnard Rd 102 DV79
Windus Rd, N16 66 DT60
Windus Wk, N16 66 DT60
Windward Cl, Enf. EN3
off Bullsmoor La 31 DX35
Windycroft Cl, Pur. CR8 159 DK113
Windy Hill, Brwd. (Hutt.) CM13 55 GC46
Windy Ridge, Brom. BR1 144 EL95
Windyridge Cl, SW19 119 CX92
Wine Cl, E1 202 F1
Wine Office Ct, EC4 196 E8
Winern Glebe, W.Byf. (Byfleet) KT14 152 BK113
Winery La, Kings.T. KT1 138 CM97
Winey Cl, Chess. KT9
off Nigel Fisher Way 155 CJ108
Winfield Mobile Home Pk, Wat. WD25 24 CB39
Winford Ho, E3 85 DZ66
Winford Par, Sthl. UB1
off Telford Rd 78 CB72
Winforton St, SE10 103 EC81
Winfrith Rd, SW18 120 DC87
Wingate Cres, Croy. CR0 141 DK100
Wingate Rd, W6 99 CV76
Ilford IG1 69 EP64
Sidcup DA14 126 EW92
Wingate Trd Est, N17 46 DU52
Wing Cl, Epp. (N.Wld Bas.) CM16
off Epping Rd 18 FA27
Wingfield, Grays (Bad.Dene) RM17 110 FZ78
Wingfield Bk, Grav. (Nthflt) DA11 130 GC89
Wingfield Cl, Add. (New Haw) KT15 152 BH110
Brentwood CM13
off Pondfield La 55 GA48
Wingfield Gdns, Upmin. RM14 73 FT58
Wingfield Ms, SE15
off Wingfield St 102 DU83
Wingfield Rd, E15 68 EE64
E17 67 EB57
Gravesend DA12 131 GH87
Kingston upon Thames KT2 118 CN93
Wingfield St, SE15 102 DU83
Wingfield Way, Ruis. HA4 77 BV65
Wingford Rd, SW2 121 DL86
Wingletye La, Horn. RM11 72 FM60
Wingmore Rd, SE24 102 DQ83
Wingrave Cres, Brwd. CM14 54 FS49
Wingrave Rd, W6 99 CW79
Wingrove Dr, Purf. RM19 108 FP78
Wingrove Rd, SE6 124 EE89
Wings Cl, Sutt. SM1 158 DA105
Wing Way, Brwd. CM14
off Geary Dr 54 FW46
Winifred Av, Horn. RM12 72 FK63
Winifred Cl, Barn. EN5 27 CT44
Winifred Gro, SW11 100 DF84
Winifred Pl, N12 *off High Rd* 44 DC50
Winifred Rd, SW19 140 DA95
Coulsdon CR5 174 DG116
Dagenham RM8 70 EY61
Dartford DA1 127 FH85
Erith DA8 107 FE78
Hampton (Hmptn H.) TW12 116 CA91
Winifred St, E16 87 EM74
Winifred Ter, E13
off Victoria Rd 86 EG68
Enfield EN1
off Great Cambridge Rd 46 DT45
Winkers Cl, Ger.Cr. (Chal.St.P.) SL9 37 AZ53
Winkers La, Ger.Cr. (Chal.St.P.) SL9 37 AZ53
Winkfield Rd, E13 86 EH68
N22 45 DN53
Winkley St, E2 84 DV68
Winkworth Pl, Bans. SM7
off Bolters La 157 CZ114
Winkworth Rd, Bans. SM7 157 CZ114
Winlaton Rd, Brom. BR1 123 ED91
Winmill Rd, Dag. RM8 70 EZ62
Winnards, Wok. GU21
off Abercorn Way 166 AV118
Winn Common Rd, SE18 105 ES79
Winnett St, W1 195 M10
Winningales Ct, Ilf. IG5
off Vienna Cl 68 EL55
Winnings Wk, Nthlt. UB5
off Arnold Rd 78 BY65
Winnington Cl, N2 64 DD58
Winnington Rd, N2 64 DD59
Enfield EN3 30 DW38
Winnington Way, Wok. GU21 166 AV118
Winnipeg Dr, Orp. BR6 163 ET107
Winnipeg Way, Brox. EN10 15 DY25
Winnock Rd, West Dr. UB7 76 BK74
Winn Rd, SE12 124 EG88
Winns Av, E17 67 DY55
Winns Ms, N15
off Grove Pk Rd 66 DS56
Winns Ter, E17 47 EA54
Winsbeach, E17 67 ED55
Winscombe Cres, W5 79 CK70
Winscombe St, N19 65 DH61
Winscombe Way, Stan. HA7 41 CG50
Winsford Rd, SE6 123 DZ90
Winsford Ter, N18 46 DR50
Winsham Gro, SW11 120 DG85
Winslade Rd, SW2 121 DL85
Winslade Way, SE6
off Rushey Grn 123 EB87
Winsland Ms, W2
off London St 82 DD72
Winsland St, W2 82 DD72
Winsley St, W1 195 K8
Winslow, SE17 102 DS78
Winslow Cl, NW10
off Neasden La N 62 CS62
Pinner HA5 59 BV58
Winslow Gro, E4 48 EE47
Winslow Rd, W6 99 CW79
Winslow Way, Felt. TW13 116 BX90
Walton-on-Thames KT12 136 BW104
Winsor Ter, E6 87 EN71
Winsor Ter Roundabout, E6
off Royal Docks Rd 87 EP71
Winstanley Cl, Cob. KT11 153 BV114
Winstanley Est, SW11 100 DD83
Winstanley Rd, SW11 100 DD83
Winstanley Wk, Cob. KT11
off Winstanley Cl 153 BU114
Winstead Gdns, Dag. RM10 71 FC64
Winston Av, NW9 62 CS59
Winston Churchill Way, Wal.Cr. (Chsht) EN8 14 DW33
Winston Cl, Green. DA9 129 FT85
Harrow HA3 41 CF51
Romford RM7 71 FB56
Winston Ct, Har. HA3 40 CB52
Winston Dr, Cob. (Stoke D'Ab.) KT11 170 BY116
Winston Rd, N16 66 DR63
Winston Wk, W4
off Beaconsfield Rd 98 CR77
Winston Way, Ilf. IG1 69 EP62
Potters Bar EN6 12 DA34
Woking (Old Wok.) GU22 167 BB120
Winstre Rd, Borwd. WD6 26 CN39
Winter Av, E6 86 EL67
Winterborne Av, Orp. BR6 145 ER104
Winterbourne Gro, Wey. KT13 153 BQ107
Winterbourne Rd, SE6 123 DZ88
Dagenham RM8 70 EW61
Thornton Heath CR7 141 DN97
Winter Box Wk, Rich. TW10 98 CM84
Winterbrook Rd, SE24 122 DQ86
Winterburn Cl, N11 44 DG51
Winterdown Gdns, Esher KT10 154 BZ107
Winterdown Rd, Esher KT10 154 BZ107
Winterfold Cl, SW19 119 CY89
Wintergarden, Green. (Bluewater) DA9
off Bluewater Parkway 129 FU88
Winter Gdn Cres, Green. (Bluewater) DA9 129 FU87
Wintergreen Cl, E6
off Yarrow Cres 86 EL71
Winters Cft, Grav. DA12 131 GK93
Wintersells Rd, W.Byf. (Byfleet) KT14 152 BK110
Winters Rd, T.Ditt. KT7 137 CH101
Winterstoke Gdns, NW7 43 CU50
Winterstoke Rd, SE6 123 DZ88
Winters Way, Wal.Abb. EN9 16 EG33
Winterton Ho, E1 84 DV72
Winterton Pl, SW10
off Park Wk 100 DC79
Winterwell Rd, SW2 121 DL85
Winthorpe Rd, SW15 99 CY84
Winthrop St, E1 84 DV71
Winthrop Wk, Wem. HA9
off Everard Way 62 CL62
Winton App, Rick. (Crox.Grn) WD3 23 BQ43
Winton Av, N11 45 DJ52
Winton Cl, N9 47 DX45
Winton Cres, Rick. (Crox.Grn) WD3 23 BP43
Winton Dr, Rick. (Crox.Grn) WD3 23 BP44
Waltham Cross (Chsht) EN8 15 DY29
Winton Gdns, Edg. HA8 42 CM52

A B C D E F G H I J K L M N O P Q R S T U V

X Y Z

★ Place of interest ⇌ Railway station ⊖ London Underground station DLR Docklands Light Railway station Tra Tramlink station H Hospital Riv Pedestrian ferry landing stage

Win - Woo

Winton Rd, Orp. BR6 163 EP105
Winton Way, SW16 121 DN92
Winvale, Slou. SL1 92 AS76
Winwood, Slou. SL2 74 AW72
Wireless Rd, West. (Bigg.H.) TN16 178 EK115
Wirrall Ho, SE26 off Sydenham Hill 122 DU90
Wisbeach Rd, Croy. CR0 142 DR99
Wisborough Rd, S.Croy. CR2 160 DT109
Wisdons Cl, Dag. RM10 71 FB60
Wise La, NW7 43 CV51
West Drayton UB7 94 BK77
Wiseman Ct, SE19 122 DS92
Wiseman Rd, E10 67 EA61
Wise Rd, E15 85 ED67
Wise's La, Hat. AL9 11 CW27
Wiseton Rd, SW17 120 DE88
Wishart Rd, SE3 104 EK81
Wishbone Way, Wok. GU21 166 AT116
Wishford Ct, Ashtd. KT21 off The Marld 172 CM118
WISLEY, Wok. GU23 168 BL116
Wisley Common, Wok. GU23 168 BN117
Wisley Ct, S.Croy. CR2 off Sanderstead Rd 160 DS110
Wisley La, Wok. (Wisley) GU23 168 BL116
Wisley Rd, SW11 120 DG85
Orpington BR5 126 EU94
Wistaria Cl, Brwd. (Pilg.Hat.) CM15 54 FW43
Wistaria Dr, St.Alb. AL2 off Shenley La 9 CH26
Wisteria Cl, NW7 43 CT51
Ilford IG1 69 EP64
Orpington BR6 145 EP103
Wisteria Gdns, Swan. BR8 147 FD96
Wisteria Rd, SE13 103 ED84
Witan St, E2 84 DV69
Witches La, Sev. TN13 190 FD122
Witham Cl, Loug. IG10 32 EL44
Witham Rd, SE20 142 DW97
W13 79 CG74
Dagenham RM10 70 FA64
Isleworth TW7 97 CD81
Romford RM2 71 FH57
Withens Cl, Orp. BR5 146 EW98
Witherby Cl, Croy. CR0 160 DS106
Witherings, The, Horn. RM11 72 FL57
Witherington Rd, N5 65 DN64
Withers Cl, Chess. KT9 off Coppard Gdns 155 CJ107
Withers Mead, NW9 43 CT53
Witherston Way, SE9 125 EN89
Witheygate Av, Stai. TW18 114 BH93
Withies, The, Lthd. KT22 171 CH120
Woking (Knap.) GU21 166 AS117
Withybed Cor, Tad. KT20 173 CV123
Withycombe Rd, SW19 119 CX87
Withycroft, Slou. (Geo.Grn) SL3 74 AY72
Withy La, Ruis. HA4 59 BQ57
Withy Mead, E4 47 ED48
Withy Pl, St.Alb. (Park St) AL2 8 CC28
Witley Cres, Croy. (New Adgtn) CR0 161 EC107
Witley Gdns, Sthl. UB2 96 BZ77
Witley Pt, SW15 off Wanborough Dr 119 CV88
Witley Rd, N19 off Holloway Rd 65 DJ61
Witney Cl, Pnr. HA5 40 BZ51
Uxbridge UB10 58 BM63
Witney Path, SE23 123 DX90
Wittenham Way, E4 47 ED48
Wittering Cl, Kings.T. KT2 117 CK92
Wittering Wk, Horn. RM12 90 FJ65
Wittersham Rd, Brom. BR1 124 EF92
Wivenhoe Cl, SE15 102 DV83
Wivenhoe Ct, Houns. TW3 96 BZ84
Wivenhoe Rd, Bark. IG11 88 EU68
Wiverton Rd, SE26 122 DW93
Wixom Ho, SE3 off Romero Sq 104 EJ84
Wix Rd, Dag. RM9 88 EX67
Wixs La, SW4 101 DH84
Woburn Av, Epp. (They.B.) CM16 33 ES37
Hornchurch RM12 71 FG63
Purley CR8 off High St 159 DN111
Woburn Cl, SE28 off Summerton Way 88 EX72
SW19 off Tintern Cl 120 DC93
Bushey WD23 24 CC43
Woburn Ct, SE16 off Masters Dr 102 DV78
Woburn Hill, Add. KT15 134 BJ103
Woburn Pl, WC1 195 N4
Woburn Rd, Cars. SM5 140 DE102
Croydon CR0 142 DQ102
Woburn Sq, WC1 195 N5
Woburn Wk, WC1 195 N3
Wodehouse Av, SE5 102 DT81
Wodehouse Rd, Dart. DA1 108 FN84
Woffington Cl, Kings.T. KT1 137 CJ95
Wokindon Rd, Grays RM16 111 GH76
WOKING 167 AZ117
⇌ Woking 167 AZ117
Woking Business Pk, Wok. GU21 167 BB115
Woking Cl, SW15 99 CT84
H Woking Comm Hosp, Wok. GU22 167 AZ118
H Woking Nuffield Hosp, The, Wok. GU21 150 AY114
Wold, The, Cat. (Wold.) CR3 177 EA122
Woldham Pl, Brom. BR2 144 EJ98
Woldham Rd, Brom. BR2 144 EJ98
WOLDINGHAM, Cat. CR3 177 EB122
⇌ Woldingham 177 DX122
WOLDINGHAM GARDEN VILLAGE, Cat. CR3 177 DY121
Woldingham Rd, Cat. (Wold.) CR3 176 DV120
Wolds Dr, Orp. BR6 163 EN105
Wolfe Cl, Brom. BR2 144 EG100
Hayes UB4 off Ayles Rd 77 BV69
Wolfe Cres, SE7 104 EK78
SE16 203 H5
Wolferton Rd, E12 69 EM63
Wolffe Gdns, E15 86 EF65
Wolffram Cl, SE13 124 EE85
Wolfington Rd, SE27 121 DP91
Wolfs Hill, Oxt. RH8 188 EG131
H Wolfson Med Rehab Cen, SW20 119 CV94
Wolf's Row, Oxt. RH8 188 EH130
Wolfs Wd, Oxt. RH8 188 EG132
Wolftencroft Cl, SW11 100 DD83
Wollaston Cl, SE1 201 H8
Wolmer Cl, Edg. HA8 42 CP49
Wolmer Gdns, Edg. HA8 42 CN48
Wolseley Av, SW19 120 DA89
Wolseley Gdns, W4 98 CP79
Wolseley Rd, E7 86 EH66
N8 65 DK58
N22 45 DM53
W4 98 CQ77
Harrow HA3 61 CE55
Mitcham CR4 140 DG101
Romford RM7 71 FD59
Wolseley St, SE1 202 A5
Wolsey Av, E6 87 EN69
E17 67 DZ55
Thames Ditton KT7 137 CF99
Waltham Cross (Chsht) EN7 14 DT29
Wolsey Business Pk, Wat. WD18 39 BR45
Wolsey Cl, SW20 119 CV94
Hounslow TW3 96 CC84
Kingston upon Thames KT2 138 CP95
Southall UB2 96 CC76
Worcester Park KT4 157 CU105
Wolsey Cres, Croy. (New Adgtn) CR0 161 EC109
Morden SM4 139 CY101
Wolsey Dr, Kings.T. KT2 118 CL92
Walton-on-Thames KT12 136 BX102
Wolsey Gdns, Ilf. IG6 49 EQ51
Wolsey Gro, Edg. HA8 42 CR52
Esher KT10 154 CB105
Wolsey Ms, NW5 83 DJ65
Orpington BR6 off Osgood Av 163 ET106
Wolsey Pl Shop Cen, Wok. GU21 off Commercial Way 166 AY117
Wolsey Rd, N1 66 DR64
Ashford TW15 114 BL91
East Molesey KT8 137 CD98
Enfield EN1 30 DV40
Esher KT10 154 CB105
Hampton (Hmptn H.) TW12 116 CB93
Northwood HA6 39 BQ47
Sunbury-on-Thames TW16 115 BT94
Wolsey St, E1 off Sidney St 84 DW71
Wolsey Wk, Wok. GU21 166 AY117
Wolsey Way, Chess. KT9 156 CN106
Wolsley Cl, Dart. DA1 127 FE85
Wolstan Cl, Uxb. (Denh.) UB9 off Lindsey Rd 58 BG62
Wolstonbury, N12 44 DA50
Wolvercote Rd, SE2 106 EX75
Wolverley St, E2 off Bethnal Grn Rd 84 DV69
Wolverton, SE17 201 L10
Wolverton Av, Kings.T. KT2 138 CN95
Wolverton Gdns, W5 80 CM73
W6 99 CX77
Wolverton Rd, Stan. HA7 41 CH51
Wolverton Way, N14 29 DJ43
Wolves La, N13 45 DN52
N22 45 DN52
Wombwell Gdns, Grav. (Nthflt) DA11 130 GE89
WOMBWELL PARK, Grav. DA11 130 GD89
Womersley Rd, N8 65 DM58
Wonersh Way, Sutt. SM2 157 CX109
Wonford Cl, Kings.T. KT2 138 CS95
Tadworth KT20 183 CU126
Wontford Rd, Pur. CR8 175 DN115
Wontner Cl, N1 off Greenman St 84 DQ66
Wontner Rd, SW17 120 DF89
Wooburn Cl, Uxb. UB8 off Aldenham Dr 77 BP70
Woodall Cl, E14 off Lawless St 85 EB73
Chessington KT9 155 CK107
Woodall Rd, Enf. EN3 31 DX44
Wood Av, Purf. RM19 108 FQ77
Woodbank, Rick. WD3 22 BJ44
Woodbank Av, Ger.Cr. SL9 56 AX58
Woodbank Dr, Ch.St.G. HP8 36 AX48
Woodbank Rd, Brom. BR1 124 EF90
Woodbastwick Rd, SE26 123 DX92
Woodberry Av, N21 45 DN47
Harrow HA2 60 CB56
Woodberry Cl, NW7 43 CX52
Sunbury-on-Thames TW16 off Ashridge Way 115 BU93
Woodberry Cres, N10 65 DH55
Woodberry Down, N4 66 DQ59
Epping CM16 18 EU29
Woodberry Down Est, N4 66 DQ59
Woodberry Gdns, N12 44 DC51
Woodberry Gro, N4 66 DQ59
N12 44 DC51
Bexley DA5 127 FD90
Woodberry Way, E4 47 EC46
N12 44 DC51
Woodbine Cl, Twick. TW2 117 CD89
Waltham Abbey EN9 32 EJ35
Woodbine Gro, SE20 122 DV94
Enfield EN2 30 DR38
Woodbine La, Wor.Pk. KT4 139 CW104
Woodbine Pl, E11 68 EG58
Woodbine Rd, Sid. DA15 125 ES88
Woodbines Av, Kings.T. KT1 137 CK97
Woodbine Ter, E9 off Morning La 84 DW65
Woodborough Rd, SW15 99 CV84
Woodbourne Av, SW16 121 DK90
Woodbourne Cl, SW16 off Woodbourne Av 121 DL90
Woodbourne Dr, Esher (Clay.) KT10 155 CF107
Woodbourne Gdns, Wall. SM6 159 DH108
Woodbridge Av, Lthd. KT22 171 CG118
Woodbridge Cl, N7 65 DM61
NW2 63 CU62
Romford RM3 52 FK49
Woodbridge Ct, Wdf.Grn. IG8 48 EL52
Woodbridge Gro, Lthd. KT22 171 CG118
Woodbridge La, Rom. RM3 52 FK48
Woodbridge Rd, Bark. IG11 69 ET64
Woodbridge St, EC1 196 F4
Woodbrook Gdns, Wal.Abb. EN9 16 EE33
Woodbrook Rd, SE2 106 EU79
Woodburn Cl, NW4 63 CX57
Woodbury Cl, E11 68 EH56
Croydon CR0 142 DT103
Westerham (Bigg.H.) TN16 179 EM118
Woodbury Dr, Sutt. SM2 158 DC110
Woodbury Hill, Loug. IG10 32 EL41
Woodbury Hollow, Loug. IG10 32 EL40
Woodbury Pk Rd, W13 79 CH70
Woodbury Rd, E17 67 EB56
Westerham (Bigg.H.) TN16 179 EM118
Woodbury St, SW17 120 DE92
Woodchester Sq, W2 82 DB71
Woodchurch Cl, Sid. DA14 125 ER90
Woodchurch Dr, Brom. BR1 124 EK94
Woodchurch Rd, NW6 82 DA66
Wood Cl, E2 84 DU70
NW9 62 CR59
Bexley DA5 127 FE90
Harrow HA1 61 CD59
Woodclyffe Dr, Chis. BR7 145 EN96
Woodcock Ct, Har. HA3 62 CL59
Woodcock Dell Av, Har. HA3 61 CK59
Woodcock Hill, Har. HA3 61 CK59
Rickmansworth WD3 38 BL50
Woodcocks, E16 86 EJ71
Woodcombe Cres, SE23 122 DW88
WOODCOTE, Epsom KT18 172 CQ116
WOODCOTE, Pur. CR8 159 DK111
Woodcote Av, NW7 43 CW51
Hornchurch RM12 71 FG63
Thornton Heath CR7 141 DP98
Wallington SM6 159 DH108
Woodcote Cl, Enf. EN3 30 DW44
Epsom KT18 156 CR114
Kingston upon Thames KT2 118 CM92
Waltham Cross (Chsht) EN8 14 DW30
Woodcote Dr, Orp. BR6 145 ER102
Purley CR8 159 DK110
Woodcote End, Epsom KT18 172 CR115
Woodcote Grn, Wall. SM6 159 DJ109
Woodcote Grn Rd, Epsom KT18 172 CQ116
Woodcote Gro, Couls. CR5 159 DH112
Woodcote Gro Rd, Couls. CR5 175 DK115
Woodcote Hurst, Epsom KT18 172 CQ116
Woodcote La, Pur. CR8 159 DK111
Woodcote Ms, Loug. IG10 48 EK45
Wallington SM6 159 DH107
Woodcote Pk Av, Pur. CR8 159 DJ112
Woodcote Pk Rd, Epsom KT18 172 CQ116
Woodcote Pl, SE27 121 DP92
Woodcote Rd, E11 68 EG59
Epsom KT18 156 CR114
Purley CR8 159 DJ109
Wallington SM6 159 DH107
Woodcote Side, Epsom KT18 172 CP115
Woodcote Valley Rd, Pur. CR8 159 DK113
Woodcott Ho, SW15 off Ellisfield Dr 119 CU87
Woodcrest Rd, Pur. CR8 159 DL113
Woodcrest Wk, Reig. RH2 184 DE132
Woodcroft, N21 45 DM46
SE9 125 EM90
Greenford UB6 79 CG65
Woodcroft Av, NW7 42 CS52
Stanmore HA7 41 CF53
Woodcroft Cres, Uxb. UB10 77 BP67
Woodcroft Ms, SE8 203 K9
Woodcroft Rd, Th.Hth. CR7 141 DP99
Woodcutters Av, Grays RM16 110 GC75
Wood Dr, Chis. BR7 124 EL93
Sevenoaks TN13 190 FF126
Woodedge Cl, E4 48 EF46
Woodend, SE19 122 DQ93
Esher KT10 136 CC103
Wood End, Hayes UB3 77 BS72
St. Albans (Park St) AL2 8 CC28
Woodend, Sutt. SM1 140 DC103
Woodend, The, Wall. SM6 159 DH109
Wood End Av, Har. HA2 60 CB63
Wood End Cl, Nthlt. UB5 61 CD64
Woodend Cl, Wok. GU21 166 AU119
Woodend Gdns, Enf. EN2 29 DL42
Wood End Gdns, Nthlt. UB5 60 CC64
Wood End Grn Rd, Hayes UB3 77 BR71
Wood End La, Nthlt. UB5 78 CB65
Woodend Pk, Cob. KT11 170 BX115
Woodend Rd, E17 47 EC54
Wood End Rd, Har. HA1 61 CD63
Wood End Way, Nthlt. UB5 60 CC64
Wooder Gdns, E7 68 EF63
Wooderson Cl, SE25 142 DS98
Woodfall Av, Barn. EN5 27 CZ43
Woodfall Dr, Dart. DA1 107 FE84
Woodfall Rd, N4 65 DN60
Woodfall St, SW3 100 DF78
Woodfarrs, SE5 102 DR84
Woodfield, Ashtd. KT21 171 CK117
Woodfield Av, NW9 62 CS56
SW16 121 DK90
W5 79 CJ70
Carshalton SM5 158 DG107
Gravesend DA11 131 GH88
Northwood HA6 39 BS49
Wembley HA0 61 CJ62
Woodfield Cl, SE19 122 DQ94
Ashtead KT21 171 CK117
Woodfield Cl, Coulsdon CR5 175 DJ119
Enfield EN1 30 DS42
Redhill RH1 184 DE133
Woodfield Cres, W5 79 CJ70
Woodfield Dr, Barn. EN4 44 DG46
Romford RM2 71 FG56
Woodfield Gdns, W9 off Woodfield Rd 81 CZ71
New Malden KT3 139 CT99
Woodfield Gro, SW16 121 DK90
Woodfield Hill, Couls. CR5 175 DH119
Woodfield La, SW16 121 DK90
Ashtead KT21 172 CL116
Woodfield Pl, W9 81 CZ70
Woodfield Ri, Bushey WD23 41 CD45
Woodfield Rd, W5 79 CJ70
W9 81 CZ71
Ashtead KT21 171 CK117
Hounslow TW4 95 BV82
Radlett WD7 25 CG36
Thames Ditton KT7 137 CF103
Woodfields, Sev. TN13 190 FD122
Woodfields, The, S.Croy. CR2 160 DT111
Woodfield Ter, Epp. (Thnwd) CM16 off High Rd 18 EW25
Uxbridge (Hare.) UB9 38 BH54
Woodfield Way, N11 45 DK52
Hornchurch RM12 72 FK60
Redhill RH1 184 DE132
Woodfines, The, Horn. RM11 72 FK58
WOODFORD, Wdf.Grn. IG8 48 EH51
⊖ Woodford 48 EH51
Woodford Av, Ilf. IG2, IG4 69 EM57
Woodford Green IG8 68 EK55
WOODFORD BRIDGE, Wdf.Grn. IG8 49 EM52
Woodford Br Rd, Ilf. IG4 68 EK55
Woodford Ct, W12 off Shepherds Bush Grn 99 CX75
Waltham Abbey EN9 16 EG33
Woodford Cres, Pnr. HA5 39 BV54
WOODFORD GREEN 48 EF49
Woodford New Rd, E17 68 EE56
E18 68 EE53
Woodford Green IG8 48 EE53
Woodford Pl, Wem. HA9 62 CL60
Woodford Rd, E7 68 EH63
E18 68 EG56
Watford WD17 23 BV40
WOODFORD WELLS, Wdf.Grn. IG8 48 EH49
Woodgate, Wat. WD25 7 BV33
Woodgate Av, Chess. KT9 155 CK106
Potters Bar EN6 13 DH33
Woodgate Cres, Nthwd. HA6 39 BU51
Woodgate Dr, SW16 121 DK94
Woodgavil, Bans. SM7 173 CZ116
Woodger Rd, W12 off Goldhawk Rd 99 CW75
Woodgers Gro, Swan. BR8 147 FF96
Woodget Cl, E6 off Remington Rd 86 EL72
Woodgrange Av, N12 44 DD51
W5 80 CN74
Enfield EN1 30 DU44
Harrow HA3 61 CJ57
Woodgrange Cl, Har. HA3 61 CK57
Woodgrange Gdns, Enf. EN1 30 DU44
⇌ Woodgrange Park 68 EK64
Woodgrange Rd, E7 68 EH63
Woodgrange Ter, Enf. EN1 off Great Cambridge Rd 30 DU44
WOOD GREEN, N22 45 DL53
⊖ Wood Green 45 DM54
Woodgreen Rd, Wal.Abb. EN9 32 EJ35
Wood Grn Shop City, N22 45 DN54
Wood Grn Way, Wal.Cr. (Chsht) EN8 15 DY31
Woodhall Av, SE21 122 DT90
Pinner HA5 40 BY54
Woodhall Cl, Uxb. UB8 58 BK64
Woodhall Cres, Horn. RM11 72 FM59
Woodhall Dr, SE21 122 DT90
Pinner HA5 40 BX53
Woodhall Gate, Pnr. HA5 40 BX52
Woodhall Ho, SW18 off Fitzhugh Gro 120 DD86
Woodhall La, Rad. (Shenley) WD7 26 CL35
Watford WD19 40 BX49
Woodhall Rd, Pnr. HA5 40 BX52
WOODHAM, Add. KT15 151 BF111
Woodham Ct, E18 68 EF56
Woodham La, Add. (New Haw) KT15 152 BG110
Woking GU21 151 BB114
Woodham Pk Rd, Add. (Wdhm) KT15 151 BF109
Woodham Pk Way, Add. (Wdhm) KT15 151 BF111
Woodham Ri, Wok. GU21 151 AZ114
Woodham Rd, SE6 123 EC90
Woking GU21 166 AY115
Woodham Waye, Wok. GU21 151 BB113
Woodhatch Cl, E6 off Remington Rd 86 EL72
Woodhatch Spinney, Couls. CR5 175 DL116
Woodhaven Gdns, Ilf. IG6 off Brandville Gdns 69 EQ55
Woodhaw, Egh. TW20 113 BB91
Woodhayes Rd, SW19 119 CW94
Woodhead Dr, Orp. BR6 off Sherlies Av 145 ES103
Woodheyes Rd, NW10 62 CR64
Woodhill, SE18 104 EL77
Woodhill Av, Ger.Cr. SL9 57 BA58
Woodhill Cres, Har. HA3 61 CK58
Wood Ho, SW17 off Laurel Cl 120 DE92
Woodhouse Av, Grnf. UB6 79 CF68
Woodhouse Cl, Grnf. UB6 79 CF68
Hayes UB3 95 BS76
Woodhouse Eaves, Nthwd. HA6 39 BU50
Woodhouse Gro, E12 86 EL65
Woodhouse Rd, E11 68 EF62
N12 44 DD51
Woodhurst Av, Orp. BR5 145 EQ100
Watford WD25 24 BX35
Woodhurst Dr, Uxb. (Denh.) UB9 57 BF57
Woodhurst La, Oxt. RH8 188 EE130
Woodhurst Pk, Oxt. RH8 188 EE130
Woodhurst Rd, SE2 106 EU78
W3 80 CQ73
Woodhyrst Gdns, Ken. CR8 off Firs Rd 175 DP115
Woodington Cl, SE9 125 EN86
Woodknoll Dr, Chis. BR7 145 EM95
Woodland App, Grnf. UB6 79 CG65
Woodland Av, Brwd. (Hutt.) CM13 55 GC43
Woodland Cl, NW9 62 CQ58
SE19 off Woodland Hill 122 DS93
Brentwood (Hutt.) CM13 55 GC43
Epsom KT19 156 CS107
Uxbridge (Ickhm) UB10 59 BP61
Weybridge KT13 off Woodland Gro 153 BR105
Woodford Green IG8 48 EH48
Woodland Ct, Oxt. RH8 187 ED128
Woodland Cres, SE10 104 EE79
SE16 203 H5
Woodland Dr, Wat. WD17 23 BT39
Woodland Gdns, N10 65 DH57
Epsom KT18 173 CW117
Isleworth TW7 97 CE82
South Croydon CR2 160 DW111
Woodland Gro, SE10 104 EE78
Epping CM16 18 EU31
Weybridge KT13 153 BR105
Woodland Hill, SE19 122 DS93
Woodland La, Rick. (Chorl.) WD3 21 BD41
Woodland Ms, SW16 121 DL89
Woodland Pl, Rick. (Chorl.) WD3 21 BF42
Woodland Ri, N10 65 DH56
Greenford UB6 79 CG65
Oxted RH8 188 EE130
Sevenoaks TN15 191 FL123
Woodland Rd, E4 47 EC46
N11 45 DH50
SE19 122 DS92
Loughton IG10 32 EL41
Rickmansworth (Map.Cr.) WD3 37 BD50
Thornton Heath CR7 141 DN98
WOODLANDS, Islw. TW7 97 CE82
Woodlands, NW11 63 CY58
SW20 139 CW98
Gerrards Cross SL9 57 AZ57
Harrow HA2 60 CA56
Hatfield AL9 12 DB26
Radlett WD7 9 CG34
St. Albans (Park St) AL2 8 CC27
Woking GU22 off Constitution Hill 166 AY118
Woodlands, The, N14 45 DH46
SE13 123 ED87
SE19 122 DQ94
Beckenham BR3 143 EC95
Esher KT10 136 CC103
Isleworth TW7 97 CF82
Orpington BR6 164 EV107
Wallington SM6 159 DH109
Woodlands Av, E11 68 EH60
N3 44 DC52
W3 80 CP74
Hornchurch RM11 72 FK57
New Malden KT3 138 CQ95
Romford RM6 70 EY58
Ruislip HA4 60 BW60
Sidcup DA15 125 ES88
West Byfleet KT14 151 BF113
Worcester Park KT4 139 CT103
Woodlands Cl, NW11 63 CY57
Borehamwood WD6 26 CP42
Bromley BR1 145 EM96
Chertsey (Ott.) KT16 151 BB110
Esher (Clay.) KT10 155 CF108
Gerrards Cross SL9 57 BA58
Grays RM16 110 GE76
Swanley BR8 147 FF97
Woodlands Copse, Ashtd. KT21 171 CK116
Woodlands Ct, Wok. GU22 off Constitution Hill 166 AY119
Woodlands Dr, Kings L. WD4 7 BQ28
Stanmore HA7 41 CF51
Sunbury-on-Thames TW16 136 BW96
Woodlands Gro, Couls. CR5 174 DG117
Isleworth TW7 97 CE82
Woodlands La, Cob. (Stoke D'Ab.) KT11 170 CA117
Woodlands Par, Ashf. TW15 115 BQ93
Woodlands Pk, Add. KT15 151 BF106
Bexley DA5 127 FC91
Tadworth (Box H.) KT20 182 CP131
Woking GU21 off Blackmore Cres 151 BC114
Woodlands Pk Rd, N15 65 DP57
SE10 104 EE79
Woodlands Ri, Swan. BR8 147 FF96
Woodlands Rd, E11 68 EE61
E17 67 EC55
N9 46 DW46
SW13 99 CT83
Bexleyheath DA7 106 EY83
Bromley BR1 144 EL96
Bushey WD23 24 BY43
Enfield EN2 30 DR39
Epsom KT18 172 CN115
Harrow HA1 61 CF57
Hemel Hempstead HP3 6 BN27
Ilford IG1 69 EQ62
Isleworth TW7 97 CE82
Leatherhead KT22 171 CD117
Orpington BR6 164 EU107
Romford RM1 71 FF55
Romford (Harold Wd) RM3 52 FN53
Southall UB1 78 BX74
Surbiton KT6 137 CK101
Virginia Water GU25 132 AW98
West Byfleet KT14 151 BF114
Woodlands Rd E, Vir.W. GU25 132 AW98
Woodlands Rd W, Vir.W. GU25 132 AW97

★ Place of interest ⇌ Railway station ⊖ London Underground station DLR Docklands Light Railway station Tra Tramlink station H Hospital Riv Pedestrian ferry landing stage

★ Place of interest   ⇌ Railway station   ⊖ London Underground station   DLR Docklands Light Railway station   Tra Tramlink station   H Hospital   Rtv Pedestrian ferry landing stage

Wrights Row, Wall. SM6 . . . . . 159 DH105
Wrights Wk, SW14 . . . . 98 CR83
Wrigley Cl, E4 . . . . 47 ED50
Wriotsley Way, Add. KT15
   off Coombelands La 152 BG107
Writtle Wk, Rain. RM13 . . . . . . 89 FF67
★ Wrotham Pk, Barn. EN5 . . . . 27 CZ36
Wrotham Rd, NW1 *off Agar Pl.* 83 DJ66
  W13 *off Mattock La* 79 CH74
  Barnet EN5 . . . . 27 CY40
  Gravesend DA11, DA13 . . . 131 GG88
  Welling DA16 . . . . 106 EW81
Wroths Path, Loug. IG10 . . . . . 33 EM39
Wrottesley Rd, NW10 . . . . 81 CU68
  SE18 . . . . 105 EQ79
Wroughton Rd, SW11 . . . . . . 120 DF86
Wroughton Ter, NW4 . . . . 63 CW56
Wroxall Rd, Dag. RM9 . . . . . . 88 EW62
Wroxham Gdns, N11 . . . . 45 DJ52
  Enfield EN2 . . . . 29 DN35
  Potters Bar EN6 . . . . 11 CX31
Wroxham Rd, SE28 . . . . 88 EX73
Wroxham Way, Ilf. IG6 . . . . . . 49 EP53
Wroxton Rd, SE15 . . . . 102 DV82
WRYTHE, THE, Cars. SM5 . . . 140 DE103
Wrythe Grn, Cars. SM5
  off Wrythe Grn Rd 140 DF104
Wrythe Grn Rd, Cars. SM5 . . 140 DF104
Wrythe La, Cars. SM5 . . . . . . 140 DC102
Wulfstan St, W12 . . . . 81 CT72
Wulstan Pk, Pot.B. EN6
  off Tempest Av 12 DD32
Wyatt Cl, SE16 . . . . 203 M5
  Bushey (Bushey Hth) WD23. 41 CE45
  Feltham TW13 . . . . 116 BW88
  Hayes UB4 . . . . 77 BU71
Wyatt Dr, SW13 . . . . 99 CW80
Wyatt Pk Rd, SW2 . . . . 121 DL89
Wyatt Rd, E7 . . . . 86 EG65
  N5 . . . . 66 DQ62
  Dartford DA1 . . . . 107 FF83
  Staines TW18 . . . . 114 BG92
Wyatts Cl, Rick. (Chorl.) WD3 . 22 BG41
Wyatt's Covert Caravan Site, Uxb.
  (Denh.) UB9 . . . . 57 BE56
Wyatts La, E17 . . . . 67 EC55
Wyatts Rd, Rick. (Chorl.) WD3 . 21 BF42
Wybert St, NW1 . . . . 195 J4
Wyborne Way, NW10 . . . . 80 CQ66
Wyburn Av, Barn. EN5 . . . . . . 27 CZ41
Wyche Gro, S.Croy. CR2 . . . . 160 DQ108
Wych Elm Cl, Horn. RM11 . . . 72 FN59
Wych Elm Dr, Brom. BR1
  off London La. 124 EF94
Wych Elm Pas, Kings.T. KT2 . 118 CM94
Wych Elm Rd, Horn. RM11 . . . 72 FN58
Wych Elms, St.Alb.
  (Park St) AL2 . . . . 8 CB28
Wycherley Cl, SE3 . . . . 104 EF80
Wycherley Cres, Barn. EN5 . . . 28 DB44
Wych Hill, Wok. GU22 . . . . . . 166 AW119
Wych Hill La, Wok. GU22 . . . 166 AY119
Wych Hill Pk, Wok. GU22 . . . 166 AX119
Wych Hill Ri, Wok. GU22 . . . . 166 AW118
Wych Hill Way, Wok. GU22 . . 166 AX120
Wychwood Av, Edg. HA8 . . . . . 41 CK51
  Thornton Heath CR7 . . . . 142 DQ97
Wychwood Cl, Edg. HA8 . . . . . 41 CK51
  Sunbury-on-Thames TW16 . 115 BU93
Wychwood End, N6 . . . . 65 DJ59
Wychwood Gdns, Ilf. IG5 . . . . 69 EM56
Wychwood Way, SE19
  off Roman Ri 122 DR93
  Northwood HA6 . . . . 39 BT52
Wycliffe Cl, Well. DA16 . . . . . 105 ET81
Wycliffe Ct, Abb.L. WD5 . . . . . 7 BS32
Wycliffe Rd, SW11 . . . . 100 DG82
  SW19 . . . . 120 DB93
Wycliffe Row, Grav.
  (Nthflt) DA11 . . . . 131 GF88
Wyclif St, EC1 . . . . 196 F3
Wycombe Gdns, NW11 . . . . . . 64 DA61
Wycombe Pl, SW18 . . . . 120 DC86
Wycombe Rd, N17 . . . . 46 DU53
  Ilford IG2 . . . . 69 EN57
  Wembley HA0 . . . . 80 CN67
Wydehurst Rd, Croy. CR0 . . . 142 DU101
Wydell Cl, Mord. SM4 . . . . . . 139 CW100
Wydeville Manor Rd, SE12 . . 124 EH91
Wyecliffe Gdns, Red. RH1 . . . 185 DJ130
Wye Cl, Ashf. TW15 . . . . 115 BP91
  Orpington BR6 . . . . 145 ET101
  Ruislip HA4 . . . . 59 BQ58
Wyedale, St.Alb.
  (Lon.Col.) AL2 . . . . 10 CM27
Wyemead Cres, E4 . . . . 48 EE47
Wye Rd, Grav. DA12 . . . . 131 GK89
Wye St, SW11 . . . . 100 DD82
Wyeth's Ms, Epsom KT17 . . . 157 CT113
Wyeths Rd, Epsom KT17 . . . . 157 CT113
Wyevale Cl, Pnr. HA5 . . . . 59 BU55
Wyfields, Ilf. IG5
  off Ravensbourne Gdns . . 49 EP53
Wyfold Ho, SE2
  off Wolvercote Rd 106 EX75
Wyfold Rd, SW6 . . . . 99 CY80
Wyhill Wk, Dag. RM10 . . . . . . 89 FC65
Wyke Cl, Islw. TW7 . . . . 97 CF79
Wyke Gdns, W7 . . . . 97 CG76
Wykeham Av, Dag. RM9 . . . . . 88 EW65
  Hornchurch RM11 . . . . 72 FK58
Wykeham Cl, Grav. DA12 . . . 131 GL93
  West Drayton UB7 . . . . 94 BN78
Wykeham Grn, Dag. RM9 . . . . 88 EW65
Wykeham Hill, Wem. HA9 . . . . 62 CM60
Wykeham Ri, N20 . . . . 43 CY46
Wykeham Rd, NW4 . . . . 63 CW57
  Harrow HA3 . . . . 61 CH56
Wyke Rd, E3 . . . . 85 EA66
  SW20 . . . . 139 CW96
Wylands Rd, Slou. SL3 . . . . . . 93 BA77
Wylchin Cl, Pnr. HA5 . . . . 59 BT56
Wyldes Cl, NW11
  off Wildwood Rd 64 DC60
Wyldfield Gdns, N9 . . . . 46 DT47

Wyld Way, Wem. HA9 . . . . . . 80 CP65
Wyleu St, SE23 . . . . 123 DY87
Wylie Rd, Sthl. UB2 . . . . 96 CA76
Wyllen Cl, E1 . . . . 84 DW70
Wyllyotts Cl, Pot.B. EN6 . . . . . 11 CZ32
Wyllyotts La, Pot.B. EN6 . . . . . 11 CZ32
Wyllyotts Pl, Pot.B. EN6 . . . . . 11 CZ32
Wylo Dr, Barn. EN5 . . . . 27 CU44
Wymering Rd, W9 . . . . 82 DA69
Wymond St, SW15 . . . . 99 CW83
Wynan Rd, E14 . . . . 204 B10
Wynash Gdns, Cars. SM5 . . . 158 DE106
Wynaud Ct, N22
  off Palmerston Rd 45 DM51
Wyncham Av, Sid. DA15 . . . . 125 ES88
Wynchgate, N14 . . . . 45 DK46
  N21 . . . . 45 DL46
  Harrow HA3 . . . . 41 CE52
Wyncote Way, S.Croy. CR2 . . 161 DX109
Wyncroft Cl, Brom. BR1 . . . . 145 EM97
Wyndale Av, NW9 . . . . 62 CN58
Wyndcliff Rd, SE7 . . . . 104 EH79
Wyndcroft Cl, Enf. EN2 . . . . . 29 DP41
Wyndham Av, Cob. KT11 . . . . 153 BU113
Wyndham Cl, Orp. BR6 . . . . . 145 EQ102
  Sutton SM2 . . . . 158 DA108
Wyndham Cres, N19 . . . . 65 DJ62
  Hounslow TW4 . . . . 116 CA86
Wyndham Est, SE5 . . . . 102 DQ80
Wyndham Ms, W1 . . . . 194 D7
Wyndham Pl, W1 . . . . 194 D7
Wyndham Rd, E6 . . . . 86 EK66
  SE5 . . . . 101 DP80
  W13 . . . . 97 CH76
  Barnet EN4 . . . . 44 DF46
  Kingston upon Thames KT2 . 118 CM94
  Woking GU21 . . . . 166 AV118
Wyndham St, W1 . . . . 194 D6
Wyndham Yd, W1 . . . . 194 D7
Wyneham Rd, SE24 . . . . 122 DR85
Wynell Rd, SE23 . . . . 123 DX90
Wynford Gro, Orp. BR5 . . . . . 146 EV97
Wynford Pl, Belv. DA17 . . . . . 106 FA79
Wynford Rd, N1 . . . . 83 DM68
Wynford Way, SE9 . . . . 125 EM90
Wynlie Gdns, Pnr. HA5 . . . . . 39 BV54
Wynn Br Cl, Wdf.Grn. IG8
  off Chigwell Rd 48 EJ53
Wynndale Rd, E18 . . . . 48 EH53
Wynne Rd, SW9 . . . . 101 DN82
Wynns Av, Sid. DA15 . . . . . . 126 EU85
Wynnstay Gdns, W8 . . . . 100 DA76
Wynnstow Pk, Oxt. RH8 . . . . 188 EF131
Wynter St, SW11 . . . . 100 DC84
Wynton Gdns, SE25 . . . . 142 DT99
Wynton Gro, Walt. KT12 . . . . ✱ 135 BU104
Wynton Pl, W3 . . . . 80 CP72
Wynyard Cl, Rick.
  (Sarratt) WD3 . . . . 22 BG36
Wynyard Ter, SE11 . . . . 200 C10
Wynyatt St, EC1 . . . . 196 F3
Wyre Gro, Edg. HA8 . . . . 42 CP48
  Hayes UB3 . . . . 95 BU77
Wyresdale Cres, Grnf. UB6 . . . 79 CF69
Wyteleaf Cl, Ruis. HA4 . . . . . . 59 BQ58
Wythburn Pl, W1 . . . . 194 D9
Wythenshawe Rd, Dag. RM10 . 70 FA62
Wythens Wk, SE9 . . . . 125 EP86
Wythes Cl, Brom. BR1 . . . . . 145 EM96
Wythes Rd, E16 . . . . 86 EL74
Wythfield Rd, SE9 . . . . 125 EM86
Wyvenhoe Rd, Har. HA2 . . . . . 60 CC62
Wyvern Cl, Dart. DA1 . . . . . . 128 FJ87
  Orpington BR6 . . . . 146 EV104
Wyvern Est, N.Mal. KT3 . . . . 139 CU98
Wyvern Gro, Hayes UB3 . . . . . 95 BP80
Wyvern Pl, Add. KT15
  off Green La. 152 BH105
Wyvern Rd, Pur. CR8 . . . . . . 159 DP110
Wyvern Way, Uxb. UB8 . . . . . . 76 BH66
Wyvil Est, SW8
  off Luscombe Way 101 DL80
Wyvil Rd, SW8 . . . . 101 DL79
Wyvis St, E14 . . . . 85 EB71

Y

Yabsley St, E14. . . . . 204 E2
Yaffle Rd, Wey. KT13 . . . . . . 153 BQ110
Yalding Cl, Orp. BR5 . . . . . . 146 EX98
Yalding Rd, SE16 . . . . 202 B7
Yale Cl, Houns. TW4
  off Bramley Way. 116 BZ85
Yale Way, Horn. RM12 . . . . . . 71 FG63
Yaohan Plaza, NW9 . . . . 62 CR55
Yarborough Rd, SW19 . . . . . 140 DD95
Yarbridge Cl, Sutt. SM2 . . . . 158 DB110
Yardley Cl, E4 . . . . 31 EB43
  Reigate RH2 . . . . 184 DB132
Yardley Ct, Sutt. SM3
  off Hemingford Rd 157 CW105
Yardley La, E4 . . . . 31 EB43
Yardley St, WC1 . . . . 196 D3
Yard Mead, Egh. TW20 . . . . . 113 BA90
Yarm Cl, Lthd. KT22 . . . . 171 CJ123
Yarm Ct Rd, Lthd. KT22 . . . . 171 CJ123
Yarmouth Cres, N17 . . . . 66 DV57
Yarmouth Pl, W1 . . . . 199 H3
Yarmouth Rd, Wat. WD24 . . . . 24 BW38
Yarm Way, Lthd. KT22 . . . . . 171 CJ123
Yarnfield Sq, SE15
  off Clayton Rd 102 DU81
Yarnton Way, SE2 . . . . 106 EX75
  Erith DA18 . . . . 106 EZ76
Yarrow Cres, E6 . . . . 86 EL71
Yarrowfield, Wok. GU22 . . . . 166 AX123
Yarrowside, Amer. HP7 . . . . . 20 AV41
Yateley St, SE18 . . . . 104 EK76
Yates Ct, NW2 . . . . 81 CX65
YEADING, Hayes UB4 . . . . . . 77 BV69
Yeading Av, Har. HA2 . . . . 60 BY61
Yeading Fork, Hayes UB4 . . . . 78 BW71
Yeading Gdns, Hayes UB4 . . . 77 BV71
Yeading La, Hayes UB4 . . . . . 77 BV72
  Northolt UB5 . . . . 78 BW69
Yeames Cl, W13 . . . . 79 CG72
Yeate St, N1 . . . . 84 DR66
Yeatman Rd, N6 . . . . 64 DF58

Yeats Cl, NW10 . . . . 80 CS65
Yeats Ct, N15
  off Tynemouth Rd 66 DT56
Ye Cor, Wat. WD19 . . . . 24 BY44
Yeend Cl, W.Mol. KT8 . . . . . . 136 CA98
Yeldham Rd, W6 . . . . 99 CX78
Yellow Hammer Ct, NW9
  off Eagle Dr 42 CS54
Yellowpine Way, Chig. IG7 . . . 50 EV49
Yelverton Cl, Rom. RM3 . . . . . 52 FK53
Yelverton Rd, SW11 . . . . 100 DD82
Yenston Cl, Mord. SM4 . . . . . 140 DA100
Yeoman Cl, E6
  off Ferndale St 87 EP73
  SE27 . . . . 121 DP90
Yeoman Dr, Stai. TW19
  off Long La. 114 BL88
Yeoman Rd, Nthlt. UB5 . . . . . 78 BY66
Yeomanry Cl, Epsom KT17
  off Dirdene Gdns 157 CT112
Yeomans Acre, Ruis. HA4 . . . . 59 BU58
Yeomans Keep, Rick. (Chorl.) WD3
  off Rickmansworth Rd. . . . 21 BF41
Yeomans Meadow, Sev.
  TN13 . . . . 190 FG126
Yeoman's Ms, Islw. TW7
  off Queensbridge Pk 117 CE85
Yeoman's Row, SW3 . . . . 198 C7
Yeoman St, SE8 . . . . 203 K8
Yeomans Way, Enf. EN3 . . . . . 30 DW40
Yeomans Yd, E1
  off Chamber St 84 DT73
Yeomen Way, Ilf. IG6 . . . . 49 EQ51
Yeo St, E3 . . . . 85 EB71
Yeoveney Cl, Stai. TW19 . . . . 113 BD89
Yeovil Cl, Orp. BR6 . . . . 145 ES103
Yeovilton Pl, Kings.T. KT2 . . . 117 CJ92
Yerbury Rd, N19 . . . . 65 DK62
Yester Dr, Chis. BR7 . . . . 124 EL94
Yester Pk, Chis. BR7 . . . . 125 EM94
Yester Rd, Chis. BR7 . . . . 125 EM94
Yevele Way, Horn. RM11 . . . . 72 FL59
Yewbank Cl, Ken. CR8 . . . . . 176 DR115
Yew Cl, Buck.H. IG9 . . . . 48 EK47
  Waltham Cross EN7 . . . . . 14 DS27
Yewdale Cl, Brom. BR1 . . . . . 124 EE93
Yewdells Cl, Bet.
  (Buckland) RH3 . . . . 183 CU133
Yewfield Rd, NW10 . . . . 81 CT66
Yew Gro, NW2 . . . . 63 CX63
Yewlands Cl, Bans. SM7 . . . . 174 DC115
Yew Pl, Wey. KT13 . . . . 135 BT104
Yews, The, Ashf. TW15 . . . . . 115 BP91
  Gravesend DA12 . . . . 131 GK88
Yew Tree Bottom Rd, Epsom
  KT17, KT18 . . . . 173 CV116
Yew Tree Cl, N21 . . . . 45 DN45
  Waltham Cross EN8 . . . . . 15 DY34
  Watford WD18 . . . . 24 BW43
  West Byfleet
    (Byfleet) KT14 . . . . 152 BK112
  Westerham (Bigg.H.) TN16 . 178 EH119
  Weybridge KT13 . . . . 153 BQ105
  Woking GU22 . . . . 166 AY118
Yorkshire Cl, N16 . . . . 66 DS62
Yorkshire Gdns, N18 . . . . 46 DV50
Yorkshire Grey Pl, NW3
  off Heath St 64 DC63
Yorkshire Grey Yd, WC1 . . . . 196 B7
Yorkshire Rd, E14 . . . . 85 DY72
  Mitcham CR4 . . . . 141 DL99
York Sq, E14 . . . . 85 DY72
York St, W1 . . . . 194 E6
  Barking IG11 *off Abbey Rd* . 87 EQ67
  Mitcham CR4 . . . . 140 DG101
  Twickenham TW1 . . . . 117 CG88
York Ter, Enf. EN2 . . . . 30 DQ38
  Erith DA8 . . . . 107 FC81
York Ter E, NW1 . . . . 194 G5
York Ter W, NW1 . . . . 194 F5
Yorkton St, E2 . . . . 84 DU68
York Way, N1 . . . . 83 DL67
  N7 . . . . 83 DK65
  N20 . . . . 44 DF48
  Borehamwood WD6 . . . . . 26 CR40
  Chessington KT9 . . . . 156 CL108
  Feltham TW13 . . . . 116 BZ90
  Watford WD25 . . . . 24 BX36
York Way Ct, N1 . . . . 83 DL67
York Way Est, N7
  off York Way 83 DL65
Youngmans Cl, Enf. EN2 . . . . 30 DQ39
Young Rd, E16 . . . . 86 EJ72
Young St, W8 . . . . 100 DB75
Youngstroat La, Wok.
  GU21, GU24 . . . . 150 AY110
Young's Bldgs, EC1 . . . . 197 J4
★ Young's Ram Brewery,
  SW18 . . . . 120 DB85
Youngs Rd, Ilf. IG2 . . . . 69 ER57

Yeats Cl, NW10 . . . . 80 CS65
York Ms, Ilford IG1 *off York Rd.* 69 EN62
York Par, Brent. TW8 . . . . 97 CK78
York Pl, SW11 . . . . 100 DD83
  WC2 . . . . 200 A1
  Dagenham RM10 . . . . 89 FC65
  Grays RM17 . . . . 110 GA79
  Ilford IG1 *off York Rd* 69 EN61
York Ri, NW5 . . . . 65 DH62
  Orpington BR6 . . . . 145 ES102
York Rd, E4 . . . . 47 EA50
  E7 . . . . 86 EG65
  E10 . . . . 67 EC62
  E17 . . . . 67 DX57
  N11 . . . . 45 DK51
  N18 . . . . 46 DV51
  N21 . . . . 46 DR45
  SE1 . . . . 200 C4
  SW11 . . . . 100 DC84
  SW18 . . . . 100 DC84
  SW19 . . . . 120 DC93
  W3 . . . . 80 CQ72
  W5 . . . . 97 CJ76
  Barnet EN5 . . . . 28 DD43
  Brentford TW8 . . . . 97 CK78
  Brentwood (Shenf.) CM15 . 55 FZ45
  Croydon CR0 . . . . 141 DN101
  Dartford DA1 . . . . 128 FM87
  Epping (N.Wld Bas.) CM16 . 18 FA27
  Gravesend DA12 . . . . 131 GJ90
  Gravesend (Nthflt) DA11 . . 130 GD87
  Hounslow TW3 . . . . 96 CB83
  Ilford IG1 . . . . 69 EN62
  Kingston upon Thames KT2 . 118 CM94
  Northwood HA6 . . . . 39 BU54
  Rainham RM13 . . . . 89 FD66
  Richmond TW10
    off Albert Rd 118 CM85
  South Croydon CR2 . . . . . 161 DX110
  Sutton SM2 . . . . 158 DA107
  Teddington TW11 . . . . 117 CE91
  Uxbridge UB8 . . . . 76 BK66
  Waltham Cross EN8 . . . . . 15 DY34
  Watford WD18 . . . . 24 BW43
  West Byfleet
    (Byfleet) KT14 . . . . 152 BK112
  Westerham (Bigg.H.) TN16 . 178 EH119
  Weybridge KT13 . . . . 153 BQ105
  Woking GU22 . . . . 166 AY118
Yorkshire Cl, N16 . . . . 66 DS62
Yorkshire Gdns, N18 . . . . 46 DV50
Yorkshire Grey Pl, NW3
  off Heath St 64 DC63
Yorkshire Grey Yd, WC1 . . . . 196 B7
Yorkshire Rd, E14 . . . . 85 DY72
  Mitcham CR4 . . . . 141 DL99
York Sq, E14 . . . . 85 DY72
York St, W1 . . . . 194 E6
  Barking IG11 *off Abbey Rd* . 87 EQ67
  Mitcham CR4 . . . . 140 DG101
  Twickenham TW1 . . . . 117 CG88
York Ter, Enf. EN2 . . . . 30 DQ38
  Erith DA8 . . . . 107 FC81
York Ter E, NW1 . . . . 194 G5
York Ter W, NW1 . . . . 194 F5
Yorkton St, E2 . . . . 84 DU68
York Way, N1 . . . . 83 DL67
  N7 . . . . 83 DK65
  N20 . . . . 44 DF48
  Borehamwood WD6 . . . . . 26 CR40
  Chessington KT9 . . . . 156 CL108
  Feltham TW13 . . . . 116 BZ90
  Watford WD25 . . . . 24 BX36
York Way Ct, N1 . . . . 83 DL67
York Way Est, N7
  off York Way 83 DL65
Youngmans Cl, Enf. EN2 . . . . 30 DQ39
Young Rd, E16 . . . . 86 EJ72
Young St, W8 . . . . 100 DB75
Youngstroat La, Wok.
  GU21, GU24 . . . . 150 AY110
Young's Bldgs, EC1 . . . . 197 J4
★ Young's Ram Brewery,
  SW18 . . . . 120 DB85
Youngs Rd, Ilf. IG2 . . . . 69 ER57
Yoxley App, Ilf. IG2 . . . . 69 EQ58
Yoxley Dr, Ilf. IG2 . . . . 69 EQ58
Yukon Rd, SW12 . . . . 121 DH87
  Broxbourne EN10 . . . . 15 DY25
Yule Cl, St.Alb. (Brick.Wd) AL2 . 8 BZ30
Yuletide Cl, NW10 . . . . 80 CS66
Yunus Khan Cl, E17 . . . . 67 EA57

Z

Zambezie Dr, N9 . . . . 46 DW48
Zampa Rd, SE16 . . . . 102 DW78
Zander Ct, E2
  off St. Peter's Cl 84 DU68
Zangwill Rd, SE3 . . . . 104 EK81
Zealand Av, West Dr. UB7 . . . . 94 BK80
Zealand Rd, E3 . . . . 85 DY68
Zelah Rd, Orp. BR5 . . . . 146 EV101
Zeland Cl, NW2 . . . . 63 CW60
Zennor Rd, SW12 . . . . 121 DJ88
Zenoria St, SE22 . . . . 102 DT84
Zermatt Rd, Th.Hth. CR7 . . . . 142 DQ98
Zetland St, E14 . . . . 85 EB71
Zig Zag Rd, Ken. CR8 . . . . . . 176 DQ116
Zion Pl, Grav. DA12 . . . . 131 GH87
  Thornton Heath CR7 . . . . 142 DR98
Zion Rd, Th.Hth. CR7 . . . . . . 142 DR98
Zion St, Sev. (Seal) TN15
  off Church Rd. 191 FM121
Zoar St, SE1 . . . . 201 H2
Zodiac Business Pk, Uxb. UB8
  off Hornbill Cl. 76 BJ71
Zoffany St, N19 . . . . 65 DK61

★ Place of interest   ⇌ Railway station   ⊖ London Underground station   DLR Docklands Light Railway station   Tra Tramlink station   H Hospital   Riv Pedestrian ferry landing stage